The Developing Person
Through the Life Span

The Developing Person
Through the Life Span

NINTH EDITION

Kathleen Stassen Berger

Bronx Community College
City University of New York

WORTH PUBLISHERS
A Macmillan Higher Education Company

Publisher: Kevin Feyen

Associate Publisher: Jessica Bayne

Developmental Editor: Tom Churchill

Executive Marketing Manager: Katherine Nurre

Supplements and Media Editor: Lauren Samuelson

Director of Editing, Design, and Media Production: Tracey Kuehn

Managing Editor: Lisa Kinne

Production Editor: TSI Graphics, Inc.

Assistant Editor: Catherine Michaelsen

Interior Designer: Lissi Sigillo

Photo Treatments: Lyndall Culbertson

Photo Editor: Sheena Goldstein

Photo Researcher: Teri Stratford

Art Manager: Matthew McAdams

Illustrations: Todd Buck Illustrations, MPS Limited, TSI Graphics, Inc.

Production Manager: Barbara Seixas

Composition: TSI Graphics, Inc.

Printing and Binding: RR Donnelley

Cover Art: Roderick Chen/Getty Images

Library of Congress Control Number: 2014935218

ISBN-13: 978-1-4292-8381-6

ISBN-10: 1-4292-8381-5

ISBN-13: 978-1-4292-8393-9 (ppbk.)

ISBN-10: 1-4292-8393-9 (ppbk.)

ISBN-13: 978-1-4641-3979-6 (LL)

ISBN-10: 1-4641-3979-2 (LL)

Printed in the United States of America

First printing

Worth Publishers

41 Madison Avenue

New York, NY 10010

www.worthpublishers.com

Credit is given to the following sources for permission to use the photos indicated:

Part Openers, in part order

Jose Luis Pelaez Inc/Getty Images

Alex Cao/Getty Images

BLOOM Image/Getty Images

Ronnie Kaufman/Larry Hirshowitz/Getty Images

Tyler Edwards/Digital Vision/Getty Images

Jacqueline Veissid/Getty Images

WIN-Initiative/Getty Images

© Jacqueline Veissid/Blend Images/Corbis

Chapter Openers, in chapter order

Hugh Sitton/Corbis

Marilyn Nieves/Vetta/Getty Images

Professors Pietro M. Motta & Sayoko Makabe/Science Source

Zhang Bo/Getty Images

Terry J Alcorn/Getty Images

Jose Luis Pelaez, Inc/Blend Images/Getty Images

Bruce Yuanyue Bi/Lonely Planet/Getty Images

Fotosearch/Creatas Photos/Jupiter Images

Marcus Lindstrom/Getty Images

GM Visuals/Getty Images

Holger Winkler/Corbis

Sean Sprague/The Image Works

Hola Images RF/Getty Images

Aldo Murillo/Getty Images

Anna Wehmeyer - Germany/Getty Images

Image Source/Getty Images

© Jon Arnold Images/DanitaDelimont.com

© Exotica im/PhotosIndia.com Pvt. Ltd./Age Fotostock, Inc.

Robin Skjoldborg/Getty Images

© David Burch/Age Fotostock

Tony Anderson/Taxi/Getty Images

© Alena Brozova/Age Fotostock

© Guillem Lopez/Aurora Photos/Corbis

Nancy Rica Schiff/SuperStock

Mimmopellicola.com/Flickr/Getty Images

Brief Contents and other Silhouettes, in order of appearance

Lane Oatey/Getty Images

© John Lund/Annabelle Breakey/Blend Images/Corbis

George Doyle/Getty Images

© Vinicius Ramalho Tupinamba/iStockphoto

Mark Andersen/Getty Images

Lane Oatey/Blue Jean Images/Getty Images

Jeff Randall/Getty Images

Rubberball/Getty Images

About the Author

Kathleen Stassen Berger received her undergraduate education at Stanford University and Radcliffe College, earned an M.A.T. from Harvard University and an MS and PhD from Yeshiva University. Her broad experience as an educator includes directing a preschool, serving as chair of philosophy at the United Nations International School, teaching child and adolescent development to graduate students at Fordham University and undergraduates at Montclair State University in New Jersey and at Quinnipiac University in Connecticut, as well as teaching social psychology to inmates at Sing Sing Prison.

Throughout most of her professional career, Berger has worked at Bronx Community College of the City University of New York, first as an adjunct and for the past two decades as a full professor. She has taught introduction to psychology, child and adolescent development, adulthood and aging, social psychology, abnormal psychology, and human motivation. Her students—who come from many ethnic, economic, and educational backgrounds and who have a wide range of ages and interests—consistently honor her with the highest teaching evaluations.

Berger is also the author of *The Developing Person Through Childhood and Adolescence* and *Invitation to the Life Span*. Her developmental texts are currently being used at more than 700 colleges and universities worldwide and are available in Spanish, French, Italian, and Portuguese, as well as English. Her research interests include adolescent identity, immigration, and bullying, and she has published many articles on developmental topics in the *Wiley Encyclopedia of Psychology* and in publications of the American Association for Higher Education and the National Education Association for Higher Education. She continues teaching and learning as her four daughters and three grandsons continue to develop, as she interacts with students every semester, and as she revises each edition of her books.

WORTH PUBLISHERS

Preface   xvii

PART I The Beginnings   1

Chapter 1 The Science of Human Development   3
Chapter 2 Theories of Development   35
Chapter 3 Heredity and Environment   67
Chapter 4 Prenatal Development and Birth   93

PART II The First Two Years   125

Chapter 5 The First Two Years: Biosocial Development   127
Chapter 6 The First Two Years: Cognitive Development   155
Chapter 7 The First Two Years: Psychosocial Development   181

PART III Early Childhood   213

Chapter 8 Early Childhood: Biosocial Development   215
Chapter 9 Early Childhood: Cognitive Development   245
Chapter 10 Early Childhood: Psychosocial Development   275

PART IV Middle Childhood   307

Chapter 11 Middle Childhood: Biosocial Development   309
Chapter 12 Middle Childhood: Cognitive Development   339
Chapter 13 Middle Childhood: Psychosocial Development   367

PART V Adolescence   399

Chapter 14 Adolescence: Biosocial Development   401
Chapter 15 Adolescence: Cognitive Development   429
Chapter 16 Adolescence: Psychosocial Development   457

BRIEF CONTENTS

PART VI Emerging Adulthood   489

Chapter 17   Emerging Adulthood: Biosocial Development   491

Chapter 18   Emerging Adulthood: Cognitive Development   517

Chapter 19   Emerging Adulthood: Psychosocial Development   543

PART VII Adulthood   573

Chapter 20   Adulthood: Biosocial Development   575

Chapter 21   Adulthood: Cognitive Development   603

Chapter 22   Adulthood: Psychosocial Development   631

PART VIII Late Adulthood   665

Chapter 23   Late Adulthood: Biosocial Development   667

Chapter 24   Late Adulthood: Cognitive Development   699

Chapter 25   Late Adulthood: Psychosocial Development   729

Epilogue   Death and Dying   760

Appendix A   Supplemental Charts, Graphs, and Tables   A-1

Appendix B   More About Research Methods   B-1

Glossary   G-1

References   R-1

Name Index   NI-1

Subject Index   SI-1

CONTENTS

Preface xvii

PART I
The Beginnings 1

Chapter 1 The Science of Human Development 3

Understanding How and Why 4
The Scientific Method 4
The Nature–Nurture Debate 5

The Life-Span Perspective 5
Development Is Multidirectional 6
Development Is Multicontextual 7
Development Is Multicultural 11
OPPOSING PERSPECTIVES: Using the Word *Race* 15
Development Is Multidisciplinary 16
Development Is Plastic 19
A CASE TO STUDY: David 20

Using the Scientific Method 22
Observation 22
The Experiment 24
The Survey 24
Studying Development over the Life Span 25

Cautions and Challenges from Science 28
Correlation and Causation 29
Ethics 29
What Should We Study? 31

Chapter 2 Theories of Development 35

What Theories Do 35
Questions and Answers 36
Facts and Norms 37

Grand Theories 39
Psychoanalytic Theory:
Freud and Erikson 39
Behaviorism: Conditioning and
Social Learning 42

Cognitive Theory: Piaget and Information Processing 45
Comparing Grand Theories 48
OPPOSING PERSPECTIVES: Toilet Training—How and When? 50

Newer Theories 51
Sociocultural Theory: Vygotsky and Beyond 52
The Universal Perspective: Humanism and
Evolutionary Theory 55
A VIEW FROM SCIENCE: If Your Mate Were Unfaithful 60

What Theories Contribute 62

Chapter 3 Heredity and Environment 67

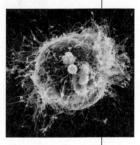

The Genetic Code 68
What Genes Are 68
Variations 69

The Beginnings of Life 70
Matching Genes 70
Male or Female? 70
New Cells, New Functions 71
OPPOSING PERSPECTIVES: Too Many Boys? 71
Twins 73
Assisted Reproduction 75

From Genotype to Phenotype 77
Epigenetics 77
Gene–Gene Interactions 78

Nature and Nurture 81
Alcoholism 82
Nearsightedness 82
Practical Applications 83

Chromosomal and Genetic Problems 84
Not Exactly 46 84
Gene Disorders 85
Genetic Counseling and Testing 87

Chapter 4 Prenatal Development and Birth 93

Prenatal Development 94
Germinal: The First 14 Days 94
Embryo: From the Third Through the
Eighth Week 95
Fetus: From the Ninth Week Until Birth 96

Birth 99
The Newborn's First Minutes 101
Medical Assistance 101
Alternatives to Hospital Technology 103

Problems and Solutions 105
Harmful Substances 105
Risk Analysis 106
Applying the Research 108
OPPOSING PERSPECTIVES: "What Do People Live to Do?" 112
Low Birthweight 113
Complications During Birth 116

The New Family 116
The Newborn 116
New Fathers 117
New Mothers 119
Parental Alliance 120
Bonding 120

PART II

The First Two Years   125

Chapter 5 The First Two Years: Biosocial Development 127

Growth in Infancy 127
Body Size 128
Brain Growth 129
A VIEW FROM SCIENCE: Face Recognition 134
Sleep 135
OPPOSING PERSPECTIVES: Where Should Babies Sleep? 135

Perceiving and Moving 137
The Senses 137
Motor Skills 140
Dynamic Sensory-Motor Systems 142

Surving in Good Health 142
Better Days Ahead 143
Immunization 144
Nutrition 145
Sudden Infant Death Syndrome 149

Chapter 6 The First Two Years: Cognitive Development 155

Sensorimotor Intelligence 155
Stages One and Two: Primary Circular Reactions 156
Stages Three and Four: Secondary Circular Reactions 157
Stages Five and Six: Tertiary Circular Reactions 159
Piaget and Modern Research 160

Information Processing 162
Affordances 163
Memory 165

Language: What Develops in the First Two Years? 168
The Universal Sequence 168
First Words 170
Cultural Differences 171
Theories of Language Learning 172
OPPOSING PERSPECTIVES: Language and Video 174

Chapter 7 The First Two Years: Psychosocial Development 181

Emotional Development 181
Early Emotions 182
Toddlers' Emotions 183

Brain and Emotions 185
Growth of the Brain 185
Temperament 187

The Development of Social Bonds 189
Synchrony 189
Attachment 190
Insecure Attachment and the Social Setting 195
Social Referencing 197
Fathers as Social Partners 197

Theories of Infant Psychosocial Development 199
Psychoanalytic Theory 199
Behaviorism 200
OPPOSING PERSPECTIVES: Proximal and Distal Parenting 201
Cognitive Theory 202
Humanism 203
Evolutionary Theory 204
Infant Day Care 205

PART III
Early Childhood 213

Chapter 8 Early Childhood: Biosocial Development 215

Body Changes 215
Growth Patterns 215
Nutrition 216
Hazards of "Just Right" 218

Brain Development 219
Speed of Thought 220
The Brain's Connected
    Hemispheres 220
Emotions and the Brain 224

Improving Motor Skills 227
Gross Motor Skills 227
A VIEW FROM SCIENCE: Eliminating Lead 230
Fine Motor Skills 232
Artistic Expression 232

Injuries and Abuse 233
Avoidable Injury 233
Prevention 235
Child Maltreatment 236
Three Levels of Prevention, Again 240

Chapter 9 Early Childhood: Cognitive Development 245

Thinking During Early Childhood 245
Piaget: Preoperational
    Thought 245
A CASE TO STUDY: Stones in
    the Belly 247
Vygotsky: Social Learning 249

A VIEW FROM SCIENCE: Research Report:
    Early Childhood and STEM 251
Children's Theories 252
Brain and Context 254

Language Learning 256
A Sensitive Time 256
The Vocabulary Explosion 257
Learning Two Languages 260

Early-Childhood Education 262
Homes and Schools 262
Child-Centered Programs 263
Teacher-Directed Programs 265
Long-Term Gains from Intensive Programs 269

Chapter 10 Early Childhood: Psychosocial Development 275

Emotional Development 275
Initiative Versus Guilt 276
Motivation 277
Culture and Emotional Control 278
Seeking Emotional Balance 279
A VIEW FROM SCIENCE: Sex Differences in
    Emotional Regulation 280

Play 280
Playmates 282
Culture and Cohort 282
Active Play 283

Challenges for Caregivers 287
Caregiving Styles 287
Cultural Variations 289
Teaching Children to Be Boys or Girls 290

Moral Development 295
Nature and Nurture 295
Empathy and Antipathy 296
Discipline 298
OPPOSING PERSPECTIVES: Is Spanking Okay? 301

PART IV

Middle Childhood 307

Chapter 11 Middle Childhood: Biosocial Development 309

A Healthy Time 309
Slower Growth, Greater Strength 310
Physical Activity 311

    Health Problems in Middle Childhood 313
    Childhood Obesity 313
    A VIEW FROM SCIENCE: What Contributes to
      Childhood Obesity? 315
    Asthma 317

    Brain Development 318
    Coordinating Connections 318
    Measuring the Mind 320

Children with Special Needs 323
Causes and Consequences 324
Attention-Deficit/Hyperactivity Disorder 325
A CASE TO STUDY: Lynda Is Getting Worse 327
Specific Learning Disorders 328
Autism Spectrum Disorder 329
Special Education 331
Gifted and Talented 333

Chapter 12 Middle Childhood: Cognitive Development 339

Building on Theory 339
    Piaget and School-Age Children 339
    Vygotsky and School-Age Children 341
    Information Processing 343
    A VIEW FROM SCIENCE:
      Balls Rolling Down 347

Language 348
    Vocabulary 348
Differences in Language Learning 350
A CASE TO STUDY: Two Immigrants 352

Teaching and Learning 353
International Schooling 353
In the United States 358
Choices and Complications 361

Chapter 13 Middle Childhood: Psychosocial Development 367

The Nature of the Child 367
Industry and Inferiority 368
Self-Concept 368
Culture and Self-Esteem 369
Resilience and Stress 370

Families and Children 373
Shared and Nonshared
    Environments 373
A VIEW FROM SCIENCE: "I Always
    Dressed One in Blue Stuff . . ." 374
Family Function and Family Structure 374
Connecting Family Structure and Function 376
A CASE TO STUDY: How Hard Is It to Be a Kid? 380
Family Trouble 381
A VIEW FROM SCIENCE: Divorce 381

The Peer Group 384
The Culture of Children 384
Friendships 385
Popular and Unpopular Children 385
Bullies and Victims 386

Children's Moral Values 389
Moral Reasoning 389
What Children Value 391

PART V

Adolescence 399

Chapter 14 Adolescence: Biosocial Development 401

Puberty Begins 401
Unseen Beginnings 402
OPPOSING PERSPECTIVES: Algebra at
    7 A.M.? Get Real 405
Age and Puberty 406
A VIEW FROM SCIENCE: Stress and
    Puberty 409
Too Early, Too Late 409

Growth and Nutrition 411
Growing Bigger and Stronger 411
Diet Deficiencies 413
Eating Disorders 414

Brain Development 416
A Need for Caution 416
A CASE TO STUDY: "What Were You Thinking?" 417
Benefits of Adolescent Brain Development 418

Sexual Maturation 419
Sexual Characteristics 419
Sexual Activity 420
Problems with Adolescent Sex 422

Chapter 15 Adolescence: Cognitive Development 429

Logic and Self 430
Egocentrism 430
Formal Operational
   Thought 431

Two Modes of Thinking 434
Intuition Versus Analysis 436
Dual Processing and the
   Brain 438

Digital Natives 440
Technology and Cognition 441
A New Addiction? 441
Cyber Danger 442

Teaching and Learning 444
Definitions and Facts 444
Middle School 445
A CASE TO STUDY: James, the High-Achieving
   Dropout 446
High School 448
OPPOSING PERSPECTIVES: Testing 449

Chapter 16 Adolescence: Psychosocial Development 457

Identity 457
Not Yet Achieved 458
Four Arenas of Identity
   Formation 459

Relationships with Adults 462
Parents 462
A VIEW FROM SCIENCE: Parents,
   Genes, and Risks 465
Other Adults 465

Peer Power 466
Peers and Parents 467
Peer Pressure 467
Romance 469
Sex Education 471

Sadness and Anger 473
Depression 473
Delinquency and Defiance 476
OPPOSING PERSPECTIVES:
   Teenage Rage: Necessary? 476

Drug Use and Abuse 478
Variations in Drug Use 479
Harm from Drugs 480
Preventing Drug Abuse:
   What Works? 481

PART VI
Emerging Adulthood 489

Chapter 17 Emerging Adulthood: Biosocial Development 491

Growth and Strength 491
Strong and Active Bodies 491
A VIEW FROM SCIENCE: Ages and Stages 493
Bodies in Balance 493
Staying Healthy 497

Sexual Activity 500
Then and Now 500
Opinions and Problems 501

Psychopathology 503
Multiple Stresses of Emerging Adults 503
Mood Disorders 504
Anxiety Disorders 505
Schizophrenia 506

Taking Risks 507
OPPOSING PERSPECTIVES: Brave or Foolish? 509
Drug Abuse 510
Social Norms 511
Implications of Risks and Norms 513

Chapter 18 Emerging Adulthood: Cognitive Development 517

Postformal Thought 517
The Practical and the Personal: A Fifth Stage? 518
Combining Subjective and Objective Thought 521
Cognitive Flexibility 522
Countering Stereotypes 523
Dialectical Thought 525

Morals and Religion 528
Which Era? What Place? 529
Dilemmas for Emerging Adults 529
Stages of Faith 531

Cognitive Growth and Higher Education 532
The Effects of College 532
A CASE TO STUDY: College Advancing Thought 535
Changes in the College Context 535
Evaluating the Changes 538

Chapter 19 Emerging Adulthood: Psychosocial Development 543

Continuity and Change 543
Identity Achieved 544
Personality in Emerging Adulthood 549

Intimacy 551
Friendship 551
The Dimensions of Love 553
OPPOSING PERSPECTIVES: Cohabitation 557
A CASE TO STUDY: My Daughters and Me 560
What Makes Relationships Succeed? 560
Conflict 561

Emerging Adults and Their Parents 564
Linked Lives 564
Financial Support 565

PART VII
Adulthood 573

Chapter 20 Adulthood: Biosocial Development 575

Senescence 576
The Experience of Aging 576
The Aging Brain 577

Outward Appearance 577
Sense Organs 579

The Sexual-Reproductive System 580
Contraception 580
Sexual Responsiveness 581
Fertility 582
Menopause 584

Health Habits and Age 586
Drug Abuse 586
Nutrition 589
Inactivity 592
A VIEW FROM SCIENCE: A Habit Is Hard to Break 593

Measuring Health 594
Mortality 594
Morbidity 596
Disability 596
Vitality 597
Correlating Income and Health 598

Chapter 21 Adulthood: Cognitive Development 603

What Is Intelligence? 603
Research on Age and Intelligence 604
Cross-Sequential Research 606

Components of Intelligence: Many and Varied 608
Two Clusters of Intelligence 608
Three Forms of Intelligence 610
Age and Culture 612
OPPOSING PERSPECTIVES: What Makes a Good Parent? 613

Selective Gains and Losses 615
Accumulating Stressors 615
A CASE TO STUDY: Coping with Katrina 619
Selective Optimization with Compensation 620
Expert Cognition 621

Chapter 22 Adulthood: Psychosocial Development 631

Personality Development in Adulthood 631
Theories of Adult Personality 631
Personality Traits 634
OPPOSING PERSPECTIVES: Local Context Versus Genes 636

Intimacy: Friends and Family 637
Friends and Acquaintances 638
Family Bonds 639

Intimacy: Romantic Partners 641
Marriage and Happiness 641
Partnerships over the Years 642
Gay and Lesbian Partners 644
Divorce and Remarriage 644

Generativity 646
Parenthood 646
Caregiving 651
Employment 654
A VIEW FROM SCIENCE:
Accommodating
Diversity 656

PART VIII

Late Adulthood 665

Chapter 23 Biosocial Development: Late Adulthood 667

Prejudice and Predictions 667
Believing the Stereotype 668
A VIEW FROM SCIENCE:
When You Think of Old People . . . 669
The Demographic Shift 673

Selective Optimization with Compensation 676
Personal Compensation: Sex 676
A CASE TO STUDY: Should Older Couples
Have More Sex? 677
Social Compensation: Driving 678
Technological Compensation: The Senses 681
Compensation for the Brain 682

Aging and Disease 684
Primary and Secondary Aging 684
Compression of Morbidity 686

Theories of Aging 688
Wear and Tear 689
Genetic Theories 689
Cellular Aging 690

The Centenarians 693
Far from Modern Life and Times 693
Maximum Life Expectancy 694

Chapter 24 Late Adulthood: Cognitive Development 699

The Aging Brain 700
New Brain Cells 700
Senescence and the Brain 701

Information Processing After Age 65 703
Input 703
Memory 704
Control Processes 705
A VIEW FROM SCIENCE: Cool Thoughts and
Hot Hands 705
Output 706
OPPOSING PERSPECTIVES: How to Measure Output 708

Neurocognitive Disorders 709
The Ageism of Words 709
Mild and Major Impairment 710
Prevalence of NCD 710
Preventing Impairment 714
Reversible Neurocognitive Disorder? 716
A CASE TO STUDY: Too Many Drugs or Too Few? 718

New Cognitive Development 719
Erikson and Maslow 719
Learning Late in Life 719
Aesthetic Sense and Creativity 721
Wisdom 723

Chapter 25 Late Adulthood 729

Theories of Late Adulthood 730
Self Theories 730
OPPOSING PERSPECTIVES: Too Sweet or
Too Sad? 733
Stratification Theories 734

Activities in Late Adulthood 737
Working 737
Home Sweet Home 739
Religious Involvement 742
Political Activism 742

Friends and Relatives 743
Long-Term Partnerships 744
Relationships with Younger Generations 744
Friendship 748

The Frail Elderly 749
Activities of Daily Life 750
A CASE TO STUDY: Preventing Frailty 751
Caring for the Frail Elderly 752

Epilogue 760

Death and Hope 761
Cultures, Epochs, and Death 761
Understanding Death Throughout
the Life Span 763
Near-Death Experiences 767

Choices in Dying 768
A Good Death 768
Better Ways to Die 770
Ethical Issues 771
OPPOSING PERSPECTIVES: The "Right to Die"? 775
Advance Directives 776

Affirmation of Life 778
Grief 778
Mourning 780
Diversity of Reactions 783
Practical Applications 783
A VIEW FROM SCIENCE: Resilience After a Death 784

Glossary   G-1
References   R-1
Name Index   NI-1
Subject Index   SI-1

Preface

My grandson, Asa, is in early childhood. He sees the world in opposites: male/female, child/grown-up, good guys/ bad guys. He considers himself one of the good guys, destroying the bad guys in his active imagination, and in karate kicks in the air.

Oscar, his father, knows better. He asked me if Asa really believes there are good guys and bad guys, or is that just a cliché. I said that most young children believe quite simple opposites.

Undeterred, Oscar told Asa that he knows some adults who were once bad guys but became good guys.

"No," Asa insisted. "That never happens."

Asa is mistaken. As he matures, his body will grow taller but become less active, and his mind will appreciate the development of human behavior as life goes on. This book describes how our thoughts and actions change over the lifespan, including that almost nothing "never happens" as humans grow older.

Oscar is not alone in realizing that people change. Many common sayings affirm development over time: People "turn over a new leaf," are "born-again"; parents are granted a "do-over" when they become grandparents; today is "the first day of the rest of your life." Adults also recognize that the past never disappears; we say, "The apple does not fall far from the tree," and many other adages that stress past influences.

Pondering My grandson, Asa, looks thoughtfully at his father, Oscar.

The complexity, the twists and turns, the endless variety of the human experience at every age is fascinating to me, which is why I wrote this book. We all have echoes of Asa in us: We want life to be simple, for people to be good guys. But life is not simple. Learning about human growth helps everyone respond to life's variations and influences, not with imaginary kicks but with wise responses. Knowledge does that. In a vivid example, Stephen Pinker (2011) finds that humans kill each other less now than they did in previous centuries; he cites education as one reason.

Education occurs in hundreds of ways. This textbook is only one of them, an aid to understanding the complexity of your life, my life, and the lives of all the estimated 18 billion humans alive now or who once lived. Nonetheless, although life experiences and thousands of other books contribute to our education, writing this text is my contribution and studying it is yours: Together we might learn how to limit the bad and increase the good in each of us as time goes on.

New Material

Every year, scientists discover and explain more concepts and research. The best of these are integrated into the text, including hundreds of new references on many topics—among them the genetics of delinquency, infant nutrition, bipolar and autistic spectrum disorders, attachment over the life span, high-stakes testing, drug use and drug addiction, brain changes throughout adulthood, and ways to die. Cognizant of the interdisciplinary nature of human development, I reflect recent research in biology, sociology, education, anthropology, political science, and more—as well as my home discipline, psychology.

Compare These with Those These children seem ideal for cross-sectional research—they are school children of both sexes and many ethnicities. Their only difference seems to be age, so a study might conclude that 6-year-olds raise their hands.

Genetics and social contexts are noted throughout. The variations and hazards of infant day care and preschool education are described; emerging adulthood is further explained in a trio of chapters; the blurry boundaries of adulthood are stressed; the various manifestations, treatments, and prevention of neurocognitive disorders (not just Alzheimer disease) are discussed; and much more.

New Pedagogical Aids

This edition incorporates learning objectives at the beginning of each chapter: The "What Will You Know?" questions indicate important concepts for students to focus on. There is also a new element at the end of each chapter: The "What Have You Learned?" questions help students assess their learning in more detail. Some further explanation follows.

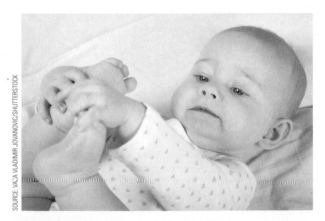

Success At 6 months, she is finally able to grab her toes. From a developmental perspective, this achievement is as significant as walking, as it requires coordination of feet and fingers. Note her expression of determination and concentration.

Learning Objectives

Much of what students learn from this course is a matter of attitude, approach, and perspective—all hard to quantify. In addition, there are specific learning objectives, which supplement the key terms that should also be learned. For the first time in this edition, two sets of objectives are listed for each chapter. The first set ("What Will You Know?"), asked at the beginning of each chapter, lists the general ideas that students might remember and apply lifelong. At the end of each chapter are more specific learning objectives ("What Have You Learned?") that connect to each major heading within that chapter.

Ideally, students answer the learning objective questions in sentences, with specifics that demonstrate knowledge. Some items on the new lists are straightforward, requiring only close attention to the chapter content. Others require comparisons, implications, or evaluations.

New *Opposing Perspectives* Boxed Feature and Updated *A View from Science* and *A Case to Study* Features

We all need to develop our critical thinking skills. Virtually every page of this book presents not only facts but also questions with divergent interpretations. A new boxed feature called *Opposing Perspectives* appears in this edition of *The Developing Person Through the Life Span* for the first time. This box focuses on exciting and controversial topics in development—from prenatal sex selection to the right to die. These high-interest sections appear in most chapters and provide information on both sides of an issue so that students can practice weighing evidence, assessing arguments, and coming to their own conclusions.

In addition, the boxes titled *A View from Science,* which explain surprising insights from recent scientific research, and *A Case to Study,* which illustrate developmental issues through the story of specific individuals, have been extensively updated. All these new features are included in the table of contents.

Visualizing Development

Also new to this edition are full-page illustrations of key topics in development. Every chapter now includes an infographic display of data on key issues ranging from the biology of twin births to the economic benefits of a college degree to the range of venues in which elders spend their last years. Many of these infographics combine global statistics, maps, charts, and photographs. Working closely with noted designer Charles Yuen, I have tried to use this visual display to reinforce and explain key ideas.

New Child Development and Nursing Career Appendices

Available online, these new resources link the content of the life-span course to key student career areas—early childhood development and nursing—by correlating the Ninth Edition and its test bank to the NAEYC (National Association for the Education of Young Children) preparation goals and the NCLEX (nursing) licensure exams.

Content Changes to the Ninth Edition

Life-span development, like all sciences, builds on past learning. Many facts and concepts are scaffolds that remain strong over time: ages and stages, norms and variations, dangers and diversities, classic theories and fascinating applications. However, the study of development is continually changed by discoveries and experiences, so no paragraph in this ninth edition is exactly what it was in the eighth edition, much less the first. Some major revisions have been made, and hundreds of new examples are cited. Highlights of this updating appear below.

Part I: The Beginnings
1. The Science of Human Development

- A new chapter opener focuses on Kathleen Berger's (embarrassing) experience at the birth of her grandson, Caleb.
- Comprehensive explanation of the *difference-equals-deficit error* is used to highlight the importance of a multicultural approach in developmental science.

Before Words The New York infant interpreting a smile is doing what babies do: trying to understand communications long before they are able to talk.

SOURCE: VIKRAM RAGHUVANSHI/GETTY IMAGES

- An Opposing Perspectives feature box introduces students to the controversies surrounding the use of the word "race" in the social sciences.
- An explanation of genetics and epigenetics now appears in this introductory chapter as an example of why the study of human development needs to take a multidisciplinary approach.
- A new section on researching the topic of depression provides students with a concrete illustration of the way a multidisciplinary approach can lead to a better understanding of a particular issue.
- Dynamic systems theory and the concept of *differential sensitivity* are used to explain the plasticity of human development.

2. Theories of Development
- The controversial text of *Battle Hymn of the Tiger Mother* is used as an example to illustrate the popularity and ubiquity of theories of human development.
- A new section on Comparing Grand Theories provides thought-provoking comparisons between psychoanalytic, behavioral, and cognitive theories.
- A new feature box on Toilet Training illustrates exactly how various theoretical schools can take radically different approaches to a particular issue.
- An expanded account of sociocultural theory explains the pervasiveness of cultural influences on individual people and the extent to which scientists now acknowledge these influences in their studies.
- A View from Science feature box explores the way evolutionary theory accounts for sexual jealousy between men and women.

3. Heredity and Environment
- New material on *copy number variations* as a type of interaction between genes that correlates with a large number of diseases and conditions.
- An expanded discussion of genetic counseling that includes criteria for determining when a pregnant woman should be informed about genetic disorders that tests have detected in her fetus.

4. Prenatal Development and Birth
- Updated data on rates of cesarean deliveries in the United States and around the world.
- A new discussion of *innate vulnerability* as a factor that influences the effects of teratogens on prenatal development.
- New material on the responsibility of doctors and scientists in advising pregnant women about avoiding various teratogens.
- Expanded discussion of problems associated with *low birthweight*, including the complementary roles of mothers and fathers.
- A new section on the way the *parental alliance* can have a healthy influence on pregnancy and birth.

Part II: The First Two Years
5. The First Two Years: Biosocial Development
- A new View from Science feature box on Face Recognition outlines the role of experience in the development of dendrites in the *fusiform face area* of the brain, which in turn gives babies the ability to recognize faces.
- New material on Harming the Infant Brain explores several sources of harm and successful interventions.
- An expanded section on Touch and Pain summarizes current scientific thought on infants' experience of pain.
- A new section on Dynamic Sensory-Motor Systems connects dynamic systems theory with a baby's growing ability to coordinate senses and skills.

SOURCE: AMY WHITT/RADIUS IMAGES/GETTY IMAGES

Bliss for Boys But not for moms. Finger painting develops fine motor skills, which is why it is part of the curriculum in early childhood. This boy shows why most stay-at-home 3-year-olds miss out on this joy.

- Updated data on infant death rates around the world show the way improved public health measures have increased infant survival rates.
- An account of Susan Beal's research into *sudden infant death syndrome* now ends this chapter, summarizing the complexity of infant care and the way many factors interact to produce any one result.

6. The First Two Years: Cognitive Development

- A new section on Piaget and Modern Research focuses on the limitations of Piaget's conclusions about Sensorimotor Intelligence that have come to light in more recent studies.
- The section called Research on Early Affordances has been updated to include new research on the influence of social context on early affordances.
- A new feature box on Language and Video discusses the connection between a toddler's interpersonal relationships and his or her intellectual growth, cautioning against the claims of certain commercial "educational" products.
- In the section on Information Processing there is more of an emphasis on the active nature of the young child's brain and the influences of experiences and memory on what the child knows.

7. The First Two Years: Psychosocial Development

- A new discussion of Social Awareness complements that on Self-Awareness in the section on the emotional development of toddlers.
- The section on brain growth and its links to this stage of child development is expanded.
- A discussion of Romanian orphans is used to illustrate the hazards associated with insecure attachment.
- A new section on Preventing Problems discusses ways of avoiding insecure attachment between new parents and their babies.
- The discussion of *proximal and distal parenting* has been expanded and highlighted by placing it in an Opposing Perspectives feature box.
- In the section on theories, there are new discussions of Humanism and Evolutionary Theory and the way they apply to this stage of development.

Part III: Early Childhood
8. Early Childhood: Biosocial Development

- Treatment of stress hormones and their effects on the limbic system is expanded.
- The discussion of Nutritional Deficiencies has been expanded to include recent research on food allergies.
- The section on prevention of avoidable injuries has been reorganized to place a greater emphasis on cultural variations.
- A new feature box describes the way scientific research encouraged the elimination of lead from paints and gasoline in the United States and the positive effects this has had on child development.

9. Early Childhood: Cognitive Development

- The discussion of Piaget's Preoperational Thought has been expanded to include the use of *symbolic thought* by young children.
- Vygotsky's Social Learning Theory is applied to the recent emphasis on STEM (Science, Technology, Engineering, Math) education and possible implications for early childhood learning.
- Under Language Learning there is new material on the activities in early childhood that aid later literacy in elementary school.
- A new section covers recent research into strategies for enhancing bilingual education in early childhood.

10. Early Childhood: Psychosocial Development

- The opening section on Emotional Development has been reorganized and rewritten to emphasize the connection with brain maturation during early childhood.
- In the section on Motivation, there is a new discussion of why young children create *imaginary friends*.
- Under Play, the discussion of the importance of culture and cohort has been significantly expanded.
- The expanded treatment of Challenges for Caregivers discusses not only parents but also other significant adults in a child's life.
- The discussion of theoretical approaches to sex and gender has been broadened to include sociocultural theory, humanism, and evolutionary theory.
- The nature/nurture controversy as it applies to early childhood behavior is treated in greater detail.
- Under the topic of discipline, there is a new Opposing Perspectives box on the pros and cons of spanking.

Part IV: Middle Childhood
Chapter 11: Middle Childhood: Biosocial Development

- Extensively updated coverage of psychopathology in childhood including updated coverage of Autism Spectrum Disorder, ADHD, and Specific Learning Disorders.
- New A Case to Study on Lynda, about a young girl with psychological difficulties, whose case is "diagnosed" by a number of professionals, leading to a critical thinking discussion of the challenges in treating and understanding childhood psychopathology.
- New section on gifted education.
- New A View from Science box on childhood obesity.

Chapter 12: Middle Childhood: Cognitive Development

- Updated and extensive section on the international contexts for the growth in childhood cognition, including an extended example of the sense of direction among children in Varanasi, a city in India.
- Updated discussion of international tests and international schooling, including material on the Finnish educational success story.
- New discussion of the Common Core standards.

Chapter 13: Middle Childhood: Psychosocial Development

- New chapter-opening vignette about an 8-year-old boy whose father says he's too young to play video games in which he kills zombies.
- Updated discussion and understanding of risk and resilience, focusing on epigenetics—and the fact that differential sensitivity may mean that what is beneficial to one child may be stressful for another.
- New A Case to Study about child neglect and how to recognize it in children in school.

Part V: Adolescence
Chapter 14: Adolescence: Biosocial Development

- New research on sleep deprivation, including the observation that the light from computers, video games, and even cell phones can interrupt circadian rhythms and interfere with teenagers' natural nighttime sleepiness.
- New coverage of new DSM-5 diagnosis of binge eating disorders.
- Updated data about the timing of adolescent sexual activity.

Chapter 15: Adolescence: Cognitive Development

- New section on the impact of technology on adolescents Digital Natives, which includes material on potential Internet and video game addiction, sexting, and cyberbullying.
- New chapter-opening vignette about the challenges of teaching sometimes "egocentric" adolescents in high school.
- Updated research, including the work of Daniel Kahneman (the Nobel Prize–winning psychologist) on logical fallacies.
- New research on what motivates students to succeed in middle and high school, including theories about students' beliefs about what causes school success.
- New material on high-stakes testing in high school, including coverage of the Common Core and updated international tests including the PISA.

Chapter 16: Adolescence: Psychosocial Development

- New material on culture and cultural differences and similarities in parent-child relationships across the world.
- Updated section and data on relationships between same-sex adolescents.
- New coverage of the impact of culture and context, particularly among Latino/Latina youths and gay youths, on depression in adolescence.
- New Opposing Perspectives box on teenage rage, asking students to think critically about whether rage and rebellion are a culturally determined or universal part of the adolescent experience.

Part VI: Emerging Adulthood
Chapter 17: Emerging Adulthood: Biosocial Development

- Material on homeostasis, organ reserve, and allostatis has been moved to this chapter.
- Significantly reorganized and updated material on psychopathology in emerging adulthood, reflecting new DSM-5 categorizations.
- New Opposing Perspectives box on risk-taking in early adulthood.
- Updated material on abuse of drugs, including coverage of energy drinks and ketamine, and social-norms theories of drug-abuse prevention.

Chapter 18: Emerging Adulthood: Cognitive Development

- Updated research on stereotype threat and its power to influence the success of college students.
- Updated data on trends in higher education, including the increasing costs of college and use of technology in the classroom (including the "flipped classroom" and MOOCs).

Chapter 19: Emerging Adulthood: Psychosocial Development

- Updated material on vocation and vocational identity in emerging adulthood, with coverage of John Holland's research and the recent economic challenges faced by young adults.
- New coverage of the importance of plasticity in emerging adulthood, including the concept of "plasticity genes," which reiterates the ongoing coverage in this book of epigenesis—the impact of environment on gene expression throughout the life span.
- Updated material on how use of the Internet and social media enhances friendships during emerging adulthood.
- New coverage of "churning" relationships which start and stop frequently and are characterized by conflict.
- Updated coverage of the relationship between emerging adults and their parents (which tends to be closer than ever before).

Part VII: Adulthood
Chapter 20: Adulthood: Biosocial Development
- Updated research on aging vision and senses.
- New material on the use of hormone replacement therapy for aging men and women, and adult obesity.

Chapter 21: Adulthood: Cognitive Development
- Updated data on IQ changes in adulthood, including cohort and generational effects.

Chapter 22: Adulthood: Psychosocial Development
- New chapter-opening vignette on Kathleen Berger's broken bones, illustrating the web of connection in adulthood.
- New material on culture and variations in adult children's relationships with their parents.
- Updated section on sibling and "fictive kin" relationships.
- Updated section on possible predictors of marital happiness and new research on same-sex marriage and adoption.
- New box focusing on diversity in the workplace and the harm caused by "microaggression" among co-workers.

Part VIII: Late Adulthood
Chapter 23: Late Adulthood: Biosocial Development
- New box on sex in later adulthood—focusing on how satisfied many older adults are with their sexuality.
- New material on driving in late adulthood, including material on policy issues and changes in our senses as we age.
- Recent research on normative brain changes in late adulthood, including coverage of brain shrinkage.
- Updated research on the theories of aging and controversies over how to delay it—including calorie restriction, sirtuins, and reversatrol.

Chapter 24: Late Adulthood: Cognitive Development
- Significantly revised and updated presentation on neurocognitive disorder to reflect the new DSM-5 categorization.
- Significantly updated and revised discussion of brain function and cognitive processes during aging, including developments in memory and executive control processes.
- New boxes on cognitive errors during adulthood, focusing on dual processing and intelligence testing in late adulthood.

Chapter 25: Late Adulthood: Psychosocial Development
- New coverage of compulsive hoarding, a new DSM-5 diagnosis.
- New Opposing Perspectives box on positive world view among elders.
- Updated section on employment in late adulthood to reflect the fact that many elders are still in the workforce, or would like to be.

Epilogue
- Updated coverage of hospice care in the U.S. and around the world.
- New material on planning for the end of life, including coverage of advanced directives.
- Updated material on bereavement and grief.

Ongoing Features

Many characteristics of this book have been acclaimed since the first edition and have been retained in this revision.

Writing That Communicates the Excitement and Challenge of the Field

An overview of the science of human development should be lively, just as real people are. Each sentence conveys tone as well as content. Chapter-opening vignettes that describe real-life situations bring student readers into the immediacy of development. Examples and explanations abound, helping students make the connections among theory, research, and their own experiences.

Coverage of Brain Research

Inclusion of the exciting results from neuroscience is now a familiar feature of this book. Brain development is the most obvious example: Every trio of chapters includes a section on the brain, often enhanced with charts and photos to help students understand its inner workings. The following list highlights some of this material.

Compare These with Those Any group, such as these 16-year-olds, in cross-sectional research may differ in a way that is not obvious—perhaps income, national origin, or culture—and that may be the underlying reason for any observed age differences.

The role of dopamine, serotonin, and growth factors such as GDNF in depression, p. 17

Epigenetics and brain function in depressed individuals, pp. 17–19

PET scans of brains of a depressed and a non-depressed person, p. 19; illustrated, p. 18

Neuroscience and the limits of Piaget's developmental theory, p. 47

Brain scans of adults with ADHD, p. 48; illustrated, p. 48

Influence of copy number variations on basic brain structures, p. 80

Prenatal growth of the brain, pp. 98–99; illustrated, pp. 98–99

Teratogenic effects on brain development, p. 106–111; illustrated, p. 107

Brain development in the first two years, pp. 129–134; illustrated, pp. 129–130

Experience-expectant and experience-dependent brain development, p. 133

Brain immaturity and cross-modal perception, p. 142

Implication of low serotonin levels in SIDS, p. 150

Limitations of Piaget's theory as revealed by brain scans, pp. 161–162

Techniques of infant brain scans, p. x; illustrated, p. 162

Mirror neurons and infant cognition, p. 162

Brain developments that support social emotions, pp. 185–186

The effect of the stress hormone cortisol on the developing brain, p. 186

Genetic influences on temperament, especially the combination of DRD4 VNTR and 5-HTTLPR genes, p. 188

Brain maturation and synchrony, p. 191

Attachment and brain development, p. 195

A View from Science: the effect of lead exposure on brain development, pp. 230–231

Brain development in early childhood (prefrontal cortex, myelination, lateralization, the limbic system), pp. 219–223; illustrated, pp. 219–220

Abnormal growth of the corpus callosum and ADHD, p. 223

Maturation of the prefrontal cortex and theory of mind, p. 254; illustrated p. 255

Cultural differences in executive function among 5-year-olds, p. 254

The influence of myelination of the limbic system and growth of the prefrontal cortex in development of emotional regulation, pp. 276–277

The effects of physical exercise on the brain, p. 311

Brain development in middle childhood, pp. 318–323

Neurological advances and selective attention, p. 319

Neurological scans confirm usefulness of information-processing approach, p. 343

Development of control processes in middle childhood, p. 346
Brain abnormality as a possible factor in bullying, p. 387
The role of the pituitary gland in hormone production, pp. 402–403
The role of the brain in regulating circadian rhythms, pp. 403–404
Adolescent brain development; heightened arousal of reward areas of the brain, pp. 416–418
Proportion of gray matter from childhood through adolescence, illustrated p. 416
Benefits of adolescent brain development, pp. 418–419
Dual processing as a result of brain maturation, pp. 438–439
Risk-taking and brain activity, p. 438; illustrated p. 439
Neurological factors as predictors of delinquency in adolescence, p. 477
Drug use and potential harm to the brain, pp. 478–479
The impact of alcohol on the adolescent brain, p. 481
Physiological responses affecting neurological patterns, p. 502
Brain development and hormones as factors in risk-taking, p. 507
Brain development and postformal thought, pp. 519–520
Brain changes from age 14 to age 25, illustrated p. 520
Lust and affection centered in different brain areas, p. 553
The aging brain: neurological changes in adulthood, p. 577
Causes of severe brain loss before age 65, p. 577
Thirty distinct brain areas involved in vision, p. 579
Complications in calculating adult IQ due to brain changes, p. 605
Fluid intelligence and overall brain health, p. 609
The effects of stress on the brain, p. 615
Multitasking and the aging brain, p. 621
Brain changes due to experience and expertise, p. 626
Correlation between brain function and personality, p. 636, illustrated p. 637
Encoding of the sense of unfairness in the brain, p. 654
Compensation strategies for brain loss in late adulthood, pp. 676–683
The aging brain: neurological changes in late adulthood, pp. 682–683
Neurogenesis in late adulthood, p. 683
Brain abnormalities in neurocognitve disorders, p. 711
Specific genes associated with Alzheimer disease; scans of progress of AD, p. 712
Correlation between vascular dementia and the ApoE4 allele, p. 712
Repeated brain trauma as a precursor of dementia, p. 714
Expression of creativity and its impact on brain health, p. 722
Opposing Perspectives: brain activity in response to disappointment: differences between old, healthy individuals; old, depressed individuals; and young individuals, p. 733; illustrated p. 733
Brain death as determining factor in declaring a person legally dead, pp. 772–773

DASHA PETRENKO/SHUTTERSTOCK

Don't Worry Contemporary teenagers, like this couple, are more likely to be seen in public hugging and kissing but are less likely to be sexually active than similar couples were 20 years ago.

Coverage of Diversity

Cross-cultural, international, multiethnic, sexual orientation, wealth, age, gender—all these words and ideas are vital to appreciating how people develop. Research uncovers surprising similarities and notable differences: We have much in common, yet each human is unique. From the discussion of social contexts in Chapter 1 to the coverage of cultural differences in mourning in the Epilogue, each chapter highlights possibilities and variations.

New research on family structures, immigrants, bilingualism, single adults, and ethnic differences in health are among the many topics that illustrate human diversity. Listed here is a smattering of the discussions of culture and diversity in this new edition. Respect for human differences is evident throughout. You will note that examples and research findings from many parts of the world are included, not as add-on highlights, but as integral parts of the description of each age.

Inclusion of all kinds of people in the study of development, p. 4

Multicontextual considerations in development (SES, cohort, family configuration, etc.), pp. 7–11

Culture defined; the need to include people of many cultures in developmental study, p. 11

Learning within a culture/cultural transmission (Vygotsky), p. 14

Race and *ethnic group* defined and discussed (includes *Opposing Perspectives*), pp. 14–16

Genetic, biochemical, and neurological differences in adults with depression versus adults without depression; international differences in incidence of depression, pp. 17–19

Age diversity in cross-sectional research and cohort diversity in cross-sequential research, pp. 25–28

Age, gender, and immigrant/nonimmigrant differences in explanation of correlation, p. 29

Ethnotheories arising from a specific culture or ethnic group, p. 35

Developmental theories reflect historical and cultural influences of their time, p. 48

Vygotsky's sociocultural theory, pp. 52–55

Genetic variations among people: alleles, p. 69

Male and female sex chromosomes, pp. 70–71

Opposing Perspectives: international differences in sex selection, pp. 71–72

Rates of cesarean births in selected countries, p. 102

Birthing practices in various cultures, pp. 103–104

Ethnic differences in the allele that causes low folic acid, p. 108

Rates of low birthweight in various countries, p. 115

Opposing Perspectives: cultural differences in co-sleeping, pp. 135–136; rates in various countries, p. 136

Infant mortality rates in various countries, p. 143

Breast-feeding and HIV-positive women in Africa, p. 146

International rates of stunting, p. 148

Malnutrition: wasting in developing nations, pp. 148–149

Cultural and family differences in infants' exposure to language and language use, pp. 171–172

Understanding of emotional content of English by non-English speakers, pp. 173–174

Separation anxiety and stranger wariness in Japan and Germany, p. 183

Cultural differences in emotions encouraged in toddlers, p. 184

Cultural differences in activation of the anterior cingulate gyrus, p. 185

Genetic and gender differences in infant/toddler temperament, p. 188

Ugandan mothers' contact-maintaining behaviors, p. 193

Influence of SES on attachment type, p. 195

Outcomes for Romanian orphans adopted by North American, European, and Australian families, p. 196

Danish father involvement with infants, p. 198

Gender differences in child care, pp. 198–199

Opposing Perspectives: proximal and distal parenting in Cameroon, Greece, and Costa Rica, pp. 201–202

International comparisons of infant caregiving differences, pp. 206–207

Parental leave policies in selected countries, p. 207

A View from Science: correlation of blood lead levels and crime in various countries, pp. 230–231

FUSE/GETTY IMAGES

Healthy? Children have high energy but small stomachs, so they enjoy frequent snacks more than bog meals. Yet snacks are typically poor sources of nutrition.

Differences in the corpus callosum between right- and left-handed people, p. 220

Culture as a determinant of how one thinks and acts (social learning, Vygotsky), pp. 249–252

Study of overimitation in South Africa, Botswana, and Australia, p. 250

Cultural differences in development of theory of mind, pp. 255–256

Bilingualism in various nations; ethnicity and bilingualism in the U.S.; English proficiency among U.S. children whose home language is not English, pp. 260–261

Ethnic breakdown on children in preschool programs, p. 268

Effects of intervention programs on low-SES children, pp. 269–270

Various cultures' goals for emotional regulation in young children, p. 278

A View from Science: sex differences in emotional regulation, p. 280

Cultural differences in young children's play, pp. 282–283

Ethnic and SES differences in children's activities, illustrated, p. 282

Cultural differences in caregiving styles, pp. 289–290

Cultural differences in child discipline, pp. 299–300

Opposing Perspectives: cultural attitudes towards spanking, pp. 301–302

Attitudes towards children's leisure time: U.S., Australia, South Korea, p. 312

Common leisure activities in various nations, p. 312

A View from Science: childhood obesity in the U.S., by ethnicity; genetic propensity toward obesity and diabetes, pp. 315–316

Childhood asthma and ethnicity in the U.S., p. 317

Cultural considerations in IQ testing, p. 322

Consideration of children with special needs, pp. 323–335

A Case to Study: difficulties in diagnosis of special needs, p. 327

Cultural differences (Vygotsky) and SES differences in school-age children's learning, pp. 341–343

Curriculum differences in various countries, pp. 353–355

Math and reading achievement in various countries, pp. 356–357

Children's second-language proficiency: Europe, Africa, Canada, the U.S., pp. 359–360

Class size and student performance in various countries, p. 362

Cultural differences in self-esteem in middle childhood, pp. 369–370

Children's reactions to stress in Louisiana (Hurricane Katrina), Sri Lanka (tsunami), and Sierra Leone (war and child soldiers), pp. 371–372

SES and resilience, p. 372

Family function within various structures, including families headed by same-sex couples, pp. 374–381

International rates of single-parent families, p. 377

Percentage of one- and two-parent families in the U.S., by ethnicity of parents, pp. 380–381

Effects of SES on family structure and function, pp. 382–383

Shyness and popularity in North America and China, p. 386

Gender differences in bullying, p. 386

Efforts to control bullying in various nations, p. 388

Age-related differences in moral reasoning, p. 392

Gender differences in children's retribution/restitution behavior, pp. 393–394

Ethnic differences in timing of puberty (U.S.), p. 406; in other nations, pp. 410–411

Ethnic differences in median age of menarche, p. 406

Influence of body fat on onset of puberty (girls): ethnic differences and international examples, pp. 406–408

Gender differences in reaction to early or late puberty, pp. 409–410

Nutritional deficiencies: U.S. ethnic and international examples, pp. 413–414

Ethnic differences in teen birth rates (U.S.); differences in other nations, p. 422

Condom use among teens in various nations, p. 425

Age differences in logical thinking, pp. 430–432

Comparison of international scores on PISA, p. 453

Parent–child communication in Hong Kong, the United States, and Australia, p. 463

Formation of ethnic identity, pp. 467–468

Adolescent same-sex relationships and gender identity, pp. 460–461, 470–471

Differences in sex education, U.S. and Europe, pp. 472–473

Gender, ethnic, and age differences in self-esteem in adolescence, pp. 473–474

Genetic and gender differences in risk of depression, p. 474

Gender differences in rates of teen parasuicide and suicide, pp. 474–475

Opposing Perspectives: Is adolescent rebellion a social construction?— international comparisons, p. 476

International comparisons: adolescent use of alcohol and cigarettes, p. 479

Differences in teen drug use by age, gender and generation, pp. 479–480

The effect of globalization on the spread of infectious diseases, including STIs, pp. 501–502

Sex differences in experience of depression, p. 505

Gender differences in prevalence of risk-taking, pp. 507–509

Homicide victims and perpetrators, by age, p. 508

Differences in substance abuse, by age, p. 510

Stereotype threat—ethnic and gender factors, p. 524

Gender differences in morality, p. 530

Rates of college graduation in various nations, pp. 535–536

Proliferation of universities in Asia and the Middle East, p. 536

Ethnic and gender diversity in college, and their effects, pp. 536–538

Ethnic identity in emerging adulthood, pp. 544–547

Gender and friendship, p. 552

National differences in acceptance and timing of cohabitation, pp. 556–557

Ethnicity as a factor in romantic relationships, p. 561

National differences in relationship of emerging adults to their parents, pp. 565–568

National and regional differences in fertility, p. 582

Cultural differences in acceptance of HRT, p. 585

Gender differences in incidence of lung cancer (U.S.), p. 587

Rates of smoking in men and women (U.S.), p. 588

International rates of overweight and obesity, p. 590

Ethnic and cultural influences on incidence of obesity, p. 591

Gender differences in rates of daily exercise, p. 592

Mortality rates by age, gender, and ethnicity, p. 594

Gender differences in life expectancy, various nations, p. 595

SES and health, pp. 589–599

Gender and age differences in intellectual abilities, p. 606

Sex differences in response to stress, pp. 616–617

Age and job effectiveness, p. 626

The influence of culture, age, and social context on personality in adulthood, pp. 634–635

Opposing Perspectives: genetic and contextual influences on adult personality, pp. 636–637

Income as a determinant of family structure for young, married couples in Thailand, p. 639

National differences in the quality of older adults' relationships with their children, p. 639

Income and education as factors in marital happiness, p. 642

Ethnic differences in likelihood of divorce, p. 643

E. HANAZAKI PHOTOGRAPHY/FLICKR RF/GETTY IMAGES

No Toys Boys in middle childhood are happiest playing outside with equipment designed for work. This wheelbarrow is perfect, especially because at any moment the pusher might tip it.

A Social Gathering Fifty years ago teens hung out on the corner or at the local drug store. Now they gather in someone's house. Each seems to be in his or her own world, but show and tell is part of technology for adolescents.

Gay and lesbian partners, p. 644

SES and ethnicity as factors in remarriage, p. 645

Ethnic differences in interdependence of family members, p. 652

Cultural determinants of family caregiving for the elderly, pp. 652–654

Evolving gender differences in the U.S workforce; ethnic make-up of the U.S. labor force, 1980 and 2012, p. 656

A *View from Science:* accommodating diversity in the workplace, p. 656

Work schedules in the U.S. and Europe, p. 658

Cultural and age differences in ageist stereotypes; differences between hearing and nonhearing Americans, pp. 669–670

Percent of population age 65 or older, selected nations, p. 673

Dependency ratio in developed and developing nations, p. 674

A *Case to Study:* gender differences in sexual desire and activity in late adulthood, pp. 677–678

Death rates by cause of death in late adulthood relative to adulthood, p. 685

Age differences in drug testing and in the efficacy of medical interventions in the old and the young, p. 685

Gender difference in incidence of chronic and acute diseases, p. 686

Breakdown of U.S. population over 55, by age and gender, p. 686

Genetic diversity: alleles that promote or compromise longevity, pp. 689–690

Correlation between high SES and high intellect in old age, p. 702

Age-related disparity in efficacy of IQ testing and tests of memory, pp. 706–708

Disparity in prevalence of neurocognitive disorders in developed and developing nations; rates in selected nations, p. 711

Gender differences in prevalence of neurocognitive disorders, p. 711

Genetic propensity to developing Alzheimer disease, p. 712

Genetic propensity to developing vascular disorder, p. 712

The impact of gender, ethnic, and SES stratification, pp. 734–736

Effects of ethnic stratification on Africa Americans and on U.S. immigrant elders, p. 735

Ethnic and age disparities in SES, p. 735

Average life expectancy compared by ethnicity and age (California), p. 735

Effects of age stratification, p. 736

SES as a factor in disengagement, p. 736

Culture and policy effects on volunteerism among the elderly, p. 739

Differences in national policies regarding care for the elderly, p. 745

Cultural differences in expectations about care of the elderly, U.S. and Asian cultures, p. 745

Cultural differences in the well-being of grandparents who raise their grandchildren, pp. 747–748

Life expectancy compared: white and black men and women with and without a high school diploma, p. 747

Cultural and national differences in care for the frail elderly, pp. 751–752

Death beliefs and practices in ancient Egypt and Greece, p. 762

Modern death beliefs and practices in different cultures/religions, p. 763

Age differences in response to death, pp. 763–767

Ethnic and national differences in the availability and use of hospice care, pp. 770–771

State, national, and cultural differences in attitudes toward and policies about euthanasia and physician-assisted suicide, pp. 773–774

Mourning rituals in various religions, pp. 780–781

Up-to-Date Coverage

My mentors welcomed curiosity, creativity, and skepticism; as a result, I am eager to read and analyze thousands of articles and books on everything from Alzheimer disease to zygosity. The recent explosion of research in neuroscience and genetics has challenged me, once again, first to understand and then to explain many complex findings and speculative leaps. My students continue to ask questions and share their experiences, always providing new perspectives and concerns.

Topical Organization Within a Chronological Framework

The book's basic organization remains unchanged. Four chapters begin the book with coverage of definitions, theories, genetics, and prenatal development. These chapters function not only as a developmental foundation but also as the structure for explaining the life-span perspective, plasticity, nature and nurture, multicultural awareness, risk analysis, gains and losses, family bonding, and many other concepts that yield insights for all of human development.

The other seven parts correspond to the major periods of development. Each part contains three chapters, one for each of the three domains: biosocial, cognitive, and psychosocial. The topical organization within a chronological framework is a useful scaffold for students' understanding of the interplay between age and domain. The chapters are color-coded with tabs on the right-hand margins. The pages of the biosocial chapters have turquoise tabs, the cognitive chapters have purple tabs, and the psychosocial chapters have green tabs.

Three Series of Integrated Features

Three series of deeper discussions appear as integral parts of the text, and only where they are relevant. Readers of earlier editions will remember *A Case to Study* and *A View from Science*; new to this edition is the *Opposing Perspectives* feature.

End-of-Chapter Summary

Each chapter ends with a summary, a list of key terms (with page numbers indicating where the word is introduced and defined), key questions, and three or four application exercises designed to help students apply concepts to everyday life. Key terms appear in boldface type in the text and are defined in the margins and again in a glossary at the back of the book. The outline on the first page of each chapter, the new learning objectives, and the system of major and minor subheads facilitate the survey-question-read-write-review (SQ3R) approach.

A "Summing Up" feature at the end of each section provides an opportunity for students to pause and reflect on what they've just read. Observation Quizzes inspire readers to look more closely at certain photographs, tables, and figures. The "Especially for . . ." questions in the margins, many of which are new to this edition, apply concepts to real-life careers and social roles.

Photographs, Tables, and Graphs That Are Integral to the Text

Students learn a great deal from this book's illustrations because Worth Publishers encourages authors to choose the photographs, tables, and graphs and to write captions that extend the content. Appendix A furthers this process by presenting numerous charts and tables that contain detailed data for further study.

MASKOT/GETTY IMAGES

Didn't Want to Marry This cohabiting couple decided to wed only after they learned that her health insurance would not cover him unless they were legally married. Two years later they had a son, who is now developing happily and well. She is pregnant with their second child, and he is searching for a house to buy. Would this have happened if they were still unmarried?

Supplements

After teaching every semester for many years, I know well that supplements can make or break a class. Students are now media savvy and instructors use tools that did not exist when they themselves were in college. Many supplements are available for both students and professors.

LaunchPad with LearningCurve Quizzing

A comprehensive web resource for teaching and learning development, LaunchPad combines rich media resources and an easy-to-use platform. For students, it is the ultimate online study guide with videos, ebook, and the LearningCurve adaptive quizzing system. For instructors, LaunchPad is a full-course space where class documents can be posted, quizzes are easily assigned and graded, and students' progress can be assessed and recorded. The LaunchPad can be previewed at www.worthpublishers.com/launchpad/bergerls9e. You'll find the following in our LaunchPad:

The **LearningCurve** quizzing system was designed based on the latest findings from learning and memory research. It combines adaptive question selection, immediate and valuable feedback, and a game-like interface to engage students in a learning experience that is unique to them. Each LearningCurve quiz is fully integrated with other resources in LaunchPad through the Personalized Study Plan, so students will be able to review with Worth's extensive library of videos and activities. And state-of-the-art question-analysis reports allow instructors to track the progress of individual students as well as their class as a whole. A team of dedicated instructors—including Jim Cuellar, Indiana University, Bloomington; Lisa Hager, Spring Hill College; Jessica Herrick, Mesa State College; Sara Lapsley, Simon Fraser University; Rosemary McCullough, Ave Maria University; Wendy Morrison, Montana State University; Emily Newton, University of California, Davis; Diana Riser, Columbus State University; Curtis Visca, Saddleback College; and Devon Werble, East Los Angeles Community College—have worked closely to develop more than 5,000 quizzing questions developed specifically for this book.

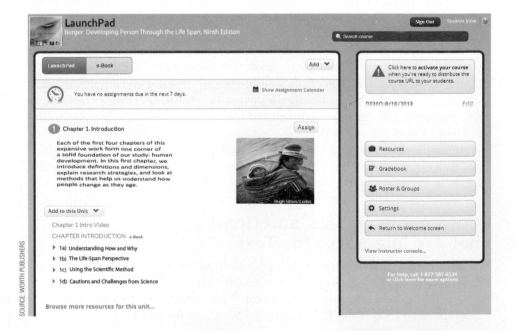

Human Development Videos

In collaboration with dozens of instructors and researchers, Worth has developed an extensive archive of video clips. This collection covers the full range of the course, from classic experiments (like the Strange Situation and Piaget's conservation tasks) to investigations of children's play, adolescent risk-taking, and the devastation of Alzheimer disease. Instructors can assign these videos to students through LaunchPad or choose one of 50 popular video activities that combine videos with short-answer and multiple-choice questions. For presentation purposes, our videos are available in a variety of formats to suit your needs, including download and flash drive.

Instructor's Resources

Now fully integrated with LaunchPad, this collection of resources written by Richard O. Straub (University of Michigan, Dearborn) has been hailed as the richest collection of instructor's resources in developmental psychology. The resources include learning objectives, springboard topics for discussion and debate, handouts for student projects, course-planning suggestions, ideas for term projects, and a guide to audiovisual and online materials.

Interactive Presentation Slides

A new extraordinary series of "next-generation" interactive presentation lectures gives instructors a dynamic yet easy-to-use new way to engage students during classroom presentations of core developmental psychology topics. Each lecture provides opportunities for discussion and interaction and enlivens the psychology classroom with an unprecedented number of embedded video clips and animations from Worth's library of videos. In addition to these animated presentations, Worth also offers a set of prebuilt slide sets with all chapter art and illustrations. These slides can be used as is or can be customized to fit individual needs.

Test Bank and Computerized Test Bank

The test bank, prepared by Jessica Siebenbruner, Winona State University, and Jillene Seiver, Bellevue College, includes at least 100 multiple-choice and 70 fill-in-the-blank, true-false, and essay questions for each chapter. Good test questions are critical to every course and we have gone through each and every one of these test questions with care. We have added more challenging questions, and questions are keyed to the textbook by topic, page number, and level of difficulty. We have also written rubrics for grading all of the short answer and essay questions in the test bank.

The Diploma computerized test bank, available on a dual-platform CD-ROM for Windows and Macintosh, guides instructors step by step through the process of creating a test. It also allows them to quickly add an unlimited number of questions; edit, scramble, or resequence items; format a test; and include pictures, equations, and media links. The accompanying gradebook enables instructors to record students' grades throughout the course and includes the capacity to sort student records, view detailed analyses of test items, curve tests, generate reports, and add weights to grades.

The CD-ROM is also the access point for Diploma Online Testing, which allows instructors to create and administer secure exams over a network or over the Internet. In addition, Diploma has the ability to restrict tests to specific computers or time blocks. Blackboard-formatted versions of each item in the test bank are available on the CD-ROM.

Thanks

I'd like to thank the academic reviewers who have read this book in every edition and who have provided suggestions, criticisms, references, and encouragement. They have all made this a better book. I want to mention especially those who have reviewed this edition:

Jackie Adamson, *Del Mar College*

MaryBeth Ahlum, *Nebraska Wesleyan University*

William Aronson, *Florida International University*

Darin Baskin, *Houston Community College*

Saundra Boyd, *Houston Community College*

Jessica Burkholder, *Georgian Court University*

David Carlston, *Midwestern State Univeristy*

Jenel Cavazos, *Cameron University*

Chris Cline, *Colorado Christian University*

Charles deWitt, *Nashville State Community College*

Faith Edwards, *University of Wisconsin, Oshkosh*

Anne Ferrari, *The College of New Rochelle*

Cass Foursha-Stevenson, *Mount Royal University*

Rod Fowers, *Highline Community College*

Tina Garrett, *Mississippi Delta Community College*

Sidney Hardyway, *Volunteer State Community College*

Janice Hartgrove-Freile, *Lone Star College, North Harris*

Julie Homb, *Loras College*

Nora Kametani, *Nunez Community College*

Kathleen Kirasic, *University of South Carolina*

Jared Lisonbee, *Weber State University*

Zena Mello, *University of Colorado, Colorado Springs*

Omar Mendez, *William Paterson University*

Robin Montvilo, *Rhode Island College*

Nyaka NiiLampti, *Queens University of Charlotte*

Reginald Rackley, *Southern University*

Sabrina Rieder, *Rockland Community College*

Hugh Riley, *Baylor University*

Holly Schofield, *Central Carolina Community College*

Jessica Siebenbruner, *Winona State University*

Brooke Spangler, *Miami University*

Asako Stone, *Central New Mexico Community College*

Andrew Supple, *The University of North Carolina, Greensboro*

Laura Thayer, *Lewis Clark State College*

Shirlen Triplett, *DePaul University*

Barbara Vail, *Rocky Mountain College*

Trish Vandiver, *University of St. Thomas*

Andrea Walker, *Oral Roberts University*

Jewel Wiesinger, *Queens University of Charlotte*

Chrysalis Wright, *University of Central Florida*

Benita Yowe, *Spartanburg Community College*

In addition, I wish to thank the instructors who participated in our online survey. We've tried to apply the insights gained from their experiences with the last edition to make this new edition even better.

Kristi Almeida-Bowin, *Moorpark College*

Kathleen Bonnelle, *Lansing Community College*

Dava Brock, *Arkansas State University, Beebe*

Deborah Carvelli, *University of Richmond*

Aileen Collins, *Chemeketa Community College*

Jonathan Durm, *Lonestar College*

Laurel End, *Mount Mary College*

Joy Fea, *Messiah College*

Angela Fiorille, *Regis University*

James Francis, *San Jacinto College, South*

Daryl Graves, *Endicott College*

Terry Holbrook, *Olympic College*

Susan Leveridge, *Northwest University*

Sarah Luckadoo, *Jeff State Community College*

Ron Madison, *Holy Family University*

Kathryn A. Markell, *Anoka-Ramsey Community College*

T. Darin Matthews, *The Citadel*

Jeannie L. McCarter, *Union College*

Ginger McElwee, *Pittsburg State University*

Kendra Miller, *Anoka Ramsey Community College*

Terry Moore, *Mississippi Delta Community College*

Bruce Mortenson, *Towson University*

Zita Mueller, *Champlain College, Lennoxville*

Mary Bess Pannel, *Mississippi Delta Community College*

Amy Pietan, *Allen Community College*

Casi Ruffo, *Northern Arizona University*

Rebecca Ryan, *Georgetown University*

Russell Searight, *Lake Superior State University*

David W. Shwalb, *Southern Utah University*

Lydia Smith, *University of North Carolina, Charlotte*

Kimberlee Taylor, *Utah State University*

Kristine Walker, *Northwest College*

Robin White-Underwood, *Schoolcraft College*

The editorial, production, and marketing people at Worth Publishers are dedicated to meeting the highest standards of excellence. Their devotion of time, effort, and talent to every aspect of publishing is a model for the industry. I particularly would like to thank Jessica Bayne, Tom Churchill, Lyndall Culbertson, John Franchak, Sheena Goldstein, Lisa Kinne, Ann Kirby-Payne, Tracey Kuehn, Rosemary McCullough, Catherine Michaelsen, Katherine Nurre, Babs Reingold, Lauren Samuelson, Barbara Seixas, and Teri Stratford.

New York, March 2014

the beginnings

The science of human development has many beginnings; each of the first four chapters of this text forms one corner of a solid foundation for our study.

Chapter 1 introduces definitions and dimensions, explaining research strategies and methods that help us understand how people change as they age. The power of culture and context, as well as the dynamic interactions of human development, are emphasized.

Without ideas we would wonder where to start. Chapter 2 provides guideposts. Five major theories, each leading to many other theories and hypotheses, are described.

Chapter 3 explains the specifics of heredity. Genes never act alone, yet no development—whether in body or brain, at any time, in anyone—is unaffected by DNA.

Chapter 4 details the early biological growth of each developing person, from one cell to a newborn. Circumstances in embryonic and fetal growth impact the entire life span; prenatal beginnings continue to echo in the final hours.

The science and the wonder of human life begin long before the first breath. Understanding the beginnings described in each of these chapters prepares us for every later time.

The Science of Human Development

- **Understanding How and Why**
  The Scientific Method
  The Nature–Nurture Controversy

- **The Life-Span Perspective**
  Development Is Multidirectional
  Development Is Multicontextual
  Development Is Multicultural
  OPPOSING PERSPECTIVES:
    Using the Word *Race*
  Development Is Multidisciplinary
  Development Is Plastic
  A CASE TO STUDY: David

- **Using the Scientific Method**
  Observation
  The Experiment
  The Survey
  Studying Development over the Life Span

- **Cautions and Challenges from Science**
  Correlation and Causation
  Ethics
  What Should We Study?

WHAT WILL YOU KNOW?

1. What are the complexities of studying growth over the life span?
2. What research methods do developmentalists use to study change over time?
3. Why do scientific conclusions need to be interpreted with caution?

At 6:11 A.M. I hold my daughter's bent right leg in place with all my strength. A nurse holds her left leg while the midwife commands, "Push . . . push . . . push." Finally, a head is visible, small and wet, but perfect. In a moment, body and limbs emerge, all 4,139 grams of Caleb, perfect as well. Every number on the monitor is good, and Caleb breathes and moves as a healthy newborn should. Bethany, smiling, begins to nurse.

This miracle makes celestial music ring in my ears. The ringing grows louder. Suddenly, I am on the floor, looking up at six medical professionals: I have fainted.

"I am fine," I insist, scrambling back onto the couch where I spent the night. Six people stare at me.

"You need to go to triage," one says.

"No, I am fine. Sorry I fainted."

"We must send you to triage, in a wheelchair."

What can I say to make them ignore me and focus on Caleb?

"You can refuse treatment," a nurse tells me.

I remember; the law requires patient consent.

I am wheeled down to Admitting; I explain that I was with my laboring daughter all night with no food or sleep. I refuse treatment.

The admitting nurse takes my blood pressure—normal—and checks with her supervisor. She lets me return before the placenta is delivered.

I am thankful, but puzzled. I understand birth, numbers, jargon, monitors, body language, medical competence, hospital cleanliness, hall noises, and more. I do not panic. I told the triage nurse that I had not slept or eaten all night—true, but I had done that before, never fainting. Why this time?

This incident is a fitting introduction for Chapter 1, which begins to explain what we know, what we don't know, and how we learn about human development. For me and other scientists, and also for you and everyone else, surprises occur as each life is lived. Emotions mix with intellect, family bonds with professional competence, contexts with cultures, personal experiences with academic knowledge, general conclusions with individual oddities.

Many details of Caleb's arrival were distinct from details of birth in other cultures and eras. Yet other aspects have always been part of the human experience. This chapter, and those that follow, will help you understand the specifics and the universals of human life.

Both Blissful One of us rests after an arduous journey, and the other rejoices after crying and fainting.

Observation Quiz What is universal and what is culture-specific about Caleb's birth? (see answer, page 5)

Left: Hugh Sitton/Corbis
Top: Lane Oatey/Getty Images

>> Understanding How and Why

science of human development The science that seeks to understand how and why people of all ages and circumstances change or remain the same over time.

The **science of human development** *seeks to understand how and why people—all kinds of people, everywhere, of every age—change over time.* The goal of this science is for all 7 billion people on Earth to fulfill their potential. Growth is *multidirectional, multicontextual, multicultural, multidisciplinary,* and *plastic,* five terms that will soon be explained.

First, however, we need to emphasize that developmental study is a *science.* It depends on theories, data, analysis, critical thinking, and sound methodology, just like every other science. All scientists ask questions and seek answers in order to ascertain "how and why."

Science is especially useful when we study people: Lives depend on it. What should pregnant women eat? How much should babies cry? When should children be punished? Under what circumstances should adults marry, or divorce, or retire, or die? People disagree, sometimes vehemently, because emotions, experiences, and cultures differ.

The Scientific Method

scientific method A way to answer questions that requires empirical research and data-based conclusions.

hypothesis A specific prediction that can be tested.

empirical evidence Evidence that is based on observation, experience, or experiment, not theory.

Facts may be misinterpreted and applications may spring from assumptions, not from data. To avoid unexamined opinions and to rein in personal biases, researchers follow the five steps of the **scientific method** (see Figure 1.1):

1. *Begin with curiosity.* On the basis of theory, prior research, or a personal observation, pose a question.
2. *Develop a hypothesis.* Shape the question into a **hypothesis,** a specific prediction to be examined.
3. *Test the hypothesis.* Design and conduct research to gather **empirical evidence** (data).
4. *Analyze the evidence gathered in the research.* Conclude whether the hypothesis is supported or not.
5. *Report the results.* Share the data, conclusions, and alternative explanations.

replication The repetition of a study, using different participants.

As you see, developmental scientists begin with curiosity and then seek the facts, drawing conclusions after careful research. **Replication**—repeating the procedures and methods of a study with different participants—may be a sixth and crucial step (Jasny et al., 2011).

Scientists study the reported procedures and results of other scientists. They read publications, attend conferences, send emails, and collaborate with others far from home. Conclusions are revised, refined, and confirmed after replication. Scientists still sometimes stray, drawing conclusions too quickly, misinterpreting data, or ignoring issues, as discussed at the end of this chapter. Nonetheless, testing hypotheses by gathering empirical data is the foundation of our study.

Process, Not Proof Built into the scientific method—in questions, hypotheses, tests, and replication—is a passion for possibilities, especially unexpected ones.

1. Curiosity

2. Hypothesis

3. Test

4. Analyze data and draw conclusions

5. Report the results

The Nature–Nurture Controversy

An easy example of the need for science concerns a great puzzle of development, the *nature–nurture debate*. **Nature** refers to the influence of the genes that people inherit. **Nurture** refers to environmental influences, beginning with the health and diet of the embryo's mother and continuing lifelong, including family, school, community, and societal experiences.

The nature–nurture debate has many other names, among them *heredity–environment* and *maturation–learning*. Under whatever name, the basic question is: *How much of any characteristic, behavior, or emotion is the result of genes, and how much is the result of experience?*

Some people believe that most traits are inborn, that children are innately good ("an innocent child") or bad ("beat the devil out of them"). Others stress nurture, crediting or blaming parents, or neighborhood, or drugs, or even food, when someone is good or bad, a hero or a criminal.

Neither belief is accurate. The question is "how much," not "which," because *both* genes and the environment affect every characteristic: Nature always affects nurture, and then nurture affects nature. Even "how much" is misleading, if it implies that nature and nurture each contribute a fixed amount (Eagly & Wood, 2013; Lock, 2013).

A further complication is that the impact of a beating, or a beer, or any other experience might be magnified because of a particular set of genes. The opposite is true as well: Something in the environment—perhaps a poison, perhaps a blessing—might stop a gene before it could be expressed. Thus each aspect of nature and nurture depends on other aspects of nature and nurture, in ways that vary for each person.

The most obvious examples occur when a virus or a drug distorts the body or brain of a child. Less obvious, but probably more important, are protective influences, such as special nurturance that helps a person avoid learning disabilities or self-destructive impulses.

A complex nature–nurture interaction is apparent for every moment of our lives. For example, I fainted at Caleb's birth because of at least ten factors (blood sugar, exhaustion, exertion, hormones, gender, age, family history, memory, relief, joy), each influenced by both nature and nurture. The combination, and no single factor, landed me on the floor.

nature A general term for the traits, capacities, and limitations that each individual inherits genetically from his or her parents at the moment of conception.

nurture A general term for all the environmental influences that affect development after an individual is conceived.

>> **Answer to Observation Quiz** (from page 3): Dozens of answers are correct. From the photo, you can see at least two universals—the family connection between grandmother and grandchild, and the relatively large head of the newborn. You can also see two specifics: the clothes we are both wearing (Caleb's little blue cap), and the setting—an urban hospital (note objects on the window sill, the view) not a humble home.

SUMMING UP

The science of human development seeks to understand how and why each individual is affected by the changes that occur over the life span. Every science, including this one, follows five steps: question, hypothesis, empirical research, conclusions based on data, and publication. A sixth step—replication—confirms, refutes, or refines conclusions. Although no human is completely objective, the scientific method is designed to avoid unexamined opinions and wishful thinking.

Both genes and environment affect every human characteristic in an explosive interaction of nature and nurture. No human behavior—whether wonderful or horrific—results from genes or experiences alone. ■

>> The Life-Span Perspective

The **life-span perspective** (Fingerman et al., 2011; Lerner et al., 2010) takes into account all phases of life and has led to a new understanding of human development as multidirectional, multicontextual, multicultural, multidisciplinary, and plastic (Baltes et al., 2006; Haase et al., 2013; Staudinger & Lindenberger, 2003).

life-span perspective An approach to the study of human development that takes into account all phases of life, not just childhood or adulthood.

TABLE 1.1 Age Ranges for Different Stages of Development

Infancy	0 to 2 years
Early childhood	2 to 6 years
Middle childhood	6 to 11 years
Adolescence	11 to 18 years
Emerging adulthood	18 to 25 years
Adulthood	25 to 65 years
Late adulthood	65 years and older

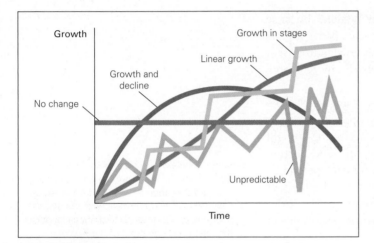

FIGURE 1.2

Patterns of Developmental Growth Many patterns of developmental growth have been discovered by careful research. Although linear (or near-linear) progress seems most common, scientists now find that almost no aspect of human change follows the linear pattern exactly.

critical period A time when a particular type of developmental growth (in body or behavior) must happen if it is ever going to happen.

Age periods (see Table 1.1) are only a rough guide, a truism particularly apparent in adulthood. For example, emerging adulthood, defined as ages 18 to 25, is not a period accepted by all scholars. Many prefer dividing adulthood into *early adulthood* for ages 20 to 40, *middle adulthood* for ages 40 to 65, and *late adulthood*, said to begin at age 60, 65, or even 70. As emphasized time and again, birthdays are an imperfect measure of aging.

As you will learn, developmentalists are reluctant to specify chronological ages for any period of development, since time is only one of many variables that affect each person. However, age is a crucial variable, and development can be segmented into periods of study. Approximate ages for each period are given here.

Development Is Multidirectional

Multiple changes, in every direction, characterize the life span. Traits appear and disappear, with increases, decreases, and zigzags (see Figure 1.2). An earlier idea—that all development advances until about age 18, steadies, and then declines—has been refuted by life-span research.

Sometimes *discontinuity* is evident: Change can occur rapidly and dramatically, as when caterpillars become butterflies. Sometimes *continuity* is found: Growth can be gradual, as when redwoods add rings over hundreds of years. Some characteristics do not seem to change at all: Almost every zygote is XY or XX, male or female, and chromosomal sex is lifelong.

Humans experience simple growth, radical transformation, improvement, and decline as well as stability, stages, and continuity—day to day, year to year, and generation to generation. Not only do the pace and direction of change vary, but each characteristic follows its own trajectory: Losses in some abilities occur simultaneously with gains in others. For example, babies lose some ability to distinguish sounds from other languages when they begin talking in whatever language they hear, and when adults quit their paid job they often become more creative.

The timing of losses and gains, impairments or improvements varies as well. Some changes are sudden and profound because of a **critical period,** which is either when something *must* occur to ensure normal development or the only time when an abnormality might occur. For instance, the human embryo grows arms and legs, hands and feet, fingers and toes, each over a critical period between 28 and 54 days after conception. After that, it is too late: Unlike some insects, humans never grow replacement limbs.

We know this fact because of a tragic episode. Between 1957 and 1961, thousands of newly pregnant women in 30 nations took *thalidomide*, an antinausea drug. This change in nurture (via the mother's bloodstream) disrupted nature (the embryo's genetic program). If an expectant woman ingested thalidomide during the 26 days of the critical period for limb formation, her newborn's arms or legs were malformed or absent (Moore & Persaud, 2007). Whether all four limbs, or just arms, or only hands were missing depended on exactly when the drug was taken. If thalidomide was ingested only before day

28 or after day 54, no harm occurred since the critical period had ended.

Life has few such dramatic critical periods. Often, however, a particular development occurs more easily—but not exclusively—at a certain time. That is called a **sensitive period.**

An example is learning language. If children do not communicate in their first language between ages 1 and 3, they might do so later (hence, these years are not critical), but their grammar is impaired (hence, these years are sensitive).

Similarly, childhood is a sensitive period for learning to pronounce a second or third language with a native accent. Many adults master a new language, but strangers still ask, "Where are you from?" Native speakers can detect an accent that reveals that the first language was something else.

Often in development, individual exceptions to general patterns occur. Sweeping generalizations, like those in the language example, do not hold true in every case. Accent-free speech *usually* must be learned before puberty, but exceptional nature and nurture (a person naturally adept at hearing and then immersed in a new language) can result in flawless second-language pronunciation (Birdsong, 2006; Munoz & Singleton, 2011).

Development Is Multicontextual

The second insight we garner from the life-span perspective is that development is multicontextual. Those many contexts are physical (climate, noise, population density, etc.), family (marital status, family size, members' age and sex), community (urban, suburban, or rural, multiethnic or not, etc.), and so on, with each context affecting everyone.

Ecological Systems

A leading developmentalist, Urie Bronfenbrenner (1917–2005), led the way to considering contexts. Just as a naturalist studying an organism examines the ecology (the relationship between the organism and its environment) of a tiger, or tree, or trout, Bronfenbrenner recommended that developmentalists take an **ecological-systems approach** (Bronfenbrenner & Morris, 2006) to understanding humans.

The ecological-systems approach recognizes three nested levels that surround individuals and affect them (see Figure 1.3). Most obvious are *microsystems*—each person's immediate surroundings, such as family and peer group. Also important are *exosystems* (local institutions such as school and church) and *macrosystems* (the larger social setting, including cultural values, economic policies, and political processes).

Two more systems are related to these three. One is the *chronosystem* (literally, "time system"), which is the historical context. The other is the *mesosystem*, consisting of the connections among the other systems.

Your Child's Teacher This 19-year-old attending Oang Ninh College in Hanoi, Vietnam, is studying to be a teacher. Emerging adulthood worldwide is a period of exploration and change: He may change professions and locations in the next six years.

sensitive period A time when a certain type of development is most likely to happen or happens most easily, although it may still happen later with more difficulty. For example, early childhood is considered a sensitive period for language learning.

ecological-systems approach The view that in the study of human development, the person should be considered in all the contexts and interactions that constitute a life. (Later renamed *bioecological theory*.)

Cat, Duck, or Dog? Nine-year-old Sun Minyi must circle the correct animal and then write "cat" in his workbook—not hard at his age. Then why is he listening so intently? He is learning English near Shanghai. His first language is Chinese.

Observation Quiz (see answer, page 8): What factors suggest this is not a U.S. classroom?

FIGURE 1.3

The Ecological Model According to developmental researcher Urie Bronfenbrenner, each person is significantly affected by interactions among a number of overlapping systems, which provide the context of development. *Microsystems*—family, peer groups, classroom, neighborhood, house of worship—intimately and immediately shape human development. Surrounding and supporting the microsystems are the *exosystems*, which include all the external networks, such as community structures and local educational, medical, employment, and communications systems, that influence the microsystems. Influencing both of these systems is the *macrosystem*, which includes cultural patterns, political philosophies, economic policies, and social conditions. *Mesosystems* refer to interactions among systems, as when parents and teachers coordinate to educate a child. Bronfenbrenner added a fifth system, the *chronosystem*, to emphasize the importance of historical time.

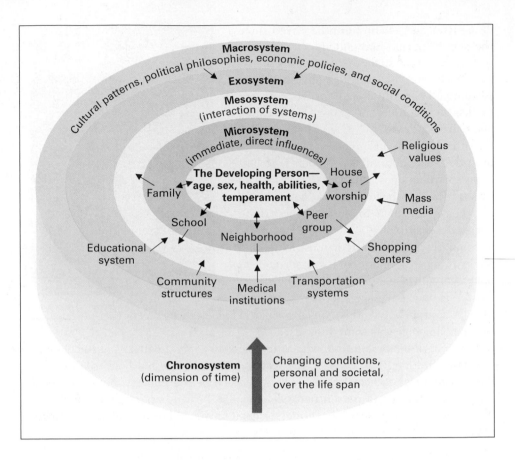

>> Answer to Observation Quiz
(from page 7): Few U.S. third-grade classes have desks set up in rows, and most U.S. teachers expect children to talk as much as listen—especially when learning a new language. In addition, class size is larger in China (an average of 37 students), which seems likely here, given the layout shown.

cohort A group defined by the shared age of its members, who, because they were born at about the same time, move through life together, experiencing the same historical events and cultural shifts.

Bronfenbrenner believed that people need to be studied in their natural contexts. He looked at children playing, or mothers putting babies to sleep, or nurses in hospitals—never asking people to come to a scientist's laboratory for a contrived experiment. Toward the end of his life, Bronfrenbrenner renamed his approach *bioecological theory* to highlight the role of biology, recognizing that systems within the body (e.g., the sexual-reproductive system, the cardiovascular system) affect the external systems (Bronfenbrenner & Morris, 2006).

Bronfenbrenner's systems perspective remains useful, as is evident in a recent discussion of climate change (Boon et al., 2012). Two contexts—the historical and the socioeconomic—are so basic to understanding people throughout the life span that we explain them now.

The Historical Context

All persons born within a few years of one another are called a **cohort**, a group defined by its members' shared age. Cohorts travel through life together, affected by the interaction of their chronological age with the values, events, technologies, and culture of the era. From the moment of birth, when parents decide the name of their baby, historical context affects what may seem like a private and personal choice (see Table 1.2).

In another life-span example, the years 18 to 25 constitute a sensitive period for consolidation of political values. Therefore, experiences and circumstances during emerging adulthood have a lifelong impact.

Consider attitudes about same-sex marriage. A few decades ago, many homosexual people were "in the closet." As a result, young heterosexual adults were totally unaware that any gay or lesbian person might want to be married, and the political leadership was decidedly homophobic.

The political climate has changed dramatically in recent years, as of February 2014, 17 U.S. states allow same-sex marriages. The present generation is more approving than the generation of a decade ago. Those who were young adults 60 years ago mostly disapprove (only 31 percent favor same-sex marriage) compared to young adults now (70 percent are in favor). As you can see from Figure 1.4, recent trends affect every cohort, but emerging adults are much more likely to be influenced by current trends than any older cohort, even the one immediately preceding them.

Sometimes demographic characteristics rather than current events reflect the historical context. For example, the baby boomers, those born between 1946 and 1964, are experiencing quite a different late adulthood than did earlier cohorts because there are so many of them. Their numbers have already led to an increase in the age at which a person qualifies for Social Security benefits in the United States; similar changes have been made to social programs in many other nations.

By contrast, the current cohort of young adults is relatively small, and their birth rate is low. That means they will have fewer children and grandchildren when they are older—perhaps a blessing, perhaps not, but certainly this trend represents a cohort change.

TABLE 1.2	Popular First Names Since 1932
Girls:	
2012: Sophia, Emma, Isabella, Olivia, Ava	
1992: Ashley, Jessica, Amanda, Brittany, Sarah	
1972: Jennifer, Michelle, Lisa, Kimberly, Amy	
1952: Linda, Mary, Patricia, Deborah, Susan	
1932: Mary, Betty, Barbara, Dorothy, Joan	
Boys:	
2012: Jacob, Mason, Ethan, Noah, William	
1992: Michael, Christopher, Matthew, Joshua, Andrew	
1972: Michael, Christopher, James, David, John	
1952: James, Robert, John, Michael, David	
1932: Robert, James, John, William, Richard	

Source: U.S. Social Security Administration

Growing Support for Same-Sex Marriage

Allowing gays and lesbians to marry legally

All Adults

58 — Oppose — 49
33 — Favor — 44

2003 — 2013

% Favor by Generation

Generation

70 — Millennial born after 1980
51 — 49 — Gen X 1965–1980
41 — 38 — Baby Boom 1946–1964
33 — 31 — Silent 1928–1945
17

2003 — 2013

PEW RESEARCH CENTER March 13–17, 2013.
2003–2012 figures based on all surveys conducted in each year.

Source: PEW RESEARCH CENTER, 2013, P.1.

© WILLIAM HAEFELI/THE NEW YORKER COLLECTION/www.cartoonbank.com

"Hey! Elbows off the table."

Twenty-First-Century Manners If he obeyed his father but kept texting, would Emily Post be pleased?

FIGURE 1.4

Same-Sex Marriage and Different Ages Support for making same-sex marriage legal shows both cohort and period effects. If the data were only from the population of all ages, not quite half are in favor. But cohort analysis reveals a generational shift, with dramatic trends among the young, much less among the rest.

Same Situation, Far Apart: Times Are Changing Elders in the twenty-first century live decades longer than did earlier cohorts, affording them opportunities that were previously unavailable. In 1950 in Peru, average life expectancy was 45. Now in Lima, newlyweds Carmen Mercado, age 74, and Jorge de la Cruz, age 74 (left), can expect a decade of wedded bliss. While they were courting, Hazel Soares (right) was studying, culminating in her graduation from Mills College in Oakland, California, at age 94.

socioeconomic status (SES) A person's position in society as determined by income, wealth, occupation, education, and place of residence. (Sometimes called *social class*.)

The Socioeconomic Context

Another pervasive context is **socioeconomic status,** abbreviated **SES.** Sometimes SES is called *social class* (as in *middle class* or *working class*). SES reflects income and much more, including occupation, education, and neighborhood.

Consider U.S. families that are composed of an infant, an unemployed mother, and a father who earns $18,000 a year. Their SES would be low if the wage earner were an illiterate dishwasher living in an urban slum, but it would be much higher if the wage earner were a postdoctoral student living on campus and teaching part-time.

As this example makes clear, income alone does not define SES, especially when the historical context is considered. Moreover, even poverty is less clearly defined than some people think. The traditional poverty level in the United States is set only by food costs and family size, although food basics have become much cheaper and housing more expensive. The traditional standards have not changed,

No Fresh Fruit? Many religious groups provide food for low-income families. Lisa Arsa is fortunate to have found this Seventh-day Adventist food pantry for herself and her son, Isaac. Unfortunately, the food donated to low-income families is usually high in salt, sugar, and fat—among the reasons why the U.S. rates of obesity and diabetes rise as income falls.

so a family of three is below the 2013 poverty threshold if their household income is under $19,530. A revision of the poverty definition is under way and takes into account housing, medical care, and various subsidies (Short, 2011).

Developmentalists note that policies and practices regarding poverty vary from nation to nation, which affects the economic context and thus the developmental path for people in each nation. For example, in the United States the gap between rich and poor has increased in the past two decades. This has led to a larger disparity in life expectancy between the rich and the poor: Richer people are living longer than they did, but poorer people are dying at about the same age as they did 20 years ago.

The socioeconomic context is also affected by the national and historical contexts, including the proportion of the population in each cohort, as Visualizing Development (p. 12) explains.

The size of the disparity in income and education within a nation varies substantially around the world, and many conditions—health, family size, and housing among them—are affected as a result. Thus, the socioeconomic context is more critical in some jurisdictions than in others, as when health care is provided to everyone equally, or is paid privately. Examples appear in almost every later chapter. Suffice it to emphasize now that cohort, nation, and SES always affect each person's development.

Development Is Multicultural

In order to learn about "all kinds of people, everywhere, at every age," it is necessary to study people of many cultures. For social scientists, **culture** is "the system of shared beliefs, conventions, norms, behaviors, expectations and symbolic representations that persist over time and prescribe social rules of conduct" (Bornstein et al., 2011, p. 30).

Thus, culture is far more than food or clothes; it is a set of ideas, beliefs, and patterns. Culture is a powerful **social construction,** that is, a concept created, or *constructed*, by a society. Social constructions affect how people think and act—what they value, ignore, and punish.

culture A system of shared beliefs, norms, behaviors, and expectations that persist over time and prescribe social behavior and assumptions.

social construction An idea that is based on shared perceptions, not on objective reality. Many age-related terms, such as *childhood*, *adolescence*, *yuppie*, and *senior citizen*, are social constructions.

KUTTIG/RF-KIDS/ALAMY

Family Pride Grandpa Charilaos is proud of his tavern in northern Greece (central Macedonia), but he is even prouder of his talented grandchildren, including Maria Soni (shown here). Note her expert fingering. Her father and mother also play instruments— is that nature or nurture, genes or culture?

Socioeconomic Status and Human Development

Globally and locally, socioeconomic status is one of the most accurate predictors of health. Poverty rates and level of education almost always correlate with health indicators (such as mortality) in just about every phase of the life span. Less developed countries typically have higher birth rates, but they also have much higher rates of mortality in the first year of life. Simply, and sadly, that means that more babies are born, and more die, in impoverished nations.

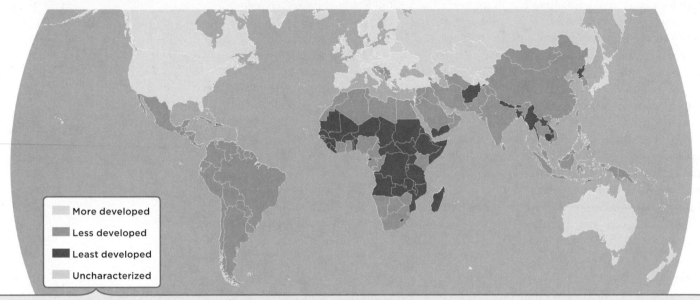

- More developed
- Less developed
- Least developed
- Uncharacterized

GLOBAL TRENDS

The United Nations categorizes nations as more, less, or least developed, based on economic growth. As indicated here, a nation's economic status correlates closely with birth rate, which itself correlates with levels of female literacy.

This is a rough guide. For example, fewer newborns die in their first year in the United States than in nations with high poverty rates, but the U.S. infant mortality rate is higher than 33 other nations, some (such as Portugal and Greece) with lower average income.

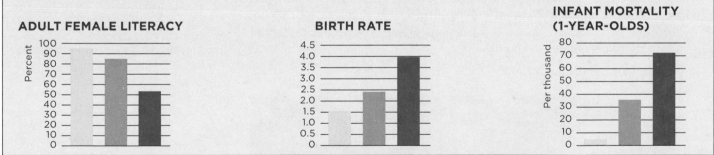

ADULT FEMALE LITERACY

BIRTH RATE

INFANT MORTALITY (1-YEAR-OLDS)

INFANT MORTALITY IN THE UNITED STATES

About two-thirds of infant deaths in the United States occur within the first 28 days of life. The single biggest cause of infant death in the United States is preterm birth.

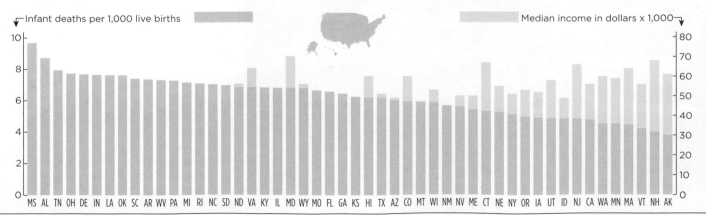

⌐Infant deaths per 1,000 live births   Median income in dollars x 1,000⌐

Source: UNITED NATIONS DEPARTMENT OF ECONOMIC AND SOCIAL AFFAIRS, 2012.

Sources: U.S. CENSUS BUREAU, CURRENT POPULATION SURVEY, 2011, 2012, AND 2013 ANNUAL SOCIAL AND ECONOMIC SUPPLEMENTS.

CDC NATIONAL VITAL STATISTICS SYSTEM, 2010 INFANT MORTALITY RATES, BY STATE, 2010.

Each family, community, and college has a particular culture, and for any one person these cultures may clash. For example, decades ago my friend from a small rural town arrived for her first college class wearing her Sunday best: a matching striped skirt, jacket, and blouse. She looked at her classmates, realized a culture clash, and went directly to a used-clothing store to buy jeans and a T-shirt. On the next day she looked like the other students, but she still was shocked by their assumptions about authority, sex, religion, and much else.

Although it is important to take a multicultural perspective, be careful. Sometime people overgeneralize, as when they speak of Asian culture or Hispanic culture. That way of generalizing invites stereotyping, as if there were no cultural differences between people from Korea and Japan, for instance, or those from Mexico and Guatemala. An additional complication is that individuals within every culture sometimes rebel against their culture's expected "beliefs, conventions, norms, behaviors."

Thus the words *culture* and *multicultural* need to be used carefully, especially when they are applied to individuals, including oneself. Cultural pride may foster happiness, but as now explained, it may harm both the person and the community (Morrison et al., 2011; Reeskens & Wright, 2011).

Deficit or Just Difference?

Humans tend to believe that they, their nation, and their culture are better than others. This way of thinking has benefits: Generally, people who like themselves are happier, prouder, and more willing to help strangers. However, that belief becomes destructive if it reduces respect and appreciation for people from another group. [**Lifespan Link:** The major discussion of ethnic identity is in Chapter 19.]

Developmentalists recognize the **difference-equals-deficit error,** which is the assumption that people unlike us (different) are inferior (deficit). Sadly, when humans realize that their way of thinking and acting is not universal, they tend to believe that those who think or act differently are to be pitied, feared, or encouraged to change.

The difference-equals-deficit error is one reason a careful multicultural approach is necessary. Being stuck in only one cultural perspective is too narrow, but it is just as narrow to assume that another culture is wrong and inferior—or the opposite, right and superior. Assumptions are dangerous, especially when they arise from culture.

A multicultural perspective allows us to see how different cultures view the same phenomenon—either as an asset or as a deficit (Marschark & Spencer, 2003). For example, cultures that discourage dissent also foster social harmony. Is harmony worth the harm of punishing rebels? The opposite is also true—cultures that encourage dissent also value independence. Whether you personally are inclined to appreciate or protest particular values, assuming that dissent is valuable or destructive, remember that the opposite reaction has merit.

The difference-equals-deficit understanding of language development goes further: In some cultures, children who talk too much are considered disrespectful. Consider the experience of one of my students:

> My mom was outside on the porch talking to my aunt. I decided to go
> outside; I guess I was being nosey. While they were talking I jumped into their
> conversation which was very rude. When I realized what I did it was too late.
> My mother slapped me in my face so hard that it took a couple of seconds to
> feel my face again.
>
> *[C., personal communication]*

Notice how much this student continues to reflect the norms of her culture, as she labels her own behavior "nosey" and "very rude." She later wrote that she expects

difference-equals-deficit error The mistaken belief that a deviation from some norm is necessarily inferior to behavior or characteristics that meet the standard.

children to be seen but not heard, and that her son makes her "very angry" when he interrupts. Might the children whose North American parents encouraged them to be talkative become misfits if they live in some other cultures?

Learning Within a Culture

Russian developmentalist Lev Vygotsky (1896–1934) was a leader in describing how cultures vary in the education they provide (Wertsch & Tulviste, 2005). He noticed that adults from the varied cultures of the Soviet Union (Asians and Europeans, representing many religions) taught their children whatever beliefs and habits they might need as adults, but specifics differed markedly. [**Lifespan Link:** A major discussion of sociocultural theory appears in Chapter 2, page 52, and a discussion of Vygotsky appears in Chapter 9.]

Vygotsky believed that *guided participation* is a universal process used by mentors to teach cultural knowledge, skills, and habits. Guided participation can occur through school instruction, but more often it happens informally, through "mutual involvement in several widespread cultural practices with great importance for learning: narratives, routines, and play" (Rogoff, 2003, p. 285). Each culture guides toward different goals.

Inspired by Vygotsky, Barbara Rogoff studied cultural transmission in Guatemalan, Mexican, Chinese, and U.S. families. Adults always guide children, but clashes occur if parents and teachers are of different cultures. In one such misunderstanding, a teacher praised a student to his mother:

> **Teacher:** Your son is talking well in class. He is speaking up a lot.
> **Mother:** I am sorry.
>
> *[Rogoff, 2003, p. 311; from Crago, 1992, p. 496]*

Of course, this does not mean that either talking or listening to children is harmful: quite the opposite. However, do not assume that any particular cultural practice is best; difference in not always deficit.

Ethnic and Racial Groups

The terms *culture, ethnicity,* and *race* are confusing, as they often overlap (see Figure 1.5). Members of an **ethnic group** almost always share ancestral heritage and often have the same national origin, religion, and language (Whitfield & McClearn, 2005). Consequently, ethnic groups often share a culture, but not necessarily. People may share ethnicity but differ culturally (e.g., people of Irish descent in Ireland, Australia, and North America), and people of one culture may come from several ethnic groups (consider British culture).

Ethnicity is a social construction, a product of the social context, not biology. It is nurture, not nature. For example, African-born people who live in North America typically consider themselves African, but African-born people living in Africa identify with a more specific ethnic group. Many Americans are puzzled by civil wars (e.g., in Syria, or Sri Lanka, or Kenya) because people of the same ethnicity seem to be bitter enemies, but those opposing sides see many ethnic differences between them.

DR. JAMES WERTSCH

Affection for Children Vygotsky lived in Russia from 1896 to 1934, when war, starvation, and revolution led to the deaths of millions. Throughout this turmoil, Vygotsky focused on learning. His love of children is suggested by this portrait: He and his daughter have their arms around each other.

ethnic group People whose ancestors were born in the same region and who often share a language, culture, and religion.

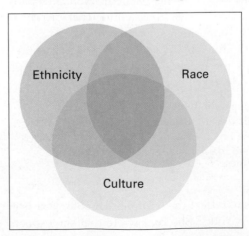

Ethnicity

Race

Culture

FIGURE 1.5

Overlap, but How Much? Ethnicity, culture, and race are three distinct concepts, but they often—though not always—overlap.

Ethnic identity flourishes when co-ethnics are nearby and outsiders emphasize differences. This is particularly obvious when racial identity is connected to ethnicity. Race is a social construction—and a misleading one. There are good reasons to abandon the term and good reasons to keep it, as the following explains.

> **race** A group of people who are regarded by themselves or by others as distinct from other groups on the basis of physical appearance, typically skin color. Social scientists think race is a misleading concept, as biological differences are not signified by outward appearance.

OPPOSING PERSPECTIVES *

Using the Word *Race*

The term **race** categorizes people on the basis of physical differences, particularly outward appearance. Historically, most North Americans believed that race was an inborn biological characteristic. Races were categorized by color: white, black, red, and yellow (Coon, 1962).

It is obvious now, but was not a few decades ago, that no one's skin is really white (like this page) or black (like these letters) or red or yellow. Social scientists are convinced that race is a social construction and that color terms exaggerate minor differences.

Genetic analysis confirms that the concept of "race" is based on a falsehood. Although most genes are identical in every human, those genetic differences that distinguish one person from another are poorly indexed by appearance (Race, Ethnicity, and Genetics Working Group of the American Society of Human Genetics, 2005). Skin color is particularly misleading because dark-skinned people with African ancestors have "high levels of genetic population diversity" (Tishkoff et al., 2009, p. 1035) and because dark-skinned people whose ancestors were not African share neither culture nor ethnicity with Africans.

Race is more than a flawed concept; it is a destructive one. It is used to justify racism, which over the years has been expressed in myriad laws and customs, with slavery, lynching, and segregation directly connected to the idea that race was real. Racism continues today in less obvious ways (some of which are highlighted later in this book), undercutting the goal of our science of human development—to help all of us fulfill our potential.

Since race is a social construction that leads to racism, some social scientists believe that the term should be abandoned. Cultural differences influence development, but racial differences do not. A study of census categories used by 141 nations found that only 15 percent use the word *race* on their census forms (Morning, 2008). Only in the United States does the census still separate race and ethnicity, stating, for example, that Hispanics "may be of any race."

Cognitively, labels encourage stereotyping (Kelly et al., 2010). As one scholar explains:

> The United States' unique conceptual distinction between race and ethnicity may unwittingly support the longstanding belief that race reflects biological difference and ethnicity stems from cultural difference. In this scheme, ethnicity is socially produced but race is an immutable fact of nature. Consequently, walling off race from ethnicity on the census may reinforce essentialist interpretations of race and preclude understanding of the ways in which racial categories are also socially constructed. [*Morning, 2008, p. 255*]

BURKE/TRIOLO PRODUCTIONS/GETTY IMAGES

Shared Laughter Humor is cultural specific: a funny comment in one community may be offensive in another. These two men may seem different in ethnicity, but they share cohort and nation, so they both are laughing.

Observation Quiz Do you see any differences between these two people that might be cultural? (see answer, page 16)

*Every page of this text includes information that requires critical thinking and evaluation. In addition, in almost every chapter you will find an Opposing Perspectives feature in which an issue that has compelling opposite perspectives is highlighted.

All of this suggests that, to avoid racism, we should abandon the word *race*.

But there is an opposite perspective, and it is a powerful one (Bliss, 2012). In a nation with a history of racial discrimination, reversing that history may require recognizing race, allowing those who have been harmed to be proud of their identity. The fact that race is a social construction, not a biological distinction, does not make it meaningless. Particularly in adolescence, people who are proud of their racial identity are likely to achieve academically, resist drug addiction, and feel better about themselves (Crosnoe & Johnson, 2010).

Furthermore, documenting ongoing racism requires data to show that many medical, educational, and economic conditions—from low birthweight to college graduation, from family income to health insurance—reflect racial disparities. To overcome such disparities, race must first be recognized.

Consider the results of one scientific study. An anonymous survey of 4,915 employees at several corporations found that when most workers endorsed color-blind sentiments, such as "Employees should downplay their racial and ethnic differences," Black employees were less proud and less engaged in their work. By contrast, when workers believed that "policies should support ethnic and racial diversity," Black employees were more committed to their jobs. According to the authors of this study, the entire organization suffered when color blindness was the norm (Plaut et al., 2009).

Similar conclusions have been reached by many social scientists, who find that to be color-blind is to be subtly racist (e.g., sociologists Marvasti & McKinney, 2011; anthropologist McCabe, 2011). Two political scientists studying the criminal justice system found that people who claim to be color-blind display "an extraordinary level of naivete" (Peffley & Hurwitz, 2010, p. 113).

As you see, strong arguments support both sides of this issue. In this book, we refer to ethnicity more often than to race, but we speak of race or color when the original data are reported that way. Appendix A shows changes in the proportions of people of various races in the United States. Would pride or depression increase if data were reported only by national origin? Racial categories may crumble someday, but not yet.

>> Answer to Observation Quiz (from page 15): One man wears a cap, the other doesn't; one laughs with wide-open mouth, only one has a moustache. Such difference could be cultural, or could be only personal preference.

Development Is Multidisciplinary

Scientists usually specialize, studying one phenomenon in one species at one age. Such specialization provides a deeper understanding of the rhythms of vocalization among 3-month-old infants, for instance, or of the effects of alcohol on adolescent mice, or of widows' relationships with their grown children. (The results of these studies inform later sections of this book.)

However, human development requires insights and information from many scientists, past and present, in many disciplines. Our understanding of every topic benefits from multidisciplinary research; scientists hesitate to apply general conclusions about human life until they are substantiated by several disciplines, each with specialization.

Genetics and Epigenetics

The need for multidisciplinary research is obvious when considering genetic analysis. When the Human Genome was first mapped, some thought that humans became whatever their genes destined them to be—heroes, killers, or ordinary people. However, multidisciplinary research quickly showed otherwise. Yes, genes affect every aspect of behavior. But even identical twins, with identical genes, differ biologically, psychologically, and socially (Poulsen et al., 2007). The reasons are many, including how they are positioned in the womb and non-DNA influences in utero, both of which affect birthweight and birth order, and dozens of other epigenetic influences throughout life (Carey, 2012). [**Lifespan Link:** Mapping of the human genome is discussed in Chapter 3, page 78.]

We now know that all important human characteristics are **epigenetic.** The prefix *epi-* means "with," "around," "above," "after," "beyond," or "near." The word *epigenetic,* therefore, refers to the factors that surround the genes, affecting genetic expression.

epigenetic Referring to the effects of environmental forces on the expression of an individual's, or a species', genetic inheritance.

"Epi" influences begin soon after conception, as bio-chemical elements silence certain genes, in a process called *methylation*. Methylation changes over the life span, affecting genetic expression (Kendler et al., 2011). Some epigenetic influences (e.g., injury, temperature extremes, drug abuse, and crowding) impede development, while others (e.g., nourishing food, loving care, and active play) facilitate it. Research far beyond the discipline of genetics, or even the broader discipline of biology, is needed to discover all the epigenetic effects. [**Lifespan Link:** The major discussion of epigenetics is in Chapter 3, page 77.]

The inevitable epigenetic interaction between genes and the environment (nature and nurture) is illustrated in Figure 1.6. That simple diagram, with arrows going up and down over time, has been redrawn and reprinted many times to emphasize that genes interact with environmental conditions again and again in each person's life (G. Gottlieb, 2010).

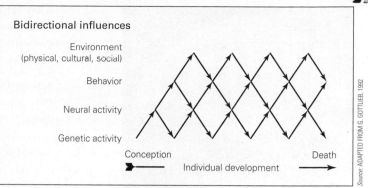

FIGURE 1.6

An Epigenetic Model of Development
Notice that there are as many arrows going down as there are going up, at all levels. Although development begins with genes at conception, it requires that all four factors interact.

Multidisciplinary Research on Depression

Consider severe depression, the cause of 65 million lost years of productive life every year worldwide (P. Y. Collins et al., 2011). Depression is partly genetic and neurological—certain inherited brain chemicals make people sad and uninterested in life. This condition is caused not only by neurotransmitters such as dopamine and serotonin but also by growth factors such as GDNF (glial cell line–derived neurotrophic factor), the product of one gene that makes neurons grow or stagnate (Uchida et al., 2011).

Depression is also developmental: It increases and decreases at certain ages (Kapornai & Vetró, 2008; Kendler et al., 2011). For instance, the incidence of clinical depression suddenly rises in early adolescence, particularly among girls (Maughan et al., 2013).

Child-rearing practices have an impact as well. Depressed mothers smile and talk to their infants less than other mothers; in turn, the infants become less active and verbal. A researcher who studies mother–infant interaction told nondepressed mothers to do the following with their 3-month-olds for only three minutes:

> to speak in a monotone, to keep their faces flat and expressionless, to slouch back in their chair, to minimize touch, and to imagine that they felt tired and blue. The infants . . . reacted strongly, . . . cycling among states of wariness, disengagement, and distress with brief bids to their mother to resume her normal affective state. Importantly, the infants continued to be distressed and disengaged . . . after the mothers resumed normal interactive behavior.

> [*Tronick, 2007, p. 306*]

Thus, even three minutes of mock-depressive behavior makes infants act depressed. If a mother is actually depressed, her baby will be, too.

When all the research is considered, whether a particular person is depressed depends on dozens of factors, each of which is the focus of a particular academic discipline. To mitigate depression, then, and to prevent those 65 million productive years from being lost to humanity each year, dozens of factors must be understood.

For adults as well as children, many genetic, biochemical, and neurological factors distinguish depressed individuals from other adults (Kanner, 2012; Poldrack et al., 2008), yet moods and behaviors are also powerfully affected by experience

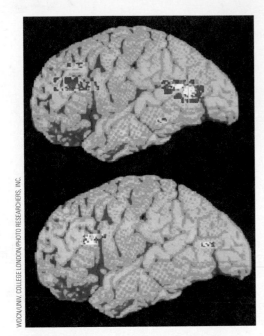

WDCN/UNIV. COLLEGE LONDON/PHOTO RESEARCHERS, INC.

Red Means Stop At top, the red areas on this PET scan show abnormally low metabolic activity and blood flow in a depressed person's brain, in contrast to the normal brain at bottom.

and cognition (Huberty, 2012; van Praag et al., 2012). Again, nature is affected by nurture. A person with depressing relationships and experiences is likely to develop the brain patterns characteristic of depression, and vice versa.

Scientists have found the following dozen factors linked to depression.

- Low serotonin in the brain, as a result of an allele of the gene for serotonin transport (*neuroscience*)
- Caregiver depression in childhood, especially postpartum depression with exclusive mother-care (*psychopathology*)
- Low exposure to daylight, as in winter in higher latitudes, causing low mood called SAD (Seasonal Affective Disorder) (*biology*)
- Malnutrition, particularly low hemoglobin (*nutrition*)
- Lack of close friends, especially when entering a new culture, school, or neighborhood (*anthropology*)
- Diseases, including Parkinson's and AIDS, and drugs to treat diseases (*medicine*)
- Disruptive social interaction, such as breakup with a romantic partner (*sociology*)
- Death of mother before age 10 (*psychology*)
- Absence of father during childhood—especially because of divorce, less so because of death or migration (*family studies*)
- Siblings with eating disorders (*genetics*)
- Poverty, especially in nations with large disparity between rich and poor (*economics*)
- Low cognitive skills, including illiteracy and lack of exposure to stimulating ideas (*education*)

As you see, discovery of each of these factors arises from research in a different discipline (italicized above in parentheses). This list is only partial; dozens more factors have been suggested as causing depression, with all scholars recognizing that some people are affected by some factors more than others. Remember that scientists learn from each other, which means that disciplines overlap. Lack of close confidants, for instance, is noted not only by anthropologists, but also by sociologists and psychologists. Furthermore, culture, climate, and politics all have an effect on depression, although the particulars are debatable. For example, consider the national differences shown in Figure 1.7. At least six explanations have been offered for the disparity between one nation and another—some genetic, some cultural, and some a combination of the two.

A multidisciplinary approach is crucial in alleviating every impairment, not only depression: Currently in the United States, a combination of cognitive therapy, family therapy, and antidepressant medication is often more effective than any one of these three alone. International research finds that depression is quite high in some populations in some places (e.g., half the women in Pakistan) and low in others (e.g., about 3 percent of the nonsmoking men in Denmark), again for a combination of reasons (Flensborg-Madsen et al., 2011; Husain et al., 2011; von dem Knesebeck et al., 2011).

No single factor determines any outcome, and no single discipline portrays the entire story of human life. Indeed, some people who experience one, and only one, of the dozen factors listed above are not depressed at all.

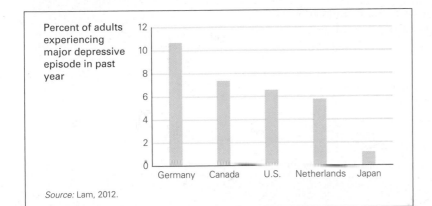

Percent of adults experiencing major depressive episode in past year

Germany Canada U.S. Netherlands Japan

Source: Lam, 2012.

FIGURE 1.7

Why? Interpretation of these data depends on the interpreter's assumption. The low rates in Japan could be caused by something wonderful in Japanese culture—close human bonds, for instance. Or it could be something negative—repression of emotions, perhaps, which would reduce the rate of diagnosed depression, but not the rate of actual depression. As with the results of most research, data often raise new questions.

Multidisciplinary research leads to better treatment. For instance, postpartum depression is linked to birth experiences, particularly drugs that medical researchers discovered to make birth easier for the mother. Without psychological research, they might never have realized that their practices could harm later development. Family studies have shown that fathers can become active, affectionate, and lively caregivers, protecting infants from maternal depression. This finding has helped psychologists, who now include fathers when treating mothers who are depressed.

Multidisciplinary research broadens and deepens the perspective of every scientist. Almost every circumstance that affects human development entails risks and benefits, which are often best understood by another discipline. That leads to the next topic, plasticity.

Development Is Plastic

The term *plasticity* denotes two complementary aspects of development: Human traits can be molded (as plastic can be), and yet people maintain a certain durability of identity (as plastic does). The concept of plasticity in development provides both hope and realism—hope because change is possible, and realism because development builds on what has come before.

Dynamic Systems

Plasticity is basic to our contemporary understanding of human development. This is evident in one of the newest approaches, called **dynamic systems.** The idea is that human development is an ongoing, ever-changing interaction between the body and mind and between the individual and every aspect of the environment, including all the systems described in the ecological approach. The dynamic-systems approach began in disciplines that focus on changes in the natural world.

> [S]easons change in ordered measure, clouds assemble and disperse, trees grow to a certain shape and size, snowflakes form and melt, minute plants and animals pass through elaborate life cycles that are invisible to us, and social groups come together and disband.
>
> *[Thelen & Smith, 2006, p. 271]*

Note the word *dynamic:* Physical contexts, emotional influences, the passage of time, each person, and every aspect of the ecosystem are always interacting, always in flux, always in motion. For instance, a new approach to developing the motor skills of children with autism spectrum disorder stresses the dynamic systems that undergird movement—the changing aspects of the physical and social contexts (Lee & Porretta, 2013). [**Lifespan Link:** The major discussion of autism spectrum disorder is in Chapter 11.]

The dynamic-systems approach builds on the multidirectional, multicontextual, multicultural, and multidisciplinary nature of development. With any developmental topic, stage, or problem, the dynamic-systems approach urges consideration of all the interrelated aspects, every social and cultural factor, over days and years. Plasticity and the need for a dynamic-systems approach are most evident when considering the actual lived experience of each individual. My nephew David is one example.

dynamic systems A view of human development as an ongoing, ever-changing interaction between the physical, cognitive, and psychosocial influences. The crucial understanding is that development is never static but is always affected by, and affects, many systems of development.

Breathe, Don't Sink Ben Schwenker is learning "drown-proofing," important for a skinny 8-year-old, since his low body fat (a physiological system) makes floating harder. Ecological systems also make this skill vital, since Ben is in Marietta, a city with thousands of pools, in Georgia, a state bordered by the Atlantic. Another system is relevant: Ben was diagnosed with autism at age 1; for him, a sense of body strength and autonomy is particular important.

A CASE TO STUDY

David*

My Brother's Children Michael, Bill, and David (left to right) are adults now, with quite different personalities, abilities, offspring (4, 2, and none), and contexts (in Massachusetts, Pennsylvania, and California). Yet despite distinct genes, prenatal life, and contexts, I see the shared influence of Glen and Dot, my brother and sister-in-law—evident here in their similar, friendly smiles.

My sister-in-law contracted rubella (also called German measles) early in her third pregnancy; it was not diagnosed until David was born, blind and dying. Immediate heart surgery saved his life, but surgery to remove a cataract destroyed one eye.

The doctor then decided the cataract on the other eye should not be removed until the virus was finally gone. But one dead eye and one thick cataract meant that David's visual system was severely impaired for the first five years of his life. That affected all his other systems. For instance, he interacted with other children by pulling their hair. Fortunately, the virus occurred prenatally after the critical period for hearing had been reached. Because the systems of the body are interrelated, David developed extraordinary listening ability.

But the virus did harm his thumbs, ankles, teeth, feet, spine, and brain. He was admitted to special preschools—for the blind, for children with cerebral palsy, for children who were intellectually disabled. At age 6, when some sight was restored, he entered regular public school, learning academics but not social skills—partly because he was excluded from physical education.

By age 10 he had blossomed intellectually: David had skipped a year of school and was a fifth-grader, reading at the eleventh-grade level. Before age 20 he learned a second and a third language. In young adulthood, he enrolled in college.

As development unfolded, the interplay of systems was evident. His family context allowed him to become a productive adult, and happy. He told me, "I try to stay in a positive mood."

Remember, plasticity cannot erase a person's genes, childhood, or permanent damage. The brain destruction and compensation from that critical period of prenatal development remain. David is now 47; he still lives with his parents. Yet his listening skills are impressive. He told me

> I am generally quite happy, but secretly a little happier lately, especially since November, because I have been consistently getting a pretty good vibrato when I am singing, not only by myself but also in congregational hymns in church. [*He explained vibrato:*] When a note bounces up and down within a quartertone either way of concert pitch, optimally between 5.5 and 8.2 times per second.

David works as a translator of German texts, which he enjoys because, as he says, "I like providing a service to scholars, giving them access to something they would otherwise not have." As his aunt, I have seen him repeatedly overcome disabilities. Plasticity is dramatically evident. This case illustrates all five aspects of the life-span perspective (see Table 1.3).

*Many chapters include the feature A Case to Study. Each person is unique, which means that generalities cannot be validly drawn from one case, but sometimes one example makes a general concept clear.

Differential Sensitivity

Plasticity emphasizes that people can and do change, that predictions are not always accurate. More accurate predictions could improve prevention of developmental problems.

Three insights gained by developmentalists have advanced the benefits of prediction. Two of them you already know: (1) Nature and nurture always interact, and (2) certain periods of life are particularly sensitive for particular developments.

TABLE 1.3	Five Characteristics of Development
Characteristic	**Application in David's Story**
Multidirectional. Change occurs in every direction, not always in a straight line. Gains and losses, predictable growth, and unexpected transformations are evident.	David's development seemed static (or even regressive, as when early surgery destroyed one eye), but then it accelerated each time he entered a new school or college.
Multidisciplinary. Numerous academic fields—especially psychology, biology, education, and sociology, but also neuroscience, economics, religion, anthropology, history, medicine, genetics, and many more—contribute insights.	Two disciplines were particularly critical: medicine (David would have died without advances in surgery on newborns) and education (special educators guided him and his parents many times).
Multicontextual. Human lives are embedded in many contexts, including historical conditions, economic constraints, and family patterns.	The high SES of David's family made it possible for him to receive daily medical and educational care. His two older brothers protected him.
Multicultural. Many cultures—not just between nations but also within them—affect how people develop.	Appalachia, where David and his family lived, has a particular culture, including acceptance of people with disabilities and willingness to help families in need. Those aspects of that culture benefited David and his family.
Plasticity. Every individual, and every trait within each individual, can be altered at any point in the life span. Change is ongoing, although it is neither random nor easy.	David's measured IQ changed from about 40 (severely intellectually disabled) to about 130 (far above average), and his physical disabilities became less crippling as he matured. Nonetheless, because of a virus contracted before he was born, his entire life will never be what it might have been.

Both of these insights were apparent in David's case. His inborn characteristics affected his ability to learn, but, unlike the case for babies born a century ago with rubella, nurture from family and professionals limited the impact of many handicaps. As for critical and sensitive periods, David's attendance in preschool may be one reason he fared so well later on, because developmentalists now know that education from birth to age 4 has profound influence on later learning.

The third factor to aid prediction and target intervention is a recent discovery, **differential sensitivity.** The idea is that because of their genes some people are more vulnerable than others to particular experiences. This vulnerability can work in both directions: The same genes affect people for better or for worse, depending on postconception experiences.

Can you remember something you heard in childhood that still affects you, perhaps a criticism that stung or a compliment that inspired? Now think of what that same comment meant to the person who uttered it or might have meant to another child. Those words stayed with you, but they might have been forgotten by others. That is differential sensitivity.

More generally, many scientists have found genes, or circumstances, that work both ways—they predispose people to being either unusually successful or severely pathological (Belsky et al., 2012; Kéri, 2009). This idea is captured in the folk saying "Genius is close to madness": The same circumstance (genius) can become a gift for an entire society, or a burden for an individual, or have no effect at all.

differential sensitivity The idea that some people are more vulnerable than others to certain experiences, usually because of genetic differences.

Differential sensitivity is apparent at every point in the life span, from prenatal development throughout old age. An experiment involved stressing pregnant rhesus monkeys and then observing how responsive those monkeys were to their newborns. The mothers who were inclined to be nurturing were even more nurturing than usual; the mothers who were already less warm were even less nurturing than usual. Stress affected those mothers in opposite ways, and then that affected their offspring, again with differential sensitivity.

To control for the influence of genes, the monkeys in utero when the mothers were stressed were compared to other monkeys born to the same mothers with unstressed pregnancies. It was apparent that the stressed nurturing mothers had babies who were superior to their siblings, and the stressed cold mothers had babies who were inferior. Thus stress affected them all, for better or worse, in differential sensitivity (Shirtcliff et al., 2013).

SUMMING UP

Development is multidirectional, with gains and losses evident at every stage. An ecological-systems perspective emphasizes the many contexts that affect each person, including the immediate family, nearby institutions, and the overall cultural values of the society. Cohort and socioeconomic status always affect each life.

Cultural influences are pervasive, albeit sometimes unrecognized. Social constructions, including ethnicity and race, are tangled with cultural values, making culture not only crucial but also complex. To untangle the influences on development, many academic disciplines provide insight on how people grow and change over time. The interaction of all the developmental contexts cannot be fully grasped by any one discipline.

Each person's development is plastic, with the basic substance of each individual life moldable by contexts and events. Genes can make a person more or less vulnerable to certain experiences, for better or for worse. ■

>> Using the Scientific Method

There are hundreds of ways to design scientific studies and analyze their results, and researchers continually try to ensure that their data and conclusions are valid. Statistical measures often help scientists discover relationships between various aspects of the data. (Some statistical perspectives are presented in Table 1.4.) Every research design, method, and statistical measure has strengths as well as weaknesses. Next we describe three basic research strategies—observation, the experiment, and the survey—and then three ways developmentalists study change over time.

Observation

Scientific observation requires researchers to record behavior systematically and objectively. Observations often occur in a naturalistic setting such as a home, where people behave normally. Scientific observation can also occur in a laboratory, where scientists record human reactions in various situations, often with wall-mounted video cameras and the scientist in another room.

Observation is crucial to develop hypotheses. However, observation provides issues to explore, not proof. For example, one study of how long parents lingered when

scientific observation A method of testing a hypothesis by unobtrusively watching and recording participants' behavior in a systematic and objective manner in a natural setting or in a laboratory; a search of archival data is another way to conduct scientific observation.

Especially for Nurses In the field of medicine, why are experiments conducted to test new drugs and treatments? (see response, page 25)

TABLE 1.4	Statistical Measures Often Used to Analyze Research Results
Measure	**Use**
Effect size	Indicates how much one variable affects another. Effect size ranges from 0 to 1: An effect size of 0.2 is called small, 0.5 moderate, and 0.8 large.
Significance	Indicates whether the results might have occurred by chance. A finding that chance would produce the results only 5 times in 100 is significant at the 0.05 level. A finding that chance would produce the results once in 100 times is significant at 0.01; once in 1,000 times is significant at 0.001.
Cost-benefit analysis	Calculates how much a particular independent variable costs versus how much it saves. This is particularly useful for analyzing public spending. For instance, one cost-benefit analysis showed that an intensive preschool program cost $15,166 per child (in 2000 dollars) but saved $215,000 (again, 2000 dollars) later on, in reduced costs of special education, unemployment, prison, and other public expenses (Belfield et al., 2006).
Odds ratio	Indicates how a particular variable compares to a standard, set at 1. For example, one study found that, although less than 1 percent of all child homicides occurred at school, the odds were similar for public and private schools. The odds of such deaths occurring in high schools, however, were 18.47 times that of elementary or middle schools (set at 1.0) (MMWR, January 18, 2008).
Factor analysis	Hundreds of variables could affect any given behavior. In addition, many variables (such as family income and parental education) may overlap. To take this into account, analysis reveals variables that can be clustered together to form a factor, which is a composite of many variables. For example, SES might become one factor, child personality another.
Meta-analysis	A "study of studies." Researchers use statistical tools to synthesize the results of previous, separate studies. Then they analyze the accumulated results, using criteria that weight each study fairly. This approach improves data analysis by combining the results of studies that were too small, or too narrow, to lead to solid conclusions.

Who Participates? For all these measures, the characteristics of the people who participate in the study (formerly called the subjects, now called the participants) are important, as is the number of people who are studied. This also is presented with statistics.

dropping off their children in preschool found that children were slower to engage with toys or friends when their parents stayed longer (Grady et al., 2013). This could mean that parental hesitancy to leave made children less social with friends. However, the opposite interpretation is also possible. Perhaps those children who were shyer and less social caused their parents to stay longer. Thus this study led to two alternative hypotheses: More research is needed to ascertain which one is more accurate.

Friendly Dogs? Dr. Sabrina Schuck is observing children with ADHD (attention-deficit/hyperactive disorder), who are singing as part of a 12-week therapy program. She notes specific disruptions (can you see that child's flailing arm?). Half the children in her study have sessions with therapy dogs—trained not to bark when the children get too lively. Those children were most likely to calm down.

The Experiment

The **experiment** establishes what causes what. In the social sciences, experimenters typically impose a particular treatment on a group of volunteer participants or expose them to a specific condition and then note whether their behavior changes.

In technical terms, the experimenters manipulate an **independent variable,** which is the imposed treatment or special condition (also called the *experimental variable*; a *variable* is anything that can vary). They note whether this independent variable affects whatever they are studying, called the **dependent variable** (which *depends* on the independent variable).

Thus, the independent variable is the new, special treatment; any change in the dependent variable is the result. The purpose of an experiment is to find out whether an independent variable affects the dependent variable. In a typical experiment (as diagrammed in Figure 1.8), two groups of participants are studied. One group, the *experimental group*, is subjected to the particular treatment or condition (the independent variable); the other group, the *comparison group* (also called the *control group*), is not.

experiment A research method in which the researcher tries to determine the cause-and-effect relationship between two variables by manipulating one (called the *independent variable*) and then observing and recording the ensuing changes in the other (called the *dependent variable*).

independent variable In an experiment, the variable that is introduced to see what effect it has on the dependent variable. (Also called *experimental variable*.)

dependent variable In an experiment, the variable that may change as a result of whatever new condition or situation the experimenter adds. In other words, the dependent variable *depends* on the independent variable.

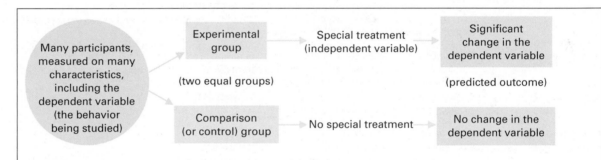

Procedure:

1. Divide participants into two groups that are matched on important characteristics, especially the behavior that is the dependent variable on which this study is focused.

2. Give special treatment, or intervention (the independent variable), to one group (the experimental group).

3. Compare the groups on the dependent variable. If they now differ, the cause of the difference was probably the independent variable.

4. Publish the results.

FIGURE 1.8

How to Conduct an Experiment The basic sequence diagrammed here applies to all experiments. Many additional features, especially the statistical measures listed in Table 1.4 and various ways of reducing experimenter bias, affect whether publication occurs. (Scientific journals reject reports of experiments that were not rigorous in method and analysis.)

The Survey

survey A research method in which information is collected from a large number of people by interviews, written questionnaires, or some other means.

A third research method is the **survey,** in which information is collected from a large number of people by interview, questionnaire, or some other means. This is a quick, direct way to obtain data.

Unfortunately, although surveys may be quick and direct, they are not necessarily accurate. When pollsters try to predict elections, they survey thousands of potential voters. They hope that the people they survey will vote as they say they will, that undecided people will follow the trends, and that people who refuse to give their opinion, or who are not included, will be similar to those surveyed. None of this is certain. Some people lie, some change their minds, some (especially those who don't have phones or who never talk to strangers) are never counted.

Furthermore, survey answers are influenced by the wording and the sequence of the questions. For instance, "climate change" and "global warming" are two ways to describe the same phenomenon according to many scientists, yet many people believe in climate change but not in global warming (McCright & Dunlap, 2011). For that reason, surveys that seem to be about the same issue may reach opposite conclusions.

Additionally, survey respondents present themselves as they would like to be perceived. For instance, every two years since 1991, high school students in the United States have been surveyed. The participants are carefully chosen to be representative of all students in the nation. The most recent survey included 15,503 students from all 50 states and from schools large and small, public and private (MMWR, June 8, 2012).

Students are asked whether they had sexual intercourse *before* age 13. Every year, compared to the twelfth-grade boys, about twice as many ninth-grade boys say they had sex before age 13 (see Figure 1.9). Do seniors forget or do ninth-graders lie? Or are some 13-year-olds proud of early sexual experience but ashamed by age 17?

To understand responses in more depth, another method can be used—the **case study,** which is an in-depth study of one person. Case studies usually require personal interviews, background information, test or questionnaire results, and more. Although in some ways case studies seem more accurate than more superficial measures, in other ways they are not: The assumptions and interpretations of the researcher are more likely to bias the results than they would a survey that includes hundreds of participants.

Even if accurate, the case study applies only to one person, who may be quite unlike other people. For instance, my report on my nephew David is a case study, but David is unique: Other embryos exposed to rubella may have quite different lives than David's.

Studying Development over the Life Span

In addition to conducting observations, experiments, and surveys, developmentalists must measure how people *change or remain the same over time*. They use one of three basic research designs: cross-sectional, longitudinal, or cross-sequential (see Figure 1.10).

Cross-Sectional Research

The quickest and least expensive way to study development over time is with **cross-sectional research,** in which groups of people of one age are compared with groups of people of another age. Such research has found, for instance, that

>> **Response for Nurses** (from page 22): Experiments are the only way to determine cause-and-effect relationships. If we want to be sure that a new drug or treatment is safe and effective, an experiment must be conducted to establish that the drug or treatment improves health.

case study An in-depth study of one person, usually requiring personal interviews to collect background information and various follow-up discussions, tests, questionnaires, and so on.

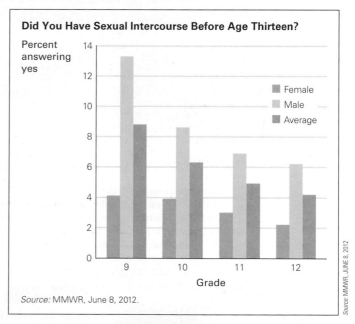

Did You Have Sexual Intercourse Before Age Thirteen?

Source: MMWR, June 8, 2012.

Source: MMWR, JUNE 8, 2012

FIGURE 1.9

I Forgot? If this were the only data available, you might conclude that ninth-graders have suddenly become more sexually active than twelfth-graders. But we have 20 years of data—those who are ninth-graders now will answer differently by twelfth grade.

cross-sectional research A research design that compares groups of people who differ in age but are similar in other important characteristics.

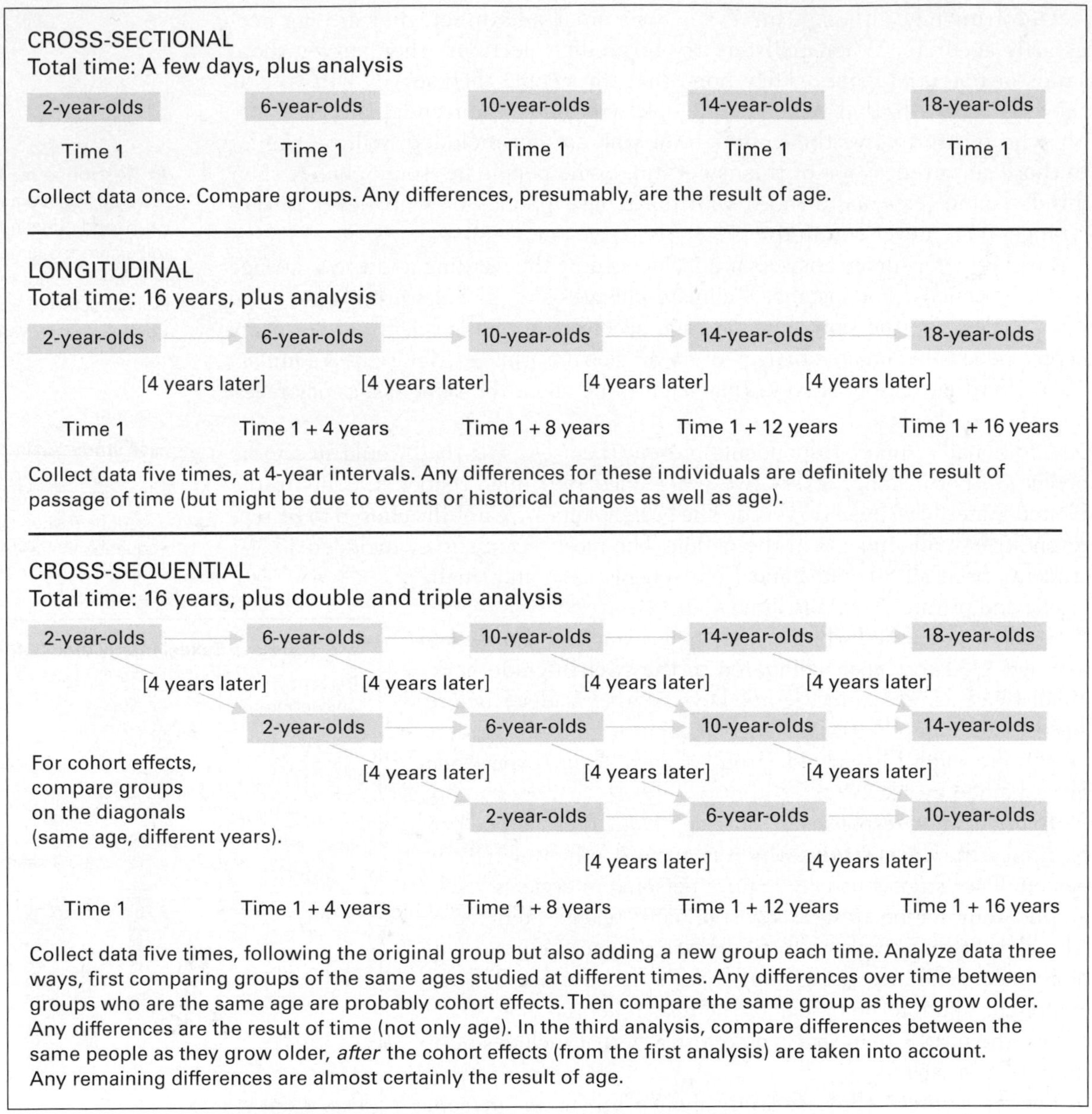

CROSS-SECTIONAL
Total time: A few days, plus analysis

| 2-year-olds | 6-year-olds | 10-year-olds | 14-year-olds | 18-year-olds |
| Time 1 | Time 1 | Time 1 | Time 1 | Time 1 |

Collect data once. Compare groups. Any differences, presumably, are the result of age.

LONGITUDINAL
Total time: 16 years, plus analysis

2-year-olds →	6-year-olds →	10-year-olds →	14-year-olds →	18-year-olds
[4 years later]	[4 years later]	[4 years later]	[4 years later]	
Time 1	Time 1 + 4 years	Time 1 + 8 years	Time 1 + 12 years	Time 1 + 16 years

Collect data five times, at 4-year intervals. Any differences for these individuals are definitely the result of passage of time (but might be due to events or historical changes as well as age).

CROSS-SEQUENTIAL
Total time: 16 years, plus double and triple analysis

2-year-olds →	6-year-olds →	10-year-olds →	14-year-olds →	18-year-olds
[4 years later]	[4 years later]	[4 years later]	[4 years later]	
	2-year-olds →	6-year-olds →	10-year-olds →	14-year-olds

For cohort effects, compare groups on the diagonals (same age, different years).

		[4 years later]	[4 years later]	[4 years later]
		2-year-olds →	6-year-olds →	10-year-olds
			[4 years later]	[4 years later]
Time 1	Time 1 + 4 years	Time 1 + 8 years	Time 1 + 12 years	Time 1 + 16 years

Collect data five times, following the original group but also adding a new group each time. Analyze data three ways, first comparing groups of the same ages studied at different times. Any differences over time between groups who are the same age are probably cohort effects. Then compare the same group as they grow older. Any differences are the result of time (not only age). In the third analysis, compare differences between the same people as they grow older, *after* the cohort effects (from the first analysis) are taken into account. Any remaining differences are almost certainly the result of age.

FIGURE 1.10

Which Approach Is Best? Cohort-sequential research is the most time-consuming and complex, but it yields the best information. One reason that hundreds of scientists conduct research on the same topics, replicating one another's work, is to gain some advantages of cohort-sequential research without waiting for decades.

in the United States in 2012, 74 percent of men aged 25 to 29 were in the labor force, but only 52 percent of those aged 60 to 64 were (U.S. Bureau of Labor Statistics, 2011). It seems that about one-third of all men stop working between age 30 and age 60. Younger adults might imagine them golfing in the sun, happy with their pensions and free time.

Cross-sectional design seems simple. However, it is difficult to ensure that the various groups being compared are similar in every way except age. In this example, the younger U.S. men, on average, had more education than the older ones. Thus, what seems to be the result of age might actually have to do with schooling: Perhaps education, not age, accounted for the

higher employment rates of the younger adults. Or perhaps age discrimination was the problem: The older adults may have wanted jobs but been unable to get them.

Longitudinal Research

To help discover whether age itself rather than cohort causes a developmental change, scientists undertake **longitudinal research.** This research requires collecting data repeatedly on the same individuals as they age. Longitudinal research is particularly useful in tracing development over many years.

Longitudinal research has several drawbacks, however. Over time, participants may withdraw, move to an unknown address, or die. Another problem is that participants become increasingly aware of the goals of the study—knowledge that makes them less typical, and thus the results become less valid.

Finally, the historical context changes, which limits the current relevance of data on people born decades ago. Results from longitudinal studies of people born in 1910 may not be applicable to people born in 2010.

Longitudinal research requires years of data. For example, alarm about possible future harm caused by ingesting *phthalates* and *bisphenol A* (BPA) (chemicals used in manufacturing) from plastic baby bottles and infant toys leads many parents to use glass baby bottles. But perhaps the risk of occasional shattered glass causes more harm than the chemicals in plastic, or perhaps the mother's use of cosmetics, which puts phthalates in breast milk, is a much greater source of the chemicals than any bottles (Wittassek et al., 2011). Could breast-feeding harm infants? Pediatricians believe that the benefits of breast milk outweigh any dangers, but we need answers now, not decades from now.

Compare These with Those These children seem ideal for cross-sectional research—they are school children of both sexes and many ethnicities. Their only difference seems to be age, so a study might conclude that 6-year-olds raise their hands but 16-year-olds do not. But any two groups in cross-sectional research may differ in ways that are not obvious— perhaps income, national origin, or culture— and that may be the underlying reason for any observed age differences.

longitudinal research A research design in which the same individuals are followed over time and their development is repeatedly assessed.

Five Stages of Life These photos show Sarah-Maria, born in 1980 in Switzerland, in infancy (age 1), early childhood (age 3), adolescence (age 15), emerging adulthood (age 19), and adulthood (age 29). Continuity (that smile) and discontinuity (her hair) are both evident in longitudinal research.

cross-sequential research A hybrid
research design in which researchers first
study several groups of people of different ages (a cross-sectional approach)
and then follow those groups over the
years (a longitudinal approach). (Also
called *cohort-sequential research or
time-sequential research*.)

Especially for Future Researchers
What is the best method for collecting data?
(see response, page 30)

Cross-Sequential Research

Scientists have found a third strategy, combining cross-sectional and longitudinal research, called **cross-sequential research** (also referred to as *cohort-sequential* or *time-sequential research*). With this design, researchers study several groups of people of different ages (a cross-sectional approach) and follow them over the years (a longitudinal approach).

With cross-sequential design, researchers compare findings for a group of, say, 18-year-olds, with findings for the same individuals at age 6-year-olds, as well as with findings for groups who were 18 a decade or two earlier and with findings for groups who are currently 6-year-olds (see Figure 1.10). Cross-sequential research is complicated, in recruitment and analysis, but it lets scientists disentangle the effects of age from the effects of history.

One well-known cross-sequential study (the *Seattle Longitudinal Study*) found that some intellectual abilities (vocabulary) increase even after age 60, whereas others (processing speed) start to decline at age 30 (Schaie, 2005).

Some recent cross-sequential research discovered that some factors affect the mental health of children more during middle childhood than infancy. Absent or unemployed fathers are among such factors (Sanson et al., 2011), a discovery that could not have been made by cross-sectional or longitudinal research in isolation.

SUMMING UP

Scientists use many methods and research designs to investigate development. Ideally, conclusions from one type of study are confirmed by other types. Careful and systematic observation can discover phenomena that were previously unnoticed, and then experiments can investigate hypotheses to uncover causes. Surveys are quick but vulnerable to bias in the questions asked and answers given. Case studies are detailed, but it is folly to draw general conclusions from the specifics of any one individual.

To study change over time, cross-sectional, longitudinal, and cross-sequential designs are used, each with advantages and disadvantages. Cross-sectional is quickest, longitudinal may be more accurate, and cross-sequential combines the two, reaching conclusions that neither cross-sectional nor longitudinal research could find in isolation. ▪

❯❯ Cautions and Challenges from Science

The scientific method illuminates and illustrates human development as nothing else does. Facts, hypotheses, and possibilities have all emerged that would not be known without science—and people of all ages are healthier, happier, and more capable than people of previous generations because of it.

For example, infectious diseases in children, illiteracy in adults, depression in late adulthood, and racism and sexism at every age are much less prevalent today than a century ago. Science deserves credit for all these advances. Even violent death is less likely, with scientific discoveries and universal education considered likely reasons (Pinker, 2011).

Developmental scientists have also discovered unexpected sources of harm. Video games, cigarettes, television, shift work, and asbestos are all less benign than people first thought. Even life-sustaining medical measures, such as restarting a stopped heart, and mechanical respirators, may sometimes impede optimal development in late adulthood.

Although the benefits of science are many, so are the pitfalls. We now discuss three potential hazards: misinterpreting correlation, depending too heavily on numbers, and ignoring ethics.

Correlation and Causation

Probably the most common mistake in interpreting research is confusing correlation with causation. A **correlation** exists between two variables if one variable is more—or less—likely to occur when the other does. A correlation is *positive* if both variables tend to increase together or decrease together, *negative* if one variable tends to increase while the other decreases, and *zero* if no connection is evident.

To illustrate: From birth to age 9, there is a positive correlation between age and height (children grow taller as they grow older), a negative correlation between age and napping (children nap less often as they grow older), and zero correlation between age and number of toes (children do not grow new toes with age). (Now try the quiz on correlation in Table 1.5.)

correlation A number that indicates the degree of relationship between two variables, expressed in terms of the likelihood that one variable will (or will not) occur when the other variable does (or does not). A correlation indicates only that two variables are related, not that one variable causes the other to occur.

TABLE 1.5	Quiz on Correlation		
Two Variables		Positive, Negative, or Zero Correlation?	Why? (Third Variable)
1. Ice cream sales and murder rate		_____	_____
2. Learning to read and number of baby teeth		_____	_____
3. Child gender and sex of parent		_____	_____

For each of these three pairs of variables, indicate whether the correlation between them is positive, negative, or nonexistent. Then try to think of a third variable that would determine the direction of the correlation. The correct answers are printed upside down below.

Answers:

1. Positive; third variable: heat

2. Negative; third variable: age

3. Zero; each child must have a parent of each sex; no third variable.

Many correlations are unexpected. For instance, first-born children are more likely to develop asthma than are later-born children, teenage girls have higher rates of mental health problems than do teenage boys, and newborns of immigrants weigh more than do newborns of nonimmigrants. All these surprising correlations are discussed later.

However, *correlation is not causation*. Just because two variables are correlated does not mean that one causes the other—even if it seems logical that it does. Correlation proves only that the variables are connected somehow. Many mistaken and even dangerous conclusions are drawn because people misunderstand correlation.

Ethics

The most important caution for all scientists, especially for those studying humans, is to uphold ethical standards in their research. Each academic discipline and every professional society involved in the study of human development has a *code of ethics* (a set of moral principles) and specific practices within a scientific culture to protect the integrity of research.

Ethical standards and codes are increasingly stringent. In the United States, most educational and medical institutions have an *Institutional Review Board* (IRB), a group that permits only research that follows certain guidelines.

Especially for Future Researchers and Science Writers Do any ethical guidelines apply when an author writes about the experiences of family members, friends, or research participants? (see response, page 31)

>> Response for Future Researchers
(from page 28): There is no best method
for collecting data. The method used
depends on many factors, such as the
age of participants (infants can't complete
questionnaires), the question being
researched, and the time frame.

Although IRBs often slow down scientific study, some research conducted more than 50 years ago, before IRBs were established, was clearly unethical, especially when the participants were children, members of minority groups, prisoners, or animals (Blum, 2002; Washington, 2006). Scientists—and everyone else—are horrified to learn about the Tuskegee study that did not treat people who had syphilis, or the Little Albert research that taught an infant to fear white furry things.

Protection of Research Participants

Ethical principles underlying all research in human development include that researchers must ensure that participation is voluntary, confidential, and will not harm the participants. This entails the *informed consent* of the participants—that is, they must understand and agree to the research procedures, knowing what risks are involved. If children are involved, consent must be obtained from the parents as well as the children, and the children must be allowed to end their participation at any time.

Although protection of participants may conflict with the goals of science, scientists now believe that protection of participants is paramount. The Canadian Psychological Association suggests four guiding principles, which are expressed in similar ways in other disciplines and other nations:

1. Respect for the dignity of persons
2. Responsible caring
3. Integrity in relationships
4. Responsibility to society

All four principles should be followed, if possible, but they are ranked in order of importance: Respect for individuals trumps social responsibility.

Implications of Research Results

Once a study has been completed, additional issues usually arise. Scientists are obligated to "promote accuracy, honesty, and truthfulness" (American Psychological Association, 2010).

Deliberate falsification is unusual. When it does occur, it leads to ostracism from the scientific community, dismissal from a teaching or research position, and, sometimes, criminal prosecution.

Another obvious breach of ethics is to "cook" the data, or distort one's findings, in order to make a particular conclusion seem to be the only reasonable one. This is not as rare as it should be. Tenure, promotion, and funding all encourage scientists to publish, and publishers seek remarkable findings. Awareness of this danger is leading to increased calls for replication (Carpenter, 2012).

Scientists are rewarded for publishing surprising results. When a hypothesis is not confirmed, that may lead to the "file drawer problem"; that is, a study is filed away and never published because the results are not exciting.

Ethical standards cannot be taken for granted. As stressed in the beginning of this chapter, researchers, like all other humans, have strong opinions that they expect research to confirm. Therefore, sometimes without even realizing it, they might try to achieve the results they want. As one team explains:

> Our job as scientists is to discover truths about the world. We generate hypotheses, collect data, and examine whether or not the data are consistent with those hypotheses . . . [but we] often lose sight of this goal, yielding to pressure to do whatever is justifiable to compile a set of studies we can publish. This is not driven by a willingness to deceive but by the self-serving interpretation of ambiguity . . .

[Simmons et al., 2011, pp. 1359, 1365]

Obviously, collaboration, replication, and transparency are essential ethical safeguards for all scientists.

What Should We Study?

Finally one crucial ethical concern should begin the process of scientific study for all developmentalists: to study issues that will help "all kinds of people, everywhere, of every age" live satisfying and productive lives. Consider these questions, for instance:

- Do we know enough about prenatal drug use to protect every fetus?
- Do we know enough about poverty to enable everyone to be healthy?
- Do we know enough about same-sex relationships, or polygamy, or single parenthood, or divorce to make sure all people develop well no matter what their family structure?
- Do we know enough about dying to enable everyone to die with dignity?

The answer to all these questions is a resounding *NO*. The reasons are many, but a major one is that these topics are controversial. Some researchers avoid them, fearing unwelcome and uninformed publicity (Kempner et al., 2005). Few funders are eager to support scientific studies of drug abuse, poverty, nonstandard families, or death, partly because people have strong opinions on these issues that may conflict with scientific findings and conclusions. Religion, politics, and ethics shape scientific research, sometimes stopping investigation before it begins. For instance, federal legislation passed in 1997 virtually prohibits federal funding for research on gun use.

The next cohort of developmental scientists will build on what is known, mindful of what needs to be explored. Remember that the goal is to help all 7 billion people on Earth fulfill their potential. Much more needs to be learned. The next 24 chapters are only a beginning.

SUMMING UP

Although science has improved human development in many ways, caution is needed in interpreting results and in designing research. Sometimes people think that correlation indicates cause. It does not.

Research on human development must subscribe to high ethical standards. Participants must be respected and must give informed consent. Political and publishing concerns can interfere with objective research. Scientists must study and report data on issues that affect the development of all people. ∎

>> **Response for Future Researchers and Science Writers** (from page 29): Yes. Anyone you write about must give consent and be fully informed about your intentions. They can be identified by name but only if they give permission. For example, family members gave permission before anecdotes about them were included in this text. My nephew David read the first draft of his story (see pages 20–21) and is proud to have his experiences used to teach others.

SUMMARY

Understanding How and Why

1. The study of human development is a science that seeks to understand how people change or remain the same over time. A scientist begins with curiosity and questions, refines them into hypotheses, then gathers empirical data, and finally draws conclusions that are shared (usually published) with other scientists. A crucial step before the conclusions are accepted is that the research be replicated, to confirm, modify, or refute the conclusions.

2. Nature and nurture always interact. Each human characteristic is affected by the interaction of both genes (nature) and environment (nurture). Gene expression is affected by the environment, beginning at the moment of conception, in a process called epigenesis.

The Life-Span Perspective

3. Development is multidirectional: Gains and losses are apparent throughout life, and change can be rapid, slow or imperceptible.

4. A multicontextual approach is ecological. That means it takes into account immediate contexts (family, school) as well as broader contexts (historical conditions, socioeconomic status). When a person is born determines their cohort, which influences development lifelong. Poverty also affects development at every age.

5. As the multicultural aspect of the life-span perspective stresses, each culture embraces values and assumptions about human life. Culture, ethnicity, and race are social constructions, that is, concepts created by society. Culture includes beliefs about life and patterns of behavior. Some social scientists want to abandon concerns about race and national origin, while others want to use those concepts to combat racism and cultural prejudice.

6. As emphasized by multidisciplinary concerns, development needs to be understood using the methods and viewpoints of many areas of study. For example, to understand the cause of psychological depression, at least a dozen factors from a dozen disciplines are helpful. Always genes, past history and current age of the person are relevant, so a particular person may be better understood via the perspective of one discipline more than another.

7. Development is plastic, which means that, although inborn traits and childhood experiences affect later development, patterns and possibilities can change throughout life. Further, in differential sensitivity, some people are particularly vulnerable, for better and for worse, to particular genes or experiences.

Using the Scientific Method

8. Several specific research designs help scientists understand human development. Scientific observation, the experiment, and the survey each provide insights and discoveries that were not apparent before the research. Each also has liabilities; before conclusions are accepted by the scientific community, several methods are typically used. Statistics, and research on dozens, sometimes hundreds, of individuals are useful in reaching objective conclusions.

9. An additional challenge for developmentalists is to study change over time. Two traditional research designs are often used: cross-sectional research (comparing people of different ages) and longitudinal research (studying the same people over time). A third method, cross-sequential research (combining the two other methods) is more complicated, expensive, and time-consuming, but many developmentalists believe it allows more reliable conclusions.

Cautions and Challenges from Science

10. A correlation shows that two variables are related. However, it does not prove that one variable causes the other: The variable thought to be the cause may actually be the consequence, or both variables may be the result of a third variable.

11. Ethical behavior is crucial in all the sciences. Not only must participants be protected and data be kept confidential, but results must be fairly reported, honestly interpreted, and replicated. Scientists must be especially mindful of the implications of their research.

12. Appropriate application of scientific research depends partly on the training and integrity of the scientists. One very important ethical question is whether scientists are designing, conducting, analyzing, publishing, and applying the research needed to help the entire human family develop well.

KEY TERMS

case study (p. 25)
cohort (p. 8)
correlation (p. 29)
critical period (p. 6)
cross-sectional research (p. 25)
cross-sequential research (p. 28)
culture (p. 11)
dependent variable (p. 24)
difference-equals-deficit error (p. 13)

differential sensitivity (p. 21)
dynamic systems (p. 19)
ecological-systems approach (p. 7)
empirical evidence (p. 5)
epigenetic (p. 16)
ethnic group (p. 14)
experiment (p. 24)
hypothesis (p. 4)
independent variable (p. 24)

life-span perspective (p. 5)
longitudinal research (p. 27)
nature (p. 5)
nurture (p. 5)
race (p. 15)
replication (p. 4)
science of human development (p. 4)
scientific method (p. 4)
scientific observation (p. 22)

sensitive period (p. 7)
social construction (p. 11)
socioeconomic status (SES) (p. 9)
survey (p. 24)

WHAT HAVE YOU LEARNED?

Understanding How and Why

1. What are the five steps of the scientific method?

2. What basic question is at the heart of the nature–nurture controversy?

The Life-Span Perspective

3. What are the concepts of discontinuity and of continuity?

4. Why is development said to be multicontextual?

5. Which components of the exosystem affect your life today?

6. What causes cohort differences between you and your parents?

7. What is a social construction and what is an example of one?

8. Define guided participation as described by Vygotsky.

9. What is the difference between race and ethnicity?

10. How do both specialization and multidisciplinary research add to our understanding of a topic?

11. What is the difference between "genetic" and "epigenetic"?

12. In what two ways is human development plastic?

13. Why is human development described as dynamic?

14. What is the concept of "differential sensitivity"?

Using the Scientific Method

15. Explain the following statement: "Observation provides issues to explore, not proof."

16. Why do experimenters use a control (or comparison) group as well as an experimental group?

17. What are the strengths and weaknesses of the survey method?

18. Why would a scientist conduct a cross-sectional study?

19. What are some advantages and disadvantages of longitudinal studies?

20. Explain the following statement: "Cross-sequential research combines cross-sectional and longitudinal research."

Cautions and Challenges from Science

21. Why is it important for academic disciplines and professional societies to follow codes of ethics?

22. What is one additional question about development that should be answered?

APPLICATIONS

1. It is said that culture is pervasive but that people are unaware of it. List 30 things you did today that you might have done differently in another culture.

2. How would your life be different if your parents were much higher or lower in SES than they are? What if you had been born in another cohort?

3. Design an experiment to answer a question you have about human development. Specify the question and the hypothesis and then describe the experiment, including the sample size and the variables. (Look first at Appendix B.)

>>ONLINE CONNECTIONS

To accompany your textbook, you have access to a number of online resources, including Learning Curve, an adaptive quizzing program, critical thinking questions, and case studies. For access to any of these links, go to www.worthpublishers .com/launchpad/bergerls9e. In addition to these resources, you'll also find links to video clips, personalized study advice, and an ebook. Some of the videos and activities available online include:

- *Ethics in Human Research: Violating One's Privacy?* This video introduces the controversies around a research project in Iceland that collects genetic and health information about private citizens.

- *What's Wrong with This Study?* This activity allows you to review some of the pitfalls in various research designs.

WORTH PUBLISHERS

Theories of Development

■ **What Theories Do**
Questions and Answers
Facts and Norms

■ **Grand Theories**
Psychoanalytic Theory: Freud and Erikson
Behaviorism: Conditioning and Social
    Learning
Cognitive Theory: Piaget and Information
    Processing
Comparing Grand Theories
OPPOSING PERSPECTIVES:
    Toilet Training—How and When?

■ **Newer Theories**
Sociocultural Theory: Vygotsky and
    Beyond
The Universal Perspective: Humanism and
    Evolutionary Theory
A VIEW FROM SCIENCE: If Your Mate
    Were Unfaithful

■ **What Theories Contribute**

WHAT WILL YOU KNOW?

1. How does a theory differ from a fact?
2. Does development occur in stages, or more gradually, day by day?
3. What limitations do Freud, Erikson, Watson, Skinner, and Piaget share?
4. Why is it better to use several theories to understand human development rather than just one?

When I was little, on special occasions we drove to my grandparents' farm, the childhood home of my father and his three brothers and one sister, all married with children. When we arrived, my brother and I played with our 12 cousins, including three other girls my age. I remember turkey, mashed potatoes, and lemon meringue pie on a big table; horses and hay in the barn; grandma in an apron; grandpa resting his big hands over a huge coffee mug; enormous wooden rocking chairs in the sitting room. But my strongest single memory is a bitter one: One Christmas, Grandma gave her three other young granddaughters and me similar dolls, precursors of Barbie. Mine had a peach-colored gown; my cousin's (the only daughter of Grandma's only daughter) had a white bride's dress and veil.

Why did I feel rejected? In hindsight, I can think of several laudable reasons for Grandma's choice. But when I was 6, my observations of my relatives led to childish conclusions about presents and brides and then to resentment. It is not surprising that I formed a simple theory: that Grandma loved my cousin more than me.

We all construct theories, sometimes called "folk theories" to indicate that they are not scientific, or "ethnotheories" when they arise from a specific culture or ethnic group. [**Lifespan Link:** Ethnotheories are discussed in Chapter 7.]

This chapter outlines five theories of human development, or actually ten, since each theory has at least two versions. Many more theories refer to the human life span; some are explained later. Before beginning, however, you should know that theorizing is part of human nature. In fact, according to "theory theory," young children spontaneously develop theories to explain whatever they observe, because that is what humans do (Gopnik & Shulz, 2007). My theory led me to conclude that Grandma loved my cousin most of all.

>> What Theories Do

Every theory is an explanation of facts and observations, a set of concepts and ideas that organize the confusing mass of experiences that each of us encounters every minute. Some theories are idiosyncratic, narrow, and useless to anyone except the people who thought of them. Others are much more elaborate and insightful, such as the major theories described in this chapter that focus on human development over the life span.

developmental theory A group of ideas, assumptions, and generalizations that interpret and illuminate the thousands of observations that have been made about human growth. A developmental theory provides a framework for explaining the patterns and problems of development.

A **developmental theory** is a systematic statement of general principles that provides a framework for understanding how and why people change as they grow older. Facts and observations are connected to patterns and explanations, weaving the details of life into a meaningful whole. A developmental theory is more than a hunch or a hypothesis, and is far more comprehensive than my childish theorizing about bride dolls. Developmental theories provide insights that are both broad and deep, and they are therefore more comprehensive than the many observations and ideas from which they arise.

As an analogy, imagine building a house. A person could have a heap of lumber, nails, and other materials, but without a plan and labor the heap cannot become a building. Furthermore, not every house is alike: People have theories (usually not explicit) about houses that lead to preferences for the number of stories, bedrooms, entrances, and so on. Likewise, the observations and empirical studies of human development are essential raw materials, but theories put them together.

Kurt Lewin (1943) once quipped, "Nothing is as practical as a good theory." Like many other scientists, he knew that theories can be insightful. Of course, theories differ; some are less comprehensive or adequate than others, some are no longer useful, some reflect one culture but not another. Nevertheless without them we have only a heap.

Questions and Answers

As we saw in Chapter 1, the first step in the science of human development is to pose a question, which often springs from a developmental theory. Among the thousands of important questions are the following, each central to one of the five theories described in this chapter:

1. Does the impact of early experience—of breast-feeding or attachment or abuse—linger into adulthood, even if the experience is seemingly forgotten?
2. Does learning depend on specific encouragement, punishment, and role models?
3. Do children develop morals, even if they are not taught right from wrong?
4. Does culture guide behavior?
5. Is survival a basic instinct, underlying all personal and social decisions?

Each of these five questions is answered "yes" by, in order, psychoanalytic theory, behaviorism, cognitive theory, sociocultural theory, and the two universal theories, humanism and evolutionary theory. Each question is answered "no" or "not necessarily" by several others. For every answer, more questions arise: Why or why not? When and how? So what? This last question is crucial; the implications and applications of the answers affect everyone's daily life.

To be more specific about what theories do:
- Theories produce *hypotheses*.
- Theories generate *discoveries*.
- Theories offer *practical guidance*.

A popular book of child-rearing advice, *Battle Hymn of the Tiger Mother* (Chua, 2011), advocates a parenting style that demands high achievement. For example, the author rejected a birthday card, hastily handmade by her 4-year-old daughter, saying:

> I don't want this. . . . I want a better one—one that you've put some thought and effort into. . . . I deserve better.

[p. 103]

Reactions to Chua's book have been either very positive or very negative. Six months after the book was published, of the first 500 reader reviews on Amazon, 42 percent gave it the highest ratings, 23 percent the lowest, and the three ratings between high and low averaged only 12 percent each. Explaining these reactions, one professional reviewer wrote:

> There was bound to be some pushback. All the years of nurturance overload simply got to be too much. The breast-feeding through toddlerhood, nonstop baby wearing, co-sleeping, "Baby Mozart" . . . . After "free range" parenting . . . [and] "simplicity parenting" [came] a kind of edgy irritation with it all: a new stance of get-tough-no-nonsense, frequently called—with no small amount of pride—being a bad mother.
>
> [*Warner, 2011, p. 11*]

Chua was surprised at the reactions, arguing that many people misinterpreted what she wrote (2011). Some of the positive comments from readers say that the book is a provocative memoir, not necessarily to be followed step by step. That makes it more like a theory than a parenting manual.

Chua's narrative shows that her strategies do not always work as she hoped. But *Tiger Mother* illustrates one fact: Everyone has theories about development, some promoted with fierce intensity. For all of us, opinions about how to respond to children, adolescents, and adults often can be traced to the five theories that we will soon describe.

Happy Family? Not always! Probably every mother of teenagers has a theory about child-rearing that her children sometimes resist, as Amy Chua (*right*) found with Lulu (*left*) and Sophia (*middle*). In this family, the result was a best-selling book, that Amy calls a "self-parody."

Facts and Norms

A **norm** is an average or usual event or experience. It is related to the word "normal," although it has a slightly different meaning. For instance, my cousin's bride dress had a long white veil because in Western culture it is a norm for brides to wear white, symbolizing purity, but in Asian culture brides wear red, symbolizing celebration.

To be abnormal (not normal) implies that something is wrong, but norms are not meant to be right or wrong. A norm is an average—not an arithmetical mean or median, but a mode, a common behavior that results from biological or social pressure. Thus, norms reflect facts in that norms can be calculated (such as the norm for babies beginning to walk or for brides wearing a certain color), but as you learned in Chapter 1, differences from the norm are not necessarily deficits.

Do not confuse theories with norms or facts. Theories raise questions and suggest hypotheses, and they lead to research to gather empirical data. **[Lifespan Link:** The scientific method is discussed in Chapter 1.] Those data are facts that suggest conclusions, which may verify or refute a theory, although other interpretations of the data and new research to investigate the theory are always possible.

Thus, theories are neither true nor false. Ideally, they are provocative and useful, leading to hypotheses and exploration. For example, some people dismiss Darwin's theory of evolution as "just a theory," while others believe it is a fact that explains all of nature since the beginning of time. No and no. Good theories should neither be dismissed as wrong nor equated with facts. Instead, theories deepen thought; they are useful (like a house plan), provoking insight, interpretation, and research.

As already explained, developmental theories are comprehensive and detailed, unlike the simple theories of children or the implicit theories that underlie the customs and assumptions of each culture. But to clarify the distinction between

norm An average, or standard, measurement, calculated from the measurements of many individuals within a specific group or population.

(a)   (b)

Backpacks or Bouquets? Children worldwide are nervous on the first day of school, but their coping reflects implicit cultural theories. Kindergartener Madelyn Ricker in Georgia shows her new backpack to her teacher, and elementary school children in Russia bring flowers to their teachers.

theory and fact, we return to the simple theory of the bride doll. My bitterness was one outcome of a dominant theory in my childhood culture—a pro-family theory. The theory led to a series of assumptions, including that marriage and motherhood were the destiny for every girl, celebrated in an elaborate, expensive wedding dress. Alternatives were sad and shameful.

The pro-family theory of my childhood led to norms, evident in my father and his four siblings, all of whom pitied my mother's two unmarried sisters (her six other sisters were married). Reflecting our culture, children played a game called Old Maid, with cards that could all be paired except for one card of an ugly woman (the old maid). That theory was reflected in the laws and assumptions of my community: Having more than one spouse was illegal (bigamists went to jail), divorce meant a "failed" marriage and "broken" family, and "only" children had psychological problems.

True to the dominant theory of my childhood, I fantasized about my wedding, named my seven possible children, and never imagined that maintaining a marriage and raising children was anything but "happy ever after." Norms have changed, reflected in statistics as well as research that singleton children (no longer called "only") are often high achievers with successful lives (Falbo et al., 2009), and that adults who never marry are often quite happy and accomplished. **[Lifespan Link:** Single adults are described in Chapter 22.]

Some say that the pro-family theory I knew as a child has been replaced, at least in Western middle-class culture, by another implicit theory, that personal happiness is the goal of life. This newer theory leads to alternate practices: Parents strive to make their children happy, dissatisfied spouses divorce, self-esteem is more important than academic success—all of which then led to the tiger-mother pushback.

Obviously, science is needed. Theories are not facts, and "each theory of developmental psychology always has a view of humans that reflects philosophical, economic, and political beliefs" (Miller, 2011, p. 17). Scientists question norms, develop hypotheses, and design studies. That leads to conclusions that undercut some theories and modify others, to the benefit of all.

Without developmental theories, we would be merely reactive and bewildered, adrift and increasingly befuddled, blindly following our culture and our prejudices, less able to help anyone with a developmental problem.

SUMMING UP

Theories provide a framework for organizing and understanding the thousands of observations and daily behaviors that occur in every aspect of development. Theories are not facts, but they allow us to question norms, suggest hypotheses, and provide guidance. Thus, theories are practical and applied: They frame and organize our millions of experiences. ∎

>> Grand Theories

In the first half of the twentieth century, two opposing theories—psychoanalytic theory and behaviorism (also called *learning theory*)—began as general theories of psychology, each with applications in the study of development. By mid-century, cognitive theory had emerged, becoming the dominant seedbed of research hypotheses. All three theories are "grand" in that they are comprehensive, enduring, and widely applied (McAdams & Pals, 2006), although they are not universally accepted (as you will soon read). To understand development we begin with these theories. Be forewarned: Grand theories are less grand than scientists once hoped.

Psychoanalytic Theory: Freud and Erikson

Inner drives, deep motives, and unconscious needs rooted in childhood are the foundation of **psychoanalytic theory.** These basic underlying forces are thought to influence every aspect of thinking and behavior, from the smallest details of daily life to the crucial choices of a lifetime.

Freud's Ideas

Psychoanalytic theory originated with Sigmund Freud (1856–1939), an Austrian physician who treated patients suffering from mental illness. He listened to their accounts of dreams and fantasies and to their uncensored streams of thought, and he constructed an elaborate, multifaceted theory.

According to Freud, development in the first six years of life occurs in three stages, each characterized by sexual interest and pleasure arising from a particular part of the body. His theory of childhood sexuality was one reason psychoanalytic theory was rejected at first, because Victorian sensibilities arose from an opposite theory, that children were innocent, asexual beings, and that even in adulthood sexual passions were shameful.

According to Freud, in infancy the erotic body part is the mouth (the *oral stage*); in early childhood it is the anus (the *anal stage*); in the preschool years it is the penis (the *phallic stage*), a source of pride and fear among boys and a reason for sadness and envy among girls. Then, after a quiet period (*latency*), the *genital stage* arrives at puberty, lasting throughout adulthood. (Table 2.1 describes stages in Freud's theory.)

Freud maintained that sensual satisfaction (from stimulation of the mouth, anus, or penis) is linked to major developmental stages, needs and challenges. During the oral stage, for example, sucking provides not only nourishment but also erotic joy and attachment to the mother. Kissing in adulthood is a vestige of the oral stage. Next, during the anal stage, pleasures arise from self-control (initially with defecation and toilet training) and so on.

psychoanalytic theory A grand theory of human development that holds that irrational, unconscious drives and motives, often originating in childhood, underlie human behavior.

Freud at Work In addition to being the world's first psychoanalyst, Sigmund Freud was a prolific writer. His many papers and case histories, primarily descriptions of his patients' symptoms and sexual urges, helped make the psychoanalytic perspective a dominant force for much of the twentieth century.

Odd or Common? The oddity here is not the biting toddler, but the old leather suitcase, or perhaps Freud's interpretation of the oral stage. Everyone who knows babies expects them to mouth whatever they can.

TABLE 2.1	Comparison of Freud's Psychosexual and Erikson's Psychosocial Stages	
Approximate Age	**Freud (Psychosexual)**	**Erikson (Psychosocial)**
Birth to 1 year	*Oral Stage* The lips, tongue, and gums are the focus of pleasurable sensations in the baby's body, and sucking and feeding are the most stimulating activities.	*Trust vs. Mistrust* Babies either trust that others will satisfy their basic needs, including nourishment, warmth, cleanliness, and physical contact, **or** develop mistrust about the care of others.
1–3 years	*Anal Stage* The anus is the focus of pleasurable sensations in the baby's body, and toilet training is the most important activity.	*Autonomy vs. Shame and Doubt* Children either become self-sufficient in many activities, including toileting, feeding, walking, exploring, and talking, **or** doubt their own abilities.
3–6 years	*Phallic Stage* The phallus, or penis, is the most important body part, and pleasure is derived from genital stimulation. Boys are proud of their penises; girls wonder why they don't have them.	*Initiative vs. Guilt* Children either try to undertake many adultlike activities **or** internalize the limits and prohibitions set by parents. They feel either adventurous **or** guilty.
6–11 years	*Latency* Not really a stage, latency is an interlude. Sexual needs are quiet; psychic energy flows into sports, schoolwork, and friendship.	*Industry vs. Inferiority* Children busily practice and then master new skills **or** feel inferior, unable to do anything well.
Adolescence	*Genital Stage* The genitals are the focus of pleasurable sensations, and the young person seeks sexual stimulation and satisfaction in heterosexual relationships.	*Identity vs. Role Confusion* Adolescents task themselves "Who am I?" They establish sexual, political, religious, and vocational identities **or** are confused about their roles.
Adulthood	Freud believed that the genital stage lasts throughout adulthood. He also said that the goal of a healthy life is "to love and to work."	*Intimacy vs. Isolation* Young adults seek companionship and love **or** become isolated from others, fearing rejection. *Generativity vs. Stagnation* Middle-aged adults contribute to future generations through work, creative activities, and parenthood **or** they stagnate. *Integrity vs. Despair* Older adults try to make sense of their lives, either seeing life as a meaningful whole **or** despairing at goals never reached.

One of Freud's most influential ideas was that each stage includes its own potential conflicts. Conflict occurs, for instance, when mothers try to wean their babies (oral stage) or when parents try to control the sexual interests of adolescents (genital stage). According to Freud, how people experience and resolve these conflicts determines personality lifelong because "the early stages provide the foundation for adult behavior" (Salkind, 2004, p. 125).

Freud did not believe that new stages occurred after puberty; rather, he believed that adult personalities and habits were influenced by earlier stages. Unconscious conflicts rooted in early life may be evident in adult behavior—for instance, smoking cigarettes (oral) or keeping a clean and orderly house (anal) or falling in love with a much older partner (phallic).

For all of us, psychoanalytic theory contends, that childhood fantasies and memories remain powerful lifelong, particularly as they affect the sex drive (which Freud called the *libido*). If you have ever wondered why lovers call each other "baby" or why many people refer to their spouse as their "old lady" or "sugar daddy," then Freud's theory provides an explanation: The parent–child relationship echoes in all later relationships.

Erikson's Ideas

Many of Freud's followers became famous theorists themselves. They acknowledged the importance of the unconscious and of early childhood experience, but each of them expanded and modified Freud's ideas. One of them, Erik Erikson (1902–1994), proposed a comprehensive developmental theory that is still respected.

Erikson's mother, pregnant with him, left her native Denmark alone by train to Germany, where she later married Erikson's pediatrician. After a traditional German education, in emerging adulthood Erikson left Germany to wander for years in Italy, as did many artistic young adults at that time. When he decided to settle down, he became an art teacher for the children of Freud's patients, who had traveled to Vienna for psychoanalysis. He met and married a Canadian, fleeing to the United States just before World War II. His temperament, his travel, and his studies of Harvard students, Boston children at play, and child-rearing among the Sioux and Yurok Indians all led Erikson to stress cultural diversity, social change, and psychological crises throughout life (Erikson, 1969).

Erikson described eight developmental stages, each characterized by a particular challenge, or *developmental crisis* (summarized in Table 2.1). Although Erikson named two polarities at each crisis, he recognized a wide range of outcomes between those opposites. For most people, development at each stage leads to neither extreme but to something in between.

In *initiative versus guilt*, for example, 3- to 6-year-olds undertake activities that exceed the limits set by their parents and culture. They jump into swimming pools, pull their pants on backwards, make cakes according to their own recipes, and wander off alone. Such efforts to act independently produce feelings of pride or failure, producing lifelong guilt if adults are too critical or if social norms are too strict. Most adults fall somewhere between unbridled initiative and crushing guilt, depending on their early childhood experiences.

As you can see from Table 2.1, Erikson's first five stages are closely related to Freud's stages. Erikson, like Freud, believed that problems of adult life echo unresolved childhood conflicts. For example, an adult who has difficulty establishing a secure, mutual relationship with a life partner may never have resolved the first crisis of early infancy, *trust versus mistrust*. Or perhaps in late adulthood, one older person may be outspoken while another avoids saying anything, because each resolved the initiative-versus-guilt stage in opposite ways. However in two crucial aspects, Erikson's stages differ significantly from Freud's:

1. Erikson's stages emphasize family and culture, not sexual urges.
2. Erikson recognizes adult development, with three stages after adolescence.

A Legendary Couple In his first 30 years, Erikson never fit into a particular local community, since he frequently changed nations, schools, and professions. Then he met Joan. In their first five decades of marriage, they raised a family and wrote several books. If he had published his theory at age 73 (when this photograph was taken) instead of in his 40s, would he still have described life as a series of crises?

Pink or Purple Hair These adolescents think they are nonconformist, and their short skirts, opaque tights, and hairstyles are certainly unlike those of their mothers or grandmothers. But they are similar to adolescents everywhere during each particular historical period—seeking to establish their own distinct identity.

Especially for Teachers Your kindergartners are talkative and always moving. They almost never sit quietly and listen to you. What would Erik Erikson recommend? (see response, page 42)

>> **Response for Teachers** (from page 41):
Erikson would note that the behavior of 5-year-olds is affected by their developmental stage and by their culture. Therefore, you might design your curriculum to accommodate active, noisy children.

An Early Behaviorist John Watson was an early proponent of learning theory. His ideas are still influential and controversial today.

ARCHIVES OF THE HISTORY OF AMERICAN PSYCHOLOGY/THE UNIVERSITY OF AKRON

Behaviorism: Conditioning and Social Learning

The second grand theory arose in direct opposition to the psychoanalytic notion of the unconscious. John B. Watson (1878–1958) argued that if psychology was to be a true science, psychologists should examine only what they could see and measure: behavior, not irrational thoughts and hidden urges. In his words:

> Why don't we make what we can *observe* the real field of psychology? Let us limit ourselves to things that can be observed, and formulate laws concerned only with those things. . . . We can observe behavior—what the organism does or says.
>
> [*Watson, 1924/1998, p. 6*]

According to Watson, if psychologists focus on behavior, they will realize that everything can be learned. He wrote:

> Give me a dozen healthy infants, well-formed, and my own specified world to bring them up in and I'll guarantee to take any one at random and train him to become any type of specialist I might select—doctor, lawyer, artist, merchant-chief, and yes, even beggar-man and thief, regardless of his talents, penchants, tendencies, abilities, vocations, and race of his ancestors.
>
> [*Watson, 1924/1998, p. 82*]

Other psychologists, especially in the United States, agreed. They developed **behaviorism** to study actual behavior, objectively and scientifically. Behaviorism is also called *learning theory* because it describes how people learn—by developing habits, bit by bit. For everyone at every age, behaviorists describe laws that describe how simple actions and environmental responses become complex competencies, such as reading a book or securing a new job.

Learning theorists believe that development occurs not in stages but in small increments: A person learns to talk, read, or anything else one tiny step at a time. Behaviorists study the laws of **conditioning,** the processes by which responses link to particular stimuli. In the first half of the twentieth century, behaviorists described only two types of conditioning: classical and operant.

Classical Conditioning

A century ago, Russian scientist Ivan Pavlov (1849–1936), after winning the Nobel Prize for his work on animal digestion, began to examine the link between stimulus and response. While studying salivation, Pavlov noted that his experimental dogs drooled not only at the smell of food but also, eventually, at the footsteps of the people bringing food. This observation led Pavlov to perform a famous experiment: He conditioned dogs to salivate when hearing a particular noise.

Pavlov began by sounding a tone just before presenting food. After a number of repetitions of the tone-then-food sequence, dogs began salivating at the sound even when there was no food. This simple experiment demonstrated **classical conditioning** (also called *respondent conditioning*).

In classical conditioning, a person or animal learns to associate a neutral stimulus with a meaningful stimulus, gradually responding to the neutral stimulus in

behaviorism A grand theory of human development that studies observable behavior. Behaviorism is also called *learning theory* because it describes the laws and processes by which behavior is learned.

conditioning According to behaviorism, the processes by which responses become linked to particular stimuli and learning takes place. The word *conditioning* is used to emphasize the importance of repeated practice, as when an athlete *conditions* his or her body to perform well by training for a long time.

classical conditioning The learning process in which a meaningful stimulus (such as the smell of food to a hungry animal) is connected with a neutral stimulus (such as the sound of a tone) that had no special meaning before conditioning. (Also called *respondent conditioning*.)

the same way as to the meaningful one. In Pavlov's original experiment, the dog associated the tone (the neutral stimulus) with food (the meaningful stimulus) and eventually responded to the tone as if it were the food itself. The conditioned response to the tone (no longer neutral but now a conditioned stimulus) was evidence that learning had occurred.

Behaviorists see dozens of examples of classical conditioning in life-span development. Infants learn to smile at their parents because they associate them with food and play; toddlers become afraid of busy streets if the noise of traffic repeatedly frightens them; college students enjoy—or fear—sitting in class, depending on past schooling; adults are relieved or terrified upon entering a hospital because of earlier associations with that experience.

One specific example of classical conditioning is called the *white coat syndrome,* when past experiences with medical professionals have conditioned someone to feel anxious. For that reason, when someone dressed in white takes their blood pressure, it is higher than it would be under normal circumstances. White coat syndrome is apparent in about half of the United States population over age 80 (Bulpitt et al., 2013). Many nurses now wear colorful blouses and many doctors wear street clothes to prevent conditioned anxiety in patients.

Observation Quiz How is Pavlov similar to Freud in appearance, and how do both look different from the other theorists pictured? (see answer, page 44)

A Contemporary of Freud Ivan Pavlov was a physiologist who received the Nobel Prize in 1904 for his research on digestive processes. It was this line of study that led to his discovery of classical conditioning, when his research on dog saliva led to insight about learning.

operant conditioning The learning process by which a particular action is followed by something desired (which makes the person or animal more likely to repeat the action) or by something unwanted (which makes the action less likely to be repeated). (Also called *instrumental conditioning*.)

Operant Conditioning

The most influential North American proponent of behaviorism was B. F. Skinner (1904–1990). Skinner agreed that psychology should focus on the science of behavior. His famous contribution was to recognize another type of conditioning—**operant conditioning** (also called *instrumental conditioning*)—in which animals (including people) act and then something follows that action. If the consequence that follows is enjoyable, the animal tends to repeat the behavior; if the consequence is unpleasant, the animal might not. Usually, learning occurs only after several repetitions with consequences.

Pleasant consequences are sometimes called *rewards,* but behaviorists do not call them that because what some other people call "punishment" may actually be a pleasant consequence and vice versa. For example, parents think they punish their children by withholding dessert, by spanking them, by not letting them play, by speaking harshly to them, and so on. But a particular child might dislike the dessert, so being deprived of it is no punishment. Or a child might not mind a spanking, especially if that is the only time the child gets parental attention. Thus, an intended punishment becomes a reward.

Similarly, teachers sometimes send misbehaving children out of the classroom and principals suspend them from school. However, if a child hates the teacher, leaving class is rewarding. In fact, research on school discipline finds that some measures, including school suspension, *increase* later misbehavior (Osher et al.,

Rats, Pigeons, and People B. F. Skinner is best known for his experiments with rats and pigeons, but he also applied his knowledge to human behavior. For his daughter, he designed a glass-enclosed crib in which temperature, humidity, and perceptual stimulation could be controlled to make her time in the crib enjoyable and educational. He encouraged her first attempts to talk by smiling and responding with words, affection, or other positive reinforcement.

>> **Answer to Observation Quiz** (from page 43): Both are balding and have white beards. Note that none of the other theorists in this chapter have beards—a cohort difference, not an ideological one.

Especially for Teachers Same problem as previously (talkative kindergartners), but what would a behaviorist recommend? (see response, page 46)

reinforcement The process by which a behavior is followed by something desired, such as food for a hungry animal or a welcoming smile for a lonely person.

Still Social Learning Even in his 80s, Albert Bandura is on the faculty at Stanford University. One reason, of course, it that he is esteemed by his peers, and another reason is that, as a proponent of social learning, he believes he can still influence many others. Social interaction is central to social learning theory.

social learning theory An extension of behaviorism that emphasizes the influence that other people have over a person's behavior. Even without specific reinforcement, every individual learns many things through observation and imitation of other people.

modeling The central process of social learning, by which a person observes the actions of others and then copies them. (Modeling is also called *observational learning*.)

2010). In order to stop misbehavior, it is more effective to encourage good behavior, to "catch them being good." The true test is the *effect* a consequence has on the individual's future actions, not whether it is intended to be a reward or a punishment. A child, or an adult, who repeats an offense may have been reinforced, not punished, for the first infraction.

Consequences that increase the frequency or strength of a particular action are called reinforcers, in a process called **reinforcement** (Skinner, 1953). Almost all of our daily behavior, from saying "Good morning" to earning a paycheck, can be understood as the result of past reinforcement, according to behaviorism, although the laws are hard to pin down.

The problem is that research on conditioning has discovered that individuals vary in their responses, as already noted with spanking. In another example, a longitudinal study of children's physical activity (playing sports, exercising, and so on) found that, for boys, the father's praise was especially important. For girls, the father's reinforcement helped, but the mother's own physical activity was the more powerful influence (Cleland et al., 2011).

Social Learning

The importance of the father and mother in our last example provides another insight. At first, behaviorists thought all behavior arose from a chain of learned responses, the result of either the association between one stimulus and another (classical conditioning) or of past reinforcement (operant conditioning). Both of those processes—classical conditioning and operant conditioning—occur, as demonstrated by many studies. However, humans are social and active, not just reactive. Instead of responding merely to their own direct experiences, "people act on the environment. They create it, preserve it, transform it, and even destroy it . . . in a socially embedded interplay" (Bandura, 2006, p. 167).

That social interplay is the foundation of **social learning theory** (see Table 2.2), which holds that humans sometimes learn without personal reinforcement. This learning often occurs through **modeling,** when people copy what they see others do (also called *observational learning*). Modeling is not simple imitation; not every role model is equal. Instead, people model only some actions, of some individuals, in some contexts.

As an example of social learning, you may know adults who, as children, saw their parents hit each other. Some such adults abuse their own partners, while others scrupulously avoid marital conflict. These two responses seem opposite, but both are the result of social learning produced by childhood observation, with

TABLE 2.2	**Three Types of Learning** Behaviorism is also called *learning theory* because it emphasizes the learning process, as shown here.	
Type of Learning	Learning Process	Result
Classical Conditioning	Learning occurs through association.	Neutral stimulus becomes conditioned response.
Operant Conditioning	Learning occurs through reinforcement and punishment.	Weak or rare responses becomes strong, frequent responses—or, with punishment, become extinct.
Social Learning	Learning occurs through modeling what others do.	Observed behaviors become copied behaviors.

one observing the benefits of abuse, the other noting the suffering. Still other adults seem unaffected by their parents' past fights: Differential susceptibility (explained in Chapter 1) may be the reason.

Generally, modeling is most likely when the observer is uncertain or inexperienced (which explains why modeling is especially powerful in childhood) and when the model is admired, powerful, nurturing, or similar to the observer (Bandura, 1986, 1997).

Social learning is common in adulthood as well. If your speech, hairstyle, or choice of shoes is similar to those of a celebrity, ask yourself why? Admiration? Similarity? Fads and fashions are most evident in adolescence and emerging adulthood because teenagers want to distinguish themselves from their parents, but they are uncertain as to how to dress or behave.

Cognitive Theory: Piaget and Information Processing

Social scientists sometimes write about the "cognitive revolution," which occurred in about 1980 when psychoanalytic and behaviorist research and therapy were overtaken by a focus on cognition. According to **cognitive theory,** thoughts and expectations profoundly affect attitudes, beliefs, values, assumptions, and actions.

This revolution was the result of increasing awareness of the power of cognition, a term that refers to thinking. Ideas, education, and language are considered part of cognition. Cognitive theory dominated psychology for decades, becoming a grand theory.

Piaget's Stages of Development

The first major cognitive theorist was the Swiss scientist Jean Piaget (1896–1980), whose academic training was in biology, with a focus on shellfish—a background that taught him to look very closely at small details. He became interested in human thought when he was hired to standardize an IQ test by noting at what age children answered each question correctly.

However, the children's wrong answers caught his attention. *How* children think is much more revealing, Piaget concluded, than *what* they know.

In the 1920s, most scientists believed that babies could not yet think. Then Piaget used scientific observation with his own three infants, finding them curious and thoughtful. Later he studied hundreds of schoolchildren. From this work Piaget formed the central thesis of cognitive theory: How children think changes with time

cognitive theory A grand theory of human development that focuses on changes in how people think over time. According to this theory, our thoughts shape our attitudes, beliefs, and behaviors.

Would You Talk to This Man? Children loved talking to Jean Piaget, and he learned by listening carefully—especially to their incorrect explanations, which no one had paid much attention to before. All his life, Piaget was absorbed with studying the way children think. He called himself a "genetic epistemologist"—one who studies how children gain knowledge about the world as they grow.

(a)   (b)   (c)

How to Think About Flowers A person's stage of cognitive growth influences how he or she thinks about everything, including flowers. (a) To an infant, in the sensorimotor stage, flowers are "known" through pulling, smelling, and even biting. (b) At the concrete operational stage, children become more logical. This boy can understand that flowers need sunlight, water, and time to grow. (c) At the adult's formal operational stage, flowers can be part of a larger, logical scheme—for instance, to earn money while cultivating beauty. As illustrated by all three photos, thinking is an active process from the beginning of life until the end.

>> **Response for Teachers** (from page 44):
Behaviorists believe that anyone can learn anything. If your goal is quiet, attentive children, begin by reinforcing a moment's quiet or a quiet child, and soon all the children will be trying to remain attentive for several minutes at a time.

cognitive equilibrium In cognitive theory, a state of mental balance in which people are not confused because they can use their existing thought processes to understand current experiences and ideas.

assimilation The reinterpretation of new experiences to fit into old ideas.

accommodation The restructuring of old ideas to include new experiences.

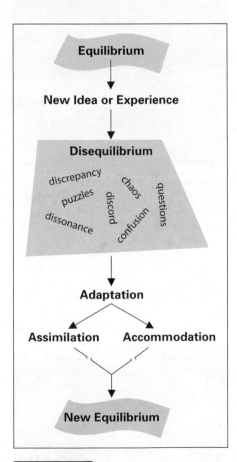

FIGURE 2.1

Challenge Me Most of us, most of the time, prefer the comfort of our conventional conclusions. According to Piaget, however, when new ideas disturb our thinking, we have an opportunity to expand our cognition with a broader and deeper understanding.

and experience, and their thought processes affect their behavior. According to cognitive theory, to understand humans one must understand thinking.

Piaget maintained that cognitive development occurs in four age-related periods, or stages: *sensorimotor, preoperational, concrete operational,* and *formal operational* (see Table 2.3). Each period fosters certain cognitive processes; for instance, infants think via their senses, and abstract logic is absent in middle childhood but possible at puberty (Inhelder & Piaget, 1958; Piaget, 1952b).

Piaget found that intellectual advancement occurs because humans at every age seek **cognitive equilibrium**—a state of mental balance. The easiest way to achieve this balance is to interpret new experiences through the lens of preexisting ideas. For example, infants grab new objects in the same way that they grasp familiar objects, children interpret their parents' behavior by assuming that adults think in the same way that children do, and adults do the same when interpreting children.

Achieving equilibrium is not always easy, however. Sometimes a new experience or question is jarring or incomprehensible. Then the individual experiences *cognitive disequilibrium,* an imbalance that creates confusion. As Figure 2.1 illustrates, disequilibrium can cause cognitive growth if people adapt their thinking. Piaget describes two types of cognitive adaptation:

- **Assimilation:** New experiences are reinterpreted to fit into, or *assimilate* old ideas.
- **Accommodation:** Old ideas are restructured to include, or *accommodate,* new experiences.

Accommodation is more difficult to achieve than assimilation, but it produces intellectual advancement. For example, if a friend's questions reveal inconsistencies in your own opinions, or if your favorite chess strategy puts you

TABLE 2.3	Piaget's Periods of Cognitive Development		
	Name of Period	Characteristics of the Period	Major Gains During the Period
Birth to 2 years	Sensorimotor	Infants use senses and motor abilities to understand the world. Learning is active, without reflection.	Infants learn that objects still exist when out of sight (*object permanence*) and begin to think through mental actions.
2–6 years	Preoperational	Children think symbolically, with language, yet children are *egocentric,* perceiving from their own perspective.	The imagination flourishes, and language becomes a significant means of self-expression and social influence.
6–11 years	Concrete operational	Children understand and apply logic. Thinking is limited by direct experience.	By applying logic, children grasp concepts of conservation, number, classification, and many other scientific ideas.
12 years through adulthood	Formal operational	Adolescents and adults use abstract and hypothetical concepts. They can use analysis, not only emotion.	Ethics, politics, and social and moral issues become fascinating as adolescents and adults use abstract, theoretical reasoning.

in checkmate, or if your mother says something completely unexpected, disequilibrium occurs. In the last example, you might *assimilate* by deciding your mother didn't mean what you heard. You might tell yourself that she was repeating something she had read or that you misheard her. However, intellectual growth would occur if, instead, you changed your view of your mother to *accommodate* a new, expanded understanding.

Ideally, when two people disagree, or when they surprise each other by what they say, adaptation is mutual. For example, when parents are startled by their children's opinions, the parents may revise their concepts of their children and even of reality, accommodating to new perceptions. If an honest discussion occurs, the children, too, might accommodate. Cognitive growth is an active process, dependent on clashing concepts that require new thought.

Information Processing

Piaget is credited with discovering that people's assumptions and perceptions affect their development, an idea now accepted by most social scientists. However, many think Piaget's theories were limited. Neuroscience, cross-cultural studies, and step-by-step understanding of cognition have revealed the limitations of Piaget's theory.

As one admirer explains, Piaget's "claims were too narrow and too broad" (Hopkins, 2011, p. 35). The narrowness comes from his focus on understanding the material world, ignoring the fact that people can be advanced in physics, biology, and math but not in other aspects of thought. The excessive broadness is reflected in his description of stages, ignoring the ongoing variability in thought. Contrary to Piaget's ideas, "intelligence is now viewed more as a modular system than as a unified system of general intelligence" (Hopkins, 2011, p. 35).

Here we introduce one newer version of cognitive theory, **information-processing theory,** inspired by the input, programming, memory, and output of a sophisticated computer. When conceptualized in that way, thinking is affected by changes throughout adulthood, as this theory describes.

Information processing is "a framework characterizing a large number of research programs" (Miller, 2011, p. 266). Instead of merely interpreting *responses* by infants and children, as Piaget did, this cognitive theory focuses on the *processes* of thought—that is, how minds work before a response and then the many ways a response might occur. The underlying theoretical basis of information processing is that the details of process shed light on the specifics of outcome.

For information-processing scientists, cognition begins with input picked up by the five senses, proceeds to brain reactions, connections, and stored memories, and concludes with some form of output. For infants, output consists of moving a hand, making a sound, or staring a split second longer at one stimulus than at another. In adults, not only words but also hesitations, neuronal activity, and bodily reactions (heartbeat, blood pressure, and the like) are studied. With the aid of sensitive technology, information-processing research has overturned some of Piaget's findings, as explained in later chapters.

However, the basic tenet of cognitive theory is true for information processing and for Piaget: Ideas matter. For instance, an information-processing study of adults who compulsively keep things that should be discarded (old papers, plastic bags, etc.) finds that they are indecisive, impulsive, and losing memory. In contrast, neuropsychological tests find that their decisiveness, impulsivity, and memory are normal (Fitch & Cougle, 2013). This is in accord with cognitive

information-processing theory A perspective that compares human thinking processes, by analogy, to computer analysis of data, including sensory input, connections, stored memories, and output.

Healthy Control Adults

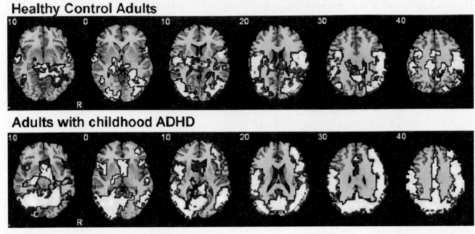

Adults with childhood ADHD

We Try Harder Details of brain scans require interpretation from neurologists, but even the novice can see that adults who have been diagnosed with ADHD (second line of images) reacted differently in this experiment when they were required to push a button only if certain letters appeared on a screen. Sustained attention to this task required more brain power (the lit areas) for those with ADHD. Notice also that certain parts of the brain were activated by the healthy adults and not by the ADHD ones. Apparently adults who had problems paying attention when they were children have learned to focus when they need to, but they do it in their own way and with more effort.

A REVIEW OF FRONTO-STRIATAL AND FRONTO-CORTICAL BRAIN ABNORMALITIES IN CHILDREN AND ADULTS WITH ATTENTION DEFICIT HYPERACTIVITY DISORDER (ADHD) AND NEW EVIDENCE FOR DYSFUNCTION IN ADULTS WITH ADHD DURING MOTIVATION AND ATTENTION BY CUBILLO ET AL, CORTEX 48 (2012) 194 E2 15, FIG. 2. WITH PERMISSION FROM ELSEVIER.

theory: A person's self-concept is crucial because it affects behavior, with cognition more influential than basic brain functions.

This approach to understanding cognition has many other applications. For example, it has long been recognized that children with ADHD (attention-deficit/hyperactivity disorder) tend to have difficulty learning in school, obeying their parents, and making friends (whether or not they are excessively active). Information processing has led to the discovery that certain brain circuits (called *fronto-striatal systems*) do not function normally in children with ADHD. Consequently, it is harder for them to read facial expressions and voice tone in order to understand emotions (Uekermann et al., 2009).

This means that children with ADHD may not know whether their father's "Come here" is an angry command or a loving suggestion, or when a classmate is hostile or friendly. Information processing helps in remediation: If a specific brain function can be improved, children may learn more, obey more, and gain friends.

Comparing Grand Theories

The grand theories have endured because they were innovative, comprehensive, and surprising. Until these theories were developed, few imagined that childhood experiences or the unconscious exert such power (psychoanalytic) or that adult behavior arises from prior reinforcement (behaviorist) or that children have quite different ways of thinking—not just less knowledge—than adults (cognitive).

These grand theories have also been soundly criticized, with many psychologists rejecting psychoanalytic theory as unscientific (Mills, 2004), behaviorism as demeaning of human potential (Chein, 1972/2008), and cognitive theory as disconnected from the social context that affects behavior. All three theories may emphasize past experiences and thoughts instead of future possibilities (Seligman et al., 2013). And, of course, they all reflect historical and cultural influences of their time (see Visualizing Development 2, p. 49).

The methods of these grand theories also differ.

- Freud and Erikson thought unconscious drives and early experiences formed the basis for later personality and behavior, so they listened to people's dreams and memories, and incorporated themes from past myths and history.
- Behaviorists instead stressed actual experiences in each individual's life, focusing on learning by association, by reinforcement, and by observation. For that reason they collected experimental data on animals of all kinds, believing that laws of behavior apply to all creatures, including humans.
- Cognitive theory held that to understand a person one must learn how that person thinks. Accordingly, Piaget gave children intellectual tasks and listened to their answers.

Highlights from Developmental Psychology over the Centuries

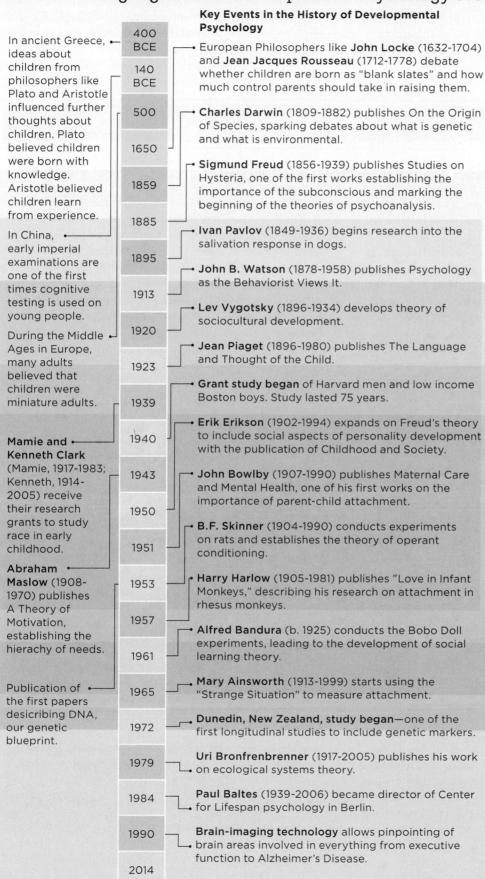

Key Events in the History of Developmental Psychology

In ancient Greece, ideas about children from philosophers like Plato and Aristotle influenced further thoughts about children. Plato believed children were born with knowledge. Aristotle believed children learn from experience.

In China, early imperial examinations are one of the first times cognitive testing is used on young people.

During the Middle Ages in Europe, many adults believed that children were miniature adults.

Mamie and Kenneth Clark (Mamie, 1917-1983; Kenneth, 1914-2005) receive their research grants to study race in early childhood.

Abraham Maslow (1908-1970) publishes A Theory of Motivation, establishing the hierachy of needs.

Publication of the first papers desicribing DNA, our genetic blueprint.

400 BCE

140 BCE

European Philosophers like **John Locke** (1632-1704) and **Jean Jacques Rousseau** (1712-1778) debate whether children are born as "blank slates" and how much control parents should take in raising them.

500

Charles Darwin (1809-1882) publishes On the Origin of Species, sparking debates about what is genetic and what is environmental.

1650

Sigmund Freud (1856-1939) publishes Studies on Hysteria, one of the first works establishing the importance of the subconscious and marking the beginning of the theories of psychoanalysis.

1859

1885

Ivan Pavlov (1849-1936) begins research into the salivation response in dogs.

1895

John B. Watson (1878-1958) publishes Psychology as the Behaviorist Views It.

1913

Lev Vygotsky (1896-1934) develops theory of sociocultural development.

1920

Jean Piaget (1896-1980) publishes The Language and Thought of the Child.

1923

Grant study began of Harvard men and low income Boston boys. Study lasted 75 years.

1939

Erik Erikson (1902-1994) expands on Freud's theory to include social aspects of personality development with the publication of Childhood and Society.

1940

John Bowlby (1907-1990) publishes Maternal Care and Mental Health, one of his first works on the importance of parent-child attachment.

1943

1950

B.F. Skinner (1904-1990) conducts experiments on rats and establishes the theory of operant conditioning.

1951

Harry Harlow (1905-1981) publishes "Love in Infant Monkeys," describing his research on attachment in rhesus monkeys.

1953

1957

Alfred Bandura (b. 1925) conducts the Bobo Doll experiments, leading to the development of social learning theory.

1961

Mary Ainsworth (1913-1999) starts using the "Strange Situation" to measure attachment.

1965

Dunedin, New Zealand, study began—one of the first longitudinal studies to include genetic markers.

1972

Uri Bronfrenbrenner (1917-2005) publishes his work on ecological systems theory.

1979

Paul Baltes (1939-2006) became director of Center for Lifespan psychology in Berlin.

1984

Brain-imaging technology allows pinpointing of brain areas involved in everything from executive function to Alzheimer's Disease.

1990

2014

Major Theories of Developmental Psychology

Psychoanalytic Theory: holds that unconscious drives, often originating in childhood, underlie human behavior.

Behaviorism: studies observable human behavior; also called learning theory because it focuses on the process of learning.

Cognitive Theories of Development: focus on how people's thoughts change as they grow older.

Humanism: stresses the potential for all human beings for self-actualization.

Cultural Theories of Development: focus on the impact of culture on human behavior.

Information Processing Theories: focus on how the mind interprets perceptions on sensory input, stored memories and output.

Evolutionary Theories of Development: focus on how human behavior developed as an adaptation between biology and envionrment.

Despite all their differences, like all good theories these three grand theories are provocative, each leading to newer theories (as shown here by Erikson, Bandura, and information processing), to hypotheses tested in thousands of experiments, and to countless applications. Here is one example.

OPPOSING PERSPECTIVES

Toilet Training—How and When?

Remember that theories are practical. For example, parents hear opposite advice about when to respond to an infant's cry. Some experts tell them that ignoring the cry will affect the infant's future happiness (psychoanalytic—advocating attachment parenting), while others tell them that responding to every cry will teach the child to be demanding and spoiled (behaviorist—advocating strong character). Neither theory directly predicts such dire results, but each underlies one side or the other of this debate.

Meanwhile, cognitive theory seeks to understand the reason for the cry. Is it a reflexive wail of hurt and hunger, or is it an expression of social pain? According to this theory, when the meaning of an action is understood, people can respond effectively. Thus all three theories have led to advise for parents—although in conflicting ways.

Another practical example is toilet training. In the nineteenth century, many parents believed that, to distinguish humans from lower animals, bodily functions should be controlled as soon as possible. Consequently, they began toilet training in the first months of life (Accardo, 2006). Then psychoanalytic theory pegged the first year as the oral stage (Freud) or the time when trust was crucial (Erikson), before the toddler's anal stage (Freud) or autonomy needs(Erikson).

What to Do? Books on infant care give contradictory advice. Even in this photo one can see that these modern mothers follow divergent parenting practices. One is breast-feeding a one-year-old, another has toilet, trained her toddler, one sits cross-legged so her baby can be on her lap, which would be impossible for another—and so on.

ANDREA MOHIN/THE NEW YORK TIMES/REDUX PICTURES

Consequently, applying psychoanalytic theory led to postponing toilet training to avoid serious personality problems later on. Soon this was part of many manuals on child rearing. For example, a leading pediatrician, Barry Brazelton, wrote a popular book for parents advising that toilet training should not begin until the child is cognitively, emotionally, and biologically ready—around age 2 for daytime training and age 3 for nighttime dryness.

As a society, we are far too concerned about pushing children to be toilet trained early. I don't even like the phrase "toilet training." It really should be toilet learning.

[*Brazelton & Sparrow, 2006, p. 193*]

By the middle of the twentieth century, many U.S. psychologists had rejected psychoanalytic theory and become behaviorists. Since they believed that learning depends primarily on conditioning, some suggested that toilet training occur whenever the parent wished, not at a particular age. In one application of behaviorism, children drank quantities of their favorite juice, sat on the potty with a parent nearby to keep them entertained, and then, when the inevitable occurred, the parent praised and rewarded them—a powerful reinforcement. Children were conditioned (in one day, according to some behaviorists) to head for the potty whenever the need arose (Azrin & Foxx, 1974).

Rejecting both of these theories, some Western parents prefer to start potty training very early. One U.S. mother began training her baby just 33 days after birth. She noticed when her son was about to defecate, held him above the toilet, and had trained him by 6 months (Sun & Rugolotto, 2004). Such early training is criticized by all of the grand theories, although each theory has a particular perspective, as now explained.

Behaviorists would say that the mother was trained, not the son. She taught herself to be sensitive to his body; she was reinforced when she read his clues correctly. Psychoanalysts would wonder what made her such an anal person, with a need for cleanliness and order that did not consider the child's needs. Cognitive theory would wonder what the mother was thinking, particularly if she had an odd fear of normal body functions.

What is best? Dueling theories and diverse parental practices have led the authors of an article for pediatricians to conclude that "despite families and physicians having addressed this issue for generations, there still is no consensus regarding the best method or even a standard definition of toilet training" (Howell et al., 2011, p. 262). One comparison study of toilet-training methods found that the behaviorist approach was best for older children with serious disabilities but that almost every method succeeded with the average young child. No method seemed to result in marked negative emotional consequences (Klassen et al., 2006). Many sources explain that because each child is different, there is no "right" way, "the best strategy for implementing training is still unknown" (Colaco et al., 2013, p. 49).

That conclusion arises from cognitive theory, which holds that each person's assumptions and ideas determine their actions. Therefore, since North American parents are from many cultures with diverse assumptions, marked variation is evident in beliefs regarding toilet training. Contemporary child-rearing advice also considers the child's own cognitive development. If the child is at the sensorimotor stage, then body sensations and reflexive actions are central to training. Later on, when language has been added to the mix, the child's intellectual awareness (evidenced in "big boy" underpants and so on) is crucial.

What values are embedded in each practice? Psychoanalytic theory focuses on later personality, behaviorism stresses conditioning of body impulses, and cognitive theory considers variation in the child's intellectual capacity and in adult values. Even the idea that each child is different, making no one method best, is the outgrowth of a theory. There is no easy answer, but many parents are firm believers in one approach or another. That confirms the statement at the beginning of this chapter, that we all have theories, sometimes strongly held, whether we know it or not.

SUMMING UP

The three grand theories originated decades ago, each pioneered by thinkers who set forth psychological frameworks so comprehensive and creative that they deserve to be called "grand." Each grand theory has a different focus: emotions (psychoanalytic theory), actions (behaviorism), and thoughts (cognitive theory).

Freud and Erikson thought unconscious drives and early experiences form later personality and behavior. Behaviorists stress experiences in the more recent past and focus on learning by association, by reinforcement, and by observation. Cognitive theory holds that to understand a person, one must learn how that person thinks, either in stages (Piaget) or in the organization and maturation of many components of the brain (information processing).

>> Newer Theories

You have surely noticed that the seminal grand theorists (Freud, Erikson, Pavlov, Skinner, Piaget) were all men, scientists from western Europe or North America, born more than a hundred years ago. These background variables are limiting. (Of course, female, non–Western, and contemporary theorists are limited by their backgrounds, too.) Despite their impressive insights, the three grand theories no longer seem as comprehensive as they once did, in part because their limitations have become more apparent.

New theories have emerged that, unlike the grand theories, are multicultural and multidisciplinary and thus are more in accord with the life-span perspective, as explained in Chapter 1. The first theory described below, sociocultural theory, draws on education, anthropology, and history. The second theory, universal theory, has two notable manifestations: humanism arises from theology, political science, and history, and evolutionary psychology from archeology, ethology, and biology.

Sociocultural Theory: Vygotsky and Beyond

sociocultural theory A newer theory that holds that development results from the dynamic interaction of each person with the surrounding social and cultural forces.

The central thesis of **sociocultural theory** is that human development results from the dynamic interaction between developing persons and their surrounding society. Culture is viewed not as something external that impinges on developing persons but as integral to their development every day via the social context (all the dynamic systems described in Chapter 1).

Social Interaction

The pioneer of the sociocultural perspective was Lev Vygotsky (1896–1934), a psychologist from the former Soviet Union, already mentioned in Chapter 1 because aspects of the sociocultural approach are now accepted by virtually all contemporary developmentalists.

Vygotsky was a leader in describing the interaction between culture and education. He noted that each community in his native Russia (comprising Asians and Europeans, of many faiths and many languages) taught children whatever beliefs and habits were valued in each culture. He studied cognitive competency in many people, including children with special needs. For example, his research included how farmers used tools, how illiterate people thought of abstract ideas, and how children learned in school. In his view, each person, schooled or not, develops with the guidance of more skilled members of his or her society, who are tutors or mentors in an **apprenticeship in thinking** (Vygotsky, 1934/1986).

apprenticeship in thinking Vygotsky's term for how cognition is stimulated and developed in people by more skilled members of society.

guided participation The process by which people learn from others who guide their experiences and explorations.

To describe this process, Vygotsky developed the concept of **guided participation,** the method used by parents, teachers, and entire societies to teach novices the skills and habits expected within their culture. Tutors engage learners (also called *apprentices*) in joint activities, offering not only instruction but also "mutual involvement in several widespread cultural practices with great importance for learning: narratives, routines, and play" (Rogoff, 2003, p. 285). Active apprenticeship is a central concept of sociocultural theory because each person depends on others to learn. This process of guided participation is informal, pervasive, and social.

For example, one of my students came to my office with her young son, who eyed my candy dish but did not take any.

> "He can have one if it's all right with you," I whispered to his mother.
> She nodded and told him, "Dr. Berger will let you have one piece of candy."
> He smiled shyly and quickly took one.
> "What do you say?" she prompted.
> "Thank you," he replied, glancing at me out of the corner of his eye.
> "You're welcome," I said.

In that brief moment, all three of us were engaged in cultural transmission. We were surrounded by cultural traditions and practices, including my authority as professor and the fact that I have an office and a candy dish (a social custom that I learned from one of my teachers). True to my culture, I deferred to the direct authority of the mother, who, true to her culture, had taught her son to be polite and obedient. As an apprentice, he needed to be reminded to say "thank you." I guided him as well, in part by saying he could have one piece (encouraging math, authority, and moderation all at once). Specifics differ, but all adults teach children skills expected in their society and culture.

All cultural patterns and beliefs are social constructions, not natural laws, according to sociocultural theorists. These theorists find customs to be powerful, shaping the development of every person, and they also find that some assumptions need to shift to allow healthier development. Vygotsky stressed this point, arguing that mentally and physically disabled children should be educated (Vygotsky, 1925/1994). This is a cultural belief that has become law in the United States but is not yet accepted in many other nations.

The Zone of Proximal Development

According to sociocultural theory, all learning is social, whether people are learning a manual skill, a social custom, or a language. As part of the apprenticeship of thinking, a mentor (parent, peer, or professional) finds the learner's zone of proximal development, which contains the skills, knowledge, and concepts that the learner is close (proximal) to acquiring but cannot yet master without help.

Through sensitive assessment of the learner, the mentor engages the mentee within that zone. Together, in a "process of joint construction," new knowledge is attained (Valsiner, 2006). The mentor must avoid two opposite dangers: boredom and failure. Some frustration is permitted, but the learner must be actively engaged, never passive or overwhelmed (see Figure 2.2).

To make this seemingly abstract process more concrete, consider an example: a father teaching his daughter to ride a bicycle. He begins by rolling her along, supporting her weight while telling her to keep her hands on the handlebars, to push the right and left pedals in rhythm, and to look straight ahead. As she becomes more comfortable and confident, he begins to roll her along more quickly, praising her for steadily pumping. Within a few lessons, he is jogging beside her, holding only the handlebars. When he senses that she could maintain her balance, he urges her to pedal faster while he loosens his grip. Perhaps without realizing it, she rides on her own.

Note that this is not instruction by preset rules or reinforcement. Sociocultural learning is active: No one learns bike-riding by reading and memorizing written instructions, and no good teacher merely repeats a prepared lesson. Because each learner has personal traits, experiences, and aspirations, education must be individualized. Learning styles vary: Some people need more assurance; some learn best by looking, others by hearing. A mentor must sense when support or freedom is needed and how peers can help (they may be the best mentors). Skilled teachers know when the zone of proximal development expands and shifts.

Home-Schooling Academic achievement tests in reading and math class may crowd out practical skills, such as how to apply proper pressure with a rolling pin. This boy is fortunate that his mother guides him in mastering the domestic arts. He also is learning other skills in regular school.

CULTURA/FRANK AND HELENA/GETTY IMAGES

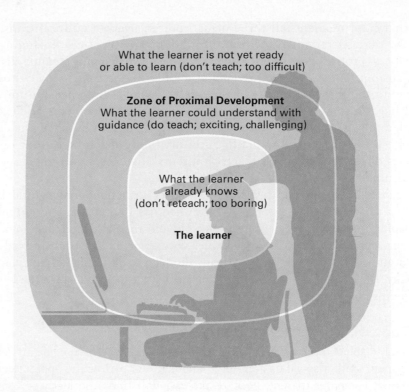

FIGURE 2.2

The Magic Middle Somewhere between the boring and the impossible is the zone of proximal development, where interaction between teacher and learner results in knowledge never before grasped or skills not already mastered. The intellectual excitement of that zone is the origin of the joy that both instruction and study can bring.

Excursions into and through the zone of proximal development, as illustrated by the boy prompted to say "thank you" and the girl learning to balance on a bike, are commonplace for all of us. Examples are everywhere. At the thousand or so science museums in the United States, children ask numerous questions, and adults guide their scientific knowledge (Haden, 2010). Physical therapists tailor exercises to the particular patient and the surrounding context. For example, when physical therapists provide exercise for patients in intensive care, they not only take into account the illness but also the culture of the ICU (Pawlik & Kress, 2013).

In general, mentors, attuned to ever-shifting abilities and motivation, continually urge a new competence—the next level, not the moon. For their part, learners ask questions, show interest, and demonstrate progress, which guides and inspires the mentors. When education goes well, both are fully engaged and productive within the zone of proximal development. Particular skills and processes vary enormously, but the overall interaction is the same.

Taking Culture into Account

The sociocultural perspective has led contemporary scientists to consider social context in every study. Earlier theorists and researchers are criticized for failing to do so. This newer approach considers not only differences between one nation and another, but also differences between one region and another, between one cohort and another, between one ethnic group and another, and so on. This has led to a wealth of provocative findings, many described later. Here we briefly present only a few:

- Context counts: Children who attend multiethnic schools are less ethnically prejudiced than other children (Killen at al., 2010).
- Among adults, acceptance of same-sex marriage has increased in recent years. This new attitude is true in all cohorts (see Figure 1.4 in the previous chapter) but is particularly evident among certain groups. The reason most often given is sociocultural: Many people say they know people who are homosexual, and that has changed their minds. Of course, the fact that more gay and lesbian adults make public their sexual orientation is itself a sociocultural phenomenon (Pew, 2013).
- The proportion of U.S. elders in nursing homes has declined (now less than 4 percent of those over age 65), again reflecting a sociocultural shift.
- Cultures differ not only in values but also in how strictly or loosely those values are held. People in cultures that accept nonconformists consider themselves more creative and tolerant; others consider them lax and permissive (Gelfand, 2012).

Finally, culture needs to be considered person by person as each individual participates in some aspects of the culture while rejecting or modifying others. Consider two sisters.

> When the local constables knocked on Chona's parents' door with their wooden staffs, searching for children to send to the school, her parents hid their children under the wooden bed just inside the door and told the constables that the children did not exist. But Chona's sister Susana, ever rebellious, leaped out from under the bed and yelled . . . "I want to go to school."
>
> *[Rogoff, 2011, p. 5]*

These two sisters, both speaking a local language, raised in the same tribal culture (Mayan, in San Pedro, Guatemala), nevertheless followed distinct cultural paths. Later Susana refused an arranged marriage and moved to a nearby town, unlike her unschooled sister who married a man she did not like and stayed close to her childhood home all her life. Culture shapes everyone, but each person experiences it differently.

Especially for Adoptive Families Does the importance of genetics mean that adopted children will not bond securely with nonbiological caregivers? (see response, page 57)

The Universal Perspective: Humanism and Evolutionary Theory

No developmentalist doubts that each person is unique. Yet many social scientists contend that the sociocultural focus on differences (cultural, ethnic, sexual, economic) depicts a fractured understanding of development. Moreover, no developmentalist doubts that nonhuman animals can help us understand humans, but many think that earlier theories rested too heavily on animal drives and instincts, ignoring the aspects of development that characterize humans.

Universal theories hold that all people share impulses and motivations, which they express in ways most other animals cannot. A universal perspective has been articulated in many developmental theories, each expressed in particular ways but always contending that humans are similar to each other.

Here we describe two of the most prominent of such perspectives: humanism and evolutionary theory. These two may seem to be opposite, in that humanism emphasizes the heights of human striving and evolutionary theory begins with quite simple instincts, but several recent scholars find many similarities in these theories, specifically that the "hierarchy of human motives" (humanism) can be anchored "firmly in the bedrock of modern evolutionary theory" (Kendrik et al., 2010, p. 292).

Humanism

Many scientists are convinced that there is something hopeful, unifying, and noble in the human spirit, something ignored by psychoanalytic theory (which stresses the selfish id and childhood sexuality) and by behaviorism (which seems to ignore free will). The limits of those two major theories were especially apparent to two Americans: Abraham Maslow (1908–1970) and Carl Rogers (1902–1987), both deeply religious men. They had witnessed the Great Depression and two world wars and concluded that traditional psychological theories underrated human potential by focusing on evil, not good. They founded a theory called **humanism** that became prominent after World War II, as millions read Maslow's *Toward a Psychology of Being* (1962/1998) and Rogers's *On Becoming a Person* (1961/2004).

Hope and Laughter Maslow studied law before psychology, and he enjoyed deep discussions with many psychoanalytic theorists who escaped Nazi Europe. Nonetheless, he believed the human spirit could overcome oppression and reach self-actualization, where faith, hope, and humor abound.

Maslow believed that all people—no matter what their culture, gender, or background—have the same basic needs. He arranged these needs in a hierarchy (see Figure 2.3):

1. Physiological: needing food, water, warmth, and air
2. Safety: feeling protected from injury and death
3. Love and belonging: having friends, family, and a community (often religious)
4. Esteem: being respected by the wider community as well as by oneself
5. Self-actualization: becoming truly oneself, fulfilling one's unique potential while appreciating all of humanity

humanism A theory that stresses the potential of all humans for good and the belief that all people have the same basic needs, regardless of culture, gender, or background.

This pyramid caught on almost immediately; it was one of the most "contagious ideas of behavioral science" since it seemed insightful about human psychology (Kendrick et al., 2010, p. 292). At the highest level, when basic needs have been met, people can be fully themselves—creative, spiritual, curious, appreciative of nature, able to respect everyone else.

One sign of self-actualization is that the person has "peak experiences" when life is so intensely joyful that time stops and self-seeking disappears. Given the stresses and deprivations of modern life, humanists believe that relatively few people reach the self-actualization of level 5. But everyone *can*—that is the universality of humanism. [**Lifespan Link:** An extension of this is apparent in self-theory in late adulthood, which appears in Chapter 25.]

Rogers also stressed the need to accept and respect one's own personhood as well as that of everyone else. He thought that people should give each other *unconditional positive regard*, which means that they should see (regard) each other with appreciation (positive) without conditions (unconditional).

If parents do not have unconditional positive regard for their children, the danger is that the children will have long-lasting problems with intimacy and self-acceptance (Roth & Assor, 2012). Rogers spent the last years of his life trying to reconcile the factions in Northern Ireland, South Africa, and Russia; he believed all sides need to listen to each other.

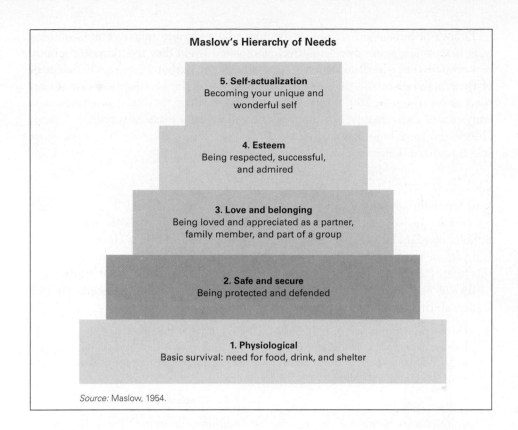

Maslow's Hierarchy of Needs

5. Self-actualization
Becoming your unique and wonderful self

4. Esteem
Being respected, successful, and admired

3. Love and belonging
Being loved and appreciated as a partner, family member, and part of a group

2. Safe and secure
Being protected and defended

1. Physiological
Basic survival: need for food, drink, and shelter

Source: Maslow, 1954.

FIGURE 2.3

Moving Up, Not Looking Back Maslow's hierarchy is like a ladder: Once a person stands firmly on a higher rung, the lower rungs are no longer needed. Thus, someone who has arrived at step 4 might devalue safety (step 2) and be willing to risk personal safety to gain respect.

As you can see, humanists emphasize what all people have in common, not their national, ethnic, or cultural differences. Maslow contended that everyone must satisfy each lower level of the hierarchy of needs before moving higher. A starving man, for instance, may not be concerned for his own safety when he seeks food (level 1 precedes level 2), or an unloved woman might not care about self-respect because she needs love (level 3 precedes level 4). Destructive and inhumane actions that prevent people from self-actualization may be the consequence of unmet lower needs. At the end of his life, Maslow explained that the highest level transcended selfishness and became selflessness, when a person is able to appreciate all of humanity (Maslow, 1971).

Although humanism does not postulate developmental stages, ideally as people mature they move up the hierarchy. Babies seek food and comfort, and not until adulthood can a person focus wholeheartedly on success and esteem, beyond the immediate approval of friends and family.

Satisfaction of childhood needs is crucial for later self-acceptance, according to Maslow. Thus, when babies cry in hunger, their basic need should be satisfied. People may become thieves or even killers, unable to reach their potential, to self-actualize, if they were unsafe or unloved as children.

Rogers agreed that adults who were deprived of unconditional positive regard in childhood might become selfish and antisocial. He developed a widely used method of psychological therapy to help people become more accepting of themselves and therefore of other people.

This theory is still prominent among medical professionals because they now realize that pain is not always physical (the first two levels), it can be social (the next two) (Majercsik, 2005; Zalenski & Raspa, 2006). Even the very sick need love and belonging (family should be with them) and esteem (the dying need respect).

>> Response for Adoptive Families (from page 55): No. Attachment is the result of a relationship between one person and another, not biology. In some cultures, many children are adopted from infancy, and the emotional ties to their caregivers are no less strong than are the ties of other children.

Especially for Nurses Maslow's hierarchy is often taught in health sciences because it alerts medical staff to the needs of patients. What specific hospital procedures might help? (see response, page 58)

>> **Response for Nurses** (from page 57): Reassurance from nurses (explaining procedures, including specifics and reasons) helps with the first two of Maslow's needs; and visitors, cards, and calls might help with the next two. Obviously, specifics depend on the patient, but everyone needs respect as well as physical care.

Echoes of humanism are also evident in education and sports: The basic idea here is that people are more effectively motivated when they try to master a body of knowledge or a skill to achieve a "personal best"—that is, to reach the peak of their own potential—than when they strive to be the best in their class or on their team (Ravizza, 2007). One criticism of the theory is that it promotes selfishness and individuality, but that may be unfair: In a massive survey in China, elders who were high in social participation, sharing in common life, were most self-actualized (Chen & Gao, 2013).

Evolutionary Theory

You are familiar with Darwin and his ideas, first published 150 years ago: Essentially he showed that plants, insects, birds, and animals developed over billions of years, as life evolved from primitive cells to humans (Darwin, 1859). But you may not realize that serious research on human development inspired by this theory does not focus primarily on lower creatures, but instead studies the history of human characteristics. Evolutionary psychology is quite recent. As two leaders in this field write:

> During the last two decades, the study of the evolutionary foundations of human nature has grown at an exponential rate. In fact, it is now a booming interdisciplinary scientific enterprise, one that sits at the cutting edge of the social and behavioral sciences.

> *[Gangestad & Simpson, 2007, p. 2]*

Evolutionary theory has intriguing explanations for many issues in human development, including women's nausea in pregnancy, 1-year-olds' attachment to their parents, rebellion in adolescence, and the growing obesity epidemic. According to this theory, many human impulses, needs, and behaviors evolved to help humans survive and thrive many millennia ago (Konner, 2010).

To understand human development, this theory contends that humans should acknowledge the lives of our early ancestors. For example, many people are terrified of snakes, screaming and breaking into a cold sweat upon seeing one. However, virtually no one is terrified of automobiles. Yet snakes cause less than 1 death in a million, while cars cause more than a hundred times that. The extreme reaction to snakes derives from instinctive fears that evolved over millennia, when snakes were common killers. Thus,

> Evolutionarily ancient dangers such as snakes, spiders, heights, and strangers appear on lists of common phobias far more often than do evolutionarily modern dangers such as cars and guns, even though cars and guns are more dangerous to survival in the modern environment (Confer et al., 2010, p. 111).

Since our fears have not caught up to modern inventions, we use our minds to protect ourselves with laws regarding seat belts, red lights, and speed limits. Humanity is succeeding in such measures: The U.S. motor-vehicle death rate has been cut in half over the past 20 years. Other modern killers—climate change, drug addiction, obesity, pollution—also require social management because instincts are contrary to knowledge. Evolutionary theory contends that once we recognizing the origins of destructive urges—such as the deadly desire to eat calorie-dense chocolate cake—we will be better able to control them (King, 2013).

According to evolutionary theory, every species has two long-standing, biologically-based drives: survival and reproduction. Understanding these two drives provides insight into protective parenthood, the death of newborns, infant dependency, child immaturity, the onset of puberty, and much more (Konner, 2010).

Especially for Teachers and Counselors of Teenagers Teen pregnancy is destructive of adolescent education, family life, and sometimes even health. According to evolutionary theory, what can be done about this problem? (see response, page 60)

Later chapters will explain these, but here is one example. Adults consider babies cute—despite the reality that babies have little hair, no chins, stubby legs, and round stomachs—all of which are considered ugly in adults. The reason, evolutionary theory contends, is that adults of all species are instinctually attuned to protect and cherish the young. For some, a competing instinct is to perpetuate their own heirs, and that might lead to infanticide, again explained by evolutionary theory (Hrdy, 2009)

A basic idea from evolutionary theory—**selective adaptation**—proposes that humans today react in ways that helped promote survival and reproduction long ago. In one version of selective adaptation, genes for traits that aid survival and reproduction are selected over time to allow the species to thrive (see Figure 2.4). Some of the best qualities of people—cooperation, spirituality, and self-sacrifice—may have originated thousands of years ago when groups of people survived because they took care of one another. Childhood itself, particularly the long period when children depend on their parents, can be explained via evolution (Konner, 2010).

selective adaptation The process by which living creatures (including people) adjust to their environment. Genes that enhance survival and reproductive ability are selected, over the generations, to become more prevalent.

	Women With (Sex-Linked) Advantageous Gene	Women Without (Sex-Linked) Advantageous Gene
Mothers (1st generation)	👩	👩👩👩👩👩👩👩👩👩
Daughters (2nd generation)	👩　👩	👩👩👩👩👩👩👩👩👩
Granddaughters (3rd generation)	👩👩👩👩	👩👩👩👩👩👩👩👩👩
Great-granddaughters (4th generation)	👩👩👩👩👩👩👩👩	👩👩👩👩👩👩👩👩
Great-great-granddaughters (5th generation)	👩👩👩👩👩👩👩👩👩👩👩👩👩👩👩👩	👩👩👩👩👩👩👩👩

FIGURE 2.4

Selective Adaptation Illustrated Suppose only one of nine mothers happened to have a gene that improved survival. The average woman had only one surviving daughter but this gene mutation might meant more births and more surviving children, such that each woman who had the gene bore two girls who survived to womanhood instead of one. As you see, in 100 years, the "odd" gene becomes more common, making it a new normal.

The process of selective adaptation works as follows: If one person happens to have a gene that makes survival more likely, that gene is likely to be passed on to the next generation because that person survives long enough to reproduce. Such a beneficial gene might have arisen as a mutation, or it might simply be a genetic combination that results in one end of the natural variation in height, body type, anxiety, or any other characteristic. Anyone who inherits such genes has an increased chance of growing up, finding a mate, and bearing children—half of whom would inherit that desirable gene.

For example, originally all humans probably got sick after drinking cow's milk; that is, they were *lactose intolerant* (Suchy, 2010). Then in a few regions thousands of years ago, cattle were domesticated and raised for their meat. In those places, "killing the fatted calf" provided a rare feast for the entire community when a major celebration occurred.

Although more than half of all babies died of malnutrition in ancient times, in cattle-raising regions, if a hungry child chanced to have an aberrant gene for the enzyme that allowed digestion of cow's milk, and drank some milk intended for a calf, he or she was likely to survive long enough to have children. Indeed, a girl who could digest milk would become fat, experience early puberty, then sustain many pregnancies, and then breast-feed her thriving babies longer than her lactose-intolerant, skinny, malnourished sisters. In that way, the next generation would include more people who inherited that gene.

Got Milk! Many people in Sweden (like this barefoot preschooler at her summer cottage) drink cow's milk and eat many kinds of cheese. That may be because selective adaptation allowed individuals who could digest lactose to survive in the long Northern winters when no crops grew.

>> Response for Teachers and Counselors of Teenagers (from page 58): Evolutionary theory stresses the need for reproduction, which gives teenagers a powerful sex drive. Thus, informing teenagers of the difficulty of newborn care is unlikely to stop the sex drive. Better methods would make pregnancy impossible—for instance, with constant supervision or excellent, available contraception.

This process of selective adaptation continues over many generations. An odd gene allowing digestion of cow's milk became widespread where plant proteins were scarce and cow's milk meant survival. This might explain why few Scandinavians are lactose-intolerant but many Africans are—a useful fact for Wisconsin dairy farmers who want to ship milk to starving children in Senegal. Once it was understood that milk might make some children sick, better ways to relieve hunger were found. Although malnutrition is still a global problem, fewer children are malnourished than a few decades ago, partly because nutritionists now know which foods are digestible and nourishing for whom.

For groups as well as individuals, the interaction of genes and environment affects survival and reproduction, the two basic drives recognized by evolutionary theory. Genetic variations are particularly beneficial when the environment changes, which is one reason the genetic diversity of humans throughout the world benefits humanity as a whole. If a species' gene pool does not include variants that allow survival in difficult circumstances (such as exposure to a new disease or to an environmental toxin), the entire species becomes extinct. This explains why biologists worry when a particular species becomes inbred—diversity is protective.

Genetic variation among humans, differential sensitivity, and plasticity (explained in Chapter 1) enable humans to survive and multiply. This statement is true not only for biological traits (such as digestion of milk) but also for psychological traits that originate in the brain (Confer et al., 2010; Tomasello, 2009).

Evolutionary theory contends that certain epigenetic factors foster socialization, parenthood, communication, and language, all of which helped humans a hundred thousand years ago and allowed societies a few thousand years ago to develop writing, then books, and then universities. As a result, humans learn from history and from strangers in distant continents. The fact that you are reading this book, accepting some ideas and rejecting others, is part of the human heritage that will aid future generations, according to evolutionary theory.

In recent years, "evolutionary psychology has grown from being viewed as a fringe theoretical perspective to occupying a central place within psychological science" (Confer et al., 2010). This theory is insightful and intriguing, but some interpretations are hotly disputed.

For instance, an evolutionary account of mental disorders suggests that some symptoms (such as an overactive imagination or a crushing anxiety) are normal extremes of adaptive traits. This implies that few people should be considered mentally ill, an implication rejected by many psychologists. Also controversial are explanations of sex differences, as the following explains.

A VIEW FROM SCIENCE

If Your Mate Were Unfaithful

Men seek more sexual partners than women do. Brides are younger, on average, than grooms. These are norms, not followed in every case, but apparent in every culture. Why?

An evolutionary explanation begins with biology. Since females, not males, become pregnant and breast-feed, in most of human history mothers needed mature, strong men to keep predators away. That helped women fulfill their evolutionary destiny, to bear children who would live long enough to reproduce. Consequently, women chose men who were big and strong, and then kept them nearby with home cooking and sex.

The evolutionary reasons that men acquiesced, sometimes becoming faithful partners to one woman despite their inclinations, included that men needed to keep rivals away in order to protect their children (Lukas & Clutton-Brock, 2013). Men tried to show women that they were powerful, worthy mates, a trait that now fuels gang wars and dangerous driving. For their part, women tried to show men that they could satisfy sexual desires, a trait that led to sexualization of teenage girls.

A historic conflict occurred because men were more able to father many children if they removed their rivals and had multiple sexual partners—all young, curvaceous, and healthy—who would birth many surviving babies. According to this theory, that explains why powerful kings had many young wives and concubines. Those ancient needs may have led to male/female hormonal differences, so even today males are attracted to young women, while women seek one steady marriage partner.

Does this interpretation have empirical, research support? Evolutionary scientists have asked people of many ages, nationalities, and religions to imagine their romantic partner either "forming a deep emotional attachment" or "enjoying passionate sexual intercourse" with someone else. After imagining that, people are asked which of those two possibilities is more distressing. The men generally are more upset at sexual infidelity while the women are more upset with emotional infidelity (Buss et al., 2004).

For example, one study involved 212 college students, all U.S. citizens, whose parents were born in Mexico (Cramer et al., 2009). As with other populations, more women (60 percent) were distressed at the emotional infidelity and more men (66 percent) at the sexual infidelity.

Evolutionary theory explains this oft-replicated result by noting that for centuries a woman has needed a soul mate to be emotionally committed, to ensure that he will provide for her and her children, whereas a man has needed a woman to be sexually faithful to ensure that her children are also his.

Indeed, worldwide, men are more likely to go into a jealous rage if they suspect infidelity, sometimes beating their partner to death, which wives never do (Mize et al., 2009). The evolutionary explanation is not universally accepted, yet some sex differences, including this one, call out for theory and research.

Many women reject the evolutionary explanation for sex differences. They contend that hypothetical scenarios do not reflect actual experience, and that patriarchy and sexism, not genes, produce mating attitudes and patterns (Vandernassen, 2005; Varga et al., 2011).

Similar controversies arise with other applications of evolutionary theory. People do not always act as evolutionary theory predicts: Parents sometimes abandon newborns, adults sometimes handle snakes, and so on. In the survey of Mexican American college students that was cited in A View from Science, more than one-third did not follow the typical pattern for their gender (Cramer et al., 2009).

Nonetheless, evolutionary theorists contend that humans need to understand the universal, biological impulses within our species, in order to control destructive reactions (e.g., we need to make "crimes of passion" illegal) and to promote constructive ones (to protect against newer dangers, by manufacturing safer cars and guns).

SUMMING UP

Newer theories of development are more multicultural, expansive, and multidisciplinary than the earlier, grand theories. Sociocultural theory emphasizes the varied cultural contexts of development. Learning occurs within the zone of proximal development, as the result of sensitive collaboration between a teacher (who could be a parent or a peer) and a learner who is ready for the next step.

Universal theories include humanism and evolutionary theory, both of which stress that all people have the same underlying needs. Humanism holds that everyone merits respect and positive regard in order to become self-actualized. Evolutionary theory contends that thousands of years of selective adaptation have led humans to experience emotions and impulses that have satisfied two universal needs of every species: to survive and to reproduce.

>> What Theories Contribute

Each major theory discussed in this chapter has contributed to our understanding of human development (see Table 2.4):

- *Psychoanalytic theories* make us aware of the impact of early-childhood experiences, remembered or not, on subsequent development.
- *Behaviorism* shows the effect that immediate responses, associations, and examples have on learning, moment by moment and over time.
- *Cognitive theories* bring an understanding of intellectual processes, including that thoughts and beliefs affect every aspect of our development.
- *Sociocultural theories* remind us that development is embedded in a rich and multifaceted cultural context, evident in every social interaction.
- *Universal theories* stress that human differences are less significant than characteristics that are shared by all humans, in every place and era.

No comprehensive view of development can ignore any of these theories, yet each has encountered severe criticism. Psychoanalytic theory has been faulted for being too subjective; behaviorism, for being too mechanistic; cognitive theory, for undervaluing emotions; sociocultural theory, for neglecting individuals; and universal theories, for slighting cultural, gender, and economic variations. Most developmentalists prefer an **eclectic perspective,** choosing what they consider the best aspects of each theories. Rather than adopt any one of these theories exclusively, they make selective use of all of them.

Being eclectic, not tied to any one theory, is beneficial because everyone, scientist as well as layperson, tends to be biased. It is easy to dismiss alternative

eclectic perspective The approach taken by most developmentalists, in which they apply aspects of each of the various theories of development rather than adhering exclusively to one theory.

TABLE 2.4	Five Perspectives on Human Development		
Theory	Area of Focus	Fundamental Depiction of What People Do	Relative Emphasis on Nature or Nurture?
Psychoanalytic theory	Psychosexual (Freud) or psychosocial (Erikson) stages	Battle unconscious impulses and overcome major crises.	More nature (biological, sexual impulses, and parent–child bonds)
Behaviorism	Conditioning through stimulus and response	Respond to stimuli, reinforcement, and models.	More nurture (direct environment produces various behaviors)
Cognitive theory	Thinking, remembering, analyzing	Seek to understand experiences while forming concepts.	More nature (mental activity and motivation are key)
Sociocultural theory	Social context, expressed through people, language, customs	Learn the tools, skills, and values of society through apprenticeships.	More nurture (interaction of mentor and learner, within contexts)
Universal perspective	Needs and impulses that all humans share as a species	Develop impulses, interests, and patterns to survive and reproduce.	More nature (needs and impulses apply to all humans)

points of view, but using all five theories opens our eyes and minds to aspects of development that we might otherwise ignore. As one overview of seven developmental theories (including those explained here) concludes, "Because no one theory satisfactorily explains development, it is critical that developmentalists be able to draw on the content, methods, and theoretical concepts of many theories" (Miller, 2011, p. 437).

As you will see in many later chapters, theories provide a fresh look at behavior. Imagine a parent and a teacher discussing a child's actions. Each suggests a possible explanation that makes the other say, "I never thought of that." If they listen to each other with an open mind, together they understand the child better. Having five theories is like having five perceptive observers. All five are not always on target, but it is better to use theory to expand perception than to stay in one narrow groove. A hand functions best with five fingers, although each finger is different and some fingers are more useful than others.

SUMMING UP

Theories are needed to suggest hypotheses, to spur investigation, and, finally, to collect data and form conclusions so that empirical evidence can replace untested assumptions. All five of the major theories have met with valid criticism, but each has also advanced our understanding of human development. Most developmentalists are eclectic, making selective use of all these theories and others. This helps guard against bias and keeps scientists, parents, students, and everyone else open to alternative explanations for the complexity of human life. ∎

SUMMARY

What Theories Do

1. A theory provides a framework of general principles to guide research and to explain observations. Each of the five major developmental theories—psychoanalytic, behaviorist, cognitive, sociocultural, and universal—interprets human development from a distinct perspective, together interpreting human experience and behavior.

2. Theories are neither true nor false. They are not facts; they suggest hypotheses to be tested. Good theories are practical: They aid inquiry, interpretation, and daily life.

3. A norm is a usual standard of behavior. Norms are not theories, although they may result from theories if a theory suggests that a certain behavior is proper. Norms are not necessarily good or bad, although sometimes differences from the norm are falsely considered deficits.

Grand Theories

4. Psychoanalytic theory emphasizes that human actions and thoughts originate from unconscious impulses and childhood conflicts. Freud theorized that sexual urges arise during three stages of childhood development—oral, anal, and phallic—and continue, after latency, in the genital stage.

5. Erikson described psychosocial, not psychosexual, stages. He described eight successive stages of development, each involving a crisis as people mature within their context. Societies, cultures, and family members shape each person's development.

6. All psychoanalytic theories stress the legacy of childhood. Conflicts associated with children's erotic impulses have a lasting impact on adult personality, according to Freud. Erikson thought that the resolution of each crisis affects adult development.

7. Behaviorists, or learning theorists, believe that scientists should study observable and measurable behavior. Behaviorism emphasizes conditioning—a lifelong learning process, in which an association between one stimulus and another (classical conditioning) or the consequences of reinforcement and punishment (operant conditioning) guide behavior.

8. Social learning theory recognizes that people learn by observing others. Children are particularly susceptible to social learning, but all humans are affected by other people.

9. Cognitive theorists believe that thoughts and beliefs powerfully affect attitudes, actions, and perceptions. Piaget proposed four age-related periods of cognition, propelled by an active search for cognitive equilibrium. Information processing focuses on each aspect of cognitive input, processing, and output.

Newer Theories

10. Sociocultural theory explains human development in terms of the guidance, support, and structure provided by knowledgeable members of the society through culture and mentoring. Vygotsky described how learning occurs through social interactions, when mentors guide learners through their zone of proximal development.

11. The universal perspective focuses on the shared impulses and common needs of all humanity. One universal theory is humanism. Maslow believed that humans have five basic needs, which he arranged in sequence beginning with survival and ending with self-actualization. Rogers believed that each person merits respect and appreciation, with unconditional positive regard.

12. Evolutionary theory contends that contemporary humans inherit genetic tendencies that have fostered survival and reproduction of the human species for tens of thousands of years. Many hypotheses arising from this theory are intriguing but controversial.

What Theories Contribute

13. Psychoanalytic, behavioral, cognitive, sociocultural, and universal theories have each aided our understanding of human development, yet no single theory describes the full complexity and diversity of human experience. Most developmentalists are eclectic, drawing upon many theories.

KEY TERMS

accommodation (p. 46)
apprenticeship in thinking (p. 52)
assimilation (p. 46)
behaviorism (p. 42)
classical conditioning (p. 42)

cognitive equilibrium (p. 46)
cognitive theory (p. 45)
conditioning (p. 42)
developmental theory (p. 36)
eclectic perspective (p. 62)
guided participation (p. 52)

humanism (p. 56)
information-processing theory (p. 47)
modeling (p. 44)
norm (p. 37)
operant conditioning (p. 43)

psychoanalytic theory (p. 39)
reinforcement (p. 44)
selective adaptation (p. 59)
social learning theory (p. 44)
sociocultural theory (p. 52)

WHAT HAVE YOU LEARNED?

1. How can a theory be practical?
2. What is the relationship between norms and facts?
3. How do theories differ from facts?
4. What is the basic idea of psychoanalytic theory?
5. What is Freud's theory of childhood sexuality?
6. What body parts are connected to the oral, anal, and phallic stages?
7. In what two ways does Erikson's theory differ from Freud's?
8. What is the basic idea of behaviorism?
9. How does behaviorism oppose psychoanalytic theory?
10. How do classical and operant conditioning differ?
11. What reinforcers are emphasized by social learning theory?
12. What is the basic idea of cognitive theory?
13. How do Piaget's stages compare to Freud's stages?
14. What are assimilation and accommodation and how are they similar?
15. Why is information processing not a stage theory?
16. What are the underlying differences between the newer theories and the grand theories?
17. How is "apprenticeship in thinking" an example of sociocultural theory?
18. What do mentors do when mentees are in their zone of proximal development?
19. What did Carl Rogers and Abraham Maslow stress in humanism?
20. How does Maslow's hierarchy of needs differ from Erikson's stages?
21. How does evolutionary psychology explain human instincts?
22. Why are aspects of evolutionary theory of human emotions controversial?
23. What does the idea of selective adaptation imply about the nature–nurture controversy?
24. What are the key criticism and key contribution of psychoanalytic theory?
25. What are the key criticism and key contribution of behaviorism?
26. What are the key criticism and key contribution of cognitive theory?
27. What are the key criticism and key contribution of sociocultural theory?
28. What are the key criticism and key contribution of universal theories?
29. What are the advantages of an eclectic perspective?

APPLICATIONS

1. Developmentalists sometimes talk about "folk theories," which are theories developed by ordinary people, who may not know that they are theorizing. Choose three sayings commonly used in your culture, such as (from the dominant U.S. culture) "A penny saved is a penny earned" or "As the twig is bent, so grows the tree." Explain the underlying assumption, or theory, that each saying reflects.

2. Behaviorism has been used to change personal habits. Think of a habit you'd like to change (e.g., stop smoking, exercise more, watch less TV). Count the frequency of that behavior for a week, noting the reinforcers for each instance. Then, and only then, develop a substitute behavior, reinforcing yourself for it. Keep careful data for several days. What did you learn?

3. Ask three people to tell you their theories about male–female differences in mating and sexual behaviors. Which of the theories described in this chapter is closest to each explanation, and which theory is not mentioned?

>>ONLINE CONNECTIONS

To accompany your textbook, you have access to a number of online resources, including Learning Curve, an adaptive quizzing program, critical thinking questions, and case studies. For access to any of these links, go to www.worthpublishers.com/launchpad/bergerls9e. In addition to these resources, you'll also find links to video clips, personalized study advice, and an ebook. Some of the videos and activities available online include:

- *Modeling: Learning from Observation.* This activity includes clips from Albert Bandura's classic Bobo doll experiment on observational learning.

- *Mother Love: The Work of Harry Harlow.* Original footage from Harry Harlow's lab and interviews with Harlow discussing his work.

COURTESY OF ALBERT BANDURA

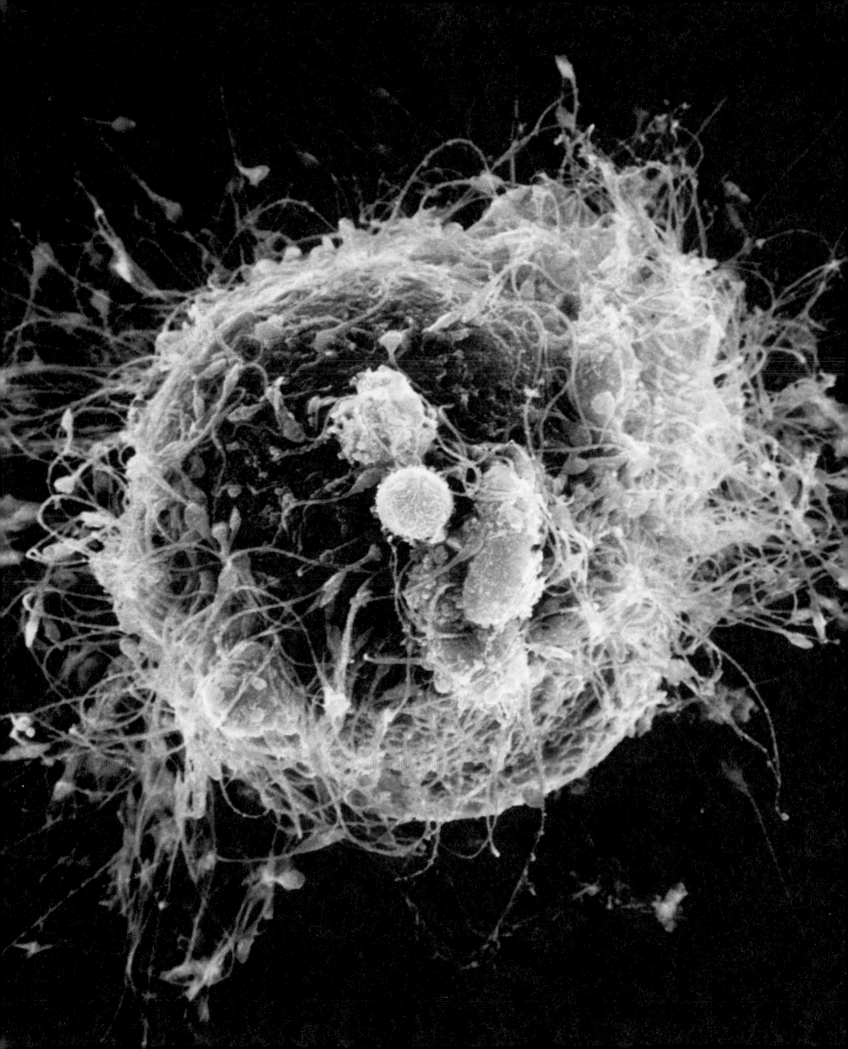

Heredity and Environment

- **The Genetic Code**
  What Genes Are
  Variations

- **The Beginnings of Life**
  Matching Genes
  Male or Female?
  New Cells, New Functions
  OPPOSING PERSPECTIVES:
  Too Many Boys?
  Twins
  Assisted Reproduction

- **From Genotype to Phenotype**
  Epigenetics
  Gene–Gene Interactions

- **Nature and Nurture**
  Alcoholism
  Nearsightedness
  Practical Applications

- **Chromosomal and Genetic Problems**
  Not Exactly 46
  Gene Disorders
  Genetic Counseling and Testing

WHAT WILL YOU KNOW?

1. What is the relationship between genes and chromosomes?

2. Do sex differences result from chromosomes or culture?

3. How can a child have genetic traits that are not obvious in either parent?

4. If both parents are alcoholics, will their children be alcoholics too?

5. Why are some children born with Down syndrome, and what can be done for them?

"She needs a special school. She cannot come back next year," Elissa's middle school principal told us.

Martin and I were stunned. Apparently the school staff thought that our wonderful daughter, bright and bubbly (Martin called her "frothy"), was learning-disabled. They had a specific phrase for it, "severely spatially disorganized." We had noticed that she misplaced homework, got lost, left books at school, forgot where each class met on which day—but we thought that insignificant compared to her strengths in reading, analyzing, and friendship.

I knew the first lesson from genetics: Genes affect everything, not just physical appearance, diseases, and cognitive abilities, so I wondered whether Elissa had inherited her behavior patterns from us. Our desks were covered with papers, and our home had assorted objects everywhere. If we needed masking tape, or working scissors, or silver candle sticks, we had to search in several places. Could that be why we were oblivious to Elissa's failings?

The second lesson from genetics is that nurture always matters. My husband and I had both learned to compensate for innate organizational weaknesses. Since he often got lost, Martin did not hesitate to ask strangers for directions; since I was prone to mislaying important documents, I kept my students' papers in clearly marked folders at my office. Despite our genes, we both were successful; we thought Elissa was fine.

Once we recognized our daughter's nature, we changed her nurture. We devoted much more attention to her homework and learning patterns; we hired a tutor who taught Elissa to list her homework assignments, check them off when done, put them carefully in her bag, and then take the bag to school. We reinforced those habits and did our part to change her social context. For instance, Martin attached her bus pass to her backpack; I wrote an impassioned letter telling the principal it would be unethical to expel her; Elissa herself began to study diligently when she realized she might need to leave her friends.

Success! Elissa aced her final exams, and the principal allowed her to return. She became a master organizer; 25 years later, she is an accomplished professional.

This chapter begins with nature and then emphasizes nurture. Throughout, we note some ethical and practical choices regarding the interaction of genes and environments. I hope you recognize the implications long before you have a seventh-grade daughter.

Observation Quiz In the chapter opening photograph (page 66), can you distinguish the Y sperm from the X sperm? (see answer, page 69)

Left: Professors Pietro M. Motta & Sayoko Makabe/Science Source
Top: Lane Oatey/Getty Images

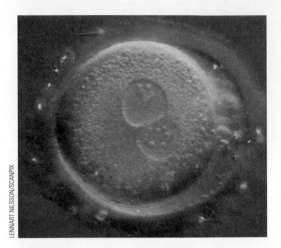

The Moment of Conception This ovum is about to become a zygote. It has been penetrated by a single sperm, whose nucleus now lies next to the nucleus of the ovum. Soon, the two nuclei will fuse, bringing together about 20,000 genes to guide development.

LENNART NILSSON/SCANPIX

Especially for Scientists A hundred years ago, it was believed that humans had 48 chromosomes, not 46; 20 years ago, it was thought that humans had 100,000 genes, not 20,000 or so. Why? (see response, page 70)

gamete A reproductive cell; that is, a sperm or ovum that can produce a new individual if it combines with a gamete from the other sex to make a zygote.

zygote The single cell formed from the union of two gametes, a sperm and an ovum.

deoxyribonucleic acid (DNA) The chemical composition of the molecules that contain the genes, which are the chemical instructions for cells to manufacture various proteins.

chromosome One of the 46 molecules of DNA (in 23 pairs) that virtually each cell of the human body contains and that, together, contain all the genes. Other species have more or fewer chromosomes.

gene A small section of a chromosome; the basic unit for the transmission of heredity. A gene consists of a string of chemicals that provide instructions for the cell to manufacture certain proteins.

allele A variation that makes a gene different in some way from other genes for the same characteristics. Many genes never vary; others have several possible alleles.

>> The Genetic Code

A reproductive cell is called a **gamete.** Every person begins life as a single cell, called a **zygote;** the zygote is the combination of two gametes, one sperm (sperm is an abbreviation of spermatozoon, plural spermatozoa, from the Greek word for seed) and one ovum (plural, ova, from the Greek for egg). The zygote contains all a person's genes, which affect every aspect of development lifelong. Many people have misconceptions about heredity, so the beginning of this chapter is crucial to understanding human development.

What Genes Are

First, we review some biology. All living things are composed of cells. The work of cells is done by *proteins*. Each cell manufactures certain proteins according to instructions stored by molecules of **deoxyribonucleic acid (DNA)** at the heart of each cell. These coding DNA molecules are on a **chromosome.**

Humans have 23 pairs of chromosomes (46 in all), which contain the instructions to make all the proteins that a person needs for life and growth (see Figure 3.1). The instructions in the 46 chromosomes are organized into genes, with each **gene** usually located at a specific spot on a particular chromosome. Humans have between 18,000 and 23,000 genes, and each gene directs the formation of specific proteins made from a string of 20 amino acids.

The instructions for making those amino acids are on about 3 billion pairs of chemicals, called base pairs, arranged in precise order. A small variation—such as repeated pairs, or one missing pair—changes the gene a tiny bit. Although all humans have most of the same genes with identical codes, those tiny variations of certain genes make each person unique. Each variation of a particular gene is called an **allele** of that gene.

RNA (ribonucleic acid, another molecule) and additional DNA surround each gene. In a process called *methylation,* this additional material enhances, transcribes,

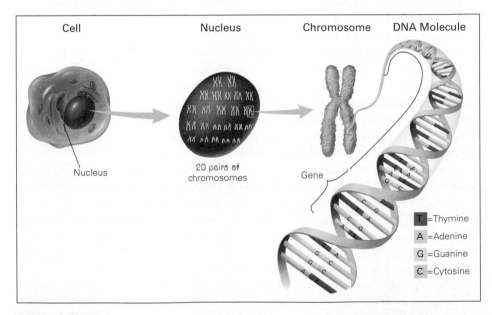

=Thymine
=Adenine
=Guanine
=Cytosine

FIGURE 3.1

How Proteins Are Made The genes on the chromosomes in the nucleus of each cell instruct the cell to manufacture the proteins needed to sustain life and development. The code for a protein is the particular combination of four bases, T-A-G-C (thymine, adenine, guanine, and cytosine).

connects, empowers, silences, and alters genetic instructions (Shapiro, 2009). This nongenetic material used to be called *junk*—but no longer. Thousands of scientists are now seeking to discover exactly what these molecules do (Wright & Bruford, 2011; Volders et al., 2013). We do know that methylation continues throughout life, and it can alter a gene's expression, not only prenatally but after birth as well. This is part of epigenetics, mentioned in Chapter 1 as well as later in this chapter.

Variations

It is human nature for people to notice differences more than commonalities. Hence many scientists seek genetic reasons for the fact that no two people look or act exactly alike. Differences begin with alleles, which can be caused by transpositions, deletions, or repetitions of those base pairs, making some genes *polymorphic* (literally, "many forms") or, more formally, *single-nucleotide polymorphisms* (abbreviated SNPs, pronounced "snips").

Usually genes have only one set of instructions (no alleles), but polymorphic genes can have two, three, or more versions. Most alleles seem inconsequential; some cause only minor differences (such as the shape of an eyebrow or the shade of the skin); and a few are notable, even devastating, but the devastating ones are rare. Several destructive alleles in combination with specific epigenetic conditions make a person develop schizophrenia, or diabetes, or whatever (Plomin et al., 2012).

Some variation springs from the simple fact that it takes two people to make one new person. Each parent contributes half the genetic material; the 23 chromosomes with their thousands of genes from one parent match up with the 23 from the other, forming identical or nearly identical pairs. Thus chromosome 1 from the sperm connects with chromosome 1 from the ovum, chromosome 2 with chromosome 2, and so on.

Each gene pairs with a counterpart gene from the other parent, and the interaction between the two members of each pair determines the inherited traits of the future person. Since the alleles from the father often differ from the alleles from the mother, their combination may be different from either parent. Thus each new person is a product of both parents but unlike either one.

Diversity at conception is increased by another fact: When a man or woman makes sperm or ova, and then their chromosomes pair up when they join, some genetic material is transferred from one chromosome to the other, so that "even if two siblings get the same chromosome from their mother, their chromosomes aren't identical" (Zimmer, 2009, p. 1254). All these kinds of genetic diversity help societies, because creativity and even species survival is enhanced when one person is unlike another, although there are benefits when genes are shared as well (Ashraf & Galor, 2011).

The entire packet of instructions to make a living organism is called the **genome.** There is a genome for every species and variety of plant and animal—even for every bacteria and virus. Knowing the genome of the human species is only a start (it was decoded in 2001) at understanding the genetics of people, since each individual has a slightly different set of those 3 billion base pairs.

SUMMING UP

The human genome contains approximately 20,000 genes on 46 chromosomes, using 3 million base pairs of code to make a person. Some genes, called alleles, are polymorphic. Because of small differences in their genetic codes, each person is unlike any other. The result is that each person is unique yet similar to all other humans. The entire instruction code is the genome, contained in a single cell, the zygote. ∎

>>**Answer to Observation Quiz** (from page 67): Probably not. The Y sperm are slightly smaller, which can be detected via scientific analysis (using such analysis, some cattle breeders raise only steers), but visual inspection, even magnified as in this photo, may be inaccurate. Further, these may all be Y sperm, as those may swim faster—but they may not necessarily be more successful at entering the ovum.

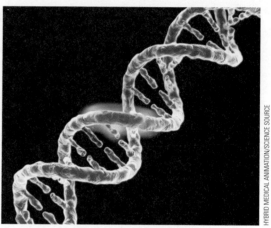

HYBRID MEDICAL ANIMATION/SCIENCE SOURCE

Twelve of 3 Billion Pairs This is a computer illustration of a small segment of one gene. Even a small difference in one gene can cause major changes in a person's phenotype.

genome The full set of genes that are the instructions to make an individual member of a certain species.

>> Response for Scientists (from page 68): There was some scientific evidence for the wrong numbers (e.g., chimpanzees have 48 chromosomes), but the reality is that humans tend to overestimate many things, from the number of genes to their grade on the next test. Scientists are very human: They tend to overestimate until the data prove them wrong.

genotype An organism's entire genetic inheritance, or genetic potential.

homozygous Referring to two genes of one pair that are exactly the same in every letter of their code. Most gene pairs are homozygous.

heterozygous Referring to two genes of one pair that differ in some way. Typically one allele has only a few base pairs that differ from the other member of the pair.

23rd pair The chromosome pair that, in humans, determines sex. The other 22 pairs are autosomes, inherited equally by males and females.

XX A 23rd chromosome pair that consists of two X-shaped chromosomes, one each from the mother and the father. XX zygotes become females.

XY A 23rd chromosome pair that consists of an X-shaped chromosome from the mother and a Y-shaped chromosome from the father. XY zygotes become males.

Uncertain Sex Every now and then, a baby is born with "ambiguous genitals," meaning that the child's sex is not abundantly clear. When this happens, a quick analysis of the chromosomes is needed, to make sure there are exactly 46 and to see whether the 23rd pair is XY or XX. The karyotypes shown here indicate a normal baby boy (*left*) and girl (*right*).

>> The Beginnings of Life

The one-celled zygote copies itself again and again, changing names as it multiplies—from morula to blastocyst, from embryo to fetus—and finally, at birth, baby. [**Lifespan Link:** Prenatal growth is described in Chapter 4.] By adulthood, a person has between 50 trillion and 100 trillion cells, each with the same 46 chromosomes and the same thousands of genes of the original zygote.

The particular member of each chromosome pair from each parent on a given gamete is randomly selected. A man or woman can produce 2^{23} different gametes—more than 8 million versions of his or her own 46 chromosomes. If a given couple conceived a billion zygotes, each would be genetically unique because of the chromosomes of the particular sperm that fertilized that particular ovum. Interacting alleles, methylation, and other genetic forces add more variations to the zygote. Epigenetics silence some genes and increase others. Nurture creates even more variations.

Matching Genes

The genes on the chromosomes constitute the organism's genetic inheritance, or **genotype,** which endures throughout life. Growth requires duplication again and again of the code of the original cell.

In 22 of the 23 pairs of chromosomes, both members of the pair are closely matched. Each of these 44 chromosomes is called an *autosome*, which means that it is independent (*auto* means "self") of the sex chromosomes (the 23rd pair). Each autosome, from number 1 to number 22, contains hundreds of genes in the same positions and sequence. If the code of the gene from one parent is exactly like the code on the same gene from the other parent, the gene pair is **homozygous** (literally, "same-zygote").

The match is not always letter perfect because the mother might have a different allele for a particular gene than the father has. If a gene's code differs from that of its counterpart, the two genes still pair up, but the zygote (and, later, the person) is **heterozygous.** This can occur with any of the gene pairs, but the most dramatic example of a heterozygous pairing is chromosomal, not genetic, with the 23rd pair.

Male or Female?

The chromosomes that make up the **23rd pair** are the sex chromosomes. In females, the 23rd pair is composed of two X-shaped chromosomes. Accordingly, it is called **XX.** In males, the 23rd pair has one X-shaped chromosome and one Y-shaped chromosome. It is called **XY.**

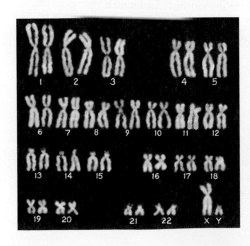
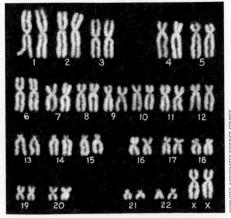

BIOPHOTO ASSOCIATES/SCIENCE SOURCE

Because a female's 23rd pair is XX, all her ova contain either one X or the other—but always an X. And because a male's 23rd pair is XY, half of his sperm carry an X chromosome and half a Y. The X chromosome is bigger and has more genes, but the Y chromosome has a crucial gene, called *SRY*, that directs the embryo to make male hormones and organs. Thus, sex depends on which sperm penetrates the ovum—a Y sperm with the SRY gene, creating a boy (XY), or an X sperm, creating a girl (XX) (see Figure 3.2).

In some other species, sex is not determined at conception. In certain reptiles, for instance, temperature during incubation of the fertilized egg affects the sex of the embryo (Hare & Cree, 2010). However, for humans, the zygote is either XX or XY, a fact that in the past was not revealed to anyone until the baby was born. Today sex can be known much earlier: Parents choose names, decorate nurseries, and bond with the future boy or girl—or not, as the opposing perspective explains.

New Cells, New Functions

Within hours after conception, the zygote begins *duplication* and *division*. First, the 23 pairs of chromosomes carrying all the genes duplicate, forming two complete sets of the genome. These two sets move toward opposite sides of the zygote,

FIGURE 3.2

One Species, a Billion Variations Dogs immediately recognize other dogs, even from a distance, despite dramatic differences in size, shape, coloring (of tongues and eyes as well as coats), and, as shown here, in hair. Minor code variations become marked fur differences— long or short, curly or straight, wiry or limp.

OPPOSING PERSPECTIVES

Too Many Boys?

Parents can choose to give birth to only boys or only girls; millions of couples have done it. Is this a problem?

Historically, in every culture, some newborns were killed because they were female. One of the moral advances of Islam, founded in the seventh century, was to forbid female infanticide. Currently, the birth of a child of unwanted sex can be prevented long before birth in three ways: by inactivating X or Y sperm before conception; by inserting only the male or female zygotes after in vitro conception; or by aborting XX or XY fetuses. Should that be now banned as immoral?

In China, a "one-child" policy implemented in about 1979 cut the birth rate in half. That achieved the intended goal: Severe poverty was almost eliminated. Unanticipated results included (1) increased abortions of female fetuses, (2) millions of newborn girls available for adoption, and, recently, (3) far more unmarried young men than women. In 1993, the Chinese government forbade prenatal testing for sex selection; in 2013, China rescinded the one-child policy.

That policy change may be too late. Routine sonograms reveal sex, and the sex ratio of newborns in many regions

My Strength, My Daughter That's the slogan these girls in New Delhi are shouting at a demonstration against abortion of female fetuses in India. The current sex ratio of children in India suggests that this campaign has not convinced every couple.

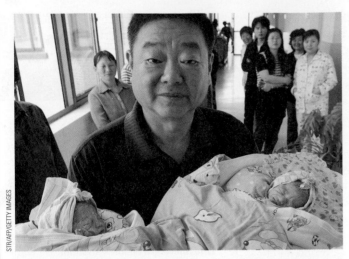

Mama Is 60 Wu Jingzhou holds his newborn twin daughters, born to his 60-year-old wife after in vitro fertilization. Ordinarily, it is illegal in China, as in most other nations, for women to have children after menopause. But an exception was made for this couple since the death of their only child, a young woman named Tinglin, in a gas poisoning accident.

of Asia (not only in China) is as high as four boys born for every three girls. One elderly Indian man said, "We should have at least four children per family, three of them boys" (quoted in Khanna, 2010, p. 66). The preference for boys occurs partly because in many East Asian cultures, sons are expected to care for their aged parents. Thus parents want to have a boy.

Couples of Asian ancestry in the United States also prefer boys (Puri et al., 2011). In some Western nations, including Germany, girls are preferred—both as newborns and as caregivers of the old (Wilhelm et al., 2013).

The most common argument in favor of sex selection is freedom to choose. Some fertility doctors and parents believe that sex selection is a reproductive right and that couples should be able to decide to have either a boy or a girl (Puri & Nachtigall, 2009). Some people who themselves would not abort a fetus nonetheless favor allowing personal freedom—in this case, freedom to "balance" the family.

Why would anyone object to freedom? The Chinese experience shows that sex selection can have unanticipated consequences. For instance, now many more young Chinese men than women die prematurely. The developmental explanation is that unmarried young men in every culture take risks to attract women and become depressed if they remain single.

Other problems may occur: Males are more likely to be learning disabled, drug addicted, and criminal, as well as to start wars and suffer heart attacks. Any nation with more men than women will risk increases in all these problems.

But wait: Chromosomes and genes do not determine behavior. Every sex difference is a product of culture. Even traits that originate with biology, such as the propensity to heart attacks, are affected more by environment (in this case, diet and cigarettes) than by XX or XY chromosomes. Perhaps nurture could change if nature produced more males than females, and then societies would not suffer. The frequency of sex selection is influenced by national policy and cultural values (Park et al., 2012).

Might laws against prenatal sex choices be unnecessary if culture could shift? "Might" . . . "if" . . . Critical thinking needed.

and the single cell splits neatly down the middle into two cells, each containing the original genetic code. These two cells duplicate and divide, becoming four, which duplicate and divide, becoming eight, and so on.

Every Cell the Same

By the time a baby is born, the zygote has become about 5 trillion cells, all influenced by material surrounding the genes (once called junk DNA) and by whatever nutrients, drugs, hormones, viruses, and so on came to the embryo from the pregnant woman. Almost every human cell carries a complete copy of the genetic instructions of the one-celled zygote. This explains why DNA testing of any body cell, even from a drop of blood or a snip of hair, can identify "the real father," "the guilty criminal," "the long-lost brother."

DNA lingers long after death. This fact is evident in living African Americans who claimed Thomas Jefferson as an ancestor: DNA testing proved some of them right and some of them wrong (Foster et al., 1998).

Indeed, because the Y chromosome is passed down to every male descendant, and because the genes on the Y typically do not change from one generation to another, men have the Y of one of their male ancestors who died thousands of years ago. Tracing that Y chromosome suggests that thousands of East Asian men may be descendants of Genghis Khan—although that twelfth-century leader's bones and thus his DNA have never been found (Stoneking & Delfin, 2010). Such genetic sleuthing is not totally reliable: It is quite possible to trace ancestry for several generations; it is much more complex to go back for hundreds of years.

Stem Cells

The cells that result from the early duplication and division are called **stem cells;** these cells are able to produce any other cell and thus to become a complete person. Indeed, as later described, sometimes those cells split apart and each becomes an identical twin.

After about the eight-cell stage, although duplication and division continue, a third process, *differentiation*, begins. In differentiation, cells specialize, taking different forms and reproducing at various rates depending on where they are located. For instance, some cells become part of an eye, others part of a finger, still others part of the brain. They are no longer stem cells. Blood cells in the umbilical cord, however, may act like stem cells.

Scientists have discovered ways to add genes to certain differentiated cells in a laboratory process that reprograms those cells, making them like stem cells again. However, scientists do not yet know how to use reprogrammed stem cells to cure genetic conditions without harming other cells. One use of reprogrammed cells has been found: to test drugs to treat diseases caused by genes, either directly (such as sickle-cell anemia) or indirectly (such as heart disease, diabetes, and dementia) (Zhu & Huangfu, 2013; Vogel, 2010).

Some U.S. restrictions on stem cell research were lifted in 2009, and some states (e.g., California) and nations (e.g., South Korea) allow more extensive research, but everywhere many ethical and practical issues remain (Nguyen et al., 2013). As the head of the Michael J. Fox Foundation for Parkinson's Research said, "All my exposure was pop media. I thought it was all about stem cells. I have not totally lost hope on cell replacement, I just don't think it's a near-term hope" (Hood, quoted in Holden, 2009).

Twins

One "near-term hope" four decades ago has become reality, beginning with the birth of Louise Brown in England in 1978. Millions of infertile couples now have babies, often twins, increasing the demand for twin strollers and rhyming names—and also increasing the number of tiny, preterm newborns fighting for life in hospital intensive-care nurseries. Such multiple births from more than one ovum and sperm are usually the result of fertilization outside the mother's body. To understand twin conceptions, you need to know the difference between monozygotic and dizygotic twins (see Visualizing Development 3, p. 74).

Monozygotic Twins

Although every zygote is genetically unique, about once in 250 human conceptions, duplication results in one or more complete splits, creating two, or four, or even eight separate zygotes, each identical to the first single cell. This kind of split is illegal for humans in a laboratory, but nature does it occasionally in the womb. (An incomplete split creates *conjoined twins*, formerly called Siamese twins.)

If each of those separated cells from one zygote then duplicates, divides, differentiates, implants, grows, and survives, multiple births occur. One separation results in **monozygotic (MZ) twins**, from one (*mono*) zygote (also called *identical twins*). Two or three separations create monozygotic quadruplets or octuplets. Because monozygotic multiples originate from the same zygote, they

stem cells Cells from which any other specialized type of cell can form.

monozygotic (MZ) twins Twins who originate from one zygote that splits apart very early in development. (Also called *identical twins*.) Other monozygotic multiple births (such as triplets and quadruplets) can occur as well.

One Baby or More

Humans usually have one baby at a time, but sometimes twins are born. Most often they are from two ova fertilized by two sperm (lower left), resulting in dizygotic twins. Sometimes, however, one zygote splits in two (lower right), resulting in monozygotic twins; if each of these zygotes splits again, the result is monozygotic quadruplets.

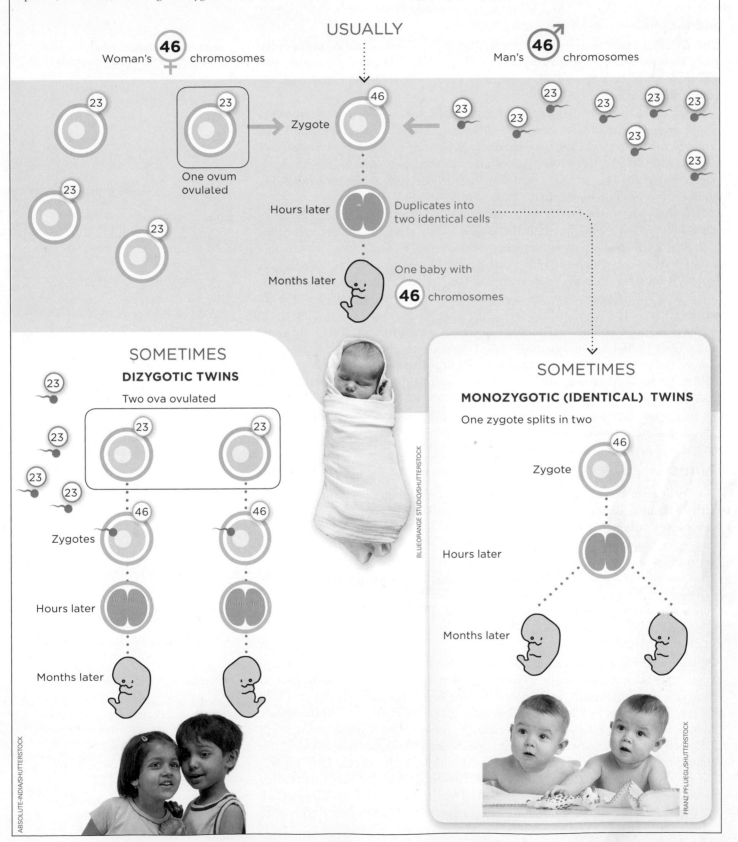

USUALLY

Woman's **46** chromosomes

Man's **46** chromosomes

23

23   One ovum ovulated   →   Zygote   46   ←   23

23   23   23   23

23   23   23

23   23

Hours later   Duplicates into two identical cells

Months later   One baby with **46** chromosomes

SOMETIMES

DIZYGOTIC TWINS

Two ova ovulated

23

23

23

23

23   23

Zygotes   46   46

Hours later

Months later

BLUEORANGE STUDIO/SHUTTERSTOCK

SOMETIMES

MONOZYGOTIC (IDENTICAL) TWINS

One zygote splits in two

Zygote   46

Hours later

Months later

ABSOLUTE-INDIA/SHUTTERSTOCK

FRANZ PFLUEGL/SHUTTERSTOCK

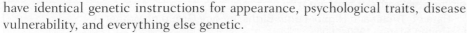

have identical genetic instructions for appearance, psychological traits, disease vulnerability, and everything else genetic.

Monozygotic twins are blessed in some ways: they can donate a kidney or other organ to their twin with no organ rejection, thus avoiding the major complication with surgical transplants. On a lighter note, they can also befuddle their parents and teachers, who may use special signs (such as different earrings) to tell them apart. Usually, the twins themselves find their own identities while enjoying twinship. They might enjoy inherited athletic ability, for instance, with one playing basketball and the other soccer.

As one monozygotic twin writes:

> Twins put into high relief *the* central challenge for all of us: self-definition. How do we each plant our stake in the ground, decide how sensitive, callous, ambitious, cautious, or conciliatory we want to be every day? . . . Twins come with a built-in constant comparison, but defining oneself against one's twin is just an amped-up version of every person's life-long challenge: to individuate, to create a distinctive persona in the world.

> *[Pogrebin, 2010, p. 9]*

Dizygotic Twins

Among naturally-conceived twins, only about one in three pairs is monozygotic. Most are **dizygotic (DZ),** also called *fraternal twins*. They began life as two separate zygotes created by two ova fertilized by two sperm at the same time. (Usually, women release only one ovum per month, but sometimes double or triple ovulation occurs, a tendency that is affected by genes.) Note that dizygotic twinning depends on multiple ovulation, so the likelihood of a woman bearing twins depends on her genes, not the father's. However, a man has half his genes from his mother. If multiple ovulation is in his family, he will not produce twins, but his daughters might.

When dizygotic twinning occurs naturally, the incidence varies by ethnicity. For example, about 1 in 11 Yorubas in Nigeria is a twin, as are about 1 in 45 European Americans, 1 in 75 Japanese and Koreans, and 1 in 150 Chinese. Age matters, too: Older women more often double-ovulate and thus have more twins. After twins are conceived, their chance of survival until birth depends on the prenatal circumstances: An early sonogram might reveal two developing organisms, but later only one embryo continues to grow. This *vanishing twin* phenomenon may occur in about 12 percent of pregnancies (Giuffrè et al., 2012).

Like all full siblings, DZ twins have about half of their genes in common. They can differ markedly in appearance, or they can look so much alike that only genetic tests can determine whether they are monozygotic or dizygotic. Chance determines which sperm fertilizes each ovum, so about half are same-sex pairs and half are boy–girl pairs.

Assisted Reproduction

When couples are infertile (a condition affecting about 12 percent of U.S. couples), they have many choices. **[Lifespan Link:** Causes and choices of infertility are discussed in Chapter 20.] To better understand conception, one choice is explained here, **assisted reproductive technology (ART)**. A woman can take drugs to cause ovulation, often of several ova, which may lead to multiple births (see Figure 3.3). Or ova can be surgically removed from an ovary, fertilized in a lab dish, and then inserted into the uterus. This procedure is known as **in vitro fertilization (IVF)**—*in vitro* means "in glass." Younger women are more

dizygotic (DZ) twins Twins who are formed when two separate ova are fertilized by two separate sperm at roughly the same time. (Also called *fraternal twins*.)

assisted reproductive technology (ART) A general term for the techniques designed to help infertile couples conceive and then sustain a pregnancy.

in vitro fertilization (IVF) Fertilization that takes place outside a woman's body (as in a glass laboratory dish). The procedure involves mixing sperm with ova that have been surgically removed from the woman's ovary. If a zygote is produced, it is inserted into a woman's uterus, where it may implant and develop into a baby.

FIGURE 3.3

Why More Multiple Births? Historically in the United States, the natural rate of multiple births tended to increase as mothers aged. Women in their mid to late 30s were more likely to have twins or triplets than those who were younger. The advent of assisted reproductive technology (ART) led to a dramatic increase in multiple births overall starting in the early 1990s; it is now women aged 40 and over who are most likely to experience this phenomenon. After peaking in the late 1990s, rates of triplet births declined, as the hazards of multiple births are more apparent.

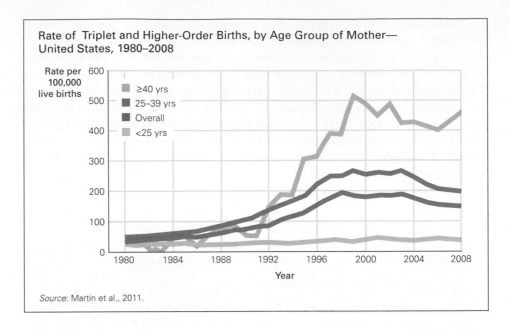

Rate of Triplet and Higher-Order Births, by Age Group of Mother— United States, 1980–2008

Source: Martin et al., 2011.

intra-cytoplasmic injection (ICSI) An in vitro fertilization technique in which a single sperm cell is injected directly into an ovum.

likely to have successful IVF pregnancies, but even among healthy young women, less than half of IVF cycles result in a baby.

In IVF a sperm often is inserted directly into each ovum to improve the odds of fertilization, in a procedure called **intra-cytoplasmic sperm injection (ICSI).** Zygotes that fail to duplicate, or blastocysts tested positive for serious genetic diseases, are rejected. Then, after two to six days of development outside the uterus, technicians insert the normally developing cells, either one blastocyst or several, into the uterus. Between 1 and 3 percent of all newborns in developed nations and thousands more in developing nations are the result of IVF.

ART has enabled millions of couples to have children. Indeed, some parents have children who are not genetically or biologically theirs if others donate the sperm, the ova, and/or the womb (Almeling, 2011). The word *donate* may be misleading, since people—often college students—are paid for their sperm, ova, or pregnancy. Most people who become parents via IVF are heterosexual, with one partner infertile, but a sizable minority are same-sex couples.

Although donors are screened for serious genetic problems, birth defects and later illnesses increase slightly with IVF. The risk is small: About 97 percent of all IVF newborns have no apparent defects. Not small, however, is the risk of prematurity and low birthweight. [**Lifespan Link:** The problems of low birthweight are discussed in Chapter 4.] In the United States, almost half of all IVF babies are twins or triplets (MMWR, November 2, 2012).

Most European nations limit the numbers of blastocysts inserted into the uterus at one time, partly because national health care pays for both IVF and newborn care. If only one blastocyst is inserted, others are usually frozen for later insertion if the first one does not develop. According to research in seven nations, inserting just one blastocyst results in as many successful pregnancies as inserting multiple blastocysts, but fewer low-birthweight newborns (7 percent compared to 30 percent), primarily because each fetus develops alone (Grady et al., 2012).

SUMMING UP

People usually have 23 chromosomes from their mother and 23 from their father, with all the genes and chromosomes matched up into mother–father pairs—although the match may not be letter perfect because of alleles. The father's 23rd chromosome

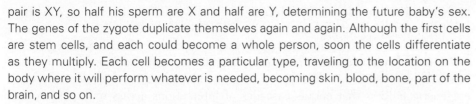

pair is XY, so half his sperm are X and half are Y, determining the future baby's sex. The genes of the zygote duplicate themselves again and again. Although the first cells are stem cells, and each could become a whole person, soon the cells differentiate as they multiply. Each cell becomes a particular type, traveling to the location on the body where it will perform whatever is needed, becoming skin, blood, bone, part of the brain, and so on.

Twins are monozygotic (one zygote, from the same stem cells) or dizygotic (two zygotes). Assisted reproductive technology has increased the rate of multiple births. Modern reproductive measures, including IVF, have led to millions of much-wanted, healthy infants but also to new dilemmas, including whether people should be able to choose the sex, the genetic and biological parentage, and the number of newborns they have. ■

>> From Genotype to Phenotype

As already explained, when a sperm and an ovum combine into a zygote, they establish the *genotype:* all the genes that the developing person has. Creation of a person from one cell involves several complex processes to form the **phenotype**— the person's appearance, behavior, and brain and body functions. Nothing is totally genetic, not even such obvious traits as height or hair color, but nothing is untouched by genes, not even behavior such as voting Republican or Democrat, working overtime or not at all, wanting or refusing a divorce (Plomin et al., 2013).

The genotype instigates body and brain formation, but the phenotype depends on many genes and on the environment, influenced from the moment of conception until the moment of death through "the organism's encounters with its prenatal and postnatal environments" (Gilbert, 2010, p. 26). Most traits are **polygenic** (affected by many genes) and **multifactorial** (influenced by many factors). A zygote might have the genes for becoming, say, a musical genius, but that potential may never be expressed. Completely accurate prediction of a person's phenotype is impossible, even if the genotype is entirely known (Lehner, 2013).

Almost daily, researchers describe additional complexities in polygenic and multifactorial interaction. It is apparent that "phenotypic variation . . . results from multiple interactions among numerous genetic and environmental factors." To describe this "fundamental problem of interrelating genotype and phenotype in complex traits" (Nadeau & Dudley, 2011, p. 1015), we begin with epigenetics.

phenotype The observable characteristics of a person, including appearance, personality, intelligence, and all other traits.

polygenic Referring to a trait that is influenced by many genes.

multifactorial Referring to a trait that is affected by many factors, both genetic and environmental, that enhance, halt, shape, or alter the expression of genes, resulting in a phenotype that may differ markedly from the genotype.

Epigenetics

As you learned in Chapter 1, all important human characteristics are *epigenetic,* including diseases known to be inherited such as cancer, schizophrenia, and autism (Kundu, 2013; Plomin et al., 2013).

Diabetes is a notable example. People who inherit genes that put them at risk might nonetheless never develop diabetes. Alternatively, at some point, factors in the diet might activate that genetic risk, causing the person to become diabetic. Once that happens, epigenetic changes in the genes make diabetes irreversible: diet and insulin may control the disease, allowing the person to live a normal life, but the pre-diabetic state never returns (Reddy & Natarajan, 2013).

The same may be true for other developmental changes over the life span. Certain environmental influences (such as injury, temperature extremes, drug abuse, and crowding) can impede healthy development, whereas others (nourishing food, loving care, play) can facilitate it, all because of differential susceptibility. A recent discovery is that some epigenetic factors that suppress or release genes are cognitive, not

Human Genome Project An international effort to map the complete human genetic code. This effort was essentially completed in 2001, though analysis is ongoing.

Especially for Future Parents Suppose you wanted your daughters to be short and your sons to be tall. Could you achieve that? (see response, page 80)

MARCO C. PEREIRA/SARA WONG/ASEE/REDUX

Hidden Husband Shyness is inherited, but this mother seems not to have the gene. Probably her husband is the shy one—unless nurture has taught the daughter to be shy and the mother to be outgoing.

dominant–recessive pattern The interaction of a heterozygous pair of alleles in such a way that the phenotype reflects one allele (the dominant gene) more than the other (the recessive gene).

carrier A person whose genotype includes a gene that is not expressed in the phenotype. The carried gene occurs in half of the carrier's gametes and thus is passed on to half of the carrier's children. If such a gene is inherited from both parents, the characteristic appears in the phenotype.

biological. For example, if a person feels lonely and rejected, that feeling can affect the RNA (organic material that enables DNA to function), which allows genetic potential for heart disease or social anxiety to be expressed (Slavich & Cole, 2013).

No trait—even one with strong, proven, genetic origins, such as blood pressure or severe depression—is determined by genes alone because "development is an epigenetic process that entails cascades of interactions across multiple levels of causation, from genes to environments" (Spencer et al., 2009, p. 80). Because epigenetic influences occur lifelong, latent genes can become activated at any point.

A surprising example might be political ideology: Several researchers report that a particular allele of a dopamine receptor gene (DRD4-R7) correlates with being liberal, but only if a person has many friends. Loners, even with the liberal-leaning allele, are more conservative (Settle et al., 2010).

Gene–Gene Interactions

Many discoveries have followed the completion of the **Human Genome Project** in 2001. One of the first surprises was that humans have far fewer than 100,000 genes, the number often cited in the twentieth century. The total number of genes in a person is between 18,000 and 23,000. The precise number is elusive because—another surprise—it is not always easy to figure out where one gene starts and another ends, or even if a particular stretch of DNA is actually a gene (Rouchka & Cha, 2009). Nor is it always easy to predict exactly how the genes from one parent will interact with the genes from the other. We do, however, know some basics of genetic interaction, which we describe now.

Additive Heredity

Some alleles are *additive* because their effects *add up* to influence the phenotype. When genes interact additively, the phenotype usually reflects the contributions of every gene that is involved. Height, hair curliness, and skin color, for instance, are usually the result of additive genes. Indeed, height is probably influenced by 180 genes, each contributing a very small amount (Enserink, 2011).

Most people have ancestors of varied height, hair curliness, skin color, and so on, so their children's phenotype does not mirror the parents' phenotypes (although the phenotype does always reflect their genotypes). I see this in my family: Our daughter Rachel is of average height, shorter than her father or me, but taller than either of our mothers. She apparently inherited some of her grandmothers' height genes from us. And none of my children have exactly my skin color—apparent when we borrow clothes from each other and are distressed that a particular shade is attractive on one but ugly on another.

How any additive trait turns out depends partly on all the genes a child happens to inherit (half from each parent, which means one-fourth from each grandparent). Some genes amplify or dampen the effects of other genes, aided by all the other DNA and RNA (not junk!) in the zygote (Pauler et al., 2012).

Dominant–Recessive Heredity

Not all genes are additive. In one nonadditive form, alleles interact in a **dominant–recessive pattern,** when one allele, the *dominant gene*, is more influential than the other, the *recessive gene*. The dominant gene controls the characteristic even when a recessive gene is the other half of a pair. Every person has recessive genes that are not apparent in their phenotype. A person is said to be a **carrier** of that recessive gene because it is *carried* on the genotype.

Most recessive genes are harmless. For example, blue eyes are determined by a recessive allele and brown eyes by a dominant one, so a child conceived by a blue-eyed parent (who always has two recessive blue-eye genes) and a brown-eyed parent will usually have brown eyes.

"Usually have brown eyes" is accurate because sometimes a brown-eyed person is a carrier of the blue-eye gene. In that case, in a blue-eye/brown-eye couple, every child has at least one blue-eye gene (from the blue-eyed parent) and half of them will have a blue-eye recessive gene (from the brown-eyed parent). Then half of those will have blue eyes because they have no dominant brown-eye gene. The other half will have a brown-eye dominant gene and thus have brown eyes but be carriers, like their brown-eyed parent.

This gets tricky if both parents are carriers. Thus if two brown-eyed parents both have the blue-eye recessive gene, they could have a blue-eyed child (one chance in four). No one should raise doubts about the child's paternity (see Figure 3.4). The same pattern is found for all recessive genes: Most are harmless (like the genes for blue eyes) but some are lethal (like those that cause serious diseases, discussed at the end of this chapter.)

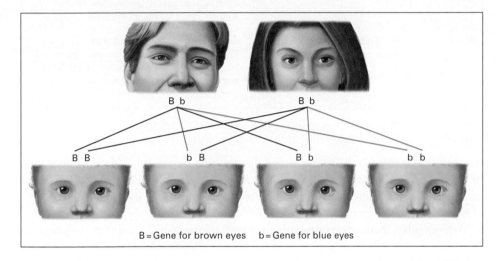

B = Gene for brown eyes   b = Gene for blue eyes

FIGURE 3.4

Changeling? No. If two brown-eyed parents both carry the blue-eye gene, they have one chance in four of having a blue-eyed child. Other recessive genes include the genes for red hair, Rh negative blood, and many genetic diseases.

A special case of the dominant–recessive pattern occurs with genes that are **X-linked** (located on the X chromosome). If an X-linked gene is recessive—as are the genes for most forms of color blindness, many allergies, several diseases, and some learning disabilities—the fact that it is on the X chromosome is critical in determining whether it will be expressed in the phenotype (see Table 3.1).

To understand the inheritance of X-linked traits, you need to remember that the Y chromosome is much smaller than the X, so genes on the X almost never have a counterpart on the Y. Therefore, recessive traits carried on the X affect the phenotypes of sons more often than daughters because the daughters have another X chromosome, usually with the dominant gene. This explains why males with an X-linked disorder inherited it from their mothers, not their fathers. Because of their mothers, 20 times more boys than girls are color-blind (McIntyre, 2002).

X-linked A gene carried on the X chromosome. If a male inherits an X-linked recessive trait from his mother, he expresses that trait because the Y from his father has no counteracting gene. Females are more likely to be carriers of X-linked traits but are less likely to express them.

Copy Number Variations

For any living creature, the outcomes of all the interactions involved in heredity are difficult to predict. A small deletion, repetition, or transposition in any of the 3 billion base pairs may be inconsequential, lethal, or something in between.

When the human genome was first mapped in 2001, it was hoped that a specific additive, recessive, or dominant gene could be located for each genetic disorder and that a cure would soon follow. That "one gene/one disorder" hope proved to be fantasy, disappointing many doctors who hoped that personalized medicine

TABLE 3.1	The 23rd Pair and X-Linked Color Blindness		
23rd Pair	**Phenotype**	**Genotype**	**Next Generation**
1. XX	Normal woman	Not a carrier	No color blindness from mother
2. XY	Normal man	Normal X from mother	No color blindness from father
3. XX	Normal woman	Carrier from father	Half her children will inherit her X. The girls with her X will be carriers; the boys with her X will be color-blind.
4. XX	Normal woman	Carrier from mother	Half her children will inherit her X. The girls with her X will be carriers; the boys with her X will be color-blind.
5. XY	Color-blind man	Inherited from mother	All his daughters will have his X. None of his sons will have his X. All his children will have normal vision, unless their mother also had an X for color blindness.
6. XX	Color-blind woman (rare)	Inherited from both parents	Every child will have one X from her. Therefore, every son will be color-blind. Daughters will be only carriers, unless they also inherit an X from the father, as their mother did.

was imminent (Marshall, 2011). Molecular analysis found, instead, that thousands of seemingly minor variations in base pairs turn out to be influential—each in small ways. Since there are 3 billion combinations of base pairs, accumulated variations have notable impact.

Attention has focused on **copy number variations,** which are genes with repeats (from one to hundreds) or deletions of base pairs. Copy number variations correlate with almost every disease and condition, including heart disease, impaired intellectual abilities, mental illness, and many cancers. Such variations are partly developmental in that they are particularly influential prenatally as basic brain structures are formed. But remember plasticity—changes can occur lifelong (Chaignat et al., 2011).

Copy number variations are "abundant"—we all have some of them (Mills et al., 2011). Detecting and interpreting such variations may be crucial for personalized medicine in the future. For instance, many drugs work differently depending on the genetic structure of the recipient. These specific factors lead directly to effective treatment of individual patients (Marshall, 2011).

Researchers are just beginning to understand the implications of copy number variations, although many hope that soon such genetic information will help target drugs and other medical measures. Even that may be a hopeful fantasy. Since epigenetics shows that environmental influences can actually change genetic expression, personalized medicine must consider each individual's habits of mind and life at least as much as their genes (Horowitz et al., 2013)

To further complicate matters, sometimes one-half of a gene pair switches off completely, allowing the other free rein but potentially causing a problem if that remaining gene has a deleterious variation. For girls, one X of the 23rd pair is deactivated early in prenatal life. The implications of that shut-off are not well understand, but it is known that sometimes that X is from the ovum, sometimes from the sperm. Boys, of course, have only one X, so it always is activated.

copy number variations Genes with various repeats or deletions of base pairs.

>> **Response for Future Parents** (from page 78): Possibly, but you wouldn't want to. You would have to choose one mate for your sons and another for your daughters, and you would have to use sex-selection methods. Even so, it might not work, given all the genes on your genotype. More important, the effort would be unethical, unnatural, and possibly illegal.

She Laughs Too Much No, not the smiling sister, but the 10-year-old on the right, who has Angelman syndrome. She inherited it from her mother's chromosome 15. Fortunately, her two siblings inherited the mother's other chromosome 15 and are normal. If she had inherited the identical deletion on her father's chromosome 15, she would have developed Prader-Willi syndrome, which would cause her to be overweight, hungry, and often angry. With Angelman syndrome, however, laughing, even at someone's pain, is a symptom.

That is not the only case that is affected by sex. Sometimes the same gene affects male and female embryos differently. It also matters whether a gene came from the mother or the father, a phenomenon called *parental imprinting*.

The best-known example of parental imprinting occurs with a small deletion on chromosome 15. If that deletion came from the father's chromosome 15, the child may develop Prader-Willi syndrome and be obese, slow moving, and stubborn. If that deletion came from the mother's chromosome 15, the child will have Angelman syndrome and be thin, hyperactive, and happy—sometimes too happy, laughing when no one else does. In both cases, intellectual development is impaired, though in somewhat distinct ways.

Parental imprinting is quite common. Early in prenatal development (day 15), an estimated 553 genes act differently if they come from the mother or from the father—a much higher frequency than previously thought (Gregg, 2010). Imprinting may be affected by the sex of the embryo as well as the sex of the parent. For instance, women develop multiple sclerosis more often than men, and they usually inherit it from their mothers, not their fathers, probably for genetic as well as epigenetic reasons (Huynh & Casaccia, 2013).

SUMMING UP

The distinction between genotype (heredity) and phenotype (manifest appearance and observed behavior) is one of the many complexities in genetics and development. All traits are epigenetic, the product of genetic and nongenetic influences, beginning with methylation at conception and continuing lifelong. Furthermore, most traits are polygenic, the result of many genes that interact—some additively and some in a dominant–recessive pattern, with thousands of minor variations in base pairs, all of which may be affected by the sex of the parent and the zygote. ∎

>> Nature and Nurture

The goal of this chapter is to help every reader grasp the complex interaction between genotype and phenotype. This is not easy. For decades in many nations, millions of scientists have struggled to understand this complexity. Each year brings advances in statistics and molecular analysis, new data to uncover various patterns, all resulting in hypotheses to be explored.

Now we examine two complex traits: addiction and visual acuity. As you will see, understanding the progression from genotype to phenotype has many practical implications.

Alcoholism

At various times throughout history, people have considered the abuse of alcohol and other drugs to be a moral weakness, a social scourge, or a personality defect. Historically and internationally, the focus has been on alcohol, since people everywhere discovered fermentation thousands of years ago. Alcohol has been declared illegal (as in the United States from 1919 to 1933) or considered sacred (as in many Judeo-Christian rituals), and alcoholics have been jailed, jeered, or burned at the stake. We now know that inherited biochemistry affects alcohol metabolism; punishing those with the genes does not stop addiction.

To be more specific, genes create an addictive pull that can be overpowering, extremely weak, or somewhere in between, as each person's biochemistry reacts to alcohol by causing sleep, nausea, aggression, joy, relaxation, forgetfulness, sex urges, or tears. Metabolism allows some people to "hold their liquor" and therefore drink too much, whereas others (including many East Asians) sweat and become red-faced after just a few sips, an embarrassing response that may lead to abstinence. There is no single alcoholic gene, but genes and alleles that make alcoholism more likely have been identified on every chromosome except the Y (Epps & Holt, 2011). Every research scientist agrees: Alcoholism is polygenic and culture is crucial.

Although the emphasis at first was on the genes that cause biological addiction, we now know that genes that affect personality traits may be pivotal (Macgregor et al., 2009). Temperamental traits known to be inherited, among them a quick temper, sensation-seeking, and high anxiety, all encourage drinking. Moreover, some contexts (such as fraternity parties) make it hard to avoid alcohol; other contexts (a church social in a "dry" county) make it difficult to swallow anything stronger than lemonade.

Sex (biology—XX or XY) and gender (cultural) also affect the risk of alcoholism. For biological reasons (body size, fat composition, metabolism), women become drunk on less alcohol than men, but how much a woman drinks depends on her social context. For example, in Japan, both sexes have the same genes for metabolizing alcohol, yet women drink only about one-tenth as much as men. When women of Japanese ancestry live in the United States, their alcohol consumption increases about fivefold (Higuchi et al., 1996). Apparently, Americans of Asian descent try to adopt the drinking patterns of their new culture (Makimoto, 1998).

Nearsightedness

Age, genes, and culture affect vision as well.

First consider age. Newborns focus only on things within 1 to 3 feet of their eyes; vision improves steadily until about age 10. The eyeball changes shape at puberty, increasing nearsightedness (myopia), and again in middle age, decreasing myopia.

Heritable?

Now consider genes. A study of British twins found that the Pax6 gene, which governs eye formation, has many alleles that make people somewhat nearsighted (Hammond et al., 2004). This research found *heritability* of almost 90 percent, which means that if one monozygotic twin was nearsighted, the other twin was almost always nearsighted, too.

However, **heritability** indicates only how much of the variation in a particular trait *within a particular population* in a particular context and era can be traced to genes. For example, the heritability of height is very high (about 95 percent) when

Especially for Drug Counselors Is the wish for excitement likely to lead to addiction? (see response, page 84)

heritability A statistic that indicates what percentage of the variation in a particular trait within a particular population, in a particular context and era, can be traced to genes.

children receive good medical care and nutrition, but low (about 20 percent) when children are malnourished. Thus, the 90 percent heritability of nearsightedness among the British may not apply elsewhere.

Indeed, it does not. In some African communities, vision heritability is close to zero because severe vitamin A deficiency makes vision depend much more on diet than on genes. If a child has no vitamin A, that child may have poor vision, even if the genotype is programmed for great vision. Scientists are working to develop a strain of maize (the local staple) high in vitamin A. If they succeed, heritability will increase and overall vision will improve (Harjes et al., 2008). But what about children who are well nourished? Is their vision entirely inherited? Cross-cultural research suggests that it is not.

One report claimed that "myopia is increasing at an 'epidemic' rate, particularly in East Asia" (Park & Congdon, 2004, p. 21). The first published research on this phenomenon appeared in 1992, when scholars noticed that, in army-mandated medical exams of all 17-year-old males in Singapore, 26 percent were nearsighted in 1980 but 43 percent were nearsighted in 1990 (Tay et al., 1992). A recent article in the leading British medical journal suggests that, although genes are to blame for most cases of severe myopia, "any genetic differences may be small" for the common nearsightedness of Asian school children (Morgan et al., 2012, p. 1739). Nurture must somehow be involved. But how?

Outdoor Play?

One possible culprit is homework. As Chapter 12 describes, contemporary East Asian children are amazingly proficient in math and science. Fifty years ago, most Asian children were working; now almost all are diligent students. As their developing eyes focus on their books, those with a genetic vulnerability to myopia may lose acuity for objects far away—which is exactly what nearsightedness means.

A study of Singaporean 10- to 12-year-olds found a positive correlation between nearsightedness (measured by optometric exams) and high achievement, especially in language (presumably reflecting more reading). Correlation is not proof, but the odds ratio was 2.5 and the significance was 0.001, which makes this data impossible to ignore (Saw et al., 2007). Data from the United States on children playing sports has led some ophthalmologists to suggest that the underlying cause is not time spent studying but inadequate time spent in daylight (Morgan et al., 2012). Perhaps if children spent more time outside playing, walking, or relaxing, fewer would need glasses.

Between the early 1970s and the early 2000s, nearsightedness in the U.S. population increased from 25 to 42 percent (Vitale et al., 2009). Urbanization, television, and fear of strangers have kept many U.S. children indoors most of the time, unlike earlier generations who played outside for hours each day. One ophthalmologist comments that "we're kind of a dim indoors people nowadays" (Mutti, 2010, p. 17). Genetically vulnerable children once did not necessarily become nearsighted; now they do.

LONELY PLANET IMAGES/GETTY IMAGES

No Time for Play Chinese children spend most of their time in school, at home doing school work, or in school activities, such as this parade in Wan Chai.

Observation Quiz Focus on education is one reason for China's economic success, but these children wear one of the negative consequences. (see answer, page 84)

Practical Applications

Since genes affect every disorder, no one should be blamed or punished for inherited problems. However, knowing that genes never act in isolation allows prevention after birth. For instance, if alcoholism is in the genes, parents can keep alcohol out of their home, hoping their children become cognitively and socially mature before imbibing. If nearsightedness runs in the family, parents can make sure that children play outdoors every day.

Of course, outdoor play and abstention from alcohol are recommended for every child, as are dozens of other behaviors, such as flossing, saying "please," getting enough sleep, eating vegetables, and writing thank-you notes. However, no parent can enforce every recommendation. Awareness of genetic risks helps parents set priorities.

Ignoring the nature–nurture interaction can be lethal. Consider baseball superstar Mickey Mantle, who hit more home runs in World Series baseball than any other player. Most of his male relatives were alcoholics and died before middle age, including his father, who died of Hodgkin disease (a form of cancer) at age 39. Mantle became "a notorious alcoholic [because he] believed a family history of early mortality meant he would die young" (Jaffe, 2004, p. 37). He ignored his genetic predisposition to alcoholism.

At age 46 Mantle said, "If I knew I was going to live this long, I would have taken better care of myself." He never developed Hodgkin disease, and if he had, chemotherapy discovered and developed since his father's death would likely have saved him—an example of environment prevailing over genes.

However, drinking destroyed Mantle's liver. He understood too late what he had done. When he was dying, he told his fans at Yankee Stadium: "Please don't do drugs and alcohol. God gave us only one body, keep it healthy. If you want to do something great, be an organ donor" (quoted in Begos, 2010). Despite a last-minute liver transplant, he died at age 63—15 years younger than most men of his time.

SUMMING UP

Genes affect every trait—whether it is something wonderful, such as a wacky sense of humor; something fearful, such as a violent temper; or something quite ordinary, such as a tendency to be bored. The environment affects every trait as well, in ways that change as maturational, cultural, and historical processes unfold. Genes themselves can be modified through epigenetic factors, not only biological ones but also psychological ones. This is apparent in height, alcoholism, nearsightedness, and almost every other physical and psychological condition. All have genetic roots, developmental patterns, and environmental triggers. ▪

>> Chromosomal and Genetic Problems

We now focus on conditions caused by an extra chromosome or a single destructive gene. These are abnormalities in that they are not the norm (hence called *ab*normal). Three factors make these conditions relevant to human development:

1. They provide insight into the complexities of nature and nurture.
2. Knowing their origins helps limit their effects.
3. Information combats prejudice: Difference is not always deficit.

Not Exactly 46

As you know, each sperm or ovum usually has 23 chromosomes, creating a zygote with 46 chromosomes and eventually a person. However, cells do not always split exactly in half to make those reproductive cells. One variable known to correlate with chromosomal abnormalities is the parents' age, particularly the age of the mother. A suggested explanation is that, since ova begin to form before a girl is born, older mothers have older ova. When the 46 chromosomes of the mother splits to make ova, usually the split is even, 23/23. But older women are more likely to release some ova that are 22/24. Sperm also are diminished in quantity and normality with age.

Miscounts are not rare. One estimate is that 5 to 10 percent of all zygotes have more or fewer than 46 chromosomes (Brooker, 2009); another estimate suggests that the rate is as high as 50 percent (Fragiouli & Wells, 2011). Far fewer of these zygotes develop to birth (only less than 1 percent of newborns have other than 46 chromosomes) primarily because most odd-numbered organisms never duplicate, divide, differentiate, and implant.

If implantation does occur, many are aborted, spontaneously (miscarried) or by choice. Birth itself is hazardous; about 5 percent of stillborn (dead-at-birth) babies have 47 chromosomes (O. J. Miller & Therman, 2001), and many abnormal but living newborns die within the first few days. Once in about every 200 births, a newborn survives with 45, 47, or, rarely, 48 or 49 chromosomes.

Down Syndrome

Each abnormality leads to a recognizable *syndrome*, a cluster of distinct characteristics that tend to occur together. Usually the cause is three chromosomes at a particular location instead of the usual two (a condition called a *trisomy*). The most common extra-chromosome condition that results in a surviving child is **Down syndrome,** also called *trisomy-21* because the person has three copies of chromosome 21.

Some 300 distinct characteristics can result from that third chromosome 21. No individual with Down syndrome is identical to another, but trisomy usually produces specific facial characteristics—a thick tongue, round face, slanted eyes—as well as distinctive hands, feet, and fingerprints.

Many people with Down syndrome also have hearing problems, heart abnormalities, muscle weakness, and short stature. They are usually slower to develop intellectually, especially in language, and they reach their maximum intellectual potential at about age 15 (Rondal, 2010). Some are severely intellectually disabled; others are of average or above-average intelligence. That extra chromosome affects the person lifelong, but family context, educational efforts, and possibly medication can decrease the harm (Kuehn, 2011).

Problems of the 23rd Pair

Every human has at least 44 autosomes and one X chromosome; an embryo cannot develop without those 45. However, about 1 in every 500 infants is born with only one sex chromosome (no Y) or with three or more (not just two) (Hamerton & Evans, 2005) (see Table 3.2). Most conceptions in which there are serious chromosomal abnormalities are aborted spontaneously.

Having an odd number of sex chromosomes impairs cognition and sexual maturation, with varied specifics depending on both genes and nurture. Sometimes only part of the 23rd pair is missing, or a person with an extra chromosome is relatively unaffected by it. In such cases, the person seems to be a normal adult but typically is infertile (Mazzocco & Ross, 2007).

Gene Disorders

Everyone carries alleles that *could* produce serious diseases or handicaps in the next generation. Most such genes have no serious consequences because they are recessive. The phenotype is affected only when the inherited gene is dominant or when a zygote is homozygous for a particular recessive condition, that is, when the zygote has received the recessive gene from both parents.

Down Syndrome A condition in which a person has 47 chromosomes instead of the usual 46, with 3 rather than 2 chromosomes at the 21st site. People with Down syndrome typically have distinctive characteristics, including unusual facial features, heart abnormalities, and language difficulties. (Also called trisomy-21.)

REUTERS/CLAUDIA DAUT/LANDOV

Universal Happiness All young children delight in painting brightly colored pictures on a big canvas, but this scene is unusual for two reasons: Daniel has trisomy-21, and this photograph was taken at the only school in Chile where normal and special-needs children share classrooms.

Especially for Teachers Suppose you know that one of your students has a sibling who has Down syndrome. What special actions should you take? (see response, page 86)

Especially for Future Doctors Might a patient who is worried about his or her sexuality have an undiagnosed abnormality of the sex chromosome? (see response, page 86)

>> **Response for Teachers** (from page 85): As the text says, "information combats prejudice." Your first step would be to make sure you know about Down syndrome, reading material about it. You would learn, among other things, that it is not usually inherited (your student need not worry about his or her progeny) and that some children with Down syndrome need extra medical and educational attention. This might mean you need to pay special attention to your student, whose parents might focus on the sibling.

TABLE 3.2	Common Abnormalities Involving the Sex Chromosomes		
Chromosomal Pattern	Physical Appearance	Psychological Characteristics	Incidence*
XXY (Klinefelter Syndrome)	Males. Usual male characteristics at puberty do not develop—penis does not grow, voice does not deepen. Usually sterile. Breasts may develop.	Can have some learning disabilities, especially in language skills.	1 in 700 males
XYY (Jacob's Syndrome)	Males. Typically tall.	Risk of intellectual impairment, especially in language skills.	1 in 1,000 males
XXX (Triple X Syndrome)	Females. Normal Appearance.	Impaired in most intellectual skills.	1 in 500 females
XO (only one sex chromosome) (Turner Syndrome)	Females. Short, often "webbed" neck. Secondary sex characteristics (breasts, menstruation) do not develop.	Some learning disabilities, especially related to math and spatial understanding; difficulty recognizing facial expressions of emotion.	1 in 2,000 females

*Incidence is approximate at birth.
Source: Hamerton & Evans, 2005; Aksglaede et al., 2013; Powell, 2013; Stocholm et al., 2013

>> **Response for Future Doctors** (from page 85): That is highly unlikely. Chromosomal abnormalities are evident long before adulthood. It is quite normal for adults to be worried about sexuality for social, not biological, reasons. You could test the karyotype, but that may be needlessly alarmist.

fragile X syndrome A genetic disorder in which part of the X chromosome seems to be attached to the rest of it by a very thin string of molecules. The cause is a single gene that has more than 200 repetitions of one triplet.

Dominant Disorders

Most of the 7,000 *known* single-gene disorders are dominant (always expressed) (Milunsky, 2011). Severe dominant disorders are rare because people with such disorders usually die in childhood and thus do not pass the gene on to children.

Dominant disorders become common only when they are latent in childhood; they appear when an adult is old enough to have had several children. That is the case with *Huntington disease,* a fatal central nervous system disorder caused by a copy number variation—more than 35 repetitions of a particular set of three base pairs. The symptoms first appear in middle age, when a person could have had several children, as did the original Mr. Huntington (Bates et al., 2002). Another exception is a rare but severe form of Alzheimer's disease that causes dementia before age 60.

Recessive Disorders

Recessive diseases are more numerous because they are passed down from one generation to the next. Some such recessive conditions are X-linked, including hemophilia, Duchenne muscular dystrophy, and **fragile X syndrome**, caused by more than 200 repetitions on one gene (Plomin et al., 2013). (Some repetitions are normal, but not this many.) The cognitive deficits caused by fragile X syndrome are the most common form of *inherited* intellectual disability (many other forms, such as trisomy-21, are not inherited). Boys are much more often impaired by fragile X than girls.

Most recessive disorders are on the autosomes and thus are not X-linked (Milunsky, 2011). Carrier detection is possible for about 500 of them, a number that increases every month (Kingsmore et al., 2011). Although most recessive diseases are rare, about 1 in 12 North American men and women carries an allele for cystic fibrosis, thalassemia, or sickle-cell anemia, all equally common and devastating in children of both sexes. That high incidence occurs because carriers benefit from the gene (Brooker, 2009).

The most studied example of the benefits of recessive genes is sickle-cell anemia. Carriers of the sickle-cell gene die less often from malaria, which is still prevalent in parts of Africa. Indeed, four distinct alleles cause sickle-cell anemia, each originating in a malaria-prone region. Selective adaptation allowed the gene to become widespread because it protected more people (the carriers, who had only one copy of the gene) than it killed (those who actually had the disease because they had inherited the recessive gene from both parents). About 11 percent of Americans with African ancestors are carriers.

Similarly, cystic fibrosis is more common among Americans with ancestors from northern Europe; carriers may have been protected from cholera. Another allele provides some protection from HIV, although that allele is not yet common because, unlike malaria and cholera, HIV has become widespread only in the past decades.

Genetic Counseling and Testing

Until recently, after the birth of a child with a severe disorder, couples blamed witches or fate, not genes or chromosomes. Today, many young adults worry about their genes long before they marry. Virtually everyone has a relative with a serious condition and wonders what their children will inherit. People are also curious about their own future health. Many pay for commercial genetic testing, which often provides misleading information.

This misinformation is particularly the case for psychological disorders, such as depression, schizophrenia, and autism. No doubt genes are a factor in all of these conditions (Plomin et al, 2013). Yet, as with addiction and vision, the environment is crucial for every disorder—not only what the parents do but also what the community and governments do.

For dizygotic twins and other siblings, if one develops schizophrenia, chances are that about 12 percent of their siblings also develop the disease—a risk higher than the 1 percent incidence of schizophrenia for people who have no relatives with the disease. The detailed correlations leave no doubt that genes are one factor, but that environment is also key (Castle & Morgan, 2008).

If a monozygotic twin becomes schizophrenic, often—but not always—the other identical twin also develops a psychological disorder, with the particular disorder influenced by nurture. Since even monozygotic twins differ, this means that schizophrenia is not entirely genetic.

This nature–nurture interaction was confirmed by a study of the entire population of Denmark. If both parents developed schizophrenia, 27 percent of their children developed it; if one parent had it, 7 percent of their children developed it. These same statistics can be presented another way: Even if both parents developed the disease, almost three-fourths (73 percent) of their children never did (Gottesman et al., 2010). Some of them developed other psychological disorders, again providing evidence for epigenetics.

Numerous studies have identified environmental influences on schizophrenia, including fetal malnutrition, birth in the summer, adolescent use of psychoactive drugs, emigration in young adulthood, and family emotionality during adulthood. Because environment is crucial, few scientists advocate genetic testing for schizophrenia. They fear that a positive test would itself lead to depression and stress that might be groundless, as well as more stigma for those who do develop mental illness (Mitchell et al., 2010).

genetic counseling Consultation and testing by trained experts that enable individuals to learn about their genetic heritage, including harmful conditions that they might pass along to any children they may conceive.

"The Hardest Decision I Ever Had to Make" That's how this woman described her decision to terminate her third pregnancy when genetic testing revealed that the fetus had Down syndrome. She soon became pregnant again with a male fetus that had the normal 46 chromosomes; her two daughters also had the normal number, and so will her fourth child, not yet born when this photo was taken. Many personal factors influence such decisions. Do you think she and her husband would have made the same choice if they had no other children?

Nations, scientists, and the general public have many opinions about genetic testing (Plows, 2011). The problem is that science has revealed much more about genes than anyone imagined a decade ago. Laws and ethics have not kept up with the possibilities.

Professionals trained to provide **genetic counseling** help prospective parents understand their genetic risk so that they can make informed decisions about their pregnancy. The genetic counselor's task is complicated, for many reasons. One is that testing is now possible for hundreds of conditions, but it is not always accurate. Sometimes a particular gene increases the risk by only a tiny amount, perhaps 0.1 percent. Further, every adult is a carrier for something. It is therefore crucial to explain the results carefully, since many people misinterpret words such as *risks* and *probability*, especially when considering personal and emotional information (O'Doherty, 2006).

Even doctors do not always understand genetics. Consider the experience of one of my students. A month before she became pregnant, Jeannette was required to have a rubella vaccination for her job. Hearing that she had had the shot, her prenatal care doctor gave her the following prognosis:

My baby would be born with many defects, his ears would not be normal, he would be intellectually disabled. . . . I went home and cried for hours and hours. . . .
I finally went to see a genetic counselor. Everything was fine, thank the Lord, thank you, my beautiful baby is okay.

[Jeannette, personal communication]

It is possible that Jeannette misunderstood what she was told, but genetic counselors are trained to make information clear. If sensitive counseling is available, then preconception, prenatal, or even prenuptial (before marriage) testing is especially useful for:

- Individuals who have a parent, sibling, or child with a serious genetic condition
- Couples who have had several spontaneous abortions or stillbirths
- Couples who are infertile
- Couples from the same ethnic group, particularly if they are relatives
- Women over age 35 and men over age 40

Genetic counselors follow two ethical rules: (1) tests are confidential, beyond the reach of insurance companies and public records, and (2) decisions are made by the clients, not by the counselors.

However, these guidelines are not always easy to follow (Parker, 2012). One quandary arises when parents already have a child with a recessive disease, but tests reveal that the husband does not carry that gene. Should the counselor tell the couple that their next child will not have this disease because the husband is not the biological father of the first?

Another quandary arises when DNA is collected for one purpose—say, to assess the risk of sickle-cell disease—and analysis reveals another quite different problem, such as an extra sex chromosome or a high risk of breast cancer. This problem is new: Even a few years ago, testing was so expensive that research did not discover any conditions except those for which they were testing. This is no longer the case: Because of genome sequencing, many counselors will soon learn about thousands of conditions that were not suspected and are not treatable (Kaiser, 2013). Must they inform the person?

The current consensus is that information should be shared if:

1. the person wants to hear it
2. the risk is severe and verified
3. an experienced counselor explains the data
4. treatment is available (Couzin-Frankel, 2011)

A group of experts recently advocated informing patients of any serious genetic disorder, whether or not the person wants to know (Couzin-Frankel, 2013). Even so, scientists and physicians disagree about severity, certainty, and treatment.

One more complication is that individuals also differ in their willingness to hear bad news. What if one person wants to know, but other family members—perhaps a parent or a monozygotic twin who has the same condition—do not. We all are carriers. Do we all want specifics?

Sometimes couples make a decision (such as to begin or to abort a pregnancy) that reflects a mistaken calculation of the risk, at least as the professional interprets it (Parker, 2012). Even with careful counseling, people with identical genetic conditions often make opposite choices. For instance, 108 women who already had one child with fragile X syndrome were told they had a 50 percent chance of having another such child. Most (77 percent) decided to avoid pregnancy with sterilization or excellent contraception, but some (20 percent) deliberately had another child (Raspberry & Skinner, 2011). Always the professional explains facts and probabilities; always the clients decide.

Counseling must be individualized because each adult's perceptions are affected by his or her partner, present and future children, work, religion, and community (McConkie-Rosell & O'Daniel, 2007). Without careful explanation and comprehension checking, misunderstanding is common. For example, half of a large group of women misinterpreted an explanation (written for the general public) about tests for genes that make breast cancer more likely (Hanoch et al., 2010).

Many developmentalists stress that changes in the environment, not in the genes, are the most promising direction for "disease prevention and more effective health maintenance" (Schwartz & Collins, 2007, p. 696). In fact, some believe that the twenty-first-century emphasis on genes is a way to avoid focus on poverty, pollution, pesticides, and so on, even though such factors cause more health problems than genes do (Plows, 2011).

As you have read many times in this chapter, genes are part of the human story, influencing every page of it, but they do not determine the plot or the final paragraph. The rest of this book describes the rest of the story.

Reach for the Sky Gavin and Jake Barder both have cystic fibrosis, which would have meant early death had they been born 50 years ago. Now their parents pound on their chests twice a day to loosen phlegm—and they can enjoy jumping on the trampoline while wearing special pneumatic vests under their shirts.

SUMMING UP

Every person is a carrier for some serious genetic conditions. Most of them are rare, which makes it unlikely that the combination of sperm and ovum will produce severe disabilities. A few exceptional recessive-gene diseases are common because carriers were protected by a recessive gene against some lethal conditions in their communities. They survived to reproduce, and the gene spread throughout the population. Most serious dominant diseases disappear because the affected person dies before having children, but a few dominant conditions continue because their effects are not evident until after a person enters their childbearing years.

Often a zygote does not have 46 chromosomes. Such zygotes rarely develop to birth, with two primary exceptions: those with Down syndrome (trisomy-21) and those with abnormalities of the sex chromosomes. Genetic counseling helps couples clarify their values and understand the genetic risks, but every fact and decision raises ethical questions. Counselors try to explain probabilities. The final decision is made by those directly involved. ∎

SUMMARY

The Genetic Code

1. Genes are the foundation for all development, first instructing the living creature to form the body and brain and then influencing thought and behavior. Human conception occurs when two gametes (an ovum and a sperm, each with 23 chromosomes) combine to form a zygote, 46 chromosomes in a single cell.

2. Genes and chromosomes from each parent match up to make the zygote. The match is not always perfect because of genetic variations called alleles.

The Beginnings of Life

3. The sex of an embryo depends on the sperm: A Y sperm creates an XY (male) embryo; an X sperm creates an XX (female) embryo. Virtually every cell of every living creature has the unique genetic code of the zygote that began that life. The human genome contains about 20,000 genes in all.

4. Twins occur if a zygote splits into two separate beings (monozygotic, or identical, twins) or if two ova are fertilized in the same cycle by two sperm (dizygotic, or fraternal, twins). Monozygotic multiples are genetically the same. Dizygotic multiples have only half of their genes in common, as do all siblings who have the same parents.

5. Assisted reproductive technology (ART), including drugs and in vitro fertilization, has led not only to the birth of millions of much-wanted babies but also to an increase in multiple births and infants who have a higher rate of medical problems. Several aspects of ART raise ethical and medical questions.

From Genotype to Phenotype

6. Genes interact in various ways—sometimes additively, with each gene contributing to development, and sometimes in a dominant–recessive pattern. Environmental factors influence the phenotype as well. Epigenetics is the study of all the environmental factors that affect the expression of genes, including the DNA and RNA that surrounds the genes at conception.

7. The environment interacts with the genetic instructions for every trait. Every aspect of a person is almost always multifactorial and polygenic.

8. The first few divisions of a zygote are stem cells, capable of becoming any part of a person. Then cells differentiate, specializing in a particular function.

9. Combinations of chromosomes, interactions among genes, and myriad influences from the environment all ensure both similarity and diversity within and between species. This aids health and survival.

Nature and Nurture

10. Environmental influences are crucial for almost every complex trait, with each person experiencing different environments. Customs and contexts differ markedly.

11. Genetic makeup can make a person susceptible to a variety of conditions; nongenetic factors also affect susceptibility. Examples include alcoholism and nearsightedness. Cultural and familial differences affecting both of these problems are dramatic evidence for the role of nurture.

12. Knowing the impact of genes and the environment can be helpful. People are less likely to blame someone for a characteristic that is inherited; realizing that someone is at risk of a serious condition helps with prevention.

Chromosomal and Genetic Problems

13. Often a gamete has fewer or more than 23 chromosomes. Usually zygotes with other than 46 chromosomes do not develop.

14. Infants may survive if they have three chromosomes at the 21st location (Down syndrome, or trisomy-21) or one, three, or more sex chromosomes instead of two. Affected individuals have lifelong physical and cognitive problems but can live a nearly normal life.

15. Everyone is a carrier for genetic abnormalities. Genetic disorders are usually recessive (not affecting the phenotype unless inherited from both parents). If a disorder is dominant, the trait is usually mild, varied, or inconsequential until late adulthood.

16. Genetic testing and counseling can help many couples. Testing usually provides information about possibilities, not actualities. Couples, counselors, and cultures differ in the decisions they make when risks are known.

KEY TERMS

23rd pair (p. 70)
allele (p. 68)
assisted reproductive technology (ART) (p. 75)
carrier (p. 78)
chromosome (p. 68)
copy number variations (p. 80)
deoxyribonucleic acid (DNA) (p. 68)

dizygotic (DZ) twins (p. 75)
dominant–recessive pattern (p. 78)
Down syndrome (p. 85)
fragile X syndrome (p. 86)
gamete (p. 68)
gene (p. 68)
genetic counseling (p. 88)
genome (p. 69)

genotype (p. 70)
heritability (p. 82)
heterozygous (p. 70)
homozygous (p. 70)
Human Genome Project (p. 78)
in vitro fertilization (IVF) (p. 75)
intra-cytoplasmic injection (ICSI) (p. 76)
monozygotic (MZ) twins (p. 73)

multifactorial (p. 77)
phenotype (p. 77)
polygenic (p. 77)
stem cells (p. 73)
X-linked (p. 79)
XX (p. 70)
XY (p. 70)
zygote (p. 68)

WHAT HAVE YOU LEARNED?

1. How many pairs of chromosomes and how many genes does a person usually have?

2. What is the relationship among genes, base pairs, and alleles?

3. What determines a person's sex?

4. What are the advantages and disadvantages of being a monozygotic twin?

5. Why does in vitro fertilization increase the incidence of dizygotic twins?

6. Why is a person's genotype not usually apparent in the phenotype?

7. What is the difference between an epigenetic characteristic and a multifactorial one?

8. Why do polygenic traits suggest that additive genes are more common than dominant–recessive ones?

9. What surprises came from the Human Genome Project?

10. Regarding heritability, why is it important to know which population at what historical time provided the data?

11. What nature and nurture reasons encourage one person to become an alcoholic and another not?

12. What nature and nurture reasons make one person near-sighted and another not?

13. What can be learned about the nature-nurture connection from Mickey Mantle's life?

14. Why does this textbook on normal development include information about abnormal development?

15. What usually happens when a zygote has fewer or more than 46 chromosomes?

16. What are the consequences if a newborn is born with trisomy-21?

17. Why are so few genetic conditions dominant?

18. Why are a few recessive traits (such as sickle-cell) quite common?

19. What are the advantages and disadvantages of genetic testing?

20. Why do people need genetic counselors rather than fact sheets about genetic conditions?

APPLICATIONS

1. Pick one of your traits, and explain the influences that both nature *and* nurture have on it. For example, if you have a short temper, explain its origins in your genetics, your culture, and your childhood experiences.

2. Many adults have a preference for having a son or a daughter. Interview adults of several ages and backgrounds about their preferences. If they give the socially preferable answer ("It does not matter"), ask how they think the two sexes differ. Listen and take notes—don't debate. Analyze the implications of the responses you get.

3. Draw a genetic chart of your biological relatives, going back as many generations as you can, listing all serious illnesses and causes of death. Include ancestors who died in infancy. Do you see any genetic susceptibility? If so, how can you overcome it?

4. List a dozen people you know who need glasses (or other corrective lenses) and a dozen who do not. Are there any patterns? Is this correlation or causation?

>>ONLINE CONNECTIONS

To accompany your textbook, you have access to a number of online resources, including Learning Curve, an adaptive quiz-zing program, critical thinking questions, and case studies. For access to any of these links, go to www.worthpublishers .com/launchpad/bergerls9e. In addition to these resources, you'll also find links to video clips, personalized study advice, and an ebook. Some of the videos and activities available online include:

- *Genetics and Early Prenatal Development.* This activity includes animations of our earliest development.

- *Identical Twins: Growing Up Apart.* This video features footage of two identical twins, separated at birth and unknown to each other until adulthood.

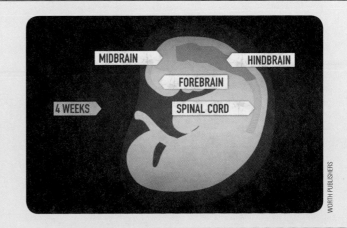

Prenatal Development and Birth

- **Prenatal Development**
  Germinal: The First 14 Days
  Embryo: From the Third Through the Eighth Week
  Fetus: From the Ninth Week Until Birth

- **Birth**
  The Newborn's First Minutes
  Medical Assistance
  Alternatives to Hospital Technology

- **Problems and Solutions**
  Harmful Substances
  Risk Analysis
  Applying the Research
  OPPOSING PERSPECTIVES: "What Do People Live to Do?"
  Low Birthweight
  Complications During Birth

- **The New Family**
  The Newborn
  New Fathers
  New Mothers
  Parental Alliance
  Bonding

WHAT WILL YOU KNOW?

1. What are the three stages of pregnancy, and what are the major developmental changes in each stage?

2. What usually occurs in the first few minutes of a newborn's life?

3. What factors determine whether a potentially harmful substance or circumstance will actually have detrimental effects on the developing fetus? What are the causes and consequences of low birth weight?

4. What kinds of changes does the birth of a child cause in family relationships, and what can couples do to help ensure they adjust to these changes in ways that are best for the child?

Birthdays are important. A day or two before every February 28, I send a birthday card to my older brother, a 6-foot-tall grandfather of six, born in 1936.

Prenatal care is important, too. Although my brother was full term, he was born underweight because my mother was told to be hungry when she was expecting. Seventy-three years later, when my daughter was pregnant, she was told to eat as much as she wanted. In mid-pregnancy she baked a cake for her husband's birthday and decorated it with a metal figure of Superman. She wrapped Superman's legs in plastic before sticking it on the cake because she worried the figurine might be made of lead and wanted to ensure that she could eat a slice.

I think both my mother and my daughter were irrational mothers-to-be. There are other foolish warnings—no spicy foods, no reaching, no sex, no exercise—that pregnant women have followed over the years. I took some needless precautions and stupid risks myself. There is one universal: Women everywhere and in every cohort want healthy and happy babies, and they change their habits to that end.

My brother often asked what time he was born. My mother always answered that she didn't remember. Finally, when she was in her 90s, he told her "a story."

> When your first precious baby was beginning to be born, it was February 28th. But labor was slow, so he was born on the 29th. You felt sorry for your little boy, with a birthday only once in four years, so you persuaded the doctor to lie.
>
> "Yes," Mom replied. "That is just what happened."

Glen told me that with a smile; he had long suspected my mother's memory of his time of birth was intact, a few hours past midnight, and that her claim of forgetfulness was to protect a lie. But I was shocked. I thought my scrupulously honest mother would never lie, much less persuade a doctor to sign a false birth

germinal period The first two weeks of prenatal development after conception, characterized by rapid cell division and the beginning of cell differentiation.

embryonic period The stage of prenatal development from approximately the third through the eighth week after conception, during which the basic forms of all body structures, including internal organs, develop.

fetal period The stage of prenatal development from the ninth week after conception until birth, during which the fetus gains about 7 pounds (more than 3,000 grams) and organs become more mature, gradually able to function on their own.

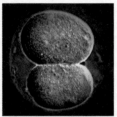
(a)

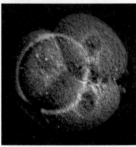
(b)

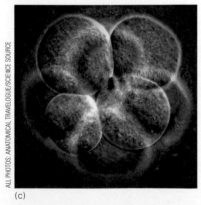
(c)

ALL PHOTOS: ANATOMICAL TRAVELOGUE/SCIENCE SOURCE

First Stages of the Germinal Period The original zygote as it divides into (a) two cells, (b) four cells, and (c) eight cells. Occasionally at this early stage, the cells separate completely, forming the beginning of monozygotic twins, quadruplets, or octuplets.

certificate. But this illustrates another universal truth: Parents imagine their newborns' future lives and try to protect them.

In this chapter, you will learn about the amazing growth of the embryo and fetus, and you will learn how family members and medical professionals safeguard newborns. Possible harm is noted, too—causes and consequences of diseases, malnutrition, drugs, pollution, stress, and so on. Birth locations vary: a high-tech operating room or a lowly hut or tub at home or a bed in a birthing center. Practices vary too. Despite such variety, remember the universals: Humans all develop for months before birth, nurtured by women's bodies and by thousands of others, who have hopes, plans, and fantasies for each person's future.

>> Prenatal Development

The most dramatic and extensive transformation of one's entire life occurs before birth. To make it easier to study, prenatal development is often divided into three main periods. The first two weeks are called the **germinal period**; the third through the eighth week is the **embryonic period**; from then until birth is the **fetal period**. (Alternative terms are presented in Table 4.1.)

Germinal: The First 14 Days

You learned in Chapter 3 that the one-celled zygote duplicates and multiplies. Soon after the 16-cell stage, differentiation begins as those early cells take on distinct characteristics and gravitate toward particular locations.

About a week after conception, the cell mass, now called a *blastocyst*, forms two distinct parts—a shell that will become the *placenta* and a nucleus that will become the embryo.

TABLE 4.1	Timing and Terminology

Popular and professional books use various phrases to segment the stages of pregnancy. The following comments may help to clarify the phrases used.

- *Beginning of pregnancy:* Pregnancy begins at conception, which is also the starting point of *gestational age*. However, the organism does not become an *embryo* until about two weeks later, and pregnancy does not affect the woman (and is not confirmed by blood or urine testing) until implantation. Perhaps because the exact date of conception is usually unknown, some obstetricians and publications count from the woman's last menstrual period (LMP), usually about 14 days *before* conception.

- *Length of pregnancy:* Full-term pregnancies last 266 days, or 38 weeks, or 9 months. If the LMP is used as the starting time, pregnancy lasts 40 weeks, sometimes expressed as 10 lunar months. (A lunar month is 28 days long.)

- *Trimesters:* Instead of *germinal period*, *embryonic period*, and *fetal period*, as used in this text, some writers divide pregnancy into three-month periods called *trimesters*. Months 1, 2, and 3 are called the *first trimester*; months 4, 5, and 6, the *second trimester*; and months 7, 8, and 9, the *third trimester*.

- *Due date:* Although a specific due date based on the LMP is calculated, only 5 percent of babies are born on that exact day. Babies born between three weeks before and two weeks after that date are considered *full term*, although labor is often induced if the baby has not arrived within 7 days of the due date. Babies born more than three weeks early are *preterm*, a more accurate term than *premature*.

The first task of the outer cells is to achieve **implantation**—that is, to embed themselves in the nurturing lining of the uterus (see Figure 4.1). This process is far from automatic; about half of natural conceptions and an even larger proportion of in vitro conceptions never implant (see Table 4.2): Most new life ends before an embryo begins (Sadler, 2010).

implantation The process, beginning about 10 days after conception, in which the developing organism burrows into the placenta that lines the uterus, where it can be nourished and protected as it continues to develop.

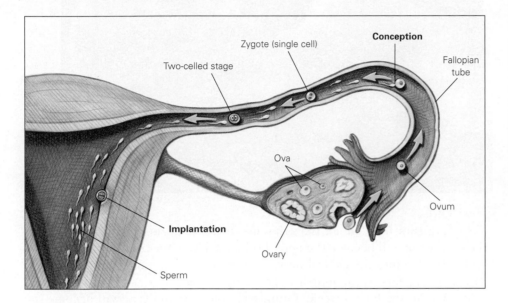

FIGURE 4.1

The Most Dangerous Journey In the first 10 days after conception, the organism does not increase in size because it is not yet nourished by the mother. However, the number of cells increases rapidly as the organism prepares for implantation, which occurs successfully not quite half of the time.

TABLE 4.2	Vulnerability During Prenatal Development

The Germinal Period

An estimated 60 percent of all zygotes do not grow or implant properly and thus do not survive the germinal period. Many of these organisms are abnormal; few women realize they were pregnant.

The Embryonic Period

About 20 percent of all embryos are aborted spontaneously, most often because of chromosomal abnormalities. This is usually called an early *miscarriage*.

The Fetal Period

About 5 percent of all fetuses are aborted spontaneously before viability at 22 weeks or are *stillborn*, defined as born dead after 22 weeks. This is much more common in poor nations.

Birth

Because of all these factors, only about 31 percent of all zygotes grow and survive to become living newborn babies. Age is crucial. One estimate is that less than 3 percent of all conceptions after age 40 result in live births.

Sources: Bentley & Mascie-Taylor, 2000; Corda et al., 2012; Laurino et al., 2005.

Embryo: From the Third Through the Eighth Week

The start of the third week after conception initiates the *embryonic period*, during which the formless mass of cells becomes a distinct being—not yet recognizably human but worthy of a new name, **embryo.** (The word *embryo* is often used loosely, but each stage of development has a particular name; here, embryo refers to the developing human from day 14 to day 56.)

embryo The name for a developing human organism from about the third through the eighth week after conception.

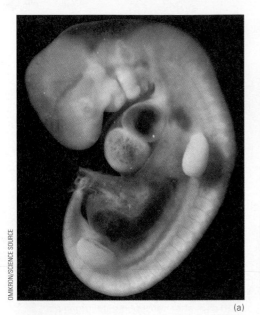

OMIKRON/SCIENCE SOURCE

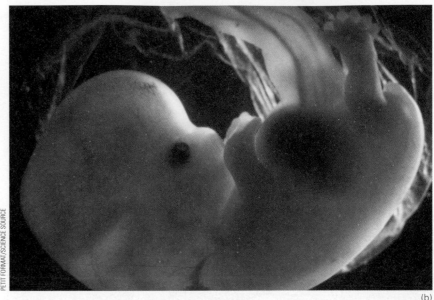

PETIT FORMAT/SCIENCE SOURCE

(a)

(b)

The Embryonic Period (*a*) At 4 weeks past conception, the embryo is only about 1/8 inch (3 millimeters) long, but already the head has taken shape. (*b*) By 7 weeks, the organism is somewhat less than an inch (2 centimeters) long. Eyes, nose, the digestive system, and even the first stage of toe formation can be seen.

fetus The name for a developing human organism from the start of the ninth week after conception until birth.

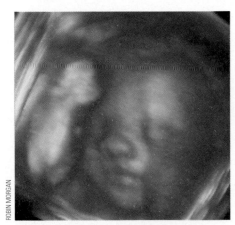

ROBIN MORGAN

There's Your Baby For many parents, their first glimpse of their future child is an ultrasound image. This is Alice, 63 days before birth.

First, a thin line (called the *primitive streak*) appears down the middle of the embryo; it will become the neural tube 22 days after conception and eventually develop into the central nervous system (the brain and spinal column). The head appears in the fourth week, as eyes, ears, nose, and mouth start to form. Also in the fourth week, a minuscule blood vessel that will become the heart begins to pulsate.

By the fifth week, buds that will become arms and legs emerge. The upper arms and then forearms, palms, and webbed fingers grow. Legs, knees, feet, and webbed toes, in that order, are apparent a few days later, each having the beginning of a skeletal structure. Then, 52 and 54 days after conception, respectively, the fingers and toes separate (Sadler, 2010).

As you can see, prenatally, the head develops first, in a *cephalocaudal* (literally, "head-to-tail") pattern, and the extremities form last, in a *proximodistal* (literally, "near-to-far") pattern. At the end of the eighth week after conception (56 days), the embryo weighs just one-thirtieth of an ounce (1 gram) and is about 1 inch (2½ centimeters) long. It has all the basic organs and body parts (except sex organs) of a human being, including elbows and knees. It moves frequently, about 150 times per hour, but this movement is random and imperceptible.

Fetus: From the Ninth Week Until Birth

The organism is called a **fetus** from the beginning of the ninth week after conception until birth. The fetal period encompasses dramatic change, from a tiny, sexless creature smaller than the final joint of your thumb to a boy or girl about 20 inches (51 centimeters) long.

The Third Month

If the 23rd chromosomes are XY, the SRY gene on the Y triggers the development of male sexual organs. Otherwise, female organs develop. The male fetus experiences a rush of the hormone testosterone, affecting many structures and connections in the brain (Filová et al., 2013). Of course, the range of brain and behavioral variations *among* males and *among* females is greater than the variations *between* the average man and woman. Nonetheless, some neurological sex differences begin early in prenatal development.

By the end of the third month, the sex organs may be visible via **ultrasound** (in a *sonogram*), which is similar to an X-ray but uses sound waves instead of radiation. The 3-month-old fetus weighs about 3 ounces (87 grams) and is about 3 inches (7.5 centimeters) long. Early prenatal growth is very rapid, with considerable variation, especially in body weight. The numbers just given—3 months, 3 ounces, 3 inches—are rounded off for easy recollection. (Metric measures—100 days, 100 grams, 100 millimeters—are similarly imprecise yet useful.)

The Middle Three Months

In the fourth, fifth, and sixth months, the heartbeat becomes stronger. Digestive and excretory systems develop. Fingernails, toenails, and buds for teeth form, and hair grows (including eyelashes). The brain increases about six times in size and develops many new neurons (*neurogenesis*) and synapses (*synaptogenesis*). Indeed, up to half a million brain cells per minute are created at peak growth during mid-pregnancy (Dowling, 2004). Following the proximodistal sequence, first the brain stem above the back of the neck, then the midbrain, and finally the cortex develop and connect.

Brain development occurs in every prenatal month, but these middle three months may be the most crucial (Johnson, 2010). Brain growth is critical at this point because the entire central nervous system becomes responsive during mid-pregnancy, beginning to regulate basic body functions such as breathing and sucking. Advances in neurological functioning allow the fetus to reach the **age of viability**, when a preterm newborn can survive.

With intensive medical care, some babies survive at 22 weeks past conception, although many hospitals worldwide do not routinely initiate intensive care unless the fetus is at least 25 weeks old. The age of viability decreased dramatically in the twentieth century, but it now seems stuck at about 22 weeks (Pignotti, 2010) because even the most advanced technology cannot maintain life without some brain response. (Reports of survivors born before 22 weeks are suspect because the date of conception is unknown.)

As the brain matures, the organs of the body begin to work in harmony. The heart beats faster during activity; fetal movement as well as heart rate quiet down during rest (not necessarily when the mother wants to sleep).

ultrasound An image of a fetus (or an internal organ) produced by using high-frequency sound waves. (Also called *sonogram*.)

Especially for Biologists Many people believe that the differences between the sexes are sociocultural, not biological. Is there any prenatal support for that view? (see response, page 98)

age of viability The age (about 22 weeks after conception) at which a fetus might survive outside the mother's uterus if specialized medical care is available.

LENNART NILSSON/SCANPIX

Viability This fetus is in mid-pregnancy, a few weeks shy of viability. As you can see, the body is completely formed. Unseen is the extent of brain and lung development; it will take at least another month for these organs to become sufficiently mature to allow for survival.

>>Response for Biologists (from page 97): Only one of the 46 human chromosomes determines sex, and the genitals develop last in the prenatal sequence, suggesting that dramatic male–female differences are cultural. On the other hand, several sex differences develop before birth.

FIGURE 4.2

Prenatal Growth of the Brain Just 25 days after conception *(a)*, the central nervous system is already evident. The brain looks distinctly human by day 100 *(c)*. By the 28th week of gestation *(e)*, at the very time brain activity begins, the various sections of the brain are recognizable. When the fetus is full term *(f)*, all the parts of the brain, including the cortex (the outer layers), are formed, folding over one another and becoming more convoluted, or wrinkled, as the number of brain cells increases.

The Final Three Months

Reaching viability simply means that life outside the womb is *possible*. Each day of the final three months improves the odds, not only of survival but also of life without disability (Iacovidou et al., 2010). (More on viability is presented later in this chapter.)

A preterm infant born in the seventh month is a tiny creature requiring intensive care for each gram of nourishment and every shallow breath. By contrast, after nine months or so, the typical full-term newborn is ready to thrive at home on mother's milk—no expert help, oxygenated air, or special feeding required. For thousands of years, that is how humans survived: We would not be alive if any of our ancestors had required intense newborn care.

The critical difference between life and death, or between a fragile preterm newborn and a robust one, is maturation of the neurological, respiratory, and cardiovascular systems. In the final three months of prenatal life, the lungs begin to expand and contract, and breathing muscles are exercised as the fetus swallows and spits out amniotic fluid. The valves of the heart go through a final maturation, as do the arteries and veins throughout the body. Among other things, this helps to prevent "brain bleeds," one of the hazards of preterm birth in which paper-thin blood vessels in the skull collapse.

The fetus usually gains at least 4½ pounds (2.1 kilograms) in the third trimester, increasing to almost 7½ pounds (about 3.4 kilograms) at birth. By full term, human brain growth is so extensive that the *cortex* (the brain's advanced outer layers) forms several folds in order to fit into the skull (see Figure 4.2). Although some large

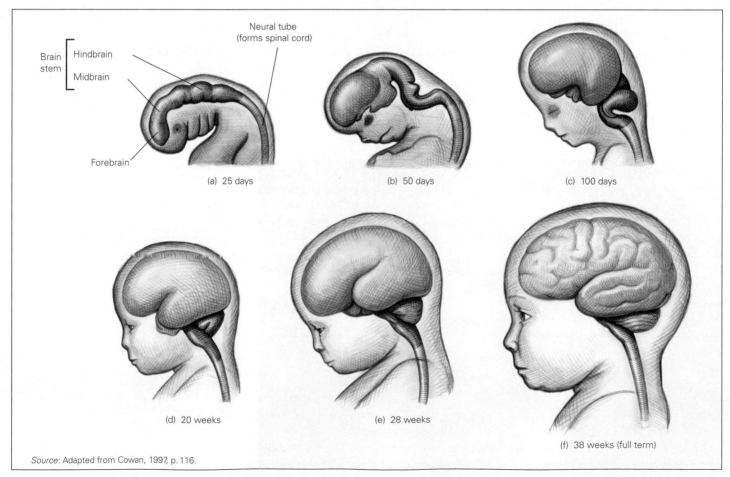

Brain stem { Hindbrain, Midbrain

Neural tube (forms spinal cord)

Forebrain

(a) 25 days

(b) 50 days

(c) 100 days

(d) 20 weeks

(e) 28 weeks

(f) 38 weeks (full term)

Source: Adapted from Cowan, 1997, p. 116.

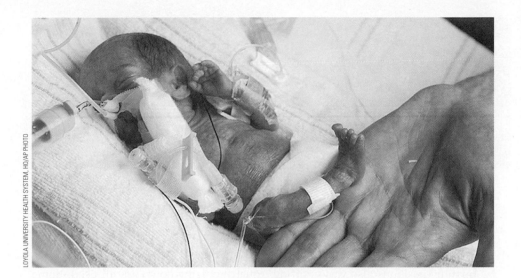

One of the Tiniest Rumaisa Rahman was born after 26 weeks and 6 days, weighing only 8.6 ounces (244 grams). Nevertheless, she has a good chance of living a full, normal life. Rumaisa gained 5 pounds (2,270 grams) in the hospital and then, 6 months after her birth, went home. Her twin sister, Hiba, who weighed 1.3 pounds (590 grams) at birth, had gone home two months earlier. At their one-year birthday, the twins seemed normal, with Rumaisa weighing 15 pounds (6,800 grams) and Hiba 17 (7,711 grams) (CBS News, 2005).

mammals (whales, for instance) have bigger brains than humans, no other creature needs as many folds because, relative to size, the human cortex contains much more material than the brains of nonhumans.

The relationship between mother and child intensifies during the final three months as the fetus's size and movement make the pregnant woman very aware of it. In turn, her sounds, the tastes of her food (via amniotic fluid), and her behavior patterns become part of fetal consciousness.

Auditory communication from mother to child begins at the 28th week and improves each week as fetal hearing (or newborn hearing if a baby is born early) becomes more acute (Bisiacchi et al., 2009). The fetus startles and kicks at loud noises, listens to the mother's heartbeat and voice, and is comforted by rhythmic music and movement, such as when the mother sings as she walks. If the mother is fearful or anxious, the fetal heart beats faster and body movements increase (DiPietro et al., 2002).

Can He Hear? A fetus, just about at the age of viability, is shown fingering his ear. Such gestures are probably random; but yes, he can hear.

SUMMING UP

In two weeks of rapid cell duplication, differentiation, and finally implantation, the newly conceived organism is transformed from a one-celled zygote to a many-celled embryo. The embryo soon develops the beginning of the central nervous system (3 weeks), a heart and a face (4 weeks), arms and legs (5 weeks), hands and feet (6 weeks), and fingers and toes (7 weeks) while the inner organs take shape. By 8 weeks, all the body structures, except male and female sex organs, are in place. Fetal growth then proceeds rapidly, including mid-trimester weight gain (about 2 pounds, almost 1,000 grams) and brain maturation, which make viability possible. By full term, all the organs function well in the 35- to 40-week newborn, who usually weighs between 6 and 9 pounds, or between 2,700 and 4,000 grams. ∎

>> Birth

About 38 weeks (266 days) after conception, the fetal brain signals the release of hormones, specifically *oxytocin*, which prepares the fetus for delivery and starts labor, as well as increases the mother's urge to nurture the baby. The average baby is born after 12 hours of active labor for first births and 7 hours for subsequent births, although often birth takes twice or half as long, with biological,

Choice, Culture, or Cohort? Why do it that way? Both of these women (in Peru, on the *left*, in England, on the *right*) chose methods of labor that are unusual in the United States, where birth stools and birthing pools are uncommon. However, in all three nations, most births occur in hospitals—a rare choice a century ago.

psychological, and social circumstances all significant. The definition of "active" labor varies, which is one reason some women believe they are in active labor for days and others say 10 minutes.

Birthing positions also vary—sitting, squatting, lying down are all used. Some women give birth while immersed in warm water, which helps the woman relax; some cultures expect women to be upright, supported by family members during birth; and some doctors insist that women be lying down. Figure 4.3 shows the universal stages of birth.

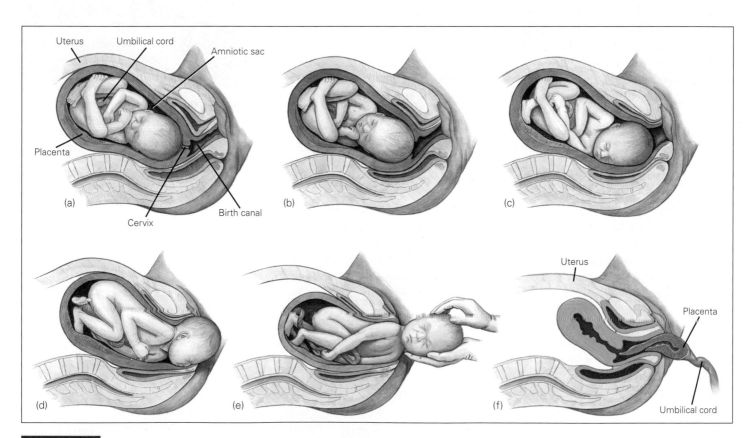

FIGURE 4.3

A Normal, Uncomplicated Birth *(a)* The baby's position as the birth process begins. *(b)* The first stage of labor: The cervix dilates to allow passage of the baby's head. *(c)* Transition: The baby's head moves into the "birth canal," the vagina. *(d)* The second stage of labor: The baby's head moves through the opening of the vagina (the baby's head "crowns") and *(e)* emerges completely. *(f)* The third stage of labor is the expulsion of the placenta. This usually occurs naturally, but the entire placenta must be expelled, so birth attendants check carefully. In some cultures, the placenta is ceremonially buried, to commemorate its life-giving role.

The Newborn's First Minutes

Newborns usually breathe and cry on their own. Between spontaneous cries, the first breaths of air bring oxygen to the lungs and blood, and the infant's color changes from bluish to pinkish. (Pinkish refers to blood color, visible beneath the skin, and applies to newborns of all hues.) Eyes open wide; tiny fingers grab; even tinier toes stretch and retract. The newborn is instantly, zestfully, ready for life.

Nevertheless, there is much to be done. If birth occurs with a Western-trained professional, mucus in the baby's throat is removed, especially if the first breaths seem shallow or strained. The umbilical cord is cut to detach the placenta, leaving an inch or so of the cord, which dries up and falls off to leave the belly button. The infant is examined, weighed, and given to the mother to preserve its body heat and to breast-feed a first meal of colostrum, a thick substance that helps the newborn's digestive and immune systems.

One widely used assessment of infant health is the **Apgar scale** (see Table 4.3), first developed by Dr. Virginia Apgar. When she graduated from Columbia medical school with her M.D. in 1933, Apgar wanted to work in a hospital but was told that only men did surgery. Consequently, she became an anesthesiologist. She saw that "delivery room doctors focused on mothers and paid little attention to babies. Those who were small and struggling were often left to die" (Beck, 2009, p. D-1).

Apgar scale A quick assessment of a newborn's health. The baby's color, heart rate, reflexes, muscle tone, and respiratory effort are given a score of 0, 1, or 2 twice—at one minute and five minutes after birth—and each time the total of all five scores is compared with the maximum score of 10 (rarely attained).

TABLE 4.3	Criteria and Scoring of the Apgar Scale				
Five Vital Signs					
Score	Color	Heartbeat	Reflex Irritability	Muscle Tone	Respiratory Effort
0	Blue, pale	Absent	No response	Flaccid, limp	Absent
1	Body pink, extremities blue	Slow (below 100)	Grimace	Weak, inactive	Irregular, slow
2	Entirely pink	Rapid (over 100)	Coughing, sneezing, crying	Strong, active	Good; baby is crying

Source: Apgar, 1953.

To save those young lives, Apgar developed a simple rating scale of five vital signs—color, heart rate, cry, muscle tone, and breathing—to alert doctors to newborn health. Since 1950, birth attendants worldwide have used the Apgar (often using an acronym: Appearance, Pulse, Grimace, Activity, and Respiration) at one minute and again at five minutes after birth, assigning each vital sign a score of 0, 1, or 2. (See also Visualizing Development, p. 118.)

If the five-minute Apgar is 7 or higher, all is well. If the five-minute total is below 7, emergency help is needed (the hospital loudspeaker may say "paging Dr. Apgar").

Medical Assistance

How closely any particular birth matches the foregoing description depends on the parents' preparation, the position and size of the fetus, and the customs of the culture. In developed nations, births almost always include sterile procedures, electronic monitoring, and drugs to dull pain or speed contractions.

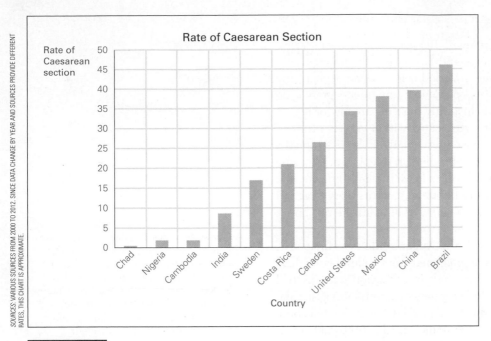

SOURCES: VARIOUS SOURCES FROM 2000 TO 2012. SINCE DATA CHANGE BY YEAR AND SOURCES PROVIDE DIFFERENT RATES, THIS CHART IS APPROXIMATE.

FIGURE 4.4

Too Many Cesareans or Too Few? Rates of cesarean deliveries vary widely from nation to nation. Latin America has the highest rates in the world (note that 40 percent of all births in Chile are by cesarean), and sub-Saharan Africa has the lowest (the rate in Chad is less than half of 1 percent). The underlying issue is whether some women who should have cesareans do not get them, while other women have unnecessary cesareans.

cesarean section (c-section) A surgical birth, in which incisions through the mother's abdomen and uterus allow the fetus to be removed quickly, instead of being delivered through the vagina. (Also called simply *section*.)

Surgery

Midwives are as skilled at delivering babies as physicians, but only medical doctors are licensed to perform surgery. More than one-third of U.S. births occur via **cesarean section** (**c-section**, or simply *section*), whereby the fetus is removed through incisions in the mother's abdomen. Cesareans are controversial: The World Health Organization suggested that c-sections are medically indicated in only 15 percent of births.

Most nations have fewer cesareans than the United States, but some—especially in Latin America—have more (see Figure 4.4). The rate has stabilized in the United States, but in many countries the rate is increasing. The most dramatic increases are in China, where the rate was 5 percent in 1991, 20 percent by 2001, and 46 percent in 2008, as the surgery has become safer and more indicators of possible problems are used (Guo et al., 2013; Juan, 2010).

In the United States, the rate rose every year between 1996 and 2008 (from 21 percent to 34 percent) before stabilizing. Variation is dramatic from one hospital to another—from 7 to 70 percent (Kozhimannil et al., 2013). Cesareans are usually safe for mother and baby and have many advantages for hospitals (they are easier to schedule, quicker, and—when insurance pays surgeons and pays for days in hospitals—more expensive than vaginal deliveries). They also increase complications after birth and reduce breast-feeding (Malloy, 2009). By age 3, children born by cesarean have double the rate of childhood obesity: 16 percent compared to 8 percent (Huh et al., 2012). This obesity connection could be correlation or causation.

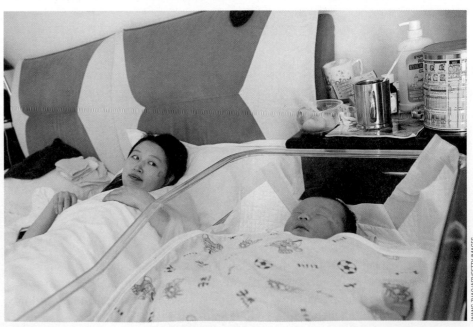

Pick Up Your Baby! Probably she can't. In this maternity ward in Beijing, China, most patients are recovering from Cesarean sections, making it difficult to cradle, breast-feed, or carry a newborn until the incision heals.

Less studied is the *epidural,* an injection in a particular part of the spine of the laboring woman to alleviate pain. Epidurals are often used in hospital births, but they increase the rate of cesarean sections and decrease the readiness of newborn infants to suck immediately after birth (Bell et al., 2010). Another medical intervention is *induced labor,* in which labor is started, speeded up, or strengthened with a drug. The rate of induced labor in the United States tripled between 1990 and 2010, and is close to 20 percent. Starting labor before it begins spontaneously increases the incidence of cesarean birth (Jonsson et al., 2013).

Newborn Survival

A century ago, at least 5 of every 100 newborns in the United States died (De Lee, 1938), as did more than half of newborns in developing nations. In the least developed nations, the rate of newborn death may still be about 1 in 20, although some rural newborn deaths are not tallied. One estimate is that worldwide almost 2 million newborns (1 in 70) die each year (Rajaratnam et al., 2010).

Currently in the United States, newborn mortality is about 1 in 250—a statistic that includes very fragile newborns weighing only 1 pound. That rate is far too high; about forty nations have better rates of newborn survival than the United States. Nonetheless, considering rates in past decades, medical measures have saved the lives of billions of babies.

Several aspects of birth arise from custom or politics, not from necessity (Stone & Selin, 2009). A particular issue in medically-advanced nations concerns the attention lavished on "miracle babies" who require intensive care, microsurgery, and weeks in the hospital (Longo, 2013). Those who survive often, but not always, need special care all their lives. Only happy outcomes are published, but critics note the public expense of keeping them alive and then the private burden borne lifelong by the parents.

The American Academy of Pediatrics recommends careful and honest counseling for parents of very preterm babies so that they understand the consequences of each medical measure. As an obstetrics team writes, "We should be frank with ourselves, with parents and with society, that there are gaps of knowledge concerning the management of infants born at very low gestational ages . . . including ethical decisions such as . . . when to provide intensive care and how extensive this should be" (Iacovidou et al., 2010, p. 133).

Alternatives to Hospital Technology

Questions of costs—emotional as well as financial—abound. For instance, c-section and epidural rates vary more by doctor, hospital, day of the week, and region than by the circumstances of the birth—even in Sweden, where obstetric care is paid for by the government (Schytt & Walderenström, 2010). A rare complication (uterine rupture), which sometimes happens when women give birth vaginally after a previous cesarean, has caused most doctors to insist that, after one cesarean, subsequent births be cesarean. Many women and some experts think this is unnecessarily cautious, but juries blame doctors for inaction more than for action. To avoid lawsuits, doctors intervene.

Most U.S. births now take place in hospital labor rooms with high-tech operating rooms nearby in case they are needed. Another 5 percent of U.S. births occur in *birthing centers* (not in a hospital), and less than 1 percent occur at home (home births are illegal in some jurisdictions). About half of the home births are planned and half not, because of unexpectedly rapid labor. The unplanned ones are hazardous if no one is nearby to rescue a newborn in distress.

Especially for Conservatives and Liberals Do people's attitudes about medical intervention at birth reflect their attitudes about medicine at other points in their life span, in such areas as assisted reproductive technology (ART), immunization, and life support? (see response, page 105)

Birth in Afghanistan The Afghan doctor is explaining why this woman, who is pregnant with twins, will have an induced labor. Unfortunately, neither baby is expected to survive—a devastating blow this woman has already faced, having twice lost a baby less than a week old.

doula A woman who helps with the birth process. Traditionally in Latin America, a doula was the only professional who attended childbirth. Now doulas are likely to arrive at the woman's home during early labor and later work alongside a hospital's staff.

Compared with the United States, planned *home* births are more common in many other developed nations (2 percent in England, 30 percent in the Netherlands) where midwives are paid by the government. In the Netherlands, special ambulances called *flying storks* speed mother and newborn to a hospital if needed. Dutch research finds home births better for mothers and no worse for infants than hospital births (de Jonge et al., 2013).

One crucial question is how supportive the medical professionals are. One committee of obstetricians decided that planned home births are acceptable because women have "a right to make a medically informed decision about delivery," but they also insisted that a trained midwife or doctor be present, that the woman not be high-risk (e.g., no previous cesarean), and that speedy transportation to a hospital be ready (American College of Obstetricians and Gynecologists Committee on Obstetric Practice, 2011).

Historically, women in hospitals labored by themselves until birth was imminent; fathers and other family members were kept away. Almost everyone now agrees that a laboring woman should never be alone. However, family members may not know how to help, and professionals focus more on the medical than the psychological aspects of birth. As a result, some women do not get adequate emotional support. Many women now have a **doula**, a woman trained to support the laboring woman, Doulas time contractions, use massage, provide encouragement, and do whatever else is helpful.

Often doulas begin their work before active labor begins. When the actual birth is imminent, they work beside the midwives or doctors. Many studies have found that doulas benefit low-income women with no partner, decreasing the disparity in birth outcomes between middle-class and poor women (Vonderheid et al., 2011). Indeed, doulas benefit anyone giving birth, rich or poor, married or not. For example, in one study 420 middle-class married women were randomly assigned a doula or not (McGrath & Kennell, 2008). Those with doulas needed less medical intervention.

Pressure Point Many U.S. couples, like this one, benefit from a doula's gentle touch, strong pressure, and sensitive understanding—all of which make doula births less likely to include medical intervention.

SUMMING UP

Most newborns weigh about 7½ pounds (3.4 kilograms), score at least 7 out of 10 on the Apgar scale, and thrive without medical assistance. If necessary, neonatal surgery and intensive care save lives. Although modern medicine has reduced maternal and newborn deaths, many critics deplore treating birth as a medical crisis rather than a natural event. Responses to this critique include women choosing to give birth in hospital labor rooms rather than operating rooms, in birthing centers instead of hospitals, or even at home. The assistance of a doula is another recent practice that reduces medical intervention. ∎

>> Problems and Solutions

The early days of life place the developing newborn on the path toward health and success—or not. Fortunately, healthy newborns are the norm, not the exception. However, if something is amiss, it is often part of a cascade that may become overwhelming.

Harmful Substances

Such a cascade begins before the woman realizes she is pregnant, as many toxins, illnesses, and experiences can cause harm early in pregnancy. Every week, scientists discover an unexpected **teratogen**, which is anything—drugs, viruses, pollutants, malnutrition, stress, and more—that increases the risk of prenatal abnormalities. But do not be alarmed. Many abnormalities can be avoided, many potential teratogens do no harm, and much damage can be remedied. Thus, prenatal life is not a dangerous period to be feared; it is a natural process to be protected.

Some teratogens cause no physical defects but affect the brain, making a child hyperactive, antisocial, or learning-disabled. These are **behavioral teratogens**. About 20 percent of all children have difficulties that *could* be connected to behavioral teratogens, although the link is not straightforward: The cascade is murky. One of my students wrote:

> I was nine years old when my mother announced she was pregnant. I was the one who was most excited. . . . My mother was a heavy smoker, Colt 45 beer drinker and a strong caffeine coffee drinker.
> One day my mother was sitting at the dining room table smoking cigarettes one after the other. I asked "Isn't smoking bad for the baby? She made a face and said "Yes, so what?" I said " So why are you doing it?" She said, "I don't know.". . .
> During this time I was in the fifth grade and we saw a film about birth defects. My biggest fear was that my mother was going to give birth to a fetal alcohol syndrome (FAS) infant. . . . My baby brother was born right on schedule. The doctors claimed a healthy newborn. . . . Once I heard healthy, I thought everything was going to be fine. I was wrong, then again I was just a child. . . . My baby brother never showed any interest in toys . . . he just cannot get the right words out of his mouth . . . he has no common sense . . .
> Why hurt those who cannot defend themselves?

> *[J., personal communication]*

As you remember from Chapter 1, one case proves nothing. J. blames her mother, although genes, postnatal experiences, and lack of preventive information and services may be part of the cascade as well. Nonetheless, J. rightly wonders why her mother took a chance.

>> Response for Conservatives and Liberals (from page 103): Yes, some people are much more likely to want nature to take its course. However, personal experience often trumps political attitudes about birth and death; several of those who advocate hospital births are also in favor of spending one's final days at home.

teratogen An agent or condition, including viruses, drugs, and chemicals, that can impair prenatal development and result in birth defects or even death.

behavioral teratogens Agents and conditions that can harm the prenatal brain, impairing the future child's intellectual and emotional functioning.

GILES MINGASSON/GETTY IMAGES

Swing High and Low Adopted by loving parents but born with fetal alcohol syndrome, Philip, shown here at age 11, sometimes threatened to kill his family members. His parents sent him to this residential ranch in Eureka, Montana (nonprofit, tuition $3,500 a month) for children like him. This moment during recess is a happy one; it is not known whether he learned to control his fury.

Especially for Judges and Juries
How much protection, if any, should the legal system provide for fetuses? Should alcoholic women who are pregnant be jailed to prevent them from drinking? What about people who enable them to drink, such as their partners, their parents, bar owners, and bartenders? (see response, page 108)

Behavioral teratogens can be subtle, yet their effects may last a lifetime. That is one conclusion from research on the babies born to pregnant women exposed to flu in 1918. By middle age, although some of these babies grew up to be rich and brilliant, on average those born in flu-ravaged regions had less education, employment, and income than those born a year earlier (Almond, 2006).

Risk Analysis

Life requires risks: We analyze which chances to take and how to minimize harm. To pick an easy example: Crossing the street is risky, yet it would be worse to avoid all street crossing. Knowing the danger, we cross carefully, looking both ways.

Sixty years ago no one analyzed the risks of prenatal development. It was assumed that the placenta screened out all harmful substances. Then two tragic episodes showed otherwise. First, on an Australian military base, an increase in the number of babies born blind was linked to a rubella (German measles) epidemic on the same base seven months earlier (Gregg, 1941; reprinted in Persaud et al., 1985). Second, a sudden rise in British newborns with deformed limbs was traced to maternal use of thalidomide, a new drug for nausea that was widely prescribed in Europe in the late 1950s (Schardein, 1976).

Thus began teratology, a science of risk analysis. Although all teratogens increase the *risk* of harm, none *always* cause damage. The impact of teratogens depends on the interplay of many factors, both destructive and protective, an example of the dynamic-systems perspective described in Chapter 1.

The Critical Time

Timing is crucial. Some teratogens cause damage only during a *critical period* (see Figure 4.5). [**Lifespan Link:** Critical and sensitive periods are described in Chapter 1.] Obstetricians recommend that *before* pregnancy occurs, women should avoid drugs (especially alcohol), supplement a balanced diet with extra folic acid and iron, and update their immunizations. Indeed, preconception health is at least as important as postconception health (see Table 4.4).

The first days and weeks after conception (the germinal and embryonic periods) are critical for body formation, but health during the entire fetal period affects the brain. Some teratogens that cause preterm birth or low birthweight are particularly harmful in the second half of pregnancy. In fact, one study found that although smoking cigarettes throughout prenatal development can harm the fetus, smokers who quit early in pregnancy had no higher risks of birth complications than did women who never smoked (McCowan et al., 2009).

Timing may be important in another way. When pregnancy occurs soon after a previous pregnancy, risk increases. For example, one study found that second-born children are twice as likely to be autistic if they are born within a year of the first-born (Cheslac-Postava et al., 2011).

How Much Is Too Much?

A second factor affecting the harm from teratogens is the dose and/or frequency of exposure. Some teratogens have a **threshold effect**; they are virtually harmless until exposure reaches a certain level, at which point they "cross the threshold" and become damaging. This threshold is not a fixed boundary: Dose, timing, frequency, and other teratogens affect when the threshold is crossed (O'Leary et al., 2010).

threshold effect In prenatal development, when a teratogen is relatively harmless in small doses but becomes harmful once exposure reaches a certain level (the threshold).

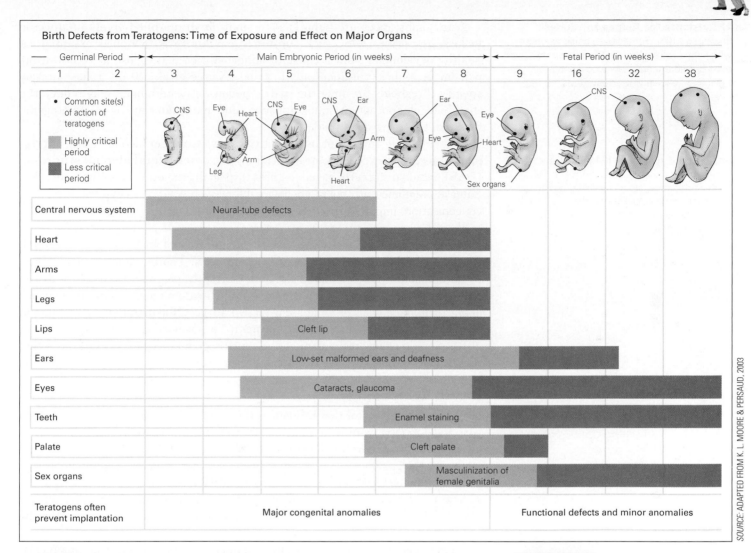

Birth Defects from Teratogens: Time of Exposure and Effect on Major Organs

SOURCE: ADAPTED FROM K. L. MOORE & PERSAUD, 2003

FIGURE 4.5

Critical Periods in Human Development
The most serious damage from teratogens (green bars) is likely to occur early in prenatal development. However, significant damage (purple bars) to many vital parts of the body, including the brain, eyes, and genitals, can occur during the last months of pregnancy as well.

TABLE 4.4	Before Pregnancy
What Prospective Mothers Should Do	**What Prospective Mothers Really Do (U.S. Data)**
1. Plan the pregnancy.	1. At least a third of all pregnancies are not intended.
2. Take a daily multivitamin with folic acid.	2. About 60 percent of women aged 18 to 45 do not take multivitamins.
3. Avoid binge-drinking (defined as four or more drinks in a row).	3. One in seven women in their childbearing years binge-drink.
4. Update immunizations against all teratogenic viruses, especially rubella.	4. Unlike in many developing nations, relatively few pregnant women in the United States lack basic immunizations.
5. Gain or lose weight, as appropriate.	5. About one-third of all U.S. women of childbearing age are obese, and about 5 percent are underweight. Both extremes increase complications.
6. Reassess use of prescription drugs.	6. Ninety percent of pregnant women take prescription drugs (not counting vitamins).
7. Develop daily exercise habits.	7. More than half of women of childbearing age do not exercise.

Sources: Bombard et al., 2013; MMWR, (July 20, 2012); Mitchell et al., 2012; Mosher et al, 2012; U.S. Department of Health and Human Services, 2012.

>> Response for Judges and Juries
(from page 106): Some laws punish women
who jeopardize the health of their fetuses,
but a developmental view would consider
the micro-, exo-, and macrosystems.

fetal alcohol syndrome (FAS) A cluster of
birth defects, including abnormal facial
characteristics, slow physical growth, and
reduced intellectual ability, that may occur
in the fetus of a woman who drinks alcohol while pregnant.

A few substances are beneficial in small amounts but fiercely teratogenic
in large quantities. One such substance is vitamin A, which is essential for
healthy development but a cause of abnormalities if the dose is 50,000 units
per day or higher (obtained only in pills) (Naudé et al., 2007). Experts rarely
specify thresholds for any drug, partly because one teratogen may reduce the
threshold of another. Alcohol, tobacco, and marijuana are more teratogenic
when all three are combined.

Is there a safe amount of psychoactive drugs? Consider alcohol. Early in pregnancy, an embryo exposed to heavy drinking can develop **fetal alcohol syndrome
(FAS)**, which distorts the facial features (especially the eyes, ears, and upper lip).
Later in pregnancy, alcohol is a behavioral teratogen, leading to hyperactivity, poor
concentration, impaired spatial reasoning, and slow learning (Niccols, 2007; Riley
et al., 2011).

Some pregnant women, however, drink some alcohol with no evident harm to
the fetus. If drinking during pregnancy always caused harm, almost everyone born
in Europe before 1980 would be affected. Currently, pregnant women are advised
to avoid all alcohol, but women in the United Kingdom receive conflicting advice
about drinking a glass of wine a day or two a week (Raymond et al., 2009), and
French women are told to abstain but many do not heed that message (Toutain,
2010). Should all women who might become pregnant avoid a legal substance that
most men use routinely? Wise? Probably. Necessary?

Innate Vulnerability

Genes are a third factor that influences the effects of teratogens. When a woman
carrying dizygotic twins drinks alcohol, for example, the twins' blood alcohol levels
are equal; yet one twin may be more severely affected than the other because their
alleles for the enzyme that metabolizes alcohol differ. Genetic vulnerability is suspected for many birth defects (Sadler et al., 2010).

The Y chromosome may be crucial in some differential sensitivity. Male fetuses
are more likely to be spontaneously aborted or stillborn and also more likely to be
harmed by teratogens than female fetuses.

Genes may be important not only at conception but also during pregnancy.
One maternal allele results in low levels of folic acid in a woman's bloodstream
and hence in the embryo, which can produce *neural-tube defects*—either *spina
bifida*, in which the tail of the spine is not enclosed properly (enclosure normally occurs at about week 7), or *anencephaly,* when part of the brain is missing. Neural-tube defects are more common in certain ethnic groups (Irish,
English, and Egyptian), but the crucial maternal allele is rare among Asians
and sub-Saharan Africans (Mills et al., 1995).

Since 1998 in the United States, every packaged cereal has added folic acid,
an intervention that reduced neural-tube defects by 26 percent in the first three
years after the law went into effect (MMWR, September 13, 2002). But some
women rarely eat cereal and do not take vitamins. Data by region is not always
available, but in 2010 in Appalachia (where many women are of British descent),
about 1 newborn in 1,000 had a neural-tube defect.

Especially for Nutritionists Is it beneficial
that most breakfast cereals are fortified
with vitamins and minerals? (see response,
page 110)

Applying the Research

Risk analysis cannot precisely predict the results of teratogenic exposure in individual cases. However, much is known more generally about destructive and
damaging teratogens and what can be done by individuals and society to reduce
the risks. Table 4.5 lists some teratogens and their possible effects, as well as
preventive measures.

TABLE 4.5	Teratogens: Effects of Exposure and Prevention of Damage*	
Teratogens	Effects of Exposure on Fetus	Measures for Preventing Damage (Laws, doctors, and individuals can all increase prevention)
Diseases		
Rubella (German measles)	In embryonic period, causes blindness and deafness; in first and second trimesters, causes brain damage.	Immunization before becoming pregnant.
Toxoplasmosis	Brain damage, loss of vision, intellectual disabilities.	Avoid eating undercooked meat and handling cat feces, garden dirt during pregnancy.
Measles, chicken pox, influenza	May impair brain functioning.	Immunization of all children and adults.
Syphilis	Baby is born with syphilis, which, untreated, leads to brain and bone damage and eventual death.	Early prenatal diagnosis and treatment with antibiotics.
HIV	Baby may catch the virus. Without treatment, illness and death are likely during childhood.	Prenatal drugs and cesarean birth make HIV transmission rare.
Other sexually transmitted infections, including gonorrhea and chlamydia	Not usually harmful during pregnancy but may cause blindness and infections if transmitted during birth.	Early diagnosis and treatment; if necessary, cesarean section, treatment of newborn.
Infections, including infections of urinary tract, gums, and teeth	May cause premature labor, which increases vulnerability to brain damage.	Good, inexpensive medical care before pregnancy.
Pollutants		
Lead, mercury, PCBs (polychlorinated biphenyls); dioxin; and some pesticides, herbicides, and cleaning compounds	May cause spontaneous abortion, preterm labor, and brain damage.	May be harmless in small doses, but pregnant women should avoid exposure, such as drinking well water, eating unwashed fruits or vegetables, using chemicals, eating fish from polluted waters.
Radiation		
Massive or repeated exposure to radiation, as in medical X-rays	May cause small brains (microcephaly) and intellectual disabilities. Background radiation probably harmless.	Sonograms, not X-rays, during pregnancy. Pregnant women who work directly with radiation need special protection.
Social and Behavioral Factors		
Very high stress	May cause cleft lip or cleft palate, spontaneous abortion, or preterm labor.	Adequate relaxation, rest, and sleep; reduce intensity of employment, housework and child care.
Malnutrition	When severe, interferes with conception, implantation, normal fetal development.	Eat a balanced diet, normal weight before pregnancy, gain 25–35 lbs (10–15 kg) during pregnancy.
Excessive, exhausting exercise	Can harm fetal growth if it interferes with woman's sleep, digestion, or nutrition.	Regular, moderate exercise is best for everyone.
Medicinal Drugs		
Lithium	Can cause heart abnormalities.	Avoid all medicines, whether prescription or over the counter, during pregnancy unless given by a medical professional who knows recent research on teratogens.
Tetracycline	Can harm teeth.	
Retinoic acid	Can cause limb deformities.	
Streptomycin	Can cause deafness.	
ACE inhibitors	Can harm digestive organs.	
Phenobarbital	Can affect brain development.	
Thalidomide	Can stop ear and limb formation.	

continued on page 110

TABLE 4.5	(Continued)	
Teratogens	**Effects of Exposure on Fetus**	**Measures for Preventing Damage (Laws, doctors, and individuals can all increase prevention)**
Psychoactive Drugs		
Caffeine	Normal, modest use poses no problem.	Avoid excessive use. (Note that coffee, tea, cola drinks, chocolate all contain caffeine).
Alcohol	May cause fetal alcohol syndrome (FAS) or fetal alcohol effects (FAE).	Stop or severely limit alcohol consumption; especially dangerous are three or more drinks a day or four or more drinks on one occasion.
Tobacco	Reduces birthweight, increases risk of malformations of limbs and urinary tract, and may affect the baby's lungs.	Ideally, stop smoking before pregnancy. Stopping during pregnancy also beneficial.
Marijuana	Heavy exposure affects central nervous system; when smoked, may hinder fetal growth.	Avoid or strictly limit marijuana consumption.
Heroin	Slows fetal growth, increases prematurity. Addicted newborns need treatment to control withdrawal.	Treatment needed before pregnancy but if already pregnant, gradual withdrawal on methadone is better than continued use of heroin.
Cocaine	Slows fetal growth, increases prematurity and then learning problems.	Stop before pregnancy; if not, babies need special medical and educational attention in their early years.
Inhaled solvents (glue or aerosol)	May cause abnormally small head, crossed eyes, and other indications of brain damage.	Stop before becoming pregnant; damage can occur before a woman knows she is pregnant.

* The field of toxicology advances daily. Research on new substances begins with their effects on nonhuman species, which provides suggestive (though not conclusive) evidence. This table is a primer; it is no substitute for careful consultation with a knowledgeable professional.

>> **Response for Nutritionists** (from page 108): Useful, yes; optimal, no. Some essential vitamins are missing (too expensive), and individual nutritional needs differ, depending on age, sex, health, genes, and eating habits. The reduction in neural-tube defects is good, but many women don't eat cereal or take vitamin supplements before becoming pregnant.

General health during pregnancy matters. Women are advised to maintain good nutrition and especially to avoid drugs and teratogenic chemicals (which are often found in pesticides, cleaning fluids, and cosmetics). Some medications are necessary (e.g., for women with epilepsy, diabetes, and severe depression), but caution and consultation should begin *before* pregnancy is confirmed.

Sadly, the cascade of teratogens is most likely to begin with women who are already vulnerable. For example, cigarette smokers are more often drinkers (as was J.'s mother); and those whose jobs require exposure to chemicals and pesticides are more often malnourished (Ahmed & Jaakkola, 2007; Hougaard & Hansen, 2007).

Advice from Doctors

Although prenatal care is helpful in protecting the developing fetus, even doctors are not always careful. One study of 152,000 new mothers in eight U.S. health maintenance organizations (HMOs) found that, during pregnancy, 40 percent of the women were given prescriptions for drugs that had not been declared safe during pregnancy, and 2 percent were prescribed drugs with proven risks to fetuses (Andrade et al., 2004). Perhaps these physicians did not know their patients were pregnant, but even a few of the wrong pills early in pregnancy may do harm.

Worse still is the failure of some doctors to advise women about harmful life patterns. For example, one Maryland study found that almost one-third of pregnant women were not asked about their alcohol use (Cheng et al., 2011). Those who were over age 35 and college-educated were least likely to be queried. Did their doctors assume they knew the dangers? Wrong. In this study, they were also most likely to drink during pregnancy.

Advice from Scientists

Scientists interpret research in contradictory ways. For instance, pregnant women in the United States are told to eat less fish, but those in the United Kingdom are told to increase fish consumption. The reason for these opposite messages is that fish contains both mercury (a teratogen) and DHA (an omega-3 fatty acid needed for fetal brain development) (Oken & Bellinger, 2008; Ramón et al., 2009). Scientists weigh the benefits and risks of fish differently, and few women are able to assess the possible harm from each mouthful, which would require them to know each kind of fish and where it swam.

Another dispute involves bisphenol A (commonly used in plastics), banned in Canada but allowed in the United States. The effect of bisphenol A is disputed because research on mice, not humans, finds it teratogenic. Should people be guided by mouse studies?

Undisputed epidemiological research on humans is logistically difficult because exposure must be measured at several different time points, including early gestation, but the outcome may not manifest itself for many years. No doubt pregnant women are more exposed to bisphenol A than they were a decade ago, and exposure correlates with hyperactive 2-year-olds, but those facts can be interpreted in at least a dozen ways (Braun et al., 2011; Diamanti-Kandarakis et al., 2009).

It is certain that prenatal teratogens can cause behavioral problems, reproductive impairment, and several diseases. Almost every common disease, almost every food additive, most prescription and nonprescription drugs (even caffeine and aspirin), many minerals in the air and water, emotional stress, exhaustion, and poor nutrition *might* impair prenatal development—but only at some times, in some amounts, in some mammals.

Most research is conducted with mice; harm to humans is rarely proven to everyone's satisfaction. Even when evidence seems clear, the proper social response is controversial. If a pregnant woman uses alcohol or other psychoactive drugs, should she be jailed for abusing her fetus, as is legal in five U.S. states (Minnesota, North Dakota, Oklahoma, South Dakota, and Wisconsin)? If a baby is stillborn, should the mother be convicted of murder, as occurred for an Oklahoma woman, Theresa Hernandez, who took meth while pregnant and was sentenced to 15 years? (Fentiman, 2009)

Prenatal Diagnosis

Early prenatal care has many benefits: Women learn what to eat, what to do, and what to avoid. Some serious conditions, syphilis and HIV among them, can be diagnosed and treated before any harm to the fetus occurs. In addition, prenatal tests (of blood, urine, and fetal heart rate as well as ultrasound) reassure parents, facilitating the crucial parent-child bond, long before fetal movement is apparent.

In general, early care protects fetal growth, makes birth easier, and renders parents better able to cope. When complications (such as twins, gestational diabetes, and infections) arise, early recognition increases the chance of a healthy birth.

Unfortunately, however, about 20 percent of early pregnancy tests *raise* anxiety instead of reducing it. For instance, the level of alpha-fetoprotein (AFP) may be too high or too low, or ultrasound may indicate multiple fetuses, abnormal growth, Down syndrome, or a mother's narrow pelvis. Many such warnings are **false positives**; that is, they falsely suggest a problem that does not exist. Any warning, whether false or true, requires further testing but also leads to worry and soul-searching. Some choose to abort, some not, with neither option easy. Consider the following.

Especially for Social Workers When is it most important to convince women to be tested for HIV: before pregnancy, after conception, or immediately after birth? (see response, page 113)

false positive The result of a laboratory test that reports something as true when in fact it is not true. This can occur for pregnancy tests, when a woman might not be pregnant even though the test says she is, or during pregnancy when a problem is reported that actually does not exist.

"What Do People Live to Do?"

John and Martha, both under age 35, were expecting their second child. Martha's initial prenatal screening revealed low alpha-fetoprotein, which could indicate Down syndrome.

> Another blood test was scheduled. . . . John asked:
>
> "What exactly is the problem?" . . .
>
> "We've got a one in eight hundred and ninety-five shot at a retarded baby."
>
> John smiled, "I can live with those odds."
>
> "I'm still a little scared."
>
> He reached across the table for my hand. "Sure," he said, "that's understandable. But even if there is a problem, we've caught it in time. . . . The worst-case scenario is that you might have to have an abortion, and that's a long shot. Everything's going to be fine." . . .

Happy Boy Martha Beck not only loves her son Adam (shown here), but she also writes about the special experiences he has brought into the whole family's life—hers, John's, and their other children's. She is "pro-choice"; he is a chosen child.

COURTESY KAREN GERDES

> "I might *have to have* an abortion?" The chill inside me was gone. Instead I could feel my face flushing hot with anger. "Since when do you decide what I *have* to do with my body?"
>
> John looked surprised. "I never said I was going to decide anything," he protested. "It's just that if the tests show something wrong with the baby, of course we'll abort. We've talked about this."
>
> "What we've talked about," I told John in a low, dangerous voice, "is that I am pro-choice. That means I decide whether or not I'd abort a baby with a birth defect. . . . I'm not so sure of this."
>
> "You used to be," said John.
>
> "I know I used to be." I rubbed my eyes. I felt terribly confused. "But now . . . look, John, it's not as though we're deciding whether or not to have a baby. We're deciding what *kind* of baby we're willing to accept. If it's perfect in every way, we keep it. If it doesn't fit the right specifications, whoosh! Out it goes." . . .
>
> John was looking more and more confused. "Martha, why are you on this soapbox? What's your point?"
>
> "My point is," I said, "that I'm trying to get you to tell me what you think constitutes a 'defective' baby. What about . . . oh, I don't know, a hyperactive baby? Or an ugly one?"
>
> "They can't test for those things and—"
>
> "Well, what if they could?" I said. "Medicine can do all kinds of magical tricks these days. Pretty soon we're going to be aborting babies because they have the gene for alcoholism, or homosexuality, or manic depression. . . . Did you know that in China they abort a lot of fetuses just because they're female?" I growled. "Is being a girl 'defective' enough for you?"
>
> "Look," he said, "I know I can't always see things from your perspective. And I'm sorry about that. But the way I see it, if a baby is going to be deformed or something, abortion is a way to keep everyone from suffering—*especially* the baby. It's like shooting a horse that's broken its leg. . . . A lame horse dies slowly, you know? . . . It dies in terrible pain. And it can't run anymore. So it can't enjoy life even if it doesn't die. Horses live to run; that's what they do. If a baby is born not being able to do what other people do, I think it's better not to prolong its suffering."
>
> ". . . And what is it," I said softly, more to myself than to John, "what is it that people do? What do we live to do, the way a horse lives to run?"

[Beck, 1999, pp. 132–133, 135]

The second AFP test was in the normal range, "meaning there was no reason to fear . . . Down syndrome" (p. 137).

As you read in Chapter 3, genetic counselors help couples discuss their choices *before* becoming pregnant. John and Martha had had no counseling because the pregnancy was unplanned and their risk for Down syndrome was low. The opposite of a false positive is a false negative, a mistaken assurance that all is well. Amniocentesis later revealed that the second AFP was a false negative. Their fetus had Down syndrome after all. Martha decided against abortion.

Low Birthweight

Some newborns are small and immature. With modern hospital care, tiny infants usually survive, but it would be better for everyone—mother, father, baby, and society—if all newborns were in the womb for at least 35 weeks and weighed more than 2,500 grams (5½ pounds). (Usually, this text gives pounds before grams, but hospitals worldwide report birthweight using the metric system, so grams precede pounds and ounces here.)

The World Health Organization defines **low birthweight (LBW)** as under 2,500 grams. LBW babies are further grouped into **very low birthweight (VLBW)**, under 1,500 grams (3 pounds, 5 ounces), and **extremely low birthweight (ELBW)**, under 1,000 grams (2 pounds, 3 ounces). Some newborns weigh as little as 500 grams, and they are the most vulnerable—about half of them die even with excellent care (Lau et al., 2013).

Maternal Behavior and Low Birthweight

Remember that fetal weight normally doubles in the last trimester of pregnancy, with 900 grams (about 2 pounds) of that gain occurring in the final three weeks. Thus, a baby born **preterm** (three or more weeks early; no longer called *premature*) is usually, but not always, LBW. Preterm birth correlates with many of the teratogens already mentioned, part of the cascade.

Not every low-birthweight baby is preterm. Some fetuses gain weight slowly throughout pregnancy and are *small-for-dates,* or **small for gestational age (SGA).** A full-term baby weighing only 2,600 grams and a 30-week-old fetus weighing only 1,000 grams are both SGA, even though the first is not technically low birthweight. Maternal or fetal illness might cause SGA, but maternal drug use is a more common cause. Every psychoactive drug slows fetal growth, with tobacco implicated in 25 percent of all low-birthweight births worldwide.

Another common reason for slow fetal growth is malnutrition. Women who begin pregnancy underweight, who eat poorly during pregnancy, or who gain less than 3 pounds (1.3 kilograms) per month in the last six months more often have underweight infants.

Unfortunately, many risk factors—underweight, undereating, underage, and smoking—tend to occur together. To make it worse, many such mothers live in poor neighborhoods, where pollution is high—another risk factor for low birthweight (Stieb et al., 2012).

What About the Father?

The causes of low birthweight just mentioned rightly focus on the pregnant woman. However, fathers—and grandmothers, neighbors, and communities—are often crucial. As an editorial in a journal for obstetricians explains: "Fathers' attitudes regarding the pregnancy, fathers' behaviors during the prenatal period, and the relationship between fathers and mothers . . . may indirectly influence risk for adverse birth outcomes" (Misra et al., 2010, p. 99).

As already explained in Chapter 1, each person is embedded in a social network. Since the future mother's behavior impacts the fetus, everyone who affects her also affects the fetus. For instance, unintended pregnancies increase the incidence of low birthweight (Shah et al., 2011). Obviously, intentions are in the mother's mind, not her body, and they are affected by the father. Thus, the father's intentions affect her diet, drug use, prenatal care, and so on.

Not only fathers but also the entire social network and culture are crucial (Lewallen, 2011). This is most apparent in what is called the *immigrant paradox.* Many immigrants have difficulty getting well-paid jobs, and thus are of low

low birthweight (LBW) A body weight at birth of less than 5½ pounds (2,500 grams).

very low birthweight (VLBW) A body weight at birth of less than 3 pounds, 5 ounces (1,500 grams).

extremely low birthweight (ELBW) A body weight at birth of less than 2 pounds, 3 ounces (1,000 grams).

preterm A birth that occurs 3 or more weeks before the full 38 weeks of the typical pregnancy—that is, at 35 or fewer weeks after conception.

small for gestational age (SGA) A term for a baby whose birthweight is significantly lower than expected, given the time since conception. For example, a 5-pound (2,265-gram) newborn is considered SGA if born on time but not SGA if born two months early. (Also called *small-for-dates.*)

>> Response for Social Workers (from page 111): Testing and then treatment are useful at any time because women who know they are HIV-positive are more likely to get treatment, reduce the risk of transmission, or avoid pregnancy. If pregnancy does occur, early diagnosis is best. Getting tested after birth is too late for the baby.

socioeconomic status. Low SES correlates with low birthweight. Thus, their new-borns should be more often underweight. But, paradoxically, newborns born in the United States to immigrants are generally healthier in every way, including birthweight, than newborns of U.S.-born women of the same gene pool (Coll & Marks, 2012).

This paradox was first recognized among Hispanics, who are the main immi-grant group in the U.S., and it was called the Hispanic paradox. Thus, although U.S. residents born in Mexico or South America average lower SES than Hispan-ics born in the United States, their newborns have fewer problems. Why? Perhaps fathers and grandparents keep pregnant immigrant women drug-free and healthy. The same is now apparent for immigrants from the Caribbean, from Africa, from Eastern Europe, and from Asia compared to U.S.-born women of those ethnicities.

Consequences of Low Birthweight

You have already read that life itself is uncertain for the smallest newborns. Ranking worse than most developed nations—and similar to Poland and Malaysia—the U.S. infant mortality rate (death in the first year) is about 6 per 1,000, primarily because of low birthweight.

Moreover, the death rate of the tiniest babies seems to be rising, not falling, even as fewer slightly older newborns die, which is why U.S. infant mortality rates are not falling as fast as they are in other nations (Lau et al., 2013). For survi-vors who are born very low birthweight, every developmental milestone—smiling, holding a bottle, walking, talking—is later, even when babies are compared on the basis of age since conception, not birth age.

Low-birthweight babies also experience cognitive difficulties as well as vi-sual and hearing impairments. High-risk newborns become infants and chil-dren who cry more, pay attention less, disobey, and experience language delays (Aarnoudse-Moens et al., 2009; Spinillo et al., 2009).

Longitudinal research from many nations finds that, in middle childhood, children who were at the extremes of SGA or preterm have many neurologi-cal problems, including smaller brain volume, lower IQs, and behavioral dif-ficulties (Hutchinson et al., 2013; van Soelen et al., 2010). Even in adulthood, risks persist: Adults who were LBW are more likely to develop diabetes and heart disease.

Longitudinal data provide both hope and caution. Remember that risk analysis gives odds, not certainties—averages that are not true in every case. By age 4, some ELBW infants are normal in brain development and overall (Claas et al., 2011; Spittle et al., 2009). Those may be the ones who would have been above average if they had stayed in the womb a few more weeks.

Comparing Nations

In some northern European nations, only 4 percent of newborns weigh under 2,500 grams; in several South Asian nations, more than 20 percent do. Worldwide, far fewer low-birthweight babies are born than two decades ago; as a result, neonatal deaths have been reduced by one-third (Rajaratnam et al., 2010).

Some nations, China and Chile among them, have improved markedly. In 1970, about half of Chinese newborns were LBW; recent estimates put that number at 4 percent (UNICEF, 2010). In some nations, community health programs aid the growth of low-birthweight infants. That makes a notable difference, according to one study provocatively titled *Low birth weight outcomes: Why better in Cuba than Alabama?* (Neggars & Crowe, 2013).

In some nations, notably in sub-Saharan Africa, the LBW rate is rising because global warming, HIV, food shortages, wars, and other problems affect pregnancy. Another nation with troubling rates of LBW rate is the United States, where the rate fell throughout most of the twentieth century, reaching a low of 7.0 percent in 1990. But then it rose again, with the 2010 rate at 8.1 percent, ranging from under 6 percent in Alaska to over 12 percent in Mississippi. The U.S. rate is higher than that of virtually every other developed nation (see Figure 4.6 for a sampling).

Many scientists have developed hypotheses to explain the U.S. rates. One logical possibility is assisted reproduction, since ART often leads to low-birthweight twins and triplets. However, LBW rates rose for naturally conceived babies as well (Pinborg et al., 2004), so ART cannot be the only explanation. Added to the puzzle is the fact that several changes in maternal ethnicity, age, and health since 1990 should have decreased LBW, not increased it.

For example, African Americans have LBW newborns twice as often as the national average (almost 14 percent compared with 7 percent), and younger teenagers have smaller babies than do women in their 20s. However, the birth rate among both groups was much lower in 2010 than it was in 1990. Furthermore, maternal obesity and diabetes are increasing; both lead to heavier babies, not lighter ones.

Something else must be amiss. One possibility is nutrition. Nations with many small newborns are also nations where hunger is prevalent, and increasing hunger correlates with increasing LBW. In both Chile and China, LBW fell as nutrition improved.

As for the United States, the U.S. Department of Agriculture found an increase in *food insecurity* (measured by skipped meals, use of food stamps, and outright hunger) between 2000 and 2007. Food insecurity directly affects LBW, and it also increases chronic illness, which itself correlates with LBW (Seligman & Schillinger, 2010).

In 2008, about 15 percent of U.S. households were considered food insecure, with rates higher among women in their prime reproductive years than among middle-aged women or men of any age. These rates increased with the economic recession of 2008–2010; if this hypothesis is accurate, rates of LBW will continue to increase.

Another possibility is drug use. As you will see in Chapter 16, the rate of smoking, drinking, and other drug use among high school girls reached a low in 1992, then increased, then decreased. Most U.S. women giving birth in the first decade of the 20th century are in a cohort that experienced rising drug use; they may still suffer the effects. If that is the reason, the recent decrease in drug use among teenagers will result in fewer LBW in the second decade of the 21st century. Sadly, in developing nations, more young women are smoking and drinking than a decade ago, including in China. Will rates rise in China soon?

A third possibility is pollution. Air pollution is increasing in China, but decreasing in the United States. If pollution is the cause, low birth rate in those nations may change in the next decade. Looking at trends in various nations will help developmentalists understand how to prevent LBW in the future.

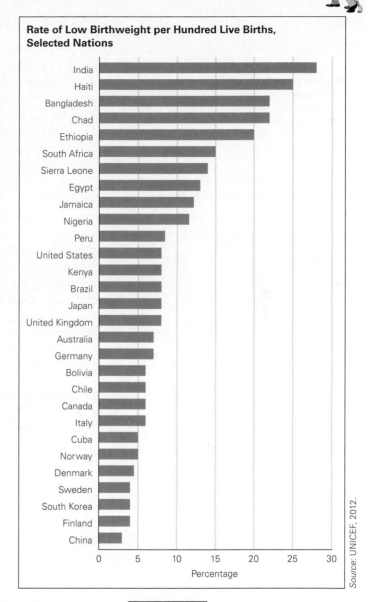

Rate of Low Birthweight per Hundred Live Births, Selected Nations

Source: UNICEF, 2012.

FIGURE 4.6

Getting Better Some public health experts consider the rate of low birthweight to be indicative of national health, since both are affected by the same causes. If that is true, the world is getting healthier, since the LBW world average was 28 percent in 2009 but 16 percent in 2012. When all nations are included, 47 report LBW at 6 per 100 or lower (United States and United Kingdom are not among them).

Complications During Birth

Any birth complication usually has multiple causes: a fetus is low birthweight, preterm, or exposed to teratogens and a mother is unusually young, old, small, or ill. As an example, **cerebral palsy** (a disease marked by difficulties with movement) was once thought to be caused solely by birth procedures (excessive medication, slow breech birth, or use of forceps to pull the fetal head through the birth canal). However, we now know that cerebral palsy results from genetic vulnerability, teratogens, and maternal infection (J. R. Mann et al., 2009), worsened by insufficient oxygen to the fetal brain at birth.

A lack of oxygen is **anoxia**. Anoxia often occurs for a second or two during birth, indicated by a slower fetal heart rate, with no harm done. To prevent prolonged anoxia, the fetal heart rate is monitored during labor and the Apgar is used immediately after birth. How long anoxia can continue without harming the brain depends on genes, birthweight, gestational age, drugs in the bloodstream (either taken by the mother before birth or given during birth), and many other factors. Thus, anoxia is part of a cascade that may cause cerebral palsy. The same cascade applies to almost every other birth complication.

cerebral palsy A disorder that results from damage to the brain's motor centers. People with cerebral palsy have difficulty with muscle control, so their speech and/or body movements are impaired.

anoxia A lack of oxygen that, if prolonged, can cause brain damage or death.

SUMMING UP

Risk analysis is complex but necessary to protect every fetus. Many factors reduce risk, including the mother's health and nourishment before pregnancy, her early prenatal care and drug use, and the father's support. The timing of exposure to teratogens, the amount of toxin ingested, and the genes of the mother and fetus may be crucial. Low birthweight, slow growth, and preterm birth increase vulnerability. The birth process itself can worsen the effects of any vulnerability, especially if anoxia lasts more than a moment or two. ▪

>> The New Family

Humans are social creatures, seeking interaction with their families and their societies. We have already seen how crucial social support is during pregnancy; social interaction may become even more important once the child is born.

The Newborn

Before birth, developing humans already affect their families through fetal movements and hormones that trigger maternal nurturance (food aversions, increased sleep, and more). At birth, a newborn's appearance (big hairless head, tiny feet, and so on) stirs the human heart, as becomes evident in adults' brain activity and heart rate. Fathers are often enraptured by their scraggly newborn and protective of the exhausted mothers, who may appreciate their husbands more than before, for hormonal as well as practical reasons.

Newborns are responsive social creatures in the first hours of life (Zeifman, 2013). They listen, stare, cry, stop crying, and cuddle. In the first day or two a professional might administer the **Brazelton Neonatal Behavioral Assessment Scale (NBAS)**, which records 46 behaviors, including 20 reflexes. Parents watching this assessment are amazed at the newborn's responses—and this fosters early parent–child connection (Hawthorne, 2009).

Technically, a **reflex** is an involuntary response to a particular stimulus. That definition makes reflexes seem automatic, with the person having no role. Actually, the strength of reflexes varies from one newborn to the next, an early indication that each person is unique. Humans of every age instinctively protect themselves

Brazelton Neonatal Behavioral Assessment Scale (NBAS) A test often administered to newborns that measures responsiveness and records 46 behaviors, including 20 reflexes.

reflex An unlearned, involuntary action or movement in response to a stimulus. A reflex occurs without conscious thought.

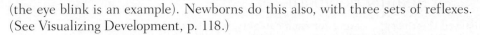

(the eye blink is an example). Newborns do this also, with three sets of reflexes. (See Visualizing Development, p. 118.)

- *Reflexes that maintain oxygen supply.* The *breathing reflex* begins even before the umbilical cord, with its supply of oxygen, is cut. Additional reflexes that maintain oxygen are reflexive *hiccups* and *sneezes,* as well as *thrashing* (moving the arms and legs about) to escape something that covers the face.
- *Reflexes that maintain constant body temperature.* When infants are cold, they *cry, shiver,* and *tuck their legs* close to their bodies. When they are hot, they try to *push away* blankets and then stay still.
- *Reflexes that manage feeding.* The *sucking reflex* causes newborns to suck anything that touches their lips—fingers, toes, blankets, and rattles, as well as natural and artificial nipples of various textures and shapes. In the *rooting reflex,* babies turn their mouths toward anything that brushes against their cheeks—a reflexive search for a nipple—and start to suck. *Swallowing* also aids feeding, as does *crying* when the stomach is empty and *spitting up* when too much is swallowed quickly.

Other reflexes are not necessary for survival but signify the state of brain and body functions. Among them are the:

- *Babinski reflex.* When a newborn's feet are stroked, the toes fan upward.
- *Stepping reflex.* When newborns are held upright, feet touching a flat surface, they move their legs as if to walk.
- *Swimming reflex.* When held horizontally on their stomachs, newborns stretch out their arms and legs.
- *Palmar grasping reflex.* When something touches newborns' palms, they grip it tightly.
- *Moro reflex.* When someone bangs on the table they are lying on, newborns fling their arms outward and then bring them together on their chests, crying with wide-open eyes.

These reflexes are responses to experiences, not unlike an adult's sudden fear, or lust, or anger.

The senses are also responsive: New babies listen more to voices than to traffic, for instance. Thus, in many ways newborns connect with the people of their world, who are predisposed to respond (Zeifman, 2013). If the baby performing these actions on the Brazelton NBAS were your own, you would be proud and amazed; that is part of being human.

New Fathers

As we have seen, fathers-to-be help mothers-to-be stay healthy, nourished, and drug-free. The father's role in birth may also be crucial.

Being There

At birth, the father's presence reduces complications, in part because he reassures his wife. I observed this with my own daughter, whose anxiety rose when the doctor and midwife discussed a possible cesarean without asking her opinion. Her husband told her, "All you need to do is relax between contractions and push when a contraction comes. I will do the rest." She listened. He did. No cesarean.

Whether or not he is present at the birth, the father's legal acceptance of the birth is important to mother and newborn. A study of all live single births in Milwaukee from 1993 to 2006 (151,869 babies!) found that complications correlated with several expected variables (e.g., maternal cigarette smoking) and one unexpected one—no father listed on the birth record. This connection was especially apparent for

Especially for Scientists Research with animals can benefit people, but it is sometimes wrongly used to support conclusions about people. When does that happen? (see response, page 119)

Especially for Nurses in Obstetrics Can the father be of any practical help in the birth process? (see response, page 119)

A Healthy Newborn

Just moments after birth, babies are administered their very first test. The APGAR score is an assessement tool used by doctors and nurses to determine whether a newborn requires any medical intervention. It tests five specific criteria of health, and the medical professional assigns a score of 0, 1, or 2 for each category. A perfect score of 10 is rare—most babies will show some minor deficits at the 1 minute mark, and many will still lose points at the 5 minute mark.

GRIMACE RESPONSE/REFLEXES

(2) A healthy baby will indicate his displeasure when his airways are suctioned—he'll grimace, pull away, cough, or sneeze

(1) Baby will grimace during suctioning

(0) Baby shows no response to being suctioned and requires immediate medical attention

RESPIRATION

(2) A good strong cry indicates a normal breathing rate

(1) A weak cry or whimper, or slow/irregular breathing

(0) Baby is not breathing and requires immediate medical intervention

PULSE

(2) A heartbeat of 100 or more beats per minute is healthy for a newborn

(1) Fewer than 100 beats per minute

(0) A baby with no heartbeat requires immediate medical attention

APPEARANCE/COLOR

(2) Body and extremities should show good color, with pink undertones indicating good circulation

(1) Some blueness in the palms and soles of the feet. Many babies exhibit some blueness at both the 1 and 5 minute mark; most warm up soon after

(0) A baby whose entire body is blue, grey, or very pale requires immediate medical intervention

ACTIVITY AND MUSCLE TONE

(2) Baby exhibits active motion of arms, legs, body

(1) Baby shows some movement of arms and legs

(0) A baby who is limp and motionless requires immediate medical attention

REFLEXES IN INFANTS

Never underestimate the power of a reflex. For developmentalists, newborn reflexes are mechanism for survival, indicators of brain maturation, and vestiges of evolutionary history. For parents, they are mostly delightful and sometimes amazing.

THE SUCKING REFLEX A newborn, just a few minutes old, demonstrates that he is ready to nurse by sucking on a doctor's finger.

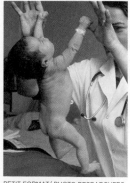

THE GRASPING REFLEX When the doctor places a finger on the palm of a healthy infant, and he or she will so tightly that the baby's legs can dangle in space.

THE STEP REFLEX A one-day-old girl steps eagerly forward long on legs too tiny to support her body.

European American births: When the mother did not list the father, she was more likely to have long labor, a cesarean section, and so on (Ngui et al., 2009).

Currently, about half of all U.S. women are not married when their baby is born (U.S. Bureau of the Census, 2010), but fathers may still be on the birth certificate. When fathers acknowledge their role, birth is better for mother and child.

Couvade

Fathers may experience pregnancy and birth biologically, not just psychologically. For example, levels of the stress hormone *cortisol* correlate between expectant fathers and mothers, probably because they make each other anxious or relaxed (Berg & Wynne-Edwards, 2002). Beyond that, many fathers experience symptoms of pregnancy and birth, including weight gain and indigestion during pregnancy and pain during labor (Leavitt, 2009). Among the Papua in New Guinea and the Basques in Spain, husbands used to build a hut when birth was imminent and then lie down to writhe in mock labor (Klein, 1991).

Paternal experiences of pregnancy and birth are called **couvade**; they are expected in some cultures, a normal variation in many, and considered pathological in others (M. Sloan, 2009). In developed nations, couvade is unnoticed and unstudied, but many fathers are intensely involved with the early development of their future child (Brennan et al., 2007).

couvade Symptoms of pregnancy and birth experienced by fathers.

New Mothers

About half of all women experience physical problems soon after birth, such as healing from a c-section, or painfully sore nipples, or problems with urination (Danel et al., 2003). However, worse than any physical problems are psychological ones. When the birth hormones decrease, between 8 and 15 percent of women experience **postpartum depression**, a sense of inadequacy and sadness (called *baby blues* in the mild version and *postpartum psychosis* in the most severe form) (Perfetti et al., 2004).

postpartum depression A new mother's feelings of inadequacy and sadness in the days and weeks after giving birth.

With postpartum depression, baby care (feeding, diapering, bathing) feels very burdensome. The newborn cry may not compel the mother to carry and nurse her infant. Instead, the mother may have thoughts of neglecting or abusing the infant, a thought so terrifying that she is afraid of herself.

The first sign that something is amiss may be euphoria after birth. A new mother may be unable to sleep, or stop talking, or push aside irrational worries. Some of this behavior is normal, but family members and medical personnel need to be alert to the mother's emotions. After the initial high, severe depression may set in, with a long-term impact on the child. Fathers are usually the first responders; they may be instrumental in getting the support the mother and baby need (Cuijpers et al., 2010; Goodman & Gotlib, 2002). But fathers are vulnerable to depression, too; other people need to help.

From a developmental perspective, some causes of postpartum depression (such as financial stress) predate the pregnancy; others (such as marital problems) occur during pregnancy; others correlate with birth (especially if the mother is alone and imagined a different birth than actually occurred); and still others are specific to the particular infant (such as health, feeding, or sleeping problems). Successful breast-feeding mitigates maternal depression, one of the many reasons a lactation consultant is an important part of the new mother's support team.

>> **Response for Scientists** (from page 117): Animal research should not, by itself, confirm an assertion that has popular appeal but no scientific evidence. This occurred in the social construction that physical contact was crucial for parent–infant bonding.

>> **Response for Nurses in Obstetrics** (from page 117): Usually not, unless he is experienced, well taught, or has expert guidance. But his presence provides emotional support for the woman, which makes the birth process easier and healthier for mother and baby.

Parental Alliance

Remember John and Martha, the young couple whose amniocentesis revealed that their fetus had trisomy-21 (Down syndrome)? One night at 3:00 A.M., after about seven months of pregnancy, Martha was crying uncontrollably. She told John she was scared.

> "Scared of what?" he said. "Of a little baby who's not as perfect as you think he ought to be?"
>
> "I didn't say I wanted him to be perfect," I said. "I just want him to be normal. That's all I want. Just normal."
>
> "That is total bullshit. . . . You don't want this baby to be normal. You'd throw him in a dumpster if he just turned out to be normal. What you really want is for him to be superhuman."
>
> "For your information," I said in my most acid tone, "I was the one who decided to keep this baby, even though he's got Down's. You were the one who wanted to throw him in a dumpster."
>
> "How would you know?" John's voice was still gaining volume. "You never asked me what I wanted, did you? No. You never even asked me."
>
> *[Beck, 1999, p. 255]*

This episode ended well, with a long, warm, and honest conversation between the two prospective parents. Each learned what their fetus meant to the other, a taboo topic until that night. Adam, their future son, became an important part of their relationship.

Their lack of communication up to this point, and the sudden eruption of unexpressed emotions, is not unusual, because pregnancy itself raises memories from childhood and fears about the future. Yet honest and intimate communication is crucial throughout pregnancy, birth, and child rearing. Such early communication between new parents helps to form a **parental alliance,** a commitment by both parents to cooperate in raising their child.

The parental alliance is especially beneficial when the infant is physically vulnerable, such as having a low birthweight. The converse is also true: Family conflict when a newborn needs extra care increases the risk of child maladjustment and parental divorce (Whiteside-Mansell et al., 2009).

parental alliance Cooperation between a mother and a father based on their mutual commitment to their children. In a parental alliance, the parents support each other in their shared parental roles.

Bonding

To what extent are the first hours after birth crucial for the **parent–infant bond,** the strong, loving connection that forms as parents hold, examine, and feed their newborn? It has been claimed that this bond develops in the first hours after birth when a mother touches her naked baby, just as sheep and goats must immediately smell and nuzzle their newborns if they are to nurture them (Klaus & Kennell, 1976).

However, the hypothesis that early skin-to-skin contact is *essential* for human nurturance has been proven false (Eyer, 1992; Lamb, 1982). In fact, substantial research on monkeys begins with *cross-fostering*, a strategy in which newborns are removed from their biological mothers in the first days of life and raised by another female or even a male. A strong and beneficial relationship sometimes develops (Suomi, 2002).

This finding does not contradict the generalization that prospective parents' active involvement in pregnancy, birth, and care of the newborn benefits all three. Factors that encourage parents (biological or adoptive) to nurture their newborns may have lifelong benefits, as has been proven with mice, monkeys, and humans (Champagne & Curley, 2010).

parent–infant bond The strong, loving connection that forms as parents hold, examine, and feed their newborn.

ROLEX DELA PENA/EPA/NEWSCOM

Better Care Kangaroo care benefits mothers, babies, and hospitals, saving space and medical costs in this ward in Manila. Kangaroo care is one reason Filipino infant mortality in 2010 is only one fifth of what it was in 1950.

The role of early contact has become apparent with **kangaroo care,** in which the newborn lies between the mother's breasts, skin-to-skin, listening to her heartbeat and feeling her body heat. Many studies find that kangaroo-care newborns sleep more deeply, gain weight more quickly, and spend more time alert than do infants with standard care (Feldman et al., 2002; Ferber & Makhoul, 2004; Gathwala et al., 2010). Father involvement may also be important, including father–infant kangaroo care (Feeley et al., 2013).

Kangaroo care benefits babies, not only in the hospital but months later, either because of improved infant adjustment to life outside the womb or because of increased parental sensitivity and effectiveness. Which of these two is the explanation? Probably both.

Implementation of many strategies, especially for fragile infants and their parents, is especially needed in developing nations, where kangaroo care and other measures could reduce deaths by 20 to 40 percent (Bhutta et al., 2008). From a developmental perspective, the most difficult time for high-risk infants occurs when they leave the hospital, weeks after birth. At this juncture, measures to involve parents in early care are crucial. As we will see in later chapters, the relationship between parent and child develops over months, not merely hours. Birth is one step of a lifelong journey.

kangaroo care A form of newborn care in which mothers (and sometimes fathers) rest their babies on their naked chests, like kangaroo mothers that carry their immature newborns in a pouch on their abdomen.

SUMMING UP

Every member of the new family contributes to their shared connection, enabling them all to thrive. The new baby has responsive senses and many reflexes. Close observation and reflection reveal how much the new baby can do. The father's support may be crucial for a healthy, happy newborn and mother. Postpartum depression is not rare; factors before and after birth affect how serious and long-lasting it is. Family relationships begin before conception, may be strengthened throughout pregnancy and birth, and continue throughout the life span.

SUMMARY

Prenatal Development

1. The first two weeks of prenatal growth are called the germinal period. During this time, the single-celled zygote multiplies into more than 100 cells that will eventually form both the placenta and the embryo. The growing organism travels down the fallopian tube to implant in the uterus.

2. From the third through the eighth week after conception is the embryonic period. The heart begins to beat, and the eyes, ears, nose, and mouth form. By the eighth week, the embryo has the basic organs and features of a human, with the exception of the sex organs.

3. The fetal period extends from the ninth week until birth. In the ninth week, the sexual organs develop. By the end of the third month, all the organs and body structures have formed. The fetus attains viability at 22 weeks, when the brain can regulate basic body functions. Babies born before the 26th week are at high risk of death or disability.

4. The average fetus gains approximately 5 pounds (2,268 grams) from the 6th to the 9th month, weighing 7 1/2 pounds (3,400 grams) at birth. Maturation of brain, lungs, and heart ensures survival of more than 99 percent of all full-term babies born in developed nations.

Birth

5. Birth typically begins with contractions that push the fetus out of the uterus and then through the vagina. The Apgar scale, which rates the newborn at one minute and again at five minutes after birth, provides a quick evaluation of the infant's health.

6. Medical assistance can speed contractions, dull pain, and save lives. However, many aspects of medicalized birth have been criticized as impersonal and unnecessary, including about half the cesareans performed in the United States. Contemporary birthing practices are aimed at finding a balance and protecting the baby, but also allowing more parental involvement and control.

Problems and Solutions

7. Some teratogens (diseases, drugs, and pollutants) cause physical impairment. Others, called behavioral teratogens, harm the brain and therefore impair cognitive abilities and affect personality.

8. Whether a teratogen harms an embryo or fetus depends on timing, dose, and genes. Public and personal health practices can protect against prenatal complications, with some specifics debatable. Always, however, family members affect the pregnant woman's health.

9. Low birthweight (under 5½ pounds, or 2,500 grams) may arise from multiple births, placental problems, maternal illness, malnutrition, smoking, drinking, illicit drug use, and age. Compared with full-term newborns, preterm and underweight babies experience more medical difficulties and psychological problems for many years. Babies that are small for gestational age (SGA) are especially vulnerable.

10. Birth complications, such as unusually long and stressful labor that includes anoxia (a lack of oxygen to the fetus), have many causes. Long-term handicaps are not inevitable for high-risk children, but careful nurturing from their parents and society may be needed.

The New Family

11. Humans are social animals, from the moment of birth. The Brazelton Neonatal Behavioral Assessment Scale measures 46 newborn behaviors, 20 of which are reflexes.

12. Fathers can be supportive during pregnancy as well as helpful in birth. Paternal support correlates with shorter labor and fewer complications. Some fathers become so involved with the pregnancy and birth that they experience couvade.

13. Many women feel unhappy, incompetent, or unwell after giving birth. Postpartum depression gradually disappears with appropriate help; fathers may be crucial for mother and child. Ideally, a parental alliance forms to help the child develop well.

14. Kangaroo care benefits all babies but especially those who are vulnerable. Mother–newborn interaction should be encouraged, although the parent–infant bond depends on many factors in addition to birth practices.

KEY TERMS

age of viability (p. 97)
anoxia (p. 116)
Apgar scale (p. 101)
behavioral teratogens (p. 105)
Brazelton Neonatal Behavioral Assessment Scale (NBAS) (p. 116)
cerebral palsy (p. 116)
cesarean section (c-section) (p. 102)

couvade (p. 119)
doula (p. 104)
embryo (p. 95)
embryonic period (p. 96)
extremely low birthweight (ELBW) (p. 113)
false positive (p. 111)
fetal alcohol syndrome (FAS) (p. 108)
fetal period (p. 94)

fetus (p. 96)
germinal period (p. 94)
implantation (p. 95)
kangaroo care (p. 121)
low birthweight (LBW) (p. 113)
parental alliance (p. 120)
parent–infant bond (p. 120)
postpartum depression (p. 119)
preterm (p. 113)
reflex (p. 116)

small for gestational age (SGA) (p. 113)
teratogen (p. 105)
threshold effect (p. 106)
ultrasound (p. 97)
very low birthweight (VLBW) (p. 113)

WHAT HAVE YOU LEARNED?

1. What are three major developments in the germinal period?

2. What body parts develop during the embryonic period?

3. What major milestone is reached about halfway through the fetal period?

4. What are three major reasons pregnancy continues months after the fetus could live outside the uterus?

5. How has the Apgar scale increased newborns' survival rate?

6. Why has the rate of cesarean sections increased?

7. Why are developmentalists concerned that surgery is often part of birth?

8. Why is the newborn mortality rate much higher in some countries than in others?

9. What are the differences among a doula, a midwife, and a doctor?

10. What teratogens may harm the fetus's developing body structure?

11. Why is it difficult to establish the impact of behavioral teratogens?

12. How does timing affect the risk of harm to the fetus?

13. Why does risk analysis fail to precisely predict damage to a fetus?

14. What factors increase or decrease the risk of spina bifida?

15. What are the potential consequences of drinking alcohol during pregnancy?

16. What are the differences among LBW, VLBW, and ELBW?

17. List four reasons a baby might be born LBW.

18. How have U.S. LBW rates changed in the past decade?

19. What is the long-term prediction for the health of a very tiny or vulnerable newborn who survives?

20. How do culture and customs affect one's exposure to teratogens?

21. What do newborns do to aid their survival?

22. What impact do fathers have during and after birth?

23. How do fathers experience pregnancy?

24. What are the signs of postpartum depression?

25. What affects the parent–infant bond?

26. What are the results of kangaroo care?

APPLICATIONS

1. Go to a nearby greeting-card store and analyze the cards about pregnancy and birth. Do you see any cultural attitudes (e.g., variations depending on the sex of the newborn or of the parent)? If possible, compare those cards with cards from a store that caters to another economic or ethnic group.

2. Interview three mothers of varied backgrounds about their birth experiences. Make your interviews open-ended—let them choose what to tell you, as long as they give at least a 10-minute description. Then compare and contrast the three accounts, noting especially any influences of culture, personality, circumstances, and cohort.

3. People sometimes wonder how any pregnant woman could jeopardize the health of her fetus. Consider your own health-related behavior in the past month—exercise, sleep, nutrition, drug use, medical and dental care, disease avoidance, and so on. Would you change your behavior if you were pregnant? Would it make a difference if you, your family, and your partner did not want a baby?

>>ONLINE CONNECTIONS

To accompany your textbook, you have access to a number of online resources, including Learning Curve, an adaptive quizzing program, critical thinking questions, and case studies. For access to any of these links, go to www.worthpublishers .com/launchpad/bergerls9e. In addition to these resources, you'll also find links to video clips, personalized study advice, and an ebook. Some of the videos and activities available online include:

- *Brain Development: In the Beginning.* Three-dimensional animation follows brain development from the formation of the neural tube until birth. Animations of microscopic changes in the brain including synaptic pruning.

- *Periods of Prenatal Development.* A series of detailed animations shows the stages of prenatal development from fertilization to birth.

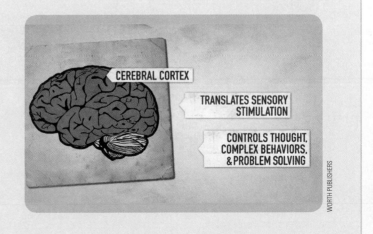

CEREBRAL CORTEX

TRANSLATES SENSORY STIMULATION

CONTROLS THOUGHT, COMPLEX BEHAVIORS, & PROBLEM SOLVING

WORTH PUBLISHERS

the first two years

Adults don't change much in a year or two. They might have longer, grayer, or thinner hair; they might gain or lose weight; they might learn something new. But if you saw friends you hadn't seen for a few years, you'd recognize them immediately.

Imagine caring for a newborn 24/7 for a month and then leaving for two years. On your return, you might not recognize him or her. The baby would have quadrupled in weight, grown a foot taller, and sprouted a new head of hair. Behavior and emotions change, too—less crying, but new laughter and fear—including fear of you.

A year or two is not much compared with the 80 or so years of the average life. However, in their first two years humans reach half their adult height, learn to talk in sentences, and express almost every emotion—not just joy and fear but also love, jealousy, and shame. Invisible changes in the brain are even more crucial, setting the pattern for the life span. The next three chapters describe these radical and awesome changes.

Left: Alex Cao/Getty Images
Right: © John Lund/Annabelle Breakey/Blend Images/Corbis

The First Two Years: Biosocial Development

WHAT WILL YOU KNOW?

1. What part of an infant grows most in the first two years?
2. How do newborn humans differ from newborn kittens?
3. Does immunization protect or harm babies?

■ Growth in Infancy
Body Size
Brain Growth
A VIEW FROM SCIENCE: Face Recognition
Sleep
OPPOSING PERSPECTIVES: Where Should
Babies Sleep?

■ Perceiving and Moving
The Senses
Motor Skills
Dynamic Sensory-Motor Systems

■ Surviving in Good Health
Better Days Ahead
Immunization
Nutrition
Sudden Infant Death Syndrome

Our first child, Bethany, was born when I was in graduate school. I memorized developmental norms, including walking and talking at 12 months. I was delighted to hear her babble and say "mama," but at 14 months, Bethany had not yet taken her first step.

To reassure myself, I told my husband that genes were more influential than anything we did. I had read that babies in Paris are among the latest walkers in the world, and my grandmother was French. To my relief, Bethany soon began walking, and by age 5 she was the fastest runner in her kindergarten. My genetic explanation was bolstered when our next two children, Rachel and Elissa, were also slow to walk. And my students with ancestors from Guatemala and Ghana had infants who walked before a year; those from China and Europe walked later. Genetic, I thought.

Fourteen years after Bethany, Sarah was born. I could afford a full-time caregiver, Mrs. Todd, from Jamaica. She thought Sarah was the most advanced baby she had ever known, except for her own daughter, Gillian. I told her that Berger children walk late.

"She'll be walking by a year," Mrs. Todd told me. "Gillian walked at 10 months."

"We'll see," I graciously replied, confident of my genetic explanation.

I underestimated Mrs. Todd. She bounced my delighted baby on her lap, day after day, and spent hours giving her "walking practice." Sarah took her first step at 12 months, late for a Todd, early for a Berger, and a humbling lesson for me.

As a scientist, I know that a single case proves nothing. My genetic explanation might be valid, since Sarah shares only half her genes with Bethany and since my daughters are only one-eighth French, a fraction I had ignored when they were infants.

Nonetheless, I see the influence of caretakers in every aspect of biosocial growth. As you read about development, you also will see that caregiving enables babies to grow, move, and learn. Development is not as straightforward and automatic, nor as genetically determined, as it once seemed. It is multidirectional and multicontextual, multicultural and plastic.

>> Growth in Infancy

In infancy, growth is so rapid and the consequences of neglect are so severe that gains are closely monitored. Medical checkups, including measurement of height, weight, and head circumference, occur often in developed nations because these measurements provide the first clues as to whether an infant is progressing as expected—or not.

Body Size

Newborns lose several ounces in the first three days and then gain an ounce a day for months. Birthweight typically doubles by 4 months and triples by a year. An average 7-pound newborn will be 21 pounds at 12 months (9,525 grams, up from 3,175 grams at birth). Height increases too: A typical baby grows 10 inches (24 centimeters) in a year.

Physical growth then slows, but not by much. Most 24-month-old children weigh almost 28 pounds (13 kilograms) and have added another 4 inches (10 centimeters) or so. Typically, 2-year-olds are half their adult height and about one-fifth their adult weight, four times heavier than they were at birth (see Figure 5.1).

Each of these numbers is a norm, which is an average, or standard, for a particular population. The "particular population" for the norms just cited is United States infants in about 1970.

At each well-baby checkup (monthly at first), a doctor or nurse measures growth and compares it to that baby's previous numbers. Often measurements are expressed as a **percentile,** from 0 to 100. Percentiles indicate where an individual ranks on a particular measure. Percentiles are often used for school achievement; here they are used for an infant's rank on weight and height compared to other babies of the same age. Thus, weight at the 30th percentile means that 30 percent of all babies weigh less and 70 percent weigh more.

For a baby who has always been average (50th percentile), something is amiss if the percentile changes a lot, either up or down. If an average baby suddenly grows more slowly, that could be the first sign of a medical condition called *failure to thrive.* If weight gain is much above the norm, that may be a warning for later obesity.

Abnormal growth in either direction was once blamed on parents. For small babies, it was thought that parents made feeding stressful, leading to "nonorganic failure to thrive." Now dozens of medical conditions have been discovered that cause failure to thrive. Pediatricians consider it "outmoded" to blame parents (Jaffe, 2011, p. 100).

percentile A point on a ranking scale of 0 to 100. The 50th percentile is the midpoint; half the people in the population being studied rank higher and half rank lower.

FIGURE 5.1

Eat and Sleep The rate of increasing weight in the first weeks of life makes it obvious why new babies need to be fed day and night.

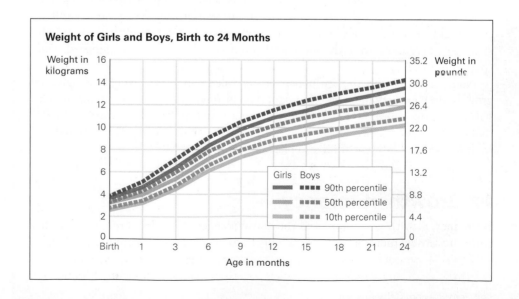

CECILIA VARAS

Same Boy, Much Changed All three photos show Conor: first at 3 months, then at 12 months, and finally at 24 months. Note the rapid growth in the first two years, especially apparent in the changing proportions of the head compared to the body and use of the legs.

Brain Growth

Prenatal and postnatal brain growth (measured by head circumference) affects later cognition (Gilles & Nelson, 2012). If teething or a stuffed-up nose temporarily slows weight gain, nature slows growth of the body but not the brain, a phenomenon called **head-sparing.** Sadly, prolonged malnutrition eventually affects the brain, as explained later.

From two weeks after conception to two years after birth, the brain grows more rapidly than any other organ, being about 25 percent of adult weight at birth and almost 75 percent at age 2 (see Figure 5.2). Over the same period, head circumference increases from about 14 to 19 inches.

The brain develops lifelong; it is mentioned in every chapter of this book. We begin with the basics—neurons, axons, dendrites, neurotransmitters, synapses, and the cortex, especially the prefrontal cortex.

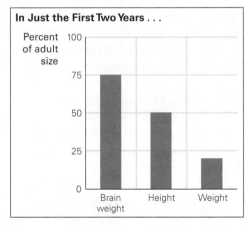

In Just the First Two Years . . .

Percent of adult size

(Bar chart showing: Brain weight ≈ 75, Height ≈ 50, Weight ≈ 20)

head-sparing A biological mechanism that protects the brain when malnutrition disrupts body growth. The brain is the last part of the body to be damaged by malnutrition.

FIGURE 5.2

Growing Up Two-year-olds are totally dependent on adults, but they have already reached half their adult height and three-fourths of their adult brain size.

Neurons Connecting

Communication within the central nervous system (CNS)—the brain and spinal cord—begins with nerve cells, called **neurons,** which proliferate in the last half of fetal life. The brain continues to grow rapidly after birth, protected by the skull, which has two "soft spots" (fontenelles) to allow it to squeeze through the vagina. Even so, the newborn head is proportionally the biggest part of the body, which is why birthing the head takes hours; only a few moments are needed for birth of the rest of the body.

The newborn brain has billions of neurons, about 70 percent of them in the **cortex,** the brain's six outer layers (see Figure 5.3). Most thinking, feeling, and sensing occur in the cortex (Johnson, 2010).

The final part of the brain to mature is the **prefrontal cortex,** the area for anticipation, planning, and impulse control. It is not, as once thought, "functionally

neuron One of billions of nerve cells in the central nervous system, especially in the brain.

cortex The outer layers of the brain in humans and other mammals. Most thinking, feeling, and sensing involves the cortex.

prefrontal cortex The area of the cortex at the very front of the brain that specializes in anticipation, planning, and impulse control.

FIGURE 5.3

The Developing Cortex The infant's cortex consists of four to six thin layers of tissue that cover the rest of the brain. The cortex contains virtually all the neurons that make conscious thought possible. Some areas, such as those devoted to the senses, mature relatively early. Others, such as the prefrontal cortex, mature quite late.

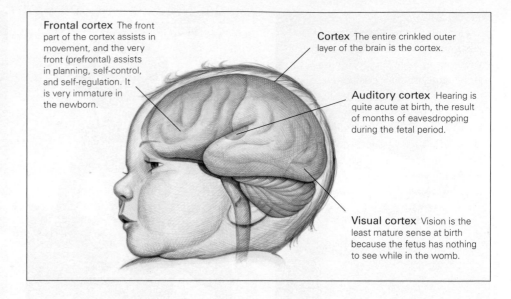

Frontal cortex The front part of the cortex assists in movement, and the very front (prefrontal) assists in planning, self-control, and self-regulation. It is very immature in the newborn.

Cortex The entire crinkled outer layer of the brain is the cortex.

Auditory cortex Hearing is quite acute at birth, the result of months of eavesdropping during the fetal period.

Visual cortex Vision is the least mature sense at birth because the fetus has nothing to see while in the womb.

silent during most of infancy" (Grossmann, 2013, p. 303). Nonetheless, many of the connections between emotions and thought have not yet formed. The prefrontal cortex gradually becomes more efficient over the next two decades (Wahlstrom et al., 2010). **[Lifespan Link:** Major discussion of the growth of the prefrontal cortex is in Chapter 14.]

All areas of the brain specialize, becoming fully functioning at different ages. Some regions deep within the skull maintain breathing and heartbeat, and thus are able to sustain life by seven months after conception. Some areas in the midbrain underlie emotions and impulses. These functions are apparent in the first year of life and are shared with many other animals, although emotional regulation and impulse control continue to develop throughout childhood. Finally, some regions in the cortex allow perception and cognition, first cognition of exciting, social interactions and later cognition of more abstract thoughts (Grossmann, 2013). These areas reach final maturation in adulthood.

Examples of this specialization are the areas of the cortex: a visual cortex, an auditory cortex, and an area dedicated to the sense of touch for each body part—including each finger of a person and each whisker of a rat (Barnett et al., 2006). The senses require maturation and learning, but all are present at birth. Humans have a much larger frontal cortex relative to body size than any other animal: That is why people can plan and create better than any mouse, whale, or chimpanzee.

Within and between areas of the central nervous system, neurons are connected to other neurons by intricate networks of nerve fibers called **axons** and **dendrites.** Each neuron has a single axon and numerous dendrites, which spread out like the branches of a tree. The axon of one neuron meets the dendrites of other neurons at intersections called **synapses,** which are critical communication links within the brain.

To be more specific, neurons communicate by sending electrochemical impulses through their axons to synapses, to be picked up by the dendrites of other neurons. The dendrites bring messages to the cell bodies of their neurons, which, in turn, convey the messages via their axons to the dendrites of other neurons (see Visualizing Development, p. 131).

Axons and dendrites do not quite touch at synapses. Instead, the electrical impulses in axons typically cause the release of chemicals called **neurotransmitters,** which carry information from the axon of the sending neuron, across a **synaptic gap,** to the dendrites of the receiving neuron (see Figure 5.4).

axon A fiber that extends from a neuron and transmits electrochemical impulses from that neuron to the dendrites of other neurons.

dendrite A fiber that extends from a neuron and receives electrochemical impulses transmitted from other neurons via their axons.

synapse The intersection between the axon of one neuron and the dendrites of other neurons.

neurotransmitter A brain chemical that carries information from the axon of a sending neuron to the dendrites of a receiving neuron.

synaptic gap The pathway across which neurotransmitters carry information from the axon of the sending neuron to the dendrites of the receiving neuron.

Nature, Nurture, and the Brain

The mechanics of neurological functioning are varied and complex; neuroscientists hypothesize, experiment, and discover more each day. Brain development begins with genes and other biological elements, but hundreds of epigenetic factors affect brain development from the first to the final minutes of life. Particularly important in human development are experiences: plasticity means that dendrites form or atrophy is response to nutrients and events. The effects of early nurturing experiences are lifelong, as proven many times in mice; research on humans suggest similar effects.

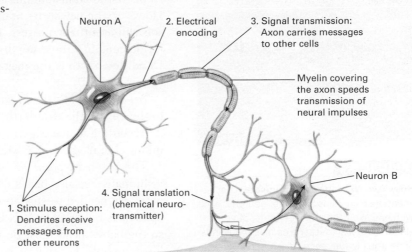

1. Stimulus reception: Dendrites receive messages from other neurons
2. Electrical encoding
3. Signal transmission: Axon carries messages to other cells
Myelin covering the axon speeds transmission of neural impulses
Neuron A
Neuron B
4. Signal translation (chemical neuro-transmitter)

NATURE

The link between one neuron and another is shown in this simplified diagram. The infant brain contains billions of neurons, each with one axon and many dendrites. Every electrochemical message to or from the brain causes thousands of neurons to fire simultaneously, each transmitting the message across the synapse to neighboring neurons.

Synapse   Dendrite
Axon
Neuron B
Neuron A
Neurotransmitters

In the synapse—an intersection between axon and dendrite—neurotransmitters carry information from one neuron to another.

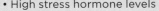

NURTURE

In experiments with baby mice, those that were frequently licked and nuzzled by their mothers exhibited very different behaviors from those that were neglected.

Low Maternal Licking and Grooming	High Maternal Licking and Grooming
• High stress hormone levels • High anxiety	• Low stress hormone levels • Low anxiety

PHOTO: ANYAIVANOVA/ISTOCK/THINKSTOCK

THE BRAIN

Social scientists now believe that every aspect of early life affects brain patterns: Each experience activates and prunes neurons, such that the firing patterns from one axon to another dendrite reflect the past. When a mother mouse licks her newborn babies, that reduces methylation of a gene (called Nr3c1), allowing increased serotonin to be released by the hypothalamus. That serotonin not only increases momentary pleasure (mice love being licked) but also starts a chain of epigenetic responses that reduce stress hormones from many parts of the brain and body, including the adrenal glands. The effects are lifelong, as proven many times in mice. In humans, a mother's gentle stroking and cuddling of her newborn seem to affect the baby similarly.

PHOTO: RUBBERBALL/NICOLE HILL/ALAMY

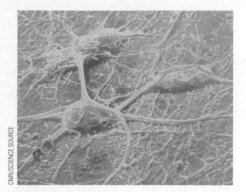

CNRI/SCIENCE SOURCE

FIGURE 5.4

How Two Neurons Communicate The infant brain contains billions of neurons, each with one axon and many dendrites. Every electrochemical message causes thousands of neurons to fire, each transmitting the message across the synapse to neighboring neurons. This electron micrograph shows neurons greatly magnified, with their tangled but highly organized and well-coordinated sets of dendrites and axons.

transient exuberance The great but temporary increase in the number of dendrites that develop in an infant's brain during the first two years of life.

pruning When applied to brain development, the process by which unused connections in the brain atrophy and die.

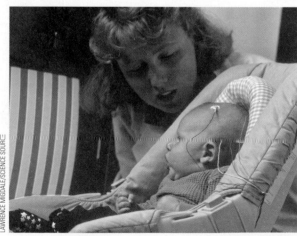

LAWRENCE MIGDALE/SCIENCE SOURCE

Electric Excitement Are those stripes exciting? Researchers at University of California, Berkeley, know that the neurons in this eight-week-old boy's brain will show changes in brain activity as the patterns on the screen change. Electrodes on his head map those changes as he undergoes a color vision test. Every month of life up until age 2 shows increased electrical excitement in an infants' brain.

Experiences and Pruning

At birth, the brain contains at least 100 billion neurons, more than a person needs. However, the newborn's brain has far fewer dendrites and synapses than the person will eventually possess. During the first months and years, rapid growth and refinement in axons, dendrites, and synapses occurs, especially in the cortex. Dendrite growth is the major reason that brain weight triples from birth to age 2 (Johnson, 2010).

An estimated fivefold increase in the number of dendrites in the cortex occurs in the 24 months after birth, with about 100 trillion synapses being present at age 2. According to one expert, "40,000 new synapses are formed every second in the infant's brain" (Schore & McIntosh, 2011, p. 502).

This extensive *postnatal* brain growth is highly unusual for mammals. It occurs in humans because heads cannot grow enough before birth to contain the brain networks needed to sustain human development. Although prenatal brain development is remarkable, it is limited because the human pelvis is relatively small, so the baby's head must be much smaller than an adult's head in order to make birth possible. For that reason, unlike other mammals, humans must nurture and protect their offspring for more than a decade while the child's brain continues to develop (Konner, 2010).

Early dendrite growth is called **transient exuberance:** *exuberant* because it is so rapid and *transient* because some of it is temporary. The expansive growth of dendrites is followed by **pruning.** Just as a gardener might prune a rose bush by cutting away some growth to enable more, or more beautiful, roses to bloom, unused brain connections atrophy and die, enabling the brain to develop in accord with the sociocultural context (Stiles & Jernigan, 2010).

The details of brain structure and growth depend on genes and maturation but even more on experience (Stiles & Jernigan, 2010). Some dendrites wither away because they are never used—that is, no experiences have caused them to send a message to other neurons. Expansion and pruning of dendrites occur for every aspect of early experience, from noticing musical rhythms to understanding emotions (Scott et al., 2007).

Strangely enough, this loss of dendrites increases brainpower. The space between neurons in human brains, for instance—especially in regions for advanced, abstract thought—is far greater than the space in chimpanzee brains (Miller, 2010). The densely packed neurons of chimps make them less intelligent than people, probably because humans have more space for dendrite formation. This spacing allows more complex thinking, as well as learning that is specific to the particular culture each baby is born into.

Some children with intellectual disabilities have "a persistent failure of normal synapse pruning" (Irwin et al., 2002, p. 194). That makes thinking and learning difficult. One sign of autism is rapid brain growth, suggesting too little pruning (Hazlett et al., 2011). Indeed, studies of brain development in autistic children suggest that their brains develop normally for the first six months, but then synapses do not develop as they should, so that by the second year of life symptoms of autism become evident (Landa et al., 2013).

Yet just as too little pruning creates problems, so does too much pruning. Brain sculpting is attuned to experience: The appropriate links in the brain need to be established, protected, and strengthened while inappropriate ones are eliminated. One group of scientists speculates that "lack of normative experiences may lead to overpruning of neurons and synapses, both of which may lead to reduction of brain activity" (Moulson et al., 2009, p. 1051).

Another group suggests that infants who are often hungry, or hurt, or neglected may develop brains that compensate—and cannot be reprogrammed even if circumstances change. The hungry baby becomes the obese adult, the abused child rejects attention, and so on, always with the interaction of nature and nurture (van IJzendoorn et al., 2012).

Harm and Protection

Most infants develop well within their culture, and head-sparing usually ensures that baby brains are sufficiently nourished. For normal brain development, a baby could hear French or Farsi, or see emotions displayed dramatically or subtly (e.g., throwing oneself to the floor or merely pursing the lips, a cultural difference). However, infant brains do not develop well without essential experiences that all humans need.

Those essential experiences are called *expectant* because the brain requires them to develop normally and therefore "expects" them to be provided in much the same way the stomach expects food. That contrasts with *dependent* experiences, which vary from family to family.

Experience-dependent brain development is variable because circumstances vary: For example, a baby's main caregiver could be a biological or adoptive mother or father, or a grandparent, or a hired baby nurse. Happy and successful babies have been raised by each of those types of caregivers, although obviously the children are affected by their particular caregiver, whomever that might be. All that is experience-dependent.

Experience-expectant brain development occurs because of circumstances that all human babies should have. For example, every baby needs at least one steady caregiver: Without that stability the brain might not develop normal emotional responses. [**Lifespan Link:** Neglected children are discussed in Chapter 8.]

Another essential experience that every infant brain expects is sensory stimulation. Playing with a young baby, allowing varied sights, sounds, touches, and movements (arm waving in the early months, walking later on) are all fodder for brain connections. Severe lack of stimulation (e.g., a baby who never hears speech) stunts the brain. As one review of early brain development explains, "enrichment and deprivation studies provide powerful evidence of . . . widespread effects of experience on the complexity and function of the developing system" (Stiles & Jernigan, 2010, p. 345).

This does not mean that babies require spinning, buzzing, multitextured, and multicolored toys. In fact, such toys may be a waste of money. Infants are fascinated by simple objects and facial expressions. Fortunately, although elaborate infant toys are not needed, there is no evidence that they harm the brain; babies prevent overstimulation by ignoring them. A simple application of what has been learned about the prefrontal cortex is that hundreds of objects, from the very simple to the quite complex, can capture an infant's attention.

However, because the prefrontal cortex is underdeveloped in infancy, the brain is not yet under thoughtful control. For instance, it is useless to insist that an infant stop crying: Babies are too immature to *decide* to stop crying, as adults do. If adults do not understand this fact, the results can be tragic.

If a frustrated caregiver shakes a crying baby sharply and quickly, that can cause **shaken baby syndrome,** a life-threatening condition. Because the brain is still developing, shaking stops the crying because blood vessels in the brain rupture and neural connections break. Shaken baby syndrome is an example of *abusive head trauma* (Christian et al., 2009). Death is the worst consequence; life-long intellectual impairment is the more likely one.

Especially for Parents of Grown Children Suppose you realize that you seldom talked to your children until they talked to you and that you often put them in cribs and playpens. Did you limit their brain growth and their sensory capacity? (see response, page 134)

experience-dependant brain functions Brain functions depend on particular, variable experiences and therefore may or may not develop in a particular infant.

experience-expectant brain functions Brain functions require certain basic common experiences (which an infant can be expected to have) in order to develop normally.

shaken baby syndrome A life-threatening injury that occurs when an infant is forcefully shaken back and forth, a motion that ruptures blood vessels in the brain and breaks neural connections.

>> Response for Parents of Grown Children (from page 133): Probably not. Brain development is programmed to occur for all infants, requiring only the stimulation that virtually all families provide—warmth, reassuring touch, overheard conversation, facial expressions, movement. Extras such as baby talk, music, exercise, mobiles, and massage may be beneficial but are not essential.

self-righting The inborn drive to remedy a developmental deficit; literally, to return to sitting or standing upright after being tipped over. People of all ages have self-righting impulses, for emotional as well as physical imbalance.

The fact that infant brains respond to their circumstances suggests that waiting for evidence of child mistreatment is waiting too long. In the first months of life babies adjust to their world, becoming withdrawn and quiet if their caregivers are depressed, or becoming loud and demanding if that is the only way they can get fed. In both these circumstances, they learn destructive habits. Thus, since development is dynamic and interactive, caregivers need help from the start, not when harmful systems are established (Tronick & Beeghly, 2011).

The word *systems* is crucial here. Almost every baby experiences something stressful—a caregiver yelling, or a fall off the bed, or a painful stomachache. Fortunately, **self-righting**—an inborn drive to remedy deficits—is built into the human system. For example, infants with no toys develop their brains by using whatever objects are available, and infants with neglectful mothers may bond with a father, grandparent, or stranger who provides daily affection and stimulation. Human brains are designed to grow and adapt; plasticity is apparent from the beginning (Tomalski & Johnson, 2010). It is the patterns, not the moments, of neglect or maltreatment that harm the brain.

A VIEW FROM SCIENCE

Face Recognition

Unless you have *prosopagnosia* (face blindness, relatively uncommon), the *fusiform face area* of your brain is astonishingly adept at face recognition. This area is primed among newborns, who are quicker to recognize a face they have just seen once than older children and adults (Zeifman, 2013). However, every face is fascinating early in life: Babies stare at pictures of monkey faces and photos of human ones, at drawings and toys with faces, as well as at live faces.

Soon, experiences refine perception (De Heering et al., 2010). By 3 months, babies smile more readily at familiar people and are more accurate at differentiating faces from their own ethnic group (called the *own-race effect*). Babies are not prejudiced: The own-race effect results from limited multiethnic experience. Indeed, children of one ethnicity, adopted and raised exclusively among people of another ethnicity, recognize differences among people of their adopted group more readily than differences among people of their biological group.

The importance of early experience is confirmed by two studies. From 6 to 9 months, infants were repeatedly shown a book with pictures of six monkey faces, each with a name written on the page (see photo). One-third of the parents read the names while showing the pictures; another one-third said only "monkey" as they turned each page; the final one-third simply turned the pages with no labeling.

At 9 months, infants in all three groups viewed pictures of six *unfamiliar* monkeys. The infants who had heard names of monkeys were better at distinguishing one new monkey from another than were the infants who saw the same picture book but did not hear each monkey's name (Scott & Monesson, 2010).

Many children and adults do not notice the individuality of newborns. Some even claim that "all babies look alike." However, the second interesting study found that 3-year-olds with younger siblings were much better at recognizing differences between photos of unfamiliar newborns than were 3-year-olds with no younger brothers or sisters (Cassia et al., 2009). This finding shows again that experience matters, contributing to development of dendrites in the fusiform face area.

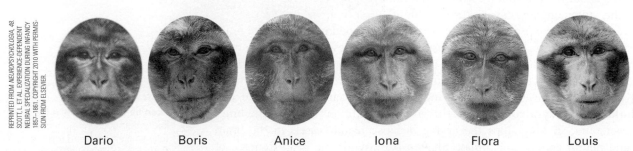

Dario   Boris   Anice   Iona   Flora   Louis

Iona Is Not Flora If you heard that Dario was not Louis or Boris, would you stare at unfamiliar monkey faces more closely in the future? For 6-month-olds, the answer is yes.

Sleep

One consequence of brain maturation is the ability to sleep through the night. Newborns cannot do this. Normally, they sleep 15 to 17 hours a day, in one- to three-hour segments. Hours of sleep decrease rapidly with maturity: The norm per day for the first 2 months is 14¼ hours; for the next 3 months, 13¼ hours; for 6 to 17 months, 12¾ hours.

Wide variation is particularly apparent in the early weeks. As reported by parents (who might exaggerate), one new baby in 20 sleeps 9 hours or fewer per day and one in 20 sleeps 19 hours or more (Sadeh et al., 2009).

Sleep specifics vary not only because of biology (age and genes) but also because of the social environment. Full-term newborns sleep more than low-birthweight babies, who are hungry every two hours. Babies who are fed cow's milk and cereal sleep more soundly—easier for parents but not ideal for the baby. Such feeding practices arise from the interaction between infant and culture. The social context also has a direct effect: If parents respond to predawn cries with food and play, babies wake up early each morning (Sadeh et al., 2009).

Over the first months, the relative amount of time in various stages of sleep changes. Babies born preterm may always seem to be dozing. About half of the sleep of full-term newborns is **REM (rapid eye movement) sleep**, with closed lids but flickering eyes and rapid brain waves, indicating dreaming. REM sleep declines over the early weeks, as does "transitional sleep," the dozing, half-awake stage. At 3 or 4 months, quiet sleep (also called *slow-wave sleep*) increases, as does time alert and wide awake.

Overall, 25 percent of children under age 3 have sleeping problems, according to parents surveyed in an Internet study of more than 5,000 North Americans (Sadeh et al., 2009). Sleep problems are more troubling for parents than for infants. This does not render the problems insignificant, however; overtired parents may be less patient and responsive (Bayer et al., 2007).

One problem for parents is that advice about where infants should sleep varies. Some suggest that infants should sleep beside their parents—who must immediately respond to every cry (Nicholson & Parker, 2009). Others advise that infants need their own room, should be allowed to "cry it out" so they will not be spoiled, and can learn to soothe themselves. Both sets of advice make sense, as the following explains.

REM (rapid eye movement) sleep A stage of sleep characterized by flickering eyes behind closed lids, dreaming, and rapid brain waves.

co-sleeping A custom in which parents and their children (usually infants) sleep together in the same room.

OPPOSING PERSPECTIVES

Where Should Babies Sleep?

Traditionally, most middle-class U.S. infants slept in cribs in their own rooms; it was feared that they would be traumatized by their parents' sexual interactions. By contrast, most infants in Asia, Africa, and Latin America slept near their parents, a practice called **co-sleeping.** People in those cultures believed that parent–child separation at night was cruel.

Even today, at baby's bedtime, Asian and African mothers worry more about separation, whereas European and North American mothers worry more about lack of privacy. A 19-nation survey found that parents act on these fears: The extremes were 82 percent of babies in Vietnam sleeping with their parents compared with 6 percent in New Zealand (Mindell et al., 2010) (see Figure 5.5).

This difference in practice may seem related to income, since low-SES families are less likely to have an extra room. But even wealthy Japanese families often co-sleep. By contrast, many poor North American families find a separate space for their children at night. Co-sleeping results from culture and custom, not merely income (Kohyama et al., 2011).

The argument for co-sleeping is that it makes it easier to respond to a baby in the middle of the night, especially if he or she is hungry or scared. When parents opt for co-sleeping, they are less exhausted since they can reach over to feed or comfort their baby. Breast-feeding, often done every hour or two at first, is easier if it does not require walking to another room.

Yet the argument against co-sleeping rests on a chilling statistic: Sudden infant death is more common when babies sleep beside their parents (Gettler & McKenna, 2010; Ruys et al., 2007). (Sudden infant death syndrome [SIDS] is discussed at the end of this chapter.) Many young parents occasionally go to sleep after drinking or drugging. If their baby is beside them, bed-sharing (not merely co-sleeping), is dangerous.

One reason for opposite practices is that adults are affected by their own early experiences. This phenomenon is called *ghosts in the nursery* because new parents bring decades-old memories into the bedrooms of their children. Those ghosts can encourage either co-sleeping or separate rooms.

For example, compared with Israeli adults who had slept near their parents as infants, those who had slept communally with other infants (as sometimes occurred on kibbutzim) were more likely to interpret their own infants' nighttime cries as distress, requiring comfort (Tikotzky et al., 2010). That is how a ghost affects current behavior: If parents think their crying babies are frightened, lonely, and distressed, they want to respond. Quick responses are easier with co-sleeping.

But remember that infants learn from their earliest experiences. If babies become accustomed to bed-sharing, they will crawl into their parents' bed long past infancy. Parents might lose sleep for years because they wanted more sleep when their babies were small.

Developmentalists hesitate to declare any particular pattern best because the issue is "tricky and complex" (Gettler & McKenna, 2010, p. 77). Sleeping alone may encourage independence—a trait appreciated in some cultures, abhorred in others. Past experiences (ghosts in the nursery) affect us all: Should some ghosts be welcomed and others banned?

Australia
Canada
China
Hong Kong
Indonesia
Japan
Malaysia
New Zealand
Philippines
Thailand
Taiwan
United Kingdom
United States
Vietnam

0 10 20 30 40 50 60 70 80 90

Percent co-sleeping

Source: Mindell et al., 2010.

FIGURE 5.5

Awake at Night Why the disparity between Asian and non-Asian rates of co-sleeping? It may be that Western parents use a variety of gadgets and objects—monitors, night lights, pacifiers, cuddle cloths, sound machines—to accomplish the same things Asian parents do by having their infant next to them.

YAGI STUDIO/GETTY IMAGES.

Infant at Risk? Sleeping in the parents' bed is a risk factor for SIDS in the United States, but don't worry about this Japanese girl. In Japan, 97 percent of infants sleep next to their parents, yet infant mortality is only 3 per 1,000—compared with 7 per 1,000 in the United States. Is this bed, or this mother, or this sleeping position protective?

Especially for New Parents You are aware of cultural differences in sleeping practices, which raises a very practical issue: Should your newborn sleep in bed with you? (see response, page 138)

SUMMING UP

Weight and height increase markedly in the first two years. Babies triple their birth weight by age 1 and add more than a foot between birth and age 2. Norms for height and weight are expressed in percentiles, because children who are relatively big or small typically continue on that path.

Brain development is rapid during infancy, particularly development of the axons, dendrites, and synapses within the cortex. The timing of brain growth is under genetic control, as various parts of the cortex mature on schedule. Experience—both expected and varied—shapes the infant brain, as pruning eliminates unused connections. Pruning helps children respond to their experiences; a lack of pruning indicates pathology. All babies sleep and dream a great deal in the first years; the specifics of where and how much they sleep is shaped not only by brain maturation but also by family and culture. ∎

>> Perceiving and Moving

People might think that infants are passive creatures at first, unable to do much. But that is far from the truth: Developmentalists have traced the rapid development of every sense and skill.

The Senses

Every sense functions at birth. Newborns have open eyes, sensitive ears, and responsive noses, tongues, and skin. Indeed, very young babies seem to use their senses to attend to everything without much judgment. For instance, in the first months of life, they smile at strangers and suck almost anything in their mouths.

Why are new infants not more discriminating? Because sensation precedes perception. Then perception leads to cognition. Thus, in order to learn, babies begin by responding to every sensation that might be significant.

Sensation occurs when a sensory system detects a stimulus, as when the inner ear reverberates with sound or the retina and pupil of the eye intercept light. Thus, sensations begin when an outer organ (eye, ear, nose, tongue, or skin) meets anything that can be seen, heard, smelled, tasted, or touched.

Genetic selection over more than 100,000 years affects all the senses. Humans cannot hear what mice hear, or see what bats see, or smell what puppies smell; humans do not need those sensory abilities. However, survival requires babies to respond to people, and newborns innately do so with every sense they have (Konner, 2010; Zeifman, 2013).

Perception occurs when the brain processes a sensation. This happens in the cortex, usually as the result of a message from one of the sensing organs, such as from the eye to the visual cortex. If a particular sensation occurs often, it connects with past experience, making a particular sight worth interpreting (M. E. Diamond, 2007).

Some sensations are beyond a baby's comprehension at first. A newborn has no idea that the letters on a page might have significance, that Mother's face should be distinguished from Father's, or that the smells of roses and garlic have different connotations. Perceptions require experience.

Infants' brains are especially attuned to their own repeated social experiences; that is where evidence of perception first appears. You already saw this with face recognition.

Thus, perception follows sensation, when sensory stimuli are interpreted in the brain. Then cognition follows perception, when people think about what they have perceived. (Later, cognition no longer depends on sensation: People imagine, fantasize, hypothesize.) The sequence from sensation to perception to cognition requires that an infant's sense organs function. No wonder the parts of the cortex dedicated to hearing, seeing, and so on develop rapidly: That is the prerequisite for human intellect. Now some specifics.

sensation The response of a sensory system (eyes, ears, skin, tongue, nose) when it detects a stimulus.

perception The mental processing of sensory information when the brain interprets a sensation.

>> Response for New Parents (from page 136): From the psychological and cultural perspectives, babies can sleep anywhere as long as the parents can hear them if they cry. The main consideration is safety: Infants should not sleep on a mattress that is too soft, nor beside an adult who is drunk or drugged. Otherwise, each family should decide for itself.

binocular vision The ability to focus the two eyes in a coordinated manner in order to see one image.

Especially for Nurses and Pediatricians
The parents of a 6-month-old have just been told that their child is deaf. They don't believe it because, as they tell you, the baby babbles as much as their other children did. What do you tell them? (see response, page 142)

Hearing and Seeing

The sense of hearing develops during the last trimester of pregnancy; fetuses hear sounds. At birth, familiar, rhythmic sounds such as a heartbeat are soothing: That is one reason kangaroo care reduces newborn stress (see Chapter 4). If a newborn is deaf (many states require testing at birth), early remediation—either a cochlear implant or sign language—allows language and cognition to develop normally.

In the early weeks, babies come to expect the familiar rhythms, segmentation, and cadence of the words they hear long before they understand their meaning (Minagawa-Kawai et al., 2011). By 14 months, they not only prefer their native speech, but they like strangers better who speak whatever language they have often heard —even if they understand nothing of the content of the talking (Buttelmann et al., 2013).

By contrast, vision is immature at birth. Although in mid-pregnancy the eyes open and are sensitive to bright light (if the pregnant woman is sunbathing in a bikini, for instance), the fetus has nothing much to see. Consequently, newborns are legally blind; they focus only on things between 4 and 30 inches (10 and 75 centimeters) away (Bornstein et al., 2005).

Almost immediately, experience combines with maturation of the visual cortex to improve the ability to see shapes and then notice details. Vision improves so rapidly that researchers are hard-pressed to describe the day-by-day improvements (Dobson et al., 2009). By 2 months, infants not only stare at faces but also, after perception and then cognition, smile. (Smiling can occur earlier but not because of perception.)

As perception builds, visual scanning improves. Thus, 3-month-olds look closely at the eyes and mouth, smiling more at smiling faces than at angry or expressionless ones. They pay attention to patterns, colors, and motion (Kellman & Arterberry, 2006).

Because **binocular vision** (coordinating both eyes to see one image) is impossible in the womb (nothing is far enough away to need two eyes), many newborns seem to use their eyes independently, momentarily appearing wall-eyed or cross-eyed. Normally, experience leads to rapid focus and binocular vision. Usually between 2 and 4 months, both eyes focus on a single thing (Wang & Candy, 2010).

This ability aids in the development of depth perception, which has been demonstrated in 3-month-olds, although it was once thought to develop much later. Experienced crawlers and walkers are very adept at deciding if a given path is safe to cross upright, thereby illustrating the coordination of the senses and motor skills (Kretch & Adolph, 2013). (This does not mean that toddlers can be trusted not to fall off tables or out of windows.)

Tasting and Smelling

As with vision and hearing, smell and taste function at birth and rapidly adapt to the social world. Infants learn to appreciate what their mothers eat, first through breast milk and then through smells and spoonfuls of the family dinner.

Some herbs and plants contain natural substances that are medicinal. The foods of a particular culture may aid survival: For example, bitter foods provide some defense against malaria, hot spices help preserve food and thus work against food poisoning, and so on (Krebs, 2009). Thus, for 1-year-olds, developing a taste for their family cuisine may save their lives.

Adaptation also occurs for the sense of smell. When breast-feeding mothers used a chamomile balm to ease cracked nipples during the first days of their baby's lives, those babies preferred that smell almost two years later, compared with babies whose mothers used an odorless ointment (Delaunay-El Allam et al., 2010).

Learning About a Lime As with every other normal infant, Jacqueline's curiosity leads to taste and then to a slow reaction, from puzzlement to tongue-out disgust. Jacqueline's responses demonstrate that the sense of taste is acute in infancy and that quick brain perceptions are still to come.

As babies learn to recognize each person's scent, they prefer to sleep next to their caregivers, and they nuzzle into their caregivers chests—especially when the adults are shirtless. One way to help infants who are frightened of the bath (some love bathing, some hate it) is for the parent to get in the tub with the baby. The smells of the adult's body mix with the smell of soap, making the experience comforting.

Touch and Pain

The sense of touch is acute in infants. Wrapping, rubbing, massaging, and cradling are each soothing to many new babies. Even when their eyes are closed, some infants stop crying and visibly relax when held by their caregivers. The ability to be comforted by touch is one of the skills tested in the Brazelton Neonatal Behavioral Assessment Scale (NBAS, described in Chapter 4).

Pain and temperature are not among the five senses, but they are often connected to touch. Some babies cry when being changed because sudden coldness on their skin is distressing. Some touches seem intrusive and distressful—such as a poke, a pinch, or a pat—although this varies from one baby to another, and some adults do not realize that their friendly touch may not be perceived as such.

Scientists are not certain about infant pain. Some experiences that are painful to adults (circumcision, setting of a broken bone) are much less so to newborns. For many newborn medical procedures, from a pinprick to minor surgery, a taste of sugar right before the event is an anesthetic. An empirical study conducted with an experimental group and a control group found that newborns typically cry lustily when their heel is pricked (to get a blood sample, routine after birth) but not if they have had a drop of sucrose beforehand (Harrison et al., 2010).

Some people imagine that the fetus feels pain; others say that the sense of pain does not mature until months after birth. Many young infants cry inconsolably for 10 minutes or more; digestive pain is the usual explanation. Often infants fuss before their first tooth erupts: Teething is said to be painful. However, these explanations are unproven; infant crying may not indicate pain (nor does adult crying, necessarily).

Many physiological measures, including stress hormones, erratic heartbeats, and rapid brain waves, are studied to assess pain in preterm infants, who typically undergo many procedures that would be painful to an adult (Holsti et al., 2011). But infant brains are immature: We cannot assume that they do, or do not, feel pain.

AT ABOUT THIS TIME

Age Norms (in Months) for Fine Gross Skills

	When 50% of All Babies Master the Skill	When 90% of All Babies Master the Skill
Sit unsupported	6	7.5
Stands holding on	7.4	9.4
Crawls (creeps)	8	10
Stands not holding	10.8	13.4
Walking well	12.0	14.4
Walk Backward	15	17
Run	18	20
Jump up	26	29

Note: As the text explains, age norms are affected by culture and cohort. The first five norms are based on babies in five continents (Brazil, Ghana, Norway, USA, Oman, and India). WHO (World Health Organization), 2006. The next three are from a USA-only source (Coovadia & Wittenberg, 2004; based on Denver II (Frankenburg et al., 1992). Mastering skills a few weeks earlier or later does not indicate health or intelligence. Being very late, however, is a cause for concern.

Observation Quiz Which of these skills has the greatest variation in age of acquisition? Why? (see answer, page 142)

motor skill The learned abilities to move some part of the body, in actions ranging from a large leap to a flicker of the eyelid. (The word *motor* here refers to movement of muscles.)

gross motor skill Physical abilities involving large body movements, such as walking and jumping. (The word *gross* here means "big.")

Young Expert This infant is an adept crawler. Note the coordination between hands and knees as well as the arm and leg strength needed to support the body in this early version of push-ups. This boy will probably become an expert walker and runner.

Motor Skills

The most dramatic **motor skill** (any movement ability) is independent walking, which explains why I worried when Bethany did not take a step. All the motor skills, from the newborn's head-lifting to the toddler's stair-climbing, develop over the first two years.

The first evidence of motor skills is in the reflexes, explained in Chapter 4. Although the definition of reflexes implies that they are automatic, their strength and duration vary from one baby to another. Most newborn reflexes disappear by 3 months, but some morph into more advanced motor skills.

Caregiving and culture matter. Reflexes become skills if they are practiced and encouraged. As you saw in the chapter's beginning, the foundation for my fourth child's walking was set by Mrs. Todd when Sarah was only a few months old. Similarly, some very young babies can swim—if adults have helped them in the water.

Gross Motor Skills

Deliberate actions that coordinate many parts of the body, producing large movements, are called **gross motor skills.** These skills emerge directly from reflexes and proceed in a *cephalocaudal* (head-down) and *proximodistal* (center-out) direction. Infants first control their heads, lifting them up to look around. Then they control their upper bodies, their arms, and finally their legs and feet (see At About This Time).

Sitting develops gradually; it is a matter of developing the muscles to steady the top half of the body. By 3 months, most babies can sit propped up in someone's lap. By 6 months, they can usually sit unsupported.

Crawling is another example of the head-down and center-out direction of skill mastery. When placed on their stomachs, many newborns reflexively try to lift their heads and move their arms as if they were swimming. As they gain muscle strength, infants wiggle, attempting to move forward by pushing their arms, shoulders, and upper bodies against whatever surface they are lying on.

Usually by 5 months, infants add their legs to this effort, inching forward (or backward) on their bellies. Exactly when this occurs depends partly on how much "tummy time" the infant has had, which is affected by culture (Zachry & Kitzmann, 2011).

Between 8 and 10 months after birth, most infants lift their midsections and crawl (or *creep*, as the British call it) on "all fours," coordinating the movements of their hands and knees. Crawling depends on experience as well as maturation. Some normal babies never do it, especially if the floor is cold, hot, or rough, or if they have always lain on their backs (Pin et al., 2007). It is not true that babies *must* crawl to develop normally.

All babies find some way to move before they can walk (inching, bear-walking, scooting, creeping, or crawling), but many resist being placed on their stomachs (Adolph & Berger, 2005). Overweight babies master gross motor skills later than thinner ones: Practice and balance is harder when the body is heavy (Slining et al., 2010).

CATHARINA VAN DEN DIKKENBERG/ISTOCKPHOTO

As soon as they are able, babies walk, falling frequently but getting up undaunted and trying again, because walking is much quicker than crawling, and it has another advantage—free hands (Adolph et al., 2012).

The dynamic system underlying every motor skill has three interacting elements. We illustrate those three here with walking.

1. *Muscle strength.* Newborns with skinny legs and 3-month-olds buoyed by water make stepping movements, but 6-month-olds on dry land do not; their legs are too chubby for their underdeveloped muscles. As they gain strength, they stand and then walk.
2. *Brain maturation.* The first leg movements—kicking (alternating legs at birth and then both legs together or one leg repeatedly at about 3 months)—occur without much thought. As the brain matures, deliberate leg action becomes possible.
3. *Practice.* Unbalanced, wide-legged, short strides become a steady, smooth gait.

This last item, *practice,* is powerfully affected by caregiving before the first independent step. Some adults spend hours helping infants walk (holding their hands or the back of their shirts) or providing walkers (dangerous if not supervised).

Once toddlers are able to walk by themselves, they practice obsessively, barefoot or not, at home or in stores, on sidewalks or streets, on lawns or in mud. They fall often, but that does not stop them—"they average between 500 and 1,500 walking steps per hour so that by the end of each day, they have taken 9,000 walking steps and traveled the length of 29 football fields" (Adolph et al., 2003, p. 494).

Fine Motor Skills

Small body movements are called **fine motor skills.** The most valued fine motor skills are finger movements, enabling humans to write, draw, type, tie, and so on. Movements of the tongue, jaw, lips, and toes are fine movements, too.

Actually, mouth skills precede finger skills by many months (newborns can suck; chewing precedes drawing by a year or more). Since every culture encourages finger dexterity, children practice finger movements, and adults teach using spoons, or chopsticks, or markers. By contrast, skilled spitting or chewing is not praised; only other children admire blowing bubbles with gum.

Regarding hand skills, newborns have a strong reflexive grasp but lack control. During their first 2 months, babies excitedly stare and wave their arms at objects dangling within reach. By 3 months, they can usually touch such objects, but they cannot yet grab and hold on unless an object is placed in their hands, because of limited eye–hand coordination.

By 4 months, infants sometimes grab, but their timing is off: They close their hands too early or too late. Finally, by 6 months, with a concentrated, deliberate stare, most babies can reach, grab, and grasp almost any object that is of the right size. Some can even transfer an object from one hand to the other. Almost all can hold a bottle, shake a rattle, and yank a sister's braids. Toward the end of the first year and throughout the second, finger skills improve as babies master the pincer movement (using thumb and forefinger to pick up tiny objects) and self-feeding (first with hands, then fingers, then utensils) (Ho, 2010). (See At About This Time.)

As with gross motor skills, fine motor skills are shaped by culture and opportunity. For example, when given "sticky mittens" (with Velcro) that allow grabbing, infants master hand skills sooner than usual. Their perception advances as well (Libertus et al., 2010; Soska et al., 2010). As with the senses, each motor skill expands the baby's cognitive awareness.

Bossa Nova Baby? This boy in Brazil demonstrates his joy at acquiring the gross motor skill of walking, which quickly becomes dancing whenever music plays.

fine motor skills Physical abilities involving small body movements, especially of the hands and fingers, such as drawing and picking up a coin. (The word *fine* here means "small.")

Success At 6 months, this baby is finally able to grab her toes. From a developmental perspective, this achievement is as significant as walking, as it requires coordination of feet and fingers. Note her expression of determination and concentration.

AT ABOUT THIS TIME

Age Norms (in Months) for Fine Motor Skills

	When 50% of All Babies Master the Skill	When 90% of All Babies Master the Skill
Grasps rattle when placed in hand	3	4
Reaches to hold an object	4.5	6
Thumb and finger grasp	8	10
Stacks two blocks	15	21
Imitates vertical line	30	39

Source: WHO (World Health Organization), 2006.

>> **Response for Nurses and Pediatricians** (from page 138): Urge the parents to begin learning sign language and investigate the possibility of cochlear implants. Babbling has a biological basis and begins at a specified time, in deaf as well as hearing babies. If their infant can hear, sign language does no harm. If the child is deaf, however, noncommunication may be destructive.

>> **Answer to Observation Quiz** (from page 140): Jumping up, with a three-month age range for acquisition. The reason is that the older an infant is, the more impact both nature and nurture have.

In the second year, grasping becomes more selective. Toddlers learn when *not* to pull at a sister's braids, or Mommy's earrings, or Daddy's glasses.

Dynamic Sensory-Motor Systems

Young human infants are, physiologically, an unusual combination of motor immaturity (they cannot walk for many months), sensory acuteness (all senses function at birth), and curiosity (Konner, 2010). What a contrast to kittens, for instance, who are born deaf, with eyes sealed shut, and who stay beside their mother although they can walk.

Human newborns listen and look from day 1, eager to practice every motor skill as soon as possible. An amusing example is rolling over. At about 3 months, infants can roll over from their stomachs to their backs, but not vice versa because their arms are no help when they are not on their stomachs. Once they can roll from stomach to back, many babies do so and then fuss, turtle-like, with limbs flailing. When some kind person flips them back on their stomachs, they immediately roll over again, only to fuss once more.

The most important experiences are perceived with interacting senses and skills, in dynamic systems. Breast milk, for instance, is a mild sedative, so the newborn literally feels happier at Mother's breast, connecting that pleasure with taste, touch, smell, and sight. But in order for all those joys to occur, the infant must actively suck at the nipple (an inborn motor skill, which becomes more efficient with practice). Because of brain immaturity, *cross-modal perception* (using several senses to understand the same experience) is particularly common in young infants.

By 6 months babies have learned to coordinate senses and skills, expecting another person's lip movements to synchronize with speech, for instance (Lewkowicz, 2010). For toddlers, crawling and walking are dynamic systems that allow exploration. Piaget named the first two years of cognition "sensorimotor" for good reason. The next chapter will describe some of the specifics. But first, there is one obvious prerequisite for all the growth already described—staying alive.

SUMMING UP

All the senses function at birth, with hearing the most acute sense and vision the least developed. Every sense allows perception to develop and furthers social understanding. Caregivers are soon recognized by sight, touch, smell, and voice.

Gross motor skills follow a genetic timetable for maturation; they are also affected by practice and experience. Fine motor skills develop with time and experience, combining with the senses as part of dynamic systems. All the skills are practiced relentlessly as soon as possible, advancing learning and thinking. ■

>> Surviving in Good Health

Although precise worldwide statistics are unavailable, at least 9 billion children were born between 1950 and 2010. More than 1 billion of them died before age 5. Although 1 billion is far too many, twice that many would have died without

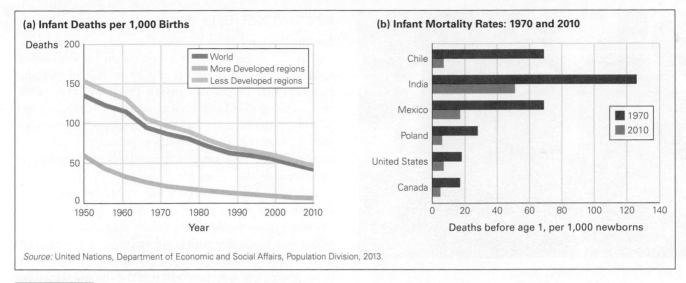

(a) Infant Deaths per 1,000 Births

Deaths 200

- World
- More Developed regions
- Less Developed regions

150

100

50

0

1950 1960 1970 1980 1990 2000 2010

Year

(b) Infant Mortality Rates: 1970 and 2010

Chile

India

Mexico

Poland

United States

Canada

- 1970
- 2010

0   20   40   60   80   100   120   140

Deaths before age 1, per 1,000 newborns

Source: United Nations, Department of Economic and Social Affairs, Population Division, 2013.

FIGURE 5.6

More Babies Are Surviving Improvements in public health—better nutrition, cleaner water, more widespread immunization—over the past three decades have meant millions of survivors.

recent public health measures. One young child in 5 died in 1950, as did 1 child in 17 in 2010 (United Nations, 2012). Those are official statistics; probably millions more died in the poorest nations without being counted. In earlier centuries more than half of all newborns died in infancy.

Better Days Ahead

In the twenty-first century in developed nations, 99.9 percent of newborns who survive the first month live to adulthood. Even in the poorest nations, where a few decades ago infant mortality was accepted as part of the human experience, now about 93 percent live (see Figure 5.6a). Some nations have seen dramatic improvement. For instance, Chile's rate of infant mortality was almost 4 times higher than the rate in the United States in 1970; now the two rates are even (see Figure 5.6b).

The world death rate in the first five years of life has dropped about 2 percent per year since 1990 (Rajaratnam et al., 2010). Public health measures (clean water, nourishing food, immunization) deserve most of the credit. Further, as more children survive, parents focus more effort on each child.

For example, when parents expect every newborn to live, they have fewer babies. That advances the national economy, which can provide better schools and health care. Infant survival and maternal education are the two main reasons the world's 2010 fertility rate is half what the rate was in 1950 (Bloom, 2011; Lutz & K. C., 2011).

If public health professionals were more available, the current infant death rate would be cut in half again, because public health includes measures to help parents as well as children, via better food distribution, less violence, more education, cleaner water, and more widespread immunization (Farahani et al., 2009).

Well Protected Disease and early death are common in Africa, where this photo was taken, but neither is likely for 2-year-old Salem. He is protected not only by the nutrition and antibodies in his mother's milk but also by the large blue net that surrounds them. Treated bed nets, like this one provided by the Carter Center and the Ethiopian Health Ministry, are often large enough for families to eat, read, as well as sleep in together, without fear of malaria-infected mosquitoes.

True Dedication This young Buddhist monk lives in a remote region of Nepal, where, until recently, measles was a fatal disease. Fortunately, a UNICEF porter carried the vaccine over mountain trails for two days so that this boy—and his whole community—could be immunized.

immunization A process that stimulates the body's immune system by causing production of antibodies to defend against attack by a particular contagious disease. Creation of antibodies may be accomplished either naturally (by having the disease), by injection, by drops that are swallowed, or by a nasal spray. (These imposed methods are also called *vaccination*.)

Especially for Nurses and Pediatricians A mother refuses to have her baby immunized because she wants to prevent side effects. She wants your signature for a religious exemption, which in some jurisdictions allows the mother to refuse vaccination. What should you do? (see response, page 146)

Immunization

Immunization primes the body's immune system to resist a particular disease. Immunization (often via *vaccination*) is said to have had "a greater impact on human mortality reduction and population growth than any other public health intervention besides clean water" (J. P. Baker, 2000, p. 199). Immunization has been developed for measles, mumps, whooping cough, smallpox, pneumonia, polio, and rotavirus, which no longer kill hundreds of thousands of children each year.

It used to be that the only way to become immune to these diseases was to catch them, sicken, and recover. The immune system would then produce antibodies to prevent recurrence. Beginning with smallpox in the nineteenth century, doctors discovered that giving a small dose of the virus to healthy people who have not had the disease stimulates the same antibodies. (Immunization schedules, with U.S. recommendations, appear in Appendix A. Most of the vaccines listed reduce the risk of child death in every nation. However, specifics vary; caregivers need to heed local health authorities.)

Success and Survival

Stunning successes in immunization include the following:

- Smallpox, the most lethal disease for children in the past, was eradicated worldwide as of 1980. Vaccination against smallpox is no longer needed.
- Polio, a crippling and sometimes fatal disease, is rare. Widespread vaccination, begun in 1955, eliminated polio in the Americas. Only 784 cases were reported anywhere in the world in 2003. In the same year, however, rumors halted immunization in northern Nigeria. Polio reappeared, sickening 1,948 people in 2005, almost all of them in West Africa. Then public health workers and community leaders campaigned to increase immunization, and Nigeria's polio rate fell again to 21 in 2010. However, poverty and wars in South Asia prevented immunization: Worldwide, 650 cases were reported in 2011, primarily in Afghanistan, India, Nigeria, and Pakistan (De Cock, 2011; World Health Organization, 2012; Roberts, 2013). (See Figure 5.7.)
- Measles (rubeola, not rubella) is disappearing, thanks to a vaccine developed in 1963. Prior to that time, 3 to 4 million cases occurred each year in the United States alone (Centers for Disease Control and Prevention, 2007). In 2010 in the United States, only 61 people had measles, most of them born in nations without widespread immunization (MMWR, January 7, 2011). The number of reported cases rose again in 2011, when 222 were reported to have measles, 17 of which were brought into the United States from other countries, including countries in Europe and Asia. The other 215 occurred because too many children are unvaccinated (MMWR, April 20, 2012).

Immunization protects not only from temporary sickness or death but also from complications, including deafness, blindness, sterility, and meningitis. Sometimes the damage from illness is not apparent until decades later. Having mumps in childhood, for instance, can cause sterility and doubles the risk of schizophrenia in adulthood (Dalman et al., 2008).

Some people cannot be safely immunized, including the following:
- Embryos, who may be born blind, deaf, and brain-damaged if their pregnant mother contracts rubella (German measles)

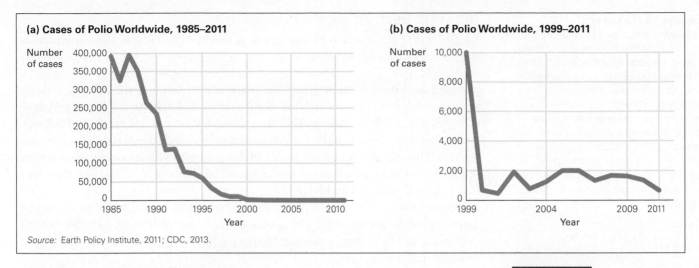

(a) Cases of Polio Worldwide, 1985–2011

(b) Cases of Polio Worldwide, 1999–2011

Source: Earth Policy Institute, 2011; CDC, 2013.

- Newborns, who may die from a disease that is mild in older children
- People with impaired immune systems (HIV-positive, aged, or undergoing chemotherapy), who can become deathly ill

Fortunately, each vaccinated child stops transmission of the disease and thus protects others, a phenomenon called *herd immunity*. Although specifics vary by disease, usually if 90 percent of the people in a community (a herd) are immunized, the disease does not spread to those who are vulnerable. Without herd immunity, some community members die of a "childhood" disease.

Problems with Immunization

Infants may react to immunization by being irritable or even feverish for a day or so, to the distress of their parents. However, parents do not notice if their child does *not* get polio, measles, or so on. Before the varicella (chicken pox) vaccine, more than 100 people in the United States died each year from that disease, and 1 million were itchy and feverish for a week. Now almost no one dies of varicella, and far fewer get chicken pox.

Many parents are concerned about the potential side effects of vaccines. Whenever something seems to go amiss with vaccination, the media broadcasts it, which frightens parents. As a result, the rate of missed vaccinations in the United States has been rising over the past decade. This horrifies public health workers, who, taking a longitudinal and society-wide perspective, realize that the risks of the diseases are far greater than the risks from immunization. A hypothesis that the MMR (measles-mumps-rubella) vaccine causes autism has been repeatedly disproved (Shattuck, 2006; Mrozek-Budzyn et al., 2010; MMWR, 2013). [**Lifespan Link:** The major discussion of autism appears in Chapter 11.]

Doctors agree that vaccines "are one of the most cost-effective, successful interventions in the history of public health" and lament that that success has made parents, physicians, and governments less vigilant (Hannan et al., 2009, p. S571). For example, lack of immunization is blamed for a spike in infant whooping cough deaths in 2010 in California, which declared a whooping cough epidemic (McKinley, 2010).

Nutrition

Infant mortality worldwide has plummeted in recent years. Several reasons have already been mentioned. One more measure has made a huge difference: better nutrition.

FIGURE 5.7

Not Yet Zero Many public health advocates hope polio will be the next infectious disease to be eliminated worldwide, as is the case in almost all of North America. The number of cases has fallen dramatically worldwide (a). However, there was a discouraging increase in polio rates from 2003 to 2005 (b).

>> Response for Nurses and Pediatricians (from page 144): It is difficult to convince people that their method of child rearing is wrong, although you should try. In this case, listen respectfully and then describe specific instances of serious illness or death from a childhood disease. Suggest that the mother ask her grandparents if they knew anyone who had polio, tuberculosis, or tetanus (they probably did). If you cannot convince this mother, do not despair: Vaccination of 95 percent of toddlers helps protect the other 5 percent. If the mother has genuine religious reasons, talk to her clergy adviser.

Breast Is Best

Ideally, nutrition starts with *colostrum,* a thick, high-calorie fluid secreted by the mother's breasts at birth. After about three days, the breasts begin to produce milk.

Compared with formula based on cow's milk, human milk is sterile; always at body temperature; and rich in many essential nutrients for brain and body (Drover et al., 2009). Babies who are exclusively breast-fed are less often sick, partly because breast milk provides antibodies and decreases allergies and asthma. Disease protection continues lifelong: Babies who are exclusively breast-fed in the early months become obese less often (Huh et al., 2011) and thus have lower rates of diabetes and heart disease.

Breast-feeding is especially protective for preterm babies; if a tiny baby's mother cannot provide breast milk, physicians recommend milk from another woman (Schanler, 2011). (Once a woman has given birth, her breasts can continue to produce milk for decades.)

The specific fats and sugars in breast milk make it more digestible and better for the brain than any substitute (Drover et al., 2009; Riordan, 2005). The composition of breast milk adjusts to the age of the baby, with milk for premature babies distinct from that for older infants. Quantity increases to meet the demand: Twins and even triplets can grow strong while being exclusively breast-fed for months.

Formula-feeding is preferable only in unusual cases, such as when the mother is HIV-positive or uses toxic or addictive drugs. Even then, however, breast milk without supplementation may be advised, depending on the risks and the alternatives. For example, in some African nations, HIV-positive women are encouraged to breast-feed because their infants' risk of catching HIV from their mothers is lower than the risk of dying from infections, diarrhea, or malnutrition as a result of bottle-feeding (Cohen, 2007; Kuhn et al., 2009).

For all these reasons, doctors worldwide recommend breast-feeding with no other foods—not even juice. (Table 5.1 lists some of the benefits of breast-feeding.) Some pediatricians suggest adding foods (rice cereal and bananas) at 4 months; others want mothers to wait until 6 months (Fewtrell et al., 2011). For breast milk to meet the baby's nutritional needs, the mother must be well fed and hydrated (which is especially important in hot climates) and should avoid alcohol, cigarettes, and other drugs.

Same Situation, Far Apart: Breast-feeding Breast-feeding is universal. None of us would exist if our fore-mothers had not successfully breast-fed their babies for millennia. Currently, breast-feeding is practiced worldwide, but it is no longer the only way to feed infants, and each culture has particular practices.

TABLE 5.1	The Benefits of Breast-Feeding

For the Baby	For the Mother
Balance of nutrition (fat, protein, etc.) adjusts to age of baby	Easier bonding with baby
Breast milk has micronutrients not found in formula	Reduced risk of breast cancer and osteoporosis
Less infant illness, including allergies, ear infections, stomach upsets	Natural contraception (with exclusive breast-feeding, for several months)
Less childhood asthma	Pleasure of breast stimulation
Better childhood vision	Satisfaction of meeting infant's basic need
Less adult illness, including diabetes, cancer, heart disease	No formula to prepare; no sterilization
Protection against many childhood diseases, since breast milk contains antibodies from the mother	Easier travel with the baby
Stronger jaws, fewer cavities, advanced breathing reflexes (less SIDS)	**For the Family**
Higher IQ, less likely to drop out of school, more likely to attend college	Increased survival of other children (because of spacing of births)
Later puberty, fewer teenage pregnancies	Increased family income (because formula and medical care are expensive)
Less likely to become obese or hypertensive by age 12	Less stress on father, especially at night

Sources: Beilin & Huang, 2008; Riordan & Wambach, 2009; Schanler, 2011; U.S. Department of Health and Human Services, 2011.

Breast-feeding was once universal, but by the middle of the twentieth century many mothers thought formula was better because it was more modern. Fortunately, that has changed again. In the United States, 77 percent of infants are breast-fed at birth, 48 percent at 6 months (most with other food as well), and 25 percent at a year (virtually all with other food and drink) (see Figure 5.8)

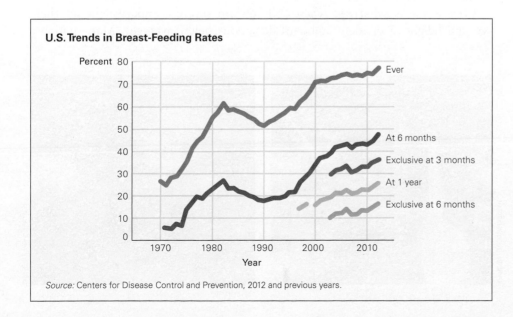

U.S. Trends in Breast-Feeding Rates

Source: Centers for Disease Control and Prevention, 2012 and previous years.

FIGURE 5.8

A Smart Choice In 1970, educated women were taught that formula was the smart, modern way to provide nutrition—but no longer. Today, more education for women correlates with more breast milk for babies. About half of U.S. women with college degrees now manage three months of *exclusive* breast-feeding—no juice, no water, and certainly no cereal.

FIGURE 5.9

Genetic? The data show that basic nutrition is still unavailable to many children in the developing world. Some critics contend that Asian children are genetically small and therefore that Western norms make it appear as if India and Africa have more stunted children than they really do. However, children of Asian and African descent born and nurtured in North America are as tall as those of European descent. Thus, malnutrition, not genes, accounts for most stunting worldwide.

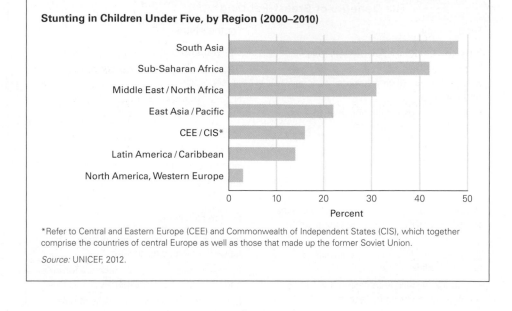

Stunting in Children Under Five, by Region (2000–2010)

*Refer to Central and Eastern Europe (CEE) and Commonwealth of Independent States (CIS), which together comprise the countries of central Europe as well as those that made up the former Soviet Union.

Source: UNICEF, 2012.

(U.S. Department of Health and Human Services, 2011). Worldwide, about half of all 2-year-olds are still nursing, usually at night.

Since formula-feeding may seem easier for the mother, particularly in the early weeks, encouragement of breast-feeding and help from family members, especially new fathers, are crucial. Ideally, nurses visit new mothers weekly at home; such visits (routine in some nations, rare in others) increase the likelihood that breast-feeding will continue.

Malnutrition

protein-calorie malnutrition A condition in which a person does not consume sufficient food of any kind. This deprivation can result in several illnesses, severe weight loss, and even death.

stunting The failure of children to grow to a normal height for their age due to severe and chronic malnutrition.

wasting The tendency for children to be severely underweight for their age as a result of malnutrition.

Protein-calorie malnutrition occurs when a person does not consume enough food to sustain normal growth. That form of malnutrition affects roughly one-third of the world's children in developing nations: They suffer from **stunting,** being short for their age because chronic malnutrition kept them from growing (World Bank, 2010). Stunting is most common in the poorest nations (see Figure 5.9).

Even worse is **wasting,** when children are severely underweight for their age and height (2 or more standard deviations below average). Many nations,

Same Situation, Far Apart: Children Still Malnourished Infant malnutrition is common in refugees (like this baby now living in Thailand, right) or in countries with conflict or crop failure (like Niger, at left). Relief programs reach only some of the children in need around the world. The children in these photographs are among the lucky ones who are being fed.

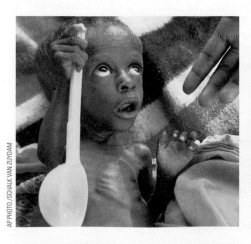
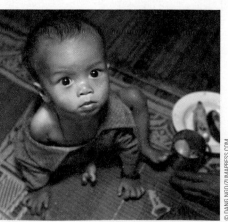

especially in East Asia, Latin America, and central Europe, have seen improvement in child nutrition in the past decades, with an accompanying decrease in wasting and stunting.

In some other nations, however, primarily in Africa, wasting has increased. And in several nations in South Asia, about half the children over age 5 are stunted and half of them are also wasted, at least for a year (World Bank, 2010). In some nations, the traditional diet for young children does not provide sufficient vitamins, fat, and protein for robust health. As a result, energy is reduced and normal curiosity is absent (Osorio, 2011). Young children naturally want to understand whatever they can: A child with no energy is also a child who is not learning.

Chronically malnourished infants and children suffer in three additional ways (World Bank, 2010):

1. Their brains may not develop normally. If malnutrition has continued long enough to affect height, it may also have affected the brain.
2. Malnourished children have no body reserves to protect them against common diseases. About half of all childhood deaths occur because malnutrition makes a childhood disease lethal.
3. Some diseases result directly from malnutrition—both **marasmus** during the first year, when body tissues waste away, and **kwashiorkor** after age 1, when growth slows down, hair becomes thin, skin becomes splotchy, and the face, legs, and abdomen swell with fluid (edema).

> **marasmus** A disease of severe protein-calorie malnutrition during early infancy, in which growth stops, body tissues waste away, and the infant eventually dies.
>
> **kwashiorkor** A disease of chronic malnutrition during childhood, in which a protein deficiency makes the child more vulnerable to other diseases, such as measles, diarrhea, and influenza.

Prevention, more than treatment, is needed. Sadly, some children hospitalized for marasmus or kwashiorkor die even after feeding because their digestive systems are already failing (Smith et al., 2013). Ideally, prenatal nutrition, then breast-feeding, and then supplemental iron and vitamin A stop malnutrition before it starts.

A study of two of the poorest African nations (Niger and Gambia) found several specific factors that reduced the likelihood of wasting and stunting: breast-feeding, both parents at home, water piped to the house, a tile (not dirt) floor, a toilet, electricity, immunization, a radio, and the mother's secondary education (Oyekale & Oyekale, 2009). Overall, "a mother's education is key in determining whether her children will survive their first five years of life" (United Nations, 2011, p. 26). This conclusion has been found in other research as well: Apparently mothers worldwide try to nurture their children well, but sometimes they do not know how to do it and some cultural practices—as you already saw with avoidance of immunization—harm children's health.

But we should not close this chapter by blaming the mothers or the cultures. Sometimes culture helps, as you will now see.

Sudden Infant Death Syndrome

Every year until the mid-1990s, tens of thousands of infants died of **sudden infant death syndrome (SIDS)**, called *crib death* in North America and *cot death* in England. Tiny infants smiled at their caregivers, waved their arms at rattles that their small fingers could not yet grab, went to sleep, and never woke up. As parents mourned, scientists tested hypotheses (the cat? the quilt? natural honey? homicide? spoiled milk?) to no avail: Sudden infant death was a mystery.

One scientist named Susan Beal studied every SIDS death in South Australia for years, noting dozens of circumstances, seeking factors that increased the risk.

> **sudden infant death syndrome (SIDS)** A situation in which a seemingly healthy infant, usually between 2 and 6 months old, suddenly stops breathing and dies unexpectedly while asleep.

PETER SOLNESS/GETTY IMAGES

Protective Sleeping It matters little what infants sleep in—bassinet, cradle, crib, or Billum bag made from local plants in Papua New Guinea, as shown here. In fact, this kind of bag is very useful since babies can easily be carried in it. It can also be used for carrying food, tools, and much else. What does matter is the infant's sleeping position— always on the back, like this healthy infant.

Some things did not matter (such as birth order), and others increased the risk (such as maternal smoking and lambskin blankets).

Beal discovered an ethnic variation: Australian babies of Chinese descent died of SIDS far less often than did Australian babies of European descent. Genetic? Most experts thought so. But Beal's scientific observation led her to note that Chinese babies slept on their backs, contrary to the European or American custom of stomach-sleeping. The Chinese mothers, many of whom had no formal education, said that back-sleeping is what their mothers and grandmothers advised.

Beal thought of a new hypothesis: that sleeping position mattered. To test that hypothesis, she convinced a large group of non-Chinese parents to put their newborns to sleep on their backs. Almost none of them died suddenly. After several years of data, comparing them with a control group who put babies to sleep on their stomachs, Beal reached a surprising conclusion: Back-sleeping protected against SIDS.

Her published reports (Beal, 1988) caught the attention of doctors in the Netherlands, one of the many Western nations where babies almost always slept on their stomachs. Two Dutch scientists (Engelberts & de Jong, 1990) recommended back-sleeping, and parents took heed. SIDS was reduced in Holland by 40 percent in one year, a stunning replication.

Replication and application spread. By 1994, a "Back to Sleep" campaign in nation after nation cut the SIDS rate dramatically (Kinney & Thach, 2009; Mitchell, 2009). In the United States, in 1984, SIDS killed 5,245 babies; in 1996 it was down to 3,050; and since 2000, about 2,000 a year (see Figure 5.10). The campaign has been so successful that physical therapists report that babies crawl later than they used to, and so they advocate *tummy time*—putting awake infants on their stomachs to develop their muscles (Zachry & Kitzmann, 2011).

We close with the saga of SIDS because it is a dramatic example of many themes of this chapter. First, infant care is complex, with many factors interacting to produce each accomplishment. Stomach-sleeping is a proven, replicated risk,

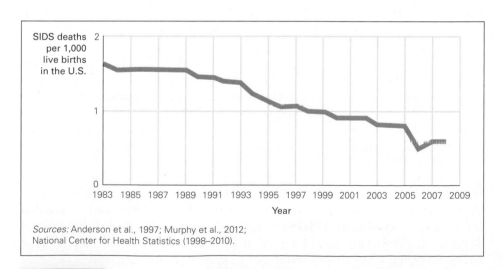

Sources: Anderson et al., 1997; Murphy et al., 2012; National Center for Health Statistics (1998–2010).

FIGURE 5.10

Before and After Detailed U.S. data on SIDS are available only for the past 25 years, but as best we know, the rate was steady at about 1 baby in every 700 throughout most of the twentieth century and has been even lower after 2008, at about 1 baby in every 2000.

but it is not the only one: SIDS still occurs. Researchers are discovering other risks: low birthweight, a brain-stem abnormality that produces too little serotonin, cigarette smoking in the household, soft blankets or pillows, and bed-sharing (Duncan et al., 2010; Ostfeld et al., 2010).

The success in reducing SIDS underscores several themes first described in Chapter 1. Because of developmental science, with a multidisciplinary and multi-cultural perspective, in the United States alone about 40,000 children and young adults are alive today because they were born after 1990 and thus escaped sudden infant death.

SUMMING UP

Various public health measures have saved billions of infants in the past century. Immunization protects those who are inoculated and also halts the spread of contagious diseases (via herd immunity). Smallpox has been eliminated, and many other diseases are rare except in regions of the world that public health professionals have not reached.

Breast milk is the ideal infant food, improving development for decades and reducing infant malnutrition and death. Fortunately, rates of breast-feeding are increasing in developing nations; most underdeveloped nations have always had high rates of breast-feeding. Malnutrition has not been eliminated, however. If a breast-feeding mother is severely malnourished, or if a toddler does not get sufficient nourishment, diseases flourish and learning diminishes. ■

SUMMARY

Growth in Infancy

1. In the first two years of life, infants grow taller, gain weight, and increase in head circumference—all indicative of development. Birthweight doubles by 4 months, triples by 1 year, and quadruples by 2 years, when toddlers weigh about 28 pounds (12.7 kilograms).

2. Brain size increases even more dramatically, from about 25 to 75 percent of adult weight in the first two years. Complexity increases as well, with cell growth, development of dendrites, and formation of synapses. Both growth and pruning aid cognition. Experience is vital for brain development.

3. The amount of time a child sleeps gradually decreases over the first two years. As with all areas of development, variations in sleep patterns are normal, caused by both nature and nurture. Bed-sharing is the norm in many developing nations, and co-sleeping is increasingly common in developed ones.

Perceiving and Moving

4. At birth, the senses already respond to stimuli. Prenatal experience makes hearing the most mature sense. Vision is the least mature sense at birth, but it improves quickly. Infants use all their senses to strengthen their early social interactions.

5. Infants gradually improve their motor skills as they begin to grow and brain maturation increases. Gross motor skills are soon evident, from rolling over to sitting up (at about 6 months), from standing to walking (at about 1 year), from climbing to running (before age 2).

6. Babies gradually develop the fine motor skills to grab, aim, and manipulate almost anything within reach. Experience, time, and motivation allow infants to advance in all their motor skills.

Surviving in Good Health

7. About 2 billion infant deaths have been prevented in the past half-century because of improved health care. One major innovation is immunization, which has eradicated smallpox and virtually eliminated polio and measles. More medical professionals are needed to prevent, diagnose, and treat the diseases that still cause many infant deaths in poor nations.

8. Breast-feeding is best for infants, partly because breast milk helps them resist disease and promotes growth of every kind. Most babies are breast-fed at birth, but in North America only one-third are exclusively breast-fed for three months, as doctors worldwide recommend.

9. Severe malnutrition stunts growth and can cause death, both directly through marasmus or kwashiorkor and indirectly through vulnerability if a child catches measles, an intestinal virus, or some other illness.

10. Careful scientific research and multicultural awareness have led to a dramatic reduction worldwide in sudden infant deaths (SIDS). The specific practice that has saved thousands of infants is putting babies to sleep on their backs, not their stomachs.

KEY TERMS

axon (p. 130)
binocular vision (p. 138)
cortex (p. 129)
co-sleeping (p. 135)
dendrite (p. 130)
experience-dependent (p. 133)
experience-expectant (p. 133)
fine motor skills (p. 141)
gross motor skills (p. 140)

head-sparing (p. 129)
immunization (p. 144)
kwashiorkor (p. 149)
marasmus (p. 149)
motor skill (p. 140)
neuron (p. 129)
neurotransmitter (p. 130)
percentile (p. 128)
perception (p. 137)

prefrontal cortex (p. 129)
protein-calorie malnutrition (p. 148)
pruning (p. 132)
REM (rapid eye movement) sleep (p. 135)
self-righting (p. 134)
sensation (p. 137)
shaken baby syndrome (p. 133)

stunting (p. 148)
sudden infant death syndrome (SIDS) (p. 149)
synapses (p. 130)
synaptic gap (p. 130)
transient exuberance (p. 132)
wasting (p. 148)

WHAT HAVE YOU LEARNED?

1. In what ways do a baby's weight and height change in the first two years?

2. Describe the process of communication within the central nervous system.

3. Why is pruning an essential part of brain development?

4. What should caregivers remember about brain development when an infant cries?

5. How does a baby's sleep patterns change over the first 18 months?

6. What is the relationship among perception, sensation, and cognition?

7. How does an infant's vision change over the first three months?

8. Describe how an infant's gross motor skills develop over the first year.

9. Describe how a baby's hand skills develop over the first two years.

10. Why has there been a decrease in infant mortality rates? What other measures could lead to a further decrease?

11. What is the purpose of immunization?

12. In what ways does herd immunity save lives?

13. Why has the rate of immunization in the U.S. decreased over the past decade?

14. What are the reasons for and against breast-feeding until a child is at least 1 year old?

15. In what ways does malnutrition affect infants and children?

APPLICATIONS

1. Immunization regulations and practices vary, partly for social and political reasons. Ask at least two faculty or administrative staff members what immunizations the students at your college must have and why. If you hear, "It's a law," ask why.

2. Observe three infants (whom you do not know) in public places such as a store, playground, or bus. Look closely at body size and motor skills, especially how much control each baby has over legs and hands. From that, estimate the age in months, and then ask the caregiver how old the infant is.

3. *This project can be done alone, but it is more informative if several students pool responses.* Ask 3 to 10 adults whether they were bottle-fed or breast-fed and, if breast-fed, for how long. If anyone does not know, or if anyone expresses embarrassment about how long they were breast-fed, that itself is worth noting. Do you see any correlation between adult body size and infant feeding?

>>ONLINE CONNECTIONS

To accompany your textbook, you have access to a number of online resources, including Learning Curve, an adaptive quizzing program, critical thinking questions, and case studies. For access to any of these links, go to www.worthpublishers .com/launchpad/bergerls9e. In addition to these resources, you'll also find links to video clips, personalized study advice, and an ebook. Some of the videos and activities available online include:

- *Infant Reflexes.* Watch video clips of some of the most common infant reflexes, from the Babinski to the Moro.

- *Brain Development: Infants and Toddlers.* Interactive animations show the neural pruning and development in a child's growing brain.

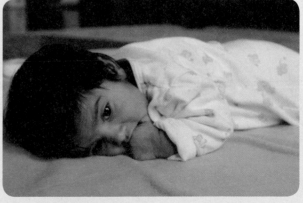

WORTH PUBLISHERS

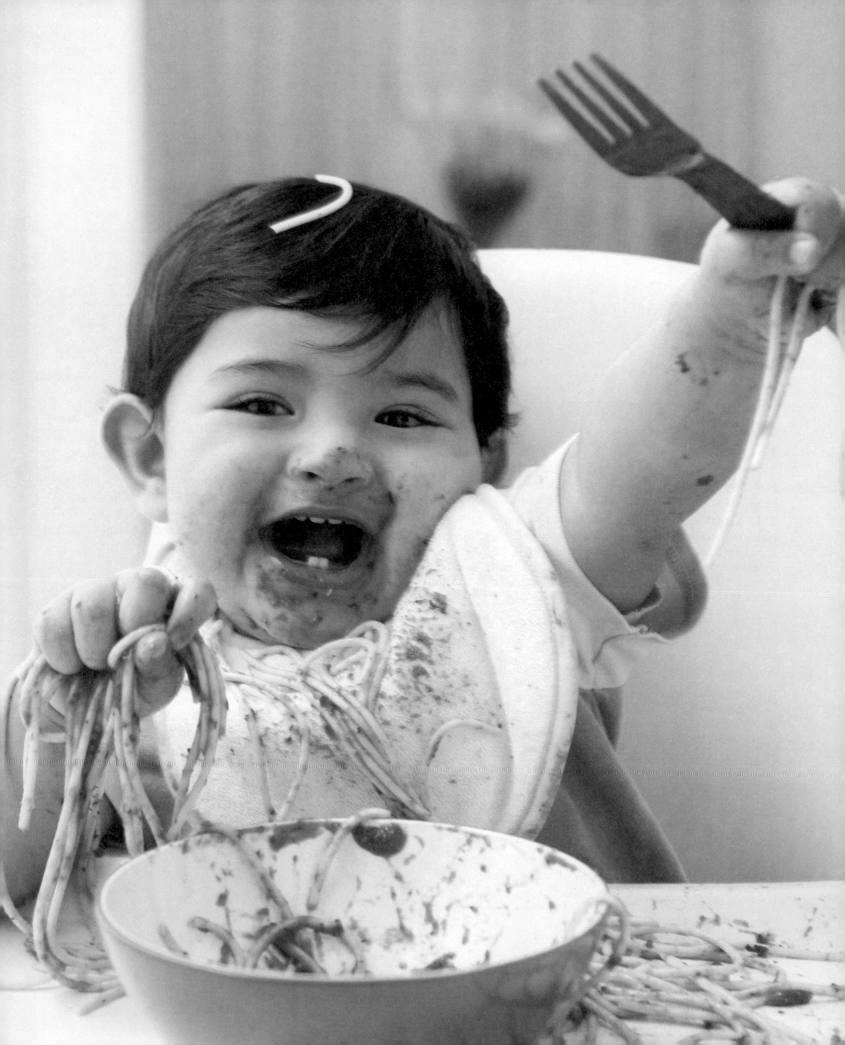

The First Two Years: Cognitive Development

- **Sensorimotor Intelligence**
  Stages One and Two: Primary Circular Reactions
  Stages Three and Four: Secondary Circular Reactions
  Stages Five and Six: Tertiary Circular Reactions
  Piaget and Modern Research

- **Information Processing**
  Affordances
  Memory

- **Language: What Develops in the First Two Years?**
  The Universal Sequence
  First Words
  Cultural Differences
  Theories of Language Learning
  OPPOSING PERSPECTIVES: Language and Video

WHAT WILL YOU KNOW?

1. Why did Piaget compare 1-year-olds to scientists?

2. Why isn't Piaget's theory of sensorimotor intelligence universally recognized as insightful?

3. What factors influence whether infants remember what happens to them before they can talk?

4. When and how do infants learn to talk?

My Aunt Anna's husband, Uncle Henry, boasted that he did nothing with his three children—all boys—until they were smart enough to talk. He may have found an excuse to avoid diapering, burping, and bathing, but he was wrong about infant cognition.

Babies are smart from the first days of life; they think about people and things, communicating long before they say their first words. His sons grew up to be devoted to their mother and much more interactive with their own infants than Uncle Henry had been with them. The research presented in this chapter explains why his sons' approach represents a marked improvement in fathering.

Newborns seem to know nothing. Two years later they can make a wish, say it out loud, and blow out their birthday candles. Thousands of developmentalists have traced this rapid progression, finding that preverbal infants know much more than adults once realized and that every month brings new cognitive developments.

We begin with Piaget's overall understanding of early cognition, specifically his six stages of intellectual progression over the first two years. We then describe another approach to infant cognition, information processing, with some intriguing research that reveals preverbal memory and communication, using methods such as habituation and brain scans. The most dramatic evidence of early intellectual growth—the talking that Uncle Henry waited for—is then described.

The final topic of this chapter may be most important of all: How do early cognitive accomplishments, particularly language, occur? The implications for caregivers are many—none of which Uncle Henry understood.

>> Sensorimotor Intelligence

As you remember from Chapter 2, Jean Piaget was a Swiss scientist who earned his doctorate in 1918, when most scientists thought infants ate, cried, and slept but did not yet learn. When Piaget became a father, he used his scientific observation skills with his own babies, and, contrary to conventional wisdom (including that of Uncle Henry), he realized that infants are active learners, adapting to experience. His theories and observations have earned Piaget the admiration of developmentalists ever since. [**Lifespan Link:** See Chapter 2.]

TABLE 6.1	The Six Stages of Sensorimotor Intelligence

For an overview of the stages of sensorimotor thought, it helps to group the six stages into pairs. The first two stages involve the infant's responses to its own body.

Primary Circular Reactions

Stage One (birth to 1 month)	*Reflexes:* sucking, grasping, staring, listening
Stage Two (1–4 months)	*The first acquired adaptations:* accommodation and coordination of reflexes *Examples:* sucking a pacifier differently from a nipple; attempting to hold a bottle to suck it

The next two stages involve the infant's responses to objects and people.

Secondary Circular Reactions

Stage Three (4–8 months)	*Making interesting events last:* responding to people and objects *Example:* clapping hands when mother says "patty-cake"
Stage Four (8–12 months)	*New adaptation and anticipation:* becoming more deliberate and purposeful in responding to people and objects *Example:* putting mother's hands together in order to make her start playing patty-cake

The last two stages are the most creative, first with action and then with ideas.

Tertiary Circular Reactions

Stage Five (12–18 months)	*New means through active experimentation:* experimentation and creativity in the actions of the "little scientist" *Example:* putting a teddy bear in the toilet and flushing it
Stage Six (18–24 months)	*New means through mental combinations:* thinking before doing, new ways of achieving a goal without resorting to trial and error. *Example:* before flushing the teddy bear, hesitating because of the memory of the toilet overflowing and mother's anger

sensorimotor intelligence Piaget's term for the way infants think—by using their senses and motor skills—during the first period of cognitive development.

Piaget called cognition in the first two years **sensorimotor intelligence.** The reflexes, senses, and motor skills described in Chapters 4 and 5 are used by infants to develop their minds, adapting to experience. Sensorimotor intelligence is subdivided into six stages (see Table 6.1).

Stages One and Two: Primary Circular Reactions

Piaget described the interplay of sensation, perception, and cognition as *circular reactions,* emphasizing that, as in a circle, there is no beginning and no end because each experience leads to the next, which loops back (see Figure 6.1). The first two stages of sensorimotor intelligence are **primary circular reactions,** involving the infant's body.

Stage one, called the *stage of reflexes,* lasts only a month. It includes senses as well as motor reflexes, the foundations of infant thought. Soon reflexes become deliberate; sensation leads to perception, perception leads to cognition, and then cognition leads back to sensation.

primary circular reactions The first of three types of feedback loops in sensorimotor intelligence, this one involving the infant's own body. The infant senses motion, sucking, noise, and other stimuli and tries to understand them.

Stage two, *first acquired adaptations* (also called *stage of first habits*), begins because reflexes adjust to whatever responses they elicit. Adaptation is cognitive; it includes both assimilation and accommodation. [**Lifespan Link:** See Chapter 2.] Infants adapt their reflexes as their responses teach them about what the body does and how each action feels.

Here is one example. In a powerful reflex, full-term newborns suck anything that touches their lips. By about 1 month, infants adapt this reflex to bottles or

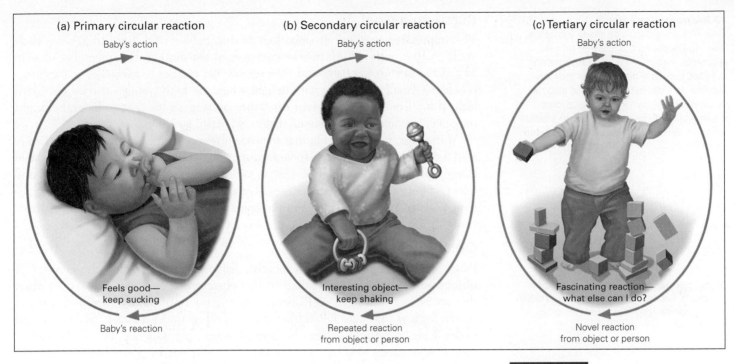

(a) Primary circular reaction

Baby's action

Feels good—
keep sucking

Baby's reaction

(b) Secondary circular reaction

Baby's action

Interesting object—
keep shaking

Repeated reaction
from object or person

(c) Tertiary circular reaction

Baby's action

Fascinating reaction—
what else can I do?

Novel reaction
from object or person

FIGURE 6.1

Never Ending Circular reactions keep going because each action produces pleasure that encourages more action.

breasts, pacifiers or fingers, each requiring specific types of tongue pushing. This adaptation is a sign that infants have begun to interpret their perceptions; as they accommodate to pacifiers, they are "thinking."

During stage two, which Piaget pegged from about 1 to 4 months of age, additional adaptation of the sucking reflex begins. Infant cognition leads babies to suck in some ways for hunger, in other ways for comfort—and not to suck fuzzy blankets or large balls. Once adaptation occurs, it sticks.

For instance, breast-fed babies may reject milk from the nipple of a bottle if they have never experienced it early on. If parents of a 4-month-old thumb-sucker then decide that a pacifier would be better, it may be too late. Their baby may refuse to readapt, a refusal that is evident when the baby spits out the pacifier and finds the thumb instead. Piaget believed that people of all ages tend to be stuck in their ways for cognitive reasons; early adaptation is one example.

Stages Three and Four: Secondary Circular Reactions

In stages three and four, development advances from primary to **secondary circular reactions.** Those reactions extend beyond the infant's body; they are a circular reaction between the baby and something else.

During stage three (4 to 8 months), infants attempt to produce exciting experiences, *making interesting events last.* Realizing that rattles make noise, for example, they wave their arms and laugh whenever someone puts a rattle in their hand. The sight of something delightful—a favorite book, a smiling parent—can trigger active efforts for interaction.

Next comes stage four (8 months to 1 year), *new adaptation and anticipation* (also called the *means to the end*). Babies may ask for help (fussing, pointing, gesturing) to accomplish what they want. Thinking is more innovative because adaptation is more complex. For instance, instead of always smiling at Daddy, an infant might first assess his mood. Stage-three babies know how to continue an experience; stage-four babies initiate and anticipate.

FSTOP/PUNCHSTOCK

Time for Adaptation Sucking is a reflex at first, but adaptation begins as soon as an infant differentiates a pacifier from her mother's breast or realizes that her hand has grown too big to fit into her mouth. This infant's expression of concentration suggests that she is about to make that adaptation and suck just her thumb from now on.

secondary circular reactions The second of three types of feedback loops in sensorimotor intelligence, this one involving people and objects. Infants respond to other people, to toys, and to any other object they can touch or move.

Especially for Parents When should parents decide whether to feed their baby only by breast, only by bottle, or using some combination of the two? When should they decide whether or not to let their baby use a pacifier? (see response, page 158)

>> **Response for Parents** (from page 157): Both decisions should be made within the first month, during the stage of reflexes. If parents wait until the infant is 4 months or older, they may discover that they are too late. It is difficult to introduce a bottle to a 4-month-old who has never sucked on an artificial nipple or a pacifier to a baby who has already adapted the sucking reflex to a thumb.

object permanence The realization that objects (including people) still exist when they can no longer be seen, touched, or heard.

Family Fun Peek-a-boo makes all three happy, each for cognitive reasons. The 9-month-old is discovering object permanence, his sister (at the concrete operational stage) enjoys making brother laugh, and their mother understands more abstract ideas—such as family bonding.

BAMBU PRODUCTIONS/GETTY IMAGES

Pursuing a Goal

The impressive attribute of stage four is that babies work hard to achieve their goals. A 10-month-old girl might crawl over to her mother, bringing a bar of soap as a signal to start her bath, and then remove her clothes to make her wishes crystal clear—finally squealing with delight when the bath water is turned on. Similarly, if a 10-month-old boy sees his father putting on his coat to leave, he might drag over his own jacket to signal that he wants to go along.

At that age, babies indicate that they are hungry—and keep their mouths firmly shut if the food on the spoon is something they do not like. If the caregivers have been using sign language, among the first signs learned by 10-month-olds are "eat" and "more." These cognitive advances benefit from new motor skills (e.g., crawling, grabbing, hand gestures), which result from brain maturation—dynamic systems again.

Object Permanence

Piaget thought that, at about 8 months, babies first understand the concept of **object permanence**—the realization that objects or people continue to exist when they are no longer in sight. As Piaget discovered, not until about 8 months do infants search for toys that have fallen from the crib, rolled under a couch, or disappeared under a blanket. Blind babies also acquire object permanence toward the end of their first year, reaching for an object that they hear nearby (Fazzi et al., 2011).

As they grow older, toddlers become better at seeking hidden objects, which Piaget again considered symptomatic of sensorimotor advances. Piaget developed a basic experiment to measure object permanence: An adult shows an infant an interesting toy, covers it with a lightweight cloth, and observes the response. The results:

- Infants younger than 8 months do not search for the object (by removing the cloth).
- At about 8 months, infants search immediately (removing the cloth) after the object is covered but not if they have to wait a few seconds.
- At 18 months, they search quite well, but not if they have seen the object put first in one place and then moved to another. They search in the first place, a mistake called A-not-B.
- By 2 years, children fully understand object permanence, progressing through several stages of ever-advanced cognition (Piaget, 1954).

This research provides many practical suggestions. If young infants fuss because they see something they cannot have (keys, a cigarette, candy), put that coveted object out of sight. Fussing stops.

By contrast, for toddlers, hiding a forbidden object is not enough. It must be securely locked up or discarded, lest the child later retrieve it, climbing onto the kitchen counter or under the bathroom sink to do so. Since object permanence develops gradually, games such as peek-a-boo and hide-and-seek are too advanced in the first months, but they are fun once object permanence is newly understood. As comprehension of hidden objects matures, peek-a-boo becomes boring, but hide-and-seek becomes more elaborate (longer waiting, more imaginative hiding).

Piaget believed that failure to search before 8 months of age meant that infants had no concept of object permanence—that "out of sight" literally means "out of mind." That belief has been questioned. As one researcher points out,

"Amid his acute observation and brilliant theorizing, Piaget . . . mistook infants' motor incompetence for conceptual incompetence" (Mandler, 2004, p. 17). A series of clever experiments in which objects seemed to disappear behind a screen while researchers traced babies' eye movements and brain activity revealed that long before 8 months infants are surprised if an object vanishes (Baillargeon & DeVos, 1991; Spelke, 1993).

Further research on object permanence continues to raise questions and produce surprises. For instance, many other creatures (cats, monkeys, dogs, birds) develop object permanence at younger ages than Piaget found. Does this reflect slower development of the human brain or simply slower maturation of motor skills (Bruce & Muhammad, 2009)?

Stages Five and Six: Tertiary Circular Reactions

In their second year, infants start experimenting in thought and deed—or, rather, in the opposite sequence, deed and thought. They act first (stage five) and think later (stage six).

Tertiary circular reactions begin when 1-year-olds take independent actions to discover the properties of other people, animals, and things. Infants no longer respond only to their own bodies (primary reactions) or to other people or objects (secondary reactions). Their cognition is more like a spiral than a closed circle, increasingly creative with each discovery.

Piaget's stage five (ages 12 to 18 months), *new means through active experimentation,* builds on the accomplishments of stage four. Now goal-directed and purposeful activities become more expansive.

Toddlers delight in squeezing all the toothpaste out of the tube, taking apart an iPod, or uncovering an anthill, activities they have never seen an adult do. Piaget referred to the stage-five toddler as a "**little scientist**" who "experiments in order to see." Their scientific method is trial and error. Their devotion to discovery is familiar to every adult scientist—and to every parent.

Finally, in the sixth stage (ages 18 to 24 months), toddlers use *mental combinations,* intellectual experimentation via imagination that can supersede the active experimentation of stage five. Thankfully, the stage-six sequence may begin with thought (especially if the toddler remembers that something was forbidden) and then move on to action. Of course, the urge to explore may overtake memories of prohibition: Things that are truly dangerous (poisons, swimming pools, open windows) need to be locked and gated, not simply forbidden.

Another major cognitive accomplishment at the sixth stage is that toddlers can pretend. For instance, they know that a doll is not a real baby, but they can belt it into a stroller and take it for a walk. At 22 months my grandson gave me imaginary "shoe ice cream" and laughed when I pretended to eat it.

Because they combine ideas, stage-six toddlers think about consequences, hesitating a moment before yanking the cat's tail or dropping a raw egg on the floor. Of course, their strong drive to discover may overwhelm reflection; they do not always choose wisely.

Piaget describes another stage-six intellectual accomplishment involving both thinking and memory. **Deferred imitation** occurs when infants copy behavior

ARIEL SKELLEY/AGE FOTOSTOCK

tertiary circular reactions The third of three types of feedback loops in sensorimotor intelligence, this one involving active exploration and experimentation. Infants explore a range of new activities, varying their responses as a way of learning about the world.

"little scientist" The stage-five toddler (age 12 to 18 months) who experiments without anticipating the results, using trial and error in active and creative exploration.

deferred imitation A sequence in which an infant first perceives something done by someone else and then performs the same action hours or even days later.

Especially for Parents One parent wants to put all the breakable or dangerous objects away because their toddler is able to move around independently. The other parent says that the baby should learn not to touch certain things. Who is right? (see response, page 161)

Exploration at 15 Months One of the best ways to investigate food is to squish it in your hands, observe changes in color and texture, and listen for sounds. Taste and smell are primary senses for adults when eating, but it looks as if Jonathan has already had his fill of those.

TOOGA PRODUCTIONS, INC./GETTY IMAGES.

Push Another Button Little scientists "experiment in order to see" as this 14-month-old does. Many parents realize, to their distress, that their infant has deleted a crucial file, or called a distant relative on a cell phone, because the toddler wants to see what happens.

they noticed hours or even days earlier (Piaget, 1945/1962). Piaget described his daughter, Jacqueline, who observed another child

> who got into a terrible temper. He screamed as he tried to get out of a playpen and pushed it backward, stamping his feet. Jacqueline stood watching him in amazement, never having witnessed such a scene before. The next day, she herself screamed in her playpen and tried to move it, stamping her foot lightly several times in succession.
>
> *[Piaget, 1945/1962, p. 63]*

Piaget and Modern Research

As detailed by hundreds of developmentalists, many infants reach the stages of sensorimotor intelligence earlier than Piaget predicted (Oakes et al., 2011). Not only do 5-month-olds show surprise when objects seem to disappear (evidence of object permanence before 8 months) but babies younger than 1 year pretend and defer imitation (both stage-six abilities, according to Piaget) (Bauer, 2006; Fagard & Lockman, 2010; Hayne & Simcock, 2009; Meltzoff & Moore, 1999). How could a gifted scientist be so wrong? There are at least three reasons.

Sample Too Small

First, Piaget's original insights were based on his own infants. Direct observation of three children is a start, and Piaget was an extraordinarily meticulous and creative observer, but no contemporary researcher would stop there. Given the immaturity and variability of babies, dozens of infants must be studied. For instance, as evidence for early object permanence, Baillargeon (2000) listed 30 studies involving more than a thousand infants younger than 6 months old.

Methods Too Simple

Second, infants are not easy to study; there are problems with "fidelity and credibility" (Bornstein et al., 2005, p. 287). To overcome these problems, modern researchers use innovative statistics, research designs, sample sizes, and strategies that were not available to Piaget—often finding that object permanence, deferred imitation, and other sensorimotor accomplishments occur earlier, and with more variation, than Piaget had assumed (Hartmann & Pelzel, 2005; Kolling et al., 2009). For instance, if an infant looks a few milliseconds longer when an object seems to have vanished, is that evidence of object permanence? Many researchers believe the answer is yes—but only advanced cameras, programmed by computers, can measure it.

One particular research strategy has been a boon to scientists, confirming the powerful curiosity of very young babies. That research method is called **habituation** (from the word *habit*). Habituation refers to getting accustomed to an experience after repeated exposure, as when the school cafeteria serves macaroni day after day or when infants repeatedly encounter the same sound, sight, toy, or so on. Evidence of habituation is loss of interest (or, for macaroni, loss of appetite).

Using habituation as a research strategy with infants involves repeating one stimulus until babies lose interest and then presenting another, slightly different stimulus (a new sound, sight, or other sensation). Babies indicate that they detect a difference between the two stimuli with a longer or more focused gaze; a faster or slower heart rate; more or less muscle tension around the lips; a change in the rate, rhythm, or pressure of suction on a nipple. Such subtle indicators are recorded by technology that was unavailable to Piaget (such as eye-gaze cameras and heart monitors).

habituation The process of becoming accustomed to an object or event through repeated exposure to it, and thus becoming less interested in it.

By inducing habituation and then presenting a new stimulus, scientists have learned that even 1-month-olds can detect the difference between a *pah* sound and a *bah* sound, between a circle with two dots inside it and a circle without any dots, and much more. Babies younger than 6 months perceive far more than Piaget imagined.

Brain Activity Unseen

Third, several ways of measuring brain activity now allow scientists to record infant cognition long before any observable evidence is found (see Table 6.2) (Johnson, 2010). In **fMRI** (functional magnetic resonance imaging), a burst of electrical activity measured by blood flow within the brain is recorded, indicating that neurons are firing. This leads researchers to conclude that a particular stimulus has been noticed and processed. Moreover, scientists now know exactly which parts of the brain signify what sensations or thoughts, so electrical activity in the face area, for instance, means that the infants is processing a face.

>> Response for Parents (from page 159): It is easier and safer to babyproof the house because toddlers, being "little scientists," want to explore. However, it is important for both parents to encourage and guide the baby, so it is preferable to leave out a few untouchable items if that will help prevent a major conflict between the adults.

fMRI Functional magnetic resonance imaging, a measuring technique in which the brain's electrical excitement indicates activation anywhere in the brain; fMRI helps researchers locate neurological responses to stimuli.

TABLE 6.2   **Some Techniques Used by Neuroscientists to Understand Brain Function**

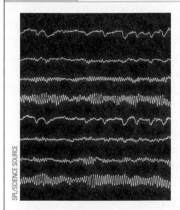

EEG, normal brain

Technique

EEG (electroencephalogram)

Use

Measures electrical activity in the top layers of the brain, where the cortex is.

Limitations

Especially in infancy, much brain activity of interest occurs below the cortex.

ERP when listening

Technique

ERP (event-related potential)

Use

Notes the amplitude and frequency of electrical activity (as shown by brain waves) in specific parts of the cortex in reaction to various stimuli.

Limitations

Reaction within the cortex signifies perception, but interpretation of the amplitude and timing of brain waves is not straightforward.

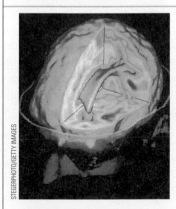

fMRI when talking

Technique

fMRI (functional magnetic resonance imaging)

Use

Measures changes in blood flow anywhere in the brain (not just the outer layers).

Limitations

Signifies brain activity, but infants are notoriously active, which can make fMRIs useless.

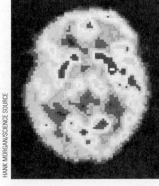

PET scan of sleep

Technique

PET (positron emission tomography)

Use

PET (like fMRI) reveals activity in various parts of the brain. Locations can be pinpointed with precision, but PET requires injection of radioactive dye to light up the active parts of the brain.

Limitations

Many parents and researchers hesitate to inject radioactive dye into an infant's brain unless a serious abnormality is suspected.

For both practical and ethical reasons, it is difficult to use these techniques on large, representative samples. One of the challenges of neuroscience is to develop methods that are harmless, quick, acceptable to parents and babies, and comprehensive. A more immediate challenge is to depict the data in ways that are easy to interpret and understand.

As time goes on, milliseconds of gaze, or blood flow in the brain, indicate that habitation has occurred. Based on advanced methods, scientists are convinced that infants have memories, goals, deferred imitation, and even mental combinations well in advance of Piaget's stages (Bauer et al., 2010; Morasch & Bell, 2009).

Brain imagery of normal children is not only difficult and expensive, with interpretation sometimes controversial, but any scans of the head raise questions about long-term effects (Schenkman, 2011). Brain scans may provide crucial information if an infant is ill or injured, but many parents refuse to allow such measures with healthy infants. Such caution is understandable, even admirable, but it slows down neurological confirmation of infant cognition.

However, brain scans of non-human primates has revealed much about the human brain. That includes the discovery of **mirror neurons.** About two decades ago, scientists noticed that when a one monkey saw another reach for a banana, the same brain areas were activated (lit up in brain scans) in both monkeys. Those brain areas in the F5 area of the observing macaque's premotor cortex were dubbed mirror neurons, because they reflected what was observed. Using increasingly advanced technology, neuroscientists have now found mirror neurons in several parts of the adult human brain (Keysers & Gazzola, 2010).

Many scientists have suggested that mirror neurons lead to exciting implications for infant cognition. Perhaps avid watching and listening enable babies to understand objects, language, and other people learn long before Piaget realized (Diamond & Amso, 2008; Rossi et al., 2011; Virji-Babul et al., 2012). A baby's learning by observation may actually involved brain activity that mirrors what was seen and heard, so that as soon as physiological maturation makes it possible, the baby knows exactly what to do. He or she has already done it many times before—in the brain.

mirror neurons Cells in an observer's brain that respond to an action performed by someone else in the same way they would if the observer were actually performing that action.

SUMMING UP

Piaget discovered, studied, and then celebrated active infant learning, which he described in six stages of sensorimotor intelligence. Babies use senses and motor skills to understand their world, first with reflexes and then by adapting through assimilation and accommodation. Piaget's detailed descriptions contrasted with earlier assumptions that babies did not think until they could talk. Thousands of researchers followed his lead, using advanced technology to demonstrate the rapid cognitive development of the early months.

We now know that object permanence, pursuit of goals, and deferred imitation all develop before the ages that Piaget assigned to his stages. The infant is a "little scientist" not only at 1 year, as Piaget described, but months earlier. Brain scans and measurement of eye movements indicate that thinking develops before infants have the motor skills to demonstrate their thoughts. Mirror neurons might be part of the reason.

>> Information Processing

As explained in Chapter 2, Piaget's sweeping overview of four periods of cognition contrasts with information-processing theory, a perspective originally modeled after computer functioning, including input, memory, programs, analysis, and output. Just as input connects with a program and then leads to output on a computer, sensation leads to perception, which may produce cognition. Those links are detailed in information-processing theory.

For infants, output might be moving a hand to uncover a toy (object permanence), saying a word to signify recognition (e.g., *mama*), or looking at one photo longer than another (habituation). Some recent studies examine changes in brain waves when infants see a picture (Koulder et al., 2013), research that both confirms and refutes Piaget's theory.

To understand the many aspects of information processing in infancy, consider the baby's reaction to feeling hungry. A newborn simply cries with hunger pangs as a reflex, but an older hungry infant hears its mother's voice, looks for her, reaches to be picked up, and then nuzzles at her breast, or, at an even older age, signs or says something to indicate hunger. Each step of this process requires information to be processed. Older infants are much more thoughtful and effective than newborns because of more advanced information processing. Advances occur week by week or even day by day in the first year, contrary to Piaget's notion of six discrete stages (Cohen & Cashon, 2006).

The information-processing perspective, aided by modern technology, has uncovered many aspects of infant cognition. As one researcher summarizes, "Rather than bumbling babies, they are individuals who . . . can learn surprisingly fast about the patterns of nature" (Keil, 2011, p. 1023). Concepts and categories seem to develop in infants' brains by 6 months or earlier (Mandler & DeLoach, 2012).

Consider the concept of number. Habituation and brain scans reveal that 6-month-olds can detect the difference between displays of 8 and 16 dots. By 9 months, they can do even better, differentiating between 8 and 12 dots (Lipton & Spelke, 2003). This suggests that not only that vision is more perceptive, but also that infants have some mental apparatus that registers more or less.

The information-processing perspective helps tie together many aspects of infant cognition. Indeed, if adults want to know how intelligent a particular baby is, the best way probably is to measure speed of information processing. Rapid habituation is an encouraging sign; babies like novelty.

In earlier decades, infant intelligence was measured via age of sitting up, grasping, and so on, but we now know that, unless a child is severely impaired, age of achieving motor skills does not correlate with later intellectual achievement. However, information-processing research seems to find that early attention and habituation correlate with later intelligence. Babies who focus intently on new stimuli, and then quickly become habituated, may be more intelligent (Bornstein & Columbo, 2012).

Now let us look at two specific aspects of infant cognition that illustrate the information-processing approach: affordances and memory. Affordances concern perception or, by analogy, input. Memory concerns brain organization and output—that is, storage and retrieval.

Affordances

Perception, remember, is the processing of information that arrives at the brain from the sense organs. Decades of thought and research led Eleanor and James Gibson to conclude that perception is far from automatic (E. J. Gibson, 1969; J. J. Gibson, 1979). Perception—for infants, as for the rest of us—is a cognitive accomplishment that requires selectivity: "Perceiving is active, a process of obtaining information about the world . . . We don't simply see, we look" (E. J. Gibson, 1988, p. 5). Or, as one neuroscientist said, "You see what you expect or are trained to see, not what is there" (Freeman, quoted in Bower, 2007, p. 106).

The environment (people, places, and objects) *affords*, or offers, many opportunities to interact with whatever is perceived (E. J. Gibson, 1997). Each of these opportunities is called an **affordance.** Which particular affordance is perceived and acted on depends on four factors: sensory awareness, immediate motivation, current level of development, and past experience.

What Next? Information-processing research asks what these babies are thinking as they both pull on the same block. Will those thoughts lead to hitting, crying, or sharing?

Especially for Computer Experts In what way is the human mind not like a computer? (see response, page 164)

affordance An opportunity for perception and interaction that is offered by a person, place, or object in the environment.

>> Response for Computer Experts
(from page 163): In dozens of ways, including speed of calculation, ability to network across the world, and vulnerability to viruses. In at least one crucial way, the human mind is better: Computers become obsolete or fail within a few years, while human minds keep advancing for decades.

visual cliff An experimental apparatus that gives the illusion of a sudden drop-off between one horizontal surface and another.

MARK RICHARDS/PHOTOEDIT

Depth Perception This toddler in a laboratory in Berkeley, California, is crawling on the experimental apparatus called a visual cliff. She stops at the edge of what she perceives as a drop-off.

Especially for Parents of Infants When should you be particularly worried that your baby will fall off the bed or down the stairs? (see response, page 166)

As an example, imagine that you are lost in an unfamiliar city. You need to ask directions. Of whom? Not the first person you see. You want someone knowledgeable and approachable. Affordance is what you seek, and you scan facial expression, body language, gender, dress, and more of the passersby (Miles, 2009).

Age of the perceiver affects what affordances are perceived. For example, since toddlers enjoy running as soon as their legs allow it, every open space affords running: a meadow, a building's long hall, a highway. To adults, affordance of running is much more limited, as they notice a bull grazing in the meadow, neighbors behind the hallway doors, or traffic on the road. Furthermore, because motivation is pivotal in affordances, toddlers start moving when most adults prefer to stay put.

Selective perception of affordances depends not only on age, motivation, and context but also on culture. Just as a baby might be oblivious to something adults consider crucial—or vice versa—an American in, say, Cambodia might miss an important sign of the social network. In every nation, foreigners behave in ways considered rude, but their behavior may simply indicate that their affordances differ from those of the native people.

Variation in affordance is also apparent within cultures. City-dwellers complain that visitors from rural areas walk too slowly, yet visitors complain that the natives are always in a hurry. Sidewalks afford either fast motion or views of urban architecture, depending on the perceiver.

Research on Early Affordances

Experience affects which affordances are perceived. This is obvious in studies of depth perception. Research demonstrating this began with an apparatus called the **visual cliff,** designed to provide the illusion of a sudden drop-off between one horizontal surface and another (see photo). Six-month-olds, urged forward by their mothers, wiggled toward mom over the supposed edge of the cliff, but 10-month-olds, even with mothers' encouragement, fearfully refused to budge (E. J. Gibson & Walk, 1960).

Scientists once thought that a visual deficit—specifically, inadequate depth perception—prevented 6-month-olds from seeing the drop, which was why they crawled forward. According to this hypothesis, as the visual cortex matured, 10-month-olds perceived that crawling over a cliff afforded falling. Later research (using more advanced technology) disproved that interpretation. Even 3-month-olds notice the drop: Their heart rate slows, and their eyes open wide when they are placed over the cliff. Their depth perception is in place, but until they can crawl, they do not realize that crawling over an edge affords falling.

This awareness of the visual cliff hazard depends on experience. The difference is in processing, not input; in affordance, not sensory ability. Further research on affordances of the visual cliff includes the social context, with the tone of the mother's encouragement indicating whether or not the cliff affords crawling (Kim et al., 2010).

A similar sequence happens with fear. By 9 months, infants attend to snakes and spiders more readily than to other similar images, but they do not yet fear them. A few months later, perhaps because they have learned from others, they are afraid of such creatures. Thus perception is a prerequisite, but it does not always lead to affordance (LoBue, 2013).

Movement

Despite all the variations from one person to another in affordances perceived, all babies are attracted to things that move. They stare at passing cars, flickering images on a screen, mobiles—because of their inborn information-processing

programs. As soon as they can, they move their bodies—grabbing, scooting, crawling, walking—which changes what the world affords them. As a result, infants strive to master each motor skill (Adolph, 2012).

Other creatures that move, especially an infant's own caregivers, afford pleasure to every infant. It's almost impossible to teach a baby *not* to chase and grab moving creatures, including dogs, cats, or even bugs. Universally, moving objects are more attractive than static ones.

The infant's interest in motion was the inspiration for another experiment (van Hof et al., 2008). A ball was moved at various speeds in front of infants aged 3 to 9 months. Most tried to touch or catch the ball as it passed within reach. However, they differed in their perception of whether the balls afforded catching.

Sometimes younger infants did not reach for slow-moving balls, yet tried to grasp the faster balls. They failed, touching the ball only about 20 percent of the time. By contrast, the 9-month-olds knew when a ball afforded catching. They grabbed the slower balls and did not try to catch the fastest ones; their success rate was almost 100 percent. This finding "follows directly from one of the key concepts of ecological psychology, that animals perceive the environment in terms of action possibilities or affordances" (van Hof et al., 2008, p. 193).

Grab Him As with most babies, she loves grabbing any creature, hoping for a reaction. To recognize that people change over time, imagine these two a few years or decades older. She would not grab him, and if she did, he would not be placid.

Memory

The term *infant amnesia* refers to the belief that infants remember nothing until about age 2, an idea once accepted by most adults. Information processing has revealed otherwise; memory is evident in very young babies.

However, memory is fragile in the first months of life. Both a certain amount of experience and a certain amount of brain maturation are required in order to process and remember anything (Bauer et al., 2010).

Infants have difficulty storing new memories in their first year, and older children are often unable to describe events that occurred when they were younger. One reason is linguistic: People use words to store (and sometimes distort) memories, so preverbal children have difficulty with recall (Richardson & Hayne, 2007), while adults cannot access early memories because they did not have words to solidify them.

Selective Amnesia As we grow older, we forget about spitting up, nursing, crying, and almost everything else from our early years. However, strong emotions (love, fear, mistrust) may leave lifelong traces.

COURTESY OF CAROLYN ROVEE-COLLIER

He Remembers! In this demonstration of Rovee-Collier's experiment, a young infant immediately remembers how to make the familiar mobile move. (Unfamiliar mobiles do not provoke the same reaction.) He kicks his right leg and flails both arms, just as he learned to do several weeks ago.

>> Response for Parents of Infants (from page 164): Constant vigilance is necessary for the first few years of a child's life, but the most dangerous age is from about 4 to 8 months, when infants can move but do not yet fear falling over an edge.

reminder session A perceptual experience that helps a person recollect an idea, a thing, or an experience.

Who is thinking? They all are. Julie is stretching her sensorimotor intelligence as she rotates a piece to make it fit, while her mother decides if her 2-year-old is ready for a puzzle with 20 cardboard pieces. But the champion thinker may be baby Samara, as her mirror neurons reflect actions she can think but not yet do.

LUCAS OLENIUK/TORONTO STAR VIA GETTY IMAGES

A series of experiments, however, reveals that very young infants *can* remember, even if they cannot later put memories into words. Memories are particularly evident if:

- Motivation is high.
- Retrieval is strengthened by reminders and repetition.

The most dramatic proof of infant memory comes from innovative experiments in which 3-month-olds learned to move a mobile by kicking their legs (Rovee-Collier, 1987, 1990). The infants lay on their backs connected to a mobile by means of a ribbon tied to one foot (see photo). Virtually every baby began making occasional kicks (as well as random arm movements and noises) and realized, that kicking made the mobile move. They then kicked more vigorously and frequently, sometimes laughing at their accomplishment. So far, this is no surprise—observing self-activated movement is highly reinforcing to infants, a dynamic system. [**Lifespan Link:** Chapter 1.]

When some infants had the mobile-and-ribbon apparatus reinstalled and reconnected *one week later,* most started to kick immediately. Their reaction indicated that they remembered their previous experience. But when other 3-month-old infants were retested *two weeks later,* they began with only random kicks. Apparently they had forgotten what they had learned—evidence that memory is fragile early in life. But that conclusion needs revision, or at least qualification.

Reminders and Repetition

The lead researcher, Carolyn Rovee-Collier, developed another experiment demonstrating that 3-month-old infants *could* remember after two weeks *if* they had a brief reminder session before being retested (Rovee-Collier & Hayne, 1987). A **reminder session** is any experience that helps people recollect an idea, a thing, or an event.

In this particular reminder session, *two weeks* after the initial training, the infants watched the mobile move but were *not* tied to it and were positioned so that they could *not* kick. The next day, when they were again connected to the mobile and positioned so that they *could* move their legs, they kicked as they had learned to do two weeks earlier. Apparently, watching the mobile move on the previous day had revived their faded memory. The information about making the mobile move was stored in their brains, but they needed processing time to retrieve it. The reminder session provided that time.

Other research finds that repeated reminders are more powerful than single reminders and that context is crucial, especially for infants younger than 9 months old: Being tested in the same room as the initial experience aids memory (Rovee-Collier & Cuevas, 2009a).

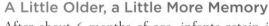

A Little Older, a Little More Memory

After about 6 months of age, infants retain information for a longer time than younger babies do, with less training or reminding. Toward the end of the first year, many kinds of memory are apparent. For example, suppose a 9-month-old watches someone playing with a toy he or she has never seen. The next day, if given the toy, the 9-month-old will play with it in the same way as he or she had observed. Younger infants will not.

Many experiments show that toddlers can transfer learning from one object or experience to another and that they learn from various people and events—from parents and strangers, from other babies and older siblings, from picture books and family photographs (Hayne & Simcock, 2009). The dendrites and neurons of the brain change to reflect their experiences and memories even in the first years of life. [**Lifespan Link:** Experience-related brain growth is described in Chapter 5.]

Note that these experiments are further evidence of several facts already mentioned: Babies observe affordances carefully, they are especially attuned to movement, and deferred imitation is possible before Piaget's stage six begins.

One reason earlier scientists underestimated memory is that they failed to distinguish between **implicit memory** and **explicit memory.** Implicit memory is memory that remains hidden until a particular stimulus brings it to mind (like the mobile reminder session), whereas explicit memory is memory that can be recalled on demand. Explicit memories are usually verbal, and therefore "although explicit memory *emerges* sometime between 6 and 12 months, it is far from fully developed" (Nelson, de Haan et al., 2006, p. 23).

The particular part of the brain on which explicit memory depends is the hippocampus, present at birth but very immature until about age 5 or 6. [**Lifespan Link:** The function of the hippocampus is explained in Chapter 8.] It is no surprise that this timing coincides with the beginning of formal education, because children are much better at memorizing at that age.

Implicit memories, by contrast, begin before birth. Implicit memories are evident in all the examples just mentioned, when evidence of memory comes from the situation, not from the answer to a spoken question.

For instance, adults who knew a language in childhood often have no explicit memory of it: They claim to have forgotten all the Spanish, French, Chinese, or whatever. When asked the word for a common object in that language, they honestly reply that they do not know (Bowers et al., 2009). Moreover, when first tested, such adults are no better at comprehension than those who never heard the language.

However, repeated exposure uncovers implicit memories from infancy. Thus, a student who has forgotten childhood Spanish catches on more quickly in Spanish class than does the student who never knew Spanish as an infant. Apparently, the first weeks of class serve as a reminder session. Reminders may also explain the phenomenon of déjà vu; people, places, and smells sometimes seem familiar or emotionally evocative, even if they were never experienced before, because something very similar occurred in infancy and was stored implicitly.

Infants probably store in their brains many emotions and sensations that they cannot readily retrieve. The information-processing approach finds that infant memory is crucial for later development—far more so than are other components of early thought, such as attention and processing speed (Rose et al., 2009). Extensive research finds that memories help in early word learning, and those words in turn help encode later memories (Richardson & Hayne, 2007). People need to talk to babies, long before the babies can talk back.

The crucial insight from information processing is that the brain is a very active organ, even in early infancy. Therefore, the particulars of experiences and memory are critically important in determining what a child knows or does not know. Soon generalization is possible. In one study, after 6-month-olds had had only two half-hour sessions with a novel puppet, a month later they remembered the experience—an amazing feat of memory for babies who could not talk or even stand up (Giles & Rovee-Collier, 2011).

Many studies show that infants remember not only specific events and objects but also patterns and general goals (Keil, 2011). Some examples come from research, such as memory of what syllables and rhythms are heard and how objects move in relation to other objects. Additional examples arise from

implicit memory Unconscious or automatic memory that is usually stored via habits, emotional responses, routine procedures, and various sensations.

explicit memory Memory that is easy to retrieve on demand (as in a specific test). Most explicit memory involves consciously learned words, data, and concepts.

Especially for Teachers People of every age remember best when they are active learners. If you had to teach fractions to a class of 8-year-olds, how would you do it? (see response, page 168)

>> Response for Teachers
(from page 167): Remember the three principles of infant memory: real life, motivation, and repetition. Find something children already enjoy that involves fractions—even if they don't realize it. Perhaps get a pizza and ask them to divide it in half, quarters, eighths, sixteenths, and so on.

close observations of babies at home, such as what they expect from Mommy as compared to Daddy or what details indicate bedtime. Every day of their young lives, infants are processing information and storing conclusions.

SUMMING UP

Information processing analyzes each component of how thoughts begin; how they are organized, remembered, and expressed; and how cognition builds, day by day. Infants' perception is powerfully influenced by particular experiences and motivation; affordances perceived by one infant differ from those perceived by another. Memory depends on brain maturation and on experience. For that reason, memory is fragile in the first year (though it can be triggered by reminders) and becomes more evident, although still fragile, in the second year. ▪

>> Language: What Develops in the First Two Years?

The brains of no other species have anything approaching the neurons and networks that support the 6,000 or so human languages. Many other animals communicate, but the human linguistic ability at age 2 far surpasses that of full-grown adults from every other species. How do babies do it?

The Universal Sequence

The sequence of language development is the same worldwide (see At About This Time). Some children learn several languages, some only one, some learn rapidly and others slowly, but they all follow the same path. Even deaf infants who become able to hear (thanks to cochlear implants) follow the sequence, catching up to their age-mates unless they have multiple disabilities (Fazzi et al., 2011). Those who learn sign language also begin with one word at a time, and then sign sentences of increasing length and complexity.

Listening and Responding

Language learning begins before birth (Dirix et al., 2009). Newborns prefer to listen to the language their mother spoke when they were in the womb, not because they understand the words, of course, but because they are familiar with the rhythm, the sounds, and the cadence.

Surprisingly, newborns of bilingual mothers differentiate between both languages (Heinlein et al., 2010). Data were collected on 94 newborns (0 to 5 days old) in a large hospital in Vancouver, Canada. Half were born to mothers who spoke both English and Tagalog (the native language of Filipinos), one-third to mothers who spoke only English, and one-sixth to mothers who spoke English and Chinese. The bilingual mothers used English in more formal contexts and non-English with family.

The infants in all three groups sucked as they listened to 10 minutes of recorded sentences in English or Tagalog matched for pitch, duration, and number of syllables. Most of them with bilingual mothers preferred Tagalog, whereas those with monolingual mothers preferred English. The Chinese bilingual babies (who had never heard Tagalog) nonetheless preferred it. The researchers believe that they liked Tagalog because the rhythm of that Asian language is more similar to Chinese than to English (Heinlein et al., 2010).

Who Is Babbling? Probably both the 6-month-old and the 27-year-old. During every day of infancy, mothers and babies communicate with noises, movements (notice the hands), and expressions.

ARIEL SKELLEY/GETTY IMAGES

AT ABOUT THIS TIME

The Development of Spoken Language in the First Two Years

Age*	Means of Communication
Newborn	Reflexive communication—cries, movements, facial expressions.
2 months	A range of meaningful noises—cooing, fussing, crying, laughing.
3–6 months	New sounds, including squeals, growls, croons, trills, vowel sounds.
6–10 months	Babbling, including both consonant and vowel sounds repeated in syllables.
10–12 months	Comprehension of simple words; speechlike intonations; specific vocalizations that have meaning to those who know the infant well. Deaf babies express their first signs; hearing babies also use specific gestures (e.g., pointing) to communicate.
12 months	First spoken words that are recognizably part of the native language.
13–18 months	Slow growth of vocabulary, up to about 50 words.
18 months	Naming explosion—three or more words learned per day. Much variation: Some toddlers do not yet speak.
21 months	First two-word sentence.
24 months	Multiword sentences. Half the toddler's utterances are two or more words long.

*The ages in this table reflect norms. Many healthy, intelligent children attain each linguistic accomplishment earlier or later than indicated here.

Young infants attend to voices more than to mechanical sounds (a clock ticking) and look closely at the facial expressions of someone talking to them (Minagawa-Kawai et al., 2011). By 6 months, simply by seeing someone's mouth movements (no sound), infants can distinguish whether or not that person is speaking their native language (Weikum et al., 2007). By 1 year, even when they don't understand the actual content of the speech, they are more likely to imitate the actions of a stranger speaking their native language than those of a person who speaks another language (Buttelmann et al., 2013).

Infants' ability to distinguish sounds in the language they hear improves, whereas the ability to hear sounds never spoken in their native language (such as how an "r" or an "l" is pronounced) deteriorates (Narayan et al., 2010). If parents want a child to speak two languages, they must speak both of them to their infant.

In every language, adults use higher pitch, simple words, repetition, varied speed, and exaggerated emotional tone when talking to infants (Bryant & Barrett, 2007). This special language form is sometimes called *baby talk*, since it is directed to babies, and sometimes called *motherese*, since mothers universally speak it. Non-mothers speak it as well. For that reason, scientists prefer the more formal designation, **child-directed speech**.

No matter what term is used, child-directed speech fosters learning, and babies communicate as best they can. By 4 months, they squeal, growl, gurgle, grunt, croon, and yell, telling everyone what is on their minds in response to both their own internal state and their caregivers' words. At 7 months, infants begin to recognize words that are highly distinctive (Singh, 2008): *Bottle, dog,* and *mama,* for instance, might be differentiated, but words that sound alike (*baby, Bobbie,* and *Barbie*) are not.

child-directed speech The high-pitched, simplified, and repetitive way adults speak to infants and children. (Also called *baby talk* or *motherese*.)

Especially for Nurses and Pediatricians
The parents of a 6-month-old have just been told that their child is deaf. They don't believe it because, as they tell you, the baby babbles as much as their other children did. What do you tell them? (see response, page 172)

babbling An infant's repetition of certain syllables, such as *ba-ba-ba*, that begins when babies are between 6 and 9 months old.

Show Me Where Pointing is one of the earliest forms of communication, emerging at about 10 months. As you see here, pointing is useful lifelong for humans.

holophrase A single word that is used to express a complete, meaningful thought.

Not only do infants prefer child-directed speech, but they also like alliteration, rhymes, repetition, rhythm, and varied pitch (Hayes & Slater, 2008; Schön et al., 2008). Think of your favorite lullaby (itself an alliterative word); obviously, babies prefer sounds over content.

Babbling

Between 6 and 9 months, babies repeat certain syllables (*ma-ma-ma, da-da-da, ba-ba-ba*), a vocalization called **babbling** because of the way it sounds. Babbling is experience-expectant; all babies babble, even deaf ones. Since babies like to "make interesting sights last," babbling increases in response to child-directed speech. Deaf babies stop babbling but increasingly engage in responsive gesturing.

Toward the end of the first year, babbling begins to sound like the infant's native language; infants imitate accents, cadence, consonants, and so on. Videotapes of deaf infants whose parents sign to them show that 10-month-olds use about a dozen distinct hand gestures in a repetitive manner similar to babbling.

Many caregivers, recognizing the power of gestures, teach "baby signs" to their 6- to 12-month-olds, who communicate with hand signs months before they can master moving their tongues, lips, and jaws to make specific words. There is no evidence that baby signing accelerates talking (as had been claimed), but it does seem to make mothers more responsive, which itself is an advantage (Kirk et al., 2013).

One early gesture is pointing, an advanced social gesture that requires understanding another person's perspective. Most animals cannot interpret pointing; most 10-month-old humans look toward wherever someone else points and can already use a tiny index finger (not just a full hand) to point themselves, even to a place where an object belongs but is not yet there (Liszkowski et al., 2009; Liszkowski & Tomasello, 2011). Pointing is well developed by 12 months, especially when the person who is pointing also speaks (e.g., "look at that") (Daum et al., 2013).

First Words

Finally, at about 1 year, the average baby utters a few words, understood by caregivers if not by strangers. For example, at 13 months, a child named Kyle knew standard words such as *mama,* but he also knew *da, ba, tam, opma,* and *daes,* which his parents knew to be, respectively, "downstairs," "bottle," "tummy," "oatmeal," and "starfish." He also had a special sound that he used to call squirrels (Lewis et al., 1999).

Gradual Beginnings

In the first months of the second year, spoken vocabulary increases gradually (perhaps one new word a week). However, meanings are learned rapidly; babies understand about 10 times more words than they can say. Initially, the first words are merely labels for familiar things (*mama* and *dada* are common), but early words are soon accompanied by gestures, facial expressions, and nuances of tone, loudness, and cadence (Saxton, 2010). Imagine meaningful communication in "Dada," "Dada?" and "Dada!" Each is a **holophrase,** a single word that expresses an entire thought.

Intonation (variation in tone and pitch) is extensive in both babbling and holophrases, but it is temporarily reduced at about 12 months. Apparently, at that point infants reorganize their vocalization from universal to language-specific (Snow, 2006). They are no longer just making noises; they are trying to communicate in a specific language. Uttering meaningful words takes all their attention—none is left over for intonation.

Careful tracing of early language finds other times when vocalization slows before a burst of new talking begins; perception affects action (Pulvermüller & Fadiga, 2010). Thus neurological advances may temporarily inhibit vocalization (Parladé & Iverson, 2011).

The Naming Explosion

Spoken vocabulary builds rapidly once the first 50 words are mastered, with 21-month-olds typically saying twice as many words as 18-month-olds (Adamson & Bakeman, 2006). This language spurt is called the **naming explosion** because many early words are nouns, that is, names of persons, places, or things.

Between 12 and 18 months almost every infant learns the name of each significant caregiver (often *dada, mama, nana, papa, baba, tata*) and sibling (and sometimes each pet). (See Appendix A.) Other frequently uttered words refer to the child's favorite foods (*nana* can mean "banana" as well as "grandma") and to elimination (*pee-pee, wee-wee, poo-poo, ka-ka, doo-doo*).

Notice that all these words have two identical syllables, each a consonant followed by a vowel sound. Many words follow that pattern—not just *baba* but also *bobo, bebe, bubu, bibi*. Other early words are only slightly more complicated—*mame, ama,* and so on. The meaning of such words varies by language, but every baby says such words, and everywhere, culture assigns meaning to them.

Cultural Differences

Cultures and families vary in how much child-directed speech children hear. Some parents read to their infants, teach them signs, and respond to every burp or fart as if it were an attempt to talk. Other parents are much less verbal. They use gestures and touch; they say "hush" and "no" instead of expanding vocabulary.

By 5-months, babies prefer adults who often use child-directed speech, even when those talkative adults are temporarily silent. Apparently, just as infants seek to master motor skills as soon as they can, they seek to learn language from the best teachers available (Schachner & Hannon, 2011). They soon favor the words, accents, and even musical rhythms of their culture (Soley & Hannon, 2010).

naming explosion A sudden increase in an infant's vocabulary, especially in the number of nouns, that begins at about 18 months of age.

Especially for Caregivers A toddler calls two people "Mama." Is this a sign of confusion? (see response, page 173)

Cultural Values If they are typical of most families in the relatively taciturn Otavalo culture of Ecuador, these three children hear significantly less conversation than children elsewhere. In most Western cultures, that might be called neglect, a form of maltreatment. However, each culture encourages the qualities it values, and verbal fluency is not a priority in this community. In fact, people who talk more than listen are ostracized, and those who keep secrets are valued, so encouragement of child talk may be maltreatment in Otavalo.

WOLFGANG KAEHLER/CORBIS

>> Response for Nurses and Pediatricians (from page 170): Urge the parents to learn sign language and investigate cochlear implants. Babbling has a biological basis and begins at a specified time, in deaf as well as in hearing babies. However, deaf babies eventually begin to use gestures more and to vocalize less than hearing babies. If their infant can hear, sign language does no harm. If the child is deaf, however, lack of communication may be devastating.

grammar All the methods—word order, verb forms, and so on—that languages use to communicate meaning, apart from the words themselves.

mean length of utterance (MLU) The average number of words in a typical sentence (called utterance, because children may not talk in complete sentences). MLU is often used to indicate how advanced a child's language development is.

Parts of Speech

Although all new talkers say names, use similar sounds, and prefer nouns more than other parts of speech, the ratio of nouns to verbs and adjectives varies from place to place. For example, by 18 months, the ratio of nouns to verbs is higher in English-speaking infants than Chinese or Korean infants. Why?

One explanation goes back to the language itself. Chinese and Korean are "verb-friendly" in that verbs are placed at the beginning or end of sentences. That facilitates learning. English verbs occur anywhere in a sentence, and their forms change in illogical ways (e.g., *go, gone, will go, went*). This irregularity makes English verbs harder to learn.

An alternative explanation considers the entire social context: Playing with a variety of toys and learning about dozens of objects are routine in North America, whereas East Asian cultures emphasize human interactions—specifically, how one person responds to another. Accordingly, North American infants are expected to name many objects, whereas Asian infants are expected to act on objects (as explained in Chapter 1) and respond to people. Thus, Chinese toddlers might learn the equivalent of *come, play, love, carry, run,* and so on early in life.

A simpler explanation is that young children are sensitive to sounds. Verbs are learned more easily if they sound like the action (Imai et al., 2008), and such verbs are more common in some languages than others.

English does not have many onomatopoeic verbs, which makes verb-learning difficult. (*Jump, kiss,* and *poop*—all learned early on—are exceptions.) When the same word could be a noun or a verb, English-speaking mothers say them differently: kiss, for instance, is emphasized more as a noun than a verb, so babies learn the noun before the verb (Conwell & Morgan, 2012). The infant's focus on sounds explains why many toddlers who have never been on a farm know that cows "moo" and ducks "quack."

Putting Words Together

Grammar includes all the methods that languages use to communicate meaning. Word order, prefixes, suffixes, intonation, verb forms, pronouns and negations, prepositions and articles—all of these are aspects of grammar. Grammar can be discerned in holophrases but it becomes obvious between 18 and 24 months, when babies begin to use two-word combinations (Bremner et al., 2010).

For example, "Baby cry" and "More juice" follow grammatical word order. No child asks, "Juice more," and even toddlers know that "cry baby" is not the same as "baby cry." By age 2, children combine three words. English grammar uses subject–verb–object order; for example, toddlers say "Mommy read book," rather than any of the five other possible sequences of those three words.

Children's grammar correlates with the length of their sentences, which is why in every language **mean length of utterance (MLU)** is considered an accurate way to measure a child's language progress (e.g., Miyata et al., 2013). The child who says "Baby is crying" is advanced in language development compared with the child who says "Baby crying" or simply the holophrase "Baby."

Young children can master two languages, not just one. Children are statisticians: They implicitly track the number of words and phrases and learn those expressed most often, in one, two, or more languages (Johnson & Tyler, 2010). [**Lifespan Link:** Bilingual learning is discussed in detail in Chapter 9.]

Theories of Language Learning

Worldwide, people who are not yet 2 years old already speak their native tongue. They continue to learn rapidly: Some teenagers compose lyrics or deliver orations that move thousands of their co-linguists. How is language learned so easily and so well?

Answers come from three schools of thought, each of which is connected to a theory introduced in Chapter 2: behaviorism, sociocultural theory, and evolutionary psychology. The first theory says that infants are directly taught, the second that social impulses propel infants to communicate, and the third that infants understand language because of brain advances thousands of years ago that allowed survival of our species.

Theory One: Infants Need to Be Taught

The seeds of the first perspective were planted more than 50 years ago, when the dominant theory in North American psychology was behaviorism, or learning theory. The essential idea was that all learning is acquired, step-by-step, through association and reinforcement. Just as Pavlov's dogs learned to associate sound with food, infants may associate objects with words, especially if reinforcement occurs.

B. F. Skinner (1957) noticed that spontaneous babbling is usually reinforced. Typically, every time the baby says "ma-ma-ma-ma," a grinning mother appears, repeating the sound and showering the baby with attention, praise, and perhaps food. The baby learns affordances and repeats "ma-ma-ma-ma" when lonely or hungry; through operant conditioning, talking begins.

Skinner believed that most parents are excellent instructors, responding to their infants' gestures and sounds, thus reinforcing speech (Saxton, 2010). Even in preliterate societies, parents use child-directed speech, responding quickly with high pitch, short sentences, stressed nouns, and simple grammar—exactly the techniques that behaviorists would recommend.

The core ideas of this theory are the following:
- Parents are expert teachers, although other caregivers help.
- Frequent repetition is instructive, especially when linked to daily life.
- Well-taught infants become well-spoken children.

Behaviorists note that some 3-year-olds converse in elaborate sentences; others just barely put one simple word with another. Such variations correlate with the amount of language each child has heard. Parents of the most verbal children teach language throughout infancy—singing, explaining, listening, responding, and reading to their children every day, even before age 1 (Forget-Dubois et al., 2009) (see Figure 6.2).

Theory Two: Social Impulses Foster Infant Language

The second theory is called *social-pragmatic*. It arises from the sociocultural reason for language: communication. According to this perspective, infants communicate because humans are social beings, dependent on one another for

>> Response for Caregivers
(from page 171): Not at all. Toddlers hear several people called "Mama" (their own mother, their grandmothers, their cousins' and friends' mothers) and experience mothering from several people, so it is not surprising if they use "Mama" too broadly. They will eventually narrow the label down to one person.

Especially for Educators An infant day-care center has a new child whose parents speak a language other than the one the teachers speak. Should the teachers learn basic words in the new language, or should they expect the baby to learn the majority language? (see response, page 175)

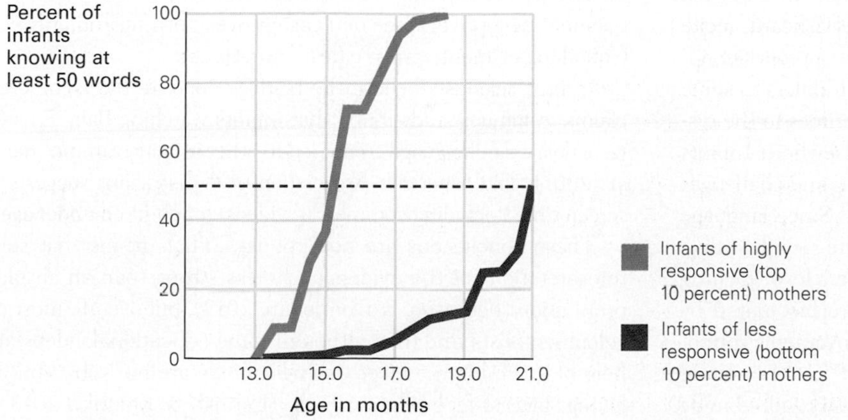

Percent of infants knowing at least 50 words

Age in months

Infants of highly responsive (top 10 percent) mothers

Infants of less responsive (bottom 10 percent) mothers

Source: Adapted from Tamis-LeMonda et al., 2001, p. 761.

FIGURE 6.2

Maternal Responsiveness and Infants' Language Acquisition Learning the first 50 words is a milestone in early language acquisition, as it predicts the arrival of the naming explosion and the multiword sentence a few weeks later. Researchers found that the 9-month-old infants of highly responsive mothers (top 10 percent) reached this milestone as early as 15 months. The infants of nonresponsive mothers (bottom 10 percent) lagged significantly behind.

survival and joy. Each culture has practices that further social interaction; talking is one of those practices. Thus, all infants (and no chimpanzees) master words and grammar to join the social world in which they find themselves (Tomasello & Herrmann, 2010).

According to this perspective, it is the emotional messages of speech, not the words, that propel communication. In one study, people who had never heard English (Shuar hunter-gatherers living in isolation near the Andes Mountains) listened to tapes of North American mothers talking to their babies. The Shuar successfully distinguished speech conveying comfort, approval, attention, and prohibition, without knowing any of the words (Bryant & Barrett, 2007). This study suggests that the social content of speech is universal, and since babies are social creatures, they learn whatever specifics their culture provides.

Evidence for social learning comes from educational programs for children. Many 1-year-olds enjoy watching television and videos, but they learn from it only when adults are actively involved in teaching (see Opposing Perspectives: Language and Video, below). In a controlled experiment, 1-year-olds learned vocabulary much better when someone taught them directly than when the same person gave the same lesson on video (Roseberry et al., 2009).

Same Situation, Far Apart: Before Words The Polish babies learning sign language (*top*) and the New York infant interpreting a smile (*bottom*) are all doing what babies do: trying to understand communication long before they are able to talk.

OPPOSING PERSPECTIVES

Language and Video

Toddlers can learn to swim in the ocean, throw a ball into a basket, walk on a narrow path beside a precipice, use an iPad, cut with a sharp knife, play a guitar, say a word on a flashcard, recite a poem, utter a curse and much else—if provided appropriate opportunity, encouragement, and practice. Indeed, toddlers in some parts of the world do each of these things—sometimes to the dismay, disapproval, and even shock of adults from elsewhere. Infants do what others do, a trait that fosters rapid learning and challenges caregivers, who try to keep "little scientists" safe. Since language learning is crucial, many parents hope to accelerate such learning.

Commercial companies recognize that toddlers love learning and that parents are eager to teach. Infants are fascinated by dynamic activity, especially when it includes movement, sound, and people. This explains the popularity of child-directed videos—"like crack for babies," as one mother said (quoted in de Loache et al., 2010, p. 1572). Such products are named to appeal to parents, such as *Baby Einstein, Brainy Baby,* and *Mozart for*

Mommies and Daddies—Jumpstart your Newborn's I.Q., and are advertised with testimonials. Scientists consider such an advertisement deceptive, since one case proves nothing and only controlled experiments prove cause and effect.

In fact, scientists believe the truth is opposite the commercial claims. A famous study found that infants watching Baby Einstein were delayed in language compared to other infants (Zimmerman et al., 2007). The American Association of Pediatricians suggests no screen time (including commercial videos) for children under age 2.

These conclusions are not "robust." That means that some interpretations of the evidence are less strong than an absolute prohibition (Ferguson, & Donnellan, 2013), but overall, most developmentalists find that, although some educational videos may help older children, videos during infancy are no "substitute for loving, face-to-face relationships" (Lemish & Kolunki, 2013, p. 335). The crucial factor for intellectual growth seems to be caregiver responsiveness to the individual child (Richert et al., 2011).

One product, *My Baby Can Read,* was pulled off the market in 2012 because experts repeatedly attacked its claims, and the cost of defending lawsuits was too high (Ryan, 2012). But many such products are still sold, and new ones appear continually. The owners of Baby Einstein lost a lawsuit in 2009, promised not to claim it was educational, and offered a refund, yet, as one critic notes:

> The bottom line is that this industry exists to capitalize on the national preoccupation with creating intelligent children as early as

possible, and it has become a multi-million dollar enterprise. Even after . . . the Baby Einstein Company itself admitted its products are not educational, Baby Einstein products continue to fly off of the shelves.

> *[Ryan, 2012, p. 784]*

This seems to be a battle between child experts and business leaders, with parents on both sides and infants caught in the middle. Which side are you on? More importantly, why?

Theory Three: Infants Teach Themselves

A third theory holds that language learning is genetically programmed to begin at a certain age; adults need not teach it, nor is it a by-product of social interaction (theories one and two). It arises from the universal human impulse to imitate. As already explained in the research on memory, infants and toddlers observe what they see and they apply it—not slavishly but according to their own concepts and intentions, which develop as the brain matures. Theory three proposes that this is exactly what they do with the language they hear (Saxton, 2010).

This perspective began soon after Skinner proposed his theory of verbal learning. Noam Chomsky (1968, 1980) and his followers felt that language is too complex to be mastered merely through step-by-step conditioning. Although behaviorists focus on variations among children in vocabulary size, Chomsky focused on similarities in language acquisition—the universals, not the differences.

Noting that all young children master basic grammar according to a schedule, Chomsky cited this *universal grammar* as evidence that humans are born with a mental structure that prepares them to seek some elements of human language. For example, everywhere a raised tone indicates a question.

Chomsky labeled this hypothesized mental structure the **language acquisition device (LAD).** The LAD enables children, as their brains develop, to derive the rules of grammar quickly and effectively from the speech they hear every day, regardless of whether their native language is English, Thai, or Urdu.

Other scholars agree with Chomsky that all infants seek to use their minds to understand and speak whatever language they hear. They are eager learners, and language may be considered one more aspect of neurological maturation (Wagner & Lakusta, 2009). This idea does not strip languages and cultures of their differences in sounds, grammar, and almost everything else, but the basic idea is that "language is a window on human nature, exposing deep and universal features of our thoughts and feelings" (Pinker, 2007, p. 148).

The various languages of the world are all logical, coherent, and systematic. Infants are primed to grasp the particular language they are exposed to, making caregiver speech "not a 'trigger' but a 'nutrient'" (Slobin, 2001, p. 438). There is no need for a trigger, according to theory three, because words are expected by the developing brain, which quickly and efficiently connects neurons to support whichever language the infant hears. Thus, language itself is experience-expectant, although obviously the specific words are experience-dependent.

A Hybrid Theory

Which of these three perspectives is correct? Perhaps all of them. In one monograph that included details and results of 12 experiments, the authors presented a hybrid (which literally means "a new creature, formed by combining other living things") of previous theories (Hollich et al., 2000). Since infants learn language to do numerous things—to indicate intention, call objects by name, put words together, talk to family members, sing to themselves, express their wishes, remember the

>> **Response for Educators** (from page 173): Probably both. Infants love to communicate, and they seek every possible way to do so. Therefore, the teachers should try to understand the baby and the baby's parents, but they should also start teaching the baby the majority language of the school.

Especially for Nurses and Pediatricians Bob and Joan have been reading about language development in children. They are convinced that because language develops naturally, they need not talk to their 6-month-old son. How do you respond? (see response, page 176)

language acquisition device (LAD) Chomsky's term for a hypothesized mental structure that enables humans to learn language, including the basic aspects of grammar, vocabulary, and intonation.

>> Response for Nurses and Pediatricians (from page 175): Although humans may be naturally inclined to communicate with words, exposure to language is necessary. You may not convince Bob and Joan, but at least convince them that their baby will be happier if they talk to him.

past, and much more—some aspects of language learning may be best explained by one theory at one age and other aspects by another theory at another age.

Although originally developed to explain acquisition of first words, mostly nouns, this theory also explains learning verbs: Perceptual, social, and linguistic abilities combine to make that possible (Golinkoff & Hirsh-Pasek, 2008). Linguists seek to understand how most children acquire more than one language; it seems that many strategies help (Canagarajah & Wurr, 2011).

After intensive study, yet another group of scientists also endorsed a hybrid theory, concluding that "multiple attentional, social and linguistic cues" contribute to early language (Tsao et al., 2004, p. 1081). It makes logical and practical sense for nature to provide several paths toward language learning and for various theorists to emphasize one or another of them (Sebastián-Gallés, 2007).

It also seems that some children learn better one way, and others, another way (Goodman et al., 2008). Parents need to talk often to their infants (theory one), encourage social interaction (theory two), and appreciate the innate abilities of the child (theory three).

As one expert concludes:

> In the current view, our best hope for unraveling some of the mysteries of language acquisition rests with approaches that incorporate multiple factors, that is, with approaches that incorporate not only some explicit linguistic model, but also the full range of biological, cultural, and psycholinguistic processes involved.
>
> *[Tomasello, 2006, pp. 292–293]*

The idea that every theory is correct in some way seems idealistic. However, scientists working on extending and interpreting research on language acquisition arrived at a similar conclusion. They contend that language learning is neither the direct product of repeated input (behaviorism) nor the result of a specific human neurological capacity (LAD). Rather, from an evolutionary perspective, "different elements of the language apparatus may have evolved in different ways," and thus a "piecemeal and empirical" approach is needed (Marcus & Rabagliati, 2009, p. 281). In other words, no single theory can explain how babies learn language: Humans accomplish this feat in many ways.

What conclusion can we draw from research on infant cognition? That infants are active learners of language and concepts, that they seek to experiment with objects and find ways to achieve their goals. This is the cognitive version of the biosocial developments noted in Chapter 5, that babies strive to roll over, crawl, walk, and so on as soon as they can. (See Visualizing Development, p. 177.)

Now back to Uncle Henry: My cousins loved their mother because she knew instinctively that her babies wanted to learn. When they grew up they realized, as developmentalists recognize, that caregivers in the first weeks of life—fathers as well as mothers—can be the first, and perhaps the best, teachers.

SUMMING UP

From the first days of life, babies attend to words and expressions, responding as well as their limited abilities allow—crying, cooing, and soon babbling. Before age 1, they understand simple words and communicate with gestures. At 1 year, most infants speak. Vocabulary accumulates slowly at first, but then more rapidly with the naming explosion and with the emergence of the holophrase and the two-word sentence.

The impressive language learning of the first two years can be explained in many ways: that caregivers must teach language, that infants learn because they are social beings, that inborn cognitive capacity propels infants to acquire language as soon as maturation makes that possible. Because infants vary in culture, learning style, and social context, a hybrid theory contends that each theory may be valid for explaining some aspects of language learning at different ages.

▪

Early Communication and Language Development

A COMMUNICATION MILESTONES: THE FIRST TWO YEARS

Months	Communication Milestone
0	Reflexive communication—cries, movements, facial expressions
1	Recognizes some sounds Makes several different cries and sounds Turns toward familiar sounds
3	A range of meaningful noises—cooing, fussing, crying, laughing. Social smile well established Laughter begins Imitates movements Enjoys interaction with others
6	New sounds, including squeals, growls, croons, trills, vowel sounds Meaningful gestures including showing excitement (waving arms and legs) Deaf babies express their first signs Recognizes and reacts to own name Expresses negative feelings (with face and arms) Capable of distinguishing emotion by tone of voice Responds to noises by making sounds Uses noise to express joy and unhappiness Babbles, including both consonant and vowel sounds repeated in syllables
10	Makes simple gestures, like raising arms for "pick me up" Recognizes pointing Makes a sound (not in recognizable language) to indicate a particular thing Responds to simple requests
12	Attends to speech More gestures, such as shaking head for "no" Babbles with inflection Names familiar people (like "mama", "dada", "nana") Uses exclamations, such as "oh-oh!" Tries to imitate words Points and responds to pointing First spoken words that are recognizably part of the native language
18	Combines 2 words (like "Daddy bye-bye") Slow growth of vocabulary, up to about 50 words Language use focuses on 10-30 holophrases Uses nouns and verbs Uses movement, including running and throwing, to indicate emotion Naming explosion may begin; three or more words learned per day Much variation: Some toddlers do not yet speak
24	Combines 3 or 4 words together. Half the toddler's utterances are two or more words long. Uses adjectives and adverbs ("blue", "big", "gentle") Sings simple songs

SOURCE: AMERICAN ACADEMY OF PEDIATRICS

SOURCES & CREDITS LISTED ON P. SC-1

B UNIVERSAL FIRST WORDS

Across cultures, babies' first words are remarkably similar. The words for mother and father are recognizable in almost any language. Most children will learn to name their immediate family and caregivers between the ages of 12 and 18 months.

Language	Mother	Father
English	mama, mommy	dada. daddy
Spanish	mama	papa
French	maman, mama	papa
Italian	mamma	bebbo, papa
Latvian	mama	te-te
Syrian Arabic	mama	babe
Bantu	be-mama	taata
Swahili	mama	baba
Sanskit	nana	tata
Hebrew	ema	abba
Korean	oma	apa

PHOTO: R. EKO BINTORO/ISTOCK/THINKSTOCK

C MASTERING LANGUAGE

Childrens' use of language becomes more complex as they acquire more words and begin to master grammar and usage. A child's utterances, or utterances, are broken down into the smallest units of language to determine their length and complexity:

SAMPLES OF UTTERANCES

"Doggie!" = **1**

"Doggie + Sleep = **2**

"Doggie + Sleep + ing" = **3**

"Shh! + Doggie + Sleep + ing" = **4**

"Shh! + Doggie + is + Sleep + ing" = **5**

"Shh! + The + Doggie + is + Sleep + ing = **6**

simple ← → complex

SOURCE: COURTESY OF MONICA KALFUR, SLP

SUMMARY

Sensorimotor Intelligence

1. Piaget realized that very young infants are active learners who seek to understand their complex observations and experiences. The six stages of sensorimotor intelligence involve early adaptation to experience.

2. Sensorimotor intelligence begins with reflexes and ends with mental combinations. The six stages occur in pairs, with each pair characterized by a circular reaction; infants first react to their own bodies (primary), then respond to other people and things (secondary), and finally, in the stage of tertiary circular reactions, infants become more goal-oriented, creative, and experimental as "little scientists."

3. Infants gradually develop an understanding of objects. As shown in Piaget's classic experiments, infants understand object permanence and begin to search for hidden objects at about 8 months. Newer research, using brain scans and other new methods, finds that Piaget underestimated infant cognition, including his conclusions about when infants understand object permanence and when they defer imitation.

Information Processing

4. Another approach to understanding infant cognition involves information-processing theory, which looks at each step of the thinking process, from input to output. The perceptions of a young infant are attuned to the particular affordances, or opportunities for action, that are present in the infant's world.

5. Objects, creatures and especially people that move are particularly interesting to infants, because they afford many possibilities for interaction and perception. Early affordances are evidence of early cognition.

6. Infant memory is fragile but not completely absent. Reminder sessions help trigger memories, and young brains learn motor sequences and respond to repeated emotions (their own and those of other people) long before they can remember with words. Memory is multifaceted; explicit memories are rare in infancy.

Language: What Develops in the First Two Years?

7. Language learning, which distinguishes the human species from other animals, may be the most impressive cognitive accomplishment of infants. The universal sequence of early language development is well known; there are alternative explanations for how early language is learned.

8. Eager attempts to communicate are apparent in the first weeks and months. Infants babble at about 6 months, understand words and gestures by 10 months, and speak their first words at about 1 year. Deaf infants make their first signs before a year.

9. Vocabulary builds slowly until the infant knows approximately 50 words. Then the naming explosion begins. Toward the end of the second year, toddlers put words together in short sentences. The tone of holophrases is evidence of grammar, but putting two or three words together in the proper sequence is proof.

10. Various theories explain how infants learn language as quickly as they do. The three main theories emphasize different aspects of early language learning: that infants must be taught, that their social impulses foster language learning, and that their brains are genetically attuned to language as soon as the requisite maturation has occurred.

11. Each theory of language learning is confirmed by some research. The challenge for developmental scientists has been to formulate a hybrid theory that uses all the insights and research on early language learning. The challenge for caregivers is to respond to the infant's early attempts to communicate, expecting neither too much nor too little.

KEY TERMS

affordance (p. 163)
babbling (p. 170)
child-directed speech (p. 169)
deferred imitation (p. 159)
explicit memory (p. 167)
fMRI (p. 161)
grammar (p. 172)

habituation (p. 160)
holophrase (p. 170)
implicit memory (p. 167)
language acquisition device (LAD) (p. 175)
"little scientist" (p. 159)

mean length of utterance (MLU) (p. 172)
mirror neurons (p. 162)
naming explosion (p. 171)
object permanence (p. 158)
primary circular reactions (p. 156)
reminder session (p. 166)

secondary circular reactions (p. 157)
sensorimotor intelligence (p. 156)
tertiary circular reactions (p. 159)
visual cliff (p. 164)

WHAT HAVE YOU LEARNED?

1. Why did Piaget call his first stage of cognition *sensorimotor* intelligence?

2. How do the first two sensorimotor stages illustrate primary circular reactions?

3. How is object permanence an example of stage four of sensorimotor intelligence?

4. What is the difference between stages five and six in sensorimotor intelligence?

5. What steps of the scientific method does the "little scientist" follow?

6. What caused Piaget to underestimate how rapidly early cognition occurs?

7. Explain how the affordances of this book differ to a baby at age 1 month, 12 months, and 20 years?

8. What hypotheses have been offered to explain why infants refuse to crawl over visual cliffs?

9. What strategies help 3-month-old babies to remember something?

10. What is the crucial difference between implicit and explicit memory?

11. Why is explicit memory difficult for babies under age 2?

12. What communication abilities do infants have at 6 months?

13. What aspects of early language development are universal, apparent in babies of every culture and family?

14. What is typical kind of the first words that infants speak?

15. What have developmentalists discovered about the way adults talk to babies?

16. What are the early signs of grammar in infant speech?

17. According to behaviorism, how do adults teach infants to talk?

18. According to sociocultural theory, why do infants try to communicate?

19. What is Chomsky's theory about how young children learn language?

20. What does the idea that language development results from brain maturation imply for caregivers?

21. How does the hybrid theory of language development compare to the eclectic approach to developmental study described in Chapter 2?

APPLICATIONS

1. Elicit vocalizations from an infant—babbling if the baby is under age 1, words if the baby is older. Write down all the baby's communication for 10 minutes. Then ask the primary caregiver to elicit vocalizations for 10 minutes, and write these down. What differences are apparent between the baby's two attempts at communication? Compare your findings with the norms described in the chapter.

2. Piaget's definition of intelligence is adaptation. Others consider a good memory or an extensive vocabulary to be a sign of intelligence. How would you define intelligence? Give examples.

3. Many educators recommend that parents read to babies every day, even before one year of age. What theory of language development does this reflect and why? Ask several parents if they did so, and why or why not.

4. Test an infant's ability to search for a hidden object. Ideally, the infant should be about 7 or 8 months old, and you should retest over a period of weeks. If the infant can immediately find the object, make the task harder by pausing between hiding and searching or by moving the object from one hiding place to another.

>>ONLINE CONNECTIONS

To accompany your textbook, you have access to a number of online resources, including Learning Curve, an adaptive quizzing program, critical thinking questions, and case studies. For access to any of these links, go to www.worthpublishers.com/launchpad/bergerls9e. In addition to these resources, you'll also find links to video clips, personalized study advice, and an ebook. Some of the videos and activities available online include:

■ *Language Development in Infancy.* How easy is it to understand a newborn's coos? Or a 6-month old's babbling? But we can almost all make out the voice of a toddler singing "Twinkle, Twinkle." Video clips from a variety of real-life contexts bring to life the development of children's language.

WORTH PUBLISHERS

The First Two Years: Psychosocial Development

■ Emotional Development
Early Emotions
Toddlers' Emotions

■ Brain and Emotions
Growth of the Brain
Temperament

■ The Development of Social Bonds
Synchrony
Attachment
Insecure Attachment and the Social Setting
Social Referencing
Fathers as Social Partners

■ Theories of Infant Psychosocial Development
Psychoanalytic Theory
Behaviorism
OPPOSING PERSPECTIVES: Proximal and Distal Parenting
Cognitive Theory
Humanism
Evolutionary Theory
Infant Day Care

WHAT WILL YOU LEARN?

1. How do smiles, tears, anger, and fear change from birth to age 2?
2. Does a baby's temperament predict lifelong personality?
3. What are the signs of a healthy parent–infant relationship?
4. Do human cultures differ in their understanding of infant emotions and caregiving practices?

My 1-week-old grandson cried. Often. Again and again. Day and night. For a long time. Again. He and his parents stayed with me for a few months. I was not the caregiver, so I didn't mind the crying for myself. But I did mind for my sleep-deprived daughter.

And I worried about her husband. He spent many hours, day and night, carrying my grandson while my daughter slept.

"It seems to me that you do most of the baby-comforting," I told him.

"That's because Elissa does most of the breast-feeding," he answered with a smile.

This chapter opens by tracing infants' emotions as their brains mature and their experiences accumulate, and it notes temperamental and cultural differences. All babies cry early on, but soon their emotions take many forms. This discussion leads to an exploration of caregiver–infant interaction, particularly *synchrony, attachment,* and *social referencing.* For every aspect of caregiving, fathers as well as mothers are included.

COURTESY OF KATHLEEN BERGER

Then we apply each of the five theories introduced in Chapter 2 not only to understand infant emotions but also to a controversial topic: Who should be the caregiver? As this chapter explains, although temperaments and caregivers vary, most infants (including my now-happy grandson) thrive, as long as their basic physical and emotional needs are met.

Now Happy Asa How does a crying baby become a happy toddler? A clue is here: devoted father and grandfather.

>> Emotional Development

In their first two years, infants progress from reactive pain and pleasure to complex patterns of social awareness (see At About This Time) (Lewis, 2010). This is a period of "high emotional responsiveness" (Izard et al., 2002, p. 767),

AT ABOUT THIS TIME

Developing Emotions

Birth	Distress; contentment
6 weeks	Social smile
3 months	Laughter; curiosity
4 months	Full, responsive smiles
4–8 months	Anger
9–14 months	Fear of social events (strangers, separation from caregiver)
12 months	Fear of unexpected sights and sounds
18 months	Self-awareness; pride; shame; embarrassment

As always, culture and experience influence the norms of development. This is especially true for emotional development after the first eight months.

social smile A smile evoked by a human face, normally first evident in infants about 6 weeks after birth.

Smiles All Around Joy is universal when an infant smiles at her beaming grandparents—a smile made even better when the tongue joins in. This particular scene took place in Kazakhstan in central Asia, an independent nation only since 1991.

cortisol The primary stress hormone; fluctuations in the body's cortisol level affect human emotion.

expressed in speedy, uncensored reactions—crying, startling, laughing, raging—and, by toddlerhood, in complex responses, from self-satisfied grins to mournful pouts.

Early Emotions

At first there is pleasure and pain. Newborns are happy and relaxed when fed and drifting off to sleep. They cry when they are hurt or hungry, tired or frightened (as by a loud noise or a sudden loss of support). Some infants have bouts of uncontrollable crying, called *colic*—probably the result of immature digestion. About 20 percent of babies cry "excessively," defined as more than three hours a day, for more than three days a week, for more than three weeks (J. S. Kim, 2011).

Smiling and Laughing

Soon, additional emotions become recognizable (Lavelli & Fogel, 2005). Curiosity is evident as infants (and people of all ages) respond to objects and experiences that are new but not too novel. Happiness is expressed by the **social smile**, evoked by a human face at about 6 weeks. Preterm babies smile a few weeks later because the social smile is affected by age since conception.

Infants worldwide express social joy, even laughter, between 2 and 4 months (Konner, 2007; Lewis, 2011). Laughter builds as curiosity does; a typical 6-month-old laughs loudly upon discovering new things, particularly social experiences that have the right balance between familiarity and surprise, such as Daddy making a funny face. They prefer looking at happy faces over sad ones, even if the happy faces are not looking at them (Kim et al., 2013).

Anger and Sadness

The positive emotions of joy and contentment are soon joined by negative emotions, which are expressed more often in infancy than later on (Izard, 2009). Anger is evident at 6 months, usually triggered by frustration, such as when infants are prevented from moving or grabbing. It is usually easy to see when an infant is angry.

To learn how infants responded to frustration, researchers "crouched behind the child and gently restrained his or her arms for 2 minutes or until 20 seconds of hard crying ensued" (Mills-Koonce et al., 2011, p. 390). "Hard crying" is not infrequent: Infants hate to be strapped in, caged in, closed in, or even just held in place when they want to explore.

In infancy, anger is a healthy response to frustration, unlike sadness, which also appears in the first months. Sadness indicates withdrawal and is accompanied by an increase in the body's production of **cortisol**, the primary stress hormone.

This conclusion comes from experiments in which 4-month-olds were taught to pull a string to see a picture, which they enjoyed—not unlike the leg-kicking study to move the mobile, described in Chapter 6. Then the string was disconnected. Most babies reacted by angrily jerking the string. Some, however, quit trying and looked sad (Lewis & Ramsay, 2005); as a consequence, their cortisol increased. This suggests that anger relieves stress but that some babies learn, to their sorrow, to repress their anger.

Since sadness produces physiological stress (measured by cortisol levels), sorrow negatively impacts the infant. All social emotions, particularly sadness and fear, probably shape the brain (Fries & Pollak, 2007; M. H. Johnson, 2011). As you learned in Chapter 5, experience matters. Too much sadness early in life correlates with depression in later years.

Fear

Fear in response to some person, thing, or situation (not just being startled in surprise) is evident at about 9 months and soon becomes more frequent and obvious (Witherington et al., 2004). Two kinds of social fear are typical:

Separation anxiety—clinging and crying when a familiar caregiver is about to leave

Stranger wariness—fear of unfamiliar people, especially when they move too close, too quickly

Separation anxiety is normal at age 1, intensifies by age 2, and usually subsides after that. Fear of separation interferes with infant sleep. For example, infants who fall asleep next to familiar people may wake up terrified if they are alone (Sadeh et al., 2010). Some babies become accustomed to a "transitional object," such as a teddy bear or blanket that comforts them as they transition from sleeping in their parents' arms to sleeping alone.

Transitional objects are not pathological; they are the infant's way of coping with anxiety. However, if separation anxiety remains strong after age 3 and impairs the child's ability to leave home, go to school, or play with friends, it is considered an emotional disorder. Separation anxiety as a disorder can be diagnosed up to age 18 (DSM-5, 2013), although some clinicians find it can appear in adulthood as well (Bögels et al., 2013).

Strangers—especially those who do not resemble or move like familiar caregivers—merit stares, not smiles, at age 1. This is a good sign: Infant memory is active and engaged.

Many 1-year-olds fear not only strangers but also anything unexpected, from the flush of the toilet to the pop of a jack-in-the-box, from closing elevator doors to the tail-wagging approach of a dog. With repeated experience and reassurance, older infants might enjoy flushing the toilet (again and again) or calling the dog (and might cry if the dog does *not* come).

Every aspect of early emotional development interacts with cultural beliefs, expressed in parental actions. There seems to be more separation anxiety and stranger wariness in Japan than in Germany because Japanese infants "have very few experiences with separation from the mother," whereas in German towns, "infants are frequently left alone outside of stores or supermarkets" while their mothers shop (Saarni et al., 2006, p. 237).

Toddlers' Emotions

Emotions take on new strength during toddlerhood (Izard, 2009). For example, throughout the second year and beyond, anger and fear become less frequent but more focused, targeted toward infuriating or terrifying experiences. Similarly, laughing and crying are louder and more discriminating.

The new strength of emotions is apparent in temper tantrums. Toddlers are famous for fury. When something angers them they might yell, scream, cry, hit, and throw themselves on the floor. Logic is beyond them; if adults respond with anger or teasing, that makes it worse. Soon sadness comes to the fore, and then comfort (not acquiescence or punishment) is helpful (Green et al., 2011).

separation anxiety An infant's distress when a familiar caregiver leaves; most obvious between 9 and 14 months.

stranger wariness An infant's expression of concern—a quiet stare while clinging to a familiar person, or a look of fear—when a stranger appears.

Developmentally Correct Both Santa's smile and Olivia's grimace are appropriate reactions for people of their age. Adults playing Santa must smile no matter what, and if Olivia smiled that would be troubling to anyone who knows about 7-month-olds. But why did someone scare this infant by putting her in the grip of an oddly dressed, bearded stranger?

Especially for Nurses and Pediatricians Parents come to you concerned that their 1-year-old hides her face and holds onto them tightly whenever a stranger appears. What do you tell them? (see response, page 184)

>> **Response for Nurses and Pediatricians** (from page 183): Stranger wariness is normal up to about 14 months. This baby's behavior actually might indicate secure attachment!

self-awareness A person's realization that he or she is a distinct individual whose body, mind, and actions are separate from those of other people.

STEPHEN CHIANG/GETTY IMAGES

Glad to Meet You She enjoys meeting another baby, even if that baby is herself in the mirror. Later, at about 18 months, she will realize that the mirror image is herself.

Social Awareness

Temper can be seen as an expression of selfhood. So can new toddler emotions: pride, shame, embarrassment, disgust, and guilt (Stevenson et al., 2010; Thompson, 2006). These emotions require social awareness, which emerges from family interactions, shaped by the culture (Mesquita & Leu, 2007).

For example, many North American parents encourage toddler pride (saying, "You did it yourself"—even when that is untrue), but Asian families typically discourage pride. Instead, they cultivate modesty and shame (Rogoff, 2003). Such differences may still be apparent in adult personality and judgment, as some criticize people who brag but others criticize those who are too self-deprecating.

Disgust is also strongly influenced by other people and age. According to a study that involved many children of various ages, many 18-month-olds (but not younger infants) express disgust at touching a dead animal. None, however, are yet disgusted when a teenager curses at an elderly person—something that parents and older children often find disgusting (Stevenson et al., 2010).

Self-Awareness

In addition to social awareness, another foundation for emotional growth is **self-awareness**, the realization that one's body, mind, and activities are distinct from those of other people (Kopp, 2011). Closely following the new mobility that results from walking is an emerging sense of "me" and "mine" that leads the infant to develop a new consciousness of others at about age 1.

Very young infants have no sense of self—at least of *self* as most people define it, but self-awareness grows during toddlerhood with

> self-referential emotions . . . By the end of the second year [age 1] and increasingly in the third [age 2], the simple joy of success becomes accompanied by looking and smiling to an adult and calling attention to the feat; the simple sadness of failure becomes accompanied either by avoidance of eye contact with the adult and turning away or by reparative activity and confession.
>
> *[Thompson, 2006, p. 79]*

In a classic experiment (Lewis & Brooks, 1978), 9- to 24-month-olds looked into a mirror after a dot of rouge had been surreptitiously put on their noses. If they reacted by touching the red dot on their noses, that meant they knew the mirror showed their own faces. None of the babies younger than 12 months did that, although they sometimes smiled and touched the dot on the "other" baby in the mirror.

However, between 15 and 24 months, babies became self-aware, touching their noses with curiosity and puzzlement. Self-recognition in the mirror/rouge test (and in photographs) usually emerges at about 18 months, along with two other advances: pretending and using first-person pronouns (I, *me, mine, myself, my*) (Lewis, 2010).

SUMMING UP

A newborn's emotions are distress and contentment, expressed by crying or looking relaxed. The social smile is evident at about 6 weeks. Soon curiosity, laughter, anger (when infants are kept from something they want), and fear (when something unexpected occurs) appear, becoming evident in the latter half of the first year. Toddlers become aware of themselves, and that allows them to experience and express many emotions that indicate awareness of themselves and other people's reactions to them. Throughout infancy, cultural expectations and parental actions shape emotions. ■

>> Brain and Emotions

Brain maturation is involved in the emotional developments just described because all emotional reactions begin in the brain (Johnson, 2010). Experience promotes specific connections between neurons and emotions.

Links between expressed emotions and brain growth are complex and thus difficult to assess and describe (Lewis, 2011). Compared with the emotions of adults, discrete emotions during early infancy are murky and unpredictable. For instance, an infant's cry can be triggered by pain, fear, tiredness, surprise, or excitement; laughter can quickly turn to tears.

Furthermore, infant emotions may erupt, increase, or disappear for unknown reasons (Camras & Shutter, 2010). The growth of synapses and dendrites is a likely explanation, the result of past experiences and ongoing maturation.

Growth of the Brain

Many specific aspects of brain development support social emotions (Lloyd-Fox et al., 2009). For instance, the social smile and laughter appear as the cortex matures (Konner, 2010). The same is probably true for fear, self-awareness, and anger. The maturation of a particular part of the cortex (the anterior cingulate gyrus) is directly connected to emotional self-regulation, allowing a child to express or hide feelings (Posner et al., 2007).

Cultural differences become encoded in the infant brain, called "a cultural sponge" by one group of scientists (Ambady & Bharucha, 2009, p. 342). It is difficult to measure how infant brains are molded by their context. However, one study (Zhu et al., 2007) of adults—half born in the United States and half in China—found that a particular area of the brain (the medial prefrontal cortex) was activated when the adults judged whether certain adjectives applied to them. However, only in the Chinese was that area also activated when they were asked whether those adjectives applied to their mothers.

Researchers consider this finding to be "neuroimaging evidence that culture shapes the functional anatomy of self-representation" (Zhu et al., 2007, p. 1310). They speculate that brain activation occurs because the Chinese participants learned, as babies, that they are closely aligned with their mothers, whereas the Americans learned to be independent. (A related cultural difference is explored in the Opposing Perspectives feature about proximal and distal parenting later in this chapter.)

Learning About Others

The tentative social smile the infant gives to every face soon becomes a quicker and fuller smile when he or she sees a familiar, loving caregiver. This occurs because, with repeated experience, the neurons that fire together become more closely and quickly connected to each other (via dendrites and neurotransmitters).

Social preferences form in the early months and are connected not only with an individual's face, but also with the person's voice, touch, and smell. This is one reason adopted children are placed with their new parents in the first days of life whenever possible (a marked change from 100 years ago, when adoptions began after age 1).

Social awareness is also a reason to respect an infant's reaction to a babysitter: If a 6-month-old screams and clings to the parent when the sitter arrives, another caregiver probably needs to be found. (Do not confuse this reaction with separation anxiety at 12 months—a normal, expected reaction.)

Every experience that a person has—especially in the early days and months—activates and prunes neurons, such that the firing patterns from one axon to another dendrite reflect past learning. As illustrated in Visualizing Development in Chapter 5, p. 131, this was first shown dramatically with baby mice: Some were licked and nuzzled by their mothers almost constantly, and some were neglected. A mother mouse's licking of her newborn babies reduced methylation of a gene (Nr3c1), which allowed more serotonin (a neurotransmitter) to be released by the hypothalamus (a region of the brain discussed in Chapter 8).

Serotonin not only increased momentary pleasure (mice love being licked) but also started a chain of epigenetic responses to reduce stress hormones from many parts of the brain and body, including the adrenal glands. The effects on both brain and behavior are lifelong for mice and probably for humans as well.

For many humans, social anxiety is stronger than any other anxieties. Certainly to some extent this is genetic, but as epigenetic research finds, parenting behavior is a factor as well.

If the infant of an anxious biological mother is raised by a responsive but not anxious adoptive mother, the inherited anxiety does not materialize (Natsuaki et al., 2013). Parents need to be comforting (as with the nuzzled baby mice) but not overprotective. Fearful mothers tend to raise fearful children, but fathers who offer their infants exciting but not dangerous challenges (such as a game of chase, crawling on the floor) reduce later anxiety (Majdandži et al., 2013).

Stress

Emotions are connected to brain activity and hormones, but the connections are complicated; they are affected by genes, past experiences, and additional hormones and neurotransmitters not yet understood (Lewis, 2011). One link is clear: Excessive stress (which increases cortisol) harms the developing brain (Adam et al., 2007). The hypothalamus (discussed further in Chapter 8), in particular, grows more slowly if an infant is often frightened.

Brain scans of children who were maltreated in infancy show abnormal responses to stress, anger, and other emotions—and even to photographs of frightened people (Gordis et al., 2008; Masten et al., 2008). Some children seem resilient, but it is also evident that brains are affected by abuse, especially if the maltreatment begins in infancy (Cicchetti, 2013).

The likelihood that early caregiving affects the brain lifelong leads to obvious applications (Belsky & de Haan, 2011). Since infants learn emotional responses, caregivers need to be consistent and reassuring. This is not always easy—remember that some infants cry inconsolably in the early weeks. As one researcher notes:

> An infant's crying has 2 possible consequences: It may elicit tenderness and desire to soothe, or helplessness and rage. It can be a signal that encourages attachment or one that jeopardizes the early relationship by triggering depression and, in some cases, even neglect or abuse.

> *[J. S. Kim, 2011, p. 229]*

Sometimes mothers are blamed, or blame themselves, when an infant cries. This attitude is not helpful: A mother who feels guilty or incompetent may become angry at her baby, which leads to unresponsive parenting, an unhappy child, and then hostile interactions. Years later, first-grade classmates and teachers are likely to consider such children disruptive and aggressive (Lorber & Egeland, 2011).

But the opposite may occur if early crying produces solicitous parenting. Then, when the baby outgrows the crying, the parent–child bond may be exceptionally strong.

Hush Now Babies cry and parents soothe them the world over, while contexts shape both crying and soothing. The little girl (left) will probably quiet soon, as she is held snuggly next to her father's body. The boy (right) is less likely to settle down, as he is surrounded by strangers in a Ukrainian contest to see which baby can crawl fastest.

Temperament

Temperament is defined as the "biologically based core of individual differences in style of approach and response to the environment that is stable across time and situations" (van den Akker et al., 2010, p. 485). "Biologically based" means that these traits originate with nature, not nurture. Confirmation that temperament arises from the inborn brain comes from an analysis of the tone, duration, and intensity of infant cries after the first inoculation, before much experience outside the womb. Cry variations at this very early stage correlate with later temperament (Jong et al., 2010).

Temperament is not the same as personality, although temperamental inclinations may lead to personality differences. Generally, personality traits (e.g., honesty and humility) are learned, whereas temperamental traits (e.g., shyness and aggression) are genetic. Of course, for every trait, nature and nurture interact.

In laboratory studies of temperament, infants are exposed to events that are frightening or attractive. Four-month-olds might see spinning mobiles or hear unusual sounds. Older babies might confront a noisy, moving robot or a clown who quickly moves close to them. During such experiences, some children laugh, some cry, others are quiet, and still others exhibit some combination of these reactions that might be signs of one of four types of babies: easy (40%), difficult (10%), slow-to-warm-up (15%), and hard-to-classify (35%).

These categories originate from the *New York Longitudinal Study* (NYLS). Begun in the 1960s, the NYLS was the first large study to recognize that each newborn has distinct inborn traits (Thomas & Chess, 1977). According to the NYLS, by 3 months, infants manifest nine traits that cluster into the four categories just listed.

Although the NYLS began a rich research endeavor, its nine dimensions have not held up in later studies (Caspi & Shiner, 2006; Zentner & Bates, 2008). Generally, only three (not nine) dimensions of temperament are found (Else-Quest et al., 2006; van den Akker et al., 2010; Degnan et al., 2011). The following three dimensions of temperament are apparent:

> Effortful control (able to regulate attention and emotion, to self-soothe)
> Negative mood (fearful, angry, unhappy)
> Exuberant (active, social, not shy)

Each of these dimensions is associated with distinctive brain patterns as well as behavior, and each affects later personality. [**Lifespan Link:** Personality is discussed in Chapter 22.]

temperament Inborn differences between one person and another in emotions, activity, and self-regulation. It is measured by the person's typical responses to the environment.

Especially for Nurses Parents come to you with their fussy 3-month-old. They say they have read that temperament is "fixed" before birth, and they are worried that their child will always be difficult. What do you tell them? (see response, page 188)

>> **Response for Nurses** (from page 187):
It's too soon to tell. Temperament is not truly "fixed" but variable, especially in the first few months. Many "difficult" infants become happy, successful adolescents and adults, if their parents are responsive.

Since these temperamental traits are thought to be inborn, some developmentalists seek to discover which alleles affect specific emotions (M. H. Johnson & Fearon, 2011). For example, researchers have found that the 7-repeat allele of the DRD4 VNTR gene, when combined with the 5-HTTLPR genotype, results in 6-month-olds who are difficult—they cry often, are hard to distract, and are slow to laugh (Holmboe et al., 2011). You need not remember the letters of these alleles, but remember that infant emotions vary, partly for genetic reasons.

One longitudinal study analyzed temperament in the same children at 4, 9, 14, 24, and 48 months; again in middle childhood; and again at adolescence. The scientists designed laboratory experiments with specifics appropriate for the age of the children; collected detailed reports from the mothers and later from the participants themselves; and gathered observational data and physiological evidence, including brain scans. Each time, past data was reevaluated, and cross-sectional and international studies were considered (Fox et al., 2001, 2005, 2013; Hane et al., 2008; L. R. Williams et al., 2010).

Half of the participants did not change much over time, reacting the same way and having similar brain-wave patterns when confronted with frightening experiences. Curiously, the participants most likely to change from infancy to age 4 were the inhibited, fearful ones. Least likely to change were the exuberant babies (see Figure 7.1). Apparently, adults coax frightened infants to be brave but encourage exuberant children to stay happy.

The researchers found unexpected gender differences. As teenagers, the formerly inhibited boys were more likely than the average adolescent to use drugs, but the inhibited girls were less likely to do so (L. R. Williams et al., 2010). The most likely explanation is cultural: Shy boys seek to become less anxious by using drugs, but shy girls are more accepted as they are.

Continuity and change were also found in another study that described temperament using three traits (expressive, typical, and fearful). Again, typical infants stayed typical, but fearful infants were most likely to change. Only about one-third (5 percent overall) who earlier had been fearful still seemed afraid at age 3 (van den Akker et al., 2010). Parental attitudes and actions influenced these changes.

Other studies confirm that difficult infants often become easier—*if* their parents provide excellent, patient care (Belsky & Pluess, 2009). How could this be? Some scientists suggest that, since fussy and scared children often come to the parents for comfort or reassurance, they are particularly likely to flourish with responsive parenting but they wither if their parents are rejecting (Stupica et al., 2011). This is differential sensitivity again. **[Lifespan Link:** Differential sensitivity is discussed in Chapter 1.]

Here is one very specific example. Researchers selected 32 difficult newborns (they cried quickly and loudly when an examiner tested their reflexes) and 52 somewhat difficult ones. The quality of their caregiving and bonding was measured (via attachment, soon described) at age 1. These 84 infants were assessed at 18 and 24 months on their ability to explore new objects and respond to strangers—two skills that promote learning in toddlerhood.

Highly irritable infants who received responsive parenting (secure attachment) were *more* social,

FIGURE 7.1

Do Babies' Temperaments Change?
Sometimes—especially if they were fearful babies. Adults who are reassuring help children overcome fearfulness. If fearful children do not change, it is not known whether that's because their parents are not sufficiently reassuring (nurture) or because the babies themselves are temperamentally more fearful (nature).

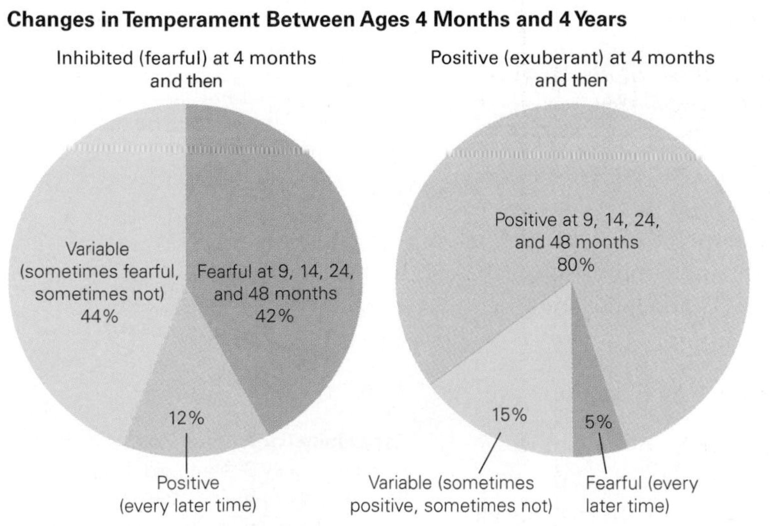

Changes in Temperament Between Ages 4 Months and 4 Years

Inhibited (fearful) at 4 months and then

- Variable (sometimes fearful, sometimes not) 44%
- Fearful at 9, 14, 24, and 48 months 42%
- Positive (every later time) 12%

Positive (exuberant) at 4 months and then

- Positive at 9, 14, 24, and 48 months 80%
- Variable (sometimes positive, sometimes not) 15%
- Fearful (every later time) 5%

Source: Adapted from Fox et al., 2001.

and no less adept at exploration, than the other toddlers. By contrast, all the infants with less good care (insecure attachment) were markedly less social and less skilled than average at exploring. Impairment was especially strong for the ones who were very irritable newborns (Stupica et al., 2011).

The two patterns evident in all these studies—continuity and improvement—have been replicated in many longitudinal studies of infant temperament, especially for antisocial personality traits. Difficult babies tend to become difficult children, but family and culture sometimes mitigate negative outcomes (Kagan et al., 2007; Zentner & Bates, 2008).

SUMMING UP

Brain maturation underlies much of emotional development in the first two years. The circumstances of an infant's life affect emotions and sculpt the brain, with long-lasting effects. Early maltreatment can be particularly devastating to later emotional expression. Some babies are more difficult, which can begin a cascade of hostile relationships or can eventually increase the mutual responsiveness of caregiver and child.

Temperament is inborn, with some babies much easier and others more difficult, some more social and others more shy. Such differences are partly genetic and therefore lifelong, but caregiver responses channel temperament into useful or destructive traits.

>> The Development of Social Bonds

As you see, the social context has a powerful impact on development. So does the infant's age, via brain maturation. With regard to emotional development, the age of the baby determines specific social interactions that lead to growth—first synchrony, then attachment, and finally social referencing (see Visualizing Development, p. 191).

Synchrony

Early parent–child interactions are described as **synchrony**, a mutual exchange that requires split-second timing. Synchrony is evident in the first three months, becoming more frequent and elaborate as the infant matures (Feldman, 2007).

synchrony A coordinated, rapid, and smooth exchange of responses between a caregiver and an infant.

Both Partners Active

Detailed research reveals the symbiosis of adult–infant partnerships. Adults rarely smile at young infants until the infants smile at them, several weeks after birth. That tentative baby smile is like a switch that turns on the adults, who usually grin broadly and talk animatedly (Lavelli & Fogel, 2005).

Synchrony is evident not only in direct observation, as when watching a caregiver play with an infant too young to talk, but also via computer measurement of the millisecond timing of smiles, arched eyebrows, and so on (Messinger et al., 2010). Synchrony is a powerful learning experience for the new human. In every episode, infants read others' emotions and develop social skills, such as taking turns and watching expressions.

One study found that mothers who took longer to bathe, feed, and diaper their infants were also most responsive. Apparently, some parents combine

Tell Me More Synchrony lets infants and caregivers communicate the crucial messages that one person seeks to share with another. Is the message here "I love you" or "How delightful!" or simply "Tell me more"? The father probably knows; we can only guess.

still-face technique An experimental practice in which an adult keeps his or her face unmoving and expressionless in face-to-face interaction with an infant.

caregiving with emotional play, which takes longer but also allows more synchrony.

Synchrony usually begins with adults imitating infants (not vice versa) (Lavelli & Fogel, 2005), with tone and rhythm (Van Puyvelde et al., 2010). Metaphors for synchrony are often musical—a waltz, a jazz duet—to emphasize that each partner must be attuned to the other.

Adults respond to nuances of infant facial expressions and body motions. This helps infants connect their internal state with behaviors that are understood within their culture. Synchrony is particularly apparent in Asian cultures, perhaps because of a cultural focus on interpersonal sensitivity (Morelli & Rothbaum, 2007).

In Western cultures as well, parents and infants become partners. This relationship is crucial when the infant is at medical risk. The need for time-consuming physical care might overwhelm concern about psychosocial needs, yet those needs are as important for long-term health as are the more obvious needs (Newnham et al., 2009).

Neglected Synchrony

Is synchrony necessary? If no one plays with an infant, what will happen? Experiments involving the **still-face technique** have addressed these questions (Tronick, 1989; Tronick & Weinberg, 1997).

In still-face studies, an infant faces an adult who responds normally while two video cameras simultaneously record their interpersonal reactions. Frame-by-frame analysis reveals that parents instinctively synchronize their responses to the infants' movements, with exaggerated tone and expression. Babies reciprocate with smiles and flailing limbs.

To be specific, long before they can reach out and grab, infants respond excitedly to caregiver attention by waving their arms. They are delighted if the adult moves closer so that a waving arm touches the face or, even better, a hand grabs hair. You read about this eagerness for interaction (when infants try to "make interesting sights last") in Chapter 6. In response, adults open their eyes wide, raise their eyebrows, smack their lips, and emit nonsense sounds.

In still-face experiments, on cue the adult erases all facial expression, staring quietly with a "still face" for a minute or two. Sometimes by 2 months, and clearly by 6 months, infants are upset when their parents are unresponsive. Babies frown, fuss, drool, look away, kick, cry, or suck their fingers. By 5 months, they also vocalize, as if to say, "React to me" (Goldstein et al., 2009).

Many studies reach the same conclusion: Synchrony is expected. Responsiveness aids psychosocial and biological development, evident in heart rate, weight gain, and brain maturation (Moore & Calkins, 2004; Newnham et al., 2009). Particularly in the first year, babies of depressed mothers suffer unless someone else is a sensitive partner (Bagner et al., 2010).

Attachment

Toward the end of the first year, face-to-face synchrony almost disappears. Once infants can walk, they are no longer content to respond, moment by moment, to adult facial expressions and vocalizations.

Instead **attachment** becomes evident. Actually, attachment is lifelong, beginning before birth and influencing relationships throughout life (see At About This Time). Thousands of researchers on every continent have studied attachment;

attachment According to Ainsworth, "an affectional tie" that an infant forms with a caregiver—a tie that binds them together in space and endures over time.

Developing Attachment

Attachment begins at birth and can influences relationships throughout the life span. But maturation, context, and past experience also play a role. Much depends not only on the ways in which parents and babies bond, but also on the qual-ity and consistency of caregiving, the safety and security of the home environment, and individual and family experi-ence. While the patterns set in infancy may echo in later life, they are not determinative.

1 EARLY ATTACHMENT

clinging, crying, hitting

extreme separation distress and anxiety experienced

NO

Is the caregiver near, affectionate, responsive?

YES

child is relaxed, playing

creative play, smiling, social

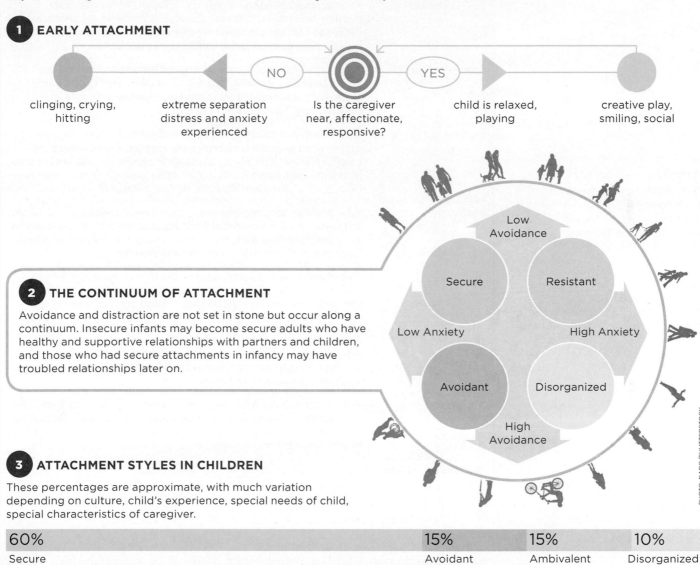

Low Avoidance

Secure

Resistant

Low Anxiety

High Anxiety

Avoidant

Disorganized

High Avoidance

PHOTO: DARQ/SHUTTERSTOCK

2 THE CONTINUUM OF ATTACHMENT

Avoidance and distraction are not set in stone but occur along a continuum. Insecure infants may become secure adults who have healthy and supportive relationships with partners and children, and those who had secure attachments in infancy may have troubled relationships later on.

3 ATTACHMENT STYLES IN CHILDREN

These percentages are approximate, with much variation depending on culture, child's experience, special needs of child, special characteristics of caregiver.

60%	15%	15%	10%
Secure	Avoidant	Ambivalent	Disorganized

4 ATTACHMENT THROUGH THE LIFESPAN

Attachment patterns formed in the first two years continue to influence personality and behaviors throughout the life span, although later experiences also play a role.

Compounding factors include social and physical environment, physical and mental health, family structures and dynamics, and the quality and consistency of care during childhood.

		As Children	As Adults
Securely Attached [Type B]		Able to separate from caregiver but prefers caregiver to strangers	Tends to have good relationships and good self-esteem
Insecurely Attached	**Avoidant [Type A]**	Avoids connection with caregiver	May be anxious, fearful, clingy or depressed
	Resistant/Ambivalent [Type C]	Is anxious and uncertain when separated from caregiver	May be dismissive, loners, angry; relationships can be stormy.
	Disorganized [Type D]	Is unhappy, angry, may cry, may cling	May display erratic, abusive, and/or pathological behaviors

SOURCES & CREDITS LISTED ON P. SC-1

AT ABOUT THIS TIME

Stages of Attachment

Birth to 6 weeks	*Preattachment.* Newborns signal, via crying and body movements, that they need others. When people respond positively, the newborn is comforted and learns to seek more interaction. Newborns are also primed by brain patterns to recognize familiar voices and faces.
6 weeks to 8 months	*Attachment in the making.* Infants respond preferentially to familiar people by smiling, laughing, babbling. Their caregivers' voices, touch, expressions, and gestures are comforting, often overriding the infant's impulse to cry. Trust (Erikson) develops.
8 months to 2 years	*Classic secure attachment.* Infants greet the primary caregiver, play happily when he or she is present, show separation anxiety when the caregiver leaves. Both infant and caregiver seek to be close to each other (proximity) and frequently look at each other (contact). In many caregiver–infant pairs, physical touch (patting, holding, caressing) is frequent.
2 to 6 years	*Attachment as launching pad.* Young children seek their caregiver's praise and reassurance as their social world expands. Interactive conversations and games (hide-and-seek, object play, reading, pretending) are common. Children expect caregivers to comfort and entertain.
6 to 12 years	*Mutual attachment.* Children seek to make their caregivers proud by learning whatever adults want them to learn, and adults reciprocate. In concrete operational thought (Piaget), specific accomplishments are valued by adults and children.
12 to 18 years	*New attachment figures.* Teenagers explore and make friendships independent from parents, using their working models of earlier attachments as a base. With formal operational thinking (Piaget), shared ideals and goals become influential.
18 years on	*Attachment revisited.* Adults develop relationships with others, especially relationships with romantic partners and their own children, influenced by earlier attachment patterns. Past insecure attachments from childhood can be repaired rather than repeated, although this does not always happen.

Source: Adapted from Grobman, 2008.

all of these studies were inspired first by John Bowlby's theories and then by Mary Ainsworth, who described mother–infant relationships in central Africa 60 years ago (Ainsworth, 1967).

Signs of Attachment

Infants show their attachment through *proximity-seeking* (such as approaching and following their caregivers) and through *contact-maintaining* (such as touching, snuggling, and holding). Proximity-seeking is evident when a baby cries if the mother closes the door when she goes to the bathroom or if a back-facing car seat prevents the baby from seeing the parent.

To maintain contact in the car and to reassure the baby, some caregivers in the front seat reach back to give a hand, or install a mirror so they can see the baby and the baby can see them as they drive. As in this example, maintaining contact need not be physical: Visual or verbal connections are often sufficient.

Caregivers also are attached. They keep a watchful eye on their baby, and they initiate interactions with expressions, gestures, and sounds. Before going to sleep at midnight they might tiptoe to the crib to gaze at their sleeping infant, or, in daytime, absentmindedly smooth their toddler's hair.

Attachment is universal, being part of the inborn social nature of the human species, but specific manifestations vary depending on the culture as well as the age of the people who are attached to each other. For instance, Ugandan mothers never kiss their infants, but they often massage them, contrary to Westerners, who rarely massage except when they are putting on lotion.

American adults might remain in contact via daily phone calls, e-mails, or texts and keep in proximity by sitting in the same room as each reads quietly, whereas in other cultures adults often hold hands with each other. Some scholars believe that attachment with infants, not only of mothers but also of fathers, grandparents, and nonrelatives, is the reason that *Homo sapiens* thrived when other species became extinct (Hrdy, 2009).

Secure and Insecure Attachment

Attachment is classified into four types: A, B, C, and D (see Table 7.1). Infants with **secure attachment** (type B) feel comfortable and confident. The caregiver is a *base for exploration*, providing assurance and enabling discovery. A toddler might, for example, scramble down from the caregiver's lap to play with an intriguing toy but periodically look back and vocalize (contact-maintaining) or bring the toy to the caregiver for inspection (proximity-seeking).

By contrast, insecure attachment (types A and C) is characterized by fear, anxiety, anger, or indifference. Some insecure children play independently without maintaining contact; this is **insecure-avoidant attachment** (type A). The opposite reaction is **insecure-resistant/ambivalent attachment** (type C). Children with this type of attachment cling to caregiver and are angry at being left.

Ainsworth's original schema differentiated only types A, B, and C. Later researchers discovered a fourth category (type D), **disorganized attachment**. Type D infants may shift suddenly from hitting to kissing their mothers, from staring blankly to crying hysterically, from pinching themselves to freezing in place.

Among the general population, almost two-thirds of infants are secure (type B). Their mothers' presence gives them courage to explore; her departure causes distress; her return elicits positive social contact (such as smiling or hugging) and then more playing. The infant's balanced reaction—being concerned but not overwhelmed by comings and goings—indicates security. Early research was only

secure attachment A relationship in which an infant obtains both comfort and confidence from the presence of his or her caregiver.

insecure-avoidant attachment A pattern of attachment in which an infant avoids connection with the caregiver, as when the infant seems not to care about the caregiver's presence, departure, or return.

insecure-resistant/ambivalent attachment A pattern of attachment in which an infant's anxiety and uncertainty are evident, as when the infant becomes very upset at separation from the caregiver and both resists and seeks contact on reunion.

disorganized attachment A type of attachment that is marked by an infant's inconsistent reactions to the caregiver's departure and return.

TABLE 7.1	Patterns of Infant Attachment				
Type	Name of Pattern	In Play Room	Mother Leaves	Mother Returns	Toddlers in Category (%)
A	Insecure-avoidant	Child plays happily.	Child continues playing.	Child ignores her.	10–20
B	Secure	Child plays happily.	Child pauses, is not as happy.	Child welcomes her, returns to play.	50–70
C	Insecure-resistant/ ambivalent	Child clings, is preoccupied with mother.	Child is unhappy, may stop playing.	Child is angry; may cry, hit mother, cling.	10–20
D	Disorganized	Child is cautious.	Child may stare or yell; looks scared, confused.	Child acts oddly— may scream, hit self, throw things.	5–10

on mothers; later, fathers and other caregivers were included, since they also could have secure or insecure attachments to an infant.

About one-third of infants are insecure, either indifferent (type A) or unduly anxious (type C). About 5 to 10 percent of infants fit into none of these categories; they are disorganized (type D), with no consistent strategy for social interaction, even avoidance or resistance. Sometimes they become hostile and aggressive, difficult for anyone to relate to (Lyons-Ruth et al., 1999). Unlike the first three types, disorganized infants have elevated levels of cortisol in reaction to stress (Bernard & Dozier, 2010).

Measuring Attachment

Strange Situation A laboratory procedure for measuring attachment by evoking infants' reactions to the stress of various adults' comings and goings in an unfamiliar playroom.

Ainsworth (1973) developed a now-classic laboratory procedure called the **Strange Situation** to measure attachment. In a well-equipped playroom, an infant is observed for eight episodes, each lasting three minutes. First, the child and mother are together. Next, according to a set sequence, the mother and then a stranger come and go. Infants' responses to their mother indicate which type of attachment they have formed.

Researchers are trained to distinguish types A, B, C, and D. They focus on the following:

> *Exploration of the toys.* A secure toddler plays happily.
> *Reaction to the caregiver's departure.* A secure toddler notices when the caregiver leaves and shows some sign of missing him or her.
> *Reaction to the caregiver's return.* A secure toddler welcomes the caregiver's reappearance, usually seeking contact, and then plays again.

Attachment is not always measured via the Strange Situation; surveys and interviews are also used. Sometimes parents answer 90 questions about their children's characteristics, and sometimes adults are interviewed extensively (according to a detailed protocol) about their relationships with their own parents, again with various specific measurements (Fortuna & Roisman, 2008).

Research measuring attachment has revealed that some behaviors that might seem normal are, in fact, a sign of insecurity. For instance, an infant who clings to the caregiver and refuses to explore the toys might be type A. Likewise, adults who say their childhood was happy and their mother was a saint, especially if they provide few specific memories, might be insecure. And young children who

Excited, Troubled, Comforted This sequence is repeated daily for 1-year-olds, which is why the same sequence is replicated to measure attachment. As you see, toys are no substitute for mother's comfort if the infant or toddler is secure, as this one seems to be. Some, however, cry inconsolably or throw toys angrily when left alone.

are immediately friendly to strangers may never have formed a secure attachment (Tarullo et al., 2011).

Assessments of attachment that were developed and validated for middle-class North Americans may be less useful in other cultures. Infants who seem dismissive or clingy may not always be insecure. Everywhere, however, parents and infants are attached to each other, and everywhere secure attachment predicts academic success and emotional stability (Erdman & Ng, 2010; Molitor & Hsu, 2011; Rothbaum et al., 2011).

Insecure Attachment and the Social Setting

At first, developmentalists expected secure attachment to "predict all the outcomes reasonably expected from a well-functioning personality" (R. A. Thompson & Raikes, 2003, p. 708). But this expectation turned out to be naive.

Harsh contexts, especially the stresses of poverty, reduce the incidence of secure attachment (Seifer et al., 2004; van IJzendoorn & Bakermans-Kranenburg, 2010), and insecure attachment correlates with many later problems. However, correlation is not causation, and thus insecure attachment may be a sign but may not be the direct cause of those problems.

Securely attached infants *are* more likely to become secure toddlers, socially competent preschoolers, high-achieving schoolchildren, and capable parents. Attachment affects early brain development, one reason these later outcomes occur (Diamond & Fagundes, 2010). But insecure infants are not doomed to failure later on.

Although attachment patterns form in infancy (see Table 7.2), they are not necessarily set in stone; they may change when the family context changes, such as abuse or income loss. Many aspects of low SES increase the risk of low school achievement, hostile children, and fearful adults. The underlying premise—that responsive early parenting leads to secure attachment, which buffers stress and encourages exploration—is at least partly true, but attachment behaviors in the Strange Situation provide only one indication of the quality of the parent–child relationship.

TABLE 7.2	Predictors of Attachment Type

Secure attachment (type B) is more likely if:

- The parent is usually sensitive and responsive to the infant's needs.
- The infant–parent relationship is high in synchrony.
- The infant's temperament is "easy."
- The parents are not stressed about income, other children, or their marriage.
- The parents have a working model of secure attachment to their own parents.

Insecure attachment is more likely if:

- The parent mistreats the child. (Neglect increases type A; abuse increases types C and D.)
- The mother is mentally ill. (Paranoia increases type D; depression increases type C.)
- The parents are highly stressed about income, other children, or their marriage. (Parental stress increases types A and D.)
- The parents are intrusive and controlling. (Parental domination increases type A.)
- The parents are active alcoholics. (Alcoholic father increases type A; alcoholic mother increases type D.)
- The child's temperament is "difficult." (Difficult children tend to be type C.)
- The child's temperament is "slow to warm up." (This correlates with type A.)

Insights from Romania

No scholar doubts that close human relationships should develop in the first year of life and that the lack of such relationships risks dire consequences. Unfortunately, thousands of children born in Romania are proof.

When Romanian dictator Nicolae Ceausescu forbade birth control and abortions in the 1980s, illegal abortions became the leading cause of death for Romanian women aged 15 to 45 (Verona, 2003), and more than 100,000 children were abandoned to crowded, impersonal, state-run orphanages. The children experienced severe deprivation, including virtually no normal interaction, play, or conversation (Rutter et al., 2007).

In the two years after Ceausescu was ousted and killed in 1989, thousands of those children were adopted by North American, western European, and Australian families. Those who were adopted before 6 months of age fared best; synchrony was established via play and caregiving. Most of them developed normally.

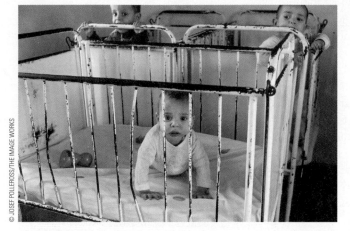

For those adopted after 6 months, and especially after 12 months, early signs were encouraging: Skinny infants gained weight and grew faster than other 1-year-olds, developing motor skills they had lacked (H. Park et al., 2011). However, their early social deprivation soon became evident in their emotions and cognition. Many were overly friendly to strangers throughout childhood, a sign of insecure attachment (Tarullo et al., 2011). At age 11, their average IQ was only 85, 15 points below normal (Rutter et al., 2010).

These children are now young adults, many with serious emotional or conduct problems. The cause is more social than biological. Even those who were well nourished, or who caught up to normal growth, often became impulsive and angry teenagers. Apparently, the stresses of adolescence and emerging adulthood have exacerbated the cognitive and social strains on these young people and their families (Merz & McCall, 2011).

Romanian infants are no longer available for international adoption, even though some remain abandoned. Research confirms that early emotional deprivation, not genes or nutrition, is their greatest problem. Romanian infants develop best in their own families, second best in foster families, and worst in institutions (Nelson et al., 2007). As best we know, this applies to infants everywhere: Families usually care for their babies better than strangers who are paid to care for many infants at once.

Fortunately, institutions have improved or been shuttered; more recent adoptees are not as impaired as those Romanian orphans (Merz & McCall, 2011). However, some infants in every nation are deprived of healthy interaction. The early months are a sensitive period for emotional development. Children need responsive parents, biological or not (McCall et al., 2011).

Danger Ongoing Look closely and you can see danger. That bent crib bar could strangle an infant, and that chipped paint could contain lead. (Lead tastes sweet; is that why two of the children are biting it?) Fortunately, these three Romanian infants (photographed in 1990) escaped those dangers to be raised in loving adoptive homes. Unfortunately, the damage of social isolation (note the sheet around the crib) could not be completely overcome: Some young adults who spent their first year in an institution like this still carry emotional scars.

Preventing Problems

All infants need love and stimulation; all seek synchrony and then attachment—secure if possible, insecure if not. Without some adult support, infants become disorganized and adrift, emotionally troubled. Extreme early social deprivation is difficult to overcome.

Since synchrony and attachment develop over the first year, and since more than one-third of all parents have difficulty establishing secure attachments, many developmentalists have sought to discover what particularly impairs these parents and what can be done to improve their parenting. We know that secure attachment is more difficult to achieve when the parents were abused as children, when families are socially isolated, when mothers are young adolescents, or when infants are unusually difficult (Zeanah et al., 2011). If biological parents do not care for their newborns, foster or adoptive parents need to be found quickly so that synchrony and attachment can develop (McCall et al., 2011).

Some birth parents, fearing that they cannot provide responsive parenting, choose adoptive parents for their newborns. If high-risk birth parents believe they can provide good care, early support may prevent later problems. Success has been reported when skilled professionals come to the home to nurture relationships between infant and caregiver (Lowell et al., 2011). If a professional helps parents in the first days after birth, perhaps by using the Brazelton Neonatal Behavioral Assessment Scale (mentioned in Chapter 4) to encourage bonding, then problems need never start (e.g., Nugent et al., 2009).

Social Referencing

Social referencing refers to seeking emotional responses or information from other people, much as a student might consult a dictionary or other reference work. Someone's reassuring glance or cautionary words; a facial expression of alarm, pleasure, or dismay—those are social references.

After age 1, when infants can walk and are "little scientists," their need to consult others becomes urgent. Social referencing is constant, as toddlers search for clues in gazes, faces, and body position, paying close attention to emotions and intentions. They focus on their familiar caregivers, but they also use relatives, other children, and even strangers to help them assess objects and events. They are remarkably selective: Even at 16 months, they notice which strangers are reliable references and which are not (Poulin-Dubois & Chow, 2009).

Social referencing has many practical applications. Consider mealtime. Caregivers the world over smack their lips, pretend to taste, and say "yum-yum," encouraging toddlers to eat their first beets, liver, or spinach. For their part, toddlers become astute at reading expressions, insisting on the foods that the adults *really* like.

Through this process, some children may develop a taste for raw fish or curried goat or smelly cheese—foods that children in other cultures refuse. Similarly, toddlers use social cues to understand the difference between real and pretend eating (Nishida & Lillard, 2007), as well as to understand which toys, emotions, and activities are encouraged or forbidden.

social referencing Seeking information about how to react to an unfamiliar or ambiguous object or event by observing someone else's expressions and reactions. That other person becomes a social reference.

Rotini Pasta? Look again. Every family teaches their children to relish delicacies that other people avoid. Examples are bacon (not in Arab nations), hamburgers (not in India), and, as shown here, a witchetty grub. This Australian aboriginal boy is about to swallow an insect larva.

Fathers as Social Partners

Fathers enhance their children's social and emotional development in many ways (Lamb, 2010). Synchrony, attachment, and social referencing are sometimes more apparent with fathers than with mothers. This notion was doubted until research found that some infants are securely attached to their fathers but not to their mothers (Bretherton, 2010). Furthermore, fathers elicit more smiles and laughter from their infants than mothers do, probably because they play more exciting games, while mothers do more caregiving and comforting (Fletcher et al., 2013).

Close father–infant relationships can teach infants (especially boys) appropriate expressions of emotion (Boyce et al., 2006), particularly anger. The results may endure: Teenagers are less likely to lash out at friends and authorities if, as infants, they experienced a warm, responsive relationship with their father

Same Situation, Far Apart: Bonded That fathers enjoy their sons is not surprising, but notice the infants' hands—one clutching Dad's hair tightly and the other reaching for Dad's face. At this age, infants show their trust in adults by grabbing and reaching. Synchrony and attachment are mutual, in Ireland *(left)*, Kenya *(right)*, and in your own neighborhood.

(Hoeve et al., 2011). Close relationships with infants help the men, too, reducing a man's risk of depression (Borke et al., 2007; Bronte-Tinkew et al., 2007).

In most cultures and ethnic groups, fathers spend much less time with infants than mothers do (Parke & Buriel, 2006; Tudge, 2008). National cultures and parental attitudes are influential: Some women are gatekeepers, believing that child care is their special domain (Gaertner et al., 2007) and excluding fathers (perhaps indirectly, saying, "You're not holding her right"). Some fathers think it unmanly to dote on an infant.

That is not equally true everywhere. For example, Denmark has high rates of father involvement. At birth, 97 percent of Danish fathers are present, and five months later, most Danish fathers say that *every day* they change diapers (83 percent), feed (61 percent), and play with (98 percent) their infants (Munck, 2009).

Less rigid sex roles seem to be developing in every nation. One U.S. example of historical change is the number of married women with children under age 6 who are employed. In 1970, 30 percent of married mothers of young children earned paychecks; in 2012, 60 percent did, almost all in dual-earner families (U.S. Department of Labor Statistics, 2013). These statistics include many mothers of infants.

Note the reference to "married" mothers: About half the mothers of infants in the United States are not married, and their employment rates are higher than their married counterparts. As detailed later in this chapter, often fathers—not necessarily married—care for infants when mothers are at the job.

One sex difference seems to persist: "Mothers engage in more caregiving and comforting, and fathers in more high intensity play" (Kochanska et al., 2008, p. 41). When asked to play with their baby, mothers typically caress, read, sing, or play traditional games such as peek-a-boo. Fathers are more exciting: They move their infant's limbs in imitation of walking, kicking, or climbing, or they swing the baby through the air, sideways, or even upside down.

Mothers might say, "Don't drop him"; fathers and babies laugh with joy. In this way, fathers tend to help children become less fearful. Over the past 20 years, father–infant research has tried to answer three questions:

1. Can men provide the same care as women?
2. Is father–infant interaction different from mother–infant interaction?
3. How do fathers and mothers cooperate to provide infant care?

Many studies over the past two decades have answered yes to the first two questions. A baby fed, bathed, and diapered by Dad is just as happy and clean as when Mom does it. Gender differences are sometimes found in specifics, but they are not harmful.

On the third question, the answer depends on the family (Bretherton, 2010). Usually, mothers are caregivers and fathers are playmates, but not always. Each couple, given their circumstances (which might include being immigrant, low-income, or same-sex), finds their own way to complement each other to help their infant thrive (Lamb, 2010).

A constructive parental alliance cannot be assumed, whether or not the parents are legally wed. Sometimes neither parent is happy with their infant, with themselves, or with each other. One study reported that 7 percent of fathers of 1-year-olds were depressed, and they were four times as likely to spank as were nondepressed fathers (40 percent versus 10 percent) (Davis et al., 2011) (see Figure 7.2).

Family members affect each other's moods: Paternal depression correlates with maternal depression and with sad, angry, and disobedient toddlers. Cause and consequence are intertwined. When any one is depressed or hostile, everyone (mother, father, baby) needs help.

SUMMING UP

Caregivers and young infants engage in split-second interaction, which is evidence of synchrony. Still-face research has found that infants depend on such responsiveness. Attachment between people is universal; it is apparent in infancy with contact-maintaining and proximity-seeking behaviors as 1-year-olds explore their world. Such early patterns may persist lifelong. Toddlers use other people as social references, to guide them in their exploration. Fathers are as capable as mothers in social partnerships with infants, although they may favor physical, creative play more than mothers do. Every family member affects all the others; ideally, they cooperate to create a caregivers' alliance to support every baby's development. ■

>> Theories of Infant Psychosocial Development

Consider again the theories discussed in Chapter 2. As you will see, theories lead to insight and applications that are relevant for the final topic of this chapter, infant day care.

Psychoanalytic Theory

Psychoanalytic theory connects biosocial and psychosocial development. Sigmund Freud and Erik Erikson each described two distinct stages of early development, one in the first year and one beginning in the second.

Freud: Oral and Anal Stages

According to Freud (1935, 1940/1964) the first year of life is the *oral stage,* so named because the mouth is the young infant's primary source of gratification. In the second year, with the *anal stage,* pleasure comes from the anus—particularly from the sensual satisfaction of bowel movements and, eventually, the psychological pleasure of controlling them.

Freud believed that the oral and anal stages are fraught with potential conflicts. If a mother frustrates her infant's urge to suck—weaning too early or too late, for example, or preventing the baby from sucking a thumb or a pacifier—that may

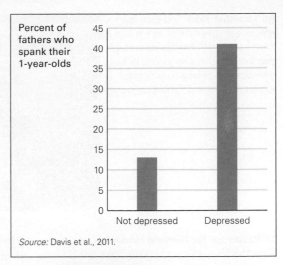

FIGURE 7.2

Shame on Who? Not on the toddlers, who are naturally curious and careless, but maybe not on the fathers either. Both depression and spanking are affected by financial stress, marital conflict, and cultural norms; who is responsible for those?

Especially for Nursing Mothers You have heard that if you wean your child too early he or she will overeat or become an alcoholic. Is it true? (see response, page 200)

All Together Now Toddlers in an employees' day-care program at a flower farm in Colombia learn to use the potty on a schedule. Will this experience lead to later personality problems? Probably not.

>> **Response for Nursing Mothers** (from page 199): Freud thought so, but there is no experimental evidence that weaning, even when ill-timed, has such dire long-term effects.

trust versus mistrust Erikson's first crisis of psychosocial development. Infants learn basic trust if the world is a secure place where their basic needs (for food, comfort, attention, and so on) are met.

autonomy versus shame and doubt Erikson's second crisis of psychosocial development. Toddlers either succeed or fail in gaining a sense of self-rule over their actions and their bodies.

later lead to an *oral fixation*. Such a person is stuck (fixated) at the oral stage, and therefore, as an adult, he or she eats, drinks, chews, bites, or talks excessively, still seeking the mouth-related pleasures of infancy.

Similarly, if toilet training is overly strict or if it begins before the infant is mature enough, then the toddler's refusal—or inability—to comply will clash with the wishes of the adult, who denies the infant normal anal pleasures. That may lead to an anal personality—an adult who seeks self-control, with an unusually strong need for regularity and cleanliness in all aspects of life. [**Lifespan Link:** Theory of toilet training was discussed in Chapter 2.]

Erikson: Trust and Autonomy

According to Erikson, the first crisis of life is **trust versus mistrust**, when infants learn whether or not the world can be trusted to satisfy basic needs. Babies feel secure when food and comfort are provided with "consistency, continuity, and sameness of experience" (Erikson, 1963, p. 247). If social interaction inspires trust, the child (later the adult) confidently explores the social world.

The second crisis is **autonomy versus shame and doubt**, beginning at about 18 months, when self-awareness emerges. Toddlers want autonomy (self-rule) over their own actions and bodies. Without it, they feel ashamed and doubtful. Like Freud, Erikson believed that problems in early infancy could last a lifetime, creating adults who are suspicious and pessimistic (mistrusting) or easily shamed (lacking autonomy).

Erikson was aware of cultural variations. He knew that mistrust and shame could be destructive or not, depending on local norms and expectations. Westerners expect toddlers to go through the stubborn and defiant "terrible twos"; that is a sign of the urge for autonomy. Parents elsewhere expect toddlers to be docile and obedient, and "shame is a normative emotion that develops as parents use explicit shaming techniques" to encourage children's loyalty and harmony within their families (Mascolo et al., 2003, p. 402).

Behaviorism

From the perspective of behaviorism, emotions and personality are molded as parents reinforce or punish a child. Behaviorists believe that parents who respond joyously to every glimmer of a grin will have children with a sunny disposition. The opposite is also true:

> Failure to bring up a happy child, a well-adjusted child—assuming bodily health—falls squarely upon the parents' shoulders. [By the time the child is 3] parents have already determined . . . [whether the child] is to grow into a happy person, wholesome and good-natured, whether he is to be a whining, complaining neurotic, an anger-driven, vindictive, over-bearing slave driver, or one whose every move in life is definitely controlled by fear.

> [Watson, 1928, pp. 7, 45]

social learning The acquisition of behavior patterns by observing the behavior of others.

Later behaviorists recognized that infants' behavior also has an element of **social learning**, as infants learn from other people. Albert Bandura conducted a famous experiment (Bandura, 1977) in which young children were frustrated by

Hammering Bobo These images are stills from the film of Bandura's original study of social learning, in which frustrated 4-year-olds imitated the behavior they had observed an adult perform. The children used the same weapon as the adult, with the same intent—whether that involved hitting the doll with a hammer, shooting it with a toy gun, or throwing a large ball at it.

being told they could not play with some attractive toys. They were then left alone with a mallet and a rubber clown (Bobo) after seeing an adult hit Bobo. Both boys and girls pounded and kicked Bobo as the adult had done, indicating that they had learned from observation.

Since that experiment, developmentalists have demonstrated that social learning occurs throughout life (Morris et al., 2007; Rendell et al., 2011). Toddlers express emotions in various ways—from giggling to cursing—just as their parents or older siblings do.

For example, a boy might develop a hot temper if his father's outbursts seem to win his mother's respect; a girl might be coy, or passive-aggressive, if that is what she has seen at home. These examples are deliberately sexist: gender roles, in particular, are learned, according to social learning.

Parents often unwittingly encourage certain traits in their children. This is evident in the effects of proximal versus distal parenting, explained below.

proximal parenting Caregiving practices that involve being physically close to the baby, with frequent holding and touching.

distal parenting Caregiving practices that involve remaining distant from the baby, providing toys, food, and face-to-face communication with minimal holding and touching.

OPPOSING PERSPECTIVES

Proximal and Distal Parenting

Should parents carry infants most of the time, or will that spoil them? Should babies have many toys, or will that make them too materialistic?

Answers to these questions refer to the distinction between **proximal parenting** (being physically close to a baby, often holding and touching) and **distal parenting** (keeping some distance—providing toys, encouraging self-feeding, talking face to face instead of communicating by touch). Caregivers tend to behave in proximal or distal ways very early, when infants are only 2 months old (Kärtner et al., 2010). The cultural patterns that push parents to be proximal or distal also illustrate the importance of social learning—parents learn what to do with babies, and then the babies learn what their culture teaches.

The research finds notable variation in parenting approach (Keller et al., 2010). For example, in a longitudinal study (H. Keller et al., 2004) comparing child-rearing methods of the Nso people of Cameroon with those of Greeks in Athens, 78 mothers were videotaped playing with their 3-month-olds.

Coders (who did not know the study's hypothesis) counted frequency of proximal play (e.g., carrying, swinging, caressing, exercising the child's body) and distal play (e.g., face-to-face talking) (see Table 7.3). The Nso mothers were proximal, holding their babies all the time and almost never using toys or bottles. The Greek mothers were more distal.

The researchers hypothesized that proximal parenting would result in toddlers who were less self-aware but more compliant—traits needed in an interdependent and cooperative

Especially for Statisticians Note the sizes of the samples: 78 mother–infant pairs in Cameroon and Greece. Are these samples large enough to draw conclusions? (see response, page 202)

Especially for Pediatricians A mother complains that her toddler refuses to stay in the car seat, spits out disliked foods, and almost never does what she says. How should you respond? (see response, page 202)

>> **Response for Statisticians** (from page 201): Probably not. These studies are reported here because the results were dramatic (see Table 7.3) and because the two studies pointed in the same direction. Nevertheless, replication by other researchers is needed.

>> **Response for Pediatricians** (from page 201): Consider the origins of the misbehavior—probably a combination of the child's inborn temperament and the mother's distal parenting. Acceptance and consistent responses (e.g. avoiding disliked foods but always using the car seat) is more warranted than anger. Perhaps this mother is expressing hostility toward the child—a sign that intervention may be needed. Find out.

society such as that of rural Cameroon. By contrast, distal parenting might produce children who were aware of their personal uniqueness but less obedient, as needed in cultures that value independence.

TABLE 7.3	Infants in Rural Cameroon and Urban Greece	
	Cameroon	Athens, Greece
I. Infant–mother play at 3 months		
Percent of time held by mother	100%	31%
Percent of time playing with objects	3%	40%
II. Toddler behavior at 18 months		
Self-recognition	3%	68%
Immediate compliance with request	72%	2%

Source: Adapted from Keller et al., 2004.

The predictions were accurate. At 18 months, these same infants were tested on self-awareness (via the mirror/rouge test) and obedience to their parents. The average African toddler (proximal) didn't recognize him- or herself in the mirror but were compliant; the opposite was true of the Greek toddlers (distal).

The researchers then reanalyzed all their data, child by child. They found that, even apart from culture, proximal or distal play at 3 months was highly predictive: Greek mothers who, unlike most of their peers, were proximal parents had more obedient toddlers. Further research in other nations confirmed these conclusions (Borke et al., 2007; Kärtner et al., 2011).

Cultural attitudes shape every aspect of infant care. Is independence valued over dependence? Is autonomy more important than compliance? Cultures differ because values differ. If toddlers are asked to put away toys that they did not use (a task measuring compliance), and they do so without protest, is that wonderful or disturbing?

Should you pick up your crying baby (proximal) or give her a pacifier (distal)? Should you breast-feed until age 2 or longer (proximal) or switch to bottle-feeding before 6 months (distal)? Of course, as detailed in Appendix A, many factors influence parental actions, and breast-feeding is only one example of parental behavior. But every parental response is influenced by whatever assumptions the culture holds.

Her Personal Best How much time do you think the baby in the stroller spends cradled by his mother, with her sunglasses off, no words, just an expression of silent bliss?

TOM PRETTYMAN/PHOTO EDIT

Cognitive Theory

Cognitive theory holds that ideas, concepts and assumptions determine a person's perspective. Early experiences are important because beliefs, perceptions, and memories make them so, not because they are buried in the unconscious (psychoanalytic theory) or burned into the brain's patterns (behaviorism).

According to many cognitive theorists, early experiences help infants develop a **working model**, which is a set of assumptions that become a frame of reference

working model In cognitive theory, a set of assumptions that the individual uses to organize perceptions and experiences. For example, a person might assume that other people are trustworthy and be surprised by an incident in which this working model of human behavior is erroneous.

for later life (Johnson et al., 2010). It is a "model" because early relationships form a prototype, or blueprint; it is "working" because, although it is used, it is not necessarily fixed or final.

Ideally, infants develop "a working model of the self as valued, loved, and competent" and "a working model of parents as emotionally available, loving, sensitive and supportive" (Harter, 2006, p. 519). However, reality does not always conform to this ideal. A 1-year-old girl might develop a model, based on her parents' inconsistent responses to her, that people are unpredictable. She will continue to apply that model to everyone: Her childhood friendships will be insecure, and her adult relationships will be guarded.

The crucial idea, according to cognitive theory, is that an infant's early experiences themselves are not necessarily pivotal, but the interpretation of those experiences is (Olson & Dweck, 2009). Children may misinterpret their experiences, or parents may offer inaccurate explanations, and these form ideas that affect later thinking and behavior.

In this way, working models formed in childhood echo lifelong. A hopeful message from cognitive theory is that people can rethink and reorganize their thoughts, developing new models. Our mistrustful girl might marry a faithful and loving man and gradually develop a new working model.

Humanism

Remember from Chapter 2 that Maslow described a hierarchy of needs (physiological, safety/security, love/belonging, success/esteem, and self-actualization), with the lower levels being prerequisites for higher ones. Infants begin at the first level: Their emotions serve to ensure that physiological needs are met. That's why babies cry when they are hungry or hurt, as adults usually do not. Basic survival needs must be satisfied to enable the person to reach higher levels (Silton et al., 2011).

Humanism reminds us that caregivers also have needs and that their needs influence how they respond to infants. Self-actualized people (level 5) no longer demand their children's love and respect, so they can guide an infant well even if the child is momentarily angry (as when getting the child immunized). But most young parents are at level 3 or 4, seeking love or respect. They may be troubled by "ghosts in the nursery" (first mentioned in Chapter 5 in the discussion of infant sleep). Their own babyhood experiences includes unmet needs, and their early distress interferes with their ability to nurture the next generation.

For example, while all experts endorse breast-feeding as the best way to meet infants' physiological needs, many mothers quit breast-feeding after trying for a few days, and many fathers feel excluded if the mother spends most of her time and attention on nursing. This may puzzle the experts but not the humanist theorists, who realize that a parent's needs may clash with the infant's needs (Mulder & Johnson, 2010).

For example, one mother of a 1-year-old said:

> My son couldn't latch so I was pumping and my breasts were massive and I'm a pretty small woman with big breasts and they were enormous during pregnancy. It has always been a sore spot for me and I've never loved my breasts. And that has been hard for me in not feeling good about myself. And I stopped pumping in January and slowly they are going back and I'm beginning to feel some confidence again and that definitely helps. Because I felt overweight, your boobs are not your own and you are exhausted and your body is strange it's just really hard to want to share that with someone. They think you are beautiful, they love it and love you the way you are but it is not necessarily what you feel.

[quoted in Shapiro, 2011, p. 18]

This woman's need for self-respect was overwhelming, causing her to stop breast-feeding in order to feel some confidence about her shape. Neither her husband's love of her body nor her son's need for breast milk helped because she was not past level 3 (love and belonging). Her "strange" body attacked her self-esteem (level 4).

Her personal needs may have been unmet since puberty (she says, "I've never loved my breasts"). She blames her husband for not understanding her feelings and her son who "couldn't latch." Since all babies learn to latch with time and help, this woman's saying that her son couldn't latch suggests something amiss in synchrony and attachment—unmet baby needs because of unmet mother needs.

By contrast, some parents understand their baby's need for safety and security (level 2) even if they themselves are far beyond that stage. Kevin is an example.

> Kevin is a very active, outgoing person who loves to try new things. Today he takes his 11-month-old daughter, Tyra, to the park for the first time. Tyra is playing alone in the sandbox, when a group of toddlers joins her. At first, Tyra smiles and eagerly watches them play. But as the toddlers become more active and noisy, Tyra's smiles turn quickly to tears. She . . . reaches for Kevin, who picks her up and comforts her. But then Kevin goes a step further. After Tyra calms down, Kevin gently encourages her to play near the other children. He sits at her side, talking and playing with her. Soon Tyra is slowly creeping closer to the group of toddlers, curiously watching their moves.
>
> [Lerner & Dombro, 2004, p. 42]

Evolutionary Theory

Remember that evolutionary theory stresses two needs: survival and reproduction. Human brains are extraordinarily adept at those tasks. However, it takes about 20 years of maturation before the human brain is fully functioning. A child must be nourished, protected, and taught by adults much longer than offspring of any other species. Infant and parent emotions ensure this lengthy protection (Hrdy, 2009).

Emotions for Survival

Infant emotions are part of the evolutionary mandate. All the reactions described in the first part of this chapter—from the hunger cry to the temper tantrum—can be seen from this perspective (Konner, 2010).

For example, newborns are extraordinarily dependent, unable to walk or talk or even sit up and feed themselves for months after birth. They must attract adult devotion—and they do. That first smile, the sound of infant laughter, and their role in synchrony are all powerfully attractive to adults—especially to parents.

Adults call their hairless, chinless, round-faced, small-limbed creatures "cute," "handsome," "beautiful," "adorable," and willingly spend hours carrying, feeding, changing, and cleaning them. Adaptation is evident: Men have the genetic potential to be caregivers, and grandparents have done it before, but specific survival demands dictate adaptation of such potential, turning busy adults into devoted caregivers.

If humans were motivated merely by financial reward, no one would have children. Yet evolution has created adults who find parenting worth every sacrifice. The costs are substantial: food (even breast milk requires the mother to eat more), diapers, clothes, furniture, medical bills, toys, and child care (whether paid or unpaid) are just a start. Before a child becomes independent, many parents have paid for a bigger home, for education, for vacations, and much more. These are just the financial costs; the emotional costs are even greater.

Reproductive nurturance depends on years of self-sacrificing investment, and humans have evolved to provide it. Hormones—specifically, oxytocin—do much more than trigger birth and promote breast-feeding; they increase the impulse to bond with others, especially one's children. Both men and women have oxytocin in their blood and saliva, and this hormone continues to be produced as needed for caregiving (Feldman et al., 2011).

Evolutionary theory holds that, over human history, attachment, with proximity-seeking and contact-maintaining, promoted species survival by keeping toddlers near their caregivers and keeping caregivers vigilant. Infants fuss at still faces, they fear separation, and they laugh when adults play with them, all to sustain parent–child interdependence. We inherited these emotional reactions from our great-great- . . . grandparents, who would have died without them.

As explained in Chapter 4, human bonding is unlike that of goats and sheep—a mother does not need to nuzzle her newborn immediately. Bonding followed by synchrony and then attachment are greater and more durable for humans than for other animals. Toddlers attend to adult expressions (social referencing) to establish the relationships between self and others.

allocare The care of children by people other than their biological parents.

Allocare

Evolutionary social scientists note that if mothers were the exclusive caregivers of each child until children were adults, a given woman could rear only one or two offspring—not enough for the species to survive. Instead, before the introduction of reliable birth control, the average interval between births for humans was two to four years. Humans birth children at relatively short intervals and raise them successfully because of **allocare**—the care of children by people other than the biological parents (Hrdy, 2009). Allocare is essential for *Homo sapiens* survival.

Compared with many other species, human mothers have evolved to let other people help with child care, and other people are usually eager to do so (Kachel et al., 2011). Throughout the centuries, the particular person to provide allocare has varied by culture and ecological conditions.

Often fathers helped but not always: Some men were far away, fighting, hunting, or seeking work; some had several wives and a dozen or more children. In those situations, other women (daughters, grandmothers, sisters, friends) and sometimes other men provided allocare (Hrdy, 2009).

Infant Day Care

Cultural variations in allocare are vast, and each theory just described can be used to justify or criticize certain variations. This makes infant day care a controversial topic. No theory directly endorses any particular position. Nonetheless, theories are made to be useful, so we will include some discussion about the day-care implications of various theories.

It is estimated that about 134 million babies will be born each year from 2010 to 2021 (United Nations, 2013). Most newborns will be cared for primarily or exclusively by their mothers, and then allocare will increase as the baby gets older. Fathers and grandmothers are usually the first nonmaternal caregivers; only about 15 percent of infants (birth to age 2) receive daily care from a nonrelative who is paid and trained to provide it.

Statistics on the precise incidence and consequences of various forms of infant care in each nation are difficult to find or interpret because "informal in-family arrangements speak to the ingenuity of parents trying to cope but bedevil child care statistics" (Leach, 2009, p. 44). Furthermore, patterns of infant care are part of a complex web of child rearing: It is difficult to connect any one particular pattern with one particular outcome.

Same Situation, Far Apart: Safekeeping Historically, grandmothers were sometimes crucial for child survival. Now, even though medical care has reduced child mortality, grandmothers still do their part to keep children safe, as shown by these two—in the eastern United States *(top)* and western China *(bottom)*.

TABLE 7.4	High-Quality Day Care

High-quality day care during infancy has five essential characteristics:

1. *Adequate attention to each infant.* A small group of infants (no more than five) needs two reliable, familiar, loving caregivers. Continuity of care is crucial.

2. *Encouragement of language and sensorimotor development.* Infants need language—songs, conversations, and positive talk— and easily manipulated toys.

3. *Attention to health and safety.* Cleanliness routines (e.g., handwashing), accident prevention (e.g., no small objects), and safe areas to explore are essential.

4. *Professional caregivers.* Caregivers should have experience and degrees/ certificates in early-childhood education. Turnover should be low, morale high, and enthusiasm evident.

5. *Warm and responsive caregivers.* Providers should engage the children in active play and guide them in problem solving. Quiet, obedient children may indicate unresponsive care.

Observation Quiz What three cultural differences do you see in the pictures below? (see answer, page 208)

Same Situation, Far Apart: Instead of Mothers Casper, Wyoming *(left)*, is on the opposite side of the earth from Dhaka, Bangladesh *(right)*, but day care is needed in both places, as shown here.

Many people believe that the practices of their own family or culture are best and that other patterns harm either the infant or the mother. This is another example of the difference-equals-deficit error. Without evidence, assumptions flourish.

International Comparisons

Center-based infant care is common in France, Israel, China, and Sweden, where it is heavily subsidized by the governments, and scarce in South Asia, Africa, and Latin America, where it is not. North America is in between these extremes, but variations from place to place are apparent. No matter where center day care is located, though, there are certain factors that indicate a high-quality day-care environment (see Table 7.4).

Involvement of relatives also varies. Worldwide, fathers increasingly take part in baby care. Most nations provide some paid leave for mothers; some also provide paid leave for fathers; and several nations provide paid family leave that can be taken by either parent or shared between them. The length of paid leave varies from a few days to about 15 months (see Figure 7.3).

When all the developed nations are considered, the United States is one of the few without paid leave. Note, however, practices do not necessarily align with policies. In many nations, parents have unregulated employment and take off only a day or two for birth, although national policy is more generous. The reverse is also true: some fathers and mothers hesitate to take allowed parental leave, because it may undercut their advancement.

Underlying every national policy and private practices are theories about what is best for infants. When nations mandate paid leave, the belief is that infants need maternal care and that employers should encourage such care to occur.

In the United States, marked variations are apparent by state and by employer, with some employers far more generous than the law requires. Federal policy mandates that a job be held for a parent who takes unpaid leave of up to 12 weeks unless the company has fewer than 50 employees. Almost no company pays for paternal leave, with one exception: The U.S. military allows 10 days of paid leave for fathers.

In the United States, only 20 percent of infants are cared for *exclusively* by their mothers (i.e., no other relatives or babysitters are involved in baby care) throughout their first year. This is in contrast to Canada, which is similar to the United States in ethnic diversity but has lower rates of maternal employment: in the first year of life, 60 percent of Canadians are cared for only by their mothers (Babchishin, et al., 2013).

Obviously, these differences are affected by culture more than by the universal psychosocial needs of babies and parents. Changes occur through economic and political pressures—which means that data on infant care in 2015 will differ from the numbers reported here.

One might hope that centuries of maternal care, paternal care, and allocare would provide clear conclusions about the best practices. Unfortunately, the evidence is mixed. In most nations and centuries, infants were more likely to survive if their grandmothers were nearby, especially during the time immediately after weaning (Sear & Mace, 2008). This is thought to have been because the grandmothers provided essential nourishment and protection.

However, in at least one community (northern Germany, 1720–1874), having a living grandmother, especially a paternal grandmother, had a negative effect on infant survival (Beise & Voland, 2002). The authors speculate that living with mothers-in-law (which was the norm) increased the stress on pregnant daughters-in-law and diminished expectant fathers' protective devotion, which led to more frequent preterm births.

Evidence on the effects of early nonmaternal care suggests that national policies, cultural expectations, and family income are at least as significant as the actual hours in care and who provides it (Côté et al., 2013; Solheim et al., 2013).

No matter what form of care is chosen or what theory is endorsed, responsive, individualized care with stable caregivers seems best (Morrissey, 2009). Caregiver change is especially problematic for infants because each simple gesture or sound that a baby makes not only merits an encouraging response but also requires interpretation by someone who knows that particular baby well.

For example, "baba" could mean bottle, baby, blanket, banana, or some other word that does not even begin with *b*. This example is an easy one, but similar communication efforts—requiring individualized emotional responses—are evident throughout infancy. If you have any doubts, remember the importance of synchrony and the troubled lives of the Romanian orphans who received excellent care after adoption but not in their first year.

Some babies seem far more affected than others by the quality of their care (Phillips et al., 2011; Pluess & Belsky, 2009). In fact, if the home environment is poor—neglectful, hostile, unresponsive—then day care may be an improvement. The main concern is that some infants with extensive nonmaternal care will become more aggressive and hyperactive later on (Jacob, 2009; Babchishin et al., 2013). This seems particularly likely for unregulated care (i.e., care with no requirements as to infant-caregiver ratio and teacher training).

As one review explained: "This evidence now indicates that early nonparental care environments sometimes pose risks to young children and sometimes confer benefits" (Phillips et al., 2011). Differential sensitivity is evident: For genetic and familial reasons, the choice about how best to provide care for an infant varies from case to case.

Maternal Employment in Infancy

Closely tied to the issue of infant day care is the issue of maternal employment. Until recent history it was assumed that mothers should stay home with their children. That is the recommendation of both psychoanalytic and behaviorist theory. That assumption has been challenged, partly by the idea that mothers have

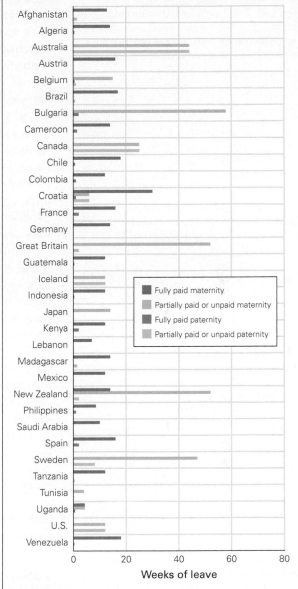

Source: ILO Database on Conditions of Work and Employment Laws, 2011.

Note: In some cases, leave can be shared between parents or other family members.

FIGURE 7.3

A Changing World No one was offered maternity leave a century ago because the only jobs that mothers had were unregulated ones. Now, virtually every nation has a maternity leave policy, revised every decade or so. As of 2012 only Australia, Iceland, and Canada offered policies reflecting gender equality. That may be the next innovation in many nations.

Especially for Day-Care Providers A mother who brings her child to you for day care says that she knows she is harming her baby, but economic necessity compels her to work. What do you say? (see response, page 208)

>> Answer to Observation Quiz (from page 206): The Bangladeshi children are dressed alike, are the same age, and are all seated around toy balls in a net—there's not a book in sight, unlike in the Wyoming setting.

needs that merit attention (humanism) and by historical evidence that allocare was typical over the centuries (evolutionary theory).

A summary of the longitudinal outcomes of nonmaternal infant care finds "externalizing behavior is predicted from a constellation of variables in multiple contexts . . . and no study has found that children of employed mothers develop serious emotional or other problems *solely* because their mothers are working outside the home" (McCartney et al., 2010, pp. 1, 16).

Indeed, research from the United States indicates that children generally benefit if their mothers are employed (Goldberg et al., 2008). The most likely reasons are that maternal income reduces parental depression and increases family wealth, both of which correlate with happier and more successful children.

That is a comforting conclusion for employed mothers, but again, other interpretations are possible. It may be that the women who were able to find worthwhile work were also more capable of providing good infant care than women who were unemployed.

Marital relationships benefit from shared activities, so couples who rarely spend time together are likely to be less dedicated to each other. Sharing child care—with both partners together playing with the baby—seems to benefit all three; husbands who are active and involved fathers tend also to be devoted to their wives. Father involvement correlates with child happiness and success. The opposite is also true.

As you see, every study reflects many variables, just as every theory has a different perspective on infant care. Given that, and given divergent cultural assumptions, it is not surprising that researchers find mixed evidence on infant care and caregivers. Many factors are relevant: infant gender and temperament, family income and education, and especially the quality of care at home and elsewhere.

Thus, as is true of many topics in child development, questions remain. But one fact is without question: Each infant needs personal responsiveness—ideally from both mother and father, but another relative or even a nonrelative can suffice. Someone should serve as a partner in the synchrony duet, a base for secure attachment, and a social reference who encourages exploration. Then infant emotions and experiences—cries and laughter, fears and joys—will ensure that psychosocial development goes well.

SUMMING UP

All theories recognize that infant care is crucial: Psychosocial development depends on it. Psychoanalytic theory stresses early caregiving routines, developing oral or anal characteristics according to Freud and trust and autonomy according to Erikson. Behaviorists emphasize early learning, with parents' reinforcing or punishing infant reactions. Cognitive theories emphasize working models. In all these theories, lifelong patterns are said to begin in infancy, but later change is possible. Culture is crucial.

Humanists consider the basic needs of adults as well as infants. Consequently, they acknowledge the parental side of the parent–infant interaction. According to evolutionary theory, inborn impulses provide the interdependence that humans have always needed. Since human brains and thoughts take many years to mature, allocare has been essential for the survival of the species, as has understanding each other's emotional messages.

The psychosocial impact of infant day care depends on many factors, including the culture. Although many nations pay mothers of infants to stay home with their babies, maternal employment does not seem harmful if someone else provides responsive care. Continuity is crucial; mothers, fathers, and others can all be good caregivers. ■

>> Response for Day-Care Providers (from page 207): Reassure the mother that you will keep her baby safe and will help to develop the baby's mind and social skills by fostering synchrony and attachment. Also tell her that the quality of mother–infant interaction at home is more important than anything else for psychosocial development; mothers who are employed full time usually have wonderful, secure relationships with their infants. If the mother wishes, you can discuss ways to be a responsive mother.

SUMMARY

Emotional Development

1. Two emotions, contentment and distress, appear as soon as an infant is born. Smiles and laughter are evident in the early months. Anger emerges in reaction to restriction and frustration, between 4 and 8 months of age, and becomes stronger by age 1.

2. Reflexive fear is apparent in very young infants. Fear of something specific, including fear of strangers and of separation, is typically strong toward the end of the first year.

3. In the second year, social awareness produces more selective fear, anger, and joy. As infants become increasingly self-aware, emotions emerge that encourage an interface between the self and others—specifically, pride, shame, and affection. Self-recognition (on the mirror/rouge test) emerges at about 18 months.

Brain and Emotions

4. Stress impedes early brain and emotional development. Some infants are particularly vulnerable to the effects of early maltreatment.

5. Temperament is a set of genetic traits whose expression is influenced by the context. Inborn temperament is linked to later personality, although plasticity is also evident.

The Development of Social Bonds

6. Often by 2 months, and clearly by 6 months, infants become more responsive and social, and synchrony is evident. Infants are disturbed by a still face because they expect and need social interaction.

7. Attachment, measured by the baby's reaction to the caregiver's presence, departure, and return in the Strange Situation, is crucial. Some infants seem indifferent (type A attachment—insecure-avoidant) or overly dependent (type C—insecure-resistant/ambivalent), instead of secure (type B).

Disorganized attachment (type D) is the most worrisome. Secure attachment provides encouragement for infant exploration.

8. As they play, toddlers engage in social referencing, looking to other people's facial expressions and body language to detect what is safe, frightening, or fun.

9. Infants frequently use fathers as partners in synchrony, attachment figures, and social references, developing emotions and exploring their world via father caregiving.

Theories of Infant Psychosocial Development

10. According to all major theories, caregiver behavior is especially influential in the first two years. Freud stressed the mother's impact on oral and anal pleasure; Erikson emphasized trust and autonomy. The impact of these is lifelong.

11. Behaviorists focus on learning; parents teach their babies many things, including when to be fearful or joyful. Cognitive theory holds that infants develop working models based on their experiences. Both these theories suggest that later developments can modify early experiences.

12. Humanism notes that some adults are stuck in their own unfinished development, which impairs their ability to give infants the loving responses they need.

13. Evolutionary theorists recognize that both infants and caregivers have impulses and emotions, developed over millennia, that foster the survival of each new member of the human species.

14. The impact of nonmaternal care depends on many factors; it varies from one nation, one family, and even one child to another. Although each theory has a somewhat different emphasis, all agree that quality of care (responsive, individualized) is crucial, particularly in infancy, no matter who provides that care.

KEY TERMS

allocare (p. 205)
attachment (p. 191)
autonomy versus shame and doubt (p. 200)
cortisol (p. 182)
disorganized attachment (p. 193)

distal parenting (p. 201)
insecure-avoidant attachment (p. 193)
insecure-resistant/ambivalent attachment (p. 193)
proximal parenting (p. 201)
secure attachment (p. 193)

self-awareness (p. 184)
separation anxiety (p. 183)
social learning (p. 200)
social referencing (p. 197)
social smile (p. 182)
still-face technique (p. 191)
Strange Situation (p. 194)

stranger wariness (p. 183)
synchrony (p. 189)
temperament (p. 187)
trust versus mistrust (p. 200)
working model (p. 202)

WHAT HAVE YOU LEARNED?

1. What are the first emotions to appear in infants?

2. What experiences trigger anger and sadness in infants?

3. What do typical 1-year-olds fear?

4. How do emotions differ between the first and second year of life?

5. How do family interactions and culture shape a toddler's emotions?

6. What is known and unknown about the impact of brain maturation on emotions?

7. How are memory and emotion connected?

8. How does stress affect early brain development?

9. Why are temperamental traits more apparent in some people than in others?

10. How might synchrony affect early emotional development?

11. Give examples of how infants and caregivers demonstrate proximity-seeking and contact-maintaining behaviors.

12. Describe the four types of attachment. How might each affect later life?

13. What can be done to improve the parent–child bond for high-risk parents?

14. How is social referencing important in infancy?

15. How does father involvement affect infants?

16. What might happen if a person is stuck in the oral or anal stage of development?

17. How might the crisis of "trust versus mistrust" affect later life?

18. How might the crisis of "autonomy versus shame and doubt" affect later life?

19. How do behaviorists explain the development of emotions and personality?

20. Why does the concept of a "working model" arise from cognitive theory?

21. According to humanism, how might caregivers' own needs affect their response to an infant?

22. How does evolution explain the parent–child bond?

23. Why is allocare necessary for survival of the human species?

24. What are the advantages and disadvantages of nonmaternal infant care?

25. Compare the costs and benefits of infant care by relatives versus center day care.

26. Why is it difficult to draw conclusions about infant day care?

27. What are the benefits and problems for infants if their mothers are employed?

APPLICATIONS

1. One cultural factor influencing infant development is how infants are carried from place to place. Ask four mothers whose infants were born in each of the past four decades how they transported them—front or back carriers, facing out or in, strollers or carriages, in car seats or on mother's laps, and so on. Why did they choose the mode(s) they chose? What are their opinions and yours on how such cultural practices might affect infants' development?

2. Observe synchrony for three minutes. Ideally, ask the parent of an infant under 8 months of age to play with the infant. If no infant is available, observe a pair of lovers as they converse. Note the sequence and timing of every facial expression, sound, and gesture of both partners.

3. Telephone several day-care centers to try to assess the quality of care they provide. Ask about factors such as adult/child ratio, group size, and training for caregivers of children of various ages. Is there a minimum age? Why or why not? Analyze the answers, using Table 7.4 as a guide.

>>**ONLINE CONNECTIONS**

To accompany your textbook, you have access to a number of online resources, including Learning Curve, an adaptive quizzing program, critical thinking questions, and case studies. For access to any of these links, go to www.worthpublishers.com/launchpad/bergerls9e. In addition to these resources, you'll also find links to video clips, personalized study advice, and an ebook. Some of the videos and activities available online include:

- *Attachment Behaviors in the Strange Situation.* You'll get a chance to watch—and take your best guess about attachment states—as some infants are left in the company of strangers.

WORTH PUBLISHERS

PART II The Developing Person So Far:

The First Two Years

BIOSOCIAL

Growth in Infancy Over the first two years, body weight quadruples and brain weight triples. Connections between brain cells grow dense, with complex networks of dendrites and axons. Experiences that are universal (experience-expectant) and culture-bound (experience-dependent) aid brain growth, partly by pruning unused connections between neurons.

Perceiving and Moving Brain maturation as well as culture underlies the development of all the senses. Seeing, hearing, and mobility progress from reflexes to coordinated voluntary actions, including focusing, grasping, and walking.

Surviving in Good Health Infant health depends on immunization, parental practices (including "back to sleep"), and nutrition. Breast milk protects health. Survival rates are much higher today than even a few decades ago.

COGNITIVE

Sensorimotor Intelligence As Piaget describes it, in the first two years, infants progress from knowing their world through immediate sensory experiences to "experimenting" on that world through actions and mental images.

Information Processing Information-processing theory stresses the links between sensory experiences and perception. Infants develop their own ideas regarding the possibilities offered by the objects and events of the world.

Language: What Develops in the First Two Years? Interaction with responsive adults exposes infants to the structures of communication and language. By age 1, infants usually speak a word or two; by age 2, language has exploded—toddlers talk in short sentences and add vocabulary each day.

PSYCHOSOCIAL

Emotional Development Babies soon progress to smiling and laughing at pleasurable objects and events, and experience anger, sadness, and fear. Toddlers develop self-awareness and social awareness, and experience new emotions: pride, shame, embarrassment, disgust, and guilt. All emotional reactions begin in the brain, but the links between expressed emotions and brain growth are complex.

The Development of Social Bonds Parents and infants respond to each other by synchronizing their behavior. Toward the end of the first year, secure attachment to the parent sets the stage for the child's increasingly independent exploration of the world. Insecure attachment—avoidant, resistant, or disorganized—signifies a parent–child relationship that hinders learning. Infants' self-awareness and independence are shaped by parents. Much of basic temperament is inborn and apparent throughout life. Sociocultural theory stresses cultural norms, evident in parents' ethnotheories in raising their infants; some parents are more proximal (encouraging touch), others more distal (encouraging cognition). All provide allocare, essential for survival.

early
childhood

From age 2 to age 6, children spend most of their waking hours discovering, creating, laughing, and imagining, as they acquire the skills they need. They chase each other and attempt new challenges (developing their bodies); they play with sounds, words, and ideas (developing their minds); they invent games and dramatize fantasies (learning social skills and morals).

These years once were called the *preschool years* because school started in first grade. But now most children begin school during these years. Therefore, we use the traditional term *early childhood*.

Of course, these could also be called the play years, since young children love to play, whether quietly tracking a beetle through the grass or riotously turning a bedroom into a shambles. Their words and minds are playful, too; they explain that "a bald man has a barefoot head" or that "the sun shines so children can go outside to play."

Early childhood—by whatever name—is a time of extraordinary growth, impressive learning, and spontaneous play, joyful not only for young children but also for anyone who knows them.

Early Childhood: Biosocial Development

■ **Body Changes**
Growth Patterns
Nutrition
Hazards of "Just Right"

■ **Brain Development**
Speed of Thought
The Brain's Connected Hemispheres
Emotions and the Brain

■ **Improving Motor Skills**
Gross Motor Skills
A VIEW FROM SCIENCE: Eliminating Lead
Fine Motor Skills
Artistic Expression

■ **Injuries and Abuse**
Avoidable Injury
Prevention
Child Maltreatment
Three Levels of Prevention, Again

WHAT WILL YOU KNOW?

1. Do children eat too much, too little, or just the right amount?
2. How does brain maturation affect emotional development in early childhood?
3. What do children need for their gross motor skills to develop?
4. When and how should child abuse be prevented?

When I was 4, I jumped off the back of our couch again and again, trying to fly. I did it many times because I tried it with and without a cape, with and without flapping my arms. My laughing mother wondered whether she had made a mistake in letting me see *Peter Pan*. An older woman warned that jumping would hurt my uterus. I didn't know what a uterus was, I didn't heed that lady, and I didn't stop until I decided I could not fly because I had no pixie dust.

When you were 4, I hope you also wanted to fly and someone laughed while keeping you safe. Protection, appreciation, and fantasy are all needed in early childhood. Do you remember trying to skip, climb a tree, or write your name? Young children try, fail, and try again. They become skilled and wise, eventually understanding some of life's limitations, including that humans have no wings. Advances in body and brain, and the need for adult protection, are themes of this chapter. Amazing growth, unexpected injury, and sobering maltreatment are all described.

>> Body Changes

In early childhood as in infancy, the body and brain develop according to powerful epigenetic forces, biologically driven and socially guided, experience-expectant and experience-dependent. [**Lifespan Link:** Experience-expectant and experience-dependent brain development are explained in Chapter 5.] Bodies and brains mature in size and function.

Growth Patterns

Compare a toddling, unsteady 1-year-old with a cartwheeling 6-year-old. Body differences are obvious. During early childhood, children slim down as the lower body lengthens and fat turns to muscle.

In fact, the average body mass index (BMI, the ratio of weight to height) is lower at ages 5 and 6 than at any other time of life. Gone are the infant's protruding belly, round face, short limbs, and large head. The center of gravity moves from the breast to the belly, enabling cartwheels, somersaults, and many other motor skills. The joys of dancing, gymnastics, and pumping a swing become

Size and Balance These cousins are only four years apart, but note the doubling in leg length and marked improvement in balance. The 2-year-old needs to plant both legs on the sand, while the 6-year-old cavorts on one foot.

Victory! He's on his way. This boy participates in a British effort to combat childhood obesity; mother and son exercising in Liverpool Park is part of the solution. Harder to implement are dietary changes—many parents let children eat as much as they want.

possible; changing proportions enable new achievements. [**Lifespan Link:** Body mass index is discussed in Chapter 11.]

Increases in weight and height are apparent as well. Over each year of early childhood, well-nourished children gain about 4½ pounds (2 kilograms) and grow almost 3 inches (about 7 centimeters). By age 6, the average child in a developed nation:

- Weighs between 40 and 50 pounds (between 18 and 22 kilograms)
- Is at least 3½ feet tall (more than 100 centimeters)
- Looks lean, not chubby (ages 5 to 6 are lowest in body fat)
- Has adult-like body proportions (legs constitute about half the total height)

When many ethnic groups live together in a nation with abundant food and adequate medical care, children of African descent tend to be tallest, followed by those of European descent, then Asians, and then Latinos. However, height differences are greater *within* ethnic groups than *between* groups, evidence again that ethnicity is not determined by genes.

Nutrition

Although they rarely starve, preschool children sometimes suffer from poor nutrition. The main reason for preschool malnourishment in developed nations is that too often young children's small appetites are satiated with unhealthy foods, crowding out needed vitamins.

Adults often encourage children to eat, protecting them against famine that was common a century ago. Unfortunately, that encouragement is destructive when food is abundant. This is true in many nations: In Brazil 30 years ago, the most common nutritional problem was undernutrition; now it is overnutrition (Monteiro et al., 2004), with low-income Brazilians particularly vulnerable (Monteiro et al., 2007).

A detailed study of 2- to 4-year-olds in low-income families in New York City found many overweight children, with an increase in weight as family income fell (J. A. Nelson et al., 2004) and as children grew older (14 percent at age 2; 27 percent at age 4). This age pattern suggests that eating habits, not genes, were the cause. In that New York study, overweight children were more often of Hispanic (27 percent) or Asian American (22 percent) descent rather than of African (14 percent) or European (11 percent) descent.

One explanation for North American ethnic differences is that many low-income children live with grandmothers who knew firsthand the dangers of malnutrition. Indeed, immigrant Latino and Asian American grandparents are unlikely to be obese themselves but often have overweight grandchildren (Bates et al., 2008). For every ethnic group, the reality of food availability for young children has changed faster than traditions have.

Overfed children often become overweight adults. An article in *The Lancet* (the leading medical journal in England) predicted that by 2020, 228 million adults worldwide will have diabetes (more in India than in any other nation) as a result of unhealthy eating habits acquired in childhood. This article suggests that measures to reduce childhood overeating in the United States have been inadequate and that "U.S. children could become the first generation in more than a century to have shorter life spans than their parents if current trends of excessive weight and obesity continue" (Devi 2008, p. 105).

Appetite decreases between ages 2 and 6 because young children need fewer calories per pound than they did as infants. This is especially true for the current generation since children get much less exercise than former generations did. They do not tend the farm animals, walk long distances to school, or even play outside for hours. However, instead of accepting this generational change, many of the older generations fret, threaten, and cajole children to overeat ("Eat all your dinner and you can have ice cream"). Pediatricians have found that most parents of infants, toddlers, and preschoolers believe that relatively thin children are less healthy than relatively heavy ones, a false belief that leads to overfeeding (Laraway et al., 2010).

Nutritional Deficiencies

Although most children in developed nations consume more than enough calories, they do not always obtain adequate iron, zinc, and calcium. For example, children now drink less milk than formerly, which means less calcium and weaker bones later on. Another problem is sugar. Many customs entice children to eat sweets—in birthday cake, holiday candy, desserts, and other treats.

Sweetened cereals and drinks (advertised as containing 100 percent of daily vitamins) are a poor substitute for a balanced, varied diet, partly because some nutrients have not yet been identified, much less listed on food labels. The lack of micronutrients is severe in poor nations, but vitamin pills and added supplements do not always help (Ramakrishnan et al., 2011).

Eating a wide variety of fresh foods may therefore be essential for optimal health. Compared with the average child, those preschoolers who eat more dark-green and orange vegetables and less fried food benefit in many ways. They gain bone mass but not fat, according to a study that controlled for other factors that might correlate with body fat, such as gender (girls have more), ethnicity (people of some ethnic groups are genetically thinner), and income (poor children have worse diets) (Wosje et al., 2010).

An added complication is that an estimated 3 to 8 percent of all young children are allergic to a specific food—and almost always a common, healthy food: Cow's milk, eggs, peanuts, tree nuts, soy, wheat, fish, and shellfish are the usual culprits. Diagnostic standards vary (which explains the range of estimates), and treatment varies even more (Chafen et al., 2010).

Some experts advocate total avoidance of the offending food—there are peanut-free schools, where no one is allowed to bring a peanut butter sandwich for lunch—but other experts suggest that tolerance should be gradually increased, beginning by giving babies a tiny bit of peanut butter (Reche et al., 2011). Fortunately, many childhood food allergies are outgrown, but since young children are already at nutritional risk, allergies make a balanced diet even harder.

Oral Health

Too much sugar and too little fiber cause tooth decay, the most common disease of young children in developed nations. More than one-third of all U.S. children under age 6 already have at least one cavity (Brickhouse et al., 2008). Sugary fruit drinks and soda are prime causes, and sugar-free soda contains acid that makes decay more likely (Holtzman, 2009).

Fortunately, "baby" teeth are replaced naturally at about ages 6 to 10. The schedule is primarily genetic, with girls averaging a few months ahead of boys. However, tooth care should not be postponed until the permanent teeth erupt. Severe tooth decay in early childhood harms those permanent teeth (which form below the first teeth) and can cause jaw malformation, chewing difficulties, and speech problems.

Especially for Nutritionists
A parent complains that she prepares a variety of vegetables and fruits, but her 4-year-old wants only French fries and cake. What should you advise? (see response, page 218)

"I'm not hungry, I ate with Rover."

Eat Your Veggies On their own, children do not always eat wisely.

Especially for Early-Childhood Teachers
You know that young children are upset if forced to eat a food they hate, but you have eight 3-year-olds with eight different preferences. What do you do? (see response, page 218)

>> Response for Nutritionists
(from page 217): The nutritionally wise advice would be to offer only fruits, vegetables, and other nourishing, low-fat foods, counting on the child's eventual hunger to drive him or her to eat them. However, centuries of cultural custom make such wisdom difficult. A physical checkup, with a blood test, may be warranted to make sure the child is healthy.

>> Response for Early-Childhood Teachers (from page 217): Remember to keep food simple and familiar. Offer every child the same food, allowing refusal but no substitutes—unless for all eight. Children do not expect school and home routines to be identical; they eventually taste whatever other children enjoy.

Teeth are affected by diet and illness, which means that the state of a young child's teeth can alert adults to other health problems. The process works in reverse as well: infected teeth can affect the rest of the child's body.

Most preschoolers visit the dentist if they have U.S.-born, middle-class parents, However, the less education parents have, the less likely they are to know the importance of early dental care (Horowitz et al., 2013). Many young and low-income parents are overwhelmed with work and child care and do not realize that tooth-brushing is a vital habit, best learned early in life (Mofidi et al., 2009; Niji et al., 2010).

If the parent was raised in a nation with inadequate dental care (sometimes visible in the number of toothless elders), they may not get dental care for their children. However, in many countries, ignorance is not the problem; access and income are. In the United States, free dentistry is not available to most poor parents, who "want to do better" for their children's teeth than they did for their own (Lewis et al., 2010).

Hazards of "Just Right"

Many young children are compulsive about their daily routines, insisting that bedtime be preceded by tooth-brushing, a book, and prayers—or by a snack, sitting on the toilet, and a song. Whatever the routine, children expect it and are upset if someone puts them to bed without it. Similarly, mealtime can become a time for certain foods, prepared and placed in a particular way, on a specific plate.

The early childhood wish for routines, known as the "just right" or "just so" phenomenon, might signify an obsessive-compulsive disorder in older children. For that reason, adults should help older children reduce their anxiety (Flessner et al., 2011). However, among young children, a wish for continuity and sameness is normal and widespread (Evans et al., 2006; Pietrefesa & Evans, 2007). As a team of experts explains: "Most, if not all, children exhibit normal age-dependent obsessive-compulsive behaviors [that are] usually gone by middle childhood" (March et al., 2004, p. 216).

Overeating can become a serious problem: Indulgence and patience for "just right" becomes destructive if the result is an overweight child. [**Lifespan Link:** Obesity is discussed in detail in Chapter 11, and Chapter 20.]

Pediatricians need to provide parents of 2- to 5-year-olds with "anticipatory guidance" (Collins et al., 2004), since prevention is better than putting a 6-year-old on a diet (as some pediatricians do). Pre-school educators (sometimes via guidelines for parents or requests to food providers) can also influence children's nutritional intake, giving them time to eat and talk—and providing only nutritious food.

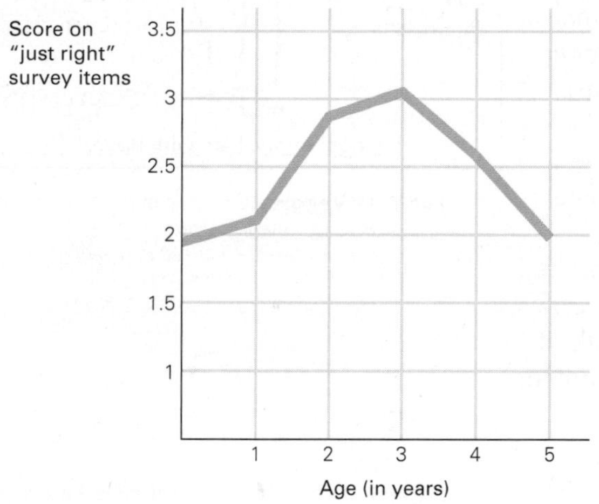

Source: Evans et al., 1997.

FIGURE 8.1

Young Children's Insistence on Routine This chart shows the average scores of children (who are rated by their parents) on a survey indicating the child's desire to have certain things—including food selection and preparation—done "just right." Such strong preferences for rigid routines tend to fade by age 6.

SUMMING UP

Between ages 2 and 6, children grow taller and proportionately thinner, with variations depending on genes, nutrition, income, and ethnicity. Nutrition and oral health are serious concerns, as many children eat unhealthy foods, developing cavities and too much body fat. Young children usually have small appetites and picky eating habits. Unfortunately, many adults encourage overeating, not realizing that being overweight leads to life-threatening illness.

>> Brain Development

Brains grow rapidly before birth and throughout infancy, as you saw in Chapter 5. By age 2, most neurons have connected to other neurons and substantial pruning has occurred. The 2-year-old's brain already weighs 75 percent of what it will weigh in adulthood; the 6-year-old's brain is 90 percent of adult weight. (The major structures of the brain are diagrammed in Figure 8.2).

Since most of the brain is already present and functioning by age 2, what remains to develop? The most important parts!

> Although the brains and bodies of other primates seem better than humans in some ways (they climb trees better, for instance) and although many animals have abilities humans lack (smell in dogs, for instance), humans have intellectual capacities far beyond any other animal. Considered from an evolutionary perspective, our brains allowed the human species to develop "a mode of living built on social cohesion, cooperation and efficient planning . . . survival of the smartest" seems more accurate than survival of the fittest (Corballis, 2011, p. 194).

The social understanding that develops as the prefrontal cortex matures distinguishes humans from other primates. For example, a careful series of tests given to 106 chimpanzees, 32 orangutans, and 105 human 2½-year-olds found that young children were "equivalent . . . to chimpanzees on tasks of physical cognition but far outstripped both chimpanzees and orangutans on tasks of social cognition" such as pointing or following someone's gaze (Herrmann et al., 2007, p. 1365).

FIGURE 8.2

Connections A few of the dozens of named parts of the brain are shown here. Although each area has particular functions, the entire brain is interconnected. The processing of emotions, for example, occurs primarily in the limbic system, where many brain areas are involved, including the amygdala, hippocampus, and hypothalamus.

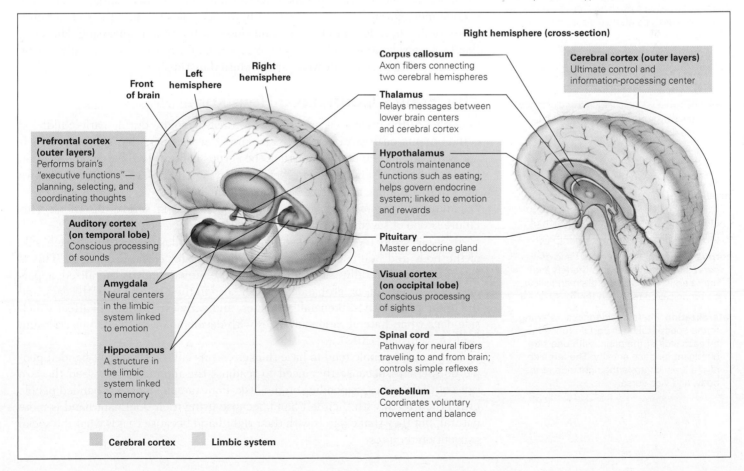

Right hemisphere (cross-section)

Corpus callosum
Axon fibers connecting two cerebral hemispheres

Cerebral cortex (outer layers)
Ultimate control and information-processing center

Thalamus
Relays messages between lower brain centers and cerebral cortex

Front of brain

Left hemisphere

Right hemisphere

Prefrontal cortex (outer layers)
Performs brain's "executive functions"—planning, selecting, and coordinating thoughts

Hypothalamus
Controls maintenance functions such as eating; helps govern endocrine system; linked to emotion and rewards

Auditory cortex (on temporal lobe)
Conscious processing of sounds

Pituitary
Master endocrine gland

Amygdala
Neural centers in the limbic system linked to emotion

Visual cortex (on occipital lobe)
Conscious processing of sights

Hippocampus
A structure in the limbic system linked to memory

Spinal cord
Pathway for neural fibers traveling to and from brain; controls simple reflexes

Cerebellum
Coordinates voluntary movement and balance

■ Cerebral cortex   ■ Limbic system

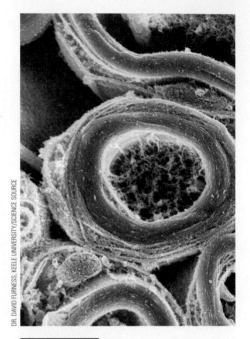

DR. DAVID FURNESS, KEELE UNIVERSITY/SCIENCE SOURCE

FIGURE 8.3

Faster and Faster Myelination is a lifelong process. Shown here is a cross section of an axon (dark middle) coated with many layers of Schwann cells, as more and more myelin wraps around the axon throughout childhood. Age-related slowdowns in late adulthood are caused by gradual disappearance of myelin layers.

Especially for Early-Childhood Teachers You know you should be patient, but frustration rises when your young charges dawdle on the walk to the playground a block away. What should you do? (see response, page 222)

myelination The process by which axons become coated with myelin, a fatty substance that speeds the transmission of nerve impulses from neuron to neuron.

corpus callosum A long, thick band of nerve fibers that connects the left and right hemispheres of the brain and allows communication between them.

lateralization Literally, sidedness, referring to the specialization in certain functions by each side of the brain, with one side dominant for each activity. The left side of the brain controls the right side of the body, and vice versa.

As their brains mature, children become better at controlling their emotions. For example, when a stranger greets them, many 2-year-olds are speechless, hiding behind their mothers if possible. Adults may feel equally shy, but they bravely respond. Brain scans of the prefrontal cortex and amygdala (soon described) taken at age 18 may show inhibition, but most inhibited people no longer act in extremely anxious ways (Schwartz et al., 2010). [**Lifespan Link:** Emotional regulation is further discussed in Chapter 10.]

Speed of Thought

After infancy, some brain growth is the result of proliferation of the communication pathways (dendrites and axons). However, most increased brain weight occurs because of **myelination.** *Myelin* (sometimes called the *white matter* of the brain) is a fatty coating on the axons that speeds signals between neurons (see Figure 8.3).

Although myelination continues for decades, the effects are especially apparent in early childhood (Silk & Wood, 2011). The areas of the brain that show greatest early myelination are the motor and sensory areas (Kolb & Whishaw, 2013).

Speed of thought from axon to neuron becomes pivotal when several thoughts must occur in rapid succession. By age 6, most children can see an object and immediately name it, catch a ball and throw it, write their ABCs in proper sequence, and so on. In fact, rapid naming of letters and objects—possible only when myelination is extensive—is a crucial indicator of later reading ability (Shanahan & Lonigan, 2010).

Of course, adults must be patient when listening to young children talk, helping them get dressed, or watching them write each letter of their names. Everything is done more slowly by 6-year-olds than by 16-year-olds because the younger children's brains have less myelination, and slower information processing. However, thanks to myelination, older preschoolers are much quicker than toddlers, who sometimes forget what they were doing before they finish.

The Brain's Connected Hemispheres

One part of the brain that grows and myelinates rapidly during early childhood is the **corpus callosum,** a long, thick band of nerve fibers that connects the left and right sides of the brain. Growth of the corpus callosum makes communication between the hemispheres more efficient, allowing children to coordinate the two sides of their brains, and hence both sides of their bodies.

Failure of the corpus callosum to develop results in serious disorders: This failure is one of several possible causes of autism (Frazier et al., 2012).

To understand the significance of the corpus callosum, note that each side of the body and brain specializes, being dominant for certain functions. This is **lateralization,** literally, "sidedness." The entire human body is lateralized, apparent not only in right- or left-handedness but also in the feet, the eyes, the ears, and the brain itself. Genes, prenatal hormones, and early experiences all affect which side does what. Lateralization advances with development of the corpus callosum (Kolb & Whishaw, 2013).

Left-handed people tend to have thicker corpus callosa than right-handed people do, perhaps because they need to readjust the interaction between the two sides of their bodies, depending on the task. For example, most left-handed people brush their teeth with their left hand because using their dominant hand is more natural, but they shake hands with their right hand because that is what the social convention requires.

The Left-Handed Child

Infants and toddlers usually prefer one hand to the other for grabbing spoons and rattles. By age 2 most children have a dominant hand used for scribbling and throwing. Preschool teachers notice that about 1 child in 10 prefers the left hand. Handedness is partly genetic (Goymer, 2007), but many cultures have tried to make everyone right-handed, with some success. When left-handed children were forced to use their right hands, most learned to write right-handedly. However, neurological success was incomplete: Their brains were only partly reprogrammed (Klöppel et al., 2007).

Even today, many cultures endorse the belief that being right-handed is best, an example of the *difference-equals-deficit error,* explained in Chapter 1. Consider language: In English, a "left-handed compliment" is insincere, and no one wants to have "two left feet" or to be "out in left field." In Latin, *dexter* (as in *dexterity*) means "right" and *sinister* means "left" (and also "evil"). *Gauche,* the French word for *left,* means "socially awkward" in English. Many languages are written from left to right, which is easier for right-handed people.

The design of doorknobs, scissors, baseball mitts, instrument panels, and other objects favor the right hand. (Some manufacturers have special versions for lefties, but few young children know to ask for them.) In many Asian and African cultures, the left hand is used only for wiping after defecation; it is an insult to give someone anything with that "dirty" hand.

Developmentalists advise against switching a child's handedness, not only because this causes adult–child conflicts and may create neurological confusion but also because left lateralization is an advantage in some professions, especially those involving creativity and split-second actions. A disproportionate number of artists, musicians, and sports stars were/are left-handed, including Jimi Hendrix, Bill Gates, Oprah Winfrey, Lady Gaga, and Justin Bieber. Five of the past six presidents of the United States were/are lefties: Gerald Ford, Ronald Reagan, George H.W. Bush, Bill Clinton, and Barack Obama.

Acceptance of left-handedness is more widespread now than a century ago. More adults in Great Britain and the United States claim to be left-handed today (about 10 percent) than in 1900 (about 3 percent) (McManus et al., 2010). There also seem to be more left-handed men than women, as well as more left-handers in North America than elsewhere.

The Whole Brain

Astonishing studies of humans whose corpus callosa were severed to relieve severe epilepsy, as well as research on humans and other vertebrates with intact corpus callosa, have revealed how the brain's hemispheres specialize. Typically, the brain's left half controls the body's right side as well as areas dedicated to logical reasoning, detailed analysis, and the basics of language. Then the brain's right half controls the body's left side and areas dedicated to emotional and creative impulses, including appreciation of music, art, and poetry. Thus, the left side notices details and the right side grasps the big picture.

This left–right distinction has been exaggerated, especially when broadly applied to people (Hugdahl & Westerhausen, 2010). No one is exclusively left-brained or right-brained (except severely brain-damaged individuals); moreover, the brain is plastic [**Lifespan Link:** Brain plasticity is discussed in Chapter 1], especially in childhood, so a lost function in one hemisphere is sometimes replaced in the other hemisphere.

STOCKBYTE/GETTY IMAGES

Smarter than Most? Beware of stereotypes. Obviously, this student is a girl, Asian, left-handed, and attending a structured school (note the uniform). Each of these four characteristics leads some to conclude that she is more intelligent than other 7-year-olds. But all children have brains with the potential to learn: Specific teaching, not innate characteristics, is crucial.

>> Response for Early-Childhood Teachers (from page 220): One solution is to remind yourself that the children's brains are not yet myelinated enough to enable them to quickly walk, talk, or even button their jackets. Maturation has a major effect, as you will observe if you can schedule excursions in September and again in November. Progress, while still slow, will be a few seconds faster.

Further, both sides of the brain are usually involved in every skill. That is why the corpus callosum is crucial. As myelination progresses, signals between the two hemispheres become quicker and clearer, enabling children to become better thinkers and less clumsy.

To pick an easy example: No 2-year-old has the balance to hop on one foot, but most 6-year-olds can do it—an example of brain balancing. Many songs, dances, and games that young children love involve moving their bodies in some coordinated way—difficult, but fun because of that.

Maturation of the Prefrontal Cortex

The entire frontal lobe continues to develop for many years after early childhood; dendrite density and myelination are still increasing in emerging adulthood (Johnson, 2010). Nonetheless, neurological control advances significantly every year between ages 2 and 6, as is evident in several ways:

- Sleep becomes more regular.
- Emotions become more nuanced and responsive.
- Temper tantrums subside.
- Uncontrollable laughter and tears are less common.

One example of the maturing brain is in the game *Simon Says*. Players are supposed to follow the leader *only* when orders are preceded by the words "Simon says." Thus, if leaders touch their noses and say, "Simon says touch your nose," players are supposed to touch their noses; but when leaders touch their noses and say, "Touch your nose," no one is supposed to follow the example. Young children lose at this game because they impulsively do what they see and hear. Older children can think before acting. The prefrontal cortex works!

Such advances can be observed in every child, but might personal experience rather than brain maturation be the reason? A convincing demonstration that something neurological, not experiential, is the primary reason for these changes comes from a series of experiments.

These experiments begin with young children given a set of cards with clear outlines of trucks or flowers, some red and some blue. They are asked to "play the shape game," putting trucks in one pile and flowers in another. Three-year-olds (and even some 2-year-olds) can do this correctly.

Then children are asked to "play the color game," sorting the cards by color. Most children under age 4 fail. Instead they sort by shape, as they had done before. This basic test has been replicated in many nations; 3-year-olds usually get stuck in their initial sorting pattern. By age 5 (and sometimes age 4). most children make the switch.

When this result was first obtained, experimenters thought perhaps the children didn't have enough experience to know their colors; so the scientists switched the order, first playing "the color game." Most 3-year-olds did that correctly, because most 3-year-olds know colors. Then, when these children were asked to play "the shape game," they sorted by color! Even with a new set of cards, such as yellow and green or rabbits and boats, 3-year-olds still tend to sort however they did originally, either by color or shape.

Researchers are looking into many possible explanations for this result (Müller et al., 2006; Marcovitch et al., 2010; Ramscar et al., 2013). All agree, however, that something in the brain must mature before children are able to switch from one way of sorting objects to another. [**Lifespan Link:** Maturation of the prefrontal cortex is also discussed in Chapter 5, Chapter 11, and Chapter 14.]

Impulsiveness and Perseveration

Neurons have only two kinds of impulses: on–off, or activate–inhibit. Each is signaled by biochemical messages from dendrites to axons to neurons. Both activation and inhibition are necessary for thoughtful adults, who neither leap too quickly nor hesitate too long. A balanced brain is best throughout life: One sign of cognitive loss in late adulthood is that people become too cautious or too impulsive.

Many young children are notably unbalanced. They are impulsive, flitting from one activity to another. That explains why many 3-year-olds cannot stay quietly on one task, even in "circle time" in preschool, where each child is supposed to sit in place, not talking or touching anyone else. Poor **impulse control** signifies a personality disorder in adulthood but not in early childhood. Few 3-year-olds are capable of sustained attention, as required in primary school.

During the same age period, the see-saw tips in the opposite direction, as some children play with a single toy for hours. **Perseveration** refers to the tendency to persevere in, or stick to, one thought or action, as evident in the card-sorting study just described (Hanania, 2010).

Many explanations are plausible, but the tendency is unmistakable. Often young children repeat one phrase or question again and again, and often once they start giggling they find it hard to stop. Another example of perseveration occurs when a child has a tantrum when told to stop an activity. (Wise teachers give a warning—"Cleanup in 5 minutes"—which may help.) The tantrum itself may perseverate. Crying may become uncontrollable, because the child is stuck in the emotion that triggered the tantrum.

Impulsiveness and perseveration are opposite manifestations of the same underlying cause: immaturity of the prefrontal cortex. No young child is perfect at regulating attention; impulsiveness and perseveration are evident in every 2-year-old (Else-Quest et al., 2006).

Over the years of childhood, from ages 2 to 12, brain maturation (innate) and emotional regulation (learned) increase: Most older children can pay attention and switch activities as needed. By early adolescence, children change tasks at the sound of the bell—no perseveration allowed.

Exceptions include children diagnosed with attention-deficit/hyperactivity disorder (ADHD), who are too impulsive for their age. An imbalance between the left and right sides of the prefrontal cortex and abnormal growth of the corpus callosum seem to underlie (and perhaps cause) ADHD (Gilliam et al., 2011).

As with all biological maturation, development of impulse control and behavioral flexibility is related to culture—hence the reason this chapter is called *biosocial development,* not simply *physical development.* A study of Korean preschoolers found that they developed impulse control and reduced perseveration sooner than a comparable group of English children (Oh & Lewis, 2008).

This study included the shape–color task: Of the 3-year-olds, 40 percent of Korean children but only 14 percent of British children successfully shifted from sorting by shape to sorting by color. The researchers considered many possible reasons and finally concluded that "a cultural explanation is more likely" (page 96).

impulse control The ability to postpone or deny the immediate response to an idea or behavior.

perseveration The tendency to persevere in, or stick to, one thought or action for a long time.

Ashes to Ashes, Dust to Dust Many religious rituals have sustained humans of all ages for centuries, including listening quietly in church on Ash Wednesday—as Nailah Pierre tries to do. Sitting quietly is developmentally difficult for young children, but for three reasons she probably will succeed: (1) gender (girls mature earlier than boys), (2) experience (she has been in church many times), and (3) social context (she is one of 750 students in her school attending a special service at Nativity Catholic church).

SKIP O'ROURKE/TAMPA BAY TIMES/ZUMAPRESS.COM

Emotions and the Brain

Now that we have considered the prefrontal cortex, we turn to another region of the brain, sometimes called the *limbic system,* the major system for emotions. Emotional expression and emotional regulation advance during early childhood. [**Lifespan Link:** Emotional regulation is discussed further in Chapter 10 and Chapter 15.] Crucial to that advance are three parts of the brain—the amygdala, the hippocampus, and the hypothalamus.

The Limbic System

The **amygdala** is a tiny structure deep in the brain, about the same shape and size as an almond. It registers emotions, both positive and negative, especially fear (Kolb & Whishaw, 2013). Increased amygdala activity is one reason some young children have terrifying nightmares or sudden terrors, overwhelming the prefrontal cortex. A child may refuse to enter an elevator or may hide from a nightmare. The amygdala responds to comfort but not to logic. If a child is terrified of, say, a dream of a lion in the closet, an adult should not laugh but might open the closet door and command the lion to go home.

Another structure in the emotional network is the **hippocampus,** located right next to the amygdala. A central processor of memory, especially memory for locations, the hippocampus responds to the anxieties of the amygdala by summoning memory. A child can remember, for instance, whether previous elevator-riding was scary or fun.

Early memories of location are fragile because the hippocampus is still developing. Nonetheless, emotional memories from early childhood can interfere with expressed, rational thinking: An adult might have a panic attack but not know why.

The interaction of the amygdala and the hippocampus is sometimes helpful, sometimes not; fear can be constructive or destructive (LaBar, 2007). Studies performed on some animals show that when the amygdala is surgically removed, the animals are fearless in situations that should scare them. For instance, a cat without an amygdala will stroll nonchalantly past monkeys—something no normal cat would do (Kolb & Whishaw, 2013).

A third part of the limbic system, the **hypothalamus,** responds to signals from the amygdala (arousing) and to signals from the hippocampus (usually dampening) by producing cortisol, oxytocin, and other hormones that activate parts of the brain and body (see Figure 8.4). Ideally, this hormone production occurs in moderation (Tarullo & Gunnar, 2006).

As the limbic system develops, young children watch their parents' emotions closely. If a parent looks worried when entering an elevator, the child may fearfully cling to the parent when the elevator moves. If this sequence recurs often enough, the child may become hypersensitive to elevators, as fear from the amygdala joins memories from the hippocampus, increasing cortisol via the hypothalamus. If, instead, the parent makes elevator riding fun (letting the child push the buttons, for instance), initial feelings of fear subside, and the child's brain will be aroused to enjoy elevators—even when there is no need to go from floor to floor.

Knowing the varieties of fears and joys is helpful when a teacher takes a group of young children on a trip. To stick with the elevator example, one child might be terrified while another child might rush forward, pushing the close button before the teacher enters. Every experience (elevators, fire engines, subways, animals at the zoo, a police officer) is likely to trigger a range of emotions, without much reflection, in a group of 3-year-olds: A trip needs several adults, ready to respond to whatever reactions the children have.

amygdala A tiny brain structure that registers emotions, particularly fear and anxiety.

hippocampus A brain structure that is a central processor of memory, especially memory for locations.

hypothalamus A brain area that responds to the amygdala and the hippocampus to produce hormones that activate other parts of the brain and body.

Especially for Neurologists Why do many experts think the limbic system is an oversimplified explanation of brain function? (see response, page 225)

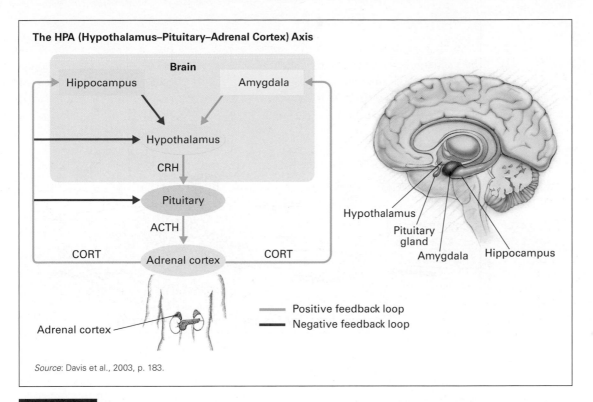

The HPA (Hypothalamus–Pituitary–Adrenal Cortex) Axis

Brain

Hippocampus   Amygdala

Hypothalamus

CRH

Pituitary

ACTH

CORT   Adrenal cortex   CORT

Adrenal cortex

━━━ Positive feedback loop
━━━ Negative feedback loop

Hypothalamus
Pituitary gland
Amygdala   Hippocampus

Source: Davis et al., 2003, p. 183.

FIGURE 8.4

A Hormonal Feedback Loop This diagram simplifies a hormonal linkage, the HPA (hypothalamus–pituitary–adrenal) axis. Both the hippocampus and the amygdala stimulate the hypothalamus to produce CRH (corticotropin-releasing hormone), which in turn signals the pituitary gland to produce ACTH (adrenocorticotropic hormone). ACTH then triggers the production of CORT (glucocorticoids) by the adrenal cortex (the outer layers of the adrenal glands, atop the kidneys). Fear may either build or disappear, depending on other factors, including how the various parts of the brain interpret that first alert from the amygdala.

Stress Hormones

Cortisol, which is the primary stress hormone, may flood the brain and destroy part of the hippocampus. Does that mean a young child's life should be stress-free? No, some cortisol is needed for normal development. However, there is "extensive evidence of the disruptive impacts of toxic stress" (Siegel et al., 2013). Too much cortisol early in life may lead to permanent deficits in learning and health, with major depression, post-traumatic stress disorder, and attention-deficit/hyperactivity in childhood and adolescence.

Yet, stress may sometimes be helpful. Ongoing research seeks to discover exactly how and when stress harms the human brain. Emotionally-arousing experiences—meeting new friends, entering school, visiting a strange place—seem beneficial if a young child has someone or something to moderate the stress. Parent support and child personality at age 3 (such as a child who is not too fearful, and thus becomes accustomed to new experiences) are crucial moderators. When past support and experience are in place, cortisol will not be overwhelming during stressful events at age 6.

In an experiment conducted by Teoh and Lamb (2013), brain scans and hormone measurements were taken of 4- to 6-year-olds immediately after a fire alarm. As measured by their levels of cortisol, some children were upset and some were not. Two weeks later, either a friendly or a stern adult questioned them about the event. Those with higher cortisol reactions to the alarm remembered more details than did those with less stress, which suggests that some stress aided memory.

>> **Response for Neurologists** (from page 224): The more we discover about the brain, the more complex we realize it is. Each part has specific functions and is connected to every other part.

BARBARA SMALLER/THE NEW YORKER COLLECTION/CARTOONBANK.COM

"I would share, but I'm not there developmentally."

Good Excuse It is true that emotional control of selfish instincts is difficult for young children because the prefrontal cortex is not yet mature enough to regulate some emotions. However, family practices can advance social understanding.

Another study found that children remembered more when they were interrogated by a friendly interviewer (Quas et al., 2004). Generally, a child's memory is more accurate when an interviewer is warm and attentive. This finding is particularly useful if a child witnesses a crime (Teoh & Lamb, 2013).

Context is always crucial: Stress can facilitate memory and learning if adults are reassuring. Because of individual variations in genes and early childhood, a study of 5- and 6-year-olds exposed to a stressful experience found that cortisol rose dramatically in some children but not at all in others (de Weerth et al., 2013).

In addition to such individual differences, a crucial factor is past history, specifically whether or not the children experienced chronic early stress. A young child who experienced neglect or abuse day after day may become unable to use his or her brain/cortisol connection to adjust to stress later on (Evans & Kim, 2013).

Studies of children who have been maltreated suggest that excessive stress hormones in early childhood may permanently damage the brain, blunting or accelerating emotional responses lifelong (Wilson et al., 2011). Sadly, this topic leads again to research on those adopted Romanian children mentioned in Chapter 7. When they saw pictures of happy, sad, frightened, or angry faces, their limbic systems were less reactive than were those of Romanian children living with their biological parents. Their brains were also less lateralized, suggesting less specialized, less efficient thinking (Parker & Nelson, 2005). Thus early stress had probably damaged their brains.

Romania no longer permits wholesale international adoptions. Nonetheless, as mentioned earlier, some Romanian children are raised in institutions. In one study, several of them were randomly assigned to foster homes at about age 2. By age 4, they were smarter (by about 10 IQ points) than those who remained institutionalized (Nelson et al., 2007). This research suggests that ages 2 to 4 constitute a sensitive time for brain growth, as measured by tests of language and memory.

SUMMING UP

The brain continues to mature during early childhood. Myelination is notable in several crucial areas. One is the corpus callosum, which connects the two sides of the brain and therefore allows control of the two sides of the body. Increased myelination speeds up actions and

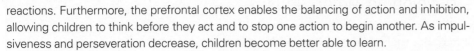

reactions. Furthermore, the prefrontal cortex enables the balancing of action and inhibition, allowing children to think before they act and to stop one action to begin another. As impulsiveness and perseveration decrease, children become better able to learn.

Several key areas of the brain—including the amygdala, the hippocampus, and the hypothalamus—are involved in emotions. Children whose early experiences are highly stressful and who lack nurturing caregivers may be impaired in emotional regulation and expression. ∎

>> Improving Motor Skills

Maturation of the prefrontal cortex allows impulse control, whereas myelination of the corpus callosum and lateralization of the brain permit better physical coordination. No wonder children move with greater speed, agility, and grace as they age. (See Visualizing Development, p. 228.)

Mastery of gross and fine motor skills results not only from maturation but also from extensive, active play. A study in Brazil, Kenya, and the United States tracked how young children spend their time. Cultural variations and differences based on socioeconomic status (SES) emerged. For example, middle-class European American children did the most talking with adults, and working-class Kenyan children did the most chores. But at every income level in all three nations, children spent more time playing than doing anything else—chores, lessons, or conversations (Tudge et al., 2006).

Gross Motor Skills

Gross motor skills improve dramatically. When playing, many 2-year-olds fall down and bump clumsily into each other. By contrast, some 5-year-olds are skilled and graceful, performing coordinated dance steps or sports moves.

Specific Skills

Many North American 5-year-olds can ride a tricycle, climb a ladder, and pump a swing, as well as throw, catch, and kick a ball. A few can do these things by age 3, and some 5-year-olds can already skate, ski, dive, and ride a bike—activities that demand balanced coordination and use of both brain hemispheres. Elsewhere, some 5-year-olds swim in oceans or climb cliffs. Brain maturation, motivation, and guided practice undergird all motor skills.

Adults need to make sure children have a safe space, time, appropriate equipment, and playmates. Children learn best from peers who demonstrate whatever the child is ready to try, from catching a ball to climbing a tree. Of course, culture and locale influence particulars: Some small children learn to ski, others to sail.

AT ABOUT THIS TIME

Motor Skills at Ages 2–6*

Approximate Age	Skill or Achievement
2 years	Run for pleasure without falling (but bumping into things) Climb chairs, tables, beds, out of cribs Walk up stairs Feed self with spoon Draw lines, spirals
3 years	Kick and throw a ball Jump with both feet off the floor Pedal a tricycle Copy simple shapes (e.g., circle, rectangle) Walk down stairs Climb ladders
4 years	Catch a ball (not too small or thrown too fast) Use scissors to cut Hop on either foot Feed self with fork Dress self (no tiny buttons, no ties) Copy most letters Pour juice without spilling Brush teeth
5 years	Skip and gallop in rhythm Clap, bang, sing in rhythm Copy difficult shapes and letters (e.g., diamond shape, letter S) Climb trees, jump over things Use knife to cut Tie a bow Throw a ball Wash face, comb hair
6 years	Draw and paint with preferred hand Write simple words Scan a page of print, moving the eyes systematically in the appropriate direction Ride a bicycle Do a cartwheel Tie shoes Catch a ball

*Context and culture are crucial for acquisition of all these skills. For example, many 6-year-olds cannot tie shoelaces because they have no shoes with laces.

Developing Motor Skills

Every child can do more with each passing year. These examples detail what one child might be expected to accomplish from ages 2 to 6. But each child is unique, and much depends on culture, practice, and maturity.

SKILLS

AVERAGE HEIGHT IN INCHES
BOYS 45.5   GIRLS 45.0

Draw and paint recognizable images
Write simple words
Read a page of print   **6 years**
Tie shoes
Catch a small ball

BOYS 43.0   GIRLS 42.5

Skip and gallop in rhythm
Clap, bang, sing in rhythm
Copy difficult shapes and letters
Climb trees, jump over things   **5 years**
Use a knife to cut
Wash face, comb hair

BOYS 40.5   GIRLS 40.0

Catch a beach ball
Use scissors
Hop on either foot
Feed self with fork
Dress self   **4 years**
Copy most letters
Pour juice without spilling
Brush teeth

BOYS 37.5   GIRLS 37.0

Kick and throw a ball
Jump with both feet
Pedal a tricycle
Copy simple shapes   **3 years**
Walk down stairs
Climb ladders

BOYS 34.1   GIRLS 33.5

Run without falling
Climb out of crib
Walk up stairs   **2 years**
Feed self with spoon
Draw spirals

Practice with the Big Kids Ava is unable to stand as Carlyann can (*left*) but she is thrilled to be wearing her tutu in Central Park, New York, with 230 other dancers in a highly organized attempt to break a record for the most ballerinas on pointe at the same moment. Motor skills are developing in exactly the same way on the other side of the world (right) despite superficial opposites (boys, Japan, soccer, pick-up game).

Recent urbanization concerns many developmentalists. A century ago children with varied skill levels played together in empty lots or fields without adult supervision, but now more than half the world's children live in cities. Many of these are "megacities . . . overwhelmed with burgeoning slums and environmental problems" (Ash et al., 2008, p. 739).

Crowded, violent streets not only impede development of gross motor skills but also add to the natural fears of the immature amygdala, responding to the learned fears of adults. Gone are the days when parents told their children to go out and play, to return when hunger, rain, or nightfall brought them home. Now many parents fear strangers and traffic, keeping their 3- to 5-year-olds inside (Taylor et al., 2009).

Environmental Hazards

Observable dangers are not the only problem. Children who breathe heavily polluted air tend to be impaired in brain development. Is this correlation or causation? Such children often live in low-SES households, in crowded neighborhoods, and attend poor schools. Some rarely play outside. Are we certain that dirty air is one cause of learning problems?

Scientists have grappled with this question and answered yes: Environmental substances cause problems in young children at every SES level, but especially those in lower-income families. This conclusion is easiest to demonstrate with asthma, which reduces oxygen to the brain. In the United States, asthma is far more prevalent among children who live in poverty than among those who do not (U.S. Department of Health and Human Services, 2012).

As you already know, the dynamic systems approach to development means that every impairment has many causes, both in the immediate context and in the impact of past genetic and environmental factors. Nonetheless, a recent study conducted in British Columbia, where universal public health care and detailed birth records allow solid research, showed that air pollution from traffic and industry early in life was one cause, not just a correlate, of asthma (Clark et al., 2010).

This study began with all births in 1999 and 2000 in southwest British Columbia (which includes a major city, Vancouver). For three years, 37,401 children were studied, 3,482 of whom were diagnosed with asthma by age 3. Each of those 3,482 was matched on SES, gender, and so on with five other children from the same group.

Exposure to air pollution, (including carbon monoxide, nitric oxide, nitrogen dioxide, particulate matter, ozone, sulfur dioxide, black carbon, wood smoke, car exhausts, and smoke from parents' cigarettes) was carefully measured.

One finding was that parents could not always protect their children, partly because they did not always know when substances caused poor health. For example, although carbon monoxide emissions are not apparent, when compared to their five matched peers who did not have asthma, those children who were diagnosed with asthma were more likely to live near major highways, where carbon monoxide is more prevalent. Conversely, because wood smoke is easy to see and smell, some parents tried to avoid it, but burning wood did not increase asthma.

Respiratory problems are not the only early-childhood complications caused by pollution. Research on lower animals suggests that hundreds of substances in the air, food, and water affect the brain and thus impede balance, finger dexterity, and motivation. Many substances have not been tested, but some—including lead in the water and air, pesticides in the soil or on clothing, bisphenol A (BPA) in plastic, and secondhand cigarette smoke—are proven harmful.

The administrator of environmental public health for the state of Oregon said, "We simply do not know—as scientists, as regulators, as health professionals— the health impacts of the soup of chemicals to which we expose human beings" (Shibley, quoted in Johnson, 2011). Whether you think Shibley is needlessly alarmist or is simply stating the obvious depends on your own perspective—and maybe on your amygdala.

Lead, however, has been thoroughly researched. The history of lead exposure in the United States illustrates the long path from science to practice, as the following A View from Science illustrates.

A VIEW FROM SCIENCE

Eliminating Lead

Lead was targeted as a poison a century ago (Hamilton, 1914). The symptoms of *plumbism,* as lead poisoning is called, were obvious—intellectual disability, hyperactivity, and even death if the level reached 70 micrograms per deciliter of blood.

The lead industry defended the heavy metal as an additive, arguing that low levels were harmless, and blamed parents for letting their children eat flaking chips of lead paint (which tastes sweet). Further, since children with high levels of lead in their blood were often from low-SES families, some argued that malnutrition, inadequate schools, family conditions, or a host of other causes were the reason for their reduced IQ (Scarr, 1985).

Consequently, lead remained a major ingredient in paint (it speeds drying) and in gasoline (it raises octane) for most of the twentieth century. The fact that babies in lead-painted cribs, that preschoolers living near traffic, and that children in lead-painted homes near industrial waste were intellectually impaired and hyperactive was claimed to be correlation, not causation.

Finally, chemical analysis of blood and teeth, with careful longitudinal and replicated research, proved that lead was indeed a poison for all children (Needleman et al., 1990; Needleman & Gatsonis, 1990). The United States banned the use of lead in paint (in 1978) and automobile fuel (in 1996). The blood level that caused plumbism was set at 40 micrograms per deciliter, then 20, then 10 (and recently danger is thought to begin at 5 micrograms), with no level proven to be risk-free (MMWR, April 5, 2013).

Regulation has made a difference: The percentage of U.S. 1- to 5-year-olds with more than 5 micrograms of lead per deciliter of blood was 8.6 percent in 1999–2001, 4.1% in 2003–2006, and 2.6 percent in 2007–2010 (see Figure 8.5). Children who are young, low-SES, and/or living in old housing tend to have higher levels (MMWR, April 5, 2013).

Parents are beginning to do their part: They are increasing their children's calcium intake, wiping window ledges clean, testing drinking water, avoiding lead-based medicines and crockery (available in some other nations), and making sure children never eat chips of lead-based paint.

In some states (e.g., Colorado and Wyoming), average lead levels for young children are close to zero. In other states that once had extensive lead-based manufacturing, young children are still at risk, probably because of lead in the soil and dust. In 2010, Pennsylvania documented 509 children under age 6 with more than 20 micrograms per deciliter in their blood; Ohio had 417; and Michigan had 254 (National Center for Environmental Health, 2012).

Remember from Chapter 1 that scientists sometimes use data collected for other reasons to draw new conclusions. This is the case with lead. About 15 years after the sharp decline in blood lead levels in preschool children, the rate of violent crime committed by teenagers and young adults fell sharply.

As some nations reduced lead in the environment sooner or later than others, year-by-year correlations became apparent: People who had less lead in their blood as infants commit fewer crimes as teenagers.

A scientist comparing these two trends concluded that some teenagers commit impulsive, violent crimes because their brains were poisoned by lead when they were preschoolers. The correlation is found not only in the United States but also in every nation that has reliable data on lead and crime—Canada, Germany, Italy, Australia, New Zealand, France, and Finland (Nevin, 2007). Not everyone is convinced, but there is no doubt that chemicals in the air, food, and water sometimes affect developing brains.

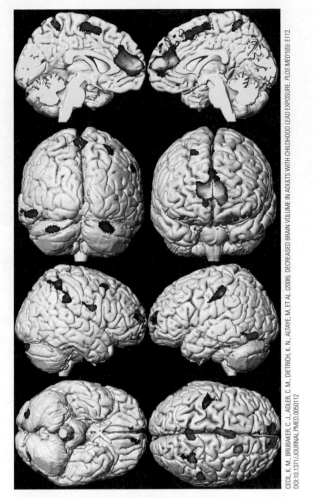

CECIL, K. M., BRUBAKER, C. J., ADLER, C. M., DIETRICH, K. N., ALTAYE, M., ET AL. (2008). DECREASED BRAIN VOLUME IN ADULTS WITH CHILDHOOD LEAD EXPOSURE. *PLOS MED* 5(5): E112. DOI:10.1371/JOURNAL.PMED.0050112

Toxic Shrinkage A composite of 157 brains of adults—who, as children, had high lead levels in their blood—shows reduced volume. The red and yellow hot spots are all areas that are smaller than areas in a normal brain. No wonder lead-exposed children have multiple intellectual and behavioral problems.

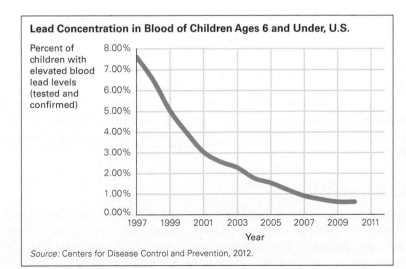

Lead Concentration in Blood of Children Ages 6 and Under, U.S.

Percent of children with elevated blood lead levels (tested and confirmed)

Source: Centers for Disease Control and Prevention, 2012.

FIGURE 8.5

Dramatic Improvement in a Decade Once researchers established the perils of high lead levels in children's blood, the percentage of children suffering from plumbism fell by more than 300 percent. Levels are higher in states that once had heavy manufacturing and lower in mountain and Pacific states.

Source: MMWR (April 5, 2013). Blood lead levels in children aged 1–5 Years—United States, 1999–2010. *62, 245–248.*

Same Situation, Far Apart: Finger Skills
Children learn whatever motor skills their culture teaches. Some master chopsticks, with fingers to spare; others cut sausage with a knife and fork. Unlike these children in Japan (left) and Germany (right), some never master either, because about one-third of adults worldwide eat directly with their hands.

Especially for Immigrant Parents
You and your family eat with chopsticks at home, but you want your children to feel comfortable in Western culture. Should you change your family's eating customs? (see response, page 234)

Fine Motor Skills

Fine motor skills are harder to master than gross motor skills. Whistling, winking, and especially writing are difficult actions. Pouring juice into a glass, cutting food with a knife and fork, and achieving anything more artful than a scribble with a pencil all require a level of muscular control, patience, and judgment that is beyond most 2-year-olds.

Many fine motor skills involve two hands and thus both sides of the brain: The fork stabs the meat while the knife cuts it; one hand steadies the paper while the other writes; tying shoes, buttoning shirts, cutting paper, and zipping zippers require both hands.

Limited myelination of the corpus callosum may be the underlying reason that shoelaces get knotted, paper gets ripped, and zippers get stuck. Short, stubby fingers add to the problem. As with gross motor skills, practice and maturation are key; using glue, markers, and scraps of cloth are part of the preschool curriculum. Puzzles—with large pieces of splinter-proof wood—are essential supplies.

Traditional academic learning depends on fine motor skills and body control. Writing requires finger control, reading a line of print requires eye control, sitting for hours at a desk requires bladder control, and so on. These are beyond most young children, so even the brightest 3-year-old is not allowed in first grade.

Slow maturation is one reason some 6-year-olds are frustrated if their teachers expect them to write neatly and cut straight. Some educators suggest waiting until a child is "ready" for school; some suggest that preschools should focus on readiness; still others suggest that schools should adjust to the immaturity of the child, instead of trying to make the child adjust. This controversy is explored in the next chapter.

Fine motor skills—like many other biological characteristics, such as bones, brains, and teeth—typically mature about six months earlier in girls than in boys. This may be one reason that girls typically outperform boys on tests of reading and writing.

Artistic Expression

Young children are imaginative, creative, and not yet self-critical. They love to express themselves, especially if their parents applaud their performances, display their artwork, and otherwise communicate approval. The fact that their fine motor skills are immature, and thus their drawings lack precision, is irrelevant. Perhaps the immaturity of the prefrontal cortex is a blessing: It allows creativity without self-criticism.

All forms of artistic expression blossom during early childhood; 2- to 6-year-olds love to dance around the room, build an elaborate tower of blocks, make music by pounding in rhythm, and put bright marks on shiny paper. In every artistic domain, skill takes both practice and maturation.

For example, when drawing a person, 2- to 3-year-olds usually draw a "tadpole"—a circle head, dots for eyes, sometimes a smiling mouth, and then a line or two beneath to indicate the rest of the body. Gradually, tadpoles get bodies, limbs, hair, and so on.

Cultural and cohort differences are apparent. For the most part, Chinese culture incorporates the idea that drawing benefits from instruction, so young children are guided in how best to draw a person, a house, and—most important for the Chinese—a word. Consequently, by age 9, Chinese children draw more advanced pictures than children of other cultures. Adult encouragement, child practice, and developing technical skill correlate with more mature, creative drawings a few years later (Chan & Zhao, 2010; Huntsinger et al., 2011).

Bliss for Boys But not for moms. Finger painting develops fine motor skills, which is part of the preschool curriculum in early childhood. This boy shows why most stay-home 3-year-olds miss out on this joy.

AMY WHITT/RADIUS IMAGES/GETTY IMAGES

SUMMING UP

Maturation of the brain leads to better hand and body control. Gross motor skills advance every year as long as young children have space to play, older children to emulate, and freedom from environmental toxins. Sadly, pollution, crowding, and fear of strangers reduce the opportunities many contemporary children have to develop gross motor skills, and may affect their overall learning as well.

Young children also develop their fine motor skills, preparing them for formal education. They love to dance, draw, and build, all of which helps in the gradual mastery of finger movements, which will in turn be essential when they start to write. ∎

>> Injuries and Abuse

In almost all families of every income, ethnicity, and nation, parents want to protect their children while fostering their growth. Yet more children die from violence—either accidental or deliberate—than from any specific disease.

The contrast between disease and accidental death is most obvious in developed nations, where medical prevention, diagnosis, and treatment make fatal illness rare until late adulthood. In the United States in 2010, almost six times as many 1- to 4-year-olds died of accidents or homicide than died of cancer (National Center for Health Statistics, 2013).

Avoidable Injury

Worldwide, injuries cause millions of premature deaths among adults as well as children: Not until age 40 does any specific disease overtake accidents as a cause of mortality, and 14 percent of all life-years lost worldwide are caused by injury (World Health Organization, 2010).

In some nations, malnutrition, malaria, and other infectious diseases *combined* cause more infant and child deaths than injuries do, but nations with high rates of child disease also have high rates of child injury. India, for example, has one of the highest rates worldwide of child motor-vehicle deaths; most children who die in such accidents are pedestrians (Naci et al., 2009). Everywhere, 2- to 6-year-olds

>> **Response for Immigrant Parents**
(from page 232): Children develop the motor skills that they see and practice. They will soon learn to use forks, spoons, and knives. Do not abandon chopsticks completely, because young children can learn several ways of doing things, and the ability to eat with chopsticks is a social asset.

injury control/harm reduction Practices that are aimed at anticipating, controlling, and preventing dangerous activities; these practices reflect the beliefs that accidents are not random and that injuries can be made less harmful if proper controls are in place.

Same Situation, Far Apart: Keeping Everyone Safe Preventing child accidents requires action by both adults and children. In the United States (*below left*), adults passed laws and bought safety seats—and here two sisters have taught each other how to buckle themselves in. In France (*below right*), teachers stop cars while children hold hands to cross the street—each child keeping his or her partner moving ahead.

are at greater risk than slightly older children. In the United States, for instance, children are more than twice as likely to be seriously hurt in early childhood as in middle childhood.

Age-Related Dangers

Why are 2- to 6-year-olds so vulnerable? Some of the reasons have just been explained. Immaturity of the prefrontal cortex makes young children impulsive; they plunge into danger. Unlike infants, their motor skills allow them to run, leap, scramble, and grab in a flash. Their curiosity is boundless; their impulses uninhibited. If they do something that becomes dangerous, such as playing with matches, fear and stress might make them slow to get help.

Age-related trends are apparent in particulars. Falls are more often fatal for the youngest (under 24 months) and oldest (over 80 years); preschoolers have high rates of poisoning and drowning; motor vehicle deaths peak during ages 15–25.

Injury Control

Instead of using the term *accident prevention*, public health experts prefer **injury control** (or **harm reduction**). Consider the implications. *Accident* implies that an injury is random, unpredictable; if anyone is at fault, it's a careless parent or an accident-prone child. This is called the "accident paradigm"—as if "injuries will occur despite our best efforts," allowing the public to feel blameless (Benjamin, 2004, p. 521).

A better phrase is *injury control*, which implies that harm can be minimized with appropriate controls. Minor mishaps (scratches and bruises) are bound to occur, but serious injury is unlikely if a child falls on a safety surface instead of on concrete, if a car seat protects the body in a crash, if a bicycle helmet cracks instead of a skull, or if swallowed pills come from a tiny bottle.

Less than half as many 1- to 5-year-olds in the United States were fatally injured in 2012 as in 1982, thanks to laws that limit poisons, prevent fires, and regulate

cars. Control has not yet caught up with newer hazards, however. For instance, many homes in California, Florida, Texas, and Arizona now have swimming pools: In those states drowning is a leading cause of child death.

Prevention

Prevention begins long before any particular child, parent, or legislator does something foolish. Unfortunately, no one notices injuries and deaths that did not happen. For developmentalists, two types of analysis are useful to predict danger and prevent it.

One is called an *accident autopsy*. Whenever a child is seriously injured, analysis can find causes in the microsystem and exosystem as well as in the macrosystem, and thus protect children in the future. For example, when a child is hit by a car and dies, an autopsy might point not only to parental neglect (microsystem), but also to the lack of parks, speed limits, traffic lights, sidewalks, or curbs (exosystem) or to the fact that the entire nation values fast cars over slow pedestrians (macrosystem).

The second type of analysis involves looking at statistics. For example, the rate of childhood poisoning decreased markedly when pill manufacturers adopted bottles with safety caps that are difficult for 2-year-olds to open; such a statistic goes a long way in countering complaints about the inconvenience of the bottles. New statistics show a rise in the number of children being poisoned by taking adult recreational drugs, such as cocaine, which has become another target for prevention.

Levels of Prevention

Three levels of prevention apply to every health and safety issue.

- In **primary prevention,** the overall situation is structured to make harm less likely. Primary prevention fosters conditions that reduce everyone's chance of injury.
- **Secondary prevention** is more specific, averting harm in high-risk situations or for vulnerable individuals.
- **Tertiary prevention** begins after an injury has already occurred, limiting damage.

In general, tertiary prevention is the most visible of the three levels, but primary prevention is the most effective (Cohen et al., 2010). An example comes from data on pedestrian deaths. Fewer people in the United States die after being hit by a motor vehicle than did 35 years ago (see Figure 8.6). How does each level of prevention contribute?

Primary prevention includes sidewalks, speed bumps, pedestrian overpasses, streetlights, and traffic circles. Cars have been redesigned (e.g., better headlights, windows, and brakes), and

primary prevention Actions that change overall background conditions to prevent some unwanted event or circumstance, such as injury, disease, or abuse.

secondary prevention Actions that avert harm in a high-risk situation, such as stopping a car before it hits a pedestrian.

tertiary prevention Actions, such as immediate and effective medical treatment, that are taken after an adverse event (such as illness or injury) and that are aimed at reducing harm or preventing disability.

FIGURE 8.6

While the Population Grew This chart shows dramatic evidence that prevention measures are succeeding in the United States. Over the same time period, the total population has increased by about one-third, making these results even more impressive.

Source: United States Department of Transportation, 2012.

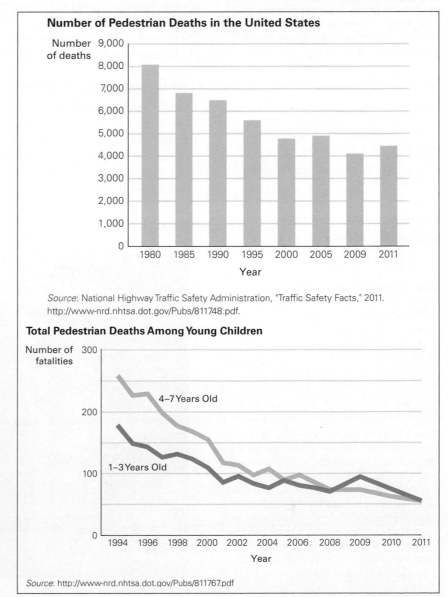

Number of Pedestrian Deaths in the United States

Source: National Highway Traffic Safety Administration, "Traffic Safety Facts," 2011. http://www-nrd.nhtsa.dot.gov/Pubs/811748.pdf.

Total Pedestrian Deaths Among Young Children

Source: http://www-nrd.nhtsa.dot.gov/Pubs/811767.pdf

drivers' competence has improved (e.g., with stronger drunk-driving penalties). Reduction of traffic via improved mass transit provides additional primary prevention.

Secondary prevention reduces danger in high-risk situations. School crossing guards and flashing lights on stopped school buses are secondary prevention as are salt on icy roads, warning signs before blind curves, speed bumps, and walk/don't walk signals at busy intersections.

Finally, *tertiary prevention* reduces damage after an accident. Examples include laws against hit-and-run drivers, speedy ambulances, efficient emergency room procedures, and effective rehabilitation, all of which have been improved from decades ago. Medical personnel speak of the *golden hour,* the hour following an accident, when a victim should get to emergency care. Of course, there is nothing magical about 60 minutes in contrast to 61 minutes, but the faster an injury victim reaches a trauma center, the better the chance of survival (Bansal et al., 2009).

Child Maltreatment

Until about 1960, people thought child maltreatment was rare and consisted of a sudden attack by a disturbed stranger. Today we know better, thanks to a pioneering study based on careful observation in one Boston hospital (Kempe & Kempe, 1978). Maltreatment is neither rare nor sudden, and the perpetrators are usually one or both of the child's own parents. That makes it much worse: Ongoing maltreatment, with no protector, is much more damaging than a single incident, however injurious.

Definitions and Statistics

Child maltreatment now refers to all intentional harm to, or avoidable endangerment of, anyone under 18 years of age. Thus, child maltreatment includes both **child abuse,** which is deliberate action that is harmful to a child's physical, emotional, or sexual well-being, and **child neglect,** which is failure to meet essential physical or emotional needs.

The more that researchers study the long-term effects of maltreatment, the worse neglect seems to be, especially in early childhood. It also is increasingly common. Data on cases of *substantiated* maltreatment from all 50 U.S. states in 2010 found that 78 percent were cases of neglect, 18 percent physical abuse, and 9 percent sexual abuse (a few were tallied in two categories) (U.S. Department of Health and Human Services, 2012).

Substantiated maltreatment means that a case has been reported, investigated, and verified (see Figure 8.7). The U.S. rate was about 700,000 in 2011; almost 200,000 of these incidents occurred during the victims' preschool years. Annually about 1 in every 90 young children, aged 2 to 5 years old, is substantiated as a maltreatment victim.

Reported maltreatment means simply that the authorities have been informed. Since 1993, the number of children *reported* as maltreated in the United States has ranged from about 2.7 million to 3.6 million per year.

CHRISTOPHER SADOWSKI/SPLASH NEWS/NEWSCOM

Especially for Urban Planners Describe a neighborhood park that would benefit 2- to 5-year-olds. (see response, page 239)

Especially for Criminal Justice Professionals Over the past decade, the rate of sexual abuse has gone down by almost 20 percent. What are three possible explanations? (see response, page 239)

child maltreatment Intentional harm to or avoidable endangerment of anyone under 18 years of age.

child abuse Deliberate action that is harmful to a child's physical, emotional, or sexual well-being.

child neglect Failure to meet a child's basic physical, educational, or emotional needs.

substantiated maltreatment Harm or endangerment that has been reported, investigated, and verified.

reported maltreatment Harm or endangerment about which someone has notified the authorities.

Abuse Victim? Fair-skinned Anna, age 5, told the school nurse she was sunburned because her mommy, Patricia, took her to a tanning salon. Patricia said Anna was gardening in the sun; Anna's father and brother (shown here) said all three waited outside the salon while Patricia tanned inside. The story led to an arrest for child endangerment, a court trial, and a media frenzy. Was the media abusive, the nurse intrusive, or the opposite? If your child is sunburned, is it your fault?

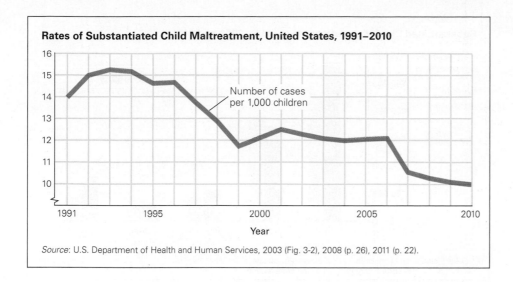

Rates of Substantiated Child Maltreatment, United States, 1991–2010

Number of cases per 1,000 children

Source: U.S. Department of Health and Human Services, 2003 (Fig. 3-2), 2008 (p. 26), 2011 (p. 22).

Still Far Too Many The number of substantiated cases of maltreatment of children under age 18 in the United States is too high, but there is some good news: The rate has declined significantly from its peak in 1993.

Source: U.S. Department of Health and Human Services, 2003 (Fig. 3-2), 2008 (p. 26), 2011 (p. 22)

Observation Quiz The data point for 2010 is close to the bottom of the graph. Does that mean it is close to zero? (see answer, page 239)

Especially for Nurses While weighing a 4-year-old, you notice several bruises on the child's legs. When you ask about them, the child says nothing and the parent says the child bumps into things. What should you do? (see response, page 239)

The three-to-one ratio of reported versus substantiated cases occurs because:

1. Each child is counted only once. Thus, five verified reports about a single child can result in one substantiated case.
2. Substantiation requires proof. Not every investigation finds unmistakable injuries, severe malnutrition, or a witness willing to testify.
3. Many professionals are *mandated reporters,* required to report any signs of possible maltreatment. Some signs are caused by something that could be maltreatment, but investigation finds another cause (Pietrantonio et al., 2013).
4. A report may be false or deliberately misleading (though few are) (Kohl et al., 2009).

Frequency of Maltreatment

How often does maltreatment actually occur? No one knows. Not all cases are noticed; not all that are noticed are reported; and not all reports are substantiated. Similar issues apply in every nation, city, and town, with marked variations in reports and confirmations.

If we rely on official U.S. statistics, interesting trends are apparent. Officially, substantiated child maltreatment increased from about 1960 to 1990 but decreased thereafter (see Figure 8.8). Physical and sexual abuse declined but neglect did not. Other sources also report declines over the past two decades. That seems to be good news; perhaps national awareness of child abuse led to better reporting and then better prevention.

Unfortunately official reports leave room for doubt. For example, Pennsylvania and Maine reported almost identical numbers of substantiated victims in 2010 (3,388 and 3,270, respectively), but the child population of Pennsylvania is ten times that of Maine. No one thinks that Maine children suffer ten times more than Pennsylvania children; something in reporting or substantiating must differ between those two states. Whether or not maltreatment is reported is powerfully influenced by culture (one of my students asked, "When is a child too old to be beaten?") and by personal willingness to report. The United States has become more culturally diverse; could that be why reports are down?

Getting Better? As you can see, the number of victims of child maltreatment in the United States has declined in the past decade. The legal and social-work responses to serious maltreatment have improved over the years, which is a likely explanation for the decline. Other, less sanguine explanations are possible, however.

Source: U.S. Bureau of the Census, 2011b.

Observation Quiz Have all types of maltreatment declined since 2000? (see answer, page 240)

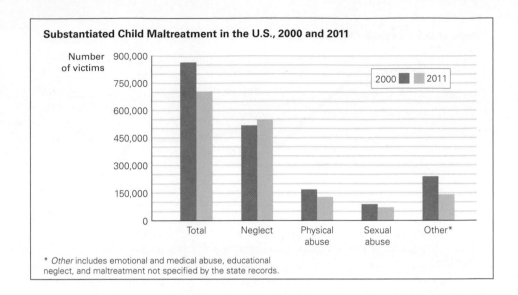

Substantiated Child Maltreatment in the U.S., 2000 and 2011

Number of victims

* *Other* includes emotional and medical abuse, educational neglect, and maltreatment not specified by the state records.

In a confidential nationwide survey of young adults in the United States, 1 in 4 said they had been physically abused ("slapped, hit, or kicked" by a parent or other adult caregiver) before sixth grade, and 1 in 22 had been sexually abused ("touched or forced to touch someone else in a sexual way") (Hussey et al., 2006). Almost never had their abuse been reported. The authors of this study think these rates are *underestimates* (Hussey et al., 2006)!

One reason for these high rates may be that the respondents were asked if they had *ever* been mistreated by someone who was caring for them; most other sources report annual rates. Another reason is that few children report their own abuse. Indeed, many children do not realize that they are mistreated until later, when they compare their experiences with those of their friends. Even then, some adults who were slapped, hit, or kicked in childhood do not think they were abused.

Warning Signs

Often the first sign of maltreatment is delayed development, such as slow growth, immature communication, lack of curiosity, or unusual social interactions. All these difficulties may be evident even at age 1 (Valentino et al., 2006).

During early childhood, maltreated children may seem fearful, startled by noise, defensive and quick to attack, and confused between fantasy and reality. These are symptoms of **post-traumatic stress disorder (PTSD),** first identified in combat veterans, then in adults who had experienced some emotional injury or shock (after a serious accident, natural disaster, or violent crime), and more recently in some maltreated children, who suffer neurologically, emotionally, and behaviorally (Neigh et al., 2009; Weiss et al., 2013). Table 8.1 lists signs of child maltreatment, both neglect and abuse. None of these signs are proof that a child has been abused, but whenever any of them occurs, it signifies trouble.

Consequences of Maltreatment

The impact of any child-rearing practice is affected by the cultural context. Certain customs (such as circumcision, pierced ears, and spanking) are considered abusive in some cultures but not in others; their effects vary accordingly. Children suffer if their parents seem to love them less than most parents in their neighborhood. If a parent forbids something other children have (from candy to cell phones) or punishes more severely or not at all, children might feel unloved. However, although culture is always relevant, there is no doubt that the impact of maltreatment is multifaceted and long-lasting.

post-traumatic stress disorder (PTSD) An anxiety disorder that develops as a delayed reaction to having experienced or witnessed a profoundly shocking or frightening event, such as rape, severe beating, war, or natural disaster. Its symptoms may include flashbacks to the event, hyperactivity and hypervigilance, displaced anger, sleeplessness, nightmares, sudden terror or anxiety, and confusion between fantasy and reality.

TABLE 8.1	Signs of Maltreatment in Children Aged 2 to 10

Injuries that are unlikely to be accidents, such as bruises on both sides of the face or body; burns with a clear line between burned and unburned skin

Repeated injuries, especially broken bones not properly tended (visible on X-ray)

Fantasy play, with dominant themes of violence or sex

Slow physical growth

Unusual appetite or lack of appetite

Ongoing physical complaints, such as stomachaches, headaches, genital pain, sleepiness

Reluctance to talk, to play, or to move, especially if development is slow

No close friendships; hostility toward others; bullying of smaller children

Hypervigilance, with quick, impulsive reactions, such as cringing, startling, or hitting

Frequent absence from school

Frequent change of address

Frequent change in caregivers

Child seems fearful, not joyful, on seeing caregiver

The biological and academic impairment resulting from maltreatment is substantial and thus relatively easy to notice, as when a teacher sees when a child is bruised, broken, shivering, or failing. However, when researchers follow maltreated children over the years, enduring deficits in social skills usually seem more crippling than physical damages. Some research finds that maltreated children tend to hate themselves, and then hate everyone else, with effects still evident in adulthood (Sperry & Widom, 2013).

Hate is corrosive. A warm and enduring friendship might repair some of the damage, but maltreatment itself makes such a friendship unlikely. Many studies have found that mistreated children typically regard other people as hostile and exploitative; hence, abused children are less friendly, more aggressive, and more isolated than other children. The earlier the abuse starts and the longer it continues, the worse their peer relationships are (Scannapieco & Connell-Carrick, 2005). Neglected children may have greater social deficits than abused ones because they never had healthy relationships with their parents (Stevenson, 2007).

Deficits are lifelong. Maltreated children may become bullies or victims or both, not only in childhood and adolescence but also in adulthood. They tend to dissociate, that is, to disconnect their memories from their understanding of themselves (Valentino et al., 2008). Adults who were severely maltreated as children (physically, sexually, or emotionally) often abuse drugs or alcohol, enter unsupportive relationships, become victims or aggressors, sabotage their own careers, eat too much or too little, and engage in other self-destructive behavior (Sperry & Widom, 2013). They also have a much higher risk of emotional disorders and suicide attempts, even after other risk factors (e.g., poverty) are considered (Afifi et al., 2008).

In the current economic climate, finding and keeping a job is a critical aspect of adult well-being; adults who were maltreated suffer with regard to employment as well. One study carefully matched 807 children who had experienced substantiated abuse with other children who were of the same sex, ethnicity, and family SES. About 35 years later, long after the maltreatment had stopped, those who had been mistreated were 14 percent less likely to be employed than those who had not been abused. The researchers concluded: "abused and neglected children experience large and enduring economic consequences" (Currie & Widom, 2010, p. 111). In this study, the women were more impaired than the men: The reason may be that

>> **Response for Urban Planners** (from page 236): The adult idea of a park—a large, grassy open place—is not best for young children. For them, you would design an enclosed area, small enough and with adequate seating to allow caregivers to socialize while watching their children. The playground surface would have to be protective (since young children are clumsy), with equipment that encourages motor skills. Teenagers and dogs should have their own designated area, far from the youngest children.

>> **Response for Criminal Justice Professionals** (from page 236): Hopefully, more adults or children are aware of sexual abuse and stop it before it starts. A second possibility is that sexual abuse is less often reported and substantiated because the culture is more accepting of teenage sex (most victims of sexual abuse are between ages 10 and 18). A third possible explanation is that the increase in the number of single mothers means that fathers have less access to children (fathers are the most frequent sexual abusers).

>> **Response for Nurses** (from page 237): Any suspicion of child maltreatment must be reported, and these bruises are suspicious. Someone in authority must find out what is happening so that the parent as well as the child can be helped.

>> **Answer to Observation Quiz** (from page 237): No. The number is actually 10.0 per 1,000. Note the little squiggle on the graph's vertical axis below the number 10. This means that numbers between 0 and 9 are not shown.

>> **Answer to Observation Quiz**
(from page 238) Most types of abuse are declining, but not neglect. This kind of maltreatment may be the most harmful because the psychological wounds last for decades.

permanency planning An effort by child-welfare authorities to find a long-term living situation that will provide stability and support for a maltreated child. A goal is to avoid repeated changes of caregiver or school, which can be particularly harmful to the child.

foster care A legal, publicly supported system in which a maltreated child is removed from the parents' custody and entrusted to another adult or family, which is reimbursed for expenses incurred in meeting the child's needs.

Mother–Daughter Love, Finally After a difficult childhood, 7-year-old Alexia is now safe and happy in her mother's arms. Maria Luz Martinez was her foster parent and has now become her adoptive mother.

self-esteem, emotional stability, and social skills are even more important for female than for male workers.

This study is just one of hundreds of longitudinal studies, all of which find that maltreatment affects children decades after the broken bones, or skinny bodies, or medical neglect disappear. To protect the health of the entire society in the future, we need to stop maltreatment now.

Three Levels of Prevention, Again

Just as with injury control, the ultimate goal with regard to child maltreatment is *primary prevention,* in which a changed social context makes parents and neighbors more likely to protect every child. Neighborhood stability, parental education, income support, and fewer unwanted children all reduce the rate of maltreatment.

Secondary prevention involves spotting warning signs and intervening to keep a risky situation from getting worse (Giardino & Alexander, 2011). For example, insecure attachment, especially of the disorganized type, is a sign of a disrupted parent–child relationship. [**Lifespan Link:** Attachment types are explained in detail in Chapter 7].

Maltreatment is reduced by home visits from helpful nurses or social workers and by high-quality day care that gives vulnerable parents a break and helps children make friends. Families with several young children are at higher risk, especially when the head of the family is a single parent with money problems. If a nation has free health care for everyone, and if every health worker is a mandated reporter, children can be protected before serious harm occurs.

Tertiary prevention is geared to the limitation of harm after maltreatment has occurred. Reporting and substantiating abuse are the first steps. Often the caregiver needs help in providing better care. Sometimes the child needs another home. If hospitalization is required, that signifies failure: Intervention should have begun much earlier. At that point, treatment is very expensive, harm has already been done, and hospitalization itself further strains the parent–child bond (Rovi et al., 2004).

Children need caregivers they trust, in safe and stable homes, whether they live with their biological parents, a foster family, or an adoptive family. Whenever a child is removed from an abusive or neglectful home, **permanency planning** must begin, through which a family is found to nurture the child until adulthood.

This requires cooperation among social workers, judges, and psychologists as well as the caregivers themselves (Edwards, 2007). Sometimes the child's original family can become better caregivers; sometimes a relative can be found who will provide good care; sometimes a stranger is the best caregiver.

Similar problems arise for homeless children, who often not only move from place to place but also move in and out of the foster care system (Zlotnick et al., 2012). The best ways to help such children are not obvious, as research-based solutions are rarely tested, but it is clear that children whose parents cannot care for them need a permanent family who will guide them throughout childhood.

In **foster care,** children are officially taken from their parents and entrusted to another adult or family; foster parents are reimbursed for the expenses they incur in meeting the children's needs. In every year from 2000 to 2011, about half a million children in the United States were in foster care. More than half of them were in a special version of foster care called **kinship care,** in which a relative—usually a grandmother—becomes the caregiver. This estimate is for official kinship care; three times as many children are unofficially cared for by relatives.

In every nation, most foster children are from low-income, ethnic-minority families, a statistic that reveals problems in the macrosystem as well as the microsystem. In the United States, children in foster care often have experienced severe maltreatment and multiple physical, intellectual, and emotional problems (Jones & Morris, 2012). Despite these problems, most develop better in foster care (including kinship care) than with their original abusive families if a supervising agency provides ongoing financial support and counseling (MacMillan et al., 2009; Oosterman et al., 2007).

Adequate support is not typical, however. One obvious failing is that many children move from one foster home to another for reasons that are unrelated to the child's behavior or wishes (Jones & Morris, 2012). Each move increases the risk of a poor outcome (Oosterman et al., 2007). Another problem is that kinship care is sometimes used as an easy, less expensive solution. Kinship care may be better than stranger care, but supportive services are especially needed since the grandparent who gets the child is also the parent of the abusive adult (Edwards, 2010; Fechter-Leggett & O'Brien, 2010).

Adoption (when an adult or couple is legally granted parenthood) is the best permanent option when a child should not be returned to a parent. However, adoption is difficult for many reasons, among the following:

- Judges and biological parents are reluctant to release children for adoption.
- Most adoptive parents prefer infants.
- Some agencies screen out families not headed by a heterosexual married couple.
- Some professionals insist that adoptive parents be of the same ethnicity and religion as the child.
- Some adults who want to adopt are not ready for the responsibilities entailed.

As detailed many times in this chapter, caring for young children is not easy, whether it involves making them brush their teeth or keeping them safe from harm. Parents shoulder most of the burden, and their love and protection usually result in strong and happy children. Teachers can be crucial during these years, working closely with the parents. Beyond the microsystem, however, complications abound. Parents and teachers are failing with at least a million young children in the United States. The benefit to the entire community of well-nurtured children is obvious; the ways for the society to achieve that goal seem less clear.

kinship care A form of foster care in which a relative of a maltreated child, usually a grandparent, becomes the approved caregiver.

adoption A legal proceeding in which an adult or couple is granted the joys and obligations of being that child's parent(s).

SUMMING UP

As they move with more speed and agility, young children encounter new dangers. Compared to older children, they are more often injured, abused, or neglected. Maltreatment has lifelong consequences, with neglect often worse than abuse, and social and emotional deficits harder to remedy that physical harm.

Overall in the United States, official rates of substantiated maltreatment have decreased in the past 25 years but more needs to be done. In primary prevention, laws and customs need to protect everyone; in secondary prevention, supervision, forethought, and protective care can prevent harm to those at risk. When injury or maltreatment occurs, quick and effective medical and psychosocial intervention is needed (tertiary prevention). Foster care and adoption are sometimes best for children, but these options are not as available as they need to be. Putting an end to maltreatment of all kinds is urgent but complex because changes are needed in families, cultures, communities, and laws.

SUMMARY

Body Changes

1. Well nourished children continue to gain weight and add height during early childhood. Unfortunately, however, many adults overfeed children, not realizing that young children are naturally quite thin.

2. Culture, income, and family customs all affect children's growth. In contrast to past decades, children of low-income families are twice as likely to be overweight as their wealthier counterparts. Worldwide, an increasing number of children are eating too much, which puts them at risk for heart disease and diabetes.

3. Many young children consume too much sugar and too little calcium and other nutrients. One consequence is poor oral health. Children need to brush their teeth and visit the dentist years before their permanent teeth erupt.

Brain Development

4. The brain continues to grow in early childhood, reaching 75 percent of its adult weight at age 2 and 90 percent by age 6.

5. Myelination is substantial during early childhood, speeding messages from one part of the brain to another. The corpus callosum becomes thicker and functions much more effectively. The prefrontal cortex, known as the executive of the brain, is strengthened as well.

6. Brain changes enable more reflective, coordinated thought and memory, better planning, and quicker responses. Left–right specialization is apparent in the brain as well as in the body, although the entire brain and the entire body work together to perform most skills.

7. The expression and regulation of emotions are fostered by several brain areas, including the amygdala, the hippocampus, and the hypothalamus. Childhood abuse may create a flood of stress hormones (especially cortisol) that damage the brain and interfere with learning. However, some stress aids learning if reassurance is also present.

Improving Motor Skills

8. Gross motor skills continue to develop; clumsy 2-year-olds become 6-year-olds who move their bodies well, guided by their culture. Children's main activity is play. By playing with other children in safe places, they practice the skills needed for formal education.

9. Urbanization and chemical pollutants are two factors that hamper development. More research is needed, but it is already apparent that high lead levels in the blood can impair the brain and that opportunities to develop gross motor skills are restricted when play space is scarce.

10. Fine motor skills are difficult to master during early childhood. Young children enjoy expressing themselves artistically, developing their body and finger control as well as self-expression. Fortunately, self-criticism is not yet strong.

Injuries and Abuse

11. Accidents cause more child deaths than diseases, with young children more likely to suffer a serious injury or premature death than older children. Close supervision and public safeguards can protect young children from their own eager, impulsive curiosity.

12. Injury control occurs on many levels, including long before and immediately after each harmful incident. Primary prevention protects everyone. Secondary prevention that focuses on high risk conditions and people, and tertiary prevention that occurs after an injury, are needed.

13. Child maltreatment includes ongoing abuse and neglect, usually by a child's own parents. Each year, about 3 million cases of child maltreatment are reported in the United States; fewer than 1 million are substantiated, with rates decreasing in recent years.

14. Physical abuse is the most obvious form of maltreatment, but neglect is more common and more harmful. Health, learning, and social skills are all impeded by abuse and neglect, not only during childhood but also decades later.

15. Tertiary prevention may include placement of a child in foster care, including kinship care. Adoption is much less common, although often it is the best solution for the child.

16. Permanency planning is required because frequent changes of home environment are harmful to children. Primary and secondary prevention help parents care for their children and reduce the need for tertiary prevention.

KEY TERMS

adoption (p. 241)
amygdala (p. 224)
child abuse (p. 236)
child maltreatment (p. 236)
child neglect (p. 236)
corpus callosum (p. 220)
foster care (p. 240)

hippocampus (p. 224)
hypothalamus (p. 224)
impulse control (p. 223)
injury control/harm reduction (p. 234)
kinship care (p. 241)
lateralization (p. 220)

myelination (p. 220)
permanency planning (p. 240)
perseveration (p. 223)
post-traumatic stress disorder (PTSD) (p. 238)
primary prevention (p. 235)

reported maltreatment (p. 236)
secondary prevention (p. 235)
substantiated maltreatment (p. 236)
tertiary prevention (p. 235)

WHAT HAVE YOU LEARNED?

1. About how much does a well-nourished child grow in height and weight from ages 2 to 6?

2. Why do many parents overfeed their children?

3. Childhood obesity increases the incidence of what adult diseases?

4. What specific measures should be part of oral health in early childhood?

5. When is it normal for children to be picky about eating and other daily routines?

6. How much does the brain grow from ages 2 to 6?

7. Why is *myelination* important for thinking and motor skills?

8. What is the function of the corpus callosum?

9. What should parents do if their toddler seems left-handed?

10. How does the prefrontal cortex affect impulsivity and perseveration?

11. What are the three functions of three areas of the brain that are part of the limbic system?

12. Is stress beneficial or harmful to young children?

13. What three factors help children develop their motor skills?

14. What is known and unknown about the effects on young children of chemicals in food, air, and water?

15. How does brain and body maturation affect children's artistic expression?

16. Why is the term *injury control* preferred over the term *accident prevention*?

17. What primary measures may prevent childhood injury, abuse, and neglect?

18. What secondary measures may prevent childhood injury, abuse, and neglect?

19. What tertiary measures may prevent further childhood injury, abuse, and neglect?

20. Why did few people recognize childhood maltreatment 50 years ago?

21. Why is neglect in childhood considered more harmful than abuse in the long term?

22. Why is it difficult to know exactly how often childhood maltreatment occurs?

23. What are the common signs that indicate a child may be maltreated?

24. What are the long-term consequences of childhood maltreatment?

25. Why would a child be placed in foster care?

APPLICATIONS

1. Keep a food diary for 24 hours, writing down what you eat, how much, when, how, and why. Then think about nutrition and eating habits in early childhood. Do you see any evidence in yourself of imbalance (e.g., not enough fruits and vegetables, too much sugar or fat, eating when you are not really hungry)? Did your food habits originate in early childhood, in adolescence, or at some other time?

2. Go to a playground or other place where young children play. Note the motor skills that the children demonstrate, including abilities and inabilities, and keep track of age and sex. What differences do you see among the children?

3. Ask several parents to describe each accidental injury of each of their children, particularly how it happened and what the consequences were. What primary, secondary, or tertiary prevention measures would have made a difference?

4. Think back to your childhood and the friends you had at that time. Was there any maltreatment? Considering what you have learned in this chapter, why or why not?

>>ONLINE CONNECTIONS

To accompany your textbook, you have access to a number of online resources, including Learning Curve, an adaptive quizzing program, critical thinking questions, and case studies. For access to any of these links, go to www.worthpublishers.com/launchpad/bergerls9e. In addition to these resources, you'll also find links to video clips, personalized study advice, and an ebook. Some of the videos and activities available online include:

- *Brain Development in Early Childhood.* Animations illustrate the macroscopic and microscopic changes as children's brains grow.

- *Stolen Childhoods.* Some children, because of poverty or abuse, never have the opportunities for schooling and nurture that many of us take for granted. Children in a variety of difficult circumstances, from sex work to work in carpet factories, tell their stories in a variety of video clips.

WORTH PUBLISHERS

Early Childhood: Cognitive Development

- **Thinking During Early Childhood**
  Piaget: Preoperational Thought
  A Case to Study: Stones in the Belly
  Vygotsky: Social Learning
  A VIEW FROM SCIENCE:
    Early Childhood and STEM
  Children's Theories
  Brain and Context

- **Language Learning**
  A Sensitive Time
  The Vocabulary Explosion
  Learning Two Languages

- **Early-Childhood Education**
  Homes and Schools
  Child-Centered Programs
  Teacher-Directed Programs
  Head Start
  Long-Term Gains from Intensive Programs

WHAT WILL YOU KNOW?

1. Are young children selfish or just self-centered?
2. How should adults answer when children ask, "Why?"
3. Does it confuse young children if they hear two or more languages?
4. What do children learn in preschool?

Asa, not yet 3 feet tall, held a large rubber ball. He wanted me to play basketball with him.

"We can't play basketball; we don't have a hoop," I said.

"We can imagine a hoop," he answered, throwing up the ball.

"I got it in," he said happily. "You try."

I did.

"You got it in, too," he announced, and did a little dance.

Soon I was tired, and sat down.

"I want to sit and think my thoughts," I told him.

"Get up," he urged. "You can play basketball and think your thoughts."

Asa is typical. Imagination comes easily to him, and he aspires to the skills of older, taller people in his culture. He thinks by doing, and his vocabulary is impressive, but he does not yet understand that my feelings differ from his, that I would rather sit than throw imaginary baskets. He does know, however, that I am likely to respond to his requests.

This chapter describes those characteristics of the young child—imagination, active learning, vocabulary, and some difficulty understanding another person's perspective. I hope it also conveys the joy of understanding the thinking of young children. When that happens, you might do what I did: get up to play.

>> Thinking During Early Childhood

You have just learned that every year of early childhood advances motor skills, brain development, and impulse control. Each of these affects cognition, as first described by Jean Piaget and Lev Vygotsky, already mentioned in Chapter 1.

Piaget: Preoperational Thought

Early childhood is the time of **preoperational intelligence**, the second of Piaget's four periods of cognitive development. He called early-childhood thinking *pre*operational because children do not yet use logical operations (reasoning processes) (Inhelder & Piaget, 1964).

However, preoperational children are past sensorimotor intelligence because they can think in symbols, not just via senses and motor skills. In **symbolic thought**, an object or word can stand for something else, including something

preoperational intelligence Piaget's term for cognitive development between the ages of about 2 and 6; it includes language and imagination (which involve symbolic thought), but logical, operational thinking is not yet possible at this stage.

symbolic thought A major accomplishment of preoperational intelligence that allows a child to think symbolically, including understanding that words can refer to things not seen and that an item, such as a flag, can symbolize something else (in this case, for instance, a country).

not seen, or pretended. That is more advanced than thinking only via the senses, because using words makes it possible to think about many more things at once. However, although vocabulary and imagination can soar, logical connections between ideas are not yet active, not yet *operational*.

The word *dog,* for instance, is at first only the family dog sniffing at the child, not yet a symbol (Callaghan, 2013). By age 2, the word becomes a symbol: It can refer to a remembered dog, or a plastic dog, or an imagined dog. Symbolic thought allows for the language explosion (detailed later in this chapter), which enables children to talk about thoughts and memories. However, since thought is preoperational, it is hard for young children to understand the historical connections, similarities, and differences between dogs and wolves, or even between a cocker spaniel and a collie.

animism The belief that natural objects and phenomena are alive.

Symbolic thought helps explain **animism**, the belief of many young children that natural objects (such as a tree or a cloud) are alive and that nonhuman animals have the same characteristics as the child. Many children's stories include animals or objects that talk and listen (Aesop's fables, *Winnie-the-Pooh*, *Goodnight Moon*, *The Day the Crayons Quit*). Preoperational thought is symbolic and magical, not logical and realistic. Animism gradually disappears as the mind becomes more mature (Kesselring & Müller, 2011).

Obstacles to Logic

Piaget described symbolic thought as characteristic of preoperational thought. He also described four limitations that make logic difficult until about age 6: centration, focus on appearance, static reasoning, and irreversibility.

centration A characteristic of preoperational thought in which a young child focuses (centers) on one idea, excluding all others.

egocentrism Piaget's term for children's tendency to think about the world entirely from their own personal perspective.

Centration is the tendency to focus on one aspect of a situation to the exclusion of all others. Young children may, for example, insist that Daddy is a father, not a brother, because they center on the role that he fills for them.

The daddy example illustrates a particular type of centration that Piaget called **egocentrism**—literally, "self-centeredness." Egocentric children contemplate the world exclusively from their personal perspective.

Egocentrism is not selfishness, however. One 3-year-old chose to buy a model car as a birthday present for his mother: His "behavior was not selfish or greedy; he carefully wrapped the present and gave it to his mother with an expression that clearly showed that he expected her to love it" (Crain, 2005, p. 108).

focus on appearance A characteristic of preoperational thought in which a young child ignores all attributes that are not apparent.

A second characteristic of preoperational thought is a **focus on appearance** to the exclusion of other attributes. For instance, a girl given a short haircut might worry that she has turned into a boy. In preoperational thought, a thing is whatever it appears to be—evident in the joy young children have in wearing the hats or shoes of a grown-up.

static reasoning A characteristic of preoperational thought in which a young child thinks that nothing changes. Whatever is now has always been and always will be.

Third, preoperational children use **static reasoning**, believing that the world is unchanging, always in the state in which they currently encounter it. Many children cannot imagine that their own parents were ever children. If they are told that Grandma is their mother's mother, they still do not understand how people change with maturation. One preschooler wanted his grandmother to tell his mother to never spank him because "she has to do what her mother says."

irreversibility A characteristic of preoperational thought in which a young child thinks that nothing can be undone. A thing cannot be restored to the way it was before a change occurred.

The fourth characteristic of preoperational thought is **irreversibility**. Preoperational thinkers fail to recognize that reversing a process sometimes restores whatever existed before. A young girl might cry because her mother put lettuce on her sandwich. Overwhelmed by her desire to have things "just right," she might reject the food even after the lettuce is removed because she believes that what is done cannot be undone.

A CASE TO STUDY

Stones in the Belly

As we were reading a book about dinosaurs, 3-year-old Caleb told me that some dinosaurs (*sauropods*) have stones in their bellies. It helps them digest their food and then poop and pee.

I was amazed, never having known this before.

"I didn't know that dinosaurs ate stones," I said.

"They don't eat them."

"Then how do they get the stones in their bellies? They must swallow them."

"They don't eat them."

"Then how do they get in their bellies?"

"They are just there."

"How did they get there?"

"They don't eat them," said Caleb. "Stones are dirty. We don't eat them."

I dropped it, but my question apparently puzzled him. Later he asked his mother, "Do dinosaurs eat stones?"

"Yes, they eat stones so they can grind their food," she answered. At that, Caleb was quiet.

In all of this, preschool cognition is evident. Caleb's vocabulary is impressive, although he uses the word *belly* for *stomach*, since belly is easier for children to say. He can name several kinds of dinosaurs, as can many young children. He also shares with many other children a fascination with defecation and large animals, topics no longer intriguing to adults.

But logic eludes Caleb, as it does most young children. It seems obvious that dinosaurs must somehow have gotten the stones into their bellies. However, in his static thinking, Caleb said the stones "were just there." In his typical egocentrism, he rejects the thought that they ate them, because he knows that stones are too dirty for him to eat. Should I have expected him to tell me that I was right, when his mother agreed with me?

Conservation and Logic

Piaget highlighted several ways in which preoperational intelligence disregards logic. A famous set of experiments involved **conservation**, the notion that the amount of something remains the same (is conserved) despite changes in its appearance.

Suppose two identical glasses contain the same amount of pink lemonade, and the liquid from one of these glasses is poured into a taller, narrower glass. If young children are asked whether one glass contains more or both glasses contain the same amount, they will insist that the narrower glass (with the higher level) has more. (See Figure 9.1 for other examples.)

All four characteristics of preoperational thought are evident in this mistake. Young children fail to understand conservation because they focus (*center*) on

conservation The principle that the amount of a substance remains the same (i.e., is conserved) even when its appearance changes.

Especially for Nutritionists How can Piaget's theory help you encourage children to eat healthy foods? (see response, page 249)

Easy Question; Obvious Answer (below, left) Sadie, age 5, carefully makes sure both glasses contain the same amount. (below, right) When one glass of pink lemonade is poured into a wide jar, she triumphantly points to the tall glass as having more. Sadie is like all 5-year-olds—only a development psychologist or a 7-year-old child knows better.

WORTH PUBLISHERS

Tests of Various Types of Conservation

Type of Conservation	Initial Presentation	Transformation	Question	Preoperational Child's Answer
Volume	Two equal glasses of liquid.	Pour one into a taller, narrower glass.	Which glass contains more?	The taller one.
Number	Two equal lines of checkers.	Increase spacing of checkers in one line.	Which line has more checkers?	The longer one.
Matter	Two equal balls of clay.	Squeeze one ball into a long, thin shape.	Which piece has more clay?	The long one.
Length	Two sticks of equal length.	Move one stick.	Which stick is longer?	The one that is farther to the right.

FIGURE 9.1

Conservation, Please According to Piaget, until children grasp the concept of conservation at (he believed) about age 6 or 7, they cannot understand that the transformations shown here do not change the total amount of liquid, checkers, clay, and wood.

what they see (*appearance*), noticing only the immediate (*static*) condition. It does not occur to them that they could reverse the process and re-create the level of a moment earlier (*irreversibility*).

Piaget's original tests of conservation required children to respond verbally to an adult's questions. Later research has found that when the tests of logic are simplified or made playful, young children may succeed. In many ways, children indicate via eye movements or gestures that they know something before they can say it in words (Goldin-Meadow, 2009).

As with sensorimotor intelligence in infancy, Piaget underestimated what preoperational children could understand. Piaget was right that young children are not as logical as older children, but he did not realize how much they could learn.

Brain scans, videos measured in milliseconds, and the computer programs that developmentalists now use were not available to him. Studies from the past 20 years show intellectual activity before age 6 that was not previously known, although they also show that Piaget was perceptive about many aspects of cognition (Crone & Ridderinkhof, 2011).

Given the new data, it is easy to be critical of Piaget. However, note that many adults make the same mistakes as children. For instance, the shape of boxes and bottles in the grocery store undermine adults' sense of conservation (package designers know that an ounce does not always appear to be an ounce). Animism is evident in many religious and cultural myths that include talking, thinking animals.

Indeed, most adults encourage children to believe in Santa Claus, the Tooth Fairy, and so on (Barrett, 2008). If preschoolers are foolish to imagine that animals and plants have human traits, what are adults who talk to their pets and who mourn the death of a tree? And why do some adults take it personally when it rains unexpectedly?

Vygotsky: Social Learning

For decades, the magical, illogical, and self-centered aspects of cognition dominated our concepts of early-childhood thought. Scientists were understandably awed by Piaget. His description of egocentrism and magical thinking was confirmed daily by anecdotes of young children's behavior.

Vygotsky emphasized another side of early cognition—that each person's thinking is shaped by other people's wishes and goals. He emphasized the social aspects of development, a contrast to Piaget's emphasis on the individual. That led Vygotsky to notice the power of culture, acknowledging that "the culturally specific nature of experience is an integral part of how the person thinks and acts," as several developmentalists explain (Gauvain et al., 2011).

Mentors

Vygotsky believed that cognitive development is embedded in a social context at every age (Vygotsky, 1934/1987). He stressed that children are curious and observant. They ask questions—about how machines work, why weather changes, where the sky ends—and seek answers from more knowledgeable mentors, who might be their parents, teachers, older siblings, or just a stranger. These answers are affected by the mentors' perceptions and assumptions—that is, their culture—which shapes their thought.

As you remember from Chapter 2, children learn through *guided participation,* as mentors teach them. Parents are the first guides, although children are guided by many others too. For example, the verbal proficiency of children in day-care centers is affected by the language of their playmates, who teach vocabulary without consciously doing so (Mashburn et al., 2009).

According to Vygotsky, children learn because their mentors do the following:

- Present challenges.
- Offer assistance (without taking over).
- Add crucial information.
- Encourage motivation.

Overall, the ability to learn from mentors indicates intelligence; according to Vygotsky: "What children can do with the assistance of others might be in some sense even more indicative of their mental development than what they can do alone" (1934/1987, p. 5).

Scaffolding

Vygotsky believed that all individuals learn within their **zone of proximal development (ZPD)**, an intellectual arena in which new ideas and skills can be mastered. *Proximal* means "near," so the ZPD includes the ideas children are close to understanding as well as the skills they can almost master but are not yet able to demonstrate independently. How and when children learn depends, in part, on the wisdom and willingness of mentors to provide **scaffolding**, or temporary sensitive support, to help them within their developmental zone.

>> Response for Nutritionists
(from page 247): Take each of the four characteristics of preoperational thought into account. Because of egocentrism, having a special place and plate might assure the child that this food is exclusively his or hers. Since appearance is important, food should look tasty. Since static thinking dominates, if something healthy is added (e.g., grate carrots into the cake, add milk to the soup), do it before the food is given to the child. In the reversibility example in the text, the lettuce should be removed out of the child's sight and the "new" hamburger presented.

CORBIS RF/AGE FOOTSTOCK

Words Fail Me Could you describe how to tie shoes? The limitations of verbal tests of cognitive understanding are apparent in the explanation of many skills.

Observation Quiz What three sociocultural factors make it likely that the child pictured above will learn? (see answer, page 250)

zone of proximal development (ZPD) Vygotsky's term for the skills—cognitive as well as physical—that a person can exercise only with assistance, not yet independently.

scaffolding Temporary support that is tailored to a learner's needs and abilities and aimed at helping the learner master the next task in a given learning process.

TIM HALL/GETTY IMAGES

Count by Tens A large, attractive abacus could be a scaffold. However, in this toy store the position of the balls suggests that no mentor is nearby. Children are unlikely to grasp the number system without a motivating guide.

Observation Quiz Is the girl above right- or left-handed? (see answer, page 252)

overimitation When a person imitates an action that is not a relevant part of the behavior to be learned. Overimitation is common among 2- to 6-year-olds when they imitate adult actions that are irrelevant and inefficient.

>> Answer to Observation Quiz
(from page 249): Motivation (this father and son are from Spain, where yellow running shoes are popular); human relationships (note the physical touching of father and son); and materials (the long laces make tying them easier).

Especially for Driving Instructors
Sometimes your students cry, curse, or quit. How would Vygotsky advise you to proceed? (see response, page 252)

Good mentors provide plenty of scaffolding, encouraging children to look both ways before crossing the street (while holding the child's hand) or letting them stir the cake batter (perhaps while covering the child's hand on the spoon handle, in guided participation).

Sometimes scaffolding is inadvertent, as when children observe something said or done and then try to do likewise—even if it is something that adults would rather the child not do. Young children curse, kick, and do even worse because someone else showed them how.

More benignly, children imitate habits and customs that are meaningless, a trait called **overimitation**, evident in humans but not in other animals. This stems from the child's eagerness to learn from mentors, allowing "rapid, high-fidelity intergenerational transmission of cultural forms" (Nielsen & Tomaselli, 2010, p. 735).

Overimitation was demonstrated in an experiment with 2- to 6-year-olds, 61 of them from Bushman communities in South Africa and Botswana and, for comparison, 16 from Australia. Australian adults often scaffold for children with words and actions, but Bushman adults rarely do. The researchers expected the Australian children to follow adult demonstrations, since they were accustomed to learning in that way. They did not expect the Bushman children to do so (Nielsen & Tomaselli, 2010).

One by one, all the Australian and half of the Bushman children observed an adult perform irrelevant actions, such as waving a red stick above a box three times and then using that stick to push down a knob to open the box, which could be easily and more efficiently opened by merely pulling down the same knob by hand. Then children were given the stick and the box. No matter what their cultural background, the children followed the adult example, waving the stick three times and not using their hands directly on the knob.

Other Bushman children did not see the demonstration. When they were given the stick and asked to open the box, they simply pulled the knob. Then they observed an adult do the stick-waving opening—and they did something odd: They copied those inefficient actions, even though they already knew the easy way to open the box.

Apparently, children everywhere learn from others through observation, even if they have not been taught to do so. They even learn to do things contrary to their prior learning. Thus, scaffolding occurs through observation as well as explicit guidance. Across cultures, "similarity of performance is profound" (Nielsen & Tomaselli, 2010, p. 734), with children everywhere strongly inclined to learn whatever adults from their culture do. That is exactly what Vygotsky explained.

As always, cultural differences are crucial. Consider book-reading, for instance. In many North American families, when an adult reads to a child, the adult scaffolds—explaining, pointing, listening—within the child's zone of development. A sensitive adult reader does not tell the child to be quiet but might instead prolong the session by expanding on the child's questions and the pictures in the book.

By contrast, book-reading in middle-class Peruvian families includes teaching the child to listen when adults talk, so that a 2-year-old who interrupts is lovingly taught to be quiet (Melzi & Caspe, 2005). Obviously, scaffolded behaviors and processes in Peru differ because the goal is a respectful child, not a talkative one.

Same or Different? Which do you see? Most people focus on differences, such as ethnicity or sex. But a developmental perspective appreciates similarities: book reading to a pre-literate child cradled on a parent's lap.

Words, Cultures, and Math

Vygotsky particularly stressed the role of language to advance thought. He wrote that *private speech,* which is talking to oneself either out loud or in one's mind, is an important road to cognitive development. That seems to be especially true in early childhood (Al-Namlah et al., 2012). Young children talk to themselves when they are alone in their beds, to their toys, and to their parents, even when the parents are pushing their strollers and unable to hear them. All this private speech, Vygotsky believed, develops their minds.

A VIEW FROM SCIENCE

Research Report: Early Childhood and STEM

A practical use of Vygotsky's theory concerns the current emphasis on STEM (Science, Technology, Engineering, Math) education. Because finding more young people to specialize in those fields is crucial for economic growth, educators and political leaders are continually seeking ways to make STEM fields attractive to adolescents and young adults of all ethnicities (Rogers-Chapman, 2013; Wang, 2013).

Research on early childhood suggests that STEM education actually begins long before high school. This is increasingly recognized by experts, who note that most parents and teachers have much to learn about math and science if they wish to teach these subjects to young children (Hong et al., 2013; Bers et al., 2013)

For example, learning about numbers is possible very early in life. Even babies have a sense of whether one, two, or three objects are in a display, although exactly what infants understand about numbers is controversial (Varga et al., 2010). If Vygotsky is correct that words are tools, toddlers need to hear number words and science concepts (not just counting and shapes, but fractions and science principles, such as the laws of motion) early so that other knowledge becomes accessible. In math understanding, it is evident that preschoolers gradually learn to:

- Count objects, with one number per item (called *one-to-one correspondence*).

- Remember times and ages (bedtime at 8, a child is 4 years old, and so on).

- Understand sequence (first child wins, last child loses).

- Know what numbers are higher than others (it is not obvious to young children that 7 is more than 4).

These and many other cognitive accomplishments of young children have been the subject of extensive research: Mentoring and language are always found to be pivotal.

Culture affects language and may foster math knowledge. For example, English-speaking and Chinese-speaking preschoolers seem to have equal comprehension of 1 to 10, but the Chinese are ahead in their understanding of 11 to 19. Among the many possible explanations is a linguistic one: In all the Chinese dialects, the names for 11 to 19 are logical and direct, the equivalent of ten-one, ten-two, ten-three, and so on. This system is easier for young children to understand than eleven, twelve, thirteen, and so on.

German-speaking children may be slower to master numbers from 20 to 99, since they say the equivalent of one-and-twenty, two-and-twenty, and so on, not twenty-one, twenty-two, and so on. In these and many other ways, cultural restraints and routines affect young children's understanding of math (Göbel et al., 2011).

By age 3 or 4, children's brains are mature enough to comprehend numbers, store memories, and recognize routines.

Whether or not children actually demonstrate such understanding depends on what they hear and how they participate in various activities within their families, schools, and cultures.

Some 2-year-olds hear sentences such as "One, two, three, takeoff," and "Here are two cookies," and "Dinner in five minutes" several times a day. They are shown an interesting bit of moss, or are alerted to the phases of the moon, or learn about the relationship between pace and the steepness of a hill. Others never hear such comments—and they have a harder time with math in first grade, with science in the third grade, and with STEM subjects when they are older. According to Vygotsky, words mediate between brain potential and comprehension, and this process begins long before formal education.

>> Answer to Observation Quiz
(from page 250): Right-handed. Her dominant hand is engaged in something more comforting than exploring the abacus.

theory-theory The idea that children attempt to explain everything they see and hear by constructing theories.

>> Response for Driving Instructors
(from page 250): Use guided participation to scaffold the instruction so that your students are not overwhelmed. Be sure to provide lots of praise and days of practice. If emotion erupts, do not take it as an attack on you.

Children's Theories

Piaget and Vygotsky both recognized that children work to understand their world. No contemporary developmental scientist doubts that. How do children acquire their impressive knowledge? Part of the answer is that children do more than gain words and concepts—they develop theories to help them understand and remember.

Theory-Theory

Humans of all ages want explanations. **Theory-theory** refers to the idea that children naturally construct theories to explain whatever they see and hear. In other words, the theory about how children think is that they construct a theory. All people

> search for causal regularities in the world around us. We are perpetually driven to look for deeper explanations of our experience, and broader and more reliable predictions about it . . . Children seem, quite literally, to be born with . . . the desire to understand the world and the desire to discover how to behave in it.
>
> [Gopnik, 2001, p. 66]

According to theory-theory, the best explanation for cognition is that humans seek reasons, causes, and underlying principles to make sense of their experience. That requires curiosity and thought, connecting bits of knowledge and observations, which is what young children do. Humans always want theories, even false ones.

Exactly how do children seek explanations? They ask questions, and, if they are not satisfied with the answers, they develop their own theories. This is particularly evident in children's understanding of God and religion. One child thought his grandpa died because God was lonely; another thought thunder occurred because God was rearranging the furniture.

Theories do not appear randomly. Children wonder about the underlying purpose of whatever they observe, and they note how often a particular event occurs in order to develop a theory about what causes what and why (Gopnik & Wellman, 2012). Of course, their theories are not always correct.

For instance, when I was a young child, I noticed that my father never carried an umbrella. Since I looked up to him, I assumed he must have had a good reason. Consequently, throughout all my adult years, I never carried an umbrella. Neither did my brother, which confirmed for me that my father was right.

Over time I developed many reasons for my father's behavior. He must have realized, I decided, that umbrellas poke people in the eye, get forgotten, blow away, and are lost. Then, when Dad was in his 80s, my brother asked him why he didn't like umbrellas. The answer was "Chamberlain." Neville Chamberlain was famous for carrying an umbrella when he was prime minister of England from 1937 to 1940; and he was photographed with his black umbrella after signing the Munich Agreement in 1938, when he announced that Hitler would not attack England. For Dad, umbrellas symbolized foolish trust. All my theories were imagined to justify something I did not understand. That is theory-theory.

A series of experiments that explored when and how 3-year-olds imitate others provides research support for theory-theory (Williamson et al., 2008). Children figure out *why* adults act as they do before deciding to copy those actions. If an adult intends to accomplish something and succeeds, a child is likely to follow the example, but if the same action and result seem inadvertent or accidental, the child is less likely to copy it.

Indeed, even when asked to repeat something ungrammatical that an adult says, children often correct the grammar. They theorize that the adult intended to speak grammatically but failed to do so (Over & Gattis, 2010). This is another example of a general principle: Children develop theories about intentions before they employ their impressive ability to imitate; they do not mindlessly copy whatever they observe. As you have read, when children saw an adult wave a stick before opening a box, the children theorized that, since the adult did it deliberately, stick-waving was somehow important.

Theory of Mind

Mental processes—thoughts, emotions, beliefs, motives, and intentions—are among the most complicated and puzzling phenomena that humans encounter every day. Adults wonder why people fall in love with the particular persons they do, why they vote for the candidates they do, or why they make foolish choices—from taking on a huge mortgage to buying an overripe cucumber. Children are puzzled about a playmate's unexpected anger, a sibling's generosity, or an aunt's too-wet kiss.

To know what goes on in another's mind, people develop a *folk psychology,* which includes ideas about other people's thinking, called **theory of mind**. Theory of mind is an emergent ability, slow to develop but typically beginning in most children at about age 4 (Sterck & Begeer, 2010).

Realizing that thoughts do not mirror reality is beyond very young children, but that realization dawns on them sometime after age 3. It then occurs to them that

theory of mind A person's theory of what other people might be thinking. In order to have a theory of mind, children must realize that other people are not necessarily thinking the same thoughts that they themselves are. That realization seldom occurs before age 4.

WORTH PUBLISHERS

Candies in the Crayon Box Any one would expect crayons in a crayon box, but once a child sees that candy is inside, he expects that everyone else will also know that candies are inside!

people can be deliberately deceived or fooled—an idea that requires some theory of mind.

In one of several false-belief tests that researchers have developed, a child watches a puppet named Max put a toy dog into a red box. Then Max leaves and the child sees the dog taken out of the red box and put in a blue box. When Max returns, the child is asked, "Where will Max look for the dog?" Most 3-year-olds confidently say, "In the blue box"; most 6-year-olds correctly say, "In the red box," a pattern found in a dozen nations (Wellman et al., 2001).

Indeed, 3-year-olds almost always confuse what they recently learned with what they once thought and what someone else might think. Another way of describing this is to say that they are "cursed" by their own knowledge (Birch & Bloom, 2003), too egocentric to grasp others' perspectives. Asa did that in the vignette at the start of this chapter when he failed to understand that I was tired of throwing imaginary baskets and wanted to sit. He thought I didn't know that a person could think while standing!

The development of theory of mind can be seen when young children try to escape punishment by lying. Their face often betrays them: worried or shifting eyes, pursed lips, and so on. Parents sometimes say, "I know when you are lying," and, to the consternation of most 3-year-olds, parents are usually right.

In one experiment, 247 children, aged 3 to 5, were left alone at a table that had an upside-down cup covering dozens of candies (Evans et al., 2011). The children were told *not* to peek, and the experimenter left the room. For 142 children (57 percent), curiosity overcame obedience. They peeked, spilling so many candies onto the table that they could not put them back under the cup. The examiner returned, asking how the candies got on the table. Only one-fourth of the participants (more often the younger ones) told the truth.

The rest lied, with increasing skill. The 3-year-olds typically told hopeless lies (e.g., "The candies got out by themselves"); the 4-year-olds told unlikely lies (e.g., "Other children came in and knocked over the cup"). Some of the 5-year-olds, however, told plausible lies (e.g., "My elbow knocked over the cup accidentally").

This particular study was done in Beijing, China, but the results seem universal: Older children are better liars. Beyond the age differences, the experimenters found that the more logical liars were also more advanced in theory of mind and executive functioning (Evans et al., 2011), which indicates a more mature prefrontal cortex (see Figure 9.2).

Especially for Social Scientists
Can you think of any connection between Piaget's theory of preoperational thought and 3-year-olds' errors in this theory-of-mind task? (see response, page 256)

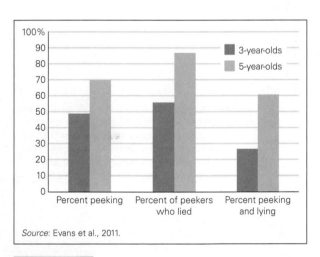

Source: Evans et al., 2011.

FIGURE 9.2

Better with Age? Could an obedient and honest 3-year-old become a disobedient and lying 5-year-old? Apparently yes, as the proportion of peekers and liars in this study more than doubled over those two years. Does maturation make children more able to think for themselves or less trustworthy?

Brain and Context

Many studies have found that a child's ability to develop theories correlates with the maturity of the prefrontal cortex and with advances in executive processing (Mar, 2011). This brain connection was further suggested by research on 8- to 16-year-olds. Their readiness to lie did not correlate with age or brain maturation (they were old enough to realize that a lie was possible, but whether they actually lied depended on their expectations and values); but if they did lie, their executive abilities correlated with the sophistication of their lies (Evans & Lee, 2011).

Additional evidence for the crucial role of the prefrontal cortex in development of theory of mind comes from the other study of 3- to 5-year-olds just cited. The experimenters tested the children's ability to say "day" when they saw a picture of the moon and "night" when they saw a picture of the sun. The ability to do this indicates advanced *executive function*, which correlates with maturation of the prefrontal cortex.

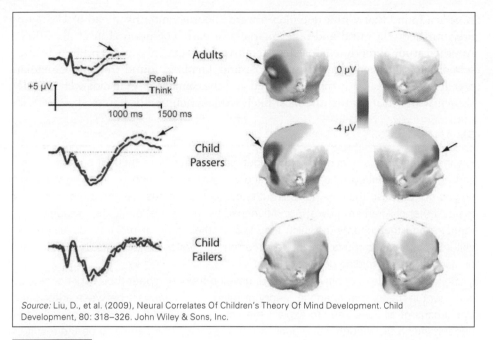

Source: Liu, D., et al. (2009), Neural Correlates Of Children's Theory Of Mind Development. Child Development, 80: 318–326. John Wiley & Sons, Inc.

FIGURE 9.3

Brains at Work Neuroscience confirms the critical role of the prefrontal cortex in development of theory of mind. Adults and 4- to 6-year-olds were questioned on 40 theory-of-mind examples. The adults answered correctly, as did some 4- to 6-year-olds (passers), though not all (failers). The leftmost images are brain-wave patterns; the other images are fMRI scans—the middle ones represent brain activity when confronted with questions about social interaction (active brains in children and adults) and the rightmost ones show mental activity when distinguishing between reality and belief (needed to pass theory-of-mind questions). Adult brain waves show quick answers, and the contrast *(right)* shows that they answered quickly with little effort; but the child passers needed to think longer before they answered, and the child failers didn't give the questions much thought, because they didn't recognize the problem. The authors concluded that "social cognition and the brain develop together" (Liu et al., 2009, pp. 318, 325).

Brothers and Sisters When every family had many children, as in this Western Australian family, even 3-year-olds had to learn when a brother was to be trusted not to move the chair.

Even when children were the same age, those who failed the day–night tests typically told impossible lies, whereas their age-mates who were high in executive function told more plausible lies (Evans et al., 2011).

Does the crucial role of brain maturation make context irrelevant? No (Sterck & Begeer, 2010); nurture is always important. For instance, research finds that language development fosters theory of mind, especially when mother–child conversations involve thoughts and wishes (Ontai & Thompson, 2008). Furthermore, social interactions with other children advance a child's thinking process. As one expert quipped, "Two older siblings are worth about a year of chronological age" (Perner, 2000, p. 383).

As brothers and sisters argue, agree, compete, and cooperate, and as older siblings fool younger ones, it dawns on 3-year-olds that not everyone thinks as they do. By age 5, children with siblings have figured out how to how to persuade their younger siblings to give them a toy, and they've learned how to gain parental sympathy by acting as if they are victims of their older brothers and sisters. Parents, beware: Asking "Who started it?" may be irrelevant.

Finally, the exosystem also influences development of theory of mind. A meta-analysis of 254 studies in China and North

America found that Chinese children were about six months ahead of U.S. children in theory of mind and other markers of early cognition (Liu et al., 2008). Another study directly comparing executive function in young children in preschools in Canada, India, Peru, Samoa, and Thailand found that the Canadian 5-year-olds were slightly more advanced and the Samoan 5-year-olds were slightly slower, with social context the most likely explanation (Callaghan et al., 2005).

SUMMING UP

Preoperational children, according to Piaget, can use symbolic thought but are illogical and egocentric, limited by appearance and immediate experience. Their egocentrism occurs not because they are selfish, but because their minds are immature. Vygotsky realized that children are powerfully influenced by their social contexts, including their mentors and the cultures in which they live. In their zone of proximal development, children are ready to move beyond their current understanding, especially if deliberate or inadvertent scaffolding occurs.

Children use their cognitive abilities to develop theories about their experiences, as is evident in theory-theory and in theory of mind, which appears between ages 3 and 5. Humans of all ages seek to explain their observations and become more adept at understanding the thoughts and goals of other people. This seems to be the result of both brain maturation and experience. ■

>> Language Learning

Learning language is the premier cognitive accomplishment of early childhood. Two-year-olds use short, telegraphic sentences ("Want cookie," "Where Daddy go?"), omitting adjectives, adverbs, and articles. By contrast, 5-year-olds seem able to say almost anything (see At About This Time).

AT ABOUT THIS TIME

Language in Early Childhood

Approximate Age	Characteristic or Achievement in First Language
2 years	*Vocabulary:* 100–2,000 words *Sentence length:* 2–6 words *Grammar:* Plurals; pronouns; many nouns, verbs, adjectives *Questions:* Many "What's that?" questions
3 years	*Vocabulary:* 1,000–5,000 words *Sentence length:* 3–8 words *Grammar:* Conjunctions, adverbs, articles *Questions:* Many "Why?" questions
4 years	*Vocabulary:* 3,000–10,000 words *Sentence length:* 5–20 words *Grammar:* Dependent clauses, tags at sentence end ("...didn't I?" "...won't you?") *Questions:* Peak of "Why?" questions; many "How?" and "When?" questions
6 years	*Vocabulary:* 5,000–30,000 words *Sentence length:* Some seem unending ("...and...who...and...that...and...") *Grammar:* Complex, depending on what the child has heard. Some children correctly use the passive voice ("Man bitten by dog") and subjunctive ("If I were..."). *Questions:* Some about social differences (male–female, old–young, rich–poor) and many other issues

A Sensitive Time

Brain maturation, myelination, scaffolding, and social interaction make early childhood ideal for learning language. As you remember from Chapter 1, scientists once thought that early childhood was a *critical period* for language learning—the *only* time when a first language could be mastered and the best time for a second or third one.

It is easy to understand why they thought so. Young children have powerful motivation and ability to sort words and sounds into meaning (theory-theory), which makes them impressive language learners. For that reason, teachers and parents should converse with children many hours each day. However, the critical-period hypothesis is false: Many people learn languages after age 6 (Singleton & Munoz, 2011).

Instead, early childhood is a *sensitive period* for language learning—for rapidly and easily mastering vocabulary, grammar, and pronunciation. Young children are called "language sponges" because they soak up every drop of language they encounter.

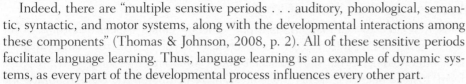

Indeed, there are "multiple sensitive periods . . . auditory, phonological, semantic, syntactic, and motor systems, along with the developmental interactions among these components" (Thomas & Johnson, 2008, p. 2). All of these sensitive periods facilitate language learning. Thus, language learning is an example of dynamic systems, as every part of the developmental process influences every other part.

Preoperational thinking—which is not logical—helps with language. For example, in a conversation I had with Asa, he said a toy lion was a mother. I said it couldn't be a mother because it had a mane. Rather than realizing that I might know more about sex differences in lions than he did, or questioning the new word (mane), he confidently insisted that this particular lion was a mother with a mane.

Asa is not alone. One of the valuable (and sometimes frustrating) traits of young children is that they talk about many things to adults, to each other, to themselves, to their toys—unfazed by misuse, mispronunciation, ignorance, stuttering, and so on (Marazita & Merriman, 2011). Language comes easily partly because preoperational children are not self-critical about what they say. Egocentrism has advantages; this is one of them.

The Vocabulary Explosion

The average child knows about 500 words at age 2 and more than 10,000 at age 6 (Herschensohn, 2007). That's more than six new words a day. These are averages. Estimates of vocabulary size at age 6 vary from 5,000 to 30,000: Some children learn six times as many words as others. Always, however, vocabulary builds quickly, and comprehension is more extensive than speech.

Fast-Mapping

After painstakingly learning one word at a time between 12 and 18 months of age, children develop interconnected categories for words, a kind of grid or mental map that makes speedy vocabulary acquisition possible. The process is called **fast-mapping** (Woodward & Markman, 1998) because, rather than figuring out the exact definition after hearing a word used in several contexts, children hear a word once and quickly stick it into a category in their mental language grid.

Language mapping is not precise. For example, children rapidly connect new animal names close to already-known animal names, without knowing all the details. Thus, *tiger* is easy to map if you know *lion*, but a leopard might be called a tiger. A trip to the zoo facilitates fast-mapping of animal names because zoos scaffold learning by placing similar animals near each other.

Picture books offer many opportunities for scaffolding and fast-mapping as well. A mentor might point out the next steps in the child's ZPD, such as that tigers have stripes and leopards spots, or, for an older child, that calico cats are almost always female and that lions with manes are always male.

Fast-mapping begins before age 2, and accelerates over childhood, as each new word makes it easier to map other words (Gershkoff-Stowe & Hahn, 2007). Generally, the more linguistic clues children have, the better their fast-mapping is (Mintz, 2005).

This process explains children's learning of color words. Generally, 2-year-olds already know some color words, but they fast-map them (Wagner et al., 2013). For instance, "blue" could be used for some greens or greys. It is not that children cannot see the hues. Instead, they apply words they know to broad categories, and they have not yet learned the boundaries that adults use. Thus, all women may be called mothers, all cats can be kitties, and all bright colors red. As one team of scientists explains, adult color words are the result of slow-mapping (Wagner et al., 2013), which is not what young children do.

fast-mapping The speedy and sometimes imprecise way in which children learn new words by tentatively placing them in mental categories according to their perceived meaning.

Words and the Limits of Logic

Closely related to fast-mapping is a phenomenon called *logical extension*: After learning a word, children use it to describe other objects in the same category. One child told her father she had seen some "Dalmatian cows" on a school trip to a farm. Instead of criticizing her foolishness, he remembered the Dalmatian dog she had petted the weekend before.

Bilingual children who don't know a word in the language they are speaking often insert a word from the other language. That may be considered wrong, but actually that is an example of the child's drive to communicate. To call it "Spanglish" when a Spanish-speaking person uses some English words deprecates a logical way to explain something (Otheguy & Stern, 2010). Soon children realize who understands which language—and they avoid substitutions when speaking to a monolingual person.

Some English words are particularly difficult for every child —*who/whom, have been/had been, here/there, yesterday/tomorrow*. More than one child has awakened on Christmas morning and asked, "Is it tomorrow yet?" A child told to "stay there" or "come here" may not follow instructions because the terms are confusing. Better might be to say, "Stay there on that bench" or "Come here to hold my hand." Other languages also have difficult concepts that are expressed in words; children everywhere learn them eventually.

Extensive study of children's language abilities finds that fast-mapping is only one of many techniques that children use to learn language: When a word does not refer to an object on the mental map, children find other ways to master it (Carey, 2010). If a word does not refer to anything the child can see or otherwise sense or act on, it may be ignored. Always, however, action helps. A hole is to dig; love is hugging; hearts beat.

Listening, Talking, and Reading

Because understanding the printed word is crucial, a meta-analysis of about 300 studies analyzed which activities in early childhood aided reading later on. Both vocabulary and phonics (precise awareness of the sounds of words) predicted literacy (Shanahan & Lonigan, 2010). Five specific strategies and experiences were particularly effective for children of all income levels and ethnicities:

1. *Code-focused teaching.* In order for children to read, they must "break the code" from spoken to written words. It helps if they learn the letters and sounds of the alphabet (e.g., "A, alligators all around" or, conventionally, "B is for baby").
2. *Book reading.* Vocabulary as well as familiarity with pages and print will increase when adults read to children, allowing questions and conversation.
3. *Parent education.* When teachers and other professionals teach parents how to stimulate cognition (as in book reading), children become better readers. Adults need to use words to expand vocabulary much more often than to control behavior.
4. *Language enhancement.* Within each child's zone of proximal development, mentors can expand vocabulary and grammar, based on the child's knowledge and experience.
5. *Preschool programs.* Children learn from teachers, songs, excursions, and other children. (We discuss the pros and cons of early education soon, but every study finds that language advances for children who attend preschool.)

Acquiring Grammar

We noted in Chapter 6 that *grammar* includes structures, techniques, and rules that communicate meaning. Knowledge of grammar is essential for learning to speak, read, and write. A large vocabulary is useless unless a person knows how to put words together.

By age 2, children understand the basics. For example, English-speaking children know word order (subject/verb/object), saying, "I eat apple," rather than any of the five other possible sequences of those three words. They use plurals, tenses (past, present, and future), and nominative, objective, and possessive pronouns (*I, me,* and *mine* or *my*).

Some 3-year-olds use articles (*the, a, an*) correctly, although proper article use in English is bewilderingly complex. Each aspect of language acquisition (grammar, vocabulary, pronunciation, etc.) follows a particular learning path as the months roll by.

One reason for variation in particulars of language learning is that several parts of the brain are involved, each myelinating at a distinct rate. Furthermore, many genes and alleles affect comprehension and expression. In general, genes affect *expressive* (spoken or written) language more than *receptive* (heard or read) language. Thus, some children are relatively talkative or quiet because they inherit that tendency, but experience (not genes) determines what they understand (Kovas et al., 2005).

Learning the Rules

Children are eager to apply rules of grammar as soon as they learn them. For example, English-speaking children quickly learn to add an *s* to form the plural: Toddlers follow that rule when they ask for two cookies or more blocks.

Soon they add an *s* to make the plural of words they have never heard before, even nonsense words. If preschoolers are shown a drawing of an abstract shape, told it is called a *wug,* and are then shown two of these shapes, they say there are two *wugs.* In keeping with the distinction between reception and expression, very young children realize words have a singular and a plural before they can express it (Zapf & Smith, 2007).

However, sometimes children apply the rules of grammar when they should not. This error is called **overregularization**. By age 4, many children overregularize that final *s,* talking about *foots, tooths,* and *mouses.* This signifies knowledge, not stupidity: Many children first say words correctly (*feet, teeth, mice*), repeating what they have heard. Later, they apply the rules of grammar, and overregularize, assuming that all constructions follow the rules (Ramscar & Dye, 2011).

More difficult to learn is an aspect of language called **pragmatics**—knowing which words, tones, and grammatical forms to use with which person (Siegal & Surian, 2012). In some languages, it is essential to know which set of words to use when a person is older, or not a close friend or family member.

For example, French children learn the difference between *tu* and *vous* in early childhood. Although both words mean "you," *tu* is used with familiar people, while *vous* is the more formal expression. In other languages, children learn that there are two words for grandmother, depending on whose mother it is.

English does not make those distinctions, but pragmatics are important for early-childhood learning nonetheless. Children learn that there are many practical differences in vocabulary and tone on the context and, once theory of mind is established, on the audience. Knowledge of pragmatics is evident when a 4-year-old is pretending to be a doctor, a teacher, or a parent. Each role requires different speech.

overregularization The application of rules of grammar even when exceptions occur, making the language seem more "regular" than it actually is.

pragmatics The practical use of language that includes the ability to adjust language communication according to audience and context.

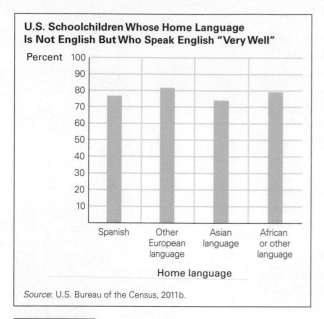

U.S. Schoolchildren Whose Home Language Is Not English But Who Speak English "Very Well"

Source: U.S. Bureau of the Census, 2011b.

FIGURE 9.4

Mastering English: The Younger, the Better Of all the schoolchildren whose home language is not English, this is the proportion who, according to their parents, speak English well. Immigrant children who attend school almost always master English within five years.

Source: U.S. Bureau of the Census, 2011b.

Learning Two Languages

Language-minority people (those who speak a language that is not their nation's dominant one) suffer if they do not also speak the majority language. In the United States, those who are not proficient in English have lower school achievement, diminished self-esteem, and inadequate employment, as well as many other problems. Fluency in English can erase these liabilities; fluency in another language then becomes an asset.

In the United States in 2011, 22 percent of schoolchildren spoke a language other than English at home, with most of them (77 percent) also speaking English well, according to their parents (U.S. Bureau of the Census, 2011b) (see Figure 9.4).

The percentage of bilingual children is higher in many other nations. In Canada and many African, Asian, and European nations, by sixth grade most schoolchildren are bilingual, and some are trilingual. Language learning is aided by school instruction, but generally, the earlier a child learns a second language, the more easily and quickly the learning occurs.

How and Why

Unlike a century ago, everyone now seeking U.S. citizenship must be able to speak English. Some people believe that national unity is threatened by language-minority speakers. By contrast, other people emphasize that international understanding is crucial and that ideally everyone should speak several languages.

Should a nation have one official language, several, or none? Individuals and nations have divergent answers. Switzerland has three official languages; Canada has two; India has one national language [Hindi], but many states of India also have their own, for a total of 28 official languages; the United States has none.

Some adults have expressed the concern that young children who are taught two languages might become semilingual, not bilingual, "at risk for delayed, incomplete, and possibly even impaired language development" (Genesee, 2008, p. 17). Others have used their own experience to argue the opposite, that "there is absolutely no evidence that children get confused if they learn two languages" (Genesee, 2008, p. 18).

This second position has gained increasing research support in the past decade. Soon after the vocabulary explosion, children who have heard two languages since birth usually master two distinct sets of words and grammar, along with each language's pauses, pronunciations, intonations, and gestures. Proficiency is directly related to how much language they hear (Hoff et al., 2013).

No doubt early childhood is the best time to learn a language or languages. Neuroscience finds that in adults who learned a second language when they were young, both languages are located in the same areas of the brain. They manage to keep the two languages separate, activating one and temporarily inhibiting the other when speaking to a monolingual person (Crinion et al., 2006). They may be a millisecond slower to respond when they switch languages, but their brains function better overall. Being bilingual in childhood may even provide some resistance to Alzheimer's dementia in old age (Bialystok et al., 2009).

Learning a second language in high school or college, as required of most U.S. children, is too late for fluency. After childhood, the logic of language is quite possible to grasp, so adults can learn the rules of forming the past tense, for instance, but metaphors and exceptions to the rules are particularly elusive after puberty. The human brain is designed to learn language best in childhood.

Pronunciation is particularly hard to master after childhood, in any language. However, do not equate pronunciation and spoken fluency with comprehension and reading ability. Many adults who speak the majority language with an accent are quite knowledgeable in the language and culture (difference is not deficit). From infancy on, hearing is more acute than vocalization. Almost all young children mispronounce whatever language they speak, blithely unaware of their mistakes.

In early childhood, all children transpose sounds (*magazine* becomes *mazagine*), drop consonants (*truck* becomes *ruck*), convert difficult sounds to easier ones (*father* becomes *fadder*), and drop complex sounds (*cherry* become *terry*). Mispronunciation does not impair fluency primarily because young children are more receptive than expressive—they hear better than they talk. For instance, when 4-year-old Rachel asked for a "yeyo yayipop," her father repeated, "You want a yeyo yayipop?" She replied, "Daddy, sometimes you talk funny."

Language Loss and Gains

Schools in all nations stress the dominant language, and language-minority parents fear that their children will make a *language shift,* becoming more fluent in the school language than in their home language. Language shift occurs everywhere, if theory-theory leads children to conclude that their first language is inferior to the new one (Bhatia & Ritchie, 2013).

Some language-minority children in Mexico shift to Spanish, some First Nations (as native tribes are called) children in Canada shift to English, some Chinese-speaking children in the United States shift to English. In China, all speak Chinese, but some shift from one dialect to another. No shift is inevitable: The attitudes and practices of parents and the community are crucial.

Remember that young children are preoperational: They center on the immediate status of their language (not on future usefulness or past glory), on appearance more than substance. No wonder many shift toward the language of the dominant culture. Since language is integral to culture, if a child is to become fluently bilingual, everyone who speaks with the child should show appreciation of both cultures.

Becoming a **balanced bilingual**, which means speaking two languages equally well with no audible hint of the other language, is accomplished by millions of young children in many nations. This ability benefits their intellectual flexibility (Bialystok & Viswanathan, 2009; Pearson, 2008).

The basics of language learning—the naming and vocabulary explosions, fast-mapping, overregularization, scaffolding—apply to every language children learn. Although skills in one language can be transferred to make learning another easier, "transfer is neither automatic nor inevitable" (Snow & Kang, 2006, p. 97). To become balanced bilinguals, children need to hear twice as much talk as usual (Hoff et al., 2013).

The same practices can make a child fluently trilingual, as some 5-year-olds are. One parent might spend hours each day talking and reading to a child in French, for instance, the other parent in English, and that child might play with friends at a Spanish-speaking preschool. The result is a child who speaks three languages without an accent—except whatever accent their mother, father, and friends have.

Bilingual children and adults are advanced in theory of mind and executive functioning, probably because they need to be more reflective and strategic when they speak. However, sheer linguistic proficiency does not necessarily lead to cognitive advances (Bialystok & Barac, 2011). Cognition depends on many aspects of education, as described in the following section.

Bilingual Learners These are Chinese children learning a second language. Could this be in the United States? No, this is a class in the first Chinese-Hungarian school in Budapest. There are three clues: the spacious classroom, the trees outside, and the letters on the book.

ATTILA KISBENEDEK/AFP/GETTY IMAGES

balanced bilingual A person who is fluent in two languages, not favoring one over the other.

Especially for Immigrant Parents
You want your children to be fluent in the language of your family's new country, even though you do not speak that language well. Should you speak to your children in your native tongue or in the new language? (see response, page 262)

>> **Response for Immigrant Parents**
(from page 261): Children learn by listening, so it is important to speak with them often. Depending on how comfortable you are with the new language, you might prefer to read to your children, sing to them, and converse with them primarily in your native language and find a good preschool where they will learn the new language. The worst thing you could do would be to restrict speech in either tongue.

SUMMING UP

Children learn language rapidly and well during early childhood, with an explosion of vocabulary and mastery of many grammatical constructions. Fast-mapping is one way children learn. Overregularization, mispronunciation, and errors in precision are common and are not problematic at this age.

Young children can learn two languages almost as easily as one if adults talk frequently, listen carefully, and value both languages. However, this is not necessarily the case; some children undergo a language shift, abandoning their first language. Others never master a second language because they were not exposed to one during the sensitive time for language learning. ■

>> Early-Childhood Education

A hundred years ago, children had no formal education until first grade, which, as mentioned earlier, is why it was called "first" and why young children were "*pre*schoolers." Today, virtually every nation provides some early-childhood education, sometimes financed by the government, sometimes privately (Britto et al., 2011). In some countries, most 3- to 6-year-olds are in school (see Figure 9.5 for U.S. trends), not only because of changing family and economic patterns but also because research has verified that young children can accomplish a great deal of cognitive advance and language learning.

Homes and Schools

One robust research conclusion about children's learning is that the quality of the learning context matters. If home education is poor, a good preschool program aids health, cognition, and social skills (Hindman et al., 2010). However, if a family provides extensive learning opportunities and encouragement, the quality of the preschool is less crucial. It is better for the young children to be at such a home than in a stressful, overcrowded preschool.

It is difficult to judge the quality of homes and schools in the United States because of the "stunning variability and fragmentation" of public and private schools (Pianta et al., 2009, p. 50) and the changing configuration of home care. It is a mistake to conclude that care by the mother is better than care by another relative or nonrelative—or vice versa. Mother care varies: Some mothers are fabulous, others disastrous.

Observation Quiz At what point did the percentage of 3- to 4-year-olds in school exceed that of 18- to 19-year-olds in college? (see answer, page 264)

FIGURE 9.5

Changing Times Because research increasingly finds that preschool education provides a foundation for later learning, most young children are enrolled in educational programs. Note the contrast with the proportion of 18- to 19-year-olds in college (not shown are the 18- to 19-year-olds still in high school—about 15 percent).

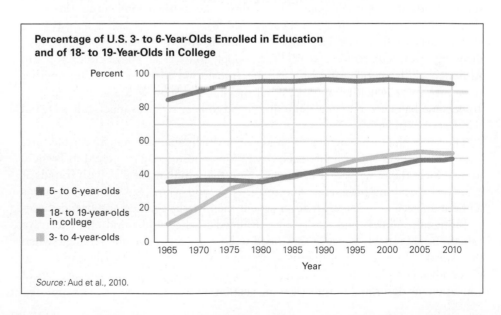

Percentage of U.S. 3- to 6-Year-Olds Enrolled in Education and of 18- to 19-Year-Olds in College

- 5- to 6-year-olds
- 18- to 19-year-olds in college
- 3- to 4-year-olds

Source: Aud et al., 2010.

Group care also varies, both in name and practice. Educational institutions for young children are called preschools, nursery schools, day-care centers, pre-primary programs, pre-K classes. Sometimes the sponsoring agencies are noted: public, private, church, corporation. None of these labels reliably indicates quality (A. S. Fuligni et al., 2009). Each early-childhood program (and sometimes each teacher) emphasizes different skills, goals, and methods.

Early-childhood education can be considered to be child-centered or teacher-directed. Remember, however, that the quality of the home and the effectiveness of the teachers have greater impact on young children than does the label or professed philosophy. Also remember that young children are shaped by their culture and differentiated by their genes, so a child who flourishes in one setting might languish in another, and some contexts work only for certain children. Parents need to find a good fit for their child, their values, and their income—not an easy task.

Child-Centered Programs

Many programs are called *developmental,* or *child-centered,* because they stress each child's development and growth. Teachers in such programs believe children need to follow their own interests rather than adult directions. For example, they agree that "children should be allowed to select many of their own activities from a variety of learning areas that the teacher has prepared" (Lara-Cinisomo et al., 2011). The physical space and the materials (such as dress-up clothing, art supplies, puzzles, blocks, other toys) are arranged to allow self-paced exploration.

Most child-centered programs encourage artistic expression. Some educators argue that young children "are all poets" in that they are gifted in seeing the world more imaginatively than older people do. According to advocates of child-centered programs, this peak of creative vision should be encouraged; children are given many opportunities to tell stories, draw pictures, dance, and make music for their own delight.

That does not mean that academics are ignored. Advocates of math learning, for instance, believe that children have a natural interest in numbers and that child-centered schools can guide those interests as children grow (Stipek, 2013).

Especially for Teachers In trying to find a preschool program, what should parents look for? (see response, page 265)

Especially for Unemployed Early-Childhood Teachers You are offered a job in a program that has 10 3-year-olds for every 1 adult. You know that is too many, but you want a job. What should you do? (see response, page 265)

"We teach them that the world can be an unpredictable, dangerous, and sometimes frightening place, while being careful not to spoil their lovely innocence. It's tricky."

Tricky Indeed Young children are omnivorous learners, picking up habits, curses, and attitudes that adults would rather not transmit. Deciding what to teach—by actions more than words—is essential.

Tibet, China, India, and . . . Italy? Over the past half-century, as China increased its control of Tibet, thousands of refugees fled to northern India. Tibet traditionally had no preschools, but young children adapt quickly, as in this preschool program in Ladakh, India. This Tibetan boy is working a classic Montessori board.

>> Answer to Observation Quiz
(from page 262): Between 1985 and 1990. The exact year (not shown) was 1988.

Montessori schools Schools that offer early-childhood education based on the philosophy of Maria Montessori, which emphasizes careful work and tasks that each young child can do.

Child-Centered Pride How could Rachel Koepke, a 3-year-old from a Wisconsin town called Pleasant Prairie, seem so pleased that her hands (and cuffs) are blue? The answer arises from northern Italy—Rachel attended a Reggio Emilia preschool that encourages creative expression.

Reggio Emilia A program of early-childhood education that originated in the town of Reggio Emilia, Italy, and that encourages each child's creativity in a carefully designed setting.

Child-centered programs are often influenced by Piaget, who emphasized that each child will discover new ideas, and by Vygotsky, who thought that children learn from other children, with adult guidance (Bodrova & Leong, 2005). Trained teachers are crucial: A child-centered program requires appropriate activities for each child and teachers who guide and scaffold so that each child advances (Dominguez et al., 2010).

Montessori Schools

One type of child-centered school began more than 100 years ago, when Maria Montessori opened nursery schools for poor children in Rome. She believed that children needed structured, individualized projects to give them a sense of accomplishment. Her students completed puzzles, used sponges and water to clean tables, traced shapes, and so on.

Contemporary **Montessori schools** still emphasize individual pride and achievement, presenting many literacy-related tasks (e.g., outlining letters and looking at books) to young children (Lillard, 2005). Specific materials differ from those that Montessori developed, but the underlying philosophy is the same. Children seek out learning tasks; they do not sit quietly in groups while a teacher instructs them. That makes Montessori programs child-centered (Lillard, 2013).

This philosophy seems to work. A study of 5-year-olds in inner-city Milwaukee who were chosen by lottery to attend Montessori programs found that the children were advanced in prereading (such as recognizing letters), math, and theory of mind, compared with their peers in other schools (Lillard & Else-Quest, 2006). Some benefits became more apparent by middle school (called a *sleeper effect*, because the benefits seem to hibernate for a while) (Lillard, 2013). The probable explanation: Montessori tasks lead to self-confidence, curiosity, and exploration, which eventually motivate learning to read, calculate, and so on.

Reggio Emilia

Another form of early-childhood education is **Reggio Emilia**, named after the town in Italy where it began. In Reggio Emilia, children are encouraged to master skills that are not usually taught in North American schools until age 7 or so, such as writing and using tools (hammers, knives, and so on).

Reggio schools do not provide large-group instruction, with lessons in, say, forming letters or cutting paper. Instead, "Every child is a creative child, full of potential" (Gandini et al., 2005, p. 1), with personal learning needs and artistic drive.

Measurement of achievement, such as standardized testing to see whether children have learned their letters, is not part of the core belief that each child should explore and learn in his or her own way (Lewin-Benham, 2008).

Appreciation of the arts is evident. Every Reggio Emilia school has a studio, an artist, and space to encourage creativity. Consequently, Reggio Emilia schools have a large central room with many hubs of activity and a low child/adult ratio. Children's art is displayed on white walls and hung from high ceilings, and floor-to-ceiling windows open to a spacious, plant-filled playground. Big mirrors are part of the schools' décor—again, with the idea of fostering individuality and self-expression.

The curious little scientist is encouraged with materials to explore. One analysis of Reggio Emilia in the United States found "a science-rich context that triggered and supported preschoolers' inquiries and effectively engaged preschoolers' hands, heads, and hearts with science" (Inan et al., 2010, p. 1186).

Teacher-Directed Programs

Teacher-directed preschools stress academics, often taught by one adult to the entire group. The curriculum includes learning the names of letters, numbers, shapes, and colors according to a set timetable; every child naps, snacks, and goes to the bathroom on schedule as well. Children learn to sit quietly and listen to the teacher. Praise and other reinforcements are given for good behavior, and time-outs (brief separation from activities) are imposed to punish misbehavior.

In teacher-directed programs, the serious work of schooling is distinguished from the unstructured play of home. According to a study of preschool educators, some teachers endorse ideas that indicate their teacher-directed philosophy, such as that children should form letters correctly before they are allowed to write a story (Lara-Cinisomo et al., 2011).

The goal of teacher-directed programs is to make all children "ready to learn" when they enter elementary school. For that reason, basic skills are stressed, including precursors to reading, writing, and arithmetic, perhaps through teachers asking questions that children answer together in unison.

Children practice forming letters, sounding out words, counting objects, and writing their names. If a 4-year-old learns to read, that is success. (In a child-centered program, that might arouse suspicion that there was too little time to play or socialize.) Good behavior, not informal social interaction, is rewarded—leading one critic to suggest that "readiness" is too narrowly defined (Winter, 2011).

>> **Response for Teachers** (from page 263):
Tell parents to look at the people more than the program. Parents should see the children in action and note whether the teachers show warmth and respect for each child.

>> **Response for Unemployed Early-Childhood Teachers** (from page 263):
It would be best for you to wait for a job in a program where children learn well, organized along the lines explained in this chapter. You would be happier, as well as learn more, in a workplace that is good for children. Realistically, though, you might feel compelled to take the job. If you do, change the child/adult ratio—find a helper, perhaps a college intern or a volunteer grandmother. But choose carefully—some adults are not helpful at all. Before you take the job, remember that children need continuity: You can't leave simply because you find something better.

Learning from One Another Every nation creates its own version of early education. In this scene at a nursery school in Kuala Lumpur, Malaysia, note the head coverings, uniforms, and distance between the sexes. None of these elements would be found in most early-childhood-education classrooms in North America or Europe.

MOHD RASFAN/AFP/GETTY IMAGES

Many teacher-directed programs were inspired by behaviorism, which emphasizes step-by-step learning and repetition, with reinforcement (praise, gold stars, prizes) for accomplishment. Another inspiration for teacher-directed programs comes from research indicating that children who have not learned basic vocabulary and listening skills by kindergarten often fall behind in primary school. Many state legislatures mandate that preschoolers learn particular concepts, an outcome best achieved by teacher-directed learning (Bracken & Crawford, 2010).

Most developmentalists and most teachers advocate child-centered programs. But studies show that teachers' classroom behaviors do not always correlate with their beliefs (Tonyan et al., 2013). In fact, most teachers lead more than follow the children's lead (see Figure 9.6). This was true even among teachers who said they took a child-centered approach—especially if they were novice teachers. For instance, they might say they are child-centered but tell children what to do instead of asking them their ideas). Teachers with more experience or training were more likely to be consistent in belief and behavior (Wen et al., 2011).

FIGURE 9.6

Don't Blame the Teacher Children develop their own ideas best when adults listen, encourage, and play, but most adults give directions, provide information, and ask questions they know the answer to. This is true for parents, strangers, and as shown here, even teachers who try to be child-centered.

Source: Wen, Elicker, and McMullen (2011).

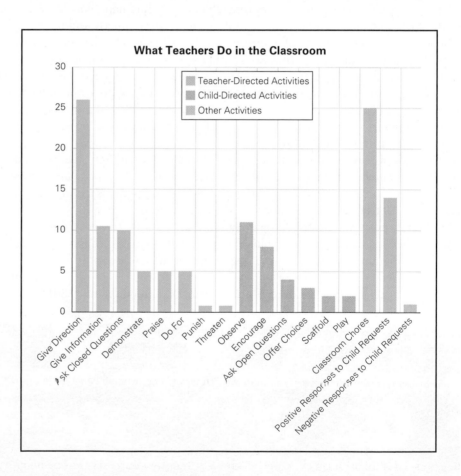

Head Start

In the early 1960s, millions of young children in the United States were thought to need a "head start" on their formal education to help foster better health and cognition before first grade. Early education was considered to be a necessary intervention for poor children of all ethnicities. Consequently, since 1965 the federal government has funded a massive program for 4-year-olds called **Head Start**.

Head Start A federally funded early-childhood intervention program for low-income children of preschool age.

The goals for Head Start have changed over the decades, from lifting families out of poverty to promoting literacy, from providing dental care and immunizations to teaching Standard English. Although initially most Head Start programs were child-centered, they have become increasingly teacher-directed as waves of legislators have approved and shaped them. Children have learned whatever their Head Start teachers and curricula emphasize.

For example, many low-income 3- and 4-year-olds in the United States are not normally exposed to math. After one Head Start program engaged children in a board game with numbers, their mathematical understanding advanced significantly (Siegler, 2009). A congressional reauthorization of funding for Head Start included a requirement for extensive evaluation to answer two questions:

1. What difference does Head Start make to key outcomes of development and learning (in particular, school readiness) for low-income children? How does Head Start affect parental practices?
2. Under what circumstances and for whom does Head Start achieve the greatest impact?

The answers were not as dramatic as either advocates or detractors had hoped (U.S. Department of Health and Human Services, 2010). Head Start improved literacy and math skills, oral health, and parental responsiveness. However, many academic benefits faded by first grade. One explanation is that, unlike when Head Start began, many children in the comparison group were enrolled in other early-childhood programs—sometimes excellent ones, sometimes not.

The research found that benefits were strongest for children with the lowest family incomes, for those living in rural areas, and for those with disabilities (U.S. Department of Health and Human Services, 2010). These children are least likely to find other sources of early education. Most Head Start children advanced in language and social skills, but by elementary school the comparison children often caught up, with one exception: Head Start children were still ahead in vocabulary.

That finding also supports what you have just read about early childhood as a sensitive period for language learning. Any good preschool will introduce children to words they would not learn at home. Children will fast-map those words, gaining a linguistic knowledge base that facilitates expanded vocabulary throughout life.

The Need for Structure

Many developmentalists resist legislative prescriptions (such as those in some current Head Start regulations) regarding what 3- and 4-year-olds should learn. Some teachers want to do whatever they believe is best, resulting in a happy hodgepodge of strategies and rules. However, this approach may confuse children and parents. Differences may reflect culture, not what theory and research suggest is best.

For example, in a detailed study in the Netherlands, native-born Dutch teachers emphasized individual achievement (child-centered) more than did the teachers from the Caribbean or Mediterranean, who stressed proper behavior and group learning (teacher-directed) (Huijbregts et al., 2009). Teachers of either background who had worked together for years shared more beliefs and practices than new teachers did (Huijbregts et al., 2009). Hopefully, they had learned from one another.

Similar discrepancies were found in a study of U.S. preschool teachers. Those who were younger and had more education often differed from those who were older and had more experience—yet both groups thought their way was best (Tonyan et al., 2013).

As many studies have shown, children can learn whatever academic and social skills are taught to them; those who attend preschool advance in cognitive skills because such skills are emphasized (Camilli et al., 2010; Chambers et al., 2010). But no matter what the curriculum, all young children need personal attention, consistency, and continuity: It does not help when every adult applies idiosyncratic rules and routines.

Disaster Recovery The success of Head Start led to Early Head Start for children such as this 2-year-old in Biloxi, Mississippi. When Hurricane Katrina destroyed most of the community, it was the first educational program to reopen. Since a family is a system, not just a collection of individuals, this Head Start program is helping parents as well as entire families recover.

For this reason, among many others, parents and teachers should communicate and cooperate with each other in teaching young children, a strategy Head Start has emphasized from the early days. It also is true that a warm teacher–child relationship fosters learning no matter what kind of curriculum or strategy is used (Howes et al., 2013).

Bilingual Education

The need for a coherent strategy is apparent in bilingual education. Successful strategies need to vary depending on the child, the home background, and national values. As one review concludes, "It is highly unlikely that one approach will be equally effective for all **DLLs (dual language learners)**" (Hammer et al., 2011), but some strategy is needed.

U.S. research has focused on young children of Hispanic heritage. In general, programs that combine English and Spanish instruction, sometimes with half a day for each, are more successful at teaching English while advancing Spanish than are programs that simply immerse the Spanish-speaking children in an English-only setting (Barnett et al., 2007) or keep Spanish as the sole language of instruction.

Unfortunately, for political, cultural, and economic reasons, Hispanic American children are among the young children who are least likely to attend preschool in the United States (see Figure 9.7). After decades of steady gains in preschool education, enrollment of Hispanic American children decreased in the United States during the economic recession, which coincided with increased rates of deportation of the 11 million undocumented immigrants (Fuller & Kim, 2011). This is especially troubling for children from Spanish-speaking homes: As discussed earlier, learning a second language is easiest before age 4.

Head Start now requires that all children in the program be from low-income families. Many Hispanic children qualify and hence could take advantage of free early education. However, even in Head Start, Hispanic children are less likely to be enrolled than other low-income children.

One reason for the low attendance of young Spanish-speaking children (most of whom are U.S. citizens) is their parents' fear of deportation if anyone in the extended family is undocumented. Another reason is custom: The evidence that young children benefit from preschool is familiar to most English-speaking adults, but not to most immigrants.

Added problems are that many Head Start programs are limited to three hours a day, few teachers are native Spanish speakers, and the mothers least likely to

Dual Language Learners (DDLs) Children who develop skills in two languages are dual language learners. Ideally education fosters proficiency in two languages rather than creating a language shift.

FIGURE 9.7

Early Advantage Since even the critics agree that early education advances language and literacy, it is troubling that the children who most need language learning are least likely to be in pre-primary programs of any kind - public, private, or church related.

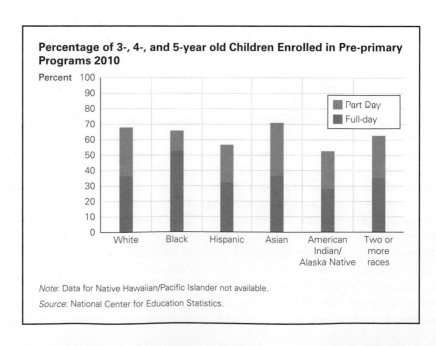

Percentage of 3-, 4-, and 5-year old Children Enrolled in Pre-primary Programs 2010

Note: Data for Native Hawaiian/Pacific Islander not available.

Source: National Center for Education Statistics.

have jobs are those who speak only Spanish. For all these reasons, many families choose mothers or grandmothers to provide child care until kindergarten, not realizing the impact of Spanish-only care on later education.

The percentage of Hispanics in early education would be even lower if the statistics included noncitizen children. Almost none of them are eligible for public preschool, although all of them can attend public school once they reach age 6. Consequently, each year, almost a million children enter first grade in the United States with poor English skills, often because they had no early education.

Of course, not all immigrant children have similar needs. Spanish-speaking children whose origins are Puerto Rican, Cuban, or other Latino have experiences that are unlike Mexican-origin children. Further, each local jurisdiction (each state in the U.S. and each nation elsewhere) has distinct policies—some welcoming, some not. Moreover, many ELLs are not Hispanic. Their parents have distinct expectations and attitudes. Home-school communication is crucial for all young children; they learn best when all the adults share strategies and goals.

Long-Term Gains from Intensive Programs

This discussion of philosophies, practices, and programs may give the impression that the research on early childhood cognition is contradictory. That is not true. Specifics are debatable, but empirical evidence and longitudinal evaluation find that preschool education advances learning. Ideally, each program has a curriculum that guides practice, all the adults collaborate, and experienced teachers respond to each child.

The best evidence comes from three longitudinal programs that enrolled children for years, sometimes beginning with home visits in infancy, sometimes continuing in after-school programs through first grade. One program, called *Perry* (or *High/Scope*), was spearheaded in Michigan (Schweinhart & Weikart, 1997); another, called *Abecedarian*, got its start in North Carolina (Campbell et al., 2001); a third, called *Child–Parent Centers*, began in Chicago (Reynolds, 2000). Because of the political context when these programs began, all were focused on children from low-SES families.

All three programs compared experimental groups of children with matched control groups, and all reached the same conclusion: Early education has substantial long-term benefits that become most apparent when children are in the third grade or later. By age 10, children who had been enrolled in any one of these three programs scored higher on math and reading achievement tests than did other children from the same backgrounds, schools, and neighborhoods. They were less likely to be placed in special classes for slow or disruptive children or to repeat a year of school.

An advantage of longitudinal research over the decades is that teenagers and adults who received early education can be compared with those who did not. For all three programs, early investment paid off. In adolescence, the children who had undergone intensive preschool education had higher aspirations, possessed a greater sense of achievement, and were less likely to have been abused. As young adults, they were more likely to attend college and less likely to go to jail. As middle-aged adults, they were more often employed, paying taxes and not needing government subsidies (Reynolds & Ou, 2011; Schweinhart et al., 2005).

Early education affected every aspect of adult life. One review concluded that "early cognitive and scholastic advantages lead to social and motivational gains that culminate in enhanced well-being" (Reynolds & Ou, 2011, p. 578).

All three research projects found that providing direct cognitive training (rather than simply letting children play), with specific instruction in various school-readiness skills, was useful. Each child's needs and talents were considered—a circumstance made possible because the child/adult ratio was low. The curricular approach combined child-centered and teacher-directed programs, with all the teachers trained together, so children were not confused. Teachers involved parents in their children's education, and each program included strategies to enhance the home–school connection.

These programs were expensive (ranging from $6,000 to $18,000 annually per young child in 2014 dollars). From a developmental perspective, the decreased need for special education and other social services makes early education a "wise investment" (Duncan & Magnusson, 2013, p. 128). The benefits to society over the child's lifetime, including increased employment, taxes, and reduced crime, are much more than that.

The greatest lifetime return came from boys from high-poverty neighborhoods in the Chicago preschool program: The social benefit over their lifetime was more than 12 times the cost (Reynolds et al., 2011). Unfortunately costs are immediate and benefits are long term. Consequently, some legislators and voters are unwilling to fund expensive intervention programs that do not pay off until decades later.

That is changing. Most states sponsor public education for young children—although usually only for low-income 4-year-olds. In 2009–2010, more than a million children (1,292,310) attended state-sponsored preschools—double the number a decade earlier (Barnett et al., 2010). Since 4 million (actually, 4,268,000) children were born in 2006, that is slightly more than one child in three. Although early education is free in some nations, most U.S. parents pay for it. That is one reason why families in the highest income quartile are more likely to have their 3- and 4-year-old in an educational program (see Visualizing Development, p. 271).

From a developmental perspective, the leading state is Oklahoma, which provides full-day kindergarten and preschool education for all children. Attendance is voluntary, but most children are enrolled. The Oklahoma curriculum emphasizes literacy and math; benefits are particularly strong for children whose home language is Spanish (Phillips et al., 2009).

Although developmentalists are pleased that the public finally recognizes the benefits of early education, the message that quality matters does not seem to be understood. For the 40 states that sponsor early education, the average funding is less than $5,000 per year per student. That is not enough to pay for a low child/adult ratio, teachers with college degrees, and professional mentoring in a safe, well-equipped space.

Note also that the initial research was on low-income children. Most developmentalists think that the findings apply to all children, but that is controversial—especially when funding for education at all levels is diminishing.

The same dilemma is apparent for many aspects of early cognition. Much more is known now than formerly about what children can learn, and there is no doubt that 2- and 3-year-olds are capable of learning languages, concepts, and much else. A hundred years ago, that was not understood. Piaget was a leader in recognizing the abilities of the child. Now Piaget's work has been eclipsed by new research: What a child learns before age 6 is pivotal for later schooling and adult life, yet many children do not learn what they need to know.

This theme continues in the next chapter, where we talk about the interaction between children and all the systems that surround them.

SUMMING UP

Young children can learn a great deal before kindergarten, in either a child-centered or teacher-directed preschool, or in an excellent home setting. Montessori and Reggio Emilia schools advance children's learning. Both emphasize individual accomplishments and child development.

Teacher-directed programs stress readiness for school, emphasizing letters and numbers that all children should understand. Head Start and other programs advance learning for low-income children. Longitudinal research finds that some of the benefits are evident in adulthood. However, quality and accessibility are variable. The best programs are expensive; the benefits are apparent only decades later. ■

Early Childhood Education

Preschool can be an academic and social benefit to children. Around the world, increasing numbers of children are enrolled in early childhood education programs.

Early childhood education programs are described as "teacher-directed" or "child-centered," but in reality, most teachers's styles reflect a combination of both approaches. Some students benefit more from the order and structure of a teacher-directed classroom, while others work better in a more collaborative and creative environment.

TEACHER-DIRECTED APPROACH

Focused on Getting Preschoolers Ready to Learn

Direct instruction

Teacher as formal authority

Students learn passively

Classroom is orderly and quiet

Teacher fully manages lesssons

Fosters independence

Encourages academics

Students learn from teacher

STUDENT-CENTERED APPROACH

Focused on Individual Development and Growth

Teacher as facilitator

Teacher as delegator

Students learn actively

Classroom is designed for collaborative work

Students direct content

Fosters collaboration

Encourages artistic expression

Students learn from other students

PHOTO: WORTH PUBLISHERS

CHARACTERISTICS OF U.S. PRESCHOOLERS

Proportion of children who are enrolled in preschool, by ethnicity and parents' education. You'll see a larger proportion of children whose parents have a graduate degree go to preschool than those whose parents have only a high school diploma.

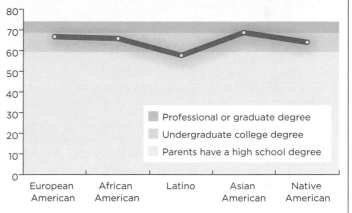

Legend:
- Professional or graduate degree
- Undergraduate college degree
- Parents have a high school degree

X-axis: European American, African American, Latino, Asian American, Native American

Y-axis: 0 to 80

DIFFERENT STUDENTS, DIFFERENT TEACHERS

There is clearly no "one right way" to teach children. Each approach has potential benefits and pitfalls. A classroom full of independent, self-motivated students can thrive when a gifted teacher acts as a competent facilitator. But students who are distracted or annoyed by noise, or who are shy or intimidated by other children, can blossom under an engaging and encouraging teacher in a more traditional environment.

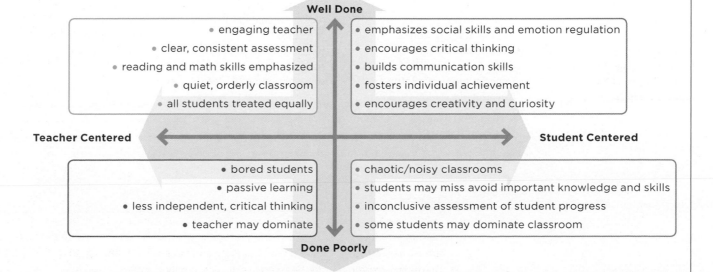

Well Done

- engaging teacher
- clear, consistent assessment
- reading and math skills emphasized
- quiet, orderly classroom
- all students treated equally

- emphasizes social skills and emotion regulation
- encourages critical thinking
- builds communication skills
- fosters individual achievement
- encourages creativity and curiosity

Teacher Centered ← → **Student Centered**

- bored students
- passive learning
- less independent, critical thinking
- teacher may dominate

- chaotic/noisy classrooms
- students may miss avoid important knowledge and skills
- inconclusive assessment of student progress
- some students may dominate classroom

Done Poorly

SUMMARY

Thinking During Early Childhood

1. Piaget stressed the egocentric and illogical aspects of thought during the play years. He called this stage of thinking preoperational intelligence because young children do not yet use logical operations to think about their observations and experiences.

2. Young children, according to Piaget, sometimes focus on only one thing (centration) and see things only from their own viewpoint (egocentrism), remaining stuck on appearances and current reality. They may believe that living spirits reside in inanimate objects, a belief called animism.

3. Vygotsky stressed the social aspects of childhood cognition, noting that children learn by participating in various experiences, guided by more knowledgeable adults or peers. Such guidance assists learning within the zone of proximal development, which encompasses the knowledge children are close to understanding and the skills they can almost master.

4. According to Vygotsky, the best teachers use various hints, guidelines, and other tools to provide a child with a scaffold for new learning. Language is a bridge that provides social mediation between the knowledge that the child already has and the learning that the society hopes to impart. For Vygotsky, words are tools for learning.

5. Children develop theories, especially to explain the purpose of life and their role in it. One theory about children's thinking is called "theory-theory"—the hypothesis that children develop theories because all humans innately seek explanations for everything they observe.

6. An example of the developing cognition of young children is theory of mind—an understanding of what others may be thinking. Theory of mind begins at around age 4, partly the result of maturation of the brain. Culture and experiences also influence its development.

Language Learning

7. Language develops rapidly during early childhood, a sensitive period but not a critical one for language learning. Vocabulary increases dramatically, with thousands of words added between ages 2 and 6. In addition, basic grammar is mastered.

8. Many children learn to speak more than one language, gaining cognitive as well as social advantages. Ideally, children become balanced bilinguals, equally proficient in two languages, by age 6.

Early-Childhood Education

9. Organized educational programs during early childhood advance cognitive and social skills, although specifics vary a great deal. Montessori and Reggio Emilia are two child-centered programs that began in Italy and are now offered in many nations. Behaviorist principles led to many specific practices of teacher-directed programs.

10. Head Start is a U.S. federal government program primarily for low-income children. Longitudinal research finds that early-childhood education reduces the risk of later problems, such as needing special education. High-quality programs increase the likelihood that a child will become a law-abiding, gainfully employed adult.

11. Many types of preschool programs are successful. It is the quality of early education that matters. Children learn best if teachers follow a defined curriculum and if the child/adult ratio is low. The training, warmth, and continuity of early-childhood teachers benefit the children in many ways.

KEY TERMS

animism (p. 246)
balanced bilingual (p. 261)
centration (p. 246)
conservation (p. 247)
Dual Language Learners (DLLs) (p. 268)
egocentrism (p. 246)

fast-mapping (p. 257)
focus on appearance (p. 246)
Head Start (p. 266)
irreversibility (p. 246)
Montessori schools (p. 264)
overimitation (p. 250)
overregularization (p. 259)

pragmatics (p. 259)
preoperational intelligence (p. 245)
Reggio Emilia (p. 264)
scaffolding (p. 249)
static reasoning (p. 246)
symbolic thought (p. 245)

theory of mind (p. 253)
theory-theory (p. 252)
zone of proximal development (ZPD) (p. 249)

WHAT HAVE YOU LEARNED?

1. What are the strengths of preoperational thought?

2. What is the difference between egocentrism in a child and selfishness in an adult?

3. How does guided participation increase a child's zone of proximal development?

4. Why did Vygotsky think that talking to oneself is not a sign of illness but an aid to cognition?

5. What factors spur the development of theory of mind?

6. What is the evidence that early childhood is a sensitive time for learning language?

7. How does fast-mapping aid the language explosion?

8. How does overregularization signify a cognitive advance?

9. What evidence in language learning shows the limitations of logic in early childhood?

10. What are the advantages of teaching a child two languages?

11. How can native language loss be avoided in children?

12. What do most preschools provide for children that most homes do not?

13. In child-centered programs, what do the teachers do?

14. What makes the Reggio Emilia program different from most other preschool programs?

15. Why are Montessori schools still functioning, 100 years after the first such schools opened?

16. What are the advantages and disadvantages of teacher-directed preschools?

17. What are the goals of Head Start?

18. Why have various evaluations of Head Start reached different conclusions?

19. What are the long-term results of intervention preschools?

APPLICATIONS

The best way to understand thinking in early childhood is to listen to a child, as applications 1 and 2 require. If some students have no access to children, they should do application 3 or 4.

1. Replicate one of Piaget's conservation experiments. The easiest one is conservation of liquids (Figure 9.1). Work with a child under age 5 who tells you that two identically shaped glasses contain the same amount of liquid. Then carefully pour one glass of liquid into a narrower, taller glass. Ask the child if one glass now contains more or if the glasses contain the same amount.

2. To demonstrate how rapidly language is learned, show a preschool child several objects and label one with a nonsense word the child has never heard. (*Toma* is often used; so is *wug*.) Or choose a word the child does not know, such as *wrench*,

spatula, or the name of a coin from another nation. Test the child's fast-mapping.

3. Theory of mind emerges at about age 4, but many adults still have trouble understanding other people's thoughts and motives. Ask several people why someone in the news did whatever he or she did (e.g., a scandal, a crime, a heroic act). Then ask your informants how sure they are of their explanation. Compare and analyze the reasons as well as the degrees of certainty. (One person may be sure of an explanation that someone else thinks is impossible.)

4. Think about an experience in which you learned something that was initially difficult. To what extent do Vygotsky's concepts (guided participation, zone of proximal development) explain the experience? Write a detailed, step-by-step account of your learning process as Vygotsky would have described it.

Early Childhood: Psychosocial Development

- Emotional Development
  Initiative versus Guilt
  Motivation
  Culture and Emotional Control
  Seeking Emotional Balance

- Play
  Playmates
  Culture and Cohort
  Active Play

- Challenges for Caregivers
  Caregiving Styles
  Cultural Variations
  Teaching Children to Be Boys or Girls

- Moral Development
  Nature and Nurture
  Empathy and Antipathy
  Discipline
  OPPOSING PERSPECTIVES:
  Is Spanking Okay?

WHAT WILL YOU KNOW?

1. Why do 2-year-olds have more sudden tempers, tears, and terrors than 6-year-olds?
2. If a child never plays, is that a problem?
3. What happens if parents let their children do whatever they want?
4. What are the long-term effects of spanking children?

It was a hot summer afternoon. Rachel, almost 3, and Bethany, age 4, were with me in the kitchen, which was in one corner of our living/dining area. Rachel opened the refrigerator and grabbed a bottle of orange juice. The sticky bottle slipped, shattering on the tile floor. My stunned daughters looked at me, at the shards, at the spreading juice with extra pulp. I picked my girls up and plopped them on the couch.

"Stay there," I yelled.

They did, quiet, wide-eyed, and puzzled at my fury; Rachel had not deliberately dropped the juice, and Bethany had done nothing wrong. As they watched me pick, sweep, and mop, I understood how parents could hit their kids. By the end of the chapter, I hope you also realize that a moment like this—in the summer heat, with two small children causing unexpected and difficult work—can turn a loving, patient parent into something else. It is not easy, day after day, being the guide and model that parents should be.

Fortunately, many safeguards prevented me from serious maltreatment: The girls had learned when to obey, I knew not to punish in anger, my finances made buying more juice easy. I hugged them when I took them off the couch. As children learn to manage their emotions, as parents learn to guide their children, as the macrosystem and microsystem (beliefs and income) influence adult–child interaction, many aspects of psychosocial development affect how children develop from ages 2 to 6. This chapter describes all that.

>> Emotional Development

Children gradually learn when and how to express emotions, becoming more capable in every aspect of their lives (Buckley & Saarni, 2009; Morrison et al., 2010). Controlling the expression of emotions, called **emotional regulation**, is the preeminent psychosocial task between ages 2 and 6 (N. Eisenberg et al., 2004).

Such regulation is virtually impossible in infancy, but when the emotional hot spots of the limbic system connect to the prefrontal cortex, children become better able to control their reactions. This is not easy; it requires practice, maturation, and work, called **effortful control**. By age 6, children can usually be angry but not explosive, frightened but not terrified, sad but not inconsolable, anxious but not withdrawn, proud but not boastful. Depending on each child's temperament,

emotional regulation The ability to control when and how emotions are expressed.

effortful control The ability to regulate one's emotions and actions through effort, not simply through natural inclination.

some emotions are easier to control than others, but even temperamentally angry or fearful children can learn to modify the expression of their emotions (Moran et al., 2013, Tan et al., 2013).

Emotional regulation is a lifelong necessity; no one does it perfectly all the time. When Rachel dropped the orange juice, I should not have yelled. Fortunately, my unregulated expression of anger stopped there. Learning to regulate emotion is a long process; it begins during early childhood, from ages 3 to 5 (Lewis, 2013).

Initiative versus Guilt

initiative versus guilt Erikson's third psychosocial crisis, in which children undertake new skills and activities and feel guilty when they do not succeed at them.

During Erikson's third developmental stage, **initiative versus guilt**, children acquire many skills and competencies in addition to emotional regulation. *Initiative* can mean several things—saying something new, expanding an ability, beginning a project. Depending on the outcome (especially reactions from other people), children feel proud or guilty.

Usually, North American parents encourage enthusiasm, effort, and pride in their 2- to 6-year-olds, as well as prevent guilt from becoming self-hatred. If, instead, parents ignore rather than guide emotions, a child may not learn emotional regulation (Morris et al., 2007).

Protective Optimism

self-concept A person's understanding of who he or she is, in relation to self-esteem, appearance, personality, and various traits.

Children's beliefs about their worth are connected to parental confirmation, especially when parents remind their children of their positive accomplishments ("You helped Daddy sweep the sidewalk. You made it very clean.").

Remember that Erikson described autonomy at ages 1 and 2, a stage often characterized by stubbornness and nicknamed "the terrible twos." By age 3, autonomy is transformed to become initiative, as children act on their eagerness to learn new skills (Rubin et al., 2009).

This chapter's opening anecdote is an example: Rachel was learning to get juice when she was thirsty. Both autonomy and initiative are more prized in Western cultures than in Eastern ones, where children learn to be socially attuned and interdependent (Keller & Otto, 2011).

Children in North America and Europe develop a strong **self-concept**, an understanding of themselves. For example, young children are given choices: "Apple or banana?" "Blue pajamas or red ones?" Choosing makes people believe they are independent agents (Kim & Chu, 2011). In the United States, self-concept quickly includes gender and size. Girls are usually happy to be girls; boys to be boys; both are glad they aren't babies. "Crybaby" is an insult; praise for being "a big kid" is welcomed.

© ENIGMA/ALAMY

A Poet and We Know It She is the proud winner of a national poetry contest. Is she as surprised, humbled, and thankful as an adult winner would be?

Erikson recognized that young children are not realistic. They believe that they are strong, smart, and good-looking—and thus that any goal is achievable. Whatever they are (self-concept) is thought to be good.

For instance, young children not only believe that their nation and religion are best, they feel sorry for children who do not belong to their country or church. At this age, a protective optimism encourages children to try unfamiliar activities, make friends, begin school, and so on (Boseovski, 2010). The same is true for mastering skills: They learn to pour juice, zip pants, and climb trees, undeterred by overflowing juice, stuck zippers, or a perch too high. Faith in themselves helps them persist.

Brain Maturation

The new initiative that Erikson describes results from myelination of the limbic system, growth of the prefrontal cortex, and a longer attention span—all made possible by neurological maturation. [**Lifespan Link:** Brain maturation is described in detail in Chapter 5 and Chapter 8.] Emotional regulation and cognitive maturation develop together, each enabling the other to advance (Bell & Calkins, 2011; Lewis, 2013).

Normally, neurological advances in the prefrontal cortex at about age 4 or 5 make children less likely to throw tantrums, provoke attacks, or giggle during prayer (Kagan & Herschkowitz, 2005). Throughout early childhood, violent outbursts, uncontrolled crying, and terrifying *phobias* (irrational, crippling fears) diminish. The capacity for self-control—such as not opening a present immediately if asked to wait and not expressing disappointment at an undesirable gift—becomes more evident.

For example, in one study researchers asked children to wait 8 minutes while their mothers did some paperwork before opening a wrapped present in front of them (Cole, Tan et al., 2011). The children used strategies to help them wait, including distractions and private speech.

Keisha was one of the study participants:

> "Are you done, Mom?" . . . "I wonder what's in it" . . . "Can I open it now?"
>
> Each time her mother reminds Keisha to wait, eventually adding, "If you keep interrupting me, I can't finish and if I don't finish . . ." Keisha plops in her chair, frustrated. "I really want it," she laments, aloud but to herself. "I want to talk to mommy so I won't open it. If I talk, Mommy won't finish. If she doesn't finish, I can't have it." She sighs deeply, folds her arms, and scans the room . . . The research assistant returns. Keisha looks at her mother with excited anticipation. Her mother says, "OK, now." Keisha tears open the gift.
>
> [Cole, Armstrong et al., 2011, p. 59]

Motivation

Motivation (the impulse that propels someone to act) comes either from a person's own desires or from the social context.

Intrinsic motivation occurs when people do something for the joy of doing it: A musician might enjoy making music even when no one else hears it. **Extrinsic motivation** comes from outside the person, when people do something to gain praise (or some other reinforcement): A musician might play for applause or money.

Intrinsic motivation is crucial for young children (Cheng & Yeh, 2009). Fortunately, preschool children are often intrinsically motivated, eager to play and practice, whether or not someone else wants them to. Child-centered preschools, as described in Chapter 9, depend on the reality that children love to talk, play, and move. Praise and prizes might be appreciated, but that's not why children work at what they do. When playing a game, they might not keep score; the fun is in the activity (intrinsic), not the winning.

Imaginary Friends

Intrinsic motivation is apparent when children invent dialogues for their toys, concentrate on creating a work of art or architecture, and converse with **imaginary friends**. Such conversations with invisible creatures are rarely encouraged by adults (i.e., there is no extrinsic motivation), but imaginary friends are nonetheless increasingly common over the years of early childhood. Children know their imaginary friends are invisible and pretend, but conjuring them up meets various psychosocial needs (Taylor et al., 2009).

For example, imaginary friends may help with emotional regulation: Children use them to control their fears and temper as well as to provide comfort and companionship. One girl's friend named Elephant was "7 inches tall, gray color, black

Proud Peruvian In rural Peru, a program of early education (Pronoei) encourages community involvement and traditional culture. Preschoolers, like this girl in a holiday parade, are proud to be themselves, and that helps them become healthy and strong.

© MIKE THEISS/NATIONAL GEOGRAPHIC SOCIETY/CORBIS

Especially for College Students
Is extrinsic or intrinsic motivation more influential in your study efforts? (see response, page 282)

intrinsic motivation A drive, or reason to pursue a goal, that comes from inside a person, such as the desire to feel smart or competent.

extrinsic motivation A drive, or reason to pursue a goal, that arises from the need to have one's achievements rewarded from outside, perhaps by receiving material possessions or another person's esteem.

imaginary friends Make-believe friends who exist only in a child's imagination; increasingly common from ages 3 through 7. They combat loneliness and aid emotional regulation.

Especially for Teachers One of your students tells you about a child who plays, sleeps, and talks with an imaginary friend. Does this mean that that child is emotionally disturbed? (see response, page 280)

Especially for Teachers of Young Children Should you put gold stars on children's work? (see response, page 282)

eyes, wears tank top and shorts . . . sometimes is mean" (Taylor et al., 2004, p. 1178). By having a companion who "sometimes is mean," this girl was developing strategies to deal with mean people.

An Experiment in Motivation

In a classic experiment, preschool children were given markers and paper for drawing and assigned to one of three groups who received, respectively: (1) no award, (2) an expected award (they were told *before* they had drawn anything that they would get a certificate), and (3) an unexpected award (*after* they had drawn something, they heard, "You were a big help," and got a certificate) (Lepper et al., 1973).

Later, observers noted how often children in each group chose to draw on their own. Those who received the expected award were less likely to draw than those who were unexpectedly rewarded. The interpretation was that extrinsic motivation (condition #2) undercut intrinsic motivation.

This research triggered a flood of studies seeking to understand whether, when, and how positive reinforcement should be given. The consensus is that praising or paying a person *after* an accomplishment sometimes encourages that behavior. However, if payment is promised in advance, that extrinsic reinforcement may backfire (Deci et al., 1999; Cameron & Pierce, 2002; Gottfried et al., 2009).

Praise is effective when it is connected to the particular production, not to a general trait ("You did a good drawing," not "You are a great artist") because then the child believes that effort paid off, which motivates a repeat performance (Zentall & Morris, 2010).

Culture and Emotional Control

As you know, cultural differences are apparent in every aspect of development. This is quite obvious in emotional expression. Children may be encouraged to laugh/cry/yell or, the opposite, to hide their emotions (H. S. Kim et al., 2008). Some adults guffaw, slap their knees, and stomp their feet for joy; others cover their mouths with their hands if a smile spontaneously appears. Children learn to do the same.

Control strategies vary as well (Matsumoto, 2004). Peers, parents, and strangers sometimes ignore emotional outbursts, sometimes deflect them, sometimes punish them. Shame is used when social reputation is a priority. In some cultures, "pride goeth before a fall" and people who "have no shame" are considered mentally ill (Stein, 2006).

Finally, certain families, cultures, and nations differ as to which emotions most need to be regulated. Although individuals may disagree with the following generalizations, developmentalists suggest that nations emphasize regulation as follows:

- Fear (United States)
- Anger (Puerto Rico)
- Pride (China)
- Selfishness (Japan)
- Impatience (many Native American communities)
- Defiance (Mexico)
- Moodiness (the Netherlands)

(Chen, 2011; Harkness et al., 2011; J. G. Miller, 2004; Stubben, 2001)

Of course, this list is oversimplified. Temperaments vary, which makes people within the same culture unlike one another. "Cultures are inevitably more complicated than the framework that is supposed to explain them" (Harkness et al., 2011, p. 92). Nonetheless, parents everywhere teach emotional regulation, hoping their children will adapt to the norms of their culture.

Seeking Emotional Balance

At every age, in all cultures and cohorts, caregivers try to prevent **psychopathology**, an illness or disorder (-*pathology*) of the mind (*psycho-*). Although symptoms and diagnoses are influenced by culture (rebellion is expected in some cultures and pathological in others), impaired emotional regulation universally signals mental imbalance. Parents guide young children toward "an optimal balance" between emotional expression and emotional control (Blair & Dennis, 2011; Trommsdorff & Cole, 2011).

Without adequate regulation, emotions are overwhelming. Intense reactions can occur in opposite ways, as you might expect from the activate/inhibit nature of neurons.

Some people have **externalizing problems**: Their powerful feelings burst out uncontrollably. They externalize rage, for example, by lashing out or breaking things. Without emotional regulation, an angry child might flail at another person or lie down screaming and kicking. By age 5, children usually have learned more self-control, perhaps pouting or cursing, not hitting and screaming.

Other people have **internalizing problems**: They are fearful and withdrawn, turning distress inward. Emotions may be internalized via headaches or stomachaches. Although the cause is psychological, the ache is real.

Again, with maturity, the extreme fears of some 2-year-olds (e.g., terror of the bathtub drain, of an imagined tidal wave, of a stranger on crutches) diminish. The fear isn't gone, but expression is regulated: A child might be afraid of kindergarten, for instance, but bravely let go of Mother's hand anyway.

Both undercontrol, which produces externalizing behavior, and overcontrol, which leads to internalizing behavior, are much more common in 3-year-olds than 5-year-olds. Experiences during those years interact with brain maturation, ideally strengthening emotional regulation (Lewis, 2013).

Sex differences in internalizing and externalizing behavior are traditionally assumed to be biological, but a cultural explanation is also possible. Does prenatal testosterone shape boys' brains, making them more likely to develop ADHD? Or do parents and cultures teach young girls to restrain their externalizing actions, while teaching boys to avoid internalizing? (See Visualizing Development, page 281). Trying to understand the causes of sex or gender differences is a concern of thousands of researchers (Eagly & Wood, 2013). Conflicting theories and evidence are presented later in this chapter.

psychopathology Literally, an illness of the mind, or psyche. Various cultures and groups within cultures have different concepts of a specific psychopathology. A recent compendium of symptoms and disorders in the United States is in the DSM-5. Many other nations use an international set of categories, the ICD-10.

externalizing problems Difficulty with emotional regulation that involves expressing powerful feelings through uncontrolled physical or verbal outbursts, as by lashing out at other people or breaking things.

internalizing problems Difficulty with emotional regulation that involves turning one's emotional distress inward, as by feeling excessively guilty, ashamed, or worthless.

KOICHI SAITO/AMANAIMA/AGE FOTOSTOCK

Age or Gender? Probably both. Brother and sister are reacting typically for their age and sex, as the 4-year old boy moves his book away from his sister, who cries rather than grabbing it. Culture may be a factor, too, as these sibling are in Korea, where physical fighting between siblings is not allowed.

SUMMING UP

Emotional regulation is the crucial psychosocial task in early childhood. Erikson thought young children are naturally motivated to take initiative, with joy at new tasks. He also thought that during early childhood, guilt feelings may come to the fore, as parents criticize unrestrained emotional expression. Brain maturation and family guidance help children regulate their emotions, avoiding either extreme externalizing or internalizing reactions. Universally, 3- to 5-year-olds become better able to regulate their emotions, but cultures differ in which emotions should be controlled and how emotions should be expressed.

Sex Differences in Emotional Regulation

On average, young girls are advanced in controlling their emotions, particularly anger, compared with boys. (Visualizing Development, p. 281, illustrates gender differences and similarities in several areas of development.) Research on childhood and adolescence traditionally focused on boys. More recently girls have been studied, and it seems that girls' aggression is more often directed at themselves or at people in their immediate social circle, whereas boys can be aggressive with strangers as well (Loeber et al., 2013). What is the origin of such sex differences? Data from early childhood can be used to support either biological or cultural explanations.

Consider one study (also noted in Visualizing Development) in detail. Researchers gave eighty-two 5-year-olds two toy figures and told them the beginning of a story (Zahn-Waxler et al., 2008): The two toy children (named Mark and Scott for the boys, Mary and Sarah for the girls) were said to start yelling at each other. The 5-year-olds were asked to show what happened next.

Many boys showed Mark and Scott hitting and kicking each other. Boys whose externalizing behavior worsened between ages 5 and 9 (as rated by teachers and parents) were the most likely to dramatize such attacks at age 5. They became aggressive 9-year-olds—"problem children" according to the adults.

By contrast, 5-year-old girls often had Mary and Sarah discuss the conflict or change the subject. Curiously, however, those 5-year-old girls who immediately had Mary and Sarah engage in "reparative behavior" (repairing the relationship, such as having Mary hug Sarah and say, "I'm sorry") were more likely to be disruptive at age 9 than the other girls, and hence were "problem children." Their quickness to repair the conflict may have signaled too much guilt or shame, which could erupt later on.

The authors of the study wrote:

> Gender-role stereotypes or exaggerations of masculine qualities (e.g., impulsive, aggressive, uncaring) and feminine qualities (submissive, unassertive, socially sensitive) are reflected not only in the types of problems males and females tend to develop but also in different forms of expression.

> *[Zahn-Waxler et al., 2008, p. 114]*

These researchers suggest that extreme externalization or extreme internalization predicts future psychopathology. Because of cultural expectations, mistreated boys are likely to externalize and mistreated girls to internalize.

An alternative explanation is that something in the hormones or brain structures of boys and girls pushes them in opposite directions. In any case, it seems clear that, unless children master emotional regulation during early childhood, boys throw and hit, and girls sob or hide.

FLORESCO PRODUCTIONS CULTURA/NEWSCOM

Cute or Too Shy? Cute, of course. Universally, girls and women are expected to be reticent. They cling more to their mothers in kindergarten, they wait to be asked to dance or date, they talk less in co-ed groups. If she were a he, would he be considered too shy?

>> Response for Teachers (from page 278): No, unless the child is over age 10. In fact, imaginary friends are quite common, especially among creative children. The child may be somewhat lonely, though; you could help him or her find a friend.

>> Play

Play is timeless and universal—apparent in every part of the world for thousands of years. Many developmentalists believe that play is the most productive as well as the most enjoyable activity that children undertake (Elkind, 2007; Frost, 2009; P. K. Smith, 2010). Whether play is essential for normal growth or is merely fun is "a controversial topic of study" (Pellegrini, 2011, p. 3).

There are echoes of this controversy in preschool education, as explained in Chapter 9. Some educators want children to focus on reading and math; others predict emotional and academic problems for children who rarely play

VISUALIZING DEVELOPMENT

Sex Differences and Similarities

Humans tend to exaggerate differences and forget how much we have in common. Despite the common phrase "opposite sex," most of our biological characteristics except sex organs are the same. The studies presented below are complex, but the bottom line is the same as the top: Whenever sex differences appear, be cautious—remember, sex similarities are more apparent than differences, and every study shows overlap. The two sexes are never opposites. As you can see from the photo of six children, all close in age, for height age is much more important than gender.

DIFFERENCES IN PSYCHOPATHOLOGY

For children under age 10, boys have higher rates of psychopathology, although specific ratios vary by cohort and location. The most dramatic gender difference in rates of psychopathology is found with attention-deficit/hyperactivity disorder, as shown on the right. Most children do not have ADHD, but almost three times as many boys as girls do.

4.8% 12.1%

Attention-deficit/hyperactivity disorder

PHOTO: GELPI JM/SHUTTERSTOCK

CENTERS FOR DISEASE CONTROL, 2011

SOME COMPLICATIONS

Every study that details sex differences in children's behavior reports a complex picture.

1 Perhaps between ages 5 and 10, boys *learn* to become more aggressive and girls *learn* to apologize more often. In one study teachers and parents judged the behavior of children from ages 5 to 9 (Zahn-Wexler et al., 2008). Most improved over those 4 years, but some (called "problem children") did not. A marked shift occurred between ages 5 and 7, when all the children used dolls to show what might happen in several conflict situations. The "problem children" were more aggressive. Most boys continued to be aggressive, but girls were more likely to try to repair the situation.

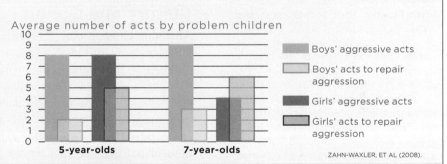

Average number of acts by problem children

■ Boys' aggressive acts
■ Boys' acts to repair aggression
■ Girls' aggressive acts
■ Girls' acts to repair aggression

ZAHN-WAXLER, ET AL (2008).

2 Many adults generalize that boys have externalizing problems (they act out by hitting, breaking things, etc.) while girls have internalizing problems (they withdraw, cry, blame themselves). But, as you see here, the actual picture is more complex, with many children having both kinds of problems. Also note that mothers, fathers, and teachers rated the same children but often did not agree. When adults were asked to rate a specific child, more than half the children were not rated as problematic (note percentages on the left); however, when parents were asked to rate a specific child, they were more likely to see problems than teachers were. Adults did not agree about sex differences.

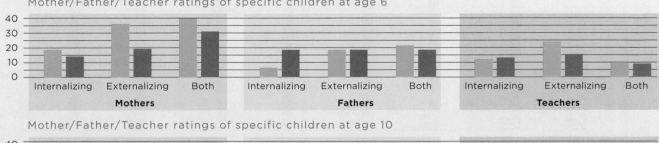

Mother/Father/Teacher ratings of specific children at age 6

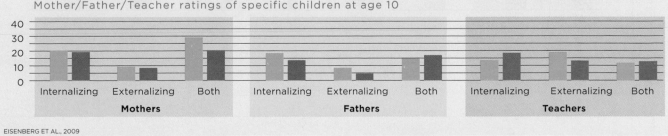

Mother/Father/Teacher ratings of specific children at age 10

SOURCES & CREDITS LISTED ON P. SC-1

EISENBERG ET AL., 2009

FIGURE 10.1

Mostly Playing When researchers studied 3-year-olds in the United States, Brazil, and Kenya, they found that, on average, the children spent more than half their time playing. Note the low percentages of both middle- and working-class Brazilian children in the Lessons category, which included all intentional efforts to teach children something. There is a cultural explanation: Unlike parents in Kenya and the United States, most Brazilian parents believe that children of this age learn without instruction.

(Hirsh-Pasek et al., 2009; Pellegrini, 2009; Rubin et al., 2009). It does seem to be true that children who are deprived of activity for a long period tend to play more vigorously when they finally have the chance (Pellegrini et al., 2013).

Playmates

Young children play best with *peers,* that is, people of about the same age and social status. Although even infants are intrigued by other small children, most infant play is either solitary or with a parent. Some maturation is required for social play with peers.

At first, children are too self-absorbed to be good playmates, but they learn quickly over the years of early childhood. By age 6, most are quite skilled: They know how to join a peer group, manage conflict, take turns, find friends, and keep playmates. Over the childhood years, social play teaches emotional regulation, empathy, and cultural understanding (Göncü & Gaskins, 2011).

Parents have an obvious task in this regard: Find peers and arrange play dates. Of course, some parents play with their children, which benefits both of them. But even the most playful parent is outmatched by another child at negotiating the rules of tag, at play-fighting, at pretending to be sick, at killing dragons. Specifics vary, but "play with peers is one of the most important areas in which children develop positive social skills" (Xu, 2010, p. 496).

Culture and Cohort

All young children play; "everywhere, a child playing is a sign of healthy development" (Gosso, 2010, p. 95). Everywhere, play is the prime activity of even very young children, as illustrated in Figure 10.1. Basic play is similar in every culture, such as throwing and catching; pretending to be adults; drawing with chalk, markers, sticks, or what have you. Accordingly, developmentalists think play is *experience-expectant.*

Some specifics are *experience-dependent,* however, reflecting culture and SES. **[Lifespan Link:** Experience-expectant and experience-dependent brain development is explained in Chapter 5.] Chinese children fly kites, Alaskan natives

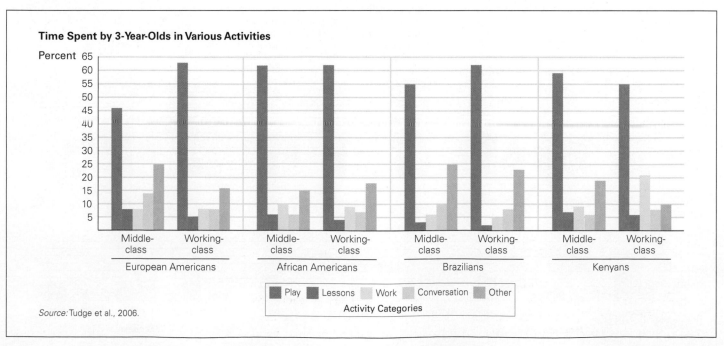

Time Spent by 3-Year-Olds in Various Activities

Source: Tudge et al., 2006.

tell dreams and stories, Lapp children pretend to be reindeer, Cameroon children hunt mice, and so on. Parents in some cultures consider play important and willingly engage in games and dramas. In other places, sheer survival takes time and energy, and children must help by doing chores. In those places, if children have any time for play, it is with each other, not with adults (Kalliala, 2006; Roopnarine, 2011).

As children grow older, play becomes more social, influenced by brain maturation, playmate availability, and the physical setting. One developmentalist bemoans the twenty-first century's "swift and pervasive rise of electronic media" and adults who lean "more toward control than freedom" (Chudacoff, 2011, p. 108). He praises children who find places to play independently and "conspire ways to elude adult management."

This opinion may be extreme, but it is echoed in more common concerns. As you remember, one dispute in preschool education is the proper balance between unstructured, creative play and teacher-directed learning. Before the electronic age, and in places where technology was rare, most families had several children and few mothers worked outside the home. Then young children played outside with nearby children, often of several ages.

That was true in the United States a century ago. In 1932 the American sociologist Mildred Parten described the development of five kinds of social play, each more advanced than the previous one:

1. *Solitary play:* A child plays alone, unaware of any other children playing nearby.
2. *Onlooker play:* A child watches other children play.
3. *Parallel play:* Children play with similar objects in similar ways but not together.
4. *Associative play:* Children interact, sharing material, but their play is not reciprocal.
5. *Cooperative play:* Children play together, creating dramas or taking turns.

Parten thought that progress in social play was age-related, with 1-year-olds usually playing alone and 6-year-olds usually cooperatively.

Research on contemporary children finds much more age variation. Many Asian parents successfully teach 3-year-olds to take turns, share, and otherwise cooperate. Many North American children, encouraged to be individuals, still engage in parallel play at this age. Given all the social, political, and economic changes over the past century, many forms of social play (not necessarily in Parten's sequence) are normal for children at each age (Xu, 2010).

Play Ball! In every nation, young children play with balls, but the specific games they play vary with the culture. Soccer is the favorite game in many countries, including Brazil, where these children are practicing their dribbling on Copacabana Beach in Rio de Janeiro.

Observation Quiz Does kicking a soccer ball, as shown above, require fine or gross motor skills? (see answer, page 284)

No Grabbing Maybe the child on the left or the right will soon try to grab. If sharing continues, is it because these children have been raised within Asian families.

Active Play

Children need physical activity to develop muscle strength and control. Peers provide an audience, role models, and sometimes competition. For instance, running skills develop best when children chase or race each other, not when a child runs alone. Gross motor play is favored among young children, who enjoy climbing, kicking, and tumbling (Case-Smith & Kuhaneck, 2008).

Active social play—not solitary play—correlates with peer acceptance and a healthy self-concept (Nelson et al., 2008; P. K. Smith, 2010) and may help regulate emotions (Sutton-Smith, 2011). Adults need to remember this when

>> **Answer to Observation Quiz**
(from page 283): Although controlling the
trajectory of a ball with feet is a fine motor
skill, these boys are using gross motor
skills—their entire bodies (arms, torsos,
even heads)—to run to the ball.

they want children to sit still and be quiet. Among nonhuman primates, deprivation of social play warps later life, rendering some monkeys unable to mate, to make friends, or even to survive alongside other monkeys (Herman et al., 2011; Palagi, 2011).

Active play advances planning and self-control. Two-year-olds merely chase and catch each other, but older children keep the interaction fair, long-lasting, and fun. In tag, for instance, they set rules (adjusted to location), and each child decides how far to venture from base. If one child is "It" for too long, another child (often a friend) makes it easy to be caught.

Rough-and-Tumble Play

rough-and-tumble play Play that mimics aggression through wrestling, chasing, or hitting, but in which there is no intent to harm.

The most common form of active play is called **rough-and-tumble play** because it looks quite rough and because the children seem to tumble over one another. The term was coined by British scientists who studied primates in East Africa (Blurton-Jones, 1976). They noticed that monkeys often chased, attacked, rolled over in the dirt, and wrestled quite roughly, but without hurting one another.

If a young male monkey wanted to play, he would simply catch the eye of a peer and then run a few feet away. This invitation to rough-and-tumble play was almost always accepted, with a *play face* (smiling, not angry). Puppies, kittens, and chimps behave similarly.

When the scientists returned to London, they saw that human youngsters, like baby monkeys, also enjoy rough-and-tumble play, signified by the play face. Children chase, wrestle, and grab each other, developing games like tag and cops-and-robbers, with various conventions, expressions, and gestures that children use to signify "just pretend."

Rough-and-tumble play happens everywhere (although cops-and-robbers can be "robots-and-humans" or many other iterations). It is two or three times more as common among boys than girls and flourishes in ample space with minimal supervision (Berenbaum et al., 2008; Hassett et al., 2008, Pellegrini, 2013).

Many scientists think that rough-and-tumble play helps the prefrontal cortex develop, as children learn to regulate emotions, practice social skills, and strengthen their bodies (Pellis & Pellis, 2011). Indeed, some believe that play in childhood, especially rough-and-tumble play between father and son, may prevent antisocial behavior (even murder) later on (Wenner, 2009).

sociodramatic play Pretend play in which children act out various roles and themes in stories that they create.

Joy Supreme Pretend play in early childhood is thrilling and powerful. For this 7-year-old from Park Slope, Brooklyn, pretend play overwhelms mundane realities, such as an odd scarf or awkward arm.

WORTH PUBLISHERS

Drama and Pretending

Another major type of active play is **sociodramatic play**, in which children act out various roles and plots. Through such acting, children:

- Explore and rehearse social roles
- Learn to explain their ideas and persuade playmates
- Practice emotional regulation by pretending to be afraid, angry, brave, and so on
- Develop self-concept in a nonthreatening context

Sociodramatic play builds on pretending, which emerges in toddlerhood. But preschoolers do more than pretend; they combine their imagination with that of their friends, advancing in theory of mind (Kavanaugh, 2011). The beginnings of sociodramatic play are illustrated by the following pair, a 3-year-old girl and a 2-year-old boy. The girl wanted to act out the role of a baby, and she persuaded a boy in her nursery school to be the parent.

Boy: Not good. You bad.
Girl: Why?
Boy: 'Cause you spill your milk.
Girl: No. 'Cause I bit somebody.
Boy: Yes, you did.
Girl: Say, "Go to sleep. Put your head down."
Boy: Put your head down.
Girl: No.
Boy: Yes.
Girl: No.
Boy: Yes. Okay, I will spank you. Bad boy. *[Spanks her, not hard]*
Girl: No. My head is up. *[Giggles]* I want my teddy bear.
Boy: No. Your teddy bear go away.
[At this point she asked if he was really going to take the teddy bear away.]

[from Garvey, reported in Cohen, 2006, p. 72]

Note the social interaction in this form of play, with the 3-year-old clearly more mature than the 2-year-old. She created, directed and played her part, sometimes accepting what the boy said and sometimes not. The boy took direction, yet also made up his own dialogue and actions ("Bad boy"). It is noteworthy that the 2-year-old boy was willing to cooperate; when children are a few years older than these two, sex segregation is almost universal (Leaper, 2013).

A slightly older girl might want to play with the boys, but the older boys usually do not allow her (Pellegrini, 2013). Boy-versus-girl play emerges later, at puberty, but toward the end of early childhood both sexes stick to their own unless a particular neighborhood group has no other girls or no other boys.

Older preschoolers are not only more gender conscious, their sociodramatic play is much more elaborate. This was evident in four boys, about age 5, in a day-care center in Finland. Joni plays the role of the evil one who menaces the other boys; Tuomas directs the drama and acts in it as well.

Tuomas: And now he [Joni] would take me and would hang me . . . This would be the end of all of me.
Joni: Hands behind.
Tuomas: I can't help it. I have to. *[The two other boys follow his example.]*
Joni: I would put fire all around them.
[All three brave boys lie on the floor with hands tied behind their backs. Joni piles mattresses on them, and pretends to light a fire, which crackles closer and closer.]
Tuomas: Everything is lost.
[One boy starts to laugh.]
Petterl: Better not to laugh, soon we will all be dead. . . . I am saying my last words.
Tuomas: Now you can say your last wish. . . . And now I say I wish we can be terribly strong.
[At that point, the three boys suddenly gain extraordinary strength, pushing off the mattresses and extinguishing the fire. Good triumphs over evil, but not until the last moment, because, as one boy explains, "Otherwise this playing is not exciting at all."]

[adapted from Kalliala, 2006, p. 83]

Good versus evil is a favorite theme of boys' sociodramatic play, with danger part of the plot but victory in the end. By contrast, girls often act out domestic scenes, with themselves as the adults. In the same day-care center where Joni

FIGURE 10.2

Learning by Playing Fifty years ago, the average child spent three hours a day in outdoor play. Video games and television have largely replaced that play time, especially in cities. Children seem safer if parents can keep an eye on them, but what are the long-term effects on brain and body?

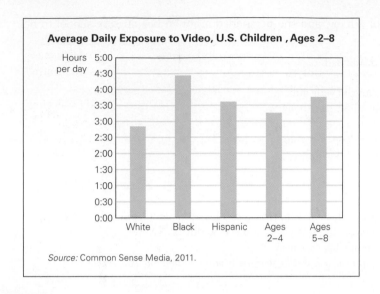

Average Daily Exposure to Video, U.S. Children, Ages 2–8

Source: Common Sense Media, 2011.

A Toy Machine Gun These boys in Liberia are doing what young children everywhere do—following adult example. Whenever countries are at war, children play soldiers, rebels, heroes, or spies. From their perspective, there is only one problem with such play—no one wants to be the enemy.

"Why don't you get off the computer and watch some TV?"

piled mattresses on his playmates, the girls say their play is "more beautiful and peaceful . . . [but] boys play all kinds of violent games" (Kalliala, 2006, p. 110).

The prevalence of sociodramatic play varies by family. Some cultures find it frivolous and discourage it; in other cultures, parents teach toddlers to be lions, or robots, or ladies drinking tea. Then children elaborate on those themes (Kavanaugh, 2011). Some children are avid television watchers, and they then act out superhero themes.

Television arouses concern among many developmentalists, who prefer that children's dramas come from their own imagination, not from the media. Of course, some children learn from television and educational videos, especially if adults watch with them and reinforce the lessons. However, children on their own rarely select educational programs over fast-paced cartoons, in which characters hit, shoot, and kick.

Six major organizations (the American Psychological Association, the American Academy of Pediatrics, the American Medical Association, the American Academy of Child and Adolescent Psychiatry, the American Academy of Family Physicians, and the American Psychiatric Association) recommend no electronic media at all for children under age 2 and strict limitations after that. The problem is not only that violent media teach aggression but also that all media take time from constructive interaction and creative play (see Figure 10.2).

SUMMING UP

All children everywhere in every era play during early childhood, which makes many developmentalists think play is essential for healthy development. Children benefit from play with peers, even more than from solitary play or play with adults. Specific forms of play vary by culture, gender, and SES. Rough-and-tumble play is active play that boys usually enjoy; sociodramatic play is common in children of both sexes, although the specific types of drama often differ by gender. Boys tend to prefer good-versus-evil dramas, with themselves conquering the bad guys; girls prefer domestic scenes, with themselves as the adults.

>> Challenges for Caregivers

We have seen that young children's emotions and actions are affected by many factors, including brain maturation, culture, and peers. Now we focus on another primary influence on young children: their caregivers.

For all children "parental involvement plays an important role in the development of both social and cognitive competence" (Parke & Buriel, 2006, p. 437). As more and more children spend long hours during early childhood with other adults, alternate caregivers become pivotal as well.

Caregiving Styles

Many researchers have studied the effects of parenting strategies and adult emotions. Although the temperament of the child and the patterns of the culture are always influential, adults vary a great deal in how they respond to children, with some parental practices leading to psychopathology while others encourage children to become outgoing, caring adults (Deater-Deckard, 2013).

Baumrind's Three Styles of Caregiving

Although thousands of researchers have traced the effects of parenting on child development, the work of one person, 50 years ago, continues to be influential. In her original research, Diana Baumrind (1967, 1971) studied 100 preschool children, all from California, almost all middle-class European Americans. (The cohort and cultural limitations of this sample were not obvious at the time.)

Baumrind found that parents differed on four important dimensions:

1. *Expressions of warmth.* Some parents are warm and affectionate; others, cold and critical.
2. *Strategies for discipline.* Parents vary in how they explain, criticize, persuade, and punish.
3. *Communication.* Some parents listen patiently; others demand silence.
4. *Expectations for maturity.* Parents vary in expectations for responsibility and self-control.

On the basis of these dimensions, Baumrind identified three parenting styles (summarized in Table 10.1).

Authoritarian parenting. The authoritarian parent's word is law, not to be questioned. Misconduct brings strict punishment, usually physical. Authoritarian parents set down clear rules and hold high standards. They do not expect children to offer opinions; discussion about emotions is especially rare. (One adult from such a family said that "How do you feel?" had only two possible answers: "Fine" and "Tired.") Authoritarian parents seem cold, rarely showing affection.

authoritarian parenting An approach to child rearing that is characterized by high behavioral standards, strict punishment for misconduct, and little communication from child to parent.

TABLE 10.1	Characteristics of Parenting Styles Identified by Baumrind				
				Communication	
Style	Warmth	Discipline	Expectations of Maturity	Parent to Child	Child to Parent
Authoritarian	Low	Strict, often physical	High	High	Low
Permissive	High	Rare	Low	Low	High
Authoritative	High	Moderate, with much discussion	Moderate	High	High

Protect Me from the Water Buffalo These two are at the Carabao Kneeling Festival. In rural Philippines, hundreds of these large but docile animals kneel on the steps of the church, part of a day of gratitude for the harvest.

Observation Quiz Is the father above authoritarian, authoritative, or permissive? (see answer, page 290)

Especially for Political Scientists Many observers contend that children learn their political attitudes at home, from the way their parents teach them. Is this true? (see response, page 290)

"He's just doing that to get attention."

Pay Attention Children develop best with lots of love and attention. They shouldn't have to ask for it!

permissive parenting An approach to child rearing that is characterized by high nurturance and communication but little discipline, guidance, or control. (Also called *indulgent parenting*.)

authoritative parenting An approach to child rearing in which the parents set limits but listen to the child and are flexible.

neglectful/uninvolved parenting An approach to child rearing in which the parents are indifferent toward their children and unaware of what is going on in their children's lives.

Permissive parenting. Permissive parents (also called *indulgent*) make few demands, hiding any impatience they feel. Discipline is lax, partly because they have low expectations for maturity. Permissive parents are nurturing and accepting, listening to whatever their offspring say, even if it is profanity or criticism of the parent.

Authoritative parenting. Authoritative parents set limits, but they are flexible. They encourage maturity, but they usually listen and forgive (not punish) if the child falls short. They consider themselves guides, not authorities (unlike authoritarian parents) and not friends (unlike permissive parents).

Other researchers describe a fourth style, called **neglectful/ uninvolved parenting,** which may be confused with permissive but is quite different (Steinberg, 2001). The similarity is that neither permissive nor neglectful parents use physical punishment. However, neglectful parents are oblivious to their children's behavior; they seem not to care. By contrast, permissive parents care very much: They defend their children, arrange play dates, and sacrifice to buy coveted toys.

The following long-term effects of parenting styles have been reported, not only in the United States but in many other nations as well (Baumrind, 2005; Baumrind et al., 2010; Chan & Koo, 2011; Huver et al., 2010; Rothrauff et al., 2009; Deater-Deckard, 2013).

- *Authoritarian* parents raise children who become conscientious, obedient, and quiet but not especially happy. Such children tend to feel guilty or depressed, internalizing their frustrations and blaming themselves when things don't go well. As adolescents, they sometimes rebel, leaving home before age 20.
- *Permissive* parents raise unhappy children who lack self-control, especially in the give-and-take of peer relationships. Inadequate emotional regulation makes them immature and impedes friendships, which is the main reason for their unhappiness. They tend to continue to live at home, still dependent on their parents, in early adulthood.
- *Authoritative* parents raise children who are successful, articulate, happy with themselves, and generous with others. These children are usually liked by teachers and peers, especially in cultures that value individual initiative (e.g., the United States).
- *Neglectful/uninvolved* parents raise children who are immature, sad, lonely, and at risk of injury and abuse, not only in early childhood but also lifelong.

Problems with Baumrind's Styles

Baumrind's classification schema is often criticized. Problems include the following:

- Her participants were not diverse in SES, ethnicity, or culture.
- She focused more on adult attitudes than on adult actions.
- She overlooked children's temperamental differences.
- She did not recognize that some "authoritarian" parents are also affectionate.
- She did not realize that some "permissive" parents provide extensive verbal guidance.

We now know that a child's temperament and the culture's standards powerfully affect caregivers, as do the consequences of one style or another (Cipriano & Stifter, 2010). This is as it should be.

Fearful or impulsive children require particular styles (an emphasis on reassurance for the fearful ones and quite strict standards for the impulsive ones) that may seem permissive or authoritarian. Of course, every child needs guidance and protection, but not too much: Overprotection and hypervigilance seem to be both cause and consequence of childhood anxiety (McShane & Hastings, 2009; Deater-Deckard, 2013). Much depends on the particular characteristics of the child, as the concept of differential sensitivity makes clear.

A study of parenting at age 2 and children's competence in kindergarten (including emotional regulation and friendships) found "multiple developmental pathways," with the best outcomes dependent on both the child and the adult (Blandon et al., 2010). Such studies suggest that simplistic advice from a book, a professional, or a neighbor who does not know the temperament of the child may be misguided: Scientific observation of parent–child interactions is needed before discerning whether an adult provides appropriate guidance without being overly controlling.

Cultural Variations

The significance of the context is particularly obvious when children of various ethnic groups are compared. It may be that certain alleles are more common in children of one group or another, and that difference may affect their temperament. However, much more influential are the attitudes and actions of adult caregivers.

U.S. parents of Chinese, Caribbean, or African heritage are often stricter than those of European backgrounds, yet their children develop better than if the parents were easygoing (Chao, 2001; Parke & Buriel, 2006). Latino parents are sometimes thought to be too intrusive, other times too permissive—but their children seem to be happier than the children of European American parents who behave the same way (García & Gracia, 2009; Ispa et al., 2004). A three-way interaction seems to influence the outcome of any parenting style: the child's temperament, the parent's personality, and the social context.

In a detailed study of 1,477 instances in which Mexican American mothers of 4-year-olds tried to get their children to do something they were not doing, most of the time the mothers simply uttered a command and the children complied (Livas-Dlott et al., 2010). This simple strategy, with the mother asserting authority and the children obeying without question, might be considered authoritarian. Almost never, however, did the mothers use physical punishment or even harsh threats when the children did not immediately do as they were told—which happened 14 percent of the time. For example,

> Hailey [the 4-year-old] decided to look for another doll and started digging through her toys, throwing them behind her as she dug. Maricruz [the mother] told Hailey she should not throw her toys. Hailey continued to throw toys, and Maricruz said her name to remind her to stop. Hailey continued her misbehavior, and her mother repeated "Hailey" once more. When Hailey continued, Maricruz raised her voice but calmly directed, "Hailey, look at me." Hailey continued but then looked at Maricruz as she explained, "You don't throw toys; you could hurt someone." Finally, Hailey complied and stopped.
>
> [Livas-Dlott et al., 2010, p. 572]

Note that the mother's first three efforts failed, and then a look accompanied by an explanation (albeit inaccurate in that setting, as no one could be hurt) succeeded. The researchers explain that these Mexican American families did not fit any of Baumrind's categories; respect for adult authority did not mean a cold mother–child relationship. Instead, the relationship shows evident *cariono* (caring) (Livas-Dlott et al., 2010). That warmth is crucial: Other research also

>>Answer to Observation Quiz (from page 288): It is impossible to be certain based on one moment, but the best guess is authoritative. He seems patient and protective, providing comfort and guidance, neither forcing (authoritarian) nor letting the child do whatever he wants (permissive).

>> Response for Political Scientists (from page 288): There are many parenting styles, and it is difficult to determine each one's impact on children's personalities. At this point, attempts to connect early child rearing with later political outlook are speculative.

finds that parental affection and warmth allow children to develop self-respect and to become compassionate adults, and this can occur in any of the three common parenting styles (Deater-Deckard, 2013; Eisenberg et al., 2013).

Given a multicultural and multicontextual perspective, developmentalists hesitate to be too specific in recommending any particular parenting style (Dishion & Bullock, 2002; J. G. Miller, 2004). That does not mean that all families function equally well—far from it. Signs of trouble, including a child's anxiety, aggression, and inability to play with others, are indicative. Ineffective, abusive, and neglectful parents are one cause of such trouble, but not the only one.

Teaching Children to Be Boys or Girls

Biology determines whether a child is male or female. As you remember from Chapter 4, at about 8 weeks after conception, the SRY gene directs the reproductive organs to develop externally, and then male hormones exert subtle control over the brain, body, and later behavior. Without that gene, the fetus develops female organs, which produce female hormones that also affect the brain and behavior.

It is possible for sex hormones to be unexpressed prenatally, in which case the child does not develop like the typical boy or girl (Hines, 2013). That is very rare; most children are male or female in all three ways: chromosomes, genitals, and hormones. That is their nature, but obviously nurture affects their sexual development from birth until death.

During early childhood, sex patterns and preferences become important to children and apparent to adults. At age 2, children apply gender labels (*Mrs., Mr., lady, man*) consistently. By age 4, children are convinced that certain toys (such as dolls or trucks) and roles (not just Daddy or Mommy, but also nurse, teacher, police officer, soldier) are "best suited" for one sex or the other.

At least in the United States, sexual stereotypes are obvious and rigid between ages 3 and 6. Dynamic-systems theory suggests that concepts of male and female behavior are affected by many developmental aspects of biology and culture, changing as humans grow older (Martin & Ruble, 2010).

Same Situation, Far Apart: Culture Clash? He wears the orange robes of a Buddhist monk and she wears the hijab of a Muslim girl. Although he is at a week-long spiritual retreat led by the Dalai Lama and she is in an alley in Pakistan, both carry universal toys—a pop gun and a bride doll, identical to those found almost everywhere.

Sex and Gender

Many scientists distinguish **sex differences,** which are biological differences between males and females, from **gender differences,** which are culturally-prescribed roles and behaviors. In theory, this distinction seems straightforward, but, as with every nature–nurture distinction, the interaction between sex and gender makes it hard to separate the two. Scientists need to "treat culture and biology not as separate influences but as interacting components of nature and nurture" (Eagly & Wood, 2013, p. 349).

Young children are often confused about male-female differences. One little girl said she would grow a penis when she got older, and one little boy offered to buy his mother one. Ignorance about biology was demonstrated by a 3-year-old who went with his father to see a neighbor's newborn kittens. Returning home, the child told his mother that there were three girl kittens and two boy kittens. "How do you know?" she asked. "Daddy picked them up and read what was written on their tummies," he replied.

In recent years, sex and gender issues have become increasingly complex—to the outrage of some and the joy of others. Adults may be lesbian, gay, bi, trans, "mostly straight," or totally heterosexual (Thompson & Morgan, 2008, p. 15).

Despite the increasing acceptance of sexual diversity, many preschoolers become remarkably rigid in their ideas of male and female. Already by age 3, boys reject pink toys and girls prefer them (LoBue & DeLoache, 2011). If young boys need new shoes, but the only ones that fit them are pink, most would rather go barefoot.

As already mentioned, girls tend to play with other girls and boys with other boys. Despite their parents' and teachers' wishes, children say, "No girls [or boys] allowed." Most older children consider ethnic discrimination immoral, but they accept some sex discrimination (Møller & Tenenbaum, 2011). Why?

A dynamic-systems approach reminds us that attitudes, roles, and even the biology of gender differences change from one developmental period to the next. Theories about how and why this occurs change as well (Martin & Ruble, 2010; Leaper, 2013). We reviewed the five broad theories described in Chapter 2 to understand the range of explanations for the apparent sexism of many 5-year-olds.

Psychoanalytic Theory

Freud (1938) called the period from about ages 3 to 6 the **phallic stage,** named after the *phallus,* the Greek word for penis. At about 3 or 4 years of age, said Freud, boys become aware of their male sexual organ. They masturbate, fear castration, and develop sexual feelings toward their mother.

These feelings make every young boy jealous of his father—so jealous, according to Freud, that he wants to replace his dad. Freud called this the **Oedipus complex,** after Oedipus, son of a king in Greek mythology. Abandoned as an infant and raised in a distant kingdom, Oedipus returned to his birthplace and, without realizing it, killed his father and married his mother. When he discovered the horror, he blinded himself.

Freud believed that this ancient story dramatizes the overwhelming emotions that all boys feel about their parents—both love and hate. Every male feels guilty about his unconscious incestuous and murderous impulses. In self-defense, he develops a powerful conscience called the **superego,** which is quick to judge and punish.

That marks the beginning of morality, according to psychoanalytic theory. This theory contends that a boy's fascination with superheroes, guns, kung fu, and the like arises from his unconscious impulse to kill his father. Further, an adult man's homosexuality, homophobia, or obsession with guns, sins, and guilt arises from problems at the phallic stage.

sex differences Biological differences between males and females, in organs, hormones, and body type.

gender differences Differences in the roles and behaviors of males and females that are prescribed by the culture.

phallic stage Freud's third stage of development, when the penis becomes the focus of concern and pleasure.

Oedipus complex The unconscious desire of young boys to replace their father and win their mother's romantic love.

superego In psychoanalytic theory, the judgmental part of the personality that internalizes the moral standards of the parents.

Electra complex The unconscious desire of girls to replace their mother and win their father's romantic love.

identification An attempt to defend one's self-concept by taking on the behaviors and attitudes of someone else.

Freud offered several descriptions of the moral development of girls. One centers on the **Electra complex** (also named after a figure in classical mythology). The Electra complex is similar to the Oedipus complex in that the little girl wants to eliminate the same-sex parent (her mother) and become intimate with the opposite-sex parent (her father). That may also lead girls to develop a superego.

According to psychoanalytic theory, at the phallic stage children cope with guilt and fear through **identification;** that is, they try to become like the same-sex parent. Consequently, young boys copy their fathers' mannerisms, opinions, and actions, and girls copy their mothers'. Both sexes exaggerate the male or female role, which is why 5-year-olds are so sexist.

Since the superego arises from the phallic stage, and since Freud believed that sexual identity and expression are crucial for mental health, his theory suggests that parents encourage children to accept and follow gender roles. Many social scientists disagree. They contend that the psychoanalytic explanation of sexual and moral development "flies in the face of sociological and historical evidence" (David et al., 2004, p. 139).

Accordingly, I learned in graduate school that Freud was unscientific. However, as explained in Chapter 2, developmental scientists seek to connect research, theory, and experience. My own experience has made me rethink my rejection of Freud, as episodes with my four daughters illustrate.

My rethinking began with a conversation with my eldest daughter, Bethany, when she was about 4 years old:

> **Bethany:** When I grow up, I'm going to marry Daddy.
> **Me:** But Daddy's married to me.
> **Bethany:** That's all right. When I grow up, you'll probably be dead.
> **Me:** [*Determined to stick up for myself*] Daddy's older than me, so when I'm dead, he'll probably be dead, too.
> **Bethany:** That's OK. I'll marry him when he gets born again.

I was dumbfounded, without a good reply. I had no idea where she had gotten the concept of reincarnation. Bethany saw my face fall, and she took pity on me:

> **Bethany:** Don't worry, Mommy. After you get born again, you can be our baby.

The second episode was a conversation I had with my daughter Rachel when she was about 5:

> **Rachel:** When I get married, I'm going to marry Daddy.
> **Me:** Daddy's already married to me.
> **Rachel:** [*With the joy of having discovered a wonderful solution*] Then we can have a double wedding!

The third episode was considerably more graphic. It took the form of a "Valentine" left on my husband's pillow on February 14th by my daughter Elissa (see Figure 10.3).

Finally, when Sarah turned 5, she also said she would marry her father. I told her she couldn't, because he was married to me. Her response revealed one more hazard of watching TV: "Oh, yes, a man can have two wives. I saw it on television."

As you remember from Chapter 1, a single example (or four daughters from one family) does not prove that Freud was correct. I still think Freud was wrong on many counts. But his description of the phallic stage seems less bizarre than I once thought.

Other Theories of Gender Development

Although most psychologists have rejected Freud's theory regarding sex and gender, many other theories explain the young child's sex and gender awareness.

FIGURE 10.3

Pillow Talk Elissa placed this artwork on my husband's pillow. My pillow, beside it, had a less colorful, less elaborate note—an afterthought. It read, "Dear Mom, I love you too."

COURTESY KATHLEEN STASSEN BERGER

Behaviorists believe that virtually all roles, values, and morals are learned. To behaviorists, gender distinctions are the product of ongoing reinforcement and punishment, as well as social learning. Parents, peers, and teachers all reward behavior that is "gender appropriate" more than behavior that is "gender inappropriate" (Berenbaum et al., 2008).

For example, "adults compliment a girl when she wears a dress but not when she wears pants" (Ruble et al., 2006, p. 897), and a boy who asks for both a train and a doll for his birthday is likely to get the train. Boys are rewarded for boyish requests, not for girlish ones. Indeed, the parental push toward traditional gender behavior in play and chores is among the most robust findings of decades of research on this topic (Eagly & Wood, 2013).

Social learning is considered an extension of behaviorism. According to that theory, people model themselves after people they perceive to be nurturing, powerful, and yet similar to themselves. For young children, those people are usually their parents. As it happens, adults are the most sex-typed of their entire lives when they are raising young children. If an employed woman is ever to leave the labor market to become a housewife, it is when her children are young.

Furthermore, although national policies (e.g., subsidizing preschool) impact gender roles and many fathers are involved caregivers, women in every nation do much more child care, house cleaning, and meal preparation than do men (Hook, 2010). Children follow those examples, unaware that the examples they see are caused partly by their very existence: Before children are born, many couples share domestic work.

Cognitive theory offers an alternative explanation for the strong gender identity that becomes apparent at about age 5. Remember that cognitive theorists focus on how children understand various ideas. A **gender schema** is the child's understanding of male-female differences (Kohlberg et al., 1983; Martin et al., 2011; Renk et al., 2006).

Young children have many gender-related experiences but not much cognitive depth. They see the world in simple, egocentric terms, as explained in Chapter 9. For this reason, their gender schema categorize male and female as opposites. Nuances, complexities, exceptions, and gradations about gender (as well as just about everything else) are beyond them.

Remember that for preoperational children, appearance is crucial. When they see men and women style their hair, use makeup, and wear clothes in distinct, gender-typed ways, static preoperational thinking makes them conclude that what they see is permanent, irreversible.

Sociocultural theory stresses the importance of cultural values and customs. Some cultural aspects are transmitted through the parents, as explained with behaviorism, but much more arises from the larger community. This varies from place to place and time to time, as would be expected for any cultural value.

Consider a meta-analysis of research from many nations. Traditional mate preferences—including men's preference for younger, more attractive women, and women's for older, more established men—change somewhat when nations treat men and women more equally (Zenter & Mitura, 2012).

Thus national culture affects even personal adult choices such as marriage partners. Children are influenced by norms—that more men than women are soldiers, or engineers, or football players. As children try to make sense of their culture, they encounter numerous customs, taboos, and terminologies that echo gender norms.

This explains cultural differences in the strength of sexism, in that male/female divisions are much more dominant in some places than others. Specifics vary (a man holding the hand of another man is either taboo or expected, depending

gender schema A cognitive concept or general belief based on one's experiences—in this case, a child's understanding of sex differences.

on local customs), but everywhere young children try to conform to what they observe as the norms of their culture.

Humanism stresses the hierarchy of needs, beginning with survival, then safety, then love and belonging. The final two needs—respect and self-actualization—are not considered priorities for people until the earlier ones have been satisfied.

Ideally, babies have all their basic needs met, and toddlers learn to feel safe, which makes love and belonging crucial during early childhood. Children increasingly strive for admiration from their peers. Therefore, the girls seek to be one of the girls and the boys to be one of the boys.

In a study of slightly older children, participants wanted to be part of same-sex groups, not because they disliked the other sex, but because that satisfied their need to belong (Zosuls et al., 2010). As we have already seen, children increasingly prefer to play with boys or girls, as the case may be, again because humans are social beings who want to be validated for who they are.

Evolutionary theory holds that sexual attraction is crucial for humankind's most basic urge, to reproduce. For this reason, males and females try to look attractive to the other sex, walking, talking, and laughing in gendered ways. If girls see their mothers wearing make-up and high heels, they want to do likewise.

According to evolutionary theory, the species' need to reproduce is part of everyone's genetic heritage, so young boys and girls practice becoming attractive to the other sex. This behavior ensures that they will be ready after puberty to find each other and that a new generation will be born, as evolution requires.

Thus, according to this explanation, over millennia of human history, particular genes, chromosomes, and hormones have evolved to allow the species to flourish. It is natural for boys to be more active (rough-and-tumble play) and girls more domestic (sociodramatic play) because that is what humans need to do. To deny that is to deny nature.

What Is Best?

Each of the major developmental theories strives to explain the ideas that young children express and the roles they follow. No consensus has been reached. Regarding sex or gender, those who contend that nature is more important than nurture, or vice versa, tend to design, cite, and believe studies that endorse their perspective. Only recently has a true interactionist perspective been endorsed (Eagly & Wood, 2013).

These theories raise important questions: What gender or sex patterns *should* parents and other caregivers teach? Should every child learn to combine the best of both sexes (called *androgyny*), thereby causing gender stereotypes to eventually disappear as children become more mature, as happens with their belief in Santa Claus and the Tooth Fairy? Or should male–female distinctions be encouraged as essential for human reproduction and family life?

Answers vary among developmentalists as well as among parents and cultures. This section refers to "challenges" for caregivers. Determining how to raise children who are happy with themselves but not prejudiced against those of the other sex is one challenge that all caregivers face.

SUMMING UP

Caregiving styles vary, ranging from very strict, cold, and demanding to very lax, warm, and permissive. Baumrind's classic research categorized parenting as authoritarian, authoritative, and permissive; these categories still seem relevant, even though the original research was limited in many ways. In general, a middle ground—neither strict nor lax—seems best, and parental warmth seems more crucial than other aspects of style.

One difficult question for parents is how to respond to the young child's ideas and stereotypes about males and females, which tend to be quite rigid during early childhood. Norms are changing, which means that old theories and traditional responses may not be helpful. Freud's ideas are no longer endorsed by most developmentalists. However, theorists differ in their explanations and interpretations of gender differences. Caregivers' responses depend not only on their culture, but also on whether they believe the primary impetus for boy/girl behavior is nature or nurture. ∎

>> Moral Development

Emotional regulation, moral development, and the emergence of empathy are intertwined, as "morality is multifaceted and includes affective, cognitive, and behavioral components" (Smetana, 2013). Thus moral development is evident in many of the topics already discussed.

Rough-and-tumble play, for instance, teaches children not to hurt their playmates. Concern for helping other people is also apparent in sociodramatic play, especially the rescue fantasies and caregiving routines that are commonly acted out. Children learn to take turns and to share—and they believe it unfair when another child does not do so (Utendale & Hastings, 2011).

Children develop increasingly complex moral values, judgments, and behaviors as they mature. Social bonds and theory of mind provide the foundation for more advanced moral action. [**Lifespan Link:** Development of social bonds is discussed in Chapter 7 and theory of mind in Chapter 9.] Piaget thought that moral development began when children learned games with rules, which he connected with concrete operational thought at about age 7 (Piaget, 1932/1997).

We now know that Piaget was mistaken: Both games with rules and moral development are evident much earlier. Some precursors of morality appear in infancy (Narvaez & Lapsley, 2009). With maturation and adult guidance, children develop guilt (as Erikson explained) and self-control. That helps them behave in ethical ways (Kochanska et al., 2009; Konner, 2010).

Nature and Nurture

Many parents, teachers, and other adults consider children's "good" behavior more important than any other advancement already described in previous chapters (physical strength, motor skills, intelligence, language, etc.). Perhaps for this reason, debate rages over how children internalize standards, develop virtues, and avoid vices. Scholars in many social sciences hold conflicting perspectives—nature versus nurture again.

The *nature* perspective suggests that morality is genetic, an outgrowth of natural bonding, attachment, and cognitive maturation. That would explain why young children help and defend their parents, no matter what the parents do, and punish other children who violate moral rules. Even infants have a sense of what is fair and not, expecting adults to reward effort (Sloane et al., 2012).

Morality, if defined as behavior that helps others without immediate reward to oneself, may be in our DNA. According to evolutionary theory, humans protect, cooperate, and even sacrifice for one another because our bodies are defenseless and vulnerable to weather, strangers, and wild animals. To survive, people need to rely on other people, and from that need springs a moral sense (Dunning, 2011). Hormones, specifically oxytocin, that are produced by the body, may naturally push people toward trusting and loving each other (Zak, 2012).

The *nurture* perspective contends that culture is crucial to the development of morality. That would explain why young children emulate people who follow the rules of their community, even if the actual behavior is not innately good or bad. Although children understand the intellectual difference between morality and custom, some children believe that people who eat raw fish, or hamburgers, or bacon, or dogs are immoral (Turiel, 2002).

Developmentalists distinguish between ethical behavior (seeking not to harm others) and conventional behavior (seeking to follow norms), but that distinction is not always apparent. Consider gun use, abortion, the death penalty, disobeying an elder, stealing food—all considered immoral in some cultures, conventional in others, and a moral right (not wrong) in some communities under particular circumstances.

Both nature and nurture are always influential in standards of conduct, and the interaction between the two is crucial—and well worth discussion and debate. Beyond that truism, specifics cannot be settled here. However, we can explore two moral issues that arise from age 2 to age 6: children's aggression and adults' disciplinary practices. Nature and nurture are evident in both.

Empathy and Antipathy

Moral emotions are evident as children play with one another. With increasing social experiences and decreasing egocentrism, children develop **empathy,** an understanding of other people's feelings and concerns, and **antipathy,** a feeling of dislike or even hatred.

Prosocial Behavior

Scientists studying young humans and other primates report spontaneous efforts to help others who are hurt, crying, or in need of help: That is evidence of empathy and compassion, which then lead to **prosocial behavior**—extending helpfulness and kindness without any obvious benefit to oneself (Warneken & Tomasello, 2009).

Expressing concern, offering to share, and including a shy child in a game or conversation are examples of prosocial behavior among young children. Jack, age 3, showed empathy when he "refused to bring snacks with peanuts to school because another boy had to sit alone during snack because he was allergic to nuts. Jack wanted to sit with him" (Lovecky, 2009, p. 161).

Prosocial behavior seems to result more from emotion than from intellect, more from empathy than from theory of mind (Eggum et al., 2011). The origins of prosocial behavior may arise from parents helping their children become aware of emotions, not from parents informing children what emotions others might have (Brownell et al., 2013).

Prosocial reactions are not automatic. Some children limit empathy by "avoiding contact with the person in need [which illustrates] . . . the importance of emotion development and regulation in the development of prosocial behavior" and the critical influence of cultural norms (Trommsdorff & Cole, 2011, p. 136). Feeling distress may be a part of nature; responding to distress may be nurture.

Antisocial Actions

Antipathy can lead to **antisocial behavior**—deliberately hurting another person, including people who have done nothing wrong. Antisocial actions include verbal insults, social exclusion, and physical assaults (Calkins & Keane, 2009). An antisocial 4-year-old might look another child in the eye, scowl, and then kick him hard without provocation.

empathy The ability to understand the emotions and concerns of another person, especially when they differ from one's own.

antipathy Feelings of dislike or even hatred for another person.

prosocial behavior Actions that are helpful and kind but are of no obvious benefit to oneself.

antisocial behavior Actions that are deliberately hurtful or destructive to another person.

Pinch, Poke, or Pat Antisocial and prosocial responses are actually a sign of maturation: Babies do not recognize the impact of their actions. These children have much more to learn, but they already are quite social.

In some ways, antisocial behavior comes naturally (Seguin & Tremblay, 2013). Even letting another child use a crayon that a child has already used is hard at age 2. Most 5-year-olds have learned to do it. Much depends on the child's family and preschool education: With guidance, children balance giving and taking. The result is more prosocial and fewer antisocial actions as children mature (Ramani et al., 2010).

Aggression

Not surprisingly, given the moral sensibilities of young children, 5-year-olds already judge whether another child's aggression is justified or antisocial (Etchu, 2007). Children are particularly focused on effects, not motives: A child who accidentally spilled water on another's painting may be the target of that child's justified anger. As with adults, self-defense is more readily forgiven than is a deliberate, unprovoked attack.

Do not assume, however, that bullies realize when they are wrong: At every age, aggressors feel they have a reason to do what they did. The young child's emphasis on effects more than intentions may make more sense than the adult's readiness to consider reasons.

Researchers recognize four general types of aggression, all of which are evident in early childhood (see Table 10.2). **Instrumental aggression** is common

instrumental aggression Behavior that hurts someone else because the aggressor wants to get or keep a possession or a privilege.

TABLE 10.2	The Four Forms of Aggression	
Type of Aggression	**Definition**	**Comments**
Instrumental aggression	Hurtful behavior that is aimed at gaining something (such as a toy, a place in line, or a turn on the swing) that someone else has	Often increases from age 2 to 6; involves objects more than people; quite normal; more egocentric than antisocial.
Reactive aggression	An impulsive retaliation for a hurt (intentional or accidental) that can be verbal or physical	Indicates a lack of emotional regulation, characteristic of 2-year-olds. A 5-year-old can usually stop and think before reacting.
Relational aggression	Nonphysical acts, such as insults or social rejection, aimed at harming the social connections between the victim and others	Involves a personal attack and thus is directly antisocial; can be very hurtful; more common as children become socially aware.
Bullying aggression	Unprovoked, repeated physical or verbal attack, especially on victims who are unlikely to defend themselves	In both bullies and victims, a sign of poor emotional regulation; adults should intervene before the school years. (Bullying is discussed in Chapter 8.)

reactive aggression An impulsive retaliation for another person's intentional or accidental action, verbal or physical.

relational aggression Nonphysical acts, such as insults or social rejection, aimed at harming the social connection between the victim and other people.

bullying aggression Unprovoked, repeated physical or verbal attacks, especially on victims who are unlikely to defend themselves.

among 2-year-olds, who often want something they do not have and simply try to take it. An aggressive reaction from the other child—crying, hitting, and resisting the grab of the instrumentally aggressive child—is also more typical at age 2 than earlier or later.

Reactive aggression is therefore common among young children; almost every child reacts when hurt, whether or not the hurt was deliberate. Children are less likely to respond with physical aggression as they develop emotional control and theory of mind (Olson et al., 2011).

Relational aggression (usually verbal) destroys another child's self-esteem and disrupts the victim's social networks, becoming more hurtful as children mature. A young child might tell another, "You can't be my friend" or "You are fat," hurting another's feelings. These examples are relational aggression.

The fourth and most ominous type is **bullying aggression**, done to dominate someone else. It is not rare among young children but should be stopped before school age, when it becomes particularly destructive. Not only does it destroy the self-esteem of victims, it impairs the later development of the bullies, who learn patterns that will harm them in adulthood. [**Lifespan Link:** An in-depth discussion of bullying appears in Chapter 13.]

All forms of aggression usually become less common from ages 2 to 6, as the brain matures and empathy increases. Parents, peers, and preschool teachers are pivotal mentors in this process. It is a mistake to expect children to regulate their emotions on their own; without guidance they may develop destructive patterns. It is also a mistake to punish the aggressor too harshly because that may remove them from their zone of proximal development, where they can learn to regulate their anger.

In other words, although there is evidence that preschool children spontaneously judge others who harm people, with the emphasis on the actual hurt more than the intention, there also is evidence that prosocial and antisocial behavior is learned (Smetana, 2013).

Discipline

Adults' values, temperament, and experiences affect their responses when their children misbehave. Of course, those values and disciplinary strategies are influenced by culture.

Ideally, adults guide children toward good behavior and internalized standards of morality so that children always behave well. But this is not reality: Misbehavior cannot always be prevented.

Lest anyone imagine that, with benevolent parents, children will always be good, consider a study of mothers and 3-year-olds during late afternoon (a stressful time). Conflicts (including verbal disagreements) arose about every two minutes (Laible et al., 2008). Here is one example that began with an activity recommended for every parent; the mother was about to take her daughter for a walk:

> **Child:** I want my other shoes.
> **Mother:** You don't need your other shoes. You wear your Pooh sandals when we go for a walk.
> **Child:** Noooooo.
> **Mother:** [*Child's name*]! You don't need your other shoes.
> **Child:** [*Cries loudly*]
> **Mother:** No, you don't need your other shoes. You wear your Pooh sandals when we go for a walk.

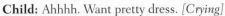

Child: Ahhhh. Want pretty dress. *[Crying]*

Mother: Your pretty dress!

Child: Yeah.

Mother: You can wear them some other day.

Child: Noooooo. *[Crying]*

[from Laible et al., 2008, pp. 442–443]

In this study, those 3-year-olds who had been securely attached at age 1 (an indication of responsive parenting) had as many conflicts as those who had been insecurely attached. Obviously, good parenting does not always produce good children, if by good children we mean those who are peaceful and obedient.

However, unlike the situation in the snippet above, the mothers of securely-attached children were more likely to compromise and explain (Laible et al., 2008). Is that the best response? Should this mother have offered reasons why the other shoes were not appropriate, or should she have let her daughter wear them? Alternatively, should she have slapped the child for crying, or said "I don't want to walk with you if you fuss"?

Physical Punishment

In the United States, young children are slapped, spanked, or beaten more often than are infants or older children, and more often than children in Canada or western Europe. Not only in the United States but also in many developing nations, adults remember being physically punished and think it works. In some ways, they are correct: Physical punishment (called **corporal punishment** because it hurts the body) succeeds at the moment—spanking stops misbehavior.

Longitudinal research finds, however, that children who are physically punished are more likely to become bullies, delinquents, and then abusive adults. They are also less likely to learn quickly in school or attend college (Straus & Paschall, 2009). In fact, although children who misbehave in externalizing ways (hitting, yelling, throwing things) are more likely to be spanked, longitudinal research finds that if they are not spanked they learn to control their acting out. On the other hand, the more children are spanked, the more likely they are to continue misbehaving (Gershoff et al., 2012).

In several nations of Europe, corporal punishment is illegal; in many nations on other continents, it is the norm. In the United States, it is legal and parents use it often. Even in U.S. schools, paddling is legal (but rarely used) in 19 of the 50 states. Most of those states are in the Southeast, and most of the children who are paddled are African American boys, which raises questions about the effectiveness and justice of the punishment (Morones, 2013).

Although some adults believe that physical punishment will "teach a lesson" of obedience, the lesson that children learn may be that "might makes right." When they become bigger and stronger, they use corporal punishment on others. Parents who were hit as children usually become hitters themselves.

Many studies of children from all family constellations find that physical punishment of young children correlates with delayed theory of mind and increased aggression (Olson et al., 2011). To prove cause without a doubt would require parents of monozygotic twins to raise them identically, except that one twin would be spanked often and the other never. Of course, that is unethical as well as impossible.

Especially for Parents of 3-Year-Olds How could a parent compromise with a child who wants to wear "other shoes"? (see response, page 300)

corporal punishment Punishment that physically hurts the body, such as slapping, spanking, etc.

Especially for Parents Suppose you agree that spanking is destructive, but you sometimes get so angry at your child's behavior that you hit him or her. Is your reaction appropriate? (see response, page 300)

Smack Will the doll learn never to disobey her mother again?

>> Response for Parents of 3-Year-Olds
(from page 299): Remember, authoritative
parents listen but do not usually give in.
A parent could ask why the child did not
want the Pooh sandals (ugly? too tight? old?)
and explain why the "other shoes" were
not appropriate (raining? save for special
occasions? hard to walk in?). A promise
for the future (e.g., "Let's save your other
shoes and pretty dress for the birthday party
tomorrow") might stop the "Noooo."

>> Response for Parents (from page 299):
No. The worst time to spank a child is when
you are angry. You might seriously hurt the
child, and the child will associate anger
with violence. You would do better to learn
to control your anger and develop other
strategies for discipline and for prevention of
misbehavior.

psychological control A disciplinary
technique that involves threatening to
withdraw love and support and that relies
on a child's feelings of guilt and gratitude
to the parents.

time-out A disciplinary technique in which a
child is separated from other people for a
specified time.

SW PRODUCTIONS/AGE FOTOSTOCK

Bad Boy or Bad Parent? For some children
and in some cultures, sitting alone is an
effective form of punishment. Sometimes,
however, it produces an angry child without
changing the child's behavior.

Nonetheless, many developmentalists wonder why parents would take the chance. The best argument in favor of spanking is that alternative punishments are often worse (Larzelere et al., 2010). Let us consider some of those alternatives.

Psychological Control

Another common method of discipline is called **psychological control**, in which children's shame, guilt, and gratitude are used to control their behavior (Barber, 2002). Psychological control may reduce academic achievement and emotional intelligence, just as spanking is thought to do (Alegre, 2011).

Consider the results of a study of an entire cohort (the best way to obtain an unbiased sample) of children born in Finland (Aunola & Nurmi, 2004). Their parents were asked 20 questions about their approach to child rearing. The following four items, which the parents rated from 1 ("Not at all like me") to 5 ("Very much like me"), measured psychological control:

1. "My child should be aware of how much I have done for him/her."
2. "I let my child see how disappointed and shamed I am if he/she misbehaves."
3. "My child should be aware of how much I sacrifice for him/her."
4. "I expect my child to be grateful and appreciate all the advantages he/she has."

The higher the parents scored on these four measures of psychological control, the lower the children's math scores were—and this connection grew stronger over time. Surprisingly, math achievement suffered most if parents were high not only in psychological control but also in affection (e.g., they frequently hugged their children) (Aunola & Nurmi, 2004). One explanation is that affection increased the child's fear of disappointing the parent, which slowed down their willingness to learn new ideas.

Other research also finds that psychological control can depress children's achievement, creativity, and social acceptance (Soenens & Vansteenkiste, 2010). Compared with corporal punishment, children punished with psychological control seem less likely to be physical bullies but more likely to be relationally aggressive (Kuppens et al., 2009), depressed, and anxious (Gershoff et al., 2010).

The disciplinary technique most often used with young children in North America is the **time-out**, in which an adult requires a misbehaving child to sit quietly, without toys or playmates, for a short time (Barkin et al., 2007). Time-out is favored by many experts in the United States. For example, in the large, longitudinal evaluation of the Head Start program highlighted in Chapter 5, an increase in time-outs and a decrease in spankings were considered signs of improved parental discipline (U.S. Department of Health and Human Services, 2010).

Another alternative to physical punishment and psychological control is *induction,* in which the parents talk extensively with the offender, helping the child understand why his or her behavior was wrong. Ideally, parents listen as children articulate their emotions and then encourage the children to imagine what they might have done instead of what they did do.

Such conversation helps children internalize standards, but induction takes time and patience. Since 3-year-olds confuse causes with consequences, they cannot answer an angry "Why did you do that?" or appreciate a lengthy explanation of why the behavior was wrong. Simple induction ("You made him sad") may be more appropriate, but even that is hard before theory of mind is possible.

Is Spanking Okay?

Worldwide, cultural differences in child discipline are apparent. For example, only half as many Canadian parents as U.S. parents slap, pinch, or smack their children (Oldershaw, 2002). Although many U.S. school districts forbid corporal punishment in schools, the U.S. Supreme Court decided in 2004 that teachers and parents could use "reasonable force" to punish children (Bugental & Grusec, 2006).

By contrast, physical punishment by anyone—parent, teacher, sibling, stranger—is illegal in many other developed nations (including Austria, Croatia, Cyprus, Denmark, Finland, Germany, Israel, Italy, Norway, New Zealand, and Sweden). It is considered a violation of human rights (Bitensky, 2006).

Opinions about spanking are influenced by past experiences and cultural norms, making it hard for opposing perspectives to be understood by people on the other side. For that reason, consider why a person might or might not put hot sauce on a child's tongue. Then see if those reasons apply to other forms of corporal punishment.

In a book titled *Creative Correction* (Whelchel, 2005), an evangelical Christian suggests hot sauce (which burns) as punishment for forbidden speech, such as curses or sexual slang. (Many other methods, including spanking, are also suggested therein.)

Readers seem to be strongly for or against this suggestion. Of the 198 comments on the book that were posted on Amazon.com through November 2012, half were highly favorable (97 readers rated it 5), 34 percent were highly unfavorable (71 rated it 1), and only 15 percent were in between (at 2, 3, or 4). One woman wrote:

> Putting hot sauce on your child's tongue? I bet the author wouldn't ever dare to do that to herself & look at all the hate spewing out of her mouth. As a born-again believer & mother, I'd never follow anything in this book. It's so unchristlike that it's sickening. There's nothing "creative" about her correction ideas—it's just plain mean & a newer version of old abuse tactics that our parents used to do.

An opposing perspective came from another woman:

> I haven't had the need for the Tabasco trick yet, but I'm not above using it. It would make a strong impression and wouldn't require a repeat dose, I'm quite sure. Child abuse? Hardly. Giving a child free reign over the TV, internet and the house IS child abuse. Ask any elementary school teacher who her problem child is and it'll be the kid with no discipline at home. A well-behaved child grows into a well-behaved adult. This world certainly needs more of those.

Back to spanking: If both of the above comments seem extreme, consider whether your attitudes about spanking are also more extreme than they might be. The research finds that many methods of discipline, including spanking, affect the child's later level of anxiety and aggression (Gershoff et al., 2010). Developmentalists themselves suggest many opposing strategies.

The parents' underlying attitude may be crucial. One study of African American mothers found that if they disapproved of spanking but did it nonetheless, their children were likely to be depressed. However, their children were not harmed if spanking mothers were convinced that spanking was the correct thing to do (McLoyd et al., 2007).

Similarly, Chinese American parents who used physical punishment and shame raised children who were relatively happy and well adjusted *if* the parents used those methods because they agreed with the Chinese ideology that led to them (Fung & Lau, 2009). Remember, parental affection and warmth are more influential than any disciplinary strategy.

What might be wrong with spanking? One problem is not only the attitudes but also the emotions of the adult. Angry spankers might become abusive. Another problem is the child's thoughts, as he or she may not understand the reasoning behind the spanking. Parents assume the transgression is obvious, but many children think the parents' emotions, not the child's actions, triggered the spanking (Harkness et al., 2011).

She understands? Children who are spanked remember the pain and anger, but not the reason for the punishment. It is better for parents to explain what the misbehavior was. However, sometimes explanations are not understood.

Further complications can occur. Children vary in temperament; some may suffer from spanking and some may not care. Parents vary in personality; some spank while out of control. Cultures differ as well. Harmful effects are reduced, but do not necessarily disappear, if children believe the punishment is fair because similar punishments happen to every child they know (Vittrup & Holden, 2010).

A U.S. study of parents who attend religiously conservative Protestant churches found that, as expected, they spanked their children more often than other parents did. However, unexpectedly, children spanked during early (but not middle) childhood did not seem to develop the lower self-esteem and increased aggression that has been found with other spanked children (Ellison et al., 2011). Indeed, the opposite was more likely.

The authors of the study suggest that, since spanking was the norm and since most religious leaders also tell parents to explain transgressions (induction), to assure children that they are loved, and to never hit in anger, conservative Protestant children do not perceive being spanked as stigmatizing or demeaning. To the contrary, children may view mild-to-moderate corporal punishment as legitimate, appropriate, and even a sign of parental involvement, commitment, and concern (Ellison et al., 2011, p. 957).

As I write these words, I realize that the opposing perspective is mine. As you saw in the opening of this chapter, I believe that children should never be hit. I am one of many developmentalists convinced that alternatives to spanking are better for the child as well as a safeguard against abuse. But a dynamic-systems view considers discipline as one aspect of a complex web. I know I am influenced by my background and context; I also know that I am not always right.

SUMMING UP

Children's moral development often advances during early childhood, usually gaining empathy as their theory of mind advances and their emotions become better regulated. New empathy usually helps a child act prosocially, making the child able to share, take turns, and so on. Children can also increasingly develop antipathy, which leads some to be aggressive without a self-protective reason (i.e., bullies), unlike those who engage in instrumental or reactive aggression. Parents, guided by their culture, teach morality in many ways, including the strategies they choose for discipline.

Every means of punishment may have long-term effects, with physical punishment especially criticized for encouraging aggression. ■

SUMMARY

Emotional Development

1. Learning to regulate and control emotions is crucial during early childhood. Emotional regulation is made possible by maturation of the brain, particularly of the prefrontal cortex, as well as by experiences with parents and peers.

2. In Erikson's psychosocial theory, the crisis of initiative versus guilt occurs during early childhood. Children normally feel pride, sometimes mixed with feelings of guilt. Shame is also evident, particularly in some cultures.

3. Both externalizing and internalizing problems signify impaired self-control. Some emotional problems that indicate psychopathology are first evident during early childhood, with boys more often manifesting externalizing behaviors and girls exhibiting internalizing behaviors.

Play

4. All young children enjoy playing—preferably with other children of the same sex, who teach them lessons in social interaction that their parents do not. Some experts believe that play is essential for healthy psychosocial development.

5. Active play takes many forms, with rough-and-tumble play fostering social skills and sociodramatic play developing emotional regulation.

Challenges for Caregivers

6. Three classic styles of parenting have been identified: authoritarian, permissive, and authoritative. Generally, children are more successful and happier when their parents are authoritative, expressing warmth and setting guidelines.

7. A fourth style of parenting, neglectful/uninvolved, is always harmful. The particulars of parenting reflect the culture as well as the temperament of the child.

8. Children are prime consumers of many kinds of media. The problems that arise from media exposure include increased aggression and less creative play. In addition, time spent watching television is time taken away from more productive activities.

9. Even 2-year-olds correctly use sex-specific labels. Young children become aware of gender differences in clothes, toys, playmates, and future careers, and typically are more gender stereotyped than their parents.

10. Freud emphasized that children are attracted to the opposite-sex parent and eventually seek to identify, or align themselves, with the same-sex parent. Behaviorists hold that gender-related behaviors are learned through reinforcement and punishment (especially for males) and social modeling. Parents are crucial teachers of gender roles.

11. Cognitive theorists note that simplistic preoperational thinking leads to gender schemas and therefore stereotypes. Humanists stress the powerful need of all humans to belong to their group. Evolutionary theory contends that sex and gender differences are crucial for the survival and reproduction of the species.

12. Each of the major developmental theories strives to explain the gender roles and sexist stereotypes that young children express, but no consensus has been reached as to which theory is best. Recent scholarship endorses an interactionist perspective.

Moral Development

13. Both nature and nurture play a role in moral development, which is intertwined with emotional regulation and the emergence of empathy. Moral development includes affective, cognitive, and behavioral components.

14. Prosocial emotions lead to caring for others; antisocial emotions lead to behaviors that are harmful to others, including instrumental, reactive, relational, and bullying aggression.

15. The type of punishment parents use can have long-term consequences, with both corporal punishment and psychological control having potentially adverse effects. Alternative forms of discipline, such as the time-out and induction, may be more effective.

KEY TERMS

antipathy (p. 296)
antisocial behavior (p. 296)
authoritarian parenting (p. 287)
authoritative parenting (p. 288)
bullying aggression (p. 298)
corporal punishment (p. 299)
effortful control (p. 275)
Electra complex (p. 292)
emotional regulation (p. 275)

empathy (p. 296)
externalizing problems (p. 279)
extrinsic motivation (p. 277)
gender differences (p. 291)
gender schema (p. 293)
identification (p. 292)
imaginary friends (p. 277)
initiative versus guilt (p. 276)
instrumental aggression (p. 297)

internalizing problems (p. 279)
intrinsic motivation (p. 277)
neglectful/uninvolved parenting (p. 288)
Oedipus complex (p. 291)
permissive parenting (p. 288)
phallic stage (p. 291)
prosocial behavior (p. 296)
psychological control (p. 300)

psychopathology (p. 279)
reactive aggression (p. 298)
relational aggression (p. 298)
rough-and-tumble play (p. 284)
self-concept (p. 276)
sex differences (p. 291)
sociodramatic play (p. 284)
superego (p. 291)
time-out (p. 300)

WHAT HAVE YOU LEARNED?

1. How might protective optimism lead to a child's acquisition of new skills and competencies?

2. What is an example of an intrinsic motivation and an extrinsic motivation for reading a book?

3. What is the connection between psychopathology and emotional regulation?

4. In what ways might playing with peers teach emotional regulation, empathy, and cultural understanding?

5. How does culture affect the development of social play?

6. Why might children's muscle strength and control develop better when playing with peers than when playing alone?

7. What do children learn from rough-and-tumble play?

8. What do children learn from sociodramatic play?

9. Which parenting style seems to promote the happiest, most successful children?

10. Why do American childhood professionals advise limitations on electronic media for young children?

11. What does psychoanalytic theory say about the origins of sex differences and gender roles?

12. What do behaviorists say about the origins of sex differences and gender roles?

13. How does evolutionary theory explain why children follow gender norms?

14. What did Piaget believe about the moral development of children?

15. How might evolutionary theory explain moral development?

16. What is the nature perspective on how people develop morals? What is the nurture perspective?

17. How might children develop empathy and antipathy as they play with one another?

18. What is the connection between empathy and prosocial behavior?

19. What are the four kinds of aggression?

20. How does moral development relate to discipline?

21. Why have many nations made corporal punishment illegal?

22. How might a parent use time-out as an effective form of discipline?

23. What are the benefits of induction as a form of discipline? What are its challenges?

APPLICATIONS

1. Children's television programming is rife with stereotypes about ethnicity, gender, and morality. Watch an hour of children's TV, especially on a Saturday morning, and describe the content of both the programs and the commercials. Draw some conclusions about stereotyping in the material you watched, citing specific evidence (rather than merely reporting your impressions).

2. Gender indicators often go unnoticed. Go to a public place (park, restaurant, busy street) and spend at least 10 minutes recording examples of gender differentiation, such as articles of clothing, mannerisms, interaction patterns, and activities. Quantify what you see, such as baseball hats on eight males and two females. Or (better, but more difficult) describe four male–female conversations, indicating gender differences in length and frequency of talking, interruptions, vocabulary, and so on.

3. Ask three parents about punishment, including their preferred type, at what age, for what misdeeds, and by whom. Ask your three informants how they were punished as children and how that affected them. If your sources all agree, find a parent (or a classmate) who has a different view.

To accompany your textbook, you have access to a number of online resources, including quizzes for every chapter of the book, flashcards (in English and Spanish), critical thinking questions, and case studies. For access to any of these links, go to www.worthpublishers.com/launchpad/bergerls9e. In addition to these free resources, you'll also find links to podcasts, video clips, diagnostic quizzing with personalized study advice, and an ebook. Some of the videos and activities available online include:

■ *Children at Play.* Watch video clips of children at play, identify the types of play you see, and review how each type contributes to children's development.

■ *Bullying.* With video clips of bullying, this activity covers physical and relational aggression, gender differences in bullying, and the impact on victims. It presents causes and preventive measures.

Early Childhood

BIOSOCIAL

Body Changes Children continue to grow from ages 2 to 6, but at a slower rate. Normally, the BMI (body mass index) is lower at about ages 5 and 6 than at any other time of life. Children often eat too much unhealthy food and refuse to eat certain other foods altogether, insisting that food and other routines be "just right."

Brain Development The proliferation of neural pathways and myelination continues. Parts of the brain (e.g., the corpus callosum, prefrontal cortex, amygdala, hippocampus, and hypothalamus) connect, which allows lateralization of the brain's left and right hemispheres and better coordination of the left and right sides of the body; it also leads to a decline in impulsivity and perseveration.

Improving Motor Skills Maturation of the prefrontal cortex allows for impulse control; ongoing myelination of the corpus callosum and lateralization of the brain permit better physical coordination.

Injuries and Abuse Far more children worldwide die of avoidable accidents than of diseases. Child abuse and neglect require primary, secondary, and tertiary prevention.

COGNITIVE

Thinking During Early Childhood Piaget stressed the young child's egocentric, illogical perspective, which prevents the child from grasping concepts such as conservation. Vygotsky stressed the cultural context, noting that children learn from mentors—which include parents, teachers, peers—and from the social context. Children develop their own theories, including a theory of mind, as they realize that not everyone thinks as they do.

Language Learning Language develops rapidly. By age 6, the average child knows 10,000 words and demonstrates extensive grammatical knowledge. Young children can become balanced bilinguals during these years if their social context is encouraging.

Early-Childhood Education Young children are avid learners. Child-centered, teacher-directed, and intervention programs, such as Head Start, can all nurture learning.

PSYCHOSOCIAL

Emotional Development Self-esteem is usually high during early childhood. Self-concept emerges in Erikson's stage of initiative versus guilt, as does the ability to regulate emotions. Externalizing problems may be the result of too little emotional regulation; internalizing problems may result from too much control.

Play All young children play, and they play best with peers. Play helps children develop physically and teaches emotional regulation, empathy, and cultural understanding.

Challenges for Caregivers A caregiving style that is warm and encouraging, with good communication as well as high expectations (called authoritative), is most effective in promoting the child's self-esteem, autonomy, and self-control. The authoritarian and permissive styles are less beneficial, although cultural variations are apparent.

Moral Development Morality becomes more evident during early childhood. Empathy produces prosocial behavior; antipathy leads to antisocial actions. Aggression takes many forms; bullying aggression is ominous. Every method of parental discipline affects children's emotional development.

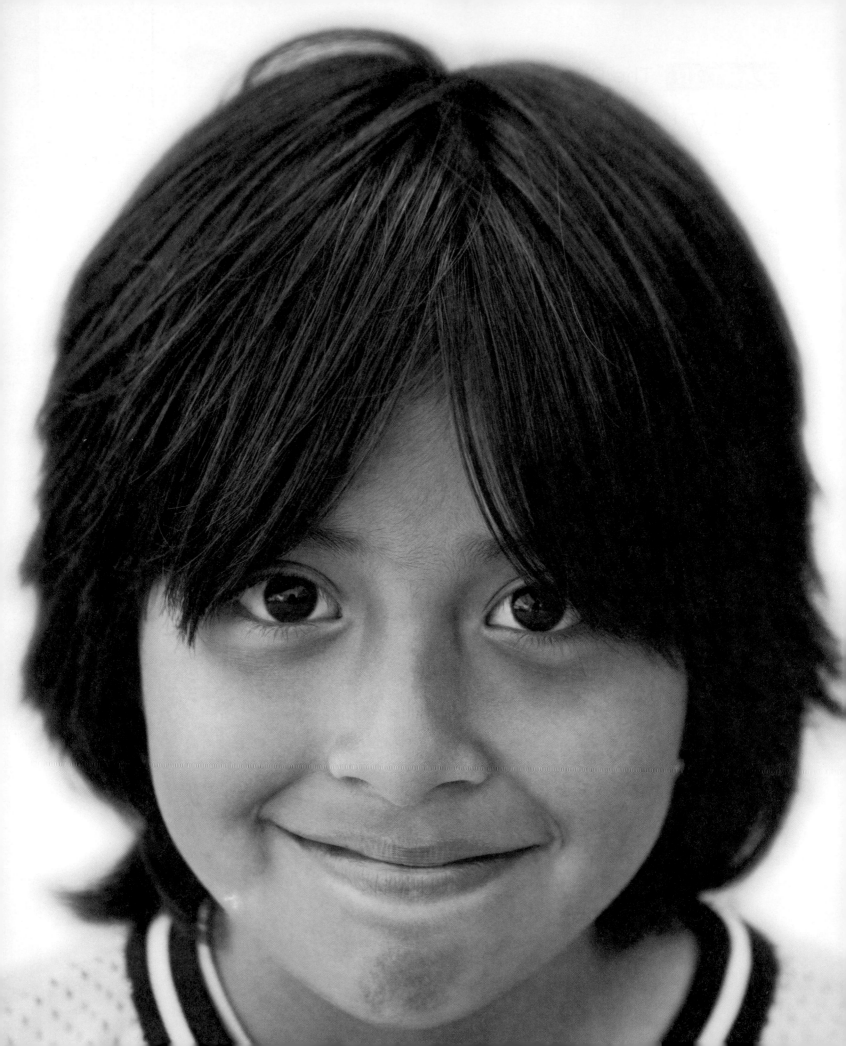

P A R T

IV

CHAPTERS 11•12•13

middle childhood

Every age has joys and sorrows, gains and losses. But if you were pushed to choose one best time, you might select ages 6 to 11, when many people experience good health and steady growth as they master new athletic skills, learn thousands of words, and become less dependent on families. Usually, they appreciate their parents, make new friends, and proudly learn about their nation and religion. Life is safe and happy, the dangers of adolescence (drugs, early sex, violence) are not yet on the horizon.

Yet some adults remember these years as the worst, not the best. Some children may hate school, live in destructive families, have no permanent home, or contend with obesity, asthma, learning disabilities, or bullies. The next three chapters celebrate the joys and acknowledge the difficulties of ages 6 to 11.

Middle Childhood: Biosocial Development

■ A Healthy Time
Slower Growth, Greater Strength
Physical Activity

■ Health Problems in Middle Childhood
Childhood Obesity
A VIEW FROM SCIENCE: What Contributes to Childhood Obesity?
Asthma

■ Brain Development
Coordinating Connections
Measuring the Mind

■ Children with Special Needs
Causes and Consequences
Attention-Deficit/Hyperactivity Disorder
A CASE TO STUDY: Lynda Is Getting Worse
Specific Learning Disorders
Autism Spectrum Disorder
Special Education
Gifted and Talented

WHAT WILL YOU KNOW?

1. What would happen if more parents let their children "go out and play"?
2. Should the epidemic of childhood obesity be blamed on parents, schools, or policies?
3. Why are IQ tests not used as often as they were a few decades ago?
4. How helpful are diagnosis, special education, and medication for children with special needs?

In the middle of the second grade, my family and I moved a thousand miles. I entered a new school where my accent was odd; I was self-conscious and lonely. Cynthia had a friendly smile, freckles, and red hair. More important, she talked to me; I asked her to be my friend.

> "We cannot be friends," she said, "because I am a Democrat."
> "So am I," I answered. (I knew my family believed in democracy.)
> "No, you're not. You are a Republican," she said.
> I was stunned and sad. We never became friends.

Neither Cynthia nor I realized that all children are unusual in some way (perhaps because of appearance, culture, or family) and yet capable of friendship with children unlike themselves. Cynthia and I could have been good friends, but neither of us knew it. Her parents had told her something about my parents' politics that I did not understand. Cynthia left the school later that year, friendless; I made other friends.

This chapter describes not only the similarities among all school-age children but also differences that may become significant—in size, health, learning ability, and more. At the end of this chapter, we focus on children with special needs—children who need friends but have trouble finding them.

>> A Healthy Time

Genes and environment safeguard **middle childhood**, as the years from about 6 to 11 are called (Konner, 2010). Fatal diseases or accidents are rare; both nature and nurture make these years the healthiest of the entire life span (see Figure 11.1).

Genetic diseases are more threatening in early infancy or old age than in middle childhood, and serious accidents and fatal illnesses are less common, even compared with a few decades ago. This is true virtually everywhere. For example, in the United States in 1950 the death rate per 100,000 children aged 5 to 14 was 70; in 2010, it was 13. Even the incidence of minor illnesses, such as ear infections, infected tonsils, and flu, has been reduced, in part because of better medicine and immunization (National Center for Health Statistics, 2013)

middle childhood The period between early childhood and early adolescence, approximately from ages 6 to 11.

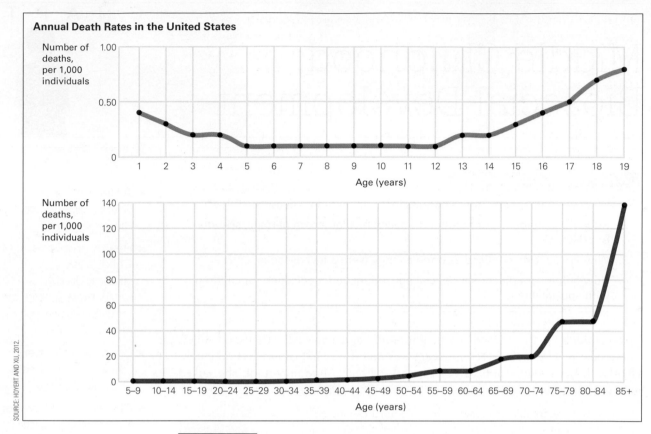

Annual Death Rates in the United States

SOURCE: HOYERT AND XU, 2012.

FIGURE 11.1

Death at an Early Age? Almost Never! Schoolchildren are remarkably hardy, as measured in many ways. These charts show that death rates for 6- to 11-year-olds are lower than those for children younger than 6 or older than 11 and are about 100 times lower than those for adults.

Observation Quiz From the bottom graph, it looks as if ages 9 and 19 are equally healthy, but they are dramatically different in the top graph. What is the explanation for this? (see answer, page 312)

Slower Growth, Greater Strength

Unlike infants or adolescents, school-age children grow slowly and steadily. Self-care is easy—from dressing to hair washing, from making lunch to walking to school. Brain maturation allows schoolchildren to sit and do their work without breaking their pencils, tearing their papers, or elbowing their classmates. In these middle years, children are much more self-sufficient than younger children but not yet buffeted by adolescent body changes.

Teeth

Important to the individual child is the loss of baby teeth, with the entire set replaced by permanent teeth beginning at about age 6 (with girls a few months ahead of boys) and complete by puberty.

Important to society is oral health overall. Sixty years ago, many children neither brushed their teeth nor saw a dentist, and fluoride was almost never added to water. That's why many elders have missing teeth. In developed nations, they usually have dentures; in poor nations, they have gaps in their mouths or very visible gold teeth—a sign of wealth in nations where good dentistry is scarce.

Currently in developed nations, school-age children brush their teeth, and most communities—including all the larger cites—add fluoride to drinking water. According to a national survey, about 75 percent of U.S. children saw a dentist for preventive care in the past year, and for 70 percent the condition of their teeth was rated very good (Hiroko & Rozier, 2013). Children with poor oral health are likely to have parents who are low SES do not speak English. In addition, they are likely to live in neighborhoods where adults do not help or trust each other—apparently one thing that good neighbors do for each other is encourage visits to the dentist! (Hiroko & Rozier, 2013)

Children's Health Habits

Good childhood habits protect later adult health. For example, the more regular exercise children get, the less likely they are to suffer a stroke or a heart attack in adulthood (Branca et al., 2007). The health that most school-age children naturally enjoy may either continue or be disrupted, depending on daily practices—such as eating a balanced diet, getting enough exercise and sleep, and breathing clean air. Unfortunately, children who have poor health for economic or social reasons (such as those with no regular medical care) are vulnerable lifelong, even if their socioeconomic status (SES) improves later on (G. E. Miller et al., 2010).

Children's habits during these years are strongly affected by peers and parents. When children see others routinely care for their health, social learning pushes them to do the same. Camps for children with asthma, cancer, diabetes, sickle cell anemia, and other chronic illnesses are particularly beneficial because the example of other children, and the guidance of knowledgeable adults, helps children care for themselves. Establishing good health habits is vital before adolescence, because teenage rebellion leads some children with chronic diseases to ignore special diets, pills, warning signs, and doctors unless the children themselves have incorporated such habits into daily life (Dean et al., 2010; Suris et al., 2008).

Physical Activity

Beyond the sheer fun of playing, the benefits of physical activity—especially games with rules, which school-age children are now able to follow—can last a lifetime. Exercise not only improves physical health, it may also improve academic achievement (Carlson et al., 2008).

How could body movement improve brain functioning? A review of the research suggests several possible mechanisms, including direct benefits of better cerebral blood flow and increased neurotransmitters, as well as the indirect results of better mood and thus improved concentration (Singh et al., 2012). In addition, playing games with other children teaches cooperation, problem solving, and respect for teammates and opponents of many backgrounds.

Where can children reap these benefits?

Expert Eye–Hand Coordination The specifics of motor-skill development in middle childhood depend on the culture. These flute players are carrying on the European Baroque musical tradition that thrives among the poor, remote Guarayo people of Bolivia.

Neighborhood Games

Neighborhood play is flexible. Rules and boundaries are adapted to the context (out of bounds is "past the tree" or "behind the parked truck"). Stickball, touch football, tag, hide-and-seek, and dozens of other running and catching games go on forever—or at least until dark. The play is active, interactive, and inclusive—ideal for children. It also teaches ethics. As one scholar notes:

> Children play tag, hide and seek, or pickup basketball. They compete with one another but always according to rules, and rules that they enforce themselves without recourse to an impartial judge. The penalty for not playing by the rules is not playing, that is, social exclusion.

[Gillespie, 2010, p. 398]

>> Answer to Observation Quiz
(from page 310): Look at the vertical axes.
From age 1 to 20, the annual death rate is
less than 1 in 1,000.

Idyllic Two 8-year-olds, each with a 6-year-old sister, all four day-dreaming or exploring in a very old tree beside a lake in Denmark—what could be better? Ideally, all the world's children would be so fortunate, but most are not.

For school-age children, "social exclusion" is a steep price to pay for insisting on their own way. Instead, they learn to cooperate. Unfortunately, modern life has undercut informal neighborhood games. Vacant lots and empty fields have largely disappeared.

An additional problem is that parents fear "stranger danger"—although one expert writes that "there is a much greater chance that your child is going to be dangerously overweight from staying inside than that he is going to be abducted" (quoted in Layden, 2004, p. 86). Indoor activities such as homework, television, and video games compete with outdoor play in every nation, perhaps especially in the United States. According to an Australian scholar:

> Australian children are lucky. Here the dominant view is that children's after school time is leisure time. In the United States, it seems that leisure time is available to fewer and fewer children. If a child performs poorly in school, recreation time rapidly becomes remediation time. For high achievers, after school time is often spent in academic enrichment.
>
> [Vered, 2008, p. 170]

The United States is not the greatest offending nation in terms of using after-school time as study time instead of play time. South Korea in particular is known for the intensity of "shadow education," which is extra tutoring that parents find for their children, hoping to improve their test grades later on (Lee & Shouse, 2011).

Many parents around the world enroll their children in neighborhood organizations that offer additional opportunities for play. Culture and family affect the specifics: Some children learn golf, others tennis, others boxing. Cricket and rugby are common in England and in former British colonies such as India, Australia, and Jamaica; baseball is common in Japan, the United States, Cuba, Panama, and the Dominican Republic; soccer is central in many European, African, and Latin American nations.

Unfortunately, organized teams are less likely to include children of low SES or children with disabilities. As a result, the children most likely to benefit are least likely to participate, even when enrollment is free. The reasons are many; the consequences sad (Dearing et al., 2009).

Exercise in School

When opportunities for neighborhood play are scarce, physical education in school is a logical alternative. However, because schools are pressured to focus on test scores in academic subjects, time for physical education and recess has declined. A study of Texas elementary schools found that 24 percent had no recess at all and only 1 percent had recess several times a day (W. Zhu et al., 2010).

Texas, unfortunately, is no exception. A survey of U. S. teachers of more than 10,000 third-graders nationwide found that about one-third of all children had less than 15 minutes of recess each day. Children deprived of recess were more often lower SES, in classes that were "hard to manage," in public schools, and in cities. They also had fewer scheduled gym periods.

Many researchers note that "many children from disadvantaged backgrounds are not free to roam their neighborhoods or even their own yards unless they are accompanied by adults. For many of these children, recess periods may

"Just remember, son, it doesn't matter whether you win or lose—unless you want Daddy's love."

be the only opportunity for them to practice their social skills with other children" (Barros et al., 2009, p. 434). Thus school exercise is least likely for children most likely to need it—city-dwellers who live in poor neighborhoods, where fearful parents do not let them go outside to play (Barros et al., 2009).

When school districts require gym, classes may be too crowded to allow active play for all the children. Ironically, schools in Japan, where many children score well on international tests, usually have several recess breaks totaling more than an hour each day. It is common for Japanese public schools to have an indoor gym and a pool.

After-school sports teams affiliated with schools or other organizations are not always ideal for 6- to 11-year-olds. Sometimes they push children to excel at sports that are better suited to adults, such as baseball, basketball, and football.

National organizations are developing guidelines to prevent concussions among 7- and 8-year-olds in football practice as well as to halt full-body impact among children under age 12 playing ice hockey. The fact that regulations are needed to protect children from serious harm is sobering (Toporek, 2012).

Why Helmets? Sports organized by adults, such as this football team of 7- to 8-year-old boys sponsored by the Lyons and Police Athletic League of Detroit, may be harmful to children. The best games are those that require lots of running and teamwork—but no pushing or shoving.

SUMMING UP

School-age children are usually healthy, strong, and capable. Genes as well as immunization protect them against contagious diseases, and medical awareness and care have improved over the past decades. Moreover, children's maturation adds strength, understanding, and coordination and enables them to undertake self-care, allowing them to learn health habits to sustain them lifelong. Although neighborhood play, school physical education, and community sports leagues all provide needed activity, energetic play is much more likely for some children than for others. Unfortunately, those who need it most are the least likely to have it.

Especially for Physical Education Teachers A group of parents of fourth- and fifth-graders have asked for your help in persuading the school administration to sponsor a competitive sports team. How should you advise the group to proceed? (see response, page 315)

>> Health Problems in Middle Childhood

Chronic conditions become more troubling if they interfere with school, play, and friendships. Some conditions—including Tourette syndrome, stuttering, and allergies—often worsen during the school years. Even minor problems—wearing glasses, repeatedly coughing or blowing one's nose, or having a visible birthmark—can make children self-conscious.

Researchers increasingly recognize that every physical and psychological problem is affected by the social context and, in turn, affects that context (Jackson & Tester, 2008). Parents and children are not merely reactive: In a dynamic-systems manner, individuals and contexts influence each other. [**Lifespan Link:** Dynamic-systems theory is discussed in Chapter 1.] We now focus on two examples: obesity and asthma.

Childhood Obesity

Body mass index (BMI) is the ratio of weight to height. **Childhood overweight** is usually defined as a BMI above the 85th percentile, and **childhood obesity** is defined as a BMI above the 95th percentile of children a particular age. In 2010, 18 percent of 6- to 9-year-olds in the United States were obese (Ogden et al., 2012).

childhood overweight In a child, having a BMI above the 85th percentile, according to the U.S. Centers for Disease Control's 1980 standards for children of a given age.

childhood obesity In a child, having a BMI above the 95th percentile, according to the U.S. Centers for Disease Control's 1980 standards for children of a given age.

Childhood Obesity Around the Globe

Obesity now causes more deaths worldwide than malnutrition. There are more than 42 million overweight children around the world. Obesity is caused by factors in every system—biological, familial, social, and cultural. One specific example is advertisements for unhealthy foods, often marketed directly to children (see below).

There is hope. A multifaceted prevention effort—including mothers, preschools, pediatricians, grocery stores, and even the White House—has reduced obesity in the United States for 2-5 year olds. It was 13.9 percent in 2002 and was 8.4 percent in 2012. However, obesity rates from age 6 to 60 remain higher in the United States than in most nations.

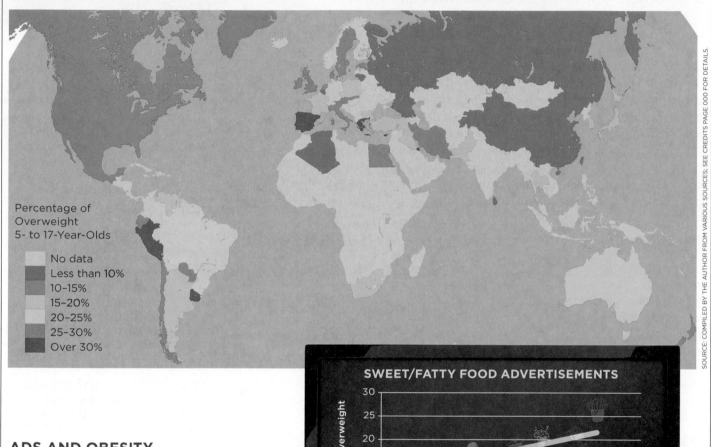

Percentage of Overweight 5- to 17-Year-Olds

- No data
- Less than 10%
- 10–15%
- 15–20%
- 20–25%
- 25–30%
- Over 30%

SOURCE: COMPILED BY THE AUTHOR FROM VARIOUS SOURCES; SEE CREDITS PAGE 000 FOR DETAILS.

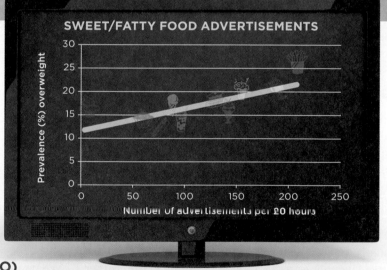

SWEET/FATTY FOOD ADVERTISEMENTS

Prevalence (%) overweight

Number of advertisements per 20 hours

PHOTO: HERO30/ISTOCK/THINKSTOCK

ADS AND OBESITY

Nations differ not only in obesity rates but also in children's exposure to television ads for unhealthy food. The amount of advertising of unhealthy foods on television correlates with childhood obesity— except in nations where few children watch TV.

SOURCE: LOBSTEIN, TIM, & DIBB (2005)

WORLD HEALTH ORGANIZATION (WHO) RECOMMENDATIONS FOR PHYSICAL ACTIVITY FOR CHILDREN

1

Children ages 5 to 17 should be active for at least an hour a day.

2

More than an hour of exercise brings additional benefits.

3

Most physical activity should be aerobic. Vigorous activities should occur 3 times per week or more.

WHO also recommends daily exercise for adults of every age—including centenarians.

WORLD HEALTH ORGANIZATION. (2010)

Childhood obesity is increasing worldwide, having more than doubled since 1980 in all three nations of North America (Mexico, the United States, and Canada) (Ogden et al., 2011). Since 2000, rates seem to have leveled off in the U.S., but they have but increased in China (Ji et al., 2013). The World Health Organization uses lower cutoffs between healthy and excess weight, and thus some international statistics report even more childhood obesity (Shields & Tremblay, 2010) (see Visualizing Development, p. 314).

Although rates have stabilized in the United States, the current plateau is far too high. About one-third of 6- to 11-year-old children are overweight, and more than half of those are obese (Ogden et al., 2012) (see Figure 11.2).

Childhood overweight correlates with asthma, high blood pressure, and elevated cholesterol (especially LDL, the "lousy" cholesterol). As excessive weight builds, school achievement often decreases, self-esteem falls, and loneliness rises (Harris et al., 2012). If obese children stay heavy, they become adults who are less likely to marry, attend college, or find work that reflects their ability (Han et al., 2011; Sobal & Hanson, 2012).

>> Response for Physical Education Teachers (from page 313): Discuss with the parents their reasons for wanting the team. Children need physical activity, but some aspects of competitive sports are better suited to adults than to children.

Especially for Teachers A child in your class is overweight, but you are hesitant to say anything to the parents, who are also overweight, because you do not want to offend them. What should you do? (see response, page 318)

Observation Quiz Generally, rates of obesity increase every year from ages 2 to 19, but boys and girls in one group here seem less likely to be overweight in adolescence than in middle childhood. Which group, and why? (see answer, page 318)

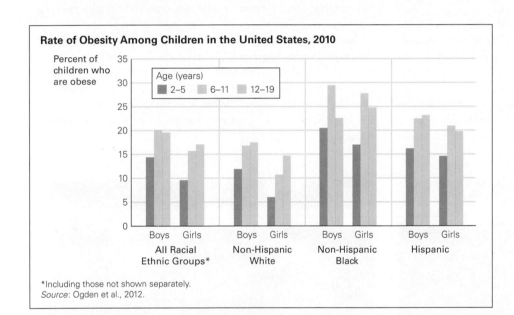

Rate of Obesity Among Children in the United States, 2010

*Including those not shown separately.
Source: Ogden et al., 2012.

FIGURE 11.2

Fatter and Fatter As you see, the incidence of obesity (defined here as a BMI above the 95th percentile, according to the Centers for Disease Control and Prevention 2000 growth charts) increases as children grow older. Not shown is the rate in infancy, which is significantly lower for every group. The "All Groups" rate includes children of groups not shown separately, such as biracial, Asian, Hawaiian, Alaskan native, and American Indian.

A VIEW FROM SCIENCE

What Contributes to Childhood Obesity?

There are "hundreds if not thousands of contributing factors" for childhood obesity, from the cells of the body to the norms of the society (Harrison et al., 2011, p. 51). One way to think of it is to consider the many opportunities and practices that might mitigate obesity in six domains that begin with the letter C— cell, child, clan, community, country, culture (see Appendix A). Heredity (cell), family (child and clan), and society (community, country, and culture) are all causes of overweight.

More than 200 genes affect weight by influencing activity level, hunger, food preferences, body type, and metabolism (Gluckman & Hanson, 2006). Having two copies of an allele called FTO (inherited by 16 percent of all European Americans) increases the likelihood of both obesity and diabetes (Frayling et al., 2007). New genes and alleles that affect obesity, never acting alone, are discovered virtually every month (Dunmore, 2013).

Knowing that genes are involved may slow down the impulse to blame fat people for their weight, but problems at the cellular level are epigenetic, and they represent only one of the six categories of causes mentioned above. Further, genes cannot be the reason for *increases* in obesity, since genes change little from one generation to the next (Harrison et al., 2011).

Family practices, however, can change, and they have in the past decades. Obesity is more common in infants who are not breast-fed; in preschoolers who watch TV and drink soda; and in school-age children who are driven to school, sleep too little, and rarely play outside (Hart et al., 2011; Institute of Medicine, 2006; Rhee, 2008).

During middle childhood, children themselves contribute to their weight gain. They have *pester power*—the ability to get adults to do what they want (Powell et al., 2011). Often they pester their parents to give them calorie-dense foods, although children who learn about health from their teacher or a nurse can pester in the opposite direction—to play outside, to join a sports team, and so on.

On average, family contexts changed for the worse toward the end of the twentieth century in North America and are now spreading worldwide. For instance, pester power increases as family size decreases. That makes childhood obesity collateral damage from improvements in contraception.

Attempts to restrict foods that are high in sugar and fat clash with the sales efforts corporations that sell snacks for a profit. Some success, however, has occurred in policies within schools that increasingly serve healthy foods and monitor the location and contents of vending machines.

Communities and countries can affect the prevalence of parks, bike paths, and sidewalks and decrease subsidies for corn oil and sugar. Simply offering healthy food is not enough to convince children to change their diet; context and culture are crucial (Hanks et al., 2013).

Cultural sensitivity is crucial, since each ethnic group has preferred foods and family patterns. To work against culture is foolish, but working within cultures can protect the children.

For example, African Americans may consider fried fish part of their culture, but so are baked fish and a variety of greens; Mexican Americans may relish rice and beans, but those can be cooked without added fat. Immigrants who want to "eat American" may need to learn that fast-food restaurants correlate with childhood obesity (Alviola et al., 2013). In fact, in the United States, adults born elsewhere have lower rates of obesity than do the native born, yet children of immigrants have higher obesity rates—a statistic that should give everyone pause.

Rather than trying to zero in on any single factor, a dynamic-systems approach is needed: Many factors, over time, make a child overweight (Harrison et al., 2011); changing just one of them is not sufficient to resolve the problem. The answer to the second "What Will You Know?" question at the beginning of this chapter is that everyone is at least a tiny bit at fault.

Same Situation, Far Apart Children have high energy but small stomachs, so they enjoy frequent snacks more than big meals. Yet snacks are typically poor sources of nutrition. Who is healthier: the Latin American children eating lollypops at a theme park in Florida or the Japanese children eating *takoyaki* (an octopus dumpling) as part of a traditional celebration near Tokyo?

Asthma

Asthma is a chronic inflammatory disorder of the airways that makes breathing difficult. Sufferers have periodic attacks, sometimes requiring a rush to the hospital emergency room, a frightening experience for children. Although people of every age experience asthma, rates are highest among school-age children (Cruz et al., 2010).

In the United States, child asthma rates have tripled since 1980. (See Figure 11.3 for current rates for those younger than 18 years old.) Parents report that 10.2 percent of U.S. 5- to 9-year-olds currently have asthma; 6.2 percent have had an attack within the past year (National Center for Health Statistics, 2013).

Researchers have long sought to find the causes of asthma. A few alleles have been identified as contributing factors, but none acts in isolation (Akinbami et al., 2010; Bossé & Hudson, 2007). Some make asthma difficult to control, while others cause milder, more controllable asthma (Almomani et al., 2013). Several aspects of modern life—carpets, pollution, house pets, airtight windows, parental smoking, cockroaches, less outdoor play—contribute to the increased rates of asthma (Tamay et al., 2007), but again no single factor is the sole trigger, and some children are more susceptible to certain allergens than others.

Some experts suggest a *hygiene hypothesis*: that "the immune system needs to tangle with microbes when we are young" (Leslie, 2012, p. 1428), that children are overprotected from viruses and bacteria. In their concern about hygiene, parents keep young children from exposure to minor infections and diseases that would strengthen their immunity. This hypothesis is supported by data showing that (1) first-born children develop asthma more often than later-born ones; (2) farm children have less asthma and other allergies; and (3) children born by cesarean delivery (very sterile) have a greater incidence of asthma.

None of these factors, however, *proves* the hygiene hypothesis. Perhaps farm children are protected by drinking unpasteurized milk, by outdoor chores, or by genes that are more common in farm families, rather than by being more often exposed to a range of bacteria (von Mutius & Vercelli, 2010).

The incidence of asthma increases as nations get richer, dramatically evident since 2000 in Brazil and China. Better hygiene for wealthier children is one

Pride and Prejudice In some city schools, asthma is so common that using an inhaler is a sign of pride, as suggested by the facial expressions of these two boys. The "prejudice" is beyond the walls of this school nurse's room, in a society that allows high rates of childhood asthma.

asthma A chronic disease of the respiratory system in which inflammation narrows the airways from the nose and mouth to the lungs, causing difficulty in breathing. Signs and symptoms include wheezing, shortness of breath, chest tightness, and coughing.

Especially for Parents Suppose that you always serve dinner with the television on, tuned to a news broadcast. Your hope is that your children will learn about the world as they eat. Can this practice be harmful? (see response, page 318)

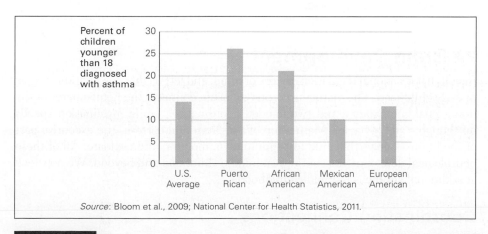

Source: Bloom et al., 2009; National Center for Health Statistics, 2011.

FIGURE 11.3

Not Breathing Easy Of all U.S. children younger than 18, 14 percent have been diagnosed at least once with asthma. Why are Puerto Rican and African American children more likely to have asthma? Does the answer have to do with nature or nurture, genetics or pollution?

>> **Response for Teachers** (from page 315): Speak to the parents, not accusingly (because you know that genes and culture have a major influence on body weight) but helpfully. Alert them to the potential social and health problems their child's weight poses. Most parents are very concerned about their child's well-being and will work with you to improve the child's snacks and exercise levels.

>> **Answer to Observation Quiz** (from page 315): Non-Hispanic blacks. The reasons are not known, but one possibility is that African American teenagers become more aware of the larger society and more able to make their own food choices than they were when younger. Note, however, that children and adolescents of every group carry more excess weight than is healthy.

>> **Response for Parents** (from page 317): Habitual TV watching correlates with obesity, so you may be damaging your children's health rather than improving their intellect. Your children would probably profit more if you were to make dinner a time for family conversation about world events.

explanation, but so is increasing urbanization, which correlates with more cars, more pollution, more allergens, and better medical diagnoses (Cruz et al., 2010). One review of the hygiene hypothesis notes that "the picture can be dishearteningly complex" (Couzin-Frankel, 2010, p. 1168).

Since developmentalists realize that every day of school absence—and every exercise opportunity not taken—harms health and happiness in middle childhood, the increase in childhood asthma is disheartening. But improvement may be possible.

Consider a study of 133 Latino adult smokers, all caregivers of children with asthma. They were not necessarily willing to quit cigarettes, but they agreed to allow a Spanish-speaking counselor come repeatedly to their homes (Borrelli et al., 2010). The counselor placed a smoke monitor in the child's bedroom. A week later she told the caregiver how much smoke exposure the child had experienced. Then, in three sessions, she provided specific suggestions on how to quit smoking, based on research on addiction, with particular sensitivity to Latino values.

Three months later, one-fourth of the caregivers had quit smoking completely, and many of the rest had cut down. The average child's exposure to smoke was cut in half, and asthma attacks diminished (Borrelli et al., 2010). Note that having data on their child and getting personal encouragement were helpful to these parents.

Other research confirms that most parents want to provide good care (many wonder how) and that many adults, including those who are neither parents nor Latino, want to protect children but do not know how. Air pollution, for instance, is considered a general environmental problem, but many adults do not realize the impact it has on children.

SUMMING UP

Some children have chronic health problems that interfere with school and friendship. Among these are obesity and asthma, both of which are increasing in every nation and have genetic and environmental causes. Childhood obesity may seem harmless, but it leads to social problems among classmates and severe health problems later on. Asthma's harm is more immediate: Asthmatic children often miss school and are rushed to emergency rooms, gasping for air. Although genes predispose some children to each particular health problem, family practices and neighborhood context can increase rates of obesity and asthma, and many society-wide policies and cultural customs make the problems worse. ▪

>> Brain Development

Recall that emotional regulation, theory of mind, and left–right coordination emerge in early childhood. The maturing corpus callosum connects the hemispheres of the brain, enabling balance and two-handed coordination, while myelination speeds up thoughts and behavior. Maturation of the prefrontal cortex—the executive part of the brain—allows the child to begin to plan, monitor, and evaluate. All of these neurological developments continue in middle childhood and beyond. We now look at additional advances in middle childhood.

Coordinating Connections

Increasing maturation results "by 7 or 8 years of age, in a massively interconnected brain" (Kagan & Herschkowitz, 2005, p. 220). Such connections are crucial for the complex tasks that children must master, which require "smooth coordination of large numbers of neurons (Stern, 2013, p. 577). One example is learning to read, perhaps the most important intellectual accomplishment of the school-age child. Reading is not instinctual: Our ancestors never did it, and until recent centuries only a few scribes and scholars were expected to make sense of those marks on paper. Consequently, the brain has no areas dedicated to reading, the way it does for talking or gesturing (Gabrieli, 2009).

How do humans read without brain-specific structures? The answer is "a massively interconnected brain." Reading uses several parts of the brain—one for sounds, another for recognizing letters, another for sequencing, another for comprehension, and so on (Booth, 2007).

Those massive interconnections are needed for many social skills as well—deciding whom to trust, figuring out what is fair, interpreting ambiguous gestures and expressions. Younger children are not proficient at interpreting social cues (that's why they are told, "Don't talk to strangers"). During middle childhood, parts of the brain connect to allow better social decisions. (Crone & Westenberg, 2009).

The prefrontal cortex takes decades to mature. For children who want to be rocket scientists, billionaire stock analysts, or brain surgeons, connecting those distant goals with current behavior or social reality is not yet possible. Nonetheless, connections between one part of the brain and another may be crucial because some neuroscientists believe that "social or linguistic disorders could be caused by disruptions in the pathways" of brain connections, not in the neurons themselves (Minogue, 2010, p. 747).

Think Quick; Too Slow

Advance planning and impulse control are aided by faster **reaction time**, which is how long it takes to respond to a stimulus. Increasing myelination reduces reaction time every year from birth until about age 16.

A simple example is being able to kick a speeding soccer ball toward a teammate; a more complex example is being able to calculate when to utter a witty remark and when to stay quiet. That depends on four quick reactions, not only (1) to realize that a comment could be made and (2) to decide what it could be, but also (3) to think about the other person's possible response, and in that split second (4) to realize when something should NOT be said.

Pay Attention

Neurological advances allow children not only to process information quickly but also to pay special heed to the most important elements of their environment. **Selective attention**, the ability to concentrate on some stimuli while ignoring others, improves markedly at about age 7. School-age children not only notice various stimuli (which is one form of attention) but also select appropriate responses when several possibilities conflict (Wendelken et al., 2011).

In the classroom, selective attention allows children to listen, take concise notes, and ignore distractions (all difficult at age 6, easier by age 10). In the din of the cafeteria, children can understand one another's gestures and expressions and respond. On the baseball diamond, older batters ignore the other team's attempts to distract them, and fielders start moving into position as soon as the bat hits a ball.

Indeed, selective attention underlies all the abilities that gradually mature during the school years. "Networks of collaborating cortical regions" (M. H. Johnson et al., 2009, p. 151) are required.

reaction time The time it takes to respond to a stimulus, either physically (with a reflexive movement such as an eyeblink) or cognitively (with a thought).

selective attention The ability to concentrate on some stimuli while ignoring others.

Pay Attention Some adults think that computers can make children lazy, because they can look up whatever they don't know. But imagine the facial expressions of these children if they were sitting at their desks with 30 classmates, listening to a lecture.

PRESSMASTER/SHUTTERSTOCK

Automatic

One final advance in brain function in middle childhood is **automatization**, the process by which a sequence of thoughts and actions is repeated until it becomes automatic and routine. At first, almost all behaviors under conscious control require careful thought. After many repetitions, as neurons fire in sequence, actions become automatic and patterned. Less thinking is needed because the firing of one neuron sets off a chain reaction: That is automatization.

Consider again learning to read. At first, eyes (sometimes aided by a guiding finger) focus intensely, painstakingly making out letters and sounding out each one. This leads to the perception of syllables and then words. Eventually, the process becomes so automatic that, for instance, as you read this text, automatization allows you to concentrate on concepts without thinking about the letters, and as you drive down the highway, you read billboards that you do not want to read.

Automatization aids every skill. Learning to speak a second language, to recite the multiplication tables, and to write one's name are all slow at first but gradually become automatic. Habits and routines learned in childhood are useful lifelong—and when they are not, they are hard to break. That's automatization.

Measuring the Mind

In ancient times, if adults were strong and fertile, that was usually enough. A few wise men were admired, but most people were not expected to think quickly and profoundly. By the twentieth century, however, a stupid person, even if strong and fertile, was less admired. Because intelligence became increasingly significant, many ways to measure it were developed. As you will see, no method is considered completely accurate.

Aptitude, Achievement, and IQ

In theory, **aptitude** is the potential to master a specific skill or to learn a certain body of knowledge. The brain functions just described—reaction time, selective attention, and automatization—may be the foundation of aptitude, but traditionally intellectual aptitude is measured not by brain scans but by **IQ tests**. The underlying assumption is that there is one general thing called *intelligence* (often referred to as *g*, for general intelligence) and that IQ tests measure that general aptitude.

Originally, an IQ score was literally an Intelligence Quotient: Mental age (the average chronological age of children who attained a particular score on an IQ tests) was divided by a particular child's chronological age, and the result of that division (the quotient) was multiplied by 100. Obviously, if a child's mental age was the same as that child's chronological age, the quotient would be 1. In that case, the child's IQ would be 100, exactly average for children of that age.

Thus, the IQ of a 6-year-old with a mind typical for 6-year-olds would be ⁶⁄₆ × 100 = 100. If a 6-year-old answered the questions as well as a typical 8-year-old, the score would be ⁸⁄₆ × 100, or 133. The current method of calculating IQ is more complex, but an IQ within one standard deviation of 100 (between 85 and 115) is still considered average (see Figure 11.4).

In theory, achievement is what has actually been learned, not potential (aptitude). **Achievement tests** in school compare scores to norms established for each grade. For example, third-grade students whose reading is typical of third-grade students everywhere (achievement tests typically have national norms) would be at the third-grade level in reading achievement. [**Lifespan Link:** Achievement tests are discussed in Chapter 12.]

automatization A process in which repetition of a sequence of thoughts and actions makes the sequence routine, so that it no longer requires conscious thought.

aptitude The potential to master a specific skill or to learn a certain body of knowledge.

IQ test A test designed to measure intellectual aptitude, or ability to learn in school. Originally, intelligence was defined as mental age divided by chronological age, times 100—hence the term *intelligence quotient*, or *IQ*.

Observation Quiz If a person's IQ is 110, what category is he or she in? (see answer, page 322)

achievement test A measure of mastery or proficiency in reading, mathematics, writing, science, or some other subject.

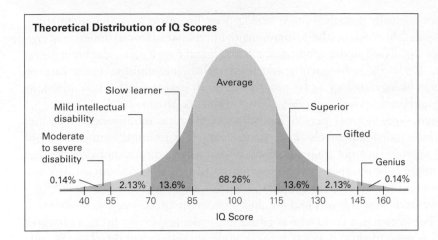

Theoretical Distribution of IQ Scores

Mild intellectual disability

Moderate to severe disability

Slow learner

Average

Superior

Gifted

Genius

0.14%   2.13%   13.6%   68.26%   13.6%   2.13%   0.14%

40   55   70   85   100   115   130   145   160

IQ Score

FIGURE 11.4

In Theory, Most People Are Average Almost 70 percent of IQ scores fall within the normal range. Note, however, that this is a norm-referenced test. In fact, actual IQ scores have risen in many nations; 100 is no longer exactly the midpoint. Furthermore, in practice, scores below 50 are slightly more frequent than indicated by the normal curve shown here because severe disability is the result not of normal distribution, but of genetic and prenatal factors.

Note, however, that children who read at the third-grade level could be of any age. If they are, in fact, in the third grade, their reading achievement is exactly on grade level, whether they are 7, 8, or 9 years old. IQ tests take age into account, but achievement tests do not.

The words *in theory* precede the definitions of *aptitude* and *achievement tests* because, although potential and accomplishment are supposed to be distinct, the data find substantial overlap. IQ and achievement scores are strongly correlated for individuals, for groups of children, and for nations (Lynn & Mikk, 2007).

It was once assumed that aptitude was a fixed characteristic, present at birth. Longitudinal data show that this is not the case. Young children with a low IQ can become above average or even gifted adults, like my nephew David (discussed in Chapter 1). Indeed, the average IQ scores of entire nations have risen substantially every decade for the past century—a phenomenon called the **Flynn effect**, named after the researcher who first described it (Flynn, 1999, 2012).

Most psychologists now agree that the brain is like a muscle, affected by mental exercise—which often is encouraged or discouraged by the social setting. Brain scans show that the neurological structures within each person's brain grow or shrink depending on past learning in language and music, and probably in other areas as well (Zatorre, 2013).

The idea that intelligence changes over the years is now accepted by almost every expert, whether or not they believe there is such a thing as *g*, general intelligence. During middle childhood, speed of thought is particularly crucial for high IQ, with working memory also a foundation for intelligence (Demetriou et al., 2013). Both speed and memory are affected by experience.

Flynn effect The rise in average IQ scores that has occurred over the decades in many nations.

Criticisms of Testing

The reality that scores change over time makes IQ tests much less definitive than they were once thought to be. A more fundamental question is whether any single test can measure the complexities of the human brain. This criticism has been targeted particularly at IQ tests, because those tests assume that there is g, one general aptitude. According to some experts, children instead inherit many abilities, some high and some low, rather than any g (e.g., Q. Zhu et al., 2010).

Two leading developmentalists (Sternberg and Gardner) are among those who believe that humans have **multiple intelligences**, not just one. [**Lifespan Link:** Sternberg's three intelligences are discussed in Chapter 21.] Gardner's concepts are directly relevant to middle childhood, because these concepts influence the curriculum in many primary schools. For instance, children might be allowed to demonstrate their understanding of a historical event via a poster with drawings, not a paper with a bibliography.

multiple intelligences The idea that human intelligence is composed of a varied set of abilities rather than a single, all-encompassing one.

>> Answer to Observation Quiz
(from page 320): He or she is average.
Anyone with a score between 85 and 115 has
an average IQ.

Especially for Teachers What are the
advantages and disadvantages of using
Gardner's nine intelligences to guide your
classroom curriculum? (see response,
page 324)

Gardner originally described seven intelligences: linguistic, logical-mathematical, musical, spatial, bodily-kinesthetic (movement), interpersonal (social understanding), and intrapersonal (self-understanding), each associated with a particular brain region (Gardner, 1983). He subsequently added an eighth (naturalistic: understanding nature, as in biology, zoology, or farming) and a ninth (spiritual/existential: thinking about life and death) (Gardner, 1999, 2006; Gardner & Moran, 2006).

Although every normal person has some of all nine intelligences, Gardner believes each individual excels in particular ones. For example, someone might be gifted spatially but not linguistically (a visual artist who cannot describe her work) or might have interpersonal but not naturalistic intelligence (an astute clinical psychologist whose houseplants die).

Gardner finds that cultures and families dampen or encourage particular intelligences. For instance, a child who is gifted musically and grows up in a family of musicians is more likely to develop musical intelligence than a child whose parents are tone deaf.

Another criticism of the IQ test arises from multicultural understanding. Every test reflects the culture of the people who create, administer, and take it. This is obviously true for achievement tests: A child may score low because of the school, the teacher, the family, or the culture, not because of ability. Indeed, one reason IQ tests are still used is that achievement tests do not necessarily reflect aptitude.

However, scores on aptitude tests are also influenced by culture. Some experts have tried to develop tests that are culture-free asking children to identify pictures, draw shapes, repeat stories, hop on one foot, name their classmates, sort objects, and so on.

Even with such tests, culture is relevant. One group reports that Sudanese children averaged 40 points lower when IQ tests required that they use a pencil to write answers. The reason: They had no experience with pencils (Wicherts et al., 2010). By contrast, most American children begin using markers before age 2; by school age, automatization allows them to write without thinking about how to hold and push a writing implement. Even such a crucial aspect of testing as answering questions from a stranger is culturally biased.

Brain Scans

One way to indicate aptitude is to measure the brain directly, avoiding the pitfalls of written exams or individual questions. Neurological measures do not necessarily correlate with written IQ tests, which leads some neuroscientists to consider IQ scores inaccurate. Yet interpretation of brain scans is not straightforward either. For example, although it seems logical that less brain activity means less intelligence, such a conclusion is mistaken.

In fact, many areas of a young child's brain are activated simultaneously, and then, with practice, automatization reduces the need for brain activity, so the smartest children might have less active brains. Some research finds that a thick cortex correlates with higher ability but also that thickness develops more slowly in gifted children (Karama et al., 2009; Miller, 2006). Further, brain patterns in children who are highly creative differ from those who are highly intelligent (Jung & Ryman, 2013). The gifted patterns are puzzling—but so is much brain research.

Neuroscientists agree, however, on three conclusions:

1. Brain development depends on a person's specific experiences because "brain, body, and environment are . . . dynamically coupled" (Marshall, 2009, p. 119), and thus any brain scan is accurate only for the moment it is done.

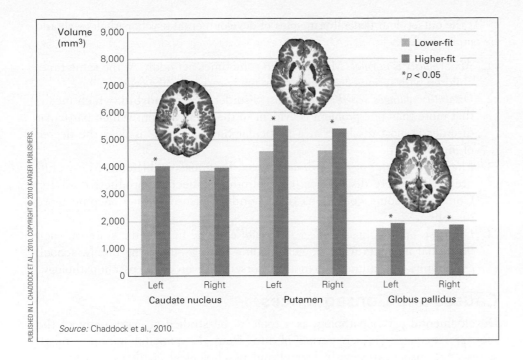

Source: Chaddock et al., 2010.

Brain Fitness Aerobic fitness was measured (by VO_2—volume of oxygen expelled after exercise) in 59 children (average age 10, none of whom had ADHD or were pubescent); then the children's brains were scanned. Overall brain size did not correlate with fitness—genes and early nutrition are more important for that. However, the volume of crucial areas for cognitive control (attention, contextualizing, planning) was significantly greater in the children who were in better shape. This is one more reason to go biking, running, or swimming with your child.

2. Brain development continues throughout life. Middle childhood is crucial, but developments before and after these years are also significant.
3. Children with disorders often have unusual brain patterns, and training their brains may help. However, brain complexity and normal variation mean that neuroscience diagnosis and remediation are far from perfect.

This leads to the final topic of this chapter, children with special needs.

SUMMING UP

During middle childhood, neurological maturation allows faster, more automatic reactions. Selective attention enables focused concentration in school and in play. Aptitude tests, including IQ tests, compare mental age to chronological age, while actual learning is measured by achievement tests.

IQ scores change much more than was originally imagined, as children and cultures adapt to changing contexts. Some scientists believe that certain abilities, perhaps speed of thought and working memory, undergird general intelligence, known as *g*.

The concept that intelligence arises from one underlying aptitude is challenged by several scientists who believe that people have not just one type of intelligence but multiple intelligences. Further challenges to traditional IQ tests come from social scientists, who find marked cultural differences in what children are taught to do, and from neuroscientists, who see that brain activity does not reliably correlate with IQ scores. ■

>> Children with Special Needs

Developmental psychopathology links the study of usual development with the study of disorders (Cicchetti, 2013). Every topic already described, including "genetics, neuroscience, developmental psychology, . . . must be combined to understand how psychopathology develops and can be prevented" (Dodge, 2009, p. 413).

developmental psychopathology
The field that uses insights into typical development to understand and remediate developmental disorders.

>> Response for Teachers (from page 322): The advantages are that all the children learn more aspects of human knowledge and that many children can develop their talents. Art, music, and sports should be an integral part of education, not just a break from academics. The disadvantage is that they take time and attention away from reading and math, which might lead to less proficiency in those subjects on standard tests and thus to criticism from parents and supervisors.

comorbid Refers to the presence of two or more unrelated disease conditions at the same time in the same person.

At the outset, four general principles of developmental psychopathology should be emphasized.

1. *Abnormality is normal.* Most children sometimes act oddly. At the same time, children with serious disorders are, in many respects, like everyone else.
2. *Disability changes year by year.* Most disorders are **comorbid**, which means that more than one problem is evident in the same person. Which particular disorder is most disabling at a particular time changes, as does the degree of impairment.
3. *Life may be better or worse in adulthood.* Prognosis is difficult. Many children with severe disabilities (e.g., blindness) become productive adults. Conversely, some conditions (e.g., conduct disorder) may become more disabling.
4. *Diagnosis and treatment reflect the social context.* In dynamic systems, each individual interacts with the surrounding setting—including family, school, community, and culture—to modify, worsen, or even create psychopathology.

Causes and Consequences

Developmental psychopathology is a topic to be studied at every point of the life span because "[e]ach period of life, from the prenatal period through senescence, ushers in new biological and psychological challenges, strengths, and vulnerabilities" (Cicchetti, 2013, p. 458). Turning points, opportunities, and the influence of prior burdens appear at every age, as already noted in our discussion of epigenetics, of three forms of prevention, of environmental toxins, and of much else.

However, it is in middle childhood that children are first grouped by age and expected to start learning on schedule. For some parents and children, it suddenly becomes obvious that a particular child differs markedly from others the same age. Fortunately, most abnormalities can be mitigated if treatment is early and properly targeted.

Therein lies a problem: Although early treatment is more successful, early and accurate diagnosis is difficult, not only because many disorders are comorbid but also because symptoms differ by age. As you learned in Chapter 7, infants have temperamental differences that might or might not become problems, and Chapter 10 explained that some aggression is normal. When does unusual behavior signify a serious problem? Difference is not necessarily deficit—but not all differences are benign.

multifinality A basic principle of developmental psychopathology that holds that one cause can have many (multiple) final manifestations.

Two basic principles of developmental psychopathology lead to caution in diagnosis and treatment (Cicchetti & Toth, 2009; Cicchetti, 2013). First is **multifinality**, which means that one cause can have many (multiple) final manifestations. For example, an infant who has been flooded with stress hormones may become a hypervigilant or unusually calm kindergartener, may be easily angered or quick to cry, or may not be affected at all.

equifinality A basic principle of developmental psychopathology that holds that one symptom can have many causes.

The second principle is **equifinality** (equal in final form), which means that one symptom can have many causes. For instance, a nonverbal child may be autistic, hard of hearing, not comfortable in the dominant language, or pathologically shy.

The complexity of diagnosis is evident in the *Diagnostic and Statistical Manual of Mental Disorders*, 5th edition (American Psychiatric Association, 2013), often referred to as DSM-5. We focus now on only three disorders (attention-deficit/hyperactivity disorder, learning disability, and autism spectrum disorder) to illustrate the general principles just set forth. Appendix A lists the DSM-5 criteria for these three.

Attention-Deficit/Hyperactivity Disorder

Someone with **attention-deficit/hyperactivity disorder (ADHD)** consistently demonstrates a pattern of inattentiveness and may be unusually active and impulsive to the point of compromising their functioning or development. Compared with earlier criteria, the description of ADHD in DSM-5 allows more people to be diagnosed as having this disorder. For such a diagnosis, symptoms once had to start before age 7; now they must start before age 12. Earlier, ADHD had to *impair* daily life; now daily life simply needs to be *impacted*.

Essentially a child with ADHD is more easily distracted and more often in motion than the average child. For instance, when sitting down to do schoolwork, the child might look up, ask questions, get a drink, fidget, squirm, tap the table, jiggle his or her legs, and go to the bathroom—and then start the whole sequence again. This may be tolerated by parents but not by teachers in a crowded classroom. Not surprisingly, such children tend to have academic difficulties; they are less likely to graduate from high school and college, and as adults they are likely to suffer when employment demands sitting at a desk.

A River Is Better Than a School People must be quick and active to avoid capsizing in white-water rafting, but these children are up to the task. They have been diagnosed with ADHD, but they are quite able to respond to fast-changing currents.

attention-deficit/hyperactivity disorder (ADHD) A condition characterized by a persistent pattern of inattention and/or by hyperactive or impulsive behaviors; ADHD interferes with a person's functioning or development.

Problems with Diagnosis

A major problem in diagnosing ADHD is that there is no biological marker for it (such as a substance in the blood or an abnormality in the brain), yet some children find it almost impossible to sit quietly and concentrate. Those children might be punished and excluded because they are not like other children.

Moreover, ADHD is comorbid with many other conditions, including biological problems such as sleep deprivation or allergic reactions, and psychological disorders, including those soon to be discussed (Miklowitz & Cicchetti, 2010). This is an example of equifinality in that explosive rages and, later, deep regret are typical for children with many disorders, including ADHD.

Although the U.S. rates were about 5 percent in 1980, recent data find that 7 percent of all 4- to 9-year-olds, 13 percent of all 10- to 13-year-olds, and 15 percent of all 14- to 17-year-olds have been diagnosed with ADHD (Schwartz & Cohen, 2013). These numbers, called "astronomical" by a pediatric neurologist who is a professor at the Yale School of Medicine (Graf, quoted in Schwarz & Cohen, 2013), do not include children who are not yet diagnosed or whose primary diagnosis is something other than ADHD.

Rates of ADHD in most other nations are lower than in the United States, but they are rising everywhere (e.g., Al-Yagon et al., 2013; Hsia & Maclennan, 2009; van den Ban et al., 2010). Increases in ADHD diagnosis are worrisome for at least three reasons.

- *Misdiagnosis.* If ADHD is diagnosed when another disorder is the problem, treatment might make the problem worse, not better (Miklowitz & Cicchetti, 2010). Many psychoactive drugs alter moods, so a child with bipolar disorder (formerly called manic-depressive disorder) might be harmed by drugs that help children with ADHD.
- *Drug abuse.* Although alleviating the symptoms of ADHD with drugs actually reduces the incidence of later drug abuse, some adolescents may seek a diagnosis of ADHD in order to legally obtain amphetamines, which are often abused.

Especially for Health Workers Parents ask that some medication be prescribed for their kindergarten child, who they say is much too active for them to handle. How do you respond? (see response, page 328)

■ *Normal behavior considered pathological.* In young children, high activity, impulsiveness, and curiosity are normal but may be disruptive to parents or teachers. Some normal children, who will become more mature in time, may be convinced that they are abnormal. ADHD is at least twice as common among boys than among girls—might some unconscious sexism affect the diagnosis?

Treatment for ADHD involves (1) counseling and training for the family and the child, (2) showing teachers how to help the children learn, and (3) medication. But, as equifinality suggests, most disorders vary in causes so that treatment that helps one child does not necessarily work for another (Mulligan et al., 2013). Because many adults are upset by what young children normally do and because any physician can write a prescription to quiet a child, developmentalists fear that thousands of children are overmedicated.

Drug Treatment for ADHD and Other Disorders

The most common and also the most controversial treatment for many childhood disorders is medication. In the United States, more than 2 million people younger than 18 take prescription drugs to regulate their emotions and behavior. The rate is about 14 percent for teenagers (Merikangas et al., 2013), about 10 percent for 6- to 11-year-olds, and less than 1 percent for 2- to 5-year-olds (Olfson et al., 2010).

The most commonly prescribed drug for ADHD is Ritalin, but at least 20 other psychoactive drugs treat depression, anxiety, developmental delay, autism, bipolar disorder, and many other conditions in middle childhood. Because few psychoactive drugs have been adequately tested for children, many drugs are prescribed "off label"—that is, they are not approved for patients of a particular age or condition. Much of the American public is suspicious of any childhood psychiatric medicine (Moldavsky & Sayal, 2013; Rose, 2008), as are people worldwide. In China, for instance, parents rarely use psychoactive medication for children: A Chinese child with ADHD symptoms is thought to need correction rather than medication (Rongwang et al., 2013).

Many child psychologists believe that drugs can be helpful, and they worry that the public is oblivious to the devastation and lost learning that occur when a child's serious disorder is not recognized or treated. But they also raise concerns (Mayes et al., 2009). Finding the best drug at the right strength is difficult, in part because each child's genes and personality are unique.

Moreover, since weight and metabolism change every year, the right dose at one time is wrong at another. Only half of all children who take psychoactive drugs are evaluated and monitored by a mental health professional (Olfson et al., 2010).

Most developmentalists accept the research showing that medication helps children with emotional problems, particularly ADHD (Epstein et al., 2010). Many also believe that contextual interventions (instructing parents and teachers on child management) should be tried first (Daley et al., 2009; Leventhal, 2013; Pelham & Fabiano, 2008). Careful, individualized treatment is needed to find the right medication for each child.

By contrast, parents tend to be either pro-drug or antidrug and not in between. One study of parents whose children were diagnosed with ADHD found that about 20 percent believed drugs should *never* be used for children and that about 29 percent believed that drugs were *necessary* to treat illnesses (dosReis et al., 2009). Another study found that only about half (56 percent) of the parents of U.S. children who are diagnosed with ADHD give them medication every day (Scheffler et al., 2009).

African American and Hispanic children are less likely to be diagnosed with ADHD, especially when they do not have health insurance. When they are diagnosed, their parents are less likely to give them medication (Morgan et al., 2013). The reasons include fragmented medical care and distrust of doctors (Miller et al., 2009).

As a result of the discrepancy between public attitudes and research data, some children who would benefit from drugs are never medicated, and other children take medication without the necessary monitoring. Even with medication, problems may continue.

For example, a group of children with ADHD from many cities in the United States and Canada were given appropriate medication, carefully calibrated, and their symptoms improved. However, eight years later, many had stopped taking their medicine. At this follow-up, both those on medication and those who had stopped taking it often had learning difficulties (Molina et al., 2009).

When appropriately used, drugs for ADHD may help children make friends, learn in school, feel happier, and behave better. These drugs also seem to help adolescents and adults with ADHD (Surman et al., 2013). However, as the just cited longitudinal study of ADHD children found, problems do not disappear: adolescents and adults who were diagnosed with ADHD as children are less successful academically and personally, whether or not they were medicated (Brooke et al., 2013). Drugs may help, but they are not the solution. The following A Case to Study makes this clear.

A CASE TO STUDY

Lynda Is Getting Worse

Even experts differ in diagnosis and treatment. For instance, one study asked 158 child psychologists to diagnose an 11-year-old girl with the following symptoms.

> Parents say Lynda has been hyperactive, with poor boundaries and disinhibited behavior since she was a toddler. . . . Lynda has taken several stimulants since age 8. She is behind in her school work, but IQ normal. . . . At school she is oppositional and "lazy" but not disruptive in class. Psychological testing, age 8, described frequent impulsivity, tendencies to discuss topics unrelated to tasks she was completing, intermittent expression of anger and anxiety, significantly elevated levels of physical activity, difficulties sitting still, and touching everything. Over the past year Lynda has become very angry, irritable, destructive and capricious. She is provocative and can be cruel to pets and small children. She has been sexually inappropriate with peers and families, including expressing interest in lewd material on the Internet, Play Girl magazine, hugging and kissing peers. She appears to be grandiose, telling her family that she will be attending medical school, or will become a record producer, a professional wrestler, or an acrobat. Throughout this period there have been substantial marital difficulties between the parents.
>
> [Dubicka et al., 2008, appendix p. 3]

What is the problem here? Most (81 percent) of the clinicians diagnosing Lynda thought she had ADHD, and most thought she had another disorder as well. In this study, about half of the clinicians were British, and half American.

The Americans were much more likely to suggest a second and third disorder, with 75 percent of them specifying bipolar disorder. Only 33 percent of the British psychologists agreed, although they were more likely to diagnose an adjustment disorder (Dubicka et al., 2008).

From a developmental perspective, it is noteworthy, but not unusual, that the family context or teacher's attitudes do not seem to be reflected in the diagnoses of the clinicians. Testing at age 8 seems to have focused only on Lynda, not on the parents. Lynda is in regular classes at school. In fact, for both nature and nurture reasons, parents who have ADHD or mood disorders are more likely to have children with disorders, and it would have made sense for the parents to be tested and perhaps treated.

In this case, her parents thought Lynda had ADHD since toddlerhood; a pediatrician agreed and at age 8 put her on drugs. Now, at age 11, she seems to be getting worse, not better, while her parents are increasingly hostile to each other. The experts differ, partly because of cultural differences.

It is impossible to know what would have happened if intensive intervention had taken place for the entire family when Lynda was a toddler. Using a family-systems, life-span perspective, it is possible that marital problems would not have appeared if a parental alliance had developed early on to help Lynda. In any case, the four principles of developmental psychopathology suggest that developmental patterns and social contexts needed to be considered. That might have led to improvement, as apparently three years of medication did not.

>> Response for Health Workers
(from page 326): Medication helps some
hyperactive children but not all. It might
be useful for this child, but other forms of
intervention should be tried first. Compliment
the parents on their concern about their child,
but refer them to an expert in early childhood
for an evaluation and recommendations.
Behavior-management techniques geared to
the particular situation, not medication, is the
first strategy.

**specific learning disorder (learning
disability)** A marked deficit in a particular
area of learning that is not caused by
an apparent physical disability, by an
intellectual disability, or by an unusually
stressful home environment.

dyslexia Unusual difficulty with reading;
thought to be the result of some neurological underdevelopment.

Happy Reading Those large prism glasses
keep the letters from jumping around on the
page, a boon for this 8-year-old French boy.
Unfortunately, each child with dyslexia needs
individualized treatment: These glasses
help some, but not most, children who find
reading difficult.

dyscalculia Unusual difficulty with math,
probably originating from a distinct part of
the brain.

Specific Learning Disorders

The DSM-5 diagnosis of **specific learning disorder** now includes deficits in
both perception and processing of information, which leads to lower achievement than expected in any of several academic areas. Learning disorders make
it difficult for someone to master a particular skill that most other people
acquire easily. According to Gardner's view of multiple intelligences, almost
everyone has a specific inadequacy or two. Perhaps one person is clumsy (low
in kinesthetic intelligence), while another sings loudly but off key (low in
musical intelligence).

Most learning disorders are not debilitating (e.g., the off-key singer learns to
be quiet in chorus), but every schoolchild is expected to learn reading and math.
Disabilities in either of these two subjects undercut academic achievement and
make a child feel inadequate, ashamed, and stupid. Hopefully, such children find
(or are taught) ways to compensate: They learn coping strategies, and in adulthood their other abilities shine. Winston Churchill, Albert Einstein, and Hans
Christian Andersen are all said to have had learning disabilities as children.

Dyslexia

The most commonly diagnosed learning disability is **dyslexia**—unusual difficulty with reading. No single test accurately diagnoses dyslexia (or any learning
disability) because every academic achievement involves many distinct factors
(Riccio & Rodriguez, 2007). One child with a reading disability
might have trouble sounding out words but might excel in comprehension and memory of printed text; another child might have
the opposite problem. Dozens of types and causes of dyslexia
have been identified.

Early theories hypothesized that visual difficulties—for example, reversals of letters (reading *was* instead of *saw*) and mirror writing (*b* instead of *d*)—were the cause of dyslexia, but we
now know that dyslexia often originates with speech and hearing
difficulties (Gabrieli, 2009). An early warning occurs if a 3-year-
old does not talk clearly or has not exhibited a naming explosion.
[**Lifespan Link:** The naming explosion and the sequence of language acquisition are explained in Chapter 6.] Not only might
early speech therapy improve talking, but it might also reduce or
prevent later dyslexia.

Traditionally, dyslexia was diagnosed only if a child had difficulty reading despite normal IQ, normal hearing and sight, and normal behavior.
However, DSM-5 allows comorbid diagnosis, and many children with ADHD are
diagnosed with a learning disability (DuPaul et al., 2013). Indeed, in the United
States, children with ADHD are not granted special education but children with
speech or learning disabilities are, so a comorbid diagnosis is often sought.

Dyscalculia

Similar suggestions apply to learning disabilities in math, called **dyscalculia**.
Dyslexia and dyscalculia are often comorbid, although each originates from a distinct part of the brain. Early help with counting and math concepts (long before
first grade) can help prevent the emotional anxiety that occurs if a child is made to
feel stupid (Butterworth et al., 2011).

Remember that in early childhood most children can look at a series of dots
and estimate how many there are. Perhaps even in infancy, a child with dyscalculia cannot estimate how many dots are present. Basic number sense is deficient

in children with dyscalculia, which provides a clue for early remediation (Piazza et al., 2010).

When a young child has trouble performing math tasks that other children can do easily, dyscalculia is suspected. For example, a second-grader, when asked to estimate the height of a normal room, might answer "200 feet" or, when asked whether the 5 or the 8 of Hearts is higher, might correctly answer 8—but only after counting the number of hearts on each card (Butterworth et al., 2011). Some children with dyscalculia improve when computer programs are designed to improve their number understanding, but—remember equifinality—this does not help every child.

Every person, learning disabled or not, has strengths and interests, and almost everyone can learn basic skills if they have extensive and specific help, encouragement, and practice. The problem with learning disabilities is that most children are not diagnosed early enough, with sufficient detail, or given individualized education.

Autism Spectrum Disorder

Of all the children with special needs, those with **autism spectrum disorder (ASD)** are probably the most troubling. Their problems are severe and the causes of and treatments for autism are hotly disputed.

Most children with autism can be spotted in the first year of life, but some seem normal and only later does autism become evident. Many children with symptoms of autism but who learned to talk on time were formerly considered to have Asperger syndrome. Now the diagnosis would be "autism spectrum disorder without language or intellectual impairment" (DSM-5, p. 32).

Symptoms

Autism is characterized by woefully inadequate social understanding. Almost a century ago, it was considered a single, rare disorder affecting fewer than 1 in 1,000 children with "an extreme aloneness that, whenever possible, disregards, ignores, shuts out anything . . . from the outside" (Kanner, 1943). Children who developed slowly but were not so withdrawn were diagnosed as being mentally retarded or as having a "pervasive developmental disorder." (Note that the term "mental retardation," which was used in DSM-4, has been replaced with "intellectual disability" in DSM-5.)

Much has changed in the past decades. Now many children who would have been considered intellectually disabled are said to have an autism spectrum disorder, which characterizes as many as 1 in every 88 children (almost five times as many boys as girls and about a third more European Americans than Hispanic, Asian, or African Americans) (Lord & Bishop, 2010). Some children "on the spectrum" do not seem to be intellectually delayed.

The two main signs of an autism spectrum disorder are: (1) problems in social interaction and the social use of language, and (2) restricted, repetitive patterns of behavior, interests, and activities. Children with any form of ASD find it difficult to understand the emotions of others, which makes them feel alien, like "an anthropologist on Mars," as Temple Grandin, an educator and writer with autism, expressed it (quoted in Sacks, 1995). Consequently, they are less likely to talk, play, or otherwise interact with anyone, and they usually are delayed in developing a theory of mind (Senju et al., 2010).

Autism spectrum disorders include many symptoms of varied severity. Some children never speak, rarely smile, and often play for hours with one object (such as a spinning top or a toy train). Others are called "high functioning";

autism spectrum disorder A developmental disorder marked by difficulty with social communication and interaction—including difficulty seeing things from another person's point of view—and restricted, repetitive patterns of behavior, interests, or activities.

Precious Gifts Many children with autism are gifted artists. This boy attends a school in Montmoreau, France, that features workshops in which children with autism develop social, play, and learning skills.

they are often extremely talented in some specialized area, such as drawing or geometry. Many are brilliant in unusual ways (Dawson et al., 2007), including Grandin, a well-respected expert on animal care (Grandin & Johnson, 2009). However, social interaction is always impaired. Grandin was bewildered by romantic love.

Most children with autism spectrum disorder show signs in early infancy (no social smile, for example, or less gazing at faces). Some improve by age 3, whereas others deteriorate. Amazingly, 40 percent of parents who were told their child has autism said later that their child no longer had it (Kogan et al., 2009). On the other hand, late onset of autism spectrum disorder occurs with *Rett syndrome,* in which a newborn girl (never a boy; they do not survive if they have the X-linked Rett gene) has "apparently normal psychomotor development through the first 5 months after birth," but then her brain develops much more slowly than normal, severely limiting movement and language (Bienvenu, 2005).

Many children with autism have an opposite problem—too much neurological activity, not too little. Their heads are slightly larger than average, and parts of their brain (especially the limbic system) are unusually sensitive to noise, light, and other sensations (Schumann et al., 2004).

Far more children have autism spectrum disorders now than in 1990, either because the incidence of this disorder has increased or because more children receive that diagnosis. The new criteria in DSM-5 will probably decrease the number of children who fit the category, especially those who function well in most situations (Bauminger-Zviely, 2013).

Underlying that estimate is the reality that no definitive measure diagnoses autistic spectrum disorder: Many adults are socially inept, insensitive to other people's emotions, and poor at communication—are they all on the spectrum?

Treatment

When a child is diagnosed with ASD, parents' responses vary from irrational hope to deep despair, from blaming doctors and chemical additives to feeling guilty for what they did wrong. Developmentalists generally believe that genes are one factor in autism but that parents are not at fault. Parents and teachers can be very helpful, however, if they cooperate with one another while the child is young. Even when all the adults work in harmony, treatment is complicated.

Equifinality certainly applies to autism: A child can have autistic symptoms for many reasons, which makes treatment difficult, as an intervention that seems to help one child proves worthless for another. It is known, however, that biology is crucial (genes, birth complications, prenatal injury, or perhaps chemicals) and that family nurture is not the cause (G. Dawson, 2010). One family factor may be influential, however: having one baby soon after another. Children born less than a year after a previous birth are more than twice as likely to be diagnosed as autistic compared with children born three or more years later (Cheslack-Postava et al., 2011).

A vast number of treatments have been used to help children with autism spectrum disorders, but none of them has been completely successful. Some parents are convinced that a particular treatment helped their child, whereas other parents say that the same treatment failed.

Scientists disagree as well. For instance, one popular treatment is putting the child in a hyperbaric chamber to breathe more concentrated oxygen than is found in everyday air. Two studies of hyperbaric treatments—both randomized in participant selection and both with control groups—reported contradictory results, either benefits (Rossignol et al., 2009) or no effect (Granpeesheh et al., 2010).

Treatment is further complicated when parents and medical professionals disagree, as illustrated by the controversy about thimerosal, an antiseptic containing mercury that was formerly used in childhood immunizations. Many parents of children with the symptoms of autism first noticed their infants' impairments after their vaccinations and believed thimerosal was the cause. No scientist who examines the evidence agrees: Extensive research has disproven the immunization hypothesis many times (Offit, 2008).

More than a decade ago thimerosal was removed from vaccines given to infants, but the rates of autism are still rising. Many doctors fear that parents who cling to this hypothesis are not only wrong but are also harming millions of children who suffer needless illnesses because their parents refuse to immunize them.

Some children with autism are treated biologically, with special diets, vitamin supplements, hormones (oxytocin), or psychoactive drugs. Each of these strategies is used by some advocates who find symptoms improving, but none has proven successful at relieving the basic condition.

Many behavioral methods to improve talking and socialization have also been tried, again with mixed results (Granpeesheh et al., 2009; Hayward et al., 2009; Howlin et al., 2009). Early and individualized education of both the child and the parents has had some success.

All Together Now Kiemel Lamb (top center) leads autistic children in song, a major accomplishment. For many autistic children, music is soothing, words are difficult, and handholding in a group is almost impossible.

Special Education

The overlap of the biosocial, cognitive, and psychosocial domains is evident to developmentalists, who envision each child's growth in every area as affected by the other areas. However, whether or not a child is designated as needing special education is not straightforward, nor is it closely related to specific special needs.

Changing Laws and Practices

In the United States, recognition that the distinction between normal and abnormal is not clear-cut (the first principle of developmental psychopathology) led to a series of reforms in the treatment and education of children with special needs. According to the 1975 Education of All Handicapped Children Act, children with special needs must be educated in the **least restrictive environment (LRE).**

LRE has usually meant educating children with special needs in a regular class, a practice once called *mainstreaming,* rather than in a special classroom or school. Sometimes a child is sent to a *resource room,* with a teacher who provides targeted tutoring. Sometimes a class is an *inclusion class,* which means that children with special needs are "included" in the general classroom, with "appropriate aids and services" (ideally from a trained teacher who works with the regular teacher) (Kalambouka et al., 2007).

The latest educational strategy in the United States is called **response to intervention (RTI)** (Fletcher & Vaughn, 2009; Shapiro et al., 2011; Ikeda, 2012). All children in the early grades who are below average in achievement (which may

least restrictive environment (LRE) A legal requirement that children with special needs be assigned to the most general educational context in which they can be expected to learn.

response to intervention (RTI) An educational strategy intended to help children who demonstrate below-average achievement in early grades, using special intervention.

THE TUSCALOOSA NEWS, DUSTY COMPTON/AP PHOTO

individual education plan (IEP) A document that specifies educational goals and plans for a child with special needs.

be half the class) are given some special intervention. Most of them respond by improving their achievement, but for those who do not, more intervention occurs. If there is no response to repeated intervention, the child is referred for testing and observation to diagnose the problem.

Professionals use a battery of tests (not just IQ or achievement tests) to reach their diagnosis and develop recommendations. If they find that a child has special needs, they discuss an **individual education plan (IEP)** with the parents, to specify educational goals for the child.

Cohort and Culture

Developmentalists consider a child's biological and brain development as the starting point for whatever special assistance will allow the child to reach his or her full potential. Thus home and school practices are crucial.

Among all the children in the United States who are recognized by educators as having special needs, historical shifts are notable. As Figure 11.5 shows, the proportion of children designated with special needs rose in the United States from 10 percent in 1980 to 13 percent in 2011, primarily because more children are considered learning disabled (National Center for Education Statistics, 2013). In 1975 the number was only 8 percent.

In 1980 almost one in 5 of the children that the school system categorized as having special needs was intellectually disabled. That category continues to shrink: in 2011 only one child in 14 was so designated. Autism and developmental delay were not recognized in 1980, but these diagnoses have increased notably since they were first introduced. Children with these disorders in 1980 were probably categorized as intellectually disabled (then called mentally retarded).

FIGURE 11.5

Percent of 3- to 21-Year Old Children with Special Educational Needs (Compared to Total Public School Enrollment)
Nature or Nurture Communities have always has some children with special needs, with physical, emotional, and neurological disorders of many kinds. In some eras, and even today in some nations, the education of such children was neglected. Indeed, many children were excluded from normal life even before they quit trying. Now in the United States every child is entitled to school. As you see, the specific label for such children has changed over the past decades, probably because of nurture, not nature. Thus teratogens before and after birth, coupled with changing parental and community practice, probably caused the rise in autism and developmental delay, the decrease in intellectual disability, and the fluctuation in learning disabilities apparent here.

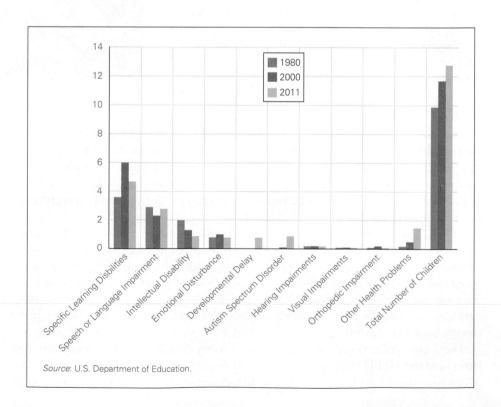

Source: U.S. Department of Education.

It is possible that contemporary children have a markedly different mix of special needs, but it is more likely that some rates have changed because the labels have changed. Note that there is still no separate category for ADHD. To receive special services, children with ADHD usually have to prove they are learning disabled.

In the international arena, the connection between special needs and education varies for cultural reasons, not child-related ones. In many African and Latin American nations, no children are given special education; in many Asian nations, diagnosis refers primarily to physically disability. As a result, in Taiwan, for example, less than 1 percent of the students receive special education of any kind (Tzeng, 2007).

Gifted and Talented

Children who are unusually gifted are often thought to have special needs as well, but they are not covered by the federal laws. Instead, each state of the United States selects and educates gifted and talented children in a particular way, a variation that leads to controversy.

A scholar writes: "The term *gifted* . . . has never been more problematic than it is today" (Dai, 2011, p. 8). Educators, political leaders, scientists, and everyone else argue about who is gifted and what should be done about them. Are gifted children unusually intelligent, or talented, or creative? Should they be skipped, segregated, enriched, or left alone?

A hundred years ago, the definition of gifted was simple: high IQ. A famous longitudinal study followed a thousand "genius" children, all of whom scored about 140 on the Stanford-Binet IQ test (Terman, 1925). Even today, some school systems define gifted as having an IQ of 130 or above (attained by 1 child in 50), or sometimes as 145 and above (1 child in 1,000).

A hundred years ago, school placement was simple, too: The gifted were taught with children who were their mental age, not their chronological age. This practice was called **acceleration**. Today that is rarely done because many accelerated children were bullied, unhappy, and never learned how to get along with others. As one woman remembers:

> Nine-year-old little girls are so cruel to younger girls. I was much smaller than them, of course, and would have done anything to have a friend. Although I could cope with the academic work very easily, emotionally I wasn't up to it. Maybe it was my fault and I was asking to be picked on. I was a weed at the edge of the playground.
>
> *[Rachel, quoted in Freeman, 2010, p. 27]*

Weeds grow no matter where they are planted, and research on thousands of children has found that while the gifted learn differently from other children, they are neither more nor less likely to need emotional and social education. Educating the whole child, not just the mind, is required (Winner, 1996).

Another type of special child is designated *precocious* in one of Gardner's nine intelligences. Such children are often called talented instead of gifted. Mozart was one, composing music at age 3; so was Pablo Picasso, creating works of art at age 4.

Historically, many famous musicians, artists, and scientists were child prodigies whose fathers recognized their talent (often because the father was talented) and taught them. Mozart's father transcribed his earliest pieces and toured Europe with his gifted son. Picasso's father removed him from school

acceleration Educating gifted children alongside other children of the same mental, not chronological, age.

Gifted. Then What? Mercan Türkoğlu holds her Bambi, the German equivalent of an Oscar, awarded for her star performance in the film *Three Quarter Moon*. She is German of Turkish ancestry, Muslim, and a talented actress. What education will best prepare her for adulthood?

in second grade so he could create all day (Pablo said he never learned to read or write).

Although such intense early education nourished talent, neither Mozart nor Picasso had happy adult lives. Similar patterns are still apparent, as exemplified by gifted athletes (e.g., Tiger Woods and Steffi Graf) as well as those in more erudite specialties. Here is one example:

> Sufiah Yusof started her maths degree at Oxford [the leading University in England] in 2000, at the age of 13. She too had been dominated and taught by her father. But she ran away the day after her final exam. She was found by police but refused to go home, demanding of her father in an email: "Has it ever crossed your mind that the reason I left home was because I've finally had enough of 15 years of physical and emotional abuse?" Her father claimed she'd been abducted and brainwashed. She refuses to communicate with him. She is now a very happy, high-class, high-earning prostitute.
>
> *[Freeman, 2010, p. 286]*

A third kind of child who might need special education is the unusually creative one (Sternberg et al., 2011). They are *divergent thinkers*, finding many solutions and even more questions for every problem. Such students joke in class, resist drudgery, ignore homework, and bedevil their teachers. They may become innovators, inventors, and creative forces of the future.

Creative children do not conform to social standards. They are not *convergent thinkers,* who choose the correct answer on school exams. One such person was Charles Darwin, whose "school reports complained unendingly that he wasn't interested in studying, only shooting, riding, and beetle-collecting" (Freeman, 2010, p. 283). Other creative geniuses who were poor students are Einstein, Freud, Newton, and almost every contemporary innovator. What should be done about them in school?

Since both acceleration and intense parental tutoring have led to later problems, a third education strategy has become popular, at least in the United States. Children who are bright, talented, and/or creative—all the same age but each with special abilities—are taught as a special group in their own classroom. Ideally, such children are neither bored nor lonely; each is challenged and appreciated by their classmates.

Neuroscience has recently discovered another advantage to gifted classes: brain development. Children who practice musical talents in early childhood develop specialized brain structures, as do child athletes and mathematicians. This suggests that neurological specialization occurs for every form of giftedness. Since plasticity means that all children learn whatever their context teaches, talents may be developed, not wasted, with special education.

Classes for gifted students require unusual teachers, bright and creative, able to appreciate divergent thinking and challenge the very bright. They must be flexible: providing a 7-year-old artist freedom, guidance, and inspiration for magnificent art and simultaneously providing patient, step-by-step reading instruction if that same child is a typical new reader. Similarly, a 7-year-old who reads at the twelfth-grade level might have immature social skills, needing a teacher who finds another child to befriend him or her, and who then helps both of them share, compromise, and take turns.

Flexible teachers must be carefully selected and chosen for gifted and talented children. However, every child may need such teachers, no matter what the child's abilities or disabilities may be.

Some nations educate all children together, assuming that intelligence is not a matter of some children being unusually gifted as much as some children putting more effort into learning. Thus the teacher's job is to motivate and challenge every child. Some gifted children benefit from special recognition in school, and some would be much better off if they were left alone, without teachers or parents expecting them to excel (Freeman, 2010).

As the Education of All Handicapped Children law states, all children can learn. But not all schools and teachers successfully teach them. Every special and ordinary form of education can benefit from what we know about children's minds and how they learn (De Corte, 2013). That is the topic of the next chapter.

SUMMING UP

Many children have special learning needs that originate with problems in the development of their brains. Developmental psychopathologists emphasize that no one is typical in every way; the passage of time sometimes brings improvement to children with special needs and sometimes not. Children with attention-deficit/hyperactivity disorder, learning disabilities, and autism spectrum disorders may function adequately as adults or may have lifelong problems, depending on many variables, including (1) the severity of the problem, (2) family support, (3) school strategies (4) comorbid conditions. Specifics of diagnosis, prognosis, medication, and education are debatable; no child learns or behaves exactly like another, and no educational strategy always succeeds. Various strategies are apparent not only for children with disabilities but also for those who are unusually gifted and talented. ∎

SUMMARY

A Healthy Time

1. Middle childhood is a time of steady growth and few serious illnesses. Increasing independence and self-care allow most school-age children to be relatively happy and competent.

2. Advances in medical care, including effective immunization, have reduced childhood sickness and death.

3. Physical activity aids health and joy in many ways. However, current social and environmental conditions make informal neighborhood play rare and school physical education less prevalent.

Health Problems in Middle Childhood

4. Childhood obesity is a worldwide epidemic. Although genes are part of the problem, too little exercise and the greater availability of unhealthy foods are the main reasons today's youth are heavier than their counterparts of 50 years ago. Parents and policies share the blame.

5. The incidence of asthma is increasing overall, with notable ethnic differences. The origins of asthma are genetic; the triggers are specific environmental allergens. Preventive measures include longer breast-feeding, increased outdoor play, and less air pollution, particularly from cars.

Brain Development

6. Brain development continues during middle childhood, enhancing every aspect of development. Notable are advances in reaction time and automatization, allowing faster and better coordination of many parts of the brain.

7. IQ tests quantify intellectual aptitude. Most such tests emphasize language and logic ability and predict school achievement. IQ scores sometimes change over time, partly because of maturation but primarily because of experience.

8. Achievement tests measure accomplishment, often in specific academic areas. Aptitude and achievement are correlated, both for individuals and for nations, and have risen in the past decades.

9. Critics contend that intelligence is manifested in multiple ways, which makes conventional IQ tests too narrow and limited. Multiple intelligences include creative and practical abilities as well as many skills not usually valued in typical North American schools.

Children with Special Needs

10. Developmental psychopathology uses an understanding of normal development to inform the study of unusual development. Four general lessons have emerged: Abnormality is normal; disability changes over time; a condition may get better or worse in adolescence and adulthood; diagnosis depends on context.

11. Children with attention-deficit/hyperactivity disorder (ADHD) have potential problems in three areas: inattention, impulsiveness, and overactivity. Stimulant medication often helps children with ADHD to learn, but any drug use by children must be carefully monitored.

12. People with a specific learning disability have unusual difficulty in mastering a specific skill or skills that other people learn easily. The most common learning disabilities that impair achievement in middle childhood are dyslexia, unusual difficulty with reading, and dyscalculia, difficulty with math.

13. Children with autism spectrum disorder typically have problems with social interactions and the social use of language. They often exhibit restricted, repetitive patterns of behavior, interests, and activities. Many causes are hypothesized. Autism is partly genetic; no one now views autism as primarily the result of inadequate parenting. Treatments are diverse: All are controversial and none are certain to help.

14. About 13 percent of all school-age children in the United States receive special education services. These services begin with an IEP (individual education plan) and assignment to the least restrictive environment (LRE), usually the regular classroom.

15. Some children are unusually intelligent, talented, or creative, and states and nations provide special education for them. Specifics of that education vary and are controversial.

KEY TERMS

acceleration (p. 333)
achievement test (p. 320)
aptitude (p. 320)
attention-deficit/hyperactivity disorder (ADHD) (p. 325)
asthma (p. 317)
autism spectrum disorder (p. 329)
automatization (p. 320)

childhood obesity (p. 313)
childhood overweight (p. 313)
comorbid (p. 324)
developmental psychopathology (p. 323)
dyscalculia (p. 328)
dyslexia (p. 328)
equifinality (p. 324)

Flynn effect (p. 321)
individual education plan (IEP) (p. 332)
IQ test (p. 320)
least restrictive environment (LRE) (p. 331)
middle childhood (p. 309)
multifinality (p. 324)

multiple intelligences (p. 321)
reaction time (p. 319)
response to intervention (RTI) (p. 331)
selective attention (p. 319)
specific learning disorder (learning disability) (p. 328)

WHAT HAVE YOU LEARNED?

1. What physical abilities emerge from age 6 to age 11?

2. How do childhood health habits affect adult health?

3. What are the main advantages and disadvantages of physical play during middle childhood?

4. How do children benefit from physical education in school?

5. What are the national and cohort differences in childhood obesity?

6. Why does a thin 6-year-old have no need to fatten up?

7. What roles do nature and nurture play in childhood asthma?

8. What would be primary prevention for childhood obesity?

9. Why does good tertiary prevention for childhood asthma not reach every child who needs it?

10. Why does quicker reaction time improve the ability to learn?

11. How does selective attention make it easier for a child to sit in a classroom?

12. When would a teacher give an aptitude test instead of an achievement test?

13. If the theory of multiple intelligences is correct, should IQ tests be discarded? Why or why not?

14. Which intellectual abilities are more valued than others? Give examples.

15. Should brain scans replace traditional intelligence tests? Why or why not?

16. How does normal childhood behavior differ between the United States and Asia?

17. What is the difference between multifinality and equifinality?

18. Why is medication recommended for children with ADHD?

19. Why might parents ask a doctor to prescribe Ritalin for their child?

20. What are dyslexia and dyscalculia?

21. When might an adult have a learning disability that has never been diagnosed?

22. If an adult with autism spectrum disorder is high-functioning, what kind of profession and what sort of family life would you expect him or her to have?

23. What are the three primary signs of autism spectrum disorder?

APPLICATIONS

1. Compare play spaces for children in different neighborhoods—ideally, urban, suburban, and rural areas. Note size, safety, and use. How might children's weight and motor skills be affected by the differences you observe?

2. Developmental psychologists believe that every teacher should be skilled at teaching children with a wide variety of needs. Does the teacher-training curriculum at your college or university reflect this goal? Should all teachers take the same courses, or should some teachers be specialized? Give reasons for your opinions.

3. Internet sources on any topic vary in quality, but this may be particularly true of websites designed for parents of children with special needs. Pick one childhood disability or disease and find several Web sources devoted to that condition. How might parents evaluate the information provided?

4. Special education teachers are in great demand. In your local public school, what is the ratio of regular to special education teachers? How many of those special education teachers are in self-contained classrooms, resource rooms, and inclusion classrooms? What do your data reveal about the education of children with special needs in your community?

>> ONLINE CONNECTIONS

To accompany your textbook, you have access to a number of online resources, including Learning Curve, an adaptive quizzing program, critical thinking questions, and case studies. For access to any of these links, go to www.worthpublishers.com/launchpad/bergerls9e. In addition to these resources, you'll also find links to video clips, personalized study advice, and an ebook. Some of the videos and activities available online include:

- *Educating the Girls of the World.* Girls around the world talk about the challenges that hinder their enrolment in all levels of education. Highlights initiatives for change.

WORTH PUBLISHERS

Middle Childhood: Cognitive Development

■ Building on Theory
Piaget and School-Age Children
Vygotsky and School-Age Children
Information Processing
A VIEW FROM SCIENCE:
Balls Rolling Down

■ Language
Vocabulary
Differences in Language Learning
A CASE TO STUDY: Two Immigrants

■ Teaching and Learning
International Schooling
In the United States
Choices and Complications

WHAT WILL YOU KNOW?

1. Does cognition improve naturally with age, or is teaching crucial to its development?

2. Do children learn best from experience or from explicit instruction?

3. Why do children use slang, curses words, and bad grammar?

4. What type of school is best during middle childhood?

At age 9, I wanted a puppy. My parents said no, we already had Dusty, our family dog. I dashed off a poem, promising "to brush his hair as smooth as silk" and "to feed him milk." Twice wrong. Not only poor cadence, but also puppies get sick on cow's milk. But my father praised my poem; I got Taffy, a blonde cocker spaniel.

At age 10, Sarah wanted her ears pierced. I said no, it would be unfair to her three older sisters, who had had to wait for ear piercing until they were teenagers. Sarah wrote an affidavit and persuaded all three to sign "no objection." She got gold posts.

Our wishes differed by cohort and our strategies by family. Sarah knew I wouldn't budge for doggerel but that signed documents might work. However, we were both typical school-age children, mastering whatever circumstances offer. Depending on the context, children learn to divide fractions, text friends, memorize baseball stats, load rifles, and persuade parents.

This chapter describes those cognitive accomplishments. We begin with Piaget, Vygotsky, and information processing. Then we discuss applications of those theories to language and formal education, nationally and internationally. Everyone agrees that extensive learning occurs; adults disagree sharply about how best to teach.

>> Building on Theory

Learning is rapid. By age 11, some children beat their elders at chess, play music that adults pay to hear, publish poems, win trophies. Others survive on the streets or kill in wars, learning lessons that no child should know. How do they learn so quickly?

Piaget and School-Age Children

Piaget called the cognition of middle childhood **concrete operational thought**, characterized by new concepts that enable children to use logic. *Operational* comes from the Latin word *operare*, meaning "to work; to produce." By calling this period operational, Piaget emphasized productive thinking.

The school-age child, no longer limited by egocentrism, performs logical operations. Children apply their new reasoning skills to *concrete* situations. Those are situations that are concrete, like a

concrete operational thought Piaget's term for the ability to reason logically about direct experiences and perceptions.

Product of Cognition Concrete thinking is specific, such as caring for a lamb until it becomes an award-winning sheep, as this New Jersey 4-H member did.

Left: Holger Winkler/Corbis
Top: George Doyle/Getty Images

cement sidewalk; they are visible, tangible, and real (not abstract). A shift from preoperational to concrete operational occurs between ages 5 and 7: Children become more systematic, objective, scientific—and educable.

A Hierarchy of Categories

classification The logical principle that things can be organized into groups (or categories or classes) according to some characteristic they have in common.

One logical operation is **classification**, the organization of things into groups (or *categories* or *classes*) according to some characteristic that they share. For example, *family* includes parents, siblings, and cousins. Other common classes are animals, toys, and food. Each class includes some elements and excludes others; each is part of a hierarchy.

Food, for instance, is an overarching category, with the next-lower level of the hierarchy being meat, grains, fruits, and so on. Most subclasses can be further divided: Meat includes poultry, beef, and pork, each of which can be divided again. Adults realize that items at the bottom of a classification hierarchy belong to every higher level: Bacon is always pork, meat, and food, but most food, meat, and pork are not bacon. However, the mental operation of moving up and down the hierarchy are beyond preoperational children.

Piaget devised many classification experiments. For example, a child is shown a bunch of nine flowers—seven yellow daisies and two white roses. Then the child is asked: "Are there more daisies or more flowers?"

Until about age 7, most children answer, "More daisies." The youngest children offer no justification, but some 6-year-olds explain that "there are more yellow ones than white ones" or "because daisies are daisies, they aren't flowers" (Piaget et al., 2001). By age 8, most children can classify: "More flowers than daisies," they say.

seriation The concept that things can be arranged in a logical series, such as the number sequence or the alphabet.

Other Logical Concepts

Several logical concepts were already discussed in Chapter 9 in the explanation of ideas that are beyond preoperational children, such as conservation and reversibility.

Another example of concrete logic is **seriation**, the knowledge that things can be arranged in a logical *series*. Seriation is crucial for using (not merely memorizing) the alphabet or the number sequence. By age 5, most children can count up to 100, but because they do not yet grasp seriation they cannot correctly estimate where any particular two-digit number would be placed on a line that starts at 0 and ends at 100 (Meadows, 2006).

Concrete operational thought correlates with primary school math achievement, although many other factors contribute (Desoete et al., 2009). For example, logic helps with arithmetic: Children at the stage of concrete operational thought eventually understand that $12 + 3 = 3 + 12$, and that 15 is always 15 (both conservation), that all the numbers from 20 to 29 are in the 20s (classification), that 134 is lower than 143 (seriation), and that if $5 \times 3 = 15$, then $15 \div 5$ is 3 (reversibility). [**Lifespan Link:** These four concepts are explained in Chapter 9.]

Math and Money Third-grader Perry Akootchook understands basic math, so he might beat his mother at "spinning for money," shown here. Compare his concrete operational skills with that of a typical preoperational child, who would not be able to play this game and might give a dime for a nickel.

The Significance of Piaget's Findings

Although logic connects to math, researchers find more continuity than discontinuity as children master number skills. Thus, Piaget's stage idea was mistaken: There is no sudden shift between preoperational and concrete operational intelligence.

Nonetheless, Piaget's experiments revealed something important. School-age children use mental categories and subcategories more flexibly, inductively, and simultaneously than younger children can. They are more advanced thinkers, capable in ways that younger children are not.

Vygotsky and School-Age Children

Like Piaget, Vygotsky felt that educators should consider children's thought processes, not just the outcomes. He appreciated the fact that children are curious, creative learners. For that reason, Vygotsky believed that an educational system based on rote memorization rendered the child "helpless in the face of any sensible attempt to apply any of this acquired knowledge" (Vygotsky, 1934/1994, pp. 356–357).

The Role of Instruction

Unlike Piaget, Vygotsky stressed the centrality of instruction. For Vygotsky, school can be crucial for cognitive growth. He thought that peers and teachers provide the bridge between developmental potential and needed skills via guided participation and scaffolding, in the zone of proximal development. [**Lifespan Link:** Vygotsky's theory is discussed in Chapters 2 and 9.]

Confirmation of the role of social interaction and instruction comes from a U.S. study of children who, because of their school's entry-date cutoff, are either relatively old kindergartners or quite young first-graders. At the end of the school year, achievement scores of the 6-year-old first-graders far exceeded those of kindergarten 6-year-olds who were only one month younger (Lincove & Painter, 2006). Obviously, they had learned a great deal from first grade.

Internationally as well, children who begin first grade earlier tend to be ahead in academic achievement compared to those who enter later, an effect noted even at age 15. The author of this study noted that Vygotsky's explanation is not the only one, and that these results were not found in every nation (Sprietsma, 2010). However, no matter what explanation is correct, children's academic achievement seems influenced by social context.

Vygotsky would certainly agree with that, and he would explain those national differences by noting that the education of some nations is far better than others. Remember that Vygotsky believed education occurs everywhere, not only in school. Children learn as they play with peers, watch television, eat with their families, walk down the street. Every experience, from birth on, teaches them something, with some contexts much more educational than others.

For instance, a study of the reading and math achievement of more than a thousand third- and fifth-grade children from ten U.S. cities found that high-scoring primary school children were likely to have had extensive cognitive stimulation. There were three main sources of intellectual activity:

1. Families (e.g., parents read to them daily when they were toddlers)
2. Preschool programs (e.g., a variety of learning activities)
3. First-grade curriculum (e.g., emphasis on literacy with individual evaluation)

In this study, although most children from families of low socioeconomic status did not experience all three sources of stimulation, those who did showed more cognitive advances by fifth grade than the average high-SES child (Crosnoe et al., 2010).

Generally, poverty reduces children's achievement because they are less likely to have these three. However, for low-SES children especially, maternal education makes a notable difference in academic achievement—presumably because educated mothers read, listen, and talk to their children more, and find a preschool with a curriculum that encourages learning.

Especially for Teachers How might Piaget's and Vygotsky's ideas help in teaching geography to a class of third-graders? (see response, page 342)

Girls Can't Do It As Vygotsky recognized, children learn whatever their culture teaches. Fifty years ago girls were in cooking and sewing classes. No longer. This 2012 photo shows 10-year-olds Kamrin and Caitlin in a Kentucky school, preparing for a future quite different from that of their grandmothers.

MIRANDA PEDERSON/DAILY NEWS/ASSOCIATED PRESS

>> Response for Teachers (from page 341): Here are two of the most obvious ways. (1) Use logic. Once children can grasp classification and class inclusion, they can understand cities within states, states within nations, and nations within continents. Organize your instruction to make logical categorization easier. (2) Make use of children's need for concrete and personal involvement. You might have the children learn first about their own location, then about the places where relatives and friends live, and finally about places beyond their personal experience (via books, photographs, videos, and guest speakers).

Never Lost These children of Varanasi sleep beside the Ganges in the daytime. At night they use their excellent sense of direction to guide devotees from elsewhere.

International Contexts

In general, Vygotsky's emphasis on sociocultural contexts contrasts with Piaget's maturational, self-discovery approach. Vygotsky believed that cultures (tools, customs, and mentors) teach. For example, if a child is surrounded by reading adults, by full bookcases, by daily newspapers, and by street signs, that child will read better than a child who has had little exposure to print, even if both are in the same classroom.

The same applies to math. If children learn math in school, they are proficient at school math; if they learn math out of school, they are adept at solving mathematical problems in situations similar to the context in which they learned (Abreu, 2008). Ideally, though, children learn math both in and out of school.

Context affects more than academic learning. A stunning example of knowledge acquired from the social context comes from Varanasi, a city in northeast India. Many Varanasi children have an extraordinary sense of spatial orientation: They know whether they are facing north or south, even when they are inside a room with no windows. In one experiment, children were blindfolded, spun around, and led to a second room, yet many still knew which way they were now facing (Mishra et al., 2009). How did they know?

In Varanasi, everyone refers to the spatial orientation to locate objects. (The U.S. equivalent might be, not that the dog is sleeping by the door, but that the dog is sleeping southeast.) From their early days, children learned north/south/east/west, in order to communicate with others. By middle childhood, their internal sense of direction was acute.

Culture affects how children learn, not just what they learn. This was evident in a two-session study in California of 80 Mexican American children, each with a sibling (Silva et al., 2010). Half of the sibling pairs were from indigenous Indian families, in which children learn by watching, guided by other children. The other half were from families more acculturated to U.S. norms, learning by direct instruction, not observation. Those children had learned that they should work independently, sitting at desks, not collaboratively, not crowding around a teacher.

In the first session of this study, a Spanish-speaking "toy lady" showed each child how to make a toy while his or her sibling sat nearby. First, the younger sibling waited while the older sibling made a toy mouse, and then the older sibling waited while the younger sibling made a toy frog. Each waiting child's behavior was videotaped and coded every 5 seconds as *sustained attention* (alert and focused on the activity), *glancing* (sporadic interest, but primary focus elsewhere), or *not attending* (looking away).

A week later, each child individually was told there was some extra material to make the toy that his or her sibling had made the week before, and encouraged to make the mouse or the frog (whichever one that child had not already made.) In this second session, the toy lady did not give the children step-by-step instructions as she had for the sibling a week earlier, but she had a long list of possible hints if the child needed help.

The purpose of this experiment was to see how much the children had learned by observation the week before. The children from indigenous backgrounds scored higher, needing fewer hints, because they had been more attentive when their siblings made the toy (Silva et al., 2010) (see Figure 12.1).

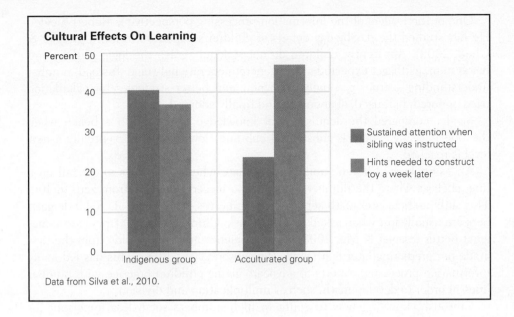

Cultural Effects On Learning

Percent

Sustained attention when sibling was instructed

Hints needed to construct toy a week later

Indigenous group   Acculturated group

Data from Silva et al., 2010.

FIGURE 12.1

Two Ways to Learn Even when children currently live in the same settings and attend the same schools, they follow family cultural traditions in the way they learn.

The same conclusions have been found in other research. For example, in another study, children born and raised in the United States who are accustomed to learning by observation (as in some American Indian cultures) were more proficient at remembering an overheard folktale (Tsethlikai & Rogoff, 2013).

Information Processing

Today's educators and psychologists regard both Piaget and Vygotsky as insightful. International research confirms the merits of their theories. Piaget described universal changes; Vygotsky noted cultural impact.

A third, and more recent, approach to understanding cognition adds crucial insight. The *information-processing perspective* benefits from technology that allows much more detailed data and analysis than was possible 50 years ago. [**Lifespan Link:** Information processing is introduced in Chapter 2.]

Thousands of researchers who study cognition can be said to use the information-processing approach. Not all of them would identify themselves as such because some people contend that "information processing is not a single theory but, rather, a framework characterizing a large number of research programs" (Miller, 2011, p. 266).

The basic assumption of all those research programs is that, like computers, people can access large amounts of information. They then: (1) seek specific units of information (as a search engine does), (2) analyze (as software programs do), and (3) express their conclusions so that another person can understand (as a networked computer or a printout might do). By tracing the paths and links of each of these functions, scientists better understand the learning process.

The brain's gradual growth, now seen in neurological scans, confirms the usefulness of the information-processing perspective. So does data on children's school achievement: Absences, vacations, new schools, and even new teachers may set back a child's learning because learning each day builds on the previous day. Brain connections and pathways are forged from repeated experiences, allowing advances in processing. Without careful building and repetition of various skills, fragile connections between neurons break.

Skills of the Street Children In many nations, children sell to visitors, using math and business skills that few North American children know. This boy was offering necklaces to visitors at the Blue Mosque in Afghanistan.

sensory memory The component of the information-processing system in which incoming stimulus information is stored for a split second to allow it to be processed. (Also called the *sensory register.*)

working memory The component of the information-processing system in which current conscious mental activity occurs. (Formerly called *short-term memory.*)

One of the leaders of the information-processing perspective is Robert Siegler. He has studied the day-by-day details of children's cognition in math (Siegler & Chen, 2008). Apparently, children do not suddenly grasp the logic of the number system, as Piaget expected at the concrete operational stage. Instead, number understanding accrues gradually, with new and better strategies for calculation tried, ignored, half-used, abandoned, and finally adopted.

Siegler compared the acquisition of knowledge to waves on a beach when the tide is rising. There is substantial ebb and flow, although eventually a new level is reached.

An example is children's ability to estimate where a number might fall on a line, such as where the number 53 would be placed on a line from zero to 100. This skill predicts later math achievement (Libertus et al., 2013). U.S. kindergartners are usually lost when asked to do this task; Chinese kindergartners are somewhat better (Siegler & Mu, 2008), but proficiency gradually builds from the first grade on, predicting later math skills (Feigenson et al., 2013). This has led many information-processing experts to advocate giving children practice with number lines in order to develop math, such as multiplication and division.

Curiously, knowing how to count to high numbers seem less important for math mastery than these estimates of magnitude (Thompson & Siegler, 2010). For example, understanding the size of fractions (e.g., that 3/16 is smaller than 1/4) is connected to a thorough understanding of the relationship between one number and another (Siegler et al., 2011). Overall, information processing guides teachers who want to know exactly which concepts and skills are crucial foundations for mastery, not only for math but for reading and writing as well.

Memory

Many scientists who study memory take an information-processing approach. They have learned that various methods of input, storage, and retrieval affect the increasing cognitive ability of the schoolchild. Each of the three major steps in the memory process—sensory memory, working memory, and long-term memory—is affected by both maturation and experience.

Sensory memory (also called the *sensory register*) is the first component of the human information-processing system. It stores incoming stimuli for a split second, with sounds retained slightly longer than sights. To use terms explained in Chapter 5, *sensations* are retained for a moment, and then some become *perceptions*. This first step of sensory awareness is already quite good in early childhood. Sensory memory improves slightly until about age 10, and remains adequate until late adulthood.

Once some sensations become perceptions, the brain selects the meaningful ones and transfers them to working memory for further analysis. It is in **working memory** (formerly called *short-term memory*) that current, conscious mental activity occurs. Processing, not mere exposure, is essential for getting information into working memory; for this reason, working memory improves markedly in middle childhood (Cowan & Alloway, 2009) (see Table 12.1).

As Siegler's waves metaphor suggests, memory strategies do not appear suddenly. Gradual improvement occurs from toddlerhood through adolescence (Schneider & Lockl, 2008). Children develop strategies to increase working memory (Camos & Barrouillet, 2011), and they use these strategies occasionally at first, then consistently.

Cultural differences are evident. For example, many Muslim children are taught to memorize all 80,000 words of the Quran, so they learn strategies to remember long passages—strategies unknown to non-Muslim children. A very

TABLE 12.1	Advances in Memory from Infancy to Age 11
Child's Age	Memory Capabilities
Under 2 years	Infants remember actions and routines that involve them. Memory is implicit, triggered by sights and sounds (an interactive toy, a caregiver's voice).
2–5 years	Words are now used to encode and retrieve memories. Explicit memory begins, although children do not yet use memory strategies. Children remember things by rote (their phone number, nursery rhymes).
5–7 years	Children realize they need to remember some things, and they try to do so, usually via rehearsal (repeating an item again and again). This is not the most efficient strategy, but repetition can lead to automatization.
7–9 years	Children can learn new strategies, including visual clues (remembering how a particular spelling word looks) and auditory hints (rhymes, letters), evidence of brain functions called the visual-spatial sketchpad and phonological loop. Children benefit from organizing things to be remembered.
9–11 years	Memory becomes more adaptive and strategic as children become able to learn various memory techniques from teachers and other children. They can organize material themselves, developing their own memory aids.

Source: Based on Meadows, 2006.

different example is the ability to draw a face, an ability admired by U.S. children. They learn strategies to improve their drawing, such as remembering the ratios of distance involving forehead, eyes, mouth, and chin. (Few spontaneously draw the eyes mid-face, rather than at the top, but most learn to do so.)

Finally, information from working memory may be transferred **long-term memory**, where it is stored for minutes, hours, days, months, or years. The capacity of long-term memory—how much can be crammed into one brain—is huge by the end of middle childhood. Together with sensory memory and working memory, long-term memory organizes ideas and reactions, with more effective brain functioning over the years (Wendelken et al., 2011).

Crucial to long-term memory is not merely *storage* (how much material has been deposited) but also *retrieval* (how readily past learning can be brought into working memory). For everyone, at every age, retrieval is easier for some memories (especially memories of vivid, emotional experiences) than for others. And for everyone, long-term memory is imperfect: We all forget and distort memories, with strategies needed for accurate recall. [**Lifespan Link:** See Chapter 24 for discussion of memory and memory strategies in late adulthood.]

Knowledge

Research on information processing finds that the more people already know, the more information they can learn. Having an extensive **knowledge base**, or a broad body of knowledge in a particular subject, makes it easier to remember and understand related new information. As children gain knowledge during the school years, they become better able to understand what is true or not, what is worth remembering, and what is insignificant (Woolley & Ghossainy, 2013)

Three factors facilitate increases in the knowledge base: past experience, current opportunity, and personal motivation. The last item in this list explains why children's knowledge base is not what their parents or teachers prefer. Some schoolchildren memorize words and rhythms of hit songs, know plots and characters of television programs, or can recite the names and histories of basketball players, and yet do not know whether World War I was in the nineteenth or twentieth century, or whether Pakistan is in Asia or Africa.

long-term memory The component of the information-processing system in which virtually limitless amounts of information can be stored indefinitely.

Especially for Teachers How might your understanding of memory help you teach a 2,000-word vocabulary list to a class of fourth-graders? (see response, page 346)

knowledge base A body of knowledge in a particular area that makes it easier to master new information in that area.

>> Response for Teachers (from page 345):
Children this age can be taught strategies for remembering by forming links between working memory and long-term memory. You might break down the vocabulary list into word clusters, grouped according to root words, connections to the children's existing knowledge, applications, or (as a last resort) first letters or rhymes. Active, social learning is useful; perhaps in groups the students could write a story each day that incorporates 15 new words. Each group could read its story aloud to the class.

control processes Mechanisms (including selective attention, metacognition, and emotional regulation) that combine memory, processing speed, and knowledge to regulate the analysis flow of information within the information-processing system. (Also called *executive processes*.)

metacognition "Thinking about thinking," or the ability to evaluate a cognitive task in order to determine how best to accomplish it, and then to monitor and adjust one's performance on that task.

Motivation provides a clue for teachers: New concepts are learned best if they are connected to personal and emotional experiences. Children who themselves are from South Asia, or who have friends who are, learn the boundaries of Pakistan more readily.

Control Processes

The mechanisms that put memory, processing speed, and the knowledge base together are **control processes**; they regulate the analysis and flow of information within the system. Control processes include *emotional regulation* and *selective attention* (explained in Chapters 10 and 11, respectively).

Equally important is **metacognition**, sometimes defined as "thinking about thinking." Metacognition is the ultimate control process because it allows a person to evaluate a cognitive task, determine how to accomplish it, monitor performance, and then make adjustments. According to scholars of cognition, "Middle childhood may be crucial for the development of metacognitive monitoring and study of control processes" (Metcalfe & Finn, 2013, p. 19).

Control processes require the brain to organize, prioritize, and direct mental operations, much as the CEO (chief executive officer) of a business organizes, prioritizes, and directs business operations. For that reason, control processes are also called *executive processes*. These processes are evident whenever people concentrate on only the relevant parts of a task, using their knowledge base to connect new information or to apply memory strategies.

Executive processes are more evident among 10-year-olds than among 4- or 6-year-olds (Bjorklund et al., 2009). Fourth-grade students can listen to the teacher talk about the river Nile, ignoring classmates who are chewing gum or passing notes. That deliberate selectivity is control.

Both metacognition and control processes improve with age and experience. For instance, in one study, children took a fill-in-the-blanks test and indicated how confident they were of each answer. Then they were allowed to delete some questions, with the remaining ones counting more. Already by age 9, they were able to estimate correctness; by age 11, they were skilled at knowing what to delete (Roebers et al., 2009).

Sometimes experience is not directly related, but it nonetheless has an impact. This seems to be true for fluently bilingual children, who must learn to inhibit one language while using another. They are advanced in control processes, obviously in language but also in more abstract measures of control (Bialystok, 2010).

Such processes develop spontaneously, as the prefrontal cortex matures, but they can be taught. Sometimes teaching is explicit, more so in some nations (e.g., Germany) than in others (e.g., the United States) (Bjorklund et al., 2009). Examples that may be familiar include spelling rules ("*i* before *e* except after *c*") and ways to remember how to turn a lightbulb (lefty, loosey, righty, tighty). Preschoolers ignore such rules or use them only on command, 7-year-olds begin to use them, and 9-year-olds can create and master more complicated rules.

Many factors beyond specific instruction affect learning. For example, if children do not master emotional control in early childhood, their school achievement is likely to suffer for years (Bornstein et al., 2013).

Given the complexity of factors and goals, educators disagree as to what should be deliberately taught versus what is best discovered by the child. However, understanding the early steps that lead to later knowledge, as information processing seeks to do, may guide instruction and hence improve learning. That is one possible conclusion from an interesting experiment (see a View from Science).

Balls Rolling Down

Should metacognition be taught, or should children develop it spontaneously when they are old enough? This question has been the focus of decades of research (Lee & Anderson, 2013; Orlich et al., 2009; Pressley & Hilden, 2006). Scholars have considered both "discovery" learning (inspired by Piaget) and explicit teaching (from an information-processing perspective), always with awareness of cultural differences (as Vygotsky stressed).

The answer depends partly on cultural goals and methods. Some cultures value single-minded concentration, others multitasking; some stress direct instruction, others self-exploration, and still others social learning.

Most U. S. schools now focus on achievement as measured by tests. That has led to emphasis on instruction and research to support the strategy of explicit teaching. In one study, researchers sought to teach children that a scientific experiment must measure variables one at a time in order to be valid (Klahr & Nigam, 2004). The researchers showed 112 third- and fourth-graders two balls that could roll down several ramps (see Figure 12.2). There were four variables: golf or rubber ball, steep or shallow slope, smooth or rough ramp, long or short downhill run.

First, the children were asked to design four experiments on their own: two to determine the effect of distance and two to determine the effect of steepness. Only 8 of the 112 children designed experiments that controlled the variables. For example, in an uncontrolled experiment, a child might use a golf ball on a long ramp and a rubber ball on a short ramp. With the variables uncontrolled, the results would be confounded (inappropriately combined).

The 104 children who did not spontaneously control the variables were then divided into two groups. Half were told to continue to create their own experiments; the other half received explicit instruction by watching an experimenter create pairs of demonstrations. For that half, the experimenter asked the children whether a demonstrated pair allowed them to "tell for sure" how a particular variable affected the distance traveled by the ball. After each response, the experimenter provided the correct answer and explained it, emphasizing the importance of testing one variable at a time.

Then all 104 children were asked to design four experiments, as before. Far more children who received direct instruction (40 of 52) correctly isolated the variables than did children who explored on their own (12 of 52).

A week later, those children who seemed to understand (the 40 and the 12) were asked to examine two science posters ostensibly created by 11-year-olds. The researcher asked the children for suggestions that would make the posters "good enough to enter in a state science fair." The 40 children who had been instructed were virtually as perceptive in their critiques as the 12 who had learned through discovery. This study suggests that strategy can be taught—if the teacher actively engages the students. That is exactly what information-processing theory would predict.

Of course, scientific understanding is about more than understanding variables: It is about questioning conclusions and realizing that answers can and do change. How children develop this ability—whether by discovery and personal exploration as Piaget might expect, or whether by explicit instruction as information-processing theory suggests—is a matter of intense concern to educators.

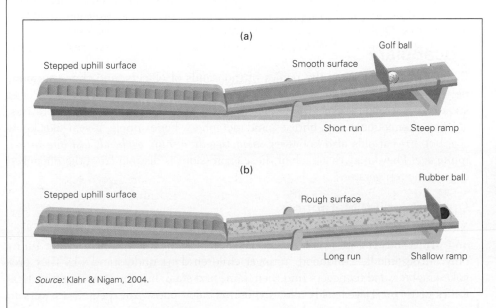

Source: Klahr & Nigam, 2004.

FIGURE 12.2

Confounded Experiment On each of these two ramps, children could vary the steepness, surface, and length of the ramp as well as the type of ball. The confounded experiment depicted here contrasts *(a)* a golf ball on a steep, smooth, short ramp with *(b)* a rubber ball on a shallow, rough, long ramp.

A recent experiment involving computer simulation with several classes of German 13-year-olds found that some explicit instruction helped, but that "'too much' instructional support can constrain knowledge acquisition" (Eckhardt et al., 2013, p. 120). The proper balance between self-propelled discovery and teacher-provided instruction may depend on exactly what is being taught by whom and to whom.

Many educators fear that the current political climate stresses specific facts, taught explicitly, over broader concepts, grasped by discovery. Psychologists see merit in both strategies, as well as in learning by observation (Lee & Anderson, 2013; Tsethlikai & Rogoff, 2013). What do you think? And, as Vygotsky would ask, "How does your cultural heritage and political persuasion affect your answer?"

SUMMING UP

Every theory of cognitive development recognizes that school-age children are avid learners who actively build on the knowledge they already have. Piaget emphasized children's own logic, with maturation and experience allowing them to reach the stage he called concrete operational. Research inspired by Vygotsky and the sociocultural perspective reveals that cultural differences can be powerful: Both what is learned and how it is learned are influenced by the context of instruction and everyday experience.

An information-processing analysis highlights the many components of thinking that advance, step-by-step, during middle childhood. Although sensory and long-term memory do not change much during these years, the speed and efficiency of working memory improve dramatically, making school-age children better thinkers as well as more strategic learners as they grow older. With every passing year children expand their knowledge base, which makes new material easier to connect with past learning and thus easier to learn. As control processes and metacognition advance, children are better able to direct their minds toward whatever they want to learn. ■

>> Language

As you will remember, many aspects of language advance during early childhood. By age 6, children have mastered the basic vocabulary and grammar of their first language. Many also speak a second language fluently. Those linguistic abilities form a strong knowledge base, enabling some school-age children to learn up to 20 new words a day and to apply complex grammar rules. Here are some specifics.

Vocabulary

By age 6, children know the names of thousands of objects, and they use many parts of speech—adjectives and adverbs as well as nouns and verbs. As Piaget stressed, they soon become more flexible and logical; they can understand prefixes, suffixes, compound words, phrases, and metaphors. For example, 2-year-olds know *egg*, but 10-year-olds also know *egg salad, egg-drop soup, egghead, last one in is a rotten egg*. They know that each of these expressions is distinct from the uncooked eggs in the refrigerator.

Understanding Metaphors

Metaphors, jokes, and puns are finally comprehended. Some jokes ("What is black and white and read all over?" "Why did the chicken cross the road?") are funny only during middle childhood. Younger children don't understand why they provoke laughter, and teenagers find them lame and stale, but the new cognitive flexibility of 6- to- 11-year-olds allows them to enjoy puns, unexpected answers to normal questions, and metaphors.

Indeed, a lack of metaphorical understanding, even if a child has a large vocabulary, signifies cognitive problems (Thomas et al., 2010). Humor, or lack of it, is a diagnostic tool.

Many adults do not realize how difficult it is for young children or adults who are learning a new language to grasp figures of speech. The humorist James Thurber remembered

> the enchanted private world of my early boyhood. . . . In this world, business-men who phoned their wives to say they were tied up at the office sat roped to their swivel chairs, and probably gagged, unable to move or speak except some-how, miraculously, to telephone. . . . Then there was the man who left town under a cloud. Sometimes I saw him all wrapped up in the cloud and invisible. . . . At other times it floated, about the size of a sofa, above him wherever he went. . . . [I remember] the old lady who was always up in the air, the husband who did not seem able to put his foot down, the man who lost his head during a fire but was still able to run out of the house yelling.

> *[Thurber, 1999, p. 40]*

Metaphors are context specific, building on the knowledge base. An American who lives in China notes phrases that U.S. children learn but that children in cultures without baseball do not, including "dropped the ball," "on the ball," "play ball," "throw a curve," "strike out" (Davis, 1999). If a teacher says "keep your eyes on the ball," some immigrant children might not pay attention because they are looking for that ball.

Because school-age children can create metaphors, asking them to do so reveals emotions that they do not express in other ways. For instance, in a study of how children felt about their asthma, one 11-year-old said that his asthma

> is like a jellyfish, which has a deadly sting and vicious bite and tentacles which could squeeze your throat and make your bronchioles get smaller and make breathing harder. Or like a boa constrictor squeezing life out of you.

> *[quoted in Peterson & Sterling, 2009, p. 97]*

That boy was terrified of his disease, which he considered evil and dangerous—and beyond his parents' help. Other children in the same study responded differently. One girl thought asthma would attack her only if she was not good and that her "guardian angel" would keep it away as long as she behaved herself. Adults who want to know how a child feels about something might ask for a metaphor.

Adjusting Vocabulary to the Context

One aspect of language that advances markedly in middle childhood is pragmatics, already defined in Chapter 9. Pragmatics is evident when we are comparing how children talk formally with teachers (never calling them a *rotten egg*) and informally with friends (who can be rotten eggs or worse). As children master pragmatics, they become more adept at making friends. Shy 6-year-olds cope far better with the social pressures of school if they use pragmatics well (Coplan & Weeks, 2009).

Mastery of pragmatics allows children to change styles of speech, or "linguistic codes," depending on their audience. Each code includes many aspects of language—tone, pronunciation, gestures, sentence length, idioms, vocabulary, and grammar. Sometimes the switch is between *formal code* (used in academic contexts) and *informal code* (used with friends); sometimes it is between standard (or proper) speech and dialect or vernacular (used on the street). Code used in texting—numbers (411), abbreviations (LOL), emoticons (:-D), and spelling (r u ok?)—shows exemplary pragmatics.

Especially for Parents You've had an exhausting day but are setting out to buy groceries. Your 7-year-old son wants to go with you. Should you explain that you are so tired that you want to make a quick solo trip to the supermarket this time? (see response, page 351)

Typical Yet Unusual It's not unusual that these children are texting in French—they live in Bordeaux, and children everywhere text their friends. The oddity is that a girl and a boy are lying head to head, which rarely occurs in middle childhood. The explanation? They are siblings. Like dogs and cats that grow up together, familiarity overtakes hostility.

BSIP/PHOTO RESEARCHERS, INC.

Some children may not realize that such expressions are wrong in formal language. All children need instruction to become fluent in the formal code because the logic of grammar (whether *who* or *whom* is correct or how to spell *you*) is almost impossible to deduce. The peer group teaches the informal code, and each local community transmits dialect, metaphors, and pronunciation. Educators must teach the formal code without making children feel that their code's grammar or pronunciation is shameful.

Code changes are obvious when children speak one language at home and another at school. Every nation includes many such children; most of the world's 6,000 languages are not school languages. For instance, English is the language of instruction in Australia, but 17 percent of the children speak one of 246 other languages at home (Centre for Community Child Health, 2009).

In the United States, almost 1 school-age child in 4 speaks a language other than English at home; most of them also speak English well (see Figure 12.3). In addition, many children speak a dialect of English at home that differs from the pronunciation and grammar taught at school. All these alternate codes have distinct patterns of timing, grammar, and emphasis, as well as vocabulary.

ELLs (English Language Learners) Children in the United States whose proficiency in English is low—usually below a cutoff score on an oral or written test. Many children who speak a non-English language at home are also capable in English; they are *not* ELLs.

Some children of every ethnicity are called **ELLs**, or **English Language Learners**, based on their proficiency in English. Among U.S. children with Latin American heritage, those who speak English well are much better at reading than those who do not, but even they are less adept at reading than the average European American child (Garcia & Miller, 2008). Culture may be the reason, as their learning style may not be the same as their teachers' teaching style, even though they speak English.

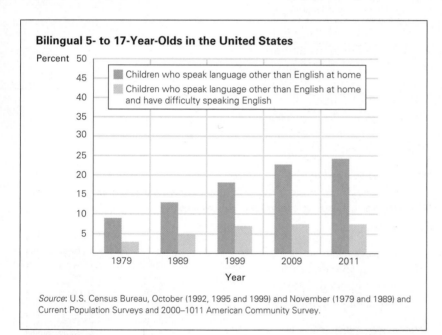

Bilingual 5- to 17-Year-Olds in the United States

Percent

- Children who speak language other than English at home
- Children who speak language other than English at home and have difficulty speaking English

Source: U.S. Census Bureau, October (1992, 1995 and 1999) and November (1979 and 1989) and Current Population Surveys and 2000–1011 American Community Survey.

FIGURE 12.3

Hurray for Teachers More children in the United States are now bilingual and more of them speak English well, from about 40 percent in 1980 to 82 percent in 2011.

Source: Federal Interagency Forum.

The information-processing perspective shows that each aspect of language learning follows a distinct developmental path. Between ages 5 and 8, for children who speak Spanish at home and English in school, the length of each sentence in English (average number of words) dips during summer vacation but fluency improves steadily (words per minute). Their knowledge of Spanish follows another trajectory. It does not improve much at all during kindergarten and first grade (presumably because the child was focused on learning English), and then it advances markedly at the end of second grade (Rojas & Iglesias, 2013). These are averages; specifics depend on the particular experiences of the child at home and school.

Differences in Language Learning

Learning to speak, read, and write the school language is pivotal for primary school education. Some differences may be innate: A child with a language disability has trouble with both the school and home languages. It is a mistake to assume that a child who does not speak English well is learning disabled (difference is not deficit), but it is also is a mistake to assume that such a child's only problem is lack of English knowledge (deficits do occur among all children, no matter what their culture).

Nonetheless, most of the language gap between one child and another is the result of the social context, not brain abnormality. Two crucial factors are the family's SES and everyone's expectations for the child's learning.

Socioeconomic Status

Decades of research throughout the world have found a strong correlation between academic achievement and socioeconomic status. Language is a major reason. Not only do children from low-SES families usually have smaller vocabularies than those from higher-SES families, but their grammar is also simpler (fewer compound sentences, dependent clauses, and conditional verbs) and their sentences are shorter (Hart & Risley, 1995; E. Hoff, 2006).

With regard to language learning, the information-processing perspective focuses on specifics that might affect the brain and thus the ability to learn. Possibilities abound—inadequate prenatal care, exposure to lead, no breakfast, overcrowded households, few books at home, teenage parents, authoritarian child rearing, inexperienced teachers . . . the list could go on and on. All of these conditions correlate with low SES and less learning, but none has been proven to be the major cause (not merely a correlate) of low achievement during primary school.

In addition, a child's early exposure to words has been proven to affect language learning. Unlike most parents who have attended college, many less-educated parents do not provide varied and extensive language exposure to their infants and young children. Daily book reading to 2-year-olds, for instance, occurs for 24 percent of the children of mothers with less than a high school education as opposed to 70 percent of the children of mothers with at least a BA (National Center for Education Statistics, 2009) (see Figure 12.4). Even independent of income and social class, research has shown that children who grow up in homes with many books accumulate, on average, three years more schooling than children who grow up in homes with no books (Evans et al., 2010).

Book reading is not the only way to increase language exposure in children—some families do not read to their children but engage them in conversation about the interesting sights around them—but in the United States book reading often indicates how much verbal input a child receives. Another way to increase language exposure is to sing to a child, not just a few simple songs, but dozens of songs.

Ideally, parents read to, sing to, and converse with each child daily, as well as provide extensive vocabulary about various activities, such as walking down the street: "The sidewalk is narrow [or wide, or cracked, or cement] here. See the wilted rose. Is it red or magenta or maroon? That truck has six huge tires. Why does it have so many?."

As already noted, slow language development correlates with low income, but language exposure is the likely reason. Indeed, children from high-SES families who rarely hear language also do poorly in school.

Studies that track how much language young children hear from adults find vast differences from one home to another—some children hear ten times as many words as others do. Some high-SES parents rarely talk to their children, whereas the opposite is also sometimes true (Greenwood et al., 2011; Hart & Risley, 1995). Remember that dendrites grow to reflect children's experiences. Children in nontalking families fall behind, first in reading and then in other school subjects. Eventually their brains signal linguistic weaknesses (Hackman & Farah, 2009).

>> Response for Parents (from page 349): Your son would understand your explanation, but you should take him along if you can do so without losing patience. You wouldn't ignore his need for food or medicine, so don't ignore his need for learning. While shopping, you can teach vocabulary (does he know pimientos, pepperoni, polenta?), categories (root vegetables, freshwater fish), and math (which size box of cereal is cheaper?). Explain in advance that you need him to help you find items and carry them and that he can choose only one item that you wouldn't normally buy. Seven-year-olds can understand rules, and they enjoy being helpful.

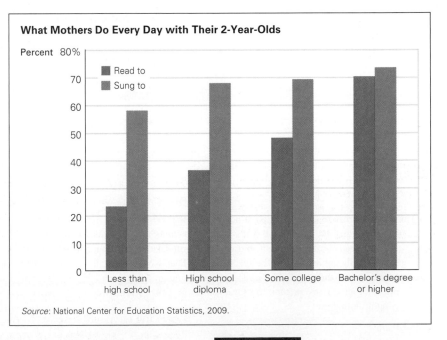

FIGURE 12.4

Red Fish, Blue Fish As you can see, most mothers sing to their little children, but the college-educated mothers are much more likely to know that book reading is important. Simply knowing how to turn a page or hearing new word combinations (hop on pop?) correlates with reading ability later on.

Expectations

A second cause of low achievement in middle childhood in many nations of the world is teachers' and parents' expectations (Melhuish et al., 2008; Phillipson & Phillipson, 2007; Rosenthal, 1991; Rubie-Davies, 2007). Expectations are related to another factor: whether or not a child is taught advanced words and concepts, especially the vocabulary words that are the foundation for later learning, such as *negotiate, evolve, respiration, allegation, deficit* (Snow et al., 2007).

Recent research has repeatedly found that expectations do not necessarily follow along income lines. For low-SES Latinos especially, family expectations for learning can be high, and children try to meet those expectations (Fuller & Garcia Coll, 2010).

International achievement test scores (discussed in the last section of this chapter) indicate that the income gap and the consequent variations in school resources and student achievement are much greater in some nations than in others. One of the largest gaps is in the United States, where the fourth-grade math scores for the public schools with the largest number of low-income children is 91 points below the average for the public schools with the fewest poor children (Provasnik et al., 2012). For comparison, 91 points is more than the difference between the U.S. average (541) and that of Thailand (458) or Armenia (451).

The worst part of adults' low expectations is that they are transmitted to the child. Schoolchildren who internalize their parents' or teachers' expectation that they will not learn much probably won't learn much. A child's expectations and motivation (discussed earlier) go hand in hand.

Expectations are crucial at every stage of life. A study of learning among college students found that, after controlling for family background and high

---

A CASE TO STUDY

Two Immigrants

Two children, both Mexican American, describe their experiences in their local public school in California.

Yolanda:
When I got here [from Mexico at age 7], I didn't want to stay here, 'cause I didn't like the school. And after a little while, in third grade, I started getting the hint of it and everything and I tried real hard in it. I really got along with the teachers. . . . They would start talking to me, or they kinda like pulled me up some grades, or moved me to other classes, or took me somewhere. And they were always congratulating me.

Paul:
I grew up . . . ditching school, just getting in trouble, trying to make a dollar, that's it, you know? Just go to school, steal from the store, and go sell candies at school. And that's what I was doing in the third or fourth grade. . . . I was always getting in the principal's office, suspended, kicked out, everything, starting from the third grade.

[quoted in Nieto, 2000, pp. 220, 249]

Note that initially Yolanda didn't like the United States because of school, but her teachers "kind of pulled me up." By third grade, she was beginning to get "the hint of it." For Paul, school was where he sold stolen candy and where his third-grade teacher sent him to the principal, who suspended him. Ms. Nelson's fifth grade was "a good year," but it was too late—he had already learned he was "just a mess-up," and his expectations for himself were low. Paul was later sent to a special school, and the text implies that he was in jail by age 18. Yolanda became a successful young woman, fluently bilingual.

It would be easy to conclude that the difference was gender, since girls generally do better in school than boys. But that is too simple: Some Mexican-born boys do well in California schools—which raises the question of how teachers impact children: What could the third-grade teacher have done for Paul?

school grades, the colleges where professors expected students to study, and who therefore gave longer reading and writing assignments, advanced student learning (Arum & Roksa, 2011). A person's expectations influence more than just academics: Adults who expect to live a long life take better care of their health. [**Lifespan Link:** The impact of health habits on longevity is discussed in Chapter 20.]

SUMMING UP

Children continue to learn language rapidly during the school years. They become more flexible, logical, and knowledgeable, figuring out the meanings of new words and grasping metaphors, jokes, and compound words. Many converse with friends using informal speech and master formal code in school. They learn whatever grammar and vocabulary they are taught, and they succeed at pragmatics—the practical task of adjusting their language to friends, teachers, or family. Millions become proficient in a second language, a process facilitated by teachers and peers. For academic achievement during middle childhood, both past exposure to language and adults' expectations are influential. ∎

>> Teaching and Learning

As we have just described, school-age children are great learners, using logic, developing strategies, accumulating knowledge, and expanding their language proficiency. In every century and nation, new responsibilities and formal instruction begin in middle childhood because that is when the human body and brain are ready. Traditionally, this learning occurred at home, but now more than 95 percent of the world's 7-year-olds are in school; that is where their parents and political leaders want them to be (Cohen & Malin, 2010).

International Schooling

Everywhere in the world children are taught to read, write, and do arithmetic. Because of brain maturation and sequenced learning, 6-year-olds are not expected to multiply three-digit numbers or read paragraphs fluently out loud, but every nation teaches 10-year-olds to do so. Some of the sequences recognized universally are listed in the accompanying At About This Time tables (see next page).

Nations also want their children to be good citizens. However, citizenship is not easy to teach. There is no consensus as to what that means or what developmental paths should be followed (Cohen & Malin, 2010).

Differences by Nation

Although literacy and numeracy (reading and math, respectively) are valued everywhere, many curriculum specifics vary by nation, by community, and by school. These variations are evident in the results of international tests, in the mix of school subjects, and in the relative power of parents, educators, and political leaders.

For example, daily physical activity is mandated in some schools but not in others. Many schools in Japan have swimming pools; virtually no schools in Africa or Latin America do. As you read in Chapter 11, some U.S. schools have no recess at all.

Geography, music, and art are essential in some places, not in others. Half of all U.S. 18- to 24-year-olds say they had no arts education in childhood, either in school or anywhere else (Rabkin & Hedberg, 2011) (see Figure 12.5).

AT ABOUT THIS TIME

Math

Age	Norms and Expectations
4–5 years	■ Count to 20. ■ Understand one-to-one correspondence of objects and numbers. ■ Understand *more* and *less*. ■ Recognize and name shapes.
6 years	■ Count to 100. ■ Understand *bigger* and *smaller*. ■ Add and subtract one-digit numbers.
8 years	■ Add and subtract two-digit numbers. ■ Understand simple multiplication and division. ■ Understand word problems with two variables.
10 years	■ Add, subtract, multiply, and divide multidigit numbers. ■ Understand simple fractions, percentages, area, and perimeter of shapes. ■ Understand word problems with three variables.
12 years	■ Begin to use abstract concepts, such as formulas, algebra.

Math learning depends heavily on direct instruction and repeated practice, which means that some children advance more quickly than others. This list is only a rough guide, meant to illustrate the importance of sequence.

AT ABOUT THIS TIME

Reading

Age	Norms and Expectations
4–5 years	■ Understand basic book concepts. For instance, children learning English and many other languages understand that books are written from front to back, with print from left to right, and that letters make words that describe pictures. ■ Recognize letters—name the letters on sight. ■ Recognize and spell own name.
6–7 years	■ Know the sounds of the consonants and vowels, including those that have two sounds (e.g., *c, g, o*). ■ Use sounds to figure out words. ■ Read simple words, such as *cat, sit, ball, jump*.
8 years	■ Read simple sentences out loud, 50 words per minute, including words of two syllables. ■ Understand basic punctuation, consonant–vowel blends. ■ Comprehend what is read.
9–10 years	■ Read and understand paragraphs and chapters, including advanced punctuation (e.g., the colon). ■ Answer comprehension questions about concepts as well as facts. ■ Read polysyllabic words (e.g., *vegetarian, population, multiplication*).
11–12 years	■ Demonstrate rapid and fluent oral reading (more than 100 words per minute). ■ Vocabulary includes words that have specialized meaning in various fields. For example, in civics, *liberties, federal, parliament,* and *environment* all have special meanings. ■ Comprehend paragraphs about unfamiliar topics. ■ Sound out new words, figuring out meaning using cognates and context. ■ Read for pleasure.
13+ years	■ Continue to build vocabulary, with greater emphasis on comprehension than on speech. Understand textbooks.

Reading is a complex mix of skills, dependent on brain maturation, education, and culture. The sequence given here is approximate; it should not be taken as a standard to measure any particular child.

FIGURE 12.5

Focus on Facts As achievement test scores become the measure of learning, education in art, music, and movement has been squeezed out. Artists worry that creativity and imagination may be lost as well.

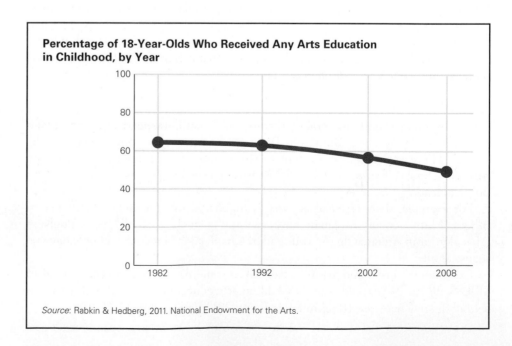

Percentage of 18-Year-Olds Who Received Any Arts Education in Childhood, by Year

Source: Rabkin & Hedberg, 2011. National Endowment for the Arts.

Educational practices may differ even between nations that are geographically and culturally close. For example, the average child in a primary school in Germany spends three times as much school time studying science as does the average child across the border, in the Netherlands (Snyder & Dillow, 2010).

Differences between one nation and another, and, in the United States, between one school and another, are notable in aspects of the **hidden curriculum**, which includes implicit values and assumptions evident in course selection, schedules, tracking, teacher characteristics, discipline, teaching methods, sports competition, student government, extracurricular activities, and so on.

Whether students should be quiet or talkative in the classroom is part of the hidden curriculum, taught from kindergarten on. I realized this particular hidden curriculum difference when I taught at the United Nations high school. One student, newly arrived from India, never spoke in class so I called on him. He immediately stood up to answer—to the surprise of his classmates. Soon he learned to stay seated, but he never spoke spontaneously.

More generally, if teachers' gender, ethnicity, or economic background is unlike that of the students, children may conclude that education is irrelevant for them. If the school has gifted classes, the hidden message may be that most students are not very capable.

The physical setting of the school also sends a message. Some schools have spacious classrooms, wide hallways, and large, grassy playgrounds, others have cramped, poorly equipped rooms and cement play yards. In some nations, school is held outdoors, with no chairs, desks, or books, and sessions are canceled when it rains. What does that tell the students?

Same Situation, Far Apart: Spot the Hidden Curriculum Literacy is central to the curriculum for schoolchildren everywhere, no matter how far apart they live. However, in the U.S. classroom at the left, boys and girls learn together, clothes are casual, history books are paperback and illustrated, and children of every background read the same stories with the same patriotic—but not religious—themes. The hidden curriculum is quite different for the boy memorizing his holy book on the right.

hidden curriculum The unofficial, unstated, or implicit rules and priorities that influence the academic curriculum and every other aspect of learning in a school.

Observation Quiz What three differences do you see between recess in New York City (left) and Santa Rosa, California (right)? (see answer, page 356)

Having Fun? Not necessarily.

>> **Answer to Observation Quiz** (from page 355): The most obvious is the play equipment, but there are two others that make some New York children eager for recess to end. Did you notice the concrete play surface and the winter jackets?

Trends in Math and Science Study (TIMSS) An international assessment of the math and science skills of fourth- and eighth-graders. Although the TIMSS is very useful, different countries' scores are not always comparable because sample selection, test administration, and content validity are hard to keep uniform.

Progress in International Reading Literacy Study (PIRLS) Inaugurated in 2001, a planned five-year cycle of international trend studies in the reading ability of fourth-graders.

International Testing

Over the past two decades, more than 50 nations have participated in at least one massive international test of educational achievement. Longitudinal data reveal that, if achievement rises, the national economy advances with it; this sequence seems causal, not merely correlational (Hanushek & Woessmann, 2009). Apparently, better-educated adults become more productive workers.

Science and math achievement are tested in the **Trends in Math and Science Study (TIMSS)**. The main test of reading is the **Progress in International Reading Literacy Study (PIRLS)**. These tests are given every few years, with East Asian nations usually ranking at the top and the United States' rank rising, but it is still not as high as many other nations (see Tables 12.2 and 12.3). Most developing nations do not give these tests, but when they do, their scores are low.

After a wholesale reform of the educational system, Finland's scores increased dramatically from about 1990 to 2001 (Sahlberg, 2011). Changes occurred over several years, from the abolition of ability grouping in 1985 to curriculum

TABLE 12.2 TIMSS Ranking and Average Scores of Math Achievement for Fourth-Graders, 2011

Rank*	Country	Score
1.	Singapore	606
2.	Korea	605
3.	Hong Kong	602
4.	Chinese Taipei	591
5.	Japan	585
6.	N. Ireland	562
7.	Belgium	549
8.	Finland	545
9.	England	542
10.	Russia	542
11.	United States	541
12.	Netherlands	540
	Canada (Quebec)	533
	Germany	528
	Canada (Ontario)	518
	Australia	516
	Italy	508
	Sweden	504
	New Zealand	486
	Iran	431
	Yemen	248

*The top 12 groups are listed in order, but after that, not all the jurisdictions that took the test are listed. Some nations have improved over the past 15 years (notably, Hong Kong, England) and some have declined (Austria, Netherlands), but most continue about where they have always been.

Source: Provasnik et al., 2012; TIMSS 2011 International Mathematics Report.

TABLE 12.3 PIRLS Distribution of Reading Achievement

Country	Score
Hong Kong	571
Russia	568
Finland	568
Singapore	567
N. Ireland	558
United States	556
Denmark	554
Chinese Taipei	553
Ireland	552
England	552
Canada	548
Italy	541
Germany	541
Israel	541
New Zealand	531
Australia	527
Poland	526
France	520
Spain	513
Iran	457
Colombia	448
Indonesia	428
Morocco	310

Source: Adapted from Mullis et al., 2012.

reform in 1994 that encouraged collaboration and active learning. Strict requirements for becoming a teacher may be key. Only the top 3 percent of high school graduates are admitted to teachers' colleges, where they receive five years of free education, including a master's degree in education theory and practice.

Finnish teachers are also granted more autonomy within their classrooms than is typical in other systems, and since the 1990s they have time and encouragement to work with colleagues (Sahlberg, 2011). Buildings are designed to foster collaboration, with comfortable teacher's lounges in place (Sparks, 2012), reflecting a hidden curriculum.

Respect for teaching might be the reason for Finland's success, or perhaps something more basic regarding Finland's size, population, culture, or history may be responsible. Or it may come from considering every child to have strengths and weaknesses: Few are designated as having special needs because *all* are given individualized attention.

International test results may be related to educational approaches in various nations. TIMSS experts videotaped 231 math classes in three nations—Japan, Germany, and the United States (Stigler & Hiebert, 1999/2009). The U.S. teachers taught math at a lower level than did their German and Japanese counterparts, presenting more definitions but not connecting those definitions to prior learning. Few U.S. students seemed interested, because they felt the teachers themselves were not overly interested: "teachers seem to believe that learning terms and practicing skills is not very exciting" (p. 89).

By contrast, the Japanese teachers were excited about math instruction, working collaboratively and structuring lessons so that the children developed proofs and alternative solutions, both alone and in groups. Teachers used social interaction and followed an orderly sequence (building lessons on previous knowledge). Such teaching reflected all three theories of cognition: problem-solving from Piaget, collaborative learning from Vygotsky, and sequencing from information processing. Remember that Japanese students excel on the TIMSS, which suggests that all three theories may be relevant.

Sharing Answers After individually subtracting 269 from 573, these two third-graders check their answers two ways—first by adding and then by showing their work to each other. As you can see, he is not embarrassed at his mistake because students in this class enjoy learning from each other.

Problems with International Benchmarks

Elaborate and extensive measures are in place to make the PIRLS and the TIMSS valid. For instance, test items are designed to be fair and culture-free, and participating children represent the diversity (income, ethnic, etc.) of the child population. Consequently, most social scientists worldwide respect the data gathered from these tests.

The tests are far from perfect, however. Designing test items that are equally challenging to all students is impossible. Should fourth-graders be expected to understand fractions, graphs, and simple geometry, or should the test focus only on basic operations with whole numbers? Once those general questions are decided, specific items may nonetheless be unfair. One item testing fourth-grade math was the following:

> Al wanted to find out how much his cat weighed. He weighed himself and noted that the scale read 57 kg. He then stepped on the scale holding his cat and found that it read 62 kg. What was the weight of the cat in kilograms?
>
> Answer: _____ kilograms

This problem involves simple subtraction. Yet, 40 percent of U.S. fourth-graders got it wrong. Were they unable to subtract 57 from 62, or did they not understand the example, or did the abbreviation for kilograms confuse them because—unlike children in most nations—they are more familiar with pounds? On this item, children from Yemen were at the bottom, with 95 percent of them failing. Is that because few of them have cats for pets or weigh themselves on a scale?

In the United States

Although some national tests indicate improvements in U.S. children's academic performance, when U.S. children are compared with children in other nations, not much has changed in reading or math scores in the past two decades. A particular concern is that a child's achievement seems to be more influenced by income and ethnicity in the United States than in other nations, some of which have more diversity and more immigrants than the United States.

Also in the United States, although many educators and political leaders have attempted to eradicate performance disparities linked to a child's background, the gap between fourth-grade European Americans and their Latino and African American peers is as wide as it was 15 years ago. Furthermore, the gap between low- and high-income U.S. students is widening, as is the gap between American Indians and other groups (Maxwell, 2012; National Center for Education Statistics, 2012).

National Standards

International comparisons and disparities within the United States led to passage of the **No Child Left Behind Act** in 2001 (NCLB), a federal law promoting high national standards for public schools. One controversial aspect of the law is its requirement of frequent testing to measure whether standards are being met. Low-scoring schools lose funding and may be closed. An unfortunate result is that children of middling achievement are pushed hard to make sure they meet the benchmark, while children far above or far below standards may be ignored.

Most people agree with the NCLB goals (accountability and higher achievement) but not with the strategies that must be used (Frey et al., 2012). NCLB troubles those who value the arts, social studies, or physical education because those subjects are often squeezed out when reading and math achievement is the priority (Dee et al., 2013). States have been granted substantial power of implementation, teacher preparation has increased but class size has not decreased, and the tests, and testing, remain controversial (Frey et al., 2012; Dee et al., 2013).

Federally sponsored tests called the **National Assessment of Educational Progress (NAEP)** measure achievement in reading, mathematics, and other subjects. Many critics believe that the NAEP is better than state tests (Applegate et al., 2009), basing their conclusion on the fact that the NAEP labels fewer children proficient than do state tests.

Disagreement about state tests and standards led the governors of all 50 states to designate a group of experts who developed a *Common Core* of standards, finalized in 2010, for use nationwide. The standards, higher than most state standards, are quite explicit, with half a dozen or more specific expectations for achievement in each subject for each grade. (Table 12.4 provides a sample of the specific standards.) As of 2013, forty-five states have adopted this Common Core for both reading and math; Minnesota is a partial adopter, in reading but not in math; and four states—Texas, Virginia, Alaska, and Nebraska—have opted out of the Common Core.

The issue of how best to teach children to learn what they need, and what exactly that learning is, continues to be controversial in almost every nation.

MIKE TWOHY/THE NEW YORKER COLLECTION/WWW.CARTOONBANK.COM

"Big deal, an A in math. That would be a D in any other country."

No Child Left Behind Act A U.S. law enacted in 2001 that was intended to increase accountability in education by requiring states to qualify for federal educational funding by administering standardized tests to measure school achievement.

National Assessment of Educational Progress (NAEP) An ongoing and nationally representative measure of U.S. children's achievement in reading, mathematics, and other subjects over time; nicknamed "the Nation's Report Card."

TABLE 12.4	The Common Core: Sample Items for Each Grade	
Grade	Reading and Writing	Math
Kindergarten	Pronounce the primary sound for each consonant	Know number names and the count sequence
First	Decode regularly spelled one-syllable words	Relate counting to addition and subtraction (e.g., by counting 2 more to add 2)
Second	Decode words with common prefixes and suffixes	Measure the length of an object twice, using different units of length for the two measurements; describe how the two measurements relate to the size of the unit chosen
Third	Decode multisyllabic words	Understand division as an unknown-factor problem; for example, find $32 \div 8$ by finding the number that makes 32 when multiplied by 8
Fourth	Use combined knowledge of all letter–sound correspondences, syllable patterns, and morphology (e.g., roots and affixes) to read accurately unfamiliar multisyllabic words in context and out of context	Apply and extend previous understandings of multiplication to multiply a fraction by a whole number
Fifth	With guidance and support from peers and adults, develop and strengthen writing as needed by planning, revising, editing, rewriting, or trying a new approach	Graph points on the coordinate plane to solve real-world and mathematical problems

Source: National Governors Association, 2010.

Learning a Second Language

One example of such a controversy involves determining when, how, to whom, and whether schools should provide second-language instruction, a question answered in opposite ways from nation to nation. Some nations teach two or more languages throughout elementary school, and others punish children who utter any word in any language other than the majority one.

In the United States, less than 5 percent of children under age 11 study a language other than English in school (Robelen, 2011). (In secondary school, almost every U.S. student takes a year or two of a language other than English, but studies of brain maturation suggest that this is too late for efficient language learning.)

Some U.S. educators note that almost every child speaks two languages by age 10 in Canada and most nations of Europe, where children are taught two languages throughout middle childhood. African children who are talented and fortunate enough to reach high school often speak three languages. The implications of this for U.S. language instruction are often ignored because of debates about immigration and globalization. Instead of trying to teach English-speaking children a second language during the years when they are best able to learn it, educators in the United States debate how best to teach English to children who do not speak it.

Teaching approaches range from **immersion**, in which instruction occurs entirely in the new language, to the opposite, in which children are taught in their first language until the second language can be taught as a "foreign" tongue (a strategy rare in the United States but common elsewhere). Between these extremes lies **bilingual schooling**, with instruction in two languages, and **ESL (English as a second language)**, with all non-English speakers taught English in one multilingual group. ESL is intended to be a short and intense program to prepare students for regular classes.

Methods for teaching a second language sometimes succeed and sometimes fail, with the research not yet clear as to which approach is best (Gandara & Rumberger, 2009). The success of any method seems to depend on the literacy of the home environment (frequent reading, writing, and listening in any language helps);

immersion A strategy in which instruction in all school subjects occurs in the second (usually the majority) language that a child is learning.

bilingual schooling A strategy in which school subjects are taught in both the learner's original language and the second (majority) language.

ESL (English as a Second Language) A U.S. approach to teaching English that gathers all the non-English speakers together and provides intense instruction in English. Their first language is never used; the goal is to prepare them for regular classes in English.

All the Same These five children all speak a language other than English at home and are now learning English as a new language at school. Although such classes should ideally be taught to true English language learners (ELLs), children who already speak English are sometimes mistakenly included in them (like 8-year-old Elena, from Mexico).

FIGURE 12.6

Where'd You Go to School? Note that although home schooling is still the least-chosen option, the number of home-schooled children is increasing, while the number of children attending zoned public schools is slightly decreasing. Although any child can be home-schooled, more detailed data indicate that the typical home-schooled child is a 7-year-old European American girl living in a rural area of the South with an employed father and a stay-at-home mother.

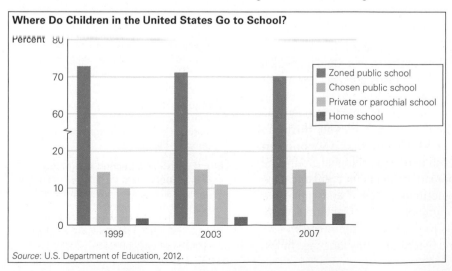

Where Do Children in the United States Go to School?

Source: U.S. Department of Education, 2012.

the warmth, training, and skill of the teacher; and the national context. In some schools, every teacher is bilingual; in other schools, none are—and children notice that hidden curriculum. ELLs are more likely than other students to underachieve and then drop out.

Children and parents born outside the United States may not be accustomed to the teaching norms: For instance, should students be quiet or vocal? Should students work in groups or independently?

Many immigrants to the United States are raised in families in which survival depended on cooperation, and thus the competition and individuality within U.S. classrooms are disconcerting. At the same time, they often greatly respect education and teachers, so they are aghast if a student refuses to do homework or talks back to a teacher.

To further complicate matters, generalities (including those just described) about immigrants and cultures may be stereotypes. For instance, although the political rhetoric sometimes implies that all U.S. immigrant children are from Mexico, many Latino immigrants are not Mexican, and many immigrants are not Latino. Although immigrants from Latin America account for more than half of the foreign-born population of the United States (53 percent), only 29 percent of foreigners have come from Mexico, roughly the same as have come from Asia (28 percent). Other Latino immigrants have come from elsewhere in Central America (8 percent), South America (7 percent), and the Caribbean (9 percent) (United States Census Bureau, 2012).

Further, differences are vast within every group. Asian immigrants to the United States are from China, India, and many other Asian nations—each with a distinct culture that affects learning. And, of course, many families with Hispanic names have lived in the United States for centuries: Spanish may be a foreign language for them.

Cognitive research leaves no doubt that school-age children *can* learn a second language if they are taught logically, step-by-step, and they *can* maintain their original language. Whether they do so, however, is affected by factors beyond cognitive research: SES, family ethnotheories, expectations, and national policies.

Who Determines Educational Practice?

An underlying issue for almost any national or international educational dispute is the role of parents. In most nations, matters regarding public education—curriculum, funding, teacher training, and so on—are set by the central government. Almost all children attend their local school, whose resources and standards are similar to all the other schools in that nation.

In contrast, local U.S. jurisdictions provide most of the funds and guidelines. Parents affect education by talking to their child's teacher, by parent–teacher associations (PTAs), by moving to a particular school zone, or by electing local officials. Moreover, while most parents send their children to a nearby public school, almost a third do not. They choose a public charter school, a private school, or home schooling (see Figure 12.6).

Choices and Complications

Charter schools are public schools funded and licensed by states or local districts. Typically, they also have private money and sponsors. They are exempt from some regulations, especially those negotiated by unions, and they have some control over admissions and expulsions. For that reason, they often are more ethnically segregated and enroll fewer children with special needs. On average, teachers are younger and work longer hours, and school size is smaller than in traditional public schools.

Some charter schools are remarkably successful; others are not (Peyser, 2011). A major criticism is that not every child who enters a charter school stays to graduate; one scholar reports that "the dropout rate for African American males is shocking" (Miron, quoted in Zehr, 2011, p. 1). Overall, children and teachers leave charter schools more often than they leave regular public schools, a disturbing statistic. However, the explanation may be that because teachers and parents actively choose charter schools, such people may be more selective, or more critical by nature, and thus more willing to leave a school if their expectations are not met.

Private schools are funded by tuition, endowments, and church sponsors. Traditionally in the United States, most private schools were parochial (church related), organized by the Catholic Church to teach religion and to resist the anti-Catholic rhetoric of many public schools. Tuition was low since teachers were nuns who earned little pay. Recently, though, many parochial schools have closed, and more independent private schools have opened. A major concern is economic: Higher tuition means that few private-school children are poor or even middle class.

To solve that problem, some U.S. jurisdictions issue **vouchers**, money that parents can use to pay some or all of the tuition at a private school, including a church-sponsored one. This practice is controversial, not only because it decreases public school support but also because public funds go to religious institutions. That is contrary to the U.S. principle of separation of church and state. Advocates say that vouchers increase competition and improve all schools; critics counter that they weaken public schools and are costly to taxpayers.

Home schooling occurs when parents avoid both public and private schools by educating their children at home. This solution is becoming more common, but only about 1 child in 35 (more girls than boys, more preadolescents than teenagers) is home-schooled (Snyder & Dillow, 2012). A prerequisite is an adult at home, typically the mother in a two-parent family, who is willing to teach the children. Authorities set standards for what a child must learn, but home-schooling families decide specifics of curriculum, schedules, and discipline.

The major problem with home schooling is not academic (some mothers are conscientious teachers and some home-schooled children score high on achievement tests) but social: Children have no interaction with classmates. To compensate, many home-schooling parents plan activities with other home-schooling families. This practice reflects local culture: Home schooling is more common in some parts of the United States (in the South and the Northwest more than in the Northeast or Midwest), which affects how readily parents can find other home-schooled children.

The underlying problem with all these options is that people disagree about the best education for a 6- to 11-year-old, and how to measure it. For example, many parents consider class size to be a major issue: They may choose private school, if they can afford it, because fewer students are in each class. They also insist that children have homework, beginning in the first grade. Yet many developmentalists are not convinced that small classes and daily homework are essential during middle childhood.

Mom or Teacher? Don't be fooled by the warm hug from a former student, congratulating Diane Palmer for winning $25,000 as an outstanding teacher. Teacher quality is more crucial for learning than whether the school is public or private.

charter school A public school with its own set of standards that is funded and licensed by the state or local district in which it is located.

private school A school funded by tuition charges, endowments, and often religious or other nonprofit sponsors.

voucher Public subsidy for tuition payment at a nonpublic school. Vouchers vary a great deal from place to place, not only in amount and availability but also in restrictions as to who gets them and what schools accept them.

home schooling Education in which children are taught at home, usually by their parents.

Especially for School Administrators Children who wear uniforms in school tend to score higher on reading tests. Why? (see response, page 362)

>> Response for School Administrators
(from page 361): The relationship reflects correlation, not causation. Wearing uniforms is more common when the culture of the school emphasizes achievement and study, with strict discipline in class and a policy of expelling disruptive students.

Mixed evidence comes from nations where children score high on international tests. Sometimes they have large student-teacher ratios (Korea's average is 28 to 1) and sometimes small (Finland's is 14 to 1). Fourth-graders with no homework sometimes have higher achievement scores than those with homework (Snyder & Dillow, 2010). This does not prove that small classes and extensive homework are worthless. Perhaps weaker students are assigned to smaller classes with more homework, so the data on homework or class size may be the results of low-scoring children, not vice versa. Nevertheless, these correlations raise legitimate doubts.

Who should decide what children should learn and how? Every developmental theory can lead to suggestions for teaching and learning (Farrar & Al-Qatawneh, 2010), but none endorses one curriculum or method to the exclusion of all others. Parents, politicians, and developmental experts all agree that school is vital and that some children learn much more than others, but disagreement about teachers and curriculum—hidden or overt—abound.

SUMMING UP

Societies throughout the world recognize that school-age children are avid learners and that educated citizens are essential to economic development. That has led to increased school enrollment: Almost all of the world's 6- to 11-year-olds are in school. Schools differ in what and how children are taught, and international tests find that some nations are far more successful than others in educating their young. Test scores, as well as the nature and content of education, raise ideological and political passions. Teachers are crucial, and so are parents, who foster children's basic skills and motivation. ■

Education in Middle Childhood Around the World

Only a decade ago, gender differences in education around the world were stark, with far fewer girls in school than boys. Now girls have almost caught up, but recent data finds that the best predictor of childhood health is an educated mother. Many of today's children suffer from decades of inequality.

WORLDWIDE PRIMARY SCHOOL ENROLLMENT, 2011

Enrollments in elementary school are increasing around the world, but poor countries still lag behind more wealthy ones and in all countries, more boys attend school than boys.

BARBARA DELGADO/SHUTTERSTOCK

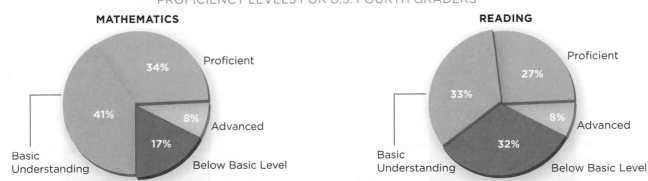

SOURCE: THE WORLD BANK, 2013

WORLDWIDE, BASIC ELEMENTARY EDUCATION LEADS TO:

LESS −
- Child and maternal mortality
- Transmission of HIV
- Early marriage and childbirth
- War

MORE +
- Better paying jobs
- Agricultural productivity
- Use of medical care
- Voting

SOURCE: THE WORLD BANK, 2013

HOW ARE U.S. FOURTH GRADERS DOING?

Primary school enrollment is high in the United States, but not every student is learning. While numbers are improving, less than half of fourth graders are proficient in math and reading.

PROFICIENCY LEVELS FOR U.S. FOURTH GRADERS

MATHEMATICS

- Proficient 34%
- Advanced 8%
- Below Basic Level 17%
- Basic Understanding 41%

READING

- Proficient 27%
- Advanced 8%
- Below Basic Level 32%
- Basic Understanding 33%

SOURCE: ADAPTED FROM NAEP 2013, FIGURES 4 AND 5.

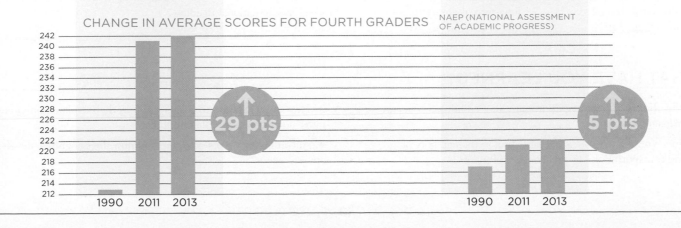

CHANGE IN AVERAGE SCORES FOR FOURTH GRADERS   NAEP (NATIONAL ASSESSMENT OF ACADEMIC PROGRESS)

29 pts   5 pts

1990 2011 2013   1990 2011 2013

SOURCE: NAEP 2013, FIGURE 1.

SOURCES & CREDITS LISTED ON P. SC-1

SUMMARY

Building on Theory

1. According to Piaget, middle childhood is the time of concrete operational thought, when egocentrism diminishes and logical thinking begins. School-age children can understand classification, conservation, and seriation.

2. Vygotsky stressed the social context of learning, including the specific lessons of school and learning from peers and adults. Culture affects not only what children learn but also how they learn.

3. An information-processing approach examines each step of the thinking process, from input to output, using the computer as a model. This approach is useful for understanding memory, perception, and expression.

4. Memory begins with information that reaches the brain from the sense organs. Then selection processes, benefiting from past experience, allow some information to reach working memory. Finally, long-term memory indefinitely stores images and ideas that can be retrieved when needed.

5. A broader knowledge base, logical strategies for retrieval, and faster processing advance every aspect of memory and cognition. Control processes are crucial. Children become better at controlling and directing their thinking as the prefrontal cortex matures. Metacognition improves over the years of middle childhood and beyond.

Language

6. Language learning advances in many practical ways, including expanded vocabulary, as words are logically linked together and as an understanding of metaphors begins.

7. Children excel at pragmatics during middle childhood, often using one code with their friends and another in school. Many children become fluent in the school language while speaking their first language at home.

8. Children of low SES are usually lower in linguistic skills, primarily because they hear less language at home and because adult expectations for their learning are low. This is not inevitable for low-SES families, however.

Teaching and Learning

9. Nations and experts agree that education is critical during middle childhood. Almost all the world's children now attend primary school. Schools differ in what and how they teach, especially with regard to religion, languages, and the arts.

10. International assessments are useful as comparisons, partly because few objective measures of learning are available. Reading is assessed with the PIRLS, math and science with the TIMSS. On both measures, children in East Asia excel and children in the United States are in the middle ranks.

11. In the United States, the No Child Left Behind Act and the National Assessment of Educational Progress (NAEP) attempt to raise the standard of education, with mixed success. The Common Core, developed with the sponsorship of the governors of the 50 states, is an effort to raise national standards and improve accountability.

12. Disagreements about education are frequent; some parents choose charter schools, others prefer private schools, and still others opt for home schooling. However, parents value some aspects of schooling (class size, homework) more than do many educators, and nations differ in how much national control they seek for public education. More research is needed to discover the best way for children to learn.

KEY TERMS

bilingual schooling (p. 359)
charter school (p. 361)
classification (p. 340)
concrete operational thought (p. 339)
control processes (p. 346)
ELLs (English Language Learners) (p. 350)

ESL (English as a Second Language) (p. 359)
hidden curriculum (p. 355)
home schooling (p. 361)
immersion (p. 359)
knowledge base (p. 345)
long-term memory (p. 345)
metacognition (p. 346)

National Assessment of Educational Progress (NAEP) (p. 358)
No Child Left Behind Act (p. 358)
private school (p. 361)
Progress in International Reading Literacy Study (PIRLS) (p. 356)

sensory memory (p. 344)
seriation (p. 340)
Trends in Math and Science Study (TIMSS) (p. 356)
voucher (p. 361)
working memory (p. 344)

WHAT HAVE YOU LEARNED?

1. Why did Piaget call cognition in middle childhood *concrete operational* thought?

2. How would one express classification in the category of ground transportation? In the category of plants?

3. How do Vygotsky and Piaget differ in their explanation of cognitive advances in middle childhood?

4. According to Vygotsky, where and how does cognitive development occur?

5. How does information processing differ from traditional theories of cognitive development?

6. According to information processing, how do children learn math concepts?

7. What aspects of memory improve markedly during middle childhood?

8. How might metacognitive skills help a student?

9. How does the process of learning language progress between the ages of 3 and 10?

10. How does a child's age affect the understanding of metaphors and jokes?

11. Why is the understanding of prefixes and suffixes so useful in expanding vocabulary?

12. Why would a child's linguistic code be criticized by teachers but admired by friends?

13. What factors in a child's home life affect his or her ability to learn grammar and advanced vocabulary?

14. How and why does low-SES affect language learning?

15. What do all nations have in common regarding education in middle childhood?

16. How does the hidden curriculum differ from the stated school curriculum?

17. What are the three different ways in which English language learners are taught English in school?

18. What are the TIMSS and the PIRLS?

19. What are the main goals and outcomes of the No Child Left Behind Act?

20. What problems does the Common Core Standards attempt to solve?

21. What are the differences among charter schools, private schools, and home schools?

APPLICATIONS

1. Visit a local elementary school and look for the hidden curriculum. For example, do the children line up? Why or why not, when and how? Does gender, age, ability, or talent affect the grouping of children or the selection of staff? What is on the walls? Are parents involved? If so, how? For everything you observe, speculate about the underlying assumptions.

2. Interview a 6- to 11-year-old child to find out what he or she knows *and understands* about mathematics. Relate both correct and incorrect responses to the logic of concrete operational thought.

3. What do you remember about how you learned to read? Compare your memories with those of two other people, one at least 10 years older and the other at least 5 years younger than you are. Can you draw any conclusions about effective reading instruction? If so, what are they? If not, why not?

4. Talk to two parents of primary school children. What do they think are the best and worst parts of their children's education? Ask specific questions and analyze the results.

>>ONLINE CONNECTIONS

To accompany your textbook, you have access to a number of online resources, including Learning Curve, an adaptive quizzing program, critical thinking questions, and case studies. For access to any of these links, go to www.worthpublishers .com/launchpad/bergerls9e. In addition to these resources, you'll also find links to video clips, personalized study advice, and an ebook. Some of the videos and activities available online include:

- *Achieving Conservation.* Half empty or half full? Watch as children of different ages perform the Piagetian conservation-of-liquid task, and note the differences as they explain their reasoning.

- *Moral Reasoning.* What would you have done if your wife was dying and you couldn't afford the medication that might save her? Watch children of various ages respond to the Heinz dilemma.

WORTH PUBLISHERS

Middle Childhood: Psychosocial Development

- **The Nature of the Child**
  Industry and Inferiority
  Self-Concept
  Culture and Self-Esteem
  Resilience and Stress

- **Families and Children**
  Shared and Nonshared Environments
  A VIEW FROM SCIENCE: "I Always Dressed One in Blue Stuff . . ."
  Family Function and Family Structure
  Connecting Family Structure and Function
  A CASE TO STUDY: How Hard Is It to Be a Kid?
  Family Trouble
  A VIEW FROM SCIENCE: Divorce

- **The Peer Group**
  The Culture of Children
  Friendships
  Popular and Unpopular Children
  Bullies and Victims

- **Children's Moral Values**
  Moral Reasoning
  What Children Value

WHAT WILL YOU KNOW?

1. What helps some children thrive in difficult family or neighborhood conditions?
2. Should parents marry, risking divorce, or not marry and thus avoid divorce?
3. What can be done to stop a bully?
4. When would children lie to adults to protect a friend?

> "But Dad, that's not fair! Why does Keaton get to kill zombies and I can't?"
>
> "Well, because you are too young to kill zombies. Your cousin Keaton is older than you, so that's why he can do it. You'll get nightmares."
>
> "That's soooo not fair."
>
> "Next year, after your birthday, I'll let you kill zombies."
>
> *[adapted from Asma, 2013]*

This conversation between a professor and his 8-year-old illustrates psychosocial development in middle childhood, explained in this chapter. All children want to do what the bigger children do, and all parents seek to protect their children, sometimes ineffectively. Throughout middle childhood, issues of parents and peers, fairness and justice, inclusion and exclusion are pervasive. Morality is the final topic of this chapter, but even the first topic, the nature of the child, raises ethical as well as psychosocial questions.

>> The Nature of the Child

As explained in the previous two chapters, steady growth, brain maturation, and intellectual advances make middle childhood a time for more independence (see At About This Time). Children acquire an "increasing ability to regulate themselves, to take responsibility, and to exercise self-control" (Huston & Ripke, 2006, p. 9).

One practical result is that between ages 6 and 11, children learn to care for themselves. They not only hold their own spoon but also make their own dinner, not only zip their own pants but also pack their own suitcases, not only walk to school but also organize games with friends. They venture outdoors alone. Boys are especially likely to engage in

JOE POLILLO/GETTY IMAGES

Adults Stay Out In middle childhood, children want to do things themselves. What if parents grabbed each child's hand and wanted to jump in, too? That would spoil the fun.

Left: Sean Sprague/The Image Works
Top: George Doyle/Getty Images

AT ABOUT THIS TIME

Signs of Psychosocial Maturation over the Years of Middle Childhood*

Children responsibly perform specific chores.
Children make decisions about a weekly allowance.
Children can tell time, and they have set times for various activities.
Children have homework, including some assignments over several days.
Children are less often punished than when they were younger.
Children try to conform to peers in clothes, language, and so on.
Children voice preferences about their after-school care, lessons, and activities.
Children are responsible for younger children, pets, and, in some places, work.
Children strive for independence from parents.

*Of course, culture is crucial. For example, giving a child an allowance is typical for middle class children in developed nations since about 1960. It was rare, or completely absent , in earlier times and other places.

industry versus inferiority The fourth of Erikson's eight psychosocial crises, during which children attempt to master many skills, developing a sense of themselves as either industrious or inferior, competent or incompetent.

latency Freud's term for middle childhood, during which children's emotional drives and psychosexual needs are quiet (latent). Freud thought that sexual conflicts from earlier stages are only temporarily submerged, bursting forth again at puberty.

activities without their parents' awareness or approval (Munroe & Romney, 2006). This budding independence fosters growth.

Industry and Inferiority

Throughout the centuries and in every culture, school-age children are industrious. They busily master whatever skills their culture values. Their mental and physical maturation, described in the previous two chapters, makes such activity possible.

Erikson's Insights

With regard to his fourth psychosocial crisis, **industry versus inferiority**, Erikson noted that the child "must forget past hopes and wishes, while his exuberant imagination is tamed and harnessed to the laws of impersonal things," becoming "ready to apply himself to given skills and tasks" (Erikson, 1963, pp. 258, 259).

Think of learning to read and add, both of which are painstaking and boring tasks. For instance, slowly sounding out "Jane has a dog" or writing "3 + 4 = 7" for the hundredth time is not exciting. Yet school-age children busily practice reading and math: They are intrinsically motivated to read a page, finish a worksheet, memorize a spelling word, color a map, and so on. Similarly, they enjoy collecting, categorizing, and counting whatever they gather—perhaps stamps, stickers, stones, or seashells. That is industry.

Overall, children judge themselves as either *industrious* or *inferior*—deciding whether they are competent or incompetent, productive or useless, winners or losers. Self-pride depends not necessarily on actual accomplishments, but on how others, especially peers, view one's accomplishments. Social rejection is both a cause and a consequence of feeling inferior (Rubin et al., 2013).

Freud on Latency

Sigmund Freud described this period as **latency**, a time when emotional drives are quiet (latent) and unconscious sexual conflicts are submerged. Some experts complain that "middle childhood has been neglected at least since Freud relegated these years to the status of an uninteresting 'latency period'" (Huston & Ripke, 2006, p. 7).

But in one sense, at least, Freud was correct: Sexual impulses are absent, or at least hidden. Even when children were betrothed before age 12 (rare today but common in earlier eras), the young husband and wife had little interaction. Everywhere, boys and girls typically choose to be with others of their own sex. Indeed, boys who write "Girls stay out!" and girls who complain that "boys stink" are typical.

Self-Concept

As children mature, they develop their *self-concept*, which is their idea about themselves, including their intelligence, personality, abilities, gender, and ethnic background. As you remember, the very notion that they are individuals is a discovery in toddlerhood, and a positive, global self-concept is typical in early childhood. Not so in middle childhood. The self-concept gradually becomes more specific and logical, the result of increases in cognitive development and social awareness.

Crucial during middle childhood is **social comparison**—comparing one's self to others (Davis-Kean et al., 2009; Dweck, 2013). Ideally, social comparison helps school-age children value themselves and abandon the imaginary, rosy self-evaluation of preschoolers. The self-concept becomes more realistic, incorporating comparison to peers and judgments from the overall society (Davis-Kean et al., 2009).

This means that some children—especially those from minority ethnic or religious groups—become newly aware of social prejudices they need to overcome (Kiang & Harter, 2008; McKown & Strambler, 2009). Children also become aware of gender discrimination, with girls complaining that they are not allowed to play tougher sports and boys complaining that teachers favor the girls (Brown et al., 2011).

For all children, this increasing self-understanding and social awareness come at a price. Self-criticism and self-consciousness rise from ages 6 to 11, and "by middle childhood this [earlier] overestimate of their ability or judgments decreases" (Davis-Kean et al., 2009, p. 184) while self-esteem falls. Children's self-concept becomes influenced by the opinions of others, even by other children whom they do not know (Thomaes et al., 2010).

In addition, because children think concretely during middle childhood, materialism increases, and attributes that adults might find superficial (hair texture, sock patterns) become important, making self-esteem fragile (Chaplin & John, 2007). Insecure 10-year-olds might desperately want the latest jackets, cell phones, and so on.

social comparison The tendency to assess one's abilities, achievements, social status, and other attributes by measuring them against other people, especially one's peers.

Culture and Self-Esteem

Academic and social competence are aided by realistic self-perception. Unrealistically high self-esteem reduces effortful control (deliberately modifying one's impulses and emotions), and less effortful control leads to lower achievement and increased aggression.

The same consequences occur if self-esteem is too low. Obviously then, the goal is to find a middle ground. This is not easy: children may be too self-critical or not self-critical enough. Cultures differ on what that the middle ground is.

Same Situation, Far Apart: Helping at Home Sichuan, in China, and Virginia, in the United States, provide vastly different contexts for child development. For instance, in some American suburbs, laws require recycling and forbid hanging laundry outside—but not in rural China. Nonetheless, everywhere children help their families with household chores, as these two do.

High self-esteem is neither universally valued nor universally criticized (Yamaguchi et al., 2007). Many cultures expect children to be modest, not prideful. For example, Australians say that "tall poppies are cut down," the Chinese say "the nail that sticks up is hammered," and the Japanese discourage social comparison aimed at making oneself feel superior. This makes self-esteem a moral issue as well as a practical one: *Should* people believe that they are better than other people, as is typical in the United States? Answers vary (Robins et al., 2012; Buhrmester et al., 2011).

Often in the United States, children's successes are praised and teachers are wary of being critical, especially in middle childhood. For example, some schools issue report cards with grades ranging from "Excellent" to "Needs improvement" instead of from A to F. An opposite trend is found in the national reforms of education, explained in Chapter 12. Because of the No Child Left Behind Act, some schools are rated as failing. Obviously culture, cohort, and age all influence attitudes toward high self-esteem: The effects are debatable.

One crucial component of self-concept has received considerable research attention (Dweck, 2013). As children become more self-aware, they benefit from praise for their process, not for their person: for *how* they learn, *how* they relate to others, and so on, not for static qualities such as intelligence and popularity. This encourages growth.

For example, children who fail a test are devastated if failure means they are not smart. However, process-oriented children consider failure a "learning opportunity," a time to figure out how to study the next time.

Resilience and Stress

In infancy and early childhood, children depend on their immediate families for food, learning, and life itself. Then "experiences in middle childhood can sustain, magnify, or reverse the advantages or disadvantages that children acquire in the preschool years" (Huston & Ripke, 2006, p. 2). Some children continue to benefit from supportive families, and others escape destructive family influences by finding their own niche in the larger world.

Surprisingly, some children seem unscathed by early experiences. They have been called "resilient" or even "invincible." Current thinking about resilience (see Table 13.1), with insights from dynamic-systems theory, emphasizes that no one is impervious to past history or current context (Jenson & Fraser, 2006; Luthar et al., 2003; Masten, 2013), but some cope better than others.

Differential sensitivity is apparent, not only because of genes but also because of early child rearing, preschool education, and sociocultural values. Some children are hardy, more like dandelions than orchids, but all are influenced by their situation (Ellis & Boyce, 2008).

resilience The capacity to adapt well to significant adversity and to overcome serious stress.

Resilience has been defined as "a dynamic process encompassing positive adaptation within the context of significant adversity" (Luthar et al., 2000, p. 543). Note the three parts of this definition:

- Resilience is *dynamic,* not a stable trait. That means a given person may be resilient at some periods but not others.
- Resilience is a *positive adaptation* to stress. For example, if parental rejection leads a child to a closer relationship with another adult, that is positive adaptation, not mere passive endurance. That child is resilient.
- Adversity must be *significant.* Some adversities are comparatively minor (large class size, poor vision), and some are major (victimization, neglect). Children need to cope with both kinds, but not all coping qualifies them as resilient.

TABLE 13.1	Dominant Ideas About Resilience, 1965–Present
1965	All children have the same needs for healthy development.
1970	Some conditions or circumstances—such as "absent father," "teenage mother," "working mom," and "day care"—are harmful for every child.
1975	All children are *not* the same. Some children are resilient, coping easily with stressors that cause harm in other children.
1980	Nothing inevitably causes harm. All the factors thought to be risks in 1970 (e.g., day care) are sometimes beneficial.
1985	Factors beyond the family, both in the child (low birthweight, prenatal alcohol exposure, aggressive temperament) and in the community (poverty, violence), can harm children.
1990	Risk–benefit analysis finds that some children are "invulnerable" to, or even benefit from, circumstances that destroy others.
1995	No child is invincibly resilient. Risks are always harmful—if not in education, then in emotions; if not immediately, then long term.
2000	Risk–benefit analysis involves the interplay among many biological, cognitive, and social factors, some within the child (genes, disability, temperament), the family (function as well as structure), and the community (including neighborhood, school, church, and culture).
2005	Focus on strengths, not risks. Assets in child (intelligence, personality), family (secure attachment, warmth), community (schools, after-school programs), and nation (income support, health care) are crucial.
2010	Strengths vary by culture and national values. Both universal needs and local variations must be recognized and respected.
2012	Genes, family structures, and cultural practices can be either strengths or weaknesses. Differential sensitivity means identical stressors can benefit one child and harm another.

Cumulative Stress

One important discovery is that accumulated stresses over time, including minor ones (called "daily hassles"), are more devastating than an isolated major stress. Almost every child can withstand one trauma, but repeated stresses make resilience difficult (Jaffee et al., 2007).

One international example comes from Sri Lanka, where many children in the first decade of the twenty-first century were exposed to war, a tsunami, poverty, deaths of relatives, and relocation. A study of the Sri Lankan children found that accumulated stresses, more than any single problem, increased pathology and decreased achievement. The authors point to "the importance of multiple contextual, past, and current factors in influencing children's adaptation" (Catani et al., 2010, p. 1188).

The social context, especially supportive adults who do not blame the child, is crucial. A chilling example comes from the "child soldiers" in the 1991–2002 civil war in Sierra Leone (Betancourt et al., 2013). Children witnessed and often participated in murder, rape, and other traumas. When the war was over, 529 war-affected

Death and Disruption Children are astonishingly resilient. This girl is in a refugee camp in Northern Syria in 2013, having fled the civil war that killed thousands in her community. Nonetheless, she is with her family and is adequately fed and clothed, and that is enough for a smile.

AAMIR QURESHI/AFP/GETTY IMAGES

youth, then aged 10 to 17, were interviewed. Many were pathologically depressed or anxious, as one might expect.

These war-damaged children were interviewed again two and six years later. Surprisingly, many had overcome their trauma and were functioning normally. Recovery was more likely if they were in middle childhood, not adolescence, when the war occurred. If at least one caregiver survived, if their communities did not reject them, and if their daily routines were restored, the children usually regained emotional normality.

Cognitive Coping

Obviously, this example from Sierra Leone is extreme, but the general finding appears in other research as well. Disasters take a toll, but resilience is possible. Factors in the child (especially problem-solving ability), in the family (consistency and care), and in the community (good schools and welcoming churches) all help children recover (Masten, 2013).

One pivotal factor is the child's own interpretation of events. Cortisol (the stress hormone) increases in low-income children *if* they interpret events connected to their family's poverty as a personal threat and *if* the family lacks order and routines (thus increasing daily hassles) (E. Chen et al., 2010). When low-SES children do not take things personally and their family is not chaotic, they are more likely to be resilient. Think of people you know: Many adults whose childhood family income was low did not consider themselves poor. In that case, poverty may not have harmed them.

In general, a child's interpretation of a family situation (poverty, divorce, and so on) determines how it affects him or her (Olson & Dweck, 2008). Some children consider the family they were born into a temporary hardship; they look forward to the day when they can leave childhood behind. The opposite reaction is called *parentification*, when children feel responsible for the entire family, acting as parents who take care of everyone, including their actual parents (Byng-Hall, 2008).

In another example, children who endured hurricane Katrina were affected by their thoughts, positive and negative, more than by factors one might expect, such as their caregivers' distress (Kilmer & Gil-Rivas, 2010). Interestingly, religious faith is sometimes crucial in helping children cope because faith is thought to provide hope and meaning (Masten, 2013).

Same Situation, Far Apart: Praying Hands Differences are obvious between the Northern Indian girls entering their Hindu school and the West African boy in a Christian church, even in their clothes and hand positions. But underlying similarities are more important. In every culture, many 8-year-olds are more devout than their elders.

Children gain in maturity and responsibility during the school years. According to Erikson, the crisis of industry versus inferiority generates feelings of confidence or self-doubt as children try to accomplish whatever their family, school, and culture set out for them to do. Freud thought latency enables children to master new skills because sexual impulses are quiet.

Often children develop more realistic self-concepts, with the help of their families and their own attitudes. Resilience to major adversity is apparent in some children in middle childhood, especially if the stress is temporary and coping measures and social support are available. School achievement, helpful adults, and religious beliefs help many children overcome whatever problems they face.

>> Families and Children

No one doubts that genes affect personality as well as ability, that peers are vital, and that schools and cultures influence what, and how much, children learn. Some go farther, suggesting that genes, peers, and communities have so much influence that parenting has little impact—unless it is grossly abusive (Harris, 1998, 2002; McLeod et al., 2007). This suggestion arose from studies about the impact of the environment on child development.

Shared and Nonshared Environments

Many studies have found that children are much less affected by *shared environment* (influences that arise from being in the same environment, such as for two siblings living in one home, raised by their parents) than by *nonshared environment* (e.g., the different experiences of two siblings).

Most personality traits and intellectual characteristics can be traced to genes and nonshared environments, with little left over for the shared influence of being raised by the same parents. Even psychopathology, happiness, and sexual orientation (Burt, 2009; Långström et al., 2010; Bartels et al., 2013) arise primarily from genes and nonshared environment.

Since many research studies find that shared environment has little impact, could it be that parents are merely caretakers, necessary for providing basic care (food, shelter) but inconsequential no matter what rules, routines, or responses they provide? If a child becomes a murderer or a hero, don't blame or credit the parents!

Recent findings, however, reassert parent power. The analysis of shared and nonshared influences was correct, but the conclusion was based on a false assumption. Siblings raised together do *not* share the same environment.

For example, if relocation, divorce, unemployment, or a new job occurs in a family, the impact depends on each child's age, genes, resilience, and gender. Moving to another town upsets a school-age child more than an infant, divorce harms boys more than girls, poverty may hurt the preschoolers the most, and so on.

The age and gender variations above do not apply for all siblings: Differential sensitivity means that one child is more affected, for better or worse, than another (Pluess & Belsky, 2010). When siblings are raised together, the mix of genes, age, and gender may lead one child to become antisocial, another to have a personality disorder, and a third to be resilient, capable, and strong (Beauchaine et al., 2009). This applies even to monozygotic twins, as the following explains.

Family Unity Thinking about any family—even a happy, wealthy family like this one—makes it apparent that each child's family experiences differ. For instance, would you expect this 5-year-old boy to be treated the same way as his two older sisters? And how about each child's feelings toward the parents? Even though the 12-year-olds are twins, one may favor her mother while the other favors her father.

Especially for Scientists How would you determine whether or not parents treat all their children the same? (see response, page 374)

A VIEW FROM SCIENCE

"I Always Dressed One in Blue Stuff . . ."

An expert team of scientists compared 1,000 sets of mono-zygotic twins reared by their biological parents (Caspi et al., 2004). Obviously, the pairs were identical in genes, sex, and age. The researchers asked the mothers to describe each twin. Descriptions ranged from very positive ("my ray of sunshine") to very negative ("I wish I never had her. . . . She's a cow, I hate her") (quoted in Caspi et al., 2004, p. 153). Many mothers noted personality differences between their twins. For example, one mother said:

> Susan can be very sweet. She loves babies . . . she can be insecure . . . she flutters and dances around. . . . There's not much between her ears. . . . She's exceptionally vain, more so than Ann. Ann loves any game involving a ball, very sporty, climbs trees, very much a tomboy. One is a serious tomboy and one's a serious girlie girl. Even when they were babies I always dressed one in blue stuff and one in pink stuff.
>
> *[quoted in Caspi et al., 2004, p. 156]*

Some mothers rejected one twin but not the other:

> He was in the hospital and everyone was all "poor Jeff, poor Jeff" and I started thinking, "Well, what about me? I'm the one's just had twins. I'm the one's going through this, he's a seven-week-old baby and doesn't know a thing about it" . . . I sort of detached and plowed my emotions into Mike.
>
> *[quoted in Caspi et al., 2004, p. 156]*

This mother blamed Jeff for favoring his father: "Jeff would do anything for Don but he wouldn't for me, and no matter what I did for either of them [Don or Jeff] it wouldn't be right" (p. 157). She said Mike was much more lovable.

The researchers measured personality at age 5 (assessing, among other things, antisocial behavior as reported by kinder-garten teachers) and then measured each twin's personality two years later. They found that if the mothers were more negative toward one of their twins, that twin *became* more antisocial, more likely to fight, steal, and hurt others at age 7 than at age 5, unlike the favored twin.

These researchers acknowledge that many other nonshared factors—peers, teachers, and so on—are significant. But this difference in monozygotic twins confirms that parents matter. If you have a brother or a sister, you know that children from the same family do not neces-sarily share the same experiences, at home or elsewhere.

---

family structure The legal and genetic relationships among relatives living in the same home; includes nuclear family, extended family, stepfamily, and so on.

family function The way a family works to meet the needs of its members. Children need families to provide basic material necessities, to encourage learning, to help them develop self-respect, to nurture friendships, and to foster harmony and stability.

>> Response for Scientists
(from page 373): Proof is very difficult when human interaction is the subject of investigation, since random assignment is impossible. Ideally, researchers would find identical twins being raised together and would then observe the parents' behavior over the years.

Family Function and Family Structure

Family structure refers to the legal and genetic connections among related people living in the same household. Families are single-parent families, or step-families, or three-generational families, and so on. **Family function** refers to how a family cares for its members: Some families function well, others are dysfunctional.

Function is more important than structure; everyone always needs family love and encouragement, which can come from parents, grandparents, siblings, or any other family member. Beyond that, people's needs differ depending on how old they are: Infants need responsive caregiving, teenagers need guidance, young adults need freedom, the aged need respect.

The Needs of Children in Middle Childhood

What do school-age children need? Ideally, families provide five things:

1. *Physical necessities.* Although 6- to 11-year-olds eat, dress, and go to sleep without help, families provide food, clothing, and shelter.
2. *Learning.* These are prime learning years: Families support, encourage, and guide education.
3. *Self-respect.* Because children at about age 6 become much more self-critical and socially aware, families provide opportunities for success (in sports, the arts, or other arenas if academic success is difficult).

4. *Peer relationships.* Families choose schools and neighborhoods with friendly children, and then arrange play dates, group activities, overnights, and so on.

5. *Harmony and stability.* Families provide protective, predictable routines with a home that is a safe, peaceful haven.

The final item on the list above is especially crucial in middle childhood: Children cherish safety and stability, not change (Turner et al., 2013). Ironically, many parents move from one neighborhood or school to another during these years. Children who move frequently are significantly harmed, academically and psychologically, but resilience is possible (Cutuli et al., 2013).

The problems arising from instability are evident for U.S. children in military families. Enlisted parents tend to have higher incomes, better health care, and more education than do civilians from the same backgrounds. But they have one major disadvantage. Military children (dubbed "military brats") have more emotional problems and lower school achievement than do their peers from civilian families for the following reason:

> Military parents are continually leaving, returning, leaving again. School work suffers, more for boys than for girls, and . . . reports of depression and behavioral problems go up when a parent is deployed.

> *[Hall, 2008, p. 52]*

The U.S. military has instituted a special program to help children whose parents are deployed. Caregivers of such children are encouraged to avoid changes in the child's life: no new homes, new rules, or new schools (Lester et al., 2011).

Diverse Structures

Worldwide today there are more single-parent households, more divorces and remarriages, and fewer children per family than in the past (see Visualizing Development, p. 377). The specifics vary from decade to decade and nation to nation (see Figure 13.1). Nevertheless, although the proportions differ, the problems are similar worldwide.

Almost two-thirds of all U.S. school-age children live with two married parents (see Table 13.2, p. 376), most often their biological parents. A **nuclear family** is a family composed only of children and their biological parents (married or not). Other two-parent structures include adoptive, foster, grandparents without parents, stepfamilies, and same-sex couples.

Rates of single-parenthood vary greatly worldwide (see Visualizing Development); about 31 percent of all U.S. 6-to-11 year olds live in a **single-parent family**. Some observers think more than 31 percent of U. S. children are in single-parent families since more than half of all contemporary U.S. children will live in a single-parent family before they reach age 18. However, as far as we can deduce, at any given moment most 6- to 11-year-olds are living with two parents.

The distinction between one-parent, two-parent, and **extended families** is not as simple in practice as it is on paper. Many young parents live near relatives who provide meals, emotional support, money, and child care, functioning as an extended family. The opposite is true as well, especially in developing nations: Some extended families share a household, but create separate living quarters for each set of parents and children, making these units somewhat like two-parent families (Georgas et al., 2006).

In many nations, the **polygamous family** (one husband with two or more wives) is an acceptable family structure. Generally in polygamous families, income per child is reduced, and education, especially for the girls, is limited (Omariba & Boyle, 2007). Polygamy is rare—and illegal—in the United States. Even in nations where it is allowed, polygamy is less common than it was 30 years ago. In Ghana, for example, men with several wives and a dozen children are now a rarity (Heaton & Darkwah, 2011).

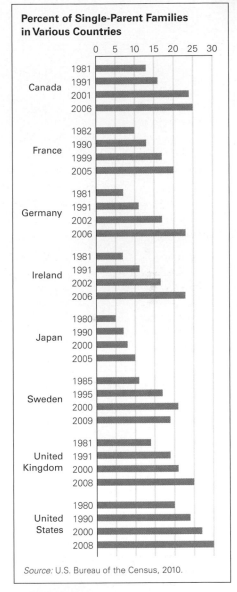

Percent of Single-Parent Families in Various Countries

Source: U.S. Bureau of the Census, 2010.

FIGURE 13.1

Single Parents Of all the households with children, a rising percentage of them are headed by a single parent. In some countries, many households are headed by two unmarried parents, a structure not shown here.

nuclear family A family that consists of a father, a mother, and their biological children under age 18.

single-parent family A family that consists of only one parent and his or her biological children under age 18.

extended family A family of three or more generations living in one household.

polygamous family A family consisting of one man, several wives, and their children.

TABLE 13.2	Family Structures (percent of U.S. 6- to 11-year-olds in each type)*

Two-Parent Families (69%)

1. **Nuclear family** (46%). Named after the nucleus (the tightly connected core particles of an atom), the nuclear family consists of a man and a woman and their biological offspring under 18 years of age. Almost half of all children live in nuclear families in middle childhood.

2. **Extended family** (10%). If both biological parents are present and other relatives live with them (usually a grandparent, sometimes an aunt or uncle), that is an extended family. About 10 percent of school-age children live in such families.

3. **Stepparent family** (9%). Divorced fathers usually remarry; divorced mothers remarry about half the time. When children from a former relationship live with the new couple, it makes a stepparent family. If the stepparent family includes children born to two or more couples (such as children from the spouses' previous marriages and/or children of the new couple), that is called a *blended family*.

4. **Adoptive family** (2%). Although as many as one-third of infertile married couples adopt children, few adoptable children are available, and so most adoptive couples have only one or two children. Thus, only 2 percent of children are adopted, although the overall percentage of adoptive families is higher than that.

5. **Both grandparents, no parents** (1%). Grandparents take on parenting for some children when biological parents are absent (dead, imprisoned, sick, addicted, etc.).

6. **Two same-sex parents** (1%). Some two-parent families are headed by a same-sex couple, whose legal status (married or not) varies.

Single-Parent Families (31%)

One-parent families are increasing, but they average fewer children than two-parent families, so in middle childhood, only 31 percent of children have a lone parent.

1. **Single mother—never married** (13%). More than half of all U. S. women under age 30 who gave birth in 2010 or later were unmarried. However, by the time their children reach middle childhood, often the mothers have married or the children are cared for by someone else. At any given moment, about 13 percent of 6- to 11-year-olds are with their never-married mothers.

2. **Single mother—divorced, separated, or widowed** (12%). Although many marriages end in divorce (almost half in the United States, fewer in other nations), many divorcing couples have no children. Others remarry. Thus, only 12 percent of school-age children currently live with single, formerly married mothers.

3. **Single father** (4%). About 1 father in 25 has physical custody of his children and raises them without their mother or a new wife. This category increased at the start of the twenty-first century but has decreased since 2005.

4. **Grandparent alone** (2%). Sometimes a single grandparent (usually the grandmother) becomes the sole caregiving adult for a child.

*Less than 1 percent of U.S. children live without any caregiving adult; they are not included in this table.

Source: The percentages in this table are estimates, based on data in U.S. Bureau of the Census, *Statistical Abstract* and Current Population Reports, *America's Families and Living Arrangements*, and Pew Research Center reports. The category "extended family" in this table is higher than in most published statistics, since some families do not tell official authorities about relatives living with them.

Connecting Family Structure and Function

More important for the children is not the structure of their family but how that family functions. The two are related; structure influences (but does not determine) function. The crucial question is whether the structure makes it more or less likely that the five family functions mentioned earlier (physical necessities, learning, self-respect, friendship, and harmony/stability) will be fulfilled.

A Wedding, or Not? Family Structures Around the World

Children fare best when both parents actively care for them every day. This is most likely to occur if the parents are married, although there are many exceptions. Many developmentalists now focus on the rate of single parenthood, shown on this map. Some single parents raise children well, but the risk of neglect, poverty, and instability in single-parent households increases the chances of child problems.

RATES OF SINGLE PARENTHOOD

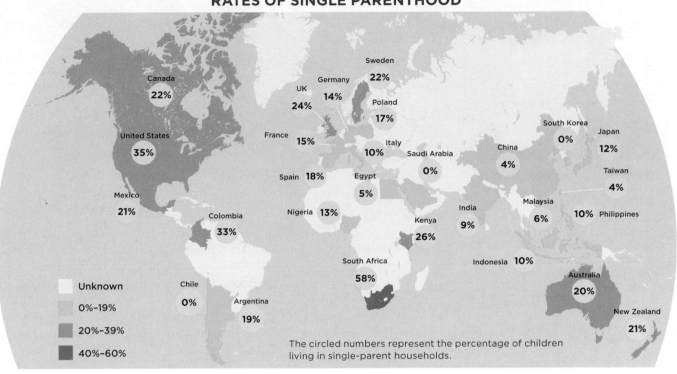

Canada 22%
Sweden 22%
Germany 14%
UK 24%
Poland 17%
United States 35%
France 15%
Italy 10%
Saudi Arabia 0%
China 4%
South Korea 0%
Japan 12%
Taiwan 4%
Spain 18%
Egypt 5%
Mexico 21%
Nigeria 13%
India 9%
Malaysia 6%
Philippines 10%
Colombia 33%
Kenya 26%
Indonesia 10%
South Africa 58%
Australia 20%
Chile 0%
Argentina 19%
New Zealand 21%

Unknown
0%–19%
20%–39%
40%–60%

The circled numbers represent the percentage of children living in single-parent households.

SOURCE: SOCIAL TRENDS INSTITUTE, 2012.

A young couple in love and committed to each other—*what next?*

IN THE UNITED STATES:

Influence of family and religion:
relatively weak

Likelihood of cohabitation:
70%

Likelihood of woman's marriage before age 25:
40%

IN NIGERIA:

influence of family and religion:
relatively strong

(Islam in Northern Nigeria, evangelical Christianity in Eastern Nigeria)

Likelihood of cohabitation:
1%

Likelihood of woman's marriage before age 25:
80%

COPEN, ET AL (2012); US CENSUS BUREAU (2012);

Cohabitation and marriage rates change from year to year and from culture to culture. These two examples are illustrative and approximate. Family-structure statistics like these often focus on marital status and may make it seem as if Nigerian children are more fortunate than American children. However, actual household functioning is more complex than that, and involves many other factors.

Same Situation, Far Apart: Happy Families
The boys in both photos are about 4 years old. Roberto (left) lives with his single mother in Chicago. She pays $360 a month for her two children to attend a day-care center. The youngest child in the Balmedina family (right) lives with his nuclear family—no day care needed—in the Philippines. Which boy has the better life? The answer is not known; family function is more crucial than family structure.

Two-Parent Families

On average, nuclear families function best; children in the nuclear structure tend to achieve better in school with fewer psychological problems. A scholar who summarized dozens of studies concludes: "Children living with two biological married parents experience better educational, social, cognitive, and behavioral outcomes than do other children" (Brown, 2010, p. 1062). Why? Does this mean that parents should all marry and stay married? Not necessarily: Some benefits are correlates, not causes.

Education, earning potential, and emotional maturity all make it more likely that people will marry, have children, stay married, and establish a nuclear family. Thus, brides and grooms tend to have personal assets *before* they marry, and those assets are brought to their new family. That means that the correlation between child success and married parents occurs partly because of who marries, not because of the wedding.

Income also correlates with family structure. Usually, if everyone can afford it, relatives live independently, apart from the married couple. That means that, at least in the United States, an extended family suggests that someone is financially dependent.

These two factors explain some of the correlation, but not all of it. After marriage, ideally, mutual affection encourages both partners to become wealthier and healthier than either would be alone. This often occurs—the selection effects noted in the previous paragraph are not the entire story (Amato, 2005; Brown, 2010). A *parental alliance,* whereby mother and father support each other in their mutual commitment to the child, is crucial. [**Lifespan Link:** The parental alliance and its importance were discussed in Chapter 4.]

Shared parenting decreases the risk of child maltreatment and makes it more likely that children will have someone to read to them, check their homework, invite their friends over, buy them new clothes, and save for their education. Of course, having two married parents does not guarantee an alliance. One of my students wrote:

> My mother externalized her feelings with outbursts of rage, lashing out and breaking things, while my father internalized his feelings by withdrawing, being silent and looking the other way. One could say I was being raised by bipolar parents. Growing up, I would describe my mom as the Tasmanian devil and my father as the ostrich, with his head in the sand. . . . My mother disciplined with corporal punishment as well as with psychological control, while my father was permissive. What a pair.

[C., 2013]

This student is now a single parent, having twice married, given birth, and divorced. She is one example of a general finding. The effects of a childhood family can echo in adulthood. For college students, this effect may be financial as well as psychological. A survey of college tuition payments found that nuclear families provided the most money for college.

This was not simply because two-parent families are wealthier, on average, than one-parent families. Even remarried parents, whose family income is comparable to that of nuclear parents, contribute less, on average, to children from their first marriage (Turley & Desmond, 2011).

Adoptive and same-sex parents function well for children, as do stepfamilies if a single biological parent chooses a new partner who will be a good parent. Especially when children are under age 2 and the stepparent forms a close and loving relationship with the biological parent, the children may thrive (Ganong et al., 2011). Of course, no structure always functions well, but circumstances (such as biological connections, or adoptive choices) nudge in the right direction.

Considerable research has focused on stepparent families. The primary advantage of this family structure is financial, especially when compared with most single-parent families. The primary disadvantage is in meeting the fifth family function listed earlier—providing harmony and stability.

Stability is threatened not only by the inevitable instability of having a new parent. Compared with other two-parent families, stepfamilies move more often, older stepchildren are more likely to leave, babies who are half-brothers or sisters may capture parental attention and affection, and divorce is more common (Teachman, 2008a).

Harmony is difficult to achieve (Martin-Uzzi, & Duval-Tsioles, 2013). Often the child's loyalty to both biological parents is challenged by ongoing disputes between them. A solid parental alliance is elusive when it includes three adults—two of whom disliked each other enough to divorce, plus another adult who is a newcomer to the child.

Children who are given a stepparent may be angry or sad; they often create problems, and hence disagreements, for their remarried parents. Further, disputes between half-siblings in blended families are common. Remember, however, that structure affects function but does not determine it. Some stepparent families are difficult for children, but others function well for everyone (van Eeden-Moorefield & Pasley, 2013).

Finally, when grandparents provide full-time care without parents present (called a *skipped-generation family*, the most common form of foster care), the hope is that their experience and maturity will benefit the children. However, on average, grandparent families have lower incomes, more health problems, and less stability than other two-parent families. The children often have ADHD or learning disabilities.

Skipped-generation families are less likely to get services for children with special needs, to find responsive judges, schools, and social workers, or even to find neighbors and friends to share child care (Baker & Mutchler, 2010; Hayslip & Smith, 2013). This is true when both grandparents are caregivers; it is even more true when a grandmother alone is the caregiver, which is the usual case.

Middle American Family This photo seems to show a typical breakfast in Brunswick, Ohio—Cheerios for 1-year-old Carson, pancakes that 7-year-old Carter does not finish eating, and family photos crowded on the far table. The one apparent difference—that both parents are women—does not necessarily create or avoid children's problems.

DAVID MAXWELL/THE NEW YORK TIMES/REDUX

Especially for Single Parents You have heard that children raised in one-parent families will have difficulty in establishing intimate relationships as adolescents and adults. What can you do about this possibility? (see response, page 382)

Single-Parent Families

On average, the single-parent structure functions less well for children because single parents have less income and stability than two-parent families. Most single parents fill many roles—including wage earner, daughter or son (single parents often depend on their own parents), and lover (many seek a new partner)—which makes it hard for them to provide steady emotional and academic support for their schoolchildren. If they are depressed (and many are), they are less available to meet their children's needs. Neesha in the following case is an example.

One correlate of support is whether or not the community, ethnic group, or nation helps single parents. More than half of African American 6- to 11-year-olds live with only one parent (Figure 13.2). They might be less isolated and dysfunctional because their experience is so common (Cain & Combs-Orme, 2005; Taylor et al., 2008), and often relatives and friends help.

In some European nations, single parents are given many public resources; in other nations, they are shamed as well as unsupported. Children benefit or suffer accordingly.

A CASE TO STUDY

How Hard Is It to Be a Kid?

Neesha's fourth-grade teacher referred her to the school guidance team because Neesha often fell asleep in class, was late 51 days, and was absent 15 days. Testing found Neesha at the seventh-grade level in reading and writing and at the fifth-grade level in math. Since achievement was not Neesha's problem, something psychosocial might be amiss.

The counselor spoke to Neesha's mother, Tanya, a single parent who was depressed and worried about paying the rent on a tiny apartment where she had moved when Neesha's father left three years earlier. He lived with his girlfriend, now with a baby. Tanya said she had no problems with Neesha, who was "more like a little mother than a kid," unlike her 15-year-old son, Tyrone, who suffered from fetal alcohol effects and whose behavior worsened when his father left.

Tyrone was recently beaten up badly as part of a gang initiation, a group he considered "like a family." He was currently in juvenile detention, after being arrested for stealing bicycle parts. Note the nonshared environment here: Although the siblings grew up together and their father left them both, 12-year-old Tyrone became rebellious whereas 7-year-old Neesha became "a little mother."

The school counselor also spoke with Neesha.

Neesha volunteered that she worried a lot about things and that sometimes when she worries she has a hard time falling asleep. . . . she got in trouble for being late so many times, but it was hard to wake up. Her mom was sleeping late because she was working more nights cleaning offices. . . . Neesha said she got so far behind that she just gave up. She was also having problems with the other girls in the class, who were starting to tease her about sleeping in class and

not doing her work. She said they called her names like "Sleepy" and "Dummy." She said that at first it made her very sad, and then it made her very mad. That's when she started to hit them to make them stop.

[Wilmhurst, 2011, pp. 152–153]

Neesha is coping with poverty, a depressed mother, an absent father, a delinquent brother, and classmate bullying. She showed resilience—her achievement scores are impressive—but shortly after Neesha was interviewed,

The school principal received a call from Neesha's mother, who asked that her daughter not be sent home from school because she was going to kill herself. She was holding a loaded gun in her hand and she had to do it, because she was not going to make this month's rent. She could not take it any longer, but she did not want Neesha to come home and find her dead. . . . While the guidance counselor continued to keep the mother talking, the school contacted the police, who apprehended [the] mom while she was talking on her cell phone. . . . The loaded gun was on her lap. . . . The mother was taken to the local psychiatric facility.

[Wilmhurst, 2011, pp. 154–155]

Whether Neesha's resilience will continue depends on her ability to find support beyond her family. Perhaps the school counselor will help:

When asked if she would like to meet with the school psychologist once in a while, just to talk about her worries, Neesha said she would like that very much. After she left the office, she turned and thanked the psychologist for working with her, and added, "You know, sometimes it's hard being a kid."

[Wilmhurst, 2011, p. 154]

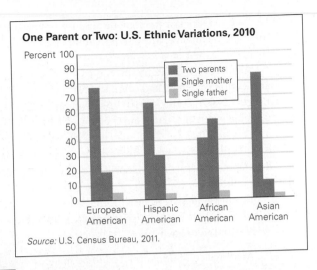

One Parent or Two: U.S. Ethnic Variations, 2010

Legend:
- Two parents
- Single mother
- Single father

Categories: European American, Hispanic American, African American, Asian American

Source: U.S. Census Bureau, 2011.

FIGURE 13.2

Diverse Families The fact that family structure is affected partly by ethnicity has implications for everyone in the family. It is easier to be a single parent if there are others of the same background who are also single parents.

All these are generalities: Contrary to the averages, thousands of nuclear families are destructive, thousands of stepparents provide excellent care, and thousands of single-parent families are wonderful. Structure may encourage or undercut healthy function, but many parents overcome structural problems to support their children, as explained now.

Family Trouble

Two factors interfere with family function in every structure, ethnic group, and nation: low income and high conflict. Many families experience both because financial stress increases conflict and vice versa (McLanahan, 2009).

A VIEW FROM SCIENCE

Divorce

Scientists try to provide analysis and insight, based on empirical data (of course), but the task goes far beyond reporting facts. Regarding divorce, thousands of studies and several opposing opinions need to be considered, analyzed, and combined—no easy task. One scholar who has attempted this analysis is Andrew Cherlin, who has written 13 books and over 200 articles since 1988.

Among the facts that need analysis are these:

1. The United States leads the world in the rates of marriage, divorce, and remarriage, with almost half of all marriages ending in divorce. Why?

2. Single parents, cohabiting parents, and stepparents sometimes provide good care, but children tend to do best in nuclear families with married parents. Why?

3. Divorce often impairs children's academic achievement and psychosocial development for years, even decades. Why?

The problem, Cherlin (2009) contends, is that U.S. culture is conflicted: Marriage is idolized, but so is personal freedom. As a result, many people assert their independence by marrying without consulting their parents or community. Then, when child care becomes overwhelming and family or public support is lacking, the marriage becomes strained, so they divorce.

Didn't Want to Marry This cohabiting couple decided to wed only after they learned that her health insurance would not cover him unless they were legally married. Two years later they had a son, who is now developing happily and well. She is pregnant with their second child, and he is searching for a house to buy. Would this have happened if they were still unmarried?

Because marriage remains the ideal, they blame their former mate or their own poor decision, not the institution.

Consequently, they seek another marriage, which may lead to another divorce. (Divorced people are more likely to remarry than single people their age are to marry, but second marriages fail more often than first marriages.) All this is in accord with personal freedom, but repeated transitions harm children.

This leads to a related insight. Cherlin suggests that the main reason children are harmed by divorce—as well as by cohabitation, single parenthood, and stepparenthood—is not the legal status of their parents but the lack of stability. For example, divorces typically include numerous disruptions: in residence, in school, in family members, and—this may be crucial—in the relationship between child and parent. Divorced parents may become too strict or too lenient, impose premature responsibility or independence, or trouble the child by sharing confidences that relieve their own loneliness.

Scholars now describe divorce as a process, with transitions and conflicts before and after the formal event (Magnuson & Berger, 2009; Potter, 2010). As you remember, resilience is difficult when the child must contend with repeated changes and ongoing hassles—yet that is what divorce brings. Coping is particularly hard when children are at an age that involves a developmental transition, such as entering first grade or beginning puberty.

Beyond analysis and insight, the other task of developmental science is to provide practical suggestions. Most scholars would agree with the following:

1. Marriage commitments need to be made slowly and carefully, to minimize the risk of divorce. It takes time to develop intimacy and commitment.
2. Once married, couples need to work to keep the relationship strong. Often happiness dips after the birth of the first child. Knowing that, new parents need to do together what they love—dancing, traveling, praying, whatever.
3. Divorcing parents need to minimize transitions and maintain a child's relationships with both parents. Often a mediator—who advocates for the child, not for either parent—can help. (Mediators are required in some U.S. jurisdictions.)
4. In middle childhood, schools can provide vital support. Routines, friendships, and academic success may be especially crucial when a child's family is chaotic.

This may sound idealistic. However, another scientist, who has also studied divorced families for decades, writes:

> Although divorce leads to an increase in stressful life events, such as poverty, psychological and health problems in parents, and inept parenting, it also may be associated with escape from conflict, the building of new more harmonious fulfilling relationships, and the opportunity for personal growth and individuation.
>
> [Hetherington, 2006, p. 204]

Not every parent should marry, not every marriage should continue, and not every child is devastated by divorce. However, every child benefits from all five family functions. Adults can provide that. Scientists hope they do.

Wealth and Poverty

Family income correlates with both function and structure. Marriage rates fall in times of recession, and divorce correlates with unemployment. The effects of poverty are cumulative; low socioeconomic status (SES) may be especially damaging for children if it begins in infancy and continues in middle childhood (Duncan et al., 2010).

Several scholars have developed the *family-stress model*, which holds that any risk factor (such as low income, divorce, single parenthood, unemployment) damages a family if, and only if, it increases stress. Poverty is less stressful *if* low

>> **Response for Single Parents** (from page 380): Do not get married mainly to provide a second parent for your child. If you were to do so, things would probably get worse rather than better. Do make an effort to have friends of both sexes with whom your child can interact.

income is temporary and the family's net worth (home ownership, investments, and so on) buffers the strain (Yeung & Conley, 2008). However, if economic hardship is ongoing and parents have little education, the result is increased stress. Adults become tense and hostile toward their partners and children (Conger et al., 2002). Thus, the *reaction* to poverty is crucial.

Reaction to wealth may also cause problems. Children in high-income families develop more than their share of developmental problems. One reason may be parental pressure on the children to excel, which creates externalizing and internalizing problems in middle childhood that lead to drug use, delinquency, and poor academic performance (Ansary & Luthar, 2009).

Remember the dynamic-systems perspective described in Chapter 1? That perspective applies to income: Multigenerational research finds that poverty is both a cause and a symptom of emotional and learning problems.

Adults whose upbringing included less education and impaired emotional control are more likely to have difficulty finding employment and raising their children, and then low income adds to their difficulties (Schofield et al., 2011). Health problems in infancy may lead to "biologically embedded" stresses that impair adult well-being, and that affects the next generation (Masten, 2013).

If all this is so, more income means better family functioning. For example, children in single-mother households do much better if their father pays child support, even if he is not actively involved in the child's daily life (Huang, 2009). Nations that subsidize single parents (e.g., Austria and Iceland) also have smaller achievement gaps between low- and middle-SES children on the TIMSS. This finding is suggestive, but controversial and value-laden. Some developmentalists report that raising income does *not,* by itself, improve parenting (L. M. Berger et al., 2009).

Conflict

There is no controversy about conflict: Every researcher agrees that family conflict harms children, especially when adults fight about child rearing. Such fights are more common in stepfamilies, divorced families, and extended families, but nuclear families are not immune. In every family, children suffer not only if they are abused, physically or emotionally, but also if they are merely witness to their parents' fighting. Fights between siblings can be harmful, too (Turner et al., 2013).

Researchers wonder whether one reason that children are emotionally troubled in families with feuding parents is inherited tendencies, instead of directly caused by seeing the parents fight. The idea is that the parents' genes lead to marital problems, and that those same genes lead to children's difficulties. If that is the case, then it doesn't matter if children are aware of their parents' conflicts.

This idea was tested in a longitudinal study of 867 twin pairs (388 monozygotic pairs and 479 dizygotic pairs), all married with an adolescent child. Each adolescent was compared to his or her cousin, the child of one parent's twin (Schermerhorn et al., 2011). Thus, this study had data on family conflict from 5,202 individuals—one-third of them adult twins, one-third of them spouses of twins, and one-third of them adolescents.

The researchers found that, although genes had some effect, witnessing conflict itself had a powerful effect on the children, causing externalizing problems in the boys and internalizing problems in the girls. In this study, quiet disagreements did not much harm the child, but open conflict (such as yelling when children could hear) or divorce did (Schermerhorn et al., 2011). That leads to an obvious conclusion: Parents should not fight in front of the children.

SUMMING UP

Families serve five crucial functions for school-age children: to supply basic necessities, to encourage learning, to develop self-respect, to nurture friendships, and to provide harmony and stability.

The nuclear, two-parent family is the most common family structure, with other two-parent families possible. Many families are headed by a single parent, usually the mother—half because she never married and half because she divorced. Nuclear families (headed by two biological parents) tend to provide more income, stability, and parental attention, all of which benefit children. Other family types (grandparent, single mother, single father, stepparent, same-sex, or adoptive) often raise successful children, although each type has vulnerabilities. Although structures affect function, no structure inevitably harms children, and no structure (including nuclear) guarantees optimal function. Poverty and wealth can both cause stress, which interferes with family function. Conflict between the parents affects the children, no matter what the family structure.

>> The Peer Group

Peers become increasingly important in middle childhood. School-age children are painfully aware of their classmates' opinions, judgments, and accomplishments.

The Culture of Children

child culture The particular habits, styles, and values that reflect the set of rules and rituals that characterize children as distinct from adult society.

Peer relationships, unlike adult–child relationships, involve partners who negotiate, compromise, share, and defend themselves as equals. Consequently, children learn social lessons from one another that grown-ups cannot teach (Rubin et al., 2013). Adults sometimes command obedience, sometimes are subservient, but they are always much older and bigger, with their own values and experiences, which are not the child's.

Child culture includes the customs, rules, and rituals that are passed down to younger children from slightly older ones. Jump-rope rhymes, insults, and superstitions are often part of peer society. Even nursery games echo child culture. For instance, "Ring around the rosy/Pocketful of posy/Ashes, ashes/We all fall down," may have originated as children coped with the Black Death, which killed half the population of Europe in the fourteenth century (Kastenbaum, 2006). (*Rosy* may be short for *rosary*.)

Throughout the world, child culture encourages independence from adults. Many children reject clothes that parents buy as too loose, too tight, too long, too short, or wrong in color, style, brand, decoration, or some other aspect that adults might not notice.

Appearance is important for child culture, but more important are relationships with adults. Classmates pity those (especially boys) whose parents kiss them ("mama's boy"), tease children who please the teachers ("teacher's pet," "suck-up"), and despise those who betray children to adults ("tattletale," "grasser," "snitch," "rat"). Keeping secrets from parents and teachers is a moral mandate (Gillis, 2008).

The culture of children is not always benign. For example, because communication with peers is vital, children learn the necessary languages. Parents proudly note how well their bilingual children speak a second language, but parents are distressed when their children spout their peers' curses, accents, and slang. Seeking independence from parents, children find friends who defy authority, sometimes harmlessly (passing a note in class), sometimes not (shoplifting, smoking).

No Toys Boys in middle childhood are happiest playing outside with equipment designed for work. This wheelbarrow is perfect, especially because at any moment the pusher might tip it.

E. HANAZAKI PHOTOGRAPHY/FLICKR RF/GETTY IMAGES

Friendships

Teachers may try to separate friends, but most developmentalists realize that friends help each other learn both academic and social skills (Bagwell & Schmidt, 2012). Friends affect attitudes as well as behavior. It is mistake to assume that friends are a distraction, or a source of trouble, although obviously each relationship is distinct. Aggressive friends are sought out by other aggressive children, and then they both are mean to outsiders, but they may learn loyalty via the friendship (Rubin et al., 2013).

Remember Yolanda and Paul from Chapter 12? Their friends guided them:

Yolanda:
There's one friend . . . she's always been with me, in bad or good . . . She's always telling me, "Keep on going and your dreams are gonna come true."

Paul:
I think right now about going Christian, right? Just going Christian, trying to do good, you know? Stay away from drugs, everything. And every time it seems like I think about that, I think about the homeboys. And it's a trip because a lot of the homeboys are my family, too, you know?

[quoted in Nieto, 2000, pp. 220, 149]

Yolanda went to college; Paul went to jail.

Children want to be liked; consequently they learn faster and feel happier when they have friends. If they had to choose between being friendless but popular (looked up to by many peers) or having close friends but being unpopular (ignored by peers), most would choose to have friends (Bagwell & Schmidt, 2012). A wise choice.

Friendships become more intense and intimate over the years of middle childhood, as social cognition and effortful control advance. Six-year-olds may be friends with anyone of the same sex and age who is willing to play with them cooperatively. By age 10, children demand more of their friends. They share secrets, change friends less often, become more upset when a friendship breaks up, and find it harder to make new friends.

Older children tend to choose friends whose interests, values, and backgrounds are similar to their own. By the end of middle childhood, close friendships are almost always between children of the same sex, age, ethnicity, and socioeconomic status (Rubin et al., 2013). This occurs not because children naturally become more prejudiced over the course of middle childhood (they do not) but because they seek friends who understand and agree with them.

Gender differences persist in activities (girls converse more whereas boys play more active games), but both boys and girls want best friends and usually find them. Having no close friends at age 11 predicts depression at age 13 (Brendgen et al., 2010).

Popular and Unpopular Children

In North American culture, shy children are not popular, but a 1990 survey in Shanghai found that shy children were liked and respected (X. Chen et al., 1992). Twelve years later, assertiveness became more valued in China: A survey from the same schools found shy children less popular than their shy predecessors had been (X. Chen et al., 2005). A few years later, a third study in rural China found shyness still valued; it predicted adult adjustment (X. Chen et al., 2009). Obviously, cohort and context matter.

Recently in the United States, two types of popular children and three types of unpopular children have become apparent in middle childhood. First, at every age, children who are "kind, trustworthy, cooperative" are well liked. By the end of middle childhood, the second type of popularity begins: children who are "athletic, cool, dominant, arrogant, and . . . aggressive" (Cillessen & Mayeux, 2004a, p. 147; Rodkin & Roisman, 2010).

As for the three types of unpopular children, some are *neglected*, not rejected; they are ignored, but not shunned. The other two types are actively rejected, either **aggressive-rejected**, disliked because they are antagonistic and confrontational, or **withdrawn-rejected**, disliked because they are timid and anxious. Rejected children of both types often misinterpret social situations, lack emotional regulation, and are mistreated by their parents. They may become bullies and victims.

Bullies and Victims

Bullying is defined as repeated, systematic attacks intended to harm those who are unable or unlikely to defend themselves. It occurs in every nation, in every community, and in every kind of school (religious or secular, public or private, progressive or traditional, large or small) and perhaps in every child. As one girl said, "There's a little bit of bully in everyone" (Guerra et al., 2011, p. 303).

Bullying may be of four types:
- *Physical* (hitting, pinching, shoving, or kicking)
- *Verbal* (teasing, taunting, or name-calling)
- *Relational* (destroying peer acceptance)
- *Cyberbullying* (using electronic means to harm another)

The first three types are common in primary school and begin even earlier, in preschool. Cyberbullying is more common later on. [**Lifespan Link:** Cyberbullying is discussed in Chapter 15.]

A key word in the definition of bullying is *repeated*. Almost every child experiences an isolated attack or is called a derogatory name at some point. Victims of bullying, however, endure shameful experiences again and again—being forced to hand over lunch money, laugh at insults, drink milk mixed with detergent, and so on—with no

aggressive-rejected Rejected by peers because of antagonistic, confrontational behavior.

withdrawn-rejected Rejected by peers because of timid, withdrawn, and anxious behavior.

bullying Repeated, systematic efforts to inflict harm through physical, verbal, or social attack on a weaker person.

Who Suffers More? The 12-year-old girl and the 10-year-old boy both seem to be bullying younger children, but their attacks differ. Some developmentalists think a verbal assault is more painful than a physical one because it lingers for years.

one defending them. Victims tend to be "cautious, sensitive, quiet . . . lonely and abandoned at school. As a rule, they do not have a single good friend in their class" (Olweus et al., 1999, p. 15).

Although it is often thought that victims are particularly ugly or odd, this is not usually the case. Victims are chosen because of their emotional vulnerability and social isolation, not their appearance. Children who are new to a school, or children whose background and therefore home culture are unlike that of their peers, are especially vulnerable.

As one boy said,
> You can get bullied because you are weak or annoying or because you are different. Kids with big ears get bullied. Dorks get bullied. You can also get bullied because you think too much of yourself and try to show off. Teacher's pet gets bullied. If you say the right answer too many times in class you can get bullied. There are lots of popular groups who bully each other and other groups, but you can get bullied within your group too. If you do not want to get bullied, you have to stay under the radar, but then you might feel sad because no one pays attention to you.

[*quoted in Guerra et al., 2011, p. 306*]

Remember the three types of unpopular children? Neglected children are not victimized; they are ignored, "under the radar." If their family relationships are good, they suffer less even if they are bullied (which they usually are not) Bowes et al., 2010).

Withdrawn-rejected children are often victims; they are isolated, feel depressed, and are friendless. Aggressive-rejected children are called **bully-victims** (or *provocative victims*), with neither friends nor sympathizers. They suffer the most, because they strike back ineffectively, which increases the bullying (Dukes et al., 2009).

Unlike bully-victims, most bullies are *not* rejected. Although some have low self-esteem, others are proud; they are pleased with themselves, they have friends who admire them and classmates who fear them (Guerra et al., 2011). Often they are socially perceptive, picking victims who are rejected by most classmates (Veenstra et al., 2010). Over the years of middle childhood, they become skilled at avoiding adult awareness, attacking victims who will not resist or tell.

Boys bully more than girls, usually physically attacking smaller, weaker boys. Girl bullies usually use words to attack shyer, more soft-spoken girls. Young boys can sometimes bully girls, but by puberty (about age 11), boys who bully girls are not admired (Veenstra et al., 2010), although sexual teasing is. Especially in the final years of middle childhood, boys who are thought to be gay become targets, with suicide attempts one consequence (Hong et al., 2012).

Causes and Consequences of Bullying

Bullying may originate with a genetic predisposition or a brain abnormality, but when a toddler is aggressive, parents, teachers, and peers usually teach emotional regulation and effortful control. If home life is stressful, discipline is ineffectual, siblings are hostile, or attachment is insecure, those lessons are not learned. Instead, young children develop externalizing and internalizing problems, becoming bullies or victims (Turner et al., 2013).

Peers are crucial. Some peer groups approve of relational bullying, and then children entertain their classmates by mocking and insulting each other (N. E. Werner & Hill, 2010). On the other hand, when students themselves disapprove of bullying, its incidence is reduced (Guerra & Williams, 2010). Age is also an important factor. For most of childhood, bullies are disliked, but a switch occurs at about age 11, when bullying becomes a way to gain social status (Caravita & Cillessen, 2012).

bully-victim Someone who attacks others and who is attacked as well. (Also called *provocative victims* because they do things that elicit bullying.)

The consequences of bullying can echo for years, worsening with age. Many victims become depressed; many bullies become increasingly cruel. However, bullies and victims can be identified in first grade and get "active guidance and remediation" before their behavior becomes truly destructive (Leadbeater & Hoglund, 2009, p. 857).

Unless bullies are deterred, they and their victims risk impaired social understanding, lower school achievement, and relationship difficulties. Decades later they have higher rates of mental illness (Copeland et al., 2013; Ma et al., 2009; Pepler et al., 2004). Compared to other adults the same age, former bullies are more likely to die young, be jailed, or have destructive marriages. Bystanders suffer, too, learning less when bullying is common (Monks & Coyne, 2011; Nishina & Juvonen, 2005; Rivers et al., 2009).

Can Bullying Be Stopped?

Most victimized children find ways to halt ongoing bullying—by ignoring, retaliating, defusing, or avoiding. Friends defend each other and restore self-esteem (Bagwell & Schmidt, 2012). Friendships help individual victims, but what can be done to halt a culture of bullying?

We know what does *not* work: simply increasing students' awareness of bullying, instituting zero tolerance for fighting, or putting bullies together in a therapy group or a classroom (Baldry & Farrington, 2007; Monks, & Coyne, 2011). This last measure tends to make daily life easier for some teachers, but it increases aggression. Since one cause of bullying is poor parent–child interaction, talking to the bully's or victim's parents may "create even more problems for the child, for the parents, and for their relationship" (Rubin et al., 2013, p. 267).

The school community as a whole—teachers and bystanders, parents and aides, bullies and victims—needs to change. In fact, the entire school can either increase the rate of bullying or decrease it. For example, a Colorado study found that, when the overall school climate encouraged learning and cooperation, children with high self-esteem were unlikely to be bullies; when the school climate was hostile, those with high self-esteem were often bullies (Gendron et al., 2011).

Peers are crucial: If they simply notice bullying, becoming aware without doing anything that provides no help. In fact, some bystanders feel morally disengaged from the victims, which increases bullying. Others are sympathetic but feel powerless (Thornberg & Jungert, 2013). However, if they empathize with victims, feel effective (high in effortful control), and refuse to admire bullies, classroom aggression is reduced (Salmivalli, 2010).

Efforts to change the entire school—bystanders, teachers, and aides—are credited with recent successful efforts to decrease bullying in 29 schools in England (Cross et al., 2011), throughout Norway, in Finland (Kärnä et al., 2011), and often in the United States (Allen, 2010; Limber, 2011).

A review of ways to halt bullying (Berger, 2007) finds that:
- Everyone in the school must change, not just the identified bullies.
- Intervention is more effective in the earlier grades.
- Evaluation is critical: Programs that seem good might be harmful.

This final point merits emphasis. Longitudinal research on whole-school efforts finds that some programs make a difference and some do not, with variations depending on the age of the children and the indicators (peer report of bullying or victimization, teacher report of incidents reported, and so on). Objective follow-up efforts suggest that bullying can be reduced but not eliminated.

Especially for Parents of an Accused Bully Another parent has told you that your child is a bully. Your child denies it and explains that the other child doesn't mind being teased. (see response, page 390)

SUMMING UP

School-age children develop their own culture, with customs that encourage them to be loyal to one another. All 6- to 11-year-olds want and need social acceptance and close, mutual friendships to protect against loneliness and depression. Children of all ages value peers who are kind and outgoing; by the end of middle childhood, peers who are self-assured and aggressive may be admired as well. Friendship is more valued than popularity; being rejected is painful.

Most children experience occasional peer rejection. However, some children are victims, repeatedly rejected and friendless, and experience physical, verbal, or relational bullying. Bullies may have friends and social power in middle childhood and early adolescence, but they are likely to suffer in adulthood. Some efforts to reduce bullying succeed and some do not. A whole-school approach seems best, with the bystanders crucial to establishing an anti-bullying culture. ∎

>> Children's Moral Values

The origins of morality are debatable (see Chapter 10), but there is no doubt that middle childhood is prime time for moral development. These are:

> years of eager, lively searching on the part of children . . . as they try to understand things, to figure them out, but also to weigh the rights and wrongs. . . . This is the time for growth of the moral imagination, fueled constantly by the willingness, the eagerness of children to put themselves in the shoes of others.

> *[Coles, 1997, p. 99]*

Many forces drive children's growing interest in moral issues. Three of them are (1) child culture, (2) personal experience, and (3) empathy. As already explained, the culture of children includes moral values, such as loyalty to friends and keeping secrets. Personal experiences also matter.

For example, students in multiethnic schools are better able to use morality to combat prejudice than students in more ethnically homogeneous schools (Killen et al., 2006). For all children, empathy increases in middle childhood because children become more socially perceptive.

This increasing perception can backfire, however. One example was just described: Bullies become adept at picking victims (Veenstra et al., 2010). An increase in social understanding makes noticing and defending rejected children possible, but in a social context that allows bullying, bystanders may decide to be self-protective rather than intervening (Pozzoli & Gini, 2013).

Children who are slow to develop theory of mind—which, as discussed in Chapter 9, is affected by family and culture—are also slow to develop empathy (Caravita et al., 2010). The authors of a study of 7-year-olds "conclude that moral *competence* may be a universal human characteristic, but that it takes a situation with specific demand characteristics to translate this competence into actual prosocial performance" (van Ijzendoorn et al., 2010, p. 1). In other words, school-age children can think and act morally, but they do not always do so.

Moral Reasoning

Much of the developmental research on children's moral thinking began with Piaget's descriptions of the rules used by children as they play (Piaget, 1932/1997). This work led to a famous description of cognitive stages of morality (Kohlberg, 1963).

Wonderfully Conventional Krysta Caltabiano displays her poster, "Ways to Be a Good Citizen," which won the Good Citizenship Contest sponsored by the Connecticut Secretary of State.

Kohlberg's Levels of Moral Thought

Lawrence Kohlberg described three levels of moral reasoning and two stages at each level (see Table 13.3), with parallels to Piaget's stages of cognition.

- **Preconventional moral reasoning** is similar to preoperational thought in that it is egocentric, with children most interested in their personal pleasure or avoiding punishment.
- **Conventional moral reasoning** parallels concrete operational thought in that it relates to current, observable practices: Children watch what their parents, teachers, and friends do, and try to follow suit.
- **Postconventional moral reasoning** is similar to formal operational thought because it uses abstractions, going beyond what is concretely observed, willing to question "what is" in order to decide "what should be."

According to Kohlberg, intellectual maturation advances moral thinking. During middle childhood, children's answers shift from being primarily preconventional to being more conventional: Concrete thought and peer experiences help children move past the first two stages (level I) to the next two (level II). Postconventional reasoning is not usually present until adolescence or adulthood, if then.

Kohlberg posed moral dilemmas to school-age boys (and eventually girls, teenagers, and adults). The most famous example of these dilemmas involves a

preconventional moral reasoning Kohlberg's first level of moral reasoning, emphasizing rewards and punishments.

conventional moral reasoning Kohlberg's second level of moral reasoning, emphasizing social rules.

postconventional moral reasoning Kohlberg's third level of moral reasoning, emphasizing moral principles.

>> Response for Parents of an Accused Bully (from page 388): The future is ominous if the charges are true. Your child's denial is a sign that there is a problem. (An innocent child would be worried about the misperception instead of categorically denying that any problem exists.) You might ask the teacher what the school is doing about bullying. Family counseling might help. Because bullies often have friends who egg them on, you may need to monitor your child's friendships and perhaps befriend the victim. Talk matters over with your child. Ignoring the situation might lead to heartache later on.

TABLE 13.3	Kohlberg's Three Levels and Six Stages of Moral Reasoning

Level I: Preconventional Moral Reasoning

The goal is to get rewards and avoid punishments; this is a self-centered level.

- *Stage one: Might makes right* (a punishment-and-obedience orientation). The most important value is to maintain the appearance of obedience to authority, avoiding punishment while still advancing self-interest. Don't get caught!

- *Stage two: Look out for number one* (an instrumental and relativist orientation). Each person tries to take care of his or her own needs. Be nice to other people so that they will be nice to you.

Level II: Conventional Moral Reasoning

Emphasis on social rules; this is a family, community, and cultural level.

- *Stage three: Good girl and nice boy.* Proper behavior pleases other people. Social approval is more important than any specific reward.

- *Stage four: Law and order.* Proper behavior means being a dutiful citizen and obeying the laws set down by society, even when no police are nearby.

Level III: Postconventional Moral Reasoning

Emphasis is placed on moral principles; this level is centered on ideals.

- *Stage five: Social contract.* Social rules are obeyed when they benefit everyone and are established by mutual agreement. If the rules become destructive or if one party doesn't live up to the agreement, the contract is no longer binding. Under those circumstances, disobeying the law may be moral.

- *Stage six: Universal ethical principles.* Universal principles, not individual situations (level I) or community practices (level II), determine right and wrong. Ethical values (such as "life is sacred") are established by thought and prayer. They may contradict egocentric (level I) or social and community (level II) values.

poor man named Heinz, whose wife was dying. He could not pay for the only drug that could cure his wife, a drug that a local druggist sold for 10 times what it cost to make.

> Heinz went to everyone he knew to borrow the money, but he could only get together about half of what it cost. He told the druggist that his wife was dying and asked him to sell it cheaper or let him pay later. But the druggist said "no." The husband got desperate and broke into the man's store to steal the drug for his wife. Should the husband have done that? Why?

[Kohlberg, 1963, p. 19]

The crucial element in Kohlberg's assessment of moral stages is not what a person answers but the reasons given.

For instance, suppose someone says that Heinz should steal the drugs. The reason could be that Heinz needs his wife to care for him (preconventional), or that people will blame him if he lets his wife die (conventional), or that a human life is more important than obeying a law (postconventional).

Or suppose someone says Heinz should not steal. The reason could be that he will go to jail (preconventional) or that business owners will blame him (conventional) or that for a community to function, no one should take another person's livelihood (postconventional).

Criticisms of Kohlberg

Kohlberg has been criticized for not appreciating cultural or gender differences. For example, loyalty to family overrides any other value in some cultures, so some people might avoid postconventional actions that hurt their family. Also, Kohlberg's original participants were all boys, which may have led him to discount female values of nurturance and relationships (Gilligan, 1982). Overall, Kohlberg seemed to value abstract principles more than individual needs, but caring for individuals may be no less moral than impartial justice (Sherblom, 2008).

Furthermore, Kohlberg did not seem to recognize that although children's morality differs from that of adults, they may be quite moral. School-age children tend to question or ignore adult rules that seem unfair (Turiel, 2006, 2008), and that may indicate postconventional thinking.

In one respect, however, Kohlberg was undeniably correct. He was right in noting that children use their intellectual abilities to justify their moral actions. In one experiment, children aged 8 to 18 were grouped with two others about the same age, were allotted some money, and were asked to decide how much to share with another trio of children.

There were no age trends in the actual decisions: Some groups chose to share equally; other groups were more selfish. However, there were age differences in the reasons. Older children suggested more complex rationalizations for their choices, both selfish and altruistic (Gummerum et al., 2008).

What Children Value

Many lines of research have shown that children develop their own morality, guided by peers, parents, and culture (Killen & Smetana, 2014). Some prosocial values are evident in early childhood. Among these values are caring for close family members, cooperating with other children, and not hurting anyone intentionally. Even very young children think stealing is wrong.

As children become more aware of themselves and others in middle childhood, they realize that one person's values may conflict with another's. Concrete operational cognition, which gives children the ability to understand and to use logic, propels them to think about morality and to try to behave ethically (Turiel, 2006). As part of growing up, children become conscious of immorality in their peers (Abrams et al., 2008) and, later on, in their parents, themselves, and their culture.

Adults Versus Peers

When child culture conflicts with adult morality, children often align themselves with peers. A child might lie to protect a friend, for instance. Friendship itself has a hostile side: Many close friends resist other children who want to join in (Rubin et al., 2013).

The conflict between the morality of children and that of adults is evident in the value that children place on education. Adults usually prize school, but children may encourage one another to play hooky, cheat on tests, or drop out. Peer values may outweigh adult values. Consider another comment from Paul:

> I try not to get influenced too much, pulled into what I don't want to be into. But mostly, it's hard. You don't want people to be saying you're stupid. "Why do you want to go to school and get a job? . . . Drop out."

> *[quoted in Nieto, 2000, p. 252]*

Not surprisingly, Paul later left school.

Three common moral imperatives among 6- to 11-year-olds are the following:
- Protect your friends.
- Don't tell adults what is happening.
- Conform to peer standards of dress, talk, behavior.

These three can explain both apparent boredom and overt defiance, as well as standards of dress that mystify adults (such as jeans so loose that they fall off or so tight that they impede digestion—both styles worn by my children, who grew up in different cohorts). Given what is known about middle childhood, it is no surprise that children do not echo adult morality.

Before criticizing children for conforming to other children, notice adults. For example, many Americans homeowners spend time and money growing lawns, which need fertilizer, watering, and mowing, not because they enjoy it but because all the neighbors have lawns. At least that is the opinion of one blogger who wrote that lawns are "Wasteful, Unquestioned Totems of Conformity." (Godlike Productions, 2012).

Fortunately, peers during adulthood as well as childhood help one another develop morals. Research finds that children are better at stopping bullying than adults are, because children sometimes defend the victim and isolate the bully. Since bullies tend to be low on empathy, they need peers to teach them that their actions are not admired (many bullies believe people admire their aggression). During middle childhood, morality can be scaffolded just as cognitive skills are, with mentors—peers or adults—using moral dilemmas to advance moral understanding (Nucci, 2009; Turner & Berkowitz, 2005).

Not Victims An outsider might worry that these two boys would be bullied, one because he is a member of a minority group in this New Jersey school, and the other because he is disabled. But both are well liked for the characteristics shown here: friendship and willingness to help and be helped.

Developing Moral Values

Throughout middle childhood, moral judgment becomes more comprehensive, taking into account psychological as well as physical harm, intentions as well as consequences. For example, when 5- to 11-year-olds were presented with anecdotes that differed in whether the harm done was intended to prevent further harm, or was simply mean, the younger children judged based on results but the older children considered intention: They rated justifiable harm as less bad and unjustifiable harm as worse than the younger children did (Jambon & Smetana, 2013).

A detailed examination of the effect of peers on morality began with an update on one of Piaget's moral issues: whether punishment should seek *retribution* (hurting the transgressor) or *restitution* (restoring what was lost). Piaget found that children advance from retribution to restitution between ages 8 and 10 (Piaget, 1932).

To learn how this occurs, researchers asked 133 9-year-olds:

> Late one afternoon there was a boy who was playing with a ball on his own in the garden. His dad saw him playing with it and asked him not to play with it so near the house because it might break a window. The boy didn't really listen to his dad, and carried on playing near the house. Then suddenly, the ball bounced up high and broke the window in the boy's room. His dad heard the noise and came to see what had happened. The father wonders what would be the fairest way to punish the boy. He thinks of two punishments. The first is to say: "Now, you didn't do as I asked. You will have to pay for the window to be mended, and I am going to take the money from your pocket money." The second is to say: "Now, you didn't do as I asked. As a punishment you have to go to your room and stay there for the rest of the evening." Which of these punishments do you think is the fairest?
>
> *[Leman & Björnberg, 2010, p. 962]*

The children were split almost equally in their answers. Then 24 pairs were formed of children who had opposite views. Each pair was asked to discuss the issue, trying to reach agreement. (The other children did not discuss it). Six pairs were boy–boy, six were boy–girl with the boy favoring restitution, six were boy–girl with the girl favoring restitution, and six were girl–girl.

The conversations typically took only five minutes, and the retribution side was more often chosen—which Piaget would consider a moral backslide, since more restitution than retribution advocates switched. However, two weeks and eight weeks later all the children were queried again, and their responses changed toward the more advanced, restitution thinking (see Figure 13.3). This advance

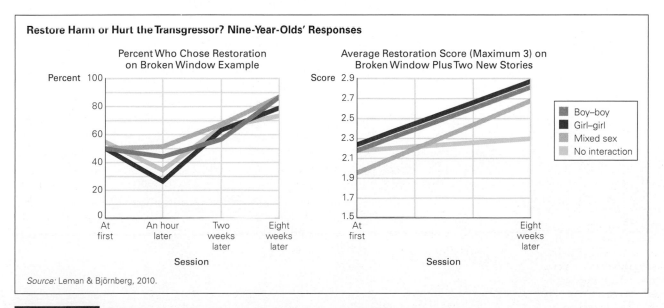

Source: Leman & Björnberg, 2010.

FIGURE 13.3

Benefits of Time and Talking The graph on the left shows that most children, immediately after their initial punitive response, became even more likely to seek punishment rather than to repair damage. However, after some time and reflection, they affirmed the response Piaget considered more mature. The graph on the right indicates that children who had talked about the broken window example moved toward restorative justice even in examples they had not heard before, which was not true for those who had not talked about the first story.

occurred even for the children who merely thought about the dilemma again, but children who had discussed it with another child were particularly likely to decide that restitution was best.

The main conclusion from this study was that "conversation on a topic may stimulate a process of individual reflection that triggers developmental advances" (Leman & Björnberg, 2010, p. 969). Parents and teachers take note: Raising moral issues, and letting children talk about them, may advance morality—not immediately, but soon.

Think again about the opening anecdote for this chapter (killing zombies) or the previous chapter (piercing ears). In both cases, the parent used age as a criterion, and in both cases the child rejected that argument. A better argument might raise a higher standard; in the first example, for instance, that killing is never justified. The child might disagree, but such conversations might help the child think more deeply about moral values, as happened in this experiment. That deeper thought might protect the child during adolescence, when life-changing moral issues arise, described in the next three chapters.

SUMMING UP

Moral issues are of great interest to children in middle childhood, who are affected by their cultures, by their parents, and particularly by their peers. Kohlberg's stages of moral thought parallel Piaget's stages of development, suggesting that the highest level of morality transcends the norms of any particular nation. Kohlberg has been criticized for not having a multicultural understanding, but it is true that moral judgment advances from ages 6 to 11. Children develop moral standards that they try to follow, although these may differ from adult morals, in part because children's morality includes loyalty to peers. Maturation, reflection, and discussion all foster moral development. ▪

SUMMARY

The Nature of the Child

1. All theories of development acknowledge that school-age children become more independent and capable in many ways.

2. Erikson emphasized industry, when children busily strive to master various tasks. If they are unable to do so, they feel inferior. Freud described latency, when psychosexual needs are quiet.

3. Children develop their self-concept during middle childhood, basing it on a more realistic assessment of their competence than they had in earlier years.

4. Self-respect is always helpful, but high self-esteem may reduce effort and is not valued in every culture. Low self-esteem is also harmful.

5. Both daily hassles and major stresses take a toll on children, with accumulated stresses more likely to impair development than any single event on its own. Resilience is aided by the child's interpretation of the situation and the availability of supportive adults, peers, and institutions.

Families and Children

6. Families influence children in many ways, as do genes and peers. Although most siblings share a childhood home and parents, each sibling experiences different (nonshared) circumstances within the family.

7. The five functions of a supportive family are to satisfy children's physical needs; to encourage learning; to support friendships; to protect self-respect; and to provide a safe, stable, and harmonious home.

8. The most common family structure worldwide is the nuclear family, usually with other relatives nearby and supportive. Other two-parent families include adoptive, same-sex, grandparent, and stepfamilies, each of which sometimes functions well for children. However, each of these also has vulnerabilities.

9. On average, children have fewer emotional problems and learn more in school if they live with two parents rather than one, especially if the two have a good parental alliance, so that both adults are caregivers.

10. Single-parent families have higher rates of change—for example, in where they live and who belongs to the family. On average, such families have less income, which may cause stress. Nonetheless, some single parents are better parents than they would be if the child's other parent were in the household.

11. Income affects family function, for two-parent as well as single-parent households. Poor children are at greater risk for emotional and behavioral problems because the stresses that often accompany poverty hinder effective parenting.

12. No matter what the family SES, instability and conflict are harmful. Children suffer even when the conflict does not involve them directly but their parents or siblings fight.

The Peer Group

13. Peers teach crucial social skills during middle childhood. Each cohort of children has a culture, passed down from slightly older children. Close friends are wanted and needed.

14. Popular children may be cooperative and easy to get along with or may be competitive and aggressive. Much depends on the age and culture of the children.

15. Rejected children may be neglected, aggressive, or withdrawn. Aggressive and withdrawn children have difficulty with social cognition; their interpretation of the normal give-and-take of childhood is impaired.

16. Bullying is common among school-age children and has long-term consequences for both bullies and victims. Bullies themselves may be admired, which makes their behavior more difficult to stop.

17. Overall, a multifaceted, long-term, whole-school approach—with parents, teachers, and bystanders working together—seems the best way to halt bullying.

Children's Moral Values

18. School-age children seek to differentiate right from wrong. Peer values, cultural standards, and family practices are all part of their personal morality.

19. Children advance in moral thinking as they mature. Kohlberg described three levels of moral reasoning, each related to cognitive maturity. His description has been criticized for ignoring cultural and gender differences.

20. When values conflict, children often choose loyalty to peers over adult standards of behavior. When children discuss moral issues with other children, they develop more thoughtful answers to moral questions.

KEY TERMS

aggressive-rejected (p. 386)
bullying (p. 386)
bully-victim (p. 387)
child culture (p. 384)
conventional moral reasoning (p. 390)

extended family (p. 375)
family function (p. 374)
family structure (p. 374)
industry versus inferiority (p. 368)
latency (p. 368)

nuclear family (p. 375)
polygamous family (p. 375)
postconventional moral reasoning (p. 390)
preconventional moral reasoning (p. 390)

resilience (p. 370)
single-parent family (p. 375)
social comparison (p. 369)
withdrawn-rejected (p. 386)

WHAT HAVE YOU LEARNED?

1. How do Erikson's stages for preschool and school-age children differ?

2. Why is social comparison particularly powerful during middle childhood?

3. Why do cultures differ in how they value pride or modesty?

4. Why and when might minor stresses be more harmful than major stresses?

5. How might a child's interpretation of events help him or her cope with repeated stress?

6. How is it that siblings raised together do not share the exact same environment?

7. What is the difference between family structure and family function?

8. Why is a harmonious, stable home particularly important during middle childhood?

9. Describe the characteristics of four different family structures.

10. What are the advantages for children in a nuclear family structure?

11. List three reasons why the single-parent structure might function less well than other family structures.

12. In what ways are family structure and family function affected by culture?

13. Using the family-stress model, explain how low family income might affect family function.

14. How does what children wear reflect the culture of children?

15. In what ways are friendships at the end of middle childhood different from those at the beginning of middle childhood?

16. How is a child's popularity affected by culture and cohort?

17. What are the similarities and differences between boy bullies and girl bullies?

18. How might bullying be reduced?

19. Using Kohlberg's levels of moral reasoning, explain how cognition advances morality.

20. What are the main criticisms of Kohlberg's theory of moral development?

21. What three values are common among school-age children?

APPLICATIONS

1. Go someplace where school-age children congregate (such as a schoolyard, a park, or a community center) and use naturalistic observation for at least half an hour. Describe what popular, average, withdrawn, and rejected children do. Note at least one potential conflict (bullying, rough-and-tumble play, etc.). Describe the sequence and the outcome.

2. Focusing on verbal bullying, describe at least two times when someone said something hurtful to you and two times when you said something that might have been hurtful to someone else. What are the differences between the two types of situations?

3. How would your childhood have been different if your family structure had been different, such as if you had (or had not) lived with your grandparents, if your parents had (or had not) gotten divorced, if you had (or had not) been adopted?

PART IV The Developing Person So Far:

Middle Childhood

BIOSOCIAL

A Healthy Time During middle childhood, children grow more slowly than they did earlier or than they will during adolescence. Physical play is crucial for health and happiness. Genes as well as immunization protect them against contagious diseases, and medical awareness and care have improved over the past decades.

Obesity and asthma, have genetic roots and psychosocial consequences.

Brain Development Brain maturation continues, leading to faster reactions and better self-control. The specific skills that are mastered depend largely on culture, gender, and inherited ability, all of which are reflected in intelligence tests. Children have multiple intellectual abilities, most of which are not reflected in standard IQ tests.

Children with Special Needs Many children have special learning needs. Early recognition, targeted education, and psychological support can help them.

COGNITIVE

Building on Theory Beginning at about age 7, Piaget noted, children attain concrete operational thought, including the ability to understand the logical principles of classification and transitive inference. Vygotsky emphasized that children become more open to learning from mentors, both teachers and peers. Information-processing abilities increase, including greater memory, knowledge, control, and metacognition.

Language Children's increasing ability to understand the structures and possibilities of language enables them to extend the range of their cognitive powers and to become more analytical and expressive in vocabulary. Children have the cognitive capacity to become bilingual and bicultural, although much depends on the teacher.

Teaching and Learning International comparisons reveal marked variations in the overt and hidden curriculums, as well as in learning, between one nation and another. In recent years, traditional educational approaches have been pitted against a more holistic approach to learning.

PSYCHOSOCIAL

The Nature of the Child Theorists agree that many school-age children develop competencies, emotional control, and attitudes to defend against stress. Some children are resilient, coping well with problems and finding support in friends, family, school, religion, and community.

Families and Children Parents continue to influence children, especially as they exacerbate or buffer problems in school and the community. During these years, families need to meet basic needs, encourage learning, foster self-respect, nurture friendship, and—most important—provide harmony and stability. Nuclear families often provide this, but one-parent, foster, same-sex, or grandparent families can also function well for children. Household income, little conflict, and family stability benefit children of all ages.

The Peer Group Children depend less on their parents and more on friends for help, loyalty, and sharing of mutual interests. Rejection and bullying become serious problems.

Children's Moral Values Moral development, influenced by peers, advances during these years. Children develop moral standards that they try to follow, although these may differ from the moral standards of adults.

adolescence

A century ago, puberty began at age 15 or so. Soon after that age, most girls married and most boys found work. It is said that *adolescence begins with biology and ends with culture*. If so, then a hundred years ago adolescence lasted a few months. Now adolescence lasts many years. Puberty starts before the teen years and adult responsibilities are often postponed until emerging adulthood or later.

In the next three chapters (covering ages 11 to 18), we begin with biology (this chapter), consider cognition (Chapter 15), and then discuss culture (Chapter 16). Adolescence attracts extremes, arousing the highest hopes and the worst fears of parents, teachers, police officers, social workers, and children themselves. Patterns and events can catapult a teenager to destruction or celebration. Understanding this phase of development is the first step toward ensuring a fulfilling, not devastating, adolescence.

Adolescence: Biosocial Development

- **Puberty Begins**
  Unseen Beginnings
  OPPOSING PERSPECTIVES: Algebra at 7 A.M.? Get Real
  Age and Puberty
  A VIEW FROM SCIENCE: Stress and Puberty
  Too Early, Too Late

- **Growth and Nutrition**
  Growing Bigger and Stronger
  Diet Deficiencies
  Eating Disorders

- **Brain Development**
  A Need for Caution
  A CASE TO STUDY: "What Were You Thinking?"
  Benefits of Adolescent Brain Development

- **Sexual Maturation**
  Sexual Characteristics
  Sexual Activity
  Problems with Adolescent Sex

WHAT WILL YOU KNOW?

1. Since puberty begins anytime from age 8 to 14, how can onset be predicted for a particular child?

2. Why do some teenagers starve themselves and others overeat?

3. Since adolescent sexual impulses are powerful and inevitable, why is there so much variation in rates of teen pregnancy and STIs?

I overheard a conversation among three teenagers, including my daughter Rachel, all of them past their awkward years and now becoming beautiful. They were discussing the imperfections of their bodies. One spoke of her fat stomach (what stomach? I could not see it), another of her long neck (hidden by her silky, shoulder-length hair). Rachel complained not only about a bent pinky finger but also about her feet!

The reality that children grow into men and women is no shock to any adult. But for teenagers, heightened self-awareness often triggers surprise or even horror, joy, and despair at the specifics of their development. Like these three, adolescents pay attention to details of their growth.

This chapter describes the biosocial specifics of growing bodies and emerging sexuality. It all begins with hormones, but other invisible changes may be even more potent—such as the timing of neurological maturation that does not yet allow adolescents like these three to realize that minor imperfections are insignificant.

>> Puberty Begins

Puberty refers to the years of rapid physical growth and sexual maturation that end childhood, producing a person of adult size, shape, and sexuality. The forces of puberty are unleashed by a cascade of hormones that produce external growth and internal changes, including heightened emotions and sexual desires.

The process of puberty normally starts between ages 8 and 14. Most physical growth and maturation ends about four years after the first signs appear, although some individuals (especially boys) add height, weight, and muscle until age 20 or so.

For girls, the observable changes of puberty usually begin with nipple growth. Soon a few pubic hairs are visible, followed by a peak growth spurt, widening of the hips, the first menstrual period (**menarche**), a full pubic-hair pattern, and breast maturation (Susman et al., 2010). The average age of menarche among normal-weight girls is about 12 years, 8 months (Rosenfield et al., 2009), although variation in timing is quite normal.

For boys, the usual sequence is growth of the testes, initial pubic-hair growth, growth of the penis, first ejaculation of seminal fluid (**spermarche**), appearance

puberty The time between the first onrush of hormones and full adult physical development. Puberty usually lasts three to five years. Many more years are required to achieve psychosocial maturity.

menarche A girl's first menstrual period, signaling that she has begun ovulation. Pregnancy is biologically possible, but ovulation and menstruation are often irregular for years after menarche.

spermarche A boy's first ejaculation of sperm. Erections can occur as early as infancy, but ejaculation signals sperm production. Spermarche may occur during sleep (in a "wet dream") or via direct stimulation.

Left: Hola Images RF/Getty Images
Top: Mark Anderson/Getty Images

Especially for Parents of Teenagers
Why would parents blame adolescent moods on hormones? (see response, page 404)

hormone An organic chemical substance that is produced by one body tissue and conveyed via the bloodstream to another to affect some physiological function.

pituitary A gland in the brain that responds to a signal from the hypothalamus by producing many hormones, including those that regulate growth and that control other glands, among them the adrenal and sex glands.

adrenal glands Two glands, located above the kidneys, that produce hormones (including the "stress hormones" epinephrine [adrenaline] and norepinephrine).

HPA (hypothalamus–pituitary–adrenal) axis A sequence of hormone production originating in the hypothalamus and moving to the pituitary and then to the adrenal glands.

of facial hair, a peak growth spurt, deepening of the voice, and final pubic-hair growth (Biro et al., 2001; Herman-Giddens et al., 2012; Susman et al., 2010). The typical age of spermarche is just under 13 years, close to the age for menarche.

Unseen Beginnings

These are the visible changes of puberty, but the entire process begins with an invisible event, a marked increase in hormones. **Hormones** are body chemicals that regulate hunger, sleep, moods, stress, sexual desire, immunity, reproduction, and many other bodily functions, including puberty. Throughout adolescence, hormone levels correlate with physiological changes and self-reported developments (Shirtcliff et al., 2009).

You learned in Chapter 8 that the production of many hormones is regulated deep within the brain, where biochemical signals from the hypothalamus signal another brain structure, the **pituitary**, to go into action. The pituitary produces hormones that stimulate the **adrenal glands**, located above the kidneys at either side of the lower back. The adrenal glands produce more hormones.

Many hormones that regulate puberty follow this route, known as the **HPA (hypothalamus–pituitary–adrenal) axis** (see Figure 14.1). Abnormalities of the HPA axis in adolescence are associated with eating disorders, anxiety, and depression. These conditions and many other types of psychopathology, appearing for the first time or worsening at puberty, are connected to hormones and genes (Dahl & Gunnar, 2009).

Indeed, abnormalities of the HPA axis probably cause the sudden increases in clinical depression in early adolescence (Guerry & Hastings, 2011), HPA disruptions are one result of childhood sexual abuse (discussed soon) (Trickett et al., 2011).

Same Situation, Far Apart: Eye Openers Nature often grows eyelashes straight or slightly curly, but adolescent girls want them curlier. The main difference between these two settings is not the goal but the equipment. Girls in Pinellas Park, Florida, have large mirrors and metal tools designed for lash curling—both are rare in Beijing, China.

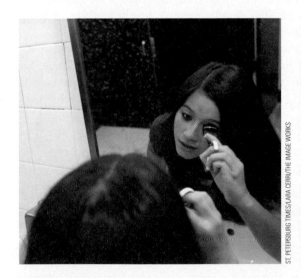

ST. PETERSBURG TIMES/LARA CERRI/THE IMAGE WORKS

JASON LEE/REUTERS/LANDOV

FIGURE 14.1

Biological Sequence of Puberty Puberty begins with a hormonal signal from the hypothalamus to the pituitary gland, both deep within the brain. The pituitary, in turn, sends a hormonal message through the blood stream to the adrenal glands and the gonads to produce more hormones.

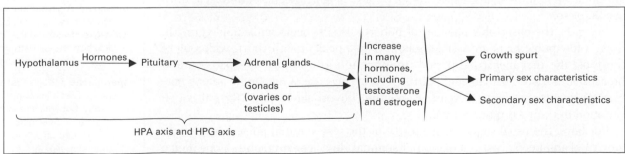

Hypothalamus —Hormones→ Pituitary → Adrenal glands → / Gonads (ovaries or testicles) → Increase in many hormones, including testosterone and estrogen → Growth spurt / Primary sex characteristics / Secondary sex characteristics

HPA axis and HPG axis

Sex Hormones

At adolescence, the pituitary activates not only the adrenal glands but also the **gonads**, or sex glands (ovaries in females; testes, or testicles, in males), following another sequence called the **HPG (hypothalamus–pituitary–gonad) axis**. One hormone in particular, GnRH (gonadotropin-releasing hormone), causes the gonads to enlarge and dramatically increase their production of sex hormones, chiefly **estradiol** in girls and **testosterone** in boys. These hormones affect the body's shape and function, producing additional hormones that regulate stress and immunity (E. A. Young et al., 2008).

Estrogens (including estradiol) are female hormones and *androgens* (including testosterone) are male hormones, although both sexes have some of both. The biochemical messages from the HPG axis activate the ovaries to produce high levels of estrogens and the testes to produce dramatic increases in androgens. This "surge of hormones" affects bodies, brains, and behavior before any visible signs of puberty appear, "well before the teens" (Peper & Dahl, 2013, p. 134).

The activated gonads eventually produce mature sperm or ova, released in menarche or spermarche. That signifies the potential for conception, although peak fertility occurs four to six years later. Hormonal increases and differences may also underlie sex differences in psychopathology (Naninck et al., 2011; Steiner & Young, 2008). That is one explanation for two notable facts: Compared to their peers of the other sex, males are twice as likely to become schizophrenic and females are twice as likely to become depressed.

However, the most obvious psychological effect of hormones at puberty is to awaken and increase interest in sex. The first sexual objects are usually unattainable—a film star, a teacher, someone's older sibling—but by mid-adolescence, fantasies typically settle on another teenager.

Not only are bodies and brains affected by hormones, behavior is as well—flirting, crying, slamming doors, and more. Puberty is an example of a dynamic system that includes every aspect of development, each affecting the other.

Emotional surges and lustful impulses may begin with hormones, but then thoughts themselves can *cause* physiological and neurological processes, not just result from them. The hormones of puberty make young adolescents more vulnerable to stress, and thus quicker to become angry or upset (Goddings et al., 2012; Klein & Romeo, 2013). Then those emotions increase hormone levels. For example, other people's reactions to emerging breasts, beards, or body shapes evoke adolescent thoughts and frustrations that result in increased hormone production and emotional outbursts, each increasing the other.

Body Rhythms

The brain of every living creature responds to the environment with natural rhythms that rise and fall by the hours, days, and seasons. For example, body weight and height are affected by time of year: The rate of child growth increases for height in summer and for weight in winter. Some *biorhythms* are on a day–night cycle that occurs approximately every 24 hours, called the **circadian rhythm**. (*Circadian* means "about a day.") Puberty affects both seasonal and daily biorhythms.

The hypothalamus and the pituitary regulate the hormones that affect patterns of stress, appetite, sleep, and so on. These hormones at puberty cause a *phase delay* in the circadian sleep–wake cycles. The delay is in the body's reaction to daylight and dark. For most people, morning light awakens the brain.

---

gonads The paired sex glands (ovaries in females, testicles in males). The gonads produce hormones and gametes.

HPG (hypothalamus–pituitary–gonad) axis A sequence of hormone production originating in the hypothalamus and moving to the pituitary and then to the gonads.

estradiol A sex hormone, considered the chief estrogen. Females produce much more estradiol than males do.

testosterone A sex hormone, the best known of the androgens (male hormones); secreted in far greater amounts by males than by females.

Especially for Teenagers Some 14-year-olds have unprotected sex and then are relieved to realize that conception did not occur. Does this mean they do not need to worry about contraception? (see response, page 404)

circadian rhythm A day–night cycle of biological activity that occurs approximately every 24 hours (*circadian* means "about a day").

I Covered That Teachers everywhere complain that students don't remember what they were taught. Maybe schedules, not daydreaming, are to blame.

>> Response for Parents of Teenagers (from page 402): If something causes adolescents to shout "I hate you," to slam doors, or to cry inconsolably, parents may decide that hormones are the problem. This makes it easy to disclaim personal responsibility for the teenager's anger. However, research on stress and hormones suggests that this comforting attribution is too simplistic.

>> Response for Teenagers (from page 403): No. Early sex has many hazards, but it is true that pregnancy is less likely (although quite possible) before age 15. However, this may lead to a false sense of security: Conception is more likely in the late teens than at any other period in the life span.

Observation Quiz As you see, the problems are worse for the girls. Why is that? (see answer, page 406)

That's why people fighting jet lag are urged to take a morning walk. However, at puberty, the circadian rhythm is delayed, so many teens are wide awake and hungry at midnight but half asleep, with little appetite or energy, all morning.

Added to the adolescent day–night pattern, some individuals (especially males) are naturally more alert in the evening than in the morning, a genetic trait called *eveningness*. Exacerbated by the pubescent phase delay, eveningness puts adolescents at risk for antisocial activities because they are awake when adults are asleep. Another result of eveningness and the overall change in circadian rhythm in a society that schedules for adults, not teenagers, is that adolescents are increasingly sleep-deprived with each year of high school (Carskadon, 2011).

To make it worse, "the blue spectrum light from TV, computer, and personal-device screens may have particularly strong effects on the human circadian system" (Peper & Dahl, 2013, p. 137). Watching late-night TV, working on the computer, or texting friends at 10 P.M. interferes with normal nighttime sleepiness. Sleeping late on weekend mornings is a sign of deprivation, not compensation.

Sleep deprivation and irregular sleep schedules lead to several specific dangers, including insomnia, nightmares, mood disorders (depression, conduct disorder, anxiety), and falling asleep while driving. In addition, individuals who are sleepy do not think or learn as well as they might when rested.

Sleep deprivation is particularly likely among adolescents, not only in the United States but also in many other nations (Eaten et al., 2010; Roenneberg et al., 2012). Every year of high school, fewer students get even 8 hours of sleep, the minimum needed by a young body (see Figure 14.2). Many adults ignore the implications, as the following Opposing Perspectives explains.

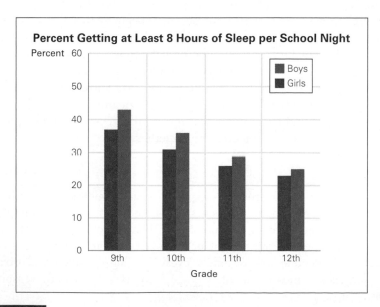

Percent Getting at Least 8 Hours of Sleep per School Night

FIGURE 14.2

Sleepyheads Three of every four high school seniors are sleep deprived. Even if they go to sleep at midnight, as many do, they must get up before 8, as almost all do. Then all day they are tired.

OPPOSING PERSPECTIVES

Algebra at 7 A.M.? Get Real

Parents sometimes fight biology. They might command their wide-awake teen to "go to sleep" or to hang up on a classmate who phones after 10:00 P.M., they may set early curfews and stay awake until their teenager comes home, or they may drag their child out of bed for school—the same child who, a decade earlier, was told to stay in bed until 7 A.M.

Meanwhile, adolescents fight parents. Among the reasons is their circadian rhythm that makes early bedtime and early rising almost impossible. Sleep-deprived teenagers fall asleep in school (see Figure 14.3) and abuse drugs (sometimes to stay awake or go to sleep) (Mueller et al., 2011; Patrick & Schulenberg, 2011).

Data on the circadian rhythm and the teenage brain convinced social scientists at the University of Minnesota to ask 17 school districts to start high school at 8:30 A.M. or later. Parents disagreed. Many (42 percent) thought high school should begin before 8:00 A.M. Some (20 percent) wanted their teenagers out of the house by 7:15 A.M., as did only 1 percent of parents with younger children (Wahlstrom, 2002).

Other adults had their own reasons for wanting high school to begin early. Teachers generally thought that learning was more efficient in the morning; bus drivers hated rush hour; cafeteria workers liked to be done by mid-afternoon; police wanted teenagers off the streets by 4:00 P.M.; coaches needed after-school sports events to end before dark; business owners hired teens for the early evening shift; community groups wanted the school gyms available in the late afternoon.

Only one school district tried a later start time. In Edina, Minnesota, high school schedules changed from 7:25 A.M.–2:05 P.M. to 8:30 A.M.–3:10 P.M. After a trial year, most parents (93 percent) and virtually all students liked the new schedule. One student said, "I have only fallen asleep in school once this whole year, and last year I fell asleep about three times a week" (quoted in Wahlstrom, 2002, p. 190). Fewer students were absent, late, disruptive, or sick (the school nurse became an advocate). Grades rose.

Other school districts noticed. Minneapolis high schools changed their start time from 7:15 A.M. to 8:40 A.M. Again, attendance and graduation rates improved. School boards in South Burlington (Vermont), West Des Moines (Iowa), Tulsa (Oklahoma), Arlington (Virginia), Palo Alto (California), and Milwaukee (Wisconsin) voted to start high school later, from an average of 7:45 A.M. to 8:30 A.M. (Tonn, 2006; Snider, 2012), as did one private school in Rhode Island (Owens et al., 2010). Unexpected advantages appeared: more efficient energy use, less adolescent depression, and, in Tulsa, unprecedented athletic championships.

Many school districts stick to their traditional schedules, set to allow school buses to take teenagers to school and then come back for the younger children. That was before the hazards of sleep deprivation were known. Now the evidence is clear, "the science is there, the will to change is not" (Snider, 2012).

From 1990 to 2009, the community of Fairfax (Virginia) argued, forming two opposing groups: SLEEP (Start Later for Excellence in Education Proposal) versus WAKE (Worried About Keeping Extra-Curriculars). One sports reporter argued:

> The later start would hinder teams without lighted practice fields. Hinder kids who work after-school jobs to save for college or to help support their families. Hinder teachers who work second jobs or take late-afternoon college classes. Hinder commuters who would get stopped behind more buses during peak traffic times. Hinder kids who might otherwise seek after-school academic help, or club or team affiliation. Hinder families that depend on high school children to watch younger siblings after school. Hinder community groups that use school and park facilities in the late afternoons and evenings.
>
> [Williams, 2009]

This writer wrote that science was on the side of change but reality was not. To developmentalists, of course, science *is* reality. However, in 2009 the Fairfax school board voted to keep high school start at 7:20 A.M. The advocates kept trying. On the eighth try, the Fairfax school board in 2012 finally set a goal: High schools should not start before 8 A.M. They hired a team to figure out how to implement that goal.

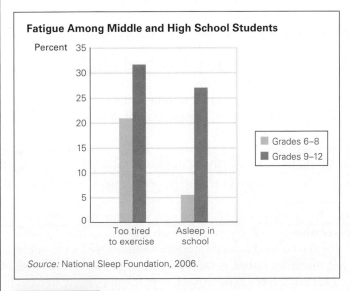

Fatigue Among Middle and High School Students

Legend: Grades 6–8, Grades 9–12

Source: National Sleep Foundation, 2006.

FIGURE 14.3

Dreaming and Learning? This graph shows the percentage of U.S. students who, once a week or more, fall asleep in class or are too tired to exercise. Not shown are those who are too tired overall (59 percent of high school students) or who doze in class "almost every day" (8 percent).

Brothers, but Not Twins These brothers are close in age, and both exhibit the emotional excitement that accompanies the hormones of puberty. The past year has led to many rapid physical changes, especially for the older boy.

Observation Quiz What three body differences that show adolescent growth do you see? (see answer, page 408)

>> **Answer to Observation Quiz** (from page 404): Girls tend to spend more time studying, talking to friends, and getting ready in the morning. Other data show that many girls get less than 7 hours of sleep per night.

secular trend The long-term upward or downward direction of a certain set of statistical measurements, as opposed to a smaller, shorter cyclical variation. As an example, over the last two centuries, because of improved nutrition and medical care, children have tended to reach their adult height earlier and their adult height has increased.

Age and Puberty

Normally, hormones increase between age 8 and 14, and visible signs of puberty appear a year later. That six-year range is too great for many parents, teachers, and children, who want to pinpoint a more precise age. Fortunately, if a person knows a child's genes, gender, body fat, and stress, it is possible to predict timing of puberty (see Visualizing Development, p. 407).

Genes and Gender

About two-thirds of the variation in age of puberty is genetic, evident not only in families but also in ethnic groups (Dvornyk & Waqar-ul-Haq, 2012; Susman et al., 2010). African Americans reach puberty about seven months earlier than European or Hispanic Americans, while Chinese Americans average several months later. Ethnic differences are apparent on other continents as well. For instance, northern European girls reach menarche at 13 years, 4 months, on average; southern European girls do so at 12 years, 5 months (Alsaker & Flammer, 2006).

The sex chromosomes have a marked effect. In height, the average girl is about two years ahead of the average boy. However, the female height spurt occurs before menarche, whereas for boys, the increase in height is relatively late, after spermarche. Thus, when it comes to hormonal and sexual changes, girls are less than a year ahead of boys (Hughes & Gore, 2007). A sixth-grade boy with sexual fantasies about the taller girls in his class is neither perverted nor precocious; his hormones are ahead of his visible growth.

Body Fat

Another major influence on the onset of puberty is body fat, at least in girls. Heavy girls reach menarche years earlier than malnourished ones do. Most girls must weigh at least 100 pounds (45 kilograms) before they experience their first period (Berkey et al., 2000). Although malnutrition always delays puberty, body fat may not be as necessary for well-fed boys: One study found that overweight U.S. boys reach puberty later, not earlier, than others (J. M. Lee et al., 2010).

Worldwide, urban children are more often overfed and underexercised compared with rural children. That is probably why puberty starts earlier in the cities of India and China than it does in their more remote villages, a year earlier in Warsaw than in rural Poland, and earlier in Athens than in other parts of Greece (Malina et al., 2004).

Body fat also explains why youths reach puberty at age 15 or later in some parts of Africa, although their genetic relatives in North America mature much earlier. Similarly, malnutrition may explain why puberty began at about age 17 in sixteenth-century Europe.

Since then, puberty has occurred at younger and younger ages (an example of what is called the **secular trend**, the trend for changes in human growth as nutrition improved). Increased food availability has led to weight gain in childhood, and that has led to earlier puberty and taller average height. Because of the secular trend, for centuries every generation has reached puberty before the previous one (Floud et al., 2011; Fogel et al., 2011).

One curious bit of evidence of the secular trend is that U.S. presidents are taller in recent decades than they were earlier (James Madison, the fourth president, was shortest at 5 feet, 4 inches; Barack Obama is 6 feet, 1 inch tall). The secular trend has stopped in developed nations, because now nutrition allows everyone to attain their genetic potential. Currently, young men no longer usually look down at

VISUALIZING DEVELOPMENT

The Timing of Puberty

The process of puberty can take years—and varies widely from child to child. Puberty begins for healthy children sometime between ages 8 and 14, with apparent ethnic and gender differ- ences. The sequence is usually the same, with the entire prcess lasting about 5 years.

THE SEQUENCE OF PUBERTY

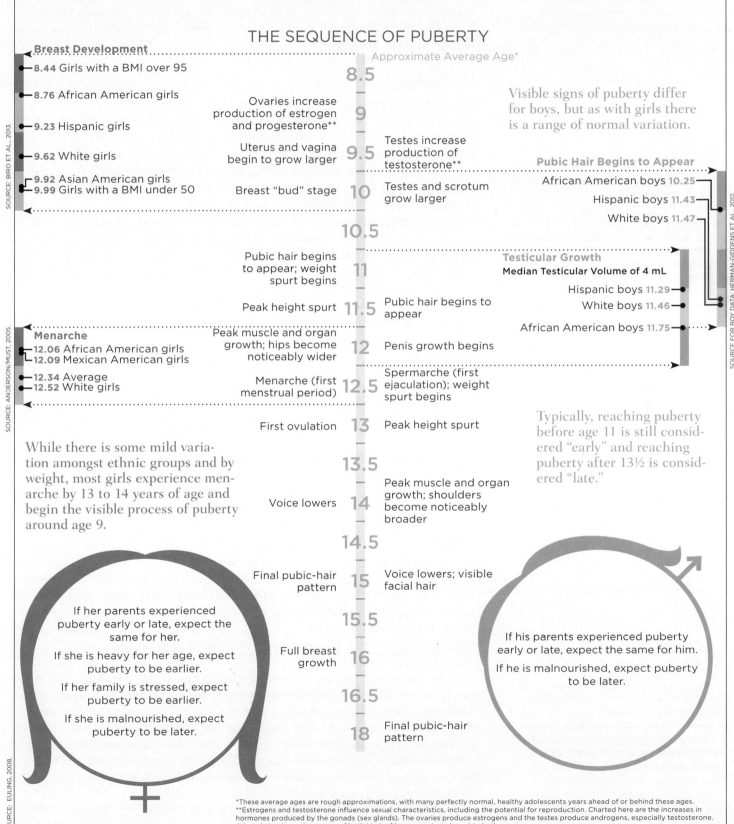

Approximate Average Age*

Breast Development
- **8.44** Girls with a BMI over 95
- **8.76** African American girls
- **9.23** Hispanic girls
- **9.62** White girls
- **9.92** Asian American girls
- **9.99** Girls with a BMI under 50

SOURCE: BIRO ET AL., 2013.

Ovaries increase production of estrogen and progesterone**

Uterus and vagina begin to grow larger

Breast "bud" stage

Pubic hair begins to appear; weight spurt begins

Peak height spurt

Menarche
- **12.06** African American girls
- **12.09** Mexican American girls
- **12.34** Average
- **12.52** White girls

SOURCE: ANDERSON/MUST, 2005.

Peak muscle and organ growth; hips become noticeably wider

Menarche (first menstrual period)

First ovulation

While there is some mild varia- tion amongst ethnic groups and by weight, most girls experience men- arche by 13 to 14 years of age and begin the visible process of puberty around age 9.

Voice lowers

Final pubic-hair pattern

If her parents experienced puberty early or late, expect the same for her.

If she is heavy for her age, expect puberty to be earlier.

If her family is stressed, expect puberty to be earlier.

If she is malnourished, expect puberty to be later.

Full breast growth

Final pubic-hair pattern

SOURCE: EULING, 2008.

8.5
9
9.5
10
10.5
11
11.5
12
12.5
13
13.5
14
14.5
15
15.5
16
16.5
18

Visible signs of puberty differ for boys, but as with girls there is a range of normal variation.

Testes increase production of testosterone**

Testes and scrotum grow larger

Penis growth begins

Spermarche (first ejaculation); weight spurt begins

Peak height spurt

Peak muscle and organ growth; shoulders become noticeably broader

Voice lowers; visible facial hair

Pubic Hair Begins to Appear
- African American boys 10.25
- Hispanic boys 11.43
- White boys 11.47

Testicular Growth
Median Testicular Volume of 4 mL
- Hispanic boys 11.29
- White boys 11.46
- African American boys 11.75

SOURCE FOR BOY DATA: HERMAN-GIDDENS ET AL., 2012.

Typically, reaching puberty before age 11 is still consid- ered "early" and reaching puberty after 13½ is consid- ered "late."

If his parents experienced puberty early or late, expect the same for him.

If he is malnourished, expect puberty to be later.

*These average ages are rough approximations, with many perfectly normal, healthy adolescents years ahead of or behind these ages.
**Estrogens and testosterone influence sexual characteristics, including the potential for reproduction. Charted here are the increases in hormones produced by the gonads (sex glands). The ovaries produce estrogens and the testes produce androgens, especially testosterone. Adrenal glands produce some of both kinds of hormones (not shown) in both sexes.

Especially for Parents Worried About Early Puberty Suppose your cousin's 9-year-old daughter has just had her first period, and your cousin blames hormones in the food supply for this "precocious" puberty. Should you change your young daughter's diet? (see response, page 410)

leptin A hormone that affects appetite and is believed to affect the onset of puberty. Leptin levels increase during childhood and peak at around age 12.

their short fathers, or girls at their little mothers, unless they were born in Asia or Africa, where the secular trend continues.

There is one possible exception in developed nations to the statement "the secular trend has stopped." Puberty that begins before age 8, called *precocious puberty*, seems more common, although still rare (perhaps 2 percent). The increase may be caused by more childhood obesity or by new chemicals. Experts disagree about both prevalence and causes.

Hormones

Of course, hormones as well as genes affect sex differences, height, and weight, but additional factors may directly trigger the onset of puberty. Many scientists suspect that precocious or delayed puberty is caused by substances in the food supply. Cattle are fed steroids to increase bulk and milk, and hundreds of chemicals and hormones are used to produce most of the food and drink that children consume. All these *might* affect appetite, body fat, and sex hormones, with effects particularly apparent at puberty (Wang et al., 2005).

One hormone naturally produced by the body definitely affects the onset of puberty. That hormone is **leptin**, which regulates appetite and energy. Without leptin, puberty does not occur. However, abnormally high levels of leptin correlate with obesity. A girl with this problem is likely to experience early puberty that ends relatively soon, stopping growth. Thus the fattest girl may become the tallest 5th grader and then the shortest high school graduate.

Normally, body fat produces leptin (one reason puberty is delayed is if a person overexercises or undereats), and starvation usually increases leptin so the hungry person seeks food. Once weight is gained, higher levels of leptin decrease the appetite (Elias & Purohit, 2013). Most of the research on leptin has been done with mice, which become fat or thin depending on the levels of this hormone, but the picture is more complicated for humans.

The precise impact of all the chemicals in the air, water, or diet on the human sexual-reproductive system is not yet known. It seems that the female system is especially sensitive not only to leptin but also to factors in the environment, perhaps because pregnancy and prenatal growth occur in female bodies. Leptin is one factor in the onset of puberty, but many other hormones, chemicals, genes, and psychosocial forces are involved (Elias, 2012).

Stress

Stress hastens the hormonal onset of puberty, especially if a child's parents are sick, drug addicted, or divorced, or if the neighborhood is violent and impoverished. One study of sexually abused girls found that they began puberty seven months earlier, on average, than did a matched comparison group (Trickett et al., 2011). Particularly for girls who are genetically sensitive, puberty comes early if their family interaction is stressful but late if their family is supportive (Ellis et al., 2011; James et al., 2012).

>> Answer to Observation Quiz (from page 406): Actually, puberty affects every part of the body, so far more than three changes are visible, including longer arms, legs, and torso; more arm and leg muscle; visible nipples; less round head; and a more mature facial expression. The younger boy will change soon—as evidenced by his big feet.

Thus the age of menarche is influenced by the child's genes as well as by the family situation, as differential sensitivity would predict. [**Lifespan Link:** Differential sensitivity was explained in Chapter 1.] Minor stresses—first day of a new school, summer camp away from home, a fight with a best friend—also trigger menarche in a girl whose body is ready. Twenty years ago many scientists were skeptical about a link between stress and puberty, suggesting that maybe early puberty caused stress rather than the other way around, but now the link seems clear. (See A View from Science.)

A VIEW FROM SCIENCE

Stress and Puberty

Hypothetically, stress effects on puberty could be indirect, a marker for other factors, not a direct cause of early puberty. For example, it is possible that children in dysfunctional families eat more unhealthy food (thus gaining excessive weight), or they inherit genes from their distressed mothers for early puberty, and those genes led the mothers to become divorced. Either of those possibilities could be the cause of early puberty.

However, several longitudinal studies show a direct link between stress and early puberty. For example, one study of 756 children found that early menarche correlated with harsh parenting a decade earlier. Their parents tended to demand respect, spank often, and rarely hug them as babies (Belsky et al., 2007). It is known that such early parenting might increase the level of the stress hormone, cortisol, and it is also known that cortisol affects puberty, so the link between stress and puberty is plausible.

A further study of the same girls at age 15, controlled for genetic differences, found that harsh treatment in childhood increased sexual risk (more sex partners, pregnancies, sex-related diseases) but not other risks (drugs, crime) (Belsky et al., 2010). This finding suggests that stress triggers earlier onset of sex hormones (which makes sexual activity more compelling) but that stress does not increase generalized rebellion. The direct impact of stress on puberty seems evident.

Why would higher cortisol trigger puberty? Given what is known about optimal development, it makes more sense for stress to *delay* puberty. If puberty were delayed, then young teens would still look and act childlike, which might evoke adult protection for the child rather than lust or anger at the teenager. Protection is especially needed in conflict-ridden or single-parent homes, yet such homes produce earlier puberty and less parental nurturance.

One explanation comes from evolutionary theory:

Maturing quickly and breeding promiscuously would enhance reproductive fitness more than would delaying development, mating cautiously, and investing heavily in parenting. The latter strategy, in contrast, would make biological sense, for virtually the same reproductive-fitness-enhancing reasons, under conditions of contextual support and nurturance.

[Belsky et al., 2010, p. 121]

In other words, historically, when harsh conditions threatened survival of the species, it was crucial that adolescents reproduce early and often. Natural selection would hasten puberty to increase the birth rate, especially if many adults died before their reproductive years were over.

By contrast, in peaceful times, puberty could occur later, allowing children to postpone maturity and instead enjoy extra years of nurturance from parents and grandparents. Genes evolved to respond differentially to war and peace.

Of course, this evolutionary rationale no longer applies. Today, early sexual activity and reproduction are more likely to destroy societies than protect the species. However, the genome has been shaped over millennia; if there is a puberty-starting allele that responds to social conditions, it will respond in the twenty-first century as it did thousands of years ago.

Too Early, Too Late

For most adolescents, the link between puberty and hormones is irrelevant. Only one aspect of pubertal timing is important: their friends' schedules. Puberty can enhance or diminish a person's status with peers. No one wants to be too early or too late.

Girls

Think about the early-maturing girl. If she has visible breasts at age 10, the boys her age tease her; they are unnerved by the sexual creature in their midst. She must fit her developing body into a school chair designed for smaller children; she might hide her breasts in large T-shirts and bulky sweaters; she might refuse to undress for gym. Early-maturing girls tend to have lower self-esteem, more depression, and poorer body image than do other girls (Compian et al., 2009).

All the Same? All four girls are 13, all from the same community in England. But as you see, each is on her own timetable, and that affects the clothes and expressions. Why is one in a tank top and shorts while another is in a heavy shirt and pants?

Observation Quiz Who is least developed and who is most? (see answer, page 412)

>> Response for Parents Worried About Early Puberty (from page 408): Probably not. If she is overweight, her diet should change, but the hormone hypothesis is speculative. Genes are the main factor; she shares only one-eighth of her genes with her cousin.

Sometimes early-maturing girls have older boyfriends, who are attracted to their womanly shape and girlish innocence. Having an older boyfriend gives these girls status, but it also increases their risk of drug and alcohol use (Weichold et al., 2003), relational bullying, and physical violence (from that same boyfriend) (Schreck et al., 2007).

Early-maturing girls enter abusive relationships more often than other girls do, perhaps because they are lonely and their social judgment is immature. Depression and suicide are also risks for early-maturing girls, especially if they are genetically predisposed to eveningness and are sleep deprived (Negriff et al., 2011).

Boys

Research over the past 100 years has always found that early female maturation is more harmful than helpful, but cohort seems crucial for males. Early-maturing boys who were born around 1930 often became leaders in high school and earned more money as adults (M. C. Jones, 1965; Taga et al., 2006). Since about 1960, however, the risks associated with early male maturation have outweighed the benefits.

In the twenty-first century, early-maturing boys are more aggressive, lawbreaking, and alcohol abusing than are later-maturing boys (Biehl et al., 2007; Lynne et al., 2007). This is not surprising: a boy who is experiencing rapid increases in testosterone, and whose body looks more like a man than a child, is likely to cause trouble with parents, schools, and the police.

For both sexes, early puberty correlates with sexual activity and teenage parenthood, which in turn correlate with depression and other psychosocial problems (B. Brown, 2004; Siebenbruner et al., 2007). Not only is early puberty stressful, but speed of change is difficult as well: The boys most likely to become depressed are those for whom puberty was both early and quick (Mendle et al., 2010). In adolescence, depression is often masked as anger. That fuming, flailing 12-year-old boy may be more sad than mad.

Late puberty may also be difficult, especially for boys (Benoit et al., 2013). Slow-developing boys tend to be more anxious, depressed, and afraid of sex. Girls are less attracted to them, coaches less often want them on their teams.

Every adolescent wants to hit puberty "on time." They often overestimate or underestimate their maturation, or become depressed, if they are not average (Conley & Rudolph, 2009; Shirtcliff et al., 2009; Benoit et al., 2013). However, the effects are not caused by biology alone; family contexts and especially peer pressure can make early and late puberty worse (Mendle et al., 2012; Benoit et al., 2013).

Ethnic Differences

Puberty that is late by world norms, at age 14 or so, is not troubling if one's friends are late as well. Well-nourished Africans tend to experience puberty a few months earlier and Asians a few months later than Europeans, but they all develop well if their classmates are on the same schedule (Al Sahab et al., 2010). This is true within those continents, as well as within nations, such as the United States and Canada, home to many teenagers with roots elsewhere. For adolescents of all ethnic backgrounds, peer approval is more important than adult approval or historic understanding (Green et al., 2006; Sentse et al., 2010).

Variable timing may add to intergroup tensions in multiethnic schools. For instance, in one New England high school, the shorter and thinner "quiet Asian boys" were teased, much to their dismay. When one larger Asian American boy fought back at an ethnic insult, he was a hero to his Asian peers, even though school authorities punished him for his actions (Lei, 2003). In a California high school, Samoan students were a small minority of the school population but advanced in puberty. That earned them respect from their classmates. They were accepted as peacemakers between the two more numerous groups, African and Mexican Americans (Staiger, 2006).

Size and maturation are important for adolescents in every nation. For example, a study of more than 3,000 Australian students, primarily of English heritage, found that late developers had four times the rate of self-harm (cutting or poisoning themselves) as did other students. Certainly this is a marked indication of serious depression (Patton et al., 2007).

Further studies have confirmed the correlation between off-time puberty and depression in both sexes. These studies also find that other factors—especially peer and parental relationships—make off-time puberty worse (Benoit et al., 2013).

SUMMING UP

Puberty usually begins between ages 8 and 14 (typically around age 11) in response to a chain reaction of hormones from the hypothalamus to the pituitary to the adrenal and sex glands. Hormones affect emotions as well as the body: Adolescent outbursts of sudden anger, sadness, and lust are caused not only by hormones, but also by reactions from other people to the young person's changing body. Those reactions cause emotional responses in the young person, and then emotions affect hormones, which triggers additional behavior.

The dynamic interaction among hormones, genes, adolescent behavior, and social regulations is evident in the circadian rhythm and high school schedules. Many teenagers are sleep deprived, which affects their learning and emotions.

Genes, body fat, hormones, and stress affect the onset of puberty, especially among girls. For both sexes, early or late puberty is less desirable than puberty at the same age as one's peers; off-time maturation may lead to depression, drug abuse, and other problems.

>> Growth and Nutrition

Puberty entails transformation of every part of the body, each change affecting the others. Here we discuss biological growth, the nutrition that fuels that growth, and the eating disorders that disrupt it. Next we will focus on the two other aspects of pubertal transformation, brain reorganization and sexual maturation.

Growing Bigger and Stronger

The first set of changes is called the **growth spurt**—a sudden, uneven jump in the size of almost every body part, turning children into adults. Growth proceeds from the extremities to the core (the opposite of the earlier proximodistal growth). Thus, fingers and toes lengthen before hands and feet, hands and feet before arms and legs, arms and legs before the torso. This growth is not always symmetrical: One foot, one breast, or even one ear may grow later than the other.

Because the torso is the last body part to grow, many pubescent children are temporarily big-footed, long-legged, and short-wasted. If young teenagers complain that their jeans don't fit, they are probably correct, even if those same jeans fit

growth spurt The relatively sudden and rapid physical growth that occurs during puberty. Each body part increases in size on a schedule: Weight usually precedes height, and growth of the limbs precedes growth of the torso.

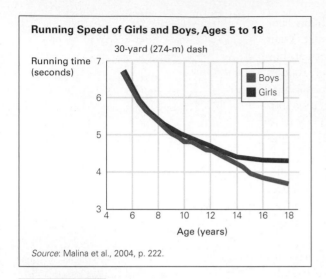

Running Speed of Girls and Boys, Ages 5 to 18

30-yard (27.4-m) dash

Running time (seconds)

Boys
Girls

Age (years)

Source: Malina et al., 2004, p. 222.

FIGURE 14.4

Little Difference Both sexes develop longer and stronger legs during puberty.

>> **Answer to Observation Quiz** (from page 410): Impossible to be sure, but it seems as if the only one smiling is the least developed (note the size of her hands, the narrowness of her hips, and her height); the one on the left is the most developed (note hips, facial expression, height, and—most revealing—her choice of clothes).

when their parents paid for them a month earlier. (Advance warning about rapid body growth occurs when parents have to buy their children's shoes in the adult section).

Sequence: Weight, Height, Muscles

As the growth spurt begins, children eat more and gain weight. Exactly when, where, and how much weight they gain depends on heredity, hormones, diet, exercise, and gender. By age 17, the average girl has twice the percentage of body fat as her male classmate, whose increased weight is mostly muscle (Roche & Sun, 2003).

A height spurt follows the weight spurt; then a year or two later a muscle spurt occurs. Thus, the pudginess and clumsiness of early puberty are usually gone by late adolescence. Arm muscles develop particularly in boys, doubling in strength from age 8 to 18. Other muscles are gender-neutral. For instance, both sexes run faster with each year of adolescence, with boys not much faster than girls (unless the girls choose to slow down) (see Figure 14.4).

Organ Growth

In both sexes organs mature in much the same way. Lungs triple in weight; consequently, adolescents breathe more deeply and slowly. The heart doubles in size as the heartbeat slows, decreasing the pulse rate while increasing blood pressure (Malina et al., 2004). Consequently, endurance improves: Some teenagers can run for miles or dance for hours. Red blood cells increase in both sexes, but dramatically more so in boys, which aids oxygen transport during intense exercise.

Both weight and height increase *before* muscles and internal organs: Athletic training and weight lifting should be tailored to an adolescent's size the previous year, to protect immature muscles and organs. Sports injuries are the most common school accidents, and they increase at puberty. One reason is that the height spurt precedes increases in bone mass, making young adolescents particularly vulnerable to fractures (Mathison & Agrawal, 2011).

One organ system, the lymphoid system (which includes the tonsils and adenoids), *decreases* in size, so teenagers are less susceptible to respiratory ailments. Mild asthma, for example, often switches off at puberty—half as many teenagers as children are asthmatic (MMWR, June 8, 2012). In addition, teenagers have fewer colds and allergies than younger children. This reduction in susceptibility is aided by growth of the larynx, which also gives deeper voices to both sexes, dramatically noticeable in boys.

Another organ system, the skin, becomes oilier, sweatier, and more prone to acne. Hair also changes, becoming coarser and darker. New hair grows under arms, on faces, and over sex organs (pubic hair, from the same Latin root as *puberty*). Visible facial and chest hair is sometimes considered a sign of manliness, although hairiness in either sex depends on genes as well as on hormones. Girls pluck or dye any facial hair they see and shave their legs, while boys proudly grow sideburns, soul patches, chinstraps, moustaches, and so on—with specifics dependent on culture and cohort.

Often teenagers cut, style, or grow their hair in ways their parents do not like, as a sign of independence. To become more attractive, many adolescents spend considerable time, money, and thought on their visible hair—growing, gelling, shaving, curling, straightening, highlighting, brushing, combing, styling, dyeing, wetting, drying. . . . In many ways, hair is far more than a growth characteristic; it is a display of sexuality.

Diet Deficiencies

All the changes of puberty depend on adequate nourishment, yet many adolescents do not eat well. Teenagers often skip breakfast, binge at midnight, guzzle down soda, and munch on salty, processed snacks. One reason for their eating patterns is that their hormones affect their diurnal rhythms, including their appetites; another reason is that their drive for independence makes them avoid family dinners and refuse to eat what their mother says they should.

Cohort and age are crucial. In the United States, each new generation eats less well than the previous one, and each 18-year-old tends to eat a less balanced diet than he or she did at age 10 (N. I. Larson et al., 2007). Most adolescents consume enough calories, but in 2011 only 15 percent of high school seniors ate the recommended three or more servings of vegetables a day (MMWR, June 8, 2012).

Deficiencies of iron, calcium, zinc, and other minerals are especially common during adolescence. Because menstruation depletes iron, anemia is more likely among adolescent girls than among any other age group. This is true everywhere, especially in South Asia and sub-Saharan Africa, where teenage girls rarely eat iron-rich meat and green vegetables.

Reliable laboratory analysis of blood iron on a large sample of young girls in developing nations is not available, but a study of 18- to 23-year-old women in Saudi Arabian colleges found that 24 percent were clinically anemic and another 26 percent had insufficient iron, although not technically anemic (Al-Sayes et al., 2011). These numbers are especially troubling since virtually all college women in Saudi Arabia are in good health, come from wealthy families, and have never been pregnant. They should be iron-rich, not iron-poor.

Boys everywhere may also be iron-deficient if they engage in physical labor or intensive sports: Muscles need iron for growth and strength. The cutoff for anemia (i.e., the blood level of iron) is higher for boys than for girls because boys naturally require more iron to be healthy (Morón & Viteri, 2009). Yet many adolescents of both sexes spurn iron-rich foods (green vegetables, eggs, and meat) in favor of iron-poor chips, sweets, and fries.

Similarly, although the daily recommended intake of calcium for teenagers is 1,300 milligrams, the average U.S. teen consumes less than 500 milligrams a day. About half of adult bone mass is acquired from ages 10 to 20, which means many contemporary teenagers will develop osteoporosis (fragile bones), a major cause of disability, injury, and death in late adulthood. [**Lifespan Link:** Osteoporosis is discussed in Chapter 23.]

One reason for calcium deficiency is that milk drinking has declined. In 1961, most North American children drank at least 24 ounces (about ¾ liter) of milk each day, providing almost all (about 900 milligrams) of their daily calcium requirement. Fifty years later, only 15 percent of high school students drank that much milk (MMWR, June 8, 2012). In the twenty-first century, the beverage most often consumed by 2- to 18-year-olds is soda (Dietary Guidelines for Americans, 2010). No iron or calcium in soft drinks.

Choices Made

Many economists advocate a "nudge" to encourage people to make better choices, not only in nutrition but also in all other aspects of their lives (Thaler & Sunstein, 2008). Teenagers are often nudged in the wrong direction. Nutritional deficiencies result from the food choices that young adolescents are enticed to make.

Fast-food establishments cluster around high schools, often with extra seating that encourages teenagers to eat and socialize. This is especially true for high

Diet Worldwide, adolescent obesity is increasing. Parental responses differ, from indifference to major focus. For some U.S. parents the response is to spend thousands trying to change their children, as for the parents of these girls, eating breakfast at Wellspring, a California boarding school for overweight teenagers which costs $6,250 a month. Every day, these girls exercise more than 10,000 steps (tracked with a pedometer) and eat less than 20 grams of fat (normal is more than 60 grams).

body image A person's idea of how his or her body looks.

schools with large Hispanic populations, the group most at risk for obesity (Taber et al., 2011). Price influences food choices, especially for adolescents, and healthy foods are more expensive than unhealthy ones. To cite one specific example: In 2014, a McDonald's salad cost much more than a hamburger.

Furthermore, nutritional deficiencies increase when schools have vending machines that offer soda and snacks, especially for middle school students (Rovner et al., 2011). A constructive nudge of higher prices for, and less attractive placement of, junk foods as well as healthier selections for in-school vending machines would improve adolescent nutrition.

A more drastic strategy would be to ban the purchase of unhealthy foods in schools altogether—a strategy used by 29 percent of U.S. high schools in 2002 and 69 percent in 2008. An increasing number of laws require schools to encourage healthy eating, and many more schools do this voluntarily (Masse et al., 2013). More measures appear in elementary schools than high schools.

Not surprisingly, rates of obesity are falling in childhood but not in adolescence. Only three U.S. states (Kentucky, Mississippi, Tennessee) had high school obesity rates at 15 percent or more in 2003; 12 states were that high in 2011.

Body Image

One reason for poor nutrition among teenagers is anxiety about **body image**—that is, a person's idea of how his or her body looks. Few teenagers welcome every change in their bodies. Instead, they tend to focus on and exaggerate imperfections (as did the three girls in the anecdote that opens this chapter). Two-thirds of U.S. high school girls are trying to lose weight, even though only one-fourth are actually overweight or obese (MMWR, June 8, 2011).

Few adolescents are happy with their bodies, partly because almost none look like the bodies portrayed in magazines, videos, and so on marketed to teenagers (Bell & Dittmar, 2010). Unhappiness with appearance is worldwide. A longitudinal study in Korea found that body image dissatisfaction began at about age 10 and increased until age 15 or so, increasing depression and thoughts of suicide (Kim & Kim, 2009). Adolescents in China have anxieties about weight gain similar to those of U.S. teenagers (Chen & Jackson, 2009).

Eating Disorders

Dissatisfaction with body image can be dangerous, even deadly. Many teenagers, mostly girls, eat erratically or ingest drugs (especially diet pills) to lose weight; others, mostly boys, take steroids to increase muscle mass. Eating disorders are rare in childhood but increase dramatically at puberty, accompanied by distorted body image, food obsession, and depression (Bulik et al., 2008; Hrabosky & Thomas, 2008). Such disorders are often unrecognized and untreated until they get worse in adulthood.

Adolescents sometimes switch from obsessive dieting to overeating to overexercising and back again. Obesity is an eating disorder at every age. [**Lifespan Link:** Obesity is discussed in Chapter 8, Chapter 17, and Chapter 20.] Here we describe two other eating disorders that are particularly likely to begin in adolescence.

Anorexia Nervosa

A body mass index (BMI) of 18 or lower, or loss of more than 10 percent of body weight within a month or two, indicates **anorexia nervosa**, a disorder characterized by voluntary starvation. The person becomes very thin, risking death by organ failure. Staying too thin becomes an obsession. People suffering from anorexia refuse to eat normally because their body image is severely distorted; they may believe they are too fat when actually they are dangerously underweight.

Although anorexia existed earlier, it was not identified until about 1950, when some high-achieving, upper-class young women became so emaciated that they died. Soon anorexia was evident among younger women (the rate spikes at puberty and again in emerging adulthood) of every income, nation, and ethnicity, and among men (Chao et al., 2008). Certain alleles increase the risk (J. K. Young, 2010), with higher risk among girls with close relatives who suffer from eating disorders or severe depression.

Binge Eating

About three times as common as anorexia is **bulimia nervosa** (also called the *binge–purge syndrome*). This disorder is clinically present in 1 to 3 percent of female teenagers and young adults in the United States. They overeat compulsively, wolfing down thousands of calories within an hour or two, and then purge through vomiting or laxatives. Most are close to normal in weight and therefore unlikely to starve. However, they risk serious health problems, including damage to their gastrointestinal systems and cardiac arrest from electrolyte imbalance.

Binging and purging are common among adolescents. For instance, a survey found that *in the last 30 days* of 2012, 6 percent of U.S. high school girls and 3 percent of the boys vomited or took laxatives to lose weight, with marked variation by state, from 4 percent in Oklahoma to 10 percent in Louisiana (MMWR, June 8, 2012).

Some adolescents periodically and compulsively overeat, quickly consuming large amounts of ice cream, cake, or any snack food until their stomachs hurt. Such binging is typically done in private, at least weekly for several months. The sufferer does not purge (hence this is not bulimia) but feels out of control, distressed, and depressed. This is a new disorder recognized in DSM 5 as *binge eating disorder*.

All adolescents are vulnerable to eating disorders of many kinds. They try new diets, go without food for 24 hours (as did 13 percent of U.S. high school girls in the last month in 2011), or take diet drugs (6 percent) (MMWR, June 8, 2012). Many eat oddly (e.g., only rice or only carrots) or begin unusual diets.

Each episode of bingeing, purging, or fasting makes the next one easier. A combination of causes leads to obesity, anorexia, bulimia, or bingeing, with at least five general elements—cultural images, stress, puberty, hormones, and childhood patterns—making disordered eating more likely.

As might be expected from a developmental perspective, healthy eating begins with childhood habits and family routines. Most overweight or underweight infants never develop nutritional problems, but children who are overweight or underweight are at greater risk. Particularly in adolescence, family-based therapy for eating disorders is more successful than therapy that focuses only on the individual (Couturier et al., 2013).

anorexia nervosa An eating disorder characterized by self-starvation. Affected individuals voluntarily undereat and often overexercise, depriving their vital organs of nutrition. Anorexia can be fatal.

Not just dieting. Now sitting in a café in France, Elize believed that she developed anorexia after she went on an extreme diet when she was eating just 1200 calories a day.

bulimia nervosa An eating disorder characterized by binge eating and subsequent purging, usually by induced vomiting and/or use of laxatives.

SUMMING UP

The transformations of puberty are dramatic. Boys and girls become men or women, both physically and neurologically. Growth proceeds from the extremities to the center, so the limbs grow before the internal organs do. Increase in weight precedes that in height, which precedes growth of the muscles and of the internal organs.

All adolescents are vulnerable to poor nutrition; few are well nourished. Insufficient consumption of iron and calcium is particularly common as fast food and nutrient-poor snacks often replace family meals. Both boys and girls often choose junk food instead of a balanced diet, in part because they and their peers are concerned about physical appearance and social acceptance. The combination of nutritional deficiencies, peer culture, and anxiety about body image sometimes causes obesity, anorexia, or bulimia, influenced by heredity and childhood patterns. All adolescent nutrition problems have lifelong, life-threatening consequences. ■

>> Brain Development

Like the other parts of the body, different parts of the brain grow at different rates. Myelination and maturation occur in sequence, proceeding from the inner brain to the cortex and from back to front (Sowell et al., 2007). That means that the limbic system, including the amygdala, the site of intense fear and excitement, matures before the prefrontal cortex, where planning, emotional regulation, and impulse control occur.

Furthermore, pubertal hormones target the amygdala and other crucial parts of the HPA axis directly (Romeo, 2013), but full functioning of the cortex requires maturation beyond the teen years. For both of these reasons, the instinctual and emotional areas of the adolescent brain develop ahead of the reflective, analytic areas. Early puberty means emotional rushes, unchecked by caution.

A Need for Caution

Brain scans confirm that emotional control, revealed by fMRI studies, is not fully developed until adulthood, because the prefrontal cortex is limited in connections and engagement (Luna et al., 2013). When compared with the brains of emerging adults, adolescent brains show heightened arousal in the brain's reward centers.

FIGURE 14.5

Same People, But Not the Same Brain
These brain scans are part of a longitudinal study that repeatedly compared the proportion of gray matter from childhood through adolescence. (Gray matter refers to the cell bodies of neurons, which are less prominent with age as some neurons are unused.) Gray matter is reduced as white matter increases, in part because pruning during the teen years (the last two pairs of images here) allows intellectual connections to build. As the authors of one study that included this chart explained, teenagers may "look like an adult, but cognitively they are not there yet" (K. Powell, 2006, p. 865).

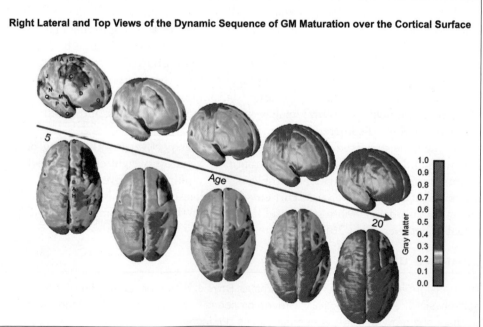

Right Lateral and Top Views of the Dynamic Sequence of GM Maturation over the Cortical Surface

Teens seek excitement and pleasure, especially the social pleasure of a peer's admiration (Galvan, 2013). In fact, when others are watching, teens find it thrilling to take dramatic risks that produce social acclaim, risks they would not dare take alone (Albert et al., 2013).

Many types of psychopathology increase at puberty, especially when puberty is early, bringing extreme stress before the prefrontal cortex matures. Two experts explain, "higher rates of psychopathology among early maturers are expected because their slow-developing neurocognitive systems are mismatched with the fast-approaching social and affective challenges at the onset of puberty" (Ge & Natsuaki, 2009, p. 329).

The fact that the frontal lobes (prefrontal cortex) are the last to mature may explain something that has long bewildered adults: Many adolescents are driven by the excitement of new experiences, sensations, and peers—forgetting the caution that their parents have tried to instill. The following is one example.

Especially for Health Practitioners How might you encourage adolescents to seek treatment for STIs? (see response, page 418)

A CASE TO STUDY

"What Were You Thinking?"

Laurence Steinberg is a noted expert on adolescence. He is also a father.

> When my son, Benjamin, was 14, he and three of his friends decided to sneak out of the house where they were spending the night and visit one of their girlfriends at around two in the morning. When they arrived at the girl's house, they positioned themselves under her bedroom window, threw pebbles against her windowpanes, and tried to scale the side of the house. Modern technology, unfortunately, has made it harder to play Romeo these days. The boys set off the house's burglar alarm, which activated a siren and simultaneously sent a direct notification to the local police station, which dispatched a patrol car. When the siren went off, the boys ran down the street and right smack into the police car, which was heading to the girl's home. Instead of stopping and explaining their activity, Ben and his friends scattered and ran off in different directions through the neighborhood. One of the boys was caught by the police and taken back to his home, where his parents were awakened and the boy questioned.

> I found out about this affair the following morning, when the girl's mother called our home to tell us what Ben had done. . . . After his near brush with the local police, Ben had returned to the house out of which he had snuck, where he slept soundly until I awakened him with an angry telephone call, telling him to gather his clothes and wait for me in front of his friend's house. On our drive home, after delivering a long lecture about what he had done and about the dangers of running from armed police in the dark when they believe they may have interrupted a burglary, I paused.

"What were you thinking?" I asked.
"That's the problem, Dad," Ben replied, "I wasn't."

[Steinberg, 2004, pp. 51, 52]

Steinberg realized that his son was right: When emotions are intense, especially when friends are nearby, the logical part of the brain shuts down. This shutdown is not reflected in questionnaires that require teenagers to respond to paper-and-pencil questions regarding hypothetical dilemmas. On those tests, most teenagers think carefully and answer correctly. In fact, when strong emotions are not activated, teenagers may be more logical than adults (Casey & Caudle, 2013). They remember facts they have learned in biology or health class about sex and drugs. However,

> the prospect of visiting a hypothetical girl from class cannot possibly carry the excitement about the possibility of surprising someone you have a crush on with a visit in the middle of the night. It is easier to put on a hypothetical condom during an act of hypothetical sex than it is to put on a real one when one is in the throes of passion. It is easier to just say no to a hypothetical beer than it is to a cold frosty one on a summer night.

[Steinberg, 2004, p. 53]

Ben reached adulthood safely. Some other teenagers, with less cautious police or less diligent parents, do not. Brain immaturity is not the origin of every "troublesome adolescent behavior," but teenage brains have underdeveloped "response inhibition, emotional regulation, and organization" (Sowell et al., 2007, p. 59). That makes teenagers vulnerable to social pressures and stresses, which typically bombard young people today (Casey & Caudle, 2013).

>> Response for Health Practitioners
(from page 417): Many adolescents are intensely concerned about privacy and fearful of adult interference. This means your first task is to convince the teenagers that you are nonjudgmental and that everything is confidential.

The normal sequence of brain maturation (limbic system at puberty, then prefrontal cortex sometime in the early 20s) combined with the early onset of puberty means that, for contemporary teenagers, emotions rule behavior for years. The limbic system, unchecked by the slower-maturing prefrontal cortex, makes powerful sensations—loud music, speeding cars, strong drugs—compelling.

It is not that the prefrontal cortex shuts down. Actually, it continues to mature throughout childhood and adolescence, and, when they think about it, adolescents are able to assess risks better than children are (Pfeiffer et al., 2011). It is the balance and coordination between the various parts of the brain that is off-kilter, not the brain itself (Casey et al., 2011).

When stress, arousal, passion, sensory bombardment, drug intoxication, or deprivation is extreme, the adolescent brain is flooded with impulses that might shame adults. Teenagers brag about being so drunk, they were "wasted," "bombed," "smashed"—a state most adults try to avoid and would not admit. [**Lifespan Link:** Abuse of alcohol and other drug abuse are discussed in Chapter 16.]

Also, unlike adults, some teenagers choose to spend a night without sleep, to eat nothing all day, to exercise in pain, or to risk parenthood or an STI by avoiding a condom. The parts of the brain dedicated to analysis are immature until years after the first hormonal rushes and sexual urges, while teenagers have access to fast cars, lethal weapons, and dangerous drugs. My friend said to his neighbor, who gave his son a red convertible for high school graduation, "Why didn't you just give him a loaded gun?"

One example of the cautious part of the brain being overwhelmed by the emotions of the moment comes from teens sending text messages while they are driving. In one survey, 64 percent of U.S. 16- to 17-year-olds said they had been in a car when the driver was texting, as occurs in every state and nation even though it is illegal almost everywhere (Madden & Lenhart, 2009). More generally, despite quicker reflexes and better vision than at later ages, far more teenagers die in motor-vehicle accidents than adults do. Thoughtless impulses and poor decisions are almost always to blame.

Any decision, from whether to eat a peach to where to go to college, requires balancing risk and reward, caution and attraction. Experiences, memories, emotions, and the prefrontal cortex help all of us choose to avoid some actions and perform others. Since the reward parts of adolescents' brains (the parts that respond to excitement and pleasure) are stronger than the inhibition parts (the parts that urge caution) (Luna et al., 2013), many adolescents act in ways that seem foolhardy to adults.

Benefits of Adolescent Brain Development

It is easy to be critical of adolescent behavior and blame it on hormones, peers, culture, or brains. Yet remember from Chapter 1 that difference is not always deficit, and that gains as well as losses are part of every stage of life. There are benefits as well as hazards in every development, including in the brain.

With increased myelination and slower inhibition, reactions become lightning fast. Such speed is valuable. For instance, adolescent athletes are potential superstars, quick and fearless as they steal a base, tackle a fullback, or sprint when their lungs feel about to burst. Ideally, coaches have the wisdom to channel such bravery.

Furthermore, as the brain's reward areas activate positive neurotransmitters, teenagers become happier. A new love, a first job, a college acceptance, or even an A on a term paper can produce a rush of joy, to be remembered and cherished lifelong.

There are constructive good evolutionary reasons for adolescents to question tradition. As social and ecological circumstances change, someone needs to ask whether having lots of children, or eating bacon every breakfast, or burning fossil fuels, is still a good practice. If every tradition were accepted uncritically, social practices would ossify and societies would die.

Further, it is beneficial that teenagers take risks and learn new things, because "the fundamental task of adolescence—to achieve adult levels of social competence—requires a great deal of learning about the social complexities of human social interactions" (Peper & Dahl, 2013, p. 135). That is exactly what teenagers' brains enable adolescents to do.

Synaptic growth enhances moral development as well. Adolescents question their elders and forge their own standards. Values embraced during adolescence are more likely to endure than those acquired later, after brain connections are firmly established. This is an asset if adolescent values are less self-centered than those of children or are more culturally attuned than those of older generations.

Yes, Not No Diving into cold water with your friends is thrilling if you are a teenage boy and a girl is watching. Adult prohibition increases the joy.

The fact that the prefrontal cortex is still developing "confers benefits as well as risks. It helps explain the creativity of adolescence and early adulthood, before the brain becomes set in its ways" (Monastersky, 2007, p. A17). The emotional intensity of adolescents "intertwines with the highest levels of human endeavor: passion for ideas and ideals, passion for beauty, passion to create music and art" (Dahl, 2004, p. 21). As a practical application, since adolescents are learning lessons about life, those who care about the next generation need to help make sure those lessons are good ones.

SUMMING UP

The brain develops unevenly during adolescence, with the limbic system ahead of the prefrontal cortex. That makes the brain's reward centers more active than the cautionary areas, especially when adolescents are with each other. As a result, adolescents are quick to react, before having second thoughts or considering consequences. Without impulse control, anger can lead to hurtful words or even serious injury, lust can lead to disease or pregnancy, self-hatred can lead to self-destruction. These same brain qualities can be positive, as adolescents fall in love, throw themselves into work or study, question social traditions that are no longer relevant. Adolescent brain development allows joy and despair; teenagers are vulnerable to some of the best, as well as the worst, experiences life has to offer. ∎

>> Sexual Maturation

Sexuality is a complex aspect of human development. Here we consider biological changes at puberty and some of the cultural variations and implications. Variations are discussed again in later chapters.

Sexual Characteristics

The body characteristics that are directly involved in conception and pregnancy are called **primary sex characteristics**. During puberty, every primary sex organ (the ovaries, the uterus, the penis, and the testes) increases dramatically in size and matures in function. By the end of the process, reproduction is possible.

primary sex characteristics The parts of the body that are directly involved in reproduction, including the vagina, uterus, ovaries, testicles, and penis.

secondary sex characteristics Physical traits that are not directly involved in reproduction but that indicate sexual maturity, such as a man's beard and a woman's breasts.

At the same time that maturation of the primary sex characteristics occurs, secondary sex characteristics develop. **Secondary sex characteristics** are bodily features that do not directly affect reproduction (hence they are secondary) but that signify masculinity or femininity.

One secondary characteristic is shape. Young boys and girls have similar shapes, but at puberty males widen at the shoulders and grow about 5 inches taller than females, while girls develop breasts and wider hips. Those female curves are often considered signs of womanhood, but neither breasts nor wide hips are required for conception; thus, they are secondary, not primary, sex characteristics.

The pattern of hair growth at the scalp line (widow's peak), the prominence of the larynx (Adam's apple), and several other anatomical features differ for men and women; all are secondary sex characteristics that few people notice. As previously explained, facial hair increases in both sexes, affected by sex hormones as well as genes.

Secondary sex characteristics such as hair are important psychologically, if not biologically. Breasts are an obvious example. Many adolescent girls buy "minimizer," "maximizer," "training," or "shaping" bras in the hope that their breasts conform to an idealized body image. During the same years, many boys are horrified to notice a swelling around their nipples—a temporary result of the erratic hormones of early puberty. If a boy's breast growth is very disturbing, tamoxifen or plastic surgery can reduce the swelling, although many doctors prefer to let time deal with the problem (Morcos & Kizy, 2012).

Sexual Activity

The primary and secondary sex characteristics just described are not the only manifestations of the sex hormones. Fantasizing, flirting, hand-holding, staring, standing, sitting, walking, displaying, and touching are all done in particular ways to reflect gender, availability, and culture. As already explained, hormones trigger thoughts and emotions, but the social context shapes thoughts into enjoyable fantasies, shameful preoccupations, frightening impulses, or actual contact (see Figure 14.6).

A recent study on sexual behaviors such as hand-holding and cuddling among young adolescents found that biological maturation was only one factor in whether

FIGURE 14.6

Boys and Girls Together Boys tend to be somewhat more sexually experienced than girls during the high school years, but since the Youth Risk Behavior Survey began in 1991, the overall trend has been toward equality in rates of sexual activity.

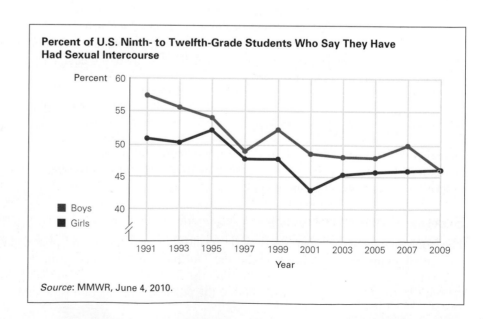

Percent of U.S. Ninth- to Twelfth-Grade Students Who Say They Have Had Sexual Intercourse

■ Boys
■ Girls

Source: MMWR, June 4, 2010.

or not such activities occurred: Especially among young European Americans, those girls with lower self-esteem were more likely to engage in sexual intimacy (Hipwell et al., 2010).

Regarding sex-related impulses, some experts believe that boys are more influenced by hormones and girls by culture (Baumeister & Blackhart, 2007). Perhaps. If a relationship includes sexual intimacy, girls seem more concerned than boys are about the depth of the romance (Zani & Cicognani, 2006). Girls hope their partners say, "I'll love you forever"; boys like to hear, "I want you now."

Everyone, however, is influenced by hormones and society, biology and culture. All adolescents have sexual interests they did not previously have (biology), which produce behaviors that teenagers in other nations would not engage in (culture). Since only girls can become pregnant, their wish for long-term commitment may be a consequence of biology, not culture. If this is so, the gender difference (girls wanting love versus boys seeking sex) may disappear as contraception makes unwanted pregnancy rare.

For whatever reason, the gender gap in experience is narrowing. It has already been reversed in some European nations, including Norway where sex education begins in childhood. By adolescence, Norwegian teenagers currently know how to prevent the unwanted consequences of intercourse. In 1987, Norwegian boys had their first sexual intercourse almost a year younger than girls did; by 2002, the sexes flipped, with girls averaging half a year younger than boys (Stigum et al., 2009).

It may seem that choosing sexual partners and activities is a private and personal matter. Yet culture and cohort dominate, as data on age at first sexual experience make clear.

In some nations girls' first partners are significantly older, and in other nations that is more true for boys. For most of the twentieth century, surveys in North America reported sexual activity among adolescents of both sexes at younger and younger ages. That trend has reversed in recent decades: first sex is now at older ages.

One statistic illustrates this new trend. In 1991, 62 percent of U.S. eleventh-graders said they had had intercourse, but in 2011 only 53 percent said so. Rates vary by state as well, from a low of 37 percent of Hawaiian high school students (ninth to twelfth grade) to a high of 59 percent in Delaware (MMWR, June 8, 2012), both less than earlier.

The trend toward later sexual activity among adolescents is worldwide, although in many nations, as marriage age has become later, premarital sex is more common—including among teens. Nonetheless, more teenagers worldwide are virgins, a trend documented in China, where, unlike before 2000, first intercourse does not occur until age 20, on average (Yu et al., 2013).

During the same time period, the *double standard* (boys expected to be more sexually active than girls) narrowed in every ethnic group. Ethnic differences in sexual activity are narrowing as well, with every group less sexually active. Between 1991 and 2011, intercourse experience among African American high school students decreased 26 percent (from 81 to 60); among European Americans, it was down 12 percent (from 50 to 44); and among Latinos, it was down 7.5 percent (from 53 to 49) (MMWR, June 8, 2012).

All these examples demonstrate that a universal experience (rising hormones) that produces another universal experience (growth of primary and secondary sex characteristics) is influenced by cohort, gender, and culture. Other research finds that the most powerful influence on adolescent sexual activity is close friends, not national norms for their sexual or ethnic group. [**Lifespan Link:** The influence of peers on adolescent sexual activity is discussed in Chapter 16.]

Prom and Proper This prom picture shows a happy young couple from Michigan who reflect the standards of their community. Note the matching clothes and flowers, and consider that in many cultures of the world, a 17-year old girl would never publicly cling so tightly to a classmate.

Don't Worry Contemporary teenagers, like this couple, are more likely to be seen in public hugging and kissing but are less likely to be sexually active than similar couples were 20 years ago.

Problems with Adolescent Sex

Sexual interest and interaction are part of adolescence; healthy adult relationships are more likely to develop when adolescent impulses have not been haunted by shame and fear (Tolman & McClelland, 2011). Although guidance is needed, teenagers are healthy and normal, not depraved or evil, in experiencing sexual urges. Before focusing on the hazards of adolescent sex, we should note that several "problems" are less troubling now than in earlier decades. Here are three specifics:

- *Teen births have decreased in every nation.* Teen births have been declining in most countries over the past few decades (World Health Organization, March 19, 2012). In the U.S., births to teenaged mothers (aged 15 to 19) decreased 25 percent between 2007 and 2011 across race and ethnicity, with the biggest drop among Hispanic teens (Martin et al., 2010; CDC, 2013). Similar declines are evident in other nations. In China, the teen pregnancy rate was cut in half from 1960 to 2010 (reducing the United Nations' projections of the world's population in 2050 by about 1 billion).
- *The use of "protection" has risen.* Contraception, particularly condom use among adolescent boys, has increased markedly in most nations since 1990 (Santelli & Melnikas, 2010). The U.S. Youth Risk Behavior Survey found that 67 percent of sexually active ninth-grade boys had used a condom during their most recent intercourse (MMWR, June 8, 2012).
- *The teen abortion rate is down.* In general, the teen abortion rate in the United States has declined every year since abortion became legal. The rate today is about half that of 20 years earlier (Kost et al., 2013), even as the rate among older women has increased. Internationally, however, abortion rates among teenagers are very difficult to track. An estimated three million girls aged 15 to 19 undergo unsafe abortions each year, mostly in low- and middle-income countries (WHO, 2012).

These are positive trends, but many aspects of adolescent sexual activity remain problematic.

Sex Too Soon

Sex can, of course, be thrilling and affirming, providing a bonding experience. However, compared to a century ago, adolescent sexual activity—especially if it results in birth—is more hazardous because four circumstances have changed:

1. Earlier puberty and weaker social taboos mean teens have sexual experiences at younger ages. Early sex correlates with depression and drug abuse.
2. Most teenage mothers have no husbands to help them. A century ago, teenage mothers were married; now, in the United States, 85 percent are unwed.
3. Raising a child has become more complex and expensive, and most young grandmothers are employed, so fewer of them can help.
4. Sexually transmitted infections are more common and dangerous.

As you just read, teen births are declining, as are teen abortions. However, the U.S. rate of adolescent pregnancy is the highest of any developed nation (true among every ethnic group). Such pregnancies are risky. If a pregnant girl is under 16 (most are not), she is more likely than teenagers who are a year or two older to experience complications—including spontaneous or induced abortion, high blood pressure, stillbirth, preterm birth, and an underweight newborn. Older

See the Joy Some young mothers are wonderful as seems the case here. This mother-infant pair have many advantages, not only their mutual love but also a supportive community. (Note the floor of the play room—colorful, non-toxic and soft—perfect for toddlers)

teens also have higher rates of medical, educational, and social problems lifelong if they become pregnant.

There are many reasons in addition to age for these hazards. Poverty and lack of education correlate with teenage pregnancy and with every problem just listed (Santelli & Melnikas, 2010). Beyond that, younger pregnant teenagers are often malnourished and postpone prenatal care (Borkowski et al., 2007). After birth, adolescents are less often the responsive mothers that newborns need, so insecure attachment is more common. [**Lifespan Link:** Attachment types and the importance of early attachment were discussed in Chapter 7.]

Even without pregnancy, teenagers who have early intercourse risk psychosocial problems. A study of 3,923 adult women in the United States found that those who *voluntarily* had sex before age 16 were more likely to divorce later on, whether or not they became pregnant or later married their first sexual partner. The same study found that adolescents of any age whose first sexual experience was unwanted (either "really didn't want it" or "had mixed feelings about it") were also more likely to later experience divorce (Paik, 2011).

Forced sex is much worse, of course, as now explained.

Sexual Abuse

Teenage births are risky, but sexual abuse is devastating: It harms development lifelong. **Child sexual abuse** is defined as any sexual activity (including fondling and photographing) between a juvenile and an adult, with age 18 the usual demarcation (although legal age varies by state). Girls are particularly vulnerable, although pubescent boys are also at risk.

The rate of sexual abuse increases at puberty, a particularly sensitive time because many young adolescents are confused about their own sexual urges and identity (Graber et al., 2010). Virtually every adolescent problem, including pregnancy, drug abuse, eating disorders, and suicide, is more frequent in adolescents who are sexually abused.

This is true worldwide. The United Nations reports that millions of girls in their early teens are forced into marriage or prostitution (often across national

child sexual abuse Any erotic activity that arouses an adult and excites, shames, or confuses a child, whether or not the victim protests and whether or not genital contact is involved.

Especially for Parents Worried About Their Teenager's Risk Taking You remember the risky things you did at the same age, and you are alarmed by the possibility that your child will follow in your footsteps. What should you do? (see response, page 424)

>> Response for Parents Worried About Their Teenager's Risk Taking (from page 423): You are right to be concerned, but you cannot keep your child locked up for the next decade or so. Since you know that some rebellion and irrationality are likely, try to minimize them by not boasting about your own youthful exploits, by reacting sternly to minor infractions to nip worse behavior in the bud, and by making allies of your child's teachers.

borders) each year (Pinheiro, 2006). Almost every nation has laws against child sexual abuse, but these laws are rarely enforced, and sensationalism about a single horrific case often crowds out systemic efforts to prevent, monitor, and eliminate sexual trafficking (Davidson, 2005).

Unfortunately, the people most likely to sexually abuse a young person are family members, who typically isolate the victim, depriving him or her of the friendships and romances that aid in developing a healthy and satisfying life. Young people who are sexually exploited tend to fear sex and to devalue themselves lifelong.

A longitudinal study of 84 reported victims (all girls) of child sex abuse included interviews with each of them six times over 23 years (Trickett et al., 2011). In order to isolate the effects of abuse, the researchers also followed the development of individuals from the same backgrounds (SES, ethnicity, and so on) who were not sexually abused.

Every trait examined (from those directly involving sex to more general social or cognitive accomplishments) showed a far higher incidence of problems in the victims than in their nonvictimized peers. Problems included attitudes directly related to abuse (e.g., most of those abused by their biological fathers thought of sex as dirty, shameful, and dangerous) and behaviors seemingly unconnected (e.g., although their body weight was in the normal range in childhood, 42 percent were obese in their 20s). Cognitive development—school achievement as well as language use—was also impaired. Among the most troubling results were much higher rates of self-harm, aggression, and repeated victimization—both sexual and physical abuse (Trickett et al., 2011).

Almost half of the girls who were abused became mothers. They had a total of 78 children, 3 of whom died in infancy and 9 of whom were permanently removed from their mothers, who had severely maltreated them. These rates were much higher than rates among the non-victimized mothers from the same income and ethnic groups.

Early in this chapter, we noted that the HPA system regulates puberty and many other physiological responses. Many of the formerly abused women had abnormal HPA regulation, with alteration of their cortisol responses. That condition produced heightened stress reactions in early adolescence but then abnormally low-stress responses in adulthood. Fortunately, now that sexual abuse is reported more often, it has become less common, with "large declines in sexual abuse from 1992 to 2010" in the United States (Finkelhor & Jones, 2012, p. 3). Worldwide, about 13 percent of women say they were sexually abused as children (Stoltenborgh et al., 2011). Of course, even one instance is too many.

sexually transmitted infection (STI) A disease spread by sexual contact, including syphilis, gonorrhea, genital herpes, chlamydia, and HIV.

Sexually Transmitted Infections

Unlike teen pregnancy and sexual abuse, the other major problem of teenage sex shows no signs of abating. A **sexually transmitted infection (STI)** (sometimes referred to as sexually transmitted disease [STD] or venereal disease [VD]) is any infection transmitted through sexual contact. Worldwide, sexually active teenagers have higher rates of the most common STIs—gonorrhea, genital herpes, and chlamydia—than do sexually active people of any other age group.

In the United States, half of all new STIs occur in people ages 15 to 25, even though this age group has less than one-fourth of the sexually active people (Satterwhite et al., 2013). One reason is biological. Pubescent girls are particularly likely to catch an STI compared to fully developed women, probably because women have more sexual secretions, although of

GODDARD, CLIVE/CARTOONSTOCK.COM

course they also need to practice safe sex. Further, if symptoms appear, teens are less likely to alert their partners or seek treatment unless pain requires it.

There are hundreds of STIs (see Appendix A). *Chlamydia* is the most frequently reported one; it often begins without symptoms, yet it can cause permanent infertility. Worse is *human papillomavirus (HPV)*, which has no immediate consequences but later increases a woman's risk of uterine cancer and death. Immunization before the first intercourse has reduced the rate of HPV, but many parents hesitate to immunize their virginal 11- and 12-year-olds, worried that immunization might increase the risk of early sex even as it decreases the risk of cancer.

National variations in laws and rates of STIs are large. Rates among U.S. teenagers higher than those in any other medically advanced nation, but lower than rates in some developing nations.

Internationally, a comparison of 30 nations found that French teenagers were among the most likely to use condoms, while those in the United States were least likely to do so (MMWR, June 8, 2012; Nic Gabhainn et al., 2009) (see Table 14.1). One reason French teenagers make greater use of condoms may be that, by law, every French high school (including Catholic ones) must offer free, confidential medical care and condoms. By contrast, providing either is illegal at many U.S. schools.

Once again, it is apparent that a universal experience (the biology of puberty) varies remarkably depending on the culture. As we stated earlier, adolescence begins with biology and ends with culture. You will see that again in the next chapter, as schools for adolescents vary a great deal in how and what they teach.

TABLE 14.1	Condom Use Among 15-Year-Olds (Tenth Grade)	
Country	Sexually Active (% of total)	Used Condom at Last Intercourse (% of those sexually active)
France	20	84
Israel	14	72
Canada	23	78
United States	41	68
England	29	83
Russia	33	75

Sources: MMWR, June 4, 2010; Nic Gabhainn et al., 2009.

SUMMING UP

Sexual differentiation is another example of the dramatic transformations of puberty. Primary sex characteristics, which are directly connected to reproduction, develop; so do secondary sex characteristics, which signify masculinity or femininity but are not necessary for pregnancy. Sexual interest increases as bodies mature and hormone levels rise. Early parenthood, sexual abuse, and sexually transmitted infections are increasingly hazardous. The first two of these are becoming less frequent, but sexually transmitted infections are alarmingly common among teenagers, especially in the United States. Some of these lead to lifelong infertility, while others lead to death in adulthood. Some nations have policies in place to protect adolescents from such hazards, but many others do not.

SUMMARY

Puberty Begins

1. Puberty refers to the various changes that transform a child's body into an adult one. Even before the teenage years, biochemical signals from the hypothalamus to the pituitary gland to the adrenal glands (the HPA axis) increase production of testosterone, estrogen, and various other hormones, which causes the body to grow rapidly and become capable of reproduction.

2. Some emotional reactions, such as quick mood shifts, are directly caused by hormones, as are thoughts about sex. The reactions of others to adolescents and their own reactions to the physical changes they are undergoing also trigger emotional responses, which, in turn, affect hormones.

3. Hormones regulate all the body rhythms of life, by day, by season, and by year. Changes in these rhythms in adolescence often result in sleep deprivation, partly because the natural circadian rhythm makes teenagers wide awake at night.

4. Puberty normally begins anytime from about age 8 to about age 14, most often between ages 10 and 13. The young person's sex, genetic background, body fat, and level of stress all contribute to this variation in timing.

5. Girls generally begin and end puberty before boys do, although the time gap in sexual maturity is much shorter than the two-year gender gap in reaching peak height.

6. Adolescents who reach puberty earlier or later than their friends experience additional stresses. Generally (depending on culture, community, and cohort), early-maturing girls and late-maturing boys have a particularly difficult time.

Growth and Nutrition

7. The growth spurt is an acceleration of growth in every part of the body. Peak weight usually precedes peak height, which is then followed by peak muscle growth. The lungs and the heart also increase in size and capacity.

8. All the changes of puberty depend on adequate nourishment, yet adolescents do not always make healthy food choices. One reason for poor nutrition is the desire to lose (or, less often, gain) weight because of anxiety about body image. This is a worldwide problem, involving cultural as well as biological factors.

9. Although serious eating disorders such as anorexia and bulimia are not usually diagnosed until emerging adulthood, their precursors are evident during puberty. Many adolescents eat too much of the wrong foods or too little food overall, with bingeing and obesity common.

Brain Development

10. Because of the sequence of brain development, many adolescents seek intense emotional experiences, unhindered by rational thought. For the same reason, adolescents are quick to react, explore, and learn. As a result, adolescents take risks, bravely or foolishly, with potential for harm as well as for good.

11. Various parts of the brain mature during puberty and in the following decade. The regions dedicated to emotional arousal (including the amygdala) mature before those that regulate and rationalize emotional expression (the prefrontal cortex).

Sexual Maturation

12. Male–female differences become apparent at puberty. The maturation of primary sex characteristics means that by age 13 or so, after experiencing menarche or spermarche, teenagers are capable of reproducing.

13. Secondary sex characteristics are not directly involved in reproduction but signify that the child is becoming a man or a woman. Body shape, breasts, voice, body hair, and numerous other features differentiate males from females. Sexual activity is influenced more by culture than by physiology.

14. Among the problems that adolescents face is the tendency to become sexually active before their bodies and minds are ready. Pregnancy before age 16 takes a physical toll on a growing girl, and STIs at any age can lead to infertility and even death.

15. Sexual abuse, which includes any sexually provocative activity that involves a juvenile and an adult, is more likely to occur in early adolescence than at other ages. Girls are more often the victims than boys are; the perpetrators are often family members.

KEY TERMS

adrenal glands (p. 402)
anorexia nervosa (p. 415)
body image (p. 414)
bulimia nervosa (p. 415)
child sexual abuse (p. 423)
circadian rhythm (p. 403)
estradiol (p. 403)
gonads (p. 403)

growth spurt (p. 411)
hormone (p. 402)
HPA (hypothalamus–pituitary–adrenal) axis (p. 402)
HPG (hypothalamus–pituitary–gonad) axis (p. 403)
leptin (p. 408)
menarche (p. 401)

pituitary (p. 402)
primary sex characteristics (p. 419)
puberty (p. 401)
secondary sex characteristics (p. 420)
secular trend (p. 406)
spermarche (p. 401)

testosterone (p. 403)
sexually transmitted infection (STI) (p. 424)

WHAT HAVE YOU LEARNED?

1. What are the first visible signs of puberty?

2. What body parts of a teenage boy or girl are the last to reach full growth?

3. How do hormones affect the physical and psychological aspects of puberty?

4. Why do adolescents experience sudden, intense emotions?

5. Why is eveningness a particular problem during adolescence?

6. Why might some high schools decide to adopt later start times?

7. What are the gender differences in the growth spurt?

8. What are the ethnic and cultural differences in the timing of the changes of puberty?

9. How would society be affected if puberty occurred for everyone a few years later?

10. Why is early puberty more difficult for girls than for boys?

11. Why is late puberty more difficult for boys than for girls?

12. What is the pattern of growth in adolescent bodies?

13. What problems result from the growth spurt sequence (weight/height/muscles)?

14. Why are young adolescents particularly vulnerable to bone fractures?

15. Why are most adolescents unhappy with their appearance?

16. Why would anyone voluntarily starve herself or himself to death?

17. Why would anyone make herself or himself throw up?

18. What problems might occur if adolescents do not get enough iron or calcium?

19. Since adolescents have quicker reflexes and better vision than adults, why are they more likely to die in a motor vehicle accident than from any other cause?

20. How might the timing of brain maturation during adolescence create problems?

21. In what ways is adolescent brain functioning better than adult brain functioning?

22. What is the crucial difference between primary sex characteristics and secondary sex characteristics? Give examples of each.

23. Why is adolescent sexuality more hazardous now than it was five decades ago?

24. Among sexually active people, why do adolescents have more STIs than adults?

25. What are positive changes in adolescent sexuality over the past five decades?

26. What are some long-term effects of child sexual abuse?

APPLICATIONS

1. Visit a fifth-, sixth-, or seventh-grade class. Note variations in the size and maturity of the students. Do you see any patterns related to gender, ethnicity, body fat, or self-confidence?

2. Interview two to four of your friends who are in their late teens or early 20s about their memories of menarche or spermarche, including their memories of others' reactions. Do their comments indicate that these events are, or are not, emotionally troubling for young people?

3. Talk with someone who became a teenage parent. Were there any problems with the pregnancy, the birth, or the first years of

parenthood? Would the person recommend teen parenthood? What would have been different had the baby been born three years earlier or three years later?

4. Find two or three adults who, as adolescents, acted impulsively and did something that could have potentially caused great harm to themselves and/or other people. What do they recall about their thinking at the time of the incident? How would their actions differ now? What do their answers reveal about the adolescent mind?

WORTH PUBLISHERS

Adolescence: Cognitive Development

- **Logic and Self**
  Egocentrism
  Formal Operational Thought

- **Two Modes of Thinking**
  Intuition Versus Analysis
  Dual Processing and the Brain

- **Digital Natives**
  Technology and Cognition
  A New Addiction?
  Cyber Danger

- **Teaching and Learning**
  Definitions and Facts
  Middle School
  A CASE TO STUDY: James, the High-
    Achieving Dropout
  High School
  OPPOSING PERSPECTIVES: Testing

WHAT WILL YOU KNOW?

1. Why do most young adolescents think everyone else is focused on them?

2. Why don't adolescents use their new cognitive ability to think logically?

3. How do computers and cell phones affect adolescent learning?

4. Which adolescents (age and background) in which schools (size and type) are most likely to feel lost and ignored?

I have taught at four universities, educating thousands of college students. Most of the content of my courses is standard. That allows me to focus on updating, adding current examples to, and adjusting each class session. I can decide the best strategy for the particular topic and class (lecture, discussion, polls, groups, video clip, pair/share, role play, written responses, quizzes, and more).

No class is exactly like any other. Not only is the group dynamic in one class unlike the next, but also each student is unique. Ideally I know who needs encouragement ("Good question"), who needs prompts ("Do you agree with —"), who should think before they speak ("What is your evidence?"), whose particular background is instructive ("Is that what it was like when you were a child in . . . ?"). Deciding who should learn what, when, and how is my challenge and my joy.

A few years ago, I taught a course for college credit to advanced high school students. They grasped concepts quickly, they studied diligently, they completed papers on time—in all those ways, they were easy to teach. But in other ways they presented difficulties unlike my college students. For example, one day I was explaining Freud's stages.

> **Student:** I don't agree with Freud.
> **Me:** You don't have to agree, just learn the terms and concepts.
> **Student:** Why should I do that?
> **Me:** You need to understand Freud, so you can then disagree.
> **Student:** But I have my own ideas, and I like them better than Freud's.

I was taken aback. None of my college students had ever been so egocentric as to claim that their own ideas were so good that they didn't need to bother with Freud. This is not to say they all agreed with Freud: some of them offered insightful criticism. But none resisted learning about Freud, especially by deciding in advance that they liked their ideas better. Then I remembered: Bright as they were, these students were adolescents. I adjusted my teaching accordingly.

This chapter describes adolescent cognition, sometimes impressively brilliant, sometimes surprisingly abstract, and sometimes amazingly egocentric. Then we describe how adolescents are taught—in middle school, in high school, and around the world—and how that aligns or clashes with adolescent cognition.

Every Detail Appearance has always been important to young adolescents, but each cohort is distinct. Thin, waxed eyebrows, blue hair and nails, and a checkered shirt over stripes would all have been anathema to this girl's grandmother at age 15, who might have examined her own rosy cheeks in a large, living-room mirror.

adolescent egocentrism A characteristic of adolescent thinking that leads young people (ages 10 to 13) to focus on themselves to the exclusion of others.

personal fable An aspect of adolescent egocentrism characterized by an adolescent's belief that his or her thoughts, feelings, and experiences are unique, more wonderful, or more awful than anyone else's.

invincibility fable An adolescent's egocentric conviction that he or she cannot be overcome or even harmed by anything that might defeat a normal mortal, such as unprotected sex, drug abuse, or high-speed driving.

>> Logic and Self

Brain maturation, additional years of schooling, moral challenges, increased independence, and intense conversations all occur between the ages of 11 and 18. These aspects of the adolescent's development propel impressive cognitive growth, as teenagers move from egocentrism to abstract logic.

Egocentrism

During puberty, young people center on themselves, in part because maturation of the brain heightens self-consciousness (Sebastian et al., 2008). Young adolescents grapple with conflicting feelings about their parents and friends, thinking deeply (but not always realistically) about their future. Adolescents ruminate (via phone, text, and private talk) about each nuance of everything they have done, are doing, and might do.

Adolescent egocentrism—thinking intensely about themselves and about what others think of them—was first described by David Elkind (1967). Egocentrism is evident throughout adolescence, especially in teenagers who have problems such as delinquency, aggression, or eating disorders, or when entering a new educational institution (middle school, high school, or college) (Schwartz et al., 2008).

In egocentrism, adolescents regard themselves as much more unique, special, and admired or disliked than they actually are. For example, few adolescent girls are attracted to boys with pimples and braces, but Edgar was so eager to be recognized as growing up that he did not realize this, according to his older sister:

> Now in the 8th grade, Edgar has this idea that all the girls are looking at him in school. He got his first pimple about three months ago. I told him to wash it with my face soap but he refused, saying, "Not until I go to school to show it off." He called the dentist, begging him to approve his braces now instead of waiting for a year. The perfect gifts for him have changed from action figures to a bottle of cologne, a chain, and a fitted baseball hat like the rappers wear.

> *[adapted from Eva, personal communication]*

Egocentrism leads adolescents to interpret everyone else's behavior as if it were a judgment on them. A stranger's frown or a teacher's critique can make a teenager conclude that "No one likes me" and then deduce that "I am unlovable" or even "I can't leave the house." More positive casual reactions—a smile from a sales clerk or an extra-big hug from a younger brother—could lead to "I am great" or "Everyone loves me," with similarly distorted self-perception.

Acute self-consciousness about physical appearance is probably more prevalent between the ages of 10 and 14 than at any other time in one's life (Rankin et al., 2004). Most young adolescents would rather not stand out from their peers, hoping instead to blend in, although they may want to flaunt adult standards. Conformity rules.

Fables

The **personal fable** is the belief that one is unique, destined to have a heroic, fabled, even legendary life. Some 12-year-olds plan to star in the NBA, or to become billionaires, or to cure cancer. Others believe they are destined to die an early, tragic death; for them smoking, eating junk food, or other habits that could lead to midlife cancer or heart disease are no problem. This fable may coexist with the **invincibility fable**, the idea that death will not occur unless destiny allows it, and therefore fast driving, unprotected sex, or addictive drugs will do no harm.

In every nation, most volunteers for military service—hoping that they will be sent into combat—are under the age of 20. Young recruits take risks more often than older, more experienced soldiers (Killgore et al., 2006). Another example of the invincibility fable comes from online chat rooms: despite adult warnings, teenagers reveal personal information to electronic "friends" (McCarty et al., 2011).

PICTURE PARTNERS/ALAMY

The Imaginary Audience

Egocentrism creates an **imaginary audience** in the minds of many adolescents. They believe they are at center stage, with all eyes on them, and they imagine how others might react to their appearance and behavior.

One woman remembers:

> When I was 14 and in the 8th grade, I received an award at the end-of-year school assembly. Walking across the stage, I lost my footing and stumbled in front of the entire student body. To be clear, this was not falling flat on one's face, spraining an ankle, or knocking over the school principal—it was a small misstep noticeable only to those in the audience who were paying close attention. As I rushed off the stage, my heart pounded with embarrassment and self-consciousness, and weeks of speculation about the consequence of this missed step were set into motion. There were tears and loss of sleep. Did my friends notice? Would they stop wanting to hang out with me? Would a reputation for clumsiness follow me to high school?

[*Somerville, 2013, p. 212*]

This woman went on to become an expert on the adolescent brain; she knew from personal experience that "adolescents are hyperaware of other's evaluations and feel they are under constant scrutiny by an imaginary audience" (Somerville, 2013, p. 124).

Egocentrism Reassessed

Egocentrism is sometimes blamed for every foolish action an adolescent takes (Leather, 2009). However, that is too simple a generalization. First, some adolescents do not feel they are invincible at all; instead they have exaggerated perceptions of risks (Mills et al., 2008). Neurological studies show that in some ways adolescents are fearless. Yet, particularly regarding social disapproval, adolescents are more anxious than people of any other age (Pattwell et al., 2013).

Second, egocentrism may be protective when "an individual enters into a new environmental context or dramatically new life situation" (Schwartz et al., 2008, p. 447) because being sensitive to social cues speeds adjustment. The egocentrism of adolescents brings psychic benefits as well as dangers (Martin & Sokol, 2011).

Formal Operational Thought

Piaget described a shift to **formal operational thought**, as adolescents move past concrete operational thinking and consider abstractions, including "assumptions that have no necessary relation to reality" (Piaget, 1972, p. 148).

One way to distinguish formal from concrete thinking is to compare curricula in primary school and high school. Here are three examples:

1. *Math.* Younger children multiply real numbers, such as $4 \times 3 \times 8$; adolescents can multiply unreal numbers, such as $(2x)(3y)$ or even $(25xy^2)(-3zy^3)$.
2. *Social studies.* Younger children study other cultures by considering daily life—drinking goat's milk or building an igloo, for instance. Adolescents can consider the effect of "gross national product" and "fertility rate" on global politics.
3. *Science.* Younger students water plants; adolescents test H_2O in the lab.

Each of these examples shows that teachers realize what their students can understand.

Piaget's Experiments

Piaget and his colleagues devised a number of tasks to assess formal operational thought (Inhelder & Piaget, 1958); "in contrast to concrete operational children, formal operational adolescents imagine all possible determinants . . . [and] systematically vary the factors one by one, observe the results correctly, keep track of the results, and draw the appropriate conclusions" (P. H. Miller, 2011, p. 57).

AP PHOTO

Ready for Battle? As uniformed Russian draftees, Yevgeny and Alexei might imagine that an audience sees them as tough men. They would be mortified to know how boyishly naive they appear.

imaginary audience The other people who, in an adolescent's egocentric belief, are watching and taking note of his or her appearance, ideas, and behavior. This belief makes many teenagers very self-conscious.

formal operational thought In Piaget's theory, the fourth and final stage of cognitive development, characterized by more systematic logical thinking and by the ability to understand and systematically manipulate abstract concepts.

AP PHOTO/LAS CRUCES SUN-NEWS, VLADIMIR CHALOUPKA

A Proud Teacher "Is it possible to train a cockroach?" This hypothetical question, an example of formal operational thought, was posed by 15-year-old Tristan Williams of New Mexico. In his award-winning science project, he succeeded in conditioning Madagascar cockroaches to hiss at the sight of a permanent marker. (His parents' logic about sharing their home with 600 cockroaches is unknown.)

How to Balance a Scale Piaget's balance-scale test of formal reasoning, as it is attempted by *(a)* a 4-year-old, *(b)* a 7-year-old, *(c)* a 10-year-old, and *(d)* a 14-year-old. The key to balancing the scale is to make weight times distance from the center equal on both sides of the center; the realization of that principle requires formal operational thought.

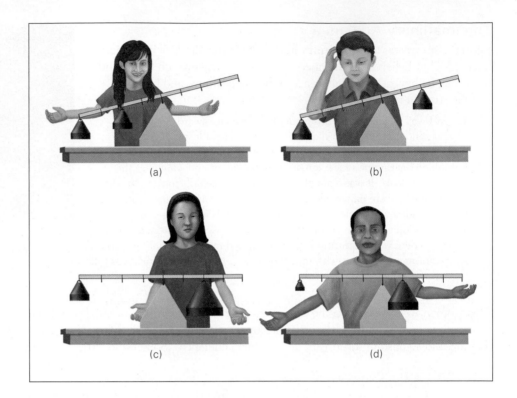

One of their experiments (diagrammed in Figure 15.1) required balancing a scale by hooking weights onto the scale's arms. To master this task, a person must realize the reciprocal interaction between distance and the weights' heaviness. Therefore, a heavy weight close to the center can be counterbalanced with a light weight far from the center on the other side.

Balancing was not understood by the 3- to 5-year-olds. By age 7, children balanced the scale by putting the same amount of weight on each arm, but they didn't realize that the distance from the center mattered. By age 10, children experimented with location and weight, using trial and error, not logic. Finally, by about age 13 or 14, some children hypothesized about the reciprocal relationship, developing the correct formula (Piaget & Inhelder, 1969).

Hypothetical-Deductive Reasoning

One hallmark of formal operational thought is the capacity to think of possibility, not just reality. "Here and now" is only one of many possibilities, including "there and then," "long, long ago," "not yet," and "never." As Piaget said:

> The adolescent . . . thinks beyond the present and forms theories about everything, delighting especially in considerations of that which is not . . .
>
> [*Piaget, 1972, p. 148*]

hypothetical thought Reasoning that includes propositions and possibilities that may not reflect reality.

Adolescents are therefore primed to engage in **hypothetical thought**, reasoning about *if–then* propositions that do not reflect reality. For example, consider this question (adapted from De Neys & Van Gelder, 2009):

> If all mammals can walk,
> And whales are mammals,
> Can whales walk?

Children answer "No!" They know that whales swim, not walk; the logic escapes them. Some adolescents answer "Yes." They understand the concept of *if*, and therefore the counterfactual phase "if all mammals."

Possibility no longer appears merely as an extension of an empirical situation or of action actually performed. Instead, it is *reality* that is now secondary to *possibility*.

[Inhelder & Piaget, 1958, p. 251; emphasis in original]

Hypothetical thought transforms perceptions, but not necessarily for the better. Adolescents might criticize everything from their mother's spaghetti (it's not *al dente*) to the Gregorian calendar (it's not the Chinese or Jewish one). They criticize what *is* because of their hypothetical thinking about what might be and their growing awareness that other families and cultures differ from their own. That complicates decision making when it comes to immediate, practical questions (Moshman, 2011).

In developing the capacity to think hypothetically, by age 14 or so adolescents become capable of **deductive reasoning**, or *top-down reasoning*, which begins with an abstract idea or premise and then uses logic to draw specific conclusions. In the example above, "if all mammals can walk" is a premise. By contrast, **inductive reasoning**, or *bottom-up reasoning*, predominates during the school years, as children accumulate facts and experiences (the knowledge base) to aid their thinking. Since they know whales cannot walk, that trumps the logic.

In essence, a child's reasoning goes like this: "This creature waddles and quacks. Ducks waddle and quack. Therefore, this must be a duck." This reasoning is inductive: It progresses from particulars ("waddles" and "quacks") to a general conclusion ("a duck"). By contrast, deduction progresses from the general to the specific: "If it's a duck, it will waddle and quack" (see Figure 15.2).

An example of the progress toward deductive reasoning comes from how children, adolescents, and adults change in their understanding of the causes of racism. Even before adolescence, almost everyone is aware that racism exists—and almost everyone opposes it. However, children tend to think the core problem is that some people are prejudiced. Using inductive reasoning, they think that the remedy is to argue against racism when they hear other people express it. By contrast, older adolescents think, deductively, that racism is a society-wide problem that requires policy solutions.

This example arises from a study of adolescent agreement or disagreement with policies to remedy racial discrimination (Hughes & Bigler, 2011). Not surprisingly, most students of all ages in an interracial U.S. high school recognized disparities between African and European Americans and believed that racism was a major cause.

However, the age of the students made a difference. Among those who recognized marked inequalities, older adolescents (ages 16 to 17) more often supported systemic solutions (e.g., affirmative action and desegregation) than did younger adolescents (ages 14 to 15). Hughes and Bigler wrote: "during adolescence, cognitive development facilitates the understanding that discrimination exists at the social-systemic level . . . [and] racial awareness begins to inform views of race-conscious policies during middle adolescence" (2011, p. 489).

Triple Winners Sharing the scholarship check of $100,000, these high school students are not only high achievers, but they also have learned to collaborate within a comprehensive public school (Hewlett). They were taught much more than formal operational logic.

deductive reasoning Reasoning from a general statement, premise, or principle, through logical steps, to figure out (deduce) specifics. (Also called *top-down reasoning*.)

inductive reasoning Reasoning from one or more specific experiences or facts to reach (induce) a general conclusion. (Also called *bottom-up reasoning*.)

Especially for Natural Scientists Some ideas that were once universally accepted, such as the belief that the sun moved around the Earth, have been disproved. Is it a failure of inductive or deductive reasoning that leads to false conclusions? (see response, page 434)

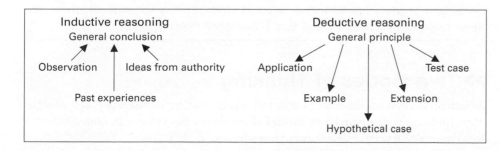

Inductive reasoning
General conclusion
Observation　　Ideas from authority
Past experiences

Deductive reasoning
General principle
Application　　　　Test case
Example　　Extension
Hypothetical case

FIGURE 15.2

Bottom Up or Top Down? Children, as concrete operational thinkers, are likely to draw conclusions on the basis of their own experiences and what they have been told. This is called inductive, or bottom-up, reasoning. Adolescents can think deductively, from the top down.

>> **Response for Natural Scientists**
(from page 433): Probably both. Our false assumptions are not logically tested because we do not realize that they might need testing.

sunk cost fallacy The mistaken belief that if money, time, or effort that cannot be recovered (a "sunk cost," in economic terms) has already been invested in some endeavor, then more should be invested in an effort to reach the goal. Because of this fallacy, people spend money trying to fix a "lemon" of a car or send more troops to fight a losing battle.

base rate neglect A common fallacy in which a person ignores the overall frequency of some behavior or characteristic (called the *base rate*) in making a decision. For example, a person might bet on a "lucky" lottery number without considering the odds that that number will be selected.

Logical Fallacies

Many cognitive scientists study how people of all ages sometimes think illogically. Such failures are apparent throughout adolescence (Albert & Steinberg, 2011), but there is one age-related difference: younger adolescents are more confident of their illogical ideas than older adolescents are (De Neys, 2013).

One example is the **sunk cost fallacy**: the belief of people who have spent if money, time, or effort that cannot be recovered (a cost already "sunk") that they must continue to pursue their goal because otherwise all previous effort in reaching that goal will be wasted (Cunha & Caldieraro, 2009). It is this fallacy that leads people to pour money into repairing a "lemon" of a car, remain in a class they are failing, stay in an abusive relationship, and so on.

Another common fallacy is **base rate neglect** (Kahneman, 2011), in which people ignore information about the frequency of a phenomenon. For example (cited by Kahneman, 2011, p. 151), if a stranger on the subway is reading the *New York Times*, which is more likely?

> She does not have a college degree.
> She has a Ph.D.

The answer is no college degree. Far more subway riders have no degree than have a Ph.D. (perhaps 50:1). But people tend to ignore that base rate, and instead conclude that a Ph.D. recipient is more likely to read the *New York Times* than someone without a degree. That is base rate neglect.

Egocentrism makes base rate neglect more likely and more personal. For instance, a teen might not wear a bicycle helmet, feeling invincible despite statistics, until a friend is brain-damaged in a biking accident. "When adolescents take unjustified risks, it is often because of the weakness of their analytic systems, which provide an inadequate check on impulsive or ill-considered decisions" (Sunstein, 2008, p. 145).

Not only adolescents but also adults sometimes reason like concrete operational or even preoperational children. Logical fallacies occur at every age, and "No contemporary scholarly reviewer of research evidence endorses the emergence of a discrete new cognitive structure at adolescence that closely resembles . . . formal operations" (Kuhn & Franklin, 2006, p. 954). Nonetheless, something shifts in cognition after puberty: Piaget was correct when he concluded that most older adolescents can think differently than most children do.

SUMMING UP

Thinking reaches heightened self-consciousness at puberty. Some adolescents are egocentric, with unrealistic notions about their place in the social world, as evidenced by the personal fable and the imaginary audience. They often imagine themselves to be invincible, unique, and the center of attention. Adolescent egocentrism is an exaggerated focus on oneself, which is typical of adolescents.

Piaget's fourth and final stage of intelligence, called *formal operational thought*, begins in adolescence. He found that adolescents' deductive logic and hypothetical reasoning improve. Other scholars note logical lapses at every age and much more variability in adolescent thought than Piaget's description implies. ▪

dual-process model The notion that two networks exist within the human brain, one for emotional and one for analytical processing of stimuli.

>> Two Modes of Thinking

Advanced logic in adolescence is counterbalanced by the increasing power of intuitive thinking. A **dual-process model** of cognition has been formulated (Dustin & Steinberg, 2011) (see Visualizing Development, p. 435).

Thinking in Adolescence

We are able to think both intuitively and analytically, but adolescents tend to rely more on intuitive thinking than do adults. As we age, we move toward more analytical processing.

INDUCTIVE vs. DEDUCTIVE REASONING

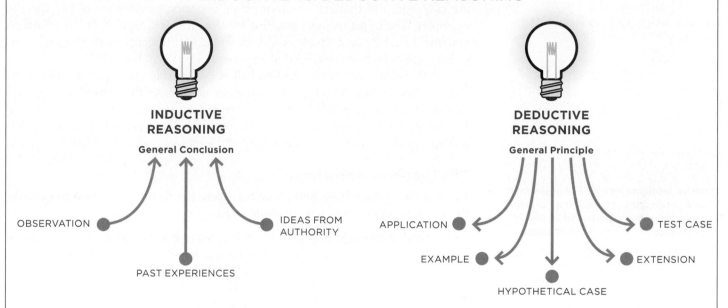

INDUCTIVE REASONING

General Conclusion

OBSERVATION

PAST EXPERIENCES

IDEAS FROM AUTHORITY

DEDUCTIVE REASONING

General Principle

APPLICATION

EXAMPLE

HYPOTHETICAL CASE

TEST CASE

EXTENSION

CHANGES IN AGE

As people age, their thinking tends to move from intuitive processing to more analytical processing. Virtually all cognitive psychologists note these two alternative processes and describe a developmental progression toward more dispassionate logic with maturity. However, the terms used and the boundaries between the two vary. They are roughly analogous to Kahneman's System 1 (which "operates automatically and quickly") and System 2 ("the conscious, reasoning self") (Kahneman, 2011, pp. 20–21), as well as to the traditional distinction between inductive and deductive reasoning, and to Piaget's concrete operational versus formal operational thought. Although experts vary in their descriptions, and individuals vary in when and how they use these two processes, overall adolescents tend to favor intuitive rather than analytic thinking.

INTUITIVE THINKING

ANALYTIC THINKING

age

YOUNGER

OLDER

INTUITIVE

This beat and sound moves me = I'll listen

ANALYTICAL

This singer sometimes writes her own songs

She makes clever videos

She is socially aware = I'll listen

She shares my values

Intuition Versus Analysis

At least two modes characterize reasoning, which we refer to here as intuitive and analytical. Although they interact and can overlap, each is independent of the other (Kuhn, 2013). Although most cognitive psychologists recognize that there are two modes of thought, the terms they use vary, as do some of the specific examples. The terms include: intuitive/analytic, implicit/explicit, creative/factual, systems 1 and 2, contextualized/decontextualized, unconscious/conscious, gist/quantitative, emotional/intellectual, experiential/rational, hot/cold.

The thinking described by the first half of each pair is easier, preferred in everyday life. Sometimes, however, circumstances necessitate the second mode, when deeper thought is demanded. The discrepancy between the maturation of the limbic system and the prefrontal cortex reflects this duality. [**Lifespan Link:** Timing differences in maturation of various parts of the brain was discussed in Chapter 14.]

The Irrational Adolescent

Particularly in describing adolescent cognition, the terms often used to describe these two modes of thinking are intuitive/analytic:

- **Intuitive thought** begins with a belief, assumption, or general rule (called a *heuristic*) rather than logic. Intuition is quick and powerful; it feels "right."
- **Analytic thought** is the formal, logical, hypothetical-deductive thinking described by Piaget. It involves rational analysis of many factors whose interactions must be calculated, as in the scale-balancing problem.

intuitive thought Thought that arises from an emotion or a hunch, beyond rational explanation, and is influenced by past experiences and cultural assumptions.

analytic thought Thought that results from analysis, such as a systematic ranking of pros and cons, risks and consequences, possibilities and facts. Analytic thought depends on logic and rationality.

Adolescents are quick thinkers; their reaction time is shorter than at any other time of life. That typically makes them "fast and furious" intuitive thinkers, unlike their teachers and parents, who prefer slower, more analytic thinking.

Of course, when the two modes of thinking conflict, people of all ages sometimes use one mode and sometimes the other: We are all "predictably irrational" at times (Ariely, 2009). Although older adults may prefer the more thoughtful responses, it is possible to overthink a decision, to become so entangled in possibilities that no action is taken. Adolescents are impatient with adult logic, but they also can overthink. They more often err in another direction, however, with quick illogical action.

Experiences and role models influence choices, not only what action to take but also what intellectual process to use to decide what to do. Conversations, observations, and debate all move thinking forward, leading to conclusions that consider more of the facts (Kuhn, 2013).

AP PHOTO/GREGORY SMITH

Impressive Connections This robot is about to compete in the Robotics Competition in Atlanta, Georgia, but much more impressive are the brains of the Oregon high school team (including Melissa, shown here) who designed the robot.

Observation Quiz Above, Melissa seems to working by herself, but what sign do you see that suggests she is part of a team who built this robot? (see answer, page 438)

Paul Klaczynski has conducted dozens of studies comparing the thinking of children, young adolescents, and older adolescents (usually 9-, 12-, and 15-year-olds) (Holland & Klaczynski, 2009; Klaczynski, 2001, 2011; Klaczynski et al., 2009). In one study he presented 19 logic problems to children and adolescents. For example:

Timothy is very good-looking, strong, and does not smoke. He likes hanging around with his male friends, watching sports on TV, and driving his Ford Mustang convertible. He's very concerned with how he looks and with being in good shape. He is a high school senior now and is trying to get a college scholarship.

Based on this [description], rank each statement in terms of how likely it is to be true. . . . The most likely statement should get a 1. The least likely statement should get a 6.

_____	Timothy has a girlfriend.
_____	Timothy is an athlete.
_____	Timothy is popular and an athlete.
_____	Timothy is a teacher's pet and has a girlfriend.
_____	Timothy is a teacher's pet.
_____	Timothy is popular.

In ranking these statements, most adolescents (73 percent) made at least one analytic error, ranking a double statement (e.g., popular *and* an athlete) as more likely than either of the single statements included in it (popular *or* an athlete). They intuitively jumped to the more inclusive statement rather than sticking to logic. Klaczynski found that almost every adolescent was analytical and logical on some of the 19 problems but not on others, with some scoring high on the same questions that others scored low on. Logical thinking improved with age and education, although not with IQ.

In other words, being smarter as measured by an intelligence test did not advance logic as much as did having more experience, in school and in life. Klaczynski (2001) concluded that, even though teenagers *can* use logic, "most adolescents do not demonstrate a level of performance commensurate with their abilities" (p. 854).

Preferring Emotions

What would motivate adolescents to use—or fail to use—their formal operational thinking? Klaczynski's participants had all learned the scientific method in school, and they knew that scientists use empirical evidence and deductive reasoning. But they did not always think like scientists. Why not?

Dozens of experiments and extensive theorizing have found some answers (Albert & Steinberg, 2011). Essentially, logic is more difficult than intuition, and it requires questioning ideas that are comforting and familiar. Once people of any age reach an emotional conclusion (sometimes called a "gut feeling"), they resist changing their minds. Prejudice does not quickly disappear, because it is not seen as prejudice.

As people gain experience in making decisions and thinking things through, they become better at knowing when analysis is needed (Milkman et al., 2009). For example, in contrast to younger students, when judging whether a rule is legitimate, older adolescents are more suspicious of authority and more likely to consider mitigating circumstances (Klaczynski, 2011). Both suspicion of authority and awareness of context signify advances in reasoning, but both also complicate simple issues—sometimes to the exasperation of their parents.

Rational judgment is especially difficult when egocentrism dominates. One psychologist discovered this personally when her teenage son phoned to be picked up from a party that had "gotten out of hand." The boy heard

> his frustrated father lament "drinking and trouble—haven't you figured out the connection?" Despite the late hour and his shaky state, the teenager advanced a lengthy argument to the effect that his father had the causality all wrong and the trouble should be attributed to other covariates, among them bad luck.
>
> *[Kuhn & Franklin, 2006, p. 966]*

Better Thinking

Sometimes adults conclude that more mature thought processes are wiser, since they lead to caution (as in the father's connection between "drinking and trouble"). Adults are particularly critical when egocentrism leads an impulsive teenager to risk future addiction by experimenting with drugs, or to risk pregnancy and AIDS by not using a condom.

>> **Answer to Observation Quiz** (from page 436): The flag on the robot matches her T-shirt. Often teenagers wear matching shirts to signify their joint identity.

But adults may themselves be egocentric in making such judgments if they assume that adolescents share their values. Parents want healthy, long-lived children, so they think that adolescents use faulty reasoning when they risk their lives. Adolescents, however, value social warmth and friendship, and their hormones and brains are more attuned to those values than to long-term consequences (Crone & Dahl, 2012).

A 15-year-old who is offered a cigarette, for example, might rationally choose social acceptance and maybe romance over the distant risk of cancer. Think of a teenager who wants to be "cool" or "bad," and then think of one who says "my mother wouldn't approve."

Weighing alternatives and thinking of possibilities can be paralyzing. The systematic, analytic thought that Piaget described is slow and costly, not fast and frugal, wasting precious time when a young person wants to act. Some risks are taken impulsively and foolishly, but others are premeditated, leading adolescents to make choices unlike those the parent would wish (Maslowsky et al., 2011).

As the knowledge base increases and the brain matures, as impulses become less insistent and past experiences accumulate, both modes of thought become more forceful. With maturity, education, and conversation with those who disagree, adolescents are neither paralyzed by too much analysis nor plummeted into danger via intuition. Logic increases from adolescence to adulthood (and then decreases somewhat in old age) (De Neys & Van Gelder, 2009; Kuhn, 2013).

Dual Processing and the Brain

The brain maturation process described in Chapter 14 seems to be directly related to the dual processes just explained (Steinberg, 2010). Because the limbic system is activated by puberty but the prefrontal cortex matures more gradually over time, it is easy to understand why adolescents are swayed by their intuition instead of by analysis.

Since adolescent brains respond quickly and deeply to social rejection, it is not surprising that teens might readily follow impulses that will bring social approval. Consider the results of experiments in which adults and adolescents, alone or with peers, played a video game in which taking risks might lead to crashes or gaining points. Compared to the adults, the adolescents were much more likely to take risks and crash, especially when they were with peers (Albert et al., 2013) (see Figure 15.3).

This explains why motor vehicle accidents in adolescence result in more deaths per vehicle than crashes in adulthood—teenage drivers seek the admiration of their passengers by speeding, by passing trucks, by trying to beat the train at the railroad crossing. Chances are about 10 times greater that the driver in a fatal motor vehicle accident is under 20 than over the age of 25 (Winston et al., 2008). Don't blame it only on inexperience; blame it on the need for acclaim. Some states now prohibit teen drivers from transporting other teenagers, a law that reduces deaths.

In the risk-taking video experiment, brain activity, (specifically in that part of the brain called the *ventral striatum*) showed an marked discrepancy between the adolescents and the adults: The adults' brains gave more signals of caution (inhibition) when with other adults—the opposite reaction of adolescents' brains when they were with peers.

Because experiments that include brain scans are expensive, they rarely include many participants. However, other research methods confirm these results. One longitudinal survey repeatedly queried over than 7,000 adolescents, beginning at age 12 and ending at age 24. The results were "consistent with neurobiological research indicating that cortical regions involved in impulse control and planning continue to mature through early adulthood [and that] subcortical

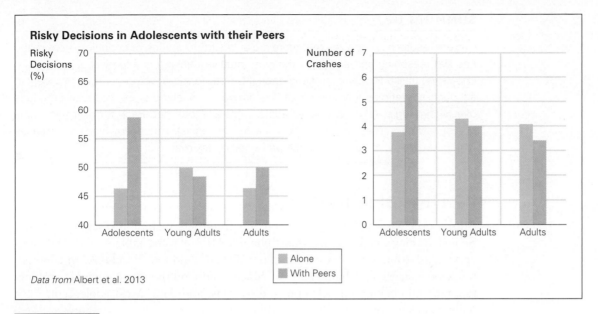

Risky Decisions in Adolescents with their Peers

Risky Decisions (%) — left chart, y-axis 40 to 70, categories: Adolescents, Young Adults, Adults

Number of Crashes — right chart, y-axis 0 to 7, categories: Adolescents, Young Adults, Adults

Legend: Alone | With Peers

Data from Albert et al. 2013

FIGURE 15.3

Losing Is Winning In this game, risk-taking led to more crashes and fewer points. As you see, adolescents were strongly influenced by the presence of peers, so much so that they lost points they would have kept if they had played alone. In fact, sometimes they laughed when they crashed, instead of bemoaning their loss. Note the contrast with emerging adults, who were more likely to take risks when alone.

regions that respond to emotional novelty and reward are more responsive in middle adolescence than in either children or adults" (Harden & Tucker-Drob, 2011, p. 743).

Specifically, this longitudinal survey traced sensation-seeking (e.g., "I enjoy new and exciting experiences") from early adolescence to the mid-20s. Increases were notable from ages 12 to 14 (see Figure 15.4). Sensation-seeking leads to intuitive thinking, direct from the gut to the brain. The researchers also studied impulsivity, as indicated by agreement with statements such as "I often get in a jam because I do things without thinking." A decline in impulsive action occurs as analytic thinking increases.

A burst of sensation seeking at puberty and the slow decline of impulsivity over the years of adolescence were the general trends in this study. However, trajectories varied individually: The decline in sensation seeking did not correlate with the decline in impulsivity. Thus, biology (the HPA system) is not necessarily linked to experience (which affects decision making of the prefrontal cortex) (Harden & Tucker-Drob, 2011).

For example, hormone rushes in two adolescents might produce intense and identical drives for sex, but one teenager might have had experiences (direct or via role models) that taught him or her to curb that desire, while the other has had the opposite experiences. For the first, impulsivity would decline rapidly, as practice at saying no increases. This would not be true for the second adolescent, who would seek sexual pleasure as he or she had seen on a video, heard from a friend, or had experienced before. Thus both might experience equal sensation-seeking impulses, but how they act on those impulses would vary.

FIGURE 15.4

Look Before You Leap As you can see, adolescents become less impulsive as they mature, but they still enjoy the thrill of a new sensation.

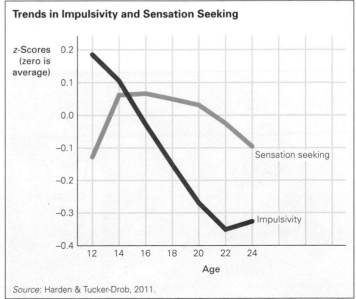

Trends in Impulsivity and Sensation Seeking

z-Scores (zero is average), y-axis −0.4 to 0.2, x-axis Age 12 to 24. Lines labeled Sensation seeking and Impulsivity.

Source: Harden & Tucker-Drob, 2011.

SUMMING UP

Current research recognizes that there are at least two modes of cognition, here called intuitive reasoning and analytical thought. Intuitive thinking is experiential, quick, and impulsive, unlike formal operational thought. Both forms develop during adolescence, although sometimes intuitive processes crowd out analytic ones, because emotions overwhelm logic, especially when adolescents are together. Each form of thinking is appropriate in some contexts. The capacity for logical, reflective thinking increases with neurological maturation, as the prefrontal cortex matures.   ▪

>> Digital Natives

Adults over age 40 grew up without the Internet, instant messaging, Twitter, Snapchat, blogs, cell phones, smart phones, MP3 players, tablets, or digital cameras. Until 2006, only students at elite colleges could join Facebook. In contrast, today's teenagers are "digital natives." Since childhood they have been networking, texting, and clicking for definitions, directions, and data. Most adolescents have mobile devices within reach, day and night.

The gap between those with and without computers was bemoaned a decade ago; it divided boys from girls and rich from poor (Dijk, 2005; Norris, 2001). However, within nations, that *digital divide* is shrinking, though *digital differences* remain. Low-income families continue to be less likely to have high-speed Internet at home, and adolescents from low-SES neighborhoods are less likely to use the Internet.

However, the arrival of lower-cost smartphones has narrowed this gap. Smartphone owners who are from minority ethnic groups and/or low SES often rely on their phones for Internet access (Madden et al., 2013). In developed nations, virtually every school and library is connected to the Internet, as are many in developing nations. No doubt this opens up new ideas and allows access to like-minded friends, both especially important for teens who feel isolated within their communities.

Today's adolescents and emerging adults take technology for granted. Most own computers; some own companies. The most notable digital divide is now age: In 2011, 95 percent of teenagers were online compared to only 41 percent of those over the age of 65 (Zickuhr and Smith, April 13, 2012). **[Lifespan Link:** Use of technology in late adulthood is discussed in Chapter 25.**]** No wonder most critics of technology are older adults.

Observation Quiz Is teenage conformity more evident in the photo in Shanghai (right) or in Texas (left)? (see answer, page 442)

Same Situation, Far Apart: Alone Together Adults sometimes worry that technology isolates users, but that is rarely the case. Worldwide, texting is more likely to bring people together.

Technology and Cognition

In general, educators accept, even welcome, digital natives. In many high schools, teachers use laptops, smartphones, and so on as tools for learning. In some districts, students are required to take at least one class completely online. There are "virtual" schools, in which students earn all their credits online, never entering a school building.

Recall that research conducted before the technology explosion found that education, conversation, and experience advance adolescent thought. Social networking via technology may speed up this process, as teens communicate daily with dozens—perhaps even hundreds or thousands—of "friends" via e-mail, texting, and cell phone.

Most secondary students check facts, read explanations, view videos, and thus grasp concepts they would not have understood without technology. For some adolescents, the Internet is their only source of information about health and sex. Students use the Internet for research, finding it quicker and more extensive than books on library shelves.

Teachers use it, too, not only for research and assignments, but also to judge whether or not a student's paper is plagiarized. Educators claim that the most difficult aspect of technology is teaching students how to evaluate sources, some reputable, some nonsensical. To this end, teachers explain the significance of .com, .org, .edu, and .gov (O'Hanlon, 2013).

A New Addiction?

Parents worry about sexual abuse via the Internet. There is reassuring research here: Although sexual predators lurk online, most teens avoid them, just as most adults avoid distasteful ads and pornography. Sexual abuse is a serious problem, but social networking does not increase the risk (Wolak et al., 2008).

Technology does present some dangers, however. It encourages rapid shifts of attention, multitasking without reflection, and visual learning instead of invisible analysis (Greenfield, 2009). Video games with violent content promote aggression (Gentile, 2011). For some adolescents, chat rooms, video games, and Internet gambling are addictive, taking time from needed play, schoolwork, and friendship.

This is not mere speculation. A study of almost two thousand older children and adolescents in the United States found that the *average* person played video games two hours a day. Some played much more, and only 3 percent of the boys and 21 percent of the girls never played (Gentile, 2011) (see Figure 15.5). Another survey found that almost one-third of all high school students use technology more than 3 hours a day (this does not include using computers at school), with use higher among boys and non-whites (MMWR, June 10, 2012). The rate has been increasing steadily since 1990.

Many adolescents in the first survey admit that video game playing takes time away from household chores and homework. Worse, one-fourth used video games to escape from problems, and one-fifth had "done poorly on a school assignment or test" because of spending too much time on video games. The heaviest users got lower school grades and had more physical fights than did the average users. Sadly, the data from this research may underestimate the problem, since adolescents reported on themselves.

Using criteria for addiction developed by psychiatrists for other addictions (gambling, drugs, and so on), one study found that 12 percent of the boys and 3 percent of the girls were addicted to playing video games. Remember that correlation is

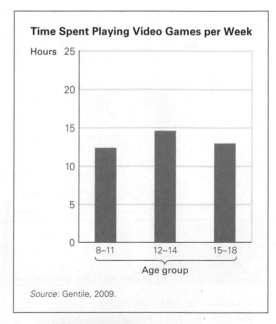

Time Spent Playing Video Games per Week

Source: Gentile, 2009.

FIGURE 15.5

More Than Eating The average adolescent boy spends more time playing video games than reading, eating, doing homework, talking with friends, playing sports, or almost anything else except sleeping or sitting in class. Indeed, some skip school or postpone sleep to finish a game.

>> **Answer to Observation Quiz** (from page 440): Probably in Texas . . . but do both Chinese teens really like the same flavor and size of ice cream cone? The Texas trio all wear faded blue jeans, short-sleeved shirts, and part their long straight hair in the middle. Might they all be texting the same person?

not causation, so perhaps low school achievement led to video game playing rather than vice versa. However, another study began with younger boys whose parents intended to buy them a video game system. Randomly, half of them were given the system, and the other half had to wait four months. Those who received the video game system had lower reading and writing achievement after 4 months than did their peers who waited (Weis & Ccrankosky, 2010).

Most screen time occurs at home, often in the child's own bedroom. About half of all parents do not impose restrictions on what kind of technology their adolescents use, when they use it, or for how long at a sitting. Some suggest that technology should be banned from schools and bedrooms, but, as one critic writes, "we don't ban pencils and paper because students pass notes" (Shuler, 2009, p. 35). Some teachers confiscate computers and cell phones used in class, others ignore them, and still others include them in the curriculum.

Whether extensive use of the Internet qualifies as an addiction is controversial. The psychiatrists who wrote the new DSM 5, after consideration, did not include it as an addiction. On the other hand, authors of studies in many nations found that a sizable minority of high school students (e.g., Turkey, 15 percent, and India, 12 percent) were addicted to computer use (Şaşmaz et al., 2014; Yadav et al., 2013). Whether a psychological disorder or not, overuse of technology is problematic for some adolescents.

cyberbullying Bullying that occurs when one person spreads insults or rumors about another by means of emails, text messages, or cell phone videos.

Cyber Danger

When a person is bullied via electronic devices, usually via e-mail, text messages, or cell phone videos, that is **cyberbullying** (Tokunaga, 2010). The adolescents most involved in cyberbullying are usually already bullies or victims or both, with bully victims the most likely to engage in, and suffer from, cyberbullying. [**Lifespan Link:** For a discussion of bullying, see Chapter 13.] Although technology does not create bullies, it gives them another means to act and wider access.

Worst in Adolescence

Texted and emailed rumors and insults can "go viral," reaching thousands, transmitted day and night. The imaginary audience magnifies the shame (Englander et al., 2009). Not only words but also photos can be easily sent: Some adolescents photograph others drunk, naked, or crying and send the photo to dozens of others, who may send it to yet others. Since adolescents are quick-acting but judgment is weak, cyberbulling is particularly prevalent between ages 11–14.

Fake Face in Georgia Alex stands behind a phony Facebook page that portrays her as a racist, sexually-active drug user. She is 14, a late developer, which may be why she became a cyberbullying target. Also shown are her parents, Amy and Chris Boston, who are suing her classmates for libel. No matter what happens in court, the worst has already happened: Alex thought those girls were her friends.

While the causes of all forms of bullying are similar, each form has its own sting: cyberbullying may be worst when the imaginary audience is strong, the identity is forming, and impulsive thoughts precede analytic ones. Adolescent victims are likely to suffer from depression and may commit suicide (Bonannor & Hymel, 2013).

The school climate affects all forms of bullying. When students consider their school a good place to be—with supportive teachers, friendly students, opportunities for growth (clubs, sports, theater, music), and the like—those with high self-esteem are not only less likely to engage in cyberbullying but also are more likely to disapprove of it. That reduces the incidences. However, when the school climate is negative, those with high self-esteem are often bullies (Gendron et al., 2011). Some students believe that cyberbullying is unstoppable. Nonetheless, teens themselves use successful strategies, including deleting messages without reading them (Parris et al., 2011).

A complication is that most adolescents trust technology while many adults ignore it. Parents and teachers are often unaware of cyberbullying, and few laws and policies successfully prevent it. Some school administrators insist that, since cyberbullying does not emanate from school computers, they cannot stop it. However, cyberbullying usually occurs among classmates and can poison the school climate, and thus educators must be concerned. Adolescents are vulnerable, needing more protection than adults realize.

Sexting

The vulnerability of adolescence was tragically evident in the suicide of a California 15-year-old, Audrie Pott (Sulik, 2013). At a sleepover, Audrie and her friends found alcohol. She got so drunk that she blacked out, or passed out. When she came to, she realized she had been raped. On the next school day, three boys in her school were bragging that they had sex with her, showing pictures to classmates. The next weekend, Audrie hanged herself. Only then did her parents learn what had happened.

One aspect of this tragedy will come as no surprise to adolescents: "sexting," as sending sexual photographs is called. Willingly or not, almost 3 percent of a national sample of 10- to 17-year-olds say that a photo of themselves wearing few or no clothes has been sent electronically, and 7 percent have received such a picture (Mitchel et al., 2012). That may be an outdated estimate.

Other studies report as many as 30 percent of adolescents report having received sexting photos, although variation by school, gender, and ethnicity is evident (Temple et al., 2014). Adults are seldom aware of this activity, which technically is child pornography.

Every study finds that sexting has two dangers; (1) the pictures are often forwarded without the naked person's knowledge, and (2) senders risk serious depression if the reaction is not what they wished (Temple et al., 2014). Remember that body image formation is crucial during early adolescence, and that many teens have distorted self-concepts—no wonder sexting is fraught with trouble.

The other destructive side of Internet connections is that it allows adolescents to connect with others who share their prejudices and self-destructive obsessions, such as anorexia, or cutting. The people they connect with are those who confirm and inform their twisted cognition. This suggests that parents and teachers need to continue their close relationships with their adolescents. Note the absence of parents at Audrie's alcoholic sleepover, the rape, cyberbullying, and suicide. (Parent/child relationships are a central theme of the next chapter.)

The danger of all forms of technology lies not in the equipment but in the cognition of the user. As is true of many aspects of adolescence (puberty, brain development, egocentric thought, contraception, and so on), context, adults, peers, and the adolescent's own personality and temperament "shape, mediate, and/or modify effects" of technology (Oakes, 2009, p. 1142).

Teens are intuitive, impulsive, and egocentric, and they often have difficulty analyzing the impact of whatever they send or limiting the power of whatever they read. Adults should know better, but all of us are sometimes illogical and emotional: It takes time and experience to use technology wisely.

SUMMING UP

In fostering adolescent cognition, technology has many positive aspects: A computer is a tool for learning, and online connections promote social outreach and reduce isolation, especially for those who feel marginalized. Friends often connect via texting and email, and social-networking sites expand the social circle. However, technology also has a dark side, especially evident in cyberbullying, sexting, and video game addiction. This negative aspect of technology can interfere with education and friendship rather than enhance them. ∎

>> Teaching and Learning

What does our knowledge of adolescent thought imply about school? Educators, developmentalists, political leaders, and parents wonder exactly which curricula and school structures are best for 11- to 18-year-olds. There are dozens of options: academic knowledge versus vocational skills, single sex or co-ed, competitive or cooperative, large or small, public or private—and more.

To further complicate matters, adolescents are far from a homogeneous group. As a result, "some students thrive at school, enjoying and benefiting from most of their experiences there; others muddle along and cope as best they can with the stress and demands of the moment; and still others find school an alienating and unpleasant place to be" (Eccles & Roeser, 2011, p. 225).

Given all these variations, no single school structure or style of pedagogy seems best for everyone. Various scientists, nations, schools, and teachers try many strategies, some based on opposite, but logical, hypotheses. To analyze these strategies, we present definitions, facts, issues, and possibilities.

Definitions and Facts

Each year of schooling advances human potential, a fact recognized by leaders and scholars in every nation and discipline. As you have read, adolescents are capable of deep and wide-ranging thought, no longer limited by concrete experience, yet they are often egocentric, impulsive, and intuitive. The quality of education matters: A year can propel thinking forward or can have little impact (Hanushek & Woessmann, 2010).

Secondary education—traditionally grades 7 through 12—denotes the school years after elementary or grade school (known as *primary education*) and before college or university (known as *tertiary education*). Adults are healthier and wealthier if they complete primary education, learning to read and write, and then continue on through secondary and tertiary education.

Even such a seemingly unrelated condition as obesity among adult women in the United States is much higher among those with no high school diploma as it is among those with B.A. degrees (43 percent versus 25 percent) (National Center for Health Statistics, 2012). This is just one example from one nation, but data on almost every ailment, from every nation and every ethnic group, confirm that high school graduation correlates with better health, wealth, and family life. Some of the reasons are indirectly related to education (e.g., income and place of residence), but even when poverty and toxic neighborhoods are equalized, education confers benefits.

Partly because political leaders recognize that educated adults advance national wealth and health, every nation is increasing the number of students in secondary schools. Education is compulsory until at least age 12 almost everywhere, and new high schools and colleges open almost daily in developing nations. The two most populous countries, China and India, show dramatic growth. In India, for example, less than 1 percent of the population graduated from high school in 1950;

secondary education Literally, the period after primary education (elementary or grade school) and before tertiary education (college). It usually occurs from about ages 12 to 18, although there is some variation by school and by nation.

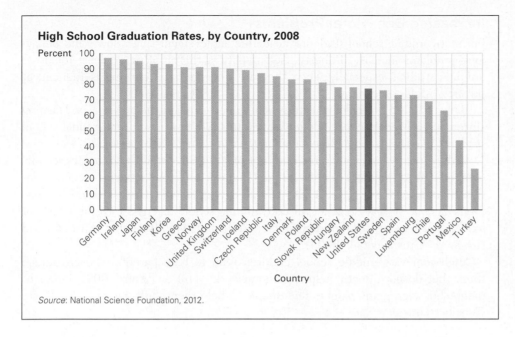

High School Graduation Rates, by Country, 2008

Percent

Source: National Science Foundation, 2012.

Countries (x-axis): Germany, Ireland, Japan, Finland, Korea, Greece, Norway, United Kingdom, Switzerland, Iceland, Czech Republic, Italy, Denmark, Poland, Slovak Republic, Hungary, New Zealand, United States, Sweden, Spain, Luxembourg, Chile, Portugal, Mexico, Turkey

FIGURE 15.6

Children Left Behind High school graduation rates in almost every nation and ethnic group are improving. However, the United States still lags behind other nations, and ethnic differences persist, with the rate among Native-Americans lowest and among Asian-Americans highest. High school diplomas are only one sign of educational accomplishment: Nations at the top of this chart tend also to rank highest in preschool attendance, in middle school achievement, and in college graduation. Raising the graduation rate involves the entire educational system, not simply more rigorous or more lenient graduation standards.

the 2002 rate was 37 percent; the 2010 rate was 50 percent; now it is even higher (Bagla & Stone, 2013).

Often, two levels of secondary education are provided. Traditionally, secondary education was divided into junior high (usually grades 7 and 8) and senior high (usually grades 9 through 12). As the average age of puberty declined, **middle schools** were created for grades 6 to 8, and sometimes for grades 5 to 8.

Every nation seeks to educate its citizens. As reviewed in Chapter 12, two international tests, the TIMSS (Trends in International Mathematics and Science Study) and the PIRLS (Progress in International Reading Literacy Study), find that the United States is only middling among developed nations in student learning. A third set of international tests, the PISA (Programme for International Student Assessment), to be explained soon, places U.S. students even lower.

In many nations, scores on those three international tests as well as other metrics compel reexamination of school policies and practices. That certainly is true in the United States, which lags behind other developed nations in high school graduation rate (see Figure 15.6).

middle school A school for children in the grades between elementary and high school. Middle school usually begins with grade 6 and ends with grade 8.

Middle School

School dropout rates are affected by middle school. As one scholar wrote: "Long-term academic trajectories—the choice to stay in school or to drop out and the selection in high school of academic college-prep courses versus basic-level courses—are strongly influenced by experience in grades 6–8" (Snow et al., 2007, p. 72).

Many developmentalists find middle schools to be "developmentally regressive" (Eccles & Roesner, 2010, p. 13), which means learning goes backward. Entering a new school is particularly stressful during the growth spurt or the onset of sexual characteristics (Riglin et al., 2013). Adjusting to middle school is bound to be stressful, as teachers, classmates, and expectations all change.

Same Situation, Far Apart: No Romance Here. Young adolescents around the globe, such as these in California (left) and Pakistan (right), attend middle school but what they learn differs. Many North American schools encourage collaboration and hands-on learning (these girls are dissecting a squid), whereas many south Asian schools stress individual writing. Note that both classrooms are single-sex—unusual in the United States but standard in many developing nations. What do students learn from that?

Especially for Teachers You are stumped by a question your student asks. What do you do? (see response, page 447)

Increasing Behavioral Problems

For many middle school students, academic achievement slows down and behavioral problems increase. Puberty itself is part of the problem. At least for other animals studied, especially when they are under stress, learning is reduced at puberty (McCormick et al., 2010).

Biological and psychological stresses of puberty are not the only reason learning suffers in early adolescence. Cognition matters too: how much new middle school students like their school affects how much they learn (Riglin et al., 2013).

Unfortunately, many students have reasons to dislike middle school, especially compared to elementary school. Middle schools undercut student–teacher relationships (Meece & Eccles, 2010). Unlike earlier school years, when each classroom has one primary teacher all year, middle school teachers have hundreds of students. This makes them impersonal and distant: Their students learn less and risk more (Crosnoe et al., 2004).

High-achieving middle school children tend to have parents who encourage them (but do not directly help with homework) (Hill & Tyson, 2009). Unfortunately, however, many parents feel unable to help their adult-size children learn. Consider James.

A CASE TO STUDY

James, the High-Achieving Dropout

A longitudinal study in Massachusetts followed children from preschool through high school. James was one of the most promising of these students. In his early school years, he was an excellent reader whose mother took great pride in him, her only child. Once James entered middle school, however, something changed:

> Although still performing well academically, James began acting out. At first his actions could be described as merely mischievous, but later he engaged in much more serious acts, such as drinking and fighting, which resulted in his being suspended from school.
>
> *[Snow et al., 2007, p. 59]*

Family problems increased. James and his father blamed each other for their poor relationship, and his mother bragged "about how independent James was for being able to be left alone to fend for himself," while James "described himself as isolated and closed off" (Snow et al., 2007, p. 59).

James said, "The kids were definitely afraid of me but that didn't stop them" from associating with him (Snow et al., 2007, p. 59). James's experience is not unusual. Generally, aggressive and drug-using students are admired in middle school more than those who are conscientious and studious—a marked difference from elementary school (Rubin et al., 2013). Students dislike those who are unlike them, which may mean general antipathy toward those who excel (Laursen et al., 2010). Some adolescents sacrifice academics to avoid social exclusion.

This is not true only for African American boys like James. Research from Germany, Canada, and Israel found that mathematically gifted girls are particularly likely to underachieve (Boehnke, 2008). But girls have one advantage over boys in secondary school—they are less likely to quit. Although the population of the United States has slightly more males than females until about age 55, for the past four decades (since 1977) more girls have graduated from high school than boys. In 2011, 18 percent more boys dropped out of high school than girls (National Center for Education Statistics, 2012).

At the end of primary school, James planned to go to college; in middle school, he said he had "a complete lack of motivation"; in tenth grade, he left school.

As was true for James, the early signs of a future high school dropout are found in middle school. Those students who leave without graduating tend to be low-SES boys from minority ethnic groups, yet almost no middle school has male guidance counselors or teachers from those groups. Given the egocentric and intuitive way that young adolescents think, many stop trying to achieve in middle school if they do not see role models of successful, educated men (Morris and Morris, 2013).

Finding Acclaim

To pinpoint the developmental mismatch between students' needs and the middle school context, note that just when egocentrism leads young people to feelings of shame or fantasies of stardom (the imaginary audience), schools typically require them to change rooms, teachers, and classmates every 40 minutes or so. That makes both public acclaim and new friendships difficult to achieve.

Recognition for academic excellence is especially elusive because middle school teachers mark more harshly than their primary school counterparts. Effort per se is not recognized, and achievement that was earlier called outstanding is now only average. Acclaim for after-school activities is also elusive, because many art, drama, dance, and other programs put adolescents of all ages together, and those who are 11 to 13 years old are not as skilled as older adolescents. Finally, athletic teams become competitive, so those with fragile egos avoid them altogether.

Since public acclaim escapes them, many middle school students seek acceptance from their peers. Bullying increases, physical appearance becomes more important, status symbols are displayed (from gang colors to trendy sunglasses), expensive clothes are coveted, and sexual conquests are flaunted. Of course, much depends on the cultural context, but almost every middle school student seeks peer approval in ways that adults disapprove (Véronneau & Dishion, 2010).

Coping with Middle School

One way to cope with stress is directly cognitive, that is, blaming classmates, teachers, parents, governments for any problems. This may explain the surprising results of a Los Angeles study: Students in schools that were *more* ethnically mixed felt safer and *less* lonely. They did not necessarily have friends from other groups, but students who felt rejected could "attribute their plight to the prejudice of other people" rather than blame themselves (Juvonen et al., 2006, p. 398). Furthermore, since each group was a minority, the students tended to support and defend other members of their group, so each individual had some natural allies.

Some students avoid failure by simply not making an effort; that way, they can blame a low grade on a lack of trying ("I didn't study") rather than on stupidity. Pivotal is their understanding of their own potential.

If they hold to the **entity theory of intelligence** (i.e., believing that ability is innate, a fixed quantity present at birth), then nothing they do can improve their academic skill. They consider themselves as innately incompetent at math, or reading, or whatever, and mask that reality by claiming not to study, try, or care. Thus, entity belief reduces stress, but it also reduces learning.

By contrast, if adolescents adopt the **incremental theory of intelligence** (i.e., believing that intelligence can increase if they try to master whatever they seek to learn), they will pay attention, participate in class, study, complete their homework, and learn. That is also called *mastery motivation,* an example of intrinsic motivation. [**Lifespan Link:** Intrinsic and extrinsic motivation were discussed in Chapter 10.]

This is not just a hypothesis. In the first year of middle school, students with entity beliefs do not achieve much, whereas those with mastery motivation improve academically. In one study, students in their first year of middle school were taught eight lessons (such as ways to "grow your intelligence") designed to convey the idea that being smart is incremental. Especially if they had formerly held the entity theory, their performance improved compared to the students in other classes (Blackwell et al., 2007).

>> **Response for Teachers** (from page 446): Praise a student by saying, "What a great question!" Egos are fragile, so it's best to always validate the question. Seek student engagement, perhaps asking whether any classmates know the answer or telling the student to discover the answer online or saying you will find out. Whatever you do, don't fake it—if students lose faith in your credibility, you may lose them completely.

entity theory of intelligence An approach to understanding intelligence that sees ability as innate, a fixed quantity present at birth; those who hold this view do not believe that effort enhances achievement.

incremental theory of intelligence An approach to understanding intelligence that holds that intelligence can be directly increased by effort; those who subscribe to this view believe they can master whatever they seek to learn if they pay attention, participate in class, study, complete their homework, and so on.

Especially for Middle School Teachers You think your lectures are interesting and you know you care about your students, yet many of them cut class, come late, or seem to sleep through it. What do you do? (see response, page 448)

**>> Response for Middle School
Teachers** (from page 447): Students need
both challenge and involvement; avoid
lessons that are too easy or too passive.
Create small groups; assign oral reports,
debates, and role-plays; and so on.
Remember that adolescents like to hear one
another's thoughts and their own voices.

Teachers themselves were surprised at the effect. A "typical" comment came from a teacher who explained that a boy

> who never puts in any extra effort and doesn't turn in homework on time actually stayed up late working for hours to finish an assignment early so I could review it and give him a chance to revise it. He earned a B+ . . . he had been getting C's and lower.

[quoted in Blackwell et al., 2007, p. 256]

The idea that skills can be mastered motivates the learning of social skills as well as academic subjects (Dweck, 2013). Social skills are particularly important in adolescence because students want to know how to improve their peer relationships.

The contrast between entity and incremental theories is apparent not only for individual adolescents but also for teachers, parents, schools, and cultures. If the hidden curriculum endorses competition among students, then everyone believes the entity theory, and students are unlikely to help each other (Eccles & Roeser, 2011). If a teacher believes that children cannot learn much, then they won't.

International comparisons reveal that educational systems that track students into higher or lower classes, that expel low-achieving students, and that allow competition between schools for the brightest students (all reflecting entity, not incremental, theory) also show lower average achievement and a larger gap between the scores of students at the highest and lowest score quartiles (OECD, 2011).

High School

Many of the patterns and problems of middle school continue in high school. As we have seen, adolescents can think abstractly, analytically, hypothetically, and logically as well as personally, emotionally, intuitively, and experientially. The curriculum and teaching style in high school often require the former mode.

**Same Situation, Far Apart: How to
Learn** Although developmental psychologists find that adolescents learn best when they are actively engaged with ideas, most teenagers are easier to control when they are taking tests (left, Winston-Salem, North Carolina, United States) or reciting scripture (right, Kabul, Afghanistan).

The College-Bound

From a developmental perspective, the fact that high schools emphasize formal thinking makes sense, since many older adolescents are capable of abstract logic. High school teachers typically assume that their pupils have mastered formal thinking and do not attempt to teach them how to think that way (Kuhn & Franklin, 2006). That lack of instruction might hinder them in college, when formal thinking is expected.

The United States is trying to raise standards so that all high school graduates will be ready for college. For that reason, schools are increasing the number of students who take classes that are assessed by externally scored exams, either the IB (International Baccalaureate) or the AP (Advanced Placement). Such classes have high standards and satisfy a number of college requirements.

Especially for High School Teachers You
are much more interested in the nuances and
controversies than in the basic facts of your
subject, but you know that your students will
take high-stakes tests on the basics and that
their scores will have a major impact on their
futures. What should you do? (see response,
page 449)

Unfortunately, merely taking an AP class does not necessarily lead to college readiness (Sadler et al., 2010). Some students are discouraged from taking the AP exams. However, of the students who graduated from U.S. high schools in 2012, 32 percent had taken at least one AP exam and one-third of them failed. Far fewer take the IB exams, but, again, few receive the highest scores. Students who score well on AP or IB tests tend to do well in college, but this may be correlation, not causation. Since the most capable and motivated students take advanced courses, later success in college may be the result of who they are, not what they have learned (Pope, 2013).

Of course, college credit is not the only measure of high school rigor. Another indicator is an increase in the requirements to receive an academic diploma. (In many U.S. schools, no one is allowed to earn a vocational or general diploma unless parents request it.) Graduation requirements usually include two years of math beyond algebra, two years of laboratory science, three years of history, and four years of English. Learning a language other than English is often required as well.

In addition to these required courses, many U.S. states now also require students to pass a **high-stakes test** in order to graduate; a decade ago no state had such a test as a graduation requirement. (Any exam for which the consequences of failing are severe is called a high-stakes test.) Because the more populous states are likely to have high-stakes tests, 74 percent of U.S. high school students must take exit exams before graduation. This requirement is controversial, as the following explains.

>> Response for High School Teachers (from page 448): It would be nice to follow your instincts, but the appropriate response depends partly on pressures within the school and on the expectations of the parents and administration. A comforting fact is that adolescents can think about and learn almost anything if they feel a personal connection to it. Look for ways to teach the facts your students need for the tests as the foundation for the exciting and innovative topics you want to teach. Everyone will learn more, and the tests will be less intimidating to your students.

high-stakes test An evaluation that is critical in determining success or failure. If a single test determines whether a student will graduate or be promoted, it is a high-stakes test.

OPPOSING PERSPECTIVES

Testing

Students in the United States take many more tests than they did even a decade ago. This includes many high-stakes tests—not only the tests to earn a high school diploma, but also tests to get into college (the SAT and ACT, achievement and aptitude) and tests to earn college credits while in high school.

Testing begins long before high school: many students take high-stakes tests to pass eighth, fifth, and third grades, and some take tests to enter special kindergarten classes. Further, the Common Core, explained in Chapter 12, requires students to take tests in reading and math, with tests in science, history, and geography planned as well.

All tests are also high stakes for teachers, who can earn extra pay or lose their job based on what their students have learned, and for schools, which may gain resources, or be closed, because of test scores. Opposing perspectives on testing are voiced in many schools, parent groups, and state legislatures. In 2013, Alabama dropped its high stakes test for graduation while Pennsylvania instituted such a test. In the same year Texas reduced the number of tests required for graduation from 15 (the result of a 2007 law) to 4 (Rich, 2013).

Overall, high school graduation rates in the United States have increased every year for the past decade, reaching 78 percent in 2010 (see Figure 15.7). Some say that tests and standards are part of the reason.

However, others fear that students who do not graduate are discouraged. This is a particular concern for students with learning disabilities, one-third of whom do not graduate (Samuels, 2013).

Even those who pass may be less excited about education. A panel of experts found that too much testing reduces learning rather than advances it (Hout & Elliot, 2011). But how much is "too much"?

One expert recommends "using tests to motivate students and teachers for better performance" (Walberg, 2011, p. 7). He believes that well-constructed tests benefit everyone—teachers, students, and the taxpayers who fund public education. Other experts contend that the most important learning is deeper and more enduring than any machine-scored test can measure (Au & Tempel, 2012; David, 2011).

Ironically, just when more U.S. schools are raising requirements, many East Asian nations, including China, Singapore, and Japan (all with high scores on international tests), are moving in the opposite direction. Particularly in Singapore, national high-stakes tests are being phased out, and local autonomy is increasing (Hargreaves, 2012). On the other hand, some nations, including Australia and the United Kingdom, instituted high-stakes tests since 2000, amid the same opposing views.

A team of Australian educators reviewed all the evidence and concluded:

What emerges consistently across this range of studies are serious concerns regarding the impact of high stakes testing on student health and well-being, learning, teaching and curriculum.

[Polesel et al., 2012, p. 5]

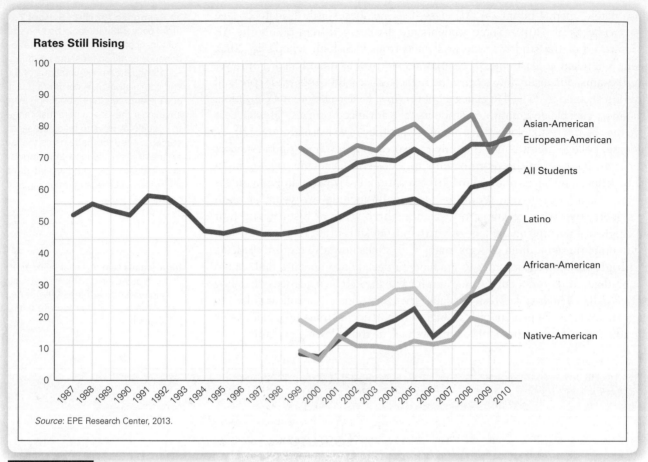

Rates Still Rising

Source: EPE Research Center, 2013.

Graduation Rates on the Rebound The U.S. graduation rate has reached its highest point thus far. Every racial and ethnic group posted solid gains in recent years. The gap between Asian/White and the three other groups is almost always the result of differences in socioeconomic status—that is, poor families live in communities with poor schools.

International data support both sides of this controversy. One nation whose children generally score well is South Korea, where high-stakes tests have resulted in extensive studying. Many South Korean parents hire tutors to teach their children after school and on weekends to improve their test scores (Lee & Shouse, 2011).

On the opposite side of the globe, students in Finland also score very well on international tests, and yet they have no national tests until the end of high school. Nor do they spend much time on homework or after-school education. A Finnish expert proudly states that "schoolteachers teach in order to help their students learn, not to pass tests" (Sahlberg, 2011, p. 26). He believes that teachers do their best with each child because there is no external standard that makes them "teach to the test."

Soon data may clarify if U.S. testing has gone too far. If Finland and Singapore continue to do well, and improvement lags in North America, that suggests that tests are not helping. Ideally, either those who support high-stakes tests or those opposed to them will change their minds.

Those Who Do Not Go to College

Many high school graduates (about 70 percent) enter college. However, only a fourth of those entering public community colleges complete their Associate degree within three years, and almost half of those entering public or private four-year schools do not earn degrees. Even 10 years after the usual age for high school graduation, only 34 percent of U.S. young adults have earned a bachelor's degree (National Center for Education Statistics, 2013).

These sobering statistics underlie another debate among educators. Should students be encouraged to "dream big" early in high school, aspiring for tertiary learning? This suggestion originates from studies that find a correlation between dreaming big in early adolescence and going to college years later (Domina et al., 2011a, 2011b). Others suggest that college is a "fairy tale dream" that may lead to low self-esteem (Rosenbaum, 2011). If adolescents fail academic classes, will they feel bored, stupid, and disengaged?

Business leaders have another concern: that high school graduates are not ready for the demands of work because their education has been too abstract. They have not learned enough through discussion, emotional maturation, and real-world experience. As one executive of Boeing (which hired 33,000 new employees in two years) wrote:

> We believe that professional success today and in the future is more likely for those who have practical experience, work well with others, build strong relationships, and are able to think and do, not just look things up on the Internet.

> *[Stephens & Richey, 2013]*

In the United States, some 2,500 *career academies* (small institutions of about 300 students each) prepare students for specific jobs. Seven years after graduation, students who were in career academies earn about $100 more a month than do other students who applied but could not enroll because there was no room (Kemple, 2008). They are also more likely to be married (38 percent versus 34 percent) and living with their children (51 percent versus 44 percent).

These programs are available to relatively few high school students, in part because the focus is on college for all. Indeed, suggesting that a student should head away from college is often considered racist, classist, sexist, or worse. Everyone agrees that adolescents need to be educated for life as well as college, but it is difficult to decide what that means.

Measuring Practical Cognition

Employers usually provide on-the-job training, which is much more specific and current than what high schools provide. They hope their future employees will have learned in secondary school how to think, explain, write, concentrate, and get along with other people. Those skills are hard to measure, especially on national high-stakes tests or on the two international tests explained in Chapter 12, the PIRLS and the TIMSS.

A third set of international tests of math, science, and reading is the **PISA (Programme for International Student Assessment),** taken by 15-year-olds, an age chosen because some 15-year-olds are close to the end of their formal school career. The questions are written to be practical, measuring knowledge that might apply at home or on the job. As a PISA report described it:

PISA (Programme for International Student Assessment) An international test taken by 15-year-olds in 50 nations that is designed to measure problem solving and cognition in daily life.

> The tests are designed to generate measures of the extent to which students can make effective use of what they have learned in school to deal with various problems and challenges they are likely to experience in everyday life.

> *[PISA, 2009, p. 12]*

For example, among the 2012 math questions is this one:

> Chris has just received her car driving license and wants to buy her first car. This table below shows the details of four cars she finds at a local car dealer.

Model	Alpha	Bolte	Castel	Dezal
Year	2003	2000	2001	1999
Advertised price (zeds)	4800	4450	4250	3990
Distance travelled (kilometers)	105 000	115 000	128 000	109 000
Engine capacity (liters)	1.79	1.796	1.82	1.783

> What car's engine capacity is the smallest?
>
> A. Alpha   B. Bolte   C. Castel   D. Dezal.

For that and the other questions on the PISA, the calculations are quite simple—most 10-year-olds can do them; no calculus, calculators, or complex formulas required. However, almost half of the 15-year-olds worldwide got that question wrong (the answer is D). Decimals may be difficult when a practical question is asked. Even in Singapore and Hongkong, one out of five 15-year-olds got it wrong.

Overall, the U.S. students did worse on the PISA than on the PIRLS or TIMSS. In the latest PISA overall results (for reading, science, and math), China, Singapore, and South Korea were at the top; Finland improved dramatically to rank close to the top, followed immediately by Canada. The United States scored near average or below average in math, reading, and science (see Table 15.1). Four factors correlate with high achievement (OECD, 2010, p. 6):

1. Leaders, parents, and citizens overall value education, with individualized approaches to learning so that all students learn what they need.
2. Standards are high and clear, so every student knows what he or she must do, with a "focus on the acquisition of complex, higher-order thinking skills."
3. Teachers and administrators are valued, given "considerable discretion . . . in determining content" and sufficient salary as well as time for collaboration.
4. Learning is prioritized "across the entire system," with high-quality teachers working in the most challenging environments.

The PISA and international comparisons of high school dropout rates suggest that U.S. secondary education can be improved, especially for those who do not go to college. Surprisingly, students who are capable of passing their classes, at least as measured on IQ tests, drop out almost as often as those who are less capable. Persistence, engagement, and motivation seem more crucial than intellectual ability (Archambault et al., 2009; Tough, 2012).

An added complication in deciding what are the best middle schools and high schools comes from the variation among adolescents: some thoughtful, some impulsive, some ready for analytic challenges, some egocentric, and all needing personal encouragement. A study of student emotional and academic engagement from the fifth to the eighth grade found that, as expected, the overall average was a slow and steady decline of engagement, but a distinctive group (about 18 percent) were highly engaged throughout, and another distinctive group (about 5 percent) experienced precipitous disengagement year by year (Li & Lerner, 2011).

Thus schools and teachers need many strategies to educate adolescents, since they themselves vary. Now let us return to general conclusions for this chapter.

TABLE 15.1	Selected Scores on the Math PISA, 2012 and 2009					
Education System	**Average Score 2012**	**Average Score 2009**	**Education System**	**Average Score 2012**	**Average Score 2009**
Shanghai-China	613	600	Iceland	493	507
Singapore	573	562	Norway	489	498
Hong Kong-China	561	555	Portugal	487	487
South Korea	554	546	Italy	485	483
Japan	536	529	Spain	484	483
Switzerland	531	*534*	Russian Federation	482	468
Netherlands	523	*526*	**United States**	**481**	**487**
Finland	519	541	Sweden	478	494
Canada	518	527	Hungary	477	490
Poland	518	495	Florida	467	n/a
Belgium	515	515	Israel	466	447
Germany	514	513	Turkey	448	445
Austria	506	496	Chile	423	421
Australia	504	514	Mexico	413	419
Ireland	501	487	Uruguay	409	427
Denmark	500	503	Brazil	391	386
New Zealand	500	519	Argentina	388	388
Czech Republic	499	493	Tunisia	388	371
France	495	497	Jordan	386	387
United Kingdom	494	492	Indonesia	375	371

Source: Organization for Economic Cooperation and Development (OECD), Program for International Student Assessment (PISA), 2012.

The cognitive skills that boost national economic development and personal happiness are creativity, flexibility, relationship building, and analytic ability. Whether or not an adolescent is college bound, those skills are exactly what adolescents can develop—with proper education and guidance.

As you have read, every researcher believes that the logical, social, and creative potential of the adolescent mind is not always realized, but that it can be. Does that belief mean that this chapter ends on a hopeful note?

SUMMING UP

Middle schools tend to be less personal, less flexible, and more tightly regulated than elementary schools, which may contribute to a general finding: declining student achievement. Teachers grade more harshly, students are more rebellious, and every teacher has far more students—all of which works against what young adolescents need most, an adult who cares about their education. Ideally, secondary education advances thinking, but this is not always the case. Variations in the structure and testing in high schools are vast, nationally and internationally. On international tests and measures, the United States is far from the top. Most students try college, but many do not graduate. Of those who do not attend college, many are even less prepared with the skills needed for a happy and productive adulthood. ∎

SUMMARY

Logic and Self

1. Cognition in early adolescence may be egocentric, a kind of self-centered thinking. Adolescent egocentrism gives rise to the personal fable, the invincibility fable, and the imaginary audience.

2. *Formal operational thought* is Piaget's term for the last of his four periods of cognitive development. He tested and demonstrated formal operational thought with various problems that students in a high school science or math class might encounter.

3. Piaget realized that adolescents are no longer earthbound and concrete in their thinking; they imagine the possible, the probable, and even the impossible, instead of focusing only on what is real. They develop hypotheses and explore, using deductive reasoning. However, few developmentalists find that adolescents move suddenly from concrete to formal thinking.

Two Modes of Thinking

4. Intuitive thinking becomes more forceful during adolescence. Few teenagers always use logic, although they are capable of doing so. Emotional, intuitive thinking is quicker and more satisfying, and sometimes better, than analytic thought.

5. Neurological as well as survey research find that adolescent thinking is characterized by more rapid development of the limbic system and slower development of the prefrontal cortex. This explains the imbalance evident in dual processing.

Digital Natives

6. Adolescents use technology, particularly the Internet, more than people of any other age. They reap many educational benefits, and many teachers welcome the accessibility of information and the research advances made possible by the Internet. Social connections are encouraged as well.

7. However, technology can be destructive for many adolescents. Some are addicted to video games, some use cell phone and instant messages for cyberbullying, some find like-minded peers to support eating disorders and other pathologies.

Teaching and Learning

8. Achievement in secondary education—after primary education (grade school) and before tertiary education (college)—correlates with the health and wealth of individuals and nations.

9. In middle school, many students struggle both socially and academically. One reason may be that middle schools are not structured to accommodate egocentrism or intuitive thinking. Students' beliefs about the nature of intelligence may also affect their learning.

10. Many forms of psychopathology increase during the transitions to middle school, to high school, and to college. Experiencing school changes may be particularly difficult in adolescence, when young people must also adjust to biological and family changes.

11. Education in high school emphasizes formal operational thinking. In the United States the demand for more accountability has led to an increase in the requirements for graduation and to more Advanced Placement (AP) classes and high-stakes testing. There is concern that all these requirements may undermine creativity and innovation.

12. A sizable number of high school students do not graduate or go on to college, and many more leave college without a degree. Current high school education does not seem to meet their needs.

13. The PISA test taken by many 15-year-olds in 50 nations measures how well they can apply the knowledge they have been taught. Students in the United States seem to have particular difficulty with such tests.

KEY TERMS

adolescent egocentrism (p. 430)
analytic thought (p. 436)
base rate neglect (p. 434)
cyberbullying (p. 442)
deductive reasoning (p. 433)
dual-process model (p. 434)

entity theory of intelligence (p. 447)
formal operational thought (p. 431)
high-stakes test (p. 449)
hypothetical thought (p. 432)

imaginary audience (p. 431)
incremental theory of intelligence (p. 447)
inductive reasoning (p. 433)
intuitive thought (p. 436)
invincibility fable (p. 430)

middle school (p. 445)
personal fable (p. 430)
PISA (Programme for International Student Assessment) (p. 451)
secondary education (p. 444)
sunk cost fallacy (p. 434)

WHAT HAVE YOU LEARNED?

1. How does adolescent egocentrism differ from early childhood egocentrism?

2. What are the main perceptions that arise from belief in the imaginary audience?

3. Why are the personal fable and the invincibility fable called "fables"?

4. How does formal operational thinking differ from concrete operational thinking?

5. What are the advantages and disadvantages of using inductive rather than deductive reasoning??

6. How certain are contemporary developmentalists that Piaget accurately described adolescent cognition?

7. When might intuition and analysis lead to contrasting conclusions?

8. What mode of thinking—intuitive or analytic—do most people prefer, and why?

9. How does personal experience increase the probability of base rate neglect?

10. How does egocentrism account for the clashing priorities of parents and adolescents?

11. When is intuitive thinking better than analytic thinking?

12. What benefits come from adolescents' use of technology?

13. How do video games affect student learning?

14. Who is most apt and least apt likely to be involved in cyberbullying?

15. Why have most junior high schools disappeared?

16. What characteristics of middle schools make them more difficult for students than elementary schools?

17. How does being a young adolescent affect a person's ability to learn?

18. How do individual beliefs about intelligence affect motivation and learning?

19. Why are school transitions a particular concern for educators?

20. Why is the first year of attendance at a new school more stressful than the second year?

21. How are educational standards changing in the United States?

22. What are the advantages and disadvantages of high-stakes testing?

23. How does the PISA differ from other international tests?

24. How does having students with strong school achievement advance a nation's economy?

APPLICATIONS

1. Describe a time when you overestimated how much other people were thinking about you. How was your mistake similar to and different from adolescent egocentrism?

2. Talk to a teenager about politics, families, school, religion, or any other topic that might reveal the way he or she thinks. Do you hear any adolescent egocentrism? Intuitive thinking? Systematic thought? Flexibility? Cite examples.

3. Think of a life-changing decision you have made. How did logic and emotion interact? What would have changed if you had given the matter more thought—or less?

4. Describe what happened and what you thought in the first year you attended a middle school or high school. What made it better or worse than later years in that school?

>>ONLINE CONNECTIONS

To accompany your textbook, you have access to a number of online resources, including Learning Curve, an adaptive quizzing program, critical thinking questions, and case studies. For access to any of these links, go to www.worthpublishers .com/launchpad/bergerls9e. In addition to these resources, you'll also find links to video clips, personalized study advice, and an ebook. Some of the videos and activities available online include:

- *HIV/AIDS.* A brief history of the global spread of HIV and the successful promotion of educational intervention in Sri Lanka. Videos let affected children with HIV tell their stories. tell their stories.

- *The Balance Scale Problem*: Adolescents have remarkable cognitive abilities. Watch them demonstrate problem-solving skills in the balance scale problem.

WORTH PUBLISHERS

Adolescence: Psychosocial Development

- Identity
  Not Yet Achieved
  Four Arenas of Identity Formation

- Relationships with Adults
  Parents
  A VIEW FROM SCIENCE:
    Parents, Genes, and Risks
  Other Adults

- Peer Power
  Peers and Parents
  Peer Pressure
  Romance
  Sex Education

- Sadness and Anger
  Depression
  Delinquency and Defiance
  OPPOSING PERSPECTIVES:
    Teenage Rage: Necessary?

- Drug Use and Abuse
  Variations in Drug Use
  Harm from Drugs
  Preventing Drug Abuse: What Works?

WHAT WILL YOU KNOW?

1. Why do some teenagers seem to markedly change their appearance, their behavior, and their goals from one year to the next?

2. When teenagers disagree with their parents on every issue, is it time for the parents to give up, become stricter, or do something else?

3. Does knowing about sex make it more likely that a teenager will be sexually active?

4. Is delinquency a temporary phase or a sign that a person is likely to commit serious crimes in adulthood?

5. Since most adolescents try alcohol, why do laws forbid it?

It's not easy being a teenager, as the previous chapters make clear, but neither is it easy being the parent of a teenager. Sometimes I was too lenient. For example, once my daughter came home late; I was worried, angry, and upset, but I did not think about punishing her until she asked, "How long am I grounded?" And sometimes I was too strict. For years I insisted that my daughters and their friends wash the dinner dishes until all my children told me that none of their friends had such mean mothers.

At times all parents probably ricochet, surprised by their adolescents. When our children were infants, my husband Martin and I had discussed and decided how we would raise them when they became teenagers: We were ready to be firm and consistent regarding illicit drug use, unsafe sex, and serious law-breaking—but none of those issues ever became a problem for us. Instead, our children presented unanticipated challenges and we reacted, sometimes at cross-purposes. As Martin said, "I knew they would become adolescents some day. I didn't know we would become parents of adolescents."

This chapter is about adolescent behavior and relationships with friends, parents, and the larger society. As you see, it begins with identity and ends with drugs, both of which might appear to be matters of private and personal choice, but both of which are strongly affected by the social context. My children's actions, my reactions, and the results were affected at every moment by past history (I washed had dishes for my family, as was the norm when I was young) and by my children's current social world (their friends did not).

>> Identity

Psychosocial development during adolescence is often understood to be a search for a consistent understanding of oneself. Self-expression and self-concept become increasingly important at puberty, as the egocentrism described in Chapter 15 illustrates. Each young person wants to know, "Who am I?"

identity versus role confusion Erikson's term for the fifth stage of development, in which the person tries to figure out "Who am I?" but is confused as to which of many possible roles to adopt.

identity achievement Erikson's term for the attainment of identity, or the point at which a person understands who he or she is as a unique individual, in accord with past experiences and future plans.

role confusion A situation in which an adolescent does not seem to know or care what his or her identity is. (Sometimes called *identity* or *role diffusion.*)

foreclosure Erikson's term for premature identity formation, which occurs when an adolescent adopts parents' or society's roles and values wholesale, without questioning or analysis.

moratorium An adolescent's choice of a socially acceptable way to postpone making identity-achievement decisions. Going to college is a common example.

No Role Confusion These are high school students in Junior ROTC training camp. For many youths who cannot afford college, the military offers a temporary identity, complete with haircut, uniform, and comrades.

According to Erik Erikson, life's fifth psychosocial crisis is **identity versus role confusion**: The complexities of finding one's own identity are the primary task of adolescence (Erikson, 1968). He said this crisis is resolved with **identity achievement**, when adolescents have reconsidered the goals and values of their parents and culture, accepting some and discarding others, forging their own identity.

The result is neither wholesale rejection nor unquestioning acceptance of social norms (Côté, 2009). With their new autonomy, teenagers maintain continuity with the past so that they can move to the future. Each person must achieve his or her own identity. Simply adopting parental norms does not work, because the social context of each generation differs, and everyone has a unique combination of genes and alleles.

Not Yet Achieved

Erikson's insights have inspired thousands of researchers. Notable among those he influenced was James Marcia, who described and measured four specific ways young people cope with the identity crisis: (1) role confusion, (2) foreclosure, (3) moratorium, and finally (4) identity achievement (Marcia, 1966).

Over the past half-century, major psychosocial shifts have lengthened the duration of adolescence and made identity achievement more complex (Côté, 2006; Kroger et al., 2010; Meeus, 2011). However, the three waystations on the road to identity achievement still seem evident.

Role confusion is the opposite of identity achievement. It is characterized by lack of commitment to any goals or values. It is sometimes called *identity diffusion* to emphasize that some adolescents seem diffuse, unfocused, and unconcerned about their future (Phillips & Pittman, 2007).

Even usual social demands—putting away clothes, making friends, completing school assignments, and thinking about college or career—are beyond role-confused adolescents. Instead, they might sleep too much, immerse themselves in video games or television, and turn from one flirtation to another. Their thinking is disorganized, they procrastinate, and they avoid issues and actions (Côté, 2009).

Identity **foreclosure** occurs when, in order to avoid the confusion of not knowing who they are, young people accept traditional roles and values (Marcia, 1966; Marcia et al., 1993). They might follow customs transmitted from their parents or culture, never exploring alternatives. Or they might foreclose on an oppositional, *negative identity*—the direct opposite of whatever their parents want—again without thoughtful questioning. Foreclosure is comfortable. For many, it is a temporary shelter, a time for commitment to a particular identity, soon followed by more exploration (Meeus, 2011).

A more mature shelter is the **moratorium**, a time-out that includes some exploration, either in breadth (trying many things) or in depth (following one path after a tentative, temporary commitment) (Meeus, 2011). In high school, a student might become focused on playing in a band, not expecting this to be a lifelong career; in the next stage, emerging adulthood, moratoria might lead to signing up for the army. Moratoria are more common at age 19 than younger, because some maturity is required (Kroger et al., 2010).

Several aspects of the search for identity, especially sexual and vocational identity, have become more arduous than they were when Erikson described them, and establishing a personal identity is more difficult. Fifty years ago, the drive to become independent and autonomous was thought to be the "key normative psychosocial task of adolescence" (Zimmer-Gembeck &

Collins, 2003, p. 177). Adolescents still begin the search for identity, but a review of longitudinal "studies among adults revealed that identity is a life-long process" (Meeus, 2011, p. 88).

Four Arenas of Identity Formation

Erikson (1968) highlighted four aspects of identity: religious, political, vocational, and sexual. Terminology and emphasis have changed for all four, as has timing. In fact, if an 18-year-old is no longer open to new possibilities in any of these four areas, that may indicate foreclosure, not achievement—and identity might shift again.

None of these four identity statuses occurs in social isolation: Parents and peers are influential, as detailed later in this chapter, and the ever-changing chronosystem (historical context) makes identity dynamic. Nonetheless, each of these four arenas remains integral to adolescence. [**Lifespan Link:** Discussion of Bronfenbrenner's ecological-systems approach, which includes the chronosystem, is in Chapter 1.]

Religious Identity

For most adolescents, their *religious identity* is similar to that of their parents and community. Few adolescents totally reject religion if they've grown up following a particular faith, especially if they have a good relationship with their parents (Kim-Spoon et al., 2012).

Past parental practices influence adolescent religious identity, although some adolescents express that identity in ways that their parents did not anticipate: A Muslim girl might start to wear a headscarf, a Catholic boy might study for the priesthood, or a Baptist teenager might join a Pentecostal youth group, each surprising their less devout parents.

Such new practices are relatively minor, not evidence of a totally new religious identity. Almost no young Muslims convert to Judaism, and almost no teenage Baptists become Hindu—although such conversions can occur in adulthood. Most adolescents question specific beliefs as their cognitive processes allow more analytic thinking, but few teenagers have a crisis of faith unless unusual circumstances propel it (King & Roeser, 2009).

Same Situation, Far Apart: Chosen, Saved, or Just Another Teenager? An Orthodox Jewish boy lighting Hanukkah candles in Israel and an evangelical Christian girl at a religious rally in Michigan are much alike, despite distance and appearance. Many teenagers express such evident religious devotion that outsiders consider them fanatics.

SPENCER PLATT/GETTY IMAGES

Rebels Not Prophets Teenagers are often on the forefront of political activism, especially if their parents have instilled values that make them want to do something dramatic to help earthquake victims, or reverse abortion laws, or, as with these Egyptians in Tahrir Square, topple a repressive regime. However, their political sentiments are not yet the product of their own identity achievement: Given the cognition of adolescence as described in Chapter 15, joining a group protest may be based more on emotion than analysis.

Political Identity

Parents also influence their children's *political identity.* In the twenty-first century in the United States, party identification is weakening among adults, with more of them saying they are independent rather than Republican, Democratic, or some other party. Their teenage children reflect this new independence; some proudly say they do not care about politics, actually echoing their parents without realizing it. In any case, their political leanings are likely to continue in adulthood (Côté, 2009).

A word here about political terrorism and religious extremism: Those under age 30 are often on the front lines of terrorism or are converts to groups that their elders consider cults. Fanatical political and religious movements have much in common—age of new adherents is one of them (L. L. Dawson, 2010).

However, adolescents are rarely drawn to these groups unless personal loneliness or family background (such as a parent's death caused by an opposing group) compels them. It is myth that every teenager is potentially a suicide bomber or a willing martyr. The risk-taking of extreme political or religious groups is more attractive to emerging adults than to adolescents.

Vocational Identity

Vocational identity originally meant envisioning oneself as a worker in a particular occupation. Choosing a future career made sense for teenagers a century ago, when most girls became housewives and most boys became farmers, small businessmen, or factory workers. Those few in professions were generalists (doctors did family medicine, lawyers handled all kinds of cases, teachers taught all subjects).

Obviously, early vocational identity is no longer appropriate. No teenager can be expected to choose among the tens of thousands of careers; most adults change vocations (not just employers) many times. Vocational identity takes years to establish, and most jobs demand quite specific skills and knowledge that are best learned on the job.

Although some adults hope that employment will keep teenagers out of trouble as they identify as workers, the opposite is more likely (Staff & Schulenberg, 2010). Adolescents who work more than 20 hours a week during the school year tend to quit school, fight with parents, smoke cigarettes, and hate their jobs—both when they are teenagers and when they become adults. This research controlled for SES. Typically, teenagers with a paycheck spend their wages on clothes, cars, drugs, and concerts, not on supporting their families or saving for college. Grades fall: Employment interferes with homework and school attendance (see Figure 16.1).

Sexual Identity

Achieving *sexual identity* is also a lifelong task, in part because norms of sexuality and attitudes about it keep changing (see Figure 16.2). Increasing numbers of young adults are single, gay, and cohabiting, providing teenagers with new role models and choices and thus making sexual identity more confusing.

Above and Below Grade Average

z-score

-0.4 -0.3 -0.2 -0.1 0.0 0.1 0.2 0.3 0.4

Work over 20 hr/wk

Work 20 or fewer hr/wk

Not employed but wish for >20 hr/wk

Not employed but wish for <20 hr/wk

Not employed and don't want to work

Grade 8
Grade 10
Grade 12

Source: Staff et al., 2009.

FIGURE 16.1

Don't Think About It There was a time when high school employment correlated with lifetime success. This is no longer true. The surprise is that even wanting a full-time job (and the extra income it would bring) reduces achievement—or is it the other way around? The scores in the chart above are z-scores, or standard scores, which show the difference from the group average. A z-score of 2 is a dramatic difference; a z-score of 3 is extreme.

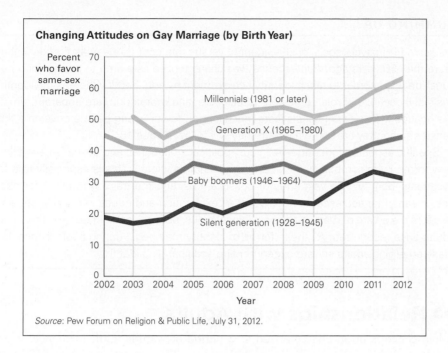

Changing Attitudes on Gay Marriage (by Birth Year)

Percent who favor same-sex marriage (y-axis: 0 to 70)

Millennials (1981 or later)
Generation X (1965–1980)
Baby boomers (1946–1964)
Silent generation (1928–1945)

Year (x-axis: 2002 to 2012)

Source: Pew Forum on Religion & Public Life, July 31, 2012.

FIGURE 16.2

Young and Old Everyone knows that attitudes about same-sex relationships are changing. Less well known is that cohort differences are greater than the historical shifts.

A half-century ago, Erikson and other theorists thought of the two sexes as opposites (P. Y. Miller & Simon, 1980). They assumed that adolescents who were confused about sexual identity would soon adopt "proper" male or female roles (Erikson, 1968; A. Freud, 1958/2000). Adolescence was once a time for "gender intensification," when people increasingly identified as male or female—no longer (Priess et al., 2009).

As you remember from Chapter 10, for social scientists *sex* and *sexual* refer to biological characteristics, whereas *gender* refers to cultural and social attributes that differentiate males and females. Erikson's term *sexual identity* has been replaced by **gender identity** (Denny & Pittman, 2007), which refers primarily to a person's self-definition as male or female. Gender identity often (not always) begins with the person's biological sex and leads to a gender role that society considers appropriate.

Gender roles once meant that only men were employed; they were *breadwinners* (good providers) and women were *housewives* (married to their houses). As women entered the labor market, gender roles expanded but were still apparent (nurse/doctor, secretary/businessman, pink collar/blue collar). That is changing—with the degree, rate, and direction of change varying dramatically from culture to culture. There is no culture, however, that does not distinguish male and female roles.

What also has not changed is the adolescent's experience of a strong sexual drive as hormone levels increase. As Erikson recognized, many are confused regarding when, how, and with whom to express those drives. Some adolescents foreclose by exaggerating male or female roles; others seek a moratorium by avoiding all sexual contact. If adolescents feel their gender identity is fragile, they are more likely to aspire to a gender-stereotypic vocation (Sinclair & Carlsson, 2013), which is another reason why settling on a vocational identity during adolescence may be premature.

gender identity A person's acceptance of the roles and behaviors that society associates with the biological categories of male and female.

Who and Where? As Erikson explained in 1968, the pride of self-discovery is universal for adolescents: These could be teenagers anywhere. But a closer look reveals gay teenagers in Atlanta, Georgia, where this march would not have occurred 50 years ago.

SUMMING UP

Erikson's fifth psychosocial crisis—identity versus role confusion—was first described more than 50 years ago. Adolescence was characterized as a time to search for a personal identity in order to reach identity achievement by adulthood. Whereas the identity crisis still occurs and role confusion, foreclosure, and moratorium are apparent, timing has changed. The identity crisis lasts much longer; fewer young people develop a firm sense of who they are and what path they will follow by age 18.

Specific aspects of identity—religious, political, vocational, and sexual—have taken new forms, with complexities that Erikson did not anticipate. This is especially true for vocational identity: The vast array of possible jobs, and the training required for each one, means that adolescents need years of exploration and education. Likewise, adolescents are aware of many more possible religious, political, and gender identities than adults once recognized. All these forms of identity may begin during adolescence, but many emerging adults still are experimenting and changing identity. ▪

>> Relationships with Adults

Adolescence is often characterized as a period of waning adult influence, when children distance themselves from their elders. This picture is not always accurate. Adult influence is less immediate but no less important.

Parents

The fact that parent–adolescent relationships are pivotal does not mean that they are peaceful (Eisenberg et al., 2008; Laursen & Collins, 2009). Disputes are common because the adolescent's drive for independence, arising from biological as well as psychological impulses, clashes with the parents' desire to maintain control.

Normally, conflict peaks in early adolescence, especially between mothers and daughters, usually in *bickering*—repeated, petty arguments (more nagging than fighting) about routine, day-to-day concerns such as cleanliness, clothes, chores, and schedules (Eisenberg et al., 2008). Each generation misjudges the other: Parents think their offspring resent them more than they actually do, and adolescents imagine their parents want to dominate them more than they actually do (Sillars et al., 2010).

Unspoken concerns need to be aired so both generations better understand each other. Imagine a parent seeing dirty socks on the floor. The parent might think that is a deliberate mark of adolescent disrespect and therefore react angrily. But perhaps the adolescent was merely distracted, oblivious to the parent's desire for a neat house. If so, then the parent could merely sigh and put the socks in laundry.

Some bickering may indicate a healthy family, since close relationships almost always include conflict. The parent-child relationship usually improves with time. By age 18, many teenagers appreciate their parents more than they did at puberty (remembering that parents want the socks in the hamper), and many parents have adjusted to their child's independence (allowing the adolescent to leave socks on the floor in his own room) (Masche, 2010). A study of modern Chinese American adolescents, exposed to clashing values (respect for elders versus adolescent autonomy), found that conflict was not necessarily problematic if communication was good (Juang et al., 2012).

"So I blame you for everything—whose fault is that?"

BARBARA SMALLER/THE NEW YORKER COLLECTION/CARTOONBANK.COM

You have already learned that authoritative parenting is usually best for children and that uninvolved parenting is worst. [**Lifespan Link:** Parenting styles were discussed in Chapter 10.] The same holds true in adolescence. Although teenagers sometimes say their parents are irrelevant, that is not true. Neglect is always destructive and authoritarian parenting can boomerang, resulting in children who lie, leave, or learn to deceive their parents.

Cultural Differences

Expectations vary by culture, as do justifications (Brown & Bakken, 2011). For example, in Chile, adolescents usually obey their parents, but if they do something their parents might not like, they keep it secret (Darling et al., 2008). By contrast, many U.S. adolescents deliberately provoke an argument by boldly announcing what they think is permissible, even if it is something they themselves would not do (Cumsille et al., 2010). Filipino adolescents expect autonomy in daily choices but not in life goals: Parental advice is sought and usually followed in the four aspects of identity explained earlier (Russel et al., 2010).

Several researchers have compared parent–child relationships in Hong Kong, the United States, and Australia. Although these areas exemplify many cultural differences in assumptions about parental roles, in all three places, parent–child communication and encouragement benefit teenagers, reducing depression, suicide, and low self-esteem and increasing aspirations and achievements (e.g., Kwok & Shek, 2010; Leung et al., 2010; Qin et al., 2009).

Yet culture also has an impact, as demonstrated in a study of pubescent Hong Kong students who were proficient in both Chinese and English (they spoke Chinese with their parents, but their education was in English) (Wang et al., 2010).

In this study, bilingual researchers asked questions in English to half the children and in Chinese to the other half. All the children replied, in the language the questioner used, about their memories, self-concept, and values. Coders judged the children's answers as being either about themselves alone (such as "I enjoy books," "My eyes are dark") or about themselves as one of a group or as a person connected to others (such as "I am a student," "My family loves me"), and tallied the social descriptors.

Especially in early adolescence, descriptions in Chinese were more social while descriptions in English were more individualistic. It was not the words themselves that influenced the children, of course, but rather the ideological framework evoked when a researcher spoke English or Chinese (e.g., Hong Kong's centuries of British heritage or the millennia of mainland Chinese culture). The researchers interpreted these results to mean that adolescents are strongly influenced by their culture, thinking as well as talking as the culture expects.

Closeness Within the Family

More important than family conflict or individualism may be family closeness, which has four aspects:

1. Communication (Do family members talk openly with one another?)
2. Support (Do they rely on one another?)
3. Connectedness (How emotionally close are they?)
4. Control (Do parents encourage or limit adolescent autonomy?)

No social scientist doubts that the first two, communication and support, are helpful, perhaps essential, for healthy development. Patterns set in place during childhood continue, ideally buffering some of the turbulence of adolescence (Cleveland et al., 2005; Laursen & Collins, 2009). Regarding the next two, connectedness and control, consequences vary and observers differ in what they see. How do you react to this example, written by one of my students?

> I got pregnant when I was sixteen years old, and if it weren't for the support of my parents, I would probably not have my son. And if they hadn't taken care of him, I wouldn't have been able to finish high school or attend college. My parents also helped me overcome the shame that I felt when . . . my aunts, uncles, and especially my grandparents found out that I was pregnant.

[I., personal communication]

My student is grateful to her parents, but you might wonder whether teenage motherhood gave her parents too much control, requiring her dependence when she should have been seeking her own identity. Indeed, had they somehow allowed her to become pregnant, by permitting her to have time alone with a boy but not educating her about birth control?

An added complexity is that this young woman's parents had emigrated from South America. Cultural expectations affect everyone's responses, so her dependence may have been normative for her culture but not elsewhere. A longitudinal study of nonimmigrant adolescent mothers in the U. S. found that most (not all) fared best if their parents were supportive but did not take over child care (Borkowski et al., 2007). Whether this is true in other nations has not been reported.

A related issue is **parental monitoring**—that is, parental knowledge about each child's whereabouts, activities, and companions. Many studies have shown that, when parental knowledge is the result of a warm, supportive relationship, adolescents are likely to become confident, well-educated adults, avoiding drugs and risky sex. But adolescents play an active role in their own monitoring: Some happily tell parents about their activities, whereas others are secretive (Vieno et al., 2009). Most disclose only part of the truth, selectively omitting things their parents would not approve of (Brown & Bakken, 2011).

A Study in Contrasts? These two teenagers appear to be opposites: one yelling at his mother and the other conscientiously helping his father. However, adolescent moods can change in a flash, especially with parents. Later in the day, these two might switch roles.

parental monitoring Parents' ongoing awareness of what their children are doing, where, and with whom.

Thus, monitoring may signify a mutual, close interaction (Kerr et al., 2010). However, monitoring may be harmful when it derives from suspicion instead of from a warm connection. Especially in early adolescence, if adolescents resist telling their parents much of anything, they are more likely to develop problems such as aggression against peers, law-breaking, and drug abuse (Laird et al., 2013).

Control is another aspect of parenting that can backfire. Adolescents expect parents to exert some control, especially over moral issues. However, overly restrictive and controlling parenting correlates with many adolescent problems, including depression (Brown & Bakken, 2011). Decreasing control over the years of adolescence is best, according to a longitudinal study of 12- to 14-year-olds in the suburbs of Chicago and Hong Kong. In both cultures, adolescents were given more autonomy over personal choices as they grew older; in both cultures increasing autonomy correlated with better emotional functioning (Qin et al., 2009).

Parents, Genes, and Risks

Research on human development has many practical applications. This was evident in a longitudinal study (first mentioned in Chapter 1) of African American families in rural Georgia that involved 611 parents and their 11-year-olds (Brody et al., 2009). Half of them were assigned to the comparison group, with no special intervention. The other half were invited to seven two-hour training sessions. Groups were small, and leaders were well prepared and selected to be likely role models. Parents and their 11-year-olds were taught in two separate groups for an hour and then brought together.

The parents learned the following:

- The importance of being nurturing and involved
- The importance of conveying pride in being African American (called racial socialization)
- How monitoring and control benefit adolescents
- Why clear norms and expectations reduce substance use
- Strategies for communication about sex

The 11-year-olds learned the following:

- The importance of having household rules
- Adaptive behaviors when encountering racism
- The need for making plans for the future
- The differences between them and peers who use alcohol

After that first hour, the parents and 11-year-olds were led in games, structured interactions, and modeling, designed to improve family communication and cohesion. Three years after the intervention, both the experimental and comparison groups were reassessed regarding sex and alcohol/drug activity. The results were disappointing: The intervention helped but not very much.

Then, four years after the study began, the researchers read new research that found heightened risks of depression, delinquency, and other problems for people with the short allele of the 5-HTTLPR gene. To see whether this applied to their African American teenagers, they collected and analyzed the DNA of

16-year-olds who had been, at age 11, in either the special training group or the comparison group. As Figure 16.3 shows, the training had virtually no impact on those with the long allele, but it had a major impact on those with the short one.

That 14 hours or fewer of training (some families skipped sessions) had an impact on genetically sensitive boys is amazing, given all the other influences surrounding these boys over the years. Apparently, since the parent–child relationship is crucial throughout adolescence, those seven sessions provided insights and connections that affected each vulnerable dyad from then on.

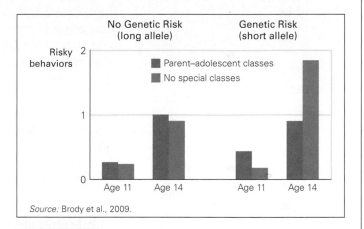

Source: Brody et al., 2009.

FIGURE 16.3

Not Yet The risk score was a simple one point for each of the following: had drunk alcohol, had smoked marijuana, had had sex. As shown, most of the 11-year-olds had done none of these. By age 14, most had done one (usually had drunk beer or wine)—except for those at genetic risk who did not have the seven-session training. Some of them had done all three, and many had done at least two. As you see, for those youths without genetic risk, the usual parenting was no better or worse than the parenting that benefited from the special classes: The average 14-year-old in either group had tried only one risky behavior. But for those at genetic risk, the special program made a decided difference.

Other Adults

Parents are important to an adolescent, but so are many other adults. One of the admirable characteristics of most adolescents is that they know many people, sometimes seeking advice and help from neighbors, teachers, relatives and so on.

Impact is notable when an adult takes time to listen to a child. For many youths, the most patient advisors are family members—older siblings, cousins, aunts and uncles, grandparents. Sometimes parents delegate a sibling (the adolescent's aunt or uncle) to discuss taboo topics, such as sex or delinquency (Milardo, 2009).

Links between teenagers and relatives are especially common in developing nations and among immigrant groups for two reasons: (1) Relatives often live together or nearby, and (2) cultural values make family central.

In addition, adults with no biological relationship to the young person can be significant (Chang et al., 2010; Scales et al., 2006). For instance, regarding the four arenas of identity development (religion, politics, vocation, gender), clergy can affect a young person's faith, political leaders can mold values, school counselors can influence vocational aspirations, and adults in satisfying sexual relationships can be role models (Lerner & Steinberg, 2009). In addition, many adolescents admire celebrities—in sports, music, and film—and try to be like them.

SUMMING UP

Relationships with adults are essential during adolescence. Parents and adolescents often bicker over small things, especially in the first years after puberty, but squabbling does not mean that the relationship is destructive. In fact, parental guidance and ongoing communication promote adolescents' psychosocial health. Among the signs of a healthy parent–adolescent relationship are that parents know what their child is doing (parental monitoring) and that adolescents talk with their parents about their concerns. Both of these factors are affected by culture, by past relationships, and by the adolescent's maturity. Either extreme neglect or excessive control can lead to adolescent rebellion. The firm but flexible guidance of authoritative parenting continues to be effective. Other relatives and non-relatives also sometimes become guides and mentors, especially when parental advice is limited or resisted.   ▪

Observation Quiz There are dramatic differences among teenagers in these two nations as well. What three differences can you see? (See answer, page 468)

Same Situation, Far Apart: Friends Together Teenagers in the middle of the United States (Illinois) and in the middle of Sudan (Khartoum) prefer to spend their free time with peers (these are all 15- to 17-year-olds), not with adults. Generational loyalty is stronger during these years than during any other stage of life.

>> Peer Power

Adolescents rely on peers to help them navigate the physical changes of puberty, the intellectual challenges of high school, and the social changes of leaving childhood. Friendships are important at every stage, but during early adolescence popularity is most coveted (LaFontana & Cillessen, 2010).

Peers and Parents

Adults are sometimes unaware of adolescents' desire for respect from their contemporaries. I did not recognize this at the time with my own children:

- Our oldest daughter wore the same pair of jeans in tenth grade, day after day. She washed them each night by hand and asked me to put them in the dryer early each morning. My husband was bewildered. "Is this some weird female ritual?" he asked. Years later, she explained that she was afraid that if she wore different pants each day, her classmates would think she cared about her clothes and then criticize her choices.
- Our second daughter, at 16, pierced her ears for the third time. When I asked if this meant she would do drugs, she laughed at my ignorance. I later noticed that many of her friends had multiple holes in their ear lobes.
- At age 15, our third daughter was diagnosed with cancer. My husband and I weighed opinions from four physicians, each explaining treatment that would minimize the risk of death. She had other priorities: "I don't care what you choose, as long as I keep my hair." (Now her health is good, and her hair grew back.)
- Our youngest, in sixth grade, refused to wear her jacket (it was new; she had chosen it), even in midwinter. Not until high school did she tell me she did it so that her middle school classmates would think she was tough.

In retrospect, I am amazed that I was unaware of the power of peers.

Sometimes adults conceptualize adolescence as a time when peers and parents are at odds, or worse, as a time when peer influence overtakes parental influence. This is not true. Relationships with parents are the prototype for peer relationships: Healthy communication and support from parents make constructive peer relationships more likely.

Parents and peers are often mutually reinforcing, although many adolescents downplay the influence of their parents and many parents are unaware of the influence of peers, as I was. Only when parents are harsh or neglectful does peer influence reign alone (Bakken & Brown, 2011).

Peer Pressure

For every adolescent, peer opinions and friends are vital. One high school boy said:

> A lot of times I wake up in the morning and I don't want to go to school, and then I'm like, you know, I have got this class and these friends are in it, and I am going to have fun. That is a big part of my day—my friends.

> [quoted in Hamm & Faircloth, 2005, p. 72]

Adults sometimes fear **peer pressure**; that is, they fear that peers will push an adolescent to use drugs, break the law, or do other things their child would never do alone. But peers are more helpful than harmful (Audrey et al., 2006; Nelson & DeBacker, 2008), especially in early adolescence, when biological and social stresses can be overwhelming. In later adolescence, teenagers are less susceptible to peer pressure, either positive or negative (Monahan et al., 2009).

Peers may be particularly helpful for adolescents of minority and immigrant groups as they strive to achieve ethnic identity, attaining their own firm (not confused or foreclosed) understanding of what it means to be Asian, African, Latino, and so on. The larger society provides stereotypes and prejudice, and parents ideally describe ethnic heroes and reasons to be proud (Umana-Taylor et al., 2010), but each young person must fashion his or her own identity, distinct from that of either society or parents (Fuligni et al., 2009). For this, peers may be pivotal (Whitehead et al., 2009).

peer pressure Encouragement to conform to one's friends or contemporaries in behavior, dress, and attitude; usually considered a negative force, as when adolescent peers encourage one another to defy adult authority.

COURTESY RICHARD RONAY

Watch Me Fall Peers can be helpful or harmful, but they are never ignored. Adolescent boys in a skate park were videotaped in two circumstances: with an attractive female stranger sitting on a bench nearby and with no one watching. (The camera was hidden.) When the female observer was present, the boys took more risks and fell more often (Ronay & von Hippel, 2010).

>> Answer to Observation Quiz (from page 466: (1) The U.S. friends are of both sexes; it's all boys in Sudan. (2) Recreational use of inner tubes in the United States; inner tubes are used only for tires in Sudan. (3) The boys in Sudan are excited to show off their cell phones, which would be unlikely in the United States. There are also many differences in clothing, as you can see.

The social context is especially crucial. For example, in large schools with many ethnic groups, friends from the same background help adolescents avoid feeling adrift and alone, as they resist social prejudice and yet distance themselves from the patterns and attitudes of their parents (Kiang et al., 2009).

Social Networking

You read in Chapter 15 about the dangers of technology. Remember, however, that although some adolescents seem addicted to video games or the Internet, most are not. Technology is a tool, which might exacerbate depression or self-destruction, but it does not cause the problem (Yom-Tov et al., 2012).

Despite adult fears to the contrary, technology usually brings friends together in adolescence (Mesch & Talmud, 2010). This is obvious with texting and email, but also occurs with video games. Many games now pit one player against another, or require cooperation among several players (Collins & Freeman, 2013). Technology users, including video game players, are usually at least as extraverted and socially connected as other adolescents.

Although most social networking is between friends who know each other well, the Internet may be a lifeline for teenagers who are isolated because of their sexual orientation, culture, religion, or native language. Furthermore, online resources for teens struggling with depression, addiction, and countless other issues are sometimes particularly helpful, partly because they are frequently anonymous—parents and classmates need not know.

A Social Gathering Fifty years ago teens hung out on the corner or at the local drug store. Now they gather in someone's house. Each seems to be in his or her own world, but show and tell is part of technology for adolescents.

JGI/JAMIE GRILL/BLEND IMAGES/GETTY IMAGES

A particular niche is found within technology for adolescents with special health needs. During these years, many of them refuse to follow special diets, take medication, see doctors monthly, do exercises, or whatever. Technology can literally save lives, as shown with teenagers who have diabetes: They monitor their insulin via cell phone, talk to the doctor via Skype, and talk to other young people with diabetes via Internet chat (Harris et al., 2012).

Selecting Friends

Peers are often beneficial, but they *can* lead one another into trouble. Collectively, peers sometimes provide **deviancy training**, whereby one person shows another how to rebel against social norms (Dishion et al., 2001). However, innocent teens are not corrupted by deviant friends. Adolescents choose their friends and models—not always wisely, but never randomly.

A developmental progression can be traced: The combination of "problem behavior, school marginalization, and low academic performance" at age 11 leads to gang involvement two years later, deviancy training two years after that, and violent behavior at age 18 or 19 (Dishion et al., 2010, p. 603). This cascade is not inevitable; adults need to engage marginalized 11-year-olds instead of blaming their friends years later.

To further understand the impact of peers, examination of two concepts is helpful: *selection* and *facilitation*. Teenagers *select* friends whose values and interests they share, abandoning former friends who follow other paths. Then friends *facilitate* destructive or constructive behaviors. It is easier to do wrong ("Let's all skip school on Friday") or right ("Let's study together for the chem exam") with friends. Peer facilitation helps adolescents act in ways they are unlikely to act on their own.

Thus, adolescents select and facilitate, choose and are chosen. Happy, energetic, and successful teens have close friends who themselves are high achievers, with no major emotional problems. The opposite also holds: Those who are drug users, sexually active, and alienated from school choose compatible friends.

For instance, one U.S. study found that "tough" and "alternative" crowds felt that teenagers should question every adult rule, whereas the "prep" crowd thought that parental authority was usually legitimate (Daddis, 2010). A study in Finland found that students with high grades criticized those who prioritized sports or did not study, who reciprocated by disliking the honors crowd (Laursen et al., 2010).

A study of identical twins from ages 14 to 17 found that selection typically preceded facilitation, rather than the other way around. Those who *later* rebelled chose lawbreaking friends at age 14 more than did their more conventional twin (Burt et al., 2009). A study of teenage use of cigarettes also found that selection preceded peer pressure (Kiuru et al., 2010). Peers provide opportunity and encouragement for what adolescents already want to do.

Romance

Half a century ago, Dexter Dunphy (1963) described the sequence of male–female relationships during childhood and adolescence:

1. Groups of friends, exclusively one sex or the other
2. A loose association of girls and boys, with public interactions within a crowd
3. Small mixed-sex groups of the advanced members of the crowd
4. Formation of couples, with private intimacies

Culture affects the timing and manifestation of each step on Dunphy's list, but subsequent research in many nations validates the sequence. Heterosexual youths worldwide (and even the young of other primates) avoid the other sex in

Especially for Parents of a Teenager
Your 13-year-old comes home after a sleepover at a friend's house with a new, weird hairstyle—perhaps cut or colored in a bizarre manner. What do you say and do? (see response, page 471)

deviancy training Destructive peer support in which one person shows another how to rebel against authority or social norms.

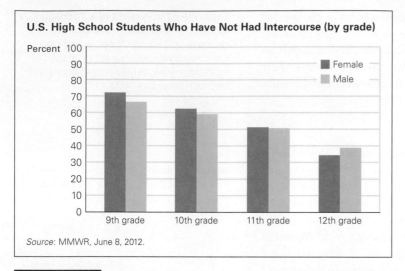

U.S. High School Students Who Have Not Had Intercourse (by grade)

Source: MMWR, June 8, 2012.

FIGURE 16.4

Many Virgins For 30 years, the Youth Risk Behavior Survey has asked high school students from all over the United States dozens of confidential questions about their behavior. As you can see, about one-third of all students have already had sex by the ninth grade, and about one-third have not yet had sex by their senior year—a group whose ranks have been increasing in recent years. Other research finds that sexual behaviors are influenced by peers, with members of some groups all sexually experienced by age 14 and members of others not until age 18 or older.

sexual orientation A term that refers to whether a person is sexually and romantically attracted to others of the same sex, the opposite sex, or both sexes.

Girls Together These two girls from Sweden seem comfortable lying close to one another. Many boys of this age wouldn't be want their photograph taken if they were this close together. Around the world, there are cultural and gender norms about what is acceptable physical expression of affection among friends during adolescence.

childhood and are attracted to them by adulthood. This universal pattern suggests that biology underlies this sequence.

The peer group is part of this process. Romantic partners, especially in early adolescence, are selected not for their individual traits as much as for the traits that peers admire. If the leader of a girls' group of close friends pairs with the leader of a boys' group, the unattached members of the two cliques tend to pair off as well. A classic example is football players and cheerleaders: They often date each other. Pairing of groups allows easy double or triple dating, makes it easier to have a mixed-sex party, and helps explain why adolescent romantic partners tend to have less in common, in personality and attitudes, than adult couples do (Zimmer-Gembeck & Ducat, 2010).

First Love

Teens' first romances typically occur in high school, with girls having a steady partner more often than boys do. Exclusive commitment is desired, but "cheating," flirting, switching, and disloyalty are rife. Breakups are common, as are unreciprocated crushes. All of this can be devastating, with emotions such as hatred and despair leading to irrational revenge or impulsive suicide. In such cases, peer support can be a lifesaver; friends help adolescents cope with romantic ups and downs (Mehta & Strough, 2009).

Contrary to adult fears, many teenage romances do not include sexual intercourse. In the United States in 2011, even though about one-third of all high school students were sexually experienced by the tenth grade, about another one-third were virgins at high school graduation (see Figure 16.4). Norms vary markedly from group to group, school to school, city to city, and nation to nation.

For instance, twice as many ninth- to twelfth-graders in Memphis as in San Francisco say they have had intercourse (62 percent versus 28 percent) (MMWR, June 8, 2012). Obviously, within every city are many subgroups, each with their own norms. Parents have an impact. Thus, when parent–child relationships are good, girls from religious families tend to be romantically involved with boys from religious families, and their shared values typically slow down sexual activity (Kim-Spoon et al., 2012).

Same-Sex Romances

Some adolescents are attracted to peers of the same sex. **Sexual orientation** refers to the direction of a person's erotic desires. One meaning of *orient* is to "turn toward"; thus, sexual orientation refers to whether a person is romantically attracted to (turned on by) people of the other sex, the same sex, or both sexes. Sexual orientation can be strong, weak, overt, secret, or unconscious.

Currently in North America and western Europe, not just two discrete orientations (homosexual and heterosexual) but a range of orientations—including bisexual, asexual, mostly homosexual, adamantly heterosexual, transgender and so on— are possible (Denny & Pittman, 2007). The DSM-5 no longer has a category called gender identity disorder, and instead has gender dysphoria—for people who are distressed at whatever gender or orientation they have.

Obviously, culture and cohort are powerful. In many nations of Africa and the Middle East, non-heterosexual behavior is considered criminal. Worldwide, many gay youths date members of the other sex to hide their orientation, and they are at higher risk for binge-drinking, suicidal thoughts, and drug use. Hiding one's orientation is less common in communities in which same-sex partnerships are accepted, especially when parents affirm their offspring's sexuality. At least in the United States, adolescents have similar problems and strengths whether they are gay or straight (Saewyc, 2011).

Sexual orientation is surprisingly fluid among adolescents. Girls are particularly likely to decide their orientation only after they have had sexual experiences; many adult lesbian women had other-sex relationships in adolescence (Saewyc, 2011).

Among sexually active teenagers in New York City, 10 percent had had same-sex partners, but more than one-third of that 10 percent nonetheless identified themselves as straight (Pathela & Schillinger, 2010). In that study, those most at risk of sexual violence and sexually transmitted infections (STIs) were those who had partners of both sexes.

Sex Education

Many adolescents have strong sexual urges but minimal logic about pregnancy and disease, as might be expected from the 10-year interval between maturation of the body and of the brain. Millions of teenagers worry that they are oversexed, undersexed, or deviant, unaware that thousands, maybe millions, of people are just like them.

As a result, "students seem to waffle their way through sexually relevant encounters driven both by the allure of reward and the fear of negative consequences" (Wagner, 2011, p. 193). They have much to learn. Where do they learn it?

From the Media

Many adolescents learn about sex from the media. The Internet is a common source. Unfortunately websites are often frightening (featuring pictures of diseased sexual organs) or mesmerizing (containing pornography), and the youngest adolescents are particularly naïve.

TV watching peaks at puberty, and the shows most watched by teenagers include sexual content almost seven times per hour (Steinberg & Monahan, 2011). That content is alluring: Almost never does a television character develop an STI, deal with an unwanted pregnancy, or mention (much less use) a condom. Magazines may be even worse. One study found that men's magazines convince teenage boys that maleness means sexual conquests (Ward et al., 2011).

Adolescents with intense exposure to sexual content on the screen and in music are more often sexually active, but this correlation is controversial (Collins et al., 2011; Steinberg & Monahan, 2011). Do teenagers watch sexy TV because they are sexually active, or does the media cause them to be sexually involved? One analysis concludes that "the most important influences on adolescents' sexual behavior may be closer to home than Hollywood" (Sternberg & Monahan, 2011, p. 575).

From Parents and Peers

As that quote implies, sex education begins at home. Every study finds that explicit parental communication influences adolescents' behavior (Longmore et al., 2009). However, many parents wait too long to discuss sex. They tend to express clichés

>> **Response for Parents of a Teenager** (from page 469): Remember: Communicate, do not control. Let your child talk about the meaning of the hairstyle. Remind yourself that a hairstyle in itself is harmless. Don't say "What will people think?" or "Are you on drugs?" or anything that might give your child reason to stop communicating.

Especially for Sex Educators Suppose adults in your community never talk to their children about sex or puberty. Is that a mistake? (see response, page 472)

>> Response for Sex Educators (from page 471): Yes, but forgive them. Ideally, parents should talk to their children about sex, presenting honest information and listening to the child's concerns. However, many parents find it very difficult to do so because they feel embarrassed and ignorant. You might schedule separate sessions for adults over 30, for emerging adults, and for adolescents.

and generalities, unaware of their adolescents' sexuality. Three studies of quite different groups illustrate the problem.

1. Parents of 12-year-old girls were asked whether their daughters had hugged or kissed a boy "for a long time" or hung out with older boys (signs that sex information is urgently needed). Only 5 percent of the parents said yes, as did 38 percent of the girls (O'Donnell et al., 2008).

2. African and Hmong American 14- to 19-year-olds rarely tell their parents about their romantic encounters. For example, one girl said she was going to the movies with her girlfriend (true) but not that their boyfriends were coming, too (Brown & Bakken, 2011).

3. Mexican American mothers told their teenagers *cuidate*, "take care of yourself," which their teenagers interpreted as advice about health, not contraception. Some of the girls became pregnant, to the mothers distress and surprise. They thought they had warned their daughters and sons to use condoms if they had sex (Moncloa et al., 2010).

What should parents say? That is the wrong question, according to a longitudinal study of thousands of adolescents. Those teens who became sexually active and who were most likely to develop an STI had parents who warned them to stay away from sex. In contrast, adolescents were more likely to remain virgins if they had a warm relationship with their parents—specific information was less important than open communication (Deptula et al., 2010).

Especially when parents are silent, forbidding, or vague, adolescent sexual behavior is strongly influenced by peers. Boys are likely to learn about sex from other boys (Henry et al., 2012). Partners also teach each other. However, their lessons are more about pleasure than consequences: Most U.S. adolescent couples do not decide together *before* they have sex how they will prevent pregnancy and disease, and what they will do if their prevention efforts fail.

From Educators

Sex education varies dramatically by nation. The curriculum for middle schools in most European schools includes information about masturbation, same-sex romance, oral and anal sex, specific uses and failures of various methods of contraception—subjects almost never covered in U.S. classes, even in high school. Rates of teenage pregnancy in most European nations are less than half those in the United States. Perhaps curriculum is the reason, although obviously curriculum is part of the larger culture, and cultural differences regarding sex are vast.

Within the United States, the timing and content of sex education vary by state and community. Some high schools provide comprehensive education, free condoms, and medical treatment; others provide nothing.

Some schools begin sex education in the sixth grade; others wait until senior year. If they begin early, many sex-education programs successfully delay the age at which adolescents become sexually active, and they increase condom use, but some programs have no impact (Hamilton et al., 2013; Kirby & Laris, 2009).

One controversy centers on whether abstinence should be taught as the only sexual strategy for adolescents. It is true, of course, that abstaining from sex (including oral sex) prevents STIs and pregnancy, but longitudinal data on several abstinence-only programs, four to six years after adolescents had participated, was disappointing. For instance, about half the students in both experimental (abstinence-only) and control groups (more comprehensive sex education) had had sex by age 16 (Trenholm et al., 2007). Students in the control groups knew slightly more about preventing disease and pregnancy, but their sexual activity was similar in those who had abstinence-only education.

SUMMING UP

Contrary to what some adults may think, peer pressure can be positive. Many adolescents rely on friends of both sexes to help them with the concerns and troubles of the teen years. Romances are typical in high school, but early, exclusive, long-lasting romances are more often a sign of emotional trouble than of maturity. Some adolescents are romantically attracted to others of their own sex; the psychological impact of same-sex orientation depends on the adolescent's family and community.

The media and peers are the most common sources for sex information, but not the most accurate. Parents are influential role models, but few provide detailed and current information before adolescents begin experimenting with sex. School instruction may be helpful, but not every curriculum is equally effective, and schools vary in what and when they teach about sex. ∎

>> Sadness and Anger

Adolescence is usually a wonderful time, perhaps better for current generations than for any generation before. Nonetheless, troubles plague about 20 percent of youths. Most disorders are *comorbid*, with several problems occurring at once. Distinguishing between pathology and normal moodiness, between behavior that is seriously troubled versus merely unsettling, is complex.

It is typical for an adolescent to be momentarily less happy and more angry than younger children, but teen emotions often change quickly (Neumann et al., 2011). For a few, however, negative emotions cloud every moment, becoming intense, chronic, even deadly.

Depression

The general emotional trend from late childhood through adolescence is toward less confidence. A dip in self-esteem at puberty is found for children of every ethnicity and gender (Fredricks & Eccles, 2002; Greene & Way, 2005; Kutob et al., 2009; Zeiders et al., 2013). Some studies report rising self-esteem thereafter (especially for African American girls and European American boys), but reports vary, and every study finds notable individual differences.

On average, however, self-esteem is lower in girls than boys, lower in Asian Americans than European Americans who themselves are lower than African Americans, and lower in younger adolescents than older adolescents (Bachman et al., 2011). Many studies report a gradual rise in self-esteem from early adolescence through at least age 30, but all find notable variability from one person to another, and some find continuity within each person. Severe depression may lessen, but it rarely disappears (Huang, 2010).

Parents and peers affect self-esteem, and some communities have lower rates of depression because they promote strong and supportive relationships between teenagers and adults. Differential sensitivity means that some adolescents are particularly vulnerable, while others are not. When mothers are belligerent, disapproving, and contemptuous, some of their daughters are suicidal,

familism The belief that family members should support one another, sacrificing individual freedom and success, if necessary, in order to preserve family unity and protect the family from outside sources.

clinical depression Feelings of hopelessness, lethargy, and worthlessness that last two weeks or more.

rumination Repeatedly thinking and talking about past experiences; can contribute to depression.

suicidal ideation Thinking about suicide, usually with some serious emotional and intellectual or cognitive overtones.

Hanging Out These three adolescents live on the Rosebud Sioux Reservation in South Dakota. Adolescence can be challenging for all teenagers, but the suicide rate among Native American teenagers is more than three times the rate for US adolescents overall. Tribal officials in South Dakota are trying to improve the lives of young people so they feel more hope for the future.

while others are genetically protected from the self-blame such mothers cause (Whittle et al., 2011).

Cultural contexts are influential. One cultural norm is **familism**—the belief that family members should sacrifice personal freedom and success to care for one another. For Latino youth, self-esteem and ethnic pride are higher than for most other groups and usually rise after puberty. This is particularly true for girls (Zeiders et al., 2013). Perhaps adolescent girls are able to help their families in many ways as they mature, and that expression of familism brings pride.

However, if a Latino family is characterized by fighting and fragmentation, that reduces self-esteem even more than do similar circumstances for non-Latino adolescents (Smokowski et al., 2010). Similarly for gay adolescents, family rejection markedly increases the risk of suicide (Saewyc, 2011). Adolescents of any background with low self-esteem because of family rejection are likely to turn to drugs, sex, cutting, and dieting—all of which often make depression worse.

Clinical Depression

Some adolescents sink into **clinical depression,** a deep sadness and hopelessness that disrupts all normal, regular activities. The causes, including genes and early care, predate adolescence. Then the onset of puberty—with its myriad physical and emotional ups and downs—pushes some vulnerable children, especially girls, into despair. The rate of clinical depression more than doubles during this time, to an estimated 15 percent, affecting about 1 in 5 girls and 1 in 10 boys.

Sex hormones are probably part of the reason, but girls also experience social pressures from their families, peers, and cultures that boys do not (Naninck et al., 2011). Perhaps the combination of biological and psychosocial stresses causes some to slide into depression. Genes are involved as well.

One study found that the short allele of the serotonin transporter promoter gene (5-HTTLPR) increased the rate of depression among girls everywhere but increased depression among boys only if they lived in low-SES communities (Uddin et al., 2010). It is not surprising that certain genes make depression more likely, but it is puzzling that neighborhoods affected boys more than girls. Perhaps the social context factors that depress girls are in the culture, and hence affect girls no matter where they live, but boys are protected unless they live in a place where jobs, successful male role models, and encouragement are scarce.

A cognitive explanation for gender differences in depression focuses on **rumination**—talking about, remembering, and mentally replaying past experiences. Girls ruminate much more than boys, and rumination often leads to depression (Michl et al., 2013). For that reason, close mother–daughter relationships may be depressing if the pair ruminate about the mother's problems (Waller & Rose, 2010).

Suicide

Serious, distressing thoughts about killing oneself (called **suicidal ideation**) are most common at about age 15. The 2011 Youth Risk Behavior Survey revealed that more than one-third (36 percent) of U.S. high school girls

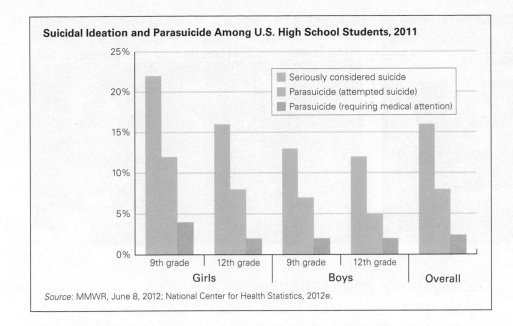

Suicidal Ideation and Parasuicide Among U.S. High School Students, 2011

Legend:
- Seriously considered suicide
- Parasuicide (attempted suicide)
- Parasuicide (requiring medical attention)

Source: MMWR, June 8, 2012; National Center for Health Statistics, 2012e.

FIGURE 16.5

Sad Thoughts Completed suicide is rare in adolescence, but serious thoughts about killing oneself are frequent. Depression and parasuicide are more common in girls than in boys, but rates are high even in boys. There are three reasons to suspect the rates for boys are underestimates: Boys tend to be less willing to divulge their emotions, boys consider it unmanly to try but fail to kill themselves, and completed suicide is higher in males than in females.

felt so hopeless that they stopped doing some usual activities for two weeks or more in the previous year, and almost one-fifth (19.3 percent) seriously thought about suicide. The corresponding rates for boys were 22 percent and 12.5 percent (MMWR, June 8, 2012).

Suicidal ideation can lead to **parasuicide**, also called *attempted suicide* or *failed suicide*. Parasuicide includes any deliberate self-harm that could have been lethal. *Parasuicide* is the best word to use because "failed" suicide implies that to die is to succeed (!); suicide "attempt" is likewise misleading because, especially in adolescence, the difference between attempt and actual suicide may be luck and prompt treatment, not intent.

As you see in Figure 16.5, parasuicide can be divided according to those who require medical attention (surgery, pumped stomachs, etc.) and those who do not, but any parasuicide is a warning. If there is a next time, the person may die.

Internationally, rates of teenage parasuicide range between 6 and 20 percent. Among U.S. high school students in 2011, 9 percent of the girls and 6 percent of the boys tried to kill themselves in the previous year (MMWR, June 8, 2012; see Figure 16.5).

While suicidal ideation during adolescence is common, completed suicides are not. The U.S. annual rate of completed suicide for people aged 15 to 19 (in school or not) is about 8 per 100,000, or 0.008 percent, half the rate for adults aged 20 and older.

Because they are not logical and analytical, adolescents are particularly affected when they hear about a suicide, either through the media or from peers (Insel & Gould, 2008). That makes them susceptible to **cluster suicides**, a term for the occurrence of several suicides within a group over a brief span of time.

In every large nation except China, girls are more likely to attempt suicide but boys are more likely to complete it. In the United States, adolescent boys kill themselves four times more often than girls (National Center for Health Statistics, 2012). The reason may be method: Males typically jump from high places or shoot themselves (immediately lethal), whereas females often swallow pills or cut their wrists, which allows time for conversation, intervention, and second thoughts.

parasuicide Any potentially lethal action against the self that does not result in death. (Also called *attempted suicide* or *failed suicide*.)

cluster suicides Several suicides committed by members of a group within a brief period of time.

Especially for Journalists You just heard that a teenage cheerleader jumped off a tall building and died. How should you report the story? (see response, page 477)

Hope and Anger Adolescents and young adults everywhere demonstrate against adult authority, with varied strategies and results. In Cairo's Tahrir Square *(left)*, this young man flashes the peace sign hours before President Mubarak's resignation. French students *(right)* protested cuts in high school staff, but their demands were resisted by the government. Worldwide, social change is fueled by youthful aspirations—sometimes leading to victory, sometimes to despair, and often (as in Egypt) with high emotions that seem unrealistic later on. The French students *(right)* seem to have lost all hope—a sign of political despair.

Delinquency and Defiance

Like low self-esteem and suicidal ideation, bouts of anger are common in adolescence. In fact, the moody adolescent could be both depressed and delinquent because externalizing and internalizing behavior are more closely connected in adolescence than at any other age (Loeber & Burke, 2011). Teenagers jailed for assault (externalizing) are suicide risks (internalizing).

Externalizing actions are obvious. Many adolescents slam doors, curse parents, and tell friends exactly how badly other teenagers (or siblings or teachers) have behaved. Some teenagers—particularly boys—"act out" by breaking laws. They steal, damage property, or injure others.

OPPOSING PERSPECTIVES

Teenage Rage: Necessary?

Is it normal for adolescents to challenge and disobey authority? Perhaps teenagers need to break some laws, curse some adults, rebel against their parents in order to establish their own identity and become independent adults. The best-known proponent of this perspective was Anna Freud (Sigmund's daughter, herself a prominent psychoanalyst), who wrote that adolescent resistance to parental authority was "welcome . . . beneficial . . . inevitable." She explained:

> We all know individual children who, as late as the ages of fourteen, fifteen or sixteen, show no such outer evidence of inner unrest. They remain, as they have been during the latency period, "good" children, wrapped up in their family relationships, considerate sons of their mothers, submissive to their fathers, in accord with the atmosphere, idea and ideal of their childhood background. Convenient as this may be, it signifies a delay of their normal development and is, as such, a sign to be taken seriously.
>
> [A. Freud, 1958/2000, p. 263]

Contrary to Freud, many psychologists, most teachers, and almost all parents are quite happy with well-behaved, considerate teenagers. Most teenagers usually obey the law, and their lawfulness does not predict a later explosion or breakdown. In fact, according to the 30-year New Zealand study first mentioned in Chapter 1, by age 26, men who had never been arrested usually earned degrees, "held high-status jobs, and expressed optimism about their own futures" (Moffitt, 2003, p. 61). Some psychologists suggest that adolescent rebellion is a social construction, an idea created and endorsed by many Western adults but not expected or usual in Asian nations (Russell et al., 2010).

Dozens of longitudinal studies confirm that most adolescents learn to express their anger in acceptable ways. Only a minority are explosive: breaking something, hurting someone. Those who are not rebellious develop well, and those who are explosive can still learn to modify their anger.

Which view do you hold? Does your personal experience, remembering your adolescence, indicate that rebellion is normal? Or do you think that respect for adults, especially parents, is a common occurrence during adolescence, leading to a healthy adulthood?

Breaking the Law

Both the prevalence (how widespread) and the incidence (how frequent) of criminal actions are more common during adolescence than earlier or later. Arrest statistics in every nation reflect this fact, and confidential self-reports reveal that virtually every adolescent breaks the law at least once before age 20. Only about one-fourth of young lawbreakers are caught, and most of those are warned and released (Dodge et al., 2006).

In one study of 1,559 urban seventh-graders (both sexes, all races, from parochial as well as public schools), more than three-fourths had committed at least one offense (stolen something, damaged property, or hurt someone physically). Usually, however, adolescents are not chronic offenders: In the same study, fewer than one-third had committed five or more such acts (Nichols et al., 2006). To put this in perspective, remember that buying cigarettes or a beer, having sex with someone underage, skipping school, and breaking a local curfew are all illegal for those under age 18.

Research on confessions to a crime negates the notion that adolescents are often serious criminals. In the United States, about 20 percent of confessions are false: That is, a person confesses to a crime he or she did not commit. False confessions are more likely in adolescence, partly because of brain immaturity and partly because young people want to help their family members and please adults—including the police (Owen-Kostelnik et al., 2006; Steinberg, 2009).

A leading researcher on juvenile delinquency says that we need to distinguish two kinds of teenage lawbreakers. Most juvenile delinquents are **adolescence-limited offenders**, adolescents whose criminal activity stops by age 21 (Moffitt, 2003). They break the law with their friends, facilitated by their chosen antisocial peers. More boys than girls are in this group, but some gangs include both sexes (the gender gap in law-breaking is narrower in late adolescence than earlier) (Moffitt et al., 2001).

The other kind of delinquents are **life-course-persistent offenders** (Moffitt et al., 2001), people who break the law before and after adolescence as well as during it. Their law breaking is more often alone than as part of a gang, and the cause of their problems is neurological impairment (either inborn or caused by early experiences), the symptoms of which include problems with language and learning from childhood.

The criminal records of both types of teenagers may be similar. However, if adolescence-limited delinquents can be protected from various snares (such as quitting school, entering prison, drug addiction, early parenthood), they outgrow their criminal behavior. This is confirmed by other research: Few delinquent youths who are not imprisoned continue to be criminals in early adulthood (Monahan et al., 2009).

Causes of Delinquency

One way to analyze the likelihood of adolescent crime is to consider earlier patterns and stop delinquency before the police become involved. Parents and schools need to develop strong and protective relationships with children, teaching them emotional regulation and prosocial behavior,

>> **Response for Journalists** (from page 475): Since teenagers seek admiration from their peers, be careful not to glorify the victim's life or death. Facts are needed, as is, perhaps, inclusion of warning signs that were missed or cautions about alcohol abuse. Avoid prominent headlines or anything that might encourage another teenager to do the same thing.

adolescence-limited offender A person whose criminal activity stops by age 21.

life-course-persistent offender A person whose criminal activity typically begins in early adolescence and continues throughout life; a career criminal.

What Next? Jenelle Evans, famous as *Teen Mom 2*, has photographers following her even to court. Here she returns to court with her then boyfriend, Kieffer Delp, both accused of breaking and entering and drug possession. Those charges were dropped, but the judge sentenced her to two days in jail because she tested positive for marijuana. Limited or persistent?

AARON ST. CLAIR/SPLASH NEWS/NEWSCOM

as explained in earlier chapters. In adolescence, three pathways to dire consequences can be seen:

1. Stubbornness can lead to defiance, which can lead to running away—runaways are often victims as well as criminals (e.g., falling in with prostitutes and petty thieves).
2. Shoplifting can lead to arson and burglary.
3. Bullying can lead to assault, rape, and murder.

Each of these pathways demands a different response. The rebelliousness of the first can be channeled or limited until more maturation and less impulsive anger prevail. Those on the second pathway require stronger human relationships and moral education. Those on the third present the most serious problem; Their bullying should have been stopped earlier, as Chapters 10 and 13 explained. In all cases, early warning signs are present, and intervention is more effective earlier than later (Loeber & Burke, 2011).

Adolescent crime in the United States and many other nations has decreased in the past 20 years. Only half as many juveniles under age 18 are currently arrested for murder than was true in 1990. For almost every crime, boys are arrested at least twice as often as girls are.

No explanations for this declining rate or for gender differences are accepted by all scholars. Regarding gender, it is true that boys are more overtly aggressive and rebellious at every age, but this may be nurture, not nature (Loeber et al., 2013). Some studies find that female aggression is typically limited to family and friends, and therefore less likely to lead to an arrest.

Regarding the drop in adolescent crime, many possibilities have been suggested: fewer high school dropouts (more education means less crime); wiser judges (who now have community service as an option); better policing (arrests for misdemeanors are up, which may warn parents); smaller families (parents are more attentive to each of two children than each of twelve); better contraception and legal abortion (wanted children are less likely to become criminals); stricter drug laws (binge drinking and crack use increase crime); more immigrants (who are more law abiding); less lead (early lead poisoning reduces brain functioning); and more.

Nonetheless, adolescents are more likely to break the law than adults are. To be specific, the arrest rate for 15- to 17-year-olds is twice that for those over 18. The disproportion is true for almost every crime (fraud, forgery, and embezzlement are exceptions) (FBI, 2013). Jail may increase the chance that a temporary rebellion will become a lifetime pattern, but, as with depression, angry adolescents cannot be ignored.

SUMMING UP

Compared with people of other ages, many adolescents experience sudden and extreme emotions that lead to powerful sadness and explosive anger. Supportive families, friends, neighborhoods, and cultures usually contain and channel such feelings. For some teenagers, however, emotions are unchecked or intensified by their social contexts. This situation can lead to parasuicide (especially for girls), to minor lawbreaking (for both sexes), and, less often, to completed suicide or jail (especially for boys). Pathways to crime can be seen in childhood and early adolescence: Intervention is most effective then as well.

>> Drug Use and Abuse

Hormonal surges, the brain's reward centers, and cognitive immaturity make adolescents particularly attracted to the sensations produced by drugs. But their immature bodies and brains make drug use especially hazardous.

Variations in Drug Use

Most teenagers try *psychoactive drugs,* that is, drugs that activate the brain. To a developmentalist (but not to a police officer), cigarettes, alcohol, and many prescription medicines are as addictive and damaging as illegal drugs such as marijuana, cocaine, and heroin.

Age Trends

Both the prevalence and incidence of drug use increase from about ages 10 to 25 and then decrease, with use before age 18 being the best predictor of later abuse. Many studies find that use of alcohol and cigarettes before age 15 is an ominous sign: It correlates with depression, sexual abuse, bullying, and later addiction (Merikangas & McClaire, 2012; Mennis & Mason, 2012). Girls under age 15 who have boyfriends are particularly vulnerable to early substance use and later addiction (Poulin et al., 2011).

Use of only one drug category decreases with age—inhalants (fumes from aerosol containers, glue, cleaning fluid, etc.), which can cause brain damage and even death. Sadly, the youngest adolescents—among whom inhalant use is greatest—are least able, cognitively, to analyze risks. Close family relationships are protective (Baltazar et al., 2013), but many parents are unaware of their children's inhalant use.

Variations by Place, Generation, and Gender

Nations vary markedly in drug use. Consider the most common drugs: alcohol and tobacco. In most European nations, alcohol is part of every dinner, and children as well as adults partake. In much of the Middle East, alcohol is illegal, and teenagers almost never drink. The only alcohol available is concocted illegally, and is distasteful and dangerous—in one recent incident, 7 young Iranian men died from drinking it (Erdblink, 2013).

Cigarettes are available everywhere, but national differences are dramatic. In many Asian nations, anyone anywhere may smoke cigarettes; in the United States, adolescents are forbidden to buy or smoke them, and smoking by anyone of any age is prohibited in many places. Nonetheless, 40 percent of U.S. high school seniors have smoked (Johnston et al., 2012). In Canada, cigarette advertising is outlawed, and cigarettes packs have graphic pictures of diseased lungs, rotting teeth, and so on; only 14 percent of Canadian 15- to 19-year-olds smoke.

Variations within nations are also marked. In the United States, most high school seniors have tried alcohol (70 percent), and almost half have smoked cigarettes or marijuana—but a significant minority (about 25 percent) have never used any drugs.

Cohort differences are evident, even over a few years. Use of most drugs has decreased in the United States since 1976 (see Figure 16.6, p. 480), with the most notable decreases in marijuana and the most recent decreases in synthetic narcotics and prescription drugs (Johnson et al., 2012).

Longitudinal data show that the availability of drugs does not have much impact on use: Most high school students say they could easily get alcohol, cigarettes, and marijuana if they wish (MMWR, June 8, 2012). However, perception of risks varies from cohort to cohort, and that has a large effect on use.

Especially for Police Officers You see some 15-year-olds drinking beer in a local park when they belong in school. What do you do? (see response, page 480)

How to Escape Imagine living where these boys do, on the streets in the capital city (Tegucigalpa) of Honduras, the nation with the highest murder rate in the world. These homeless teenagers are sniffing paint thinner for a dangerous moment of joy.

SPENCER PLATT/GETTY IMAGES

FIGURE 16.6

Rise and Fall By asking the same questions year after year, the Monitoring the Future study shows notable historical effects. It is encouraging that something in society, not in the adolescent, makes drug use increase and decrease and that the most recent data show a decline in use. However, as Chapter 1 emphasized, survey research cannot prove what causes change.

>> Response for Police Officers (from page 479): Avoid both extremes: Don't let them think this situation is either harmless or serious. You might take them to the police station and call their parents. These adolescents are probably not life-course-persistent offenders; jailing them or grouping them with other lawbreakers might encourage more crime.

Drug Use by U.S. High School Seniors in the Past Year

Percent reporting use of drug

Legend: Alcohol, Illicit drugs other than Marijuana, Amphetamines, Cocaine, Marijuana, Any Prescription Drug, Vicodin, OxyContin, Ritalin

Source: Johnston et al., 2012.

With some exceptions, adolescent boys use more drugs, and use them more often, than girls do, especially outside the United States (Mennis & Mason, 2012). For example, an international survey of 13- to 15-year-olds in 131 nations found that more boys are smokers (except in a few European nations), including three times as many boys as girls in Southeast Asia (Warren et al., 2006).

These gender differences are reinforced by social constructions about proper male and female behavior. In Indonesia, for instance, 38 percent of the boys smoke cigarettes, but only 5 percent of the girls do. One Indonesian boy explained, "If I don't smoke, I'm not a real man" (quoted in Ng et al., 2007).

A Man Now This boy in Tibet is proud to be a smoker—in many Asian nations, smoking is considered manly.

In the United States, females smoke cigarettes less than males (for high school seniors the rates are 15 and 21 percent), but they drink alcohol at younger ages (Johnston et al., 2010). Body image is important for both sexes, leading to drug differences: Boys use steroids and girls use diet drugs. [**Lifespan Link:** The impact of body image on development was discussed in Chapter 14.]

Harm from Drugs

Many researchers find that drug use before maturity is particularly likely to harm body and brain growth. However, adolescents are especially likely to deny that they ever could become addicted to drugs. Few adolescents notice when they or their friends move past *use* (experimenting) to *abuse* (experiencing harm) and then to *addiction* (needing the drug to avoid feeling nervous, anxious, sick, or in pain).

Each drug is harmful in a particular way. An obvious negative effect of *tobacco* is that it impairs digestion and nutrition, slowing down growth. This is true for bidis, cigars, pipes, and chewing tobacco as well as for cigarettes. Since internal organs continue to mature after the height spurt, drug-using teenagers who appear to be fully grown may damage their developing hearts, lungs, brains, and reproductive systems.

Alcohol is the most frequently abused drug in North America. Heavy drinking impairs memory and self-control by damaging the hippocampus and the prefrontal cortex, perhaps distorting the reward circuits of the brain life-long (Guerri & Pascual, 2010). Adolescence is a particularly sensitive period, because the regions of the brain that are connected to pleasure are more strongly affected by alcohol during adolescence than at later ages. That makes teenagers less conscious of the "intoxicating, aversive, and sedative effects" (Spear, 2013, p. 155). The effects drinking has on the brain during adolescence have been proven with controlled research on mice, and the results seem to extend to humans as well.

Marijuana seems harmless to many people (especially teenagers), partly because users seem more relaxed than inebriated. Yet adolescents who regularly smoke marijuana are more likely to drop out of school, become teenage parents, be depressed, and later be unemployed.

Marijuana affects memory, language proficiency, and motivation (Lane et al., 2005)—all of which are especially crucial during adolescence. An Australian study found that even occasional marijuana use (once a week) before age 20 affected development up to 10 years later (Degenhardt et al., 2010).

Some researchers wonder whether these are correlations, not causes. It is true that depressed and abused adolescents are more likely to use drugs, and that later these same people are likely to be more depressed and further abused. Maybe the stresses of adolescence lead to drug use, not vice versa.

However, longitudinal research suggests that drug use *causes* more problems than it solves, often *preceding* anxiety disorders, depression, and rebellion (Chassin et al., 2009; Meririnne et al., 2010). Longitudinal studies of twins (which allow control of genetics and family influences) find that, although many problems predate drug use, drugs themselves add to the problems (Lynskey et al., 2012; Korhonen et al., 2012).

Marijuana is often the drug of choice among wealthier adolescents, who then become less motivated to achieve in school and more likely to develop other problems (Ansary & Luthar, 2009). It seems as if, rather than lack of ambition leading to marijuana use, marijuana destroys ambition.

Especially for Parents Who Drink Socially You have heard that parents should allow their children to drink at home, to teach them to drink responsibly and not get drunk elsewhere. Is that wise? (see response, page 483)

Preventing Drug Abuse: What Works?

Drug use is a progression, beginning with a social occasion and ending in a solitary place. The first use usually occurs with friends; occasional use seems to be a common expression of friendship or generational solidarity. An early sign of trouble is lower school achievement, but few notice that as early as they should (see Visualizing Development, p. 482, for school dropout rates).

However, the Monitoring the Future study found that in 2012:
- 24 percent of high school seniors report having had five drinks in a row in the past two weeks.
- 9 percent smoked cigarettes every day for the past month.
- 6.5 percent smoked marijuana every day.

[Johnston et al., 2012]

How Many Adolescents Are in School?

Attendance in secondary school is a psychosocial topic as much as a cognitive one. Whether or not an adolescent is in school reflects every aspect of the social context, including national policies, family support, peer pressures, employment prospects, and other economic concerns. Rates of violence, delinquency, poverty, and births to girls younger than 17 increase as school attendance decreases.

PERCENTAGE OF YOUNG ADOLESCENTS (AGES 12–15) NOT IN SCHOOL

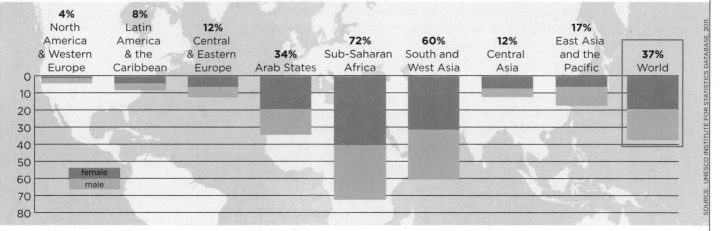

SOURCE: UNESCO INSTITUTE FOR STATISTICS DATABASE, 2011.

SELECTED SECONDARY SCHOOL GRADUATION RATES

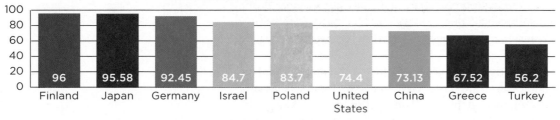

Finland	Japan	Germany	Israel	Poland	United States	China	Greece	Turkey
96	95.58	92.45	84.7	83.7	74.4	73.13	67.52	56.2

SOURCE: OECD, 2013

U.S. HIGH SCHOOL GRADUATION RATE, CLASS OF 2010

In the United States, the poorest students are five times more likely to drop out of school than the wealthiest.

SOURCE: RUMBERGER (2013).

Almost a third of U.S. girls who drop out of school do so because they are pregnant. This is both a cause and a consequence.

SOURCE: SHUGER (2012).

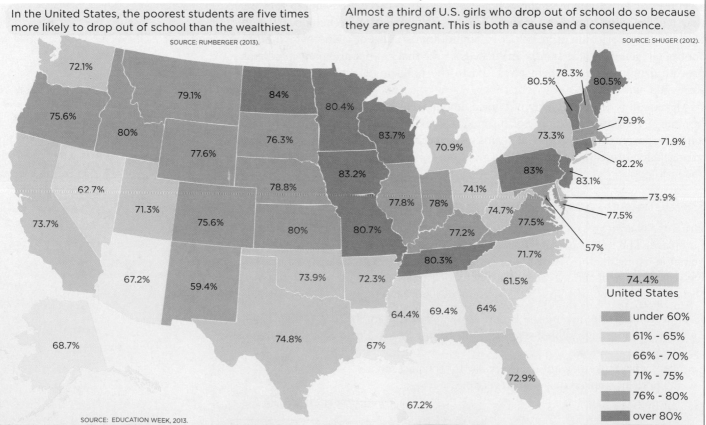

74.4% United States

- under 60%
- 61% - 65%
- 66% - 70%
- 71% - 75%
- 76% - 80%
- over 80%

SOURCE: EDUCATION WEEK, 2013.

These figures are ominous, suggesting that addiction is the next step. Another problem is synthetic marijuana ("spice"), which was not widely available until 2009 and was used by 11 percent of high school seniors in 2011 (Johnston et al., 2012). And although prescription drug use may seem harmless, since the source originally was a physician, many adolescents are already addicted to prescription drugs.

Remember that most adolescents think they are exceptions, sometimes feeling invincible, sometimes extremely fearful of social disapproval, but almost never worried that they themselves will become addicts. They rarely realize that every psychoactive drug excites the limbic system and interferes with the prefrontal cortex.

Because of these neurological reactions, drug users are more emotional (varying from ecstasy to terror, from paranoia to rage) than they would otherwise be, as well as less reflective—both problems for adolescence even when they are drug-free. Every hazard—including car crashes, unsafe sex, and suicide—is more common among teens who have taken a psychoactive drug.

With harmful drugs, as with many other aspects of life, each generation prefers to learn things for themselves. A common phenomenon is **generational forgetting**, the idea that each new generation forgets what the previous generation learned (Chassin et al., 2009; Johnston et al., 2012). Mistrust of the older generation, added to loyalty to one's peers, leads not only to generational forgetting but also to a backlash. If a friend passes out from drug use, adolescents try to protect the friend from adult awareness rather than getting medical help. If adults forbid something, that may be a reason to try it.

Some antidrug curricula and advertisements using scare tactics (such as D.A.R.E. initiatives or the TV commercial that showed eggs in a hot frying pan as "This is your brain on drugs") have no effect. Instead, they make drugs seem exciting. Antismoking announcements produced by cigarette companies (such as a clean-cut young person advising viewers to think before they smoke) actually increase use (Strasburger et al., 2008).

This does not mean that trying to halt early drug use is hopeless. Massive ad campaigns by public health advocates in Florida and California cut adolescent smoking almost in half, in part because the publicity appealed to the young. One effective ad depicted young people dumping 1,200 body bags in front of the corporate headquarters of a tobacco company to highlight the number of smoking-related deaths that occur in the United States each day (Farrelly et al., 2005). The anticorporation video, with grainy black-and-white footage (as if a teen had shot it a decade ago), had an impact.

Both parental example and social changes make a difference. Throughout the United States, higher prices, targeted warnings, and better law enforcement have led to a marked decline in cigarette smoking among younger adolescents. In 2012, only 5 percent of eighth-graders had smoked cigarettes in the past month, compared with 21 percent in 1996 (Johnston et al., 2012). (Use of other drugs has not declined as much.)

Looking broadly at the past three chapters and the past 40 years in the United States, we see that the universal biological processes do not lead to universal psychosocial problems. Sharply declining rates of teenage births and abortions (Chapter 14), increasing numbers graduating from high school (Chapter 15), and less use

>> **Response for Parents Who Drink Socially** (from page 481): No. Alcohol is particularly harmful for young brains. It is best to drink only when your children are not around. Children who are encouraged to drink with their parents are more likely to drink when no adults are present. It is true that adolescents are rebellious, and they may drink even if you forbid it. But if you allow alcohol, they might rebel with other drugs.

generational forgetting The idea that each new generation forgets what the previous generation learned. As used here, the term refers to knowledge about the harm drugs can do.

Serious Treatment A nurse checks Steve Duffer's blood pressure after a dose of Naltrexone, a drug with many side effects that combats severe addiction, in this case addiction to heroin. Steve is now 24.

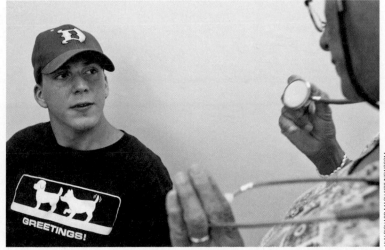

HUY RICHARD MACH/KRT/NEWSCOM

of legal and illegal drugs are apparent in many nations. Adolescence starts with puberty, that much is universal. But what happens next depends on parents, peers, culture, and society.

SUMMING UP

Most adolescents worldwide try drugs, usually cigarettes and alcohol. Drug use and abuse vary depending on age, culture, cohort, laws, and gender, with almost all adolescents in some nations using drugs that are never tried in other nations. Drug use early in adolescence is especially risky, since many drugs reduce learning and growth, harm the developing brain, and make later addiction more likely. Generational forgetting is one reason each cohort has distinctive drug-use patterns and many efforts to stop drug use have failed, but other efforts have succeeded, such as well-designed ads, public education, and package design. The overall trend is positive: Drug use is lower in the United States and in many other nations (though not for all drugs) than it was a few decades ago. ▪

SUMMARY

Identity

1. Adolescence is a time for self-discovery. According to Erikson, adolescents seek their own identity, sorting through the traditions and values of their families and cultures.

2. Many young adolescents foreclose on their options without exploring possibilities or experience role confusion. Older adolescents might seek a moratorium. Identity achievement takes longer for contemporary adolescents than it did half a century ago when Erikson first described it.

3. Identity achievement occurs in many domains, including religion, politics, vocation, and sex. Each of these remains important over the life span, but timing, contexts, and often terminology have changed since Erikson and Marcia first described them. Vocational and gender identity are particularly difficult in adolescence.

Relationships with Adults

4. Parents continue to influence their growing children, despite bickering over minor issues. Ideally, communication and warmth remain high within the family, while parental control decreases and adolescents develop autonomy.

5. There are cultural differences in the timing of conflicts and in the particulars of parental monitoring. Too much parental control is harmful, as is neglect. Parents need to find a balance between granting freedom and providing guidance.

6. Adults other than parents sometimes provide important mentoring and modeling for adolescents. Adult relatives, teachers, religious and community leaders, and even public figures can be influential.

Peer Power

7. Peers and peer pressure can be beneficial or harmful, depending on the particular friends. Adolescents select their friends, including friends of the other sex, who then facilitate constructive and/or destructive behavior.

8. Adolescents seek the approval of their peers, sometimes engaging in risky behavior to gain such approval.

9. Like adults, adolescents experience diverse sexual needs and may be involved in short-term or long-term romances, depending in part on their peer group. Finding a life partner is a long process,

typically involving emotional ups and downs. Early, exclusive sexual relationships are often a sign of emotional immaturity.

10. The sexual orientation of some youths is toward same-sex romance. Depending on the culture and cohort, they may have a more difficult adolescence than others, risking bullying or worse.

11. Many adolescents learn about sex from peers and the media—sources that do not provide a balanced picture. Ideally parents are the best teachers about sex, but many are silent and naïve.

12. Most parents want schools to teach adolescents about sex. Education varies from nation to nation, with some nations providing comprehensive education beginning in the early grades. In the United States, no curriculum (including abstinence-only programs) markedly changes the age at which adolescents become sexually active, although some help reduce rates of pregnancy and STIs.

Sadness and Anger

13. Almost all adolescents become self-conscious and self-critical. A few become chronically sad and depressed. Many adolescents (especially girls) think about suicide, and some attempt it. Few adolescents actually kill themselves; most who do so are boys.

14. At least in Western societies, almost all adolescents become more independent and angry as part of growing up, although most still respect their parents. Lawbreaking as well as momentary rage are common; boys are more likely to be arrested for violent offenses than are girls.

15. Adolescence-limited delinquents should be prevented from hurting themselves or others; their criminal behavior will disappear with maturation. Life-course-persistent offenders are aggressive in childhood and may continue to be so in adulthood.

Drug Use and Abuse

16. Most adolescents experiment with drugs, especially alcohol and tobacco, although such substances impair growth of the body and the brain. National culture has a powerful influence on which specific drugs are used as well as on frequency of use. Age, gender, community, and parental factors are also influential.

17. Prevention and moderation of adolescent drug use and abuse are possible. Antidrug programs and messages need to be carefully designed to avoid a backlash or generational forgetting.

KEY TERMS

adolescence-limited offender (p. 477)
clinical depression (p. 474)
cluster suicides (p. 475)
deviancy training (p. 469)
familism (p. 474)

foreclosure (p. 458)
gender identity (p. 461)
generational forgetting (p. 483)
identity achievement (p. 458)
identity versus role confusion (p. 458)

life-course-persistent offender (p. 477)
moratorium (p. 458)
parasuicide (p. 475)
parental monitoring (p. 464)
peer pressure (p. 467)

role confusion (p. 458)
rumination (p. 474)
sexual orientation (p. 470)
suicidal ideation (p. 474)

WHAT HAVE YOU LEARNED?

1. What is Erikson's fifth psychosocial crisis, and how is it resolved during adolescence?

2. How does identity foreclosure differ from identity moratorium?

3. Why is identity foreclosure considered a less mature option than identity achievement?

4. Why is it premature for today's adolescents to achieve their vocational identity?

5. What role do parents play in the formation of an adolescent's religious and political identity?

6. What assumptions about sexual identity did most adults hold 50 years ago?

7. Why do parents and adolescents often bicker?

8. When is parental monitoring a sign of a healthy parent-adolescent relationship, and when is it not?

9. How does the influence of parents and non-parent adults differ for adolescents?

10. How does the influence of peers and parents differ for adolescents?

11. Why do many adults misunderstand the role of peer pressure?

12. What is the role of parents, peers, and society in helping an adolescent develop an ethnic identity?

13. How do friendships differ during adolescence and adulthood?

14. When is an adolescent romance healthy, and when is it not?

15. How does culture affect the development of sexual orientation?

16. From whom do adolescents usually learn about sex?

17. What variations are there in sex education in schools, and how does this affect adolescent sexual behavior?

18. What is the difference between adolescent sadness and clinical depression?

19. Why do many adults think adolescent suicide is more common than it is?

20. How can rumination contribute to gender differences in depression and suicide?

21. Why are cluster suicides more common in adolescence than in later life?

22. What are the similarities between life-course-persistent and adolescence-limited offenders?

23. Why are psychoactive drugs particularly attractive in adolescence?

24. Why are psychoactive drugs particularly destructive in adolescence?

APPLICATIONS

1. Interview people who spent their teenage years in U.S. schools of various sizes, or in another nation, about the peer relationships in their high schools. Describe and discuss any differences you find.

2. Locate a news article about a teenager who committed suicide. Can you find evidence in the article that there were warning signs that were ignored? Does the report inadvertently encourage cluster suicides?

3. Research suggests that most adolescents have broken the law but that few have been arrested or incarcerated. Ask 10 of

your fellow students whether they broke the law when they were under 18 and, if so, how often, in what ways, and with what consequences. (Assure them of confidentiality.) What hypothesis arises about lawbreaking in your cohort?

4. Cultures have different standards for drug use among children, adolescents, and adults. Interview three people from different cultures (not necessarily from different nations; each occupation, generation, or religion can be said to have a culture) about their culture's drug-use standards. Ask your respondents to explain the reasons for any differences.

>>**ONLINE CONNECTIONS**

To accompany your textbook, you have access to a number of online resources, including Learning Curve, an adaptive quizzing program, critical thinking questions, and case studies. For access to any of these links, go to www.worthpublishers.com/launchpad/bergerls9e. In addition to these resources, you'll also find links to video clips, personalized study advice, and an ebook. Some of the videos and activities available online include:

▪ *Who Am I?* Reviews pathways to identity achievement and Marcia's dimensions of exploration and commitment. Teens talk about identity. The embedded questionnaire lets you gauge your progress in identity formation.

WORTH PUBLISHERS

Adolescence

BIOSOCIAL

Puberty Begins Puberty begins adolescence, as the child's body becomes much bigger (the growth spurt) and more sexual. Hormones of the HPA and HPG axes influence growth and sexual maturation as well as body rhythms, which change so that adolescents are more wakeful at night. The normal range for the beginning of puberty is age 8 to age 14.

Growth and Nutrition Many teens do not get enough iron or calcium because they often consume fast food and soda instead of family meals and milk. Some suffer from serious eating disorders such as anorexia and bulimia. The limbic system typically matures faster than the prefrontal cortex. As a result, adolescents are more likely to act impulsively.

Sexual Maturation Both sexes experience increased hormones, new reproductive potential, and primary as well as secondary sexual characteristics. Every adolescent is more interested in sexual activities, with possible hazards of early pregnancy and sexual abuse.

COGNITIVE

Logic and Self Adolescents think differently than younger children do. Piaget stressed the adolescent's new analytical ability—using abstract logic (part of formal operational thought). Adolescents use two modes of cognition, intuitive reasoning and analytic thought. Intuitive thinking is experiential, quick, and impulsive, unlike formal operational thought; intuitive processes sometimes crowd out analytical ones. Technology has both positive and negative aspects. Positives include enhancement of learning and promotion of social outreach and reduced isolation through online connections. Negatives are evident in cyberbullying and video game addiction.

Teaching and Learning Secondary education promotes individual and national success. International tests find marked differences in achievement. In the United States, high-stakes tests and more rigorous course requirements before high school graduation are intended to improve standards.

PSYCHOSOCIAL

Identity Adolescent development includes a search for identity, as Erikson described. Adolescents combine childhood experiences, cultural values, and their unique aspirations in forming an identity. The contexts of identity are religion, politics/ethnicity, vocation, and sex/gender.

Relationships Families continue to be influential, despite rebellion and bickering. Adolescents seek autonomy but also rely on parental support. Parental guidance and ongoing communication promote adolescents' psychosocial health. Friends and peers of both sexes are increasingly important.

Sadness and Anger Depression and rebellion become serious problems for a minority of adolescents. Many adolescents break the law, but their delinquency is limited to their adolescent years; the great majority eventually become law-abiding adults. Some, however, are life-course-persistent offenders. Adolescents are attracted to psychoactive drugs yet such drugs are particularly harmful during the teen years.

VI

emerging adulthood

Until very recent history, three roles traditionally signified adulthood: employee, spouse, and parent. Those roles were coveted, once puberty was over. But in the past few decades, millions of young people have found themselves on the border between adolescence and adulthood. Their bodies were fully grown by about age 18, but they did not want to plunge into adulthood.

Postponing adult roles was first evident among college students in rich nations. Their stage of life was labeled "youth" or "late adolescence" or "early adulthood." But millions more young people now hover before full adulthood. The world's teen birth rate has plummeted, marriage age has increased, and more than a billion people hope to attend college or are already there, expecting to work in their preferred occupation someday—but not yet.

Consequently a major shift has occurred in the study of life-span development. A new stage has appeared, worthy of a new name, **emerging adulthood.**

emerging adulthood The period of life between the ages of 18 and 25. Emerging adulthood is now widely thought of as a distinct developmental stage.

Emerging Adulthood: Biosocial Development

■ Growth and Strength
Strong and Active Bodies
A VIEW FROM SCIENCE: Ages and Stages
Bodies in Balance
Staying Healthy

■ Sexual Activity
Then and Now
Opinions and Problems

■ Psychopathology
Multiple Stresses of Emerging Adults
Mood Disorders
Anxiety Disorders
Schizophrenia

■ Taking Risks
OPPOSING PERSPECTIVES: Brave or
   Foolish?
Drug Abuse
Social Norms
Implications of Risks and Norms

WHAT WILL YOU KNOW?

1. Why do emerging adults want sex but not marriage?
2. Why are emerging adults unlikely to go to doctors for checkups?
3. Why would anyone risk his or her life unnecessarily?
4. How can drug abuse among college students be reduced?

"How does it feel to be your age?" Elissa asked me at my birthday dinner.

"I don't feel old," I said, "but the number makes me think that I am."

"Twenty-five is old, too," Sarah said. (She had turned 25 two weeks earlier.)

We laughed, but we all understood. Although 18 or 21 was once considered the beginning of adulthood, age 25 has become the new turning point. By about age 18, the biological changes of adolescence are complete: A person is literally "grown up." But many people do not consider themselves adults (which is what Sarah meant by *old*) until age 25 or later.

As this chapter explains, emerging adults share particular biosocial characteristics. Their bodies are ready for hard work and reproduction. However, physical growth now allows dangerous risks, and sexual maturation could mean baby after baby. As bodies mature and health improves, new vulnerabilities appear, all described in this chapter.

>> Growth and Strength

Biologically, the years from ages 18 to 25 are prime time for hard physical work and safe reproduction. However, as you will see, the ability of an emerging adult to move stones, plow fields, or haul water better than older adults is no longer admired, and if a contemporary young couple had a baby every year, their neighbors would be more appalled than approving.

Strong and Active Bodies

Maximum height is usually reached by age 16 for girls and 18 for boys, except for a few late-maturing boys who gain another inch or two by age 21. Maximum strength soon follows. During emerging adulthood, muscles grow, bones strengthen, and shape changes, with males gaining more arm muscle and females more fat (Whitbourne & Whitbourne, 2011). By age 22, women have developed adult breasts and hips and men have reached full shoulder width and upper-arm strength.

Peak Performance Because this is a soccer match, of course we see skilled feet and strong legs—but also notice the arms, torsos, and feats of balance. Deniz Naki and Luis Gustavo, now in their early twenties, are German soccer team members in better shape than most emerging adults, but imagine these two a decade earlier or later and you will realize why, physiologically, the early 20s are considered the prime of life.

Left: Image Source/Getty Images
Top: Lane Oatey/Blue Jean Images/Getty Images

491

Especially for a Competitive Young Man Given the variations in aging muscle, how might a 20-year-old respond if he loses an arm-wrestling contest against his father? (see response, page 495)

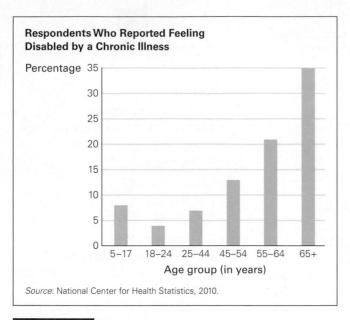

Respondents Who Reported Feeling Disabled by a Chronic Illness

Source: National Center for Health Statistics, 2010.

FIGURE 17.1

Strong and Independent Looking at this graph, do you wonder why twice as many 5- to 17-year-olds as 18- to 24-year-olds are said to be limited in daily activities? The answer relates to who reports the limitations. Parents answer for children; adults answer for themselves. Parents tend to be more protective, reporting that chronic conditions (mostly ADHD and asthma) limit what their children can do. Emerging adults are strong and capable—and they say they are even when they are not.

For both sexes, muscles can be powerful. Emerging adults are more able than people of any other age to race up a flight of stairs, lift a heavy load, or grip an object with maximum force. Strength gradually decreases over the decades of adulthood, with some muscles weakening more quickly than others. Back and leg muscles shrink faster than the arm muscles, for instance (McCarter, 2006). This is apparent in older baseball players who still hit home runs long after they no longer steal bases.

Every body system—including the digestive, respiratory, circulatory, and sexual-reproductive systems—functions optimally at the beginning of adulthood. Serious diseases are not yet apparent, and some childhood ailments are outgrown.

In a large survey, 96.1 percent of young adults (aged 18 to 24) in the United States rated their health as good, very good, or excellent, whereas only 3.9 percent rated it as fair or poor (National Center for Health Statistics, 2012). Similarly, 95.3 percent of 18- to 24-year-olds reported no limitations on their activities due to chronic health conditions, a rate far better than that of any other age group (see Figure 17.1).

However, some emerging adults have health problems that they may ignore. Doctors have told 15 percent of 18- to 29-year-olds that they have a chronic disease—most often asthma, arthritis, diabetes, or high blood pressure (National Center for Health Statistics, 2010). These diseases are not usually severe until middle age or later, but their prevalence suggests that health for many emerging adults is not as good as it might be.

Lifelong, many serious conditions can be avoided or ameliorated with preventive medicine. If this were the only way to be healthy, then most emerging adults would be sick, because they avoid medical professionals unless they are injured or pregnant. Thirty percent of this age group in the United States has no usual source of medical care (National Center for Health Statistics, 2012). Perhaps as a result, the average emerging adult sees a health professional once a year, compared with about 10 annual medical visits for the typical adult aged 75 or older. In fact, one-fifth of all young men do not see a doctor or other health professional even once (National Center for Health Statistics, 2012).

Emblematic of the carelessness of emerging adults regarding health is hand washing among students at a college in Ontario, where a viral epidemic led the school's administration to advocate—by using signs in bathrooms, public announcements, and so on—frequent, careful, time-consuming, hand washing. Most students (85 percent) claimed they practiced proper hand hygiene, but observers discovered that only 17 percent actually did (Surgeoner et al., 2009).

Dirty Hands Once men avoided hand washing—it was too ladylike. Then scientists proved that hand contact spread every virus, from the common cold to SARS. Here famed Ferrari driver Fernando Alonso joins a UNICEF hand-washing day, showing a young lad in India that he should wash his knuckles too.

Similarly, while the Centers for Disease Control recommends the flu shot each year for everyone over 6 months of age, only about one-fourth of adults have had the shot in the past year (National Center for Health Statistics, 2012). Young adults especially avoid the flu shot, unless their college requires it. Their reasons? It's not guaranteed and it takes time (ignoring the time saved by preventing the flu, which it does for most vaccinated young adults).

A VIEW FROM SCIENCE

Ages and Stages

In many ways, a person aged 18 to 25 is no different from a person a few years younger or older. The age parameters of emerging adulthood are somewhat arbitrary, unlike earlier in life, when physical maturation is closely tied to chronological age and developmental stage

Earlier in life, age signifies growth and abilities. No one would mistake a 3-month-old for a 3-year-old or expect a 6-year-old to learn in the same way an 11-year-old does, much less a 16-year-old.

For adults, however, chronological age is an imperfect guide. A 40-year-old could have a body that functions like that of a typical person a decade older or younger. The same is true for intellect: College students are held to the same academic standards whether they are 18 or 80.

Nor do adult social roles follow strict age parameters. Virtually all children live with their parents and go to school, but a cross section of 40-year-olds would include many lifestyles and household patterns. Some hope never to marry, some are divorced several times, some expect their first child, some are grandparents, some employed, some not, some living alone, some with a dozen relatives.

Then why do developmental scientists cluster adults into chronological age groups, reporting differences between one group and another? Every researcher in developmental psychology does that, as do textbooks such as this one. One indication of the fluidity of adult age boundaries is that textbooks use various ages to indicate the beginning of adulthood or late adulthood.

Nonetheless, chronological ages are always given. Why?

There are three reasons. The first is that age matters to adults as they live their lives. People note birthdays, especially the ones ending in 5 or 0, and say "I'm too old to . . . " or "It's about time for you to. . . ."

The second reason is that cohort matters. For example, because the Internet, cell phones, and social networking are relatively new, the emerging adult generation has a different life pattern than older adults did. Indeed, almost all young people meet potential dates and many meet marriage partners online. That has changed courtship patterns, changes that are reflected in any discussion of this generation.

Finally, maturation and experience accumulate. Of course, some people age faster than others, but every aspect of the body and brain is affected by time. Despite variability, many characteristics (vision, hearing, reaction time) of young adults differ from those of people in middle or late adulthood. The study of human development must delineate the impact of maturation.

The goal of developmental study remains to understand change over time in order to help all people fulfill their potential. Since people follow patterns that vary by birthdays, cohort, and maturation, we need to know what those patterns are. Chronological boundaries help with that. (See Visualizing Development, p. 494, for the average age of important life events for the current cohort of emerging adults.)

Bodies in Balance

Fortunately, bodies are naturally healthy during emerging adulthood. The immune system is strong, fighting off everything from the sniffles to cancer and responding well to vaccines (Grubeck-Loebenstein, 2010). Usually, blood pressure is normal, teeth have no new cavities, heart rate is steady, the brain functions well, and lung capacity is sufficient.

Rates of illness are so low that many diagnostic tests, such as PSA (for prostate cancer), mammograms (for breast cancer), and colonoscopies (for colon cancer), are not recommended until middle age or later, unless family history or warning signs suggest otherwise. These tests are more likely to be harmful to young adults because of false positives than to benefit them because of early detection. Fatal disease is rare worldwide during emerging adulthood, as Table 17.1 details for the United States. (see page 495).

This does not mean that emerging adults are unaffected by the passing years. The process of aging, called senescence, begins in late adolescence. [**Lifespan Link:** Senescence is discussed in more detail in Chapter 20.] However, because of three biological processes we now describe—organ reserve, homeostasis, and allostasis—few emerging adults are aware that their organs and cells are aging.

VISUALIZING DEVELOPMENT

Highlights in the Journey to Adulthood

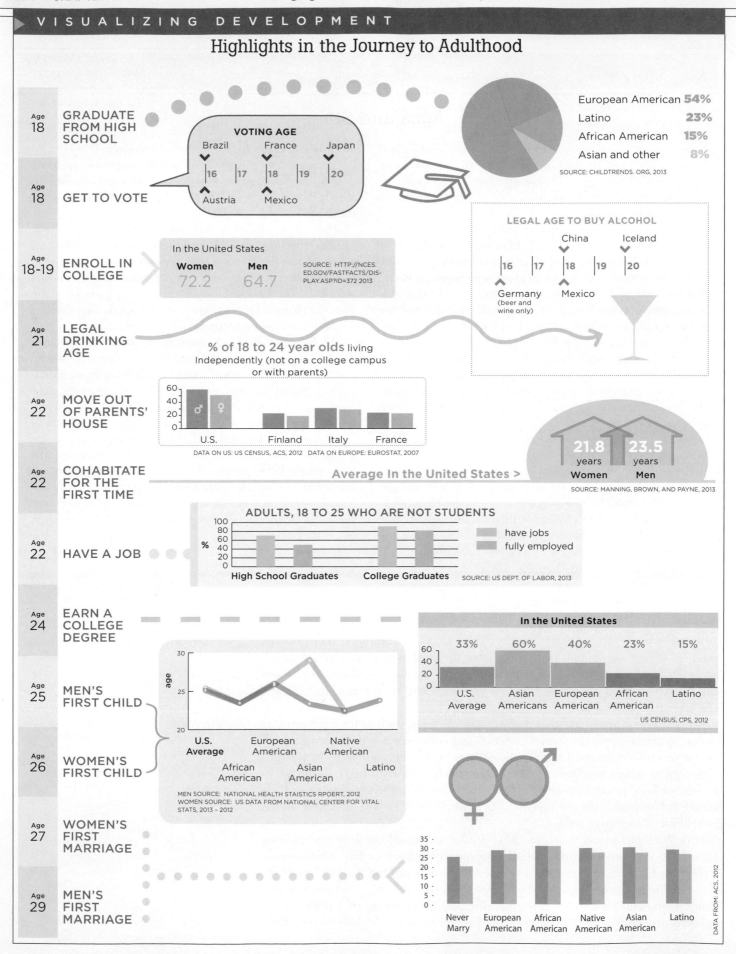

Age 18 GRADUATE FROM HIGH SCHOOL

Age 18 GET TO VOTE

VOTING AGE
Brazil | France | Japan
16 | 17 | 18 | 19 | 20
Austria | Mexico

European American **54%**
Latino **23%**
African American **15%**
Asian and other **8%**
SOURCE: CHILDTRENDS. ORG, 2013

Age 18-19 ENROLL IN COLLEGE

In the United States
Women **72.2** | Men **64.7**
SOURCE: HTTP://NCES. ED.GOV/FASTFACTS/DIS-PLAY.ASP?ID=372 2013

LEGAL AGE TO BUY ALCOHOL
China | Iceland
16 | 17 | 18 | 19 | 20
Germany (beer and wine only) | Mexico

Age 21 LEGAL DRINKING AGE

% of 18 to 24 year olds living Independently (not on a college campus or with parents)

Age 22 MOVE OUT OF PARENTS' HOUSE

60 40 20 0
U.S. | Finland | Italy | France
DATA ON US: US CENSUS, ACS, 2012   DATA ON EUROPE: EUROSTAT, 2007

21.8 years Women | **23.5** years Men
Average In the United States >
SOURCE: MANNING, BROWN, AND PAYNE, 2013

Age 22 COHABITATE FOR THE FIRST TIME

ADULTS, 18 TO 25 WHO ARE NOT STUDENTS
100 80 60 40 20 0
%
High School Graduates | College Graduates
have jobs
fully employed
SOURCE: US DEPT. OF LABOR, 2013

Age 22 HAVE A JOB

Age 24 EARN A COLLEGE DEGREE

In the United States
33% | 60% | 40% | 23% | 15%
60 40 20 0
U.S. Average | Asian Americans | European American | African American | Latino
US CENSUS, CPS, 2012

Age 25 MEN'S FIRST CHILD

30 25 20
age
U.S. Average | European American | Native American
African American | Asian American | Latino

Age 26 WOMEN'S FIRST CHILD

MEN SOURCE: NATIONAL HEALTH STAISTICS RPOERT, 2012
WOMEN SOURCE: US DATA FROM NATIONAL CENTER FOR VITAL STATS, 2013 – 2012

Age 27 WOMEN'S FIRST MARRIAGE

35 30 25 20 15 10 5 0
Never Marry | European American | African American | Native American | Asian American | Latino

Age 29 MEN'S FIRST MARRIAGE

DATA FROM: ACS, 2012

Organ Reserve

Organ reserve refers to the extra power that every organ is capable of producing when needed. That reserve power decreases each year, but it usually does not matter because people rarely need to draw on it. Bodies function well unless major stress, genetic weakness, or aging has caused that extra strength to be used up.

Bodies have a muscle reserve as well, directly related to physical strength. Maximum strength *potential* typically begins to decline by age 25. However, few adults develop all their possible strength, and even if they did, 50-year-olds retain 90 percent of the muscle they had at age 20 (Rice & Cunningham, 2002). Indeed, if a 50-year-old couch potato begins lifting weights, he or she may become stronger than ever.

The most important muscle of all, the heart, shows a similar pattern. The heart is amazingly strong during emerging adulthood: Only 1 in 50,000 North American young adults dies of heart disease each year. The average *maximum* heart rate—the number of times the heart can beat per minute under extreme stress—declines as the organ reserve is reduced, beginning at about age 25. But the *resting* heart rate remains very stable.

Homeostasis

All the parts of the body work in harmony. **Homeostasis**—a balance between various parts of the body systems—keeps every physical function in sync with every other. For example, if the air temperature rises, people sweat, move slowly, and thirst for cold drinks— three aspects of body functioning that allow them to cool off. If it gets chilly, pores constrict and people automatically walk faster and shiver to increase body heat. If they are really cold, their teeth chatter too, a more intense form of shivering.

Homeostasis works most quickly and efficiently during emerging adulthood. Thus, as long as they get enough sleep and nourishment, emerging adults are less likely to be sick, fatigued, or obese than older adults. When they catch a cold, they are down for a day or two; older adults often complain that they cannot "shake" a virus.

Each person's homeostatic systems are affected by age and past experiences, as well as by genes. For example, reaction to weather depends partly on childhood climate (an African may be cold when her roommate from northern Europe is warm), and younger people are generally warmer than older ones. If two people share a bed, one may want more blankets, which is why modern electric blankets have dual controls. Your mother may tell *you* to put on a sweater because *she* is cold.

Allostasis

Related to homeostasis is **allostasis**, a dynamic body adjustment that affects overall physiology. The main difference between homeostasis and allostasis is time: Homeostasis requires an immediate response from the body systems, whereas allostasis refers to longer-term adjustment.

For example, how much a person eats daily is affected by many factors related to appetite—that is the homeostatic "set point." An empty stomach triggers hormones, stomach pains, digestion, and so on, all of which lead a person to eat again. If an overweight person begins a serious diet, rapid weight loss soon triggers short-term, homeostatic reactions, making it harder to lose weight (Tremblay & Chaput, 2012).

Eating is related to a broader set of human needs: how emotionally satisfied or distressed a person is. Many people overeat when they are upset, and eat less when they have recently exercised—those responses could be considered part of homeostasis as well. Our bodies are designed to be comfortable, with many mechanisms to relieve

TABLE 17.1	U.S. Deaths from the Top Three Causes (Heart Disease, Stroke, and Cancer)
Age Group	Annual Rate per 100,000
15 – 24	6
25 – 34	17
35 – 44	59
45 – 54	205
55 – 64	515
65 – 74	1,157
75 – 84	2,662
85 +	7,009

Source: National Center for Health Statistics, 2013.

organ reserve The capacity of organs to allow the body to cope with stress, via extra, unused functioning ability.

homeostasis The adjustment of all the body's systems to keep physiological functions in a state of equilibrium. As the body ages, it takes longer for these homeostatic adjustments to occur, so it becomes harder for older bodies to adapt to stress.

>> Response for a Competitive Young Man (from page 492): He might propose a stair-climbing race and win, since leg strength declines faster than arm strength. Of course, intergenerational competition has psychological ramifications; perhaps the son should simply say "congratulations" and leave it at that.

allostasis A dynamic body adjustment, related to homeostasis, that affects overall physiology over time. The main difference is that homeostasis requires an immediate response whereas allostasis requires longer-term adjustment.

A Moment or a Lifetime These three in New Delhi enjoy free pizza at the opening of the 600th Domino's in India, just one of more than 5,000 outside the United States. Cheese and pepperoni may satisfy the homeostatic drive, but they now increase the allostatic load in every nation.

the pains of hunger, low oxygen, thirst, and so on. Those reactions are short term—that makes them part of homeostasis.

Over the longer term, allostasis adjusts to whatever the person eats, breathes, exercises, and so on. If a person is hungry for several weeks, the body adjusts. That allostatic adjustment is why a heavy meal suddenly consumed by a starving person might result in vomiting or diarrhea. Allostasis for a starving person requires gradual readjustment (small, digestible meals) when food is plentiful. Similarly, if a long-term vegan eats a healthy portion of meat, that might cause indigestion.

Over the years, allostasis becomes more crucial: If a person overeats or starves day after day, the body adjusts, but that takes a toll on health. In medical terminology, that person has an increased *allostatic load* because the body's adjustment results in a burden that may impair long-term health. Obesity is one cause of diabetes, heart disease, high blood pressure, and so on—all the result of physiological adjustment (allostasis) to long-term daily overeating (Sterling, 2012).

Thus, overeating and underexercising require not just adjustment for each moment (homeostasis) but also adjustment over decades. One heavy meal reduces appetite for the next few hours (homeostasis); years of obesity put increasing pressure on the allostatic system, so a new stress (such as running up three flights of stairs) may cause a major breakdown (such as a heart attack).

All Three Together

Add organ reserve to homeostasis and allostasis and it is clear why health habits in emerging adulthood affect vitality in old age. Because of organ reserve, a heart attack is unlikely before midlife, but years of physical stresses affect overall body functioning. Thus a person may have a heart attack at age 50 because of obesity and smoking that began at age 20.

Young adults rarely experience serious illness because all three aspects of body functioning—organ reserve, homeostasis, and allostasis—work in harmony. Senescence gradually reduces the capacity of each organ and slows down homeostasis, eventually increasing allostatic load. The increased physiological burden is usually imperceptible (except in laboratory analysis) and rarely affects daily life until old age.

Even in the smaller changes of aging, such as the wearing down of the teeth or loss of cartilage in the knees, serious reductions are not normally evident until later in life. For example, brushing and flossing the teeth reduces bacteria of the mouth, but all three aspects of body functioning prevent gum disease in emerging adulthood even with poor oral hygiene and never seeing a dentist. The consequences appear much later, when tooth loss reflects decades of taking teeth for granted.

For everyone, the immune system is a strong and vital part of homeostasis, which is why emerging adults are so healthy. But don't make the mistake of thinking that eventual illness is simply the result of age and fate. Daily life makes a difference, as proven by astronauts. Those chosen to fly in space are relatively young and in excellent health, with strong immune systems. However, after a space flight, the immune system shows temporary but severe loss. That proves that the body is affected by much more than genes and aging (Crucian et al., 2013).

Appearance

Partly because of their overall health, strength, and activity, most emerging adults look vital and attractive. The oily hair, pimpled faces, and awkward limbs of adolescence are gone, and the wrinkles and hair loss of middle adulthood have not yet appeared. Obesity is less common during emerging adulthood than in adulthood.

The organ that protects people from the elements, the skin, is clear and taut, characteristics that "can change quite drastically" with time (Whitbourne & Whitbourne, 2011, p. 66). The attractiveness of youth is one reason that newly prominent fashion models, popular singers, and film stars tend to be in their early 20s, looking fresh and glamorous.

Vanity about personal appearance is not admired, so few emerging adults admit that they are intensely concerned about their looks. That was one conclusion from a study of 19- to 26-year-olds in the United States, New Zealand, India, and China (Durvasula et al., 2001). Yet this age group spends more money on clothes and shoes than adults of any other age. When they exercise, their main reason is to maintain—or attain—fit, slender, attractive bodies, unlike exercising older adults, whose main motivation is to maintain or achieve good health. New students in college, no matter what their ethnicity, usually care a great deal about looking good (Gillen & Lefkowitz, 2012).

Concern about appearance may be connected to sexual drives, since appearance attracts sexual interest, and young adults hope to be attractive. Furthermore, in these years many people seek employment. Attractiveness (in clothing, body, and face) correlates with better jobs and higher pay (Fletcher, 2009). Women particularly focus on appearance, especially weight, because how they look is important for both dating and employment (Fikkan & Rothblum, 2012; Morgan et al., 2012).

No wonder emerging adults try to look their best. Usually they succeed.

Staying Healthy

Emerging adults experiment and select from many options. We focus now on two vital choices that help emerging adults stay healthy: exercise and nutrition.

Exercise

Exercise at every stage of life protects against serious illness, even if a person smokes and overeats. Exercise reduces blood pressure, strengthens the heart and lungs, and makes depression, osteoporosis, heart disease, arthritis, and even some cancers less likely. Health benefits from exercise are substantial for men and women, old and young, former sports stars and those who never joined an athletic team.

By contrast, sitting for long hours correlates with almost every chronic illness, especially heart disease and diabetes, both of which pose additional health hazards. Even a little movement—gardening, light housework, walking up the stairs or to the bus—helps. Walking briskly for 30 minutes a day, five days a week, is good; more intense exercise (swimming, jogging, bicycling, and the like) is better, and adding muscle-strengthening exercise is best.

The health consequences of inactivity in early adulthood have been found in dozens of studies. One of the best is CARDIA (Coronary Artery Risk Development in Adulthood) that began with over four thousand healthy 18- to 30-year-olds. Most (3,154) were reexamined 7 and 20 years later. Those who were the least fit at the first assessment were four times more likely to have diabetes and high blood pressure in middle age. Problems began, unnoticed, and continued to worsen unless the unfit person changed habits, which rarely occurred (Camhi et al., 2013).

Boot Camp for Beauties *Dangerously Fit* offers high-intensity exercise in 20 outdoors locations in Australia, claimed to be good for body and soul. Why are all the souls here women age 18 to 30, and why is developing a "killer shape" also promised?

WILLIAM WEST/AFP/GETTY IMAGES

Fortunately, most emerging adults are quite active, getting aerobic exercise by climbing stairs, jogging to the store, joining intramural college and company athletic teams, playing at local parks, biking, hiking, swimming, and so on. In the United States, emerging adults walk more and drive less than older adults, and 61 percent of them reach the standard of exercising 30 minutes a day, five days a week. That 61 percent is higher than any other age group, and higher than the percentage of young adults who achieved that standard a decade ago (52 percent).

Past generations quit exercising when marriage, parenthood, and career became more demanding. Young adults today, aware of this tendency, can choose friends and communities that support, rather than preclude, staying active. Two factors can encourage activity:

1. *Friendship.* People exercise more if their friends do so, too. Because social networks typically shrink with age, adults need to maintain, or begin, friendships that include movement, such as meeting a friend for a jog instead of a beer or playing tennis instead of going to a movie.
2. *Communities.* Some neighborhoods have walking and biking paths, ample fields and parks, and subsidized pools and gyms. Most colleges provide these amenities, which increases the exercise of students. Health experts cite extensive research showing that community design can have a positive effect on the levels of obesity, hypertension, and depression (Bors et al., 2009).

Eating Well

Nutrition is another lifelong habit embedded in culture. At every stage of life, diet affects future development. For example, a program in Guatemala that provided adequate nutrition to pregnant women and children under age 3 had benefits for emerging adults 20 years later—the children of these women had more education and better jobs than a comparable group of emerging adults who had not been such fortunate babies (Martorell et al., 2010).

For body weight, there is a homeostatic **set point**, or settling point, that makes people eat when hungry and stop eating when full. Of course, extreme dieting may alter the set point: Eating disorders such as anorexia and bulimia nervosa may worsen in early adulthood, and death from such disorders is more likely in the 20s than in the teens. Or people may routinely overeat, again shortening their life span. [**Lifespan Link:** Eating disorders were discussed in detail in Chapter 14.]

The **body mass index (BMI)**—the ratio between weight and height (see Table 17.2)—is used to determine whether a person is below, at, or above normal weight. A BMI below 18 is a symptom of anorexia, between 20 and 25 indicates a normal weight, above 25 is considered overweight, and 30 or more is called obese. Emerging adulthood correlates with healthy weight.

About half of all emerging U.S. adults are within the normal BMI range, as are less than one-third of adults aged 25 to 65. Emerging adulthood is also the time when the lowest proportion of the daily diet comes from fat: less fat is another sign of good nutrition (National Center for Health Statistics, 2012).

Once emerging adults become independent, they can change childhood eating patterns. Sometimes they do. As a generation, U.S. young adults consume more bottled water, organic foods, and nonmeat diets than do older adults, and many become more fit than their parents were at the same age. A large British study found that about one-half of those who were obese as children become normal-weight young adults, with healthier eating and social patterns (Viner & Cole, 2005).

Especially for Emerging Adults Seeking a New Place to Live People move more often between the ages of 18 and 25 than at any later time. Currently, real estate agents describe sunlight, parking, and privacy as top priorities for their young clients. What else might emerging adults ask when seeking a new home? (see response, page 500)

set point A particular body weight that an individual's homeostatic processes strive to maintain.

body mass index (BMI) The ratio of a person's weight in kilograms divided by his or her height in meters squared.

| TABLE 17.2 | Body Mass Index (BMI) |

To find your BMI, locate your height in the first column; then look across that row. Your BMI appears at the top of the column that contains your weight.

BMI	19	20	21	22	23	24	25	26	27	28	29	30	35	40
Height (in feet and inches)							Weight (in pounds)							
4'10"	91	96	100	105	110	115	119	124	129	134	138	143	167	191
4'11"	94	99	104	109	114	119	124	128	133	138	143	148	173	198
5'0"	97	102	107	112	118	123	128	133	138	143	148	153	179	204
5'1"	100	106	111	116	122	127	132	137	143	148	153	158	185	211
5'2"	104	109	115	120	126	131	136	142	147	153	158	164	191	218
5'3"	107	113	118	124	130	135	141	146	152	158	163	169	197	225
5'4"	110	116	122	128	134	140	145	151	157	163	169	174	204	232
5'5"	114	120	126	132	138	144	150	156	162	168	174	180	210	240
5'6"	118	124	130	136	142	148	155	161	167	173	179	186	216	247
5'7"	121	127	134	140	146	153	159	166	172	178	185	191	223	255
5'8"	125	131	138	144	151	158	164	171	177	183	190	197	230	262
5'9"	128	135	142	149	155	162	169	176	182	189	196	203	236	270
5'10"	132	139	146	153	160	167	174	181	188	195	202	207	243	278
5'11"	136	143	150	157	165	172	179	186	193	200	208	215	250	286
6'0"	140	147	154	162	169	177	184	191	199	206	213	221	258	294
6'1"	144	151	159	166	174	182	189	197	204	212	219	227	265	302
6'2"	148	155	163	171	179	186	194	202	210	218	225	233	272	311
6'3"	152	160	168	176	184	192	200	208	216	224	232	240	279	319
6'4"	156	164	172	180	189	197	205	213	221	230	238	246	287	328
	Normal						*Overweight*					*Obese*		

Source: National Heart, Lung, and Blood Institute.

A study in the United States found that emerging adults who lived on college campuses ate a more balanced, healthier diet than those living with their parents (Laska et al., 2010). The effect of home cooking continues, however, no matter where the person lives: The strongest influence on fruit and vegetable consumption in emerging adulthood is family patterns at home during childhood (Larson et al., 2012).

Obviously, better eating is not automatic. Although some emerging adults lose excess weight, others gain. According to the British study cited above, 12 percent of normal-weight teenagers become obese by age 30 (Viner & Cole, 2005). Further, many nutritionists note that the fruit and vegetable consumption of young adults is about half of what it should be (Larson et al., 2012). Almost everyone could improve. Just as health in emerging adulthood is affected by consumption 20 years earlier, so is health in middle age affected by consumption during early adulthood.

Particular nutritional hazards await young adults who are immigrants or children of immigrants. If they decide to "eat American," they might avoid curry, hot peppers, or wasabi—each of which has been discovered to have health

>> Response for Emerging Adults Seeking a New Place to Live (from page 498): Since neighborhoods have a powerful impact on health, a person could ask to see the nearest park, to meet a neighbor who walks to work, or to contact a neighborhood sports league.

benefits—and indulge in fast food, which tends to be high in fat, sugar, and salt. Although older immigrants overall are healthier than native-born Americans, their young-adult offspring have significantly higher rates of obesity and diabetes than their parents, particularly if their national origin is African or South Asian (Oza-Frank & Narayan, 2010).

No matter what their ancestry, today's emerging adults are fatter than past cohorts, and as they age they gain weight—about a pound a year, according to the CARDIA study. Specifics of diet matter: CARDIA found that fast foods, high-fat diets, and diet soda each had independent effects, with the overall result affecting not only body weight but also other health factors indicated by laboratory tests (Duffey et al., 2012). [**Lifespan Link:** Adult obesity is discussed in Chapter 20.]

SUMMING UP

Emerging adulthood is a distinct period of life, often defined as between ages 18 and 25, when most people are strong, healthy, and attractive. They have well-functioning organ systems, protected by homeostasis, allostasis, and organ reserve. Exercise and eating habits established in emerging adulthood affect health in the rest of adulthood. Young adults tend to move more, and eat less fat, than older adults, but there still is substantial room for improvement in their diets. ■

Observation Quiz Why is Single's Day on November 11ᵗʰ each year? (see answer, page 502)

>> Sexual Activity

As already mentioned, the sexual-reproductive system is at its most efficient during emerging adulthood. Conception is quicker; miscarriage is less common; serious birth complications are unusual; orgasms are more frequent; and testosterone (the hormone associated with sexual desire) is higher for both sexes at age 20 than at age 40. Whether this is a blessing or a curse depends on context.

Then and Now

Historically, most babies were born to women under 25 years old, and peak newborn survival occurred when mothers were aged 18 to 25. Women married in late adolescence, partly so that couples could proudly bear many children.

Not Married But... Postponing parenthood does not mean postponing contact, although each culture does it differently. Amanda Hawn and Nate Larsen (left) have just moved in to their California apartment, and two emerging adults in Beijing (right) keep their balloon from falling during "Singles Day," a new Chinese custom celebrated on November 11ᵗʰ.

However, these physiological assets are liabilities for today's emerging adults because their hormones want sex but their minds know they are not ready for parenthood. For many, the solution is reliable birth control.

Because of improvements in the past twenty years, long-acting contraception (implant, IUD, Depo-Provera) almost never fails (about 1 failure in 400 women per year), whereas shorter-acting measures (pill, patch, or ring) fail for 1 in 20 (Winner et al., 2012). Condoms, correctly used, are good—a failure rate of 1 in 50—but they often are used incorrectly and that results in a higher failure rate.

Compare these to rates for emerging adults with unprotected intercourse: For them, pregnancy occurs within three months, on average. That would mean 4 pregnancies per women per year—but obviously, once a woman is pregnant, she does not ovulate until after the birth. In former centuries, some couples were happy to have a baby every year or two. No longer.

Now early motherhood and large families are considered burdens more than blessings, which has dramatically reduced family size. Between 1960 and 2010 the birth rate fell from 4.9 to 2.45 worldwide (United Nations, 2011). In the United States, the 2010 birth rate for every major ethnic group was only half that in the 1960s. Emerging adults are the reason for this shift. In the United States as well as worldwide, women over age 30 are having *more* children than they did 20 years earlier, while emerging adults are having far fewer (United Nations, 2012).

Most nations do not keep accurate records on abortions, but in the United States women aged 20 to 24 have the highest rate of abortions of any age group. Worldwide, fewer babies are born to teenagers and more to women in their late 20s and older than was the case even a decade ago, including in the two most populous nations, China and India.

Another set of statistics again shows that emerging adults are postponing the traditional sequence of marriage and then parenthood. Most new mothers younger than age 30 in the United States are not married (National Center for Health Statistics, 2013).

Opinions and Problems

Attitudes toward premarital sex and single motherhood are changing, with most adults over age 65 believing that premarital sex and extramarital childbirth are wrong (in 2007 their disapproval rates were 60 percent and 75 percent, respectively). Only about one-fourth of emerging adults disapproved of premarital sex (Pew Research Center, 2007).

Sexually Transmitted Infections

There is no controversy, however, about another consequence of sexual freedom: the rise of sexually transmitted infections (STIs). Half of all new cases worldwide occur in people younger than 26 (Gewirtzman et al., 2011).

The single best way to prevent STIs is *lifelong monogamy*, because most STIs, including HIV/AIDS, are transmitted primarily via sex with more than one partner. STIs would also be limited if sexually active people, after the end of a monogamous relationship, were celibate for six months and then tested, treated, and cured for any STI before having a new partner (Mah & Halperin, 2010). However, current practice is far from that ideal. Most emerging adults practice *serial monogamy*, beginning a new relationship soon after one ends. At times a new sexual liaison overlaps an existing one, and sometimes a steady relationship is interspersed with a fling with someone else. Rapid transmission of STIs occurs.

In addition, globalization fuels the spread of every contagious disease (Herring & Swedlund, 2010). With international travel, an STI caught from an infected sex

>> **Answer to Observation Quiz** (from page 500): November 11th is written 11/11. In China singles are supposed to stay upright but close.

Especially for Nurses When should you suspect that a patient has an untreated STI? (see response, page 504)

worker in one place quickly arrives in another nation. HIV, for instance, has several variants, each of which is prevalent in a specific part of the world—but all variants are found in every nation. Primarily because of the sexual activities of young adults, AIDS has become a worldwide epidemic, with more heterosexual females than gay males testing positive for HIV (Davis & Squire, 2010). Emerging adults are prime STI vectors (those who spread disease) as well as the most common victims.

Emotional Stress

Another possible problem caused by the sexual patterns among emerging adults is increased anxiety and depression. New relationships tend to make people happy, but breakups are depressing.

Remember that contemporary emerging adults have more sexual partners than do somewhat older adults. Human physiological responses affect neurological patterns as well as vice versa, which means that sexual relationships trigger the brain system for attachment (as well as for romantic love), leading to "complex, unanticipated emotional entanglement" (H. E. Fisher, 2006, p. 12).

"Unanticipated emotional entanglement" produces unanticipated stress because people disagree about sex and reproduction. Generally speaking, attitudes about the purpose of sex fall into one of three categories (Laumann & Michael, 2001):

1. *Reproduction.* About one-fourth of all people in the United States (more women than men; more older adults than younger ones) believe that the primary purpose of sex is reproduction. Emerging adults with this perspective are likely to marry young, pressured not only by their parents but also by their values and sexual desires.

2. *Relationship.* Half of the people in the United States (more women than men) believe that the main purpose of sex is to strengthen pair bonding. This is the dominant belief among emerging adults. Their preferred sequence is dating, falling in love, deciding to be faithful, having sex, perhaps living together, and finally (if both are "ready"), marriage and parenthood.

3. *Recreation.* About one-fourth of all adults (more men than women, especially young men) believe that sex is "a fundamental human drive and a highly pleasurable physical and mental experience" (Cockerham, 2006, p. 25), sought primarily for enjoyment. Ideally, both partners achieve orgasm, without commitment. As already explained, this attitude is difficult to sustain because sex usually leads to attachment.

Assumptions about the purpose of sex are most often mutual when partners share a religion and culture. In that case, both partners share attitudes about fidelity, pregnancy, love, and abortion, and no debate is necessary. Currently, however, many emerging adults leave their childhood community and "have a number of love partners in their late teens and early twenties before settling on someone to marry" (Arnett, 2004, p. 73). Each partner may hold a worldview that the other does not understand.

Partners may feel misused and misled because "choices about sex are not the disassociated, disembodied, hedonistic and sensuous affairs of the fantasy world; they are linked, and rather tightly linked by their social embeddedness, to other domains of our lives" (Laumann & Michael, 2001, p. 22). An unplanned pregnancy may make one partner assume that marriage is the solution and the other partner expect an abortion. Each might be shocked at their lover's reaction. Further, whenever a close relationship dissolves, at least one of the partners feels rejected.

An added complication is gender identity (discussed in Chapter 16). Whereas former generations identified as either male or female, either heterosexual or homosexual,

Especially for Couples Counselors Sex is no longer the main reason for divorce—money is. If you are counseling a cohabiting couple who want to marry, do you still need to ask them about sex? (see response, page 504)

some emerging adults refuse to categorize themselves, saying they fall under all, or none, of these categories (Savin-Williams, 2005). Obviously, this complicates bonding.

If partners hold differing assumptions about the purpose of sex or the nature of gender, emotional pain and frustration are likely to follow. One might accuse the other of betrayal, an accusation the other considers patently unfair. Romantic breakups often result from such disagreements and may lead to depression, especially among adolescents and emerging adults (Davila, 2008). The more partners a person has from ages 18 to 25, the more breakups occur—each stressful. This may contribute to the rise of psychopathology in emerging adulthood, our next topic.

SUMMING UP

Although they avoid marriage and parenthood, emerging adults typically satisfy their strong sexual appetites with a series of relationships that may last months or years. They are much more likely to engage in premarital sex, and much more likely to use contraception, than older adults are. Two hazards of this new pattern, not always anticipated, are emotional distress and sexually transmitted infections; worldwide, some STIs, including HIV/AIDS, have become epidemic. Individuals, religions, and cultures disagree about the purpose of sex and parenthood, which can lead to additional stress in couples from divergent backgrounds. ■

>> Psychopathology

Most emerging adults enjoy the freedom that modern life has given them. Not all do, however. Although physical health peaks during these years, with almost no new, serious diseases, the same is not true for psychological health. Average well-being rises, but so does the incidence of psychopathology.

Multiple Stresses of Emerging Adults

Except for dementia, emerging adults experience more of every diagnosed psychological disorder (sometimes called *mental illness*) than any older group. Their rate of serious mental illness is almost double that of adults over age 25 (SAMHSA, 2009). Most serious disorders start in adolescence and emerging adulthood, and most are comorbid and untreated. That means, for instance, that an overly anxious young adult is also likely to be depressed (comorbid) and to have no professional help for either disorder (untreated) (Wittchen, 2012).

The first signs of future illness often appear in childhood, and symptoms typically worsen in adolescence. However, the full disorder often becomes evident and thus diagnosed for the first time during adulthood. This was one conclusion from research on psychological disorders in people in 14 nations (Kessler et al., 2012).

The burden falls not only on individuals and their families, but on societies as well. Although "mental disorders cause fewer deaths than infectious diseases, they cause as much or more disability because they strike early and can last a long time" (G. Miller, January 2006, p. 459).

Why does an increase take place in emerging adulthood? One reason may be the sexual freedom just described, which sometimes causes anxiety, depression, and disease. In addition, parents are less involved in the day-to-day life of their adult offspring than they were earlier, which means that disturbed young adults are on a tightrope without the safety net of parental protection. Further, especially in today's economy, emerging adults are the age group most likely to be unemployed. They lack the steadiness of a job, and instead experience rejection after rejection—obviously a difficult condition for someone still forming an identity.

>> Response for Nurses (from page 502): Always. In this context, "suspect" refers to a healthy skepticism, not to prejudice or disapproval. Your attitude should be professional rather than judgmental, but be aware that education, gender, self-confidence, and income do not necessarily mean that a given patient is free of an STI.

diathesis–stress model The view that psychological disorders, such as schizophrenia, are produced by the interaction of a genetic vulnerability (the diathesis) and stressful environmental factors and life events.

Most people can withstand uncertainly in one domain of their lives, but many emerging adults are hit from several directions. Multiple identity crises are likely to cause depression and anxiety (Crocetti et al., 2012). Vocational, financial, educational, and interpersonal stresses may combine during these years because

> for the first time in their lives, young adults are faced with independence and its inherent rights and responsibilities. Given the novelty of these challenges, young adults may lack the requisite skills to effectively cope and subsequently experience negative mental health outcomes, including depression and anxiety.
>
> [Cronce & Corbin, 2010, p. 92]

Most psychologists and psychiatrists accept the **diathesis–stress model**, which "views psychopathology as the consequence of stress interacting with an underlying predisposition (biological, psychosocial, or sociocultural) to produce a specific disorder" (Hooley, 2004, p. 204). You will recognize this model as related to the dynamic-systems model described in Chapter 1—that all the systems of the body, mind, and social context interact and influence one another as time goes on.

College counselors report an increasing number of students with serious psychological problems (Sander, 2013). This is particularly true for students at small, private, four-year colleges, where about 18 percent of the student body consult college therapists at least once during their four years. Only half as many students go to the counseling center at large public universities. The reason for this difference is unknown. It could have to do with the counseling center itself, or the college support for counseling, or the attitudes of the students. Or it could be the ecological setting: Most students at small private colleges are far from home, living on campus, unmarried, with large debts and uncertain future employment. That combination may be overwhelming.

Strength in any one domain of an emerging adult's life is protective; the combination of stressors causes the breakdown. Certainly family context has an effect, for better or worse. Having a job may be pivotal, at least according to results from a program to secure employment for adolescents, young adults, and older adults with serious mental disorders. Benefits were particularly apparent for the emerging adults (Burke-Miller et al., 2011).

Thus, the demands of emerging adulthood may cause psychopathology when added to preexisting vulnerability. As a result, many disorders appear: Some (e.g., anorexia and bulimia) we have already discussed, and others (extreme risk-taking and drug abuse) are discussed soon. First we note three traditional categories of psychopathology: mood disorders, anxiety disorders, and schizophrenia.

Mood Disorders

Before they reach age 30, 8 percent of U.S. residents suffer from a mood disorder: mania, bipolar disorder, or severe depression. Mood disorders often appear, disappear, and reappear—which means that the individual, the family, and the society suffer repeatedly. The social cost of mood disorders is estimated to be higher than that of most physical illnesses, including cancer and heart disease, since mood disorders may begin in early adulthood (or before) and can prevent a person from fully functioning for decades (Wittchen, 2012).

The most common mood disorder is major depressive disorder, signaled by a loss of interest or lack of pleasure in nearly all activities for two weeks or more. Other difficulties—in sleeping, concentrating, eating, carrying on friendships, and feeling hopeful—are also present (American Psychiatric Association, 2013). About one-fourth of mood disorders begin in adolescence, and another one-fourth first appear in young adulthood.

>> Response for Marriage Counselors (from page 502): Yes. The specifics of sex—frequency, positions, preferences—are no longer a taboo topic for most couples, but the couple still needs to discuss exactly what sex means to each of them. Issues of contraception, fidelity, and abortion can drive partners apart, each believing that he or she is right and the other is rigid, or loose, or immoral, or hidebound, or irresponsible, or unloving, and so on.

Major depression may be rooted in biochemistry, specifically in neurotransmitters and hormones. However, as the diathesis–stress model explains, problems that are more prevalent in late adolescence and emerging adulthood (e.g., romantic breakups, arrests) can trigger latent depression that would not emerge if life were less stressful.

Women at all ages are more often depressed than men, but according to research on thousands of young adults in 15 nations, men are particularly vulnerable to depression from loss of a romantic partner. Marriage typically relieves male depression, but divorce may plummet men into despair (Scott et al., 2009; Seedat et al., 2009). However, day-to-day relationship interaction is particularly important for women, who can be depressed even within a romantic partnership (Whitton & Kuryluk, 2012).

Depression may be debilitating in emerging adulthood because it undercuts accomplishments—higher education, vocational choices, romantic commitment—that normally occur by age 25. Thus, depression at this stage makes the rest of adulthood more difficult (Howard et al., 2010; Zarate, 2010).

Failure to get treatment for depression is common among emerging adults (Zarate, 2010). They distance themselves from anyone who might know them well enough to realize that professional help is needed. Furthermore, depressed people of all ages characteristically believe that nothing will help. For that reason, although effective treatment lifts most depression, sufferers are unlikely to seek it on their own.

Anxiety Disorders

Another major set of disorders, evident in one-fourth of all U.S. residents below the age of 25, is anxiety disorders. These include panic attacks, post-traumatic stress disorder (PTSD), and obsessive-compulsive disorder (OCD).

Anxiety disorders are even more prevalent than depression. This is true worldwide, according to the World Mental Health surveys of the World Health Organization (Kessler et al., 2009). Incidence statistics vary from study to study, depending partly on definition and cutoff score, but all research finds that many emerging adults are anxious about themselves, their relationships, and their future.

Age and genetic vulnerability shape the symptoms of anxiety disorders. For instance, everyone with PTSD has had a frightening experience—such as a near-death encounter in battle or a rape at knifepoint—yet most people who have had frightening experiences do not develop PTSD. Young adults, especially if they have no support from close friends or relatives, are more likely to develop the disorder than are people of other ages (Grant & Potenza, 2010). This is not surprising because young adults face a higher rate of trauma (military combat, rape, serious accidents) and are less protected by parents or spouses (Odlaug et al., 2010).

Similarly, every anxiety disorder is affected by culture and context. In the United States, social phobia—fear of talking to other people—is a common anxiety disorder, one that keeps young adults away from college, unable to make new friends, and hesitant to apply for jobs. In some Latin American cultures, anxiety takes the form of a physical sickness, such as headaches or stomach upsets (Bravo & Roca, 2013).

In Japan, a severe social phobia has appeared that may affect more than 100,000 young adults. It is called **hikiko-mori**, or "pull away" (Teo, 2010). The hikikomori sufferer stays in his (or, less often, her) room almost all the time for six months or more, a reaction to extreme anxiety about the social and academic pressures of high school and college. The close connection between Japanese mothers and children—and the fact that Japanese parents usually have only one or

hikikomori A Japanese word literally meaning "pull away"; it is the name of an anxiety disorder common among young adults in Japan. Sufferers isolate themselves from the outside world by staying inside their homes for months or even years at a time.

Don't Worry Isaiah Schaffer was wounded twice as a soldier in Iraq and now suffers from PTSD. Evident in the photo are two ways he is learning to readjust to civilian life. He is buying a book for his young daughter, and he has his trusty service dog, Meghan, by his side. Meghan calms him when being in public suddenly triggers a panic attack.

EVELYN HOCKSTEIN/POLARIS

Recovering A young Japanese man sits alone in his room, which until recently was his self-imposed prison. He is one of thousands of Japanese young people (80 percent of whom are male) who have the anxiety disorder known as *hikikomori*.

two children—makes this particular social phobia more common in that culture. Complications with attachment, coupled with shyness, are thought to cause the problem (Krieg & Dickie, 2013).

It is easier to see how a culture in a distant nation (Japan) enables a particular anxiety disorder (hikikomori) than it is to recognize how one's own culture raises anxiety in emerging adults. However, the severe anxiety about food and weight that underlies eating disorders seems more common in the United States than elsewhere. Anxiety seems to rise in emerging adulthood everywhere. Symptoms vary, but the emotion is universal.

Schizophrenia

About 1 percent of all adults experience schizophrenia, becoming overwhelmed by disorganized and bizarre thoughts, delusions, hallucinations, and emotions (American Psychiatric Association, 2013). Schizophrenia is found in every nation, but some cultures and contexts have much higher rates than others (Anjum et al., 2010).

No doubt the cause of schizophrenia is partly genetic, although most people with this disorder have no immediate family members diagnosed with it. Beyond genetics, several other risk factors are known (McGrath & Murray, 2011). One is malnutrition when the brain is developing: Women who are severely malnourished in the early months of pregnancy are twice as likely to have a child with schizophrenia.

Another is extensive social pressure. Schizophrenia is higher among immigrants than among their relatives who stayed in the home country, and the rate triples when young immigrant adults have no familial supports (Bourque et al., 2011). Drug use also increases the risk, another reason the incidence peaks in emerging adulthood, since during these years many people try psychoactive drugs.

The first symptoms of schizophrenia typically begin in adolescence. Diagnosis is most common from ages 18 to 24, with men particularly vulnerable. Men who have had no symptoms by age 35 almost never develop schizophrenia. Women who develop schizophrenia are also usually young adults, but some older women are diagnosed as well (Anjum et al., 2010).

Especially for Immigrants What can you do in your adopted country to avoid or relieve the psychological stresses of immigration? (see response, page 508)

This raises the question: Does something in the body, mind, or social surroundings trigger schizophrenia in emerging adults? The diathesis–stress model of mental illness suggests that the answer is yes for all three.

SUMMING UP

Most emerging adults enjoy their independence. However, those with inborn vulnerability, and with added emotional and cognitive burdens, may experience a serious disorder during emerging adulthood. Mood disorders, anxiety disorders, and schizophrenia are all diagnosed more often before age 25 than later, partly because the stresses of this period occur when family supports are less available. ∎

>> Taking Risks

Many emerging adults bravely, or foolishly, risk their lives. Extreme risk-taking is not usually considered pathological, but accidents, homicides, and suicides are the three leading causes of death among people aged 15 to 25—killing more of them than all diseases combined. This is true even in nations where infectious diseases and malnutrition are rampant. It is also true historically: Young males have always experienced what demographers call an *accident hump* at about age 20 (Goldstein, 2011).

Destructive risks are numerous, including having sex without a condom, driving without a seat belt, carrying a loaded gun, and abusing drugs. The attraction of an adrenaline rush is one reason people commit crimes or gamble (Cosgrave, 2010). The worst results of risk-taking are serious injury or death, but arrest is also common. About one-third of emerging adults in the United States have been arrested at least once, usually for drug-related offenses and usually between ages 18 and 21 (Brame et al., 2012).

The reasons for such risk-taking are both social and biological. Although the arrest statistics above include both sexes, the rate of risk-taking is much higher in males than females, again for social and biological reasons.

The social reason is that young men vie for status among other males and for female attention by showing off and destroying other young men, sometimes figuratively and sometimes literally. It seems hard for them to react to an insult from another man, or even an accidental push, by walking away. That is one explanation for the statistics about homicide, since both the victim and the perpetrator are usually emerging adult males (see Figure 17.2). Increased competition for mates may be the reason that the violent death rate of emerging adults in China seems to be increasing, an unexpected consequence of the one-child policy that produced more young men than young women.

The biological reason is that young men's hormones, energy, and brain development, which once propelled them to engage in strenuous physical work, now need another outlet. The most popular outlets are sports such as football, wrestling, and the newer **extreme sports**. One example of an extreme sport is *freestyle motocross*—riding a motorcycle off a ramp, catching "big air," doing tricks while falling, and hoping to land upright.

Many young adults are fans or participants of extreme sports; they find golf, bowling, and so on too tame (Breivik, 2010). As the authors of one study of dirt-bikers (off-road motorcyclists) explain, particularly from ages 18 to 24 there is a "developmental lag between impulse control and cognitive evaluation of risk" (Dwane, 2012, p. 62). Thrill overwhelms reason.

The conclusion that risk-taking is biological, wired into the male of the species, is suggested by research on another primate, the orangutan. As they leap from branch to branch, male orangutans are more likely than females to grab onto flimsy branches that might break—even though males weigh much more, which means the risk of falling is much greater (Myatt & Thorpe, 2011).

extreme sports Forms of recreation that include apparent risk of injury or death and that are attractive and thrilling as a result. Motocross is one example.

Anywhere In some ways, life in China is radically different from life elsewhere, but universals are also apparent. This emerging-adult couple poses in front of the Beijing stadium. Any risk-taking here?

© ULANA SWITUCHA/AGE FOTOSTOCK

Observation Quiz One detail in the young man's hands suggests that he is taking a risk in Asia, not North America. What is it? (see answer, page 508)

Seven Serious Years It may seem as if two adult groups include almost as many offenders and victims as the green emerging adult group, but notice the age span. The adult groups are ten and fifteen years. A person is more than twice as likely to be raped, murdered, or seriously wounded (usually by an emerging adult) at age 20 than age 40).

>> **Response for Immigrants** (from page 506): Maintain your social supports. Ideally, emigrate with members of your close family, and join a religious or cultural community where you will find emotional understanding.

>> **Answer to Observation Quiz** (from page 507): The cigarette (not the camera). Most young men in Canada and the United States do not smoke, especially publicly and casually, as this man does.

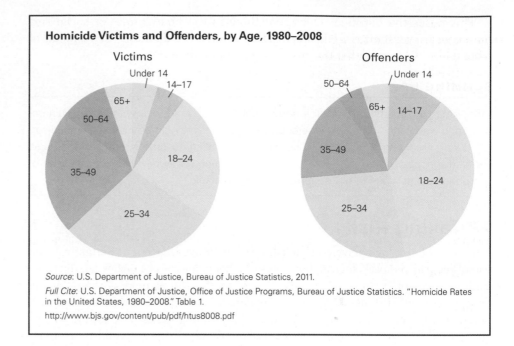

Homicide Victims and Offenders, by Age, 1980–2008

Victims — Under 14, 14–17, 18–24, 25–34, 35–49, 50–64, 65+

Offenders — Under 14, 14–17, 18–24, 25–34, 35–49, 50–64, 65+

Source: U.S. Department of Justice, Bureau of Justice Statistics, 2011.

Full Cite: U.S. Department of Justice, Office of Justice Programs, Bureau of Justice Statistics. "Homicide Rates in the United States, 1980–2008." Table 1.

http://www.bjs.gov/content/pub/pdf/htus8008.pdf

Dangerous Pleasure Here Travis Pastrana prepares to defy death once again as a NASCAR driver. Two days later, his first child was born, and two months later, he declared his race record disappointing. At age 30 he quit, declaring on Facebook that he would devote himself to his wife and family. Is that maturation, fatherhood, or failure?

drug abuse The ingestion of a drug to the extent that it impairs the user's biological or psychological well-being.

For people, think about this example. A 22-year-old named Travis Pastrana won the 2006 X Games MotoX Freestyle event with a double back flip because, as he explained, "The two main things are that I've been healthy and able to train at my fullest, and a lot of guys have had major crashes this year" (Higgins, 2006, D7).

"Major crashes" are part of every sport Pastrana likes. Four years later, in 2010, he set a new record for leaping through big air in an automobile, speeding off a ramp on the California shore and over the ocean, to a barge more than 250 feet out. He crashed into a barrier on the boat, emerging, ecstatic and unhurt, to the thunderous cheers of thousands of other young adults (Roberts, 2010).

In 2011, a broken ankle temporarily stopped him, but soon he was back risking his life to the acclaim of his cohort, winning races rife with flips and other hazards. In 2013, after some more serious injuries, he said he was "still a couple of surgeries away" from being able to race on a motorcycle, but he decided to race at NASCAR. (But see caption on the left.)

Pastrana is far from the only one attracted to extreme sports. These events attract thousands of adults, who travel long distances and spend large sums of money to jump off famous bridges (base jumping, with parachute), climb the sheer or icy sides of mountains, ride dangerous waves (on a surf board or body surfing), and so on. Such adventure has become a significant niche of tourism (Allman et al., 2009).

Drug Abuse

Although risk-taking has many benefits, the risk-taking impulse sometimes goes awry. The most studied example is substance abuse, recognized as a psychological disorder in the DSM-5.

Drug abuse occurs whenever a person uses a drug that is harmful to physical, cognitive, or psychosocial well-being. Given what is known about health and tobacco, even occasional smoking can be abuse. Some drug use—legal or not—is harmless and is therefore not abuse. However, many abusers think they

Brave or Foolish?

As you might guess, I am not a fan of extreme sports; I find them not only dangerous but also irrational. Many adults, especially women like me, find young adult risk-taking foolish, perhaps pathological. However, there is an opposite perspective.

Societies as well as individuals benefit precisely because emerging adults take chances. Enrolling in college, moving to a new state or nation, getting married, having a baby—all these endeavors are risky. So are starting a business, filming a documentary, entering an athletic contest, enlisting in the military, and joining the Peace Corps. Emerging adults take these risks, and the rest of society is grateful.

Many occupations are filled with risk-takers—police officers, military recruits, financial traders, firefighters, construction workers, and forest rangers among them. These jobs may require some bravery, and it is good that some young men want such work. (Some women and older men also engage in these jobs, and do them well, but generally, young males are more attracted to risks.) If a young man cannot find work that satisfies his need for danger, he might climb mountains, sail oceans, skydive, and so on, activities that celebrate risk but not stupidity.

Extreme sports may seem irrational from a distance, but not for the participant. One study found that facing fear was exhilarating and transformative, improving the individual's self-esteem without harming anyone. The researchers suggest that "extreme sports are good for your health" (Brymer & Schweitzer, 2013, p. 477).

Consider again the developmental need to experiment and explore. We would all suffer if young adults were always timid, traditional, and afraid of innovation. They need to befriend strangers, try new foods, explore ideas, travel abroad, and sometimes risk their lives.

Whenever I find myself critical of something that millions of other people admire, I wonder if my perspective is too narrow, too culture-bound. I know that many young adults cause themselves serious injury because they are not cautious and careful. And I know that some things that people enjoy—from eating potato chips to shooting heroin—are harmful to healthy development.

But just because I don't want to ride into big air, or even watch a game in which men in helmets tackle each other, does not mean that I should criticize those who do. Super Bowl Sunday attracts more TV viewers than any other show, and advertisers spend 4 million dollars for a 30-second commercial. Apparently my perspective is not the only one.

Getting High Climbing may be the most sober way to enjoy the thrills of emerging adulthood. The impulse to do so is universal, illustrated with two examples here: an artificial rock-climbing wall in Somerville, Massachusetts and an Art of Motion festival in Santorini, Greece.

drug addiction A condition of drug dependence in which the absence of the given drug in the individual's system produces a drive—physiological, psychological, or both—to ingest more of the drug.

What the F— Happened? That's what 30-year-old Reggie Colby asks. He says he had a happy childhood, tried heroin at age 18, married and dropped out of college, joined the army, and became addicted after an injury in Afghanistan. Since then he has been dishonorably discharged, divorced, and estranged from his daughter. Now he is sheltered by an overpass in Camden, New Jersey, two days after serving time in jail for stealing food. "What happened?" is the right question. Did the stress of emerging adulthood have anything to do with it?

are merely users, so this distinction is tricky. Denial is common, and harmful, in abusers.

Drug abuse can lead to **drug addiction**, a condition of dependence in which the absence of a drug causes intense cravings to satisfy a need. The need may be either physical (e.g., to stop the shakes, settle one's stomach, or sleep) or psychological (e.g., to quiet anxiety or lift depression). Withdrawal symptoms are the telltale signs of addiction.

Although cigarettes and alcohol can be as addictive and destructive as illegal drugs, from an emerging-adult perspective, part of the lure of illegal drugs is that they are against the law: There is a risk-taking thrill in buying, carrying, and using, knowing that arrest and prison are dangers. No wonder illegal drug use peaks between ages 18 to 25 and then declines more sharply than use of cigarettes and alcohol (see Figure 17.3).

It may be surprising, however, that drug abuse—particularly of alcohol and marijuana, not cocaine or heroin—is more common among college students than among their peers who are not in college. The overall binge-drinking rate among U.S. college students in 2010 was 37 percent, compared to 28 percent for their age-mates who were not in college (Johnston et al., 2011). That high rate of binge drinking arises from the same drive as extreme sports or other risks—with the same possible consequence (death).

Being with peers, especially for college men, seems to encourage many kinds of drug abuse. The opposite is also true. In fact, the emerging adults least likely to abuse drugs are women who are not in college, living with their parents. Patterns of use, abuse, and addiction are also affected by historical trends; they vary from time to time and from nation to nation. However, the overall trend is curvilinear everywhere, rising during emerging adulthood and then falling with maturity.

With drugs as with many other risks, the immediate benefits obscure the eventual costs. Most young adults use alcohol to reduce social anxiety—a problem for many emerging adults as they enter college, start a new job, speak to strangers, or embark on a romance. It does not occur to them that they might become alcoholics.

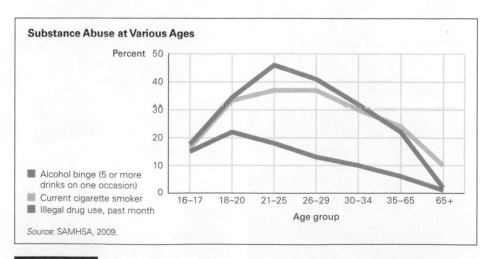

Substance Abuse at Various Ages

Source: SAMHSA, 2009.

■ Alcohol binge (5 or more drinks on one occasion)
■ Current cigarette smoker
■ Illegal drug use, past month

FIGURE 17.3

Too Old for That As you can see, emerging adults are the biggest substance abusers, but illegal drug use drops much faster than cigarette smoking or binge drinking. This graph depicts drug use at one time in one nation (the United States in 2008), but these trends are universal.

Similarly, more than half of all college students and more than half of all U.S. soldiers in Afghanistan use "energy drinks," with high doses of caffeine, to stay awake. They are unaware that such drinks correlate with sexual assault and dangerous driving, and that high doses of caffeine can be lethal (Sepkowitz, 2013).

Indeed, no matter what the drug, crossing the line between use and abuse does not always ring alarms in the user. This was apparent in a study of ketamine use among young adults in England, who justified its use—"a bargain"—even after signs of addiction were apparent (Moore & Measham, 2008). (Ketamine has medical uses, but it is often used as a recreational drug.) A complication with ketamine and many other drugs is that they are potent mood changers: many depressed or anxious emerging adults self-medicate, treating one psychological problem by creating another (Duman & Aghajanian, 2012).

Although family members often try to stop drug abuse, intervention is least likely during emerging adulthood. During these years, parents keep their distance and drug users are unlikely to marry, so abuse can continue unchecked for years.

Yet longitudinal data show that early drug abuse impairs later life in many ways. Those who use drugs heavily in high school are less likely to go to college, and those who begin heavy drug use in college are less likely to earn a degree, find a good job, or sustain a romance (Johnston et al., 2009). Drug abuse during early adulthood may lead to serious physical and mental ailments later in life. Longitudinal research comes to this conclusion in every nation. For instance, a 21-year study in Scotland found that young-adult men who drank heavily doubled their risk of dying by middle age (Hart et al., 1999).

Social Norms

One discovery from the study of human development that might help the health of emerging adults is the power of *social norms,* which are customs for usual behavior within a particular society. Social norms exert a particularly strong influence on college students. They want the approval of their new peers; social norms matter.

Some social norms work well for emerging adults. This is evident from rates of obesity, since young adults watch their weight in order to be attractive to others, and from rates of exercise, since young adults join sports teams and gyms partly because norms encourage it. However, some norms push emerging adults in destructive directions.

Base Rate Neglect

In Chapter 15 you read about the logical error that humans often make called base rate neglect—the tendency to overlook or ignore the frequency of a specific factor when making a judgment or decision, even in the face of overwhelming odds. Compounding this fallacy is something called the *availability error,* which occurs when people remember most easily the events or people who make a dramatic impact, not the quiet people or everyday events that might make a quieter impact (Kahneman, 2011).

An example from college students is that they notice the flashy, noisy, unusual classmate, and might mistakenly assume such behavior is far more typical than it is. You probably have noticed such prejudice in other people, who judge everyone of a certain ethnic or national background because of what one member of that group has done. In the same ways, base rate neglect and availability error may lead to risk-taking.

Emerging adults are immersed in social settings (colleges, parties, concerts, sports events) where risk-takers are admired. They notice the risk-takers—such as the classmate who brags that he waited until the last minute and wrote a term paper in one night or the star athlete who did something dangerous and unex-

Especially for Substance Abuse Counselors Can you think of three possible explanations for the more precipitous drop in the use of illegal drugs compared to legal ones? (see response, page 512)

>> Response for Substance Abuse Counselors (from page 511): Legal drugs could be more addictive, or the thrill of illegality may diminish with age, or the fear of arrest may increase. In any case, treatment for young-adult substance abusers may need to differ from that for older ones.

social norms approach A method of reducing risky behavior that uses emerging adults' desire to follow social norms by making them aware, through the use of surveys, of the prevalence of various behaviors within their peer group.

pected. Because of base rate neglect, they may conclude that such people are not unusual. That might make them overestimate the prevalence of drug use and then follow that example.

For instance, in one experiment, several small groups of college students were offered as much alcohol as they wanted while they socialized with one another. In some groups, one student was secretly recruited in advance to drink heavily; in others, one student was assigned to drink very little; in a third condition, there was no student confederate. In those groups with a designated drinker, participants followed the norm set by the heavy drinker, increasing the average amount of alcohol they consumed, but their drinking was unaffected by the light drinker (reported in W. R. Miller & Carroll, 2006).

The power of social norms as well as the "liquid courage" of alcohol is evident at concerts and sports events when a crowd of people suddenly moves so quickly that some are crushed and trampled, or when a new extreme sport becomes popular. For instance, a small group of young-adult British men formed the Dangerous Sports Club. They told the press they would try bungee jumping on April Fools' Day in 1979. On that day, they all backed off, telling the press it was a foolish joke. But later, after drinking, one was filmed bungee jumping. Thousands saw the video; then bungee jumping became a fad.

A similar story holds for other extreme sports—hang gliding, ice climbing, pond swooping, base jumping—that were never imagined until one daredevil young adult inspired thousands of others. Media coverage (especially photos and videos) and social networking create a rush, and people follow the trend without thinking about dangers.

Norms and Drugs

An understanding of the perceptions and needs of emerging adults, as well as the realization that college students abuse drugs even more than others their age, has led to a promising effort to reduce alcohol abuse on college campuses. This is the **social norms approach**, using surveys to make students aware of the true prevalence of various behaviors.

About half the colleges in the United States have surveyed alcohol use on their campuses and reported the results. Almost always, students not only overestimate how much the average student drinks, but they also underestimate how their peers feel about the loud, late talking and other behaviors of drunk students (C. M. Lee et al., 2010). Ironically, those who exaggerate the quantity of drinking are often those who are relatively isolated and depressed. They then drink to be like everyone else, and they only become more depressed.

In general, when survey results are reported and college students realize that most of their classmates study hard, avoid binge drinking, refuse drugs, and are sexually abstinent, faithful, or protected, they are more likely to follow these social norms. This is especially true if the survey is conducted and reported on the Web (not a paper questionnaire with written responses) and if the students are not living with many heavy drinkers (Ward & Gryczynski, 2009). In the latter case, the social norm of their immediate residence may be more powerful than information about students overall.

Recent research continues to find that emerging adults are influenced by perceived norms, including not only how much people drink but also by what the negative consequences might be. The relationship is not always simple—some people and some ideas are much more influential than others—but the general effect of social norms has been found again and again (Wardell & Read, 2013).

An interesting caveat is that when people are drinking and using drugs with other people who are drinking and using drugs, they tend to perceive the positive effects more than the negative ones (Brie et al., 2011). They do not realize that they are keeping others awake; they do not know that someone who has passed out may need medical attention; they think they can drive, or think, or walk when they cannot. That may explain why people who are trying to stop a habit need to avoid people and contexts that might encourage the habit they want to break. [**Lifespan Link:** The challenges of breaking a habit are discussed in A View from Science, Chapter 20.]

Implications of Risks and Norms

One of my older students, John, told the class about his experience as an emerging adult. At first, he spoke with amused pride. But by the end of his narrative, he was troubled, partly because John was now the father of a little boy he adored, and he realized that his son might become an equally reckless young man.

John told us that, during a vacation break in his first year of college, he and two of his male friends were sitting, bored, on a beach. One friend proposed swimming to an island, which was barely visible on the horizon. They immediately set out. After swimming for a long time, John realized that he was only about one-third of the way there, that he was tired, that the island was merely an empty spit of sand, and that he would have to swim back. He turned around and swam to shore. The friend who made the proposal eventually reached the island. The third boy became exhausted and almost drowned (a passing boat rescued him).

What does this episode signify about the biosocial development of emerging adults? It is easy to understand why John started swimming. Male ego, camaraderie, boredom, and the overall context made this an attractive adventure. Young men like to be active, feeling their strong arms, legs, and lungs.

Like John, many adults fondly remember past risks. They forget the friends who caught STIs, who had abortions or unwanted births, who became addicts or alcoholics, or who died young; they ignore the fact that their younger siblings and children might do the same. Emerging adulthood is a strong and healthy age, but not without serious risks. Why swim to a distant island? More thinking is needed, as described in the next chapter.

SUMMING UP

Risk-taking is common during young adulthood. Some risks are beneficial, others are not. Leaving a childhood home, starting a new job, and developing a new relationship all entail some risks but are important development tasks for emerging adults. However, some risks are more problematic—extreme sports, law breaking, drug use.

In general, males take more risks than females; admiration from peers of both sexes may be part of the motivation. Emerging adults—especially those in college—have high rates of drug and alcohol abuse, which may undermine their college achievement. Social norms are powerful influences, particularly for college students. Knowledge about others' behavior and attitudes may help reduce alcohol abuse and other problems. ∎

SUMMARY

Growth and Strength

1. Emerging adulthood, from about age 18 to age 25, is a newly recognized period of development characterized by postponing parenthood, marriage, and career commitment, while attaining additional education.

2. Most emerging adults are strong and healthy. All the body systems function optimally during these years; immunity is strong; death from disease is rare.

3. Organ reserve, homeostasis, and allostasis help ensure that emerging adults recover quickly from infections and injuries. The gradual slowdowns of senescence begin as soon as puberty is complete but are not yet noticed.

4. Emerging adults are usually physically and sexually attractive, more concerned with their appearance than they will be later in life. Such concerns may be related to sexual drives as well as the need for employment, as attractive appearance correlates to better jobs and higher pay.

5. Emerging adults tend to eat well and exercise often, but poor eating or exercise habits may continue. Habits established in emerging adulthood affect health in the rest of adulthood.

6. More emerging adults have a healthy body mass index (BMI) than adults over age 25, but some have serious eating disorders.

Sexual Activity

7. Reproduction is most successful during emerging adulthood because both male and female bodies are at their most fertile. However, most emerging adults want to postpone parenthood.

8. Most young adults believe that sexual relationships before marriage are acceptable, but their sexual activity may arouse unexpected emotions and arguments about the purpose of sex—reproduction, relationship, or recreation.

9. Sexually transmitted infections are much more common among emerging adults now than in earlier generations, as well as more common than among sexually active older adults.

Psychopathology

10. Generally, well-being increases during emerging adulthood, but so does the incidence of psychological disorders. Although the roots of such problems begin earlier, the stresses of this stage push some people over the edge.

11. Mood and anxiety disorders are apparent at every period of life, but some of the social contexts that are more prevalent during emerging adulthood tend to worsen these problems. Therapy can help, but many young adults do not seek it.

12. Schizophrenia is an example of the diathesis–stress model. Genes underlie the vulnerability, and prenatal nutrition is protective, but the expression of this disorder occurs most often during emerging adulthood.

Taking Risks

13. Risk-taking increases during emerging adulthood, particularly among young men. Some risks are worth taking, but many—including drug abuse and addiction, unprotected sex, and extreme sports—are life threatening.

14. Context is crucial for risk-taking, with social norms particularly powerful during these years. Dangerous risks can be reduced when young adults are aware of social norms and attitudes.

KEY TERMS

allostasis (p. 495)
body mass index (BMI) (p. 498)
diathesis–stress model (p. 504)

drug abuse (p. 508)
drug addiction (p. 510)
emerging adulthood (p. 489)

extreme sports (p. 507)
hikikomori (p. 505)
homeostasis (p. 495)

organ reserve (p. 495)
set point (p. 498)
social norms approach (p. 512)

WHAT HAVE YOU LEARNED?

1. Why is maximum physical strength usually attained in emerging adulthood?

2. How are homeostasis and allostasis apparent in the human need for nutrition?

3. How does organ reserve protect against heart attacks?

4. What advantages do emerging adults have in their physical appearance?

5. Why is the nutrition of emerging adults often better than that of other adults?

6. How does exercise in early adulthood affect a person's health in late adulthood?

7 What cohort differences are evident in people's attitudes toward premarital sex?

8. Why do so few 20-year-old men and women want to get married?

9. Biologically, what is the best age to have a baby?

10. Why are STIs more common today than they were 50 years ago?

11. What is the usual pattern of well-being during emerging adulthood?

12. Why do depressed people tend not to seek help?

13. What is one common anxiety disorder in the United States?

14. What evidence suggests that schizophrenia is not based solely on genes?

15. What are the social benefits of risk-taking?

16. Why are risk sports more attractive to emerging adults than to other adults?

17. Why are serious accidents more common during emerging adulthood than later in adulthood?

18. Who is more likely to abuse drugs: college students or emerging adults who are not in college?

19. How does addiction differ from drug abuse?

20. Why are social norms particularly powerful in emerging adulthood?

APPLICATIONS

1. Describe an incident during your emerging adulthood when taking a risk could have led to disaster. What were your feelings at the time? What would you do if you knew that a child of yours was about to do the same thing?

2. Describe the daily patterns of someone you know who has unhealthy habits related to eating, exercise, drug abuse, risk-taking, or some other aspect of lifestyle. What would it take for that person to change his or her habits? Consider the impact of time, experience, medical advice, and fear.

3. Use the library or the Internet to investigate changes over the past 50 years in the lives of young adults in a particular nation or ethnic group. What caused those changes? Are they similar to the changes reported in this text?

>>ONLINE CONNECTIONS

To accompany your textbook, you have access to a number of online resources, including quizzes for every chapter of the book, flashcards (in English and Spanish), critical thinking questions, and case studies. For access to any of these links, go to www.worthpublishers.com/launchpad/bergerls9e. In addition to these free resources, you'll also find links to the podcasts, video clips, diagnostic quizzing with personalized study advice, and an ebook. Some of the videos and activities available online include:

- *Eating Disorders.* This activity covers the signs, symptoms, and impact of living with eating disorders. It also looks at cultural and gender differences.

- *The Effects of Psychological Stress.* What is stress, and how can it be managed? Activities let you measure your vulnerability to stress and determine your current stress level.

WORTH PUBLISHERS

Emerging Adulthood: Cognitive Development

- **Postformal Thought**
  The Practical and the Personal:
   A Fifth Stage?
  Combining Subjective and Objective
   Thought
  Cognitive Flexibility
  Countering Stereotypes
  Dialectical Thought

- **Morals and Religion**
  Which Era? What Place?
  Dilemmas for Emerging Adults
  Stages of Faith

- **Cognitive Growth and Higher Education**
  The Effects of College
  A CASE TO STUDY: College Advancing
   Thought
  Changes in the College Context
  Evaluating the Changes

WHAT WILL YOU KNOW?

1. How is adults' thinking about problems different from that of adolescents?

2. Is there evidence that adults are more moral than adolescents?

3. What nation has the highest proportion of young adults who graduate from college?

4. How does college affect a person's thinking processes?

What did you learn today?

When I asked my young children this question, I sometimes heard their excitement about new discoveries (that the sun does not really move in the sky) but also about things of no interest to me (like how a bunny eats a carrot). When I asked my adolescents this same question, I sometimes heard emotional truths (did you know that slaves were not counted as whole people in the Constitution?), but often I got silence. The children gave details; the adolescents might say "Nothing."

How would you answer if someone asked you now? You might respond with ideas or information, something thoughtful, new to me as well as to you. In adulthood, cognition changes in quality, quantity, speed, efficiency, and depth, reflecting values, interests, and skills, as well as an awareness of what other people know. When and how these changes take place is explained in each of this book's three chapters on adult cognition, Chapters 18, 21, and 24.

Cognitive development has been studied using many approaches:

- The *stage approach* describes shifts in the nature of thought, as in a postformal stage that follows the formal stage discussed in Chapter 15.
- The *psychometric approach* analyzes intelligence via IQ tests and other measures.
- The *information-processing approach* studies how the brain encodes, stores, and retrieves information.

All three approaches provide valuable insights into the complex patterns of adult cognition. Yet, as emphasized in Chapter 17, chronological age is an imperfect boundary in adulthood. This chapter focuses on postformal thought, Chapter 21 on psychometrics, and Chapter 24 on information processing. For all three, some examples extend beyond chronological age boundaries.

Each cognitive chapter also includes age-related topics: college education here, expertise in Chapter 21, and dementia in Chapter 24. But boundaries are fluid, as evidenced by the many college students who are long past emerging adulthood.

>> Postformal Thought

Thinking in adulthood differs from earlier thinking in three major ways: It is more practical, more flexible, and more *dialectical* (that is, it is able to consider and integrate opposing or conflicting ideas). Taken together, these characteristics may constitute a fifth stage of cognitive development, combining a new "ordering of formal operations" with a "necessary subjectivity" (Sinnott, 1998, p. 24).

If postformal thought occurs, its appearance is gradual, not tied to any particular year or decade. Emerging adulthood is the usual, but not the only, time that people develop the ability to think as adults.

The Practical and the Personal: A Fifth Stage?

postformal thought A proposed adult stage of cognitive development, following Piaget's four stages, that goes beyond adolescent thinking by being more practical, more flexible, and more dialectical (that is, more capable of combining contradictory elements into a comprehensive whole).

The term **postformal thought** originated because several developmentalists agreed that Piaget's fourth stage, *formal operational thought*, was inadequate to describe adult thinking. They proposed a fifth stage. As one group of scholars explained, in postformal thought "one can conceive of multiple logics, choices, or perceptions . . . in order to better understand the complexities and inherent biases in 'truth'" (Griffin et al., 2009, p. 173).

Postformal thinkers do not wait for someone else to present a problem to solve. They take a flexible and comprehensive approach, considering various aspects of a situation beforehand, anticipating problems, dealing with difficulties in a timely manner rather than denying, avoiding, or procrastinating. As a result, postformal thought is more practical as well as more creative and imaginative than earlier thinking is (Kallio, 2011; Su, 2011).

As you remember, adolescents use two modes of thought, but combining them is difficult. High school students may use formal analysis to distill universal truths, develop arguments, and resolve the world's problems, or they may think spontaneously and emotionally, but they rarely combine the two. They *can* analyze, but they may not anticipate the consequences of their actions. [**Lifespan Link:** The dual processing that characterizes adolescent thought is discussed in Chapter 15.]

Time Management

Crammed Together Students flock to the Titan Student Union at Cal State Fullerton for the biannual All Night Study before final exams, making cramming a social experience. This is contrary to what scientific evidence has shown is the best way to learn—that is, through distributed practice, which means studying consistently throughout the semester, not bunching it all at the end. Is cramming simply the result of poor time management or is it a rational choice?

ROSS PALMISANO/THE ORANGE COUNTY REGISTER/ZUMAPRESS.COM

One way to contrast postformal and formal thinking is to understand how adolescents and adults think about time. In adulthood, intellectual skills are harnessed to real educational, occupational, and interpersonal concerns. Conclusions and consequences matter; setting priorities includes postponing some tasks in order to accomplish others.

Interestingly, good time management is characteristic of successful, conscientious, part-time college students more than of full-time students, probably because part-time students must balance more conflicting demands on their time (McCann et al., 2012). Using logic to balance personal priorities and external demands (in this case family, job, and academics) is characteristic of postformal thought.

Another example of priorities is evident in the first week of college classes: most professors (in contrast to high school teachers) announce assignments and due dates for the entire semester and expect students "to decide for themselves when to do [the work], . . . invoking that dreaded phrase *time management*" (Howard, 2005, p. 15). Emerging adults struggle with procrastination: time management is a challenge that adults gradually master as their cognition matures (Berg, 2008).

Generally, in the process of developing postformal thought, adults accept and adapt to the many contradictions and inconsistencies of everyday experience, becoming less playful and more practical. They consider most of life's answers to be provisional, not necessarily permanent; they take irrational and emotional factors into account.

To give an example from time management, planning when to work on a term paper that is due in a month may include personal emotions and traits (e.g., anxiety, perfectionism), other obligations (at home and at work), and practical considerations (rewriting, library reserves, computer and printer availability, formatting). Adolescents might ignore all this until the last moment; emerging adults hopefully know better.

No one always plans well for the future, however. A common logical error is **delay discounting**—the tendency to undervalue (discount) future events. If offered $100 now or $110 later, people usually discount the delayed reward and choose the immediate one. Delay discounting occurs at every age. For example, lottery winners usually choose to take half of their winnings immediately, forfeiting the other half, rather than taking all in installments. Delay discounting, in effect, is an example of the difficulty of postponing immediate gratification.

Gradually, as the prefrontal cortex matures, people become better able to plan ahead. Delay discounting is reduced with age (Löckenhoff et al., 2011), but adolescents are particularly likely to underestimate delayed consequences.

This tendency explains a paradox described in the previous chapter. As a result of school classes and media messages, almost all 18-year-olds know the life-threatening risks of drug abuse and unprotected sex. And yet many consume addictive drugs and have sex with partners whose history they do not know. Why? The answer is delay discounting. Ironically, the use of psychoactive drugs (especially alcohol and marijuana) distorts the sense of time and makes delay discounting more likely, even long after the immediate effects of the drug have worn off.

Objectively, the oldest adults might be more likely to choose immediate gratification since they have fewer future years for any postponed pleasure. But the opposite is true, because postformal thinking allows better planning (Löckenhoff et al., 2011). Postformal thought is more practical, creative, and imaginative than thought in previous stages (Wu & Chiou, 2008). Investment bankers, corporation heads, surgeons, and police detectives all need to combine many modes of thought, which is one reason even the smartest young person is not chosen for those roles (Kahneman, 2011).

Really a Stage?

As you have read, some developmentalists doubt Piaget's stage theory of childhood cognition. Many more question this fifth stage. As two scholars writing about emerging adulthood wrote, "Who needs stages anyway?" (Kloep & Hendry, 2011).

Piaget himself never labeled or described postformal cognition. Certainly, if cognitive *stage* means attaining a new set of intellectual abilities (such as the symbolic use of language that distinguishes sensorimotor from preoperational thought), then adulthood has no stages.

However, as described in Chapter 15, the prefrontal cortex is not fully mature until the early 20s, and new dendrites connect throughout life. As more is understood about brain development after adolescence, it seems that the characteristics of postformal thought (practical, flexible, dialectical) are more evident as the brain matures (Lemieux, 2012).

Moreover, the prefrontal cortex seems particularly connected to social understanding (Barbey et al., 2009): Several studies find that adults tend to think in ways that adolescents do not, partly because they benefit from a wider understanding and greater experience of the social world.

delay discounting The tendency to undervalue, or downright ignore, future consequences and rewards in favor of more immediate gratification.

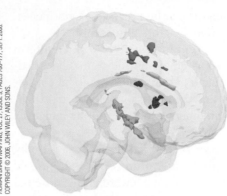

IMAGE COURTESY CRAIG BENNETT & ABIGAIL BAIRD, FROM ANATOMICAL CHANGES IN THE EMERGING ADULT BRAIN (ABIGAIL BAIRD, CRAIG BENNETT), *HUMAN BRAIN MAPPING*, VOL. 27, ISSUE 9, PAGES 766–777, SEPT. 2006. COPYRIGHT © 2006, JOHN WILEY AND SONS.

Thinking Away from Home Entering a residential college means experiencing new foods, new friends, and new neurons. A longitudinal study of 18-year-old students at the beginning and end of their first year in college (Dartmouth) found increases in the brain areas that integrate emotion and cognition—namely, the cingulate cortex (blue and yellow), caudate nucleus (red), and insula (orange). Researchers also studied one-year changes in the brains of students over age 25 at the same college and found no dramatic growth.

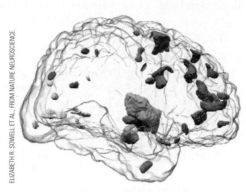

ELIZABETH R. SOWELL ET AL., FROM NATURE NEUROSCIENCE.

More Purple Means More Planning Shown here are the areas of one person's brain changes from age 14 to age 25. The frontal cortex (purple) demonstrated many changes in particular parts, as did the areas for processing speech (green and blue)—a crucial aspect of young adult learning. Areas for visual processing (yellow) showed less change. Researchers now know that brains mature in many ways between adolescence and adulthood; scientists are not yet sure of the cognitive implications.

For instance, one study of people aged 13 to 45 found that logical skills improved from adolescence to emerging adulthood and then remained steady, as might be expected as formal operational thinking becomes well established. However, social understanding continued to advance (Demetriou & Bakracevic, 2009). (Social understanding includes knowing how best to interact with other people—making and keeping good friends, responding to social slights, helping others effectively, and so on.)

Of course, context and culture are crucial: A 30-year-old in one place and time may think quite differently from someone the same age in another place and at a different time. But non-Western as well as Western cultures describe adult thought as qualitatively different from adolescent thought.

In one U.S. study, researchers asked adolescents and adults to describe themselves (Labouvie-Vief, 2006). Then coders read the descriptions and, without knowing the participants' ages, categorized self-descriptions as *protective* (high in self-involvement, low in self-doubt), *dysregulated* (fragmented, overwhelmed by emotions or problems), *complex* (valuing openness and independence above all), or *integrated* (able to regulate emotions and logic).

As life experiences accumulated, adults expressed themselves differently. No one under age 20 was at the advanced "integrated" stage (see Figure 18.1). The largest shift occurred between adolescence and emerging adulthood. As the lead researcher wrote, adult thinking "can be ordered in terms of increasing levels of complexity and integration" (Labouvie-Vief et al., 2009, p. 182).

Thus, many scholars find that thinking changes both qualitatively and quantitatively during adulthood (Bosworth & Hertzog, 2009, Lemieux, 2012; Kallio, 2011). The term *fifth stage* may be a misnomer, and *postformal* may imply a depth of intellectual thought that few people attain, but adults can and often do reach a new cognitive level when their brains and life circumstances allow it.

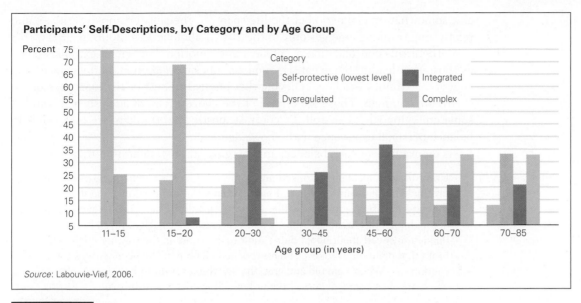

Participants' Self-Descriptions, by Category and by Age Group

Category
- Self-protective (lowest level)
- Dysregulated
- Integrated
- Complex

Age group (in years): 11–15, 15–20, 20–30, 30–45, 45–60, 60–70, 70–85

Percent axis: 5 to 75

Source: Labouvie-Vief, 2006.

FIGURE 18.1

Talk About Yourself People gradually became less self-centered and less confused as they described themselves over the years of adulthood. Many adults, but no children or adolescents, achieved a level of self-acceptance at which emotions and reason were integrated.

Combining Subjective and Objective Thought

One of the practical skills of postformal thinking is the ability to combine subjective and objective thought. **Subjective thought** arises from personal experiences and perceptions; **objective thought** follows abstract, impersonal logic. Traditional models of formal operational thinking value impersonal logic (such as, on Piaget's balance scale, the mathematical relationship between weight and distance) and devalue subjective feelings, personal faith, and emotional experience.

Purely objective, logical thinking may be maladaptive when one is navigating the complexities and commitments of daily life, especially for the social understanding needed for productive families, workplaces, and neighborhoods. Subjective feelings and individual experiences must be taken into account because objective reasoning alone is too limited, rigid, and impractical.

Yet subjective thinking is also limited. Truly mature thought involves an interaction between abstract, objective forms of processing and expressive, subjective forms, the dual processing described in Chapter 15. Adult thought does not abandon objectivity; instead, "postformal logic combines subjectivity and objectivity" (Sinnott, 1998, p. 55) to become personal and practical.

Solving the complex problem of combining emotion and logic is the crucial practical challenge for adults: "Emerging adulthood truly does emerge

subjective thought Thinking that is strongly influenced by personal qualities of the individual thinker, such as past experiences, cultural assumptions, and goals for the future.

objective thought Thinking that is not influenced by the thinker's personal qualities but instead involves facts and numbers that are universally considered true and valid.

What Would It Take for You to March for a Cure? You know that breast cancer is a serious and all-too-common disease (affecting about one woman in eight) and that more research on it is needed. That is an intellectual understanding. But when emotions combine with intellect, as happens in adulthood, the combination leads to action. That happened to Gabrielle Union when her close friend was diagnosed with metastatic breast cancer at age 32. She moved dialectically from abstraction to despair and then to advocacy, first for her friend and then for an entire cause.

as a somewhat crucial period of the life span . . . [because] complex, critical, and relativizing thinking emerges only in the 20s" (Labouvie-Vief, 2006, p. 78).

Without this consolidation of intellect and emotion, behavioral extremes (such as those that lead to binge eating, anorexia, obesity, addiction, and violence) and cognitive extremes (such as believing that one is the best or the worst person on earth) are common. Those are typical of the egocentrism of adolescence—and of some emerging adults as well. By contrast, postformal thinkers are better able to balance personal experience with knowledge.

As an example of such balance, an emerging adult student of mine wrote:

> Unfortunately, alcoholism runs in my family. . . . I have seen it tear apart not only my uncle but my family also. . . . I have gotten sick from drinking, and it was the most horrifying night of my life. I know that I didn't have alcohol poisoning or anything, but I drank too quickly and was getting sick. All of these images flooded my head about how I didn't want to ever end up the way my uncle was. From that point on, whenever I have touched alcohol, it has been with extreme caution. . . . When I am old and gray, the last thing I want to be thinking about is where my next beer will come from or how I'll need a liver transplant.

> *[Laura, personal communication]*

Laura's thinking about alcohol is postformal in that it combines knowledge (e.g., of alcohol poisoning) with emotions (images flooding her head). Note that she is cautious, not abstinent; she can combine the objective awareness of her genetic potential with the subjective experience of wanting to be part of the crowd. She can combine both modes of thought to reach a conclusion that works for her, without needing searing personal experiences (becoming an active alcoholic and reaching despair) and then going to the other logical extreme (avoiding even one sip, as recovering alcoholics must).

This development of postformal thought regarding alcohol is seen in most U.S. adults over time. As explained in the previous chapter, those in their early 20s are more likely than people of any other age to abuse alcohol and other drugs. With personal experience and learning from others (social norms), however, cognitive maturity leads most adults to drink occasionally and moderately from then on (Schulenberg et al., 2005). Looking at all the research makes it apparent that adolescents tend to use either objective *or* subjective reasoning, but adults combine the two.

Especially for Someone Who Has to Make an Important Decision Which is better: to go with your gut feelings or to consider pros and cons as objectively as you can? (see response, page 524)

Cognitive Flexibility

The ability to be practical—to predict, to plan, and to combine objective and subjective mental processes—is valuable; it is fortunate that adults can reach that postformal level. However, plans can go awry.

For example: Corporate restructuring might require finding another job; a failure of birth control might mean an unwanted pregnancy; a parent's illness might require changing plans for higher education; an economic collapse might make a mortgage impossible to sustain.

Almost every adult experiences unanticipated events such as these. Cognitive flexibility allows the adult to avoid retreating into either emotions or intellect. Research on practical problem-solving finds that adults, given a complex problem with no pat solution (such as what to do if your landlord will not pay for expensive repairs?), reflect on their options, combine emotions and reason, and then select the best course of action (Berg, 2008).

Thus, a hallmark of postformal cognition is intellectual flexibility, a characteristic that is far more typical of emerging adults than of younger people. The "fundamental flux of emerging adulthood" (Tanner et al., 2009, p. 34) comes from the realization that each perspective is only one of many, that each problem has several solutions, and that knowledge is dynamic, not static. Emerging adults begin to realize that "there are multiple views of the same phenomenon" (Baltes et al., 1998, p. 1093). Listening to others, considering diverse opinions, is a sign of flexibility.

Working Together

Consider this problem:

> Every card in a pack has a letter on one side and a number on the other. Imagine that you are presented with the following four cards, each of which has some-thing on the back. Turn over only those cards that will confirm or disconfirm this proposition: *If a card has a vowel on one side, then it always has an even number on the other side.*
>
> E 7 K 4
>
> Which cards must be turned over?

The difficulty of this puzzle is "notorious in the literature of human reasoning" (Moshman, 2011, p. 50). Fewer than 10 percent of college students solve it when working independently. Almost everyone wants to turn over the E and the 4—and almost everyone is mistaken.

However, when groups of college students who had guessed wrong on their own then had a chance to discuss the problem together, 75 percent got it right: They avoided the 4 card (even if it has a consonant on the other side, the statement could still be true) and selected the E and the 7 cards (if the 7 has a vowel on the other side, the proposition is proved false).

As in this example, adults can think things through, and change their minds after listening (Moshman, 2011). Think about a time when you thought one thing, which is opposite to what you now think. Probably a combination of logic and social experience caused you to develop your new view. This is cognitive flexibility.

Alternate Solutions

Such data on behavioral change could be attributed to many factors other than cognitive flexibility. However, research that specifically examines adult cognition finds that adults are more likely than children to imagine several solutions for every problem and then to take care in selecting the best one.

For example, young, middle-aged, and older adults in a particular study were asked to suggest solutions to various life problems (Artistico et al., 2010). Most participants found several possible solutions for each dilemma, as postformal thinkers (but not concrete or formal operational thinkers) usually do. The more familiar the problem, the more possibilities were suggested. For instance, the problem of losing motivation to finish a college degree evoked more solutions from younger adults, but the problem of relatives not visiting as often as desired got more solutions from older adults.

Countering Stereotypes

Cognitive flexibility, particularly the ability to change childhood assumptions, is needed to counter stereotypes. Daily life for young adults shows many signs of such flexibility. The very fact that emerging adults marry and become parents years later than their parents did means that, couple by couple, thinking processes lead to conclusions other than those their parents arrived at and to assumptions

>> **Response for Someone Who Has to Make an Important Decision** (from page 522): Both are necessary. Mature thinking requires a combination of emotions and logic. To make sure you use both, take your time (don't just act on your first impulse) and talk with people you trust. Ultimately, you will have to live with your decision, so do not ignore either intuitive or logical thought.

stereotype threat The thought in a person's mind that one's appearance or behavior will be misread to confirm another person's oversimplified, prejudiced attitudes.

different from past social assumptions. Of course, early experiences are influential, but for postformal thinkers they are not determinative.

Research on racial prejudice in adulthood merits closer study. Many American children and adults harbor some implicit bias against African Americans, detectable in their slower reaction time when mentally processing photos of African Americans as compared with photos of European Americans (Baron & Banaji, 2006). This implicit bias may be in the unconscious minds of African Americans themselves, harming their health and well-being (Chae et al., 2012).

By contrast, most people say and believe that they are not racially prejudiced, and their behavior reveals no overt bias. Thus, many adults have both unconscious prejudice and rational nonprejudice—even about themselves—an example of dual-processing thinking. Cognitive flexibility allows adults to recognize their emotional biases and then to change their thoughts. That requires openness, insight, and flexibility.

An intriguing discovery regarding unconscious emotions is called **stereotype threat**, the worry that other people assume that you yourself are stupid, lazy, oversexed, or worse because of your race, sex, age, or appearance. Note that the worry is the threat, quite apart from the behaviors that are based on prejudice.

The mere *possibility* of being negatively stereotyped arouses emotions that can disrupt cognition as well as emotional regulation. This has been shown with hundreds of studies on dozens of stereotyped groups, of every ethnicity, sex and sexual orientation, and age (Inzlicht & Schmader 2012).

Stereotype threat is likely when circumstances remind a person of a possible threat "in the air," not an overt threat (Steele, 1997). To stick with the original example, African American men have lower grades in high school and earn only half as many college degrees as their genetic peers, African American women. This disparity has many possible causes; stereotype threat is one of them.

If African American males are aware of the stereotype that they are poor scholars, they might become anxious. That anxiety would reduce their ability to focus on academics. Then, if they underachieve, they might denigrate academic success in order to protect their pride. That would lead to disengagement from studying and ultimately to even lower achievement. The more threatening the learning and testing context is, the worse they will do (Taylor & Walton, 2011).

Indeed, that downward pattern seems to occur exactly, not only for African American men. Hundreds of studies show that almost all humans are harmed by stereotype threat: Women underperform in math, older people are more forgetful, bilingual students stumble with English, and every member of a stigmatized minority in every nation performs less well. Even those sometimes thought to be on top—White men—do less well in math if they think they will be negatively compared with Asian men. Not only academic performance but also athletic prowess and health habits may be impaired if stereotype threat makes people anxious (Aronson et al., 2013).

The worst part of stereotype threat is that it is self-handicapping. People alert to the possibility of prejudice and discrimination are not only hypersensitive when it occurs, but they also allow it to hijack their mind, undercutting their ability. Eventually they disengage, but their initial reaction may be to try harder to prove the stereotype wrong, and that extra effort may backfire (Mangels et al., 2012; Aronson et al., 2013).

© CORBIS

The Threat of Bias If students fear that others expect them to do poorly in school because of their ethnicity or gender, they might not identify with academic achievement and therefore do worse on exams than they otherwise would have.

Observation Quiz Which of these three college students taking an exam is least vulnerable to stereotype threat? (see answer, page 526)

How do unconscious prejudices relate to postformal thought? Since everyone has some childhood stereotypes hidden in the brain, adults need flexible cognition to overcome them, abandoning the prejudices they learned earlier. Many programs attempt to increase the achievement of individuals whose potential seems unrealized.

Surprisingly successful are colleges that are predominantly for women or African Americans. Such colleges not only have higher graduation rates but also their students tend to be more successful as adults than similar students in colleges where they may be self-conscious minorities. Could one reason be that if every student is from the same group, individuals do not experience stereotype threat?

Can stereotype threat be reduced when students are a minority? One multiracial team of scientists had a hypothesis: that stereotype threat will decrease and achievement will increase if people *internalize* (believe wholeheartedly, not just intellectually) that intelligence is plastic, not inborn. These scientists used a series of measures that convinced African American college students at Stanford University that their ability depended on their personal efforts. That reduced stereotype threat and led to higher grades (Aronson et al., 2002).

This study was the first of many. Books written for the general population, not for academics, often tell the same story of people who notice their own self-handicapping prejudice and then overcome it. Sheryl Sandburg (2013, p. 8) writes that "we internalize the negative messages we get throughout our lives," and then she explains how she overcame her own biases to become the chief operating officer of Facebook.

Stereotype threat can create a vicious spiral: Some college admissions personnel wonder if it interferes with college acceptance (Soares, 2012). If minority college applicants fear stereotyping, anxiety may make them too quiet or too talkative in the interview. That may lead to a prejudicial reaction from the admissions officer. If applicants are rejected, they can correctly blame a stereotype, not realizing that they themselves set it in motion.

Postformal thinking allows people to overcome fear and anxiety, no longer denying such unconscious emotions. Is this wishful thinking, or can you recall prejudices you held about others, or about yourself, that no longer impair your thoughts?

Dialectical Thought

Postformal thought, at its best, becomes **dialectical thought**, which may be the most advanced cognitive process (Basseches, 1984, 1989; Riegel, 1975). The word *dialectic* refers to the philosophical concept, developed by Hegel two centuries ago, that every idea or truth bears within itself the opposite idea or truth.

To use the words of philosophers, each idea, or **thesis**, implies an opposing idea, or **antithesis**. Dialectical thought involves considering both these poles of an idea simultaneously and then forging them into a **synthesis**—that is, a new idea that integrates the original and its opposite. Note that the synthesis is not a compromise; it is a new concept that incorporates both original ones in some transformative way (Lemieux, 2012).

For example, many young children idolize their parents (thesis), many adolescents are highly critical of their parents (antithesis), and many emerging adults appreciate their parents and forgive their shortcomings, which they attribute to their parents' background, historical conditions, and age (synthesis).

Because ideas can engender their opposites, the possibility of change is continuous. Each new synthesis deepens and refines the thesis and antithesis that

dialectical thought The most advanced cognitive process, characterized by the ability to consider a thesis and its antithesis simultaneously and thus to arrive at a synthesis. Dialectical thought makes possible an ongoing awareness of pros and cons, advantages and disadvantages, possibilities and limitations.

thesis A proposition or statement of belief; the first stage of the process of dialectical thinking.

antithesis A proposition or statement of belief that opposes the thesis; the second stage of the process of dialectical thinking.

synthesis A new idea that integrates the thesis and its antithesis, thus representing a new and more comprehensive level of truth; the third stage of the process of dialectical thinking.

>> Answer to Observation Quiz
(from page 524): Anyone could experience stereotype threat, depending on what is being tested and on the students' history. White males are generally least vulnerable, but if the test is about literature and if the male student has been told that men are deficient at interpreting poetry and fiction, his performance on the exam might be affected by that stereotype.

initiated it, with "cognitive development as the dance of adaptive transformation" (Sinnott, 2009, p. 103). Thus, dialectical thinking involves the constant integration of beliefs and experiences with all the contradictions and inconsistencies of daily life. Change throughout the life span is multidirectional, ongoing, and often surprising—a dynamic, dialectical process.

Appreciation that life is a series of thesis/antithesis/synthesis is found in the work of every great developmentalist. For instance:

- Educators who agree with Vygotsky that learning is a social interaction within the zone of proximal development (with learners and mentors continually adjusting to each other) take a dialectical approach to education (Vianna & Stetsenko, 2006).
- Piaget could be considered a dialectical thinker, too, in that he thought conflict between new and old ideas was the fuel that fired a new stage of development (Lemieux, 2012).
- Dialectical processes are readily observable by life-span researchers, who believe that "the occurrence and effective mastery of crises and conflicts represent not only risks, but also opportunities for new development" (Baltes et al., 1998, p. 1041).
- Arnett, who coined the term *emerging adulthood*, wrote that brain organization allows the young adult to move past dualism to multiplicity (Tanner & Arnett, 2011), which can be seen as moving past thesis and antithesis, arriving at a synthesis that recognizes the many aspects of truth.

A "Broken" Marriage

Let's look at an example of dialectical thought familiar to many: the end of a love affair. A nondialectical thinker might believe that each person has stable, enduring, independent traits. Faced with a troubled romance, then, a nondialectical thinker concludes that one partner (or the other) is at fault, or perhaps the relationship was a mistake from the beginning because the two were a bad match.

By contrast, dialectical thinkers see people and relationships as constantly evolving; partners are changed by time as well as by their interaction. Therefore, a romance becomes troubled not because the partners are fundamentally incompatible, or because one or the other is bad, but because they have changed without adapting to each other. Marriages do not "break" or "fail"; they either continue to develop over time (dialectically) or they stagnate as the two people move apart.

Does this happen in practice as well as in theory? Possibly. Certainly marriages are more likely to end if the couple married as teenagers rather than as adults, perhaps because few adolescents think dialectically. People of all ages are upset when a romance fades, but neurological immaturity makes a young person overcome by jealousy or despair unable to find the synthesis (Fisher, 2006). Older couples think more dialectically and therefore move from thesis ("I love you because you are perfect") to antithesis ("I hate you—you can't do anything right") to synthesis ("Neither of us is perfect, but together we can grow").

New demands, roles, responsibilities, and even conflicts become learning opportunities for the dialectical thinker. Students might take a class in an unfamiliar subject, employees might apply for an unexpected promotion, young adults might leave their parents' household and move to another town or nation. In such situations, when comfort collides with the desire for growth, dialectical thinkers find a new synthesis, gaining insight. This basic idea underlies all continuing education—that people of all ages must keep learning as new challenges require new education (Su, 2011).

Culture and Dialectics

Several researchers have compared cognition in Asian and American adults, focusing on dialectical thought. It may be that ancient Greek philosophy led Europeans and North Americans to use analytic, absolutist logic—to take sides in a battle between right and wrong, good and evil—whereas Confucianism and Taoism led the Chinese and other Asians to seek compromise, the "Middle Way."

For whatever reason, Asians tend to think holistically, about the whole rather than the parts, seeking the synthesis because "in place of logic, the Chinese developed a dialectic" (Nisbett et al., 2001, p. 305). One example is in judging emotions: Westerners are more likely to pay close attention to facial expressions, and Asians are more likely to consider the context, such as surrounding circumstances (Matsumoto et al., 2012).

This leaves Asians open to more possibilities and makes them less likely to conclude that one answer is the only correct one. For example, a study of Canadians, some of them immigrants from China and others native born, found that the Asian Canadians were more tolerant of ambivalence. As a result, when presented with a one-sided argument, they were less likely to conclude that the argument was correct.

A series of studies compared three groups of students: Koreans in Seoul, South Korea; Korean Americans who had lived most of their lives in the United States; and U.S.-born European Americans. Individuals in all three groups were told the following:

> Suppose you are the police officer in charge of a case involving a graduate
> student who murdered a professor. . . . As a police officer, you must
> establish motive.

> *[Choi et al., 2003]*

Participants were given a list of 97 items of information and were asked to identify the ones they would want to know as they looked for the killer's motive. Some of the 97 items were clearly relevant (e.g., whether the professor had publicly ridiculed the graduate student), and virtually everyone in all three groups chose them. Some were clearly irrelevant (e.g., the student's favorite color), and almost everyone left them out.

Other items were questionable (e.g., what the professor was doing that fateful night; how the professor was dressed). Compared with both groups of Americans, the students in Korea asked for 15 more items, on average. The researchers suggest that their culture had taught them to include the entire context in order to find a holistic synthesis (Choi et al., 2003).

Researchers agree that notable differences between Eastern and Western thought are the result of nurture, not nature—that "cognitive differences have ecological, historical and sociological origins" (Choi et al., 2003, p. 47), not genetic ones.

Do not conclude that one way of thinking (either Eastern or Western) is always better. Indeed, the notion that there is one "best way" is not dialectical; most developmentalists think that reflecting flexibly is more advanced than simply sticking to one thesis.

SUMMING UP

A fifth stage of cognition, called postformal thought, may follow Piaget's fourth stage, formal operational thought. Adults may be better able to combine emotion and logic, both halves of the dual processing of adolescents. Postformal thinking is practical, flexible, and dialectical.

Cognition advances in adulthood partly because adults have responsibilities that require both logical analysis and emotional reactions, so problem solving is likely to encourage adults to think of many solutions before they select the best one for the particular circumstances. Cognitive advances and flexibility may allow adults to overcome their stereotypes, move beyond stereotype threat, and adapt their long-term relationships. Some adults think dialectically, with thesis leading to antithesis and then to synthesis. This ever-changing, dynamic cognition of intellectually advanced adults may be more evident in some contexts and cultures—especially Asian cultures—than in others. ∎

>> Morals and Religion

As already explained in earlier chapters, the process of developing morals begins in childhood. Children combine the values of their parents, their culture, and their peers with their own sensibilities as they mature. However, that is only the beginning. Many researchers believe that adult responsibilities, experiences, and education are crucial in shaping a person's ethics. The idea that emerging adulthood is pivotal for a process that continues through middle age has been supported by research over the past decades. As one expert said:

> Dramatic and extensive changes occur in young adulthood (the 20s and 30s) in the basic problem-solving strategies used to deal with ethical issues. . . . These changes are linked to fundamental reconceptualizations in how the person understands society and his or her stake in it.

[Rest, 1993, p. 201]

This expert has found that college education is one stimulus for young adults' shifts in moral reasoning, especially if coursework includes extensive discussion of moral issues or if the student's future profession (such as law or medicine) requires ethical decisions. Even without college, another researcher finds that people in early adolescence are least likely to make moral decisions and that the incidence of moral decision making rises as people mature and confront various issues (Nucci & Turiel, 2009).

There is a paradoxical connection between attending religious services, which becomes less frequent during emerging adulthood, and developing religious convictions, which becomes more frequent (Barry et al., 2012). Emerging adults are interested in developing prosocial values, but they are less interested in hearing a religious leader express the received wisdom of their faith.

Paths to Enlightenment Tolerance and openness are characteristic of emerging adults. Probably actress Dafne Fernandez (center, left) doing yoga in Barcelona, and the choir members (right) shouting hallelujah seven times in a London church, would respect each other's spiritual practices.

Which Era? What Place?

As discussed in earlier chapters, moral values are powerfully affected by circumstances, including national background, culture, and era.

The power of culture makes it difficult to assess how adult morality changes with age because changing opinions can be judged as improvements or declines. For example, compared to younger adults in the United States, older people tend to be less supportive of gay marriage and more troubled by divorce and yet more supportive of public money for mass transit and health.

Do these age trends suggest that adults become more or less moral? Or are older people more stuck in their ways, using morality to justify their intransigence instead of shifting when popular opinion and practice cause others to rethink their moral position? Indeed, more older than younger people think that various issues are moral ones, a position that allows them to stick to an outmoded opinion "on moral grounds." Is that intransigence, or is that integrity? (See Figure 18.2.)

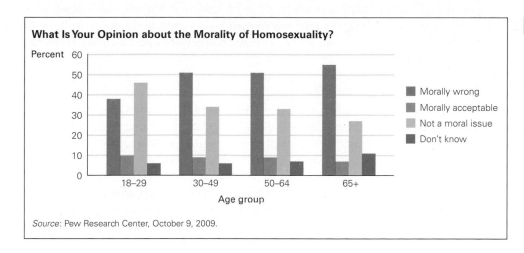

What Is Your Opinion about the Morality of Homosexuality?

Source: Pew Research Center, October 9, 2009.

FIGURE 18.2

Don't Judge Me On many issues, not only this one, older adults are more likely to judge something as right or wrong than are younger adults. Your own judgment may reflect your age and personal experience more than anything else. The specifics on this is issue keeps changing, with far fewer people of every age thinking homosexuality is morally wrong, but at every age on almost every issue, older adults see more moral issues than younger ones do.

Despite such concerns, the research does indicate that the process (though not necessarily the outcome) of moral thinking improves with age. At least adult thinking may be more flexible than adolescent thinking. As one scholar explains it, "The evolved human brain has provided humans with cognitive capacity that is so flexible and creative that every conceivable moral principle generates opposition and counter principles" (Kendler, 2002, p. 503).

Evidence for moral growth abounds in biographical and autobiographical literature. Most readers of this book probably know someone (or might *be* that someone) who had a narrow, shallow outlook on the world at age 18 and then developed a broader, deeper perspective and empathy between adolescence and adulthood (Eisenberg et al., 2005).

Many people would consider more open, dialectical, and flexible thinking (as in the postformal thinking just described) to also be more ethical. A study of the relationship between postformal thinking and concepts of God found that a more complex, multifaceted concept correlated with more postformal thought (Benovenli et al., 2011).

Dilemmas for Emerging Adults

It is fortunate that adolescent egocentrism ebbs because emerging adults often experience dilemmas that raise moral issues that egocentrism would interfere with resolving. Most adults are no longer bound by their parents' rules or by their childhood culture, but they are not yet connected to a family of their own. As a result, they must decide for themselves what to do about sex, drugs, education, vocation, and many other matters.

morality of care In Gilligan's view, moral principles that reflect the tendency of females to be reluctant to judge right and wrong in absolute terms because they are socialized to be nurturing, compassionate, and nonjudgmental.

morality of justice In Gilligan's view, moral principles that reflect the tendency of males to emphasize justice over compassion, judging right and wrong in absolute terms.

Defining Issues Test (DIT) A series of questions developed by James Rest and designed to assess respondents' level of moral development by having them rank possible solutions to moral dilemmas.

Gender Differences

There is widespread disagreement about whether gender differences in morality exist. Carol Gilligan, a Harvard professor who challenged some of Kohlberg's work, believes that decisions about reproduction advance moral thinking, especially for women (Gilligan, 1981; Gilligan et al., 1990). According to Gilligan, the two sexes think differently about parenthood, abortion, and so on. Girls are raised to develop a **morality of care**. They give human needs and relationships the highest priority. In contrast, boys develop a **morality of justice**; they are taught to distinguish right from wrong.

No other research has found gender differences in moral thinking. Factors such as education, specific dilemmas (some situations evoke care and some justice), and culture correlate more strongly than gender with whether a person's moral judgments emphasize relationships or absolutes (Juujärvi, 2005; Vikan et al., 2005; Walker, 1984).

For example, a longitudinal study of high school students who were exceptionally talented in math found that, as adults, the men were more likely to have advanced degrees in science and math and to be leaders in various fields of science, whereas many of the equally talented women had chosen to devote more time to their families (Ferriman et al., 2009). Is that a moral difference, a cultural pattern, or a gender difference?

Measuring Moral Growth

How can we assess whether a person uses postformal thinking regarding moral choices? In Kohlberg's scheme, people discuss standard moral dilemmas, responding to various probes. Over decades of longitudinal research, Kohlberg noted that during young adulthood, some respondents seemed to regress from postconventional to conventional thought. On further analysis of the responses, this shift could be an advance because the young adults incorporated human social concerns (Labouvie-Vief, 2006). [**Lifespan Link:** Kohlberg's levels of moral thought were discussed in Chapter 13.]

The **Defining Issues Test (DIT)** is another way to measure moral thinking. The DIT presents a series of questions with specific choices. For example, in one DIT dilemma, a news reporter must decide whether to publish some old personal information that will damage a political candidate. Respondents rank their priorities from personal benefits ("credit for investigative reporting") to higher goals ("serving society").

In the DIT, the ranking of items leads to a number score, which correlates with other aspects of adult cognition, experience, and life satisfaction (Schiller, 1998). These correlations suggest that people who are more caring about other people are also more satisfied with their lives, but of course correlations are provocative, not proof. In general, DIT scores rise with age because adults gradually become less doctrinaire and self-serving and more flexible and altruistic (Rest et al., 1999).

A study of adolescents and young adults in the Netherlands found intriguing results when they were given the DIT (Raaijmakers, 2005). Although many individual differences were found, some age trends were apparent: The responses of the participants shifted from justification for past behavior (adolescents) to guidance for future behavior (emerging adults). DIT scores gradually rose among adolescents who rarely broke the law. However, for delinquents, DIT scores rose as they grew older but *preceded* a drop in delinquency. For emerging adults, then, moral thinking may produce moral behavior, not just vice versa.

Many critics, however, complain that the DIT measures only some parts of moral development (Hannah et al., 2011). Factors such as religious conviction, postformal thought, moral courage, and social support are crucial in moral decisions. The problem, of course, is that it is difficult to measure all these factors, especially because one person's moral choice may be the opposite of another's. The same problem appears with faith development, as you will now see.

Stages of Faith

Spiritual struggles—including "questioning one's religious/spiritual beliefs; feeling unsettled about religious or spiritual matters; struggling to understand evil, illness, and death; and feeling angry at God" (Bryant & Astin, 2008, p. 3)—are not unusual for emerging adults. Maturation may move them past the doctrinaire religion of childhood to a more flexible, dialectical, postformal faith.

To describe this process, James Fowler (1981, 1986) developed a now-classic sequence of six stages of faith, building on the work of Piaget and Kohlberg:

- *Stage 1: Intuitive-projective faith.* Faith is magical, illogical, imaginative, and filled with fantasy, especially about the power of God and the mysteries of birth and death. It is typical of children ages 3 to 7.
- *Stage 2: Mythic-literal faith.* Individuals take the myths and stories of religion literally, believing simplistically in the power of symbols. God is seen as rewarding those who follow divine laws and punishing others. Stage 2 is typical from ages 7 to 11, but it also characterizes some adults. Fowler cites a woman who says extra prayers at every opportunity, to put them "in the bank."
- *Stage 3: Synthetic-conventional faith.* This is a conformist stage. Faith is conventional, reflecting concern about other people and favoring "what feels right" over what makes intellectual sense. Fowler quotes a man whose personal rules include "being truthful with my family. Not trying to cheat them out of anything. . . . I'm not saying that God or anybody else set my rules. I really don't know. It's what I feel is right."
- *Stage 4: Individual-reflective faith.* Faith is characterized by intellectual detachment from the values of the culture and from the approval of other people. College may be a springboard to stage 4, as the young person learns to question the authority of parents, teachers, and other powerful figures and to rely instead on his or her own understanding of the world. Faith becomes an active commitment.
- *Stage 5: Conjunctive faith.* Faith incorporates both powerful emotional ideas (such as the power of prayer and the love of God) and rational conscious values (such as the worth of life compared with that of property). People are willing to accept contradictions, obviously a postformal manner of thinking. Fowler says that this cosmic perspective is seldom achieved before middle age.
- *Stage 6: Universalizing faith.* People at this stage have a powerful vision of universal compassion, justice, and love that compels them to live their lives in a way that others may think is either saintly or foolish. A transforming experience is often the gateway to stage 6, as happened to Moses, Muhammad, the Buddha, and Paul of Tarsus, as well as more recently to Mohandas Gandhi, Martin Luther King Jr., and Mother Teresa. Stage 6 is rarely achieved.

If Fowler is correct, faith, like other aspects of cognition, progresses from a simple, self-centered, one-sided perspective to a more complex, altruistic (unselfish), and many-sided view. Other evidence also suggests that faith develops over the years of adulthood, with emerging adults less likely than those in their 30s and older to attend religious services and to pray (Wilhelm et al., 2007), even though most consider themselves at least as spiritual as they were when younger (Smith & Snell, 2009).

SUMMING UP

Moral issues challenge cognitive processes as people move beyond the acceptance of authority (typical in childhood) and past reactive rebellion (characteristic of adolescents). Cultural values always shape beliefs; whether women's traditional emphasis on relationships and men's traditional emphasis on absolutes are the result of sex (biological) or gender (cultural) is not certain. Age and cultural differences are more evident than male/female differences.

Education in Process These students, checking the Internet on the steps in San Miguel de Allende in Mexico (top) and discussing Pakistan on the quad at Brown University in the United States (bottom), illustrate why some scholars claim that college students learn more from each other than from their professors.

Some people become more open and reflective, and less self-centered in their moral judgments and religious faith as they mature. This can be measured in a test called the Defining Issues Test (DIT). Life experience is crucial: As emerging adults encounter people of different cultures, values, and religions, new questions and doubts arise. The result may be more flexibility and tolerance, not only in moral judgment but also in religious conviction, although not everyone agrees that such postformal maturity is evidence of advanced morality and faith.   ■

>> Cognitive Growth and Higher Education

Many readers of this textbook have a personal interest in the final topic of this chapter, the relationship between college education and cognition. All the evidence is positive: College graduates are not only healthier and wealthier than other adults, on average, but also deeper and more flexible thinkers. These conclusions are so powerful that scientists wonder if selection effects or historical trends, rather than college education itself, lead to such encouraging correlations. Let us look at the data.

The Effects of College

Contemporary students attend college primarily to secure better jobs and to learn specific skills (especially in knowledge and service industries, such as information technology, global business, and health care). Among the "very important" reasons students in the United States enroll in college are "to get a better job" (88 percent) and to make more money (75 percent) (see Figure 18.3).

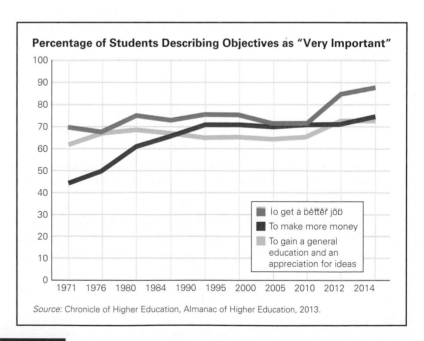

Percentage of Students Describing Objectives as "Very Important"

Legend:
- To get a better job
- To make more money
- To gain a general education and an appreciation for ideas

Source: Chronicle of Higher Education, Almanac of Higher Education, 2013.

FIGURE 18.3

Cohort Shift Decades before this study was done, students thought new ideas and a philosophy of life were prime reasons to go to college—they were less interested in jobs than were students in 2012. If this thinking causes a conflict between student motivation and professors' goals, who should adjust?

Gaining a general education and an appreciation of ideas is a secondary goal; this is "very important" to most students (73 percent) but clearly not as important as the financial goals (Pryor et al., 2012). This is true not only in the United States, but also in many other nations (Jongbloed et al., 1999).

One of my 18-year-old students is typical:

> A higher education provides me with the ability to make adequate money so I can provide for my future. An education also provides me with the ability to be a mature thinker and to attain a better understanding of myself. . . . An education provides the means for a better job after college, which will support me and allow me to have a stable, comfortable retirement.

> *[E., personal communication]*

Such worries about future costs and retirement may seem premature, but E. is not alone. About 80 percent of students are employed, yet only 20 percent of all students or their parents can pay for college. About two-thirds of U.S. students take out loans, and about two-thirds have scholarships or grants (The Chronicle of Higher Education, 2012). For most of them, their investment in college will pay off, since the average 25- to 34-year-old makes $15,000 a year more with only a B.A. compared to those with only a high school diploma (National Center for Education Statistics, 2012).

College also correlates with better health: College graduates everywhere smoke less, eat better, exercise more, and live longer. They are also more likely to be married, homeowners, and parents of healthy children. Does something gained in college—perhaps knowledge, self-control, confidence, better job prospects—account for these benefits?

Looking specifically at cognitive development, does college make people more likely to combine the subjective and objective in a flexible, dialectical way? Perhaps. College improves verbal and quantitative abilities, adds knowledge of specific subject areas, teaches skills in various professions, and fosters reasoning and reflection. According to one comprehensive review:

> Compared to freshmen, seniors have better oral and written communication skills, are better abstract reasoners or critical thinkers, are more skilled at using reason and evidence to address ill-structured problems for which there are no verifiably correct answers, have greater intellectual flexibility in that they are better able to understand more than one side of a complex issue, and can develop more sophisticated abstract frameworks to deal with complexity.

> *[Pascarella & Terenzini, 1991, p. 155]*

Note that many of these abilities characterize postformal thinking.

Some research finds that thinking becomes more reflective and expansive with *each year* of college. First-year students believe that clear and perfect truths exist; they are distressed if their professors do not explain these truths. Freshmen tend to gather knowledge as if facts were nuggets of gold, each one separate from other bits of knowledge and each one pure and true. One first-year student said he was like a squirrel, "gleaning little acorns of knowledge and burying them for later use" (quoted in Bozik, 2002, p. 145).

This initial phase is followed by a wholesale questioning of personal and social values, including doubts about the idea of truth itself. If a professor makes an assertion without extensive analysis and evidence, upper-level students are skeptical. No fact is taken at face value, much less stored intact (like an acorn) for future use.

Finally, as graduation approaches, after considering many ideas, students become committed to certain values, while they realize their opinions might change (Pascarella & Terenzini, 1991; Rest et al., 1999). Facts have become neither gold nor dross, but rather useful steps toward a greater understanding.

ANDREW HARRER/BLOOMBERG VIA GETTY IMAGES

Educating Congress Justin Neisler is a medical student, about to testify before Congress. As an openly gay man, he hopes to serve LGBTQ youth, a group with many unmet medical needs. However, he and all his classmates have a major problem: The clash between their idealism and the money they owe for their education—a median of $170,000 for new MDs in 2012.

TABLE 18.1		Perry's Scheme of Cognitive and Ethical Development During College
Dualism modified	Position 1	Authorities know, and if we work hard, read every word, and learn Right Answers, all will be well.
	Transition	But what about those Others I hear about? And different opinions? And Uncertainties? Some of our own Authorities disagree with each other or don't seem to know, and some give us problems instead of Answers.
	Position 2	True Authorities must be Right, the others are frauds. We remain Right. Others must be different and Wrong. Good Authorities give us problems so we can learn to find the Right Answer by our own independent thought.
	Transition	But even Good Authorities admit they don't know all the answers yet!
	Position 3	Then some uncertainties and different opinions are real and legitimate temporarily, even for Authorities. They're working on them to get to the Truth.
	Transition	But there are so many things they don't know the Answers to! And they won't for a long time.
Relativism discovered	Position 4a	Where Authorities don't know the Right Answers, everyone has a right to his own opinion; no one is wrong!
	Transition	Then what right have They to grade us? About what?
	Position 4b	In certain courses, Authorities are not asking for the Right Answer. They want us to think about things in a certain way, supporting opinion with data. That's what they grade us on.
	Position 5	Then all thinking must be like this, even for Them. Everything is relative but not equally valid. You have to understand how each context works. Theories are not Truth but metaphors to interpret data with. You have to think about your thinking.
	Transition	But if everything is relative, am I relative, too? How can I know I'm making the Right Choice?
	Position 6	I see I'm going to have to make my own decisions in an uncertain world with no one to tell me I'm Right.
	Transition	I'm lost if I don't. When I decide on my career (or marriage or values), everything will straighten out.
Commitments in relativism developed	Position 7	Well, I've made my first Commitment!
	Transition	Why didn't that settle everything?
	Position 8	I've made several commitments. I've got to balance them—how many, how deep? How certain, how tentative?
	Transition	Things are getting contradictory. I can't make logical sense out of life's dilemmas.
Seniors	Position 9	This is how life will be. I must be wholehearted while tentative, fight for my values yet respect others, believe my deepest values right, yet be ready to learn. I see that I shall be retracing this whole journey over and over—but, I hope, more wisely.

Source: Perry, 1981, 1999.

According to one classic study (Perry, 1981, 1999), thinking progresses through nine levels of complexity over the four years that lead to a bachelor's degree, moving from a simplistic either/or dualism (right or wrong, success or failure) to a relativism that recognizes a multiplicity of perspectives (see Table 18.1).

Perry found that the college experience itself causes this progression: Peers, professors, books, and class discussion all stimulate new questions and thoughts. In general, the more years of higher education and of life experience a person has, the deeper and more dialectical that person's reasoning becomes (Pascarella & Terenzini, 1991).

Which aspect of college is the primary catalyst for such growth? Is it the challenging academic work, professors' lectures, peer discussions, the new setting, or living away from home? All are possible. Every scientist finds that social interaction and intellectual challenge advance thinking.

College students expect classes and conversations to further their thinking—which is exactly what occurs (Kuh et al., 2005). This is not surprising, since development is a dialectical process between individuals and social structures, and college is an institution dedicated to fostering cognitive growth. Teachers and students alike can achieve postformal thought because of college, as the following suggests.

Especially for Those Considering Studying Abroad Given the effects of college, would it be better for a student to study abroad in the first year or last year of a college education? (see response, page 536)

College Advancing Thought

One of the leading thinkers in adult cognition is Jan Sinnott, a professor and past editor of the *Journal of Adult Development*. She describes the first course she taught:

> I did not think in a postformal way. . . . Teaching was good for passing information from the informed to the uninformed. . . . I decided to create a course in the psychology of aging . . . with a fellow graduate student. Being compulsive graduate students had paid off in our careers so far, so my colleague and I continued on that path. Articles and books and photocopies began to take over my house. And having found all this information, we seem to have unconsciously sworn to use all of it. . . .
>
> Each class day, my colleague and I would arrive with reams of notes and articles and lecture, lecture, lecture. Rapidly! . . . The discussion of death and dying came close to the end of the term (naturally). As I gave my usual jam-packed lecture, the sound of note taking was intense. But toward the end of the class . . . an extremely capable student burst into tears and said she had to drop the class. . . . Unknown to me, she had been the caretaker

of an older relative who had just died in the past few days. She had not said anything about this significant experience when we lectured on caretaking. . . . How could she? . . . We never stopped talking. "I wish I could tell people what it's really like," she said.

> [*Sinnott, 2008, pp. 54–55*]

Sinnott changed her lesson plan. In the next class, the student told her story.

> In the end, the students agreed that this was a class when they . . . synthesized material and analyzed research and theory critically.
>
> [*Sinnott, 2008, p. 56*]

Sinnott writes that she still lectures and gives multiple-choice exams, but she also realizes the impact of the personal story. She combines analysis and emotion; she includes the personal experiences of the students. Her teaching became postformal, dialectical, and responsive.

Changes in the College Context

You probably noticed that many of the references in the previous pages are decades old. Perry's study was first published in 1981. His conclusions may no longer apply, especially because both sides of the dialectic—students and faculty—have changed, as have the institutions in which they learn. Many recent books criticize colleges. Administrators and faculty still hope for intellectual growth, but the college context is not what it was. Has cognition suffered because of it?

Changes in the Students

College is no longer for the elite few.

To improve health and increase productivity, every nation has increased the number of students enrolled in college. This growth in enrollment has led to **massification**—the idea that college could benefit everyone (the masses) (Altbach et al., 2010). The United States was the first major nation to accept that idea, establishing thousands of institutions of higher learning and boasting millions of college students by the middle of the twentieth century.

The United States no longer leads in massification, however. In some nations, more than half of all 25- to 34-year-olds are college graduates (for example, in Canada, Korea, Russia, and Japan), with at least an Associates degree. One reason for the large college population in those nations is that tuition is lower because of heavy government subsidies, as was true in former decades in the United States.

As for a Bachelor's degree earned by 25- to 34-years-olds, the United States ranks 11th among the major nations of the world (National Center for Education Statistics, 2012). The percentages are far lower in Latin America, Africa, and Asia, but the

Especially for High School Teachers One of your brightest students doesn't want to go to college. She would rather keep waitressing in a restaurant, where she makes good money in tips. What do you say? (see response, page 536)

massification The idea that establishing institutions of higher learning and encouraging college enrollment can benefit everyone (the masses).

>> Response for Those Considering Studying Abroad (from page 534):
Since one result of college is that students become more open to other perspectives while developing their commitment to their own values, foreign study might be most beneficial after several years of college. If they study abroad too early, some students might be either too narrowly patriotic (they are not yet open) or too quick to reject everything about their national heritage (they have not yet developed their own commitments).

>> Response for High School Teachers (from page 535): Even more than ability, motivation is crucial for college success, so don't insist that she attend college immediately. Since your student has money and a steady job (prime goals for today's college-bound youth), she may not realize what she would be missing. Ask her what she hopes for, in work and lifestyle, over the decades ahead.

rates of college graduation in those places have multiplied in the past few decades. In 2010, China had more college graduates than the United States (but avoid base rate neglect— the proportion of graduates in the United States is higher). Especially in the United States, background factors such as family income and ethnicity affect college enrollment and graduation (see Visualizing Development, p. 537).

Not only have the numbers increased, but so have the characteristics of the students. The most obvious change is gender: In 1970, most college students were male; now in every developed nation (except Germany) most students are female. In addition, ethnic, economic, religious, and cultural backgrounds are varied. Compared to 1970, more students are parents, are older than age 24, attend school part time, and live and work off-campus—all true worldwide.

Student experiences, histories, skills, and goals are changing as well. Most students are technologically savvy, having spent more hours using computers than watching television or reading. Personal blogs, chat rooms, Facebook pages, and YouTube videos have exploded, often unbeknownst to college staff. Dozens of new networking sites have appeared. Students spend less than one-fourth of their waking time studying or in class and much more time socializing—either face-to-face or online (Arum & Roksa, 2011).

The courses that require more reading and writing are unpopular, as are the majors—such as English or History—that require such effort. Instead, the most popular major is business, which also requires the least student effort (Arum & Roksa, 2011). Of course, majoring in business also seems most likely to lead to a secure financial future, which has become more important to current students and their parents.

The rising importance of material possessions is considered part of the "dark side of emerging adulthood," as one book describes it (Smith et al., 2012). The same seems true of adults without a college degree: Living well is defined more by financial security and having admirable possessions than by health or caring for the community (Beutler, 2012).

Changes in the Institutions

As massification increases, more colleges are available. Some nations, including China and Saudi Arabia, have recently built huge new universities. In 1955 in the United States, only 275 junior colleges existed; in 2010 there were 1,920 such colleges, now called community colleges. For-profit colleges were scarce until about 1980; in 2010 the United States had 1,216 of them.

The facilities of the institutions have also changed. Dorms are more luxurious, rooms are larger, athletic facilities more impressive. Prices have increased. For almost half of four-year colleges, tuition (not including room and board) costs more than $30,000 per year (*Chronicle of Higher Education*, 2012).

Other changes are evident. Compared with earlier decades, colleges today offer more career programs and hire more part-time faculty, more women, and more minorities. The proportion of tenured full professors who are European American males has decreased, although they still predominate partly because they earned tenure decades ago. The trend toward more non-White and part-time faculty is worldwide.

Public colleges have grown, with more than 25,000 undergraduates at *each* of 100 public universities in the United States. Private colleges still outnumber public ones by a ratio of about 3 to 2, but most U.S. college students (75 percent, or about 14 million) attend publicly-sponsored institutions. They are less expensive for students than private colleges, but no U.S. college is free. Even students on full scholarships (rare) must pay for many items, including transportation.

Income, not ability, continues to be the most significant influence on whether a particular emerging adult will attend college and, once enrolled, will graduate

Why Study?

From a life-span perspective, college graduation is a good investment, for individuals (they become healthier and wealthier) and for nations (national income rises). That long-term perspective is the main reason why nations that control enrollment, such as China, have opened dozens of new colleges in the past two decades. However, when the effort and cost of higher education depend on immediate choices made by students and families, as in the United States, many decide it is not worth it, as illustrated by the number of people who earn BAs.

EDUCATION IN THE U.S.

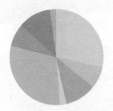   

10-year-olds in school (98.5%) **High school graduates (75%)** **Enrolled in college (52%)** **BA earned (19%)**

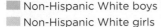 Non-Hispanic White boys   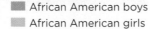 African American boys   Hispanic boys   Asian boys
Non-Hispanic White girls   African American girls   Hispanic girls   Asian girls

SOURCE: U.S. CENSUS BUREAU, 2012 AND
EDUCATION WEEK, 2013

AMONG ALL ADULTS

The percentage of U.S. residents with high school and college diplomas is increasing as more of the oldest cohort (often without degrees) dies and the youngest cohorts aim for college. However, many people are insufficiently educated and less likely to find good jobs. It is not surprising that in the recent recession, college enrollment increased. These data can be seen as encouraging or disappointing. The encouraging perspective is that rates are rising for everyone, with the only exception being associate degrees for Asian Americans, and the reason for that is itself encouraging—more of them are earning BAs. The discouraging perspective is that almost two-thirds of all adults and more than four-fifths of all Hispanics have no college degrees. International data find that many European and East Asian nations have higher rates of degree holders than the U.S.

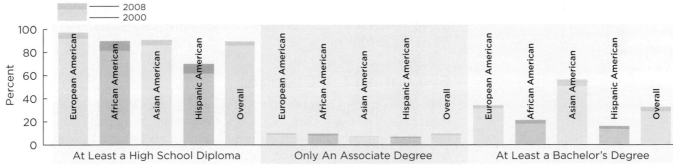

2008
2000

Percent

100
80
60
40
20
0

European American African American Asian American Hispanic American Overall

At Least a High School Diploma   Only An Associate Degree   At Least a Bachelor's Degree

SOURCE: ROBELEN, 2010.

INCOME IMPACT

Over an average of 40 years of employment, someone who completes a master's degree earns $500,000 more than someone who leaves school in eleventh grade. That translates into about $90,000 for each year of education from twelfth grade to a master's. The earnings gap is even wider than those numbers indicate because this chart includes only adults who have jobs, yet finding work is more difficult for those with less education.

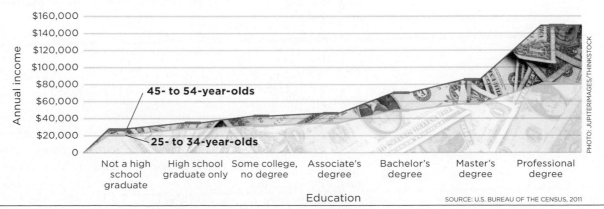

$160,000
$140,000
$120,000
$100,000
$80,000
$60,000
$40,000
$20,000
0

Annual income

45- to 54-year-olds
25- to 34-year-olds

Not a high school graduate   High school graduate only   Some college, no degree   Associate's degree   Bachelor's degree   Master's degree   Professional degree

Education

SOURCE: U.S. BUREAU OF THE CENSUS, 2011

PHOTO: JUPITERIMAGES/THINKSTOCK

SOURCES & CREDITS LISTED ON P. SC-1

Unlike Their Parents Both photos show large urban colleges in the U.S., with advantages the older college generations did not have: wireless technology (in use by all three on the left) and classmates from 50 nations (evident in the two on the right).

Observation Quiz Which is a community college? (see answer, page 539)

(Bowen et al., 2009). Non-completion is particularly high among community college students. When they enroll, 80 percent say they are likely to earn a bachelor's degree; only about 20 percent do. Access to higher education is high in the United States, but the gap between entering and graduation is huge, which is "an important alarm about the viability of college for many young people" (Settersten 2012, p. 20).

There is also a clear "mismatch between reality and expectations" for students at four-year colleges, with almost all expecting to graduate in four years but only half doing so (Pryor et al., 2012, p. 5). The chance of leaving college without a degree becomes greater as income falls, as the size of the college increases, and as other life obligations (such as employment and parenthood) accumulate (Bowen et al., 2009).

Evaluating the Changes

This situation again raises the question of what today's students get out of attending college. The major changes just described might mean that college no longer produces the "greater intellectual flexibility" that earlier research found (Pascarella & Terenzini, 1991). What do the data indicate?

All the evidence on cognition suggests that interactions with people of different backgrounds and various views lead to intellectual challenges and deeper thought, as well as more creative ideas. This occurs most easily if students themselves are bicultural, as an increasing number of United States students are, but simply working with and talking to people of various backgrounds broadens one's cognitive and cultural perspective (Nguyen & Benet-Martínez, 2013; Tadmor et al., 2012).

Thus, the increased diversity of the student body may encourage cognitive development. Colleges that make use of their diversity—through curricula, class assignments, discussions, cooperative education, learning communities, and so on—help stretch students' understanding not only of differences and similarities among people but also of themselves. Indeed, more and more faculty are moving away from the lecture format and are instead using learning methods (1) that require interaction among the students and (2) that fosters learning.

Of course, many students (and their parents) choose colleges because the student body is similar to the prospective student. Most (81 percent) U.S. freshmen attend a college in their home state. However, every college has some people who are from far away (in the U.S., 3.4 percent come from another nation).

Moreover, since each individual has unique genes and experiences, even homogeneous colleges include people with diverse opinions.

A special benefit may come from students who are parents, are employed, attend school part time, and are older than 30. They can enliven conversations and discussions with their fellow students. Some research suggests that those from the least wealthy backgrounds are most likely to benefit, financially and cognitively, from a college degree. However, they are also the most likely to leave before graduation (Bowen et al., 2009).

Two new pedagogical techniques may foster greater learning. One is called the *flipped class*, in which students are required to watch videos of a lecture on their computers before class, and then class time is used for discussion, with the professor prodding and encouraging but not lecturing. The other technique is classes that are totally online, including **massive open online courses (MOOCs)**. A student can enroll in such a class and do all the work off campus.

MOOCs are most likely to be instructive if a student is highly motivated and is adept at computer use, but it also helps if the student has another classmate, or an expert, as a personal guide: Face-to-face interaction seems to help motivation and learning (Breslow et al., 2013). The MOOC saves money and commuting time; educators disagree as to how much the typical student learns in a MOOC.

The data suggests that college still advances thinking. A valid comparison can be made with young adults who never attend college. When 18-year-old high school graduates of similar backgrounds and abilities are compared, those who begin jobs rather than higher education eventually achieve less and are less satisfied by middle age than those who earned a college degree (Hout, 2012). The benefits of college seem particularly strong for ethnic minorities or low-income families.

Even by age 24, those who attended college and postponed parenthood are more thoughtful and more secure, and seem to be better positioned for a successful adulthood. For this new stage of development—emerging adulthood—college seems to provide what is needed: a chance to postpone commitment while exploring new ideas and preparing for adulthood.

For many readers of this textbook, none of these findings are surprising. Tertiary education stimulates thought, no matter how old the student is. From first-year orientation to graduation, emerging adults do more than learn facts and skills pertaining to their majors: They learn to think deeply and reflectively, as postformal thinkers do.

Answer to Observation Quiz
(from page 538): The one with the flags is Kingsborough Community College, in Brooklyn; the one with a colonnade is UCLA (University of California in Los Angeles). If you guessed right, what clues did you use?

massive open online course (MOOC) A course that is offered solely online for college credit. Typically, tuition is very low, and thousands of students enroll.

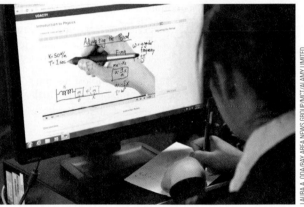

Writing on the Wall In Oakland, California, Selina Wong is learning physics online from a MOOC offered by San Jose University. The most common criticism of online courses is that they are not interactive, but, as you see, this is not always true.

SUMMING UP

Many life experiences advance thinking processes. College is one of these experiences, as years of classroom discussion, guided reading, and conversations with fellow students from diverse backgrounds lead students to develop more dynamic and dialectical reasoning. The evidence for this is solid for college education twenty years ago, but today's students and the institutions that teach them have changed. Students are more interested in jobs than philosophy, and college enrollments have increased in numbers and diversity, with women students now outnumbering men. In many nations other than the United States, an increasing number of young adults are in college, usually with substantial government subsidies. Nonetheless, despite many differences compared to decades ago, the evidence suggests that college education still promotes cognitive development. ∎

SUMMARY

Postformal Thought

1. Adult cognition can be studied in any of several ways: using a stage approach, a psychometric approach, or an information-processing approach. This chapter focuses on postformal thinking, a term used to describe adult cognitive development that may follow Piaget's four stages.

2. Many researchers believe that in adulthood the complex and conflicting demands of daily life produce a new cognitive perspective. Postformal thinking is not the automatic result of maturation, so it is not a traditional "stage," but it is a higher level of thought.

3. Postformal thought is practical, flexible, and dialectical (that is, more capable of combining contradictory elements into a comprehensive whole). Adults use their minds to solve the problems that they encounter, anticipating and deflecting difficulties.

4. One hallmark of adult thought is the ability to combine emotions and rational analysis. This ability is particularly useful in responding to social understanding and actions, because each relationship requires complex and flexible responses.

5. Stereotypes and stereotype threat interrupt thinking processes and thus can make people seem intellectually less capable. Ideally, adults find ways to overcome such liabilities.

6. Dialectical thinking synthesizes complexities and contradictions. Instead of seeking absolute, immutable truths, dialectical thought recognizes that people and situations are dynamic, ever-changing.

Morals and Religion

7. Thinking about questions of morality, faith, and ethics may also progress in adulthood. Specific moral opinions are strongly influenced by culture and context, but adults generally become less self-centered as they mature.

8. As people mature, life confronts them with ethical decisions, including many related to human relationships and the diversity of humankind. According to Fowler, religious faith also moves beyond culture-bound concepts toward universal principles.

Cognitive Growth and Higher Education

9. Research over the past several decades indicates not only that college graduates are wealthier and healthier than other adults but also that they think at a more advanced level. Over the years of college, students gradually become less inclined to seek absolute truths from authorities and more interested in making their own decisions.

10. Today's college students are unlike those of a few decades ago. In every nation, the sheer number of students has multiplied, and students' backgrounds are more diverse ethnically, economically, and in every other way.

11. Colleges as institutions have also changed, becoming larger and catering more to students who are focused on careers in business rather than on ideas and theories. In addition, enrollment in publicly funded institutions has increased. The cost of college has become a major consideration for many in the United States.

12. Students and institutions have changed, but college education still seems to benefit emerging adults, intellectually and financially. Some changes, particularly the increased diversity among students and faculty, are likely to foster deeper thinking.

KEY TERMS

antithesis (p. 525)
Defining Issues Test (DIT) (p. 530)
delay discounting (p. 519)
dialectical thought (p. 525)
massification (p. 535)
massive open online course (MOOC) (p. 539)
morality of care (p. 530)
morality of justice (p. 530)
objective thought (p. 521)
postformal thought (p. 518)
stereotype threat (p. 524)
subjective thought (p. 521)
synthesis (p. 525)
thesis (p. 525)

WHAT HAVE YOU LEARNED?

1. Why did scholars choose the term *postformal* to describe the fifth stage of cognition?

2. How does postformal thinking differ from typical adolescent thought?

3. Why is time management a cognitive issue?

4. How does delay discounting relate to eating or exercising?

5. How does the maturation of the prefrontal cortex affect social understanding?

6. What is the relationship between subjective and objective thought?

7. How does listening to opposing opinions demonstrate cognitive flexibility?

8. How could stereotype threat affect a person's cognition?

9. Which groups of people are vulnerable to stereotype threat and why?

10. Why does the term "broken home" indicate a lack of dialectical thought?

11. What differences are apparent in characteristically Asian and Western thinking?

12. Why do adults make more decisions involving morality than adolescents do?

13. Why do people disagree about whether or not something is a moral issue?

14. How does Carol Gilligan differentiate between male and female morality?

15. Why would decisions about reproduction be a catalyst for moral thought?

16. How are Fowler's stages similar to Piaget's and Kohlberg's stages?

17. Why might a devout person criticize Fowler's concept of the stages of faith?

18. What do most students hope to gain from a college education?

19. According to Perry, what changes occur in students' thinking during their college career?

20. How do current college enrollment patterns differ from those of 50 years ago?

21. How do public and private colleges differ in the United States?

APPLICATIONS

1. Read a biography or autobiography that includes information about the person's thinking from age 18 to 60, paying particular attention to practical, flexible, or dialectical thought. How did personal experiences, education, and ideas affect the person's thinking?

2. Some ethical principles are thought to be universal, respected by people of every culture. Think of one such idea and analyze whether it is accepted by each of the world's major religions.

3. Statistics on changes in students and in colleges are fascinating, but only a few are reported here. Compare your nation, state, or province with another. Analyze the data and discuss causes and implications of differences.

4. One way to assess cognitive development during college is to study yourself or your classmates, comparing thoughts and decisions at the beginning and end of college. Since case studies are provocative but not definitive, identify some hypotheses that you might examine and explain how you would do so.

>>ONLINE CONNECTIONS

To accompany your textbook, you have access to a number of online resources, including Learning Curve, an adaptive quizzing program, critical thinking questions, and case studies. For access to any of these links, go to www.worth publishers.com/launchpad/bergerls9e. In addition to these resources, you'll also find links to video clips, personalized study advice, and an ebook. Some of the videos and activities available online include:

■ *Characteristics of Formal Thought.* Emerging adults are thinking more analytically. Activities and video clips demonstrate some of the hallmarks of formal and postformal thought.

WORTH PUBLISHERS

19
CHAPTER

Emerging Adulthood: Psychosocial Development

WHAT WILL YOU KNOW?

1. What typically happens to a shy child's temperament when he or she grows up?

2. Does cohabitation before marriage make a marriage happier?

3. In cases of spouse abuse, is it better for partners to be counseled or to separate?

4. Why do some emerging adults live with their parents?

- ■ **Continuity and Change**
  Identity Achieved
  Personality in Emerging Adulthood

- ■ **Intimacy**
  Friendship
  The Dimensions of Love
  OPPOSING PERSPECTIVES: Cohabitation
  A CASE TO STUDY: My Daughters and Me
  What Makes Relationships Succeed?
  Conflict

- ■ **Emerging Adults and Their Parents**
  Linked Lives
  Financial Support

Looking back, I now see many signs of emerging adulthood in my life. When I was 20, Phoebe and Peggy were my two closest friends. As both our parents and culture expected, we anticipated becoming happy brides, wives, and mothers, even describing our wedding dresses to each other and naming our imagined children. Our anticipations were dashed by social change.

As adults the three of us had three husbands and five children—collectively, about average for our culture and cohort. But Phoebe never married or gave birth. She started her own business and became a millionaire who now owns a house near the Pacific Ocean. Peggy married, divorced, remarried, and had one child at age 40. She earned a Ph.D. and, after many academic jobs, finally found the work she loves, as a massage therapist. I married and gave birth while working and learning, a new pattern for my generation. Another woman, a stranger I met at a party, on hearing that I had four children, asked incredulously, "All from the same husband?" Yes, an odd path, part traditional (my grandmother had 12 children) and part modern (all my daughters are full-time, salaried workers).

The culture shifted just when we became adults; none of us did what was expected when we were girls. Years ago, adults used to check their developmental timing using the **social clock**, a timetable based on social norms. These norms set "best" ages for people to finish school, marry, start a career, and have children.

Ten years ago, I complained to Phoebe that, even though they were all past age 20, none of my four grown daughters were wives or mothers. She smiled, put her hand on mine, and said, "Please notice. I never married or had children. Yet I am happy." So is Peggy. So am I. As the researchers now are learning, emerging adults do not necessarily marry, secure lifelong careers, or become parents, but that does not mean their lives will be sad and lonely. Far from it.

social clock A timetable based on social norms for accomplishing certain life events such as when to finish school, marry, start a career, have children, and retire.

>> Continuity and Change

A theme of human development is that continuity and change are evident throughout life. In emerging adulthood, the legacy of childhood is apparent amidst new achievement. Erikson recognized this in his description of the fifth of his eight stages, identity versus role confusion. As you remember, the identity crisis begins in adolescence, but it is not usually resolved until adulthood.

Left: © Exotica im/PhotosIndia.com Pvt. Ltd./age fotostock, Inc.
Top: Lane Oatey/Blue Jean Images/Getty Images

543

TABLE 19.1	Erikson's Eight Stages of Development	
Stage	Virtue/Pathology	Possible in Emerging Adulthood If Not Successfully Resolved
Trust vs. mistrust	Hope / withdrawal	Suspicious of others, making close relationships difficult
Autonomy vs. shame and doubt	Will / compulsion	Obsessively driven, single-minded, not socially responsive
Initiative vs. guilt	Purpose / inhibition	Fearful, regretful (e.g., very homesick in college)
Industry vs. inferiority	Competence / inertia	Self-critical of any endeavor, procrastinating, perfectionistic
Identity vs. role confusion	Fidelity / repudiation	Uncertain and negative about values, lifestyle, friendships
Intimacy vs. isolation	Love / exclusivity	Anxious about close relationships, jealous, lonely
Generativity vs. stagnation	Care / rejection	[In the future] Fear of failure
Integrity vs. despair	Wisdom / disdain	[In the future] No "mindfulness," no life plan

Source: Erikson, 1982.

Past as Prologue In elaborating his eight stages of development, Erikson associated each stage with a particular virtue and a type of psychopathology, as shown here. He also thought that earlier crises could reemerge, taking a specific form at each stage. Listed are some possible problems (not directly from Erikson) that could occur in emerging adulthood if earlier crises were not resolved.

Just Like Me Emerging adults of every ethnicity take pride in their culture. In Japan, adulthood begins with a celebration at age 20, to the evident joy of these young women on Coming of Age Day, a national holiday.

Identity Achieved

Erikson believed that the outcome of earlier crises provides the foundation of each new stage. The identity crisis is an example (see Table 19.1). Worldwide, emerging adults ponder all four arenas of identity—religious commitments, gender roles, political loyalties, and career options—trying to reconcile plans for the future with beliefs acquired in the past.

As explained in Chapter 16, the identity crisis sometimes causes confusion or foreclosure. A more mature response is to seek a moratorium, postponing identity achievement while exploring possibilities. For instance, earning a college degree is a socially acceptable way to delay marriage and parenthood.

Societies offer many other moratoria: the military, religious mission work, apprenticeships, and various internships in government, academe, and industry. These reduce the pressure to achieve identity, offering a ready rejoinder to an older relative who urges settling down (see Visualizing Development, p. 545).

Emerging adults in moratoria do what is required (as student, soldier, missionary, or whatever), which explains why a moratorium is considered more mature than role confusion. However, they also postpone identity achievement. This respite gives emerging adults some time to achieve in the two arenas that are particularly difficult in current times—political/ethnic identity and vocational identity.

Cultural Identity

As you remember from Chapter 16, aspects of identity change as the historical context changes, even as the search for self determination continues. One expert explains "identity development . . . from the teenage years to the early 20s, if not through adulthood, . . . has been extended to explain the development of ethnic and racial identity" (Whitbourne et al., 2009, p. 1328). Ethnic identity includes Erikson's political and religious identities, both crucial in our modern multiethnic world.

Ethnic identity becomes pivotal when the young person prepares for adulthood. For example, high school senior Natasha Scott "just realized that my race is something I have to think about" (Saulny & Steinberg, 2011, p. A-1). Her mother is Asian and her father is African American, which was not an issue as she was growing up. However, college applications (and the U.S. Census) require people to make choices regarding ethnic identity.

Marital Status in the United States

Adults seek committed partners, but do not always find them—age, cohort, and culture are always influential. Some choose to avoid marriage, more commonly in northern Europe and less commonly in North Africa than in the United States. As you see, in 2010, U.S. emerging adults were unlikely to marry, middle-aged adults had the highest rates of separation or divorce, and widows often chose to stay alone while widowers often remarried.

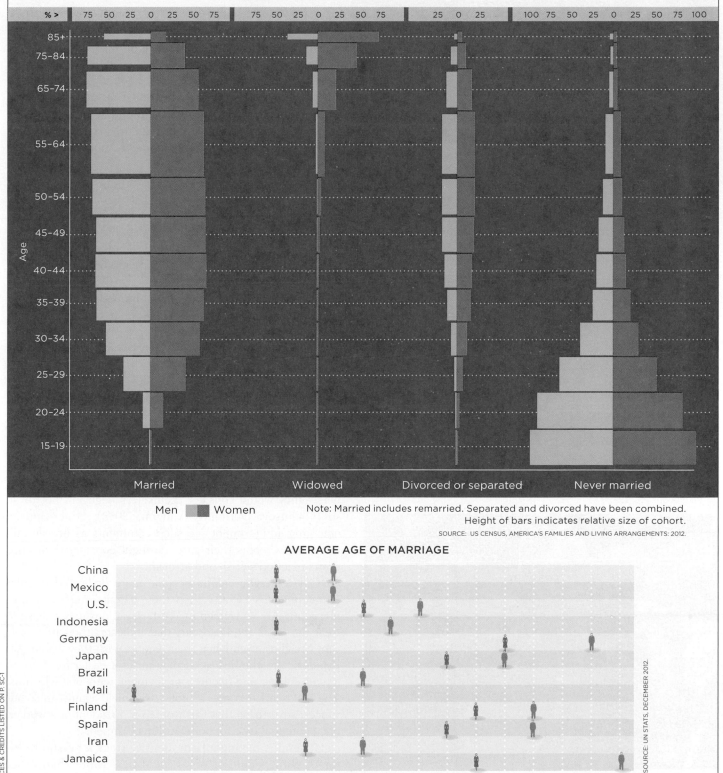

MARITAL STATUS IN THE UNITED STATES

Men ■ Women — Note: Married includes remarried. Separated and divorced have been combined. Height of bars indicates relative size of cohort.

SOURCE: US CENSUS, AMERICA'S FAMILIES AND LIVING ARRANGEMENTS: 2012.

AVERAGE AGE OF MARRIAGE

SOURCE: UN STATS, DECEMBER 2012.

SOURCES & CREDITS LISTED ON P. SC-1

One of Many Combining tradition and adventure, as these Boston tourists from the United Arab Emirates do, is the task for many emerging adults.

Confused Identity? Bruno chose Mars as his last name because "I'm out of this world." It represents an inspired combination of his parents' ethnicities: Filipino, Hungarian, Ukrainian, and Puerto Rican. His music is rock, rap, soul, R & B, and hip-hop, a mixture that made him a global superstar.

Natasha is not alone. In the United States and Canada, almost half of 18- to 25-year-olds are of African, Asian, Latino, or Native American (or, in Canada, First Nations) heritage. Many of them identify as Americans or Canadians and also as something else, as they have ancestors of more than one ethnic group.

For an increasing number of emerging adults, those diverse ancestors are their parents. Intermarriage (between adults from diverse racial groups) in the United States was less than 7 percent in 1980, more than 15 percent in 2010 (Wang, 2012). Their children are typically proudly bicultural. Beyond that are millions of other emerging adults whose heritage includes more than one nation. Bicultural identity correlates with healthy psychosocial development, not the opposite (Nguyen & Benet-Martínez, 2013).

No matter what their background is, college students who explore their ethnic identity experience less anger and anxiety, although, as is true of every other aspect of identity, some people become stuck trying to figure out what it means to be themselves (Richie et al., 2013). One study found that Hispanic college students who resisted both assimilation and alienation fared best: They were most likely to maintain their ethnic identity, deflect stereotype threat, and become good students (Rivas-Drake & Mooney, 2009).

Young adults whose parents were immigrants have an immediate challenge—they must reconcile their heritage with their new social context. Conflicts arise not only in choosing a vocation or partner (an issue for every emerging adult) but also in making a more basic choice: between family loyalty and personal autonomy. Parents expect their children to be proud of their ethnic roots—and many are—but peers expect them to make independent choices. They encounter attitudes from the native-born that make them reexamine themselves (Rodriguez et al., 2010).

One example is whether or not young adults listen to their parents' advice. In mainstream American culture, unsolicited parental advice is not welcome. Yet among many cultures (including some American subcultures) family members offer opinions about everything from clothing styles to marriage partners—they would consider themselves negligent not to do so (Chentsova-Dutton & Vaughn, 2012). Americanized emerging adults might see such comments as hostile and intrusive, whereas their parents might consider their children's reaction selfish and arrogant.

Some emerging adults become more dedicated to their ethnic/religious identity than their parents are. For example, young Arabic women in Western nations may choose to wear the *hijab*, the headscarf that indicates they are observant Muslims, even when their parents wish they would not. Paradoxically, the headscarf may make it easier for them to attend college and secure employment with non-Muslims. The headscarf becomes a protective shield against male advances, advertising that this woman is a student or a worker, not a potential date for non-Muslims (Ahmed, 2011).

Generally, having a firm identity frees a person to interact with people of other identities. More than other age groups, emerging adults tend to have friends and acquaintances of many backgrounds. As they do so, they become more aware of history, customs, and prejudices. Many refuse to limit themselves to one ethnicity, one culture, one nation: Some defiantly write "human" when a questionnaire asks, "Race?"

As emerging adults undergo cognitive development, many of them strive to combine objective and subjective identity: They take courses in history, ethnic studies, and sociology, and they also seek close friends, lovers, and affinity groups whose identity struggles are similar to their own. Emerging adults strive to combine academic and personal connections in their ethnic identity, similar to their struggle to achieve sexual identity, as described in Chapter 16.

Vocational Identity

Establishing a vocational identity is considered part of growing up, not only by developmental psychologists influenced by Erikson but also by emerging adults themselves. Many go to college to prepare for a good job. Emerging adulthood is a "critical stage for the acquisition of resources"—including the education, skills, and experience needed for lifelong family and career success (Tanner et al., 2009, p. 34) (see Table 19.2).

Unfortunately, achieving vocational identity is more difficult than ever. Children tend to want work that fewer than one in a million of them will ever obtain—rock star, sports hero, U.S. president—and adults often encourage such fantasies. By emerging adulthood, however, more practical concerns arise, as they seek to determine what employment is actually available and how enjoyable, remunerative, and demanding it is.

For such practical concerns, adults are of little help. Parents usually know only their particular work, not what labor-market projections in the next decade will be. High school guidance counselors in the United States have an *average* caseload of 367 students a year, many of whom want to apply to a dozen colleges as well as some who need time-consuming emotional support to prevent violence, suicide, or drug addiction (The College Board, 2012).

Counselors often have neither the time nor the expertise to offer vocational guidance (Zehr, 2011). College counselors may be more skillful than their high school counterparts, but many are overwhelmed by the need to counsel students with serious emotional problems, as detailed in Chapter 17.

Thus many emerging adults contemplating future careers are left on their own. John Holland's description (1997) of six possible interests (see Figure 19.1, p. 548) offers some help to these students. Unfortunately, however, even if they know what they want and they earn their degree, many are unable to find the work they want. This has been particularly true since the economic downturn that began in 2008: Emerging adults are the age group with the highest rate of unemployment (Draut & Rueschin, 2013).

Today's job market has made development of vocational identity particularly difficult for emerging adults. A life-span perspective suggests that young adults may still be affected when the financial picture improves (M. K. Johnson et al., 2011). The experiences, habits, and fears of early adulthood are not easily forgotten.

Many young people take a series of temporary jobs. Between ages 18 and 25, the average U.S. worker has held six jobs, with the college-educated changing jobs even more than average (U.S. Bureau of Labor Statistics, 2012). Part of this change occurs because many college students have summer jobs—a different one

TABLE 19.2	Top Six "Very Important" Objectives in Life*
Being well off financially	78%
Raising a family	75%
Making more money	71%
Helping others	69%
Becoming an authority in my field	59%
Obtaining recognition in my special field	56%

*Based on a national survey of students entering four-year colleges in the United States in the fall of 2010.
Source: Chronicle of Higher Education, 2010.

Look Again This research was already mentioned in Chapter 18, but now compare the cited objectives to the reality of the job market. Contemporary emerging adults are finding it difficult to achieve vocational identity. If projections prove accurate, many of them will not consider themselves "well-off financially."

Ordinary Workers Most children and adolescents want to be sports heroes, entertainment stars, billionaires, or world leaders—yet fewer than one in 1 million succeed in doing so.

FIGURE 19.1

Happy at Work John Holland's six-part diagram helps job seekers realize that income and benefits are not the only goals of employment. Workers have healthier hearts and minds if their job fits their personal preferences.

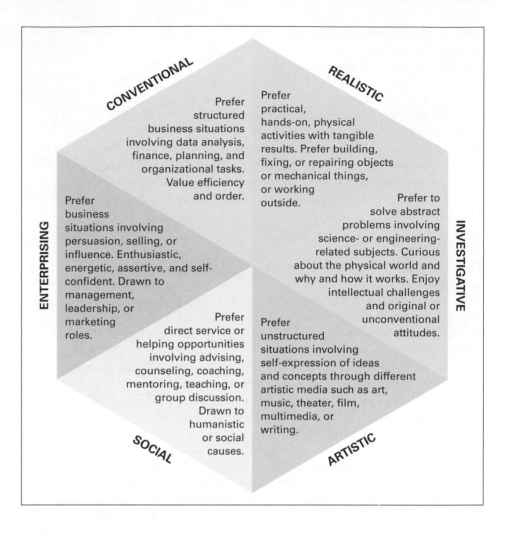

CONVENTIONAL
Prefer structured business situations involving data analysis, finance, planning, and organizational tasks. Value efficiency and order.

REALISTIC
Prefer practical, hands-on, physical activities with tangible results. Prefer building, fixing, or repairing objects or mechanical things, or working outside.

ENTERPRISING
Prefer business situations involving persuasion, selling, or influence. Enthusiastic, energetic, assertive, and self-confident. Drawn to management, leadership, or marketing roles.

INVESTIGATIVE
Prefer to solve abstract problems involving science- or engineering-related subjects. Curious about the physical world and why and how it works. Enjoy intellectual challenges and original or unconventional attitudes.

SOCIAL
Prefer direct service or helping opportunities involving advising, counseling, coaching, mentoring, teaching, or group discussion. Drawn to humanistic or social causes.

ARTISTIC
Prefer unstructured situations involving self-expression of ideas and concepts through different artistic media such as art, music, theater, film, multimedia, or writing.

Same Situation, Far Apart: Connecting with Their Generation Neither of these young women considers her job a vocation, but both use skills and knowledge that few older adults have. The DJ *(left)* mixes music for emerging adults who crowd thousands of clubs in China to drink, dance, and socialize despite regulations that attempt to close down such establishments. More than 10,000 Apple Store "geniuses" *(right)* work at low pay to meet the booming young-adult demand for the latest social networking tools.

each summer. Beyond that, however, emerging adults do not yet seek to climb, rung by rung, a career ladder: They would rather try various kinds of work. For them "the process of identifying with society's work ethic, the core of this issue [identity achievement] in Erikson's scheme, continues to evolve throughout early adulthood" (Whitbourne et al., 2009, p. 1329).

Personality in Emerging Adulthood

Continuity and change are evident in personality as well (McAdams & Olson, 2010). Of course, personality is shaped lifelong by genes and early experiences:

If self-doubt, anxiety, depression, and so on are present in adolescence, they are typically evident years later. Traits present at age 18 rarely disappear by age 25.

Yet personality is not static. After adolescence, new personality dimensions may appear. As the preceding two chapters emphasize, emerging adults make choices that break with the past. Unlike youth in previous generations, contemporary youth are more likely to pursue higher education and postpone marriage and parenthood. Their freedom from a settled lifestyle allows shifts in attitude and personality.

Many researchers study what factors lead a young adult to thrive in secondary and tertiary education. Background and genes are influential, but so is personality. Not only is success in school affected *by* personality but it also *affects* personality (Klimstra et al., 2012). In other words, college success can change personality traits for the better.

Rising Self-Esteem

One team of researchers traced the experiences of 3,912 U.S. high school seniors until age 23 or 24. Generally, chosen transitions (entering college, starting a job, getting married) increased well-being. In the United States, those who lived away from home in college showed the largest gains, and those who had become single parents or who still lived with their own parents showed the least. Even the latter, however, tended to be happier than they had been in high school (see Figure 19.2) (Schulenberg et al., 2005).

Some increasing happiness may be part of becoming more adult: Young adults in western Canada, repeatedly questioned from ages 18 to 25, reported increasing self-esteem (Galambos et al., 2006), as did German emerging adults (Wagner et al., 2013).

Logically, the many stresses and transitions of emerging adulthood might be expected to reduce self-esteem. However, only a minority experienced a decline in self-esteem during these years (Nelson & Padilla-Walker, 2013). As detailed in Chapter 17, some emerging adults develop serious psychological disorders (Twenge et al., 2010), but most do not.

Worrisome Children Grow Up

Shifts toward positive development were also found in another longitudinal study that began with 4-year-olds who were at the extremes of either of the two traits known to have strong genetic roots: extreme shyness and marked aggression. Those two traits continued to be evident throughout childhood. But by emerging adulthood many of these children had changed for the better (Asendorpf et al., 2008).

This is not to say that old patterns disappeared. For example, those who had been aggressive 4-year-olds continued to have conflicts with their parents and friends. They were more likely to quit school and leave jobs before age 25. Half had been arrested at least once, another sign of their unusually aggressive personalities.

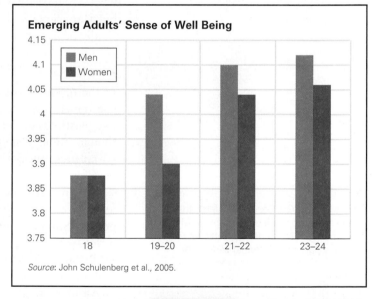

Emerging Adults' Sense of Well Being

Source: John Schulenberg et al., 2005.

FIGURE 19.2

Worthy People This graph shows a steady, although small, rise in young adults' sense of well-being from age 18 to age 24, as measured by respondents' ratings of statements such as "I feel I am a person of worth." The ratings ranged from 1 (complete disagreement) to 5 (complete agreement). The average rating was actually quite high at age 18, and it increased steadily over the years of emerging adulthood.

Source: Schulenberg et al., 2005, p. 424.

Yet, unexpectedly, these aggressive young adults had as many friends as their average peers did. They wanted more education than they already had, and their self-rating on conscientiousness was at least equal to the self-ratings of a control group who had been less aggressive as children. Their arrests were usually for minor offenses, typically adolescent-limited, not life-course-persistent. As emerging adults, most seemed to be developing well, controlling their anger and putting their childhood problems behind them. [**Lifespan Link:** Adolescence-limited and life-course-persistent offenders are discussed in Chapter 16.]

As for the emerging adults who had been shy, they were "cautious, reserved adults" (Asendorpf et al., 2008, p. 1007), slower than average to secure a job, choose a career, or find a romance (at age 23, two-thirds had no current partner). However, they were no more anxious or depressed than others of their cohort, and their self-esteem was *not* low. They had many friends, whom they saw often. Their delayed employment and later marriage were accepted, even envied, by their peers. The personality trait (shyness) that was a handicap in childhood had become an asset.

A major reason for the increasing self-esteem of many emerging adults is that they are able to set their own goals, make their own friends, and work toward whatever goals they seek. They are no longer the actors in someone else's drama but the agents and authors of their own lives, which is what young adults can finally be as they break away from earlier limits (McAdams, 2013).

Plasticity

In the research just discussed and in other research as well, plasticity (which, as you remember, refers to the idea that development is both moldable and durable, like plastic) is evident. Personality is not fixed by age 5, or 15, or 20, as it was once thought to be. Emerging adults are open to new experiences (a reflection of their adventuresome spirit), an attitude that allows personality shifts as well as eagerness for more education (McAdams & Olson, 2010; Tanner et al., 2009).

Clearly, genes do not determine behavior, but they do make a person more or less susceptible to environmental forces. Some genes have been called **plasticity genes** (Simons et al., 2013). A person who inherits them is affected, for better or for worse, by going to college, leaving home, becoming independent, stopping drug abuse, moving to a new city, finding satisfying work and performing it well, making new friends, committing to a partner.

Although total change does not occur, since genes, childhood experiences, and family circumstances affect people lifelong, personality can shift in adulthood. Increased well-being may underlie another shift: Emerging adults become less self-centered and more caring of others (Eisenberg et al., 2005, Padilla Walker et al., 2008). This can be the foundation of the next psychosocial stage of development, which we now discuss.

plasticity genes Genes and alleles that make people more susceptible to environmental influences, for better or worse. This is part of differential sensitivity.

SUMMING UP

The identity crisis continues in emerging adulthood as young people seek to establish and follow their own unique path. Achieving ethnic identity is important but difficult, especially for those who realize they are a minority within their nation. Vocational identity is also an ongoing search. Most emerging adults hold many jobs between the ages of 18 and 25, but few feel they have established a career identity. Personality traits endure lifelong, partly because genes and early childhood are influential, but emerging adults modify some traits and develop others.

∎

>> Intimacy

In Erikson's theory, after achieving identity, people experience the crisis of **intimacy versus isolation.** This crisis arises from the powerful desire to share one's personal life with someone else. Without intimacy, adults suffer from loneliness. Erikson explains:

> The young adult, emerging from the search for and the insistence on identity, is eager and willing to fuse his identity with others. He is ready for intimacy, that is, the capacity to commit himself to concrete affiliations and partnerships and to develop the ethical strength to abide by such commitments, even though they call for significant sacrifices and compromises.
>
> *[Erikson, 1963, p. 263]*

As will be explained in Chapter 22, other theorists have different words for the same human need: *affiliation, affection, interdependence, communion, belonging, love.* All agree that adults seek to become friends, lovers, companions, and partners, with the "significant sacrifices and compromises" that entails. The urge for social connection is a powerful human impulse, one reason our species has thrived.

All intimate relationships have much in common—not only in the psychic needs they satisfy but also in the behaviors they require. Intimacy progresses from attraction, to close connection, to ongoing commitment. Each relationship demands some personal sacrifice, including vulnerability that brings deeper self-understanding and shatters the isolation of too much self-protection. To establish intimacy, the young adult must

> face the fear of ego loss in situations which call for self-abandon: in the solidarity of close affiliations [and] sexual unions, in close friendship and in physical combat, in experiences of inspiration by teachers and of intuition from the recesses of the self. The avoidance of such experiences . . . may lead to a deep sense of isolation and consequent self-absorption.
>
> *[Erikson, 1963, pp. 163–164]*

intimacy versus isolation The sixth of Erikson's eight stages of development. Adults seek someone with whom to share their lives in an enduring and self-sacrificing commitment. Without such commitment, they risk profound aloneness and isolation.

Friendship

According to a more recent theory, an important aspect of close human connections is *self-expansion*—that each of us enlarges our understanding, experiences, and resources through our intimate friends and lovers (Aron et al., 2005).

Whether or not friends expand our minds, it is certain that friends strengthen our mental and physical health (Seyfarth & Cheney, 2012). Unlike relatives, friends are chosen (not inherited). Friends seek understanding, tolerance, loyalty, affection, humor from one another—all qualities that make friends trustworthy, supportive, and enjoyable.

Friends in Emerging Adulthood

Friendships "reach their peak of functional significance during emerging adulthood" (Tanner & Arnett, 2011, p. 27). Since fewer emerging adults have the family obligations that come with spouses, children, or frail parents, their friends provide needed companionship and critical support.

Friends comfort each other when romance turns sour, and they share experiences and information about everything from what college to attend to what socks to wear. One crucial question for emerging adults is what and how to tell parents news that might upset them: Friends help with that, too.

People tend to make more friends during emerging adulthood than at any later period, and they rely on them. They often use social media to extend and deepen friendships that begin face to face, becoming more aware of the day-to-day tribulations of their friends (Burstein, 2013). Fears that increasing Internet use would diminish the number or quality of friendships have been proven to be false. If anything, heavy Internet users tend to have more face-to-face friends than do nonusers (Wang & Wellman, 2010).

Gender and Friendship

It is a mistake to imagine that men and women have opposite friendship needs. All humans seek intimacy, throughout their lives. Claiming that men are from Mars and women are from Venus ignores reality: People are from Earth (Hyde, 2007).

Nonetheless, for cultural and biological reasons, some sex differences can be found. Men tend to share activities and interests, and they talk about external matters—sports, work, politics, cars. They are less likely to tell other men of their failures, emotional problems, and relationship dilemmas; if they do, they expect practical advice, not sympathy.

A meta-analysis of 37 studies found some sex differences in friendship (Hall, 2011). Women's friendships are typically more intimate and emotional. Women expect to share secrets with their friends and engage in self-disclosing talk, including difficulties with their health, romances, and relatives. Women reveal their weaknesses and problems and receive an attentive and sympathetic ear, a shoulder to cry on.

By contrast, men are less likely to touch each other except in aggressive activities, such as competitive athletics or military combat. The butt-slapping or body-slamming immediately after a sports victory, or the sobbing in a buddy's arms in the aftermath of a battlefield loss, are less likely in everyday life. By contrast, many women routinely hug friends in greeting or farewell.

Lest this discussion seem to imply that female friendships are better because they are closer, research finds that men are more tolerant; they demand less from their friendships than women do, and thus they have more friends (Benenson et al., 2011). One specific detail from college dormitories is revealing: When strangers of the same sex are assigned as roommates (as occurs for first-year students at residential colleges), more women than men request a change (Benenson et al., 2009).

Male–Female Friendships

As already noted, these gender differences may be cultural, not biological, and are changing. One sign of such changes is the frequency of male–female friendships—they are no longer rare (Lewis et al., 2011).

Cross-sex friendships are not usually preludes to romance. In fact, physical attraction to one's other-sex friend is more often considered a problem than an asset (Bleske-Rechek et al., 2011). Male–female friendships are less common for people at the extremes of gender identity (the very feminine girl or super-masculine boy), perhaps because it is more difficult for them to keep the relationship platonic (Lenton & Webber, 2006). When women want advice about a dating relationship,

Not Unisex Sex roles are less rigid worldwide: College men have close male friends and college women play basketball. Noticing such changes makes it harder to see gender differences that remain. Imagine eight women playing pick-up basketball, as these Maryland men do, or four men sharing a secret as these Jordanian women do.

JONATHAN NEWTON/THE WASHINGTON POST VIA GETTY IMAGES

JODI COBB/NATIONAL GEOGRAPHIC/GETTY IMAGES

they are more likely to turn to a male friend, especially a gay man, than they are to another woman or to a straight man (Russell et al., 2013).

Problems arise if outsiders assume that every male–female relationship is sexual. For this reason, when heterosexual couples are romantically committed to each other, they tend to have fewer cross-sex friendships in order to avoid partner jealousy (S. Williams, 2005). Keeping a relationship "just friendly" may be difficult, and, if it becomes sexual, romance with a third person is almost impossible to sustain (Bleske-Rechek et al., 2012).

Humans apparently find it difficult to sustain more than one sexual/romantic relationship at a time. Indeed, even in nations where polygamy is accepted, 90 percent of husbands have only one wife (Georgas et al., 2006). A study of couples in Kenya, where polygamy is legal, found that actual or suspected sexual infidelity was the most common reason for breaking up (Clark et al., 2010), and a study in the United States found that emerging adults thought sexual fidelity was crucial for a good, enduring relationship (Meier et al., 2009).

The Dimensions of Love

"Love" itself has many manifestations. In a classic analysis, Robert Sternberg (1988) described three distinct aspects of love: passion, intimacy, and commitment. The presence or absence of these three gives rise to seven different forms of love (see Table 19.3).

Early in a relationship, *passion* is evident in "falling in love," an intense physical, cognitive, and emotional onslaught characterized by excitement, ecstasy, and euphoria. The entire body and mind, hormones and neurons, are activated (Aron, 2010). Such moonstruck joy can become bittersweet as intimacy and commitment increase. As one observer explains, "Falling in love is absolutely no way of getting to know someone" (Sullivan, 1999, p. 225).

Intimacy is knowing someone well, sharing secrets as well as sex. This aspect of a romance is reciprocal, with each partner gradually revealing more of himself or herself as well as accepting more of the other's revelations.

The research is not clear about the best schedule for passion and intimacy, whether they should progress slowly or quickly, for instance. According to some research, they are not always connected, as lust arises from a different part of the brain than affection (Langeslag et al., 2013).

Commitment takes time and effort, at least for those who follow the current Western pattern of love and marriage. It grows through decisions to be together, mutual caregiving, shared possessions, and forgiveness (Schoebi et al., 2012). Social forces strengthen or undermine commitment; that's why in-laws are often the topic of jokes and arguments, and why a spouse might be unhappy with their mate's close friends.

Commitment is also affected by the culture. In fact, when cultures endorse arranged marriages, commitment occurs early on, before passion or intimacy (Georgas et al., 2006). Having friends and acquaintances who do, or do not, endorse the value of committed relationship affects each couple.

For example, in Sweden couples who lived in detached houses (with yards between them) broke up more often than did couples living in attached dwellings (such as apartments). Perhaps "single-family housing might have deleterious effects on couple stability due to the isolating lack of social support for couples staying together" (Lauster, 2008, p. 901). In other words, suburban couples may be too far from their neighbors to receive helpful advice when conflicts arise.

>> Especially for Young Men Why would you want at least one close friend who is a woman? (see response, page 554)

TABLE 19.3	Sternberg's Seven Forms of Love		
	Present in the Relationship?		
Form of Love	Passion	Intimacy	Commitment
Liking	No	Yes	No
Infatuation	Yes	No	No
Empty love	No	No	Yes
Romantic love	Yes	Yes	No
Fatuous love	Yes	No	Yes
Companionate love	No	Yes	Yes
Consummate love	Yes	Yes	Yes

Source: Sternberg, 1988.

>> **Response for Young Men** (from page 553): Not for sex! Women friends are particularly responsive to deep conversations about family relationships, personal weaknesses, and emotional confusion. But women friends might be offended by sexual advances, bragging, or advice giving. Save these for a future romance.

When children are born, passion seems to fade for both partners, but commitment increases. This may be one reason why most sexually active young adults try to avoid pregnancy unless they believe their partner is a lifelong mate. [**Lifespan Link:** The relationship of parenthood to marital satisfaction is discussed in Chapter 22.]

The Ideal and the Real

In Europe in the Middle Ages, love, passion, and marriage were considered to be distinct phenomena, with "courtly love" disconnected from romance, which was also distinct from lifelong commitment (Singer, 2009). Currently, however, the Western ideal of consummate love includes all three components: passion, intimacy, and commitment.

For developmental reasons, this ideal is difficult to achieve. Passion seems to be sparked by unfamiliarity, uncertainty, and risk, all of which are diminished by the familiarity and security that contribute to intimacy and by the time needed for commitment.

In short, with time, passion may fade, intimacy may grow and stabilize, and commitment may develop. This pattern occurs for all types of couples—married, unmarried, and remarried; gay, lesbian, and straight; young, middle-aged, and old; in arranged, guided, and self-initiated relationships.

Emerging adults refer to "friends with benefits," implying that sexual passion is less significant (an extra benefit, not the core attraction) than the friendship. As with other friendships, shared confidences and loyalty are the important parts of the relationship, with sexual interactions almost an afterthought. To use Sternberg's triadic theory, the relationship is intimate but not passionate.

However, if a friendship becomes sexual, complications arise (Owen & Fincham, 2011). Once the hormones of sexual intimacy are activated, people may become more emotionally involved than they expected. Such involvement may be more welcomed than feared. Young adults who add sex to a friendship may hope for romance (Mongeau et al., 2011).

Hookups Without Commitment

hookup A sexual encounter between two people who are not in a romantic relationship. Neither intimacy nor commitment is expected.

A sexual relationship that is not intended to become a romance, with no true intimacy or commitment, is a **hookup**. When this relationship occurred in prior generations, it was either prostitution or illicit, as in a "fling" or a "dirty secret." No longer. It is estimated that about half of all emerging adults have hooked up. Hookups often involve intercourse but not necessarily: The crucial factor is that sexual interaction of some sort occurs between partners who do not know each other well, perhaps having met just a few hours before.

Hookups are more common among first-year college students than among those about to graduate, perhaps because older students want partners, and, as one put it, "if you hook up with someone it probably is just a hookup and nothing is going to come of it" (quoted in Bogle, 2008, p. 38). People who are lonely are more likely to hook up, which may be more common for students new to a college (Owen et al., 2011).

The desire for physical intimacy without emotional commitment is stronger in young men than in young women, either for hormonal (testosterone) or cultural (women want committed fathers if children are born) reasons. One sociologist writes:

> While women are preparing for adult life, guys are in a holding pattern. They're hooking up rather than forming the kind of intimate romantic relationships that will ready them for a serious commitment; taking their time choosing careers that will enable them to support a family; and postponing marriage, it seems, for as long as they possibly can.
>
> [Kimmel, 2008, p. 259]

As contraception, employment, and college education have changed women's lives, this "guy" pattern includes more females. Nonetheless, by age 25, more women than men have married (44 percent compared to 31 percent) (Copen et al., 2012). Interestingly, emerging adults of both sexes who want a serious relationship with someone state that they are less likely to hook up with them, preferring to get to know them first.

Finding Each Other and Living Together

One major innovation of the current cohort of emerging adults is the use of social networks, as the online connections between dozens or hundreds of people are called. Almost all (83 percent) U.S. 18- to 29-year-olds use social networking sites to keep in contact (Duggan, Maeve, & Brenner, 2013). Such sites often indicate whether an individual is, or is not, in a committed relationship.

Many young adults seeking romance join one or more matchmaking Web sites that provide dozens of potential partners to meet and evaluate. A problem with such matches is that passion is hard to assess without meeting in person. As one journalist puts it, many people face "profound disappointment when the process ends in a face-to-face meeting with an actual, flawed human being who doesn't look like a JPEG or talk like an email message" (D. Jones, 2006, p. 13).

Emerging adults overcome this problem by filtering their online connections, meeting only those who seem promising, and then arranging a second meeting with only a few. Often physical attraction is the gateway to a relationship, but intimacy and then commitment require much more. When online connections lead to face-to-face interactions and then to marriage (true for about one-third of all marriages in the U.S. between 2008 and 2012), the likelihood of happy marriages is as high as or higher than when the first contact was made in person (Cacioppo et al., 2013).

The large number of possible partners young adults find—the thousands of fellow students at most colleges or the hundreds of suggestions that some matchmaking sites provide—cause a potential problem, **choice overload**, when too many options are available. Choice overload makes some people unable to choose and increases second thoughts after a selection is made (Iyengar & Lepper, 2000; Reutskaja & Hogarth, 2009).

choice overload Having so many possibilities that a thoughtful choice becomes difficult. This is particularly apparent when social networking and other technology make many potential romantic partners available.

Modern Match-ups These couples stare into each other's eyes as part of a singles meeting in Manhattan. Maybe some of them will end up like couples gaze into Alex and Sarah (right) who met online and are now among the 2 million US residents who met online and married in 2011.

FIGURE 19.3

More Together, Fewer Married As you see, the number of cohabiting male–female households in the United States has increased dramatically over the past decades. These numbers are an underestimate: Couples who do not tell the U.S. Census takers that they are living together, or who cohabit within their parents' households, or who are same-sex couples (not tallied until 2000) are not included here. In addition, most emerging adults who are not now cohabiting may begin to do so within a few years.

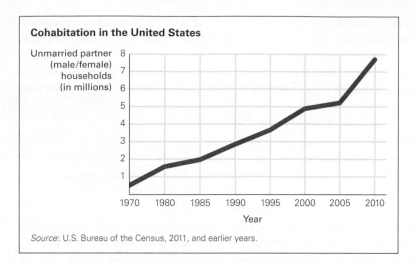

Cohabitation in the United States

Source: U.S. Bureau of the Census, 2011, and earlier years.

cohabitation An arrangement in which a couple live together in a committed romantic relationship but are not formally married.

Choice overload occurs with many consumer goods—jams, chocolates, pens, restaurants—but it may apply to mate selection as well. Having many complex options that require weighing present and future advantages and disadvantages (trade-offs are inevitable in partner selection) may be overwhelming (Scheibehenne et al., 2010). That may contribute to divorce rates, which are higher for first marriages between young adults (who have more choices) than for those over age 30. Too many choices slows down analysis; when people feel rushed, they tend to have later regrets (Inbar et al., 2011).

A second major innovation among emerging adults is **cohabitation,** the term for living together in a romantic partnership without being married. Cohabitation was relatively unusual 40 years ago: In the United States, less than 1 percent of all households were comprised of a cohabiting man and woman (see Figure 19.3). Between 2008 and 2012, 60 percent of all adults cohabited before they married, and another 11 percent continued to cohabit, perhaps never to marry (Copen et al., 2013).

Cohabitation rates vary from nation to nation: It is the norm in the United States, Canada, northern Europe, England, and Australia but not in other nations—including Japan, Ireland, Italy and Spain. However, that is changing rapidly. One-third of

Probably Married This couple with two young children could be cohabiting or married, but probably the latter—because this is Germany, where two-thirds of the children are born to married parents. If they were in France, they would probably be cohabiting, since more than half of French newborns have unmarried parents.

all Spanish couples now live together before they marry, a pattern that is not only accepted but also preferred (Dominguez-Folgueras & Castro-Martin, 2013).

Variation is also apparent in the purpose of cohabitation (Jose et al., 2010). About half of all cohabiting couples in the United States consider living together a prelude to marrying, which they expect to do when they are financially and emotionally ready. Many reach that point within three years. To be specific, a U.S. survey from 2006 to 2010 found that 40 percent of women in a first premarital cohabitation transitioned to marriage within three years, 32 percent were still cohabiting, and 27 percent had separated.

Overall, the quality of adult romantic relationships reflects early attachment styles, both anxious (too clingy and jealous) and avoidant (too distancing and secretive) (Collins & Gillath, 2012; Li & Chan, 2012). Adults who were securely attached infants are more likely to have secure relationships with their spouses as well as with their own children. Of course, plasticity is evident lifelong; early attachment affects adult relationships, but it does not determine them.

RICHARD TSONG-TAATARII/MCT/NEWSCOM

Not Married Andrew and Jessica decided to raise their daughter together but not to marry. They live in White Bear Lake, Minnesota, a relatively conservative area, but cohabiting couples are increasingly common everywhere.

OPPOSING PERSPECTIVES

Cohabitation

Many emerging adults consider cohabitation to be a wise prelude to marriage, a way for people to make sure they are compatible before tying the knot and thus reducing the chance of divorce. However, research suggests the opposite.

Contrary to widespread belief, living together before marriage does not prevent problems that might arise after a wedding. In a meta-analysis, a team of researchers examined the results of 26 scientific studies of the consequences of cohabitation for the subsequent stability and quality of marriages and found that those who had lived together were more likely to divorce (Jose et al., 2010).

Another study looked at the effects of dating, cohabitation, and marriage on happiness, as assessed by participants' answers to four questions (rated on a scale of 1 to 7) about how "ideal," "excellent," "satisfying," and "accomplished" their life was (Soons et al., 2009). At the start of any romantic relationship—dating, cohabiting, or marriage—happiness on all four indicators increased; at the end of any of these, happiness decreased. Compared to cohabitation, happiness of married couples increased more in the beginning and decreased more at separation. This suggests that cohabitation is neither the ideal nor the marriage equivalent that many emerging adults believe.

Particularly problematic is *churning,* when couples live together, then break up, then come back together. Churning relationships have high rates of verbal and physical abuse (Halpern-Meekin et al., 2013) (see Figure 19.4, p. 558). Cohabitation is fertile ground for churning because the couple are not as committed to each other as they would be in marriage, but they cannot slow down their relationship as easily as dating couples can.

Although the research suggests many problems with cohabitation, most emerging adults engage in this lifestyle. Of course, humans tend to justify whatever they do. In this case, cohabiting adults typically think they have found intimacy without the restrictions of marriage, but they may be fooling themselves.

However, most published research on the long-term effects of cohabitation are based on people who cohabited 10 or 20 years ago. They might have been more rebellious and less religious than today's cohabitants; that might explain why they were less happy in their eventual marriages compared to people who did not cohabit.

More-current research suggests the effects of cohabitation are less negative (Copen et al., 2013). Perhaps fewer cohabitants who marry will divorce than did a decade ago.

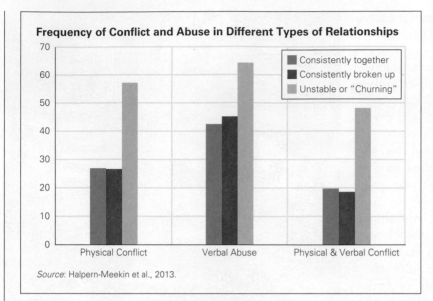

Frequency of Conflict and Abuse in Different Types of Relationships

Source: Halpern-Meekin et al., 2013.

FIGURE 19.4

Love You, Love You Not In a random sample of unmarried emerging adults (half men, half from two-parent homes, two-thirds European American, all from Toledo, Ohio) who had had a serious dating or cohabiting relationship in the past 2 years, some (15 percent) had broken up and not reunited, some (41 percent) had been together without breaking up, and some (44 percent) were churners, defined as having broken up and gotten together again with their partner. As you see, young adult relationships are often problematic, but churning correlates with the stormiest relationships, with half of churners fighting both physically and verbally.

Of course, cohabitation has one decided advantage: People save money by living together. Since the economic downturn has affected emerging adults more than older adults, this may be one reason for the current popularity of cohabitation.

National culture matters as well. Research in 30 nations finds that acceptance of cohabitation within the nation affects the happiness of those who cohabit. Within each of those 30 nations, demographic differences (such as education, income, age, and religion among the married and cohabitants) affect the happiness gap between cohabitation and marriage (Soons & Kalmijn, 2009). Another international study found that in Austria, Belgium, Denmark, New Zealand, Poland, Germany, and Norway, cohabitants were happier than married people (Lee & Ono, 2012).

All this suggests caution—neither the popularity of cohabitation nor the immediate happiness of those who move in together proves that cohabitation is beneficial over the long term. Yet in 2012, more than 16 million U.S. residents (7,845 couples) were in cohabiting relationships (United States Census, 2013).

Those 16 million chose a living arrangement other than the one that most research considers best. Do they know something that past research has not yet discovered?

Changing Historical Patterns

Love, romance, and lasting commitment are all of primary importance for emerging adults, although many specifics have changed. As already mentioned, a defining characteristic of emerging adults is that they marry later: In the United States the average age at first marriage was 29 for men and 27 for women in 2012. This was three years later than in 2000 and six years later than in 1950.

Marriage is not what it once was—a legal and religious arrangement that couples sought as the exclusive avenue for sexual expression, the only legitimate prelude to childbearing, and a lifelong source of intimacy and support. The tie between marriage and childbearing is loosening. As many babies are born to unmarried as to married couples in many nations. Most emerging adults (52 percent in 2011) think "being a good parent" is one of the most important things in life; less than one-third (30 percent) say the same about a good marriage (Wang & Taylor, 2011).

Further evidence is found in U.S. statistics (U.S. Bureau of the Census, 2013):

- Only half of all adults are married, living with their spouse.
- Only 12 percent of all emerging adults, ages 18–25, are married.

- The divorce rate is about half the marriage rate, not because more people are divorcing but because fewer people are marrying.
- Women having their first baby under age 30, are more often unmarried than married.

Such statistics make some fear that marriage is a dying institution. However, few developmentalists agree with that assessment, partly because emerging adults may be postponing, not abandoning, marriage. In fact, it seems that they have higher expectations for marriage than previous cohorts did, and they still see marriage as a marker of maturity and success (Cherlin, 2009). The efforts gay and lesbian couples have made to achieve marriage equality, and the backlash in "defense of marriage," suggest the power of the institution (Obocock, 2013).

What does seem to have occurred, however, is a change in the relationship between love and marriage. Three distinct patterns were evident in the twentieth century.

In about one-third of the world's families, love did not lead to marriage because parents arranged marriages that joined two families together. In roughly another one-third of families, adolescents met only a select group (single-sex schools keep them from unsuitable mates). Some then decided to marry, and young men asked the young women's fathers for "her hand in marriage." Parents supervised interactions and then bestowed their blessing. (When parents disapproved, young people separated or eloped—neither of which occurs often today.)

The "one-third" suggested for each of these two types is a rough approximation. In former times, nearly all marriages were of the first type, and the rest were of the second type; young people almost never met and married people unknown to their parents (Apostolou, 2007).

Currently, the practice in developing nations often blends these two types. For example, in modern India most brides believe they have a choice, but many meet their future husbands a few days before the wedding via parental arrangement. Typically, the man has more say in the union than the woman. The woman can refuse the match, but that is unusual (Desai & Andrist, 2010).

The final pattern is relatively new, although familiar to most readers of this book, and is becoming the most common one. Young people socialize with hundreds of others and are expected to fall in love but not marry until they are able to be independent, both financially and emotionally. Their choices tilt toward personal qualities observable at the moment—appearance, hygiene, sexuality, a sense of humor—and not to qualities that parents value, such as similar religion, ethnicity, and evidence of long-term stability.

For instance, a person who has been married and divorced is seen much more negatively by parents than by unpartnered adults (Buunk et al., 2008). In parts of India, love marriages have become more popular than arranged marriages, but marrying someone of a higher or lower caste is still much more troubling to the parents than to the emerging adults (Allendorf, 2013).

For Western emerging adults, love is considered a prerequisite for marriage, according to a survey of 14,121 individuals of many ethnic groups and sexual orientations (Meier et al., 2009). They were asked to rate from 1 to 10 the importance of money, same racial background, long-term commitment, love, and faithfulness for a successful marriage or a serious, committed relationship. Faithfulness was the most important of all (rated 10 by 89 percent) and love was almost as high (rated 10 by 86 percent). By contrast, most thought being the same race was not important (57 percent rated it 1, 2, or 3).

This survey was conducted in North America, but emerging adults worldwide share similar values. Halfway around the world, emerging adults in Kenya also reported that love was the main reason for couples to form and endure; money was less important (Clark et al., 2010). Elsewhere in Africa, although parental approval is more important than in the U.S., love between the couple is nonetheless crucial (Cole & Thomas, 2009).

Especially for Social Scientists Suppose your 25-year-old Canadian friend, never married, says, "Look at the statistics. If I marry now, there is a 50/50 chance I will get divorced." What three statistical facts allow you to insist, "Your odds of divorce are much lower"? (see response, page 560)

My Daughters and Me

I take some comfort in the idea that later marriages occur between people who want more from each other. I married late for my cohort (at age 25) and had children even later (two by age 30 and another two by age 40). Of my four children, only one is married—and she and her husband decided to marry so they could both have health insurance. My other three daughters are older than I was when I married and they are still single. I am proud of all four; they are admirable women working in professions that I respect. But I also wish those three would marry.

For those reasons, I pay close attention to my students' thoughts about love and marriage. Emerging adult Kerri wrote:

> All young girls have their perfect guy in mind, their Prince Charming. For me he will be tall, dark, and handsome. He will be well educated and have a career with a strong future . . . a great personality, and the same sense of humor as I do. I'm not sure I can do much to ensure that I meet my soul mate. I believe that is what is implied by the term *soul mate*; you will meet them no matter what you do. Part of me is hoping this is true, but another part tells me the idea of soul mates is just a fable.
>
> *[Personal communication]*

Kerri's classmate Chelsea, also an emerging adult, wrote:

> I dreamt of being married. The husband didn't matter specifically, as long as he was rich and famous and I had a long, off-the-shoulder wedding dress. Thankfully, my views since then have changed. . . . I have a fantastic boyfriend of almost two years who I could see myself marrying, as we are extremely compatible. Although we are different, we have mastered . . . communication and compromise. . . . I think I will be able to cope with the trials and tribulations life brings.
>
> *[Personal communication]*

Neither of these students is naive. Kerri uses the words *Prince Charming* and *fable* to express her awareness that these ideas may be childish, and Chelsea seems to have moved beyond her "long, off-the-shoulder wedding dress." I wish them both well, and I know my daughters are wise and wonderful. As a scientist, I read about divorce statistics and the pain of separation; I do not want that for my children or my students. They are wise to be wary of marriage.

But as a mother, I wish they would all have loving partners. I even imagine them owning houses with lawns, picket fences, children, and pets. My wishes are not logical. Postformal thinking makes me aware that I am stuck in traditional norms and that such homes are bad for the planet. My daughters' ideas and practices are more suited to the twenty-first century than mine.

>> Response for Social Scientists
(from page 559): First, Canada's divorce rate is not as high as the United States. Second, the divorce rate in the United States comes from dividing the number of divorces by the number of marriages. Because some people are married and divorced many times, that minority provides data that drive up the ratio and skew the average. (Actually, even in the United States, only one first marriage in three—not one in two—ends in divorce.) Finally, teenage marriages are especially likely to end: older brides and grooms are less likely to divorce. The odds of your friend getting divorced are about one in five.

What Makes Relationships Succeed?

As already stated, friendships and romances have much in common. They satisfy the need for intimacy. Friends and mates are selected in similar ways, with mutual commitments gradually increasing until someone becomes a lifelong best friend or a chosen partner. Best friends sometimes part, and long-term marriages may end in divorce, but that is neither the plan nor the usual sequence.

Another similarity is that close friendships and happy marriages aid self-esteem over the decades while providing practical support, including health benefits. Most of the research has focused on marriage, so that is what is reported here. However, similar findings apply to other intimate relationships as well.

Changes over Time

From a developmental perspective, note that marriages evolve over time, sometimes getting better and sometimes worse. Among the factors that lead to improvement are good communication, financial security (more income or new employment), and the end of addiction or illness. Children are an added stress, with adolescents particularly trying for both parents (Cui & Donnellan, 2009).

Another developmental factor is maturity. In general, the younger the partners, the more likely they are to fight and separate, perhaps because, as Erikson recognized, intimacy is elusive before identity is achieved. An emerging adult who finally achieves identity might think, "I finally know who I am, and the person I am does not belong with the person you are."

Similarities and Differences

Similarity tends to solidify commitment, probably because similar people are likely to understand each other. Anthropologists distinguish between **homogamy,** or marriage within the same tribe or ethnic group, and **heterogamy,** marriage outside the group.

Traditionally, homogamy meant marriage between people of the same cohort, religion, SES, and ethnicity. For contemporary partners, homogamy and heterogamy also refer to similarity in interests, attitudes, and goals. Educational and economic similarity are becoming increasingly important, and ethnic similarity less so (Clark et al., 2010; Hamplova, 2009; Schoen & Cheng, 2006).

The data are clear on this issue. One in seven current marriages in the United States is officially counted as interethnic (Wang, 2012). Very broad ethnic categories are used. For example, Black people from Africa, the Caribbean, and America were considered one ethnic group; Asians from more than a dozen nations were another ethnicity; European ancestry was a third category, lumping eastern, western, northern, and southern Europe together.

Thus, a marriage between a Pakistani and a Chinese person would *not* be categorized as interethnic. Nor would a marriage between a person of Greek heritage and one of Norwegian ancestry, even though the couple might be well aware of ethnic differences. Given the reality of cultural differences, perhaps most marriages in the U.S. are not homogamous.

One thorny issue that arises among couples who live together involves the allocation of domestic work, which varies dramatically by culture. In some cultures and in the United States in earlier decades, if the husband had a good job and the wife kept the household running smoothly, each partner was content. This is no longer the case.

Many twenty-first century U. S. wives work outside the home and want their husbands to do much more housework than the men would prefer. On the other hand, many fathers want to be actively involved in child rearing, something women once assumed was their domain.

Today, partners expect each other to be friends, lovers, and confidants as well as wage earners and caregivers, with both partners cooking, cleaning, and caring for children—a worldwide trend, with notable cultural differences (Wong & Goodwin, 2009). Happier relationships are those in which both partners are hardworking as well as adept at emotional perception and expression.

As women earn more money and men do more housework, increased shared responsibilities may increase marital satisfaction. Although many aspects of marriage have changed over the decades (some increasing happiness, some not), in general, couples seem as happy with their relationship as they ever were (Amato et al., 2003). Indeed, the U.S. divorce rate for first marriages seems to have decreased since 2000.

Conflict

Every intimate relationship has the potential to be destructive. The most extreme example comes from homicide statistics: When a civilian person is killed, the perpetrator is usually a friend, an acquaintance, or a relative—especially a husband or wife (see Figure 19.5, p. 562). Of course, that level of violence is rare; usually friends who seriously disagree go their separate ways.

Amicable distancing is less acceptable and more painful for married couples. We focus here on factors that make typical couples less happy than they might be and then on intimate partner violence. Some conclusions apply to friendships as well.

homogamy Defined by developmentalists as marriage between individuals who tend to be similar with respect to such variables as attitudes, interests, goals, socioeconomic status, religion, ethnic background, and local origin.

heterogamy Defined by developmentalists as marriage between individuals who tend to be dissimilar with respect to such variables as attitudes, interests, goals, socioeconomic status, religion, ethnic background, and local origin.

FIGURE 19.5

Fair Fight? Close relationships include passion and intimacy, which almost always leads to conflict at some point. Ideally, arguments should be dealt with using humor and love, yet if a woman is murdered, most likely her lover/husband is the killer.

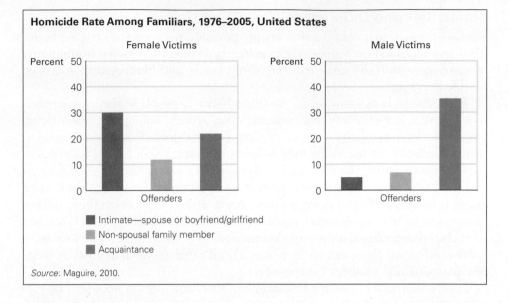

Homicide Rate Among Familiars, 1976–2005, United States

Source: Maguire, 2010.

Learning to Listen

No relationship is always smooth; each individual has unique preferences and habits. I know this personally. My husband was much more bothered by disorganization than I was, something we had not realized when we were dating. But early in our marriage, he bought a plastic container that fit in a drawer in the top of our kitchen cabinet, and organized all the silverware, separating salad and dinner forks, soup and table spoons, and so on. I was furious; I liked my way, resented his actions, and blurted out half a dozen reasons why he was wrong and I was right. Fortunately, we figured out what was beneath my anger, and that fight became a joke in later decades.

If a couple "fights fair," using humor and attending to each other's emotions as they disagree, conflict can contribute to commitment and intimacy (Gottman et al., 2002). According to John Gottman, who has videotaped and studied thousands of couples, conflict is less predictive of separation than disgust because disgust closes down intimacy.

Not every researcher agrees. Some studies of young couples (dating, cohabiting, and married) report that conflict undermines the relationship. However, every social scientist agrees that communication skills are crucial (Wadsworth & Markman, 2012). Much depends on how the conflict ends—with better understanding, with resentment, or, worst of all, with a breakup that neither partner wanted (Halpern-Meeken et al., 2013).

demand/withdraw interaction A situation in a romantic relationship wherein one partner wants to address an issue and the other refuses, resulting in opposite reactions—one insistent on talk while the other cuts short the conversation.

One particularly destructive pattern is called **demand/withdraw interaction**—when one partner insists and the other retreats (e.g., "We need to talk about this" is met with "No—I'm too busy"). This pattern is part of a downward spiral, as increased demanding leads to slammed doors and angry exits (Merrill & Afifi, 2012).

An international study of young adults in romantic relationships (again, some dating, some cohabiting, some married) in Brazil, Italy, Taiwan, and the United States found that women were more likely *demand* and men *withdraw*, although even when sex roles were reversed, the pattern was harmful. The authors explain:

> If couples cannot resolve their differences, then demand/withdraw interaction is likely not only to persist but also to become extreme. We believe that demand and withdraw may potentiate each other so that demanding leads to greater withdrawal and withdrawal leads to greater demanding. This repeated but frustrating and painful interaction can then damage relationship satisfaction.

[*Christensen et al., 2006, p. 1040*]

Intimate Partner Violence

An unmet demand may cause domestic abuse, which obviously is far worse than mere "damage to relationship satisfaction." In some abusive relationships, constructive communication is impossible; in others, mediation can teach both partners how to improve their relationship.

Young couples especially need such help because emerging adults are more likely to be victims and perpetrators of domestic abuse than people of any other age. For example, a large longitudinal study (Add Health) that began with a cross section of thousands of adolescents in the United States, most of them not in serious romantic relationships. In their early 20s, many were dating, cohabiting, or married, They were asked if there was verbal ("You're ugly"; "You're stupid") or physical (slapping, beating, kicking) abuse. Close to half (41 percent) said yes. Because this study is large and prospective, that 41 percent is probably accurate.

Surveys from other nations report even higher rates of serious abuse. In China, 14 percent of women experienced "severe physical abuse" (hitting, kicking, beating, strangling, choking, burning, or use of a weapon) in their lifetime, with 6 percent reporting such abuse in the past year (almost always at the hands of their husbands) (Xu et al., 2005). In Iran, women reported widespread abuse by their husbands, including physical abuse (44 percent), sexual abuse (31 percent), and psychological abuse (83 percent) (Vakili et al., 2010). When verbal abuse was included (hostile or insulting comments) a study of a New Zealand cohort of 25-year-olds found that 70 percent of those in relationships (married or not) experienced abuse (Fergusson et al., 2005).

It is difficult to compare rates among nations, or even cohorts, since much depends on the survey questions, how they are asked, and to whom. For example, some studies of intimate partner violence among Hispanics in the U.S. report higher rates than among European Americans; other studies report lower rates (Cunradi, 2009). Both results are plausible. However, everyone agrees that the rates everywhere are much too high, that spouse abuse is almost the norm in some cultures, and that alcohol and drugs make violence more severe.

Traditionally, women, not men, were asked if they experienced domestic abuse because it was assumed that women were victims and men were abusers. It is true that more women are seriously injured or killed by male lovers than vice versa, evident in every hospital emergency room or police summary. However, when the definition of abuse includes threats, insults, and slaps as well as physical battering, some studies find *more* abusive women than men (Archer, 2000; Fergusson et al., 2005; Swan et al., 2008).

The original, mistaken male-abuser/female-victim assumption occurred because abusive men are physically stronger, thus causing more injury. Moreover men are reluctant to admit that they are victims, and outsiders are less likely to believe them. Likewise, same-sex couples hesitate to publicly acknowledge conflict, although in domestic violence and most other aspects of relationships, they are very similar to heterosexual couples (Kurdek, 2006; Langhinrichsen-Rohling, 2009).

Social scientists have identified numerous causes of domestic violence, including youth, poverty, personality (such as poor impulse control), mental illness (such as antisocial disorders), and drug or alcohol addiction. Developmentalists note that many children who are harshly punished, sexually abused, or witness domestic assault grow up to become abusers or victims themselves. Neighborhood chaos is also a factor, as is the cultural acceptance of violence (Olsen et al., 2010).

Knowing these causes points toward prevention. Halting child maltreatment, for instance, averts some later abuse. It is also useful to learn more about each abusive relationship. Researchers differentiate two forms of partner abuse:

1. situational couple violence
2. intimate terrorism

Context Changes Shirley Hendricks signs documents sealing the deal on her new life. A former drug addict, victim, and perpetrator of couple violence, Shirley is now safe from abuse—much to the joy of her parole officer (in back). She has a new job and she and her son now have a new home.

situational couple violence Fighting between romantic partners that is brought on more by the situation than by the deep personality problems of the individuals. Both partners are typically victims and abusers.

intimate terrorism A violent and demeaning form of abuse in a romantic relationship, in which the victim (usually female) is frightened to fight back, seek help, or withdraw. In this case, the victim is in danger of physical as well as psychological harm.

linked lives Lives in which the success, health, and well-being of each family member are connected to those of other members, including those of another generation, as in the relationship between parents and children.

Each of these has distinct causes, patterns, and means of prevention (M. P. Johnson, 2008; M. P. Johnson & Ferraro, 2000; Swan et al., 2008).

Situational couple violence occurs when both partners fight—with words, slaps, and exclusion (leaving home, refusing sex, and so on)—and yet both partners are sometimes caring and affectionate. The *situation* brings out the anger, and then the partners abuse each other. This is the most common form of domestic conflict, with women at least as active in situational violence as men.

Situational couple violence can be reduced with maturation and counseling; both partners need to learn how to interact without violence. Often the roots are in the culture, not primarily in the individuals, which makes it possible for adults who love each other to learn how to overcome the culture of violence (Olsen et al., 2010).

Intimate terrorism is more violent, more demeaning, and more likely to lead to serious harm. Usually intimate terrorism involves a male abuser and female victim, although the sex roles can be reversed (Dutton, 2012). Terrorism is dangerous to the victim and to anyone who intervenes. It is also difficult to treat because the terrorist gets some satisfaction from abuse, and the victim often submits and apologizes. Social isolation makes it hard for outsiders to know what is happening, much less to stop it. With intimate terrorism, the victim needs to be immediately separated from the abuser, relocated in a safe place, and given help to restore independence.

>> Emerging Adults and Their Parents

It is hard to overestimate the importance of the family during any time of the life span. Although a family is composed of individuals, it is much more than the persons who belong to it. In the dynamic synergy of a well-functioning family, children grow, adults find support, and everyone is part of an unit that gives meaning to, and provides models for, his or her aspirations and decisions.

If anything, parents today are more important to emerging adults than ever. Two experts in human development write, "with delays in marriage, more Americans choosing to remain single, and high divorce rates, a tie to a parent may be the most important bond in a young adult's life" (Fingerman & Furstenberg, 2012).

Linked Lives

Emerging adults set out on their own, leaving their childhood home and parents behind. They strive for independence. It might seem as if they no longer need parental support and guidance, but the data show that parents continue to be crucial. Fewer emerging adults than in the past have established their own families, secured high-paying jobs, or achieved a definitive understanding of their identity and their goals.

All members of each family have **linked lives**; that is, the experiences and needs of family members at one stage of life are affected by those at other stages (Macmillan & Copher, 2005). We have seen this in earlier chapters: Children are affected by their parents' relationship, even if the children are not directly involved in their parents' domestic disputes, financial stresses, parental alliances, and so on. Brothers and sisters can be abusers or protectors, role models for good or for ill.

The same historical conditions that gave rise to the stage now called emerging adulthood have produced stronger links between parents and their adult children. Because of demographic changes over the past few decades, most middle-aged parents have only one or two offspring, and no young children who need constant care.

Brilliant, Unemployed, and Laughing Not an unusual combination for contemporary college graduates. Melissa, in Missoula, Montana, graduated summa cum laude from George Washington University and was one of many college graduates who lived with their parents. The arrangement provides many financial and family benefits, but who cooked dinner and who will wash the dishes?

Many emerging adults still live at home, though the percentage varies from nation to nation. Almost all unmarried young adults in Italy and Japan live with their parents. Fewer do so in the United States, but many parents under-write their young-adult children's independent living if they can afford to do so (Furstenberg, 2010). When they do not live at home, emerging adults see their parents, on average, several times a week and phone them even more often (Fingerman et al., 2012b).

Strong links between emerging adults and their parents are evident in attitudes as well. A detailed Dutch study found substantial agreement between parents and their adult children on contentious issues: cohabitation, same-sex partnerships, and divorce. Some generational differences appeared, but when parents were compared with their own children (not young adults in general), "intergenerational convergence" was apparent, especially when the adult children lived with their parents, as did about one-fourth of the sample (Bucx et al., 2010, p. 131).

Especially for Family Therapists More emerging-adult children today live with their parents than ever before, yet you have learned that families often function better when young adults live on their own. What would you advise? (see response, page 566)

How Old Is He? Appropriate financial planning is one of the skills of adulthood that is beyond the grasp of many emerging adults.

Financial Support

Parents of all income levels in the United States provide substantial help to their adult children, for many reasons. A major one is that the parent generation has more income. On average, households with the highest average income are headed by someone aged 45 to 54 (U.S. Bureau of the Census, 2012). Often parents of emerging adults are employed, with some seniority, and are not yet pay-ing for their own health or retirement. In nations such as the United States, where neither college nor preschool education is free, parental financial help may be crucial (Furstenberg, 2010).

This observation is not meant to criticize earlier cohorts; parents have always wanted to help their offspring. Now, however, more of them are able to give both money and time. For example, very few young college students pay all their tuition and living expenses on their own. Parents provide support; loans, part-time employment, and partial scholarships also contribute.

"Don't give me too much, I'm not good with money."

>> Response for Family Therapists (from page 565): Remember that family function is more important than family structure. Sharing a home can work out well if contentious issues—like sexual privacy, money, and household chores—are clarified before resentments arise. You might offer a three-session preparation package, to explore assumptions and guidelines.

FIGURE 19.6

Valuable, but Increasingly Unaffordable This chart shows percent of increase, compared to 1983 (set at 100 percent), when public education was supported primarily by public funds, with low tuition for students.

Cultural Differences

About one-half of all emerging adults receive cash from their parents in addition to tuition, medical care, food, and other material support. Most are also given substantial gifts of time, such as help with laundry, moving, household repairs, and, if the young adult becomes a parent, free child care. Earning a college degree is especially hard without family help.

In most European nations college tuition is free or less expensive, early childhood education is considered a public right, and housing and health care are less costly. Accordingly, emerging adults in Europe are less likely to need parental financial support. However, parents support their adult children in many other ways—it seems that the urge to support grown children is universal, with the specifics dependent on what is needed and on what the parents can afford (Brandt & Deindl, 2013).

Cultures differ in when and how families are destructive or helpful. For example, a study of enmeshment (e.g., parents involved in the thoughts and actions of their children) found that British emerging adults were less happy and successful when their parents were too intrusive. However, emerging adults in Italy seemed to remain close to their parents without hindering their own development (Manzi et al., 2006).

Some Westerners believe that family dependence is more evident in developing nations. There is some truth in this belief. For example, many African young adults marry someone approved by their parents and work to support their many relatives—siblings, parents, cousins, uncles, and so on. Individuals sacrifice personal goals for family concerns, and "collectivism often takes precedence and overrides individual needs and interests," which makes "the family a source of both collective identity and tension" (Wilson & Ngige, 2006, p. 248).

In cultures with arranged marriages, parents not only provide practical support (such as child care) and emotional encouragement, they may also protect their child. If the relationship is a disaster (for instance, the husband severely beats the wife, the wife refuses sex, the husband never works, or the wife never cooks), then the parents intervene. Again, each couple within each culture judges intervention differently: What is expected in, say, Cambodia, would be unacceptable in, say, Colorado.

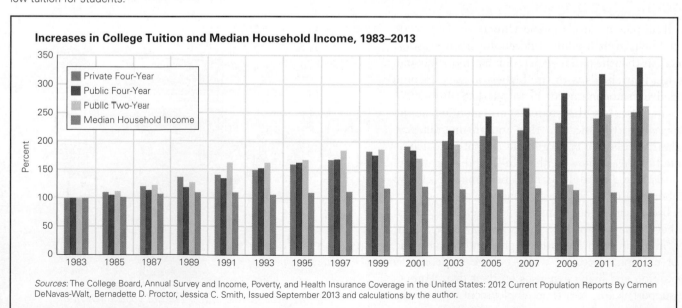

Increases in College Tuition and Median Household Income, 1983–2013

Sources: The College Board, Annual Survey and Income, Poverty, and Health Insurance Coverage in the United States: 2012 Current Population Reports By Carmen DeNavas-Walt, Bernadette D. Proctor, Jessica C. Smith, Issued September 2013 and calculations by the author.

Problems with Parental Support

Young adults from low-income families are likely to remain within the low-SES population because their parents cannot pay for college and living expenses during emerging adulthood (Fingerman et al., 2012b). Children in foster care face a particular problem: At age 18, they are considered adults, able to take their place in society. Given all that is now known about emerging adults, this is far too young (Avery & Freundlich, 2009); most 18-year-olds are not ready to manage life on their own.

There is a downside to parental support: It may impede independence. The most dramatic example is the so-called **helicopter parents,** hovering over their emerging adult child, ready to swoop down if any problem arises (Fingerman et al., 2012a).

The rise in the number of college students living at home, or attending colleges near home, could be ascribed to financial concerns, and that certainly is part of it. But it also could result from parental reluctance to let go. Parents do many things for their emerging adult college students—washing their laundry, sending them cookies, editing their college papers, paying their phone bills—but these very efforts may keep the child dependent, not learning from their mistakes.

One mother explains that her son doesn't come home from college as often as she would like, but when he does, he bring bags of dirty laundry that she washes and

> I always send him back with some food and maybe a little bit of money as well. . . . I just feel he is my baby, and I feel as though I am still providing for him if I at least know he is eating right and has enough money.

> *[quoted in Kloep & Hendry, 2011, p. 84]*

Parent assistance to emerging adults not only slows down maturation, it may create another problem. If a family has more than one child, the children may perceive favoritism. Often one sibling seems to receive more encouragement, money, or practical help from the parents. Differential treatment because of gender or age seems unfair to the less favored child.

In addition, mothers are more protective of a child who is emotionally dependent, and fathers seem more pleased with a more successful one. Interestingly, although most adults feel closer to their mothers than to their fathers, fathers are particularly influential for emerging adults, for good or ill (Schwartz et al., 2009).

From the parents' perspective, each child has different needs, and that means different treatment. But such variations may not only be resented; they may reduce sibling closeness, increase conflict, and lead to depression, in the favored as well as the less favored child (Jensen et al., 2013).

Family involvement has many advantages, especially if the young adult becomes a parent and the new grandparents provide care. Free infant care from relatively young parents may be one reason why parenthood begins much earlier in poor nations. By contrast, parenthood before age 25 in the United States is a major impediment to higher education and career success, which may explain why emerging adults postpone it (Furstenberg, 2010).

BRIAN RAY/AP PHOTO

Who decides? Ariana's first day at the University of Iowa seems to bewilder her but not her parents, who figure out what goes where in her dorm room.

helicopter parents The label used for parents who hover (like a helicopter) over their emerging adult children. The term is pejorative, but parental involvement is sometimes helpful.

Nationally and internationally, it is a mistake to put too much emphasis on whether or not a young adult still lives at home. Sharing living quarters is not the best indicator of a supportive relationship. Emerging adults who live independently but who previously had close relationships with their parents are as likely to avoid serious risks to their health and safety as those who never left.

As we think about the experiences of emerging adults overall, it is apparent that this stage of life has many pitfalls as well as benefits. These years may be crucial to long-term well-being as "decisions made during the transition to adulthood have a particularly long-lasting influence on the remainder of the life course because they set individuals on paths that are sometimes difficult to change" (Thornton et al., 2007, p. 13).

Fortunately, most emerging adults, like humans of all ages, have strengths as well as liabilities. Many survive risks, overcome substance abuse, combat loneliness, and deal with other problems through further education, maturation, friends, and family. If they postpone marriage, prevent parenthood, and avoid a set career until their identity is firmly established and their education is complete, they may be ready and eager for all the commitments and responsibilities of adulthood (described in the next chapters).

SUMMING UP

Intimacy needs are universal for all young adults, but specifics vary by culture and cohort. In developed nations in the twenty-first century, most emerging adults have many friends, including some of the other sex, and a series of romantic relationships before marriage. Cohabitation is common, although it does not necessarily further the passion, intimacy, or commitment that emerging adults seek. In some nations, arranged marriages are common. Parental support and linked lives are typical everywhere, and emerging adults are often dependent on their parents for college tuition and living expenses. For emerging adults, being too dependent on parents presents complications, but it is far better to have supportive than neglectful parents. ■

SUMMARY

Continuity and Change

1. Although Erikson thought that most people achieved identity by the end of adolescence, for today's youth the identity crisis continues into adulthood.

2. For emerging adults in multiethnic nations, ethnic identity becomes important but difficult to achieve, and requires complex psychosocial adjustment.

3. Vocational identity requires knowing what career one will have. Few young adults are certain about their career goals. Many societies offer some moratoria on identity achievement (such as college) that allows postponement of vocational identity.

4. In today's job market, many adults of all ages switch jobs, with turnover particularly quick in emerging adulthood. Most short-term jobs are not connected to the young person's skills or ambitions. Vocational identity, as Erikson conceived it, is elusive.

5. Personality can change in emerging adulthood, but continuity is also apparent. Many emerging adults find an appropriate combination of education, friendship, and achievement that improves their self-esteem. Even unusually aggressive or shy children can become quite happy adults.

Intimacy

6. Close friendships typically include some other-sex as well as same-sex friends. Gender separation is less common than it once was, but women still exchange more confidences and physical affection than men do.

7. Romantic love is complex, involving passion, intimacy, and commitment. In some nations, commitment is crucial and parents arrange marriages with that in mind. Among emerging adults in developed nations, passion is more important but does not necessarily lead to marriage.

8. Many emerging adults use social networking and matchmaking sites on the Internet to expand and deepen their friendship circles and mating options. This has advantages and disadvantages.

9. Cohabitation is increasingly common, with marked national variations. This arrangement does not necessarily improve marital happiness or stability.

10. Marriages work best if couples are able to communicate well and share responsibilities. Changes in relationships between spouses are evident over the past decades, with some positive as well as negative results.

11. Conflict is part of many intimate relationships. The pattern called demand/withdraw interaction harms a partnership. Domestic abuse is common worldwide; it takes a variety of forms and is perpetrated by both genders.

Emerging Adults and Their Parents

12. Family support is needed lifelong. Family members have linked lives, always affected by one another and often helping one another at every age.

13. In most nations, emerging adults and their parents are closely connected. Sometimes this means living in the same household, but even when it does not, complete separation of the two generations is unusual and impairs young adults' achievement.

14. Especially in nations with less public support for young adults, parents often pay college costs, provide free child care, and contribute in other ways to their young-adult children's welfare.

15. Parental support for emerging adult children usually is helpful, but it may also impede independence. The actual effect of parental care depends on cultural support for education, infant care, and so on.

KEY TERMS

choice overload (p. 555)	helicopter parents (p. 567)	intimacy versus isolation (p. 551)	plasticity genes (p. 550)
cohabitation (p. 556)	heterogamy (p. 561)		situational couple violence (p. 564)
demand/withdraw interaction (p. 562)	homogamy (p. 561)	intimate terrorism (p. 564)	
	hookup (p. 554)	linked lives (p. 564)	social clock (p. 543)

WHAT HAVE YOU LEARNED?

1. How is attending college a moratorium?

2. How does a person's ethnic pride typically change from early adolescence to adulthood?

3. Why are many emerging adults quite specific about their ethnic heritage?

4. How are romantic preferences related to ethnicity?

5. How does college help or hinder the development of vocational identity?

6. Why might vocational identity be an outdated social construction?

7. How might maturation and experience influence changes in personality?

8. What is the general trend of self-esteem during emerging adulthood?

9. How does the Internet affect friendship?

10. What are some typical gender differences in friendship?

11. What are the advantages and disadvantages of male–female friendships?

12. What do emerging adults seek in a romantic partner?

13. What are the three dimensions of love, according to Sternberg?

14. How has social networking changed the process of mate selection?

15. Why do many emerging adults cohabit instead of marrying?

16. What does most research conclude about the long-term effects of cohabitation?

17. What often happens when a person chooses a partner who is unlike himself or herself?

18. Why is demand/withdraw interaction particularly destructive of a relationship?

19. When are counseling and mediation most apt to succeed in ending intimate partner violence?

20. When is immediate protection and separation needed in intimate partner violence?

21. How does intimate partner violence differ by gender?

22. What kinds of support do parents provide their young-adult children?

23. How is family interaction affected when young adults live in their parents' homes?

APPLICATIONS

1. Talk to three people you would expect to have contrasting views on love and marriage (differences in age, gender, upbringing, experience, and religion might affect attitudes). Ask each the same questions and then compare their answers.

2. Analyze 50 marriage announcements (with photographs of the couples) in the newspaper. How much homogamy and heterogamy are evident?

3. Vocational identity is fluid in early adulthood. Talk with several people over age 30 about their work history. Are they doing what they expected they'd be doing when they were younger? Are they settled in their vocation and job? Pay attention to their age when they decided on their jobs. Was age 25 a turning point?

4. Observe couples walking together on your campus. Do your observation systematically, such as describing every third couple who walk past a particular spot. Can you tell the difference in body position or facial expression between men and women and between lovers, friends, and acquaintances? Once you have an answer, test your hypothesis by asking several of your observed couples what their relationship is.

>>ONLINE CONNECTIONS

To accompany your textbook, you have access to a number of online resources, including quizzes for every chapter of the book, flashcards (in English and Spanish), critical thinking questions, and case studies. For access to any of these links, go to www.worthpublishers.com/launchpad/bergerls9e. In addition to these free resources, you'll also find links to the podcasts, video clips, diagnostic quizzing with personalized study advice, and an ebook. Some of the videos and activities available online include:

■ *Transition to Parenthood.* Videos of couples in various stages of parenthood highlight the physical, emotional, social, household, and vocational changes that accompany this new responsibility.

■ *Homosexuality: Genes versus Environment.* What makes someone gay? This video shows how the nature–nurture debate plays out when applied to this question.

WORTH PUBLISHERS

Emerging Adulthood

BIOSOCIAL

Growth and Strength Bodies are generally strong, healthy, and active. Well-functioning organ systems provide protection through homeostasis, allostasis, and organ reserve. Good health habits include improving nutrition, increasing exercise, and avoiding dangerous risks and addictive drugs. Unfortunately, many emerging adults struggle to maintain good habits. Death due to disease in emerging adulthood is rare.

Sexual Activity Sexual and reproductive potential are at their peak. Emerging adults typically satisfy their strong sexual appetites with a series of relationships that may last months or years. Sexually transmitted infections are a particular risk for this age group.

Psychopathology Although most cope well with their new freedom, for some the stresses of this period make psychopathology more common, including major depression, anxiety, and schizophrenia.

Taking Risks Risk-taking is common during emerging adulthood, with men more prone to taking risks than women. Some risk-taking is involved in developmental tasks such as leaving home or starting a new job. Some risks are beneficial, others are not.

COGNITIVE

Postformal Thought Emerging adults may reach a fifth stage of cognition, called postformal thought, characterized by practical, flexible, and dialectical reasoning.

Morals and Religion Adults learn to balance emotions and logic, and the experiences of adulthood move individuals toward deeper reflection and moral analysis. Religious faith may become more mature.

Cognitive Growth and Higher Education Tertiary education aims to advance critical thinking as well as to develop communication and practical skills. Usually these goals are achieved. More and more emerging adults attend college, a trend particularly apparent among women (who traditionally achieved less education than men), members of minority groups, and in developing nations—especially in Asia and Africa. As a result, emerging adults everywhere are exposed to a wider range of ideas and values.

PSYCHOSOCIAL

Continuity and Change Emerging adults continue on the path toward identity achievement, finding vocational and ethnic identity particularly difficult as economic pressures and ethnic diversity increase. Personality patterns, inherited or developed in childhood, become more stable—although change is possible at every stage.

Intimacy Friendships become very important as a buffer against the stresses of emerging adulthood, and as a way to find romantic partners. Many emerging adults cohabit with a partner, with the intent of getting married someday (but not just yet). Relationship problems, including domestic violence, are more common in emerging adulthood than later on.

Emerging Adults and Their Parents Families of origin continue to be supportive of their emerging-adult children, offering financial and emotional help and often providing a home as well. The impact of living with one's parents depends not only on the habits and personality of the emerging adult, but also on cultural norms.

adulthood

We now begin the seventh part of this text. These three chapters cover 40 years (ages 25 to 65), years when bodies mature, minds master new material, and people work productively.

Adulthood spans such a long period because no particular year is a logical divider. Adults of all ages marry; raise children; care for aging parents; are hired and fired; grow richer or poorer; experience births, deaths, weddings, divorces, illness, and recovery. Thus, adulthood is punctuated by many events, joyful and sorrowful, which may occur at any time during those 40 years.

These events are not programmed by age, but they are not random: Adults build on their past development and create their own ecological niche. They choose people, activities, communities, and habits. For the most part, these are good years, when each person's goals become more attainable as people make decisions about their lives.

Culture and context are always crucial. Indeed, the very concept that people choose their niche is assumed in North America but not in places where families, finances, and past history shape almost every aspect of life. Divorce, for instance, is a chosen sequel for more than one-third of the marriages in the United States and several other nations, but until recently divorce was not legal in three nations (Chile, Malta, and the Philippines). Some experiences once thought to be part of adulthood—midlife crisis, sandwich generation, and empty nest among them—are unusual for today's middle-aged adults, no matter where they live. These three chapters describe what is universal, what is usual, and what is not.

Left: WIN-Initiative/Getty Images
Right: Jeff Randall/Getty Images

Adulthood: Biosocial Development

- **Senescence**
  The Experience of Aging
  The Aging Brain
  Outward Appearance
  Sense Organs

- **The Sexual-Reproductive System**
  Contraception
  Sexual Responsiveness
  Fertility
  Menopause

- **Health Habits and Age**
  Drug Abuse
  Nutrition
  Inactivity
  A VIEW FROM SCIENCE:
   A Habit Is Hard to Break

- **Measuring Health**
  Mortality
  Morbidity
  Disability
  Vitality
  Correlating Income and Health

WHAT WILL YOU KNOW?

1. When does a person start to show his or her age?
2. Which of the senses declines before age 65?
3. Should a woman bear children before age 30, 40, or 50?
4. How can a person be vitally healthy *and* severely disabled?

Jenny was in her early 30s, a star student in my human development class. She told told us all that she was divorced, raising her 7-year-old son, 10-year-old daughter, and two orphaned nephews in public housing in the South Bronx, infamous for guns, gangs, and drugs. She spoke enthusiastically about free activities for her children—public parks, museums, the zoo, Fresh Air camp. We were awed by her creativity, optimism, and energy.

A year later, Jenny came to my office to speak privately. She was about to graduate with honors and had found a job that would enable her family to leave their dangerous neighborhood. She sought my advice because she was four weeks pregnant. The father, Billy, was a married man who told her he would not leave his wife but would pay for an abortion. She loved him and feared he might end their relationship if she did not terminate the pregnancy.

I did not advise her, but I listened intently. Her son had a speech impediment; she thought she was too old to have another infant; she was a carrier for sickle-cell anemia, which had complicated her other pregnancies; her crowded apartment was no longer "babyproof"; she was not opposed to abortion. She was eager to get on with her adult life.

After a long conversation, Jenny thanked me profusely—although I had only asked questions, provided facts, and nodded. Then she surprised me.

"I'll have the baby," she said. "Men come and go, but children are always with you." I had thought her narrative was leading to another conclusion, but I realized she was planning her life, not mine. We all make choices about our bodies and our futures.

Despite feeling "too old" to have another baby, Jenny was relatively young. Nonetheless, she was a typical adult in many ways. Wondering about bearing and rearing children is common among adults, as are worries about genes, health, and aging.

This chapter explains the choices people make about all that. We begin with physiological changes in strength, appearance, and body functioning. Many people are concerned about some aspects of vision, hearing, and disease that occur long before they are senior citizens. Then we explain issues of sex, health habits, and medical care. At the end of this chapter, you will read how Jenny's adulthood unfolded after she left my office.

>> Senescence

senescence The process of aging, whereby the body becomes less strong and efficient.

Everyone ages. As soon as growth stops, **senescence,** a gradual physical aging over time, begins. Senescence affects every part of the body, visible and invisible.

In a culture that devalues the elderly, senescence has a negative connotation, but aging can be positive. From a developmental perspective, every period of life is multidirectional. Our scientific study of life-span development helps us see the gains and losses of adulthood.

The Experience of Aging

Although we are all aging, senescence often goes unacknowledged until age 60 or so. Typically, adults feel 5 to 10 years younger than their chronological age and think that "old" describes people significantly older than they themselves are (Pew Research Center, 2009a) (see Figure 20.1). Most adults feel strong, capable, healthy, and "in their prime."

They are not wrong. Although senescence affects every part of the body, and although some parts of the body function less well because of it, senescence does not necessarily cause illness or even impairment.

This notion is clearer with an example. With age, both blood pressure and low-density lipoprotein (LDL) cholesterol increase in everyone. The higher they get, the more likely heart disease becomes. Thus, coronary heart disease correlates with *hypertension* (high blood pressure) and cholesterol, which correlate with senescence. However, senescence does not directly *cause* heart disease. The hearts of most 25- to 65-year-olds beat strong, even as blood pressure and LDL rise.

In fact, some physiological aspects of aging protect adults. Senescence slows down the growth of cancer, although aging makes cancer more likely to occur (Rodier & Campisi, 2011). Health is further protected by organ reserve, which allows normal functioning throughout the adult years: People rarely notice that their hearts, lungs, and so on are losing reserve capacity.

Slowing Down with Age? Senescence slows everyone down, but most adults have unused reserves. Consider Lizzy Hawker, about 100 pounds and 5′4″ tall, who entered her first race at age 28 and has been running longer and faster every year since. Here she is a mile and a half above sea level (2632 meters) in the Swiss Alpine Marathon, which she won in 2007. Five years later, at age 37 she ran 100 miles around Mount Blanc, again winning.

Homeostasis and allostasis also help each part of the body adjust to accommodate changes in other parts, so the aging of some aspects of the brain, bloodstream, and cells is balanced by other factors that sustain life. For instance, if the stored level of iron in the blood is low, homeostasis increases iron absorption from the diet (Ganz & Nemeth, 2012).

In another example, the lungs automatically maintain oxygen levels whether a person is old or young, awake or asleep, exercising or resting (Dominelli & Sheel, 2012). Because of gradually diminished organ reserve, oxygen dispersal into the bloodstream from the lungs drops about 4 percent per decade after age 20. Thus, older adults may become "winded" after running fast, or pause after climbing a long flight of stairs to "catch their breath." Those are minor inconveniences, not a serious threat to the feeling that one is in good shape.

These processes are not fail-safe. If the loss of organ reserve with age is severe, homeostasis is severely pressured, or allostatic load becomes too heavy, life may be threatened. In the short term, physiological measures counterbalance psychological stresses (people might eat junk food, or abuse drugs to deal with depression or social discrimination, for instance), but some of the body's adjustments may not lead to a happy and healthy old age (Krieger, 2012; Kiecolt et al., 2009). [**Lifespan Link:** Organ reserve, homeostasis, and allostasis were explained in Chapter 17.]

At What Age Does the Average Person Become Old?

Age of becoming old	
	60
	69
	72
	74

Age of respondents ■ 18–29 ■ 30–49 ■ 50–64 ■ 65+

Source: Pew Research Center, 2009a.

FIGURE 20.1

Not Old Yet When people are asked when someone is "old," their answers depend on how old they themselves are. The trend continues—my mother, in her 80s and living in a senior residence, complained that she did not belong there because too many of the people were old.

Crucial to well-being in adulthood are setting goals and then working to accomplish them. Suppose a 50-year-old wants to run a marathon. That's quite possible—if he or she spends a year or more doing practice runs, eating and sleeping well, and maintaining good health by avoiding tobacco, following good preventive medicine, and so on. Thus physical health and strength are usually good throughout the forty years of adulthood, but habits as well as aging take a toll.

The Aging Brain

Like every other body part, the brain slows down with age. Neurons fire more slowly, and reaction time lengthens because messages from the axon of one neuron are not picked up as quickly by the dendrites of other neurons. New neurons and dendrites appear, but others atrophy: Brain size decreases, with fewer neurons and synapses in middle adulthood than earlier.

As a result, multitasking becomes harder, processing takes longer, and some complex working-memory tasks (e.g., repeating a series of eight numbers, then adding the first four, deleting the fifth one, subtracting the next two, and multiplying the new total by the last one—all in your head) may become impossible (Fabiani & Gratton, 2009).

For the most part, however, such losses are not noticed. A few individuals (less than 1 percent under age 65) experience significant brain loss with age, just as a few lose notable muscle strength. Those few are unusual, and the reason is pathology, not normal cognitive decline (Schaie, 2013). [**Lifespan Link:** Dementia is discussed in Chapter 24.]

For most adults, neurological reserves, homeostasis, and allostasis protect the brain. Adults can perform the brain equivalent of a marathon; that is one reason that judges, bishops, and world leaders are usually at least 50 years old. If severe loss occurs before age 65, the cause is not senescence but one of the following:

- *Drug abuse.* All psychoactive drugs can harm the brain, especially alcohol abuse over decades, which can cause Wernicke-Korsakoff syndrome ("wet brain").
- *Poor circulation.* Everything that impairs blood flow—such as hypertension and cigarette smoking—impairs cognition.
- *Viruses.* The brain is protected from most viruses by a so-called *blood–brain barrier,* but a few viruses—including HIV and the prion that causes mad cow disease—destroy neurons.
- *Genes.* About one in one thousand persons inherits a dominant gene for dementia.

These four factors are common physiological causes of brain slowdown in adulthood; adult cognitive function is described in the next chapter.

Especially for Drivers A number of states have passed laws requiring that hands-free technology be used by people who use cell phones while driving. Do those measures cut down on accidents? (see response, page 578)

Outward Appearance

As you see, senescence of the vital organs is not usually devastating in adulthood: Bodies function quite well at age 30 or 60. However, changes in the skin, hair, agility, and body shape are problematic in an age-conscious society. Few adults want to look old. Yet eventually they all will.

Skin and Hair

The first visible changes are in the skin, which becomes dryer, rougher, and less regular in color. Collagen, the main component of the connective tissue of the body, decreases by about 1 percent per year, starting at age 20. By age 30, the skin is thinner and less flexible, the cells just beneath the surface are more variable,

>> **Response for Drivers** (from page 577): No. Car accidents occur when the mind is distracted, not the hands.

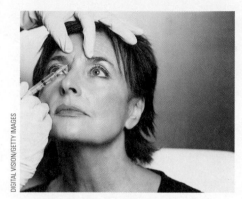

No Wrinkles An injection of Botox to beneath her eyebrows is what this woman thinks she needs, although she is quite beautiful and shows no signs of aging.

and wrinkles become visible, particularly around the eyes. Diet has an effect—fat slows down wrinkling—but aging is apparent in every layer of the skin (Nagata et al., 2010).

Wrinkles are not the only sign of skin senescence. Especially on the face (the body part most exposed to sun, rain, heat, cold, and pollution), skin becomes less firm. Age spots, tiny blood vessels, and other imperfections appear. These are visible by age 40 in people who work outside most of their lives (usually men who are farmers, sailors, and construction workers), but they are more troubling to people (usually women) who associate youth with sexual attractiveness.

In addition, veins on the legs and wrists become more prominent, and toenails and fingernails become thicker (Whitbourne & Whitbourne, 2011). Changes in appearance are barely noticeable from one year to the next, but if you meet a typical pair of siblings, one age 18 and the other 28, their skin tells you who is older. By age 60, all faces have aged significantly—some much more than others. The smooth, taut, young face is gone.

Hair usually becomes gray and thinner, first at the temples by age 40 and then over the rest of the scalp. This change does not affect health, but since hair is a visible sign of aging, many adults spend substantial amounts of money and time on coloring, thickening, styling, and more. Body hair (on the arms, legs, and pubic area) also becomes less dense. An occasional thick, unwanted hair may appear on the chin, inside the nose, or in some other place.

Shape and Agility

The body changes shape between ages 25 and 65. A "middle-age spread" increases waist circumference; all the muscles weaken; pockets of fat settle on the abdomen, the upper arms, the buttocks, and the chin; people stoop slightly when they stand (Whitbourne & Whitbourne, 2011).

By late middle age, even if they stretch to their tallest, adults are shorter than they were, because back muscles, connective tissue, and bones lose density, making the vertebrae in the spine shrink. People lose about an inch (2 to 3 centimeters) by age 65, a loss in the trunk, not the leg bones, as cushioning between spinal disks is reduced, another reason that waists widen.

Muscles shrink; joints lose flexibility; stiffness is more evident; bending is harder. As a result, agility is reduced. Rising from sitting on the floor, twisting in a dance, or even walking "with a spring in your step" is more difficult. A strained back, neck, or other muscle may occur.

Genes and exercise cause marked variation in aging not only from person to person but within each person. Muscles are particularly dependent on use—even a few weeks of bed rest weakens them substantially. The fibers for Type II muscles (the fast ones needed for forceful actions) are reduced much faster than Type I fibers (for slower, more routine movement) (Nilwik et al., 2013). That means that adults become less able to win a 100-meter dash than a marathon, or less able to lift heavy rocks for a few minutes than to pick vegetables for hours. Particularly for type II muscles, exercise has a marked effect (Nilwik et al., 2013).

The aging of the body is most evident in sports that require strength, agility, and speed: Gymnasts, boxers, and basketball players are among the athletes who benefit from youth but who experience slowdowns even by age 20. Of course, these are physiological slowdowns: The intellectual and emotional gains of adulthood may compensate for the physical changes; some 30-year-olds are more valuable teammates than younger athletes.

Age Advantage Young athletes are fast and furious—they steal bases. But older athletes keep their composure under stress. Marino Rivera (here thanking his fans when he retired at age 44) was a "closer" pitcher, famous for saving games that the Yankees might have lost.

Sense Organs

All the senses become less acute with each decade, with losses in any one sense affecting the others. One obvious example is that taste depends substantially on smell, which becomes less acute as people age (Aldwin & Gilmer, 2013). Similarly, conversation is best understood when people can see as well as hear the person who is talking. Now we describe some details of vision and hearing loss.

Vision

Not only does the rate of senescence vary from person to person and organ to organ, but each part of each organ is on its own timetable. Vision is an example, as some 30 distinct brain areas as well as at least a dozen aspects of the eye combine to allow people to see. Peripheral vision (at the sides) narrows faster than frontal vision; some colors fade more than others; nearsightedness and farsightedness follow different paths. Some aspects of vision seem unimpaired by age. Lifestyle and genes make a dramatic difference (Owsley, 2011).

One notable variation is nearsightedness (difficulty seeing objects at a distance), which is powerfully affected by genes and age. Nearsightedness increases gradually in childhood and adolescence, but in midlife the process reverses. Nearsightedness is reduced but farsightedness (difficulty seeing objects that are close) increases—because the lens of the eye changes shape. This explains why 40-year-olds hold the newspaper much farther away than 20-year-olds do: Their near focus is blurry but far focus is better (Aldwin & Glimer, 2013).

Other aspects of vision are also affected by age. It takes longer for the eyes to adjust to darkness (as when entering a dark theater after being in daylight) or to adjust to glare (as when headlights of an oncoming car cause temporarily blindness) (Aldwin & Gilmer, 2013). Motion perception (how fast is that car approaching?) and contrast sensitivity (is that a bear, a tree, or a person?) slows down (Olsley, 2011). The lens of the eyes thickens; brighter lighting is needed.

As these examples show, senescence affects the vision needed for driving, even when a person can read the letters on a vision chart. Driver license renewals at every age should include multifaceted vision tests because most adults see quite well but some need new glasses, cataract surgery, or other intervention decades before old age.

Hearing

Hearing is most acute at about age 10, again with specific intrapersonal variations. Sounds at high frequencies (a small child's voice) are lost earlier than sounds at low frequencies (a man's voice). Although some middle-aged people hear much better than others, no one hears perfectly.

Actually, hearing is always a matter of degree. No one hears a conversation a hundred feet away; "shouting distance" is limited. Because deafness is rarely absolute, gradual losses are not noticed. **Presbycusis** (literally, "aging hearing") is rarely diagnosed until about age 60, even if whispers were inaudible years before.

An alarming study finds that presbycusis may soon become apparent before old age. High school students (1,512 of them) reported whether they experienced any symptoms of hearing loss (ringing, muffled sounds, temporary deafness). Almost one-third said yes, unaware that loud music on their headphones or

presbycusis A significant loss of hearing associated with senescence. Presbycusis usually is not apparent until after age 60.

Gains and Losses In his 20s, Phil Collins was the drummer for the band Genesis, becoming a star solo singer and songwriter by age 30. A midlife ear infection and a spinal injury resulted in major sensory loss, making drumming impossible and new harmonies more difficult—but Collins adjusted. His *Going Back* album, released at age 59, reached the top of the charts. Most adults are neither so impaired nor so successful, but losses occur between ages 25 and 65 for everyone, and then gains can compensate.

at concerts might damage the hairs of the inner ear (Vogel et al., 2010). Many nations mandate ear protection for construction workers, but no laws protect against loud music.

SUMMING UP

Senescence is the process of aging, evident in every body part from the moment growth ends. However, changes are much less consequential today than in earlier centuries, when adults needed physical strength to complete their daily work. For most adults, the body and brain continue to function well, as organ reserve and homeostasis compensate for momentary stress. Activities that require peak performance of many body parts, such as major athletic contests, reveal aging in adulthood.

Appearance reflects age: Skin becomes less smooth, hair grays and thins, bodies add fat, shape changes. Such external changes have little impact on physical health, but many adults worry about them and try to look young. All the senses become less acute, with some aspects declining much faster than others. Genes and experiences affect sensory senescence.

■

>> The Sexual-Reproductive System

As you just read, although senescence affects every body part, 60-year-olds can usually accomplish almost everything 30-year-olds can, albeit more slowly and carefully. However, one critical activity becomes virtually impossible for women and difficult for men as they approach age 50—reproduction.

Contraception

The aging of the sexual-reproductive system is universal. Whether or not that matters to an individual depends on historical context (including medical advances) and local values; the most obvious example is birth control. Without it, many women avoided sex because they did not want pregnancy. Now contraception has transformed female sexuality, affecting men as well.

Local values shape contraceptive patterns. For example, couples in India rely on female sterilization to control family size but virtually never use male sterilization (Sunita & Rathnamala, 2013). In the United States almost two-thirds of sexually active women over age 35 are sterilized, with an overall female-to-male ratio of about 2:1. That ratio varies by ethnicity: Among African Americans and Latinos, far more women than men (about 6:1) are sterilized (U.S. Center for Health Statistics, 2012).

The most popular contraception for younger women in the United States and France is the birth control pill, but the pill is almost never used in Japan except to regulate menstruation (Matsumoto et al., 2011). No contraception is available in some poor nations, even though unwanted or poorly spaced births are a major cause of mortality (Cleland et al., 2012).

With no contraception allowed in Bangladesh, couples use early abortion (without calling it abortion) to control family size (Gipson & Hindin, 2008). Worldwide, abortion is illegal in some nations and readily available in others. The United States is between these extremes in practice but politically polarized, as is evident in state-by-state differences in abortion access.

Such marked variation in preferred ways to prevent unwanted births is an example of the disconnect between human biology and psychology. This disconnect is also dramatic in sexual arousal, orgasm, fertility, and menopause—all biological, but the effects, and even the occurrence, are strongly influenced by the mind (Pfaus et al., 2014). As many say: "The most important human sexual organ is between the . . . ears."

Sexual Responsiveness

Sexual arousal occurs more slowly with age, and orgasm takes longer. For some couples, these slowdowns are counterbalanced by reduced anxiety and better communication, as partners become more familiar with their own bodies and those of their mates. Distress at slower responsiveness seems less connected to physiological aging than to troubled interpersonal relationships and unrealistic fears and expectations (Burri & Spector, 2011; LaMater, 2012).

Most people are sexually active throughout adulthood. One study found that, on average, sexual intercourse (the most studied expression of sexual activity) stopped at age 60 for women and 65 for men. That was the *average,* but many stop before 60 and others are sexually active in their 80s (Lindau & Gavrilova, 2010). A study of German adults, ages 18 to 93, confirmed that sexual desire and activity are reduced with age for both sexes. Partner availability is key. In addition, unemployment reduced male desire and past sexual trauma (abuse, rape) affected female desire (Beutel et al., 2008).

Some adults say that sexual responsiveness may improve with age. Could that be? Is faster not always better? At least there is no proof that sexual responsiveness worsens; arousal and orgasm can continue throughout life.

According to a study of Chicago couples conducted in the early 1990s, most adults of all ages enjoyed "very high levels of emotional satisfaction and physical pleasure from sex within their relationships" (Laumann & Michael, 2000, p. 250). That study found that most men and women reported that they were "extremely satisfied" with sex if they were in a committed, monogamous partnership—a circumstance more likely after age 30 (Laumann & Michael, 2000).

Improved sexuality with age may be a cohort change, not a physiological one. For some people, especially those born before 1950, sex was considered shameful and dirty when they reached puberty. Then, as contraception improved and mores changed, sex was seen as fulfilling and positive. As attitudes changed, sex became more satisfying.

Is it still true that some adolescents and younger adults are anxious and confused about sexuality and terrified of accidental pregnancy? In adulthood, do

His Arm Around Her Whether in formal wear (the Akha pair in Thailand) or casual North American clothes, at every adult age couples delight in being close to each other, physically and emotionally.

people still become more secure in their sexuality and more confident of family planning? If the answer to both questions is yes, then sexual responsiveness would become better as adulthood progressed because fear and guilt would be diminished and slower climax would allow longer and more varied lovemaking.

A study of women aged 40 and older found, as expected, that sexual activity decreased each decade but that satisfaction did not (Trompeter et al., 2012). That study may not reflect a universal pattern, since participants were mostly upper-middle-class European American women, and the data was collected via questionnaires. For political reasons a valid, longitudinal, representative, large-scale study of sexual responsiveness has not been done.

It is likely, however, that cohort changes are improving sexual responsiveness. Even a few decades ago, sex was furtive or forbidden for adults who were gay, lesbian, divorced, or never married. That is less true today, at least in the United States, where adults in any of those four groups are more accepted. Adults may experience increased sexual responsiveness with age.

Fertility

infertility The inability to conceive a child after trying for at least a year.

Although sexual activity is understudied, considerable research has been done on **infertility**, often defined as being unable to conceive after trying for at least a year, although the definition varies from nation to nation (Gurunath et al., 2011; Hayden & Hallstein, 2010). For couples who want children but have none, aging adds to their regret; for couples who prefer to remain childless, age brings relief.

Infertility rises when medical care is scarce (Gurunath et al., 2011) and thus varies from nation to nation. In the United States, about 12 percent of all adult couples are infertile, partly because many postpone childbearing long past adolescence. Another group (perhaps 10 percent of all adult women in Germany, the United Kingdom, and the United States—and far fewer in most other nations) chooses to avoid motherhood (Basten, 2009).

If North American couples in their 40s try to conceive, about half fail and the other half risk various complications. Of course, risk is not reality: In 2011 in the United States, 116,000 babies were born to women age 40 and older, the only age group in which the birth rate is rising (Hamilton et al., 2012). One-fourth of these were first births. Although complications increase with age, almost all babies born to older women become healthy children.

As explained in Chapter 17, fertility peaks in late adolescence. From a biological (not psychosocial) perspective, women should try to conceive before age 25 and men before age 30. If they are unsuccessful, medical intervention usually helps if they are still relatively young.

Causes of Infertility

When couples are infertile, the cause is in the man about one-third of the time, in the woman another third, and a mystery in the final third. Now some specifics.

A common reason for male infertility is a low sperm count. Conception is most likely if a man ejaculates more than 20 million sperm per milliliter of semen, two-thirds of them mobile and viable, because each sperm's journey through the cervix and uterus is aided by millions of fellow travelers. Sperm count may have declined over the past century, but the count varies a great deal from place to place—higher in southern France than in Paris, in New York than in California, in Finland than in Sweden—for reasons that may be more connected to the specifics of the sample than to the health or age of the men (Merzenich et al., 2010).

Depending on the man's age, each day about 100 million sperm reach maturity after a developmental process that lasts about 75 days. Anything that impairs body functioning over those 75 days (e.g., fever, radiation, prescribed and nonprescribed drugs, time in a sauna, stress, environmental toxins, alcohol, cigarettes) reduces sperm number, shape, and motility (activity), making conception less likely. Sedentary behavior, perhaps particularly watching television, also correlates with lower sperm count (Gaskins et al., 2013).

Age reduces sperm count, the probable explanation for an interesting statistic: Men take five times as many months to impregnate a woman when they are over 45 as when they are under 25 (Hassan & Killick, 2003). (This study controlled for frequency of sex and age of the woman.) Overall, low sperm count is common but often easy to remedy.

As with men, women's fertility is affected by anything that impairs physical functioning—such as disease, smoking, extreme dieting, and obesity. As with men, age itself also slows down every step of female reproduction—ovulation, implantation, fetal growth, labor, and birth. Many infertile women do not even realize they have contracted one specific disease that causes infertility—*pelvic inflammatory disease (PID)*. PID creates scar tissue that sometimes blocks a woman's fallopian tubes, preventing sperm from reaching an ovum.

Fertility Treatments

In the past 50 years, medical advances have solved about half of all fertility problems. Surgery repairs reproductive systems, and *assisted reproductive technology* (ART) overcomes obstacles such as a low sperm count and blocked fallopian tubes. Some ART procedures, including in vitro fertilization (IVF), which has led to an estimated 5 million births (Fisher & Guidice, 2013), were explained in Chapter 3.

Donor sperm, donor ova, and donor wombs can help individuals whose partner is infertile or who have no partner of the other sex: Birth through all of these means is biologically possible, and together they have led to tens of thousands of children as well as to dozens of moral questions.

Some uses of ART are morally acceptable to virtually everyone, especially when couples anticipate disease-related infertility. For example, many cancer patients freeze their sperm or ova before chemotherapy or radiation, allowing conception after they recover.

In another example, before 2000, doctors recommended sterilization and predicted early death for those with HIV; Now such individuals almost always use condoms for sex (to protect the uninfected partner) and live for decades. If the woman has the virus, drugs and a Cesarean can almost always protect the fetus; if the man is HIV-positive, sperm can be collected and washed in the laboratory to rid them of the virus, and, via IVF, pregnancy can occur (Sauer et al., 2009).

All ART procedures need expensive medical assistance, not usually covered by insurance. IVF also requires both biological parents to undergo special procedures. The woman takes hormones to increase the number of ova ready to be surgically removed, and the man must ejaculate into a receptacle. Then technicians combine the ova and sperm, typically choosing one active sperm to insert into each normal ovum. Ideally, zygotes form and duplicate. Then one or more healthy blastocysts are inserted into the uterus, which is ready for implantation via additional drugs.

Even with careful preparation, less than half of the inserted blastocysts implant and grow to become newborns. Some young women freeze their ova for IVF years later because the age of the ova is crucial (MacDougall et al., 2013). Miscarriages (perhaps one in three implanted embryos) increase with age.

In most European nations, public insurance covers the cost of ART, although some nations require proof of infertility, proof of marriage, and so on. In the United States, private insurance rarely covers ART, but federal military insurance does. That increases the rate of IVF among infertile African and European Americans,

Especially for Young Men A young man who impregnates a woman is often proud of his manhood. Is this reaction valid? (see response, page 584)

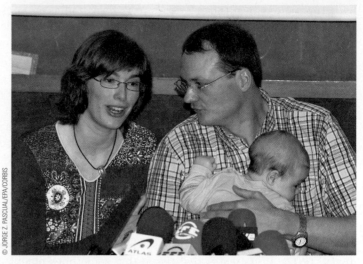

IVF to the Rescue In every nation some babies begin life in a laboratory dish, as IVF overcomes blocked Fallopian tubes, low sperm count, and other common fertility impediments. IVF now solves uncommon problems as well. In Kentucky, Avery Kennedy *(left)* began life via a donated frozen ovum, fertilized by Jared (shown here) and implanted in Wendy's uterus. In Spain (right), a few hours after Roger's conception, one stem cell was removed and tested for the gene for Huntington's chorea. Since one of his parents (shown here) has that dominant gene, Roger had a 50/50 chance of inheriting it. Obviously, he did not.

>> Response for Young Men (from page 583): The answer depends on a person's definition of what a man is. No developmentalist would define a man simply as someone who has a high sperm count.

menopause The time in middle age, usually around age 50, when a woman's menstrual periods cease and the production of estrogen, progesterone, and testosterone drops. Strictly speaking, menopause is dated one year after a woman's last menstrual period, although many months before and after that date are menopausal.

but not among Hispanics (McCarthy-Keith et al., 2010). More African and Latin Americans are infertile than European Americans, but their rate of ART is lower, for many economic and cultural reasons (Greil et al., 2011).

When IVF children are not low birthweight, they develop as well as other children, not only in health, intelligence, and school achievement, but also in self-reported emotional development as teenagers (Wagenaar et al., 2013).

Parents may be more responsive to IVF children. This is suggested by a study in Jamaica, where IVF parents are more authoritative and less permissive or authoritarian than parents whose children were conceived spontaneously (Pottinger & – Palmer, 2013). There are at least two possible explanations: that the parents tend to be more mature, and that the children tend to be strongly wanted.

Menopause

During adulthood, the level of sex hormones circulating in the bloodstream declines—suddenly in women, gradually in men. As a result, sexual desire, frequency of intercourse, and odds of reproduction decrease. The specifics differ for women and men.

Women in Middle Age

For women, sometime between ages 42 and 58 (the average age is 51), ovulation and menstruation stop because of a marked drop in production of several hormones. This is **menopause.** The age of natural menopause is affected primarily by genes (17 have been identified; see Morris et al., 2011; Stolk et al., 2012) but also by smoking (earlier menopause) and exercise (later).

In the United States, one in four women has a *hysterectomy* (surgical removal of the uterus), which often includes removal of her ovaries. If she was premenopausal, removal of the ovaries causes menopausal symptoms—vaginal dryness and body temperature disturbance, including hot flashes (feeling hot), hot flushes (looking hot), and cold sweats (feeling chilled). Natural menopause produces the same reactions, but not as suddenly and not in everyone. Early menopause, surgical or not, increases the risk of various health problems later on (Hunter, 2012).

The psychological consequences of menopause vary more than the physiological ones. Anthropologist Margaret Mead famously said, "There is no more creative force in the world than the menopausal woman with zest." Some menopausal women have erratic moods, others are more energetic, still others become depressed (Judd et al., 2012).

Pausing, Not Stopping During the years of menopause, these two women experienced more than physiological changes: Jane Goodall *(left)* was widowed and Ellen Johnson-Sirleaf *(right)* was imprisoned. Both, however, are proof that postmenopausal women can be productive. After age 50, Goodall (shown visiting a German zoo at age 70) founded and led several organizations that educate children and protect animals, and Johnson-Sirleaf (shown speaking to the International Labor Organization at age 68) became the president of Liberia.

Over the past 30 years, millions of postmenopausal women used **hormone replacement therapy (HRT).** Some did so to alleviate symptoms of menopause; others, to prevent osteoporosis (fragile bones), heart disease, strokes, or dementia. Correlational studies found that these diseases occurred less often among women taking HRT.

Researchers now believe that, since women with more education and money were more likely to use HRT, the lower rate of disease was primarily the result of higher SES. In controlled longitudinal studies, the U.S. Women's Health Initiative found that taking estrogen and progesterone *increased* the risk of heart disease, stroke, and breast cancer and did not prevent dementia (U.S. Preventive Services Task Force, 2002). A large observational study confirms the breast cancer risk: Women who took HRT were more likely to develop breast cancer (at the rate of 6 per 1,000 compared to 4 per 1,000) (Chlebowski et al., 2013).

HRT *does* reduce hot flashes and decrease the incidence of osteoporosis, but women who want those benefits need to weigh the costs. Surprisingly, culture seems more influential than cost-benefit analysis. For instance, Australian researchers confirm that estrogen reduces osteoporosis, so many Australian women take the hormone (Geelhoed et al., 2010). A study in Germany found that doctors hesitated to prescribe HRT, but at menopause most female gynecologists used HRT and male gynecologists gave it to their wives (Buhling et al., 2012).

hormone replacement therapy (HRT) Taking hormones (in pills, patches, or injections) to compensate for hormone reduction. HRT is most common in women at menopause or after removal of the ovaries, but it is also used by men as their testosterone decreases. HRT has some medical uses but also carries health risks.

Men in Middle Age

Do men undergo anything like menopause? Some say yes, suggesting that the word **andropause** should be used to signify age-related lower testosterone, which reduces sexual desire, erections, and muscle mass (Samaras et al., 2012). Even with erection-inducing drugs such as Viagra and Levitra, sexual desire and speed of orgasm decline with age, as do many other physiological and cognitive functions.

But most experts think that the term *andropause* (or *male menopause*) is misleading because it implies a sudden drop in reproductive ability or hormones. That does not occur in men, some of whom produce viable sperm lifelong. Sexual inactivity and anxiety reduce testosterone—with a result superficially similar to menopause but with a psychological, not physiological, cause.

To combat the natural decline in testosterone, some middle-aged as well as older men have turned to hormone replacement (Samaras et al., 2012). Some women also take smaller amounts of testosterone to increase their sexual desire. But at least one longitudinal study with both sexes comparing testosterone supplements

andropause A term coined to signify a drop in testosterone levels in older men, which normally results in reduced sexual desire, erections, and muscle mass. (Also called *male menopause*.)

with a placebo found no benefits (sexual or otherwise) (Nair et al., 2006). Indeed, male HRT may cause heart disease and other problems (Handelsman, 2011).

About 2 percent of older men have very low testosterone levels and benefit from supplemental hormones. For most men, however, physicians are skeptical of benefits (Handelsman, 2011). One writes that men would be better off learning about "the health benefits of physical activity. . . . Tell them to take the $1,200 they'll spend on testosterone per year and join a health club; buy a Stairmaster—they'll have money left over for their new clothes" (Casey, 2008, p. 48).

All the evidence for both sexes finds that adult health depends more on health habits than on HRT. We discuss that next.

SUMMING UP

The efficiency of the sexual-reproductive system declines with age, beginning in the 20s. As middle age approaches, many couples notice it takes longer to reach orgasm, frequency of sexual intercourse declines, and fertility is reduced—although psychological aspects of sexual interaction may improve. About 12 percent of couples in the United States are infertile; age is one of many reasons. Assisted reproduction has helped millions of infertile couples give birth, although the process may be difficult, with no guarantee of conception.

At age 51, on average, women experience menopause, a drop in estrogen that makes ovulation and menstruation cease. Hormone production also declines in men with age, although many elderly men continue to produce viable sperm. Hormone replacement therapy for either sex is controversial: Many U.S. physicians fear possible health risks for both men and women, although many women elsewhere and many men in the U.S. take hormones. ▪

≫ Health Habits and Age

Each person's routines and habits, from childhood on, powerfully affect every disease and chronic condition. This is particularly true for problems associated with aging—from arthritis to varicose veins—that may first appear after age 50 but begin decades before. In fact, some adult conditions are affected by maternal health when the adult was an embryo (Haas et al., 2013).

Virtually every fatal disease becomes more common with every decade of adulthood. Cancer is a classic example (see chart). However, most cancers are related to lifestyle behaviors that increase allostatic load every year. Although genes make a person more vulnerable to specific cancers, environment always makes a difference, with about one-third of cancer deaths connected to smoking, another one-third to diet, and the final one-third to various toxins. We now examine adult habits, with the goal of understanding which habits contribute to or diminish ongoing vitality.

Drug Abuse

As described in Chapter 17, drug abuse, especially of illegal drugs, decreases markedly over adulthood—usually before age 25 and almost always by age 40. Of the illegal drugs, marijuana use is slowest to decline. In the United States, about 11 percent of 25- to 34-year-olds still smoke it (National Center for Health Statistics, 2013). As it becomes legal in several states, rates rise.

Although illegal drug use declines in adulthood, abuse of prescribed medication increases. One reason is that such drugs are first given to reduce pain,

Half a Century of Cancer Deaths in the United States: Annual rate per 100,000 people in age group

Age	1960	2010
1–4	10	2
5–14	7	2
15–24	8	4
25–34	20	9
35–44	60	29
45–54	177	12
55–64	397	300
65–74	714	666
75–84	1127	1202
85+	1450	1730

As you see, primarily because of earlier diagnosis and better treatment, cancer deaths are dramatically reduced for those under age 35, and somewhat reduced for adults aged 35 to 75. However, the rate has increased for the elderly, partly because when they were younger, they were more likely to smoke cigarettes and eat high-fat processed food than people in earlier cohorts. It remains to be seen whether adults in the first half of the twenty-first century will also suffer the consequences of a high allostatic load.

insomnia, or psychological distress, and adults do not realize when they become addicted. However, in the United States, by far the addictive drugs most often abused are the two legal ones, sold to any adult at hundreds of thousands of stores—tobacco and alcohol.

Tobacco

Death rates for lung cancer (the leading cause of cancer deaths in North America) reflect smoking patterns of years earlier. About 70 percent of the lung cancer deaths worldwide, and 90 percent in industrialized nations, are caused by cigarettes (Ezzati & Riboli, 2012). Because North American men have been quitting for decades, the rate of lung cancer deaths for males has declined significantly since 1980, and the lung cancer–related death rate among 45- to 64-year-old males is now far lower than it is for older adults. In 2010, the median age for diagnosis of lung cancer was 70 years (National Cancer Institute, 2013). Rates for adult men continue to decline.

Relatively few women smoked in the first half of the twentieth century, but then their smoking increased and only recently has it declined. Consequently, in the United States, during the same years that male lung cancer deaths declined, the rates for females increased. Fifty years ago, more women died from the "female cancers" (breast, uterine, or ovarian) than from lung cancer; by contrast in 2010, almost twice as many adult women died from lung cancer as from the combined total of those other three (National Center for Health Statistics, 2013).

At risk in Bangalore A man puffs on a bidi, a flavored cigarette. He is at risk of being among the 1 million Indians who die each year of smoking-related causes.

Fortunately, cigarette smoking has been declining over the past decade in North America (the United States, Canada, and Mexico) for every age and gender group. In 1970, one-half of U.S. adult men and one-third of women smoked, but by 2010 only 22 percent of men and 18 percent of women did, with almost as many adult former smokers as current smokers. It is not yet time for celebration, however, because "cigarette smoking remains the leading cause of preventable morbidity and mortality in the United States" (MMWR, 2013, p. 81).

North American projections suggest a brighter future. Women are following the male pattern of quitting, and many offices, homes, and public places are now smoke-free. The percentage of adult smokers seems to be stuck at about 20 percent over the past decade, with much lower rates after age 65 (see Figure 20.2, p. 588). It is not known if that is because many adults quit in late middle age or because most of the heaviest smokers have died.

Worldwide trends are less encouraging. Almost half the adults in Germany, Denmark, Poland, Holland, Switzerland, and Spain are smokers. In developing nations, rates of smoking are rising, especially among women. The World Health Organization calls tobacco "the single largest preventable cause of death and chronic disease in the world today" (Blas & Kurup, 2010, p. 199). One billion smoking-related deaths are projected to occur in the world between 2010 and 2050.

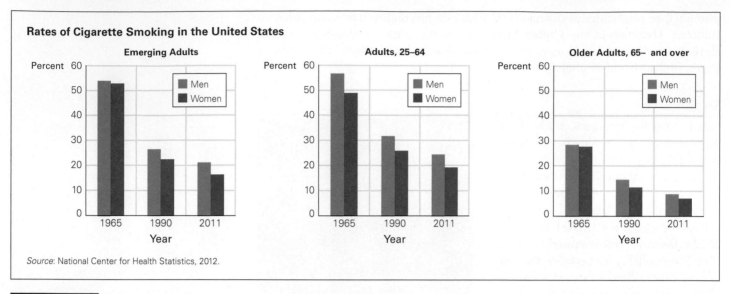

Rates of Cigarette Smoking in the United States

Source: National Center for Health Statistics, 2012.

FIGURE 20.2

Older and Wiser Everyone can see the obvious good news here: In the United States (not worldwide), far fewer people of any age are smoking than in 1965. But look closely with a developmental perspective: More than half of the people now over age 65 were smokers when they were young adults. Cigarettes are said to be as addictive as heroin, and quit-rates increase with every year of adulthood. Thus, this figure shows that about one hundred thousand Americans have kicked a powerful, destructive habit.

Source: National Center for Health Statistics, 2013.

Especially for Doctors and Nurses If you had to choose between recommending various screening tests and recommending various lifestyle changes to a 35-year-old, which would you do? (see response, page 591)

Alcohol Abuse

The harm from cigarettes is dose-related: Each puff, each day, each breath of secondhand smoke makes cancer, heart disease, strokes, and emphysema more likely. No such linear harm results from drinking alcohol. In fact, alcohol can be beneficial: People who drink wine, beer, or spirits *in moderation*—never more than two drinks a day—live longer than abstainers. Drinking more than that is harmful.

The primary reason for the benefit is that alcohol reduces coronary heart disease and strokes. It increases HDL (high-density lipoprotein), the "good" form of cholesterol, and reduces LDL (low-density lipoprotein), the "bad" cholesterol that causes clogged arteries and blood clots. An occasional drink may also lower blood pressure and glucose (Klatsky, 2009).

However, moderation is impossible for some people, and lack of moderation is dangerous. Alcoholics find it easier to abstain than to have one, and only one, drink a day. Binge drinking increases the risk of strokes and high blood pressure.

Furthermore, alcohol abuse destroys brain cells; contributes to osteoporosis; decreases fertility; and accompanies many suicides, homicides, and accidents—while wreaking havoc in many families. It is implicated in 60 diseases, not only liver damage but also cancer of the breast, stomach, and throat.

There are stark international variations in alcohol abuse. It is rare in Muslim nations where alcohol is illegal, but it causes about half the deaths of Russian men under the age of 60 (Leon et al., 2007). For U.S. adults, binge drinking is dangerous and common: About 32 percent of people 25 to 44 years of age and 18 percent of those between 45 and 64 had five or more drinks on a single occasion in the past year (National Center for Health Statistics, 2013). The U.S. had 88,000 alcohol-related deaths between 2006 and 2010 (MMWR, March 14, 2014)

From 1980 to 2010 in the United States, various laws and community practices cut in half the rate of motor vehicle deaths caused by drunk drivers. In many nations, the risk of accidental death because of drinking is more common among younger adults, but the ongoing harm to families is more prevalent when an alcoholic is middle-aged (Blas & Kurup, 2010).

In general, low-income nations have more abstainers, more abusers, and fewer moderate drinkers than more affluent nations (Blas & Kurup, 2010). In poor nations, prevention and treatment strategies for alcohol abuse have not been established, regulation is rare, and laws have not caught up with abuse (Bollyky, 2012). Thus, alcohol becomes particularly lethal as national income falls.

Nutrition

Metabolism decreases by one-third between ages 20 and 60, and digestion become less efficient. To stay the same weight, adults need to eat less and move more as they age. Further, since overall calories must decline, more fruits and vegetables and fewer sweets and fats must be consumed each year. That is not what happens.

Prevalence of Obesity

In the United States, adults now gain an average of one to two pounds each year, much more than prior generations did. Over the 40 years of adulthood, that adds 40 to 80 pounds. As a result, two-thirds of U.S. adults are overweight, defined as a body mass index (BMI) of 25 or more. Indeed, almost one-third of all U.S. men and more than one-third of all U.S. women age 25 to 65 are obese (with a BMI over 30), with 12 percent of those men and 20 percent of those women morbidly obese (with a BMI over 40) (National Center for Health Statistics, 2013). [Lifespan Link: BMI was explained in Chapter 17.]

If BMI numbers seem abstract, picture a person who is 5 feet, 8 inches tall. If that person weighs 150 pounds, BMI is about 23, a normal weight. If he or she weighs 200 pounds, the BMI is 30, which makes that person obese. If he or she weighs more than 260 pounds, the BMI is over 40, making that person morbidly obese.

If you spend most of your time among 20-year-old college students, you may be unaware of the prevalence of obesity because people in their 20s have lower rates of obesity than those in their 40s or 50s. Further, those who are obese are less likely to go out, so you do not see them as often as you see the thinner ones.

Half a billion people worldwide are obese. Rates seem to have reached a plateau in the United States, but many developing nations are reporting rapidly increasing rates (see Visualizing Development, page 590). This is particularly true in Africa and Asia, where malnutrition once was the most prevalent nutritional problem; now obesity is (World Health Organization, 2013).

Consequences of Obesity

A recent meta-analysis found that mortality rates by age for adults who were somewhat overweight were *lower* than the rates for people who were thinner, a conclusion that comforted many portly adults (Flegal et al., 2013). However, BMI of 25 or 26 may be okay, but no research finds that obesity is healthy. Excess body fat increases the risk of almost every chronic disease.

One example is diabetes, which is rapidly becoming more common and causes eye, heart, and foot problems as well as early death. Although diabetes is partly genetic, the genetic tendency is exacerbated by excess fat. The United States is the world leader in both obesity and diabetes.

The consequences of obesity are psychological as well as physical, since adults who are obese are targets of scorn and prejudice. They are less likely to be chosen as marriage partners, as employees, and even as friends. The stigma endured by fat people leads them to avoid medical checkups, to eat more, and to exercise less—with the result that their health is far more impaired than the mere fact of their weight would predict (Puhl & Heuer, 2010).

Adult Overweight Around the Globe

A century ago, being overweight was a sign of affluence, as the poor were less likely to enjoy a calorie-rich diet and more likely to be engaged in physical labor. Today, that link is less clear. Overweight—defined as having a body mass index (BMI) over 25—is common across socioeconomic groups and across borders, and obesity (a BMI over 30) is a growing health threat worldwide.

OVERWEIGHT AND GDP

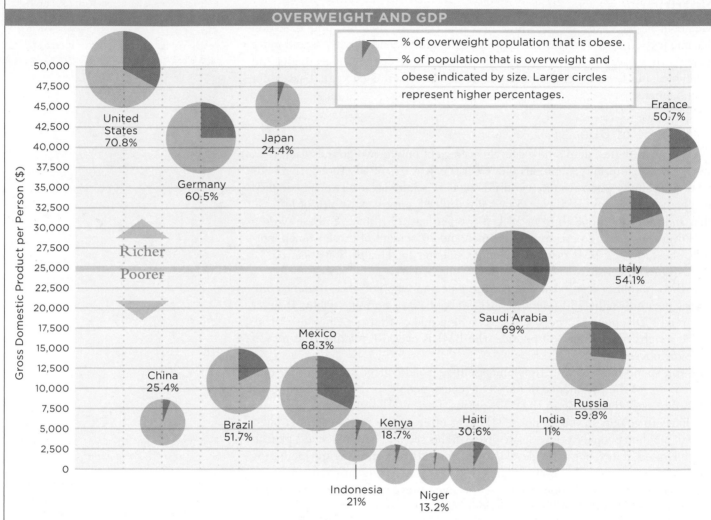

% of overweight population that is obese.

% of population that is overweight and obese indicated by size. Larger circles represent higher percentages.

Gross Domestic Product per Person ($)

Richer

Poorer

United States 70.8%

Germany 60.5%

Japan 24.4%

France 50.7%

Italy 54.1%

Saudi Arabia 69%

Russia 59.8%

Mexico 68.3%

China 25.4%

Brazil 51.7%

Kenya 18.7%

Haiti 30.6%

India 11%

Indonesia 21%

Niger 13.2%

International cutoff weights for overweight and obesity are set at various levels. These numbers show proportions of adults whose BMI is over 25.

SOURCES: WORLD HEALTH ORGANIZATION (2013); WORLD BANK (2013).

OBESITY IN THE UNITED STATES

While common wisdom holds that overweight and obesity correlate with income, recent data suggests that culture and gender may play a bigger role. Obesity tends to be less prevalent among wealthy American women; for men, the patterns are less consistent.

Male   Female

$$$ = Income 350%+ of poverty level
$$ = Income 130% - 349% of poverty level
$ = Income less than 130% of poverty level

OBESITY RATES (U.S.)

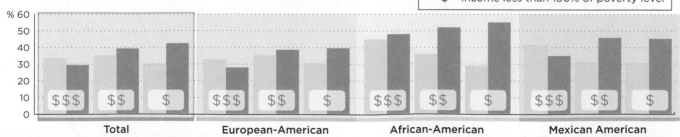

% 60

Total

European-American

African-American

Mexican American

SOURCE: PEW RESEARCH CENTER (2013).

Perhaps the goal for people whose health is damaged by their weight should be to lose enough pounds to protect their health rather than to reach normal weight. The culture's emphasis on an ideal BMI, particularly in women, may encourage unhealthy dieting and then eating disorders, including overeating (Shai & Stampfer, 2009). This may explain why more women than men are of healthy weight (they care more) or obese (they give up if they can't stay thin).

Healthy eating and good health care are important for all adults, whether or not they are overweight. Indeed, some people may be genetically destined to be outside the boundaries of normal weight. In the United States, Asian American adults have significantly lower rates of obesity (11 percent) and African Americans higher rates (48 percent). It is possible that the BMI cutoffs should be altered for these groups. It is also possible that weight is an important factor in the higher rates of premature death among African Americans.

The relationship between culture and obesity is crucial, although not completely understood. For instance, scientists collected many biophysiological measures (including weight, height, blood pressure, and cholesterol and glucose levels) on 5,000 adults, half of them with Inuit ancestry and half with European forebears, all living in the far Northwest of North America. Although the Inuit tended to have higher BMIs, their weight-related health risk was significantly lower than that of the Europeans. Centuries of adaptation to the Arctic may have produced body fat as insulation, without creating the mortality risk usually associated with excess fat (Young et al., 2007).

In another study, adaption to national conditions lowered the health risk. In Cuba from 1991 to 1995, a national economic crisis led to less meat and more exercise, resulting not only in an average weight loss of 14 pounds but also a decrease in the incidence of diabetes and heart disease. When the crisis was over, people regained the weight and the diabetes rate doubled (Franco et al., 2013).

Obviously, we should not rely on genes or hope for an economic crisis. However, many people do not seem able to control their eating before it becomes dangerous. For the morbidly obese, bariatric surgery may be the best option.

About 200,000 United States residents undergo gastric bypass or gastric banding surgery to lose weight each year. The rate of complications is quite high, with about 2 percent dying during or soon after the operation, and about 10 percent needing additional surgery.

Over time, however, surgery that reduces obesity saves lives because morbid obesity is a serious risk to survival (Adams et al., 2012; Schauer et al., 2010). The greatest benefits seem to occur for people with diabetes: 70 percent find that their diabetes disappears, usually not to return (Arterburn et al., 2013).

Causes of Weight Gain

Why is obesity so prevalent in the United States? In previous chapters we noted two culprits, advertising and peer pressure; here we focus more specifically on what people eat.

The typical U.S. family consumes more meat and fat and less fiber than people in other parts of the world. For example, the Chinese traditionally ate many vegetables mixed with small bits of meat or fish; in general, they did not have a weight problem. Some blame the recent weight increase in China on the new taste for American food.

One specific culprit in weight gain may be sugar, either sucrose or fructose (added to many packaged foods and beverages through corn syrup). A study that reduced sugar in foods found that people lost weight, and another study in 175 nations found a correlation between national sugar consumption and diabetes (Te Morenga et al, 2013; Basu et al., 2013).

>> Response for Doctors and Nurses (from page 588): Obviously, much depends on the specific patient. Overall, however, far more people develop a disease or die because of years of poor health habits than because of various illnesses not spotted early. With some exceptions, age 35 is too early to detect incipient cancers or circulatory problems, but it's prime time for stopping cigarette smoking, curbing alcohol abuse, and improving exercise and diet.

Cocaine or Coffee Cake? Could this be as dangerous as shooting up in a crack house? Few people are troubled by an overweight office worker drinking coffee and munching cake made with white flour, butter, and sugar. Yet more adult deaths occur because millions snack unhealthily than because thousands are addicted to cocaine. It is far easier to criticize people with bad habits than it is to change our own behavior.

Hope It Helps Ideally, this is part of her daily exercise routine, and no one will complain about a fire hazard. More likely, though, her back hurts from hunching over her desk in an uncomfortable chair, her supervisor questions her undignified behavior, and no one in the adjoining cubicles asks to borrow her ball. Social norms make exercise difficult.

Scientists and physicians agree that nutrition is a factor in almost every adult ailment. Although some specifics have not yet been proven (sugar may not be the worst villain), a healthy diet is undoubtedly protective for every adult. Common in Greece and Italy is the so-called Mediterranean diet, which is high in fiber, fish, and olive oil. This diet has been proven to protect against heart disease without adding weight (Estruch et al., 2013). Unfortunately, though, almost no one eats as well as they should.

Inactivity

Regular physical activity at every stage of life protects against serious illness even if a person has other undesirable health habits such as smoking and overeating. Exercise reduces blood pressure; strengthens the heart and lungs; and makes depression, osteoporosis, heart disease, arthritis, and even some cancers less likely. Health benefits from exercise are substantial for men and women, old and young, former sports stars and those who never joined a team (Aldwin & Gilmer, 2013).

By contrast, sitting for long hours correlates with almost every unhealthy condition, especially heart disease and diabetes, both of which carry additional health hazards beyond the disease itself. Even a little movement—gardening, light housework, walking up the stairs or to the bus—helps.

As explained in Chapter 17, walking briskly for at least 30 minutes a day, five days a week, is a reasonable goal. More intense exercise (e.g., swimming, jogging, bicycling) and muscle strengthening workouts are ideal. It is possible to exercise too much, but almost no adult does. In fact, one study that used objective assessment of adult movement (electronic monitors) found that fewer than 5 percent of adults in the United States and England get even 30 minutes per day of exercise (Weiler & Stamatakis, 2010). (Self-reports put the number at about 30 percent, not 5 percent; see Figure 20.3.)

The close connection between exercise and both physical and mental health is well known, as is the influence of family, friends, and neighborhoods. Exercise-friendly communities have lower rates of obesity, hypertension, and depression (Lee et al., 2009). Neighborhoods high in walkability (paths, sidewalks, etc.) reduce time spent driving and watching television (Kozo et al., 2012). This relationship between the surroundings, exercise, and health is causal, not merely correlational: People who are more active and fit have stronger immune systems, so they resist disease. Moreover, they feel energetic, which itself increases good health habits.

Many social scientists seek to encourage exercise and other good health habits among adults. Maintaining a healthy habit lifelong is the hardest part, as the following explains.

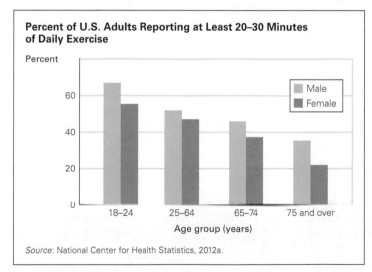

Percent of U.S. Adults Reporting at Least 20–30 Minutes of Daily Exercise

Source: National Center for Health Statistics, 2012a.

FIGURE 20.3

Older and Lazier Exercise is important at every age, but increasingly so as people get older. Why do people who need it most move the least?

A VIEW FROM SCIENCE

A Habit Is Hard to Break

Everyone knows that smoking cigarettes, abusing alcohol, overeating, and underexercising are harmful, yet almost everyone has at least one destructive habit. Why don't we all shape up and live right? Breaking New Year's resolutions; criticizing those whose bad habits are not our own; feeling guilty for consuming sugar, salt, fried foods, cigarettes, or alcohol; buying gym memberships that go unused or exercise equipment that becomes a coat rack or dust-gathering sculpture—these behaviors are common.

Many social scientists have focused on this conundrum (Martin et al., 2010; Luszczynska et al., 2011; Conner, 2008; Shumaker et al., 2009). First, we need to realize that changing a habit is a long, multistep process: Tactics that work at one step fail at another. Different strategies are needed at each stage. One list of these steps is: (1) denial, (2) awareness, (3) planning, (4) implementation, and (5) maintenance.

1. *Denial* occurs because all bad habits begin and are maintained for a reason. That makes denial a reasonable act of self-defense. For example, with cigarettes, most smokers begin as teenagers in order to be socially accepted, to appear mature, and/or to control weight—all especially important during adolescence. Before the teenager realizes it, nicotine creates addiction, and without the drug, smokers become anxious, confused, angry, and depressed. No wonder denial emerges.

With many life-threatening addictions (including smoking), being told how bad it is often leads to *more* smoking, drinking, and so on (Ben-Zur & Zeidner, 2009). People glorify destructive habits, they brag about being the "baddest." Denial is especially strong when an authority figure criticizes their habit. For instance, one out of eight smokers lies to his or her doctor about the habit, with adults aged 25 to 34 especially likely to lie (Curry et al., 2013). Obese people cannot lie about being overweight; instead they avoid doctors and strangers. Denial protects against stress; so does believing that change is impossible; so does additional drug use.

2. *Awareness* is attained by the person him- or herself, not from someone else. Sometimes awareness comes after a particularly dramatic event—a doctor predicting death from continued smoking, a night in jail because of drinking, tipping the scale at 200 pounds (which seems much more than 199).

Although other people may be counterproductive when they state facts or criticize (do you know that smoking causes lung cancer), *motivational interviewing* (asking the individual to explain the costs and benefits of the habit) may help. Often people fluctuate between denial and dawning awareness; a good listener can tip the balance by affirming what the person says about the downside of the habit and reiterating that the person can decide what to do. Self-efficacy—the belief that one can quit the drug, change the routine, and so on—is pivotal (Martin et al., 2010).

3. *Planning* is best when it is specific, such as setting a date for quitting and putting strategies in place to overcome the many obstacles. A series of studies has found that humans tend to underestimate the power of their own impulses, which arise from brain patterns, not logic (Belin et al., 2013). Thus, plans need to include strategies to defend against momentary wavering. Overconfidence makes it difficult to break a habit. This seems true for smokers, dieters, and everyone else.

In one experiment, researchers gave students who were entering or leaving a college cafeteria a choice of packaged snacks and promised to give each of them about $10 (and the snack) if they did not eat it for a week. Those who were entering the cafeteria, presumably aware of the demands of hunger, planned to avoid temptation by choosing a less desirable snack. Most of them (61 percent) earned the money. However, those who had just eaten apparently underestimated their hunger. They chose a more desirable snack and often ate it before the week was up; only 39 percent of this group earned the money (Nordgren et al., 2009).

4. *Implementation* is quitting the habit according to the plan. One crucial factor in achieving success is social support, such as (1) letting others know the specifics of the plan and enlisting their help, (2) finding a buddy, or (3) joining a group (Weight Watchers, Alcoholics Anonymous, or another 12-step program). Better yet, all three. Private efforts often fail. Implementation succeeds best with one habit at a time: Quitting cigarettes on the same day as beginning an exercise routine is ambitious but likely to be short-lived.

At the same time, past successes increase one's faith in self-efficacy. Going without a drug for a day is a reason for celebration, as well as proof that another day is possible. Checking off days on a calendar, rewarding oneself with a gift bought with the money saved from cigarettes not bought, listing past accomplishments—all these make success more likely.

5. *Maintenance* is the step that most people ignore. Although quitting any entrenched habit is difficult and sometimes painful, many addicts have quit many times, only to relapse. Dieters go on and off diets so often that this pattern has a name—yo-yo dieting. Sadly, once implementation succeeds, people are overconfident. They forget the power of temptation.

Willpower is thought to be like a muscle, slowly gaining strength with activity but subject to muscle fatigue if overused (Baumeister & Tierney, 2012). The recovered alcoholic might go out with friends who drink, confident that he will stick to juice instead of beer; the dieter will serve dessert to the rest of the family, certain she'll be able to resist a taste herself; the person who joined the gym will skip a day, planning to do twice as much the next day. Such actions are far more dangerous than people realize. The dieter who skips the dessert uses so much willpower that he or she is helpless at midnight, when the leftover cake beckons.

Any stress is likely to undercut resolve and restart the habit. For example, in one study dieters who were given a stressful task (remembering a nine-digit number) entered a room that had been set, seemingly at random, with either some tempting foods or a scale and a diet book. They were asked to taste a milkshake and give their opinion; they were also told they could drink as much as they wanted. Those who saw eating clues drank more than those who saw dieting clues (Mann & Ward, 2007).

This is called *attention myopia*, indicating that resolve (maintenance ability) fades when faced with stress. Many people who restart a bad habit explain that they did so under stress—a divorce, a new job, a rebellious teenager. Of course, sooner or later every adult is stressed; that is why maintenance strategies are crucial.

When the context encourages a slip, people mistakenly think that one cigarette, one drink, one slice of cake, one more swallow of milkshake, and so on, is inconsequential—which it would

be if the person stopped there. Unfortunately, the human mind is geared toward all or nothing. Neurons switch on or off, not halfway. For that reason, one puff makes the next one more likely, one potato chip awakens the compulsion for another, and so on. With alcohol, the drink itself scrambles the mind; people are less aware of their cognitive lapses under the influence and thus drink more after they have had that first drink (Sayette et al., 2009).

Maintenance depends a great deal on the ecological context, which makes the habits of other people and the circumstances of daily life crucial. A glass of wine poured when the recovered alcoholic wasn't looking, rain that makes jogging difficult, a calorie-dense cookie on the counter when the dieter is hungry—these are toxic to the person who is not prepared for them. Once a person is aware of a destructive problem (step two), it is relatively easy to plan and implement a better habit (steps three and four), but sticking to it (step five) is difficult if the context includes an unanticipated push in the opposite direction.

"The fresh mountain air is starting to depress me."

Just Give Me the Usual Even bad habits feel comfortable—that's what makes them habits.

mortality Death. As a measure of health, mortality usually refers to the number of deaths each year per hundred thousand members of a given population.

SUMMING UP

During adulthood, health habits are crucial. In nations with good medical care, if no one smoked, drank too much, overate, or underexercised, almost everyone would reach age 65 ready for decades more of active, happy life. Unfortunately, studies of bad habits over the decades of adulthood and over the years of the twenty-first century are not always encouraging. Cigarette smoking is decreasing in North America but not in many other nations. The United States includes a higher proportion of overweight, diabetic adults than almost any other nation. Alcohol abuse, obesity, and inactivity were not recognized as problems a few decades ago; now they are, but most adults find them hard to reverse. In many nations, better economic circumstances may, ironically, increase destructive health habits. ▪

>> Measuring Health

Far more money is spent preventing death among people who are already sick (tertiary prevention) than on wellness before anyone gets sick. [**Lifespan Link:** The three levels of prevention are discussed in Chapter 8.]

In contrast, primary and secondary prevention are the goals of most public health workers and developmentalists. To measure the effectiveness of various efforts, four indicators are used: mortality, morbidity, disability, and vitality.

Mortality

Death is the ultimate loss of health. **Mortality** is usually expressed as the annual number of deaths per hundred thousand in the population. The figure for various age, gender, and racial groups in the United States ranges from about 8 (Asian American girls aged 5 to 14 have 1 chance in 12,000 of dying within a year) to 15,640 (European American men over age 85 have about 1 chance in 6 of dying within a year) (National Center for Health Statistics, 2013).

To compare health among nations, age-adjusted mortality rates are needed; otherwise, a nation with many people over age 80 will have an artificially high mortality rate. The age-adjusted mortality rate among people in the United States in 2010 was 757 per 100,000—much better than 40 years earlier, when it was 1,230.

Mortality statistics are compiled from death certificates, which indicate age, sex, and immediate cause of death. This practice allows valid international and historical comparisons because deaths have been counted and recorded for decades—sometimes for centuries. Japan has the world's lowest age-adjusted mortality rate (about 500 per 100,000) and Sierra Leone the highest (about 3,500 per 100,000); both of these rates are markedly lower than they were a few decades ago.

Mortality is lower for women (see Figure 20.4). Worldwide, women live 4 years longer than men, though that figure varies from place to place (United Nations, 2013). For example, men die an average of 13 years earlier than women in Russia (61 versus 74) but at the same age in Sierra Leone (both at 44). Worldwide, old women outnumber old men (by 2 to 1 at age 85), primarily because more young men and boys die. The sex ratio favors boys at birth, is about equal at age 50, and tilts toward women from then on (United Nations, 2013).

This gender difference in mortality might be biological—the second X chromosome, more estrogen, or less testosterone could protect women. Or it might be cultural, since women tend to have more friends and take better care of themselves. One public health expert wrote:

> Men are socialized to project strength, individuality, autonomy, dominance, stoicism, and physical aggression, and to avoid demonstrations of emotion or vulnerability that could be construed as weakness. These [characteristics] . . . combine to increase health risks.

[D. R. Williams, 2003, p. 726]

Mortality rates also vary by ethnicity, income, and place of residence, within nations as well as between them. For example, the overall risk of dying for a U.S. resident at some point between ages 25 and 65 is about 15 percent, but for some it is as high as 50 percent (e.g., Sioux men in South Dakota) or less than 2 percent (Asian women in Connecticut) (Lewis & Bird-Sharps, 2010).

FIGURE 20.4

Not So Many Old Men International comparisons of life expectancy are useful for raising questions (why is the United States more similar to Mexico than to Japan?) and for highlighting universals (females live longer, no matter what their culture or health-care system).

Source: United Nations, Department of Economic and Social Affairs, Population Division (2013).

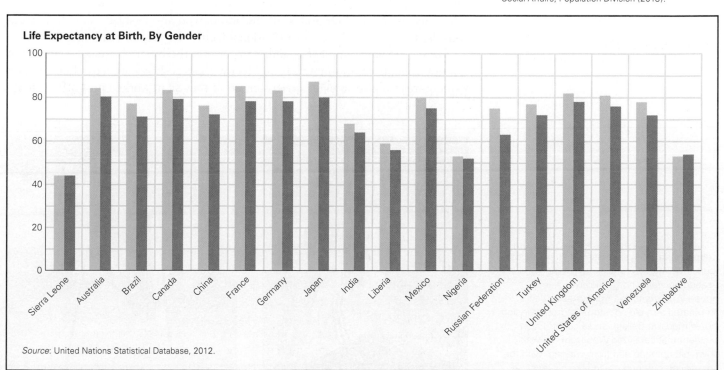

Life Expectancy at Birth, By Gender

Source: United Nations Statistical Database, 2012.

Morbidity

morbidity Disease. As a measure of health, morbidity usually refers to the rate of diseases in a given population—physical and emotional, acute (sudden) and chronic (ongoing).

Another measure of health is **morbidity** (from the Latin word for "disease"), which refers to illnesses and impairments of all kinds—acute and chronic, physical and psychological.

Morbidity does not necessarily correlate with mortality. In the United States, almost half of older women have osteoarthritis; none die of it. Compared to men the same age, adult women have lower rates of mortality but higher rates of morbidity for almost every chronic disease.

Worldwide, as mortality decreases, morbidity *increases*. For instance, heart disease and cancer have been the leading causes of death for decades, but now they are also common causes of morbidity. The very measures that have saved lives—screening, drugs, surgery—have also reduced health.

A recent example is the PSA blood test for prostate cancer. Some research finds that screening adds a day to the average man's life—the reason being that if early diagnosis stalls or prevents death, adding a year of life to one man while 364 screened men are not helped would average to about one day of extended life.

However, if a significant number of those 364 suffer from overdiagnosis, biopsies, and unnecessary surgery, producing increased morbidity (incontinence, impotence, crippling anxiety), then the screening was more destructive than beneficial. That is why the American Council of Physicians notes the "limited potential benefits and substantial harm of screening for prostate cancer" (Quaseem et al., 2013).

Likewise, mammograms for women under age 50 produce many false positives, and then needless biopsies and anxiety. Overall, when risks of both mortality and morbidity are considered, mammograms for many women may be more harmful than helpful (Woloshin & Schwartz, 2010).

Disability

disability Difficulty in performing normal activities of daily life because of some physical, mental, or emotional condition.

Disability refers to difficulty in performing "activities of daily life" because of a "physical, mental, or emotional condition." Limitation in functioning (not severity of disease) is the hallmark of disability. Disability does not necessarily equal morbidity: In the United States, of the adults who are disabled, only 30 percent consider their health fair or poor (National Center for Health Statistics, 2013).

Normal activities, and hence ability to perform them, vary by social context. For example, people who cannot walk 200 feet without resting have a disability if their job requires walking (a mail carrier) but not if they sit at work (a post office clerk).

Keep Moving Physical disabilities need not reduce vitality, as French long-jumper Arnaud Assoumani *(left)* and Canadian architect Robert Woo *(right)* exemplify. Assoumani's amputated arm did not stop him from winning a gold medal in Beijing, and a construction accident that paralyzed Woo from the waist down did not stop him from walking, with the help of computer commands to his legs.

Disability-adjusted life years, or **DALYs,** are one way to measure a person's degree of impairment due to a disability. The assumption is that a disabled person has somewhat less than a full life; Thus, a person born with a disability that reduces functioning by about 10 percent, who then lives to age 70, would be said to have 63 DALYs because the disability is considered to have cost that person 7 healthy, active years (10 percent of 70). As you might imagine, many disabled people do not like the idea of DALYs; they do not consider their lives diminished.

Nonetheless, DALYs are useful in comparing nations and in examining trends. An analysis of DALYs in 21 regions of the world found that noncommunicable diseases are now the most common cause of disability, with heart disease first on the list (Murray et al., 2012). As communicable diseases (for example, malaria) have decreased, the DALYs of mental illness, especially depression, have increased. That means that, internationally, public health measures such as immunization have reduced diseases that one person catches from another, but economic and cultural stresses have increased psychological disability.

Vitality

The final measure of health, **vitality,** refers to how healthy and energetic—physically, intellectually, and socially—an individual feels. Vitality is *joie de vivre,* zest for living, love of life (Gigante, 2007). A person can feel terrific despite having a serious disease or disability.

For example, a study of older women in the United States with chronic diseases found that many felt energetic and vital, at least some of the time (Crawford Shearer et al., 2009). Vitality is affected more by personality and social affirmation than by biology. A longitudinal study of young adults who had been born weighing less than 3 pounds found that they were shorter and less athletic, and had higher risk of disease than a matched control group, but their vitality was as high as that of their peers (Baumgardt et al., 2011).

One way to measure vitality is to calculate **quality-adjusted life years (QALYs).** If people are fully vital, their quality of life is 100 percent, which means that a year of their life equals one QALY. A healthy, happy, energetic person who lives 70 years has 70 QALYs. If one year included surgery and a difficult recovery, with an estimated 50 percent reduction in quality of life, then that person's QALY would be 69½.

Calculating DALYs or QALYs helps in allocating public funds. No society spends enough to enable everyone to live life to the fullest. Without some equitable and calculable measure of disability and vitality, the best health care goes to whoever has the most money, or whatever tugs hardest at the public heartstrings.

This raises ethical issues. For example, should taxpayers subsidize kidney dialysis for young college students or intensive care for severely disabled 80-year-olds? If care of the elderly costs $100,000 per year of life saved, but dialysis costs $10,000 per year of life saved, then dialysis would be the priority. Would it matter, though, if those damaged kidneys were the result of drug abuse, or if that older person was a former president?

That example is hypothetical; real choices are not that simple, and personal values push societies in directions that are not reflected in DALYs. Age is a factor: Many people think saving the life of a newborn is worth more than saving the life of a old person—a calculus that may benefit from understanding QALYs. But that may be ageist. [**Lifespan Link:** Ageism is discussed in Chapter 23.]

Individuals differ in how they value life, health, and appearance. As you read earlier, for some people, visibly growing older reduces their quality of life. They might avoid all social contact, and then temporarily lower their QALYs with cosmetic surgery, hoping to gain a higher quality of life. Other people would consider that foolish, because appearance does not impair their QALY.

DALYs (disability-adjusted life years) A measure of the reduced quality of life caused by disability.

vitality A measure of health that refers to how healthy and energetic—physically, intellectually, and socially—an individual actually feels.

QALYs (quality-adjusted life years) A way of comparing mere survival without vitality to survival with good health. A full year of health is a full QALY; people with less than full health have a fraction of QALY each year. Thus, their total QALY is less than the total years they live.

This discussion leads to issues of public health and human development. If the focus is only on mortality and morbidity, prevention is tertiary (saving the seriously ill from dying) or secondary (spotting early symptoms). If the goal is less disability and more vitality, then factors (such as pollution, drug abuse, and global warming) that reduce QALY by a tiny bit for millions of people merit attention.

Correlating Income and Health

Money and education protect health. Well-educated, financially secure adults live longer and avoid morbidity and disability more than their fellow citizens. National health care reduces some of the SES disparities in health but not all of them: Even in nations with good universal health-care insurance, the poorest people have shorter lives, on average. It is not clear whether income or education is the main reason.

Perhaps education teaches healthy habits. Obesity and cigarette smoking in the United States are almost twice as common among adults with the least education compared to those with post-college degrees. Or perhaps higher income allows access to better medical care as well as a home far from pollution and crime.

For whatever reason, the differences can be dramatic. The 10 million U.S. residents with the highest SES (and the best health care) outlive—by about 30 years—the 10 million with the lowest SES, who live in rundown areas (Lewis & Burd-Sharpes, 2010).

SES has been shown to be protective of health in comparisons made both between and within nations. Compared to developing nations, rich countries have lower rates of disease, injury, and early death. For example, a baby born in 2010 in Northern Europe can expect to live to age 80; a baby born in central Africa can expect to live only to age 51 (United Nations, 2013).

Without doubt, low SES harms human development in every way, evident in statistics on mortality, morbidity, disability, and vitality. The data show that babies born poor are unlikely to escape their SES, as their education, health care, job prospects, and so on are all likely to work against them. They enter adulthood already impaired. Is there any hope?

That question returns us to Jenny, whose story began this chapter. When I first met her, she was among the poorest 10 million people in the United States, living in a Bronx neighborhood known as "Gunsmoke Territory" because of its high homicide rate. She was also African American (did you guess that from the sickle-cell trait?), and people of that ethnic group tend to have a higher allostatic load.

Observation Quiz The differences between the two scenes below are less about national culture than about neighborhood SES. What three signs suggest that the Brazilians are in a low-income neighborhood? (see answer, page 599)

Playground? Cities that create play space for people of all ages keep the residents active, like these young men in Hong Kong *(left)* and Rio de Janeiro *(right)*.

Her decision to have another baby—with no promise of marriage or of the father's support—made me fear she would never escape from poverty. This is not a stereotype: The data show that lifelong poverty is the usual future for low-income mothers who have another child, out of wedlock, with a married man.

But statistics do not reflect Jenny's intelligence, creativity, and practical expertise. She applied what she learned. She knew she should be honest with Billy, and asked him to be tested for sickle cell (it was negative). She made her apartment "baby proof," locking up the poisons, covering the electric outlets, getting her landlord to put guards on the windows.

She made the best of available government help. Her tuition was paid by a Pell grant, she lived in public housing, her children went to public schools, and she found parks and museums where her children could play and learn.

More important, she knew when and how to access social support, evidenced by her seeking me out. I saw her help her children with their homework, befriend their teachers, find speech therapy for her son, and provide love, supervision, and protection for all of them. After giving birth to a healthy, full-term baby girl, she found work tutoring children in her home, so she could earn some money while caring for her newborn.

When the baby was a little older, she went back to college, earning her B.A. on a full scholarship. Her professors recognized her intelligence and chose her to give the graduation speech. She then found work as a receptionist in a city hospital, a union job that provided medical insurance for her family. That allowed her to move her family to a safer part of the Bronx. While Jenny is exceptional, she is not unique: Some low-income people are able to overcome the potential stressors of poverty (Chen & Miller, 2012).

Billy would sometimes visit her and the daughter he did not want, providing emotional and financial support. His wife became suspicious, hired a private investigator to follow him, and then delivered an ultimatum: Stop seeing Jenny or obtain a divorce. He chose Jenny. Soon after that, Billy married Jenny, and they moved to Florida.

Jenny continues to do well, though she has not completely escaped the toll of her early life (she developed diabetes, and must watch her diet carefully). But she bikes, swims, and gardens almost every day. She works full time in education, having earned a master's degree. She and Billy seem happy together. Recently, I met the son who had a speech impediment: he had earned a PhD and is an assistant professor. Jenny's daughters are college graduates.

This example might give the impression that escaping from poverty is easy; all the longitudinal data shows that it is not. Nor do most poor children thrive as Jenny's children did. But the study of human development is not only about the contexts that affect each person. Each person is buffeted by all the habits, conditions, and circumstances described in this chapter, but each is also able to make choices that affect the future. The next chapter, on cognition in adulthood, describes some of those choices.

SUMMING UP

Health can be measured in at least four ways. Mortality is the easiest way to compare nations and cohorts, since keeping track of deaths is straightforward. Morbidity measures chronic illness, requiring diagnosis and ideally leading to treatment. Morbidity is more common in women than in men. Disability is indicated by difficulty performing daily tasks. Worldwide, disability is increasingly recognized as including psychological difficulties that make it hard to live a full life. Finally, vitality is the joy in living. Vitality is sought by everyone, affected by culture and personal choices, and may be independent of mortality and morbidity. SES within nations and among nations has a dramatic impact on health. Yet individuals sometimes find ways to overcome the strikes against them. ∎

>> Answer to Observation Quiz (from page 598): The play space is smaller, the residences seem less elegant, and, most important, the Brazilians are shoeless—even though their sport demands running on cement and kicking the ball.

SUMMARY

Senescence

1. Senescence causes a universal slowdown of body systems during adulthood, but the changes due to aging are often imperceptible because organ reserve maintains capacity. The entire body adjusts to changes in the short term (homeostasis) and the long term (allostasis).

2. The brain slows down and begins a gradual decline that is not usually initially perceptible. In addition to measures that protect overall health, the brain is also affected by psychoactive drugs, poor circulation, viruses, and genetics.

3. A person's appearance undergoes gradual but noticeable changes as middle age progresses, including more wrinkles, less hair, and more fat, particularly around the abdomen. With the exception of excessive weight gain and related conditions, changes in appearance have little impact on health.

4. The rate of senescence is most apparent in the sense organs. Vision becomes less sharp with age, with both nearsightedness and farsightedness increasing gradually beginning in the 20s. Hearing also becomes less acute.

The Sexual-Reproductive System

5. Sexual responsiveness slows down with age, as does speed of recovery after orgasm. This is only a physical decline; many couples find that, overall, sexual interaction improves with age.

6. Fertility problems become more common with increased age, for many reasons. The most common one for men is a reduced number of sperm, and for women, ovulation failure or blocked fallopian tubes. For both sexes, not only youth but also overall good health—especially sexual health—correlates with fertility.

7. A number of assisted reproductive technology (ART) procedures, including IVF (in vitro fertilization), offer potential solutions to infertility. Donor sperm, donor ova, and/or donor wombs have helped thousands of infertile couples become parents.

8. At menopause, as a woman's menstrual cycle stops, ovulation ceases and levels of estrogen are markedly reduced. This

hormonal change produces various symptoms in some women, including vaginal dryness and body temperature disturbance as well as erratic moods, energy surges, and depression. Other women seem unaffected.

9. Hormone production declines in men, too, though not as suddenly as in women. For both sexes, hormone replacement therapy (HRT) should be used cautiously, if at all.

Health Habits and Age

10. Adults in North America are smoking far less than they once did, and rates of lung cancer and other diseases are falling, largely for that reason. Alcohol abuse remains a major health problem worldwide.

11. Good health habits include exercising regularly and proper nutrition. On both of these counts, today's adults worldwide are faring worse than did previous generations. This is especially true in the United States. There is a worldwide "epidemic of obesity," as more people have access to abundant food and overeat as a result.

Measuring Health

12. Variations in health can be measured in terms of mortality, morbidity, disability, and vitality. Although death and disease are easier to quantify, disability and vitality may be more significant in terms of the health of a population. Quality-adjusted life years (QALYs) and disability-adjusted life years (DALYs) help doctors and public health advocates figure out how to allocate limited resources.

13. Aging and health status can be greatly affected by SES. In general, those who have more education and money are more likely to live longer and avoid illness than their poorer counterparts. However, low SES does not inevitably lead to poor health since genes and health habits are protective. Avoiding drugs and obesity is possible at any income level.

KEY TERMS

andropause (p. 585)
disability (p. 596)
disability-adjusted life years (DALYs) (p. 597)
hormone replacement therapy (HRT) (p. 585)
infertility (p. 582)
menopause (p. 584)
morbidity (p. 596)
mortality (p. 594)
presbycusis (p. 579)
quality-adjusted life years (QALYs) (p. 597)
senescence (p. 576)
vitality (p. 597)

WHAT HAVE YOU LEARNED?

1. What is the connection between senescence and serious disease?

2. How often and why do people lose significant brain function before age 65?

3. What are the visible changes in the skin between ages 25 and 65?

4. What are the visible changes in the hair between ages 25 and 65?

5. What are the visible changes in the body shape between ages 25 and 65?

6. How does aging affect nearsightedness and farsightedness?

7. Why are hearing losses expected to increase in the next generation?

8. How are men and women affected by the changes in sexual responsiveness with age?

9. When a couple is infertile, which sex is usually responsible?

10. What are the advantages and disadvantages of HRT for women? Are there any advantages/disadvantages for men?

11. What are the trends in cigarette smoking in North America?

12. How much alcohol should an adult drink and why?

13. What factors in the diet affect the rate of obesity?

14. What nonfood factors affect the rate of obesity?

15. What diseases and conditions are less likely in people who exercise every day?

16. What are the advantages and disadvantages of using mortality as a measure of health?

17. What are the advantages and disadvantages of using morbidity as a measure of health?

18. How do men and women compare in mortality and morbidity?

19. Why would a disabled person object to measuring DALYs?

20. What factors would increase a person's QALYs?

21. Are economic or educational factors more important in the correlation between SES and illness?

22. Why are there no more diseases of affluence?

APPLICATIONS

1. Guess the age of five people you know, and then ask them how old they are. Analyze the clues you used for your guesses and the people's reactions to your question.

2. Find a specialist willing to come to your class who is an expert on weight loss, adult health, smoking, or drinking. Write a one-page proposal explaining why you think this speaker would be good and what topics he or she should address. Give this proposal to your instructor, with contact information for your speaker. The instructor will call the potential speakers, thank them for their willingness, and decide whether or not to actually invite them to speak.

3. Attend a gathering for people who want to stop a bad habit or start a good one—an open meeting of Alcoholics Anonymous or another 12-step program, an introductory session of Weight Watchers or SmokEnders, or a meeting of prospective gym members. Report on who attended, what you learned, and what your reactions were.

>>ONLINE CONNECTIONS

To accompany your textbook, you have access to a number of online resources, including Learning Curve, an adaptive quizzing program, critical thinking questions, and case studies. For access to any of these links, go to www.worthpublishers.com /launchpad/bergerls9e. In addition to these resources, you'll also find links to video clips, personalized study advice, and an ebook. Some of the videos and activities available online include:

- *Brain Development: Middle Adulthood.* Animations show age-related loss of brain volume and compensatory increase in size of the ventricles and volume of cerebrospinal fluid

- *Signs of Aging.* Video, audio, and illustrations demonstrate the physical and sensory changes that come with aging and older people's reactions to the process.

WORTH PUBLISHERS

Adulthood: Cognitive Development

- What Is Intelligence?
  Research on Age and Intelligence
  Cross-Sequential Research
- Components of Intelligence: Many and Varied
  Two Clusters of Intelligence
  Three Forms of Intelligence
  Age and Culture
  OPPOSING PERSPECTIVES: What Makes a Good Parent?
- Selective Gains and Losses
  Accumulating Stressors
  A CASE TO STUDY: Coping with Katrina
  Optimization with Compensation
  Expert Cognition

WHAT WILL YOU KNOW?

1. Why does each generation think it is smarter than earlier generations?
2. Why does each older generation think it knows more than younger generations?
3. What aspects of thinking improve during the years of adulthood?
4. Is everyone an expert at something?

One of my daughters was on the search committee for selecting the new college president and is delighted with the chosen new leader. He came from outside academia and took a huge pay cut to accept the appointment. He is improving the institution in many ways.

> "You must be glad they selected the one you wanted," I said.
> "He's not the one I wanted. I didn't even want to interview him. Others on the committee outvoted me; I am glad they did."

She was unimpressed with his paper resume because she is a scholar and he had few publications. But she listened to others' assessments, thought again about her criteria, and now is thrilled with his performance.

Her approach during the selection process illustrates adult cognition at its best. Adults have ideas, quite logical ones, but they also learn to listen to other people. We each have areas of knowledge in which we are experts, but as adults we consider other minds, experiences, and emotions.

As you read this chapter, you will realize that cognition is multifaceted. Some abilities improve with age; others do not. Each person becomes an expert at particular skills and knowledge, downplaying other abilities. Ideally, cognition improves, and we all become better able to appreciate our own intelligence and that of everyone else.

Remember that many research strategies are used to describe cognition beginning at age 18 and extending into old age. Chapter 18 described postformal thinking as well as the impact of college. Chapter 24 will take an information-processing perspective, highlighting the aspects of processing that slow down, and describing dementia. This chapter takes a psychometric approach (*metric* means "measure"; *psychometric* refers to the measurement of psychological characteristics) and considers various kinds of intelligence, including those that produce experts of one sort or another.

I am proud that my adult daughter realized that the new leader is smart and talented in many ways, just not in the areas familiar to her. That is part of expertise.

>> What Is Intelligence?

For most of the twentieth century, everyone—scientists and the general public alike—assumed that there was such a thing as "intelligence"; that is, they assumed that some people are smarter than others because they have more intelligence than others. This affects people lifelong. Scores on IQ tests can change from childhood to adulthood, sometimes markedly, but they generally predict education, income, and longevity (Calvin et al., 2011), all of which vary from person to person.

As one scholar begins a book on intelligence:

> Homer and Shakespeare lived in very different times, more than two thousand years apart, but they both captured the same idea: we are not all equally intelligent. I suspect that anyone who has failed to notice this is somewhat out of touch with the species.
>
> *[Hunt, 2011, p. 1]*

general intelligence (*g*) The idea of *g* assumes that intelligence is one basic trait, underlying all cognitive abilities. According to this concept, people have varying levels of this general ability.

One leading theoretician, Charles Spearman (1927), proposed that there is a single entity, **general intelligence**, which he called **g**. Spearman contended that, although *g* cannot be measured directly, it can be inferred from various abilities, such as vocabulary, memory, and reasoning.

IQ tests had already been developed to identify children who needed special instruction, but Spearman promoted the idea that everyone's overall intelligence could be measured by combining test scores on a diverse mix of items. A summary IQ number could reveal whether a person is a superior, typical, or slow learner, or, using labels of 100 years ago that are no longer used, a genius, imbecile, or idiot.

The belief that there is a *g* continues to influence thinking on intelligence (Nisbett et al., 2012). Many neuroscientists search for genetic underpinnings of intellectual capacity, although they have not yet succeeded in finding *g* (Deary et al., 2010; Haier et al., 2009). Some aspects of brain function, particularly in the prefrontal cortex, hold promise (Barbey et al., 2013; Roca et al., 2010). Many other scientists also seek one common factor that undergirds IQ—perhaps prenatal brain development, experiences in infancy, or physical health.

Research on Age and Intelligence

Although psychometricians throughout the twentieth century believed that intelligence could be measured and quantified via IQ tests, they disagreed about interpreting the data—especially about whether *g* rises or falls after age 20 or so (Hertzog, 2011). Methodology was one reason for that disagreement. Consider the implications of the three methods used for studying human development mentioned in Chapter 1: cross-sectional, longitudinal, and cross-sequential.

Cross-Sectional Declines

For the first half of the twentieth century, psychologists believed that intelligence increases in childhood, peaks in adolescence, and then gradually declines. Younger people were considered smarter than older ones. This belief was based on the best evidence then available.

Smart Enough for the Trenches? These young men were drafted to fight in World War I. Younger men (about age 17 or 18) did better on the military's intelligence tests than slightly older ones did.

Observation Quiz Beyond the test itself, what conditions of the testing favored the younger men? (see answer, page 606)

For instance, the U.S. Army tested the aptitude of all draftees in World War I. When the scores of men of various ages were compared, it seemed apparent that intellectual ability reached its peak at about age 18, stayed at that level until the mid-20s, and then declined (Yerkes, 1923).

Hundreds of other cross-sectional studies of IQ in many nations confirmed that younger adults outscored older adults. The case for an age-related decline in IQ was considered proven. The two classic IQ tests, the Stanford-Binet and the WISC/WAIS, are still normed for scores to peak in late adolescence. **[Lifespan Link:** IQ tests are discussed in Chapter 11.]

Longitudinal Improvements

Shortly after the middle of the twentieth century, Nancy Bayley and Melita Oden (1955) analyzed the intelligence of the adults who had been originally selected as child geniuses by Lewis Terman decades earlier. Bayley was an expert in intelligence testing. She knew that "invariable findings had indicated that most intellectual functions decrease after about 21 years of age" (Bayley, 1966, p. 117). Instead she found that the IQ scores of these gifted individuals *increased* between ages 20 and 50.

Bayley wondered if their high intelligence in childhood somehow protected them from the expected age-related declines. To find out, she retested adults who had been selected and tested in infancy as representative (mostly average, but also including some higher or lower in IQ) of the population of Berkeley, California. Their IQ scores also improved after age 21.

Why did these new data contradict previous conclusions? As you remember from Chapter 1, cross-sectional research can be misleading because each cohort has unique life experiences. The quality and extent of adult education, cultural opportunities (travel, movies), and sources of information (newspapers, radio, and later, television and the Internet) change every decade. No wonder adults studied longitudinally showed intellectual growth.

Earlier cross-sectional research did not take into account the fact that most of the older adults had left school before eighth grade. It was unfair to compare their IQ at age 70 to that of 20-year-olds, almost all of whom attended high school. In retrospect, it is not surprising that the older military volunteers scored lower, not because their minds were declining but because their education was inferior. Cross-sectional comparisons would show younger generations scoring better than the older ones, but longitudinal data might nonetheless find that most individuals increase in IQ from age 20 to age 60.

Powerful evidence that younger adults score higher because of education and health, not because of youth, comes from longitudinal research from many nations. Recent cohorts always outscore previous ones. As you remember from Chapter 11, this is the *Flynn effect*.

It is unfair—and scientifically invalid—to compare the IQ scores of a cross section of adults to learn about age-related changes. Older adults will score lower, but that does not mean that they have lost intellectual power. Longitudinal research finds that most gain, not lose.

Longitudinal studies are more accurate than cross-sectional ones in measuring development over the decades. However, longitudinal research on IQ has three drawbacks:

1. Repeated testing provides practice, and that itself may improve scores.
2. Some participants move without forwarding addresses, or refuse to be retested, or die. They tend to be those whose IQ is declining, which skews the results of longitudinal research.
3. Unusual events (e.g., a major war or a breakthrough in public health) affect each cohort, and more mundane changes—such as widespread use of the Internet or less secondhand smoke—make it hard to predict the future based on the history of the past.

Will babies born today be smarter adults than babies born in 1990? Probably. But that is not guaranteed: Cohort effects might make a new generation score lower, not higher, than their elders. New data on the Flynn effect finds that generational increases have slowed down in developed nations, albeit not in developing ones (Meisenberg & Woodley, 2013). Thus health and educational benefits may be less dramatic for the next generation than they were 50 years ago.

Cross-Sequential Research

The best method to understand the effects of aging without the complications of historical change is to combine cross-sectional and longitudinal research, a combination called *cross-sequential research*.

The Seattle Longitudinal Study

At the University of Washington in 1956, K. Warner Schaie tested a cross section of 500 adults, aged 20 to 50, on five standard primary mental abilities considered to be the foundation of intelligence: (1) verbal meaning (vocabulary), (2) spatial orientation, (3) inductive reasoning, (4) number ability, and (5) word fluency (rapid verbal associations). His cross-sectional results showed age-related decline in all five abilities, as others had found before him. He planned to replicate Bayley's research by retesting his population seven years later.

Schaie then had a brilliant idea, to use both longitudinal and cross-sectional methods. He not only retested his initial participants but also tested a new group who were the same age that his earlier sample had been. Then he could compare people not only to their own earlier scores, but also to people currently as old as his original group had been when first tested.

By retesting and adding a new group every seven years, Schaie obtained a more accurate view of development than was possible from either longitudinal or cross-sectional research alone. Known as the **Seattle Longitudinal Study**, this was the first cross-sequential study of adult intelligence.

With cross-sequential research, researchers can analyze the impact of retesting, cohort, and experience. Schaie confirmed and extended what others had found: People improve in most mental abilities during adulthood (Schaie 2013, 2005). As Figure 21.1 shows, each particular ability at each age and for each gender has a

Seattle Longitudinal Study The first cross-sequential study of adult intelligence. This study began in 1956 and is repeated every 7 years.

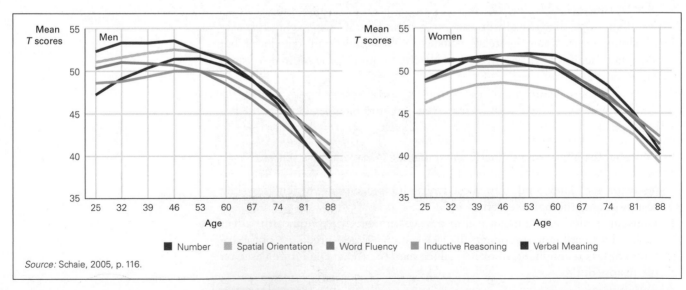

Source: Schaie, 2005, p. 116.

FIGURE 21.1

Age Differences in Intellectual Abilities Cross-sectional data on intellectual abilities at various ages would show much steeper declines. Longitudinal research, in contrast, would show more notable rises. Because Schaie's research is cross-sequential, the trajectories it depicts are more revealing: None of the average scores for the five abilities at any age are above 55 or below 35. Because the methodology takes into account the cohort and historical effects, the purely age-related differences from ages 25 to 60 are very small.

distinct pattern. Note the gradual rise and the eventual decline of all abilities. Men are initially better at number skills and women at verbal skills, but the two sexes grow closer over time. Schaie found that everyone declined by age 60 in at least one of the basic abilities, but not until age 88 did everyone decline in all five skills.

Other researchers from many nations find similar trends, although the specific abilities and trajectories differ (Hunt, 2011). Adulthood is typically a time of increasing, or at least maintaining, IQ, with dramatic individual differences: Some people and some abilities show declines at age 40; others, not until decades later (Johnson et al., 2014; Kremen et al., 2014).

Schaie discovered more detailed cohort changes than the Flynn effect. Each successive cohort (born at seven-year intervals from 1889 to 1973) scored higher in adulthood than did the previous generations in verbal memory and inductive reasoning, but number ability (math) peaked for those born in 1924 and then declined slowly in future cohorts until about 1970, when it no longer fell with each generation (Schaie, 2013). School curricula may explain these differences: By the mid-twentieth century, reading, writing, and self-expression were more emphasized than in the beginning of the twentieth and the twenty-first centuries.

Another cohort effect is that the age-related declines, though still evident, now appear about a decade later than they used to (Schaie, 2013). The likely explanation is that the later-born population, on average, has more education and better health.

One correlate of higher ability for every cohort is having work or a personal life that challenges the mind. Schaie found that recent cohorts of adults more often have intellectually challenging jobs and thus higher intellectual ability. That had a marked effect on female IQ, since women used to stay home or had routine jobs. Now that more women are employed in challenging work, women score higher than did women their age 50 years ago.

Other research also finds that challenging work fosters high intelligence. One team found that retiring from difficult jobs often reduced intellectual power, but leaving dull jobs increased it (Finkel et al., 2009). This depends on activities after retirement: Intellectually demanding tasks, paid or not, keep the mind working (Schooler, 2009; Schaie, 2013).

Many studies using sophisticated designs and statistics have supplanted early cross-sectional and longitudinal studies. None are perfect because "no design can fully sanitize a study so as to solve the age-cohort-period identification problem" (Herzog, 2010, p. 5). Cultures, eras, and individuals vary substantially regarding which cognitive abilities are nurtured and tested. From about age 20 to 70, national values, specific genes, and education are all more influential on IQ scores than chronological age (Johnson et al., 2014).

It is hard to predict intelligence for any particular adult, even if genes and age are known. For instance, a study of Swedish twins aged 41 to 84 found differences in verbal ability among the monozygotic twins with equal education. In theory, scores should have been identical, but they were not. As expected, however, age had an effect: Memory and spatial ability declined over time (Finkel et al., 2009).

Considering all the research, adult intellectual abilities measured on IQ tests sometimes rise, fall, zigzag, or stay the same as age increases. Specific patterns are affected by each person's experiences, with "virtually every possible permutation of individual profiles" (Schaie, 2013, p. 497). This illustrates the life-span perspective: Intelligence is multidirectional, multicultural, multicontextual, and plastic. Although scores on several subtests decline, especially on timed tests, overall ability is usually maintained until late adulthood.

Especially for Older Brothers and Sisters If your younger siblings mock your ignorance of current TV shows and beat you at the latest video games, does that mean your intellect is fading? (see response, page 608)

>> **Response for Older Brothers and Sisters** (from page 607): No. While it is true that each new cohort might be smarter than the previous one in some ways, cross-sequential research suggests that you are smarter than you used to be. Knowing that might help you respond wisely—smiling quietly rather than insisting that you are superior.

SUMMING UP

Intelligence as a concept is controversial, with some experts believing that there is one general intelligence, that individuals have more or less of it, and that each ability separately rises or falls. Psychometricians once believed that intelligence decreased beginning at about age 20: that is what cross-sectional data revealed. Then longitudinal testing demonstrated that many adults advance in intelligence with age. Cross-sequential research provides a more nuanced picture, finding that some abilities decrease and others increase throughout adulthood. Many factors—including challenging work, a stimulating personal life, past education, and good health—protect intelligence and postpone decline. Individual variations are dramatic, with some people showing no decrements even at age 60. ▪

>> Components of Intelligence: Many and Varied

Responding to all these data, developmentalists are now looking closely at patterns of cognitive gain and loss. They contend that, because virtually every pattern is possible, it is misleading to ask whether intelligence either increases or decreases; it does not move in lockstep. There may be "vast domains of cognitive performance . . . that may not follow a common, age-linked trajectory of decline" (Dannefer & Patterson, 2009, p. 116).

Many psychologists describe distinct intellectual abilities, each of which independently rises and falls. Math slowdowns are apparent even by age 40, but verbal ability keeps rising until the 60s (Schaie, 2013). Most current researchers agree that there are many forms of intelligence (Roberts & Lipnevich, 2012).

We consider here only two proposals, one that posits two distinct abilities and the other, three. [**Lifespan Link:** Gardner's theory of multiple intelligences describes nine abilities, an idea with implications for childhood education, as explained in Chapter 11.]

Two Clusters of Intelligence

In the 1960s, a leading personality researcher, Raymond Cattell, teamed up with a promising graduate student, John Horn, to study intelligence tests. They concluded that adult intelligence is best understood by grouping various measures into two categories, which they called fluid and crystallized.

Fluid Intelligence

fluid intelligence Those types of basic intelligence that make learning of all sorts quick and thorough. Abilities such as short-term memory, abstract thought, and speed of thinking are all usually considered part of fluid intelligence.

As its name implies, **fluid intelligence** is like water, flowing to its own level no matter where it happens to be. Fluid intelligence is quick and flexible, enabling people to learn anything, even things that are unfamiliar and unconnected to what they already know. Curiosity, learning for the joy of it, solving abstract puzzles, and the thrill at discovering something new are marks of fluid intelligence (Silvia & Sanders, 2010).

People high in fluid abilities can draw inferences, understand relationships between concepts, and readily process new ideas and facts in part because their working memory is large and flexible. Someone high in fluid intelligence is quick and creative with words and numbers and enjoys intellectual puzzles. The kinds of questions that test fluid intelligence among Western adults might be:

What comes next in each of these two series?*

4 9 16 25 3
V X Z B D

---

* The correct answers are 6 and F. The clue is to think of multiplication (squares) and the alphabet: Some series are much more difficult to complete.

Puzzles are often used to measure fluid intelligence, with speedy solutions given bonus points (as on many IQ tests). Immediate recall—of nonsense words, of numbers, of a sentence just read—is one indicator because working memory is crucial for fluid intelligence, especially in timed tests (Chuderski, 2013; Nisbett et al., 2012).

Since fluid intelligence appears to be disconnected from past learning, it may seem impractical—not so. A study of adults aged 34 to 83 found that stressors did not vary by age but did vary by fluid intelligence. People high in fluid intelligence were more exposed to stress but were less likely to suffer from it: They used their intellect to turn stressors into positive experiences (Stawski et al., 2010).

The ability to detoxify stress may be one reason that high fluid intelligence in emerging adulthood leads to longer life and higher IQ later on. Fluid intelligence is associated with openness to new experiences and overall brain health (Batterham et al., 2009; Silvia & Sanders, 2010). (Ways to cope with stress are discussed later in this chapter, when you will see that adaptive cognition provides the best defense against the problems of life.)

Crystallized Intelligence

The accumulation of facts, information, and knowledge as a result of education and experience is called **crystallized intelligence**. The size of a person's vocabulary, the knowledge of chemical formulas, and the long-term memory for dates in history all indicate crystallized intelligence. Tests designed to measure this intelligence might include questions like these:

> What is the meaning of the word *eleemosynary*?
> Who was Descartes?
> Explain the difference between a tangent and a triangle.
> Why does the city of Peking no longer exist?

Although such questions seem to measure achievement more than aptitude, these two are connected, especially in adulthood. Intelligent adults read widely, think deeply, and remember what they learn, so their achievement reflects their aptitude. Thus crystallized intelligence is an outgrowth of fluid intelligence (Nisbett et al., 2012).

Vocabulary, for example, improves with reading. Using the words *joy, ecstasy, bliss,* and *delight*—each appropriately, with distinct nuances (quite apart from the drugs, perfumes, or yogurts that use these names)—is a sign of intelligence. Remember the knowledge base (Chapter 12): As people know more, they learn more. That explains why a person's extent of education is considered a rough indicator of adult IQ (Nisbett et al., 2012).

crystallized intelligence Those types of intellectual ability that reflect accumulated learning. Vocabulary and general information are examples. Some developmental psychologists think crystallized intelligence increases with age, while fluid intelligence declines.

Think Before Acting Both of these adults need to combine fluid and crystallized intelligence, insight and intuition, logic and experience. One *(left)* is a surgeon, studying X-rays before picking up her scalpel. The other *(right)* is a court reporter for a TV station, jotting notes during a lunch recess before delivering her on-camera report on a trial.

Both Together Now

To reflect the total picture of a person's intellectual aptitude, both fluid and crystallized intelligence must be measured (Hunt, 2011). Age complicates the IQ calculation because scores on items measuring fluid intelligence decrease with age, whereas scores on items measuring crystallized intelligence increase.

Scores on subtests tend to increase or decrease over time. Typically, speed and verbal ability change in opposite ways. The combination makes IQ fairly steady from ages 30 to 70. Although brain slowdown begins at age 20 or so, it is rarely apparent until massive declines in fluid intelligence affect crystallized intelligence. Only then do overall IQ scores fall.

Horn and Cattell (1967) wrote that they had:

> shown intelligence to both increase and decrease with age—depending upon the definition of intelligence adopted, fluid or crystallized! Our results illustrate an essential fallacy implicit in the construction of omnibus measures of intelligence.

[Horn & Cattell, p. 124]

In other words, it may be foolish to try to measure *g*, a single omnibus intelligence, because components need to be measured separately. In testing for *g*, real developmental changes will be masked because fluid and crystallized abilities cancel each other out.

Three Forms of Intelligence: Sternberg

Robert Sternberg (1988, 2003, 2011) agrees that a single intelligence score is misleading. As first mentioned in Chapter 11, Sternberg proposed three fundamental forms of intelligence: analytic, creative, and practical, each of which can be tested. (See Table 21.1.)

analytic intelligence A form of intelligence that involves such mental processes as abstract planning, strategy selection, focused attention, and information processing, as well as verbal and logical skills.

creative intelligence A form of intelligence that involves the capacity to be intellectually flexible and innovative.

Analytic intelligence includes all the mental processes that foster academic proficiency by making efficient learning, remembering, and thinking possible. Thus, it draws on abstract planning, strategy selection, focused attention, and information processing, as well as on verbal and logical skills.

Strengths in those areas are valuable in emerging adulthood, particularly in college, and in graduate school. Multiple-choice tests and brief essays that call forth remembered information, with only one right answer, indicate analytic intelligence.

Creative intelligence involves the capacity to be intellectually flexible and innovative. Creative thinking is divergent rather than convergent, valuing the unexpected, imaginative, and unusual, rather than standard and conventional answers. Sternberg developed tests of creative intelligence that include writing a short story titled "The Octopus's Sneakers" or planning

TABLE 21.1	Sternberg's Three Forms of Intelligence		
Related Issues	**Analytic Intelligence**	**Creative Intelligence**	**Practical Intelligence**
Mental processes involved	▪ Abstract planning ▪ Strategizing ▪ Focused attention ▪ Information processing ▪ Verbal skills ▪ Logic	▪ Imagination ▪ Appreciation of the unexpected or unusual ▪ Originality ▪ Vision	▪ Ability to adapt behaviors ▪ Understanding and assessing real problems ▪ Ability to apply knowledge and skills
Valued for	▪ Analyzing ▪ Learning and understanding ▪ Remembering ▪ Thinking	▪ Intellectual flexibility ▪ Originality ▪ Future Hopes ▪ Artists, musicians	▪ Adaptability ▪ Concrete knowledge ▪ Real-world challenges
Indicated by	▪ Multiple-choice tests ▪ Brief essays ▪ Recall of information	▪ Inventiveness ▪ Innovation ▪ Resourcefulness ▪ Ingenuity	▪ Performance in real situations ▪ "Street smarts" ▪ Survival skills

Source: Based on Sternberg, 1988, 2003, 2011.

an advertising campaign for a new doorknob. Those with many unusual ideas earn high scores.

Practical intelligence involves the capacity to adapt one's behavior to the demands of a given situation. This capacity includes an accurate grasp of the expectations and needs of the people involved and an awareness of the particular skills that are called for, along with the ability to use these insights effectively. Practical intelligence is sometimes called *tacit intelligence* because it is not obvious on tests. Instead it comes from "the school of hard knocks" and is sometimes called "street smarts," not "book smarts."

The Three Intelligences in Adulthood

The benefits of practical intelligence in adult life are obvious once we recall the cognitive tasks of adulthood. Few adults need to define obscure words or deduce the next element in a number sequence (analytic intelligence); and few need to write a new type of music, restructure local government, or invent a new gadget (creative intelligence). Ideally, those few have already found a niche for themselves and have learned to rely on people with practical intelligence to implement their analytic or creative ideas.

Almost every adult, however, must solve real-world challenges: maintaining a home; advancing a career; managing family finances; sifting information from media, mail, and the Internet; addressing the emotional needs of family members, neighbors, and colleagues (Blanchard-Fields, 2007). Schaie found that scores on tests of practical intelligence were steadier than scores on other kinds of tests from age 20 to 70, with no notable decrement, in part because these skills are needed throughout life (Schaie, 2005).

Practical intelligence is very useful. Without it, a solution found by analytic intelligence will fail because people resist academic brilliance as unrealistic and elite, as the term *ivory tower* implies. Similarly, a stunningly creative idea may be rejected as ridiculous and weird rather than serious and sensible—if it is not accompanied by practical intelligence.

For example, imagine a business manager, a school principal, a political leader, or a parent without practical intelligence trying to change routine practices—perhaps for a good reason, because the old way was inefficient or destructive. If the new procedures are not compatible with the group and are misunderstood, then the workers, teachers, voters, or family members will misinterpret them, predict failure, and refuse to change.

Smart Farmer; Smart Teacher This school field trip is not to a museum or a fire station but to a wheat field, where children study grains that will become bread. Like this creative teacher, modern farmers use every kind of intelligence. To succeed, they need to analyze soil, fertilizer, and pests (analytic intelligence); to anticipate market prices and food fads (creative intelligence); and to know what crops and seed varieties grow in each acre of their land as they manage their workers (practical intelligence).

practical intelligence The intellectual skills used in everyday problem solving. (Sometimes called *tacit intelligence*.)

Same Situation, Far Apart: Men at Work The balloon vendor in Pakistan *(left),* and the construction supervisor in Beijing, China *(right),* have much in common: They work outdoors, use practical intelligence, and have good jobs in nations where many people do not. Context is crucial. If they were to trade places, each would be lost at first. However, practical intelligence could save the day—intensive instruction might enable them to master their new role.

Flexibility is needed for practical intelligence (K. Sloan, 2009). As you remember from Chapter 18, this develops during emerging adulthood. Ideally, practical intelligence continues to be refined throughout adulthood as each new experience provides practice. Failures can be either defeats or *learning opportunities*.

No abstract test can assess practical intelligence because context is crucial. Instead, to measure this kind of intelligence, adults need to be observed coping with daily life. In hiring a new employee, the hiring committee might describe an actual situation and ask how the applicant would handle it. Many companies use such situational tests to hire a manager (Salter & Highhouse, 2009). For instance, the prospective employee is asked:

> *You assign a new project to one of your subordinates, who protests, saying it cannot be done without more resources and time. Rank your possible responses, from best to worst. Explain your reasoning.*
>
> a. *You find someone else to do the job.*
> b. *You ask your subordinate to figure out how it can be done with current constraints.*
> c. *You reallocate work, to give your subordinate more time.*
> d. *You fire the subordinate.*
> e. *You ask your supervisor what to do.*
> f. *You postpone the new task until you find more resources.*

Situational tests can be used in many fields. They are often used in the medical professions: review books have been made for would-be doctors preparing for tests (e.g., Varain & Cartwright, 2013). Because practical intelligence is crucial on the job, probationary periods, internships, and apprenticeships are common.

Sternberg (2011) emphasizes that analytic intelligence is neither the only one nor always the best, and that everyone should deploy the strengths and guard against the limitations of each type. Choosing which intelligence to use takes wisdom, which Sternberg considers a fourth ingredient of successful intelligence:

> One needs creativity to generate novel ideas, analytical intelligence to ascertain whether they are good ideas, practical intelligence to implement the ideas and persuade others of their value, and wisdom to ensure that the ideas help reach a common goal.
>
> *[Sternberg, 2012, p. 21]*

[Lifespan Link: Wisdom is discussed in Chapter 24.]

Age and Culture

Which kind of intelligence is most needed and valued depends partly on age and partly on culture. Think about Sternberg's three types. Analytic intelligence is usually valued in high school and college, as students try to remember and analyze various ideas. However, although people considered "smart" usually have analytic intelligence, that is not enough in adulthood. As Sternberg argues: "many very smart people turn a blind eye to the wars, poverty, government atrocities, starvation, and disease that affect others around them" (Sternberg, 2013, p. 188).

Creative intelligence is prized if life circumstances change and new challenges arise; it is much more valued in some cultures and countries than in others (Kaufman & Sternberg, 2006). In times of social upheaval, or in certain professions (such as the arts), creativity is a better predictor of accomplishment than is IQ. However, creativity can be so innovative and out of touch that creative people are scorned, ignored, or even killed. The contributions of many creative geniuses went unrecognized until years after their death.

Think about these three intelligences cross-culturally. Creative individuals would be critical of tradition and so would be tolerated only in some political environments. Analytic individuals might be seen as absentminded, head-in-the-clouds dreamers. Practical intelligence, though valued less within school settings, might be most useful. Yet practical intelligence could be used for evil as well as good. Wisdom is then essential.

Difficult as it is to determine who is truly smart, it is even more difficult to judge which nation is smartest, in part because each culture has its own standards to determine the combination of abilities that comprises intelligence (Sternberg, 2013). A controversial idea from Earl Hunt, a psychologist who studies intelligence, is that the nations with the most advanced economies and greatest national wealth are those that make best use of **cognitive artifacts**—that is, ways to amplify and extend general cognitive ability (Hunt, 2012).

Historically, written language, the number system, universities, and the scientific method were cognitive artifacts. Each of these artifacts extended human intellectual abilities by helping people interact to learn more. Sheer survival (in earlier centuries, more newborns died than lived) and longer life (few people survived to age 50) resulted from cognitive artifacts. The germ theory of disease, for instance, was developed because doctors were able to do research and then learn from each other (Hunt, 2011).

In more recent times, universal education and preventive health care, clean water, electricity, global travel, and the Internet have resulted in advanced societies. According to this idea, smart people are better able to use the cognitive artifacts of their society to advance their own intelligence. Then they develop more cognitive artifacts, and the whole community benefits.

For instance, developed nations provide preschool and kindergarten to all children. That increases the IQ of the new generation, which eventually advances the nation. By contrast, some nations value fertility more than health, expose children to lead and other toxins, and censure information. All those practices undercut the full intellectual development of the people (Hunt, 2011). In thinking about adult intellectual growth, does the specific context of any particular man or woman limit or expand their mind?

cognitive artifacts Intellectual tools passed down from generation to generation which may assist in learning within societies.

Especially for Prospective Parents In terms of the intellectual challenge, what type of intelligence is most needed for effective parenthood? (see response, page 615)

OPPOSING PERSPECTIVES

What Makes a Good Parent?

"Are pacifiers bad for babies?"
"How much should a 4-year-old eat?"
"When do you tell children about sex?"

My students ask me such questions often. I answer based on my knowledge of human development and my experience raising my children. But I wonder how much my answers reflect my culture, and not research. Similar doubts can be raised about almost anything adults know. Our perspective may not be adaptive to some cultural contexts. One definition of intelligence is that it is the ability to adapt to current conditions. Might my intelligence be far more limited than my students assume?

Tests of good infant care have been developed, based primarily on analytic, not practical, child rearing (e.g., McCall et al., 2010). One of the most common scales is the *Knowledge of Infant Development Inventory* (KIDI) (MacPhee, 1981). KIDI measures how much caregivers know about infant senses, motor skills, and communication—such as at what age an infant is expected to sit up or whether parents should talk to preverbal babies.

Such knowledge seems helpful. For example, mothers and fathers who score higher on the KIDI are less depressed and more likely to provide responsive baby care (Howard, 2010; Zolotor et al., 2008). Many researchers believe that knowledge of infant development causes (not merely correlates with) good care.

Should we worry when mothers do not know about their babies' growth? Perhaps. For instance, in one study only 29 percent of immigrant mothers knew that 2-month-olds can distinguish one speech sound from another, an item on the KIDI. The researchers suggest that those mothers are less likely to advance their infants' language and social skills, handicapping the children later on (Bornstein & Cote, 2007).

The opposing perspective suggests that knowledge of infant development does not matter in caregiving. A study supporting this view found that an immigrant child's later cognitive development was best predicted *not* by KIDI scores or other measures of parenting, but by parents' SES and language use. In this longitudinal study, the mothers' KIDI scores did not predict later school success for Asian American or Latino children; it did so only for European American children (Han et al., 2012). That suggests that culture was crucial to the outcome.

In another study, researchers provided supportive, encouraging visitors to low-income, unmarried mothers—many of whom did not plan or want their babies (Katz et al., 2011). Compared with a control group with no visits, and even compared with mothers in the intervention group who had relatively few home visits, mothers who were visited 30 or more times became better infant caregivers. However, both before and after many visits, the KIDI scores of the mothers were low. The authors of the study write:

> A significant impact of this intervention was its effect on the mothers' ability to create home environments more suitable for the needs of their infants . . . despite lack of measurable change in mothers' knowledge of infant development.

[Katz et al., 2011, p. S81]

In other words, advances in practical skills, not analytic ones, made a difference.

Knowledge may not improve parenting. Instead, warmth and patience, responsiveness (without expecting an infant to reciprocate), mental health, or social support networks may be more critical than knowledge. IQ correlates with positive personal attributes, but it does not determine them (Dunkel, 2013).

Part of the underlying reason why tests of knowledge do not always predict good parenting is that cultures vary in what they believe about infant development. Such beliefs may be beneficial to babies in some contexts but not in others. For example, an anthropologist from the United States studied the Ache in Paraguay. The Ache tribal people were respectful and deferential to her on repeated visits, until she and her husband

> arrived at their study site in the forest of Paraguay with their infant daughter in tow. The Ache greeted her in a whole new way. They took her aside and in friendly and intimate but no-nonsense terms told her all the things she was doing wrong as a mother. . . . [She gave one example:] This older woman sat with me and told me I *must* sleep with my daughter. They were horrified that I brought a basket with me for her to sleep in. Here was a group of forest hunter-gatherers, people living in what Westerners would call basic conditions, giving instructions to a highly educated woman from a technologically sophisticated culture.

[Small, 1998, p. 213]

How important to quality care is accurate knowledge of child development? I am not neutral on this question; I have devoted much of my life to teaching about development. I believe knowledge is power, and I am grateful that I know what I know.

Yet the most important aspect of good parenting may not ·be information. Similarly, the sign of an intelligent adult may be something other than analytic intelligence. This box raises these issues. Education is a cultural artifact; I think everyone benefits from it. If I were convinced that responsiveness is more important than knowledge, I would teach responsiveness. Is that a contradiction?

Keep Him Close Mothers everywhere keep their toddlers nearby, but it is particularly important in an environment where poisonous spiders and plants thrive. Thus, you can see why this Ache mother physically protects her son much more than would a wise North American mother—who might instead watch her son explore freely on the floor of the house after removing small objects and covering the electric outlets.

SUMMING UP

Intelligence may be not a single entity (*g*) but rather a combination of different abilities, sometimes categorized as fluid and crystallized or as analytic, creative, and practical. These abilities rise and fall partly because of events in each person's life, partly because of culture and cohort, and partly because of age. The overall picture of adult intelligence, as measured by various tests, is complex. In general, verbal intelligence increases and timed tests of intelligence show declines as the decades of adult life go by.

One controversy underlying all the psychometric approaches to intelligence regards the definition of intelligence, with scholars disagreeing about what to measure, how, and why. It is clear that the specific intellectual abilities needed for success depend, at least in part, on context and culture. ■

>> Selective Gains and Losses

Aging neurons, cultural pressures, historical conditions, and past education all affect adult cognition. None of these can be controlled directly by an individual adult. Nonetheless, many researchers believe that adults make crucial choices about their intellectual development.

For example, why have number skills declined more for recent cohorts than for earlier ones? The reason may not be past math curricula (as was suggested) but rather modern adults' reliance on calculators instead of paper-and-pencil (or mental) calculations. If adults decided to trash their calculators, their math skills might improve. Of course, most adults would consider that strange: Spending more time on math might help number skills, but few modern adults want to do double-digit division in their heads.

Similarly, memory would improve if we did not use directories and speed dial to phone or text our friends. But do the cultural artifacts of modern life make us lazy intellectually? Or have people merely focused on new challenges?

Accumulating Stressors

Many health decisions that adults make prioritize immediate comfort over long-term health. That impairs cognition because anything that slows down blood circulation slows down the brain. That affects speed of thought and leads to brain shrinkage. Drug abuse, high blood pressure, diabetes, obesity, alcoholism, lack of exercise, and cigarette smoking—all chosen by many adults—impair thought.

Now we focus on another factor that slows down cognition: stress. Every life is stressful. Some stresses become stressors. A **stressor** is an experience, circumstance, or condition that affects a person. Thus a stress is external; if stresses are internalized, they become stressors.

Between ages 25 and 65, family members die, disasters destroy homes, jobs disappear, and even welcome events—a new marriage, birth, or job, for instance—cause stress. In addition, daily life is filled with minor stresses called *hassles*—traffic jams, spilled food, noise at night, rude strangers, aches and pains, dirty pots, and much more. Daily hassles and major stresses can become stressors, destroying health.

If organ reserves are depleted, the physiological toll of stress can lower immunity, increase blood pressure, speed up the heart, reduce sleep, and produce many other

>> Response for Prospective Parents
(from page 613): Because parenthood demands flexibility and patience, Sternberg's practical intelligence is probably most needed. Anything that involves finding a single correct answer, such as analytic intelligence or number ability, would not be much help.

stressor Any situation, event, experience, or other stimulus that causes a person to feel stressed. Many circumstances that seem to be stresses become stressors for some people but not for others.

Same Situation, Far Apart: Two 2013 Disasters In the Boston marathon *(left)*, three people were killed and more than 200 injured when a terrorist bomb exploded, and in South Africa *(right)*, 34 striking mine workers were shot dead when police opened fire. Despite the obvious differences, survivors everywhere cope by crying and holding each other

reactions that can lead to cognitive loss as allostatic load increases. Similar to organ reserve, there is a cognitive reserve: Although the mind benefits from ongoing use, when people must suddenly perform difficult cognitive tasks they are less able to think clearly. They may make impulsive decisions, and those decisions may be destructive.

Humans have always experienced stresses, some of which becomes stressors, and they have developed ways to cope with them, sometimes with biological homeostasis and allostasis, sometimes more directly with cognitive strategies. As you will see, the choice as to which coping method to use may lead to intellectual strength or impairment.

Coping Methods

Stressors increase all the bad habits described in Chapter 20—drug use, overeating, underexercising—sometimes ostensibly to relieve the stress but eventually making things worse. Stress does not merely correlate with illness—it *causes* illness. In an experiment, volunteers first indicated how stressed they felt and then agreed to have a cold virus squirted up their nostrils. A week later, some of them were stuffed, sneezing, and feverish. Others were fine. Stress was a crucial factor (S. Cohen et al., 1993).

Similarly, stress hormones not only undercut thinking in the moment, but can also reduce mental ability for the future. Stress affects more than logic; chronic stress increases depression and other psychological illnesses that impair thinking, and it attacks the brain itself (Marin et al., 2011; McEwen & Gianaros, 2011).

Reactions to stress can cause yet more stress, which means that stressors accumulate. For example, a longitudinal study of married couples in their 30s found that if the husband's health deteriorated, the chance of divorce increased. Thus one reaction to the stress of illness was to do something that increased stress. This effect was apparent with all couples, particularly for well-educated European Americans (Teachman, 2010).

The rate of divorce also increases when parents have children with special needs (Price, 2010). Conversely, for some couples having a child with serious problems brings partners closer together (Solomon, 2012). Apparently having a child with special needs is always stressful, and thus creates a stressor. But how people then cope with that stressor is crucial to their mental health.

Coping involves cognition because people choose what to do. Abuse of alcohol and other drugs is one form of **avoidant coping**. Ignoring a problem, either literally forgetting it or hiding it (one person who owed back taxes threw all official letters under his bed, unopened), is the worst way of coping—it increases depression and the risk of suicide.

Psychologists distinguish two positive ways of coping with stress. In **problem-focused coping**, people attack the stressor directly—for instance, by confronting a difficult boss, or by moving out of a noisy neighborhood. In **emotion-focused coping**, people try to change their emotional reactions—for instance, from anger to acceptance, making the stressor disappear and becoming stronger and more empathic because of it. Many adults who work to help others (therapists, human service workers, teachers) do so because of their own past experiences in overcoming serious stress.

Biologically and culturally, the two sexes may respond differently to stress. Men tend to be problem-focused, reacting in a "fight-or-flight" manner. Their sympathetic nervous system (faster heart rate, increased adrenaline) prepares them for attack or escape. Their testosterone level rises when they confront a problem and decreases if they fail. From childhood, boys are encouraged to fight back, and adult men are more likely to rage openly, use force, or disappear.

Women, however, are more emotion-focused and are likely to "tend and befriend"—that is, to seek the company of other people when they are under pressure. Their bodies produce oxytocin, a hormone that leads them to seek confidential

---

Especially for Doctors and Nurses
A patient complains of a headache or stomachache, but laboratory tests and CAT scans find no physical cause. What could it be? (see response, page 619)

avoidant coping A method of responding to a stressor by ignoring, forgetting, or hiding it.

problem-focused coping A strategy to deal with stress by tackling a stressful situation directly.

emotion-focused coping A strategy to deal with stress by changing feelings about the stressor rather than changing the stressor itself.

and caring interactions (S. E. Taylor, 2006; S. E. Taylor et al., 2000). Their first reaction when something goes wrong is to call a friend.

This gender difference in coping explains why a woman might get upset if a man doesn't want to talk about his problems and why a man might get upset if a woman just wants to talk instead of taking action. Both problem- and emotion-focused coping can be effective; everyone should sometimes fight and sometimes befriend.

Choosing Methods

Not only do people need to figure out the best strategy to deal with each particular problem, but they also need to figure out when other people will help and when they will not (Aldwin, 2007). Getting social support is generally a good strategy—other people provide suggestions, lighten a load, and add humor or perspective (Fiori & Dencklar, 2012). But sometimes other people criticize, distract, or delay a person's coping.

The best coping strategy depends on the situation. Worse than either problem- or emotion-focused coping is no strategy—denying a problem until it escalates or takes a physical toll, such as causing high blood pressure, digestive difficulties, or even a heart attack. Avoidance causes homeostasis and allostatic load. [**Lifespan Link:** Homeostatis and allostatic load were discussed in Chapter 17.]

The stress that a person endures in childhood and adolescence may become evident in morbidity during the adult years. A U.S. study of 65,000 adults compared many signs of poor health, such as hypertension and insulin resistance. The gradual accumulation of such biochemical stressors is called **weathering**, and this study found that weathering happened faster among African Americans—by age 60 their average biological age was 10 years older than that of European Americans. The authors believe this was the result of the "chronic stress" of living in a "race-conscious society" (Geronimus et al., 2006, p. 832). Social support?

weathering The gradual accumulation of stressors over a long period of time, wearing down a person's resilience and resistance.

The average life span of African American adults is about 4 years shorter than that of European Americans until about age 80, when some data find a "cross over," with African Americans living longer. Curiously, Latinos live longer than either group (National Center for Health Statistics, 2013). Social support?

Weathering has a direct impact on intelligence. In studies conducted in the United States in the 1980s, the average IQ score of African Americans was 15 points lower than the average score for European Americans (Neisser et al., 1996). Earlier researchers hypothesized that these differences were genetic. However, later research suggests that stress may be the cause. Specifically:

1. The Black–White IQ gap narrowed, from about 15 points to about 10 between 1972 and 2002 (Dickens & Flynn, 2006) and continues to shrink—more in some abilities than others.
2. The racial differences are apparent in vocabulary but not in learning ability (Fagan & Holland, 2007).
3. The racial differences are less dramatic at age 4 and most dramatic at about age 25.

All three of these findings suggest that stress may reduce the IQ of African Americans. Note that the IQ gap is most evident in early adulthood.

Ideally, with age and experience adults learn to respond wisely. Over the years of adulthood, a more positive attitude toward life develops, which makes it easier to reinterpret stresses so that they do not fester (Charles & Carstensen, 2010). Often,

> [o]lder individuals have had the opportunity to learn how to cope with stressful experiences and how to adjust their expectations. . . . On the basis of age and experience, older persons have developed more effective skills with which to manage stressful life events and to reduce emotional stress.
>
> *[Penninx & Deeg, 2000]*

Stress in Adulthood

Stresses and coping strategies differ from generation to generation. Developmentalists believe that emerging adults today may have more stresses than in the past because education is increasingly important and unemployment is higher. However, adults without jobs or supportive families may be more stressed than emerging adults since they feel more responsible for their problems. Fortunately, the ability to cope may improve with age.

Just as there are many ways to cope with stress, there are many ways to measure it. One common one is to simply ask people what stresses them and another way is experience sampling (beeping people at random times to find out what they are doing and feeling at the moment). As you see from the charts below, the results may differ.

STRESS OVER THE LIFE SPAN

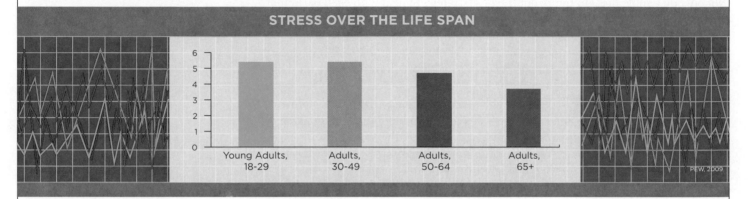

PEW, 2009

WHAT CAUSES STRESS IN DAILY LIFE

Depending on exactly how the question is phrased, adults identify different triggers for their daily stress. For many, it is work, family, health, and safety concerns that worry them.

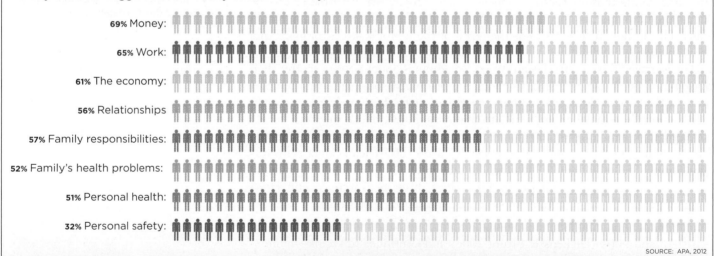

- **69%** Money:
- **65%** Work:
- **61%** The economy:
- **56%** Relationships
- **57%** Family responsibilities:
- **52%** Family's health problems:
- **51%** Personal health:
- **32%** Personal safety:

SOURCE: APA, 2012

ACTIVITIES THAT ARE LEAST STRESSFUL, RANKED BY WOMEN IN TEXAS, 2004

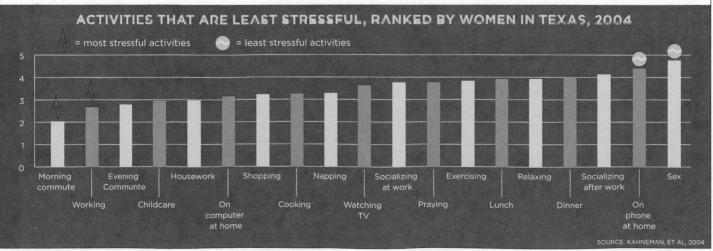

= most stressful activities   = least stressful activities

Morning commute · Working · Evening Commute · Childcare · Housework · On computer at home · Shopping · Cooking · Napping · Watching TV · Socializing at work · Praying · Exercising · Lunch · Relaxing · Dinner · Socializing after work · On phone at home · Sex

SOURCE: KAHNEMAN, ET AL, 2004

For people of every background, age brings another advantage. Emerging adult-hood is "a time of heightened hassles." Once life settles down, some stresses (dating, job hunting, moving) occur less frequently. Adults "are more adept at arranging their lives to minimize the occurrence of stressors" (Aldwin, 2007, p. 298). (Visualizing Development, p. 618, compares stress in different age groups.)

Remember that attitude sometimes determines whether or not an event be-comes a stressor, and whether that stressor decreases over time. For instance, post-traumatic stress disorder (PTSD) is a common response to combat, especially if the person suffering the disorder saw others seriously wounded or killed. The stressor can continue long after the stressful event. That is one explanation for a surprising statistic: In 2012 more U.S. soldiers died of suicide (349, often after coming home) than died in battle in Afghanistan (245). But most veterans readjust well; less than half of those with combat experience develop PTSD.

Some people respond to their stressors with **religious coping**, believing that there is some divine purpose for the problem. Social scientists find that religious coping is particularly likely when people have unexpected illnesses or disasters. As with other forms of coping, sometimes religious coping mitigates a stressor, other times it makes it worse (Burke et al., 2013; Thuné-Boyle et al., 2013). During adulthood, religious faith and practice tend to increase; past experience coping with stress may be the reason.

Of course, natural disasters, such as earthquakes, and personal tragedies, such as the death of a loved one, are always stressful at the time. The surprise is that they are usually overcome, with many adults ignoring some disruption and reinter-preting events. Instead of dwelling on their misfortune, they emphasize their good fortune—not "why me?" but "it could have been worse." Some adults reinterpret stress as challenges, not stressors, even if outsiders would consider them threats (Reich et al., 2010).

When challenges are successfully met, not only do people feel more effective and powerful, but the body's damaging responses to stressors—increased heart and breathing rates, hormonal changes, immune system breakdowns, cognitive lapses, and so on—are averted. Indeed, effective coping may strengthen the immune system and promote health (Bandura, 1997). For adults potential stressors can become posi-tive turning points (Reich et al., 2010), as may have happened in the following case.

>> **Response for Doctors and Nurses**
(from page 616): Stressors increase allostatic load, so the headache or stomachache could be caused by stress. Be careful, however, because both you and the patient may be engaged in avoidant coping. The patient may deny the stress and blame you for suggesting it, and you yourself may be avoiding responsibility. Emotional and contextual problems impact physical health, so medical experts cannot dismiss them.

religious coping The process of turning to faith as a method of coping with stress.

A CASE TO STUDY

Coping with Katrina

Developmentalists are following the hundreds of thousands of peo-ple in Louisiana and Mississippi who were uprooted by Hurricane Katrina in 2005. Many of them lost homes and jobs, went with-out food and water, and knew people who died. Not surprisingly, their stressors increased. For instance, one study of survivors from New Orleans six months after the flood found that most of them had stress reactions: Almost all were irritable and had upsetting thoughts, and half had nightmares (see Figure 21.2.).

The accumulation of stressors led to many physical and psychological difficulties. One in nine suffered serious mental health problems, twice as many as before the hurricane. An-other 20 percent had mild to moderate mental illness, again double the earlier rate (Kessler et al., 2006). Given the trauma of the storm (a major stress) and the inept official response (which led to ongoing hassles), this is not surprising.

However, longitudinal studies found that the same stressors also led to increased resilience, with three out of four people re-porting that they found a deeper sense of purpose after Katrina. Only one person in 250 had made a plan for suicide, which was one-tenth the rate before the storm, perhaps because they no longer felt personally responsible for their depression and be-cause others were more understanding (Kessler et al., 2006). Adults aged 40 to 65 were particularly likely to cope well with the trauma.

A college student who traveled to Mississippi to help survivors provides a firsthand account. She was expecting to see people defeated by their losses. In her words:

> Three hundred college students from Ohio traveled to Mississippi to help survivors of Katrina. Arriving six months after the devastation, they saw rusted cars, shells of homes, and even clothing still stuck to tree branches. But they also met hundreds of people putting their lives together, including teachers at a head start program, who eagerly got back to work within a few weeks after the storm. One student was awed by the "resilient optimism rising above the rubble." She quoted a local volunteer who said "You make a living with what you earn; you make a life with what you give."

> [Feerasta, 2006]

Although the actual hurricane occurred years ago, those who experienced it continue to cope with the aftermath. Social scientists continue to study them. One team considered religious beliefs before and after Katrina. Those caught in Katrina who believed that God is vengeful and punishing were more likely to suffer, but those who believed that God is caring and benevolent coped well, experiencing *post-traumatic growth*, not PTSD (Chan & Rhodes, 2013).

Humans seem to have a recovery reserve that is activated under stress, similar to the organ reserve explained in Chapter 17. According to a related set of studies, it seems that extra effort and alertness are summoned when emergencies arise, even if those affected are overtired and in a noisy environment. This reserve works well for the moments of the emergency, especially if people feel there is something they can do. No wonder the teachers in New Orleans after Katrina wanted to get back to work.

This may explain a familiar reaction to final exams: Some students study intensely, perform well . . . and then collapse, maybe even getting sick after their last exam. More research is needed, but it seems possible that adults gradually develop better coping methods to adapt to the vicissitudes of life (Masten & Wright, 2010; Aldwin & Gilmer, 2013).

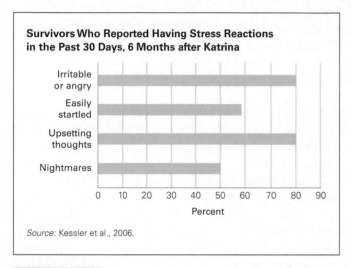

Survivors Who Reported Having Stress Reactions in the Past 30 Days, 6 Months after Katrina

Source: Kessler et al., 2006.

FIGURE 21.2

Lingering Effects of Hurricane Katrina Typically, most people involved in a natural disaster recover within weeks, but as the chart shows, most Katrina victims were still feeling the psychological effects six months later. Two years after the hurricane, death rates in New Orleans from all causes, from heart attacks to homicide, were double what they had been before the storm.

Optimization with Compensation

selective optimization with compensation The theory, developed by Paul and Margaret Baltes, that people try to maintain a balance in their lives by looking for the best way to compensate for physical and cognitive losses and to become more proficient in activities they can already do well.

Paul and Margret Baltes (1990) developed a theory called **selective optimization with compensation** to describe the "general process of systematic function" (P. B. Baltes, 2003, p. 25) by which people maintain a balance in their lives as they grow older. They believe that people seek to *optimize* their development, *selecting* the best way to *compensate* for physical and cognitive losses, becoming more proficient at activities they want to perform well.

Selective optimization with compensation applies to every aspect of life, ranging from choosing friends to playing baseball. Each adult seeks to maximize gains and minimize losses, practicing some abilities and ignoring others. Choices are critical, because any ability can be enhanced or diminished, depending on how, when, and why a person uses it. It is possible to "teach an old dog new tricks," but learning requires that adults want to learn those new tricks.

When adults are motivated to do well, few age-related deficits are apparent. However, compared with younger adults, older adults are less motivated to put forth their best effort when the task at hand is not particularly engaging (Hess et al., 2009). That works against them if they take an IQ test.

As Baltes and Baltes (1990) explain, selective optimization means that each adult selects certain aspects of intelligence to optimize and neglects the rest. If the ignored aspects happen to be the ones measured on intelligence tests, then IQ scores will fall, even if the adult's selection improves (optimizes) other aspects of intellect. The brain is plastic over the entire life span, developing new dendrites and activation sequences, adjusting to whatever the person chooses to learn (Smith & Baltes, 2013; Karmiloff-Smith, 2010; Macdonald et al., 2009).

For example, suppose someone who is highly motivated to learn about a particular area of the world (perhaps the Rocky Mountains) notices that aging affects his or her vision, making it hard to read fine print. That person might get reading glasses, increase computer type size (compensation), and read closely every article about the Rockies, ignoring news articles about everything else (selectivity). If an IQ vocabulary item happened to be *avalanche*, the person might score correctly, but he or she would fail most questions of general knowledge. In that way, knowledge increases (optimization) in depth but decreases in breadth.

Multitasking

One example of selective optimization is multitasking, which becomes more difficult with every passing decade (Reuter-Lorenz & Sylvester, 2005). Actually, multitasking slows down everyone of every age, but awareness of the slowdown is more acute with age.

This fact is obvious when people drive a car while talking on a cell phone. Such behavior is particularly dangerous for older drivers because as the brain focuses on the conversation, the neurological shift needed to react to a darting pedestrian is slower (Asbridge et al., 2013). Some jurisdictions require drivers to use hands-free phones, as if the distraction originates in the arms. These misguided laws have not reduced traffic accidents resulting from cell phone use because the multitasking brain is the problem, not the arms.

Some say that passenger conversation is as distracting as cell phone talk, but that is not true: Years of practice have taught adult passengers (though not young children) when to stop talking so that the driver can focus on the road (S. G. Charlton, 2009). If passengers do not quiet down on their own, experienced drivers stop listening and replying because they know they must concentrate.

This is why statements such as "I can't do everything at once" and "Don't rush me" are more often said by older adults than teenagers. Adults compensate for slower thinking by selecting one task at a time. Resources within the brain are increasingly limited with age, but compensation allows optimal functioning (Freund, 2008).

One father tried to explain this concept to his son as follows:

Focus It might seem as if Cindy Fay, shown here, has too many distractions to get anything done, but this scene actually depicts her intense, productive focus. She is a meteorologist for the National Weather Service, predicting the weather in the next 24 hours in Hastings, Nebraska. The monitors, phones, keyboards, and notes on her expansive desk are all carefully selected to optimize her forecasting ability.

> *I told my son: triage*
> *Is the main art of aging.*
> *At midlife, everything*
> *Sings of it. In law*
> *Or healing, learning or play,*
> *Buying or selling—above all*
> *In remembering—the rule is*
> *Cut losses, let profits ring.*
> *Specifics rise and fall*
> *By selection.*

[Hamill, 1991]

Expert Cognition

Another way to describe gains and losses is to say that everyone develops **expertise**, becoming a selective expert, specializing in activities that are personally meaningful, anything from car repair to gourmet cooking, from illness diagnosis to fly fishing. As people develop expertise in some areas, they pay less attention

expertise Specialized skills and knowledge developed around a particular activity or area of specific interest.

Same Situation, Far Apart: Don't Be Afraid The police officer in Toronto collecting slugs and the violinist in Jakarta collecting donations have both spent years refining their skills. Many adults would fear being that close to a murder victim, or that close to thousands of rushing commuters, but both these men have learned to practice their vocation no matter where they are. They are now experts: the cop discovered that two guns were used, and this musician earns more than $5 a day (the average for street musicians in Indonesia).

to others. For example, each adult usually elects to watch just some channels on television and ignoring vast realms of experience. Each adult has no interest in attending certain events for which others wait in line for hours.

Culture and context guide us in selecting areas of expertise. Many adults born 60 years ago are much better than more recent cohorts at writing letters with distinctive and legible handwriting. In childhood they practiced penmanship, became expert in it, and maintained that expertise. Today's schools and, consequently, children make other choices: Reading, for instance, is now crucial for every child, unlike a century ago when adult illiteracy was common.

Experts, as cognitive scientists define them, are not necessarily people with rare and outstanding proficiency. Although sometimes the term *expert* connotes an extraordinary genius, to researchers it means more—and less—than that. Expertise is not innate, although people with inherited abilities often select those abilities to develop.

An expert is not simply someone who knows more or who is talented in a particular way. That is only the beginning. At a certain point, accumulated knowledge, practice, and experience become transformative, putting the expert in a different league from others. The quality as well as the quantity of cognition is advanced. Expert thought is (1) intuitive, (2) automatic, (3) strategic, and (4) flexible, as we now describe.

Intuitive

Novices follow formal procedures and rules. Experts rely more on past experiences and immediate contexts; their actions are therefore more intuitive and less stereotypic than those of the novice. The role of experience and intuition is evident, for example, during surgery. Outsiders might think medicine is straightforward, but experts understand the reality:

> Hospitals are filled with varieties of knives and poisons. Every time a medication is prescribed, there is potential for an unintended side effect. In surgery, collateral damage is inherent. External tissue must be cut to allow internal access so that a diseased organ may be removed, or some other manipulation may be performed to return the patient to better health.

> [Dominguez, 2001, p. 287]

In one study, many surgeons saw the same videotape of a gallbladder operation and were asked to talk about it. The experienced surgeons anticipated and described problems twice as often as did the residents (who had also removed gallbladders, just not as many) (Dominguez, 2001). Data on physicians indicate that the single most important question to ask a surgeon is, "How often have you performed this operation?" The novice, even with the best, most recent training, is less skilled than the expert.

This is true in psychotherapy as well, according to a study that compared novices and experts—all with the requisite academic knowledge. The therapists were asked to talk aloud as they analyzed a hypothetical case. The experts did more "forward thinking," using inferences and developing a possible treatment plan. The novices were less likely to think about the social relationships of the person, and more likely to stick to a description of *what is* rather than wonder about what might be (Eells et al., 2011).

Another example of expert intuition is *chicken-sexing*—the ability to tell whether a newborn chicken is male or female. As David Myers (2002) tells it:

> Poultry owners once had to wait five to six weeks before the appearance of adult feathers enabled them to separate cockerels (males) from pullets (hens). Egg producers wanted to buy and feed only pullets, so they were intrigued to hear

that some Japanese had developed an uncanny ability to sex day-old chicks. . . . Hatcheries elsewhere then gave some of their workers apprenticeships under the Japanese. . . . After months of training and experience, the best Americans and Australians could almost match the Japanese, by sexing 800 to 1,000 chicks per hour with 99 percent accuracy. But don't ask them how they do it. The sex difference, as any chicken-sexer can tell you, is too subtle to explain.

[Myers, p. 55]

One experiment that studied the relationship between expertise and intuition involved 486 college students who were asked to predict the winners of soccer games not yet played. The students who were avid fans (the experts) made better predictions when they had a few minutes of unconscious thought instead of when they had the same number of minutes to mull over their choice (see Figure 21.3). Those who didn't care much about soccer (the nonexperts) did worse overall, but they did especially poorly when they had time to use unconscious intuition (Dijksterhuis et al., 2009).

The details of this experiment are intriguing. For 20 seconds, all participants were shown a computer screen with four soon-to-be-played soccer matches and were asked to predict the winners. One-third of the predictions were made immediately, one-third were made after two minutes of conscious thought, and one-third were made after two minutes when *only* unconscious thought could occur—because people randomly assigned to that group were required to calculate a series of mind-taxing math questions during those two minutes.

Nonexperts did no better than chance. They did worse after thinking about their answer, especially when the thought was unconscious. Perhaps the stress of doing math interfered with their thinking. By contrast, the predictions of the experts were not much better than those of the nonexperts when they guessed immediately, a little better when they had two minutes to think, and best of all after unconscious thought. Apparently, the experts' knowledge of soccer helped them most when they were consciously thinking of something else.

Automatic

This experiment with soccer experts and nonexperts also confirms that many elements of expert performance are automatic; that is, the complex action and thought required by most people have become routine for experts, making it appear that most aspects of the task are performed instinctively. Experts process incoming information quickly, analyze it efficiently, and then act in well-rehearsed ways that make their efforts appear unconscious. In fact, some automatic actions are no longer accessible to the conscious mind.

For example, adults are much better at tying their shoelaces than children are (adults can do it in the dark), but they are much worse at describing how they do it (McLeod et al., 2005). When experts think, they engage in "automatic weighting" of various unverbalized factors. This automatic thinking can be disrupted by the words that nonexperts use, which distort rather than clarify the thinking process (Dijksterhuis et al., 2009, p. 1382).

This is apparent if you are an experienced driver and try to teach someone else to drive. Excellent drivers who are inexperienced instructors find it hard to recognize or verbalize things that have become automatic—such as noticing pedestrians and cyclists on the far side of the road, or feeling the car shift gears as it heads up an incline, or hearing the tires lose traction on a bit of sand. Yet such factors differentiate the expert from the novice.

This may explain why, despite powerful motivation, quicker reactions, and better vision, teenagers have three times the rate of fatal car accidents as adults do (Insurance

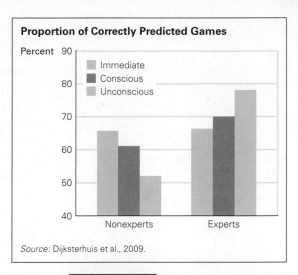

Source: Dijksterhuis et al., 2009.

FIGURE 21.3

If You Don't Know, Don't Think!
Undergraduates at the University of Amsterdam were asked to predict winners of four World Cup soccer matches in one of three conditions: (1) immediate—as soon as they saw the names of the nations that were competing in each of the contests, (2) conscious—after thinking for two minutes about their answers, and (3) unconscious—after two minutes of solving distracting math tasks. As you can see, the experts were better at predicting winners after unconscious processing, but the nonexperts became less accurate when they thought about their answers, either consciously or unconsciously.

Institute, 2012). Sometimes teenage drivers deliberately take risks (speeding, running a red light, drinking, and so on), but they more often simply misjudge and misperceive conditions that a more experienced driver would automatically notice.

The same gap between knowledge and instruction occurs when a computer expert tries to teach a novice what to do, as I know myself when my daughters try to help me with the finer points of Excel. They are unable to verbalize what they know, although they can do it very well with the computer. It is much easier to click the mouse or do the keystroke oneself than to teach what has become automatic.

automatic processing Thinking that occurs without deliberate, conscious thought. Experts process most tasks automatically, saving conscious thought for unfamiliar challenges.

Automatic processing is thought to explain why expert chess and Go players are much better than novices. They see a configuration of game pieces and automatically encode it as a whole, rather than analyzing it bit by bit.

A study of expert chess players (aged 17 to 81) found minor age-related declines, but expertise was much more important than age. This was particularly apparent for speedy recognition that the king was threatened: Older experts did that almost as quickly as younger adults (in a fraction of a second) despite steep, age-related declines on standard tests of memory and speed (Jastrzembski et al., 2006).

When something—such as an audience, a stressor, or too much conscious thought—interferes with automatic processing, the result may be clumsy performance. This is thought to be the problem when some experienced athletes "choke under pressure"—their automatic actions are hijacked (Caro et al., 2011).

Strategic

Experts have more and better strategies, especially when problems are unexpected. Indeed, strategy may be the pivotal difference between a skilled and an unskilled person. Expert chess players have general strategies for winning, and far better specific strategies for the particular responses after a move that is their specialty (Bilalić et al., 2009).

Similarly, a strategy used by expert team leaders in both the military and civilian arenas is ongoing communication, especially during slow times. Therefore, when stress builds, no team member misinterprets the previously rehearsed plans, commands, and requirements. You have witnessed the same phenomenon in expert professors: In the beginning of the semester they institute routines and policies, strategies which avoid problems later in the term.

Of course, strategies themselves need to be updated as situations change—and no chess game, or battle, or class is exactly like another. The monthly fire drill required by some schools, the standard lecture given by some professors, and the pat safety instructions read by airline attendants before takeoff become less effective over time. I recently heard a flight attendant precede his standard talk with, "For those of you who have not ridden in an automobile since 1960, this is how you buckle a seat belt." In that pre-flight monologue I actually listened.

The superior strategies of the expert permit selective optimization with compensation. That is evident in studies of airplane pilots, a group for whom age-related declines in skill could lead to thousands of fatalities.

In one study, trained pilots were given directions by air traffic controllers in a flight simulation (Morrow et al., 2003). Experienced pilots took more accurate and complete notes and used their own shorthand to illustrate and emphasize what they heard. For instance, they had more graphic symbols (such as arrows) than did pilots who were trained to understand air traffic instructions but who had little flight experience. Thus, even though nonexperts were trained and had the tools (note paper, pencil), they did not use them the way the experts did.

In actual flights, too, older pilots take more notes than younger ones do because they have mastered this strategy, perhaps to compensate for slower working memory. Another series of studies of pilots tested repeatedly over three years confirmed that expertise fostered better strategies, as expected (Taylor et al., 2007, 2011). But unexpected was the conclusion that experience was particularly beneficial for those whose age and genes produced slower thinking.

In those longitudinal studies, some deficits in memory and reaction time began to appear as the pilots aged. But expertise meant their judgment regarding piloting a plane was still good, far better than that of pilots with less experience (Taylor et al., 2007, 2011). People show age-related losses in many studies, but experts of all ages often maintain their proficiency at their chosen occupation for years after other abilities decline. That's selective optimization.

Flexible

Finally, perhaps because they are intuitive, automatic, and strategic, experts are also more flexible in their thinking. The expert artist, musician, or scientist is creative and curious, deliberately experimenting and enjoying the challenge when things do not go according to plan (Csikszentmihalyi, 1996).

Consider the expert surgeon, who takes the most complex cases and prefers unusual patients to typical ones because operating on the unusual ones might reveal sudden, unexpected complications. Compared with the novice, the expert surgeon is not only more likely to notice telltale signs (an unexpected lesion, an oddly shaped organ, a rise or drop in a vital sign) that may signal a problem but is also more flexible and willing to deviate from standard textbook procedures if those procedures seem ineffective (Patel et al., 1999).

In the same way, experts in all walks of life adapt to individual cases and exceptions—much as an expert chef will adjust ingredients, temperature, technique, and timing as a dish develops, tasting to see if a little more spice is needed, seldom following a recipe exactly. Standards are high: Some chefs throw food in the garbage rather than serve a dish that many people would happily eat. Expert chess players, auto mechanics, and violinists are similarly aware of nuances that might escape the novice.

In the field of education, best practices for the educator now emphasize flexibility and strategy, as each group of students has distinct and often erroneous assumptions. It is not helpful to simply teach the right answers; flexibility requires matching the instruction to the individual students, discovering what learning is needed (Ford & Nove, 2011).

A review of expertise finds that flexibility includes understanding which particular skills are necessary to become an expert in each profession. For example, repeated practice is needed in typing, sports, and games; collaboration skills are needed for leadership; and task management strategies are needed for aviation (Morrow et al., 2009).

Expertise and Age

The relationship between expertise and age is not straightforward. One of the essential requirements for expertise is time.

People who become experts need months—or even years—of practice (depending on the task) to develop that expertise (Ericsson et al., 2006). Some researchers think practice must be extensive, several hours a day for at least 10 years (Charness et al., 1996; Ericsson, 1996), but that is true in only some areas. Circumstances, training, genes, ability, practice, and age all affect expertise, which means that experts in one specific field are often quite inexpert in other areas.

Expertise may counteract some effects of aging (Krampe & Charness, 2006). Much depends on the task: The young have an advantage when speed is needed, but they are less adept at vocabulary. Further, they have less experience, which may be crucial for some tasks. An interesting example comes from perfumers: They need an acute sense of smell as they seek to develop new scents. Although the sense of smell typically is reduced with age, not so for perfumers. Experts outdid younger nonexperts: they had significantly developed those parts of the brain that were attuned to smell (Delon-Martin et al., 2013).

This illustrates a general conclusion from research on cognitive plasticity: Experienced adults often use selective optimization with compensation, becoming expert. This is apparent in many workplaces. The best employees may be the older, more experienced ones—if they are motivated to do their best.

Complicated work requires more cognitive practice and expertise than routine work; as a result, such work may have intellectual benefits for the workers themselves. In the Seattle Longitudinal Study, the cognitive demands of the occupations of more than 500 workers were measured, including the complexities involved in the interactions with other people, with things, and with data. In all three occupational challenges, older workers maintained their intellectual prowess (Schaie, 2005).

One final example of the relationship between age and job effectiveness comes from an occupation familiar to all of us: driving a taxi. In major cities, taxi drivers must find the best route (factoring in traffic, construction, time of day, and many other details), all while knowing where new passengers are likely to be found and how to relate to customers, some of whom might want to talk, others not.

Research in England—where taxi drivers "have to learn the layout of 25,000 streets in London and the locations of thousands of places of interest, and pass stringent examinations" (Woollett et al., 2009, p. 1407)—found not only that the drivers became more expert with time, but also that their brains adjusted to the need for particular knowledge. Some regions of their brains (areas dedicated to spatial representation) were more extensive and active than those of an average person (Woollett et al., 2009). On ordinary IQ tests, the taxi drivers' scores were average, but in navigating London, their expertise was apparent.

Other studies also show that people become more expert, and their brains adapt, as they practice various skills (Park & Reuter-Lorenz, 2009). This development occurs not only for motor skills—playing the violin, dancing, driving a taxi—but also for logic and other reasoning skills (Zatorre et al., 2012). The human brain is plastic lifelong; new learning is always possible, and practice is crucial.

Family Skills

This discussion of expertise has focused on occupations—surgeons, pilots, taxi drivers—that once had far more male than female workers. In recent years, two important shifts have occurred that add to this topic.

First, more women are working in occupations traditionally reserved for men. Remember from Chapter 4 that Virginia Apgar, when she earned her MD in 1933, was told she could not be a surgeon because only men were surgeons. Fortunately for the world, she became an anesthesiologist and her scale has saved millions of newborns. Today that assumption has changed; almost half the new MDs in the United States are women, and many of them have become surgeons (see Figure 21.4). More generally, most college women expect to have careers, husbands, and children, and many do so (Hoffnung & Williams, 2013).

The second major shift is that women's work has gained new respect. In earlier generations, women sometimes said they were "just a housewife" or "a nonworking mom." Recently, however, the importance of work at home is increasingly recognized, and men as well as women do it. We now know that not all women are good mothers or housekeepers, and that some men are expert in domestic and emotional work that was once women's exclusive domain. Couples who switch

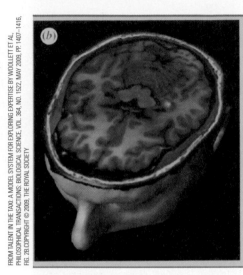

FROM TALENT IN THE TAXI: A MODEL SYSTEM FOR EXPLORING EXPERTISE BY WOOLLETT ET AL., PHILOSOPHICAL TRANSACTIONS: BIOLOGICAL SCIENCE. VOL 364, NO. 1522, MAY 2009, PP. 1407–1416, FIG. 2B.COPYRIGHT © 2009, THE ROYAL SOCIETY

Red Means Go! The red shows the activated brain areas in London taxi drivers as they navigated the busy London streets. Not only were these areas more active than the same areas in the average person's brain, but they also had more dendrites. In addition, the longer a cabby had been driving, the more brain growth was evident. This research confirms plasticity, implying that we all could develop new skills, not only by remembering but also by engaging in activities that change the very structures of our brains.

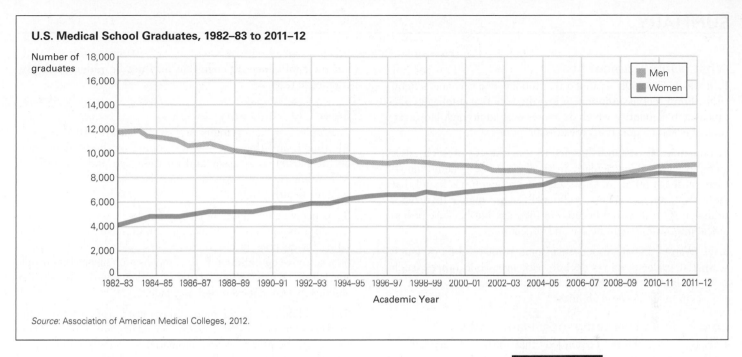

U.S. Medical School Graduates, 1982–83 to 2011–12

Source: Association of American Medical Colleges, 2012.

traditional roles are no longer rare. Most believe that for children, it is best that the father have major responsibility for child rearing (Dunn et al., 2013)

It is no longer assumed that a "maternal instinct" is innate to every mother; many mothers experience postpartum depression, financial stress, or bursts of anger and do not provide responsive child care. Certainly in some families, fathers and grandparents provide better care for children than biological mothers do. As with other adult tasks, motivation and experience are crucial for caregiving.

The skill, flexibility, and strategies needed to raise a family are a manifestation of expertise. Here again age as well as gender is important. As noted in previous chapters, in their late teens and early 20s both sexes are at their most fertile, and young women have the fewest complications of pregnancy. But conception is only a start: In general, older parents are more patient, with lower rates of child abuse as well as more successful offspring.

This is especially true if the parents have learned from experience and can listen well, as mature parents more often do. With such parents, teenagers are more likely to avoid drug addiction and other hazards. Developmentalists have not yet identified all the components necessary to become expert in child rearing, but at least we know that such expertise exists. Some parents are far more skilled than others.

FIGURE 21.4

Expect a Woman Next time you hear "The doctor will see you now," the physician is as likely to be a woman as a man—unless the doctor is over age 40.

Source: Association of American Medical Colleges, 2012.

SUMMING UP

Gains and losses occur during adulthood. Every adult experiences stress and must cope with it, with some coping methods more likely to turn stress into ongoing stressors that impair health, and other strategies able to turn stresses into productive experiences.

Adults choose to become adept at some cognitive aspects and skills, charting their course by using selective optimization with compensation. As a result, they can use their cognitive resources wisely, gaining intellectual power in areas that they choose. Choices and practice over time produce expertise, which is intuitive, automatic, strategic, and flexible. Expertise allows people to continue performing well in their work and their family life throughout adulthood. ∎

SUMMARY

What Is Intelligence?

1. It was traditionally assumed that intelligence was one general entity. From that assumption sprung the idea that intelligence in a measurable quantity, which decreases over adulthood. However, current evidence questions these assumptions.

2. Longitudinal research has found that the IQ of each adult tends to increase, particularly in vocabulary and general knowledge, until age 60 or so. Cross-sectional research has found that the reason younger adults traditionally score higher than older adults on IQ tests is not because of their age but because of historical improvements in health and education.

3. K. Warner Schaie found that some primary abilities (such as spatial understanding) decline with age while others (such as vocabulary) increase. Education, vocation, and family, as well as age, seem to affect these abilities.

Components of Intelligence: Many and Varied

4. Cattell and Horn concluded that although crystallized intelligence—which is based on accumulated knowledge—increases over time, a person's fluid, flexible reasoning skills decline with age.

5. Sternberg proposed three fundamental forms of intelligence: analytic, creative, and practical. Most research finds that, although analytic and creative abilities decline with age, practical intelligence may improve.

6. Overall, cultural values and the changing demands that come with age develop some cognitive abilities more than others. Each person and each culture responds to these demands, but their influence on cognition may not be reflected in psychometric tests.

Selective Gains and Losses

7. People experience many stressors over the 40+ years of adulthood, and they use various coping methods, depending on the particular stressor and on their age and background. A combination of stressors increases allostatic load and reduces health.

8. As people grow older, they choose to focus on certain aspects of their lives, optimizing development in those areas and compensating for declines in others, as necessary. As applied to cognition, selective optimization with compensation means that people specialize in whatever intellectual skills they choose. Meanwhile, abilities that are not exercised may fade.

9. In addition to being more experienced, experts are better thinkers than novices for four reasons. They are more intuitive; their cognitive processes are automatic, often seeming to require little conscious thought; they use more and better strategies to perform whatever task is required; they are more flexible.

10. Expertise in adulthood is particularly apparent in the workplace, as evidenced by doctors, airplane pilots, and taxi drivers. Experienced workers often outperform younger workers because they specialize, compensating for any losses that may appear.

11. Raising children and responding well to the emotional complexities and unanticipated challenges of family life are now recognized and valued as expert work. Experience and maturation increase the likelihood of family expertise.

KEY TERMS

analytic intelligence (p. 610)
automatic processing (p. 624)
avoidant coping (p. 616)
cognitive artifacts (p. 613)
creative intelligence (p. 610)

crystallized intelligence (p. 609)
emotion-focused coping (p. 616)
expertise (p. 621)
fluid intelligence (p. 608)
general intelligence (g) (p. 604)

practical intelligence (p. 611)
problem-focused coping (p. 616)
religious coping (p. 619)
Seattle Longitudinal Study (p. 606)

selective optimization with compensation (p. 620)
stressor (p. 615)
weathering (p. 617)

WHAT HAVE YOU LEARNED?

1. Many neuroscientists have searched for a genetic underpinning of g; how successful have they been?

2. What does cross-sectional research on IQ scores throughout adulthood usually find?

3. What does longitudinal research on IQ scores throughout adulthood usually find?

4. In what ways are younger generations more intelligent than older ones, according to cross-sequential research?

5. How do historical changes affect the results of longitudinal research?

6. How does cross-sequential research control for cohort effects?

7. What factors does K. Warner Schaie think have the most significant impact on adult intelligence?

8. Why would a person prefer to have greater crystallized intelligence than fluid intelligence?

9. Why would a person prefer to have greater fluid intelligence than crystallized intelligence?

10. If you want to convince your professors that you are smart, what might you do and what intelligence does that involve?

11. If you want to convince your neighbors to compost their food and yard waste, what might you do and what kind of intelligence does that involve?

12. What kinds of tests could measure creative intelligence?

13. In what situations is emotion-focused coping the best?

14. In what situations is problem-focused coping the best?

15. Why is religious coping more common in adulthood than in adolescence?

16. What might a person do to optimize ability in some area *not* discussed in the book, such as playing the flute, or growing tomatoes, or building a cabinet?

17. How might a person compensate for fading memory skills?

18. How does the saying, "Can't see the forest for the trees," relate to what you have learned about adult cognition?

19. Think of an area of expertise that you have and most people do not. What mistakes do people who are not experts in your area tend to make?

20. How does automatic processing contribute to expertise?

21. Explain how intuition might help or diminish ability.

22. In what occupations would age be an asset, and why?

23. In what occupations would age be a liability, and why?

APPLICATIONS

1. The importance of context and culture is illustrated by the things that people think are basic knowledge. With a partner from the class, write four questions that you think are hard but fair as measures of general intelligence. Then give your test to your partner, and answer the four questions which that person has prepared for you. What did you learn from the results?

2. Skill at video games is sometimes thought to reflect intelligence. Interview three or four people who play such games. What abilities do they think video games require? What do you think these games reflect in terms of experience, age, and motivation?

3. Some people assume that almost any high school graduate can become a teacher, since most adults know the basic reading and math skills that elementary children need to learn. Describe aspects of expertise that experienced teachers need to master, with examples from your own experience.

>>ONLINE CONNECTIONS

To accompany your textbook, you have access to a number of online resources, including Learning Curve, an adaptive quizzing program, critical thinking questions, and case studies. For access to any of these links, go to www .worthpublishers.com/launchpad/bergerls9e. In addition to these resources, you'll also find links to video clips, personalized study advice, and an ebook. Some of the videos and activities available online include:

- *Research Methods and Cognitive Aging.* Provides animated demonstrations of limitations of early IQ tests and illustrates Schaie's breakthrough use of sequential studies.

WORTH PUBLISHERS

Adulthood: Psychosocial Development

■ **Personality Development in Adulthood**
Theories of Adult Personality
Personality Traits
OPPOSING PERSPECTIVES: Local Context Versus Genes

■ **Intimacy: Family and Friends**
Friends and Acquaintances
Family Bonds

■ **Intimacy: Romantic Partners**
Marriage and Happiness
Partnerships over the Years
Gay and Lesbian Partners
Divorce and Remarriage

■ **Generativity**
Parenthood
Caregiving
Employment
A VIEW FROM SCIENCE: Accommodating Diversity

WHAT WILL YOU KNOW?

1. Do adults still have the personality they had as infants?
2. When is it better to divorce than to stay married?
3. When is it better to be unemployed than to have a job?

I broke two small bones in my pelvis—a mishap I caused myself: I was rushing, wearing old smooth-soled shoes, carrying papers, in the rain, after dark, stepping up a curb. I fell hard on the sidewalk. That led to a 911 call, an ambulance, five hospital days, five rehab days, heartfelt admiration for the physical therapists who got me walking, and deep appreciation of colleagues who taught my classes for two weeks.

I mention that minor event because it spotlights generativity. My four children, adults now, cared for me far beyond what I thought I needed. The two nearby daughters, Elissa and Sarah, were at the emergency room within an hour. Rachel flew in from Minnesota and bought me new shoes with slip-proof treads. Bethany drove down from Connecticut with planters, dirt, flowers, and trees to beautify my home. That was not all. They brought me books and my computer; questioned nurses and doctors; repeatedly phoned insurance providers; filled prescriptions; rearranged my bathroom; scheduled taxis; pushed my wheelchair; did laundry, shopping, cooking, cleaning.

It was hard to accept help. I told my friends, "No visitors." One laughed, "You are stuck in bed, I am coming." I hoped to return quickly to the classroom because I said "my students need me." But after several days, I realized I needed them as much as, or more, than vice versa. I now am glad my friend overruled me and grateful that my daughters did all they did.

Again and again I was reminded that generativity is mutual: People need to receive as well as to give.

That is a theme of this chapter, which focuses on the many interactions that mark adult lives: partnering and parenting, mating and mentoring. Each individual charts his or her own path, always aided by everyone else. We begin, then, with the personality traits that endure, we continue with some of the ways people support each other, and we end with the complexities of combining work and family.

>> Personality Development in Adulthood

A mixture of genes, experiences, and contexts results in personality, which includes each person's unique actions and attitudes. Continuity is evident: Few people develop characteristics that are opposite their childhood temperament. But personality can change, usually for the better, as people overcome earlier adversity and confusion.

Theories of Adult Personality

To organize this mix of embryonic beginnings, childhood experiences, and adulthood contexts, we begin with theories.

Erikson and Maslow

Erikson originally envisioned eight stages of development, three after adolescence. He is praised as "the one thinker who changed our minds about what it means to live as a person who has arrived at a chronologically mature position and yet continues to grow, to change, and to develop" (Hoare, 2002, p. 3).

Erikson's first four stages, already explained, are each tied to a particular chronological period. But adult stages do not occur in lockstep. Adults of many ages can be in the fifth stage, *identity versus role confusion*, or in any of the three adult stages—*intimacy versus isolation, generativity versus stagnation*, and *integrity versus despair* (McAdams, 2006) (see Table 22.1). Erikson saw adulthood as the continuation of the search for identity, via exploring intimacy and generativity, a vision confirmed by current research (Beaumont & Pratt, 2011).

Similarly, Abraham Maslow (1954) refused to link chronological age and adult development when he described his five stages. Thus, people of many ages can be in Maslow's third level (*love and belonging*, similar to Erikson's *intimacy versus isolation*).

At that stage, the priority for people is to be loved and accepted by partners, family members, and friends. Without affection, people might stay stuck, needing love but never feeling that they have enough of it. They might ignore other needs in order to be loved. By contrast, those who experience abundant love are able to move to the next level, *success and esteem*. The dominant adult need at this fourth stage is to be respected and admired.

For humanists like Maslow, these five needs characterize all people, with most adults seeking love or respect (levels three and four), and a few reaching

---

TABLE 22.1	**Erikson's Stages of Adulthood**

Unlike Freud or other early theorists who thought adults simply worked through the legacy of their childhood, Erikson described psychosocial needs after puberty in half of his eight stages. His most famous book, *Childhood and Society* (1963), devoted only two pages to each adult stage, but published and unpublished elaborations in later works led to a much richer depiction (Hoare, 2002).

Identity versus Role Confusion

Although Erikson originally situated the identity crisis during adolescence, he realized that identity concerns could be lifelong. Identity combines values and traditions from childhood with the current social context. Since contexts keep evolving, many adults reassess all four types of identity (sexual/gender, vocational/work, religious/spiritual, and political/ethnic).

Intimacy versus Isolation

Adults seek intimacy—a close, reciprocal connection with another human being. Intimacy is mutual, not self-absorbed, which means that adults need to devote time and energy to one another. This process begins in emerging adulthood and continues lifelong. Isolation is especially likely when divorce or death disrupts established intimate relationships.

Generativity versus Stagnation

Adults need to care for the next generation, either by raising their own children or by mentoring, teaching, and helping others. Erikson's first description of this stage focused on parenthood, but later he included other ways to achieve generativity. Adults extend the legacy of their culture and their generation with ongoing care, creativity, and sacrifice.

Integrity versus Despair

When Erikson himself was in his 70s, he decided that integrity, with the goal of combating prejudice and helping all humanity, was too important to be left to the elderly. He also thought that each person's entire life could be directed toward connecting a personal journey with the historical and cultural purpose of human society, the ultimate achievement of integrity.

Same Situation, Far Apart: Caution to the Winds Generally, risk taking decreases with age, but modern technology allows older adults to put their bodies on the line. This 80-year-old Israeli woman *(left)* has just skydived, and this man in his 50s *(right)* chases tornados with a "Doppler on Wheels."

self-actualization (level five). Unless mired in poverty, war, or severe early trauma, people move past Maslow's lower two stages (safety and basic needs) by adulthood. **[Lifespan Link:** Maslow's and Erikson's theories are discussed in Chapter 2.]

Other theorists agree, sometimes describing *affiliation* and *achievement*, sometimes using other labels. We will use Erikson's terms, intimacy and generativity, as a scaffold to describe these two universal needs. Every theory of adult personality recognizes both.

The Midlife Crisis

No current theorist sets chronological boundaries for specific stages of adult development. Middle age, if it exists, can begin at age 35 or 50.

This contradicts the notion of the **midlife crisis**, thought to be a time of anxiety and radical change as age 40 approaches. Men, in particular, were said to leave their wives, buy red sports cars, and quit their jobs. The midlife crisis was popularized by Gail Sheehy (1976), who called it "the age 40 crucible," and by Daniel Levinson (1978), who said men experienced

> tumultuous struggles within the self and with the external world. . . . Every aspect of their lives comes into question, and they are horrified by much that is revealed. They are full of recriminations against themselves and others.
>
> *[Levinson, 1978, p. 199]*

The midlife crisis continues to be referenced in popular movies, books, and songs. A 2013 Google search found more than 2 million hits, including a *Wall Street Journal* article about wealthy, successful, middle-aged men in crisis (Clements, 2005) and the song "Midlife Crisis" sung by the rock band Faith No More. However, no large study over the past three decades has found a normative midlife crisis. How could earlier observers have been so wrong?

In hindsight, it is easy to see where they went astray. Levinson studied only 40 men, all from one cohort. The data were then analyzed by men who were also middle-aged. (That would no longer be considered good science.) Sheehy is not a scientist; she summarized Levinson's research and then supplemented it by interviewing people she chose. Neither Sheehy nor Levinson used replicated, multimethod, longitudinal research on a diverse population, which now forms the bedrock of developmental science.

Even imperfect and limited data, however, might contain clues for new trends. Case studies and personal experiences may start scientists on a path of discovery. With the midlife crisis, however, every attempt at large-scale replication has failed. Why?

Remember cohort effects. Middle-class men who reached age 40 in about 1970 were affected by historic upheavals. Many began marriages and careers in the

midlife crisis A supposed period of unusual anxiety, radical self-reexamination, and sudden transformation that was once widely associated with middle age but that actually had more to do with developmental history than with chronological age.

Especially for People in Their 20s Will future "decade" birthdays—30, 40, 50, and so on—be major turning points in your life? (see response, page 634)

>> Response for People in Their 20s
(from page 633): Probably not. While many younger people associate certain ages with particular attitudes or accomplishments, few people find those ages significant when they actually live through them.

1950s, expecting grateful family members and employers. When they reached middle age, their wives were in the first wave of feminism (some called men "sexist pigs") and their teenagers thought their fathers were irrelevant (some said, "Don't trust anyone over 30").

No wonder these men were troubled. But their crisis was caused by personal reflections, family pressures, and historical circumstances, not by chronological age. Many adults, male or female, have moments when they question their earlier choices of career, or mate, or residence. Some make dramatic changes at age 30 or 40 or 50. However, few experience a classic midlife crisis.

Personality Traits

Remember from Chapter 7 that each baby has a distinct temperament. Some are shy, others outgoing; some are frightened, others fearless. Such traits begin with genes, but they are affected by experiences.

The Big Five

Temperament is partly genetic; it does not vanish. There are hundreds of examples, some of which are surprising. One recent study found, for instance, that temperament at age 3 predicted gambling addiction at age 32 (Slutske et al., 2012).

Longitudinal, cross-sectional, and multicultural research has identified five clusters of personality traits that appear in every culture and era, called the **Big Five**. (To remember the Big Five, the acronym OCEAN is useful.)

Young Stephen King

Personality Endures Fearfulness is likely to endure from childhood temperament through adult personality. Some children are terrified even by Disney movies and fairy tales and become adults who double-lock their doors. Others enjoy the thrill of fear.

Big Five The five basic clusters of personality traits that remain quite stable throughout adulthood: openness, conscientiousness, extroversion, agreeableness, and neuroticism.

ecological niche The particular lifestyle and social context that adults settle into because it is compatible with their individual personality needs and interests.

- *Openness*: imaginative, curious, artistic, creative, open to new experiences
- *Conscientiousness*: organized, deliberate, conforming, self-disciplined
- *Extroversion*: outgoing, assertive, active
- *Agreeableness*: kind, helpful, easygoing, generous
- *Neuroticism*: anxious, moody, self-punishing, critical

Each person's personality is somewhere between extremely high and extremely low on each of these five. The low end might be described, in the same order as above, with these five adjectives: *closed, careless, introverted, hard to please,* and *placid*.

Adults choose their social context, or **ecological niche**, selecting vocations, hobbies, health habits, mates, and neighborhoods in part because of personality traits. Personality affects almost everything, from whether a young adult develops an eating disorder to whether an older adult retires (Sansone & Sansone, 2013; Robinson et al., 2010).

Among the events, conditions, and attitudes linked to the Big Five are education (conscientious people are more likely to complete college), marriage (extroverts are more likely to marry), divorce (more often for neurotics), fertility (lower for women in recent cohorts who are more conscientious), IQ (higher in people who are more open), verbal fluency (again, openness and extroversion), and even political views (conservatives are less open) (Duckworth et al., 2007; Gerber et al., 2011; Jokela, 2012; Pedersen et al., 2005; Silvia & Sanders, 2010).

International research confirms that human personality traits (there are hundreds of them) can be grouped in the Big Five. Of course, personality and behavior are influenced by many other factors, not only by gender and cohort but also by culture. A test of the Big Five among a group in rural Bolivia—people who were largely illiterate and who made their living by agriculture—failed to replicate results found in urban, developed nations (Gurven et al., 2013). Even in

 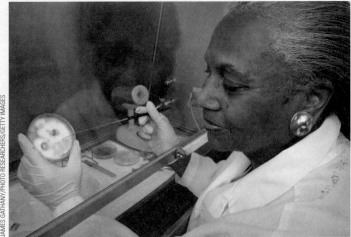

the United States it would be foolish to predict college graduation or voting behavior or anything else based *solely* on a person's ranking in the Big Five.

Age and Cohort

Many researchers who study personality find that personality shifts slightly with age, but the rank order stays the same. In other words, those highest in extroversion at age 20 are still highest at age 80, compared to others their own age, although not necessarily compared to 20-year-olds. The general age trend is positive. Traits that are considered pathological, such as neuroticism, tend to be modified as people mature (L. A. Clark, 2009). By contrast, traits that are valued, such as conscientiousness, increase slightly.

That is exactly what was found in a massive study of midlife North Americans (called MIDUS). Agreeableness and conscientiousness increased slightly overall while neuroticism decreased (Lachman & Bertrand, 2001) (see Figure 22.1). This pattern was also found in other research (Allemand et al., 2008; Donnellan & Lucas, 2008; Lehman et al., 2013).

Not surprisingly, then, self-esteem rises from early adulthood until about age 60, as people develop whatever personality is most appreciated within their culture (Orth et al., 2010). Of course, the same temperament can lead to opposite choices in people from different cohorts, as is evident in the relationship between personality and fertility.

For both men and women born in 1920, those high in openness had about the same number of children as those low in that trait because the entire culture valued fertility. For those born in 1960, people high in openness had far fewer children than average. Their openness may have encouraged them to learn about family planning and over-population, and to consider non-traditional roles, so some chose to have just one child or none (Jokela, 2012).

Same Situation, Far Apart: Scientists at Work Most scientists are open-minded and conscientious (two of the Big Five personality traits), as both of these women are. Culture and social context are crucial, however. If the woman on the right were in Tanzania, would she be a doctor surrounded by patients in the open air, as the woman on the left is? Or is she so accustomed to her North American laboratory, protected by gloves and a screen, that she could not adjust? The answer depends on personality, not knowledge.

Especially for Immigrants and Children of Immigrants Poverty and persecution are the main reasons some people leave their home for another country, but personality is also influential. Which of the Big Five personality traits do you think is most characteristic of immigrants? (see response, page 637)

Adult Personality: Stability Within Change

Personality   ⟶

Quite stable overall, but with minor ups and downs:

Openness   ↘

Conscientiousness   ↗

Extroversion   ↘

Agreeableness   ↗

Neuroticism   ↘

FIGURE 22.1

Trends, Not Rules Overall stability and some marked variation from person to person make up the main story for the Big Five over the decades of adulthood. In addition, each trait tends to shift slightly, as depicted here.

OPPOSING PERSPECTIVES

Local Context Versus Genes

Some people believe that personality is powerfully shaped by regional culture, so that a baby will have a quite different personality if born and raised, say, on the coast of Mexico or in the north of Canada. The opposite hypothesis is that personality is innate, fixed at birth and impervious to social pressures, with only minor, temporary impact from culture.

Evidence that personality is innate includes the fact that the same Big Five traits are found almost everywhere, with similar age trends. A 70-year-old grandfather in Iceland has a lot in common with a 70-year-old grandfather in Thailand. Some research suggests that supposed national differences in personality may be "unfounded stereotypes" (McCrae & Terracciano, 2006, p. 156).

Further evidence that personality is inborn rather than formed by culture is that each person usually has the same personality throughout adulthood. Personality changes, if they occur, happen more often early or late in life, not in the middle (Specht et al., 2011). Extroverted young adults become outgoing grandmothers with many friends from early adulthood and with more new friends each decade. Other traits likewise endure, sometimes changing a little but never reversing.

Nonetheless, some research finds that the environment affects personality, or, as one team wrote, "personality may acculturate" (Güngör et al., 2013, p. 713). One study compared the Big Five in three groups: Japanese, Japanese Americans, and European Americans. In general, the Japanese Americans were between the other two groups in self-rated personality.

For example, in extroversion, the average among European Americans was highest, followed by the Japanese Americans and then the Japanese. Perhaps local conditions, such as the greater density of people per square mile in Japan than in the U.S., make the Japanese more likely to seek social harmony and therefore result in less extroversion.

Another study focused on extroversion in 28 countries and reported a curious correlation between self-rated extroversion, well-being, and self-esteem. Essentially people were happiest if their own personality traits matched the norms of their surroundings. Extroversion was relatively high in Canada and low in Japan, and both the Canadians and the Japanese were happiest if their personal high or low ratings were consistent with their cultural norms (Fulmer et al., 2010).

The idea that context shapes personality also comes from the Big Five scores of adults in the 50 U.S. states (Rentfrow et al., 2010). According to 619,397 respondents on an Internet survey, New Yorkers are highest in openness, New Mexicans highest in conscientiousness, North Dakotans highest in both extroversion and agreeableness, and West Virginians highest in neuroticism. Lowest in these five traits are, in order, residents of North Dakota, Alaska, Maryland, Alaska (again), and Utah.

This survey suggests that local norms, institutions, history, and geography have an impact. Let us hypothesize how this could be. Those who live in Utah are surrounded by Mormons (no drugs, large families, generally good health) and awesome mountains. That might make them less anxious, more serene, and thus lowest in neuroticism. This study found that many aspects of adults' lives, including criminal behavior, morbidity, education, intelligence, and political preference, sprang from regional differences in personality (Rentfrow, 2008; Pesta et al., 2012).

Not only within the United States but also in England, physical surroundings seem to affect people. The English who lived near parks, gardens, and other greenery were less distressed. This study controlled for many factors, including age and income, and even traced people who moved from, or to, a plant-rich neighborhood (White et al., 2013).

Before concluding from this study that environment shapes personality, note the focus on distress, not personality. Do people who are less distressed also develop more agreeable, less neurotic personalities? Maybe. Or is distress superficial?

Someone who believes personality is innate might also question the U.S. data. Instead of people being affected by their surroundings, maybe people move to a community where their inborn traits are appreciated. For example, a North Dakotan college student who, unlike his neighbors, is genetically high in openness might relocate to New York. If people move to be with similar others, then regional differences would reflect personalities, not create them.

One review suggests that both nature and nurture are relevant, with the power of each affected by the age of the person. People under the age of 30 may seek an ecological niche—including finding a place to live—to fit their innate personality: They "actively try to change their environment." Later in life, context shapes traits, because once adults settle somewhere, they "change the self to fit the environment" (Kandler, 2012, p. 294).

A consensus regarding the relationship between culture, surroundings, genes, and personality has not yet emerged (Church, 2010). As you see, both opposing views are plausible. Which seems most accurate for you, your family, and friends? Do you "seek greener pastures" or "bloom where you are planted"? Does your culture affect your personality?

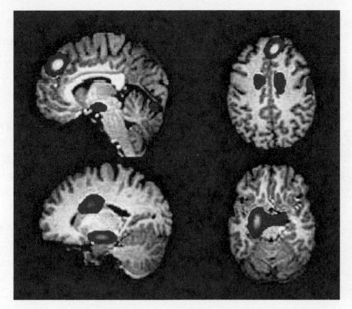

Active Brains, Active Personality The hypothesis that individual personality traits originate in the brain was tested by scientists who sought to find correlations between brain activity (shown in red) and personality traits. People who rated themselves high in four of the Big Five (conscientiousness, extroversion, agreeableness, neuroticism—but not openness) also had more activity in brain regions that are known to relate to those traits. Here are two side views *(left)* and a top and bottom view *(right)* of brains of people high in neuroticism. Their brain regions known to be especially sensitive to stress, depression, threat, and punishment (yellow bull's-eyes) were more active than the same brain regions in people low in neuroticism (DeYoung et al., 2010).

DEYOUNG, ET. AL. TESTING PREDICTIONS FROM PERSONALITY NEUROSCIENCE: BRAIN STRUCTURE AND THE BIG FIVE PSYCHOLOGICAL SCIENCE JUNE 2010 21: 820–828, FIRST PUBLISHED ON APRIL 30, 2010 DOI:10.1177/0956797610370159

SUMMING UP

As all the theories of adult development describe, adults seek to have close friends and family as well as to be productive in society. Various theorists have many words for these needs: Erikson described intimacy and generativity, whereas Maslow wrote about love and belonging. Adult personality shows both continuity and change in reaction to life circumstances, and links to childhood temperament. The Big Five personality traits (openness, conscientiousness, extroversion, agreeableness, and neuroticism) are evident lifelong and worldwide. One reason for the continuity of traits is that adults choose their ecological niche: finding partners, jobs, communities, and life patterns that are compatible with their inborn temperament. On the other hand, the expression of personality can change during adulthood, usually for the better. ∎

>> Response for Immigrants and Children of Immigrants (from page 635): Extroversion and neuroticism, according to one study (Silventoinen et al., 2008). Because these traits decrease over adulthood, fewer older adults migrate.

>> Intimacy: Friends and Family

Every adult experiences the crisis Erikson called intimacy versus isolation, seeking to connect with other people, as already described in Chapter 19. Specifics vary. Some adults are distant from their parents but close to partners and friends; others rely on family but not on others. The need for intimacy is universal yet dynamic: Each adult regulates closeness and reciprocity with everyone else (Lang et al., 2009).

Each person is part of a **social convoy**. The term *convoy* originally referred to a group of travelers in hostile territory, such as the pioneers in ox-drawn wagons headed for California or soldiers marching across unfamiliar terrain. Individuals were strengthened by the convoy, sharing difficult conditions and defending one another.

As people move through life, their social convoy metaphorically functions as those earlier convoys did, i.e., as a group of people who "provide a protective layer of social relations to guide, encourage, and socialize individuals as they go through life" (Antonucci et al., 2001, p. 572). Paradoxically, the current historical context (globalization, longevity, diversity) makes the social convoy more essential than ever (Antonucci et al., 2007).

social convoy Collectively, the family members, friends, acquaintances, and even strangers who move through life beside each individual.

Dinner Every Night Not only does the Shilts family eat together at 6:00 p.m. every night, but all six adults and five children also sleep under the same roof. The elderly couple is on the ground floor and both adult daughters, with husband and children, have a wing on the second floor.

consequential strangers People who are not in a person's closest friendship circle but nonetheless have an impact.

Strangers No More Leanne Kennedy *(right)* was dying from kidney failure, barely surviving with daily dialysis, four years on the waiting list for a donor kidney. Nonetheless, she accepted Shawn Stefanovic's marriage proposal. He offered his kidney—but it was no match. Then Stuart Kilgannan *(left)*, a consequential stranger to Leanne but Shawn's best man, offered his. A match! How will the new couple repay him? "Name a baby after me," he said.

Friends and Acquaintances

Friends are part of the social convoy; they are chosen for the traits that make them reliable fellow travelers. Mutual loyalty and aid are expected from friends: A relationship that is unbalanced (one giving and the other taking) often ends because both parties are uneasy.

Of course, sometimes a friend needs care and cannot reciprocate at the time, but it is understood that at some later day, the roles will be reversed. Friends provide practical help and useful advice when serious problems—death of a family member, personal illness, job loss—arise, and companionship, information, and laughter in daily life.

People consult their friends about mundane issues as well: how to get children to eat their vegetables, whether to remodel or replace the kitchen cabinets, when to ask for a raise, why a particular acquaintance is unreasonable. Just talking with friends lightens the load.

Friendship and Human Development

A comprehensive study found that friendships improve with age. To be specific, adolescents and young adults consider a significant minority of their friendships *ambivalent* or *problematic*. By adulthood, most friendships are rated *close,* few are ambivalent, and almost none are problematic (Fingerman et al., 2004). Unlike family members, if friends are not supportive, the relationship ends.

Friendship aids mental health throughout life (Bowers & Lerner, 2013). Friends also protect physical health, encouraging one another to eat better, to quit smoking, to exercise, and so on. The reverse is also true: If someone gains weight over the years of adulthood, his or her best friend is likely to do so as well. In fact, although most friendships last for decades, conflicting health habits may end a relationship (O'Malley & Christakis, 2011). For instance, a chain smoker and a friend who quits smoking are likely to part ways.

If an adult has no close and positive friends, health suffers (Couzin, 2009; Fuller-Iglesias et al., 2013). This seems as true in poor nations as in rich ones: Universally, humans are healthier with social support, and sicker when socially isolated (Kumar et al., 2012).

Acquaintances

In addition to friends, people have hundreds of casual acquaintances, who provide information, support, social integration, and new ideas (Fingerman, 2009). Such acquaintances—neighbors, coworkers, store clerks, local police officers, members of religious or community groups, and so on—are called **consequential strangers**, people who are not in a person's close circle but who nonetheless have an impact.

The consequential strangers in your life might include:

- Several other dog owners if you walk your dog
- Your barber or beautician if you regularly get your hair cut
- The street vendor from whom you buy a muffin every day
- The parent of your child's friend

A consequential stranger may even be literally a stranger: someone who sits next to you on an airplane, or directs you when you are lost, or gives you a seat on the bus. Not all such people are "consequential"; it depends on whether or not they have an impact on you.

Acquaintances differ from most close friends and family members in that they include people of diverse religions, ethnic groups, ages, and political opinions—and diversity is one reason they may be consequential, particularly in current times (Fingerman, 2009). Of course, close friends may also have such differences, but shared values, lifestyles, and background are often the glue that keeps a friendship close.

That is one reason strangers add to one's life: they expand one's perspective. This benefit need not be face-to-face. Many people believe that the Internet strengthens friendships and adds consequential strangers (Stern & Adams, 2010; Wang & Wellman, 2010).

Regular acquaintances are often part of each person's peripheral social network. With age, the number of such peripheral friends usually decreases. For example, one study found that the average emerging adult had 16 peripheral friends but the average middle-aged adult had 12. However, contrary to the trend, some people added people to their social network over the years (Zhang et al., 2011).

Family Bonds

People with close friends also tend to have good relationships with their family and to be affected by them. Developmentalists agree that families have linked lives—that the events or conditions that affect one family member tend to affect them all (Wickrama et al., 2013). Which particular family members become intimates varies for many reasons, as one might expect, but everyone is linked in some way.

Whether family members are considered friends depends on cultural norms. For example, in both Germany and Hong Kong, adults listed about the same number of close confidantes, but the Germans tended to include more nonfamily friends, whereas the Chinese included more family members (Fung et al., 2008).

The idea that family connections influence a person lifelong is supported by an intriguing study of the entire population of Denmark. Twins married less often than single-born adults, but those who wed were less likely to divorce. According to the researchers, twins may be less likely to need a spouse, since they have each other, but they have also learned from childhood how to get along with a close companion (Petersen et al., 2011).

Adult Children and Their Parents

Although most contemporary adults leave their parents' homes to establish their own households, a study of 7,578 adults in seven nations found that physical separation did not necessarily weaken family ties. It seemed that intergenerational relationships are becoming stronger, not weaker, as more adult children live apart from their parents (Treas & Gubernskaya, 2012). Other research agrees. Between parents and adult children, "the intergenerational support network is both durable and flexible" (Bucx et al., 2012, p. 101).

Household composition is a poor measure of family closeness, not only in developed nations. In rural Thailand, for example, income, not affection, determines whether a young married couple lives with the wife's parents (as traditional) or establishes their own household (Piotrowski, 2008). Remittances voluntarily sent back by adult children working in other nations typically boost family income, enabling couples to live in their own households. In this example, family closeness endures despite siblings living far apart.

Similar results are found in another nation, Ghana. The traditional West African household, with dozens of relatives living within one compound, is being replaced by many nuclear families, each with their own dwelling far from their

Family Harmony It is not easy to craft and sell stringed instruments, especially if you are a Black man in the mountains of northern Italy, as these two are. But they succeed, partly because they support each other. They are father and son.

DIEGO CERVO/BLEND IMAGES RM/GETTY IMAGES

childhood home. However, despite distance, reciprocity and family loyalty are enduring values, buffering financial stress, and correlating with happiness (Tsai & Dzorgbo, 2012).

Worldwide, when adult children have serious financial, legal, or marital problems, parents try to help. In Western nations this has always been evident for young, single adults, but the 2008–2011 economic recession resulted in parental support over a longer period. Specifically, in the United States, only 11 percent of 25- to 34-year-olds lived with their parents in 1980 but 29 percent did for at least several months in this economic recession. Moreover, three-fourths of them were comfortable staying with their parents when they needed to (Parker, 2012).

All the research shows that parents provide more financial and emotional support to their adult children than vice versa. Although such support is often needed and welcome, financial subsidies to adult children who are no longer in college correlate with symptoms of depression in the offspring (Johnson, 2013). For the parent generation, happiness is strongly affected by their adult children, with the most troubled offspring having more impact on parental well-being than the happy, successful ones (Fingerman et al., 2012).

Siblings

With adulthood often comes "marriage and childbearing, both of which have the potential to enhance closeness in sibling relationships or exacerbate previous difficulties" (Conger & Little, 2010, p. 89). Parenthood often increases closeness between siblings, partly because adults realize that children benefit from knowing their aunts, uncles, and cousins. Even if adult siblings have no children, they typically become closer to each other than they were as adolescents, because adulthood frees them from the intensity of a shared household (often with shared rooms, computers, schools, and so on), thus finally allowing them to differ without fighting.

In several South Asian nations, brothers are obligated to bestow gifts on their sisters, who in turn are expected to cook for and nurture their brothers (Conger & Little, 2010). Such patterns may impede individual growth, but they reduce poverty and strengthen family bonds. Encouraging siblings to care for one another helps satisfy needs for intimacy.

One factor that decreases sibling closeness is parental favoritism of one adult child over another. Particularly when fathers show favoritism, both the favored and nonfavored children are likely to be distressed (Jensen et al., 2013).

Close and affectionate family relationships seem to form more easily when the government pays for many services (e.g., health care, senior residences, child care) than when family members are obligated to pay for each other. When adults do not argue over material needs, they are likely to seek emotional intimacy, independent of practical necessity.

Regardless of public policy, most family members support each other. However, some adults avoid their blood relatives because they find them toxic. Sometimes, adults become **fictive kin** in another family, often brought in by a family member who says this person is "like a sister" or "my brother" and so on. They are not technically related (hence fictive), but they are accepted and treated like a family member (hence kin).

Fictive kin can be a lifeline to those adults who are rejected by their original family (perhaps because of their sexual orientation), or are far from home (perhaps immigrants), or are changing their habits (such as stopping addiction) (Ebaugh & Curry, 2000; Heslin et al., 2011; Kim, 2009; Muraco, 2006). Adults benefit from kin, fictive or not.

STEFANO G. PAVESI/CONTRASTO/REDUX

Arch Rivals or Blood Brothers? Both. Fernando and Humberto Campana are designers, shown here at an exhibit of their work in Spain, far from their native Brazil. As with many siblings, competition and collaboration have inspired them all their lives.

fictive kin Someone who becomes accepted as part of a family to which he or she has no blood relation.

Every adult has powerful intimacy needs, which are met by social support and companionship as the decades roll by. Friends and consequential strangers are part of the social convoy that helps adults navigate their lives. How crucial relatives are to a particular person depends on past history, cultural values, and current situation. In some cases, individuals seek to distance themselves from their family. ∎

>> Intimacy: Romantic Partners

Social scientists often make a distinction between "family of origin" (the family each person is born into) and "family of choice" (the family one creates for oneself as an adult). Family of choice typically begins with a commitment to a romantic partner.

As detailed in the chapters on emerging adulthood, adults today take longer than previous generations did to publicly commit to one long-term sexual partner. Nonetheless, although specifics differ (marriage at age 20 is late in some cultures and far too early in others), adults everywhere seek long-term partners to help meet their needs for intimacy as well as to raise children, share resources, and provide care when needed.

Almost all U.S. residents born before 1940 married (96 percent). Fewer of those born between 1940 and 1960 married (89 percent), and a significant number of them are now divorced and not remarried (16 percent) (U.S. Bureau of the Census, 2011a). Similar trends are found worldwide. Consider the data from Japan. Almost every Japanese adult was married in 1950, with many marrying before age 20. Now those Japanese who marry do so later (average age 30) and an estimated 20 percent will never marry (Raymo, 2013).

Marriage and Happiness

From a developmental perspective, marriage is a useful institution. Adults thrive if another person is committed to their well-being; children benefit when they have two parents who are legally as well as emotionally dedicated to them; societies are stronger if individuals sort themselves into families.

Share My Life Marriage often requires one partner to support the other's aspirations. That is evident in the French couple *(left)*, as Nicole embraces her husband, Alain Maignan, who just completed a six-month solo sail around the world. For twenty years, he spent most of his money and time building his 10-meter boat. Less is known about the Nebraska couple *(right)*, but many farm wives forgo the pleasures of city life in order to support the men they love.

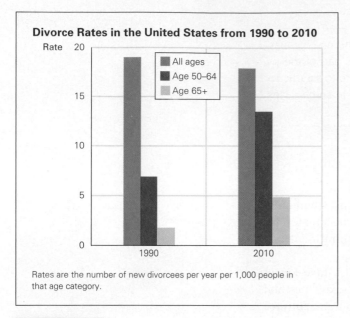

Divorce Rates in the United States from 1990 to 2010

Rates are the number of new divorcees per year per 1,000 people in that age category.

FIGURE 22.2

After All Those Years Newly married teen-agers and emerging adults continue to be the groups most likely to divorce, but older married people are twice as likely to divorce as people their age were a few decades ago. In 1990 only one in ten newly divorced men or women was over age 50; now it is 1 in 4.

Especially for Young Couples Suppose you are one-half of a turbulent relationship in which moments of intimacy alternate with episodes of abuse. Should you break up? (see response, page 644)

One Love, Two Homes Their friends and family know that Jonathan and Diana are a couple, happy together day and night, year after year. But one detail distinguishes them from most couples: Each owns a house. They commute 10 miles and are living apart together—LAT.

FRANK BARON/CAMERA PRESS/GUARDIAN/REDUX

From an individual perspective, the consequences of marriage are more mixed. There is no doubt that a satisfying marriage improves health, wealth, and happiness, but some marriages are not satisfying (Fincham & Beach, 2010; Miller et al., 2013). Overall, married people are a little happier, healthier, and richer than never-married ones—but not by much.

For this reason, it is misleading to lump all marriages together to find the average. Some marriages are very happy over the years, most marriages are moderately happy, and some marriages are not (see Figure 22.2). The least happy marriages do not always end with divorce—some unhappy adults stay married and some quite happy adults divorce. Husbands and wives in the happiest marriages tend to agree that their marriage is a good one, but in unhappy marriages it is not unusual for one spouse to be content and the other not (Brown et al., 2012).

Many factors correlate with happiness, especially adequate income and college education. Factors that correlate with un-happiness are premarital births, prior cohabitation, and a high neuroticism on the Big Five personality inventory.

Historically, women have had higher expectations for marriage and thus greater disillusionment, but that is changing by cohort and varies by culture (Stavrova et al., 2012). Women with more education and higher income are not only more likely to have happy marriages, they are "more likely to . . . stay in good marriages and leave bad marriages" (Kreager et al., 2013, p. 580).

Partnership does not always mean marriage. Cohabiters who expect to marry are quite different from those who slide into living together because of convenience. If the latter couple eventually marries, their chances of a happy marriage are less than average. The same is true for couples who have sex within the first month of being together (Sassler et al., 2012).[**Lifespan Link**: Cohabitation is discussed on Chapter 19.]

Some couples cohabit as a step in commitment and mutual trust, fully intending to marry. Then each year of the marriage increases their public and personal commitment to each other and makes divorce less likely. Many signs indicate that such couples differ from those who drift into marriage. For instance, compared to less committed couples, they have more children, the man earns more than comparable unmarried men, and the wife spends more time on household tasks (Kuperberg, 2012).

A sizable number of adults have found a third way to have a steady romantic partner: *living apart together* (LAT). They have separate residences, but especially when the partners are older than 30, they may function as a couple for decades (Duncan & Phillips, 2010).

A couple's decision to marry, to cohabit, or to LAT is influenced by many people in addition to the individuals who are romantically connected. Children born to an earlier partnership, even if those children are themselves adults, are particularly influential. Many parents choose to live apart from their partners because they do not want to upset their children (de Jong Gierveld & Merz, 2013).

Partnerships over the Years

The three boxes that questionnaires provide—married, single, divorced—do not reflect personal happiness or love, especially cross-culturally or over the decades of adulthood. Love is complex, a matter of relationship function, not structure. This has been described by many psychologists in recent years. One of them wrote:

> My whole life I have been searching for love. At a personal level, after a number of false starts, I have found it. In my research—initiated when a love relationship in my personal life was failing—I have tried to come closer to understanding what love is, how it develops, and why it succeeds or fails.

[Sternberg, 2013, p. 98]

Since 1986, Sternberg has studied three aspects of love: passion, intimacy, and commitment, and many other scientists have explored that topic (Sternberg and Weiss, 2006). As explained in Chapter 17, currently passion is usually first, then shared confidences create intimacy, and finally commitment leads to an enduring relationship. When all three are evident, that is consummate love—an ideal that is only sometimes attained in marriage.

A wealth of research finds that for most people commitment is crucial. A long-term committed partnership correlates with health and happiness throughout life (Miller et al., 2013). The reasons for this correlation range from the deep human need for someone who listens, understands, and shares one's goals to the mundane details of a mate who monitors daily diet and exercise, and insists that pain and symptoms need medical attention.

The passage of time also makes a difference. In general, the honeymoon period tends to be happy, but frustration increases as conflicts arise (see At About This Time) (H. K. Kim et al., 2008). Partnerships (including heterosexual married couples, committed cohabiters, same-sex couples, LAT couples) tend to be less happy when the first child is born, and again when children reach puberty (Umberson et al., 2010). Divorce risk rises in these years and then falls.

Remember, however, that averages obscure individual differences. Sometimes data is segmented by ethnicity. In the United States Asian Americans are much less likely to divorce than European Americans, and African Americans are more likely to do so. The ethnic differences are partly cultural and partly economic, making any broad effort to encourage marriage for everyone doomed to disappoint the politicians, social workers, and individuals involved (Johnson, 2012).

For cultural reasons, some unhappy couples stay married, and may have a long-lasting, conflict-filled relationship. As already noted, the divorce risk falls with age, but that does not mean that older couples never divorce. In 1990, 8 percent of the divorces were of people age 50 and older; in 2010, 25 percent were that old, often in marriages that had lasted 20 years or more (Brown & Lin, 2013).

On the other hand, although cohabiting couples separate more often than married couples, some cohabitants are deeply committed to each other, happily raising children together. As always with development, trends and tendencies are useful to know, but not every individual follows them.

Contrary to outdated impressions, the **empty nest**—when parents are alone again after the children have left—is usually a time for improved relationships. Simply spending time together, without crying babies, demanding children, or rebellious teenagers, improves intimacy. Partners can focus on their mates and on what they both enjoy.

Of course, time does not fix every relationship. Economic stress causes marital friction no matter how many years a couple has been together (Conger et al., 2010). Under the weight of major crises—particularly financial (such as a foreclosed home, a stretch of unemployment) or relational (such as demanding in-laws or an extramarital affair)—a long-standing relationship might well crumble.

AT ABOUT THIS TIME	
Marital Happiness over the Years	
Interval after Wedding	Characterization
First 6 months	Honeymoon period—happiest of all
6 months to 5 years	Happiness dips; divorce is more common now than later in marriage
5 to 10 years	Happiness holds steady
10 to 20 years	Happiness dips as children reach puberty
20 to 30 years	Happiness rises when children leave the nest
30 to 50 years	Happiness is high and steady, barring serious health problems

Not Always These are trends, often masked by more pressing events. For example, some couples stay together because of the children, so the empty nest stage becomes a time of conflict or divorce.

empty nest The time in the lives of parents when their children have left the family home to pursue their own lives.

Why Marry? Because many young people question the need for a wedding, marriage rates are down overall, but states that allow same-sex couples to wed find a sudden increase in rates. Miriam Brown and Carol Anastasio were among the 16,046 people to marry in New York City on July 24, 2011, the first day such marriages were legal. Extra judges and courtrooms were pressed into service.

Gay and Lesbian Partners

Almost everything just described applies to gay and lesbian partners as well as to heterosexual ones (Biblarz & Savci, 2010; Cherlin, 2013; Herek, 2006). Some same-sex couples are faithful and supportive of each other; their emotional well-being thrives on their intimacy. Others are conflicted, with problems of finances, communication, and domestic abuse resembling those in heterosexual marriages.

Political and cultural contexts for same-sex couples are changing markedly. As of this writing many nations, including Canada and Spain, recognize same-sex marriage. In the U.S., Washington, D.C., and 17 states (California, Connecticut, Delaware, Hawaii, Illinois, Iowa, Maine, Maryland, Massachusetts, Minnesota, New Hampshire, New Jersey, New Mexico, New York, Rhode Island, Vermont, and Washington) do so. Many other nations and U.S. states are ambivalent, and most countries, as well as many states, explicitly outlaw same-sex marriage. Attitudes are fluid and seem to be changing very rapidly, so that research that is even a few years old may be inaccurate.

One finding seems particularly relevant for all partnerships. In every relationship, connections to family of origin remain important. The importance of family ties, quite apart from the legal benefits of marriage, is illustrated by same-sex couples who have cohabited for years and who decide to marry now that laws are changing.

Although legal, moral, and financial arguments (health insurance, child rearing, and the like) are usually cited in public debate about same-sex marriage, often such couples marry not for the sake of legality but for the intimate needs of the couple. Partners want recognition in society, from their close relatives as well as from consequential strangers.

In a study of gay married couples in Iowa, one man decided to marry because, as he wrote about his mother: "I had a partner that I lived with . . . and I think that, as much as she accepted him, it wasn't anything permanent in her eyes" (Ocobock, 2013, p. 196). Another man wrote about his father: "He told us how proud of us he was that we were taking this step, and now he didn't have three sons, he had four sons, and it was enough to make you cry" (p. 197).

In this study, most of the family members were supportive, but some were not—again eliciting deep emotional reactions in the newly married men. One said, "Sometimes . . . a chasm forms that can't be crossed any more" (p. 200). In heterosexual marriages as well, in-laws usually welcome the new spouse, but when they do not, the partnership is more likely to be troubled. Family influences are hard to ignore.

Current and longitudinal research with a large, randomly selected sample of people in gay or lesbian marriages in the United States is not yet available. Many studies are designed to prove that same-sex marriage is either beneficial or harmful. Thus the studies make it difficult to draw objective conclusions.

For example, some research says divorce is less common for same-sex marriages, other research says more common, and still other research claims divorce is more common for male than female couples. A review of 15 years of same-sex marriages in Denmark, Sweden, and Norway finds that neither the greatest fears nor the greatest hopes for such unions are realized (Biblarz & Stacey, 2010).

Divorce and Remarriage

Throughout this text, developmental events that seem isolated, personal, and transitory are shown to be interconnected, socially mediated, with enduring consequences. Relationships never improve or end in a vacuum; they are influenced by the social and political context. For example, a study of many nations found that the happiness as well as the likelihood of separation of married and cohabiting

>> Response for Young Couples (from page 642): There is no simple answer, but you should bear in mind that, while abuse usually decreases with age, breakups become more difficult with every year, especially if children are involved.

couples was powerfully influenced by national norms (most benign in Norway, most hostile in Romania) (Wiik et al., 2012).

Divorce occurs because at least one partner believes that he or she would be happier not married. That conclusion is reached fairly often in the United States: Since 1980, almost half as many divorces or permanent separations have occurred as marriages. (More than one-third of first marriages end in divorce, and with each subsequent marriage, the odds of divorce increase.)

Typically, people divorce because some aspects of the marriage have become difficult to endure. Often, however, they are unaware of the impact divorce will have. Among the future problems are reduced income, lost friendships, and weaker relationships with the children, immediately and when they grow up (Kalmijn, 2010; Mustonen et al., 2011).

Family problems arise not only with children (usually custodial parents become stricter, and noncustodial parents feel excluded) but also with other relatives. The divorced adult's parents may be financially supportive, but often they are emotionally critical. Some married adults have good relationships with in-laws; this closeness almost always disappears when the couple splits, causing the loss of part of the social convoy.

For all these reasons, intimacy needs are less often met when couples separate. Sometimes divorced adults confide in their children, which may help the adults but not the children. Even if adults avoid that attractive trap, children need more emotional support just when the parents are often consumed by their own emotions (H. S. Kim, 2011).

Some research finds that women suffer from divorce more than men do (their income, in particular, is lower), but men's intimacy needs are especially at risk. Some husbands rely on their wives for companionship and social interaction; they are unaccustomed to inviting friends over or chatting on the phone. Divorced fathers are often lonely, alienated from their adult children and grandchildren (Lin, 2008a).

Usually, both former partners in a severed relationship attempt to reestablish friendships and resume dating. About half of all U.S. marriages are remarriages for at least one partner. Remarriage is more common as SES rises, and less common among those who are already parents. Ethnicity is also a factor; in the United States, divorced African American mothers, especially those with less than a high school education, rarely remarry (McNamee & Raley, 2011).

Initially, remarriage restores intimacy, health, and financial security. For fathers, bonds with their new stepchildren or with a new baby may replace strained relationships with their children from the earlier marriage, a benefit for the men but not for the children (Noel-Miller, 2013a).

Divorce usually increases depression and loneliness; repartnering brings relief. Most remarried adults are quite happy immediately after the wedding (Blekesaune, 2008). However, their happiness may not last. Because personality does not change much, people who were chronically unhappy in their first marriage often become unhappy in their second as well.

This research on divorce is sobering. As with all aspects of adult development, the shifting social context may have improved life for the formerly married, and even without that some people escape the usual patterns. If divorce ends an abusive, destructive relationship (as it does about one-third of the time), it usually benefits at least one spouse and the children (Amato, 2010).

Surprised? Many brides and grooms hope to rescue and reform their partners, but they should know better. Changing another person's habits, values, or addictions is very difficult.

"But you knew I was addicted to bad men when you married me."

Furthermore, some divorces lead to stronger and warmer mother–child and/or father–child relationships. That helps children cope, not only immediately but also for years to come (Vélez et al., 2011). This is not the usual outcome, however.

SUMMING UP

Family of origin (as distinct from chosen family) relationships usually remain important throughout adulthood as a source of social support, especially between parents and adult children and between siblings. Most adults seek, and find, a romantic partner who becomes an intimate companion. Each relationship follows its own path, but generally happiness ebbs and flows, with highs in the first months of a new relationship and lows when children are very young or teenagers. This is true for other-sex and same-sex marriages, for partners in cohabiting relationships, and for living-apart-together partners. Ending an intimate relationship, particularly in divorce, is almost always difficult. Remarriage can bring new happiness and new problems, especially if stepchildren are involved. ■

>> Generativity

According to Erikson, after the stage of *intimacy versus isolation* comes that of **generativity versus stagnation**, when adults seek to be productive in a caring way. Without generativity, adults experience "a pervading sense of stagnation and personal impoverishment" (Erikson, 1963, p. 267). Adults satisfy their need to be generative in many ways, especially through parenthood, caregiving, and employment.

Parenthood

Although generativity can take many forms, its chief form is "establishing and guiding the next generation" (Erikson, 1963, p. 267). Many adults pass along their values as they respond to the hundreds of requests and unspoken needs of their children each day, thus becoming generative.

All the child accomplishments already explained in this text, from the Brazelton Neonatal Behavioral Assessment Scale (Chapter 4) to the first words (Chapter 6),

generativity versus stagnation The seventh of Erikson's eight stages of development. Adults seek to be productive in a caring way, often as parents but, perhaps through art, caregiving, and employment.

Never Easy These two men both want the best for their children. The affluent German dad (left) seems to be more able to provide it than the Afghani dad (right), who has just lost his asylum case and, with his Belgium-born daughter, is about to be deported. However, both fathers seem to have a warm relationship with their children, which may be beneficial for all involved.

from theory of mind (Chapter 9) to school achievement (Chapter 12), are celebrated by astute parents—no matter how parenting came about. For such accomplishments, continuity of care is crucial.

For example, knowing one particular baby is essential in interpreting those first mispronounced words and in reading those early emotional expressions. Similarly, knowing a child's personality as well as intellectual prowess is required to find the zone of proximal development and then zeroing in on exactly when and how to help with schoolwork. In many ways, not only biological parents but also good foster parents are intensely committed to a particular, unique human being—and from that commitment both the joys and the concerns of parenting arise.

Biological Parenthood

The impact of parenting on children has been discussed many times in this text. Now we concentrate on the adult half of this interaction—the impact of parenting on the parents themselves. Children affect their parents by their personalities, needs, and sheer existence. As Erikson (1963) says, "The fashionable insistence on dramatizing the dependence of children on adults often blinds us to the dependence of the older generation on the younger one"(p. 266).

Most people underestimate how hard it is to be a good parent (Senior, 2014). Indeed, "having a child is perhaps the most stressful experience in a family's life" (LeMasters, cited in McClain, 2011). Understandably, parenthood is particularly difficult when intimacy, not generativity, is a person's primary psychosocial need. As already noted, marital happiness dips when the first baby arrives because intimacy needs must sometimes be postponed. Worse yet is having a baby as part of the search for identity, as teenagers discover too late.

Ideally, after establishing intimacy, many adults seek generativity, choosing parenthood, willingly coping with the many stresses that come with that role. Bearing and rearing children are labor-intensive expressions of generativity, "a transformative experience" with more costs than benefits when children are young (Umberson et al., 2010).

Children may reorder adult perspectives as adults become less focused on their personal identity or intimate relationships. One sign of a good parent is the parent's realization that the infant's cries are communicative, not selfish, and that adults need to care for children more than vice versa (Katz et al., 2011).

Care can be expressed in many ways. A study of men and women who had been in the top .01 percent in math ability according to achievement tests administered when they were in high school, and who had earned graduate degrees decades later, found that both sexes were changed by parenthood. The fathers worked harder to achieve more status and income, while the mothers became more communal, focusing on community and family (Ferriman et al., 2009).

The dynamic experience of raising children tests every parent. Just when adults think they have mastered the art of parenting, children become a little older, presenting new challenges. Over the decades of family life, parents must adjust to new babies, school pressures, and teenage autonomy. Privacy and income almost never seem adequate, and almost every child needs extra care and attention at some point. A positive correlation between family size and family problems is apparent worldwide, at least until the children are grown (Margolis & Myrskylä, 2011).

An added joy and burden occurs when adult children have children themselves. Grandparenthood begins, on average, when adults are about age 50, and it continues for decades. [**Lifespan Link:** The complexities of grandparenthood are discussed in Chapter 25.]

Especially when children's parents are troubled, grandparents worldwide believe their work includes helping their grandchildren (Herlofson & Hagestad, 2012). That becomes another source of generativity for them, affected by national policies and customs, gender, parent–child relationships, and the financial resources of both adult generations.

For the generativity of parenthood, biological parents have an advantage because they know they are intimately, genetically connected to their children. Especially if the pregnancy is intended (about one-third of all U.S. pregnancies are not) and if both parents want the child (some fathers deny paternity and leave the mother, especially when commitment is low) (Guzzo, 2013), raising children satisfies adult needs. Even for unplanned births, however, a strong generative love can develop that sustains both the parents.

Roughly one-third of all North American adults become adoptive, step-, or foster parents. Does this also express generativity? Yes, sometimes. Nonbiological parents have abundant opportunities for generativity, but they also experience distinct vulnerabilities as they meet the challenges of raising a child.

Adoptive Parents

Compared to foster parents and stepparents, adoptive parents have several advantages: They are legally connected to their child for life, and they desperately wanted the child. Current adoptions are usually "open," which means that the biological parents decided that someone else would be a better parent, yet they still want some connection to the child. The child knows about this arrangement, which proves an advantage for both sets of adults as well as for the child.

Strong parent–child attachments are often evident with adoption, especially when children are adopted as infants. Secure bonds can also develop if adoption occurs when the children are older (ages 4 to 7), especially when the adopting mother was strongly attached to her own mother (Pace et al., 2011).

Carry Me Every 3-year-old wants to be carried, but not every father enjoys it as much as this one seems to do, as he marches in a Korean American parade in midtown Manhattan. Many adoptive parents go out of their way to encourage their children to be proud of their heritage.

However, some adopted children have spent their early years in an institution, never attached to anyone, which makes it more difficult for the adoptive parent. Some such children are afraid to love anyone (St. Petersburg–USA Orphanage Research Team, 2008). The DSM-5 recognizes such children with the new diagnosis of reactive attachment disorder, a problem that can occur with biological children as well, but less often does so.

As you remember, adolescence—the time when teenagers seek their own identity—can stress any family. This stage is particularly problematic for adoptive families because all teenagers want to know their genetic and ethnic roots. One college student who feels well loved and cared for by her adoptive parents explains:

> In attempts to upset my parents sometimes I would (foolishly) say that I wish I was given to another family, but I never really meant it. Still when I did meet my birth family I could definitely tell we were related—I fit in with them so well. I guess I have a very similar attitude and make the same faces as my birth mother! It really makes me consider nature to be very strong in personality.

[A, 2012, personal communication]

A longitudinal study of parent–adoptive child relationships found that the parents' response to adolescent behavior was crucial. Neither overly strict nor overly permissive parenting helps the adopted teenager, but consistent, supportive parenting does (Klahr et al., 2011).

Attitudes in the larger culture often increase tensions between adoptive parents and children. For example, the mistaken notion that the "real" parents are the biological ones is a common social construction that hinders a secure relationship. International and interethnic adoptions are controversial because some people fear that such adoptions will result in children losing their heritage.

Adoptive parents who undergo the complications of international or interethnic adoption are usually intensely dedicated to their children. They are very much "real" parents, attempting to protect their children from discrimination that they might not have noticed before it affected their child. For example, one White couple adopted a mixed-race baby and three years later requested a second baby. This time they said, "We made a commitment to our daughter that we would have a brown or black baby. So we turned down a couple of situations because they were not right." These parents had noticed strangers' stares and didn't want their first child to be the only dark-skinned family member (Sweeney, 2013, p. 51).

Many such adoptive parents seek multiethnic family friends and educate their children about their heritage and the prejudice they will likely face. Similar "racial socialization" often occurs within minority families for their biological children.

In fact, all parents seek to defend their children against the stresses of discrimination. When adoptive parents do so, their adolescents who encounter frequent prejudice (but not those who encounter less prejudice) experience less stress because their adoptive parents have prepared them (Leslie et al., 2013).

Stepparents

Parents of stepchildren often find the experience far more complicated than they had expected. The average new stepchild is 9 years old. Typically, he or she has spent some time with both biological parents, and then time with a single parent, a grandparent, their nonresident parent, other relatives, and/or a paid caregiver.

Changes are always disruptive for children (Goodnight et al., 2013), and the effects are cumulative, with many children typically erupting emotionally in adolescence. Becoming a stepparent to such a child, especially if the child is dealing with a change of schools, a change of friends, or the changes of puberty, is difficult. Children sometimes react to such changes by maintaining a strong, emotional attachment to their birth parents.

This reaction is normal and beneficial, but it hinders connections to stepparents. Any new adult who tries to be a child's parent or friend and who simultaneously captures the love, care, and attention of the child's biological parent is understandably suspect.

Stepmothers may hope to heal a broken family through love and understanding, whereas stepfathers may believe their new children will welcome a benevolent disciplinarian. Often the biological parent chose the new partner partly to give their children a better father or mother than the original one. The new stepparent may look forward to the role, in part because he or she learned about the other parent from a biased reporter, their new spouse. Both newlyweds may expect their stepchildren to respond well to the new family.

Mother/Stepmother Remarriage gave Susan Heise (far right) a husband and a bigger family. Erika, 16, converses with her at the table, while Richard, 10, plays his trumpet, and Annie, 8, exercises in the doorway.

Observation Quiz Which one is a stepchild? (see answer, page 651)

Children rarely fulfill these hopes. Often they are hostile or distant (Ganong, 2011). Young stepchildren get sick, lost, injured accidentally, or become disruptive in school; teenage stepchildren may get pregnant, drunk, or arrested. These are all signs that the child needs special attention—and they may understandably make stepparents angry and resentful rather than caring and patient. If the adults either overreact to or are indifferent to such situations, the two generations become further alienated (Coleman et al., 2007).

High hopes and expectations are common in new stepparents, but few adults—biological parents or not—are able to live up to the generative ideal, day after day

(Ganong, 2011). Some stepparents go to the other extreme, remaining aloof from the children—not a good way to create a happy household.

Stepparents know that their connection to their stepchildren depends on their relationship with their new spouse, and they realize that criticizing the children or the way their mate relates to them may undercut their marriage. Some establish a good relationship with the children, although even if the marriage dissolves, as about half of all second marriages do, they will lose their connection to their stepchildren (Noel-Miller, 2013b).

It is not surprising that stepchildren add unexpected stresses to a marriage (Sweeney, 2010). One theory is that because laws and norms are unclear about the role of stepparents, adults fight about what they expect each other to do or not do (Pollet, 2010). None of this means that stepparents cannot become generative; it does, however, warn of the many difficulties.

Foster Parents

Foster parents undertake the most difficult form of parenting of all and thus have the greatest opportunity for generativity. Foster children typically have emotional and behavioral needs that require intense involvement. Consequently, foster parents need to spend far more time and effort on each child than biological parents do, and yet the social context tends to devalue their efforts (Smith et al., 2013). Their reasons to become foster parents are more often psychosocial than financial (Geiger et al., 2013). Problems arise from both the context and the children.

First, let's look at the situation. Although an estimated 400,650 children were in foster care in the United States in 2011 (Child Welfare Information Gateway, 2013), sometimes saving them from severe abuse, the general public criticizes and demeans foster parents (Smith et al., 2013). Foster parents are paid for their care, but they typically earn far less than a babysitter or than they would in a conventional job. Most foster parents feel that they are not sufficiently prepared or supported in their role and are appalled at the publicity that focuses on the atypical foster home.

Further, most foster children are in their care for less than a year, as the goal for about half the children is reunification with the birth parent, with adoption planned for many others. Foster children are often moved from one placement to another, or from foster care back to the maltreating family, for reasons unrelated to the wishes, competence, or emotions of the foster parents. This makes it doubly hard for the foster parent to develop a generative attachment to their children, and doubly admirable when they do.

The children themselves add to the difficulty. The average child entering the foster care system is 7 years old (Child Welfare Information Gateway, 2013). Many spent their early years with their birth families and are attached to them. Such human bonding is normally beneficial, not only for the children but also for the adults.

However, if birth parents are so neglectful or abusive that the children are seriously harmed by their care, the children's early attachment to their birth parents impedes relationships with the foster parent. Furthermore, the children also know that their connection to their foster parent can be severed for reasons unrelated to caregiving quality or relationship strength. Since most foster children have experienced long-standing maltreatment and have witnessed violence, they are usually suspicious of any adult (Dorsey et al., 2013).

As a result, adult caregivers of such children, either in foster families or institutions, face the dilemma of "whether to 'love' the children or maintain a cool, aloof posture with minimal sensitive or responsive interactions" (St. Petersburg–USA

Orphanage Research Team, 2008, p. 15). A loving bond is better for both the foster parent and the child, but if that bond forms, separation will be painful to both.

Generative caring does not occur in the abstract; it involves a particular caregiver and care receiver, so everything needs to be done to encourage attachment between the foster parent and child. Adults who recognize developmental norms—not expecting a child to be wiser or better behaved than children of the same age usually are—are more likely to delight in their foster children, which bodes well for the relationship (Bernard & Dozier, 2011).

Caregiving

Caregiving is a lifelong process, as "life begins with care and ends with care" (Tally & Montgomery, 2013, p. 3). As just reviewed, parenting is a prime example, but not the only one.

As Erikson (1963) wrote, a mature adult "needs to be needed" (p. 266). Some caregiving requires meeting physical needs—feeding, cleaning, and so on—but much of it involves fulfilling another person's psychological needs. That person could be a child, a spouse, a parent, or someone else, but whoever the recipient might be, caregiving is part of generative adulthood.

> This is not simple, nor should it be taken for granted. As one study concludes:
> The time and energy required to provide emotional support to others must
> be reconceptualized as an important aspect of the *work* that takes place in
> families. . . . Caregiving, in whatever form, does not just emanate from within,
> but must be managed, focused, and directed so as to have the intended effect
> on the care recipient.
>
> *[Erickson, 2005, p. 349]*

Thus, caregiving includes responding to the emotions of people who need a confidante, a cheerleader, a counselor, or a close friend. Parents and children care for one another, as do partners. Neighbors, friends, and distant relatives can be caregivers as well.

Kinkeepers

Most extended families include a **kinkeeper**, a caregiver who takes responsibility for maintaining communication. The kinkeeper gathers everyone for holidays; spreads the word about anyone's illness, relocation, or accomplishments; buys gifts for special occasions; and reminds family members of one another's birthdays and anniversaries (Sinardet & Mortelmans, 2009). Guided by their kinkeeper, all the family members become more generative.

Fifty years ago, kinkeepers were almost always women, usually the mother or grandmother of a large family. Now families are smaller and gender equity is more apparent, so some men or young women are kinkeepers.

Generally, however, the kinkeeper is still a middle-aged or older mother with several adult children. This role may seem burdensome, but caregiving provides both satisfaction and power (Mitchell, 2010). The best caregivers share the work; shared kinkeeping is an example of generativity.

Sometimes one family member is called on to do more than keep the family together. Because of their position in the generational hierarchy, middle-aged adults are expected to help both the older and younger generations.

Middle-aged adults have been called the **sandwich generation**, a term that evokes an image of a layer of filling pressed between two slices of bread. This analogy suggests that the middle generation is squeezed between the needs

>> Answer to Observation Quiz (from page 649): Erika. There are two clues: The ages of the children make it more likely that the eldest is from the father's first marriage, and biological children often try to grab their mother's attention if she seems to focus on another child.

kinkeeper A caregiver who takes responsibility for maintaining communication among family members.

sandwich generation The generation of middle-aged people who are supposedly "squeezed" by the needs of the younger and older members of their families. In reality, some adults do feel pressured by these obligations, but most are not burdened by them, either because they enjoy fulfilling them or because they choose to take on only some of them or none of them.

of younger and older relatives. This sandwich metaphor is vivid, but it gives a false impression (Gonyea, 2013; Grundy & Henretta, 2006). (See Visualizing Development, p. 653.)

Far from being squeezed, older adults who provide some financial and emotional help to their adult children are *less* likely to be depressed than those adults whose children no longer relate to them (Byers et al., 2008). Meanwhile, those of the young adult generation, who are thought to be squeezing their parents, are caregivers themselves. Their care is not usually financial, but cultural. They help their parents understand music, media, and technology, programming their cell phones, sending electronic photos, fixing computer glitches.

As for caregiving from middle-aged adults to their parents, this is not usually the case. Most of the over-60 generation are still quite proud and capable of caring for themselves. If they need care, it is typically provided by a spouse, by another elderly person, or by a paid caregiver. Thus adult children and grandchildren are part of the caregiving team but are not stuck in the middle of a sandwich. [**Lifespan Link:** Caring for the elderly is discussed in detail in Chapter 25.]

Shared caregiving keeps families together; wise kinkeepers typically make sure that happens.

Culture and Family Caregiving

The specifics of family bonds depend on many factors, including childhood attachments, cultural norms, and the financial and practical resources of each generation. Some cultures assume that elderly parents should live with their children; others believe that elders should live alone as long as possible and then enter some care-providing residence (Parveen, 2009; Ron, 2009).

Ethnic variations are evident in how interdependent family members are expected to be. Generally, ethnic minorities are more closely connected to family members than are ethnic majorities. They see each other more often, and they share food, money, child care, and so on. Although people may assume that closeness means affection, particularly for minorities closeness sometimes increases conflict (Voorpostel & Schans, 2011).

Everybody Contributes A large four-generation family such as this one helps meet the human need for love and belonging, the middle level of Maslow's hierarchy. When social scientists trace who contributes what to whom, the results show that everyone does their part but the flow is more down than up: Grandparents give more money and advice to younger generations than vice versa.

JODI COBB/NATIONAL GEOGRAPHIC/GETTY IMAGES

Caregiving in Adulthood

Longer life expectancies for elders and a challenging economy means that more adults than ever are meeting the needs of their aging parents, children, and even their grandchildren. While children account for most of the financial strain, caring for adult parents often involves the stresses, and rewards, of hands-on caregiving. Despite these burdens, and the stress that comes with them, those stuck in the middle are just as happy as those who are not, suggesting, perhaps, that the benefits of close family relationships outweigh the stress of responsibilities.

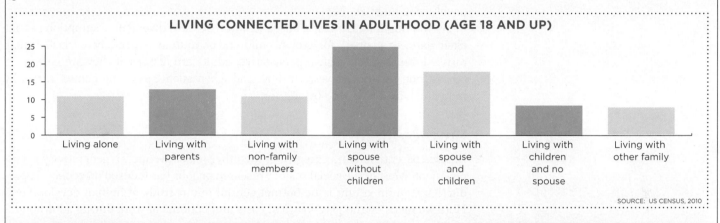

LIVING CONNECTED LIVES IN ADULTHOOD (AGE 18 AND UP)

SOURCE: US CENSUS, 2010

SUPPORTING FAMILY MEMBERS

More adults are supporting their children, grandchildren, and parents.

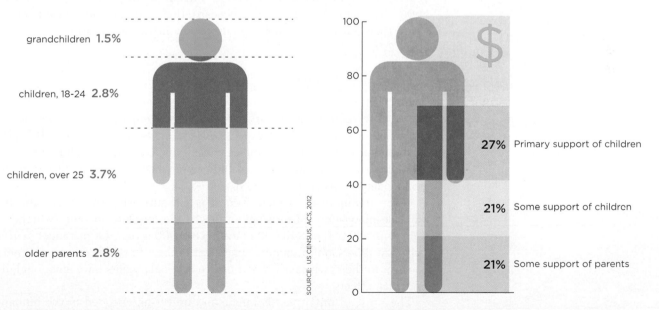

grandchildren **1.5%**

children, 18-24 **2.8%**

children, over 25 **3.7%**

older parents **2.8%**

SOURCE: US CENSUS, ACS, 2012

Almost half of adults (age 25 to 65) are providing some financial support for their grown children or their parents

27% Primary support of children

21% Some support of children

21% Some support of parents

SOURCE: US CENSUS, 2010

16% of adults under 65 are provide some care for those over 65. The relationship between the two vary.

4.3% spouse or partner
19.1% grandparent
20.7% another relative
25% friend
42.4% parents

0   10   20   30   40   50

SOURCE: DATA FROM US BUREAU OF LABOR STATISTICS, 2012

Cultures also differ as to whether sons or daughters are responsible for elder care. The assumption in traditional Asian nations is that sons provide for parents; this is unlike the assumption in most Western nations. However, the emphasis on caregiving sons (and daughters-in-law) varies from one family to another and may differ by nation as well. For instance, in mainland China, if an elderly person lives with an adult child, it is usually with a son, but in Taiwan it is usually with a daughter (Chu et al., 2011).

As you might imagine, if a husband and wife have divergent assumptions about elder care, or support for grown children, or mutual dependence, clashes may result. From a psychological perspective, adults are happier if they are caring for others, not just themselves, but how and when such caregiving occurs varies by individual, by family, and by culture.

Employment

Besides parenthood and caregiving, the other major avenue for generativity is employment. Most of the social science research on jobs has focused on economic productivity, an important issue but not central to our study of human development. Here we focus on the psychological costs and benefits of work during adulthood.

As is evident from many of the terms used to describe healthy adult development—*generativity, success and esteem, instrumental,* and *achievement*—adults have many psychosocial needs that employment can fill. The converse is also true: Unemployment is associated with behaviors and conditions that indicate psychological needs are not being met—higher rates of child abuse, alcoholism, depression, and many other social and mental health problems (Freisthler et al., 2006; Wanberg, 2012). Adults who can't find work are 60 percent more likely to die than other people their age, especially if they are younger than 40 (Roelfs et al., 2011).

Wages and Benefits

Income pays living expenses, but it does far more than that. Beginning with Thorstein Veblen (1899/2008), sociologists have described *conspicuous consumption,* whereby people buy things—such as expensive cars, hip sunglasses, and MP3 players—primarily to show them off. Families move to more affluent neighborhoods not only for safety but also for status. People buy more when they are depressed; money is a mood-changer (Cryder et al., 2008).

Given this human characteristic, it is not surprising that raises and bonuses increase motivation. Surprisingly, though, the absolute income (whether a person earns $30,000 or $40,000 or even $100,000 a year, for instance) matters less than how a person's income compares with others in their profession or neighborhood, or to their own salary a year or two ago. Salary cuts have emotional, not just financial, effects.

The sense of unfairness is innate and universal, encoded in the human brain (Hsu et al., 2008). Awareness of this fact helps explain some of the attitudes of adults about their pay. A detailed longitudinal study of nursing assistants who stayed or left their jobs over a one-year period found that respect, coworker relations, and health benefits were significant factors in their decision to stay or to leave, but pay was not (Rosen et al., 2011).

In the United States, many are offended by the extremely high salaries of corporate executives. That explains why the slogan, "We are the 99 percent," had such power before the 2012 presidential election. Resentment arises not directly from wages, benefits, and working conditions but from how they are determined: If workers have a role in setting fair wages, they are more satisfied (Choshen-Hillel & Yaniv, 2011).

If those deciding salary level seem to have favorites, especially if it seems as if sexual favors or family connections are more valued than merit, workers become distressed.

It is part of human nature to believe other people are unfairly advantaged. Women complain that men are better paid, members of one ethnic group may resent other groups for their income or benefits, some younger workers resent the seniority of older workers who themselves may complain that the young are less dedicated, and so on. This is not to deny that discrimination exists: All these complaints arise from reality as well as from human nature, but part of the human mind seems hypersensitive to perceived inequality.

A related problem is that people want to hold onto whatever they have rather than risk losing it for something better (Kahneman, 2011). This characteristic, called *risk aversion*, explains why seniors who receive medical care paid by the government (Medicare) are fiercely protective of that benefit and fear that extending that same benefit to younger adults might diminish their own care. Any change in employment conditions that benefits many people but harms a few is likely to be resisted by the few more than welcomed by the many.

To understand human development, we must go beyond income and consider also the generative aspects of work—and how people might respond if generative employment is impossible.

Work provides a structure for daily life, a setting for human interaction, a source of social status and fulfillment. In addition, work meets generativity needs by allowing people to do the following:

- Develop and use their personal skills.
- Express their creative energy.
- Aid and advise coworkers, as mentor or friend.
- Support the education and health of their families.
- Contribute to the community by providing goods or services.

These facts highlight the distinction between the **extrinsic rewards of work** (the tangible benefits such as salary, health insurance, and pension) and the **intrinsic rewards of work** (the intangible gratifications of actually doing the job). Generativity is intrinsic.

The power of these rewards may be affected by age. Extrinsic rewards tend to be more important when young people are first hired (Kooij et al., 2011). After a few years, in a developmental shift, the "intrinsic rewards of work—satisfaction, relationships with coworkers, and a sense of participation in meaningful activity—become more important as an individual ages" (Sterns & Huyck, 2001, p. 452).

The power of intrinsic rewards explains why older employees are, on average, less frequently absent or late and more committed to doing a good job than younger workers are (Landy & Conte, 2007). They also have more control over what they do, as well as when and how they do it. The autonomy that often comes with age reduces strain and increases dedication.

Employers, however, seem to favor younger workers—for at least one good reason: Older workers are usually better paid. Employers considering the costs and benefits of an older workforce should consider the cost of retraining and the advantages of keeping an older worker on part time by providing "bridge" employment, which is half way between full-time work and retirement (Kanfer et al., 2013). From a developmental perspective, that would be best.

Lowered Expectations It was once realistic, a "secular trend," for adults to expect to be better off than their parents had been, but hard times have reduced the socioeconomic status of many adults.

extrinsic rewards of work The tangible benefits, usually in the form of compensation (e.g., salary, health insurance, pension), that one receives for doing a job.

intrinsic rewards of work The intangible gratifications (e.g., job satisfaction, self-esteem, pride) that come from within oneself as a result of doing a job.

The Changing Workplace

Obviously, work is changing in many ways that affect adult development. We focus here on only three—diversity among workers, job changes, and alternate schedules. Dramatic shifts have occurred in who has a job and what they do. This is true everywhere: we use statistics for the United States as an obvious example.

Fifty years ago, the U. S. civilian labor force was 74 percent male and 89 percent non-Hispanic White. In 2012, it was 53 percent male and 65 percent non-Hispanic White (16 percent were Hispanic, 12 percent African American, 5 percent Asian, and 2 percent multiracial) (see Figure 22.3). The military also has become more diverse, from having a negligible percentage of women and minorities on active duty in the first half of the twentieth century to including 15 percent female and 37 percent from minority groups in 2011 (U.S. Department of Defense, 2012).

This increased diversity is also apparent within occupations. For example, in 1960 male nurses and female police officers were very rare, perhaps 1 percent. Now 13 percent of registered nurses are men and 9 percent of police officers are women—still an unbalanced ratio, but a dramatic shift. Employment discrimination in gender and ethnicity obviously still exists—but much less than it did.

This change benefits millions of adults who would have been jobless in previous decades, but it also requires workers and employers to be sensitive to differences they did not notice. Younger adults may have an advantage because they are more likely to accept diversity—a 25-year-old employee is not surprised to have a female boss. Older people have their own advantage if their life experience has sensitized them to ethnic and other differences. However, even today workers may be troubled by the well-intentioned but misplaced words and actions of people of other groups, as the following explains.

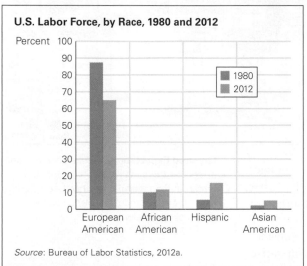

U.S. Labor Force, by Race, 1980 and 2012

Source: Bureau of Labor Statistics, 2012a.

FIGURE 22.3

Diversity at Work The U.S. labor force is increasingly non-White, even according to Labor Department statistics (which exclude some low-wage workers). The next challenge is for women and people of all ethnic groups to be more proportionally distributed in various vocations, management positions, and workplaces.

A VIEW FROM SCIENCE

Accommodating Diversity

Accommodating the various sensitivities and needs of a diverse workforce requires far more than reconsidering the cafeteria menu and the holiday schedule. Private rooms for breast-feeding, revised uniform guidelines, new office design, and revised management practices may be required. Exactly what is needed depends on the particular culture of the workers: Some are satisfied with conditions that others would reject.

Certain words, policies, jokes, or mannerisms may seem innocuous to one group but hostile to people of another group. For example, women object to sexy pin-up calendars in construction offices—something male workers accepted as routine. Researchers have begun to explore *micro-aggressions*—small things unnoticed by one person that seem aggressive to another person (Sue, 2010).

Micro-aggressions can be felt by anyone who feels different because of ethnicity, age, gender, sexual orientation, religion, or anything else. For example, one research group found that older workers were particularly likely to experience micro-aggressions at their workplace, but that some young men also noticed micro-aggressions aimed at them (Chou & Choi, 2011).

Comments about "senior moments" or being "color-blind" or the "fair sex" or "the model minority" can be perceived as aggressive, even though the person making such comments believes they are helpful, not hurtful. Workers and employers need to notice not only overt racism or sexism but also comments or actions that might be interpreted as biased.

The second change is in employment stability. Today's workers change jobs more often than workers did because resignations, firings, and hirings occur more often. Employers constantly downsize, reorganize, relocate, outsource, or merge. Loyalty between employee and employer, once heralded, seems quaint.

This flexibility of the job market may increase corporate profits, worker benefits, and consumer choices. However, churning employment affects human development, not usually for the better. Work friendships are disrupted and stress increases with every change. One study found that people who frequently changed jobs by age 36 were three times more likely to have health problems by age 42 (Kinnunen et al., 2005). This study controlled for smoking and drinking; if it had not, the health impact would have been greater.

As adults grow older, losing a job becomes increasingly stressful for several reasons (Rix, 2011):

1. Seniority brings higher salaries, more respect, and greater expertise; workers who leave a job they have had for years lose these advantages.
2. Many skills required for employment were not taught decades ago, so older job seekers are less likely to be hired.
3. Age discrimination is illegal, but workers believe it is widespread. Even if it does not exist, stereotype threat undercuts successful job searching.
4. Relocation reduces long-standing intimacy and generativity.

From a developmental perspective, this last factor is crucial. Imagine that you are a 40-year-old adult who has always lived in Michigan, and your employer goes out of business. You try to find work, but no one hires you, partly because unemployment in Michigan is among the highest in the nation. Would you move a thousand miles west to North Dakota, where the unemployment rate is only one-fourth as high?

If you were unemployed and in debt, and a new job was guaranteed, you might make the move. You would leave your friends and community, but at least you would have a paycheck. But would your spouse and children quit their jobs, schools, and social networks to move with you? If not, you would be cut off from all your social support, but if they did, their food and housing would be expensive, their schools would be overcrowded, and their lives would be lonely (at least initially). For you and anyone who comes with you, moving means losing intimacy—harmful for psychosocial development.

If You Had to Choose Which is more important, a high salary or comfortable working conditions? These workers in Mumbai, India *(left)* talk to North Americans who are confused about their computers, their bills, or their online orders, while the two men at the right are on an oil rig, spending months or even years off shore, far from their homes. Their pay is five times greater than that of the Indians. Do extrinsic rewards matter to you more than intrinsic ones?

Such difficulties are magnified for immigrants, who make up about 15 percent of the U.S. adult workforce and 22 percent of Canada's. Many of them depend on other immigrants for housing, work, and social support (García Coll & Marks, 2012). That meets some of their intimacy and generativity needs, but their connections to their family of origin and friends are strained by distance; the climate, the food, and the language are not comforting.

These developmental needs are ignored by many business owners and workers themselves. Adults' intimacy and generativity needs are met by a thriving social network; without that, psychological and physical health suffer.

Work Schedules

No longer does work always follow a 9-to-5, Monday-through-Friday schedule. In the United States, only about half of all employees work on that traditional schedule, with young parents particularly likely to work nonstandard shifts.

One crucial variable for job satisfaction is whether employees can choose their own hours. Workers who volunteer for paid overtime are usually satisfied, but workers who are *required* to work overtime are not (Beckers et al., 2008). This is true no matter how experienced the workers are, what their occupation is, or where they live.

For instance, a nationwide study of 53,851 nurses, ages 20 to 59, found that *required* overtime was one of the few factors that reduced job satisfaction in every cohort (Klaus et al., 2012). Similarly, a study of office workers in China also found that the extent of required overtime correlated with less satisfaction and poorer health (Houdmont et al., 2011). Apparently, although work (paid or unpaid) is satisfying to every adult, working too long and not by choice undercuts the psychological and physical benefits.

Weekend work, especially with mandatory overtime, is particularly difficult for father–child relationships, because "normal rhythms of family life are impinged upon by irregular schedules" (Hook, 2012, p. 631). Some nations impose limits on what employers can demand of employees who are parents; this is not true of the United States (Gornick & Meyers, 2003).

In theory, part-time work and self-employment might allow adults to balance conflicting demands. But reality does not conform to the theory. In many nations (except the Netherlands, where half the workers are part time), part-time work is typically underpaid, and in many nations benefits such as health care or pensions accrue only to full-time employees. Thus, workers avoid part-time employment if they can.

About one-third of all working couples who have young children and nonstandard schedules choose to have one parent at home while the other is at work. Mothers, particularly, are likely to rearrange meal and sleeping schedules so that they spend time with their children (Hook et al., 2012). However, night work and other nonstandard work schedules, especially when combined with overwork, correlate with personal, relational, and child-rearing difficulties (K. D. Davis et al., 2008; H. Liu et al., 2011).

Combining Intimacy and Generativity

A large study of adult Canadians found that about half of the variation in their distress was related to employment (working conditions, support at work, occupation, job security), but at least as

Especially for Entrepreneurs Suppose you are starting a business. In what ways would middle-aged adults be helpful to you? (see response, page 660)

No Perfect Job Colin Drummond is an independent photographer who earns a good living. He does most of his work here at home in Virginia, where he lives with his wife and children. Sounds ideal, but no job is perfect: Sometimes he must stand for hours outside in the rain; his profession is highly competitive so he does not know if he will earn any money next year. He is one of those photographers known as paparazzi.

MARVIN JOSEPH/THE WASHINGTON POST VIA GETTY IMAGES

much was related to family issues (having children younger than 5, support at home) and feelings of personal competence (Marchand et al., 2012).

To find an ideal balance, at least three factors are helpful: adequate income, chosen schedules, and social support. As an example of linked lives, husbands and wives usually adjust to each other's needs, which allows them to function better as a couple even than they did as singles (Abele & Volmer, 2011). For instance, after marriage men spend, on average, more hours on the job and women more hours on the home. As a result, five years after marriage the man's salary is notably higher than it would have been if he were single, while their shared home is notably more accommodating (Kuperberg, 2012).

If they have children, couples adjust their work and child-care hours, usually with the mother cutting back on employment, but not always—sometimes the father has fewer labor market hours and the mother has more. When mothers work full time, often fathers spend far more time with their children, and mothers do less housework (Abele & Volmer, 2011). If job loss threatens, both partners often prepare for their changed lives (Sweet & Moen, 2012). These adjustments reduce adult depression, especially in women.

Perhaps men, women, and children are better off with today's dual-income families, variable schedules, and so on. There are more ways to arrange their lives so that the family works well as a unit (Bianchi & Milkie, 2010).

At the same time, many couples feel overwhelmed with the simultaneous demands of parenting and employment. Often they postpone births; often the mother is employed sooner or more extensively than she would wish. This varies by nation, with government policies regarding maternity leave, child care, and health insurance influential in people's decision making (Lyonette et al., 2011; Nieuwenhuis et al., 2012).

Overall, it is debatable whether adults fare better or worse in today's economic climate and with today's social norms. Diversity, job change, and flexible schedules have benefits as well as costs. Maternal employment is more likely to benefit families than not, but children still need parental attention—so children suffer if their mothers or fathers have no time for them.

Because personality is enduring and variable, opinions about current adult development reflect personality as well as objective research. Some people are optimists—high in extroversion and agreeableness—and they tend to believe that adulthood is better now than it used to be. Others are pessimists—high in

Never Easy Juggling job responsibilities and child care simultaneously is difficult. Which is more complicated, caring for an infant while farming in South East Asia or supervising a teenager while conferring with a client? At times these two mothers might want to trade places or wish that men did as much child care as women. At other times, they would have it no other way.

>> Response for Entrepreneurs (from page 658): As employees and as customers. Middle-aged workers are steady, with few absences and good "people skills," and they like to work. In addition, household income is likely to be higher at about age 50 than at any other time, so middle-aged adults will probably be able to afford your products or services.

neuroticism and low in openness—and they are likely to conclude that adult life was better before the rise of cohabitation, LATs, divorce, and economic stress, when almost all couples married, had children, and mothers stayed home while fathers worked 9-to-5 in one job that supported the family.

The data support both perspectives—suicide is less common than it used to be, for instance, but poverty is increasing. From a developmental perspective, it is clear that intimacy and generativity continue to be important. Every adult benefits from friends and family, caregiving and satisfying work. Whether a satisfying combination is easier or more difficult at this historical moment is debatable.

As the next three chapters detail, there are many possible perspectives on life in late adulthood as well. Some view the last years of life with horror, others consider them the golden years. Neither view is quite accurate, as you will soon see.

SUMMING UP

Adults strive to meet their generativity needs, primarily through raising children, caring for others, and being productive members of society. Parenthood of all kinds is difficult yet rewarding, with foster, step-, and adoptive parents facing special challenges. Caregivers are generative, with each adult caring for other family members. Most adults still support their children, emotionally and financially, after the children are grown, and family members of all generations maintain connections with each other. Despite the phrase "sandwich generation," most middle-aged adults do not need to provide major support for their aging parents.

Employment ideally aids generativity through productivity and social networks. Diversity and flexibility characterize the current job market. Many young parents work nonstandard schedules, which disrupts family life. Many parents combine child rearing and employment, with mixed success. ▪

SUMMARY

Personality Development in Adulthood

1. The personalities of adults remain quite stable, and the midlife crisis is more myth than fact, more a cohort effect than a universal experience. Nonetheless, some individuals experience notable shifts, and many become more mature, as described by Erikson and Maslow.

2. The Big Five personality traits—openness, conscientiousness, extroversion, agreeableness, and neuroticism—are typically fairly stable in each individual over the decades of adulthood, as each person chooses a particular ecological niche. Culture and context affect everyone, with neuroticism most likely to be reduced with maturity.

Intimacy: Family and Friends

3. Every adult has powerful intimacy needs, which are met by social support and companionship as the decades roll by. Friends and consequential strangers are part of the social convoy that helps adults navigate their lives.

4. Family relationships remain important throughout adulthood as a source of social support, especially between parents and adult children and between siblings. How crucial relatives are to a particular person depends on past history, cultural values, and current situation.

5. Family members have linked lives, continuing to affect one another as they all grow older. In the U.S., they are less likely to live together than in earlier times and in other nations, but family members are often mutually supportive, both emotionally and financially. Siblings typically become closer over the years of adulthood, and adult children and their parents continue to help one another in practical and emotional ways.

Intimacy: Romantic Partners

6 . Marriage typically occurs later than it did in previous decades, but most adults still seek a partner (same sex or other sex) with whom to share life. Marital happiness often dips after the honeymoon period but improves over time, especially once children are grown.

7. Divorce is difficult for both partners as well as for their family members, not only immediately but also for years before and after the event. As divorce becomes more frequent, it may become less disruptive.

8. Remarriage is common, especially for men, and solves some of the problems (particularly financial and intimacy troubles) that many divorced adults experience—but remarriage is complicated and may end in a second divorce.

Generativity

9. Adults seek to feel generative, achieving, successful, instrumental—all words used to describe the major psychosocial need of generativity. This need is met through creative work, caregiving, and employment.

10. Caring for partners, parents, children, and others is a major expression of generativity. Often one family member becomes the chief kinkeeper and caregiver, usually by choice.

11. Parenthood is a common expression of adult caregiving. Even wanted and planned biological children pose challenges to their parents; stepchildren, foster children, and adoptive children bring additional stresses. Adults usually consider this aspect of caregiving rewarding as well as challenging.

12. Many adults feel special concern for other adult members of their families. Caregiving is more likely to flow from the older generations to the younger ones, rather than vice versa. The "sandwich generation" metaphor is misleading.

13. Employment brings many rewards to adults, particularly intrinsic benefits such as pride and friendship. Changes in employment pattern—including job switches, shift work, and the diversity of fellow workers—can affect other aspects of adult development.

14. Combining work schedules, caregiving requirements, and intimacy needs is not easy, and consequences are mixed. Some adults benefit from the diversity of employment; others find that new patterns of work impair family well-being.

KEY TERMS

Big Five (p. 634)
consequential strangers (p. 638)
ecological niche (p. 634)
empty nest (p. 643)

extrinsic rewards of work (p. 655)
fictive kin (p. 640)
generativity versus stagnation
  (p. 646)

intrinsic rewards of work (p. 655)
kinkeeper (p. 651)
midlife crisis (p. 633)

sandwich generation (p. 651)
social convoy (p. 637)

WHAT HAVE YOU LEARNED?

1. Describe the two basic needs of middle adulthood according to Erikson.

2. How might the midlife crisis reflect cohort rather than maturational changes?

3. How would each of the Big Five personality traits influence an adult's choice of jobs, mates, and neighborhoods?

4. Explain the concept of a social convoy.

5. What roles do friends play in a person's life?

6. What are the differences between friends and consequential strangers?

7. What is the usual relationship between adult children and their parents? What factors might explain this relationship?

8. What usually happens to sibling relationships over the course of adulthood?

9. Why do people have fictive kin?

10. What needs do long-term partners meet?

11. How and why does marital happiness change from the time of the wedding through old age?

12. What evidence is there that political and cultural attitudes toward same-sex partnerships are changing?

13. What are the usual consequences of divorce?

14. Many people who repartner are happy at first, but their happiness may not last. Why might this be the case?

15. What is the basic idea of generativity?

16. In what ways does parenthood satisfy an adult's need to be generative?

17. What factors might make it difficult for foster children and foster parents to bond?

18. How might each of the Big Five personality traits make it easier or more difficult to develop positive relationships with stepchildren?

19. What advantages do adoptive parents have over foster parents or stepparents?

20. Women are more often kinkeepers and caregivers than are men. How is these roles both a blessing and a burden?

21. Why are middle-aged adults sometimes called the "sandwich generation"? Why might this metaphor create a false impression?

22. What are some extrinsic and intrinsic rewards of work?

23. What are the advantages of greater ethnic diversity at work?

24. List four reasons why changing jobs is stressful.

25. What innovations in work scheduling have helped families? What innovations have hurt families?

26. Why might men and women be happier with current employment patterns than earlier ones?

APPLICATIONS

1. Describe a relationship that you know of in which a middle-aged person and a younger adult learned from each other.

2. Did your parents' marital and employment status affect you? How would you have fared if they had chosen other marriage or work patterns?

3. Imagine becoming a foster or adoptive parent yourself. What do you see as the personal benefits and costs?

4. Ask several people how their personalities have changed in the past decade. The research suggests that changes are usually minor. Is that what you found?

>> ONLINE CONNECTIONS

To accompany your textbook, you have access to a number of online resources, including Learning Curve, an adaptive quizzing program, critical thinking questions, and case studies. For access to any of these links, go to www.worth publishers.com/launchpad/bergerls9e. In addition to these resources, you'll also find links to video clips, personalized study advice, and an ebook. Some of the videos and activities available online include:

- *Development of Expertise.* It involves analytic, creative, and practical intelligence, but what makes it happen? Research shows that talent is not enough—practice, practice, practice!

WORTH PUBLISHERS

PART VII The Developing Person So Far:

Adulthood

BIOSOCIAL

Senescence As bodies age, internal as well as external organs show the effects of senescence. The brain slows down; skin becomes more wrinkled; the senses become less acute; lungs reduce capacity. Bodies change shape, with more fat in the middle and less strength in the muscles.

The Sexual-Reproductive System Sexual responsiveness and reproductive potential are reduced over adulthood. Women experience a dramatic drop in estrogen at menopause, which stops ovulation; men experience a more gradual decline in testosterone, which makes fatherhood less likely but not impossible in later adulthood.

Health Habits and Age Cigarette smoking is decreasing in North America but not in many other nations. Alcohol abuse, obesity, and inactivity are now recognized as problems, but most adults find them hard to reverse.

Measuring Health There are many ways to measure health, whether by calculating mortality, morbidity, disability, or vitality. Overall health is partly dependent on heredity, but much depends on daily habits.

COGNITIVE

What Is Intelligence? Researchers describe adult intelligence in many ways, noting that some intellectual abilities increase with age and others decline. Longitudinal research shows intelligence increasing over the years of adulthood, whereas cross-sectional research finds a decline. Over time, fluid intelligence declines and crystallized intelligence (especially vocabulary) improves. Practical intelligence, particularly social understanding, is increasingly needed through life's ups and downs.

Selective Gains and Losses Selective compensation with optimization is apparent in adulthood, as people become experts in areas of life that they choose to specialize in. In general, people are more intuitive, automatic, strategic, and flexible when dealing with problems in their area of expertise than they are in other areas.

PSYCHOSOCIAL

Personality Development in Adulthood All the major theories of adult development note that people maintain personality traits yet show some change. For instance, people become more conscientious and less neurotic with age. The Big Five traits reflect culture and are strengthened by a person's chosen lifestyle and ecological niche.

Intimacy: Family and Friends Adults depend on friends and family. They usually find good friends and have rewarding relationships with their adult children and their aging parents. However, such rewarding social relationships do not always occur: Divorce and separation are common, and difficult for all concerned. Adults depend to a great degree on their life partners, and many maintain fulfilling relationships with close partners, whether of the same sex or the other sex.

Generativity Caregiving is part of the joy as well as the obligation of adulthood. Many adults spend time and money on child rearing. Filial obligation is strong, with some adults caring for older family members. However, the sandwich generation concept is more myth than reality, and intergenerational support is usually mutual. Older generations usually provide financial and emotional support for younger generations. Employment is satisfying for many adults, although some trends, such as shift work and job change, harm optimal psychosocial development.

ROBIN SKJOLDBORG/GETTY IMAGES

© DAVID BURCH/AGE FOTOSTOCK

TONY ANDERSON/TAXI/GETTY IMAGES

late adulthood

What emotions do you anticipate as you read about late adulthood? Sadness, depression, resignation, sympathy, sorrow? Expect instead surprise and joy. You will learn that many older adults are active, alert, and self-sufficient; marked intellectual decline ("senility") is unusual; and older adults are happier than younger ones. That does not mean mindless contentment. Earlier personality and social patterns continue; the complexities of human life are evident. Joy is mixed with sorrow, and poverty, loneliness, and chronic illness are debilitating. However, most older adults, most of the time, are active and independent.

Unfortunately, late adulthood, more than any other part of life, is a magnet for misinformation and prejudice. If your first thought was a sad one as you approached these chapters, you are not alone. Why? Think about that as you read.

Biosocial Development: Late Adulthood

- **Prejudice and Predictions**
  Believing the Stereotype
  A VIEW FROM SCIENCE: When You Think of Old People . . .
  The Demographic Shift

- **Selective Optimization with Compensation**
  Personal Compensation: Sex
  A CASE TO STUDY: Should Older Couples Have More Sex?
  Social Compensation: Driving
  Technological Compensation: The Senses
  Compensation for the Brain

- **Aging and Disease**
  Primary and Secondary Aging
  Compression of Morbidity

- **Theories of Aging**
  Wear and Tear
  Genetic Theories
  Cellular Aging

- **The Centenarians**
  Far from Modern Life and Times
  Maximum Life Expectancy

WHAT WILL YOU KNOW?

1. How is ageism like racism?
2. What percentage of older people are in nursing homes?
3. Can people slow down the aging process?
4. Why would anyone want to live to 100?

I took Asa, age 1, to the playground. One mother, watching her son, warned that the sandbox would soon be crowded because the children from a nearby day-care center were coming. I asked questions, and to my delight she explained details of the center's curriculum, staffing, scheduling, and tuition as if she assumed I was Asa's mother, weighing my future options.

Soon I realized she was merely being polite, because a girl too young to be graciously ageist glanced at me and asked:

"Is that your grandchild?"
I nodded.
"Where is the mother?" was her next question.

Later that afternoon came the final blow. As I opened the gate for a middle-aged man, he said, "Thank you, young lady." I don't think I look old, but no one would imagine I was young. That "young lady" was benevolent, but it made me realize that my pleasure at the first woman's words was a sign of my own self-deceptive prejudice.

Now we begin our study of the last phase of life, from age 65 or so until death. This chapter starts by exploring the prejudices that surround aging. We describe biosocial changes—and what can be done to mitigate them. Then we provide a perspective on diseases, an exploration of the causes of aging, and finally a celebration of centenarians.

This is not a medical textbook, but various ailments that are common in the elderly—insomnia, heart disease, diabetes, osteoporosis, arthritis, erectile dysfunction, poor vision, deafness, hypertension, pneumonia, influenza, and accidental death—are all described in context, as examples of primary or secondary aging, selective optimization, the compression of morbidity, acute or chronic illness, and so on.

>> Prejudice and Predictions

Prejudice about late adulthood is common among people of all ages, including young children and older adults. That is a reflection of **ageism**, the idea that age determines who you are. Stereotyping makes ageism "a social disease, much like racism and sexism . . . [causing] needless fear, waste, illness, and misery" (Palmore, 2005, p. 90).

ageism A prejudice whereby people are categorized and judged solely on the basis of their chronological age.

667

Ageism can target people of any age, but it is not recognized as readily as racism or sexism. Consider curfew laws that require every teenager to be off the streets by 10 P.M.: that is ageist. Imagine the outcry if a curfew targeted all non-whites or all males. Why is ageism accepted, especially in regard to the old?

One expert contends that

> there is no other group like the elderly about which we feel free to openly express stereotypes and even subtle hostility. . . . Most of us . . . believe that we aren't really expressing negative stereotypes or prejudice, but merely expressing true statements about older people when we utter our stereotypes (Nelson, 2011, p. 40).

Nelson believes that ageism is institutionalized in our culture and has become pervasive in the media, employment, and retirement communities.

Another reason people accept ageism is that it often seems complimentary ("young lady") or solicitous (Bugental & Hehman, 2007). However, the effects of ageism, whether benevolent or not, are insidious, seeping into and eroding the older person's feelings of competence. The resulting self-doubt fosters anxiety, morbidity, and even mortality.

Believing the Stereotype

Parents protect their children from racism via racial socialization, teaching them to recognize and counter bias while encouraging them to be proud of who they are. However, when children express an ageist thought, few people teach them otherwise. Later on, their long-standing prejudice is "extremely resistant to change," undercutting their own health and intellect (Golub & Langer, 2007, pp. 12–13).

For example, in one study, adults younger than age 50 expressed opinions about the elderly, such as agreeing or not that "old people are helpless." Thirty years later, those who were least ageist were half as likely to have serious heart disease compared to those who were most ageist (Levy et al., 2009). Attitudes about aging vary from culture to culture, with deadly consequences.

Attitudes toward aging may be one reason longevity varies markedly depending on where a person lives. (The estimated life span for people born in various nations was shown in Figure 20.4, page 595). Japan has the highest life expectancy

Not in the West Korea *(left)* and Viet Nam *(right)* are more than two thousand miles apart, each with a distinct culture, but their people share appreciation of exercise and of the elderly. These women are among many doing Tai Chi each morning in Hanoi. Can you picture dozens of women exercising in a public plaza in a Western City?

in the world—a newborn girl in 2013 is expected to live well into her eighties (United Nations, 2013)—perhaps because of cultural practices such as *Respect for the Aged Day*.

Many contend, however, that ageism is now prevalent worldwide, even in Japan (North & Fiske, 2012). Perhaps only nations with few old people can afford to venerate them.

Ageist Elders

Ageism becomes a self-fulfilling prophecy, a prediction that comes true because people believe it. For example, most people older than 70 believe they are doing better than other people their age—who, they say, have worse problems and are too self-absorbed (Cruikshank, 2009; Townsend et al., 2006). Underlying that belief is the idea that age destroys vitality.

If the elderly attribute their problems to the inevitability of age, they will not try to change themselves or the situation. For example, if they forget something, they laugh it off as a "senior moment," not realizing the ageism of that reaction. When hearing an ageist phrase—"dirty old man" or "second childhood," or patronizing compliments such as "spry" or "having all her marbles"—elders themselves miss the insult.

Asked how old they feel, typical 80-year-olds lop a decade or more off their age (Pew Research, 2009). Yet if *most* 80-year-olds feel like they imagine the average 70-year-old feels, then that feeling is, in fact, typical for 80-year-olds. Thus they reject their own ageist stereotype of 80-year-olds, although they feel the same way most 80-year-olds actually do.

It is illogical for all the 80-year-olds to feel like 70-year-olds, but in an ageist culture thinking you feel younger than your chronological age is protective. Indeed, "feeling youthful is more strongly predictive of health than any other factors including commonly noted ones like chronological age, gender, marital status and socioeconomic status" (Barrett, 2012, p. 3).

Stereotype threat can be as debilitating for the aged as for other groups (Hummert, 2011). [**Lifespan Link:** Stereotype threat was discussed in detail in Chapter 18.] If the elderly fear they are losing their minds, that fear itself may undermine cognitive competence (Hess et al., 2009). Internalized ageism is much worse than an ageist comment from someone else, as the following view from science illustrates.

A VIEW FROM SCIENCE

When You Think of Old People . . .

The effect of internalized ageism was apparent in a classic study (Levy & Langer, 1994). The researchers selected three groups. Two were thought to be less exposed to ageism: residents of China, where the old were traditionally venerated, and North Americans who were deaf lifelong. The third group was composed of North Americans with typical hearing, who presumably had heard ageist comments all their lives. In each of these three groups, half the participants were young and half were old.

Memory tests were given to everyone, six clusters in all. Elders in all three groups (Chinese, deaf Americans, and hearing Americans) scored lower than their younger counterparts.

This was expected; age differences are common in laboratory tests of memory, as will be explained in detail in Chapter 24.

The purpose of this study, however, was not to replicate earlier research, but to see if ageism affected memory. It did. The gap in scores between younger and older hearing North Americans (most exposed to ageism) was double that between younger and older deaf North Americans and five times wider than the age gap in the Chinese (see Figure 23.1). Ageism undercut ability, a conclusion also found in many later studies (Levy, 2009).

Sadly, later studies have found that modernization has made many Asian cultures more ageist than they used to be (Chen & Powell, 2012; Nelson, 2011). And numerous studies continue to

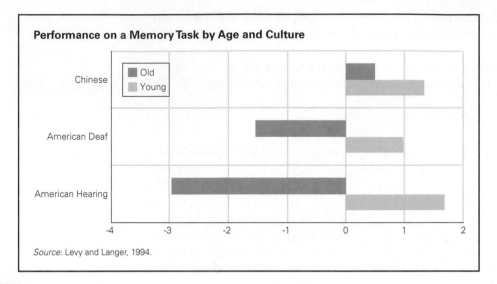

Performance on a Memory Task by Age and Culture

Source: Levy and Langer, 1994.

FIGURE 23.1

The Widest Gap The bars show how the six groups score on a memory test, with the overall average right in the middle, at 0. Age slows down memory—no surprise—but culture has a marked effect. Not only do the Chinese score higher (their culture values memorizing), but the gap between old and young is greatest among the hearing Americans. Have decades of listening to ageist remarks within the U.S. culture reduced memory?

find that an older person's attitude about aging affects, for good or ill, their mental performance, social life, and even physical health.

For example, positive concepts of aging correlate with faster recovery from disability (Levy et al., 2012). This study began with 598 healthy people age 70 or older, followed for more than 10 years. Initially they were asked, "When you think of old persons, what are the first five words or phrases that come to mind?" Their answers were rated from most negative (e.g., decrepit, demented) to most positive (e.g., wise, spry). From this a score of attitudes was calculated for each person.

Over the years of the study, many of the participants experienced disabilities, including some so severe that they temporarily could not walk, feed themselves, go to the toilet, or even get out of bed. Some had major surgery or were hospitalized, sometimes requiring intensive care. Then most recovered, at least somewhat. Their resilience depended partly on other illnesses, on income, and on many other factors, as one might predict.

However, when all those factors were taken into account, how quickly and completely people recovered from disability was affected by their earlier attitudes about the old. The most dramatic difference was found in those people who experienced severe disabilities: Compared to those with the most negative stereotypes, those with positive associations about aging became completely independent again 44 percent more often (Levy et al., 2012).

Old Lady Few young people realize that many of the most active people they know are in their 60s and 70s. Tina Turner, born in 1939, had a sold-out international tour when she was officially a senior citizen, and she married her long-time companion when she was 73. Her talent is extraordinary, but her active life is not exceptional.

When older people believe that they are independent and in control of their own lives, they are likely to be healthier—mentally, as well as physically—than others their age. Of course some need special care. Elders must find "a delicate balance . . . knowing when to persist and when to switch gears, . . . [and] some aspects of aging are out of one's control" (Lachman et al., 2011, p. 186). If an older person is struggling to carry a heavy bag, help might be appreciated. But do not assume; ask first, don't grab the bag.

Sleep and Exercise

Ageism impairs the routines of daily life. It prevents depressed older people from seeking help because they resign themselves to infirmity.

Ageism also leads others to undermine an elder's vitality and health. For instance, health professionals are less aggressive in treating disease in older patients, researchers testing new prescription drugs enroll few older adults (who are most likely to use those drugs), and caregivers diminish independence by helping the elderly too much (Cruikshank, 2009; Herrera, 2010; Peron & Ruby, 2011–2012).

One specific example is sleep. The day–night circadian rhythm diminishes with age: Many older people wake before dawn and are sleepy during the day. Older adults spend more time in bed, take longer to fall asleep, and wake frequently (about 10 times per night) (Ayalon & Ancoli-Israel, 2009). They also are more likely to nap. All this is normal: If they choose their own sleep schedules, elders feel less tired than young adults.

In one study, older adults complaining of sleep problems were mailed six booklets (one each week) (Morgan et al., 2012). The booklets described normal sleep patterns for people their age and gave suggestions to relieve insomnia. Compared to similar older people who did not get the booklets, the informed elders used less sleep medication and reported better quality sleep. Even 6 months after the last booklet, they were more satisfied with their sleep.

The booklets told elders what to do about their sleep. For uninformed elders, ageism can lead to distress over normal sleep; doctors might prescribe narcotics, or people might drink alcohol. These remedies can overwhelm an aging body, causing heavy sleep, confusion, nausea, depression, and unsteadiness.

A similar downward spiral is apparent with regard to exercise. In the United States, only 35 percent of those over age 64 meet the recommended guidelines for aerobic exercise, compared with 56 percent for adults aged 18 to 44 (National Center for Health Statistics, 2013) (see Figure 23.2). Meeting the guidelines for muscle strengthening was worse; only 16 percent of the aged did so.

An ageist culture assumes that the patterns of the young are ideal. Consequently, team sports are organized in ways that emerging adults prefer; traditional dancing assumes a balanced sex ratio; many yoga, aerobic, and other classes are paced and designed for people in their 20s. If an old man tries to join a pick-up basketball game, the reaction of the young players might be rejection or sympathy. If an old woman dons running shorts and jogs around the park, others might snicker. No wonder some elders exercise less.

Added to the problems caused by the ageism of the culture is self-imposed ageism, which reduces movement. That increases stiffness and reduces range of motion while impairing circulation, digestion, and thinking. Balance is decreased, necessitating a slower gait, a cane, or a walker. A better reaction to aging would be

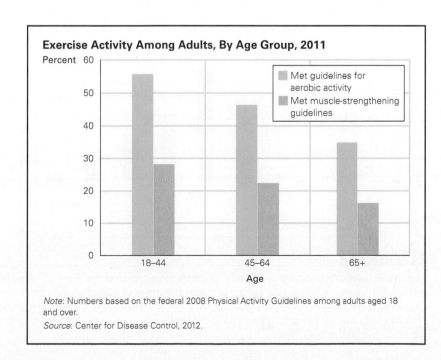

Note: Numbers based on the federal 2008 Physical Activity Guidelines among adults aged 18 and over.

Source: Center for Disease Control, 2012.

FIGURE 23.2

Heart, Lungs, and Legs As you see, most of the elderly do not meet the minimum exercise standards recommended by the Centers for Disease Control—150 minutes of aerobic exercise a week and muscle-strengthening exercises twice a week. This is especially troubling since those activities have been proven many times to safeguard the health of all the major organs, as well as to correlate with intelligence, memory, and joy.

Especially for Young Adults Should you always speak louder and slower when talking to a senior citizen? (see response, page 674)

elderspeak A condescending way of speaking to older adults that resembles baby talk, with simple and short sentences, exaggerated emphasis, repetition, and a slower rate and a higher pitch than used in normal speech.

to increase activity, and that would add healthy years, reduce depression, prevent heart disease, and more (Mullen et al., 2012; de Fina et al., 2013).

Many people think they are compassionate when they infantilize the elderly, regarding them as if they were children ("so cute," "second childhood") (Albert & Freedman, 2010). Some of the elderly accept the stereotype. It is easier not to protest: At every age and for every preconceived idea, changing someone else's attitudes and assumptions is difficult.

Among the professionals most likely to harbor stereotypes are nurses, doctors, and other care workers. Their ageism is difficult to erase (Eymard & Douglas, 2012), partly because it is based on their experience in treating older patients who are sick and dependent. Understandably, some professionals generalize based on their experiences and treat all elderly as if they were feeble (Williams et al., 2009).

A specific example is **elderspeak**—the way people talk to the old (Nelson, 2011). Like baby talk, elderspeak uses simple and short sentences, slower talk, higher pitch, louder volume, and frequent repetition. Elderspeak is especially patronizing when people call an older person "honey" or "dear," or use a nickname instead of a surname ("Billy," not "Mr. White").

Ironically, elderspeak reduces communication. Higher frequencies are harder for the elderly to hear, stretching out words makes comprehension worse, shouting causes anxiety, and simplified vocabulary reduces the precision of language.

Destructive Protection

Some younger adults and the media discourage the elderly from leaving home. For example, whenever an older person is robbed, raped, or assaulted, sensational headlines add to fear and consequently promote ageism. In fact, street crime targets young adults, not old ones (see Figure 23.3).

The homicide rate (the most reliable indicator of violent crime, since reluctance to report is not an issue) of those over age 65 is less than one-fifth the rate for those aged 25 to 34 (see Figure 17.2 on page 508) (U.S. Department of Justice, Bureau of Justice Statistics, 2011). To protect our relatives, perhaps we should insist that our young adults never leave the house alone—a ridiculous suggestion that makes it obvious why telling older adults to stay home is shortsighted.

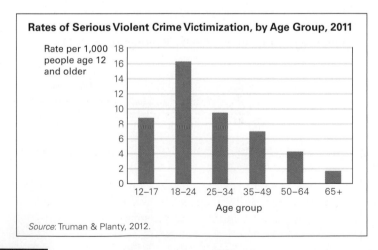

Rates of Serious Violent Crime Victimization, by Age Group, 2011

Source: Truman & Planty, 2012.

FIGURE 23.3

Victims of Crime As people grow older, they are less likely to be crime victims. These figures come from personal interviews in which respondents were asked whether they had been the victim of a violent crime—assault, sexual assault, rape, or robbery—in the past several months. This approach yields more accurate results than official crime statistics because many crimes are never reported to the police.

Although advertisements induce younger adults to buy medic-alert devices for older relatives, it might be better to go biking with them. Lest you think that bikes are only for children, a study of five nations (Germany, Italy, Finland, Hungary, and the Netherlands) found that 15 percent of Europeans *older than* 75 ride their bicycles *every day* (Tacken & van Lamoen, 2005).

In the United States, few elders ride bikes. Protected bike paths are scarce and many bikes are designed for speed, not stability. Laws requiring bike helmets often apply only to children—another example of ageism.

The Demographic Shift

Demography is the science that describes populations, including population by cohort, age, gender, or region. Demographers describe "the greatest demographic upheaval in human history" (Bloom, 2011, p. 562), a **demographic shift** in the proportions of the population of various ages. In an earlier era, there were 20 times more children than older people, and only 50 years ago the world had 7 times more people under age 15 than over age 64. This is no longer true.

The World's Aging Population

The United Nations estimates that nearly 8 percent of the world's population in 2010 was 65 or older, compared with only 2 percent a century earlier. This number is expected to double by the year 2050. Already 13 percent in the United States are that old, as are 14 percent in Canada and Australia, 20 percent in Italy, and 23 percent in Japan (United Nations, 2012).

As you saw in Chapter 1, demographers often depict the age structure of a population as a series of stacked bars, one bar for each age group, with the bar for the youngest at the bottom and the bar for the oldest at the top (refer to Visualizing Development, p. 680). Historically, the shape was a *demographic pyramid*. Like a wedding cake, it was widest at the base, and each higher level was narrower than the one beneath it, for three reasons—none of which is currently true:

1. More children were born than the replacement rate of one per adult, so each new generation had more people than the previous one. NOW FALSE
2. Many babies died, which made the bottom bar much wider than later ones. NOW FALSE
3. Serious illness was almost always fatal, reducing the size of older groups. NOW FALSE

Sometimes unusual events caused a deviation from this wedding-cake pattern. For example, the Great Depression and World War II reduced the number of births. Then postwar prosperity and the soldiers' return caused a baby boom between 1946 and 1964, just when infant survival increased. The mushrooming birth and survival rates led many demographers to predict a population explosion, with mass starvation by the year 2000 (Ehrlich, 1968).

That fear evaporated as new data emerged. Birth rates fell and a "green revolution" doubled the food supply. Early death has become rare; demographic stacks have become rectangles, not pyramids. Indeed, some people worry about another demographic shift: fewer babies and more elders, which will greatly affect world health and politics (Albert & Freedman, 2010).

This flipped demographic pattern is not yet starkly evident everywhere. Most nations still have more people under age 15 than over age 64. Worldwide, children outnumber elders more than 3 to 1—but not 20 to 1 as they once did. United Nations predictions for 2015 are for 1,904,088,000 people younger than 15 and 603,986,000 older than 64. Not until 2075 is the ratio projected to be 1 to 1 (United Nations, 2013).

ASHLEY COOPER/CORBIS

Speed Demon? Road rage? No. Neither his bike nor his garb is designed for speed, and anger is far more common in the young than in those over age 75, as this man is. He seems faster and happier than the drivers on his right, stuck in traffic in central London.

demographic shift A shift in the proportions of the populations of various ages.

Same Situation, Far Apart: Keep Smiling Good humor seems to be a cause of longevity, and vice versa. This is true for both sexes, including the British men on Founder's Day *(left)* and the two Indian women on an ordinary sunny day in Dwarka *(right)*.

>> **Response for Young Adults** (from page 672): No. Some seniors hear well, and they would resent it.

dependency ratio A calculation of the number of self-sufficient productive adults compared with the number of dependents (children and the elderly) in a given population.

Statistics that Frighten

Unfortunately, demographic data are sometimes reported in ways designed to alarm. For instance, have you heard that people aged 80 and older are the fastest-growing age group? Or that the number of people with Alzheimer disease is increasing rapidly? Both true; both misleading.

In 2010 in the United States there were more than 4 times as many people 80 and older than there were 50 years earlier (11.8 million compared with 2.7 million). The risk of Alzheimer disease increases dramatically with age. Stating the facts that way triggers ageist fears of a nation burdened by hungry hordes of frail and confused elders, requiring billions of dollars of health care in crowded hospitals and nursing homes.

But stop and think. The population has also grown. The percent of U.S. residents age 80 and older has doubled, not quadrupled (increasing between 1960 and 2010 from 1.6 percent to 3.8 percent). That does not overwhelm the other 96.2 percent. What percent of them are in nursing homes or hospitals? (Guess—the answer will be presented soon.) Since Alzheimer rates increase with age, the absolute numbers are rising—but not the proportions at each age. Indeed, the rate may be decreasing, as Chapter 24 explains.

Statisticians sometimes report the **dependency ratio**, estimating the proportion of the population that *depends* on care from others. This ratio is calculated by comparing the number of dependents (defined as those under age 15 or over 64) to the number of people in the middle, aged 15 to 64.

In 2010, the nation with the highest dependency ratio was Uganda, 1:0.98, with more dependents than adults; the lowest was Bahrain, 1:3.5, with one dependent per three and a half adults. In most nations, including the United States, the dependency ratio is about 1:2, that is, one person under 15 or over 64 for two people in between (United Nations, 2012).

But this way of calculating the dependency ratio assumes that older adults are dependent. This mistake is echoed in those dire predictions of what will happen when baby boomers age: supposedly a shrinking number of working adults will carry a crushing burden of senility and fragility. Social Security, Medicare, and public hospitals will be bankrupt, according to some. That specter is alarmist, ageist, and untrue.

The truth is that most elders are fiercely independent. They are more often care*givers*, not care receivers, caring not only for each other but also for the young, those other "dependents."

Only 10 percent of those over age 64 depend on other people for basic care. Those who do need help are more likely to get it from close relatives than tax-paying strangers. In the United States in 2012, only 3 percent of people over 64 were currently in nursing homes or hospitals (that is down from 5 percent in 1990). Less than one-half of 1 percent of the total population are in such medical institutions (Centers for Medicaid and Medicare Services, 2013).

As more and more people reach old age, the proportion (not the number) of elders who are in nursing homes and hospitals is decreasing, not increasing. Most older adults live completely independently, alone or with an aging spouse; a minority are living with adult children, and even fewer are in institutions.

The stereotype is not completely false. It is true that dependency increases after age 80. But it also is true that many very old people remain independent. Compared to most other nations, more people are in long-term hospitals and nursing homes in the United States, yet less than 10 percent of U.S. residents over age 80 are in such facilities at any given time. (Is that what you guessed?)

Some are admitted to a hospital for a short-term stay, but not for long. For those age 85 and older, each year 22 percent are admitted to the hospital, with an average stay of 6 days (National Center for Health Statistics, 2012). Most then go home, some go to a rehab facility for a few weeks, and very few go to a nursing home for years of care.

Young, Old, And Oldest

If you guessed that far more than 10 percent of the very old were in nursing homes, do not feel foolish. Almost everyone overestimates because people tend to notice only the feeble, not recognizing the rest. This is a characteristic of human thought—the memorable case is thought to be typical.

Other developmental examples of the distortion of the memorable case is thinking of teenagers as delinquents, of single mothers as neglectful, of divorced fathers as deadbeats. When you hear such stereotypes, you probably reject them as ignorant. Hopefully you now recognize that the same distorting tendency feeds ageism.

Gerontologists distinguish among the *young-old*, the *old-old*, and the *oldest-old*.
- The **young-old** are the largest group of older adults. They are healthy, active, financially secure, and independent. Few people notice them or realize their age.
- The **old-old** suffer some losses in body, mind, or social support, but they proudly care for themselves.
- Only the **oldest-old** are dependent, and they are the most noticeable.

Ages are sometimes used to demarcate these three groups. Many of the young-old are aged 65 to 75, old-old 75 to 85, and oldest-old over 85. However, age itself does not indicate dependency. A young-old person could be 70 or 90; an old-old person can be 65 or 100. Actually, an elder of any age could be any of these. For well-being and independence, which are characteristic of the young-old, attitude is more important than age (O'Rourke et al., 2010a).

The reality that most people over age 64 are quite capable of caring for themselves does not mean that they are unaffected by time. The processes of senescence, described in Chapter 20, continue lifelong. Faces wrinkle, bodies shrink, hearing fades. As you remember, such age changes vary a great deal from person to person; good health habits slow down senescence. But aging is ongoing; no 80-year-old has the physical stamina, appearance, or strength of the average 20-year-old, or of him or herself even 10 years earlier.

young-old Healthy, vigorous, financially secure older adults (generally, those aged 65 to 75) who are well integrated into the lives of their families and communities.

old-old Older adults (generally, those over age 75) who suffer from physical, mental, or social deficits.

oldest-old Elderly adults (generally, those over age 85) who are dependent on others for almost everything, requiring supportive services such as nursing homes and hospital stays.

SUMMING UP

Ageism is stereotyping based on age, a prejudice that leads to less competent and less confident elders. Ageism is evident in people of all walks of life and all ages, but it is particularly harmful when it is present in health professionals and in the elderly themselves. Elderspeak is one example.

Demographic changes have resulted in a higher proportion of elders and a lower proportion of children in every nation. In theory, as nations have more elderly people and fewer children, the dependency ratio should stay the same, but this is inaccurate. Basing the dependency ratio on everyone under age 15 and over age 65 is a distortion. Most elders are quite independent and few need full-time care. A distinction needs to be made between the young-old, who are the self-sufficient majority, the old-old, who show some signs of failing, and the oldest-old, who need help in daily life. ■

>> Selective Optimization with Compensation

Ageism distorts reality, but senescence is real. We need to push aside the distortions of ageism and instead look at the actual changes of aging and what can be done about them. As already described in Chapter 20, every part of the body is affected by the passage of time.

How does a person reach old age and still be vital? Several strategies were described in detail in Chapters 17, 20, and 21, specifically: decreasing allostatic load by exercising daily, eating well but not too much, avoiding cigarettes and other drugs, and coping with stress in such a way as to reduce or eliminate stressors. All these are as important in late adulthood as at any other time, perhaps even more so.

Now we highlight another strategy: *selective optimization with compensation*. The same principles that apply to it apply also to biological vitality. The elderly can compensate for the impairments of senescence and then can perform (optimize) whatever specific tasks they select. [**Lifespan Link:** Selective optimization with compensation is first described in Chapter 21.]

Every compensatory strategy involves personal choice, societal practices, and technological options. This will be clear with three examples: sexual intercourse, driving, and the senses.

Personal Compensation: Sex

Most people are sexually active throughout adulthood. Some continue to have intercourse long past age 65 (Lindau & Gavrilova, 2010) (see Figure 23.4), but generally intercourse becomes less frequent, and sometimes stops completely. Nonetheless, sexual satisfaction often increases after middle age (Heiman et al., 2011). How can that be?

Many older adults reject the idea that intercourse is the only, or best, measure of sexual experience. Instead, cuddling, kissing, caressing, desiring, and fantasizing become more important (Chao et al., 2011). A five-nation study (United States, Germany, Japan, Brazil, Spain) found that kissing and hugging, not intercourse, predicted happiness in long-lasting romances (Heiman et al., 2011). Is that optimization, compensation, or both?

The following in-depth study of couples might provide some answers.

FIGURE 23.4

Your Reaction Older adults who consider their health good (most of them) were asked if they had had sexual intercourse within the past year. If they answered yes, they were considered sexually active. What is your reaction to the data? Some young adults might be surprised that many adults, aged 60 to 80, still experience sexual intercourse. Other people might be saddened that most healthy adults over age 80 do not. However, neither reaction is appropriate. For many elders, sexual affection is expressed in many ways, and it continues lifelong.

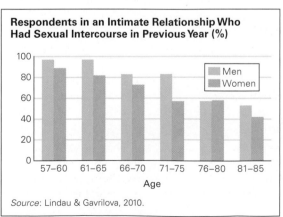

Respondents in an Intimate Relationship Who Had Sexual Intercourse in Previous Year (%)

Source: Lindau & Gavrilova, 2010.

To Have and to Hold In McMinnville, Oregon (left) and in Montevideo, Uruguay (right) these married couples, like many other elderly ones, enjoy their physical as well as psychological closeness.

A CASE TO STUDY

Should Older Couples Have More Sex?

Usually, case studies are of one or two individuals and seek to provide suggestions to be researched through surveys and experiments with hundreds of participants. **[Lifespan Link:** The major methods of scientific research are discussed in Chapter 1.] However, research on sex may be an exception. A laboratory experiment on intimate sex between two lovers, or a survey about sex worded so that everyone would give accurate answers, is difficult to design and undertake.

Two researchers wanted to study sexual activity among the elderly, but they feared that laboratory measures of sexual arousal might be calibrated on young bodies and that questions about sex might be misinterpreted by the elderly (Lodge & Umberson, 2012).

Accordingly, they used a method called *grounded theory*. They found 17 couples, aged 50 to 86, most married for decades, and interviewed each person privately, transcribing all 34 interviews. Next they read and reread all the transcripts, identifying topics that came up repeatedly. Then they tallied those topics in the transcripts, line by line, sorted by age and gender, to learn about aging sexual relationships.

From their study they concluded that sexual activity was more a social construction than a biological event (Lodge &

Umberson, 2012). They reported that everyone said that sex was less frequent with age, including four couples for whom intercourse stopped completely because of the husband's health. Despite sex being less frequent, more of the respondents said that their sex life had improved than said it deteriorated (44 percent compared to 30 percent).

Surprisingly, the middle-aged couples, who were more likely to have sex, were also more likely to be in that 30 percent, while the older couples were likely to say that their sex lives were better than before.

The middle-aged husbands and wives had different concerns. The men were troubled by difficulty maintaining an erection, and the women were worried that they were less attractive. The solution for several middle-aged couples was for the man to take Viagra, typically at the woman's suggestion.

One woman said:

All of a sudden, we didn't have sex after I got skinny. And I couldn't figure that out. I look really good now and we're not having sex. It turns out that he was going through a major physical thing at that point and just had lost his sex drive. It didn't have anything to do with me, but I thought it did. I went through years thinking it was my fault. So, let's go make sure it's your fault (laughs) or let's find out what the problem is instead of me just assuming the blame.

[Irene, quoted in Lodge & Umberson, 2012, p. 435]

The authors believe that "images of masculine sexuality are premised on high, almost uncontrollable levels of penis-driven sexual desire" (p. 430), while the cultural ideals of feminine sexuality emphasize women's passivity and yet "implore women to be both desirable and receptive to men's sexual desires and impulses," deeming "older women and their bodies unattractive" (430). Thus when people in middle age first realize that aging has changed them, their reaction is distress, with men distressed about their erections and women distressed about their appearance. Both men and women attempt to reverse aging, through drugs, hormones, lubricants, diet, hairstyles, clothes, and so on.

A few years later, as couples grew older (over age 70), the study showed they realized that the young idea of good sex (which many still thought of as intercourse) was not relevant. Instead they *compensated* for physical changes by *optimizing* their relationship in other ways. As one man said:

I think the intimacy is a lot stronger even though the sex is bad. Probably more often now we do things like holding hands and wanting to be close to each other or touch each other. It's probably more important now than sex is.

[Jim, quoted in Lodge & Umberson, 2012, p. 438]

A woman said her marriage improved because

[w]e have more opportunities and more motivation. Sex was wonderful. It got thwarted, with . . . the medication he is on. And he hasn't been functional since. The doctors just said that it is going to be this way, so we have learned to accept that. But we have also learned long before that there are more ways than one to share your love.

[Helen, quoted in Lodge & Umberson, 2012, p. 437]

The authors point out that their findings may not be true for all couples in the future. This cohort grew up with the social construction that men were rapacious and women had to be restrained but attractive. Both sexes were taught when they were young that sexual desire stopped before old age. It was considered deviant (dirty old man) or ridiculous (why is she wearing that tight skirt?) if an older adult still felt sexy.

Then this cohort witnessed the sexual revolution. Sex was suddenly accepted: Unmarried adults and old people were now considered happier and healthier if they had active sex lives. Although nursing homes and assisted living quarters had been constructed to make intercourse rare or impossible, social scientists suggested that they be redesigned to encourage sex (Frankowski & Clark, 2009). No wonder these middle-aged couples were distressed.

The next cohort of older adults may have other attitudes; the male/female and midlife/older differences evident with these 17 couples may not apply. These cases do suggest, however, that preconceptions about sex and older adults may be mistaken.

Married couples adjust to whatever biological changes occur in their sexual arousal, but many also improve their relationship in the process (Lodge & Umberson, 2012). This is an example of selective optimization with compensation. A similar process occurs for individuals after divorce or death of a partner. Since the sex drive varies from person to person, some single elders consider sex a thing of the past, some cohabit, some begin LAT (living apart together) with a new partner, and some remarry. That is selective optimization—each older person choosing whether and how to be sexual.

Neither the old myth, that no normal older person wants sex, nor the new myth, that all older people have strong sexual desires, is accepted by elderly people themselves. Of course, with every social construction, society makes some options difficult, which leads to the next topic.

Social Compensation: Driving

A life-span perspective reminds us that "aging is a process, socially constructed to be a problem" (Cruikshank, 2009, p. 8). The process is biological, but the problem begins in the social world. That means selective optimization with compensation is needed by societies, too, not just by individuals. One example is driving.

How Individuals Respond

With age, reading road signs takes longer, turning the head becomes harder, reaction time slows, and night vision worsens. The elderly compensate: Many drive slowly and reduce driving in the dark.

Relying on individuals to decide when and whether to stop driving is foolhardy, however. In the United States, driving one's car is a source of independence, so the elderly are understandably reluctant to quit. In addition, some critics are ageist, not accurate (Satariano et al, 2012). Consequently, many old people who have driven all their lives insist they are still good drivers and resent age-based restriction. They do not want to diminish their lives.

Because they are cautious and limit themselves, elderly drivers have fewer accidents than 20-year-olds. That sometimes convinces them that they drive better than younger people.

Although older drivers try to compensate, many do not realize how significant their losses are. For instance, one common problem is a reduced ability to estimate speed of oncoming cars. Without that, it is difficult to safely merge into highway traffic. How can an older adult know that speed estimation is reduced? Must that knowledge wait until a near or real collision?

What Jurisdictions Can Do

Societies need to compensate for age-related reduction in driving ability, yet often they do not. For instance, many jurisdictions renew licenses by mail, even at age 80. If an older adult causes a crash, the aging individual is blamed, not the lack of social compensation (Satariano, 2006).

If testing is required before license renewal, it often focuses on answering multiple-choice questions about stop signs and parking, and on reading letters on a well-lit chart. Anyone who fails such tests should have stopped driving long ago, but proficiency on these exams does not guarantee competent driving. For instance, judgment and reaction time are more important than book knowledge, and peripheral vision is a stronger predictor of accidents than acuity on a chart straight ahead (Johnson & Wilkinson, 2010; Wood, 2002).

Technology has now come up with a way to solve this problem. A national panel recommends simulated driving via a computer and video screen, with the prospective driver seated with a steering wheel, accelerator, and brakes (Sifrit, 2012). The results of this test could allow some 80-year-olds to renew their license, some to have their licenses revoked, and many to recognize that they are less proficient than they thought. Sadly, this test is not yet required.

Beyond retesting, there is much else that societies can do. Larger-print signs before an exit, mirrors that replace the need to turn the neck, illuminated side streets and driveways, nonglaring headlights and hazard flashes, and warnings of ice or fog ahead would reduce accidents. Well-designed cars, roads, signs, lights, and guard rails, as well as appropriate laws and enforcement, would allow for selective optimization: Competent elderly drivers could thus maintain independence, and dangerous drivers (of all ages) could be kept off the road.

Another society-wide initiative is sorely needed. Efficient and inexpensive public transportation, in suburban and rural areas as well as in cities, would benefit everyone. This is particularly true for the aged, as was discovered when a British law gave free bus passes to the elderly. That increased their walking and social activity, and it reduced their driving (Coronini-Cronberg et al., 2012). Social compensation and optimization again.

And On Icy Curves . . . Everywhere in the world, the elderly want to keep driving. Some nations require extensive training for license renewals. This is a special safety class for elderly drivers in Germany.

AXEL HEIMKEN/PICTURE-ALLIANCE/DPA/AP IMAGES

Social Comparison: Elders Behind the Wheel

Older people often change their driving habits in order to compensate for their slowing reaction time. Many states have initiated restrictions, including requiring older drivers to renew their licenses in person, to make sure older drivers stay safe. Because most older drivers limit themselves (they avoid night, rainy, and distance driving), their crash rate is low overall, but not when measured by the rate per miles driven.

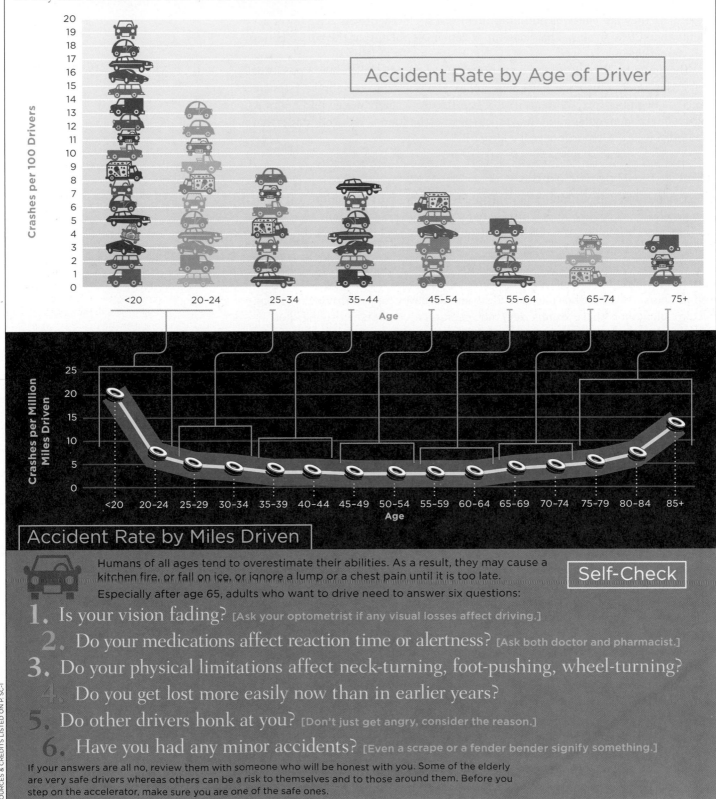

Accident Rate by Age of Driver

Crashes per 100 Drivers

Age: <20, 20–24, 25–34, 35–44, 45–54, 55–64, 65–74, 75+

Accident Rate by Miles Driven

Crashes per Million Miles Driven

Age: <20, 20–24, 25–29, 30–34, 35–39, 40–44, 45–49, 50–54, 55–59, 60–64, 65–69, 70–74, 75–79, 80–84, 85+

Humans of all ages tend to overestimate their abilities. As a result, they may cause a kitchen fire, or fall on ice, or ignore a lump or a chest pain until it is too late. Especially after age 65, adults who want to drive need to answer six questions:

Self-Check

1. Is your vision fading? [Ask your optometrist if any visual losses affect driving.]

2. Do your medications affect reaction time or alertness? [Ask both doctor and pharmacist.]

3. Do your physical limitations affect neck-turning, foot-pushing, wheel-turning?

4. Do you get lost more easily now than in earlier years?

5. Do other drivers honk at you? [Don't just get angry, consider the reason.]

6. Have you had any minor accidents? [Even a scrape or a fender bender signify something.]

If your answers are all no, review them with someone who will be honest with you. Some of the elderly are very safe drivers whereas others can be a risk to themselves and to those around them. Before you step on the accelerator, make sure you are one of the safe ones.

SOURCES & CREDITS LISTED ON P. SC-1

Technological Compensation: The Senses

Every sense becomes slower and less sharp with each passing decade. This is true for touch (particularly in fingers and toes), pain, taste (particularly for sour and bitter), smell, as well as for sight and hearing. Hundreds of manufactured devices compensate for sensory loss, from eyeglasses (first invented in the thirteenth century) to tiny video cameras worn on the forehead that connect directly to the brain, allowing people who are blind to process images (not yet commercially available).

Vision

Only 10 percent of people of either sex over age 65 see well without glasses (see Table 23.1), but selective optimization allows almost everyone to use their remaining sight quite well. Changing the environment—brighter lights, large and darker print—is a simple first step. Corrective lenses and magnifying glasses help. For those who are totally blind, dogs, canes, and audio devices have for decades allowed mobility and cognition.

Hearing

By age 90 the average man is almost deaf, as are about half the women. That may be an overestimate. Since deafness is a matter of degree, it is hard to know where to draw the line. The Gallaudet Research Institute puts hearing difficulties at 29 percent over age 65; a scholar who examined U.S. Census records suggests about half that, 16 percent (Mitchell, 2006).

TABLE 23.1	Common Vision Impairments among the Elderly

- *Cataracts.* As early as age 50, about 10 percent of adults have cataracts, a thickening of the lens, causing vision to become cloudy, opaque, and distorted. By age 70, 30 percent have cataracts. They can be removed in outpatient surgery and replaced with an artificial lens.

- *Glaucoma.* About 1 percent of those in their 70s and 10 percent in their 90s have glaucoma, a buildup of fluid within the eye that damages the optic nerve. Early stages have no symptoms. Without treatment, glaucoma causes blindness, but the damage can be prevented. Testing is crucial, particularly for African Americans and people with diabetes, since the first signs of glaucoma may occur for them as early as age 40.

- *Macular degeneration.* About 4 percent of those in their 60s and about 12 percent over age 80 have a deterioration of the retina, called macular degeneration. An early warning occurs when vision is spotty (e.g., some letters missing when reading). Again, early treatment—in this case, medication—can restore some vision, but without treatment, blindness occurs about five years after macular degeneration starts.

Everyone agrees, however, that hearing impairment increases dramatically with age and that deafness is far more common in men than in women. For all sensory deficits, an active effort to compensate—not accept—is needed. Unfortunately, ageism leads elders to avoid bifocals and hearing aids, leaving them to squint and mishear until blindness or deafness is imminent (Meisami et al., 2007).

(a)

(b)

(c)

(d)

Through Different Eyes These photographs depict the same scene as it would be perceived by a person with **(a)** normal vision, **(b)** cataracts, **(c)** glaucoma, or **(d)** macular degeneration. Think about how difficult it would be to find your own car if you had one of these disorders. That may help you remember to have your vision checked regularly.

© ANNA STOWE/ALAMY

Ageism affects whether a society provides technological help. A dramatic improvement in the ability of deaf people to enjoy concerts, plays, museums, and so on results from a "hearing loop," a small device in a room that enables people with hearing aids to hear the words or music they want, without the distracting clatter. Installing a loop requires someone to realize that it is worth the cost. David Myers, himself now hearing impaired, explains:

> The Americans with Disabilities Act does, however, mandate hearing assistance in public settings with 50 or more fixed seats. Such assistance typically takes the form of a checkout FM or infrared receiver with earphones. Alas, because well-meaning sound engineers fail to consider the human factor—how real people interact with technology—most such units sit unused in storage closets.
>
> To empathize, imagine yourself struggling to carve meaning out of sound as you watch a movie, attend worship, listen to a lecture, strain to hear an airport announcement, or stand at a ticket window. Which of these hearing solutions would you prefer?
>
> 1. Taking the initiative to locate, check out, wear, and return special equipment (typically a conspicuous headset that delivers generic sound)?
> 2. Pushing a button that transforms your hearing aid (or cochlear implant) into wireless loudspeakers that deliver sound customized to your own needs?
>
> Solution 1—the hearing-aid-incompatible solution—has been America's prevalent assistive-listening technology. Solution 2—the hearing-aid-compatible solution—has spread to Scandinavian countries and across the United Kingdom, where it now exists in most cathedrals and churches, in the back seats of all London taxis, and at 11,500 post offices and countless train and ticket windows.
>
> [Myers, 2011, pp. 1–2]

universal design The creation of settings and equipment that can be used by everyone, whether or not they are able-bodied and sensory-acute.

Disability advocates hope more designers and engineers will think of **universal design**, which is the creation of settings and equipment that can be used by everyone, whether or not able-bodied and sensory-acute (Hussein et al., 2013; Holt, 2013). At the moment, just about everything, from houses to fashionable shoes, is designed for adults with no impairments. Many disabilities would disappear with better design.

Look around at the "built" environment (stores, streets, colleges, and homes); notice the print on medicine bottles; listen to the public address systems in train stations; ask why most homes have entry stairs and narrow bathrooms, why most buses and cars require a big step up to enter, why smelling remains the usual way to detect a gas leak. Then look for signs that indicate accessibility or hearing loop availability, and find out how accurate those signs are. Too often elevators are not in service, curb cuts are not smooth, ramps are hidden, and so on.

Sensory loss need not lead to morbidity or cognitive loss, but without compensation, any disability, including deafness and blindness, can lead to isolation, less movement, and reduced intellectual stimulation. Often illness increases and cognition declines as the senses fade.

Compensation for the Brain

For the three topics just mentioned in relation to physiological problems of aging—sex, driving, the senses—the critical organ of senescence is the brain. In every aspect of aging, it is the brain that selects, optimizes, and compensates.

Thus, a person must decide that sexual touch is as rewarding as intercourse. Sexual arousal begins in the brain, not the genitals, which is why a dream, a photograph, or a voice on the phone can trigger arousal and why ageism can reduce desire.

Likewise, people must realize that their senses are fading, must decide to use technology, must find the appropriate device, and then must learn to use it. Many

MARICE COHN BAND/MCT/NEWSCOM

No Quitter When hearing fades, many older people avoid social interaction. Not so for Don Shula, former head coach of the Miami Dolphins, who led his team to two Super Bowl victories. He kept his players fighting, often surging ahead from behind. Here he proudly displays his hearing aid.

hearing aids stay in boxes beside the bed because the person does not know how to make them work properly.

The United States Department of Transportation has analyzed crash risk among the elderly and found that the biggest risk is in cognition, not in vision or motor skills (Sifrit, 2012). To forget which pedal is the brake is far worse than the loss of some foot strength, which might prevent an older person from pushing the brake as hard as a younger driver. The most common reason for a fatal crash with an elderly driver is that the driver turned left at an intersection into oncoming traffic—obviously a matter of judgment, not ability.

What then happens to the brain as humans age? It slows down, and connections between parts weaken, so people take longer to understand what is needed in a particular situation. Comprehension becomes more difficult because the white and gray matter of the brain are reduced. For instance, reading rate slows and conversation partners need to talk more slowly.

The volume of the brain decreases with each passing year—less than 1 percent per year through most of adulthood but accelerating after age 60 (Hedman et al., 2012). The brain volume of a typical 80-year-old is about 20 percent less than that of a typical 30-year-old.

More detailed research finds that brain shrinkage is most evident in particular regions: more in the neocortex than in more primitive parts of the brain, and especially notable in the hippocampus, the part of the brain that stores memories, and the prefrontal cortex, where decision making and planning occur. New neurons form as well, and cognitive reserve allows some brains to function well even when aging has continued for years. However, neither of these processes completely compensates for brain senescence (Stern, 2013).

Brain shrinkage and cell loss are particularly notable among the oldest-old. A comparative study finds that brain aging is similar in all primates, but humans experience losses relatively earlier in the life span than chimpanzees do—at the beginning of late adulthood instead of right before death (Chen et al., 2013). The authors speculate that as medical measures have increased the life span, the human brain survives longer than it may have been designed to do.

The brain is critical for all compensatory mechanisms just described. A person must think before any optimization occurs. Perhaps the brain is the organ that most needs the personal, social, or technological assistance described above.

The crucial question is: Can anything be done to compensate for brain losses in old age, to optimize thinking as people can optimize sex, or driving ability, or sensory acuteness? The answer is *yes, sometimes.* Brain plasticity is possible throughout life (e.g., Ram et al., 2011; Erickson et al., 2013). The same factors that protect the rest of the body protect the brain, especially exercise, nutrition, and avoiding drugs (including cigarettes). Beyond that, many specifics about memory and cognition affect late-life thinking. This is a major topic of the next chapter.

Not All Average A team of neuroscientists in Scotland (Farrell et al., 2009) published these images of the brains of healthy 65- to 70-year-olds. The images show normal brain loss (the white areas) from the lowest (5th percentile) to the highest (95th percentile). Some atrophy is inevitable (even younger brains atrophy), but few elders are merely average.

|(a)|(b)|(c)|(d)|(e)|

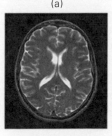 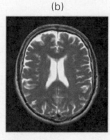 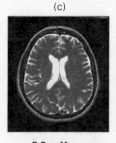 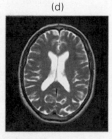 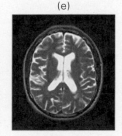

Lowest **25th Percentile** **Median** **75th Percentile** **Highest**

Atrophy Ranking

SUMMING UP

Selective optimization with compensation applies to every aspect of senescence. Older adults do not have the same sexual activity, driving ability, or sensory acuteness as younger adults. In every case, however, measures can counteract these deficits if they are recognized and understood. Some of those measures come from the awareness of the individuals themselves. For instance, many older couples enjoy their sexual interaction, even though it is not what it was when they were younger. Other compensation comes from technology, *if* individuals and societies choose to use it. Driver license tests are one example: Few jurisdictions currently test the elderly for the skills that are known to be crucial for avoiding accidents. Most sensory losses can be prevented or ameliorated, but many of the elderly do not get medical treatment or use the aids that are available. The master organ that can orchestrate all the necessary adjustments is the brain, which itself shrinks and slows with age.   ■

>> Aging and Disease

As you know from Chapters 17 and 20, with each passing decade homeostasis takes longer and allostatic load builds. Skin, hair, and body shape show unmistakable signs of senescence, while every internal organ ages. A stress to which younger bodies quickly adjust, such as a string of hot days or extra effort shoveling snow, could be lethal for the old.

Primary and Secondary Aging

primary aging The universal and irreversible physical changes that occur to all living creatures as they grow older.

secondary aging The specific physical illnesses or conditions that become more common with aging but are caused by health habits, genes, and other influences that vary from person to person.

Gerontologists distinguish between **primary aging**, which involves universal changes that occur with the passage of time, and **secondary aging**, which are the consequences of particular inherited weaknesses, chosen health habits, and environmental conditions. One researcher explains:

> Primary aging is defined as the universal changes occurring with age that are not caused by diseases or environmental influences. Secondary aging is defined as changes involving interactions of primary aging processes with environmental influences and disease processes.
>
> *[Masoro, 2006, p. 46]*

Primary aging does not directly cause illness, but it makes almost every disease more likely. The combination of primary and secondary aging causes morbidity and mortality.

For example, with age the heart pumps more slowly and the vascular network is less flexible, increasing the risk of stroke and heart attack. The lungs take in and expel less air with each breath, so that blood oxygen is reduced and chronic obstructive pulmonary disease is more common. Digestion slows. The kidneys become less efficient, increasing problems if people become dehydrated because they drink less—either because homeostasis is less efficient and thirst signals are muted, or perhaps in a deliberate attempt to reduce incontinence, which itself is caused by an aging renal/urinary system.

Furthermore, because of age, healing takes longer when an illness or an accident occurs. That is why young adults who contract pneumonia usually recover completely in a few weeks, but in the very old pneumonia can overwhelm a weakened body. Indeed, pneumonia often is listed as the cause of death for the oldest-old, although the underlying cause is primary and secondary aging.

The same is true for accidents of all kinds, from falls, crashes, fires, and poisons. Younger people are much more likely to recover from such insults, but 41 million people in the United States over age 65 died accidentally in 2010, making the accidental death rate for the elderly higher than for people of any other age (National Center for Health Statistics, 2012).

The data in the previous paragraph may bewilder you, since you learned in earlier chapters that more children, adolescents, and emerging adults die of accidents than of any other cause. The explanation centers on other causes of death. Because heart disease, cancers, strokes, and so on are rare earlier in life but common in late adulthood, accidents are the first cause of death from age 1 to 44 but only the eighth after age 65. Older people are more cautious than younger ones, but when injury occurs, death is more likely after age 65.

A developmental view of the relationship between primary and secondary aging harkens back to the lifelong toll of stress, as explained in Chapters 17 and 21. *Allostatic load* is measured by 10, or sometimes 16, biomarkers—including cortisol, C-reactive protein, systolic and diastolic blood pressure, waste-hip ratio, and insulin resistance. All of these indicate stress on the body, all increase with age, and all impair health.

Thus, measurement of allostatic load assesses the combined, long-term effect of many indicators, none of which is necessarily dangerous alone. If many of these biomarkers are outside the normal range, people become sick and die, especially when aging already has reduced organ reserve (see Figure 23.5). Thus, lifelong responses to stress create a biological burden, a load that becomes lethal.

Treatment of the Elderly: Examples—Flu and Hypertension

Because of primary aging, medical intervention affects the old differently than the young. For this reason, drugs, surgeries, and so on that have been validated on young adults may be less effective on the elderly. Two examples are treatments for flu and hypertension, or high blood pressure.

The specific strains of flu that circulate are slightly different each year, so the vaccine is redesigned annually to fight whatever strains are predicted. That's why people need flu shots every fall for the following winter. Annual immunization is particularly recommended for those over age 65, because their other infirmities make flu sometimes fatal.

The 2012–2013 vaccine protected the elderly reasonably well against the B strains of flu but provided almost no protection against the A strain, even though it protected the young (Kelvin & Farooqui, 2013). Obviously, the vaccine needs to be calibrated for age.

The importance of considering age when designing disease prevention is also apparent with medication to reduce hypertension. If systolic blood pressure in a middle-aged person is above 140, the first recommendation is diet (low salt), weight loss, and exercise. If that does not lower it, most doctors prescribe daily medication to reduce blood pressure, thus reducing the risk of strokes and heart attacks. However, the same blood pressure may affect the oldest-old differently (Sabayan et al., 2012).

Surprisingly, for some of the elderly, hypertension is protective; drugs may increase the risk of death, not decrease it. When physicians decide whether to prescribe pressure-lowering medication, they must consider the health and vitality of the person (Odden et al., 2012). The young-old may benefit; the oldest-old may not, perhaps because they are likely to experience a sudden drop in blood pressure that homeostasis is slow to fix, and that is less damaging if the drop is from high to average than from average to low.

Variation in hypertension may be one reason that anesthesia may damage an older person's brain or cause the heart to stop. Drugs to reduce pain may also affect the elderly differently from the young. That may explain why temporary hallucinations and delirium after surgery are far more common for the old than for the young.

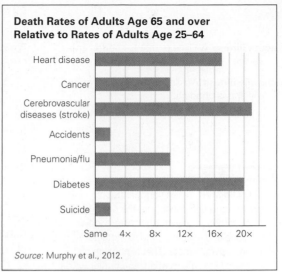

Death Rates of Adults Age 65 and over Relative to Rates of Adults Age 25–64

Source: Murphy et al., 2012.

FIGURE 23.5

More Years to Live Even compared with a decade ago, fewer people die before age 65, which means that, for many causes, death is far more likely in old age. Most of the underlying conditions for these diseases were present in middle age.

Chronic and Acute Disease: Example—The Heart

It is important to understand the distinction between acute and chronic illness. An **acute illness** is sudden and severe. A **chronic illness** is gradual and ongoing. Consider the leading cause of death in the United States, coronary heart disease.

A heart attack is acute. A person feels fine, and then suddenly breath becomes shallow; or an arm, jaw, or shoulder hurts; or the person feels nauseous or heaviness around the heart (like an elephant standing on your chest). All these symptoms are signs of a heart attack—if one occurs, do not wait to see if it goes away. Usually if medical intervention begins within an hour, the person survives, but because this is acute, every minute is crucial.

By contrast, heart disease is chronic. The arteries are clogged, so blood pressure is high, or the heartbeat becomes unsteady. Exercise leads to exhaustion or shortness of breath. The heart gradually weakens. Many adults are unaware of any disability but have high blood pressure or high LDL cholesterol—both signs of chronic heart disease.

Heart problems are the most common cause of death for both men and women. However, in general, women are more likely to have chronic diseases and men to have acute ones. More men die of heart attacks, more women die of heart disease.

The same gender difference is apparent for many other conditions: Women have far more arthritis, lupus, type 2 diabetes, depression, and osteoporosis, for instance. Men are not exempt from these conditions and women also die of acute illnesses, but gender rates differ worldwide.

Women live for years with chronic illness; men are more likely to die quickly when they become seriously ill. That is one reason the sex ratio in U.S. nursing homes is about 3 women for every man, even though the overall population of those over age 65 is only about 1.3 women for every man (Figure 23.6).

This distinction is problematic because hospitals, many doctors, and research funding target acute illnesses—the emergencies that have sirens wailing and surgeons running, hoping to save a life. Meanwhile, women suffer for years, with lower DALYs (disability life years), but without effective medical treatment.

Quite apart from sexism, there are historical reasons for the neglect of chronic conditions. For most of human history, when people died at much younger ages, most died of acute illness. Saving heart attack victims, preventing blood poisoning, vaccinating against typhoid—those were obvious goals that have changed. Dealing with chronic illness is the major medical challenge now.

Compression of Morbidity

Ideally, prevention of disease begins in childhood and continues lifelong, so "the target of public health and aging efforts is not just the older adults of today but the children and adults who are the future elders" (Albert & Freedman, 2010, pp. 31–32). Illness can be limited by establishing good childhood habits and continuing them lifelong, allowing people to be vital in old age, with few days of disability or morbidity. [**Lifespan Link:** Vitality, morbidity, and disability are explained in Chapter 20.]

The name for this extension of vitality into old age is **compression of morbidity**, which is the reduction (compression) of sickness before death. Ideally, a person is in

---

acute illness An illness that is sudden and severe.

chronic illness An illness that begins gradually and is ongoing.

FIGURE 23.6

Lonely Old Men When younger people notice the sex ratio in late adulthood, they often pity the old women, many of whom are widows living alone and unable to find (or not interested in finding) a mate. That is not true of older men: Most are married, and if their wives die they remarry far more often than women do. But the data suggests that older women are closer to their friends, their relatives, and especially to their children than older men are. Indeed, their social network may be the reason they are far less likely to commit suicide or die of a heart attack than men their age.

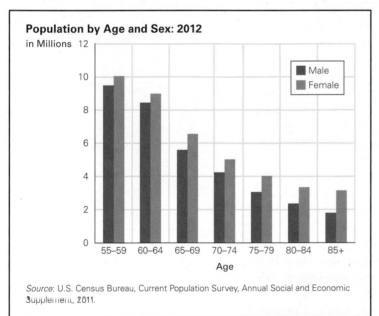

Population by Age and Sex: 2012

Source: U.S. Census Bureau, Current Population Survey, Annual Social and Economic Supplement, 2011.

compression of morbidity A shortening of the time a person spends ill or infirm, accomplished by postponing illness.

good health for decades after age 65, and then, within a few days or months, experiences serious illnesses that lead to death. Years of frailty are avoided.

Morbidity has been compressed even as mortality is postponed. For instance, unlike 30 years ago, most people diagnosed today with cancer, diabetes, or a heart condition continue to be vital for decades. The World Health Organization and many experts recognize that disability is the result of person–environment interaction, so changing the environment limits disability (Phillipson, 2013). Cultures, schools, and technology can extend the optimal aging of the young–old, forestalling the morbidity of the oldest–old (Thompson et al., 2012).

The need for compression of morbidity is apparent with **osteoporosis** (fragile bones). Primary aging makes bones more porous as cells that build bone (osteoblasts) are outnumbered by cells that reabsorb bone (osteoclasts) (Rachner et al., 2011). Osteoporosis is particularly common in underweight women with European ancestry, although men and people of other ethnic groups sometimes experience it.

The result of this chronic condition can be deadly, not just disabling. A fall that would have merely bruised a young person may result in a broken hip or a spine fracture, neither of which is lethal in itself but may potentially start a cascade of medical problems. Such a fall leads to death for 10 percent of osteoporosis sufferers within a year. According to The Center for Disease Control, a broken hip was "a leading cause of excess mortality among older adults" (MMWR, March 31, 2000). The problem was that half the people who broke their hips never walked again, and immobility causes many body systems to deteriorate.

Now let's return to compression of morbidity. Note the 2000 date above. Now a more recent report: "In the 21st century, osteoporosis, a disease once considered an inevitable consequence of aging, is both diagnosable and treatable" (Black et al., 2012, p. 2051).

How was this compression of morbidity achieved? Early diagnosis via a bone density test (not available a few decades ago) can detect bone weakening long before the first fracture. Prevention can begin in middle age, or even earlier, with weight-bearing and muscle-strengthening exercise, and a lifelong diet with sufficient calcium and vitamin D. In addition, a dozen drug treatments (including HRT) reduce bone loss.

Because a focus on chronic conditions is relatively new and treatment of osteoporosis is newer yet, scientists do not know the consequences of ingesting preventive drugs over many years. The data suggest caution (Brown et al., 2012). As you know, drugs that prevent one problem may eventually cause another. **[Lifespan Link:** HRT (hormone replacement therapy) is discussed in Chapter 20.**]** Nonetheless, the 44 million people over age 50 in the United States who have weak bones need not experience the disabling breaks that those with osteoporosis once did. That is compression of morbidity.

Hearts and bones are only two examples. For almost every condition, morbidity can be compressed, although many people do not realize it. For instance, half the elderly population has arthritis, but few know that their stiffness and immobility can be reduced (Hootman et al., 2012). The same is true for diabetes, which often goes undiagnosed until it leads to other chronic problems of the heart, kidney, feet, eyes, and more (Caspersen et al., 2012).

Consider also breast cancer. That kills African American women at one and a half times the rate of European Americans, primarily because it is diagnosed too late, causing months of morbidity and then death rather than shorter morbidity and then recovery.

Gerontologists now agree that the goal is not simply to live a long life, but to live a long, healthy life; not to add years to life but to add life to years, via health habits, early treatment, and so on (Gremeaux et al., 2012). Demographers now

osteoporosis A disease whose symptoms are low bone mass and deterioration of bone tissue, which lead to increasingly fragile bones and greater risk of fracture.

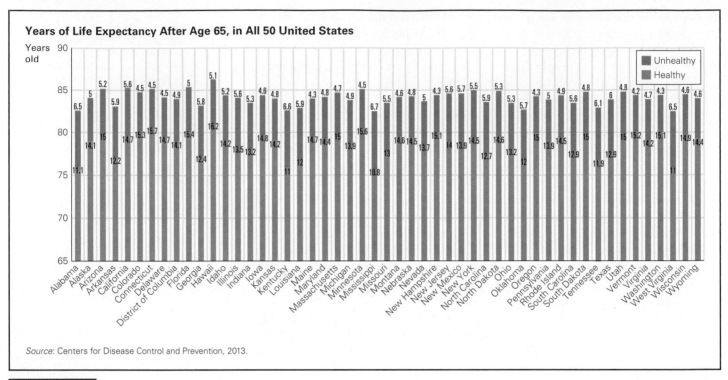

Years of Life Expectancy After Age 65, in All 50 United States

Source: Centers for Disease Control and Prevention, 2013.

FIGURE 23.7

Life Expectancy after Age 65 Another Reason to Live in Hawaii After age 65, people in Hawaii have 18 more healthy years compared to only 11 in Mississippi, or maybe go to Oregon, with only 4 unhealthy years before death, on average, at age 84.

calculate the number of healthy years. This has been done for each state of the United States (MMWR, July 19, 2013) (see Figure 23.7).

The U.S. data as well as the data from other nations show that there is no set age when people become frail. The correlation between sheer longevity and healthy longevity is positive; further compression of morbidity seems a realistic goal.

SUMMING UP

Primary aging is inevitable and universal, the direct result of years gone by. Secondary aging involves diseases that result from poor health habits, genetic vulnerability, infections, and environmental toxins that often exacerbate the losses associated with primary aging. Some of the most troubling morbidities relate to the senses, particularly vision and hearing, because sensory impairment leads to depression and social isolation. Acute illnesses are sudden, and medical measures have reduced them markedly. The next goal is to reduce debilitation caused by chronic diseases, a goal called compression of morbidity. As illustrated with osteoporosis, aging need not be accompanied by years of debilitating disease. ▪

>> Theories of Aging

Underlying all the conditions and diseases just reviewed is a fundamental question: Why do people age? If we could stop senescence, we could stop primary aging, reducing all the diseases of the old—most cancers, most heart diseases, most strokes, and so on. Hundreds of theories and thousands of scientists have sought to understand why aging occurs. To simplify, these theories can be grouped in three clusters: wear and tear, genetic adaptation, and cellular aging.

Wear and Tear

The oldest, most general theory of aging is known as **wear-and-tear theory**. The idea is that the body wears out, part by part, after years of use. Organ reserve and repair processes are exhausted as the decades pass (Gavrilov & Gavrilova, 2006).

Is this accurate? For some body parts, yes. Athletes who put repeated stress on their shoulders or knees often have chronically painful joints by middle adulthood; workers who inhale asbestos and smoke cigarettes damage their lungs; repeated blows to the head destroy the brain.

Sometimes the body wears out because of exposure to the elements, or things in the diet, or pollution, or radiation. For instance, skin cancer is caused partly by too much sun, clogged arteries are caused partly by too much animal fat, and some cancer tumors may result from too many oxygen-free radicals, which may be caused by pollution and radiation.

However, wear-and-tear theory does not account for many facts. Some body functions benefit from use. Exercise improves heart and lung functioning; tai chi improves balance; weight training increases muscle mass; sexual activity stimulates the sexual-reproductive system; foods that require intestinal activity benefit the digestive system. Thus, although the wear-and-tear theory applies to some body parts, few scientists now believe it explains aging overall.

In fact, an overreliance on the wear-and-tear hypothesis may be harmful: People are more likely to "rust out" from disuse than to wear out. Exercise is beneficial for every organ. Eating many vegetable and fruits (rich in anti-oxidants) is helpful, but excessive use of anti-oxidant vitamins (A, C, E, selenium) may be destructive, although the research is mixed on this (Bjelakovic et al., 2012).

Genetic Theories

A second cluster of theories focuses on genes (Sutphin & Kaeberlein, 2011). Humans may have a **genetic clock**, a mechanism in the DNA of cells that regulates life, growth, and aging. Just as genes trigger the beginning of puberty at about age 10, genes may also switch on to cause aging. For instance, when an older person is injured, aging genes increase the damage so that an infection spreads rather than being halted and healed as it was earlier (Borgens & Liu-Snyder, 2011).

Evidence for genetic aging comes from premature aging. Children born with Hutchinson-Gilford syndrome (a genetic disease also called *progeria*) stop growing at about age 5 and begin to look old, with wrinkled skin and balding heads. These children die in their teens of heart diseases typically found in people five times their age.

Other genes seem to program an extraordinarily long and healthy life. People who reach age 100 usually have alleles that other people do not (Halaschek-Wiener et al., 2009; Sierra et al., 2009). Some protective alleles are common. For instance, 12 percent of men in their 70s have allele 2 of the *ApoE* gene, but 17 percent of men older than 85 have it, which suggests that those 12 percent are less likely to die.

There are also common genes that seem to trigger an early death. Almost every illness of secondary aging tends to occur in families, suggesting a genetic link. Another allele of the ApoE gene, *ApoE4*, increases the rate of death by heart disease, stroke, dementia, and—if a person is HIV-positive—by AIDS (Kuhlmann et al., 2010).

wear-and-tear theory A view of aging as a process by which the human body wears out because of the passage of time and exposure to environmental stressors.

Especially for Biologists What are some immediate practical uses for research on the causes of aging? (see response, page 690)

© REUTERS/CORBIS

Skin Deep Those spots on former president Bush's face are signs of an anti-aging treatment, specifically nitrogen to freeze the damaged cells on his skin. For him as well as for everyone else, aging that results from wear and tear can be treated, unlike the aging that is genetic or cellular.

genetic clock A purported mechanism in the DNA of cells that regulates the aging process by triggering hormonal changes and controlling cellular reproduction and repair.

>> Response for Biologists (from page 689): Although ageism and ambivalence limit the funding of research on the causes of aging, the applications include prevention of AIDS, cancer, neurocognitive disorders, and physical damage from pollution—all urgent social priorities.

cellular aging The cumulative effect of stress and toxins, causing first cellular damage and eventually the death of cells.

Hayflick limit The number of times a human cell is capable of dividing into two new cells. The limit for most human cells is approximately 50 divisions, an indication that the life span is limited by our genetic program.

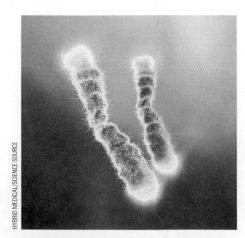

Old Caterpillars? No, these are young chromosomes, stained to show the glowing white telomeres at the ends.

Hundreds of genes hasten the aging of one body part or another, such as genes for hypertension or for many forms of cancer. Certain alleles—SIR2, def-2, among them—directly accelerate aging and death (Finch, 2010). As you know, secondary aging (the actions people take) is part of the disease process, and many bad health habits correlate with specific genes that seem to push people to drink, drug, overeat, and so on.

Primary aging also is genetic. Diabetes, a disease that accelerates many signs of senescence, is one example. Type 1 diabetes (childhood onset), seems entirely genetic. Type 2 (adult onset) is triggered by excess weight, but genes are also a factor. Actually, dozens of genes are relevant. Some diabetes genes are shared across ethnic groups and some are more common among African Americans, who have higher rates of type 2 diabetes than other U.S. groups (Palmer et al., 2012).

Surely you have noticed that most overweight people do not become diabetic; their genes protect them. Unfortunately, some people with normal weight do develop diabetes—again for genetic reasons. That is one explanation for a troubling statistic: Asians tend to develop diabetes at younger ages and lower weights than Europeans (Hu, 2011).

Why would human genes promote aging? Evolutionary theory provides an explanation (Hughes, 2010). Societies need young adults to reproduce the next generation and then need elders to die (leaving their genes behind) so that scarce resources were devoted to the reproduction and rearing of the new generation. Thus, genetic aging may be harsh to older individuals but benevolent for communities.

Cellular Aging

The third cluster of theories examines **cellular aging**, focusing on molecules and cells. Toxins damage cells over time, so minor errors in copying accumulate (remember, cells replace themselves many times). The job of the cells of the immune system is to recognize pathogens and destroy them, but the immune system weakens with age as well as with repeated stresses and infections (Wolf, 2010).

Eventually the organism can no longer repair every cellular error, resulting in senescence. This process is first apparent in the skin, an organ that replaces itself often. The skin becomes wrinkled and rough, eventually developing "age spots" when cell rejuvenation slows down. The longer that cells are exposed to toxins, the more they break down. For example, the skin on your hands is rougher than the skin on your belly—but that was not true when you were newborn.

Cellular aging also occurs inside the body, notably in cancer, which involves duplication of rogue cells. Every type of cancer becomes more common with age because the body is increasingly unable to control the cells. Some research suggests that the cells are not the actual cause of aging, but that the mitochrondria surrounding the cells mutate with time and trigger aging of the cells, thus causing aging of the body. This process may begin in childhood, or even in the womb, depending on the mother's diet (Khrapko, 2011).

Even without specific infections or stresses, healthy cells stop replicating at a certain point. This point is referred to as the **Hayflick limit**, named after the scientist who discovered it. One cellular change over time occurs with telomeres—material at the ends of the chromosome that becomes shorter with each duplication. Eventually, at the Hayflick limit, the telomere is gone, duplication stops, and the creature dies (Aviv, 2011).

The length of telomeres, which is related to cellular aging and death, is also affected by stress. The more stress a person experiences, from childhood on, the shorter their telomeres are in late adulthood and the sooner they will die (Lin et al., 2012).

Hayflick himself believes that the Hayflick limit, and therefore aging, is caused primarily by a natural loss of molecular fidelity—that is, by inevitable errors in transcription as each cell reproduces itself. He believes that aging is built into the very cells of our species, affected by stress, drugs, and so on (Hayflick, 2004). Although lifestyle factors can accelerate the aging process, no human is impervious to the stresses of life, and no human lives forever.

Research finds that telomere length is about the same in newborns of both sexes and all ethnic groups, but by late adulthood telomeres are longer in women than in men, and longer in European Americans than in African Americans (Aviv, 2011). There are many possible causes, but cellular aging theorists focus on the consequences: Women outlive men, and European Americans outlive African Americans.

Calorie Restriction

Could eating and digesting food be stressful in some way to the body? **Calorie restriction**—the drastic reduction in the usual number of calories consumed daily while still maintaining ample vitamins, minerals, and other important nutrients—slows down aging in many living organisms. The benefits of calorie restriction have been demonstrated by careful research with dozens of creatures, from fruit flies to chimpanzees.

Much remains to be understood; application to humans is controversial. Calorie restriction has been called "a fact in search of a theory." It seems to work at the cellular level, but "the molecular mechanisms by which such a simple intervention has such a stunning effect have eluded researchers for decades" (Masoro & Austad, 2011, p. xi).

Generally, compared with no restrictions, underfeeding a living organism (the early research was on fruit flies) extends the life span of many lower animals and insects in controlled laboratory conditions. The specifics of diet and timing may be crucial, although they are not yet understood.

Application to humans and other primates is particularly complicated: Some research on monkeys finds that calorie restriction extends life, but other studies do not (Mattison et al., 2012).

Looking at all the research, we find that rats seem to receive more benefit than mice, and that some species of mice do *not* live longer on restricted diets. Indeed, undereating shortens the life of some kinds of mice rather than extending it (Swindell, 2012). The results may depend on small genetic differences between one strain of mouse and another, but specifics are not known. Longevity may depend on the details of the restricted diet, but again scientists do not know what those details might be.

The result from lower animals, and data from the 7,000 people who voluntarily undereat and belong to a group in the Calorie Restriction Society, are intriguing (Roth & Polotsky, 2012). Their rate of diabetes, for instance, is almost zero. But obviously people who join the group are not a cross section of humans. Proof would require controlled experiments.

Consider what would be needed to perform a valid study. First researchers would need hundreds of participants, from all SES levels and ethnic groups. Then half would be randomly assigned to eat 1,800 calories daily, while the other half would eat normally, about 3,000 calories a day.

"If you give up alcohol, cigarettes, sex, red meat, cakes and chocolate, and don't get too excited, you can enjoy life for a few more years yet."

calorie restriction The practice of limiting dietary energy intake (while consuming sufficient quantities of vitamins, minerals, and other important nutrients) for the purpose of improving health and slowing down the aging process.

No Time to Wait for Science Kacy Collins here makes a salad as part of her daily diet of less than 2,000 calories. She is among the thousands of American volunteers in studies of Calorie Restriction. Controlled, randomized, experimental proof is still years away, but researchers hope that these diets will help people like Kacy live until at least 90.

People in both groups would be studied for decades, to see when and why they sickened and died. Periodic checks would ensure they were sticking to their diets and also measure heart rate, breathing, and dozens of biomarkers in their blood, urine, and so on. The checks would be objective, by technicians who did not know who was in which group, or even what the study was about.

No one under 21 or potentially pregnant would be included. All the participants would be told that their calorie restriction would reduce their sex drive, cause infertility, weaken bones and muscles, affect moods, decrease energy, and affect other body functions. The advantage would be to prevent diabetes and early death, but no promises could be made—that is why the experiment is necessary.

Given all that, it would be difficult to recruit even a dozen people from the general population. However, in several places (e.g., Okinawa, Denmark, and Norway), wartime occupation by an enemy forced severe calorie reduction plus healthy diets (mostly fresh vegetables) on entire populations. The result was a markedly lower death rate (Fontana et al., 2011).

Similar results were reported from Cuba, as already mentioned in Chapter 20. Cuba's main export is sugar, and a sugar embargo by the United States led to food and gas shortages from 1991 to 1995. As a result, people ate local fruits and vegetables, walked more, and lost weight—losing an average of 12 pounds over 5 years. Mortality, particularly due to heart disease and diabetes, was reduced (Franco et al., 2013).

The economic crisis ended in Cuba in 1996, and in the 15 years since then the rates of obesity, diabetes, heart disease, and death have risen (Franco et al., 2013). Apparently, the Cubans were glad they could drive their cars and eat more, but doctors and scientists were discouraged. Perhaps people want the comforts of life more than longer lives.

How to Stop the Clock

Many scientists, as well as older people, seek a way to extend life without sacrifice. Exciting results have been reported for drugs that increase *sirtuins*. They may extend life, but once again, recent research raises questions (Couzin-Frankel, 2011).

Sirtuins are proteins (mammals have 7 sirtuins naturally) that extend the life of yeast, fruit flies, and mice—sometimes. They are called a "protective cavalry of enzymes" (Hall et al., 2013, p. 973), but this particular cavalry does not always come to the rescue. Even for mice, gender and genes make a difference: Sometimes sirtuins have no effect (Kanfi et al., 2012).

Some researchers still believe sirtuins slow the progress of various diseases that affect the brain, including Alzheimer's and Parkinson's (Herskovits & Guarente, 2013). The mechanism by which sirtuins operate is thought to be cellular, with effects similar to calorie restriction but without the need for dieting. That may be, but the history of research on anti-aging finds repeatedly that methods and products thought to extend life do not actually do so.

All the theories of aging, and all the research on genes, cells, calorie restriction, sirtuins, anti-oxidants, and so on, have not yet led to any straightforward way to stop senescence. Researchers are following numerous leads because many are convinced that something that affects the cells is a critical part of the aging process.

Many people hope for some drug or food (blueberries? red wine? fish oil?) to slow down aging. However, many middle-aged adults ignore the known factors that slow senescence—exercise, a moderate diet, and avoiding harmful drugs (especially cigarettes). What does that tell us about ourselves?

SUMMING UP

There are hundreds of theories of aging. The wear-and-tear theory proposes that bodies wear out with age, but this theory does not explain the entire aging process. Genetic theories note that some genes seem to postpone primary aging, and others make secondary aging more likely. One genetic theory holds that selective adaptation may have required, or at least allowed, humans to inherit genes for aging and death that did not become active until after the age at which they could produce and raise children to replace themselves.

Cellular theories focus on damage from oxygen-free radicals, on accumulated errors in cell duplication, on telomere shortening, and/or on the cells of the immune system. Methods to stop or slow cellular aging include calorie restriction (which works with some creatures but not all), drugs (with disputed results), and diet (with fruits and vegetables).

>> The Centenarians

There is one more source of knowledge about longevity: people who live a long time. Do they do something that others do not?

Far from Modern Life and Times

In the 1970s, three remote places—one in the Republic of Georgia, one in Pakistan, and one in Ecuador—were in the news because many vigorous old people lived there. Some were over 100 years old. One researcher wrote:

> Most of the aged [older than age 90] work regularly. . . . Some even continue to chop wood and haul water. Close to 40 percent of the aged men and 30 percent of the aged women report good vision; that is, that they do not need glasses for any sort of work, including reading or threading a needle. Between 40 and 50 percent have reasonably good hearing. Most have their own teeth. Their posture is unusually erect, even into advanced age. Many take walks of more than two miles a day and swim in mountain streams.

[Benet, 1974]

Guess Their Age Someone who has not read this chapter would be surprised to learn that Bessie Cooper *(left)* was 114 and Jiroemon Kimura *(right)* was 112 when these photos were taken. The pictures are not the most current, however: She was the oldest woman alive until her death at age 116 in 2012, and he turned 115 the same year—the oldest man to have lived so long. Some of the reasons for longevity are visible: genes (note their smooth skin), caregivers (note her carefully coiffed hair and his pristine white shirt), technology (glasses and hearing aid), and attitude (proud smiles). Not visible is their independence (she lived alone on a Georgia farm from ages 67 to 105) or many descendants (over 60 for Jiroemon, including that infant great-great-grandchild on the right).

More comprehensive studies (Pitskhelauri, 1982; Buettner, 2008) found that lifestyles in all three of these regions were similar in four ways:

1. *Diet.* People ate mostly fresh vegetables and herbs, with little meat or fat. They thought it better to be a little bit hungry than too full.
2. *Work.* Even the very old did farm work, household tasks, and child care.
3. *Family and community.* The elderly were well integrated into families of several generations and interacted frequently with friends and neighbors.
4. *Exercise and relaxation.* Most took a walk every morning and evening (often up and down mountains), napped midday, and socialized in the evening.

Perhaps these factors—diet, work, social interaction, and exercise—lengthen life.

The theory that the social context promotes longevity is buttressed by evidence from bumblebees. Genetically, worker bees and queen bees are the same, but worker bees live about three months while queen bees, fed special food and treated with deference, live about five years. When a queen dies, a worker bee is chosen to become a queen, thereby living 20 times longer than that bee otherwise would have.

Maximum Life Expectancy

Surely your suspicions were raised by the preceding paragraphs. Humans have almost nothing in common with bumblebees, and the information about those long-lived people was published decades ago.

Indeed, the three regions famous for long-lived humans lack verifiable birth or marriage records. Everyone who claimed to be a centenarian was probably exaggerating, and every researcher who believed them was too eager to accept the idea that life would be long and wonderful if only the ills of modern civilization were absent (Thorson, 1995). Some people still move to those remote places in order to live longer (e.g., Volkwein-Caplan, 2012), but most scientists consider that foolish.

As for preventing the ills of old age, it does seem that exercise, diet, and social integration add a few years to the average life—but not decades. It is important to distinguish the *average* life span from the *maximum*.

Genes seem to bestow on every species an inherent **maximum life span**, defined as the oldest possible age that members of that species can attain (Wolf, 2010). Under ideal circumstances, the maximum that rats live seems to be 4 years; rabbits, 13; tigers, 26; house cats, 30; brown bats, 34; brown bears, 37; chimpanzees, 55; Indian elephants, 70; finback whales, 80; humans, 122; lake sturgeon, 150; giant tortoises, 180.

Maximum life span is quite different from **average life expectancy**, which is the average life span of individuals in a particular group. In human groups, average life expectancy varies a great deal, depending on historical, cultural, and socioeconomic factors as well as on genes (Sierra et al., 2009).

In the United States the average has doubled in the past century and continues to rise. In 2012, average life expectancy at birth was about 76 years for men and 81 years for women. That is four years longer than it was 30 years ago, and it is projected to be another five years longer in 2050 (United Nations, 2012).

In most of the twentieth century, dramatic increases in average life expectancy in every nation occurred because public health measures (clean water, immunization, and so on) prevented the deaths of many infants and children. Recent increases in life expectancy are attributed to the reduction in deaths in middle

© CHRIS RANK/CORBIS

To the Max Fred Hale, here with three of his 11 great-great grandchildren on his 113th birthday, was the oldest living man for nine months until he died in his sleep a few days shy of his 114th birthday. Until a few years earlier, he lived independently in his home in Maine, shoveling snow off his roof at age 103.

maximum life span The oldest possible age that members of a species can live under ideal circumstances. For humans, that age is approximately 122 years.

average life expectancy The number of years the average newborn in a particular population group is likely to live.

age from adult diseases (heart attack, pneumonia, cancer, etc.). The average has increased; the maximum probably has not.

Now the challenge is to increase the life span of the very old. Gerontologists are engaged in a "fiery debate" as to whether the average life span will keep rising, and whether the maximum is genetically fixed (Couzin-Frankel, 2011b, p. 549). It is known that the oldest well-documented life ended at age 122, when Jeanne Calment died in southern France in 1997. No one has yet been proven to have outlived her, despite documented birth dates for a billion people who have died since then. That suggests that the maximum is set at 122, although some disagree.

Everyone agrees, however, that the last years of life can be good ones. Those who study centenarians find many quite happy (Jopp & Rott, 2006; Paúl et al., 2013). Jeanne Calment enjoyed a glass of red wine and some olive oil each day. "I will die laughing," she said.

Disease, disability, depression, and dementia may eventually set in; studies disagree about how common these problems are past age 100. Some studies find fewer physical and mental health problems after age 100 than before. For example, in Sweden, where medical care is free, centenarians were less likely to take antidepressants, but more likely to use pain medication, than those who were aged 80 or so (Wastesson et al., 2012).

Could centenarians be happier than octogenarians, as these Swedish data suggest? That is not known. However, it is true that more and more people live past 100, and many of them are energetic, alert, and optimistic (Perls, 2008; Poon, 2008). Social relationships in particular correlate with robust mental health (Margrett et al., 2011). Centenarians tend to be upbeat about life.

That could be considered the theme of this chapter: Attitude is crucial as senescence continues. As noted in the beginning of the chapter, ageism shortens life and makes the final years less satisfying. Don't let it. As thousands of centenarians demonstrate, a long life can be a happy one.

SUMMING UP

Many scientists seek to understand why aging occurs. If senescence could be stopped or slowed down, all the diseases that increase with aging would be reduced as well. In general, the wear-and-tear theory of aging seems inadequate, genetic theories are valid but not the entire story, and cellular theories are the most promising as well as the most disappointing. The number of centenarians is increasing. Also increasing is the average life span, although the maximum life span seems not to have changed much, if at all, over the past century. Many people who live far longer than average seem happy and remarkably independent.

SUMMARY

Prejudice and Predictions

1. Contrary to ageist stereotypes, most older adults are quite happy, healthy, and active. Ageism, which includes stereotyping and behaviors like elderspeak, is prevalent in both the young and old, and can lead to self-fulfilling prophecies regarding health and well-being as we age.

2. An increasing percentage of the population is over age 65, but the impact of this is sometimes distorted in the media. Currently, about 13 percent of people in the U.S. population are elderly, and 90 percent of them are self-sufficient and productive.

3. Gerontologists sometimes distinguish among the young-old, the old-old, and the oldest-old, according to each group's relative degree of dependency. Only 10 percent of the elderly are dependent (the oldest-old), and only 3 percent of the elderly are in nursing homes or hospitals.

Aging and Disease

4. The many apparent changes in skin, hair, and body shape that began earlier in adulthood continue. The senses all become less acute. Vision losses are common and critical: many elders have cataracts, glaucoma, or macular degeneration. Hearing also declines: Most older men are significantly hard-of-hearing.

5. Selective optimization with compensation for sensory losses requires a combination of technology, specialist advice, and personal determination. These three have been underutilized in the past (exemplified by the underuse of hearing aids).

6. Primary aging happens to everyone, reducing organ reserve in body and brain. Although the particulars differ depending on the individual's past health habits and genes, eventually morbidity, disability, and risk of mortality increase. Compensation is possible and brings many benefits, including compression of morbidity.

Theories of Aging

7. Hundreds of theories address the causes of aging. Wear-and-tear theory suggests that living wears out the body; it applies to some parts of the body but not to overall aging.

8. Another theory is that genes allow humans to survive through the reproductive years but then become seriously ill and inevitably die. Some individuals have genes or alleles that lead to long life, others to shorter lives.

9. Cellular theories of aging include the idea that the processes of DNA duplication and repair are affected by aging, making repair of errors more difficult.

10. Age-related decline in the immune system may cause aging, as it contributes to elderly people's increasing vulnerability to disease.

11. Cells stop duplicating at a certain point, called the Hayflick limit. This stoppage seems to occur when the telomeres shorten and then disappear.

The Centenarians

12. In geographic regions noted for long, active lives among residents, some patterns of behavior suggest that lifestyle can impact life expectancy. It appears that four specific factors—diet, work, social interaction, and exercise—may lengthen life.

13. Each species seems to have a genetic timetable for decline and death. Although the average life span has clearly increased, it is disputed whether the maximum can increase.

14. The number of centenarians is increasing, and many of them are quite healthy and happy. The personalities and attitudes of the very old suggest that long-term survival may be welcomed more than feared.

KEY TERMS

acute illness (p. 686)
ageism (p. 667)
average life expectancy (p. 694)
calorie restriction (p. 691)
cellular aging (p. 690)

chronic illness (p. 686)
compression of morbidity (p. 686)
demographic shift (p. 673)
dependency ratio (p. 674)
elderspeak (p. 672)

genetic clock (p. 689)
Hayflick limit (p. 690)
maximum life span (p. 694)
oldest-old (p. 675)
old-old (p. 675)
osteoporosis (p. 687)

primary aging (p. 684)
secondary aging (p. 684)
universal design (p. 682)
wear-and-tear theory (p. 689)
young-old (p. 675)

WHAT HAVE YOU LEARNED?

1. What are the similarities among ageism, racism, and sexism?

2. What are the differences among ageism, racism, and sexism?

3. Is there any harm in being especially kind to people who are old?

4. Why don't the elderly exercise as much as the young?

5. How is elderspeak similar to baby talk?

6. How is the demographic pyramid changing?

7. What are the differences among young-old, old-old, and oldest-old?

8. How does heart disease represent both primary and secondary aging?

9. How does diabetes represent both primary and secondary aging?

10. Why don't we know if diseases of the elderly are more common now than in the past?

11. Describe the differences in the sleep patterns of old adults and young adults.

12. How should it be decided whether or not an elderly person should drive?

13. How is compression of morbidity related to mortality?

14. How is compression of morbidity good for society as well as the individual?

15. Why are falls a serious health problem in old age?

16. How can an older person compensate for declines in vision?

17. How can an older person compensate for hearing loss?

18. How might the decrease in the senses of touch, taste, and smell harm an older person?

19. Why is the wear-and-tear theory of aging no longer considered accurate?

20. According to the genetic theory of aging, what is the maximum human life span?

21. Why is the average life span so many decades lower than the maximum?

22. How does evolutionary theory explain why there are more diseases of aging than diseases that occur during a person's younger years?

23. What damages cells as they age?

24. How can immune system failure cause aging?

25. Why would people lie about their age by adding years to it?

26. What do studies of the very old suggest about the attitudes of other people toward elders?

APPLICATIONS

1. Analyze websites that have information about aging for evidence of ageism, anti-aging measures, and exaggeration of longevity.

2. Compensating for sensory losses is difficult because it involves learning new habits. To better understand the experience, reduce your hearing or vision for a day by wearing earplugs or dark glasses that let in only bright lights. (Use caution and common sense: Don't drive a car while wearing earplugs or cross streets while wearing dark glasses.) Report on your emotions, the responses of others, and your conclusions.

3. Ask five people of various ages if they want to live to age 100 and record their responses. Would they be willing to eat half as much, exercise much more, experience weekly dialysis, or undergo other procedures in order to extend life? Analyze the responses.

>>ONLINE CONNECTIONS

To accompany your textbook, you have access to a number of online resources, including Learning Curve, an adaptive quizzing program, critical thinking questions, and case studies. For access to any of these links, go to www.worthpublishers.com/launchpad/bergerls9e. In addition to these resources, you'll also find links to video clips, personalized study advice, and an ebook. Some of the videos and activities available online include:

- *Brain Development: Late Adulthood.* Animated illustrations show normal age-related brain changes and changes associated with different types of neurocognitive disorder.

WORTH PUBLISHERS

Late Adulthood: Cognitive Development

- **The Aging Brain**
  New Brain Cells
  Senescence and the Brain

- **Information Processing After Age 65**
  Input
  Memory
  Control Processes
  A VIEW FROM SCIENCE: Cool Thoughts and Hot Hands
  Output
  OPPOSING PERSPECTIVES: How to Measure Output

- **Neurocognitive Disorders**
  The Ageism of Words
  Mild and Major Impairment
  Prevalence of NCD
  Preventing Impairment
  Reversible Neurocognitive Disorder?
  A CASE TO STUDY: Too Many Drugs or Too Few?

- **New Cognitive Development**
  Erikson and Maslow
  Learning Late in Life
  Aesthetic Sense and Creativity
  Wisdom

WHAT WILL YOU KNOW?

1. How does the brain simultaneously grow and shrink in old age?

2. What kinds of memory are least apt to fade in old age? What kinds are the most apt to fade?

3. What is the difference between these four terms: Alzheimer, senility, dementia, and neurocognitive disorders?

4. What gains in cognition occur in late adulthood?

I have eaten many dinners sponsored by large organizations. I am tired of them. No longer do I enjoy church suppers with lasagna and Jell-O/marshmallow salad; no longer do I appreciate chicken and chocolates at nonprofit fundraisers; I am not impressed with a choice of red or white wine and rare or well-done roast beef at corporate events.

But recently hundreds of other people and I attended an organization's dinner that was unlike the rest. The appetizer was a cold kale and nut salad; the fish entrée was passed around family style; and the guests were mostly young, lean, and earnest. It was a celebration of 40 years of a group that works for pedestrian safety, protected bike lanes, and metered parking. Most of the patrons arrived by foot, subway, or bicycle.

This chapter on cognition in late adulthood begins with this event because each generation has its own concept of how things should be. Challenging our conceptions is one of the things people of other ages do for us.

My assumptions were challenged and my ideas grew, not only by the menu but also by the conversation and the speeches. Piaget thought intelligence was the ability to expand the mind whenever disequilibrium requires new thinking. Of course, Piaget's fourth and final major intellectual expansion was formal operational thought during adolescence. But his insight applies to late adulthood as well: New experiences require deeper, better thinking. That is what research on the brain suggests.

I have not changed my basic values, but that dinner did expand my understanding. Cognitive development is a lifelong process, propelled by new experiences and reassessments.

This chapter describes the many intellectual losses of late adulthood in sensory input, memory, and output. But there are gains as well, including gains in thought and expression. You will also learn about neurological diseases that become more frequent as people grow older, including Alzheimer disease. Understanding them will entail some disequilibrium as you read: Many people have distorted ideas about aging, as is evident from the use of "senility," a word that itself is a distortion.

One theme is evident throughout: Older people can become wiser, but they do not always do so. Intellectual prowess after age 65 requires that people attend to aspects of life that require new concepts or skills. As you will see, this may include playing video games, or lifting weights, or storytelling, or painting, or singing, or staying on the job. For me, it included going to dinner.

Still at Work Roger Lesch (a) is shown here at age 65, the age when police in Rockport, Massachusetts must retire. Two decades earlier Lesch started protecting the elderly from scams and safeguarding those who wandered. He turned down a promotion which would have halted his senior work. Neither he nor anyone else wanted him to quit, so Rockport appointed him "special officer for elder affairs," which allowed him to continue working in uniform. Eric Headley (b), here age 74, drives a van for his job in London, He can no longer be forced to quit: A 2011 English law forbade mandatory retirement.

(a)   (b)

Especially for People Who Are Proud of Their Intellect What can you do to keep your mind sharp all your life? (see response, page 702)

>> The Aging Brain

Ageism impairs elders in many ways, but the most feared and insidious impairment involves the mind, not the body. As with many stereotypes, the notion of cognitive decline in late adulthood begins with a half-truth and then stops too soon. In fact, "although many 70- to 80-year-old adults show evidence of age-related decline, some continue to maintain very high levels of cognitive performance" (Nyberg & Bäckman, 2011). The fear is worse than the facts.

New Brain Cells

The most exciting news regarding brain development in later life is that neurons form and dendrites grow in adulthood. That surprised many scientists when it was first discovered. Almost everyone thought that humans developed no new brain cells after infancy.

We now know that neurons develop in the adult brain particularly in two specific areas, the olfactory region (smelling) and the hippocampus (remembering).

Some antidepressants create new neurons that repair damage to the hippocampus caused by earlier stress hormones (Serget et al., 2011). In addition, old neurons can develop new dendrites, allowing adults to shake the grip of depression and anxiety (Mateus-Pinheiro et al., 2013).

Although neurogenesis may occur in many living things, an evolutionary perspective suggests that the generation of new neurons in humans may occur for unique reasons (Kempermann, 2012). When agriculture began (widely believed to be approximately 10,000 years ago), adult life started to require more planning, remembering, and strategizing than was previously necessary. People faced more complexities in nourishing the population than was the case with the nomadic hunting and gathering that earlier humans did and that wild animals still do. Further, the brain adjusted as humans faced the new challenges of gathering in towns, which meant they had to interact with much larger social groups.

The idea that the complex social interactions of human life led to new brain development is an attractive one. As one scholar suggests, "moving actively in a changing world and dealing with novelty and complexity regulate adult neurogenesis. New neurons might thus provide the cognitive adaptability to conquer ecological niches rich with challenging stimuli" (Kempermann, 2012, p. 727).

As you remember from Chapter 21, in the twentieth century the evidence suggests that the intellectual ability of each new cohort is better than that of the previous one. Perhaps the increasing complexity of modern life requires continuing improvement, with urbanization and globalization demanding intellectual expansion. Thus older people who continue to cope with challenges will continue to grow neurons.

The positive finding that neurons are created is tempered by a more negative fact—growth of the brain in late adulthood is slow and limited (Lee et al., 2012), and treatment for various illnesses may kill neurons without creating new ones (Monje & Dietrich, 2012; Mashour & Avidan, 2013). New neurons develop, but their creation and growth are less robust than earlier in life, and not sufficient to restore the aging brain to its earlier state.

Senescence and the Brain

The cold fact that senescence affects the brain has been known for decades. Recent research has brought the good news that new brain cells and dendrites can develop, but the old news is still true—brains slow down with age.

Slower Thinking

Senescence reduces the production of neurotransmitters—glutamate, acetylcholine, serotonin, and especially dopamine—that allow a nerve impulse to jump quickly across the synaptic gap from one neuron to another. Neural fluid decreases, myelination thins, and cerebral blood circulates more slowly. The result is an overall slowdown of the brain, evident in reaction time, movement, speech, and thought.

This slowdown can prove a severe drain on the intellect because speed is crucial for many aspects of cognition. In fact, some experts believe that processing speed is the g mentioned in Chapter 21—the intellectual ability that underlies all other aspects of intelligence (Salthouse, 2004).

Deterioration of cognition correlates with slower movement as well as with almost every kind of physical disability (Kuo et al., 2007; Salthouse, 2010). For example, gait speed correlates strongly with many measures of intellect (Hausdorff & Buchman, 2013). Walks slow? Talks slow? Oh no—thinks slow!

Smaller Brains

Brain aging is evident not only in processing speed but also in size, as the total volume of the brain becomes smaller. Shrinkage is particularly notable in the hippocampus and the areas of the prefrontal cortex that are needed for planning, inhibiting unwanted responses, and coordinating thoughts (Rodrigue & Kennedy, 2011).

In every part of the brain, the volume of gray matter (crucial for processing new experiences) is reduced, in part because the cortex becomes thinner with every decade of adulthood (Zhou et al., 2013). As a consequence, many people must use their cognitive reserve (Park & Reuter-Lorenz, 2009). White matter generally is reduced as well, slowing the mind. However, white matter also increases in an odd way: Bright white spots appear on MRIs after age 50 or so.

These white matter lesions are thought to result from tiny impairments in blood flow. They increase the time it takes for a thought to be processed in the brain (Rodrigue & Kennedy, 2011). Slowed transmission from one neuron to another is not the only problem. With age, transmission of impulses from entire regions of the brain, specifically from parts of the cortex and the cerebellum, is disrupted. Specifics correlate more with cognitive ability than with age (Bernard et al., 2013).

>> Response for People Who Are Proud of Their Intellect (from page 700): If you answered, "Use it or lose it" or "Do crossword puzzles," you need to read more carefully. No specific brain activity has proved to prevent brain slowdown. Overall health is good for the brain as well as for the body, so exercise, a balanced diet, and well-controlled blood pressure are some smart answers.

Observation Quiz In the figure below, how much were the 9-year-olds affected by doing both tasks at once? (see answer, page 704)

FIGURE 24.1

One Task at a Time Doing two things at once impairs performance. In this study, researchers compared the speed of a sensorimotor task (walking) and a cognitive task (naming objects within a category—for example, naming as many colors, spices, insects, crimes, four-legged animals as possible within a minute or two). The participants did each task separately first, and then they did both at once. Performing them both at once resulted in performance losses for everyone. Note, however, that the eldest seemed to safeguard verbal fluency (only a 3 percent slowdown) at the expense of significantly slower walking.

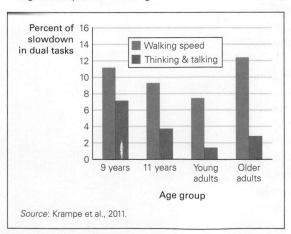

Source: Krampe et al., 2011.

Variation in Brain Efficiency

As with every other organ, all the aspects of brain senescence vary markedly from individual to individual, in part because of the individual's health and habits. Higher education and vocational status correlate with less cognitive decline. There are three plausible hypotheses for the connection between high SES and high intellect:

1. High-SES people began late adulthood with more robust and flexible minds, so their losses are not as noticeable.
2. Keeping the mind active is protective.
3. High-SES people generally avoid pollution and drugs, and have better medical care than low-SES people.

The first hypothesis seems to have the greatest amount of research support. The intellectually gifted may lose cognitive speed at the same rate as other people, but they began late adulthood as such quick thinkers that the slowdown is less apparent (Puccioni & Vallesi, 2012). But the second hypothesis also has support: The intellectually gifted are more open to new ideas, and that openness produces a more active mind (Hogan et al., 2012). This is the "use it or lose it" hypothesis, an attractive idea that has many of the elderly doing crossword puzzles and Sudoku, but not one that researchers have proven.

Finally, no one doubts that health is crucial. Exercise, nutrition, and normal blood pressure are powerful influences on brain health, and these factors predict intelligence in old age. Some experts contend that with good health habits and favorable genes, no intellectual decrement will occur (Greenwood & Parasuraman, 2012).

Variation is also evident in which parts of the brain shut down first. Names are forgotten faster than faces, spatial representation (where did I put that?) faster than vocabulary (what is that called?). This variation may be strictly biological (hypothesis one) or a matter of practice (hypothesis two). No doubt it is affected by blood circulation in the brain (hypothesis three).

Using More of the Brain

A curious finding from PET and fMRI scans is that, compared with younger adults, older adults use more parts of their brains, including both hemispheres, to solve problems. This may be compensation: Using only one brain region may no longer be sufficient if that part has shrunk, so the older brain automatically activates more parts.

Consequently, older adults are as intellectually sharp as they always were on many tasks. However, in performing difficult tasks that require younger adults to use all their cognitive resources, older adults are less proficient, perhaps because they already are using their brains to the max (Cappell et al., 2010).

Brain shrinkage interferes with multitasking even more than with other cognitive challenges. No one is intellectually as efficient with two tasks as with one, but young children and old adults are particularly impaired by doing several tasks (Krampe et al., 2011) (see Figure 24.1). Recognizing this fact, many elders are selective; they sequence tasks rather than try to do two things at once.

Suppose that a man is interrupted by his grandchild's questions while reading the newspaper, or that grandchild asks grandma which bus to take while she is getting dressed. A wise man puts down the newspaper and then answers, and grandmother will first dress and then think about transportation (avoiding mismatched shoes).

SUMMING UP

The human brain is constantly changing and developing as long as a person is alive, even adding new cells and growing new dendrites. However, like every other body part, the brain shows signs of age. It becomes smaller overall. Some parts are particularly likely to shrink, especially gray matter, the prefrontal cortex, and the hippocampus. Neurotransmitters, myelination, and white matter are also reduced, with new, intense white spots. The result of all these changes is that the transmission of messages from one neuron to another slows, which is evident in how fast people move their bodies (such as walking) and how quickly they remember a name.

Remarkable plasticity is also apparent, with wide variation in the rate and specifics of brain slowdown. In general, older adults use more of their brains, not less, to do various tasks, and they prefer doing one task at a time, avoiding multitasking. ■

>> Information Processing After Age 65

Given the complexity, variation, and diversity of late-life cognition, we need to examine specifics to combat general stereotypes. For this purpose, the information-processing approach is useful, with details of input (sensing), memory (storage), control processes (programming), and output.

Input

The first step in information processing is input, in which the brain receives information from the senses, but, as Chapters 20 and 23 explain, no sense is as sharp at age 65 as at age 15. Glasses and hearing aids mitigate severe sensory losses, but more subtle deficits impair cognition as well. In order to be perceived, information must cross the *sensory threshold*—the divide between what is sensed and what is not. [**Lifespan Link:** Sensory memory is explained in Chapter 12.]

A person may not recognize sensory losses because the brain automatically fills in missed sights and sounds. People of all ages believe they look at the eyes of their conversation partner, yet a study that examined the ability to follow a gaze found that older adults were less adept at knowing where someone was looking (Slessor et al., 2008). That creates a disadvantage in social interactions. Another study found that already by age 50, adults were less adept at reading emotions by looking at the eyes (Pardini & Nichelli, 2009).

Acute hearing is another way to detect emotional nuances. Older adults are less able to decipher the emotional content in speech, even when they hear the words correctly (Dupuis & Pichora-Fuller, 2010). Particularly for them, understanding speech is impaired when vision is impaired (Tye-Murray et al., 2011), probably because watching lips and facial expressions aids understanding. Thus, small sensory losses—not noticed by the person or family but inevitable with age—impair cognition.

I know a father—not elderly but already with fading eyesight—who was scolding his 6-year-old daughter. Without his glasses, he could not see that her lip had started to quiver. He was surprised when she cried; he did not realize how harsh his words seemed to her.

The cognition of almost 2,000 intellectually normal older adults, average age 77, was repeatedly tested 5, 8, 10, and 11 years after the initial intake (Lin et al., 2013). At the 5-year retesting, an audiologist assessed their hearing. Between the start of the study and 11 years later, the average cognitive scores of the adults with hearing loss (who were often unaware of it) were down 7 percent, while those with normal hearing lost 5 percent.

>> **Answer to Observation Quiz** (from page 702): Nine-year-olds were the only group to slow down significantly in both tasks. Impairment was about 11 percent in walking and 7 percent in naming within a category.

Especially for Students If you want to remember something you learn in class for the rest of your life, what should you do? (see response, page 706)

That 2 percent difference seems small, but statistically it was highly significant (.004). Furthermore, greater hearing losses correlated with greater cognitive declines (Lin et al., 2013). Many other researchers likewise find that small input losses have a notable effect on output.

Memory

After input, the second step is processing whatever input has come from the senses. Stereotype threat impedes this processing. [**Lifespan Link:** Stereotype threat was discussed in Chapter 18.] If older people suspect memory loss, anxiety itself impairs their memory (Ossher et al., 2013). Worse than that, simply knowing that they are taking a memory test makes them feel years older (Hughes et al., 2013). As you learned in Chapter 23, feeling old itself impairs health.

The more psychologists study memory, the more they realize that memory is not one function but many, each with a specific pattern of loss. Some losses of the elderly are quite normal and others pathological (Markowitsch & Staniloiu, 2012). The inability to recall a word or a name is a normal loss of one aspect of memory, and does not indicate that memory, overall, is fading.

Generally, explicit memory (recall of learned material) shows more loss than implicit memory (recognition and habits). That means that names are harder to remember than actions. Grandpa can still swim, ride a bike, and drive a car, even if he cannot name both U.S. senators from his state.

One memory deficit is *source amnesia*—forgetting the origin of a fact, idea, or snippet of conversation. Source amnesia is particularly problematic in the twenty-first century, as video, audio, and print information bombard the mind.

In practical terms, source amnesia means that elders might believe a rumor or political advertisement because they forget the source. Compensation requires deliberate attention to the reason behind a message before accepting a con artist's promises or the politics of a TV ad. However, elders are less likely than younger adults to analyze, or even notice, information surrounding the material they remember (Boywitt et al., 2012).

Another crucial type of memory is called *prospective memory*—remembering to do something in the future (to take a pill, to meet someone for lunch, to buy milk). Prospective memory also fades notably with age (Kliegel et al., 2008). This loss becomes dangerous if, for instance, a person cooking dinner forgets to turn off the stove, or if someone is driving on the thruway in the far lane when the exit appears.

The crucial aspect of prospective memory seems to be the ability to shift the mind quickly from one task to another: Older adults get immersed in one thought and have trouble changing gears (Schnitzspahn et al., 2013). For that reason, many elders follow routine sequences (brush teeth, take medicine, get the paper) and set an alarm to remind them to leave for a doctor's appointment. That is compensation.

Working memory (remembering information for a moment before evaluating, calculating, and inferring its significance) also declines with age. Speed is critical: Some older individuals take longer to perceive and process sensations, which reduces working memory because some items fade before they can be considered (Stawski et al., 2013).

For example, a common test of working memory is to have someone repeat backwards a string of digits just heard, but if the digits are said quickly, a slow-thinking person may be unable to process each number and then hold them all in memory. Speed of processing would explain why memory for vocabulary

(especially recognition memory, not recall) is often unaffected by age. For instance, speed is irrelevant in knowing that *chartreuse* is a color, not an animal.

Some research finds that when older people have adequate time, working memory does not fade. Speed is crucial when comparing working memory between one older adult and another, but paying attention becomes the critical factor when a person is tested repeatedly over several days (Stawski et al., 2013).

Thus adequate time and careful attention are both crucial. This explains interesting results from a study of reading ability. In that research, older people reread phrases more often than younger people did, but when both groups had ample time to pay attention, comprehension was not impaired by age (Stine-Morrow et al., 2010).

Control Processes

The next step in information processing involves control processes (discussed in Chapter 12). Many scholars believe that the underlying impairment of cognition in late adulthood is in this step, as information from all parts of the brain is analyzed by the prefrontal cortex. Control processes include selective attention, strategic judgment, and then appropriate action—the so-called *executive function* of the brain.

Instead of using analysis and forethought, the elderly tend to rely on prior knowledge, general principles, familiarity, and rules of thumb as they make decisions (Peters et al., 2011), basing actions on past experiences and current emotions.

For example, casinos have noticed that elderly gamblers gravitate to slot machines rather than to games where analysis is helpful. The reason, according to a study of brain scans of young and old slot players, is that the activated parts of older brains are less often the regions in which analysis occurs (McCarrey et al., 2012). When gamblers are able to analyze the odds, as younger players do, they spend less time with slots.

A VIEW FROM SCIENCE

Cool Thoughts and Hot Hands

As you remember from the discussion of dual processing in Chapter 15, experiential, emotional thinking is not always faulty, but sometimes analytic thinking is needed to control impulsive, thoughtless reactions.

This was apparent in a study of belief in the "hot hand," which is the idea that athletes are more likely to score if they scored in the immediately previous attempts. One study found that most people (91 percent) believe that players can be "on a roll" or that teams can have "a winning streak" (Gilovitch et al., 1985).

Most people are wrong about this; the hot hand is an illusion. Of course, the best players are more likely to score than the worst ones, but statistical analysis from basketball, golf, and other sports finds that one successful shot does not affect the chance that a particular player will make the next one.

People want to believe in streaks, so they forget when streaks do not occur. This misperception has become a classic example of the human tendency to ignore data that conflicts with assumptions (Kahneman, 2011).

Do people become more or less likely to follow their preconceptions rather than using logic to consider new information as they age? In one study, 455 people aged 22 to 90 were told that, overall, about half the time basketball shots miss. That was supposed to remind them to think analytically, not emotionally. Then they were asked two questions:

Does a basketball player have a better chance of making a shot after having just made the last two or three shots than after missing the last two or three shots?
Is it important to pass the ball to someone who has just made several shots in a row?

The correct answer to both questions is *No*, but in this study, elders were particularly likely to say *Yes*, sticking to their hot hand belief (Castel et al., 2012) (see Figure 24.2).

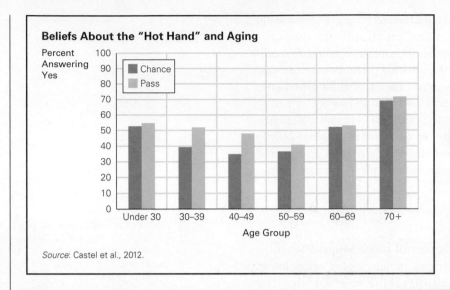

Beliefs About the "Hot Hand" and Aging

Source: Castel et al., 2012.

FIGURE 24.2

Hard to Chill This shows the percent of adults who answered "Yes" to the two questions, which meant that they were not thinking analytically. As you see, the oldest participants were most likely to stick to their "hot hand" prejudice. However, also notice that about one-fourth of those over 70 answered correctly and almost half of the younger adults did not. In this and every other study, age is only one of many factors that influence cognition.

>> Response for Students (from page 704): Learn it very well now, and you will probably remember it in 50 years, with a little review.

One particular control process is development of strategies for retrieval. Some developmentalists believe that impaired retrieval is an underlying cause of intellectual lapses in old age because elders have many thoughts and memories that they cannot access. Since deep thinking requires recognizing and comparing the similarities and differences in various experiences, if a person cannot retrieve memories of the past, new thinking is more shallow than it might otherwise be.

Inadequate control processes may explain why many older adults have extensive vocabularies (measured by written tests) but limited fluency (when they write or talk), why they are much better at recognition than recall, why tip-of-the-tongue forgetfulness is common, and why spelling is poorer than pronunciation.

Many gerontologists think elders would benefit by learning better control strategies. Unfortunately, even though "a high sense of control is associated with being happy, healthy, and wise," many older adults resist suggested strategies because they believe that declines are "inevitable or irreversible" and that no strategy can help (Lachman et al., 2009, p. 144). Efforts to improve their use of control strategies are often discouraging (McDaniel & Bugg, 2012).

Output

The final step in information processing is output. In daily life, output is usually verbal. If the timbre and speed of a person's speech sounds old, ageism might cause listeners to dismiss the content without realizing that the substance may be profound. Then, if elders realize that what they say is ignored, they talk less. Output is diminished. This provides guidance for anyone who wants to respect and learn from someone else: We all talk more if we think someone is listening appreciatively.

Scientists usually measure output through use of standardized tests of mental ability. As already noted, if older adults think their memory is being tested, that alone impairs them (Hughes et al., 2013). Even without stereotype threat, output on cognitive tests may not reflect ability, as you will now see.

Cognitive Tests

In the Seattle Longitudinal Study (described in Chapter 21), the measured output of all five primary mental abilities—verbal meaning, spatial orientation, inductive reasoning, number ability, and word fluency—declined, beginning at about

age 60. This decline was particularly notable in spatial perception and processing speed (Schaie, 2013).

Similar results are found in many tests of cognition: Thus, the usual path of cognition in late adulthood as measured by psychological tests is gradual decline, at least in output (Salthouse, 2010). However, such tests are normed and validated via the output of younger adults. To avoid cultural bias, many questions are quite abstract and timed, since speed of thinking correlates with intelligence for younger adults. A smart person is said to be a "quick" thinker, the opposite of someone who is "slow."

But abstract thinking and processing speed are the aspects of cognition that fade most with age. Is there a better way to measure output in late adulthood?

Ecological Validity

Perhaps ability should be measured in everyday tasks and circumstances, not as laboratory tests assess it. To do measurements in everyday settings is to seek **ecological validity**, which may be particularly important when measuring cognition in the elderly (Marsiske & Margrett, 2006).

For example, because of changes in their circadian rhythm, older adults are at their best in the early morning, when adolescents are half asleep. If a study were to compare 85-year-olds and 15-year-olds, both tested either at 8 A.M. or at 4 P.M., comparisons would reflect time of day, not just mental ability. Ecological validity might require different testing times for each age group.

Similarly, if intellectual ability were to be assessed via a timed test, then faster thinkers (usually young) would score higher than slower thinkers (usually old), even if the slower ones would be more accurate with a few more seconds to think. Furthermore, contextual effects might cause anxiety, for instance, if the test occurred in a college laboratory.

Indeed, age differences in prospective memory are readily apparent in laboratory tests but disappear in some naturalistic settings, a phenomenon called the "prospective memory-paradox" (Schnitzspahn et al., 2011). Motivation seems crucial; elders are less likely to forget whatever they believe is important—phoning a child on their birthday, for instance.

Similarly, as already noted, older adults are not as accurate as younger adults when tested on the ability to read emotions by looking at someone's face or listening to someone's voice. But seeing and hearing are less acute with age, so they may not be the best way to measure empathy in older adults. Accordingly, a team decided to measure empathy when visual contact was impossible.

Their study included a hundred couples who had been together for years, and each of the participants was repeatedly asked to indicate their own emotions (how happy, enthusiastic, balanced, content, angry, downcast, disappointed, nervous they were) and to guess the emotions of their partner at that moment. Technology helped with this: The participants were beeped at various times, and indicated their answers on a smart phone they kept with them. Sometimes they happened to be with their partner, sometimes not.

When the partner was present, accuracy was higher for the younger couples, presumably because they could see and hear their mate. But when the partner was absent, the older participants were as good as the younger ones (see Figure 24.3). Could you

> predict a social partner's feelings when that person is absent? Your judgment would probably be better than chance, and although many abilities deteriorate with aging, this particular ability may remain reliable throughout your life.

[*Rauers et al., 2013, p. 2215*]

ecological validity The idea that cognition should be measured in settings and conditions that are as realistic as possible and that the abilities measured should be those needed in real life.

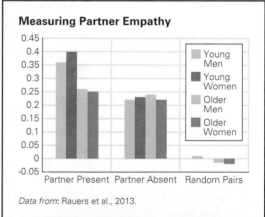

Measuring Partner Empathy

Data from: Rauers et al., 2013.

FIGURE 24.3

Always on My Mind When they were together, younger partners were more accurate than older ones at knowing their partner's emotions, but older partners were as good as younger ones when they were apart. This study used "smart phone experience sampling," buzzing both partners simultaneously to ask how they and their partner felt. Interestingly, differences were found with age but not length of relationship—five, ten, twenty, or thirty years of togetherness did not necessarily increase empathy when apart, but men who were in their 70s were better at absent mood assessment than men in their 20s.

The fundamental ecological issue for developmentalists is what should be assessed—pure, abstract thinking or practical, contextual thought, depersonalized abilities, or everyday actions? Traditional tests of cognition emphasize fluid abilities, but problem solving and emotional sensitivity may be more crucial. Those practical abilities are not measured by traditional cognitive tests.

Awareness of the need for ecological validity has helped scientists restructure research on memory. Restructured studies find fewer deficits than originally thought. However, any test may overestimate or underestimate ability. For instance, what is an accurate test of long-term memory? Many older people recount, in vivid detail, events that occurred decades ago. That is impressive . . . if the memories are accurate.

Unfortunately, "there is no objective way to evaluate the degree of ecological validity . . . because ecological validity is a subjective concept" (Salthouse, 2010, p. 77). It is impossible to be totally objective in assessing memory; memory is always subjective.

OPPOSING PERSPECTIVES

How to Measure Output

Finding the best way to measure cognition is particularly important if a decision is to be made as to whether an older person is able to live independently. An increasing number of the elderly live alone. Is this safe? Might they forget to turn off the stove, or ignore symptoms of a heart attack, or fall prey to a stranger who wants them to invest their money in a harebrained scheme? Many people seek to protect the elderly from failing cognition while allowing as much independence as possible.

Recently, tests have been developed to measure practical problem solving (Law et al., 2012). Some involve short-term memory with no delay between facts and conclusions. In one such test, for instance, a person reads relevant facts; then the paper is removed and the person is asked to solve a problem based on those facts. Other tests pose practical problems, such as what to do if your refrigerator is warm or if a favorite sweater has a hole in it.

Scores on such tests show less discrepancy between the old and the young than scores on abstract memory tests. Perhaps only when an older person living alone fails practical tests is it time for intervention.

Unfortunately, even tests that attempt to be ecologically valid may be inaccurate (Law et al., 2012). Perhaps the best way to test cognitive ability is to be quite direct, asking questions about missed appointments, lost keys, and so on of a person or of someone who knows them well. Yet even direct questions may not be answered accurately, in part because many of the elderly do not want to admit memory loss. Added to that, many family members and professionals, themselves growing older, do not want to admit to their memory loss—or they may exaggerate it in someone else. Objective measurement might help.

Which of these three measures is best? A study that compared self-assessment, spousal assessment, and tests of intellectual ability found poor correlation among them (Volz-Sidiropoulou & Gauggel, 2012). People did not accurately assess their own memories or those of their partner—with whom they had lived for an average of 30 years.

In that study, the self-assessment questions were ecologically valid, asking practical questions such as how often the person loses things around the house (Volz-Sidiropoulou & Gauggel, 2012). The formal tests of memory were also valid and well established. For instance, the examiner read a list of 15 words and asked the older person to repeat them.

Inaccurate self-assessment is characteristic of people with serious mental illness, as the study authors explain. Those who reported few memory difficulties tended to score poorly on the formal tests; this mistake was thought to be an example of "self-serving bias"—the human tendency to think we are better than we are. That could be dangerous if people are allowed to live alone until they themselves realize they should not. But read the final paragraph of this box before accepting this conclusion.

By contrast, some people in this study reported many memory problems: They typically did better on the formal tests than their self-assessment. The study authors thought this might have been their "way to protect their self-concept by claiming self-handicapping" (Volz-Sidiropoulou & Gauggel, 2012, p. 446). Thus the perspective of researchers was that the elderly are poor at assessing their own cognition.

But wait. Consider an opposing perspective. Is the gap between self-assessment and laboratory results evidence of self-serving bias or self-concept protection, whether the self-assessment is high or low? Or are the tests biased, not the people?

We know that stereotypes are insidious, that global assessments are over-simplified, that emotions affect output. We know that individuals vary, and that some but not all kinds of memory show notable age-related loss.

The final ecological question is, "What is memory for?" Older adults usually think they remember well enough. Fear of memory loss is more typical at age 60 than at age 80. Unless they develop a brain condition such as Alzheimer disease (soon described), elders are correct: They remember how to live their daily lives. Is that enough?

SUMMING UP

Every step in information processing is affected by age. As the senses become less acute, people miss some input. Some stimuli never arrive in the brain, and thus cannot inform thought. Memory also is slower, especially memory for names and places. However, some memories seem intact, including memory for words, emotions, and automatic (implicit) skills.

Impairment in control processes—especially retrieval strategies—may underlie the cognitive deficits of age. Anxiety interferes with every step in information processing. For all these reasons, output is reduced. Every test of cognitive ability shows age-related losses, but in daily life most of the elderly think well enough. ■

>> Neurocognitive Disorders

The patterns of cognitive aging challenge another assumption: that older people always lose the ability to think and remember. That is not true. Many older people are less sharp than they were, but most are still quite capable of intellectual activity. Others experience serious decline.

The Ageism of Words

It is undeniable that the rate of neurocognitive impairment increases with every decade after age 70. To understand that and prevent the worst of it, caution is needed in using words.

Senile means "old." If senility is used to mean severe mental impairment, that falsely implies that age always brings intellectual failure. *Dementia* was a better term than *senility* for irreversible, pathological loss of brain functioning, but dementia also has inaccurate connotations (e.g., "mad" or "insane").

The DSM-5 replaces the term *dementia* with **neurocognitive disorders (NCDs)**. Either *major neurocognitive disorder* or *mild neurocognitive disorder*, depending upon severity of symptoms, is a better way of capturing the range of cognitive impairment and providing the opportunity for early detection and treatment. We use NCD here.

Memory impairment is common in every cognitive disorder. Symptoms of neurocognitive disorders include many more impairments, especially in learning new material, using language, moving the body, and responding to people. Practical examples include getting lost, becoming confused about using common objects like a telephone or toothbrush, or having extreme emotional reactions.

The lines between normal age-related problems, mild disorder, and major disorder are not clearly defined, and the symptoms vary depending on the specifics of brain loss and context. Making distinctions more difficult is that the former word—*dementia*—is still often used in research, and the inaccurate word—*senility*—is used in common speech. Variation is evident in origin as well: more than 70 diseases can cause neurocognitive disorders, each with particular symptoms, sequence, and severity. Equifinality (see Chapter 11) is evident.

neurocognitive disorders (NCDs)
Impairment of intellectual functioning caused by organic brain damage or disease. NCDs may be diagnosed as *major* or *mild*, depending on the severity of symptoms. They become more common with age, but they are abnormal and pathological even in the very old.

The problem of ageist terminology has been recognized internationally. In Japanese, the traditional word for neurocognitive disorder was *chihou*, translated as "foolish" or "stupid." As more people reached old age, the Japanese decided on a new word, *ninchihou*, which means "cognitive syndrome" (George & Whitehouse, 2010). That is similar to the changes in English terminology over the past decades, from senility to dementia to neurocognitive disorder.

Mild and Major Impairment

Many instances of memory loss are not necessarily ominous signs of severe loss to come. Older adults who have significant problems with memory, but who still function well at work and home, might be diagnosed with mild NCD, formerly called *mild cognitive impairment (MCI)*. Although some of them will develop major disorders, about half will be mildly impaired for decades or will regain cognitive abilities. For instance, a detailed study of African Americans diagnosed with MCI found that each year, 6 percent developed major losses but 18 percent reverted back to normal (S. Gao et al., 2013).

Many tests are designed to measure mild loss, including one that takes less than 10 minutes—the quick MCI (qmci) (O'Caoimh et al., 2013). The problem with every test is that scores are affected by many factors, with no universally accepted cutoff between normal, mild, and major impairment.

Many scientists seek biological indicators (called *biomarkers*, such as substances in the blood or cerebrospinal fluid) or brain indicators (as found in brain scans) that predict major memory loss. However, although abnormal scores on many tests (biological, neurological, or psychological) indicate possible problems, an examination of 24 such measures found no single test, and no combination of tests, to be 100 percent accurate (Ewers et al., 2012).

The final determinant of neurocognitive disorders is the clinical judgment of a professional who considers all the markers and symptoms—everything from uncontrolled impulses to memory lapses. Any diagnosis may focus too much on losses and not enough on individual strengths. As the previous two sections on brain aging and information processing explain, no very old persons are as intellectually sharp as they once were, so almost everyone could be considered mildly impaired. Opinions are always subjective; objective data can be discounted or overemphasized by both professionals and patients. Diagnosis is complex.

Prevalence of NCD

As you remember from Chapter 23, ageism leads to presentation of statistics in ways that make younger adults recoil with horror. One example is in data about the rising numbers of old people with cognitive problems. We need a more rational understanding.

To find out how many people are truly suffering from cognitive disorders in their older years, researchers selected a representative sample of people 70 years of age and older from every part of the United States, interviewed and examined each one, and spoke with someone who knew them well (usually an immediate relative). They combined this information with test results, medical records, and clinical judgment, and found that 14 percent had some form of major impairment (Plassman et al., 2007) (see Figure 24.4). Extrapolated to the overall population, about 4 million U.S. residents have a serious neurocognitive disorder.

FIGURE 24.4

Not Everyone Gets It Most elderly people never experience a neurocognitive disorder. Among people in their 70s, only 1 person in 20 does, and even by age 90 or 100, most people still think well enough. Presented another way, the prevalent data sound more dire: Almost 4 million people in the United States have a major neurocognitive disorder. (This study used the former term, *dementia*.)

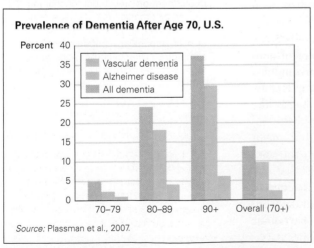

Prevalence of Dementia After Age 70, U.S.

Legend:
- Vascular dementia
- Alzheimer disease
- All dementia

Source: Plassman et al., 2007.

Rates vary by nation, from about 2 to 25 percent of elders, with an estimated 35 million people affected by NCD worldwide (Kalaria et al., 2008; WHO, 2010). Developing nations have lower rates, but that may be because people in the early stages are not counted or because health care overall is poor. (See Visualizing Development, p. 725)

How would poor health care lead to less, not more, impairment? Because many people die before any neurocognitive problems are apparent. People with diabetes, Parkinson's, strokes, and heart surgery are more likely to lose intellectual capacity in old age, but in poor nations many people with those conditions die before age 70.

Improvements in health care can reduce cognitive impairment, even as the incidences rise. The three ideal public health goals are (1) better physical health, (2) less mental disorder, and (3) longer lives. That is becoming a reality in some nations.

In England and Wales the rate of dementia for people over age 65 was 8.3 percent in 1991 but only 6.5 percent in 2011 (Matthews et al., 2013). Sweden had a similar decline (Qie et al., 2011). In China, rates were much higher in rural areas than in urban ones, probably because rural Chinese had less education (Jia et al., 2014). This again suggests that NCD will be reduced as more people understand how to stay healthy.

A comparable survey has not been done in North America, but some signs suggest improvement. Of course, reduction in rate does not necessarily mean reduction in number, since more people live to old age. In England over the past 20 years, the number of people with dementia stayed about the same (Matthews et al., 2013) even while the rate has declined.

Genetics and social context affect rates, but it is not known by how much (Bondi et al., 2009). For example, more older women than men are diagnosed with neurocognitive disorders, which may be genetic, educational, or stress-related. Or it may be simply that women live longer than men (Alzheimer's Association, 2012). Now consider some specific types of age-related neurocognitive disorders.

Alzheimer Disease

In 1906, a physician named Dr. Alois Alzheimer performed an autopsy on a patient who had lost her memory. He found unusual material in her brain; he was uncertain whether it specified a distinct disease (George & Whitehouse, 2010). Others, convinced that he had discovered a disease, named it after him. In the past century, millions of people in every large nation have been diagnosed with **Alzheimer disease (AD)** (now formally referred to as major or mild NCD due to Alzheimer disease). In China, for example, 5.7 million people have Alzheimer disease (Chan et al., 2013).

As Dr. Alzheimer discovered, autopsies reveal that some aging brains have many plaques and tangles in the cerebral cortex. These abnormalities destroy the ability of neurons to communicate with one another, causing severe cognitive loss.

Plaques are clumps of a protein called *beta-amyloid*, found in tissues surrounding the neurons; **tangles** are twisted masses of threads made of a protein called *tau* within the neurons. A normal brain contains some beta-amyloid and some tau, but in brains with AD these plaques and tangles proliferate, especially in the hippocampus, the brain structure crucial for memory. Forgetfulness is the dominant symptom; working memory disappears first.

Although finding massive brain plaques and tangles at autopsy proves that a person diagnosed with NCD had Alzheimer disease, between 20 and 30 percent of cognitively normal elders have, at autopsy, the same levels of plaques in their brains as people who had been diagnosed with AD (Jack et al., 2009). Possibly the normal elders had compensated by using other parts of their brains; possibly they were in the early stages, not yet suspected of having AD; possibly plaques are a symptom, not a cause.

Alzheimer disease (AD) The most common cause of dementia, characterized by gradual deterioration of memory and personality and marked by the formation of plaques of beta-amyloid protein and tangles of tau in the brain. (Sometimes called *senile dementia of the Alzheimer type*.)

plaques Clumps of a protein called *beta-amyloid*, found in brain tissues surrounding the neurons.

tangles Twisted masses of threads made of a protein called *tau* within the neurons of the brain.

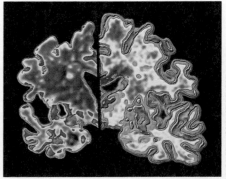

A. PAKIEKA/SCIENCE SOURCE

The Alzheimer Brain This computer graphic shows a vertical slice through a brain ravaged by Alzheimer disease (*left*) compared with a similar slice of a normal brain (*right*). The diseased brain is shrunken because neurons have degenerated. The red indicates plaques and tangles.

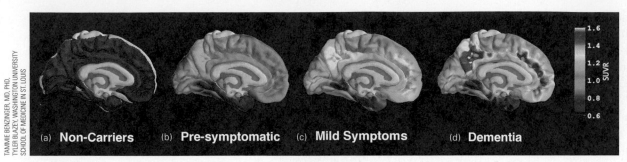

(a) **Non-Carriers**   (b) **Pre-symptomatic**   (c) **Mild Symptoms**   (d) **Dementia**

Hopeful Brains Even the brain without symptoms *(a)* might eventually develop Alzheimer disease, but people with a certain dominant gene definitely will. They have no symptoms in early adulthood *(b)*, some symptoms in middle adulthood *(c)*, and stage-five Alzheimer disease *(d)* before old age. Research finds early brain markers (such as those shown here) that predict the disease. This is not always accurate, but may soon lead to early treatment that halts AD, not only in those genetically vulnerable, but also in everyone.

Especially for Genetic Counselors Would you perform a test for *ApoE4* if someone asked for it? (see response, page 714)

vascular dementia (VaD) A form of neurocognitive disorder characterized by sporadic, and progressive, loss of intellectual functioning caused by repeated infarcts, or temporary obstructions of blood vessels, which prevent sufficient blood from reaching the brain.

Alzheimer disease is partly genetic. If it develops in middle age, the affected person either has trisomy-21 (Down syndrome) or has inherited one of three genes: amyloid precursor protein (APP), presenilin 1, or presenilin 2. For these people, the disease progresses quickly, reaching the last phase within three to five years.

Most cases begin much later, at age 75 or so. Many genes have some impact, including *SORL1* and *ApoE4* (allele 4 of the *ApoE* gene). People who inherit one copy of *ApoE4* (as about one-fifth of all U.S. residents do) have about a 50/50 chance of developing AD. Those who inherit two copies almost always develop the disorder if they live long enough.

Vascular NCD

The second most common cause of neurocognitive disorder is a *stroke* (a temporary obstruction of a blood vessel in the brain) or a series of strokes, called *transient ischemic attacks* (TIAs, or ministrokes). The interruption in blood flow reduces oxygen, destroying part of the brain. Symptoms (blurred vision, weak or paralyzed limbs, slurred speech, and mental confusion) suddenly appear.

In a TIA, symptoms may vanish quickly, unnoticed. However, unless it is recognized and preventive action taken, another is likely. Repeated TIAs produce a type of NCD sometimes called **vascular dementia (VaD)**, or *multi-infarct dementia*. The progression of vascular disorder differs from Alzheimer disease, but the final result is similar (see Figure 24.5).

Neurocognitive disorders caused by vascular disease are apparent in many of the oldest-old worldwide. VaD is more common than Alzheimer disease for those over age 90 but not for the young-old. Vascular disorders correlate with the *ApoE4* allele (Cramer & Procaccio, 2012) and, for some of the elderly, are caused by surgery that requires general anesthesia. This may cause a ministroke, which, added to reduced cognitive reserve, damages the brain (Stern, 2013).

FIGURE 24.5

The Progression of Two NCDs: Alzheimer Disease and Vascular Dementia Cognitive decline is apparent in both Alzheimer disease (AD) and vascular dementia (VaD). However, the pattern of decline for each disease is different. Victims of AD show steady, gradual decline, while those who suffer from VaD get suddenly worse, improve somewhat, and then experience another serious loss.

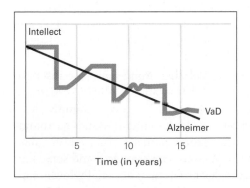

frontal lobe disorder Deterioration of the amygdala and frontal lobes, which may be the cause of 15 percent of all dementias. (Also called *frontotemporal lobar degeneration* and, in the DSM-5, *frontotemporal NCD*).

Frontal Lobe Disorders

Several types of neurocognitive disorders are called **frontal lobe disorders**, or *frontotemporal lobar degeneration* (Pick disease is the most common form). These disorders cause perhaps 15 percent of all cases of NCD in the United States. It is particularly likely to occur at relatively young ages (under age 70), unlike Alzheimer or vascular diseases, which typically begin later (Seelaar et al., 2011).

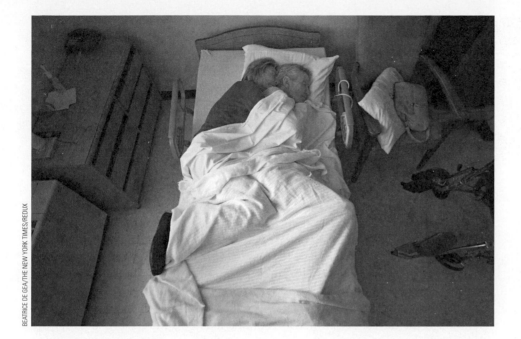

To Have and to Hold Ruth wanted to divorce Michael until she realized he suffered from frontal lobe disorder. Now she provides body warmth and comfort in his nursing home bed.

In frontal lobe disorders, parts of the brain that regulate emotions and social behavior (especially the amygdala and prefrontal cortex) deteriorate. Emotional and personality changes are the main symptoms (Seelaar et al., 2011). A loving mother with frontal lobe degeneration might reject her children, or a formerly astute businessman might invest in a harebrained scheme.

Frontal lobe problems may be worse than more obvious types of neurocognitive disease in that compassion, self-awareness, and judgment fade in a person who otherwise seems normal. One wife, Ruth French, was furious because her husband

> threw away tax documents, got a ticket for trying to pass an ambulance, and bought stock in companies that were obviously in trouble. Once a good cook, he burned every pot in the house. He became withdrawn and silent, and no longer spoke to his wife over dinner. That same failure to communicate got him fired from his job.

> *[Grady, 2012, p. A1]*

Finally, he was diagnosed with frontal lobe disorder. Ruth asked him to forgive her fury. It is not clear that he understood either her anger or her apology.

Although there are many forms and causes of frontal lobe disorders—including a dozen or so alleles—it usually progresses rapidly, leading to death in about five years.

Other Disorders

Many other brain diseases begin with impaired motor control (shaking when picking up a coffee cup, falling when trying to walk), not with impaired thinking. The most common of these is **Parkinson's disease**, the cause of about 3 percent of all cases of NCD (Aarsland et al., 2005).

Parkinson's disease starts with rigidity or tremor of the muscles as dopamine-producing neurons degenerate, affecting movement long before cognition. Younger adults with Parkinson's disease usually have sufficient cognitive reserve to avoid major intellectual loss, although about one-third have mild impairment (Gao et al., 2013). Older people with Parkinson's develop cognitive problems sooner (Pfeiffer, 2012). If people with Parkinson's live 10 years or more, major neurocognitive impairment almost always occurs (Pahwa & Lyons, 2013).

Parkinson's disease A chronic, progressive disease that is characterized by muscle tremor and rigidity, and sometimes dementia; caused by a reduction of dopamine production in the brain.

>> Response for Genetic Counselors
(from page 712): A general guideline for genetic counselors is to provide clients with whatever information they seek, but because of both the uncertainty of diagnosis and the devastation of Alzheimer disease, the *ApoE4* test is not available at present. This may change (as was the case with the test for HIV) if early methods of prevention and treatment become more effective.

Lewy bodies Deposits of a particular kind of protein in the brain that interfere with communication between neurons; Lewy bodies cause neurocognitive disorder.

Who Are You? Ralph Wenzel was a football guard for 7 years in the National Football League, a handsome catch for his wife, Eleanor, shown here. He lost his memory, did not recognize her, and died two years after this photo. His autopsied brain showed CTE, and Eleanor became an advocate for safer football.

Another 3 percent of people with NCD in the United States suffer from an excess of **Lewy bodies**: deposits of a particular kind of protein in their brains. Lewy bodies are also present in Parkinson's disease, but in Lewy body disorder they are more numerous and dispersed throughout the brain, interfering with communication between neurons. As a result, movement and cognition are both impacted. Motor effects are less severe than in Parkinson's disease and memory loss is not as dramatic as in Alzheimer disease (Bondi et al., 2009). The main Lewy body symptom is loss of inhibition: A person might gamble or become hypersexual.

Comorbidity is common with all these disorders. For instance, most people with Alzheimer disease also show signs of vascular impairment (Doraiswamy, 2012). Parkinson, Alzheimer, and Lewy body disorders can occur together: People who have all three experience more rapid and severe cognitive loss (Compta et al., 2011).

Some other types of NCD begin in middle age or even earlier, caused by Huntington disease, multiple sclerosis, a severe head injury, syphilis, AIDS, or bovine spongiform encephalitis (BSE, or mad cow disease). Repeated blows to the head, even without concussions, can cause chronic traumatic encephalopathy (CTE), which first causes memory loss and emotional changes (Voosen, 2013).

Although the rate of NCD increases dramatically with every decade after age 60, brain disease can occur at any age, as revealed by the autopsies of a number of young professional athletes. For them, prevention includes better helmets and fewer body blows. Already, tackling is avoided in professional (NFL) practices.

Changes like these have come too late for thousands of adults, including Derek Boogaard, a star National Hockey League enforcer, who died of a drug overdose at age 28. His autopsied brain showed traumatic brain injury, chronic traumatic encephalopathy.

For Boogaard, CTE may have been one cause of his drug addiction and would have become a major neurocognitive disorder if he had lived longer. Instead, NCD may have already occurred, undiagnosed. Another hockey player said of him, "His demeanor, his personality, it just left him. He didn't have a personality anymore" (John Scott, quoted in Branch, 2011, p. B13). Obviously, senility and senescence are not synonyms for neurocognitive disorder.

Preventing Impairment

Since aging increases the rate of cognitive impairment, slowing down senescence may postpone major NCD, and ameliorating mild losses may prevent worse ones. That may have occurred in the decreasing rates of major NCD documented in England (Matthews et al., 2013).

Epigenetic research is particularly likely to lead to better prevention, because "the brain contains an epigenetic 'hotspot' with a unique potential to not only better understand its most complex functions, but also to treat its most vicious diseases" (Gräff et al., 2011, p. 603). Genes are always influential. Some are expressed, affecting development, and some are latent unless circumstances change. The reasons are epigenetic: Factors beyond the genes are crucial (Issa, 2011; Skipper, 2011).

The most important nongenetic factor is exercise. Because brain plasticity is lifelong, exercise that improves blood circulation not only prevents cognitive loss but also builds capacity and repairs damage. The benefits of exercise have been repeatedly cited in this text. Now we simply emphasize that physical exercise—even more than good nutrition and mental exercise—prevents, postpones, and slows cognitive loss of all kinds (Erickson et al., 2012; Gregory et al., 2012; Lövdén et al., 2013).

(a)   (b)

Same Situation, Far Apart: Strong Legs, Long Life As this woman in a Brooklyn seniors center (a) and this man on a Greek beach (b) seem to realize, exercise that strengthens the legs is particularly beneficial for body, mind, and spirit in late adulthood.

Medication to prevent stroke also protects against neurocognitive disorders. In a Finnish study, half of a large group of older Finns were given drugs to reduce lipids in their system (primarily cholesterol). Years later, fewer of them had developed NCD than did a comparable group who were not given the drug (Solomon et al., 2010).

Avoiding specific pathogens is critical. For example, beef can be tested to ensure that it does not have BSE, condoms can protect against AIDS, syphilis can be cured with antibiotics. For most cognitive disorders, however, despite the efforts of thousands of scientists and millions of older people, no foolproof prevention or cure has been found. Avoiding toxins (lead, aluminum, copper, and pesticides) or adding supplements (hormones, aspirin, coffee, insulin, antioxidants, red wine, blueberries, and statins) have been tried as preventatives but have not proven effective in controlled, scientific research.

Thousands of scientists have sought to halt beta-amyloid production in the brain and have had some success in mice but not yet in humans. One current goal is to diagnose Alzheimer disease 10 or 15 years before the first outward signs appear, in order to prevent brain damage. That is one reason for the interest in mild neurocognitive disorders: They often (though not always) progress to major problems. If it were known why some mild losses do not lead to major ones, prevention might become found.

Among professionals, hope is replacing despair. Earlier diagnosis seems possible; many drug and lifestyle treatments are under review (Hampel et al., 2012; Lane et al., 2011). Hope comes from contemplating the success that has been achieved in combating other diseases. Heart attacks, for instance, were once the leading cause of death for middle-aged men. That is no longer the case.

As with heart disease, the first step in prevention and treatment of NCD is to improve overall health. High blood pressure, diabetes, arteriosclerosis, and emphysema all impair cognition, because they disrupt the flow of oxygen to the brain. Each type of neurocognitive disorder, each slowdown, and all chronic diseases interact, so progress in one area may reduce incidence and severity in another. A healthy diet, social interaction, and especially exercise decrease cognitive

(a)

(b)

Where to Live? People with major neuro-cognitive disorders cannot live alone. When 83-year-old Herb Winokar (a) developed Parkinson's and NCD, his daughter took him into her New Jersey home, with her husband, two children, an au pair, and two caregivers. Here Herb's 12-year-old grandson tries to calm him when he is agitated and wants to leave. When the Franciscan Sisters in Germany designed a home (b) for those with cognitive losses, they duplicated the layout and even the refrigerator of 50 years ago. Several dozen people (some of them volunteers) care for 27 residents. Here Nicole Gross talks with Magdalene Seufort, making Werner Tietz laugh.

impairment of every kind, affecting brain chemicals and encouraging improvement in other health habits.

Early, accurate diagnosis, years before obvious symptoms appear, leads to more effective treatment. Drugs do not cure NCD, but some slow progression. Sometimes surgery or stem cell therapy is beneficial. The U.S. Pentagon estimates that more than 200,000 U.S. soldiers who were in Iraq or Afghanistan suffered traumatic brain injury, predisposing them to major neurocognitive disorder before age 60 (Miller, 2012). Measures to remedy their brain damage may help the aged as well.

Reversible Neurocognitive Disorder?

Care improves when everyone knows that a disease is undermining intellectual capacity. Accurate diagnosis is even more crucial when memory problems do *not* arise from a neurocognitive disorder. Brain diseases destroy parts of the brain, but many older people are thought to be permanently "losing their minds," when a reversible condition is at fault.

Depression and Anxiety

The most common reversible condition that is mistaken for neurocognitive disorder is depression. Normally, older people tend to be quite happy; frequent sadness or anxiety is not normal. Ongoing, untreated depression increases the risk of dementia (Y. Gao et al., 2013).

Ironically, people with untreated anxiety or depression may exaggerate minor memory losses or refuse to talk. Quite the opposite reaction occurs with early Alzheimer disease, as victims are often surprised when they cannot answer questions, or with Lewy body or frontal lobe disorders, when people talk without thinking.

Specifics provide other clues. People with neurocognitive loss might forget what they just said, heard, or did because current brain activity is impaired, but they might repeatedly describe details of something that happened long ago. The opposite may be true for emotional disorders, when memory of the past is impaired but short-term memory is not.

Nutrition

Malnutrition and dehydration can also cause symptoms that may seem like brain disease. The aging digestive system is less efficient but needs more nutrients and fewer calories. This requires new habits, less fast food, and more grocery money (which many do not have).

Some elderly people deliberately drink less because they want to avoid frequent urination, yet adequate liquid in the body is needed for cell health. Since homeostasis slows with age, older people are less likely to recognize and remedy their hunger and thirst, and thus may inadvertently impair their cognition.

Beyond the need to drink water and eat vegetables, several specific vitamins have been suggested as decreasing the rate of dementia, including anti-oxidants (C, A, E) and vitamin B-12. High levels of homocysteine (from animal fat) seem to increase dementia (Perez et al., 2012; Whalley et al., 2013). Obviously, any food that increases the risk of heart disease also increases the risk of stroke and hence vascular disease. In addition, some prescribed drugs destroy certain nutrients, although specifics require more research (Jyrkkä, et al., 2012).

Indeed, well-controlled longitudinal research on the relationship between particular aspects of nutrition and NCD has not been done. It is known, however, that people who already suffer from NCD tend to forget to eat or choose unhealthy foods, and that hastens their mental deterioration. It is also known that alcohol abuse interferes with nutrition, directly (reducing eating and hydration) and indirectly (by destroying some vitamins).

Polypharmacy

At home as well as in the hospital, most elderly people take numerous drugs—not only prescribed medications, but also over-the-counter preparations and herbal remedies—a situation known as **polypharmacy** (Hajjar et al., 2007). Excessive reliance on drugs can occur on doctor's orders as well as patient ignorance.

Unfortunately, recommended doses of many drugs are determined primarily by clinical trials with younger adults, for whom homeostasis usually eliminates excess medication (Herrera et al., 2010). When homeostasis slows down, excess may linger. In addition, most trials to test safety of a new drug exclude people who have more than one disease. That means drugs are not tested on many of the elderly who will use them.

The average elderly person in the United States sees a physician eight times a year (Schiller et al., 2012). Typically, each doctor follows "clinical practice guidelines," which are recommendations for one specific condition. A "prescribing cascade" (when many interacting drugs are prescribed) may occur.

In one disturbing case, a doctor prescribed medication to raise his patient's blood pressure, and another doctor, noting the raised blood pressure, prescribed a drug to lower it (McLendon & Shelton, 2011–2012). Usually, doctors ask patients what medications they are taking and why, which could prevent such an error. However, people who are sick and confused may not give accurate responses.

Another problem is that people of every age forget when to take which drugs (before, during, or after meals? after dinner or at bedtime?), a problem multiplied as more drugs are prescribed (Bosworth & Ayotte, 2009). Short-term memory loss makes this worse.

Even when medications are taken as prescribed and the right dose reaches the bloodstream, drug interactions can cause confusion and memory loss. Cognitive side effects can occur with almost any drug, especially those drugs intended to reduce anxiety and depression. They often affect memory or reasoning.

Finally, following recommendations from the radio, friends, and television ads, many of the elderly try supplements, compounds, and herbal preparations that contain mind-altering toxins. Some of the elderly believe that only illegal drugs are harmful to the mind, which makes alcoholism and pill addiction harder to recognize in the elderly. For many reasons, polypharmacy can be dangerous, as the following describes.

polypharmacy Refers to a situation in which elderly people are prescribed several medications. The various side effects and interactions of those medications can result in dementia symptoms.

A CASE TO STUDY

Too Many Drugs or Too Few?

The case for medication is persuasive. Thousands of drugs have been proven effective, many of them responsible for longer and healthier lives. It is estimated that, on doctor's orders, 20 percent of older people take 10 or more drugs on a regular basis (Boyd et al., 2005). Common examples of life-saving drugs are insulin to halt the ravages of diabetes, statins to prevent strokes, and antidepressants to reduce despair.

In addition, many older people take supplements, drink alcohol, and swallow vitamins and other nonprescription drugs daily. The combination of doctor-ordered and self-administered drugs may lengthen life, but may do the opposite. For example,

A 70-year-old widow named Audrey was covered with large black bruises and burns from her kitchen stove. Audrey no longer had an appetite, so she ate little and was emaciated. One night she passed out in her driveway and scraped her face. The next morning, her neighbor found her face down on the pavement in her nightgown.

Audrey couldn't be trusted with the grandchildren anymore, so family visits were fewer and farther between. She rarely showered and spent most days sitting in a chair alternating between drinking, sleeping, and watching television. She stopped calling friends, and social invitations had long since ceased.

Audrey obtained prescriptions for Valium, a tranquilizer, and Placidyl, a sleep inducer. Both medications, which are addictive and have more adverse effects in patients over age 60, should only be used for short periods of time. Audrey had taken both medications for years at three to four times the prescribed dosage. She mixed them with large quantities of alcohol. She was a full-fledged addict . . . close to death.

Her children knew she had a problem, but they . . . couldn't agree among themselves on the best way to help her. Over time, they became desensitized to the seriousness of her problem—until it progressed to a dangerously advanced stage. Luckily for Audrey, she was referred to a new doctor who recognized her addiction. . . . Once Audrey was in treatment and weaned off the alcohol and drugs, she bloomed. Audrey's memory improved; her appetite returned; she regained her energy; and she started walking, swimming and exercising every day. Now, a decade later, Audrey plays an important role in her grandchildren's lives, gardens, and lives creatively and with meaning.

[Colleran & Jay, 2003, p. 11]

Audrey is a stunning example of the danger of ageist assumptions as well as of polypharmacy. Her children did not realize that she was capable of an intellectually and socially productive life.

The solution seems simple: Discontinue drugs. However, that may increase both disease and dementia. One expert warns of polypharmacy but adds that "underuse of medications in older adults can have comparable adverse effects on quality of life" (Miller, 2011–2012, p. 21).

For instance, untreated diabetes and hypertension cause cognitive loss. Lack of drug treatment for those conditions may be one reason why low-income elders experience more illness, more dementia, and earlier death than do high-income elders: They may not be able to afford good medical care or life-saving drugs.

Obviously, money complicates the issue: Prescription drugs are expensive, which increases profits for drug companies, but they can also reduce surgery and hospitalization, thus saving money. As one observer notes, the discussion about spending for prescription drugs is highly polarized, emotionally loaded, with little useful debate. A war is waged over the cost of prescriptions for older people, and it is a "gloves-off, stab-you-in-the-guts, struggle to the death" (Sloan, 2011–2012, p. 56).

Which is it—too many drugs or too few? Any general answer may be too glib, since specifics depend on the health and values of each patient as well as on caregivers—some who are antidrug and others who want drugs to control symptoms (e.g., insomnia, anger, sadness) that the patient might not want to medicate. Which is better: to be suspicious of every drug, herb, or supplement or to hope that medication will protect or restore health?

The current policy is to let the doctor and the patient decide. Even family members are not consulted or informed unless the patient agrees. That seems like a wise protection of privacy. But remember Audrey.

SUMMING UP

Many elderly people experience some cognitive impairment, which may lead to neurocognitive disorder (NCD), still often referred to as dementia. Among the many types of NCD, each with distinct symptoms, are four common diseases of the elderly: Alzheimer, vascular, frontal lobe, and Parkinson's. No cure for NCD has yet been found, but treatment may slow its progression and sometimes prevent its onset. The inclusion of minor NCD in the DSM-5 is in part intended to allow for very early identification, slowing of symptoms, and prevention. The best prevention and treatment is exercise, although drugs, nutrition, and other measures may also be helpful. The elderly are sometimes thought to suffer from NCD when in fact they have other problems, especially depression, alcoholism, malnutrition, or polypharmacy. ∎

>> New Cognitive Development

You have learned that most older adults maintain adequate intellectual power. Some losses—in rapid reactions, for instance—are quite manageable, and only a minority of elders suffer a major neurocognitive disorder. Beyond that, the life-span perspective holds that gains as well as losses occur during every period. [**Lifespan Link:** The multidirectional characteristic of development is discussed in Chapter 1.] Are there cognitive gains in late adulthood? Yes, according to many developmentalists. New depth, enhanced creativity, and even wisdom are possible.

Erikson and Maslow

Both Erik Erikson and Abraham Maslow were particularly interested in the elderly, interviewing older people to understand their views. Erikson's final book, *Vital Involvement in Old Age* (Erikson et al., 1986), written when he was in his 90s, was based on responses from other 90-year-olds—the cohort who had been studied since they were babies in Berkeley, California.

Erikson found that in old age many people gained interest in the arts, in children, and in human experience as a whole. He observed that elders are "social witnesses," aware of the interdependence of the generations as well as of all of human experience. His eighth stage, *integrity versus despair*, marks the time when life comes together in a "re-synthesis of all the resilience and strengths already developed" (Erikson et al., 1986, p. 40).

Maslow maintained that older adults are more likely than younger people to reach what he originally thought was the highest stage of development, **self-actualization**. Remember that Maslow rejected an age-based sequence of life, refusing to confine self-actualization to the old. However, Maslow also believed that life experience helps people move forward, so more of the old reach the final stage.

The stage of self-actualization is characterized by aesthetic, creative, philosophical, and spiritual understanding (Maslow, 1970). A self-actualized person might have a deeper spirituality than ever; might be especially appreciative of nature; or might find life more amusing, laughing often at himself or herself.

This seems characteristic of many of the elderly. As you read in Chapter 23, studies of centenarians find that they often have a deep spiritual grounding and a surprising sense of humor—surprising, that is, if one assumes that people with limited sight, poor hearing, and frequent pain have nothing to laugh about.

Learning Late in Life

Many people have tried to improve the intellectual abilities of older adults by teaching or training them in various tasks (Lustig et al., 2009; Stine-Morrow & Basak, 2011). Success has been reported in specific abilities. In one part of the Seattle Longitudinal Study, 60-year-olds who had lost some spatial understanding had five sessions of personalized training and practice. As a result, they returned to the skill level of 14 years earlier (Schaie, 2005).

Another group of researchers (Basak et al., 2008) targeted control processes. Volunteers with an average age of 69 and no signs of any cognitive disorder were

SEAN CAFFREY/LONELY PLANET IMAGES/GETTY IMAGES

Long Past Warring Many of the oldest men in Mali, like this Imam, are revered. Unfortunately, Mali has experienced violent civil wars and two national coups in recent years, perhaps because 75 percent of the male population are under age 30 and less than 2 percent are over age 70.

self-actualization The final stage in Maslow's hierarchy of needs, characterized by aesthetic, creative, philosophical, and spiritual understanding.

Excited Neurons As you see, this nursing home in New Mexico has a large, impersonal assembly room, where some residents sit in isolation. However, that deficit may be offset for others by the energetic Activities Director (Cyndi Bolen, left), who provided Wii Sports bowling on a wide screen. At least one of the oldest-old (Mildred Secrest, right) was thrilled when she got a spare.

divided into an experimental group and a control group. Everyone took a battery of cognitive tests to measure executive function. None were video-game players.

The experimental group was taught to play a video game that was preset to begin at the easiest level. After each round, they were told their score, and another round began—more challenging in pace and memory if the earlier one was too easy. The participants seemed to enjoy trying to raise their score. After 20 hours of game playing over several weeks, the cognitive tests were given again. Compared with the control group, the experimental group improved in mental activities that were *not* exactly the ones required by the video game.

Similar results have been found in many nations in which elders have been taught a specific skill. As a result, almost all researchers have accepted the conclusion that people younger than 80 can advance in cognition if the educational process is carefully targeted to their motivation and ability.

For instance, in one study in southern Europe people who were cognitively intact but were living in senior residences were taught memory strategies and attended motivational discussions to help them understand why and how memory was important for daily functioning. Their memory improved compared to a control group, and the improvements were still evident 6 months later (Vranica et al., 2013).

What about the oldest-old? Learning is more difficult for them, but it is still possible. The older people are, the harder it is for them to master new skills and then apply what they know (Stine-Morrow & Basak, 2011). Older adults sometimes learn cognitive strategies and skills and maintain that learning if the strategies and skills are frequently used, but they may quickly forget new learning if it is not applied (Park & Bischoff, 2013). They revert back to familiar, and often inferior, cognitive patterns.

Let's return to the question of cognitive gains in late adulthood. In many nations, education programs have been created for the old, called Universities

Screen to Brain Although elders are least likely to have Internet connection at home, they may be most likely to benefit from it. Video games may improve cognition in late adulthood. Even better may be videoconferencing with a grandchild, as shown here. Mental flexibility and family joy correlate with a long and happy life.

MONICA ALMEIDA/THE NEW YORK TIMES/REDUX

Alaska Learning Martha Wroe *(right)* of Gainesville, Florida is one of 14 seniors who travelled to Alaska on an Elderhostel excursion. "I wanted an adventure," she said. Adventures in late adulthood expand cognition.

Observation Quiz Which is more likely to advance Martha's thinking, the walrus tusk or Maryann Mendernhal *(left)*, who shot the animal? (see answer, page 722)

for the Third Age in Europe and Australia, and Exploritas (formerly Elderhostel) in the United States. Classes for seniors must take into account the range of needs and motivations: Some want intellectually challenging courses and others want practical skills (Villar & Celdrán, 2012). All the research finds that, when motivated, older adults can learn.

Aesthetic Sense and Creativity

Robert Butler was a geriatrician responsible for popularizing the study of aging in the United States. He coined the word *ageism*, and wrote a book, *Why Survive: Being Old in America*, first published in 1975. Partly because his grandparents were crucial in his life, Butler understood that society needs to recognize the potential of the elderly.

Butler explained that "old age can be a time of emotional sensory awareness and enjoyment" (Butler et al., 1998, p. 65). For example, some of the elderly take up gardening, bird watching, sculpting, painting, or making music, even if they have never done so before.

Elderly Artists

A well-known example of late creative development is Anna Moses, who was a farm wife in rural New York. For most of her life, she expressed her artistic impulses by stitching quilts and embroidering in winter, when farm work was slow. At age 75, arthritis made needlework impossible, so she took to "dabbling in oil."

Four years later, three of her paintings, displayed in a local drugstore, caught the eye of a New York City art dealer who happened to be driving through town. He bought them, drove to her house, and bought 15 more.

The following year, at age 80, "Grandma Moses" had a one-woman show, receiving international recognition for her unique "primitive" style. She continued to paint, and her work "developed and changed considerably over the course of her

PIERRE BESSARD/REA/REDUX

© RODRIGO TORRES/GLOWIMAGES/CORBIS

Exercise and the Mind Creative activity may improve the intellect, especially when it involves social activity. Both the woman in a French ceramics class *(top)*, subsidized by the government for residents of Grenoble over age 60, and the man playing the tuba in a band in Cuba *(bottom)* are gaining much more than the obvious finger or lung exercise.

History of My People When they were young they were imprisoned here, in a California internment camp for Japanese-Americans. They wanted to see it again, not only for their own life review, but also to put their experiences in context for the new generation.

>> **Answer to Observation Quiz** (from page 721): Most likely meeting a native grandmother, not holding the tusk, will prompt her thinking. Human relationships are particularly important for many older adults.

life review An examination of one's own life and one's role in the history of human life, engaged in by many elderly people.

twenty-year career" (Cardinal, 2001). Anna Moses died at age 101.

Other well-known artists continue to work in late adulthood, sometimes producing their best work. Michelangelo painted the awe-inspiring frescoes in the Sistine Chapel at age 75; Verdi composed the opera *Falstaff* when he was 80; Frank Lloyd Wright completed the design of New York City's Guggenheim Museum when he was 91.

In a study of extraordinarily creative people, almost none felt that their ability, their goals, or the quality of their work had been much impaired by age. The leader of that study observed, "In their seventies, eighties, and nineties, they may lack the fiery ambition of earlier years, but they are just as focused, efficient, and committed as before . . . perhaps more so" (Csikszentmihalyi, 1996, p. 503).

But an older artist does not need to be extraordinarily talented. Some of the elderly learn to play an instrument, and many enjoy singing. In China people gather spontaneously in public parks to sing together. The groups are intergenerational—but a disproportionate number are elderly (Wei, 2013).

Music and singing are often used to reduce anxiety in those who suffer from neurocognitive impairment, because the ability to appreciate music is preserved in the brain when other functions fail (Ueda et al., 2013). Many experts believe that creative activities—poetry and pottery, jewelry making and quilting, music and sculpture—benefit all the elderly (Flood & Phillips, 2007; Malchodi, 2012). Artistic expression may aid social skills, resilience, and even brain health (McFadden & Basting, 2010).

The Life Review

In the **life review**, elders provide an account of their personal journey by writing or telling their story. They want others to know their history, not only their personal experiences but also those of their family, cohort, or ethnic group. According to Robert Butler:

> We have been taught that this nostalgia represents living in the past and a preoccupation with self and that it is generally boring, meaningless, and time-consuming. Yet as a natural healing process it represents one of the underlying human capacities on which all psychotherapy depends. The life review should be recognized as a necessary and healthy process in daily life as well as a useful tool in the mental health care of older people.
>
> *[R. N. Butler et al., 1998, p. 91]*

Hundreds of developmentalists, picking up on Butler's suggestions, have guided elderly people in self-review. Sometimes the elderly write down their thoughts, and sometimes they simply tell their story, responding to questions from the listener.

The result of the life review is almost always quite positive, especially for the person who tells the story. For instance, of 202 elderly people in the Netherlands, half were randomly assigned to a life review process. For them, depression and anxiety were markedly reduced compared to the control group (Korte et al., 2013).

Wise or Foolish? His family (in the background) is likely to think grandfather is wise, but he probably just enjoys zipping on this home-made wire.

Wisdom

It is possible that "older adults . . . understand who they are in a newly emerging stage of life, discovering the wisdom that they have to offer" (Bateson, 2011, p. 9). A massive international survey of 26 nations from every corner of the world found that most people everywhere agree that wisdom is a characteristic of the elderly (Löckenhoff et al., 2009).

Contrary to these wishes and opinions, most objective research finds that wisdom does not necessarily increase with age. Starting at age 25 or so, some adults of every age are wise, but most, even at age 80, are not (Staudinger & Glück, 2011).

An underlying research quandary is that a universal definition of wisdom is elusive: Each culture and each cohort has its own concept, with fools sometimes seeming wise (as happens in some of Shakespeare's plays) and those who are supposed to be wise sometimes acting foolishly (provide your own examples). Older and younger adults differ in how they make decisions; one interpretation of these differences is that the older adults are wiser, but not every younger adult would agree (Worthy et al., 2011).

One summary describes wisdom as an "expert knowledge system dealing with the conduct and understanding of life" (P. B. Baltes & Smith, 2008, p. 58). Several factors just mentioned, including self-reflective honesty (as in integrity), perspective on past living (the life review), and the ability to put aside one's personal needs (as in self-actualization), are considered part of wisdom.

If this is true, the elderly may have an advantage in developing wisdom, particularly if they have: (1) dedicated their lives to the "understanding of life," (2) learned from their experiences, and (3) become more mature and integrated (Ardelt, 2011, p. 283). That may be why popes and Supreme Court judges are usually quite old.

As two psychologists explain:

> Wisdom is one domain in which some older individuals excel. . . . [They have] a combination of psychosocial characteristics and life history factors, including openness to experience, generativity, cognitive style, contact with excellent mentors, and some exposure to structured and critical life experiences.

[P. B. Baltes & Smith, 2008, p. 60]

These researchers posed life dilemmas to adults of various ages and asked others (who had no clue as to how old the participants were) to judge whether the responses were wise. They found that wisdom is rare at any age, but, unlike physical strength and cognitive quickness, wisdom does not fade with maturity. Thus, some people of every age were judged as wise.

Similarly, the author of a detailed longitudinal study of 814 people concludes that wisdom is not reserved for the old, and yet humor, perspective, and altruism increase over the decades, gradually making people wiser. He then wrote:

> To be wise about wisdom we need to accept that wisdom does—and wisdom does not—increase with age. . . . Winston Churchill, that master of wise simplicity and simple wisdom, reminds us, "We are all happier in many ways when we are old than when we are young. The young sow wild oats. The old grow sage."
>
> *[Vaillant, 2002, p. 256]*

SUMMING UP

Many older adults continue to learn and grow, and studies have shown that training can reverse cognitive losses. On balance, mental processes are adaptive and creative, as people seek integrity and self-actualization. Some famous artists are more creative and passionate about their work in later adulthood than they were in younger years. Many other people, who were not particularly gifted artistically, develop a strong aesthetic sense as well as an appreciation of music in old age. Another development common in old age is the life review, when elders tell their life story, which may inspire both teller and listener. Although many people believe that the old are wise, wisdom does not seem reserved for the old, nor are all older people wise. Nonetheless, many are insightful, creative, and reflective, using their life experience wisely. ∎

Neurocognitive Disorders in Late Adulthood

While neurocognitive disorders like Alzheimer disease are common in later adulthood, they aren't an inevitable part of aging. But these diseases are now the biggest cause of disability in developed countries and are growing in prevalence around the world. The different types of neurocognitive disorders differ in their biological origins (some are strongly genetic, like Huntington's disease; others, like Parkinson's disease, may have environmental risk factors) and in their underlying brain pathology. Common types of neurocognitive disorder include Alzheimer disease, NCD with Lewy bodies (which may cause up to 30 percent of NCDs in older adults), vascular neurocognitive disorder (cognitive loss caused by a cerebrovascular event such as a stroke, vascular disease), Parkinson's disease, and Huntington's disease.

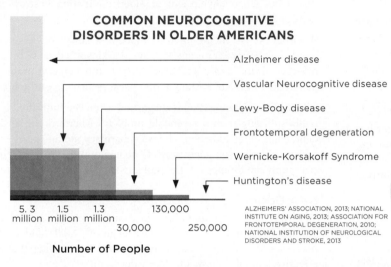

COMMON NEUROCOGNITIVE DISORDERS IN OLDER AMERICANS

— Alzheimer disease
— Vascular Neurocognitive disease
— Lewy-Body disease
— Frontotemporal degeneration
— Wernicke-Korsakoff Syndrome
— Huntington's disease

5. 3 million   1.5 million   1.3 million   130,000   30,000   250,000

Number of People

ALZHEIMERS' ASSOCIATION, 2013; NATIONAL INSTITUTE ON AGING, 2013; ASSOCIATION FOR FRONTOTEMPORAL DEGENERATION, 2010; NATIONAL INSTITUTION OF NEUROLOGICAL DISORDERS AND STROKE, 2013

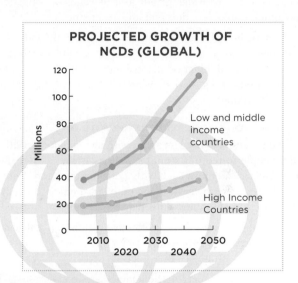

PROJECTED GROWTH OF NCDs (GLOBAL)

Millions

120
100
80
60
40
20
0

Low and middle income countries

High Income Countries

2010   2020   2030   2040   2050

DISTRIBUTION OF NEUROCOGNITIVE DISORDERS

More than 8% of people over 60
6-7% of people over 60
5-6% of people over 60
4-5% of people over 60
Fewer than 4% of people over 60

SOURCE: WHO, 2012

SOURCE: WHO, 2012

MAJOR NEUROCOGNITIVE DISORDERS INCREASE AS ADULTS AGE, UNITED STATES

The numbers of people with neurocognitive disorders rises as adults age, and the rates become particularly pronounced over age 85.

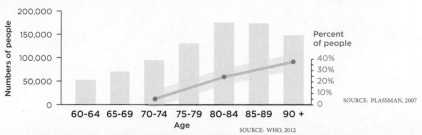

Numbers of people

200,000
150,000
100,000
50,000
0

Percent of people

40%
30%
20%
10%
0

60-64   65-69   70-74   75-79   80-84   85-89   90 +
Age

SOURCE: PLASSMAN, 2007

SOURCE: WHO, 2012

SUMMARY

The Aging Brain

1. The human brain continues to add new cells and to grow new dendrites as people age, but it also becomes smaller and slower. The effects of senescence are apparent not only in motor skills (such as speed of walking) but also in cognitive skills (such as how quickly an older adult remembers a name).

2. Remarkable plasticity is also apparent, with wide variation from person to person in the rate and specifics of brain slow-down. In general, older adults use more of their brains, not less, to do various tasks, and they prefer doing one task at a time, not multitasking.

Information Processing after Age 65

3. The senses become less acute with age, making it difficult for older people to register stimuli. Memory is slower, but there are many types of memory, each with a distinct trajectory. Source and prospective memory are less accurate but memory for semantics, emotions, and automatic skills may be strong.

4. Control processes are less effective with age, as retrieval strategies become less efficient. Anxiety may prevent older people from using the strategies they need.

5. In daily life, most of the elderly are not seriously handicapped by cognitive difficulties. The need for ecologically valid, real-life measures of cognition is increasingly apparent to developmental scientists.

Neurocognitive Disorders

6. Neurocognitive disorders (NCD), formerly (and now informally) called *dementia*, are characterized by cognitive loss—at first minor lapses, then more serious impairments, and finally major losses. Even recognition of family members, or remembering how to eat or talk, may fade.

7. The most common cause of cognitive loss among the elderly in the United States is Alzheimer disease, an incurable ailment that worsens over time, as plaques and tangles increase.

8. Vascular disorders (also called multi-infarct dementia) result from a series of ministrokes (transient ischemic attacks, or TIAs) that occur when impairment of blood circulation destroys portions of brain tissue.

9. Other NCDs, including frontal lobe and Lewy body disorders, also become more common with age. Parkinson's disease reduces muscle control, and it can also cause neurocognitive problems, particularly in the old. Many other diseases also affect the brain.

10. NCD may be mistakenly diagnosed when the individual is actually suffering from a reversible problem. Malnutrition, anxiety, depression, drug addiction, and polypharmacy are among the reasons an older person might seem to be cognitively impaired. These symptoms can disappear if the problem is recognized and treated.

New Cognitive Development

11. Older adults can and often do continue to learn as they age. Training and practice can increase cognitive skills and control processes in the aged. Surprising to some is the fact that one effective kind of training involves video games.

12. Many people become more interested and adept in creative endeavors, as well as more philosophical, as they grow older. The life review is a personal reflection that many older people undertake, remembering earlier experiences, putting their entire lives into perspective, and achieving integrity or self-actualization.

13. Wisdom does not necessarily increase as a result of age, but some elderly people are unusually wise or insightful. Learning from experience can occur at any age, but the old have an advantage in that they have had many experiences.

KEY TERMS

Alzheimer disease (AD) (p. 711)
ecological validity (p. 707)
frontal lobe disorder (p. 712)
Lewy bodies (p. 714)

life review (p. 722)
neurocognitive disorders (NCDs) (p. 709)

Parkinson's disease (p. 713)
plaques (p. 711)
polypharmacy (p. 717)

self-actualization (p. 719)
tangles (p. 711)
vascular dementia (VaD) (p. 712)

WHAT HAVE YOU LEARNED?

1. What aspects of the brain slow down with age?

2. Why must the elderly use more parts of their brains simultaneously?

3. Why is multitasking particularly difficult in late adulthood?

4. How does sensory loss affect cognition?

5. Which kinds of things are harder to remember with age?

6. Why do some elderly people resist learning strategies for memory retrieval?

7. Why is ecological validity especially important for prospective memory?

8. What diseases or conditions correlate with loss of cognition?

9. In what specific ways does exercise affect the brain?

10. How and why does training in cognitive skills help the elderly?

11. Why has the language surrounding neurocognitive disorder changed in recent years?

12. What proof is there that Alzheimer disease is partly genetic?

13. Why are most people unaware of the early stages of vascular NCD?

14. In what ways is frontal lobe dementia worse than Alzheimer disease?

15. If a person has Parkinson disease, what effect does that person's age have on the effects of the disorder?

16. Why is Lewy body dementia sometimes mistaken for Parkinson's disease?

17. How successful are scientists at preventing dementia?

18. How can older people help to improve their own cognitive abilities?

19. Why might older people become more creative, musical, and spiritual than they previously were?

20. Why do scientists hesitate to say that wisdom comes with age?

APPLICATIONS

1. At all ages, memory is selective. People forget much more than they remember. Choose someone—a sibling, a former classmate, or a current friend—who went through some public event that you did. Sit down together, write separate lists of all the details each of you remembers about the event, and then compare your accounts. What insight does this exercise give you into the kinds of things adults remember and forget?

2. Many factors affect intellectual sharpness. Think of an occasion when you felt stupid and an occasion when you felt smart. How did the contexts of the two experiences differ? How might those differences affect the performance of elderly and young adults who go to a university laboratory for testing?

3. Visit someone in a hospital. Note all the elements in the environment—such as noise, lights, schedules, and personnel—that might cause an elderly patient to feel confused.

>>ONLINE CONNECTIONS

To accompany your textbook, you have access to a number of online resources, including Learning Curve, an adaptive quizzing program, critical thinking questions, and case studies. For access to any of these links, go to www.worth publishers.com/launchpad/bergerls9e. In addition to these resources, you'll also find links to video clips, personalized study advice, and an ebook. Some of the videos and activities available online include:

- *Alzheimer Disease.* Outlines the progressive course of Alzheimer disease, as well as the types and limits of treatments. Includes video about the effects of chronic stress on caregivers.

WORTH PUBLISHERS

Late Adulthood

- **Theories of Late Adulthood**
  Self Theories
  OPPOSING PERSPECTIVES: Too Sweet or Too Sad?
  Stratification Theories

- **Activities in Late Adulthood**
  Working
  Retirement
  Home Sweet Home
  Religious Involvement
  Political Activism

- **Friends and Relatives**
  Long-Term Partnerships
  Relationships with Younger Generations
  Friendship

- **The Frail Elderly**
  Activities of Daily Life
  A CASE TO STUDY: Preventing Frailty
  Caring for the Frail Elderly

WHAT WILL YOU KNOW?

1. Do older people become more pessimistic or optimistic as time goes by?
2. Do most elderly people want to move to a distant, warm place?
3. What do adult children owe their elderly parents?
4. Is home care better than nursing home care?

Almost every week I walk with Doris, a widow in her 80s, to a meeting we both attend. The walk is short, through a park. On the way, she greets several people of all backgrounds, including a few homeless men and a woman who owns the nearby hotel. One person she often greets is Colin, who plays his piano (on wheels) in the park on sunny days. A year ago, the park police ticketed him for not having a permit.

Doris organized a protest. The ticket was withdrawn and Community Board 2 (she is the oldest member, reappointed every two years) passed a resolution about free speech. The Parks Department amended its guidelines.

Babies and animals love her, according to Doris. She may be right: Squirrels scamper up to grab peanuts from her hand, and sometimes pigeons perch on her arm. She dresses well, appropriately for the season, but one August day she wore a long-sleeved blouse. She proudly told me the reason: Her arm was scratched because two pigeons fought over the same spot.

Often we stop at the mailbox for her to mail a timely greeting card: She corresponds with hundreds. I have become one of them. Colorful envelopes arrive in my box—green for St. Patrick's Day, orange for Halloween, gray for Thanksgiving, festooned with stickers for Christmas, July 4th, my birthday, and more.

Usually friends have much in common, but Doris and I are not alike. I never send cards, feed squirrels, or protect pianists (although Doris did get me to help Colin). We are members of opposing political parties. She has no children; I have four.

How did we become friends? Five years ago, Doris had knee surgery and needed volunteers to wheel her to her many meetings, appointments, and social engagements. Dozens of people offered their services, including me—for the weekly event we both attend. Soon she became capable of walking alone, but we have walked together ever since. I have come to enjoy her anecdotes, her outgoing nature, her attitudes.

Recently Doris broke her hip. The rehab soon gave her a private room because her younger roommate complained that Doris had too many visitors at all times of the day. They came because they like her, not because they agree with her. She often is the only dissenting vote on Community Board resolutions.

Back at home, Doris continues to be active, social, and appreciated by many. Her life defies stereotyping, which makes her an illustration of the theme of this chapter: the variability and complexity of development in later life. Some of the elderly are frail, lonely, and vulnerable to abuse because of private circumstances

Not a Puppet One park regular is a puppeteer, Ricky Syers, who entertains hundreds of tourists with an array of puppets. He recently made one of Doris, one more bit of evidence that the real Doris is beloved by many—and not controlled by anyone.

and public failures. For most, however, psychosocial development includes working and socializing, concern for others as well as self-care. Doris does all this admirably. I hope to be like her someday.

>> Theories of Late Adulthood

Development in late adulthood may be more diverse than at any other age: Some elderly people run marathons and lead nations; others no longer walk or talk. Social scientists theorize about these variations.

Self Theories

self theories Theories of late adulthood that emphasize the core self, or the search to maintain one's integrity and identity.

Some theories of late adulthood are **self theories**; they focus on individuals' self-concepts and their response to challenges to their identity. The awareness of one's self begins, as you remember, before age 2, and it builds throughout childhood and adolescence. In those early decades, self image is greatly affected by physical appearance and by other people's perceptions (Harter & Bukowski, 2012), both of which become less crucial with age.

The Self and Aging

Perhaps people become more truly themselves as they grow old, as Anna Quindlen found:

> It's odd when I think of the arc of my life from child to young woman to aging adult. First I was who I was, then I didn't know who I was, then I invented someone and became her, then I began to like what I'd invented, and finally I was what I was again. It turned out I wasn't alone in that particular progression.
>
> *[Quindlen, 2012, ix]*

integrity versus despair The final stage of Erik Erikson's developmental sequence, in which older adults seek to integrate their unique experiences with their vision of community.

Older adults need to maintain their self-concept despite all the changes of senescence, as appearance and social status are altered in ways that might undercut self-esteem. In late adulthood, the "creation and maintenance of identity is a key aspect of healthy living" (Resnick, 2011, p. 10). Even the oldest-old and those who suffer from neurocognitive disorders preserve their sense of self, although memory, ability, and health fade (Klein, 2012).

A central idea of self theories is that each person ultimately depends on himself or herself. As one woman explained:

> I actually think I value my sense of self more importantly than my family or relationships or health or wealth or wisdom. I do see myself as on my own, ultimately. . . . Statistics certainly show that older women are likely to end up being alone, so I really do value my own self when it comes right down to things in the end.
>
> *[quoted in J. Kroger, 2007, p. 203]*

Integrity

The most comprehensive self theory came from Erik Erikson. His eighth and final stage of development, **integrity versus despair**, occurs when adults seek to integrate their unique experiences with their vision of community (Erikson et al., 1986). The word *integrity* is often used to mean honesty, but it also means a feeling of being whole, not scattered, comfortable with oneself.

As an example of integrity, many older people are proud of their personal history. They glorify their past, even when it includes events such as skipping school, taking drugs, escaping arrest, or being physically abused. Psychologists sometimes call

Always a Mother In this photo, in Nepal, a volunteer gives food to an elderly woman in an Aama Ghar, a home for elderly mothers. Is such an institution an example of self theory (identity as mother endures decades after children are independent) or stratification theory (older people segregated from ordinary life)?

this the "sucker to saint" *phenomenon*—that is, people interpret their experiences as signs of their nobility (saintly), not their stupidity (Jordan & Monin, 2008).

As Erikson explains it, such self-glorifying distortions are far better than despair because "time is now short, too short for the attempt to start another life" (Erikson, 1963, p. 269). As at other stages, the tension between the two opposing aspects (integrity and despair) propels growth. In this last stage,

> life brings many, quite realistic reasons for experiencing despair: aspects of the present that cause unremitting pain; aspects of a future that are uncertain and frightening. And, of course, there remains inescapable death, that one aspect of the future which is both wholly certain and wholly unknowable. Thus, some despair must be acknowledged and integrated as a component of old age.
>
> *[Erikson et al., 1986, p. 72]*

Integration of death and the self is an important accomplishment of this stage. The life review and the acceptance of death (explained in the Epilogue) are crucial aspects of the integrity envisioned by Erikson (Zimmerman, 2012). **[Lifespan Link:** The life review was discussed in Chapter 24.]

Self theory may explain why many of the elderly strive to maintain childhood cultural and religious practices. For instance, grandparents may painstakingly teach a grandchild a language that is rarely used in their current community, or encourage the child to repeat rituals and prayers they themselves learned as children. In cultures that emphasize newness, elders worry that their values will be lost and thus that they themselves will disappear.

As Erikson (1963) wrote, the older person

> knows that an individual life is the accidental coincidence of but one life cycle with but one segment of history and that for him all human integrity stands or falls with the one style of integrity of which he partakes. . . . In such a final consolation, death loses its sting.
>
> *[Erikson, p. 268]*

Holding On to the Self

Most older people consider their personalities and attitudes quite stable over their life span, even as they acknowledge physical changes in their bodies and gaps in their minds (Klein, 2012). One 103-year-old woman observed, "My core has stayed the same. Everything else has changed" (quoted in Troll & Skaff, 1997, p. 166).

The need to maintain the self may explain behavior that seems foolish to some. For example, many elders hate to give up driving a car because "the loss felt, for men in particular, is deeper than that of simply not being able to get from A to B; it is a loss of a sense of self, of the meaning of manhood" (Davidson, 2008, p. 46).

Similarly, many older people refuse to move from drafty and dangerous dwellings into smaller, safer apartments because abandoning familiar places means abandoning personal history. Likewise, they may avoid surgery or reject medicine because they fear anything that might distort their thinking or emotions: Their priority is self-protection, even if it shortens life (S. W. Miller, 2011–2012).

The insistence on protecting the self may explain a behavior that many find pathological: **compulsive hoarding**, the urge to save papers, books, mementos, and so on. In a new chapter titled "Obsessive-Compulsive and Related Disorders," the DSM-5 now specifies criteria for a diagnosis of *hoarding disorder* (DSM-5, pp. 247–251). Most elderly hoarders saved things when they were much younger and want to keep doing so. With time, hoarding takes over all available space: Things accumulate because possessions are part of self-expression, and the elderly resist self-destruction (Ayers et al., 2010).

compulsive hoarding The urge to accumulate and hold on to familiar objects and possessions, sometimes to the point of their becoming health and/or safety hazards. This impulse tends to increase with age.

Trash or Treasure? Tryphona Flood, threatened with eviction, admitted she's a hoarder and got help from Megan Tolen, shown here discussing what in this four-room apartment can be discarded. Flood sits on the only spot of her bed that is not covered with stuff. This photo was taken midway through a three-year effort to clean out the apartment—the clutter was worse a year earlier.

Socioemotional Selectivity Theory

socioemotional selectivity theory The theory that older people prioritize regulation of their own emotions and seek familiar social contacts who reinforce generativity, pride, and joy.

Another self theory is **socioemotional selectivity theory** (Carstensen, 1993). The idea is that older people prioritize their emotional regulation, seeking familiar social contacts who reinforce their generativity, pride, and joy. As socioemotional theory would predict, when people believe that their future time is limited, they think about the meaning of their life. Then they decide that they should be more appreciative of family and friends, thus furthering their happiness (Hicks et al., 2012).

A slightly different version of the same idea comes from *selective optimization with compensation,* which you read about in Chapters 21 and 23. As senescence changes external appearance, older adults select the key aspects of themselves and optimize them. This is central to self-theories. Individuals set personal goals, assess their abilities, and figure out how to accomplish their goals despite limitations. When older people are resilient, they maintain their identity despite wrinkles, slowdowns, and losses. That correlates with well-being (Resnick et al., 2010).

positivity effect The tendency for elderly people to perceive, prefer, and remember positive images and experiences more than negative ones.

An outgrowth of both socioemotional selectivity and selective optimization is known as the **positivity effect** (Penningroth & Scott, 2012). Elderly people are more likely to perceive, prefer, and remember positive images and experiences than negative ones (Carstensen et al., 2006). Compensation occurs via selective recall: Unpleasant experiences are reinterpreted as inconsequential. People select positive emotions, perceptions, and memories.

For example, with age, stressful events (economic loss, serious illness, death of friends or relatives) become less central to one's identity. That enables the elderly to maintain emotional health through positive self-perception (Boals et al., 2012). A person becomes more optimistic than pessimistic and is happier because of it.

The positivity effect may explain why, in every nation and religion, older people tend to be more patriotic and devout than younger ones. They see their national history and religious beliefs in positive terms, and they are proud to be themselves—Canadian, Czech, Chinese, or whatever. Of course, this same trait can keep them mired in their earlier prejudices—racist, or sexist, or homophobic, for instance.

Anna Quindlen was quoted just a few pages ago as saying she was glad she "was what I was again." This trait has both positive and negative implications, as the following suggests.

OPPOSING PERSPECTIVES

Too Sweet or Too Sad?

When I was young, I liked movies that were gritty, dramatic, violent. My mother criticized my choices; I told her I wanted reality. She liked romantic comedies that made her laugh; I told her that was frivolous.

Now my youngest daughter wants me to read dystopian novels in order to be aware of current culture. *Hunger Games* is an example. I tell her there is enough poverty and conflict in the world without having to read about imaginary killings. Notice the developmental shift. Is the positivity effect a distortion or a welcome perspective?

Many researchers have found that a positive worldview increases with age and that it correlates with believing that life is meaningful. Those elders who are happy, not frustrated or depressed, are likely to agree strongly that their life has a purpose (e.g., "I have a system of values that guides my daily activities" and "I am at peace with my past") (Hicks et al., 2012). Meaningfulness and positivity correlate with a long and healthy life.

When a gamble doesn't succeed, does frustration interfere with your judgment? If you are an emerging adult, the answer is often yes, but not if you are an older adult. The elderly are quicker to let go of disappointments, thinking positively about going forward. As a result, many studies have found "an increase in emotional well-being from middle age onward, whereas the experience of anger declines" (Brassen et al., 2012, p. 614).

Researchers have measured reactions to disappointment, not only in attitudes and actions, but also in brain activity and heart rate. One study compared three groups: young adults, healthy older adults, and older adults with late-life depression. The brains, bodies, and behavior of the depressed elders were more like those of the younger adults, but brain scans as well as behavior showed that the healthy older adults were able to move past disappointment. The conclusion: "emotionally healthy aging is associated with a reduced responsiveness to regretful events" (Brassen et al., 2012, p. 614) (see Figure 25.1).

In another study, adults of several ages were asked to recall recent examples of personal confrontation and then to explain what they did, why, and how they felt later (Sorkin & Rook, 2006). Of those who were over age 65, many (39 percent) could not think of any confrontation. Among those who remembered conflicts, most of the elders, but not the younger participants, said that their primary goal was to maintain goodwill. Only a few of those over age 65 sought to change the other person's behavior (see Figure 25.2).

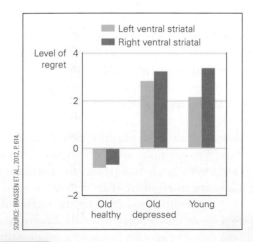

SOURCE: BRASSEN ET AL., 2012, P. 614.

FIGURE 25.1

Let Bygones Be Bygones Areas of the brain (the ventral striatal) are activated when a person feels regret. In this experiment, brain activation correlated with past loss and then unwise choices, with participants repeating behavior that had just failed. Older adults were usually wiser, evident in brain activation as well as actions. However, elders who had been diagnosed as depressed seemed to dwell on past losses. The positivity effect had passed them by.

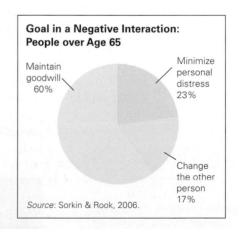

FIGURE 25.2

Keep the Peace When someone does something mean or unpleasant, what is your goal in your interaction with that person? If your goal is to maintain goodwill, as was the case for a majority of studies on older adults, you are likely to be quicker to forgive and forget.

Since their goal was to achieve harmony, the elderly were more likely to compromise instead of insisting that they were correct. This led to a happier outcome.

Participants whose primary coping goal was to preserve goodwill reported the highest levels of perceived success and the least intense and shortest duration of distress. In contrast, participants whose . . . goal was to change the other person reported the lowest levels of perceived success and the most intense and longest lasting distress.

[Sorkin & Rook, 2006, p. 723]

It could be argued that anger and frustration are useful emotions and that the positivity effect is too rosy, ignoring reality. It is distressing to try to change other people, but that doesn't mean that people should accept whatever disturbs them. My daughter recently apologized for a criticism she had of me. I replied, honestly, that I had forgotten her critique.. My response might have made her frustrated. The positivity effect is not always appreciated.

However, having a positive outlook not only makes a person happier, but it also might avoid "lasting distress." Was my mother right?

IMAGINECHINA/AP IMAGES

Twice Fortunate Ageism takes many forms. Some cultures are youth-oriented, devaluing the old, while others are the opposite. These twin sisters are lucky to be alive: They were born in rural China in 1905, a period when most female twins died. When this photo was taken, they were age 103, and fortunate again, venerated because they have lived so long.

stratification theories Theories that emphasize that social forces, particularly those related to a person's social stratum or social category, limit individual choices and affect a person's ability to function in late adulthood because past stratification continues to limit life in various ways.

Stratification Theories

A second set of theories, called **stratification theories**, emphasizes social forces (1) that position each person in a social stratum or level and (2) that create disadvantages for people in some groups and advantages for people in other groups. Stratification begins in the womb, as "individuals are born into a society that is already stratified—that is differentiated—along key dimensions, including sex, race, and SES" (Lynch & Brown, 2011, p. 107).

Stratification by Gender, Ethnicity, and SES

Every form of stereotyping makes it more difficult for people to break free from social institutions that assign them to a particular path. The results are cumulative, over the entire life span (Brandt et al., 2012).

For instance, as described in many of the preceding chapters, children who are both African American and poor are more likely to be low birthweight, less likely to talk at age 1, less likely to read before age 6, more likely to drop out of school, less likely to obtain a college degree, less likely to be employed, less likely to marry, and finally, more likely to develop cancer, diabetes, and all other serious health problems. This is true when a child is compared to children of other ethnic groups, and when compared to other African American children who are not poor (see Figure 25.3).

Each stereotype adds to stratification and thus adds to the risk of problems, perhaps putting those who are female, nonwhite, and poor in triple jeopardy. However, you will see at the end of this section that not everyone agrees with that conclusion (Rosenfeld, 2012).

First consider gender. Irrational, gender-based fear may limit female independence from infancy to old age. For example, adult children are more likely to persuade their widowed mothers to live with them than their widowed fathers. In fact, however, men living alone are more likely than women to have a sudden health crisis or to be the victim of a violent crime (5 percent versus 2 percent).

STUART FREEDMAN/IN PICTURES/CORBIS

Twice-Abandoned Widows Traditionally in India, widows walked into the funeral pyre that cremated their husband's body, a suicide called sati. If they hesitated, his relatives would sometimes push. Currently, sati is outlawed, but many Indian widows experience a social death: They are forbidden to meet men and remarry, except sometimes to the dead man's brother. Hundreds go to the sacred city of Vrindavan, where they are paid a pittance to chant prayers all day, as this woman does.

In another example of gender stratification, young women typically marry men a few years older and then outlive them. Especially in former years, many married women relied on their husbands to manage money and to keep up with politics. Thus, past gender stratification led to decades of isolation, poverty, and dependence among the oldest-old widows.

Why do women outlive men? This could be biological, but it could result from lifelong

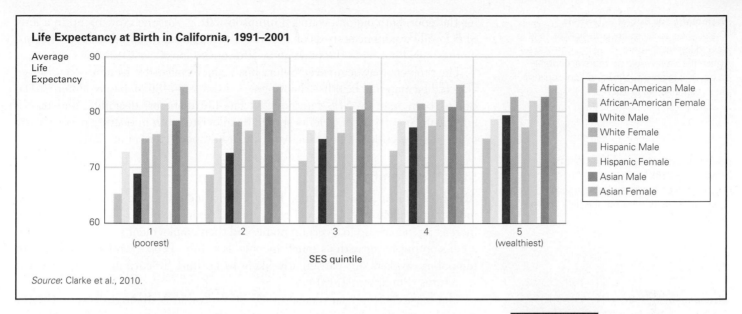

Life Expectancy at Birth in California, 1991–2001

Legend:
- African-American Male
- African-American Female
- White Male
- White Female
- Hispanic Male
- Hispanic Female
- Asian Male
- Asian Female

X-axis: SES quintile — 1 (poorest) to 5 (wealthiest)
Y-axis: Average Life Expectancy — 60 to 90

Source: Clarke et al., 2010.

FIGURE 25.3

Gender, Ethnicity, and SES These life-expectancy data provide obvious evidence for ethnic and income stratification, but sex differences are more puzzling. One possibility is that stratification by sex favors women. However, older women are more often disabled and are poorer than men the same age, which supports the original triple jeopardy concept.

Observation Quiz Which group's life span is most affected by poverty, and which is least affected? (see answer, page 736)

stratification that works against males. Boys are taught to be stoic, repressing emotions and avoiding medical attention. In this way, both sexes may suffer from gender stratification, the men by dying too soon and the women by being widowed too long.

Ethnic stratification also harms people. For instance, past racism may cause weathering in African Americans, increasing allostatic load and shortening healthy life (Thrasher et al., 2012). The fact that health problems result from a lifetime of stratification "suggests multiple intervention points at which disparities can be reduced," beginning before birth (Haas et al., 2012, p. 238). [**Lifespan Link:** Weathering is explained in Chapter 21 in the section *Accumulating Stressors*.]

Past ethnic discrimination also affects income in many ways. Consider home ownership, a source of financial security for many seniors. Fifty years ago, stratification prevented many African Americans from buying homes. Laws passed since then have reduced housing discrimination, but a disproportionate number of non-whites lost homes in the foreclosure crisis that began in 2007. Is this a new example of an old story, stratification causing poverty? (Saegert et al., 2012)

A particular form of ethnic stratification affects immigrant elders. Many cultures expect younger generations to care for the elderly, but U.S. homes are designed for nuclear families. Pensions and Social Security are given to employees who worked for decades, which leaves many older immigrants (without U.S. work history) poor, lonely, and dependent on their children, who live in homes and apartments not designed for extended families and who themselves must contend with stereotypes about immigrants.

Finally, the most harmful effect of stratification may be financial, first the direct effects of poverty, then magnified by gender, ethnicity, and age. As one reviewer explains, "[W]omen . . . are much more likely to live in households that fall below the federal poverty line. Black and Hispanic women are particularly vulnerable" (J. S. Jackson et al., 2011, p. 93). One crucial factor is past employment. Many of the poorest elderly never held jobs that paid Social Security. Thus, an important source of income is absent. When ethnic discrimination affects employment opportunity, old-age poverty is particularly likely.

Low-SES white men are also at risk, as they are more likely to have less education, worse health, and a spottier work history (more unemployment, fewer benefits, no pensions) than men of higher SES. The current economic crisis in the United States, England, and elsewhere results in less governmental social support

FRANCK FIFE/AFP/GETTY IMAGES

Memories Older adults often provide links between the past and present. Toni Morrison won a Pulitzer Prize for her novel *Beloved*, published when she was 56. It provided insight into the emotional horror of slavery for women who died long ago. Here, in Paris at age 81, Morrison dedicates a bench commemorating slavery's abolition.

Especially for Social Scientists
The various social science disciplines tend to favor different theories of aging. Can you tell which theories would be more acceptable to psychologists and which to sociologists? (see response, page 738)

>> Answer to Observation Quiz
(from page 735): White males the most, Asian females the least. There is much speculation as to why, but the data provide no answer.

disengagement theory The view that aging makes a person's social sphere increasingly narrow, resulting in role relinquishment, withdrawal, and passivity.

activity theory The view that elderly people want and need to remain active in a variety of social spheres—with relatives, friends, and community groups—and become withdrawn only unwillingly, as a result of ageism.

for the poor, both old and young (Phillipson, 2013). Anyone growing up in a low-SES family experiences stress of all kinds and accumulates disadvantages that are increasingly limiting as the years go by (Bowen & González, 2010).

The problem may begin even before birth, since epigenetic factors—themselves affected by maternal health—shape genetic expression (Shanahan & Hofer, 2011). Babies born into low-SES families risk late-life diabetes, disability, and death. Obviously, poverty among elders should be alleviated, but mitigating poverty early in life may be critical for well-being in late adulthood (Herd et al., 2011).

Stratification by Age

Ageism is, of course, stratification by age. Age affects a person's life in many ways, including income and health. For example, seniority builds in the workplace, increasing income up to a certain point, and then employment stops, perhaps with a pension but never with as much income as before. People who are unskilled or temporary workers are particularly likely to be hurt by current old-age pension structures (Phillipson, 2013).

The most controversial version of age stratification is **disengagement theory** (Cumming & Henry, 1961), which holds that as people age, traditional roles become unavailable, the social circle shrinks, coworkers stop relying on them, and adult children turn away to focus on their own children. According to this theory, disengagement is a mutual process, chosen by both generations. Thus, younger people disengage from the old, who themselves voluntarily disengage from younger adults, withdrawing from life's action.

Disengagement theory provoked a storm of protest. Many gerontologists insisted that older people need and want new involvements. Some developed an opposing theory, called **activity theory**, which holds that the elderly seek to remain active with relatives, friends, and community groups. Activity theorists contended that if the elderly disengage, they do so unwillingly and suffer because of it (J. R. Kelly, 1993; Rosow, 1985).

Later research finds that being active correlates with happiness, intelligence, and health. This is true at younger ages as well, but the correlation between activity and well-being is particularly strong at older ages (Potocnik & Sonnentag, 2012; Bielak et al., 2012).

Generally, happier and healthier elders are quite active—continuing as worker, wife, husband, mother, father, neighbor. They attend concerts, read newspapers, take classes. Disengagement is more likely among those low in SES, and thus may be the result of past stratification (Clarke, 2011). Literally being active—bustling around the house, climbing stairs, walking to work—lengthens life and increases satisfaction.

Both disengagement and activity theories need to be applied with caution, however. Disengagement in one aspect of life (e.g., retirement) does not necessarily mean disengagement overall: Many retirees disengage from work but find new roles and activities (Freund et al., 2009). The positivity effect may mean that an older person disengages from emotional events that cause anger, regret, and sadness, while actively enjoying other experiences. Certainly some elders who never graduated from 8th grade are nonetheless vital pillars of their community.

Critique of Stratification Theories

Women, ethnic minorities, and low-income people may develop habits and attitudes by old age that protect them from the worst effects of stratification (Rosenfield, 2012). Evidence is spotty, and low SES and ill health are harmful at every age, but perhaps gender, ethnicity, or low SES are less damaging for the very old than they are earlier in life.

Both age-related stratification theories—that all the elderly want to withdraw and that they all should stay active—may arise from cultural stereotypes. The particular needs of an older person may not conform to either theory. Similarly, the fact that older women live longer than older men, and that they usually have closer relationships with friends and families, suggests that they might be less disadvantaged in late adulthood than earlier.

Cautionary data about lifelong discrimination also comes from comparing ethnic groups. Although a Black/White disparity in survival and self-esteem is evident for the young-old, it disappears at about age 80 and then reverses. The average Black centenarian lives seven months longer than does the average non-Black one.

Elderly Hispanics also seem to have a longevity advantage over elderly non-Hispanics in the United States. One explanation for this *race crossover* is called selective survival—the idea that only extremely healthy non-European Americans reach old age. Other interpretations are possible. Perhaps ethnic inequality diminishes because very old age is a powerful "leveler," overwhelming ethnic and SES stratification (Bird et al., 2010; Robert et al., 2009).

SUMMING UP

Theories of development throughout the life span can apply to late adulthood as well as to earlier stages. Two sets of theories are particularly relevant to development in old age.

Self theories stress that people try to remain themselves, achieving integrity and not despairing, as Erikson explains. Other theories that can be considered self-theories are socioemotional selectivity and selective optimization with compensation. Both describe ways that older people shift their priorities in order to protect their core identity. The positivity effect protects the self, as elders take pleasure and pride in who they are, although this same impulse can lead to hoarding and ethnocentrism.

Stratification theories contend that social stereotypes continue lifelong, affecting the elderly by preventing financial independence and good health for reasons related to their gender, ethnicity, and past SES. Ageism adds to these other stereotypes. Disengagement theory suggests that the elderly relinquish past roles and withdraw from life. Activity theory holds the opposite idea, suggesting that societies should encourage activity in old age.

>> Activities in Late Adulthood

Many elders complain that they do not have enough time each day to do all they want to do. This might surprise young college students, who see few gray hairs at sports events, political rallies, job sites, or midnight concerts. But most of the elderly are far from inactive.

Working

Work provides social support and status. Many elders are reluctant to give that up (see Figure 25.4); others enjoy retirement. **[Lifespan Link:** The importance of work is discussed in Chapter 22.]

Paid Work

Past employment history affects the current health and happiness of older adults (Wahrendorf et al., 2013). Those who lost their jobs because of structural changes (a factory closing, a corporate division eliminated) are, decades later, likely to be in poor health (Schröder, 2013). Income matters as well: Those who have sufficient savings from prior employment and an adequate pension are much more likely to enjoy old age.

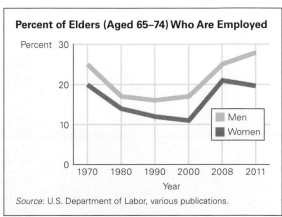

Percent of Elders (Aged 65–74) Who Are Employed

Source: U.S. Department of Labor, various publications.

FIGURE 25.4

Along with Everyone Else Although younger adults might imagine that older people stop work as soon as they can, this is clearly not the case for everyone.

Same Situation, Far Apart: Satisfying Work In Nice, France *(left)*, two paleontologists examine a skull bone, and in Arizona, the United States *(right)*, a woman said to be over 100 years old prepares wool for weaving. Note their facial expressions: Elders are often happier when they continue working.

>> Response for Social Scientists (from page 736): In general, psychologists favor self theories, and sociologists favor stratification theories. Of course, each discipline respects the other, but each believes that its perspective is more honest and accurate.

In every nation the employment rate for older workers has risen since 2005, primarily because many workers hold on to their jobs, worried about the cost of not working. Some private pensions have been eliminated, and many governments are reducing national pensions. For example, in 2010 the French raised the pension age from 60 to 62, a move reversed in 2012 for those who have worked at least 40 years. In the United States, full Social Security benefits begin at age 65 for those born before 1938, but now those born after 1959 must be age 67 for full Social Security.

The decision to quit work is affected by dozens of factors; some workers retire at age 55, and others are working full time in their 70s. Most retire in their 60s. For example, in 2012 only 13 percent of Canadians over age 64 were employed (Statistics Canada).

Nonunionized low-wage workers (who need the income) and professionals (who welcome the status) are likely to stay employed in their 60s (Komp et al., 2010). Especially for the low-wage worker, worries about retirement income are increasing: 41 percent of U.S. workers ages 45 to 65 worry they will not have enough money after retirement (Morin & Fry, 2012).

Retirement

Adequate income and poor health are the two primary reasons some people retire relatively early, younger than age 60 (Alavinia & Burdorf, 2008). Job dissatisfaction is also a factor, as is parenthood—fathers tend to work a little longer than other men, mothers tend to retire a little earlier, at least in Europe (Hank & Korbmacher, 2013). Being a grandparent is also a reason for earlier retirement (Hochman & Lewin-Epstein, 2013).

Many retirees hope to work part time or become self-employed, with small businesses or consulting work (Rix, 2011). Although such work is more difficult to find than employed adults imagine, those who succeed tend to be happier than those who work full time or quit completely (Pagán, 2011). Some employers provide "bridge" jobs, enabling older workers to transition from full employment. Of course, this requires the employer to realize that older workers are more reliable and skilled than new hires (James et al., 2011).

When retirement is precipitated by poor health or fading competence, it correlates with illness (A. Shapiro & Yarborough-Hayes, 2008), and when it leads to

disengagement from cognitive challenge it results in mental decline (Mazzonna & Peracchi, 2012; Rohwedder & Willis, 2010). However, if retirees voluntarily leave their jobs and engage in activities and intellectual challenges, they become healthier and happier than they were before (Coe & Zamarro, 2011).

Volunteer Work

Volunteering offers some of the benefits of paid employment (generativity, social connections, less depression). Longitudinal as well as cross-sectional research finds a strong link between health and volunteering (Cutler et al., 2011; Kahana et al., 2013).

As self theory would predict, volunteer work attracts older people who always were strongly committed to their community and had more social contacts (Pilkington et al., 2012). Beyond that, volunteering itself protects health, even for the very old (Okun et al., 2011). For example, one study of people in rural areas who did not drive reported that the death rate among those who volunteered was half the rate of those who did not volunteer (S. J. Lee et al., 2011).

Culture or national policy affects volunteering: Nordic elders (in Sweden and Norway) volunteer more often than their Mediterranean counterparts (in Italy and Greece), differences that persist when illness is taken into account (Hank & Erlinghagen, 2006). The microsystem also has an effect. Being married to a volunteer makes a person more likely to volunteer. Volunteering fosters social connections, which improves health as well as encourages more volunteering (Pilkington et al., 2012).

The data reveal two areas of concern, however. First, older retirees may be *less* likely to volunteer than middle-aged, employed people (see Figure 25.5). Second, less than one-third of adults of any age volunteer.

Perhaps the definition of volunteering is too narrow. Indeed, most of the elderly give money and time to relatives. A longitudinal study of the Wisconsin high school graduates of 1957 found that, by late adulthood, 96 percent of the women and 92 percent of the men provided help to someone else, not including their spouse (Kahn et al., 2011). This study did not include financial help; if it did, the rate would be almost 100 percent. That bodes well: People of all ages are happier when they help other people.

Home Sweet Home

One of the favorite activities of many retirees is caring for their own homes. Typically, both men and women do more housework and meal preparation (less fast food, more fresh ingredients) after retirement (Luengo-Prado & Sevilla, 2012). Both sexes also do yard work, redecorate, build shelves, hang pictures, rearrange furniture.

Gardening is popular: More than half the elderly in the United States do it (see Figure 25.6). Tending flowers, herbs, and vegetables is productive because it involves both exercise and social interaction (Schupp & Sharp, 2012).

Warming Her Heart Volunteers are likely to be happier and healthier than those who do not volunteer, especially if they feel their special experiences are valued. That could be the case for 72-year-old Mary Phillips, who sits in a display organized by Friends of the Earth. She is in an outdoor living room, protesting low government subsidies for home heating.

Especially for Social Workers Your agency needs more personnel but does not have money to hire anyone. Should you go to your local senior-citizen center and recruit volunteers? (see response, page 740)

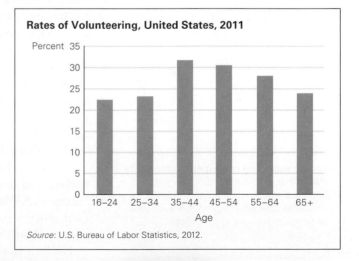

Rates of Volunteering, United States, 2011

Source: U.S. Bureau of Labor Statistics, 2012.

FIGURE 25.5

Official Volunteers As you can see, older adults volunteer less often than do middle-aged adults, according to official statistics. However, this counts people who volunteer for organizations—schools, churches, social service groups, and so on. Not counted is help given to friends, family members, neighbors, and even strangers. If that were counted, would elders have higher rates than everyone else?

FIGURE 25.6

Dirty Fingernails Almost three times as many 60-year-olds as 20-year-olds are gardeners. What is it about dirt, growth, and time that makes gardening an increasingly popular hobby as people age?

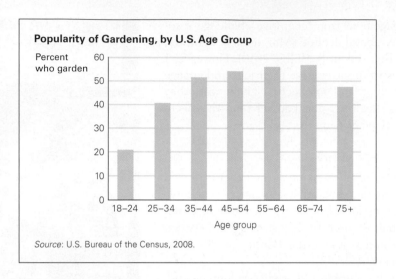

Popularity of Gardening, by U.S. Age Group

Source: U.S. Bureau of the Census, 2008.

age in place To remain in the same home and community in later life, adjusting but not leaving when health fades.

naturally occurring retirement community (NORC) A neighborhood or apartment complex whose population is mostly retired people who moved to the location as younger adults and never left.

>> Response for Social Workers
(from page 739): Yes, but be careful. If people want to volunteer and are just waiting for an opportunity, you will probably benefit from their help and they will also benefit. But if you convince reluctant seniors to help you, the experience may benefit no one.

In keeping up with household tasks and maintaining their property, many older people prefer to **age in place** rather than move. That is the plan of many middle-aged adults, too: 83 percent of those aged 55 to 64 hope to stay in their own homes when they retire (Koppen, 2009).

If they must move, most elders want to remain nearby, perhaps in a smaller apartment with an elevator, but not in another city or state. That is wise: Elders fare best surrounded by long-term friends and acquaintances. Gerontologists believe that "interrupting social connections . . . might be harmful, especially for women and the frailest" (Berkman et al., 2011, p. 347).

The preference for aging in place is evident in state statistics. Of the 50 states, Florida has the largest percentage of people over age 65, but the next three states highest in that proportion—Maine, West Virginia, and Pennsylvania—are places where older people have always lived.

Fortunately, some houses are built or remodeled to suit aging people. About 4,000 consultants are now certified by the National Association of Homebuilders to advise about *universal design*. [**Lifespan Link:** Universal design is defined in Chapter 23.] That includes dozens of details that make a home livable for people who find it hard to reach the top shelves, to climb stairs, to respond quickly to the doorbell. Non-design aspects of housing also allow aging in place, such as bright lights without dangling cords, carpets affixed to the floor, and seats in the shower.

A neighborhood or an apartment complex can become a **naturally occurring retirement community (NORC)**, where young adults stayed as they aged. People in NORCs are often content to live alone, after children left and partners died. They enjoy home repair, housework, and gardening partly because their life-long neighbors notice the new curtains, the polished door, the blooming rosebush.

NORCs can be granted public money to replace after-school karate with senior centers, or piano teachers with visiting nurses, if that is what the community needs (Greenfield et al., 2012). If a low-income elder lives in a high-crime neighborhood (and many do), they and their neighbors sometimes form a protective social network.

Public and private institutions can encourage aging in place (A. E. Smith, 2009). That is true for my friend Doris, described in this chapter's introduction as having "many meetings, appointments, and social engagements." She lives alone and has been a widow for decades. She is actively engaged in many organizations, and the community in which she has lived for 50 years knows and appreciates her. (Visualizing Development, p. 741, provides an overview of living arrangements after age 65.)

SOURCE: NATIONAL VITAL STATISTICS REPORTS, OLV 61, NO. 4, MAY 8, 2013

VISUALIZING DEVELOPMENT

Life After 65: Living Independently

Most people who reach age 65 not only survive a decade or more, but will also live independently.

AGE 65 Of 100 people:

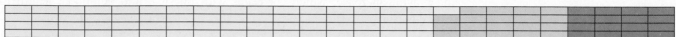

87 will survive another decade. Most will spend that time caring for all their basic needs. But 35 will be unable to take care of at least one instrumental activity of daily living (IADL) like household chores, shopping, or taking care of finances, or one activity of daily living (ADL) like bathing, dressing, eating, or getting in and out of bed. And 16 are so impaired that they are also in a long term care situation like a nursing home.

AGE 75 Of the 87 people who survived from age 65:

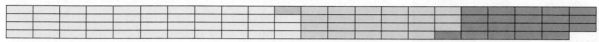

56 will survive another decade. About half will not need help caring for their basic needs. But 43 will be unable to take care of at least one instrumental activity of daily living (IADL) like household chores, shopping, or taking care of finances, or one activity of daily living (ADL) like bathing, dressing, eating, or getting in and out of bed. And 20 are so impaired that they are also in a long-term care situation like a nursing home.

AGE 85 Of the 56 people who survived from age 75:

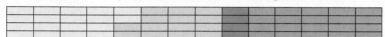

Only 11 will survive another decade. And most need help caring for their basic needs. 42 will be unable to take care of at least one instrumental activity of daily living (IADL) like household chores, shopping, or taking care of finances, or one activity of daily living (ADL) like bathing, dressing, eating, or getting in and out of bed. And 24 are so impaired that they are also in a long-term care situation like a nursing home.

AGE 95

Those who reach 95 tend to be unusually healthy and usually live for about 4 more years. Almost three-quarters now need some help caring for their basic needs and about half are in a long-term care situation like a nursing home.

KEY

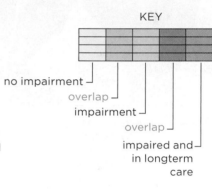

no impairment
overlap
impairment
overlap
impaired and in longterm care

With whom?

Only about 15 percent of those over age 65 move in with an adult child or live in a nursing home or hospital.

LIVING ARRANGEMENTS OF PERSONS 65+, 2010

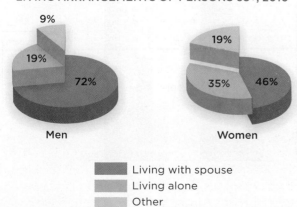

Men: 9%, 19%, 72%
Women: 19%, 35%, 46%

Living with spouse
Living alone
Other

Where?

Not necessarily in a warm state or with caregivers.

PERSONS 65+ AS A PERCENTAGE OF TOTAL POPULATION, 2010

Over 14%
12% to 14%
10% to 12%
less than 10%

SOURCE: US CENSUS BUREAU, 2011

Religious Involvement

Older adults attend fewer religious services than do the middle-aged, but faith and praying increase, which correlates with physical and emotional health for several reasons:

1. Religious prohibitions encourage good habits (e.g., less drug use).
2. Faith communities promote caring relationships.
3. Beliefs give meaning for life and death, thus reducing stress (Atchley, 2009; Lim & Putnam, 2010).

Religious identity and institutions are especially important for older members of minority groups, many of whom are more strongly committed to their religious heritage than to their national or ethnic background. A nearby house of worship, with familiar words, music, and rituals, is one reason American elders prefer to age in place.

Faith may explain an oddity in mortality statistics, specifically in suicide data (Chatters et al., 2011). In the United States, suicide after age 65 among elderly European American men occurs 50 times more often than among African American women. A possible explanation is that African American women's religious faith is often very strong, making them less depressed about their daily lives (Colbert et al., 2009).

Welcome the Stranger Anti-immigrant passions erupted violently in South Africa, to the dismay of many of the elderly who believe their nation should continue to welcome those who are suffering in their homeland. The women shown here held a prayer vigil on the site where an immigrant man was burned to death.

Especially for Religious Leaders Why might the elderly have strong faith but poor church attendance? (see response, page 744)

Political Activism

It is easy to imagine that elders are not political activists. Fewer older people turn out for rallies, and only about 2 percent volunteer in political campaigns. In 2011, only 7 percent of U.S. residents older than 65 gave time for any political, civic, international, or professional group (Bureau of Labor Statistics, 2012b). This is not good news, since democracy depends on involvement.

By other measures, however, the elderly are very political. More than any other age group, they write letters to their representatives, identify with a political party, and vote (see Figure 25.7).

FIGURE 25.7

When It Counts People over age 64 vote three times as often as those under age 25 when voting matters most—in the non-Presidential years when all of Congress and one-third of the U.S. Senate is elected. Note that some of the elderly have trouble standing in line, seeing fine print, and even getting to their polling place, but that does not stop them from being politically active.

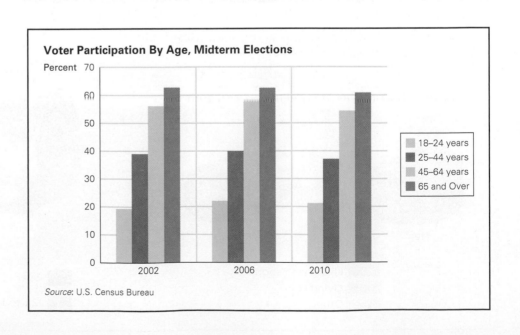

Voter Participation By Age, Midterm Elections

Percent

Legend: 18–24 years, 25–44 years, 45–64 years, 65 and Over

Source: U.S. Census Bureau

In addition, the elderly are more likely than younger adults to keep up with the news. For example, the Pew Research Center for the People and the Press periodically asks U.S. residents questions on current events. The elderly always best the young. They also know political history. In 2011, elders (65 and older) beat the youngest (aged 18 to 30) by a ratio of about 3-to-2 in knowing the political party of each of these four: Nancy Pelosi, John Boehner, Franklin Roosevelt, and Abraham Lincoln (Pew Research Center, 2012).

Many government policies affect the elderly, especially those regarding housing, pensions, prescription drugs, and medical costs. However, members of this age group do not necessarily vote their own economic interests, or vote as a bloc. Instead they are divided on most national issues, including global warming, military conflicts, and public education.

Political scientists believe the idea of "gray power" (that the elderly vote as a bloc) is a myth, promulgated to reduce support for programs that benefit the old (Walker, 2012). Given that ageism zigzags from hostile to benign—and is often based on beliefs that are far from reality—it is not surprising that "older persons [are] attacked as too powerful and, at the same time, as a burdensome responsibility" (Schulz & Binstock, 2008, p. 8).

SUMMING UP

The elderly remain active in many ways, sometimes staying in the labor force when it is not financially necessary, but more often retiring in order to do things they enjoy.

Some of the elderly volunteer, benefiting their own health as well as their community. Almost all care for neighbors and family members if they can. Elders prefer to "age in place," not moving from their community. Many keep their home in good repair and their garden flourishing. They also tend to be devout, politically active (at least in voting), and knowledgeable about current events and political issues. The idea that they exert "gray power" is a myth: They do not vote as a bloc, even on issues that directly concern them.

>> Friends and Relatives

Humans are social animals, dependent on one another for survival and drawn to one another for joy. This is as true in late life as in infancy and at every stage in between.

Every person travels through life with their social convoy. Thus companions are particularly important in old age. As socioemotional theory predicts, the size of the social circle may shrink with age, but close relationships become more crucial.

A Lover's Kiss Ralph Young awakens Ruth (a) with a kiss each day, as he has for most of the 78 years of their marriage. Here they are both 99, sharing a room in their Indiana residence, "more in love than ever." Half a world away, in Ukraine (b), more kisses occur, with 70 newly married couples and one couple celebrating their golden anniversary. Developmental data suggests that now, several years after these photos, the two old couples are more likely to be happily married than the 70 young ones.

(a) (b)

>> Response for Religious Leaders
(from page 742): There are many possible
answers, including the specifics of getting
to church (transportation, stairs), physical
comfort in church (acoustics, temperature),
and content (unfamiliar hymns and language).

Bonds formed over the years allow people to share triumphs and tragedies with others who understand. Siblings, old friends, and spouses are ideal convoy members. [**Lifespan Link:** The social convoy is discussed in Chapter 22.]

Long-Term Partnerships

For most of the current cohort of elders, their spouse is the central convoy member, a buffer against the problems of old age. Married older adults are healthier, wealthier, and happier than unmarried people their age. Spouses affect each other: One healthy and happy partner improves the other's well-being (Ruthig et al., 2012).

Obviously, not every marriage is good: About one in every six long-term marriages decreases health and happiness (Waldinger & Schulz, 2010). However, often happiness increases with the length of an intimate relationship—an association more apparent in longitudinal than in cross-sectional research (Proulx et al., 2007; Scarf, 2008). A lifetime of shared experiences—living together, raising children, and dealing with financial and emotional crises—brings partners closer. Often couples develop "an exceedingly positive portrayal" (O'Rourke et al., 2010b) of their mate, seeing their partner's personality as better than their own.

Older couples have learned how to disagree, resolving conflicts in discussions, not fights. I know one example personally.

Irma and Bill are both politically active, proud parents of two adult children, devoted grandparents, and up on current events. They seem happily married and they cooperate admirably when caring for their 2- and 4-year-old grandsons. Yet they almost always vote for opposing candidates. I was puzzled until Irma explained: "We sit together on the fence, seeing both perspectives, and then, when it is time to vote, Bob and I fall on opposite sides." I can always predict who falls on which side, but for them, the discussion is productive. Their long-term affection keeps disagreements from becoming fights.

Outsiders might judge many long-term marriages as unequal, since one or the other spouse usually provides most of the money, or needs most of the care, or does most of the housework. Yet such disparities do not bother older partners, who accept each other's dependencies, remembering times (perhaps decades ago) when the situation was reversed.

One crucial factor is that the challenges of child rearing, home ownership, economic crises, and so on require cooperation. The importance of past sharing is suggested by research that finds that older husbands and wives with mutual close friends are more likely to help each other if special needs arise (Cornwell, 2012).

Given the importance of relationship building over the life span, it is not surprising that elders who are disabled (e.g., have difficulty walking, bathing, and so on) are less depressed and anxious if they are in a close marital relationship (Mancini & Bonanno, 2006). A couple together can achieve selective optimization with compensation: The one who is bedbound but alert can keep track of what the mobile but confused one must do, for instance.

Relationships with Younger Generations

In past centuries, many adults died before their grandchildren were born. For 10-year-olds in 1900, only one in twenty-five had all four grandparents alive; in 2000 close to half (41 percent) did (Hagestad & Uhlenberg, 2007). Some families currently span five generations. Most families are closely connected across the generations (Szydlik, 2012).

Since the average couple now has fewer children, the *beanpole family*, representing multiple generations but with only a few members in each, is

"They grow old too fast."

Ignorant? Each generation has much to teach as well as much to learn.

MIKE BALDWIN/CARTOONSTOCK.COM

becoming more common (Murphy, 2011) (see Figure 25.8). Some of the youngest have no cousins, brothers, or sisters but a dozen elderly relatives.

Intergenerational Support

For the most part, family members support one another. As you remember, *familism* prompts family caregiving among all the relatives. One manifestation is **filial responsibility**, the obligation of adult children to care for their aging parents. This is a value in every nation, stronger in some cultures than in others (Saraceno, 2010).

As family size shrinks, many older parents continue to feel responsible for their grown children. This can strain a long-lasting marriage. For example:

> When my daughter divorced, they nearly lost the house to foreclosure, so I went on the loan and signed for them. But then again they nearly foreclosed, so my husband and I bought it. . . . So now I have to make the payment on my own house and most of the payment on my daughter's house, and that is hard. . . . I am hoping to get that money back from our daughter, to quell my husband's sense that the kids are all just taking and no one is giving back. He sometimes feels used and abused.

> *[quoted in Meyer, 2012, p. 83]*

Emotional support between older adults and their grown children brings additional complexities, often increasing when money is less needed (Herlofson & Hagestad, 2012). Expectations vary. Some children want and others reject emotional help, and some elders resent exactly the same behaviors that other elders expect from their children—such as visiting frequently, giving presents, or cleaning the refrigerator.

Research finds no evidence that recent changes in family structure (including divorce) reduce the sense of filial responsibility. One study found that younger cohorts (born in the 1950s and 1960s) endorsed *more* responsibility toward older generations, "regardless of the sacrifices involved," than did earlier cohorts (born in the 1930s and 1940s) (Gans & Silverstein, 2006).

Likewise, almost all elders believe the older generation should help the younger ones, although specifics vary by culture. When the government provides significant financial help for the aged (housing, pensions, and so on), the generations are *more* involved with each other than when government support is minimal (Herlofson & Hagestad, 2012).

In the United States, every generation values independence. That is why, after midlife and especially after the death of their own parents, members of the older generation are *less* likely to agree that children should provide substantial care for their parents and more likely to strive to be helpful to their children. A team who has studied this phenomenon suggests that adults of all ages like to be needed more than needy (Gans & Silverstein, 2006).

This may not be true in Asian cultures. Often the first-born son encourages his elderly parents to move in with him, and they expect to do so. Indeed, a study in rural China found depression more common among the elderly people whose daughters took care of them instead of their daughters-in-law (Cong & Silverstein, 2008). Asian daughters-in-law seem to experience similar frustrations and joys in caregiving as European American daughters do (Pinquart & Sörensen, 2011).

Intergenerational Tensions

Although elderly people's relationships with members of younger generations are usually positive, they can also include tension and conflict. In some families intergenerational respect and harmony abound, whereas in others relatives refuse

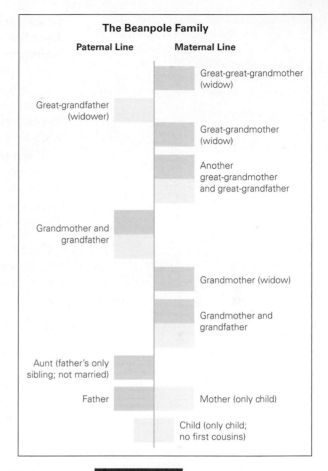

The Beanpole Family

Paternal Line   Maternal Line

Great-great-grandmother (widow)

Great-grandfather (widower)

Great-grandmother (widow)

Another great-grandmother and great-grandfather

Grandmother and grandfather

Grandmother (widow)

Grandmother and grandfather

Aunt (father's only sibling; not married)

Father   Mother (only child)

Child (only child; no first cousins)

FIGURE 25.8

Many Households, Few Members The traditional nuclear family consists of two parents and their children living together. Today, as couples have fewer children, the beanpole family is becoming more common. This kind of family has many generations, each typically living in its own household, with only a few members in each generation.

filial responsibility The obligation of adult children to care for their aging parents.

to see each other. Each culture and each family has patterns and expectations regarding interactions between generations (Herlofson & Hagestad, 2011). Some conflict is common.

A good relationship with successful grown children enhances a parent's well-being, especially when both generations do whatever the other generation expects. By contrast, a poor relationship makes life worse for everyone. Ironically, conflict is more likely in emotionally close relationships than in distant ones (Silverstein et al., 2010), especially when either generation becomes dependent on the other (Birditt et al., 2009).

It is a mistake to think of the strength of the relationship as merely the middle generation paying back the older one for past sacrifices. Instead, family norms—either for intergenerational dependence or for autonomy—predict how family members interact in late adulthood (Bucx et al., 2012; Henretta et al., 2011). Extensive research finds many factors that affect intergenerational relationships:

- Assistance arises from both need and ability to provide.
- Frequency of contact is related to geographical proximity, not affection.
- Love is influenced by childhood memories.
- Sons feel stronger obligation; daughters feel stronger affection.

Grandparents and Great-Grandparents

Eighty-five percent of U.S. elders currently older than 65 are grandparents. (The rate was lower in some previous cohorts because the birth rate fell during the 1930s, and it is expected to be lower again.)

As with parents and children, specifics of the grandparent–grandchild relationship depend partly on the personality and partly on the age of both generations. Grandparents typically delight in the youngest children, provide material support for the school-age children, and sometimes offer advice, encouragement, and example for the older grandchildren. One of my college students realized this when she wrote:

> Brian and Brianna are twins and are turning 13 years old this coming June. Over the spring break my family celebrated my grandmother's 80th birthday and I overheard the twins' talking about how important it was for them to still have grandma around because she was the only one who would give them money if they really wanted something their mom wasn't able to give them. . . . I lashed out . . . how lucky we were to have her around and that they were two selfish little brats. . . . Now that I am older, I learned to appreciate her for what she really is. She's the rock of the family, and "the bank" is the least important of her attributes now.
>
> [*Giovanna, 2010*]

Same Situation, Far Apart: Happy Grandfathers No matter where they are, grandparents and grandchildren often enjoy each other partly because conflict is less likely, as grandparents are usually not as strict as parents are. Indeed, Sam Levinson quipped, "The reason grandparents and grandchild get along so well is that they have a common enemy."

Grandparents fill one of four roles:

1. *Remote grandparents* (sometimes called *distant grandparents*) are emotionally distant from their grandchildren. They are esteemed elders who are honored, respected, and obeyed, expecting to get help whenever they need it.
2. *Companionate grandparents* (sometimes called *"fun-loving" grandparents*) entertain and "spoil" their grandchildren—especially in ways that the parents would not.
3. *Involved grandparents* are active in the day-to-day lives of their grandchildren. They live near them and see them daily.
4. *Surrogate parents* raise their grandchildren, usually because the parents are unable or unwilling to do so.

Currently in developed nations, most grandparents are companionate, partly because all three generations expect them to be companions, not authorities. Contemporary elders usually enjoy their own independence. They provide babysitting and financial help but not advice or discipline (May et al., 2012). If grandparents become too involved and intrusive, parents tend to be forgiving but not appreciative (Pratt et al., 2008).

When grandparents become surrogates, the family structure is called the *skipped generation* because the middle generation is absent. The number of such grandparents is rising; it was 2.8 million in the United States in 2010. Social workers often seek grandparents for kinship foster care because foster children fare as well as or better with grandparents than with nonrelatives, but surrogate parenting is stressful for every generation.

One reason is that both old and young are sad about the missing middle generation; another is that difficult grandchildren (such as drug-affected infants and rebellious school-age boys) are more likely to live with grandparents; a third is that surrogate grandparents tend to be the most vulnerable elders, usually grandmothers burdened by past stratification. In North America and Europe, grandparents who are totally responsible for grandchildren experience more illness, depression, and marital problems than do other elders (Shakya et al., 2012; Muller & Litwin, 2011).

Furthermore, children of skipped-generation families are less likely to graduate from high school than are children of the same SES and ethnicity in other family structures (Monserud & Elder, 2011). This has lifelong consequences: The average life span of European Americans who have not graduated from high school has actually decreased since 1990 (Olshansky et al., 2012) (see Figure 25.9). That makes the trend toward more skipped-generation families a sad one for children as well as for older adults.

FIGURE 25.9

Too Young to Die Medical advances and improving health habits mean that most adults live longer than their parents did: The average life span has increased every decade for both sexes, for all ethnic groups, in every nation. However, in the United States those without a high school diploma find that steady work is increasingly scarce, which takes a toll on survival.

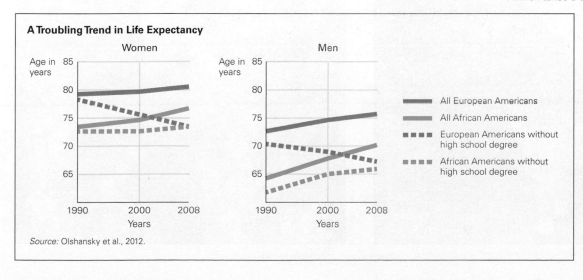

A Troubling Trend in Life Expectancy

All European Americans
All African Americans
European Americans without high school degree
African Americans without high school degree

Source: Olshansky et al., 2012.

But before concluding that grandparents suffer when they are responsible for grandchildren, consider China, where many grandparents become full-time caregivers because the middle generation is working in the cities, unable to take children with them. The working parents typically make sure the grandparents want to be caregivers, and then they send money and visit when they can. For those grandparents, caring for their grandchildren actually improves their physical and psychological health (Baker & Silverstein, 2012).

However, skipped-generation grandparents are the minority, perhaps 2 percent of all elders in the United States. Grandparenting is not always wonderful but most grandparents enjoy their role, gain generativity from it, and are appreciated by younger family members (C. L. Kemp, 2005; Thiele & Whelan, 2008). Some are even rhapsodic and spiritual about the experience. As one writes:

> Not until my grandson was born did I realize that babies are actually miniature angels assigned to break through our knee-jerk habits of resistance and to remind us that love is the real reason we're here.

[*Golden, 2010, p. 125*]

Friendship

Friendship networks typically become smaller with each decade. Emerging adults tend to average the most friends. By late adulthood, the number of people considered friends is notably smaller than it was earlier in life (Wrzus et al., 2013). Added to the normal shrinkage are two circumstances: Some older friends die, and retirement usually means losing contact with most work friends. Many older adults consider their spouse or grown children their best friends. This may create problems in the future.

Based on several U.S. Bureau of the Census documents, it appears that approximately 90 percent of people older than 75 in the United States in 2010 had been married, making this oldest generation the most-married cohort in history. Each younger generation has more people who never married: 5 percent for those aged 65 to 74, 8 percent for those 55 to 64, and 12 percent for those 45 to 54.

Same Situation, Far Apart: Partners Whether at the Vietnam memorial in Washington, D.C. *(left)* or in the Philippines *(right)*, elderly people support each other in joy and sorrow. These women are dancing together, and these men are tracing the name of one of their buddies who died forty years earlier.

Obviously, the next cohort of elders will include far fewer married people. Furthermore, more middle-aged adults, married or not, have no children, hence more elders will have no grandchildren. Accordingly, this next generation will have fewer immediate family members and they will lose some non-family friends. Will they be lonely and lack social support?

Not necessarily. Recent data finds that the young-old who never married are usually quite content, not lonely. Some of them have partners, of the same sex or other sex, and are cohabiting or LAT, seemingly just as happy as traditionally married people (Brown & Kawamura, 2010). Further, having a smaller friendship circle is not a problem if a person has at least a few close friends—as most of the aged do (Wrzus et al., 2013).

This is not to say that recent widowhood or divorce is easy, although widowhood is not as hard if one's mate was seriously ill for years or if the marriage was not a close one (Schann, 2013). Similarly, losing a close friend, through death or relocation, is difficult.

Los Amigos Some cultures seem to encourage male friendships. These men in Santa Fe de Antioquia, Colombia, are not afraid to show their closeness in the public square.

However, elderly people who have spent years without a romantic partner usually have close friendships, meaningful activities, and social connections that keep them busy and happy (DePaulo, 2006). A study of 85 single elders found that their level of well-being was similar to that of people in long-term equitable marriages, and they were happier than either recent widows or the married adults in inequitable marriages (Hagedoorn et al., 2006).

Successful aging requires that people not be socially isolated, and many elders who have lived in the same community for years have found long-term friends. A family who urges their distant parents to move closer to them may not appreciate the social networks that surround most older people.

SUMMING UP

Social connections are crucial for people at every age, including late adulthood. Long-term partnerships are beneficial; married people average longer, healthier, and happier lives than unmarried ones. Adults who have never married tend to have strong friendships, sometimes faring better than those who have been divorced or widowed. Children and grandchildren are important parts of the social network for many elders, who more often give care than receive it from the younger generations. Family relationships are complex and varied, with most of the middle generation believing they should help the older ones but most of the older ones cherishing independence. Ties to grandchildren are rewarding, but when grandparents raise grandchildren without the middle generation, all three generations may suffer. ■

>> The Frail Elderly

Now that we have dispelled stereotypes by describing aging adults who are active and enjoy supportive friends and family, we can turn to the **frail elderly**— those who are infirm, inactive, seriously disabled, or cognitively impaired.

frail elderly People over age 65, and often over age 85, who are physically infirm, very ill, or cognitively disabled.

JEFF GREENBERG/PHOTO EDIT

An Odd Couple This tiny short-haired Chihuahua and big, mustached man may seem an odd pair, but what you see here is admirable self-protection. The cognitive demands of a mobile wheelchair and the physical demands of a dog are likely to prevent frailty for years to come.

activities of daily life (ADLs) Typically identified as five tasks of self-care that are important to independent living: eating, bathing, toileting, dressing, and transferring from a bed to a chair. The inability to perform any of these tasks is a sign of frailty.

instrumental activities of daily life (IADLs) Actions (for example, paying bills and car maintenance) that are important to independent living and that require some intellectual competence and forethought. The ability to perform these tasks may be even more critical to self-sufficiency than ADL ability.

Frailty is not defined by any single disease, no matter how serious, but by an overall loss of energy and strength. It is systemic, often accompanied by weight loss and exhaustion.

The frail are not the majority. Typically, older people are happy and active for decades, but eventually about one-third will be frail for at least a year before they die.

Activities of Daily Life

One way to measure frailty, according to insurance standards and medical professionals, is by assessing a person's level of difficulty in performing the tasks of self-care to maintain independence. Gerontologists often assess five physical **activities of daily life (ADLs)**: eating, bathing, toileting, dressing, and moving (transferring) from a bed to a chair.

Equally important may be the **instrumental activities of daily life (IADLs)**, which require intellectual competence and forethought. Indeed, problems with IADLs often precede problems with ADLs since planning and problem solving help frail elders maintain self-care.

IADLs vary from culture to culture. In developed nations, IADLs may include evaluating nutrition, preparing income tax forms, using modern appliances, and keeping appointments (see Table 25.1), although even within developed nations, professionals vary in their lists of IADLs (Chan et al., 2012). In rural areas of developing nations, feeding the chickens, cultivating the garden, mending clothes, getting water from the well, and making dinner might be IADLs.

TABLE 25.1	Instrumental Activities of Daily Life (IADLs)
Domain	**Exemplar Task**
Managing medical care	Keeping current on check-ups, including teeth and eyes
	Assessing supplements as good, worthless, or harmful
Food preparation	Evaluating nutritional information on food labels
	Preparing and storing food to eliminate spoilage
Transportation	Comparing costs of car, taxi, bus, and train
	Determining quick and safe walking routes
Communication	Knowing when and whether to use landline, cell, texting, mail, e-mail
	Programming speed-dial for friends, emergencies
Maintaining household	Following instructions for operating an appliance
	Keeping safety devices (fire extinguishers, CO_2 alarms) active
Managing one's finances	Budgeting future expenses (housing, utilities, etc.)
	Completing timely income tax returns

Whose Responsibility?

There are marked cultural differences in care for the frail elderly. Many African and Asian cultures hold sons responsible for the care of their parents, and men and their wives take elders into their home, providing meals, medical care, and conversation. Indeed, many couples wanted at least one son in order to have a caregiver when they became old. **[Lifespan Link:** Sex selection is discussed in Chapter 3.]

Demographics have changed, and that change has an impact on filial responsibility. Some people still romanticize elder care, believing that frail older adults should live with their children, who should care for them. That assumption worked when the demographic pyramid meant that each surviving elder had many descendants, but it does not work for beanpole families.

Now some middle-aged couples, neither with siblings, may have a dozen living ancestors (four elderly parents and eight grandparents). They would be responsible for fewer elders if some died before age 85, but even more if some of the older generation remarried, or if a childless aunt or uncle was still alive. At least one of the oldest generation is likely to be frail, and several others may need daily help. If that middle-aged couple followed traditional practices, they would have several elders living with them.

A CASE TO STUDY

Preventing Frailty

The best solution is to prevent frailty in the first place, a goal best achieved when individuals, families, and the larger community all do their part. For example, everyone's leg muscles weaken in old age. That can lead to frailty, or not.

If elders are terrified of falling, they might not walk much. Aging in place might mean staying in a home with steep stairs and a kitchen and bathroom far from the bedroom. Then an overly solicitous caregiver might bring them meals, put a portable toilet in their room, and buy a remote control for their large bedroom TV. The community may contribute to the fear of going outside if sidewalks are lacking and if the TV news highlights violent crime.

To prevent frailty, the individual, the family, and the community could change. The person could exercise daily, walking with family members on pathways built to be safe and pleasant. A physical therapist—paid by the individual, the family, or the government—could individualize the exercise and select appropriate equipment (a walker? a cane? special shoes?). The house could be redesigned, or the elder could move to a place where walking was safe and encouraged.

Thus, all three—the elder, the family, and the community— could prevent or at least postpone frailty. Consider another example, this one not theoretical:

> A 70-year-old Hispanic man went to his family doctor following a visit to his family in Colombia, where he had appeared to be disoriented (he said he believed he was in the United States, and he did not recognize places that were known to be familiar to him). He was very agitated, especially at night. An interview with the patient and a family member revealed a history that had progressed over the past six years, at least, of gradual worsening cognitive deficit, which that family had interpreted as part of normal aging. Recently his symptoms had included difficulty operating simple appliances, misplacement of items, and difficulty finding words, with the latter attributed to his having learned English in his late 20s. . . . [His] family had been very protective and increasingly had compensated for his cognitive problems.
>
> . . . He had a lapse of more than five years without proper control of his medical problems [hypertension and diabetes] because of difficulty gaining access to medical care. . . .
>
> Based on the medical history, a cognitive exam, . . . and a magnetic resonance imaging of the brain, . . . the diagnosis of moderate Alzheimer disease was made. Treatment with ChEI [cholinesterase inhibitors] was started. . . . His family noted that his apathy improved and that he was feeling more connected with the environment.
>
> [Griffith & Lopez, 2009]

Both the community (those five years without treatment for hypertension and diabetes) and the family (making excuses, protecting him) contributed to dementia that could have been delayed, if not prevented altogether. The man himself was not blameless. He did not take care of his health, and travelling to Colombia was the worst thing he could have done: Disorientation is worsened in an unfamiliar place. With many types of failing physical and mental health, delay, moderation, and sometimes prevention are possible.

Caring for the Frail Elderly

Prevention is best, but not always sufficient. Caregivers themselves are usually elderly, and they are particularly likely to have health problems and inadequate physical strength and immune systems (Lovell & Wetherell, 2011). Thus an aging spouse who cares for the other spouse is likely to need help.

Helping may be harder for a person with failing IADLs than with failing ADLs. After listing the problems and frustrations of caring for someone who is mentally incapacitated but physically strong, the authors of one overview note:

> The effects of these stresses on family caregivers can be catastrophic. . . .
> They may include increased levels of depression and anxiety as well as higher use of psychotropic medicine such as tranquilizers, poorer self-reported health, compromised immune function, and increased mortality.

[*Gitlin et al., 2003, p. 362*]

Not What You Think This photo is a stereotype check: What do you think is happening here? In fact, the hairdresser is a volunteer, the place is a nursing home, and the country is Haiti. Do any of these surprise you?

Remember variability, however. Some caregivers feel they are repaying past caregiving, and sometimes everyone else, including the care receiver, expresses appreciation. That relieves resentment, and makes caregiving easier. In fact, a longitudinal study found that when caregivers feel supported by their family, with practical help as well as emotional encouragement, stress diminishes as time goes on—even as the frail person's needs increase (Roth et al., 2005).

The designated caregiver of a frail elderly person is chosen less for practical reasons (e.g., the relative with the most patience, time, and skill) than for cultural ones. Currently in the United States, the usual caregiver is the spouse (the wife twice as often as the husband), who often has no prior experience caring for a frail elder.

In northern European nations, most elder care is provided through a social safety net of senior day-care centers, senior homes, and skilled nurses. In some cultures an older person who is dying is taken to a hospital; in other cultures such intervention is seen as interference with the natural order.

A tradition of caregiving may explain why at least one study found that caregiving African Americans are less depressed than caregivers of other ethnicities (Roth et al., 2008). As always, ethnic generalities may obscure many individual variations: Some caregivers of every group are abusive and depressed; others are uplifted by the role.

Even in ideal circumstances, family members disagree about appropriate nutrition, medical help, and dependence. Public agencies rarely provide services unless a crisis arises. This troubles developmentalists, who study "change over time." From a life-span perspective, caregiver exhaustion and elder abuse are predictable and preventable.

If elders require extensive care, ideally skilled people provide it, helping family members to do their part. But many elders themselves are terrified of nursing homes and suspicious of strangers. Since people tend to focus on the worst, most memorable examples of every kind of problem, from complications of pregnancy to the contexts of dying, it is not surprising that people and their families sometimes regard nursing homes as worse than death, and feel shame when a frail person enters one. However, home care can be destructive for everyone.

Elder Abuse

When caregiving results in resentment and social isolation, the risk of depression, poor health, and abuse (of either the frail person or the caregiver) escalates (Smith et al., 2011). Abuse is likely if:

- the *caregiver* suffers from emotional problems or substance abuse
- the *care receiver* is frail, confused, and demanding
- the *care location* is isolated, where visitors are few

Ironically, although relatives are less prepared to cope with difficult patients than professionals are, they often provide round-the-clock care with little outside help or supervision. Ideally other family members provide respite, but they may avoid visiting. Some caregivers overmedicate, lock doors, and use physical restraints, all of which are considered elder abuse. The next step may be inadequate feeding, neglect, or rough treatment.

Extensive public and personal safety nets are needed. Most social workers and medical professionals are suspicious if an elder is unexpectedly quiet, or losing weight, or injured. They are currently "mandated reporters," which means they must alert the authorities if they believe abuse is occurring. Elder abuse may be financial, yet bankers, lawyers, and investment advisors are not trained to recognize it or obligated to respond (S. L. Jackson & Hafemeister, 2011).

A major problem is awareness: Professionals and relatives alike hesitate to criticize a family caregiver who spends the Social Security check, disrespects the elder, or does not comply with the elder's demands. At what point is this abuse? Typically, abuse begins gradually and continues for years, unnoticed. Political and legal definitions and remedies are not clear-cut (Dong & Simon, 2011).

About 5 percent of dependent elders say they are abused, and many more are probably abused but ashamed to admit it (Cooper et al., 2008). Accurate incidence data are complicated by definitions: If an elder feels abused, but a caregiver disagrees, who is right? Abused elders are often depressed, ill, and suffering from cognitive disorders, but that neither proves abuse nor absolves abusers (Dong et al., 2011).

Sometimes caregivers become victims, attacked by a confused elderly person. As with other forms of abuse, the dependency of the victim makes prosecution difficult (Mellor & Brownell, 2006). Sometimes secrecy, suspicion, and family pride keep outsiders away. Social isolation makes abuse possible; fear of professionals may makes problems worse.

Sweet But Sad Family support is evident here, as an older sister (Lillian, age 75) escorts the younger sister (Julia, age 71) to the doctor. Unseen is how family support wrecked their lives: The sisters lost their life savings and their childhood home because their nephew was addicted to crack.

NICOLE BENGIVENO/THE NEW YORK TIMES/REDUX

Long-Term Care

Fortunately, outright abuse is now rare in nursing homes. Laws forbid the use of physical restraints except temporarily in specific, extraordinary circumstances. Some nursing homes provide individualized, humane care, allowing residents to decide what to eat, where to walk, whether to have a pet. In the United States, nursing homes are frequently visited by government inspectors to "stop dreadful things from happening" (Baker, 2007).

In North America good nursing-home care is available for those who can afford it and know what to look for. Some nonprofit homes are subsidized by religious organizations, and these may be excellent. In some European nations, the federal government subsidizes care for anyone (rich or poor) who needs it. Good care allows independence, individual choice, and privacy. As with day care for young children, continuity of care is crucial: An institution with a high rate of staff turnover is to be avoided.

The training and the workload of the staff, especially of the aides who provide frequent personal care, are crucial: Such simple tasks as helping a frail person out of bed can be done clumsily, painfully, or skillfully. The difference depends on proficiency, experience, and patience—all possible with a sufficient number of well-trained and well-paid staff. Currently, however, most front-line workers have little training, low pay, and many patients—and almost half leave each year (Golant, 2011).

Especially for Those Uncertain about Future Careers Would you like to work in a nursing home? (see response, page 755)

Same Situation, Far Apart: Diversity Continues No matter where they live, elders thrive with individualized care and social interaction, as is apparent here. Lenore Walker *(left)* celebrates her 100th birthday in a Florida nursing home with her younger sister nearby, and an elderly chess player in a senior residence in Kosovo *(right)* contemplates protecting his king. Both photos show, in details such as the women's earrings and the men's head coverings, that these elders maintain their individuality.

Quality care is much more labor-intensive and expensive than most people realize. The average annual nursing home cost in the United States in 2011 was $85,775 for a private room. Variations are dramatic, primarily because of the cost of personnel. In Alaska, it costs $177,755 a year for a room shared with one other person; in Louisiana, it's only $50,370 (John Hancock Life & Health Insurance Company, 2011). Most people think that Medicare, Medicaid, or long-term insurance covers the entire cost—another misconception.

In the United States, the trend over the past 20 years has been toward a lower proportion of those over age 60 residing in nursing homes (in 2011 about 1.3 million people nationwide), and those few are usually over 80 years old, frail and confused, with several medical problems (Moore et al., 2012).

Another trend is toward smaller nursing homes with more individualized care and nurses and aides who work more closely together, especially in homes designated as Eden Alternative or Green, named after exemplars that stress individual autonomy (Sharkey et al., 2011).

Although 90 percent of elders are independent and live in the community at any given moment, half of them will need some nursing-home care, usually for less than a month after a few days in a hospital. Some need such care for more than a year, and a very few stay for 10 years or more (Stone, 2006).

Alternative Care

An ageist stereotype is that older people are either completely capable of self-care or completely dependent on others. In actuality, everyone of every age is on a continuum, with some self-care and yet needing some help.

Once that is understood a range of options can be envisioned. Remember the study cited in Chapter 24 that found that dementia is less common in England than it used to be? That study also found that the percentage of people with neurocognitive disorders in nursing homes has risen, from 56 percent in 1991 to 65 percent in 2011, primarily because of a rise in the number of oldest-old women in such places (Matthews et al., 2013).

That means that more British elderly who need some care are now in the community. This is good news for the elderly, for developmentalists, and for the community, because aging in place, assisted living, and other options are less costly and more individualized than institutions.

The number of assisted-living facilities has increased as nursing homes have decreased. Typically, assisted-living residences provide private apartments for each

Many Possibilities This couple in Wyoming *(left)* sold their Georgia house and now live in this RV, and this Cuban woman *(right)* continues to live in her familiar home. Ideally, all the elderly have a range of choices—and when that is true, almost no one needs nursing home care.

person and allow pets and furnishings as in a traditional home. The assisted aspects vary, often consisting of one daily communal meal, special transportation and activities, household cleaning, and medical assistance such as supervision of pill-taking, monitoring of blood pressure or diabetes, with a nurse, doctor, and ambulance at the ready if needed.

Assisted-living facilities range from group homes for three or four elderly people to large apartment or townhouse developments for hundreds (Golant, 2011). Almost every state, province, or nation has its own standards for assisted-living facilities, but many such places are unlicensed. Some regions of the world (e.g., northern Europe) have many assisted living options, while others (e.g., sub-Saharan Africa) have almost none.

Another form of elder care is sometimes called *village care*. Although not really a village, it is so named because of the African proverb, "It takes a whole village to raise a child." In village care, elderly people who live near each other pool their resources, staying in their homes but also getting special assistance when they need it. Such communities require that the elderly contribute financially and that they be relatively competent, so village care is not suited for everyone. However, for some it is ideal (Scharlach et al., 2012).

Another option is for elders to remain at home or at a home of a family member. While these arrangements can be rewarding for the caregiver, they can also be stressful. Caregivers, and the elders they care for, often benefit from respite care. For example, the caregivers may get a temporary break when the care receiver has a short stay in an assisted-living community or receives intensive short-term in-home care provided by a professional. Either form of respite care can help restore the caregiver and help them better weather the stress of managing the welfare of their family member.

Overall, as with many other aspects of aging, the emphasis in living arrangements is on selective optimization with compensation. Elders need settings that allow them to be safe, social, and respected, and as independent as possible. Housing solutions vary depending not only on ADLs and IADLs, but also the elder's personality and social network of family and friends. One expert explains: "There is no one-size-fits-all set of optimum residential activities, experiences, and situations" (Golant, 2011).

>> Response for Those Uncertain about Future Careers (from page 753): Why not? The demand for good workers will obviously increase as the population ages, and the working conditions are likely to improve. An important problem is that the quality of nursing homes varies, so you need to make sure you work in one whose policies incorporate the view that the elderly can be quite capable, social, and independent.

We close with an example of family care and nursing-home care at their best. A young adult named Rob related that his 98-year-old great-grandmother "began to fail. We . . . thought, well, maybe she is growing old" (quoted in L. P. Adler, 1995, p. 242). All three younger generations decided that she should move to a nearby nursing home, leaving the place she had lived in for decades. She reluctantly agreed.

Fortunately, this nursing home did not assume that decline is always a sign of "final failing." (Rob's phrase). The doctors discovered that her pacemaker was not working properly. Rob tells what happened next:

> We were very concerned to have her undergo surgery at her age, but we finally agreed. . . . Soon she was back to being herself, a strong, spirited, energetic, independent woman. It was the pacemaker that was wearing out, not Great-grandmother.
>
> *[quoted in L. P. Adler, 1995, p. 242]*

This story contains a lesson repeated throughout this book. Whenever a toddler does not talk, a preschooler grabs a toy, a teenager gets drunk, an emerging adult takes risks, an adult seeks divorce, or an older person becomes frail, it is easy to conclude that this is normal. Indeed, each of these possible problems is common at the ages mentioned and may be appropriate and acceptable for some individuals.

But none should simply be accepted without question. Any one of these should alert people to encourage talking, sharing, moderation, caution, communication, or self-care. The life-span perspective holds that, at every age, people can be "strong, spirited, and energetic."

SUMMING UP

The frail elderly are weak, tired, and fading in many ways. They are unable or unwilling to perform activities of daily life (ADLs) such as feeding, dressing, and bathing themselves, or to carry out the instrumental activities of daily life (IADLs) that require some intellectual competence. Families, communities, and the elderly themselves can postpone or prevent frailty, although they often do not.

Caregiving of the frail elderly can be depressing or satisfying, depending partly on support from professionals, family members, and the care receiver. Help is needed from many people; elder abuse is common—a sign of social isolation and overburdened caregivers. The best care for the frail elderly depends on many factors and can range from aging in place with support from visiting nurses and family members to living with younger relatives, to assisted-living facilities, to nursing homes and hospitals. Much depends not only on the specifics of frailty, but also on the people directly involved. ▪

SUMMARY

Theories of Late Adulthood

1. Several self theories hold that adults make personal choices in ways that allow them to become fully themselves. Erikson believed that individuals seek integrity that connects them to the human community, present and past.

2. Longitudinal research finds substantial continuity in personality traits over the life span, as well as a positivity effect, an elder's more positive view of themselves and others. Some elders cherish personal papers and objects to help them maintain identity—risking a disorder called hoarding

3. Stratification theories maintain that social forces—such as ageism, racism, and sexism—limit personal choices throughout the life span. The effects are cumulative, with deprivation early in life resulting in a cascade of problems lifelong.

4. Disengagement theory suggests that older adults are stratified by age, and willingly disengage. This theory is opposed by activity theory, which holds that older people are happier and healthier when they are active.

Activities in Late Adulthood

5. At every age, employment can provide social and personal satisfaction as well as needed income. However, retirement may be welcomed by the elderly who find other ways to stay active.

6. Some elderly people perform volunteer work, and many are active politically—writing letters to political leaders, voting, staying informed. These activities enhance health and well-being and benefit the larger society.

7. Common among elders is an increase in religious activity (but not necessarily attendance at services), which correlates with longer life.

8. Many of the elderly engage in home improvement or redecoration, preferring to stay in their own homes. If they move, they are likely to stay in the same neighborhood, near old friends and religious institutions.

Friends and Relatives

9. A spouse is the most important member of a person's social convoy. Older adults in long-standing marriages tend to be satisfied with their relationships and to safeguard each other's health. As a result, married elders tend to live longer, happier, and healthier lives than unmarried ones.

10. Many of the elderly, especially those who have spent many years unmarried, have a supportive network of friends. They fare better than those who have recently been divorced or widowed.

11. Relationships with adult children and grandchildren are usually mutually supportive. If the elderly become full-time caregivers of grandchildren, this may have benefits for society and for the people involved, but it also adds stress to the older generation.

The Frail Elderly

12. Some elderly people eventually become frail. They need help with activities of daily life, either with physical tasks (ADLs, such as eating and bathing) or with instrumental ones (IADLs, such as paying bills and arranging transportation).

13. Care of the frail elderly is usually undertaken by adult children or spouses, who are often elderly themselves. Most families have a strong sense of filial responsibility, although elder abuse may occur when caregiving stress is great and social support is weak.

14. Nursing homes, assisted living, and home care are of varying quality and availability. Each of these arrangements can provide necessary and beneficial care, with the need for many variations available and many people to be involved.

KEY TERMS

activities of daily life (ADLs) (p. 750)
activity theory (p. 736)
age in place (p. 740)
compulsive hoarding (p. 731)

disengagement theory (p. 736)
filial responsibility (p. 745)
frail elderly (p. 749)
instrumental activities of daily life (IADLs) (p. 750)

integrity versus despair (p. 730)
naturally occurring retirement community (NORC) (p. 740)
positivity effect (p. 732)
self theories (p. 730)

socioemotional selectivity theory (p. 732)
stratification theories (p. 734)

WHAT HAVE YOU LEARNED?

1. How does Erikson's use of the word *integrity* differ from its usual meaning?

2. How does hoarding relate to self theory?

3. What are the advantages of the positivity effect?

4. What are the disadvantages of the positivity effect?

5. How can disengagement be a mutual process?

6. What does activity theory suggest older adults should do?

7. What are the problems with being female, according to stratification theory?

8. What are the problems with being male, according to stratification theory?

9. According to stratification theory, how is old age difficult for members of minority groups?

10. How is self-theory reflected in older adults' desire to age in place?

11. How does retirement affect the health of people who have worked all their lives?

12. Why would a person choose not to retire?

13. What does age affect how likely someone is to choose to volunteer?

14. What are four common reasons why elderly people do not volunteer?

15. What are the benefits and liabilities for elders who want to age in place?

16. How does religion affect the well-being of the aged?

17. How does the political activism of older and younger adults differ?

18. What is the usual relationship between older adults who have been partners for decades?

19. Who benefits from relationships between older adults and their grown children?

20. Which type of grandparenting seems to benefit both generations the most?

21. Why do older people tend to have fewer friends as they age?

22. Why is the inability to perform ADLs indicative of frailty?

23. Why are IADLs considered even more important than ADLs in assessing frailty in an elderly person?

24. What three factors increase the likelihood of elder abuse?

25. What are the advantages and disadvantages of assisted living for the elderly?

26. When is a nursing home a good solution for the problems of the frail elderly?

APPLICATIONS

1. Attitudes about disabilities are influential. Visit the disability office on your campus, asking both staff and students what they see as the effects of attitude on performance. How do your findings relate to the elderly?

2. People of different ages, cultures, and experiences vary in their values regarding family caregiving, including the need for safety, privacy, independence, and professional help. Find four people whose backgrounds (age, ethnicity, SES) differ. Ask their opinions, and analyze the results.

3. Visit a nursing home or assisted-living residence in your community. Record details about the physical setting, the social interactions of the residents, and the activities of the staff. Would you like to work or live in this place? Why or why not?

>> ONLINE CONNECTIONS

To accompany your textbook, you have access to a number of online resources, including Learning Curve, an adaptive quizzing program, critical thinking questions, and case studies. For access to any of these links, go to www.worth publishers.com/launchpad/bergerls9e. In addition to these resources, you'll also find links to video clips, personalized study advice, and an ebook. Some of the videos and activities available online include:

- *85 plus! Case studies* of olders highlight the contributions elders can make to their communities and how activity doesn't stop after 85.

Late Adulthood

BIOSOCIAL

Ageism Prejudice based on age is common and harmful in late adulthood. Many younger adults, and even older people themselves, underestimate the health and vitality of the old.

The best strategy for coping with aging seems to be selective optimization with compensation. Physiological functions change over time, but such changes can be taken in stride if individuals and communities adjust.

Disease and Aging Virtually every disease and disability becomes more common in late adulthood. Impairment of the senses occurs to almost everyone and can result in serious losses. Every condition is affected by genes and by health habits decades earlier, and most can be mitigated by early detection and treatment. The optimal goal is compression of morbidity.

Longevity Wear and tear, genes, and cellular damage all seem relevant to some aspect of aging but none has led to proven measures that halt aging. The maximum life span for every species is determined by genes. Calorie restriction succeeds in prolonging life in some species; application to humans is unproven. People who live more than 100 years have good genes and health habits and seem unusually active, happy and supported by their community.

COGNITIVE

Brains and Thinking Some brain areas shrink with age, some kinds of memory fade, and thinking processes slow down, but new learning can produce new neurons and dendrites, and verbal memory is often unimpaired until very late in life. Sensory losses reduce input; remediating problems with vision and hearing may improve cognition. Ecologically valid cognitive assessments show most elders are able to use their minds to remain vital and independent.

Neurocognitive Disorders Neurocognitive disorders become more common with age as cognitive reserves shrink. Alzheimer disease is the most common one in the U.S. It is rare until age 70, but the rate increases every decade after that. Another common NCD is caused by a series of strokes, each destroying part of the brain. There are many other causes, each with distinct symptoms. Some reversible problems, such as depression and polypharmacy, also cause cognitive problems.

New Cognitive Development In later adulthood, many people develop their creativity via the arts or the life review. Some elders also become wise, but wisdom is not guaranteed in the old or completely absent in the young

PSYCHOSOCIAL

Theories, Activities, and Family Self and stratification theories note that it is not easy to maintain vitality and joy in late adulthood, but most elders remain active, caring about political and religious concerns. Some move to a smaller residence or assisted-living quarters, but most prefer to age in place. Relationships with mates, children, and grandchildren continue to be important for well-being.

The Frail Elderly A minority of elders are termed "frail": weak and failing, unable to maintain the activities of daily life or the instrumental activities. Frailty is partly the result of aging bodies and minds and partly the result of lack of self-care, the misguided care of other people and of neglectful communities.

Epilogue

- **Death and Hope**
  Cultures, Epochs, and Death
  Understanding Death Throughout the
    Life Span
  Near-Death Experiences

- **Choices in Dying**
  A Good Death
  Better Ways to Die
  Ethical Issues
  OPPOSING PERSPECTIVES:
    The "Right to Die"?
  Advance Directives

- **Affirmation of Life**
  Grief
  Mourning
  Diversity of Reactions
  Practical Applications
  A VIEW FROM SCIENCE: Resilience
    after a Death

WHAT WILL YOU KNOW?

1. Why is death a topic of hope, not despair?
2. What is the difference between a good death and a bad one?
3. How does mourning help with grief?

A nearby hospital (St. Vincent's) closed two years ago, the victim of budget cuts. Six other hospitals have been shuttered this year in New York City for the same reason. St. Vincent's closure struck the local community hard—emotions are still hot. Yesterday, at a rally at the hospital site, the editor of a local newspaper slapped our state senator, who responded with surprise and compassion (Taylor, 2013).

Why did that slap happen? The editor said his wife died recently in a Bronx hospital, and if St. Vincent's were still open, "I could have walked two blocks and spent time with her through the last hours of her life" (Taylor, 2013, p. A-16). Of course, that is no excuse for violence, but mourners want to blame someone—a hospital, a senator, a doctor, the dying person. Men tend to get rageful, women depressed (Corr & Corr, 2013). People say, "It didn't have to happen," even though they know that death, whether two blocks or a long subway ride away, is part of life.

That editor is not the only irrational one. When Joan Didion's husband died, she experienced a "year of magical thinking," including keeping his shoes in the closet because he would need them if he came back (Didion, 2005). Mourners are not always logical.

This chapter acknowledges the emotions that accompany a death, and helps us understand dying, death, grief, and bereavement. We can expect powerful feelings to surface; hopefully they can be directed toward help for the living. Tears yes; slaps, no. There is *hope* in death, *choices* in dying, and *affirmation* in mourning, as the three sections of this chapter describe.

>> Death and Hope

A multicultural life-span perspective reveals that reactions to death are filtered through many cultural prisms, affected by historical changes and regional variations, and by the age of both the dying and the bereaved.

One emotion is constant, however: hope. It appears in many ways: hope for life after death, hope that the world is better because someone lived, hope that death occurred for a reason, hope that survivors rededicate themselves to whatever they deem meaningful in life.

Cultures, Epochs, and Death

Few people in developed nations have witnessed someone die. This was not always the case (see Table EP.1). If someone reached age 50 in 1900 in the United States and had had 20 high school classmates, at least six of those fellow students

TABLE EP.1	How Death Has Changed in the Past 100 Years
Death occurs later. A century ago, the average life span worldwide was less than 40 years (47 in the rapidly industrializing United States). Half of the world's babies died before age 5. Now newborns are expected to live to age 71 (79 in the U.S.); in many nations, centenarians are the fastest-growing age group.	
Dying takes longer. In the early 1900s, death was usually fast and unstoppable; once the brain, the heart, or any other vital organ failed, the rest of the body quickly followed. Now death can often be postponed for years through medical technology: Hearts can beat for years after the brain stops functioning, respirators can replace lungs, dialysis does the work of failing kidneys.	
Death often occurs in hospitals. For most of our ancestors, death occurred at home, with family nearby. Now many deaths occur in hospitals, with the dying surrounded by medical personnel and machines.	
The causes of death have changed. People of all ages once usually died of infectious diseases (tuberculosis, typhoid, smallpox), or, for many women and infants, in childbirth. Now disease deaths before age 50 are rare, and in developed nations most newborns (99 percent) and their mothers (99.99 percent) live.	
And after death . . . People once knew about life after death. Some believed in heaven and hell; others, in reincarnation; others, in the spirit world. Prayers were repeated—some on behalf of the souls of the deceased, some for remembrance, some to the dead asking for protection. Believers were certain that their prayers were heard. People now are aware of cultural and religious diversity; many raise doubts that never occurred to their ancestors.	

would have already died. The survivors would have visited and reassured friends who were dying at home, promising to see them in heaven. Almost everyone believed in life after death.

Now few die before old age, and if a young person dies, most often it occurs too quickly to say goodbye. Ironically, death has become more feared as dying has become less familiar (Carr, 2012). Accordingly, we begin by describing traditional responses when familiarity with death was common.

Ancient Times

Paleontologists believe that 100,000 years ago, the Neanderthals buried their dead with tools, bowls, or jewelry, signifying belief in an afterlife (Hayden, 2012). The date is controversial: Burial could have begun over 200,000 years ago or more recently—but it is certain that long ago death was an occasion for hope, mourning, and remembrance. Two Western civilizations with written records—Egypt and Greece—had elaborate death rituals.

The ancient Egyptians built magnificent pyramids, refined mummification, and scripted instructions (called the *Book of the Dead*) to aid the soul (*ka*), personality (*ba*), and shadow (*akh*) in reuniting after death so that the dead could bless and protect the living (Taylor, 2010).

The fate of dead Egyptians depended partly on their actions while alive, partly on the circumstances of death, and partly on proper burial. Death was a reason to live morally and to honor the past. If the dead were not appropriately cared for, the living would suffer.

Another set of beliefs comes from the Greeks. Again, continuity between life and death was evident, with hope for this world and the next. The fate of a dead person depended on past deeds. A few would have a blissful afterlife, a few were condemned to torture in Hades, and most would enter a shadow world until they were reincarnated.

Three themes are apparent in all the known ancient societies, not only in Greece and Egypt, but also in the Mayan, Chinese, Indian, and African cultures.

- Actions during life were thought to affect destiny after death.
- An afterlife was more than a hope; it was assumed.
- Mourners said particular prayers and made specific offerings, in part to prevent the spirit of the dead from haunting and hurting them.

Contemporary Religions

Now consider contemporary religions. Each faith seems distinct in its practices surrounding death. One review states: "Rituals in the world's religions, especially those for the major tragic and significant events of bereavement and death, have a bewildering diversity" (Idler, 2006, p. 285).

Some details illustrate this diversity. According to one expert, in Hinduism the casket is always open, in Islam, never (Gilbert, 2013). In many Muslim and Hindu cultures the dead person is bathed by the next of kin; among some Native Americans (e.g., the Navajo) no family member touches the dead person. Specific rituals vary as much by region as by religion. In North America, Christians of all sects often follow local traditions. Similarly, there are more than 500 Indian tribes, each with its own heritage: It is a mistake to assume that Native Americans all have the same customs (Cacciatore, 2009).

According to many branches of Hinduism a person should die on the floor, surrounded by family, who neither eat nor wash until the funeral pyre is extinguished. By contrast, among some (but not all) Christians today, the very sick should be taken to the hospital; if they die, then mourners gather to eat and drink, often with music and dancing.

Diversity is also evident in Buddhism. The First Noble Truth of Buddhism is that life is suffering. Some rituals help believers accept death and detach from grieving in order to decrease the suffering that living without the deceased person entails. Other rituals help people connect to the dead as part of the continuity between life and death (Cuevas & Stone, 2011). Thus some Buddhists let the dying alone; other Buddhists hover nearby.

Religious practices change as historical conditions do. One example comes from Korea. Koreans traditionally opposed autopsies because the body is a sacred gift. However, Koreans value science education. This created a dilemma because medical schools need bodies to autopsy in order to teach. The solution was to start a new custom: a special religious service honoring the dead who have given their body for medical education (J-T. Park et al., 2011). The result: a dramatic increase in the number of bodies donated for research.

Autopsies create problems in the United States as well. Autopsies may be legally required and yet be considered a religious sacrilege. For instance, for the Hmong in Cambodia, any mutilation of the dead body has "horrifying meanings" and "dire consequences for . . . the spiritual well-being of the surviving family and community" (Rosenblatt, 2013, p. 125). In Minnesota, however, where many Hmong now live, the family does not need to be told about, much less give permission for, an autopsy if the coroner has "any question about the cause of death."

Ideas about death are expressed differently in various cultures. For example, many people believe that the spirits of ancestors visit the living. Spirits are particularly likely to appear during the Hungry Ghost Festival (in many East Asian nations), on the Day of the Dead (in many Latin American nations), or on All Souls Day (in many European nations).

Consequently, do not get distracted by death customs or beliefs that may seem odd to you, such as mummies, hungry ghosts, reincarnation, or hell. Instead, notice that death has always inspired strong emotions, often benevolent ones. It is the *denial* of death that leads to despair (Wong & Tomer, 2011). In all faiths and cultures, death is considered a passage, not an endpoint, a reason for families and strangers to come together.

Understanding Death Throughout the Life Span

Thoughts about death—as about everything else—are influenced by each person's cognitive maturation and past experiences. Here are some of the specifics.

Sorrow All Around When a 5-day-old baby died in Santa Rosa, Guatemala, the entire neighborhood mourned. Symbols and a procession help with grief: The coffin is white to indicate that the infant was without sin and will therefore be in heaven.

Death in Childhood

Some adults think children are oblivious to death; others believe children should participate in funerals and other rituals, just as adults do (Talwar et al., 2011). You know from your study of childhood cognition that neither view is completely correct. Very young children have some understanding of death, but their perspective differs from that of older people. They may believe that the dead can come alive again. For that reason, a child might not immediately be sad when someone dies. Later, moments of profound sorrow might occur when reality sinks in, or simply when the child realizes that a dead parent will never again tuck them into bed at night.

Children are affected by the attitudes of others. If a child encounters death, adults should listen with full attention, neither ignoring the child's concerns nor expecting adult-like reactions (Doering, 2010). Because the limbic system matures more rapidly than the prefrontal cortex, children may seem happy one day and morbidly depressed the next.

Young children who themselves are fatally ill typically fear that death means being abandoned (Wolchik et al., 2008). Consequently, parents should stay with a dying child, holding, reading, singing, and sleeping. A frequent and caring presence is more important than logic. By school age, many children seek independence. Parents and professionals can be too solicitous; older children do not want to be babied. Often they want facts and a role in "management of illness and treatment decisions" (Varga & Paletti, 2013, p. 27).

Children who lose a friend, a relative, or a pet might, or might not, seem sad, lonely, or angry. For example, one 7-year-old boy seemed unfazed by the loss of three grandparents and an uncle within two years. However, he was extremely upset when his dog, Twick, died. That boy's parents, each grieving for a dead mother, were taken aback by the depth of his emotions. The boy was angry that he was not taken to the animal hospital before the dog was euthanized. He refused to go back to school, saying, "I wanted to see him one more time. . . . You don't understand" (quoted in K. R. Kaufman & Kaufman, 2006, pp. 65–66).

Because the loss of a particular companion is a young child's concern, it is not helpful to say that a dog can be replaced. Even a 1-year-old knows that a new puppy is not the same dog. Nor should a child be told that Grandma is sleeping, that God wanted sister in heaven, or that Grandpa went on a trip. The child may take such explanations literally, wanting to wake up Grandma, complain to God, or phone Grandpa to say "Come home."

If a child realizes that adults are afraid to say that death has occurred, the child might decide that death is so horrible that adults cannot talk about it—a terrifying conclusion (Doering, 2010). Even worse is the idea that adults are not trustworthy: They lie to children.

Remember how cognition changes with development. Egocentric preschoolers might fear that they, personally, caused death with their unkind words. [**Lifespan Link:** Egocentrism is discussed in Chapter 9.]

As children become concrete operational thinkers, they seek facts, such as exactly how a person died and where he or she is now. They want something to do: bring flowers, repeat a prayer, write a letter. The boy whose dog died went back to school after his parents framed and hung a poem he wrote to Twick. Children see no contradiction between biological death and spiritual afterlife, as long as adults neither lie nor disregard the child's concerns (Talwar et al., 2011).

Death in Adolescence and Emerging Adulthood

Adolescents may be self-absorbed, philosophical, analytic, or distraught—or all four at different moments. [**Lifespan Link:** Adolescent dual processing is discussed in Chapter 15.] Counselors emphasize that adults must listen to teenagers. Self-expression is part of the search for identity; death of a loved one does not put an end to that search. Some adolescents use the Internet to write to the dead person or to vent their grief—an effective way to express their personal identity concerns (DeGroot, 2012).

"Live fast, die young, and leave a good-looking corpse" is advice often attributed to actor James Dean, who died in a car crash at age 24. At what stage would a person be most likely to agree? Emerging adulthood, of course. Worldwide, older teenagers and emerging adults control their anxiety about death by taking risks (de Bruin et al., 2007; Luxmoore, 2012).

Terror management theory explains some illogical responses to death, including why young people take death-defying risks (Mosher & Danoff-Burg, 2007). By surviving, they manage their terror by proving that death cannot get them. Especially when people aged 15 to 24 have access to guns and cars, this developmental tendency can be deadly (see Figure EP.1). Cluster suicides, foolish dares, fatal gang fights, and drug-impaired driving are more common during those years than later. Three attitudes typical of older adolescents are correlated: ageism, terror management, risk-taking (Popham et al., 2011b).

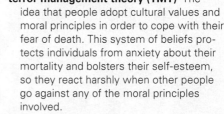

terror management theory (TMT) The idea that people adopt cultural values and moral principles in order to cope with their fear of death. This system of beliefs protects individuals from anxiety about their mortality and bolsters their self-esteem, so they react harshly when other people go against any of the moral principles involved.

Many studies have found that messages about the deadly consequences of smoking may provoke smokers to *increase* their consumption (Arndt et al., 2013). One study found that college students who were told that binge drinking is sometimes fatal were more willing to binge, not less so (Jessop & Wade, 2008). Thus teenagers and young adults may protect their pride and self-esteem by defying death and resisting the advice of adults.

Other research in many nations finds that when adolescents and emerging adults think about death, they sometimes become more patriotic and religious but less tolerant of other worldviews and less generous to people of other nations (Ellis & Wahab, 2013; Jonas et al., 2013). Apparently, people want to convince themselves that loyal, conscientious members of their own group (including themselves) are especially worthy of living.

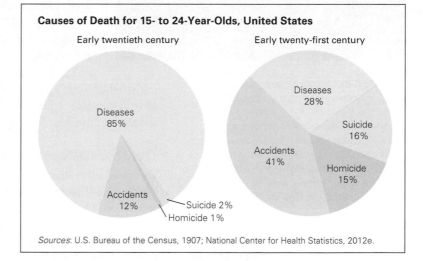

Causes of Death for 15- to 24-Year-Olds, United States

Early twentieth century

Diseases 85%
Accidents 12%
Suicide 2%
Homicide 1%

Early twenty-first century

Diseases 28%
Suicide 16%
Homicide 15%
Accidents 41%

Sources: U.S. Bureau of the Census, 1907; National Center for Health Statistics, 2012e.

FIGURE EP.1

Typhoid Versus Driving into a Tree
In 1905, most young adults in the United States who died were victims of diseases, usually infectious ones like tuberculosis and typhoid. In 2012, 3 times more died violently (accidents, homicide, suicide) than of all diseases combined.

Death in Adulthood

When adults become responsible for work and family, attitudes shift. Death is not romanticized. Many adults quit addictive drugs, start wearing seat belts, and adopt other death-avoiding behaviors when they become parents. One of my students eagerly anticipated the thrill of her first skydive, paying in advance. However, the day before the scheduled dive she learned she was pregnant. She forfeited the money and shopped for prenatal vitamins.

To defend against the fear of aging and untimely death, adults do not readily accept the death of others. When Dylan Thomas was about age 30, he wrote to his dying father: "Do not go gentle into that good night/Rage, rage against the dying of the light" (D. Thomas, 1957). Nor do adults readily accept their own death. A woman diagnosed at age 42 with a rare and almost always fatal cancer (a sarcoma) wrote:

> I hate stories about people dying of cancer, no matter how graceful, noble, or beautiful.
> . . . I refuse to accept that I am dying; I prefer denial, anger, even desperation.

[Robson, 2010, pp. 19, 27]

When adults hear about another's death, their reaction depends on the dead person's age. Death in the prime of life is particularly disturbing. Michael Jackson and Whitney Houston were mourned by millions, in part because they were not yet old. Older entertainers who die are less mourned.

"For My Kids" Randy Pausch was a brilliant, innovative scientist at Carnegie Mellon University. When he was diagnosed with terminal pancreatic cancer, he gave a talk titled "The Last Lecture: Really Achieving Your Childhood Dreams" that became famous worldwide. He devoted the final 10 months of his life to his family—his wife Jai and their children Chloë, Dylan, and Logan.

FIGURE EP.2

A Toothache Worse Than Death? A cohort of young adults (average age 21) and old adults (average age 74) were divided into three groups. One group wrote about their musings of their own death (giving them overt thoughts about dying), another did a puzzle with some words about death (giving them unconscious thoughts about death), and the third wrote about dental pain (they were the control group). Then they all judged how harshly people should be punished for various moral transgressions. Those who wrote about dental pain are represented by the zero point on this graph. Compared with them, those older adults who thought about death were less punitive, but younger adults were more so. The difference in the ratings of the young and old was more pronounced if their thoughts were unconscious than if they were overt.

Reactions to one's own mortality differ depending on the developmental stage as well. In adulthood, from ages 25 to 65, terminally ill people worry about leaving something undone or abandoning family members, especially children.

One dying middle-aged adult was Randy Pausch, a 47-year-old professor and father of three. Ten months before he died of cancer in 2008, he delivered a famous last lecture, detailing his childhood dreams and saluting those who would continue his work. After advising his students to follow their own dreams, he concluded, "This talk is not for you, it's for my kids" (Pausch, 2008). Not surprisingly, that message was embraced by his wife, also in mid-adulthood, who wrote her own book, titled *Dream New Dreams*, which deals with overcoming death by focusing on life (J. Pausch, 2012).

Adult attitudes about death are often irrational. Logically, adults should work to change social factors that increase the risk of mortality—such as air pollution, junk foods, and unsafe transportation. Instead, many people react more strongly to events that rarely cause death, such as anthrax and avalanches. They particularly fear deaths that seem random.

For example, people fear travel by plane more than by car. In fact, flying is safer: In 2008 only 11 commercial airplanes crashed in the entire world, killing 587, but 84,000 people were killed by motor vehicles in the United States alone (U.S. Bureau of the Census, 2011b). Ironically, when four airplanes crashed on 9/11, 2001, many North Americans drove long distances instead of flying. In the next few months, 2,300 more U.S. residents died in car crashes than usual (Blalock et al., 2009). Not logical, but very human.

Death in Late Adulthood

In late adulthood, attitudes shift again. Anxiety decreases; hope rises (De Raedt et al., 2013). Life-threatening illnesses reduce life satisfaction more among the middle-aged than the elderly (Wurm et al., 2008). Terror-management irrationality diminishes (Maxfield et al., 2007) (see Figure EP.2).

Some older people are quite happy even when they are fatally ill, which is beneficial. Indeed, many developmentalists believe that one sign of mental health among older adults is acceptance of mortality, which increases concern for others. Some elders engage in *legacy work*, trying to leave something meaningful for later generations (Lattanzi-Licht, 2013).

As evidence of this attitude change, older people seek to reconcile with estranged family members and tie up loose ends that most young adults leave hanging (Kastenbaum, 2012). Some people are troubled when their parents or grandparents allocate heirlooms, discuss end-of-life treatments, or buy a burial plot, but all those actions are developmentally appropriate.

Acceptance of death does not mean that the elderly give up on living; rather, their priorities shift. In an intriguing series of studies (Carstensen, 2011), people were presented with the following scenario:

> Imagine that in carrying out the activities of everyday life, you find that you have half an hour of free time, with no pressing commitments. You have decided that you'd like to spend this time with another person. Assuming that the following

Thoughts About Death and Severity of Punishment

Source: Maxfield et al., 2007.

three persons are available to you, whom would you want to spend that
time with?

- A member of your immediate family
- The author of a book you have just read
- An acquaintance with whom you seem to have much in common

Older adults, more than younger ones, choose the family member. The researchers explain that family becomes more important when death seems near.
This is supported by a study of 329 people of various ages who had recently been
diagnosed with cancer and a matched group of 170 people (of the same ages)
who had no serious illness (Pinquart & Silbereisen, 2006). The most marked
difference was between those with and without cancer, regardless of age (see
Figure EP.3). Attitudes change when death becomes more salient.

Near-Death Experiences

Even coming close to death may be an occasion for hope. This is most obvious in what is called a *near-death experience,* in which a person almost dies. Survivors sometimes report having left the body and moving toward a bright light while
feeling peace and joy. The following classic report is typical:

> I was in a coma for approximately a week. . . . I felt as though I were lifted right
> up, just as though I didn't have a physical body at all. A brilliant white light
> appeared. . . . The most wonderful feelings came over me—feelings of peace,
> tranquility, a vanishing of all worries.
>
> *[quoted in R. A. Moody, 1975, p. 56]*

Near-death experiences often include religious elements (angels seen, celestial
music heard). Survivors often become more spiritual, less materialistic. To some,
near-death experiences prove that "Heaven is for real" (Burpo & Vincent, 2010).
Most scientists are skeptical, claiming that

> there is no evidence that what happens when a person really dies and "stays
> dead" has any relationship to the experience reported by those who have
> recovered from a life-threatening episode. In fact, it is difficult to imagine how
> there could ever be such evidence.
>
> *[Kastenbaum, 2006, p. 448]*

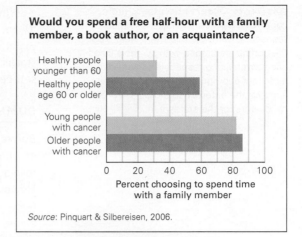

Would you spend a free half-hour with a family member, a book author, or an acquaintance?

Percent choosing to spend time with a family member

Source: Pinquart & Silbereisen, 2006.

FIGURE EP.3

Turning to Family as Death Approaches
Both young and old people diagnosed with
cancer (one-fourth of whom died within five
years) more often preferred to spend a free
half-hour with a family member rather than
with an interesting person whom they did
not know well. For healthy people, age mattered most in deciding their preference.

Observation Quiz What three similarities
do you see in these funerals? (see answer,
page 768)

Praise Famous Men The funerals of two
men, Chris Kelly (left) half of the Kriss Kross
rap duo, and Paul Celluci (right), former gov-
erner of Massachusetts, show cultural contrasts and underlying universals.

Answer to Observation Quiz (from page 767): Clothes, symbols, and ritual respect. In both, the mourners wear black, the coffins are draped with symbols (flags and flowers), and respect is conveyed in a manner appropriate for each—a rousing song for the entertainer and State Police pallbearers for the statesman.

Especially For Relatives of a Person Who Is Dying Why would a healthy person want the attention of hospice caregivers? (see response, page 771)

Nevertheless, a reviewer of near-death experiences is struck by their similarity to religious beliefs about death. In every culture, "all varieties of the dying experience" move people toward the same realizations: (1) the limitations of social status, (2) the insignificance of material possessions, and (3) the narrowness of self-centeredness (Greyson, 2009).

SUMMING UP

Before the twentieth century, everyone knew several adults who died young, and everyone had religious understandings of that event. Ancient cultures and current world religions have various customs about death, sometimes prescribing opposite actions. However, the general impact is to help survivors live better lives as they respond with hope. Age matters as well: Reaction to death depends partly on the developmental stage, with older adults less anxious about death than younger ones. Terror management theory finds that people sometimes react to death with defiance and intolerance. Near-death experiences are criticized by scholars, yet they may make people more spiritual, less materialistic, and more appreciative of others. ■

>> Choices in Dying

Do you recoil at the heading "Choices in Dying"? If so, you may be living in the wrong century. Every twenty-first-century death involves choices, beginning with risks taken or avoided, habits sustained, and specific measures to postpone or hasten death.

A Good Death

People everywhere hope for a good death (Vogel, 2011), one that is:

- At the end of a long life
- Peaceful
- Quick
- In familiar surroundings
- With family and friends present
- Without pain, confusion, or discomfort

Many would add that *control over circumstances* and *acceptance of the outcome* are also characteristic of a good death, but cultures and individuals differ. Some dying individuals willingly cede control to doctors or caregivers, and others fight every sign that death is near.

Modern Medicine

In some ways, modern medicine makes a good death more likely. The first item on the list has become the norm: Death usually occurs at the end of a long life. Younger people still get sick, but surgery, drugs, radiation, and rehabilitation typically mean that, in developed countries, the ill go to the hospital and then return home. If young people die, death is typically quick (before medical intervention could save them), which, although it does not meet the criteria set out above, may actually be a painless death for them, if not for their loved ones.

In other ways, however, contemporary medical advances have made a bad death more likely. When a cure is impossible, physical and emotional comfort may deteriorate (Kastenbaum, 2012). Instead of acceptance, people fight death with surgery and drugs that prolong pain and confusion. Hospitals may exclude visitors at the most critical point, and patients may become delirious or unconscious, unable to die in peace.

The underlying problem may be medical care itself, which is so focused on life-saving that dying invites "the dangers of well-intentioned over 'medicalization'"

(Ashby, 2009, p. 94). Dying involves emotions, values, and a community—not just a heart that might stop beating. Fortunately, three factors that make a good death more likely have increased: honest conversation, the hospice, and palliative care.

Honest Conversation

In about 1960, researcher Elisabeth Kübler-Ross (1969, 1975) asked the administrator of a large Chicago hospital for permission to speak with dying patients. He told her that no one in the hospital was dying! Eventually, she found a few terminally ill patients who, to everyone's surprise, wanted very much to talk.

From ongoing interviews, Kübler-Ross identified emotions experienced by dying people, and by their loved ones. She divided these emotions into five sequential stages.

1. Denial ("I am not really dying.")
2. Anger ("I blame my doctors, or my family, or God for my death.")
3. Bargaining ("I will be good from now on if I can live.")
4. Depression ("I don't care about anything; nothing matters anymore.")
5. Acceptance ("I accept my death as part of life.")

Another set of stages of dying is based on Abraham Maslow's hierarchy of needs; as applied to the dying, Maslow's hierarchy can be characterized as follows (Zalenski & Raspa, 2006):

1. Physiological needs (freedom from pain)
2. Safety (no abandonment)
3. Love and acceptance (from close family and friends)
4. Respect (from caregivers)
5. Self-actualization (appreciating one's unique past and present)

[Lifespan Link: Maslow's hierarchy of needs is discussed in Chapter 2.]

Maslow later suggested a possible sixth stage, *self-transcendence* (Koltko-Rivera, 2006), which emphasizes the acceptance of death.

Other researchers have *not* found these sequential stages. Remember the woman dying of a sarcoma, cited earlier? She said that she would never accept death and that Kübler-Ross should have included desperation as a stage. Kübler-Ross herself later said that her stages have been misunderstood, as "our grief is as individual as our lives. . . . Not everyone goes through all of them or goes in a prescribed order" (Kübler-Ross & Kessler, 2005, p. 7).

Nevertheless, both lists remind caregivers that each dying person has strong emotions and needs that may be unlike that same person's emotions and needs a few days or weeks earlier. Furthermore, those emotions may differ from those of the caregivers, who themselves may each have their own emotions.

It is important for everyone—doctors, nurses, family, friends, and the patient—to know that a person is dying; then, appropriate care is more likely (Lundquist et al., 2011). Unfortunately, even if a patient is dying, most doctors never ask what end-of-life care the patient wants, and the result is not longer life but more pain, more procedures, and higher hospital bills in the final week of life. One study found that patients who had spoken with their doctors about terminal care had a final bill 36 percent lower than those who had not (Zhang et al., 2009).

Most dying people want to be with loved ones and to talk honestly with medical and religious professionals. Individual differences continue, of course. Some people do *not* want the whole truth, some want every possible medical intervention to occur, some do *not* want many visitors. In many Asian families, telling people they are dying is thought to destroy hope (Corr & Corr, 2013).

Better Ways to Die

Several practices have become more prevalent since the contrast between a good death and the usual hospital death has become clear. The hospice and the palliative-care specialty are examples.

Same Situation, Far Apart: As It Should Be Dying individuals and their families benefit from physical touch but suffer from medical practices (gowns, tubes, isolation) that restrict movement and prevent contact. For these two patients—a man with his family in a Catholic hospice in Andhra Pradesh, India *(top)*, and a husband with his wife in their hotel room in North Carolina *(bottom)*.

hospice An institution or program in which terminally ill patients receive palliative care to reduce suffering; family and friends of the dying are helped as well.

Hospice

In 1950s London, Cecily Saunders opened the first modern **hospice,** where terminally ill people could spend their last days in comfort (Saunders, 1978). Thousands of other hospices have opened in many nations, and hundreds of thousands of hospice caregivers bring medication and care to dying people where they live. In the United States, half of all hospice deaths occur at home (National Center for Health Statistics, 2011).

Hospice professionals relieve discomfort, avoiding measures that merely delay death; their aim is to make dying easier. There are two principles for hospice care:

- Each patient's autonomy and decisions are respected. For example, pain medication is readily available, not on a schedule or minimal dosage. Most hospice patients use less medication than a doctor might prescribe, but they decide.
- Family members and friends are counseled before the death, taught to provide care, and guided in mourning. Their needs are as important as those of the patient. Death is thought to happen to a family, not just to an individual.

Unfortunately, hospice does not reach many dying people (see Table EP.2), even in wealthy nations, much less in developing ones (Kiernan, 2010). Hospice care is more common in England than in mainland Europe, more common in the western part of the United States than the southeastern part, and rare in poor nations. Everywhere, those of higher SES are more likely to receive hospice

TABLE EP.2	Barriers to Entering Hospice Care

- Hospice patients must be terminally ill, with death anticipated within six months, but predictions are difficult. For example, in one study of noncancer patients, physician predictions were 90 percent accurate for those who died within a week but only 13 percent accurate when death was predicted in three to six weeks (usually the patients died sooner) (Brandt et al., 2006).

- Patients and caregivers must accept death. Traditionally, entering a hospice meant the end of curative treatment (chemotherapy, dialysis, and so on). This is no longer true. Now treatment can continue, and death is estimated to occur within six months without treatment. That means many hospice patients survive for longer than six months, and some get so much better that they are discharged (Salpeter et al., 2012).

- Hospice care is costly. Skilled workers—doctors, nurses, psychologists, social workers, clergy, music therapists, and so on—provide individualized care day and night.

- Availability varies. Hospice care is more common in England than in mainland Europe and is a luxury in poor nations. In the United States, western states have more hospices than southern states do. Even in one region (northern California) and among clients of one insurance company (Kaiser), the likelihood that people with terminal cancer will enter hospice depends on exactly where they live (N. L. Keating et al., 2006).

care. In the U.S. there are ethnic differences as well. For example, when African Americans enter hospice, they are more often admitted from a hospital than a home and are likely to die relatively quickly (one week, on average) (K. S. Johnson et al., 2011).

Currently in the United States, 60 percent of people die without hospice; of the 40 percent in hospice, one-third die within a week (National Center for Health Statistics, 2011). That is too soon for the personal medical and emotional needs of a dying person and their loved ones to be assessed and met.

Entering hospice means that comfort takes precedence over cure, but sometimes that itself extends life. In fact, 16 percent of U.S. hospice patients are discharged alive. Comfort can include measures that some hospitals forbid: acupuncture, special foods, flexible schedules, visitors when the patient wants them (which could be 2 A.M.), massage, aromatic oils, and so on (Doka, 2013).

Hospice care is expensive if it occurs in a separate institution where many skilled workers—doctors, nurses, psychologists, social workers, clergy, music therapists, and so on—provide individualized care day and night. Until recently, most insurance companies (including Medicare) did not cover hospice care unless no curative measures were included. That either/or restriction has been lifted, but many new hospice programs are for-profit, which may undercut the quality of care.

Home hospice care is less expensive, but it requires family or friends trained by hospice workers to provide care. Although this has led to an increase of "good deaths" at home, most deaths still occur in hospitals, and many others occur in nursing homes (see Figure EP.4).

Palliative Care

In 2006 the American Medical Association approved a new specialty, **palliative care**, which focuses on relieving pain and suffering. Palliative-care doctors are trained to discuss options with patients and their families. Some interventions may be refused if people understand the risks and benefits (Mynatt & Mowery, 2013). Palliative-care doctors also prescribe powerful drugs and procedures that make patients comfortable.

Morphine and other opiates have a **double effect**: They relieve pain (a positive effect), but they also slow down respiration (a negative effect). A painkiller that reduces both pain and breathing is allowed by law, ethics, and medical practice. In England, for instance, although it is illegal to cause death, even of a terminally ill patient who repeatedly asks to die, it is legal to prescribe drugs that have a double effect. One-third of all English deaths include such drugs. This itself raises the issue of whether some narcotics are used to hasten death more than to relieve pain (Billings, 2011).

Heavy sedation is another method sometimes used to alleviate pain. Concerns have been raised that this sometimes merely delays death rather than prolonging meaningful life, since the patient becomes unconscious, unable to think or feel (Raus et al., 2011).

Ethical Issues

As you see, the success of medicine has created new dilemmas. Death is no longer the natural outcome of age and disease; when and how death occurs involves human choices.

>> Response for Relatives of a Person Who Is Dying (from page 768): Death affects the entire family, including children and grandchildren. I learned this myself when my mother was dying. A hospice nurse not only gave her her pain medication (which made it easier for me to be with her) but also counseled me. At the nurse's suggestion, I asked for forgiveness. My mother indicated that there was nothing to forgive. We both felt a peace that would have eluded us without hospice care.

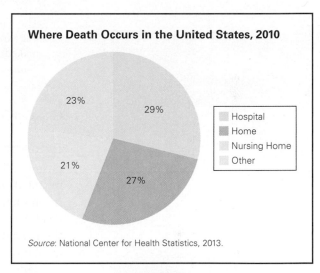

Where Death Occurs in the United States, 2010

- 29% Hospital
- 27% Home
- 21% Nursing Home
- 23% Other

Source: National Center for Health Statistics, 2013.

FIGURE EP.4

Not with Family Almost everyone prefers to die at home, yet most people die in an institution, often surrounded by medical personnel and high-tech equipment, not by the voices and touch of loved ones. The "other" category is even worse, as it includes most lethal accidents or homicides. But don't be too saddened by this chart—improvement is possible. Twenty years ago the proportion of home deaths was notably lower.

palliative care Care designed not to treat an illness but to provide physical and emotional comfort to the patient and support and guidance to his or her family.

double effect A situation in which an action (such as administering opiates) has both a positive effect (relieving a terminally ill person's pain) and a negative effect (hastening death by suppressing respiration).

Deciding When Death Occurs

No longer does death necessarily occur when a vital organ stops. Breathing continues with respirators, stopped hearts are restarted, stomach tubes provide calories, drugs fight pneumonia. At what point, if ever, should intervention stop to allow death?

Almost every life-threatening condition results in treatments started, stopped, or avoided, with death postponed, prevented, or welcomed. This has fostered impassioned arguments about ethics, both between nations (evidenced by radically different laws) and within them. Religious advisers, doctors, and lawyers disagree with colleagues within their respective professions, family members disagree with one another, and members of each group disagree with members of the other groups (Ball, 2012; Engelhardt, 2012; Prado, 2008).

One physician, a specialist in palliative care, advised his colleagues:

> The highway of aggressive medical treatment runs fast, is heavily travelled, but can lack landmarks and the signage necessary to know when it is time to make for the exit ramp. . . . These signs are there and it is your responsibility to communicate them to patients and families.

[Fins, 2006, p. 73]

Good advice, hard to follow.

Evidence of Death

Historically, death was determined by listening to a person's chest: No heartbeat meant death. To make sure, a feather was put to the person's nose to indicate respiration—a person who had no heartbeat and did not exhale was pronounced dead. Very rarely, but widely publicized when it happened, death was declared but the person was still alive. Modern medicine has changed that: Hearts and lungs need not function on their own.

Many life-support measures and medical interventions circumvent the diseases and organ failures that once caused death. Checking breathing with feathers is a curiosity that, thankfully, is never used today. But how do we know when death has happened? In the late 1970s, a group of Harvard physicians concluded that death occurred when brain waves ceased, a definition now used worldwide (Wijdicks et al., 2010). However, many doctors believe that death can occur even if primitive brain waves continue (Kellehear, 2008; Truog, 2007) (see Table EP.3).

TABLE EP.3   Dead or Not? Yes, No, and Maybe
Brain death: Prolonged cessation of all brain activity with complete absence of voluntary movements; no spontaneous breathing; no response to pain, noise, and other stimuli. Brain waves have ceased; the electroencephalogram is flat; *the person is dead*.
Locked-in syndrome: The person cannot move, except for the eyes, but normal brain waves are still apparent; *the person is not dead*.
Coma: A state of deep unconsciousness from which the person cannot be aroused. Some people awaken spontaneously from a coma; others enter a vegetative state; *the person is not yet dead*.
Vegetative state: A state of deep unconsciousness in which all cognitive functions are absent, although eyes may open, sounds may be emitted, and breathing may continue; *the person is not yet dead*. The vegetative state can be *transient, persistent,* or *permanent*. No one has ever recovered after two years; most who recover (about 15 percent) improve within three weeks (Preston & Kelly, 2006). After sufficient time has elapsed, the person may, effectively, be dead, although exactly how many days that requires has not yet been determined (Wijdicks et al., 2010).

It is critical to know when people are in a permanent vegetative state (and thus will never regain the ability to think) and when they are merely in a coma but might recover. One crucial factor is whether the person could ever again breathe without a respirator, but that is hard to guarantee if "ever again" includes 10 or 20 years hence.

In 2008, the American Academy of Neurology gathered experts to conduct a meta-analysis of recent studies regarding end-of-life brain functioning. They found 38 empirical articles. Two experts independently read each one, noting measures used to determine death and how much time elapsed between lack of sentient brain function and pronouncement of death. They found no consensus. Only two indicators were confirmed: Dead people no longer breathe spontaneously, and their eyes no longer respond to pain.

As this article points out, everyone needs to know when a person is brain-dead, but there is not yet a definitive, instant test because there are "severe limitations in the current evidence base" (Wijdicks et al., 2010, p. 1914). Thus, family members may spend months hoping for life long after medical experts believe no recovery is possible. Consequently, a person who wanted to donate organs after death is unable to do so because so much time elapsed between death and donation that the organs are no longer usable.

Euthanasia

Euthanasia, common for pets but rare for people, is very controversial. Many people see a major distinction between active and passive euthanasia (sometimes called mercy killing), although the final result is the same. In **passive euthanasia**, a person near death is allowed to die. They may have a **DNR (do not resuscitate) order**, instructing medical staff not to restore breathing or restart the heart if breathing or pulsating stops.

Passive euthanasia is legal everywhere if the dying person chooses it, but many emergency personnel start artificial respiration and stimulate hearts without asking whether a patient has a DNR. That might make passive euthanasia impossible.

Active euthanasia is deliberately doing something to cause death, such as turning off a respirator or giving a lethal drug. Some physicians condone active euthanasia when three conditions occur: (1) suffering that cannot be relieved, (2) incurable illness and (3) a patient who wants to die. Active euthanasia is legal in the Netherlands, Belgium, Luxembourg, and Switzerland, and illegal (but rarely prosecuted) elsewhere.

Attitudes may be changing. For example, over the past decade in Austria doctors in training have increasingly valued patients' autonomy, which has led to more acceptance of active euthanasia (Stronegger et al., 2011) (see Figure EP.5).

In every nation surveyed, some physicians would never perform active euthanasia, but others have done so. Opinions from the public vary as well, although generally nations in eastern Europe are less accepting than those in western Europe (Cohen et al., 2013).

The Doctor's Role

Between passive and active euthanasia is another option: A doctor may provide the means for patients to end their own lives in what is sometimes

passive euthanasia A situation in which a seriously ill person is allowed to die naturally, through the cessation of medical intervention.

DNR (do not resuscitate) order A written order from a physician (sometimes initiated by a patient's advance directive or by a health care proxy's request) that no attempt should be made to revive a patient if he or she suffers cardiac or respiratory arrest.

active euthanasia A situation in which someone takes action to bring about another person's death, with the intention of ending that person's suffering.

FIGURE EP.5

Theory and Practice Active euthanasia remains controversial, among doctors as well as lay people. As you see from this survey of young Austrian doctors, the medical profession overall is more accepting than it used to be. As you know, surveys do not always reflect behavior: Some physicians who do not accept active euthanasia in theory find themselves helping patients who want to die.

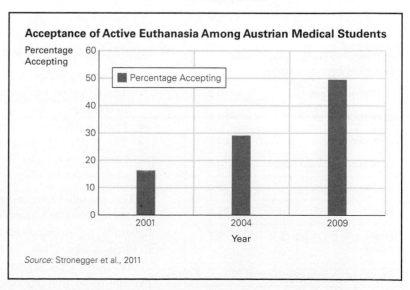

Acceptance of Active Euthanasia Among Austrian Medical Students

Source: Stronegger et al., 2011

Liberté or Death In many nations most people approve of death with dignity but most legislators do not. This woman's sign says 94 percent of her fellow citizens approve legalizing euthanasia.

physician-assisted suicide A form of active euthanasia in which a doctor provides the means for someone to end his or her own life.

Observation Quiz Where did this rally take place? (see answer, page 777)

TABLE EP.4	Oregon Residents' Reasons for Requesting Physician Assistance in Dying, 1998–2012
Percent of Patients Giving Reason (most had several reasons)	
Loss of autonomy	91.2
Less able to enjoy life	88.8
Loss of dignity	82.0
Loss of control over body	51.6
Burden on others	38.6
Pain	23.5
Financial implications of treatment	2.7

Source: Oregon Public Health Division, 2013.

called **physician-assisted suicide**, typically by prescribing lethal medication. The state of Oregon has legalized this practice, explicitly asserting that such deaths should be called "death with dignity," not suicide. No matter what the name, acceptance varies markedly by culture (Prado, 2008). Reasons have less to do with people's personal experience than with religion, education, and local values (Verbakel & Jaspers, 2010).

For example, some cultures believe that suicide may be noble: Buddhist monks publicly burned themselves to death to advocate Tibetan independence from China; everywhere, some people choose to die for the honor of their nation or themselves. However, in the United States physicians of Asian religions are *less* likely to condone physician-assisted suicide than are non-Asian physicians (Wohlenberg et al., 2013; Curlin et al., 2008).

This reluctance of Asian doctors to speed death helps explain a practice in Thailand: When it becomes apparent that a hospitalized patient will die soon, an ambulance takes that person back home, where death occurs naturally. Then the person and the family can benefit from a better understanding of life, suffering, and death (Stonington, 2012).

Pain: Physical and Psychological

The Netherlands has permitted active euthanasia and physician-assisted suicide since 1980, and they extended the law in 2002. The patient must be clear and aware in making the request, and the goal is to halt "unbearable suffering" (Buiting et al., 2009). Consequently, Dutch physicians first try to make the suffering bearable via better medication.

However, a qualitative analysis found that "fatigue, pain, decline, negative feelings, loss of self, fear of future suffering, dependency, loss of autonomy, being worn out, being a burden, loneliness, loss of all that makes life worth living, hopelessness, pointlessness and being tired of living were constituent elements of unbearable suffering" (Dees et al., 2011, p. 727). Obviously, medication cannot alleviate those states of mind.

Oregon voters approved physician-assisted "death with dignity" (but not other forms of active euthanasia) in 1994 and again in 1997. The first such legal deaths occurred in 1998. The law requires the following:

- The dying person must be an Oregon resident, over age 17.
- The dying person must request the lethal drugs twice orally and once in writing.
- Fifteen days must elapse between the first request and the prescription.
- Two physicians must confirm that the person is terminally ill, has less than six months to live, and is competent (i.e., not mentally impaired or depressed).

The law also requires record-keeping and annual reporting. About one-third of the requests are granted, and about one-third of those who are approved die naturally, never using the drugs. Between 1998 and 2012, about 200,000 people in Oregon died. Only 738 of them died after taking the prescribed lethal drugs.

As Table EP.4 shows, Oregon residents requested the drugs primarily for psychological, not biological, reasons—they were more concerned about their autonomy than their pain. In 2012, 115 Oregonians obtained lethal prescriptions, and 77 legally used drugs to die. Most of the rest died naturally, but some were alive in January 2013 and expected to use the drug in the future (about 10 percent use their prescriptions the year after obtaining them) (Oregon Department of Human Services, 2013).

slippery slope The argument that a given action will start a chain of events that will culminate in an undesirable outcome.

OPPOSING PERSPECTIVES

The "Right to Die"?

Many people fear that legalizing euthanasia or physician-assisted suicide creates a **slippery slope**, that hastening death for the dying who request it will cause a slide toward killing people who are *not* ready to die—especially the disabled, the old, the minorities, and the poor. The data refute that concern.

In Oregon and the Netherlands, the oldest-old, the poor, and those of non-European heritage are *less* likely to use fatal prescriptions. In fact, in Oregon almost all of those who have done so were European American (97 percent), had health insurance, and were well educated (81 percent had some college). There is no evidence of ageism: Most had lived a long life (average age is 71) (see Figure EP.6). Almost all (97 percent) died at home, with close friends or family nearby.

All these statistics refute both the slippery-slope and the social-abuse arguments because the ones who actually die with physician assistance are not likely to slide anywhere they do not wish to go, nor are they likely to be pushed to die. Nonetheless, even those who believe that people should decide their own medical care are not sure they themselves will choose death if given the choice. African Americans are particularly mistrustful of hospices, euthanasia, and physician-assisted suicide (Wicher & Meeker, 2012).

The 1980 Netherlands law was revised in 2002 to allow euthanasia not only when a person is terminally ill but also when a person is chronically ill and in pain. The number of Dutch people who choose euthanasia is increasing; it accounted for about 1 in 30 deaths in 2012. Is this a slippery slope? Some people think so, especially those who believe that God alone decides the moment of death and that anyone who interferes is defying God.

Arguing against that perspective, a cancer specialist writes:

> To be forced to continue living a life that one deems intolerable when there are doctors who are willing either to end one's life or to assist one in ending one's own life, is an unspeakable violation of an individual's freedom to live—and to die—as he or she sees fit. Those who would deny patients a legal right to euthanasia or assisted suicide typically appeal to two arguments: a "slippery slope" argument, and an argument about the dangers of abuse. Both are scare tactics, the rhetorical force of which exceeds their logical strength.
>
> [Benatar, 2011, p. 206]

Yet not everyone agrees with that cancer specialist. Might the decision to die itself be evidence of depression that should prohibit physicians from prescribing lethal drugs (Finlay & George, 2011)? Declining ability to enjoy life was cited by 89 percent of Oregonians who requested physician-assisted suicide in 2012 (see Table EP.4). Is that a sign of sanity or depression?

Acceptance of death signifies mental health in the aged but not necessarily in the young: Should death with dignity be allowed only after age 54? That would have excluded 11 percent of Oregonians who have used the act thus far. Is the idea that only the old should be allowed to choose death an ageist idea, perhaps assuming that the young don't understand what they are choosing, or that the old are the ones for whom life is over?

The number of people who die by taking advantage of Oregon's law has increased steadily, from 16 in 1998 (the first year) to 77 in 2012. Some might see that as evidence of a slippery slope. Others consider it proof that the practice is useful though rare—only 1 in 200 Oregon deaths involves physician assistance (Oregon Public Health Division, 2013).

People with disabling, painful, and terminal conditions who die after choosing futile measures to prolong life are eulogized as "fighters" who "never gave up." That indicates social approval of such choices. This same attitude about life and death is held by most voters and lawmakers around the world. The majority opposes laws that allow physician-assisted suicide.

However, that majority is not evident everywhere. In the state of Washington, just north of Oregon, 58 percent of the voters approved a Death with Dignity law in November 2008; in 2009, Luxembourg joined the Netherlands and Belgium in allowing active euthanasia; in 2011, the Montana senate refused to forbid physician-assisted suicide; and in 2012, a legal scholar contended that the U.S. Constitution's defense of liberty includes the freedom to decide how to die (Ball, 2012).

All that might seem like a growing trend, but proposals to legalize physician-assisted suicide have been defeated in several U.S. states and other nations. Most jurisdictions recognize the dilemma: They do not prosecute doctors who help people die as long as it is done privately and quietly. Opposing perspectives, and opposite choices, are evident.

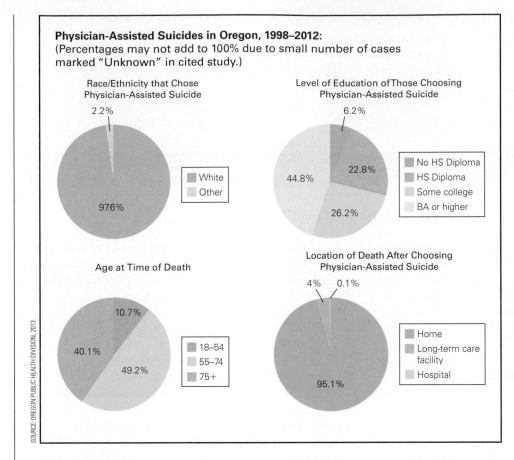

Physician-Assisted Suicides in Oregon, 1998–2012:
(Percentages may not add to 100% due to small number of cases marked "Unknown" in cited study.)

Race/Ethnicity that Chose Physician-Assisted Suicide

2.2%
97.6%

- White
- Other

Level of Education of Those Choosing Physician-Assisted Suicide

6.2%
22.8%
44.8%
26.2%

- No HS Diploma
- HS Diploma
- Some college
- BA or higher

Age at Time of Death

10.7%
40.1%
49.2%

- 18–54
- 55–74
- 75+

Location of Death After Choosing Physician-Assisted Suicide

4%   0.1%
95.1%

- Home
- Long-term care facility
- Hospital

SOURCE: OREGON PUBLIC HEALTH DIVISION, 2013.

FIGURE EP.6

Death with Dignity The data on who chooses Death with Dignity in Oregon do not suggest that people who are low in socioeconomic status are unfairly pushed to die. In fact, quite the opposite—people who choose physician-assisted suicide tend to be among the older, better educated, more affluent citizens.

Advance Directives

advance directives Any description of what people want to happen as they die and after they die. This can include medical measures, choosing whom to allow as visitors, funeral arrangements, cremation, and so on.

Advance directives can describe everything regarding end-of-life care; this includes where people want to die and what should happen to their body after death, but the main focus is on medical measures. Should artificial feeding, breathing, or heart stimulation be used? Are antibiotics that might merely prolong life or pain medication that causes coma or hallucinations desired? Is religious music or clergy welcome? The legality of such directives varies by jurisdiction: Sometimes a lawyer is needed to ensure documents are legal; sometimes a written request, signed and witnessed, is adequate.

Many people want personal choice about death, and thus approve advance directives in theory, but are uncertain about specifics. For example, few know that restarting the heart may extend life for decades in a young, healthy adult but may result in dementia, or merely prolong dying, in an elderly person whose health is failing.

Added to the complications are personal specifics, such as other morbidities, timing, mobility. For example, sometimes cardio resuscitation is harmful, partly based on how long the heart has stopped (Buss, 2013). Data on overall averages is contradictory (Elliot et al., 2011). Furthermore, data on outcome is usually for survivors, not for those who die after various interventions, so advance directives may be based on faulty assumptions.

Even talking about choices is controversial. Originally, the U.S. health care bill passed in 2010 allowed doctors to be paid for describing treatment options (e.g., Kettl, 2010). Opponents called those "death panels," an accusation that almost torpedoed the entire package. As a result, that measure was scrapped: Physicians cannot bill for time spent explaining palliative care, options for treatment, or dying.

Wills and Proxies

Advance directives often include a living will and/or a health care proxy. Hospitals and hospices strongly recommend both of these. Nonetheless, most people resist: A study of cancer patients in a leading hospital found that only 16 percent had living wills and only 48 percent had designated a proxy (Halpern et al., 2011).

A **living will** indicates what sort of medical intervention a person wants or does not want in the event that he or she becomes unable to express his or her preferences. (If the person is conscious, hospital personnel ask about each specific procedure, often requiring written consent before surgery. Patients who are conscious and lucid can choose to override any instructions they wrote earlier in their living will.)

The reason that people might want to override their own earlier wishes is that living wills include phrases such as "incurable," "reasonable chance of recovery," and "extraordinary measures," and it is difficult to know what those phrases mean until a specific issue arises. Even then, medical judgments vary. Doctors and family members also disagree about what is "extraordinary" or "reasonable."

Some people designate a **health care proxy**—another person to make medical decisions for them if they become unable to do so. That seems logical, but unfortunately neither a living will nor a health care proxy guarantees that medical care will be exactly what a person would choose. For one thing, proxies often find it difficult to allow a loved one to die. A larger problem is that few people—experts included—understand the risks, benefits, and alternatives to every medical procedure. That makes it difficult to decide for oneself, much less for a family member, exactly when the risks outweigh the benefits.

Medical professionals advocate advance directives, but they also acknowledge there are problems with them. As one couple wrote:

> Working within the reality of mortality, coming to death is then an inevitable part of life, an event to be lived rather than a problem to be solved. Ideally, we would live the end of our life from the same values that have given meaning to the story of our life up to that time. But in a medical crisis, there is little time, language, or ritual to guide patients and their families in conceptualizing or expressing their values and goals.

[Farber & Farber, 2014, p. 109]

The Schiavo Case

A heartbreaking example of the need for a health care proxy occurred with Theresa (Terri) Schiavo, who was 26 years old when her heart suddenly stopped. Emergency personnel restarted her heart, but she fell into a deep coma. Like almost everyone her age, Terri had no advance directives. A court designated Michael, her husband of six years, as her proxy.

Michael attempted many measures to bring back his wife, but after 11 years he accepted her doctors' repeated diagnosis: Terri was in a persistent vegetative state. He petitioned to have her feeding tube removed. The court agreed, noting the testimony of witnesses who said that Terri had told them that she never wanted to be on life support. Terri's parents appealed the decision but lost. They then pleaded with the public.

The Florida legislature responded, passing a law that required that the tube be reinserted. After three more years of legal wrangling, the U.S. Supreme Court ruled that the lower courts were correct. By this point, every North American newspaper and TV station was following the case. Congress passed a law requiring that artificial feeding be continued, but that law, too, was overturned as unconstitutional.

Answer to Observation Quiz (from page 774): Paris, France. Two clues: That is the Eiffel tower in the background, and François Hollande was elected President of France in 2012.

living will A document that indicates what medical intervention an individual prefers if he or she is not conscious when a decision is to be made. For example, some do not want to be given mechanical breathing.

health care proxy A person chosen by another person to make medical decisions if the second person becomes unable to do so.

Especially for People Without Advance Directives Why do very few young adults have advance directives? (see response, page 779)

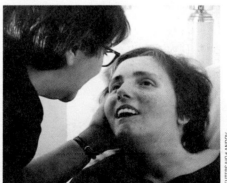

Is She Thinking? This photo of Terri Schiavo with her mother was released by those who believed Terri could recover. Other photos (not released) and other signs told the opposite story. Although autopsy showed that Terri's brain had shrunk markedly, remember that hope is part of being human. That helps explain why some people were passionately opposed to removal of Terri's stomach tube.

The stomach tube was removed, and Terri died on March 31, 2005—although some maintained that she had really died 15 years earlier. An autopsy revealed that her brain had shrunk markedly; she had not been able to think for at least a decade.

Partly because of the conflicts among family members, and between appointed judges and elected politicians, Terri's case caught media attention, inspiring vigils and protests. Lost in that blitz are the thousands of other mothers and fathers, husbands and wives, sons and daughters, judges and legislators, doctors and nurses who struggle less publicly with similar issues.

Advance directives may help make death "an event to be lived . . . [with] the same values that have given meaning to the story of our life" (Farber & Farber, 2014, p.109) and provide caregivers some peace. But, as the Schiavo case makes clear, discussion with every family member is needed long before a crisis occurs (Rogne & McCune, 2014).

SUMMING UP

Modern medicine has made some aspects of a good death more likely but has also added complexities. People can be kept alive long after their brains fail, via respirators, feeding tubes, and so on. Honest conversation, hospice care, and palliative medicine have made dying easier than when almost everyone died alone, in hospitals. However, passive and active euthanasia and assisted suicide are controversial. Part of the problem is that it is not always obvious when a dying person cannot recover, or even when death has occurred.

Various advance directives, including living wills and health care proxies in combination with honest conversation, can prevent some family conflicts and help people die as they wish and have their wishes for what happens after death honored. However, others often disagree about what a patient would want, and medical ethics, laws, and religious practices do not always provide guidance. ▪

>> Affirmation of Life

Grief and mourning are part of living. Human relationships are life sustaining, but every adult loses someone they love. That can lead to depression or to a life lived more deeply.

Grief

grief The deep sorrow that people feel at the death of another. Grief is personal and unpredictable.

Grief is the powerful sorrow that an individual feels at a profound loss, especially when a loved one dies. Grief is deep and personal, an anguish that can overtake daily life.

Normal Grief

The first thing to understand about grief is that it is a normal human emotion, even when it leads to unusual actions and thoughts. Grief is manifested in uncontrollable crying, sleeplessness, and irrational and delusional thoughts—the "magical thinking" Joan Didion described:

> Grief has no distance. Grief comes in waves, paroxysms, sudden apprehensions that weaken the knees and blind the eyes and obliterate the dailiness of life. . . . I see now that my insistence on spending that first night alone was more complicated than it seemed, a primitive instinct. . . . There was a level on which I believed that what had happened remained reversible. That is why I needed to be alone. . . . I needed to be alone so that he could come back. This was the beginning of my year of magical thinking.

[Didion, 2005, pp. 27, 32, 33]

When a loved one dies, loneliness, denial, anger, and sorrow come in rapid waves, overtaking normal human needs—to sleep, to eat, to think. Grief usually hits hardest in the first week after death and then lingers—with much of its impact dependent on the details of mourning, soon to be discussed. But first, let us recognize that grief is not always normal (Qualls & Kasl-Godley, 2010; van der Houwen et al., 2010).

Complicated Grief

In recent times, death has become more private, and for many people less religious. Emblematic of this change are funeral trends in the United States: Whereas older generations may prefer burial after a traditional funeral, younger generations are likely to prefer a memorial service after cremation.

Cremation may seem a simpler, more rational way to deal with death, but grief is neither simple nor rational: Decisions about what to do with the ashes after cremation may be fraught with denial and controversy and thus add complexity (Cranwell, 2010). About 10 percent of all mourners experience **complicated grief**, a type of grief that impedes the person's future life (Neimeyer & Jordan, 2013).

Perhaps surprisingly, one type of complication is called **absent grief**, when a bereaved person does not seem to grieve. This is a common first reaction, but if it continues, absent grief can trigger physical or psychological symptoms—for instance, trouble breathing or walking, sudden panic attacks, or depression. If such symptoms appear for no reason, the underlying cause might be grief that was never expressed.

Absent grief may be more common in modern society than it was earlier. The laws of some nations—China, Chile, and Spain, for example—mandate paid bereavement leave, but this is not true in the United States (Meagher, 2013). People who live and work where no one knows their personal lives have no community or recognized customs to help them grieve.

Indeed, for workers at large corporations or students in universities, grief becomes "an unwelcome intrusion (or violent intercession) into the normal efficient running of everyday life" (M. Anderson, 2001, p. 141). This leads to isolation—exactly the opposite of what bereaved people need.

Modern life also increases the incidence of **disenfranchised grief**, which is "not merely unnoticed, forgotten, or hidden; it is socially disallowed and unsupported" (Corr & Corr, 2013b, p. 135). For instance, many laws rule that only a current spouse or close blood relative may decide on funeral arrangements, disposal of the body, and other matters. This made sense when all adults were close to their relatives, but it may result in "gagged grief and beleaguered bereavement" when, for instance, a long-time but unmarried partner is excluded (L. Green & Grant, 2008, p. 275).

Many people are disenfranchised; they feel powerful grief but cannot express it. The deceased's unmarried lover (of the same or other sex), a divorced spouse, young children, and close friends at work may be prevented by the family, either deliberately or through thoughtlessness or ignorance, from saying goodbye, viewing the corpse, or participating in the aftermath of death. Parents who lose a fetus or newborn may be disenfranchised by those who say, "You never knew that baby; you can have another."

Another complication is **incomplete grief**. Normally grief is a process, intense at first, diminishing over time, eventually reaching closure. Customs such as viewing the dead, or throwing dirt on the grave, or scattering ashes, all move the process of grief. However, many circumstances can interfere with completion of the process.

Traumatic death is always unexpected, and that makes denial, anger, and depression undercut the emotions of grief (Kauffman, 2013). Murders and suicides

>> **Response for People Without Advance Directives** (from page 777): Young adults tend to avoid thinking realistically about their own deaths. This attitude is emotional, not rational. The actual task of preparing the documents is easy (the forms can be downloaded; no lawyer is needed). Young adults have no trouble doing other future-oriented things, such as getting a tetanus shot or enrolling in a pension plan.

complicated grief A type of grief that impedes a person's future life, usually because the person clings to sorrow or is buffeted by contradictory emotions.

absent grief A situation in which mourners do not grieve, either because other people do not allow grief to be expressed or because the mourners do not allow themselves to feel sadness.

disenfranchised grief A situation in which certain people, although they are bereaved, are prevented from mourning publicly by cultural customs or social restrictions.

incomplete grief A situation in which circumstances, such as a police investigation or an autopsy, interfere with the process of grieving.

Survivor? Two days after the typhoon Haiyan struck the Philippines, this woman mourns her husband, one of over 6,000 dead. She herself is at risk, as disease and stress will mount as she and her neighbors try and rebuild their community. That makes her much more likely to sicken and die in the coming year than in the past one.

Empty Boots The body of a young army corporal killed near Baghdad has been shipped home to his family in Mississippi for a funeral and burial, but his fellow soldiers in Iraq also need to express their grief. The custom is to hold an informal memorial service, placing the dead soldier's boots, helmet, and rifle in the middle of a circle of mourners, who weep, pray, and reminisce.

mourning The ceremonies and behaviors that a religion or culture prescribes for people to employ in expressing their bereavement after a death.

often trigger police investigations and reporters when mourners need to grieve instead of answering questions. An autopsy may prevent closure if the griever believes that the body will rise, or that the soul does not immediately leave the body. Inability to recover a body, as with soldiers who are missing in action or victims of a major flood or fire, may prevent grief from being expressed and thereby hinder completion.

After natural or human-caused disasters, including hurricanes and wars, incomplete grief is common because procuring the basics of life—food, shelter, and so on—takes precedence over emotional needs. One result of incomplete grief is that people die of causes not directly attributable to the trauma, becoming victims of the indifference of others and of their own diminished self-care.

Mourning

Grief splinters people into jumbled pieces, making them vulnerable. Mourning reassembles them, making them whole again and able to rejoin the larger community. To be more specific, **mourning** is the public and ritualistic expression of bereavement, the ceremonies and behaviors that a religion or culture prescribes to honor the dead.

How Mourning Helps

Mourning is needed because, as you just read, the grief-stricken are vulnerable not only to irrational thoughts but also to self-destructive acts. Some eat too little or drink too much, some forget caution as they drive or even as they walk across the street. Physical and mental health dips in the recently bereaved, and the rate of suicide increases. The death of a child is particularly hard on the parents, who may either distance themselves from one another or become closer. Shared mourning rituals are one way families help each other.

A large study in Sweden of those who had experienced the death of a brother or sister found that, even years later, their risk of death was higher than for other Swedes. That was true even if the siblings had not committed suicide, but if they had, their siblings were three times more likely to kill themselves than other Swedish adults of the same background (Rostila et al., 2013).

All the research shows that the mourning process is particularly needed by survivors after suicide. Survivors tend to blame themselves or feel angry at the deceased, which makes traditional mourning more difficult.

Customs are designed to help people move from grief toward reaffirmation (Harlow, 2005; Corr & Corr, 2013). For this reason, eulogies emphasize the dead person's good qualities; people who did not personally know the deceased person attend wakes, funerals, or memorial services to comfort the survivors. If the dead person was a public figure, mourners may include thousands, even millions. They express their sorrow to one another, stare at photos, and listen to music that reminds them of the dead person, weeping as they watch funerals on television. Mourners often pledge to affirm the best of the deceased, forgetting any criticisms they might have had in the past.

One function of mourning is to allow public expression of grief to channel and contain private grief. Examples include the Jewish custom of sitting Shiva at home for a week, or the three days of active sorrow among some Muslim groups, or the 10 days of ceremonies beginning at the next full moon following a Hindu death.

Memories often return to the immediate relatives and friends on the anniversary of a death, so cultures include annual rituals such as visiting a grave or lighting a candle in memory. Many people who have distanced themselves from the religious rituals of their community find solace in returning to them when a person dies (Rosenblatt, 2013).

As you have read, beliefs about death vary a great deal, and beliefs affect mourning rituals. Some religions believe in reincarnation—that a dead person is reborn and that the new life depends on the person's character in the past life. Other religions believe that souls are judged and then sent to heaven or hell.

Mourners do whatever they think will help the deceased. Certain prayers may be repeated to ensure a good afterlife. Some religions contend that the spirits of the dead remain on earth and affect those still living; mourners who believe this typically provide food and other comforts to the dead so that their spirits will be benevolent. Some religions hold that the dead live on only in memory: The custom may be to name a baby after a dead person or to honor the dead on a particular memorial day.

The Western practice of building a memorial, dedicating a plaque, or naming a location for a dead person is antithetical to some Eastern cultures. Indeed, some Asians believe that the spirit should be allowed to leave in peace, and thus all possessions, signs, and other evidence of the dead are removed after proper prayers.

This created a cultural clash when terrorist bombs in Bali killed 38 Indonesians and 164 foreigners (mostly Australian and British). The Indonesians prayed intensely and then destroyed all reminders; the Australians raised money to build a memorial (Jonge, 2011). The Indonesian officials posed many obstacles that infuriated the Australians, and the memorial was not built. Neither group understood the deep emotions of the other.

In recent decades, many people everywhere have become less religiously devout, and mourning practices are less ritualized. Has death then become a source of despair, not hope? Maybe not. People worldwide become more spiritual when confronted with death (Lattanzi-Licht, 2013). This is true even for people who do not consider themselves religious (Heflick & Goldenberg, 2012).

Psychologists contend that human cognition naturally leads to belief in life after death (Pereira et al., 2012). Societal undermining of the expression of grief and the customs of mourning may interfere with individual and community health.

Same Situation, Far Apart: Gateway to Heaven or Final Rest Many differences are obvious between a Roman Catholic burial in Mbongolwane, South Africa *(left)*, and a Hindu cremation procession in Bali, Indonesia *(right)*. The Africans believe the soul goes to heaven, the Indonesians believe the body returns to the elements. In both places, however, friends and neighbors gather to honor the dead and comfort their relatives.

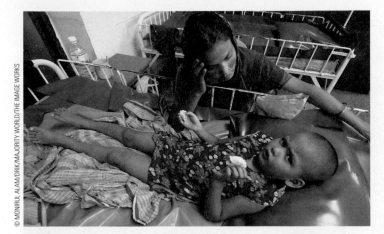

Life in the Balance The death of a young child is especially devastating to families. This girl is in a hospital in Bangladesh; she suffered from diarrhoeal disease, which kills more than 2,000 children a year worldwide, most of them in areas with unsafe water supplies.

Observation Quiz Is this girl likely to die? (see answer, page 784)

Placing Blame and Seeking Meaning

A common impulse after death is for the survivors to assess blame—for medical measures not taken, for laws not enforced, for unhealthy habits not changed. The bereaved sometimes blame the dead person, sometimes themselves, and sometimes others. In November 2011, Michael Jackson's personal doctor, Conrad Murray, was found guilty and jailed for prescribing the drugs that led to his death. Many fans and family members cheered at the verdict; Murray was one of the few who blamed Jackson, not himself.

For public tragedies, nations accuse one another. Blame is not rational or proportional to guilt. For instance, outrage at the assassination of Archduke Francis Ferdinand of Austria by a Serbian terrorist in 1914 provoked a conflict between Austria and Serbia—soon joined by a dozen other nations—that led to the four years and 16 million deaths of World War I.

As you remember, denial and anger appear first on Kübler-Ross's list of reactions to dying and death; ideally, people move on to acceptance. Finding meaning may be crucial to the reaffirmation that follows grief. In some cases, this search starts with preserving memories: Displaying photographs and personal effects and telling anecdotes about the dead person are central to many memorial services.

When death occurs from a major disaster survivors often seek to honor the memory of the dead. Many people believe that Israel would not have been created without the Holocaust, or that same-sex marriage would not have been be legalized if the AIDS epidemic had not occurred.

Mourners may be helped by strangers who have experienced a similar loss. This explains groups of parents of murdered children, of mothers whose teenagers were killed by drunk drivers, of widows of firefighters who died at the World Trade Center on 9/11, of relatives of passengers who died in the same plane crash, and many more.

Mourners sometimes want strangers to know about a death. Pages of paid obituaries are found in every major newspaper, and spontaneous memorials (graffiti, murals, stuffed animals, flowers) appear in public spaces, such as at a spot on a roadside where a fatal crash occurred. This practice was once discouraged, but no longer. Authorities realize that public commemoration aids grief and mourning, building community: Public markers of bouquets and so on are dismantled only when flowers fade and time has passed (Dickinson & Hoffmann, 2010).

Organizations that are devoted to combating a particular problem (such as breast cancer or handguns) find their most dedicated donors, marchers, and advocates among people who have lost a loved one to that specific danger. When someone dies, survivors often designate a charity that is connected to the deceased. Then mourners contribute, and the death has led to some good.

Another way people find meaning in death is to gather in vigils, rallies, or protests, typically seeking some particular redress:

- When a truck killed a 9-year-old in Germany, neighbors and strangers blocked the street for days until new safeguards were installed.
- When a cyclist was killed by a car, other cyclists erected "ghost bikes" and ritualistically raised their bicycles, leading to a plethora of new bike lanes in New York City (Rulfs, 2011; Dobler, 2011).

The impulse to assign blame and seek meaning is powerful but not always constructive. Revenge may arise, leading to long-standing and often fatal feuds between one family, one gang, or one cultural, ethnic, or religious group and another. Nations go to war because some people in one nation killed some from another. Ideally, counselors, politicians, and clergy can steer grief-stricken survivors toward beneficial ends.

Diversity of Reactions

As you see, how someone deals with bereavement depends on the customs and attitudes of their community. Particulars vary. For example, mourners who keep the dead person's possessions, talk to the deceased, and frequently review memories are notably *less* well adjusted than other mourners 18 months after the death if they live in the United States, but they are *better* adjusted if they live in China (Lalande & Bonanno, 2006).

Mommy's Memorial Praying beside the ghost bike at the spot where an 18-wheeler killed cyclist Kathryn Rickson may help these two grieve and then recover. Grief is less likely to destroy survivors when markers or rituals are observed.

Past experiences affect bereavement. Children who lost their parents might be more distraught decades later when someone else dies. Attachment history matters (Stroebe et al., 2010). Older adults who were securely attached as children may be more likely to experience normal grief; those whose attachment was insecure-avoidant may have absent grief; and those who were insecure-resistant may become stuck, unable to find meaning in death and thus unable to reaffirm their own lives.

Reaffirmation does not mean forgetting; *continuing bonds* are evident years after death (Stroebe et al., 2012). Such bonds may help or hinder reaffirmation, depending on the past relationship between the individuals and on the circumstances of the death.

In Western nations hallucinations (seeing ghosts, hearing voices) are a sign of complicated grief, but ongoing memories and thoughts of the dead person as a role model are "linked to greater personal growth" (Field & Filanosky, 2009, p. 20). Often survivors write letters or talk to the deceased person, or consider events—a sunrise, a butterfly, a rainstorm—as messages of comfort.

Bereavement theory once held that mourners should grieve and then move on, realizing that the dead person is gone forever. It was thought that if this progression did not take place, pathological grief could result, with the person either not grieving enough (absent grief) or grieving too long (incomplete grief). Current research finds a much wider variety of reactions (Rubin, 2012), with continuing bonds a normal occurrence.

On the other hand, psychologists now recognize that bereavement may be a stressor that results in major depression. For example, although DSM-4 had a "bereavement exclusion," stating that major depression could not be diagnosed within two months of the death of a loved one, DSM-5 changed that. Some people experience major depression when someone dies, and then treatment is warranted.

Practical Applications

The research suggests that many people experience powerful, complicated, and unexpected emotions when death occurs. To help the griever, a friend should listen and sympathize, never implying that the person is either too grief-stricken or not grief-stricken enough.

A VIEW FROM SCIENCE

Resilience after a Death

Earlier studies overestimated the frequency of pathological grief. For obvious reasons, scientists usually began research on mourning with mourners—that is, with people who had recently experienced the death of a loved one. With mourners, it was impossible to backtrack and study personality before the death.

Furthermore, psychologists often treated people who had difficulty dealing with a death. Some patients experienced absent grief; others felt disenfranchised grief; some were overcome by unremitting sadness many months after the loss; still others could not find meaning in a violent, sudden, unexpected death. All these people consulted therapists, who often helped them by describing the problems and the solutions.

We now know that personality has a major affect on grief and mourning (Boyraz, 2012). Pathological mourners are *not* typical. Almost everyone experiences several deaths over a lifetime—of parents and grandparents, of a spouse or close friend. Most feel sadness at first but then resume their customary activities, functioning as well a few months later as they did before. Only a small subset, about 10 to 15 percent, exhibit extreme or complicated grief (Bonanno & Lilienfeld, 2008).

The variety of reactions to death was evident in a longitudinal study that began by assessing married older adults in greater Detroit. Over several years, 319 became widows or widowers. Most were reinterviewed at 6 and 18 months after the death of their spouse, and about one-third were seen again four years later (Boerner et al., 2004, 2005).

General trends were evident. Almost all the widows and widowers idealized their past marriages, remembering them more positively after the death than they had experienced them years earlier at the first interview, which occurred before the death. This idealization is a normal phenomenon that other research finds connected to psychological health, not pathology (O'Rourke et al., 2010b). After the death, many thought of

their spouse several times each day. With time, such thoughts became less frequent, as expected with mourning.

This longitudinal study found notable variations in widows' and widowers' reactions. Four types of responses were evident (Galatzer-Levy & Bonanno, 2012):

1. Sixty-six percent were resilient. They were sad at first, but 6 months later they were about as happy and productive as they had been before the death.
2. Fifteen percent were depressed at every assessment, before as well as years after the death. If this research had begun only after the death, it might seem that the loss caused depression. However, the pre-loss assessment suggests that these people were chronically depressed, not stuck in grief.
3. Ten percent were *less* depressed after the death than before, often because they had been caregivers for their seriously ill partners.
4. Nine percent were slow to recover, functioning poorly at 18 months. By four years after the death, however, they functioned almost as well as they had before.

The slow recovery of this fourth group suggests that some of them experienced complicated grief. Note, however, that they were far from the majority of the participants.

Many studies show that grief and then recovery are the usual pattern, with only about 10 percent (here 9 percent) needing professional help to deal with a death. A person's health, finances, and personality all contribute to postmortem reactions.

Crucial are the person's beliefs before the death (Mancini et al., 2011). If someone tends to have a positive perspective, believing that justice will prevail and that life has meaning, then the death of a close family member may deepen, not weaken, those beliefs. Depression is less likely if a person has already accepted the reality of death.

>> Answer to Observation Quiz (from page 782): No. She is in a hospital, where she can receive the oral rehydration that saves almost every cholera patient. She has two additional advantages: an attentive mother and no signs of malnutrition.

A bereaved person *might or might not* want to visit the grave, light a candle, cherish a memento, pray, or sob. Whatever the action, he or she may want to be alone or may want company. Those who have been taught to bear grief stoically may be doubly distressed if a friend advises them to cry but they cannot. Conversely, those whose cultures expect loud wailing may resent it if they are urged to hush.

Even absent grief—in which the bereaved person does none of these things—might be appropriate. So might the opposite reaction, when people want to talk again and again about their loss, gathering sympathy, ascribing blame, and finding meaning.

As you see, assumptions might be inaccurate; people's reactions are much more varied than simple explanations of grief might suggest. One researcher cited an example of a 13-year-old girl who refused to leave home after her 17-year-old brother was shot dead going to school. The therapist was supposed to get her to go to school again.

It would have been easy to assume that she was afraid of dying on the street, and to arrange for a friend to accompany her on her way to school. But careful listening revealed the real reason she stayed home: She worried that her depressed mother might kill herself if she were left alone (Crenshaw, 2013). To help the daughter, the mother had to be helped.

No matter what fears arise, what rituals are followed, or what grief entails, the result of mourning may be to give the living a deeper appreciation of themselves and others. In fact, a theme frequently sounded by those who work with the dying and the bereaved is that death leads to a greater appreciation of life, especially of the value of intimate, caring relationships.

George Vaillant is a psychiatrist who studied a group of men from the time they were Harvard students through old age. He writes this about funerals: "With tears of remembrance running down our cheeks. . . . Remembered love lives triumphantly today" (Vaillant, 2008, p. 133).

It is fitting to end this Epilogue, and this book, with a reminder of the creative work of living. As first described in Chapter 1, the study of human development is a science, with topics to be researched, understood, and explained. But the process of living is an art as well as a science, with strands of love and sorrow woven into each person's unique tapestry. Death, when it leads to hope; dying, when it is accepted; and grief, when it fosters affirmation—all add meaning to birth, growth, development, and love.

Universal Emotions Grief is universal, as evidenced by the reaction of Petrus Vaalbooi, a leader of the Khoisan in Namibia, when his friend, Oom Kawid Kruiper died. Many Khoisan believe the spirit of the dead protect the living. Like many beliefs of people around the world, this one may give meaning to death and thus may soon comfort Petrus.

SUMMING UP

Grief is an overpowering and irrational emotion, a normal reaction when a loved one dies. Grief can be complicated—continuing too long, absent, or disenfranchised. Mourning is a social and cultural process to help people move past grief and reaffirm life. Modern life may make it more difficult for people to mourn, yet mourning customs help survivors find meaning in death and then in their lives.

Among the common reactions to death is the impulse to blame someone and to seek meaning in the death. These can be either helpful or destructive. When death occurs at the end of a long life, it is easier for the mourners to move on; grief is common, mourning is helpful, and then most people reaffirm life and community. ■

SUMMARY

Death and Hope

1. Death and dying have always led to strong emotions. However, in many parts of the world the experience of death is not what it was. For example, fewer people have personally witnessed the dying process.

2. In ancient times, death was considered a connection between the living, the dead, and the spirit world. People respected the dead and tried to live their lives so that their own death and afterlife would be good.

3. Every religion includes rituals and beliefs about death. These vary a great deal, but all bring hope to the living and strengthen the community.

4. Death has various meanings, depending partly on the age of the person involved. For example, young children are concerned about being separated from those they see every day; older children want to know specifics of death.

5. Terror management theory finds that some emerging adults cope with death anxiety by defiantly doing whatever is risky. In adulthood people tend to worry about leaving something undone or abandoning family members; older adults are more accepting of death.

Choices in Dying

6. Everyone wants a good death. A death that is painless and that comes at the end of a long life may be more possible currently than a century ago. However, other aspects of a good death—quick, at home, surrounded by loved ones—is less likely than it was.

7. The emotions of people who are dying change over time. Some may move from denial to acceptance, although stages of dying are much more variable than originally proposed. Honest conversation helps many, but not all, dying persons.

8. Hospice caregivers meet the biological and psychological needs of terminally ill people and their families. This can occur at home or at a specific place. Palliative care relieves pain and other uncomfortable aspects of dying.

9. Drugs that reduce pain as well as hasten dying, producing a double effect, are acceptable by many. However, euthanasia and physician-assisted suicide are controversial. A few nations and some U.S. states condone some forms of these; most do not.

10. Since 1980, death has been defined as occurring when brain waves stop; however, many measures now prolong life when no conscious thinking occurs. The need for a more precise, updated definition is apparent, but it is not obvious what the new definition should be.

11. Advance directives, such as a living will and a health care proxy, are recommended for everyone. However, it is impossible to anticipate all possible interventions that may occur. Family members as well as professionals often disagree about specifics.

Affirmation of Life

12. Grief is overwhelming sorrow. It may be irrational and complicated, absent or disenfranchised.

13. Mourning rituals channel human grief, helping people move to affirm life. Most people are able to do this.

14. Feelings of continuing bonds with the deceased are no longer thought to be pathological, and many people with lingering depression years after a death are people who were depressed before the death.

KEY TERMS

absent grief (p. 779)
active euthanasia (p. 773)
advance directives (p. 776)
complicated grief (p. 779)
disenfranchised grief (p. 779)

DNR (do not resuscitate) order (p. 773)
double effect (p. 771)
grief (p. 778)
health care proxy (p. 777)

hospice (p. 770)
incomplete grief (p. 779)
living will (p. 777)
mourning (p. 780)
palliative care (p. 771)

passive euthanasia (p. 773)
physician-assisted suicide (p. 773)
slippery slope (p. 775)
terror management theory (TMT) (p. 765)

WHAT HAVE YOU LEARNED?

1. Why are people today less familiar with death than people were 100 years ago? What impact might this have?

2. According to the ancient Egyptians and Greeks, what determined a person's fate after death?

3. What is one example of contrasting rituals about death?

4. What should parents remember when talking with children about death?

5. How does terror management theory explain young people's risk taking?

6. How does parenthood affect people's thoughts about their own death?

7. How do attitudes about death shift in late adulthood? What evidence is there of this shift?

8. In what ways do people change after a near-death experience?

9. What is a good death?

10. According to Kübler-Ross, what are the five stages of emotions associated with dying? Why doesn't everyone agree with Kübler-Ross's stages?

11. What determines whether a dying person will receive hospice care? What are the guiding principles of hospice care, and why is each one important?

12. Why is the double effect legal everywhere, even though it speeds death?

13. What differences of opinion are there regarding the definition of death?

14. What is the difference between passive and active euthanasia?

15. What are the four conditions of physician-assisted "death with dignity" in Oregon? Why is each condition important?

16. Why would a person who has a living will also need a health care proxy?

17. What is grief, and what are some of its signs?

18. List three types of complicated grief. Why is each type considered "complicated"?

19. What are the differences among grief, mourning, and bereavement?

20. How can a grieving person find meaning in death?

21. How might talking to the deceased make it easier or more difficult to adjust to the death of a loved one?

22. If a person still feels a loss six months after a death, is that pathological?

23. What should friends and relatives remember when helping someone who is grieving?

APPLICATIONS

1. Death is sometimes said to be hidden, even taboo. Ask 10 people if they have ever been with someone who was dying. Note not only the yes and no answers, but also the details and reactions. For instance, how many of the deaths occurred in hospitals?

2. Find quotes about death in *Bartlett's Familiar Quotations* or a similar collection. Do you see any historical or cultural patterns of acceptance, denial, or fear?

3. Every aspect of dying is controversial in modern society. Do an Internet search for a key term such as *euthanasia* or *grief*. Analyze the information and the underlying assumptions. What is your opinion, and why?

4. People of varying ages have different attitudes toward death. Ask people of different ages (ideally, at least one person younger than 20, one adult between 20 and 60, and one older person) what thoughts they have about their own death. What differences do you find?

>>ONLINE CONNECTIONS

To accompany your textbook, you have access to a number of online resources, including Learning Curve, an adaptive quizzing program, critical thinking questions, and case studies. For access to any of these links, go to www.worth publishers.com/launchpad/bergerls9e. In addition to these resources, you'll also find links to video clips, personalized study advice, and an ebook. Some of the videos and activities available online include:

- *Bereavement.* This in-depth activity covers the four stages of the grieving process and bereavement at different points in the life span. People share their personal experiences of loss.

- *Preparing to Die.* Experts discuss the process of dying, and dying people tell their stories. Covers death at different ages, palliative and hospice care, and more.

WORTH PUBLISHERS

Appendix A

>> Supplemental Charts, Graphs, and Tables

Often, examining specific data is useful, even fascinating, to developmental researchers. The particular numbers reveal trends and nuances not apparent from a more general view. Each chart, graph or table in this appendix contains information that may challenge some of your common assumptions.

The Human Brain   A-2

Children and Elders as a Proportion of a Nation's Population   A-3

Ethnic Composition of the U.S. Population   A-4

The Genetics of Blood Types   A-5

Odds of Down Syndrome by Maternal Age and Gestational Age   A-6

Breast-Feeding in the United States   A-7

Breast-Feeding Around the World   A-7

Saving Lives: Immunization   A-8, A-9

From Babbling to Language   A-9

Height Gains from Birth to Age 18   A-10

Weight Gains from Birth to Age 18   A-11

Body Mass Index   A-12

IQ Scores   A-12

Children Are the Poorest Americans   A-13

DSM-5 Criteria for Attention-Deficit/Hyperactivity Disorder (ADHD)   A-14

DSM-5 Criteria for Autism Spectrum Disorder   A-15

Motivation or Achievement?   A-16

Major Sexually Transmitted Infections: Some Basics   A-17

Sexual Behaviors of U.S. High School Students, 2011   A-18

Smoking Behavior Among U.S. High School Students, 1991–2011   A-19

Demographic Changes   A-20

Suicide Rates in the United States   A-21

The Human Brain

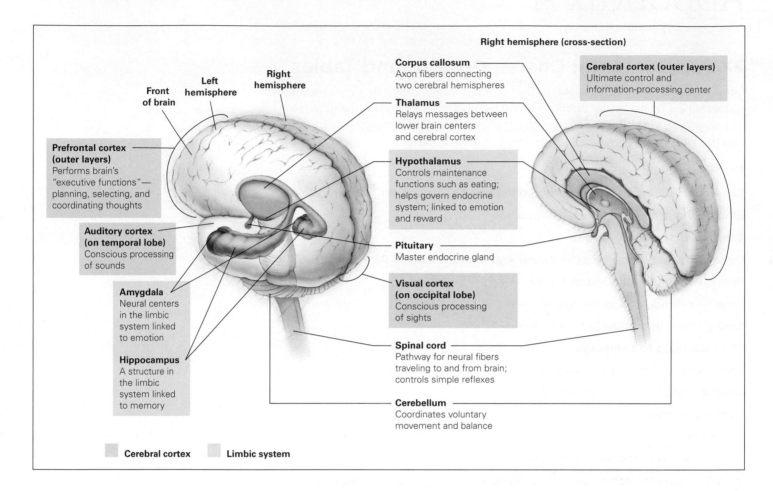

Right hemisphere (cross-section)

Prefrontal cortex (outer layers)
Performs brain's "executive functions"—planning, selecting, and coordinating thoughts

Auditory cortex (on temporal lobe)
Conscious processing of sounds

Amygdala
Neural centers in the limbic system linked to emotion

Hippocampus
A structure in the limbic system linked to memory

Front of brain
Left hemisphere
Right hemisphere

Corpus callosum
Axon fibers connecting two cerebral hemispheres

Thalamus
Relays messages between lower brain centers and cerebral cortex

Hypothalamus
Controls maintenance functions such as eating; helps govern endocrine system; linked to emotion and reward

Pituitary
Master endocrine gland

Visual cortex (on occipital lobe)
Conscious processing of sights

Spinal cord
Pathway for neural fibers traveling to and from brain; controls simple reflexes

Cerebellum
Coordinates voluntary movement and balance

Cerebral cortex (outer layers)
Ultimate control and information-processing center

▢ **Cerebral cortex**   ▢ **Limbic system**

Children and Elders as a Proportion of a Nation's Population

More Children, Fewer Elders? Nations that have high birth rates also have high death rates, short life spans, and less education. A systems approach suggests that these variables are connected. For example, the publicly funded Reggio Emilia early-childhood education program, perhaps the best in the world, originated in Italy, and Italy has one of the lowest proportions of children younger than 15. By contrast, the nations of sub-Saharan Africa have almost no government aid for children or the elderly.

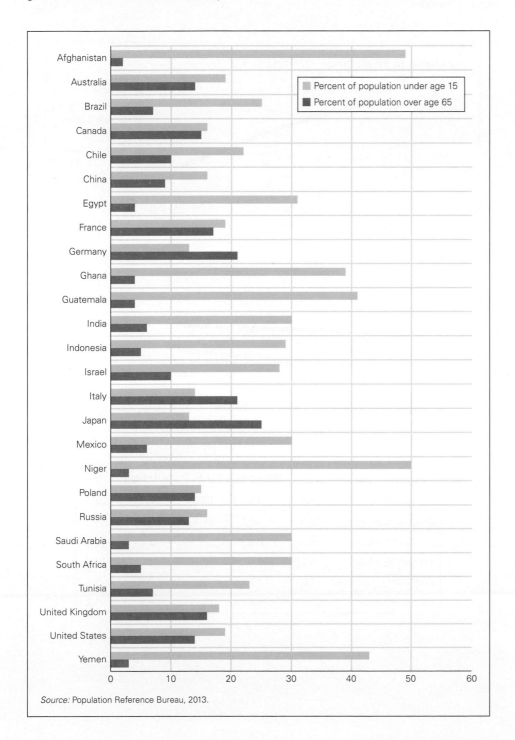

Source: Population Reference Bureau, 2013.

Ethnic Composition of the U.S. Population

Thinking about the ethnic makeup of the U.S. population helps explain the rising importance of sociocultural theory and the limitations of the concept of race. The traditional bifurcation of the population into "White" and "non-White" is increasingly irrelevant with growing numbers of Latino and Asian Americans. Every one of these broad categories includes many distinct ethnic groups. Furthermore, a growing number of people consider themselves more than one race.

Observation Quiz (see answer, page A-6): Which ethnic group is growing most rapidly in the United States?

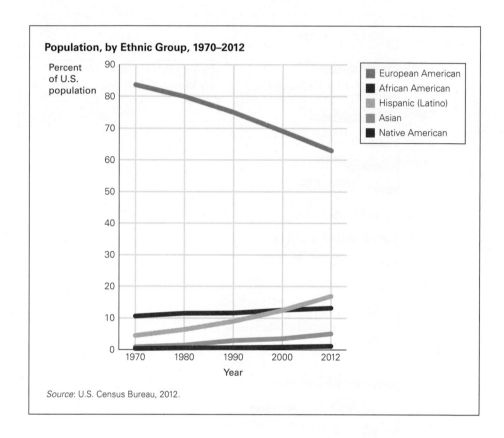

Population, by Ethnic Group, 1970–2012

Percent of U.S. population

Legend:
- European American
- African American
- Hispanic (Latino)
- Asian
- Native American

Source: U.S. Census Bureau, 2012.

		Percent of U.S. Population			
Ethnic origin	1970	1980	1990	2000	2012
European American	83.7	80	75	69.1	63
African American	10.6	11.5	12	12.5	13.1
Hispanic (Latino)	4.5	6.4	9	12.3	16.9
Asian	1.0	1.5	3	3.6	5.1
Native American	0.4	0.6	0.7	0.9	1.2

The Genetics of Blood Types

Blood types A and B are dominant traits and type O is recessive. The percentages given in the first column of this chart represent the odds that a child born to parents with the specified combinations of genotypes will have the genotype given in the second column. Note that each of the four blood phenotypes can be the outcome of at least six parental genotypes. Complex as this may seem, it is actually a very simple example. Most inheritance patterns are additive, not dominant/recessive, and even for blood types, many other factors (e.g., Rh negative or positive) may be part of the phenotype.

Genotypes of Parents*	Genotype of Offspring	Phenotype	Can Donate Blood to (Phenotype)	Can Receive Blood from (Phenotype)
AA + AA (100%) AA + AB (50%) AA + AO (50%) AB + AB (25%) AB + AO (25%) AO + AO (25%)	AA (inherits one A from each parent)	A	A or AB	A or O
AA + OO (100%) AB + OO (50%) AO + AO (50%) AO + OO (50%) AB + AO (25%) AB + BO (25%)	AO	A	A or AB	A or O
BB + BB (100%) AB + BB (50%) BB + BO (50%) AB + AB (25%) AB + BO (25%) BO + BO (25%)	BB	B	B or AB	B or O
BB + OO (100%) AB + OO (50%) BO + BO (50%) BO + OO (50%) AB + AO (25%) AB + BO (25%)	BO	B	B or AB	B or O
AA + BB (100%) AA + AB (50%) AA + BO (50%) AB + AB (50%) AB + BB (50%) AO + BB (50%) AB + BO (25%) AO + BO (25%)	AB	AB	AB only	A, B, AB, O ("universal recipient")
OO + OO (100%) AO + OO (50%) BO + OO (50%) AO + AO (25%) AO + BO (25%) BO + BO (25%)	OO	O	A, B, AB, O ("universal donor")	O only

*Blood type is not sex-linked because blood type comes equally from each parent.
Source: Adapted from Hartl & Jones, 1999.

Odds of Down Syndrome by Maternal Age and Gestational Age

The odds of any given fetus, near the end of the first trimester, having three chromosomes at the 21st site (trisomy-21) and thus having Down syndrome are shown in the 10-weeks column. These data were collected before widespread prenatal testing and induced abortion. As you see, almost half of all Down syndrome fetuses are spontaneously aborted. Also note that the odds of Down syndrome increase steadily with the age of the mother. Nonetheless, even for women giving birth in their 40s, most newborns do not have chromosomal abnormalities.

>> **Answer to Observation Quiz** (from page A-4) Asian Americans, whose share of the U.S. population has more than tripled in the past 30 years. Latinos are increasing most rapidly in numbers, but not in proportion.

Mother's age (yrs)	Weeks of Gestation 10	35	Live Births
20	1/804	1/1,464	1/1,527
21	1/793	1/1,445	1/1,507
22	1/780	1/1,421	1/1,482
23	1/762	1/1,389	1/1,448
24	1/740	1/1,348	1/1,406
25	1/712	1/1,297	1/1,352
26	1/677	1/1,233	1/1,286
27	1/635	1/1,157	1/1,206
28	1/586	1/1,068	1/1,113
29	1/531	1/967	1/1,008
30	1/471	1/858	1/895
31	1/409	1/745	1/776
32	1/347	1/632	1/659
33	1/288	1/525	1/547
34	1/235	1/427	1/446
35	1/187	1/342	1/356
36	1/148	1/269	1/280
37	1/115	1/209	1/218
38	1/88	1/160	1/167
39	1/67	1/122	1/128
40	1/51	1/93	1/97
41	1/38	1/70	1/73
42	1/29	1/52	1/55
43	1/21	1/39	1/41
44	1/16	1/29	1/30

Source: Snijders & Nicolaides, 1996.

Provisional Breast-Feeding Rates by Sociodemographic Factors, Among Children Born in 2007

	Ever breast-feeding	Breast-feeding at 6 months	Breast-feeding at 12 months
U.S. overall	75%	43%	22.40%
Race/ethnicity			
Native American	73.8	42.4	20.7
Asian or Pacific Islander	83	56.4	32.8
Hispanic or Latino	80.6	46	24.7
African American (non-Hispanic)	59.7	27.9	12.9
European (non-Hispanic)	77.7	45.1	23.6
Birth order			
First-born	74.5	44.1	23.7
Not first-born	75.6	41.8	20.8
Mother's age			
Less than 20	59.7	22.2	10.7
20-29	69.7	33.4	16.1
30+	79.3	50.5	27.1
Mother's education			
Less than high school	67	37	21.9
High school graduate	66.1	31.4	15.1
Some college	76.5	41	20.5
College graduate	88.3	59.9	31.1
Mother's marital status			
Married	81.7	51.6	27.5
Unmarried*	61.3	25.5	11.9

*Unmarried includes never married, widowed, separated, and divorced.
Source: CDC National Immunization Survey, Department of Health and Human Services, 2013, based on 2007 data for detailed sociodemographic breakdown.

Regional summaries	Exclusively Breast-fed for 6 months	Still Breast-fed 12–15 months
Africa	34	86
Sub-Saharan Africa	33	88
Eastern and Southern Africa	49	89
West and Central Africa	24	88
Middle East and North Africa	34	70
Asia	38	72
South Asia	45	87
East Asia and Pacific	29	51
Latin America and Caribbean	42	59
Central and Eastern Europe	30	59
Norway	9	46
Italy	2	24
Developing nations	37	75
Least developed nations	42	90
World	37	74

Sources: UNICEF, 2012; European Nutrition and Health Report, 2009 (for Italy and Norway).

Breast-Feeding in the United States

Differentiating excellent from less optimal mothering is not easy, once the child's basic needs for food and protection are met. However, psychosocial development depends on responsive parent–infant relationships. Breast-feeding is one sign of intimacy between mother and infant, itself one aspect of parenting. In the United States, breast-feeding overall is increasing, but some women are more likely to breast-feed than others, as seen in this detailed breakdown for babies born in 2007.

Breast-Feeding Around the World

Regions of the world differ dramatically in the rates of breast-feeding, with the highest rates in Southeast Asia, where half of all 2-year-olds are still breast-feeding. Rates vary dramatically. For example, within Europe, Norwegian babies are nearly twice as likely to be breast-fed at 1 year than are Italian babies.

Saving Lives: Immunization

Most immunizations of children are recommended worldwide and have already saved a billion or more lives. Some, however, are controversial, and some nations differ from the U.S. recommendations shown here.

Recommended Childhood Immunization Schedule, Birth to Age 6, United States, 2012

Vaccine	Birth	1 month	2 months	4 months	6 months	9 months	12 months	15 months	18 months	19–23 months	2–3 years	4–6 years
Hepatitis B	Hep B	Hep B			Hep B							
Rotavirus			RV	RV	RV							
Diphtheria, tetanus, pertussis			DTaP	DTaP	DTaP			DTaP				DTaP
Haemophilus influenzae, type B			Hib	Hib	Hib		Hib					
Pneumococcal			PCV	PCV	PCV		PCV					PPSV
Inactivated poliovirus			IPV	IPV			IPV					IPV
Influenza							Influenza (yearly)					
Measles, mumps, rubella							MMR					MMR
Varicella							Varicella					Varicella
Hepatitis A							Dose 1				HepA Series	
Meningococcal						MCV4						

■ Range of recommended ages for all children
■ Range of recommended ages for certain high-risk groups
■ Range of recommended ages for catch-up vaccination

Recommended Immunizations Schedule for U.S. Children Aged 7 Through 18 Years

Vaccine	7–10 years	11–12 years	13–18 years
Tetanus, diphtheria, pertussis	1 dose	1 dose	1 dose
Human papillomavirus		3 doses	Complete 3 dose series
Meningococcal		Dose 1	Booster
Influenza		Influenza (yearly)	
Pneumococcal			
Hepatitis A			
Hepatitis B			
Inactivated poliovirus			
Measles, mumps, rubella			
Varicella			

■ Range of recommended ages for all children
■ Range of recommendations for certain high-risk groups
■ Range of recommended ages for catch-up immunization

Recommended Immunizations for Adults, United States

Vaccine	19–21 years	22–26 years	27–49 years	50–59 years	60–64 years	65+ years
Influenza	Influenza (yearly)					
Tetanus, diphtheria, and pertussis	Get a Tdap vaccine once, then a booster every 10 years					
Varicella	2 doses					
HPV for women	HPV for women					
HPV for men	HPV for men					
Zoster (shingles)					Zoster	
Measles, mumps, rubella	MMR				MMR	
Pneumococcal	Pneumococcal					
Meningococcal						
Hepatitis A						
Hepatatis B						

Source: MMWR, January 28, 2013.

■ Range of recommended ages for all adults
■ Range of recommendations for certain high-risk groups

From Babbling to Language

Every language accommodates the abilities of toddlers. The "th" sound is difficult, so no language expects 1-year-olds to say it.

	Baby's word for:	
Language	Mother	Father
English	mama, mommy	dada, daddy
Spanish	mama	papa
French	maman, mama	papa
Italian	mamma	babbo, papa
Latvian	mama	te-te
Syrian Arabic	mama	baba
Bantu	ba-mama	taata
Swahili	mama	baba
Sanskrit	nana	tata
Hebrew	ema	abba
Korean	oma	apa

Height Gains from Birth to Age 18

The range of height (on this page) and weight (see page A-11) are for children in the United States. The columns labeled "50th" (the fiftieth percentile) show the average; the columns labeled "90th" (the ninetieth percentile) show the size of children taller and heavier than 90 percent of their contemporaries; and the columns labeled "10th" (the tenth percentile) show the size of children who are taller than only 10 percent of their peers. Note that girls are slightly shorter, on average, than boys.

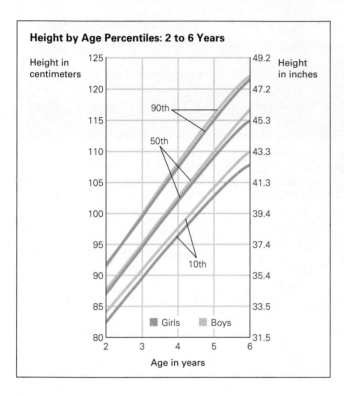

Height by Age Percentiles: 2 to 6 Years

Same Data, Different Form

The columns of numbers in the table to the right provide detailed and precise information about height ranges for every year of childhood. The illustration above shows the same information in graphic form for ages 2–6. The same is done for weight ranges on page A-11. Ages 2–6 are singled out because that is the period during which a child's eating habits are set. Which form of data presentation do you think is easier to understand?

Length in Centimeters (and Inches)

AGE	Boys: percentiles			Girls: percentiles		
	10th	50th	90th	10th	50th	90th
Birth	47.5 (18¾)	50.5 (20)	53.5 (21)	46.5 (18¼)	49.9 (19¾)	52.0 (20½)
1 month	51.3 (20¼)	54.6 (21½)	57.7 (22¾)	50.2 (19¾)	53.5 (21)	56.1 (22)
3 months	57.7 (22¾)	61.1 (24)	64.5 (25½)	56.2 (22¼)	59.5 (23½)	62.7 (24¾)
6 months	64.4 (25¼)	67.8 (26¾)	71.3 (28)	62.6 (24¾)	65.9 (26)	69.4 (27¼)
9 months	69.1 (27¼)	72.3 (28½)	75.9 (30)	67.0 (26½)	70.4 (27¾)	74.0 (29¼)
12 months	72.8 (28¾)	76.1 (30)	79.8 (31½)	70.8 (27¾)	74.3 (29¼)	78.0 (30¾)
18 months	78.7 (31)	82.4 (32½)	86.6 (34)	77.2 (30½)	80.9 (31¾)	85.0 (33½)
24 months	83.5 (32¾)	87.6 (34½)	92.2 (36¼)	82.5 (32½)	86.5 (34)	90.8 (35¾)
3 years	90.3 (35½)	94.9 (37¼)	100.1 (39½)	89.3 (35¼)	94.1 (37)	99.0 (39)
4 years	97.3 (38¼)	102.9 (40½)	108.2 (42½)	96.4 (38)	101.6 (40)	106.6 (42)
5 years	103.7 (40¾)	109.9 (43¼)	115.4 (45½)	102.7 (40½)	108.4 (42¾)	113.8 (44¾)
6 years	109.6 (43¼)	116.1 (45¾)	121.9 (48)	108.4 (42¾)	114.6 (45)	120.8 (47½)
7 years	115.0 (45¼)	121.7 (48)	127.9 (50¼)	113.6 (44¾)	120.6 (47½)	127.6 (50¼)
8 years	120.2 (47¼)	127.0 (50)	133.6 (52½)	118.7 (46¾)	126.4 (49¾)	134.2 (52¾)
9 years	125.2 (49¼)	132.2 (52)	139.4 (55)	123.9 (48¾)	132.2 (52)	140.7 (55½)
10 years	130.1 (51¼)	137.5 (54¼)	145.5 (57¼)	129.5 (51)	138.3 (54½)	147.2 (58)
11 years	135.1 (53¼)	143.33 (56½)	152.1 (60)	135.6 (53½)	144.8 (57)	153.7 (60½)
12 years	140.3 (55¼)	149.7 (59)	159.4 (62¾)	142.3 (56)	151.5 (59¾)	160.0 (63)
13 years	145.8 (57½)	156.5 (61½)	167.0 (65¾)	148.0 (58¼)	157.1 (61¾)	165.3 (65)
14 years	151.8 (59¾)	63.1 (64¼)	173.8 (68½)	151.5 (59¾)	160.4 (63¼)	168.7 (66½)
15 years	158.2 (62¼)	169.0 (66½)	178.9 (70½)	153.2 (60¼)	161.8 (63¾)	170.5 (67¼)
16 years	163.9 (64½)	173.5 (68¼)	182.4 (71¾)	154.1 (60¾)	162.4 (64)	171.1 (67¼)
17 years	167.7 (66)	176.2 (69¼)	184.4 (72½)	155.1 (61)	163.1 (64¼)	171.2 (67½)
18 years	168.7 (66½)	176.8 (69½)	185.3 (73)	156.0 (61½)	163.7 (64½)	171.0 (67¼)

Source: These data are those of the National Center for Health Statistics (NCHS), Health Resources Administration, DHHS. They were based on studies of The Fels Research Institute, Yellow Springs, Ohio. These data were first made available with the help of William M. Moore, M.D., of Ross Laboratories, who supplied the conversion from metric measurements to approximate inches and pounds. This help is gratefully acknowledged.

Weight Gains from Birth to Age 18

These height and weight charts present rough guidelines; a child might differ from these norms and be quite healthy and normal. However, if a particular child shows a discrepancy between height and weight (e.g., at the 90th percentile in height but only the 20th percentile in weight) or is much larger or smaller than most children the same age, a pediatrician should see whether disease, malnutrition, or genetic abnormality could be part of the reason.

Weight by Age Percentiles: 2 to 6 Years

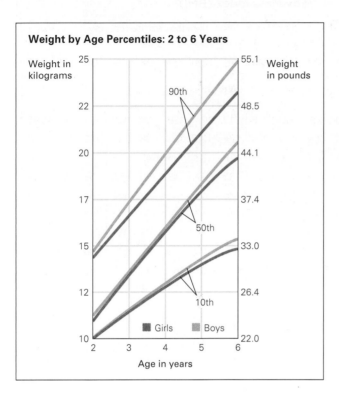

	Weight in Kilograms (and Pounds)					
	Boys: percentiles			**Girls: percentiles**		
AGE	**10th**	**50th**	**90th**	**10th**	**50th**	**90th**
Birth	2.78 (6¼)	3.27 (7¼)	3.82 (8½)	2.58 (5¾)	3.23 (7)	3.64 (8)
1 month	3.43 (7½)	4.29 (9½)	5.14 (11¼)	3.22 (7)	3.98 (8¾)	4.65 (10¼)
3 months	4.78 (10½)	5.98 (13¼)	7.14 (15¾)	4.47 (9¾)	5.40 (12)	6.39 (14)
6 months	6.61 (14½)	7.85 (17¼)	9.10 (20)	6.12 (13½)	7.21 (16)	8.38 (18½)
9 months	7.95 (17½)	9.18 (20¼)	10.49 (23¼)	7.34 (16¼)	8.56 (18¾)	9.83 (21¾)
12 months	8.84 (19½)	10.15 (22½)	11.54 (25½)	8.19 (18)	9.53 (21)	10.87 (24)
18 months	9.92 (21¾)	11.47 (25¼)	13.05 (28¾)	9.30 (20½)	10.82 (23¾)	12.30 (27)
24 months	10.85 (24)	12.59 (27¾)	14.29 (31½)	10.26 (22½)	11.90 (26¼)	13.57 (30)
3 years	12.58 (27¾)	14.62 (32¼)	16.95 (37¼)	12.26 (27)	14.10 (31)	16.54 (36½)
4 years	14.24 (31½)	16.69 (36¾)	19.32 (42½)	13.84 (30½)	15.96 (35¼)	18.93 (41¾)
5 years	15.96 (35¼)	18.67 (41¼)	21.70 (47¾)	15.26 (33¾)	17.66 (39)	21.23 (46¾)
6 years	17.72 (39)	20.69 (45½)	24.31 (53½)	16.72 (36¾)	19.52 (43)	23.89 (52¾)
7 years	19.53 (43)	22.85 (50¼)	27.36 (60¼)	18.39 (40½)	21.84 (48¼)	27.39 (60½)
8 years	21.39 (47¼)	25.30 (55¾)	31.06 (68½)	20.45 (45)	24.84 (54¾)	32.04 (70¾)
9 years	23.33 (51½)	28.13 (62)	35.57 (78½)	22.92 (50½)	28.46 (62¾)	37.60 (83)
10 years	25.52 (56¼)	31.44 (69¼)	40.80 (90)	25.76 (56¾)	32.55 (71¾)	43.70 (96¼)
11 years	28.17 (62)	35.30 (77¾)	46.57 (102¾)	28.97 (63¾)	36.95 (81½)	49.96 (110¼)
12 years	31.46 (69¼)	39.78 (87¾)	52.73 (116¼)	32.53 (71¼)	41.53 (91½)	55.99 (123½)
13 years	35.60 (78½)	44.95 (99)	59.12 (130¼)	36.35 (80¼)	46.10 (101¾)	61.45 (135½)
14 years	40.64 (89½)	50.77 (112)	65.57 (144½)	40.11 (88½)	50.28 (110¾)	66.04 (145½)
15 years	46.06 (101½)	56.71 (125)	71.91 (158½)	43.38 (95¾)	53.68 (118¼)	69.64 (153¼)
16 years	51.16 (112¾)	62.10 (137)	77.97 (172)	45.78 (101)	55.89 (123¼)	71.68 (158)
17 years	55.28 (121¾)	66.31 (146¼)	83.58 (184¼)	47.04 (103¾)	56.69 (125)	72.38 (159½)
18 years	57.89 (127½)	68.88 (151¾)	88.41 (195)	47.47 (104¾)	56.62 (124¾)	72.25 (159¼)

Source: Data are those of the National Center for Health Statistics, Health Resources Administration, DHHS, collected in its Health Examination Surveys.

Body Mass Index

BMI is a quick way to indicate weight problems. Too thin is a BMI below 19; the preferred range is 19 to 24, overweight is 25 to 29, obese is more than 30, and morbidly obese is more than 35. However, for some people, mitigating factors need to be considered before a person is advised to change his or her diet. For example, muscle is heavier than fat, so fit adults could have a BMI of 26 and still be quite healthy.

Body Mass Index (BMI)

To find your BMI, locate your height in the first column, then look across that row.
Your BMI appears at the top of the column that contains your weight.

BMI	19	20	21	22	23	24	25	26	27	28	29	30	35	40
Height (in feet and inches)							**Weight** (in pounds)							
4'10"	91	96	100	105	110	115	119	124	129	134	138	143	167	191
4'11"	94	99	104	109	114	119	124	128	133	138	143	148	173	198
5'0"	97	102	107	112	118	123	128	133	138	143	148	153	179	204
5'1"	100	106	111	116	122	127	132	137	143	148	153	158	185	211
5'2"	104	109	115	120	126	131	136	142	147	153	158	164	191	218
5'3"	107	113	118	124	130	135	141	146	152	158	163	169	197	225
5'4"	110	116	122	128	134	140	145	151	157	163	169	174	204	232
5'5"	114	120	126	132	138	144	150	156	162	168	174	180	210	240
5'6"	118	124	130	136	142	148	155	161	167	173	179	186	216	247
5'7"	121	127	134	140	146	153	159	166	172	178	185	191	223	255
5'8"	125	131	138	144	151	158	164	171	177	183	190	197	230	262
5'9"	128	135	142	149	155	162	169	176	182	189	196	203	236	270
5'10"	132	139	146	153	160	167	174	181	188	195	202	207	243	278
5'11"	136	143	150	157	165	172	179	186	193	200	208	215	250	286
6'0"	140	147	154	162	169	177	184	191	199	206	213	221	258	294
6'1"	144	151	159	166	174	182	189	197	204	212	219	227	265	302
6'2"	148	155	163	171	179	186	194	202	210	218	225	233	272	311
6'3"	152	160	168	176	184	192	200	208	216	224	232	240	279	319
6'4"	156	164	172	180	189	197	205	213	221	230	238	246	287	328
				Normal					*Overweight*				*Obese*	

Source: National Heart, Lung, and Blood Institute, n.d.

IQ Scores

Almost 70 percent of IQ scores fall within the normal range. Note, however, that this is a norm-referenced test. In fact, actual IQ scores have risen in many nations; 100 is no longer exactly the midpoint. Furthermore, in practice, scores below 50 are slightly more frequent than indicated by the normal curve shown here because severe intellectual disability is the result not of normal distribution but of genetic and prenatal factors.

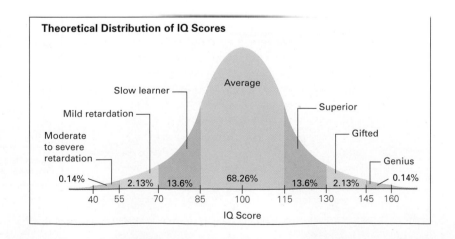

Theoretical Distribution of IQ Scores

Rates of Poverty, by State and by Age Group

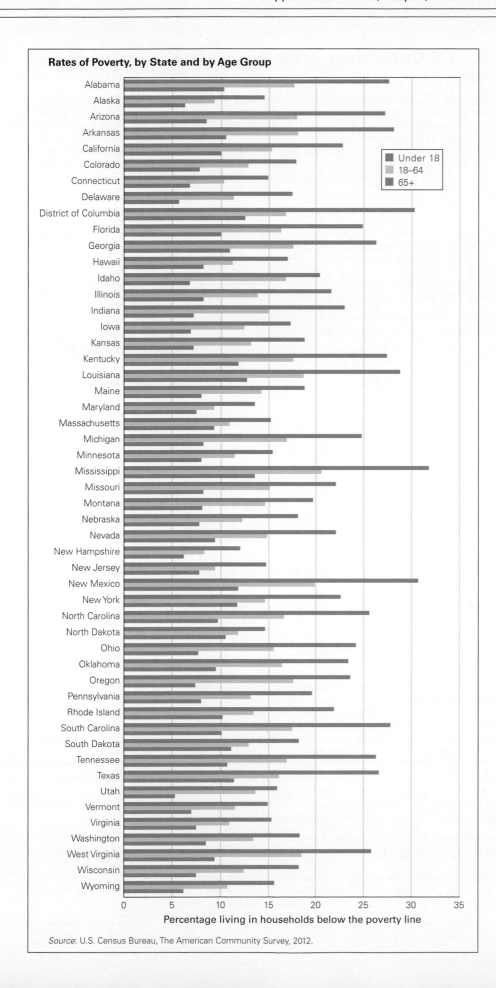

Percentage living in households below the poverty line

Legend:
- Under 18
- 18–64
- 65+

States (top to bottom): Alabama, Alaska, Arizona, Arkansas, California, Colorado, Connecticut, Delaware, District of Columbia, Florida, Georgia, Hawaii, Idaho, Illinois, Indiana, Iowa, Kansas, Kentucky, Louisiana, Maine, Maryland, Massachusetts, Michigan, Minnesota, Mississippi, Missouri, Montana, Nebraska, Nevada, New Hampshire, New Jersey, New Mexico, New York, North Carolina, North Dakota, Ohio, Oklahoma, Oregon, Pennsylvania, Rhode Island, South Carolina, South Dakota, Tennessee, Texas, Utah, Vermont, Virginia, Washington, West Virginia, Wisconsin, Wyoming

Source: U.S. Census Bureau, The American Community Survey, 2012.

Children Are the Poorest Americans

It probably comes as no surprise that the rate of poverty is twice as high in some states as in others. What is surprising is how much the rates vary among age groups within the same state.

Observation Quiz As you can see, most states have far more poor children than poor adults, unlike in most European nations. Which seven states have the most balanced poverty rates (i.e., where children are *not* twice as often poor as those over 64)? (see answer, page A-14)

>> Answer to Observation Quiz
(from page A-13) Maryland, Massachusetts, Minnesota, New Hampshire, New Jersey, North Dakota, and South Dakota. Note that those states tend to have relatively low poverty overall.

DSM-5 Criteria for Attention-Deficit/Hyperactivity Disorder (ADHD)

The Diagnostic and Statistical Manual of Mental Disorders, fifth edition (DSM-5) was written to help clinicians, researchers, and insurance companies distinguish one disorder from another, as well as to know when behavior is normal for a particular age. These are the criteria for attention-deficit/hyperactivity disorder; attention-deficit disorder is no longer a separate diagnosis in the DSM-5. The DSM-5 includes not only diagnostic criteria as shown here, but also discussion of prevalence, age and gender statistics, cultural aspects, and prognosis for hundreds of disorders or subtypes, many of which appear primarily in childhood.

Attention-Deficit/Hyperactivity Disorder

Diagnostic Criteria

A. A persistent pattern of inattention and/or hyperactivity-impulsivity that interferes with functioning or development, as characterized by (1) and/or (2):

  1. **Inattention:** Six (or more) of the following symptoms have persisted for at least 6 months to a degree that is inconsistent with developmental level and that negatively impacts directly on social and academic/occupational activities:

    Note: The symptoms are not solely a manifestation of oppositional behavior, defiance, hostility, or failure to understand tasks or instructions. For older adolescents and adults (age 17 and older), at least five symptoms are required.

    a. Often fails to give close attention to details or makes careless mistakes in schoolwork, at work, or during other activities (e.g., overlooks or misses details, work is inaccurate).

    b. Often has difficulty sustaining attention in tasks or play activities (e.g., has difficulty remaining focused during lectures, conversations, or lengthy reading).

    c. Often does not seem to listen when spoken to directly (e.g., mind seems elsewhere, even in the absence of any obvious distraction).

    d. Often does not follow through on instructions and fails to finish schoolwork, chores, or duties in the workplace (e.g., starts tasks but quickly loses focus and is easily sidetracked).

    e. Often has difficulty organizing tasks and activities (e.g., difficulty managing sequential tasks; difficulty keeping materials and belongings in order; messy, disorganized work; has poor time management; fails to meet deadlines).

    f. Often avoids, dislikes, or is reluctant to engage in tasks that require sustained mental effort (e.g., schoolwork or homework; for older adolescents and adults, preparing reports, completing forms, reviewing lengthy papers).

    g. Often loses things necessary for tasks or activities (e.g., school materials, pencils, books, tools, wallets, keys, paperwork, eyeglasses, mobile telephones).

    h. Is often easily distracted by extraneous stimuli (for older adolescents and adults, may include unrelated thoughts).

    i. Is often forgetful in daily activities (e.g., doing chores, running errands; for older adolescents and adults, returning calls, paying bills, keeping appointments).

  2. **Hyperactivity and impulsivity:** Six (or more) of the following symptoms have persisted for at least 6 months to a degree that is inconsistent with developmental level and that negatively impacts directly on social and academic/occupational activities:

    Note: The symptoms are not solely a manifestation of oppositional behavior, defiance, hostility, or a failure to understand tasks or instructions. For older adolescents and adults (age 17 and older), at least five symptoms are required.

    a. Often fidgets with or taps hands or feet or squirms in seat.

    b. Often leaves seat in situations when remaining seated is expected (e.g., leaves his or her place in the classroom, in the office or other workplace, or in other situations that require remaining in place).

    c. Often runs about or climbs in situations where it is inappropriate. (**Note:** In adolescents or adults, may be limited to feeling restless.)

    d. Often unable to play or engage in leisure activities quietly.

    e. Is often "on the go," acting as if "driven by a motor" (e.g., is unable to be or uncomfortable being still for extended time, as in restaurants, meetings; may be experienced by others as being restless or difficult to keep up with).

    f. Often talks excessively.

    g. Often blurts out an answer before a question has been completed (e.g., completes people's sentences; cannot wait for turn in conversation).

    h. Often has difficulty waiting his or her turn (e.g., while waiting in line).

    i. Often interrupts or intrudes on others (e.g., butts into conversations, games, or activities; may start using other people's things without asking or receiving permission; for adolescents and adults, may intrude into or take over what the others are doing).

B. Several inattentive or hyperactive-impulsive symptoms were present prior to age 12 years.

C. Several inattentive or hyperactive-impulsive symptoms are present in two or more settings (e.g., at home, school, or work; with friends or relatives; in other activities).

D. There is clear evidence that the symptoms interfere with, or reduce the quality of, social, academic, or occupational functioning.

E. The symptoms do not occur exclusively during the course of schizophrenia or another psychotic disorder and are not better explained by another mental disorder (e.g., mood disorder, anxiety disorder, dissociative disorder, personality disorder, substance intoxication or withdrawal).

DSM-5 Criteria on Autism Spectrum Disorder

In the fifth edition of the Diagnostic and Statistical Manual (DSM-5), autism spectrum disorder is an updated term; the disorder is marked by problems in social interaction, the ethnic use of language, and restricted, repetitive patterns of behavior.

Autism Spectrum Disorder

Diagnostic Criteria	**299.00** (F84.0)

A. Persistent deficits in social communication and social interaction across multiple contexts, as manifested by the following, currently or by history (examples are illustrative, not exhaustive; see text):

1. Deficits in social-emotional reciprocity, ranging, for example, from abnormal social approach and failure of normal back-and-forth conversation; to reduced sharing of interests, emotions, or affect; to failure to initiate or respond to social interactions.
2. Deficits in nonverbal communicative behaviors used for social interaction, ranging, for example, from poorly integrated verbal and nonverbal communication; to abnormalities in eye contact and body language or deficits in understanding and use of gestures; to a total lack of facial expressions and nonverbal communication.
3. Deficits in developing, maintaining, and understanding relationships, ranging, for example, from difficulties adjusting behavior to suit various social contexts; to difficulties in sharing imaginative play or in making friends; to absence of interest in peers.

Specify current severity:

Severity is based on social communication impairments and restricted, repetitive patterns of behavior (see Table 2).

B. Restricted, repetitive patterns of behavior, interests, or activities, as manifested by at least two of the following, currently or by history (examples are illustrative, not exhaustive; see text):

1. Stereotyped or repetitive motor movements, use of objects, or speech (e.g., simple motor stereotypes, lining up toys or flipping objects, echolalia, idiosyncratic phrases).
2. Insistence on sameness, inflexible adherence to routines, or ritualized patterns of verbal or nonverbal behavior (e.g., extreme distress at small changes, difficulties with transitions, rigid thinking patterns, greeting rituals, need to take same route or eat same food every day).
3. Highly restricted, fixated interests that are abnormal in intensity or focus (e.g., strong attachment to or preoccupation with unusual objects, excessively circumscribed or perseverative interests).
4. Hyper- or hyporeactivity to sensory input or unusual interest in sensory aspects of the environment (e.g., apparent indifference to pain/temperature, adverse response to specific sounds or textures, excessive smelling or touching of objects, visual fascination with lights or movement).

Specify current severity:

Severity is based on social communication impairments and restricted, repetitive patterns of behavior (see Table 2).

C. Symptoms must be present in the early developmental period (but may not become fully manifest until social demands exceed limited capacities, or may be masked by learned strategies in later life).
D. Symptoms cause clinically significant impairment in social, occupational, or other important areas of current functioning.
E. These disturbances are not better explained by intellectual disability (intellectual developmental disorder) or global developmental delay. Intellectual disability and autism spectrum disorder frequently co-occur; to make comorbid diagnoses of autism spectrum disorder and intellectual disability, social communication should be below that expected for general developmental level.

Note: Individuals with a well-established DSM-IV diagnosis of autistic disorder, Asperger's disorder, or pervasive developmental disorder not otherwise specified should be given the diagnosis of autism spectrum disorder. Individuals who have marked deficits in social communication, but whose symptoms do not otherwise meet criteria for autism spectrum disorder, should be evaluated for social (pragmatic) communication disorder.

Motivation or Achievement?

The PISA (Programme for International Student Assessment) is an international test of 15-year-olds' abilities to apply their knowledge. One explanation for the high scores of China and low scores of the United States is motivation of the students: Experts believe that students in the United States are not strongly motivated to learn in school—so they don't.

Science		Reading		Math	
Region	**PISA Score**	**Region**	**PISA Score**	**Region**	**PISA Score**
China	575	China	556	China	600
Finland	554	Korea	539	Singapore	562
Hong Kong	549	Finland	536	Hong Kong	555
Singapore	542	Hong Kong	533	Korea	546
Japan	539	Singapore	526	Taiwan	543
Korea	538	Canada	524	Finland	541
New Zealand	532	New Zealand	521	Liechtenstein	536
Canada	529	Japan	520	Switzerland	534
Estonia	528	Australia	515	Japan	529
Australia	527	Netherlands	508	Canada	527
Netherlands	522	Belgium	506	Netherlands	526
Taiwan	520	Norway	503	New Zealand	519
Germany	520	Estonia	501	Belgium	515
Liechtenstein	520	Switzerland	501	Australia	514
Switzerland	517	Poland	500	Germany	513
Britain	514	Iceland	500	Estonia	512
Slovenia	512	**United States**	**500**	Iceland	507
Poland	508	Liechtenstein	499	Denmark	503
Ireland	508	Sweden	497	Slovenia	501
Belgium	507	Germany	497	Norway	498
Hungary	503	Ireland	496	France	497
United States	**502**	France	496	Slovakia	497
AVERAGE SCORE*	501	Taiwan	495	AVERAGE SCORE*	497
Czech Republic	500	Denmark	495	Austria	496
Norway	500	Britain	494	Poland	495
Denmark	499	Hungary	494	Sweden	494
France	490	AVERAGE SCORE*	494	Czech Republic	493
Iceland	496	Portugal	489	Britain	492
Sweden	495	Italy	486	Hungary	490
Austria	494	Latvia	484	Luxembourg	489
Latvia	494	Slovenia	483	**United States**	**487**
Portugal	493	Greece	483	Ireland	487

*Average is based on all the students who took the test, which includes many in low-scoring nations not shown here.
Sources: OECD, 2010a, 2010b.

Major Sexually Transmitted Infections: Some Basics

These and other STIs, if left untreated, may lead to serious reproductive and other health problems or even, as with HIV/AIDS and syphilis, to death. STIs can be avoided by consistently using condoms, having sex only in a relationship with an uninfected partner, or abstaining from sex—oral, anal, and genital.

Sexually Transmitted Infection (and Cause)	Symptoms	Treatment
Chlamydia (bacterium)	The most frequently reported bacterial STI in the United States. In women, abnormal vaginal discharge or burning sensation when urinating; may be followed by pain in low abdomen or low back, nausea, fever, pain during intercourse, or bleeding between menstrual periods. In men, discharge from penis or burning sensation when urinating.	Antibiotics
Genital HPV infection (virus)	One of the most common STIs in the world. Causes no symptoms or health problems in most people, but certain types may cause genital warts and others can cause cervical cancer in women and other cancers of the genitals in both sexes.	A vaccine is now available and is recommended for 11- and 12-year-old girls who are not yet sexually active.
Genital herpes (virus)	Blisters on or around the genitals or rectum that break and leave sores, which may take 2 to 4 weeks to heal; some people may experience fever, swollen glands, and other flu-like symptoms. Later outbreaks are usually less severe and shorter. Many people never have sores and may take years to realize they are infected. May lead to potentially fatal infections in babies and makes infected person more susceptible to HIV infection.	There is no vaccine or cure, but antiviral medications can shorten and prevent outbreaks.
Gonorrhea (bacterium)	Some men and most women have no symptoms. In men, a burning sensation when urinating; a white, yellow, or green discharge from the penis; painful or swollen testicles. In women, symptoms—pain or burning during urination, increased vaginal discharge, vaginal bleeding between periods—may be so mild or nonspecific that they are mistaken for a bladder or vaginal infection. May cause pelvic inflammatory disease (PID) in women and infertility in both sexes. Infected person can more easily contract HIV.	Antibiotics
Pelvic inflammatory disease (PID) (various bacteria)	A common and serious complication in women who have certain other STIs, especially chlamydia and gonorrhea. Pain in lower abdomen, fever, unusual vaginal discharge that may have a foul odor, painful intercourse, painful urination, irregular menstrual bleeding, and (rarely) pain in the right upper abdomen. May lead to blocked fallopian tubes, causing infertility.	Administration of at least two antibiotics that are effective against a wide range of infectious agents. In severe cases, surgery.
HIV/AIDS (virus)	Infection with the human immunodeficiency virus (HIV) eventually leads to acquired immune deficiency syndrome (AIDS). Infection with other STIs increases a person's likelihood of both acquiring and transmitting HIV. Soon after exposure, some people have flu-like symptoms: fever, headache, tiredness, swollen lymph glands. Months or years later, when the virus has weakened the immune system, the person may experience lack of energy, weight loss, frequent fevers and sweats, yeast infections, skin rashes, short-term memory loss. Symptoms of full-blown AIDS include certain cancers (Kaposi's sarcoma and lymphomas), seizures, vision loss, and coma. A leading cause of death among young adults in many nations.	There is no vaccine or cure, but antiretroviral drugs can slow the growth of the virus; antibiotics can cure some secondary infections, and various treatments are available to relieve painful or unpleasant symptoms.
Syphilis (bacterium)	Symptoms may not appear for years. Primary stage: One or more sores (chancres) a few days or weeks after exposure. Secondary stage: Skin rash, lesions of mucous membranes, fever, swollen lymph glands, sore throat, patchy hair loss, headaches, weight loss, muscle aches, fatigue. Latent stage: Primary and secondary symptoms disappear, but infection remains in the body. Late stage (10 to 20 years after first infection): Damage to brain, nerves, eyes, heart, blood vessels, liver, bones, and joints, progressing to difficulty coordinating muscle movements, paralysis, numbness, blindness, dementia.	Penicillin injections will kill the syphilis bacterium and prevent further damage but cannot repair damage already done.
Trichomoniasis (*Trichomonas vaginalis*, a single-celled protozoan parasite)	Most men have no symptoms, but some may temporarily have an irritation inside the penis, mild discharge, or slight burning after urination or ejaculation. Women may have a frothy, yellow-green, strong-smelling vaginal discharge and may experience discomfort during intercourse and urination; irritation and itching of the genital area; and, rarely, lower abdominal pain.	A single oral dose of metronidazole or tinidazole

Source: Centers for Disease Control and Prevention, 2012.

Sexual Behaviors of U.S. High School Students, 2011

These percentages, as high as they may seem, are actually lower than they were in the early 1990s. (States not listed did not participate fully in the survey.) The data in this table reflect responses from students in the 9th to 12th grades. When only high school seniors are surveyed, the percentages are higher: Nationwide, 62 percent of seniors have had sexual intercourse, and 21 percent have had four or more partners.

Percentage of High School Students Who Ever Had Sexual Intercourse and Who Had Sexual Intercourse for the First Time Before Age 13, by Sex — Selected U.S. Sites, Youth Risk Behavior Survey, 2011

Site	Ever had sexual intercourse (%)			Had first sexual intercourse before age 13 years (%)			Had sexual intercourse with four or more persons during their life (%)			Currently sexually active (%)		
State surveys	Female	Male	Total	Female	Male	Total	Female	Male	Total	Female	Male	Total
Alabama	54.4	60.6	**57.6**	5.8	13.9	**10**	19	26.3	**22.8**	44.8	43.1	**44.1**
Alaska	37.3	39.3	**38.3**	2.4	6.2	**4.4**	7.5	11.8	**9.7**	26.2	24.2	**25.2**
Arizona	44.2	49.7	**46.9**	3.1	7.9	**5.4**	11.9	16.6	**14.2**	31.3	35.9	**33.5**
Arkansas	48.6	51.9	**50.3**	4.7	12.1	**8.4**	16	23	**19.5**	39.6	36.4	**38.1**
Colorado	36.1	44.5	**40.8**	2	5.4	**3.6**	11.1	14.8	**13.2**	29.2	33.5	**31.8**
Connecticut	41.8	43.7	**42.7**	3.3	6.5	**4.9**	8.6	12.6	**10.6**	31.9	29.2	**30.5**
Delaware	57.1	60.8	**59**	4.3	13.7	**8.8**	17	26.5	**21.7**	42.9	42.7	**42.9**
Florida	43.9	52.4	**48.2**	3.2	11.8	**7.6**	10.8	21.4	**16.1**	32.2	35.8	**34**
Georgia	—†	—	**—**	—	—	**—**	—§	—	**—**	—	—	**—**
Hawaii	37.4	36.7	**37**	3	7.5	**5.2**	7.4	8.7	**8**	25.9	21.7	**23.9**
Idaho	39.1	40.8	**40**	2.2	4.9	**3.6**	11	16.5	**13.8**	—	—	**—**
Illinois	45.3	44.4	**44.8**	3.4	9.1	**6.3**	10.4	14.4	**12.4**	35.2	30.3	**32.8**
Indiana	50.5	51.4	**51**	3.6	6.9	**5.2**	15.2	18.4	**16.8**	39.9	37	**38.5**
Iowa	43.5	44.3	**43.9**	2.5	5.6	**4.2**	13.1	13.1	**13.1**	34.3	31.7	**33**
Kansas	43	43.4	**43.2**	1.9	5.5	**3.7**	8.5	10.9	**9.7**	33.6	32.1	**32.8**
Kentucky	51.9	51.7	**51.8**	5.5	8.9	**7.2**	16.3	17	**16.6**	40.9	34.6	**37.7**
Louisiana	—	—	**—**	—	—	**—**	—	—	**—**	—	—	**—**
Maine	45.2	44.6	**45.1**	2.2	5.6	**4**	9.6	11.2	**10.5**	35.6	31.3	**33.6**
Maryland	—	—	**—**	—	—	**—**	—	—	**—**	—	—	**—**
Massachusetts	39.4	44.7	**42**	2.1	6.2	**4.2**	9.5	13.3	**11.4**	30.3	30.7	**30.4**
Michigan	40.4	42.1	**41.2**	2.9	5.9	**4.4**	9	12.2	**10.7**	30.9	27.2	**29.1**
Mississippi	53.3	62.5	**57.9**	4.8	19.1	**11.8**	13.7	30.6	**22.1**	38.6	45.4	**42.1**
Montana	46.6	49.1	**47.9**	2.4	6.3	**4.4**	14.5	15.5	**15**	36.8	32.6	**34.7**
Nebraska	37.2	37.2	**37.1**	2.7	4.8	**3.8**	9.9	11.3	**10.6**	28.5	25.7	**27**
New Hampshire	45.7	49.4	**47.5**	2.4	6.5	**4.5**	11.5	13.4	**12.4**	36.4	37.9	**37.1**
New Jersey	41.4	47.6	**44.6**	2.6	7.5	**5.1**	9.9	17.8	**13.9**	30.6	33.6	**32.2**
New Mexico	—	—	**—**	5.1	10.4	**7.7**	11.5	17.5	**14.5**	31.8	31.9	**31.9**
New York	39.6	44.5	**42**	4	7.6	**5.7**	11.1	15.5	**13.3**	31.1	31	**31**
North Carolina	47.1	51.4	**49.3**	5.3	12	**8.6**	14.6	18.9	**16.8**	36.7	32.9	**34.9**
North Dakota	46.2	43.4	**44.8**	3	4.4	**3.7**	14.7	11.5	**13.2**	—	—	**—**
Ohio	—	—	**—**	4.3	8	**6.1**	15.8	19	**17.5**	43.3	39.8	**41.8**
Oklahoma	50.1	51	**50.5**	2.7	7.2	**5**	14.9	18.6	**16.8**	39.2	36.4	**37.8**
Rhode Island	38.2	45.4	**41.7**	1.7	8	**4.9**	7.2	13.9	**10.5**	28.4	31.2	**29.8**
South Carolina	52	61.3	**56.6**	3.9	17.1	**10.5**	16.7	25.9	**21.3**	38.9	44.6	**41.8**
South Dakota	48.9	46.1	**47.4**	2.5	5.1	**3.8**	15.4	14.5	**14.9**	37.6	33.4	**35.4**
Tennessee	49.4	55.3	**52.4**	4	10.4	**7.2**	13.9	20.5	**17.2**	37.4	36.8	**37.1**
Texas	48.6	54.8	**51.6**	4	10.1	**7**	12.9	20.7	**16.7**	36.8	35.6	**36.2**
Utah	—	—	**—**	—	—	**—**	—	—	**—**	—	—	**—**
Vermont	—	—	**—**	2.6	5.7	**4.2**	10	12.1	**11.1**	32.8	30.7	**31.8**
Virginia	—	—	**—**	—	—	**—**	—	—	**—**	—	—	**—**
West Virginia	50.1	51.8	**50.9**	2.3	7.5	**4.9**	10.2	14.6	**12.4**	39.4	35.9	**37.6**
Wisconsin	41.4	41.7	**41.6**	2.7	6	**4.4**	9.6	10.1	**9.9**	32.9	28.8	**30.8**
Wyoming	47.4	48.5	**47.9**	4.3	7.6	**6**	16.2	18.4	**17.3**	37.8	31.6	**34.7**
Median	**45.3**	**47.6**	**46.9**	**3**	**7.5**	**5**	**11.5**	**15.5**	**13.8**	**35.4**	**33.1**	**33.8**

Source: MMWR, June 8, 2012.

Smoking Behavior Among U.S. High School Students, 1991–2011

The data in these two tables reveal many trends. For example, do you see that African American adolescents are much less likely to smoke than Hispanics or European Americans, but that this ethnic advantage is decreasing? Are you surprised to see that European American females smoke more than European American males?

Percentage of High School Students Who Reported Smoking Cigarettes								
Smoking Behavior	1991	1995	1999	2003	2005	2007	2009	2011
Lifetime (ever smoked)	70.1	71.3	70.4	58.4	54.3	50.3	46.3	44.7
Current (smoked at least once in past 30 days)	27.5	34.8	34.8	21.9	23.0	20.0	19.5	18.1
Current frequent (smoked 20 or more times in past 30 days)	12.7	16.1	16.8	9.7	9.4	8.1	7.3	6.4

Percentage of High School Students Who Reported Smoking Cigarettes, by Sex, Ethnicity, and Grade								
Characteristic	1991	1995	1999	2003	2005	2007	2009	2011
Sex								
Female	27.3	34.3	34.9	21.9	23.0	18.7	19.1	16.1
Male	27.6	35.4	34.7	21.8	22.9	21.3	19.8	19.9
Ethnicity								
European American, non-Hispanic	30.9	38.3	38.6	24.9	25.9	23.2	22.5	20.3
Female	31.7	39.8	39.1	26.6	27.0	22.5	22.8	18.9
Male	30.2	37.0	38.2	23.3	24.9	23.8	22.3	21.5
African American, non-Hispanic	12.6	19.2	19.7	15.1	12.9	11.6	9.5	10.5
Female	11.3	12.2	17.7	10.8	11.9	8.4	8.4	7.4
Male	14.1	27.8	21.8	19.3	14.0	14.9	10.7	13.7
Hispanic	25.3	34.0	32.7	18.4	22.0	16.7	18.0	17.5
Female	22.9	32.9	31.5	17.7	19.2	14.6	16.7	15.2
Male	27.9	34.9	34.0	19.1	24.8	18.7	19.4	**19.5**
Grade								
9th	23.2	31.2	27.6	17.4	19.7	14.3	13.5	13.0
10th	25.2	33.1	34.7	21.8	21.4	19.6	18.3	15.6
11th	31.6	35.9	36.0	23.6	24.3	21.6	22.3	19.3
12th	30.1	38.2	42.8	26.2	27.6	26.5	25.2	25.1

Source: MMWR, 2012.

Demographic Changes

These numbers show dramatic shifts in family planning, with teenage births continuing to fall and births after age 30 rising again. These data come from the United States, but the same trends are apparent in almost every nation. Can you tell when contraception became widely available?

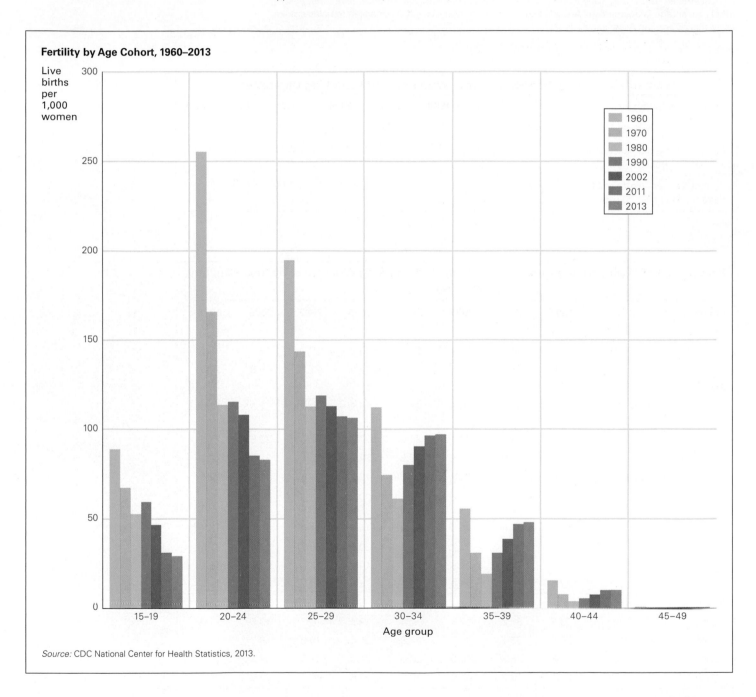

Fertility by Age Cohort, 1960–2013

Live births per 1,000 women

Legend: 1960, 1970, 1980, 1990, 2002, 2011, 2013

Age group

Source: CDC National Center for Health Statistics, 2013.

Suicide Rates in the United States

These are the rates per 100,000. When there is no bar for a given age group, that means there are too few suicides in that age group to calculate an accurate rate. Overall, the highest rates are among adult European American men.

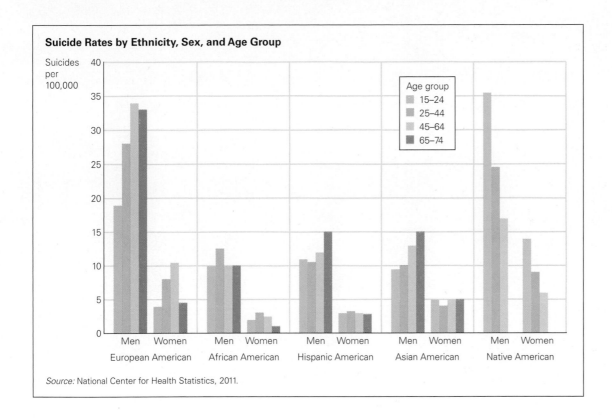

Suicide Rates by Ethnicity, Sex, and Age Group

Source: National Center for Health Statistics, 2011.

Appendix B
More About
Research Methods

This appendix explains how to learn about any topic. It is crucial that you distinguish valid conclusions from wishful thinking. Such learning begins with your personal experience.

>> Make It Personal

Think about your life, observe your behavior, and watch the people around you. Pay careful attention to details of expression, emotion, and behavior. The more you see, the more fascinated, curious, and reflective you will become. Ask questions and listen carefully and respectfully to what other people say regarding development.

Whenever you ask specific questions as part of an assignment, **remember that observing ethical standards (see Chapter 1) comes first.** *Before* you interview anyone, inform the person of your purpose and assure him or her of confidentiality. Promise not to identify the person in your report (use a pseudonym), and do not repeat any personal details that emerge in the interview to anyone (friends or strangers). Your instructor will provide further ethical guidance. If you might publish what you've learned, get in touch with your college's Institutional Review Board (IRB).

>> Read the Research

No matter how deeply you think about your own experiences, and no matter how intently you listen to others whose background is unlike yours, you also need to read scholarly published work in order to fully understand any topic that interests you. Be skeptical about magazine or newspaper reports; some are bound to be simplified, exaggerated, or biased.

Professional Journals and Books

Part of the process of science is that conclusions are not considered solid until they are corroborated in many studies, which means that you should consult several sources on any topic. **Four journals in human development are:**

- *Developmental Psychology* (published by the American Psychological Association)
- *Child Development* (Society for Research in Child Development)
- *Developmental Review* (Elsevier)
- *Human Development* (Karger)

These journals differ in the types of articles and studies they publish, but all are well respected and *peer-reviewed*, which means that other scholars review each article submitted and recommend that it be accepted, rejected, or revised. Every article includes references to other recent work.

Beyond these four are literally thousands of other professional journals, each with a particular perspective or topic. To judge them, look for journals that are peer-reviewed. Also consider the following details: the background of the author (research funded by corporations tends to favor their products); the nature of the publisher (professional organizations, as in the first two journals above, protect their reputations); how long the journal has been published (the volume number tells you that). Some interesting work does not meet these criteria, but these are guides to quality.

Many **books** cover some aspect of development. Single-author books are likely to present only one viewpoint. That view may be insightful, but it is limited. You might consult a handbook, which is a book that includes many authors and many topics. Two good handbooks in development, in their sixth and seventh editions, respectively (a sign that past scholars have found them useful), are:

- *Handbook of Child Psychology* (2006, Damon & Lerner, eds.), four volumes, published by Wiley
- *Handbook on Aging* (2011), three volumes (biology, psychology, and social sciences), published by Academic Press

Again, dozens of good handbooks are available, many of which focus on a particular age or topic.

The Internet

The **Internet** is a mixed blessing, useful to every novice and experienced researcher but dangerous as well. Every library worldwide and most homes in North America, western Europe, and East Asia have computers that provide access to journals and other information. Ask for help from the librarians; many are highly skilled. In addition, other students, friends, and even strangers can be helpful.

Virtually everything is on the Internet, not only massive national and international statistics but also very personal accounts. Photos, charts, quizzes, ongoing experiments, newspapers from around the world, videos, and much more are available at the click of a mouse. Every journal has a Web site, with tables of contents, abstracts, and sometimes full texts (an abstract gives the key findings; for the full text, you may need to consult the library's copy of the print version).

Unfortunately, you can spend many frustrating hours sifting through information that is useless, trash, or tangential. Directories (which list general topics or areas and then move you step by step in the direction you choose) and search engines (which give you all the sites that use a particular word or words) can help you select appropriate information. Each directory or search engine provides somewhat different lists; none provides only the most comprehensive and accurate sites. With experience and help, you will find the best sites for you, but you will also encounter some junk no matter how experienced you are.

Anybody can put anything on the Web, regardless of its truth or fairness, so evaluate with a very critical eye everything you find. Make sure you have several divergent sources for every "fact" you find; consider who provided the information and why. Every controversial issue has sites that forcefully advocate opposite viewpoints, sometimes with biased statistics and narrow perspectives.

Here are seven Internet sites that are quite reliable:

- *www.worthpublishers.com/launchpad/bergerls9e* Includes links to Web sites, quizzes, PowerPoint slides, and activities keyed to every chapter of the textbook.
- *embryo.soad.umich.edu* The Multidimensional Human Embryo. Presents MRI images of a human embryo at various stages of development, accompanied by brief explanations.

- *http://childdevelopmentinfo.com/* Child Development Institute. A useful site, with links and articles on child development and information on common childhood psychological disorders.
- *ericeece.org* ERIC Clearinghouse. Provides links to many education-related sites and includes brief descriptions of each.
- *http://portal.education.indiana.edu/cafs/aboutus/AdolescenceDirectoryon LineADOL.aspx* Adolescence Directory online (ADOL) is an electronic guide to information on adolescent issues. It is a service of the Center for Adolescent and Family Studies at Indiana University.
- *http://www.nia.nih.gov/* National Institute on Aging. Includes information about current research on aging.
- *www.cdc.gov/nchs/hus.htm* The National Center for Health Statistics issues an annual report on health trends, called Health, United States.

Every source—you, your interviewees, journals, books, and the Internet—is helpful. Do not depend on any particular one. Especially if you use the Web, also check print resources. Avoid plagiarism and prejudice by citing every source and noting objectivity, validity, and credibility. Your own analysis, opinions, words, and conclusions are crucial.

>> Additional Terms and Concepts

As emphasized throughout this text, the study of development is a science. Social scientists spend years in graduate school, studying methods and statistics. Chapter 1 touches on some of these matters (observation and experiments; correlation and statistical significance; independent and dependent variables; experimental and control groups; cross-sectional, longitudinal, and cross-sequential research), but there is much more. A few additional aspects of research are presented here, to help you evaluate research wherever you find it.

Who Participates?

The entire group of people about whom a scientist wants to learn is called the **population**. Generally, a research population is quite large—not usually the world's entire population of almost 8 billion, but perhaps all the 4 million babies born in the United States last year, or all the 25 million Japanese currently over age 65.

The particular individuals who are studied in a specific research project are called the **participants**. They are used as a **sample** of the larger group. Ideally, a large number of people are used as a **representative sample**, that is, a sample who reflect the entire population. Every peer-reviewed published study reports details on the sample.

Selection of the sample is crucial. Volunteers, or people with telephones, or people treated with some particular condition, are not a *random sample,* in which everyone in that population is equally likely to be selected. To avoid *selection bias,* some studies are *prospective,* beginning with an entire cluster (for instance, every baby born on a particular day) and then tracing the development of some particular characteristic.

For example, prospective studies find the antecedents of heart disease, or child abuse, or high school dropout rates—all of which are much harder to find if the study is *retrospective,* beginning with those who had heart attacks, experienced abuse, or left school. Thus, although retrospective research finds that most high school dropouts say they disliked school, prospective research finds that some who like school still decide to drop out and then later say they hated school, while others dislike school but stay to graduate. Prospective research discovers how many students are in these last two categories; retrospective research on people who have already dropped out does not.

population The entire group of individuals who are of particular concern in a scientific study, such as all the children of the world or all newborns who weigh less than 3 pounds.

participants The people who are studied in a research project.

sample A group of individuals drawn from a specified population. A sample might be the low-birthweight babies born in four particular hospitals that are representative of all hospitals.

representative sample A group of research participants who reflect the relevant characteristics of the larger population whose attributes are under study.

Research Design

Every researcher begins not only by formulating a hypothesis but also by learning what other scientists have discovered about the topic in question and what methods might be useful and ethical in designing research. Often they include measures to guard against inadvertently finding only the results they expect. For example, the people who actually gather the data may not know the purpose of the research. Scientists say that these data gatherers are **blind** to the hypothesized outcome. Participants are sometimes "blind" as well, because otherwise they might, for instance, respond the way they think they should.

Another crucial aspect of research design is to define exactly what is to be studied. Researchers establish an **operational definition** of whatever phenomenon they will be examining, defining each variable by describing specific, observable behavior. This is essential in quantitative research (see Chapter 1), but it is also useful in qualitative research. For example, if a researcher wants to know when babies begin to walk, does *walking* include steps taken while holding on? Is one unsteady step enough? Some parents say yes, but the usual operational definition of walking is "takes at least three steps without holding on." This operational definition allows comparisons worldwide, making it possible to discover, for example, that well-fed African babies tend to walk earlier than well-fed European babies.

Operational definitions are difficult but essential when personality traits are studied. How should *aggression* or *sharing* or *shyness* be defined? Lack of an operational definition leads to contradictory results. For instance, some say that infant day care makes children more aggressive, but others say it makes them less passive. Similarly, as explained in the Epilogue, the operational definition of death is the subject of heated disputes. For any scientist, operational definitions are crucial.

Reporting Results

You already know that results should be reported in sufficient detail so that another scientist can analyze the conclusions and replicate the research. Various methods, populations, and research designs may produce divergent conclusions. For that reason, handbooks, some journals, and some articles are called *reviews*: They summarize past research. Often, when studies are similar in operational definitions and methods, the review is a **meta-analysis**, combining the findings of many studies to present an overall conclusion.

Table 1.4 describes some statistical measures. One of them is *statistical significance*, which indicates whether or not a particular result could have occurred by chance.

Another statistic that is often crucial is **effect size**, a way of measuring how much impact one variable has on another. Effect size ranges from 0 (no effect) to 1 (total transformation, never found in actual studies). Effect size may be particularly important when the sample size is large, because a large sample often leads to highly "significant" results (unlikely to have occurred by chance) that have only a tiny effect on the variable of interest.

Hundreds of statistical measures are used by developmentalists. Often the same data can be presented in many ways: Some scientists examine statistical analysis intently before they accept conclusions as valid. A specific example involved methods to improve students' writing ability between grades 4 and 12. A meta-analysis found that many methods of writing instruction have a significant impact, but effect size is much larger for some methods (teaching strategies and summarizing) than for others (prewriting exercises and studying models). For teachers, this statistic is crucial, for they want to know what has a big effect, not merely what is better than chance (significant).

---

blind The condition of data gatherers (and sometimes participants as well) who are deliberately kept ignorant of the purpose of the research so that they cannot unintentionally bias the results.

operational definition A description of the specific, observable behavior that will constitute the variable that is to be studied, so that any reader will know whether that behavior occurred or not. Operational definitions may be arbitrary (e.g., an IQ score at or above 130 is operationally defined as "gifted"), but they must be precise.

meta-analysis A technique of combining results of many studies to come to an overall conclusion. Meta-analysis is powerful, in that small samples can be added together to lead to significant conclusions, although variations from study to study sometimes make combining them impossible.

effect size A way to indicate, statistically, how much of an impact the independent variable had on the dependent variable.

Numerous articles published in the past decade are meta-analyses that combine similar studies to search for general trends. Often effect sizes are also reported, which is especially helpful for meta-analysis since standard calculations almost always find some significance if the number of participants is in the thousands. Here are three recent examples, to help you grasp the use and implications of meta-analyses and effect size.

- **Twenge, Jean M., Gentile, Brittany, DeWall, C. Nathan, Ma, Debbie, Lacefield, Katharine, & Schurtz, David R.** (2010). Birth cohort increases in psychopathology among young Americans, 1938–2007: A cross-temporal meta-analysis of the MMPI. *Clinical Psychology Review*, 30, 145–154. [Using responses to the Minnesota Multiphasic Personality Inventory (the MMPI, an old chestnut, originally developed to spot psychopathology), this meta-analysis finds increasing prevalence of psychological disorders among adolescents and emerging adults in the United States. The reported effect size is large, 1.05. The authors hypothesize that contemporary culture is too materialistic and selfish, leading youth to ignore the deeper meaning of life. Note, however, that impressive statistics, as shown here, do not prove or disprove a causal explanation.]

- **Grote, Nancy K., Bridge, Jeffrey A., Gavin, Amelia R., Melville, Jennifer L., Iyengar, Satish, & Katon, Wayne J.** (2010). A meta-analysis of depression during pregnancy and the risk of preterm birth, low birthweight, and intrauterine growth restriction. *Archives of General Psychiatry*, 67, 1012–1024. [This meta-analysis confirms that pregnant women who are depressed are more likely to have low-birthweight newborns. The article also shows one of the benefits of meta-analysis—the possibility of comparing people in different contexts on the same variables. In this case, depressed women in less developed nations were more at risk, and, within the United States, maternal depression has a more marked effect on low-income women. This meta-analysis makes a very convincing case that maternal mood and fetal growth are connected. Of course, additional variables may cause both the depression and the prenatal complications.]

- **Webb, Thomas L., Joseph, Judith, Yardley, Lucy, & Michie, Susan.** (2010). Using the Internet to promote health behavior change: A systematic review and meta-analysis of the impact of theoretical basis, use of behavior change techniques, and mode of delivery on efficacy. *Journal of Medical Internet Research, 12,* e4. [The conclusion this article makes is not surprising: Messages sent via the Internet and texting can effectively promote health. Again, however, the advantages of meta-analyses are notable. In this study, the effect size of electronic messages on health was very small (d = 0.16). Such small effects might be ignored in studies with fewer participants, but a meta-analytic study can find them, with useful implications. For instance, if texting health messages annually saves only one life in 100,000, and if cost-benefit analysis finds no negative effects, then universal health texting in the United States would save 3,000 lives per year.]

Glossary

23rd pair The chromosome pair that, in humans, determines sex. The other 22 pairs are autosomes, inherited equally by males and females.

A

absent grief A situation in which mourners do not grieve, either because other people do not allow grief to be expressed or because the mourners do not allow themselves to feel sadness.

acceleration Educating gifted children alongside other children of the same mental, not chronological, age.

accommodation The restructuring of old ideas to include new experiences.

achievement test A measure of mastery or proficiency in reading, mathematics, writing, science, or some other subject.

active euthanasia A situation in which someone takes action to bring about another person's death, with the intention of ending that person's suffering.

activities of daily life (ADLs) Typically identified as five tasks of self-care that are important to independent living: eating, bathing, toileting, dressing, and transferring from a bed to a chair. The inability to perform any of these tasks is a sign of frailty.

activity theory The view that elderly people want and need to remain active in a variety of social spheres—with relatives, friends, and community groups—and become withdrawn only unwillingly, as a result of ageism.

acute illness An illness that is sudden and severe.

adolescence-limited offender A person whose criminal activity stops by age 21.

adolescent egocentrism A characteristic of adolescent thinking that leads young people (ages 10 to 13) to focus on themselves to the exclusion of others.

adoption A legal proceeding in which an adult or couple, sometimes a relative, is granted the joys and obligations of being that child's parent(s).

adrenal glands Two glands, located above the kidneys, that produce hormones (including the "stress hormones" epinephrine [adrenaline] and norepinephrine).

advance directives Any description of what people want to happen as they die and after they die. This can include medical measures, choosing whom to allow as visitors, funeral arrangements, cremation, and so on.

affordance An opportunity for perception and interaction that is offered by a person, place, or object in the environment.

age in place To remain in the same home and community in later life, adjusting but not leaving when health fades.

age of viability The age (about 22 weeks after conception) at which a fetus might survive outside the mother's uterus if specialized medical care is available.

ageism A prejudice whereby people are categorized and judged solely on the basis of their chronological age.

aggressive-rejected Rejected by peers because of antagonistic, confrontational behavior.

allele A variation that makes a gene different in some way from other genes for the same characteristics. Many genes never vary; others have several possible alleles.

allocare The care of children by people other than their biological parents.

allostasis A dynamic body adjustment, related to homeostasis, that affects overall physiology over time. The main difference is that homeostasis requires an immediate response, whereas allostasis requires longer-term adjustment.

Alzheimer disease (AD) The most common cause of dementia, characterized by gradual deterioration of memory and personality and marked by the formation of plaques of beta-amyloid protein and tangles of tau in the brain. (Sometimes called *senile dementia of the Alzheimer type*.)

amygdala A tiny brain structure that registers emotions, particularly fear and anxiety.

analytic intelligence A form of intelligence that involves such mental processes as abstract planning, strategy selection, focused attention, and information processing, as well as verbal and logical skills.

analytic thought Thought that results from analysis, such as a systematic ranking of pros and cons, risks and consequences, possibilities and facts. Analytic thought depends on logic and rationality.

andropause A term coined to signify a drop in testosterone levels in older men, which normally results in reduced sexual desire, erections, and muscle mass. (Also called *male menopause*.)

animism The belief that natural objects and phenomena are alive.

anorexia nervosa An eating disorder characterized by self-starvation. Affected individuals voluntarily undereat and often overexercise, depriving their vital organs of nutrition. Anorexia can be fatal.

anoxia A lack of oxygen that, if prolonged, can cause brain damage or death.

antipathy Feelings of dislike or even hatred for another person.

antisocial behavior Actions that are deliberately hurtful or destructive to another person.

antithesis A proposition or statement of belief that opposes the thesis; the second stage of the process of dialectical thinking.

Apgar scale A quick assessment of a newborn's health. The baby's color, heart rate, reflexes, muscle tone, and respiratory effort are given a score of 0, 1, or 2 twice—at one minute and five minutes after birth—and each time the total of all five scores is compared with the maximum score of 10 (rarely attained).

apprenticeship in thinking Vygotsky's term for how cognition is stimulated and developed in people by more skilled members of society.

aptitude The potential to master a specific skill or to learn a certain body of knowledge.

assimilation The reinterpretation of new experiences to fit into old ideas.

assisted reproductive technology (ART) A general term for the techniques designed to help infertile couples conceive and then sustain a pregnancy.

asthma A chronic disease of the respiratory system in which inflammation narrows the airways from the nose and mouth to the lungs, causing difficulty in breathing. Signs and symptoms include wheezing, shortness of breath, chest tightness, and coughing.

attachment According to Ainsworth, "an affectional tie" that an infant forms with a caregiver—a tie that binds them together in space and endures over time.

attention-deficit/hyperactivity disorder (ADHD) A condition characterized by a persistent pattern of inattention and/or by hyperactive or impulsive behaviors; ADHD interferes with a person's functioning or development.

authoritarian parenting An approach to child rearing that is characterized by high behavioral standards, strict punishment for misconduct, and little communication from child to parent.

authoritative parenting An approach to child rearing in which the parents set limits but listen to the child and are flexible.

autism spectrum disorder A developmental disorder marked by difficulty with social communication and interaction—including difficulty seeing things from another person's point of view—and restricted, repetitive patterns of behavior, interests, or activities.

automatic processing Thinking that occurs without deliberate, conscious thought. Experts process most tasks automatically, saving conscious thought for unfamiliar challenges.

automatization A process in which repetition of a sequence of thoughts and actions makes the sequence routine, so that it no longer requires conscious thought.

autonomy versus shame and doubt Erikson's second crisis of psychosocial development. Toddlers either succeed or fail in gaining a sense of self-rule over their actions and their bodies.

average life expectancy The number of years the average newborn in a particular population group is likely to live.

avoidant coping A method of responding to a stressor by ignoring, forgetting, or hiding it.

axon A fiber that extends from a neuron and transmits electrochemical impulses from that neuron to the dendrites of other neurons.

B

babbling An infant's repetition of certain syllables, such as *ba-ba-ba*, that begins when babies are between 6 and 9 months old.

balanced bilingual A person who is fluent in two languages, not favoring one over the other.

base rate neglect A common fallacy in which a person ignores the overall frequency of some behavior or characteristic (called the *base rate*) in making a decision. For example, a person might bet on a "lucky" lottery number without considering the odds that that number will be selected.

behavioral teratogens Agents and conditions that can harm the prenatal brain, impairing the future child's intellectual and emotional functioning.

behaviorism A grand theory of human development that studies observable behavior. Behaviorism is also called *learning theory* because it describes the laws and processes by which behavior is learned.

Big Five The five basic clusters of personality traits that remain quite stable throughout adulthood: openness, conscientiousness, extroversion, agreeableness, and neuroticism.

bilingual schooling A strategy in which school subjects are taught in both the learner's original language and the second (majority) language.

binocular vision The ability to focus the two eyes in a coordinated manner in order to see one image.

body image A person's idea of how his or her body looks.

body mass index (BMI) The ratio of a person's weight in kilograms divided by his or her height in meters squared.

Brazelton Neonatal Behavioral Assessment Scale (NBAS) A test often administered to newborns that measures responsiveness and records 46 behaviors, including 20 reflexes.

bulimia nervosa An eating disorder characterized by binge eating and subsequent purging, usually by induced vomiting and/or use of laxatives.

bully-victim Someone who attacks others and who is attacked as well. (Also called *provocative victims* because they do things that elicit bullying.)

bullying Repeated, systematic efforts to inflict harm through physical, verbal, or social attack on a weaker person.

bullying aggression Unprovoked, repeated physical or verbal attack, especially on victims who are unlikely to defend themselves.

C

calorie restriction The practice of limiting dietary energy intake (while consuming sufficient quantities of vitamins, minerals, and other important nutrients) for the purpose of improving health and slowing down the aging process.

carrier A person whose genotype includes a gene that is not expressed in the phenotype. The carried gene occurs in half of the carrier's gametes and thus is passed on to half of the carrier's children. If such a gene is inherited from both parents, the characteristic appears in the phenotype.

case study An in-depth study of one person, usually requiring personal interviews to collect background information and various follow-up discussions, tests, questionnaires, and so on.

cellular aging The cumulative effect of stress and toxins, causing first cellular damage and eventually the death of cells.

centration A characteristic of preoperational thought in which a young child focuses (centers) on one idea, excluding all others.

cerebral palsy A disorder that results from damage to the brain's motor centers. People with cerebral palsy have difficulty with muscle control, so their speech and/or body movements are impaired.

cesarean section (c-section) A surgical birth, in which incisions through the mother's abdomen and uterus allow the fetus to be removed quickly, instead of being delivered through the vagina. (Also called simply *section*.)

charter school A public school with its own set of standards that is funded and licensed by the state or local district in which it is located.

child abuse Deliberate action that is harmful to a child's physical, emotional, or sexual well-being.

child culture The particular habits, styles, and values that reflect the set of rules and rituals that characterize children as distinct from adult society.

child maltreatment Intentional harm to or avoidable endangerment of anyone under 18 years of age.

child neglect Failure to meet a child's basic physical, educational, or emotional needs.

child sexual abuse Any erotic activity that arouses an adult and excites, shames, or confuses a child, whether or not the victim protests and whether or not genital contact is involved.

child-directed speech The high-pitched, simplified, and repetitive way adults speak to infants and children. (Also called *baby talk* or *motherese*.)

childhood obesity In a child, having a BMI above the 95th percentile, according to the U.S. Centers for Disease Control's 1980 standards for children of a given age.

childhood overweight In a child, having a BMI above the 85th percentile, according to the U.S. Centers for Disease Control's 1980 standards for children of a given age.

choice overload Having so many possibilities that a thoughtful choice becomes difficult. This is particularly apparent when social networking and other technology make many potential romantic partners available.

chromosome One of the 46 molecules of DNA (in 23 pairs) that virtually each cell of the human body contains and that, together, contain all the genes. Other species have more or fewer chromosomes.

chronic illness An illness that begins gradually and is ongoing.

circadian rhythm A day–night cycle of biological activity that occurs approximately every 24 hours (*circadian* means "about a day").

classical conditioning The learning process in which a meaningful stimulus (such as the smell of food to a hungry animal) is connected with a neutral stimulus (such as the sound of a tone) that had no special meaning before conditioning. (Also called *respondent conditioning*.)

classification The logical principle that things can be organized into groups (or categories or classes) according to some characteristic they have in common.

clinical depression Feelings of hopelessness, lethargy, and worthlessness that last two weeks or more.

cluster suicides Several suicides committed by members of a group within a brief period of time.

cognitive artifacts Intellectual tools passed down from generation to generation which may assist in learning within societies.

cognitive equilibrium In cognitive theory, a state of mental balance in which people are not confused because they can use their existing thought processes to understand current experiences and ideas.

cognitive theory A grand theory of human development that focuses on changes in how people think over time. According to this theory, our thoughts shape our attitudes, beliefs, and behaviors.

cohabitation An arrangement in which a couple live together in a committed romantic relationship but are not formally married.

cohort A group defined by the shared age of its members, who, because they were born at about the same time, move through life together, experiencing the same historical events and cultural shifts.

comorbid Refers to the presence of two or more unrelated disease conditions at the same time in the same person.

complicated grief A type of grief that impedes a person's future life, usually because the person clings to sorrow or is buffeted by contradictory emotions.

compression of morbidity A shortening of the time a person spends ill or infirm, accomplished by postponing illness.

compulsive hoarding The urge to accumulate and hold on to familiar objects and possessions, sometimes to the point of their becoming health and/or safety hazards. This impulse tends to increase with age.

concrete operational thought Piaget's term for the ability to reason logically about direct experiences and perceptions.

conditioning According to behaviorism, the processes by which responses become linked to particular stimuli and learning takes place. The word *conditioning* is used to emphasize the importance of repeated practice, as when an athlete *conditions* his or her body to perform well by training for a long time.

consequential strangers People who are not in a person's closest friendship circle but nonetheless have an impact.

conservation The principle that the amount of a substance remains the same (i.e., is conserved) even when its appearance changes.

control processes Mechanisms (including selective attention, metacognition, and emotional regulation) that combine memory, processing speed, and knowledge to regulate the analysis flow of information within the information-processing system. (Also called *executive processes*.)

conventional moral reasoning Kohlberg's second level of moral reasoning, emphasizing social rules.

copy number variations Genes with various repeats or deletions of base pairs.

corporal punishment Punishment that physically hurts the body, such as slapping, spanking, etc.

corpus callosum A long, thick band of nerve fibers that connects the left and right hemispheres of the brain and allows communication between them.

correlation A number that indicates the degree of relationship between two variables, expressed in terms of the likelihood that one variable will (or will not) occur when the other variable does (or does not). A correlation indicates only that two variables are related, not that one variable causes the other to occur.

cortex The outer layers of the brain in humans and other mammals. Most thinking, feeling, and sensing involves the cortex.

cortisol The primary stress hormone; fluctuations in the body's cortisol level affect human emotion.

co-sleeping A custom in which parents and their children (usually infants) sleep together in the same room.

couvade Symptoms of pregnancy and birth experienced by fathers.

creative intelligence A form of intelligence that involves the capacity to be intellectually flexible and innovative.

critical period A time when a particular type of developmental growth (in body or behavior) must happen if it is ever going to happen.

cross-sectional research A research design that compares groups of people who differ in age but are similar in other important characteristics.

cross-sequential research A hybrid research design in which researchers first study several groups of people of different ages (a cross-sectional approach) and then follow those groups over the years (a longitudinal approach). (Also called *cohort-sequential research* or *time-sequential research*.)

crystallized intelligence Those types of intellectual ability that reflect accumulated learning. Vocabulary and general information are examples. Some developmental psychologists think crystallized intelligence increases with age, while fluid intelligence declines.

culture A system of shared beliefs, norms, behaviors, and expectations that persist over time and prescribe social behavior and assumptions.

cyberbullying Bullying that occurs when one person spreads insults or rumors about another by means of emails, text messages, or cell phone videos.

D

DALYs (disability-adjusted life years) A measure of the reduced quality of life caused by disability.

deductive reasoning Reasoning from a general statement, premise, or principle, through logical steps, to figure out (deduce) specifics. (Also called *top-down reasoning*.)

deferred imitation A sequence in which an infant first perceives something done by someone else and then performs the same action hours or even days later.

Defining Issues Test (DIT) A series of questions developed by James Rest and designed to assess respondents' level of moral development by having them rank possible solutions to moral dilemmas.

delay discounting The tendency to undervalue, or downright ignore, future consequences and rewards in favor of more immediate gratification.

demand/withdraw interaction A situation in a romantic relationship wherein one partner wants to address an issue and the other refuses, resulting in opposite reactions—one insistent on talk while the other cuts short the conversation.

demographic shift A shift in the proportions of the populations of various ages.

dendrite A fiber that extends from a neuron and receives electrochemical impulses transmitted from other neurons via their axons.

deoxyribonucleic acid (DNA) The chemical composition of the molecules that contain the genes, which are the chemical instructions for cells to manufacture various proteins.

dependency ratio A calculation of the number of self-sufficient productive adults compared with the number of dependents (children and the elderly) in a given population.

dependent variable In an experiment, the variable that may change as a result of whatever new condition or situation the experimenter adds. In other words, the dependent variable *depends* on the independent variable.

developmental psychopathology The field that uses insights into typical development to understand and remediate developmental disorders.

developmental theory A group of ideas, assumptions, and generalizations that interpret and illuminate the thousands of observations that have been made about human growth. A developmental theory provides a framework for explaining the patterns and problems of development.

deviancy training Destructive peer support in which one person shows another how to rebel against authority or social norms.

dialectical thought The most advanced cognitive process, characterized by the ability to consider a thesis and its antithesis simultaneously and thus to arrive at a synthesis. Dialectical thought makes possible an ongoing awareness of pros and cons, advantages and disadvantages, possibilities and limitations.

diathesis–stress model The view that psychological disorders, such as schizophrenia, are produced by the interaction of a genetic vulnerability (the diathesis) and stressful environmental factors and life events.

difference-equals-deficit error The mistaken belief that a deviation from some norm is necessarily inferior to behaviors or characteristics that meet the standard.

differential sensitivity The idea that some people are more vulnerable than others are to certain experiences, usually because of genetic differences.

disability Difficulty in performing normal activities of daily life because of some physical, mental, or emotional condition.

disenfranchised grief A situation in which certain people, although they are bereaved, are prevented from mourning publicly by cultural customs or social restrictions.

disengagement theory The view that aging makes a person's social sphere increasingly narrow, resulting in role relinquishment, withdrawal, and passivity.

disorganized attachment A type of attachment that is marked by an infant's inconsistent reactions to the caregiver's departure and return.

distal parenting Caregiving practices that involve remaining distant from the baby, providing toys, food, and face-to-face communication with minimal holding and touching.

dizygotic (DZ) twins Twins who are formed when two separate ova are fertilized by two separate sperm at roughly the same time. (Also called *fraternal twins*.)

DNR (do not resuscitate) order A written order from a physician (sometimes initiated by a patient's advance directive or by a health care proxy's request) that no attempt should be made to revive a patient if he or she suffers cardiac or respiratory arrest.

dominant–recessive pattern The interaction of a heterozygous pair of alleles in such a way that the phenotype reflects one allele (the dominant gene) more than the other (the recessive gene).

double effect A situation in which an action (such as administering opiates) has both a positive effect (relieving a terminally ill person's pain) and a negative effect (hastening death by suppressing respiration).

doula A woman who helps with the birth process. Traditionally in Latin America, a doula was the only professional who attended childbirth. Now doulas are likely to arrive at the woman's home during early labor and later work alongside a hospital's staff.

Down syndrome A condition in which a person has 47 chromosomes instead of the usual 46, with 3 rather than 2 chromosomes at the 21st site. People with Down syndrome typically have distinctive characteristics, including unusual facial features, heart abnormalities, and language difficulties. (Also called trisomy-21.)

drug abuse The ingestion of a drug to the extent that it impairs the user's biological or psychological well-being.

drug addiction A condition of drug dependence in which the absence of the given drug in the individual's system produces a drive—physiological, psychological, or both—to ingest more of the drug.

Dual Language Learners (DLLs) Children who develop skills in two languages are dual language learners. Ideally education fosters proficiency in two languages rather than creating a language shift.

dual-process model The notion that two networks exist within the human brain, one for emotional and one for analytical processing of stimuli.

dynamic systems A view of human development as an ongoing, ever-changing interaction between the physical, cognitive, and psychosocial influences. The crucial understanding is that development is never static but is always affected by, and affects, many systems of development.

dyscalculia Unusual difficulty with math, probably originating from a distinct part of the brain.

dyslexia Unusual difficulty with reading; thought to be the result of some neurological underdevelopment.

E

eclectic perspective The approach taken by most developmentalists, in which they apply aspects of each of the various theories of development rather than adhering exclusively to one theory.

ecological niche The particular lifestyle and social context that adults settle into because it is compatible with their individual personality needs and interests.

ecological validity The idea that cognition should be measured in settings and conditions that are as realistic as possible and that the abilities measured should be those needed in real life.

ecological-systems approach The view that in the study of human development, the person should be considered in all the contexts and interactions that constitute a life. (Later renamed *bioecological theory*.)

effortful control The ability to regulate one's emotions and actions through effort, not simply through natural inclination.

egocentrism Piaget's term for children's tendency to think about the world entirely from their own personal perspective.

elderspeak A condescending way of speaking to older adults that resembles baby talk, with simple and short sentences, exaggerated emphasis, repetition, and a slower rate and a higher pitch than used in normal speech.

Electra complex The unconscious desire of girls to replace their mother and win their father's romantic love.

ELLs (English Language Learners) Children in the United States whose proficiency in English is low—usually below a cutoff score on an oral or written test. Many children who primarily speak a non-English language at home are also capable in English; they are *not* ELLs.

embryo The name for a developing human organism from about the third through the eighth week after conception.

embryonic period The stage of prenatal development from approximately the third through the eighth week after conception, during which the basic forms of all body structures, including internal organs, develop.

emerging adulthood The period of life between the ages of 18 and 25. Emerging adulthood is now widely thought of as a separate developmental stage.

emotion-focused coping A strategy to deal with stress by changing feelings about the stressor rather than changing the stressor itself.

emotional regulation The ability to control when and how emotions are expressed.

empathy The ability to understand the emotions and concerns of another person, especially when they differ from one's own.

empirical evidence Evidence that is based on observation, experience, or experiment, not theory.

empty nest The time in the lives of parents when their children have left the family home to pursue their own lives.

entity theory of intelligence An approach to understanding intelligence that sees ability as innate, a fixed quantity present at birth; those who hold this view do not believe that effort enhances achievement.

epigenetic Referring to the effects of environmental forces on the expression of an individual's, or a species', genetic inheritance.

equifinality A basic principle of developmental psychopathology that holds that one symptom can have many causes.

ESL (English as a Second Language) A U.S. approach to teaching English that gathers all the non-English speakers together and provides intense instruction in English. Their first language is never used; the goal is to prepare them for regular classes in English.

estradiol A sex hormone, considered the chief estrogen. Females produce much more estradiol than males do.

ethnic group People whose ancestors were born in the same region and who often share a language, culture, and religion.

experience-dependant brain functions Brain functions that depend on particular, variable experiences and therefore may or may not develop in a particular infant.

experience-expectant brain functions Brain functions that require certain basic common experiences (which an infant can be expected to have) in order to develop normally.

experiment A research method in which the researcher tries to determine the cause-and-effect relationship between two variables by manipulating one (called the *independent variable*) and then observing and recording the ensuing changes in the other (called the *dependent variable*).

expertise Specialized skills and knowledge developed around a particular activity or area of specific interest.

explicit memory Memory that is easy to retrieve on demand (as in a specific test). Most explicit memory involves consciously learned words, data, and concepts.

extended family A family of three or more generations living in one household.

externalizing problems Difficulty with emotional regulation that involves expressing powerful feelings through uncontrolled physical or verbal outbursts, as by lashing out at other people or breaking things.

extreme sports Forms of recreation that include apparent risk of injury or death and that are attractive and thrilling as a result. Motocross is one example.

extremely low birthweight (ELBW) A body weight at birth of less than 2 pounds, 3 ounces (1,000 grams).

extrinsic motivation A drive, or reason to pursue a goal, that arises from the need to have one's achievements rewarded from outside, perhaps by receiving material possessions or another person's esteem.

extrinsic rewards of work The tangible benefits, usually in the form of compensation (e.g., salary, health insurance, pension), that one receives for doing a job.

F

false positive The result of a laboratory test that reports something as true when in fact it is not true. This can occur for pregnancy tests, when a woman might not be pregnant even though the test says she is, or during pregnancy when a problem is reported that actually does not exist.

familism The belief that family members should support one another, sacrificing individual freedom and success, if necessary, in order to preserve family unity and protect the family from outside sources.

family function The way a family works to meet the needs of its members. Children need families to provide basic material necessities, to encourage learning, to help them develop self-respect, to nurture friendships, and to foster harmony and stability.

family structure The legal and genetic relationships among relatives living in the same home; includes nuclear family, extended family, stepfamily, and so on.

fast-mapping The speedy and sometimes imprecise way in which children learn new words by tentatively placing them in mental categories according to their perceived meaning.

fetal alcohol syndrome (FAS) A cluster of birth defects, including abnormal facial characteristics, slow physical growth, and reduced intellectual ability, that may occur in the fetus of a woman who drinks alcohol while pregnant.

fetal period The stage of prenatal development from the ninth week after conception until birth, during which the fetus gains about 7 pounds (more than 3,000 grams) and organs become more mature, gradually able to function on their own.

fetus The name for a developing human organism from the start of the ninth week after conception until birth.

fictive kin Someone who becomes accepted as part of a family to which he or she has no blood relation.

filial responsibility The obligation of adult children to care for their aging parents.

fine motor skills Physical abilities involving small body movements, especially of the hands and fingers, such as drawing and picking up a coin. (The word *fine* here means "small.")

fluid intelligence Those types of basic intelligence that make learning of all sorts quick and thorough. Abilities such as short-term memory, abstract thought, and speed of thinking are all usually considered part of fluid intelligence.

Flynn effect The rise in average IQ scores that has occurred over the decades in many nations.

fMRI Functional magnetic resonance imaging, a measuring technique in which the brain's electrical excitement indicates activation anywhere in the brain; fMRI helps researchers locate neurological responses to stimuli.

focus on appearance A characteristic of preoperational thought in which a young child ignores all attributes that are not apparent.

foreclosure Erikson's term for premature identity formation, which occurs when an adolescent adopts parents' or society's roles and values wholesale, without questioning or analysis.

formal operational thought In Piaget's theory, the fourth and final stage of cognitive development, characterized by more systematic logical thinking and by the ability to understand and systematically manipulate abstract concepts.

foster care A legal, publicly supported system in which a maltreated child is removed from the parents' custody and entrusted to another adult or family, which is reimbursed for expenses incurred in meeting the child's needs.

fragile X syndrome A genetic disorder in which part of the X chromosome seems to be attached to the rest of it by a very thin string of molecules. The cause is a single gene that has more than 200 repetitions of one triplet.

frail elderly People over age 65, and often over age 85, who are physically infirm, very ill, or cognitively disabled.

frontal lobe disorder Deterioration of the amygdala and frontal lobes that may be the cause of 15 percent of all dementias. (Also called *frontotemporal lobar degeneration* and, in the DSM-5, *frontotemporal NCD*.)

G

gamete A reproductive cell; that is, a sperm or ovum that can produce a new individual if it combines with a gamete from the other sex to make a zygote.

gender differences Differences in the roles and behaviors of males and females that are prescribed by the culture.

gender identity A person's acceptance of the roles and behaviors that society associates with the biological categories of male and female.

gender schema A cognitive concept or general belief based on one's experiences—in this case, a child's understanding of sex differences.

gene A small section of a chromosome; the basic unit for the transmission of heredity. A gene consists of a string of chemicals that provide instructions for the cell to manufacture certain proteins.

general intelligence (g) The idea of *g* assumes that intelligence is one basic trait, underlying all cognitive abilities. According to this concept, people have varying levels of this general ability.

generational forgetting The idea that each new generation forgets what the previous generation learned. As used here, the term refers to knowledge about the harm drugs can do.

generativity versus stagnation The seventh of Erikson's eight stages of development. Adults seek to be productive in a caring way, perhaps through art, caregiving, and employment.

genetic clock A purported mechanism in the DNA of cells that regulates the aging process by triggering hormonal changes and controlling cellular reproduction and repair.

genetic counseling Consultation and testing by trained experts that enable individuals to learn about their genetic heritage, including harmful conditions that they might pass along to any children they may conceive.

genome The full set of genes that are the instructions to make an individual member of a certain species.

genotype An organism's entire genetic inheritance, or genetic potential.

germinal period The first two weeks of prenatal development after conception, characterized by rapid cell division and the beginning of cell differentiation.

gonads The paired sex glands (ovaries in females, testicles in males). The gonads produce hormones and gametes.

grammar All the methods—word order, verb forms, and so on—that languages use to communicate meaning, apart from the words themselves.

grief The deep sorrow that people feel at the death of another. Grief is personal and unpredictable.

gross motor skills Physical abilities involving large body movements, such as walking and jumping. (The word *gross* here means "big.")

growth spurt The relatively sudden and rapid physical growth that occurs during puberty. Each body part increases in size on a schedule: Weight usually precedes height, and growth of the limbs precedes growth of the torso.

guided participation The process by which people learn from others who guide their experiences and explorations.

H

habituation The process of becoming accustomed to an object or event through repeated exposure to it, and thus becoming less interested in it.

Hayflick limit The number of times a human cell is capable of dividing into two new cells. The limit for most human cells is approximately 50 divisions, an indication that the life span is limited by our genetic program.

Head Start A federally funded early-childhood intervention program for low-income children of preschool age.

head sparing A biological mechanism that protects the brain when malnutrition disrupts body growth. The brain is the last part of the body to be damaged by malnutrition.

health care proxy A person chosen by another person to make medical decisions if the second person becomes unable to do so.

helicopter parents The label used for parents who hover (like a helicopter) over their emerging adult children. The term is pejorative, but parental involvement is sometimes helpful.

heritability A statistic that indicates what percentage of the variation in a particular trait within a particular population, in a particular context and era, can be traced to genes.

heterogamy Defined by developmentalists as marriage between individuals who tend to be dissimilar with respect to such variables as attitudes, interests, goals, socioeconomic status, religion, ethnic background, and local origin.

heterozygous Referring to two genes of one pair that differ in some way. Typically one allele has only a few base pairs that differ from the other member of the pair.

hidden curriculum The unofficial, unstated, or implicit rules and priorities that influence the academic curriculum and every other aspect of learning in a school.

high-stakes test An evaluation that is critical in determining success or failure. If a single test determines whether a student will graduate or be promoted, it is a high-stakes test.

hikikomori A Japanese word literally meaning "pull away"; it is the name of an anxiety disorder common among young adults in Japan. Sufferers isolate themselves from the outside world by staying inside their homes for months or even years at a time.

hippocampus A brain structure that is a central processor of memory, especially memory for locations.

holophrase A single word that is used to express a complete, meaningful thought.

home schooling Education in which children are taught at home, usually by their parents.

homeostasis The adjustment of all the body's systems to keep physiological functions in a state of equilibrium. As the body ages, it takes longer for these homeostatic adjustments to occur, so it becomes harder for older bodies to adapt to stress.

homogamy Defined by developmentalists as marriage between individuals who tend to be similar with respect to such variables as attitudes, interests, goals, socioeconomic status, religion, ethnic background, and local origin.

homozygous Referring to two genes of one pair that are exactly the same in every letter of their code. Most gene pairs are homozygous.

hookup A sexual encounter between two people who are not in a romantic relationship. Neither intimacy nor commitment is expected.

hormone An organic chemical substance that is produced by one body tissue and conveyed via the bloodstream to another to affect some physiological function.

hormone replacement therapy (HRT) Taking hormones (in pills, patches, or injections) to compensate for hormone reduction. HRT is most common in women at menopause or after removal of the ovaries, but it is also used by men as their testosterone decreases. HRT has some medical uses but also carries health risks.

hospice An institution or program in which terminally ill patients receive palliative care to reduce suffering; family and friends of the dying are helped as well.

HPA (hypothalamus–pituitary–adrenal) axis A sequence of hormone production originating in the hypothalamus and moving to the pituitary and then to the adrenal glands.

HPG (hypothalamus–pituitary–gonad) axis A sequence of hormone production originating in the hypothalamus and moving to the pituitary and then to the gonads.

Human Genome Project An international effort to map the complete human genetic code. This effort was essentially completed in 2001, though analysis is ongoing.

humanism A theory that stresses the potential of all humans for good and the belief that all people have the same basic needs, regardless of culture, gender, or background.

hypothalamus A brain area that responds to the amygdala and the hippocampus to produce hormones that activate other parts of the brain and body.

hypothesis A specific prediction that can be tested.

hypothetical thought Reasoning that includes propositions and possibilities that may not reflect reality.

I

identification An attempt to defend one's self-concept by taking on the behaviors and attitudes of someone else.

identity achievement Erikson's term for the attainment of identity, or the point at which a person understands who he or she is as a unique individual, in accord with past experiences and future plans.

identity versus role confusion Erikson's term for the fifth stage of development, in which the person tries to figure out "Who am I?" but is confused as to which of many possible roles to adopt.

imaginary audience The other people who, in an adolescent's egocentric belief, are watching and taking note of his or her appearance, ideas, and behavior. This belief makes many teenagers very self-conscious.

imaginary friends Make-believe friends who exist only in a child's imagination; increasingly common from ages 3 through 7, they combat loneliness and aid emotional regulation.

immersion A strategy in which instruction in all school subjects occurs in the second (usually the majority) language that a child is learning.

immunization A process that stimulates the body's immune system by causing production of antibodies to defend against attack by a particular contagious disease. Creation of antibodies may be accomplished either naturally (by having the disease), by injection, by drops that are swallowed, or by a nasal spray. (These imposed methods are also called *vaccination*.)

implantation The process, beginning about 10 days after conception, in which the developing organism burrows into the placenta that lines the uterus, where it can be nourished and protected as it continues to develop.

implicit memory Unconscious or automatic memory that is usually stored via habits, emotional responses, routine procedures, and various sensations.

impulse control The ability to postpone or deny the immediate response to an idea or behavior.

in vitro fertilization (IVF) Fertilization that takes place outside a woman's body (as in a glass laboratory dish). The procedure involves mixing sperm with ova that have been surgically removed from the woman's ovary. If a zygote is produced, it is inserted into a woman's uterus, where it may implant and develop into a baby.

incomplete grief A situation in which circumstances, such as a police investigation or an autopsy, interfere with the process of grieving.

incremental theory of intelligence An approach to understanding intelligence that holds that intelligence can be directly increased by effort; those who subscribe to this view believe they can master whatever they seek to learn if they pay attention, participate in class, study, complete their homework, and so on.

independent variable In an experiment, the variable that is introduced to see what effect it has on the dependent variable. (Also called *experimental variable*.)

individual education plan (IEP) A document that specifies educational goals and plans for a child with special needs.

inductive reasoning Reasoning from one or more specific experiences or facts to reach (induce) a general conclusion. (Also called *bottom-up reasoning*.)

industry versus inferiority The fourth of Erikson's eight psychosocial crises, during which children attempt to master many skills, developing a sense of themselves as either industrious or inferior, competent or incompetent.

infertility The inability to conceive a child after trying for at least a year.

information-processing theory A perspective that compares human thinking processes, by analogy, to computer analysis of data, including sensory input, connections, stored memories, and output.

initiative versus guilt Erikson's third psychosocial crisis, in which children undertake new skills and activities and feel guilty when they do not succeed at them.

injury control/harm reduction Practices that are aimed at anticipating, controlling, and preventing dangerous activities; these practices reflect the beliefs that accidents are not random and that injuries can be made less harmful if proper controls are in place.

insecure-avoidant attachment A pattern of attachment in which an infant avoids connection with the caregiver, as when the infant seems not to care about the caregiver's presence, departure, or return.

insecure-resistant/ambivalent attachment A pattern of attachment in which an infant's anxiety and uncertainty are evident, as when the infant becomes very upset at separation from the caregiver and both resists and seeks contact on reunion.

instrumental activities of daily life (IADLs) Actions (for example, paying bills and driving a car) that are important to independent living and that require some intellectual competence and forethought. The ability to perform these tasks may be even more critical to self-sufficiency than ADL ability.

instrumental aggression Behavior that hurts someone else because the aggressor wants to get or keep a possession or a privilege.

integrity versus despair The final stage of Erik Erikson's developmental sequence, in which older adults seek to integrate their unique experiences with their vision of community.

internalizing problems Difficulty with emotional regulation that involves turning one's emotional distress inward, as by feeling excessively guilty, ashamed, or worthless.

intimacy versus isolation The sixth of Erikson's eight stages of development. Adults seek someone with whom to share their lives in an enduring and self-sacrificing commitment. Without such commitment, they risk profound aloneness and isolation.

intimate terrorism A violent and demeaning form of abuse in a romantic relationship, in which the victim (usually female) is frightened to fight back, seek help, or withdraw. In this case, the victim is in danger of physical as well as psychological harm.

intra-cytoplasmic sperm injection (ICSI) An in vitro fertilization technique in which a single sperm cell is injected directly into an ovum.

intrinsic motivation A drive, or reason to pursue a goal, that comes from inside a person, such as the need to feel smart or competent.

intrinsic rewards of work The intangible gratifications (e.g., job satisfaction, self-esteem, pride) that come from within oneself as a result of doing a job.

intuitive thought Thought that arises from an emotion or a hunch, beyond rational explanation, and is influenced by past experiences and cultural assumptions.

invincibility fable An adolescent's egocentric conviction that he or she cannot be overcome or even harmed by anything that might defeat a normal mortal, such as unprotected sex, drug abuse, or high-speed driving.

IQ test A test designed to measure intellectual aptitude, or ability to learn in school. Originally, intelligence was defined as mental age divided by chronological age, times 100—hence the term *intelligence quotient*, or *IQ*.

irreversibility A characteristic of preoperational thought in which a young child thinks that nothing can be undone. A thing cannot be restored to the way it was before a change occurred.

K

kangaroo care A form of newborn care in which mothers (and sometimes fathers) rest their babies on their naked chests, like kangaroo mothers that carry their immature newborns in a pouch on their abdomen.

kinkeeper A caregiver who takes responsibility for maintaining communication among family members.

kinship care A form of foster care in which a relative of a maltreated child, usually a grandparent, becomes the approved caregiver.

knowledge base A body of knowledge in a particular area that makes it easier to master new information in that area.

kwashiorkor A disease of chronic malnutrition during childhood, in which a protein deficiency makes the child more vulnerable to other diseases, such as measles, diarrhea, and influenza.

L

language acquisition device (LAD) Chomsky's term for a hypothesized mental structure that enables humans to learn language, including the basic aspects of grammar, vocabulary, and intonation.

latency Freud's term for middle childhood, during which children's emotional drives and psychosexual needs are quiet (latent). Freud thought that sexual conflicts from earlier stages are only temporarily submerged, bursting forth again at puberty.

lateralization Literally, sidedness, referring to the specialization in certain functions by each side of the brain, with one side dominant for each activity. The left side of the brain controls the right side of the body, and vice versa.

least restrictive environment (LRE) A legal requirement that children with special needs be assigned to the most general educational context in which they can be expected to learn.

leptin A hormone that affects appetite and is believed to affect the onset of puberty. Leptin levels increase during childhood and peak at around age 12.

Lewy bodies Deposits of a particular kind of protein in the brain that interfere with communication between neurons; Lewy bodies cause neurocognitive disorder.

life-course-persistent offender A person whose criminal activity typically begins in early adolescence and continues throughout life; a career criminal.

life review An examination of one's own life and one's role in the history of human life, engaged in by many elderly people.

life-span perspective An approach to the study of human development that takes into account all phases of life, not just childhood or adulthood.

linked lives Lives in which the success, health, and well-being of each family member are connected to those of other members, including those of another generation, as in the relationship between parents and children.

"little scientist" The stage-five toddler (age 12 to 18 months) who experiments without anticipating the results, using trial and error in active and creative exploration.

living will A document that indicates what medical intervention an individual prefers if he or she is not conscious when a decision is to be expressed. For example, some do not want to be given mechanical breathing.

long-term memory The component of the information-processing system in which virtually limitless amounts of information can be stored indefinitely.

longitudinal research A research design in which the same individuals are followed over time and their development is repeatedly assessed.

low birthweight (LBW) A body weight at birth of less than 5½ pounds (2,500 grams).

M

marasmus A disease of severe protein-calorie malnutrition during early infancy, in which growth stops, body tissues waste away, and the infant eventually dies.

massification The idea that establishing institutions of higher learning and encouraging college enrollment can benefit everyone (the masses).

massive open online course (MOOC) A course that is offered solely online for college credit. Typically, tuition is very low, and thousands of students enroll.

maximum life span The oldest possible age that members of a species can live under ideal circumstances. For humans, that age is approximately 122 years.

mean length of utterance (MLU) The average number of words in a typical sentence (called utterance, because children may not talk in complete sentences). MLU is often used to indicate how advanced a child's language development is.

menarche A girl's first menstrual period, signaling that she has begun ovulation. Pregnancy is biologically possible, but ovulation and menstruation are often irregular for years after menarche.

menopause The time in middle age, usually around age 50, when a woman's menstrual periods cease and the production of estrogen, progesterone, and testosterone drops. Strictly speaking, menopause is dated one year after a woman's last menstrual period, although many months before and after that date are menopausal.

metacognition "Thinking about thinking," or the ability to evaluate a cognitive task in order to determine how best to accomplish it, and then to monitor and adjust one's performance on that task.

middle childhood The period between early childhood and early adolescence, approximately from ages 6 to 11.

middle school A school for children in the grades between elementary and high school. Middle school usually begins with grade 6 and ends with grade 8.

midlife crisis A supposed period of unusual anxiety, radical self-reexamination, and sudden transformation that was once widely associated with middle age but that actually had more to do with developmental history than with chronological age.

mirror neurons Cells in an observer's brain that respond to an action performed by someone else in the same way they would if the observer were actually performing that action.

modeling The central process of social learning, by which a person observes the actions of others and then copies them. (Modeling is also called *observational learning*.)

monozygotic (MZ) twins Twins who originate from one zygote that splits apart very early in development. (Also called *identical twins*.) Other monozygotic multiple births (such as triplets and quadruplets) can occur as well.

Montessori schools Schools that offer early-childhood education based on the philosophy of Maria Montessori, which emphasizes careful work and tasks that each young child can do.

morality of care In Gilligan's view, moral principles that reflect the tendency of females to be reluctant to judge right and wrong in absolute terms because they are socialized to be nurturing, compassionate, and nonjudgmental.

morality of justice In Gilligan's view, moral principles that reflect the tendency of males to emphasize justice over compassion, judging right and wrong in absolute terms.

moratorium An adolescent's choice of a socially acceptable way to postpone making identity-achievement decisions. Going to college is a common example.

morbidity Disease. As a measure of health, morbidity usually refers to the rate of diseases in a given population—physical and emotional, acute (sudden) and chronic (ongoing).

mortality Death. As a measure of health, mortality usually refers to the number of deaths each year per 1,000 members of a given population.

motor skill The learned abilities to move some part of the body, in actions ranging from a large leap to a flicker of the eyelid. (The word *motor* here refers to movement of muscles.)

mourning The ceremonies and behaviors that a religion or culture prescribes for people to employ in expressing their bereavement after a death.

multifactorial Referring to a trait that is affected by many factors, both genetic and environmental, that enhance, halt, shape, or alter the expression of genes, resulting in a phenotype that may differ markedly from the genotype.

multifinality A basic principle of developmental psychopathology that holds that one cause can have many (multiple) final manifestations.

multiple intelligences The idea that human intelligence is composed of a varied set of abilities rather than a single, all-encompassing one.

myelination The process by which axons become coated with myelin, a fatty substance that speeds the transmission of nerve impulses from neuron to neuron.

N

naming explosion A sudden increase in an infant's vocabulary, especially in the number of nouns, that begins at about 18 months of age.

National Assessment of Educational Progress (NAEP) An ongoing and nationally representative measure of U.S. children's achievement in reading, mathematics, and other subjects over time; nicknamed "the Nation's Report Card."

naturally occurring retirement community (NORC) A neighborhood or apartment complex whose population is mostly retired people who moved to the location as younger adults and never left.

nature A general term for the traits, capacities, and limitations that each individual inherits genetically from his or her parents at the moment of conception.

neglectful/uninvolved parenting An approach to child rearing in which the parents are indifferent toward their children and unaware of what is going on in their children's lives.

neurocognitive disorders (NCDs) Impairments of intellectual functioning caused by organic brain damage or disease. NCDs may be diagnosed as *major* or *mild*, depending on the severity of symptoms. They become more common with age, but they are abnormal and pathological even in the very old.

neuron One of billions of nerve cells in the central nervous system, especially in the brain.

neurotransmitter A brain chemical that carries information from the axon of a sending neuron to the dendrites of a receiving neuron.

No Child Left Behind (NCLB) Act A U.S. law enacted in 2001 that was intended to increase accountability in education by requiring states to qualify for federal educational funding by administering standardized tests to measure school achievement.

norm An average, or standard, measurement, calculated from the measurements of many individuals within a specific group or population.

nuclear family A family that consists of a father, a mother, and their biological children under age 18.

nurture A general term for all the environmental influences that affect development after an individual is conceived.

O

object permanence The realization that objects (including people) still exist when they can no longer be seen, touched, or heard.

objective thought Thinking that is not influenced by the thinker's personal qualities but instead involves facts and numbers that are universally considered true and valid.

Oedipus complex The unconscious desire of young boys to replace their father and win their mother's romantic love.

old-old Older adults (generally, those over age 75) who suffer from physical, mental, or social deficits.

oldest-old Elderly adults (generally, those over age 85) who are dependent on others for almost everything, requiring supportive services such as nursing homes and hospital stays.

operant conditioning The learning process by which a particular action is followed by something desired (which makes the person or animal more likely to repeat the action) or by something unwanted (which makes the action less likely to be repeated). (Also called *instrumental conditioning*.)

organ reserve The capacity of organs to allow the body to cope with stress, via extra, unused functioning ability.

osteoporosis A disease whose symptoms are low bone mass and deterioration of bone tissue, which lead to increasingly fragile bones and greater risk of fracture.

overimitation When a person imitates an action that is not a relevant part of the behavior to be learned. Overimitation is common among 2- to 6-year-olds when they imitate adult actions that are irrelevant and inefficient.

overregularization The application of rules of grammar even when exceptions occur, making the language seem more "regular" than it actually is.

P

palliative care Care designed not to treat an illness but to provide physical and emotional comfort to the patient and support and guidance to his or her family.

parasuicide Any potentially lethal action against the self that does not result in death. (Also called *attempted suicide* or *failed suicide*.)

parent–infant bond The strong, loving connection that forms as parents hold, examine, and feed their newborn.

parental alliance Cooperation between a mother and a father based on their mutual commitment to their children. In a parental alliance, the parents support each other in their shared parental roles.

parental monitoring Parents' ongoing awareness of what their children are doing, where, and with whom.

Parkinson's disease A chronic, progressive disease that is characterized by muscle tremor and rigidity, and sometimes dementia; caused by a reduction of dopamine production in the brain.

passive euthanasia A situation in which a seriously ill person is allowed to die naturally, through the cessation of medical intervention.

peer pressure Encouragement to conform to one's friends or contemporaries in behavior, dress, and attitude; usually considered a negative force, as when adolescent peers encourage one another to defy adult authority.

percentile A point on a ranking scale of 0 to 100. The 50th percentile is the midpoint; half the people in the population being studied rank higher and half rank lower.

perception The mental processing of sensory information when the brain interprets a sensation.

permanency planning An effort by child-welfare authorities to find a long-term living situation that will provide stability and support for a maltreated child. A goal is to avoid repeated changes of caregiver or school, which can be particularly harmful to the child.

permissive parenting An approach to child rearing that is characterized by high nurturance and communication but little discipline, guidance, or control. (Also called *indulgent parenting*.)

perseveration The tendency to persevere in, or stick to, one thought or action for a long time.

personal fable An aspect of adolescent egocentrism characterized by an adolescent's belief that his or her thoughts, feelings, and experiences are unique, more wonderful than, or more awful than anyone else's.

phallic stage Freud's third stage of development, when the penis becomes the focus of concern and pleasure.

phenotype The observable characteristics of a person, including appearance, personality, intelligence, and all other traits.

physician-assisted suicide A form of active euthanasia in which a doctor provides the means for someone to end his or her own life.

PISA (Programme for International Student Assessment) An international test taken by 15-year-olds in 50 nations that is designed to measure problem solving and cognition in daily life.

pituitary A gland in the brain that responds to a signal from the hypothalamus by producing many hormones, including those that regulate growth and that control other glands, among them the adrenal and sex glands.

plaques Clumps of a protein called *beta-amyloid*, found in brain tissues surrounding the neurons; a normal brain contains some tau, but in brains of people with Alzheimer disease these plaques proliferate, especially in the hippocampus, a brain structure crucial for memory.

plasticity genes Genes and alleles that make people more susceptible to environmental influences, for better or worse. This is part of differential susceptibility.

polygamous family A family consisting of one man, several wives, and their children.

polygenic Referring to a trait that is influenced by many genes.

polypharmacy Refers to a situation in which elderly people have been prescribed several medications. The various side effects and interactions of those medications can result in dementia symptoms.

positivity effect The tendency for elderly people to perceive, prefer, and remember positive images and experiences more than negative ones.

post-traumatic stress disorder (PTSD) An anxiety disorder that develops as a delayed reaction to having experienced or witnessed a profoundly shocking or frightening event, such as rape, severe beating, war, or natural disaster. Its symptoms may include flashbacks to the event, hyperactivity and hypervigilance, displaced anger, sleeplessness, nightmares, sudden terror or anxiety, and confusion between fantasy and reality.

postconventional moral reasoning Kohlberg's third level of moral reasoning, emphasizing moral principles.

postformal thought A proposed adult stage of cognitive development, following Piaget's four stages, that goes beyond adolescent thinking by being more practical, more flexible, and more dialectical (that is, more capable of combining contradictory elements into a comprehensive whole).

postpartum depression A new mother's feelings of inadequacy and sadness in the days and weeks after giving birth.

practical intelligence The intellectual skills used in everyday problem solving. (Sometimes called *tacit intelligence*.)

pragmatics The practical use of language that includes the ability to adjust language communication according to audience and context.

preconventional moral reasoning Kohlberg's first level of moral reasoning, emphasizing rewards and punishments.

prefrontal cortex The area of the cortex at the very front of the brain that specializes in anticipation, planning, and impulse control.

preoperational intelligence Piaget's term for cognitive development between the ages of about 2 and 6; it includes language and imagination (which involve symbolic thought), but logical, operational thinking is not yet possible at this stage.

presbycusis A significant loss of hearing associated with senescence. Presbycusis usually is not apparent until after age 60.

preterm A birth that occurs 3 or more weeks before the full 38 weeks of the typical pregnancy—that is, at 35 or fewer weeks after conception.

primary aging The universal and irreversible physical changes that occur to all living creatures as they grow older.

primary circular reactions The first of three types of feedback loops in sensorimotor intelligence, this one involving the infant's own body. The infant senses motion, sucking, noise, and other stimuli and tries to understand them.

primary prevention Actions that change overall background conditions to prevent some unwanted event or circumstance, such as injury, disease, or abuse.

primary sex characteristics The parts of the body that are directly involved in reproduction, including the vagina, uterus, ovaries, testicles, and penis.

private school A school funded by tuition charges, endowments, and often religious or other non-profit sponsors.

problem-focused coping A strategy to deal with stress by tackling a stressful situation directly.

Progress in International Reading Literacy Study (PIRLS) Inaugurated in 2001, a planned five-year cycle of international trend studies in the reading ability of fourth-graders.

prosocial behavior Actions that are helpful and kind but are of no obvious benefit to oneself.

protein-calorie malnutrition A condition in which a person does not consume sufficient food of any kind. This deprivation can result in several illnesses, severe weight loss, and even death.

proximal parenting Caregiving practices that involve being physically close to the baby, with frequent holding and touching.

pruning When applied to brain development, the process by which unused connections in the brain atrophy and die.

psychoanalytic theory A grand theory of human development that holds that irrational, unconscious drives and motives, often originating in childhood, underlie human behavior.

psychological control A disciplinary technique that involves threatening to withdraw love and support and that relies on a child's feelings of guilt and gratitude to the parents.

psychopathology Literally, an illness of the mind, or psyche. Various cultures and groups within cultures have different concepts of a specific psychopathology. A recent compendium of symptoms and disorders in the United States is in the DSM-5. Many other nations use an international set of categories, the ICD-10.

puberty The time between the first onrush of hormones and full adult physical development. Puberty usually lasts three to five years. Many more years are required to achieve psychosocial maturity.

Q

QALYs (quality-adjusted life years) A way of comparing mere survival without vitality to survival with good health. A full year of health is a full QALY; people with less than full health have a fraction of QALY each year. Thus, their total QALY is less than the total years they live.

R

race A group of people who are regarded by themselves or by others as distinct from other groups on the basis of physical appearance, typically skin color. Social scientists think race is a misleading concept, as biological differences are not signified by outward appearance.

reaction time The time it takes to respond to a stimulus, either physically (with a reflexive movement such as an eyeblink) or cognitively (with a thought).

reactive aggression An impulsive retaliation for another person's intentional or accidental action, verbal or physical.

reflex An unlearned, involuntary action or movement in response to a stimulus. A reflex occurs without conscious thought.

Reggio Emilia A program of early-childhood education that originated in the town of Reggio Emilia, Italy, and that encourages each child's creativity in a carefully designed setting.

reinforcement The process by which a behavior is followed by something desired, such as food for a hungry animal or a welcoming smile for a lonely person.

relational aggression Nonphysical acts, such as insults or social rejection, aimed at harming the social connection between the victim and other people.

religious coping The process of turning to faith as a method of coping with stress.

REM (rapid eye movement) sleep A stage of sleep characterized by flickering eyes behind closed lids, dreaming, and rapid brain waves.

reminder session A perceptual experience that helps a person recollect an idea, a thing, or an experience.

replication The repetition of a study, using different participants.

reported maltreatment Harm or endangerment about which someone has notified the authorities.

resilience The capacity to adapt well to significant adversity and to overcome serious stress.

response to intervention (RTI) An educational strategy intended to help children who demonstrate below-average achievement in early grades, using special intervention.

role confusion A situation in which an adolescent does not seem to know or care what his or her identity is. (Sometimes called *identity* or *role diffusion*.)

rough-and-tumble play Play that mimics aggression through wrestling, chasing, or hitting, but in which there is no intent to harm.

rumination Repeatedly thinking and talking about past experiences; can contribute to depression.

S

sandwich generation The generation of middle-aged people who are supposedly "squeezed" by the needs of the younger and older members of their families. In reality, some adults do feel pressured by these obligations, but most are not burdened by them, either because they enjoy fulfilling them or because they choose to take on only some of them or none of them.

scaffolding Temporary support that is tailored to a learner's needs and abilities and aimed at helping the learner master the next task in a given learning process.

science of human development The science that seeks to understand how and why people of all ages and circumstances change or remain the same over time.

scientific method A way to answer questions that requires empirical research and data-based conclusions.

scientific observation A method of testing a hypothesis by unobtrusively watching and recording participants' behavior in a systematic and objective manner in a natural setting or in a laboratory; a search of archival data is another way to conduct scientific observation.

Seattle Longitudinal Study The first cross-sequential study of adult intelligence. This study began in 1956 and is repeated every 7 years.

secondary aging The specific physical illnesses or conditions that become more common with aging but are caused by health habits, genes, and other influences that vary from person to person.

secondary circular reactions The second of three types of feedback loops in sensorimotor intelligence, this one involving people and objects. Infants respond to other people, to toys, and to any other object they can touch or move.

secondary education Literally, the period after primary education (elementary or grade school) and before tertiary education (college). It usually occurs from about ages 12 to 18, although there is some variation by school and by nation.

secondary prevention Actions that avert harm in a high-risk situation, such as stopping a car before it hits a pedestrian.

secondary sex characteristics Physical traits that are not directly involved in reproduction but that indicate sexual maturity, such as a man's beard and a woman's breasts.

secular trend The long-term upward or downward direction of a certain set of statistical measurements, as opposed to a smaller, shorter cyclical variation. As an example, over the last two centuries, because of improved nutrition and medical care, children have tended to reach their adult height earlier and their adult height has increased.

secure attachment A relationship in which an infant obtains both comfort and confidence from the presence of his or her caregiver.

selective adaptation The process by which living creatures (including people) adjust to their environment. Genes that enhance survival and reproductive ability are selected, over the generations, to become more prevalent.

selective attention The ability to concentrate on some stimuli while ignoring others.

selective optimization with compensation The theory, developed by Paul and Margaret Baltes, that people try to maintain a balance in their lives by looking for the best way to compensate for physical and cognitive losses and to become more proficient in activities they can already do well.

self theories Theories of late adulthood that emphasize the core self, or the search to maintain one's integrity and identity.

self-actualization The final stage in Maslow's hierarchy of needs, characterized by aesthetic, creative, philosophical, and spiritual understanding.

self-awareness A person's realization that he or she is a distinct individual whose body, mind, and actions are separate from those of other people.

self-concept A person's understanding of who he or she is, in relation to self-esteem, appearance, personality, and various traits.

self-righting The inborn drive to remedy a developmental deficit; literally, to return to sitting or standing upright after being tipped over. People of all ages have self-righting impulses, for emotional as well as physical imbalance.

senescence The process of aging, whereby the body becomes less strong and efficient.

sensation The response of a sensory system (eyes, ears, skin, tongue, nose) when it detects a stimulus.

sensitive period A time when a certain type of development is most likely to happen or happens most easily, although it may still happen later with more difficulty. For example, early childhood is considered a sensitive period for language learning.

sensorimotor intelligence Piaget's term for the way infants think—by using their senses and motor skills—during the first period of cognitive development.

sensory memory The component of the information-processing system in which incoming stimulus information is stored for a split second to allow it to be processed. (Also called the *sensory register*.)

separation anxiety An infant's distress when a familiar caregiver leaves; most obvious between 9 and 14 months.

seriation The concept that things can be arranged in a logical series, such as the number sequence or the alphabet.

set point A particular body weight that an individual's homeostatic processes strive to maintain.

sex differences Biological differences between males and females, in organs, hormones, and body type.

sexual orientation A term that refers to whether a person is sexually and romantically attracted to others of the same sex, the opposite sex, or both sexes.

sexually transmitted infection (STI) A disease spread by sexual contact, including syphilis, gonorrhea, genital herpes, chlamydia, and HIV.

shaken baby syndrome A life-threatening injury that occurs when an infant is forcefully shaken back and forth, a motion that ruptures blood vessels in the brain and breaks neural connections.

single-parent family A family that consists of only one parent and his or her biological children under age 18.

situational couple violence Fighting between romantic partners that is brought on more by the situation than by the deep personality problems of the individuals. Both partners are typically victims and abusers.

slippery slope The argument that a given action will start a chain of events that will culminate in an undesirable outcome.

small for gestational age (SGA) A term for a baby whose birthweight is significantly lower than expected, given the time since conception. For example, a 5-pound (2,265-gram) newborn is considered SGA if born on time but not SGA if born two months early. (Also called *small-for-date*.)

social clock A timetable based on social norms for accomplishing certain life events such as when to finish school, marry, start a career, have children, and retire.

social comparison The tendency to assess one's abilities, achievements, social status, and other attributes by measuring them against other people, especially one's peers.

social construction An idea that is based on shared perceptions, not on objective reality. Many age-related terms, such as *childhood, adolescence, yuppie*, and *senior citizen*, are social constructions.

social convoy Collectively, the family members, friends, acquaintances, and even strangers who move through life with an individual.

social learning The acquisition of behavior patterns by observing the behavior of others.

social learning theory An extension of behaviorism that emphasizes the influence that other people have over a person's behavior. Even without specific reinforcement, every individual learns many things through observation and imitation of other people.

social norms approach A method of reducing risky behavior that uses emerging adults' desire to follow social norms by making them aware, through the use of surveys, of the prevalence of various behaviors within their peer group.

social referencing Seeking information about how to react to an unfamiliar or ambiguous object or event by observing someone else's expressions and reactions. That other person becomes a social reference.

social smile A smile evoked by a human face, normally first evident in infants about 6 weeks after birth.

sociocultural theory A newer theory that holds that development results from the dynamic interaction of each person with the surrounding social and cultural forces.

sociodramatic play Pretend play in which children act out various roles and themes in stories that they create.

socioeconomic status (SES) A person's position in society as determined by income, wealth, occupation, education, and place of residence. (Sometimes called *social class*.)

socioemotional selectivity theory The theory that older people prioritize regulation of their own emotions and seek familiar social contacts who reinforce generativity, pride, and joy.

specific learning disorder (learning disability) A marked deficit in a particular area of learning that is not caused by an apparent physical disability, by an intellectual disability, or by an unusually stressful home environment.

spermarche A boy's first ejaculation of sperm. Erections can occur as early as infancy, but ejaculation signals sperm production. Spermarche may occur during sleep (in a "wet dream") or via direct stimulation.

static reasoning A characteristic of preoperational thought in which a young child thinks that nothing changes. Whatever is now has always been and always will be.

stem cells Cells from which any other specialized type of cell can form.

stereotype threat The possibility that one's appearance or behavior will be misread to confirm another person's oversimplified, prejudiced attitudes.

still-face technique An experimental practice in which an adult keeps his or her face unmoving and expressionless in face-to-face interaction with an infant.

strange situation A laboratory procedure for measuring attachment by evoking infants' reactions to the stress of various adults' comings and goings in an unfamiliar playroom.

stranger wariness An infant's expression of concern—a quiet stare while clinging to a familiar person, or a look of fear—when a stranger appears.

stratification theories Theories that emphasize that social forces, particularly those related to a person's social stratum or social category, limit individual choices and affect a person's ability to function in late adulthood because past stratification continues to limit life in various ways.

stressor Any situation, event, experience, or other stimulus that causes a person to feel stressed. Many circumstances that seem to be stresses become stressors for some people but not for others.

stunting The failure of children to grow to a normal height for their age due to severe and chronic malnutrition.

subjective thought Thinking that is strongly influenced by personal qualities of the individual thinker, such as past experiences, cultural assumptions, and goals for the future.

substantiated maltreatment Harm or endangerment that has been reported, investigated, and verified.

sudden infant death syndrome (SIDS) A situation in which a seemingly healthy infant, usually between 2 and 6 months old, suddenly stops breathing and dies unexpectedly while asleep.

suicidal ideation Thinking about suicide, usually with some serious emotional and intellectual or cognitive overtones.

sunk cost fallacy The mistaken belief that if money, time, or effort that cannot be recovered (a "sunk cost," in economic terms) has already been invested in some endeavor, then more should be invested in an effort to reach the goal. Because of this fallacy, people spend money trying to fix a "lemon" of a car or send more troops to fight a losing battle.

superego In psychoanalytic theory, the judgmental part of the personality that internalizes the moral standards of the parents.

survey A research method in which information is collected from a large number of people by interviews, written questionnaires, or some other means.

symbolic thought A major accomplishment of preoperational intelligence that allows a child to think symbolically, including understanding that words can refer to things not seen and that an item, such as a flag, can symbolize something else (in this case, for instance, a country).

synapse The intersection between the axon of one neuron and the dendrites of other neurons.

synaptic gap The pathway across which neurotransmitters carry information from the axon of the sending neuron to the dendrites of the receiving neuron.

synchrony A coordinated, rapid, and smooth exchange of responses between a caregiver and an infant.

synthesis A new idea that integrates the thesis and its antithesis, thus representing a new and more comprehensive level of truth; the third stage of the process of dialectical thinking.

T

tangles Twisted masses of threads made of a protein called *tau* within the neurons of the brain; a normal brain contains some beta-amyloid tau, but in brains of people with Alzheimer disease these tangles proliferate, especially in the hippocampus, a brain structure crucial for memory.

temperament Inborn differences between one person and another in emotions, activity, and self-regulation. It is measured by the person's typical responses to the environment.

teratogen An agent or condition, including viruses, drugs, and chemicals, that can impair prenatal development and result in birth defects or even death.

terror management theory (TMT) The idea that people adopt cultural values and moral principles in order to cope with their fear of death. This system of beliefs protects individuals from anxiety about their mortality and bolsters their self-esteem, so they react harshly when other people go against any of the moral principles involved.

tertiary circular reactions The third of three types of feedback loops in sensorimotor intelligence, this one involving active exploration and experimentation. Infants explore a range of new activities, varying their responses as a way of learning about the world.

tertiary prevention Actions, such as immediate and effective medical treatment, that are taken after an adverse event (such as illness or injury) and that are aimed at reducing harm or preventing disability.

testosterone A sex hormone, the best known of the androgens (male hormones); secreted in far greater amounts by males than by females.

theory of mind A person's theory of what other people might be thinking. In order to have a theory of mind, children must realize that other people are not necessarily thinking the same thoughts that they themselves are. That realization seldom occurs before age 4.

theory-theory The idea that children attempt to explain everything they see and hear by constructing theories.

thesis A proposition or statement of belief; the first stage of the process of dialectical thinking.

threshold effect In prenatal development, the point at which a teratogen is relatively harmless in small doses but becomes harmful once exposure reaches a certain level (the threshold).

time-out A disciplinary technique in which a child is separated from other people for a specified time.

transient exuberance The great but temporary increase in the number of dendrites that develop in an infant's brain during the first two years of life.

Trends in Math and Science Study (TIMSS) An international assessment of the math and science skills of fourth- and eighth-graders. Although the TIMSS is very useful, different countries' scores are not always comparable because sample selection, test administration, and content validity are hard to keep uniform.

trust versus mistrust Erikson's first crisis of psychosocial development. Infants learn basic trust if the world is a secure place where their basic needs (for food, comfort, attention, and so on) are met.

U

ultrasound An image of a fetus (or an internal organ) produced by using high-frequency sound waves. (Also called *sonogram*.)

universal design The creation of settings and equipment that can be used by everyone, whether or not they are able-bodied and sensory-acute.

V

vascular dementia (VaD) A form of neurocognitive disorder characterized by sporadic, and progressive, loss of intellectual functioning caused by repeated infarcts, or temporary obstructions of blood vessels, which prevent sufficient blood from reaching the brain.

very low birthweight (VLBW) A body weight at birth of less than 3 pounds, 5 ounces (1,500 grams).

visual cliff An experimental apparatus that gives the illusion of a sudden drop-off between one horizontal surface and another.

vitality A measure of health that refers to how healthy and energetic—physically, intellectually, and socially—an individual actually feels.

voucher Public subsidy for tuition payment at a nonpublic school. Vouchers vary a great deal from place to place, not only in amount and availability but also in restrictions as to who gets them and what schools accept them.

W

wasting The tendency for children to be severely underweight for their age as a result of malnutrition.

wear-and-tear theory A view of aging as a process by which the human body wears out because of the passage of time and exposure to environmental stressors.

weathering The gradual accumulation of stressors over a long period of time, wearing down a person's resilience and resistance.

withdrawn-rejected Rejected by peers because of timid, withdrawn, and anxious behavior.

working memory The component of the information-processing system in which current conscious mental activity occurs. (Formerly called *short-term memory*.)

working model In cognitive theory, a set of assumptions that the individual uses to organize perceptions and experiences. For example, a person might assume that other people are trustworthy and be surprised by an incident in which this working model of human behavior is erroneous.

X

X-linked A gene carried on the X chromosome. If a male inherits an X-linked recessive trait from his mother, he expresses that trait because the Y from his father has no counteracting gene. Females are more likely to be carriers of X-linked traits but are less likely to express them.

XX A 23rd chromosome pair that consists of two X-shaped chromosomes, one each from the mother and the father. XX zygotes become females.

XY A 23rd chromosome pair that consists of an X-shaped chromosome from the mother and a Y-shaped chromosome from the father. XY zygotes become males.

Y

young-old Healthy, vigorous, financially secure older adults (generally, those aged 60 to 75) who are well integrated into the lives of their families and communities.

Z

zone of proximal development (ZPD) Vygotsky's term for the skills—cognitive as well as physical—that a person can exercise only with assistance, not yet independently.

zygote The single cell formed from the union of two gametes, a sperm and an ovum.

References

There are dozens of standard ways to format references. I use the style recommended by the American Psychological Association, with one major change: first names (when available) rather than initials, in order to emphasize that the authors are real people, often women. For the first time, this edition also includes DOI numbers, to ease checking on the internet.

Aarnoudse-Moens, Cornelieke S. H.; Smidts, Diana P.; Oosterlaan, Jaap; Duivenvoorden, Hugo J. and Weisglas-Kuperus, Nynke. (2009). Executive function in very preterm children at early school age. *Journal of Abnormal Child Psychology*, 37(7), 981–993. doi:10.1007/s10802-009-9327-z

Aarsland, Dag; Zaccai, Julia and Brayne, Carol. (2005). A systematic review of prevalence studies of dementia in Parkinson's disease. *Movement Disorders*, 20(10), 1255–1263. doi:10.1002/mds.20527

Abele, Andrea E. and Volmer, Judith. (2011). Dual-career couples: Specific challenges for work-life integration. In Stephan Kaiser, Max Josef Ringlstetter, Doris Ruth Eikhof and Miguel Pina e Cunha (Eds.), *Creating balance? International perspectives on the work-life integration of professionals* (pp. 173–189). Heidelberg, Germany: Springer. doi:10.1007/978-3-642-16199-5_10

Abrams, Dominic; Rutland, Adam; Ferrell, Jennifer M. and Pelletier, Joseph. (2008). Children's judgments of disloyal and immoral peer behavior: Subjective group dynamics in minimal intergroup contexts. *Child Development*, 79(2), 444–461. doi:10.1111/j.1467-8624.2007.01135.x

Abreu, Guida de. (2008). From mathematics learning out-of-school to multicultural classrooms: A cultural psychology perspective. In Lyn D. English (Ed.), *Handbook of international research in mathematics education* (2nd ed., pp. 323–353). New York, NY: Routledge.

Accardo, Pasquale. (2006). Who's training whom? *The Journal of Pediatrics*, 149(2), 151–152. doi:10.1016/j.jpeds.2006.04.026

Ackerman, Edith K. (2013). Microgenetic learning analysis: A methodology for studying knowledge in transition. *Human Development*, 56, 38–46. doi:10.1159/000345540

Adam, Emma K.; Klimes-Dougan, Bonnie and Gunnar, Megan R. (2007). Social regulation of the adrenocortical response to stress in infants, children, and adolescents: Implications for psychopathology and education. In Donna Coch, Geraldine Dawson and Kurt W. Fischer (Eds.), *Human behavior, learning, and the developing brain: Atypical development* (pp. 264–304). New York, NY: Guilford Press.

Adams, Caralee J. (2011). Popularity challenges nation's community colleges. *Education Week*, 30(34), 14–17.

Adams, Ted D.; Davidson, Lance E.; Litwin, Sheldon E.; Kolotkin, Ronette L.; LaMonte, Michael J.; Pendleton, Robert C., . . . Hunt, Steven C. (2012). Health benefits of gastric bypass surgery after 6 years. *JAMA*, 308(11), 1122–1131. doi:10.1001/2012.jama.11164

Adamson, Lauren B. and Bakeman, Roger. (2006). Development of displaced speech in early mother-child conversations. *Child Development*, 77(1), 186–200. doi:10.1111/j.1467-8624.2006.00864.x

Adler, Lynn Peters. (1995). Centenarians: The bonus years. Santa Fe, NM: Health Press.

Adolph, Karen E. and Berger, Sarah E. (2005). Physical and motor development. In Marc H. Bornstein and Michael E. Lamb (Eds.), *Developmental science: An advanced textbook* (5th ed., pp. 223–281). Mahwah, NJ: Lawrence Erlbaum Associates.

Adolph, Karen E.; Cole, Whitney G.; Komati, Meghana; Garciaguirre, Jessie S.; Badaly, Daryaneh; Lingeman, Jesse M., . . . Sotsky, Rachel B. (2012). How do you learn to walk? Thousands of steps and dozens of falls per day. *Psychological Science*, 23(11), 1387–1394. doi:10.1177/0956797612446346

Adolph, Karen E.; Vereijken, Beatrix and Shrout, Patrick E. (2003). What changes in infant walking and why. *Child Development*, 74(2), 475–497. doi:10.1111/1467-8624.7402011

Afifi, Tracie O.; Enns, Murray W.; Cox, Brian J.; Asmundson, Gordon J. G.; Stein, Murray B. and Sareen, Jitender. (2008). Population attributable fractions of psychiatric disorders and suicide ideation and attempts associated with adverse childhood experiences. *American Journal of Public Health*, 98(5), 946–952. doi:10.2105/ajph.2007.120253

Ahima, Rexford S. (2011). No Kiss1ng by leptin during puberty? *Journal of Clinical Investigation*, 121(1), 34–36. doi:10.1172/JCI45813

Ahmed, Leila. (2011). A quiet revolution: The veil's resurgence, from the Middle East to America. New Haven, CT: Yale University Press.

Ahmed, Parvez and Jaakkola, Jouni J. K. (2007). Maternal occupation and adverse pregnancy outcomes: A Finnish population-based study. *Occupational Medicine*, 57(6), 417–423. doi:10.1093/occmed/kqm038

Ainsworth, Mary D. Salter. (1967). Infancy in Uganda: Infant care and the growth of love. Baltimore, MD: Johns Hopkins Press.

Ainsworth, Mary D. Salter. (1973). The development of infant-mother attachment. In Bettye M. Caldwell and Henry N. Ricciuti (Eds.), *Child development and social policy* (pp. 1–94). Chicago, IL: University of Chicago Press.

Ajzen, Icek. (2011). Job satisfaction, effort, and performance: A reasoned action perspective. *Contemporary Economics*, 5(4), 32–43. doi:10.5709/ce.1897-9254.26

Akinbami, Lara J.; Lynch, Courtney D.; Parker, Jennifer D. and Woodruff, Tracey J. (2010). The association between childhood asthma prevalence and monitored air pollutants in metropolitan areas, United States, 2001–2004. *Environmental Research*, 110(3), 294–301. doi:10.1016/j.envres.2010.01.001

Al-Namlah, Abdulrahman S.; Meins, Elizabeth and Fernyhough, Charles. (2012). Self-regulatory private speech relates to children's recall and organization of autobiographical memories. *Early Childhood Research Quarterly*, 27(3), 441–446. doi:10.1016/j.ecresq.2012.02.005

Al-Sahab, Ban; Ardern, Chris I.; Hamadeh, Mazen J. and Tamim, Hala. (2010). Age at menarche in Canada: Results from the National Longitudinal Survey of Children & Youth. *BMC Public Health*, 10, 736–743. doi:10.1186/1471-2458-10-736

Al-Sayes, Fatin; Gari, Mamdooh; Qusti, Safaa; Bagatian, Nadiah and Abuzenadah, Adel. (2011). Prevalence of iron deficiency and iron deficiency anemia among females at university stage. *Journal of Medical Laboratory and Diagnosis*, 2(1), 5–11.

Al-Yagon, Michal; Cavendish, Wendy; Cornoldi, Cesare; Fawcett, Angela J.; Grünke, Matthias; Hung, Li-Yu, . . . Vio, Claudio. (2013). The proposed changes for DSM-5 for SLD and ADHD: International Perspectives—Australia, Germany, Greece, India, Israel, Italy, Spain, Taiwan, United Kingdom, and United States. *Journal of Learning Disabilities*, 46(1), 58–72. doi:10.1177/0022219412464353

Alavinia, Seyed Mohammad and Burdorf, Alex. (2008). Unemployment and retirement and ill-health: A cross-sectional analysis across European countries. *International Archives of Occupational and Environmental Health*, 82(1), 39–45. doi:10.1007/s00420-008-0304-6

Albert, Dustin; Chein, Jason and Steinberg, Laurence. (2013). The teenage brain: Peer influences on adolescent decision making. *Current Directions in Psychological Science*, 22(2), 114–120. doi:10.1177/0963721412471347

Albert, Dustin and Steinberg, Laurence. (2011). Judgment and decision making in adolescence. *Journal of Research on Adolescence*, 21(1), 211–224. doi:10.1111/j.1532-7795.2010.00724.x

Albert, Steven M. and Freedman, Vicki A. (2010). *Public health and aging: Maximizing function and well-being* (2nd ed.). New York, NY: Springer.

Aldwin, Carolyn M. (2007). *Stress, coping, and development: An integrative perspective* (2nd ed.). New York, NY: Guilford Press.

Aldwin, Carolyn M. and Gilmer, Diane Fox. (2013). *Health, illness, and optimal aging: Biological and psychosocial perspectives* (2nd ed.). New York, NY: Springer.

Alegre, Alberto. (2011). Parenting styles and children's emotional intelligence: What do we know? *The Family Journal, 19*(1), 56–62. doi:10.1177/1066480710387486

Alexander, Robin. (2000). Culture and pedagogy: International comparisons in primary education. Malden, MA: Blackwell.

Allemand, Mathias; Zimprich, Daniel and Martin, Mike. (2008). Long-term correlated change in personality traits in old age. *Psychology and Aging, 23*(3), 545–557. doi:10.1037/a0013239

Allen, Kathleen P. (2010). A bullying intervention system in high school: A two-year school-wide follow-up. *Studies In Educational Evaluation, 36*(3), 83–92. doi:10.1016/j.stueduc.2011.01.002

Allendorf, Keera. (2013). Schemas of marital change: From arranged marriages to eloping for love. *Journal of Marriage and Family, 75*(2), 453–469. doi:10.1111/jomf.12003

Allman, Tara L.; Mittelstaedt, Robin D.; Martin, Bruce and Goldenberg, Marni. (2009). Exploring the motivations of BASE jumpers: Extreme sport enthusiasts. *Journal of Sport & Tourism, 14*(4), 229–247. doi:10.1080/14775080903453740

Almeling, Rene. (2011). Sex cells: The medical market for eggs and sperm. Berkeley, CA: University of California Press.

Almomani, Basima; Hawwa, Ahmed F.; Millership, Jeffrey S.; Heaney, Liam; Douglas, Isabella; McElnay, James C. and Shields, Michael D. (2013). Can certain genotypes predispose to poor asthma control in children? A pharmacogenetic study of 9 candidate genes in children with difficult asthma. *PLoS ONE, 8*(4). doi:10.1371/journal.pone.0060592

Almond, Douglas. (2006). Is the 1918 influenza pandemic over? Long-term effects of in utero influenza exposure in the post-1940 U.S. population. *Journal of Political Economy, 114*(4), 672–712. doi:10.1086/507154

Alsaker, Françoise D. and Flammer, August (2006). Pubertal development. In Sandy Jackson and Luc Goossens (Eds.), *Handbook of adolescent development* (pp. 30–50). New York, NY: Psychology Press.

Altbach, Philip G.; Reisberg, Liz and Rumbley, Laura E. (2010). Tracking a global academic revolution. *Change: The Magazine of Higher Learning, 42*(2), 30–39. doi:10.1080/00091381003590845

Alviola, Pedro A.; Nayga, Rodolfo M. Jr. and Thomsen, Michael. (2013). Food desserts and childhood obesity. *Applied Economic Perspectives and Policy, 35*(1), 106–124. doi:10.1093/aepp/pps035

Alzheimer's Association. (2012). 2012 Alzheimer's disease facts and figures. *Alzheimer's & Dementia: The Journal of the Alzheimer's Association, 8*(2), 131–168. doi:10.1016/j.jalz.2012.02.001

Amato, Paul R. (2005). The impact of family formation change on the cognitive, social, and emotional well-being of the next generation. *Future of Children, 15*(2), 75–96.

Amato, Paul R. (2010). Research on divorce: Continuing trends and new developments. *Journal of Marriage and Family, 72*(3), 650–666. doi:10.1111/j.1741-3737.2010.00723.x

Amato, Paul R. (2011). Relationship sequences and trajectories: Women's family formation pathways in emerging adulthood. In Frank D. Finchman and Ming Cui (Eds.), *Romantic relationships in emerging adulthood* (pp. 27–43). New York, NY: Cambridge University Press. doi:10.1017/CBO9780511761935.004

Amato, Paul R.; Johnson, David R.; Booth, Alan and Rogers, Stacy J. (2003). Continuity and change in marital quality between 1980 and 2000. *Journal of Marriage & Family, 65*(1), 1–22. doi:10.1111/j.1741-3737.2003.00001.x

Ambady, Nalini and Bharucha, Jamshed. (2009). Culture and the brain. *Current Directions in Psychological Science, 18*(6), 342–345. doi:10.1111/j.1467-8721.2009.01664.x

American College of Obstetricians and Gynecologists Committee on Obstetric Practice. (2011). Committee opinion no. 476: Planned home birth. *Obstetrics & Gynecology, 117*(2), 425–428. doi:10.1097/AOG.0b013e31820eee20

American Psychiatric Association. (2013). *Diagnostic and statistical manual of mental disorders: DSM-5* (5th ed.). Washington, DC: American Psychiatric Association.

Anderson, Michael. (2001). 'You have to get inside the person' or making grief private: Image and metaphor in the therapeutic reconstruction of bereavement. In Jenny Hockey, Jeanne Katz and Neil Small (Eds.), *Grief, mourning, and death ritual* (pp. 135–143). Buckingham, UK: Open University Press.

Anderson, Robert N.; Kochanek, Kenneth D. and Murphy, Sherry L. (1997). Report of final mortality statistics, 1995. Hyattsville, MD: Centers for Disease Control and Prevention National Center for Health Statistics, 45. No. 11, Suppl. 2.

Andrade, Susan E.; Gurwitz, Jerry H.; Davis, Robert L.; Chan, K. Arnold; Finkelstein, Jonathan A.; Fortman, Kris, . . . Platt, Richard. (2004). Prescription drug use in pregnancy. *American Journal of Obstetrics and Gynecology, 191*, 398–407. doi:10.1016/j.ajog.2004.04.025

Anjum, Afshan; Gait, Priyanka; Cullen, Kathryn R. and White, Tonya. (2010). Schizophrenia in adolescents and young adults. In Jon E. Grant and Marc N. Potenza (Eds.), *Young adult mental health* (pp. 362–378). New York, NY: Oxford University Press.

Ansary, Nadia S. and Luthar, Suniya S. (2009). Distress and academic achievement among adolescents of affluence: A study of externalizing and internalizing problem behaviors and school performance. *Development and Psychopathology, 21*(1), 319–341. doi:10.1017/S0954579409000182

Antonucci, Toni C.; Akiyama, Hiroko and Merline, Alicia. (2001). Dynamics of social relationships in midlife. In Margie E. Lachman (Ed.), *Handbook of midlife development* (pp. 571–598). New York, NY: Wiley.

Antonucci, Toni C.; Jackson, James S. and Biggs, Simon. (2007). Intergenerational relations: Theory, research, and policy. *Journal of Social Issues, 63*(4), 679–693. doi:10.1111/j.1540-4560.2007.00530.x

Apgar, Virginia. (1953). A proposal for a new method of evaluation of the newborn infant. *Current Researches in Anesthesia and Analgesia, 32*, 260–267.

Apostolou, Menelaos. (2007). Sexual selection under parental choice: The role of parents in the evolution of human mating. *Evolution and Human Behavior, 28*(6), 403–409. doi:10.1016/j.evolhumbehav.2007.05.007

Applegate, Anthony J.; Applegate, Mary DeKonty; McGeehan, Catherine M.; Pinto, Catherine M. and Kong, Ailing. (2009). The assessment of thoughtful literacy in NAEP: Why the states aren't measuring up. *The Reading Teacher, 62*(5), 372–381. doi:10.1598/RT.62.5.1

Archambault, Isabelle; Janosz, Michel; Fallu, Jean-Sébastien and Paganim, Linda S. (2009). Student engagement and its relationship with early high school dropout. *Journal of Adolescence, 32*(3), 651–670. doi:10.1016/j.adolescence.2008.06.007

Archer, John. (2000). Sex differences in aggression between heterosexual partners: A meta-analytic review. *Psychological Bulletin, 126*(5), 651–680. doi:10.1037//0033-2909.126.5.651

Ardelt, Monika. (2011). Wisdom, age, and well-being. In K. Warner Schaie and Sherry L. Willis (Eds.), *Handbook of the psychology of aging* (7th ed., pp. 279–291). San Diego, CA: Academic Press. doi:10.1016/B978-0-12-380882-0.00018-8

Ariely, Dan. (2009). Predictably irrational: The hidden forces that shape our decisions. New York, NY: Harper.

Arndt, Jamie; Vail III, Kenneth E.; Cox, Cathy R.; Goldenberg, Jamie L.; Piasecki, Thomas M. and Gibbons, Frederick X. (2013). The interactive effect of mortality reminders and tobacco craving on smoking topography. *Health Psychology, 32*(5), 525–532. doi:10.1037/a0029201

Arnett, Jeffrey Jensen. (2004). Emerging adulthood: The winding road from the late teens through the twenties. New York, NY: Oxford University Press.

Arnold, L. Eugene; Farmer, Cristan; Kraemer, Helena Chmura; Davies, Mark; Witwer, Andrea; Chuang, Shirley, . . . Swiezy, Naomi B. (2010). Moderators, mediators, and other predictors of risperidone response in children with autistic disorder and irritability. *Journal of Child and Adolescent Psychopharmacology, 20*(2), 83–93. doi:10.1089/cap.2009.0022

Aron, Arthur; McLaughlin-Volpe, Tracy; Mashek, Debra; Lewandowski, Gary; Wright, Stephen C. and Aron, Elaine N. (2005).

Including others in the self. *European Review of Social Psychology, 15*, 101–132.

Aronson, Joshua; Burgess, Diana; Phelan, Sean M. and Juarez, Lindsay. (2013). Unhealthy interactions: The role of stereotype threat in health disparities. *American Journal of Public Health, 103*(1), 50–56. doi:10.2105/AJPH.2012.300828

Aronson, Joshua; Fried, Carrie B. and Good, Catherine. (2002). Reducing the effects of stereotype threat on African American college students by shaping theories of intelligence. *Journal of Experimental Social Psychology, 38*(2), 113–125. doi:10.1006/jesp.2001.1491

Artistico, Daniele; Orom, Heather; Cervone, Daniel; Krauss, Stephen and Houston, Eric. (2010). Everyday challenges in context: The influence of contextual factors on everyday problem solving among young, middle-aged, and older adults. *Experimental Aging Research, 36*(2), 230–247. doi:10.1080/03610731003613938

Arum, Richard and Roksa, Josipa. (2011). Academically adrift: Limited learning on college campuses. Chicago, IL: University of Chicago Press.

Asbridge, Mark; Brubacher, Jeff R. and Chan, Herbert. (2013). Cell phone use and traffic crash risk: A culpability analysis. *International Journal of Epidemiology, 42*(1), 259–267. doi:10.1093/ije/dys180

Asendorpf, Jens B.; Denissen, Jaap J. A. and van Aken, Marcel A. G. (2008). Inhibited and aggressive preschool children at 23 years of age. Personality and social transitions into adulthood. *Developmental Psychology, 44*(4), 997–1011. doi:10.1037/0012-1649.44.4.997

Ash, Caroline; Jasny, Barbara R.; Roberts, Leslie; Stone, Richard and Sugden, Andrew M. (2008). Reimagining cities. *Science, 319*(5864), 739. doi:10.1126/science.319.5864.739

Ashby, Michael. (2009). The dying human: A perspective from palliative medicine. In Allan Kellehear (Ed.), *The study of dying: From autonomy to transformation* (pp. 76–98). New York, NY: Cambridge University Press.

Ashraf, Quamrul and Galor, Oded. (2013). The 'out of Africa' hypothesis, human genetic diversity, and comparative economic development. *American Economic Review, 103*(1), 1–46. doi:10.1257/aer.103.1.1

Asma, Stephen T. (2013). Against fairness. Chicago, IL: University of Chicago Press.

Atchley, Robert C. (2009). Spirituality and aging. Baltimore, MD: Johns Hopkins University Press.

Au, Wayne and Tempel, Melissa Bollow (Eds.). (2012). Pencils down: Rethinking high-stakes testing and accountability in public schools. Milwaukee, WI: Rethinking Schools.

Aud, Susan; Hussar, William; Johnson, Frank; Kena, Grace; Roth, Erin; Manning, Eileen, . . . Zhang, Jijun. (2012). The condition of education 2012. Washington, DC: U.S. Department of Education, National Center for Education Statistics.

Aud, Susan; Hussar, William; Planty, Michael; Snyder, Thomas; Bianco, Kevin; Fox, Mary Ann, . . . Drake, Lauren. (2010).

The condition of education 2010. Washington, DC: National Center for Education Statistics, Institute of Education Sciences, U.S. Department of Education.NCES 2010-028.

Audrey, Suzanne; Holliday, Jo and Campbell, Rona. (2006). It's good to talk: Adolescent perspectives of an informal, peer-led intervention to reduce smoking. *Social Science & Medicine, 63*(2), 320–334. doi:10.1016/j.socscimed.2005.12.010

Aunola, Kaisa and Nurmi, Jari-Erik. (2004). Maternal affection moderates the impact of psychological control on a child's mathematical performance. *Developmental Psychology, 40*(6), 965–978. doi:10.1037/0012-1649.40.6.965

Avery, Rosemary J. and Freundlich, Madelyn. (2009). You're all grown up now: Termination of foster care support at age 18. *Journal of Adolescence, 32*(2), 247–257. doi:10.1016/j .adolescence.2008.03.009

Aviv, Abraham. (2011). Leukocyte telomere dynamics, human aging and life span. In Edward J. Masoro and Steven N. Austad (Eds.), *Handbook of the biology of aging* (7th ed., pp. 163–176). San Diego, CA: Academic Press.

Ayalon, Liat and Ancoli-Israel, Sonia. (2009). Normal sleep in aging. In Teofilo L. Lee-Chiong (Ed.), *Sleep medicine essentials* (pp. 173–176). Hoboken, NJ: Wiley-Blackwell.

Ayduk, Özlem and Kross, Ethan. (2008). Enhancing the pace of recovery: Self-distanced analysis of negative experiences reduces blood pressure reactivity. *Psychological Science, 19*, 229–231. doi:10.1111/j.1467-9280.2008.02073.x

Ayers, Catherine R.; Saxena, Sanjaya; Golshan, Shahrokh and Wetherell, Julie Loebach. (2010). Age at onset and clinical features of late life compulsive hoarding. *International Journal of Geriatric Psychiatry, 25*(2), 142–149. doi:10.1002/gps.2310

Azrin, Nathan H. and Foxx, Richard M. (1974). Toilet training in less than a day. New York, NY: Simon and Schuster.

Babchishin, Lyzon K.; Weegar, Kelly and Romano, Elisa. (2013). Early child care effects on later behavioral outcomes using a Canadian nation-wide sample. *Journal of Educational and Developmental Psychology, 3*(2), 15–29. doi:10.5539/jedp.v3n2p15

Bachman, Jerald G.; O'Malley, Patrick M.; Freedman-Doan, Peter; Trzesniewski, Kali H. and Donnellan, M. Brent. (2011). Adolescent self-esteem: Differences by race/ethnicity, gender, and age. *Self Identity, 10*(4), 445–473. doi:10.1080/15298861003794538

Bagla, Pallava and Stone, Richard. (2013). Science for all. *Science, 340*(6136), 1032–1036. doi:10.1126/science.340.6136.1032

Bagner, Daniel M.; Pettit, Jeremy W.; Lewinsohn, Peter M. and Seeley, John R. (2010). Effect of maternal depression on child behavior: A sensitive period? *Journal of the American Academy of Child and Adolescent Psychiatry, 49*(7), 699–707. doi:10.1016/j.jaac.2010.03.012

Bagwell, Catherine L. and Schmidt, Michelle E. (2011). Friendships in childhood & adolescence. New York, NY: Guilford Press.

Baillargeon, Renée. (2000). How do infants learn about the physical world? In Darwin Muir and Alan Slater (Eds.), Infant development: *The essential readings* (pp. 195–212). Malden, MA: Blackwell.

Baillargeon, Renée and DeVos, Julie. (1991). Object permanence in young infants: Further evidence. *Child Development, 62*(6), 1227–1246. doi:10.1111/j.1467-8624.1991.tb01602.x

Baker, Beth. (2007). Old age in a new age: The promise of transformative nursing homes. Nashville, TN: Vanderbilt University Press.

Baker, Jeffrey P. (2000). Immunization and the American way: 4 childhood vaccines. *American Journal of Public Health, 90*(2), 199–207. doi:10.2105/AJPH.90.2.199

Baker, Lindsey and Silverstein, Merril. (2012). The well-being of grandparents caring for grandchildren in rural China and the United States. In Sara Arber and Virpi Timonen (Eds.), Contemporary grandparenting: *Changing family relationships in global contexts* (pp. 51–70). Chicago, IL: Policy Press.

Baker, Lindsey A. and Mutchler, Jan E. (2010). Poverty and material hardship in grandparent-headed households. *Journal of Marriage and Family, 72*(4), 947–962. doi:10.1111/j .1741-3737.2010.00741.x

Baldry, Anna C. and Farrington, David P. (2007). Effectiveness of programs to prevent school bullying. *Victims & Offenders: An International Journal of Evidence-based Research, Policy, and Practice, 2*(2), 183–204. doi:10.1080/15564880701263155

Ball, Howard. (2012). At liberty to die: The battle for death with dignity in America. New York, NY: New York University Press.

Baltazar, Alina; Hopkins, Gary; McBride, Duane; Vanderwaal, Curt; Pepper, Sara and Mackey, Sarah. (2013). Parental influence on inhalant use. *Journal of Child & Adolescent Substance Abuse, 22*(1), 25–37. doi:10.1080/106 7828X.2012.729904

Baltes, Paul B. (2003). On the incomplete architecture of human ontogeny: Selection, optimization and compensation as foundation of developmental theory. In Ursula M. Staudinger and Ulman Lindenberger (Eds.), *Understanding human development: Dialogues with lifespan psychology* (pp. 17–43). Boston, MA: Kluwer Academic Publishers.

Baltes, Paul B. and Baltes, Margret M. (1990). Psychological perspectives on successful aging: The model of selective optimization with compensation. In Paul B. Baltes and Margret M. Baltes (Eds.), *Successful aging: Perspectives from the behavioral sciences* (pp. 1–34). New York, NY: Cambridge University Press.

Baltes, Paul B.; Lindenberger, Ulman and Staudinger, Ursula M. (1998). Life-span theory in developmental psychology. In William Damon

(Ed.), *Handbook of child psychology* (5th ed., Vol. 1, pp. 1029–1144). New York, NY: Wiley.

Baltes, Paul B.; Lindenberger, Ulman and Staudinger, Ursula M. (2006). Life span theory in developmental psychology. In William Damon and Richard M. Lerner (Eds.), *Handbook of child psychology* (6th ed., Vol. 1, pp. 569–664). Hoboken, NJ: Wiley.

Baltes, Paul B. and Smith, Jacqui. (2008). The fascination of wisdom: Its nature, ontogeny, and function. *Perspectives on Psychological Science, 3*(1), 56–64. doi:10.1111/j.1745-6916 .2008.00062.x

Bandura, Albert. (1977). Social learning theory. Englewood Cliffs, NJ: Prentice Hall.

Bandura, Albert. (1986). Social foundations of thought and action: A social cognitive theory. Englewood Cliffs, NJ: Prentice-Hall.

Bandura, Albert. (1997). The anatomy of stages of change. *American Journal of Health Promotion, 12*(1), 8–10.

Bandura, Albert. (2006). Toward a psychology of human agency. *Perspectives on Psychological Science, 1*(2), 164–180. doi:10.1111/j.1745-6916 .2006.00011.x

Banks, James and Smith, James P. (2012). International comparisons in health economics: Evidence from aging studies. *Annual Review of Economics, 4*, 57–81. doi:10.1146 /annurev-economics-080511-110944

Bansal, Vishal; Fortlage, Dale; Lee, Jeanne; Costantini, Todd; Potenza, Bruce and Coimbra, Raul. (2009). Hemorrhage is more prevalent than brain injury in early trauma deaths: The golden six hours. *European Journal of Trauma and Emergency Surgery, 35*(1), 26–30. doi:10.1007/ s00068-008-8080-2

Barac, Raluca and Bialystok, Ellen. (2011). Cognitive development of bilingual children. *Language Teaching, 44*(1), 36–54. doi:10.1017 /S0261444810000339

Barber, Brian K. (Ed.). (2002). Intrusive parenting: How psychological control affects children and adolescents. Washington, DC: American Psychological Association.

Barbey, Aron K.; Colom, Roberto; Paul, Erick J. and Grafman, Jordan. (2013). Architecture of fluid intelligence and working memory revealed by lesion mapping. Brain Structure and Function, February. doi:10.1007/s00429-013-0512-z

Barbey, Aron K.; Krueger, Frank and Grafman, Jordan. (2009). An evolutionarily adaptive neural architecture for social reasoning. *Trends in Neurosciences, 32*(12), 603–610. doi:10.1016/j.tins.2009.09.001

Barkin, Shari; Scheindlin, Benjamin; Ip, Edward H.; Richardson, Irma and Finch, Stacia. (2007). Determinants of parental discipline practices: A national sample from primary care practices. *Clinical Pediatrics, 46*(1), 64–69. doi:10.1177/0009922806292644

Barnett, Mark; Watson, Ruth and Kind, Peter. (2006). Pathways to barrel development. In Reha Erzurumlu, William Guido and Zoltán

Molnár (Eds.), *Development and plasticity in sensory thalamus and cortex* (pp. 138–157). New York, NY: Springer. doi:10.1007/978-0-387-38607-2_9

Barnett, W. Steven; Epstein, Dale J.; Carolan, Megan E.; Fitzgerald, Jen; Ackerman, Debra J. and Friedman, Allison H. (2010). The state of preschool 2010: State preschool yearbook. New Brunswick, NJ: National Institute for Early Education Research.

Barnett, W. Steven; Yarosz, Donald J.; Thomas, Jessica; Jung, Kwanghee and Blanco, Dulce. (2007). Two-way and monolingual English immersion in preschool education: An experimental comparison. *Early Childhood Research Quarterly, 22*(3), 277–293. doi:10.1016 /j.ecresq.2007.03.003

Baron, Andrew Scott and Banaji, Mahzarin R. (2006). The development of implicit attitudes: Evidence of race evaluations from ages 6 and 10 and adulthood. *Psychological Science, 17*(1), 53–58. doi:10.1111/j.1467-9280.2005.01664.x

Barrett, Anne E. (2012). Feeling young—A prescription for growing older? *Aging Today, 33*, 3–4.

Barrett, Justin L. (2008). Why Santa Claus is not a god. *Journal of Cognition and Culture, 8*(1), 149–161. doi:10.1163/156770908X289251

Barros, Romina M.; Silver, Ellen J. and Stein, Ruth E. K. (2009). School recess and group classroom behavior. *Pediatrics, 123*(2), 431–436. doi:10.1542/peds.2007-2825

Barry, Carolyn McNamara; Nelson, Larry J. and Christofferson, Jennifer L. (2013). Asocial and afraid: An examination of shyness and anxiety in emerging adulthood. *Journal of Family Studies, 19*(1), 2–18. doi:10.5172/jfs.2013.19.1.2

Barry, Carolyn McNamara; Padilla-Walker, Laura M. and Nelson, Larry J. (2012). The role of mothers and media on emerging adults' religious faith and practices by way of internalization of prosocial values. *Journal of Adult Development, 19*(2), 66–78. doi:10.1007/s10804-011-9135-x

Bartels, Meike; Cacioppo, John T.; van Beijsterveldt, Toos C. E. M. and Boomsma, Dorret I. (2013). Exploring the association between well-being and psychopathology in adolescents. *Behavior Genetics, 43*(3), 177–190. doi:10.1007/s10519-013-9589-7

Basak, Chandramallika; Boot, Walter R.; Voss, Michelle W. and Kramer, Arthur F. (2008). Can training in a real-time strategy video game attenuate cognitive decline in older adults? *Psychology and Aging, 23*(4), 765–777. doi:10.1037/a0013494

Bass, Madeline. (2011). The tough questions: Do not attempt resuscitation discussions. In Keri Thomas and Ben Lobo (Eds.), *Advance care planning in end of life care* (pp. 113–124). New York, NY: Oxford University Press.

Basseches, Michael. (1984). Dialectical thinking and adult development. Norwood, NJ: Ablex.

Basseches, Michael. (1989). Dialectical thinking as an organized whole: Comments on Irwin and Kramer. In Michael L. Commons, Jan D. Sinnott, Francis A. Richards and Cheryl Armon

(Eds.), *Adult development* (Vol. 1, pp. 161–178). New York, NY: Praeger.

Basten, Stuart. (2009). Voluntary childlessness and being childfree. St. John's College, University of Oxford, & Vienna Institute of Demography.

Basu, Sanjay; Yoffe, Paula; Hills, Nancy and Lustig, Robert H. (2013). The relationship of sugar to population-level diabetes prevalence: An econometric analysis of repeated cross-sectional data. *PLoS ONE, 8*(2), e57873. doi:10.1371 /journal.pone.0057873

Bates, Gillian; Harper, Peter S. and Jones, Lesley (Eds.). (2002). Huntington's disease (3rd ed.). New York, NY: Oxford University Press.

Bates, Lisa M.; Acevedo-Garcia, Dolores; Alegria, Margarita and Krieger, Nancy. (2008). Immigration and generational trends in body mass index and obesity in the United States: Results of the National Latino and Asian American Survey, 2002–2003. *American Journal of Public Health, 98*(1), 70–77. doi:10.2105 /ajph.2006.102814

Bateson, Mary Catherine. (2011). Composing a further life: The age of active wisdom. New York, NY: Vintage Books.

Batterham, Philip J.; Christensen, Helen and Mackinnon, Andrew J. (2009). Fluid intelligence is independently associated with all-cause mortality over 17 years in an elderly community sample: An investigation of potential mechanisms. *Intelligence, 37*(6), 551–560. doi:10.1016/j .intell.2008.10.004

Bauer, Patricia J. (2006). Event memory. In William Damon and Richard M. Lerner (Eds.), *Handbook of child psychology* (6th ed., Vol. 2, pp. 373–425). Hoboken, NJ: Wiley.

Bauer, Patricia J.; San Souci, Priscilla and Pathman, Thanujeni. (2010). Infant memory. *Wiley Interdisciplinary Reviews: Cognitive Science, 1*(2), 267–277. doi:10.1002/wcs.38

Baumeister, Roy F. and Blackhart, Ginnette C. (2007). Three perspectives on gender differences in adolescent sexual development. In Rutger C. M. E. Engels, Margaret Kerr and Håkan Stattin (Eds.), *Friends, lovers, and groups: Key relationships in adolescence* (pp. 93–104). Hoboken, NJ: Wiley.

Baumeister, Roy F. and Tierney, John. (2012). Willpower: Rediscovering the greatest human strength. New York, NY: Penguin.

Baumgardt, Melanie; Bucher, Hans Ulrich; Mieth, Romaine Arlettaz and Fauchère, Jean-Claude. (2011). Health-related quality of life of former very preterm infants in adulthood. *Acta Paediatrica, 101*(2), e59–e63. doi:10.1111/ j.1651-2227.2011.02422.x

Bauminger-Zviely, Nirit. (2013). Social and academic abilities in children with high-functioning autism spectrum disorders. New York, NY: Guilford Press.

Baumrind, Diana. (1967). Child care practices anteceding three patterns of preschool behavior. *Genetic Psychology Monographs, 75*(1), 43–88.

Baumrind, Diana. (1971). Current patterns of parental authority. *Developmental Psychology, 4*(1, Pt. 2), 1–103. doi:10.1037/h0030372

Baumrind, Diana. (2005). Patterns of parental authority and adolescent autonomy. *New Directions for Child and Adolescent Development, 2005*(108), 61–69. doi:10.1002/cd.128

Baumrind, Diana; Larzelere, Robert E. and Owens, Elizabeth B. (2010). Effects of preschool parents' power-assertive patterns and practices on adolescent development. *Parenting, 10*(3), 157–201. doi:10.1080/15295190903290790

Bayer, Jordana K.; Hiscock, Harriet; Hampton, Anne and Wake, Melissa. (2007). Sleep problems in young infants and maternal mental and physical health. *Journal of Paediatrics and Child Health, 43*(1–2), 66–73. doi:10.1111/j.1440-1754.2007.01005.x

Bayley, Nancy. (1966). Learning in adulthood: The role of intelligence. In Herbert J. Klausmeier and Chester W. Harris (Eds.), *Analyses of concept learning* (pp. 117–138). New York, NY: Academic Press.

Bayley, Nancy and Oden, Melita H. (1955). The maintenance of intellectual ability in gifted adults. *Journal of Gerontology Series B, 10*(1), 91–107. doi:10.1093/geronj/10.1.91

Beal, Susan. (1988). Sleeping position and sudden infant death syndrome. *The Medical Journal of Australia, 149*(10), 562.

Beauchaine, Theodore P.; Klein, Daniel N.; Crowell, Sheila E.; Derbidge, Christina and Gatzke-Kopp, Lisa. (2009). Multifinality in the development of personality disorders: A Biology x Sex x Environment interaction model of antisocial and borderline traits. *Development and Psychopathology, 21*(3), 735–770. doi:10.1017/S0954579409000418

Beaumont, Sherry L. and Pratt, Michael M. (2011). Identity processing styles and psychosocial balance during early and middle adulthood: The role of identity in intimacy and generativity. *Journal of Adult Development, 18*(4), 172–183. doi:10.1007/s10804-011-9125-z

Beck, Melinda. (2009, May 26). How's your baby? Recalling the Apgar score's namesake. *Wall Street Journal*, pp. D-1.

Beck, Martha Nibley. (1999). Expecting Adam: A true story of birth, rebirth, and everyday magic. New York, NY: Times Books.

Beckers, Debby G. J.; van der Linden, Dimitri; Smulders, Peter G. W.; Kompier, Michiel A. J.; Taris, Toon W. and Geurts, Sabine A. E. (2008). Voluntary or involuntary? Control over overtime and rewards for overtime in relation to fatigue and work satisfaction. *Work & Stress, 22*(1), 33–50. doi:10.1080/02678370801984927

Begos, Kevin. (2010, Winter). A wounded hero. *CR: Collaborations, Results, 5*, 30–35, 62–63.

Beilin, Lawrence and Huang, Rae-Chi. (2008). Childhood obesity, hypertension, the metabolic syndrome and adult cardiovascular disease. *Clinical and Experimental Pharmacology and Physiology, 35*(4), 409–411. doi:10.1111/j.1440-1681.2008.04887.x

Beise, Jan and Voland, Eckart. (2002). A multilevel event history analysis of the effects of grandmothers on child mortality in a historical German population: Krummhörn, Ostfriesland, 1720–1874. *Demographic Research, 7*(13), 469–498. doi:10.4054/DemRes.2002.7.13

Belfield, Clive R.; Nores, Milagros; Barnett, Steve and Schweinhart, Lawrence. (2006). The High/Scope Perry Preschool Program: Cost benefit analysis using data from the age-40 followup. *Journal of Human Resources, 41*(1), 162–190. doi:10.3368/jhr.XLI.1.162

Bell, Aleeca F.; White-Traut, Rosemary and Medoff-Cooper, Barbara. (2010). Neonatal neurobehavioral organization after exposure to maternal epidural analgesia in labor. *Journal of Obstetric, Gynecologic, & Neonatal Nursing, 39*(2), 178–190. doi:10.1111/j.1552-6909.2010.01100.x

Bell, Beth Teresa and Dittmar, Helga. (2011). Does media type matter? The role of identification in adolescent girls' media consumption and the impact of different thin-ideal media on body image. *Sex Roles, 65*(7/8), 478–490. doi:10.1007/s11199-011-9964-x

Bell, Martha Ann and Calkins, Susan D. (2012). Attentional control and emotion regulation in early development. In Michael I. Posner (Ed.), *Cognitive neuroscience of attention* (2nd ed., pp. 322–330). New York, NY: Guilford Press.

Belsky, Jay; Bakermans-Kranenburg, Marian J. and van IJzendoorn, Marinus H. (2007). For better and for worse: Differential susceptibility to environmental influences. *Current Directions in Psychological Science, 16*(6), 300–304. doi:10.1111/j.1467-8721.2007.00525.x

Belsky, Jay and de Haan, Michelle. (2011). Parenting and children's brain development: The end of the beginning. *Journal of Child Psychology and Psychiatry, 52*(4), 409–428. doi:10.1111/j.1469-7610.2010.02281.x

Belsky, Jay and Pluess, Michael. (2009). The nature (and nurture?) of plasticity in early human development. *Perspectives on Psychological Science, 4*(4), 345–351. doi:10.1111/j.1745-6924.2009.01136.x

Belsky, Jay; Schlomer, Gabriel L. and Ellis, Bruce J. (2012). Beyond cumulative risk: Distinguishing harshness and unpredictability as determinants of parenting and early life history strategy. *Developmental Psychology, 48*(3), 662–673. doi:10.1037/a0024454

Belsky, Jay; Steinberg, Laurence; Houts, Renate M. and Halpern-Felsher, Bonnie L. (2010). The development of reproductive strategy in females: Early maternal harshness to earlier menarche to increased sexual risk taking. *Developmental Psychology, 46*(1), 120–128. doi:10.1037/a0015549

Ben-Zur, Hasida and Zeidner, Moshe. (2009). Threat to life and risk-taking behaviors: A review of empirical findings and explanatory models. *Personality and Social Psychology Review, 13*(2), 109–128. doi:10.1177/1088868308330104

Benatar, David. (2011). A legal right to die: Responding to slippery slope and abuse arguments. *Current Oncology, 18*(5), 206–207.

Benenson, Joyce F.; Markovits, Henry; Fitzgerald, Caitlin; Geoffroy, Diana; Flemming, Julianne; Kahlenberg, Sonya M. and Wrangham, Richard W. (2009). Males' greater tolerance of same-sex peers. *Psychological Science, 20*(2), 184–190. doi:10.1111/j.1467-9280.2009.02269.x

Benet, Sula. (1974). Abkhasians: The long-living people of the Caucasus. New York, NY: Holt, Rinehart & Winston.

Benjamin, Georges C. (2004). The solution is injury prevention. *American Journal of Public Health, 94*(4), 521. doi:10.2105/AJPH.94.4.521

Bennett, Craig M. and Baird, Abigail A. (2006). Anatomical changes in the emerging adult brain: A voxel-based morphometry study. *Human Brain Mapping, 27*(9), 766–777. doi:10.1002/hbm.20218

Benoit, Amelie; Lacourse, Eric and Claes, Michel. (2013). Pubertal timing and depressive symptoms in late adolescence: The moderating role of individual, peer, and parental factors. *Development and Psychopathology, 25*(2), 455–471. doi:10.1017/S0954579412001174

Benovenli, Liza; Fuller, Elizabeth; Sinnot, Jan and Waterman, Sarah. (2011). Three applications of postformal thought: Wisdom, concepts of God, and success in college. *Research in the Social Scientific Study of Religion, 22*, 141–154. doi:10.1163/ej.9789004207271.i-360.23

Bentley, Gillian R. and Mascie-Taylor, C. G. Nicholas. (2000). Introduction. In Gillian R. Bentley and C. G. Nicholas Mascie-Taylor (Eds.), *Infertility in the modern world: Present and future prospects* (pp. 1–13). New York, NY: Cambridge University Press.

Berenbaum, Sheri A.; Martin, Carol Lynn; Hanish, Laura D.; Briggs, Phillip T. and Fabes, Richard A. (2008). Sex differences in children's play. In Jill B. Becker, Karen J. Berkley, Nori Geary, Elizabeth Hampson, James P. Herman and Elizabeth Young (Eds.), *Sex differences in the brain: From genes to behavior* (pp. 275–290). New York, NY: Oxford University Press.

Berg, Cynthia A. (2008). Everyday problem solving in context. In Scott M. Hofer and Duane F. Alwin (Eds.), *Handbook of cognitive aging: Interdisciplinary perspectives* (pp. 207–223). Thousand Oaks, CA: Sage.

Berg, Sandra J. and Wynne-Edwards, Katherine E. (2002). Salivary hormone concentrations in mothers and fathers becoming parents are not correlated. *Hormones & Behavior, 42*(4), 424–436. doi:10.1006/hbeh.2002.1841

Berger, Kathleen Stassen. (2007). Update on bullying at school: Science forgotten? *Developmental Review, 27*(1), 90–126. doi:10.1016/j.dr.2006.08.002

Berger, Lawrence M.; Paxson, Christina and Waldfogel, Jane. (2009). Income and child development. *Children and Youth Services Review, 31*(9), 978–989. doi:10.1016/j.childyouth.2009.04.013

Berkey, Catherine S.; Gardner, Jane D.; Frazier, A. Lindsay and Colditz, Graham A. (2000). Relation of childhood diet and body size to menarche and adolescent growth in girls. *American Journal of Epidemiology, 152*(5), 446–452. doi:10.1093/aje/152.5.446

Berkman, Lisa F.; Ertel, Karen A. and Glymour, Maria M. (2011). Aging and social intervention: Life course perspectives. In Robert H. Binstock and Linda K. George (Eds.), *Handbook of aging and the social sciences* (7th ed., pp. 337–351). San Diego, CA: Academic Press. doi:10.1016/B978-0-12-380880-6.00024-1

Bernard, Jessica A.; Peltier, Scott J.; Wiggins, Jillian Lee; Jaeggi, Susanne M.; Buschkuehl, Martin; Fling, Brett W., . . . Seidler, Rachael D. (2013). Disrupted cortico-cerebellar connectivity in older adults. *NeuroImage, 83,* 103–119. doi:10.1016/j.neuroimage.2013.06.042

Bernard, Kristin and Dozier, Mary. (2010). Examining infants' cortisol responses to laboratory tasks among children varying in attachment disorganization: Stress reactivity or return to baseline? *Developmental Psychology, 46*(6), 1771–1778. doi:10.1037/a0020660

Bernard, Kristin and Dozier, Mary. (2011). This is my baby: Foster parents' feelings of commitment and displays of delight. *Infant Mental Health Journal, 32*(2), 251–262. doi:10.1002/imhj.20293

Bers, Marina; Seddighin, Safoura and Sullivan, Amanda. (2013). Ready for robotics: Bringing together the T and E of STEM in early childhood teacher education. *Journal of Technology and Teacher Education, 21*(3), 355–377.

Betancourt, Theresa S.; McBain, Ryan; Newnham, Elizabeth A. and Brennan, Robert T. (2013). Trajectories of internalizing problems in war-affected Sierra Leonean youth: Examining conflict and postconflict factors. *Child Development, 84*(2), 455–470. doi:10.1111/j.1467-8624.2012.01861.x

Beutel, Manfred E.; Stöbel-Richter, Yve and Brähler, Elmar. (2008). Sexual desire and sexual activity of men and women across their lifespans: results from a representative German community survey. *BJU International, 101*(1), 76–82. doi:10.1111/j.1464-410X.2007.07204.x

Beutler, Ivan F. (2012). Connections to Economic Prosperity: Money aspirations from adolescence to emerging adulthood. *Journal of Financial Counseling & Planning, 23*(1), 17–32.

Bhatia, Tej K. and Ritchie, William C. (Eds.). (2013). The handbook of bilingualism and multilingualism (2nd ed.). Malden, MA: Wiley-Blackwell.

Bialystok, Ellen. (2010). Global-local and trail-making tasks by monolingual and bilingual children: Beyond inhibition. *Developmental Psychology, 46*(1), 93–105. doi:10.1037/a0015466

Bialystok, Ellen; Craik, Fergus I. M.; Green, David W. and Gollan, Tamar H. (2009). Bilingual minds. *Psychological Science in the Public Interest, 10*(3), 89–129. doi:10.1177/1529100610387084

Bialystok, Ellen and Viswanathan, Mythili. (2009). Components of executive control with advantages for bilingual children in two cultures. *Cognition, 112*(3), 494–500. doi:10.1016/j.cognition.2009.06.014

Bianchi, Suzanne M. and Milkie, Melissa A. (2010). Work and family research in the first decade of the 21st century. *Journal of Marriage and Family, 72*(3), 705–725. doi:10.1111/j.1741-3737.2010.00726.x

Biblarz, Timothy J. and Savci, Evren. (2010). Lesbian, gay, bisexual, and transgender families. *Journal of Marriage and Family, 72*(3), 480–497. doi:10.1111/j.1741-3737.2010.00714.x

Biblarz, Timothy J. and Stacey, Judith. (2010). How does the gender of parents matter? *Journal of Marriage and Family, 72*(1), 3–22. doi:10.1111/j.1741-3737.2009.00678.x

Biehl, Michael C.; Natsuaki, Misaki N. and Ge, Xiaojia. (2007). The influence of pubertal timing on alcohol use and heavy drinking trajectories. *Journal of Youth and Adolescence, 36*(2), 153–167. doi:10.1007/s10964-006-9120-z

Bielak, Allison A. M.; Anstey, Kaarin J.; Christensen, Helen and Windsor, Tim D. (2012). Activity engagement is related to level, but not change in cognitive ability across adulthood. *Psychology and Aging, 27*(1), 219–228. doi:10.1037/a0024667

Bienvenu, Thierry. (2005). Rett syndrome. In Merlin G. Butler and F. John Meaney (Eds.), *Genetics of developmental disabilities* (pp. 477–519). Boca Raton, FL: Taylor & Francis.

Bilali , Merim; McLeod, Peter and Gobet, Fernand. (2009). Specialization effect and its influence on memory and problem solving in expert chess players. *Cognitive Science, 33*(6), 1117–1143. doi:10.1111/j.1551-6709.2009.01030.x

Billings, J. Andrew. (2011). Double effect: A useful rule that alone cannot justify hastening death. *Journal of Medical Ethics, 37,* 437–440. doi:10.1136/jme.2010.041160

Birch, Susan A. J. and Bloom, Paul. (2003). Children are cursed: An asymmetric bias in mental-state attribution. *Psychological Science, 14*(3), 283–286. doi:10.1111/1467-9280.03436

Bird, Chloe E.; Seeman, Teresa; Escarce, José J.; Basurto-Dávila, Ricardo; Finch, Brian K.; Dubowitz, Tamara, . . . Lurie, Nicole. (2010). Neighbourhood socioeconomic status and biological 'wear and tear' in a nationally representative sample of US adults. *Journal of Epidemiology and Community Health, 64,* 860–865. doi:10.1136/jech.2008.084814

Birditt, Kira S.; Miller, Laura M.; Fingerman, Karen L. and Lefkowitz, Eva S. (2009). Tensions in the parent and adult child relationship: Links to solidarity and ambivalence. *Psychology and Aging, 24*(2), 287–295. doi:10.1037/a0015196

Birdsong, David. (2006). Age and second language acquisition and processing: A selective overview. *Language Learning, 56*(Suppl. 1), 9–49. doi:10.1111/j.1467-9922.2006.00353.x

Biro, Frank M.; McMahon, Robert P.; Striegel-Moore, Ruth; Crawford, Patricia B.; Obarzanek, Eva; Morrison, John A., . . . Falkner, Frank. (2001). Impact of timing of pubertal maturation on growth in black and white female adolescents: The National Heart, Lung, and Blood Institute Growth and Health Study. *Journal of Pediatrics, 138*(5), 636–643. doi:10.1067/mpd.2001.114476

Bisiacchi, Patrizia Silvia; Mento, Giovanni and Suppiej, Agnese. (2009). Cortical auditory processing in preterm newborns: An ERP study. *Biological Psychology, 82*(2), 176–185. doi:10.1016/j.biopsycho.2009.07.005

Bitensky, Susan H. (2006). Corporal punishment of children: A human rights violation. Boston, MA: Brill.

Bjelakovic, Goran; Nikolova, Dimitrinka and Gluud, Christian. (2012). Antioxidant supplements: An evidence-based approach to health benefits and risks. In Sharmila Shankar and Rakesh K. Srivastava (Eds.), *Nutrition, diet and cancer* (pp. 557–561). Netherlands: Springer. doi:10.1007/978-94-007-2923-0_22

Bjorklund, David F.; Dukes, Charles and Brown, Rhonda Douglas. (2009). The development of memory strategies. In Mary L. Courage and Nelson Cowan (Eds.), *The development of memory in infancy and childhood* (2nd ed., pp. 145–175). New York, NY: Psychology Press.

Black, Dennis M.; Bauer, Douglas C.; Schwartz, Ann V.; Cummings, Steven R. and Rosen, Clifford J. (2012). Continuing bisphosphonate treatment for osteoporosis — for whom and for how long? *New England Journal of Medicine, 366,* 2051–2053. doi:10.1056/NEJMp1202623

Blackwell, Lisa S.; Trzesniewski, Kali H. and Dweck, Carol Sorich. (2007). Implicit theories of intelligence predict achievement across an adolescent transition: A longitudinal study and an intervention. *Child Development, 78*(1), 246–263. doi:10.1111/j.1467-8624.2007.00995.x

Blair, Clancy and Dennis, Tracy. (2010). An optimal balance: The integration of emotion and cognition in context. In Susan D. Calkins and Martha Ann Bell (Eds.), *Child development at the intersection of emotion and cognition* (pp. 17–36). Washington, DC: American Psychological Association. doi:10.1037/12059-011

Blalock, Garrick; Kadiyali, Vrinda and Simon, Daniel H. (2009). Driving fatalities after 9/11: A hidden cost of terrorism. *Applied Economics, 41*(14), 1717–1729. doi:10.1080/00036840601069757

Blanchard-Fields, Fredda. (2007). Everyday problem solving and emotion: An adult developmental perspective. *Current Directions in Psychological Science, 16*(1), 26–31. doi:10.1111/j.1467-8721.2007.00469.x

Blandon, Alysia Y.; Calkins, Susan D. and Keane, Susan P. (2010). Predicting emotional and social competence during early childhood from toddler risk and maternal behavior. *Development and Psychopathology, 22*(1), 119–132. doi:10.1017/S0954579409990307

Blas, Erik and Kurup, Anand Sivasankara (Eds.). (2010). Equity, social determinants, and public health programmes. Geneva, Switzerland: World Health Organization.

Blekesaune, Morten. (2008). Partnership transitions and mental distress: Investigating temporal order. *Journal of Marriage and Family, 70*(4), 879–890. doi:10.1111/j.1741-3737.2008.00533.x

Bleske-Rechek, April; Somers, Erin; Micke, Cierra; Erickson, Leah; Matteson, Lindsay; Stocco, Corey, . . . Ritchie, Laura. (2012). Benefit or burden? Attraction in cross-sex friendship. *Journal of Social and Personal Relationships, 29*(5), 569–596. doi:10.1177/0265407512443611

Bliss, Catherine. (2012). Race decoded: The genomic fight for social justice. Stanford, CA: Stanford University Press.

Bloom, Barbara; Cohen, Robin A. and Freeman, Gulnur. (2009). Summary health statistics for U.S. children: National Health Interview Survey, 2008. Hyattsville, MD: National Center for Health Statistics, U.S. *Department of Health and Human Services, 10,* No. 244. (PHS) 2010–1572.

Bloom, David E. (2011). 7 billion and counting. *Science, 333*(6042), 562–569. doi:10.1126/science.1209290

Blum, Deborah. (2002). Love at Goon Park: Harry Harlow and the science of affection. Cambridge, MA: Perseus.

Blurton-Jones, Nicholas G. (1976). Rough-and-tumble play among nursery school children. In Jerome S. Bruner, Alison Jolly and Kathy Sylva (Eds.), *Play: Its role in development and evolution* (pp. 352–363). New York, NY: Basic Books.

Boals, Adriel; Hayslip, Bert; Knowles, Laura R. and Banks, Jonathan B. (2012). Perceiving a negative event as central to one's identity partially mediates age differences in posttraumatic stress disorder symptoms. *Journal of Aging and Health, 24*(3), 459–474. doi:10.1177/0898264311425089

Bodrova, Elena and Leong, Deborah J. (2005). High quality preschool programs: What would Vygotsky say? *Early Education and Development, 16*(4), 435–444. doi:10.1207/s15566935eed1604_4

Boehnke, Klaus. (2008). Peer pressure: a cause of scholastic underachievement? A cross-cultural study of mathematical achievement among German, Canadian, and Israeli middle school students. *Social Psychology of Education, 11*(2), 149–160. doi:10.1007/s11218-007-9041-z

Boerner, Kathrin; Schulz, Richard and Horowitz, Amy. (2004). Positive aspects of caregiving and adaptation to bereavement. *Psychology and Aging, 19*(4), 668–675. doi:10.1037/0882-7974.19.4.668

Boerner, Kathrin; Wortman, Camille B. and Bonanno, George A. (2005). Resilient or at risk? A 4-year study of older adults who initially showed high or low distress following conjugal loss. *Journals of Gerontology: Series B: Psychological Sciences and Social Sciences, 60*(2), 67–73. doi:10.1093/geronb/60.2.P67

Bögels, Susan M.; Knappe, Susanne and Clark, Lee Anna. (2013). Adult separation anxiety disorder in DSM-5. *Clinical Psychology Review, 33*(5), 663–674. doi:10.1016/j.cpr.2013.03.006

Bogle, Kathleen A. (2008). Hooking up: Sex, dating, and relationships on campus. New York, NY: New York University Press.

Bojczyk, Kathryn E.; Lehan, Tara J.; McWey, Lenore M.; Melson, Gail F. and Kaufman, Debra R. (2011). Mothers' and their adult daughters' perceptions of their relationship. *Journal of Family Issues, 32*(4), 452–481. doi:10.1177/0192513x10384073

Bollyky, Thomas J. (2012). Developing symptoms. *Foreign Affairs, 91*(3), 134–144.

Bonanno, George A. and Lilienfeld, Scott O. (2008). Let's be realistic: When grief counseling is effective and when it's not. *Professional Psychology: Research and Practice, 39*(3), 377–378. doi:10.1037/0735-7028.39.3.377

Bonanno, Rina A. and Hymel, Shelley. (2013). Cyber bullying and internalizing difficulties: Above and beyond the impact of traditional forms of bullying. *Journal of Youth and Adolescence, 42*(5), 685–697. doi:10.1007/s10964-013-9937-1

Bondi, Mark W.; Salmon, David P. and Kaszniak, Alfred W. (2009). The neuropsychology of dementia. In Igor Grant and Kenneth M. Adams (Eds.), *Neuropsychological assessment of neuropsychiatric and neuromedical disorders* (3rd ed., pp. 159–198). New York, NY: Oxford University Press.

Boon, Helen J.; Cottrell, Alison; King, David; Stevenson, Robert B. and Millar, Joanne. (2012). Bronfenbrenner's bioecological theory for modelling community resilience to natural disasters. *Natural Hazards, 60*(2), 381–408. doi:10.1007/s11069-011-0021-4

Booth, James R. (2007). Brain bases of learning and development of language and reading. In Donna Coch, Kurt W. Fischer and Geraldine Dawson (Eds.), *Human behavior, learning, and the developing brain: Typical development* (pp. 279–300). New York, NY: Guilford Press.

Borgens, Richard Ben and Liu-Snyder, Peishan. (2012). Understanding secondary injury. *The Quarterly Review of Biology, 87*(2), 89–127. doi:10.1086/665457

Borke, Jörn; Lamm, Bettina; Eickhorst, Andreas and Keller, Heidi. (2007). Father-infant interaction, paternal ideas about early child care, and their consequences for the development of children's self-recognition. *Journal of Genetic Psychology, 168*(4), 365–379. doi:10.3200/GNTP.168.4.365–380

Borkowski, John G.; Farris, Jaelyn Renee; Whitman, Thomas L.; Carothers, Shannon S.; Weed, Keri and Keogh, Deborah A. (Eds.). (2007). *Risk and resilience: Adolescent mothers and their children grow up.* Mahwah, NJ: Lawrence Erlbaum Associates.

Bornstein, Marc H.; Arterberry, Martha E. and Mash, Clay. (2005). Perceptual development. In Marc H. Bornstein and Michael E. Lamb (Eds.), *Developmental science: An advanced textbook* (5th ed., pp. 283–325). Mahwah, NJ: Lawrence Erlbaum Associates.

Bornstein, Marc H. and Colombo, John. (2012). Infant cognitive functioning and mental development. In Sabina Pauen (Ed.), Early childhood development and later outcome. New York, NY: Cambridge University Press.

Bornstein, Marc H. and Cote, Linda R. (2007). Knowledge of child development and family interactions among immigrants to America: Perspectives from developmental science. In Jennifer E. Lansford, Kirby Deater-Deckard and Marc H. Bornstein (Eds.), *Immigrant families in contemporary society* (pp. 121–136). New York, NY: Guilford Press.

Bornstein, Marc H.; Hahn, Chun-Shin and Wolke, Dieter. (2013). System and cascades in cognitive development and academic achievement. *Child Development, 84*(1), 154–162. doi:10.1111/j.1467-8624.2012.01849.x

Bornstein, Marc H.; Mortimer, Jeylan T.; Lutfey, Karen and Bradley, Robert. (2011). Theories and processes in life-span socialization. In Karen Fingerman, Cynthia Berg, Jacqui Smith and Toni Antonucci (Eds.), *Handbook of life-span development* (pp. 27–56). New York, NY: Springer.

Borrelli, Belinda; McQuaid, Elizabeth L.; Novak, Scott P.; Hammond, S. Katharine and Becker, Bruce. (2010). Motivating Latino caregivers of children with asthma to quit smoking: A randomized trial. *Journal of Consulting and Clinical Psychology, 78*(1), 34–43. doi:10.1037/a0016932

Bors, Philip; Dessauer, Mark; Bell, Rich; Wilkerson, Risa; Lee, Joanne and Strunk, Sarah L. (2009). The active living by design national program: Community initiatives and lessons learned. *American Journal of Preventive Medicine, 37*(Suppl. 2), S313-S321. doi:10.1016/j.amepre.2009.09.027

Boseovski, Janet J. (2010). Evidence for "rose-colored glasses": An examination of the positivity bias in young children's personality judgments. *Child Development Perspectives, 4*(3), 212–218. doi:10.1111/j.1750-8606.2010.00149.x

Bossé, Yohan and Hudson, Thomas J. (2007). Toward a comprehensive set of asthma susceptibility genes. *Annual Review of Medicine, 58,* 171–184. doi:10.1146/annurev.med.58.071105.111738

Bosworth, Hayden B. and Ayotte, Brian J. (2009). The role of cognitive and social function in an applied setting: Medication adherence as an example. In Hayden B. Bosworth and Christopher Hertzog (Eds.), *Aging and cognition: Research methodologies and empirical advances* (pp. 219–239). Washington, DC: American Psychological Association. doi:10.1037/11882-011

Bosworth, Hayden B. and Hertzog, Christopher. (2009). Aging and cognition: Research methodologies and empirical advances. Washington, DC: American Psychological Association. doi:10.1037/11882-000

Bourque, Francois; van der Ven, Elsje and Malla, Ashok (2011). A meta-analysis of the risk for psychotic disorders among first- and second-generation immigrants. *Psychological*

Medicine, 41(5), 897–910. doi:10.1017/S0033291710001406

Bowen, Mary Elizabeth and González, Hector M. (2010). Childhood socioeconomic position and disability in later life: Results of the health and retirement study. *American Journal of Public Health, 100*(S1), S197-S203. doi:10.2105/ajph.2009.160986

Bowen, William G.; Chingos, Matthew M.; McPherson, Michael S. and Tobin, Eugene M. (2009). Crossing the finish line: Completing college at America's public universities. Princeton, NJ: Princeton University Press.

Bower, Bruce. (2007). Net heads: Huge numbers of brain cells may navigate small worlds. *Science News, 171*(7), 104–106. doi:10.1002/scin.2007.5591710709

Bowers, Edmond P. and Lerner, Richard M. (2013). Familial and nonfamilial relationships as ecological sources of health and positive development across the life span: A view of the issues. *Research in Human Development, 10*(2), 111–115. doi:10.1080/15427609.2013.786535

Bowers, Jeffrey S.; Mattys, Sven L. and Gage, Suzanne H. (2009). Preserved implicit knowledge of a forgotten childhood language. *Psychological Science, 20*(9), 1064–1069. doi:10.1111/j.1467-9280.2009.02407.x

Bowes, Lucy; Maughan, Barbara; Caspi, Avshalom; Moffitt, Terrie E. and Arseneault, Louise. (2010). Families promote emotional and behavioural resilience to bullying: Evidence of an environmental effect. *Journal of Child Psychology and Psychiatry, 51*(7), 809–817. doi:10.1111/j.1469-7610.2010.02216.x

Boyce, W. Thomas; Essex, Marilyn J.; Alkon, Abbey; Goldsmith, H. Hill; Kraemer, Helena C. and Kupfer, David J. (2006). Early father involvement moderates biobehavioral susceptibility to mental health problems in middle childhood. *Journal of the American Academy of Child and Adolescent Psychiatry, 45*(12), 1510–1520. doi:10.1097/01.chi.0000237706.50884.8b

Boyd, Cynthia M.; Darer, Jonathan; Boult, Chad; Fried, Linda P.; Boult, Lisa and Wu, Albert W. (2005). Clinical practice guidelines and quality of care for older patients with multiple comorbid diseases: Implications for pay for performance. *Journal of the American Medical Association, 294*(6), 716–724. doi:10.1001/jama.294.6.716

Boyd, William L. (2007). The politics of privatization in American education. *Educational Policy, 21*(1), 7–14. doi:10.1177/0895904806297728

Boyraz, Guler; Horne, Sharon G. and Sayger, Thomas V. (2012). Finding meaning in loss: The mediating role of social support between personality and two construals of meaning. *Death Studies, 36*(6), 519–540. doi:10.1080/07481187.2011.553331

Boywitt, C. Dennis; Kuhlmann, Beatrice G. and Meiser, Thorsten. (2012). The role of source memory in older adults' recollective experience. *Psychology and Aging, 27*(2), 484–497. doi:10.1037/a0024729

Bozik, Mary. (2002). The college student as learner: Insight gained through metaphor analysis. *College Student Journal, 36*(1), 142–151.

Bracken, Bruce A. and Crawford, Elizabeth. (2010). Basic concepts in early childhood educational standards: A 50-state review. *Early Childhood Education Journal, 37*(5), 421–430. doi:10.1007/s10643-009-0363-7

Brame, Robert; Turner, Michael G.; Paternoster, Raymond and Bushway, Shawn D. (2012). Cumulative prevalence of arrest from ages 8 to 23 in a national sample. *Pediatrics, 129*(1), 21–27. doi:10.1542/peds.2010-3710

Branca, Francesco; Nikogosian, Haik and Lobstein, Tim (Eds.). (2007). The challenge of obesity in the WHO European Region and the strategies for response. Copenhagen, Denmark: WHO Regional Office for Europe.

Branch, John. (2011, December 5). Derek Boogaard: A brain 'going bad'. The New York Times, p. B13.

Brandt, Hella E.; Ooms, Marcel E.; Ribbe, Miel W.; van der Wal, Gerrit and Deliens, Luc. (2006). Predicted survival vs. actual survival in terminally ill noncancer patients in Dutch nursing homes. *Journal of Pain and Symptom Management, 32*(6), 560–566. doi:10.1016/j.jpainsymman.2006.06.006

Brandt, Martina and Deindl, Christian. (2013). Intergenerational transfers to adult children in Europe: Do social policies matter? *Journal of Marriage and Family, 75*(1), 235–251. doi:10.1111/j.1741-3737.2012.01028.x

Brandt, Martina; Deindl, Christian and Hank, Karsten. (2012). Tracing the origins of successful aging: The role of childhood conditions and social inequality in explaining later life health. *Social Science & Medicine, 74*(9), 1418–1425. doi:10.1016/j.socscimed.2012.01.004

Brassen, Stefanie; Gamer, Matthias; Peters, Jan; Gluth, Sebastian and Büchel, Christian. (2012). Don't look back in anger! Responsiveness to missed chances in successful and nonsuccessful aging. *Science, 336*(6081), 612–614. doi:10.1126/science.1217516

Braun, Joe M and Hauser, Russ. (2011). Bisphenol A and children's health. *Current Opinion in Pediatrics, 23*(2), 233–239. doi:10.1097/MOP.0b013e3283445675

Braun, Michael T. (2013). Obstacles to social networking website use among older adults. *Computers in Human Behavior, 29*(3), 673–680. doi:10.1016/j.chb.2012.12.004

Bravo, Irene M. and Roca, Carmen S. (2013). Assessing somatoform disorders with the Hispanic client. In Lorraine T. Benuto (Ed.), Guide to psychological assessment with Hispanics (pp. 293–307). New York, NY: Springer. doi:10.1007/978-1-4614-4412-1_19

Brazelton, T. Berry and Sparrow, Joshua D. (2006). Touchpoints, birth to 3: Your child's emotional and behavioral development (2nd ed.). Cambridge, MA: Da Capo Press.

Breaugh, James and Frye, N. Kathleen. (2008). Work-family conflict: The importance of family-friendly employment practices and family-supportive supervisors. *Journal of Business and Psychology, 22*(4), 345–353. doi:10.1007/s10869-008-9081-1

Breivik, Gunnar. (2010). Trends in adventure sports in a post-modern society. *Sport in Society: Cultures, Commerce, Media, Politics, 13*(2), 260–273. doi:10.1080/17430430903522970

Bremner, J. Gavin and Wachs, Theodore D. (Eds.). (2010). The Wiley-Blackwell handbook of infant development (Vol. 1–2). Malden, MA: Wiley-Blackwell.

Brendgen, Mara; Lamarche, Véronique; Wanner, Brigitte and Vitaro, Frank. (2010). Links between friendship relations and early adolescents' trajectories of depressed mood. *Developmental Psychology, 46*(2), 491–501. doi:10.1037/a0017413

Brennan, Arthur; Ayers, Susan; Ahmed, Hafez and Marshall-Lucette, Sylvie. (2007). A critical review of the Couvade syndrome: The pregnant male. *Journal of Reproductive and Infant Psychology, 25*(3), 173–189. doi:10.1080/02646830701467207

Breslow, Lori; Pritchard, David E.; Deboer, Jennifer; Stump, Glenda S.; Ho, Andrew D. and Seaton, Daniel T. (2013). Studying learning in the worldwide classroom research into edx's first MOOC. Research and Practice in Assessment, 8, 13–25.

Bretherton, Inge. (2010). Fathers in attachment theory and research: A review. *Early Child Development and Care, 180*(1–2), 9–23. doi:10.1080/03004430903414661

Brickhouse, Tegwyn H.; Rozier, R. Gary and Slade, Gary D. (2008). Effects of enrollment in Medicaid versus the State Children's Health Insurance Program on kindergarten children's untreated dental caries. *American Journal of Public Health, 98*(5), 876–881. doi:10.2105/ajph.2007.111468

Britto, Pia Rebello; Boller, Kimberley and Yoshikawa, Hirokazu. (2011). Quality of early childhood development programs in global contexts: Rationale for investment, conceptual framework and implications for equity. *Social Policy Report, 25*(2), 1–30.

Brody, Gene H.; Beach, Steven R. H.; Philibert, Robert A.; Chen, Yi-fu and Murry, Velma McBride. (2009). Prevention effects moderate the association of 5-HTTLPR and youth risk behavior initiation: Gene × environment hypotheses tested via a randomized prevention design. *Child Development, 80*(3), 645–661. doi:10.1111/j.1467-8624.2009.01288.x

Bronfenbrenner, Urie and Morris, Pamela A. (2006). The bioecological model of human development. In William Damon and Richard M. Lerner (Eds.), *Handbook of child psychology* (6th ed., Vol. 1, pp. 793–828). Hoboken, NJ: Wiley.

Bronte-Tinkew, Jacinta; Moore, Kristin A.; Matthews, Gregory and Carrano, Jennifer. (2007). Symptoms of major depression in a sample of fathers of infants: Sociodemographic correlates and links to father involvement. *Journal of Family Issues,* 28(1), 61–99. doi:10.1177/0192513X06293609

Brook, Judith S.; Brook, David W.; Zhang, Chenshu; Seltzer, Nathan and Finch, Stephen J. (2013). Adolescent ADHD and adult physical and mental health, work performance, and financial stress. *Pediatrics, 131*(1), 5–13. doi:10.1542/peds.2012-1725

Brooker, Robert J. (2009). Genetics: Analysis & principles (3rd ed.). New York, NY: McGraw-Hill.

Brown, B. Bradford. (2004). Adolescents' relationships with peers. In Richard M. Lerner and Laurence Steinberg (Eds.), *Handbook of adolescent psychology* (2nd ed., pp. 363–394). Hoboken, NJ: Wiley.

Brown, B. Bradford and Bakken, Jeremy P. (2011). Parenting and peer relationships: Reinvigorating research on family–peer linkages in adolescence. *Journal of Research on Adolescence, 21*(1), 153–165. doi:10.1111/j.1532-7795.2010 .00720.x

Brown, Christia Spears; Alabi, Basirat O.; Huynh, Virginia W. and Masten, Carrie L. (2011). Ethnicity and gender in late childhood and early adolescence: Group identity and awareness of bias. *Developmental Psychology, 47*(2), 463–471. doi:10.1037/a0021819

Brown, Edna; Birditt, Kira S.; Huff, Scott C. and Edwards, Lindsay L. (2012). Marital dissolution and psychological well being: Race and gender differences in the moderating role of marital relationship quality. *Research in Human Development, 9*(2), 145–164. doi:10.1080/15427609.2012 .681202

Brown, Susan L. (2010). Marriage and child well-being: Research and policy perspectives. *Journal of Marriage and Family, 72*(5), 1059–1077. doi:10.1111/j.1741-3737.2010.00750.x

Brown, Susan L. and Kawamura, Sayaka. (2010). Relationship quality among cohabitors and marrieds in older adulthood. *Social Science Research, 39*(5), 777–786. doi:10.1016/j.ssresearch .2010.04.010

Brownell, Celia A.; Svetlova, Margarita; Anderson, Ranita; Nichols, Sara R. and Drummond, Jesse. (2013). Socialization of early prosocial behavior: Parents' talk about emotions is associated with sharing and helping in toddlers. *Infancy, 18*(1), 91–119. doi:10.1111/j.1532-7078 .2012.00125.x

Bruce, Susan and Muhammad, Zayyad. (2009). The development of object permanence in children with intellectual disability, physical disability, autism, and blindness. *International Journal of Disability, Development and Education, 56*(3), 229–246. doi:10.1080/10349120903102213

Bryant, Alyssa N. and Astin, Helen S. (2008). The correlates of spiritual struggle during the college years. *Journal of Higher Education, 79*(1), 1–27. doi:10.1353/jhe.2008.0000

Bryant, Gregory A. and Barrett, H. Clark. (2007). Recognizing intentions in infant-directed speech: Evidence for universals. *Psychological Science, 18*(8), 746–751. doi:10.1111/j .1467-9280.2007.01970.x

Brymer, Eric and Schweitzer, Robert. (2013). Extreme sports are good for your health: A phenomenological understanding of fear and anxiety in extreme sport. *Journal of Health Psychology, 18*(4), 477–487. doi:10.1177/1359105312446770

Buckley, Maureen and Saarni, Carolyn. (2009). Emotion regulation: Implications for positive youth development. In Rich Gilman, Eugene Scott Huebner and Michael J. Furlong (Eds.), *Handbook of positive psychology in schools* (pp. 107–118). New York, NY: Routledge.

Bucx, Freek; Raaijmakers, Quinten and van Wel, Frits. (2010). Life course stage in young adulthood and intergenerational congruence in family attitudes. *Journal of Marriage and Family, 72*(1), 117–134. doi:10.1111/j.1741-3737 .2009.00687.x

Bucx, Freek; van Wel, Frits and Knijn, Trudie. (2012). Life course status and exchanges of support between young adults and parents. *Journal of Marriage and Family, 74*(1), 101–115. doi:10.1111/j.1741-3737.2011.00883.x

Buettner, Dan. (2012). The blue zones: Lessons for living longer from the people who've lived the longest. Washington, DC: National Geographic.

Bugental, Daphne Blunt and Grusec, Joan E. (2006). Socialization processess. In William Damon and Richard M. Lerner (Eds.), Handbook of child psychology (6th cd., Vol. 3, pp. 366–428). Hoboken, NJ: Wiley.

Bugental, Daphne Blunt and Hehman, Jessica A. (2007). Ageism: A review of research and policy implications. *Social Issues and Policy Review, 1*(1), 173–216. doi:10.1111/j.1751-2409 .2007.00007.x

Buhling, Kai J.; von Studnitz, Friederike S.G.; Jantke, Andreas; Eulenburg, Christine and Mueck, Alfred O. (2012). Use of hormone therapy by female gynecologists and female partners of male gynecologists in Germany 8 years after the Women's Health Initiative study: Results of a survey. *Menopause, 19*(10), 1088–1091. doi:10.1097/gme.0b013e318250bfda

Buhrmester, Michael D.; Blanton, Hart and Swann Jr., William B. (2011). Implicit self-esteem: Nature, measurement, and a new way forward. *Journal of Personality and Social Psychology, 100*(2), 365–385. doi:10.1037/a0021341

Buiting, Hilde; van Delden, Johannes; Onwuteaka-Philpsen, Bregje; Rietjens, Judith; Rurup, Mette; van Tol, Donald, . . . van der Heide, Agnes. (2009). Reporting of euthanasia and physician-assisted suicide in the Netherlands: Descriptive study. *BMC Medical Ethics, 10*(18). doi:10.1186/1472-6939-10-18

Bulik, Cynthia M.; Thornton, Laura; Pinheiro, Andréa Poyastro; Plotnicov, Katherine; Klump, Kelly L.; Brandt, Harry, . . . Kaye, Walter H. (2008). Suicide attempts in anorexia nervosa. *Psychosomatic Medicine, 70*(3), 378–383. doi:10.1097/PSY.0b013e3181646765

Bulpitt, Christopher J.; Beckett, Nigel; Peters, Ruth; Staessen, Jan A.; Wang, Ji-Guang; Comsa, Marius, . . . Rajkumar, Chakravarthi. (2013). Does white coat hypertension require treatment over age 80? Results of the hypertension in the very elderly trial ambulatory blood pressure side project. *Hypertension, 61,* 89–94. doi:10.1161/ HYPERTENSIONAHA.112.191791

Bureau of Labor Statistics. (2011). The employment situation – November 2011. Washington, DC: U.S. Department of Labor.

Bureau of Labor Statistics. (2012, December 13). The employment situation—September 2012. Washington, DC: U.S. Department of Labor, 2012.

Bureau of Labor Statistics. (2012a, February 22). Volunteering in the United States, 2011. (USDL-12-0329). Washington, DC: U.S. Department of Labor.

Bureau of Labor Statistics. (2013, April 30). Employment characteristics of families, 2012. Washington, DC: U.S. Department of Labor.

Bureau of Labor Statistics. (2014, February 25). Volunteering in The United States — 2013. Washington, DC: U.S. Department of Labor. USDL-14-0314.

Burke, Laurie A.; Neimeyer, Robert A.; McDevitt-Murphy, Meghan E.; Ippolito, Maria R. and Roberts, J. Matthew. (2011). Faith in the wake of homicide: Religious coping and bereavement distress in an African American sample. *International Journal for the Psychology of Religion, 21*(4), 289–307. doi:10.1080/10508619 .2011.607416

Burke-Miller, Jane; Razzano, Lisa A.; Grey, Dennis D.; Blyler, Crystal R. and Cook, Judith A. (2012). Supported employment outcomes for transition age youth and young adults. *Psychiatric Rehabilitation Journal, 35*(3), 171–179. doi:10.2975/35.3.2012.171.179

Burpo, Todd and Vincent, Lynn. (2011). Heaven is for real: A little boy's astounding story of his trip to heaven and back. Nashville, TN: Thomas Nelson.

Burri, Andrea and Spector, Timothy. (2011). Recent and lifelong sexual dysfunction in a female UK population sample: Prevalence and risk factors. *Journal of Sexual Medicine, 8*(9), 2420–2430. doi:10.1111/j.1743-6109.2011.02341.x

Burstein, David D. (2013). Fast future: How the millennial generation is shaping our world. Boston, MA: Beacon Press.

Burt, S. Alexandra. (2009). Rethinking environmental contributions to child and adolescent psychopathology: A meta-analysis of shared environmental influences. *Psychological Bulletin, 135*(4), 608–637. doi:10.1037/a0015702

Burt, S. Alexandra; McGue, Matt and Iacono, William G. (2009). Nonshared environmental mediation of the association between deviant peer affiliation and adolescent externalizing behaviors over time: Results from a cross-lagged monozygotic twin differences design. *Developmental Psychology, 45*(6), 1752–1760. doi:10.1037/a0016687

Buss, David M. (2003). The evolution of desire: Strategies of human mating. New York, NY: Basic Books.

Butler, Robert N.; Lewis, Myrna I. and Sunderland, Trey. (1998). *Aging and mental health: Positive psychosocial and biomedical approaches* (5th ed.). Boston, MA: Allyn & Bacon.

Buttelmann, David; Zmyj, Norbert; Daum, Moritz and Carpenter, Malinda (2013). Selective imitation of in-group over out-group members in 14-month-old infants. *Child Development, 84*(2), 22–428. doi:10.1111/j.1467-8624.2012 .01860.x

Butterworth, Brian; Varma, Sashank and Laurillard, Diana. (2011). Dyscalculia: From brain to education. *Science, 332*(6033), 1049–1053. doi:10.1126/science.1201536

Buunk, Abraham P.; Park, Justin H. and Dubbs, Shelli L. (2008). Parent-offspring conflict in mate preferences. *Review of General Psychology, 12*(1), 47–62. doi:10.1037 /1089-2680.12.1.47

Byers, Amy L.; Levy, Becca R.; Allore, Heather G.; Bruce, Martha L. and Kasl, Stanislav V. (2008). When parents matter to their adult children: Filial reliance associated with parents' depressive symptoms. *The Journals of Gerontology Series B: Psychological Sciences and Social Sciences, 63*(1), P33–40. doi:10.1093 /geronb/63.1.P33

Byers-Heinlein, Krista; Burns, Tracey C. and Werker, Janet F. (2010). The roots of bilingualism in newborns. *Psychological Science, 21*(3), 343–348. doi:10.1177/0956797609360758

Byng-Hall, John. (2008). The significance of children fulfilling parental roles: Implications for family therapy. *Journal of Family Therapy, 30*(2), 147–162. doi:10.1111/j.1467-6427.2008.00423.x

Cacciatore, Joanne. (2009). Appropriate bereavement practice after the death of a Native American child. *Families in Society: The Journal of Contemporary Social Services, 90*(1), 46–50. doi:10.1606/1044-3894.3844

Cain, Daphne S. and Combs-Orme, Terri. (2005). Family structure effects on parenting stress and practices in the African American family. *Journal of Sociology & Social Welfare, 32*(2), 19–40.

Calkins, Susan D. and Keane, Susan P. (2009). Developmental origins of early antisocial behavior. *Development and Psychopathology, 21*(4), 1095–1109. doi:10.1017/S095457940999006x

Callaghan, Tara. (2013). Symbols and symbolic thought. In Philip David Zelazo (Ed.), The Oxford handbook of developmental psychology (Vol. 1). New York, NY: Oxford University Press.

Callaghan, Tara; Rochat, Philippe; Lillard, Angeline; Claux, Mary Louise; Odden, Hal; Itakura, Shoji, . . . Singh, Saraswati. (2005). Synchrony in the onset of mental-state reasoning: Evidence from five cultures. *Psychological Science, 16*(5), 378–384. doi:10.1111/j.0956-7976.2005.01544.x

Calvin, Catherine M.; Batty, G. David; Lowe, Gordon D. O. and Deary, Ian J. (2011). Childhood intelligence and midlife inflammatory and hemostatic biomarkers: The National Child Development Study (1958) cohort.

Health Psychology, 30(6), 710–718. doi:10.1037 /a0023940

Cameron, Judy and Pierce, W. David. (2002). Rewards and intrinsic motivation: Resolving the controversy. Westport, CT: Bergin & Garvey.

Camhi, Sarah M.; Katzmarzyk, Peter T.; Broyles, Stephanie; Church, Timothy S.; Hankinson, Arlene L.; Carnethon, Mercedes R., . . . Lewis, Cora E. (2013). Association of metabolic risk with longitudinal physical activity and fitness: Coronary artery risk development in young adults (CARDIA). *Metabolic Syndrome and Related Disorders, 11*(3), 195–204. doi:10.1089/ met.2012.0120

Camilli, Gregory; Vargas, Sadako; Ryan, Sharon and Barnett, W. Steven. (2010). Meta-analysis of the effects of early education interventions on cognitive and social development. *Teachers College Record, 112*(3), 579–620.

Camos, Valérie and Barrouillet, Pierre. (2011). Developmental change in working memory strategies: From passive maintenance to active refreshing. *Developmental Psychology, 47*(3), 898–904. doi:10.1037/a0023193

Campbell, Frances A.; Pungello, Elizabeth P.; Miller-Johnson, Shari; Burchinal, Margaret and Ramey, Craig T. (2001). The development of cognitive and academic abilities: Growth curves from an early childhood educational experiment. *Developmental Psychology, 37*(2), 231–242. doi:10.1037/0012-1649.37.2.231

Camras, Linda A. and Shutter, Jennifer M. (2010). Emotional facial expressions in infancy. *Emotion Review, 2*(2), 120–129. doi:10.1177/ 1754073909352529

Canadian Psychological Association. (2000). Canadian code of ethics for psychologists (3rd ed.). Ottawa, Ontario, Canada.

Canagarajah, A. Suresh and Wurr, Adrian J. (2011). Multilingual Communication and Language Acquisition: New Research Directions. *The Reading Matrix, 11*(1), 1–15.

Cappell, Katherine A.; Gmeindl, Leon and Reuter-Lorenz, Patricia A. (2010). Age differences in prefontal recruitment during verbal working memory maintenance depend on memory load. *Cortex, 46*(4), 462–473. doi:10.1016/j .cortex.2009.11.009

Caravita, Simona C. S. and Cillessen, Antonius H. N. (2012). Agentic or communal? Associations between interpersonal goals, popularity, and bullying in middle childhood and early adolescence. *Social Development, 21*(2), 376–395. doi:10.1111/j.1467-9507.2011.00632.x

Caravita, Simona C. S.; Di Blasio, Paola and Salmivalli, Christina. (2010). Early adolescents' participation in bullying: Is ToM involved? *The Journal of Early Adolescence, 30*(1), 138–170. doi:10.1177/0272431609342983

Cardinal, Roger. (2001). The sense of time and place. In Jane Kallir and Roger Cardinal (Eds.), *Grandma Moses in the 21st century* (pp. 79–102). Alexandria, VA: Art Services International.

Carey, Nessa. (2012). The epigenetics revolution: How modern biology is rewriting our

understanding of genetics, disease, and inheritance. New York, NY: Columbia University Press.

Carey, Susan. (2010). Beyond fast mapping. *Language Learning and Development, 6*(3), 184–205. doi:10.1080/15475441.2010.484379

Carlson, Susan A.; Fulton, Janet E.; Lee, Sarah M.; Maynard, L. Michele; Brown, David R.; Kohl, Harold W., III and Dietz, William H. (2008). Physical education and academic achievement in elementary school: Data from the early childhood longitudinal study. *American Journal of Public Health, 98*(4), 721–727. doi:10.2105/ajph.2007.117176

Carpenter, Siri. (2012). Psychology's bold initiative. *Science, 335*(6076), 1558–1561. doi:10.1126/ science.335.6076.1558

Carr, Deborah. (2012). Death and dying in the contemporary United States: What are the psychological implications of anticipated death? *Social and Personality Psychology Compass, 6*(2), 184–195. doi:10.1111/j.1751-9004.2011.00416.x

Carskadon, Mary A. (2011). Sleep in adolescents: The perfect storm. *Pediatric Clinics of North America, 58*(3), 637–647. doi:10.1016/j .pcl.2011.03.003

Carstensen, Laura. (2011). A long bright future: Happiness, health, and financial security in an age of increased longevity. New York, NY: PublicAffairs.

Carstensen, Laura L. (1993). Motivation for social contact across the life span. In Janis E. Jacobs (Ed.), Developmental perspectives on motivation: Nebraska Symposium on Motivation (1992) (pp. 209–254). Lincoln, NE: University of Nebraska.

Carstensen, Laura L.; Mikels, Joseph A. and Mather, Mara. (2006). Aging and the intersection of cognition, motivation, and emotion. In James E. Birren and K. Warner Schaie (Eds.), *Handbook of the psychology of aging* (6th ed., pp. 343–362). San Diego, CA: Elsevier.

Case-Smith, Jane and Kuhaneck, Heather Miller. (2008). Play preferences of typically developing children and children with developmental delays between ages 3 and 7 years. *OTJR: Occupation, Participation and Health, 28*(1), 19–29. doi:10.3928/15394492-20080101-01

Casey, B. J. and Caudle, Kristina. (2013). The teenage brain: Self control. *Current Directions in Psychological Science, 22*(2), 82–87. doi:10.1177/0963721413480170

Casey, B. J.; Jones, Rebecca M. and Somerville, Leah H. (2011). Braking and accelerating of the adolescent brain. *Journal of Research on Adolescence, 21*(1), 21–33. doi:10.1111/j .1532-7795.2010.00712.x

Casey, Richard. (2008). The use of hormonal therapy in "andropause": The con side. *Canadian Urological Association Journal, 2*(1), 47–48.

Caspersen, Carl J.; Thomas, G. Darlene; Boseman, Letia A.; Beckles, Gloria L. A. and Albright, Ann L. (2012). Aging, diabetes, and the public health system in the United States. *American Journal of Public Health, 102*(8), 1482–1497. doi:10.2105/AJPH.2011.300616

Caspi, Avshalom; Moffitt, Terrie E.; Morgan, Julia; Rutter, Michael; Taylor, Alan; Arseneault, Louise, . . . Polo-Tomas, Monica. (2004). Maternal expressed emotion predicts children's antisocial behavior problems: Using monozygotic-twin differences to identify environmental effects on behavioral development. *Developmental Psychology, 40*(2), 149–161. doi:10.1037/0012-1649.40.2.149

Caspi, Avshalom and Shiner, Rebecca L. (2006). Personality development. In William Damon and Richard M. Lerner (Eds.), *Handbook of child psychology* (6th ed., Vol. 3, pp. 300–365). Hoboken, NJ: Wiley.

Cassia, Viola Macchi; Kuefner, Dana; Picozzi, Marta and Vescovo, Elena. (2009). Early experience predicts later plasticity for face processing: Evidence for the reactivation of dormant effects. *Psychological Science, 20*(7), 853–859. doi:10.1111/j.1467-9280.2009.02376.x

Castel, Alan D.; Rossi, Aimee Drolet and McGillivray, Shannon. (2012). Beliefs about the "hot hand" in basketball across the adult life span. *Psychology and Aging, 27*(3), 601–605. doi:10.1037/a0026991

Castle, David J. and Morgan, Vera. (2008). Epidemiology. In Kim T. Mueser and Dilip V. Jeste (Eds.), *Clinical handbook of schizophrenia* (pp. 14–24). New York, NY: Guilford Press.

Catani, Claudia; Gewirtz, Abigail H.; Wieling, Elizabeth; Schauer, Elizabeth; Elbert, Thomas and Neuner, Frank. (2010). Tsunami, war, and cumulative risk in the lives of Sri Lankan schoolchildren. *Child Development, 81*(4), 1176–1191. doi:10.1111/j.1467-8624.2010.01461.x

Cecil, Kim M.; Brubaker, Christopher J.; Adler, Caleb M.; Dietrich, Kim N.; Altaye, Mekibib; Egelhoff, John C., . . . Lanphear, Bruce P. (2008). Decreased brain volume in adults with childhood lead exposure. *PloS Medicine, 5*(5), 741–750. doi:10.1371/journal.pmed.0050112

Centers For Disease Control. (2012). Health, United States, 2012. 3, Table 67.

Centers for Disease Control and Prevention (Ed.). (2007). *Epidemiology and prevention of vaccine-preventable diseases* (10th ed.). Washington, DC: Department of Health & Human Services.

Centers for Disease Control and Prevention. (2012, August). Breastfeeding report card— United States, 2012. Atlanta, GA: National Center for Chronic Disease Prevention and Health Promotion Centers for Disease Control and Prevention.

Centers for Disease Control and Prevention. (2013, February). Understanding MMR Vaccine Safety. Retrieved from http://www.cdc.gov/vaccines/hcp/patient-ed/conversations/downloads/vacsafe-mmr-bw-office.pdf.

Centers for Medicare & Medicaid Services. (2013). Nursing home data compendium 2012. Baltimore, MD: United States Department of Health and Human Services.

Centre for Community Child Health and Telethon Institute for Child Health Research. (2009). A snapshot of early childhood development in Australia: Australian Early Development Index (AEDI) national report 2009. Canberra, Australia: Australian Government Department of Education. October 24.

Chaddock, Laura; Erickson, Kirk I.; Prakash, Ruchika Shaurya; VanPatter, Matt; Voss, Michelle W.; Pontifex, Matthew B., . . . Kramer, Arthur F. (2010). Basal ganglia volume is associated with aerobic fitness in preadolescent children. *Developmental Neuroscience, 32*(3), 249–256. doi:10.1159/000316648

Chae, David H.; Nuru-Jeter, Amani M. and Adler, Nancy E. (2012). Implicit racial bias as a moderator of the association between racial discrimination and hypertension: A study of midlife African American men. *Psychosomatic Medicine, 74*(9), 961–964. doi:10.1097/psy.0b013e3182733665

Chafen, Jennifer J. Schneider; Newberry, Sydne J.; Riedl, Marc A.; Bravata, Dena M.; Maglione, Margaret; Suttorp, Marika J., . . . Shekelle, Paul G. (2010). Diagnosing and managing common food allergies. *JAMA, 303*(18), 1848–1856. doi:10.1001/jama.2010.582

Chaignat, Evelyne; Yahya-Graison, Emilie Aït; Henrichsen, Charlotte N.; Chrast, Jacqueline; Schütz, Frédéric; Pradervand, Sylvain and Reymond, Alexandre. (2011). Copy number variation modifies expression time courses. *Genome Research, 21*, 106–113. doi:10.1101/gr.112748.110

Challenge Success. (2013). The advanced placement program: Living up to its promise? Stanford, CA: Challenge Success.

Chambers, Bette; Cheung, Alan C.; Slavin, Robert E.; Smith, Dewi and Laurenzano, Mary. (2010). *Effective early childhood education programs: A systematic review.* Baltimore, MD: Johns Hopkins University, Center for Research and Reform in Education.

Chan, Christian S. and Rhodes, Jean E. (2013). Religious coping, posttraumatic stress, psychological distress, and posttraumatic growth among female survivors four years after hurricane Katrina. *Journal of Traumatic Stress, 26*(2), 257–265. doi:10.1002/jts.21801

Chan, David W. and Zhao, Yongjun. (2010). The relationship between drawing skill and artistic creativity: Do age and artistic involvement make a difference? *Creativity Research Journal, 22*(1), 27–36. doi:10.1080/10400410903579528

Chan, Kitty S.; Kasper, Judith D.; Brandt, Jason and Pezzin, Liliana E. (2012). Measurement equivalence in ADL and IADL difficulty across international surveys of aging: findings from the HRS, SHARE, and ELSA. *The Journals Of Gerontology. Series B, Psychological Sciences And Social Sciences, 67*(1), 121–132. doi:10.1093/geronb/gbr133

Chan, Kit Yee; Wang, Wei; Wu, Jing Jing; Liu, Li; Theodoratou, Evropi; Car, Josip, . . . Rudan, Igor. (2013). Epidemiology of Alzheimer's disease and other forms of dementia in China, 1990—2010: A systematic review and analysis. *The Lancet, 381*(9882), 2016–2023. doi:10.1016/S0140-6736(13)60221-4

Chan, Tak Wing and Koo, Anita. (2011). Parenting style and youth outcomes in the UK. *European Sociological Review, 27*, 385–399. doi:10.1093/esr/jcq013

Chang, Esther S.; Greenberger, Ellen; Chen, Chuansheng; Heckhausen, Jutta and Farruggia, Susan P. (2010). Nonparental adults as social resources in the transition to adulthood. *Journal of Research on Adolescence, 20*(4), 1065–1082. doi:10.1111/j.1532-7795.2010.00662.x

Chao, Jian-Kang; Lin, Yen-Chin; Ma, Mi-Chia; Lai, Chin-Jen; Ku, Yan-Chiou; Kuo, Wu-Hsien and Chao, I. Chen. (2011). Relationship among sexual desire, sexual satisfaction, and quality of life in middle-aged and older adults. *Journal of Sex & Marital Therapy, 37*(5), 386–403. doi:10.1080/0092623x.2011.607051

Chao, Ruth K. (2001). Extending research on the consequences of parenting style for Chinese Americans and European Americans. *Child Development, 72*(6), 1832–1843. doi:10.1111/1467-8624.00381

Chao, Y. May; Pisetsky, Emily M.; Dierker, Lisa C.; Dohm, Faith-Anne; Rosselli, Francine; May, Alexis M. and Striegel-Moore, Ruth H. (2008). Ethnic differences in weight control practices among U.S. adolescents from 1995 to 2005. *International Journal of Eating Disorders, 41*(2), 124–133. doi:10.1002/eat.20479

Chaplin, Lan Nguyen and John, Deborah Roedder. (2007). Growing up in a material world: Age differences in materialism in children and adolescents. *Journal of Consumer Research, 34*(4), 480–493. doi:10.1086/518546

Chapple, Alison; Swift, Chris and Ziebland, Sue. (2011). The role of spirituality and religion for those bereaved due to a traumatic death. *Mortality, 16*(1), 1–19. doi:10.1080/13576275.2011.535998

Charles, Susan T. and Carstensen, Laura L. (2010). Social and emotional aging. *Annual Review of Psychology, 61*, 383–409. doi:10.1146/annurev.psych.093008.100448

Charlton, Samuel G. (2009). Driving while conversing: Cell phones that distract and passengers who react. *Accident Analysis and Prevention, 41*(1), 160–173. doi:10.1016/j.aap.2008.10.006

Charness, Neil; Krampe, Ralf and Mayr, Ulrich. (1996). The role of practice and coaching in entrepreneurial skill domains: An international comparison of life-span chess skill acquisition. In Karl Anders Ericsson (Ed.), *The road to excellence: The acquisition of expert performance in the arts and sciences, sports, and games* (pp. 51–80). Hillsdale, NJ: Erlbaum.

Chassin, Laurie; Hussong, Andrea and Beltran, Iris. (2009). Adolescent substance use. In Richard M. Lerner and Laurence Steinberg (Eds.), Handbook of adolescent psychology (3rd ed., Vol. 1, pp. 723–763). Hoboken, NJ: Wiley.

Chatters, Linda M.; Taylor, Robert Joseph; Lincoln, Karen D.; Nguyen, Ann and Joe, Sean. (2011). Church-based social support and suicidality among African Americans and Black Caribbeans. *Archives of Suicide Research, 15*(4), 337–353. doi:10.1080/13811118.2011.615703

Chein, Isidor. (1972). The science of behavior and the image of man. New York, NY: Basic Books.

Chein, Isidor. (2008). The science of behavior and the image of man. New Brunswick, NJ: Transaction Publishers.

Chen, Edith; Cohen, Sheldon and Miller, Gregory E. (2010). How low socioeconomic status affects 2-year hormonal trajectories in children. *Psychological Science, 21*(1), 31–37. doi:10.1177/0956797609355566

Chen, Edith and Miller, Gregory E. (2012). "Shift-and-persist" strategies: Why low socioeconomic status isn't always bad for health. *Perspectives on Psychological Science, 7*(2), 135–158. doi:10.1177/1745691612436694

Chen, Gong and Gao, Yuan. (2013). Changes in social participation of older adults in Beijing. *Ageing International, 38*(1), 15–27. doi:10.1007/s12126-012-9167-y

Chen, Hong and Jackson, Todd. (2009). Predictors of changes in weight esteem among mainland Chinese adolescents: A longitudinal analysis. *Developmental Psychology, 45*(6), 1618–1629. doi:10.1037/a0016820

Chen, Sheying and Powell, Jason L. (2012). Aging in China: Implications to social policy of a changing economic state. New York, NY: Springer.

Chen, Xinyin (2011). Culture and children's socioemotional functioning: A contextual-developmental perspective. In Xinyin Chen and Kenneth H. Rubin (Eds.), *Socioemotional development in cultural context* (pp. 29–52). New York, NY: Guilford Press.

Chen, Xinyin; Cen, Guozhen; Li, Dan and He, Yunfeng. (2005). Social functioning and adjustment in Chinese children: The imprint of historical time. *Child Development, 76*(1), 182–195. doi:10.1111/j.1467-8624.2005.00838.x

Chen, Xu; Errangi, Bhargav; Li, Longchuan; Glasser, Matthew F.; Westlye, Lars T.; Fjell, Anders M., . . . Rilling, James K. (2013). Brain aging in humans, chimpanzees (Pan troglodytes), and rhesus macaques (Macaca mulatta): magnetic resonance imaging studies of macro- and microstructural changes. *Neurobiology of Aging, 31*(10), 2248–2260. doi:10.1016/j.neurobiolaging.2013.03.028

Chen, Xinyin; Rubin, Kenneth H. and Sun, Yuerong. (1992). Social reputation and peer relationships in Chinese and Canadian children: A cross-cultural study. *Child Development, 63*(6), 1336–1343. doi:10.1111/j.1467-8624.1992.tb01698.x

Chen, Xinyin; Wang, Li and Wang, Zhengyan. (2009). Shyness-sensitivity and social, school, and psychological adjustment in rural migrant and urban children in China. *Child Development, 80*(5), 1499–1513. doi:10.1111/j.1467-8624.2009.01347.x

Cheng, Diana; Kettinger, Laurie; Uduhiri, Kelechi and Hurt, Lee. (2011). Alcohol consumption during pregnancy: Prevalence and provider assessment. *Obstetrics & Gynecology, 117*(2), 212–217. doi:10.1097/AOG.0b013e3182078569

Cheng, Yi-Chia and Yeh, Hsin-Te. (2009). From concepts of motivation to its application in instructional design: Reconsidering motivation from an instructional design perspective. *British Journal of Educational Technology, 40*(4), 597–605. doi:10.1111/j.1467-8535.2008.00857.x

Chentsova-Dutton, Yulia E. and Vaughn, Alexandra. (2012). Let me tell you what to do: Cultural differences in advice-giving. *Journal of Cross-Cultural Psychology, 43*(5), 687–703. doi:10.1177/0022022111402343

Cherlin, Andrew J. (2009). The marriage-go-round: The state of marriage and the family in America today. New York, NY: Knopf.

Cherlin, Andrew J. (2013). Health, marriage, and same-sex partnerships. *Journal of Health and Social Behavior, 54*(1), 64–66. doi:10.1177/0022146512474430

Cheslack-Postava, Keely; Liu, Kayuet and Bearman, Peter S. (2011). Closely spaced pregnancies are associated with increased odds of autism in California sibling births. *Pediatrics, 127*(2), 246–253. doi:10.1542/peds.2010-2371

Chiuri, Maria Concetta and Jappelli, Tullio. (2010). Do the elderly reduce housing equity? An international comparison. *Journal of Population Economics, 23*(2), 643–663. doi:10.1007/s00148-008-0217-4

Chlebowski, Rowan T.; Manson, JoAnn E.; Anderson, Garnet L.; Cauley, Jane A.; Aragaki, Aaron K.; Stefanick, Marcia L., . . . Prentice, Ross L. (2013). Estrogen plus progestin and breast cancer incidence and mortality in the Women's Health Initiative observational study. *JNCI, 105*(8), 526–535. doi:10.1093/jnci/djt043

Choi, Incheol; Dalal, Reeshad; Kim-Prieto, Chu and Park, Hyekyung. (2003). Culture and judgment of causal relevance. *Journal of Personality & Social Psychology, 84*(1), 46–59. doi:10.1037/0022-3514.84.1.46

Chomsky, Noam. (1968). Language and mind. New York, NY: Harcourt Brace & World.

Chomsky, Noam. (1980). Rules and representations. New York, NY: Columbia University Press.

Choshen-Hillel, Shoham and Yaniv, Ilan. (2011). Agency and the construction of social preference: Between inequality aversion and prosocial behavior. *Journal of Personality and Social Psychology, 101*(6), 1253–1261. doi:10.1037/a0024557

Chou, Rita Jing-Ann and Choi, Namkee G. (2011). Prevalence and correlates of perceived workplace discrimination among older workers in the United States of America. *Ageing and Society, 31*(6), 1051–1070. doi:10.1017/S0144686X10001297

Christensen, Andrew; Eldridge, Kathleen; Catta-Preta, Adriana Bokel; Lim, Veronica R. and Santagata, Rossella. (2006). Cross-cultural consistency of the demand/withdraw interaction pattern in couples. *Journal of Marriage and Family, 68*(4), 1029–1044. doi:10.1111/j.1741-3737.2006.00311.x

Christian, Cindy W. and Block, Robert. (2009). Abusive head trauma in infants and children. *Pediatrics, 123*(5), 1409–1411. doi:10.1542/peds.2009-0408

Chronicle of Higher Education. (2010). Almanac of higher education 2010–2011. Washington, DC.

Chu, C. Y. Cyrus; Xie, Yu and Yu, Ruoh Rong. (2011). Coresidence with elderly parents: A comparative study of southeast China and Taiwan. *Journal of Marriage and Family, 73*(1), 120–135. doi:10.1111/j.1741-3737.2010.00793.x

Chua, Amy. (2011, December 24). Tiger mom's long-distance cub. The Wall Street Journal, p. 3.

Chua, Amy. (2011). Battle hymn of the tiger mother. New York, NY: Penguin.

Chudacoff, Howard P. (2011). The history of children's play in the United States. In Anthony D. Pellegrini (Ed.), The Oxford handbook of the development of play (pp. 101–109). New York, NY: Oxford University Press.

Chuderski, Adam. (2013). When are fluid intelligence and working memory isomorphic and when are they not? *Intelligence, 41*(4), 244–262. doi:10.1016/j.intell.2013.04.003

Church, A. Timothy (2010). Current perspectives in the study of personality across cultures. *Perspectives on Psychological Science, 5*(4), 441–449. doi:10.1177/1745691610375559

Cicchetti, Dante. (2013). Annual Research Review: Resilient functioning in maltreated children – past, present, and future perspectives. *Journal of Child Psychology and Psychiatry, 54*(4), 402–422. doi:10.1111/j.1469-7610.2012.02608.x

Cicchetti, Dante. (2013). An overview of developmental psychopathology. In Philip David Zelazo (Ed.), The Oxford handbook of developmental psychology (Vol. 2, pp. 455–480). New York, NY: Oxford University Press.

Cicchetti, Dante and Toth, Sheree L. (2009). The past achievements and future promises of developmental psychopathology: The coming of age of a discipline. *Journal of Child Psychology and Psychiatry, 50*(1–2), 16–25. doi:10.1111/j.1469-7610.2008.01979.x

Cillessen, Antonius H. N. and Mayeux, Lara. (2004). From censure to reinforcement: Developmental changes in the association between aggression and social status. *Child Development, 75*(1), 147–163. doi:10.1111/j.1467-8624.2004.00660.x

Cipriano, Elizabeth A. and Stifter, Cynthia A. (2010). Predicting preschool effortful control from toddler temperament and parenting behavior. *Journal of Applied Developmental Psychology, 31*(3), 221–230. doi:10.1016/j.appdev.2010.02.004

Claas, Marieke J.; de Vries, Linda S.; Bruinse, Hein W.; van Haastert, Ingrid C.; Uniken Venema, Monica M. A.; Peelen, Linda M. and Koopman, Corine. (2011). Neurodevelopmental outcome over time of preterm born children ≤750g at birth. *Early Human Development, 87*(3), 183–191. doi:10.1016/j.earlhumdev.2010.12.002

Clark, Lee Anna. (2009). Stability and change in personality disorder. *Current Directions in Psychological Science, 18*(1), 27–31. doi:10.1111/j.1467-8721.2009.01600.x

Clark, Nina Annika; Demers, Paul A.; Karr, Catherine J.; Koehoorn, Mieke; Lencar, Cornel; Tamburic, Lillian and Brauer, Michael. (2010). Effect of early life exposure to air pollution on development of childhood asthma. *Environmental Health Perspectives, 118*(2), 284–290. doi:10.1289/ehp.0900916

Clark, Shelley; Kabiru, Caroline and Mathur, Rohini. (2010). Relationship transitions among youth in urban Kenya. *Journal of Marriage and Family, 72*(1), 73–88. doi:10.1111/j.1741-3737.2009.00684.x

Clarke, Christina A.; Miller, Tim; Chang, Ellen T.; Chang, Daixin; Chang, Myles and Gomez, Scarlett L. (2011). Racial and social class gradients in life expectancy in contemporary California. *Social Science & Medicine, 70*(9), 1373–1380. doi:10.1016/j.socscimed.2010.01.003

Cleland, John; Conde-Agudelo, Agustin; Peterson, Herbert; Ross, John and Tsui, Amy. (2012). Contraception and health. *The Lancet, 380*(9837), 149–156. doi:10.1016/S0140-6736(12)60609-6

Cleland, Verity; Timperio, Anna; Salmon, Jo; Hume, Clare; Telford, Amanda and Crawford, David. (2011). A longitudinal study of the family physical activity environment and physical activity among youth. *American Journal of Health Promotion, 25*(3), 159–167. doi:10.4278/ajhp.090303-QUAN-93

Clements, Jonathan. (2005, October 5). Rich, successful—and miserable: New research probes mid-life angst. Wall Street Journal.

Cleveland, Michael J.; Gibbons, Frederick X.; Gerrard, Meg; Pomery, Elizabeth A. and Brody, Gene H. (2005). The impact of parenting on risk cognitions and risk behavior: A study of mediation and moderation in a panel of African American adolescents. *Child Development, 76*(4), 900–916. doi:10.1111/j.1467-8624.2005.00885.x

Cockerham, William C. (2006). *Society of risk-takers: Living life on the edge.* New York, NY: Worth Publishers.

Coe, Norma B. and Zamarro, Gema. (2011). Retirement effects on health in Europe. *Journal of Health Economics, 30*(1), 77–86. doi:10.1016/j.jhealeco.2010.11.002

Cohen, Alison Klebanoff and Syme, S. Leonard. (2013). Education: A missed opportunity for public health intervention. *American Journal of Public Health, 103*(6), 997–1001. doi:10.2105/AJPH.2012.300993

Cohen, David. (2006). *The development of play* (3rd ed.). New York, NY: Routledge.

Cohen, Jon. (2007). Hope on new AIDS drugs, but breast-feeding strategy backfires. *Science, 315*(5817), 1357. doi:10.1126/science.315.5817.1357

Cohen, Joachim; Van Landeghem, Paul; Carpentier, Nico and Deliens, Luc. (2013). Public acceptance of euthanasia in Europe: a survey study in 47 countries. *International Journal of Public Health, 59*(1), 143–156. doi:10.1007/s00038-013-0461-6

Cohen, Joel E. and Malin, Martin B. (Eds.). (2010). International perspectives on the goals of universal basic and secondary education. New York, NY: Routledge.

Cohen, Larry; Chávez, Vivian and Chehimi, Sana (Eds.). (2007). *Prevention is primary: Strategies for community well-being* (1st ed.). San Francisco, CA: Jossey-Bass.

Cohen, Larry; Chávez, Vivian and Chehimi, Sana (Eds.). (2010). *Prevention is primary: Strategies for community well-being* (2nd ed.). San Francisco, CA: Jossey-Bass.

Cohen, Leslie B. and Cashon, Cara H. (2006). Infant cognition. In William Damon and Richard M. Lerner (Eds.), *Handbook of child psychology* (6th ed., Vol. 2, pp. 214–251). Hoboken, NJ: Wiley.

Cohen, Sheldon; Tyrrell, David A. and Smith, Andrew P. (1993). Negative life events, perceived stress, negative affect, and susceptibility to the common cold. *Journal of Personality and Social Psychology, 64*(1), 131–140. doi:10.1037/0022-3514.64.1.131

Colaco, Marc; Johnson, Kelly; Schneider, Dona and Barone, Joseph. (2013). Toilet training method is not related to dysfunctional voiding. *Clinical Pediatrics, 52*(1), 49–53. doi:10.1177/0009922812464042

Colbert, Linda; Jefferson, Joseph; Gallo, Ralph and Davis, Ronnie. (2009). A study of religiosity and psychological well-being among African Americans: Implications for counseling and psychotherapeutic processes. *Journal of Religion and Health, 48*(3), 278–289. doi:10.1007/s10943-008-9195-9

Cole, Jennifer and Thomas, Lynn M. (Eds.). (2009). *Love in Africa.* Chicago, IL: University of Chicago Press.

Cole, Pamela M.; Armstrong, Laura Marie and Pemberton, Caroline K. (2010). The role of language in the development of emotion regulation. In Susan D. Calkins and Martha Ann Bell (Eds.), *Child development at the intersection of emotion and cognition* (pp. 59–78). Washington, DC: American Psychological Association.

Cole, Pamela M.; Tan, Patricia Z.; Hall, Sarah E.; Zhang, Yiyun; Crnic, Keith A.; Blair, Clancy B. and Li, Runze. (2011). Developmental changes in anger expression and attention focus: Learning to wait. *Developmental Psychology, 47*(4), 1078–1089. doi:10.1037/a0023813

Coleman, Marilyn; Ganong, Lawrence H. and Warzinik, Kelly. (2007). *Family life in 20th-century America.* Westport, CT: Greenwood Press.

Coles, Robert. (1997). *The moral intelligence of children: How to raise a moral child.* New York, NY: Random House.

Colleran, Carol and Jay, Debra. (2003). Surviving addiction: Audrey's story. *Aging Today, 24*(1).

Collins, Emily and Freeman, Jonathan. (2013). Do problematic and non-problematic video game players differ in extraversion, trait empathy, social capital and prosocial tendencies? *Computers in Human Behavior, 29*(5), 1933–1940. doi:10.1016/j.chb.2013.03.002

Collins, Juliet; Johnson, Susan L. and Krebs, Nancy F. (2004). Screen for and treat overweight in 2- to 5-year-olds? Yes! *Contemporary Pediatrics, 21*(10), 60–74.

Collins, Pamela Y.; Patel, Vikram; Joestl, Sarah S.; March, Dana; Insel, Thomas R.; Daar, Abdallah S., . . . Walport, Mark. (2011). Grand challenges in global mental health. *Nature, 475,* 27–30. doi:10.1038/475027a

Collins, Rebecca L.; Martino, Steven C.; Elliott, Marc N. and Miu, Angela. (2011). Relationships between adolescent sexual outcomes and exposure to sex in media: Robustness to propensity-based analysis. *Developmental Psychology, 47*(2), 585–591. doi:10.1037/a0022563

Collins, Tara J. and Gillath, Omri. (2012). Attachment, breakup strategies, and associated outcomes: The effects of security enhancement on the selection of breakup strategies. *Journal of Research in Personality, 46*(2), 210–222. doi:10.1016/j.jrp.2012.01.008

Compian, Laura J.; Gowen, L. Kris and Hayward, Chris. (2009). The interactive effects of puberty and peer victimization on weight concerns and depression symptoms among early adolescent girls. *The Journal of Early Adolescence, 29*(3), 357–375. doi:10.1177/0272431608323656

Compta, Yaroslau; Parkkinen, Laura; O'Sullivan, Sean S.; Vandrovcova, Jana; Holton, Janice L.; Collins, Catherine, . . . Revesz, Tamas. (2011). Lewy- and Alzheimer-type pathologies in Parkinson's disease dementia: Which is more important? *Brain: A Journal of Nuerology, 134*(5), 1493–1505. doi:10.1093/brain/awr031

Confer, Jaime C.; Easton, Judith A.; Fleischman, Diana S.; Goetz, Cari D.; Lewis, David M. G.; Perilloux, Carin and Buss, David M. (2010). Evolutionary psychology: Controversies, questions, prospects, and limitations. *American Psychologist, 65*(2), 110–126. doi:10.1037/a0018413

Cong, Zhen and Silverstein, Merril. (2008). Intergenerational support and depression among elders in rural China: Do daughters-in-law matter? *Journal of Marriage and Family, 70*(3), 599–612. doi:10.1111/j.1741-3737.2008.00508.x

Conger, Katherine J. and Little, Wendy M. (2010). Sibling relationships during the transition to adulthood. *Child Development Perspectives, 4*(2), 87–94. doi:10.1111/j.1750-8606.2010.00123.x

Conger, Rand D.; Conger, Katherine J. and Martin, Monica J. (2010). Socioeconomic status, family processes, and individual development. *Journal of Marriage and Family, 72*(3), 685–704. doi:10.1111/j.1741-3737.2010.00725.x

Conger, Rand D.; Wallace, Lora Ebert; Sun, Yumei; Simons, Ronald L.; McLoyd, Vonnie C. and Brody, Gene H. (2002). Economic pressure in African American families:

A replication and extension of the family stress model. *Developmental Psychology, 38*(2), 179–193. doi:10.1037/0012-1649.38.2.179

Conley, Colleen S. and Rudolph, Karen D. (2009). The emerging sex difference in adolescent depression: Interacting contributions of puberty and peer stress. *Development and Psychopathology, 21*(2), 593–620. doi:10.1017/S0954579409000327

Conner, Mark (2008). Initiation and maintenance of health behaviors. *Applied Psychology, 57*(1), 42–50. doi:10.1111/j.1464-0597.2007.00321.x

Conwell, Erin and Morgan, James L. (2012). Is it a noun or is it a verb? Resolving the ambicategoricality problem. *Language Learning and Development, 8*(2), 87–112. doi:10.1080/15475441.2011.580236

Coon, Carleton S. (1962). *The origin of races.* New York, NY: Knopf.

Cooper, Alexia and Smith, Erica L. (2011). Homicide trends in the United States, 1980–2008: Annual rates for 2009 and 2010. Washington, DC: United States Department of Justice, Bureau of Justice Statistics.

Cooper, Claudia; Selwood, Amber and Livingston, Gill. (2008). The prevalence of elder abuse and neglect: A systematic review. *Age and Ageing, 37*(2), 151–160. doi:10.1093/ageing/afm194

Coovadia, Hoosen M. and Wittenberg, Dankwart F. (Eds.). (2004). *Paediatrics and child health: A manual for health professionals in developing countries* (5th ed.). New York, NY: Oxford University Press.

Copeland, William E.; Wolke, Dieter; Angold, Adrian and Costell, E. Jane. (2013). Adult psychiatric outcomes of bullying and being bullied by peers in childhood and adolescence. *JAMA Psychiatry, 70*(4), 419–426. doi:10.1001/jamapsychiatry.2013.504

Copen, Casey E.; Daniels, Kimberly and Mosher, William D. (2013). First premarital cohabitation in the United States: 2006–2010 national survey of family growth. Hyattsville, MD: National Center for Health Statistics.

Coplan, Robert J. and Weeks, Murray. (2009). Shy and soft-spoken: Shyness, pragmatic language, and socio-emotional adjustment in early childhood. *Infant and Child Development, 18*(3), 238–254. doi:10.1002/icd.622

Corballis, Michael C. (2011). The recursive mind: The origins of human language, thought, and civilization. Princeton, NJ: Princeton University Press.

Corda, Larisa; Khanapure, Amita and Karoshi, Mahantesh. (2012). Biopanic, advanced maternal age and fertility outcomes. In Mahantesh Karoshi, Sandra Newbold, Christopher B. Lynch and Louis Keith (Eds.), A Textbook of Preconceptional Medicine and Management. London, UK: Sapiens.

Cornwell, Benjamin. (2012). Spousal network overlap as a basis for spousal support. *Journal of Marriage and Family, 74*(2), 229–238. doi:10.1111/j.1741-3737.2012.00959.x

Coronini-Cronberg, Sophie; Millett, Christopher; Laverty, Anthony A. and Webb, Elizabeth. (2012). The impact of a free older persons' bus pass on active travel and regular walking in England. *American Journal of Public Health, 102*(11), 2141–2148. doi:10.2105/AJPH.2012.300946

Corr, Charles A. and Corr, Donna M. (2013a). Culture, Socialization, and Dying. In David K. Meagher and David E. Balk (Eds.), *Handbook of thanatology: The essential body of knowledge for the study of death, dying, and bereavement* (2nd ed., pp. 3–8). New York, NY: Routledge.

Corr, Charles A. and Corr, Donna M. (2013b). Historical and contemporary perspectives on loss, grief, and mourning. In David Meagher and David E. Balk (Eds.), *Handbook of thanatology: The essential body of knowledge for the study of death, dying, and bereavement* (2nd ed., pp. 135–148). New York, NY: Routledge.

Cosgrave, James F. (2010). Embedded addiction: The social production of gambling knowledge and the development of gambling markets. *Canadian Journal of Sociology, 35*(1), 113–134.

Côté, James E. (2006). Emerging adulthood as an institutionalized moratorium: Risks and benefits to identity formation. In Jeffrey Jensen Arnett and Jennifer Lynn Tanner (Eds.), *Emerging adults in America: Coming of age in the 21st century* (pp. 85–116). Washington, DC: American Psychological Association. doi:10.1037/11381-004

Côté, James E. (2009). Identity formation and self-development in adolescence. In Richard M. Lerner and Laurence Steinberg (Eds.), *Handbook of adolescent psychology* (3rd ed., Vol. 1, pp. 266–304). Hoboken, NJ: Wiley.

Côté, Sylvana M.; Borge, Anne I.; Geoffroy, Marie-Claude; Rutter, Michael and Tremblay, Richard E. (2008). Nonmaternal care in infancy and emotional/behavioral difficulties at 4 years old: Moderation by family risk characteristics. *Developmental Psychology, 44*, 155–168. doi:10.1037/0012-1649.44.1.155

Côté, Sylvana M.; Doyle, Orla; Petitclerc, Amélie and Timmins, Lori. (2013). Child Care in Infancy and Cognitive Performance Until Middle Childhood in the Millennium Cohort Study. *Child Development, 84*(4), 191–1208. doi:10.1111/cdev.12049

Couturier, Jennifer; Kimber, Melissa and Szatmari, Peter. (2013). Efficacy of family-based treatment for adolescents with eating disorders: A systematic review and meta-analysis. *International Journal of Eating Disorders, 46*(1), 3–11. doi:10.1002/eat.22042

Couzin, Jennifer. (2009). Friendship as a health factor. *Science, 323*(5913), 454–457. doi:10.1126/science.323.5913.454

Couzin-Frankel, Jennifer. (2010). Bacteria and asthma: Untangling the links. *Science, 330*(6008), 1168–1169. doi:10.1126/science.330.6008.1168

Couzin-Frankel, Jennifer. (2011a). Aging genes: The sirtuin story unravels. *Science, 334*(6060), 1194–1198. doi:10.1126/science.334.6060.1194

Couzin-Frankel, Jennifer. (2011b). A pitched battle over life span. *Science, 333*(6042), 549–550. doi:10.1126/science.333.6042.549

Couzin-Frankel, Jennifer. (2013). Return of unexpected DNA results urged. *Science, 339*(6127), 1507–1508. doi:10.1126/science.339.6127.1507

Cowan, Nelson and Alloway, Tracy. (2009). Development of working memory in childhood. In Mary L. Courage and Nelson Cowan (Eds.), *The development of memory in infancy and childhood* (2nd ed., pp. 303–342). New York, NY: Psychology Press.

Crago, Martha B. (1992). Communicative interaction and second language. *TESOL Quarterly, 26*(3), 487–505.

Crain, William C. (2005). Theories of development: Concepts and applications (5th ed.). Upper Saddle River, NJ: Prentice Hall.

Cramer, Robert; Lipinski, Ryan; Bowman, Ashley and Carollo, Tanner. (2009). Subjective distress to violations of trust in Mexican American close relationships conforms to evolutionary principles. *Current Psychology, 28*(1), 1–11. doi:10.1007/s12144-009-9049-y

Cramer, Steven C. and Procaccio, Vincent. (2012). Correlation between genetic polymorphisms and stroke recovery: Analysis of the GAIN Americas and GAIN International Studies. *European Journal of Neurology, 19*(5), 718–724. doi:10.1111/j.1468-1331.2011.03615.x

Cranwell, Brian. (2010). Care and control: What motivates people's decisions about the disposal of ashes. *Bereavement Care, 29*(2), 10–12. doi:10.1080/02682621.2010.484929

Crawford Shearer, Nelma B.; Fleury, Julie D. and Reed, Pamela G. (2009). The rhythm of health in older women with chronic illness. *Research and Theory for Nursing Practice, 23*(2), 148–160. doi:10.1891/1541-6577.23.2.148

Crenshaw, David A. (2013). The family, larger systems, and traumatic death. In David K. Meagher and David E. Balk (Eds.), *Handbook of thanatology: The essential body of knowledge for the study of death, dying, and bereavement* (2nd ed., pp. 305–309). New York, NY: Routledge.

Crinion, Jenny; Turner, R.; Grogan, Alice; Hanakawa, Takashi; Noppeney, Uta; Devlin, Joseph T., . . . Price, C. J. (2006). Language control in the bilingual brain. *Science, 312*(5779), 1537–1540. doi:10.1126/science.1127761

Crocetti, Elisabetta; Scrignaro, Marta; Sica, Luigia and Magrin, Maria. (2012). Correlates of identity configurations: Three studies with adolescent and emerging adult cohorts. *Journal of Youth & Adolescence, 41*(6), 732–748. doi:10.1007/s10964-011-9702-2

Cronce, Jessica M. and Corbin, William R. (2010). College and career. In Jon E. Grant and Marc N. Potenza (Eds.), *Young adult mental health* (pp. 80–95). New York, NY: Oxford University Press.

Crone, Eveline A. and Dahl, Ronald E. (2012). Understanding adolescence as a period of social–affective engagement and goal flexibility. *Nature Reviews Neuroscience, 13,* 636–650. doi:10.1038/nrn3313

Crone, Eveline A. and Ridderinkhof, K. Richard. (2011). The developing brain: From theory to neuroimaging and back. *Developmental Cognitive Neuroscience, 1*(2), 101–109. doi:10.1016/j.dcn.2010.12.001

Crone, Eveline A. and Westenberg, P. Michiel. (2009). A brain-based account of developmental changes in social decision making. In Michelle de Haan and Megan R. Gunnar (Eds.), *Handbook of developmental social neuroscience* (pp. 378–396). New York, NY: Guilford Press.

Crosnoe, Robert and Johnson, Monica Kirkpatrick. (2011). Research on adolescence in the twenty-first century. *Annual Review of Sociology, 37*(1), 439–460. doi:10.1146/annurev-soc-081309-150008

Crosnoe, Robert; Johnson, Monica Kirkpatrick and Elder Jr., Glen H. (2004). Intergenerational bonding in school: The behavioral and contextual correlates of student-teacher relationship. *Sociology of Education, 77*(1), 60–81. doi:10.1177/003804070407700103

Crosnoe, Robert; Leventhal, Tama; Wirth, Robert John; Pierce, Kim M. and Pianta, Robert C. (2010). Family socioeconomic status and consistent environmental stimulation in early childhood. *Child Development, 81*(3), 972–987. doi:10.1111/j.1467-8624.2010.01446.x

Cross, Donna; Monks, Helen; Hall, Marg; Shaw, Thérèse; Pintabona, Yolanda; Erceg, Erin, . . . Lester, Leanne. (2011). Three-year results of the Friendly Schools whole-of-school intervention on children's bullying behaviour. *British Educational Research Journal, 37*(1), 105–129. doi:10.1080/01411920903420024

Crucian, Brian; Stowe, Raymond; Mehta, Satish; Uchakin, Peter; Quiriarte, Heather; Pierson, Duane and Sams, Clarence. (2013). Immune system dysregulation occurs during short duration spaceflight on board the space shuttle. *Journal Of Clinical Immunology, 33*(2), 456–465. doi:10.1007/s10875-012-9824-7

Cruikshank, Margaret. (2009). *Learning to be old: Gender, culture, and aging* (2nd ed.). Lanham, MD: Rowman & Littlefield.

Cruz, Alvaro A.; Bateman, Eric D. and Bousquet, Jean. (2010). The social determinants of asthma. *European Respiratory Journal, 35*(2), 239–242. doi:10.1183/09031936.00070309

Cryder, Cynthia E.; Lerner, Jennifer S.; Gross, James J. and Dahl, Ronald E. (2008). Misery is not miserly: Sad and self-focused individuals spend more. *Psychological Science, 19*(6), 525–530. doi:10.1111/j.1467-9280.2008.02118.x

Csikszentmihalyi, Mihaly. (1996). Creativity: Flow and the psychology of discovery and invention. New York, NY: HarperCollins.

Cuevas, Bryan J. and Stone, Jacqueline Ilyse (Eds.). (2011). The Buddhist dead: Practices, discourses, representations. Honolulu, HI: University of Hawaii Press.

Cui, Ming and Donnellan, M. Brent. (2009). Trajectories of conflict over raising adolescent children and marital satisfaction. *Journal of Marriage and Family, 71*(3), 478–494. doi:10.1111/j.1741-3737.2009.00614.x

Cuijpers, P.; van Straten, A.; van Oppen, P. and Andersson, G. (2010). Welke psychologische behandeling, uitgevoerd door wie, is het meest effectief bij depressie? *Gedragstherapie, 43,* 79–113.

Cumming, Elaine and Henry, William Earl. (1961). Growing old: The process of disengagement. New York, NY: Basic Books.

Cumsille, Patricio; Darling, Nancy and Martínez, M. Loreto. (2010). Shading the truth: The patterning of adolescents' decisions to avoid issues, disclose, or lie to parents. *Journal of Adolescence, 33*(2), 285–296. doi:10.1016/j.adolescence.2009.10.008

Cunha, Marcus Jr. and Caldieraro, Fabio. (2009). Sunk-cost effects on purely behavioral investments. *Cognitive Science, 33*(1), 105–113. doi:10.1111/j.1551-6709.2008.01005.x

Cunradi, Carol B. (2009). Intimate partner violence among Hispanic men and women: The role of drinking, neighborhood disorder, and acculturation-related factors. *Violence and Victims, 24*(1), 83–97. doi:10.1891/0886-6708.24.1.83

Curlin, Farr A.; Nwodim, Chinyere; Vance, Jennifer L.; Chin, Marshall H. and Lantos, John D. (2008). To die, to sleep: US physicians' religious and other objections to physician-assisted suicide, terminal sedation, and withdrawal of life support. *American Journal of Hospice and Palliative Medicine, 25*(2), 112–120. doi:10.1177/1049909107310141

Currie, Janet and Widom, Cathy Spatz. (2010). Long-term consequences of child abuse and neglect on adult economic well-being. *Child Maltreatment, 15*(2), 111–120. doi:10.1177/1077559509355316

Curry, Laurel Erin; Richardson, Amanda; Xiao, Haijun and Niaura, Raymond S. (2013). Nondisclosure of smoking status to health care providers among current and former smokers in the United States. *Health Education and Behavior, 40*(3), 266–273. doi:10.1177/1090198112454284

Cutler, Stephen J.; Hendricks, Jon and O'Neill, Greg. (2011). Civic engagement and aging. In Robert H. Binstock and Linda K. George (Eds.), *Handbook of aging and the social sciences* (7th ed., pp. 221–233). San Diego, CA: Academic Press. doi:10.1016/B978-0-12-380880-6.00016-2

Cutuli, J. J.; Desjardins, Christopher David; Herbers, Janette E.; Long, Jeffrey D.; Heistad, David; Chan, Chi-Keung, . . . Masten, Ann S. (2013). Academic achievement trajectories of homeless and highly mobile students: Resilience in the context of chronic and acute risk. *Child Development, 84*(3), 841–857. doi:10.1111/cdev.12013

Daddis, Christopher. (2010). Adolescent peer crowds and patterns of belief in the boundaries of personal authority. *Journal of Adolescence, 33*(5), 699–708. doi:10.1016/j.adolescence.2009.11.001

Dahl, Ronald E. (2004). Adolescent brain development: A period of vulnerabilities and opportunities, Keynote address. *Annals of the New York Academy of Sciences, 1021,* 1–22. doi:10.1196/annals.1308.001

Dahl, Ronald E. and Gunnar, Megan R. (2009). Heightened stress responsiveness and emotional reactivity during pubertal maturation: Implications for psychopathology. *Development and Psychopathology, 21*(1), 1–6. doi:10.1017/S0954579409000017

Dai, David Yun. (2010). The nature and nurture of giftedness: A new framework for understanding gifted education. New York, NY: Teachers College Press.

Daley, Dave; Jones, Karen; Hutchings, Judy and Thompson, Margaret. (2009). Attention deficit hyperactivity disorder in pre-school children: Current findings, recommended interventions and future directions. *Child: Care, Health and Development, 35*(6), 754–766. doi:10.1111/j.1365-2214.2009.00938.x

Dalman, Christina; Allebeck, Peter; Gunnell, David; Harrison, Glyn; Kristensson, Krister; Lewis, Glyn, . . . Karlsson, HakÂn. (2008). Infections in the CNS during childhood and the risk of subsequent psychotic illness: A cohort study of more than one million Swedish subjects. *American Journal of Psychiatry, 165*(1), 59–65. doi:10.1176/appi.ajp.2007.07050740

Dannefer, Dale and Patterson, Robin Shura. (2008). The missing person: Some limitations in the contemporary study of cognitive aging. In Scott M. Hofer and Duane F. Alwin (Eds.), *Handbook of cognitive aging: Interdisciplinary perspectives* (pp. 105–119). Thousand Oaks, CA: Sage.

Darling, Nancy; Cumsille, Patricio and Martinez, M. Loreto. (2008). Individual differences in adolescents' beliefs about the legitimacy of parental authority and their own obligation to obey: A longitudinal investigation. *Child Development, 79*(4), 1103–1118. doi:10.1111/j.1467-8624.2008.01178.x

Darwin, Charles. (1859). On the origin of species by means of natural selection. London, UK: J. Murray.

Daum, Moritz M.; Ulber, Julia and Gredebäck, Gustaf. (2013). The development of pointing perception in infancy: Effects of communicative signals on covert shifts of attention. *Developmental Psychology, 49*(10), 1898–1908. doi:10.1037/a0031111

David, Barbara; Grace, Diane and Ryan, Michelle K. (2004). The gender wars: A self-categorization perspective on the development of gender identity. In Mark Bennett and Fabio Sani (Eds.), *The development of the social self* (pp. 135–157). New York, NY: Psychology Press.

David, Jane L. (2011). High-stakes testing narrows the curriculum. *Educational Leadership, 68*(6), 78–80.

Davidson, Julia O'Connell. (2005). *Children in the global sex trade.* Malden, MA: Polity.

Davidson, Kate. (2008). Declining health and competence: Men facing choices about driving cessation. *Generations, 32*(1), 44–47.

Davila, Joanne. (2008). Depressive symptoms and adolescent romance: Theory, research, and implications. *Child Development Perspectives, 2*(1), 26–31. doi:10.1111/j.1750-8606.2008.00037.x

Davis, Elysia Poggi; Parker, Susan Whitmore; Tottenham, Nim and Gunnar, Megan R. (2003). Emotion, cognition, and the hypothalamic-pituitary-adrenocortical axis: A developmental perspective. In Michelle de Haan and Mark H. Johnson (Eds.), *The cognitive neuroscience of development* (pp. 181–206). New York, NY: Psychology Press.

Davis, Kelly D.; Goodman, W. Benjamin; Pirretti, Amy E. and Almeida, David M. (2008). Nonstandard work schedules, perceived family well-being, and daily stressors. *Journal of Marriage and Family, 70*(4), 991–1003. doi:10.1111/j.1741-3737.2008.00541.x

Davis, Linell (1999). Doing culture: Cross-cultural communication in action. Beijing, China: Foreign Language Teaching & Research Press.

Davis, Mark and Squire, Corinne (Eds.). (2010). *HIV treatment and prevention technologies in international perspective*. New York, NY: Palgrave Macmillan.

Davis, R. Neal; Davis, Matthew M.; Freed, Gary L. and Clark, Sarah J. (2011). Fathers' depression related to positive and negative parenting behaviors with 1-year-old children. *Pediatrics, 127*(4), 612–618. doi:10.1542/peds.2010-1779

Davis-Kean, Pamela E.; Jager, Justin and Collins, W. Andrew (2009). The self in action: An emerging link between self-beliefs and behaviors in middle childhood. *Child Development Perspectives, 3*(3), 184–188. doi:10.1111/j.1750-8606.2009.00104.x

Dawson, Geraldine. (2010). Recent advances in research on early detection, causes, biology, and treatment of autism spectrum disorders. *Current Opinion in Neurology, 23*(2), 95–96. doi:10.1097/WCO.0b013e3283377644

Dawson, Lorne L. (2010). The study of new religious movements and the radicalization of home-grown terrorists: Opening a dialogue. *Terrorism and Political Violence, 22*(1), 1–21. doi:10.1080/09546550903409163

Dawson, Michelle; Soulières, Isabelle; Gernsbacher, Morton Ann and Mottron, Laurent. (2007). The level and nature of autistic intelligence. *Psychological Science, 18*(8), 657–662. doi:10.1111/j.1467-9280.2007.01954.x

de Bruin, Wändi Bruine; Parker, Andrew M. and Fischhoff, Baruch. (2007). Can adolescents predict significant life events? *The Journal of Adolescent Health, 41*(2), 208–210. doi:10.1016/j.jadohealth.2007.03.014

De Cock, Kevin M. (2011). Trends in global health and CDC's international role, 1961–2011. 60, 104–111.Suppl. 4.

De Corte, Erik. (2013). Giftedness considered from the perspective of research on learning and instruction. *High Ability Studies, 24*(1), 3–19. doi:10.1080/13598139.2013.780967

de Heering, Adelaide; de Liedekerke, Claire; Deboni, Malorie and Rossion, Bruno. (2010). The role of experience during childhood in shaping the other-race effect. *Developmental Science, 13*(1), 181–187. doi:10.1111/j.1467-7687.2009.00876.x

de Jong Gierveld, Jenny and Merz, Eva-Maria. (2013). Parents' partnership decision making after divorce or widowhood: The role of (step) children. *Journal of Marriage and Family, 75*(5), 1098–1113. doi:10.1111/jomf.12061

de Jonge, Ank; Mesman, Jeanette A. J. M.; Manniën, Judith; Zwart, Joost J.; van Dillen, Jeroen and van Roosmalen, Jos. (2013). Severe adverse maternal outcomes among low risk women with planned home versus hospital births in the Netherlands: Nationwide cohort study. *BMJ, 346*, f3263. doi:10.1136/bmj.f3263

De Lee, Joseph Bolivar. (1938). *The principles and practice of obstetrics* (7th ed.). Philadelphia: W. B. Saunders Co.

De Neys, Wim; Cromheeke, Sofie and Osman, Magda. (2011). Biased but in doubt: Conflict and decision confidence. *PLoS ONE, 6*(2), e15954. doi:10.1371/journal.pone.0015954

De Neys, Wim and Feremans, Vicky. (2013). Development of heuristic bias detection in elementary school. *Developmental Psychology, 49*(2), 258–269. doi:10.1037/a0028320

De Neys, Wim and Van Gelder, Elke. (2009). Logic and belief across the lifespan: The rise and fall of belief inhibition during syllogistic reasoning. *Developmental Science, 12*(1), 123–130. doi:10.1111/j.1467-7687.2008.00746.x

De Raedt, Rudi; Koster, Ernst H. W. and Ryckewaert, Ruben. (2013). Aging and attentional bias for death related and general threat-related information: Less avoidance in older as compared with middle-aged adults. *The Journals of Gerontology, Series B: Psychological Sciences and Social Sciences, 68*(1), 41–48. doi:10.1093/geronb/gbs047

de Weerth, Carolina; Zijlmans, Maartje; Mack, Simon and Beijers, Roseriet. (2013). Cortisol reactions to a social evaluative paradigm in 5- and 6-year-old children. *Stress, 16*(1), 65–72. doi:10.3109/10253890.2012.684112

Dean, Angela J.; Walters, Julie and Hall, Anthony. (2010). A systematic review of interventions to enhance medication adherence in children and adolescents with chronic illness. *Archives of Disease in Childhood, 95*, 717–723. doi:10.1136/adc.2009.175125

Dearing, Eric; Wimer, Christopher; Simpkins, Sandra D.; Lund, Terese; Bouffard, Suzanne M.; Caronongan, Pia, . . . Weiss, Heather. (2009). Do neighborhood and home contexts help explain why low-income children miss opportunities to participate in activities outside of school? *Developmental Psychology, 45*(6), 1545–1562. doi:10.1037/a0017359

Deary, Ian J.; Penke, Lars and Johnson, Wendy. (2010). The neuroscience of human intelligence differences. *Nature Reviews Neuroscience, 11*, 201–211. doi:10.1038/nrn2793

Deater-Deckard, Kirby. (2013). The social environment and the development of psychopathology. In Philip David Zelazo (Ed.), *The Oxford handbook of developmental psychology* (Vol. 2, pp. 527–548). New York, NY: Oxford University Press.

DeCaro, Marci S.; Thomas, Robin D.; Albert, Neil B. and Beilock, Sian L. (2011). Choking under pressure: Multiple routes to skill failure. *Journal of Experimental Psychology, 140*(3), 390–406. doi:10.1037/a0023466

Deci, Edward L.; Koestner, Richard and Ryan, Richard M. (1999). A meta-analytic review of experiments examining the effects of extrinsic rewards on intrinsic motivation. *Psychological Bulletin, 125*(6), 627–668. doi:10.1037//0033-2909.125.6.627

Dee, Thomas; Jacob, Brian A. and Schwartz, Nathaniel. (2013). The effects of NCLB on school resources and practices. *Educational Evaluation and Policy Analysis, 35*(2), 252–279. doi:10.3102/0162373712467080

Dees, Marianne K.; Vernooij-Dassen, Myrra. J.; Dekkers, Wim. J.; Vissers, Kris. C. and van Weel, Chris. (2011). 'Unbearable suffering': A qualitative study on the perspectives of patients who request assistance in dying. *Journal of Medical Ethics, 37*, 727–734. doi:10.1136/jme.2011.045492

DeFina, Laura F.; Willis, Benjamin L.; Radford, Nina B.; Gao, Ang; Leonard, David; Haskell, William L., . . . Berry, Jarett D. (2013). The association between midlife cardiorespiratory fitness levels and later-life dementia: A cohort study. *Annals of Internal Medicine, 158*(3), 162–168. doi:10.7326/0003-4819-158-3-201302050-00005

Degenhardt, Louisa; Coffey, Carolyn; Carlin, John B.; Swift, Wendy; Moore, Elya and Patton, George C. (2010). Outcomes of occasional cannabis use in adolescence: 10-year follow-up study in Victoria, Australia. *The British Journal of Psychiatry, 196*, 290–295. doi:10.1192/bjp.bp.108.056952

Degnan, Kathryn A.; Hane, Amie Ashley; Henderson, Heather A.; Moas, Olga Lydia; Reeb-Sutherland, Bethany C. and Fox, Nathan A. (2011). Longitudinal stability of temperamental exuberance and social–emotional outcomes in early childhood. *Developmental Psychology, 47*(3), 765–780. doi:10.1037/a0021316

DeGroot, Jocelyn M. (2012). Maintaining relational continuity with the deceased on Facebook. *Omega: Journal of Death & Dying, 65*(3), 195–212. doi:10.2190/OM.65.3.c

DeLamater, John. (2012). Sexual expression in later life: A review and synthesis. *The Journal of Sex Research, 49*(2–3), 125–141. doi:10.1080/00224499.2011.603168

Delaunay-El Allam, Maryse; Soussignan, Robert; Patris, Bruno; Marlier, Luc and Schaal, Benoist. (2010). Long-lasting memory for an odor acquired at the mother's breast. *Developmental Science, 13*(6), 849–863. doi:10.1111/j.1467-7687.2009.00941.x

DeLoache, Judy S.; Chiong, Cynthia; Sherman, Kathleen; Islam, Nadia; Vanderborght, Mieke; Troseth, Georgene L., . . . O'Doherty,

Katherine. (2010). Do babies learn from baby media? *Psychological Science, 21*(11), 1570–1574. doi:10.1177/0956797610384145

Delon-Martin, Chantal; Plailly, Jane; Fonlupt, Pierre; Veyrac, Alexandra and Roye, Jean-Pierre. (2013). Perfumers' expertise induces structural reorganization in olfactory brain regions. *NeuroImage, 68,* 55–62. doi:10.1016/j.neuroimage.2012.11.044

Demetriou, Andreas and Bakracevic, Karin. (2009). Reasoning and self-awareness from adolescence to middle age: Organization and development as a function of education. *Learning and Individual Differences, 19*(2), 181–194. doi:10.1016/j.lindif.2008.10.007

Demetrioua, Andreas; Spanoudisb, George; Shayerc, Michael; Mouyid, Antigoni; Kazie, Smaragda and Platsidouf, Maria. (2013). Cycles in speed-working memory-G relations: Towards a developmental–differential theory of the mind. *Intelligence, 41*(1), 34–50. doi:10.1016/j.intell.2012.10.010

Denny, Dallas and Pittman, Cathy. (2007). Gender identity: From dualism to diversity. In Mitchell Tepper and Annette Fuglsang Owens (Eds.), *Sexual Health* (Vol. 1, pp. 205–229). Westport, CT: Praeger.

DePaulo, Bella M. (2006). *Singled out: How singles are stereotyped, stigmatized, and ignored and still live happily ever after.* New York, NY: St. Martin's Press.

Deptula, Daneen P.; Henry, David B. and Schoeny, Michael E. (2010). How can parents make a difference? Longitudinal associations with adolescent sexual behavior. *Journal of Family Psychology, 24*(6), 731–739. doi:10.1037/a0021760

Desai, Sonalde and Andrist, Lester. (2010). Gender scripts and age at marriage in India. *Demography, 47*(3), 667–687. doi:10.1353/dem.0.0118

Desoete, Annemie; Stock, Pieter; Schepens, Annemie; Baeyens, Dieter and Roeyers, Herbert. (2009). Classification, seriation, and counting in grades 1, 2, and 3 as two-year longitudinal predictors for low achieving in numerical facility and arithmetical achievement? *Journal of Psychoeducational Assessment, 27*(3), 252–264. doi:10.1177/0734282908330588

Devi, Sharmila. (2008). Progress on childhood obesity patchy in the USA. *The Lancet, 371*(9607), 105–106. doi:10.1016/S0140-6736(08)60088-4

DeYoung, Colin G.; Hirsh, Jacob B.; Shane, Matthew S.; Papademetris, Xenophon; Rajeevan, Nallakkandi and Gray, Jeremy R. (2010). Testing predictions from personality neuroscience. *Psychological Science, 21*(6), 820–828. doi:10.1177/0956797610370159

Diamanti-Kandarakis, Evanthia; Bourguignon, Jean-Pierre; Giudice, Linda C.; Hauser, Russ; Prins, Gail S.; Soto, Ana M., . . . Gore, Andrea C. (2009). Endocrine-disrupting chemicals: An endocrine society scientific statement. *Endocrine Society, 30*(4), 293–342. doi:10.1210/er.2009-0002

Diamond, Adele and Amso, Dima. (2008). Contributions of neuroscience to our understanding of cognitive development. *Current Directions in Psychological Science, 17*(2), 136–141. doi:10.1111/j.1467-8721.2008.00563.x

Diamond, Lisa M. and Fagundes, Christopher P. (2010). Psychobiological research on attachment. *Journal of Social and Personal Relationships, 27*(2), 218–225. doi:10.1177/0265407509360906

Diamond, Mathew E. (2007). Neuronal basis of perceptual intelligence. In Flavia Santoianni and Claudia Sabatano (Eds.), Brain development in learning environments: Embodied and perceptual advancements (pp. 98–108). Newcastle, UK: Cambridge Scholars Publishing.

Dickens, William T. and Flynn, James R. (2006). Black americans reduce the racial iq gap: Evidence from standardization samples. *Psychological Science, 17*(10), 913–920. doi:10.1111/j.1467–9280.2006.01802.x

Dickinson, George E. and Hoffmann, Heath C. (2010). Roadside memorial policies in the United States. *Mortality: Promoting the interdisciplinary study of death and dying, 15*(2), 154–167. doi:10.1080/13576275.2010.482775

Didion, Joan. (2005). *The year of magical thinking.* New York, NY: Knopf.

Dijk, Jan A. G. M. van (2005). *The deepening divide: Inequality in the information society.* Thousand Oaks, CA: Sage.

Dijksterhuis, Ap; Bos, Maarten W.; van der Leij, Andries and van Baaren, Rick B. (2009). Predicting soccer matches after unconscious and conscious thought as a function of expertise. *Psychological Science, 20*(11), 1381–1387. doi:10.1111/j.1467-9280.2009.02451.x

DiPietro, Janet A.; Hilton, Sterling C.; Hawkins, Melissa; Costigan, Kathleen A. and Pressman, Eva K. (2002). Maternal stress and affect influence fetal neurobehavioral development. *Developmental Psychology, 38*(5), 659–668. doi:10.1037//0012-1649.38.5.659

Dirix, Chantal E. H.; Nijhuis, Jan G.; Jongsma, Henk W. and Hornstra, Gerard. (2009). Aspects of fetal learning and memory. *Child Development, 80*(4), 1251–1258. doi:10.1111/j.1467-8624.2009.01329.x

Dishion, Thomas J. and Bullock, Bernadette Marie. (2002). Parenting and adolescent problem behavior: An ecological analysis of the nurturance hypothesis. In John G. Borkowski, Sharon Landesman Ramey and Marie Bristol-Power (Eds.), *Parenting and the child's world: Influences on academic, intellectual, and social-emotional development* (pp. 231–249). Mahwah, NJ: Erlbaum.

Dishion, Thomas J.; Poulin, François and Burraston, Bert. (2001). Peer group dynamics associated with iatrogenic effects in group interventions with high-risk young adolescents. In Douglas W. Nangle and Cynthia A. Erdley (Eds.), *New directions for child and adolescent development: No. 91. The role of friendship in psychological adjustment* (pp. 79–92). San Francisco, CA: Jossey-Bass.

Dishion, Thomas J.; Véronneau, Marie-Hélène and Myers, Michael W. (2010). Cascading peer dynamics underlying the progression from problem behavior to violence in early to late adolescence. *Development and Psychopathology, 22*(3), 603–619. doi:10.1017/S0954579410000313

Dobler, Robert Thomas. (2011). Ghost bikes: Memorialization and protest on city streets. In Peter Jan Margry and Cristina Sanchez-Carretero (Eds.), *Grassroots memorials: The politics of memorializing traumatic death* (pp. 169–187). New York, NY: Berghahn Books.

Dobson, Velma; Candy, T. Rowan; Hartmann, E. Eugenie; Mayer, D. Luisa; Miller, Joseph M. and Quinn, Graham E. (2009). Infant and child vision research: Present status and future directions. *Optometry & Vision Science, 86*(6), 559–560. doi:10.1097/OPX.0b013e3181aa06d5

Dodge, Kenneth A. (2009). Mechanisms of gene-environment interaction effects in the development of conduct disorder. *Perspectives on Psychological Science, 4*(4), 408–414. doi:10.1111/j.1745-6924.2009.01147.x

Dodge, Kenneth A.; Coie, John D. and Lynam, Donald R. (2006). Aggression and antisocial behavior in youth. In William Damon and Richard M. Lerner (Eds.), *Handbook of child psychology* (6th ed., Vol. 3, pp. 719–788). Hoboken, NJ: Wiley.

Doering, Katie. (2010). Death: The unwritten curriculum. *Encounter: Education for Meaning and Social Justice, 23*(4), 57–62.

Doka, Kenneth J. (2013). Historical and contemporary perspectives on dying. In David K. Meagher and David E. Balk (Eds.), *Handbook of thanatology: The essential body of knowledge for the study of death, dying, and bereavement* (2nd ed., pp. 17–23). New York, NY: Routledge.

Domina, Thurston; Conley, AnneMarie and Farkas, George. (2011a). The case for dreaming big. *Sociology of Education, 84*(2), 118–121. doi:10.1177/0038040711401810

Domina, Thurston; Conley, AnneMarie and Farkas, George. (2011b). The link between educational expectations and effort in the college-for-all era. *Sociology of Education, 84*(2), 93–112. doi:10.1177/1941406411401808

Dominelli, Paolo B. and Sheel, A. William. (2012). Experimental approaches to the study of the mechanics of breathing during exercise. *Respiratory Physiology & Neurobiology, 180*(2–3), 147–161. doi:10.1016/j.resp.2011.10.005

Dominguez, Cynthia O. (2001). Expertise in laparoscopic surgery: Anticipation and affordances. In Eduardo Salas and Gary A. Klein (Eds.), *Linking expertise and naturalistic decision making* (pp. 287–301). Mahwah, NJ: Erlbaum.

Dominguez, Ximena; Vitiello, Virginia E.; Maier, Michelle F. and Greenfield, Daryl B. (2010). A longitudinal examination of young children's learning behavior: Child-level and classroom-level predictors of change throughout the preschool year. *School Psychology Review, 39*(1), 29–47.

Dominguez-Folgueras, Marta and Castro-Martin, Teresa. (2013). Cohabitation in Spain: No longer a marginal path to family formation. *Journal of Marriage and Family, 75*(2), 422–437. doi:10.1111/jomf.12013

Dong, XinQi and Simon, Melissa A. (2011). Enhancing national policy and programs to address elder abuse. *Journal of the American Medical Association, 305*(23), 2460–2461. doi:10.1001/jama.2011.835

Dong, XinQi; Simon, Melissa A.; Beck, T. T.; Farran, Carol; McCann, Judith J.; Mendes de Leon, Carlos F., . . . Evans, Denis A. (2011). Elder abuse and mortality: The role of psychological and social wellbeing. *Gerontology, 57*(6), 549–558. doi:10.1159/000321881

Donnellan, M. Brent and Lucas, Richard E. (2008). Age differences in the Big Five across the life span: Evidence from two national samples. *Psychology and Aging, 23*(3), 558–566. doi:10.1037/a0012897

Doraiswamy, P. Murali. (2012). Silent cerebrovascular events and Alzheimer's disease: An overlooked opportunity for prevention? *American Journal of Psychiatry, 169*(3), 251–254. doi:10.1176/appi.ajp.2011.11121830

Dorsey, Shannon; Burns, Barbara J.; Southerland, Dannia G.; Cox, Julia Revillion; Wagner, H. Ryan, Farmer and Z., Elizabeth M. (2012). Prior trauma exposure for youth in treatment foster care. *Journal of Child and Family Studies, 21*(5), 816–824. doi:10.1007/s10826-011-9542-4

dosReis, Susan; Mychailyszyn, Matthew P.; Evans-Lacko, Sara E.; Beltran, Alicia; Riley, Anne W. and Myers, Mary Anne. (2009). The meaning of attention-deficit/hyperactivity disorder medication and parents' initiation and continuity of treatment for their child. *Journal of Child and Adolescent Psychopharmacology, 19*(4), 377–383. doi:10.1089/cap.2008.0118

dosReis, Susan and Myers, Mary Anne. (2008). Parental attitudes and involvement in psychopharmacological treatment for ADHD: A conceptual model. *International Review of Psychiatry, 20*(2), 135–141. doi:10.1080/09540260801933084

Dowling, John E. (2004). The great brain debate: Nature or nurture? Washington, DC: Joseph Henry Press.

Drover, James; Hoffman, Dennis R.; Castañeda, Yolanda S.; Morale, Sarah E. and Birch, Eileen E. (2009). Three randomized controlled trials of early long-chain polyunsaturated fatty acid supplementation on means-end problem solving in 9-month-olds. *Child Development, 80*(5), 1376–1384. doi:10.1111/j.1467-8624.2009.01339.x

Dubicka, Bernadka; Carlson, Gabrielle A.; Vail, Andy and Harrington, Richard. (2008). Prepubertal mania: Diagnostic differences between US and UK clinicians. *European Child & Adolescent Psychiatry, 17*(3), 153–161. doi:10.1007/s00787-007-0649-5

Duckworth, Angela L.; Peterson, Christopher; Matthews, Michael D. and Kelly, Dennis R. (2007). Grit: Perseverance and passion for long-term goals. *Journal of Personality and Social Psychology, 92*(6), 1087–1101. doi:10.1037/0022-3514.92.6.1087

Duffey, Kiyah J.; Steffen, Lyn M.; Van Horn, Linda; Jacobs, David R. Jr and Popkin, Barry M. (2012). Dietary patterns matter: diet beverages and cardiometabolic risks in the longitudinal Coronary Artery Risk Development in Young Adults (CARDIA) Study. *American Journal of Clinical Nutrition, 95*(4), 909–915. doi:10.3945/ajcn.111.026682

Duggan, Maeve and Brenner, Joanna. (2013). The demographics of social media users — 2011. Washington, D.C: Pew Research Center Internet & American Life Project, Pew Research Center.

Dukes, Richard L.; Stein, Judith A. and Zane, Jazmin I. (2009). Effect of relational bullying on attitudes, behavior and injury among adolescent bullies, victims and bully-victims. *The Social Science Journal, 46*(4), 671–688. doi:10.1016/j.soscij.2009.05.006

Duman, Ronald S. and Aghajanian, George K. (2012). Synaptic dysfunction in depression: Potential therapeutic targets. *Science, 338*(6103), 68–72. doi:10.1126/science.1222939

Duncan, Greg J. and Magnuson, Katherine. (2013). Investing in preschool programs. *Journal of Economic Perspectives, 27*(2), 109–132. doi:10.1257/jep.27.2.109

Duncan, Greg J.; Ziol-Guest, Kathleen M. and Kalil, Ariel. (2010). Early-childhood poverty and adult attainment, behavior, and health. *Child Development, 81*(1), 306–325. doi:10.1111/j.1467-8624.2009.01396.x

Duncan, Jhodie R.; Paterson, David S.; Hoffman, Jill M.; Mokler, David J.; Borenstein, Natalia S.; Belliveau, Richard A., . . . Kinney, Hannah C. (2010). Brainstem serotonergic deficiency in sudden infant death syndrome. *JAMA, 303*(5), 430–437. doi:10.1001/jama.2010.45

Duncan, Simon and Phillips, Miranda. (2010). People who live apart together (LATs)—How different are they? *The Sociological Review, 58*(1), 112–134. doi:10.1111/j.1467-954X.2009.01874.x

Dunkel, Curtis S. (2013). The general factor of personality and general intelligence: Evidence for substantial association. *Intelligence, 41*(5), 423–427. doi:10.1016/j.intell.2013.06.010

Dunmore, Simon J. (2013). Of fat mice and men: The rise of the adipokines. *Journal of Endocrinology, 216*(1), E1-E2. doi:10.1530/JOE-12-0513

Dunning, David. (2011). *Social motivation.* New York, NY: Psychology Press.

Dunphy, Dexter C. (1963). The social structure of urban adolescent peer groups. *Sociometry, 26*(2), 230–246. doi:10.2307/2785909

DuPaul, George J.; Gormley, Matthew J. and Laracy, Seth D. (2013). Comorbidity of LD and ADHD: Implications of DSM-5 for assessment and treatment. *Journal of Learning Disabilities, 46*(1), 43–51. doi:10.1177/0022219412464351

Dupuis, Kate and Pichora-Fuller, M. Kathleen. (2010). Use of affective prosody by young and older adults. *Psychology and Aging, 25*(1), 16–29. doi:10.1037/a0018777

Durvasula, Srinivas; Lysonski, Steven and Watson, John. (2001). Does vanity describe other cultures? A cross-cultural examination of the vanity scale. *Journal of Consumer Affairs, 35*(1), 180–199. doi:10.1111/j.1745-6606.2001.tb00108.x

Dutton, Donald G. (2012). The case against the role of gender in intimate partner violence. *Aggression and Violent Behavior, 17*(1), 99–104. doi:10.1016/j.avb.2011.09.002

Dvornyk, Volodymyr and Waqar-ul-Haq. (2012). Genetics of age at menarche: A systematic review. *Human Reproduction Update, 18*(2), 198–210. doi:10.1093/humupd/dmr050

Dwane, H. Dean. (2012). Self-control and perceived physical risk in an extreme sport. *Young Consumers: Insight and Ideas for Responsible Marketers, 13*(1), 62–73. doi:10.1108/17473611211203948

Dweck, Carol S. (2013). Social Development. In Philip David Zelazo (Ed.), The Oxford handbook of developmental psychology (Vol. 2, pp. 167–190). New York, NY: Oxford University Press.

Eagly, Alice H. and Wood, Wendy. (2013). The nature–nurture debates: 25 years of challenges in understanding the psychology of gender. *Perspectives on Psychological Science, 8*(3), 340–357. doi:10.1177/1745691613484767

Ebaugh, Helen Rose and Curry, Mary. (2000). Fictive kin as social capital in new immigrant communities. *Sociological Perspectives, 43*(2), 189–209. doi:10.2307/1389793

Eccles, Jacquelynne C. and Roeser, Robert W. (2010). An ecological view of schools and development. In Judith L. Meece and Jacquelynne S. Eccles (Eds.), Handbook of research on schools, schooling, and human development (pp. 6–22). New York, NY: Routledge.

Eccles, Jacquelynne S. and Roeser, Robert W. (2011). Schools as developmental contexts during adolescence. *Journal of Research on Adolescence, 21*(1), 225–241. doi:10.1111/j.1532-7795.2010.00725.x

Eckhardt, Marc; Urhahne, Detlef; Conrad, Olaf and Harms, Ute. (2013). How effective is instructional support for learning with computer simulations? *Instructional Science, 41*(1), 105–124. doi:10.1007/s11251-012-9220-y

Editorial Projects in Education Research Center. (2011, June 9). Diplomas count, 2011: Beyond high school, before baccalaureate. *Education Week, 30*(34).

Edwards, Judge Leonard. (2010). Relative placement in child protection cases: A judicial perspective. *Juvenile and Family Court Journal, 61*(2), 1–44. doi:10.1111/j.1755-6988.2010.01040.x

Edwards, Judge Leonard P. (2007). Achieving timely permanency in child protection courts: The importance of frontloading the court process. *Juvenile and Family Court Journal, 58*(2), 1–37. doi:10.1111/j.1755-6988.2007.tb00136.x

Eells, Tracy D.; Lombart, Kenneth G.; Salsman, Nicholas; Kendjelic, Edward M.; Schneiderman, Carolyn T. and Lucas, Cynthia P. (2011). Expert reasoning in psychotherapy case formulation. *Psychotherapy Research, 21*(4), 385–399. doi:10.1080/10503307.2010.539284

Eggum, Natalie D.; Eisenberg, Nancy; Kao, Karen; Spinrad, Tracy L.; Bolnick, Rebecca; Hofer, Claire, . . . Fabricius, William V. (2011). Emotion understanding, theory of mind, and prosocial orientation: Relations over time in early childhood. *The Journal of Positive Psychology, 6*(1), 4–16. doi:10.1080/17439760.2010.536776

Ehrlich, Paul R. (1968). *The population bomb.* New York, NY: Ballantine Books.

Eisenberg, Nancy; Cumberland, Amanda; Guthrie, Ivanna K.; Murphy, Bridget C. and Shepard, Stephanie A. (2005). Age changes in prosocial responding and moral reasoning in adolescence and early adulthood. *Journal of Research on Adolescence, 15*(3), 235–260. doi:10.1111/j.1532-7795.2005.00095.x

Eisenberg, Nancy; Fabes, Richard A. and Spinrad, Tracy L. (2006). Prosocial development. In William Damon and Richard M. Lerner (Eds.), *Handbook of child psychology* (6th ed., Vol. 3, pp. 646–718). Hoboken, NJ: Wiley.

Eisenberg, Nancy; Hofer, Claire; Spinrad, Tracy L.; Gershoff, Elizabeth T.; Valiente, Carlos; Losoya, Sandra, . . . Maxon, Elizabeth. (2008). Understanding mother-adolescent conflict discussions: Concurrent and across-time prediction from youths' dispositions and parenting. *Monographs of the Society for Research in Child Development, 73*(2), vii–viii. doi:10.1111/j.1540-5834.2008.00470.x

Eisenberg, Nancy; Hofer, Claire; Sulik, Michael J. and Liew, Jeffrey. (2013). The development of prosocial moral reasoning and a prosocial orientation in young adulthood: Concurrent and longitudinal correlates. *Developmental Psychology, 50*(1), 58–70. doi:10.1037/a0032990

Eisenberg, Nancy; Spinrad, Tracy L.; Fabes, Richard A.; Reiser, Mark; Cumberland, Amanda; Shepard, Stephanie A., . . . Thompson, Marilyn. (2004). The relations of effortful control and impulsivity to children's resiliency and adjustment. *Child Development, 75*(1), 25–46. doi:10.1111/j.1467-8624.2004.00652.x

Eisenberg, Nancy; Zhou, Qing; Losoya, Sandra H.; Fabes, Richard A.; Shepard, Stephanie A.; Murphy, Bridget C., . . . Cumberland, Amanda. (2003). The relations of parenting, effortful control, and ego control to children's emotional expressivity. *Child Development, 74*(3), 875–895. doi:10.1111/1467-8624.00573

Elias, Carol F. (2012). Leptin action in pubertal development: Recent advances and unanswered questions. *Trends in Endocrinology & Metabolism, 23*(1), 9–15. doi:10.1016/j.tem.2011.09.002

Elias, Carol F. and Purohit, Darshana. (2013). Leptin signaling and circuits in puberty and fertility. *Cellular and Molecular Life Sciences, 70*(5), 841–862. doi:10.1007/s00018-012-1095-1

Elkind, David. (1967). Egocentrism in adolescence. *Child Development, 38*(4), 1025–1034.

Elkind, David. (2007). *The power of play: How spontaneous, imaginative activities lead to happier, healthier children.* Cambridge, MA: Da Capo Press.

Elliott, Vanessa J.; Rodgers, David L. and Brett, Stephen J. (2011). Systematic review of quality of life and other patient-centred outcomes after cardiac arrest survival. *Resuscitation, 82*(3), 247–256. doi:10.1016/j.resuscitation.2010.10.030

Ellis, Bruce J. and Boyce, W. Thomas. (2008). Biological sensitivity to context. *Current Directions in Psychological Science, 17*(3), 183–187. doi:10.1111/j.1467-8721.2008.00571.x

Ellis, Bruce J.; Shirtcliff, Elizabeth A.; Boyce, W. Thomas; Deardorff, Julianna and Essex, Marilyn J. (2011). Quality of early family relationships and the timing and tempo of puberty: Effects depend on biological sensitivity to context. *Development and Psychopathology, 23*(1), 85–99. doi:10.1017/S0954579410000660

Ellis, Lee and Wahab, Eshah A. (2013). Religiosity and fear of death: A theory-oriented review of the empirical literature. *Review of Religious Research, 55*(1), 149–189. doi:10.1007/s13644-012-0064-3

Ellison, Christopher G.; Musick, Marc A. and Holden, George W. (2011). Does conservative Protestantism moderate the association between corporal punishment and child outcomes? *Journal of Marriage and Family, 73*(5), 946–961. doi:10.1111/j.1741-3737.2011.00854.x

Else-Quest, Nicole M.; Hyde, Janet Shibley; Goldsmith, H. Hill and Van Hulle, Carol A. (2006). Gender differences in temperament: A meta-analysis. *Psychological Bulletin, 132*(1), 33–72. doi:10.1037/0033-2909.132.1.33

Engelberts, Adèle C. and de Jonge, Guustaaf Adolf. (1990). Choice of sleeping position for infants: Possible association with cot death. *Archives of Disease in Childhood, 65*(4), 462–467. doi:10.1136/adc.65.4.462

Engelhardt, H. Tristram, Jr. (2012). Why clinical bioethics so rarely gives morally normative guidance. In H. Tristram Engelhardt, Jr. (Ed.), *Bioethics critically reconsidered: Having second thoughts* (pp. 151–174). New York, NY: Springer. doi:10.1007/978-94-007-2244-6_8

Englander, Elizabeth; Mills, Elizabeth and McCoy, Meghan. (2009). Cyberbullying and information exposure: User-generated content in post-secondary education. *International Journal of Contemporary Sociology, 46*(2), 215–230.

Enserink, Martin. (2011). Can this DNA sleuth help catch criminals? *Science, 331*(6019), 838–840. doi:10.1126/science.331.6019.838

Epps, Chad and Holt, Lynn. (2011). The genetic basis of addiction and relevant cellular mechanisms. *International Anesthesiology Clinics, 49*(1), 3–14. doi:10.1097/AIA.0b013e3181f2bb66

Epstein, Jeffery N.; Langberg, Joshua M.; Lichtenstein, Philip K.; Altaye, Mekibib; Brinkman, William B.; House, Katherine and Stark, Lori J. (2010). Attention-deficit/hyperactivity disorder outcomes for children treated in community-based pediatric settings. *Archives of Pediatrics & Adolescent Medicine, 164*(2), 160–165. doi:10.1001/archpediatrics.2009.263

Erdbrink, Thomas. (2013, June 3). *Seven Die in Iran After Drinking Homemade Alcohol.* The New York Times, p. A3.

Erdman, Phyllis and Ng, Kok-Mun (Eds.). (2010). *Attachment: Expanding the cultural connections.* New York, NY: Routledge.

Erickson, Kirk I.; Gildengers, Ariel G. and Butters, Meryl A. (2013). Physical activity and brain plasticity in late adulthood. *Dialogues in Clinical Neuroscience, 15*(1), 99–108. doi:10.4081/ar.2012.e6

Erickson, Kirk I.; Miller, Destiny L.; Weinstein, Andrea M.; Akl, Stephanie L. and Banducci, Sarah. (2012). Physical activity and brain plasticity in late adulthood: A conceptual and comprehensive review. *Ageing Research, 3*(1). doi:10.4081/ar.2012.e6

Erickson, Rebecca J. (2005). Why emotion work matters: Sex, gender, and the division of household labor. *Journal of Marriage and Family, 67*(2), 337–351. doi:10.1111/j.0022-2445.2005.00120.x

Ericsson, K. Anders. (1996). The acquisition of expert performance: An introduction to some of the issues. In Karl Anders Ericsson (Ed.), *The road to excellence: The acquisition of expert performance in the arts and sciences, sports, and games* (pp. 1–50). Hillsdale, NJ: Erlbaum.

Ericsson, K. Anders; Charness, Neil; Feltovich, Paul J. and Hoffman, Robert R. (Eds.). (2006). *The Cambridge handbook of expertise and expert performance.* New York, NY: Cambridge University Press.

Erikson, Erik H. (1963). *Childhood and society* (2nd ed.). New York, NY: Norton.

Erikson, Erik H. (1968). *Identity: Youth and crisis.* New York, NY: Norton.

Erikson, Erik H. (1969). *Childhood and society* (2nd ed.). New York, NY: Norton.

Erikson, Erik H.; Erikson, Joan M. and Kivnick, Helen Q. (1986). *Vital involvement in old age.* New York, NY: Norton.

Erlinghagen, Marcel and Hank, Karsten. (2006). The participation of older Europeans in volunteer work. *Ageing & Society, 26*(4), 567–584. doi:10.1017/S0144686X06004818

Estruch, Ramón; Ros, Emilio; Salas-Salvadó, Jordi; Covas, Maria-Isabel; Corella, Dolores; Arós, Fernando, . . . Martínez-González, Angel Miguel. (2013). Primary prevention of cardiovascular disease with a Mediterranean diet. *New England Journal of Medicine, 368,* 1279–1290. doi:10.1056/NEJMoa1200303

Etchu, Koji. (2007). Social context and preschoolers' judgments about aggressive behavior: Social domain theory. *Japanese Journal of Educational Psychology, 55*(2), 219–230.

Evans, Angela D. and Lee, Kang. (2011). Verbal deception from late childhood to middle adolescence and its relation to executive functioning skills. *Developmental Psychology, 47*(4), 1108–1116. doi:10.1037/a0023425

Evans, Angela D.; Xu, Fen and Lee, Kang. (2011). When all signs point to you: Lies told in the face of evidence. *Developmental Psychology, 47*(1), 39–49. doi:10.1037/a0020787

Evans, David W. and Leckman, James F. (2006). Origins of obsessive-compulsive disorder: Developmental and evolutionary perspectives. In Dante Cicchetti and Donald J. Cohen (Eds.), *Developmental psychopathology* (2nd ed., Vol. 3, pp. 404–435). Hoboken, NJ: Wiley.

Evans, Gary W. and Kim, Pilyoung. (2013). Childhood poverty, chronic stress, self-regulation, and coping. *Child Development Perspectives, 7*(1), 43–48. doi:10.1111/cdep.12013

Evans, M.D.R.; Kelley, Jonathan; Sikora, Joanna and Treiman, Donald J. (2010). Family scholarly culture and educational success: Books and schooling in 27 nations. *Research in Social Stratification and Mobility, 28*(2), 171–197. doi:10.1016/j.rssm.2010.01.002

Ewers, Michael; Walsh, Cathal; Trojanowski, John Q.; Shaw, Leslie M.; Petersen, Ronald C.; Jack, Clifford R. Jr., . . . Hampel, Harald. (2012). Prediction of conversion from mild cognitive impairment to Alzheimer's disease dementia based upon biomarkers and neuropsychological test performance. *Neurobiology of Aging, 33*(7), 1203–1214. doi:10.1016/j.neurobiolaging.2010.10.019

Eymard, Amanda Singleton and Douglas, Dianna Hutto. (2012). Ageism among health care providers and interventions to improve their attitudes toward older adults: An integrative review. *Journal of Gerontological Nursing, 38*(5), 26–35. doi:10.3928/00989134-20120307-09

Ezzati, Majid and Riboli, Elio. (2012). Can noncommunicable diseases be prevented? Lessons from studies of populations and individuals. *Science, 337*(6101), 1482–1487. doi:10.1126/science.1227001

Fabiani, Monica and Gratton, Gabriele. (2009). Brain imaging probes into the cognitive and physiological effects of aging. In Wojtek Chodzko-Zajko, Arthur F. Kramer and Leonard W. Poon (Eds.), *Enhancing cognitive functioning and brain plasticity* (Vol. 3, pp. 1–13). Champaign, IL Human Kinetics.

Fagan, Joseph F. and Holland, Cynthia R. (2007). Racial equality in intelligence: Predictions from a theory of intelligence as processing. *Intelligence, 35*(4), 319–334. doi:10.1016/j.intell.2006.08.009

Fagard, Jacqueline and Lockman, Jeffrey J. (2010). Change in imitation for object manipulation between 10 and 12 months of age. *Developmental Psychobiology, 52*(1), 90–99. doi:10.1002/dev.20416

Falbo, Toni; Kim, Sunghun and Chen, Kuan-yi. (2009). Alternate models of sibling status effects on health in later life. *Developmental Psychology, 45*(3), 677–687. doi:10.1037/a0013941

Farahani, Mansour; Subramanian, S. V. and Canning, David. (2009). The effect of changes in health sector resources on infant mortality in the short-run and the long-run: A longitudinal econometric analysis. *Social Science & Medicine, 68*(11), 1918–1925. doi:10.1016/j.socscimed.2009.03.023

Farber, Stu and Farber, Annalu. (2013). It ain't easy: Making life and death decisions before the crisis. In Leah Rogne and Susana Lauraine McCune (Eds.), *Advance care planning: Communicating about matters of life and death* (pp. 109–122). New York, NY: Springer.

Farrar, Ruth D. and Al-Qatawneh, Khalil S. (2010). Interdisciplinary theoretical foundations for literacy teaching and learning. *European Journal of Social Sciences, 13*(1), 56–66.

Farrell, C.; Chappell, F.; Armitage, P. A.; Keston, P.; MacLullich, A.; Shenkin, S. and Wardlaw, J. M. (2009). Development and initial testing of normal reference MR images for the brain at ages 65–70 and 75–80 years. *European Radiology, 19*(1), 177–183. doi:10.1007/s00330-008-1119-2

Farrelly, Matthew C.; Davis, Kevin C.; Haviland, M. Lyndon; Messeri, Peter and Healton, Cheryl G. (2005). Evidence of a dose-response relationship between "truth" antismoking ads and youth smoking prevalence. *American Journal of Public Health, 95*(3), 425–431. doi:10.2105/AJPH.2004.049692

Fazzi, Elisa; Signorini, Sabrina Giovanna; Bomba, Monica; Luparia, Antonella; Lanners, Josée and Balottin, Umberto. (2011). Reach on sound: A key to object permanence in visually impaired children. *Early Human Development, 87*(4), 289–296. doi:10.1016/j.earlhumdev.2011.01.032

FBI. (2013). Crime in the United States, 2012. Clarksburg, WV: U.S. Department of Justice, Federal Bureau of Investigation, Criminal Justice Information Services Division.

Fechter-Leggett, Molly O. and O'Brien, Kirk. (2010). The effects of kinship care on adult mental health outcomes of alumni of foster care. *Children and Youth Services Review, 32*(2), 206–213. doi:10.1016/j.childyouth.2009.08.017

Feeley, Nancy; Sherrard, Kathryn; Waitzer, Elana and Boisvert, Linda. (2013). The Father at the Bedside: Patterns of Involvement in the NICU. *Journal of Perinatal & Neonatal Nursing, 27*(1), 72–80. doi:10.1097/JPN.0b013e31827fb415

Feerasta, Aniqa. (2006, August 29). Katrina broke some racial barriers: 'A humbling truth'. *USA Today,* p. A12.

Feigenson, Lisa; Libertus, Melissa E. and Halberda, Justin. (2013). Links between the intuitive sense of number and formal mathematics ability. *Child Development Perspectives, 7*(2), 74–79. doi:10.1111/cdep.12019

Feldman, Ruth. (2007). Parent-infant synchrony and the construction of shared timing; Physiological precursors, developmental outcomes, and risk conditions. *Journal of Child Psychology and Psychiatry, 48*(3–4), 329–354. doi:10.1111/j.1469-7610.2006.01701.x

Feldman, Ruth; Gordon, Ilanit and Zagoory-Sharon, Orna. (2011). Maternal and paternal plasma, salivary, and urinary oxytocin and parent–infant synchrony: Considering stress and affiliation components of human bonding. *Developmental Science, 14*(4), 752–761. doi:10.1111/j.1467-7687.2010.01021.x

Fentiman, Linda C. (2009). Pursuing the perfect mother: Why America's criminalization of maternal substance abuse is not the answer—A comparative legal analysis. *Michigan Journal of Gender & Law, 15*(2).

Ferguson, Christopher J. and Donnellan, M. Brent. (2014). Is the association between children's baby video viewing and poor language development robust? A reanalysis of Zimmerman, Christakis, and Meltzoff (2007). *Developmental Psychology, 50*(1), 129–137. doi:10.1037/a0033628

Fergusson, David M.; Horwood, L. John and Ridder, Elizabeth M. (2005). Partner violence and mental health outcomes in a New Zealand birth cohort. *Journal of Marriage and Family, 67*(5), 1103–1119. doi:10.2307/3600298

Ferriman, Kimberley; Lubinski, David and Benbow, Camilla P. (2009). Work preferences, life values, and personal views of top math/science graduate students and the profoundly gifted: Developmental changes and gender differences during emerging adulthood and parenthood. *Journal of Personality and Social Psychology, 97*(3), 517–532. doi:10.1037/a0016030

Fewtrell, Mary; Wilson, David C.; Booth, Ian and Lucas, Alan. (2011). Six months of exclusive breast feeding: How good is the evidence? *BMJ, 342,* c5955. doi:10.1136/bmj.c5955

Field, Nigel P. and Filanosky, Charles. (2009). Continuing bonds, risk factors for complicated grief, and adjustment to bereavement. *Death Studies, 34*(1), 1–29. doi:10.1080/07481180903372269

Fikkan, Janna L. and Rothblum, Esther D. (2012). Is fat a feminist issue? Exploring the gendered nature of weight bias. *Sex Roles, 66*(9–10), 575–592. doi:10.1007/s11199-011-0022-5

Filová, Barbora; Ostatníková, Daniela; Celec, Peter and Hodosy, Július. (2013). The effect of testosterone on the formation of brain structures. *Cells Tissues Organs, 197*(3), 169–177. doi:10.1159/000345387

Finch, Caleb E. (2010). Evolution of the human lifespan and diseases of aging: Roles of infection, inflammation, and nutrition. *Proceedings of the National Academy of Sciences, 107*(Suppl. 1), 1718–1724. doi:10.1073/pnas.0909606106

Fincham, Frank D. and Beach, Steven R. H. (2010). Of memes and marriage: Toward a positive relationship science. *Journal of Family Theory & Review, 2*(1), 4–24. doi:10.1111/j.1756-2589.2010.00033.x

Fingerman, Karen L. (2009). Consequential strangers and peripheral ties: The importance of unimportant relationships. *Journal of Family Theory & Review, 1*(2), 69–86. doi:10.1111/j.1756-2589.2009.00010.x

Fingerman, Karen L.; Berg, Cynthia; Smith, Jacqui and Antonucci, Toni C. (2011). *Handbook of lifespan development.* New York, NY: Springer.

Fingerman, Karen L.; Cheng, Yen-Pi; Birditt, Kira and Zarit, Steven. (2012). Only as happy as the least happy child: Multiple grown children's problems and successes and middle-aged parents' well-being. *The Journals of Gerontology Series B: Psychological Sciences and Social Sciences, 67B*(2), 184–193. doi:10.1093/geronb/gbr086

Fingerman, Karen L.; Cheng, Yen-Pi; Tighe, Lauren; Birditt, Kira S. and Zarit, Steve. (2012b). Relationships between young adults and their parents. In Alan Booth, Susan L. Brown, Nancy S. Landale, Wendy D. Manning and Susan M. McHale (Eds.), *Early adulthood in family context* (pp. 59–85). New York, NY: Springer. doi:10.1007/978-1-4614-1436-0_5

Fingerman, Karen L.; Cheng, Yen-Pi; Wesselmann, Eric D.; Zarit, Steven; Furstenberg, Frank and Birditt, Kira S. (2012a). Helicopter parents and landing pad kids: Intense parental support of grown children. *Journal of Marriage and Family, 74*(4), 880–896. doi:10.1111/j.1741-3737.2012.00987.x

Fingerman, Karen L. and Furstenberg, Frank F. (2012, May 30). You can go home again. The New York Times, p. A29.

Fingerman, Karen L.; Hay, Elizabeth L. and Birditt, Kira S. (2004). The best of ties, the worst of ties: Close, problematic, and ambivalent social relationships. *Journal of Marriage and Family, 66*(3), 792–808. doi:10.1111/j.0022-2445.2004.00053.x

Finkel, Deborah; Andel, Ross; Gatz, Margaret and Pedersen, Nancy L. (2009). The role of occupational complexity in trajectories of cognitive aging before and after retirement. *Psychology and Aging, 24*(3), 563–573. doi:10.1037/a0015511

Finkelhor, David and Jones, Lisa (2012). Have sexual abuse and physical abuse declined since the 1990s? Durham, NH: Crimes Against Children Research Center, University of New Hampshire.

Finlay, Ilora G. and George, R. (2011). Legal physician-assisted suicide in Oregon and The Netherlands: Evidence concerning the impact on patients in vulnerable groups—Another perspective on Oregon's data. *Journal of Medical Ethics, 37*, 171–174. doi:10.1136/jme.2010.037044

Fins, Joseph. (2006). A palliative ethic of care: Clinical wisdom at life's end. Sudbury, MA: Jones and Bartlett.

Fiori, Katherine L. and Denckla, Christy A. (2012). Social support and mental health in middle-aged men and women: A multidimensional approach. *Journal of Aging and Health, 24*(3), 407–438. doi:10.1177/0898264311425087

Fisher, Helen E. (2006). Broken hearts: the nature and risks of romantic rejection. In Ann C. Crouter and Alan Booth (Eds.), *Romance and sex in adolescence and emerging adulthood: risks and opportunities* (pp. 3–28). Mahwah, N.J: Lawrence Erlbaum Associates.

Fisher, Susan J. and Giudice, Linda C. (2013). Robert G. Edwards (1925–2013). *Science, 340*(6134), 825. doi:10.1126/science.1239644

Fitch, Kristin E. and Cougle, Jesse R. (2013). Perceived and actual information processing deficits in nonclinical hoarding. *Journal of Obsessive-Compulsive and Related Disorders, 2*(2), 192–199. doi:10.1016/j.jocrd.2013.02.006

Flegal, Katherine M.; Kit, Brian K.; Orpana, Heather and Graubard, Barry I. (2013). Association of all-cause mortality with overweight and obesity using standard body mass index categories: A systematic review and meta-analysis. *JAMA, 309*(1), 71–82. doi:10.1001/jama.2012.113905

Flensborg-Madsen, Trine; Bay von Scholten, Mikael; Flachs, Esben Meulengracht; Mortensen, Erik Lykke; Prescott, Eva and Tolstrup, Janne Schurmann. (2011). Tobacco smoking as a risk factor for depression. A 26-year population-based follow-up study. *Journal of psychiatric research, 45*(2), 143–149. doi:10.1016/j.jpsychires.2010.06.006

Flessner, Christopher A.; Freeman, Jennifer B.; Sapyta, Jeffrey; Garcia, Abbe; Franklin, Martin E.; March, John S. and Foa, Edna. (2011). Predictors of parental accommodation in pediatric obsessive-compulsive disorder: Findings from the POTS trial. *Journal of the American Academy of Child & Adolescent Psychiatry, 50*(7), 716–725. doi:10.1016/j.jaac.2011.03.019

Fletcher, Jason M. (2009). Beauty vs. brains: Early labor market outcomes of high school graduates. *Economics Letters, 105*(3), 321–325. doi:10.1016/j.econlet.2009.09.006

Fletcher, Jack M. and Vaughn, Sharon. (2009). Response to intervention: Preventing and remediating academic difficulties. *Child Development Perspectives, 3*(1), 30–37. doi:10.1111/j.1750-8606.2008.00072.x

Fletcher, Richard; St. George, Jennifer and Freeman, Emily. (2013). Rough and tumble play quality: Theoretical foundations for a new measure of father–child interaction. *Early Child Development and Care, 183*(6), 746–759. doi:10.1080/03004430.2012.723439

Flood, Meredith and Phillips, Kenneth D. (2007). Creativity in older adults: A plethora of possibilities. *Issues in Mental Health Nursing, 28*(4), 389–411. doi:10.1080/01612840701252956

Floud, Roderick; Fogel, Robert W.; Harris, Bernard and Hong, Sok Chul. (2011). The changing body: Health, nutrition, and human development in the western world since 1700. New York, NY: Cambridge University Press.

Flynn, James R. (1999). Searching for justice: The discovery of IQ gains over time. *American Psychologist, 54*(1), 5–20. doi:10.1037/0003-066X.54.1.5

Flynn, James R. (2012). *Are we getting smarter?: Rising IQ in the twenty-first century.* New York, NY: Cambridge University Press.

Fontana, Luigi; Colman, Ricki J.; Holloszy, John O. and Weindruch, Richard. (2011). Calorie restriction in nonhuman and human primates. In J. Masoro Edward and N. Austad Steven (Eds.), *Handbook of the biology of aging* (7th ed., pp. 447–461). San Diego, CA: Academic Press. doi:10.1016/B978-0-12-378638-8.00021-X

Ford, Carole L. and Yore, Larry D. (2012). Toward convergence of critical thinking, metacognition, and reflection: Illustrations from natural and social sciences, teacher education, and classroom practice. In Anat Zohar and Yehudit Judy Dori (Eds.), *Metacognition in Science Education* (pp. 251–271). New York, NY: Springer. doi:10.1007/978-94-007-2132-6_11

Forget-Dubois, Nadine; Dionne, Ginette; Lemelin, Jean-Pascal; Pérusse, Daniel; Tremblay, Richard E. and Boivin, Michel. (2009). Early child language mediates the relation between home environment and school readiness. *Child Development, 80*(3), 736–749. doi:10.1111/j.1467-8624.2009.01294.x

Fortuna, Keren and Roisman, Glenn I. (2008). Insecurity, stress, and symptoms of psychopathology: Contrasting results from self-reports versus interviews of adult attachment. *Attachment & Human Development, 10*(1), 11–28. doi:10.1080/14616730701868571

Foster, Eugene A.; Jobling, Mark A.; Taylor, P. G.; Donnelly, Peter; de Knijff, Peter; Mieremet, Rene, . . . Tyler-Smith, C. (1998). Jefferson fathered slave's last child. *Nature, 396*, 27–28. doi:10.1038/23835

Fowler, James W. (1981). Stages of faith: The psychology of human development and the quest for meaning. San Francisco, CA: Harper & Row.

Fowler, James W. (1986). Faith and the structuring of meaning. In Craig Dykstra and Sharon Parks (Eds.), Faith development and Fowler (pp. 15–42). Birmingham, AL: Religious Education Press.

Fox, Nathan A.; Henderson, Heather A.; Marshall, Peter J.; Nichols, Kate E. and Ghera, Melissa M. (2005). Behavioral inhibition: Linking biology and behavior within a developmental framework. *Annual Review of Psychology, 56*, 235–262. doi:10.1146/annurev.psych.55.090902.141532

Fox, Nathan A.; Henderson, Heather A.; Rubin, Kenneth H.; Calkins, Susan D. and Schmidt, Louis A. (2001). Continuity and discontinuity of behavioral inhibition and exuberance: Psychophysiological and behavioral influences across the first four years of life. *Child Development, 72*(1), 1–21. doi:10.1111/1467-8624.00262

Fox, Nathan A.; Reeb-Sutherland; C., Bethany and Degnan, Kathryn A. (2013). Personality and emotional development. In Philip David Zelazo (Ed.), The Oxford handbook of developmental psychology (Vol. 2, pp. 15–44). New York, NY: Oxford University Press.

Fragouli, Elpida and Wells, Dagan. (2011). Aneuploidy in the human blastocyst. *Cytogenetic and Genome Research, 133*(2–4), 149–159. doi:10.1159/000323500

Franco, Manuel; Bilal, Usama; Orduñez, Pedro; Benet, Mikhail; Alain, Morejón; Benjamín, Caballero, . . . Cooper, Richard S.

(2013). Population-wide weight loss and regain in relation to diabetes burden and cardiovascular mortality in Cuba 1980–2010: Repeated cross sectional surveys and ecological comparison of secular trends. *BMJ, 346,* f1515. doi:10.1136/bmj.f1515

Frankenburg, William K.; Dodds, Josiah; Archer, Philip; Shapiro, Howard and Bresnick, Beverly. (1992). The Denver II: A major revision and restandardization of the Denver Developmental Screening Test. *Pediatrics, 89*(1), 91–97.

Frankowski, Ann Christine and Clark, Leanne J. (2009). Sexuality and intimacy in assisted living: Residents' perspectives and experiences. *Sexuality Research and Social Policy Journal of NSRC, 6*(4), 25–37. doi:10.1525 /srsp.2009.6.4.25

Frayling, Timothy M.; Timpson, Nicholas J.; Weedon, Michael N.; Zeggini, Eleftheria; Freathy, Rachel M.; Lindgren, Cecilia M., . . . McCarthy, Mark I. (2007). A common variant in the FTO gene is associated with body mass index and predisposes to childhood and adult obesity. *Science, 316*(5826), 889–894. doi:10.1126 /science.1141634

Frazier, Thomas W.; Keshavan, Matcheri S.; Minshew, Nancy J. and Hardan, Antonio Y. (2012). A two-year longitudinal MRI study of the corpus callosum in autism. *Journal of Autism and Developmental Disorders, 42*(11), 2312–2322. doi:10.1007/s10803-012-1478-z

Fredricks, Jennifer A. and Eccles, Jacquelynne S. (2002). Children's competence and value beliefs from childhood through adolescence: Growth trajectories in two male-sex-typed domains. *Developmental Psychology, 38*(4), 519–533. doi:10.1037/0012-1649.38.4.519

Freeman, Joan. (2010). *Gifted lives: What happens when gifted children grow up?* New York, NY: Routledge.

Freisthler, Bridget; Merritt, Darcey H. and LaScala, Elizabeth A. (2006). Understanding the ecology of child maltreatment: A review of the literature and directions for future research. *Child Maltreatment, 11*(3), 263–280. doi:10.1177/1077559506289524

Freud, Anna. (2000). Adolescence. In James B. McCarthy (Ed.), *Adolescent development and psychopathology* (pp. 29–52). Lanham, MD: University Press of America.

Freud, Sigmund. (1938). *The basic writings of Sigmund Freud.* New York, NY: Modern Library.

Freud, Sigmund. (1964). An outline of psychoanalysis. *The standard edition of the complete psychological works of Sigmund Freud* (Vol. 23, pp. 144–207). London, UK: Hogarth Press.

Freund, Alexandra M. (2008). Successful aging as management of resources: The role of selection, optimization, and compensation. *Research in Human Development, 5*(2), 94–106. doi:10.1080/15427600802034827

Freund, Alexandra M.; Nikitin, Jana and Ritter, Johannes O. (2009). Psychological consequences of longevity: The increasing importance of self-regulation in old age. *Human Development, 52,* 1–37. doi:10.1159/000189213

Frey, Andy J.; Mandlawitz, Myrna and Alvarez, Michelle. (2012). Leaving NCLB behind. *Children and Schools, 34*(2), 67–69. doi:10.1093/cs/cds021

Fries, Alison B. Wismer and Pollak, Seth D. (2007). Emotion processing and the developing brain. In Donna Coch, Kurt W. Fischer and Geraldine Dawson (Eds.), *Human behavior, learning, and the developing brain: Typical development* (pp. 329–361). New York, NY: Guilford Press.

Frost, Joe L. (2009). *A history of children's play and play environments: Toward a contemporary child-saving movement.* New York, NY: Routledge.

Fuligni, Andrew J.; Hughes, Diane L. and Way, Niobe. (2009). Ethnicity and immigration. In Richard M. Lerner and Laurence Steinberg (Eds.), *Handbook of adolescent psychology* (3rd ed., Vol. 2, pp. 527–569). Hoboken, NJ: Wiley.

Fuligni, Allison Sidle; Howes, Carollee; Lara-Cinisomo, Sandraluz and Karoly, Lynn A. (2009). Diverse pathways in early childhood professional development: An exploration of early educators in public preschools, private preschools, and family child care homes. *Early Education and Development, 20*(3), 507–526. doi:10.1080/10409280902783483

Fuller, Bruce and García Coll, Cynthia. (2010). Learning from Latinos: Contexts, families, and child development in motion. *Developmental Psychology, 46*(3), 559–565. doi:10.1037/a0019412

Fuller, Bruce and Kim, Anthony Y. (2011). Latino Access to Preschool Stalls after Earlier Gains. Berkeley, CA: Institute of Human Development.

Fuller-Iglesias, Heather R.; Webster, Noah J. and Antonucci, Toni C. (2013). Adult family relationships in the context of friendship. *Research in Human Development, 10*(2), 184–203. doi:10 .1080/15427609.2013.786562

Fulmer, C. Ashley; Gelfand, Micheke J.; Kruglanski, Arie W.; Kim-Prieto, Chu; Diener, Ed; Pierro, Antonio and Higgins, E.Tory. (2010). On "feeling right" in cultural contexts: How person-culture match affects self-esteem and subjective well-being. *Psychological Science, 21*(11), 1563–1569. doi:10.1177/0956797610384742

Fung, Helene H.; Stoeber, Franziska S.; Yeung, Dannii Yuen-lan and Lang, Frieder R. (2008). Cultural specificity of socioemotional selectivity: Age differences in social network composition among Germans and Hong Kong Chinese. *Journals of Gerontology Series B: Psychological Sciences and Social Sciences, 63B*(3), P156-P164. doi:10.1093/geronb/63.3.P156

Fung, Joey J. and Lau, Anna S. (2009). Punitive discipline and child behavior problems in Chinese-American immigrant families: The moderating effects of indigenous child-rearing ideologies. *International Journal of Behavioral Development, 33*(6), 520–530. doi:10.1177/0165025409343749

Furstenberg, Frank F., Jr. (2010). On a new schedule: Transitions to adulthood and family change. *Future of Children, 20*(1), 67–87. doi:10.1353/foc.0.0038

Gabrieli, John D. E. (2009). Dyslexia: A new synergy between education and cognitive neuroscience. *Science, 325*(5938), 280–283. doi:10.1126/science.1171999

Gaertner, Bridget M.; Spinrad, Tracy L.; Eisenberg, Nancy and Greving, Karissa A. (2007). Parental childrearing attitudes as correlates of father involvement during infancy. *Journal of Marriage and Family, 69*(4), 962–976. doi:10.1111/j.1741-3737.2007.00424.x

Galambos, Nancy L.; Barker, Erin T. and Krahn, Harvey J. (2006). Depression, self-esteem, and anger in emerging adulthood: Seven-year trajectories. *Developmental Psychology, 42*(2), 350–365. doi:10.1037/0012-1649.42.2.350

Galatzer-Levy, Isaac R. and Bonanno, George A. (2012). Beyond normality in the study of bereavement: Heterogeneity in depression outcomes following loss in older adults. *Social Science & Medicine, 74*(12), 1987–1994. doi:10.1016/j .socscimed.2012.02.022

Galván, Adriana. (2013). The teenage brain: Sensitivity to rewards. *Current Directions in Psychological Science, 22*(2), 88–93. doi:10.1177 /0963721413480859

Gandara, Patricia and Rumberger, Russell W. (2009). Immigration, language, and education: How does language policy structure opportunity? *Teachers College Record, 111*(3), 750–782.

Gandini, Leila; Hill, Lynn; Cadwell, Louise and Schwall, Charles (Eds.). (2005). *In the spirit of the studio: Learning from the atelier of Reggio Emilia.* New York, NY: Teachers College Press.

Gangestad, Steven W. and Simpson, Jeffry A. (Eds.). (2007). *The evolution of mind: Fundamental questions and controversies.* New York, NY: Guilford Press.

Ganong, Lawrence H.; Coleman, Marilyn and Jamison, Tyler. (2011). Patterns of stepchild–stepparent relationship development. *Journal of Marriage and Family, 73*(2), 396–413. doi:10.1111/j.1741-3737.2010.00814.x

Gans, Daphna and Silverstein, Merril. (2006). Norms of filial responsibility for aging parents across time and generations. *Journal of Marriage and Family, 68*(4), 961–976. doi:10.1111/j.1741 -3737.2006.00307.x

Ganz, Tomas and Nemeth, Elizabeta. (2012). Hepcidin and iron homeostasis. *Biochimica et Biophysica Acta (BBA) - Molecular Cell Research, 1823*(9), 1434–1443. doi:10.1016/j .bbamcr.2012.01.014

Gao, Sujuan; Unverzagt, Frederick W.; Hall, Kathleen S.; Lane, Kathleen A.; Murrell, Jill R.; Hake, Ann M., . . . Hendrie, Hugh C. (2013). Mild cognitive impairment, incidence, progression, and reversion: Findings from a community-based cohort of elderly African Americans. *The American Journal of Geriatric Psychiatry,* (In Press, Corrected Proof). doi:10.1016/j.jagp .2013.02.015

Gao, Yuan; Huang, Changquan; Zhao, Kexiang; Ma, Louyan; Qiu, Xuan; Zhang, Lei,

. . . Xiao, Qian. (2013). Depression as a risk factor for dementia and mild cognitive impairment: a meta-analysis of longitudinal studies. *International Journal of Geriatric Psychiatry, 28*(5), 441–449. doi:10.1002/gps.3845

García Coll, Cynthia T. and Marks, Amy Kerivan. (2009). Immigrant stories: Ethnicity and academics in middle childhood. New York, NY: Oxford University Press.

García Coll, Cynthia T. and Marks, Amy Kerivan. (2012). The immigrant paradox in children and adolescents: Is becoming American a developmental risk? Washington, DC: American Psychological Association.

García, Eugene E. and Miller, L. Scott. (2008). Findings and recommendations of the National Task Force on Early Childhood Education for Hispanics. *Child Development Perspectives, 2*(2), 53–58. doi:10.1111/j.1750-8606.2008.00042.x

García, Fernando and Gracia, Enrique. (2009). Is always authoritative the optimum parenting style? Evidence from Spanish families. *Adolescence, 44*(173), 101–131.

Gardner, Howard. (1983). Frames of mind: The theory of multiple intelligences. New York, NY: Basic Books.

Gardner, Howard. (1999). Are there additional intelligences? The case for naturalist, spiritual, and existential intelligences. In Jeffrey Kane (Ed.), *Education, information, and transformation: Essays on learning and thinking* (pp. 111–131). Upper Saddle River, NJ: Merrill.

Gardner, Howard. (2006). Multiple intelligences: New horizons in theory and practice. New York, NY: Basic Books.

Gardner, Howard and Moran, Seana. (2006). The science of multiple intelligences theory: A response to Lynn Waterhouse. *Educational Psychologist, 41*(4), 227–232. doi:10.1207/s15326985ep4104_2

Gaskins, Audrey Jane; Mendiola, Jaime; Afeiche, Myriam; Jørgensen, Niels; Swan, Shanna H. and Chavarro, Jorge E. (2013). Physical activity and television watching in relation to semen quality in young men. British Journal of Sports Medicine, 47. doi:10.1136/bjsports-2012-091644

Gateway, Child Welfare Information. (2013). Foster care statistics, 2011. Washington, DC: U.S. Department of Health and Human Services, Children's Bureau Retrieved from http://www.acf.hhs.gov/programs/cb/research-data-technology/statistics-research/afcars.

Gauvain, Mary; Beebe, Heidi and Zhao, Shuheng. (2011). Applying the cultural approach to cognitive development. *Journal of Cognition and Development, 12*(2), 121–133. doi:10.1080/15248372.2011.563481

Gavrilov, Leonid A. and Gavrilova, Natalia S. (2006). Reliability theory of aging and longevity. In Edward J. Masoro and Steven N. Austad (Eds.), Handbook of the biology of aging (6th ed., pp. 3–42). Amsterdam, The Netherlands: Elsevier Academic Press.

Ge, Xiaojia and Natsuaki, Misaki N. (2009). In search of explanations for early pubertal timing effects on developmental psychopathology. *Current Directions in Psychological Science, 18*(6), 327–331. doi:10.1111/j.1467-8721.2009.01661.x

Geelhoed, Elizabeth; Harris, Anthony and Prince, Richard. (1994). Cost-effectiveness analysis of hormone replacement therapy and lifestyle intervention for hip fracture. *Australian Journal of Public Health, 18*(2), 153–160. doi:10.1111/j.1753-6405.1994.tb00217.x

Geiger, Jennifer Mullins; Hayes, Megan J. and Lietz, Cynthia A. (2013). Should I stay or should I go? A mixed methods study examining the factors influencing foster parents' decisions to continue or discontinue providing foster care. *Children and Youth Services Review, 35*(9), 1356–1365. doi:10.1016/j.childyouth.2013.05.003

Gelfand, Michele J. (2012). Culture's constraints: International differences in the strength of social norms. *Current Directions in Psychological Science, 21*(6), 420–424. doi:10.1177/0963721412460048

Gendron, Brian P.; Williams, Kirk R. and Guerra, Nancy G. (2011). An analysis of bullying among students within schools: Estimating the effects of individual normative beliefs, self-esteem, and school climate. *Journal of School Violence, 10*(2), 150–164. doi:10.1080/15388220.2010.539166

Genesee, Fred. (2008). Early dual language learning. *Zero to Three, 29*(1), 17–23.

Gentile, Douglas A. (2009). Pathological video-game use among youth ages 8 to 18: A National Study. *Psychological Science, 20*(5), 594–602. doi:10.1111/j.1467-9280.2009.02340.x

Gentile, Douglas A. (2011). The multiple dimensions of video game effects. *Child Development Perspectives, 5*(2), 75–81. doi:10.1111/j.1750-8606.2011.00159.x

Georgas, James; Berry, John W.; van de Vijver, Fons J. R.; Kagitçibasi, Çigdem and Poortinga, Ype H. (Eds.). (2006). *Families across cultures: A 30-nation psychological study.* New York, NY: Cambridge University Press.

George, Danny and Whitehouse, Peter. (2010). Dementia and mild cognitive impairment in social and cultural context. In Dale Dannefer and Chris Phillipson (Eds.), *The SAGE handbook of social gerontology* (pp. 343–356). Los Angeles, CA: SAGE.

Gerber, Alan S.; Huber, Gregory A.; Doherty, David and Dowling, Conor M. (2011). The Big Five personality traits in the political arena. *Annual Review of Political Science, 14*, 265–287. doi:10.1146/annurev-polisci-051010-111659

Geronimus, Arline T.; Hicken, Margaret; Keene, Danya and Bound, John. (2006). "Weathering" and age patterns of allostatic load scores among Blacks and Whites in the United States. *American Journal of Public Health, 96*(5), 826–833. doi:10.2105/AJPH.2004.060749

Gershkoff-Stowe, Lisa and Hahn, Erin R. (2007). Fast mapping skills in the developing lexicon. *Journal of Speech, Language, and Hearing Research, 50*, 682–696. doi:10.1044/1092-4388(2007/048)

Gershoff, Elizabeth T.; Grogan-Kaylor, Andrew; Lansford, Jennifer E.; Chang, Lei; Zelli, Arnaldo; Deater-Deckard, Kirby and Dodge, Kenneth A. (2010). Parent discipline practices in an international sample: Associations with child behaviors and moderation by perceived normativeness. *Child Development, 81*(2), 487–502. doi:10.1111/j.1467-8624.2009.01409.x

Gershoff, Elizabeth T.; Lansford, Jennifer E.; Sexton, Holly R.; Davis-Kean, Pamela and Sameroff, Arnold J. (2012). Longitudinal links between spanking and children's externalizing behaviors in a national sample of white, black, hispanic, and asian american families. *Child Development, 83*(3), 838–843. doi:10.1111/j.1467-8624.2011.01732.x

Gettler, Lee T. and McKenna, James J. (2010). Never sleep with baby? Or keep me close but keep me safe: Eliminating inappropriate safe infant sleep rhetoric in the United States. *Current Pediatric Reviews, 6*(1), 71–77. doi:10.2174/157339610791317250

Gevorgyan, Ruzanna; Schmidt, Elena; Wall, Martin; Garnett, Geoffrey; Atun, Rifat; Maksimova, Svetlana, . . . Renton, Adrian. (2011). Does Russia need sex education? The views of stakeholders in three Russian regions. *Sex Education, 11*(2), 213–226. doi:10.1080/14681811.2011.558429

Gewirtzman, Aron; Bobrick, Laura; Conner, Kelly and Tyring, Stephen K. (2011). Epidemiology of sexually transmitted infections. In Gerd Gross and Stephen K. Tyring (Eds.), *Sexually transmitted infections and sexually transmitted diseases* (pp. 13–34). New York, NY: Springer.

Giardino, Angelo P. and Alexander, Randell. (2005). *Child maltreatment: A clinical guide and reference* (3th ed. Vol. 1). St. Louis, MO: G. W. Medical.

Gibson, Eleanor J. (1969). Principles of perceptual learning and development. New York, NY: Appleton-Century-Crofts.

Gibson, Eleanor J. (1988). Exploratory behavior in the development of perceiving, acting, and the acquiring of knowledge. *Annual Review of Psychology, 39*, 1–42. doi:10.1146/annurev.ps.39.020188.000245

Gibson, Eleanor J. (1997). An ecological psychologist's prolegomena for perceptual development: A functional approach. In Cathy Dent-Read and Patricia Zukow-Goldring (Eds.), *Evolving explanations of development: Ecological approaches to organism-environment systems* (1st ed., pp. 23–54). Washington, DC: American Psychological Association.

Gibson, Eleanor J. and Walk, Richard D. (1960). The "visual cliff". *Scientific American, 202*(4), 64–71. doi:10.1038/scientificamerican0460-64

Gibson, James Jerome. (1979). *The ecological approach to visual perception.* Boston, MA: Houghton Mifflin.

Gigante, Denise. (2007). Zeitgeist. *European Romantic Review, 18*(2), 265–272. doi:10.1080/10509580701298040

Gilbert, Richard B. (2013). Religion, Spirituality, and End-of-Life Decision Making. In David K. Meagher and David E. Balk (Eds.), *Handbook of thanatology: The essential body of knowledge for the study of death, dying, and bereavement* (2nd ed., pp. 63–71). New York, NY: Routledge.

Giles, Amy and Rovee-Collier, Carolyn (2011). Infant long-term memory for associations formed during mere exposure. *Infant Behavior and Development, 34*(2), 327–338. doi:10.1016/j.infbeh.2011.02.004

Gillen, Meghan M. and Lefkowitz, Eva S. (2012). Gender and racial/ethnic differences in body image development among college students. *Body Image, 9*(1), 126–130. doi:10.1016/j.bodyim.2011.09.004

Gilles, Floyd H. and Nelson, Marvin D. (2012). The developing human brain: Growth and adversities. London, UK: Mac Keith Press.

Gillespie, Michael Allen. (2010). Players and spectators: Sports and ethical training in the American university. *Debating moral education: Rethinking the role of the modern university* (pp. 293–316). Durham, NC: Duke University Press.

Gilliam, Mary; Stockman, Michael; Malek, Meaghan; Sharp, Wendy; Greenstein, Deanna; Lalonde, Francois, . . . Shaw, Philip. (2011). Developmental trajectories of the corpus callosum in attention-deficit/hyperactivity disorder. *Biological Psychiatry, 69*(9), 839–846. doi:10.1016/j.biopsych.2010.11.024

Gilligan, Carol. (1981). Moral development in the college years. In Arthur Chickering (Ed.), *The modern American college: Responding to the new realities of diverse students and a changing society* (pp. 139–156). San Francisco, CA: Jossey-Bass.

Gilligan, Carol. (1982). *In a different voice: Psychological theory and women's development.* Cambridge, MA: Harvard University Press.

Gilligan, Carol; Murphy, John Michael and Tappan, Mark B. (1990). Moral development beyond adolescence. In Charles Nathaniel Alexander and Ellen J. Langer (Eds.), *Higher stages of human development: Perspectives on adult growth* (pp. 208–225). New York, NY: Oxford University Press.

Gillis, John R. (2008). The islanding of children: Reshaping the mythical landscapes of childhood. In Marta Gutman and Ning de Coninck-Smith (Eds.), *Designing modern childhoods: History, space, and the material culture of children* (pp. 316–329). New Brunswick, NJ: Rutgers University Press.

Gilovich, Thomas; Vallone, Robert and Tversky, Amos. (1985). The hot hand in basketball: On the misperception of random sequences. *Cognitive Psychology, 17*(3), 295–314. doi:10.1016/0010-0285(85)90010-6

Gipson, Jessica D. and Hindin, Michelle J. (2008). "Having another child would be a life or death situation for her": Understanding pregnancy termination among couples in rural Bangladesh. *American Journal of Public Health, 98*(10), 1827–1832. doi:10.2105/AJPH.2007.129262

Gitlin, Laura N.; Belle, Steven H.; Burgio, Louis D.; Czaja, Sara J.; Mahoney, Diane; **Gallagher-Thompson, Dolores, . . . Ory, Marcia G.** (2003). Effect of multicomponent interventions on caregiver burden and depression: The REACH multisite initiative at 6-month follow-up. *Psychology and Aging, 18*(3), 361–374. doi:10.1037/0882-7974.18.3.361

Giuffrè, Mario; Piro, Ettore and Corsello, Giovanni. (2012). Prematurity and twinning. *Journal of Maternal-Fetal and Neonatal Medicine, 25*(3), 6–10. doi:10.3109/14767058.2012.712350

Gladwell, Malcolm. (2010, October 4). Small change: Why the revolution will not be tweeted. *The New Yorker, 86*, 42–49.

Gluckman, Peter D. and Hanson, Mark A. (2006). Developmental origins of health and disease. New York, NY: Cambridge University Press.

Göbel, Silke M.; Shaki, Samuel and Fischer, Martin H. (2011). The cultural number line: A review of cultural and linguistic influences on the development of number processing. *Journal of Cross-Cultural Psychology, 42*(4), 543–565. doi:10.1177/0022022111406251

Goddings, Anne-Lise; Heyes, Stephanie Burnett; Bird, Geoffrey; Viner, Russell M. and Blakemore, Sarah-Jayne. (2012). The relationship between puberty and social emotion processing. *Developmental Science, 15*(6), 801–811. doi:10.1111/j.1467-7687.2012.01174.x

Godlike Productions. (2012). Lawns: Wasteful, unquestioned totems of conformity. http://www.godlikeproductions.com/forum1/message1925689/pg1

Gogtay, Nitin; Giedd, Jay N.; Lusk, Leslie; Hayashi, Kiralee M.; Greenstein, Deanna; Vaituzis, A. Catherine, . . . Ungerleider, Leslie G. (2004). Dynamic mapping of human cortical development during childhood through early adulthood. *Proceedings of the National Academy of Sciences of the United States of America, 10*(21), 8174–8179. doi:10.1073/pnas.0402680101

Golant, Stephen M. (2011). The changing residential environments of older people. In Robert H. Binstock and Linda K. George (Eds.), Handbook of aging and the social sciences (7th ed., pp. 207–220). San Diego, CA: Academic Press. doi:10.1016/B978-0-12-380880-6.00015-0

Goldberg, Wendy A.; Prause, JoAnn; Lucas-Thompson, Rachel and Himsel, Amy. (2008). Maternal employment and children's achievement in context: A meta-analysis of four decades of research. *Psychological Bulletin, 134*(1), 77–108. doi:10.1037/0033-2909.134.1.77

Golden, Marita. (2010). Angel baby. In Barbara Graham (Ed.), *Eye of my heart: 27 writers reveal the hidden pleasures and perils of being a grandmother* (pp. 125–133). New York, NY: HarperCollins.

Goldin-Meadow, Susan. (2009). How gesture promotes learning throughout childhood. *Child Development Perspectives, 3*(2), 106–111. doi:10.1111/j.1750-8606.2009.00088.x

Goldstein, Joshua R. (2011). A secular trend toward earlier male sexual maturity: Evidence from shifting ages of male young adult mortality. *PLoS ONE, 6*(8), e14826. doi:10.1371/journal.pone.0014826

Goldstein, Michael H.; Schwade, Jennifer A. and Bornstein, Marc H. (2009). The value of vocalizing: Five-month-old infants associate their own noncry vocalizations with responses from caregivers. *Child Development, 80*(3), 636–644. doi:10.1111/j.1467-8624.2009.01287.x

Golinkoff, Roberta Michnick and Hirsh-Pasek, Kathy. (2008). How toddlers begin to learn verbs. *Trends in Cognitive Sciences, 12*(10), 397–403. doi:10.1016/j.tics.2008.07.003

Golub, Sarit A. and Langer, Ellen J. (2007). Challenging assumptions about adult development: Implications for the health of older adults. In Carolyn M. Aldwin, Crystal L. Park and Avron Spiro (Eds.), *Handbook of health psychology and aging* (pp. 9–29). New York, NY: Guilford Press.

Göncü, Artin and Gaskins, Suzanne. (2011). Comparing and extending Piaget's and Vygotsky's understandings of play: Symbolic play as individual, sociocultural, and educational interpretation. In Anthony D. Pellegrini (Ed.), *The Oxford handbook of the development of play* (pp. 48–57). New York, NY: Oxford University Press.

Gonyea, Judith G. (2013). Midlife, multigenerational bonds, and caregiving. In Ronda C. Talley and Lydia LaGue (Eds.), *Caregiving across the lifespan: Research, practice, policy* (pp. 105–130). New York, NY: Springer.

Goodman, Judith C.; Dale, Philip S. and Li, Ping. (2008). Does frequency count? Parental input and the acquisition of vocabulary. *Journal of Child Language, 35*(3), 515–531. doi:10.1017/S0305000907008641

Goodnight, Jackson A.; D'Onofrio, Brian M.; Cherlin, Andrew J.; Emery, Robert E.; Van Hulle, Carol A. and Lahey, Benjamin B. (2013). Effects of multiple maternal relationship transitions on offspring antisocial behavior in childhood and adolescence: A cousin-comparison analysis. *Journal of Abnormal Child Psychology, 41*(2), 185–198. doi:10.1007/s10802-012-9667-y

Gopnik, Alison. (2001). Theories, language, and culture: Whorf without wincing. In Melissa Bowerman and Stephen C. Levinson (Eds.), *Language acquisition and conceptual development* (pp. 45–69). New York, NY: Cambridge University Press.

Gopnik, Alison and Schulz, Laura Elizabeth (Eds.). (2007). *Causal learning: Psychology, philosophy, and computation.* New York, NY: Oxford University Press.

Gopnik, Alison and Wellman, Henry M. (2012). Reconstructing constructivism: Causal models, Bayesian learning mechanisms, and the theory theory. *Psychological Bulletin, 138*(6), 1085–1108. doi:10.1037/a0028044

Gordis, Elana B.; Granger, Douglas A.; Susman, Elizabeth J. and Trickett, Penelope K. (2008). Salivary alpha amylase-cortisol asymmetry in maltreated youth. *Hormones and Behavior, 53*(1), 96–103. doi:10.1016/j.yhbeh.2007.09.002

Gornick, Janet C. and Meyers, Marcia. (2003). Families that work: Policies for reconciling parenthood and employment. New York, NY: Russell Sage Foundation.

Gosso, Yumi. (2010). Play in different cultures. In Peter K. Smith (Ed.), *Children and play: Understanding children's worlds* (pp. 80–98). Malden, MA: Wiley-Blackwell.

Gottesman, Irving I.; Laursen, Thomas Munk; Bertelsen, Aksel and Mortensen, Preben Bo. (2010). Severe mental disorders in offspring with 2 psychiatrically ill parents. *Archives of General Psychiatry, 67*(3), 252–257. doi:10.1001/archgenpsychiatry.2010.1

Gottfried, Adele Eskeles; Marcoulides, George A.; Gottfried, Allen W. and Oliver, Pamella H. (2009). A latent curve model of parental motivational practices and developmental decline in math and science academic intrinsic motivation. *Journal of Educational Psychology, 101*(3), 729–739. doi:10.1037/a0015084

Gottlieb, Gilbert. (2007). Probabilistic epigenesis. *Developmental Science, 10*(1), 1–11. doi:10.1111/j.1467-7687.2007.00556.x

Gottlieb, Gilbert. (2010). Normally occurring environmental and behavioral influences on gene activity. In Kathryn E. Hood, Carolyn Tucker Halpern, Gary Greenberg and Richard M. Lerner (Eds.), *Handbook of developmental science, behavior, and genetics* (pp. 13–37). Malden, MA: Wiley.

Gottman, John Mordechai; Murray, James D.; Swanson, Catherine; Tyson, Rebecca and Swanson, Kristin R. (2002). The mathematics of marriage: Dynamic nonlinear models. Cambridge, MA: The MIT Press.

Gow, Alan J.; Bastin, Mark E.; Maniega, Susana Muñoz; Hernández, Maria C. Valdés; Morris, Zoe; Murray, Catherine, . . . Wardlaw, Joanna M. (2012). Neuroprotective lifestyles and the aging brain. *Neurology, 79*(17), 1802–1808. doi:10.1212/WNL.0b013e3182703fd2

Goymer, Patrick. (2007). Genes know their left from their right. *Nature Reviews Genetics, 8*(9), 652. doi:10.1038/nrg2194

Graber, Julia A.; Nichols, Tracy R. and Brooks-Gunn, Jeanne. (2010). Putting pubertal timing in developmental context: implications for prevention. *Developmental Psychobiology, 52*(3), 254–262. doi:10.1002/dev.20438

Grady, Denise. (2012, May 5). When illness makes a spouse a stranger. *The New York Times,* p. A1.

Grady, Jessica S.; Ale, Chelsea M. and Morris, Tracy L. (2012). A naturalistic observation of social behaviours during preschool drop-off. *Early Child Development and Care, 182*(12), 1683–1694. doi:10.1080/03004430.2011.649266

Grady, Rosheen; Alavi, Nika; Vale, Rachel; Khandwala, Mohammad and McDonald, Sarah D. (2012). Elective single embryo transfer and perinatal outcomes: A systematic review and meta-analysis. *Fertility and Sterility, 97*(2), 324–331. doi:10.1016/j.fertnstert.2011.11.033

Gräff, Johannes; Kim, Dohoon; Dobbin, Matthew M. and Tsai, Li-Huei. (2011). Epigenetic regulation of gene expression in physiological and pathological brain processes. *Physiological Reviews, 91*(2), 603–649. doi:10.1152/physrev.00012.2010

Grandin, Temple and Johnson, Catherine. (2009). *Animals make us human: Creating the best life for animals*. Boston, MA: Houghton Mifflin Harcourt.

Granic, Isabela and Patterson, Gerald R. (2006). Toward a comprehensive model of antisocial development: A dynamic systems approach. *Psychological Review, 113*(1), 101–131. doi:10.1037/0033-295X.113.1.101

Granpeesheh, Doreen; Tarbox, Jonathan and Dixon, Dennis R. (2009). Applied behavior analytic interventions for children with autism: A description and review of treatment research. *Annals of Clinical Psychiatry, 21*(3), 162–173.

Granpeesheh, Doreen; Tarbox, Jonathan; Dixon, Dennis R.; Wilke, Arthur E.; Allen, Michael S. and Bradstreet, James Jeffrey. (2010). Randomized trial of hyperbaric oxygen therapy for children with autism. *Research in Autism Spectrum Disorders, 4*(2), 268–275. doi:10.1016/j.rasd.2009.09.014

Grant, Jon E. and Potenza, Marc N. (Eds.). (2010). *Young adult mental health*. New York, NY: Oxford University Press.

Green, James A.; Whitney, Pamela G. and Potegal, Michael. (2011). Screaming, yelling, whining, and crying: Categorical and intensity differences in vocal expressions of anger and sadness in children's tantrums. *Emotion, 11*(5), 1124–1133. doi:10.1037/a0024173

Green, Lorraine and Grant, Victoria. (2008). "Gagged grief and beleaguered bereavements?" An analysis of multidisciplinary theory and research relating to same sex partnership bereavement. *Sexualities, 11*(3), 275–300. doi:10.1177/1363460708089421

Green, Melinda A.; Scott, Norman A.; DeVilder, Elizabeth L.; Zeiger, Amanda and Darr, Stacy. (2006). Relational-interdependent self-construal as a function of bulimic symptomatology. *Journal of Clinical Psychology, 62*(7), 943–951. doi:10.1002/jclp.20270

Greene, Melissa L. and Way, Niobe. (2005). Self-esteem trajectories among ethnic minority adolescents: A growth curve analysis of the patterns and predictors of change. *Journal of Research on Adolescence, 15*(2), 151–178. doi:10.1111/j.1532-7795.2005.00090.x

Greenfield, Emily A.; Scharlach, Andrew; Lehning, Amanda J. and Davitt, Joan K. (2012). A conceptual framework for examining the promise of the NORC program and Village models to promote aging in place. *Journal of Aging Studies, 26*(3), 273–284. doi:10.1016/j.jaging.2012.01.003

Greenfield, Patricia M. (2009). Technology and informal education: What is taught, what is learned. *Science, 323*(5910), 69–71. doi:10.1126/science.1167190

Greenwood, Charles R.; Thiemann-Bourque, Kathy; Walker, Dale; Buzhardt, Jay and Gilkerson, Jill. (2011). Assessing children's home language environments using automatic speech recognition technology. *Communication Disorders Quarterly, 32*(2), 83–92. doi:10.1177/1525740110367826

Greenwood, Pamela M. and Parasuraman, R. (2012). Nurturing the older brain and mind. Cambridge, MA: The MIT Press.

Gregg, Christopher. (2010). Parental control over the brain. *Science, 330*(6005), 770–771. doi:10.1126/science.1199054

Gregg, Norman McAlister. (1941). Congenital cataract following german measles in the mother. *Transactions of the Ophthalmological Society of Australia, 3*, 35–46.

Gregory, Sara M.; Parker, Beth and Thompson, Paul D. (2012). Physical activity, cognitive function, and brain health: What is the role of exercise training in the prevention of dementia? *Brain Sciences, 2*(4), 684–708. doi:10.3390/brainsci2040684

Greil, Arthur L.; McQuillan, Julia; Shreffler, Karina M.; Johnson, Katherine M. and Slauson-Blevins, Kathleen S. (2011). Race-ethnicity and medical services for infertility stratified reproduction in a population-based sample of U.S. women. *Journal of Health and Social Behavior, 52*(4), 493–509. doi:10.1177/0022146511418236

Gremeauxa, Vincent; Gaydaa, Mathieu; Leperse, Romuald; Sosnera, Philippe; Juneaua, Martin and Nigam, Anil. (2012). Exercise and longevity. *Maturitas, 73*, 312–317. doi:10.1016/j.maturitas.2012.09.012

Greyson, Bruce. (2009). Near-death experiences and deathbed visions. In Allan Kellehear (Ed.), *The study of dying: From autonomy to transformation* (pp. 253–275). New York, NY: Cambridge University Press.

Griffin, James; Gooding, Sarah; Semesky, Michael; Farmer, Brittany; Mannchen, Garrett and Sinnott, Jan. (2009). Four brief studies of relations between postformal thought and non-cognitive factors: Personality, concepts of god, political opinions, and social attitudes. *Journal of Adult Development, 16*(3), 173–182. doi:10.1007/s10804-009-9056-0

Griffith, Patrick and Lopez, Oscar. (2009). Disparities in the diagnosis and treatment of Alzheimer's disease in African American and Hispanic patients: A call to action. *Generations, 33*(1), 37–46.

Grossmann, Tobias (2013). Mapping Prefrontal Cortex Functions in Human Infancy. *Infancy, 18*(3), 303–324. doi:10.1111/infa.12016

Grubeck-Loebenstein, Beatrix. (2010). Fading immune protection in old age: Vaccination in the elderly. *Journal of Comparative Pathology, 142*(Suppl. 1), S116–S119. doi:10.1016/j.jcpa.2009.10.002

Grundy, Emily and Henretta, John C. (2006). Between elderly parents and adult children: A new look at the intergenerational care provided by the 'sandwich generation'. *Ageing & Society, 26*(5), 707–722. doi:10.1017/S0144686X06004934

Guerra, Nancy G. and Williams, Kirk R. (2010). Implementing bullying prevention in diverse settings: Geographic, economic, and cultural influences. In Eric M. Vernberg and Bridget K. Biggs (Eds.), *Preventing and treating bullying and victimization* (pp. 319–336). New York, NY: Oxford University Press.

Guerra, Nancy G.; Williams, Kirk R. and Sadek, Shelly. (2011). Understanding bullying and victimization during childhood and adolescence: A mixed methods study. *Child Development, 82*(1), 295–310. doi:10.1111/j.1467-8624.2010.01556.x

Guerri, Consuelo and Pascual, María. (2010). Mechanisms involved in the neurotoxic, cognitive, and neurobehavioral effects of alcohol consumption during adolescence. *Alcohol, 44*(1), 15–26. doi:10.1016/j.alcohol.2009.10.003

Guerry, John and Hastings, Paul. (2011). In search of HPA axis dysregulation in child and adolescent depression. *Clinical Child and Family Psychology Review, 14*(2), 135–160. doi:10.1007/s10567-011-0084-5

Gummerum, Michaela; Keller, Monika; Takezawa, Masanori and Mata, Jutta. (2008). To give or not to give: Children's and adolescents' sharing and moral negotiations in economic decision situations. *Child Development, 79*(3), 562–576. doi:10.1111/j.1467-8624.2008.01143.x

Güngör, Derya; Bornstein, Marc H.; De Leersnyder, Jozefien; Cote, Linda; Ceulemans, Eva and Mesquita, Batja. (2013). Acculturation of personality: A three-culture study of Japanese, Japanese Americans, and European Americans. *Journal of Cross-Cultural Psychology, 44*(5), 701–718. doi:10.1177/0022022112470749

Gupta, Ramesh C. (2011). Reproductive and developmental toxicology. Boston, MA: Elsevier/Academic Press.

Gurunath, S.; Pandian, Z.; Anderson, Richard A. and Bhattacharya, Siladitya. (2011). Defining infertility—A systematic review of prevalence studies. *Human Reproduction Update, 17*(5), 575–588. doi:10.1093/humupd/dmr015

Gurven, Michael; von Rueden, Christopher; Massenkoff, Maxim; Kaplan, Hillard and Lero Vie, Marino. (2013). How universal is the Big Five? Testing the five-factor model of personality variation among forager–farmers in the Bolivian Amazon. *Journal of Personality and Social Psychology, 104*(2), 354–370. doi:10.1037/a0030841

Haas, Steven A. (2013). Developmental origins of disease and health disparities: Limitations and future directions. In Nancy S. Landale, Susan M. McHale and Alan Booth (Eds.), *Families and Child Health* (pp. 23–32). New York, NY: Springer. doi:10.1007/978-1-4614-6194-4_3

Haas, Steven A.; Krueger, Patrick M. and Rohlfsen, Leah. (2012). Race/ethnic and nativity disparities in later life physical performance: The role of health and socioeconomic status over the life course. *The Journals of Gerontology Series B: Psychological Sciences and Social Sciences, 67B*(2), 238–248. doi:10.1093/geronb/gbr155

Haase, Claudia M.; Heckhausen, Jutta and Wrosch, Carsten. (2013). Developmental regulation across the life span: Toward a new synthesis. *Developmental Psychology, 49*(5), 964–972. doi:10.1037/a0029231

Hackman, Daniel A. and Farah, Martha J. (2009). Socioeconomic status and the developing brain. *Trends in Cognitive Sciences, 13*(2), 65–73. doi:10.1016/j.tics.2008.11.003

Haden, Catherine A. (2010). Talking about science in museums. *Child Development Perspectives, 4*(1), 62–67. doi:10.1111/j.1750-8606.2009.00119.x

Hagedoorn, Mariët; Van Yperen, Nico W.; Coyne, James C.; van Jaarsveld, Cornelia H. M.; Ranchor, Adelita V.; van Sonderen, Eric and Sanderman, Robbert. (2006). Does marriage protect older people from distress? The role of equity and recency of bereavement. *Psychology and Aging, 21*(3), 611–620. doi:10.1037/0882-7974.21.3.611

Hagestad, Gunhild O. and Uhlenberg, Peter. (2007). The impact of demographic changes on relations between age groups and generations: A comparative perspective. In K. Warner Schaie and Peter Uhlenberg (Eds.), *Social structures: Demographic changes and the well-being of older persons* (pp. 239–261). New York, NY: Springer.

Haier, Richard J.; Colom, Roberto; Schroeder, David H.; Condon, Christopher A.; Tang, Cheuk; Eaves, Emily and Head, Kevin. (2009). Gray matter and intelligence factors: Is there a neuro-g? *Intelligence, 37*(2), 136–144. doi:10.1016/j.intell.2008.10.011

Hajjar, Emily R.; Cafiero, Angela C. and Hanlon, Joseph T. (2007). Polypharmacy in elderly patients. *American Journal of Geriatric Pharmacotherapy, 5*(4), 345–351. doi:10.1016/j.amjopharm.2007.12.002

Halaschek-Wiener, Julius; Amirabbasi-Beik, Mahsa; Monfared, Nasim; Pieczyk, Markus; Sailer, Christian; Kollar, Anita, . . . Brooks-Wilson, Angela R. (2009). Genetic variation in healthy oldest-old. *PLoS ONE, 4*(8), e6641. doi:10.1371/journal.pone.0006641

Hall, Jessica A.; Dominy, John E.; Lee, Yoonjin and Puigserver, Pere. (2013). The sirtuin family's role in aging and age-associated pathologies. *The Journal of Clinical Investigation, 123*(3), 973–979. doi:10.1172/JCI64094

Hall, Lynn K. (2008). *Counseling military families: What mental health professionals need to know.* New York, NY: Taylor and Francis.

Halpern, Neil A.; Pastores, Stephen M.; Chou, Joanne F.; Chawla, Sanjay and Thaler, Howard T. (2011). Advance directives in an oncologic intensive care unit: A contemporary analysis of their frequency, type, and impact. *Journal of Palliative Medicine, 14*(4), 483–489. doi:10.1089/jpm.2010.0397

Halpern-Meekin, Sarah; Manning, Wendy D.; Giordano, Peggy C. and Longmore, Monica A. (2013). Relationship churning: Physical violence, and verbal abuse in young adult relationships. *Journal of Marriage and Family, 75*(1), 2–12. doi:10.1111/j.1741-3737.2012.01029.x

Hamerton, John L. and Evans, Jane A. (2005). Sex chromosome anomalies. In Merlin G. Butler and F. John Meaney (Eds.), *Genetics of developmental disabilities* (pp. 585–650). Boca Raton, FL: Taylor & Francis.

Hamill, Paul J. (1991). Triage: An essay. *The Georgia Review, 45*(3), 463–469.

Hamilton, Alice. (1914). Lead poisoning in the United States. *American Journal of Public Health, 4*(6), 477–480. doi:10.2105/AJPH.4.6.477-a

Hamilton, Brady E.; Martin, Joyce A. and Ventura, Stephanie J. (2012). Births: Preliminary data for 2011. Hyattsville, MD: Retrieved from http://www.cdc.gov/nchs/data/nvsr/nvsr61/nvsr61_05.pdf.

Hamilton, Rashea; Sanders, Megan and Anderman, Eric M. (2013). The multiple choices of sex education. *Phi Delta Kappan, 94*(5), 34–39.

Hamm, Jill V. and Faircloth, Beverly S. (2005). The role of friendship in adolescents' sense of school belonging. *New Directions for Child and Adolescent Development, 2005*(107), 61–78. doi:10.1002/cd.121

Hammer, Carol Scheffner; Jia, Gisela and Uchikoshi, Yuuko. (2011). Language and literacy development of dual language learners growing up in the United States: A call for research. *Child Development Perspectives, 5*(1), 4–9. doi:10.1111/j.1750-8606.2010.00140.x

Hammond, Christopher J.; Andrew, Toby; Mak, Ying Tat and Spector, Tim D. (2004). A susceptibility locus for myopia in the normal population is linked to the PAX6 gene region on chromosome 11: A genomewide scan of dizygotic twins. *American Journal of Human Genetics, 75*(2), 294–304. doi:10.1086/423148

Hampel, Harald; Lista, Simone and Khachaturian, Zaven S. (2012). Development of biomarkers to chart all Alzheimer's disease stages: The royal road to cutting the therapeutic Gordian Knot. *Alzheimer's & Dementia, 8*(4), 312–336. doi:10.1016/j.jalz.2012.05.2116

Hamplova, Dana. (2009). Educational homogamy among married and unmarried couples in Europe: Does context matter? *Journal of Family Issues, 30*(1), 28–52. doi:10.1177/0192513X08324576

Han, Euna; Norton, Edward C. and Powell, Lisa M. (2011). Direct and indirect effects of body weight on adult wages. *Economics & Human Biology, 9*(4), 381–392. doi:10.1016/j.ehb.2011.07.002

Han, Wen-Jui; Lee, RaeHyuck and Waldfogel, Jane. (2012). School readiness among children of immigrants in the US: Evidence from a large national birth cohort study. *Children and Youth Services Review, 34*(4), 771–782. doi:10.1016/j.childyouth.2012.01.001

Hanania, Rima. (2010). Two types of perseveration in the dimension change card sort task. *Journal of Experimental Child Psychology, 107*(3), 325–336. doi:10.1016/j.jecp.2010.05.002

Handelsman, David J. (2011). Androgen misuse and abuse. *Best Practice & Research Clinical Endocrinology & Metabolism, 25*(2), 377–389. doi:10.1016/j.beem.2010.09.005

Hane, Amie Ashley; Cheah, Charissa; Rubin, Kenneth H. and Fox, Nathan A. (2008). The role of maternal behavior in the relation between shyness and social reticence in early childhood and social withdrawal in middle childhood. *Social Development, 17*(4), 795–811. doi:10.1111/j.1467-9507.2008.00481.x

Hank, Karsten and Korbmacher, Julie M. (2013). Parenthood and retirement: Gender, cohort, and welfare regime differences. *European Societies, 15*(3), 446–461. doi:10.1080/1461669 6.2012.750731

Hanks, Andrew S.; Just, David R. and Wansink, Brian. (2013). Smarter lunchrooms can address new school lunchroom guidelines and childhood obesity. *The Journal of Pediatrics, 162*(4), 867–869. doi:10.1016/j.jpeds.2012.12.031

Hannah, Sean T.; Avolio, Bruce J. and May, Douglas R. (2011). Moral maturation and moral conation: a capacity approach to explaining moral thought and action. *Academy Management Review, 36*(4), 663–685. doi:10.5465/amr.2010.0128

Hannan, Claire; Buchanan, Anna DeBlois and Monroe, Judy. (2009). Maintaining the vaccine safety net. *Pediatrics, 124*(Suppl. 5), S571–572. doi:10.1542/peds.2009–1542U

Hanoch, Yaniv; Miron-Shatz, Talya and Himmelstein, Mary. (2010). Genetic testing and risk interpretation: How do women understand lifetime risk results? *Judgment and Decision Making, 5*(2), 116–123.

Hanushek, Eric A. and Woessmann, Ludger. (2009). Do better schools lead to more growth? Cognitive skills, economic outcomes, and causation. *Journal of Economic Growth, 17*(4), 267–321. doi:10.1007/s10887-012-9081-x

Hanushek, Eric A and Woessmann, Ludger. (2010). The high cost of low educational performance: The long-run economic impact of improving PISA outcomes. Paris: OECD Publishing. doi:10.1787/9789264077485-en

Harden, K. Paige and Tucker-Drob, Elliot M. (2011). Individual differences in the development of sensation seeking and impulsivity during adolescence: Further evidence for a dual systems model. *Developmental Psychology, 47*(3), 739–746. doi:10.1037/a0023279

Hare, Kelly M. and Cree, Alison. (2010). Incidence, causes and consequences of pregnancy failure in viviparous lizards: Implications for research and conservation settings. *Reproduction, Fertility and Development, 22*(5), 761–770. doi:10.1071/RD09195

Hargreaves, Andy. (2012). Singapore: The Fourth Way in action? *Educational Research for Policy and Practice, 11*(1), 7–17. doi:10.1007 /s10671-011-9125-6

Harjes, Carlos E.; Rocheford, Torbert R.; Bai, Ling; Brutnell, Thomas P.; Kandianis, Catherine Bermudez; Sowinski, Stephen G., . . . Buckler, Edward S. (2008). Natural genetic variation in lycopene epsilon cyclase tapped for maize biofortification. *Science, 319*(5861), 330–333. doi:10.1126/science.1150255

Harkness, Sara; Super, Charles M. and Mavridis, Caroline Johnston. (2011). Parental ethnotheories about children's socioemotional development. In Xinyin Chen and Kenneth H. Rubin (Eds.), *Socioemotional development in cultural context* (pp. 73–98). New York, NY: Guilford Press.

Harlow, Ilana. (2005). Shaping sorrow: Creative aspects of public and private mourning. In Samuel C. Heilman (Ed.), *Death, bereavement, and mourning* (pp. 33–52). New Brunswick, NJ: Transaction.

Harris, Judith Rich. (1998). The nurture assumption: Why children turn out the way they do. New York, NY: Free Press.

Harris, Judith Rich. (2002). Beyond the nurture assumption: Testing hypotheses about the child's environment. In John G. Borkowski, Sharon Landesman Ramey and Marie Bristol-Power (Eds.), *Parenting and the child's world: Influences on academic, intellectual, and social-emotional development* (pp. 3–20). Mahwah, NJ: Erlbaum.

Harris, M. A.; Hood, K. K. and Mulvaney, S. A. (2012). Pumpers, skypers, surfers and texters: technology to improve the management of diabetes in teenagers. *Diabetes, Obesity and Metabolism, 14*(11), 967–972. doi:10.1111/j.1463-1326.2012.01599.x

Harrison, Denise; Bueno, Mariana; Yamada, Janet; Adams-Webber, Thomasin and Stevens, Bonnie. (2010). Analgesic effects of sweet-tasting solutions for infants: Current state of equipoise. *Pediatrics, 126*(5), 894–902. doi:10.1542/peds .2010-1593

Harrison, Kristen; Bost, Kelly K.; McBride, Brent A.; Donovan, Sharon M.; Grigsby-Toussaint, Diana S.; Kim, Juhee, . . . Jacobsohn, Gwen Costa. (2011). Toward a developmental conceptualization of contributors to overweight and obesity in childhood: The Six-Cs model. *Child Development Perspectives, 5*(1), 50–58. doi:10.1111/j.1750-8606.2010.00150.x

Harrist, Amanda W.; Topham, Glade L.; Hubbs-Tait, Laura; Page, Melanie C.; Kennedy, Tay S. and Shriver, Lenka H. (2012). What developmental science can contribute to a transdisciplinary understanding of childhood obesity: An interpersonal and intrapersonal risk model. *Child Development Perspectives, 6*, 445–455. doi:10.1111/cdep.12004

Hart, Betty and Risley, Todd R. (1995). Meaningful differences in the everyday experience of young American children. Baltimore, MD: P.H. Brookes.

Hart, Carole L.; Smith, George Davey; Hole, David J. and Hawthorne, Victor M. (1999). Alcohol consumption and mortality from all causes, coronary heart disease, and stroke: Results from a prospective cohort study of Scottish men with 21 years of follow up. *BMJ, 318*, 1725–1729. doi:10.1136/bmj.318.7200.1725

Hart, Chantelle N.; Cairns, Alyssa and Jelalian, Elissa. (2011). Sleep and obesity in children and adolescents. *Pediatric Clinics of North America, 58*(3), 715–733. doi:10.1016/j .pcl.2011.03.007

Harter, Susan. (2006). The self. In William Damon and Richard M. Lerner (Eds.), *Handbook of child psychology* (6th ed., Vol. 3, pp. 505–570). Hoboken, NJ: Wiley.

Harter, Susan. (2012). The construction of the self: Developmental and sociocultural foundations (2nd ed.). New York, NY: Guilford Press.

Hartmann, Donald P. and Pelzel, Kelly E. (2005). Design, measurement, and analysis in developmental research. In Marc H. Bornstein and Michael E. Lamb (Eds.), *Developmental science: An advanced textbook* (5th ed., pp. 103–184). Mahwah, NJ: Lawrence Erlbaum Associates.

Hassan, Mohamed A. M. and Killick, Stephen R. (2003). Effect of male age on fertility: Evidence for the decline in male fertility with increasing age. *Fertility and Sterility, 79*(Supplement 3), 1520–1527. doi:10.1016/S0015-0282(03)00366-2

Hassett, Janice M.; Siebert, Erin R. and Wallen, Kim. (2008). Sex differences in rhesus monkey toy preferences parallel those of children. *Hormones and Behavior, 54*(3), 359–364. doi:10.1016/j.yhbeh.2008.03.008

Hausdorff, Jeffrey M. and Buchman, Aron S. (2013). What links gait speed and MCI with dementia? A fresh look at the association between motor and cognitive function. *Journals of Gerontology: Series A: Biological Sciences and Medical Sciences, 68*(4), 409–411. doi:10.1093/ gerona/glt002

Hawthorne, Joanna. (2009). Promoting development of the early parent-infant relationship using the Neonatal Behavioural Assessment Scale. In Jane Barlow and P. O. Svanberg (Eds.), *Keeping the baby in mind: Infant mental health in practice* (pp. 39–51). New York, NY: Routledge.

Hayden, Brian. (2012). Neandertal social structure? *Oxford Journal of Archaeology, 31*(1), 1–26. doi:10.1111/j.1468-0092.2011.00376.x

Hayden, Sara and Hallstein, D. Lynn O'Brien (Eds.). (2010). Contemplating maternity in an era of choice: Explorations into discourses of reproduction. Lanham, MD: Lexington Books.

Hayes, Rachel A. and Slater, Alan. (2008). Three-month-olds' detection of alliteration in syllables. *Infant Behavior & Development, 31*(1), 153–156. doi:10.1016/j.infbeh.2007.07.009

Hayflick, Leonard. (2004). "Anti-aging" is an oxymoron. *Journals of Gerontology: Series A: Biological and Medical Sciences, 59A*(6), 573–578. doi:10.1093/gerona/59.6.B573

Hayne, Harlene and Simcock, Gabrielle. (2009). Memory development in toddlers. In Mary L. Courage and Nelson Cowan (Eds.), *The development of memory in infancy and childhood* (2nd ed., pp. 43–68). New York, NY: Psychology Press.

Hayslip, Bert and Smith, Gregory C. (Eds.). (2013). Resilient grandparent caregivers: A strengths-based persepective. New York, NY: Routledge.

Hayward, Diane W.; Gale, Catherine M. and Eikeseth, Svein. (2009). Intensive behavioural intervention for young children with autism: A research-based service model. *Research in Autism Spectrum Disorders, 3*(3), 571–580. doi:10.1016/j .rasd.2008.12.002

Hazlett, Heather Cody; Poe, Michele D.; Gerig, Guido; Styner, Martin; Chappell, Chad; Smith, Rachel Gimpel, . . . Piven, Joseph. (2011). Early brain overgrowth in autism associated with an increase in cortical surface area before age 2 years. *Archives of General Psychiatry, 68*(5), 467–476. doi:10.1001/archgenpsychiatry.2011.39

Heaton, Tim B. and Darkwah, Akosua. (2011). Religious differences in modernization of the family: Family demographics trends in Ghana. *Journal of Family Issues, 32*(12), 1576–1596. doi:10.1177/0192513x11398951

Hedman, Anna M.; van Haren, Neeltje E.M.; Schnack, Hugo G.; Kahn, René S. and Hulshoff Pol, Hilleke E. (2012). Human brain changes across the life span: A review of 56 longitudinal magnetic resonance imaging studies. *Human Brain Mapping, 33*(8), 1987–2002. doi:10.1002/hbm.21334

Heflick, Nathan A. and Goldenberg, Jamie L. (2012). No atheists in foxholes: Arguments for (but not against) afterlife belief buffers mortality salience effects for atheists. *British Journal of Social Psychology, 51*(2), 385–392. doi:10.1111/j .2044-8309.2011.02058.x

Heiman, Julia R.; Long, J. Scott; Smith, Shawna N.; Fisher, William A.; Sand, Michael S. and Rosen, Raymond C. (2011). Sexual satisfaction and relationship happiness in midlife and older couples in five countries. *Archives of Sexual Behavior, 40*(4), 741–753. doi:10.1007/s10508-010-9703-3

Heine, Steven J. (2007). Culture and motivation: What motivates people to act in the ways that they do? In Shinobu Kitayama and Dov Cohen (Eds.), *Handbook of cultural psychology* (pp. 714–733). New York, NY: Guilford Press.

Hendry, Leo B. and Kloep, Marion. (2011). Lifestyles in emerging adulthood: Who needs stages anyway? In Jeffrey Jensen Arnett, Marion Kloep, Leo B. Hendry and Jennifer L. Tanner (Eds.), Debating emerging adulthood: Stage or process? (pp. 77–104). New York, NY: Oxford University Press. doi:10.1093/acprof:oso/9780199757176.003.0005

Henretta, John C.; Soldo, Beth J. and Van Voorhis, Matthew F. (2011). Why do families differ? *Children's care for an unmarried mother. Journal of Marriage and Family, 73*(2), 383–395. doi:10.1111/j.1741-3737.2010.00813.x

Henry, David B.; Deptula, Daneen P. and Schoeny, Michael E. (2012). Sexually transmitted infections and unintended pregnancy: A longitudinal analysis of risk transmission through friends and attitudes. *Social Development, 21*(1), 195–214. doi:10.1111/j.1467-9507.2011.00626.x

Herd, Pamela; Robert, Stephanie A. and House, James S. (2011). Health disparities among older adults: Life course influences and policy solutions. In Robert H. Binstock and Linda K. George (Eds.), Handbook of aging and the social sciences (7th ed., pp. 121–134). San Diego, CA: Academic Press. doi:10.1016/B978-0-12-380880-6.00009-5

Herek, Gregory M. (2006). Legal recognition of same-sex relationships in the United States: A social science perspective. *American Psychologist, 61*(6), 607–621. doi:10.1037/0003-066X.61.6.607

Herlofson, Katharina and Hagestad, Gunhild. (2011). Challenges in moving from macro to micro: Population and family structures in ageing societies. *Demographic Research, 25*(10), 337–370. doi:10.4054/DemRes.2011.25.10

Herlofson, Katharina and Hagestad, Gunhild O. (2012). Transformations in the role of grandparents across welfare states. In Sara Arber and Virpi Timonen (Eds.), Contemporary grandparenting: Changing family relationships in global contexts (pp. 27–49). Chicago, IL: Policy Press.

Herman, Khalisa N.; Paukner, Annika and Suomi, Stephen J. (2011). Gene x environment interactions and social play: Contributions from rhesus macaques. In Anthony D. Pellegrini (Ed.), *The Oxford handbook of the development of play* (pp. 58–69). New York, NY: Oxford University Press.

Herman-Giddens, Marcia E.; Steffes, Jennifer; Harris, Donna; Slora, Eric; Hussey, Michael; Dowshen, Steven A., . . . Reiter, Edward O. (2012). Secondary sexual characteristics in boys: Data from the pediatric research in office settings network. *Pediatrics, 130*(5), e1058-e1068. doi:10.1542/peds.2011–3291

Herrera, Angelica P.; Snipes, Shedra Amy; King, Denae W.; Torres-Vigil, Isabel; Goldberg, Daniel S. and Weinberg, Armin D. (2010). Disparate inclusion of older adults in clinical trials: Priorities and opportunities for policy and practice change. *American Journal of Public Health, 100*(51), S105–S112. doi:10.2105/ ajph.2009.162982

Herring, Ann and Swedlund, Alan C. (Eds.). (2010). Plagues and epidemics: Infected spaces past and present. New York, NY: Berg.

Herrmann, Esther; Call, Josep; Hernàndez-Lloreda, María Victoria; Hare, Brian and Tomasello, Michael. (2007). Humans have evolved specialized skills of social cognition: The cultural intelligence hypothesis. *Science, 317*(5843), 1360–1366. doi:10.1126/science.1146282

Herschensohn, Julia Rogers. (2007). Language development and age. New York, NY: Cambridge University Press.

Herskovits, Adrianna Z. and Guarente, Leonard. (2013). Sirtuin deacetylases in neurodegenerative diseases of aging. *Cell Research, 23*, 746–758. doi:10.1038/cr.2013.70

Hertzog, Christopher. (2011). Intelligence in adulthood. In Robert J. Sternberg and Scott Barry Kaufman (Eds.), The Cambridge handbook of intelligence (pp. 174–190). New York, NY: Cambridge University Press.

Herzog, Christopher. (2010). Regarding methods for studying behavioral development: The contributions and influence of K. Warner Schaie. *Research in Human Development: Special Issue, The Contributions and Influence of K. Warner Schaie, 7*(1), 1–8. doi:10.1080/15427600903578110

Heslin, Kevin C.; Hamilton, Alison B.; Singzon, Trudy K.; Smith, James L.; Lois, Nancy and Anderson, Ruth. (2011). Alternative families in recovery: Fictive kin relationships among residents of sober living homes. *Qualitative Health Research, 21*(4), 477–488. doi:10.1177/1049732310385826

Hess, Thomas; Hinson, Joey and Hodges, Elizabeth. (2009). Moderators of and mechanisms underlying stereotype threat effects on older adults' memory performance. *Experimental Aging Research: An International Journal Devoted to the Scientific Study of the Aging Process, 35*(2), 153–177. doi:10.1080/03610730802716413

Hess, Thomas M.; Leclerc, Christina M.; Swaim, Elizabeth and Weatherbee, Sarah R. (2009). Aging and everyday judgments: The impact of motivational and processing resource factors. *Psychology and Aging, 24*(3), 735–740. doi:10.1037/a0016340

Hetherington, E. Mavis. (2006). The influence of conflict, marital problem solving and parenting on children's adjustment in nondivorced, divorced and remarried families In Alison Clarke-Stewart and Judy Dunn (Eds.), *Families count: Effects on child and adolescent development* (pp. 203–237). New York, NY: Cambridge University Press.

Hicks, Joshua A.; Trent, Jason; Davis, William E. and King, Laura A. (2012). Positive affect, meaning in life, and future time perspective: An application of socioemotional selectivity theory. *Psychology and Aging, 27*(1), 181–189. doi:10.1037/a0023965

Higgins, Matt. (2006, August 7). A series of flips creates some serious buzz. The New York Times, p. D7.

Higuchi, Susumu; Matsushita, Sachio; Muramatsu, Taro; Murayama, Masanobu and Hayashida, Motoi. (1996). Alcohol and aldehyde dehydrogenase genotypes and drinking behavior in Japanese. *Alcoholism: Clinical and Experimental Research, 20*(3), 493–497. doi:10.1111/j.1530-0277.1996.tb01080.x

Hill, Nancy E. and Tyson, Diana F. (2009). Parental involvement in middle school: A meta-analytic assessment of the strategies that promote achievement. *Developmental Psychology, 45*(3), 740–763. doi:10.1037/a0015362

Hindman, Annemarie H.; Skibbe, Lori E.; Miller, Alison and Zimmerman, Marc. (2010). Ecological contexts and early learning: Contributions of child, family, and classroom factors during Head Start, to literacy and mathematics growth through first grade. *Early Childhood Research Quarterly, 25*(2), 235–250. doi:10.1016/j .ecresq.2009.11.003

Hines, Melissa. (2013). Sex and sex differences. In Philip David Zelazo (Ed.), The Oxford handbook of developmental psychology (Vol. 1, pp. 162–201). New York, NY: Oxford University Press.

Hipwell, Alison E.; Keenan, Kate; Loeber, Rolf and Battista, Deena. (2010). Early predictors of sexually intimate behaviors in an urban sample of young girls. *Developmental Psychology, 46*(2), 366–378. doi:10.1037/a0018409

Hirsh-Pasek, Kathy; Golinkoff, Roberta Michnick; Berk, Laura E. and Singer, Dorothy G. (2009). A mandate for playful learning in preschool: Presenting the evidence. New York, NY: Oxford University Press.

Ho, Emily S. (2010). Measuring hand function in the young child. *Journal of Hand Therapy, 23*(3), 323–328. doi:10.1016/j.jht.2009.11.002

Hoare, Carol Hren. (2002). Erikson on development in adulthood: New insights from the unpublished papers. New York, NY: Oxford University Press.

Hochman, Oshrat and Lewin-Epstein, Noah. (2013). Determinants of early retirement preferences in Europe: The role of grandparenthood. *International Journal of Comparative Sociology, 54*(1), 29–47. doi:10.1177/0020715213480977

Hoeve, Machteld; Dubas, Judith Semon; Gerris, Jan R. M.; van der Laan, Peter H. and Smeenk, Wilma. (2011). Maternal and paternal parenting styles: Unique and combined links to adolescent and early adult delinquency. *Journal of Adolescence, 34*(5), 813–827. doi:10.1016/j.adolescence.2011.02.004

Hoff, David J. (2007). Not all agree on meaning of NCLB proficiency. *Education Week, 26*(33), 1, 23.

Hoff, Erika. (2006). How social contexts support and shape language development. *Developmental Review, 26*(1), 55–88. doi:10.1016/j.dr.2005.11.002

Hoff, Erika; Core, Cynthia; Place, Silvia; Rumiche, Rosario; Señor, Melissa and Parra, Marisol. (2012). Dual language exposure and early bilingual development. *Journal of Child Language, 39*(1), 1–27. doi:10.1017/S0305000910000759

Hoff, Erika and Tian, Chunyan. (2005). Socioeconomic status and cultural influences on language. *Journal of Communication Disorders, 38*(4), 271–278. doi:10.1016/j.jcomdis.2005.02.003

Hogan, Michael J.; Staff, Roger T.; Bunting, Brendan P.; Deary, Ian J. and Whalley, Lawrence J. (2012). Openness to experience and activity engagement facilitate the maintenance of verbal ability in older adults. *Psychology and Aging, 27*(4), 849–854. doi:10.1037/a0029066

Hogeboom, David L.; McDermott, Robert J.; Perrin, Karen M.; Osman, Hana and Bell-Ellison, Bethany A. (2010). Internet use and social networking among middle aged and older adults. *Educational Gerontology, 36*(2), 93–111. doi:10.1080/03601270903058507

Holden, Constance. (2009). Fetal cells again? *Science, 326*(5951), 358–359. doi:10.1126/science.326_358

Holland, James D. and Klaczynski, Paul A. (2009). Intuitive risk taking during adolescence. *Prevention Researcher, 16*(2), 8–11.

Hollich, George J.; Hirsh-Pasek, Kathy; Golinkoff, Roberta Michnick; Brand, Rebecca J.; Brown, Ellie; Chung, He Len, . . . Rocroi, Camille. (2000). Breaking the language barrier: An emergentist coalition model for the origins of word learning (Vol. 65, No. 3). Malden, MA: Blackwell.

Hollos, Marida; Larsen, Ulla; Obono, Oka and Whitehouse, Bruce. (2009). The problem of infertility in high fertility populations: Meanings, consequences and coping mechanisms in two Nigerian communities. *Social Science & Medicine, 68*(11), 2061–2068. doi:10.1016/j.socscimed.2009.03.008

Holmboe, K.; Nemoda, Z.; Fearon, R. M. P.; Sasvari-Szekely, M. and Johnson, M. H. (2011). Dopamine D4 receptor and serotonin transporter gene effects on the longitudinal development of infant temperament. *Genes, Brain and Behavior, 10*(5), 513–522. doi:10.1111/j.1601-183X.2010.00669.x

Holsti, Liisa; Grunau, Ruth E. and Shany, Eilon. (2011). Assessing pain in preterm infants in the neonatal intensive care unit: Moving to a brain-oriented approach. *Pain Management, 1*(2), 171–179. doi:10.2217/pmt.10.19

Holt, Raymond. (2013). Design for the ages: Universal design as a rehabilitation strategy (Book Review). *Disability & Society, 28*(1), 142–144. doi:10.1080/09687599.2012.739364

Holtzman, Jennifer. (2009). Simple, effective—and inexpensive—strategies to reduce tooth decay in children. *ICAN: Infant, Child, & Adolescent Nutrition, 1*(4), 225–231. doi:10.1177/1941406409338861

Hong, Jun Sung and Garbarino, James. (2012). Risk and protective factors for homophobic bullying in schools: An application of the social–ecological framework. *Educational Psychology Review, 24*(2), 271–285. doi:10.1007/s10648-012-9194-y

Hong, Soo-Young; Torquati, Julia and Molfese, Victoria J. (2013). Theory guided professional development in early childhood science education. In Lynn E. Cohen and Sandra Waite-Stupiansky (Eds.), Learning across the early childhood curriculum (pp. 1–32). Bingley, UK: Emerald.

Hook, Jennifer L. (2010). Gender inequality in the welfare state: Sex segregation in housework, 1965–2003. *American Journal of Sociology, 115*(5), 1480–1523. doi:10.1086/651384

Hook, Jennifer L. (2012). Working on the weekend: Fathers' time with family in the United Kingdom. *Journal of Marriage and Family, 74*(4), 631–642. doi:10.1111/j.1741-3737.2012.00986.x

Hooley, Jill M. (2004). Do psychiatric patients do better clinically if they live with certain kinds of families? *Current Directions in Psychological Science, 13*(5), 202–205. doi:10.1111/j.0963-7214.2004.00308.x

Hootman, Jennifer M.; Helmick, Charles G. and Brady, Teresa J. (2012). A public health approach to addressing arthritis in older adults: The most common cause of disability. *American Journal of Public Health, 102*(3), 426–433. doi:10.2105/AJPH.2011.300423

Hopkins, J. Roy. (2011). The enduring influence of Jean Piaget. *Observer, 24*(10).

Horn, John L. and Cattell, Raymond B. (1967). Age differences in fluid and crystallized intelligence. *Acta Psychologica, 26*, 107–129.

Horowitz, Alice M.; Kleinman, Dushanka V. and Wang, Min Qi. (2013). What Maryland adults with young children know and do about preventing dental caries. *American Journal of Public Health, 103*(6), e69-e76. doi:10.2105/AJPH.2012.301038

Horwitz, Ralph I.; Cullen, Mark R.; Abell, Jill and Christian, Jennifer B. (2013). (De)Personalized medicine. *Science, 339*(6124), 1155–1156. doi:10.1126/science.1234106

Houdmont, Jonathan; Zhou, Jieming and Hassard, Juliet. (2011). Overtime and psychological well-being among Chinese office workers. *Occupational Medicine, 61*(4), 270–273. doi:10.1093/occmed/kqr029

Hougaard, Karin S. and Hansen, Åse M. (2007). Enhancement of developmental toxicity effects of chemicals by gestational stress: A review. *Neurotoxicology and Teratology, 29*(4), 425–445. doi:10.1016/j.ntt.2007.02.003

Hout, Michael. (2012). Social and economic returns to college education in the United States. *Annual Review of Sociology, 39*, 379–400. doi:10.1146/annurev.soc.012809.102503

Hout, Michael and Elliott, Stuart W. (Eds.). (2011). Incentives and test-based accountability in education. Washington, DC: National Academies Press.

Howard, Andrea L.; Galambos, Nancy L. and Krahn, Harvey J. (2010). Paths to success in young adulthood from mental health and life transitions in emerging adulthood. *International Journal of Behavioral Development, 34*(6), 538–546. doi:10.1177/0165025410365803

Howard, Jeffrey A. (2005). Why should we care about student expectations? In Thomas E. Miller, Barbara E. Bender and John H. Schuh (Eds.), Promoting reasonable expectations: Aligning student and institutional views of the college experience (pp. 10–33). San Francisco, CA: Jossey-Bass.

Howard, Kimberly S. (2010). Paternal attachment, parenting beliefs and children's attachment. *Early Child Development and Care, 180*(1–2), 157–171. doi:10.1080/03004430903415031

Howell, Diane M.; Wysocki, Karen and Steiner, Michael J. (2010). Toilet training. *Pediatrics in Review, 31*(6), 262–263. doi:10.1542/pir.31-6-262

Howes, Carollee; Fuligni, Allison Sidle; Hong, Sandra Soliday; Huang, Yiching D. and Lara-Cinisomo, Sandraluz. (2013). The Preschool Instructional Context and Child–Teacher Relationships. *Early Education & Development, 24*(3), 273–291. doi:10.1080/10409289.2011.649664

Howlin, Patricia; Magiati, Iliana; Charman, Tony and MacLean, William E., Jr. (2009). Systematic review of early intensive behavioral interventions for children with autism. *American Journal on Intellectual and Developmental Disabilities, 114*(1), 23–41. doi:10.1352/2009.114:23-41

Hoyert, Donna L. and Xu, Jiaquan. (2012). Deaths: Preliminary data for 2011. Hyattsville,

MD: National Center for Health Statistics, U.S. Department of Health and Human Services.

Hrabosky, Joshua I. and Thomas, Jennifer J. (2008). Elucidating the relationship between obesity and depression: Recommendations for future research. *Clinical Psychology: Science and Practice, 15*(1), 28–34. doi:10.1111/j.1468-2850.2008.00108.x

Hrdy, Sarah Blaffer. (2009). Mothers and others: The evolutionary origins of mutual understanding. Cambridge, MA: Harvard University Press.

Hsia, Yingfen and Maclennan, Karyn. (2009). Rise in psychotropic drug prescribing in children and adolescents during 1992–2001: A population-based study in the UK. *European Journal of Epidemiology, 24*(4), 211–216. doi:10.1007/s10654-009-9321-3

Hsu, Ming; Anen, Cedric and Quartz, Steven R. (2008). The right and the good: Distributive justice and neural encoding of equity and efficiency. *Science, 320*(5879), 1092–1095. doi:10.1126/science.1153651

Hu, Frank B. (2011). Globalization of diabetes: The role of diet, lifestyle, and genes. *Diabetes Care, 34*(6), 1249–1257. doi:10.2337/dc11-0442

Huang, Chiungjung. (2010). Mean-level change in self-esteem from childhood through adulthood: Meta-analysis of longitudinal studies. *Review of General Psychology, 14*(3), 251–260. doi:10.1037/a0020543

Huang, Chien-Chung. (2009). Mothers' reports of nonresident fathers' involvement with their children: Revisiting the relationship between child support payment and visitation. *Family Relations, 58*(1), 54–64. doi:10.1111/j.1741-3729.2008.00534.x

Huberty, Thomas J. (2012). Anxiety and depression in children and adolescents: Assessment, intervention, and prevention. New York, NY: Springer.

Hugdahl, Kenneth and Westerhausen, René (Eds.). (2010). The two halves of the brain: Information processing in the cerebral hemispheres. Cambridge, MA: MIT Press.

Hughes, Diane; Rodriguez, James; Smith, Emilie P.; Johnson, Deborah J.; Stevenson, Howard C. and Spicer, Paul. (2006). Parents' ethnic-racial socialization practices: A review of research and directions for future study. *Developmental Psychology, 42*(5), 747–770. doi:10.1037/0012-1649.42.5.747

Hughes, Julie Milligan and Bigler, Rebecca S. (2011). Predictors of African American and European American adolescents' endorsement of race-conscious social policies. *Developmental Psychology, 47*(2), 479–492. doi:10.1037/a0021309

Hughes, Kimberly A. (2010). Mutation and the evolution of ageing: From biometrics to system genetics. *Philosophical Transactions of the Royal Society B: Biological Sciences, 365*(1544), 1273–1279. doi:10.1098/rstb.2009.0265

Hughes, Sonya M. and Gore, Andrea C. (2007). How the brain controls puberty, and implications for sex and ethnic differences. *Family & Community Health, 30*(Suppl 1), S112–S114.

Huh, Susanna Y.; Rifas-Shiman, Sheryl L.; Taveras, Elsie M.; Oken, Emily and Gillman, Matthew W. (2011). Timing of solid food introduction and risk of obesity in preschool-aged children. *Pediatrics, 127*(3), e544–e551. doi:10.1542/peds.2010-0740

Huh, Susanna Y.; Rifas-Shiman, Sheryl L.; Zera, Chloe A.; Edwards, Janet W. Rich; Oken, Emily; Weiss, Scott T. and Gillman, Matthew W. (2012). Delivery by caesarean section and risk of obesity in preschool age children: A prospective cohort study. *Archives of the Diseases of Childhood, 97*, 610–616. doi:10.1136/archdischild-2011-301141

Huijbregts, Sanne K.; Tavecchio, Louis; Leseman, Paul and Hoffenaar, Peter. (2009). Child rearing in a group setting: Beliefs of Dutch, Caribbean Dutch, and Mediterranean Dutch caregivers in center-based child care. *Journal of Cross-Cultural Psychology, 40*(5), 797–815. doi:10.1177/0022022109338623

Hummert, Mary Lee. (2011). Age stereotypes and aging. In K. Warner Schaie and Sherry L. Willis (Eds.), Handbook of the psychology of aging (7th ed., pp. 249–262). San Diego, CA: Elsevier/Academic Press.

Hunter, Myra Sally. (2012). Long-term impacts of early and surgical menopause. *Menopause, 19*(3), 253–254. doi:10.1097/gme.0b013e31823e9b2e

Huntsinger, Carol S.; Jose, Paul E.; Krieg, Dana Balsink and Luo, Zupei. (2011). Cultural differences in Chinese American and European American children's drawing skills over time. *Early Childhood Research Quarterly, 26*(1), 134–145. doi:10.1016/j.ecresq.2010.04.002

Husain, Nusrat; Chaudhry, Nasim; Tomenson, Barbara; Jackson, Judy; Gater, Richard and Creed, Francis. (2011). Depressive disorder and social stress in Pakistan compared to people of Pakistani origin in the UK. *Social Psychiatry and Psychiatric Epidemiology, 46*(11), 1153–1159. doi:10.1007/s00127-010-0279-y

Husain, N.; Creed, Frances and Tomenson, B. (2000). Depression and social stress in Pakistan. *Psychological Medicine, 30*(2), 395–402. doi:10.1017/S0033291700001707

Hussain, Amjad; Case, Keith; Marshall, Russell and Summerskill, Steve J. (2013). An inclusive design method for addressing human variability and work performance issues. *International Journal of Engineering and Technology Innovation, 3*(3), 144–155.

Hussey, Jon M.; Chang, Jen Jen and Kotch, Jonathan B. (2006). Child maltreatment in the United States: Prevalence, risk factors, and adolescent health consequences. *Pediatrics, 118*(3), 933–942. doi:10.1542/peds.2005-2452

Huston, Aletha C. and Aronson, Stacey Rosenkrantz. (2005). Mothers' time with infant and time in employment as predictors of mother-child relationships and children's early development. *Child Development, 76*(2), 467–482. doi:10.1111/j.1467-8624.2005.00857.x

Huston, Aletha C. and Ripke, Marika N. (2006). Middle childhood: Contexts of development. In Aletha C. Huston and Marika N. Ripke

(Eds.), Developmental contexts in middle childhood: Bridges to adolescence and adulthood (pp. 1–22). New York, NY: Cambridge University Press.

Hutchinson, Esther A.; De Luca, Cinzia R.; Doyle, Lex W.; Roberts, Gehan and Anderson, Peter J. (2013). School-age Outcomes of Extremely Preterm or Extremely Low Birth Weight Children. *Pediatrics, 131*(4), e1053–e1061. doi:10.1542/peds.2012-2311

Huver, Rose M. E.; Otten, Roy; de Vries, Hein and Engels, Rutger C. M. E. (2010). Personality and parenting style in parents of adolescents. *Journal of Adolescence, 33*(3), 395–402. doi:10.1016/j.adolescence.2009.07.012

Huynh, Jimmy L. and Casaccia, Patrizia. (2013). Epigenetic mechanisms in multiple sclerosis: implications for pathogenesis and treatment. *The Lancet Neurology, 12*(2), 195–206. doi:10.1016/S1474-4422(12)70309-5

Hyde, Janet Shibley. (2007). New directions in the study of gender similarities and differences. *Current Directions in Psychological Science, 16*(5), 259–263. doi:10.1111/j.1467-8721.2007.00516.x

Iacovidou, Nicoletta; Varsami, Marianna and Syggellou, Angeliki. (2010). Neonatal outcome of preterm delivery. *Annals of the New York Academy of Sciences, 1205*, 130–134. doi:10.1111/j.1749-6632.2010.05657.x

Idler, Ellen. (2006). Religion and aging. In Robert H. Binstock and Linda K. George (Eds.), Handbook of aging and the social sciences (6th ed., pp. 277–300). Amsterdam, The Netherlands: Elsevier.

Iida, Hiroko and Rozier, R. Gary. (2013). Mother-perceived social capital and children's oral health and use of dental care in the United States. *American Journal of Public Health, 103*(3), 480–487. doi:10.2105/AJPH.2012.300845

Ikeda, Martin J. (2012). Policy and practice considerations for response to intervention: Reflections and commentary. *Journal of Learning Disabilities, 45*(3), 274–277. doi:10.1177/0022219412442170

ILO. (2011). Database of conditions of work and employment laws: from International Labour Organization. http://www.ilo.org/dyn/travail/travmain.home

Imai, Mutsumi; Kita, Sotaro; Nagumo, Miho and Okada, Hiroyuki. (2008). Sound symbolism facilitates early verb learning. *Cognition, 109*(1), 54–65. doi:10.1016/j.cognition.2008.07.015

Inan, Hatice Zeynep; Trundle, Kathy Cabe and Kantor, Rebecca. (2010). Understanding natural sciences education in a Reggio Emilia-inspired preschool. *Journal of Research in Science Teaching, 47*(10), 1186–1208. doi:10.1002/tea.20375

Inbar, Yoel; Botti, Simona and Hanko, Karlene. (2011). Decision speed and choice regret: When haste feels like waste. *Journal of Experimental Social Psychology, 47*(3), 533–540. doi:10.1016/j.jesp.2011.01.011

Inhelder, Bärbel and Piaget, Jean. (1958). The growth of logical thinking from childhood to adolescence: An essay on the construction of formal operational structures. New York, NY: Basic Books.

Inhelder, Bärbel and Piaget, Jean. (1964). The early growth of logic in the child. New York, NY: Harper & Row.

Insel, Beverly J. and Gould, Madelyn S. (2008). Impact of modeling on adolescent suicidal behavior. *Psychiatric Clinics of North America, 31*(2), 293–316. doi:10.1016/j.psc.2008.01.007

Institute, National Cancer. (2013). SEER stat fact sheets: Lung and bronchus cancer. Bethesda, MD: Surveillance, Epidemiology, and End Results Program, National Cancer Institute.

Institute of Medicine Committee on Food Marketing and the Diets of Children and Youth. (2006). *Food marketing to children and youth: Threat or opportunity?* Washington, DC: National Academies Press.

Inzlicht, Michael and Schmader, Toni. (2012). Stereotype threat: Theory, process, and application. New York, NY: Oxford University Press.

Irwin, Scott; Galvez, Roberto; Weiler, Ivan Jeanne; Beckel-Mitchener, Andrea and Greenough, William. (2002). Brain structure and the functions of FMR1 protein. In Randi Jenssen Hagerman and Paul J. Hagerman (Eds.), *Fragile X syndrome: Diagnosis, treatment, and research* (3rd ed., pp. 191–205). Baltimore, MD: Johns Hopkins University Press.

Ispa, Jean M.; Fine, Mark A.; Halgunseth, Linda C.; Harper, Scott; Robinson, JoAnn; Boyce, Lisa, . . . Brady-Smith, Christy. (2004). Maternal intrusiveness, maternal warmth, and mother-toddler relationship outcomes: Variations across low-income ethnic and acculturation groups. *Child Development, 75*(6), 1613–1631. doi:10.1111/j.1467-8624.2004.00806.x

Issa, Jean-Pierre. (2011). Epigenetic variation and cellular Darwinism. *Nature Genetics, 43,* 724–726. doi:10.1038/ng.897

Iyengar, Sheena S. and Lepper, Mark R. (2000). When choice is demotivating: Can one desire too much of a good thing? *Journal of Personality and Social Psychology, 79*(6), 995–1006. doi:10.1037//0022-3514.79.6.995

Izard, Carroll E. (2009). Emotion theory and research: Highlights, unanswered questions, and emerging issues. *Annual Review of Psychology, 60,* 1–25. doi:10.1146/annurev.psych.60.110707.163539

Izard, Carroll E.; Fine, Sarah; Mostow, Allison; Trentacosta, Christopher and Campbell, Jan. (2002). Emotion processes in normal and abnormal development and preventive intervention. *Development & Psychopathology, 14*(4), 761–787. doi:10.1017/S0954579402004066

Jack, Clifford R. Jr.; Lowe, Val J.; Weigand, Stephen D.; Wiste, Heather J.; Senjem, Matthew L.; Knopman, David S., . . . Petersen, Ronald C. (2009). Serial PIB and MRI in normal, mild cognitive impairment and Alzheimer's disease: Implications for sequence of pathological events in Alzheimer's disease. *Brain, 132*(5), 1355–1365. doi:10.1093/brain/awp062

Jackson, James S.; Govia, Ishtar O. and Sellers, Sherrill L. (2011). Racial and ethnic influences over the life course. In Robert H. Binstock and Linda K. George (Eds.), *Handbook of aging and the social sciences* (7th ed., pp. 91–103). San Diego, CA: Academic Press. doi:10.1016/B978-0-12-380880-6.00007-1

Jackson, Richard J. J. and Tester, June. (2008). Environment shapes health, including children's mental health. *Journal of the American Academy of Child & Adolescent Psychiatry, 47*(2), 129–131. doi:10.1097/chi.0b013e31815d6944

Jackson, Shelly L. and Hafemeister, Thomas L. (2011). Risk factors associated with elder abuse: The importance of differentiating by type of elder maltreatment. *Violence and Victims, 26*(6), 738–757. doi:10.1891/0886-6708.26.6.738

Jacob, Jenet I. (2009). The socio-emotional effects of non-maternal childcare on children in the USA: A critical review of recent studies. *Early Child Development and Care, 179*(5), 559–570. doi:10.1080/03004430701292988

Jaffe, Arthur C. (2011). Failure to Thrive: Current Clinical Concepts. *Pediatrics in Review, 32*(3), 100–108. doi:10.1542/pir.32-3-100

Jaffe, Eric. (2004). Mickey Mantle's greatest error: Yankee star's false belief may have cost him years. *Observer, 17*(9), 37.

Jaffee, Sara R.; Caspi, Avshalom; Moffitt, Terrie E.; Polo-Tomás, Monica and Taylor, Alan. (2007). Individual, family, and neighborhood factors distinguish resilient from non-resilient maltreated children: A cumulative stressors model. *Child Abuse & Neglect, 31*(3), 231–253. doi:10.1016/j.chiabu.2006.03.011

Jambon, Marc and Smetana, Judith G. (2014). Moral complexity in middle childhood: Children's evaluations of necessary harm. *Developmental Psychology, 50*(1), 22–33. doi:10.1037/a0032992

James, Jenée; Ellis, Bruce J.; Schlomer, Gabriel L. and Garber, Judy. (2012). Sex-specific pathways to early puberty, sexual debut, and sexual risk taking: Tests of an integrated evolutionary–developmental model. *Developmental Psychology, 48*(3), 687–702. doi:10.1037/a0026427

James, Jacquelyn Boone; McKechnie, Sharon and Swanberg, Jennifer. (2011). Predicting employee engagement in an age-diverse retail workforce. *Journal of Organizational Behavior, 32*(2), 173–196. doi:10.1002/job.681

Jasny, Barbara R.; Chin, Gilbert; Chong, Lisa and Vignieri, Sacha. (2011). Again, and again, and again . . . *Science, 334*(6060), 1225. doi:10.1126/science.334.6060.1225

Jastrzembski, Tiffany S.; Charness, Neil and Vasyukova, Catherine. (2006). Expertise and age effects on knowledge activation in chess. *Psychology and Aging, 21*(2), 401–405. doi:10.1037/0882-7974.21.2.401

Jenson, Jeffrey M. and Fraser, Mark W. (Eds.). (2006). Social policy for children & families: A risk and resilience perspective. Thousand Oaks, CA: Sage.

Jessop, Donna C. and Wade, Jennifer. (2008). Fear appeals and binge drinking: A terror management theory perspective. *British Journal of Health Psychology, 13*(4), 773–788. doi:10.1348/135910707X272790

Ji, Cheng Ye; Chen, Tian Jiao and Working Group on Obesity in China (WGOC). (2013). Empirical changes in the prevalence of overweight and obesity among Chinese students from 1985 to 2010 and corresponding preventive strategies. *Biomedical and Environmental Sciences, 26*(1), 1–12. doi:10.3967/0895-3988.2013.01.001

John Hancock Life & Health Insurance Company. (2011). John Hancock 2011 Cost of Care Survey. Boston, MA.

Johnson, Chris A. and Wilkinson, Mark E. (2010). Vision and driving: The United States. *Journal of Neuro-Ophthalmology, 30*(2), 170–176. doi:10.1097/WNO.0b013e3181df30d4

Johnson, Elizabeth K. and Tyler, Michael D. (2010). Testing the limits of statistical learning for word segmentation. *Developmental Science, 13*(2), 339–345. doi:10.1111/j.1467-7687.2009.00886.x

Johnson, Kimberly S.; Kuchibhatla, Maragatha and Tulsky, James A. (2011). Racial differences in location before hospice enrollment and association with hospice length of stay. *Journal of the American Geriatrics Society, 59*(4), 732–737. doi:10.1111/j.1532-5415.2011.03326.x

Johnson, Matthew D. (2012). Healthy marriage initiatives: On the need for empiricism in policy implementation. *American Psychologist, 67*(4), 296–308. doi:10.1037/a0027743

Johnson, Mark H. (2011). Developmental cognitive neuroscience: An introduction (3rd ed.). Malden, MA: Wiley-Blackwell.

Johnson, Mark H. and Fearon, R. M. Pasco. (2011). Commentary: Disengaging the infant mind: Genetic dissociation of attention and cognitive skills in infants – Reflections on Leppänen et al. (2011). *Journal of Child Psychology and Psychiatry, 52*(11), 1153–1154. doi:10.1111/j.1469-7610.2011.02433.x

Johnson, Mark H.; Grossmann, Tobias and Kadosh, Kathrin Cohen. (2009). Mapping functional brain development: Building a social brain through interactive specialization. *Developmental Psychology, 45*(1), 151–159. doi:10.1037/a0014548

Johnson, Monica Kirkpatrick. (2013). Parental financial assistance and young adults' relationship with parents and well-being. *Journal of Marriage and Family, 75*(3), 713–733. doi:10.1111/jomf.12029

Johnson, Michael P. (2008). A typology of domestic violence: Intimate terrorism, violent resistance, and situational couple violence. Hanover, NH: Northeastern University Press.

Johnson, Michael P. and Ferraro, Kathleen J. (2000). Research on domestic violence in the 1990s: Making distinctions. *Journal of Marriage and Family, 62*(4), 948–963. doi:10.1111/j.1741-3737.2000.00948.x

Johnson, Susan C.; Dweck, Carol S.; Chen, Frances S.; Stern, Hilarie L.; Ok, Su-Jeong and Barth, Maria. (2010). At the intersection of social and cognitive development: Internal working models of attachment in infancy. *Cognitive*

Science, 34(5), 807–825. doi:10.1111/j.1551 -6709.2010.01112.x

Johnson, Teddi Dineley. (2011). Report calls for examination of chemical safety: National coalition notes difficulty determining exposures. *The Nation's Health, 41*(9).

Johnson, Wendy; McGue, Matt and Deary, Ian J. (2014). Normative cognitive aging. In Deborah Finkel and Chandra A. Reynolds (Eds.), *Behavior genetics of cognition across the lifespan: Advances in behavior genetics* (Vol. 1, pp. 135–167). New York, NY: Springer. doi:10.1007/978-1 -4614-7447-0_5

Johnston, Lloyd D.; O'Malley, Patrick M.; Bachman, Jerald G. and Schulenberg, John E. (2009). *Monitoring the future national survey results on drug use, 1975–2008: College students and adults ages 19–50.* Bethesda, MD: National Institute on Drug Abuse.

Johnston, Lloyd D.; O'Malley, Patrick M.; Bachman, Jerald G. and Schulenberg, John E. (2011). *Monitoring the future national survey results on drug use, 1975–2010.* Ann Arbor: Institute for Social Research, The University of Michigan.

Jokela, Markus. (2012). Birth-cohort effects in the association between personality and fertility. *Psychological Science, 23*(8), 835–841. doi:10.1177/0956797612439067

Jonas, Eva; Sullivan, Daniel and Greenberg, Jeff. (2013). Generosity, greed, norms, and death – Differential effects of mortality salience on charitable behavior. *Journal of Economic Psychology, 35,* 47–57. doi:10.1016/j.joep.2012.12.005

Jones, Andrea M. and Morris, Tracy L. (2012). Psychological adjustment of children in foster care: Review and implications for best practice. *Journal of Public Child Welfare, 6*(2), 129–148. doi:10.1080/15548732.2011.617272

Jones, Daniel. (2006, February 12). You're not sick, you're just in love. *The New York Times,* pp. H1, H13.

Jones, Mary Cover. (1965). Psychological correlates of somatic development. *Child Development, 36*(4), 899–911.

Jong, Jyh-Tsorng; Kao, Tsair; Lee, Liang-Yi; Huang, Hung-Hsuan; Lo, Po-Tsung and Wang, Hui-Chung. (2010). Can temperament be understood at birth? *The relationship between neonatal pain cry and their temperament: A preliminary study. Infant Behavior and Development, 33*(3), 266–272. doi:10.1016/j.infbeh.2010.02.001

Jongbloed, Ben W. A.; Maassen, Peter A. M. and Neave, Guy R. (Eds.). (1999). *From the eye of the storm: Higher education's changing institution.* Dordrecht, The Netherlands: Kluwer Academic Publishers.

Jonge, Huub de. (2011). Purification and remembrance: Eastern and western ways to deal with the Bali bombing. In Peter Jan Margry and Cristina Sánchez-Carretero (Eds.), *Grassroots memorials: The politics of memorializing traumatic death* (pp. 262–284). New York, NY: Berghahn Books.

Jonsson, Maria; Cnattingius, Sven and Wikström, Anna-Karin. (2013). Elective induction of labor and the risk of cesarean section in low-risk parous women: A cohort study. *Acta Obstetricia et Gynecologica Scandinavica, 92*(2), 198–203. doi:10.1111/aogs.12043

Jopp, Daniela and Rott, Christoph. (2006). Adaptation in very old age: Exploring the role of resources, beliefs, and attitudes for centenarians' happiness. *Psychology and Aging, 21*(2), 266–280. doi:10.1037/0882-7974.21.2.266

Jordan, Alexander H. and Monin, Benoît. (2008). From sucker to saint: Moralization in response to self-threat. *Psychological Science, 19*(8), 809–815. doi:10.1111/j.1467-9280.2008.02161.x

Jose, Anita; Daniel O'Leary, K. and Moyer, Anne. (2010). Does premarital cohabitation predict subsequent marital stability and marital quality? A meta-analysis. *Journal of Marriage and Family, 72*(1), 105–116. doi:10.1111/j.1741 -3737.2009.00686.x

Juan, Shan. (2010, January 14). C-section epidemic hits China: WHO. *China Daily.*

Juang, Linda P.; Syed, Moin and Cookston, Jeffrey T. (2012). Acculturation-based and everyday parent–adolescent conflict among Chinese American adolescents: Longitudinal trajectories and implications for mental health. *Journal of Family Psychology, 26*(6), 916–926. doi:10.1037/ a0030057

Judd, Fiona K.; Hickey, Martha and Bryant, Christina. (2012). Depression and midlife: Are we overpathologising the menopause? *Journal of Affective Disorders, 136*(3), 199–211. doi:10.1016/j.jad.2010.12.010

Jung, Rex E. and Ryman, Sephira G. (2013). Imaging creativity. In Kyung Hee Kim, James C. Kaufman, John Baer and Bharath Sriraman (Eds.), *Creatively gifted students are not like other gifted students: Research, theory, and practice* (pp. 69–87). Rotterdam, The Netherlands: SensePublishers. doi:10.1007/978-94-6209 -149-8_6

Juujärvi, Soile. (2005). Care and justice in real-life moral reasoning. *Journal of Adult Development, 12*(4), 199–210. doi:10.1007/s10804-005-7088-7

Juvonen, Jaana; Nishina, Adrienne and Graham, Sandra. (2006). Ethnic diversity and perceptions of safety in urban middle schools. *Psychological Science, 17*(5), 393–400. doi:10.1111/j.1467-9280.2006.01718.x

Jyrkkä, Johanna; Mursu, Jaakko; Enlund, Hannes and Lönnroos, Eija. (2012). Polypharmacy and nutritional status in elderly people. *Current Opinion in Clinical Nutrition & Metabolic Care, 15*(1), 1–6. doi:10.1097/MCO .0b013e32834d155a

Kachel, A. Friederike; Premo, Luke S. and Hublin, Jean-Jacques. (2011). Modeling the effects of weaning age on length of female reproductive period: Implications for the evolution of human life history. *American Journal of Human Biology, 23*(4), 479–487. doi:10.1002/ajhb.21157

Kagan, Jerome and Herschkowitz, Norbert. (2005). Young mind in a growing brain. Mahwah, NJ: Lawrence Erlbaum.

Kagan, Jerome; Snidman, Nancy; Kahn, Vali and Towsley, Sara. (2007). The preservation of two infant temperaments into adolescence. *Monographs of the Society for Research in Child Development, 72*(2), 1–95.

Kahana, Eva; Bhatta, Tirth; Lovegreen, Loren D.; Kahana, Boaz and Midlarsky, Elizabeth. (2013). Altruism, helping, and volunteering: Pathways to well-being in late life. *Journal of Aging and Health, 25*(1), 159–187. doi:10.1177/0898264312469665

Kahn, Joan R.; McGill, Brittany S. and Bianchi, Suzanne M. (2011). Help to family and friends: Are there gender differences at older ages? *Journal of Marriage and Family, 73*(1), 77–92. doi:10.1111/j.1741-3737.2010.00790.x

Kahneman, Daniel. (2011). Thinking, fast and slow. New York, NY: Farrar, Straus and Giroux.

Kaiser, Jocelyn. (2013). Researchers to explore promise, risks of sequencing newborns' DNA. *Science, 341*(6151), 1163. doi:10.1126/science.341 .6151.1163

Kalambouka, Afroditi; Farrell, Peter; Dyson, Alan and Kaplan, Ian. (2007). The impact of placing pupils with special educational needs in mainstream schools on the achievement of their peers. *Educational Research, 49*(4), 365–382. doi:10.1080/00131880701717222

Kalaria, Raj N.; Maestre, Gladys E.; Arizaga, Raul; Friedland, Robert P.; Galasko, Doug; Hall, Kathleen, . . . Antuono, Piero. (2008). Alzheimer's disease and vascular dementia in developing countries: Prevalence, management, and risk factors. *The Lancet Neurology, 7*(9), 812–826. doi:10.1016/S1474-4422(08)70169-8

Kalliala, Marjatta. (2006). Play culture in a changing world. Maidenhead, UK: Open University Press.

Kallio, Eeva. (2011). Integrative thinking is the key: An evaluation of current research into the development of adult thinking. *Theory Psychology, 21*(6), 785–801. doi:10.1177/0959354310388344

Kalmijn, Matthijs. (2010). Country differences in the effects of divorce on well-being: The role of norms, support, and selectivity. *European Sociological Review, 26*(4), 475–490. doi:10.1093/ esr/jcp035

Kandler, Christian. (2012). Nature and nurture in personality development: The case of neuroticism and extraversion. *Current Directions in Psychological Science, 21*(5), 290–296. doi:10.1177/0963721412452557

Kanfer, Ruth; Beier, Margaret E. and Ackerman, Phillip L. (2013). Goals and motivation related to work in later adulthood: An organizing framework. *European Journal of Work and Organizational Psychology, 22*(3), 253–264. doi:10 .1080/1359432X.2012.734298

Kanfi, Yariv; Naiman, Shoshana; Amir, Gail; Peshti, Victoria; Zinman, Guy; Nahum, Liat, . . . Cohen, Haim Y. (2012). The sirtuin SIRT6

regulates lifespan in male mice. *Nature, 483,* 218–221. doi:10.1038/nature10815

Kanner, Andres M. (2012). Depression in neurologic disorders: Diagnosis and management. Chichester, West Sussex: Wiley.

Kanner, Leo. (1943). Autistic disturbances of affective contact. *Nervous Child, 2,* 217–250.

Kapornai, Krisztina and Vetró, Ágnes. (2008). Depression in children. *Current Opinion in Psychiatry, 21*(1), 1–7. doi:10.1097/YCO.0b013e3282f25b01

Karama, Sherif; Ad-Dab'bagh, Yasser; Haier, Richard J.; Deary, Ian J.; Lyttelton, Oliver C.; Lepage, Claude and Evans, Alan C. (2009). Positive association between cognitive ability and cortical thickness in a representative US sample of healthy 6 to 18-year-olds. *Intelligence, 37*(2), 145–155. doi:10.1016/j.intell.2008.09.006

Karmiloff-Smith, Annette. (2010). A developmental perspective on modularity. In Britt Glatzeder, Vinod Goel and Albrecht Müller (Eds.), *Towards a theory of thinking* (pp. 179–187). Heidelberg, Germany: Springer. doi:10.1007/978-3-642-03129-8_12

Kärnä, Antti; Voeten, Marinus; Little, Todd D.; Poskiparta, Elisa; Kaljonen, Anne and Salmivalli, Christina. (2011). A large-scale evaluation of the KiVa antibullying program: Grades 4–6. *Child Development, 82*(1), 311–330. doi:10.1111/j.1467-8624.2010.01557.x

Kärtner, Joscha; Borke, Jörn; Maasmeier, Kathrin; Keller, Heidi and Kleis, Astrid. (2011). Sociocultural influences on the development of self-recognition and self-regulation in Costa Rican and Mexican toddlers. *Journal of Cognitive Education and Psychology, 10*(1), 96–112.

Kärtner, Joscha; Keller, Heidi and Yovsi, Relindis D. (2010). Mother–infant interaction during the first 3 months: The emergence of culture-specific contingency patterns. *Child Development, 81*(2), 540–554. doi:10.1111/j.1467-8624.2009.01414.x

Kastenbaum, Robert J. (2006). *Death, society, and human experience* (9th ed.). Boston, MA: Pearson.

Kastenbaum, Robert J. (2012). *Death, society, and human experience* (11th ed.). Boston, MA: Pearson.

Katz, Kathy S.; Jarrett, Marian H.; El-Mohandes, Ayman A. E.; Schneider, Susan; McNeely-Johnson, Doris and Kiely, Michele. (2011). Effectiveness of a combined home visiting and group intervention for low income African American mothers: The Pride in Parenting program. *Maternal and Child Health Journal, 15*(Suppl. 1), 75–84. doi:10.1007/s10995-011-0858-x

Kaufman, James C. and Sternberg, Robert J. (Eds.). (2006). *The international handbook of creativity.* New York, NY: Cambridge University Press.

Kaufman, Kenneth R. and Kaufman, Nathaniel D. (2006). And then the dog died. *Death Studies, 30*(1), 61–76. doi:10.1080/07481180500348811

Kavanaugh, Robert D. (2011). Origins and consequences of social pretend play. In Anthony D. Pellegrini (Ed.), *The Oxford handbook of the development of play* (pp. 296–307). New York, NY: Oxford University Press.

Keating, Nancy L.; Herrinton, Lisa J.; Zaslavsky, Alan M.; Liu, Liyan and Ayanian, John Z. (2006). Variations in hospice use among cancer patients. *Journal of the National Cancer Institute, 98*(15), 1053–1059. doi:10.1093/jnci/djj298

Keil, Frank C. (2011). Science starts early. *Science, 331*(6020), 1022–1023. doi:10.1126/science.1195221

Kellehear, Allan. (2008). Dying as a social relationship: A sociological review of debates on the determination of death. *Social Science & Medicine, 66*(7), 1533–1544. doi:10.1016/j.socscimed.2007.12.023

Keller, Heidi; Borke, Jörn; Chaudhary, Nandita; Lamm, Bettina and Kleis, Astrid. (2010). Continuity in parenting strategies: A cross-cultural comparison. *Journal of Cross-Cultural Psychology, 41*(3), 391–409. doi:10.1177/0022022109359690

Keller, Heidi and Otto, Hiltrud. (2011). Different faces of autonomy. In Xinyin Chen and Kenneth H. Rubin (Eds.), *Socioemotional development in cultural context* (pp. 164–185). New York, NY: Guilford Press.

Keller, Heidi; Yovsi, Relindis; Borke, Joern; Kärtner, Joscha; Jensen, Henning and Papaligoura, Zaira. (2004). Developmental consequences of early parenting experiences: Self-recognition and self-regulation in three cultural communities. *Child Development, 75*(6), 1745–1760. doi:10.1111/j.1467-8624.2004.00814.x

Kellman, Philip J. and Arterberry, Martha E. (2006). Infant visual perception. In William Damon and Richard M. Lerner (Eds.), *Handbook of child psychology* (6th ed., Vol. 2, pp. 109–160). Hoboken, NJ: Wiley.

Kelly, Daniel; Faucher, Luc and Machery, Edouard. (2010). Getting rid of racism: Assessing three proposals in light of psychological evidence. *Journal of Social Philosophy, 41*(3), 293–322. doi:10.1111/j.1467-9833.2010.01495.x

Kelly, John R. (1993). *Activity and aging: Staying involved in later life.* Newbury Park, CA: Sage.

Kelvin, David J. and Farooqui, Amber. (2013). Extremely low vaccine effectiveness against influenza H3N2 in the elderly during the 2012/2013 flu season. *Journal of Infection in Developing Countries, 7*(3), 299–301.

Kemp, Candace L. (2005). Dimensions of grandparent-adult grandchild relationships: From family ties to intergenerational friendships. *Canadian Journal on Aging, 24*(2), 161–177.

Kempe, Ruth S. and Kempe, C. Henry. (1978). *Child abuse.* Cambridge, MA: Harvard University Press.

Kempermann, Gerd. (2012). New neurons for 'survival of the fittest'. *Nature Reviews Neuroscience, 13*(10), 727–736. doi:10.1038/nrn3319

Kemple, James J. (2008). *Career academies: Long-term impacts on labor market outcomes, educational attainment, and transitions to adulthood.* New York, NY: MDRC.

Kempner, Joanna; Perlis, Clifford S. and Merz, Jon F. (2005). Forbidden knowledge. *Science, 307*(5711), 854. doi:10.1126/science.1107576

Kendler, Howard H. (2002). Unified knowledge: Fantasy or reality? *Contemporary Psychology: APA Review of Books, 47*(5), 501–503. doi:10.1037/001200

Kendler, Kenneth S.; Eaves, Lindon J.; Loken, Erik K.; Pedersen, Nancy L.; Middeldorp, Christel M.; Reynolds, Chandra, . . . Gardner, Charles O. (2011). The impact of environmental experiences on symptoms of anxiety and depression across the life span. *Psychological Science, 22*(10), 1343–1352. doi:10.1177/0956797611417255

Kenrick, Douglas T.; Griskevicius, Vladas; Neuberg, Steven L. and Schaller, Mark. (2010). Renovating the pyramid of needs: Contemporary extensions built upon ancient foundations. *Perspectives on Psychological Science, 5*(3), 292–314. doi:10.1177/1745691610369469

Kéri, Szabolcs. (2009). Genes for psychosis and creativity: A promoter polymorphism of the neuregulin 1 gene is related to creativity in people with high intellectual achievement. *Psychological Science, 20*(9), 1070–1073. doi:10.1111/j.1467-9280.2009.02398.x

Kerr, Margaret; Stattin, Håkan and Burk, William J. (2010). A reinterpretation of parental monitoring in longitudinal perspective. *Journal of Research on Adolescence, 20*(1), 39–64. doi:10.1111/j.1532-7795.2009.00623.x

Kesselring, Thomas and Müller, Ulrich. (2011). The concept of egocentrism in the context of Piaget's theory. *New Ideas in Psychology, 29*(3), 327–345. doi:10.1016/j.newideapsych.2010.03.008

Kessler, Ronald C.; Aguilar-Gaxiola, Sergio; Alonso, Jordi; Chatterji, Somnath; Lee, Sing; Ormel, Johan, . . . Wang, Philip S. (2009). The global burden of mental disorders: An update from the WHO World Mental Health (WMH) Surveys. *Epidemiologia e Psichiatria Sociale, 18*(1), 23–33. doi:10.1017/S1121189X00001421

Kessler, Ronald C.; Galea, Sandro; Jones, Russell T. and Parker, Holly A. (2006). Mental illness and suicidality after Hurricane Katrina. *Bulletin of the World Health Organization, 84*(12), 930–939. doi:10.2471/BLT.06.033011

Kessler, Ronald C.; Petukhova, Maria and Zaslavsky, Alan M. (2011). The role of latent internalizing and externalizing predispositions in accounting for the development of comorbidity among common mental disorders. *Current Opinion in Psychiatry, 24*(4), 307–312. doi:10.1097/YCO.0b013e3283477b22

Kettl, Paul. (2010). One vote for death panels. *Journal of the American Medical Association, 303*(13), 1234–1235. doi:10.1001/jama.2010.376

Keysers, Christian and Gazzola, Valeria. (2010). Social neuroscience: Mirror neurons recorded in humans. *Current Biology, 20*(8), R353–R354. doi:10.1016/j.cub.2010.03.013

Khanna, Sunil K. (2010). *Fetal/fatal knowledge: New reproductive technologies and family-building strategies in India.* Belmont, CA: Wadsworth/Cengage Learning.

Khrapko, Konstantin. (2011). The timing of mitochondrial DNA mutations in aging. *Nature Genetics, 43*(8), 726–727. doi:10.1038/ng.895

Kiang, Lisa and Harter, Susan. (2008). Do pieces of the self-puzzle fit? Integrated/fragmented selves in biculturally-identified Chinese Americans. *Journal of Research in Personality, 42*(6), 1657–1662. doi:10.1016/j.jrp.2008.07.010

Kiang, Lisa; Witkow, Melissa; Baldelomar, Oscar and Fuligni, Andrew. (2010). Change in ethnic identity across the high school years among adolescents with Latin American, Asian, and European backgrounds. *Journal of Youth and Adolescence, 39*(6), 683–693. doi:10.1007/s10964-009-9429-5

Kiecolt, K. Jill; Hughes, Michael and Keith, Verna M. (2009). Can a high sense of control and John Henryism be bad for mental health? *The Sociological Quarterly, 50*(4), 693–714. doi:10.1111/j.1533-8525.2009.01152.x

Kiernan, Stephen P. (2010). The transformation of death in America. In Nan Bauer Maglin and Donna Marie Perry (Eds.), *Final acts: Death, dying, and the choices we make* (pp. 163–182). New Brunswick, NJ: Rutgers University Press.

Killen, Melanie; Kelly, Megan Clark; Richardson, Cameron; Crystal, David and Ruck, Martin. (2010). European American children's and adolescents' evaluations of interracial exclusion. *Group Processes Intergroup Relations, 13*(3), 283–300. doi:10.1177/1368430209346700

Killen, Melanie; Margie, Nancy Geyelin and Sinno, Stefanie. (2006). Morality in the context of intergroup relationships. In Melanie Killen and Judith G. Smetana (Eds.), *Handbook of moral development* (pp. 155–183). Mahwah, NJ: Lawrence Erlbaum Associates.

Killen, Melanie and Smetana, Judith G. (Eds.). (2014). *Handbook of moral development* (2nd ed.). New York, NY: Psychology Press.

Killgore, William D. S.; Vo, Alexander H.; Castro, Carl A. and Hoge, Charles W. (2006). Assessing risk propensity in American soldiers: Preliminary reliability and validity of the Evaluation of Risks (EVAR) scale—English version. *Military Medicine, 171*(3), 233–239.

Kilmer, Ryan P. and Gil-Rivas, Virginia. (2010). Exploring posttraumatic growth in children impacted by Hurricane Katrina: Correlates of the phenomenon and developmental considerations. *Child Development, 81*(4), 1211–1227. doi:10.1111/j.1467-8624.2010.01463.x

Kim, Dong-Sik and Kim, Hyun-Sun. (2009). Body-image dissatisfaction as a predictor of suicidal ideation among Korean boys and girls in different stages of adolescence: A two-year longitudinal study. *The Journal of Adolescent Health, 45*(1), 47–54. doi:10.1016/j.jadohealth.2008.11.017

Kim, Esther Chihye. (2009). "Mama's family": Fictive kinship and undocumented immigrant restaurant workers. *Ethnography, 10*(4), 497–513. doi:10.1177/1466138109347000

Kim, Geunyoung; Walden, Tedra A. and Knieps, Linda J. (2010). Impact and characteristics of positive and fearful emotional messages during infant social referencing. *Infant Behavior and Development, 33*(2), 189–195. doi:10.1016/j.infbeh.2009.12.009

Kim, Geunyoung; Walden, Tedra A. and Knieps, Linda J. (2013). Impact and characteristics of positive and fearful emotional messages during infant social referencing. *Infant Behavior and Development, 33*(2), 189–195. doi:10.1016/j.infbeh.2009.12.009

Kim, Hojin I. and Johnson, Scott P. (2013). Do young infants prefer an infant-directed face or a happy face? *International Journal of Behavioral Development, 37*(2), 125–130. doi:10.1177/0165025413475972

Kim, Hyoun K.; Laurent, Heidemarie K.; Capaldi, Deborah M. and Feingold, Alan (2008). Men's aggression toward women: A 10-year panel study. *Journal of Marriage and Family, 70*(5), 1169–1187. doi:10.1111/j.1741-3737.2008.00558.x

Kim, Hyun Sik. (2011). Consequences of parental divorce for child development. *American Sociological Review, 76*(3), 487–511. doi:10.1177/0003122411407748

Kim, Heejung S. and Chu, Thai Q. (2011). Cultural variation in the motivation of self-expression. In David Dunning (Ed.), *Social motivation* (pp. 57–78). New York, NY: Psychology Press.

Kim, Heejung S.; Sherman, David K. and Taylor, Shelley E. (2008). Culture and social support. *American Psychologist, 63*(6), 518–526. doi:10.1037/0003-066X

Kim, Joon Sik. (2011). Excessive crying: Behavioral and emotional regulation disorder in infancy. *Korean Journal of Pediatrics, 54*(6), 229–233. doi:10.3345/kjp.2011.54.6.229

Kim-Spoon, Jungmeen; Longo, Gregory S. and McCullough, Michael E. (2012). Parent-adolescent relationship quality as a moderator for the influences of parents' religiousness on adolescents' religiousness and adjustment. *Journal of Youth and Adolescence, 41*(12), 1576–1587. doi:10.1007/s10964-012-9796-1

Kimmel, Michael S. (2008). *Guyland: The perilous world where boys become men.* New York, NY: HarperCollins.

King, Bruce M. (2013). The modern obesity epidemic, ancestral hunter-gatherers, and the sensory/reward control of food intake. *American Psychologist, 68*(2), 88–96. doi:10.1037/a0030684

King, Pamela Ebstyne and Roeser, Robert W. (2009). Religion and spirituality in adolescent development. In Richard M. Lerner and Laurence Steinberg (Eds.), *Handbook of adolescent psychology* (3rd ed., Vol. 1, pp. 435–478). Hoboken, NJ: Wiley.

Kingsmore, Stephen F.; Dinwiddie, Darrell L.; Miller, Neil A.; Soden, Sarah E. and Saunders, Carol J. (2011). Adopting orphans: comprehensive genetic testing of Mendelian diseases of childhood by next-generation sequencing. *Expert Review of Molecular Diagnostics, 11*(8), 855–868. doi:10.1586/erm.11.70

Kinney, Hannah C. and Thach, Bradley T. (2009). The sudden infant death syndrome. *New England Journal of Medicine, 361,* 795–805. doi:10.1056/NEJMra0803836

Kinnunen, Marja-Liisa; Kaprio, Jaakko and Pulkkinen, Lea. (2005). Allostatic load of men and women in early middle age. *Journal of Individual Differences, 26*(1), 20–28. doi:10.1027/1614-0001.26.1.20

Kirby, Douglas and Laris, B. A. (2009). Effective curriculum-based sex and STD/HIV education programs for adolescents. *Child Development Perspectives, 3*(1), 21–29. doi:10.1111/j.1750-8606.2008.00071.x

Kirk, Elizabeth; Howlett, Neil; Pine, Karen J. and Fletcher, Ben. (2013). To sign or not to sign? The impact of encouraging infants to gesture on infant language and maternal mind-mindedness. *Child Development, 84*(2), 574–590. doi:10.1111/j.1467-8624.2012.01874.x

Kiuru, Noona; Burk, William J.; Laursen, Brett; Salmela-Aro, Katariina and Nurmi, Jari-Erik. (2010). Pressure to drink but not to smoke: Disentangling selection and socialization in adolescent peer networks and peer groups. *Journal of Adolescence, 33*(6), 801–812. doi:10.1016/j.adolescence.2010.07.006

Klaczynski, Paul; Daniel, David B. and Keller, Peggy S. (2009). Appearance idealization, body esteem, causal attributions, and ethnic variations in the development of obesity stereotypes. *Journal of Applied Developmental Psychology, 30*(4), 537–551. doi:10.1016/j.appdev.2008.12.031

Klaczynski, Paul A. (2001). Analytic and heuristic processing influences on adolescent reasoning and decision-making. *Child Development, 72*(3), 844–861. doi:10.1111/1467-8624.00319

Klaczynski, Paul A. (2011). Age differences in understanding precedent-setting decisions and authorities' responses to violations of deontic rules. *Journal of Experimental Child Psychology, 109*(1), 1–24. doi:10.1016/j.jecp.2010.10.010

Klahr, Ashlea M.; McGue, Matt; Iacono, William G. and Burt, S. Alexandra. (2011). The association between parent-child conflict and adolescent conduct problems over time: Results from a longitudinal adoption study. *Journal of Abnormal Psychology, 120*(1), 46–56. doi:10.1037/a0021350

Klahr, David and Nigam, Milena. (2004). The equivalence of learning paths in early science instruction: Effects of direct instruction and discovery learning. *Psychological Science, 15*(10), 661–667. doi:10.1111/j.0956-7976.2004.00737.x

Klassen, Terry P.; Kiddoo, Darcie; Lang, Mia E.; Friesen, Carol; Russell, Kelly; Spooner, Carol and Vandermeer, Ben. (2006). *The effectiveness of different methods of toilet training for bowel and bladder control.* Rockville, MD: Agency for Healthcare Research and Quality, U.S. Dept. of Health and Human Services.

Klatsky, Arthur L. (2009). Alcohol and cardio-vascular diseases. *Expert Review of Cardiovascular Therapy, 7*(5), 499–506. doi:10.1586/erc.09.22

Klaus, Susan F.; Ekerdt, David J. and Gajewski, Byron. (2012). Job satisfaction in birth cohorts of nurses. *Journal of Nursing Management, 20*(4), 461–471. doi:10.1111/j.1365-2834.2011.01283.x

Klein, Hilary (1991). Couvade Syndrome: Male Counterpart to Pregnancy. *International Journal of Psychiatry in Medicine, 21*(1), 57–69. doi:10.2190/FLE0-92JM-C4CN-J83T

Klein, Stanley B. (2012). The two selves: The self of conscious experience and its brain. In Mark R. Leary and June Price Tangney (Eds.), *Handbook of self and identity* (pp. 617–637). New York, NY: Guilford Press.

Klein, Zoe A. and Romeo, Russell D. (2013). Changes in hypothalamic–pituitary–adrenal stress responsiveness before and after puberty in rats. *Hormones and Behavior, 64*(2), 357–363. doi:10.1016/j.yhbeh.2013.01.012

Kliegel, Matthias; Jäger, Theodor and Phillips, Louise H. (2008). Adult age differences in event-based prospective memory: A meta-analysis on the role of focal versus nonfocal cues. *Psychology and Aging, 23*(1), 203–208. doi:10.1037/0882-7974.23.1.203

Klimstra, Theo A.; Luyckx, Koen; Germeijs, Veerle; Meeus, Wim H. J. and Goossens, Luc. (2012). Personality traits and educational identity formation in late adolescents: Longitudinal associations and academic progress. *Journal of Youth and Adolescence, 41*(3), 346–361. doi:10.1007/s10964-011-9734-7

Klöppel, Stefan; Vongerichten, Anna; Eimeren, Thilo van; Frackowiak, Richard S. J. and Siebner, Hartwig R. (2007). Can left-handedness be switched? Insights from an early switch of handwriting. *Journal of Neuroscience, 27*(29), 7847–7853. doi:10.1523/jneurosci.1299-07.2007

Kochanska, Grazyna; Aksan, Nazan; Prisco, Theresa R. and Adams, Erin E. (2008). Mother-child and father-child mutually responsive orientation in the first 2 years and children's outcomes at preschool age: Mechanisms of influence. *Child Development, 79*(1), 30–44. doi:10.1111/j.1467-8624.2007.01109.x

Kochanska, Grazyna; Barry, Robin A.; Jimenez, Natasha B.; Hollatz, Amanda L. and Woodard, Jarilyn. (2009). Guilt and effortful control: Two mechanisms that prevent disruptive developmental trajectories. *Journal of Personality and Social Psychology, 97*(2), 322–333. doi:10.1037/a0015471

Kogan, Michael D.; Blumberg, Stephen J.; Schieve, Laura A.; Boyle, Coleen A.; Perrin, James M.; Ghandour, Reem M., . . . van Dyck, Peter C. (2009). Prevalence of parent-reported diagnosis of autism spectrum disorder among children in the US, 2007. *Pediatrics, 124*(5), 1395–1403. doi:10.1542/peds.2009-1522

Kohl, Patricia L.; Jonson-Reid, Melissa and Drake, Brett. (2009). Time to leave substantiation behind: Findings from a national probability study. *Child Maltreatment, 14*(1), 17–26. doi:10.1177/1077559508326030

Kohlberg, Lawrence. (1963). The development of children's orientations toward a moral order: I. *Sequence in the development of moral thought.* Vita Humana, 6, 11–33. doi:10.1159/000269667

Kohlberg, Lawrence; Levine, Charles and Hewer, Alexandra. (1983). *Moral stages: A current formulation and a response to critics.* New York, NY: Karger.

Kohyama, Jun; Mindell, Jodi A. and Sadeh, Avi. (2011). Sleep characteristics of young children in Japan: Internet study and comparison with other Asian countries. *Pediatrics International, 53*(5), 649–655. doi:10.1111/j.1442-200X.2010.03318.x

Kolb, Bryan and Whishaw, Ian Q. (2013). *An introduction to brain and behavior* (4th ed.). New York, NY: Worth.

Kolling, Thorsten; Goertz, Claudia; Frahsek, Stefanie and Knopf, Monika. (2009). Stability of deferred imitation in 12- to 18-month-old infants: A closer look into developmental dynamics. *European Journal of Developmental Psychology, 6*(5), 615–640. doi:10.1080/17405620701533200

Koltko-Rivera, Mark E. (2006). Rediscovering the later version of Maslow's hierarchy of needs: Self-transcendence and opportunities for theory, research, and unification. *Review of General Psychology, 10*(4), 302–317. doi:10.1037/1089-2680.10.4.302

Komp, Kathrin; van Tilburg, Theo and van Groenou, Marjolein Broese. (2010). Paid work between age 60 and 70 years in Europe: A matter of socio-economic status? *International Journal of Ageing and Later Life, 5*(1), 45–75. doi:10.3384/ijal.1652-8670.105145

Konner, Melvin. (2007). Evolutionary foundations of cultural psychology. In Shinobu Kitayama and Dov Cohen (Eds.), *Handbook of Cultural Psychology* (pp. 77–105). New York, NY: Guilford Press.

Konner, Melvin. (2010). *The evolution of childhood: Relationships, emotion, mind.* Cambridge, MA: Harvard University Press.

Kooij, Dorien T. A. M.; Annet, H. D. E.; Lange, Paul G. W.; Jansen, Ruth Kanfer and Dikkers, Josje S. E. (2011). Age and work-related motives: Results of a meta-analysis. *Journal of Organizational Behavior, 225*(2), 197–225. doi:10.1002/job.665

Kopp, Claire B. (2011). Development in the early years: Socialization, motor development, and consciousness. *Annual Review of Psychology, 62*, 165–187. doi:10.1146/annurev.psych.121208.131625

Koppen, Jean. (2009). Effect of the economy on housing choices. Washington, DC: AARP.

Korhonen, Tellervo; Latvala, Antti; Dick, Danielle M.; Pulkkinen, Lea; Rose, Richard J.; Kaprio, Jaakko and Huizink, Anja C. (2012). Genetic and environmental influences underlying externalizing behaviors, cigarette smoking and illicit drug use across adolescence. *Behavior Genetics, 42*(4), 614–625. doi:10.1007/s10519-012-9528-z

Korte, J.; Bohlmeijer, E. T.; Cappeliez, P.; Smit, F. and Westerhof, G. J. (2012). Life review therapy for older adults with moderate depressive symptomatology: A pragmatic randomized controlled trial. *Psychological Medicine, 42*(6), 1163–1173. doi:10.1017/S0033291711002042

Kossowsky, Joe; Wilhelm, Frank H.; Roth, Walton T. and Schneider, Silvia. (2012). Separation anxiety disorder in children: Disorder-specific responses to experimental separation from the mother. *Journal of Child Psychology and Psychiatry, 53*, 178–187. doi:10.1111/j.1469-7610.2011.02465.x

Kouider, Sid; Stahlhut, Carsten; Gelskov, Sofie V.; Barbosa, Leonardo S.; Dutat, Michel; de Gardelle, Vincent, . . . Dehaene-Lambertz, Ghislaine. (2013). A neural marker of perceptual consciousness in infants. *Science, 340*(6130), 376–380. doi:10.1126/science.1232509

Kovas, Yulia; Hayiou-Thomas, Marianna E.; Oliver, Bonamy; Dale, Philip S.; Bishop, Dorothy V. M. and Plomin, Robert. (2005). Genetic influences in different aspects of language development: The etiology of language skills in 4.5-year-old twins. *Child Development, 76*(3), 632–651. doi:10.1111/j.1467-8624.2005.00868.x

Kozhimannil, Katy Backes; Law, Michael R. and Virnig, Beth A. (2013). Cesarean Delivery Rates Vary Tenfold Among US Hospitals; Reducing Variation May Address Quality And Cost Issues. *Health Affairs, 32*(3), 527–535. doi:10.1377/hlthaff.2012.1030

Kozo, Justine; Sallis, James F.; Conway, Terry L.; Kerr, Jacqueline; Cain, Kelli; Saelens, Brian E., . . . Owen, Neville. (2012). Sedentary behaviors of adults in relation to neighborhood walkability and income. *Health Psychology, 31*(6), 704–713. doi:10.1037/a0027874

Krampe, Ralf Th. and Charness, Neil. (2006). Aging and expertise. In K. Anders Ericsson, Neil Charness, Paul J. Feltovich and Robert R. Hoffman (Eds.), *The Cambridge handbook of expertise and expert performance* (pp. 723–742). New York, NY: Cambridge University Press.

Krampe, Ralf Th.; Schaefer, Sabine; Lindenberger, Ulman and Baltes, Paul B. (2011). Lifespan changes in multi-tasking: Concurrent walking and memory search in children, young, and older adults. *Gait & Posture, 33*(3), 401–405. doi:10.1016/j.gaitpost.2010.12.012

Krause, Neal. (2006). Social relationships in late life. In Robert H. Binstock and Linda K. George (Eds.), *Handbook of aging and the social sciences* (6th ed., pp. 181–200). Amsterdam, The Netherlands: Elsevier.

Kreager, Derek; Felson, Richard B.; Warner, Cody and Wenger, Marin R. (2013). Women's education, marital violence, and divorce: A social exchange perspective. *Journal of Marriage and Family, 75*(3), 565–581. doi:10.1111/jomf.12018

Krebs, John R. (2009). The gourmet ape: Evolution and human food preferences. *American Journal of Clinical Nutrition, 90*(3), 707S–711S. doi:10.3945/ajcn.2009.27462B

Kremen, William S.; Moore, Caitlin S.; Franz, Carol E.; Panizzon, Matthew S. and Lyons, Michael J. (2014). Cognition in middle adulthood. In Deborah Finkel and Chandra A. Reynolds (Eds.), *Behavior genetics of cognition across the lifespan: Advances in behavior genetics* (Vol. 1, pp. 105–134). New York, NY: Springer. doi:10.1007/978-1-4614-7447-0_4

Kretch, Kari S. and Adolph, Karen E. (2013). No bridge too high: Infants decide whether to cross based on the probability of falling, not the severity of the potential fall. *Developmental Science, 16*(3), 336–351. doi:10.1111/desc.12045

Krieg, Alexander and Dickie, Jane R. (2013). Attachment and hikikomori: A psychosocial developmental model. *International Journal of Social Psychiatry, 59*(1), 61–72. doi:10.1177/0020764011423182

Krieger, Nancy. (2012). Methods for the scientific study of discrimination and health: An ecosocial approach. *American Journal of Public Health, 102*(5), 936–944. doi:10.2105/AJPH.2011.300544

Kroger, Jane. (2007). *Identity development: Adolescence through adulthood* (2nd ed.). Thousand Oaks, CA: Sage.

Kroger, Jane; Martinussen, Monica and Marcia, James E. (2010). Identity status change during adolescence and young adulthood: A meta-analysis. *Journal of Adolescence, 33*(5), 683–698. doi:10.1016/j.adolescence.2009.11.002

Kübler-Ross, Elisabeth. (1969). *On death and dying.* New York, NY: Macmillan.

Kübler-Ross, Elisabeth. (1975). *Death: The final stage of growth.* Englewood Cliffs, NJ: Prentice-Hall.

Kübler-Ross, Elisabeth and Kessler, David. (2005). On grief and grieving: Finding the meaning of grief through the five stages of loss. New York, NY: Scribner.

Kuehn, Bridget M. (2011). Scientists find promising therapies for fragile x and Down syndromes. *JAMA, 305*(4), 344–346. doi:10.1001/jama.2010.1960

Kuh, George D.; Gonyea, Robert M. and Williams, Julie M. (2005). What students expect from college and what they get. In Thomas E. Miller, Barbara E. Bender and John H. Schuh (Eds.), *Promoting reasonable expectations: Aligning student and institutional views of the college experience* (pp. 34–64). San Francisco, CA: Jossey-Bass.

Kuhlmann, Inga; Minihane, Anne; Huebbe, Patricia; Nebel, Almut and Rimbach, Gerald. (2010). Apolipoprotein E genotype and hepatitis C, HIV and herpes simplex disease risk: A literature review. *Lipids in Health and Disease, 9*(1), 8. doi:10.1186/1476-511X-9-8

Kuhn, Deanna. (2013). Reasoning. In Philip David Zelazo (Ed.), *The Oxford handbook of developmental psychology* (Vol. 1, pp. 744–764). New York, NY: Oxford University Press.

Kuhn, Deanna and Franklin, Sam. (2006). The second decade: What develops (and how). In William Damon and Richard M. Lerner (Eds.), *Handbook of child psychology* (6th ed., Vol. 2, pp. 953–993). Hoboken, NJ: Wiley.

Kuhn, Louise; Reitz, Cordula and Abrams, Elaine J. (2009). Breastfeeding and AIDS in the developing world. *Current Opinion in Pediatrics, 21*(1), 83–93. doi:10.1097/MOP.0b013e328320d894

Kumar, Santosh; Calvo, Rocio; Avendano, Mauricio; Sivaramakrishnan, Kavita and Berkman, Lisa F. (2012). Social support, volunteering and health around the world: Cross-national evidence from 139 countries. *Social Science & Medicine, 74*(5), 696–706. doi:10.1016/j.socscimed.2011.11.017

Kundu, Tapas K. (Ed.). (2013). *Epigenetics: Development and disease.* New York, NY: Springer. doi:10.1007/978-94-007-4525-4

Kuo, Hsu-Ko; Leveille, Suzanne G.; Yu, Yau-Hua and Milber, William P. (2007). Cognitive function, habitual gait speed, and late-life disability in the National Health and Nutrition Examination Survey (NHANES) 1999–2002. *Gerontology, 53,* 102–110. doi:10.1159/000096792

Kuperberg, Arielle. (2012). Reassessing differences in work and income in cohabitation and marriage. *Journal of Marriage and Family, 74*(4), 688–707. doi:10.1111/j.1741-3737.2012.00993.x

Kuppens, Sofie; Grietens, Hans; Onghena, Patrick and Michiels, Daisy. (2009). Associations between parental control and children's overt and relational aggression. *British Journal of Developmental Psychology, 27*(3), 607–623. doi:10.1348/026151008X345591

Kurdek, Lawrence A. (2006). Differences between partners from heterosexual, gay, and lesbian cohabiting couples. *Journal of Marriage and Family, 68*(2), 509–528. doi:10.1111/j.1741-3737.2006.00268.x

Kutob, Randa M.; Senf, Janet H.; Crago, Marjorie and Shisslak, Catherine M. (2010). Concurrent and longitudinal predictors of self-esteem in elementary and middle school girls. *Journal of School Health, 80*(5), 240–248. doi:10.1111/j.1746-1561.2010.00496.x

Kwok, Sylvia Y. C. Lai and Shek, Daniel T. L. (2010). Hopelessness, parent-adolescent communication, and suicidal ideation among Chinese adolescents in Hong Kong. *Suicide and Life-Threatening Behavior, 40*(3), 224–233. doi:10.1521/suli.2010.40.3.224

LaBar, Kevin S. (2007). Beyond fear: Emotional memory mechanisms in the human brain. *Current Directions in Psychological Science, 16*(4), 173–177. doi:10.1111/j.1467-8721.2007.00498.x

Labouvie-Vief, Gisela. (1990). Wisdom as integrated thought: Historical and developmental perspectives. In Robert J. Sternberg (Ed.), *Wisdom: Its nature, origins, and development* (pp. 52–83). New York, NY: Cambridge University Press.

Labouvie-Vief, Gisela. (2006). Emerging structures of adult thought. In Jeffrey Jensen Arnett and Jennifer Lynn Tanner (Eds.), *Emerging adults in America: Coming of age in the 21st century* (pp. 59–84). Washington, DC: American Psychological Association.

Labouvie-Vief, Gisela; Grühn, Daniel and Mouras, Harold. (2009). Dynamic emotion-cognition interactions in adult development: Arousal, stress, and the processing of affect. In Hayden B. Bosworth and Christopher Hertzog (Eds.), *Aging and cognition: Research methodologies and empirical advances* (pp. 181–196). Washington, DC: American Psychological Association. doi:10.1037/11882-009

LaBrie, Joseph W.; Grant, Sean and Hummer, Justin F. (2011). "This would be better drunk": Alcohol expectancies become more positive while drinking in the college social environment. *Addictive Behaviors, 36*(8), 890–893. doi:10.1016/j.addbeh.2011.03.015

Lachman, Margie E. and Bertrand, Rosanna M. (2001). Personality and the self in midlife. In Margie E. Lachman (Ed.), *Handbook of midlife development* (pp. 279–309). New York, NY: Wiley.

Lachman, Margie E.; Neupert, Shevaun D. and Agrigoroaei, Stefan. (2011). The relevance of control beliefs for health and aging. In K. Warner Schaie and Sherry L. Willis (Eds.), *Handbook of the psychology of aging* (7th ed., pp. 175–190). San Diego, CA: Elsevier/Academic Press.

Lachman, Margie E.; Rosnick, Christopher B. and Röcke, Christina. (2009). The rise and fall of control beliefs and life satisfaction in adulthood: Trajectories of stability and change over ten years. In Hayden B. Bosworth and Christopher Hertzog (Eds.), *Aging and cognition: Research methodologies and empirical advances* (pp. 143–160). Washington, DC: American Psychological Association. doi:10.1037/11882-007

LaFontana, Kathryn M. and Cillessen, Antonius H. N. (2010). Developmental changes in the priority of perceived status in childhood and adolescence. *Social Development, 19*(1), 130–147. doi:10.1111/j.1467-9507.2008.00522.x

Laible, Deborah; Panfile, Tia and Makariev, Drika. (2008). The quality and frequency of mother-toddler conflict: Links with attachment and temperament. *Child Development, 79*(2), 426–443. doi:10.1111/j.1467-8624.2007.01134.x

Laird, Robert D.; Marrero, Matthew D.; Melching, Jessica A. and Kuhn, Emily S. (2013). Information management strategies in early adolescence: Developmental change in use and transactional associations with psychological adjustment. *Developmental Psychology, 49*(5), 928–937. doi:10.1037/a0028845

Lalande, Kathleen M. and Bonanno, George A. (2006). Culture and continuing bonds: A prospective comparison of bereavement in the United States and the People's Republic of China. *Death Studies, 30*(4), 303–324. doi:10.1080/07481180500544708

Lam, Raymond W. (2012). Depression (2nd ed.). Oxford, UK: Oxford University Press.

Lamb, Michael E. (Ed.). (2010). *The role of the father in child development* (5th ed.). Hoboken, NJ: Wiley.

Landa, Rebecca J.; Gross, Alden L.; Stuart, Elizabeth A. and Faherty, Ashley. (2013). Developmental Trajectories in Children With and Without Autism Spectrum Disorders: The

First 3 Years. *Child Development, 84*(2), 429–442. doi:10.1111/j.1467-8624.2012.01870.x

Landy, Frank J. and Conte, Jeffrey M. (2007). *Work in the 21st century: An introduction to industrial and organizational psychology* (2nd ed.). Malden, MA: Blackwell.

Lane, Rachel F.; Shineman, Diana W. and Fillit, Howard M. (2011). Beyond amyloid: A diverse portfolio of novel drug discovery programs for Alzheimer's disease and related dementias. *Alzheimer's Research & Therapy, 3*(36), 36. doi:10.1186/alzrt99

Lane, Scott D.; Cherek, Don R.; Pietras, Cynthia J. and Steinberg, Joel L. (2005). Performance of heavy marijuana-smoking adolescents on a laboratory measure of motivation. *Addictive Behaviors, 30*(4), 815–828. doi:10.1016/j.addbeh.2004.08.026

Lang, Frieder R.; Wagner, Jenny and Neyer, Franz J. (2009). Interpersonal functioning across the lifespan: Two principles of relationship regulation. *Advances in Life Course Research, 14*(1–2), 40–51. doi:10.1016/j.alcr.2009.03.004

Langeslag, Sandra J. E.; Muris, Peter and Franken, Ingmar H. A. (2013). Measuring romantic love: Psychometric properties of the infatuation and attachment scales. *The Journal of Sex Research, 50*(8), 739–747. doi:10.1080/00224499.2012.714011

Langhinrichsen-Rohling, Jennifer. (2010). Controversies involving gender and intimate partner violence: Response to commentators. *Sex Roles, 62*(3–4), 221–225. doi:10.1007/s11199-010-9743-0

Långström, Niklas; Rahman, Qazi; Carlström, Eva and Lichtenstein, Paul. (2010). Genetic and environmental effects on same-sex sexual behavior: A population study of twins in Sweden. *Archives of Sexual Behavior, 39*(1), 75–80. doi:10.1007/s10508-008-9386-1

Lara-Cinisomo, Sandraluz; Fuligni, Allison Sidle and Karoly, Lynn A. (2011). Preparing preschoolers for kindergarten. In DeAnna M. Laverick and Mary Renck Jalongo (Eds.), *Transitions to early care and education* (Vol. 4, pp. 93–105). New York, NY: Springer. doi:10.1007/978-94-007-0573-9_9

Laraway, Kelly A.; Birch, Leann L.; Shaffer, Michele L. and Paul, Ian M. (2010). Parent perception of healthy infant and toddler growth. *Clinical Pediatrics, 49*(4), 343–349. doi:10.1177/0009922809343717

Larson, Nicole I.; Laska, Melissa N.; Story, Mary and Neumark-Sztainer, Dianne. (2012). Predictors of fruit and vegetable intake in young adulthood. *Journal of the Academy of Nutrition & Dietetics, 112*(8), 1216–1222. doi:10.1016/j.jand.2012.03.035

Larson, Nicole I.; Neumark-Sztainer, Dianne; Hannan, Peter J. and Story, Mary. (2007). Trends in adolescent fruit and vegetable consumption, 1999–2004: Project EAT. *American Journal of Preventive Medicine, 32*(2), 147–150. doi:10.1016/j.amepre.2006.10.011

Larzelere, Robert; Cox, Ronald and Smith, Gail. (2010). Do nonphysical punishments reduce antisocial behavior more than spanking? *A comparison using the strongest previous causal evidence against spanking.* BMC Pediatrics, 10(10). doi:10.1186/1471-2431-10-10

Laska, Melissa Nelson; Larson, Nicole I.; Neumark-Sztainer, Dianne and Story, Mary. (2010). Dietary patterns and home food availability during emerging adulthood: Do they differ by living situation? *Public Health Nutrition, 13*(2), 222–228. doi:10.1017/S1368980009990760

Lattanzi-Licht, Marcia. (2013). Religion, Spirituality, and Dying. In David K. Meagher and David E. Balk (Eds.), *Handbook of thanatology: The essential body of knowledge for the study of death, dying, and bereavement* (2nd ed., pp. 9–16). New York, NY: Routledge.

Lau, Carissa; Ambalavanan, Namasivayam; Chakraborty, Hrishikesh; Wingate, Martha S. and Carlo, Waldemar A. (2013). Extremely low birth weight and infant mortality rates in the United States. *Pediatrics, 131*(5), 855–860. doi:10.1542/peds.2012-2471

Laumann, Edward O. and Michael, Robert T. (Eds.). (2000). *Sex, love, and health in America: Private choices and public policies.* Chicago, IL: University of Chicago Press.

Laumann, Edward O. and Michael, Robert T. (2001). Introduction: Setting the scene. In Edward O. Laumann and Robert T. Michael (Eds.), *Sex, love, and health in America: Private choices and public policies* (pp. 1–38). Chicago, IL: University of Chicago Press.

Laurino, Mercy Y.; Bennett, Robin L.; Saraiya, Devki S.; Baumeister, Lisa; Doyle, Debra Lochner; Leppig, Kathleen, . . . Raskind, Wendy H. (2005). Genetic evaluation and counseling of couples with recurrent miscarriage: Recommendations of the National Society of Genetic Counselors. *Journal of Genetic Counseling, 14*(3), 165–181. doi:10.1007/s10897-005-3241-5

Laursen, Brett; Bukowski, William M.; Nurmi, Jari-Eri; Marion, Donna; Salmela-Aro, Katariina and Kiuru, Noona. (2010). Opposites detract: Middle school peer group antipathies. *Journal of Experimental Child Psychology, 106*(4), 240–256. doi:10.1016/j.jecp.2010.03.001

Laursen, Brett and Collins, W. Andrew. (2009). Parent-child relationships during adolescence. In Richard M. Lerner and Laurence Steinberg (Eds.), *Handbook of adolescent psychology* (3rd ed., Vol. 2, pp. 3–42). Hoboken, NJ: Wiley.

Lauster, Nathanael T. (2008). Better homes and families: Housing markets and young couple stability in Sweden. *Journal of Marriage and Family, 70*(4), 891–903. doi:10.1111/j.1741-3737.2008.00534.x

Lavelli, Manuela and Fogel, Alan. (2005). Developmental changes in the relationship between the infant's attention and emotion during early face-to-face communication: The 2-month transition. *Developmental Psychology, 41*(1), 265–280. doi:10.1037/0012-1649.41.1.265

Law, Lawla L. F.; Barnett, Fiona; Yau, Matthew K. and Gray, Marion A. (2012). Measures of everyday competence in older adults with cognitive impairment: A systematic review. *Age and Ageing, 41*(1), 9–16. doi:10.1093/ageing/afr104

Layden, Tim. (2004, November 15). Get out and play! *Sports Illustrated, 101*, 80–93.

Leach, Penelope. (2009). *Child care today: Getting it right for everyone.* New York, NY: Knopf.

Leadbeater, Bonnie J. and Hoglund, Wendy L. G. (2009). The effects of peer victimization and physical aggression on changes in internalizing from first to third grade. *Child Development, 80*(3), 843–859. doi:10.1111/j.1467-8624.2009.01301.x

Leaper, Campbell. (2013). Gender development during childhood. In Philip David Zelazo (Ed.), *The Oxford handbook of developmental psychology* (Vol. 2, pp. 326–377). New York, NY: Oxford University Press.

Leather, Nicola C. (2009). Risk-taking behaviour in adolescence: A literature review. *Journal of Child Health Care, 13*(3), 295–304. doi:10.1177/1367493509337443

Leavitt, Judith Walzer. (2009). Make room for daddy: The journey from waiting room to birthing room. Chapel Hill, NC: University of North Carolina Press.

Lee, Christine M.; Geisner, Irene M.; Patrick, Megan E. and Neighbors, Clayton. (2010). The social norms of alcohol-related negative consequences. *Psychology of Addictive Behaviors, 24*(2), 342–348. doi:10.1037/a0018020

Lee, Hee Seung and Anderson, John R. (2013). Student learning: What has instruction got to do with it? *Annual Review of Psychology, 64*, 445–469. doi:10.1146/annurev-psych-113011-143833

Lee, I-Min; Ewing, Reid and Sesso, Howard D. (2009). The built environment and physical activity levels: The Harvard Alumni Health Study. *American Journal of Preventive Medicine, 37*(4), 293–298. doi:10.1016/j.amepre.2009.06.007

Lee, Jihyun and Porretta, David L. (2013). Enhancing the motor skills of children with autism spectrum disorders: A pool-based approach. *JOPERD: The Journal Of Physical Education, Recreation & Dance, 84*(1), 41–45. doi:10.1080/07303084.2013.746154

Lee, Joyce M.; Kaciroti, Niko; Appugliese, Danielle; Corwyn, Robert F.; Bradley, Robert H. and Lumeng, Julie C. (2010). Body mass index and timing of pubertal initiation in boys. *Archives of Pediatric and Adolescent Medicine, 164*(2), 139–144. doi:10.1001/archpediatrics.2009.258

Lee, Soojeong and Shouse, Roger C. (2011). The impact of prestige orientation on shadow education in South Korea. *Sociology of Education, 84*(3), 212–224. doi:10.1177/0038040711411278

Lee, Sei J.; Steinman, Michael A. and Tan, Erwin J. (2011). Volunteering, driving status, and mortality in U.S. retirees. *Journal of the American Geriatrics Society, 59*(2), 274–280. doi:10.1111/j.1532-5415.2010.03265.x

Lee, Star W.; Clemenson, Gregory D. and Gage, Fred H. (2012). New neurons in an aged brain. *Behavioural Brain Research, 227*(2), 497–507. doi:10.1016/j.bbr.2011.10.009

Leger, Damien; Beck, François; Richard, Jean-Baptiste and Godeau, Emmanuelle. (2012). Total sleep time severely drops during adolescence. *PLoS ONE, 7*(10), e45204. doi:10.1371/journal.pone.0045204

Lehmann, Martin and Hasselhorn, Marcus. (2010). The dynamics of free recall and their relation to rehearsal between 8 and 10 years of age. *Child Development, 81*(3), 1006–1020. doi:10.1111/j.1467-8624.2010.01448.x

Lehmann, Regula; Denissen, Jaap J. A.; Allemand, Mathias and Penke, Lars. (2013). Age and gender differences in motivational manifestations of the Big Five from age 16 to 60. *Developmental Psychology, 49*(2), 365–383. doi:10.1037/a0028277

Lehner, Ben (2013). Genotype to phenotype: Lessons from model organisms for human genetics. *Nature Reviews Genetics, 14*(3), 168–178. doi:10.1038/nrg3404

Lei, Joy L. (2003). (Un)necessary toughness?: Those "loud black girls" and those "quiet Asian boys". *Anthropology & Education Quarterly, 34*(2), 158–181. doi:10.1525/aeq.2003.34.2.158

Leman, Patrick J. and Björnberg, Marina. (2010). Conversation, development, and gender: A study of changes in children's concepts of punishment. *Child Development, 81*(3), 958–971. doi:10.1111/j.1467-8624.2010.01445.x

Lemieux, André. (2012). Post-formal thought in gerontagogy or beyond Piaget, *Journal of Behavioral and Brain Science, 2*, 399–406. doi:10.4236/jbbs.2012.23046

Lemish, Daphna and Kolucki, Barbara. (2013). Media and early childhood development. In Pia Rebello Britto, Patrice L. Engle and Charles M. Super (Eds.), *Handbook of early childhood development research and its impact on global policy*. New York, NY: Oxford University Press.

Lenton, Alison and Webber, Laura. (2006). Cross-sex friendships: Who has more? *Sex Roles, 54*(11–12), 809–820. doi:10.1007/s11199-006-9048-5

Leon, David A.; Saburova, Ludmila; Tomkins, Susannah; Andreev, Evgueni M.; Kiryanov, Nikolay; McKee, Martin and Shkolnikov, Vladimir M. (2007). Hazardous alcohol drinking and premature mortality in Russia: A population based case-control study. *The Lancet, 369*(9578), 2001–2009. doi:10.1016/S0140-6736(07)60941-6

Lepper, Mark R.; Greene, David and Nisbett, Richard E. (1973). Undermining children's intrinsic interest with extrinsic reward: A test of the "overjustification" hypothesis. *Journal of Personality & Social Psychology, 28*(1), 129–137. doi:10.1037/h0035519

Lerner, Claire and Dombro, Amy Laura. (2004). Finding your fit: Some temperament tips for parents. *Zero to Three, 24*(4), 42–45.

Lerner, Richard M. and Overton, F. Willis. (2010). *The handbook of life-span development*. Hoboken, NJ: Wiley.

Lerner, Richard M. and Steinberg, Laurence D. (Eds.). (2009). *Handbook of adolescent psychology* (3rd ed.). Hoboken, NJ: Wiley.

Leslie, Leigh A.; Smith, Jocelyn R.; Hrapczynski, Katie M. and Riley, Debbie. (2013). Racial socialization in transracial adoptive families: Does it help adolescents deal with discriminative stress? *Family Relations, 62*(1), 72–81. doi:10.1111/j.1741-3729.2012.00744.x

Leslie, Mitch. (2012). Gut microbes keep rare immune cells in line. *Science, 335*(6075), 1428. doi:10.1126/science.335.6075.1428

Lester, Patricia; Leskin, Gregory; Woodward, Kirsten; Saltzman, William; Nash, William; Mogil, Catherine, . . . Beardslee, William. (2011). Wartime deployment and military children: Applying prevention science to enhance family resilience. In Shelley MacDermid Wadsworth and David Riggs (Eds.), *Risk and resilience in U.S. military families* (pp. 149–174). New York, NY: Springer.

Leung, Angel Nga-Man; Wong, Stephanie Siu-fong; Wong, Iris Wai-yin and McBride-Chang, Catherine. (2010). Filial piety and psychosocial adjustment in Hong Kong Chinese early adolescents. *The Journal of Early Adolescence, 30*(5), 651–667. doi:10.1177/0272431609341046

Leventhal, Bennett L. (2013). Complementary and alternative medicine: Not many compliments but lots of alternatives. *Journal of Child and Adolescent Psychopharmacology, 23*(1), 54–56. doi:10.1089/cap.2013.2312

Levinson, Daniel J. (1978). The seasons of a man's life. New York, NY: Knopf.

Levy, Becca. (2009). Stereotype embodiment: A psychosocial approach to aging. *Current Directions in Psychological Science, 18*(6), 332–336. doi:10.1111/j.1467-8721.2009.01662.x

Levy, Becca and Langer, Ellen. (1994). Aging free from negative stereotypes: Successful memory in China among the American deaf. *Journal of Personality & Social Psychology, 66*(6), 989–997. doi:10.1037/0022-3514.66.6.989

Levy, Becca R.; Slade, Martin D.; Murphy, Terrence E. and Gill, Thomas M. (2012). Association between positive age stereotypes and recovery from disability in older persons. *JAMA, 308*(19), 1972–1973. doi:10.1001/jama.2012.14541

Lewallen, Lynne Porter. (2011). The importance of culture in childbearing. *Journal of Obstetric, Gynecologic, & Neonatal Nursing, 40*(1), 4–8. doi:10.1111/j.1552-6909.2010.01209.x

Lewin, Kurt. (1943). Psychology and the process of group living. *Journal of Social Psychology, 17*(1), 113–131. doi:10.1080/00224545.1943.9712269

Lewin-Benham, Ann. (2008). *Powerful children: Understanding how to teach and learn using the Reggio approach*. New York, NY: Teachers College Press.

Lewis, Charlotte W.; Linsenmayer, Kristi A. and Williams, Alexis. (2010). Wanting better: A qualitative study of low-income parents about their children's oral health. *Pediatric Dentistry, 32*(7), 518–524.

Lewis, David M. G.; Conroy-Beam, Daniel; Al-Shawaf, Laith; Raja, Annia; DeKay, Todd and Buss, David M. (2011). Friends with benefits: The evolved psychology of same- and opposite-sex friendships. *Evolutionary Psychology, 9*(4), 543–563.

Lewis, Kristen and Burd-Sharps, Sarah. (2010). The measure of America 2010–2011: *Mapping risks and resilience*. New York, NY: New York University Press.

Lewis, Lawrence B.; Antone, Carol and Johnson, Jacqueline S. (1999). Effects of prosodic stress and serial position on syllable omission in first words. *Developmental Psychology, 35*(1), 45–59. doi:10.1037//0012-1649.35.1.45

Lewis, Michael. (2010). The emergence of human emotions. In Michael Lewis, Jeannette M. Haviland-Jones and Lisa Feldman Barrett (Eds.), *Handbook of emotions* (3rd ed.). New York, NY: Guilford Press.

Lewis, Michael and Brooks, Jeanne. (1978). Self-knowledge and emotional development. In Michael Lewis and L. A. Rosenblum (Eds.), *Genesis of behavior* (Vol. 1, pp. 205–226). New York, NY: Plenum Press.

Lewis, Michael and Ramsay, Douglas. (2005). Infant emotional and cortisol responses to goal blockage. *Child Development, 76*(2), 518–530. doi:10.1111/j.1467-8624.2005.00860.x

Lewis, Marc D. (2013). The development of emotional regulation: Integrating normative and individual differences through developmental neuroscience. In Philip David Zelazo (Ed.), *The Oxford handbook of developmental psychology* (Vol. 2, pp. 81–97). New York, NY: Oxford University Press.

Lewis, Sam and Ariyachandra, Thilini. (2011). Seniors and social networking. *Journal of Information Systems Applied Research, 4*(2), 4–18.

Lewkowicz, David J. (2010). Infant perception of audio-visual speech synchrony. *Developmental Psychology, 46*(1), 66–77. doi:10.1037/a0015579

Li, Tianyuan and Chan, Darius K. S. (2012). How anxious and avoidant attachment affect romantic relationship quality differently: A meta-analytic review. *European Journal of Social Psychology, 42*(4), 406–419. doi:10.1002/ejsp.1842

Li, Yibing and Lerner, Richard M. (2011). Trajectories of school engagement during adolescence: Implications for grades, depression, delinquency, and substance use. *Developmental Psychology, 47*(1), 233–247. doi:10.1037/a0021307

Libertus, Klaus and Needham, Amy. (2010). Teach to reach: The effects of active vs. passive reaching experiences on action and perception. *Vision Research, 50*(24), 2750–2757. doi:10.1016/j.visres.2010.09.001

Libertus, Melissa E.; Feigenson, Lisa and Halberda, Justin. (2013). Is approximate number precision a stable predictor of math ability? *Learning and Individual Differences, 25*, 126–133. doi:10.1016/j.lindif.2013.02.001

Lillard, Angeline and Else-Quest, Nicole. (2006). Evaluating Montessori education. *Science, 313*(5795), 1893–1894. doi:10.1126/science.1132362

Lillard, Angeline Stoll. (2005). *Montessori: The science behind the genius*. New York, NY: Oxford University Press.

Lillard, Angeline S. (2013). Playful learning and Montessori education. *American Journal of Play,* 5(2), 157–186.

Lim, Chaeyoon and Putnam, Robert D. (2010). Religion, social networks, and life satisfaction. *American Sociological Review,* 75(6), 914–933. doi: 10.1177/0003122410386686

Limber, Susan P. (2011). Development, evaluation, and future directions of the Olweus Bullying Prevention Program. *Journal of School Violence,* 10(1), 71–87. doi: 10.1080/15388220.2010.519375

Lin, Frank R.; Yaffe, Kristine; Xia, Jin; Xue, Qian-Li; Harris, Tamara B.; Purchase-Helzner, Elizabeth, . . . Simonsick, Eleanor M. (2013). Hearing loss and cognitive decline in older adults. *JAMA Internal Medicine,* 173(4), 293–299. doi: 10.1001/jamainternmed.2013.1868

Lin, I-Fen. (2008a). Consequences of parental divorce for adult children's support of their frail parents. *Journal of Marriage and Family,* 70(1), 113–128. doi: 10.1111/j.1741-3737.2007.00465.x

Lin, Jue; Epel, Elissa and Blackburn, Elizabeth. (2012). Telomeres and lifestyle factors: Roles in cellular aging. *Mutation Research/ Fundamental and Molecular Mechanisms of Mutagenesis,* 730(1–2), 85–89. doi: 10.1016/j.mrfmmm.2011.08.003

Lincove, Jane A. and Painter, Gary. (2006). Does the age that children start kindergarten matter? *Evidence of long-term educational and social outcomes. Educational Evaluation and Policy Analysis,* 28(2), 153–179 doi:10.3102/01623737028002153

Lindau, Stacy Tessler and Gavrilova, Natalia. (2010). Sex, health, and years of sexually active life gained due to good health: Evidence from two US population based cross sectional surveys of ageing. *BMJ,* 340(c810). doi:10.1136/bmj.c810

Linden, Ashley N. and Lau-Barraco, Cathy. (2013). Depressive symptomology and alcohol use among college students: the role of perceived drinking norms. *Mental Health and Substance Use,* 6(4), 303–314. doi:10.1080/17523281.2012.739193

Lipton, Jennifer S. and Spelke, Elizabeth S. (2003). Origins of number sense: Large-number discrimination in human infants. *Psychological Science,* 14(5), 396–401. doi:10.1111/1467-9280.01453

Liszkowski, Ulf; Schäfer, Marie; Carpenter, Malinda and Tomasello, Michael. (2009). Prelinguistic infants, but not chimpanzees, communicate about absent entities. *Psychological Science,* 20(5), 654–660. doi:10.1111/j.1467-9280.2009.02346.x

Liszkowski, Ulf and Tomasello, Michael. (2011). Individual differences in social, cognitive, and morphological aspects of infant pointing. *Cognitive Development,* 26(1), 16–29. doi:10.1016/j.cogdev.2010.10.001

Litwin, Howard and Stoeckel, Kimberly J. (2013). Social networks and subjective wellbeing among older Europeans: Does age make a difference? *Ageing and Society,* 33(7), 1263–1281. doi:10.1017/S0144686X12000645

Liu, David; Sabbagh, Mark A.; Gehring, William J. and Wellman, Henry M. (2009). Neural correlates of children's theory of mind development. *Child Development,* 80(2), 318–326. doi:10.1111/j.1467-8624.2009.01262.x

Liu, David; Wellman, Henry M.; Tardif, Twila and Sabbagh, Mark A. (2008). Theory of mind development in Chinese children: A meta-analysis of false-belief understanding across cultures and languages. *Developmental Psychology,* 44(2), 523–531. doi:10.1037/0012-1649.44.2.523

Liu, Hui; Wang, Qiu; Keesler, Venessa and Schneider, Barbara. (2011). Non-standard work schedules, work-family conflict and parental well-being: A comparison of married and cohabiting unions. *Social Science Research,* 40(2), 473–484. doi:10.1016/j.ssresearch.2010.10.008

Livas-Dlott, Alejandra; Fuller, Bruce; Stein, Gabriela L.; Bridges, Margaret; Mangual Figueroa, Ariana and Mireles, Laurie. (2010). Commands, competence, and *cariño:* Maternal socialization practices in Mexican American families. *Developmental Psychology,* 46(3), 566–578. doi:10.1037/a0018016

Lloyd-Fox, Sarah; Blasi, Anna; Volein, Agnes; Everdell, Nick; Elwell, Claire E. and Johnson, Mark H. (2009). Social perception in infancy: A near infrared spectroscopy study. *Child Development,* 80(4), 986–999. doi:10.1111/j.1467-8624.2009.01312.x

LoBue, Vanessa. (2013). What are we so afraid of? How early attention shapes our most common fears. *Child Development Perspectives,* 7(1), 38–42. doi:10.1111/cdep.12012

LoBue, Vanessa and DeLoache, Judy S. (2011). Pretty in pink: The early development of gender-stereotyped colour preferences. *British Journal of Developmental Psychology,* 29(3), 656–667. doi:10.1111/j.2044-835X.2011.02027.x

Lock, Margaret. (2013). The lure of the epigenome. *The Lancet,* 381(9881), 1896–1897. doi:10.1016/S0140-6736(13)61149-6

Löckenhoff, Corinna E.; De Fruyt, Filip; Terracciano, Antonio; McCrae, Robert R.; De Bolle, Marleen; Costa Jr, Paul T., . . . Yik, Michelle. (2009). Perceptions of aging across 26 cultures and their culture-level associates. *Psychology and Aging,* 24(4), 941–954. doi:10.1037/a0016901

Löckenhoff, Corinna E.; O'Donoghue, Ted and Dunning, David. (2011). Age differences in temporal discounting: The role of dispositional affect and anticipated emotions. *Psychology and Aging,* 26(2), 274–284. doi:10.1037/a0023280

Lodge, Amy C. and Umberson, Debra. (2012). All shook up: Sexuality of mid- to later life married couples. *Journal of Marriage & Family,* 74(3), 428–443. doi:10.1111/j.1741-3737.2012.00969.x

Loeber, Rolf and Burke, Jeffrey D. (2011). Developmental pathways in juvenile externalizing and internalizing problems. *Journal of Research on Adolescence,* 21(1), 34–46. doi:10.1111/j.1532-7795.2010.00713.x

Loeber, Rolf; Capaldi, Deborah M. and Costello, Elizabeth. (2013). Gender and the development of aggression, disruptive behavior, and delinquency from childhood to early adulthood. In Patrick H. Tolan and Bennett L. Leventhal (Eds.), *Disruptive behavior disorders* (pp. 137–160). New York, NY: Springer. doi:10.1007/978-1-4614-7557-6_6

Longmore, Monica; Eng, Abbey; Giordano, Peggy and Manning, Wendy. (2009). Parenting and adolescents' sexual initiation. *Journal of Marriage and Family,* 71(4), 969–982. doi:10.1111/j.1741-3737.2009.00647.x

Longo, Lawrence D. (2013). The rise of fetal and neonatal physiology: Basic science to clinical care. New York, NY: Springer.

Lopez Turley, Ruth N. and Desmond, Matthew. (2011). Contributions to college costs by married, divorced, and remarried parents. *Journal of Family Issues,* 32(6), 767–790. doi:10.1177/0192513x10388013

Lorber, Michael F. and Egeland, Byron. (2011). Parenting and infant difficulty: Testing a mutual exacerbation hypothesis to predict early onset conduct problems. *Child Development,* 82(6), 2006–2020. doi:10.1111/j.1467-8624.2011.01652.x

Lord, Catherine and Bishop, Somer L. (2010). Autism spectrum disorders: Diagnosis, prevalence, and services for children and families. *Social Policy Report,* 24(2), 1–26.

Lövdén, Martin; Xu, Weili and Wang, Hui-Xin. (2013). Lifestyle change and the prevention of cognitive decline and dementia: what is the evidence? *Current Opinion in Psychiatry,* 26(3), 239–243. doi:10.1097/YCO.0b013e32835f4135

Lovecky, Deirdre V. (2009). Moral sensitivity in young gifted children. In Tracy Cross and Don Ambrose (Eds.), *Morality, ethics, and gifted minds* (pp. 161–176). New York, NY: Springer. doi:10.1007/978-0-387-89368-6_13

Lovell, Brian and Wetherell, Mark A. (2011). The cost of caregiving: Endocrine and immune implications in elderly and non elderly caregivers. *Neuroscience & Biobehavioral Reviews,* 35(6), 1342–1352. doi:10.1016/j.neubiorev.2011.02.007

Lowell, Darcy I.; Carter, Alice S.; Godoy, Leandra; Paulicin, Belinda and Briggs-Gowan, Margaret J. (2011). A randomized controlled trial of Child FIRST: A comprehensive home-based intervention translating research into early childhood practice. *Child Development,* 82(1), 193–208. doi:10.1111/j.1467-8624.2010.01550.x

Luengo-Prado, María José and Sevilla, Almudena. (2012). Time to cook: Expenditure at retirement in Spain. *The Economic Journal,* 123(569), 764–789. doi:10.1111/j.1468-0297.2012.02546.x

Luna, Beatriz; Paulsen, David J.; Padmanabhan, Aarthi and Geier, Charles. (2013). The teenage brain: Cognitive control and motivation. *Current Directions in Psychological Science,* 22(2), 94–100. doi:10.1177/0963721413478416

Lundquist, Gunilla; Rasmussen, Birgit H. and Axelsson, Bertil. (2011). Information of imminent death or not: Does it make a difference? *Journal of Clinical Oncology,* 29(29), 3927–3931. doi:10.1200/JCO.2011.34.6247

Lustig, Cindy; Shah, Priti; Seidler, Rachael and Reuter-Lorenz, Patricia A. (2009). Aging, training, and the brain: A review and future directions. *Neuropsychology Review, 19*(4), 504–522. doi:10.1007/s11065-009-9119-9

Luszczynska, Aleksandra; Schwarzer, Ralf; Lippke, Sonia and Mazurkiewicz, Magda. (2011). Self-efficacy as a moderator of the planning–behaviour relationship in interventions designed to promote physical activity. *Psychology & Health, 26*(2), 151–166. doi:10.1080/08870446.2011.531571

Luthar, Suniya S.; Cicchetti, Dante and Becker, Bronwyn. (2000). The construct of resilience: A critical evaluation and guidelines for future work. *Child Development, 71*(3), 543–562. doi:10.1111/1467-8624.00164

Luthar, Suniya S.; D'Avanzo, Karen and Hites, Sarah. (2003). Maternal drug abuse versus other psychological disturbances: Risks and resilience among children. In Suniya S. Luthar (Ed.), Resilience and vulnerability: *Adaptation in the context of childhood adversities* (pp. 104–129). New York, NY: Cambridge University Press.

Lutz, Wolfgang and K. C., Samir. (2011). Global human capital: Integrating education and population. *Science, 333*(6042), 587–592. doi:10.1126/science.1206964

Luxmoore, Nick. (2012). Young people, death, and the unfairness of everything. London, UK: Jessica Kingsley.

Lynch, Scott M. and Brown, J. Scott. (2011). Stratification and inequality over the life course. In Robert H. Binstock and Linda K. George (Eds.), Handbook of aging and the social sciences (7th ed., pp. 105–117). San Diego, CA: Academic Press. doi:10.1016/B978-0-12-380880-6.00008-3

Lynn, Richard and Mikk, Jaan. (2007). National differences in intelligence and educational attainment. *Intelligence, 35*(2), 115–121. doi:10.1016/j.intell.2006.06.001

Lynne, Sarah D.; Graber, Julia A.; Nichols, Tracy R.; Brooks-Gunn, Jeanne and Botvin, Gilbert J. (2007). Links between pubertal timing, peer influences, and externalizing behaviors among urban students followed through middle school. *Journal of Adolescent Health, 40*(2), 181.e187–181.e113. doi:10.1016/j.jadohealth.2006.09.008

Lynskey, Michael T.; Agrawal, Arpana; Henders, Anjali; Nelson, Elliot C.; Madden, Pamela A. F. and Martin, Nicholas G. (2012). An Australian twin study of cannabis and other illicit drug use and misuse, and other psychopathology. *Twin Research and Human Genetics, 15*(5), 631–641. doi:10.1017/thg.2012.41

Lyonette, Clare; Kaufman, Gayle and Crompton, Rosemary. (2011). 'We both need to work: Maternal employment, childcare and health care in Britain and the USA. *Work Employment & Society, 25*(1), 34–50. doi:10.1177/0950017010389243

Lyons-Ruth, Karlen; Bronfman, Elisa and Parsons, Elizabeth. (1999). Maternal frightened, frightening, or atypical behavior and disorganized infant attachment patterns. *Monographs of the Society for Research in Child Development, 64*(3), 67–96. doi:10.1111/1540-5834.00034

Ma, Lang; Phelps, Erin; Lerner, Jacqueline V. and Lerner, Richard M. (2009). Academic competence for adolescents who bully and who are bullied: Findings from the 4-H Study of Positive Youth Development. *The Journal of Early Adolescence, 29*(6), 862–897. doi:10.1177/0272431609332667

Mac Dougall, K.; Beyene, Y. and Nachtigall, R.D. (2013). Age shock: misperceptions of the impact of age on fertility before and after IVF in women who conceived after age 40. *Human Reproduction, 28*(2), 350–356. doi:10.1093/humrep/des409

MacCann, Carolyn; Fogarty, Gerard J. and Roberts, Richard D. (2012). Strategies for success in education: Time management is more important for part-time than full-time community college students. *Learning and Individual Differences, 22*(5), 618–623. doi:10.1016/j.lindif.2011.09.015

Macgregor, Stuart; Lind, Penelope A.; Bucholz, Kathleen K.; Hansell, Narelle K.; Madden, Pamela A. F.; Richter, Melinda M., . . . Whitfield, John B. (2009). Associations of ADH and ALDH2 gene variation with self report alcohol reactions, consumption and dependence: An integrated analysis. *Human Molecular Genetics, 18*(3), 580–593. doi:10.1093/hmg/ddn372

MacMillan, Harriet L.; Wathen, C. Nadine; Barlow, Jane; Fergusson, David M.; Leventhal, John M. and Taussig, Heather N. (2009). Interventions to prevent child maltreatment and associated impairment. *The Lancet, 373*(9659), 250–266. doi:10.1016/s0140-6736(08)61708-0

Macmillan, Ross and Copher, Ronda. (2005). Families in the life course: Interdependency of roles, role configurations, and pathways. *Journal of Marriage and Family, 67*(4), 858–879. doi:10.1111/j.1741-3737.2005.00180.x

MacPhee, David. (1981). Knowledge of Infant Development Inventory (KIDI). Unpublished manuscript. Educational Testing Service. Ewing, NJ.

Madden, Mary and Lenhart, Amanda. (2009). *Teens and distracted driving: Texting, talking and other uses of the cell phone behind the wheel.* Washington, DC: Pew Internet & American Life Project.

Madden, Mary; Lenhart, Amanda; Duggan, Maeve; Cortesi, Sandra and Gasser, Urs. (2013). Teens and Technology 2013. Pew Research Center: Pew Internet & American Life Project.

Magnuson, Katherine and Berger, Lawrence M. (2009). Family structure states and transitions: Associations with children's well-being during middle childhood. *Journal of Marriage and Family, 71*(3), 575–591. doi:10.1111/j.1741-3737.2009.00620.x

Maguire, Kathleen. (2010). Sourcebook of criminal justice statistics. Washington, DC: U.S. Department of Justice, 2010, November 18.

Mah, Timothy and Halperin, Daniel. (2010). Concurrent sexual partnerships and the HIV epidemics in Africa: Evidence to move forward. *AIDS and Behavior, 14*(1), 11–16. doi:10.1007/s10461-008-9433-x

Majdandažić, Mirjana; Möller, Eline L.; de Vente, Wieke; Bögels, Susan M. and van den Boom, Dymphna C. (2013). Fathers' challenging parenting behavior prevents social anxiety development in their 4-year-old children: A longitudinal observational study. *Journal of Abnormal Child Psychology, 42*(2), 301–310. doi:10.1007/s10802-013-9774-4

Majercsik, Eszter. (2005). Hierarchy of needs of geriatric patients. *Gerontology, 51,* 170–173. doi:10.1159/000083989

Makimoto, Kiyoko. (1998). Drinking patterns and drinking problems among Asian-Americans and Pacific Islanders. *Alcohol Health and Research World, 22*(4), 270–275.

Malchiodi, Cathy A. (2012). Creativity and aging: An art therapy perspective. In Cathy A. Malchiodi (Ed.), Handbook of art therapy (pp. 275–287). New York, NY: Guilford Press.

Malina, Robert M.; Bouchard, Claude and Bar-Or, Oded. (2004). Growth, maturation, and physical activity (2nd ed.). Champaign, IL: Human Kinetics.

Malloy, Michael H. (2009). Impact of cesarean section on intermediate and late preterm births: United States, 2000–2003. *Birth, 36*(1), 26–33. doi:10.1111/j.1523-536X.2008.00292.x

Mancini, Anthony D. and Bonanno, George A. (2006). Marital closeness, functional disability, and adjustment in late life. *Psychology and Aging, 21*(3), 600–610. doi:10.1037/0882-7974.21.3.600

Mancini, Anthony D.; Prati, Gabriele and Bonanno, George A. (2011). Do shattered worldviews lead to complicated grief? Prospective and longitudinal analyses. *Journal of Social and Clinical Psychology, 30*(2), 184–215. doi:10.1521/jscp.2011.30.2.184

Mandler, Jean Matter. (2004). *The foundations of mind: Origins of conceptual thought.* New York, NY: Oxford University Press.

Mandler, Jean M. and DeLoache, Judy. (2012). The beginnings of conceptual development. In Sabina M. Pauen (Ed.), *Early childhood development and later outcome.* New York, NY: Cambridge University Press.

Mangels, Jennifer A.; Good, Catherine; Whiteman, Ronald C.; Maniscalco, Brian and Dweck, Carol S. (2012). Emotion blocks the path to learning under stereotype threat. *Social Cognitive Affective Neuroscience, 7*(2), 230–241. doi:10.1093/scan/nsq100

Mann, Joshua R.; McDermott, Suzanne; Bao, Haikun and Bersabe, Adrian. (2009). Maternal genitourinary infection and risk of cerebral palsy. *Developmental Medicine & Child Neurology, 51*(4), 282–288. doi:10.1111/j.1469-8749.2008.03226.x

Mann, Traci and Ward, Andrew. (2007). Attention, self-control, and health behaviors. *Current Directions in Psychological Science, 16*(5), 280–283. doi:10.1111/j.1467-8721.2007.00520.x

Manuck, Stephen B. and McCaffery, Jeanne M. (2014). Gene-environment interaction.

Annual Review of Psychology, 65, 41–70. doi:10.1146/annurev-psych-010213-115100

Manzi, Claudia; Vignoles, Vivian L.; Regalia, Camillo and Scabini, Eugenia. (2006). Cohesion and enmeshment revisited: Differentiation, identity, and well-being in two European cultures. *Journal of Marriage and Family, 68*(3), 673–689. doi: 10.1111/j.1741-3737.2006.00282.x

Mar, Raymond A. (2011). The neural bases of social cognition and story comprehension. *Annual Review of Psychology, 62,* 103–134. doi:10.1146/annurev-psych-120709-145406

Mar, Raymond A.; Tackett, Jennifer L. and Moore, Chris. (2010). Exposure to media and theory-of-mind development in preschoolers. *Cognitive Development, 25*(1), 69–78. doi: 10.1016/j.cogdev.2009.11.002

Marazita, John M. and Merriman, William E. (2010). Verifying one's knowledge of a name without retrieving it: A u-shaped relation to vocabulary size in early childhood. *Language Learning and Development, 7*(1), 40–54. doi:10.1080/15475441.2010.496099

March, John S.; Franklin, Martin E.; Leonard, Henrietta L. and Foa, Edna B. (2004). Obsessive-compulsive disorder. In Tracy L. Morris and John S. March (Eds.), *Anxiety disorders in children and adolescents* (2nd ed., pp. 212–240). New York, NY: Guilford Press.

Marchand, Alain; Drapeau, Aline and Beaulieu-Prévost, Dominic. (2012). Psychological distress in Canada: The role of employment and reasons for non-employment. *International Journal of Social Psychiatry, 58*(6), 596–604. doi:10.1177/0020764011418404

Marcia, James E. (1966). Development and validation of ego-identity status. *Journal of Personality & Social Psychology, 3*(5), 551–558. doi:10.1037/h0023281

Marcia, James E.; Waterman, Alan S.; Matteson, David R.; Archer, Sally L. and Orlofsky, Jacob L. (1993). *Ego identity: A handbook for psychosocial research.* New York, NY: Springer-Verlag.

Marcovitch, Stuart; Boseovski, Janet J.; Knapp, Robin J. and Kane, Michael J. (2010). Goal neglect and working memory capacity in 4- to 6-year-old children. *Child Development, 81*(6), 1687–1695. doi:10.1111/j.1467-8624.2010.01503.x

Marcus, Gary F. and Rabagliati, Hugh. (2009). Language acquisition, domain specificity, and descent with modification. In John Colombo, Peggy McCardle and Lisa Freund (Eds.), *Infant pathways to language: Methods, models, and research disorders* (pp. 267–285). New York, NY: Psychology Press.

Margolis, Rachel and Myrskylä, Mikko. (2011). A global perspective on happiness and fertility. *Population and Development Review, 37*(1), 29–56. doi:10.1111/j.1728-4457.2011.00389.x

Margrett, Jennifer A.; Daugherty, Kate; Martin, Peter; MacDonald, Maurice; Davey, Adam; Woodard, John L., . . . Poon, Leonard W.

(2011). Affect and loneliness among centenarians and the oldest old: The role of individual and social resources. *Aging & Mental Health, 15*(3), 385–396. doi:10.1080/13607863.2010.519327

Marin, Marie-France; Lord, Catherine; Andrews, Julie; Juster, Robert-Paul; Sindi, Shireen; Arsenault-Lapierre, Geneviève, . . . Lupien, Sonia J. (2011). Chronic stress, cognitive functioning and mental health. *Neurobiology of Learning and Memory, 96*(4), 583–595. doi:10.1016/j.nlm.2011.02.016

Markowitsch, Hans J. and Staniloiu, Angelica. (2012). Amnesic disorders. *The Lancet, 380*(9851), 1429–1440. doi:10.1016/S0140-6736(11)61304-4

Marschark, Marc and Spencer, Patricia Elizabeth. (2003). What we know, what we don't know, and what we should know. In Marc Marschark and Patricia Elizabeth Spencer (Eds.), *Oxford handbook of deaf studies, language, and education* (pp. 491–494). New York, NY: Oxford University Press.

Marshall, Eliot. (2011). Waiting for the revolution. *Science, 331*(6017), 526–529. doi:10.1126/science.331.6017.526

Marshall, Peter J. (2009). Relating psychology and neuroscience: Taking up the challenges. *Perspectives on Psychological Science, 4*(2), 113–125. doi:10.1111/j.1745-6924.2009.01111.x

Marsiske, Michael and Margrett, Jennifer A. (2006). Everyday problem solving and decision making. In James E. Birren and K. Warren Schaie (Eds.), *Handbook of the psychology of aging* (6th ed., pp. 315–342). San Diego, CA: Elsevier Academic Press. doi:10.1016/B978-012101264-9/50017-3

Martin, Carol; Fabes, Richard; Hanish, Laura; Leonard, Stacie and Dinella, Lisa. (2011). Experienced and expected similarity to same-gender peers: Moving toward a comprehensive model of gender segregation. *Sex Roles, 65*(5–6), 421–434. doi:10.1007/s11199-011-0029-y

Martin, Carol Lynn and Ruble, Diane N. (2010). Patterns of gender development. *Annual Review of Psychology, 61,* 353–381. doi:10.1146/annurev.psych.093008.100511

Martin, Jack and Sokol, Bryan. (2011). Generalized others and imaginary audiences: A neo-Meadian approach to adolescent egocentrism. *New Ideas in Psychology, 29*(3), 364–375. doi:10.1016/j.newideapsych.2010.03.006

Martin, Joyce A.; Hamilton, Brady E.; Sutton, Paul D.; Ventura, Stephanie J.; Mathews, T. J. and Osterman, Michelle J. K. (2010). Births: Final data for 2008. Hyattsville, MD: Centers for Disease Control and Prevention National Center for Health Statistics.(PHS) 2011–1120.

Martin, Leslie R.; Haskard-Zolnierek, Kelly B. and DiMatteo, M. Robin. (2010). Health behavior change and treatment adherence: Evidence-based guidelines for improving healthcare. New York, NY: Oxford University Press.

Martin-Uzzi, Michele and Duval-Tsioles, Denise. (2013). The experience of remarried couples in blended families. *Journal of Divorce &*

Remarriage, 54(1), 43–57. doi:10.1080/10502556.2012.743828

Martorell, Reynaldo; Melgar, Paul; Maluccio, John A.; Stein, Aryeh D. and Rivera, Juan A. (2010). The nutrition intervention improved adult human capital and economic productivity. *The Journal of Nutrition, 140*(2), 411–414. doi:10.3945/jn.109.114504

Marvasti, Amir B. and McKinney, Karyn D. (2011). Does diversity mean assimilation? *Critical Sociology, 37*(5), 631–650. doi:10.1177/0896920510380071

Masche, J. Gowert. (2010). Explanation of normative declines in parents' knowledge about their adolescent children. *Journal of Adolescence, 33*(2), 271–284. doi:10.1016/j.adolescence.2009.08.002

Mascolo, Michael F.; Fischer, Kurt W. and Li, Jin. (2003). Dynamic development of component systems of emotions: Pride, shame, and guilt in China and the United States. In Richard J. Davidson, Klaus R. Scherer and H. Hill Goldsmith (Eds.), *Handbook of affective sciences* (pp. 375–408). New York, NY: Oxford University Press.

Mashburn, Andrew J.; Justice, Laura M.; Downer, Jason T. and Pianta, Robert C. (2009). Peer effects on children's language achievement during pre-kindergarten. *Child Development, 80*(3), 686–702. doi: 10.1111/j.1467-8624.2009.01291.x

Mashour, George A. and Avidan, Michael (Eds.). (2013). *Neurologic outcomes of surgery and anesthesia.* New York, NY: Oxford University Press.

Maslow, Abraham H. (1954). *Motivation and personality.* New York, NY: Harper.

Maslow, Abraham H. (1970). *Motivation and personality* (2nd ed.). New York, NY: Harper & Row.

Maslow, Abraham H. (1971). *The farther reaches of human nature.* New York, NY: Viking Press.

Maslow, Abraham H. (1999). *Toward a psychology of being* (3rd ed.). New York, NY: Wiley.

Maslowsky, Julie; Keating, Daniel P.; Monk, Christopher S. and Schulenberg, John. (2011). Planned versus unplanned risks: Neurocognitive predictors of subtypes of adolescents' risk behavior. *International Journal of Behavioral Development, 35*(2), 152–160. doi:10.1177/0165025410378069

Masoro, Edward J. (2006). Are age-associated diseases an integral part of aging? In Edward J. Masoro and Steven N. Austad (Eds.), *Handbook of the biology of aging* (6th ed., pp. 43–62). Amsterdam, The Netherlands: Elsevier Academic Press.

Masoro, Edward J. and Austad, Steven N. (2011). Preface. In Edward J. Masoro and Steven N. Austad (Eds.), *Handbook of the biology of aging* (7th ed., pp. xiii-xiv). San Diego, CA: Academic Press.

Masten, Ann S. (2013). Risk and resilience in development. In Philip David Zelazo (Ed.), *The Oxford handbook of developmental psychology* (Vol. 2, pp. 579–607). New York, NY: Oxford University Press.

Masten, Ann S. and Wright, Margaret O'Dougherty. (2010). Resilience over the lifespan: Developmental perspectives on resistance, recovery, and transformation. In John W. Reich, Alex J. Zautra and John Stuart Hall (Eds.), *Handbook of adult resilience* (pp. 213–237). New York, NY: Guilford Press.

Masten, Carrie L.; Guyer, Amanda E.; Hodgdon, Hilary B.; McClure, Erin B.; Charney, Dennis S.; Ernst, Monique, . . . Monk, Christopher S. (2008). Recognition of facial emotions among maltreated children with high rates of post-traumatic stress disorder. *Child Abuse & Neglect, 32*(1), 139–153. doi:10.1016/j.chiabu.2007.09.006

Mateus-Pinheiro, A.; Patrício, P.; Bessa, J. M.; Sousa, N. and Pinto, L. (2013). Cell genesis and dendritic plasticity: A neuroplastic pas de deux in the onset and remission from depression. *Molecular Psychiatry, 18*(7), 748–750. doi:10.1038/mp.2013.56

Mathison, David J. and Agrawal, Dewesh. (2010). An update on the epidemiology of pediatric fractures. *Pediatric Emergency Care, 26*(8), 594–603. doi:10.1097/PEC.0b013e3181eb838d

Matsumoto, David. (2004). Reflections on culture and competence. In Robert J. Sternberg and Elena L. Grigorenko (Eds.), Culture and competence: *Contexts of life success* (pp. 273–282). Washington, DC: American Psychological Association.

Matsumoto, David; Hwang, Hyi Sung and Yamada, Hiroshi. (2012). Cultural differences in the relative contributions of face and context to judgments of emotion. *Journal of Cross-Cultural Psychology, 43*(2), 198–218. doi:10.1177/0022022110387426

Matsumoto, Yasuyo; Yamabe, Shingo; Sugishima, Toru and Geronazzo, Dan. (2011). Perception of oral contraceptives among women of reproductive age in Japan: A comparison with the USA and France. *Journal of Obstetrics and Gynaecology Research, 37*(7), 887–892. doi:10.1111/j.1447-0756.2010.01461.x

Matthews, Fiona E.; Arthur, Antony; Barnes, Linda E.; Bond, John; Jagger, Carol; Robinson, Louise and Brayne, Carol. (2013). A two-decade comparison of prevalence of dementia in individuals aged 65 years and older from three geographical areas of England: Results of the Cognitive Function and Ageing Study I and II. *The Lancet, 382*(9902), 1405–1412. doi:10.1016/S0140-6736(13)61570-6

Mattison, Julie A.; Roth, George S.; Beasley, T. Mark; Tilmont, Edward M.; Handy, April M.; Herbert, Richard L., . . . de Cabo, Rafael. (2012). Impact of caloric restriction on health and survival in rhesus monkeys from the NIA study. *Nature, 489,* 318–321. doi:10.1038/nature11432

Maughan, Barbara; Collishaw, Stephan and Stringaris, Argyris. (2013). Depression in childhood and adolescence. *Journal of the Canadian Academy of Child & Adolescent Psychiatry, 22*(1), 35–40.

Maxfield, Molly; Pyszczynski, Tom; Kluck, Benjamin; Cox, Cathy R.; Greenberg, Jeff; Solomon, Sheldon and Weise, David. (2007). Age-related differences in responses to thoughts of one's own death: Mortality salience and judgments of moral transgressions. *Psychology and Aging, 22*(2), 341–353. doi:10.1037/0882-7974.22.2.341

Maxwell, Lesli A. (2012). Achievement gaps tied to income found widening. *Education Week, 31*(23), 1, 22–23.

May, Vanessa; Mason, Jennifer and Clarke, Lynda. (2012). Being there, yet not interfering: The paradoxes of grandparenting. In Sara Arber and Virpi Timonen (Eds.), *Contemporary grandparenting: Changing family relationships in global contexts* (pp. 139–158). Chicago, IL: Policy Press.

Mayes, Rick; Bagwell, Catherine and Erkulwater, Jennifer L. (2009). *Medicating children: ADHD and pediatric mental health.* Cambridge, MA: Harvard University Press.

Mazzocco, Michèle M. M. and Ross, Judith L. (Eds.). (2007). *Neurogenetic developmental disorders: Variation of manifestation in childhood.* Cambridge, MA: The MIT Press.

Mazzonnaa, Fabrizio and Peracchi, Franco. (2012). Ageing, cognitive abilities and retirement. *European Economic Review, 56*(4), 691–710. doi:10.1016/j.euroecorev.2012.03.004

McAdams, Dan P. (2006). The redemptive self: Generativity and the stories Americans live by. *Research in Human Development, 3*(2–3), 81–100. doi:10.1080/15427609.2006.9683363

McAdams, Dan P. (2013). The psychological self as actor, agent, and author. *Perspectives on Psychological Science, 8*(3), 272–295. doi:10.1177/1745691612464657

McAdams, Dan P. and Olson, Bradley D. (2010). Personality development: Continuity and change over the life course. *Annual Review of Psychology, 61,* 517–542. doi:10.1146/annurev.psych.093008.100507

McAdams, Dan P. and Pals, Jennifer L. (2006). A new big five: Fundamental principles for an integrative science of personality. *American Psychologist, 61*(3), 204–217. doi: 10.1037/0003-066X.61.3.204

McCabe, Janice. (2011). Doing multiculturalism: An interactionist analysis of the practices of a multicultural sorority. *Journal of Contemporary Ethnography, 40*(5), 521–549. doi:10.1177/0891241611403588

McCall, Robert B. (2011). Research, practice, and policy perspectives on issues of children without permanent parental care. In Robert B. McCall and Harold D. Grotevant (Eds.), *Children without permanent parents: Research, practice and policy.* Boston, MA: Wiley-Blackwell.

McCall, Robert B.; Groark, Christina J. and Fish, Larry. (2010). A caregiver–child socioemotional and relationship rating scale. *Infant Mental Health Journal, 31*(2), 201–219. doi: 10.1002/imhj.20252

McCarrey, Anna C.; Henry, Julie D.; von Hippel, William; Weidemann, Gabrielle; Sachdev, Perminder S.; Wohl, Michael J. A. and Williams, Mark. (2012). Age differences in neural activity during slot machine gambling: An fMRI study. *PLoS ONE, 7*(11), e49787. doi:10.1371/journal.pone.0049787

McCarter, Roger J. M. (2006). Differential aging among skeletal muscles. In Edward J. Masoro and Steven N. Austad (Eds.), *Handbook of the biology of aging* (6th ed., pp. 470–497). Amsterdam, The Netherlands: Elsevier Academic Press.

McCarthy-Keith, Desireé M.; Schisterman, Enrique F.; Robinson, Randal D.; O'Leary, Kathleen; Lucidi, Richard S. and Armstrong, Alicia Y. (2010). Will decreasing assisted reproduction technology costs improve utilization and outcomes among minority women? *Fertility and Sterility, 94*(7), 2587–2589. doi:10.1016/j.fertnstert.2010.02.021

McCartney, Kathleen; Burchinal, Margaret; Clarke-Stewart, Alison; Bub, Kristen L.; Owen, Margaret T. and Belsky, Jay. (2010). Testing a series of causal propositions relating time in child care to children's externalizing behavior. *Developmental Psychology, 46*(1), 1–17. doi:10.1037/a0017886

McCarty, Cheryl; Prawitz, Aimee D.; Derscheid, Linda E. and Montgomery, Bette. (2011). Perceived safety and teen risk taking in online chat sites. *Cyberpsychology, Behavior, and Social Networking, 14*(3), 169–174. doi:10.1089/cyber.2010.0050

McClain, Lauren Rinelli. (2011). Better parents, more stable partners: Union transitions among cohabiting parents. *Journal of Marriage and Family, 73*(5), 889–901. doi: 10.1111/j.1741-3737.2011.00859.x

McConkie-Rosell, Allyn and O'Daniel, Julianne. (2007). Beyond the diagnosis: The process of genetic counseling. In Michèle M. M. Mazzocco and Judith L. Ross (Eds.), *Neurogenetic developmental disorders: Variation of manifestation in childhood* (pp. 367–389). Cambridge, MA: The MIT Press.

McCormick, Cheryl M.; Mathews, Iva Z.; Thomas, Catherine and Waters, Patti. (2010). Investigations of HPA function and the enduring consequences of stressors in adolescence in animal models. *Brain and Cognition, 72*(1), 73–85. doi:10.1016/j.bandc.2009.06.003

McCowan, Lesley M. E.; Dekker, Gustaaf A.; Chan, Eliza; Stewart, Alistair; Chappell, Lucy C.; Hunter, Misty, . . . North, Robyn A. (2009). Spontaneous preterm birth and small for gestational age infants in women who stop smoking early in pregnancy: Prospective cohort study. *BMJ, 338,* b1081. doi:10.1136/bmj.b1081

McCrae, Robert R. and Terracciano, Antonio. (2006). National character and personality. *Current Directions in Psychological Science, 15*(4), 156–161. doi:10.1111/j.1467-8721.2006.00427.x

McCright, Aaron M. and Dunlap, Riley E. (2011). The politicization of climate change and polarization in the American public's views of global warming, 2001–2010. *Sociological Quarterly, 52*(2), 155–194. doi:10.1111/j.1533-8525.2011.01198.x

McDaniel, Mark A. and Bugg, Julie M. (2012). Memory training interventions: What has been forgotten? *Journal of Applied Research in Memory and Cognition, 1*(1), 45–50. doi:10.1016/j.jarmac.2011.11.002

McEwen, Bruce S. and Gianaros, Peter J. (2011). Stress- and allostasis-induced brain plasticity. *Annual Review of Medicine, 62,* 431–445. doi:10.1146/annurev-med-052209-100430

McFadden, Susan H. and Basting, Anne D. (2010). Healthy aging persons and their brains: Promoting resilience through creative engagement. *Clinics in Geriatric Medicine, 26*(1), 149–161. doi:10.1016/j.cger.2009.11.004

McGrath, John J. and Murray, Robin M. (2011). Environmental risk factors for schizophrenia. In Daniel R. Weinberger and Paul J. Harrison (Eds.), Schizophrenia (3rd ed., pp. 226–244). Hoboken, NJ: Wiley. doi:10.1002/9781444327298.ch11

McGrath, Susan K. and Kennell, John H. (2008). A randomized controlled trial of continuous labor support for middle-class couples: Effect on cesarean delivery rates. *Birth, 35*(2), 92–97. doi:10.1111/j.1523-536X.2008.00221.x

McIntyre, Donald A. (2002). Colour blindness: *Causes and effects.* Chester, UK: Dalton Publishing.

McKinley, Jesse. (2010, June 24). Illness kills 5 in California, state declares an epidemic. The New York Times, p. A15.

McKown, Clark and Strambler, Michael J. (2009). Developmental antecedents and social and academic consequences of stereotype-consciousness in middle childhood. *Child Development, 80*(6), 1643–1659. doi:10.1111/j.1467-8624.2009.01359.x

McLanahan, Sara. (2009). Fragile families and the reproduction of poverty. *The ANNALS of the American Academy of Political and Social Science, 621*(1), 111–131. doi:10.1177/0002716208324862

McLendon, Amber and Shelton, Penny. (2011–2012). New symptoms in older adults: Disease or drug? *Generations, 35*(4), 25–30.

McLeod, Bryce D.; Wood, Jeffrey J. and Weisz, John R. (2007). Examining the association between parenting and childhood anxiety: A meta-analysis. *Clinical Psychology Review, 27*(2), 155–172. doi:10.1016/j.cpr.2006.09.002

McLeod, Jane D.; Pescosolido, Bernice A.; Takeuchi, David T. and Falkenberg White, Terry (2004). Public attitudes toward the use of psychiatric medications for children. *Journal of Health and Social Behavior, 45*(1), 53–67. doi:10.1177/002214650404500104

McLeod, Peter; Sommerville, Peter and Reed, Nick. (2005). Are automated actions beyond conscious access? In John Duncan, Peter McLeod and Louise H. Phillips (Eds.), *Measuring the mind: Speed, control, and age* (pp. 359–372). New York, NY: Oxford University Press.

McLoyd, Vonnie C.; Kaplan, Rachel; Hardaway, Cecily R. and Wood, Dana. (2007). Does endorsement of physical discipline matter? *Assessing moderating influences on the maternal and child psychological correlates of physical discipline in African American families.* Journal of Family Psychology, 21(2), 165–175. doi:10.1037/0893-3200.21.2.165

McManus, I. Chris; Moore, James; Freegard, Matthew and Rawles, Richard. (2010). Science in the making: Right Hand, Left Hand. III: Estimating historical rates of left-handedness. *Laterality: Asymmetries of Body, Brain and Cognition, 15*(1–2), 186–208. doi:10.1080/13576500802565313

McNamee, Catherine and Raley, Kelly. (2011). A note on race, ethnicity and nativity differentials in remarriage in the United States. *Demographic Research, 24*(13), 293–312. doi:10.4054/DemRes.2011.24.13

McShane, Kelly E. and Hastings, Paul D. (2009). The New Friends Vignettes: Measuring parental psychological control that confers risk for anxious adjustment in preschoolers. *International Journal of Behavioral Development, 33*(6), 481–495. doi:10.1177/0165025409103874

Meadows, Sara. (2006). *The child as thinker: The development and acquisition of cognition in childhood* (2nd ed.). New York, NY: Routledge.

Meaney, Michael J. (2010). Epigenetics and the biological definition of gene x environment interactions. *Child Development, 81*(1), 41–79. doi:10.1111/j.1467-8624.2009.01381.x

Meece, Judith L. and Eccles, Jacquelynne S. (Eds.). (2010). *Handbook of research on schools, schooling, and human development.* New York, NY: Routledge.

Meeus, Wim. (2011). The study of adolescent identity formation 2000–2010: A review of longitudinal research. *Journal of Research on Adolescence, 21*(1), 75–94. doi:10.1111/j.1532-7795.2010.00716.x

Mehta, Clare M. and Strough, JoNell. (2009). Sex segregation in friendships and normative contexts across the life span. *Developmental Review, 29*(3), 201–220. doi:10.1016/j.dr.2009.06.001

Meier, Ann; Hull, Kathleen E. and Ortyl, Timothy A. (2009). Young adult relationship values at the intersection of gender and sexuality. *Journal of Marriage and Family, 71*(3), 510–525. doi:10.1111/j.1741-3737.2009.00616.x

Meisami, Esmail; Brown, Chester M. and Emerle, Henry F. (2007). Sensory systems: Normal aging, disorders, and treatments of vision and hearing in humans. In Paola S. Timiras (Ed.), *Physiological basis of aging and geriatrics* (4th ed., pp. 109–136). New York, NY: Informa Healthcare.

Meisenberg, Gerhard and Woodley, Michael A. (2013). Are cognitive differences between countries diminishing? *Evidence from TIMSS and PISA. Intelligence, 41*(6), 808–816. doi:10.1016/j.intell.2013.03.009

Melhuish, Edward C.; Phan, Mai B.; Sylva, Kathy; Sammons, Pam; Siraj-Blatchford, Iram and Taggart, Brenda. (2008). Effects of the home learning environment and preschool center experience upon literacy and numeracy development in early primary school. *Journal of Social Issues, 64*(1), 95–114. doi:10.1111/j.1540-4560.2008.00550.x

Mellor, M. Joanna and Brownell, Patricia J. (Eds.). (2006). *Elder abuse and mistreatment: Policy, practice, and research.* New York, NY: Haworth Press.

Meltzoff, Andrew N. and Moore, M. Keith. (1999). A new foundation for cognitive development in infancy: The birth of the representational infant. In Ellin Kofsky Scholnick, Katherine Nelson, Susan A. Gelman and Patricia H. Miller (Eds.), *Conceptual*

development: Piaget's legacy (pp. 53–78). Mahwah, NJ: Lawrence Erlbaum Associates.

Melzi, Gigliana and Caspe, Margaret. (2005). Variations in maternal narrative styles during book reading interactions. *Narrative Inquiry, 15*(1), 101–125. doi:10.1075/ni.15.1.06mel

Mendle, Jane; Harden, K. Paige; Brooks-Gunn, Jeanne and Graber, Julia A. (2010). Development's tortoise and hare: Pubertal timing, pubertal tempo, and depressive symptoms in boys and girls. *Developmental Psychology, 46*(5), 1341–1353. doi:10.1037/a0020205

Mendle, Jane; Harden, K. Paige; Brooks-Gunn, Jeanne and Graber, Julia A. (2012). Peer relationships and depressive symptomatology in boys at puberty. *Developmental Psychology, 48*(2), 429–435. doi:10.1037/a0026425

Mennis, Jeremy and Mason, Michael J. (2012). Social and geographic contexts of adolescent substance use: The moderating effects of age and gender. *Social Networks, 34*(1), 150–157. doi:10.1016/j.socnet.2010.10.003

Merikangas, Kathleen R.; He, Jian-ping; Rapoport, Judith; Vitiello, Benedetto and Olfson, Mark. (2012). Medication use in US youth with mental disorders. *JAMA Pediatrics, 167*(2), 141–148. doi:10.1001/jamapediatrics.2013.431

Merikangas, Kathleen R. and McClair, Vetisha L. (2012). Epidemiology of substance use disorders. *Human Genetics, 131*(6), 779–789. doi:10.1007/s00439-012-1168-0

Meririnne, Esa; Kiviruusu, Olli; Karlsson, Linnea; Pelkonen, Mirjami; Ruuttu, Titta; Tuisku, Virpi and Marttunen, Mauri. (2010). Brief report: Excessive alcohol use negatively affects the course of adolescent depression—One year naturalistic follow-up study. *Journal of Adolescence, 33*(1), 221–226. doi:10.1016/j.adolescence.2009.07.010

Merrill, Anne F. and Afifi, Tamara D. (2012). Examining the bidirectional nature of topic avoidance and relationship dissatisfaction: The moderating role of communication skills. *Communication Monographs, 79*(4), 499–521. doi:10.1080/03637751.2012.723809

Mervis, Jeffrey. (2008). Expert panel lays out the path to algebra—and why it matters. *Science, 319*(5870), 1605. doi:10.1126/science.319.5870.1605

Merz, Emily C. and McCall, Robert B. (2011). Parent ratings of executive functioning in children adopted from psychosocially depriving institutions. *Journal of Child Psychology and Psychiatry, 52*(5), 537–546. doi:10.1111/j.1469-7610.2010.02335.x

Merzenich, Hiltrud; Zeeb, Hajo and Blettner, Maria. (2010). Decreasing sperm quality: A global problem? *BMC Public Health, 10*(24). doi:10.1186/1471-2458-10-24

Mesch, Gustavo S. and Talmud, Ilan. (2010). Wired youth: *The social world of adolescence in the information age.* New York, NY: Routledge.

Mesquita, Batja and Leu, Janxin. (2007). The cultural psychology of emotion. In Shinobu Kitayama and Dov Cohen (Eds.), *Handbook of cultural psychology* (pp. 734–759). New York, NY: Guilford Press.

Messinger, Daniel M.; Ruvolo, Paul; Ekas, Naomi V. and Fogel, Alan. (2010). Applying machine learning to infant interaction: The development is in the details. *Neural Networks, 23*(8–9), 1004–1016. doi:10.1016/j.neunet.2010.08.008

Metcalfe, Janet and Finn, Bridgid. (2013). Metacognition and control of study choice in children. *Metacognition and Learning, 8*(1), 19–46. doi:10.1007/s11409-013-9094-7

Meyer, Madonna Harrington. (2012). Grandmothers juggling work and grandchildren in the United States. In Sara Arber and Virpi Timonen (Eds.), *Contemporary grandparenting: Changing family relationships in global contexts* (pp. 71–90). Chicago, IL: Policy Press.

Michl, Louisa C.; McLaughlin, Katie A.; Shepherd, Kathrine and Nolen-Hoeksema, Susan. (2013). Rumination as a mechanism linking stressful life events to symptoms of depression and anxiety: Longitudinal evidence in early adolescents and adults. *Journal of Abnormal Psychology, 122*(2), 339–352. doi:10.1037/a0031994

Miklowitz, David Jay and Cicchetti, Dante (Eds.). (2010). *Understanding bipolar disorder: A developmental psychopathology perspective.* New York, NY: Guilford Press.

Milardo, Robert M. (2010). *The forgotten kin: Aunts and uncles.* New York, NY: Cambridge University Press.

Miles, Lynden K. (2009). Who is approachable? *Journal of Experimental Social Psychology, 45*(1), 262–266. doi:10.1016/j.jesp.2008.08.010

Milkman, Katherine L.; Chugh, Dolly and Bazerman, Max H. (2009). How can decision making be improved? *Perspectives on Psychological Science, 4*(4), 379–383. doi:10.1111/j.1745-6924.2009.01142.x

Miller, Greg. (2006). The unseen: Mental illness's global toll. *Science, 311*(5760), 458–461. doi:10.1126/science.311.5760.458

Miller, Greg. (2006). The thick and thin of brainpower: Developmental timing linked to IQ. *Science, 311*(5769), 1851. doi:10.1126/science.311.5769.1851

Miller, Greg. (2010). New clues about what makes the human brain special. *Science, 330*(6008), 1167. doi:10.1126/science.330.6008.1167

Miller, Greg. (2012). Engineering a new line of attack on a signature war injury. *Science, 335*(6064), 33–35. doi:10.1126/science.335.6064.33

Miller, Gregory E. and Chen, Edith. (2010). Harsh family climate in early life: Presages the emergence of a proinflammatory phenotype in adolescence. *Psychological Science, 21*(6), 848–856. doi:10.1177/0956797610370161

Miller, Joan G. (2004). The cultural deep structure of psychological theories of social development. In Robert J. Sternberg and Elena L. Grigorenko (Eds.), *Culture and competence: Contexts of life success* (pp. 111–138). Washington, DC: American Psychological Association.

Miller, Orlando J. and Therman, Eeva. (2001). *Human chromosomes* (4th ed.). New York, NY: Springer.

Miller, Patricia H. (2011). *Theories of developmental psychology* (5th ed.). New York, NY: Worth Publishers.

Miller, Patricia Y. and Simon, William. (1980). The development of sexuality in adolescence. In Joseph Adelson (Ed.), *Handbook of adolescent psychology* (pp. 383–407). New York, NY: Wiley.

Miller, Richard B.; Hollist, Cody S.; Olsen, Joseph and Law, David. (2013). Marital quality and health over 20 years: A growth curve analysis. *Journal of Marriage and Family, 75*(3), 667–680. doi:10.1111/jomf.12025

Miller, Susan W. (2011–2012). Medications and elders: Quality of care or quality of life? *Generations, 35*(4), 19–24.

Miller, Torri W.; Nigg, Joel T. and Miller, Robin L. (2009). Attention deficit hyperactivity disorder in African American children: What can be concluded from the past ten years? *Clinical Psychology Review, 29*(1), 77–86. doi:10.1016/j.cpr.2008.10.001

Miller, William R. and Carroll, Kathleen (Eds.). (2006). *Rethinking substance abuse: What the science shows, and what we should do about it.* New York, NY: Guilford Press.

Mills, Britain; Reyna, Valerie F. and Estrada, Steven. (2008). Explaining contradictory relations between risk perception and risk taking. *Psychological Science, 19*(5), 429–433. doi:10.1111/j.1467-9280.2008.02104.x

Mills, Jon (Ed.). (2004). *Psychoanalysis at the limit: Epistemology, mind, and the question of science.* Albany, NY: State University of New York Press.

Mills, James L.; McPartlin, Joseph M.; Kirke, Peadar N.; Lee, Young J.; Conley, Mary R.; Weir, Donald G. and Scott, John M. (1995). Homocysteine metabolism in pregnancies complicated by neural-tube defects. *Lancet, 345*(8943), 149–151. doi:10.1016/S0140-6736(95)90165-5

Mills, Ryan E.; Walter, Klaudia; Stewart, Chip; Handsaker, Robert E.; Chen, Ken; Alkan, Can, . . . Korbel, Jan O. (2011). Mapping copy number variation by population-scale genome sequencing. *Nature, 470,* 59–65. doi:10.1038/nature09708

Mills-Koonce, W. Roger; Garrett-Peters, Patricia; Barnett, Melissa; Granger, Douglas A.; Blair, Clancy and Cox, Martha J. (2011). Father contributions to cortisol responses in infancy and toddlerhood. *Developmental Psychology, 47*(2), 388–395. doi:10.1037/a0021066

Milunsky, Aubrey. (2011). *Your genes, your health: A critical family guide that could save your life.* New York, NY: Oxford University Press.

Minagawa-Kawai, Yasuyo; van der Lely, Heather; Ramus, Franck; Sato, Yutaka; Mazuka, Reiko and Dupoux, Emmanuel. (2011). Optical brain imaging reveals general auditory and language-specific processing in early infant development. *Cerebral Cortex, 21*(2), 254–261. doi:10.1093/cercor/bhq082

Mindell, Jodi A.; Sadeh, Avi; Wiegand, Benjamin; How, Ti Hwei and Goh, Daniel Y. T. (2010). Cross-cultural differences in infant and toddler sleep. *Sleep Medicine, 11*(3), 274–280.

Minogue, Kristen. (2010). China's brain mappers zoom in on neural connections. *Science, 330*(6005), 747. doi:10.1126/science.330.6005.747

Mintz, Toben H. (2005). Linguistic and conceptual influences on adjective acquisition in 24- and 36-month-olds. *Developmental Psychology, 41*(1), 17–29. doi:10.1037/0012-1649.41.1.17

Mishra, Ramesh C.; Singh, Sunita and Dasen, Pierre R. (2009). Geocentric dead reckoning in Sanskrit- and Hindi-medium school children. *Culture & Psychology, 15*(3), 386–408. doi:10.1177/1354067x09343330

Misra, Dawn P.; Caldwell, Cleopatra; Young, Alford A. and Abelson, Sara. (2010). Do fathers matter? *Paternal contributions to birth outcomes and racial disparities. American Journal of Obstetrics and Gynecology, 202*(2), 99–100. doi:10.1016/j.ajog.2009.11.031

Mitchell, Barbara A. (2010). Happiness in midlife parental roles: A contextual mixed methods analysis. *Family Relations, 59*(3), 326–339. doi:10.1111/j.1741-3729.2010.00605.x

Mitchell, Edwin A. (2009). SIDS: Past, present and future. *Acta Pædiatrica, 98*(11), 1712–1719. doi:10.1111/j.1651-2227.2009.01503.x

Mitchell, Kimberly J.; Finkelhor, David; Jones, Lisa M. and Wolak, Janis. (2012). Prevalence and characteristics of youth sexting: A national study. *Pediatrics, 129*(1), 13–20. doi:10.1542/peds.2011-1730

Mitchell, Philip B.; Meiser, Bettina; Wilde, Alex; Fullerton, Janice; Donald, Jennifer; Wilhelm, Kay and Schofield, Peter R. (2010). Predictive and diagnostic genetic testing in psychiatry. *Psychiatric Clinics of North America, 33*(1), 225–243. doi:10.1016/j.psc.2009.10.001

Mitchell, Ross E. (2006). How many deaf people are there in the United States? Estimates from the survey of income and program participation. *Journal of Deaf Studies and Deaf Education, 11*(1), 112–119. doi:10.1093/deafed/enj004

Miyata, Susanne; MacWhinney, Brian; Otomo, Kiyoshi; Sirai, Hidetosi; Oshima-Takane, Yuriko; Hirakawa, Makiko, . . . Itoh, Keiko. (2013). Developmental sentence scoring for Japanese. *First Language, 33*(2), 200–216. doi:10.1177/0142723713479436

Mize, Krystal D.; Shackelford, Todd K. and Shackelford, Viviana A. (2009). Hands-on killing of intimate partners as a function of sex and relationship status/state. *Journal of Family Violence, 24*(7), 463–470. doi:10.1007/s10896-009-9244-5

MMWR. (2000, March 31). Reducing falls and resulting hip fractures among older women. *Centers for Disease Control and Prevention, 49,* 1–12.RR02.

MMWR. (2002, September 13). Folic acid and prevention of spina bifida and anencephaly: 10 years after the U.S. public health service recommendation. *MMWR Recommendations and Reports, 51*(RR13), 1–3.

MMWR. (2008, January 18). School-associated student homicides—United States, 1992–2006. *Morbidity and Mortality Weekly Report, 57*(2), 33–36.

MMWR. (2010, June 4). Youth risk behavior surveillance—United States, 2009. Atlanta, GA: *Centers for Disease Control and Prevention, 59,* 1–142.SS05.

MMWR. (2011, February 25). Abortion surveillance —United States, 2007. Atlanta, GA: *Centers for Disease Control and Prevention, 60,* 1–39.SS1.

MMWR. (2011, January 7). Notifiable diseases and mortality tables. *Morbidity and Mortality Weekly Report, 59*(52), 1704–1717.

MMWR. (2012, April 20). Measles—United States, 2011. *Morbidity and Mortality Weekly Report, 61*(15), 253–257.

MMWR. (2012, July 20). Alcohol Use and Binge Drinking Among Women of Childbearing Age—United States, 2006–2010. *Morbidity and Mortality Weekly Report, 61*(28), 534–538.

MMWR. (2012, June 8). Youth risk behavior surveillance—United States, 2011. *Centers for Disease Control and Prevention, 61,* 1–162.

MMWR. (2012, March 30). Prevalence of autism spectrum disorders—Autism and developmental disabilities monitoring network, 14 sites, United States, 2008. *Morbidity and Mortality Weekly Report, 61*(3).

MMWR. (2012, November 2). Assisted reproductive technology surveillance — United States, 2009. *U.S. Department of Health and Human Services, Centers for Disease Control and Prevention, 61,* No. 7.

MMWR. (2013, April 5). Blood lead levels in children aged 1–5 Years—United States, 1999–2010. *Morbidity and Mortality Weekly Report, 62*(13), 245–248.

MMWR. (2013, February 8). Vital signs: Current cigarette smoking among adults aged ≥18 years with mental illness—United States, 2009–2011. *Atlanta, GA: Centers for Disease Control and Prevention, 62*(5), 81–87.

MMWR. (2013, July 19). State-specific healthy life expectancy at age 65 years—United States, 2007–2009. *Centers for Disease Control and Prevention, 62,* 561–566.28.

Moffitt, Terrie E. (2003). Life-course-persistent and adolescence-limited antisocial behavior: A 10-year research review and a research agenda. In Benjamin B. Lahey, Terrie E. Moffitt and Avshalom Caspi (Eds.), *Causes of conduct disorder and juvenile delinquency* (pp. 49–75). New York, NY: Guilford Press.

Moffitt, Terrie E.; Caspi, Avshalom; Rutter, Michael and Silva, Phil A. (2001). *Sex differences in antisocial behaviour: Conduct disorder, delinquency, and violence in the Dunedin Longitudinal Study.* New York, NY: Cambridge University Press.

Mofidi, Mahyar; Zeldin, Leslie P. and Rozier, R. Gary. (2009). Oral health of Early Head Start children: A qualitative study of staff, parents, and pregnant women. *American Journal of Public Health, 99*(2), 245–251. doi:10.2105/ajph.2008.133827

Moldavsky, Maria and Sayal, Kapil. (2013). Knowledge and attitudes about attention-deficit/hyperactivity disorder (ADHD) and its treatment: The views of children, adolescents, parents, teachers and healthcare professionals. *Current Psychiatry Reports, 15,* 377. doi: 10.1007/s11920-013-0377-0

Molina, Brooke S. G.; Hinshaw, Stephen P.; Swanson, James W.; Arnold, L. Eugene; Vitiello, Benedetto; Jensen, Peter S., . . . Houck, Patricia R. (2009). The MTA at 8 years: Prospective follow-up of children treated for combined-type ADHD in a multisite study. *Journal of the American Academy of Child & Adolescent Psychiatry, 48*(5), 484–500. doi:10.1097/CHI.0b013e31819c23d0

Molitor, Adriana and Hsu, Hui-Chin. (2011). Child development across cultures: Contemporary themes and perspectives. In Kenneth D. Keith (Ed.), *Cross-cultural psychology: Contemporary themes and perspectives* (pp. 75–109). Malden, MA: Wiley-Blackwell.

Mollenkopf, John; Waters, Mary C.; Holdaway, Jennifer and Kasinitz, Philip. (2005). The ever-winding path: ethnic and racial diversity in the transition to adulthood. In Richard A. Settersten, Frank F. Furstenberg and Rubén G. Rumbaut (Eds.), *On the frontier of adulthood: Theory, research, and public policy* (pp. 454–497). Chicago, IL: University of Chicago Press.

Møller, Signe J. and Tenenbaum, Harriet R. (2011). Danish majority children's reasoning about exclusion based on gender and ethnicity. *Child Development, 82*(2), 520–532. doi:10.1111/j.1467-8624.2010.01568.x

Monahan, Kathryn C.; Steinberg, Laurence and Cauffman, Elizabeth. (2009). Affiliation with antisocial peers, susceptibility to peer influence, and antisocial behavior during the transition to adulthood. *Developmental Psychology, 45*(6), 1520–1530. doi:10.1037/a0017417

Monastersky, Richard. (2007). Who's minding the teenage brain? *Chronicle of Higher Education, 53*(19), A14-A18.

Moncloa, Fe; Wilkinson-Lee, Ada M. and Russell, Stephen T. (2010). Cuídate sin pena: Mexican mother-adolescent sexuality communication. *Journal of Ethnic And Cultural Diversity in Social Work, 19*(3), 217–234. doi:10.1080/15313204.2010.499325

Mongeau, Paul A.; Knight, Kendra; Williams, Jade; Eden, Jennifer and Shaw, Christina. (2013). Identifying and explicating variation among friends with benefits relationships. *The Journal of Sex Research, 50*(1), 37–47. doi:10.1080/00224499.2011.623797

Monje, Michelle and Dietrich, Jörg. (2012). Cognitive side effects of cancer therapy demonstrate a functional role for adult neurogenesis. *Behavioural Brain Research, 227*(2), 376–379. doi:10.1016/j.bbr.2011.05.012

Monks, Claire P. and Coyne, Iain (Eds.). (2011). *Bullying in different contexts.* New York, NY: Cambridge University Press.

Monserud, Maria A. and Elder, Glen H. Jr. (2011). Household structure and children's educational attainment: A perspective on coresidence with grandparents. *Journal of Marriage and Family, 73*(5), 981–1000. doi:10.1111/j.1741-3737.2011.00858.x

Monteiro, Carlos A.; Conde, Wolney L. and Popkin, Barry M. (2004). The burden of disease from undernutrition and overnutrition in countries undergoing rapid nutrition transition: A view from Brazil. *American Journal of Public Health, 94*(3), 433–434. doi:10.2105/AJPH.94.3.433

Monteiro, Carlos A.; Conde, Wolney L. and Popkin, Barry M. (2007). Income-specific trends in obesity in Brazil: 1975–2003. *American Journal of Public Health, 97*(10), 1808–1812. doi:10.2105/ajph.2006.099630

Moody, Raymond A. (1975). Life after life: The investigation of a phenomenon—Survival of bodily death. Atlanta, GA: Mockingbird Books.

Moore, Ginger A. and Calkins, Susan D. (2004). Infants' vagal regulation in the still-face paradigm is related to dyadic coordination of mother-infant interaction. *Developmental Psychology, 40*(6), 1068–1080. doi:10.1037/0012-1649.40.6.1068

Moore, Karenza and Measham, Fiona. (2008). "It's the most fun you can have for twenty quid": Motivations, consequences and meanings of British ketamine use. *Addiction Research & Theory, 16*(3), 231–244. doi:10.1080/16066350801983681

Moore, Kelly L.; Boscardin, W. John; Steinman, Michael A. and Schwartz, Janice B. (2012). Age and sex variation in prevalence of chronic medical conditions in older residents of U.S. nursing homes. *Journal of the American Geriatrics Society, 60*(4), 756–764. doi: 10.1111/j.1532-5415.2012.03909.x

Moore, Keith L. and Persaud, Trivedi V. N. (2003). *The developing human: Clinically oriented embryology* (7th ed.). Philadelphia, PA: Saunders.

Moore, Keith L. and Persaud, Trivedi V. N. (2007). *The developing human: Clinically oriented embryology* (8th ed.). Philadelphia, PA: Saunders/Elsevier.

Moran, Lyndsey R.; Lengua, Liliana J. and Zalewski, Maureen. (2013). The interaction between negative emotionality and effortful control in early social-emotional development. *Social Development, 22*(2), 340–362. doi:10.1111/sode.12025

Morasch, Katherine C. and Bell, Martha Ann. (2009). Patterns of brain-electrical activity during declarative memory performance in 10-month-old infants. *Brain and Cognition, 71*(3), 215–222. doi:10.1016/j.bandc.2009.08.012

Morcos, Roy N. and Kizy, Thomas. (2012). Gynecomastia: When is treatment indicated? *Journal of Family Practice, 61*(12), 719–725.

Morelli, Gilda A. and Rothbaum, Fred. (2007). Situating the child in context: Attachment relationships and self-regulation in different cultures.

In Shinobu Kitayama and Dov Cohen (Eds.), *Handbook of cultural psychology* (pp. 500–527). New York, NY: Guilford Press.

Morgan, Ali Zaremba; Keiley, Margaret K.; Ryan, Aubrey E.; Radomski, Juliana Groves; Gropper, Sareen S.; Connell, Lenda Jo, . . . Ulrich, Pamela V. (2012). Eating regulation styles, appearance schemas, and body satisfaction predict changes in body fat for emerging adults. *Journal of Youth and Adolescence, 41*(9), 1127–1141. doi:10.1007/s10964-012-9757-8

Morgan, Ian G.; Ohno-Matsui, Kyoko and Saw, Seang-Mei. (2012). Myopia. *The Lancet, 379*(9827), 1739–1748. doi:10.1016/S0140-6736(12)60272-4

Morgan, Kevin; Gregory, Pamela; Tomeny, Maureen; David, Beverley M. and Gascoigne, Claire. (2012). Self-help treatment for insomnia symptoms associated with chronic conditions in older adults: A randomized controlled trial. *Journal of the American Geriatrics Society, 60*(10), 1803–1810. doi:10.1111/j.1532-5415.2012.04175.x

Morin, Rich and Fry, Richard. (2012, October 22). More Americans worry about financing retirement: Adults in their late 30s most concerned. Pew Research, Social and Demographic Trends.

Morning, Ann. (2008). Ethnic classification in global perspective: A cross-national survey of the 2000 census round. *Population Research and Policy Review, 27*(2), 239–272. doi: 10.1007/s11113-007-9062-5

Morón, Cecilio and Viteri, Fernando E. (2009). Update on common indicators of nutritional status: Food access, food consumption, and biochemical measures of iron and anemia. *Nutrition Reviews, 67*(Suppl. 1), S31-S35. doi:10.1111/j.1753-4887.2009.00156.x

Morones, Alyssa. (2013). Paddling persists in U.S. schools. *Exducation Week, 33*(9), 1, 10–11.

Morris, Amanda Sheffield; Silk, Jennifer S.; Steinberg, Laurence; Myers, Sonya S. and Robinson, Lara Rachel. (2007). The role of the family context in the development of emotion regulation. *Social Development, 16*(2), 361–388. doi:10.1111/j.1467-9507.2007.00389.x

Morris, Danielle H.; Jones, Michael E.; Schoemaker, Minouk J.; Ashworth, Alan and Swerdlow, Anthony J. (2011). Familial concordance for age at natural menopause: Results from the Breakthrough Generations Study. *Menopause, 18*(9), 956–961. doi:10.1097/gme.0b013e31820ed6d2

Morris, Vivian Gunn and Morris, Curtis L. (2013). A call for African American male teachers: The supermen expected to solve the problems of low-performing schools. In Chance W. Lewisand Ivory A. Toldson (Eds.), *Black male teachers: Diversifying the United States' teacher workforce* (pp. 151–165). Bingley, UK: Emerald Group.

Morrison, Frederick J.; Ponitz, Claire Cameron and McClelland, Megan M. (2010). Self-regulation and academic achievement in the transition to school. In Susan D. Calkins and Martha Ann Bell (Eds.), *Child development at the intersection of emotion and cognition* (pp. 203–224). Washington, DC: American Psychological Association. doi:10.1037/12059-011

Morrison, Mike; Tay, Louis and Diener, Ed. (2011). Subjective well-being and national satisfaction. *Psychological Science, 22*(2), 166–171. doi:10.1177/0956797610396224

Morrissey, Taryn. (2009). Multiple child-care arrangements and young children's behavioral outcomes. *Child Development, 80*(1), 59–76. doi:10.1111/j.1467-8624.2008.01246.x

Morrow, Daniel G.; Miller, Lisa M. Soederberg; Ridolfo, Heather E.; Magnor, Clifford; Fischer, Ute M.; Kokayeff, Nina K. and Stine-Morrow, Elizabeth A. L. (2009). Expertise and age differences in pilot decision making. *Aging, Neuropsychology, and Cognition, 16*(1), 33–55. doi:10.1080/13825580802195641

Morrow, Daniel G.; Ridolfo, Heather E.; Menard, William E.; Sanborn, Adam; Stine-Morrow, Elizabeth A. L.; Magnor, Cliff, . . . Bryant, David. (2003). Environmental support promotes expertise-based mitigation of age differences on pilot communication tasks. *Psychology & Aging, 18*(2), 268–284. doi:10.1037/0882-7974.18.2.268

Morrow-Howell, Nancy and Freedman, Marc. (2006–2007). Bringing civic engagement into sharper focus. *Generations, 30*(4), 6–9.

Mosher, Catherine E. and Danoff-Burg, Sharon. (2007). Death anxiety and cancer-related stigma: A terror management analysis. *Death Studies, 31*(10), 885–907. doi:10.1080/07481180701603360

Mosher, William D.; Jones, Jo and Abma, Joyce C. (2012, July 20). Intended and unintended births in the United States: 1982–2010. *National health statistics reports, 55*, 1–27.

Moshman, David. (2011). *Adolescent rationality and development: Cognition, morality, and identity* (3rd ed.). New York, NY: Psychology Press.

Moulson, Margaret C.; Westerlund, Alissa; Fox, Nathan A.; Zeanah, Charles H. and Nelson, Charles A. (2009). The effects of early experience on face recognition: An event-related potential study of institutionalized children in Romania. *Child Development, 80*(4), 1039–1056. doi:10.1111/j.1467-8624.2009.01315.x

Mrozek-Budzyn, Dorota; Kieltyka, Agnieszka and Majewska, Renata. (2010). Lack of association between measles-mumps-rubella vaccination and autism in children: A case-control study. *The Pediatric Infectious Disease Journal, 29*(5), 397–400 doi:10.1097/INF.0b013e3181c40a8a

Mueller, Christian E.; Bridges, Sara K. and Goddard, Michelle S. (2011). Sleep and parent-family connectedness: Links, relationships and implications for adolescent depression. *Journal of Family Studies, 17*(1), 9–23.

Mulder, Pamela J. and Johnson, Teresa S. (2010). The Beginning Breastfeeding Survey: Measuring mothers' perceptions of breastfeeding effectiveness during the postpartum hospitalization. *Research in Nursing & Health, 33*(4), 329–344. doi:10.1002/nur.20384

Mullen, Sean P.; McAuley, Edward; Satariano, William A.; Kealey, Melissa and Prohaska, Thomas R. (2012). Physical activity and functional limitations in older adults: the influence of self-efficacy and functional performance. *The Journals of Gerontology: Series B, 67B*(3), 354–361. doi:10.1093/geronb/gbs036

Müller, Ulrich; Dick, Anthony Steven; Gela, Katherine; Overton, Willis F. and Zelazo, Philip David. (2006). The role of negative priming in preschoolers' flexible rule use on the dimensional change card sort task. *Child Development, 77*(2), 395–412. doi:10.1111/j.1467-8624.2006.00878.x

Muller, Ziva and Litwin, Howard. (2011). Grandparenting and psychological well-being: how important is grandparent role centrality? *European Journal of Ageing, 8*(2), 109–118. doi:10.1007/s10433-011-0185-5

Mulligan, A.; Anney, R.; Butler, L.; O'Regan, M.; Richardson, T.; Tulewicz, E. M., . . . Gill, M. (2013). Home environment: association with hyperactivity/impulsivity in children with ADHD and their non-ADHD siblings. *Child: Care, Health & Development, 39*(2), 202–212. doi:10.1111/j.1365-2214.2011.01345.x

Mullis, Ina V. S.; Martin, Michael O.; Foy, Pierre and Arora, A. (2012b). *The TIMSS 2011 International Results in Mathematics.* Chestnut Hill, MA: TIMSS & PIRLS International Study Center, Boston College.

Mullis, Ina V. S.; Martin, Michael O.; Foy, Pierre and Drucker, Kathleen T. (2012a). *PIRLS 2011 international results in reading.* Chestnut Hill, MA: TIMSS & PIRLS International Study Center, Boston College.

Munck, Hanne. (2009). Early intervention and fatherhood: Denmark. In Kevin J. Nugent, Bonnie J. Petrauskas and T. Berry Brazelton (Eds.), The newborn as a person: *Enabling healthy infant development worldwide* (pp. 101–111). Hoboken, NJ: Wiley.

Muñoz, Carmen and Singleton, David. (2011). A critical review of age-related research on L2 ultimate attainment. *Language Teaching, 44*(1), 1–35. doi:10.1017/S0261444810000327

Munroe, Robert L. and Romney, A. Kimbal. (2006). Gender and age differences in same-sex aggregation and social behavior: A four-culture study. *Journal of Cross-Cultural Psychology, 37*(1), 3–19. doi:10.1177/0022022105282292

Muraco, Anna. (2006). Intentional families: Fictive kin ties between cross-gender, different sexual orientation friends. *Journal of Marriage and Family, 68*(5), 1313–1325. doi:10.1111/j.1741-3737.2006.00330.x

Murphy, Michael. (2011). Long-term effects of the demographic transition on family and kinship networks in Britain. *Population and Development Review, 37*(Suppl. 1), 55–80. doi:10.1111/j.1728-4457.2011.00378.x

Murphy, Sherry L.; Xu, Jiaquan and Kochanek, Kenneth D. (2012, January 11).

Deaths: Preliminary data for 2010. Hyattsville, MD: *U.S. Department of Health And Human Services Centers for Disease Control And Prevention, 60,* No.4.4.

Murray, Christopher J. L.; Vos, Theo; Lozano, Rafael; Naghavi, Mohsen; Flaxman, Abraham D.; Michaud, Catherine, . . . Lopez, Alan D. (2012). *Disability-adjusted life years (DALYs) for 291 diseases and injuries in 21 regions, 1990—2010: A systematic analysis for the Global Burden of Disease Study 2010. The Lancet, 380*(9859), 2197–2223. doi:10.1016 /S0140-6736(12)61689-4

Mustonen, Ulla; Huurre, Taina; Kiviruusu, Olli; Haukkala, Ari and Aro, Hillevi. (2011). Long-term impact of parental divorce on intimate relationship quality in adulthood and the mediating role of psychosocial resources. *Journal of Family Psychology, 25*(4), 615–619. doi:10.1037 /a0023996

Mutti, Donald. (2010). Quoted in Holden, Constance (Ed). *Random samples: Myopia out of control. Science, 327*(5961), 17. doi:10.1126 /science.327.5961.17-c

Myatt, Julia P. and Thorpe, Susannah K. S. (2011). Postural strategies employed by orangutans (Pongo abelii) during feeding in the terminal branch niche. *American Journal Of Physical Anthropology, 146*(1), 73–82. doi:10.1002/ajpa.21548

Myers, David G. (2002). *Intuition: Its powers and perils.* New Haven, CT: Yale University Press.

Myers, David G. (2011). Harnessing the human factor in hearing assistance. *Observer, 24*(8).

Mynatt, Blair Sumner and Mowery, Robyn L. (2013). The Family, Larger Systems, and End-of-Life Decision Making. In David K. Meagher and David E. Balk (Eds.), *Handbook of thanatology: The essential body of knowledge for the study of death, dying, and bereavement* (2nded., pp. 91–99). New York, NY: Routledge.

Naci, Huseyin; Chisholm, Dan and Baker, T. D. (2009). Distribution of road traffic deaths by road user group: A global comparison. *Injury Prevention, 15*(1), 55–59. doi:10.1136/ip .2008.018721

Nadeau, Joseph H. and Dudley, Aimée M. (2011). Systems genetics. *Science, 331*(6020), 1015–1016. doi:10.1126/science.1203869

Nagata, Chisato; Nakamura, Kozue; Wada, Keiko; Oba, Shino; Hayashi, Makoto; Takeda, Noriyuki and Yasuda, Keigo. (2010). Association of dietary fat, vegetables and antioxidant micronutrients with skin ageing in Japanese women. *British Journal of Nutrition, 103*(10), 1493–1498. doi:10.1017 /S0007114509993461

Nair, K. Sreekumaran; Rizza, Robert A.; O'Brien, Peter; Dhatariya, Ketan; Short, Kevin R.; Nehra, Ajay, . . . Jensen, Michael D. (2006). DHEA in elderly women and DHEA or testosterone in elderly men. *New England Journal of Medicine, 355*(16), 1647–1659. doi:10.1056 /NEJMoa054629

Naninck, Eva F. G.; Lucassen, Paul J. and Bakker, Julie. (2011). Sex differences in adolescent depression: Do sex hormones determine vulnerability? *Journal of Neuroendocrinology, 23*(5), 383–392. doi:10.1111/j.1365-2826. 2011.02125.x

Narayan, Chandan R.; Werker, Janet F. and Beddor, Patrice Speeter. (2010). The interaction between acoustic salience and language experience in developmental speech perception: Evidence from nasal place discrimination. *Developmental Science, 13*(3), 407–420. doi:10.1111/j.1467-7687.2009.00898.x

Narvaez, Darcia and Lapsley, Daniel K. (2009). Moral identity, moral functioning, and the development of moral character. *Psychology of Learning and Motivation, 50,* 237–274. doi:10.1016/S0079-7421(08)00408-8

National Center for Education Statistics. (2012). *Digest of education statistics, 2011.* Washington, DC: U.S. Department of Education, Institute of Education Sciences, U.S. Department of Education.NCES 2012–001.

National Center for Education Statistics. (2012). Median annual earnings of full-time year-round workers 25 to 34 years old, by sex, race/ethnicity, and educational attainment: Selected years, 1995 through 2011, Table 439. Washington, DC: Institute of Education Science, U.S. Department of Education.

National Center for Education Statistics. (2012). Percentage of the population 25 to 64 years old who attained a bachelor's or higher level degree, by age group and country: Selected years, 1999 through 2010, Table 469. Washington, DC: Institute of Education Science, U.S. Department of Education.

National Center for Education Statistics. (2013). Digest of education statistics, 2012. U.S. Department of Education, Institute of Education Sciences, National Center for Education Statistics. NCES 2014015.

National Center for Education Statistics Institute of Education Sciences. (2009). *The condition of education 2009.* Washington, DC: U.S. Department of Education

National Center for Environmental Health. (2012). Tested and confirmed elevated blood lead levels by state, year and blood lead level group for children <72 months. Atlanta, GA: Centers for Disease Control and Prevention.

National Center for Health Statistics. (2010). Health, United States, 2009: With special feature on medical technology. Hyattsville, MD: U.S. Department of Health and Human Services, Centers for Disease Control and Prevention.

National Center for Health Statistics. (2011). Health, United States, 2010: With special feature on death and dying. Hyattsville, MD: U.S. Department of Health and Human Services, Centers for Disease Control and Prevention.

National Center for Health Statistics. (2012). Health, United States, 2011: With special feature on socioeconomic status and health. Hyattsville, MD: U.S. Department of Health and Human Services, Centers for Disease Control and Prevention.

National Center for Health Statistics. (2013). Health, United States, 2012: With special feature on emergency care. Hyattsville, MD: U.S. Department of Health and Human Services, Centers for Disease Control and Prevention. 76–641496.

National Center for Health Statistics. (2013). Table 54, current cigarette smoking among adults aged 18 and over, by sex, race, and age: United States, selected years 1965–2011. Hyattsville, MD: U.S. Department of Health and Human Services, Centers for Disease Control and Prevention.

National Governors Association Center for Best Practices *(NGA Center) and the Council of Chief State School Officers (CCSSO).* (2010, October 25). Common core state standards initiative. Washington, DC: National Governors Association.

National Sleep Foundation. (2006). *Summary findings of the 2006 Sleep in America poll.* Washington, DC: National Sleep Foundation & WBA Market Research. 05–638.

Natsuaki, Misaki N.; Leve, Leslie D.; Neiderhiser, Jenae M.; Shaw, Daniel S.; Scaramella, Laura V.; Ge, Xiaojia and Reiss, David. (2013). Intergenerational transmission of risk for social inhibition: The interplay between parental responsiveness and genetic influences. *Development and Psychopathology, 25*(1), 261–274. doi:10.1017/S0954579412001010

Naudé, H.; Marx, J.; Pretorius, E. and Hislop-Esterhuyzen, N. (2007). Evidence of early childhood defects due to prenatal overexposure to vitamin A: A case study. *Early Child Development and Care, 177*(3), 235–253. doi:10.1080/03004430500456149

Needleman, Herbert L. and Gatsonis, Constantine A. (1990). Low-level lead exposure and the IQ of children: A meta-analysis of modern studies. *JAMA, 263*(5), 673–678. doi:10.1001 /jama.1990.03440050067035

Needleman, Herbert L.; Schell, Alan; Bellinger, David; Leviton, Alan and Allred, Elizabeth N. (1990). The long-term effects of exposure to low doses of lead in childhood. *New England Journal of Medicine, 322,* 83–88. doi:10.1056/NEJM199001113220203

Nef, Tobias; Ganeaa, Raluca L.; Müria, René M. and Mosimann, Urs P. (2013). Social networking sites and older users – a systematic review. *International Psychogeriatrics, 25*(7), 1041–1053. doi: 10.1017/S1041610213000355

Neggers, Yasmin and Crowe, Kristi. (2013). Low Birth Weight Outcomes: Why Better in Cuba Than Alabama? *Journal of the American Board of Family Medicine, 26*(2), 187–195. doi:10.3122/ jabfm.2013.02.120227

Negriff, Sonya; Dorn, Lorah D.; Pabst, Stephanie R. and Susman, Elizabeth J. (2011). Morningness/eveningness, pubertal timing, and substance use in adolescent girls. *Psychiatry Research, 185*(3), 408–413. doi:10.1016/j.psychres.2010.07.006

Neigh, Gretchen N.; Gillespie, Charles F. and Nemeroff, Charles B. (2009). The neurobiological toll of child abuse and neglect. *Trauma, Violence, & Abuse, 10*(4), 389–410. doi:10.1177/1524838009339758

Neimeyer, Robert A. and Jordan, John R. (2013). Historical and contemporary perspectives on assessment and intervention. In David K. Meagher and David E. Balk (Eds.), *Handbook of thanatology: The essential body of knowledge for the study of death, dying, and bereavement* (2nd ed., pp. 219–237). New York, NY: Routledge.

Neisser, Ulric; Boodoo, Gwyneth; Bouchard Jr., Thomas J.; Boykin, A. Wade; Brody, Nathan; Ceci, Stephen J., . . . Urbina, Susana. (1996). Intelligence: Knowns and unknowns. *American Psychologist, 51*(2), 77–101. doi:10.1037//0003-066X.51.2.77

Nelson, Charles A.; de Haan, Michelle and Thomas, Kathleen M. (2006). *Neuroscience of cognitive development: The role of experience and the developing brain.* Hoboken, NJ: Wiley.

Nelson, Charles A., III; Zeanah, Charles H.; Fox, Nathan A.; Marshall, Peter J.; Smyke, Anna T. and Guthrie, Donald. (2007). Cognitive recovery in socially deprived young children: The Bucharest Early Intervention Project. *Science, 318*(5858), 1937–1940. doi:10.1126/science.1143921

Nelson, Jennifer A.; Chiasson, Mary Ann and Ford, Viola. (2004). Childhood overweight in a New York City WIC population. *American Journal of Public Health, 94*(3), 458–462. doi:10.2105/AJPH.94.3.458

Nelson, Larry J.; Hart, Craig H. and Evans, Cortney A. (2008). Solitary-functional play and solitary-pretend play: Another look at the construct of solitary-active behavior using playground observations. *Social Development, 17*(4), 812–831. doi:10.1111/j.1467-9507.2008.00470.x

Nelson, Larry J. and Padilla-Walker, Laura M. (2013). Flourishing and floundering in emerging adult college students. *Emerging Adulthood, 1*(1), 67–78. doi:10.1177/2167696812470938

Nelson, R. Michael and DeBacker, Teresa K. (2008). Achievement motivation in adolescents: The role of peer climate and best friends. *Journal of Experimental Education, 76*(2), 170–189. doi:10.3200/JEXE.76.2.170-190

Nelson, Todd D. (2011). Ageism: The strange case of prejudice against the older you. In Richard L. Wiener and Steven L. Willborn (Eds.), *Disability and aging discrimination: Perspectives in law and psychology* (pp. 37–47). New York, NY: Springer.

Neumann, Anna; van Lier, Pol; Frijns, Tom; Meeus, Wim and Koot, Hans. (2011). Emotional dynamics in the development of early adolescent psychopathology: A one-year longitudinal study. *Journal of Abnormal Child Psychology, 39*(5), 657–669. doi:10.1007/s10802-011-9509-3

Nevin, Rick. (2007). Understanding international crime trends: The legacy of preschool lead exposure. *Environmental Research, 104*(3), 315–336. doi:10.1016/j.envres.2007.02.008

Newnham, Carol A.; Milgrom, Jeannette and Skouteris, Helen. (2009). Effectiveness of a modified mother-infant transaction program on outcomes for preterm infants from 3 to 24 months of age. *Infant Behavior and Development, 32*(1), 17–26. doi:10.1016/j.infbeh.2008.09.004

Ng, Nawi; Weinehall, Lars and Öhman, Ann. (2007). 'If I don't smoke, I'm not a real man'—Indonesian teenage boys' views about smoking. *Health Education Research, 22*(6), 794–804. doi:10.1093/her/cyl104

Ngui, Emmanuel; Cortright, Alicia and Blair, Kathleen. (2009). An investigation of paternity status and other factors associated with racial and ethnic disparities in birth outcomes in Milwaukee, Wisconsin. *Maternal and Child Health Journal, 13*(4), 467–478. doi:10.1007/s10995-008-0383-8

Nguyen, Angela-MinhTu D. and Benet-Martínez, Verónica. (2013). Biculturalism and adjustment: A meta-analysis. *Journal of Cross-Cultural Psychology, 44*(1), 122–159. doi:10.1177/0022022111435097

Nguyen, H.T.; Geens, Mieke and Spits, C. (2013). Genetic and epigenetic instability in human pluripotent stem cells. *Human Reproduction Update, 19*(2), 187–205. doi:10.1093/humupd/dms048

Nic Gabhainn, Saoirse; Baban, Adriana; Boyce, William and Godeau, Emmanuelle. (2009). How well protected are sexually active 15-year olds? Cross-national patterns in condom and contraceptive pill use 2002–2006. *International Journal of Public Health, 54*(Suppl. 2), 209–215. doi:10.1007/s00038-009-5412-x

Niccols, Alison. (2007). Fetal alcohol syndrome and the developing socio-emotional brain. *Brain and Cognition, 65*(1), 135–142. doi:10.1016/j.bandc.2007.02.009

Nichols, Tracy R.; Graber, Julia A.; Brooks-Gunn, Jeanne and Botvin, Gilbert J. (2006). Sex differences in overt aggression and delinquency among urban minority middle school students. *Journal of Applied Developmental Psychology, 27*(1), 78–91. doi:10.1016/j.appdev.2005.12.006

Nicholson, Barbara and Parker, Lysa. (2009). *Attached at the heart: 8 proven parenting principles for raising connected and compassionate children.* New York, NY: iUniverse.com.

Nielsen, Mark and Tomaselli, Keyan. (2010). Overimitation in Kalahari Bushman children and the origins of human cultural cognition. *Psychological Science, 21*(5), 729–736. doi:10.1177/0956797610368808

Nieto, Sonia. (2000). *Affirming diversity: The sociopolitical context of multicultural education* (3rd ed.). New York, NY: Longman.

Nieuwenhuis, Rense; Need, Ariana and van der Kolk, Henk. (2012). Institutional and demographic explanations of women's employment in 18 OECD countries. *Journal of Marriage and Family, 74*(3), 614–630. doi:10.1111/j.1741-3737.2012.00965.x

Niji, Rie; Arita, Kenji; Abe, Yoko; Lucas, Milanita E.; Nishino, Mizuho and Mitome, Masato. (2010). Maternal age at birth and other risk factors in early childhood caries. *Pediatric Dentistry, 32*(7), 493–498.

Nilwik, Rachel; Snijders, Tim; Leenders, Marika; Groen, Bart B. L.; van Kranenburg, Janneau; Verdijk, Lex B. and van Loon, Luc J. C. (2013). The decline in skeletal muscle mass with aging is mainly attributed to a reduction in type II muscle fiber size. *Experimental Gerontology, 48*(5), 492–498. doi:10.1016/j.exger.2013.02.012

Nisbett, Richard E.; Aronson, Joshua; Blair, Clancy; Dickens, William; Flynn, James; Halpern, Diane F. and Turkheimer, Eric. (2012). Intelligence: New findings and theoretical developments. *American Psychologist, 67*(2), 130–159. doi:10.1037/a0026699

Nisbett, Richard E.; Peng, Kaiping; Choi, Incheol and Norenzayan, Ara. (2001). Culture and systems of thought: Holistic versus analytic cognition. *Psychological Review, 108*(2), 291–310. doi:10.1037//0033-295X.108.2.291

Nishida, Tracy K. and Lillard, Angeline S. (2007). The informative value of emotional expressions: 'Social referencing' in mother-child pretense. *Developmental Science, 10*(2), 205–212. doi:10.1111/j.1467-7687.2007.00581.x

Nishina, Adrienne and Juvonen, Jaana. (2005). Daily reports of witnessing and experiencing peer harassment in middle school. *Child Development, 76*(2), 435–450. doi:10.1111/j.1467-8624.2005.00855.x

Noel-Miller, Claire M. (2013a). Repartnering following divorce: implications for older fathers' relations with their adult children. *Journal of Marriage and Family, 75*(3), 697–712. doi:10.1111/jomf.12034

Noël-Miller, Claire M. (2013b). Former stepparents' contact with their stepchildren after midlife. *The Journals of Gerontology Series B: Psychological Sciences and Social Sciences, 68*(3), 409–419. doi:10.1093/geronb/gbt021

Nordgren, Loran F.; Harreveld, Frenk van and Pligt, Joop van der. (2009). The restraint bias: How the illusion of self-restraint promotes impulsive behavior. *Psychological Science, 20*(12), 1523–1528. doi: 10.1111/j.1467-9280.2009.02468.x

Norris, Pippa. (2001). *Digital divide: Civic engagement, information poverty, and the internet worldwide.* New York, NY: Cambridge University Press.

North, Michael S. and Fiske, Susan T. (2012). An inconvenienced youth? Ageism and its potential intergenerational roots. *Psychological Bulletin, 138*(5), 982–997. doi:10.1037/a0027843

Nucci, Larry and Turiel, Elliot. (2009). Capturing the complexity of moral development and education. *Mind, Brain, and Education, 3*(3), 151–159. doi:10.1111/j.1751-228X.2009.01065.x

Nucci, Larry P. (2009). *Nice is not enough: Facilitating moral development.* Upper Saddle River, NJ: Merrill/Prentice Hall.

Nugent, J. Kevin; Petrauskas, Bonnie J. and Brazelton, T. Berry (Eds.). (2009). *The newborn as a person: Enabling healthy infant development worldwide.* Hoboken, NJ: Wiley.

Nyberg, Lars and Bäckman, Lars. (2011). Memory changes and the aging brain: A multimodal imaging approach. In K. Warner Schaie and Sherry L. Willis (Eds.), Handbook of the psychology of aging (7th ed., pp. 121–131). San Diego, CA: Academic Press. doi:10.1016/B978-0-12-380882-0.00008-5

O'Caoimh, Rónán; Gao, Yang; Gallagher, Paul Francis; Eustace, Joesph; McGlade, Ciara and Molloy, D. William. (2013). Which part of the Quick mild cognitive impairment screen (Qmci) discriminates between normal cognition, mild cognitive impairment and dementia? *Age and Ageing, 42*(3), 324–330. doi: 10.1093/ageing/aft044

O'Doherty, Kieran. (2006). Risk communication in genetic counselling: A discursive approach to probability. *Theory & Psychology, 16*(2), 225–256. doi:10.1177/0959354306062537

O'Donnell, Lydia; Stueve, Ann; Duran, Richard; Myint-U, Athi; Agronick, Gail; Doval, Alexi San and Wilson-Simmons, Renée (2008). Parenting practices, parents' underestimation of daughters' risks, and alcohol and sexual behaviors of urban girls. *Journal of Adolescent Health, 42*(5), 496–502. doi:10.1016 /j.jadohealth.2007.10.008

O'Hanlon, Leslie Harris. (2013). Teaching students the skills to be savvy researchers. *Education Week, 32*(32), s12, s15, s16.

O'Leary, Colleen M.; Nassar, Natasha; Zubrick, Stephen R.; Kurinczuk, Jennifer J.; Stanley, Fiona and Bower, Carol. (2010). Evidence of a complex association between dose, pattern and timing of prenatal alcohol exposure and child behaviour problems. *Addiction, 105*(1), 74–86. doi:10.1111/j.1360-0443.2009.02756.x

O'Malley, A. James and Christakis, Nicholas A. (2011). Longitudinal analysis of large social networks: Estimating the effect of health traits on changes in friendship ties. *Statistics in Medicine, 30*(9), 950–964. doi:10.1002/sim.4190

O'Rahilly, Ronan R. and Müller, Fabiola. (2001). *Human embryology & teratology* (3rd ed.). New York, NY: Wiley.

O'Rourke, Norm; Cappeliez, Philippe and Claxton, Amy. (2010a). Functions of reminiscence and the psychological well-being of young-old and older adults over time. *Aging & Mental Health, 15*(2), 272–281. doi:10.1080 /13607861003713281

O'Rourke, Norm; Neufeld, Eva; Claxton, Amy and Smith, JuliAnna Z. (2010b). Knowing me—knowing you: Reported personality and trait discrepancies as predictors of marital idealization between long-wed spouses. *Psychology and Aging, 25*(2), 412–421. doi:10.1037/a0017873

O'Donnell, Christopher and Nabel, Elizabeth. (2011). Genomics of cardiovascular disease. *New England Journal of Medicine, 365,* 2098–2109. doi:10.1056/NEJMra1105239

Oakes, J. Michael. (2009). The effect of media on children: A methodological assessment from a social epidemiologist. *American Behavioral Scientist, 52*(8), 1136–1151. doi:10.1177/0002764209331538

Oakes, Lisa M.; Cashon, Cara; Casasola, Marianella and Rakison, David (Eds.). (2011). Infant perception and cognition: Recent advances, emerging theories, and future directions. New York, NY: Oxford University Press. doi:10.1093 /acprof:oso/9780195366709.001.0001

Ocobock, Abigail. (2013). The power and limits of marriage: Married gay men's family relationships. *Journal of Marriage and Family, 75*(1), 191–205. doi:10.1111/j.1741-3737.2012.01032.x

Odden, Michelle C.; Peralta, Carmen A.; Haan, Mary N. and Covinsky, Kenneth E. (2012). Rethinking the association of high blood pressure with mortality in elderly adults: The impact of frailty. *Archives of Internal Medicine, 172*(15), 1162–1168. doi:10.1001/archinternmed .2012.2555

Odlaug, Brian L.; Mahmud, Waqar; Goddard, Andrew and Grant, Jon E. (2010). Anxiety disorders. In Jon E. Grant and Marc N. Potenza (Eds.), *Young adult mental health* (pp. 231–254). New York, NY: Oxford University Press.

OECD. (2010). *PISA 2009 results: Learning to learn: Student engagement, strategies and practices* (Vol. 3): PISA, OECD Publishing. doi:10.1787/9789264083943-en

OECD. (2011). Education at a glance 2011: OECD indicators. Paris: OECD.

Offit, Paul A. (2008). *Autism's false prophets: Bad science, risky medicine, and the search for a cure.* New York, NY: Columbia University Press.

Ogden, Cynthia L.; Carroll, Margaret D.; Kit, Brian K. and Flegal, Katherine M. (2012). Prevalence of obesity and trends in body mass index among US children and adolescents, 1999–2010. *Journal of the American Medical Association, 307*(5), 483–490. doi:10.1001/jama.2012.40

Ogden, Cynthia L.; Gorber, Sarah Connor; Dommarco, Juan A. Rivera; Carroll, Margaret; Shields, Margot and Flegal, Katherine. (2011). The epidemiology of childhood obesity in Canada, Mexico and the United States. In Luis A. Moreno, Iris Pigeot and Wolfgang Ahrens (Eds.), *Epidemiology of obesity in children and adolescents* (Vol. 2, pp. 69–93). New York, NY: Springer. doi:10.1007/978-1-4419-6039-9_5

Oh, Seungmi and Lewis, Charlie. (2008). Korean preschoolers' advanced inhibitory control and its relation to other executive skills and mental state understanding. *Child Development, 79*(1), 80–99. doi:10.1111/j.1467-8624.2007.01112.x

Oken, Emily and Bellinger, David C. (2008). Fish consumption, methylmercury and child neurodevelopment. *Current Opinion in Pediatrics, 20*(2), 178–183. doi: 10.1097/MOP.0b013e3282f5614c

Okun, Morris A.; Rios, Rebeca; Crawford, Aaron V. and Levy, Roy. (2011). Does the relation between volunteering and well-being vary with health and age? *The International Journal of Aging and Human Development, 72*(3), 265–287. doi:10.2190/AG.72.3.f

Oldershaw, Lynn. (2002). *A national survey of parents of young children.* Toronto, Canada: Invest in Kids.

Olfson, Mark; Crystal, Stephen; Huang, Cecilia and Gerhard, Tobias. (2010). Trends in antipsychotic drug use by very young, privately insured children. *Journal of the American Academy of Child and Adolescent Psychiatry, 49*(1), 13–23. doi:10.1016/j.jaac.2009.09.003

Olsen, James P.; Parra, Gilbert R. and Bennett, Shira A. (2010). Predicting violence in romantic relationships during adolescence and emerging adulthood: A critical review of the mechanisms by which familial and peer influences operate. *Clinical Psychology Review, 30*(4), 411–422. doi:10.1016/j.cpr.2010.02.002

Olshansky, S. Jay; Antonucci, Toni; Berkman, Lisa; Binstock, Robert H.; Boersch-Supan, Axel; Cacioppo, John T., . . . Rowe, John. (2012). Differences in life expectancy due to race and educational differences are widening, and many may not catch up. *Health Affairs, 31*(8), 1803–1813. doi:10.1377/hlthaff.2011.0746

Olson, Kristina R. and Dweck, Carol S. (2008). A blueprint for social cognitive development. *Perspectives on Psychological Science, 3*(3), 193–202. doi:10.1111/j.1745-6924.2008.00074.x

Olson, Kristina R. and Dweck, Carol S. (2009). Social cognitive development: A new look. *Child Development Perspectives, 3*(1), 60–65. doi:10.1111/j.1750-8606.2008.00078.x

Olson, Sheryl L.; Lopez-Duran, Nestor; Lunkenheimer, Erika S.; Chang, Hyein and Sameroff, Arnold J. (2011). Individual differences in the development of early peer aggression: Integrating contributions of self-regulation, theory of mind, and parenting. *Development and Psychopathology, 23*(1), 253–266. doi:10.1017 /S0954579410000775

Olweus, Dan; Limber, Sue and Mahalic, Sharon F. (1999). *Bullying prevention program.* Boulder, CO: Center for the Study and Prevention of Violence, Institute of Behavioral Science, University of Colorado at Boulder.

Omariba, D. Walter Rasugu and Boyle, Michael H. (2007). Family structure and child mortality in sub-Saharan Africa: Cross-national effects of polygyny. *Journal of Marriage and Family, 69*(2), 528–543. doi:10.1111/j.1741-3737 .2007.00381.x

Ontai, Lenna L. and Thompson, Ross A. (2008). Attachment, parent-child discourse and theory-of-mind development. *Social Development, 17*(1), 47–60. doi:10.1111/j.1467 -9507.2007.00414.x

Oosterman, Mirjam; Schuengel, Carlo; Slot, N. Wim; Bullens, Ruud A. R. and Doreleijers, Theo A. H. (2007). Disruptions in foster care: A review and meta-analysis. *Children and Youth Services Review, 29*(1), 53–76. doi:10.1016/j .childyouth.2006.07.003

Oregon Public Health Division. (2013). Oregon's Death with Dignity Act–2012: Table 1. Characteristics and end-of-life care of 673 DWDA patients who have died from ingesting a lethal dose of medication as of January 14, 2013, by year, Oregon, 1998–2012. Portland, OR: Retrieved from http://public.health.oregon.gov/ ProviderPartnerResources/EvaluationResearch/ DeathwithDignityAct/Documents/year15.pdf.

Orlich, Donald C.; Harder, Robert J.; Callahan, Richard C.; Trevisan, Michael S. and Brown, Abbie H. (2009). *Teaching strategies: A guide to effective instruction* (9th ed.). Boston, MA: Cengage Learning.

Orth, Ulrich; Trzesniewski, Kali H. and Robins, Richard W. (2010). Self-esteem development from young adulthood to old age: A cohort-sequential longitudinal study. *Journal of Personality and Social Psychology, 98*(4), 645–658. doi:10.1037/a0018769

Osgood, D. Wayne; Ruth, Gretchen; Eccles, Jacquelynne S.; Jacobs, Janis E. and Barber, Bonnie L. (2005). Six paths to adulthood: Fast starters, parents without careers, educated partners, educated singles, working singles, and slow starters. In Richard A. Settersten, Frank F. Furstenberg and Rubén G. Rumbaut (Eds.), *On the frontier of adulthood: Theory, research, and public policy* (pp. 320–355). Chicago, IL: University of Chicago Press.

Osher, David; Bear, George G.; Sprague, Jeffrey R. and Doyle, Walter. (2010). How can we improve school discipline? *Educational Researcher, 39*(1), 48–58. doi:10.3102/0013189X09357618

Osorio, Snezana Nena. (2011). Reconsidering Kwashiorkor. *Topics in Clinical Nutrition, 26*(1), 10–13. doi:10.1097/TIN.0b013e318209e3b6

Ossher, Lynn; Flegal, Kristin E. and Lustig, Cindy. (2013). Everyday memory errors in older adults. *Aging, Neuropsychology, and Cognition: A Journal on Normal and Dysfunctional Development, 20*(2), 220–242. doi:10.1080/13825585.2012.690365

Ostfeld, Barbara M.; Esposito, Linda; Perl, Harold and Hegyi, Thomas. (2010). Concurrent risks in sudden infant death syndrome. *Pediatrics, 125*(3), 447–453. doi:10.1542/peds.2009-0038

Otheguy, Ricardo and Stern, Nancy. (2011). On so-called Spanglish. *International Journal of Bilingualism, 15*(1), 85–100. doi:10.1177/1367006910379298

Over, Harriet and Gattis, Merideth. (2010). Verbal imitation is based on intention understanding. *Cognitive Development, 25*(1), 46–55. doi:10.1016/j.cogdev.2009.06.004

Owen, Jesse and Fincham, Frank D. (2011). Effects of gender and psychosocial factors on "friends with benefits" relationships among young adults. *Archives of Sexual Behavior, 40*(2), 311–320. doi:10.1007/s10508-010-9611-6

Owen, Jesse; Fincham, Frank D. and Moore, Jon. (2011). Short-term prospective study of hooking up among college students. *Archives of Sexual Behavior, 40*(2), 331–341. doi:10.1007/s10508-010-9697-x

Owen-Kostelnik, Jessica; Reppucci, N. Dickon and Meyer, Jessica R. (2006). Testimony and interrogation of minors: Assumptions about maturity and morality. *American Psychologist, 61*(4), 286–304. doi:10.1037/0003-066x.61.4.286

Owens, Judith A.; Belon, Katherine and Moss, Patricia. (2010). Impact of delaying school start time on adolescent sleep, mood, and behavior. *Archives of Pediatrics & Adolescent Medicine, 164*(7), 608–614. doi:10.1001/archpediatrics.2010.96

Owsley, Cynthia. (2011). Aging and vision. *Vision Research, 51*(13), 1610–1622. doi:10.1016/j.visres.2010.10.020

Oyekale, Abayomi Samuel and Oyekale, Tolulope Olayemi. (2009). Do mothers' educational levels matter in child malnutrition and health outcomes in Gambia and Niger? *The Social Sciences, 4*(1), 118–127.

Oza-Frank, Reena and Narayan, K. M. Venkat. (2010). Overweight and diabetes prevalence among U.S. immigrants. *American Journal of Public Health, 100*(4), 661–668. doi:10.2105/ajph.2008.149492

Pace, Cecilia Serena; Zavattini, Giulio Cesare and D'Alessio, Maria. (2011). Continuity and discontinuity of attachment patterns: A short-term longitudinal pilot study using a sample of late-adopted children and their adoptive mothers. *Attachment & Human Development, 14*(1), 45–61. doi:10.1080/14616734.2012.636658

Padilla-Walker, Laura; Nelson, Larry; Madsen, Stephanie and Barry, Carolyn. (2008). The role of perceived parental knowledge on emerging adults' risk behaviors. *Journal of Youth and Adolescence, 37*(7), 847–859. doi:10.1007/s10964-007-9268-1

Pagán-Rodríguez, Ricardo. (2011). Self-employment and job satisfaction: evidence for older people with disabilities in Europe. *European Journal of Ageing, 8*(3), 177–187. doi:10.1007/s10433-011-0194-4

Pahwa, Rajesh and Lyons, Kelly E. (Eds.). (2013). *Handbook of Parkinson's disease* (5th ed.). Boca Raton, FL: CRC Press.

Paik, Anthony. (2011). Adolescent sexuality and the risk of marital dissolution. *Journal of Marriage and Family, 73*(2), 472–485. doi:10.1111/j.1741-3737.2010.00819.x

Palagi, Elisabetta. (2011). Playing at every age: Modalities and potential functions in non-human primates. In Anthony D. Pellegrini (Ed.), *The Oxford handbook of the development of play* (pp. 70–82). New York, NY: Oxford University Press.

Palm, Glen. (2013). Fathers and early literacy. In Jyotsna Pattnaik (Ed.), *Father involvement in young children's lives: A global analysis* (pp. 13–29). New York, NY: Springer.

Palmer, Nicholette D.; McDonough, Caitrin W.; Hicks, Pamela J.; Roh, Bong H.; Wing, Maria R.; An, S. Sandy, . . . Bowden, Donald W. (2012). A genome-wide association search for type 2 diabetes genes in African Americans. *PLoS ONE, 7*(1), e29202. doi:10.1371/journal.pone.0029202

Palmore, Erdman. (2005). Three decades of research on ageism. *Generations, 29*(1), 87–90.

Pardini, Matteo and Nichelli, Paolo F. (2009). Age-related decline in mentalizing skills across adult life span. *Experimental Aging Research, 35*(1), 98–106. doi:10.1080/03610730802545259

Park, Denise C. and Bischof, Gérard N. (2013). The aging mind: Neuroplasticity in response to cognitive training. *Dialogues in Clinical Neuroscience, 15*(1), 109–119.

Park, Denise C. and Reuter-Lorenz, Patricia. (2009). The adaptive brain: Aging and neurocognitive scaffolding. *Annual Review of Psychology, 60*, 173–196. doi:10.1146/annurev.psych.59.103006.093656

Park, D. J. J. and Congdon, Nathan G. (2004). Evidence for an "epidemic" of myopia. *Annals Academy of Medicine Singapore, 33*(1), 21–26.

Park, Hyun; Bothe, Denise; Holsinger, Eva; Kirchner, H. Lester; Olness, Karen and Mandalakas, Anna. (2011). The impact of nutritional status and longitudinal recovery of motor and cognitive milestones in internationally adopted children. *International Journal of Environmental Research and Public Health, 8*(1), 105–116. doi:10.3390/ijerph8010105

Park, Jong-Tae; Jang, Yoonsun; Park, Min Sun; Pae, Calvin; Park, Jinyi; Hu, Kyung-Seok, . . . Kim, Hee-Jin. (2011). The trend of body donation for education based on Korean social and religious culture. *Anatomical Sciences Education, 4*(1), 33–38. doi:10.1002/ase.198

Parke, Ross D. and Buriel, Raymond. (2006). Socialization in the family: Ethnic and ecological perspectives. In William Damon and Richard M. Lerner (Eds.), *Handbook of child psychology* (6th ed., Vol. 3, pp. 429–504). Hoboken, N.J.: Wiley.

Parker, Andrew. (2012). *Ethical problems and genetics practice.* New York, NY: Cambridge University Press.

Parker, Kim. (2012). *The boomerang generation: Feeling OK about living with Mom and Dad.* Washington, DC: Pew Research Center.

Parker, Susan W. and Nelson, Charles A. (2005). The impact of early institutional rearing on the ability to discriminate facial expressions of emotion: An event-related potential study. *Child Development, 76*(1), 54–72. doi:10.1111/j.1467-8624.2005.00829.x

Parladé, Meaghan V. and Iverson, Jana M. (2011). The interplay between language, gesture, and affect during communicative transition: A dynamic systems approach. *Developmental Psychology, 47*(3), 820–833. doi:10.1037/a0021811

Parris, Leandra; Varjas, Kris; Meyers, Joel and Cutts, Hayley. (2012). High school students' perceptions of coping with cyberbullying. *Youth & Society, 44*(2), 284–306. doi:10.1177/0044118x11398881

Parveen, Sahdia and Morrison, Val. (2009). Predictors of familism in the caregiver role: A pilot study. *Journal of Health Psychology, 14*(8), 1135–1143. doi:10.1177/1359105309343020

Pascarella, Ernest T. (2005). Cognitive impacts of the first year of college. In Robert S. Feldman (Ed.), *Improving the first year of college: Research and practice* (pp. 111–140). Mahwah, NJ: Erlbaum.

Pascarella, Ernest T. and Terenzini, Patrick T. (1991). *How college affects students: Findings and insights from twenty years of research.* San Francisco, CA: Jossey-Bass.

Passel, Jeffrey S. (2011). Demography of immigrant youth: Past, present, and future. *The Future of Children, 21*(1), 19–41.

Patel, Vimla L.; Arocha, José F. and Kaufman, David R. (1999). Expertise and tacit knowledge in medicine. In Robert J. Sternberg and Joseph A. Horvath (Eds.), *Tacit knowledge in professional practice: Researcher and practitioner perspectives* (pp. 75–99). Mahwah, NJ: Erlbaum.

Pathela, Preeti and Schillinger, Julia A. (2010). Sexual behaviors and sexual violence: Adolescents with opposite-, same-, or both-sex partners. *Pediatrics, 126*(5), 879–886. doi:10.1542 /peds.2010-0396

Patrick, Megan E. and Schulenberg, John E. (2011). How trajectories of reasons for alcohol use relate to trajectories of binge drinking: National panel data spanning late adolescence to early adulthood. *Developmental Psychology, 47*(2), 311–317. doi:10.1037/a0021939

Patton, George C.; Hemphill, Sheryl A.; Beyers, Jennifer M.; Bond, Lyndal; Toumbourou, John W.; McMorris, Barbara J. and Catalano, Richard F. (2007). Pubertal stage and deliberate self-harm in adolescents. *Journal of the American Academy of Child & Adolescent Psychiatry, 46*(4), 508–514. doi:10.1097 /chi.0b013e31803065c7

Pattwell, Siobhan S.; Casey, B. J. and Lee, Francis S. (2013). The teenage brain: Altered fear in humans and mice. *Current Directions in Psychological Science, 22*(2), 146–151. doi:10.1177 /0963721412471323

Paúl, Constança; Teixeira, Laetitia and Ribeiro, Oscar. (2012). What about happiness in later life? In Constantinos Phellas (Ed.), *Aging in European societies: Healthy aging in Europe* (pp. 83–96). New York, NY: Springer. doi:10.1007/978-1-4419-8345-9_6

Pauler, Florian M.; Barlow, Denise P. and Hudson, Quanah J. (2012). Mechanisms of long range silencing by imprinted macro non-coding RNAs. *Current Opinion in Genetics & Development, 22*(3), 283–289. doi:10.1016 /j.gde.2012.02.005

Pausch, Jai. (2012). *Dream new dreams: Reimagining my life after loss.* New York, NY: Crown Archetype.

Pausch, Randy (Producer). (2007). Randy Pausch last lecture: Achieving your childhood dreams. [Video] Retrieved from http://www .youtube.com/watch?v=ji5_MqicxSo

Pawlik, Amy J. and Kress, John P. (2013). Issues affecting the delivery of physical therapy services for individuals with critical illness. *Physical Therapy, 93*(2), 256–265. doi:10.2522/ ptj.20110445

Pearson, Barbara Zurer. (2008). *Raising a bilingual child: A step-by-step guide for parents.* New York, NY: Living Language.

Pedersen, Nancy L.; Spotts, Erica and Kato, Kenji. (2005). Genetic influences on midlife functioning. In Sherry L. Willis and Mike Martin (Eds.), *Middle adulthood: A lifespan perspective* (pp. 65–98). Thousand Oaks, CA: Sage.

Peffley, Mark and Hurwitz, Jon. (2010). *Justice in America: The separate realities of blacks and whites.* New York, NY: Cambridge University Press.

Pelham, William E., Jr. and Fabiano, Gregory A. (2008). Evidence-based psychosocial treatments for attention-deficit/ hyperactivity disorder. *Journal of Clinical Child & Adolescent Psychology, 37*(1), 184–214. doi:10.1080/15374410701818681

Pellegrini, Anthony D. (2009). Research and policy on children's play. *Child Development Perspectives, 3*(2), 131–136. doi:10.1111/j.1750 -8606.2009.00092.x

Pellegrini, Anthony D. (2011). Introduction. In Anthony D. Pellegrini (Ed.), *The Oxford handbook of the development of play* (pp. 3–6). New York, NY: Oxford University Press.

Pellegrini, Anthony D. (2013). Play. In Philip David Zelazo (Ed.), *The Oxford handbook of developmental psychology* (Vol. 2, pp. 276–299). New York, NY: Oxford University Press.

Pellis, Sergio M. and Pellis, Vivien C. (2011). Rough-and-tumble play: Training and using the social brain. In Anthony D. Pellegrini (Ed.), *The Oxford handbook of the development of play* (pp. 245–259). New York, NY: Oxford University Press.

Penningroth, Suzanna L. and Scott, Walter D. (2012). Age-related differences in goals: Testing predictions from selection, optimization, and compensation theory and socioemotional selectivity theory. *International Journal Of Aging & Human Development, 74*(2), 87–111. doi:10.2190 /AG.74.2.a

Penninx, Brenda W. J. H. and van den Brink, S. (2000). Aging and psychological stress. In George Fink (Ed.), *Encyclopedia of stress* (Vol. 1, pp. 104–110). San Diego: Academic Press.

Peper, Jiska S. and Dahl, Ronald E. (2013). The teenage brain: Surging hormones— brain-behavior interactions during puberty. *Current Directions in Psychological Science, 22*(2), 134–139. doi:10.1177/0963721412473755

Pepler, Debra; Craig, Wendy; Yuile, Amy and Connolly, Jennifer. (2004). Girls who bully: A developmental and relational perspective. In Martha Putallaz and Karen L. Bierman (Eds.), *Aggression, antisocial behavior, and violence among girls: A developmental perspective* (pp. 90–109). New York, NY: Guilford Press.

Pereira, Vera; Faísca, Luís and de Sá-Saraiva, Rodrigo. (2012). Immortality of the soul as an intuitive idea: Towards a psychological explanation of the origins of afterlife beliefs. *Journal of Cognition and Culture, 12*(1–2), 101–127. doi:10.1163 /156853712X633956

Perez, L.; Helm, L.; Sherzai, A. Dean; Jaceldo-Siegl, K. and Sherzai, A. (2012). Nutrition and vascular dementia. *The Journal Of Nutrition, Health & Aging, 16*(4), 319–324. doi:10.1007/s12603-012-0042-z

Perls, Thomas T. (2008). Centenarians and genetics. In Catherine Y. Read, Robert C. Green and Michael A. Smyer (Eds.), *Aging, biotechnology, and the future* (pp. 89–99). Baltimore, MD: Johns Hopkins University.

Perner, Josef. (2000). Communication and representation: Why mentalistic reasoning is a lifelong endeavour. In Peter Mitchell and Kevin John Riggs (Eds.), *Children's reasoning and the mind* (pp. 367–401). Hove, UK: Psychology Press.

Peron, Emily P. and Ruby, Christine M. (2011–2012, Winter). A primer on medication use in older adults for the non-clinician. *Generations, 35*(4), 12–18.

Perry, William G., Jr. (1981). Cognitive and ethical growth: The making of meaning. In Arthur Chickering (Ed.), *The modern American college: Responding to the new realities of diverse students and a changing society* (pp. 76–116). San Francisco, CA: Jossey-Bass.

Perry, William G., Jr. (1999). *Forms of intellectual and ethical development in the college years: A scheme.* San Francisco, CA: Jossey-Bass.

Persaud, Trivedi V. N.; Chudley, Albert E. and Skalko, Richard G. (1985). *Basic concepts in teratology.* New York, NY: Liss.

Pesta, Bryan J.; Bertsch, Sharon; McDaniel, Michael A.; Mahoney, Christine B. and Poznan-ski, Peter J. (2012). Differential epidemiology: IQ, neuroticism, and chronic disease by the 50 U.S. States. *Journal of Marriage and Family, 74*(2), 107–114. doi:10.1016/j.intell .2012.01.011

Peters, Ellen; Dieckmann, Nathan F. and Weller, Joshua. (2011). Age differences in complex decision making. In K. Warner Schaie and Sherry L. Willis (Eds.), *Handbook of the psychology of aging* (7th ed., pp. 133–151). San Diego, CA: Academic Press. doi: 10.1016/B978-0-12 -380882-0.00009-7

Petersen, Inge; Martinussen, Torben; McGue, Matthew; Bingley, Paul and Christensen, Kaare. (2011). Lower marriage and divorce rates among twins than among singletons in Danish birth cohorts 1940–1964. *Twin Research and Human Genetics, 14*(2), 150–157. doi:10.1375 /twin.14.2.150

Peterson, Jane W. and Sterling, Yvonne M. (2009). Children's perceptions of asthma: African American children use metaphors to make sense of asthma. *Journal of Pediatric Health Care, 23*(2), 93–100. doi:10.1016/j.pedhc.2007.10.002

Pew Forum on Religion & Public Life. (2012, July 31). *Two-thirds of democrats now support gay marriage.* Washington, DC: Pew Research Center.

Pew Research Center. (2007, July 1). *As marriage and parenthood drift apart, public is concerned about social impact: Generation gap in values, behaviors.* Washington, DC: Pew Research Center.

Pew Research Center. (2009, June 29). *Growing old in America: Expectations vs. reality.* Washington, DC: Pew Research Center.

Pew Research Center. (2009, October 9). *Majority continues to support civil unions.* Washington, DC: Pew Research Center.

Pew Research Center. (2012, April 11). *What the public knows about the political parties: Pew Research News IQ quiz.*

Pew Research Center. (2013, August 6). *How long do you want to live? Washington, DC: Pew Research Center.*

Pew Research Center. (2013, March 13–17). *March 2013 political survey.* Washington, DC: Pew Research Center.

Pew Research Center. (2013, March 20). *Growing support for gay marriage: Changed minds and changing demographics.* Washington, DC: Pew Research Center.

Peyser, James A. (2011). Unlocking the secrets of high-performing charters. *EducationNext, 11*(4), 36–43.

Pfeifer, Jennifer H.; Masten, Carrie L.; Moore, William E.; Oswald, Tasha M.; Mazziotta, John C.; Iacoboni, Marco and Dapretto, Mirella. (2011). Entering adolescence: Resistance to peer influence, risky behavior, and neural changes in emotion reactivity. *Neuron, 69*(5), 1029–1036. doi:10.1016/j.neuron.2011.02.019

Pfeiffer, Ronald E. and Bodis-Wollner, Ivan (Eds.). (2012). *Parkinson's disease and nonmotor dysfunction.* New York, NY: Springer.

Phillips, Deborah A.; Fox, Nathan A. and Gunnar, Megan R. (2011). Same place, different experiences: Bringing individual differences to research in child care. *Child Development Perspectives, 5*(1), 44–49. doi:10.1111/j.1750-8606.2010.00155.x

Phillips, Deborah A.; Gormley, William T., Jr. and Lowenstein, Amy E. (2009). Inside the pre-kindergarten door: Classroom climate and instructional time allocation in Tulsa's pre-K programs. *Early Childhood Research Quarterly, 24*(3), 213–362. doi:10.1016/j.ecresq.2009.05.002

Phillips, Mary L. (2010). Coming of age? Neuroimaging biomarkers in youth. *American Journal of Psychiatry, 167*(1), 4–7. doi:10.1176/appi.ajp.2009.09101546

Phillips, Tommy M. and Pittman, Joe F. (2007). Adolescent psychological well-being by identity style. *Journal of Adolescence, 30*(6), 1021–1034. doi:10.1016/j.adolescence.2007.03.002

Phillipson, Chris. (2013). Ageing. Cambridge, UK: Polity Press.

Phillipson, Sivanes and Phillipson, Shane N. (2007). Academic expectations, belief of ability, and involvement by parents as predictors of child achievement: A cross-cultural comparison. *Educational Psychology: An International Journal of Experimental Educational Psychology, 27*(3), 329–348. doi:10.1080/01443410601104130

Piaget, Jean. (1932). *The moral judgment of the child.* London, UK: K. Paul, Trench, Trubner & Co.

Piaget, Jean. (1952b). *The origins of intelligence in children* (M. Cook, Trans.). Oxford, UK: International Universities Press.

Piaget, Jean. (1954). *The construction of reality in the child.* New York, NY: Basic Books.

Piaget, Jean. (1962). *Play, dreams and imitation in childhood.* New York, NY: Norton.

Piaget, Jean. (1972). *The psychology of intelligence.* Totowa, NJ: Littlefield.

Piaget, Jean. (1997). *The moral judgment of the child.* New York, NY: Simon and Schuster.

Piaget, Jean and Inhelder, Bärbel. (1969). *The psychology of the child.* New York, NY: Basic Books.

Piaget, Jean; Voelin-Liambey, Daphne and Berthoud-Papandropoulou, Ioanna. (2001). Problems of class inclusion and logical implication (Robert L. Campbell, Trans.). In Robert L. Campell (Ed.), *Studies in reflecting abstraction* (pp. 105–137). Hove, UK: Psychology Press.

Pianta, Robert C.; Barnett, W. Steven; Burchinal, Margaret and Thornburg, Kathy R. (2009). The effects of preschool education: What we know, how public policy is or is not aligned with the evidence base, and what we need to know. *Psychological Science in the Public Interest, 10*(2), 49–88. doi:10.1177/1529100610381908

Piazza, Manuela; Facoetti, Andrea; Trussardi, Anna Noemi; Berteletti, Ilaria; Conte, Stefano; Lucangeli, Daniela, . . . Zorzi, Marco. (2010). Developmental trajectory of number acuity reveals a severe impairment in developmental dyscalculia. *Cognition, 116*(1), 33–41. doi:10.1016/j.cognition.2010.03.012

Pietrantonio, Anna Marie; Wright, Elise; Gibson, Kathleen N.; Alldred, Tracy; Jacobson, Dustin and Niec, Anne. (2013). Mandatory reporting of child abuse and neglect: Crafting a positive process for health professionals and caregivers. *Child Abuse & Neglect, 37*(2–3), 102–109. doi:10.1016/j.chiabu.2012.12.007

Pietrefesa, Ashley S. and Evans, David W. (2007). Affective and neuropsychological correlates of children's rituals and compulsive-like behaviors: Continuities and discontinuities with obsessive-compulsive disorder. *Brain and Cognition, 65*(1), 36–46. doi:10.1016/j.bandc.2006.02.007

Pignotti, Maria Serenella. (2010). The definition of human viability: A historical perspective. *Acta Pædiatrica, 99*(1), 33–36. doi:10.1111/j.1651-2227.2009.01524.x

Pilkington, Pamela D.; Windsor, Tim D. and Crisp, Dimity A. (2012). Volunteering and subjective well-being in midlife and older adults: The role of supportive social networks. *The Journals of Gerontology Series B: Psychological Sciences and Social Sciences, 67B*(2), 249–260. doi:10.1093/geronb/gbr154

Pin, Tamis; Eldridge, Beverley and Galea, Mary P. (2007). A review of the effects of sleep position, play position, and equipment use on motor development in infants. *Developmental Medicine & Child Neurology, 49*(11), 858–867. doi:10.1111/j.1469-8749.2007.00858.x

Pinborg, Anja; Loft, Anne and Nyboe Andersen, Anders. (2004). Neonatal outcome in a Danish national cohort of 8602 children born after in vitro fertilization or intracytoplasmic sperm injection: The role of twin pregnancy. *Acta Obstetricia et Gynecologica Scandinavica, 83*(11), 1071–1078. doi:10.1111/j.0001-6349.2004.00476.x

Pinheiro, Paulo Sérgio. (2006). *World report on violence against children.* Geneva, Switzerland: United Nations.

Pinker, Steven. (2007). *The stuff of thought: Language as a window into human nature.* New York, NY: Viking.

Pinker, Steven. (2011). *The better angels of our nature: Why violence has declined.* New York, NY: Viking.

Pinquart, Martin and Silbereisen, Rainer K. (2006). Socioemotional selectivity in cancer patients. *Psychology and Aging, 21*(2), 419–423. doi:10.1037/0882-7974.21.2.419

Pinquart, Martin and Sörensen, Silvia. (2011). Spouses, adult children, and children-in-law as caregivers of older adults: A meta-analytic comparison. *Psychology and Aging, 26*(1), 1–14. doi:10.1037/a0021863

Piotrowski, Martin. (2008). Migrant remittances and household division: The case of Nang Rong, Thailand. *Journal of Marriage and Family, 70*(4), 1074–1087. doi:10.1111/j.1741-3737.2008.00547.x

PISA. (2007). *Highlights from PISA 2006: Performance of U.S. 15-year-old students in science and mathematics literacy in an international context.* Washington, DC: Institute of Education Sciences, National Center for Education Statistics, U.S. Department of Education.NCES 2008–016.

PISA. (2009). *Learning mathematics for life: A perspective from PISA.* Paris: OECD. doi:10.1787/9789264075009-en

Pitskhelauri, G. Z. (1982). *The longliving of Soviet Georgia.* New York, NY: Human Sciences Press.

Plassman, Brenda L.; Langa, Kenneth M.; Fisher, Gwenith G.; Heeringa, Steven G.; Weir, David R.; Ofstedal, Mary Beth, . . . Wallace, R. B. (2007). Prevalence of dementia in the United States: The Aging, Demographics, and Memory Study. *Neuroepidemiology, 29*(1–2), 125–132. doi:10.1159/000109998

Plaut, Victoria C.; Thomas, Kecia M. and Goren, Matt J. (2009). Is multiculturalism or color blindness better for minorities? *Psychological Science, 20*(4), 444–446. doi:10.1111/j.1467-9280.2009.02318.x

Plomin, Robert; DeFries, John C.; Knopik, Valerie S. and Neiderhiser, Jenae M. (2013). *Behavioral genetics.* New York, NY: Worth Publishers.

Plows, Alexandra. (2011). *Debating human genetics: Contemporary issues in public policy and ethics.* New York, NY: Routledge.

Pluess, Michael and Belsky, Jay. (2009). Differential susceptibility to rearing experience: The case of childcare. *Journal of Child Psychology and Psychiatry and Allied Disciplines, 50*(4), 396–404. doi:10.1111/j.1469-7610.2008.01992.x

Pluess, Michael and Belsky, Jay. (2010). Differential susceptibility to parenting and quality child care. *Developmental Psychology, 46*(2), 379–390. doi:10.1037/a0015203

Pogrebin, Abigail. (2009). *One and the same: My life as an identical twin and what I've learned about everyone's struggle to be singular.* New York, NY: Doubleday.

Poldrack, Russell A.; Wagner, Anthony D.; Gotlib, Ian H. and Hamilton, J. Paul. (2008). Neuroimaging and depression: Current status and unresolved issues. *Current Directions in Psychological Science, 17*(2), 159–163. doi:10.1111/j.1467-8721.2008.00567.x

Polesel, John; Dulfer, Nicky and Turnbull, Malcolm. (2012). *The experience of education: The impacts of high stakes testing on school students and their families.* Literature review. Rydalmere NSW, Australia: The Whitlam Institute within the University of Western Sydney.

Pollet, Susan L. (2010). Still a patchwork quilt: A nationwide survey of state laws regarding stepparent rights and obligations. *Family Court Review, 48*(3), 528–540. doi:10.1111/j.1744-1617.2010.01327.x

Poon, Leonard W. (2008). What can we learn from centenarians? In Catherine Y. Read, Robert C. Green and Michael A. Smyer (Eds.), *Aging, biotechnology, and the future* (pp. 100–110). Baltimore, MD: Johns Hopkins University.

Popham, Lauren E.; Kennison, Shelia M. and Bradley, Kristopher I. (2011b). Ageism, sensation-seeking, and risk-taking behavior in young adults. *Current Psychology, 30*(2), 184–193. doi:10.1007/s12144-011-9107-0

Posner, Michael I.; Rothbart, Mary K.; Sheese, Brad E. and Tang, Yiyuan. (2007). The anterior cingulate gyrus and the mechanism of self-regulation. *Cognitive, Affective & Behavioral Neuroscience, 7*(4), 391–395. doi:10.3758/CABN.7.4.391

Potocnik, Kristina and Sonnentag, Sabine. (2013). A longitudinal study of well-being in older workers and retirees: The role of engaging in different types of activities. *Journal of Occupational and Organizational Psychology, 86*(4), 497–521. doi:10.1111/joop.12003

Potter, Daniel. (2010). Psychosocial well-being and the relationship between divorce and children's academic achievement. *Journal of Marriage and Family, 72*(4), 933–946. doi:10.1111/j.1741-3737.2010.00740.x

Pottinger, Audrey M. and Palmer, Tiffany. (2013). Whither IVF assisted birth or spontaneous conception? Parenting anxiety, styles and child development in Jamaican families. *Journal of Reproductive and Infant Psychology, 31*(2), 148–159. doi:10.1080/02646838.2012.762085

Poulin, François; Denault, Anne-Sophie and Pedersen, Sara. (2011). Longitudinal associations between other-sex friendships and substance use in adolescence. *Journal of Research on Adolescence, 21*(4), 776–788. doi:10.1111/j.1532-7795.2011.00736.x

Poulin-Dubois, Diane and Chow, Virginia. (2009). The effect of a looker's past reliability on infants' reasoning about beliefs. *Developmental Psychology, 45*(6), 1576–1582. doi:10.1037/a0016715

Poulsen, Pernille; Esteller, Manel; Vaag, Allan and Fraga, Mario F. (2007). The epigenetic basis of twin discordance in age-related diseases. *Pediatric Research, 61*(5), 38R–42R. doi:10.1203/pdr.0b013e31803c7b98

Powell, Kendall. (2006). Neurodevelopment: How does the teenage brain work? *Nature, 442*, 865–867. doi:10.1038/442865a

Powell, Shaun; Langlands, Stephanie and Dodd, Chris. (2011). Feeding children's desires? Child and parental perceptions of food promotion to the "under 8s". *Young Consumers: Insight and Ideas for Responsible Marketers, 12*(2), 96–109. doi:10.1108/17473611111141560

Pozzoli, Tiziana and Gini, Gianluca. (2013). Why do bystanders of bullying help or not? A multidimensional model. *The Journal of Early Adolescence, 33*(3), 315–340. doi:10.1177/0272431612440172

Prado, Carlos G. (2008). *Choosing to die: Elective death and multiculturalism.* New York, NY: Cambridge University Press.

Pratt, Michael W.; Norris, Joan E.; Cressman, Kate; Lawford, Heather and Hebblethwaite, Shannon. (2008). Parents' stories of grandparenting concerns in the three-generational family: Generativity, optimism, and forgiveness. *Journal of Personality, 76*(3), 581–604. doi:10.1111/j.1467-6494.2008.00497.x

Pressley, Michael and Hilden, Katherine. (2006). Cognitive strategies: Production deficiencies and successful strategy instruction everywhere. In Deanna Kuhn and Robert S. Siegler (Eds.), *Handbook of child psychology* (6th ed., Vol. 2, pp. 511–556). Hoboken, NJ: Wiley.

Preston, Tom and Kelly, Michael. (2006). A medical ethics assessment of the case of Terri Schiavo. *Death Studies, 30*(2), 121–133. doi:10.1080/07481180500455608

Price, Margaret "Pegi" S. (2009). *The special needs child and divorce: A practical guide to evaluating and handling cases.* Chicago, IL: American Bar Association, Section of Family Law.

Priess, Heather A.; Lindberg, Sara M. and Hyde, Janet Shibley. (2009). Adolescent gender-role identity and mental health: Gender intensification revisited. *Child Development, 80*(5), 1531–1544. doi:10.1111/j.1467-8624.2009.01349.x

Proulx, Christine M.; Helms, Heather M. and Buehler, Cheryl. (2007). Marital quality and personal well-being: A meta-analysis. *Journal of Marriage and Family, 69*(3), 576–593. doi:10.1111/j.1741-3737.2007.00393.x

Provasnik, Stephen; Kastberg, David; Ferraro, David; Lemanski, Nita; Roey, Stephen and Jenkins, Frank. (2012). *Highlights from TIMSS 2011: Mathematics and science achievement of U.S. fourth- and eighth-grade students in an international context.* Washington, DC: National Center for Education Statistics, Institute of Education Sciences, U.S. Department of Education.

Pryor, John H.; Eagan, Kevin; Palucki Blake, Laura; Hurtado, Sylvia; Berdan, Jennifer and Case, Matthew H. (2012). *The American freshman: National norms fall 2012.* Los Angeles, CA: Higher Education Research Institute, UCLA.

Puccioni, Olga and Vallesi, Antonino. (2012). Conflict resolution and adaptation in normal aging: The role of verbal intelligence and cognitive reserve. *Psychology and Aging, 27*(4), 1018–1026. doi:10.1037/a0029106

Puhl, Rebecca M. and Heuer, Chelsea A. (2010). Obesity stigma: Important considerations for public health. *American Journal of Public Health, 100*(6), 1019–1028. doi:10.2105/AJPH.2009.159491

Pulvermüller, Friedemann and Fadiga, Luciano. (2010). Active perception: Sensorimotor circuits as a cortical basis for language. *Nature Reviews Neuroscience, 11*, 351–360. doi:10.1038/nrn2811

Puri, Sunita; Adams, Vincanne; Ivey, Susan and Nachtigall, Robert D. (2011). "There is such a thing as too many daughters, but not too many sons": A qualitative study of son preference and fetal sex selection among Indian immigrants in the United States. *Social Science & Medicine, 72*(7), 1169–1176. doi:10.1016/j.socscimed.2011.01.027

Puri, Sunita and Nachtigall, Robert D. (2010). The ethics of sex selection: A comparison of the attitudes and experiences of primary care physicians and physician providers of clinical sex selection services. *Fertility and Sterility, 93*(7), 2107–2114. doi:10.1016/j.fertnstert.2009.02.053

Qin, Lili; Pomerantz, Eva M. and Wang, Qian. (2009). Are gains in decision-making autonomy during early adolescence beneficial for emotional functioning? *The case of the United States and China. Child Development, 80*(6), 1705–1721. doi:10.1111/j.1467-8624.2009.01363.x

Qiu, Chengxuan; von Strauss, Eva; Bäckman, Lars; Winblad, Bengt and Fratiglioni, Laura. (2013). Twenty-year changes in dementia occurrence suggest decreasing incidence in central Stockholm, Sweden. *Neurology, 80*(20), 1888–1894. doi:10.1212/WNL.0b013e318292a2f9

Qualls, Sara Honn and Kasl-Godley, Julia E. (Eds.). (2010). *End-of-life issues, grief, and bereavement: What clinicians need to know.* Hoboken, NJ: Wiley.

Quas, Jodi A.; Bauer, Amy and Boyce, W. Thomas. (2004). Physiological reactivity, social support, and memory in early childhood. *Child Development, 75*(3), 797–814. doi:10.1111/j.1467-8624.2004.00707.x

Quindlen, Anna. (2012). *Lots of candles, plenty of cake.* New York, NY: Random House.

Raaijmakers, Quinten A. W.; Engels, Rutger C. M. E. and Van Hoof, Anne. (2005). Delinquency and moral reasoning in adolescence and young adulthood. *International Journal of Behavioral Development, 29*(3), 247–258. doi:10.1177/01650250544000035

Rabkin, Nick and Hedberg, Eric Christopher. (2011). *Arts education in America: What the declines mean for arts participation.* Washington, DC: National Endowment for the Arts.

Race Ethnicity and Genetics Working Group. (2005). The use of racial, ethnic, and ancestral categories in human genetics research.

American Journal of Human Genetics, 77(4), 519–532. doi:10.1086/491747

Rachner, Tilman D.; Khosla, Sundeep and Hofbauer, Lorenz C. (2011). Osteoporosis: Now and the future. *The Lancet, 377*(9773), 1276–1287. doi:10.1016/S0140-6736(10)62349-5

Rajaratnam, Julie Knoll; Marcus, Jake R.; Flaxman, Abraham D.; Wang, Haidong; Levin-Rector, Alison; Dwyer, Laura, . . . Murray, Christopher J. L. (2010). Neonatal, postneonatal, childhood, and under-5 mortality for 187 countries, 1970–2010: A systematic analysis of progress towards Millennium Development Goal 4. *The Lancet, 375*(9730), 1988–2008. doi:10.1016/S0140-6736(10)60703-9

Ram, Nilam; Gerstorf, Denis; Lindenberger, Ulman and Smith, Jacqui. (2011). Developmental change and intraindividual variability: Relating cognitive aging to cognitive plasticity, cardiovascular lability, and emotional diversity. *Psychology and Aging, 26*(2), 363–371. doi:10.1037/a0021500

Ramakrishnan, Usha; Goldenberg, Tamar and Allen, Lindsay H. (2011). Do multiple micronutrient interventions improve child health, growth, and development? *Journal of Nutrition, 141*(11), 2066–2075. doi:10.3945/jn.111.146845

Ramani, Geetha B.; Brownell, Celia A. and Campbell, Susan B. (2010). Positive and negative peer interaction in 3- and 4-year-olds in relation to regulation and dysregulation. *Journal of Genetic Psychology, 171*(3), 218–250. doi:10.1080/00221320903300353

Ramón, Rosa; Ballester, Ferran; Aguinagalde, Xabier; Amurrio, Ascensión; Vioque, Jesús; Lacasaña, Marina, . . . Iñiguez, Carmen. (2009). Fish consumption during pregnancy, prenatal mercury exposure, and anthropometric measures at birth in a prospective mother-infant cohort study in Spain. *American Journal of Clinical Nutrition, 90*(4), 1047–1055. doi:10.3945/ajcn.2009.27944

Ramscar, Michael and Dye, Melody. (2011). Learning language from the input: Why innate constraints can't explain noun compounding. *Cognitive Psychology, 62*(1), 1–40. doi:10.1016/j.cogpsych.2010.10.001

Ramscar, Michael; Dye, Melody; Gustafson, Jessica W. and Klein, Joseph. (2013). Dual routes to cognitive flexibility: Learning and response-conflict resolution in the dimensional change card sort task. *Child Development, 84*(4), 1308–1323. doi:10.1111/cdev.12044

Rankin, Jane L.; Lane, David J.; Gibbons, Frederick X. and Gerrard, Meg. (2004). Adolescent self-consciousness: Longitudinal age changes and gender differences in two cohorts. *Journal of Research on Adolescence, 14*(1), 1–21. doi:10.1111/j.1532-7795.2004.01401001.x

Raspberry, Kelly Amanda and Skinner, Debra. (2011). Negotiating desires and options: How mothers who carry the fragile X gene experience reproductive decisions. *Social Science & Medicine, 72*(6), 992–998. doi:10.1016/j.socscimed.2011.01.010

Raus, Kasper; Sterckx, Sigrid and Mortier, Freddy. (2011). Is continuous sedation at the end of life an ethically preferable alternative to physician-assisted suicide? *The American Journal of Bioethics, 11*(6), 32–40. doi:10.1080/15265161.2011.577510

Ravizza, Kenneth. (2007). Peak experiences in sport. In Daniel Smith and Michael Bar-Eli (Eds.), *Essential readings in sport and exercise psychology* (pp. 122–125). Champaign, IL: Human Kinetics.

Raymond, Neil; Beer, Charlotte; Glazebrook, Cristine and Sayal, Kapil. (2009). Pregnant women's attitudes towards alcohol consumption. *BMC Public Health, 9,* 175–183. doi:10.1186/1471-2458-9-175

Reche, Marta; Valbuena, Teresa; Fiandor, Ana; Padial, Antonia; Quirce, Santiago and Pascual, Cristina. (2011). Induction of tolerance in children with food allergy. *Current Nutrition & Food Science, 7*(1), 33–39. doi:10.2174/157340111794941085

Reddy, Marpadga A. and Natarajan, Rama. (2013). Role of epigenetic mechanisms in the vascular complications of diabetes. In Tapas K. Kundu (Ed.), *Epigenetics: Development and disease* (pp. 435–454). New York, NY: Springer. doi:10.1007/978-94-007-4525-4_19

Reece, E. Albert and Hobbins, John C. (Eds.). (2007). *Handbook of clinical obstetrics: The fetus & mother handbook* (2nd ed.). Malden, MA: Blackwell.

Reeskens, Tim and Wright, Matthew. (2011). Subjective well-being and national satisfaction: Taking seriously the "Proud of what?" question. *Psychological Science, 22*(11), 1460–1462. doi:10.1177/0956797611419673

Reich, John W.; Zautra, Alex J. and Hall, John Stuart (Eds.). (2010). *Handbook of adult resilience.* New York, NY: Guilford Press.

Reichow, Brian; Volkmar, Fred R. and Bloch, Michael H. (2013). Systematic review and meta-analysis of pharmacological treatment of the symptoms of attention-deficit/hyperactivity disorder in children with pervasive developmental disorder. *Journal of Autism and Developmental Disorders, 43*(10), 2435–2441. doi:10.1007/s10803-013-1793-z

Rendell, Luke; Fogarty, Laurel; Hoppitt, William J. E.; Morgan, Thomas J. H.; Webster, Mike M. and Laland, Kevin N. (2011). Cognitive culture: theoretical and empirical insights into social learning strategies. *Trends in Cognitive Sciences, 15*(2), 68–76. doi:10.1016/j.tics.2010.12.002

Renk, Kimberly; Donnelly, Reesa; McKinney, Cliff and Agliata, Allison Kanter. (2006). The development of gender identity: Timetables and influences. In Kam-Shing Yip (Ed.), *Psychology of gender identity: An international perspective* (pp. 49–68). Hauppauge, NY: Nova Science.

Rentfrow, Peter Jason. (2010). Statewide differences in personality: Toward a psychological geography of the United States. *American Psychologist, 65*(6), 548–558. doi:10.1037/a0018194

Rentfrow, Peter J.; Gosling, Samuel D. and Potter, Jeff. (2008). A theory of the emergence, persistence, and expression of geographic variation in psychological characteristics. *Perspectives on Psychological Science, 3*(5), 339–369. doi:10.1111/j.1745-6924.2008.00084.x

Resnick, Barbara; Gwyther, Lisa P. and Roberto, Karen A. (Eds.). (2011). *Resilience in aging: Concepts, research, and outcomes.* New York, NY: Springer.

Rest, James. (1993). Research on moral judgment in college students. In Andrew Garrod (Ed.), *Approaches to moral development: New research and emerging themes* (pp. 201–211). New York, NY: Teachers College Press.

Rest, James; Narvaez, Darcia; Bebeau, Muriel J. and Thoma, Stephen J. (1999). *Postconventional moral thinking: A neo-Kohlbergian approach.* New York, NY: Psychology Press.

Reuter-Lorenz, Patricia A. and Sylvester, Ching-Yune C. (2005). The cognitive neuroscience of working memory and aging. In Roberto Cabeza, Lars Nyberg and Denise C. Park (Eds.), *Cognitive neuroscience of aging: Linking cognitive and cerebral aging* (pp. 186–217). New York, NY: Oxford University Press.

Reutskaja, Elena and Hogarth, Robin M. (2009). Satisfaction in choice as a function of the number of alternatives: When "goods satiate". *Psychology and Marketing, 26*(3), 197–203. doi:10.1002/mar.20268

Reynolds, Arthur J. (2000). *Success in early intervention: The Chicago child-parent centers.* Lincoln, NE: University of Nebraska Press.

Reynolds, Arthur J. and Ou, Suh-Ruu. (2011). Paths of effects from preschool to adult well-being: A confirmatory analysis of the child-parent center program. *Child Development, 82*(2), 555–582. doi:10.1111/j.1467-8624.2010.01562.x

Reynolds, Arthur J.; Temple, Judy A.; White, Barry A. B.; Ou, Suh-Ruu and Robertson, Dylan L. (2011). Age 26 cost–benefit analysis of the child-parent center early education program. *Child Development, 82*(1), 379–404. doi:10.1111/j.1467-8624.2010.01563.x

Rhee, Kyung. (2008). Childhood overweight and the relationship between parent behaviors, parenting style, and family functioning. *Annals of the American Academy of Political and Social Science, 615*(1), 11–37. doi:10.1177/0002716207308400

Riccio, Cynthia A. and Rodriguez, Olga L. (2007). Integration of psychological assessment approaches in school psychology. *Psychology in the Schools, 44*(3), 243–255. doi:10.1002/pits.20220

Riccio, Cynthia A.; Sullivan, Jeremy R. and Cohen, Morris J. (2010). *Neuropsychological assessment and intervention for childhood and adolescent disorders.* Hoboken, NJ: Wiley.

Rice, Charles L. and Cunningham, David A. (2002). Aging of the neuromuscular system: Influences of gender and physical activity. In Roy J. Shephard (Ed.), *Gender, physical activity, and aging* (pp. 121–150). Boca Raton, FL: CRC Press.

Rich, Motoko. (2013, April 11). *Texas considers backtracking on testing.* The New York Times, p. 12.

Richardson, Rick and Hayne, Harlene. (2007). You can't take it with you: The translation of memory across development. *Current Directions in Psychological Science*, 16(4), 223–227. doi:10.1111/j.1467-8721.2007.00508.x

Richert, Rebekah A.; Robb, Michael B. and Smith, Erin I. (2011). Media as social partners: The social nature of young children's learning from screen media. *Child Development*, 82(1), 82–95. doi:10.1111/j.1467-8624.2010.01542.x

Riegel, Klaus F. (1975). Toward a dialectical theory of development. *Human Development*, 18(1–2), 50–64. doi:10.1159/000271475

Riglin, Lucy; Frederickson, Norah; Shelton, Katherine H. and Rice, Frances. (2013). A longitudinal study of psychological functioning and academic attainment at the transition to secondary school. *Journal of Adolescence*, 36(3), 507–517. doi:10.1016/j.adolescence.2013.03.002

Riley, Edward P.; Infante, M. Alejandra and Warren, Kenneth R. (2011). Fetal alcohol spectrum disorders: An overview. *Neuropsychology Review*, 21(2), 73–80. doi:10.1007/s11065-011-9166-x

Riordan, Jan (Ed.). (2005). *Breastfeeding and human lactation* (3rd ed.). Sudbury, MA: Jones and Bartlett.

Riordan, Jan and Wambach, Karen (Eds.). (2009). *Breastfeeding and human lactation* (4th ed.). Sudbury, MA: Jones and Bartlett Publishers.

Ritchie, Rachel A.; Meca, Alan; Madrazo, Vanessa L.; Schwartz, Seth J.; Hardy, Sam A.; Zamboanga, Byron L., . . . Lee, Richard M. (2013). Identity dimensions and related processes in emerging adulthood: Helpful or harmful? *Journal of Clinical Psychology*, 69(4), 415–432. doi:10.1002/jclp.21960

Rivas-Drake, Deborah and Mooney, Margarita. (2009). Neither colorblind nor oppositional: Perceived minority status and trajectories of academic adjustment among Latinos in elite higher education. *Developmental Psychology*, 45(3), 642–651. doi:10.1037/a0014135

Rivers, Ian; Poteat, V. Paul; Noret, Nathalie and Ashurst, Nigel. (2009). Observing bullying at school: The mental health implications of witness status. *School Psychology Quarterly*, 24(4), 211–223. doi:10.1037/a0018164

Rix, Sara E. (2011). Employment and aging. In Robert H. Binstock and Linda K. George (Eds.), *Handbook of aging and the social sciences* (7th ed., pp. 193–206). San Diego, CA: Academic Press. doi:10.1016/B978-0-12-380880-6.00014-9

Robelen, Erik W. (2011). *More students enrolling in mandarin chinese*. Education Week, 30(27), 5.

Robert, Stephanie A.; Cherepanov, Dasha; Palta, Mari; Dunham, Nancy Cross; Feeny, David and Fryback, Dennis G. (2009). Socioeconomic status and age variations in health-related quality of life: Results from the national health measurement study. *The Journals of Gerontology Series B: Psychological Sciences and Social Sciences*, 64B(3), 378–389. doi:10.1093/geronb/gbp012

Roberts, Leslie. (2013). The art of eradicating polio. *Science*, 342(6154), 28–35. doi:10.1126/science.342.6154.28

Roberts, Richard D. and Lipnevich, Anastasiya A. (2012). From general intelligence to multiple intelligences: Meanings, models, and measures. In Karen R. Harris, Steve Graham and Tim Urdan (Eds.), *APA educational psychology handbook* (Vol. 2, pp. 33–57). Washington, DC: American Psychological Association. doi:10.1037/13274-002

Roberts, Soraya. (2010, January 1). *Travis Pastrana breaks world record for longest rally car jump on New Year's Eve*. New York Daily News.

Robins, Richard W.; Trzesniewski, Kali H. and Donnellan, M. Brent. (2012). *A brief primer on self-esteem*. Prevention Researcher, 19(2), 3–7.

Robinson, Oliver C.; Demetre, James D. and Corney, Roslyn. (2010). Personality and retirement: Exploring the links between the Big Five personality traits, reasons for retirement and the experience of being retired. *Personality and Individual Differences*, 48(7), 792–797. doi:10.1016/j.paid.2010.01.014

Robson, Ruthann. (2010). Notes on my dying. In Nan Bauer Maglin and Donna Marie Perry (Eds.), *Final acts: Death, dying, and the choices we make* (pp. 19–28). New Brunswick, NJ: Rutgers University Press.

Roca, María; Parr, Alice; Thompson, Russell; Woolgar, Alexandra; Torralva, Teresa; Antoun, Nagui, . . . Duncan, John. (2010). Executive function and fluid intelligence after frontal lobe lesions. *Brain*, 133(1), 234–247. doi:10.1093/brain/awp269

Roche, Alex F. and Sun, Shumei S. (2003). *Human growth: Assessment and interpretation*. New York, NY: Cambridge University Press.

Rodier, Francis and Campisi, Judith. (2011). Four faces of cellular senescence. *The Journal Of Cell Biology*, 192(4), 547–556. doi:10.1083/jcb.201009094

Rodkin, Philip C. and Roisman, Glenn I. (2010). Antecedents and correlates of the popular-aggressive phenomenon in elementary school. *Child Development*, 81(3), 837–850. doi:10.1111/j.1467-8624.2010.01437.x

Rodrigue, Karen M. and Kennedy, Kristen M. (2011). The cognitive consequences of structural changes to the aging brain. In K. Warner Schaie and Sherry L. Willis (Eds.), *Handbook of the psychology of aging* (7th ed., pp. 73–91). San Diego, CA: Academic Press. doi:10.1016/B978-0-12-380882-0.00005-X

Rodriguez, Liliana; Schwartz, Seth J. and Whitbourne, Susan Krauss. (2010). American identity revisited: The relation between national, ethnic, and personal identity in a multiethnic sample of emerging adults. *Journal of Adolescent Research*, 25(2), 324–349. doi:10.1177/0743558409359055

Roebers, Claudia M.; Schmid, Corinne and Roderer, Thomas. (2009). Metacognitive monitoring and control processes involved in primary school children's test performance. *British Journal of Educational Psychology*, 79(4), 749–767. doi:10.1348/978185409X429842

Roelfs, David J.; Shor, Eran; Davidson, Karina W. and Schwartz, Joseph E. (2012). Losing life and livelihood: A systematic review and meta-analysis of unemployment and all-cause mortality. *Social Science Medicine*, 72(6), 840–854. doi:10.1016/j.socscimed.2011.01.005

Roenneberg, Till; Allebrandt, Karla; Merrow, Martha and Vetter, Céline (2012). Social jetlag and obesity. *Current Biology*, 22(10), 939–943. doi:10.1016/j.cub.2012.03.038

Rogers, Carl R. (2004). *On becoming a person: A therapist's view of psychotherapy*. London, UK: Constable.

Rogers-Chapman, M. Felicity. (2013). *Accessing STEM-Focused Education: Factors That Contribute to the Opportunity to Attend STEM High Schools Across the United States*. Education and Urban Society. doi:10.1177/0013124512469815

Rogoff, Barbara. (2003). *The cultural nature of human development*. New York, NY: Oxford University Press.

Rogoff, Barbara. (2011). *Developing destinies: A Mayan midwife and town*. New York, NY: Oxford University Press.

Rohwedder, Susann and Willis, Robert J. (2010). Mental retirement. *Journal of Economic Perspectives*, 24(1), 119–138. doi:10.1257/jep.24.1.119

Roiphe, Anne. (2010). Grandmothers should be seen and not heard. In Barbara Graham (Ed.), *Eye of my heart: 27 writers reveal the hidden pleasures and perils of being a grandmother* (pp. 241–250). New York, NY: HarperCollins.

Rojas, Raúl and Iglesias, Aquiles. (2013). The language growth of Spanish-speaking English Language Learners. *Child Development*, 84(2), 2630–2646. doi:10.1111/j.1467-8624.2012.01871.x

Romeo, Russell D. (2013). The teenage brain: The stress response and the adolescent brain. *Current Directions in Psychological Science*, 22(2), 140–145. doi:10.1177/0963721413475445

Ron, Pnina. (2009). Daughters as caregivers of aging parents: The shattering myth. *Journal of Gerontological Social Work*, 52(2), 135–153. doi:10.1080/01634370802561943

Ronay, Richard and von Hippel, William. (2010). The presence of an attractive woman elevates testosterone and physical risk taking in young men. *Social Psychological and Personality Science*, 1(1), 57–64. doi:10.1177/1948550609352807

Rondal, Jean A. (2010). Language in Down syndrome: A life-span perspective. In Marcia A. Barnes (Ed.), *Genes, brain, and development: The neurocognition of genetic disorders* (pp. 122–142). New York, NY: Cambridge University Press.

Roopnarine, Jaipaul L. (2011). Cultural variations in beliefs about play, parent-child play, and children's play: Meaning for childhood development. In Anthony D. Pellegrini (Ed.), *The Oxford handbook of the development of play* (pp. 19–39). New York, NY: Oxford University Press.

Rose, Steven. (2008). Drugging unruly children is a method of social control. *Nature, 451*(7178), 521. doi:10.1038/451521a

Rose, Susan A.; Feldman, Judith F. and Jankowski, Jeffery J. (2009). A cognitive approach to the development of early language. *Child Development, 80*(1), 134–150. doi:10.1111/j.1467-8624.2008.01250.x

Roseberry, Sarah; Hirsh-Pasek, Kathy; Parish-Morris, Julia and Golinkoff, Roberta M. (2009). Live action: Can young children learn verbs from video? *Child Development, 80*(5), 1360–1375. doi:10.1111/j.1467-8624.2009.01338.x

Rosen, Jules; Stiehl, Emily M.; Mittal, Vikas and Leana, Carrie R. (2011). Stayers, leavers, and switchers among certified nursing assistants in nursing homes: A longitudinal investigation of turnover intent, staff retention, and turnover. *The Gerontologist, 51*(5), 597–609. doi:10.1093/geront/gnr025

Rosenbaum, James E. (2011). The complexities of college for all. *Sociology of Education, 84*(2), 113–117. doi:10.1177/0038040711401809

Rosenberg, Rebecca; Mandell, David; Farmer, Janet; Law, J.; Marvin, Alison and Law, Paul. (2010). Psychotropic medication use among children with autism spectrum disorders enrolled in a national registry, 2007–2008. *Journal of Autism and Developmental Disorders, 40*(3), 342–351. doi:10.1007/s10803-009-0878-1

Rosenblatt, Paul C. (2013). Culture, Socialization, and Loss, Grief, and Mourning. In David K. Meagher and David E. Balk (Eds.), *Handbook of thanatology: The essential body of knowledge for the study of death, dying, and bereavement* (2nd ed., pp. 121–126). New York, NY: Routledge.

Rosenfield, Robert L.; Lipton, Rebecca B. and Drum, Melinda L. (2009). Thelarche, pubarche, and menarche attainment in children with normal and elevated body mass index. *Pediatrics, 123*(1), 84–88. doi:10.1542/peds.2008-0146

Rosenfield, Sarah. (2012). Triple jeopardy? Mental health at the intersection of gender, race, and class. *Social Science & Medicine, 74*(11), 1791–1801. doi:10.1016/j.socscimed.2011.11.010

Rosenthal, Miriam K. (1991). The relation of peer interaction among infants and toddlers in family day care to characteristics of the child care environment. *Journal of Reproductive and Infant Psychology, 9*(2–3), 151–167. doi:10.1080/02646839108403666

Rosow, Irving. (1985). Status and role change through the life cycle. In Robert H. Binstock and Ethel Shanas (Eds.), *Handbook of aging and the social sciences* (2nd ed., pp. 62–93). New York, NY: Van Nostrand Reinhold.

Ross, Colin A. (2009). Ethics of gender identity disorder. *Ethical Human Psychology and Psychiatry, 11*(3), 165–170. doi:10.1891/1559-4343.11.3.165

Rossi, Eleonora; Schippers, Marleen and Keysers, Christian. (2011). Broca's area: Linking perception and production in language and actions. In Shihui Han and Ernst Pöppel (Eds.), *Culture and neural frames of cognition and communication* (pp. 169–184). New York, NY: Springer. doi:10.1007/978-3-642-15423-2_11

Rossignol, Daniel; Rossignol, Lanier; Smith, Scott; Schneider, Cindy; Logerquist, Sally; Usman, Anju, . . . Mumper, Elizabeth. (2009). Hyperbaric treatment for children with autism: A multicenter, randomized, double-blind, controlled trial. *BMC Pediatrics, 9*(21). doi:10.1186/1471-2431-9-21

Rostila, Mikael; Saarela, Jan and Kawachi, Ichiro. (2013). Suicide following the death of a sibling: A nationwide follow-up study from Sweden. *BMJ Open, 3*, e002618. doi:10.1136/bmjopen-2013-002618

Roth, David L.; Ackerman, Michelle L.; Okonkwo, Ozioma C. and Burgio, Louis D. (2008). The four-factor model of depressive symptoms in dementia caregivers: A structural equation model of ethnic differences. *Psychology and Aging, 23*(3), 567–576. doi:10.1037/a0013287

Roth, David L.; Mittelman, Mary S.; Clay, Olivio J.; Madan, Alok and Haley, William E. (2005). Changes in social support as mediators of the impact of a psychosocial intervention for spouse caregivers of persons with Alzheimer's disease. *Psychology and Aging, 20*(4), 634–644. doi:10.1037/0882-7974.20.4.634

Roth, Guy and Assor, Avi. (2012). The costs of parental pressure to express emotions: Conditional regard and autonomy support as predictors of emotion regulation and intimacy. *Journal of Adolescence, 35*(4), 799–808. doi:10.1016/j.adolescence.2011.11.005

Roth, Lauren W. and Polotsky, Alex J. (2012). Can we live longer by eating less? A review of caloric restriction and longevity. *Maturitas, 71*, 315–319. doi:10.1016/j.maturitas.2011.12.017

Rothbaum, Fred; Morelli, Gilda and Rusk, Natalie. (2011). Attachment, learning and coping: The interplay of cultural similarities and differences. In Michele J. Gelfand, Chi-yue Chiu and Ying-yi Hong (Eds.), *Advances in culture and psychology* (Vol. 1). New York, NY: Oxford University Press.

Rothrauff, Tanja C.; Cooney, Teresa M. and An, Jeong Shin. (2009). Remembered parenting styles and adjustment in middle and late adulthood. *The Journals of Gerontology Series B: Psychological Sciences and Social Sciences, 64B*(1), 137–146. doi:10.1093/geronb/gbn008

Rouchka, Eric C. and Cha, I. Elizabeth. (2009). *Current trends in pseudogene detection and characterization. Current Bioinformatics, 4*(2), 112–119. doi:10.2174/157489309788184792

Rovee-Collier, Carolyn. (1987). Learning and memory in infancy. In Joy Doniger Osofsky (Ed.), *Handbook of infant development* (2nd ed., pp. 98–148). New York, NY: Wiley.

Rovee-Collier, Carolyn. (1990). The "memory system" of prelinguistic infants. *Annals of the New York Academy of Sciences, 608*, 517–542. doi:10.1111/j.1749-6632.1990.tb48908.x

Rovee-Collier, Carolyn and Cuevas, Kimberly. (2009a). The development of infant memory. In Mary L. Courage and Nelson Cowan (Eds.), *The development of memory in infancy and childhood* (2nd ed., pp. 11–41). New York, NY: Psychology Press.

Rovee-Collier, Carolyn and Hayne, Harlene. (1987). Reactivation of infant memory: Implications for cognitive development. In Hayne W. Reese (Ed.), *Advances in child development and behavior* (Vol. 20, pp. 185–238). London, UK: Academic Press.

Rovi, Sue; Chen, Ping-Hsin and Johnson, Mark S. (2004). The economic burden of hospitalizations associated with child abuse and neglect. *American Journal of Public Health, 94*(4), 586–590. doi:10.2105/AJPH.94.4.586

Rovner, Alisha J.; Nansel, Tonja R.; Wang, Jing and Iannotti, Ronald J. (2011). Food sold in school vending machines is associated with overall student dietary intake. *Journal of Adolescent Health, 48*(1), 13–19. doi:10.1016/j.jadohealth.2010.08.021

Rubie-Davies, Christine M. (2007). Classroom interactions: Exploring the practices of high- and low-expectation teachers. *British Journal of Educational Psychology, 77*(2), 289–306. doi:10.1348/000709906X101601

Rubin, Kenneth H.; Bowker, Julie C.; McDonald, Kristina L. and Menzer, Melissa. (2013). Peer relationships in childhood. In Philip David Zelazo (Ed.), *The Oxford handbook of developmental psychology* (Vol. 2, pp. 242–275). New York, NY: Oxford University Press.

Rubin, Kenneth H.; Coplan, Robert J. and Bowker, Julie C. (2009). Social withdrawal in childhood. *Annual Review of Psychology, 60*, 141–171. doi:10.1146/annurev.psych.60.110707.163642

Rubin, Simon Shimshon; Malkinson, Ruth and Witztum, Eliezer. (2012). *Working with the bereaved: Multiple lenses on loss and mourning.* New York, NY: Routledge.

Ruble, Diane N.; Martin, Carol Lynn and Berenbaum, Sheri. (2006). Gender development. In William Damon and Richard M. Lerner (Eds.), *Handbook of child psychology* (6th ed., Vol. 3, pp. 858–932). Hoboken, NJ: Wiley.

Ruder, Debra Bradley. (2008). *The teen brain. Harvard Magazine, 111*(1), 8–10.

Ruetschlin, Catherine and Draut, Tamara. (2013). *Stuck: Young America's persistent jobs crisis.* New York, NY.

Rulfs, Monika. (2011). Marking death: Grief, protest and politics after a fatal traffic accident. In Peter Jan Margry and Cristina Sanchez-Carretero (Eds.), *Grassroots memorials: The politics of memorializing traumatic death* (pp. 145–168). New York, NY: Berghahn Books.

Russell, Eric M.; DelPriore, Danielle J.; Butterfield, Max E. and Hill, Sarah E. (2013). Friends with benefits, but without the sex: Straight women and gay men exchange trustworthy mating advice. *Evolutionary Psychology, 11*(1), 132–147.

Russell, Stephen T.; Chu, June Y.; Crockett, Lisa J. and Lee, Sun-A. (2010). Interdependent independence: The meanings of autonomy among Chinese American and Filipino American adolescents. In Stephen Thomas Russell, Lisa J. Crockett and Ruth K. Chao (Eds.), *Asian American parenting and parent-adolescent relationships* (pp. 101–116). New York, NY: Springer. doi:10.1007/978-1-4419-5728-3_6

Ruthig, Joelle C.; Trisko, Jenna and Stewart, Tara L. (2012). The impact of spouse's health and well-being on own well-being: A dyadic study of older married couples. *Journal of Social and Clinical Psychology*, 31(5), 508–529. doi:10.1521/jscp.2012.31.5.508

Rutter, Michael; Colvert, Emma; Kreppner, Jana; Beckett, Celia; Castle, Jenny; Groothues, Christine, . . . Sonuga-Barke, Edmund J. S. (2007). Early adolescent outcomes for institutionally-deprived and non-deprived adoptees. I: Disinhibited attachment. *Journal of Child Psychology and Psychiatry*, 48(1), 17–30. doi:10.1111/j.1469-7610.2006.01688.x

Rutter, Michael; Sonuga-Barke, Edmund J.; Beckett, Celia; Castle, Jennifer; Kreppner, Jana; Kumsta, Robert, . . . Gunnar, Megan R. (2010). Deprivation-specific psychological patterns: Effects of institutional deprivation. *Monographs of the Society for Research in Child Development*, 75(1), 1–252. doi:10.1111/j.1540-5834.2010.00547.x

Rutters, Femke; Nieuwenhuizen, Arie G.; Vogels, Neeltje; Bouwman, Freek; Mariman, Edwin and Westerterp-Plantenga, Margriet S. (2008). Leptin-adiposity relationship changes, plus behavioral and parental factors, are involved in the development of body weight in a Dutch children cohort. *Physiology & Behavior*, 93(4/5), 967–974. doi:10.1016/j.physbeh.2007.12.021

Ruys, Jan H.; de Jonge, Guus A.; Brand, Ronald; Engelberts, Adèle, C. and Semmekrot, Ben A. (2007). Bed-sharing in the first four months of life: A risk factor for sudden infant death. *Acta Pædiatrica*, 96(10), 1399–1403. doi:10.1111/j.1651-2227.2007.00413.x

Ryan, Erin L. (2012). "They are kind of like magic": Why U.S. Mothers use baby videos with 12- to 24-month-olds. *Journalism and Mass Communication*, 2(7), 771–785.

Saarni, Carolyn; Campos, Joseph J.; Camras, Linda A. and Witherington, David. (2006). Emotional development: Action, communication, and understanding. In William Damon and Richard M. Lerner (Eds.), *Handbook of child psychology* (6th ed., Vol. 3, pp. 226–299). Hoboken, NJ: Wiley.

Sabayan, Behnam; Oleksik, Anna M.; Maier, Andrea B.; van Buchem, Mark A.; Poortvliet, Rosalinde K. E.; de Ruijter, Wouter, . . . Westendorp, Rudi G. J. (2012). High blood pressure and resilience to physical and cognitive decline in the oldest old: the Leiden 85-plus study. *Journal of the American Geriatrics Society*, 60(11), 2014–2019. doi:10.1111/j.1532-5415.2012.04203.x

Sacks, Oliver W. (1995). *An anthropologist on Mars: Seven paradoxical tales*. New York, NY: Knopf.

Sadeh, Avi; Mindell, Jodi A.; Luedtke, Kathryn and Wiegand, Benjamin. (2009).

Sleep and sleep ecology in the first 3 years: A web-based study. *Journal of Sleep Research*, 18(1), 60–73. doi:10.1111/j.1365-2869.2008.00699.x

Sadeh, Avi; Tikotzky, Liat and Scher, Anat. (2010). Parenting and infant sleep. *Sleep Medicine Reviews*, 14(2), 89–96. doi:10.1016/j.smrv.2009.05.003

Sadler, Philip Michael; Sonnert, Gerhard; Tai, Robert H. and Klopfenstein, Kristin (Eds.). (2010). *AP: A critical examination of the advanced placement program*. Cambridge, MA: Harvard Education Press.

Sadler, Thomas W. (2010). *Langman's medical embryology* (11th ed.). Philadelphia, PA: Lippincott Williams & Wilkins.

Sadler, Thomas W. (2012). *Langman's medical embryology* (12th ed.). Philadelphia, PA: Lippincott Williams & Wilkins.

Saegert, Susan; Fields, Desiree and Libman, Kimberly. (2011). Mortgage foreclosure and health disparities: Serial displacement as asset extraction in African American populations. *Journal of Urban Health*, 88(3), 390–402. doi:10.1007/s11524-011-9584-3

Saewyc, Elizabeth M. (2011). Research on adolescent sexual orientation: Development, health disparities, stigma, and resilience. *Journal of Research on Adolescence*, 21(1), 256–272. doi:10.1111/j.1532-7795.2010.00727.x

Sahlberg, Pasi. (2011). *Finnish lessons: What can the world learn from educational change in Finland?* New York, NY: Teachers College Press.

Salkind, Neil J. (2004). *An introduction to theories of human development*. Thousand Oaks, CA: Sage.

Salmivalli, Christina. (2010). Bullying and the peer group: A review. *Aggression and Violent Behavior*, 15(2), 112–120. doi:10.1016/j.avb.2009.08.007

Salpeter, Shelley R.; Luo, Esther J.; Malter, Dawn S. and Stuart, Brad. (2012). Systematic review of noncancer presentations with a median survival of 6 months or less. *The American Journal of Medicine*, 125(5), 512.e511–512.e516. doi:10.1016/j.amjmed.2011.07.028

Salter, Nicholas P. and Highhouse, Scott. (2009). Assessing managers' common sense using situational judgment tests. *Management Decision*, 47(3), 392–398. doi:10.1108/00251740910946660

Salthouse, Timothy A. (2010). *Major issues in cognitive aging*. New York, NY: Oxford University Press.

Samaras, N.; Frangos, E.; Forster, A.; Lang, P.-O. and Samaras, D. (2012). Andropause: A review of the definition and treatment. *European Geriatric Medicine*, 3(6), 368–373. doi:10.1016/j.eurger.2012.08.007

SAMHSA (Substance Abuse and Mental Health Services Administration). (2009). *Results from the 2008 National Survey on Drug Use and Health: National findings* Rockville, MD: U.S. Department of Health and Human Services, Office of Applied Studies, NSDUH Series H-36.

Samuels, Christina A. (2013). Study reveals gaps in graduation rates: Diplomas at risk. *Education Week*, 32(32), 5.

Sandberg, Sheryl. (2013). *Lean in: Women, work, and the will to lead.* New York, NY: Alfred A. Knopf.

Sander, Libby. (2013). Campus counseling centers see rising numbers of severe problems. *Chronicle of Higher Education*, 59(33), A18.

Sander, Thomas H. and Putnam, Robert David. (2010). Still bowling alone? The post-9/11 split. *Journal of Democracy*, 21(1), 9–16. doi:10.1353/jod.0.0153

Sanson, Ann; Smart, Diana and Misson, Sebastian. (2011). Children's socio-emotional, physical, and cognitive outcomes: Do they share the same drivers? *Australian Journal of Psychology*, 63(1), 56–74. doi:10.1111/j.1742-9536.2011.00007.x

Sansone, Randi and Sansone, Lori A. (2013). The relationship between borderline personality and obesity. *Innovations In Clinical Neuroscience*, 10(4), 36–40.

Santelli, John S. and Melnikas, Andrea J. (2010). Teen fertility in transition: Recent and historic trends in the United States. *Annual Review of Public Health*, 31, 371–383. doi:10.1146/annurev.publhealth.29.020907.090830

Saraceno, Chiara. (2010). Social inequalities in facing old-age dependency: A bi-generational perspective. *Journal of European Social Policy*, 20(1), 32–44. doi:10.1177/0958928709352540

Saracho, Olivia N. (2013). Mexican American father-child literacy interactions. In Jyotsna Pattnaik (Ed.), *Father involvement in young children's lives: A global analysis* (pp. 47–69). New York, NY: Springer.

Sassler, Sharon; Addo, Fenaba R. and Lichter, Daniel T. (2012). The tempo of sexual activity and later relationship quality. *Journal of Marriage and Family*, 74(4), 708–725. doi:10.1111/j.1741-3737.2012.00996.x

Satariano, William. (2006). *Epidemiology of aging: An ecological approach*. Sudbury, MA: Jones and Bartlett.

Satariano, William A.; Guralnik, Jack M.; Jackson, Richard J.; Marottoli, Richard A.; Phelan, Elizabeth A. and Prohaska, Thomas R. (2012). Mobility and aging: New directions for public health action. *American Journal of Public Health*, 102(8), 1508–1515. doi:10.2105/AJPH.2011.300631

Satterwhite, Catherine Lindsey; Torrone, Elizabeth; Meites, Elissa; Dunne, Eileen F.; Mahajan, Reena; Ocfemia, M. Cheryl Bañez, . . . Weinstock, Hillard. (2013). Sexually transmitted infections among US women and men: Prevalence and incidence estimates, 2008. *Sexually Transmitted Diseases*, 40(3), 187–193. doi:10.1097/OLQ.0b013e318286bb53

Sauer, Mark V.; Wang, Jeff G.; Douglas, Nataki C.; Nakhuda, Gary S.; Vardhana, Pratibashri; Jovanovic, Vuk and Guarnaccia, Michael M. (2009). Providing fertility care to men seropositive for human immunodeficiency virus: Reviewing 10 years of experience and 420 consecutive cycles of in vitro fertilization and intracytoplasmic sperm injection. *Fertility and Sterility*, 91(6), 2455–2460. doi:10.1016/j.fertnstert.2008.04.013

Saulny, Susan and Steinberg, Jacques. (2011, June 13). *On college forms, a question of race, or races, can perplex.* The New York Times, p. A1.

Saunders, Cicely M. (1978). *The management of terminal disease.* London, UK: Arnold.

Savin-Williams, Ritch C. (2005). *The new gay teenager.* Cambridge, MA: Harvard University Press.

Saw, Seang-Mei; Cheng, Angela; Fong, Allan; Gazzard, Gus; Tan, Donald T. H. and Morgan, Ian. (2007). School grades and myopia. *Ophthalmic and Physiological Optics,* 27(2), 126–129. doi:10.1111/j.1475-1313.2006.00455.x

Saxton, Matthew. (2010). *Child language: Acquisition and development.* Thousand Oaks, CA: Sage.

Sayette, Michael A.; Reichle, Erik D. and Schooler, Jonathan W. (2009). Lost in the sauce: The effects of alcohol on mind wandering. *Psychological Science,* 20(6), 747–752. doi:10.1111/j.1467-9280.2009.02351.x

Scales, Peter C.; Benson, Peter L. and Mannes, Marc. (2006). The contribution to adolescent well-being made by nonfamily adults: An examination of developmental assets as contexts and processes. *Journal of Community Psychology,* 34(4), 401–413. doi:10.1002/jcop.20106

Scannapieco, Maria and Connell-Carrick, Kelli. (2005). *Understanding child maltreatment: An ecological and developmental perspective.* New York, NY: Oxford University Press. doi:10.1093/acprof:oso/9780195156782.001.0001

Scarf, Maggie. (2008). *September songs: The good news about marriage in the later years.* New York, NY: Riverhead Books.

Scarr, Sandra. (1985). Constructing psychology: Making facts and fables for our times. *American Psychologist,* 40(5), 499–512. doi:10.1037/0003-066x.40.5.499

Schaan, Barbara. (2013). Widowhood and depression among older Europeans - The role of gender, caregiving, marital quality, and regional context. *The Journals of Gerontology Series B: Psychological Sciences and Social Sciences,* 68(3), 431–442. doi:10.1093/geronb/gbt015

Schachner, Adena and Hannon, Erin E. (2011). Infant-directed speech drives social preferences in 5 month old infants. *Developmental Psychology,* 47(1), 19–25. doi:10.1037/a0020740

Schaie, K. Warner. (2002). The impact of longitudinal studies on understanding development from young adulthood to old age. In Willard W. Hartup and Rainer K. Silbereisen (Eds.), *Growing points in developmental science: An introduction* (pp. 307–328). New York, NY: Psychology Press.

Schaie, K. Warner. (2005). *Developmental influences on adult intelligence: The Seattle longitudinal study.* New York, NY: Oxford University Press. doi:10.1093/acprof:oso/9780195156737.001.0001

Schaie, K. Warner. (2013). *Developmental influences on adult intelligence: The Seattle Longitudinal Study* (2nd ed.). New York, NY: Oxford University Press.

Schanler, Richard. J. (2011). Outcomes of human milk-fed premature infants. *Seminars in Perinatology,* 35(1), 29–33. doi:10.1053/j.semperi.2010.10.005

Schardein, James L. (1976). *Drugs as teratogens.* Cleveland, OH: CRC Press.

Scharlach, Andrew; Graham, Carrie and Lehning, Amanda. (2012). The "Village' model: A consumer-driven approach for aging in place. *The Gerontologist,* 52(3), 418–427. doi:10.1093/geront/gnr083

Schauer, Daniel P.; Arterburn, David E.; Livingston, Edward H.; Fischer, David and Eckman, Mark H. (2010). Decision modeling to estimate the impact of gastric bypass surgery on life expectancy for the treatment of morbid obesity. *Archives of Surgery,* 145(1), 57–62. doi:10.1001/archsurg.2009.240

Scheffler, Richard M.; Brown, Timothy T.; Fulton, Brent D.; Hinshaw, Stephen P.; Levine, Peter and Stone, Susan. (2009). Positive association between attention-deficit/hyperactivity disorder medication use and academic achievement during elementary school. *Pediatrics,* 123(5), 1273–1279. doi:10.1542/peds.2008-1597

Scheibehenne, Benjamin; Greifeneder, Rainer and Todd, Peter M. (2010). Can there ever be too many options? *A meta-analytic review of choice overload. Journal of Consumer Research,* 37(3), 409–425. doi:10.1086/651235

Schenkman, Lauren. (2011). Second thoughts about CT imaging. *Science,* 331(6020), 1002–1004. doi:10.1126/science.331.6020.1002

Schermerhorn, Alice C.; D'Onofrio, Brian M.; Turkheimer, Eric; Ganiban, Jody M.; Spotts, Erica L.; Lichtenstein, Paul, . . . Neiderhiser, Jenae M. (2011). A genetically informed study of associations between family functioning and child psychosocial adjustment. *Developmental Psychology,* 47(3), 707–725. doi:10.1037/a0021362

Schiefenhövel, Wulf and Grabolle, Andreas. (2005). The role of maternal grandmothers in Trobriand adoptions. In Eckart Voland, Athanasios Chasiotis and Wulf Schiefenhövel (Eds.), *Grandmotherhood: The evolutionary significance of the second half of female life* (pp. 177–193). New Brunswick, N.J.: Rutgers University Press.

Schiller, Jeannine S., Lucas, Jacqueline W., Ward, Brian W. and Peregoy, Jennifer A. (2012). Summary health statistics for U.S. adults: National Health Interview Survey, 2010. *National Center for Health Statistics,* 10.252.

Schiller, Ruth A. (1998). The relationship of developmental tasks to life satisfaction, moral reasoning, and occupational attainment at age 28. *Journal of Adult Development,* 5(4), 239–254. doi:10.1023/A:1021406426385

Schneider, Wolfgang and Lockl, Kathrin. (2008). Procedural metacognition in children: Evidence for developmental trends. In John Dunlosky and Robert A. Bjork (Eds.), *Handbook of metamemory and memory* (pp. 391–409). New York, NY: Psychology Press.

Schnitzspahn, Katharina M.; Stahl, Christoph; Zeintl, Melanie; Kaller, Christoph P. and Kliegel, Matthias. (2013). The role of shifting, updating, and inhibition in prospective memory performance in young and older adults. *Developmental Psychology,* 49(8), 1544–1553. doi:10.1037/a0030579

Schnitzspahn, Katharina M.; Ihlea, Andreas; Henrya, Julie D.; Rendella, Peter G. and Kliegela, Matthias. (2011). The age-prospective memory-paradox: An exploration of possible mechanisms. *International Psychogeriatrics,* 23(4), 583–592. doi:10.1017/S1041610210001651

Schoebi, Dominik; Karney, Benjamin R. and Bradbury, Thomas N. (2012). Stability and change in the first 10 years of marriage: Does commitment confer benefits beyond the effects of satisfaction? *Journal of Personality and Social Psychology,* 102(4), 729–742. doi:10.1037/a0026290

Schoen, Robert and Cheng, Yen-Hsin Alice. (2006). Partner choice and the differential retreat from marriage. *Journal of Marriage and Family,* 68(1), 1–10. doi: 10.1111/j.1741-3737.2006.00229.x

Schoeni, Robert F. and Ross, Karen E. (2005). Material assistance from families during the transition to adulthood. In Richard A. Settersten, Frank F. Furstenberg and Rubén G. Rumbaut (Eds.), *On the frontier of adulthood: Theory, research, and public policy* (pp. 396–416). Chicago, IL: University of Chicago Press. doi:10.7208/chicago/9780226748924.003.0012

Schofield, Thomas J.; Martin, Monica J.; Conger, Katherine J.; Neppl, Tricia M.; Donnellan, M. Brent and Conger, Rand D. (2011). Intergenerational transmission of adaptive functioning: A test of the interactionist model of SES and human development. *Child Development,* 82(1), 33–47. doi:10.1111/j.1467-8624.2010.01539.x

Schön, Daniele; Boyer, Maud; Moreno, Sylvain; Besson, Mireille; Peretz, Isabelle and Kolinsky, Régine. (2008). Songs as an aid for language acquisition. *Cognition,* 106(2), 975–983. doi:10.1016/j.cognition.2007.03.005

Schooler, Carmi. (2009). The effects of the cognitive complexity of occupational conditions and leisure-time activities on the intellectual functioning of older adults. In Wojtek Chodzko-Zajko, Arthur F. Kramer and Leonard W. Poon (Eds.), *Enhancing cognitive functioning and brain plasticity.* (Vol. 3, pp. 15–34). Champaign, IL: Human Kinetics.

Schore, Allan and McIntosh, Jennifer. (2011). Family law and the neuroscience of attachment, part I. *Family Court Review,* 49(3), 501–512. doi:10.1111/j.1744-1617.2011.01387.x

Schraagen, Jan Maarten and Leijenhorst, Henk. (2001). Searching for evidence: Knowledge and search strategies used by forensic scientists. In Eduardo Salas and Gary A. Klein (Eds.), *Linking expertise and naturalistic decision making* (pp. 263–274). Mahwah, NJ: Erlbaum.

Schreck, Christopher J.; Burek, Melissa W.; Stewart, Eric A. and Miller, J. Mitchell. (2007). Distress and violent victimization among young adolescents: Early puberty and the social interactionist explanation. *Journal of Research in Crime and Delinquency, 44*(4), 381–405. doi:10.1177/0022427807305851

Schröder, Mathis. (2013). Jobless now, sick later? Investigating the long-term consequences of involuntary job loss on health. *Advances in Life Course Research, 18*(1), 5–15. doi:10.1016/j.alcr.2012.08.001

Schulenberg, John; O'Malley, Patrick M.; Bachman, Jerald G. and Johnston, Lloyd D. (2005). Early adult transitions and their relation to well-being and substance use. In Richard A. Settersten, Frank F. Furstenberg and Rubén G. Rumbaut (Eds.), *On the frontier of adulthood: Theory, research, and public policy* (pp. 417–453). Chicago, IL: University of Chicago Press.

Schulz, James H. and Binstock, Robert H. (2008). *Aging nation: The economics and politics of growing older in America.* Baltimore, MD: Johns Hopkins University Press.

Schumann, Cynthia Mills; Hamstra, Julia; Goodlin-Jones, Beth L.; Lotspeich, Linda J.; Kwon, Hower; Buonocore, Michael H., . . . Amaral, David G. (2004). The amygdala is enlarged in children but not adolescents with autism; the hippocampus is enlarged at all ages. *Journal of Neuroscience, 24*(28), 6392–6401. doi:10.1523/JNEUROSCI.1297-04.2004

Schupp, Justin and Sharp, Jeff. (2012). Exploring the social bases of home gardening. *Agriculture and Human Values, 29*(2), 93–105. doi:10.1007/s10460-011-9321-2

Schwartz, Carl E.; Kunwar, Pratap S.; Greve, Douglas N.; Moran, Lyndsey R.; Viner, Jane C.; Covino, Jennifer M., . . . Wallace, Stuart R. (2010). Structural differences in adult orbital and ventromedial prefrontal cortex predicted by infant temperament at 4 months of age. *Archives of General Psychiatry, 67*(1), 78–84. doi:10.1001/archgenpsychiatry.2009.171

Schwartz, David and Collins, Francis. (2007). Environmental biology and human disease. *Science, 316*(5825), 695–696. doi:10.1126/science.1141331

Schwartz, Paul D.; Maynard, Amanda M. and Uzelac, Sarah M. (2008). Adolescent egocentrism: A contemporary view. *Adolescence, 43*(171), 441–448.

Schwartz, Seth J.; Zamboanga, Byron L.; Meca, Alan and Ritchie, Rachel A. (2012). Identity around the world: An overview. *New Directions for Child and Adolescent Development, 2012*(138), 1–18. doi:10.1002/cad.20019

Schwartz, Seth J.; Zamboanga, Byron L.; Ravert, Russell D.; Kim, Su Yeong; Weisskirch, Robert S.; Williams, Michelle K., . . . Finley, Gordon E. (2009). Perceived parental relationships and health-risk behaviors in college-attending emerging adults. *Journal of Marriage and Family, 71*(3), 727–740. doi:10.1111/j.1741-3737.2009.00629.x

Schwarz, Alan and Cohen, Sarah. (2013, March 31). *A.D.H.D. seen in 11‰ of U.S. children as diagnoses rise.* The New York Times.

Schweinhart, Lawrence J.; Montie, Jeanne; Xiang, Zongping; Barnett, W. Steven; Belfield, Clive R. and Nores, Milagros. (2005). *Lifetime effects: The High/Scope Perry Preschool Study through age 40.* Ypsilanti, MI: High/Scope Press.

Schweinhart, Lawrence J. and Weikart, David P. (1997). *Lasting differences: The high/scope preschool curriculum comparison study through age 23.* Ypsilanti, MI: High/Scope Educational Research Foundation.

Schytt, Erica and Waldenström, Ulla. (2010). Epidural analgesia for labor pain: Whose choice? *Acta Obstetricia et Gynecologica Scandinavica, 89*(2), 238–242. doi:10.3109/00016340903280974

Scott, Lisa S. and Monesson, Alexandra. (2010). Experience-dependent neural specialization during infancy. *Neuropsychologia, 48*(6), 1857–1861. doi:10.1016/j.neuropsychologia.2010.02.008

Scott, Lisa S.; Pascalis, Olivier and Nelson, Charles A. (2007). A domain-general theory of the development of perceptual discrimination. *Current Directions in Psychological Science, 16*(4), 197–201. doi:10.1111/j.1467-8721.2007.00503.x

Scott, Mindy E.; Schelar, Erin; Manlove, Jennifer and Cui, Carol. (2009). *Young adult attitudes about relationships and marriage: Times may have changed, but expectations remain high.* Washington, DC: Child Trends.

Sear, Rebecca and Mace, Ruth. (2008). Who keeps children alive? A review of the effects of kin on child survival. *Evolution and Human Behavior, 29*(1), 1–18. doi:10.1016/j.evolhumbehav.2007.10.001

Sebastian, Catherine; Burnett, Stephanie and Blakemore, Sarah-Jayne. (2008). Development of the self-concept during adolescence. *Trends in Cognitive Sciences, 12*(11), 441–446. doi:10.1016/j.tics.2008.07.008

Sebastián-Gallés, Núria. (2007). Biased to learn language. *Developmental Science, 10*(6), 713–718. doi:10.1111/j.1467-7687.2007.00649.x

Seedat, Soraya; Scott, Kate Margaret; Angermeyer, Matthias C.; Berglund, Patricia; Bromet, Evelyn J.; Brugha, Traolach S., . . . Kessler, Ronald C. (2009). Cross-national associations between gender and mental disorders in the world health organization world mental health surveys. *Archives of General Psychiatry, 66*(7), 785–795. doi:10.1001/archgenpsychiatry.2009.36

Seelaar, Harro; Rohrer, Jonathan D; Pijnenburg, Yolande A. L.; Fox, Nick C. and van Swieten, John C. (2011). Clinical, genetic and pathological heterogeneity of frontotemporal dementia: A review. *Journal of Neurology, Neurosurgery, & Psychiatry, 82*(5), 476–486. doi:10.1136/jnnp.2010.212225

Seguin, Jean R. and Tremblay, Richard E. (2013). Aggression and antisocial behavior: A developmental perspective. In Philip David Zelazo (Ed.), *The Oxford handbook of developmental psychology* (Vol. 2, pp. 507–526). New York, NY: Oxford University Press.

Seifer, Ronald; LaGasse, Linda L.; Lester, Barry; Bauer, Charles R.; Shankaran, Seetha; Bada, Henrietta S., . . . Liu, Jing. (2004). Attachment status in children prenatally exposed to cocaine and other substances. *Child Development, 75*(3), 850–868. doi:10.1111/j.1467-8624.2004.00710.x

Seligman, Hilary K. and Schillinger, Dean. (2010). Hunger and socioeconomic disparities in chronic disease. *New England Journal of Medicine, 363*(1), 6–9. doi:10.1056/NEJMp1000072

Seligman, Martin E. P.; Railton, Peter; Baumeister, Roy F. and Sripada, Chandra. (2013). Navigating into the future or driven by the past. *Perspectives on Psychological Science, 8*(2), 119–141. doi:10.1177/1745691612474317

Selin, Helaine and Stone, Pamela Kendall (Eds.). (2009). *Childbirth across cultures: Ideas and practices of pregnancy, childbirth and the postpartum.* New York, NY: Springer Verlag. doi:10.1007/978-90-481-2599-9

Senju, Atsushi; Southgate, Victoria; Miura, Yui; Matsui, Tomoko; Hasegawa, Toshikazu; Tojo, Yoshikuni, . . . Csibra, Gergely. (2010). Absence of spontaneous action anticipation by false belief attribution in children with autism spectrum disorder. *Development and Psychopathology, 22*(2), 353–360. doi:10.1017/S0954579410000106

Sentse, Miranda; Lindenberg, Siegwart; Omvlee, Annelies; Ormel, Johan and Veenstra, René. (2010). Rejection and acceptance across contexts: Parents and peers as risks and buffers for early adolescent psychopathology. The TRAILS Study. *Journal of Abnormal Child Psychology, 38*(1), 119–130. doi:10.1007/s10802-009-9351-z

Sepkowitz, Kent A. (2013). Energy drinks and caffeine-related adverse effects. *JAMA, 309*(3), 243–244. doi:10.1001/jama.2012.173526

Settersten, Richard A. Jr. (2012). The contemporary context of young adulthood in the USA: From demography to development, from private troubles to public issues. In Alan Booth, Susan L. Brown, Nancy S. Landale, Wendy D. Manning and Susan M. McHale (Eds.), *Early adulthood in a family context* (Vol. 2, pp. 3–26). New York, NY: Springer. doi:10.1007/978-1-4614-1436-0_1

Settle, Jaime E.; Dawes, Christopher T.; Christakis, Nicholas A. and Fowler, James H. (2010). Friendships moderate an association between a dopamine gene variant and political ideology. *The Journal of Politics, 72*(4), 1189–1198. doi:10.1017/S0022381610000617

Seyfarth, Robert M. and Cheney, Dorothy L. (2012). The evolutionary origins of friendship. *Annual Review of Psychology, 63*, 153–177. doi:10.1146/annurev-psych-120710-100337

Shah, Prakesh; Balkhair, Taiba; Ohlsson, Arne; Beyene, Joseph; Scott, Fran and Frick, Corine. (2011). Intention to become pregnant and low birth weight and preterm birth: A systematic review. *Maternal and Child Health Journal, 15*(2), 205–216. doi:10.1007/s10995-009-0546-2

Shai, Iris and Stampfer, Meir J. (2008). Weight-loss diets—Can you keep it off? *American Journal of Clinical Nutrition, 88*(5), 1185–1186.

Shakya, Holly Baker; Usita, Paula M.; Eisenberg, Christina; Weston, Joanna and Liles, Sandy. (2012). Family well-being concerns of grandparents in skipped generation families. *Journal of Gerontological Social Work, 55*(1), 39–54. doi:10.1080/01634372.2011.620072

Shanahan, Michael J. and Hofer, Scott M. (2011). Molecular genetics, aging, and well-being: Sensitive period, accumulation, and pathway models. In Robert H. Binstock and Linda K. George (Eds.), *Handbook of aging and the social sciences* (7th ed., pp. 135–147). San Diego, CA: Academic Press. doi:10.1016/B978-0-12-380880-6.00010-1

Shanahan, Timothy and Lonigan, Christopher J. (2010). The National Early Literacy Panel: A summary of the process and the report. *Educational Researcher, 39*(4), 279–285. doi:10.3102/0013189x10369172

Shapiro, Adam and Yarborough-Hayes, Raijah. (2008). Retirement and older men's health. Generations, 32(1), 49–53.

Shapiro, Edward S.; Zigmond, Naomi; Wallace, Teri and Marston, Doug (Eds.). (2011). *Models for implementing response to intervention: Tools, outcomes, and implications.* New York, NY: Guilford Press.

Shapiro, James A. (2009). Revisiting the central dogma in the 21st century. *Annals of the New York Academy of Sciences, 1178*(1), 6–28. doi:10.1111/j.1749-6632.2009.04990.x

Shapiro, Melanie Freedberg. (2011). *Mothers' feelings about physical and emotional intimacy twelve to fifteen months after the birth of a first child.* (Thesis). School for Social Work. Northampton, MA: Smith College. https://dspace.smith.edu/handle/11020/23004

Sharkey, Siobhan S.; Hudak, Sandra; Horn, Susan D.; James, Bobbie and Howes, Jessie. (2011). Frontline caregiver daily practices: A comparison study of traditional nursing homes and the Green House project sites. *Journal of the American Geriatrics Society, 59*(1), 126–131. doi:10.1111/j.1532-5415.2010.03209.x

Shattuck, Paul T. (2006). The contribution of diagnostic substitution to the growing administrative prevalence of autism in US special education. *Pediatrics, 117*(4), 1028–1037. doi:10.1542/peds.2005-1516

Sheehy, Gail. (1976). *Passages: Predictable crises of adult life.* New York, NY: Dutton.

Sheldon, Pavica. (2012). Profiling the non-users: Examination of life-position indicators, sensation seeking, shyness, and loneliness among users and non-users of social network sites. *Computers in Human Behavior, 28*(5), 1960–1965. doi:10.1016/j.chb.2012.05.016

Shepard, Thomas H. and Lemire, Ronald J. (2004). *Catalog of teratogenic agents* (11th ed.). Baltimore, MD: Johns Hopkins University Press.

Sherblom, Stephen. (2008). The legacy of the "Care challenge": Re-envisioning the outcome of the justice-care debate. *Journal of Moral Education, 37*(1), 81–98. doi:10.1080/03057240701803692

Shields, Margot and Tremblay, Mark S. (2010). Canadian childhood obesity estimates based on WHO, IOTF and CDC cut-points. *International Journal of Pediatric Obesity, 5*(3), 265–273. doi:10.3109/17477160903268282

Shirtcliff, Elizabeth A.; Dahl, Ronald E. and Pollak, Seth D. (2009). Pubertal development: Correspondence between hormonal and physical development. *Child Development, 80*(2), 327–337. doi:10.1111/j.1467-8624.2009.01263.x

Shirtcliff, Elizabeth A.; Phan, Jenny M.; Lubach, Gabriele R.; Crispen, Heather R. and Coe, Christopher L. (2013). Stability of parental care across siblings from undisturbed and challenged pregnancies: Intrinsic maternal dispositions of female rhesus monkeys. *Developmental Psychology, 49*(11). doi:10.1037/a0032050

Shonkoff, Jack P.; Siegel, Benjamin S.; Dobbins, Mary I.; Earls, Marian F.; Garner, Andrew S.; McGuinn, Laura, . . . Wood, David L. (2012). The lifelong effects of early childhood adversity and toxic stress. *Pediatrics, 129*(1), e232 -e246. doi:10.1542/peds.2011-2663

Short, Kathleen. (2011). *The Research Supplemental Poverty Measure: 2010.* Washington, DC: U.S. Census Bureau.

Shuler, Carly. (2009). *Pockets of potential: Using mobile technologies to promote children's learning.* New York, NY: The Joan Ganz Cooney Center at Sesame Workshop.

Shumaker, Sally A.; Ockene, Judith K. and Riekert, Kristin A. (Eds.). (2009). *The handbook of health behavior change* (3rd ed.). New York, NY: Springer.

Siebenbruner, Jessica; Zimmer-Gembeck, Melanie J. and Egeland, Byron. (2007). Sexual partners and contraceptive use: A 16-year prospective study predicting abstinence and risk behavior. *Journal of Research on Adolescence, 17*(1), 179–206. doi:10.1111/j.1532-7795.2007.00518.x

Siegal, Michael and Surian, Luca (Eds.). (2012). *Access to language and cognitive development.* New York, NY: Oxford University Press.

Siegler, Robert S. (2009). Improving the numerical understanding of children from low-income families. *Child Development Perspectives, 3*(2), 118–124. doi:10.1111/j.1750-8606.2009.00090.x

Siegler, Robert S. and Chen, Zhe. (2008). Differentiation and integration: Guiding principles for analyzing cognitive change. *Developmental Science, 11*(4), 433–448. doi:10.1111/j.1467-7687.2008.00689.x

Siegler, Robert S. and Mu, Yan. (2008). Chinese children excel on novel mathematics problems even before elementary school. *Psychological Science, 19*(8), 759–763. doi:10.1111/j.1467-9280.2008.02153.x

Siegler, Robert S.; Thompson, Clarissa A. and Schneider, Michael. (2011). An integrated theory of whole number and fractions development. *Cognitive Psychology, 62*(4), 273–296. doi:10.1016/j.cogpsych.2011.03.001

Sierra, Felipe; Hadley, Evan; Suzman, Richard and Hodes, Richard. (2009). Prospects for life span extension. *Annual Review of Medicine, 60,* 457–469. doi:10.1146/annurev.med.60.061607.220533

Silk, Timothy J. and Wood, Amanda G. (2011). Lessons about neurodevelopment from anatomical magnetic resonance imaging. *Journal of Developmental & Behavioral Pediatrics, 32*(2), 158–168. doi:10.1097/DBP.0b013e318206d58f

Sillars, Alan; Smith, Traci and Koerner, Ascan. (2010). Misattributions contributing to empathic (in)accuracy during parent-adolescent conflict discussions. *Journal of Social and Personal Relationships, 27*(6), 727–747. doi:10.1177/0265407510373261

Silton, Nava R.; Flannelly, Laura T.; Flannelly, Kevin J. and Galek, Kathleen. (2011). Toward a theory of holistic needs and the brain. *Holistic Nursing Practice, 25*(5), 258–265. doi:10.1097/HNP.0b013e31822a0301

Silva, Katie G.; Correa-Chávez, Maricela and Rogoff, Barbara. (2010). Mexican-heritage children's attention and learning from interactions directed to others. *Child Development, 81*(3), 898–912. doi:10.1111/j.1467-8624.2010.01441.x

Silventoinen, Karri; Hammar, Niklas; Hedlund, Ebba; Koskenvuo, Markku; Ronnemaa, Tapani and Kaprio, Jaakko. (2008). Selective international migration by social position, health behaviour and personality. *European Journal of Public Health, 18*(2), 150–155. doi:10.1093/eurpub/ckm052

Silverstein, Merril; Gans, Daphna; Lowenstein, Ariela; Giarrusso, Roseann and Bengtson, Vern L. (2010). Older parent-child relationships in six developed nations: Comparisons at the intersection of affection and conflict. *Journal of Marriage and Family, 72*(4), 1006–1021. doi: 10.1111/j.1741-3737.2010.00745.x

Silvia, Paul J. and Sanders, Camilla E. (2010). Why are smart people curious? Fluid intelligence, openness to experience, and interest. *Learning and Individual Differences, 20*(3), 242–245. doi:10.1016/j.lindif.2010.01.006

Simmons, Joseph P.; Nelson, Leif D. and Simonsohn, Uri. (2011). False-positive psychology: Undisclosed flexibility in data collection and analysis allows presenting anything as significant. *Psychological Science, 22*(11), 1359–1366. doi:10.1177/0956797611417632

Simons, Ronald L.; Simons, Leslie Gordon; Lei, Man-Kit; Beach, Steven R. H.; Brody, Gene H.; Gibbons, Frederick X. and Philibert, Robert A. (2013). Genetic moderation of the impact of parenting on hostility toward romantic partners. *Journal of Marriage and Family, 75*(2), 325–341. doi: 10.1111/jomf.12010

Sinardet, Dave and Mortelmans, Dimitri. (2009). The feminine side to Santa Claus. Women's work of kinship in contemporary gift-giving relations. *The Social*

Science Journal, 46(1), 124–142. doi:10.1016 /j.soscij.2008.12.006

Sinclair, Samantha and Carlsson, Rickard. (2013). What will I be when I grow up? The impact of gender identity threat on adolescents' occupational preferences. *Journal of Adolescence, 36*(3), 465–474. doi:10.1016/j.adolescence.2013.02.001

Singer, Irving. (2009). The nature of love. Cambridge, MA: The MIT Press.

Singh, Amika; Uijtdewilligen, Léonie; Twisk, Jos W. R.; van Mechelen, Willem and Chinapaw, Mai J. M. (2012). Physical activity and performance at school: A systematic review of the literature including a methodological quality assessment. *Archives of Pediatrics & Adolescent Medicine, 166*(1), 49–55. doi:10.1001/archpediatrics .2011.716

Singh, Leher. (2008). Influences of high and low variability on infant word recognition. *Cognition, 106*(2), 833–870. doi:10.1016/j.cognition.2007 .05.002

Singleton, David and Muñoz, Carmen. (2011). Around and beyond the critical period hypothesis. In Eli Hinkel (Ed.), *Handbook of research in second language teaching and learning* (Vol. 2, pp. 407–425). New York, NY: Routledge.

Sinnott, Jan D. (1998). The development of logic in adulthood: Postformal thought and its applications. New York, NY: Plenum Press.

Sinnott, Jan D. (2008). Cognitive and representational development in adults. In Kelly B. Cartwright (Ed.), *Literacy processes: Cognitive flexibility in learning and teaching* (pp. 42–68). New York, NY: Guilford.

Sinnott, Jan D. (2009). Cognitive development as the dance of adaptive transformation: Neo-Piagetian perspectives on adult cognitive development. In M. Cecil Smith and Nancy DeFrates-Densch (Eds.), *Handbook of research on adult learning and development* (pp. 103–134). New York, NY: Routledge.

Skinner, Burrhus Frederic. (1953). Science and human behavior. New York, NY: Macmillan.

Skinner, B. F. (1957). Verbal behavior. New York, NY: Appleton-Century-Crofts.

Skipper, Magdalena. (2011). Epigenomics: Epigenetic variation across the generations. *Nature Reviews Genetics, 12,* 740.

Slavich, George M. and Cole, Steven W. (2013). The emerging field of human social genomics. *Clinical Psychological Science, 1*(3), 331–348. doi:10.1177/2167702613478594

Slessor, Gillian; Phillips, Louise H. and Bull, Rebecca. (2008). Age-related declines in basic social perception: Evidence from tasks assessing eye-gaze processing. *Psychology and Aging, 23*(4), 812–822. doi:10.1037/a0014348

Slining, Meghan; Adair, Linda S.; Goldman, Barbara Davis; Borja, Judith B. and Bentley, Margaret. (2010). Infant overweight is associated with delayed motor development. *The Journal of Pediatrics, 157*(1), 20–25.e21. doi:10.1016/j.jpeds .2009.12.054

Sloan, John. (2011–2012). Medicating elders in the evidence-free zone. *Generations, 35*(4), 56–61.

Sloan, Ken. (2009). The role of personality in a manager's learning effectiveness. *European Journal of Social Sciences, 12*(1), 31–42.

Sloan, Mark. (2009). Birth day: A pediatrician explores the science, the history, and the wonder of childbirth. New York, NY: Ballantine Books.

Sloane, Stephanie; Baillargeon, Renée and Premack, David. (2012). Do infants have a sense of fairness? *Psychological Science, 23*(2), 196–204. doi:10.1177/0956797611422072

Slobin, Dan I. (2001). Form-function relations: How do children find out what they are? In Melissa Bowerman and Stephen C. Levinson (Eds.), *Language acquisition and conceptual development* (pp. 406–449). New York, NY: Cambridge University Press.

Slutske, Wendy S.; Moffitt, Terrie E.; Poulton, Richie and Caspi, Avshalom. (2012). Undercontrolled temperament at age 3 predicts disordered gambling at age 32: A longitudinal study of a complete birth cohort. *Psychological Science, 23*(5), 510–516. doi:10.1177/0956797611429708

Small, Meredith F. (1998). Our babies, ourselves: How biology and culture shape the way we parent. New York, NY: Anchor Books.

Smetana, Judith G. (2013). Moral development: The social domain theory view. In Philip David Zelazo (Ed.), *The Oxford handbook of developmental psychology* (Vol. 1, pp. 832–866). New York, NY: Oxford University Press.

Smith, Allison E. (2009). Ageing in urban neighbourhoods: Place attachment and social exclusion. Bristol, UK: Policy.

Smith, Christine. (2013). The "battle of the sexes" is alive in evolutionary psychology. *Sex Roles, 69*(9–10), 543–545. doi:10.1007/s11199 -012-0220-9

Smith, Christian; Christoffersen, Kari; Davidson, Hilary; Herzog, Patricia and Snell, Patricia. (2011). Lost in transition: the dark side of emerging adulthood. New York, NY: Oxford University Press.

Smith, Christian and Snell, Patricia. (2009). *Souls in transition: The religious and spiritual lives of emerging adults.* New York, NY: Oxford University Press.

Smith, G. Rush; Williamson, Gail M.; Miller, L. Stephen and Schulz, Richard. (2011). Depression and quality of informal care: A longitudinal investigation of caregiving stressors. *Psychology and Aging, 26*(3), 584–591. doi:10.1037/a0022263

Smith, Jacqueline; Boone, Anniglo; Gourdine, Ruby and Brown, Annie W. (2013). Fictions and facts about parents and parenting older first-time entrants to foster care. *Journal of Human Behavior in the Social Environment, 23*(2), 211–219. doi:10.1080/10911359.2013.747400

Smith, Michelle I.; Yatsunenko, Tanya; Manary, Mark J.; Trehan, Indi; Mkakosya, Rajhab; Cheng, Jiye, . . . Gordon, Jeffrey I. (2013). Gut Microbiomes of Malawian Twin Pairs Discordant for Kwashiorkor. *Science, 339*(6119), 548–554. doi: 10.1126/science.1229000

Smith, Peter K. (2010). Children and play: Understanding children's worlds. Malden, MA: Wiley-Blackwell.

Smokowski, Paul Richard; Rose, Roderick and Bacallao, Martica. (2010). Influence of risk factors and cultural assets on latino adolescents' trajectories of self-esteem and internalizing symptoms. *Child Psychiatry & Human Development, 41*(2), 133–155. doi:10.1007/s10578-009-0157-6

Snider, Terra Ziporyn. (2012). Later school start times are a public-health issue. *Education Week, 31*(31), 25, 27.

Snow, Catherine E. and Kang, Jennifer Yusun. (2006). Becoming bilingual, biliterate, and bicultural. In William Damon and Richard M. Lerner (Eds.), *Handbook of child psychology* (6th ed., Vol. 4, pp. 75–102). Hoboken, NJ: Wiley.

Snow, Catherine E.; Porche, Michelle V.; Tabors, Patton O. and Harris, Stephanie Ross. (2007). Is literacy enough? Pathways to academic success for adolescents. Baltimore, MD: Brookes Publishing Company.

Snyder, Thomas D. and Dillow, Sally A. (2010). Digest of education statistics, 2009. Washington, DC: National Center for Education Statistics, Institute of Education Sciences, U.S. Department of Education.

Snyder, Thomas D. and Dillow, Sally A. (2011). Digest of education statistics, 2010. Washington, DC: National Center for Education Statistics, Institute of Education Sciences, U.S. Department of Education, 2010.

Snyder, Thomas D. and Dillow, Sally A. (2012). Digest of education statistics, 2011. Washington, DC: National Center for Education Statistics, Institute of Education Sciences, U.S. Department of Education.

Soares, Joseph A. (2012). The future of college admissions: Discussion. *Educational Psychologist, 47*(1), 66–70. doi:10.1080/00461520.2011.638902

Sobal, Jeffery and Hanson, Karla L. (2011). Marital status, marital history, body weight, and obesity. *Marriage & Family Review, 47*(7), 474–504. doi:10.1080/01494929.2011.620934

Soenens, Bart and Vansteenkiste, Maarten. (2010). A theoretical upgrade of the concept of parental psychological control: Proposing new insights on the basis of self-determination theory. *Developmental Review, 30*(1), 74–99. doi:10.1016/j.dr.2009.11.001

Soley, Gaye and Hannon, Erin E. (2010). Infants prefer the musical meter of their own culture: A cross-cultural comparison. *Developmental Psychology, 46*(1), 286–292. doi:10.1037 /a0017555

Solheim, Elisabet; Wichstrøm, Lars; Belsky, Jay and Berg-Nielsen, Turid Suzanne. (2013). Do time in child care and peer group exposure predict poor socioemotional adjustment in Norway? *Child Development, 84*(5), 1701–1715. doi:10.1111/cdev.12071

Solomon, Andrew. (2012). Far from the tree: Parents, children and the search for identity. New York, NY: Scribner.

Solomon, Alina; Sippola, R.; Soininen, H.; Wolozin, B.; Tuomilehto, J.; Laatikainen, T. and Kivipelto, Miia. (2010). Lipid-lowering treatment is related to decreased risk of dementia: A population-based study (FINRISK). *Neuro-Degenerative Diseases, 7,* 180–182. doi:10.1159/000295659

Somerville, Leah H. (2013). The teenage brain: Sensitivity to social evaluation. *Current Directions in Psychological Science, 22*(2), 121–127. doi:10.1177/0963721413476512

Soons, Judith P. M. and Kalmijn, Matthijs. (2009). Is marriage more than cohabitation? Well-being differences in 30 European countries. *Journal of Marriage and Family, 71*(5), 1141–1157. doi: 10.1111/j.1741-3737.2009.00660.x

Soons, Judith P. M.; Liefbroer, Aart C. and Kalmijn, Matthijs. (2009). The long-term consequences of relationship formation for subjective well-being. *Journal of Marriage and Family, 71*(5), 1254–1270. doi:10.1111/j.1741-3737.2009.00667.x

Sorkin, Dara H. and Rook, Karen S. (2006). Dealing with negative social exchanges in later life: Coping responses, goals, and effectiveness. *Psychology and Aging, 21*(4), 715–725. doi:10.1037/0882-7974.21.4.715

Soska, Kasey C.; Adolph, Karen E. and Johnson, Scott P. (2010). Systems in development: Motor skill acquisition facilitates three-dimensional object completion. *Developmental Psychology, 46*(1), 129–138. doi:10.1037/a0014618

Sowell, Elizabeth R.; Peterson, Bradley S.; Thompson, Paul M.; Welcome, Suzanne E.; Henkenius, Amy L. and Toga, Arthur W. (2003). Mapping cortical change across the human life span. *Nature Neuroscience, 6*(3), 309–315. doi:10.1038/nn1008

Sowell, Elizabeth R.; Thompson, Paul M. and Toga, Arthur W. (2007). Mapping adolescent brain maturation using structural magnetic resonance imaging. In Daniel Romer and Elaine F. Walker (Eds.), *Adolescent psychopathology and the developing brain: Integrating brain and prevention science* (pp. 55–84). New York, NY: Oxford University Press.

Sparks, Sarah D. (2012). Form + Function = Finnish Schools. Education Week, 31(36), 9.

Spear, Linda. (2013). The teenage brain: Adolescents and alcohol. *Current Directions in Psychological Science, 22*(2), 152–157. doi:10.1177/0963721412472192

Spearman, Charles Edward. (1927). The abilities of man, their nature and measurement. New York, NY: Macmillan.

Specht, Jule; Egloff, Boris and Schmukle, Stefan C. (2011). Stability and change of personality across the life course: The impact of age and major life events on mean-level and rank-order stability of the Big Five. *Journal of Personality and Social Psychology, 101*(4), 862–882. doi:10.1037/a0024950

Spelke, Elizabeth S. (1993). Object perception. In Alvin I. Goldman (Ed.), *Readings in philosophy and cognitive science* (pp. 447–460). Cambridge, MA: The MIT Press.

Spencer, John P.; Blumberg, Mark S.; McMurray, Bob; Robinson, Scott R.; Samuelson, Larissa K. and Tomblin, J. Bruce. (2009). Short arms and talking eggs: Why we should no longer abide the nativist-empiricist debate. *Child Development Perspectives, 3*(2), 79–87. doi:10.1111/j.1750-8606.2009.00081.x

Sperry, Debbie M. and Widom, Cathy Spatz. (2013). Child abuse and neglect, social support, and psychopathology in adulthood: A prospective investigation. *Child Abuse & Neglect, 37*(6), 415–425. doi:10.1016/j.chiabu.2013.02.006

Spinillo, Arsenio; Montanari, Laura; Gardella, Barbara; Roccio, Marianna; Stronati, Mauro and Fazzi, Elisa. (2009). Infant sex, obstetric risk factors, and 2-year neurodevelopmental outcome among preterm infants. *Developmental Medicine & Child Neurology, 51*(7), 518–525. doi:10.1111/j.1469-8749.2009.03273.x

Spittle, Alicia J.; Treyvaud, Karli; Doyle, Lex W.; Roberts, Gehan; Lee, Katherine J.; Inder, Terrie E., . . . Anderson, Peter J. (2009). Early emergence of behavior and social-emotional problems in very preterm infants. *Journal of the American Academy of Child and Adolescent Psychiatry, 48*(9), 909–918. doi:10.1097/CHI.0b013e3181af8235

Sprietsma, Maresa. (2010). Effect of relative age in the first grade of primary school on long-term scholastic results: international comparative evidence using PISA 2003. *Education Economics, 18*(1), 1–32. doi:10.1080/09645290802201961

St. Petersburg-USA Orphanage Research Team. (2008). The effects of early social-emotional and relationship experience on the development of young orphanage children. *Monographs of the Society for Research in Child Development, 73*(3), 1–262.

Staff, Jeremy; Messersmith, Emily E. and Schulenberg, John E. (2009). Adolescents and the world of work. In Richard Lerner and Laurence Steinberg (Eds.), *Handbook of adolescent psychology* (pp. 270–313). Hoboken, NJ: Wiley. doi:10.1002/9780470479193.adlpsy002009

Staff, Jeremy and Schulenberg, John. (2010). Millennials and the world of work. Experiences in paid work during adolescence. *Journal of Business and Psychology, 25*(2), 247–255. doi:10.1007/s10869-010-9167-4

Staiger, Annegret Daniela. (2006). Learning difference: Race and schooling in the multiracial metropolis. Stanford, CA: Stanford University Press.

Staplin, Loren; Lococo, Kathy H.; Martell, Carol and Stutts, Jane. (2012). Taxonomy of Older Driver Behaviors and Crash Risk. Washington, DC: Office of Behavioral Safety Research National Highway Traffic Safety Administration, U.S. Department of Transportation.

Staudinger, Ursula M. and Glück, Judith. (2011). Psychological wisdom research: Commonalities and differences in a growing field. *Annual Review of Psychology, 62,* 215–241. doi:10.1146/annurev.psych.121208.131659

Staudinger, Ursula M. and Lindenberger, Ulman E. R. (2003). Why read another book on human development? Understanding human development takes a metatheory and multiple disciplines. In Ursula M. Staudinger and Ulman Lindenberger (Eds.), *Understanding human development: Dialogues with lifespan psychology* (pp. 1–13). Boston, MA: Kluwer.

Stavrova, Olga; Fetchenhauer, Detlef and Schlösser, Thomas. (2012). Cohabitation, gender, and happiness: A cross-cultural study in thirty countries. *Journal of Cross-Cultural Psychology, 43*(7), 1063–1081. doi:10.1177/0022022111419030

Stawski, Robert S.; Almeida, David M.; Lachman, Margie E.; Tun, Patricia A. and Rosnick, Christopher B. (2010). Fluid cognitive ability is associated with greater exposure and smaller reactions to daily stressors. *Psychology and Aging, 25*(2), 330–342. doi:10.1037/a0018246

Stawski, Robert S.; Sliwinski, Martin J. and Hofer, Scott M. (2013). Between-person and within-person associations among processing speed, attention switching, and working memory in younger and older adults. *Experimental Aging Research: An International Journal Devoted to the Scientific Study of the Aging Process, 39*(2), 194–214. doi:10.1080/0361073X.2013.761556

Steele, Claude M. (1997). A threat in the air: How stereotypes shape intellectual identity and performance. *American Psychologist, 52*(6), 613–629. doi:10.1037//0003-066X.52.6.613

Stein, Arlene. (2006). Shameless: Sexual dissidence in American culture. New York, NY: New York University Press.

Steinberg, Laurence. (2001). We know some things: Parent-adolescent relationships in retrospect and prospect. *Journal of Research on Adolescence, 11*(1), 1–19. doi:10.1111/1532-7795.00001

Steinberg, Laurence. (2004). Risk taking in adolescence: What changes, and why? *Annals of the New York Academy of Sciences, 1021,* 51–58. doi:10.1196/annals.1308.005

Steinberg, Laurence. (2009). Should the science of adolescent brain development inform public policy? *American Psychologist, 64*(8), 739–750. doi:10.1037/0003-066x.64.8.739

Steinberg, Laurence. (2010). A dual systems model of adolescent risk-taking. *Developmental Psychobiology, 52*(3), 216–224. doi:10.1002/dev.20445

Steinberg, Laurence and Monahan, Kathryn C. (2011). Adolescents' exposure to sexy media does not hasten the initiation of sexual intercourse. *Developmental Psychology, 47*(2), 562–576. doi:10.1037/a0020613

Steiner, Meir and Young, Elizabeth A. (2008). Hormones and mood. In Jill B. Becker, Karen J. Berkley, Nori Geary, Elizabeth Hampson, James P. Herman and Elizabeth Young (Eds.), *Sex differences in the brain: From genes to behavior* (pp. 405–426). New York, NY: Oxford University Press.

Stephens, Rick and Richey, Mike. (2013). A business view on U.S. *education*. *Science*, *340*(6130), 313–314. doi:10.1126/science.1230728

Sterck, Elisabeth H. M. and Begeer, Sander. (2010). Theory of Mind: Specialized capacity or emergent property? *European Journal of Developmental Psychology*, *7*(1), 1–16. doi:10.1080/17405620903526242

Sterling, Peter. (2012). Allostasis: A model of predictive regulation. *Physiology & Behavior*, *106*(1), 5–15. doi:10.1016/j.physbeh.2011.06.004

Stern, Michael J. and Adams, Alison E. (2010). Do rural residents really use the internet to build social capital? *An empirical investigation*. *American Behavioral Scientist*, *53*(9), 1389–1422. doi:10.1177/0002764210361692

Stern, Peter. (2013). Connection, Connection, Connection. . . . *Science*, *342*(6158), 577. doi:10.1126/science.342.6158.577

Stern, Yaakov (Ed.). (2013). Cognitive reserve: Theory and applications. New York, NY: Psychology Press.

Sternberg, Robert J. (1986). A triangular theory of love. *Psychological Review*, *93*(2), 119–135. doi:10.1037/0033-295X.93.2.119

Sternberg, Robert J. (1988). Triangulating love. In Robert J. Sternberg and Michael L. Barnes (Eds.), The psychology of love (pp. 119–138). New Haven, CT: Yale University Press.

Sternberg, Robert J. (2003). Wisdom, intelligence, and creativity synthesized. New York, NY: Cambridge University Press.

Sternberg, Robert J. (2011). The theory of successful intelligence. In Robert J. Sternberg and Scott Barry Kaufman (Eds.), The Cambridge Handbook of Intelligence (pp. 504–526). New York, NY: Cambridge University Press.

Sternberg, Robert J. (2012). Why I became an administrator . . . and why you might become one too. *Observer*, *25*(2), 21–22.

Sternberg, Robert J. (2013). Searching for love. *The Psychologist*, *26*(2), 98–101.

Sternberg, Robert J. (2013). "The intelligence of nations": smart but not wise—A comment on Hunt (2012). *Perspectives on Psychological Science*, *8*(2), 187–189. doi:10.1177/1745691612443829

Sternberg, Robert J.; Jarvin, Linda and Grigorenko, Elena L. (2011). Explorations in giftedness. New York, NY: Cambridge University Press.

Sternberg, Robert J. and Weis, Karin. (2006). The new psychology of love. New Haven, CT: Yale University Press.

Sterns, Harvey L. and Huyck, Margaret Hellie. (2001). The role of work in midlife. In Margie E. Lachman (Ed.), *Handbook of midlife development* (pp. 447–486). New York, NY: Wiley.

Stevenson, Olive. (2007). Neglected children and their families (2nd ed.). Malden, MA: Blackwell.

Stevenson, Richard J.; Oaten, Megan J.; Case, Trevor I.; Repacholi, Betty M. and Wagland, Paul. (2010). Children's response to adult disgust elicitors: Development and acquisi-tion. *Developmental Psychology*, *46*(1), 165–177. doi:10.1037/a0016692

Stieba, David M.; Chena, Li; Eshoulb, Maysoon and Judeka, Stan. (2012). Ambient air pollution, birth weight and preterm birth: A systematic review and meta-analysis. *Environmental Research*, *117*, 100–111. doi:10.1016/j.envres.2012.05.007

Stigler, James W. and Hiebert, James. (2009). The teaching gap: Best ideas from the world's teachers for improving education in the classroom. New York, NY: Free Press.

Stigum, Hein; Samuelsen, Sven-Ove and Traeen, Bente. (2010). Analysis of first coitus. *Archives of Sexual Behavior*, *39*(4), 907–914. doi:10.1007/s10508-009-9494-6

Stiles, Joan and Jernigan, Terry. (2010). The basics of brain development. *Neuropsychology Review*, *20*(4), 327–348. doi:10.1007/s11065-010-9148-4

Stine-Morrow, Elizabeth A. L. and Basak, Chandramallika. (2011). Cognitive interventions. In K. Warner Schaie and Sherry L. Willis (Eds.), *Handbook of the psychology of aging* (7th ed., pp. 153–171). San Diego, CA: Academic Press. doi:10.1016/B978-0-12-380882-0.00010-3

Stine-Morrow, Elizabeth A. L.; Noh, Soo Rim and Shake, Matthew C. (2010). Age differences in the effects of conceptual integration training on resource allocation in sentence processing. *Quarterly Journal of Experimental Psychology*, *63*(7), 1430–1455. doi:10.1080/17470210903330983

Stipek, Deborah. (2013). Mathematics in Early Childhood Education: Revolution or Evolution? *Early Education & Development*, *24*(4), 431–435. doi:10.1080/10409289.2013.777285

Stolk, Lisette; Perry, John R. B.; Chasman, Daniel I.; He, Chunyan; Mangino, Massimo; Sulem, Patrick, . . . Lunetta, Kathryn L. (2012). Meta-analyses identify 13 loci associated with age at menopause and highlight DNA repair and immune pathways. *Nature Genetics*, *44*, 260–268. doi:10.1038/ng.1051

Stoltenborgh, Marije; van IJzendoorn, Marinus H.; Euser, Eveline M. and Bakermans-Kranenburg, Marian J. (2011). A global perspective on child sexual abuse: Meta-analysis of prevalence around the world. *Child Maltreatment*, *16*(2), 79–101. doi:10.1177/1077559511403920

Stone, Robyn I. (2006). Emerging issues in long-term care. In Robert H. Binstock and Linda K. George (Eds.), *Handbook of aging and the social sciences* (6th ed., pp. 397–418). Amsterdam, The Netherlands: Elsevier

Stoneking, Mark and Delfin, Frederick. (2010). The human genetic history of East Asia: Weaving a complex tapestry. *Current Biology*, *20*(4), R188-R193. doi:10.1016/j.cub.2009.11.052

Stonington, Scott D. (2012). On ethical locations: The good death in Thailand, where ethics sit in places. *Social Science & Medicine*, *75*(5), 836–844. doi:10.1016/j.socscimed.2012.03.045

Strasburger, Victor C.; Wilson, Barbara J. and Jordan, Amy B. (2009). Children, adolescents, and the media (2nd ed.). Los Angeles, CA: Sage.

Straus, Murray A. and Paschall, Mallie J. (2009). Corporal punishment by mothers and development of children's cognitive ability: A longitudinal study of two nationally representative age cohorts. *Journal of Aggression, Maltreatment & Trauma*, *18*(5), 459–483. doi:10.1080/10926770903035168

Stroebe, Margaret; Schut, Henk and Boerner, Kathrin. (2010). Continuing bonds in adaptation to bereavement: Toward theoretical integration. *Clinical Psychology Review*, *30*(2), 259–268. doi:10.1016/j.cpr.2009.11.007

Stroebe, Margaret S.; Abakoumkin, Georgios; Stroebe, Wolfgang and Schut, Henk. (2012). Continuing bonds in adjustment to bereavement: Impact of abrupt versus gradual separation. *Personal Relationships*, *19*(2), 255–266. doi:10.1111/j.1475-6811.2011.01352.x

Stronegger, Willibald J.; Schmölzer, Christin; Rásky, Éva and Freidl, Wolfgang. (2011). Changing attitudes towards euthanasia among medical students in Austria. *Journal of Medical Ethics*, *37*, 227–229. doi:10.1136/jme.2010.039792

Stubben, Jerry D. (2001). Working with and conducting research among American Indian families. *American Behavioral Scientist*, *44*(9), 1466–1481. doi:10.1177/00027642010044009004

Stupica, Brandi; Sherman, Laura J. and Cassidy, Jude. (2011). Newborn irritability moderates the association between infant attachment security and toddler exploration and sociability. *Child Development*, *82*(5), 1381–1389. doi:10.1111/j.1467-8624.2011.01638.x

Su, Ya-Hui. (2011). The constitution of agency in developing lifelong learning ability: The 'being' mode. *Higher Education*, *62*(4), 399–412. doi:10.1007/s10734-010-9395-6

Suchy, Frederick J.; Brannon, Patsy M.; Carpenter, Thomas O.; Fernandez, Jose R.; Gilsanz, Vicente; Gould, Jeffrey B., . . . Wolf, Marshall A. (2010). National Institutes of Health Consensus Development Conference: Lactose intolerance and health. *Annals of Internal Medicine*, *152*(12), 792–796. doi:10.7326/0003-4819-152-12-201006150-00248

Sue, Derald Wing (Ed.). (2010). Microaggressions and marginality: Manifestation, dynamics, and impact. Hoboken, NJ: Wiley.

Sulek, Julia Prodis. (2013, April 30). *Audrie Pott suicide: Parents share grief, quest for justice in exclusive interview*. San Jose Mercury News.

Sullivan, Sheila. (1999). *Falling in love: A history of torment and enchantment*. London, UK: Macmillan.

Sun, Min and Rugolotto, Simone. (2004). Assisted infant toilet training in a Western family setting. *Journal of Developmental & Behavioral Pediatrics*, *25*(2), 99–101. doi:10.1097/00004703-200404000-00004

Sun, Rongjun and Liu, Yuzhi. (2008). The more engagement, the better? A study of mortality of the oldest old in China. In Zeng Yi, Dudley L. Jr. Poston, Denese Ashbaugh Vlosky and Danan Gu (Eds.), *Healthy longevity in China* (Vol. 20, pp. 177–192). Dordrecht, The Netherlands: Springer. doi:10.1007/978-1-4020-6752-5_11

Sunita, T. H. and Desai, Rathnamala M. (2013). Knowledge, attitude and practice of contraception among women attending a tertiary care hospital in India. *International Journal of Reproduction, Contraception, Obstetrics and Gynecology*, 2(2), 172–176. doi:10.5455/2320-1770.ijrcog20130612

Sunstein, Cass R. (2008). Adolescent risk-taking and social meaning: A commentary. *Developmental Review*, 28(1), 145–152. doi:10.1016/j.dr.2007.11.003

Surgeoner, Brae V.; Chapman, Benjamin J. and Powell, Douglas A. (2009). University students' hand hygiene practice during a gastrointestinal outbreak in residence: What they say they do and what they actually do. *Journal of Environmental Health*, 72(2), 24–28.

Surget, A.; Tanti, A.; Leonardo, E. D.; Laugeray, A.; Rainer.Q.; Touma, C., . . . Belzung, C. (2011). Antidepressants recruit new neurons to improve stress response regulation. *Molecular Psychiatry*, 16, 1177–1188. doi:10.1038/mp.2011.48

Suris, Joan-Carles; Michaud, Pierre-André; Akre, Christina and Sawyer, Susan M. (2008). Health risk behaviors in adolescents with chronic conditions. *Pediatrics*, 122(5), e1113-e1118. doi:10.1542/peds.2008-1479

Surman, Craig B. H.; Hammerness, Paul G.; Pion, Katie and Faraone, Stephen V. (2013). Do stimulants improve functioning in adults with ADHD?: *A review of the literature. European Neuropsychopharmacology*, 23(6), 528–533. doi:10.1016/j.euroneuro.2012.02.010

Susman, Elizabeth J.; Houts, Renate M.; Steinberg, Laurence; Belsky, Jay; Cauffman, Elizabeth; DeHart, Ganie, . . . Halpern-Felsher, Bonnie L. (2010). Longitudinal development of secondary sexual characteristics in girls and boys between ages 9–1/2 and 15–1/2 years. *Archives of Pediatrics & Adolescent Medicine*, 164(2), 166–173. doi:10.1001/archpediatrics.2009.261

Sutphin, George L. and Kaeberlein, Matt. (2011). Comparative genetics of aging. In Edward J. Masoro and Steven N. Austad (Eds.), *Handbook of the biology of aging* (7th ed., pp. 215–242). San Diego, CA: Academic Press.

Sutton-Smith, Brian. (2011). The antipathies of play. In Anthony D. Pellegrini (Ed.), *The Oxford handbook of the development of play* (pp. 110–115). New York, NY: Oxford University Press.

Swan, Suzanne C.; Gambone, Laura J.; Caldwell, Jennifer E.; Sullivan, Tami P. and Snow, David L. (2008). A review of research on women's use of violence with male intimate partners. *Violence and Victims*, 23(3), 301–314. doi:10.1891/0886-6708.23.3.301

Swanson, Christopher B. (2011). Analysis finds graduation rates moving up: Strong signs of improvement on graduation. *Education Week*, 30(34), 23–25.

Sweeney, Kathryn A. (2013). Race-conscious adoption choices, multiraciality and color-blind racial ideology. *Family Relations*, 62(1), 42–57. doi:10.1111/j.1741-3729.2012.00757.x

Sweeney, Megan M. (2010). Remarriage and stepfamilies: Strategic sites for family scholarship in the 21st century. *Journal of Marriage and Family*, 72(3), 667–684. doi:10.1111/j.1741-3737.2010.00724.x

Sweet, Stephen and Moen, Phyllis. (2012). Dual earners preparing for job loss: Agency, linked lives, and resilience. *Work and Occupations*, 39(1), 35–70. doi:10.1177/0730888411415601

Swindell, William R. (2012). Dietary restriction in rats and mice: A meta-analysis and review of the evidence for genotype-dependent effects on lifespan. *Ageing Research Reviews*, 11(2), 254–270. doi:10.1016/j.arr.2011.12.006

Szydlik, Marc. (2012). Generations: Connections across the life course. *Advances in Life Course Research*, 17(3), 100–111. doi:10.1016/j.alcr.2012.03.002

Taber, Daniel R.; Stevens, June; Evenson, Kelly R.; Ward, Dianne S.; Poole, Charles; Maciejewski, Matthew L., . . . Brownson, Ross C. (2011). State policies targeting junk food in schools: Racial/ethnic differences in the effect of policy change on soda consumption. *American Journal of Public Health*, 101(9), 1769–1775. doi:10.2105/ajph.2011.300221

Tacken, Mart and van Lamoen, Ellemieke. (2005). Transport behaviour and realised journeys and trips. In Heidrun Mollenkopf, Fiorella Marcellini, Isto Ruoppila, Zsuzsa Széman and Mart Tacken (Eds.), *Enhancing mobility in later life: Personal coping, environmental resources and technical support. The out-of-home mobility of older adults in urban and rural regions of five European countries* (pp. 105–139). Amsterdam, The Netherlands: IOS Press.

Tadmor, Carmit T.; Satterstrom, Patricia; Jang, Sujin and Polzer, Jeffrey T. (2012). Beyond individual creativity: The superadditive benefits of multicultural experience for collective creativity in culturally diverse teams. *Journal of Cross-Cultural Psychology*, 43(3), 384–392. doi:10.1177/0022022111435259

Taga, Keiko A.; Markey, Charlotte N. and Friedman, Howard S. (2006). A longitudinal investigation of associations between boys' pubertal timing and adult behavioral health and well-being. *Journal of Youth and Adolescence*, 35(3), 380–390. doi:10.1007/s10964-006-9039-4

Talley, Ronda C. and Montgomery, Rhonda J. V. (2013). Caregiving: A developmental lifelong perspective. In Ronda C. Talley and Lydia LaGue (Eds.), *Caregiving across the lifespan: Research, practice, policy* (pp. 3–10). New York, NY: Springer.

Talwar, Victoria; Harris, Paul L. and Schleifer, Michael (Eds.). (2011). *Children's understanding of death: From biological to religious conceptions*. New York, NY: Cambridge University Press.

Tamay, Zeynep; Akcay, Ahmet; Ones, Ulker; Guler, Nermin; Kilic, Gurkan and Zencir, Mehmet. (2007). Prevalence and risk factors for allergic rhinitis in primary school children. *International Journal of Pediatric Otorhinolaryngology*, 71(3), 463–471. doi:10.1016/j.ijporl.2006.11.013

Tamis-LeMonda, Catherine S.; Bornstein, Marc H. and Baumwell, Lisa. (2001). Maternal responsiveness and children's achievement of language milestones. *Child Development*, 72(3), 748–767. doi:10.1111/1467-8624.00313

Tan, Patricia Z.; Armstrong, Laura Marie and Cole, Pamela M. (2013). Relations between Temperament and Anger Regulation over Early Childhood. *Social Development*, 22(4), 755–772. doi:10.1111/j.1467-9507.2012.00674.x

Tanner, Jennifer L. and Arnett, Jeffrey Jensen. (2011). Presenting emerging adulthood: What makes emerging adulthood developmentally distinctive? In Jeffrey Jensen Arnett, Marion Kloep, Leo B. Hendry and Jennifer L. Tanner (Eds.), *Debating emerging adulthood: Stage or process?* (pp. 13–30). New York, NY: Oxford University Press. doi:10.1093/acprof:oso/9780199757176.003.0002

Tanner, Jennifer L.; Arnett, Jeffrey Jensen and Leis, Julie A. (2009). Emerging adulthood: Learning and development during the first stage of adulthood. In M. Cecil Smith and Nancy DeFrates-Densch (Eds.), *Handbook of research on adult learning and development* (pp. 34–67). New York, NY: Routledge.

Tarullo, Amanda R.; Garvin, Melissa C. and Gunnar, Megan R. (2011). Atypical EEG power correlates with indiscriminately friendly behavior in internationally adopted children. *Developmental Psychology*, 47(2), 417–431. doi:10.1037/a0021363

Tarullo, Amanda R. and Gunnar, Megan R. (2006). Child maltreatment and the developing HPA axis. *Hormones and Behavior*, 50(4), 632–639. doi: 10.1016/j.yhbeh.2006.06.010

Tay, Marc Tze-Hsin; Au Eong, Kah Guan; Ng, C. Y. and Lim, M. K. (1992). Myopia and educational attainment in 421,116 young Singaporean males. *Annals Academy of Medicine Singapore*, 21(6), 785–791.

Taylor, John H. (Ed.). (2010). *Journey through the afterlife: Ancient Egyptian book of the dead*. Cambridge, MA: Harvard University Press.

Taylor, Joy L.; Kennedy, Quinn; Adamson, Maheen M.; Lazzeroni, Laura C.; Noda, Art; Murphy Jr., Greer M. and Yesavage, Jerome A. (2011). Influences of APOE ε4 and expertise on performance of older pilots. *Psychology and Aging*, 26(2), 480–487. doi: 10.1037/a0021697

Taylor, Joy L.; Kennedy, Quinn; Noda, Art and Yesavage, Jerome A. (2007). Pilot age and expertise predict flight simulator performance: A 3-year longitudinal study. *Neurology*, 68(9), 648–654. doi:10.1212/01.wnl.0000255943.10045.c0

Taylor, Kate. (2013, August 20). *Man slaps two supporters at Quinn event*. The New York Times, p. A16.

Taylor, Marjorie; Carlson, Stephanie M.; Maring, Bayta L.; Gerow, Lynn and Charley, Carolyn M. (2004). The characteristics and correlates of fantasy in school-age children:

Imaginary companions, impersonation, and social understanding. *Developmental Psychology, 40*(6), 1173–1187. doi: 10.1037/0012-1649.40.6.1173

Taylor, Marjorie; Shawber, Alison B. and Mannering, Anne M. (2009). Children's imaginary companions: What is it like to have an invisible friend? In Keith D. Markman, William M. P. Klein and Julie A. Suhr (Eds.), Handbook of imagination and mental simulation (pp. 211–224). New York, NY: Psychology Press.

Taylor, Ronald D.; Seaton, Eleanor and Dominguez, Antonio. (2008). Kinship support, family relations, and psychological adjustment among low-income African American mothers and adolescents. *Journal of Research on Adolescence, 18*(1), 1–22. doi:10.1111/j.1532-7795.2008.00548.x

Taylor, Rachael W.; Murdoch, Linda; Carter, Philippa; Gerrard, David F.; Williams, Sheila M. and Taylor, Barry J. (2009). Longitudinal study of physical activity and inactivity in preschoolers: The FLAME study. *Medicine & Science in Sports & Exercise, 41*(1), 96–102. doi: 10.1249/MSS.0b013e3181849d81

Taylor, Shelley E. (2006). Tend and befriend: Biobehavioral bases of affiliation under stress. *Current Directions in Psychological Science, 15*(6), 273–277. doi: 10.1111/j.1467-8721.2006.00451.x

Taylor, Shelley E.; Klein, Laura Cousino; Lewis, Brian P.; Gruenewald, Tara L.; Gurung, Regan A. R. and Updegraff, John A. (2000). Biobehavioral responses to stress in females: Tend-and-befriend, not fight-or-flight. *Psychological Review, 107*(3), 411–429. doi: 10.1037//0033-295X.107.3.411

Taylor, Valerie Jones and Walton, Gregory M. (2011). Stereotype threat undermines academic learning. *Personality and Social Psychology Bulletin, 37*(8), 1055–1067. doi: 10.1177/0146167211406506

Te Morenga, Lisa; Mallard, Simonette and Mann, Jim. (2013). Dietary sugars and body weight: systematic review and meta-analyses of randomised controlled trials and cohort studies. *BMJ, 346,* e7492. doi: 10.1136/bmj.e7492

Teachman, Jay. (2008). Complex life course patterns and the risk of divorce in second marriages. *Journal of Marriage and Family, 70*(2), 294–305. doi: 10.1111/j.1741-3737.2008.00482.x

Teachman, Jay. (2010). Work-related health limitations, education, and the risk of marital disruption. *Journal of Marriage and Family, 72*(4), 919–932. doi:10.1111/j.1741-3737.2010.00739.x

Temple, Jeff R.; Le, Vi Donna; van den Berg, Patricia; Ling, Yan; Paul, Jonathan A. and Temple, Brian W. (2014). Brief report: Teen sexting and psychosocial health. *Journal of Adolescence, 37*(1), 33–36. doi:10.1016/j.adolescence.2013.10.008

Teo, Alan R. (2010). A new form of social withdrawal in Japan: A review of hikikomori. *International Journal of Social Psychiatry, 56*(2), 178–185. doi:10.1177/0020764008100629

Teoh, Yee San and Lamb, Michael E. (2013). Interviewer demeanor in forensic interviews of children. *Psychology, Crime & Law, 19*(2), 145–159. doi:10.1080/1068316X.2011.614610

Terman, Lewis M. (1925). *Genetic studies of genius.* Stanford, CA: Stanford University Press.

Thaler, Richard H. and Sunstein, Cass R. (2008). *Nudge: Improving decisions about health, wealth, and happiness.* New Haven, CT: Yale University Press.

Thelen, Esther and Smith, Linda B. (2006). Dynamic systems theories. In Richard M. Lerner and William Damon (Eds.), *Handbook of child psychology* (6th ed., Vol. 1, pp. 258–312). Hoboken, NJ: Wiley.

Thiele, Dianne M. and Whelan, Thomas A. (2008). The relationship between grandparent satisfaction, meaning, and generativity. *International Journal of Aging and Human Development, 66*(1), 21–48. doi:10.2190/AG.66.1.b

Thomaes, Sander; Reijntjes, Albert; Orobio de Castro, Bram; Bushman, Brad J.; Poorthuis, Astrid and Telch, Michael J. (2010). I like me if you like me: On the interpersonal modulation and regulation of preadolescents' state self-esteem. *Child Development, 81*(3), 811–825. doi:10.1111/j.1467-8624.2010.01435.x

Thomas, Alexander and Chess, Stella. (1977). *Temperament and development.* New York, NY: Brunner/Mazel.

Thomas, Dylan. (1957). *The collected poems of Dylan Thomas* (6th ed.). New York, NY: New Directions.

Thomas, Michael S. C. and Johnson, Mark H. (2008). New advances in understanding sensitive periods in brain development. *Current Directions in Psychological Science, 17*(1), 1–5. doi:10.1111/j.1467-8721.2008.00537.x

Thomas, Michael S. C.; Van Duuren, Mike; Purser, Harry R. M.; Mareschal, Denis; Ansari, Daniel and Karmiloff-Smith, Annette. (2010). The development of metaphorical language comprehension in typical development and in Williams syndrome. *Journal of Experimental Child Psychology, 106*(2–3), 99–114. doi:10.1016/j.jecp.2009.12.007

Thompson, Clarissa A. and Siegler, Robert S. (2010). Linear numerical-magnitude representations aid children's memory for numbers. *Psychological Science, 21*(9), 1274–1281. doi:10.1177/0956797610378309

Thompson, Elisabeth Morgan and Morgan, Elizabeth M. (2008). "Mostly straight" young women: Variations in sexual behavior and identity development. *Developmental Psychology, 44*(1), 15–21. doi:10.1037/0012-1649.44.1.15

Thompson, Ross A. (2006). The development of the person: Social understanding, relationships, conscience, self. In William Damon and Richard M. Lerner (Eds.), *Handbook of child psychology* (6th ed., Vol. 3, pp. 24–98). Hoboken, NJ: Wiley.

Thompson, Ross A. and Raikes, H. Abigail. (2003). Toward the next quarter-century: Conceptual and methodological challenges for attachment theory. *Development & Psychopathology, 15*(3), 691–718. doi:10.1017/S0954579403000348

Thompson, William W.; Zack, Matthew M.; Krahn, Gloria L.; Andresen, Elena M. and Barile, John P. (2012). Health related quality of life among older adults with and without functional limitations. *American Journal of Public Health, 102*(3), 496–502. doi:10.2105/AJPH.2011.300500

Thornberg, Robert and Jungert, Tomas. (2013). Bystander behavior in bullying situations: Basic moral sensitivity, moral disengagement and defender self-efficacy. *Journal of Adolescence, 36*(3), 475–483. doi:10.1016/j.adolescence.2013.02.003

Thornton, Arland; Axinn, William G. and Xie, Yu. (2007). *Marriage and cohabitation.* Chicago, IL: University of Chicago Press.

Thorson, James A. (1995). Aging in a changing society. Belmont, CA: Wadsworth.

Thrasher, Angela D.; Clay, Olivio J.; Ford, Chandra L. and Stewart, Anita L. (2012). Theory-guided selection of discrimination measures for racial/ethnic health disparities research among older adults. *Journal of Aging and Health, 24*(6), 1018–1043. doi:10.1177/0898264312440322

Thuné-Boyle, Ingela C. V.; Stygall, Jan; Keshtgar, Mohammed R. S.; Davidson, Tim I. and Newman, Stanton P. (2013). Religious/spiritual coping resources and their relationship with adjustment in patients newly diagnosed with breast cancer in the UK. *Psycho-Oncology, 22*(3), 646–658. doi:10.1002/pon.3048

Thurber, James. (1999). The secret life of James Thurber. *The Thurber carnival* (pp. 35–41). New York, NY: Harper Perennial.

Tikotzky, Liat; Sharabany, Ruth; Hirsch, Idit and Sadeh, Avi. (2010). "Ghosts in the Nursery:" Infant sleep and sleep-related cognitions of parents raised under communal sleeping arrangements. *Infant Mental Health Journal, 31*(3), 312–334. doi:10.1002/imhj.20258

Tishkoff, Sarah A.; Reed, Floyd A.; Friedlaender, Françoise R.; Ehret, Christopher; Ranciaro, Alessia; Froment, Alain, . . . Williams, Scott M. (2009). The genetic structure and history of Africans and African Americans. *Science, 324*(5930), 1035–1044. doi:10.1126/science.1172257

Tokunaga, Robert S. (2010). Following you home from school: A critical review and synthesis of research on cyberbullying victimization. *Computers in Human Behavior, 26*(3), 277–287. doi:10.1016/j.chb.2009.11.014

Tolman, Deborah L. and McClelland, Sara I. (2011). Normative sexuality development in adolescence: A decade in review, 2000–2009. *Journal of Research on Adolescence, 21*(1), 242–255. doi:10.1111/j.1532-7795.2010.00726.x

Tomalski, Przemyslaw and Johnson, Mark H. (2010). The effects of early adversity on the adult and developing brain. *Current Opinion in Psychiatry, 23*(3), 233–238. doi:10.1097/YCO.0b013e3283387a8c

Tomasello, Michael. (2006). Acquiring linguistic constructions. In William Damon and Richard M. Lerner (Eds.), Handbook of child psychology (6th ed., Vol. 2, pp. 255–298). Hoboken, NJ: Wiley.

Tomasello, Michael. (2009). Cultural transmission: A view from chimpanzees and human infants. In Ute Schönpflug (Ed.), *Cultural transmission: Psychological, developmental, social, and methodological aspects* (pp. 33–47). New York, NY: Cambridge University Press.

Tomasello, Michael and Herrmann, Esther. (2010). Ape and human cognition. *Current Directions in Psychological Science, 19*(1), 3–8. doi:10.1177/0963721409359300

Tonn, Jessica L. (2006). Later high school start times: A reaction to research. *Education Week, 25,* 5, 17.

Tonyan, Holli A.; Mamikonian-Zarpas, Ani and Chien, Dorothy. (2013). Do they practice what they preach? An ecocultural, multidimensional, group-based examination of the relationship between beliefs and behaviours among child care providers. *Early Child Development and Care, 183*(12), 1853–1877. doi:10.1080/03004430.2012.759949

Toossi, Mitra. (2002). A century of change: The U.S. labor force from 1950 to 2050. *Monthly Labor Review, 125*(5), 15–28.

Toporek, Bryan. (2012). Sports rules shift in light of concussion research. *Education Week, 31*(22), 8.

Tornstam, Lars. (2005). Gerotranscendence: A developmental theory of positive aging. New York, NY: Springer.

Tough, Paul. (2012). How children succeed: Grit, curiosity, and the hidden power of character. Boston, MA: Houghton Mifflin Harcourt.

Toutain, Stéphanie. (2010). What women in France say about alcohol abstinence during pregnancy. *Drug and Alcohol Review, 29*(2), 184–188. doi:10.1111/j.1465-3362.2009.00136.x

Townsend, Jean; Godfrey, Mary and Denby, Tracy. (2006). Heroines, villains and victims: Older people's perceptions of others. *Ageing & Society, 26*(6), 883–900. doi:10.1017/S0144686X06005149

Trautmann-Villalba, Patricia; Gschwendt, Miriam; Schmidt, Martin H. and Laucht, Manfred. (2006). Father-infant interaction patterns as precursors of children's later externalizing behavior problems: A longitudinal study over 11 years. *European Archives of Psychiatry and Clinical Neuroscience, 256*(6), 344–349. doi:10.1007/s00406-006-0642-x

Treas, Judith and Gubernskaya, Zoya. (2012). Farewell to moms? Maternal contact for seven countries in 1986 and 2001. *Journal of Marriage and Family, 74*(2), 297–311. doi:10.1111/j.1741-3737.2012.00956.x

Tremblay, Angelo and Chaput, Jean-Philippe. (2012). Obesity: The allostatic load of weight loss dieting. *Physiology & Behavior, 106*(1), 16–21. doi:10.1016/j.physbeh.2011.05.020

Trenholm, Christopher; Devaney, Barbara; Fortson, Ken; Quay, Lisa; Wheeler, Justin and Clark, Melissa. (2007). Impacts of four Title V, Section 510 abstinence education programs final report. Washington, DC: U.S. Department of Health and Human Services, Mathematica Policy Research, Inc.

Trickett, Penelope K.; Noll, Jennie G. and Putnam, Frank W. (2011). The impact of sexual abuse on female development: Lessons from a multigenerational, longitudinal research study. *Development and Psychopathology, 23*(2), 453–476. doi:10.1017/S0954579411000174

Troll, Lillian E. and Skaff, Marilyn McKean. (1997). Perceived continuity of self in very old age. *Psychology and Aging, 12*(1), 162–169. doi:10.1037/0882-7974.12.1.162

Trommsdorff, Gisela and Cole, Pamela M. (2011). Emotion, self-regulation, and social behavior in cultural contexts. In Xinyin Chen and Kenneth H. Rubin (Eds.), *Socioemotional development in cultural context* (pp. 131–163). New York, NY: Guilford Press.

Trompeter, Susan E.; Bettencourt, Ricki and Barrett-Connor, Elizabeth. (2012). Sexual activity and satisfaction in healthy community-dwelling older women. *The American Journal of Medicine, 125*(1), 37–43.e31. doi:10.1016/j.amjmed.2011.07.036

Tronick, Edward. (2007). The neurobehavioral and social-emotional development of infants and children. New York, NY: W. W. Norton & Co.

Tronick, Ed and Beeghly, Marjorie. (2011). Infants' meaning-making and the development of mental health problems. *American Psychologist, 66*(2), 107–119. doi:10.1037/a0021631

Tronick, Edward Z. (1989). Emotions and emotional communication in infants. *American Psychologist, 44*(2), 112–119. doi:10.1037//0003-066X.44.2.112

Tronick, Edward Z. and Weinberg, M. Katherine. (1997). Depressed mothers and infants: Failure to form dyadic states of consciousness. In Lynne Murray and Peter J. Cooper (Eds.), *Postpartum depression and child development* (pp. 54–81). New York, NY: Guilford Press.

Truog, Robert D. (2007). Brain death: Too flawed to endure, too ingrained to abandon. *The Journal of Law, Medicine & Ethics, 35*(2), 273–281. doi:10.1111/j.1748-720X.2007.00136.x

Tsai, Ming-Chang and Dzorgbo, Dan-Bright S. (2012). Family reciprocity and subjective well-being in Ghana. *Journal of Marriage and Family, 74*(1), 215–228. doi: 10.1111/j.1741-3737.2011.00874.x

Tsao, Feng-Ming; Liu, Huei-Mei and Kuhl, Patricia K. (2004). Speech perception in infancy predicts language development in the second year of life: A longitudinal study. *Child Development, 75*(4), 1067–1084. doi:10.1111/j.1467-8624.2004.00726.x

Tsethlikai, Monica and Rogoff, Barbara. (2013). Involvement in traditional cultural practices and American Indian children's incidental recall of a folktale. *Developmental Psychology, 49*(3), 568–578. doi:10.1037/a0031308

Tudge, Jonathan. (2008). *The everyday lives of young children: Culture, class, and child rearing in diverse societies.* New York, NY: Cambridge University Press.

Tudge, Jonathan R. H.; Doucet, Fabienne; Odero, Dolphine; Sperb, Tania M.; Piccinini, Cesar A. and Lopes, Rita S. (2006). A window into different cultural worlds: Young children's everyday activities in the United States, Brazil, and Kenya. *Child Development, 77*(5), 1446–1469. doi:10.1111/j.1467-8624.2006.00947.x

Turiel, Elliot. (2002). The culture of morality: Social development, context, and conflict. New York, NY: Cambridge University Press.

Turiel, Elliot. (2006). The development of morality. In William Damon and Richard M. Lerner (Eds.), *Handbook of child psychology* (6th ed., Vol. 3, pp. 789–857). Hoboken, NJ: Wiley.

Turiel, Elliot. (2008). Thought about actions in social domains: Morality, social conventions, and social interactions. *Cognitive Development, 23*(1), 136–154. doi:10.1016/j.cogdev.2007.04.001

Turner, Heather A.; Finkelhor, David; Ormrod, Richard; Hamby, Sherry; Leeb, Rebecca T.; Mercy, James A. and Holt, Melissa. (2012). Family context, victimization, and child trauma symptoms: Variations in safe, stable, and nurturing relationships during early and middle childhood. *American Journal of Orthopsychiatry, 82*(2), 209–219. doi:10.1111/j.1939-0025.2012.01147.x

Turner, Val D. and Berkowitz, Marvin W. (2005). Scaffolding morality: Positioning a socio-cultural construct. *New Ideas in Psychology, 23*(3), 174–184. doi:10.1016/j.newideapsych.2006.04.002

Twenge, Jean M.; Gentile, Brittany; DeWall, C. Nathan; Ma, Debbie; Lacefield, Katharine and Schurtz, David R. (2010). Birth cohort increases in psychopathology among young Americans, 1938–2007: A cross-temporal meta-analysis of the MMPI. *Clinical Psychology Review, 30*(2), 145–154. doi:10.1016/j.cpr.2009.10.005

Tye-Murray, Nancy; Spehar, Brent; Myerson, Joel; Sommers, Mitchell S. and Hale, Sandra. (2011). Cross-modal enhancement of speech detection in young and older adults: Does signal content matter? *Ear and Hearing, 32*(5), 650–655. doi:10.1097/AUD.0b013e31821a4578

Tzeng, Shih-Jay. (2007). Learning disabilities in Taiwan: A case of cultural constraints on the education of students with disabilities. *Learning Disabilities Research & Practice, 22*(3), 170–175. doi:10.1111/j.1540-5826.2007.00243.x

U.S. Census Bureau. Historical Time Series Tables, Washington, DC: Retrieved from http://www.census.gov/hhes/www/socdemo/voting/publications/historical/.

U.S. Census Bureau. (1992, October). *Current Population Survey.* Washington, DC: U.S. Department of Commerce, Economic and Statistics Administration, U.S. Census Bureau.

U.S. Census Bureau. (1995, October). *Current Population Survey.* Washington, DC: U.S. Department of Commerce, Economic and Statistics Administration, U.S. Census Bureau. D1-C95-OCTF-TECH.

U.S. Census Bureau. (1999, October). *Current Population Survey.* Washington, DC: U.S. Department of Commerce, Economic and Statistics Administration, U.S. Census Bureau.

U.S. Census Bureau. (2008). *Statistical abstract of the United States: 2009* (128th ed.). Washington, DC: U.S. Department of Commerce.

U.S. Census Bureau. (2009). *Statistical abstract of the United States: 2010* (129th ed.). Washington, DC: U.S. Government Printing Office.

U.S. Census Bureau. (2010). *America's families and living arrangements: 2009.* Housing and Household Economic Statistics Division, Fertility & Family Statistics Branch.November 4.

U.S. Census Bureau. (2011). *America's families and living arrangements: 2011.* Housing and Household Economic Statistics Division, Fertility & Family Statistics Branch.

U.S. Census Bureau. (2012). American Community Survey Reports: The Foreign-Born Population in the United States: 2010.

U.S. Census Bureau. (2012). *Statistical abstract of the United States: 2012* (131st ed.). Washington, DC: U.S. Government Printing Office.

U.S. Department of Agriculture and U.S. Department of Health and Human Services. (2010). *Dietary Guidelines for Americans, 2010.* Washington, DC: U.S. Government Printing Office.

U.S. Department of Health and Human Services. (2003). *Child maltreatment 2001.* Washington, DC: Administration for Children and Families Administration on Children Youth and Families Children's Bureau.

U.S. Department of Health and Human Services. (2008). *Child maltreatment 2006.* Washington, DC: Administration for Children and Families Administration on Children Youth and Families Children's Bureau.

U.S. Department of Health and Human Services. (2010). Head Start impact study: Final report. Washington, DC.

U.S. Department of Health and Human Services. (2011). The Surgeon General's call to action to support breastfeeding. Washington, DC: U.S. Department of Health and Human Services, Office of the Surgeon General.

U.S. Department of Health and Human Services. (2011). *Child maltreatment 2010.* Washington, DC: Administration for Children and Families Administration on Children Youth and Families Children's Bureau.

U.S. Department of Health and Human Services. (2012). *Child Maltreatment 2011.* Washington, DC: Administration for Children and Families Administration on Children Youth and Families Children's Bureau.

U.S. Department of Health and Human Services. (2012, November). National Surveillance of Asthma: United States, 2001–2010. Hyattsville, MD: Centers for Disease Control & Prevention, 31, Table 32.(PHS) 2013–1419.

U.S. Department of Justice Office of Justice Programs Bureau of Justice Statistics. (2011). Homicide trends in the United States, 1980–2008: Annual rates for 2009 and 2010. Washington, DC.

U.S. Department of Transportation. (2010). *Traffic safety facts: 2009 data.* Washington, DC: National Center for Statistics and Analysis.

U.S. Department of Transportation. (2013). *Traffic safety facts: 2011 data. Washington*, DC: National Center for Statistics and Analysis.

U.S. Preventive Services Task Force. (2002). Postmenopausal hormone replacement therapy for primary prevention of chronic conditions: Recommendations and rationale. *Annals of Internal Medicine, 137*(10), 834–839. doi:10.7326/0003-4819-137-10-200211190-00013

Uchida, Shusaku; Hara, Kumiko; Kobayashi, Ayumi; Otsuki, Koji; Yamagata, Hirotaka; Hobara, Teruyuki, . . . Watanabe, Yoshifumi. (2011). Epigenetic status of Gdnf in the ventral striatum determines susceptibility and adaptation to daily stressful events. *Neuron, 69*(2), 359–372. doi:10.1016/j.neuron.2010.12.023

Uddin, Monica; Koenen, Karestan C.; de los Santos, Regina; Bakshis, Erin; Aiello, Allison E. and Galea, Sandro. (2010). Gender differences in the genetic and environmental determinants of adolescent depression. *Depression and Anxiety, 27*(7), 658–666. doi:10.1002/da.20692

Ueda, Tomomi; Suzukamo, Yoshimi; Mai, Sato and Izumi, Shin-Ichi. (2013). Effects of music therapy on behavioral and psychological symptoms of dementia: A systematic review and meta-analysis. *Ageing Research Reviews, 12*(2), 628–641. doi:10.1016/j.arr.2013.02.003

Uekermann, J.; Kraemer, M.; Abdel-Hamid, M.; Schimmelmann, B. G.; Hebebrand, J.; Daum, I., . . . Kis, B. (2010). Social cognition in attention-deficit hyperactivity disorder (ADHD). *Neuroscience & Biobehavioral Reviews, 34*(5), 734–743. doi:10.1016/j.neubiorev.2009.10.009

Umana-Taylor, Adriana J. and Guimond, Amy B. (2010). A longitudinal examination of parenting behaviors and perceived discrimination predicting Latino adolescents' ethnic identity. *Developmental Psychology, 46*(3), 636–650. doi:10.1037/a0019376

Umberson, Debra; Pudrovska, Tetyana and Reczek, Corinne. (2010). Parenthood, childlessness, and well-being: A life course perspective. *Journal of Marriage and Family, 72*(3), 612–629. doi:10.1111/j.1741-3737.2010.00721.x

UNICEF. (2011). *The state of the world's children 2011: Adolescence–An age of opportunity.* New York, NY: United Nations Children's Fund.

UNICEF. (2012). *The state of the world's children 2012:* Children in an urban world. New York, NY: United Nations.

United Nations. (2011). *Population and Vital Statistics Report: Vol. 62. Series A.* New York, NY: United Nations.

United Nations. (2011). The millennium development goals report 2011. New York, NY.

United Nations. (2012). *World population prospects: The 2010 revision.* New York, NY: Population Division of the United Nations Department of Economic and Social Affairs of the United Nations Secretariat, Department of Economic and Social Affairs.

United Nations. (2013). *World population prospects:* The 2012 revision. New York, NY: Population Division of the United Nations Department of Economic and Social Affairs of the United Nations Secretariat.

United Nations Department of Social and Economic Affairs. (2013). Social indicators, Table 2a: Life expectancy. New York, NY: United Nations.

Utendale, William T. and Hastings, Paul D. (2011). Developmental changes in the relations between inhibitory control and externalizing problems during early childhood. *Infant and Child Development, 20*(2), 181–193. doi:10.1002/icd.691

Vaillant, George E. (2002). Aging well: Surprising guideposts to a happier life from the landmark Harvard Study of Adult Development. Boston, MA: Little Brown.

Vaillant, George E. (2008). Spiritual evolution: A scientific defense of faith. New York, NY: Broadway Books.

Vakili, Mahmood; Nadrian, Haidar; Fathipoor, Mohammad; Boniadi, Fatemeh and Morowatisharifabad, Mohammad Ali. (2010). Prevalence and determinants of intimate partner violence against women in Kazeroon, Islamic Republic of Iran. *Violence and Victims, 25*(1), 116–127. doi:10.1891/0886-6708.25.1.116

Valentino, Kristin; Cicchetti, Dante; Toth, Sheree L. and Rogosch, Fred A. (2006). Mother-child play and emerging social behaviors among infants from maltreating families. *Developmental Psychology, 42*(3), 474–485. doi:10.1037/0012-1649.42.3.474

Valsiner, Jaan. (2006). Developmental epistemology and implications for methodology. In Richard M. Lerner and William Damon (Eds.), *Handbook of child psychology* (6th ed., Vol. 1, pp. 166–209). Hoboken, NJ: Wiley.

van den Akker, Alithe; Dekovi , Maja; Prinzie, Peter and Asscher, Jessica. (2010). Toddlers' temperament profiles: Stability and relations to negative and positive parenting. *Journal of Abnormal Child Psychology, 38*(4), 485–495. doi:10.1007/s10802-009-9379-0

van den Ban, Els; Souverein, Patrick; Swaab, Hanna; van Engeland, Herman; Heerdink, Rob and Egberts, Toine. (2010). Trends in incidence and characteristics of children, adolescents, and adults initiating immediate- or extended-release methylphenidate or atomoxetine in the Netherlands during 2001–2006. *Journal of Child and Adolescent Psychopharmacology, 20*(1), 55–61. doi:10.1089/cap.2008.0153

van der Houwen, Karolijne; Stroebe, Margaret; Schut, Henk; Stroebe, Wolfgang and Bout, Jan van den. (2010). Mediating processes in bereavement: The role of rumination, threatening grief interpretations, and deliberate grief avoidance. *Social Science & Medicine, 71*(9), 1669–1676. doi:10.1016/j.socscimed.2010.06.047

van Eeden-Moorefield, Brad and Pasley, Kay. (2013). Remarriage and stepfamily life. In Gary W. Peterson and Kevin R. Bush (Eds.), *Handbook of Marriage and the Family* (pp. 517–546). New York, NY: Springer. doi:10.1007/978-1-4614-3987-5_22

van Hof, Paulion; van der Kamp, John and Savelsbergh, Geert J. P. (2008). The relation between infants' perception of catchableness and the control of catching. *Developmental Psychology, 44*(1), 182–194. doi:10.1037/0012-1649.44.1.182

van IJzendoorn, Marinus H. and Bakermans-Kranenburg, Marian J. (2010). Invariance of adult attachment across gender, age, culture, and socioeconomic status? *Journal of Social and Personal Relationships, 27*(2), 200–208. doi:10.1177/0265407509360908

van IJzendoorn, Marinus H.; Bakermans-Kranenburg, Marian J.; Pannebakker, Fieke and Out, Dorothée. (2010). In defence of situational morality: Genetic, dispositional and situational determinants of children's donating to charity. *Journal of Moral Education, 39*(1), 1–20. doi:10.1080/03057240903528535

Van Praag, Herman M. (2012). Enlightenment and Dimmed Enlightenment. Psychiatric Times.

Van Puyvelde, Martine; Vanfleteren, Pol; Loots, Gerrit; Deschuyffeleer, Sara; Vinck, Bart; Jacquet, Wolfgang and Verhelst, Werner. (2010). Tonal synchrony in mother-infant interaction based on harmonic and pentatonic series. *Infant Behavior and Development, 33*(4), 387–400. doi:10.1016/j.infbeh.2010.04.003

van Soelen, Inge L. C.; Brouwer, Rachel M.; Peper, Jiska S.; van Beijsterveldt, Toos C. E. M.; van Leeuwen, Marieke; de Vries, Linda S., . . . Boomsma, Dorret I. (2010). Effects of gestational age and birth weight on brain volumes in healthy 9 year-old children. *The Journal of Pediatrics, 156*(6), 896–901. doi:10.1016/j.jpeds.2009.12.052

Vandermassen, Griet. (2005). Who's afraid of Charles Darwin? Debating feminism and evolutionary theory. Lanham, MD: Rowman & Littlefield.

Varga, Colleen M.; Gee, Christina B. and Munro, Geoffrey. (2011). The effects of sample characteristics and experience with infidelity on romantic jealousy. *Sex Roles, 65*(11–12), 854–866. doi:10.1007/s11199-011-0048-8

Varga, Mary Alice and Palett, Robin. (2013). Life span issues and dying. In David K. Meagher and David E. Balk (Eds.), *Handbook of thanatology: The essential body of knowledge for the study of death, dying, and bereavement* (2nd ed., pp. 25–31). New York, NY: Routledge.

Varga, M. F.; Pavlova, O. G. and Nosova, S. V. (2010). The counting function and its representation in the parietal cortex in humans and animals. *Neuroscience and Behavioral Physiology, 40*(2), 185–196 doi:10.1007/s11055-009-9238-z

Varian, Frances and Cartwright, Lara. (2013). The situational judgement test at a glance. Hoboken, NJ: Wiley-Blackwell.

Veblen, Thorstein. (2007). The theory of the leisure class. New York, NY: Oxford University Press.

Veenstra, René; Lindenberg, Siegwart; Munniksma, Anke and Dijkstra, Jan Kornelis. (2010). The complex relation between bullying, victimization, acceptance, and rejection: Giving special attention to status, affection, and sex differences. *Child Development, 81*(2), 480–486. doi:10.1111/j.1467-8624.2009.01411.x

Vélez, Clorinda E.; Wolchik, Sharlene A.; Tein, Jenn-Yun and Sandler, Irwin. (2011). Protecting children from the consequences of divorce: A longitudinal study of the effects of parenting on children's coping processes. *Child Development, 82*(1), 244–257. doi:10.1111/j.1467-8624.2010.01553.x

Verbakel, Ellen and Jaspers, Eva. (2010). A comparative study on permissiveness toward euthanasia: Religiosity, slippery slope, autonomy, and death with dignity. *Public Opinion Quarterly, 74*(1), 109–139. doi:10.1093/poq/nfp074

Vered, Karen Orr. (2008). Children and media outside the home: Playing and learning in after-school care. New York, NY: Palgrave Macmillan.

Verona, Sergiu. (2003). Romanian policy regarding adoptions. In Victor Littel (Ed.), *Adoption update* (pp. 5–10). New York, NY: Nova Science.

Véronneau, Marie-Hélène and Dishion, Thomas. (2010). Predicting change in early adolescent problem behavior in the middle school years: A mesosystemic perspective on parenting and peer experiences. *Journal of Abnormal Child Psychology, 38*(8), 1125–1137. doi:10.1007/s10802-010-9431-0

Vianna, Eduardo and Stetsenko, Anna. (2006). Embracing history through transforming it: Contrasting Piagetian versus Vygotskian (activity) theories of learning and development to expand constructivism within a dialectical view of history. *Theory & Psychology, 16*, 81–108. doi:10.1177/0959354306060108

Vieno, Alessio; Nation, Maury; Pastore, Massimiliano and Santinello, Massimo. (2009). Parenting and antisocial behavior: A model of the relationship between adolescent self-disclosure, parental closeness, parental control, and adolescent antisocial behavior. *Developmental Psychology, 45*(6), 1509–1519. doi:10.1037/a0016929

Vikan, Arne; Camino, Cleonice and Biaggio, Angela. (2005). Note on a cross-cultural test of Gilligan's ethic of care. *Journal of Moral Education, 34*(1), 107–111. doi:10.1080/03057240500051105

Villar, Feliciano and Celdrán, Montserrat. (2012). Generativity in older age: A challenge for Universities of the Third Age (U3A). *Educational Gerontology, 38*(10), 666–677. doi:10.1080/03601277.2011.595347

Viner, Russell M. and Cole, Tim J. (2005). Adult socioeconomic, educational, social, and psychological outcomes of childhood obesity: A national birth cohort study. *BMJ, 330*(7504), 1354–1357. doi:10.1136/bmj.38453.422049.E0

Virji-Babul, Naznin; Rose, A.; Moiseeva, N. and Makan, N. (2012). Neural correlates of action understanding in infants: Influence of motor experience. *Brain and Behavior, 2*(3), 237–242. doi:10.1002/brb3.50

Vitale, Susan; Sperduto, Robert D. and Ferris, Frederick L., III. (2009). Increased prevalence of myopia in the United States between 1971–1972 and 1999–2004. *Archives of Ophthalmology, 127*(12), 1632–1639. doi:10.1001/archophthalmol.2009.303

Vittrup, Brigitte and Holden, George W. (2010). Children's assessments of corporal punishment and other disciplinary practices: The role of age, race, SES, and exposure to spanking. *Journal of Applied Developmental Psychology, 31*(3), 211–220. doi:10.1016/j.appdev.2009.11.003

Vogel, Gretchen. (2010). Diseases in a dish take off. *Science, 330*(6008), 1172–1173. doi:10.1126/science.330.6008.1172

Vogel, Ineke; Verschuure, Hans; van der Ploeg, Catharina P. B.; Brug, Johannes and Raat, Hein. (2010). Estimating adolescent risk for hearing loss based on data from a large school-based survey. *American Journal of Public Health, 100*(6), 1095–1100. doi:10.2105/ajph.2009.168690

Vogel, Lauren. (2011). Dying a "good death". *Canadian Medical Association Journal, 183*(18), 2089–2090. doi:10.1503/cmaj.109–4059

Volders, Pieter-Jan; Helsens, Kenny; Wang, Xiaowei; Menten, Björn; Martens, Lennart; Gevaert, Kris, . . . Mestdagh, Pieter. (2013). LNCipedia: A database for annotated human lncRNA transcript sequences and structures. *Nucleic Acids Research, 41*, D246-D251. doi:10.1093/nar/gks915

Volkwein-Caplan, Karin A. E. and McConatha, Jasmin Tamahseb. (2012). The social geography of healthy aging. Aachen, Germany: Meyer et Meyer Sport (UK) Ltd.

Volz-Sidiropoulou, Eftychia and Gauggel, Siegfried. (2012). Do subjective measures of attention and memory predict actual performance? *Metacognition in older couples. Psychology and Aging, 27*(2), 440–450. doi:10.1037/a0025384

von dem Knesebeck, Olaf; Pattyn, Elise and Bracke, Piet. (2011). Education and depressive symptoms in 22 European countries. *International Journal of Public Health, 56*(1), 107–110. doi:10.1007/s00038-010-0202-z

von Mutius, Erika and Vercelli, Donata. (2010). Farm living: Effects on childhood asthma and allergy. *Nature Reviews Immunology, 10*, 861–868. doi: 10.1038/nri2871

Vonderheid, Susan C.; Kishi, Rieko; Norr, Kathleen F. and Klim a, Carrie. (2011). Group prenatal care and doula care for pregnant women. In Arden Handler, Joan Kennelly and Nadine Peacock (Eds.), *Reducing racial/ethnic disparities in reproductive and perinatal outcomes: The evidence from population-based interventions* (pp. 369–400). New York, NY: Springer. doi:10.1007/978-1-4419-1499-6_15

Voorpostel, Marieke and Schans, Djamila. (2011). Sibling relationships in Dutch and immigrant families. *Ethnic and Racial Studies, 34*(12), 2027–2047. doi:10.1080/01419870.2010.496490

Voosen, Paul. (2013, July 15). A brain gone bad: Researchers clear the fog of chronic head trauma. The Chronicle Review, B6-B10.

Vranić, Andrea; Španić, Ana Marija; Carretti, Barbara and Borella, Erika. (2013). The efficacy of a multifactorial memory training program in older adults living in residential care settings. *International Psychogeriatrics, 25*(11), 1885–1897. doi:10.1017/S1041610213001154

Vygotsky, Lev S. (1986). *Thought and language.* Cambridge, MA: MIT Press.

Vygotsky, Lev Semenovič. (1987). *Thinking and speech.* In Robert W. Rieber and Aaron S. Carton (Eds.), *The collected works of L. S. Vygotsky* (Vol. 1, pp. 39–285). New York, NY: Plenum Press.

Vygotsky, Lev S. (1994). The development of academic concepts in school aged children. In René van der Veer and Jaan Valsiner (Eds.), *The Vygotsky reader* (pp. 355–370). Cambridge, MA: Blackwell.

Vygotsky, Lev S. (1994). Principles of social education for deaf and dumb children in Russia. In Rene van der Veer and Jaan Valsiner (Eds.), *The Vygotsky reader* (pp. 19–26). Cambridge, MA: Blackwell.

Waber, Deborah P. (2010). *Rethinking learning disabilities: Understanding children who struggle in school.* New York, NY: Guilford Press.

Wadsworth, Martha E. and Markman, Howard J. (2012). Where's the action? Understanding what works and why in relationship education. *Behavior Therapy, 43*(1), 99–112. doi:10.1016/j.beth.2011.01.006

Wagenaar, Karin; van Weissenbruch, Mirjam M.; van Leeuwen, Flora E.; Cohen-Kettenis, Peggy T.; Delemarre-van de Waal, Henriette A.; Schats, Roel and Huisman, Jaap. (2011). Self-reported behavioral and socioemotional functioning of 11- to 18-year-old adolescents conceived by in vitro fertilization. *Fertility and Sterility, 95*(2), 611–616. doi:10.1016/j.fertnstert.2010.04.076

Wagner, Jenny; Lüdtke, Oliver; Jonkmann, Kathrin and Trautwein, Ulrich. (2013). Cherish yourself: Longitudinal patterns and conditions of self-esteem change in the transition to young adulthood. *Journal of Personality and Social Psychology, 104*(1), 148–163. doi:10.1037/a0029680

Wagner, Katie; Dobkins, Karen and Barner, David. (2013). Slow mapping: Color word learning as a gradual inductive process. *Cognition, 127*(3), 307–317. doi:10.1016/j.cognition.2013.01.010

Wagner, Laura and Lakusta, Laura. (2009). Using language to navigate the infant mind. *Perspectives on Psychological Science, 4*(2), 177–184. doi:10.1111/j.1745-6924.2009.01117.x

Wagner, Paul A. (2011). Socio-sexual education: A practical study in formal thinking and teachable moments. *Sex Education: Sexuality, Society and Learning, 11*(2), 193–211. doi:10.1080/14681811.2011.558427

Wahlstrom, Dustin; Collins, Paul; White, Tonya and Luciana, Monica. (2010). Developmental changes in dopamine neurotransmission in adolescence: Behavioral implications and issues in assessment. *Brain and Cognition, 72*(1), 146–159. doi:10.1016/j.bandc.2009.10.013

Wahlstrom, Kyla L. (2002). Accommodating the sleep patterns of adolescents within current educational structures: An uncharted path. In Mary A. Carskadon (Ed.), *Adolescent sleep patterns: Biological, social, and psychological influences* (pp. 172–197). New York, NY: Cambridge University Press.

Wahrendorf, Morten; Blane, David; Bartley, Mel; Dragano, Nico and Siegrist, Johannes. (2013). Working conditions in mid-life and mental health in older ages. *Advances in Life Course Research, 18*(1), 16–25. doi:10.1016/j.alcr.2012.10.004

Waillet, Nastasya van der Straten and Roskam, Isabelle. (2013). Are religious tolerance and pluralism reachable ideals? A psychological perspective. *Religious Education, 108*(1), 69–87. doi:10.1080/00344087.2013.747873

Walberg, Herbert J. (2011). Tests, testing, and genuine school reform. Stanford, CA: Education Next Books.

Waldinger, Robert J. and Schulz, Marc S. (2010). What's love got to do with it? Social functioning, perceived health, and daily happiness in married octogenarians. *Psychology and Aging, 25*(2), 422–431. doi:10.1037/a0019087

Walker, Alan. (2012). The new ageism. *The Political Quarterly, 83*(4), 812–819. doi:10.1111/j.1467-923X.2012.02360.x

Walker, Lawrence J. (1984). Sex differences in the development of moral reasoning: A critical review. *Child Development, 55*(3), 677–691. doi:10.2307/1130121

Waller, Erika M. and Rose, Amanda J. (2010). Adjustment trade-offs of co-rumination in mother-adolescent relationships. *Journal of Adolescence, 33*(3), 487–497. doi:10.1016/j.adolescence.2009.06.002

Walsh, Bridget A. and Petty, Karen. (2007). Frequency of six early childhood education approaches: A 10-year content analysis of Early Childhood Education Journal. *Early Childhood Education Journal, 34*(5), 301–305. doi:10.1007/s10643-006-0080-4

Wanberg, Connie R. (2012). The individual experience of unemployment. *Annual Review of Psychology, 63*, 369–396. doi:10.1146/annurev-psych-120710-100500

Wang, Hua and Wellman, Barry. (2010). Social connectivity in America: Changes in adult friendship network size from 2002 to 2007. *American Behavioral Scientist, 53*(8), 1148–1169. doi:10.1177/0002764209356247

Wang, Jingyun and Candy, T. Rowan. (2010). The sensitivity of the 2- to 4-month-old human infant accommodation system. *Investigative Ophthalmology and Visual Science, 51*(6), 3309–3317. doi:10.1167/iovs.09-4667

Wang, Qi; Shao, Yi and Li, Yexin Jessica. (2010). "My way or mom's way?" The bilingual and bicultural self in Hong Kong Chinese children and adolescents. *Child Development, 81*(2), 555–567. doi:10.1111/j.1467-8624.2009.01415.x

Wang, Richard Y.; Needham, Larry L. and Barr, Dana B. (2005). Effects of environmental agents on the attainment of puberty: Considerations when assessing exposure to environmental chemicals in the National Children's Study. *Environmental Health Perspectives, 113*(8), 1100–1107. doi:10.1289/ehp.7615

Wang, Wendy and Taylor, Paul. (2011). For millennials, parenthood trumps marriage. Washington, DC: Pew Social & Demographic Trends.

Wang, Xueli. (2013). Modeling entrance into STEM fields of study among students beginning at community colleges and four-year institutions. *Research in Higher Education, 54*(6), 664–692. doi:10.1007/s11162-013-9291-x

Wang, Zhen; Szolnoki, Attila and Perc, Matjaž. (2013). Interdependent network reciprocity in evolutionary games. Scientific Reports, 3. doi:10.1038/srep01183

Ward, Brian W. and Gryczynski, Jan. (2009). Social learning theory and the effects of living arrangement on heavy alcohol use: Results from a national study of college students. *Journal of Studies on Alcohol and Drugs, 70*(3), 364–372.

Ward, L. Monique; Epstein, Marina; Caruthers, Allison and Merriwether, Ann. (2011). Men's media use, sexual cognitions, and sexual risk behavior: Testing a mediational model. *Developmental Psychology, 47*(2), 592–602. doi:10.1037/a0022669

Wardell, Jeffrey D. and Read, Jennifer P. (2013). Alcohol expectancies, perceived norms, and drinking behavior among college students: Examining the reciprocal determinism hypothesis. *Psychology of Addictive Behaviors, 27*(1), 191–196. doi:10.1037/a0030653

Warneken, Felix and Tomasello, Michael. (2009). The roots of human altruism. *British Journal of Psychology, 100*(3), 455–471. doi:10.1348/000712608X379061

Warner, Judith. (2011, January 11). No more Mrs. nice mom. New York Times Magazine, pp. 11–12.

Warren, Charles W.; Jones, Nathan R.; Eriksen, Michael P. and Asma, Samira. (2006). Patterns of global tobacco use in young people and implications for future chronic disease burden in adults. *The Lancet, 367*(9512), 749–753. doi:10.1016/S0140-6736(06)68192-0

Washington, Harriet A. (2006). *Medical apartheid: The dark history of medical experimentation on Black Americans from colonial times to the present.* New York, NY: Doubleday.

Wastesson, Jonas W.; Parker, Marti G.; Fastbom, Johan; Thorslund, Mats and Johnell, Kristina. (2012). Drug use in centenarians compared with nonagenarians and octogenarians in Sweden: A nationwide register-based study. *Age and Ageing, 41*(2), 218–224. doi:10.1093/ageing/afr144

Watson, John B. (1924). Behaviorism. New York, NY: The People's institute Publishing Co.

Watson, John B. (1928). Psychological care of infant and child. New York, NY: Norton.

Watson, John B. (1998). Behaviorism. New Brunswick, NJ: Transaction.

Waytz, Adam. (2013). Social connection and seeing human. In C. Nathan DeWall (Ed.), The Oxford handbook of social exclusion (pp. 251–256). New York, NY: Oxford University Press.

Wei, Si. (2013). A multitude of people singing together. *International Journal of Community Music, 6*(2), 183–188. doi:10.1386/ijcm.6.2.183_1

Weichold, Karina; Silbereisen, Rainer K. and Schmitt-Rodermund, Eva. (2003).

Short-term and long-term consequences of early versus late physical maturation in adolescents. In Chris Hayward (Ed.), *Gender differences at puberty* (pp. 241–276). New York, NY: Cambridge University Press.

Weikum, Whitney M.; Vouloumanos, Athena; Navarra, Jordi; Soto-Faraco, Salvador; Sebastian-Galles, Nuria and Werker, Janet F. (2007). Visual language discrimination in infancy. *Science, 316*(5828), 1159. doi:10.1126 /science.1137686

Weis, Robert and Cerankosky, Brittany C. (2010). Effects of video-game ownership on young boys' academic and behavioral functioning: A randomized, controlled study. *Psychological Science, 21*(4), 463–470. doi:10.1177/0956797610362670

Weissa, Nicole H.; Tullb, Matthew T.; Lavenderd, Jason and Gratzb, Kim L. (2013). Role of emotion dysregulation in the relationship between childhood abuse and probable PTSD in a sample of substance abusers. *Child Abuse & Neglect, 37*(11), 944–954. doi:10.1016/j.chiabu .2013.03.014

Wellman, Henry M.; Cross, David and Watson, Julanne. (2001). Meta-analysis of theory-of-mind development: The truth about false belief. *Child Development, 72*(3), 655–684. doi:10.1111/1467-8624.00304

Wen, Xiaoli; Elicker, James G. and McMullen, Mary B. (2011). Early childhood teachers' curriculum beliefs: Are they consistent with observed classroom practices? *Early Education & Development, 22*(6), 945–969. doi:10.1080/10409289.2010.507495

Wendelken, Carter; Baym, Carol L.; Gazzaley, Adam and Bunge, Silvia A. (2011). Neural indices of improved attentional modulation over middle childhood. *Developmental Cognitive Neuroscience, 1*(2), 175–186. doi:10.1016/j.dcn.2010.11.001

Wenner, Melinda. (2009). The serious need for play. *Scientific American Mind, 20*(1), 22–29. doi:10.1038/scientificamericanmind0209-22

Werner, Nicole E. and Hill, Laura G. (2010). Individual and peer group normative beliefs about relational aggression. *Child Development, 81*(3), 826–836. doi:10.1111/j.1467-8624.2010.01436.x

Wertsch, James V. and Tulviste, Peeter. (2005). L. S. Vygotsky and contemporary developmental psychology. In Harry Daniels (Ed.), *An introduction to Vygotsky.* New York, NY: Routledge.

Whalley, Lawrence J.; Duthie, Susan J.; Collins, Andrew R.; Starr, John M.; Deary, Ian J.; Lemmon, Helen, . . . Staff, Roger T. (2014). Homocysteine, antioxidant micronutrients and late onset dementia. *European Journal of Nutrition, 53*(1), 277–285. doi:10.1007/s00394 -013-0526-6

Whelchel, Lisa. (2005). *Creative correction: Extraordinary ideas for everyday discipline.* Wheaton, IL: Tyndale House.

Whitbourne, Susan Krauss; Sneed, Joel R. and Sayer, Aline. (2009). Psychosocial development from college through midlife: A 34-year sequential study. *Developmental Psychology, 45*(5), 1328–1340. doi:10.1037/a0016550

Whitbourne, Susan Krauss and Whitbourne, Stacey B. (2011). *Adult development and aging: Biopsychosocial perspectives* (4th ed.). Hoboken, NJ: Wiley.

White, Matthew P.; Alcock, Ian; Wheeler, Benedict W. and Depledge, Michael H. (2013). Would you be happier living in a greener urban area? *A fixed-effects analysis of panel data. Psychological Science, 24*(6), 920–1928. doi:10.1177/0956797612464659

Whitehead, Kevin A.; Ainsworth, Andrew T.; Wittig, Michele A. and Gadino, Brandy. (2009). Implications of ethnic identity exploration and ethnic identity affirmation and belonging for intergroup attitudes among adolescents. *Journal of Research on Adolescence, 19*(1), 123–135. doi:10.1111/j.1532-7795.2009.00585.x

Whitfield, Keith E. and McClearn, Gerald. (2005). Genes, environment, and race: Quantitative genetic approaches. *American Psychologist, 60*(1), 104–114. doi:10.1037/0003-066X.60.1.104

Whittle, Sarah; Yap, Marie B. H.; Sheeber, Lisa; Dudgeon, Paul; Yücel, Murat; Pantelis, Christos, . . . Allen, Nicholas B. (2011). Hippocampal volume and sensitivity to maternal aggressive behavior: A prospective study of adolescent depressive symptoms. *Development and Psychopathology, 23*(1), 115–129. doi:10.1017 /S0954579410000684

Whitton, Sarah W. and Kuryluk, Amanda D. (2013). Intrapersonal moderators of the association between relationship satisfaction and depressive symptoms: Findings from emerging adults. *Journal of Social and Personal Relationships, 30*(6), 750–770. doi:10.1177/0265407512467749

Wicher, Camille P. and Meeker, Mary Ann. (2012). What influences African American end-of-life preferences? *Journal of Health Care for the Poor and Underserved, 23*(1), 28–58. doi:10.1353/hpu.2012.0027

Wicherts, Jelte M.; Dolan, Conor V. and van der Maas, Han L. J. (2010). The dangers of unsystematic selection methods and the representativeness of 46 samples of African test-takers. *Intelligence, 38*(1), 30–37. doi:10.1016/j.intell .2009.11.003

Wickrama, K. A. S.; O'Neal, Catherine Walker and Lorenz, Fred O. (2013). Marital functioning from middle to later years: A life course–stress process framework. *Journal of Family Theory & Review, 5*(1), 15–34. doi:10.1111/ jftr.12000

Wiik, Kenneth Aarskaug; Keizer, Renske and Lappegård, Trude. (2012). Relationship quality in marital and cohabiting unions across Europe. *Journal of Marriage and Family, 74*(3), 389–398. doi:10.1111/j.1741-3737.2012.00967.x

Wijdicks, Eelco F. M.; Varelas, Panayiotis N.; Gronseth, Gary S. and Greer, David M. (2010). Evidence-based guideline update: Determining brain death in adults; Report of the quality standards subcommittee of the American Academy of Neurology. *Neurology, 74*(23), 1911–1918. doi:10.1212/WNL.0b013e3181e242a8

Wilhelm, Miriam; Dahl, Edgar; Alexander, Henry; Brähler, Elmar and Stöbel-Richter, Yve. (2013). Ethical attitudes of German specialists in reproductive medicine and legal regulation of preimplantation sex selection in Germany. *PloS, 8*(2), e56390. doi:10.1371/journal.pone.0056390

Wilhelm, Mark O.; Rooney, Patrick M. and Tempel, Eugene R. (2007). Changes in religious giving reflect changes in involvement: Age and cohort effects in religious giving, secular giving, and attendance. *Journal for the Scientific Study of Religion, 46*(2), 217–232. doi:10.1111/j.1468 -5906.2007.00352.x

Williams, David R. (2003). The health of men: Structured inequalities and opportunities. *American Journal of Public Health, 93*(5), 724–731. doi:10.2105/AJPH.93.5.724

Williams, Kristine N.; Herman, Ruth; Gajewski, Byron and Wilson, Kristel. (2009). Elderspeak communication: Impact on dementia care. *American Journal of Alzheimer's Disease and Other Dementias, 24*(1), 11–20. doi:10.1177/1533317508318472

Williams, Lela Rankin; Fox, Nathan A.; Lejuez, C. W.; Reynolds, Elizabeth K.; Henderson, Heather A.; Perez-Edgar, Koraly E., . . . Pine, Daniel S. (2010). Early temperament, propensity for risk-taking and adolescent substance-related problems: A prospective multimethod investigation. *Addictive Behaviors, 35*(2), 1148–1151. doi:10.1016/j.addbeh.2010.07.005

Williams, Preston. (2009, March 5). Teens might need to sleep more, but schools have to work efficiently. The Washington Post, p. LZ10.

Williams, Shirlan A. (2005). Jealousy in the cross-sex friendship. *Journal of Loss and Trauma, 10*(5), 471–485. doi:10.1080/15325020500193937

Williamson, Rebecca A.; Meltzoff, Andrew N. and Markman, Ellen M. (2008). Prior experiences and perceived efficacy influence 3-year-olds' imitation. *Developmental Psychology, 44*(1), 275–285. doi:10.1037/0012-1649.44.1.275

Wilmshurst, Linda. (2011). *Child and adolescent psychopathology: A casebook* (2nd ed.). Thousand Oaks, CA: Sage.

Wilson, Kathryn R.; Hansen, David J. and Li, Ming. (2011). The traumatic stress response in child maltreatment and resultant neuropsychological effects. *Aggression and Violent Behavior, 16*(2), 87–97. doi:10.1016/j.avb.2010.12.007

Wilson, Stephan M. and Ngige, Lucy W. (2006). Families in sub-Saharan Africa. In Bron B. Ingoldsby and Suzanna D. Smith (Eds.), *Families in global and multicultural perspective* (2nd ed., pp. 247–273). Thousand Oaks, CA: Sage.

Winner, Brooke; Peipert, Jeffrey F.; Zhao, Qiuhong; Buckel, Christina; Madden, Tessa; Allsworth, Jenifer E. and Secura, Gina M. (2012). Effectiveness of long-acting reversible contraception. *New England Journal of Medicine, 366*, 1998–2007. doi:10.1056/NEJMoa1110855

Winner, Ellen. (1996). Gifted children: Myths and realities. New York, NY: Basic Books.

Winston, Flaura Koplin; Kallan, Michael J.; Senserrick, Teresa M. and Elliott, Michael R. (2008). Risk factors for death among older child and teenaged motor vehicle passengers. *Archives of Pediatric and Adolescent Medicine, 162*(3), 253–260. doi:10.1001/archpediatrics.2007.52

Winter, Suzanne M. (2011). Culture, health, and school readiness. In DeAnna M. Laverick and Mary Renck Jalongo (Eds.), *Transitions to early care and education* (Vol. 4, pp. 117–133). New York, NY: Springer. doi:10.1007/978-94-007-0573-9_11

Witherington, David C.; Campos, Joseph J. and Hertenstein, Matthew J. (2004). Principles of emotion and its development in infancy. In Gavin Bremner and Alan Fogel (Eds.), *Blackwell handbook of infant development* (pp. 427–464). Malden, MA: Blackwell.

Wittassek, Matthias; Koch, Holger Martin; Angerer, Jürgen and Brüning, Thomas. (2011). Assessing exposure to phthalates – The human biomonitoring approach. *Molecular Nutrition & Food Research, 55*(1), 7–31. doi:10.1002/mnfr.201000121

Wittchen, Hans-Ulrich. (2012). The burden of mood disorders. *Science, 338*(6103), 15. doi:10.1126/science.1230817

Wolak, Janis; Finkelhor, David; Mitchell, Kimberly J. and Ybarra, Michele L. (2008). Online "predators" and their victims: Myths, realities, and implications for prevention and treatment. *American Psychologist, 63*(2), 111–128. doi:10.1037/0003-066X.63.2.111

Wolchik, Sharlene A.; Ma, Yue; Tein, Jenn-Yun; Sandler, Irwin N. and Ayers, Tim S. (2008). Parentally bereaved children's grief: Self-system beliefs as mediators of the relations between grief and stressors and caregiver-child relationship quality. *Death Studies, 32*(7), 597–620. doi:10.1080/07481180802215551

Wolenberg, Kelly M.; Yoon, John D.; Rasinski, Kenneth A. and Curlin, Farr A. (2013). Religion and United States physicians' opinions and self-predicted practices concerning artificial nutrition and hydration. *Journal of Religion and Health, 52*(4), 1051–1065. doi:10.1007/s10943-013-9740-z

Wolf, Norman S. (Ed.). (2010). Comparative biology of aging. New York, NY: Springer.

Woloshin, Steven and Schwartz, Lisa M. (2010). The benefits and harms of mammography screening: Understanding the trade-offs. *JAMA, 303*(2), 164–165. doi:10.1001/jama.2009.2007

Wong, Paul T. P. and Tomer, Adrian. (2011). Beyond terror and denial: The positive psychology of death acceptance. *Death Studies, 35*(2), 99–106. doi:10.1080/07481187.2011.535377

Wong, Sowan and Goodwin, Robin. (2009). Experiencing marital satisfaction across three cultures: A qualitative study. *Journal of Social and Personal Relationships, 26*(8), 1011–1028. doi:10.1177/0265407509347938

Wood, Joanne M. (2002). Aging, driving and vision. *Clinical and Experimental Optometry, 85*(4), 214–220. doi:10.1111/j.1444-0938.2002.tb03040.x

Woodward, Amanda L. and Markman, Ellen M. (1998). Early word learning. In Deanna Kuhn and Robert S. Siegler (Eds.), *Handbook of child psychology* (5th ed., Vol. 2, pp. 371–420). Hoboken, NJ: Wiley.

Woollett, Katherine; Spiers, Hugo J. and Maguire, Eleanor A. (2009). Talent in the taxi: A model system for exploring expertise. *Philosophical Transactions of the Royal Society of London, 364*(1522), 1407–1416. doi:10.1098/rstb.2008.0288

Woolley, Jacqueline D. and Ghossainy, Maliki E. (2013). Revisiting the fantasy–reality distinction: Children as naïve skeptics. *Child Development, 84*(5), 1496–1510. doi:10.1111/cdev.12081

World Bank. (2010). *What can we learn from nutrition impact evaluations?* Lessons from a review of interventions to reduce child malnutrition in developing countries. Washington, DC: The International Bank for Reconstruction and Development. doi:10.1596/978-0-8213-8406-0

World Health Organization. (2006). WHO Motor Development Study: Windows of achievement for six gross motor development milestones. *Acta Paediatrica, 95*(Suppl. 450), 86–95. doi:10.1111/j.1651-2227.2006.tb02379.x

World Health Organization. (2012). Early marriages, adolescent and young pregnancies: Report by the Secretariat. Geneva: *World Health Organization.*

World Health Organization. (2012, May 18). Progress Toward Interruption of Wild Poliovirus Transmission — Worldwide, January 2011–March 2012 Weekly. *Morbidity and Mortality Weekly Report, 61*(19), 353–357.

World Health Organization. (2013). World health statistics 2013. Geneva: World Health Organization.

Worthy, Darrell A.; Gorlick, Marissa A.; Pacheco, Jennifer L.; Schnyer, David M. and Maddox, W. Todd. (2011). With age comes wisdom: Decision making in younger and older adults. *Psychological Science, 22*(11), 1375–1380. doi:10.1177/0956797611420301

Wosje, Karen S.; Khoury, Philip R.; Claytor, Randal P.; Copeland, Kristen A.; Hornung, Richard W.; Daniels, Stephen R. and Kalkwarf, Heidi J. (2010). Dietary patterns associated with fat and bone mass in young children. *American Journal of Clinical Nutrition, 92*(2), 294–303. doi:10.3945/ajcn.2009.28925

Wright, Mathew W. and Bruford, Elispeth A. (2011). Naming 'junk': Human non-protein coding RNA (ncRNA) gene nomenclature. *Human Genomics, 5*(2), 90–98. doi:10.1186/1479-7364-5-2-90

Wrzus, Cornelia; Hänel, Martha; Wagner, Jenny and Neyer, Franz J. (2013). Social network changes and life events across the life span: A meta-analysis. *Psychological Bulletin, 139*(1), 53–80. doi:10.1037/a0028601

Wu, Pai-Lu and Chiou, Wen-Bin. (2008). Postformal thinking and creativity among late adolescents: A post-Piagetian approach. *Adolescence, 43*(170), 237–251.

Wurm, Susanne; Tomasik, Martin and Tesch-Römer, Clemens. (2008). Serious health events and their impact on changes in subjective health and life satisfaction: The role of age and a positive view on ageing. *European Journal of Ageing, 5*(2), 117–127. doi:10.1007/s10433-008-0077-5

Xu, Xiao; Zhu, Fengchuan; O'Campo, Patricia; Koenig, Michael A.; Mock, Victoria and Campbell, Jacquelyn. (2005). Prevalence of and risk factors for intimate partner violence in China. *American Journal of Public Health, 95*(1), 78–85. doi:10.2105/AJPH.2003.023978

Xu, Yaoying. (2010). Children's social play sequence: Parten's classic theory revisited. *Early Child Development and Care, 180*, 489–498. doi:10.1080/03004430802090430

Yadav, Priyanka; Banwari, Girish; Parmar, Chirag and Maniar, Rajesh. (2013). Internet addiction and its correlates among high school students: A preliminary study from Ahmedabad, India. *Asian Journal of Psychiatry, 6*(6), 500–505. doi:10.1016/j.ajp.2013.06.004

Yamaguchi, Susumu; Greenwald, Anthony G.; Banaji, Mahzarin R.; Murakami, Fumio; Chen, Daniel; Shiomura, Kimihiro, . . . Krendl, Anne. (2007). Apparent universality of positive implicit self-esteem. *Psychological Science, 18*(6), 498–500. doi:10.1111/j.1467-9280.2007.01928.x

Yang, Rongwang; Zhang, Suhan; Li, Rong and Zhao, Zhengyan. (2013). Parents' attitudes toward stimulants use in China. *Journal of Developmental & Behavioral Pediatrics, 34*(3), 225. doi:10.1097/DBP.0b013e318287cc27

Yerkes, Robert Mearns. (1923). Testing the human mind. *Atlantic Monthly, 131*, 358–370.

Yeung, W. Jean and Conley, Dalton. (2008). Black-White achievement gap and family wealth. *Child Development, 79*(2), 303–324. doi:10.1111/j.1467-8624.2007.01127.x

Yom-Tov, Elad; Fernandez-Luque, Luis; Weber, Ingmar and Crain, Steven P. (2012). Pro-anorexia and pro-recovery photo sharing: A tale of two warring tribes. *Journal of Medical Internet Research, 14*(6), e151. doi:10.2196/jmir.2239

Young, Elizabeth A.; Korszun, Ania; Figueiredo, Helmer F.; Banks-Solomon, Matia and Herman, James P. (2008). Sex differences in HPA axis regulation. In Jill B. Becker, Karen J. Berkley, Nori Geary, Elizabeth Hampson, James P. Herman and Elizabeth Young (Eds.), *Sex differences in the brain: From genes to behavior* (pp. 95–105). New York, NY: Oxford University Press.

Young, John K. (2010). Anorexia nervosa and estrogen: Current status of the hypothesis. *Neuroscience & Biobehavioral Reviews, 34*(8), 1195–1200. doi:10.1016/j.neubiorev.2010.01.015

Young, T. Kue; Bjerregaard, Peter; Dewailly, Eric; Risica, Patricia M.; Jorgensen, Marit E. and Ebbesson, Sven E. O. (2007). Prevalence of obesity and its metabolic correlates among the circumpolar Inuit in 3 countries. *American Journal of Public Health, 97*(4), 691–695. doi:10.2105/ajph.2005.080614

Yu, Xiao-ming; Guo, Shuai-jun and Sun, Yu-ying. (2013). Sexual behaviours and associated risks in Chinese young people: A meta-analysis. *Sexual Health, 10*(5), 424–433. doi:10.1071/SH12140

Zachry, Anne H. and Kitzmann, Katherine M. (2011). Caregiver awareness of prone play recommendations. *American Journal of Occupational Therapy, 65*(1), 101–105. doi:10.5014/ajot.2011.09100

Zahn-Waxler, Carolyn; Park, Jong-Hyo; Usher, Barbara; Belouad, Francesca; Cole, Pamela and Gruber, Reut. (2008). Young children's representations of conflict and distress: A longitudinal study of boys and girls with disruptive behavior problems. *Development and Psychopathology, 20*(1), 99–119. doi:10.1017/S0954579408000059

Zak, Paul J. (2012). *The moral molecule: the source of love and prosperity.* New York, NY: Dutton.

Zalenski, Robert J. and Raspa, Richard. (2006). Maslow's hierarchy of needs: A framework for achieving human potential in hospice. *Journal of Palliative Medicine, 9*(5), 1120–1127. doi:10.1089/jpm.2006.9.1120

Zani, Bruna and Cicognani, Elvira. (2006). Sexuality and intimate relationships in adolescence. In Sandy Jackson and Luc Goossens (Eds.), *Handbook of adolescent development* (pp. 200–222). New York, NY: Psychology Press.

Zapf, Jennifer A. and Smith, Linda B. (2007). When do children generalize the plural to novel nouns? *First Language, 27*(1), 53–73. doi:10.1177/0142723707070286

Zarate, Carlos A., Jr. (2010). Psychiatric disorders in young adults: Depression assessment and treatment. In Jon E. Grant and Marc N. Potenza (Eds.), Young adult mental health (pp. 206–230). New York, NY: Oxford University Press.

Zatorre, Robert J. (2013). Predispositions and plasticity in music and speech learning: Neural correlates and implications. *Science, 342*(6158), 585–589. doi:10.1126/science.1238414

Zatorre, Robert J.; Fields, R. Douglas and Johansen-Berg, Heidi. (2012). Plasticity in gray and white: neuroimaging changes in brain structure during learning. *Nature Neuroscience, 15*, 528–536. doi:10.1038/nn.3045

Zeanah, Charles H.; Berlin, Lisa J. and Boris, Neil W. (2011). Practitioner review: Clinical applications of attachment theory and research for infants and young children. *Journal of Child Psychology and Psychiatry, 52*(8), 819–833. doi:10.1111/j.1469-7610.2011.02399.x

Zehr, Mary Ann. (2011). Efforts Seek to Boost Counseling On Postsecondary-Study Options. *Education Week, 30*(34), 16–17.

Zehr, Mary Ann. (2011). Study stings KIPP on attrition rates. *Education Week, 30*(27), 1, 24–25.

Zeiders, Katharine H.; Umaña-Taylor, Adriana J. and Derlan, Chelsea L. (2013). Trajectories of depressive symptoms and self-esteem in Latino youths: Examining the role of gender and perceived discrimination. *Developmental Psychology, 49*(5), 951–963. doi:10.1037/a0028866

Zeifman, Debra M. (2013). Built to bond: Coevolution, coregulation, and plasticity in parent-infant bonds. In Cindy Hazan and Mary I. Campa (Eds.), *Human bonding: The science of affectional ties* (pp. 41–73). New York, NY: The Guilford Press.

Zentall, Shannon R. and Morris, Bradley J. (2010). "Good job, you're so smart": The effects of inconsistency of praise type on young children's motivation. *Journal of Experimental Child Psychology, 107*(2), 155–163. doi:10.1016/j.jecp.2010.04.015

Zentner, Marcel and Bates, John E. (2008). Child temperament: An integrative review of concepts, research programs, and measures. *European Journal of Developmental Science, 2*(1–2), 7–37.

Zentner, Marcel and Mitura, Klaudia. (2012). Stepping out of the caveman's shadow: Nations' gender gap predicts degree of sex differentiation in mate preferences. *Psychological Science, 23*(10), 1176–1185. doi:10.1177/0956797612441004

Zettel, Laura A. and Rook, Karen S. (2004). Substitution and compensation in the social networks of older widowed women. *Psychology and Aging, 19*(3), 433–443. doi:10.1037/0882-7974.19.3.433

Zhang, Baohui; Wright, Alexi A.; Huskamp, Haiden A.; Nilsson, Matthew E.; Maciejewski, Matthew L.; Earle, Craig C., . . . Prigerson, Holly G. (2009). Health care costs in the last week of life: Associations with end-of-life conversations. *Archives of Internal Medicine, 169*(5), 480–488. doi:10.1001/archinternmed.2008.587

Zhang, Xin; Yeung, Dannii Y.; Fung, Helene H. and Lang, Frieder R. (2011). Changes in peripheral social partners and loneliness over time: The moderating role of interdependence. *Psychology and Aging, 26*(4), 823–829. doi:10.1037/a0023674

Zhou, Dongming; Lebel, Catherine; Evans, Alan and Beaulieu, Christian. (2013). Cortical thickness asymmetry from childhood to older adulthood. *NeuroImage, 83*, 66–74. doi:10.1016/j.neuroimage.2013.06.073

Zhu, Qi; Song, Yiying; Hu, Siyuan; Li, Xiaobai; Tian, Moqian; Zhen, Zonglei, . . . Liu, Jia. (2010). Heritability of the specific cognitive ability of face perception. *Current Biology, 20*(2), 137–142. doi:10.1016/j.cub.2009.11.067

Zhu, Weimo; Boiarskaia, Elena A.; Welk, Gregory J. and Meredith, Marilu D. (2010). Physical education and school contextual factors relating to students' achievement and cross-grade differences in aerobic fitness and obesity. *Research Quarterly for Exercise and Sport,* 81(Suppl. 3), S53-S64. doi:10.5641/027013610X13100547898194

Zhu, Ying; Zhang, Li; Fan, Jin and Han, Shihui. (2007). Neural basis of cultural influence on self-representation. *NeuroImage, 34*(3), 1310–1316. doi:10.1016/j.neuroimage.2006.08.047

Zhu, Zengrong and Huangfu, Danwei. (2013). Human pluripotent stem cells: an emerging model in developmental biology. *Development, 140*, 705–717. doi:10.1242/dev.086165

Zickuhr, Kathryn and Smith, Aaron. (2012). Digital differences. Washington, DC: Pew Research Internet Project, Pew Research Center.

Zimmer, Carl. (2009). On the origin of sexual reproduction. *Science, 324*(5932), 1254–1256. doi:10.1126/science.324_1254

Zimmer-Gembeck, Melanie J. and Collins, W. Andrew. (2003). Autonomy development during adolescence. In Gerald R. Adams and Michael D. Berzonsky (Eds.), *Blackwell handbook of adolescence* (pp. 175–204). Malden, MA: Blackwell.

Zimmer-Gembeck, Melanie J. and Ducat, Wendy. (2010). Positive and negative romantic relationship quality: Age, familiarity, attachment and well-being as correlates of couple agreement and projection. *Journal of Adolescence, 33*(6), 879–890. doi:10.1016/j.adolescence.2010.07.008

Zimmerman, Frederick J. ; Christakis, Dimitri A. and Meltzoff, Andrew N. (2007). Associations between Media Viewing and Language Development in Children Under Age 2 Years. *The Journal of Pediatrics, 151*(4), 364–368. doi:10.1016/j.jpeds.2007.04.071

Zimmermann, Camilla. (2012). Acceptance of dying: A discourse analysis of palliative care literature. *Social Science & Medicine, 75*(1), 217–224. doi:10.1016/j.socscimed.2012.02.047

Zlotnick, Cheryl; Tam, Tammy and Zerger, Suzanne. (2012). Common needs but divergent interventions for U.S. homeless and foster care children: results from a systematic review. *Health & Social Care in the Community, 20*(5), 449–476. doi:10.1111/j.1365-2524.2011.01053.x

Zolotor, Adam J.; Burchinal, Margaret; Skinner, Debra and Rosenthal, Marjorie. (2008). Maternal psychological adjustment and knowledge of infant development as predictors of home safety practices in rural low-income communities. *Pediatrics, 121*(6), e1668-e1675. doi:10.1542/peds.2007-1255

Zosuls, Kristina M.; Martin, Carol Lynn; Ruble, Diane N.; Miller, Cindy F.; Gaertner, Bridget M.; England, Dawn E. and Hill, Alison P. (2011). "It's not that we hate you": Understanding children's gender attitudes and expectancies about peer relationships. *British Journal of Developmental Psychology, 29*(2), 288–304. doi:10.1111/j.2044-835X.2010.02023.x

Credits

Figure 1.4
Original chart, "Growing Support for Same-Sex Marriage" from "Growing Support for Gay Marriage: Changes Minds and Changing Demographics" published by the Pew Research Center for the People and the Press, March 20, 2013, provided by Pew Research Center (www.pewresearch.org) and adapted by W.H. Freeman and Company/Worth Publishers/Macmillan Higher Education or its licensees. Reproduced with permission.

Figure 1.6
From *Individual development and evolution: the genesis of novel behavior* by Gilbert Gottlieb. Copyright © 2002 by Gilbert Gottlieb. Reproduced with permission of Lawrence Erlbaum Associates via Copyright Clearance Center.

Chapter 2
Excerpt from "No More Mrs. Nice Mom" by Judith Warner, from *The New York Times Magazine*, January 16, 2011. Copyright © 2011 The New York Times. All rights reserved. Used by permission and protected by the Copyright Laws of the United States. The printing, copying, redistribution, or re-transmission of this Content without express written permission is prohibited.

Figure 4.5
Adapted from *The Developing Human: Clinically Oriented Embryology, 9E* by Keith L. Moore, T.V.N. Persaud, and Mark G. Torchia. Copyright © 2013 by Saunders, an imprint of Elsevier, Inc. Reproduced courtesy of Elsevier Limited.

Chapter 14
Excerpts from "Risk-taking in adolescence: What changes, and why?" by Laurence Steinberg. Republished with permission of New York Academy of Sciences, from *Annals of the New York Academy of Sciences,* 1021 (2004); permission conveyed through Copyright Clearance Center, Inc.

Figure 15.7
"Rates Still Rising" from "Nation's Graduation Rate Nears a Milestone" by Christopher B. Swanson and Sterling C. Lloyd, as first appeared in *Education Week,* June 6, 2013. Reproduced with permission from Editorial Projects in Education.

Chapter 18
Excerpts from "Cognitive and Representational Development in Adults" by Jan Sinnott, *from Literacy Processes: Cognitive Flexibility in Learning and Teaching,* ed. by Kelly B. Cartwright. Copyright © 2008 by The Guilford Press. Reproduced with permission of The Guilford Press.

Table 18.1
From "Cognitive and Ethical Growth: The Making of Meaning" by William Perry, in *The Modern American College: Responding to The New Realities of Diverse Students and a Changing Society,* edited by Arthur W. Chickering (1981). Republished with permission of John Wiley & Sons Incorporated; permission conveyed through Copyright Clearance Center, Inc.

Chapter 21
Excerpt from the poem, "Triage: An Essay" by Paul J. Hamill, from *The Georgia Review,* 45, pp. 463–469. Reproduced courtesy of Paul J. Hamill.

Chapter 23
Excerpt from "Harnessing the Human Factor in Hearing Assistance" by David G. Myers, from "Research on Hearing Communication and Health Gets Center Stage at NIDCD." Reproduced with permission of Association of Psychological Science, from *APS Observer,* Vol. 24, No. 8, October 2011; permission conveyed through Copyright Clearance Center.

Figure 23.1
Levy, Becca, & Langer, Ellen. (1994). Aging free from negative stereotypes: Successful memory in China among the American deaf. *Journal of Personality & Social Psychology,* 66, 989–997. Adapted with permission.

Figure 23.5
Murphy, Sherry L., Xu, Jiaquan, & Kochanek, Kenneth D. (2012). "Deaths: Preliminary data for 2010." *National Vital Statistics Reports,* 60(4). Washington, DC: U.S. Department of Health and Human Services.

Figure 24.2
Castel, Alan D., Rossi, Aimee Drolet, McGillivray, Shannon. (2012). Beliefs about the "hot hand" in basketball across the adult life span. *Psychology and Aging,* 27, 601–605. Adapted with permission.

Table A (appendix)
Reprinted with permission from the *Diagnostic and Statistical Manual of Mental Disorders, Fifth Edition,* (Copyright © 2013). American Psychiatric Association.

Name Index

A maz, et al 2014 , 442
Aarnoudse-Moens, Cornelieke S. H., 114
Aarsland, Dag, 713
Abakoumkin, Georgios, 783
Abdel-Hamid, M., 48
Abele, Andrea E., 392, 659
Abell, Jill, 80
Abelson, Sara, 113
Abrams, Elaine J., 146
Abuzenadah, Adel, 413
Accardo, Pasquale, 50
Acevedo-Garcia, Dolores, 187, 189, 216
Ackerman, Debra J., 270
Ackerman, Michelle L., 752
Ackerman, Phillip L., 655
Adair, Linda S., 140
Adam, Emma K., 186
Adams, Alison E., 639
Adams, Erin E., 198
Adams, Ted D., 591
Adamson, Lauren B., 171
Adamson, Maheen M., 524, 625
Adams-Webber, Thomasin, 139
Addo, Fenaba R., 642
Adler, Lynn Peters, 756
Adler, Nancy E., 524
Adolph, Karen E., 138, 140, 141, 165
Afeiche, Myriam, 583
Afifi, Tamara D., 562
Afifi, Tracie O., 239
Aghajanian, George K., 511
Agliata, Allison Kanter, 293
Agrawal, Arpana, 481
Agrawal, Dewesh, 412
Agrigoroaeri, Stefan, 670
Agronick, Gail, 472
Aguilar-Gaxiola, Sergio, 505
Aguinagalde, Xabier, 111
Ahmed, Hafez, 119
Ahmed, Leila, 546
Ahmed, Parvez, 110
Aiello, Allison E., 474
Ainsworth, Andrew T., 467
Ainsworth, Mary, 192
Ainsworth, Mary D. Salter, 193, 194
Akcay, Ahmet, 317, 764
Aken, Marcel A. G. van, 549, 550
Akinbami, Lara J., 317
Akiyama, Hiroko, 637
Akker, Alithe van den, 187, 188
Akl, Stephanie L., 714
Akre, Christina, 311
Aksan, Nazan, 198
Alabi, Basirat O., 369
Alain, Moreón, 591, 692
Alavi, Nika, 23, 76
Alavinia, Seyed Mohammad, 738
Albert, Dustin, 417, 434, 437, 438, 439

Albert, Steven M., 672, 673, 686
Albright, Ann L., 687
Alcock, Ian, 636
Aldwin, Carolyn M., 579, 592, 617, 619, 620
Alegre, Alberto, 300
Alegria, Margarita, 187, 189, 216
Alexander, Henry, 72
Alexander, Randell, 240
Alexander, Robin, 240
Alkan, Can, 80
Alkon, Abbey, 197
Allebeck, Peter, 144
Allebrandt, Karla, 404
Allemand, Mathias, 635
Allen, Kathleen P., 388
Allen, Lindsay H., 217
Allen, Michael S., 330
Allen, Nicholas B., 474
Allendorf, Keera, 559
Allman, Tara L., 508
Alloway, Tracy, 344
Allred, Elizabeth N., 230
Allsworth, Jenifer E., 501
Almeida, David M., 609, 658
Almeling, Rene, 76
Almomani, Basima, 317
Al-Namlah, Abdulrahman S., 251
Alonso, Jordi, 505
Alsaker, Françoise D., 406
Al-Sayes, Fatin, 362, 413
Al-Shawaf, Laith, 552
Altaye, Mekibib, 326
Altbach, Philip G., 535
Alvarez, Michelle, 358
Alviola, Pedro A., 316
Al-Yagon, Michal, 325
Alzheimer, Alois, 711
Alzheimer's Association, 711
Amaral, David G., 330
Amato, Paul R., 378, 645
Ambady, Nalini, 185
Ambalavanan, Namasivayam, 113, 114
American Academy of Child and Adolescent Psychiatry, 286
American Academy of Neurology, 773
American Academy of Pediatrics, 103, 286
American Academy of Family Physicians, 286
American College of Obstetricians and Gynecologists Committee on Obstetric Practice, 104
American Council of Physicians, 596
American Medical Association, 286
American Psychiatric Association, 324, 329, 504, 506
American Psychiatry Association, 286
American Psychological Association, 30, 286

American Society of Human Genetics, 15
Amir, Gail, 692
Amirabbasi-Beik, Mahsa, 689
Amso, Dima, 162
Amurrio, Ascensión, 111
An, Jeong Shin, 288
An, S. Sandy, 690
Anastasio, Carol, 644
Ancoli-Israel, Sonia, 671
Andel, Ross, 607
Anderman, Eric M., 472
Andersen, Hans Christian, 328
Anderson, Garnet L., 584
Anderson, John R., 347, 348
Anderson, Michael, 779
Anderson, Peter J., 114
Anderson, Ranita, 296
Anderson, Richard A., 582
Anderson, Robert N., 150
Anderson, Ruth, 640
Andersson, G., 119
Andrade, Susan E., 110
Andreev, Evgueni M., 588
Andrew, Toby, 82
Andrews, Julie, 616
Andrist, Lester, 559
Anen, Cedric, 195, 654
Angerer, Jürgen, 27
Angermeyer, Matthias C., 505
Angold, Adrian, 388
Anjum, Afshan, 506
Annet, H. D. E., 655
Anney, R., 326
Ansari, Daniel, 349
Ansary, Nadia S., 383, 481
Anstey, Kaarin J., 736
Antone, Carol, 170
Antonucci, Toni C., 5, 565, 567, 637, 638, 747
Antoun, Nagui, 604
Antuono, Piero, 711
Apgar, Virginia, 101, 626
Apostolou, Menelaos, 559
Applegate, Anthony J., 358
Applegate, Mary DeKonty, 358
Appugliese, Danielle, 406
Aragaki, Aaron K., 584
Archambault, Isabelle, 452
Archer, John, 563
Archer, Sally L., 458
Ardelt, Monika, 723
Arden, Chris I., 410
Ariely, Dan, 436
Arizaga, Raul, 711
Armstrong, Alicia Y., 584
Armstrong, Laura Marie, 276, 277
Arndt, Jamie, 765
Arnett, Jeffrey Jensen, 502, 522, 526, 547, 550, 551
Arnold, L. Eugene, 327
Arocha, José F., 625

Aron, Arthur, 551
Aron, Elaine N., 551, 553
Aronson, Joshua, 524, 525, 609
Arora, A., 356
Arós, Fernando, 592
Arsenault-Lapierre, Genevieve, 616
Arseneault, Louis, 374
Arterberry, Martha E., 138, 160
Arterburn, David E., 591
Arthur, Antony, 711, 714, 754
Artistico, Daniele, 523
Arum, Richard, 353, 536
Asbridge, Mark, 621
Asendorpf, Jens B., 549, 550
Ash, Caroline, 229
Ashby, Michael, 769
Ashraf, Quamrul, 69
Ashurst, Nigel, 388
Ashworth, Alan, 584
Asma, Samira, 480
Asma, Stephen T., 367
Asmundson, Gordon J. G., 239
Asscher, Jessica, 187, 188
Association of American Medical Colleges, 627
Assor, Avi, 56
Astin, Helen S., 531
Atchley, Robert C., 742
Au, Wayne, 449
Au Eong, Kah Guan, 83
Aud, Susan, 262, 449
Audrey, Suzanne, 467
Aunola, Kaisa, 300
Austad, Steven N., 691
Avendano, Mauricio, 638
Avery, Rosemary J., 567
Avidan, Michael, 701
Aviv, Abraham, 690, 691
Avolio, Bruce J., 530
Axelsson, Bertil, 769
Axinn, William G., 568
Ayalon, Liat, 671
Ayer, Catherine R., 731
Ayers, Susan, 119
Ayers, Tim S., 764
Ayotte, Brian J., 717
Azrin, Nathan H., 51

Baaren, Rick B. van, 623
Baban, Adriana, 425
Babchisin, Lyzon K., 207
Bacallao, Martica, 474
Bachman, Jerald G., 473, 479, 480, 481, 483, 510, 511, 522, 549
Bäckman, Lars, 700, 711
Bada, Henrietta S., 195
Badaly, Daryaneh, 141, 165
Baeyens, Dieter, 340
Bagatian, Nadiah, 413
Bagla, Pallava, 445
Bagner, Daniel M., 191
Bagwell, Catherine, 326

Bagwell, Catherine L., 385, 388
Bai, Ling, 83
Baillargeon, Renée, 159, 160, 295
Baird, Abigail A., 520
Bakeman, Roger, 171
Baker, Beth, 753
Baker, Jeffrey P., 144
Baker, Julie, 403, 474
Baker, Lindsey, 748
Baker, Lindsey A., 379
Baker, T. D., 233
Bakermans-Kranenburg, Marian J., 195, 409, 424
Bakken, Jeremy P., 463, 464, 467, 472
Bakraceyic, Karin, 520
Bakshis, Erin, 474
Baldry, Anna C., 388
Balk, David E., 779
Balkhair, Taiba, 113
Ball, Howard, 772, 775
Ballester, Ferran, 111
Balottin, Umberto, 158, 168
Baltazar, Alina, 479
Baltes, Margaret, 620–621
Baltes, Paul B., 5, 523, 526, 620–621, 621, 702
Ban, Els van den, 325
Banaji, Mahzarin R., 370, 524
Banducci, Sarah, 714
Bandura, Albert, 45, 200–201, 619
Banks, Jonathan B., 732
Banks-Solomon, Matia, 403
Bansal, Vishal, 236
Banwari, Girish, 442
Bao, Haikun, 116
Barac, Raluca, 261
Barber, Brian K., 300
Barbey, Aron K., 519, 604
Barbosa, Leonardo S., 163
Bard, Abigail, 520
Barker, Erin T., 549
Barkin, Shari, 300
Barlow, Denise P., 78
Barlow, Jane, 241
Barner, David, 257
Barnes, Linda E., 711, 714, 754
Barnett, Fiona, 708
Barnett, Mark, 130, 270
Barnett, Melissa, 182
Barnett, W. Steven, 262, 267, 268, 269
Baron, Andrew Scott, 524
Barone, Joseph, 51
Bar-Or, Oded, 406
Barr, Dana B., 408
Barrett, Anne E., 669
Barrett, H. Clark, 169, 174
Barrett, Justin L., 248
Barrett-Connor, Elizabeth, 582
Barros, Romina M., 313
Barrouillet, Pierre, 344
Barry, Carolyn, 550
Barry, Carolyn McNamara, 528
Barry, Robin A., 295
Bartels, Meike, 373
Barth, Maria, 97, 129, 132, 134, 172, 185, 203, 222, 230, 679
Bartley, Mel, 737

Basak, Chandramallika, 719, 720
Basseches, Michael, 525
Basten, Stuart, 582
Bastin, Mark E., 702
Basting, Anne D., 722
Basu, Sanjay, 591
Basurto-Dávila, Ricardo, 737
Bateman, Eric D., 318
Bates, Gillian, 86
Bates, Lisa M., 187, 189, 216
Bates, P. B., 723
Bateson, Mary Catherine, 723
Batterham, Philip J., 609
Battista, Deena, 421
Batty, G. David, 604
Bauer, Amy, 226
Bauer, Charles R., 195
Bauer, Douglas C., 687
Bauer, Patricia J., 162, 165, 421
Baumeister, Roy F., 48, 593
Baumgardt, Melanie, 597
Bauminger-Zviely, Nirit, 330
Baumrind, Diana, 287, 288, 294
Baumwell, Lisa, 174f
Bay von Scholten, Mikael, 18
Bayer, Jordana K., 135
Bayley, Nancy, 605
Baym, Carol L., 319, 345
Bazerman, Max H., 437
Bckel, Christina, 501
Beach, Steven R. H., 465, 550, 642
Beal, Susan, 149–150
Bear, George G., 43
Bearman, Peter S., 106, 330
Beasley, T. Mark, 691
Beauchaine, Theodore P., 373
Beaulieu, Christian, 701
Beaulieu-Prevost, Dominic, 659
Beaumont, Sherry L., 632
Bebeau, Muriel J., 530, 533
Beck, Martha, 101, 112, 120
Beck, T. T., 753
Beckel-Mitchener, Andrea, 132
Becker, Bruce, 318
Beckers, Debby G. J., 658
Beckett, Celia, 196
Beckett, Nigel, 43
Beckles, Gloria L. A., 687
Beddor, Patrice Speeter, 169
Beebe, Heidi, 249
Beeghly, Marjorie, 134
Beer, Charlotte, 108
Begeer, Sander, 253
Begos, Kevin, 84
Beier, Margaret E., 655
Beijers, Roseriet, 226
Beijsterveldt, Toos C. E. M. van, 114, 373
Beise, Jan, 207
Belfield, Clive R., 269
Belin, David, 593
Belin-Rauscent, Aude, 593
Bell, Aleeca F., 103
Bell, Beth Teresa, 414
Bell, Martha Ann, 162, 277
Bell, Rich, 498
Belle, Steven H., 752
Bellinger, David C., 111, 230
Belliveau, Richard A., 150

Belon, Katherine, 405
Belouad, Francesca, 280
Belsky, Jay, 21, 186, 188, 207, 208, 373, 402, 409, 715
Beltran, Alicia, 326
Benatar, David, 775
Benbow, Camilla P., 530, 647
Benenson, Joyce F., 552
Benet, Mikhail, 591, 692
Benet, Sula, 692
Benet-Martínez, Verónica, 538, 546
Bengtson, Vern L., 746
Benjamín, Caballero, 591, 692
Benjamin, Georges C., 234
Bennett, Craig, 520
Bennett, Shira A., 563, 564
Benoit, Amelie, 410, 411
Benovenli, Liza, 529
Benson, Peter L., 466
Bentley, Gillian R., 95t
Bentley, Margaret, 140
Ben-Zur, Hasida, 593
Berdan, Jennifer, 533, 538
Berenbaum, Sheri A., 284, 293
Berg, Cynthia A., 5, 119, 518, 522, 565, 567, 638
Berg, Patricia van den, 443
Berger, Kathleen Stassen, 388
Berger, Lawerence M., 382, 383
Berger, Sarah E., 140
Berglund, Patricia, 505
Berg-Nielsen, Turid Suzanne, 207, 715
Berk, Laura E., 282
Berkey, Catherine S., 406
Berkman, Lisa F., 638, 740, 747
Berkowitz, Marvin W., 392
Berlin, Lisa J., 197
Bernard, Kristin, 194, 651
Bernard, Jessica, 701
Berry, Jarett D., 672
Berry, John W., 375, 553
Bers, Marina, 251
Bersabem, Adrian, 116
Berteletti, Ilaria, 328
Bertelsen, Aksel, 87
Bertrand, Rosanna M., 635
Bertsch, Sharon, 636
Bessa, J. M., 700
Besson, Mireille, 170
Betancourt, Theresa S., 371
Bettencourt, Ricki, 582
Beutel, Manfred E., 581
Beutler, Ivan F., 536
Beyene, Joseph, 113
Beyene, Y., 583
Beyers, Jennifer M., 411
Bharucha, Jamshed, 185
Bhatia, Tej K., 261
Bhatta, Tirth, 739
Bhattacharya, Siladitya, 582
Bhutta, Zulfigar A., 121
Biaggio, Angela, 530
Bialystok, Ellen, 260, 261, 346
Bianchi, Suzanne M., 659, 739
Bianco, Kevin, 262
Biblarz, Timothy J., 644
Biehl, Michael C., 410
Bielak, Allison A. M., 736

Bienvenu, Thierry, 330
Biggs, Simon, 637
Bigler, Rebecca S., 433
Bilal, Usama, 591, 692
Bilalic, Merim, 624
Billings, J. Andrew, 771
Bingley, Paul, 639
Binstock, Robert H., 743, 747
Biovin, Michel, 173
Birch, Eileen E., 146
Birch, Leann L., 217
Birch, Susan A. J., 254
Bird, Chole E., 737
Bird, Geoffrey, 403
Birditt, Kira S., 567, 642, 687, 746
Birdsong, David, 7
Biro, Frank M., 402
Bischof, Gérard N., 626, 720
Bishop, Dorothy V. M., 259
Bishop, Somer L., 329
Bisiacchi, Patrizia Silvia, 99
Bjelakovic, Goran, 689
Bjerregaard, Peter, 591
Bjorklund, Davd F., 346
Björnberg, Marina, 393–394
Black, Dennis M., 687
Blackburn, Elizabeth, 691
Blackhart, Ginnette C., 421
Blackwell, Lisa S., 447, 448
Blair, Clancy B., 182, 277, 279, 604
Blakemore, Sarah-Jayne, 403, 430
Blalock, Garrick, 765
Blanchard-Fields, Fredda, 611
Blanco, Dulce, 268
Blandon, Alysia Y., 289
Blane, David, 737
Blanton, Hart, 370
Blas, Erik, 587, 588
Blasi, Anna, 185
Blekesaune, Morten, 645
Bleske-Rechek, April, 552, 553
Blettner, Maria, 582
Bliss, Catherine, 16
Block, Robert, 133
Bloom, Barbara, 676
Bloom, Paul, 254
Blum, Deborah, 30
Blumberg, Mark S., 78
Blumberg, Stephen J., 330
Blurton-Jones, Nicholas G., 284
Blyler, Crystal R., 504
Boals, Adriel, 732
Bobrick, Laura, 501
Bodis-Wollner, Ivan, 713
Boehnke, Klaus, 446
Boerner, Kathrin, 783
Boersch-Supan, Axel, 747
Bogart, Andy, 591
Bögels, Susan M., 183, 186
Bogle, Kathleen A., 554
Bohlmeijer, E. T., 722
Boiarskaia, Elena A., 312
Boisvert, Linda, 121
Bolen, Cyndi, 720
Boller, Kimberley, 262
Bollyky, Thomas J., 589
Bolnick, Rebecca, 296
Bomba, Monica, 158, 168
Bonanno, George A., 744, 783, 784

Bonanno, Rina A., 442
Bond, John, 711, 714, 754
Bond, Lyndal, 411
Bondi, Mark W., 711, 714
Boniadi, Fatemeh, 563
Boodoo, Gwyneth, 617
Boogaard, Derek, 714
Boom, Dymphna C. van den, 186
Boomsma, Dorret I., 114, 373
Boone, Anniglo, 650
Boot, Walter R., 719
Booth, Ian, 146
Booth, James R., 319
Borenstein, Natalia S., 150
Borge, Anne I., 207
Borgens, Richard Ben, 689
Boris, Neil W., 197
Borja, Judith B., 140
Borke, Jörn, 198, 201, 202
Borkowski, John G., 423, 464
Bornstein, Marc H., 11, 138, 160, 163, 174f, 346, 613, 636
Borrelli, Belinda, 318
Bors, Philip, 498
Bos, Maarten W., 623
Boscardin, W. John, 754
Boseman, Letia A., 687
Boseovski, Janet J., 222, 276
Bossé, Yohan, 317
Bost, Kelly K., 315, 316
Bosworth, Hayden B., 520, 717
Bothe, Denise, 196
Botti, Simona, 556
Botvin, Gilbert J., 410, 477
Bouchard, Claude, 406, 412
Bouchard, Thomas J. Jr., 617
Bouffard, Suzanne M., 312
Boult, Chad, 718
Boult, Lisa, 718
Bound, John, 617
Bourguignon, Jean-Pierre, 111
Bourque, Francois, 506
Bousquet, Jean, 318
Bout, Jan van den, 779
Bowden, Donald W., 690
Bowen, Mary Elizabeth, 736
Bowen, William G., 538, 539
Bower, Bruce, 163
Bower, Carol, 106
Bowers, Edmond P., 638
Bowers, Jeffrey S., 167, 387, 538
Bowker, Julie C., 188, 276, 282, 385, 446
Bowlby, John, 192
Bowman, Ashley, 61
Boyce, Lisa, 289
Boyce, W. Thomas, 197, 226, 370
Boyce, William, 425
Boyd, Cynthia M., 718
Boyer, Maud, 170
Boykin, A. Wade, 617
Boyle, Coleen A., 330
Boyle, Michael H., 375
Boywitt, C. Dennis, 704
Bozik, Mary, 533
Bracke, Piet, 18
Bracken, Bruce A., 266
Bradbury, Thomas N., 553
Bradley, Kristopher I., 765

Bradley, Robert H., 11, 406
Bradstreet, James Jeffrey, 330
Brady, Teresa J., 687
Brady-Smith, Christy, 289
Brähler, Elmar, 72, 581
Brame, Robert, 507
Branca, Francesco, 311
Branch, John, 714
Brand, Rebecca J., 175
Brand, Ronald, 136
Brandt, Harry, 414
Brandt, Jason, 750
Brandt, Martina, 566, 734
Brannon, Patsy M., 59
Brassen, Stefanie, 733
Brauer, Michael, 229, 553, 559, 561
Braun, Joe M., 111
Bravata, Dena M., 217
Bravo, Irene M., 505
Brazelton, Barry, 50
Brazelton, T. Berry, 197
Breivik, Gunnar, 507
Bremner, J. Gavin, 172
Brendgen, Mara, 385
Brennan, Arthur, 119
Brennan, Robert T., 371
Brenner, Joanna, 555
Breslow, Lori, 539
Bretherton, Inge, 197, 199
Brett, Stephen J., 776
Brickhouse, Tegwyn H., 217
Bridge, Jeffrey A., B-5
Bridges, Margaret, 289
Bridges, Sara K., 405
Briggs, Phillips T., 284, 293
Briggs-Gowan, Margaret J., 197
Brink, S. van den, 617
Brinkman, William B., 326
Britto, Pia Rebello, 262
Brner, ND., 404
Brody, Gene H., 383, 464, 465, 550
Brody, Nathan, 617
Bromet, Evelyn J., 505
Bronfenbrenner, Urie, 7, 8
Bronfman, Elisa, 194
Bronte-Tinkew, Jacinta, 198
Brook, David W., 327
Brook, Judith S., 327
Brooker, Robert J., 85, 87
Brooks, Jeanne, 184
Brooks-Gunn, Jeanne, 410, 423, 477
Brooks-Wilson, Angela R., 689
Brouwer, Rachel M., 114
Brown, Abbie H., 347
Brown, Annie W., 650
Brown, B. Bradford, 410, 463, 464, 467, 472
Brown, Chester M., 681
Brown, Christia Spears, 369
Brown, David R., 311
Brown, Edna, 642, 687
Brown, Ellie, 175
Brown, J. Scott, 734
Brown, Louise, 73
Brown, Miriam, 644
Brown, Rhonda Douglas, 346
Brown, Susan L., 378, 643, 749
Brown, Timothy T., 326

Brownell, Celia A., 296, 297
Brownell, Patricia, 753
Brownson, Ross C., 414
Broyles, Stephanie, 497
Brubacher, Jeff R., 621
Bruce, Susan, 159
Bruford, Elispeth A., 69
Brugha, Traolach S., 505
Bruin, Wändi de, 765
Bruinse, Hein W., 114
Brüning, Thomas, 27
Brutnell, Thomas P., 83
Bryant, Alyssa, 531
Bryant, Christina, 584
Bryant, David, 624
Bryant, Gregory A., 169, 174
Brymer, Eric, 509
Bub, Kristen L., 208
Buchanan, Anna DeBlois, 145
Büchel, Christian, 733
Buchem, Mark A. van, 685
Bucher, Hans Ulrich, 597
Buchman, Aron S., 701
Bucholz, Kathleen K., 82
Buckler, Edwards S., 83
Buckley, Maureen, 275
Bucx, Freek, 565, 639, 746
Buddha, 531
Buehler, Cheryl, 744
Bueno, Mariana, 139
Buettner, Dan, 694
Bugental, Daphne Blunt, 301, 668
Bugg, Julie M., 706
Buhling, Kai J., 585
Buhrmester, Michael D., 370
Buiting, Hilde, 774
Bukowski, William M., 446, 469, 730
Bulik, Cynthia M., 414
Bull, Rebecca, 703
Bullens, Ruud A. R. ., 241
Bullock, Bernadette Marie, 290
Bulpitt, Christopher J., 43
Bunge, Silvia A., 319, 345
Bunting, Brendan P., 702
Buonocore, Michael H., 330
Burchinal, Margaret, 208, 262, 269, 613
Burdorf, Alex, 738
Burd-Sharps, Sarah, 595, 598
Bureau of Labor Statistics, 656
Burek, Melissa W., 410
Burgess, Diana, 524
Burgio, Louis D., 752
Buriel, Raymond, 198, 287, 289
Burk, William J., 464, 469
Burke, Jeffrey D., 478, 619
Burke-Miller, Jane, 504
Burnett, Stephanie, 430
Burns, Barbara J., 650
Burns, Tracey C., 168
Burpo, Todd, 767
Burraston, Bert, 469
Burri, Andrea, 581
Burstein, David D., 552
Burt, S. Alexandra, 373, 469, 648
Buschkuehl, Martin, 701
Bush, George H. W., 689
Bushman, Brad J., 369

Bushway, Shawn D., 507
Buss, David M., 58, 60, 61, 552, 776
Butler, L., 326
Butler, Robert N., 721, 722
Buttelmann, David, 138, 169
Butterfield, Max E., 553
Butters, Meryl A., 683
Butterworth, Brian, 328, 329
Buunk, Abraham, 559, 652
Buzhardt, Jay, 351
Byers-Heinlein, Krista, 168

Cabo, Rafael de, 691
Cacciatore, Joanne, 763
Cacioppo, John T., 373, 555, 747
Cacioppo, Stephanie, 555
Cadwell, Louise, 264
Cafiero, Angela C., 717
Cain, Daphne S., 380
Cain, Kelli, 592
Cairns, Alyssa, 316
Caldieraro, Fabio, 434
Caldwell, Cleopatra, 113
Caldwell, Jennifer E., 563, 564
Calkins, Susan D., 188, 191, 277, 289, 296
Call, Josep, 173, 219
Callaghan, Tara, 246, 256
Callahan, Richard C., 347
Calmet, Jeanne, 695
Calvin, Catherine M., 604
Calvo, Rocio, 638
Cameron, Judy, 278
Camhi, Sarah M., 497
Camilli, Gregory, 267
Camino, Cleonice, 530
Camos, Valérie, 344
Campana, Fernando, 640
Campana, Humberto, 640
Campbell, Frances A., 269
Campbell, Jacquelyn, 563
Campbell, Jan, 181
Campbell, Rona, 467
Campbell, Susan B., 297
Campisi, Judith, 576
Campos, Joseph J., 183
Camras, Linda A., 183, 185
Canadian Psychological Association, 30
Canagarajah, A. Suresh, 176
Candy, T. Rowan, 138
Capaldi, Deborah M., 280, 478, 643
Cappeliez, Philippe, 675, 722
Cappell, Katherine A., 702
Car, Josip, 711
Caravita, Simona C. S., 387, 389
Cardinal, Roger, 722
Carey, Nessa, 258
Carey, Susan, 16
Cargo, Marjorie, 473
Carleson, Gabrielle A., 327
Carlin, John B., 481
Carlo, Waldemar A., 113, 114
Carlson, Susan A., 311
Carlsson, Rickard, 461
Carlstrom, Eva, 373
Carnethon, Mercedes R., 497
Carolan, Megan E., 270
Carollo, Tanner, 61

Caronongan, Pia, 312
Carothers, Shannon S., 463, 464
Carpenter, Malinda, 138, 169
Carpenter, Siri, 30
Carpenter, Thomas O., 59
Carpentier, Nico, 773
Carr, Deborah, 762
Carrano, Jennifer, 198
Carroll, Kathleen, 512
Carroll, Margaret D., 315
Carskadon, Mary A., 404
Carstensen, Laura L., 617, 732, 765
Carter, Alice S., 197
Cartwright, Lara, 612
Caruthers, Allison, 471
Casaccia, Patrizia, 81
Case, Keith, 682
Case, Matthew H., 533, 538
Case, Trevor I., 184
Case-Smith, Jane, 283
Casey, B. J., 417, 418, 431
Casey, Richard, 586
Cashon, Cara H., 163
Caspe, Margaret, 250
Caspersen, Carl J., 687
Caspi, Avshalom, 187, 371, 374, 477, 634
Cassia, Viola Macchi, 134
Cassidy, Jude, 189
Castañeda, Yolanda S., 146
Castel, Alan D., 705, 706
Castle, David J., 87
Castle, Jenny, 196
Castro, Carl A., 430
Castro-Martin, Teresa, 557
Catalano, Richard, 411
Catani, Claudia, 371
Catta-Preta, Adriana Bokel, 562
Cattell, Raymond, 608–610
Caudle, Kristina, 417
Cauffman, Elizabeth, 406, 467, 477
Cauley, Jane A., 584
Cavendish, Wendy, 325
Ceausescu, Nicolae, 196p
Ceci, Stephen J., 617
Celdrán, Montserrat, 721
Celec, Peter, 96
Celluci, Paul, 767
Cen, Guozhen, 385
Centers for Disease Control and Prevention, A-7, A-17, A-20, 144, 147, 422, 492, 671, 688
Centers for Medicaid and Medicare Services, 675
Centre for Community Child Health, 350
Cerankosky, Brittany C., 442
Cervone, Daniel, 523
Ceulemans, Eva, 636
Cha, I. Elizabeth, 78
Chaddock, Laura, 323
Chae, David H., 524
Chafen, Jennifer J. Schneider, 217
Chaignat, Evelyne, 80
Chakraborty, Hrishikesh, 113, 114
Chambers, Bette, 267
Champagne, F. A., 120
Chan, Chi-Keung, 375
Chan, Christian S., 620

Chan, Darius K. S., 557
Chan, David W., 233
Chan, Eliza, 106
Chan, Herbert, 621
Chan, K. Arnold, 110
Chan, Kit Yee, 711
Chan, Kitty S., 750
Chan, Tak Wing, 288
Chang, Daixin, 735
Chang, Ellen T., 735
Chang, Esther S., 466
Chang, Hyein, 298, 299
Chang, Jen Jen, 238
Chang, Lei, 300, 301
Chang, Myles, 735
Chao, I. Chen, 676
Chao, Jian-Kang, 676
Chao, Ruth K., 289
Chao, Y. May, 415
Chaplin, Ian Nguyen, 369
Chapman, Benjamin J., 492
Chappell, Chad, 132
Chappell, Lucy C., 106
Chaput, Jean-Philippe, 495
Charles, Susan T., 617
Charlton, Samuel G., 621
Charness, Neil, 624, 625
Charney, Dennis S., 186
Chasman, Daniel I., 584
Chassin, Laurie, 481, 483
Chatterji, Somnath, 505
Chatters, Linda M., 742
Chaudhary, Nandita, 201
Chaudhry, Nasim, 18
Chavarro, Jorge E., 583
Chávez, Vivian, 235
Chawla, Sanjay, 777
Cheah, Charissa, 188
Chehimi, Sana, 235
Chein, Isidor, 48
Chein, Jason, 417, 438, 439
Chelsea, personal communication, 560
Chen, Chuansheng, 466
Chen, Daniel, 370
Chen, Edith, 311, 599
Chen, Frances S., 97, 129, 132, 134, 172, 185, 203, 222, 230, 679
Chen, Gong, 414, 683
Chen, Ken, 80
Chen, Kuan-yi, 38
Chen, Ping-Hsin, 240
Chen, Sheying, 669
Chen, Tian Jiao, 315
Chen, Xinyin, 278, 385
Chen, Yi-Fu, 465
Cheney, Dorothy L., 551
Cheng, Angela, 83
Cheng, Diana, 110
Cheng, Yen-Hsin Alice, 561
Cheng, Yen Pi, 567
Cheng, Yi-Chia, 277
Chentsova-Dutton, Yulia E., 546
Cherek, Don R., 481
Cherepanov, Dasha, 737
Cherlin, Andrew J., 381–382, 559, 644, 649
Cheslack-Postava, Keely, 106, 330
Chess, Stella, 187

Cheung, Alan C., 267
Chiasson, Mary Ann, 216
Chien, Dorothy, 266, 267
Child Welfare Information Gateway, 650
Chin, Marshall H., 774
Chinapaw, Mai J. M., 311
Chingos, Matthew M., 538, 539
Chiong, Cynthia, 174, 291
Chiou, Wen-Bin, 519
Chisholm, Dan, 233
Chlebowski, Rowan T., 584
Choi, Incheol, 527
Choi, Namkee G., 656
Chomsky, Noam, 175
Choshen-Hillel, Shoham, 654
Chou, Joanne F., 777
Chou, Rita Jing-Ann, 656
Chow, Virginia, 197
Chrast, Jacqueline, 80
Christakis, Dimitri A., 174
Christakis, Nicholas A., 78, 638
Christensen, Andrew, 562
Christensen, Helen, 609, 736
Christensen, Kaare, 639
Christian, Cindy W., 133
Christian, Jennifer B., 80
Christoffersen, Kari, 536, 752
Christofferson, Jennifer L., 528
Chronicle of Higher Education, 533, 536, 547
Chu, C. Y. Cyrus, 654
Chu, June Y., 463, 476
Chu, Thai Q., 276
Chua, Amy, 36–37
Chudacoff, Howard P., 283
Chuderski, Adam, 609
Chugh, Dolly, 437
Chung, He Len, 175
Church, Timothy A., 636
Church, Timothy S., 497
Churchill, Winston, 328, 724
Chyen D., 404
Cicchetti, Dante, 186, 238, 239, 323, 324, 325
Cicognani, Elvira, 421
Cillessen, Antonius H. N., 386, 387, 466
Cipriano, Elizabeth, 288
Claas, Marieke J., 114
Claes, Michel, 410, 411
Clark, Leanne J., 678
Clark, Lee Anna, 183, 635
Clark, Melissa, 473
Clark, Nina Annika, 229, 553, 559, 561
Clarke, Christina A., 735, 736
Clarke, Lynda, 747
Clarke-Stewart, Alison, 208
Claux, Mary Louis, 256
Claxton, Amy, 675, 744
Clay, Olivio J., 735, 752
Claytor, Randal P., 217
Cleland, John, 580
Cleland, Verity, 44
Clements, Jonathan, 633
Cleveland, Michael J., 464
Cnattingius, Sven, 103
Cockerham, William C., 502

Coe, Christopher L., 22
Coe, Norman B., 739
Coffey, Carolyn, 481
Cohen, David, 285
Cohen, Haim Y., 692
Cohen, Joachim, 773
Cohen, Joel E., 353
Cohen, Jon, 146
Cohen, Larry, 235
Cohen, Leslie B., 163
Cohen, Robin A., 676
Cohen, Sarah, 325
Cohen, Sheldon, 616
Cohen-Kettenis, Peggy T., 584
Coimbra, Raul, 236
Colaco, Marc, 51
Colbert, Linda, 742
Colditz, Graham A., 406
Cole, Jennifer, 559
Cole, Pamela M., 276, 277, 279, 280, 296
Cole, Steven W., 78
Cole, Tim J., 498, 499
Cole, Whitney G., 141, 165
Coleman, Karen J., 591
Coleman, Marilyn, 379, 649, 650
Coles, Robert, 389
College Board
Colleran, Carol, 718
Collings, Catherine, 714
Collins, Andrew R., 717
Collins, Emily, 468
Collins, Francis, 89
Collins, Juliet, 218
Collins, Pamela Y., 17
Collins, Paul, 130
Collins, Phil, 579
Collins, Rebecca L., 471
Collins, Tara J., 557
Collins, W. Andrews, 369, 458–459, 462, 464
Collishaw, Stephan, 17
Colman, Ricki J., 692
Colom, Roberto, 604
Columbo, John, 163
Colvert, Emma, 196
Combs-Orme, Terri, 380
Compian, Laura J., 409
Compta, Yaroslau, 714
Comsa, Marius, 43
Conde, Wolney L., 216
Conde-Agudelo, Agustin, 580
Condon, Christopher A., 604
Confer, Jaime C., 58, 60
Cong, Zhen, 745
Congdon, Nathan G., 83
Conger, Katherine J., 383, 640, 643
Conger, Rand D., 383, 643
Conley, AnneMarie, 451
Conley, Colleen S., 383, 410
Conley, Mary R., 108
Connell, Lenda Jo, 497, 671
Connell-Carrick, Kelli, 239
Conner, Kelly, 501
Conner, Mark, 593
Connolly, Jennifer, 388
Conrad, Olaf, 348
Conroy-Beam, Daniel, 552
Conte, Jeffrey M., 655

Conte, Stefano, 328
Conway, Terry L., 592
Conwell, Erin, 172
Cook, Judith A., 504
Cookston, Jeffrey T., 462
Coon, Carleton S., 15
Cooney, Teresa M., 288
Cooper, Bessie, 692
Cooper, Claudia, 753
Cooper, Richard S., 591, 692
Copeland, Kristen A., 217
Copeland, William E., 388
Copen, Casey, 555, 556, 557
Coplan, Robert J., 349
Corballis, Michael C., 219
Corbin, William, 504
Core, Cynthia, 261
Corella, Dolores, 592
Corney, Roslyn, 634
Cornoldi, Cesare, 325
Cornwell, Benjamin, 744
Coronini-Cronberg, Sophie, 679
Corr, Charles A., 761, 769, 779, 780
Corr, Donna M., 761, 769, 779, 780
Correa-Chávez, Maricela, 342
Corsello, Giovanni, 75
Cortesi, Sandra, 440
Corwyn, Robert F., 406
Cosgrave, James F., 507
Costa, Paul. T. Jr., 723
Costantini, Todd, 236
Costell, E. Jane, 388
Costello, Elizabeth, 280, 478
Costigan, Kathleen A., 99
Côté, James E., 458, 460
Cote, Linda R., 613, 636
Côté, Sylvana M., 207
Cougle, Jesse R., 47
Couturier, Jennifer, 415
Couzin, Jennifer, 638
Couzin-Frankel, Jennifer, 89, 318, 692, 695
Covas, Maria-Isabel, 592
Covino, Jennifer M., 220
Covinsky, Kenneth E., 685
Cowan, Nelson, 344
Cox, Brian J., 239
Cox, Cathy R., 765, 766
Cox, Julia Revillion, 650
Cox, Martha J., 182
Cox, Ronald, 300
Coyne, Iain, 388
Coyne, James C., 749
Craig, Wendy, 388
Craik, Fergus I. M., 260
Crain, Steven P., 468
Crain, William C., 246
Cramer, Robert, 61
Cramer, Steven C., 712
Cranwell, Brian, 779
Crawford, Aaron V., 739
Crawford, David, 44
Crawford, Elizabeth, 266
Crawford, Patricia B., 402
Crawford Shearer, Nelma B., 597
Cree, Alison, 71
Creed, Francis, 18
Crenshaw, David A., 784
Cressman, Kate, 747

Crinion, Jenny, 260
Crisp, Dimity A., 739
Crispen, Heather R., 22
Crnic, Keith A., 277
Crocetti, Elisabetta, 504
Crockett, Lisa J., 463, 476
Crompton, Rosemary, 659
Cronce, Jessica M., 504
Crone, Eveline A., 248, 319, 438
Crosnoe, Robert, 16, 341, 446
Cross, David, 254
Cross, Donna, 388
Crowe, Kristi, 114
Crowell, Sheila E., 373
Crucian, Brian, 496
Cruikshank, Margaret, 669, 670, 678
Cruz, Alvaro A., 317, 318
Cryder, Cynthia E., 654
Crystal, David, 55
Crystal, Stephen, 326
Csibra, Gergely, 329
Csikszentmihalyi, Mihaly, 625, 722
Cuevas, Bryan J., 166, 763
Cui, Carol, 505
Cui, Ming, 560
Cuijpers, P., 119
Cullen, Kathryn R., 506
Cullen, Mark R., 80
Cumberland, Amanda, 275, 328, 529
Cumming, Elaine, 736
Cummings, Steven R., 687
Cumsille, Patricio, 463
Cunha, Marcus Jr., 434
Cunningham, David A., 495
Cunradi, Carol B., 563
Curley, J. P., 120
Curlin, Farr A., 774
Currie, Janet, 239
Curry, Laurel Erin, 593
Curry, Mary, 640
Cutler, Stephen J., 739
Cutts, Hayley, 443
Cutuli, J.J., 375
Czaja, Sara J., 752

Daar, Abdallah S., 17
Daddis, Christopher, 469
Dahl, Edgar, 72
Dahl, Ronald E., 402, 403, 404, 410, 419, 438, 654
Dai, David Yun, 333
Dalal, Reeshad, 527
Dale, Philip S., 119, 176, 259
D'Alessio, Maria, 648
Daley, Dave, 326
Dalman, Christina, 144
Danel, Isabella, 119
Daniel, David B., 436
Daniels, Kimberly, 555, 556, 557
Daniels, Stephen R., 217
Dannefer, Dale, 608
Danoff-Burg, Sharon, 765
Dapretto, Mirella, 418
Darer, Jonathan, 718
Darkwah, Akosua, 375
Darling, Nancy, 463
Darr, Stacy, 410
Darwin, Charles, 58, 334
Dasen, Pierre R., 342

Daugherty, Kate, 695
Daum, I., 48
Daum, Moritz M., 138, 169, 170
Davey, Adam, 695
David, Barbara, 292
David, Jane L., 449
Davidson, Hilary, 536, 752
Davidson, Julia O'Connell, 424
Davidson, Kate, 731
Davidson, Lance E., 591
Davidson, Tim I., 619
Davila, Joanne, 503
Davis, Elysia Poggi, 199
Davis, Kelly D., 658
Davis, Linell, 349
Davis, Mark, 502
Davis, Robert L., 110
Davis, Ronnie, 742
Davis, William E., 732, 733
Davis-Kean, Pamela E., 299, 369
Davitt, Joan K., 740
Dawes, Christopher T., 78
Dawson, Geraldine, 330
Dawson, Lorne L., 460
Dawson, Michelle, 329
De Bolle, Marleen, 723
De Cock, Kevin M., 144
De Corte, Erik, 335
De Fruyt, Filip, 723
De Haan, Michelle, 186
De Heering, Adelaide, 134
De Jonge, Ank, 104
De Lee, Joseph Bolivar, 103
De Leersynder, Jozefien, 636
De Luca, Cinzia R., 114
De Neys, Wim, 432, 434, 438
De Raedt, Rudi, 765
De Vries, Linda S., 114
Dean, Angela J., 311
Dean, James, 765
Dearing, Eric, 312
Deary, Ian J., 604, 607, 702, 717
Deater-Decker, Kirby, 287, 288, 289, 290, 300, 301
DeBacker, Teresa K., 467
Deboer, Jennifer, 539
Deboni, Malorie, 134
Deci, Edward L., 278
Dee, Thomas, 358
Dees, Marianne K., 774
DeFries, John C., 69, 77, 86, 87
Degenhardt, Louisa, 481
Degnan, Kathryn A., 187
DeGroot, Jocelyn M., 765
Dehaene-Lambertz, Ghislaine, 163
DeHart, Ganie, 406
Deindl, Christian, 566, 734
Dekay, Todd, 552
Dekker, Gustaaf A., 106
Dekkers, Wim J., 774
Dekovic, Maja, 187, 188
DeLamater, John, 581
Delaunay-El Allam, Maryse, 138
Delden, Johannes van, 774
Delemarre-van de Waal, Henriette A., 584
Delfin, Frederick, 73
Deliens, Luc, 773
DeLoache, Judy S., 163, 174, 291

Delon-Martin, Chantal, 626
DelPriore, Danielle J., 553
Demers, Paul A., 229, 553, 559, 561
Demetre, James D., 634
Demetriou, Andreas, 321, 520
Denault, Anne-Sophie, 479
Denby, Tracy, 669
Denckla, Christy A., 617
Denissen, Jaap J. A., 549, 550, 635
Dennis, Tracy, 279
Denny, Dallas, 461, 470
DePaulo, Bella M., 749
Depledge, Michael H., 636
Deptula, Daneen P., 472
Derbidge, Christina, 373
Derscheid, Linda E., 430
Desai, Rathnamala M., 580
Desai, Sonalde, 559
Deschuyffeleer, Sara, 191
Desjardins, Christopher David, 375
Desmond, Matthew, 379
Desoete, Annemie, 340
Dessauer, Mark, 498
Devaney, Barbara, 473
Devi, Sharmila, 216
DeVilder, Elzabeth L., 410
Devlin, Joseph T., 260
DeVos, Julie, 159
Dewailly, Eric, 591
DeWall, C. Nathan, B-5, 549
DeYoung, Colin G., 637
Dhatariya, Ketan, 586
Di Blasio, Paola, 389
Diamanti-Kandarakis, Evanthia, 111
Diamond, Adele, 162, 195
Diamond, M. E., 137
Dick, Anthony Steven, 222
Dick, Danielle M., 481
Dickens, William T., 604, 609, 617
Dickie, Jane R., 506
Dickinson, George E., 782
Didion, Joan, 761, 778
Dieckmann, Nathan F., 705
Diener, Ed, 13, 636
Dierker, Lisa C., 415
Dietary Guidelines for Americans, 413
Dietrich, Jörg, 701
Dietz, William H., 311
Dijk, Jan A. G. M. van, 440
Dijksterhuis, Ap, 623
Dijkstra, Jan Kornelis, 387, 389
Dikkers, Josje S. E., 655
Dillen, Jeroen van, 104
Dillow, Sally A., 355, 361, 362
DiMatteo, M. Robin, 422, 593
Dinella, Lisa, 76, 293, 431
Dinwiddie, Darrell L., 86
Dionne, Ginette, 173
DiPietro, Janet A., 99
Dirix, Chantal E. H., 168
Dishion, Thomas J., 290, 447, 469
Dittmar, Helga, 414
Dixon, Dennis R., 330, 331
Dobbin, Matthew M., 714
Dobkins, Karen, 257
Dobler, Robert Thomas, 782
Dobson, Velma, 138
Dodd, Chris, 316

Dodge, Kenneth A., 300, 301, 323, 477
Doering, Katie, 764
Doherty, David, 634
Dohm, Faith-Anne, 415
Doka, Kenneth J., 771
Dolan, Conor V., 322
Dombro, Amy Laura, 204
Domina, Thurston, 451
Dominelli, Paolo B., 576
Dominguez, Antonio, 380
Dominguez, Cynthia O., 622
Dominguez-Folgueras, Marta, 557
Dominy, John E., 692
Dommarco, Juan A. Rivera, 315
Donald, Jennifer, 87
Dong, XinQi, 753
Donnellan, M. Brent, 174, 370, 383, 473, 560, 635
Donnelly, Peter, 72
Donnelly, Reesa, 293
D'Onofrio, Brian M., 383, 649
Donovan, Sharon M., 315, 316
Doraiswamy, P. Murali, 714
Doreleijers, Theo A. H., 241
Dorn, Lorah D., 410
Dorsey, Shannon, 650
DosReis, Susan, 326
Doucet, Fabienne, 227, 282
Douglas, Dianna Hutto, 672
Douglas, Isabella, 317
Douglas, Nataki C., 583
Doval, Alexi San, 472
Dowling, Conor M., 634
Dowling, John E., 97
Downer, Jason T., 249
Dowshen, Steven A., 402
Doyle, Lex W., 114
Doyle, Walter, 43
Dozier, Mary, 194, 651
Dragano, Nico, 737
Drake, Brett, 237
Drake, Lauren, 262
Drapeau, Aline, 659
Draut, Tamara, 547
Drover, James, 146
Drum, Melinda L., 401
Drummond, Jesse, 296
Dubas, Judith Semon, 198
Dubbs, Shelli L., 559, 652
Dubicka, Bernadka, 327
Dubowitz, Tamara, 737
Ducat, Wendy, 470
Duckworth, Angela L., 634
Dudgeon, Paul, 474
Dudley, Aimée M., 77
Duffey, Kiyah J., 500
Duggan, Maeve, 440, 555
Duivenvoorden, Hugo J., 114
Dukes, Charles, 346
Dukes, Richard L., 387
Dulfer, Nicky, 449
Duman, Ronald S., 511
Duncan, Greg J., 270, 382
Duncan, Jhodie R., 150
Duncan, John, 604
Duncan, Simon, 642
Dunham, Nancy Cross, 737
Dunkel, Curtis S., 614

Dunlap, Riley E., 25
Dunmore, Simon J., 315
Dunn, et al., 2013, 627
Dunne, Eileen F., 424
Dunning, David, 295, 519
Dunphy, Dexter, 469
DuPaul, George J., 328
Dupoux, Emmanuel, 113, 138, 169
Dupuis, Kate, 703
Duran, Richard, 472
Durvasula, Srinivas, 497
Dustin, 434, 437
Dutat, Michel, 163
Duthie, Susan J., 717
Dutton, Donald G., 564
Duval-Tsioles, Denise, 379
Dvornyk, Volodymyr, 406
Dwane, H. Dean, 507
Dweck, Carol Sorich, 97, 129, 132, 134, 172, 185, 203, 222, 230, 369, 370, 447, 448, 524, 679
Dwyer, Laura, 103, 114, 143
Dyck, Peter C. van, 330
Dye, Melody, 222, 259
Dyson, Alan, 331
Dzorgbo, Dan-Bright S., 640

Eagan, Kevin, 533, 538
Eagly, Alice H., 5, 279, 291, 293, 294
Earle, Craig C., 769
Easton, Judith A., 58, 60
Eaton, Danice K., 404
Eaves, Emily, 604
Eaves, Lindon J., 17
Ebaugh, Helen Rose, 640
Ebbesson, Sven E. O., 591
Eccles, Jacquelynne C., 445
Eccles, Jacquelynne S., 444, 446, 448, 473
Eckhardt, Marc, 348
Eckman, Mark H., 591
Eden, Jennifer, 554
Edwards, Janet W. Rich, 102
Edwards, Judge Leonard P., 240, 241
Edwards, Lindsay L., 642, 687
Eeden-Moorefield, Brad van, 379
Eells, Tracy D., 622
Egberts, Toine, 325
Egeland, Byron, 186, 410
Eggum, Natalie D., 296
Egloff, Boris, 636
Ehret, Christopher, 15
Ehrlich, Paul R., 673
Eickhorst, Andreas, 198, 202
Eikeseth, Svein, 331
Eimeren, Thilo van, 221
Einstein, Albert, 328
Eisenberg, Christina, 747
Eisenberg, Nancy, 198, 275, 290, 296, 462, 529, 550
Ekas, Naomi V., 189
Ekerdt, David J., 658
Elbert, Thomas, 371
Elder, Glen H. Jr., 446, 747
Eldridge, Beverley, 140
Eldridge, Kathleen, 562
Elias, Carol F., 408
Elicker, James G., 266
Elkind, David, 280, 430

Elliot, Marc N., 471
Elliot, Michael R., 438
Elliot, Stuart W., 449
Elliot, Vanessa J., 776
Ellis, Bruce J., 21, 370, 408
Ellis, Lee, 765
Ellison, Christopher G., 302
El-Mohandes, Ayman A. E., 614, 647
Else-Quest, Nicole M., 187, 223, 264
Elwell, Claire E., 185
Emerle, Henry F., 681
Emery, Robert E., 649
Eng, Abbey, 471
Engeland, Herman van, 325
Engelberts, Adèle C., 136
Engelhardt, H. Tristram Jr., 772
Engels, Rutger C. M. E., 530
England, Dawn E., 294
Englander, Elizabeth, 442
Engleberts, Adéle, 150
Engles, Rutger C. M. E., 288
Enlund, Hannes, 717
Enns, Murray W., 239
Enserink, Martin, 78
EPE Research Center, 450
Epel, Elissa, 691
Epps, Chad, 82
Epstein, Dale J., 270
Epstein, Jeffery N., 326
Epstein, Marina, 471
Erceg, Erin, 388
Erdblink, Thomas, 479
Erdman, Phyllis, 195
Erickson, Kirk I., 323
Erickson, Leah, 552, 553
Ericsson, K. Anders, 625
Eriksen, Michael P., 480
Erikson, Erik, 41, 41p, 41t, 48, 50, 64, 199, 200, 208, 209, 276–277, 279, 295, 303, 368, 373, 395, 458, 459, 461, 462, 485, 543, 544, 547, 551, 560, 569, 632, 637, 646, 647, 651, 661, 719, 757
Erikson, Joan M., 719
Erikson, Kirk I., 683, 714
Erkulwater, Jennifer L., 326
Erlinghagen, Marcel, 739
Ernst, Monique, 186
Ertel, Karen A., 740
Escarce, José J., 737
Esposito, Linda, 150
Essex, Marilyn, 197
Esteller, Manel, 16
Estrada, Steven, 431
Estruch, Ramón, 592
Etchu, Koji, 297
Eulenburg, Christine, 585
European Nutrition and Health Report, A-7
Euser, Eveline M., 424
Eustace, Joesph, 710
Evans, Alan, 701
Evans, Angela D., 254, 255
Evans, Cortney A., 549
Evans, David W., 218
Evans, Denis A., 753
Evans, Gary W., 226
Evans, Jane A., 85

Evans, M. D. R., 351
Evans-Lacko, Sara E., 326
Evenson, Kelly R., 414
Ever, 120
Everdell, Nick, 185
Everitt, Barry J., 593
Ewers, Michael, 710
Ewing, Reid, 592
Eymard, Amanda Singleton, 672
Ezzati, Majid, 587

Fabes, Richard A., 76, 275, 284, 293, 431
Fabiani, Monica, 577
Fabiano, Gregory A., 326
Fabricius, William V., 296
Facoetti, Andrea, 328
Fadiga, Luciano, 171
Fagan, Joseph F., 617
Fagundes, Christopher P., 195
Faherty, Ashley, 132
Faircloth, Beverly S., 467
Faísca, Luís, 781
Falbo, Toni, 38
Falkenberg White, Terry, 623
Falkner, Frank, 402
Fallu, Jean-Sébastien, 452
Fan, Jin, 185
Farah, Martha J., 351
Faraone, Stephen V., 327
Farber, Annalu, 777, 778
Farber, Stu, 777, 778
Farkas, George, 451
Farmer, Brittany, 518
Farooqui, Amber, 685
Farran, Carol, 753
Farrar, Ruth D., 362
Farrell, Peter, 331
Farrington, David P., 388
Farris, Jaelyn Renee, 423, 464
Farruggia, Susan P., 466
Fastbom, Johan, 695
Fathipoor, Mohammad, 563
Faucher, Luc, 15
Fauchére, Jean-Claude, 597
Fawcett, Angela J., 325
Fay, Cindy, 621
Fazzi, Elisa, 114, 158, 168
FBI, 478
Fearon, R. M. Pasco, 188
Fechter-Leggett, Molly O., 241
Feeley, Nancy, 121
Feeny, David, 737
Feerasta, Aniqa, 620
Feigenson, Lisa, 344
Feingold, Alan, 643
Feldman, Judith F., 167
Feldman, Ruth, 121, 189, 205
Fels Research Institute, A-11
Felson, Richard B., 642
Feltovich, Paul J., 625
Fentiman, Linda C., 111
Ferber, S. G., 121
Ferdinand, Archduke Francis, 782
Feremans, Vicky, 434
Ferguson, Christopher J., 174
Fergusson, David M., 241, 563
Fernandez, Dafne, 528p
Fernandez, Jose R., 59

Fernandez-Luque, Luis, 468
Fernyhough, Charles, 251
Ferraro, David, 352, 356
Ferraro, Kathleen J., 564
Ferrell, Jennifer M., 392
Ferriman, Kimberley, 530, 647
Ferris, Frederick L. III, 83
Fetchenhauer, Detlef, 642
Fewtrell, Mary, 146
Fiandor, Ana, 217
Field, Nigel P., 783
Fields, Desiree, 735
Fields, R. Douglas, 626
Figueiredo, Helmer F., 403
Fikkan, Janna L., 497
Filanosky, Charles, 783
Fillit, Howard M., 715
Filová, Barbora, 96
Fina, Laura F. de, 672
Finch, Brian K., 737
Finch, Caleb E., 690
Finch, Stacia, 300
Finch, Stephen J., 327
Fincham, Frank D., 554, 642
Fine, Mark A., 289
Fine, Sarah, 181
Fingerman, Karen L., 5, 565, 567,
    638, 639, 746
Finkel, Deborah, 607
Finkelhor, David, 375, 383, 387,
    424, 441, 443
Finkelstein, Jonathan A., 110
Finlay, Ilora G., 775
Finley, Gordon E., 567
Finn, Bridgid, 346
Fins, Joseph, 772
Fiori, Katherine L., 617
Fischer, David, 591
Fischer, Kurt W., 200
Fischer, Martin H., 252
Fischhoff, Baruch, 765
Fisher, Helen E., 502, 526
Fisher, Susan J., 583
Fisher, William A., 676
Fiske, Susan T., 669
Fitch, Krisin E., 47
Fitzgerald, Caitlin, 552
Fitzgerald, Jen, 270
Flachs, Esben Meulengracht, 18
Flammer, August, 406
Flannelly, Kevin J., 203
Flannelly, Laura T., 203
Flaxman, Abraham D., 103, 114,
    143, 597
Flegal, Katherine M., 315, 589
Flegal, Kristin E., 704
Fleischman, Diana S., 58, 60
Flemming, Juliaane, 552
Flensborg-Madsen, Trine, 18
Flessner, Christopher A., 218
Fletcher, Ben, 170
Fletcher, Jack M., 331
Fletcher, Jason M., 497
Fletcher, Richard, 197
Fleury, Julie D., 597
Fling, Brett W., 701
Flood, Meredith, 722
Floud, Roderick, 406
Flynn, James R., 321, 604, 609, 617

Foa, Edna B., 218
Fogarty, Laurel, 201
Fogel, Alan, 182, 189, 191
Fogel, Robert W., 406
Fong, Allan, 83
Fonlupt, Pierre, 321, 626
Fontana, Luigi, 692
Ford, Carole L., 625
Ford, Chandra L., 735
Ford, Viola, 216
Forget-Dubois, Nadine, 173
Forster, A., 584
Fortlage, Dale, 236
Fortman, Kris, 110
Fortson, Ken, 473
Fortuna, Keren, 194
Foster, Eugene A., 72
Fowler, James H., 78, 531
Fox, Mary Ann, 262
Fox, Nathan A., 187, 188, 196, 207
Fox, Nick C., 712
Foxx, Richard M., 51
Foy, Pierre, 356
Frackowiak, Richard S. J., 221
Fraga, Mario F., 16
Frahsek, Stefanie, 160
Fraizier, A Lindsay, 406
Franco, Manuel, 591, 692
Frangos, E., 584
Franken, Ingmar H. A., 553
Franklin, Martin E., 218
Franklin, Sam, 434, 437, 448
Frankowski, Ann Christine, 678
Franz, Carol E., 607
Fraser, Mark W., 370
Fratiglioni, Laura, 711
Frayling, Timothy M., 315
Frazier, Thomas W., 220
Freathy, Rachel M., 315
Fredricks, Jennifer A., 473
Freedman, Vicki A., 672, 673, 686
Freedman-Doan, Peter, 473
Freegard, Matthew, 221
Freeman, Emily, 197
Freeman, Gulnur, 676
Freeman, Jennifer B., 218
Freeman, Joan, 163, 333, 334, 335
Freeman, Jonathan, 468
Freidl, Wolfgang, 773
Freisthler, Bridget, 654
French, Ruth, 713
Freud, Anna, 461, 476
Freud, Sigmund, 39–40, 48, 50, 64,
    199–200, 208, 209, 291–292,
    295, 303, 334, 368, 373, 395
Freund, Alexandra M., 621, 736
Freundlich, Madelyn, 567
Frey, Andy J., 358
Frick, Corine, 113
Fried, Carrie B., 525
Fried, Linda P., 718
Friedlaender, Françoise R., 15
Friedland, Robert P., 711
Friedman, Allison H., 270
Friedman, Howard S., 410
Fries, Alison B. Wismer, 183
Friesen, Carol, 51
Frijns, Tom, 473
Froment, Alain, 15

Frost, Joe L., 280
Fryback, Dennis G., 737
Fuligni, Allison Sidle, 263, 265, 738
Fuligni, Andrew, 467
Fuller, Bruce, 268, 289, 352
Fuller, Elizabeth, 529
Fuller-Iglesias, Heather R., 638
Fullerton, Janice, 87
Fulmer, C. Ashley, 636
Fulton, Brent D., 326
Fulton, Janet E., 311
Fung, Helene H., 639
Fung, Joey J., 301
Furstenberg, Frank, 567
Furstenberg, Frank F. Jr., 565, 567

Gabrieli, John D. E., 319, 328
Gadino, Brandy, 467
Gaertner, Bridget M., 198, 294
Gage, Suzanne H., 167, 387, 538
Gait, Priyanka, 506
Gajewski, Byron, 658, 672
Galambos, Nancy L., 505, 549
Galasko, Doug, 711
Galatzer-Levy, Isaac R., 784
Gale, Catherine M., 331
Galea, Mary P., 140
Galea, Sandro, 474, 619, 620
Galek, Kathleen, 203
Gallagher, Paul Francis, 710
Gallagher-Thompson, Dolores, 752
Gallaudet Research Institute, 681
Gallo, Ralph, 742
Galor, Oded, 69
Galvan, Adriana, 417
Galvez, Roberto, 132
Gambone, Laura J., 563, 564
Gamer, Matthias, 733
Gandara, Patricia, 359
Gandhi, Mohandas, 531
Gandini, Leila, 264
Gangestad, Steven W., 58
Ganiban, Jody M., 383
Ganong, Lawrence H., 379, 649, 650
Gans, Daphna, 745, 746
Ganz, Tomas, 576
Gao, Ang, 672
Gao, Sujuan, 710
Gao, Yang, 710
Gao, Yuan, 683, 713, 716
Garbarino, James, 387
Garber, Judy, 408
Garcia, Abbe, 218
García, Enrique, 289
Garcia, Eugene E., 350
Garcia, Fernando, 289
Garcia Coll, Cynthia T., 114, 352,
    658
Garciaguirre, Jessie S., 141, 165
Gardella, Barbara, 114
Gardelle, Vincent de, 163
Gardner, Charles O., 17
Gardner, Howard, 321, 322, 328, 608
Gardner, Jane D., 406
Gari, Mamdooh, 413
Garilova, Natalia, 581
Garrett-Peters, Patricia, 182
Garvey, 285
Garvin, Melissa C., 195, 196

Gaskins, Audrey Jane, 583
Gaskins, Suzanne, 282
Gasser, Urs, 440
Gater, Richard, 18
Gathwala, G., 121
Gatsonis, Constantine A., 230
Gattis, Merideth, 253
Gatz, Margaret, 607
Gatzke-Kopp, Lisa, 373
Gauggel, Siegfried, 708
Gauvain, Mary, 249
Gavin, Amelia R., B-5
Gavrilov, Leonid A., 689
Gavrilova, Natalia S., 676, 689
Gaydaa, Mathieu, 687
Gazzaley, Adam, 319, 345
Gazzard, Gus, 83
Gazzola, Valeria, 162
Ge, Xiaojia, 186, 410, 417
Gee, Christina B., 61, 251
Geelhoed, Elizabeth, 585
Geens, Mieke, 73
Gehring, William J., 255
Geier, Charles, 416, 418
Geiger, Jennifer Mullins, 650
Geisner, Irene M., 512
Gela, Katherine, 222
Gelfand, Micheke J., 55, 636
Gelskov, Sofie V., 163
Gendron, Brian P., 388, 443
Genessee, Fred, 260
Gentile, Douglas A., 441
Geoffroy, Diana, 552
Geoffroy, Marie-Claude, 207
Georgas, James, 375, 553
George, Danny, 711
George, R., 775
Gerber, Alan S., 634
Gerhard, Tobias, 326
Gerig, Guido, 132
Germeijs, Veerle, 549
Gernsbacher, Morton Ann, 329
Geronimus, Arline T., 617
Gerrard, Meg, 430, 464
Gerris, Jan R. M., 198
Gershkoff-Stowe, Lisa, 257
Gershoff, Elizabeth T., 299, 300,
    301, 462
Gerstorf, Denis, 683
Gettler, Lee T., 136
Geurts, Sabine A. E., 658
Gevaert, Kris, 69
Gewirtz, Abigail H., 371
Gewirtzman, Aron, 501
Ghandour, Reem M., 330
Ghossainy, Maliki E., 345
Gianaros, Peter J., 616
Giardino, Angelo P., 240
Giarrusso, Roseann, 746
Gibbons, Frederick X., 430, 464,
    550, 765
Gibson, Eleanor J., 163, 164
Gibson, James J., 163
Gierveld, Jenny de Jong, 642
Gigante, Denise, 597
Gilbert, Richard B., 77, 763
Gildengers, Ariel G., 683
Giles, Amy, 167
Giles, Floyd H., 129

Gilkerson, JIll, 351
Gill, M., 326
Gill, Thomas M., 670
Gillath, Omri, 557
Gillen, Meghan M., 497
Gilles, Floyd H., 129
Gillespie, Charles F., 238
Gillespie, Michael Allen, 311
Gilliam, Mary, 223
Gilligan, Carol, 391, 530
Gillis, John R., 384
Gillman, Matthew W., 102, 146
Gilmer, Diane Fox, 579, 592, 620
Gilovitch, Thomas, 705
Gilsanz, Vicente, 59
Gini, Gianluca, 389
Giordano, Peggy C., 471, 557, 562
Giovanna, 2010, 746
Gipson, Jessica D., 580
Gitlin, Laura N., 752
Giudice, Linda C., 111, 583
Giuffrè, Mario, 75
Glazebrook, Cristine, 108
Glück, Judith, 723
Gluckman, Peter D., 315
Gluth, Sebastian, 733
Gluud, Christian, 689
Glymour, Maria M., 740
Gmeindl, Leon, 702
Göbel, Silke M., 252
Gobet, Fernand, 624
Goddard, Andrew, 505
Goddard, Michelle S., 405
Goddings, Anne-Lise, 403
Godeau, Emmanuelle, 425
Godfrey, Mary, 669
Godoy, Leandra, 197
Goertz, Claudia, 160
Goetz, Cari D., 58, 60
Goh, Daniel Y. T., 135
Golant, Stephen M., 753, 755
Goldberg, Daniel S., 670, 717
Goldberg, Wendy A., 208
Golden, Marita, 748
Goldenberg, Jamie L., 765, 781
Goldenberg, Marni, 508
Goldenberg, Tamar, 217
Goldin-Meadow, Susan, 248
Goldlike Productions, 2012, 392
Goldman, Barbara Davis, 140
Goldsmith, H. Hill, 187, 197, 223
Goldstein, Joshua R., 507
Goldstein, Michael H., 191
Golinkoff, Roberta Michnick, 174, 175, 176, 282
Gollan, Tamar H., 260
Golshan, Shahrokh, 731
Golub, Sarit A., 668
Gomez, Scarlett L., 735
Göncü, Artin, 282
Gonyea, Judith G., 652
Gonyea, Robert M., 534
Gonzaga, Gian C., 555
González, Hector M., 736
Good, Catherine, 524, 525
Goodall, Jane, 584
Gooding, Sarah, 518
Goodlin-Jones, Beth L., 330
Goodman, Judith C., 119, 176

Goodman, W. Benjamin, 658
Goodnight, Jackson A., 649
Goodwin, Robin, 561
Goossens, Luc, 549
Gopnik, Alison, 252
Gorber, Sarah Connor, 315
Gordis, Elana B., 186
Gordon, Ilanit, 121, 205
Gore, Andrea C., 111, 406
Goren, Matt J., 16
Gorlick, Marissa A., 723
Gormley, Matthew J., 328
Gormley, William T. Jr., 270
Gornick, Janet C., 658
Gosling, Samuel D., 636
Gosso, Yumi, 282
Gotlib, Ian H., 17, 119
Gottesman, Irving I., 87
Gottfried, Adele Eskeles, 278
Gottfried, Allen W., 278
Gottlieb, Gilbert, 17
Gottman, John Mordechai, 562
Gould, Jeffrey B., 59
Gould, Madelyn S., 475
Gourdine, Ruby, 650
Govia, Ishtar O., 735
Gow, Alan, 702
Gowen, L. Kris, 409
Goymer, Patrick, 221
Graber, Julia A., 410, 423
Grace, Diane, 292
Grady, Denise, 713
Grady, Jessica S., 23, 76
Graf, Steffi, 325, 334
Gräff, Johannes, 714
Grafman, Jordan, 519, 604
Graham, Carrie, 755
Graham, Sandra, 447
Grandin, Temple, 329–330
Granger, Douglas A., 182, 186
Granpeesheh, Doreen, 330, 331
Grant, Jon E., 505
Grant, Sean, 513
Grant, Victoria, 779
Gratton, Gabriele, 577
Gratzb, Kim L., 238
Graugard, Barry I., 589
Gray, Jeremy R., 637
Gray, Marion A., 708
Gredebäck, Gustaf, 170
Green, David W., 260
Green, James A., 183
Green, Lorraine, 779
Green, Melissa L., 410
Greenberg, Jeff, 765, 766
Greenberger, Ellen, 466
Greene, David, 278
Greene, Melissa L., 473
Greenfield, Emily A., 740
Greenfield, Patricia M., 441
Greenough, William, 132
Greenstein, Deanna, 223
Greenwood, Charles R., 351
Greenwood, Pamela M., 702
Greer, David M., 772, 773
Greewald, Anthony G., 370
Gregg, Christopher, 81
Gregg, Norman McAlister, 106
Gregory, Sara M., 714

Greifeneder, Rainer, 556
Greil, Arthur L., 584
Gremeaux, Vincent, 687
Greve, Douglas N., 220
Greving, Karissa A., 198
Grey, Dennis D., 504
Greyson, Bruce, 768
Grietens, Hans, 300
Griffin, James, 518
Griffith, Patrick, 751
Grigsby-Toussaint, Diana S., 315, 316
Griskevicius, Vladas, 56
Grobman, K. H., 192t
Groenou, Marjolein Broese van, 738
Grogan, Alice, 260
Grogan-Kaylor, Andrew, 300
Gronseth, Gary S., 772, 773
Groothues, Christine, 196
Gropper, Sareen S., 497, 671
Gross, Alden L., 132
Gross, James J., 654
Gross, Nicole, 716
Grossmann, Tobias, 130, 319
Grote, Nancy K., B-5
Grubeck-Loebenstein, Beatrix, 493
Gruber, Reut, 280
Gruenewald, Tara L., 617
Gruhn, Daniel, 520
Grunau, Ruth E., 139
Grundy, Emily, 652
Grünke, Matthias, 325
Grusec, Joan E., 301
Gryczynski, Jan, 512
Guarente, Leonard, 692
Guarnaccia, Michael M., 583
Guerra, Nancy G., 386, 387, 388, 443
Guerri, Consuelo, 481
Guerry, John, 402
Guilherme, M. Campos, 591
Guimond, Amy B., 467
Guler, Nermin, 317, 764
Gummerum, Michaela, 391
Güngör, Derya, 636
Gunnar, Megan R., 186, 195, 196, 199, 207, 224, 402
Gunnell, David, 144
Guo, H. Y., 102
Guo, Shuai-jun, 421
Guralnik, Jack M., 679
Gurbernskaya, Zoya, 639
Gurunath, S., 582
Gurung, Regan A. R., 617
Gurven, Michael, 635
Gurwitz, Jerry H., 110
Gustafson, Jessica W., 222
Guthrie, Donald, 196
Guthrie, Ivanna K., 328, 529
Guyer, Amanda E., 186
Guzzo, Karen Benjamin, 648
Gwenith, G., 710
Gwyther, Lisa P., 730, 732

Haan, Mary N., 685
Haan, Michelle de, 167, 226
Haas, Steven A., 735
Haase, Claudia M., 5, 586
Haastert, Ingrid C. van, 114
Hackman, Daniel A., 351

Greifeneder, Rainer, 556
Haden, Catherine A., 54
Hadley, Evan, 689, 694
Hafemeister, Thomas L., 753
Hagedoorn, Mariët, 749
Hagestad, Gunhild O., 648, 744, 745, 756
Hahn, Chun-Shin, 346
Hahn, Erin R., 257
Haier, Richard J., 604
Hajjar, Emily R., 717
Hake, Ann M., 710
Halaschek-Wiener, Julius, 689
Halberda, Justin, 344
Hale, Fred, 694
Hale, Sandra, 703
Haley, William E., 752
Halgunseth, Linda C., 289
Hall, Anthony, 311
Hall, Jessica A., 552, 692
Hall, John Stuart, 619
Hall, Kathleen S., 710, 711
Hall, Lynn K., 375
Hall, Marg, 388
Hall, Sarah E., 277
Hallstein, D. Lynn O'Brien, 582
Halperin, Daniel, 501
Halpern, Diane F., 604, 609
Halpern, Neil A., 777
Halpern-Felsher, Bonnie L., 406, 409
Halpern-Meekin, Sarah, 557, 562
Hamadeh, Mazen J., 410
Hamby, Sherry, 375, 383, 387
Hamerton, John L., 85
Hamill, Paul J., 621
Hamilton, Alice, 230
Hamilton, Alison B., 640
Hamilton, Brady E., 582
Hamilton, J. Paul, 17
Hamilton, Rashea, 472
Hamm, Jill V., 467
Hammer, Carol Scheffner, 268
Hammerness, Paul G., 327
Hammond, Christopher J., 82
Hammond, S Katharine, 318
Hampel, Harald, 710, 715
Hamplova, Dana, 561
Hampton, Anne, 135
Hamstra, Julia, 330
Han, Euna, 315
Han, Shihui, 185
Han, Wen-Jui, 613
Hanakawa, Takashi, 260
Hanania, Rima, 223
Handelman, D. J., 586
Handsaker, Robert E., 80
Handy, April M., 691
Hane, Amie Ashley, 187, 188
Hänel, Martha, 748, 749
Haneuse, Sebastien, 591
Hanish, Laura D., 76, 284, 293, 431
Hank, Karsten, 734, 738, 739
Hankinson, Arlene L., 497
Hanko, Karlene, 556
Hanks, Andrew S., 316
Hanlon, Joseph T., 717
Hannah, Sean T., 530
Hannan, Claire, 145
Hannan, Peter J., 413, 499
Hannon, Erie E., 171

Hanoch, Yaniv, 89
Hansell, Narelle K., 82
Hansen, Åse M., 110
Hansen, David J., 226
Hanson, Karla L., 315
Hanson, Mark A., 315
Hanushek, Eric A., 356, 444
Hara, Kumiko, 17
Hardan, Antonio Y., 220
Hardaway, Cecily R., 301
Harden, K. Paige, 410, 439
Harder, Robert J., 347
Hare, Brian, 173, 219
Hare, Kelly M., 71
Haren, Neeltje E. M. van, 683
Hargreaves, Andy, 449
Harjes, Carlos E., 83
Harkness, Sara, 278, 301
Harlow, Ilana, 780
Harms, Ute, 348
Harper, Peter S., 86
Harper, Scott, 289
Harreveld, Frenk van, 593
Harrington, Richard, 327
Harris, Anthony, 585
Harris, Bernard, 406
Harris, Donna, 402
Harris, Judith Rich, 373
Harris, M. A., 469
Harris, Stephanie Ross, 352, 445, 446
Harris, Tamara B., 703, 704
Harris W. A., 404
Harrison, Denise, 139
Harrison, Glyn, 144
Harrison, Kristen, 315, 316
Hart, Betty, 351
Hart, Carole L., 511
Hart, Chantelle N., 316
Hart, Craig H., 549
Harter, Susan, 203, 369, 730
Hartmann, Donald P., 160
Hartmann, E. Eugenie, 138
Hasegawa, Toshikazu, 329
Haskard-Zolnierek, Kelly B., 422, 593
Haskell, William L., 672
Hassan, Mohamed A. M., 583
Hassard, Juliet, 658
Hassett, Janice M., 284
Hastings, Paul D., 289, 295, 402
Haukkala, Ari, 645
Hausdorff, Jeffrey M., 701
Hauser, Russ, 111
Hawker, Lizzy, 576
Hawkins, J., 404
Hawkins, Melissa, 99
Hawthorne, Joanna, 116
Hawthorne, Victor M., 511
Hawwa, Ahmed F., 317
Hayashi, Makoto, 578
Hayashida, Motoi, 82
Hayde, Brian, 552
Hayden, Brian, 582, 762
Hayes, Megan J., 650
Hayes, Rachel A., 170
Hayflick, Leonard, 691
Hayiou-Thomas, Marianna F., 259
Hayne, Harlene, 165, 166, 167
Hayslip, Bert, 379, 732
Hayward, Chris, 409

Hayward, Diane W., 331
Hazlett, Heather Cody, 132
He, Chunyan, 584
He, Yunfeng, 385
Head, Kevin, 604
Headley, Eric, 699
Heaney, Liam, 317
Heaton, Tim B., 375
Hebblethwaite, Shannon, 747
Hebebrand, J., 48
Heckhausen, Jutta, 5, 466, 586
Hedberg, Eric Christopher, 353
Hedman, Anna M., 683
Heerdink, Rob, 325
Heeringa, Steven G., 710
Heflick, Nathan A., 781
Hegyi, Thomas, 150
Hehman, Jessica A., 668
Heide, Agnes van der, 774
Heiman, Julia R., 676
Heise, Susan, 649
Heistad, David, 375
Helm, L., 717
Helmick, Charles G., 687
Helms, Heather M., 744
Helsens, Kenny, 69
Hemphill, Sheryl A., 411
Henders, Anjali, 481
Henderson, Heather A., 187, 188
Hendrichsen, Charlotte N., 80
Hendricks, Jon, 739
Hendricks, Shirley, 564
Hendrie, Hugh C., 710
Hendry, Leo B., 519
Henretta, John C., 652, 746
Henry, David B., 472
Henry, Julie D., 705, 707
Henry, William Earl, 736
Herbers, Janette E., 375
Herbert, Richard L., 691
Herd, Pamela, 736
Herek, Gregory M., 644
Herlofson, Katharina, 648, 745, 756
Herman, James P., 403
Herman, Khalisa N., 284
Herman, Ruth, 672
Hernandez, Lloreda, Maria Victoria, 173, 219
Hernández, Maria C. Valdés, 702
Hernandez, Theresa, 111
Hernan-Giddens, Marica E., 402
Herrera, Angelica P., 670, 717
Herring, Ann, 501
Herrmann, Esther, 173, 219
Herschensohn, Julia Rogers, 257
Herschkowitz, Norbert, 277, 318
Herskovits, Adrianna Z., 692
Hertenstein, Matthew J., 183
Hertzog, Christopher, 520, 604, 607
Herzog, Patricia, 536, 752
Heslin, Kevin C., 640
Hess, Thomas, 669
Hess, Thomas M., 620
Hetherington, E. Mavis, 382
Heuer, Chelsea A., 589
Hewer, Alexandra, 293
Heyes, Stephanie Burnett, 403
Hicken, Margaret, 617
Hickey, Martha, 584

Hicks, Joshua A., 732, 733
Hicks, Pamela J., 690
Hiebert, James, 357
Higgins, E. Tory, 636
Higgins, Matt, 508
Highhouse, Scott, 612
Higuchi, Susumu, 82
Hilden, Katherine, 347
Hill, Alison P., 294
Hill, Lynn, 264
Hill, Nancy E., 387, 446
Hill, Sarah E., 553
Hillevi, Ari, 645
Hills, Nancy, 591
Hilton, Sterling C., 99
Himmelstein, Mary, 89
Himsel, Amy, 208
Hindin, Michelle J., 580
Hindman, Annemarie H., 262
Hindy, with Kloep 2011, 567
Hines, Melissa, 290
Hinshaw, Stephen P., 326, 327
Hinson, Joey, 669
Hippel, William von, 705
Hipwell, Alison E., 421
Hirakawa, Makiko, 172
Hiroko, Iida, 311
Hirsch, Idit, 136
Hirsch-Pasek, Kathy, 174, 175, 176, 282
Hirsh, Jacob B., 637
Hiscock, Harriet, 135
Hislop-Esterhuyzen, N., 108
Ho, Andrew D., 539
Ho, Emily S., 141
Hoare, Carol Hren, 632
Hobara, Teruyuki, 17
Hochman, Oshrat, 738
Hodes, Richard, 689, 694
Hodgdon, Hilary B., 186
Hodges, Elizabeth, 669
Hodosy, Július, 96
Hoeve, Machteld, 198
Hof, Paulion van, 165
Hofbauer, Lorenz C., 687
Hofer, Claire, 290, 296, 462
Hofer, Scott M., 705, 736
Hoff, Erika, 261, 351
Hoffenaar, Peter, 267
Hoffman, Denis R., 146
Hoffman, Jill M., 150
Hoffman, Robert R., 625
Hoffmann, Heath C., 782
Hoffnung, 626
Hogan, Michael J., 702
Hogarth, Robin M., 555
Hoge, Charles W., 430
Hoglund, Wendy L. G., 388
Holden, Constance, 73, 301
Holden, George W., 301, 302
Hole, David J., 511
Holland, Cynthia R., 617
Holland, James D., 436
Holland, John, 547, 548
Hollatz, Amanda L., 295
Hollich, George J., 175
Holliday, Jo, 467
Hollist, Cody S., 642, 643
Holloszy, John O., 692

Holmboe, K., 188
Holsinger, Eva, 196
Holsti, Liisa, 139
Holt, Lynn, 82
Holt, Melissa, 375, 383, 387
Holt, Raymond, 682
Holton, Janice L., 714
Holtzman, Jennifer, 217
Hong, Jun Sung, 251, 387
Hong, Sok Chul, 406
Hood, K. K., 469
Hook, Jennifer L., 293, 658
Hooley, Jill M., 504
Hootman, Jennifer M., 687
Hopkins, Gary, 479
Hopkins, J. Roy, 47
Hoppitt, William J. E., 201
Horn, John, 608–610
Horn, Susan D., 754
Hornstra, Gerard, 168
Hornung, Richard W., 217
Horowitz, Alice M., 218
Horowitz, Ralph I., 80
Horwood, L. John, 563
Houck, Patricia R., 327
Houdmont, Jonathan, 658
Hougaard, Karin S., 110
House, James S., 736
House, Katherine, 326
Houston, Eric, 523
Houston, Whitney, 765
Houts, Renate M., 401, 402, 406, 409
Houwen, Karolijne van der, 779
How, Ti Hwei, 135
Howard, Andrea L., 505
Howard, Jeffrey A., 518
Howard, Kimberly S., 613
Howell, Diane M., 51
Howes, Carollee, 263, 738
Howes, Jessie, 754
Howlett, Neil, 170
Hrabosky, Joshua I., 414
Hrapczynski, Katie M., 649
Hrdy, Sarah Blaffer, 59, 193, 204
Hsia, Yingfen, 325
Hsu, Hui-Chin, 327
Hsu, Ming, 195, 654
Hu, Frank B., 690
Hu, Kyung-Seok, 72
Hu, Siyuan, 321
Huang, Cecilia, 326
Huang, Changquan, 713, 716
Huang, Chiungjung, 383, 473
Huang, Hung-Hsuan, 187
Huangfu, Danwei, 73
Huber, Gregory A., 634
Huberty, Thomas J., 18
Hublin, Jean-Jacques, 205
Hudak, Sandra, 754
Hudson, Quanah J., 78
Hudson, Thomas J., 317
Huebbe, Patricia, 689
Huff, Scott C., 642, 687
Hugdahl, Kenneth, 221
Hughes, Diane L., 467
Hughes, et al 2013, 704, 706
Hughes, Julie Milligan, 433

Hughes, Kimberly A., 690
Hughes, Michael, 576
Hughes, Sonya M., 406
Huh, Susanna Y., 102, 146
Huijbregts, Sanne K., 267
Huisman, Jaap, 584
Huizink, Anja C., 481
Hull, Kathleen E., 553, 559
Hulshoff Pol, Hilleke E., 683
Hume, Clare, 44
Hummer, Justin F., 513
Hummert, Mary Lee, 669
Hung, Li-Yu, 325
Hunt, Earl, 604, 607, 610, 613
Hunt, Steven C., 591
Hunter, Misty, 106
Hunter, Myra Sally, 584
Huntsinger, Carol S., 233
Hurt, Lee, 110
Hurtado, Sylvia, 533, 538
Hurwitz, Jon, 16
Husain, Nusrat, 18
Huskamp, Haiden A., 769
Hussar, William, 262, 449
Hussein, Amjad, 682
Hussey, Jon M., 238
Hussey, Michael, 402
Hussong, Andrea, 481, 483
Huston, Aletha C., 367, 368, 370
Hutchings, Judy, 326
Hutchinson, Esther A., 114
Huurre, Taina, 645
Huver, Rose M. E., 288
Huyck, Margaret Hellie, 655
Huynh, Jimmy L., 81
Huynh, Virginia W., 369
Hwanf, Hyi Sung, 527, 580
Hyde, Janet Shibley, 187, 223, 461
Hymel, Shelley, 442

Iacoboni, Marco, 418
Iacono, William G., 469, 648
Iacovidou, Nicoletta, 98, 103
Iannotti, Ronald J., 414
Idler, Ellen, 763
Iglesias, Aquiles, 350
Ihlea, Andreas, 707
IJzendoorn, Marinus H. van, 133,
    195, 389, 409, 424
Ikeda, Martin J., 331
Imai, Mutsumi, 172
Inan, Hatice Zeynep, 265
Inbar, Yoel, 556
Inder, Terrie E., 114
Infante, M. Alejandra, 108
Inhelder, Bärbel, 245, 431, 432, 433
Iñiguez, Carmen, 111
Insel, Beverly J., 475
Insel, Thomas R., 17
Insitute of Medicine, 316
Insurance Institute, 623
International Mathematics Report,
    356
Inzlicht, Michael, 524
Ip, Edward H., 300
Irwin, Scott, 132
Islam, Nadia, 174, 291
Ispa, Jean M., 289
Issa, Jean-Pierre, 714

Itakura, Shoji, 256
Ivey, Susan, 72
Iyengar, Satish, B-5
Iyengar, Sheena S., 555
Izard, Carroll E., 181, 182, 183
Izumi, Shin-Ichi, 722

Jaakkola, Jouni J. K., 110
Jaarsveld, Cornelia H. M. van, 749
Jaceldo-Siegl, K., 717
Jack, Clifford R. Jr., 710, 711
Jackson, James S., 637, 735
Jackson, Judy, 18
Jackson, Michael, 765, 782
Jackson, Richard J. J., 313, 679
Jackson, Shelly L., 753
Jackson, Todd, 414
Jacob, Brian A., 358
Jacob, Jenet I., 207
Jacobs, David R. Jr., 500
Jacobsohn, Gwen Costa, 315, 316
Jacquet, Wolfgang, 191
Jaeggi, Susanne M., 701
Jaffe, Arthur C., 128
Jaffe, Eric, 84
Jaffee, Sara R., 371
Jager, Justin, 369
Jäger, Theodor, 704
Jagger, Carol, 711, 714, 754
Jambon, Marc, 392
James, Bobbie, 754
James, Jacquelyn Boone, 738
James, Jenée, 408
Jamieson, Tyler, 379, 649, 650
Jang, Sujin, 538
Jang, Yoonsun, 72
Jankowski, Jeffery J., 167
Janosz, Michel, 452
Jansen, Ruth Kanfer, 655
Jantke, Andreas, 585
Jarrett, Marian H., 614, 647
Jasny, Barbara R., 229
Jaspers, Eva, 774
Jastrzembski, Tiffany S., 624
Jay, Debra, 718
Jefferson, Joseph, 742
Jelalian, Elissa, 316
Jenkins, Frank, 352, 356
Jensen, et al 2013, 567, 640
Jensen, Henning, 201
Jensen, Michael D., 586
Jensen, Peter S., 327
Jenson, Jeffrey M., 570
Jernigan, Terry, 132, 133
Jessop, Donna C., 765
Ji, Cheng Ye, 315
Jia, et al 2014, 711
Jia, Gisela, 268
Jimenez, Natasha B., 295
Jobling, Mark A., 72
Joe, Sean, 742
Joestl, Sarah S., 17
Johansen-Berg, Heidi, 626
John, Deborah Roedder, 369
Johnell, Kristina, 695
Johnson, Catherine, 329
Johnson, Chris A., 679
Johnson, Elizabeth, 172
Johnson, Frank, 449

Johnson, Jacqueline S., 170
Johnson, Katherine M., 584
Johnson, Kelly, 51
Johnson, Kimberly S., 771
Johnson, Mark H., 134, 183, 185,
    188, 257, 319
Johnson, Mark S., 240
Johnson, Matthew D., 643
Johnson, Michael P., 564
Johnson, Monica Kirkpatrick, 16,
    446, 547, 640
Johnson, Scott P., 141
Johnson, Susan C., 97, 129, 132,
    134, 172, 185, 203, 222, 230
Johnson, Susan L., 218
Johnson, Teresa S., 203
Johnson, Wendy, 604, 607
Johnson-Sirleaf, Ellen, 584
Johnston, Lloyd D., 479, 480, 481,
    483, 510, 511, 522, 549
Jokela, Markus, 634, 635
Jonas, Eva, 765
Jones, Andrea M., 241
Jones, Daniel, 555
Jones, Karen, 326
Jones, Lesley, 86
Jones, Lisa M., 424, 443
Jones, Mary Cover, 410
Jones, Michael E., 584
Jones, Nathan R., 480
Jones, Rebecca M., 418
Jones, Russell T., 619, 620
Jong, Jyh-Tsorng, 187
Jongbloed, Ben W. A., 533
Jonge, Guustaaf Adolf de, 136, 150
Jonge, Huub de, 781
Jongsma, Henk W., 168
Jonkmann, Kathrin, 549
Jonson-Reid, Melissa, 237
Jonsson, Maria, 103
Jopp, Daniela, 695
Jordan, Alexander H., 731
Jordan, Amy B., 483
Jordan, John R., 779
Jorgensen, Marit E., 591
Jørgensen, Niels, 583
Jose, Anita, 557
Jose, Paul E., 233
Joseph, Judith, B-5
Jovanovic, Vuk, 583
Juan, Shan, 102
Juang, Linda P., 462
Juarez, Lindsay, 524
Judd, Fiona K., 584
Jun Sung, 387
Juneau, Martin, 687
Jung, Kwanghee, 268
Jung, Rex E., 322
Jungert, Tomas, 388
Just, David R., 316
Juster, Robert-Paul, 616
Justice, Laura M., 249
Juujärvi, Soile, 530
Juvonen, Jaana, 388, 447
Jyrkkä, Johanna, 717

K. C., Samir, 143
Kachel, A. Friederike, 205
Kaciroti, Niko, 406

Kadiyali, Vrinda, 765
Kadosh, Kathrin Cohen, 319
Kaeberlein, Matt, 689
Kagan, Jerome, 189, 277, 318
Kagitcibasi, Çigdem, 375, 553
Kahana, Boaz, 739
Kahana, Eva, 739
Kahlenberg, Sonya M., 552
Kahn, Joan R., 739
Kahn, René S., 683
Kahn, Vali, 189
Kahneman, Daniel, 434, 435, 511,
    519, 655, 705
Kaiser, Jocelyn, 88
Kalambouka, Afroditi, 331
Kalaria, Raj N., 711
Kalil, Ariel, 382
Kaljonen, Anne, 388
Kalkwarf, Heidi J., 217
Kallan, Michael J., 438
Kaller, Christoph P., 704
Kalliala, Marjatta, 283, 285, 286
Kallio, Eeva, 518, 520
Kalmijn, Matthijs, 558, 645
Kamp, John van der, 165
Kandianis, Catherine Bermudez, 83
Kandler, Christian, 636
Kane, Michael J., 222
Kanfer, Ruth, 655
Kanfi, Yariv, 692
Kang, Jennifer Yusun, 261
Kanner, Andres M., 17
Kanner, Leo, 329
Kantor, Rebecca, 265
Kao, Karen, 296
Kao, Tsair, 187
Kaplan, Hillard, 635
Kaplan, Ian, 331
Kaplan, Rachel, 301
Kapornai, Krisztina, 17
Kaprio, Jaakko, 481, 657
Karama, et al, 322
Karlsson, Håkan, 144
Karlsson, Linnea, 481
Karmiloff-Smith, Annette, 349, 621
Kärnä, Antti, 388
Karney, Benjamin R., 553
Karoly, Lynn A., 263, 738
Karr, Catherine J., 229, 553, 559,
    561
Kärtner, Joscha, 201, 202
Kasl-Godley, Julia E., 779
Kasper, Judith D., 750
Kastberg, David, 352, 356
Kastenbaum, Robert J., 384, 765,
    767, 768
Kaszniak, Alfred W., 711, 714
Kato, Kenji, 634
Katon, Wayne J., B-5
Katz, Kathy S., 614, 647
Katzmarzyk, Peter T., 497
Kauffman, Kenneth K., 764, 779
Kaufman, David R., 625
Kaufman, Gayle, 659
Kaufman, James C., 612
Kaufman, Nathaniel D., 764
Kavanaugh, Robert D., 284, 286
Kawachi, Ichiro, 780
Kawamura, Sayaka, 749

Kaye, Walter H., 414
Kealey, Melissa, 672
Keane, Susan P., 289, 296
Keating, Daniel P., 438
Keenan, Kate, 421
Keene, Danya, 617
Keesler, Venessa, 658
Keil, Frank C., 163, 167
Keiley, Margaret K., 497, 671
Keith, Verna M., 576
Keizer, Renske, 645
Kellehear, Allan, 772
Keller, Heidi, 198, 201, 202, 276
Keller, Monika, 391
Keller, Peggy S., 436
Kelley, Jonathan, 351
Kellman, Philip J., 138
Kelly, Chris, 767
Kelly, Daniel, 15
Kelly, Dennis R., 634
Kelly, John R., 736
Kelly, Megan Clark, 55
Kelly, Michael, 772
Kelvin, David J., 685
Kemp, Candace L., 748
Kempe, C. Henry, 236
Kempe, Ruth S., 236
Kemperman, Gerd, 700
Kemple, James J., 451
Kempner, Joanna, 31
Kena, Grace, 449
Kendall, Pamela, 48
Kendjelic, Edward M., 622
Kendler, Howard H., 529
Kendler, Kenneth S., 17
Kendrick, Douglas T., 56
Kennedy, Kristen M., 701
Kennedy, Leanne, 638
Kennedy, Quinn, 524, 625
Kennell, John H., 104, 120
Kennison, Shelia M., 765
Keogh, Deborah A., 463, 464
Kéri, Szabolcs, 21
Kerr, Jacqueline, 592
Kerr, Margaret, 464
Keshavan, Matcheri S., 220
Keshtgar, Mohammed R. S., 619
Kesselring, Thomas, 246
Kessler, David, 769
Kessler, Ronald C., 503, 505, 619, 620
Kettinger, Laurie, 110
Kettl, Paul, 776
Keysers, Christian, 162
Khachaturian, Zaven S., 715
Khandwala, Mohammad, 23, 76
Khanna, Sunil K., 72
Khosla, Sundeep, 687
Khoury, Philip R., 217
Khrapko, Konstantin, 690
Kiang, Lisa, 369
Kiddoo, Darcie, 51
Kiecolt, K. Jill, 576
Kieltyka, Agnieszka, 145
Kiely, Michele, 614, 647
Kiernan, Stephen P., 770
Kilgannan, Stuart, 638
Kilic, Gurkan, 317, 764
Killen, Melanie, 55, 389, 391

Killgore, William D. S., 430
Killick, Stephen R., 583
Kim, Anthony Y., 268
Kim, Dohoon, 714
Kim, Dong-Sik, 414
Kim, Esther, 640
Kim, Geunyoung, 164, 182
Kim, Hee-Jin, 72
Kim, Heejung S., 276, 278
Kim, Hvoun K., 643
Kim, Hyun Sik, 645
Kim, Hyun-Sun, 414
Kim, Joon Sik, 182, 186
Kim, Juhee, 315, 316
Kim, Pilyoung, 226
Kim, Su Yeong, 567
Kim, Sunghun, 38
Kimber, Melissa, 415
Kimmel, Michael S., 554
Kim-Prieto, Chu, 527, 636
Kim-Spoon, Jungmeen, 459, 470
Kimura, Jiroemon, 692
Kinchen S., 404
Kind, Peter, 130
King, Bruce M., 58
King, Denae W., 670, 717
King, Laura A., 732, 733
King, Martin Luther, Jr., 531
King, Pamela Ebstyne, 459
Kingsmore, Stephen F., 86
Kinney, Hannah C., 150
Kinnunen, Marja-Liisa, 657
Kirby, Douglas, 472
Kirchner, H. Lester, 196
Kirk, Elizabeth, 170
Kirke, Peadar N., 108
Kiryanov, Nikolay, 588
Kis, B., 48
Kishi, Rieko, 104
Kit, Brian K., 315, 589
Kita, Sotaro, 172
Kitzmann, Katherine M., 140, 150
Kiuru, Noona, 446, 469
Kiviruusu, Olli, 481, 645
Kivnick, Helen Q., 719
Kizy, Thomas, 420
Klacyniski, Paul, 436, 436–437
Klahr, Ashlea M., 648
Klahr, David, 347
Klasky, Arthur L., 588
Klassen, Terry P., 51
Klaus, Susan F., 120, 658
Klein, Daniel N., 373
Klein, Hilary, 119
Klein, Joseph, 222
Klein, Laura Cousino, 617
Klein, Stanley, 730, 731
Klein, Zoe A., 403
Kleinman, Dushanka V., 218
Kleis, Astrid, 201, 202
Kliegel, Matthias, 704
Kliegela, Matthias, 707
Klima, Carrie, 104
Klimes-Dougan, Bonnie, 186
Klimstra, Theo A., 549
Kloep, Marion, 519, 567
Klopfenstein, Kristin, 108, 449
Klöppel, Stefan, 221
Kluck, Benjamin, 765, 766

Klump, Kelly L., 414
Knapp, Robin J., 222
Knappe, Susanne, 183
Knesebeck, Olaf von dem, 18
Knieps, Linda J., 164, 182
Knight, Kendra, 554
Knijff, Peter de, 72
Knijn, Trudie, 639, 746
Knopf, Monika, 160
Kolling, Thorsten, 160
Knopik, Valerie S., 69, 77, 86, 87
Knopman, David S., 711
Knowles, Laura R., 732
Kobayashi, Ayumi, 17
Koch, Holger Martin, 27
Kochanek, Kenneth D., 150
Kochanska, Grazyna, 198, 295
Koehoorn, Mieke, 229, 553, 559, 561
Koenen, Karestan C., 474
Koenig, Michael A., 563
Koerner, Ascan, 462
Koestner, Richard, 278
Kogan, Michael D., 330
Kohl, Harold W., III, 311
Kohl, Patricia L., 237
Kohlberg, Lawrence, 293, 389, 390–391, 395, 530, 531
Kohyama, Jun, 136
Kolb, Bryan, 220, 224
Kolinsky, Régine, 170
Kolk, Henk van deer, 659
Kollar, Anita, 689
Kolling, Thorsten, 160
Kolotkin, Ronette L., 591
Koltbo-Rivera, 2006, 769
Kolunki, Barbara, 174
Komati, Meghana, 141, 165
Komp, Kathrin, 738
Kompier, Michiel A. J., 658
Kong, Ailing, 358
Konner, Melvin, 58, 59, 132, 137, 142, 182, 185, 204, 295, 309
Koo, Anita, 288
Kooij, Dorien T. A. M., 655
Koopman, Corine, 114
Koot, Hans, 473
Kopp, Claire B., 184
Korbel, Jan O., 80
Korbmacher, Julie M., 738
Korhonen, Tellervo, 481
Korszun, Ania, 403
Korte, J., 722
Kost, K. 422
Koster, Ernst, H. W., 765
Kotch, Jonathan B., 238
Koulder, Sid, 163
Kovas, Yulia, 259
Kozhimannil, Katy Backes, 102
Kozo, Justine, 592
Kraemer, Helena C., 197
Kraemern, M., 48
Krahn, Harvey J., 505, 549
Kramer, Arthur F., 719
Krampe, Ralf, 625, 702
Kranenburg, Janneau van, 578
Krauss, Stephen, 523
Kreager, Derek, 642
Krebs, John R., 138
Krebs, Nancy F., 218

Kremen, William S., 607
Krendle, Anne, 370
Kreppner, Jana, 196
Kress, John P., 54
Kretch, Kari S., 138
Krieg, Alexander, 506
Krieg, Dana Balsink, 233
Krieger, Nancy, 187, 189, 216, 576
Kristensson, Krister, 144
Kroger, Jane, 458, 730
Krueger, Frank, 519
Krueger, Patrick M., 735
Kruglanski, Arie W., 636
Kruiper, Oom Kawid, 784
Ku, Yan-Chiou, 676
Kübler-Ross, Elisabeth, 769, 782
Kuchibhatla, Maragatha, 771
Kuefner, Dana, 134
Kuehn, Bridget M., 85
Kuh, George D., 534
Kuhaneck, Heather Miller, 283
Kuhl, Patricia K., 176
Kuhlmann, Beatrice G., 704
Kuhlmann, Inga, 689
Kuhn, Deanna, 434, 436, 437, 438, 448
Kuhn, Emily S., 464
Kuhn, Louise, 146
Kumar, Santosh, 638
Kundu, Tapas K., 77
Kunwar, Pratap S., 220
Kuo, Hsu-Ko, 701
Kuo, Wu-Hsien, 676
Kuperberg, Arielle, 642, 659
Kupfer, David J., 197
Kuppens, Sofie, 300
Kurdek, Lawrence A., 563
Kurinczuk, Jennifer J., 106
Kurup, Anand Sivasankara, 587, 588
Kuryluk, Amanda D., 505
Kutob, Randa M., 473
Kwok, Sylvia Y. C. Lai, 463
Kwon, Hower, 330

Laan, Peter H. van der, 198
LaBar, Kevin S., 224
Labouvie-Vief, Gisela, 520, 521, 522, 530
LaBrie, Joseph W., 513
Lacasaña, Marina, 111
Lacefield, Katharine, B-5, 549
Lachman, Margie E., 609, 635, 670, 706
Lacourse, Eric, 410, 411
LaFontana, Kathryn M., 466
LaGrasse, Linda L., 195
Lahey, Benjamin B., 649
Lai, Chin-Jen, 676
Laible, Deborah, 298–299
Laird, Robert D., 464
Lakusta, Laura, 175
Laland, Kevin N., 201
Lalande, Kathleen M., 783
Lalonde, Francois, 223
Lamarche, Véronique, 385
Lamb, Michael E., 120, 197, 199, 226
Lamm, Bettina, 198, 201, 202
Lamoen, Ellemieke van, 673

LaMonte, Michael J., 591
Landa, Rebecca J., 132
Landy, Frank J., 655
Lane, David J., 430
Lane, Kathleen A., 710
Lane, Rachel F., 715
Lane, Scott D., 481
Lang, Frieder R., 637, 639
Lang, Mia E., 51
Lang, P. O., 584
Langa, Kenneth M., 710
Langberg, Joshua M., 326
Lange, Paul G. W., 655
Langer, Ellen J., 668, 669, 670
Langeslag, Sandra J. E., 553
Langhinrichsen-Rohling, Jennifer, 563
Langlands, Stephanie, 316
Långstrom, Niklas, 373
Lanners, Josée, 158, 168
Lansford, Jennifer E., 299, 300, 301
Lantos, John D., 774
Lappegård, Trude, 645
Lapsley, Daniel K., 295
Lara-Cinisomo, Sandraluz, 263, 265, 738
Laracy, Seth D., 328
Laraway, Kelly A., 217
Laris, B. A., 472
Larson, Nicole I., 413, 499
Larzelere, Robert E., 288, 300
LaScala, Elizabeth A., 654
Laska, Melissa Nelson, 499
Lattanzi-Licht, Marcia, 765, 781
Latvala, Antti, 481
Lau, Anna S., 301
Lau, Carissa, 113, 114
Laumann, Edward O., 502, 581
Laurent, Heidemarie K., 643
Laurenzano, Mary, 267
Laurillard, Diana, 328, 329
Laursen, Brett, 446, 462, 464, 469
Laursen, Thomas Munk, 87
Lauster, Nathanael T., 553
Lavelli, Manuela, 182, 189, 191
Lavenderd, Jason, 238
Laverty, Anthony A., 679
Law, David, 642, 643
Law, Lawla L. F., 708
Law, Michael R., 102
Lawford, Heather, 747
Layden, Tim, 312
Lazzeroni, Laura C., 524, 625
Le, Vi Donna, 113
Leach, Penelope, 205
Leadbeater, Bonnie J., 388
Leana, Carrie R., 654
Leaper, Campbell, 285, 291
Leather, Judith Walzer, 431
Leavitt, Judith Walzer, 119
Lebel, Catherine, 701
Leckman, James F., 218
Leclerc, Christina M., 620
Lee, Christine M., 512
Lee, Francis S., 431
Lee, Hee Seung, 347, 348
Lee, I-Min, 592
Lee, Jeanne, 236
Lee, Jihyun, 19
Lee, Joanne, 498

Lee, Joyce M., 406
Lee, Kang, 254, 255
Lee, Katherine J., 114
Lee, Lian-Yi, 187
Lee, RaeHyuck, 613
Lee, Sarah M., 311
Lee, Sei J., 739
Lee, Sing, 505
Lee, Soojeong, 312, 450
Lee, Star W., 701
Lee, Sun-A, 463, 476
Lee, Yoonjin, 692
Lee, Young J., 108
Leeb, Rebecca T., 375, 383, 387
Leenders, Marika, 578
Leeuwen, Flora E. van, 584
Leeuwen, Marieke van, 114
Lefkowitz, Eva S., 497, 746
Lehman, Regula, 635
Lehner, Ben, 77
Lehning, Amanda J., 740, 755
Lei, Joy L., 411
Lei, Man-Kit, 550
Leij, Andries van der, 623
Leis, Julia A., 522, 547, 550
Lejuez, C. W., 188
Lely, Heather van der, 113
Leman, Patrick J., 393–394
Lemanski, Nita, 352, 356
Lemelin, Jean-Pascal, 173
Lemieux, André, 519, 520, 525, 526
Lemish, Daphna, 174
Lemmon, Helen, 717
Lencar, Cornel, 229, 553, 559, 561
Lengua, Liliana J., 276
Lenhart, Amanda, 418, 440
Lenton, Alison, 552
Leon, David A., 588
Leonard, David, 672
Leonard, Henrietta L., 218
Leonard, Stacie, 76, 293, 431
Leperse, Romuald, 687
Lepper, Mark R., 278, 555
Lerner, Claire, 204
Lerner, Jacqueline V., 388
Lerner, Jennifer S., 654
Lerner, Richard M., 5, 388, 452, 466, 638
Lero Vie, Marino, 635
Lesch, Roger, 699
Leseman, Paul, 267
Leslie, Leigh A., 649
Leslie, Mitch, 517
Lester, Barry, 195
Lester, Leanne, 388
Leu, Janxin, 184
Leung, Angel Nga-Man, 463
Leve, Leslie D., 186
Leveille, Suzanne G., 701
Leventhal, Bennet L., 326
Leventhal, John M., 241
Leventhal, Tama, 341
Levine, Charles, 293
Levine, Peter, 326
Levin-Rector, Alison, 103, 114, 143
Levinson, Daniel, 633
Leviton, Alan, 230
Levy, Becca R., 668, 669, 670
Levy, Roy, 739

Lewallen, Lynne Porter, 113
Lewandowski, Gary, 551
Lewin, Kurt, 36
Lewin-Benham, 265
Lewin-Epstein, Noah, 738
Lewinsohn, Peter M., 191
Lewis, Brian P., 617
Lewis, Charlie, 223
Lewis, Charlotte W., 218
Lewis, Cora E., 497
Lewis, David M. G., 58, 60, 552
Lewis, Glyn, 144
Lewis, Kristen, 595, 598
Lewis, Lawrence B., 170
Lewis, Marc D., 276, 277, 279
Lewis, Michael, 181, 182, 184, 185, 186
Lewis, Myrna I., 721, 722
Lewkowicz, David J., 142
Ley, Heather van der, 138, 169
Li, Dan, 385
Li, Jin, 200
Li, Ming, 226
Li, Ping, 119, 176
Li, Rong, 326
Li, Runze, 277
Li, Tianyuan, 557
Li, Xiaobai, 321
Li, Yexin Jessica, 463
Li, Yibing, 452
Libertus, Klaus, 141
Libertus, Melissa E., 344
Libman, Kimberly, 735
Lichtenstein, Paul, 373, 383
Lichtenstein, Philip K., 326
Lichter, Daniel T., 642
Liedekerke, Claire de, 134
Liefbroer, Aart C., 557
Lier, Pol van, 473
Lietz, Cynthia A., 650
Liew, Jeffrey, 290
Liles, Sandy, 747
Lilienfeld, Scott O., 783
Lillard, Angeline S., 197, 256, 264
Lim, Chaeyoon, 742
Lim, M. K., 83
Lim, Veronica R., 562
Limber, Susan P., 387, 388
Lin, C., 404
Lin, Frank R., 703, 704
Lin, I-Fen, 643, 645
Lin, Jue, 691
Lin, Yen-Chin, 676
Lincoln, Karen D., 742
Lincove, Jane A., 341
Lind, Penelope A., 82
Lindau, Stacy Tessler, 581, 676
Lindberg, Sara M., 461
Linden, Dimitri van der, 658
Lindenberg, Siegwart, 387, 389, 410
Lindenberger, Ulman, 5, 523, 526, 683, 702
Lindgren, Cecilia M., 315
Ling, Yan, 443
Lingeman, Jesse M., 141, 165
Linsenmayer, Kristi A., 218
Lipinski, Ryan, 61
Lipnevich, Anastasiya, 608
Lippke, Sonia, 593

Lipton, Jennifer S., 163
Lipton, Rebecca B., 401
Lista, Simone, 715
Liszkowski, Ulf, 170
Little, Todd D., 388
Little, Wendy M., 640
Litwin, Howard, 747
Litwin, Sheldon E., 591
Liu, David, 255, 256
Liu, Huei-Mei, 176
Liu, Hui, 658
Liu, Jia, 321
Liu, Jing, 195
Liu, Kayuet, 106, 330
Liu, Li, 711
Liu-Snyder, Peishan, 689
Livas-Dlott, Alejandra, 289
Livingston, Edward H., 591
Livingston, Gill, 753
Lloyd-Fox, Sarah, 185
Lo, Po-Tsung, 187
Lobstein, Tim, 311
LoBue, Vanessa, 164, 291
Löchenhoff, Corinna E., 519, 723
Lock, Margaret, 5
Lockl, Kathrin, 344
Lodge, Amy C., 677–678
Loeber, Rolf, 280, 421, 478
Loft, Anne, 115
Logerquist, Sally, 330
Lois, Nancy, 640
Loken, Erik K., 17
Lombart, Kenneth G., 622
Long, J. Scott, 676
Long, Jeffrey D., 375
Longmore, Monica A., 471, 557, 562
Longo, Gregory S., 459, 470
Longo, Lawrence D., 103
Lonigan, Christopher J., 220, 258
Lönnroos, Eija, 717
Loon, Luc J. C. van, 578
Loots, Gerrit, 191
Lopes, Rita, 227, 282
Lopez, Alan D., 597
Lopez, Oscar, 751
Lopez Turley, Ruth N., 379
Lopez-Duran, Nestor, 298, 299
Lorber, Michael F., 186
Lord, Catherine, 329, 616
Lorenz, Fred O., 639
Losoya, Sandra, 462
Lotspeich, Linda J., 330
Lövdén, Martin, 714
Lovecky, Deirdre V., 296
Lovegreen, Loren D., 739
Lovell, Brian, 752
Lowe, Gordon D. O., 604
Lowe, Val J., 711
Lowell, Darcy I., 197
Lowenstein, Amy E., 270
Lowenstein, Ariela, 746
Lowry, R., 404
Lozano, Rafael, 597
Lubach, Gabriele R., 22
Lubinski, David, 530, 647
Lucangeli, Daniela, 328
Lucas, Alan, 146
Lucas, Cynthia P., 622
Lucas, Jacqueline W., 717

Lucas, Richard E., 635
Lucassen, Paul J., 403, 474
Lucas-Thompson, Rachel, 208
Luciana, Monica, 130
Lucidi, Richard S., 584
Lüdtke, Oliver, 549
Luengo-Prado, Maria Jose, 739
Lumeng, Julie C., 406
Luna, Beatriz, 416, 418
Lund, Terese, 312
Lundquist, Gunilla, 769
Lunetta, Kathryn L., 584
Lunkenheimer, Erika S., 298, 299
Luo, Zupei, 233
Luparia, Antonella, 158, 168
Lupien, Sonia J., 616
Lurie, Nicole, 737
Lustig, Cindy, 704, 719
Lustig, Robert H., 591
Luszczynska, Aleksandra, 593
Lutfey, Karen, 11
Luthar, Suniya S., 370, 383, 481
Lutz, Wolfgang, 143
Luxmoore, Nick, 765
Luyckx, Koen, 549
Lynch, Courtney D., 317
Lynch, Scott M., 734
Lynn,Richard, 321
Lynne, Sarah D., 410
Lynskey, Michael T., 481
Lyonette, Clare, 659
Lyons, Kelly E., 713
Lyons, Michael J., 607
Lyons-Ruth, Karlen, 194
Lysonski, Steven, 497

Ma, Debbie, B-5, 549
Ma, Lang, 388
Ma, Louyan, 713, 716
Ma, Mi-Chia, 676
Ma, Yue, 764
Maas, Han L. J. van der, 322
Maasmeier, Kathrin, 201, 202, 388
Maassen, Peter A. M., 533
MacDonald, Maurice, 621, 695
MacDougall, K., 583
Mace, Ruth, 207
Macgregor, Stuart, 82
Machery, Edouard, 15
Maciejewski, Matthew L., 414, 769
Mack, Simon, 226
Mackey, Sarah, 479
Mackinnon, Andrew J., 609
Maclennan, Karyn, 325
MacMillan, Harriet L., 241
MacPhee, David, 613
MacWhinney, Brian, 172
Madan, Alok, 752
Madden, Mary, 418, 440
Madden, Pamela A. F., 82, 481
Madden, Tessa, 501
Maddox, W. Todd, 723
Madison, James, 406
Madsen, Stephanie, 550
Maestre, Gladys E., 711
Maglione, Margaret, 217
Magnor, Cliff, 624
Magnusson, Katherine, 270, 382
Magrin, Maria, 504

Maguire, Eleanor A., 626
Mah, Timothy, 501
Mahajan, Reena, 424
Mahalic, Sharon F., 387
Mahmud, Waqar, 505
Mahoney, Christine B., 636
Mahoney, Diane, 752
Mai, Sato, 722
Maier, Andrea B., 685
Maignan, Alain, 641
Maignan, Nicole, 641
Majdandzic, Mirjana, 186
Majercsik, Eszter, 57
Majewska, Renata, 145
Mak, Ying Tat, 82
Makariev, Drika, 298–299
Makhoul, I. R., 121
Makimoto, Kiyoko, 82
Malchodi, Cathy A., 722
Malek, Meaghan, 223
Malin, Martin B., 353
Malina, Robert M., 406, 412
Malkinson, Ruth, 783
Malla, Ashok, 506
Mallard, Simonette, 591
Malloy, Michael H., 102
Maluccio, John A., 498
Mamikonian-Zarpas, Ani, 266, 267
Mancini, Anthony D., 744
Mandalakas, Anna, 196
Mandlawitz, Myrna, 358
Mandler, Jean M., 159, 163
Mangels, Jennifer A., 524
Mangino, Massimo, 584
Mangual Figueroa, Ariana, 289
Maniar, Rajesh, 442
Maniega, Susana Muñoz, 702
Maniscalco, Brian, 524
Manlove, Jennifer, 505
Mann, Jim, 591
Mann, Joshua R., 116
Mann, Traci, 594
Mannchen, Garrett, 518
Mannering, Anne M., 277
Mannes, Marc, 466
Manniën, Judith, 104
Manning, Eileen, 449
Manning, Wendy D., 471, 557, 562
Manson, JoAnn E., 584
Mantle, Mickey, 84
Manzi, Claudia, 566
Marazita, John M., 257
March, Dana, 17
March, John S., 218
Marchand, Alain, 659
Marcia, James E., 458, 485
Marcoulides, George A., 278
Marcovitch, Stuart, 222
Marcus, Gary F., 176
Marcus, Jake R., 103, 114, 143
Mareschal, Denis, 349
Margie, Nancy Geyelin, 389
Margolis, Rachel, 647
Margrett, Jennifer A., 695, 707
Marin, Maria-France, 616
Marion, Donna, 446, 469
Markey, Charlotte N., 410
Markman, Ellen M., 253, 257
Markman, Howard J., 562

Markovits, Henry, 552
Markowitsch, Hans J., 704
Marks, Amy Kerivan, 114, 658
Marlier, Luc, 138
Marottoli, Richard A., 679
Marrero, Matthew D., 464
Marschark, Marc, 13
Marshall, Eliot, 80
Marshall, Peter J., 196, 322
Marshall, Russell, 682
Marshall-Lucette, Sylvie, 119
Marsiske, Michael, 707
Marston, Doug, 331
Martens, Lennart, 69
Martin, Bruce, 508
Martin, Carol Lynn, 76, 284, 290, 291, 293, 294, 431
Martin, Jack
Martin, Joyce A., 582
Martin, Leslie R., 422, 593
Martin, Michael O., 356
Martin, Monica J., 383, 643
Martin, Nicholas G., 481
Martin, Peter, 695
Martinez, M. Loreto, 463
Martinez, Maria Luz, 240p
Martínez-Gonzalez, Andel Miguel, 592
Martinm, Mike, 635
Martino, Steven C., 471
Martinussen, Monica, 458
Martinussen, Torben, 639
Martin-Uzzi, Michele, 379
Martorell, Reynaldo, 498
Marttunen, Mauri, 481
Marvasti, Amir B., 16
Marx, J.; Pretorius, E., 108
Masche, J. Gowert, 462
Mascie-Taylor, C. G. Nicholas, 95t
Mascolo, Michael F., 200
Mash, Clay, 138, 160
Mashburn, Andrew J., 249
Mashek, Debra, 551
Mashour, George A., 701
Maslow, Abraham, 56–58, 64, 203, 632, 637, 661, 719, 769
Maslowsky, Julie, 438
Mason, Jennifer, 747
Mason, Michael J., 479, 480
Masoro, Edward J., 684, 691
Massenkoff, Maxim, 635
Masses, et al 2013, 414
Masten, Ann S., 370, 375, 383, 620
Masten, Carrie L., 186, 369, 418
Mata, Jutta, 391
Mateus-Pinheiro, A., 700
Mather, Mara, 732
Mathews, Iva Z., 446
Mathison, David J., 412
Matsui, Tomoko, 329
Matsumoto, David, 278, 527, 580
Matsushita, Sachio, 82
Matteson, David R., 458
Matteson, Lindsay, 552, 553
Matthews, Fiona E., 711, 714, 754
Matthews, Gregory, 198
Matthews, Michael D., 634
Mattison, Julie A., 691
Mattys, Sven L., 167, 387, 538

Maughan, Barbara, 17
Mavridis, Caroline Johnston, 278, 301
Maxfield, Molly, 765, 766
Maxon, Elizabeth, 462
Maxwell, Molly, 358, 765, 766
May, Alexis M., 415
May, Douglas R., 530
May, Vanessa, 747
Mayer, D. Luisa, 138
Mayes, Rick, 326
Mayeux, Lara, 386
Maynard, Amanda M., 430, 431
Maynard, L. Michele, 311
Mayr, Ulrich, 481, 483, 625
Mazuka, Reiko, 113, 138, 169
Mazurkiewicz, Magda, 593
Mazziotta, John C., 418
Mazzocco, Michéle M. M., 85
Mazzonna, Fabrizio, 739
McAdams, Dan P., 39, 549, 550, 632
McAuley, Edward, 672
McBain, Ryan, 371
McBride, Brent A., 315, 316
McBride, Duane, 479
McBride-Chang, Catherine, 463
McCabe, Janice, 16
McCall, Robert B., 196, 197
McCann, Judith J., 518, 753
McCarrey, Anna C., 705
McCarter, Roger J. M., 492
McCarthy, Mark I., 315
McCarthy-Keith, Desireé, 584
McCartney, Kathleen, 208
McCarty, Cheryl, 430
McClain, Lauren Rinelli, 647
McClaire, Vetisha L., 479
McClearn, Gerald, 14
McClelland, Megan M., 275
McClelland, Sara I., 422
McClure, Erin B., 186
McConatha, Jasmin Tamahseb, 694
McConkie-Rosell, Allyn, 89
McCormick, Cherly M., 446
McCowan, Lesley M. E., 106
McCoy, Meghan, 442
McCrae, Robert R., 636, 723
McCright, Aaron M., 25
McCulloch, David, 591
McCullough, Michael E., 459, 470
McCune, Susana Lauraine, 778
McDaniel, Mark A., 706
McDaniel, Michael A., 636
McDermott, Suzanne, 116
McDonald, Kristina L., 188, 276, 282, 385, 446
McDonald, Sarah D., 23
McDonough, Caitrin W., 690
McElnay, James C., 317
McEwen, Bruce S., 616
McFadden, Susan H., 722
McGeehan, Catherine M., 358
McGill, Brittany S., 739
McGillivray, Shannon, 705, 706
McGlade, Ciara, 710
McGrath, John J., 506
McGrath, Susan K., 104
McGue, Matthew, 469, 607, 639, 648
McIntosh, Jennifer, 132

McIntyre, Donald A., 79
McKechnie, Sharon, 738
McKee, Martin, 588
McKenna, James J., 136
McKinley, Jesse, 145
McKinney, Cliff, 293
McKinney, Karyn D., 16
McKown, Clark, 369
McLanahan, Sara, 381
McLaughlin, Katie A., 474
McLaughlin-Volpe, Tracy, 551
McLendon, Amber, 717
McLeod, Bryce D., 373
McLeod, Peter, 623, 624
McLoyd, Vonnie C., 301, 383
McMahon, Robert P., 402
McManus, I. Chris, 221
McManus, T., 404
McMorris, Barbara J., 411
McMullen, Mary B., 266
McMurray, Bob, 78
McNamee, Catherine, 645
McNeely-Johnson, Doris, 614, 647
McPartlin, Joseph M., 108
McPherson, Michael S., 538, 539
McQuaid, Elizabeth L., 318
McQuillan, Julia, 584
McShane, Kelly E., 289
Mead, Margaret, 584
Meadows, Sara, 340, 345
Meagher, David K., 779
Measham, Fiona, 511
Mechelen, Willem van, 311
Medoff-Cooper, Barbara, 103
Meece, Judith L., 446
Meeker, Mary Ann, 775
Meeus, Wim, 473
Meeus, Wim H. J., 458, 459, 549
Mehta, Clare M., 470
Mehta, Satish, 496
Meier, Ann, 553, 559
Meins, Elizabeth, 251
Meisami, Esmail, 681
Meisenberg, Gerhard, 605
Meiser, Bettina, 87
Meiser, Thorsten, 704
Meites, Elissa, 424
Melgar, Paul, 498
Melhuish, Edward C., 352
Mellor, M. Joanna, 753
Melnickas, Andrea J., 422, 423
Meltzoff, Andrew N., 174, 253
Melville, Jennifer L., B-5
Melzi, Gigliana, 250
Menard, William E., 624
Mendes de Leon, Carlos F., 753
Mendiola, Jaime, 583
Mendle, Jane, 410
Mennis, Jeremy, 479, 480
Menten, Björn, 69
Mento, Giovanni, 99
Menzer, Melissa, 188, 276, 282,
    385, 446
Mercy, James A., 375, 383, 387
Meredith, Marilu D., 312
Merikangas, et al, 326
Merikangas, Kathleen R., 479
Meririnne, Esa, 481
Merline, Alicia, 637

Merrill, Anne F., 562
Merriman, William E., 257
Merritt, Darcey H., 654
Merriwether, Ann, 471
Merrow, Martha, 404
Merz, Emily C., 196
Merz, Eva-Maria, 642
Merz, Jon F., 31
Merzenich, Hiltrud, 582
Mesch, Gustavo S., 468
Mesman, Jeanette A. J. M., 104
Mesqui, Batja, 636
Mesquita, Batja, 184
Messersmith, Emily E., 460
Messinger, Daniel M., 189
Mestdagh, Pieter, 69
Metcalfe, Janet, 346
Meyer, Jessica R., 477
Meyer, Madonna Harrington, 745
Meyers, David, 622–623
Meyers, Joel, 443
Meyers, Marcia, 658
Michael, Robert T., 502, 581
Michaud, Catherine, 597
Michaud, Pierre-André, 311
Michelangelo, 722
Michie, Susan, B-5
Michiels, Daisy, 300
Michl, Louisa C., 474
Micke, Cierra, 552, 553
Middeldorp, Christel M., 17
Midlarsky, Elizabeth, 739
Mieremet, Rene, 72
Mieth, Romaine Arlettaz, 597
Mikels, Joseph A., 732
Mikk, Jaan, 321
Miklowitz, David Jay, 325
Milardo, Robert M., 465
Milber, WIlliam P., 701
Miles, Lynden K., 164
Milgrom, Jeannette, 191
Milkie, Melissa A., 659
Milkman, Katherine L., 437
Miller, Alison, 262
Miller, Cindy F., 294
Miller, Destiny L., 714
Miller, Greg, 132, 322, 503, 716
Miller, Gregory E., 311, 599
Miller, J. Mitchell, 410
Miller, Joan G., 278, 290
Miller, Joseph M., 138
Miller, L. Scott, 350
Miller, L. Stephen, 149
Miller, Laura M., 746
Miller, Neil A., 86
Miller, Orlando J., 85
Miller, Patricia H., 38, 47, 63, 343,
    432
Miller, Richard B., 642, 643
Miller, Robin L., 326
Miller, Susan W., 718, 731
Miller, Tim, 735
Miller, Torri W., 326
Miller, William R., 512
Miller-Johnson, Shari, 269
Millership, Jeffrey S., 317
Millet, Christopher, 679
Mills, Britain, 431
Mills, Elizabeth, 442

Mills, James L., 108
Mills, Jon, 48
Mills, Ryan E., 80
Mills-Koonce, W. Roger, 182
Milunsky, Aubrey, 86
Minagawa-Kawal, Yasuyo, 138, 169
Mindell, Jodi A., 135, 136
Minogue, Kristen, 319
Minshew, Nancy J., 220
Mintz, Toben H., 257
Mireles, Laurie, 289
Miron-Shatz, Talya, 89, 361
Mishra, Ramesh C., 342
Misra, Dawn P., 113
Mitchell, Barbara A., 651
Mitchell, Kimberly J., 441, 443
Mitchell, Philip B., 87
Mitchell, Ross E., 681
Mittal, Vikas, 654
Mittelstaedt, Robin D., 508
Mittleman, Mary S., 752
Mitura, Klaudia, 293, 473, 474
Miu, Angela, 471
Miura, Yui, 329
Miyata, Susanne, 172
Mize, Krystal, 61
MMWR, A-8–A-9, A-18, A-19, 144,
    145, 230, 231, 412, 413, 414,
    415, 420, 421, 422, 441, 470,
    475, 479, 587, 687, 688
Moas, Olga Lydia, 187
Mock, Victoria, 563
Moen, Phyllis, 172, 659
Moffitt, Terrie E., 371, 374, 476,
    477, 634
Mofidi, Mahyar, 218
Mokler, David J., 150
Moldavsky, Maria, 326
Molina, Brooke S. G., 327
Molitir, Adriana, 195
Moller, Eline L., 186
Møller, Signe J., 291
Molloy, D. William, 710
Monahan, Kathryn C., 467, 471,
    477
Monastersky, Richard, 419
Moncloa, Fe, 472
Monesson, Alexandra, 134, 135
Monfared, Nasim, 689
Mongeau, Paul A., 554
Monin, Benoît, 731
Monitoring the Future, 481
Monje, Michelle, 701
Monk, Christopher S., 186, 438
Monks, Claire P., 388
Monks, Helen, 388
Monroe, Judy, 145
Monserud, Maria A., 747
Montanari, Laura, 114
Monteiro, Carlos A., 216
Montessori, Maria, 264
Montgomery, Bette, 430
Montgomery, Rhonda J. V., 651
Montie, Jeanne, 269
Moody, Raymond A., 767
Mooney, Margarita, 546
Moore, Caitlin S., 607
Moore, Elya, 481
Moore, Ginger A., 191

Moore, James, 221
Moore, Jon, 554
Moore, Karenza, 511
Moore, Keith L., 6
Moore, Kelly L., 754
Moore, Kristin A., 198
Moore, William E., 418
Moore, William M., A-10, A-11
Morale, Sarah E., 146
Moran, Lyndsey R., 220, 276
Moran, Seana, 322
Morasch, C., 162
Morcos, Roy N., 420
Morelli, Gilda A., 191
Moreno, Sylvain, 170
Morgan, Ali Zaremba, 497, 671
Morgan, Elizabeth M., 291
Morgan, Ian G., 83
Morgan, James L., 172
Morgan, Julia, 374
Morgan, Thomas J. H., 201
Morgan, Vera, 87
Morin, Rich, 738
Morning, Ann, 15
Morón, Cecilio, 413
Morones, Alyssa, 299
Morowatisharifabad, Mohammas Ali,
    563
Morris, Amanda Sheffield, 201, 276
Morris, Bradley J., 278
Morris, Curtis L., 446
Morris, Daniel H., 584
Morris, Pamela A., 7, 8
Morris, Tracy L., 241
Morris, Vivian Gunn, 446
Morris, Zoe, 702
Morrison, Frederick J., 275
Morrison, John A., 402
Morrison, Mike, 13
Morrison, Toni, 735p
Morrison, Val, 652
Morrissey, Taryn, 207
Morrow, Daniel G., 624
Mortelmans, Dimitri, 651
Mortensen, Erik Lykke, 18
Mortensen, Preben Bo, 87
Mortier, Freddy, 771
Mortimer, Jeylan T., 11
Moses, 531
Moses, Anna "Grandma," 721–722
Mosher, Catherine E., 765
Mosher, William D., 555, 556, 557
Moshman, David, 433, 523
Moss, Patricia, 405
Mostow, Allison, 181
Mother Teresa, 531
Mottron, Laurent, 329
Moulson, et al, 132
Mouras, Harold, 520
Mowery, Robyn L., 771
Moyer, Anne, 557
Mozart, 334
Mrozek-Budzyn, Dorota, 145
Mu, Yan, 344
Mueck, Alfred O., 585
Mueller, Christian E., 405
Muhammad, 531
Muhammad, Zayyad, 159
Mulder, Pamela J., 203

Mullen, Sean P., 672
Müller, Ulrich, 222, 246
Muller, Ziva, 747
Mulligan, A., 326
Mullis, Ina V. S., 356
Mulvaney, S. A., 469
Mumper, Elizabeth, 330
Munck, Hanne, 198
Munniksma, Anke, 387, 389
Muñoz, Carmen, 7, 256
Munro, Geoffrey, 61, 251
Munroe, Robert L., 368
Muraco, Anna, 640
Murakami, Fumio, 370
Muramatsu, Taro, 82
Murayama, Masanobu, 82
Muris, Peter, 553
Murphy, Bridget C., 328, 529
Murphy, et al 2012, 685
Murphy, Greer M. Jr., 524, 625
Murphy, John Michael, 530
Murphy, Michael, 745
Murphy, Sherry L., 150
Murphy, Terrence E., 670
Murray, Catherine, 702
Murray, Christopher J. L., 103, 114,
    143, 597
Murray, Conrad, 782
Murray, Jennifer E., 593
Murray, Robin M., 506
Murrell, Jill R., 710
Murry, James D., 562
Murry, Velma McBride, 465
Mursu, Jaakko, 717
Musick, Marc A., 302
Mustonen, Ulla, 645
Mutcher, Jan E., 379
Mutius, Erika von, 317
Mutti, Donald, 83
Mwlching, Jessica A., 464
Myatt, Julia P., 507
Mychailyszyn, Matthew P., 326
Myers, David G., 623, 682
Myers, Mary Anne, 326
Myers, Michael W., 469
Myers, Sonya S., 201, 276
Myerson, Joel, 703
Myint-U, Athi, 472
Mynatt, Blair Sumner, 771
Myrskylä, Mikko, 647

Nachtigall, Robert D., 72, 583
Naci, Huseyin, 233
Nadeau, Joseph H., 77
Nadrian, Haidar, 563
Nagata, Chisato, 578
Naghavi, Mohsen, 597
Nagumo, Miho, 172
Nahum, Liat, 692
Naiman, Shoshana, 692
Nair, K. Sreekumaran, 586
Nakamura, Kozue, 578
Nakhuda, Gary S., 583
Naninck, Eva F. G., 403, 474
Nansel, Tonja R., 414
Narayan, Chandan R., 169
Narayan, K. M. Venkat, 500
Narvaez, Darcia, 295, 530, 533
Nassar, Natasha, 106

Natarajan, Rama, 77
Nation, Maury, 464
National Association of
    Homebuilders, 740
National Cancer Institute, 587
National Center for Education
    Statistics, 332, 351, 358, 446,
    451, 533, 535
National Center for Environmental
    Health, 231
National Center for Health
    Statistics, A-10, A-11, 233, 309,
    317, 444, 475, 492, 495, 498,
    501, 586, 587, 588, 589, 594,
    617, 671, 675, 685, 770, 771
National Governors Association, 359
National Heart, Lung, and Blood
    Institute, A-12, 499
National Science Foundation, 445
National Sleep Foundation, 405
Natsuaki, Misaki N., 186, 410, 417
Naudé, H., 108
Navarra, Jordi, 169
Nayga, Rodolfo M. Jr., 316
Neave, Guy R., 533
Nebel, Almut, 689
Need, Ariana, 659
Needham, Amy, 141
Needham, Larry L., 408
Needleman, Herbert L., 230
Neggars, Yasmin, 114
Negriff, Yasin, 410
Nehra, Ajay, 586
Neiderhiser, Jenae M., 69, 77, 86,
    87, 186, 383
Neigh, Gretchen N., 238
Neighbors, Clayton, 512
Neimeyer, Robert A., 779
Neisler, Justin, 533
Neisser, Ulric, 617
Nelson, Charles A., 132, 167, 226
Nelson, Charles A., III, 196
Nelson, Elliot C., 481
Nelson, Jennifer A., 216
Nelson, Larry J., 283, 528, 549, 550
Nelson, Leif D., 30
Nelson, Marvin D., 129
Nelson, R. Michael, 467
Nelson, Todd D., 669, 672
Nemeroff, Charles B., 238
Nemeth, Elizabeta, 576
Nemoda, Z., 188
Neppl, Tricia M., 383
Neuberg, Steven L., 56
Neufeld, Eva, 744
Neumann, Anna, 473
Neumark-Sztainer, Dianne, 413, 499
Neuner, Frank, 371
Neupert Shevaun D., 670
Nevin, 231
New York Longitudinal Study (NYLS),
    187
Newberry, Sydne J., 217
Newman, Stanton P., 619
Newnham, Carol A., 191
Newnham, Elizabeth A., 371
Newton, Sir Isaac, 334
Neyer, Franz J., 637, 748, 749
Ng, C. Y., 83

Ng, Kok-Mun, 195
Ng, Nawi, 480
Ngige, Lucy W., 566
Nguyen, Angela-MinhTu D., 73,
    538, 546
Nguyen, Ann, 742
Niaura, Raymond S., 593
Nic Gabhainn, Saoirse, 425
Niccols, Alison, 108
Nichelli, Paolo F., 703
Nichols, Sara R., 296
Nichols, Tracy R., 410, 423, 477
Nicholson, Barbara, 135
Nicolaides, A-6
Nielson, Mark, 250
Nieto, Sonia, 352, 385, 392
Nieuwenhuis, Rense, 659
Nigam, Anil, 687
Nigam, Milena, 347
Nigg, Joel T., 410
Nijhuis, Jan G., 168
Nikitin, Jana, 736
Nikogosian, Haik, 311
Nikolova, Dimitrinka, 689
Nilsson, Matthew E., 769
Nilwik, Rachel, 578
Nisbett, Richard E., 278, 527, 604,
    609
Nishida, Tracy K., 197
Nishina, Adrienne, 388, 447
Noda, Art, 524, 625
Noel-Miller, Claire, 645, 650
Noh, Soo Rim, 705
Nolen-Hoeksema, Susan, 474
Noll, Jennie G., 402, 408, 424
Noppeney, Uta, 260
Nordgren, Loran F., 578, 593
Norenzayan, Ara, 527
Nores, Milagros, 269
Noret, Nathalie, 388
Norr, Kathleen F., 104
Norris, Joan E., 747
Norris, Pippa, 440
North, Michael S., 669
North, Robyn A., 106
Norton, Edward C., 315
Novak, Scott P., 318
Nove, 625
Nucci, Larry P., 392, 528
Nugent, J. Kevin, 197
Nurmi, Jari-Erik, 300, 446, 469
Nuru-Jeter, Amani M., 524
Nwodim, Chinyere, 774
Nyberg, Lars, 700
Nyboe Andersen, Anders, 115

Oakes, J. Michael, 443
Oaten, Megan J., 184
Oba, Shino, 578
Obama, Barack, 406
Obarzanek, Eva, 402
O'Brien, Kirk, 241
O'Brien, Peter, 586
O'Campo, Patricia, 563
Ocfemia, M. Cheryl Bañez, 424
Ockene, Judith K., 593
O'Coaimh, Rónán, 710
Ocobock, Abigail, 559, 644
O'Connor, Patrick J., 591

O'Daniel, Julianne, 89
Odden, Hal, 256
Odden, Michelle C., 685
Oden, Melita, 605
Odero, Dolphine, 227, 282
Odlaug, Brian L., 505
O'Doherty, Katherine, 174
O'Doherty, Katherine, 291
O'Doherty, Kieran, 88
O'Donnell, Lydia, 472
O'Donoghue, Ted, 519
OECD, A-16, 448, 452
Offit, Paul A., 331
Ofstedal, Mary Beth, 710
Ogburn, Elizabeth L., 555
Ogden, Cynthia L., 313, 315
Oh, Seungmi, 223
O'Hanlon, Leslie Harris, 441
Ohlsson, Anne, 113
Öhman, Ann, 480
Ohno-Matsui, Kyoko, 83
Ok, Su-Jeong, 97, 129, 132, 134,
    172, 185, 203, 222, 230, 679
Okada, Hiroyuki, 172
Oken, Emily, 102, 111, 146
Okonkwo, Ozioma C., 752
Okun, Morris, 739
Oldershaw, Lynn, 301
O'Leary, Colleen M., 106
O'Leary, Kathleen, 584
O'Leary, K. Daniel, 557
Oleksik, Anna M., 685
Olfson, Mark, 326
Oliver, Bonamy, 259
Oliver, Pamella H., 278
Olness, Karen, 196
Olsen, James P., 563, 564
Olsen, Joseph, 642, 643
Olshansky, S. Jay, 747
Olson, Bradley D., 549, 550
Olson, Kristina, 203
Olson, Sheryl L., 298, 299
Olweus, Dan Limber, 387
O'Malley, A. James, 638
O'Malley, Patrick M., 473, 479, 480,
    481, 483, 510, 511, 522, 549
Omariba, D. Walter Rasugu, 375
Omvlee, Annelies, 410
O'Neal, Catherine Walker, 639
O'Neill, Greg, 739
Ones, Ulker, 317, 764
Onghena, Patrick, 300
Ontai, Lenna L., 255
Onwuteaka-Philpsen, Bregje, 774
Oosteman, Mirjam, 241
Oosterlaan, Jaap, 114
Oppen, P. van, 119
Orduñez, Pedro, 591, 692
O'Regan, M., 326
Oregon Department of Human
    Services, 775
Oregon Public Health Division,
    774, 775
Orlich, Donal C., 347
Orlofsky, Jacob L., 458
Ormel, Johan, 410, 505
Ormrod, Richard, 375, 383, 387
Orobio de Castro, Bram, 369
Orom, Heather, 523

O'Rourke, Norm, 675, 744
Orpana, Heather, 589
Orth, Ulrich, 635
Ortyl, Timothy A., 553, 559
Ory, Marcia G., 752
Osher, David, 43
Oshima-Takane, Yuriko, 172
Osorio, Snezana Nena, 149
Ossher, Lynn, 704
Ostatníková, Daniela, 96
Ostfeld, Barbara M., 150
O'Sullivan, Sean S., 714
Oswald, Tasha M., 418
Otheguy, Ricardo, 258
Otomo, Kiyoshi, 172
Otsuki, Koji, 17
Otten, Roy, 288
Otto, Hiltrud, 276
Ou, Suh-Ruu, 269
Over, Harriet, 253
Overton, Willis F., 5, 222
Owen, Jesse, 554
Owen, Margaret T., 208
Owen, Neville, 592
Owen-Kostelnik, Jessica, 477
Owens, Elizabeth B., 288
Owens, Judith A., 405
Owsley, Cynthia, 579
Oyekale, Abayomi Samuel, 149
Oyekale, Tolulope Olayemi, 149
Oza-Frank, Reena, 500

Pabst, Stephanie R., 410
Pace, Cecilia Serena, 648
Pacheco, Jennifer L., 723
Padial, Antonia, 217
Padilla-Walker, Laura M., 549, 550
Padmanabhan, Aarthi, 416, 418
Pae, Calvin, 72
Paganim, Linda S., 452
Pagán-Rodríguez, Ricardo, 738
Pahwa, Rajesh, 713
Paik, Anthony, 423
Painter, Gary, 341
Palagi, Elisabetta, 284
Paletti, Robin, 764
Palmar, Tiffany, 584
Palmer, Nicholette D., 690
Palmore, Erdman, 667
Pals, Jennifer L., 39, 632
Palta, Mari, 737
Palucki Blake, Laura, 533, 538
Pandian, Z., 582
Panfile, Tia, 298–299
Panizzon, Matthew S., 607
Pantelis, Christos, 474
Papademtris, Xenophon, 637
Papaligoura, Zaira, 201
Parasuraman, R., 702
Pardini, Matteo, 703
Parish-Morris, Julia, 174
Park, D. J. J., 83
Park, Denise C., 626, 701, 720
Park, Hyekyung, 527
Park, Hyun, 196
Park, J. T., 763
Park, Jinyi, 72
Park, Jong-Hyo, 280
Park, Jong-Tae, 72

Park, Justin H., 559, 652
Park, Min Sun, 72
Parke, Ross D., 198, 287, 289
Parker, Andrew, 88, 89
Parker, Andrew M., 765
Parker, Beth, 714
Parker, Holly A., 619, 620
Parker, Jennifer D., 317
Parker, Kim, 640
Parker, Lysa, 135
Parker, Marti G., 695
Parker, Susan Whitmore, 199, 226
Parkkinen, Laura, 714
Parmar, Chirag, 442
Parr, Alice, 604
Parra, Gilbert R., 563, 564
Parra, Marisol, 261
Parris, Leandra, 443
Parsons, Elizabeth, 194
Parten, Mildred, 283
Parveen, Sahdia, 652
Pascalis, Olivier, 132, 534, 538
Pascarella, Ernest T., 533
Paschall, Mallie J., 299
Pascual, Cristina, 217
Pascual, María, 481
Pasley, Kay, 379
Pastore, Massimiliano, 464
Pastores, Stephen M., 777
Pastrana, Travis, 508
Patel, Vikram, 17
Patel, Vimla L., 625
Paternoster, Raymond, 507
Paterson, David S., 150
Pathela, Preeti, 471
Pathman, Thanujeni, 162, 165, 421
Patricio, P., 700
Patrick, Megan E., 405, 512
Patris, Bruno, 138
Patterson, Robin Shura, 608
Patton, George C., 411, 481
Pattwell, Siobhan S., 431
Pattyn, Elise, 18
Paukner, Annika, 284
Paúl, Constança, 695
Paul, Erick J., 604
Paul, Ian M., 217
Paul, Jonathan A., 443
Paul of Tarsus, 531
Pauler, Florian M., 78
Paulicin, Belinda, 197
Paulsen, David J., 416, 418
Pausch, Randy, 763
Pavlov, Ivan, 43–44
Pawlik, Amy J., 54
Paxson, Christina, 382, 383
Pearson, Barbara Zurer, 261
Pedersen, Nancy L., 17, 607, 634
Pedersen, Sara, 479
Peelen, Linda M., 114
Peffley, Mark, 16
Peipert, Jeffrey F., 501
Pelham, William E. Jr., 326
Pelkonen, Mirjami, 481
Pellegrini, Anthony D., 280, 282, 284, 285
Pelletier, Joseph, 392
Pellis, Sergio M., 284
Pellis, Vivien C., 284

Peltier, Scott J., 701
Pelzel, Kelly E., 160
Pemberton, Caroline K., 277
Pendleton, Robert C., 591
Peng, Kaiping, 527
Penke, Lars, 604, 635
Penningroth, Suzanna L., 732
Penninx, Brenda W. J. H., 617
Peper, Jiska S., 114, 403, 404, 419
Pepler, Debra, 388
Pepper, Sara, 479
Peracchi, Franco, 739
Peralta, Carmen A., 685
Perc, Matjaz, 251
Peregoy, Jennifer A., 717
Pereira, Vera, 781
Peretz, Isabelle, 170
Perez, L., 717
Perez-Edgar, Koraly E., 188
Perfetti, Jennifer, 119
Perilloux, Carin, 58, 60
Perl, Harold, 150
Perlis, Clifford S., 31
Perls, Thomas T., 695
Perner, Josef, 255
Peron, Emily P., 670
Perrin, James M., 330
Perry, William G. Jr., 534, 535
Perry, John R. B., 584
Persaud, Trivedi V. N., 6, 106
Pérusse, Daniel, 173
Pescosolido, Bernice A., 623
Peshti, Victoria, 692
Pesta, Bryan J., 636
Peters, Ellen, 705
Peters, Jan, 733
Peters, Ruth, 43
Petersen, Inge, 639
Petersen, Ronald C., 710, 711
Peterson, Herbert, 580
Peterson, Jane W., 349
Peterson, Christopher, 634
Petrauskas, Bonnie J., 197
Pettit, Jeremy W., 191
Petukhova, Maria, 503
Pew Forum on Religion and Public Life, 461
Pew Research Center, 55, 501, 529, 576, 669, 743
Peyser, James A., 361
Pezzin, Liliana E., 750
Pfaus, et al 2014, 580
Pfeiffer, Jennifer H., 418
Pfeiffer, Ronald E., 713
Phan, Jenny M., 22
Phan, Mai B., 681
Phelan, Elizabeth A., 679
Phelan, Sean M., 524
Phelps, Erin, 388
Philibert, Robert A., 465, 550
Phillips, Deborah A., 207, 270
Phillips, Kenneth D., 722
Phillips, Louise H., 703, 704
Phillips, Mary, 739
Phillips, Miranda, 642
Phillips, Tommy M., 458
Phillipson, Chris, 736
Phillipson, Shane N., 352
Phillipson, Sivanes, 352

Piaget, Jean, 45–47, 48, 64, 142, 155–162, 156t, 167, 178, 245–249, 256, 264, 270, 272, 295, 305, 339–340, 343, 347, 348, 357, 364, 389, 393–394, 397, 431–434, 434, 435, 436, 438, 454, 487, 518, 519, 526, 531, 699
Pianta, Robert C., 249, 262, 341
Piasecki, Thomas M., 765
Piazza, Manuela, 328
Picasso, Pablo, 334
Piccinini, Cesar A., 227, 282
Pichora-Fuller, M. Kathleen, 703
Picozzi, Marta, 134
Piecyzk, Markus, 689
Pierce, Kim M., 341
Pierce, W. David, 278
Pierro, Antonio, 636
Pierson, Duane, 496
Pietrantonio, et al, 237
Pietras, Cynthia J., 481
Pietrefesa, Ashley S., 218
Pignotti, Maria Serenella, 97
Pijnenburg, Yolande A. L., 712
Pilkinton, Pamela D., 739
Pin, Tamis, 140
Pinborg, Anja, 115
Pine, Daniel S., 188
Pine, Karen J., 170
Pinheiro, Andréa Poyastro, 414
Pinheiro, Paulo Sérgio, 424
Pinker, Steven, 28, 175
Pinquart, Martin, 745, 767
Pintabona, Yolanda, 388
Pinto, Catherine M., 358
Pinto, L., 700
Pion, Katie, 327
Piotrowski, Martin, 639
Piro, Ettore, 75
Pirretti, Amy E., 658
Pisetsky, Emily M., 415
Pitskhelauri, G. Z., 694
Pittman, Cathy, 461, 470
Pittman, Joe F., 458
Piven, Joseph, 132
Place, Silvia, 261
Plailly, Jane, 321, 626
Planty, Michael, 262
Planty, w/Truman 2012, 672
Plassman, Brenda L., 710
Platt, Richard, 110
Plaut, Victoria C., 16
Pligt, Joop van der, 593
Ploeg, Catharina P. B. van der, 580
Plomin, Robert, 69, 77, 86, 87, 259
Plotnicov, Katherine, 414
Plows, Alexandra, 88, 89
Pluess, Michael, 188, 207, 373
Poe, Michele D., 132
Pogrebin, Abigail, 75
Poldrack, Russell A., 17
Polesel, John, 449
Pollak, Seth D., 183, 402, 410
Pollet, Susan L., 650
Polo-Tomas, Monica, 371, 374
Polotsky, Alex J., 691
Polzer, Jeffrey T., 538
Pomerantz, Eva M., 463, 464

Pomery, Elizabeth A., 464
Ponitz, Claire Cameron
Poole, Charles, 414
Poon, Leonard W., 695
Poorthuis, Astrid, 369
Poortinga, Ype H., 375, 553
Poortvliet, Rosalinde K. E., 685
Pope, Denise, 449
Popham, Lauren E., 765
Popkin, Barry M., 216, 500
Population Reference Bureau, A-3
Porche, Michelle V., 352, 445, 446
Porretta, David L., 19
Poskiparta, Elisa, 388
Posner, Michael I., 185
Poteat, V. Paul, 388
Potegal, Michael, 183
Potenza, Bruce, 236
Potenza, Marc N., 505
Potocnik, Kristina, 736
Pott, Audrie, 443
Potter, Audrey M., 382
Potter, Jeff, 636
Pottinger, Audrey M., 584
Poulin, François, 469, 479
Poulin-Dubois, Diane, 197
Poulsen, Pernille, 16
Poulton, Richie, 634
Powell, Douglas A., 492
Powell, Jason L., 669
Powell, Lisa M., 315
Powell, Shaun, 316
Pozan-ski, Peter J., 636
Pozzoli, Tizianna, 389
Pradervand, Sylvain, 80
Prado, Carlos G., 772, 774
Prakash, Ruchika Shaurya, 323
Pratt, Micahel W., 747
Pratt, Michael M., 632
Prause, JoAnn, 208
Prawitz, Aimee D., 430
Premack, David, 295
Premo, Luke S., 205
Prentice, Ross L., 584
Prescott, Eva, 18
Pressley, Michael, 347
Pressman, Eva K., 99
Preston, Tom, 772
Price, C. J., 260, 616
Priess, Heather A., 461
Prigerson, Holly G., 769
Prince, Richard, 585
Prins, Gail S., 111
Prinzie, Peter, 187, 188
Prisco, Theresa R., 198
Pritchard, David E., 539
Procaccio, Vincent, 712
Programme for International
    Student Assessment (PISA),
    451–453
Prohaska, Thomas R., 672, 679
Proulx, Christine M., 744
Provasnik, Stephen, 352, 356
Pryor, John H., 533, 538
Puccioni, Olga, 702
Pudrovska, Tetyana, 643, 647
Puhl, Rebecca M., 589
Puigserver, Pere, 692
Pulkkinen, Lea, 481, 657

Pulvermüller, Friedemann, 171
Pungello, Elizabeth P., 269
Purchase-Helzner, Elizabeth, 703,
    704
Puri, Sunita, 72
Purohit, Darshana, 408
Purser, Harry R. M., 349
Putnam, Frank W., 402, 408, 424
Putnam, Robert D., 742
Pyszczynski, Tom, 765, 766

Qaseem, Amir, 596
Qin, Lili, 463, 464
Qiu, Chengzuan, 711
Qiu, Xuan, 713, 716
Qualls, Sara Honn, 779
Quartz, Steven R., 195, 654
Quas, Jodi A., 226
Quay, Lisa, 473
Quindlen, Anna, 730, 732
Quinn, Graham E., 138
Quirce, Santiago, 217
Quiriarte, Heather, 496
Qusti, Safaa, 413

Raaijmakers, Quinten A. W., 530, 565
Rabagliati, Hugh, 176
Rabkin, Nick, 353
Rachner, Tilman D., 687
Radford, Nina B., 672
Radomski, Juliana Groves, 497, 671
Rahman, Qazi, 373
Rahman, Rumaisa, 99p
Raikes, H. Abigail, 195
Railton, Peter, 48
Raja, Annia, 552
Rajaratnam, Julie Knoll, 103, 114,
    143
Rajeevan, Nallakkandi, 637
Rajkumar, Chakravarthi, 43
Raley, Kelly, 645
Ram, Nilam, 683
Ramakrishnan, Usha, 217
Ramani, Geetha B., 297
Ramey, Craig T., 269
Ramón, Rosa, 111
Ramsay, Douglas, 182
Ramscar, Michael, 222, 259
Ramus, Franck; Sato, 113, 138, 169
Ranchor, Adelita V., 749
Ranciaro, Alessia, 15
Rankin, Jane L., 430
Rasinski, Kenneth A., 774
Rásky, Éva, 773
Rasmussen, Birgit H., 769
Raspa, Richard, 57, 769
Raspberry, Kelly Amanda, 89
Rauers, Antje, 707
Raus, Kasper, 771
Ravert, Russell D., 567
Ravizza, Kenneth, 58
Rawles, Richard, 221
Raymo, James, 641
Raymond, Neil, 108
Razzano, Lisa A., 504
Read, Jennifer P., 513
Reche, Marta, 217
Reczek, Corinne, 643, 647
Reddy, Marpadga A., 77

Reeb-Sutherland, Bethany C., 187
Reed, Floyd A., 15
Reed, Pamela G., 597
Reeskens, Tim, 13
Regalia, Camillo, 566
Reich, John W., 619
Reichle, Erik D., 594
Reijntjes, Albert, 369
Reisberg, Liz, 535
Reiser, Mark, 275
Reiss, David, 186
Reitz, Cordula, 146
Rendell, Luke, 201
Rendella, Peter G., 707
Renk, Kimberly, 293
Rentfrow, Peter Jason, 636
Reppucci, N. Dickson, 477
Resnick, Barbara, 730, 732
Rest, James, 528, 530, 533
Rett syndrome, 330
Reuter-Lorenz, Patricia A., 621,
    626, 701, 702, 719
Reutskaja, Elena, 555
Revesz, Tamas, 714
Reymond, Alexandre, 80
Reyna, Valerie F., 431
Reynolds, Arthur J., 269, 270
Reynolds, Chandra, 17
Reynolds, Elizabeth K., 188
Rhodes, Jean E., 620
Ribeiro, Oscar, 695
Riboli, Elio, 587
Riccio, Cynthia A., 328
Rice, Charles L., 495
Rich, Motoko, 449
Richardson, Amanda, 593
Richardson, Cameron, 55
Richardson, Irma, 300
Richardson, Rick, 165, 167
Richardson, T., 326
Richert, Rebekah A., 174
Richey, Mike, 451
Richie, Rachel A., 546
Richter, Melinda M., 82
Rickson, Kathryn, 783
Ridder, Elizabeth M., 563
Ridderinkof, K. Richard, 248
Ridolfo, Heather E., 624
Riedl, Marc A., 217
Riegel, 1975, 525
Riekert, Kristin A., 593
Rieter, Edward O., 402
Rietjens, Judith, 774
Rifas-Shiman, Sheryl L., 102, 146
Riglin, et al 2013, 445, 446
Riley, Anne W., 326
Riley, Debbie, 649
Riley, Edward P., 108
Rimbach, Gerald, 689
Riordan, Jan, 146
Rios, Rebeca, 739
Ripke, Marika N., 367, 368, 370
Risica, Patricia M., 591
Risley, Todd R., 351
Ritchie, Laura, 552, 553
Ritchie, William C., 261
Ritter, Johannes O., 736
Rivas-Drake, Deborah, 546

Rivera, Juan A., 498
Rivera, Marino, 578
Rivers, Ian, 388
Rix, Sara E., 657, 738
Rizza, Robert A., 586
Robb, Michael B., 174
Robelen, Erik W., 359
Robert, Stephanie A., 736, 737
Roberto, Karen A., 730, 732
Roberts, Gehan, 114
Roberts, Leslie, 229
Roberts, Richard D., 144, 608
Roberts, Soraya, 508
Robins, Richard W., 370, 635
Robinson, JoAnn, 289
Robinson, Lara Rachel, 201, 276
Robinson, Louise, 711, 714, 754
Robinson, Oliver C., 634
Robinson, Randal D., 584
Robinson, Scott R., 78
Robson, Ruthann, 765
Roca, Carmen S., 505
Roca, María, 604
Roccio, Marianna, 114
Rochat, Philippe, 256
Roche, Alex F., 412
Rocheford, Torbert R., 83
Rocke, Christina, 706
Rocroi, Camille, 175
Roderer, Thomas, 346
Rodgers, David L., 776
Rodier, Francis, 576
Rodkin, Philip C., 386
Rodrigue, Karen M., 701
Rodriguez, Liliana, 546
Rodriguez, Olga L., 328
Roebers, Claudia M., 346
Roenneberg, Till, 404
Roeser, Robert W., 444, 445, 448,
    459
Roey, Stephen, 352, 356
Roeyers, Herbert, 340
Rogers, Carl, 56–58, 64
Rogers-Chapman, 251
Rogne, Leah, 778
Rogoff, Barbara, 14, 55, 184, 342,
    343, 348
Rogosch, Fred A., 238, 239
Roh, Bong H., 690
Rohlfsen, Leah, 735
Rohrer, Jonathan D., 712
Rohwedder, Susann, 739
Roisman, Glenn I., 194, 386
Rojas, Raul, 350
Roksa, Josipa, 353, 536
Romano, Elisa, 207
Romeo, Russell D., 403, 416
Romney, A. Kimbal, 368
Ron, Pnina, 652
Rondal, Jean A., 85
Rook, Karen S., 733, 734
Rooney, Patrick M., 531
Roopnarine, Jaipaul L., 283
Roosmalen, Jos van, 104
Ros, Emilio, 592
Rose, Amanda J., 474
Rose, Richard J., 481
Rose, Roderick, 474
Rose, Steven, 326

Rose, Susan A., 167
Roseberry, Sarah, 174
Rosen, Clifford J., 687
Rosen, Jules, 654
Rosen, Raymond C., 676
Rosenbaum, James E., 451
Rosenblatt, Paul C., 763, 781
Rosenfield, Robert L., 401
Rosenfield, Sarah, 734, 736
Rosenthal, Marjorie, 613
Rosenthal, Miriam K., 352
Rosnick, Christopher B., 609, 706
Rosow, Irving, 736
Ross, Colin A., 85
Ross, John, 580
Ross, Judith L., 85
Ross J., 404
Rosselli, Francine, 415
Rossi, Aimee Drolet, 705, 706
Rossi, Eleonora, 162
Rossignol, Daniel, 330
Rossignol, Lanier, 330
Rossion, Bruno, 134
Rostila, Mikael, 780
Roth, David L., 752
Roth, Erin, 449
Roth, George S., 691
Roth, Guy, 56
Roth, Lauren W., 691
Rothbart, Mary K., 185
Rothbaum, Fred, 191, 195
Rothblum, Esther D., 497
Rothrauff, Tanja C., 288
Rott, Christoph, 695
Rouchka, Eric C., 78
Rovee-Collier, Carolyn, 166, 167
Rovi, Sue, 240
Rovner, Alisha J., 414
Rowe, John, 747
Royce, Jean-Pierre, 321, 626
Rozier, R. Gary, 217, 218, 311
Rubie-Davies, Christine M., 352
Rubin, Kenneth H., 188, 276, 282,
    368, 384, 385, 388, 392, 446
Rubin, Simon Shimshon, 783
Ruble, Diane N., 290, 291, 293, 294
Ruby, Christine M., 670
Ruck, Martin, 55
Rudan, Igor, 711
Rudolph, Karen D., 410
Rueden, Christopher von, 635
Rueschin, Catherine, 547
Rugolotto, Simone, 51
Ruijter, Wouter de, 685
Rulfs, Monika, 782
Rumberger, Russell W., 359
Rumbley, Laura E., 535
Rumiche, Rosario, 261
Rurup, Mette, 774
Russell, Eric M., 553
Russell, Kelly, 51
Russell, Stephen T., 463, 472, 476
Ruthig, Joelle C., 744
Rutland, Adam, 392
Rutter, Michael, 196, 207, 374, 477
Ruuttu, Titta, 481
Ruvolo, Paul, 189
Ruys, Jan H., 136
Ryan, Aubrey E., 497, 671

Ryan, Erin L., 175
Ryan, Michelle K., 292
Ryan, Richard M., 278
Ryan, Sharon, 267
Ryckewaert, Ruben, 765
Ryman, Sephira G., 322

Saarela, Jan, 780
Saarni, Carolyn, 183, 275
Sabayan, Behnam, 685
Sabbagh, Mark A., 255, 256
Saburova, Ludmila, 588
Sachdev, Perminder S., 705
Sacks, Oliver W., 329
Sadeh, Avi, 135, 136, 183
Sadek, Shelly, 386, 387
Sadler, Philip Michael, 108, 449
Sadler, Thomas W., 95, 96
Saegert, Susan, 735
Saelens, Brian E., 592
Saewyc, Elizabeth M., 471, 474
Al Sahab, Ban, 410
Sahlberg, Pasi, 356, 357, 450
Sailer, Christian, 689
Salas-Salvadó, Jordi, 592
Sallis, James F., 592
Salmela-Aro, Katariina, 446, 469
Salmivalli, Christina, 388, 389
Salmon, David P., 711, 714
Salmon, Jo, 44
Salsman, Nicholas, 622
Salter, Nicholas P., 612
Salthouse, Timothy A., 701, 702,
    707, 708
Samaras, D., 584
Samaras, N., 584
Sameroff, Arnold J., 298, 299
SAMHSA, 503, 510
Sammons, Pam, 681
Sams, Clarence, 496
Samuels, Christina A., 449
Samuelsen, Sven-Ove, 421
Samuelson, Larissa K., 78
San Souci, Priscilla, 162, 165, 421
Sanborn, Adam, 624
Sand, Michael S., 676
Sandburg, Sheryl, 525
Sander, Libby, 504
Sanderman, Robbert, 749
Sanders, Camilla E., 608, 609, 634
Sanders, Megan, 472
Sandler, Irwin N., 764
Sansone, Lori A., 634
Sansone, Randi, 634
Santagata, Rossella, 562
Santelli, John S., 422, 423
Santinello, Massimo, 464
Santos, Regina de los, 474
Sapyta, Jeffrey, 218
Saraceno, Chiara, 745
Sareen, Jitender, 239
Sá-Saraiva, Rodrigo de, 781
Sassler, Sharon, 642
Sasvari-Szekely, M., 188
Satariano, William A., 672, 679
Sato, Yutaka, 113, 138, 169
Satterstrom, Patricia, 538
Satterwhite, Catherine Lindsey, 424
Sauer, Mark V., 583

Saulny, Susan, 544
Saunders, Carol J., 86
Saunders, Cecily, 770
Savci, Evren, 644
Savelsbergh, Geert J. P., 165
Savin-Willams, Ritch C., 503
Saw, Seang-Mei, 83
Sawyer, Susan M., 311
Saxena, Sanjaya, 731
Saxton, Matthew, 170, 173, 175
Sayal, Kapil, 108, 326
Sayer, Aline, 544, 546, 548
Sayette, Michael A., 594
Scabini, Eugenia, 566
Scales, Peter C., 466
Scannapieco, Maria, 239
Scaramella, Laura V., 186
Scarf, Maggie, 744
Scarr, Sandra, 230
Schaal, Benoist, 138
Schaan, Barbara, 749
Schachner, Adena, 171
Schaefer, Sabine, 702
Schaie, K. Warner, 577, 606–607,
    608, 611, 626, 628, 707, 719
Schaller, Mark, 56
Schanler, Richard J., 146
Schans, Djamila, 652
Scharlach, Andrew, 740, 755
Schats, Roel, 584
Schauer, Daniel P., 591
Schauer, Elizabeth, 371
Scheffler, Richard M., 326
Scheibehenne, Benjamin, 556
Scheindlin, Benjamin, 300
Schelar, Erin, 505
Schell, Alan, 230
Schenkman, Lauren, 162
Schepens, Annemie, 340
Scher, Anat, 135, 183
Schermerhorn, Alice, 383
Schiavo, Robert, 777–778
Schiavo, Terri, 777–778
Schieve, Laura A., 330
Schiller, Jeannine S., 717
Schiller, Ruth A., 530
Schillinger, Dean, 115
Schillinger, John E., 471
Schimmelmann, B. G., 48
Schippers, Marleen, 162
Schisterman, Enrique F., 584
Schlomer, Gabriel L., 21, 408
Schlosser, Thomas, 642
Schmader, Toni, 524
Schmid, Corinne, 346
Schmidt, Louis A., 188
Schmidt, Michelle E., 385, 388
Schmitt-Rodermund, Eva, 410
Schmölzer, Christin, 773
Schmukle, Stefan C., 636
Schnack, Hugo G., 683
Schneider, Barbara, 658
Schneider, Cindy, 330
Schneider, Dona, 51
Schneider, Michael, 344
Schneider, Susan, 614, 647
Schneider, Wolfgang, 344
Schneiderman, Carolyn T., 622
Schnitzspahn, Katharina M., 704, 707

Schnyer, David M., 723
Schoebi, Dominik, 553
Schoemaker, Minouk J., 584
Schoen, Robert, 561
Schoeny, Michael E., 472
Schofield, Peter R., 87
Schofield, Thomas J., 383
Schön, Daniele, 170
Schooler, Carmi, 607
Schooler, Jonathan W., 594
Schore, Allan, 132
Schreck, Christopher J., 410
Schröder, Mathis, 737
Schroeder, David H., 604
Schuck, Sabrina, 23p
Schuengel, Carlo, 241
Schulenberg, John E., 405, 438,
    460, 479, 480, 481, 483, 510,
    511, 522, 549
Schulz, James H., 743, 744
Schulz, Marc S., 744
Schulz, Richard, 149
Schumann, Cynthia Mills, 330
Schupp, Justin, 739
Schurtz, David R., B-5, 549
Schut, Henk, 779, 783
Schütz, Frédéric, 80
Schwall, Charles, 264
Schwartz, Ann V., 687
Schwartz, Carl E., 220
Schwartz, David, 89
Schwartz, Janice B., 754
Schwartz, Lisa M., 596
Schwartz, Nathaniel, 358
Schwartz, Paul D., 430, 431
Schwartz, Seth J., 546, 567
Schwarz, Alan, 325
Schwarzer, Ralf, 593
Schweinhart, Lawrence J., 269
Schweitzr, Robert, 509
Schytt, Erica, 103
Scott, Fran, 113
Scott, John, 714
Scott, John M., 108
Scott, Kate Margaret, 505
Scott, Lisa S., 132, 134, 135
Scott, Mindy, 505
Scott, Norman A., 410
Scott, Walter D., 732
Scrignaro, Marta, 504
Sear, Rebecca, 207
Seaton, Daniel T., 539
Seaton, Eleanor, 380
Sebastian, Catherine, 430
Sebastián-Gallés, Núria, 169, 176
Secrest, Mildred, 720
Secura, Gina M., 501
Seddighin, Safoura, 251
Seedat, Soraya, 505
Seelaar, Harro, 712
Seeley, John R., 191
Seeman, Teresa, 737
Seguin, Jean R., 297
Seidler, Rachael D., 701, 719
Seifer, Ronald, 195
Seligman, Hilary K., 115
Seligman, Martin E. P., 48
Selin, Helaine, 103
Sellers, Sherrill L., 735

Seltzer, Nathan, 327
Selwood, Amber, 753
Semesky, Michael, 518
Semmekrot, Ben A., 136
Senf, Janet H., 473
Senjem, Matthew L., 711
Senju, Atsushi, 329
Senor, Melissa, 261
Senserrick, Teresa M., 438
Sentse, Miranda, 410
Sepkowitz, Kent A., 511
Serget, 700
Sesso, Howard D., 592
Settersten, Richard A. Jr., 538
Settle, Jaime E., 78
Seufort, Magdalene, 716
Sevilla, Almudena, 739
Sexton, Holly R., 299
Seyfarth, Robert M., 551
Shackelford, Todd K., 61
Shaffer, Michele L., 217
Shah, Prakesh, 113
Shah, Priti, 719
Shai, Iris, 591
Shake, Matthew C., 705
Shaki, Samuel, 252
Shakya, Holly Baker, 747
Shanahan, Michael J., 736
Shanahan, Timothy, 220, 258
Shane, Matthew S., 637
Shankaran, Seetha, 195
Shanklin, S., 404
Shany, Eilon, 139
Shao, Yi, 463
Shapiro, Adam, 738
Shapiro, Edward S., 331
Shapiro, James A., 69
Shapiro, Melanie Freedberg, 203
Sharabany, Ruth, 136
Sharkey, Siobhan S., 754
Sharp, Jeff, 739
Sharp, Wendy, 223
Shattuck, 145
Shaw, Christina, 554
Shaw, Daniel S., 186
Shaw, Leslie M., 710
Shaw, Philip, 223
Shaw, Thérèse, 388
Shawber, Alison B., 277
Sheeber, Lisa, 474
Sheehy, Gail, 633
Sheel, A. William, 576
Sheese, Brad E., 185
Shek, Daniel T. L., 463
Shekelle, Paul G., 217
Shelby, Joe, 591
Shelton, Penny, 717
Shepard, Stephanie A., 275, 328, 529
Shepherd, Kathrine, 474
Sherblom, Stephen, 391
Sherman, David K., 278
Sherman, Kathleen, 174, 291
Sherman, Laura J., 188
Sherrard, Kathryn, 121
Sherwood, Nancy E., 591
Sherzai, A. Dean, 717
Shibley, Janet, 230
Shields, Margot, 315
Shields, Michael D., 317

Shineman, Diana W., 715
Shiner, Rebecca L., 187
Shiomura, Kimihiro, 370
Shirtcliff, Elizabeth A., 22, 402, 410
Shisslak, Catherine M., 473
Shkolnikov, Vladimir M., 588
Short, Kathleen, 11
Short, Kevin R., 586
Shouse, Roger C., 312, 450
Shreffler, Karina M., 584
Shrout, Patrick E., 138, 141
Shula, Don, 682
Shuler, Carly, 442
Shumaker, Sally A., 593
Shutter, Jennifer M., 185
Sica, Luigia, 504
Siebenbruner, Jessica, 410
Siebert, Erin R., 284
Siebner, Hartwig R., 221
Siegal, Micahel, 259
Siegal, Robert S., 226
Siegler, Robert S., 267, 344
Siegrist, Johannes, 737
Sierra, Felipe, 689, 694
Sifrit, [2012], 679, 683
Signorini, Sabrina Giovanna, 158, 168
Sikora, Joanna, 351
Silbereisen, Rainer K., 410, 767
Silk, Jennifer S., 201, 276
Silk, Timothy J., 220
Sillars, Alan, 462
Silton, Nava R., 203
Silva, Katie G., 342
Silva, Phil A., 477
Silver, Ellen J., 313
Silverstein, Merril, 745, 746, 748
Silvia, Paul J., 608, 609, 634
Simcock, Gabrielle, 167
Simmons, Joseph P., 30
Simon, Daniel H., 765
Simon, Melissa A., 753
Simons, Leslie Gordon, 550
Simons, Ronald L., 383, 550
Simonsick, Eleanor M., 703, 704
Simonsohn, Uri, 30
Simpkins, Sandra D., 312
Simpson, Jeffry A., 58
Sinardet, Dave, 651
Sinclair, Samantha, 461
Sindi, Shireen, 616
Singer, Dorothy G., 282
Singer, Irving, 554
Singh, Amika, 311
Singh, Leher, 169
Singh, Saraswati, 256
Singh, Sunita, 342
Singleton, David, 7, 256
Singzon, Trudy K., 640
Sinno, Stefanie, 389
Sinnott, Jan D., 518, 521, 526, 529
Sirai, Hidetosi, 172
Siraj-Blatchford, Iram, 681
Sivaramakrishnan, Kavita, 638
Skaff, Marilyn McKean, 731
Skibbe, Lori E., 262
Skinner, B. F., 43–44, 173, 175
Skinner, Debra, 89, 613
Skipper, Magdalena, 714
Skouteris, Helen, 191

Slade, Gary D., 217
Slade, Martin D., 670
Slater, Alan, 170
Slauson-Blevins, Kathleen S., 584
Slavich, George M., 78
Slavin, Robert E., 267
Slessor, Gillian, 703
Slining, Meghan, 140
Sliwinski, Martin J., 704
Sloan, John, 718
Sloan, Ken, 612
Sloan, Mark, 119
Sloane, Stephanie, 295
Slobin, Dan I., 175
Slora, Eric, 402
Slot, N. Wim, 241
Slutske, Wendy S., 634
Small, Meredith F., 614
Smeenk, Wilma, 198
Smetana, Judith G., 295, 298, 392
Smidts, Diana P., 114
Smith, Aaron, 440
Smith, Alison E., 531, 740
Smith, Andrew P., 616
Smith, Christian, 536, 752
Smith, Dewi, 267
Smith, Erin I., 174
Smith, G. Rush, 149
Smith, Gail, 300
Smith, George Davey, 511
Smith, Gregory C., 379
Smith, Jacqueline, 650
Smith, Jacqui, 5, 565, 567, 621, 638, 683, 723
Smith, James L., 640
Smith, Jocelyn R., 649
Smith, Linda B., 19, 259
Smith, P. K., 280, 283
Smith, Rachel Gimpel, 132
Smith, Scott, 330
Smith, Shawna N., 676
Smith, Traci, 462
Smokowski, Paul Richard, 474
Smulders, Peter G. W., 658
Smyke, Anna T., 196
Sneed, Joel R., 544, 546, 548
Snell, Patricia, 536, 752
Snell, with Smith 2009, 531
Snider, Terra Ziporyn, 405
Snidman, Nancy, 189
Snijders, Tim, A-6, 578
Snipes, Shedra Amy, 670, 717
Snow, Catherine E., 170, 261, 352, 445, 446
Snow, David L., 563, 564
Snyder, Thomas D., 262, 355, 361, 362
Soares, Joseph A., 525
Sobal, Jeffery, 315
Soden, Sarah E., 86
Soelen, Inge L. van, 114
Soenens, Bart, 300
Sokol, Bryan, 431
Soldo, Beth J., 746
Soley, Gaye, 171
Solheim, Elisabet, 207
Solomon, Alina, 715
Solomon, Andrew, 616
Solomon, Sheldon, 765, 766

Somers, Erin, 552, 553
Somerville, Leah H., 418, 431
Sommers, Mitchell S., 703
Sonderen, Eric van, 749
Song, Yiying, 321
Sonnentag, Sabine, 736
Sonnert, Gerhard, 108, 449
Sonuga-Barke, Edmund J. S., 196
Soons, Judith P. M., 557, 558
Sörensen, Silvia, 745
Sorkin, Dara H., 733, 734
Soska, Kasey C., 141
Sosnera, Philippe, 687
Soto, Ana M., 111
Soto-Faraco, Salvador, 169
Sotsky, Rachel B., 141, 165
Soulières, Isabelle, 329
Sousa, N., 700
Soussignan, Robert, 138
Southerland, Dannoa G., 650
Southgate, Victoria, 329
Souverein, Patrick, 325
Sowell, Elizabeth R., 416, 417
Sowinski, Stephen G., 83
Sparks, Sarah D., 357
Sparrow, Joshua D., 50
Spear, Linda, 481
Spearman, Charles, 604
Specht, Jule, 636
Spector, Tim D., 82
Spector, Timothy, 581
Spehar, Brent, 703
Spelke, Elizabeth S., 159, 163
Spencer, John P., 78
Spencer, Patricia Elizabeth, 13
Sperb, Tania M., 227, 282
Sperduto, Robert D., 83
Sperry, Debbie M., 239
Spiers, Hugo J., 626
Spinillo, Arsenio, 114
Spinrad, Tracy L., 198, 275, 296, 462
Spits, C., 73
Spittle, Alicia J., 114
Spooner, Carol, 51
Spotts, Erica L., 383, 634
Sprague, Jeffrey R., 43
Sprietsma, Maresa, 341
Squire, Corinne, 502
Sripada, Chandra, 48
St. George, Jennifer, 197
St. Petersburg-USA Orphanage Research Team, 348, 648, 650
Stacey, Judith, 644
Staessen, Jan A., 43
Staff, Jeremy, 460
Staff, Roger T., 702, 717
Stahl, Christoph, 704
Stahlhut, Carsten, 163
Staiger, Annegret Daniela, 411
Stampfer, Meir J., 591
Staniloiu, Angelica, 704
Stanley, Fiona, 106
Stark, Lori J., 326
Starr, John M., 717
Statistics Canada, 738
Stattin, Håkan, 464
Staudinger, Ursula M., 5, 523, 526, 723
Stavrova, Olga, 642

Stawski, Robert S., 609, 704, 705
Steele, Claude M., 524
Stefanick, Marcia L., 584
Stefanovic, Shawn, 638
Steffen, Lyn M., 500
Steffes, Jennifer, 402
Stein, Arlene, 278
Stein, Aryeh D., 498
Stein, Gabriela L., 289
Stein, Judith A., 387
Stein, Murray B., 239
Stein, Ruth E. K., 313
Steinberg, Jacques, 544
Steinberg, Joel L., 481
Steinberg, Laurence, 201, 276, 401, 409, 417, 434, 437, 438, 439, 466, 467, 471, 477
Steiner, Meir, 403
Steiner, Michael J., 51
Steinman, Michael A., 701, 739, 754
Stephen, Sidney, 591
Stephens, Rick, 451
Sterck, Elsabeth H. M., 253
Sterckx, Sigrid, 771
Sterling, Peter, 496
Sterling, Yvonne M., 349
Stern, Hilarie L., 129, 132, 134, 172, 185, 203, 222, 230, 679
Stern, Michael J., 639
Stern, Nancy, 258
Stern, Peter, 318, 683, 712
Sternberg, Robert J., 321, 334, 553, 554, 610–612, 613, 628, 643
Sterns, Harvey L., 655
Stetsenko, Anna, 526
Stevens, Bonnie, 139
Stevens, June, 414
Stevenson, Olive, 239
Stevenson, Richard J., 184
Steward, Anita L., 735
Stewart, Alistair, 106
Stewart, Chip, 80
Stewart, Eric A., 410
Stewart, Tara L., 744
Stieb, David, 113
Stiehl, Emily M., 654
Stifter, Cynthia A., 288
Stigler, James W., 357
Stigum, Hein, 421
Stiles, Hein, 132, 133
Stine-Morrow, Elizabeth A. L., 624, 705, 719, 720
Stipek, Deborah, 203
Stöbel-Richter, Yve, 72, 581
Stocco, Corey, 552, 553
Stock, Pieter, 340
Stockman, Michael, 223
Stoeber, Franziska S., 639
Stolk, Lisette, 584
Stoltenborgh, Marije, 424
Stone, Jacqueline Ilyse, 763
Stone, Richard, 229, 445
Stone, Robyn I., 103, 754
Stone, Susan, 326
Stoneking, Mark, 73
Stonington, Scott D., 774
Story, Mary, 413, 499
Strambler, Michael J., 369
Strasburger, Victor C., 483

Straten, A. van, 119
Straus, Murray A., 299
Strauss, Eva von, 711
Striegel-Moore, Ruth, 402, 415
Stringaris, Argyris, 17
Stroebe, Margaret S., 779, 783
Stroebe, Wolfgang, 779, 783
Stronati, Mauro, 114
Stronegger, Willibald J., 773
Strough, JoNell, 470
Strowe, Raymond, 496
Strunk, Sarah L., 498
Stuart, Elizabeth A., 132
Stubben, Jerry D., 278
Studnitz, Friederike S. G. van, 585
Stueve, Ann, 472
Stump, Glenda S., 539
Stupica, Brandi, 188, 189
Stygall, Jan, 619
Styner, Martin, 132
Su, Ya-Hui, 518, 526
Suchy, Frederick J., 59
Sue, Derald Wing, 656
Sugden, Andrew M., 229
Sulek, Julia Prodis, 443
Sulem, Patrick, 584
Sulik, Michael J., 290
Sullivan, Amanda, 251
Sullivan, Daniel, 765
Sullivan, Shiela, 553
Sullivan, Tami P., 563, 564
Summerskill, Steve J., 682
Sun, Min, 51
Sun, Shumei S., 412
Sun, Yuerong, 385
Sun, Yumei, 383
Sun, Yu-ying, 421
Sunderland, Trey, 721, 722
Sunita, T. H., 580
Sunstein, Cass R., 413, 434
Suomi, Stephen J., 120, 284
Super, Charles M., 278, 301
Suppiej, Agnese, 99
Surgeoner, Brae V., 492
Surian, Luca, 259
Suris, Joan-Carles, 311
Surman, Craig B. H., 327
Susman, Elizabeth J., 186, 401, 402, 406, 410
Sutphin, George L., 689
Sutton-Smith, Brian, 283
Suttorp, Marika J., 217
Suzman, Richard, 689, 694
Suzukamo, Yoshimi, 722
Svetlova, Margarita, 296
Swaab, Hanna, 325
Swaim, Elizabeth, 620
Swan, Shanna H., 583
Swan, Suzanne C., 563, 564
Swanberg, Jennifer, 738
Swann, William B. Jr., 370
Swanson, Cathrine, 562
Swanson, James W., 327
Swanson, Kristin R., 562
Swedlund, Alan C., 501
Sweeney, Kathryn A., 649
Sweeney, Megan M., 650
Sweet, Stephen, 659
Swerdlow, Anthony J., 584

Swieten, John C. van, 712
Swift, Wendy, 481
Swindell, William R., 691
Syed, Moin, 462
Syer, Ricky, 729
Syggellou, Angeliki, 98
Sylva, Kathy, 681
Sylvester, Ching-Yune C., 621
Szatmari, Peter, 415
Szolnoki, Attila, 251
Szydlik, Marc, 744

Taber, Daniel R., 414
Tabors, Patton O., 352, 445, 446
Tacken, Mart, 673
Tadmor, Carmit T., 538
Taga, Keiko A., 410
Taggart, Brenda, 681
Tai, Robert H., 108, 449
Takeda, Noriyuki, 578
Takeuchi, David T., 623
Takezawa, Masanori, 391
Tally, Ronda C., 651
Talmud, Ilan, 468
Talwar, Zeynep, 764
Tam, Tammy, 240
Tamay, Zeynep, 317
Tamburic, Lillian, 229, 553, 559, 561
Tamin, Hala, 410
Tamis-LeMonda, Catherine S., 174f
Tan, Donald T. H., 83
Tan, Erwin J., 701, 739
Tan, Patricia Z., 276, 277
Tang, Cheuk, 604
Tang, Yiyuan, 185
Tanner, Jennifer L., 522, 526, 547, 550, 551
Tappan, Mark B., 530
Tarbox, Jonathan, 330, 331
Tardif, Twila, 256
Taris, Toon W., 658
Tarullo, Amanda R., 195, 196, 224
Taussig, Heather N., 241
Tavecchio, Louis, 267
Taveras, Elsie M., 146
Tay, Louis, 13
Tay, Marc Tze-Hsin, 83
Taylor, Alan, 371, 374
Taylor, John H., 762
Taylor, Joy L., 524, 625
Taylor, Kate, 761
Taylor, Marjorie, 277
Taylor, P. G., 72
Taylor, Paul, 558
Taylor, Robert Joseph, 742
Taylor, Ronald D., 380
Taylor, Shelley E., 278, 617
Taylor, Valerie Jones, 524
Te Morenga, Lisa, 591
Teachman, Jay, 379, 616
Tein, Jenn-Yun, 764
Teixeira, Laetitia, 695
Telch, Michael J., 369
Telford, Amanda, 44
Tempel, Eugene R., 531
Tempel, Melissa Bollow, 449
Temple, Brian W., 443
Temple, Jeff R., 443
Temple, Judy A., 270

Tenenbaum, Harriet R., 291
Teo, Alan R., 505
Teoh, Yee San, 226
Terenzini, Patrick T., 533, 534, 538
Terman, Lewis M., 333, 605
Terracciano, Antonio, 636
Terrocciano, Antonio, 723
Tesch-Römer, Clemens, 766
Tester, June, 313
Thach, Bradley T., 150
Thaler, Howard T., 777
Thaler, Richard H., 413
Theis, Mary Kay, 591
Thelen, Esther, 19
Theodoratou, Evropi, 711
Therman, Eeva, 85
Thiele, Dianne M., 748
Thiemann-Bourque, Kathy, 351
Thoma, Stephen J., 530, 533
Thomaes, Sander, 369
Thomas, Alexander, 187
Thomas, Catherine, 446
Thomas, Dylan, 765
Thomas, G. Darlene, 687
Thomas, Jennifer J., 414
Thomas, Jessica, 268
Thomas, Kathleen M., 167, 226
Thomas, Kecia M., 16
Thomas, Lynn M., 559
Thomas, Michael S. C., 257, 349
Thompson, Clarissa A., 344
Thompson, Elisabeth Morgan, 291
Thompson, Margaret, 326
Thompson, Marilyn, 275
Thompson, Melissa Emery, 552
Thompson, Paul D., 714
Thompson, Paul M., 416, 417
Thompson, Ross A., 184, 195, 255
Thompson, Russell, 604
Thomsen, Michael, 316
Thornberg, Robert, 388
Thornburg, Kathy R., 262
Thornton, Arland, 568
Thornton, Laura, 414
Thorpe, Susannah K. S., 507
Thorslund, Mats, 695
Thorson, James A., 694
Thrasher, Angela D., 735
Thuné-Boyle, Ingela C. V., 619
Thurber, James, 349
Tian, Moqian, 321
Tierney, John, 593
Tiertz, Werner, 716
Tikotzky, Liat, 135, 136, 183
Tilburg, Theo van, 738
Tilmont, Edward M., 691
Timperio, Anna, 44
Timpson, Nicholas J., 315
Tishkoff, Sarah A., 15
Tobin, Eugene M., 538, 539
Todd, Peter M., 556
Toga, Arthur W., 416, 417
Tojo, Yoshikuni, 329
Tokunaga, Robert S., 442
Tol, Donald van, 774
Tolman, Deborah L., 422
Tolstrup, Janne Schurmann, 18
Tomakski, Przemyslaw, 134
Tomaselli, Keyan, 250

Tomasello, Michael, 60, 170, 173, 176, 219, 296
Tomasik, Martin, 766
Tomblin, J. Bruce, 78
Tomenson, Barbara, 18
Tomer, Adrian, 763
Tomkins, Susannah, 588
Tonn, Jessica L., 405
Tonyan, Holli A., 266, 267
Toporek, Bryan, 313
Torralva, Teresa, 604
Torres-Vigil, Isabel, 670, 717
Torrone, Elizabeth, 424
Toth, Sheree L., 238, 239, 324
Tottenham, Nim, 199
Tough, Paul, 452
Toumbourou, John W., 411
Toutain, Stéphanie, 108
Townsend, Jean, 669
Towsley, Sara, 189
Traeen, Bente, 421
Trautwein, Ulrich, 549
Treas, Judith, 639
Treiman, Donald J., 351
Tremblay, Angelo, 495
Tremblay, Mark S., 315
Tremblay, Richard E., 173, 207, 297
Trends in Math and Science Study (TIMMS), 356, 357
Trenholm, Christopher, 473
Trent, Jason, 732, 733
Trentacosta, Christopher, 181
Trevisan, Michael S., 347
Treyvaud, Karli, 114
Trickett, Penelope K., 186, 402, 408, 424
Trisko, Jenna, 744
Trojanowski, John Q., 710
Troll, Lillian E., 731
Trommsdorff, Gisela, 279, 296
Trompeter, Susan E., 582
Tronick, Edward Z., 17, 134, 191
Troseth, Georgene L., 174, 291
Truman, Jennifer L., 672
Trundle, Kathy Cabe, 265
Truog, Robert D., 772
Trussardi, Anna Noemi, 328
Trzesniewski, Kali H., 370, 447, 448, 473, 635
Tsai, Li-Huei, 714
Tsai, Ming-Chang, 640
Tsao, Feng-Ming, 176
Tsethlikai, Monica, 343, 348
Tsui, Amy, 580
Tucker-Drob, Elliot M., 439
Tudge, Jonathan R. H., 198, 227, 282
Tuisku, Virpi, 481
Tulewicz, E. M., 326
Tullb, Matthew T., 238
Tulsky, James A., 771
Tulviste, Peeter, 14
Tun, Patricia A., 609
Turiel, Elliot, 296, 391, 392, 528
Turkheimer, Eric, 383, 604, 609
Turnbull, Malcolm, 449
Turner, Heather A., 375, 383, 387
Turner, Michael G., 507
Turner, R., 260

Turner, Tina, 670
Turner, Val D., 392
Tversky, Amos, 705
Twenge, Jean M., B-5, 549
Twisk, Jos W. R., 311
Tye-Myrray, Nancy, 703
Tyler, Michael D., 172
Tyler-Smith, C., 72
Tyring, Stephen K., 501
Tyrrell, David A., 616
Tyson, Diana F., 446
Tyson, Rebecca, 387, 562
Tzeng, Shih-Jay, 333

U. S. Bureau of Labor Statistics, 739, 742
U. S. Census Bureau, 740, 765
U. S. Department of Health and Human Resources, 147
U. S. Department of Transportation, 683
Uchakin, Peter, 496
Uchida, Shusaku, 17
Uchikoshi, Yuuko, 268
Uddin, Monica, 474
Uduhiri, Kelechi, 110
Ueda, Tomomi, 722
Uekermann, J., 48
Uhlenberg, Peter, 744
Uijtdewilligen, Léonie, 311
Ulber, Julia, 170
Ulrich, Pamela V., 497, 671
Umana-Taylor, Adriana J., 467
Umberson, Debra, 643, 677–678
UN Stats, 545
Unberson, Debra, 647
UNICEF, A-7, 114, 115f, 144p, 148
Uniken Venema, Monica M. A., 114
United Nations, 143, 149, 205, 501, 595, 669, 673, 694
United States Department of Justice Bureau of Justice Statistics, 508
Unverzagt, Frederick W., 710
Updegraff, John A., 617
Urbina, Susana, 617
Urhahne, Detlef, 348
U.S. Bureau of Labor Statistics, 547
U.S. Census Bureau, A-4, A-13, 350, 360, 381, 544, 545, 558, 565, 641, 686, 742, 765
U.S. Center for Health Statistics, 580
U.S. Department of Defense, 656
U.S. Department of Health and Human Services, A-7, 229, 236, 267, 300
U.S. Department of Justice Bureau of Justice Statistics, 672
U.S. Department of Labor Statistics, 198
U.S. Pentagon, 716
U.S. Preventive Services Task Force, 584
U.S. Women's Health Initiative, 585
Usher, Barbara, 280
Usita, Paula M., 747
Usman, Anju, 330
Utendale, William T., 295
Uzelac, Sarah M., 430, 431

Vaag, Allan, 16
Vaalbooi, Petrus, 784
Vail, Andy, 327
Vail III, Kenneth E., 765
Vaillant, George E., 724, 784
Vakili, Mahmood, 563
Valbuena, Teresa, 217
Vale, Rachel, 23, 76
Valentino, Kristin, 238, 239
Valiente, Carlos, 462
Vallesi, Antonino, 702
Vallone, Robert, 705
Valsiner, Jaan, 53
Van Duuren, Mike, 349
Van Gelder, Elke, 432, 438
Van Hoof, Anne, 530
Van Horn, Linda, 500
Van Hulle, Carol A., 187, 223, 649
Van Landeghem, Paul, 773
Van Praag, Herman M., 18
Van Puyvelde, Martine, 191
Van Voorhis, Mathew F., 746
Van Yperen, Nico W., 749
Vance, Jennifer L., 774
Vanderborght, Mieke, 174, 291
Vandermeer, Ben, 51
Vandernassen, Griet, 61
Vanderwaal, Curt, 479
VanderWeele, Tyler J., 555
Vandrovcova, Jana, 714
Vanfleteren, Pol, 191
Vansteenkiste, Maarten, 300
Varain, Frances, 612
Vardhana, Pratibashri, 583
Varelas, Panayiotis N., 772, 773
Varga, Colleen M., 61, 251
Varga, Mary Alice, 764
Vargas, Sadako, 267
Varjas, Kris, 443
Varma, Sashank, 328, 329
Varsami, Marianna, 98
Vasyukova, Catherine, 624
Vaughn, Alexandra, 546
Vaughn, Sharon, 331
Veblen, Thorstein, 654
Veenstra, René, 387, 389, 410
Ven, Elsje van der, 506
Vente, Wieke de, 186
Ventura, Stephanie J., 582
Verbakel, Ellen, 774
Vercelli, Donata, 317
Verdi, Giuseppe, 722
Verdijk, Lex B., 578
Vered, Karen Orr, 312
Vereijken, Beatrix, 138, 141
Verhelst, Werner, 191
Vernooij-Dassen, Myrra J., 774
Verona, Sergiu, 196
Véronneau, Marie-Hélène, 447, 469
Verschuure, Hans, 580
Vescovo, Elena, 134
Vetró, Ágnes, 17
Vetter, Céline, 404
Veyrac, Alexandra, 321, 626
Vianna, Eduardo, 526
Vieno, Alessio, 464
Vignoles, Vivian L., 566
Vijver, Fons J. R. van de, 375, 553
Vikan, Arne, 530

Villar, Feliciano, 721
Vincent, Lynn, 767
Vinck, Bart, 191
Viner, Jane C., 220
Viner, Russell M., 403, 498, 499
Vio, Claudio, 325
Vioque, Jesus, 111
Virji-Babul, et al, 162
Virnig, Beth A., 102
Vissers, Kris C., 774
Viswanathan, Mythili, 261
Vitale, Susan, 83
Vitaro, Frank, 385
Viteri, Fernando E., 413
Vitiello, Benedetto, 327
Vittrup, Brigitte, 301
Viviana, A., 61
Vo, Alexander H., 430
Voeten, Marinus, 388
Vogel, Gretchen, 73
Vogel, Ineke, 580
Vogel, Lauren, 768
Voland, Eckart, 207
Volders, Pieter-Jan, 69
Volein, Agnes, 185
Volkwein-Caplan, Karin A. E., 694
Volmer, Judith, 659
Volz-Sidiropoulou, Eftychia, 708
Vonderheid, Susan C., 104
Vongerichten, Anna, 221
Voorpostel, Marieke, 652
Voosen, Paul, 714
Vos, Theo, 597
Voss, Michelle W., 719
Vouloumanos, Athena, 169
Vries, Hein de, 288
Vries, Linda S. de, 114
Vygotsky, Lev, 14, 52–53, 248–252, 256, 264, 272, 305, 341, 343, 347, 348, 357, 397, 526

Wachs, Theodore D., 172
Wada, Keiko, 578
Wade, Jennifer, 765
Wadsworth, Martha E., 562
Wagenaar, Karin, 584
Wagland, Paul, 184
Wagner, Anthony D., 17
Wagner, H. Ryan Farmer, 650
Wagner, Jenny, 549, 637, 748, 749
Wagner, Katie, 257
Wagner, Laura, 175
Wagner, Paul A., 471
Wahab, Lee, 765
Wahlstrom, Dustin, 130
Wahlstrom, Kyla L., 405
Wahrendorf, Morten, 737
Waitzer, Elana, 121
Wake, Melissa, 135
Walberg, Herbert J., 449
Walden, Tedra A., 164, 182
Walderenström, Ulla, 103
Waldfogel, Jane, 382, 383, 613
Waldinger, Robert J., 744
Walk, Richard D., 164
Walker, Alan, 743
Walker, Dale, 351
Walker, Lawrence J., 530
Wallace, Lora Ebert, 383

Wallace, R. B., 710
Wallace, Stuart R., 220
Wallace, Teri, 331
Wallen, Kim, 284
Waller, Erika M., 474
Walport, Mark, 17
Walsh, Cathal, 710
Walter, Klaudia, 80
Walters, Julie, 311
Walton, Gregory, 524
Wanberg, Karen, 654
Wang, Haidong, 103, 114, 143
Wang, Hua, 552, 639
Wang, Hui-Chung, 187
Wang, Hui-Xin, 714
Wang, Jeff G., 583
Wang, Ji-Guang, 43
Wang, Jing, 414
Wang, Jingyun, 138
Wang, Li, 385
Wang, Min Qi, 218
Wang, Philip S., 505
Wang, Qian, 463, 464
Wang, Qiu, 658
Wang, Richard Y., 408
Wang, Wei, 711
Wang, Wendy, 558
Wang, Xiaowei, 69
Wang, Xueli, 546, 561
Wang, Zhen, 251
Wang, Zhengyan, 385
Wang Qian, 463
Wanner, Brigitte, 385
Wansink, Brian, 316
Waqar-ul-Haq, 406
Ward, Andrew, 594
Ward, Brian W., 512, 717
Ward, Dianne S., 414
Ward, L. Monique, 471
Wardell, Jeffrey D., 513
Wardlaw, Joanna M., 702
Warneken, Felix, 296
Warner, Cody, 642
Warner, Judith, 37
Warren, Charles W., 480
Warren, Kenneth R., 108
Warzinik, Kelly, 649
Washington, Harriet A., 30
Wastesseon, Jonas W., 695
Watanabe, Yoshifum, 17
Waterman, Alan S., 458
Waterman, Sarah, 529
Waters, Patti, 446
Wathen, C. Nadine, 241
Watson, John B., 42, 200, 497
Watson, Julanne, 254
Watson, Ruth, 130
Way, Niobe, 467, 473
Weatherbee, Sarah R., 620
Webb, Elizabeth, 679
Webb, Thomas L., B-5
Webber, Laura, 552
Weber, Ingmar, 468
Webster, Mike M., 201
Webster, Noah J., 638
Wechsler, H., 404
Weed, Keri, 463, 464
Weedon, Michael N., 315
Weegar, Kelly, 207

Weeks, Murray, 349
Weel, Chris van, 774
Weerth, Carolina de, 226
Wei, Si, 722
Weichold, Karina, 410
Weidemann, Gabrielle, 705
Weigand, Stephen D., 711
Weikart, David P., 269
Weikum, Whitney M., 169
Weiler, & Stamatakis, 592
Weiler, Ivan Jeanne, 132
Weinberg, Armin D., 670, 717
Weinberg, M. Katherine, 191
Weindruch, Richard, 692
Weinehall, Lars, 480
Weinstein, Andrea M., 714
Weinstock, Hillard, 424
Weir, David R., 710
Weir, Donald G., 108
Weis, Robert, 442
Weise, David, 765, 766
Weisglas-Kuperus, Nynke, 114
Weiss, 643
Weiss, Heather, 312
Weiss, Nicole H., 238
Weiss, Scott T., 102
Weissenbruch, Mirjam M. van, 584
Weisskirch, Robert S., 567
Weisz, John R., 373
Wel, Frits van, 565, 639, 746
Welk, Gregory J., 312
Weller, Joshua, 705
Wellman, Barry, 552, 639
Wellman, Henry M., 252, 254, 255,
   256
Wen, Xiaoli, 266
Wendelken, Carter, 319, 345
Wenger, Marin R., 642
Wenner, Melinda, 284
Werker, Janet F., 168, 169
Werner, Nicole E., 387
Wertsch, James V., 14
Wesselmann, Eric D., 567
Westenberg, P. Michiel, 319
Westendorp, Rudi G. J., 685
Westerhausen, René, 221
Westerhof, G. J., 722
Weston, Joanna, 747
Wetherell, Julie Loebach, 731
Wetherell, Mark A., 752
Whalley, Lawrence J., 702, 717
Wheeler, Benedict W., 636
Wheeler, Justin, 473
Whelan, Thomas A., 748
Whelchel, Lisa, 301
Whishaw, Ian Q., 220, 224
Whitbourne, Stacey B., 491, 497,
   578
Whitbourne, Susan Krauss, 491, 497,
   544, 546, 548, 578
White, Barry A. B., 270
White, Matthew P., 636
White, Tonya, 130, 506
Whitehead, Kevin A., 467
Whitehouse, Peter, 711
Whiteman, Ronald C., 524
Whiteside-Mansell, et al, 120
White-Traut, Rosemary, 103
Whitfield, John B., 82

Whitfield, Keith E., 14
Whitman, Thomas L., 463, 464
Whitney, Pamela G., 183
Whittle, Sarah, 474
Whittle L., 404
Whitton, Sarah W., 505
Wicher, Camille P., 775
Wicherts, Jelte M., 322
Wichstrøm, Lars, 207, 715
Wickrama, K. A. S., 639
Widom, Cathy Spatz, 239
Wiegand, Benjamin, 135
Wieling, Elizabeth, 371
Wiggins, Jillian Lee, 701
Wiik, Kenneth Aarskaug, 645
Wijdicks, Eelco F. M., 772, 773
Wikström, Anna-Karin, 103
Wilde, Alex, 87
Wilhelm, Kay, 87
Wilhelm, Mark O., 531
Wilhelm, Miriam, 72
Wilke, Arthur E., 330
Wilkerson, Risa, 498
Wilkinson, Mark E., 679
Wilkinson-Lee, Ada M., 472
Williams, Alexis, 218
Williams, D. R., 595
Williams, Jade, 554
Williams, Julie M., 534
Williams, Kirk R., 386, 387, 388, 443
Williams, Kristine N., 626, 672
Williams, Lela Rankin, 188
Williams, Mark, 705
Williams, Michelle K., 567
Williams, Preston, 405
Williams, Scott M., 15
Williams, Shirlan, 553
Williamson, Gail M., 149
Williamson, Rebecca A., 253
Willis, Benjamin L., 672
Willis, Robert J., 739
Wilmhurst, Linda, 380
Wilson, Barbara J., 483
Wilson, David C., 146
Wilson, Kathryn R., 226
Wilson, Kristel, 672
Wilson, Stephan M., 566
Wilson-Simmons, Renée, 472
Wimer, Christopher, 312
Winblad, Bengt, 711
Windsor, Tim D., 736, 739
Wing, Maria R., 690
Wingate, Martha S., 113, 114
Winner, Brooke, 501
Winner, Ellen, 333
Winokar, Herb, 716
Winston, Flaura Koplin, 438
Winter, Suzanne M., 265
Wirth, Robert John, 341
Wiste, Heather J., 711
Witherington, David C., 183
Wittassek, Matthias, 27
Wittchen, Hans-Ulrich, 503, 504
Wittig, Michele A., 467
Witztum, Eliezer, 783
Woessmann, Ludger, 356, 444
Wohl, Michael J. A., 705
Wohlenberg, Kelly M., 774
Wolak, Janis, 441, 443

Wolchik, Sharlene A., 764
Wolf, Marshall A., 59
Wolf, Norman S., 694
Wolke, Dieter, 346, 388
Woloshin, Steven, 596
Wong, Iris Wai-yin, 463
Wong, Paul T. P., 763
Wong, Sowan, 561
Wong, Stephanie Siu-fong, 463
Wood, Amanda G., 220
Wood, Dana, 301
Wood, Jeffrey J., 373
Wood, Joanne M., 679
Wood, Wendy, 5, 279, 291, 293, 294
Woodard, Jarilyn, 295
Woodard, John L., 695
Woodley, Michael A., 605
Woodruff, Travey J., 317
Woods, Tiger, 334
Woodward, Amanda L., 257
Wooley, Jacqueline D., 345
Woolgar, Alexandra, 604
Woollett, Katherine, 626
Working Group on Obesity in China
   (WGOC), 315
World Bank, 148, 149
World Health Organization, 144,
   233, 315, 422, 505, 587, 589,
   687, 711
Worthy, Darrell A., 723
Wosje, Karen S., 217
Wrangham, Richard, 552
Wrangham, Richard W., 552
Wright, Alexi A., 769
Wright, Frank Lloyd, 722
Wright, Margaret O'Dougherty, 620
Wright, Matthew W., 13, 69
Wright, Stephen C., 551
Wroe, Martha, 721
Wrosch, Carsten, 5, 586
Wrzus, Cornelia, 748, 749
Wu, Albert W., 718
Wu, Jing Jing, 711
Wu, Pai-Lu, 519
Wurm, Susanne, 766
Wurr, Adrian J., 176
Wynne-Edwards, 119
Wysocki, Karen, 51

Xia, Jin, 703, 704
Xiang, Zongping, 269
Xiao, Haijun, 593
Xiao, Qian, 713, 716
Xie, Yu, 568, 654
Xu, Fen, 255
Xu, L. Z., 102
Xu, Weili, 714
Xu, Xiao, 563
Xu, Yaoying, 282, 283
Xue, Qian-Li, 703, 704

Yadav, Priyanka, 442
Yaffe, Kristine, 703, 704
Yahya-Graison, Emilie Aït, 80
Yamada, Hiroshi, 527, 580
Yamada, Janet, 139
Yamagata, Hirotaka, 17
Yamaguchi, Susumu, 370
Yang, Rongwang, 326

Yaniv, Ilan, 654
Yap, Marie B. H., 474
Yardley, Lucy, B-5
Yarosz, Donald J., 268
Yasuda, Keigo, 578
Yau, Matthew K., 708
Ybarra, Michele L., 441
Yeh, Hsin-Te, 277
Yerkes, Robert Mearns, 604
Yesavage, Jerome A., 524, 625
Yeung, Dannii Yuen-lan, 639
Yeung, W. Jean, 383
Yik, Michelle, 723
Yoffe, Paula, 591
Yom-Tov, Elad, 468
Yoon, John D., 774
Yore, Larry D., 625
Yoshikawa, Hirokazu, 262
Young, Alford A., 113
Young, Elizabeth, 403
Young, John K., 415
Young, Ralph, 743
Young, Ruth, 743
Young, T. Kue, 591
Youth Risk Behavior Survey, 474
Yovsi, Relindis, 201
Yu, Ruoh Rong, 654
Yu, Xiao-ming, 421

Yu, Yau-Hua, 701
Yücel, Murat, 474
Yuile, Amy, 388
Yusof, Sufiah, 334

Z. Elizabeth M., 650
Zaccai, Julia, 713
Zachry, Anne H., 140, 150
Zagoory-Sharon, Orna, 121, 205
Zahn-Waxler, Carolyn, 280
Zak, Paul J., 295
Zalenski, Robert, 57, 769
Zalewski, Maureen, 276
Zamarro, Gema, 739
Zamboanga, Byron L., 567
Zane, Jazmin I., 387
Zani, Bruna, 421
Zapf, Jennifer A., 259
Zarate, Carlos A. Jr., 505
Zarite, Steven, 567
Zaslavsky, Alan M., 503
Zatorre, Robert J., 321, 626
Zautra, Alex J., 619
Zavattini, Giulio Cesare, 648
Zeanah, Charles H., 196, 197
Zeeb, Hajo, 582
Zeggini, Eleftheria, 315
Zehr, Mary Ann, 361, 547

Zeiders, Marcel, 473, 474
Zeidner, Moshe, 593
Zeifman, Debra M., 116, 117, 134, 137
Zeintl, Melanie, 704
Zelazo, Philip David, 222
Zeldin, Leslie P., 218
Zelli, Arnaldo, 300, 301
Zentall, Shanon R., 278
Zenter, Marcel, 189, 190, 293
Zera, Chloe A., 102
Zerger, Suzanne, 240
Zhang, Baohui, 769
Zhang, Chenshu, 327
Zhang, Jijun, 449
Zhang, Lei, 713, 716
Zhang, Li, 185
Zhang, Suhan, 326
Zhang, Xin, 639
Zhang, Yiyun, 277
Zhao, Kexiang, 713, 716
Zhao, Qiuhong, 501
Zhao, Shuheng, 249
Zhao, Yongjun, 233
Zhao, Zhengyan, 326
Zhen, Zonglei, 321
Zhou, Dongming, 701

Zhou, Jieming, 658
Zhu, Fengchuan, 563
Zhu, Qi, 321
Zhu, Weimo, 312
Zhu, Ying, 185
Zhu, Zengrong, 73
Zhuo, Y. M., 102
Zickuhr, Kathryn, 440
Zieger, Amanda, 410
Zigmond, Naomi, 331
Zijlmans, Maartje, 226
Zimmer, Carl, 69
Zimmer-Gembeck, Melanie J., 410, 470
Zimmerman, Camilla, 731
Zimmerman, Frederick J., 174
Zimmerman, Marc, 262
Zimmerman-Gembeck, Melanie J., 458–459
Zimprich, Daniel, 635
Zinman, Guy, 692
Ziol-Guest, Kathleen M., 382
Zmyj, Norbert, 138, 169
Zolotor, Adam J., 613
Zoltnick, Cheryl, 240
Zorzi, Marco, 328
Zosuls, Kristina M., 294
Zubrick, Stephen R., 106

Subject Index

Abecedarian, 269
Abnormality, 324, 336. *See also* Birth defects
Abortion
  in cases of birth defects, 85, 88p, 111–112
  gendered views of, 530
  legality of, 580
  rate for teens, 422
  reduction in adolescent crime due to, 478
  in Romania, 196
  sex selection by, 71
  spontaneous abortion, 85, 95, 422
  in the U.S., 501, 575
Absent grief, 779, 783, 784, 786
Abuse. *See also* Bullying; Child maltreatment; Cyberbullying; Domestic abuse; Sexual abuse; Spousal abuse
  between cohabiting couples, 558f
  of frail elderly, 752–753, 753p, 756, 757
  impact on adulthood, 36
Abusive head trauma, 133
Academic achievement. *See also* Achievement tests; International tests
  of bullies and victims, 388
  childhood overweight related to, 315
  of children in military families, 375
  of children with ADHD, 325, 327
  correlation to SES, 341, 351, 382–383
  divorce affecting, 381, 385
  employment affecting, 460, 460f
  factors correlated with high achievement, 452
  family function related to, 378, 395
  foundation in repetition, 343
  lack of behavior control affecting, 346
  learning disabilities affecting, 328–329
  marijuana use affecting, 481
  maternal education affecting, 341, 351, 351f
  in middle school, 445–446, 453
  parent-adolescent relationships affecting, 463
  personality's relationship with, 549
  physical activity affecting, 311
  psychological control and physical punishment affecting, 300
  realistic self-perception aiding, 369
  in secondary education, 454
  sexual abuse affecting, 424
  sleep deprivation inhibiting, 404–405, 404f, 404p, 405f, 411

social context affecting, 341
stereotype threat affecting, 524–525
teacher/family expectations affecting, 352–353
of video game players, 441–442
Acceleration, 333
Acceptance, 782
Accident autopsy, 235
Accident hump, 507
Accidents, 235, 507, 684–685, 685f, 765f
Accommodation, 46–47, 46f, 156, 162
ACE inhibitors, 109t
Achievement tests. *See also* International tests
  Advanced Placement, 449
  efficacy of, 320–321, 322, 323, 336, 397
  high-stakes tests, 449–450, 450f, 454
  SAT and ACT, 449
Acquaintances, 638–639, 638p, 641
Active apprenticeship, 52
Active euthanasia, 773, 774, 778
Active labor, 100
Active play, 283–284, 283p, 303
Activities. *See also* Employment; Exercise; Physical activity; Sexual activity
  activities of daily life (ADLs), 750, 756, 757
  of adolescents, 740f
  adulthood, 739f, 740f
  around the home, 739–740, 740f, 743, 757
  of children, 227, 282f
  community encouragement, 498, 592
  of the frail elderly, 750, 750t
  happiness, intelligence, and health correlated with, 736, 737
  instrumental activities of daily life (ADLs), 750, 750t
  in late adulthood, 737–743, 737f, 738p, 739f, 739p, 740f, 742f, 742p, 757
  political activism, 742–743, 742f, 757
  religious involvement, 742, 742p, 743, 757
  volunteer work, 739, 739f, 739p, 743, 757
Activities of daily life (ADLs), 750, 756, 757
Activity theory, 736, 737, 757
Acute illness, 686, 688
Adaptive cognition, 46f, 156–157, 157p, 157t, 609
Add Health, 563
Addiction. *See also* Alcoholism; Drug use and abuse; Smoking; Tobacco

to drugs, 480, 510
effect on marriages, 560
genetic/environmental contribution to, 82, 90
girls' vulnerability to, 479
to video games, chat rooms, Internet gambling, 441–442, 441f, 468, 487
Additive heredity, 78, 90
ADHD. *See* Attention-deficit/hyperactivity disorder (ADHD)
Adolescence. *See also* Puberty
  activities, 740f
  adoptive parents' response to, 648
  attachment, 192t
  attraction of extremes, 399
  brain development, 416–419, 416f, 419p, 426, 430, 436, 438, 487
  chronic illnesses in, 492t
  cognitive learning stages, 46f
  conformity in, 41p
  deaths from top three causes, 495t
  decision making, 436–437
  diet deficiencies, 413–414, 414p, 416, 426, 487
  digital natives, 440–444, 440p, 441f, 442p, 454, 487
  drug use and abuse, 405, 408, 410, 414, 415, 422, 446, 464, 478–484, 479p, 480f, 480p, 482f, 483p, 487, 510f, 519
  education during, 444–453, 445f, 445p, 448p, 453t, 487, 537f
  egocentrism of, 430–431, 430p
  enrollees in college, 262f
  Erikson's stages of development, 40t, 41
  Freud's stages of development, 39, 40t
  growth and maturation, 411–416, 412f, 414p, 415p, 426, 487
  health habits, 311
  hearing loss, 579–580
  identity formation, 457–462, 458p, 459p, 460f, 460p, 461f, 461p, 485, 487, 543
  importance of physical appearance, 730
  logic and self in, 430–434, 430p, 431p, 432f, 433f, 433p, 487
  mental health problems, 29, 324, 336, 504, 506
  motor vehicle crashes, 234, 418, 438, 439f, 483, 623
  nearsightedness, 579
  need for guidance, 374
  nutrition, 426
  obesity rates in U.S., 315f

peer relationships, 409–411, 410p, 439f, 466–473, 466p, 468p, 470f, 470p, 485, 487
pregnancy during, 58, 115, 147t, 410, 419, 422–423, 423p, 426, 464, 472, 489, 501, 647
puberty, 399, 401–411, 402p, 404f, 404p, 406p, 407f, 410p, 426, 487
relationships with adults, 462–466, 462p, 464p, 465f, 472, 473, 485, 487, 560
response to death, 764–765, 765f
sadness and anger in, 473–478, 474p, 475f, 476p, 477p
sex drive, 60
sexual activity, 25, 25f, A-18
sexual maturation, 419–426, 420f, 420p, 421p, 423p, 424p, 425f, 426, 487
smoking behaviors, 593, A-19
suicide rates, A-21
synthetic-conventional faith of, 531
time management of, 518–519
two modes of thinking, 434–440, 435f, 436p, 439f, 448, 487, 518, 520–521, 521f, 522
volunteer work, 739f
Adolescence-limited offenders, 477, 485, 550
Adolescent egocentrism, 430–431, 430p
Adolescent-adult relationships, 462–466, 462p, 464p, 465f, 485
Adoption
  difficulties of, 241
  of institutionalized children, 196, 196p, 226
  interethnic adoption, 648–649, 648p
  of maltreated children, 240p, 241, 242
  open adoption, 648
  optimal placement time, 185
Adoptive families, 375, 376t, 379, 384
Adoptive parents, 648–649, 648p, 661
Adrenal glands, 402, 402f, 411, 426
Adulthood. *See also* Death and dying; Emerging adulthood; Fathers; Late adulthood; Men; Mothers; Parents; Women
  accumulation of and response to stressors, 615–620, 615p, 618f, 620f
  activities, 739f, 740f
  attachment, 192t
  changes in eyes, 82
  chronic illnesses in, 492t

components of intelligence, 608–614, 609p, 610t, 611p, 614p, 628, 663
deaths from top three causes, 495t
decreasing strength during, 491
defined, 6, 573
drug use and abuse, 510f
echoes of childhood family life in, 379
events of, 573
expert cognition, 621–627, 622p, 623f, 626p, 627f
family bonds, 639–641, 639p, 640p, 641, 661
filial responsibility, 745, 749, 751, 757
formal operational stage, 41, 45p
Freud's stages of development, 39–40, 40t
generativity, 646–652, 646p, 647p, 648p, 649p, 652p, 653f, 654–660, 655f, 656f, 657p, 658p, 659p, 661, 663
health habits, 586–589, 586t, 587p, 588f, 590f, 591–594, 591p, 592f, 592p, 600, 663
identity achievement, 543
intelligence, 603–608, 604p, 606f, 628, 663
intimacy of friends and family, 637–641, 638p, 639p, 640p, 661, 663
intimacy of romantic partners, 641–646, 641p, 642f, 642p, 643t, 644p, 645p, 661, 663
language learning in, 260
maturation of cognition/ perception, 130
measurements of health, 594–599, 594p, 595f, 596p, 598p, 600, 663
midlife crisis, 633–634, 633p
motor vehicle crashes, 438, 439f
optimization with compensation, 620–621, 621p
peer influence in, 439f
personality development, 631–637, 632t, 633p, 634p, 635p, 636f, 637p, 661, 663
postformal thought, 517–528, 521f
postponement of, 489
relationships with adolescents, 462–466, 462p, 464p, 465–466, 465f, 485
response to death, 765–766, 766p, 786
selective cognitive gains and losses, 615–617, 615p, 616f, 618f, 619–627, 620f, 621p, 622p, 623f, 626p, 627f, 628, 663
senescence, 576f, 576p, 578–580, 578p, 579p, 600, 663
sense of well-being, 733
sexual-reproductive system, 580–586, 581p, 584p, 585p, 600, 663

short-term changes, 125
suicide rates, A-21
thinking in, 520–521, 521f
voting rates, 742f
Advance directives, 776–777, 778
Advanced Placement classes, 448–449, 454
Advanced Placement test, 449
Advertising, 591
Aesthetic sense, 721–722, 721p, 722p
Affection. *See* Intimacy; Love; Romantic love
Affiliation. *See* Intimacy
Affirmation of life
diversity of reactions to death, 783, 783p, 786
grief, 778–780, 786
mourning, 780–783, 780p, 781p, 782p, 786
practical applications, 783–785, 785p, 786
resilience, 784
Affordances, 162–165, 164p, 167, 178
Afghanistan, A-3
Africa
breast-feeding in, A-7
college graduates in, 535–536
co-sleeping in, 135
c-sections in, 102f
elder care in, 751
family relationships, 566
incidence of anemia, 413
incidence of neural tube defects, 108
infant day care in, 207
infant mortality in, 143p
languages spoken by school children, 359
left-handedness in, 221
life expectancy, 598
low birthweight in, 115, 115f
marriage in, 559
obesity in, 589
onset of puberty, 406
percentage of young adolescents not in school, 482f
physical activity in schools, 353
secular trend in, 408
special education in, 333
sports in, 312
stunting of children in, 148t
view of non-heterosexual behavior, 471
vision heritability in, 83
African Americans
average daily exposure to video in U.S., 286f
average height of children, 216
breast-feeding by, A-7
caregiving style, 289
childhood obesity, 216, 315f, 316
children's activities by socioeconomic class, 282f
communication of romantic encounters to parents, 472
death in a hospice, 771
diabetes among, 690

diagnosed with ADHD, 326
divorce rate, 643
elder care, 752
high school graduation rate, 450f
incidence of low birthweights among, 115
incidence of weathering, 617
level of education, 537f
life expectancy, 617, 691, 735f, 737, 747f
obesity rate and income, 590f, 591
onset of puberty, 406, 410
population of, A-4
prejudice against in U.S., 524
punishment of poor behavior, 301
remarriage of women, 645
self-esteem in adolescence, 473
sexual activity of adolescents, 421
single-parent families, 380
smoking behaviors in high school, A-19
sterilization of adults, 580
stratification of, 734, 735
suicide rates, 742, A-21
in U.S. workforce, 656, 656f
use of IVF, 583–584
Age. *See also* Adolescence; Adulthood; Children; Early childhood; Emerging adulthood; Infancy (first two years); Late adulthood; Middle childhood
advantages/disadvantages in workplace, 656, 657
anxiety disorders related to, 505
attachment related to, 193
attitude toward bullying related to, 387
attitudes toward high self-esteem influences by, 370
birthweight related to, 113, 122
cancer deaths by, 586t
changes in thinking related to, 520–521, 521f
chronic illnesses associated with, 492t
of college students, 536
divorce related to, 643
eating habits associated with, 413
fertility by, A-20
gamete production affected by, 84
hearing affected by, 579, 579p
homeostasis related to, 495
important life events related to, 494f
incidence of multiple births related to, 75, 76f
intelligence affected by, 604–608, 604p, 606f, 612–613, 614, 628
marriages affected by, 560
moral values related to, 529, 531
parameters for stages, 493
personality affected by, 635, 635f, 635p
physician-assisted suicide related to, 776f
prenatal development affected by, 95t

of puberty, 406–409, 406p, 407f
reduction of sperm count, 583
self-esteem in adolescence related to, 473
senescence, 576f, 576p, 578–580, 578p, 579p
size of social network affected by, 639
stratification of society by, 736
suicide rates by, A-21
trends in drug use, 479
use of coping mechanisms, 618f
vision affected by, 82, 579
weight gain associated with, 500
Age discrimination, 27. *See also* Ageism
Age in place, 740, 743, 754, 756, 757
Age of viability, 97, 97p, 98
Age periods, 6t
Age spots, 689p, 690
Age structure, 12f
Ageism
coining of term, 721
defined, 667, 676
effects of, 597, 669–670, 670f, 676, 678, 681–682, 696, 706, 710, 718, 736, 737, 743
forms of, 734
pervasiveness of, 668, 669, 676
stereotype of the elderly, 667–673, 668p, 670f, 670p, 671f, 672f, 696, 700, 754
words of, 709–710
Ageist elders, 669–670, 670f, 670p, 676
Aggression. *See also* Abuse; Bullying; Child maltreatment; Corporal punishment; Cyberbullying; Spousal abuse
of adolescents, 446, 464
boys' expression of, 280
in early childhood, 549–550
of early-maturing boys, 410
effect of high/low self-esteem, 369
effects of sexual abuse, 424
egocentrism associated with, 430
in emerging adulthood, 549–550, 569
girls' expression of, 280
of preschoolers, 297–298, 297p, 302, 303
as result of physical punishment, 299, 301, 302
as result of psychological control, 300
types of, 297p, 297t
video games promoting, 441
Aggressive-rejected children, 386, 387
Agility, 578, 578p
Aging
belief in hot hand related to, 705–706, 706f
of the brain, 683–684, 700–703, 702f, 726
calorie restriction affecting, 691–692, 691p, 692p

cause of death, 685–686, 685f
cellular aging, 690–693, 690p, 691p, 692p
chronic and acute illnesses of, 686, 696
compression of morbidity, 686–688, 688f, 696
Hutchinson-Gilford syndrome, 689
primary and secondary, 684–686, 696
self-image, 730
of senses, 681–682, 681p, 681t, 682p
theories of, 688–693, 689p, 690p, 691p, 692p, 696
Agreeableness
outlook on life, 659
as personality trait, 634, 635, 635f, 636, 637, 661
AIDS, 714
Ainsworth, Mary, 192, 193
Alaska, 282–283
Alcohol
adolescent crime associated with, 478
adolescent use of, 418, 485
adult abuse of, 288–289, 587, 600, 663
birthweight affected by, 115, 122
breast-feeding and, 146
as cause of infertility, 583
cognition affected by, 717, 718
contribution to abusive relationships, 563
early-maturing children's risk of using, 410
emerging adults' use of, 510, 511, 512, 513, 522
girls' consumption of, 480
harm to adolescent users, 481
national differences in use, 479
non-heterosexual teens use of, 471
prenatal development affected by, 105, 105–106, 105p, 107f, 108, 109t, 110–111, 110t
smoking associated with, 110
as a teratogen, 108
use by age, 510f
use in U.S., 480f
Alcoholism
as avoidant coping method, 616
effects of, 588, 615
genetic/environmental contribution to, 82, 90
in late adulthood, 719
preventative measures, 83
recovery, 593–594
unemployment contributing to, 654
All Souls Day, 763
Alleles. See also Genes
acceleration of aging and death, 690
additive heredity, 78
for alcoholism, 82
for asthma, 317
as carriers of disease, 85–86
causing sickle-cell anemia, 87

contribution to childhood obesity, 315
controlling language acquisition, 259
for cystic fibrosis, 87
defined, 68
of dopamine receptor gene, 78
for eye formation, 82
genetic diversity associated with, 70, 76, 90
for longevity, 689
for neural-tube defects, 108
single-nucleotide polymorphisms, 69
Allergies, 217, 313, 336
Allocare, 205–207, 206p, 206t, 209
Allostasis
function of, 493, 495–496, 500, 514, 571, 576, 600, 616
interaction with organ reserve and homeostasis, 496
protection of brain, 577
Allostatic load
avoidance increasing, 617, 619
behaviors increasing, 586
cancer related to, 586
cognitive loss due to, 616
in emerging adulthood, 496
increase with age, 496, 576, 580, 600, 684
measurement of, 605, 685
racism increasing, 735
reduction of, 676
sickle-cell anemia increasing, 598
stress increasing, 576, 628
Alpha-fetoprotein (AFP), 111–112
Alternative elder care, 754–756, 755p
Altruism, 724
Alzheimer, Alois, 711
Alzheimer disease (AD)
bilingual brain's resistance to, 260
brain of sufferer, 711p, 712p
causes of, 711–712
dominant genetic disorder, 86
incidence of, 674, 710f
progression of, 726, 726f
symptoms of, 716
treatment of, 692
American Academy of Pediatrics, 103
American College of Obstetricians and Gynecologists Committee on Obstetric Practice, 104
American Council of Physicians, 596
American Society of Human Genetics, 15
Americans with Disabilities Act, 682
Amphetamines, 480f
Amygdala
development of, 220, 426
effect of pubertal hormones, 416
in frontal lobe disorders, 712
functions of, 219f, 224, 227, 242, A-2
maturation in adolescence, 416
Amyloid precursor protein (APP), 712
Anal personality, 200
Anal stage, 39–40, 40t, 199–200, 200p

Analytic intelligence, 610, 610t, 611–612, 614, 628
Analytical thought, 435f, 436–438, 436p, 440, 454
Androgens, 403
Androgyny, 294
Andropause, 585–586, 663
Anemia, 413
Anencephaly, 108
Angelman syndrome, 81
Anger
in adolescence, 476–478, 476p, 477p, 485, 487
brain growth enabling, 185
decline in adulthood, 733
of early-maturing boys, 410
emphasis on regulation of in Puerto Rico, 278
girls' expression, 280
as learned response, 182–183, 184, 209
results of in adolescence, 419
as stage of dying, 769, 782
in toddlers, 183
Animals, 71, 71p
Animism, 246, 248–249, 272
Anoxia, 116, 122
Anterior cingulate gyrus, 185
Antibodies, 146, 147t
Anti-oxidants, 697, 715, 717
Antipathy, 296–297, 297t, 302, 305
Antisocial behavior
in adolescence, 404
caused by behavioral teratogens, 105
in early childhood, 284, 296–297, 297p, 297t, 305, 374
as learned behavior, 298, 374
Antithesis, 525
Anxiety
in adolescence, 549
effects of ageism, 668, 704
in emerging adulthood, 502, 503–504
HPA abnormalities causing, 402
in late adulthood, 700, 709, 716, 726
memory affected by, 704
psychological control and physical punishment causing, 300, 301
reduction of testosterone, 585
sleep deprivation causing, 404
sources of in early childhood, 289
treatment of, 722
Anxiety disorders
in emerging adulthood, 514, 571
hikikomori, 505–506, 506p
obsessive-compulsive disorder, 505
post-traumatic stress disorder, 226, 238, 505, 505p
social phobia, 505
Apgar, Virginia, 101, 626
Apgar scale, 101, 101t, 105, 116, 122
ApoE gene, 689, 712
Appearance. See Physical appearance

Appetite, 239t
Apprenticeship in thinking, 52
Aptitude, 320, 336
Aptitude tests, 320–322, 321f, 323, 336
Arab states, 482f
Argentina, 453t
Art education, 353, 354f
Arteriosclerosis, 715
Arthritis, 492, 497, 592, 596, 686, 687
Artistic expression, 232–233, 721–722, 721p, 722p
Asia. See also specific Asian country
breast-feeding in, A-7
cognition in, 527
college graduates in, 535–536
co-sleeping in, 135
early childhood play in, 283
elder care in, 751
funeral customs in, 763
incidence of anemia, 413
incidence of neural-tube defects, 108
incidence of twins, 75
low birthweights in, 114, 115f
norms for sibling roles, 640
obesity in, 589
percentage of young adolescents not in school, 482f
preferred sex of children, 71–72
scores on international tests, 356, 356t
secular trend in, 408
smoking in, 479
special education in, 333
synchrony in, 191
view of left hand in, 221
vision heritability in, 83
Asian Americans
average height of children, 216
breast-feeding by, A-7
caregiving style, 289
cognition of, 527
diabetes among, 690
divorce rate, 643
education of, 360, 450f
incidence of childhood obesity, 216
level of education, 537f
life expectancy by SES, 735f
mortality rate, 594
obesity among, 591
onset of puberty, 406, 410
parent-adolescent relationships, 462
punishment of poor behavior, 301
self-esteem in adolescence, 473
suicide rates, A-21
in U.S. workforce, 656, 656f
Asperger syndrome, 329
Assimilation, 46, 46–47, 46f, 156, 162
Assisted reproductive technology (ART), 71, 75–76, 77, 90, 115, 583, 586, 600
Assisted-living facilities, 754–755, 756, 757
Associative play, 283

Asthma
  in adolescence, 412
  childhood overweight related to, 315
  defined, 317
  development of in first-born children, 29
  effect of breast-feeding, 146, 147t, 336
  in emerging adulthood, 492
  in middle childhood, 317–318, 317f, 317p, 336, 397
  socioeconomic effect on incidence of, 229–230
Attachment
  between adopted children and parents, 648
  anxiety disorders associated with problems of, 506
  behavior associated with, 299
  classifications of, 193–194
  comorbidity of, 325
  contact-maintaining, 199, 205
  defined, 191
  disorganized attachment, 193, 193t, 194, 209
  effect on bereavement, 783
  effect on intimate relationships in adulthood, 557
  effect on temperament, 188–189
  with fathers, 197
  of foster children, 650, 651
  impact on adulthood, 36
  insecure attachment, 299, 387
  insecure-avoidant attachment, 193, 193t, 209
  insecure-resistant/ambivalent attachment, 193, 193t, 209
  measurement of, 194–195, 194p
  patterns of, 191–192, 193t
  predictors of type, 195t
  problem prevention, 196–197
  proximity-seeking, 199, 205
  reactive attachment disorder, 196, 196p, 226, 648
  response to infants' cry associated with, 50
  secure attachment, 193t, 209, 299
  sex leading to, 502
  signs of, 192–193
  social setting and, 195t, 196–197
  stages of, 192t
  as survival technique, 205
Attempted suicide. See Parasuicide
Attention, 319
Attention-deficit/hyperactivity disorder (ADHD)
  brain patterns associated with, 48, 223
  diagnosis of, 325–326
  DSM-5 criteria, A-14
  education for, 335, 397
  effect of low birthweight, 114
  perseveration and, 223
  possible causes of, 105, 108, 226, 230
  problems associated with, 336
  sex differences, 281f
  special education for, 333

  treatment of, 325p, 326–327, 336
  use of therapy dogs, 23
Attitude, 695, 696
Auditory cortex, 130, 130f, 219f, A-2
Australia
  beliefs about death, 781
  cohabitation in, 556
  demographics, 673
  high-stakes tests in, 449
  parent-adolescent relationships, 463
  play in childhood in, 312
  population of children and elders, A-3
  rate of self-harm in puberty, 411
  scaffolding in, 250
  scores on international tests, 356t, A-16
  use of HRT in, 585
  view of pride in, 370
Austria
  birth of blind babies, 106
  co-sleeping in, 136f
  euthanasia in, 773, 773f
  low birthweights in, 115f
  PISA scores, 453t, A-16
  punishment of poor behavior in, 301
Authoritarian parenting, 287, 287t, 288, 303, 409, 462, 466
Authoritative parenting, 287t, 288, 303, 462, 466, 584
Autism spectrum disorders (ASD)
  DSM-5 criteria, A-15
  dynamic systems approach to developing motor skills, 19
  as epigenetic characteristic, 77
  genetic testing for, 87
  immunizations and, 145
  possible causes of, 220, 336
  rapid brain growth in, 132
  sex differences, 281f
  special needs education for, 333
  symptoms, 329–330, 329p
  timing of birth and, 106
  treatment of, 330–331, 335, 336
Automatic processing, 624
Automatic thought, 623–624, 623f, 627, 628, 663
Automatization, 320, 322, 323, 336
Autonomy, 200, 276, 458
Autonomy vs. shame and doubt, 40t, 41, 200, 276, 544t
Autopsies, 763, 780
Availability error, 511–512
Average life expectancy, 694
Avoidant coping, 616, 617
Awareness, 593
Axons
  defined, 130
  function of, 131f, 132f
  growth and refinement in first two years, 132, 137
  myelination of, 220, 220f
  proliferation in early childhood, 220
  slowing connections in adulthood, 577

Babbling, 170, 173, 176, 178, A-9
Babies. See Infancy (first two years); Newborns

Babinski reflex, 117
Baby blues, 119
Baby boom, 673
Baby boomers, 9, 9f
Baby Einstein, 174, 175
Baby talk, 169–170
Back to Sleep campaign, 150
Back-sleeping, 150, 150p, 152
Bahrain, 674
Balanced bilingual, 261
Baltes, Margaret, 620–621
Baltes, Paul, 620–621
Bandura, Albert, 44–45
Bangladesh, 115f, 580
Bargaining, 769
Bariatric surgery, 591
Base for exploration, 193
Base pairs, 68, 69
Base rate neglect, 434, 511–512
Battle Hymn of the Tiger Mother (Chua), 36–37
Baumrind, Diana, 287
Bayley, Nancy, 605
Beal, Susan, 149–150
Beanpole family, 744–745, 745f, 751
Beck, Martha, 101, 112
Bed-sharing, 136, 150, 152
Behavior. See also Antisocial behavior; Delinquency; Prosocial behavior; Risky behavior; Self-destructive behavior
  cultural influence on, 36
  friends' facilitation of, 469, 477
  increasing problems in middle school years, 446
  in puberty, 403, 430
  self-concept's influence on, 48, 430
Behavioral teratogens, 105–106, 108, 122
Behaviorism
  application of, 50–51
  application to infant social development, 200–201, 201p, 208, 209
  classical conditioning, 42–43, 44t, 50–51, 64
  concepts of, 62f
  contribution/criticism of, 48, 62
  defined, 42, 64
  emergence of, 39
  as inspiration for teacher-directed programs, 266
  limitations of, 51–52, 56
  methodology, 48
  operant conditioning, 43–44, 43p, 44t, 64
  social learning, 44–45, 44t
  view of gender development, 293, 303
  view of language development, 173
  view of maternal employment, 207
Belgium, 356t, 453t, 773, A-16
Belonging, 56, 57, 57f, 551, 632
Benchmarks, 357
Bereavement leave, 779
Bereavement theory, 783
Beta-amyloid, 711, 715

Bias, 25, 28
Bickering, 462, 466, 485
Bicultural identity, 544, 546, 546p
Big Five personality traits, 634–636, 634p, 635p, 637, 659–660, 661, 663
Bilingual children
  academic achievement, 353
  cognitive and social benefits of, 272, 305
  control processes of, 346
  number in U.S., 350f
  parent-adolescent relationships among, 463
  reasons and process for learning two languages, 260–261, 260f, 261p, 262
  in U.S., 260f
Bilingual learning
  automatization required for, 320
  how and why, 260–261, 261p, 262
  substitution between languages, 258
Bilingual schooling
  language codes and, 350
  learning a second language, 359–360, 360p
  timing, curriculum, and students, 359
  in U.S., 268–269
Binge drinking
  by adolescents, 471, 478, 510, 510f, 512
  by adults, 588
  in childbearing years, 107
Binge eating disorder, 415
Binge-purge syndrome, 415
Binocular vision, 138
Bioecological theory. See Ecological-systems approach
Biological parenthood, 647–648
Biological parents, 661
Biomarkers, 710
Biorhythms
  circadian rhythm, 403–404, 404, 404f, 404p, 671, 707
  disruption of, 403–404, 404f, 404p, 405f, 411, 426
  seasonal, 403
Biosocial development. See also Body size; Brain; Emotions; Motor skills
  activities in late adulthood, 737–743, 737f, 738p, 739f, 739p, 740f, 742f, 742p, 757
  aging and disease in late adulthood, 684–688, 685f, 686f, 688f, 696
  body changes in early childhood, 215–218, 216p, 218f, 271f
  body size in first two years, 127–128, 128f, 129p
  brain development in adolescence, 416–419, 416f, 419p
  brain development in early childhood, 219–227, 220f, 221p, 223p, 225f
  brain development in middle childhood, 313p, 318–323, 321f, 323f

brain growth in first two years, 129–130, 129f, 130f, 131f, 132–134, 137

centenarians, 693–695, 693p, 694p, 696

child mistreatment in early childhood, 236–241, 236p, 237f, 238f, 239t, 240p

children in middle childhood with special needs, 323–335, 331p, 332f, 333p

compulsions about daily routines in early childhood, 218, 218f, 246

dynamic sensory-motor systems in first two years, 142

in early childhood, 305

frailty of the elderly, 749–756, 750p, 750t, 753p, 754p, 755p, 757

friends and relatives in late adulthood, 743–749, 743p, 744p, 745f, 746p, 747f, 748p, 749p, 757

growth and maturation in adolescence, 411–416, 412f, 414p, 415p

growth and strength in emerging adulthood, 491–493, 491p, 492p, 492p, 494f, 495–500, 495t, 496p, 497p, 499t, 571

health habits and age, 586–589, 586t, 587p, 588f, 590f, 591–594, 591p, 592f, 592p, 600, 663

health in middle childhood, 309–312, 310f, 311p, 312p, 313p, 397

health problems in middle childhood, 313, 314f, 315–318, 315f, 316p, 317f, 317p

injury in early childhood, 233–236, 234p, 235f

measurements of health in adulthood, 594–599, 594p, 595f, 596p, 598p, 600, 663

motor skills in early childhood, 227, 227t, 228f, 228p, 229–233, 231f, 231p, 232p, 233p

motor skills in first two years, 140–143, 140p, 140t, 141p

prejudice and predictions concerning late adulthood, 665, 667–676, 668p, 670f, 670p, 671f, 672f, 673p, 674p, 696

psychopathology in emerging adulthood, 503–507, 505p, 506p, 571

puberty, 401–411, 402p, 404f, 404p, 406p, 407f, 410p, 487

risk-taking in emerging adulthood, 507–513, 507p, 508f, 508p, 509p, 510f, 510p, 571

selective optimization with compensation in late adulthood, 676–684, 676f, 677p, 680f, 696

senescence, 576f, 576p, 578–580, 578p, 579p, 600, 663

senses in first two years, 137–139, 139p

sexual activity in emerging adulthood, 500–503, 500p, 571

sexual maturation in adolescence, 419–426, 420f, 420p, 421p, 423p, 424p, 425f

sexual-reproductive system in adulthood, 580–586, 581p, 584p, 585p, 600, 663

survival in first two years, 142–151, 143f, 143p, 144p, 145f, 146p, 147f, 147t, 148f, 148p, 150f, 150p

theories of aging, 688–693, 689p, 690p, 691p, 692p

theories of late adulthood, 730–737, 730p, 731p, 733f, 734p, 735f, 735p, 757

Bipolar disorder, 504

Birth
in Afghanistan, 104p
Apgar scale, 101, 101t, 122
complications during, 116, 117, 119, 122
by c-section, 102, 102f, 102p, 103, 122, 317
development at, 98
doula's support, 104, 105
epidural anesthesia, 103
full-term weight at, 98, 99, 105, 113
induced labor, 103
location of, 94, 103, 105
low birthweight, 113–115, 115f, 122
newborn survival, 103
positions for, 100
preterm delivery, 94t, 97, 98, 99p, 103, 106, 113, 116, 135
uterine rupture, 103
vaginal, 99–100, 100f, 100p, 122, 129
vulnerability during, 95t

Birth control. See Contraception

Birth defects, 20–21, 82t, 85, 88p, 106, 111–112

Birth order, A-7

Birth rate, 12f, 501

Birthdays, 93

Birthing centers, 103, 105

Birthweight, 98, 99, 105, 113. See also Low birthweight (LBW)

Bisexuals, 471

Bisphenol A (BPA), 230

Blastocyst, 95

Blind data gatherers, B-4

Blind participants, B-4

Blood pressure. See also Hypertension
alcohol use related to, 588
benefits of exercise, 497, 592
brain fitness related to, 702
effects of stress, 615
in emerging adulthood, 493
as epigenetic characteristic, 78

increase with age, 576
as symptom of heart disease, 686
of teen mothers, 422

Blood types, A-5

Blood-brain barrier, 577

Bodily-kinesthetic intelligence, 322

Body balance, 493, 494f, 495–497, 495t, 496p

Body fat
of adolescent girls, 412
effect on puberty, 406, 408, 411, 426
role of leptin, 408

Body image
of adolescents, 414, 414p, 416, 420, 426, 443
drug use associated with, 480
of early-maturing girls, 409
eating disorders associated with, 414–415, 415p, 426

Body mass index (BMI)
defined, 313
in early childhood, 215, 216p
in emerging adulthood, 498, 514
encouragement of dieting, 591
indications of anorexia nervosa, 415
indications of obesity, 589
in middle childhood, 313
percent by height and weight, 499t, A-12

Body shape
changes in adulthood, 578, 578p, 580, 600, 663
changes in puberty, 402, 420, 426
in late adulthood, 684, 696

Body size
changes in adulthood, 578
growth in adolescence, 402, 406, 411–412, 412f, 426, 487
growth in early childhood, 215–216, 216p, 217f, 218, 242, 305
growth in first two years, 128, 128f, 129p, 136, 211
growth in puberty, 406, 407f
height gain from birth to age 18, A-10
malnutrition's effect on, 148–149, 148f
in middle childhood, 310
nutrition in early childhood, 216–218, 217f
oral health and, 217–218
weight gain from birth to age 18, A-11

Body temperature, 117

Bonding, 120–121, 121p

Boogaard, Derek, 714

Book reading, 258

Books for research, B-2

Bovine spongiform encephalitis (BSE), 714, 715

Boys. See also Males
addiction to video games, 441–442, 441f
as bullies, 386p, 387
change in body shape at puberty, 401–402, 420

childhood obesity rates in U.S., 315f

delinquency of, 477, 478

depression in adolescence, 474

drug use and abuse, 480

eating disorders among adolescents, 415

emotional regulation, 279, 279p, 280p, 281f

externalization of problems, 279–280, 303, 380, 383

father's influence on, 44

growth of, 401–402, 406, 412, 491, A-10

incidence of anemia, 413

maturation of, 232

moral development of, 291, 530

puberty, 401–402, 402f, 403, 407f, 410, 426

school drop-out rates, 446

self-esteem in adolescence, 473

sex-related impulses of, 421

sexual abuse of, 423–424, 426

smoking behaviors, A-19

social effect of early and late maturation of, 410–411

sociodramatic play in early childhood, 285

suicide/parasuicide of, 475, 475f, 485

weight gain from birth to age 18, A-11

Brain. See also Cognition; Intelligence testing; specific brain structure
aging of, 577, 600, 663, 700–703, 702f, 726
of Alzheimer patients, 711–712, 711p, 712p
atrophy with age, 683, 683p
compensation for in late adulthood, 682–683, 682p, 683p, 684
connected hemispheres, 219f, 220–223, 221p, 223p
control processes, 346
development of prefrontal cortex, 254, 255f, 255p, 256
dual processing, 438–439, 439f, 440
effect of pollution, 230
effect of stress, 616
effects of alcohol, 588
function in adulthood, 580
fusiform face area, 134
language development and maturation of, 256
lateralization, 220
Lewy bodies in, 714
limbic system, 224, 225f
myelination of, 220, 220f, 226–227
neurons connecting, 129–130, 131f, 219
of Parkinson's suffers, 713
plasticity of, 134, 221, 621, 626, 683, 703, 714, 726
processing of sensations, 137
region of personality, 637p
stress hormones effect on, 186, 226
structures of, 130f, 219t, A-2

Brain death, 772t
Brain development/maturation.
  See also Limbic system;
  Prefrontal cortex
  in adolescence, 416–419, 416f,
    419p, 426, 430, 436, 487
  completion, 204
  connected hemispheres, 220–222,
    221p
  coordinating connections,
    318–320, 318p
  development of automatization,
    320
  development of selective attention,
    320
  in early childhood, 215, 219–227,
    219f, 220f, 221p, 223p,
    225f, 242, 276–277, 305
  effect of stress on, 186
  effect on play, 283
  during emerging adulthood, 507,
    519, 520f
  for emotional regulation, 224, 225f,
    226, 275–276, 276–277,
    279
  emotions and in first two years,
    185–189, 187p, 188f, 209
  environmental hazards, 229–231,
    231f, 231p
  experience-dependent development,
    132–133, 137
  experience-expectant development,
    133, 137
  in fetus, 97, 98f, 122
  of gifted and talented children,
    334
  growth in first two years, 125,
    129–130, 129f, 130f, 131f,
    132–134, 137, 152, 211
  impulse control, 223
  language acquisition and, 259
  learning about others, 186–187
  lengthening of reaction time, 320
  as lifelong process, 322
  malnutrition's effect on, 149
  maturation needed for gross motor
    skills, 141
  maturation of prefrontal cortex.
    See Prefrontal cortex
  in middle childhood, 313p,
    318–323, 321f, 323f, 336
  perseveration, 223, 223p
  pruning, 132, 134, 219
  sequence of, 416, 416f, 418
  use of drugs affecting, 480
Brain fitness, 323f
Brain function, 493
Brain scans, 321, 322–323, 323f
Brain sculpting, 132
Brain stem, 98t
Brazelton Neonatal Behavioral
    Assessment Scale (NBAS),
    116–117, 122, 139, 197
Brazil
  average age of marriage, 545f
  children's activities by socioeconomic
    class, 282f
  c-sections in, 102f
  incidence of asthma in, 317–318

  low birthweights in, 115f
  overnutrition in, 216
  overweight people in, 590f
  population of children and elders,
    A-3
  scores on PISA, 453t
Breast cancer, 521p, 687
Breast milk, 151
Breast-feeding
  benefits of, 27, 119, 142, 146–148,
    146p, 147t, 151, 152, 316
  clash with parental needs,
    203–204
  effect of c-sections on, 102, 102p
  impact on adulthood, 36
  rates by sociodemographic factors,
    A-7
  trends in U.S., 147f
Breathing, 130
Breathing reflex, 117, 147t
Bridge jobs, 655, 738
Brown, Louise, 73
Buddhism, 763
Bulimia nervosa, 415, 416, 426, 498
Bullies, 297, 386p, 387
Bullying
  causes and consequences, 386–387,
    389, 395, 478
  cyberbullying, 442, 442p, 454
  of early-maturing girls, 410
  increase in middle school years,
    392p, 397, 447
  reduction of, 387–388, 389, 392,
    395
  types of, 386
  victims of, 386
Bullying aggression, 297t, 298, 303,
    305, 386–388, 386p
Bully-victims, 387

Caffeine, 511
Caleb's birth, 3, 5
Calorie restriction, 691–692, 691p,
    692p, 693
Calorie Restriction Society, 691
Cambodia, 102f, 763
Cameroon, 201–202, 283
Camps for special needs children,
    311
Canada
  bilingual school children in, 260
  childhood obesity in, 315
  cognition in, 527
  cohabitation in, 556
  college graduates in, 535
  co-sleeping in, 136f
  c-sections in, 102f
  decline in smoking, 587
  demographics, 673
  extroverted personalities in, 636
  infant care in, 207
  infant mortality in, 143f
  languages spoken by school
    children, 359
  low birthweights in, 115f
  official languages of, 260
  population of children and elders,
    A-3
  retirement in, 738

  same-sex marriage in, 644p
  scores on international tests, 356t,
    452, 453t, A-16
  self-esteem of emerging adults,
    549
  sexually active teens/condom use,
    425f
  single-parent families in, 375f
  smoking in, 479
Cancer
  alcohol abuse related to, 588
  benefits of exercise, 497, 592
  breast cancer, 521p, 585, 687
  causes of, 77, 586, 687, 690
  copy number variations causing, 80
  correlation with age, 576
  deaths due to, 586t, 587, 685f, 695
  diagnosis and treatment of, 687
  incidence of, 596, 690
  skin cancer, 689
CARDIA (Coronary Artery
    Risk Development in
    Adulthood), 497, 500
Cardiovascular accident (CVA). *See*
    Stroke
Cardiovascular system. *See also*
    Heart; Heart attack; Heart
    disease; Stroke; Vascular
    dementia (VaD)
  aging of, 684
  development of, 98, 99
  effects of impaired blood flow on
    the brain, 577, 600
Career academies, 451
Caregivers. *See also* Doctors; Family;
    Fathers; Grandparents;
    Hospice; Mothers; Nursing
    homes; Parents
  ageism of, 672
  challenges for with children 2–6,
    287–294, 287t, 288p, 290f,
    292f, 303
  of the dying, 769, 770, 786
  elderly as, 674–675
  of elders, 752–753, 755, 756, 757
  foster care, 196, 196p, 226, 240,
    240–241, 240p, 242
  frequent changes as indicator of
    maltreatment, 239t
  as guides to moral development, 298
  kinship care, 241, 242, 376t, 747
Caregiving. *See also* Elder care;
    Family; Fathers; Filial
    responsibility; Mothers;
    Parenting; Parents
  adjustment for temperament of
    child, 288–289
  allocare, 205–207, 205p, 206p,
    206t, 209
  attachment, 191–197, 192t, 193t,
    195t, 205, 209
  Baumrind's styles of, 287–289,
    287t, 288p
  brain development affected by,
    186
  challenges of with children 2–6,
    305
  characteristics of good parents,
    613–614

  cultural variations, 289–290
  culture and family caregiving,
    652–654, 652p, 653f
  of the elderly, 670
  emotional development affected
    by, 182, 184, 185, 186
  expertise in, 626–627
  infant day care, 205–207, 206p,
    206t, 207f
  infant growth and development
    affected by, 127, 133
  infant motor skills affected by, 140
  kinkeepers, 651–652
  as lifelong process, 651
  proximal and distal parenting,
    201–202, 202p, 202t
  social anxiety affected by, 186
  styles of, 294, 303
  synchrony, 189, 190f, 191, 191p
  temperament affected by, 188–189
Careless personality, 634
Caribbean, 148f, 267, A-7
Caribbean Americans, 289
Carrier of X-linked characteristics,
    78–79, 79f, 89
Case studies
  College Advancing Thought, 635
  Coping with Katrina, 626
  David, 20–21, 25
  defined, 25
  How Hard Is It to Be a Kid? 380
  James, the High-Achieving
    Dropout, 451
  Lynda Is Getting Worse, 327
  Preventing Frailty, 751
  as research method, 25, 28
  Should Older People Have More
    Sex? 685
  Stones in the Belly (preschool
    cognition), 247
  Too May Drugs or Too Few? (elder
    care), 718
  Two Immigrants, 352
  What Makes a Relationship
    Succeed? 560
  What Were You Thinking? 417
Cataracts, 107f, 681p, 681t, 696
Categorization, 340
Causation, 29, 31, 32
Ceausescu, Nicolae, 196p
Cell phones, 493
Cells, 316
Cellular aging theory, 690–693,
    690p, 691p, 692p, 693,
    695, 696
Centenarians, 693–695, 693p,
    694p, 696, 719, 737
Central nervous system, 97, 98t,
    99, 129
Centration, 246, 272
Cephalocaudal pattern of
    development, 96, 140
Cerebellum, 219f, A-2
Cerebral cortex, 219f, A-2
Cerebral palsy, 116
Cesarean section (c-section), 102,
    102f, 103, 122, 317
Chad, 102f
Charter schools, 361, 364, 397

Chemicals, 408. *See also* Toxins
Chemotherapy patients, 145
Chewing, 141
Chickenpox, 109t, 145
Chicken-sexing, 622–623
Child abuse, 236–237, 236f, 237f, 242, 305. *See also* Child maltreatment
Child culture
  bullies and victims, 386p, 387–388, 389
  conflict with adult morality, 392
  defined, 384
  development of moral values, 389
  friendships, 385, 389
  in middle childhood, 384p, 395
  popular and unpopular children, 385–386, 389
Child maltreatment. *See also* Child abuse; Neglect
  adolescent girls affected by, 473–474
  attachment affected by, 195t, 196–197
  brain development affected by, 186, 189, 209, 226, 227
  consequences of, 238–240
  contribution to abusive relationships later in life, 563
  definitions and statistics, 236–237
  in early childhood, 233, 236–241, 236p, 237f, 238f, 239t, 240p, 242, 305
  effects of, 133
  establishment of harmful systems, 134
  foster care as remedy for, 240, 242, 650–651
  frequency of, 237–238, 237f, 238f
  impact on adulthood, 36
  levels of prevention, 240–241, 240p, 242
  by sexually abused mothers, 424
  shaken baby syndrome, 133
  shared parenting on affecting, 378
  unemployment contributing to, 654
  warning signs, 238, 239t
Child neglect, 236, 238f, 242. *See also* Child maltreatment; Neglect
Child pornography, 443
Child-centered programs
  assumptions of, 277, 305
  methodology of, 263–265, 263p, 264p
  Montessori schools, 264, 270, 272
  Reggio Emilia, 264–265, 270, 272
Child-directed speech, 169–170, 171, 173
Child-directed videos, 174–175
Childhood. *See also* Early childhood; Infancy (first two years); Middle childhood; Newborns
  attachment, 192t
  cognitive learning stages, 46f
  compression of morbidity in old age, 686–688, 688f
  concrete operational stage, 45p
  effect of low birthweight, 114

Erikson' stages of development, 40t, 41
  evolutionary theory concerning, 59
  Freud's stages of development, 39–40, 40t
  immunization, 144–145, 144p
  obesity in, 102
  signs of future psychopathology in, 503
Childhood obesity
  in adolescence, 414, 414p, 416, 426
  breast-feeding reducing risk of, 146, 147t, 316, 336
  of children born by c-section, 102
  consequences of, 315, 318
  contributing factors, 133, 315–316, 316p, 397
  in early childhood, 216–217, 216p, 218, 242, 315f
  effect on onset of puberty, 408
  by ethnicity, 315f
  indicators in infancy, 128
  in middle childhood, 313, 314f, 315–316, 315f, 316p, 318
  by nation, 314f
  role of leptin, 408
Childhood overweight, 313, 315
Child-Parent Centers, 269
Children. *See also* Bilingual children; Child abuse; Child maltreatment; Childhood; Childhood obesity; Early childhood; Infancy (first two years); Middle childhood; Special needs children
  contribution to childhood obesity, 316
  death of, 780, 782
  divorce affecting, 645–646
  effect on happiness in marriage, 643
  percentage of population by nation, A-3
  remarriage of parents affecting, 649
  response to death, 764p
Children with special needs. *See* Special needs children
Children's theories
  theory of mind, 253–254, 253p, 254f, 256, 272, 295
  theory-theory, 252–253, 256, 272
Chile
  bereavement leave in, 779
  c-sections in, 102f
  divorce in, 573
  high school graduation rate, 445f
  infant mortality in, 143, 143f
  low birthweights in, 114, 115, 115f
  parent-adolescent relationships, 463
  population of children and elders, A-3
  scores on PISA, 453t
China
  age of mothers at birth, 501
  Alzheimer rates in, 711
  artistic instruction in, 233

average age of marriage, 545f
  bereavement leave in, 779
  body image of adolescents in, 414
  cognition in, 527
  college graduates in, 536
  co-sleeping in, 136f
  c-sections in, 102, 102f, 102p
  death rate for emerging adults, 507
  diet in, 591
  education in, 444
  elder care in, 654, 745
  family bonds in, 639
  high school graduation rate, 444, 445f, 482f
  high-stakes tests in, 449
  incidence of asthma in, 317–318
  incidence of twins, 75
  infant day care in, 207
  job satisfaction in, 658
  language development in, 172
  low birthweights in, 114, 115, 115f
  mastery of numbers, 251
  one-child policy, 71
  overweight people in, 590f
  PISA scores, 452, 453t, A-16
  play in early childhood, 282
  popularity of shy children, 385
  population of children and elders, A-3
  rate of dementia in, 711
  regulation of pride, 278, 370
  respect for elderly in, 669
  school's effect on vision in, 83
  serious abuse in intimate relationships, 563
  sexual activity of adolescents in, 421
  surrogate grandparents in, 747
  teen pregnancy in, 422
  theory of the mind in children of, 255–256
  treatment of ADHD in, 326
  universities in, 536, 537f
Chinese Taipei, 356t
Chlamydia, 109t, 424, 425, A-17
Choice overload, 555–556
Choices
  in dying, 768–778, 770p, 770t, 771f, 772f, 773f, 774p, 774t, 776f, 777p
  encouragement of independence, 276
Cholesterol, 576, 588, 686
Chomsky, Noam, 175
Christianity, 763
Chromosomal sex, 6
Chromosome 15, 81
Chromosomes. *See also* Alleles; Genes; Heredity
  23rd pair (sex chromosomes), 70, 70–71, 85, 86–87, 86t, 89, 90, 406
  combinations of, 90
  at conception, 68, 68p, 70, 76, 90
  copy number variations, 79–81, 81p, 90
  deactivation of X chromosome, 80
  defined, 68, 90
  effect of excess chromosomes, 84–85, 85p, 86t, 89, 90

of normal human, 70p, 76
  role in protein synthesis, 68, 68f
Chronic illness, 684, 686, 688, 715
Chronic obstructive pulmonary disease, 684
Chronic traumatic encephalopathy (CTE), 714
Chronosystem, 7, 8, 8f. *See also* Cohort; Historical context
Chua, Amy, 36–37
Churning, 557, 558f
Cigarettes. *See* Smoking; Tobacco
Circadian rhythm
  changes in old age, 671, 707
  disruption in adolescence, 403–404, 404f, 404p, 405f, 411, 426
  effect of electronic blue-spectrum light, 404
Citing sources, B-3
Class. *See* Social class
Classical conditioning, 42–43, 44t, 50–51, 64
Classification, 340, 364
Cleaning compounds, 109t, 110
Cleft lip, 107f
Cleft palate, 107f
Climbing, 152
Clinical depression, 474
Closed personality, 634
Closeness, 637
Cluster suicides, 475, 765
Cocaine, 109t, 480f
Code-focused teaching, 258
Cognition
  adolescence in digital age, 454
  area of brain controlling, 130
  defined, 45
  dendrite pruning associated with, 132, 152
  developing motor skills affecting, 141
  effect on genetic expression, 77–78
  genetic impairment of, 85
  low birthweight's effect on, 114
  measurement of, 706–708
  measurement of practical cognition, 451–453, 453t, 726
  perception leading to, 137, 156, 162
  prenatal/postnatal brain growth affecting, 129
  of Romanian adoptees, 196
  technology and, 441
  teratogens' effect on, 105–106, 122
Cognitive artifacts, 613, 614
Cognitive development
  of adolescence in digital age, 440–444, 440p, 441f, 442p, 487
  aging of the brain in late adulthood, 700–703, 702f, 726
  approaches to study of, 517
  components of intelligence, 608–614, 609p, 610t, 611p, 614p, 628, 663
  early-childhood education, 262–270, 262f, 263p, 264p, 265p, 266f, 267p, 268f

education in middle childhood, 353, 354f, 354t, 355–362, 355p, 356t, 357p, 358p, 359t, 360f, 360p, 361p, 363f

emotional regulation enabling and enabled by, 277

higher education associated with, 520f, 532–536, 532p, 533p, 534t, 537f, 538–539, 538p, 539p, 540, 571

information processing after 65, 703–709, 706f, 707f, 726

information processing in first two years, 162–168, 163p, 164p, 165p, 166p, 178, 211, 305

information processing in middle childhood, 343–348, 344p, 345t, 347f, 397

intelligence in adulthood, 603–608, 604p, 606f, 628, 663

language development in first two years, 168–176, 168p, 169t, 170p, 171p, 173p, 174f, 178, 211

language in middle childhood, 348–353, 349p, 350f, 351f

language learning in early childhood, 256–262, 256t, 260f, 261p

in late adulthood, 725f

learning in late adulthood, 719–721, 720p, 721p

logic and self in adolescence, 430–434, 430p, 431p, 432f, 433f, 433p

morals and religion in emerging adulthood, 528–532, 528p, 529f, 540, 571

neurocognitive disorders of late adulthood, 709–719, 710f, 711p, 712f, 712p, 713p, 714p, 715p, 716p, 726

new cognitive development in late adulthood, 719–724, 719p, 720p, 721p, 722p, 723p, 726

postformal thought of emerging adulthood, 517–527, 518p, 520f, 521f, 521p, 524p, 540, 571

selective gains and losses in adulthood, 615–617, 615p, 616f, 618f, 619–627, 620f, 621p, 622p, 623f, 626p, 627f, 628, 663

self-actualization, 719

sensorimotor intelligence in first two years, 155–162, 156t, 157f, 157p, 158p, 159p, 161t, 178, 211

sexual abuse affecting, 424

teaching and learning in adolescence, 444–453, 445f, 445p, 448p, 453t

theories applied to middle childhood, 339–348, 339p, 340p, 341p, 342p, 343f, 343p, 345t, 347f

thinking during early childhood, 245–256, 247p, 248f, 249p, 253p, 254f, 255f, 255p

two modes of thinking in adolescence, 434–440, 435f, 436p, 439f

Cognitive disequilibrium, 46, 46f

Cognitive equilibrium, 46, 46f, 64

Cognitive flexibility, 522–523, 612

Cognitive reserve, 616, 683, 701

Cognitive tests, 706–709

Cognitive theory
    application of, 50–51
    application to adolescence, 431–434, 431f, 431p, 487
    application to infant social development, 202–203, 208
    application to middle childhood, 339–340, 339p, 340p
    concepts of, 45p, 62f
    contribution/criticism of, 48, 62
    emergence of, 39
    information processing, 47–48
    logic and self in adolescence, 487
    methodology, 48
    Piaget's stages of development, 45, 45–47, 64, 155–162, 156t, 157f, 157p, 158p, 159p, 161t
    on preoperational thought, 272
    social learning in early childhood and, 245–249, 247p, 248f
    view of gender development, 293, 303
    working model, 202–203

Cohabitation
    conflict within the home, 558f, 571
    correlation with unhappiness in marriage, 642
    effect on children, 381
    frequency of, 568, 569
    happiness in, 647
    in late adulthood, 749
    in Nigeria, 377f
    of same-sex partners, 644
    separating couples, 643
    in U.S., 377f, 556f, 556p, 557p
    variation in and reasons for, 556–558, 578

Cohort. See also Historical context
    attitudes toward high self-esteem influences by, 370
    defined, 8
    early maturation of boys associated with, 410
    eating habits associated with, 413
    effect on each life, 22
    fertility affected by, A-20
    filial responsibility associated with, 745
    gender stereotypes affected by, 677
    identity related to, 457, 458, 459
    impact on sexual responsiveness in adulthood, 581–582
    intelligence associated with, 605, 607, 614, 700–701
    midlife crisis related to, 633–634, 661

moral values associated with, 529

onset of puberty affected by, 406

personality related to, 634, 635, 635p

play influenced by, 282–283

popularity of children related to, 385

sexual activity in adolescence changing with, 421

special needs education and, 332

stages of life and, 493

variation in drug use, 479, 484

view of non-heterosexual behavior by, 471

views of marriage changing with, 558–559, 748–749

Cohort-sequential research, 26, 28. See also Cross-sequential research

Colic, 182

College
    brain development in first year, 520f
    changes in context, 535–539, 537f, 538p, 539p, 540
    cognitive decline correlated with, 702
    cognitive growth associated with, 532–536, 532f, 532p, 533o, 533p, 534t, 537f, 538–539, 538p, 539p, 540, 571
    drug use and abuse in, 510
    enrollment, 489, 535, 537f, 571
    financing for, 565, 566f, 568, 569
    graduation rates, 451, 454, 525, 537f, 538
    health benefits of, 533
    impediments to, 567
    motivations for enrollment, 532–533, 532f
    scheme of cognitive and ethical development during, 534, 534t

College-bound students, 448–449, 450f, 451

Colombia, 356t

Colonoscopy, 493

Colorblindness, 16, 79, 80t

Colostrum, 101, 146

Coma, 772t, 773

Commitments in relativism development, 534t, 535, 568, 569, 643

Common Core standards, 358, 359t, 364, 449

Communication
    in caregiving, 287–288, 287t
    within CNS, 129, 131f, 132f
    within families, 463–464, 466, 467
    between hemispheres of brain, 220–223, 221p, 223p
    between married partners, 560, 562
    role in childbearing/rearing, 120
    role of epigenetics, 60
    technology enabling, 440

Communion. See Intimacy

Communities
    aging affected by, 694
    contribution to abusive relationships, 563
    contribution to childhood obesity, 315, 316
    contribution to clinical depression in adolescent boys, 474
    effect of violence in, 408
    effect on bereavement, 783
    effect on self-esteem in adolescence, 473
    elder care, 751
    elements of developmental context, 7
    encouragement of activity, 498, 592
    influence on development, 10
    teaching of language, 350

Comorbid disorders
    ADHD, 325
    in adolescence, 473
    neurocognitive disorders (NCDs), 714
    psychopathological disorders as, 324, 328, 503

Companionate grandparents, 747

Companionate love, 553t

Comparison group, 24, 24f

Competition, 448

Complex personalities, 520, 521f

Complicated grief, 779–780, 783, 784, 786

Compression of morbidity, 686–688, 688f, 696

Compulsive hoarding, 731, 732p, 757

Conception
    assisted reproductive technology, 71, 75–76, 77, 90, 95, 115, 583, 586, 600
    determining date of, 94t
    division creating multiple fetus, 73–75, 74f
    genetic combination, 68, 68p, 70–76, 77, 84
    in vitro fertilization, 71, 75–76, 77, 90, 95, 583, 586, 600

Conclusions, 4, 5

Concrete operational thought
    of adolescents, 435f
    characteristics of, 45p, 46, 46f, 46t, 339–340, 339p, 340p, 364
    classification, conservation, reversibility, and seriation, 340
    formal operational thought compared to, 431
    moral development enabled by, 390, 391–392
    processes leading to, 348

Conditioning
    classical conditioning, 42–43, 44t, 50–51, 64
    defined, 42
    operant conditioning, 43–44, 43p, 44t, 64

Conduct disorder, 281f

Conflict
    within families, 383, 384, 387, 395, 408, 561–564, 567, 569, 571
    between friendships, 561–564

in marriage, 643
between parents and teens, 462
Confucianism, 527
Conjoined twins, 73
Conjunctive faith, 531
Connectedness, 463–464
Conscientiousness, 634, 635, 635f, 635p, 636, 637, 661
Consequential strangers, 638, 638p, 641, 661
Conservation
lacking in early childhood, 247–249, 247p, 340p
in middle childhood, 340, 340p, 364
types of, 248f
Conspicuous consumption, 654
Consummate love, 553t, 643
Contact-maintaining, 192, 193, 205
Contentment, 182, 182t, 209
Context. See also Culture; Exosystem; Historical context; Macrosystems; Microsystems; Social context; specific nation
role in personality development, 631, 636–637, 637p
selection of expertise affected by, 622
Continuing bonds, 783, 786
Continuity and change
in development, 6, 208
during emerging adulthood, 543–550, 544p, 544t, 545f, 546p, 547p, 547t, 548f, 548p, 549f, 569, 571
identity achievement, 544–548, 544p, 545f, 546p, 547p, 547t, 548f, 548p
in personality, 637, 757
Contraception
adolescents' use of, 422, 424f
adult use of, 580, 586
education concerning, 472
effect on sexual activity in adolescence, 421
emerging adult's use of, 501, 503
reduction in adolescent crime due to, 478
Control, 463–464
Control group, 24, 24f
Control processes, 346, 364, 705–706, 706f, 709, 726
Conventional behavior, 296
Conventional moral reasoning, 390, 390t
Convergent thinkers, 334
Conversation, 351, 430
Cooperative play, 283, 311–312
Coping methods, 616–617, 618f, 619–620, 620f
Copy number variations, 80, 86, 90
Corporal punishment, 299, 300–301, 303
Corpus callosum
defined, 220
functions of, 219f, 220–222, 221p, 226, 232, 318, A-2
myelination of, 220, 226–227, 232, 318

Correlation, 29, 31, 32
Cortex
defined, 129
emotional development related to maturity of, 185
folding of, 98–99, 98t
functions of, 129, 130f, 137, 219f
growth in first two years, 137
thinning with age, 701
Cortisol
brain development affected by, 186, 226, 242
effects of sexual abuse, 424
in low-income children, 372
mental ability affected by, 616
onset of puberty affected by, 409
production in hypothalamus, 224
sadness producing in infants, 182–183
Co-sleeping, 135–136, 136f, 136p, 152
Cosmetics, 110
Costa Rica, 102f
Cost-benefit analysis, 23t
Cot death. See Sudden infant death syndrome (SIDS)
Courtship patterns, 493
Couvade, 119, 122
Crawling, 140, 140p, 140t, 142, 150, 158, 165
Creative Correction (Whelchel), 301
Creative intelligence, 610–612, 610t, 614, 628, 724
Creativity. See also Artistic expression
of adolescents, 419
in late adulthood, 721–722, 721p, 722p, 724, 726
prefrontal cortex and, 232
Creeping, 140, 140p, 140t
Cremation, 779, 781
Crib death. See Sudden infant death syndrome (SIDS)
Crime, 231, 477, 478, 485, 636, 672f. See also Delinquency; Homicide
Critical period, 6, 6–7
Critical time, 106, 107f, 107t, 122, 256
Croatia, 301
Cross-fostering, 120
Cross-modal perception, 142
Cross-sectional research
advantages/disadvantages, 28, 604, 628
defined, 25
on intelligence, 604, 663
participants, 27p
process of, 25–27, 26f
Cross-sequential research
advantages/disadvantages, 28, 606, 608
defined, 28
on intelligence, 606–608, 606p, 663
process of, 26f
Seattle Longitudinal Study, 28, 606–607, 606p, 626, 628, 706–707, 719
Crying
in early childhood, 222, 223, 277

in early infancy, 182, 184, 647
as infant reflex, 117
responses to by caregivers, 186, 187p
as survival technique, 204
triggers for, 185
Crystallized intelligence, 609–610, 609p, 614, 663
C-section, 102, 102f, 103, 122
Cuba, 115f, 312, 591, 692
Cultural identity, 544, 544p, 546–547, 546p
Cultural patterns, 53
Cultural sponge, 185
Culture
acceptance of cohabitation, 558
adult-adolescent relationships related to, 466
anxiety disorders affected by, 505–506
aptitude test scores influenced by, 322
artistic expression associated with, 233
attachment affected by, 193
attitudes toward elderly affected by, 668, 668p
attitudes toward premarital sex, 502, 503
behavior influenced by, 36, 249, 250
beliefs about death, 763
birth and, 104, 104p
birthweight affected by, 113–114
caregiving influenced by, 288
child-rearing practices affected by, 238, 289–290, 295, 298, 300–301
of children in middle childhood, 384–389, 384p, 386p
children's opportunities for play affected by, 312
commitment to relationships impacted by, 553
contraception use determined by, 580
contribution to abusive relationships, 564
contribution to adolescent depression, 474
contribution to alcoholism, 82
contribution to childhood obesity, 315
defined, 11
as determinant of infant care, 201–202
development affected by, 11–16, 22
development of impulse control associated with, 223
dialectical thought impacted by, 527
differences in thought processes, 528
drug use associated with, 485
effect on adults, 573
emotional development affected by, 183, 184, 185, 276, 278, 279
ethnicity/race related to, 14f, 22
family caregiving expectations related to, 652, 652p, 654

funeral customs determined by, 763
gender development affected by, 293–294
gross motor development affected by, 227, 227t
growth related to, 242
HRT use determined by, 585
humor and, 15
infant day care determined by, 206–207
infant motor skills affected by, 140, 141
infant social development affected by, 208
intelligence affected by, 607, 612–613, 614, 628
language development differences, 171–172, 171p
male-female relationships affected by, 469
marriage differences, 554
math learning and, 251–252
metacognition teaching influenced by, 347
moral development and empathy associated with, 296, 391
moral values determined by, 391, 528, 531, 540
obesity related to, 591
parent-adolescent relationships related to, 463, 566
parent-emerging adult relationships related to, 565, 566, 571
perception of affordances and, 164
personality influenced by, 634–635, 636
play influenced by, 282–283, 282f
puberty affected by, 425
reporting of child maltreatment determined by, 237
role in learning process, 52, 342–343, 342p, 343f
role models determined by, 561
schooling determined by, 353–355, 355p, 364
selection of expertise affected by, 622
self-esteem of children 5-11 influenced by, 360p, 369–370
sexual activity in adolescence affected by, 421
sleep patterns related to, 135, 137
sociocultural theory, 54–55
special needs education determined by, 333
strategies for working memory development influenced by, 344–345
synchrony associated with, 191
thought processes affected by, 249, 250, 520
view of non-heterosexual behavior associated with, 471
views of death and dying, 774, 786
vision affected by, 82
volunteer work related to, 739
Curfew laws, 668
Curiosity, 182, 182t, 184

Current events, 9, 9f
Curriculum, 353–354. *See also*
   Education
Customs, 53, 242
Cutting, 411, 443, 474
Cyberbullying, 386, 442–443, 442p,
   444, 454, 487
Cyprus, 301
Cystic fibrosis, 87, 89p
Czech Republic, 445f, 453t, A-16

Daily hassles, 371
DALYs. *See* Disability-adjusted life
   years (DALYs)
DARE, 483
Darwin, Charles, 58, 334
David's story, 20–21, 20p
Day of the Dead, 763
Deafness, 107f. *See also* Hearing
Death and dying. *See also* Homicide;
   Infant mortality; Motor
   vehicle crashes; Suicide
  acceptance of, 766, 768, 769, 775,
     782, 786
  adolescents' response to, 764–765,
     765f
  adults' response to, 765–766,
     766p, 786
  advance directives, 776–777, 778,
     786
  affirmation of life, 778–785, 780p,
     781p, 782p, 785p, 786
  in ancient times, 762, 786
  causes of for adolescents and
     emerging adults, 765f
  causes of for elderly, 684–685,
     685f, 686, 687
  of children, 780, 782
  children's response to, 764, 764p,
     786
  choices in dying, 786
  death and hope, 761–768, 762t,
     764p, 765f, 766f, 766p,
     767f, 767p, 786
  diversity of reactions to, 783–785,
     783p, 784, 786
  due to illness, 145, 685f, 695,
     765f
  euthanasia, 773–775, 773f, 774f,
     774p, 776f, 778, 786
  evidence of death, 772–773, 772t,
     786
  fear of, 762
  good death, 768–769, 770p, 778,
     786
  grief, 778–780, 783–784, 786
  hospice care, 768, 770–771, 770t,
     786
  infant mortality, 595f
  infanticide, 59, 71, 71p
  integration with self, 731
  location of, 771f
  mortality rates, 594–595
  mourning, 761, 780–783, 780p,
     781p, 782p, 784, 786
  near-death experiences, 767–768,
     786
  palliative care, 771, 778, 786
  pedestrian deaths, 234, 235, 235f

physical and psychological pain of,
     774–775, 786
  physician-assisted suicide, 773–775,
     774t, 775, 776f, 786
  religious beliefs concerning, 763,
     781, 786
  response to in late adulthood,
     766–767, 766f, 767f
  Schiavo case, 777–778, 777p
  stages of, 769, 782, 786
  sudden infant death syndrome,
     136, 149–151, 150f, 152
  support of grievers, 783–784, 786
  top three causes, 495t, 685f, 686
  in United States, 235f, 310f, 770–
     771, 771f, 774, 774t
  wills and proxies, 777, 778, 786
  in youth, 768
Death with dignity, 773–775, 774t,
   776f
Decision making, 36, 436–437, 439,
   530, 683, 705
Deductive reasoning, 433, 433f,
   434, 435f, 454
Deferred imitation, 159–160, 160,
   162, 167, 178
Defiance, 278, 476–478, 476p,
   477p
Defining Issues Test (DIT), 530, 532
Dehydration, 716–717
Déjà vu, 167
Delay discounting, 519
Delinquency
  of adolescents, 476–478, 476p,
     477p, 485, 487
  causes of, 430, 465, 469, 477,
     477–478
  types of, 477
Delivery. *See also* Labor and delivery
  in birthing centers, 103, 105
  cesarean section (c-section), 102,
     102f
  complications during, 116, 117, 119
  doula's support, 104, 105
  epidural anesthesia, 103
  at home, 103–104, 104p, 105
  induced labor, 103
  low birthweight, 122
  preterm delivery, 94t, 97, 98, 99p,
     103, 106, 113, 116, 122,
     135
  vaginal, 99–101, 100f, 100p, 122,
     129
Demand/withdraw interaction, 562,
   569
Dementia, 709, 710f, 726
Demographic pyramid, 673
Demographic shift, 673–676, 686f,
   696
Demographics, 9, 10f, 696, A-20
Dendrites
  appearance and atrophy of in
     adulthood, 577
  emotional volatility related to
     growth of, 185
  experience altering, 167, 351
  function of, 130, 131f, 132
  growth and refinement in first two
     years, 132, 137, 152

growth in late adulthood,
     700–701, 726
  increased density, 222
  proliferation in early childhood,
     220
Denial, 593, 769, 782
Denmark
  family bonds in, 639
  father involvement with infants
     in, 198
  high school graduation rate, 445f
  incidence of schizophrenia in, 87
  low birthweights in, 115f
  punishment of poor behavior in,
     301
  restrictions on diet in, 692
  scores on international tests, 356t,
     453t, A-16
  smokers in, 587
Deoxyribonucleic acid (DNA). *See*
   DNA
Dependency ratio, 674, 676
Dependent experiences, 133
Dependent variable, 24, 24f
Depression
  absent grief manifesting as, 779
  in adolescence, 409, 410, 411,
     414, 473–475, 474p, 475f,
     485, 487, 549
  alcohol use associated with, 513
  avoidant coping contributing to,
     616
  benefits of exercise, 497
  bullying resulting in, 388, 442, 443
  divorce as cause of, 645
  effect of mother's on infants, 191
  in emerging adulthood, 502,
     503–504, 504–505, 571
  as epigenetic characteristic, 78
  exercise's effect, 592
  factors linked to, 18
  of fathers, 199, 199t
  of friendless teens, 385
  gender difference, 406
  genetic testing for, 87
  HPA abnormalities causing, 402
  intergenerational homes associated
     with, 640
  in late adulthood, 700, 716, 719,
     726
  from marijuana use, 481
  during menopause, 584
  of mothers, 199
  multidisciplinary research on,
     17–19, 18f, 18p
  parent-adolescent relationships
     affecting, 463
  in people with short 5-HTTLPR
     gene, 465
  percent of adults experiencing by
     country, 18f
  PET scans of brains with, 18p
  physical punishment resulting
     in, 301
  physician-assisted suicide and,
     775
  postpartum depression, 119
  psychological control exacerbating,
     300

response to death of loved one,
     783, 784, 786
  sensory impairment contributing
     to, 688
  sleep deprivation causing, 404
  as stage of dying, 769
  stress associated with, 226, 616
  of surrogate grandparents, 747
  technology associated with, 468
  in toddlers, 199
  treatment, 18–19, 722
  unemployment contributing to, 654
  use of sleep aids associated with,
     671
  volunteer work preventing, 739,
     739f, 739p
  women suffering from, 686
Depth perception, 138, 164, 164p
Despair, 731, 763
Development. *See also* Biosocial
     development; Cognitive de-
     velopment; Developmental
     theories; Psychosocial de-
     velopment; *specific life stage*
  critical period, 6–7
  differential sensitivity, 20–22, 21t
  dynamic systems, 19
  multicontextual nature of, 7–11,
     21t, 32, 127
  multicultural nature of, 11–16,
     21t, 32, 127
  multidirectional nature of, 6–7,
     21t, 22, 32, 127
  multidisciplinary nature of, 16–19,
     21t, 32
  multidisciplinary research on
     depression, 17–19, 18f, 18p
  patterns of growth, 6f
  plasticity of, 19, 21t, 32
  sensitive period, 7
  study of, 24–31, 26f, B-1–B-5
Developmental crisis, 41
Developmental level, 163–164
Developmental psychopathology,
   323, 324, 336
Developmental theories
  application to middle childhood,
     339p, 340p, 341p, 342p,
     343f, 343p, 345t, 347f,
     395, 397
  application to toilet training, 50–51
  behaviorism. *See* Behaviorism
  classical conditioning, 42–43,
     50–51
  cognitive theory. *See* Cognitive
     theory; Piaget, Jean
  concepts of, 62f
  contribution/criticism of, 62–63
  defined, 36, 62f
  eclectic perspective, 62–63
  Erikson's psychosocial theory. *See*
     Erikson, Erik; Psychosocial
     theory
  evolutionary theory. *See*
     Evolutionary theory
  facts and norms compared to, 37–39
  Freud's psychosexual theory.
     See Freud, Sigmund;
     Psychosexual theory

grand theories, 36–51, 48, 49f, 50–52, 56, 64
humanism, 55–58, 61
information processing theory. *See* Information-processing perspective
newer theories, 51–60, 64
operant conditioning, 43–44, 43p, 44t
psychoanalytic theory, 51–52, 56, 62, 64. *See also* Psychosexual theory; Psychosocial development
questions and answers of, 36–37
social learning, 64
sociocultural theory, 52–55, 54f, 61, 62, 62f, 64
theory of the mind. *See* Theory of mind
theory theory, 35, 252–253, 256, 272
universal perspective, 55–61, 62, 62f, 64. *See also* Evolutionary theory; Humanism
Deviancy training, 469
Diabetes
causes of, 216, 496, 591
cognition affected by, 715
deaths due to, 685f
diagnosis and treatment of, 687
effect of breast-feeding, 146, 147t
in emerging adulthood, 492
epigenetic influence on, 77–78
genetic contribution to, 315, 690
in immigrants' children, 500
low birthweight associated with, 114, 115
mature brain affected by, 615
obesity associated with, 589, 591
treatment of, 718
type 2 in women, 686
use of technology to monitor, 469
Diagnostic and Statistical Manual of Mental Disorders (American Psychiatric Association)
ADHD criteria, 325, A-14
autism spectrum disorders criteria, 329, 330, A-14
complexity of diagnosis, 324
depression criteria, 783
drug abuse designation, 510
gender dysphoria criteria, 471
hoarding disorder criteria, 731
learning disabilities criteria, 328
neurocognitve disorders described, 709, 718
psychopathology described, 279
reactive attachment disorder recognized, 648
separation anxiety described, 184
Dialectical thought
of adults, 528, 540, 571
application to broken marriages, 526
cultural differences, 527
defined, 517, 525
of developmentalists, 526
Diathesis-stress model of mental illness, 504, 505, 506, 514

Diet. *See also* Malnutrition; Nutrition
for adults, 589
aging affected by, 689, 691–692, 691p, 692p, 693, 694, 696
brain fitness related to, 702, 715, 716–717, 719
cancer caused by, 586
effect on skin and hair, 578
in Greece and Italy, 592
for late adulthood, 676
weight gain and, 591
Dieting, 474, 495, 498, 583, 591
Difference-equals-deficit error
concerning child care, 206
concerning left-handedness, 221
defined, 13–14
in language abilities, 350
Differential sensitivity
biological advantage of, 60
caregiving and, 289
changes in temperament associated with, 188
defined, 20–22, 373
of infants in day care, 207
multidisciplinary nature of, 22
onset of puberty, 408
in responses to stress, 370, 380
role of Y chromosome, 108
vulnerability to depression, 473–474
Differential susceptibility, 45, 77
Differentiation, 73, 77, 90, 95, 99
Digestion, 589, 617, 684, 687, 716
Digital divide, 440
Digital natives, 440–444, 440p, 441f, 442p, 454
Disability
attitude's effect on recovery, 670
changing nature of, 324, 336
cognition affecting in late adulthood, 701
as measure of health, 594, 596–597, 596p, 599, 600, 663
prevention of, 687
Disability-adjusted life years (DALYs), 597
Disappointment, response to, 733–734
Discipline
consequences of, 36, 305
physical punishment, 3, 299–300, 299p, 301–302, 301p
psychological control, 300, 300p, 302, 303
strategies for, 287–288, 287t, 289, 298–299
Discontinuity, 6
Discoveries, 36
Discrimination, 734–736
Disease. *See also* Illness; Mental illness; Psychopathology; Sexually transmitted infections (STIs); *specific disease*
immunization against, 144–145, 151, 152, 309, 331, 336, 425, 685, A-8–A-9
in late adulthood, 684–688, 685f, 686f, 688f, 696
Disenfranchised grief, 779, 784, 786
Disengagement theory, 736, 737, 757

Disequilibrium, 46f
Disgust, 184
Disorganized attachment, 193, 193t, 194, 209, 240
Distal parenting, 201–202, 202p, 202t
Distant grandparents, 747
Distress, 181–182, 182t, 184, 209, 296
Divergent thinkers, 334
Diversity
biological advantage of, 60, 90
in workplace, 656–657, 656f, 660, 661
Divorce
contributing factors, 423, 557, 616, 642, 643, 644–646, 645p, 661
effect of choice overload, 556
effect on children, 645, 663
effect on men and women, 505, 645, 661, 663
ethnicity and, 643
family structure, 376t
link to neurotic personality, 634
onset of puberty affected by, 408, 409
problems generated by, 645
rates in U.S., 545f, 559, 561, 573, 641, 642t
in United States, 641
Dizygotic (DZ) twins, 74f, 75, 77, 87, 90, 108
DLLs. *See* Dual language learners (DLLs)
DNA. *See also* Epigenetics; Genes; Heredity
nature-nurture controversy, 5
role in development, 1
role in protein synthesis, 68, 68f
testing, 72–73
DNR (do not resuscitate), 773
Doctors
age distinctions promoted by, 675, 696
ageism of, 672
clinical practice guidelines, 717
debate on life expectancy, 695
distinction between primary and secondary aging, 684
expertise of, 622, 625, 626, 628
gender of, 627f
physician-assisted suicide, 773–775, 774t, 775, 776f
views of euthanasia, 773–774
Domestic abuse, 558f, 561–564, 567, 569, 571, 645
Dominant disorders, 86
Dominant genes, 78–79, 79f, 86, 90
Dominant-recessive heredity
expression of, 81, 90
gene disorders with dominant genes, 85–86, 89, 90
gene disorders with recessive genes, 85, 86–87, 89, 90
genotype/phenotype, 78–79, 79f, 90
X-linked characteristics, 79
Dominant-recessive pattern, 78
Dominican Republic, 312

Dopamine receptor gene (DRD4-R7), 78
Double effect, 771
Doula, 104, 104p, 105
Down syndrome, 86, 86p, 89, 90, 111–112, 712, A-6
Drama, 284–286, 286f, 286p
Drawing, 232
DRD4 VNTR gene, 188
Dream New Dreams (Pausch), 765
Dress standards, 392
Driving, 678–679, 679p, 680f, 684, 696, 731
Drowning, 234, 235
Drug addiction, 510
Drug use and abuse
ADHD treatment, 325, 326
in adolescence, 405, 408, 410, 414, 415, 422, 446, 464, 478, 478–484, 479p, 480f, 480p, 482f, 483p, 485, 487, 510f, 519
by adults, 576, 577, 586–589, 587p, 588f
avoidance of, 676
as avoidant coping method, 616
birthweight affected by, 113, 115, 116, 122
breast-feeding and, 146
as cause of infertility, 583
contribution to abusive relationships, 423, 563
early sexual activity associated with, 422
early-maturing girls' risk of, 410
eating disorders associated with, 414, 415
during emerging adulthood, 507, 510–511, 510f, 510p, 514, 522
family rejection affecting, 474
girls' vulnerability to, 479
harm from, 480–481
in late adulthood, 718, 726
mature brain affected by, 577, 600, 615
by non-heterosexual teens, 471
onset of puberty affected by, 408
in palliative care, 771, 786
prenatal development affected by, 105–106, 107f, 109–110t, 110–116
prescribing cascade, 717
of prescription drugs, 480f, 483, 586
prevention of, 481, 482f, 483–484, 483p, 484, 485
for reduction of pain in elderly, 685
as risk factor for schizophrenia, 506
sleep aids, 671
sleep deprivation causing, 405
social norms affecting, 512–513
in U.S., 480f
variations in, 479–480, 479p, 480f, 480p
DSM-5. *See Diagnostic and Statistical Manual of Mental Disorders* (American Psychiatric Association)

Dual language learners (DLLs), 268
Dualism modified thinking, 534t
Dual-process model of cognition, 434–435, 435f
Due date, 94t
Dynamic sensory-motor systems, 142, 158
Dynamic-systems perspective
  approach to autism, 19
  approach to childhood obesity, 316
  defined, 19
  identity formation as, 459
  on impact of teratogens, 106
  operating in puberty, 403, 411, 426
  on socioeconomic factors affecting academic success, 383
  view of effect of past history/current context, 370
  view of sexual development, 290
Dyscalculia, 328–329, 336
Dyslexia, 328, 328p, 336
Dysregulated personalities, 520, 521f

Early adulthood, 6. See also Emerging adulthood
Early childhood
  activities by socioeconomic class and nationality, 282f
  artistic expressions, 232–233, 233p
  body changes, 215–218, 216p, 217f, 218f, 242
  brain development, 219–227, 219f, 220f, 221p, 223p, 225f, 226–227
  challenges for caregivers, 287–294, 287t, 288p, 290f, 292f
  cognitive learning stages, 46f
  compulsions about daily routines, 218, 218f
  development of emotional regulation, 130
  development of impulse control, 130
  effect of stress, 226
  emotional development, 275–280, 276p, 277p, 279p, 280p
  emotions and brain development in, 224, 225f, 226, 227
  environmental hazards, 229–231, 231f, 231p
  Erikson's stages of development, 40t, 41
  extremes of shyness or aggression, 549–550
  Freud's stages of development, 39–40, 40t
  impulsiveness and perseveration, 223, 223p
  injury in, 233–236, 234p, 235f
  intuitive-projective faith of, 531
  language learning, 256–262, 256t, 260f, 261p, 272
  left-handedness, 220–221
  limbic system of, 224, 225f
  maltreatment, 236–241, 236p, 237f, 238f, 239t, 240p
  moral development, 295–302, 297p, 297t, 299p, 300p, 301p, 391

motor skills development, 227–233, 228f, 228p, 231f, 231p, 232p, 233p
  nutrition during, 216–218, 216p, 217p
  oral health, 217–218
  play, 280, 281f, 282–286, 282f, 283p, 286f, 286p
  response to death, 764
  speed of thought, 220
  STEM education and, 251–252
  thought processes during, 245–256, 247p, 248f, 249p, 253p, 254f, 255f, 255p, 272
  as time of play and learning, 213, 214
  toilet training, 50–51
Early-childhood education
  child-centered programs, 263–265, 263p, 264p, 272, 305
  Head Start, 266–269, 267p, 268f
  homes and schools, 262–263
  long-term gains from intensive programs, 269–270, 272
  teacher-directed programs, 265–269, 265p, 266f, 267p, 268f, 272, 305
East Asia, 148f
Eastern Europe, 148f
Eating disorders. See also Obesity
  in adolescence, 414–415, 415p, 426
  anorexia nervosa, 415, 415p, 416, 426, 443, 454, 498
  associated with sexual abuse, 423
  binge eating disorder, 415
  binge-purge syndrome, 415
  bulimia nervosa, 415, 416, 426, 498
  dieting causing, 591
  egocentrism associated with, 430
  in emerging adulthood, 514
  encouragement through social networking, 443, 454
  HPA abnormalities causing, 402
  in U.S., 506
Eclectic perspective, 62–63
Ecological model, 8, 8f
Ecological niche, 634, 637, 661, 663, 700
Ecological validity, 707–708, 707f, 726
Ecological-systems approach, 7, 7–8, 8f, 22
Ecuador, 171
Education. See also Bilingual schooling; College; High school; Learning; Teaching
  of adolescents, 444–453, 445f, 445p, 448p, 450f, 453t, 454
  in art, 354f
  changing laws and practices, 331–332
  children in middle childhood with special needs, 323–335, 331p, 332f, 333p, 397
  for children of nuclear families, 379–380
  child's vs. adult's view of, 392
  cognitive decline correlated with, 702

college-bound students, 448–449, 450f
  controversy over starting age, 232
  cultural impact on, 14, 342–343, 342p, 343f
  dementia rates related to, 711
  dialectical approach to, 526
  effects of school climate on cyber-bullying, 442–443
  for elderly, 720–721
  employment affected by, 26–27
  encouragement of healthy eating, 414
  evolutionary theory concerning, 60
  exercise in schools, 312–313, 313p
  as factor in remarriage, 645
  for gifted and talented children, 333–335, 335p, 336, 355
  happiness in marriage correlated with, 642
  health affected by, 598, 600
  high school graduation rate, 444–445, 445f
  humanism in, 58
  impact on intelligence, 605, 607, 608, 609, 628
  infant mortality related to, 149
  influence on development, 10, 11
  international schooling, 353–355, 355p
  international testing, 356–357, 356t, 364
  life expectancy related to, 747f
  link to conscientious personality, 634
  maternal education's role in language learning, 351, 351f
  in middle childhood, 353, 354f, 354t, 355–362, 355p, 356t, 357p, 358p, 359t, 360f, 360p, 361p, 363f, 364
  in middle school, 445–448, 445p
  obesity related to, 444, 598
  observation vs. instruction, 342–343
  readiness for math and reading, 354t
  of recipients of physician-assisted suicide, 776f
  relationship to culture, 52
  sensitive periods, 21
  sex education, 471–473, 485, 487
  smoking related to, 598
  for special needs children, 331–333, 332f, 333p, 334p, 336
  stemming from regional differences in personality, 636
  teaching second language, 359–360, 360p
  teen pregnancy associated with, 422
  types of schools, 360f, 361–362, 361p, 364, 397, 441
  in United States, 358–360, 358p, 358t, 360f, 360p, 370
  use of technology, 441, 444, 454
  vision affected by, 83, 83p
  Vygotsky's view of, 341–343

Education of All Handicapped Children Act (1975), 331, 335
EEG (electroencephalogram), 161t
Effect size, 23t, B-4–B-5
Effortful control
  development in early childhood, 275–276, 387
  effect of high self-esteem, 369
  as inborn trait, 187–188
  reduction of bullying, 388
Egocentrism
  of adolescents, 429, 430–431, 434, 437, 446, 447, 454, 457
  aid to language learning, 257
  creation of fables, 430
  creation of imaginary audiences, 431, 431p
  of early childhood, 246, 247, 254, 256, 272, 764
  moral development related to, 296, 390
  resolution of dilemmas, 529
Egypt, 108, 115f, 762, A-3
Elder abuse, 752–753, 753p, 756, 757
Elder care, 652, 654, 745, 751, 754–756, 755p, 757
Elders/elderly. See Late adulthood
Elderspeak, 672, 676, 696
Electra complex, 292, 292f
Electroencephalogram (EEG), 161t
Electronics, 404
Elevated cholesterol, 315
Embryo, 95, 95p, 99, 122, 144
Embryonic growth, 1, 6–7
Embryonic period
  defined, 94
  development, 95–96, 96p, 99, 122
  effect of teratogens during, 106, 107f
  vulnerability during, 95t
Emerging adulthood
  age parameters of, 489, 493
  attraction of extremist groups, 460
  chronic illnesses in, 492t
  cognitive growth and higher education, 532–536, 532p, 533p, 534t, 537f, 538–539, 538p, 539p, 540, 571
  continuity and change during, 543–550, 544p, 544t, 545f, 546p, 547p, 547t, 548f, 548p, 549f, 569, 571
  deaths from top three causes, 495t
  defined, 6, 6t
  dilemmas of, 528–532
  growth and strength, 491–493, 491p, 492f, 492p, 494f, 495–500, 495t, 496p, 497p, 499t, 514, 571
  influence of current events on, 9
  intimacy during, 551–564, 552p, 553f, 555p, 556f, 556p, 557p, 558f, 560f, 564p, 568, 569, 571
  morals and religion, 528–532, 528p, 529f, 540, 571
  moratoria in, 458, 458p, 544

motor vehicle crashes, 438, 439f
need for freedom, 374
obesity rates, 589
objectives in life, 547t
peer influence in, 439f
political value consolidation, 8
postformal thought, 517–527,
518p, 520f, 521f, 521p,
524p, 540, 571
problems from unresolved
pathology, 544t
psychopathology, 503–507, 505p,
506p, 514, 571
relationships with parents, 546,
564–568, 565p, 566f,
567p, 569, 571
response to death, 765–766, 786
risk-taking, 507–513, 507p, 508f,
508p, 509p, 510f, 510p,
514, 571
roles signaling, 489
sense of well-being, 549, 549f
sexual activity, 500–503, 500p,
514, 571
smoking during, 588f
suicide rates, A-21
time management during,
518–519, 518p
trends in, 489
view of same-sex marriage, 9, 9f
voting rates, 742f
Emotional development
anger and sadness, 182–183,
182p, 182t
brain development in first two years
and, 185–189, 187p, 188f
brain maturation in early
childhood, 276–277
cultural impact on, 278
in early childhood, 275–280, 276p,
277p, 279p, 280p, 303, 305
fear, 183, 183p
in first two years, 181–184, 182p,
182t, 183p, 209, 211
imaginary friends, 277–278
initiative versus guilt, 276–277
motivation for preschoolers, 276p,
277–278
prosocial behavior, 296
protective optimism, 276, 276p
in puberty, 403
of Romanian adoptees, 196
seeking balance, 279, 279p
self-awareness, 184, 184p
smiling and laughing, 182, 182p
social awareness, 184
temperament, 187–189, 188f
Emotional problems, 239, 375
Emotional regulation
in adolescence, 416–417, 426
brain maturation required for,
416–418
as control process in information
processing, 346
cultural influences on, 185, 278
development in early childhood, 220,
223, 224, 225f, 227, 242,
275–276, 279, 303, 318, 387
effects of drugs on, 483

as foundation for moral
development, 298
in frontal lobe disorders, 712
as lifelong necessity, 276
in middle childhood, 397
moral development and empathy
associated with, 295
prioritizing in late adulthood, 732
role of play, 282, 283, 284, 303
seeking balance, 279, 279p
sex differences, 279, 279p, 280,
280p, 281f
use of imaginary friends, 276–277
Emotional stress, 502–504, 514
Emotion-focused coping, 616–617
Emotions
adolescents' reliance on, 437
brain development in early childhood and, 224, 225f, 226
development of in first two years,
125, 130
development of normal responses,
133, 222
of the dying, 769, 782, 786
grief, 778–780, 783–784
limbic system and, 224, 225f
mourning, 780–783, 780p, 781p,
782p, 784
stress hormones and, 226
for survival, 204–205
Empathy
defined, 296
development of, 297p, 302, 305
development of moral values, 389
measurement of, 707f
reduction of bullying, 388, 392
role of play in learning, 282
Emphysema, 715
Empirical evidence, 4, 5, 32
Employee benefits, 654–655, 658
Employment. See also Employee
benefits; Wages; Work
schedules; Workforce
aging affected by, 694, 696
areas of interest, 548t
changing workplace, 656–658,
656f, 657p, 660, 661
cognitive decline correlated with,
702
combining intimacy and generativity,
658–660, 659p
consequences of maltreatment in
childhood, 239
effect on mental status, 504
of the elderly, 737–738, 737f, 738p
of emerging adults, 543, 547,
547–548, 549, 550, 569
fulfillment of psychological needs,
654, 655, 661, 663
impact on intelligence, 607, 608,
628
in late adulthood, 743, 757
physical appearance associated
with, 497, 514
in teen years, 460, 460f
wages and benefits, 654–655, 655p
work schedules, 658, 658p, 660,
661
Empty love, 553t

Empty nest, 573, 643
Encouragement, 36
England. See United Kingdom
English as a second language (ESL),
359
English language learners (ELL),
350, 359–360, 360p
Enmeshment, 566
Entity theory of intelligence, 447, 448
Environment
contribution to alcoholism, 82
effect on incidence of twins, 75
influence on phenotype, 77–78,
78p, 84, 90
influence on schizophrenia, 87
Environmental hazards. See also
Toxins
gross motor development and,
229–230
lead, 230–231, 231f, 231p
Epidural anesthesia, 103
Epigenetics
contributing to childhood obesity,
315
defined, 16–17, 90
effect on genes, 70, 77–78, 84
emotional impact on, 186
influence on development, 16–17,
17f, 215, 736
prevention of neurocognitive
impairment, 714
role in socialization, parenthood,
communication, language,
60
study of development, 16–17
Equifinality, 324, 325, 330
Erikson, Erik
arenas of identity, 459
autonomy vs. shame and doubt,
200, 208, 209
on caregiving, 651
on children's effect on parents, 647
generativity vs. stagnation, 632,
632t, 637, 646, 661
identity vs. role confusion, 458,
462, 485, 543, 632, 632t
industry vs. inferiority, 368, 373,
395
initiative vs. guilt, 276–277, 277p,
279, 303
integrity vs. despair, 719, 730, 757
intimacy vs. isolation, 551, 560,
569, 637
on late adulthood, 719
photograph of, 41p
stages of psychosocial development,
40t, 41, 48, 50, 64, 199,
544t, 632, 632t, 637
view of sexes, 461
ERP (event-related potential), 161t
Esteem, 56, 57, 57f, 632
Estonia, A-16
Estradiol, 403
Estrogen, 402f, 403, 426, 554, 663
Ethical behavior, 296
Ethics
of death and dying, 771–778,
772t, 773f, 774p, 774t,
776f, 777p, 778, 786

defined, 29
development of in adulthood, 528,
540
of genetic counselors, 88–89
implications of research results,
30–31, 32
issues raised for allocation of public
health funds, 597–598
learned through neighborhood
games, 311p
of medical intervention for preterm infants, 103
postformal thought related to, 529
protection of research participants,
30
in research, 29–31, B-1
Ethiopia, 115f
Ethnic group, 14
Ethnic identity
formation in emerging adulthood,
544, 546–547, 546p, 550,
569, 571
peer pressure enabling formation
of, 467
Ethnic pride, 474
Ethnicity. See also specific ethnic
group
age of puberty related to, 407f,
410–411
breast-feeding by, A-7
caregiving expectations related
to, 652
of college students, 536
composition in U.S., A-4
contraception use and, 580
death in a hospice by, 771
diabetes and, 690
early-/late-maturing children
affected by, 410–411
education associated with, 358,
537f
employment discrimination, 656
as factor in remarriage, 645
high school graduation rate by, 450f
influence on development, 14–15
interethnic marriage, 559, 561
moral values associated with, 528
mortality rates differing by, 595
nutrition and, 217
obesity rates by in U.S., 216, 590f
onset of puberty affected by, 406
percentages of employees, 656f
physician-assisted suicide related
to, 776f
relationship to race/culture, 14f,
22
school drop-out rates related to,
446
self-esteem related to, 473
sexual activity in adolescence
related to, 421
smoking behaviors by, A-19
as social construct, 22, 216
stratification of society by, 734–736,
735f, 735p
suicide rates by, A-21
support and defense of members
of group, 447
Ethnotheories, 35

Eulogies, 780
Europe. *See also specific nation*
  alcohol consumption in, 479
  ART in, 583
  birth of thalidomide affected
    babies, 106
  cognition in, 527
  cohabitation in, 556
  education in, 566
  elder care in, 752, 754
  funeral customs in, 763
  languages spoken by school
    children, 359
  life expectancy, 598
  low birthweights in, 114, 115f
  onset of puberty, 406
  percentage of young adolescents
    not in school, 482f
  punishment of poor behavior in,
    299, 301
  self-concept of children in, 276
  sex education in, 472
  sports in, 312
  stunting in children in, 148f
European Americans
  activities of children, 227
  average daily exposure to video in
    U.S., 286f
  average height of children, 216
  breast-feeding by, A-7
  caregiving style, 289
  childhood obesity rates in U.S.,
    315f
  children's activities by
    socioeconomic class, 282f
  cognition of, 527
  diabetes among, 690
  divorce rate, 643
  extroverted personalities, 636
  gene for obesity, 315
  incidence of childhood obesity,
    216
  incidence of twins, 75
  level of education, 537f
  life expectancy, 617, 691, 735f,
    747f
  mortality rate, 594
  obesity rate and income, 590f
  onset of puberty, 406, 410
  physician-assisted suicide and,
    775, 776f
  population of, A-4
  reading ability in middle child-
    hood, 350
  self-esteem in adolescence, 473
  sexual activity in adolescence,
    420–421, 421
  smoking behaviors in high school,
    A-19
  suicide rates, A-21
  in U.S. workforce, 656, 656f
  use of IVF, 583–584
Euthanasia, 773–775, 773f, 774f,
  774p, 776f, 778, 786
Eveningness, 404, 410
Event-related potential (ERP), 161t
Evolutionary theory
  on aging, 690
  on allocare, 205, 205p

application to infant social
  development, 204–205, 209
concepts of, 55–56, 58–61, 64
on early onset of puberty, 409
on gender development, 294
on language development, 173
on maternal employment, 208
on moral development, 295
on neurogenesis, 700
responses to, 37
Excitement, 416–418, 419p,
  438–439, 439f
Executive function, 254, 705, 720
Executive processes, 346
Exercise. *See also* Physical activity;
  Play
  during adolescence, 671f
  of adults, 671f
  aging affected by, 578, 676, 687,
    694, 696
  benefits of, 311, 497, 500, 592p,
    600, 672
  brain fitness related to, 323f, 702,
    714, 714p, 715–716, 719
  effect of excessive exercise on
    fetus, 109t
  during emerging adulthood, 497,
    497p, 498, 507, 514, 571
  in late adulthood, 671–672, 671f,
    673, 673p, 676
  motivation for in adulthood, 497,
    663
  neighborhood games, 311–312, 336
  protection against illness, 592
  social norms affecting, 511
  timing of menopause affected by,
    584
Exosystem, 7, 8, 8f, 235, 255–256.
  See also Communities;
    Employment; Religion;
    Videos
Expectant experiences, 133
Expectations
  affecting language learning,
    352–353
  for math and reading goals, 354t
  of maturity in caregiving, 287–288,
    287t
Experience
  accumulation of with age, 493
  of aging, 576f, 576o, 578–579,
    578p
  bereavement affected by, 783
  brain growth associated with, 132,
    137, 152, 167, 185–186,
    322
  control processes affected by, 346
  decision making influenced by,
    436–437, 439
  dendrite growth stimulated by,
    167, 351
  development of moral values, 389
  effect of stress associated with,
    226
  fine motor skills associated with,
    152
  increase in knowledge base, 345
  intelligence influenced by, 605,
    607, 609, 614

memory affected by, 321, 344
moral development affected by,
  530–531, 532
perception of affordances and,
  163–164
perception requiring, 137
personality shaped by, 549
postformal thought affected by, 523
professional success associated
  with, 451
pruning of brain connections, 132
role in personality development, 631
speed of thought affected by, 321
temperament influenced by, 634
Experience-dependent brain development, 133, 211, 282
Experience-expectant brain development, 133, 211, 282–283
Experiment, 24, 24f, 28, 32
Experimental group, 24, 24f
Experimental variable. *See*
  Independent variable
Expert cognition, 621–627, 622p,
  623f, 626p, 627, 627f,
  628, 663
Expertise, 621, 625–626, 626p, 627,
  627f
Explicit memory, 167, 704
Expressive language, 259
Extended family, 375, 376t, 378
Externalization of problems, 279–280,
  303, 380, 383, 387, 476
Extreme sports, 507–509, 508p,
  509p, 513
Extremely low birthweight (ELBW),
  113
Extrinsic motivation, 277, 278
Extrinsic rewards of work, 655
Extroversion
  outlook on life, 659
  as personality trait, 634, 635, 635f,
    636, 637, 661
Exuberance, 187–188
Eye movements, 248
Eye-hand coordination, 141, 141p
Eyes, 138. *See also* Vision

Fables of adolescence, 430
Face recognition, 134
Facilitation of behavior, 469, 477
Factor analysis, 23t
Facts, 37–39
Failed suicide. *See* Parasuicide
Failure to thrive, 128
False negative, 112
False positive, 111
False-belief tests, 254
Familism, 474
Family. *See also* Cohabitation;
  Divorce; Family function;
  Family structure; Fathers;
  Marriage; Mothers;
  Parents; Same-sex parents
  adoption, 185, 196, 196p, 204p,
    226, 241, 242, 375, 376t,
    379, 384, 648–649, 648p
  adult children-parent relation-
    ships, 639–640, 639p, 641,
    660, 661

  adult siblings, 640, 640p, 641
  advancement of social
    understanding, 225f
  in Africa, 566
  aging affected by, 694
  beanpole family, 744–745, 745f,
    751
  benefits of breast-feeding, 147t
  bonding, 120–121, 121p
  caregiving, 651–652, 652, 652p,
    653f, 654, 658–660, 659p
  conflict within, 383, 384, 387, 408,
    561–564, 567, 569, 571
  contribution to childhood obesity,
    315, 316
  of the dying, 770
  effect of socioeconomic status,
    382–383, 384
  effect on birthweight, 122
  effect on sleep patterns, 135, 137
  effects of alcoholism, 588
  elements of developmental con-
    text, 7
  family of choice, 641–646, 641p,
    642f, 642p, 643t, 644p,
    645p
  family of origin, 641
  father's role in pregnancy and
    birth, 117, 119, 122
  fictive kin, 640
  filial responsibility, 745, 749, 751,
    757
  foster families, 196, 196p, 226,
    240, 242, 375, 567,
    650–651
  functions of, 374–375, 395, 397
  grandparent-grandchild relation-
    ships, 744–745, 744p, 757
  grandparents and great-grand-
    parents, 746–748, 746p,
    747p, 757
  homicide rates among, 562f
  impact on intelligence, 628
  importance during emerging adult-
    hood, 564–568, 565p,
    566f, 567p
  importance in late adulthood, 732,
    736, 737, 743–749, 743p,
    744p, 745f, 746p, 747f,
    748p, 749p, 766–767, 767f
  intergenerational homes, 639–640
  intergenerational support, 745
  intergenerational tensions,
    745–746
  kangaroo care, 121, 121p, 122
  kinkeepers, 651–652, 653f
  in late adulthood, 743–748, 743p,
    744p, 745f, 746p, 747f,
    749, 757
  linked lives, 564–565, 565p, 569,
    639, 659, 661
  middle childhood and, 373–384,
    373p, 375f, 376t, 377f,
    378p, 379p, 381f, 382p,
    395
  mothers following birth, 119, 122
  newborns, 116–117, 122
  parent-adolescent relationships,
    463–464, 464p, 485

parent-adult child bonds, 639–640, 639p
parental alliance, 120, 122, 199, 327, 378, 379, 395
parental favoritism, 567, 640
reduction in size, 501
relationships, 118f
response to emotional complexities of, 626–627, 628
sexual abuse within, 424
shared and unshared environments, 373, 373p, 395
skipped-generation family, 747, 749
smaller size of related to adolescent crime, 478
as source of intellectual activity, 341
as source of needs, 374–375, 384
stepfamilies, 375, 376t, 379, 380, 384, 649–650
support of same-sex partners, 644
work schedules affecting, 658
Family function
conflict, 383, 383–384, 384, 387, 395, 408, 462, 561–564, 567, 569, 571, 643
correlation with income, 382, 384, 395, 397
defined, 374
depression in adolescence related to, 474
divorce, 381–382, 382p. *See also* Divorce
eating disorders associated with, 415
effect on children in middle childhood, 380
effect on onset of puberty, 408, 409, 410
family structure and, 376, 377f, 378–381, 381f, 397
socioeconomic context, 382–383
Family of choice, 641–646, 641p, 642f, 642p, 643t, 644p, 645p
Family of origin, 641, 644
Family structure
correlation with income, 378, 382, 384, 397
defined, 372
family function and, 376, 377f, 378–381, 381f, 397
single-parent families, 375f, 377f, 380–381, 381f
two-parent families, 378–379, 378p, 379, 379p
types of, 375, 376t, 395
Family-stress model, 382–383
Farsightedness, 579p, 600
Fast-mapping, 257, 262, 267
Fathers. *See also* Parenting; Parents
baby's words for, A-9
biological response to birth, 119, 122
as caregivers, 181, 181p, 207, 626–627, 659
depression following birth, 119
effect on birth complications, 117, 119
effect on birthweight, 113–114, 116
impact of children, 647
influence on sons, 44
kangaroo care, 121

percentage who spank one-year-olds, 199t
response to infants, 116
as social partners, 197–199, 198p, 199f, 208, 209
support of mothers during/after birth, 117, 119, 121
Fatuous love, 553t
Fear. *See also* Anxiety; Anxiety disorders
brain growth enabling, 185
of death, 762
development of hypothalamus effected by, 186
effect of caregiver's response, 188–189, 188f
emphasis on regulation of in U.S., 278
as indicator of maltreatment, 239t
as learned response, 164, 182t, 183, 183p, 184, 209
persistence of, 634
regulation of, 224, 279, 416
separation anxiety, 183
stranger wariness, 183, 183p, 229, 233
in toddlers, 183
Females. *See also* Girls; Mothers
chromosomes of, 70–71, 70p
effect of child maltreatment, 239–240
innate vulnerability of, 108
literacy rates, 12f
Ferdinand, Archduke Francis, 782
Fertility
by age and cohort, A-20
causes of infertility, 582–583, 586, 588, 600
link to conscientious personality, 634
link to openness, 635
peak time, 491, 500, 514, 571, 627
treatment of infertility, 583–584, 584p, 586
Fetal alcohol syndrome (FAS), 105, 105p, 108
Fetal consciousness, 99
Fetal growth, 1
Fetal period
brain development, 129, 130
defined, 94
development, 96–99, 96p, 97p, 98p, 122
development of hearing, 138
effect of teratogens during, 105, 106, 106f, 107–108, 107f, 109–110t, 110
photographs of, 94p
third month, 96–97
vulnerability during, 95t
Fetus
defined, 96
development of, 96–99, 122
photograph of, 95p, 96p, 97p, 98p
prenatal diagnosis of problems, 111
preterm delivery, 94t, 97, 98, 99p
teratogen damage to, 105, 106f, 107–108, 107f, 109–110t, 110
Feuds, 783

Fever, 583
Fictive kin, 640
Filial responsibility, 745, 749, 751, 757
Fine motor skills
development in early childhood, 242
development in first two years, 141–142, 152
in early childhood, 232–233, 232p
norms for development, 142t
Finger movement skills, 141
Finland
average age of marriage, 545f
friendships of adolescents in, 469
high school graduation rate, 445f, 482f
high-stakes tests in, 450
low birthweights in, 115f
punishment of poor behavior in, 300, 301
scores on international tests, 356, 356t, 452, 453t, A-16
view of teaching in, 356–357
First acquired adaptations, 156–157, 156t
First names of children, 9t
First-born children, 29
First-grade curriculum, 341
First-person pronouns, 184
5-HTTLPR genotype, 188, 465, 465f, 474
Flexibility, 522–523, 612, 625, 627, 628, 663
Flipped class, 539
Flu, 685, 685f
Fluid intelligence, 608–609, 610, 614, 663
Flying storks, 104
Flynn effect, 321, 605
fMRI (functional magnetic resonance imaging), 161, 161t
Focus on appearance, 246, 247–248, 256, 272, 293
Folic acid, 108
Folk psychology, 253
Folk theories, 35
Fontanelles, 129
Food insecurity, 115
Forced retirement, 699
Forebrain, 98t
Foreclosure, 458, 459, 461, 462, 544
Formal code (language), 349–350, 353, 364
Formal operational thought
in adolescence, 431–434, 431p, 432f, 434, 435f, 448, 454, 487, 518
adult thinking compared to, 518
characteristics of, 45p, 46, 46f, 46t
hypothetical-deductive reasoning, 432–433, 433f
moral development related to, 390
Piaget's experiment, 431–432, 432f
Formula-feeding, 146, 148
Foster care
advantages over institutions, 196, 196p, 226
effect on college financing, 567
kinship care, 241, 242, 376t, 747
for maltreated children, 240, 242

Foster children, 650
Foster families, 375
Foster parents, 650–651, 661
Fowler, James, 531
Fragile X syndrome, 86, 86–87, 89
Frail elderly
abuse of, 752–753, 753p
activities of daily life indicating, 750, 750t
care of, 751, 752–756, 752p, 753p, 754p, 755p
defined, 749–750
preventing frailty, 751
France
centenarians in, 695
cohabitation in, 556
contraception in, 580
infant day care in, 207
overweight people in, 590f
population of children and elders, A-3
public pension in, 738
scores on international tests, 356t, 453t, A-16
sexually active teens/condom use, 425, 425f
single-parent families in, 375f
Fraternal twins, 74f, 75, 90
Freestyle motocross, 507–508, 508p
French, Ruth, 713
Freud, Anna, 476
Freud, Sigmund
latency of middle childhood, 368, 373, 395
oral and anal stages in infant social development, 199–200, 208, 209
phallic stage and preschoolers' sexism, 291–292, 295, 303
photograph of, 39p
psychosexual theory, 39–40, 40t, 48, 50, 51
as a student, 334
Friendships
in adulthood, 638–639, 638p, 641, 661
aging affected by, 694
aid for bullied children, 388
conflict between friends, 561–564
in emerging adulthood, 551–553, 552p, 568, 569, 661, 748
encouragement of activity, 498
facilitation of bad/good behavior, 469, 477, 485
friends with benefits, 554
hostile side of, 392
importance of in adolescence, 438, 466–467
importance of in late adulthood, 736, 737
lack of as indicator of maltreatment, 239t
in late adulthood, 729, 732, 748–749, 748p, 749p, 757
male-female friendships, 552p, 569
in middle childhood, 385, 389
in middle school setting, 447
selection of friends, 469

Frontal cortex, 130f, 219
Frontal lobe disorders, 712–713, 713p, 716, 726
Fronto-striatal systems, 48
Frontotemporal lobar degeneration, 712–713, 713f
FTO allele, 315
Functional magnetic resonance imaging (fMRI), 161, 161t
Funeral customs, 763, 779, 780–781
Fun-loving grandparents, 747
Fusiform face area of brain, 134

G (general intelligence), 320–321, 323, 604, 608, 610, 628, 701
Gamete, 68
Gang involvement, 469, 477
Gardening, 739, 740f
Gardner, Howard, 321–322, 328
Gay marriage, 9, 461f, 529, 559
Gay partners, 563, 644
Gender. See also Boys; Girls; Men; Sex; Women
  of college students, 536
  contribution to alcoholism, 82
  difference in intimate relationships, 554–555
  drug use and abuse related to, 480
  emotional regulation associated with, 279, 279p, 280, 280p, 281f
  employment discrimination, 656
  friendships related to, 552, 552p, 569
  life expectancy by ethnicity and SES, 735f
  moral values related to, 530, 531, 595
  onset of puberty affected by, 406
  personality related to, 634
  relationship to sex, 291
  response to stress associated with, 616–617
  sexual activity in adolescence affected by, 420–421
  sociodramatic play in early childhood by, 285–286
  stratification of society by, 734–736, 734p, 735f, 735p
  teaching gender roles, 290–294, 290p, 292p
Gender development
  behaviorists' view of, 293
  cognitive theory, 293
  in early childhood, 303
  evolutionary theory, 294
  genetic determination of age of onset, 406
  humanists' view of, 294
  psychoanalytic theory, 291–292
  in puberty, 406, 407f, 408–409
  sociocultural theory, 293–294
Gender differences, 291
Gender discrimination
  awareness of in middle childhood, 369
  in middle childhood, 385

of preschoolers, 285, 291–294, 294p
Gender dysphoria, 471
Gender identity, 461, 462, 485, 502–503
Gender roles
  changing patterns, 561, 626
  as social learning, 201
  teaching in early childhood, 290–294, 290p, 292p
Gender schema, 293
Gene-gene interactions, 78–81
General intelligence (g), 320–321, 323, 604, 608, 610, 628, 701
Generalizations, 13
Generational forgetting, 483, 484
Generativity
  caregiving, 651–652, 652p, 653f, 654, 660, 661, 663
  defined, 646
  employment, 654–660, 655p, 656f, 657p, 658p, 659p, 661, 663, 737–738
  parenthood, 646–651, 646p, 658–660, 659p, 661, 663
  volunteer work, 739, 739f, 739p
Generativity vs. stagnation, 40t, 41, 544t, 632, 632t, 637, 646
Genes. See also Alleles; Chromosomes; DNA; Epigenetics; Genotype
  activation of latent genes, 78
  for addiction, 82, 690
  additive heredity, 78, 81, 90
  for alcoholism, 82, 90
  for Alzheimer disease, 712
  anxiety disorders affected by, 505
  application of genetics, 83–84
  for asthma, 317, 336
  for autism, 336
  beneficial mutations of, 59–60
  for bullying, 387
  for cancer, 586
  childhood obesity affected by, 315
  computer illustration of segment of, 69p
  at conception, 69, 70
  contribution to childhood obesity, 315
  control of aging process, 578, 689–690, 690, 694, 696
  control of brain growth, 132, 137
  control of handedness, 221
  controlling language acquisition, 259
  copy number variations, 79–81, 81p
  deactivation of, 80
  defined, 68, 90
  for dementia, 577, 711
  depression caused by, 474
  for diabetes, 589
  differential sensitivity of, 20–22, 21, 22, 60, 108, 188, 207, 289, 370, 373, 380, 408, 473–474
  dominant-recessive heredity, 78–79, 79f, 80t, 85–87, 90

effect of, 84
epigenetic effect on, 70, 77–78, 84
for frontal lobe disorders, 713
for gender development, 406, 420, 426
genetic counseling and testing, 87–89, 88p
happiness affected by, 373
heterozygous genes, 70
homozygous genes, 70
hypertension caused by, 690
incidence of twins controlled by, 75
intelligence affected by, 607
interaction of, 90
mature brain affected by, 600
number in humans, 78, 90
parent-adolescent relationships affected by, 465, 465f
personality development and, 631, 636–637, 637p
personality formed by, 549
plasticity genes, 550
polymorphic genes, 69
problems caused by, 85–87, 85p, 86t, 89, 336
protein synthesis, 68, 68f
race and, 15
for schizophrenia, 506, 514
temperament influenced by, 634
teratogens effects influenced by, 108
timing of menopause directed by, 584
uniformity in cells of individuals, 72–73
vision affected by, 82–83, 84, 579
Genetic blood types, A-5
Genetic clock, 689–690
Genetic code, 68–69, 90
Genetic counseling, 88–89, 88p, 90
Genetic diseases, 309, A-6
Genetic diversity, 60, 69
Genetic selection, 137
Genetic testing, 87–88, 90
Genetic theories of aging, 689–690, 693, 695, 696
Genetic vulnerability, 108, 116, 122
Genetics, 16–17
Genital herpes, 424, A-17
Genital stage, 39–40, 40t
Genome, 69
Genome sequencing, 88
Genotype
  additive heredity, 78
  carrier of, 78–79, 79f
  copy number variations, 79–81, 81p
  creation at conception, 70, 77
  defined, 70
  dominant-recessive heredity, 78–79, 79f
  effect of, 84
  functions of, 77
  parental imprinting, 81, 81p
  X-linked characteristics, 79, 80t
Gentile, Brittany, 549, B-5
Georgia, Republic of, 693–694
Germ theory, 613
Germany

allocare in, 207
average age of marriage, 545f
family bonds in, 639
high school graduation rate, 445f, 482f
infertility rates, 582
low birthweights in, 115f
marriage in, 556
mastery of numbers, 251
overweight people in, 590f
population of children and elders, A-3
preferred sex of children, 72
primary curriculum in, 355
punishment of poor behavior in, 301
scores on international tests, 356t, 453t, A-16
self-esteem of emerging adults, 549
separation anxiety in infants from, 183
single-parent families in, 375f
smokers in, 587
use of HRT in, 585
Germinal period
  defined, 94
  development, 94p, 94t, 99, 122
  effect of teratogens during, 106, 107f
  vulnerability during, 95t
Gestational age, 94t
Gestures, 248
Ghana, 375, 639–640, A-3
Ghosts in the nursery, 136, 203
Gifted and talented children, 322, 333–335, 333p, 336, 397, 446
Girls. See also Females
  addiction to video games, 441–442, 441f
  anorexia nervosa, 415, 415p
  body image in adolescence, 409, 414, 414p
  as bullies, 386p, 387
  change in body shape at puberty, 401, 420
  childhood obesity rates in U.S., 315f
  delinquency of, 477, 478
  depression in adolescence, 474
  determining sexual orientation, 470p, 471
  drug use and abuse, 480
  emotional regulation, 279, 280, 280p, 281f
  growth of, 401–402, 406, 412, 491, A-10, A-11
  incidence of anemia, 413
  internalization of problems, 279–280, 303, 380, 383
  maturation of, 232
  moral development of, 292, 530
  mother's influence on, 44
  puberty, 399, 401, 402f, 403, 407f, 409–410, 410p, 426
  school drop-out rates, 446
  self-esteem in adolescence, 473
  sex-related impulses of, 420–421
  sexual abuse of, 408, 423–424, 426

sexual activity, 472
smoking behaviors, A-19
social effect of early or late matu-
    ration, 409–410, 410p, 411
sociodramatic play in early
    childhood, 285–286
suicidal ideation in adolescence,
    474–475
suicide/parasuicide of, 473–474,
    475, 475f, 485
underachievement in school, 446
vulnerability to drug use, 479
Glaucoma, 107f, 681p, 681t, 696
Global warming, 115
Glucose, 588
Goal setting, 577
Goals, infants' pursuit of, 158, 162
Golden hour, 236
Gonads, 403
Gonorrhea, 109t, 424, A-17
Grabbing, 152, 158, 165
Graf, Steffi, 334
Grammar
    acquisition in early childhood,
        259, 272
    advancement in middle childhood,
        349, 353
    defined, 172, 259
    overregularization, 259
Grandparenthood, 647
Grandparents
    aid to grandchildren, 648
    raising grandchildren, 375, 376t,
        379, 384, 397
    relationships with grandchildren,
        744–745, 746–747, 746p,
        749, 757
    roles of, 747, 749
Grasping, 142
Gratitude, 300
Gray power, 743
Great Britain. See United Kingdom
Great-grandparents, 746–748, 747f
Greece
    death rituals in, 762
    elderly volunteers in, 739
    high school graduation rate, 445f,
        482f
    parenting in, 201–202
    PISA scores, A-16
Greek philosophy, 527
Grief, 778–780, 783–784
Gross motor skills
    crawling, 140p
    defined, 140
    developed during play, 283–284
    development in early childhood,
        227, 228f, 229–231, 231f,
        231p, 233, 242
    development in first two years,
        140–141, 142, 152
    effect of lead, 230–231, 231f, 231p
    environmental hazards delaying,
        229–230
    motivation for learning, 165
Grounded theory, 677
Growth. See also Body size; Brain
    in adolescence, 411–416, 412f,
        414p, 415p, 426, 487, 491

aspects of, 4
in early childhood, 215–218
in first two years, 211
of muscles in emerging adulthood,
    491, 571
norms, A-10–A-11
nutrition in early childhood,
    216–218, 216p, 217f
patterns in early childhood,
    215–216, 216p, 217f, 218
patterns of developmental growth,
    6f
Growth spurt, 411–412, 487
Guatemala, 498, A-3
Guided participation, 14, 52, 249,
    249p
Guilt, 276, 295, 300, 303

Habituation, 160–161, 162, 163
Hair
    in adulthood, 578, 580, 600
    changes in puberty, 401–402, 420
    as display of sexuality, 412
    in late adulthood, 684, 696
Haiti, 115f, 590f
Hand gestures, 170, 170p, 178
Hand skills, 141, 142t
Handedness, 220–221
Happiness
    activity correlated with, 736, 737
    arising from genes and nonshared
        environment, 373
    cohabitation related to, 557–558
    in late adulthood, 732, 733–734
    in marriage, 557–558, 641–643,
        641p, 642f, 642p, 643f,
        646, 676, 744
    in retirement, 739
Hard-to-please personality, 634
Harm reduction, 234–235, 234p
Harmony, 375, 379, 397
Hassles, 615, 618
Hate, 239
Hayflick limit, 690–691, 696
Head Start
    benefits to low-income children,
        270, 272, 305
    bilingual education, 268–269
    children enrolled by race/ethnic-
        ity, 268f
    disaster recovery, 267p
    need for structure, 267–268
    regulation of, 266–267
Head-sparing, 129, 133
Healing, 684
Health
    activity correlated with, 737
    of adults, 586
    ageism's effect on, 668, 669, 670
    attitude's effect on, 669, 670
    benefits of exercise, 311, 497–498,
        497p, 672, 736
    commitment in marriage corre-
        lated with, 643
    disability, 596–597, 599, 600
    effect of friendships, 551, 638
    in emerging adulthood, 492, 492t,
        493, 494f, 495–500, 495t,
        496p, 497p, 499t, 571

impact on intelligence, 605, 607,
    608, 628
income correlated with, 598–599,
    598p
job related problems, 657, 658
level of education related to, 444
maintenance of in emerging adult-
    hood, 497–500, 497p, 499t
in middle childhood, 309–312,
    310f, 311p, 312p, 313p
morbidity rate, 596, 599, 600
mortality rate, 564–565, 595f,
    599, 600
in retirement, 739
stratification's effect on, 735
vitality, 597–598, 599, 600
volunteer work linked to, 739
Health care proxy, 777, 778, 786
Health habits
    of adults, 586–589, 586t, 587p,
        588f, 590f, 591–594, 591p,
        592f, 592p, 600, 663
    age and, 663
    breaking bad habits, 593–594, 594p
    drug abuse. See Drug use and
        abuse
    exercise. See Exercise; Physical
        activity; Play; Sports
    inactivity, 592, 592f
    in middle childhood, 311
    nutrition. See Diet; Nutrition
    obesity. See Obesity
    relationship to longevity, 353
Health problems. See also Diabetes;
        Heart attack; Heart dis-
        ease; Illness; Mental ill-
        ness; Psychopathology
    asthma, 317–318, 317f, 317p
    childhood obesity, 313, 314f,
        315–316, 316p
    chronic illness in adolescence,
        686, 688
    Internet as source for children
        with, 469
    in middle childhood, 313, 314f,
        315–318, 315f, 316p, 317f,
        317p
Hearing
    in adulthood, 579–580, 600
    area of brain controlling, 130f
    deafness, 107f
    effect of low birthweight, 114
    of elderly, 672, 681–682, 682p,
        696
    fetal development of, 99, 99p,
        138, 142, 152
    maturity at birth, 130f
Hearing loop, 682
Heart
    aging of, 576, 684
    effects of exercise, 592
    effects of stress, 615
    strength in emerging adulthood,
        495
Heart attack, 686, 695, 715
Heart disease
    benefits of exercise, 497, 592
    benefits of moderate alcohol use,
        588

causes of, 496, 576, 668
cognitive effect on, 78
copy number variations causing,
    80
deaths due to, 685f, 686
disability due to, 597
effect of breast-feeding, 146, 147t
effect of low birthweight, 114
effects of stress, 617
in elderly, 686
during emerging adulthood, 495
from HRT, 585
incidence of, 596
prevention of, 715
symptoms of, 686
Heartbeat
    area of brain controlling, 130
    irregularity as symptom of heart
        disease, 686
    rate during emerging adulthood,
        493, 495
    rate in late adulthood, 684
Helicopter parents, 567
Herbicides, 109t
Herd immunity, 145, 151
Heredity. See also Chromosomes;
        DNA; Genes; Genetic code
    activation/deactivation of genes,
        81
    of addiction, 82, 690
    additive heredity, 78, 81
    application of genetics, 83–84
    contribution to childhood obesity,
        315
    copy number variations, 79–81,
        81p
    dominant-recessive heredity,
        78–79, 79f, 80t, 81
    effect on vision, 82–83, 84, 579
    excess chromosomes, 84–85, 85p,
        86t
    genetic counseling and testing,
        87–89, 88p
    genetic disorders, 85–87, 85p, 85t
    X-linked characteristics, 79
Heredity-environment debate. See
        Nature-nurture controversy
Heritability, 82–83
Hernandez, Theresa, 111
Heroin, 109t
Heterogamy, 561
Heterozygous genes, 70
Heuristic, 436
Hiccups, 117
Hidden curriculum, 355, 360, 448
High blood pressure. See
        Hypertension
High school, 448–453, 448p, 450f,
        453t, 454, A-19
High school graduation rate,
    444–445, 445f, 449, 450f,
    454, 482f
Higher education. See College
High/Scope, 269
High-stakes tests, 449–450, 450f,
    451, 454
Hikikomori, 505–506, 506p
Hindbrain development, 98t
Hinduism, 763, 781

Hippocampus
  of Alzheimer patients, 711
  atrophy with age, 683, 701
  damage from alcohol, 481
  functions of, 219f, 224, 227, 242,
      A-2
  maturation of, 167
  new cells in late adulthood, 700
  stress hormones effect on, 226
Hispanic Americans. *See also* Latinos
  breast-feeding by, A-7
  childhood obesity, 315f, 316, 414
  diagnosed with ADHD, 326
  education of, 268–269, 268t, 360,
      450f, 537f
  as English language learners, 350
  ethnic identity of, 546
  life expectancy, 735f
  obesity rate and income, 590f
  onset of puberty, 406
  population of, A-4
  smoking behaviors in high school,.
      A-19
  suicide rates, A-21
  in U.S. workforce, 656, 656f
Historical context. *See also*
      Chronosystem; Cohort
  of acceptance of homosexuality,
      9, 9t
  of death and dying, 762–763, 786
  defined, 7, 8
  of drug use and abuse, 511
  identity related to, 458, 459, 460
  of intelligence, 605, 608, 614, 628
  of love, 558–559
  marriage differences related to,
      554, 558–559, 748
  moral values related to, 528
  of onset of puberty, 406
  relationship to other contexts, 8f
  of sexual activity, 500–501, 500p
HIV/AIDS
  breast-feeding and, 146
  effect on brain, 577
  effect on fetus, 109t, 115
  epidemic of, 502, 503
  gene for activation, 689
  genetic resistance to, 87
  immunization and, 145
  legalization of same-sex marriage
      due to, 782
  prevention of, 715
  protection of partner and fetus, 503
  symptoms and treatment, 111, A-17
  transmission of, 501–502
Hoarding, 731, 732p, 757
Holland, 565, 587
Holland, John, 547, 548f
Holophrase, 170, 176, 177, 178
Home, 262
Home birth, 103–104, 104p, 105
Home schooling, 53p, 54p, 361,
      364, 397
Homeostasis
  in adults, 576, 580, 600
  function of, 493, 495–496, 500,
      514, 571
  interaction with organ reserve and
      allostasis, 496

in late adulthood, 684, 717
  polypharmacy and, 717
  response to stress, 616
Homicide
  of adolescents and young adults,
      765f
  alcohol abuse related to, 588
  of emerging adults, 507
  grief process and, 779–780
  infanticide, 59, 71, 71p
  within intimate relationships, 561,
      562f
  rates in U.S. by age, 672, 672f
Homocysteine, 717
Homogamy, 561
Homosexual people. *See* Gay
      marriage; Gay partners;
      Lesbian partners; Same-sex
      couples; Same-sex mar-
      riage; Same-sex parents
Homosexuality, 9, 9f, 529, 529f
Homozygous genes, 70
Hong Kong, 136f, 356t, 453t, 463,
      A-16
Hookups, 554–555
Hope in dying, 761–763, 761t, 763,
      786
Hormonal feedback loop, 225f
Hormone replacement therapy (HRT),
      585, 586, 600, 663, 687
Hormones. *See also* Estrogen;
      Oxytocin; Testosterone
  decline of sex hormones in middle
      age, 584–586
  defined, 402
  effect on mood, 426
  effects during emerging adult-
      hood, 507
  passion activating, 553, 554
  regulation of, 403
  regulation of body rhythms,
      403–404, 404f, 404p, 411,
      426
  released at birth, 99
  replacement therapy, 585, 586,
      600, 663, 687
  role in sex development, 290,
      402–403, 402f, 407f, 408,
      409, 411, 420, 426
  role of in moral development, 295
  stimulation of sexual activity,
      420–421, 421p, 584–586,
      600
  stress hormones, 616. *See also*
      Cortisol
Hospice, 770–771, 770p, 771t, 778,
      786
Hot hand, 705–706, 706f
HPA axis. *See* Hypothalamus-
      pituitary-adrenal cortex axis
      (HPA axis)
HPG axis. *See* Hypothalamus-
      pituitary-gonad axis (HPG
      axis)
Human genome, 90
Human Genome mapping, 16
Human Genome Project, 78
Human papillomavirus (HPV), 425,
      A-17

Humanism
  application to infant social develop-
      ment, 203–204, 208, 209
  concepts of, 55–58, 61, 64
  view of gender development, 294
  view of maternal employment, 208
Humor, 674, 724
Hungary, 445f, 453t, A-16
Hunger, 133
Hungry Ghost Festival, 763
Hunt, Earl, 613
Huntington disease, 86, 714
Hurricane Katrina, 619–620, 620f
Hutchinson-Gilford syndrome, 689
Hygiene hypothesis, 317
Hyperactivity, 105, 108, 230. *See
      also* Attention-deficit hyper-
      activity/disorder (ADHD)
Hypertension. *See also* Blood pressure
  in adults, 576
  breast-feeding and, 147t
  causes of, 315, 496, 576, 615,
      617, 690
  effect on mature brain, 615, 715
  in emerging adulthood, 492
  treatment of, 685, 718
Hypervigilance, 239t, 289
Hypothalamus
  atrophy with age, 703
  effect of fear on development of,
      186
  functions of, 219f, 224, 227, 242,
      403, A-2
  stimulation of puberty, 402, 402f,
      411, 426
Hypothalamus-pituitary-adrenal cor-
      tex axis (HPA axis)
  abnormalities causing psychopa-
      thology in adolescence, 402
  antidepressant repair of, 700
  disruptions due to sexual abuse,
      402, 424
  hormonal feedback loop, 225f
  link to experience, 439
  stimulation of puberty, 402, 411,
      416, 426
Hypothalamus-pituitary-gonad axis
      (HPG axis), 403
Hypothesis, 4, 5, 22–23, 32, 36, 37,
      64, B-4
Hypothetical-deductive reasoning,
      432–433, 433f, 434, 436
Hysterectomy, 501

Iceland, 445f, 453t, A-16
Identical twins. *See* Monozygotic
      (MZ) twins
Identification, 292
Identity. *See also* Cultural identity;
      Ethnic identity; Political
      identity; Religious identity;
      Vocational identity
  creation and maintenance of in
      late adulthood, 730
  formation in adolescence, 457–462,
      458p, 459p, 460f, 460p,
      461f, 461p, 476, 485, 487
  formation in emerging adulthood,
      503–504, 550, 560, 569, 571

four arenas of, 459–461, 459p,
      460p, 461f, 461p, 462,
      485, 487, 544–548, 544p,
      547p, 547t, 548f, 548p
Identity achievement, 458, 462, 571
Identity crisis, 458, 462
Identity diffusion, 458
Identity vs. role confusion, 40t, 41,
      458, 462, 485, 543, 544t,
      632, 632t
Illness. *See also* Asthma;
      Diabetes; Heart disease;
      Psychopathology
  by age, 492t
  as cause of infertility, 583
  chronic and acute illnesses, 686,
      686f, 688
  chronic obstructive pulmonary
      disease, 684
  chronic traumatic encephalopathy
      (CTE), 714
  death due to in young adults, 765f
  effect on birthweight, 113, 122
  effect on marriages, 560
  effect on prenatal development,
      105–106, 107f, 109t,
      110–111
  in elderly, 684, 685f, 686
  in emerging adulthood, 492t
  in late adulthood, 684–688, 685f,
      686f, 688f, 696
  malnutrition's effect on, 149
  in middle childhood, 309, 310f
  morbidity rates, 596
  resistance in adolescence, 412
  retirement correlated with, 738–739
  stress causing, 616
  of surrogate grandparents, 747
Imaginary audience, 431, 431p, 434,
      442, 447, 454
Imaginary friends, 277–278
Imagination, 245, 246
Imitation of vertical line, 142t
Immersion teaching, 359
Immigrant paradox, 113–114
Immigrants
  adult-adolescent relationships
      among, 466
  case study of language learning,
      352
  childhood obesity rates, 316
  difficulty with figures of speech,
      319
  employment insecurity affecting,
      658
  incidence of schizophrenia, 506
  knowledge of infant language de-
      velopment, 613
  language instruction for, 359–360,
      360p
  lawfulness of, 478
  nutritional hazards for, 499–500
  peer pressure's effect on ethnic
      identity, 467
  stratification affecting, 735
  weight of newborns, 29
Immune system
  benefits of exercise, 592
  effects of stress, 615, 616

in emerging adulthood, 493, 496, 514
functions of, 690, 696
Immunization
autism and, 331
for elderly, 685
functions of, 144
for HPV, 425
problems caused by, 145
success of, 144–145, 151, 152, 309, 336
U.S. schedule for, A-8–A-9
Impatience, 278
Implantation, 95, 95f, 99, 107f
Implementation, 593
Implicit memory, 167, 704
Impulse control
of adolescents, 438–439
brain maturation required for, 416–418, 419
defined, 223
development in early childhood, 130, 223, 227, 234
of emerging adults, 507
lack of in abusive relationships, 563
reaction time aiding, 319
Impulsivity, 439, 439f, 487, 705
in vitro fertilization (IVF), 71, 75–76, 77, 90, 95, 583, 586, 600
Inactivity, 615, 663
Inclusion classes, 331
Income. *See also* Socioeconomic context (SES)
alcohol use related to, 588–589
differences in mortality rates, 595
discrimination affecting, 735
effect on growth, 242
effect on marriages, 560, 642
family structure and function correlated with, 378, 382, 383, 384, 395, 397, 639–640
financial support of emerging adults, 565, 565p, 566f, 660
happiness and intelligence correlated with, 737
health correlated with, 598–599, 598p, 737
influence on development, 10–11, 12f
level of education correlated with, 537f
nutrition and, 217
oral health and, 218
stress related to, 659
wages and benefits, 654–655, 655p
Incomplete grief, 779, 783, 786
Incontinence, 684
Incremental theory of intelligence, 447–448
Independence
in adolescence, 412, 413, 430
effect on marriages, 381–382
in late adulthood, 745

in middle childhood, 367–368, 368t, 384
parental support as impediment to, 567
Independent variable, 24, 24f
India
age of mothers at birth, 501
children killed in car accidents in, 233
contraception in, 580
c-sections in, 102f
education in, 444–445, 445f
infant mortality in, 143f
infanticide, 71p
languages of, 260
low birthweights in, 115f
marriage in, 559
overweight people in, 590f
population of children and elders, A-3
sports in, 312
Individual education plan (IEP), 332, 336
Individual-reflective faith, 531
Indonesia
average age of marriage, 545f
beliefs about death, 781
co-sleeping in, 136f
drug use and abuse in, 480
population of children and elders, A-3
scores on international tests, 356t, 453t
Induced labor, 103
Induction, 300, 302, 303
Inductive reasoning, 433, 433f, 435f, 454, 606f
Indulgent parenting, 288
Industry vs. inferiority, 40t, 41, 368, 373, 395, 544t
Infancy (first two years). *See also* Infant mortality; Newborns
affordances, 163–165, 164p
attachment, 191–197, 192t, 193t, 195t, 205, 209
bonding, 120–121
brain and emotions, 185–189, 187p, 188f, 209
brain growth, 129–130, 130f, 131f, 132–134, 137, 152
Brazelton Neonatal Behavioral Assessment Scale, 116–117, 122, 139, 197
breast-feeding, 146–148, 146p, 151
cognitive development, 211
cognitive learning stages, 46f
co-sleeping, 135–136, 136f, 136p
development of, 125
development of dynamic sensory-motor systems, 142
development of social bonds, 195t, 196p, 197p, 198p, 199f, 209, 211
effect of parental response to cries of, 50
emotional development, 181–184, 182p, 182t, 183p, 209, 211
Erikson's stages of development, 40t, 41

face recognition, 134
failure to thrive, 128
father as social partner, 197–199, 198p, 199f, 209
Freud's stages of development, 39–40, 39p, 40t
immunization, 144–145, 152
information processing theory, 162–168, 163p, 164p, 165p, 166p
kangaroo care, 121, 121p, 138
language development, 168–176, 168p, 169t, 170p, 171p, 173p, 174f, 211
low birthweight, 113–115
malnutrition, 148–149, 148f, 148p, 152
memory of, 165–168, 165p
motor skill development, 140–143, 140p, 140t, 141p, 152
need for caregiving, 374
physical growth, 125, 128, 128f, 129p, 152
senses of, 137–139, 139p, 142, 152
sensorimotor intelligence, 45p, 155–162, 156t, 157f, 157p, 158p, 159p, 161t, 178
shaken baby syndrome, 133
sleep patterns, 135, 152
social referencing, 197, 197p
sudden infant death syndrome, 136, 149–151, 150f, 152
survival of, 142–151
synchrony, 189, 190f, 191, 207, 209
theories of psychosocial development, 199–208, 200p, 201p, 202p, 202t, 205p, 206p, 206t, 207f, 211
vision during, 82
Infant amnesia, 165
Infant day care, 205–207, 206p, 206t, 207f, 209
Infant mortality
from 1950–2010, 143f
by country, 12f, 143f
due to extremely low birthweight, 113
due to shaken baby syndrome, 133
due to SIDS, 136, 149–151, 150f, 152
malnutrition associated with, 145–148
mother's education related to, 149
reduction of, 105, 121, 673
in U.S., 12f, 103, 114
Infanticide, 59, 71, 71p
Infatuation, 553t
Infection, 109t, 116. *See also* Sexually transmitted infections (STI)
Inferiority, 368
Infertility
causes of, 85, 425, 582–583, 586, 588, 600
defined, 582
treatments, 75–76, 583–584, 584p, 586
Influenza, 109t

Informal code (language), 349–350, 353, 364
Information-processing perspective
application to early childhood, 50–51
concepts of, 47–48, 64, 343, 348
control processes during middle childhood, 346
control processes in late adulthood, 705–706, 706f
defined, 47, 517
in first two years, 162–168, 163p, 164p, 165p, 166p, 178, 211
input, 703–704
knowledge in middle childhood, 345–346
language acquisition, 350, 351
memory advances from infancy to age 11, 345t
memory in first two years, 165–168, 165p, 178
memory in late adulthood, 704–705
memory in middle childhood, 344–345
metacognition, 347–348, 347p
in middle childhood, 343–348, 344p, 345t, 347f, 357, 364, 397
output, 706–709, 707f
Informed consent, 30, 31
Inhalants, 109t, 479
Inhibition, 438, 701, 714
Initiative vs. guilt, 40t, 41, 276–277, 279, 544t
Injury
avoidable injury, 233–236, 234p, 235f
control of, 234–235, 234p, 242
in early childhood, 233–236, 234p, 235f, 241, 242, 305
as indicator of maltreatment, 239t
prevention of, 235–236, 235f, 242
sports injuries, 412
Injury control, 234–235, 234p, 242
Innate vulnerability, 108
Insecure attachment
as indicator of maltreatment, 239t, 240
results of, 387
of Romanian adoptees, 196, 196p
social setting and, 195–197, 195t, 196p
teen mothers associated with, 423
types of, 209, 299
Insecure-avoidant attachment, 193, 193t, 209, 783
Insecure-resistant/ambivalent attachment, 193, 193t, 209, 783
Institutional Review Board (IRB), 29–30
Instrumental activities of daily life (IADLs), 750, 750t, 756, 757
Instrumental aggression, 297–298, 297t, 302, 303
Instrumental conditioning, 43–44, 43p

Integrated personalities, 520, 521f
Integrity, 723, 730–731, 757
Integrity vs. despair, 40t, 41, 544t, 632, 632t, 719, 730–731, 757
Intellectual impairment, 80
Intelligence
  activity correlated with, 736
  in adulthood, 603–608, 604p, 606f, 628, 663
  analytic intelligence, 610, 610t, 611–613, 612, 614, 628
  components of, 608–614, 609p, 610t, 611p, 614p, 628, 663
  creative intelligence, 610–612, 610t, 612, 614, 628
  cross-sectional research, 604, 604p, 605, 608, 628, 663
  cross-sequential research, 606–608, 606f, 628, 663
  crystallized intelligence, 609–610, 609p, 614, 628
  expert cognition, 621–627, 622p, 623f, 627, 627f, 628
  fluid intelligence, 608–609, 610, 614, 628
  impact of weathering, 617
  in late adulthood, 700–701
  longitudinal improvements, 605, 608, 614, 628
  longitudinal research, 663
  practical intelligence, 610t, 611–612, 614, 628
  selective optimization with compensation, 620–621, 621p, 628
  stemming from regional differences in personality, 636
  Sternberg's three forms of, 610–612, 610t, 611p, 628
  theories concerning, 323, 336, 603–604
  Intelligence testing, 320–322, 321f, 604–608, 604p, 606f. See also Achievement tests; International tests; IQ tests
Intensive preschool programs, 269–270, 272
Interdependence. See Intimacy
Intergenerational bonds, 639–640, 639p
Intergenerational convergence, 565
Intergenerational homes, 565, 565p, 567–568, 639–640
Intergenerational support, 745–746
Intergenerational tensions, 745–746
Internalization of problems, 279–280, 303, 380, 383, 387, 476
International Baccalaureate classes, 448–449
International Baccalaureate test, 449
International schooling, 353–355, 355p, 448–449
International tests
  International Baccalaureate test, 449
  international gaps, 352
  problems with benchmarks, 357, 357–358, 358p, 362, 397

Programme for International Student Assessment (PISA), 445, 451–452
Progress in International Reading Literacy Study (PIRLS), 356, 356t, 357, 364, 445, 451
Trends in Math and Science Study (TIMMS), 356, 356t, 357, 364, 383.445, 451
  types of, 356, 445
Internet. See also Social networking
  adolescents' use to vent grief, 765
  availability of, 440, 454
  change in life patterns, 493
  matchmaking Web sites, 555, 569
  sexual abuse via, 441
  as source for at-risk teens, 468–469, 487
  as source for research, B-2–B-3
  as source of friendships and consequential strangers, 639
  as a source of sex education, 471
Intimacy. See also Friendships; Love; Romance
  as aspect of love, 553, 643
  changing historical patterns, 558–559
  cohabitation, 556–558, 556f, 556p, 557p, 558f, 568, 569, 571
  conflict between partners, 558f, 561–564
  divorce and, 644–645, 645p
  effects of relocation, 657–658
  during emerging adulthood, 551–564, 552p, 553f, 555p, 556f, 556p, 557p, 558f, 560f, 564p, 568, 569, 571
  evolution of relationships, 560
  factors affecting success, 560–561
  family bonds, 641
  finding a partner, 555, 555p
  of friends and family in adulthood, 637–641, 638p, 639p, 640p, 641, 661, 663
  friendship in emerging adulthood, 551–553, 552p, 661
  generativity combined with, 658–660, 659p
  marriage and happiness, 641–643, 641p, 642f, 642p, 643f, 661, 663
  of romantic partners in adulthood, 641–646, 641p, 642f, 642p, 643t, 644p, 645p, 661, 663
  same-sex partners, 644, 644p
  social convoy, 637
Intimacy vs. isolation crisis
  of adulthood, 632, 632t, 637
  of emerging adulthood, 544t, 551, 569
  stage of development, 40t, 41
Intimate terrorism, 563–564
Intonation, 170
Intra-cytoplasmic sperm injection (ICSI), 76
Intrapersonal intelligence, 322
Intrinsic motivation, 277, 278, 447–448

Intrinsic rewards of work, 655
Introversion, 634
Intuitive thought
  of adolescents, 435f, 436–438, 436p, 440, 454
  of experts, 622–623, 622p, 623f, 627, 628, 663
Intuitive-projective faith, 531
Invincibility fable, 430, 434, 454
Involved grandparents, 747
IQ. See also General intelligence (g); Intelligence
  benefits of breast-feeding, 148
  drop-out rates related to, 452
  effect of ingested lead, 230
  effect of neglect, 196, 226
  effect of preterm birth, 114
  effect of weathering, 617
  effect on thought processes, 437
  link to openness, 634
IQ tests
  changes with age, 604, 628
  cross-sequential research, 606–608, 606f
  for crystallized intelligence, 609
  distribution of scores, A-12
  for fluid intelligence, 608–609
  interpretation of, 604–605, 604p
  for practical intelligence, 612
  theoretical distribution of scores, 321f
  types of, 320–322, 322p, 323, 336
Iran, 356t, 545f, 563
Ireland, 108, 375f, 445f, 453t, 556, A-16
Irreversibility, 246, 247–248, 272, 293
Islam, 71, 546, 588, 763, 781
Isolation. See also Intimacy vs. isolation crisis
  avoidance of interaction creating, 550
  of bereaved people, 779
  contribution to abusive relationships, 564, 753, 756
  disabilities contributing to, 682, 688
  effect on infants, 196
  identity formation affected by, 458
  Internet as remedy for, 444, 486
  lack of intimacy, 551
  language development and, 173
  victimization of socially isolated children, 386
Israel
  creation of, 782
  high school graduation rate, 482f
  infant day care in, 207
  location infants' sleep periods, 136
  population of children and elders, A-3
  punishment of poor behavior in, 301
  scores on international tests, 356t, 453t
  sexually active teens/condom use, 425f
Italy
  breast-feeding in, A-7
  cohabitation in, 556
  demographics, 673

elderly volunteers in, 739
emerging adulthood in, 565, 566
high school graduation rate, 445f
low birthweights in, 115f
overweight people in, 590f
population of children and elders, A-3
punishment of poor behavior in, 301
scores on international tests, 356t, 453t, A-16

Jackson, Michael, 782
Jacob's syndrome, 86t
Jail, 478
Jamaica, 115f, 312, 545f, 584
Japan
  age-adjusted mortality rate in, 595
  alcohol consumption in, 82
  average age of marriage, 545f
  cohabitation in, 556
  college graduates in, 535
  Coming of Age Day, 544p
  contraception in, 580
  co-sleeping in, 135, 136f
  demographics, 673
  emerging adulthood in, 565
  emphasis on regulation of selfishness, 278
  extroverted personalities in, 636
  high school graduation rate, 445f, 482f
  high-stakes tests in, 449
  hikikomori in, 505–506, 506p
  life expectancy, 668–669
  low birthweights in, 115f
  marriage in, 641
  obesity in, 590f
  physical activity in schools, 313, 353
  population of children and elders, A-3
  regulation of pride in, 370
  scores on international tests, 356t, 357, 453t, A-16
  separation anxiety in infants from, 183
  single-parent families in, 375f
  sports in, 312
  word for neurocognitive disorders in, 710
Japanese Americans, 636
John Hancock Life & Health Insurance Company, 754
Jordan, 453t
Judaism, 781
Jumping up, 140t
Just right phenomenon, 218, 218f, 246

Kahneman's Systems 1 and 2, 435f
Kangaroo care, 121, 121p, 122, 138
Kenya
  activities of children, 227
  children's activities by socioeconomic class, 282f
  low birthweights in, 115f
  marriage in, 553, 559
  overweight people in, 590f

Ketamine, 511
Kicking, 141
Kinkeepers, 651–652, 661
Kinship care, 241, 242, 376t, 747
Klacyniski, Paul, 436–437
Klinefelter syndrome, 86t
Knowledge acquisition, 345–348
Knowledge base, 345, 348, 364, 609
Knowledge of Infant Development Inventory (KIDI), 613
Kohlberg, Lawrence
   Fowler's work based on, 531
   levels and stages of moral thought, 390–391, 390t, 394, 395
   on measuring moral growth, 530
Korea
   body image of adolescents in, 414
   college graduates in, 535
   development of impulse control in, 223
   education in, 362
   funeral customs in, 763
   high school graduation rate, 445f
   incidence of twins, 75
   respect for elderly in, 668
   scores on international tests, 356t, A-16
Kübler-Ross, Elisabeth, 782
Kwashiorkor, 149, 152

Labor and delivery. *See also* Delivery
   in birthing centers, 103, 105
   complications during, 116, 117, 119
   c-sections, 102, 102f, 102p, 103, 122, 317
   doula's support, 104, 105
   epidural anesthesia, 103
   at home, 104, 104p, 105
   induced labor, 103
   low birthweight, 113–115, 115f, 122
   preterm delivery, 94t, 97, 98, 99p, 103, 106, 113, 116, 122, 135
   vaginal, 99–101, 100f, 100p, 122, 129
Labrador, 283
Lactation, 146–148, 146p
Lactose intolerance, 59, 59p
Lancet, The, 216
Language. *See also* Bilingual children; Bilingual learning; Bilingual schooling
   math learning and, 251–252
   in middle childhood, 348–353, 349p, 350f, 351f
   vocabulary, 348–350, 349p, 350f, 351f
Language acquisition device (LAD), 175
Language development
   associated with memory, 165, 167
   babbling, 170, 173, 177, 178
   bilingual learning, 172. *See also* Bilingual children; Bilingual learning; Bilingual schooling
   brain growth and shrinkage related to, 321
   case study of immigrants, 352
   child-directed speech, 169–170, 171, 173

cultural differences, 171–172, 171p
difference-equals-deficit error concerning, 13
differences in middle childhood, 350–353, 351f
in early childhood, 256–262, 256t, 260f, 261p, 305
expectations related to, 352–353
in first two years, 168–176, 168p, 169t, 170p, 171p, 173p, 174f, 177f, 178, 211
first words, 170–171, 177, 178
fostering of theory of mind, 255
friends and relatives, 729
grammar, 172
losses and gains, 261
low birthweight affecting, 114
mean length of utterance (MLU), 172
in middle childhood, 348–353, 349p, 350f, 351f, 364, 397
naming explosion, 171, 177, 178
parts of speech, 172
percent of infants knowing 50 words, 174f
preoperational thought and, 257
in preschools, 267
role of epigenetics, 60
sensitive period for learning, 7, 256–257, 256t
sexual abuse affecting, 424
socioeconomic context and, 350–351, 351f, 364
teacher/family expectations affecting, 352–353
theories of, 172–176, 178
universal sequence, 168–170, 169t, 178
use of first-person pronouns, 184
videos and, 174–175
vocabulary explosion, 257–259
Language explosion, 246
Language shift, 261
Language sponges, 256
Last menstrual period (LMP), 94t
Late adulthood
   activities, 737–743, 737f, 738p, 739f, 739p, 740f, 742f, 742p, 743
   aging and disease, 684–688, 685f, 686f, 688, 688f, 696
   aging of brain, 700–703, 702f, 726
   causes of death, 495t, 684–685, 685f
   centenarians, 693–695, 693p, 694p, 696
   chronic illnesses in, 492t
   compensation for brain, 682–684, 683p
   compression of morbidity, 686–688, 688f
   creativity in, 721–722, 721p, 722p, 724, 726
   defined, 6
   driving ability, 439f, 678–679, 679p, 680f, 684
   drug use and abuse, 510f
   effects of prior bad habits, 496

employment during, 737–738, 737f, 738p, 743, 757
exercise patterns, 671–672, 671f, 673, 673p
frailty, 749–756, 750p, 750t, 753p, 754p, 755p, 757
friends and relatives, 732, 737, 743–749, 743p, 744p, 745f, 746p, 747f, 748p, 749p, 757
immunizations, 145
independence of, 674–675, 676
information processing, 703–709, 706f, 707f, 726
learning in, 719–721, 720p, 721p, 724, 726
life reviews written in, 722, 722p, 724, 726
living arrangements, 741f
maximum life expectancy, 694–695, 694p
medical treatment during, 685
need for respect, 374
neurocognitive disorders of, 709–719, 710f, 711p, 712f, 712p, 713p, 714p, 715p, 716p, 726
neurogenesis in, 700–701
new cognitive development, 699–700, 719–724, 719p, 720p, 721p, 722p, 723p, 726
percentage of world population, 673, A-3
political activism, 742–743, 742f, 757
prejudice and predictions concerning, 665, 667–676, 668p, 670f, 670p, 671f, 672f, 673p, 674p, 696
primary and secondary aging, 684, 688
religious involvement, 723, 742, 742p, 757
response to death, 766–767, 766f, 767f, 786
retirement, 737–739, 743, 757
selective optimization with compensation, 676–684, 676f, 677p, 680f, 696, 732, 737, 744
senses, 681–682, 681p, 681t, 682p
sexual activity, 676–678, 676f, 677p, 684
sleep patterns, 671
suicide rates, A-21
support of younger generations, 745
theories of, 730–737, 730p, 731p, 733f, 734p, 735f, 735p, 757
theories of aging, 688–693, 689, 690p, 691p, 692p
variations in development, 730
volunteer work, 757
wisdom in, 723–724, 723p, 726
Latency, 39, 40t, 368, 373
Latent genes, 78
Lateralization, 220, 226, 227

Latin America
   anxiety disorders in, 505
   breast-feeding in, A-7
   college graduates in, 535–536
   co-sleeping in, 135
   c-sections in, 102, 102f
   funeral customs in, 763
   infant day care in, 207
   percentage of young adolescents not in school, 482f
   physical activity in schools, 353
   special education in, 333
   sports in, 312
   stunting in children in, 148f
Latinos. *See also* Hispanic Americans; Mexican Americans
   attendance at preschool, 268–269
   average daily exposure to video in U.S., 286f
   average height of children, 216
   breast-feeding by, A-7
   caregiving style, 289
   education of, 360
   expectations for learning, 352
   high school graduation rate, 450f
   incidence of childhood obesity, 216
   life expectancy, 617
   obesity rate and income, 590f
   population of, A-4
   self-esteem in adolescence, 474
   sexual activity of adolescents, 421
   sterilization of adults, 580
   use of IVF, 583–584
Latvia, A-16
Laughter
   development of, 182, 182p, 182t, 184, 185, 209
   in early childhood, 222, 223
   emotional development related to maturity of, 185
   as survival technique, 204
Law breaking
   in adolescence, 477, 485
   during emerging adulthood, 507, 508f, 510, 513
Lead
   effect on aging brain, 715
   effect on brain development, 230–231, 231f, 231p, 478
   effect on fetus, 109t
Learning. *See also* College; Early childhood education; Education; High school; Middle school; Preschool programs; Teaching
   in adolescence, 444–453, 445f, 445p, 448p, 453t, 454, 487
   becoming an expert, 621–622, 625–626
   cultural effect on, 342–343, 342p, 343f
   dependence on fine motor skills, 232
   effect of stress in early childhood, 226
   international tests, 356–357, 356t, 397
   in late adulthood, 719–721, 720p, 721p, 724, 726

malnutrition and, 149
in middle childhood, 353, 354f, 354t, 355–358, 355–362, 355p, 356t, 357p, 358p, 359t, 360f, 360p, 361p, 363f, 364, 374
national variations in curriculum, 353, 355
observation vs. instruction, 342–343
required factors, 36, 61, 64
selective optimization with compensation, 620–621, 621p, 624, 626
in United States, 358–360, 358p, 358t, 360f, 360p
use of technology, 441
Learning disabilities
ADHD, 324–327
behavioral teratogens causing, 105
Down syndrome, 85
dyscalculia, 328–329
dyslexia, 328, 328p
education for, 335
high-stakes tests and, 449
plumbism causing, 230
recessive genetic disorders associated with, 86–87
specific learning disorder, 328–329, 328p
Learning opportunities, 612
Learning theory. See Behaviorism
Least restrictive environment (LRE), 331, 336
Left-handedness, 220–221
Left-right coordination, 219f, 220–222, 226, 232, 318
Leg-tucking reflex, 117
Legacy work, 766
Leptin, 408
Lesbian partners, 644, 644p
Levinson, Daniel, 633
Lewy body disorder, 714, 714p, 716, 726
Libido, 40
Liechtenstein, A-16
Life after death, 762, 762t
Life expectancy
attitudes toward aging affecting, 668
average life expectancy, 694
by ethnicity and SES, 617, 735p
income and education related to, 598–599
maximum life expectancy, 694
for men, 595, 691, 694
by nation, 595f
in United States, 688f, 694, 747f
for women, 595, 691, 694
Life review, 722, 722p, 723, 724, 726
Life-course-persistent offenders, 477, 485
Life-span perspective, 5–6, 32
Liking, 553t
Limbic system
in autistic children, 330
effects of drugs on, 483
emotional regulation, 275–276, 276–277

functions of, 219f
maturation in adolescence, 416, 418, 419, 436, 438, 454, 487
maturation of in middle childhood, 764
myelination of, 276–277
parts of, 219f, 224, 225f
structures of, A-2
Linguistic disorders, 319
Linguistic intelligence, 322
Linked lives, 564–565, 565p, 569, 639, 659, 661
Listening, 168–170, 258
Literacy, 12f
Lithium, 109t
Little scientists, 159, 159p, 162, 178, 197
Living apart together (LAT), 642, 642p, 647, 749
Living arrangements for elderly, 741f
Living will, 777, 778, 786
Locked-in syndrome, 772t
Logic
absence in early childhood, 245–246
of adolescents, 430–434, 430p, 431p, 432f, 433f, 433p, 454, 487, 520
conservation in early childhood and, 247–249, 247p, 248f
development of in middle childhood, 339–340
of emerging adulthood, 520
obstacles to in early childhood, 246
Logical extension, 258
Logical fallacies, 434
Logical-mathematical intelligence, 322
Loneliness, 315, 551, 554, 645
Longevity. See Life expectancy
Longitudinal research
advantages/disadvantages, 28, 605
defined, 27
on intelligence, 605, 608, 628, 663
participants, 27p
process of, 26f, 27
Long-term care, 753–754, 754p
Long-term memory, 344, 345, 348, 364, 609
Love. See also Cohabitation; Intimacy; Marriage; Romance
aspects of, 553
changing historical patterns, 558–559
cohabitation, 555–558, 556–557, 556f, 556p, 557p, 558f
complexity of, 642–643
conflict between partners, 558f, 561–564
dimensions of, 553–560, 553t, 555p, 556f, 556p, 557p, 558f
factors affecting successful relationships, 560–561
finding a partner, 555
hookup without commitment, 554–555

human need of, 56, 57, 57f, 551, 632
ideal compared to real, 554
Sternberg's three forms of, 643
Low birth weight outcomes: Why better in Cuba than Alabama? (Neggars & Crowe), 114
Low birthweight (LBW)
causes, 76, 106, 113–114, 422
consequences, 114, 116, 122, 135, 597
defined, 113
national statistics compared, 114–115, 115f
Low-set malformed ears, 107f
Lungs. See also Asthma
aging of, 576, 663, 684
capacity in emerging adulthood, 493
chronic obstructive pulmonary disease, 684
effects of exercise, 592
emphysema, 715
prenatal development, 98
Lupus, 686
Lust, 419
Luxembourg, 445f, 773, 775, A-16
Lying, 254–255, 254f

Macrosystems, 7, 8, 8f, 235, 241. See also Culture; Social bonds
Macular degeneration, 681p, 681t, 696
Mad cow disease, 577, 714, 715
Magic Middle, 54f
Magical thinking, 249
Mainstreaming, 331
Maintenance, 593–594
Major neurocognitive disorders, 709, 710
Making-interesting-things-last stage, 156t, 157, 157f
Malaysia, 136f
Males. See also Boys; Fathers; Men
chromosomes of, 70–71, 70p
effect of child maltreatment, 239–240
innate vulnerability of, 108
Malnutrition
cognitive impairment related to, 716–717, 719, 726
delay of puberty, 406
effect on birthweight, 113, 122
effect on brain growth, 129, 133
effect on infant survival, 148–149, 148p, 151, 152
effect on prenatal development, 109t
as risk factor for schizophrenia, 506, 514
teen pregnancy associated with, 423
Malta, 573
Mammogram, 493, 596
Mandated reporters, 237, 240, 753
Mania, 504
Mantle, Mickey, 84
Marasmus, 149, 152
Marcia, James E., 485

Marijuana
decline of use with age, 586
effect on fetus, 109t
harm to adolescent users, 481
as a teratogen, 108
use by college students, 510
use in U.S., 479, 480f
Marital status, A-7
Marriage. See also Divorce; Family; Family function; Family structure
advantages/disadvantages of, 641–642
in Africa, 566
arrangement of, 553, 559, 566, 568, 569
average age, 545f
changing historical patterns, 558–559, 748
conflict within, 643
current trends, 641
dialectical approach to, 526
divorce, 381–382, 382p
effect on depressed men, 505
empty nest stage, 643, 643t
evolutionary theory concerning, 60–61
factors affecting successful relationships, 560–561, 569
gender differences, 554–555
in Germany, 556
happiness in, 641–643, 641p, 642f, 642p, 643f, 647, 661. See also Divorce
increase in age of, 489
in late adulthood, 744, 749, 757
link to extroversion, 634
marital status in U.S., 545f
remarriage, 645–646
same-sex marriage, 9, 9f, 644, 644p
of surrogate grandparents, 747
through matchmaking Web sites, 555
Masculinization of female genitalia, 107f
Maslow, Abraham
hierarchy of needs, 56–58, 56p, 57f, 64, 661
love and belonging, 652
love and respect, 632–633, 637
physiological needs and safety, 203
self-actualization, 632–633, 719
stages of dying, 769
Massification, 535–536
Massive open online courses (MOOCs), 539, 539p
Mastery motivation, 447–448
Materialism, 369, 536
Maternal education
breast-feeding related to, A-7
effect on child's academic achievement, 341, 351, 351f
facilitation of reading, 258
role in language learning, 351, 351f
Maternal instinct, 627
Math
acquisition of concepts, 344
automatization required for, 320

change in ability with age, 606f, 608, 614
Common Core standards, 359t
concrete operational thought necessary for, 340
cultural impact on learning, 342
dyscalculia, 328–329, 336
elementary compared to high school, 431
international test scores, 356t, 453t, A-16
national variation in teaching techniques, 353
readiness for, 354t
understanding in early childhood, 251–252
in United States, 356t, 358
Maturation, 493
Maturation-learning debate. See Nature-nurture controversy
Maximum life expectancy, 695, 696
Mean length of utterance (MLU), 172
Means to an end stage, 156t, 157–159, 158p, 159p
Measles, 109t, 144
Measurements of health, 594–599, 594p, 595f, 596p, 598p, 663. See also Life expectancy; Morbidity; Mortality; Vitality
Media, 471, 672, 696
Medial frontal cortex, 185
Mediation, 563
Medicaid, 754
Medical checkups, 127–128
Medical practices. See also specific disease for treatment
advance directives, 776–777
euthanasia, 773–775, 773f, 774f, 774p, 776f, 778, 786
good death and, 768, 778, 786
life support measures, 772, 778
for newborns/mothers, 101–103, 102p
palliative care, 771
physician-assisted suicide, 773–774, 773–775, 774t, 775, 776f
Medicare, 754, 771
Mediterranean diet, 592
Memorial services, 779, 782
Memorials, 781, 782, 783p
Memory
advances from infancy to age 11, 345t
ageism's effect on, 669, 670f
of Alzheimer patients, 711
assessment of, 708
effect of stress on, 226
experience and, 321
explicit and implicit memory, 167, 704
in first two years, 165–168, 165p, 178
of infants, 162
language and, 165
in late adulthood, 683, 704–705, 709, 710, 720, 726

long-term memory, 364
loss as symptom of neurocognitive disorders, 709
in middle childhood, 344–345, 364, 397
motivation and, 166, 166p
prospective memory, 704
relationship to intelligence, 321, 323
reminders and repetition affecting, 166, 166p
selective amnesia, 165f
sensory memory, 344, 364
working memory, 344–345, 348, 364, 608–609, 704–705
Men. See also Fathers; Males
as abusers in intimate relationships, 563
andropause, 585–586, 663
average age of marriage, 545f
college enrollment, 536
dementia rates, 711
depression following loss of romantic partner, 505
diseases afflicting, 686
effects of divorce, 645
graduates of medical school, 627f
hearing loss, 681
infertility, 582–583
intelligence changes over time, 606–607, 606f
as kinkeepers, 651
life expectancy, 595, 691, 694, 735f
midlife crisis, 633–634, 633p
moral values of, 531
morbidity rates, 596
perpetrators of homicide against, 562f
physical development in emerging adulthood, 491
reasons for hooking up, 554–555
response to stress, 616
risk-taking during emerging adulthood, 507, 513
role in the home, 626
sexual responsiveness, 581
smokers in U.S., 587, 588f
suicide rates, A-21
vulnerability to schizophrenia, 506
Menarche
age of onset, 406, 407f, 408–409, 426
defined, 401
hormones stimulating, 402f, 403, 407f, 408, 409
Menopause, 584–585, 585p, 600, 663
Menstruation, 413, 584, 600. See also Menarche
Mental combination stage, 156–160, 156t, 162
Mental health, 638, 695
Mental illness. See also Psychopathology
in adolescence, 29
bullying resulting in, 388
as cause of domestic violence, 563
diathesis-stress model of mental illness, 504, 507

factors influencing, 87, 504, 507, 597
Freud's study of, 39
genetic causes, 80
incidence in emerging adulthood, 503–504
indicators of, 708
as result of stress, 619
unemployment contributing to, 654
Mentors
facilitation of reading, 258
role in learning process, 52–54, 249, 256, 342
scaffolding of learning, 249–250, 250p, 251p, 256
scaffolding of morality, 392
Mercury, 109t
Mercy killing. See Euthanasia
Mesosystem, 7, 8, 8f
Meta-analysis, 23t, B-4–B-5
Metabolism, 589
Metacognition, 346, 347–348, 347f, 364, 397
Metaphors, 348–349, 353, 364
Methylation, 17, 68–69, 70
Mexican Americans, 472, 590f
Mexico
average age of marriage, 545f
childhood obesity in, 315
c-sections in, 102f
decline in smoking, 587
emphasis on regulation of defiance, 278
high school graduation rate, 445f
infant mortality in, 143f
overweight people in, 590f
population of children and elders, A-3
scores on PISA, 453t
Michelangelo, 722
Microaggressions, 656
Microsystems. See also Education; Family; Peer relationships; Religion
causes of car accidents, 235
effect on development, 7, 8, 8f
effect on volunteerism, 739
problems leading to foster care, 241
Mid-brain, 130
Midbrain development, 98t
Middle adulthood, 6
Middle childhood
brain development, 313p, 318–323, 321f, 323f
challenges of, 307
children with special needs, 323–335, 331p, 332f, 333p, 397
chronic illnesses in, 492t
concrete operational stage, 339–340, 339p, 340p
defined, 309
developmental theories applied to, 339p, 340p, 341p, 342p, 343f, 343p, 345t, 347f, 395, 397
education during, 353, 354f, 354t, 355–362, 355p, 356t, 357p, 358p, 359t, 360f, 360p, 361p, 363f, 397, 537f

family life, 373–384, 373p, 375f, 376t, 377f, 378p, 379p, 381f, 382p, 395, 397
growth during, 307
health problems, 313, 314f, 315–318, 315f, 316p, 317f, 317p, 397
as healthy time, 309–312, 310f, 311p, 312p, 313p, 336, 397
hearing, 579
inductive reasoning in, 433, 433f
information processing in, 343–348, 344p, 345t, 347f
language in, 348–353, 349p, 350f, 351f
maturity of the child, 397
moral development, 389–394, 390p, 390t, 392p, 393f, 395, 397
mythic-literal faith of, 531
nature of the child, 267p, 367–373, 368t, 369p, 372p, 374p, 374t, 395
nearsightedness, 579
needs of, 374–375, 395
peer group, 384–389, 384p, 386p, 395, 397
Middle East, 148f, 471, 479, 482f, A-7
Middle school, 445–448, 445p, 452, 453, 454
Midlife crisis, 573, 633–634, 633p, 661
MIDUS study, 635
Midwives, 102, 104
Mild cognitive impairment (MCI), 710
Military brats, 375
Military service
brain injury in combat, 716
as form of moratorium, 458
identity provided by, 458p
mourning for fallen friends, 780p
PTSD sufferers, 505, 505p, 619
soldiers missing in action, 780
women in, 656
Minor neurocognitive disorders, 709, 710
Mirror neurons, 162
Mirror/rouge test, 184, 184p, 202, 209
Miscarriage, 85, 95, 422, 583
Misdiagnosis, 325, 326
Mispronunciation, 261, 262
MMWR, 108
Modeling, 44, 44–45
Modesty, 184
Monozygotic (MZ) twins
differences in intelligence, 607
differential sensitivity of, 373–374
process producing, 73, 74f, 75, 77, 90
schizophrenia and, 87
Montessori, Maria, 264
Montessori schools, 264, 270, 272
Mood disorders, 404, 504–505, 514
Moodiness, 278
Moral challenges, 430
Moral competence, 389

Moral development
  in adolescence, 419
  discipline, 298–299
  in early childhood, 295–302, 297p, 297t, 299p, 300p, 301p, 303, 305
  in emerging adulthood, 528–532, 528o, 529f, 532f, 532p, 571
  empathy and antipathy, 296, 297p, 297t
  gender differences, 530
  Kohlberg's levels of moral thought, 390–391, 391t
  measures of, 530
  in middle childhood, 383f, 389–394, 390p, 390t, 392p, 393f, 395, 397
  nature-nurture interaction, 295–296
  in phallic stage, 291–292
  physical punishment, 299–300, 299p, 301–302
  psychological control, 300, 300p
Moral reasoning, 389–391, 389t
Moral values
  conflict between children and adults over, 392
  development of, 382–384, 393f
  in middle childhood, 389–394, 390p, 390t, 392p, 393f, 395, 397
Morality, 295, 684
Morality of care, 530
Morality of justice, 530
Morals
  development of, 36
  of emerging adulthood, 528–532, 528p, 529f, 540
  origins of, 389
Moratorium, 458, 461, 462, 485, 544, 549, 569
Morbidity
  compression of, 686–688, 688f, 696
  effects of ageism, 668
  effects of primary aging, 684
  as measure of health, 594, 596, 599, 600, 663
  stemming from regional differences in personality, 636
  stress in childhood contributing to, 617
Moro reflex, 117
Morocco, 356t
Mortality, 594–595, 595f, 599, 600, 663, 668, 766
Moses, Anna "Grandma," 721–722
Mother-infant interaction, 17, 116, 122
Mothers
  age and Down syndrome babies, A-6
  baby's words for, A-9
  behavior causing low birthweight in infants, 113, 116
  breast-feeding, 146–148, 146p, 147t, A-7
  as caregivers, 659

difficulties following birth, 119
  effect of depression on infants, 191
  employment with infants, 207–208
  impact of children, 647
  influence on daughters, 44
  interaction with infants, 17, 116, 122
  postpartum depression, 119, 121, 122
  relationship to fetus, 99
  response to infants, 116
  variability in care, 262
  as workers, 626–627
Motivation
  extrinsic motivation, 277, 278
  increase in knowledge base, 345–346
  intrinsic motivation, 277, 278
  for learning, 166, 166p
  perception of affordances and, 163–164
  of preschoolers, 277, 279
  source of, 277
Motivational interviewing, 593
Motor area of brain, 220
Motor skills
  artistic expressions, 232–233
  defined, 140
  development in early childhood, 227, 227t, 228f, 228p, 229–233, 231f, 231p, 232p, 233p, 242, 305
  development in first two years, 140–143, 142, 152, 211
  fine motor skills, 141–142, 142t, 152, 211, 232, 232–233, 232p
  gross motor skills, 140–141, 140p, 142, 152, 165, 211, 227, 228f, 229–231, 231f, 231p
Motor vehicle crashes
  of adolescents, 234, 418, 438, 439f, 483
  of adults vs. adolescents, 623–624
  alcohol abuse related to, 588
  of elderly, 679, 680f, 683
Mourning, 761, 780–783, 780p, 781p, 782p, 784
Mouth skills, 141
Movement, infants' attraction to, 164, 167
Mozart, Amadeus, 334
Multicontextual nature of development, 7–11, 21t, 127
Multicultural nature of development, 11–16, 21t, 127
Multidirectional nature of development, 6–7, 21t, 22, 127
Multidisciplinary nature of development, 16–19, 18f, 18p, 21t
Multifactorial traits, 77, 90
Multifinality, 324
Multi-infarct dementia, 712, 726
Multiple births
  breast-feeding and, 146
  causes of, 73–75, 74f, 76f, 77, 90. See also Twins
  low birthweights, 114, 122
Multiple intelligences, 321–322, 323, 336

Multiple sclerosis, 81, 714
Multitasking, 577, 621, 702, 726
Mumps, 144
Murray, Conrad, 782
Muscle reserve, 495
Muscle strength, 141
Music learning, 321
Musical intelligence, 322
Muslims, 546, 588, 763, 781
My Baby Can Read, 174–175
Myelin, 220
Myelination
  in early childhood, 220, 220f, 222, 226, 242, 318
  grammar acquisition and, 259
  language development and, 256
  of limbic system, 276–277
  in middle childhood, 318
  motor skills permitted by, 227, 232
  reduction of reaction time, 319
  sequence of, 416
  thinning in late adulthood, 701, 703
Myopia, 82–83, 84, 90
Mythic-literal faith, 531

Naming explosion, 171, 176, 178, 328
National Assessment of Educational Progress (NAEP), 358, 364
National Center for Health Statistics, 596
National norms, 644–645
National policies
  effect on elderly, 743
  paternity leave affected by, 206
  sex selection in pregnancy influenced by, 72
  volunteer work related to, 739
Native Americans
  breast-feeding by, A-7
  emphasis on regulation of impatience, 278
  funeral customs, 763
  high school graduation rate, 450f
  population of, A-4
  suicide rates, A-21
Naturalistic intelligence, 322
Naturally occurring retirement community (NORC), 740
Nature, 5
Nature of the child
  cognitive coping, 372, 372p, 373
  Erikson's industry and inferiority stage, 368, 373, 395
  Freud's latency stage, 368, 373, 395
  in middle childhood, 267p, 367–373, 368t, 369p, 372p, 374p, 374t, 395, 397
  resilience, 370, 371p, 371t, 373
  response to cumulative stress, 371–372, 371p, 373
  self-concept, 368–369
Nature-nurture controversy, 5
Nature-nurture interaction
  in depression, 17–19, 18f, 18p
  in development, 5, 17, 90

in education, 67
  ignorance of, 83–84
  in middle childhood, 309
  in moral development, 295–296, 303
  in personality development, 636
  predictions based on, 20–21
  in psychological disorders, 87
  relationship between genotype and phenotype, 81–84
  in sexual development, 290–294
  in temperament, 187
Near-death experiences, 767–768
Nearsightedness, 82–83, 84, 90, 579p, 600
Negative correlation, 29
Negative identity, 458
Negative mood, 187–188
Neglect. See also Child maltreatment
  of children, 237, 238f, 241, 242
  effect on attachment, 195t, 196, 196p
  effect on brain growth, 133
  responses to, 134
Neglected victims, 387
Neglectful/uninvolved parenting, 288, 303, 462, 466
Neighborhood, 10
Neighborhood games, 311–312, 313, 336
Netherlands
  emphasis in preschools in, 267
  emphasis on regulation of moodiness, 278
  euthanasia in, 773, 774, 775
  home births in, 104
  incidence of SIDS, 150
  PISA scores, 453t, A-16
  primary curriculum in, 355
  results of DIT, 530
Neural tube, 96, 98t, 99
Neural-tube defects, 107f, 108
Neurocognitive disorders (NCDs)
  AIDS, 714
  Alzheimer disease, 711–712, 711p, 712f, 712p, 716, 726
  bovine spongiform encephalitis (BSE), 714
  characteristics of, 709–710, 726
  comorbidity of, 714, 715
  dementia, 710f
  frontal lobe disorders, 712–713, 712p, 716, 726
  Huntington disease, 714
  Lewy body disorder, 714, 714p, 716, 726
  mild and major impairment, 709, 710
  multiple sclerosis, 714
  Parkinson's disease, 713
  polypharmacy inducing, 717–718, 726
  prevalence of, 710–771, 710f
  prevention of impairment, 714–716, 715p
  reversibility, 716–718, 726
  syphilis in last stages, 714
  traumatic encephalopathy, 714, 714p
  vascular dementia, 712, 712f, 726

Neurogenesis, 97, 700–701
Neurological problems, 114
Neurons
  of Alzheimer patients, 711
  appearance and atrophy of in
    adulthood, 577
  change with experience, 167
  communication, 131f, 132f
  defined, 129
  developing connections, 129, 219
  emotional development related to
    growth of, 185
  function of, 131f, 132f
  growth in late adulthood, 700–701
  kinds of impulses, 223
Neuroticism
  brain function and, 637p
  correlation with unhappiness in
    marriage, 642
  decrease with age, 635, 635f, 661
  outlook on life, 660
  as personality trait, 634, 636, 661
Neurotransmitters, 130, 131f, 132f,
  701, 703
New adaptation and anticipation
  stage, 156t, 157–159,
  158p, 159p
New Guinea, 119
New means through active experimentation stage, 156t, 159
New Zealand
  co-sleeping in, 135, 136f
  high school graduation rate, 445f
  punishment of poor behavior in,
    301
  scores on international tests, 356t,
    453t, A-16
  serious abuse in intimate relation-
    ships, 563
Newborns. See also Infancy (first
    two years)
  Apgar score, 101, 101t, 122
  attachment, 192t
  attraction of adult devotion, 204
  birth of, 99–101, 100f, 100p
  birthweight, 29, 98, 99, 105, 113,
    113–115, 114, 115f, 122
  bonding, 120–121
  brain growth, 129–130, 130f,
    131f, 132–134, 152
  Brazelton Neonatal Behavioral
    Assessment Scale, 116–
    117, 122, 139, 197
  breast-feeding, 146–148, 146p,
    151
  co-sleeping, 135–136, 136f, 136p
  effect of c-section, 102
  effect of epidural anesthesia, 103
  effect of induced labor, 103
  effect on family, 116–117
  emotional development, 181–182
  face recognition, 134
  failure to thrive, 128
  first minutes after birth, 101
  growth, 127–130
  immunization and, 145
  infant mortality, 12f, 12t, 103,
    105, 113, 114
  information processing, 163

interaction with mother, 17, 116,
  122
  kangaroo care, 121, 121p, 122, 138
  motor skill development, 140–143,
    140p, 140t, 141p
  physical growth, 152
  preterm delivery, 94t, 97, 98, 99p,
    103, 106, 113, 116
  reflexes of, 116–117
  senses of, 142
  shaken baby syndrome, 133
  sleep patterns, 135, 152
  sudden infant death syndrome,
    136, 149–151, 150f, 152
  survival of, 103, 142–151, 143f,
    143p, 152
Newton, Sir Isaac, 334
Niger, 148p, 590f, A-3
Nigeria, 75, 102f, 115f, 144, 377f
Nightmares, 224
No Child Left Behind Act, 358,
  364, 370
Nonshared environment, 373–374,
  380, 395, 567
Norms
  for body size, 128
  contribution to childhood obesity,
    315
  defined, 37, 64, 128
  for development of fine motor
    skills, 142t
  effect on gender development,
    293–294
  effect on marriage, 644–645
  for emotional development, 182t
  facts and, 37–39
  for height and weight, A-10–A-11
  for reading and math readiness,
    354t
  social norms of emerging adult-
    hood, 511–513
North Africa, 148, 148f, 149
North America. See also Canada;
    Mexico; United States
  childhood obesity in, 315
  decline in smoking, 587
  early childhood play in, 283
  funeral customs in, 763
  infant day care in, 207
  percentage of young adolescents
    not in school, 482f
  scaffolding in, 250
  self-concept of children in, 276
  stunting in children in, 148f
  theory of the mind in children of,
    255–256
Northern Ireland, 356t
Norway
  breast-feeding in, A-7
  elderly volunteers in, 739
  high school graduation rate, 445f
  low birthweights in, 115f
  PISA scores, 453t, A-16
  punishment of poor behavior in,
    301
  restrictions on diet in, 692
  sexual activity of adolescents in, 421
Nuclear family, 375, 376t, 380, 384,
  395, 397

Nursing homes
  care of the elderly, 674–675, 677,
    696, 754–755, 756, 757
  death in, 771f
Nurture, 5, 70. See also Nature-
    nurture interaction
Nutrition. See also Diet
  of adults, 576, 589, 590f, 591–
    592, 591p, 592p
  birthweight affected by, 115, 122
  brain fitness related to, 702, 715,
    716–717, 719
  breast-feeding, 27, 36, 102, 102p,
    119, 142, 146–148, 146p,
    147f, 147t, 151, 152
  deficiencies in early childhood,
    217, 217p
  diet deficiencies in adolescents,
    413–414, 414p, 416, 426,
    487
  in early childhood, 216–218, 217f,
    242
  effect of chemicals in food, 408
  in emerging adulthood, 498–500,
    514, 571
  genetic expression affected by, 77
  height affected by, 82–83
  infant mortality assoicated with,
    145–148, 152
  infant sleep patterns affected by,
    135
  oral health related to, 217–218
  prenatal development affected by,
    110, 116
  vision impacted by, 83

Obesity
  in adolescence, 414, 414p, 416, 426
  in adulthood, 499, 589, 590f,
    591–592, 591p, 592p, 594,
    600, 663
  birthweight associated with
    mother's, 115
  body mass index (BMI), 499t
  breast-feeding and, 146, 147t
  causes of weight gain, 591–592,
    591p
  of children born by c-section, 102
  consequences of, 496, 583, 589
  contributing factors, 133, 315–316
  by country, 590f
  cultural differences, 591
  in early childhood, 216–217, 216p,
    218, 242
  as eating disorder, 414
  education related to, 598
  during emerging adulthood, 497
  by ethnicity, 590f
  of immigrants' children, 500
  indicators in infancy, 128
  level of education related to, 444
  mature brain affected by, 615
  in middle childhood, 313, 314f,
    315–316, 316p, 336, 397
  onset of puberty affected by, 408
  overcoming, 593–594
  role of leptin, 408
  of sexually abused girls, 424
  social norms affecting, 511

Obituaries, 782
Object permanence, 158, 160,
  162, 178
Objective thought, 521–522
Observation, 32
Obsessive-compulsive behaviors,
  218, 218f, 505
Occupation, 10
Odds ratio, 23t
Oden, Melita, 605
Oedipus complex, 291
Okinawa, 692
Old-age pensions, 735, 736,
  737–738
Oldest-old people
  care of, 674–675, 677, 696
  cause of death, 684
  cognition of, 683
  creation and maintenance of
    identity, 730
  defined, 675, 676
  dependence of widows, 734
  learning ability, 720
  in nursing homes, 754
  physician-assisted suicide and, 775
  treatment of hypertension, 685
Old-old people, 675, 676, 696
Olfactory region of the brain, 700
On Becoming a Person (Rogers), 56
One-to-one correspondence, 251
Online chat rooms, 430
Onlooker play, 283
On-the-job training, 451
Openness
  of adults in U.S., 636
  of emerging adulthood, 528p
  outlook on life, 660
  as personality trait, 634, 635, 635f,
    635p, 637, 661
Operant conditioning, 43–44, 43p,
  44t, 64
Operational definition, B-4
Opportunity, 345
Oppositional defiance disorder, 281f
Oral fixation, 200
Oral health, 217–218
Oral stage, 39–40, 39p, 40t,
  199–200
Oregon, euthanasia law, 774–775,
  776f
Organ growth, 412, 415, 426, 481
Organ reserve
  of adults, 600
  decrease with age, 576, 580, 684,
    685, 689
  function of, 493, 500, 514, 571
  interaction with allostasis and
    homeostasis, 496
  response to stress, 615
Orphanages, 196, 196p, 226
Osteoporosis
  in adolescents, 413
  alcohol abuse related to, 588
  benefits of exercise, 497, 592
  benefits of HRT, 585
  deaths due to, 687
  diagnosis and treatment of, 687
  in women, 686
Output, 706–709, 707f

Ovaries, 403, 419
Overeating, 495–496
Overimitation, 250
Overprotection, 289
Overregularization, 259, 262
Ovulation, 584, 600, 663
Ovum
  abnormal genetic formation, 84–85, 85p, 86t
  fertilization, 68, 68p
  sex chromosomes of, 71
Own-race effect, 134
OxyContin, 480f
Oxygen dispersal, 576
Oxytocin, 99, 204–205, 224, 295, 616–617

Pacific, 148f
Pain, 139, 181–182, 774–775
Pakistan, 693–694
Palliative care, 771, 778, 786
Palmar grasping reflex, 117
Panama, 312
Panic attacks, 224
Parallel play, 283
Parasuicide, 475, 475f, 478
Parent-adolescent relationships, 466, 469, 472, 473–474, 476
Parental alliance, 120, 122, 199, 327, 378, 379, 395
Parental imprinting, 81
Parental leave, 207
Parental monitoring, 464, 466, 485
Parent-child relationships, 645–646
Parentification, 372
Parent-infant bond, 120, 121p, 122
Parenting
  adoptive parents, 648–649, 648p, 660
  biological parents, 647–648, 660
  continuity of care, 646, 646p
  foster parents, 650–651, 660
  gendered views of, 530
  as impediment to higher education, 567
  role of epigenetics, 60
  stepparents, 649–650, 649p, 660
Parents. See also Caregiving; Fathers; Mothers
  adolescents' peer relationships and, 467
  adoptive parents, 648–649, 648p, 660, 661
  attachment, 191–197, 192t, 193t, 195t, 205
  biological parents, 647–648, 660, 661
  characteristics of good parents, 613–614
  confirmation of child's worth, 276
  effect on child's personality, 373
  facilitation of reading, 258
  foster parents, 650–651, 660, 661
  as guides to moral development, 298
  influence on identity formation, 459, 460
  instinct to protect young, 58–59, 93–94

level on Maslow's hierarchy affect-ing parenting, 203–204
maltreatment of children, 236–241, 236p, 238f, 239t
  as mentors, 249, 249p
  moral development and empathy associated with, 391
  proximal and distal parenting, 201–202
  relationship with adolescent children, 462–465, 462p, 464p, 465f, 485, 487, 560
  relationship with adult children, 639, 641
  relationship with emerging-adult children, 546, 564–568, 565p, 566f, 567p, 569, 660
  role in determining educational practice, 360, 360f
  as role models, 200–201, 293
  sex education from, 471–472
  stepparents, 649–650, 649p, 660, 661
  support of emerging-adult children, 565–568, 565p, 566f, 567p, 569, 571, 660
  synchrony, 189, 190f, 191, 191p
  view of newborns, 204
Parkinson's disease, 692, 713–714
Participants in studies, 23t, 30, 31, B-3, B-4
Parts of speech, 172, 348
Passion, 553, 554, 568, 569, 643
Passive euthanasia, 773, 778
Pastrana, Travis, 508, 508p
Paternal leave, 207t
Patterns of growth, 6f
Pausch, Randy, 765
Pavlov, Ivan, 42p, 43–44
Paxó gene, 82
PCBs, 109t
Pedestrian deaths, 234, 235, 235f
Peer relationships
  in adolescence, 417, 438, 439f, 466–473, 466p, 468p, 470f, 470p, 485, 487
  bullies and victims, 386p, 387–388, 389, 395, 397
  child culture, 384, 384p, 389
  drug use encouraged by, 510
  effect on morality, 392, 393
  effect on self-esteem in adolescence, 473
  effect on sexual activity in adolescence, 421se
  facilitation of bad/good behavior, 469, 477, 485
  friendships, 385, 389, 485
  influence on identity formation, 459
  influence on sexual behavior, 472
  in middle childhood, 384–389, 384p, 386p, 395, 397
  moral development and empathy associated with, 391, 395
  as need of middle childhood, 375
  onset of puberty and, 409–411, 410p, 426
  parents and, 467

peer pressure, 467–468, 468p, 473, 591
  popular and unpopular children, 385–386, 395
  as purpose of sex, 502
  romance, 469–470, 470f
  selection of friends, 469
  sex education from, 471–472
  social networking, 468–469, 468p
  social norms affecting, 511–513
  social skills necessary for, 448
Pelvic inflammatory disease (PID), 583, A-17
Penis, 419
Percentile, 128, 136
Perception
  area of brain controlling, 130
  cross-modal perception, 142
  defined, 137, 163
  development of, 152
  in first two years, 211
  formed from sensations, 137, 344, 364
  leading to cognition, 137, 156, 162
Perfumers, 626
Permanency planning, 240, 240p, 242
Permissive parenting, 287t, 288, 303
Perry, 269
Perry, William G., Jr., 534, 534–535, 534t
Presenilin 2 gene, 712
Perseveration, 223, 223p, 227
Personal compensation: sex, 676–678, 676f, 677p, 684
Personal decisions, 36
Personal fable, 430, 434, 454
Personality
  Big Five traits, 634–635, 634p, 635f, 635p, 637, 659–660, 661, 663
  changes with frontal lobe disor-ders, 712
  continuity and change, 637, 757
  development in adulthood, 631–637, 632t, 633p, 634p, 635p, 636f, 637p, 661, 663
  in emerging adulthood, 549–550, 549f, 569, 571
  factors determining, 631, 634–636, 637, 637p
  midlife crisis, 633–634, 633p, 663
  plasticity of, 550
  theories of adult personality, 631–633, 632t, 637, 663
  vitality associated with, 597
Perspective, 724
Peru, 115f, 250
Pester-power, 316
Pesticides, 110, 230
PET scans, 18p, 161t
Phallic stage, 39–40, 40t, 291–292, 303
Phase delay, 403–405, 404f, 404p, 405f
Phenobarbital, 109t
Phenotype
  additive heredity, 78, 90
  copy number variations, 79–81, 81p

deactivation of X chromosome, 80
dominant-recessive heredity, 78–79, 79f, 90
environmental influence on, 77–78, 78p, 84, 90
functions of, 77
parental imprinting, 81, 81p
X-linked characteristics, 79, 80t
Philippines, 121p, 136f, 463, 573
Phobias, 58, 277
Physical activity. See also Exercise; Play; Sports
  in adolescence, 413, 418, 419p
  for early childhood, 283–284, 283p
  in middle childhood, 311–313, 312p, 313p, 336
  running speed during adolescence, 412f
  in schools, 354, 355p
Physical appearance
  adolescents' concern about, 414, 416, 430, 431, 447, 730
  changes in adulthood, 577–578, 577p, 580, 597, 600, 663, 675, 678, 730, 732
  of common sex chromosome abnormalities, 82t
  in emerging adulthood, 496–497, 514
  emerging adults' concern about, 514, 524, 559
  genetic determination of, 74f, 75, 76, 77, 82
  in late adulthood, 676–677
  of newborns, 117
  preoperational thought focusing on, 246–248, 256, 261, 293
  race based on, 15, 16
Physical bullying, 386
Physical context of development, 7
Physical education, 312–313, 313p, 336, 354
Physical necessities, 374
Physical punishment
  results of, 299–300, 299p, 302, 303
  spanking, 299p, 301–302, 301p
Physician-assisted suicide, 773–775, 774t, 775, 776f, 778, 786
Physiological needs, 56, 57, 57f, 769
Piaget, Jean
  acceptance of theory, 343, 347, 518, 519
  application to middle childhood, 357, 397
  on children's moral thinking, 389
  cognition sensorimotor years, 142
  concrete operational thought, 339–340, 339p, 340p, 348, 364, 435f
  definition of intelligence, 699
  dialectical approach of, 526
  formal operational thought, 431–434, 431p, 432f, 434, 435f, 436, 438, 454, 487
  Fowler's work based on, 531
  influence on child-centered programs, 264

moral development, 295
on moral issue of retribution or restitution, 393–394, 393f
new research and, 160–162, 161t, 270
preoperational thought, 245–249, 256, 272, 305
sensorimotor intelligence, 155–160, 156t, 178
stages of development, 45–47, 45p, 46t, 48, 51, 64
Picasso, Pablo, 334
Pick disease, 712
Pilots, 625, 628
Pincer movement, 141, 142t
PISA. *See* Programme for International Student Assessment (PISA)
Pituitary gland
functions of, 219f, A-2
stimulation of puberty, 402, 402f, 403, 411, 426
Placenta, 95, 100f, 101
Placid personality, 634
Plagiarism, avoiding, B-3
Planning
of adolescents, 438–439, 519
bad habit breaking, 593
brain maturation required for, 416
by elderly, 683
of emerging adults, 519, 520f
in late adulthood, 701
reaction time aiding, 319
role of active social play, 284
Plaques, 711
Plasticity
biological advantage of, 60
case study of David, 20–21
defined, 19, 32
of developmental process, 19, 22, 80, 209
education for gifted and talented children and, 334
in emerging adulthood, 550
of human brain, 134, 221, 621, 626, 683, 703, 714, 726
in late adulthood, 703
as lifelong characteristic, 557
Play
active play, 283–284, 283p
in early childhood, 227, 229p, 280, 282–286, 282f, 283p, 286f, 286p, 303
effect on vision, 83, 83p
as indicator of maltreatment, 239t
influence of culture and cohort, 282–283
in middle childhood, 311–313, 311p, 312p, 313p
percentage of time spent by SES and nationality, 282t
playmates, 282
rough-and-tumble play, 284, 295
sociodramatic play, 284–286, 286f, 286p, 295
types of social play, 283
Play face, 284
Playmates, 282
Pleasure, 182

Plumbism, 230–231, 231f, 231p
Pneumonia, 144, 684, 685f, 695
Pointing, 170, 170p
Poisoning, 234, 235, 411
Poland
high school graduation rate, 445f, 482f
infant mortality in, 143f
language development in, 173p
population of children and elders, A-3
scores on international tests, 356t, 453t, A-16
smokers in, 587
Polio, 144, 145f
Political activism, 742–743, 742f, 743, 757
Political context, 644
Political identity, 460, 460p, 462, 485, 487, 544
Political ideology, 78
Political terrorism, 460
Political views, 634, 636
Pollution
aging affected by, 689
asthma associated with, 229–230, 317, 318, 336
birthweight affected by, 113, 115
brain development affected by, 229, 230
fetus affected by, 109t
gross motor development affected by, 229, 230, 233
Polychlorinated biphenyls, 109t
Polygamous family, 375
Polygenic traits, 77, 81, 82, 90
Polymorphic genes, 69
Polypharmacy, 717–718, 719, 726
Popularity, 385–386, 389, 395, 466
Population, 686f, B-3
Portugal, 445f, 453t, A-16
Positive adaptation, 370
Positive correlation, 29
Positive effect, 732–734, 733f
Positivity bias, 276
Positron emission tomography (PET), 161t
Postconventional moral reasoning, 390, 390t
Postformal thought
cognitive flexibility of, 522–523
combination of subjective and objective thought, 521–522, 521p
countering of stereotypes, 523–525, 524p
development of in college, 533
as dialectical thought, 525–527
of emerging adulthood, 517–527, 518p, 520f, 521f, 521p, 524p, 540, 571
ethics related to, 529
practical and personal aspects of, 518–520, 518p, 520f, 521f
Postpartum depression, 119, 121, 122, 191, 627
Postpartum psychosis, 119
Post-traumatic growth, 619, 620

Post-traumatic stress disorder (PTSD)
of combat troops, 505, 505p, 619
as result of maltreatment, 238
from stress in early childhood, 226
Poverty
defined, 10–11
escape from, 598–599
increase in, 660
in late adulthood, 735
rates by state and age, A-13
Practical guidance, 36
Practical intelligence, 611–612, 611p, 614, 628, 663
Practice, 141, 142, 232
Prader-Willi syndrome, 81
Pragmatics, 259, 349–350, 353, 364
Precocious children, 333–334
Precocious puberty, 408
Preconventional moral reasoning, 390, 390t
Predictions concerning aging, 665, 667–676, 668p, 670f, 670p, 671f, 672f, 673p, 674p, 696
Prefrontal cortex
ability to develop theories, 256
atrophy with age, 683, 701, 703
damage from alcohol, 481
defined, 129
development of control processes, 346
development of in first two years, 130, 133
effects of drugs on, 483
emotional regulation, 275–276, 276–277, 303
in frontal lobe disorders, 712
functions of, 129, 130f, 219f, 227, 318, 519, 705, A-2
growth in early childhood, 276–277
injuries caused by immaturity of, 234
maturation during emerging adulthood, 519
maturation in adolescence, 416–417, 418, 419, 436, 438, 440, 454, 487
maturation in early childhood, 220, 222, 227, 232, 242, 305
maturation in middle childhood, 318–319, 364, 764
role in development of theory of the mind, 254, 255f, 255p
role of rough-and-tumble play in development of, 284
Pregnancy. *See also* Abortion; Prenatal development
advice from doctors, 110
advice from scientists, 111
assisted reproductive technology, 71, 75–76, 77, 90, 115, 583, 586, 600
associated with sexual abuse, 423, 424
avoidance of in marriage, 554
beginning of, 94t
choosing sex of zygote, 71
due date, 94t

effect of stress on incidence of in young girls, 409
effect of teratogens, 105–106, 107f, 107t, 108, 109–110t, 110–111
embryonic period, 94, 94t, 95–96, 96p, 99, 107f
father's role in, 117, 119, 122
fetal period, 96–99, 96p, 97p, 98p, 107f
first trimester. *See* Embryonic period; Germinal period
germinal period, 94–95, 94p, 94t, 95f, 99, 107f
labor and delivery, 99–104, 100f, 100p, 101f, 102f, 102p, 104p
last trimester, 98–99, 138
length of, 94t
miscarriage, 85, 95, 422, 583
outside of marriage, 558, 559
preparation for, 106, 107t
preterm delivery, 94t, 97, 98, 99p
problems and solutions, 105, 106f, 107–108, 109–110t, 110–116, 110t
second trimester, 97, 97p
stillbirth, 85, 95
in teen years, 58, 115, 147t, 410, 419, 422–423, 423p, 426, 464, 472, 489, 501, 647
third month, 96, 96p
timing between, 106
trimesters of, 94t
unplanned pregnancy, 502
in vitro fertilization, 71, 75–76, 77, 90, 95, 583, 586, 600
vulnerability during prenatal development, 95t
Prejudice
ageist stereotype, 668–673, 668p, 670f, 670p, 671f, 672f, 696
concerning late adulthood, 665, 667–676, 668p, 670f, 670p, 671f, 672f, 673p, 674p, 696
racial prejudice, 437, 447, 524
Premarital birth, 642
Prenatal care, 110, 111
Prenatal development
of brain, 129, 130
effect of teratogens, 105–106, 107f, 107t, 108, 109–110t, 110–111, 116
embryonic period, 94, 94t, 95–96, 96p, 99, 107f, 122
of eyes, 138
fetal period, 94, 94t, 96–99, 96p, 97p, 98p, 107f, 122, 129, 130
germinal period, 94–95, 94p, 94t, 95f, 99, 107f, 122
of hearing, 138
low birthweight, 113–115, 115f
risk analysis, 106–108, 107f, 116
in second trimester, 97, 97p, 122
stages of, 107f
vulnerability during, 95t

Preoperational thought
   aid to language learning, 257, 261
   characteristics of, 46, 46t
   conservation and logic, 247–249,
      247p, 248f
   defined, 245–246, 256, 272
   moral development related to, 390
   obstacles to logic, 246
   view of sexes, 293
Preoperative intelligence, 245
Presbycusis, 579
Preschool programs
   bilingual education, 268–269
   child-centered programs, 263–265,
      263p, 264p, 270, 272, 305
   children enrolled in, 262f, 266f,
      268f, 271f
   controversy over focus, 280, 283
   facilitation of reading, 258
   Head Start, 266–269, 267p, 268f
   long-term gains from intensive
      programs, 269–270, 272
   as source of intellectual activity, 341
   teacher-directed programs,
      265–266, 265p, 266f,
      267p, 268f, 270, 272, 305
   types of, 262–263
Prescribing cascade, 717
Prescription drugs, 480f, 483, 586
Presenilin 1 gene, 712
Pretending, 184, 284–286, 286f,
   286p
Preterm delivery
   age of viability, 97
   birthweight, 113, 116
   complications, 98, 116, 122
   defined, 94t, 113
   effect on emotional development,
      182
   effect on infant sleep patterns, 135
   of infant conceived by IVF, 76
   survival of infant, 99p, 103
   teen pregnancy associated with, 422
   teratogens causing, 106
Pride
   of bullies, 387
   cultural norms for development of,
      184, 276, 278, 370
   development in early childhood,
      303
   development of in first two years,
      182t
Primary aging, 684, 688, 690, 693,
   696
Primary circular reactions, 156–157,
   156t, 157f, 157p, 178
Primary education, 444, 454
Primary prevention
   of disease, 594
   of injury, 235–236, 242
   of maltreatment of children, 240,
      242
Primary sex characteristics, 419,
   425, 426
Primitive streak, 96
Prions, 577
Private schools, 361, 364, 397
Private speech, 251
Problem-focused coping, 616, 617

Problems
   externalization of, 279–280, 303,
      380, 383, 387, 476
   in families, 380, 381–384, 382p
   internalization of, 279–280, 303,
      383, 387, 476
Problem-solving ability, 708
Processing speed, 28. See also Speed
      of thought
Pro-family theory, 38
Professional journals, B-1–B-2
Progeria, 689
Programme for International Student
      Assessment (PISA), 445,
      451–452, 453t, 454, A-16
Progress in International Reading
      Literacy Study (PIRLS),
      356, 356t, 357, 364, 445,
      451, A-16
Prosocial behavior
   in adolescence, 477–478
   development in middle childhood,
      391
   development of in early childhood,
      296, 297, 302, 303, 305, 391
Prosocial values, 528
Prosopagnosia, 134
Prospective memory, 704, 726
Prospective memory-paradox, 707
Prospective studies, B-3
Protective optimism, 276
Protective personalities, 520, 521f
Protein synthesis, 68f
Protein-calorie malnutrition, 148
Proteins, 68
Provocative victims, 387
Proximal parenting, 201–202, 202p,
      202t
Proximity-seeking, 192, 193, 205
Proximodistal pattern, 96, 140
Proxy, 777, 778, 786
Pruning, 132, 137, 152, 186, 219
PSA (test for prostate cancer), 493,
      596
Psychoactive drug
   effect on birthweight, 113
   effect on prenatal development,
      108, 109t
   use for psychopathologies, 326
Psychoanalytic theory. See also
      Psychosexual theory;
      Psychosocial theory
   application of, 50–51
   application to early childhood,
      276–277, 291–292
   application to infant social develop-
      ment, 199–205, 208, 209
   application to middle childhood,
      368, 373
   concepts of, 62f
   contribution/criticism of, 48, 62
   defined, 39
   emergence of, 39
   Erikson's stages of development,
      40t, 41, 50, 51, 64, 200,
      276–277
   Freud's stages of development,
      39–40, 40t, 50, 51, 64,
      291–292

limitations of, 51–52, 56
   methodology, 48
   view of maternal employment, 207
Psychological control, 300, 300p, 303
Psychometric approach to cognitive
      development, 517
Psychopathology. See also
      Depression; Mental illness
   in adolescence, 503
   anxiety disorders, 226, 238,
      505–506, 505p, 506p
   of bullies and victims, 388
   causes and consequences, 324,
      373, 402, 619
   comorbidity of, 324, 328, 503
   contribution to abusive relationships,
      563
   copy number variations causing, 80
   defined, 279
   diagnosis and treatment of, 324
   diathesis-stress model, 504, 505,
      506, 514
   during emerging adulthood,
      503–504, 503–507, 505p,
      506p, 514, 571
   of Erikson's stages of development,
      544t
   evolutionary theory concerning, 60
   increase in puberty, 417, 454
   mood disorders, 504–505
   prognosis, 324
   schizophrenia, 77, 87, 144, 406,
      506–507, 514
   sex differences, 281f, 303, 406
Psychosexual theory
   Freud's stages of development,
      39–40, 40t, 48, 50, 51, 64
   latency in middle childhood, 368,
      373, 395
   oral and anal stages in infant social
      development, 199–200,
      200p, 208, 209
   phallic stage and preschoolers'
      sexism, 291–292, 295, 303
   stages of development, 39–40, 40t,
      48, 50, 51
Psychosocial development
   adolescent-adult relationships,
      462–466, 462p, 464p,
      465f, 487
   brain and emotions in first two
      years, 185–189, 187p,
      188f, 211
   challenges for caregivers of two-six
      year-olds, 287–294, 287t,
      288p, 290f, 292f
   continuity and change during
      emerging adulthood,
      543–550, 544p, 544t, 545f,
      546p, 547p, 547t, 548f,
      548p, 549f, 569, 571
   development of social bonds in
      first two years, 189, 190f,
      191–199, 191p, 192t, 193t,
      194p, 195t, 196p, 197p,
      198p, 199, 199f, 211
   drug use and abuse in adolescence,
      478–484, 479p, 480f, 480p,
      482f, 483p, 487

emerging adult-parental relationships,
      564–568, 565p, 566f, 567p,
      569, 571
   emotional development in early
      childhood, 275–280, 276p,
      277p, 279p, 280p, 305
   emotional development in first
      two years, 181–184, 182p,
      182t, 183p, 211
   families and children, 373–384,
      373p, 375f, 376t, 377f,
      378p, 379p, 381f, 382p, 397
   generativity in adulthood,
      646–652, 646p, 647p,
      648p, 649p, 652p, 653f,
      654–660, 655f, 656f, 657p,
      658p, 659p, 663
   identity formation in adolescence,
      457–462, 458p, 459p, 460f,
      460p, 461f, 461p, 487
   intimacy during emerging adult-
      hood, 551–564, 552p,
      553f, 555p, 556f, 556p,
      557p, 558f, 560f, 564p,
      569, 571, 663
   intimacy of friends and family in
      adulthood, 637–641, 638p,
      639p, 640p, 663
   intimacy of romantic partners in
      adulthood, 641–646, 641p,
      642f, 642p, 643t, 644p,
      645p, 663
   moral development in early child-
      hood, 295–302, 297p, 297t,
      299p, 300p, 301p, 305
   moral values of middle childhood,
      389–394, 390p, 390t,
      392p, 393f, 397
   nature of the child in middle
      childhood, 267p, 367–373,
      368t, 369p, 372p, 374p,
      374t, 397
   peer group in middle childhood,
      384–389, 384p, 386p, 397
   peer relationships in adolescence,
      466–473, 466p, 468p,
      470f, 470p, 487
   personality development in adult-
      hood, 631–637, 632t,
      633p, 634p, 635p, 636f,
      637p, 663
   play in early childhood, 280, 281f,
      282, 286, 282f, 283p, 286f,
      286p
   sadness and anger in adolescence,
      473–478, 474p, 475f,
      476p, 477p
   theories of infant psychosocial de-
      velopment, 199–205, 200p,
      201p, 202p, 202t, 205p,
      206p, 206t, 207f, 209
Psychosocial problems, 423
Psychosocial theory
   application to early childhood,
      276–277, 279, 303
   application to infant social
      development, 200
   application to middle childhood,
      368, 373

arenas of identity, 459
autonomy vs. shame and doubt, 199, 200, 208, 209
on caregiving, 651
on children's effect on parents, 647
generativity vs. stagnation, 632, 632t, 637, 646, 661
identity vs. role confusion, 458, 462, 485, 543, 632, 632t
industry vs. inferiority, 368, 373, 395
initiative vs. guilt, 276–277, 277p, 279, 303
integrity vs. despair, 719, 730, 757
intimacy vs. isolation, 551, 560, 569, 637
on late adulthood, 719
stages of psychosocial development, 40t, 41, 48, 50, 51, 64, 544t, 632, 632t, 637
view of sexes, 461
PTSD. See Post-traumatic stress disorder (PTSD)
Puberty. See also Adolescence
age of onset, 401, 406–409, 406p, 407f, 409–411, 411, 426, 487
body fat, 406, 411, 426
body rhythms, 403–405, 404f, 404p, 405f, 411
changes in eyes, 82
defined, 401
duration of, 399
effect of stress, 403, 408–409, 411, 426
effect on parent's happiness in marriage, 643
Freud's stages of development, 39–40
genes controlling age of onset, 406
hormones stimulating, 402–403, 402f, 402p, 403, 407f, 408, 411
language learning after, 260
menarche and spermarche, 401–402, 426
peer relationships, 409–411, 410p, 426, 466–473, 466p, 468p, 470f, 470p
precocious puberty, 408
rise in depression, 474
sequence of, 401–402, 407f
sexual maturation, 419–426, 420f, 420p, 421p, 423p, 424p, 425f
stress of middle school, 445–448, 445p
Public acclaim, 417, 438, 447
Public health, 143, 711
Puerto Rico, 278
Punishment. See Discipline

Quality-adjusted life years (QALYs), 597
Quindlen, Anna, 730, 732

Race, 14–16, 14f, 22. See also Ethnicity; specific ethnic group
Racial prejudice, 524

Racial socialization, 649, 668
Racism, 15–16, 433, 649, 668, 735
Radiation, 109t, 583, 689
Rahman, Rumaisa, 99p
Random sample, B-3
Rapid eye movement (REM) sleep, 135
Rational judgment, 437
Reaching, 142t
Reaction time, 319, 320
Reactive aggression, 297t, 298, 302, 303
Reactive attachment disorder, 648
Reading
    Common Core standards, 359t
    connections in the brain required for, 318–319, 320
    cultural impact on, 342
    dyslexia, 328, 328p, 336
    international test scores, 356t
    as means of teaching language, 351, 351f
    national variation in teaching techniques, 353
    Programme for International Student Assessment, 445, 451–452, 454, A-16
    Progress in International Reading Literacy Study, 356, 356t, 357, 364, 445, 451, A-16
    readiness for, 354t
    strategies facilitating, 258
    in United States, 356t, 358
Reaffirmation, 783
Receptive language, 259
Recess, 312–313, 354
Recessive disorders, 86–87, 89, 90
Recessive genes
    disorders associated with, 85, 86–87, 89, 90
    X-linked characteristics, 78–79, 79f
Reciprocity, 637
Recognition, 162
Recreation, 502
Reflexes, 116–117, 140, 156, 156t
Reflexive fear, 209
Reggio Emilia, 264, 270, 272
Reincarnation, 781
Reinforcement, 44
Relational aggression, 297t, 298, 303
Relational bullying, 386
Relativism discovered thinking, 534t
Relaxation, 694
Religion
    as aid to overcoming stress, 372, 372p
    attitudes toward premarital sex, 502, 503
    beliefs about death, 763, 781, 786
    of college students, 536, 571
    during emerging adulthood, 528p, 529f, 531, 532, 540
    involvement in late adulthood, 742, 742p, 743, 757
    near-death experiences associated with, 767–768
    political activism, 743
    stages of development, 531, 532

Religious coping, 619, 620
Religious extremism, 460
Religious identity, 459, 459p, 462, 485, 487, 544, 546
Relocation, 657–658
REM (rapid eye movement) sleep, 135
Remarriage, 645–646, 648–649, 648p, 661. See also Stepfamilies; Stepparents
Reminder session, 166
Reminders, 166
Remote grandparents, 747
Repetition, 166
Replication, 4, 5, 30–31
Reported maltreatment, 236–237
Reporting results, B-4
Representative sample, B-3
Reproduction. See also Birth; Contraception; Fertility; Sexual activity
    assisted reproductive technology, 71, 75–76, 77, 90, 95, 115, 583, 586, 600
    as biological-based drive, 58–60, 61
    decrease possibility in middle age, 580, 584–586
    maturity of system in adolescence, 419–420, 420f, 426
    as purpose of sex, 502
    readiness for in emerging adulthood, 491, 500, 514, 571
    in vitro fertilization, 71, 75–76, 77, 90, 95, 583, 586, 600
Reproductive nurturance, 204
Reprogrammed cells, 73
Research
    application of, 32
    blind gatherers, B-4
    case studies, 2, 25
    cautions and challenges, 32
    code of ethics, 28–31
    correlation and causation, 29, 32
    cross-sectional, 25–27, 26f
    cross-sequential, 26f, 28
    design of, B-4
    effect size, B-4
    experiment, 24, 24f, 28, 32
    implication of results, 30–31, 32
    Internet sources, B-2–B-3
    journals and books, B-1–B-2
    longitudinal, 26f, 27
    meta-analysis, B-4
    observation, 22–23, 32
    operational definition, B-4
    participants, B-3, B-4
    personalization of, B-1
    population, B-3
    protection of participants, 30, 32
    reporting results, B-4–B-5
    representative sample, B-3
    sample, B-3
    scientific method, 4–5, 32
    statistical measures, 23t
    study issues, 31
    survey, 24–25, 28, 32
    on teratogen damage, 108, 109–110t, 110

Resilience
    coping with stress producing, 619–620
    of the elderly, 670
    in late adulthood, 732
    in middle childhood, 370–372, 371p, 371t, 373, 380, 382, 395
Resource room, 331
Respect, 769
Respiratory development, 98
Respite care, 755
Respondent conditioning, 43–44
Response to intervention (RTI), 331
Restitution, 393, 393f
Retinoic acid, 109t
Retirement, 735, 736, 738–739, 743, 757
Retribution, 393, 393f
Retrieval of memories, 345, 364, 706, 726
Retrospective studies, B-3
Reversibility, 340
Reviews, B-4
Rewards, 43, 48p
Ribonucleic acid (RNA), 68
Right to die, 775
Risk analysis for teratogen exposure, 106, 107f, 108, 116
Risk aversion, 655
Risky behavior. See also Drug use and abuse; Excitement; Parasuicide; Self-destructive behavior; Sexual activity; Suicidal ideation; Suicide
    of adolescents, 430, 434, 437–438, 439f, 765, 786
    base rate neglect and availability error associated with, 511–512
    benefits of, 509, 513
    during emerging adulthood, 507–513, 507p, 508f, 508p, 509p, 510f, 510p, 513, 514, 571, 786
    in people with short 5-HTTLPR gene, 465, 465f
    social norms affecting, 511–513, 514
Ritalin, 326, 480f
RNA, 68, 78
Rogers, Carl, 56–58, 64
Role confusion, 458, 462, 485, 544
Role models
    academic achievement related to, 446
    effect on learning, 36
    influence on adolescents' decisions, 436, 439, 485
    for sexual identity formation, 460
Rolling over, 142, 152
Roman Catholicism, 781
Romance. See also Intimacy; Love
    in adolescence, 469–470, 470f, 473, 485
    dialectical approach to, 526
Romanian adoptees, 196, 196p, 226
Romantic love, 553t, 569, 663, 676
Romantic partners. See Cohabitation; Living apart together (LAT); Marriage

Rooting reflex, 117
Rotavirus, 144
Rough-and-tumble play, 284, 286, 295, 303
Routines, 218, 218f
Rovee-Collier, Carolyn, 166
Rubella, 20–21, 106, 109t, 144
Rubeola, 144
Rumination, 474
Running, 140t, 152
Russia
   alcohol use in, 588
   college graduates in, 535
   overweight people in, 590f
   population of children and elders, A-3
   scores on international tests, 356t, 453t
   sexually active teens/condom use, 425f

S1R2, def-2 gene, 690
Sadness
   in adolescence, 473–477, 474p, 475f, 485, 487
   development of, 182–183, 182t
   manifestations of in toddlers, 184
Safety, 56, 57, 57f, 769
Same-sex couples, 563, 644
Same-sex marriage, 9, 9f, 644, 644p, 647, 782
Same-sex parents, 375, 376t, 379, 379p, 384, 397
Same-sex romance, 470–471, 470p, 473, 485, 582
Sample, B-3
Sandwich generation, 573, 651–652, 652f, 660, 661, 663
Sati, 734
Saudi Arabia, 413, 536, 590f, A-3
Saunders, Cecily, 770
Scaffolding
   of language learning, 256, 257
   mentor-assisted learning, 249–250, 250p, 272
   in middle childhood, 341
   of morality, 392
Schaie, K. Warner, 606–607, 611, 628
Schiavo, Terri, 777–778, 777p
Schizophrenia
   caused by mumps, 144
   in emerging adulthood, 506–507, 514, 571
   as epigenetic characteristic, 77
   gender difference, 406
   genetic testing for, 87
   nature-nurture interaction, 87
School drop-out rates, 445, 446
Schools. See Education
Science, 251–252, 431, A-16
Science of human development, 4, 5
Scientific method
   application of, 22–23, 22–28, 23, 23–24, 25–28, 32
   cautions and challenges, 28–31, 29, 29–31, 31, 32
   defined, 4
   process of, 5, 32
   study of development, 32

Scientific observation, 22–23, 28
Scientists, 4
Scotland, 511
Seasonal rhythms, 403, 426
Seattle Longitudinal Study, 28, 606–607, 606f, 626, 706–707, 719
Secondary aging, 684, 688, 690, 693
Secondary circular reactions, 156t, 157–159, 158p, 178
Secondary education, 444, 453, 454. See also High school; Middle school
Secondary prevention
   of disease, 594
   of injury, 235, 236, 242
   of maltreatment of children, 240, 242
Secondary sex characteristics, 420, 425, 426
Secular trend, 406
Secure attachment, 193, 193t, 195, 195t, 209, 299, 557, 783
Sedentary behavior, 583, 585, 591, 592f
Selection bias, avoiding, B-3
Selective adaptation, 59–60, 59f, 59p, 61
Selective amnesia, 165f
Selective attention, 319, 320, 323, 346
Selective optimization with compensation
   in adulthood, 620–621, 621p, 624, 626, 627, 628, 663
   compensation for the brain, 682–683, 682p, 683p, 684
   personal compensation: sex, 676–678, 676f, 677p, 684, 696
   social compensation: driving, 678–679, 679p, 680f, 684, 696
   technical compensation: senses, 681–682, 681p, 681t, 684, 696
Selective recall, 732
Self theories of late adulthood, 730–734, 730p, 731p, 733f, 737, 739, 757
Self-acceptance, 57
Self-actualization
   in adulthood, 633
   as aspect of wisdom, 723
   characteristics of, 56, 57, 58, 61, 64, 719
   of dying, 769
   in late adulthood, 719, 719p, 724
Self-assessment, 708
Self-awareness, 182t, 184, 184p, 185, 209, 730
Self-care, 310, 336
Self-concept
   of adolescents, 430–434, 430p, 431p, 432f, 433f, 433p, 443, 457
   affect on behavior, 48
   development in early childhood, 276
   in late adulthood, 730
   in middle childhood, 368–369, 373, 395

role of active social play, 283
role of sociodramatic play, 284
Self-consciousness
   in adolescence, 430–431, 431p, 434
   emergence in middle childhood, 369
Self-control
   development in early childhood, 277
   development in middle childhood, 367
   indicators of impairment of, 303
   moral development based on, 295
   role of active social play, 284
Self-criticism, 369
Self-definition, 75
Self-destructive behavior, 239, 443, 454, 468, 474. See also Parasuicide; Risky behavior; Suicide; Suicide ideation
Self-doubt, 549, 668
Self-efficacy, 593
Self-esteem
   of bullies, 387, 388
   childhood overweight related to, 315
   cultural influences on, 360p, 369–370
   cyberbullying and, 442–443
   depression associated with low self-esteem, 473
   drop in middle childhood, 369, 395
   of early-maturing girls, 409
   effect of aggressive actions, 298
   of emerging adults, 549–550, 569
   ethnic differences, 473, 474
   relationships affecting, 463, 473
   rise in adulthood, 635
   sexual activity related to, 420–421
Self-expansion, 551
Self-expression, 457
Self-feeding, 141
Self-harm, 411, 424
Self-hatred, 419
Self-image, 730
Selfishness, 246, 278
Self-perception, 369, 732
Self-pride, 368
Self-protection, 731
Self-recognition, 184, 184p, 209
Self-respect, 290, 374, 395
Self-righting, 134
Self-theory, 56
Self-transcendence, 769
Senescence
   aging of the brain, 577, 580, 600, 663, 701–702, 702f, 726
   beginning of, 493, 514
   cognitive compensation, 676, 682–683, 682p, 683p, 684, 696
   compression of morbidity, 686–688, 688f, 696
   defined, 576, 600
   experience of aging, 576f, 576p, 578–579, 578p, 580, 600, 663, 675

outward appearance, 577–578, 577p, 580, 600, 663
   personal compensation: sex, 676–678, 676f, 677p, 684, 696
   sense organs, 579–580, 580, 600, 663, 681–682, 681t, 682p, 696
   social compensation: driving, 678–679, 679p, 680f, 684, 696
   technical compensation: senses, 681–682, 681p, 681t, 684, 696
   theories of, 688–693, 689p, 690p, 691p, 692p, 695, 696
Senility, 709
Senior citizens. See Late adulthood
Senior day-care centers, 752
Senior homes, 752
Sensation, 137, 156, 162, 344
Sensation seeking, 416–418, 419p, 438–439, 439f
Sense of unfairness, 654–655
Senses
   in adulthood, 579–580, 579p, 663
   hearing, 99, 99p, 107f, 114, 130, 130f, 138, 152, 579, 579–580, 579p, 600, 681–682, 688, 696, 703–704
   in late adulthood, 681–682, 681p, 681t, 682p, 684, 688, 696, 703, 726
   of newborns, 117, 142
   perception, 137
   presence at birth, 130
   sensations, 137
   smell, 138–139, 579
   taste, 138–139, 579
   touch, 130
   vision, 82–83, 84, 90, 130, 130f, 138, 152, 579, 600, 681, 681p, 681t, 688, 696, 703
Sensitive period
   for consolidation of political values, 8
   defined, 7
   for language learning, 256–257, 256t, 272
   predictions based on, 20–21
Sensorimotor intelligence
   characteristics of, 46, 46f, 46t
   defined, 156
   primary circular reactions, 156–157, 157f, 157p
   secondary circular reactions, 157–159, 158p
   stages of, 45p, 156t, 157f, 178, 211
   tertiary circular reactions, 159–160, 159p, 161t
Sensory area of brain, 220
Sensory awareness, 163–164
Sensory memory, 344, 348, 364
Sensory register, 344
Sensory stimulation, 133
Sensory threshold, 703–704, 709
Separation anxiety, 183, 205

Seriation, 340, 364
Serotonin, 186
Serotonin transporter promoter gene, 188, 465, 465f, 474
Set point for weight, 498
Sex. *See also* Boys; Gender; Girls; Men; Women
  chromosomes determining, 70–71, 70p, 76–77, 80, 90
  effect on genetic expression, 80–81
  effect on onset of puberty, 426
  fetal development of, 96–97
  gender development, 303
  parental choosing, 71–72
  relationship to gender, 291
  SRY gene activation, 290
  theories concerning gender development, 291–294
Sex characteristics, 419–420, 420f, 420p, 425
Sex chromosomes
  deactivation of one chromosome, 80
  problems of, 85, 86t, 89
  recessive genetic disorders associated with, 86–87
  role in puberty, 406
  sex determination, 6, 70–71, 70p, 76–77
Sex differences, 61, 291, 426
Sex drive, 60–61, 497
Sex education, 424p, 471–473, 485, 487
Sex hormones
  decline in middle age, 584–586, 600
  involvement in clinical depression, 474
  role in puberty, 402f, 403
  stimulation of sexual activity, 420–421, 421p
Sexting, 443, 444
Sexual abuse
  of adolescents, 423–424, 426, 443
  of children, 236, 237, 238, 238f, 423–424
  consequences of, 402, 408, 563, 581
  via Internet, 441
Sexual activity
  in adolescence, 420–421, 420f, 421p, 426, 485, A-18
  before age 13, 25, 25f
  aging affected by, 687
  attitudes about purpose of, 502, 503, 514
  attitudes toward premarital sex, 501
  contraception use, 422, 424f, 425, 425f, 503
  of early-maturing girls and boys, 410
  effect of sex education, 471–473
  effect of stress on age of initial encounters, 409
  effects of drug abuse, 483
  during emerging adulthood, 500–503, 500p, 507, 514, 571

family rejection affecting, 474
flaunting of in middle school years, 447
historical context, 500–501, 500p
influence on, 471–472
in late adulthood, 676–678, 676f, 677p, 682, 684
problem for adolescents, 422–425, 424p, 425f
psychopathology resulting from early encounters, 503
results of in adolescence, 419
Sexual identity, 460–461, 461f, 461p, 462, 485, 487
Sexual impulses, 368
Sexual intercourse, 25, 25f
Sexual interests, 402, 406
Sexual maturation in adolescence, 419–426, 420f, 420p, 421p, 423p, 424p, 425, 425f, 426, 487
Sexual orientation, 373, 469–470, 471p, 485
Sexual satisfaction, 676
Sexual teasing, 387, 409
Sexuality, 470–471, 470p
Sexually transmitted infections (STIs). *See also* HIV/AIDS
  in adolescence, 422, 424–425, 424p, 472
  among bisexuals, 471
  effect of stress on incidence of in young girls, 409
  effect on fetus, 109t
  in emerging adulthood, 501–502, 503, 514, 571
  types, symptoms, and treatments, A-17
Sexual-reproductive system. *See also* Birth; Labor and delivery; Pregnancy; Reproduction; Sexual activity; Sexually transmitted infections (STIs)
  of adults, 580–586, 581p, 584p, 585p, 663
  contraception, 421, 422, 424f, 472, 478, 501, 503, 580, 586
  fertility, 581–584, 584p, 586, 600
  menopause, 584–586, 585p, 600, 663
  sexual responsiveness of adults, 581–582, 581p, 586, 600
Shadow education, 312
Shaken baby syndrome, 133
Shame
  adolescent's feelings of, 447
  control behavior with, 300
  cultural norms for development of, 184, 278
  development in early childhood, 303
  development of in early childhood, 209
Shared environment, 373, 395
Sheehy, Gail, 633
Shiva, sitting, 781
Shivering, 117, 495

Short-term memory. *See* Working memory
Shyness, 549–550, 569
Siblings
  favoritism and, 567, 640
  nonshared environment, 373–374, 380, 395, 567
  relationships between, 640, 641, 661, 744
Sickle cell anemia, 87
SIDS. *See* Sudden infant death syndrome (SIDS)
Sierra Leone, 115f, 371–372, 595
Sign language, 158, 168, 170, 173p
Significance, 23t
Singapore, 356t, 449, 452, 453t, A-16
Singing, 351, 351f
Single-nucleotide polymorphisms (SNPs), 69
Single-parent families, 375, 375f, 376t, 377f, 378p, 380–381, 381f, 383, 384, 395, 397
Sinnott, Jan, 535
Sirtuins, 692
Sitting, 140, 140t, 152
Situational couple violence, 563–564
Situational tests, 612
Skin
  in adulthood, 577–578, 577p, 580, 600, 663
  during emerging adulthood, 497
  in late adulthood, 684, 696
Skin cancer, 689
Skinner, B. F., 43p, 173, 175
Skin-to-skin contact, 120–121, 121p, 139
Skipped-generation family, 375, 376t, 379, 384, 747, 749
Sleep
  effects of stress, 615
  of newborns, 135, 137, 152
  patterns in adolescents, 403–404, 404f, 404p, 405f, 411, 426
  patterns in early childhood, 222
  patterns in late adulthood, 670, 671
  problems in young children, 135
Sleep deprivation, 404, 410, 411, 426
Sleeper effect, 264
Slippery slope, 775
Slovak Republic, 445f
Slovakia, A-16
Slovenia, A-16
Slow-wave sleep, 135
Small for gestational age (SGA), 113, 122
Small-for-dates, 113
Smallpox, 144, 151
Smell, 138–139, 626
Smile
  development of, 134, 138, 182, 182p, 182t, 184, 185, 209
  as survival technique, 204
Smoking
  by age, 510f
  aging affected by, 689

alcohol associated with, 110, 588
avoidance of, 676
behavior among U.S. high school students, A-19
birth complications due to, 106, 117
breast-feeding and, 146
consequences of, 479, 481, 583, 586, 587, 600
effect of second-hand smoke, 230
effect on birthweight, 113, 115, 122
effect on mature brain, 615
effect on prenatal development, 105–106, 107f, 108, 110–111, 110t
effect on timing of menopause, 584
during emerging adulthood, 510
friends' facilitation of, 469
income related to, 598
national variation in use, 479, 480, 480p, 663
quitting, 593–594
in U.S., 480f, 485
Sneezes, 117
Social affirmation, 597
Social anxiety, 78, 78p, 186
Social awareness, 184, 184p, 202, 209
Social bonds. *See also* Family; Friendships; Parents; Peer relationships; Romantic love; Romantic partners
  attachment, 189, 190f, 191–196, 191p, 192t, 193t, 194p, 195t, 196p, 199, 205, 209
  of bullies and victims, 388
  development in first two years, 189, 190f, 191–199, 191p, 192t, 193t, 194p, 195t, 196p, 197p, 198p, 199f, 209, 211
  fathers as social partners, 197–199, 198p, 199, 199f, 209
  as foundation for moral development, 295, 296
  mental health correlated with, 695
  social referencing, 197, 197p, 199, 205, 209
  synchrony, 189, 190f, 191, 191p, 199, 205, 207, 209
  theories of psychosocial development, 211
Social class, 9–11. *See also* Socioeconomic context (SES)
Social clock, 543
Social comparison, 369
Social compensation: driving, 678–679, 679p, 680f, 684
Social competence, 369
Social constructions
  aging as, 678
  culture as, 11
  defined, 11
  ethnicity/race as, 14–15, 22
  sexual activity as, 677

Social context
  academic achievement related
      to, 341
  adjusting language for, 349–350,
      350p, 351f
  adolescent emotional stability
      associated with, 478
  adults affected by, 573
  adults' choice of, 634
  anxiety disorders associated with,
      505
  as crucial element in overcoming
      stress, 371–372, 373
  dementia rates affected by, 711
  development of theory of mind
      associated with, 255–256
  drug use and abuse related to,
      510–511
  ethnic identity achievement in, 546
  interplay of physical and psycho-
      logical problems, 313
  language learning related to,
      350–353, 351f
  learning in early childhood af-
      fected by, 248–251, 249p,
      250p, 256
  learning in middle childhood
      related to, 341–343, 341p,
      342p, 343f, 348, 357, 364
  marriage affected by, 644
  moral values related to, 540
  peer pressure in ethnic groups, 467
  popularity of children related to,
      385
  reflected in diagnosis and treatment
      of psychopathology, 324
  of risk-taking during emerging
      adulthood, 507, 514
  sleep patterns affected by, 135, 137
  social learning embedded in, 249
  stimulation of sexual activity, 420
  thought processes affected by, 520
  understanding of metaphors
      related to, 349
Social convoy, 638, 641, 657–658,
      661, 743–744
Social decisions, 36
Social deficit, 239
Social disorders, 319
Social exclusion, 311–312
Social interaction. See also Social
      bonds
  ageism's effect on, 670
  aging affected by, 694, 696, 700
  brain fitness related to, 715
  fostering of theory of mind, 255
  language development and, 256
  role of play, 284, 303
  of social learning theory, 64
  social learning theory, 44–45,
      200–201, 249–251, 249p,
      250p, 272
  sociocultural theory, 52–53
  volunteer work, 739, 739f, 739p
Social learning theory
  concepts of, 44–45, 44t, 64
  in early childhood, 200–201,
      249–251, 249p, 250p, 272
  mentors, 249, 249p

scaffolding, 249–250, 250p
view of gender development, 293
Social media, 551–552
Social network, loss of, 657–658
Social networking
  of adolescents, 440–441, 444,
      468–469, 468p
  change in life patterns, 493
  decrease with age, 498
  effect on birthweight, 113–114
  encouragement of risk-taking, 512
  matchmaking Web sites, 555, 569
  as source of friendships and conse-
      quential strangers, 639
Social norms
  base rate neglect and availability
      error, 511–512
  drug use and abuse related to,
      512–513
  of emerging adulthood, 511–513
  implications for risk-taking, 513,
      514
  timetable for important events in
      life, 543
Social norms approach, 512
Social phobia, 505
Social prejudices, 369
Social pressure, 506
Social referencing, 197, 197p, 199,
      205, 209
Social rejection, 368
Social Security benefits, 738
Social setting, 195–197, 195t, 196p
Social skills
  mastery motivation and development
      of, 448
  peer relationships teaching, 384,
      385
  role of play in learning, 282
Social smile, 182, 182t, 184, 185
Social studies, 431
Social support. See also Family;
      Friendships
  of adults, 553, 641, 659, 661
  at birth of child, 116
  to break bad habits, 593
  combining intimacy and generativity,
      659, 661
  for coping with stress, 617
  of the elderly, 749, 757
  within families, 463–464
  health related to, 638
  loss of, 657–658, 675
  mental health correlated with, 695
  for moral development, 530
  parents' need of, 599, 614
  for school age children, 373
  sources of, 638, 659, 737
Social understanding, 389, 519–520,
      663
Social witnesses, 719
Socialization, 60
Social-pragmatic theory, 173
Sociocultural theory
  accounting for culture, 54–55
  application to middle childhood,
      341–343, 341p, 342p,
      343f, 348, 357, 364
  concepts of, 61, 62f, 64

contribution/criticism of, 62
defined, 52
social interaction, 52–53
social learning in early childhood
      and, 249–252
STEM education and, 251–252
view of gender development,
      293–294
view of language development, 173
zone of proximal development,
      53–54, 54f, 61, 64, 249,
      256, 258, 272, 341, 647
Sociodramatic play, 284–286, 286f,
      286p, 295, 303
Socioeconomic status (SES). See
      also Income
  academic achievement correlated
      with, 341, 350–351, 351,
      351f, 352
  age structure and development, 12f
  alcohol use related to, 588–589
  availability of technology, 440
  birthweight affected by, 114
  children's activities by nationality,
      282f
  of college students, 536, 537f
  contribution to abusive relationships,
      563
  contribution to clinical depression
      in adolescent boys, 474
  defined, 9
  dental care related to, 311
  development affected by, 10–11,
      12f, 22
  education in U.S. determined by,
      358, 444, 567
  effect of poverty on intellectual
      achievement, 341
  environmental hazards related to,
      229, 230–231
  as factor in remarriage, 645
  family structure and function
      correlated with, 378, 382,
      382–383, 384, 639–640
  financial support of emerging
      adults, 565, 565p, 566f,
      660
  food choices base on, 414
  gross motor development affected
      by, 227
  health affected by, 598–599, 598p,
      600
  hospice care availability, 770
  intellect correlated with, 702
  language learning associated with,
      350–351, 364
  life expectancy by ethnicity and
      gender, 735f
  marriages affected by, 560, 643t
  obesity related to, 590f, 591
  onset of puberty related to, 408
  opportunities for organized play
      related to, 312
  resilience affected by, 372
  school drop-out rates related to, 446
  stratification of society by,
      734–736, 735f
  teen pregnancy associated with, 423
  treatment of disease affected by, 718

Socioemotional selectivity theory,
      732–734, 733f, 737, 743
Solitary play, 283
Sonogram, 96p, 97
SORL 1 gene, 712
Source amnesia, 704, 726
South Africa, 115f, A-3
South Asia, 148, 148f, 207
South Korea
  cognition in, 527
  high-stakes tests in, 450
  low birthweights in, 115f
  play in childhood in, 312
  scores on PISA, 452, 453t
Spain
  average age of marriage, 545f
  bereavement leave in, 779
  birth rituals in, 119
  cohabitation in, 556–557
  high school graduation rate, 445f
  same-sex marriage in, 644p
  scores on international tests, 356t,
      453t
  smokers in, 587
Spanking, 199t, 301
Spatial intelligence, 322
Spatial orientation, 606f
Special education, 331–333, 332f,
      334p, 336, 397
Special needs children
  in middle childhood, 323–335,
      331p, 332f, 333p, 397
  parental stress, 616
Specific learning disorder, 328–329,
      328p, 336
Speed of thought
  decline with age, 28
  in early childhood, 220
  in emerging adulthood, 702f
  experience and, 321
  intelligence associated with, 321,
      323
  in late adulthood, 701, 702f, 703,
      704–705, 707
  in middle childhood, 323, 336, 702f
Sperm
  abnormal genetic formation,
      84–85, 85p, 86t
  fertilization, 68, 68p
  inactivation of, 71
  sex chromosomes of, 71
Spermarche, 401, 403, 407f, 426
Spice (synthetic marijuana), 483
Spina bifida, 108
Spinal cord, 98t, 219f, A-2
Spiritual/existential intelligence, 322
Spitting up, 117
Sports
  aging affected by, 578, 689
  brain disease among athletes, 714
  during emerging adulthood, 507
  hot hand belief, 705–706, 706f
  humanism in, 58
  in middle school, 447
  prediction of game outcomes, 623,
      623f
Spousal abuse, 563
Sri Lanka, 371
SRY gene, 71, 290

Stability
  as need of middle childhood, 375, 382, 395, 397
  in permanent placement homes, 185, 240–241, 240p
  in stepfamilies, 379
Stacking blocks, 142t
Stage approach to cognitive development, 517, 540
Stage of first habits, 156–157, 156t
Stage of reflexes, 156, 156t
Stages of life, 27f
Standing, 140t, 152
Stanford-Binet IQ test, 604
Static reasoning, 246, 247
Statistical measures, 22, 23t, 32
Statistical significance, B-4
Status symbols, 447
STEM (science, technology, engineering, math), 251–252
Stem cell therapy, 716
Stem cells, 73, 77, 90
Stepfamilies, 375, 376t, 379, 380, 384
Stepparents, 649–650, 649p, 661
Stepping reflex, 117
Stereotype threat
  debilitation of elderly, 669, 704
  deflection of, 524–525, 524p, 528, 540, 546
  effect on job search, 657
Stereotypes
  as distortion of memorable cases, 675
  effects of, 737
  of the elderly, 667–676, 668p, 670f, 670p, 671f, 672f, 673p, 674p, 696, 700, 754
  of genders and gender roles, 280, 290, 294, 295, 677
  of immigrants and cultures, 360
  postformal thinking countering, 523–525, 524p, 528, 540
  of race or ethnicity, 13, 15
  stratification of society, 734
Sterilization, 580
Sternberg, Robert
  dimensions of love, 553, 553t, 554
  forms of intelligence, 610–612, 610t, 611p, 613, 628
  on love, 643
Stillbirth, 85, 95
Still-face technique, 191, 199, 209
Stomach-sleeping, 150
Storage of memories, 345, 364
Strange situation, 194, 195
Stranger wariness, 183, 183p, 229, 233, 312
Strategic thinking, 624–625, 627, 628, 663
Stratification theories, 734–737, 734p, 735p, 735p, 737, 757
Strength, 491–493, 491p, 492f, 492p, 494f, 495–500, 495t, 496p, 497p, 499t
Streptomycin, 109t
Stress
  aggressive children affected by, 387
  aging affected by, 676, 685, 691
  attachment affected by, 195, 195t

brain development affected by, 186, 209, 226, 242
as cause of infertility, 583
cognition affected by, 615
coping methods, 616–617, 618f, 619, 627, 628
effect during puberty, 403, 408–409, 411, 426, 617
effect in middle childhood, 371–372, 371p, 373, 395, 617
emotional stress in emerging adulthood, 502–504, 503, 506, 514
employment related to, 657, 658
family issues related to, 658
fetus affected by, 109t
maternal nurturing affected by, 22
of middle school, 445
religious involvement reducing, 742
response to, 609, 619, 620f
return of bad habits during, 594
as risk factor for schizophrenia, 506
sadness producing in infants, 182–183
Stress hormones, 616. See also Cortisol
Stressors
  accumulation of, 616, 628
  bereavement as, 783
  effect on cognition, 615–617, 615p, 618f, 619–620, 620f
Stroke, 585, 588, 685f, 712, 715
Study of development
  correlation and causation, 29
  cross-sectional research, 25–27, 26f
  cross-sequential research, 26f, 28
  defined, 32
  ethical issues, 29–31, 30, 30–31
  longitudinal research, 26f, 27
  scientific method, 4–5, 32, B-1–B-5
  study topics, 31
Stunting, 148–149, 148f, 152
Stuttering, 313
Subjective thought, 521–522
Substantiated maltreatment, 236, 237, 242
Success, 632
Sucker to saint phenomenon, 730–731
Sucking reflex, 117, 141, 142, 156–157, 157f, 157p
Sudden infant death syndrome (SIDS), 136, 149–151, 150f, 152
Suicidal ideation, 474–475, 474p, 475f, 478
Suicide
  of adolescents and young adults, 485, 487, 765f
  alcohol abuse related to, 588
  avoidant coping contributing to, 616
  by bullied children, 387, 443
  cluster suicides, 475
  of cyberbullied adolescents, 442
  decrease in, 660
  dissatisfaction with body image associated with, 414

drug abuse related to, 483
early-maturing girls' risk of, 410
of elderly white men, 742
during emerging adulthood, 507
of gay teens, 474
grief and mourning process following, 779–780
incidence of in U.S., 475
internalization of problems associated with, 176
of maltreated children, 239
of Native Americans, 474p
of non-heterosexual teens, 471
parent-adolescent relationships affecting, 463, 473–474
physician-assisted suicide, 773–775, 774t, 776f, 778
of PTSD sufferers, 619
rate in U.S., A-20
sati, 734
sexual abuse related to, 423, 443
Sunk cost fallacy, 434
Superego, 291–292
Surgeons, 622, 625, 626, 628, 663
Surrogate grandparents, 747
Survey, 24–25, 28, 32
Survival
  allocare, 205
  combination of genes insuring, 60, 90
  developmental theories concerning, 36
  emotions for, 204–205
  evolutionary theory concerning, 58, 59, 60, 61
  of newborns, 103, 142–151, 152
Swallowing reflexes, 117
Sweden
  centenarians in, 695
  c-sections in, 102f
  elderly volunteers in, 739
  high school graduation rate, 445f
  infant day care in, 207
  low birthweights in, 115f
  punishment of poor behavior in, 301
  rate of dementia in, 711
  scores on international tests, 356t, 453t, A-16
  single-parent families in, 375f
Swimming reflex, 117
Switzerland
  euthanasia in, 773
  high school graduation rate, 445f
  official languages of, 260
  PISA scores, 453t, A-16
  smokers in, 587
Symbolic thought, 245–246, 256
Synapses
  changes in late adulthood, 701
  decrease in adulthood, 577
  defined, 130
  emotional volatility related to growth of, 185
  function of, 131f, 132f
  growth and refinement in first two years, 132, 137, 152
  growth in adolescence, 419
Synaptic gap, 130, 131f, 132f
Synaptogenesis, 97

Synchrony
  defined, 189
  between infant and caregiver, 189, 190f, 191, 196, 197, 199, 209
  as survival technique, 204, 205, 207
Syndrome, 85
Synthesis, 525
Synthetic marijuana, 483
Synthetic-conventional faith, 531
Syphilis, 109t, 111, 714, 715, A-17

Tacit intelligence, 611–612, 611p
Taiwan, A-16
Talking, 258. See also Language development
Tangles, 711
Taoism, 527
Taste, 138–139
Tau protein, 711
Taxi drivers, 628, 663
Teacher-directed preschool programs, 265–269, 265p, 266f, 267p, 268f, 305
Teachers, 298
Teaching. See also College; Early-childhood education; Education; High school; Learning; Middle school; Preschool programs
  adolescents, 429, 444–453, 445f, 445p, 448p, 453t, 454, 487
  children in middle childhood, 353, 354f, 354t, 355–358, 355p, 356t, 357p, 364
  by experts, 623–624
  international schooling, 353–355, 354f, 354t, 355p, 356–357, 357p
  international tests, 356–358, 356t, 358p, 397
  need for flexibility, 625
  one's own children, 647
  second language, 359–360, 360p
  sex education, 472
  in the United States, 358–360, 358p, 359t, 360f, 360p
  use of technology, 441, 444
Technical compensation: senses, 681–682, 681p, 681t, 684, 696
Technology
  addiction to video games, 441–442, 441f, 444, 454
  adolescents' familiarity with, 440–441, 440p, 444, 454, 487
  college students' use of, 536
  compensation for loss of vision and hearing, 681, 681p
  cyberbullying, 442, 442p, 444, 454
  depression associated with, 468
  educational applications, 441, 444
  reduction of isolation, 487
  sexting, 443, 444
  social networking, 440–441, 444, 468–469, 468p
Teeth, 107f, 310, 493
Telomeres, 690–691, 690p, 693, 696

Temper tantrums, 183–184, 222, 223, 277
Temperament
  changes between ages 4 months and 4 years, 188f
  defined, 187, 209
  effect on attachment, 195t
  effect on child-rearing practices, 298
  factors affecting, 634
  in first two years, 187–189, 188f
  influence on caregiving, 288–289
  persistence of, 631
Temperature, infants' sensitivity to, 139
Teratogens
  advice from doctors, 110
  advice from scientists, 111
  application of research, 108, 109–110t, 110
  complications during birth associated with, 116
  critical time, 106, 107f, 122
  defined, 105
  effect on prenatal development, 105, 109–110t, 116, 122
  prenatal diagnosis, 111
  preterm delivery, 113
  prevention of damage from, 109–110t
  risk analysis, 106–108, 107f
  threshold effect, 106, 108, 122
  types, effect, and prevention, 109–110t
  what prospective mothers do, 107t
Teratology, 106
Terman, Lewis, 605
Terror management theory, 765, 786
Tertiary circular reactions, 156t, 157f, 178
Tertiary education, 444, 454, 571. See also College; Higher education
Tertiary prevention
  of disease, 594
  of injury, 235, 236, 242
  of maltreatment of children, 240, 242
Testes, 403, 419
Testosterone
  factors reducing, 585, 663
  increase in puberty, 402f, 426
  levels in emerging adulthood, 500
  response to stress, 616
  as a supplement, 585–586
Tetracycline, 109t
Texting, 418, 440, 440p, 444, 468
Thailand, 136f, 639
Thalamus, 219f, A-2
Thalassemia, 87
Thalidomide, 6–7, 106, 109t
Theories, 35–39, 63, 64. See also Children's theories; Ethnotheories; Folk theories; Theories of development; specific theory

Theories of aging, 688–693, 689p, 690p, 691p, 692p
Theories of infant psychosocial development, 199–205, 200p, 201p, 202p, 202t, 205p, 206p, 206t, 207f
Theories of late adulthood
  self theories, 730–734, 730p, 731p, 733f, 737, 739, 757
  stratification theories, 734–737, 734p, 735f, 735p, 737, 757
Theory of mind
  as cognitive development, 253–254, 253p, 254f, 256, 261, 272, 305
  development of empathy associated with, 389
  effect on corporal punishment on development of, 299
  as foundation for moral development, 295, 298
  role of sociodramatic play, 284
Theory theory, 35, 252–253, 256, 272
Therapy dogs, 23
Thesis, 525
Thimerosal, 331
Thinking
  ageism's effect on, 670
  during early childhood, 245–256, 247p, 248f, 249p, 253p, 254f, 255f, 255p, 305
  during emerging adulthood, 517–527, 518p, 520f, 521f, 521p, 524p, 540
  of experts, 621–627, 622p, 623f, 626p, 627, 627f, 628
  in late adulthood, 701
  during middle childhood, 343–348, 345f, 345t
  selective optimization with compensation, 620–621, 621p, 624, 626, 627, 628, 663, 676–684, 676f, 677p, 680f, 696, 732, 737, 744
  speed of in early childhood, 220
  two modes of in adolescence, 434–440, 435f, 436p, 439f, 448, 454, 487, 518, 520, 521, 522
Thrashing reflex, 117
Threshold effect, 106, 108
Time management, 518–519, 518p
Time-out, 300, 300p, 303
Time-sequential research. See Cross-sequential research
Tobacco
  addiction to, 593
  adolescent use of, 485
  adult use of, 587, 587p, 588f
  alcohol associated with, 110, 588
  as cause of infertility, 583
  consumption of worldwide, 479
  effect on birthweight, 113, 115, 122
  effect on fetus, 109t
  harm from, 481
  national variation in use, 480, 480p
  smoking among U.S. high school students, A-19

as a teratogen, 108
use by age, 510f
use in emerging adulthood, 510
Toe touching, 141p
Toilet training, 39, 50–51
Tolerance, 528p
Touch, 130, 139
Tourette syndrome, 313
Toward a Psychology of Being (Maslow), 56
Toxins
  as cause of cancer, 586
  as cause of neurocognitive disorders, 715
  effect on brain development, 230–231, 231f, 231p, 478
  effect on fetus, 105, 109t
  effects on children, 233, 324, 613
  role in aging, 688, 689, 690
Toxoplasmosis, 109t
Traits
  genetic/environmental effect on, 84
  multifactorial, 77, 90
  polygenic, 77, 81, 90
  temperament, 187–189, 188f
Transient exuberance, 132
Transient ischemic attacks (TIAs), 712, 726
Transitional objects, 183
Traumatic encephalopathy, 714, 714p
Trends in Math and Science Study (TIMMS), 356, 356t, 357, 364, 383, 445, 451
Trichomoniasis, A-17
Trimesters, 94t
Triple X syndrome, 86t
Trisomy, 85
Trisomy-21, 85, 85p, 89, 90, 712, A-6
Trust vs. mistrust, 40t, 200, 544t
Tummy time, 140, 150
Tunisia, 453t, A-3
Turkey, 445f, 453t, 482f
Turner syndrome, 86t
Twenge, Jean M., B-5
Twenty-first-century manners, 9f
23rd pair of chromosomes
  deactivation of one chromosome, 80
  effect on growth patterns, 406
  problems of, 85, 86t, 89
  recessive genetic disorders associated with, 86–87
  sex determination, 70–71, 70p, 76–77, 90
Twins
  breast-feeding and, 146
  conjoined, 73
  differences in intelligence, 607
  differential sensitivity of, 373–374
  dizygotic, 74f, 75, 77, 90, 108
  low birthweights, 114, 122
  marriage of, 639
  monozygotic, 73, 74f, 75, 77, 90, 373–374
  schizophrenia and, 87
  vanishing, 75
Two-parent families, 378–379, 378p, 379p

Uganda, 193, 674
Ultrasound image, 96p, 97, 111
Umbilical cord, 101
Unconditional positive regard, 56, 64
Unemployment
  effect on adult sexual responsiveness, 581
  of emerging adults, 547
  social and mental health problems associated with, 654, 663
United Kingdom
  advice to pregnant women in, 111
  cohabitation in, 556
  co-sleeping in, 136f
  development of impulse control in, 223
  emerging adulthood in, 566
  exercise by adults in, 592
  high school graduation rate, 445f
  high-stakes tests in, 449
  home births in, 104
  hospice care availability, 770
  incidence of neural-tube defects, 108
  infertility rates, 582
  influence of surroundings on personality in, 636
  ketamine use in, 511
  low birthweights in, 115f
  neurocognitive disorders in, 714
  population of children and elders, A-3
  rate of dementia in, 711
  scores on international tests, 356t, 453t, A-16
  sexually active teens/condom use, 425f
  single-parent families in, 375f
  sports in, 312
  view of left-handedness, 221
  vision heritability in, 83
United States
  abortions in, 580
  adolescent crime in, 478
  advice to pregnant women in, 110–111
  age-adjusted mortality rate in, 594
  alcohol use in, 588
  anxiety disorders in, 505
  art education in, 353, 354f
  average age of marriage, 545f
  average daily exposure to video by ethnic group and age, 286f
  bilingual school children in, 260, 260f
  body image of adolescents in, 414
  breast-feeding in, 147, 147f, A-7
  caregiving styles in, 289
  child maltreatment in, 236, 237f, 238f
  childhood obesity in, 315, 315f
  children with special needs in, 332, 332f
  children's activities by socioeconomic class, 282f
  cognition in, 527
  cohabitation in, 556, 556f, 557, 558
  contraception in, 580

co-sleeping in, 135, 136f
c-sections in, 102, 102f, 122
death in, 235f, 309, 770–771, 771f, 774, 774t
demographics, 673
dependency ratio in, 674
diet in, 591
divorce rates in, 545f, 559, 561, 573, 641, 642t, 645
eating disorders in, 415, 506
eating habits in, 413
education in, 262f, 331–332, 333, 334, 347, 358–360, 358p, 358t, 360f, 364, 370, 448, 449, 453, 535, 536, 537f, 566
emphasis in preschools in, 267
emphasis on regulation of fear, 278
employment rates of mothers in, 198
ethnic composition, A-4
exercise in, 592, 592f
family size, 501
family structures in, 375, 375f, 376t
foster care in, 240–241, 650
groups of popular and unpopular children in, 385
high school graduation rate, 445, 445f, 449, 450f, 482f
homicide by age, 672f
incidence of measles in, 144
infant care in, 207
infant mortality in, 103, 114, 143, 143f
infertility rates, 582
influence of family and religion in, 377f
language development in, 172, 173p
laws preventing injury, 234–235, 236
leave for infant care in, 207
life expectancy in, 688f, 694, 747f
low birthweights in, 115, 115f
marijuana use in, 586
marriage in, 545f, 553, 555, 558, 561, 641
morality rates for, 687
number of bilingual school children, 350f
obesity in, 216, 589, 590f, 594
official language of, 260
parent-adolescent relationships, 463, 469
physical activity in schools, 213, 353
play in childhood in, 312
population of children and elders, A-3
punishment of poor behavior in, 299
racial prejudice in, 524
rate of STIs in, 424
rates of ADHD, 325
regulation of lead, 230–231
respect for elderly in, 669
restrictions on tobacco use, 479
same-sex marriage in, 529, 644, 644p
schedule for immunizations, A-8–A-9

scores on international tests, 356, 356t, 452, 453t, 454, A-16
secular trend in, 406
serious abuse in intimate relationships, 563
sex education in, 472
sexual activity of adolescents, 421, 425, 425f, A-18
smokers in, 587, 588t, 598, A-19
teen abortion rate, 422
teen pregnancy in, 422
view of left-handedness, 221
work force, 658
workforce, 656–658, 656t, 658
Universal design, 682, 740
Universal grammar, 175
Universal perspective. See also Evolutionary theory
concepts of, 62f
contribution/criticism of, 62
humanism, 55–58, 61, 64, 203–204, 208, 209, 294
Universal sequence of language development, 168–170, 168p, 169t, 178
Universalizing faith, 531
Urbanization, 229, 242, 318
Urinary system, 684
Uruguay, 453t
U.S. Census Bureau, 748
U.S. Department of Health and Human Services, 237
U.S. Youth Risk Behavior Survey, 422
Use it or lose it hypothesis, 702
Uterine rupture, 103
Uterus, 419

Vaccination, 144–145, 685
Vanishing twin, 75
Variables, 24, 24f
Varicella, 109t, 145
Vascular dementia (VaD), 712, 712f, 726
Vegetative state, 772t, 773, 777–778, 777p
Venereal disease (VD). See Sexually transmitted infections (STIs)
Ventral striatum, 438
Verbal abilities, 606f, 608, 614. See also Language development
Verbal bullying, 386
Verbal fluency, 634
Verdi, 722
Very low birthweight (VLBW), 113
Viability, 97, 97p, 98, 99
Vicodin, 480f
Victims. See also Abuse; Child maltreatment; Domestic abuse; Sexual abuse
of bullying, 386p, 387, 388
of crime, 672f
Video games
addiction to, 440–441, 441f, 444, 454, 468
improvement of cognition in late adulthood, 720, 720p, 726

Videos
average daily exposure to by ethnic group, 286f
encouragement of risk-taking, 512
recommendations for viewing in first two years, 174–175, 286, 303
Viet Nam, 135, 136f, 668
Village care, 755
Viral infections, 577, 600
Virtues, 544t
Vision
in adulthood, 600
area of brain controlling, 130f
binocular vision, 138
changes in adulthood, 579
common impairments among elderly, 681p, 681t, 696
development of, 138, 142, 152
effect of low birthweight, 114
factors affecting acuity, 82–83, 84, 90
maturity at birth, 130
technology compensating for, 681, 696
Visual cliff, 164, 164p
Visual cortex
development of, 138
functions of, 130, 130f, 137, 219f, A-2
Vital Involvement in Old Age (Erikson), 719
Vitality
in late adulthood, 670, 676
as measure of health, 594, 597–598, 599, 600, 663
Vitamin A, 108
Vitamin supplements, 331, 691, 695, 697, 717, 718
Vocabulary. See also Language development
adjusting to context, 349–350, 349p, 350f, 351f
advancement of pragmatics, 349–350
in early childhood, 246
increase of acquisition with age, 28
understanding metaphors, 348–349, 364
Vocabulary explosion, 257–259
Vocation. See Employment
Vocational identity, 460, 460f, 462, 485, 487, 544, 547–548, 547p, 547t, 548f, 548p, 550, 569, 571
Volunteer work, 739, 739f, 739p, 743, 757
Vouchers (for schooling), 361
Vygotsky, Lev
acceptance of theory, 343, 347, 526
influence on child-centered programs, 264
international contexts, 342–343, 342p, 348
on role of instruction, 341p, 343f
social learning in early childhood, 248–251, 249p, 250p, 256, 272, 305

social learning in middle childhood, 341–343, 341p, 342p, 343f, 348, 357, 364, 397
sociocultural theory, 14, 14p, 52–53
STEM education and, 251–252

Wages, 654–655, 655p
Walking
development of motor skills for, 140, 140t, 152
learning process, 127, 141, 141p, 142
motivation for learning, 165
Warmth, expression of
in caregiving, 287–288, 287t, 289–290, 294, 301, 303
toward adolescents, 464, 472, 485
Wasting, 148, 148–149, 148p
Watson, John B., 42, 42p
Wear-and-tear theory of aging, 689, 689p, 693, 695, 696
Weathering, 617, 735
Weight gain, 591–592, 591p
Wernicke-Korsakoff syndrome, 577
White coat syndrome, 43
White matter, 220, 220f, 701, 703
White matter lesions, 701, 703
Whooping cough, 144
Why Survive: Being Old in America (Butler), 721
Widowers, 734
Widows
care of, 718, 729, 734–735, 734p
care of children, 376t
life of, 686, 740, 749, 751
sati, 734
Willpower, 593
Wills, 777, 778, 786
WISC/WAIS IQ test, 604
Wisdom, 612, 613, 723–724, 723p, 725f, 726
Withdrawn-rejected children, 386, 387
Women. See also Mothers; Parents
as abusers in intimate relationships, 563
college enrollment, 536, 571
dementia rates, 711
depression in emerging adulthood, 505
diseases afflicting, 686
effects of divorce, 645
employment discrimination, 656
expectation for marriage, 642
graduates of medical school, 627f
hearing loss, 681
infertility, 582, 583
intelligence changes over time, 606–607, 606f
as kinkeepers, 651
life expectancy, 595, 691, 694, 735f
menopause, 584–585, 585p, 600, 663
moral values of, 530, 531
morbidity rates, 596
occupations of, 626, 627
perpetrators of homicide against, 562f
physical development in emerging adulthood, 491

reasons for hooking up, 554–555
response to stress, 616–617
risk-taking during emerging
 adulthood, 507, 513
sexual responsiveness, 581
smokers in U.S., 587, 588f
suicide rates, A-21
vulnerability to schizophrenia,
 506
in workforce, 656, 659
Woods, Tiger, 334
Words, 258, 272. *See also* Language
 development
Work schedules, 658, 658p, 660,
 661, 663
Workforce, 656, 656f, 659, 661

Working memory
 of Alzheimer patients, 711
 decline with age, 704
 development of, 344–345, 348
 fluid intelligence associated with,
  608–609
 as foundation for intelligence,
  321, 323
Working model, 202–203, 208
World Health Organization, 102, 113
Worldview, 732–734
Wright, Frank Lloyd, 722
Wroe, Martha, 721

X-linked characteristics, 79, 80t
X-rays, 109t

XX chromosomes, 70, 77, 80, 90
XY chromosomes, 70, 77, 90

Y chromosome, 108
Yemen, 356t, A-3
Young-old people, 675, 676, 685, 696
Yusof, Sufiah, 334

Zero correlation, 29
Zone of proximal development (ZPD)
 defined, 53, 249
 parents' need to understand, 647
 as site of learning, 249, 256, 272, 341
 sociocultural theory, 53–54, 54f,
  61, 64
 teaching of reading, 258

Zygotes
 assisted reproductive technology,
  71, 75–76, 77, 90, 115,
  583, 586, 600
 defined, 68
 division creating twins, 73–75,
  74f
 divisions of, 73, 90, 94p, 99, 122
 duplication of, 70, 72
 fertilization, 68, 68p, 84, 90
 genes determining sex, 6, 70–71,
  70p, 76–77
 genetic code in, 69
 implantation, 94–95, 95f, 95t
 in vitro fertilization, 71, 75–76, 77,
  90, 95, 583, 586, 600